The McGraw-Hill Children's Dictionary

By the Wordsmyth Collaboratory

The Wordsmyth Reference Series

McGraw-Hill Children's Publishing
A Division of The McGraw-Hill Companies

 **Children's Publishing**

Columbus, Ohio

Library of Congress Cataloging-in-Publication Data

The McGraw-Hill children's dictionary.
　　　p. cm.
　　Summary: A dictionary with word histories, synonyms, illustrations, and spelling, grammar, and usage features.
　　ISBN 1-57768-298-X
1. English language—Dictionaries, Juvenile. [1. English language—Dictionaries.] I. Title: Children's dictionary. II. McGraw-Hill Companies.

　　PE1628.5 .M37 2002
　　423—dc21
2002018796

Children's Publishing

Send all inquiries to:
McGraw-Hill Children's Publishing
8787 Orion Place
Columbus, Ohio 43240
www.MHkids.com

ISBN 1-57768-298-X

4 5 6 7 8 9 VHJ 07 06 05 04 03

Manufactured in the United States of America.

Table of Contents

Look for special **Graphic Features** at these entry words!
*Amphibians • Birds • Body Systems • Conservation • Constellations • Dinosaurs • Earth (Natural Disasters)
Elements (Periodic Table) • Exploration • First Aid • Flowers • Insects • International (Currency) • Languages
Mammals • Metamorphosis • Musical Instruments • Native Americans • Number Systems • Reptiles • Solar System
Teeth • Time • Weapons • Weather*

Wordsmyth Collaboratory Staff

Director
Robert Q. Parks, Ph.D.

Editorial Director
Jean V. Callahan, Ph.D.

Information Architect
Aaron Weiss

Art Director
Jen Gage Sage

Editors
Gabriel Tavares, Joan Patrick, Jan Douglas,
Margaret McCasland, Jill Gorey

Contributing Editors
Maura Stephens, Lyn Broquist

Copy Editors
Michelle Mason, Maria Barry, Eunice Ferguson, Christian Zwahlen

Indexing Team
Meredith Elaine Wilson, Samantha Cooper,
Theresa Fives, Barth Myers, Pat Haines,
Shana Herron

Writers
Weena Perry, Helen Lang, Jay Wrolstadt,
Emily Johnson, Abby More, Lissa Harris,
Marla Perkins, Monica Hamill

Book Design
Brian Dudla

Art Team
Christian Wheeler, Keren Cohen, George
Sapio, Lukasz Lysakowski, Vanessa Valentine

Illustration
Keren Cohen, Jim Houghton, J. M. Barringer,
Robert (Mac) Myers, Chris Jung, Victor Lay

Photography
Douglas J. Davenport, Angela K. Horne

Consultants
Marty Kaminsky, Robert Ross, Robert Ascher,
Christopher Wright, John Culpepper, Laura
Johnson-Kelly

McGraw-Hill Children's Dictionary Team

President
Vincent F. Douglas

Publisher
Tracey E. Dils

Editor
Janet D. Sweet

Art Director
Robert Sanford

Designer
Jennifer Bowers

Production Manager
Diane Yarman

Wordsmyth would also like to acknowledge the important contributions of staff members who worked on earlier versions of the Wordsmyth database.

For a listing of staff for the Wordsmyth Educational Dictionary-Thesaurus and our electronic resources, visit our Web site at www.wordsmyth.net.

We wish to acknowledge the assistance of the children who gave their honest and helpful reactions to this Dictionary as it was being written.

Preface

Our language is our heritage and our resource for creating the future. The McGraw-Hill Children's Dictionary is designed to provide authoritative information on the meaning, usage, and spelling of words. As a collaboration of Wordsmyth Collaboratory and McGraw-Hill Children's Publishing, the text is written with respect for children's growing minds. The language is simple, but not simplistic. The style takes into account children's limited exposure to difficult words while challenging them to grasp ever more difficult ideas.

In addition to thousands of words and phrases which children ordinarily use in talking, reading, and writing, this dictionary features a host of word histories, synonyms, homophones, and word usage identifications. A spelling and pronunciation guide highlights a listing of words featuring Canadian and British spelling. Countless illustrations, diagrams, and extended graphics offer enhanced, detailed information.

A unique world reference section features a world history timeline, world population density maps, a world atlas, and the flags and currencies of the world. A North American section details the American states and presidents, as well as the Canadian provinces and prime ministers. Additional reference information includes a table of weights and measures and a unique display of symbolic and language communication. The innovative Wordsmyth Word Explorer enables children to explore the meanings of related keywords and topics.

Language is a powerful tool for life and for learning. Enjoy using the McGraw-Hill Children's Dictionary to enhance the exploration of our language.

Robert Q. Parks
Director, Wordsmyth Collaboratory

How to Use This Dictionary

Quick Reference Diagram

Guide Words identify the first and last entry words on a page.

Spelling and Look-Up Tips explain the sounds a letter can make and list frequently misspelled words.

Thumb-Index Tabs make it easy to locate words quickly.

Phrases and Expressions enhance word meanings.

Word History Notes feature extra information about the origin or usage of the word.

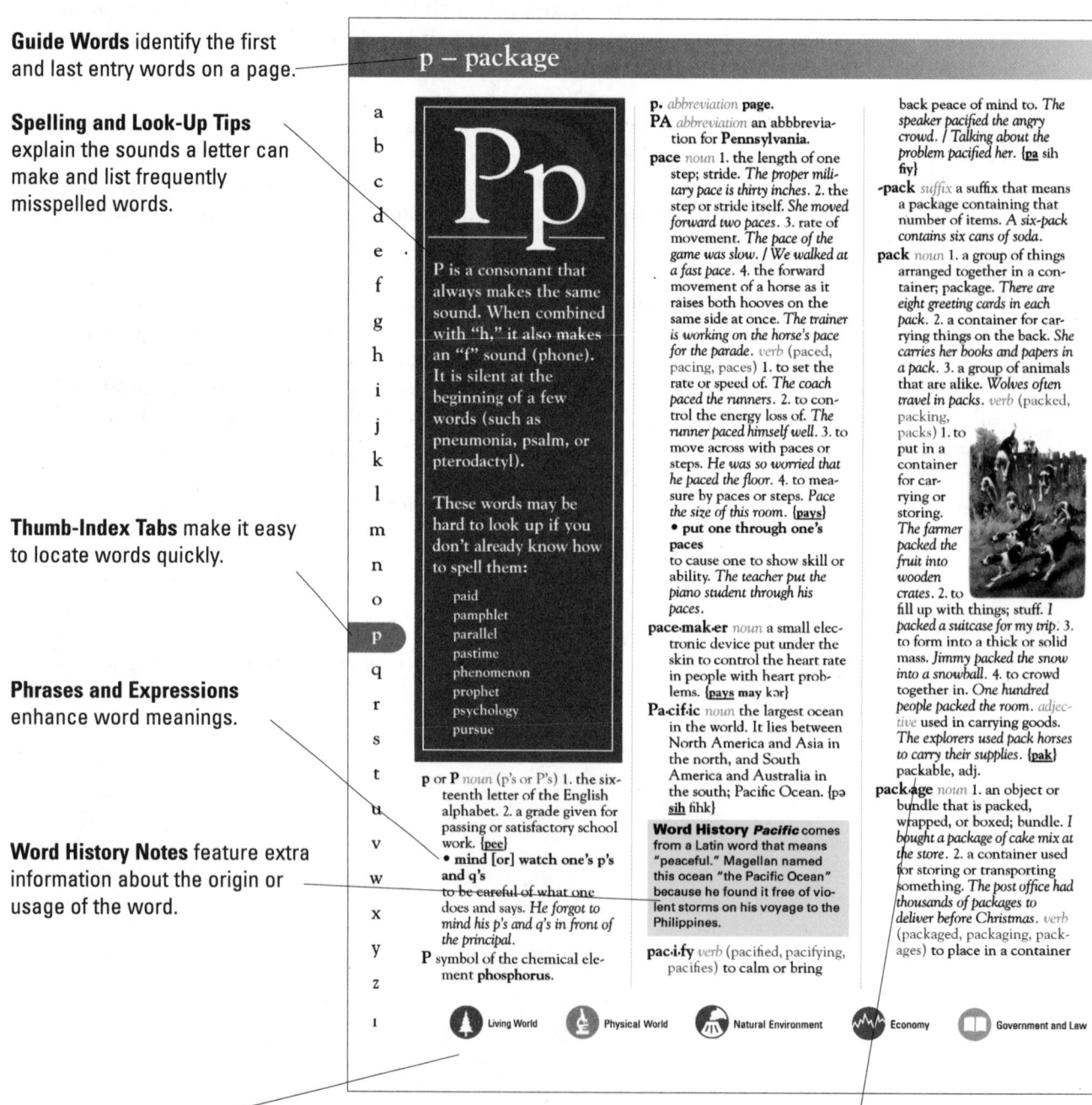

p – package

a b c d e f g h i j k l m n o **p** q r s t u v w x y z 1

P is a consonant that always makes the same sound. When combined with "h," it also makes an "f" sound (phone). It is silent at the beginning of a few words (such as pneumonia, psalm, or pterodactyl).

These words may be hard to look up if you don't already know how to spell them:

paid
pamphlet
parallel
pastime
phenomenon
prophet
psychology
pursue

p or **P** *noun* (p's or P's) 1. the sixteenth letter of the English alphabet. 2. a grade given for passing or satisfactory school work. {pee}
• **mind [or] watch one's p's and q's**
to be careful of what one does and says. *He forgot to mind his p's and q's in front of the principal.*
P symbol of the chemical element **phosphorus**.

p. *abbreviation* **page.**
PA *abbreviation* an abbbreviation for **Pennsylvania.**
pace *noun* 1. the length of one step; stride. *The proper military pace is thirty inches.* 2. the step or stride itself. *She moved forward two paces.* 3. rate of movement. *The pace of the game was slow. / We walked at a fast pace.* 4. the forward movement of a horse as it raises both hooves on the same side at once. *The trainer is working on the horse's pace for the parade.* *verb* (paced, pacing, paces) 1. to set the rate or speed of. *The coach paced the runners.* 2. to control the energy loss of. *The runner paced himself well.* 3. to move across with paces or steps. *He was so worried that he paced the floor.* 4. to measure by paces or steps. *Pace the size of this room.* {pays}
• **put one through one's paces**
to cause one to show skill or ability. *The teacher put the piano student through his paces.*
pace·mak·er *noun* a small electronic device put under the skin to control the heart rate in people with heart problems. {pays may kər}
Pa·cif·ic *noun* the largest ocean in the world. It lies between North America and Asia in the north, and South America and Australia in the south; Pacific Ocean. {pə sih fihk}

Word History *Pacific* comes from a Latin word that means "peaceful." Magellan named this ocean "the Pacific Ocean" because he found it free of violent storms on his voyage to the Philippines.

pac·i·fy *verb* (pacified, pacifying, pacifies) to calm or bring

back peace of mind to. *The speaker pacified the angry crowd. / Talking about the problem pacified her.* {pa sih fiy}
-pack *suffix* a suffix that means a package containing that number of items. *A six-pack contains six cans of soda.*
pack *noun* 1. a group of things arranged together in a container; package. *There are eight greeting cards in each pack.* 2. a container for carrying things on the back. *She carries her books and papers in a pack.* 3. a group of animals that are alike. *Wolves often travel in packs.* *verb* (packed, packing, packs) 1. to put in a container for carrying or storing. *The farmer packed the fruit into wooden crates.* 2. to fill up with things; stuff. *I packed a suitcase for my trip.* 3. to form into a thick or solid mass. *Jimmy packed the snow into a snowball.* 4. to crowd together in. *One hundred people packed the room.* *adjective* used in carrying goods. *The explorers used pack horses to carry their supplies.* {pak} packable, adj.
pack·age *noun* 1. an object or bundle that is packed, wrapped, or boxed; bundle. *I bought a package of cake mix at the store.* 2. a container used for storing or transporting something. *The post office had thousands of packages to deliver before Christmas.* *verb* (packaged, packaging, packages) to place in a container

🌲 Living World 🔬 Physical World 🏔 Natural Environment 〰 Economy 📖 Government and Law

Indexing Icons refer to advanced word search in the **Lexipedia Word Explorer**, beginning on page B48.

Derived Words identify words that can be formed from the entry word.

For a complete explanation of the various parts of an entry, see pages F8-F18 in the introduction.

Expanded definitions give detailed explanations.

Entry words in dark type feature syllable breaks.

Red italics identify parts of speech.

Blue parentheses identify inflections.

Example sentences show how a word is used.

Numbers feature the most frequently used meanings first.

Pronunciations appear in curly brackets.

Language Notes provide tips on the proper use of words.

Synonym Notes offer words that have meanings similar to the entry word.

Homophone Notes help you distinguish between words that sound alike.

Full-color illustrations

---

or in wrapping. *She packaged the gift in a red box.* {**păk** kihj}

pack·et *noun* a small bundle or parcel. *I bought her a packet of gum.* {**pak** iht}

pact *noun* 1. an agreement or a sworn promise. *We made a pact never to tell.* 2. a written agreement between or among countries; treaty. *The three countries signed a trade pact.* {**pakt**}

pad[1] ○ *noun* 1. a piece of soft material used as cushioning for protection or comfort. *Football players wear shoulder pads. I need a pad for this hard seat.* 2. a block of paper sheets glued together at one edge. *I bought a drawing pad.* 3. a cushion used for holding ink for rubber stamps. 4. a flat platform for landing or taking off. *The astronauts waited on the rocket pad.* 5. the small cushion of flesh on the bottom of the toes or feet of some animals. *verb* (padded, padding, pads) 1. to fill or protect by stuffing or to cover with soft material. *Grandmother padded her old chairs.* 2. to make longer or thicker by adding things that are not important. *She padded the report with useless information.* {**pad**}

pad·dle *noun* 1. a short oar with a wide blade. A paddle is used with both arms for moving a small boat through the water. 2. a similar, smaller device used to hit the ball in table tennis. *verb* (paddled, paddling, paddles) 1. to use a paddle to move a canoe. *We paddled down the river to our camp.* 2. to hit or spank with

a paddle or hand. *The boy cried when his father paddled him.* {**pad** əl}

paddle wheel *noun* a wheel that has boards or paddles fixed at right angles around it. A paddle wheel is used to move a river steamboat. {**pa** dəl weel}

pad·dock *noun* 1. a field surrounded by a fence, near a barn. Animals graze or exercise in a paddock. 2. an area near a race track where horses are kept before the race. {**pad** ək}

pad·dy *noun* (paddies) a flooded field for growing rice. {**pad** ee}

pad·lock *noun* a lock with a bar shaped like a U used to fasten doors, boxes, or cables. One end of the bar moves on a hinge. The other end of the bar is slipped through a ring before being snapped into the body of the lock. *verb* (padlocked, padlocking, padlocks) to fasten with a padlock. *Be sure to padlock your locker.* {**pad** lok}

pa·gan *noun* 1. a person who practices a religion that worships many gods. 2. a person outside of accepted Western religions; one who is not a Christian, Jew, or Muslim; heathen. {**pay** gən}

Word History *Pagan* comes from a Latin word that means "a villager." In later Latin it also meant "heathen." After Christianity became an established religion, those who continued to practice the old religions were usually from country villages.

page[1] *noun* one side of a sheet of printed or written paper. *verb* (paged, paging, pages) to turn pages (often fol-

---

... an area near a [...] track where horses are kept before the race. {**pad** ək}

pad·dy *noun* (paddies) a flooded field for growing rice. {**pad** ee}

pad·lock *noun* a lock with a bar shaped like a U used to fasten doors, boxes, or cables. One end of the bar moves on a hinge. The other end of the bar is slipped through a ring before being snapped into the body of the lock. *verb* (padlocked, padlocking, padlocks) to fasten with a padlock. *Be sure to padlock your locker.* {**pad** lok}

pa·gan *noun* 1. a person who practices a religion that worships many gods. 2. a person outside of accepted Western religions; one who is not a Christian, Jew, or Muslim; heathen. {**pay** gən}

Word History *Pagan* comes ... us at ... m a Latin word ...

page[2] *n* [...] who [...] pers [...] y[...]

i[...] S[...] p[...] a[...] p[...]

pag·eant *noun* a [...] tic show about events in history or legend. {**pa** jənt}

pa·go·da *noun* a religious temple of Asia that has curved roof lines at each of its many stories. {pɔ **goh** də}

paid *verb* past tense and past participle of pay. {**payd**}

pail *noun* 1. a container with steep sides and a handle; bucket. *The pail is old and rusty.* 2. an amount that will fill a pail. *How many pails of water do you need?* {**payl**}

Homophone Note Are you looking for the word *pale* (light in color)? *Pail* and *pale* sound alike but have different meanings.

pain ○ ① *noun* 1. physical hurt or discomfort t [...] caused by injur [...] Pain is the ner [...] way of telling t [...] something is w [...] helped to lessen [...] back. 2. hurt fe [...] or emotional s [...] sorrow. *Her mo[...] caused her great [...]* (plural) great c [...] *She took pains t[...]*

h
i
j
k
l
m
n
o
p
q
r
s
t

 Human Body

? Human Mind

 Everyday Life

History and Culture

Cor[...]

State-of-the-Art Graphics illustrate detailed features using contemporary photographs, drawings, and diagrams.

Insects

Insects make up the largest group of animals in the world. There are about a million different kinds of insects, and scientists find and identify more kinds every year.

wings
thorax
abdomen
head
compound eyes
antenna
mandibles (mouth parts)
legs

The monarch butterfly is a champion flyer. In the fall, large numbers of monarchs travel from Canada and the United States to Mexico. The monarchs mate and lay their eggs in Mexico. When the eggs hatch in the spring, the young butterflies journey north to Canada and the United States.

Some bees build nests called "hives". They make thousands of connected chambers out of wax where the queen lays her eggs. Each tiny chamber is in the shape of a six-sided hexagon. Some wasps build large nests out of paper. They make their own paper by chewing wood into pulp.

A female mosquito must feed on the blood of a mammal before her eggs can develop. The male sucks juice out of fruits. Mosquitos spread many serious diseases.

Most flies have only one pair of wings. They have mouth parts for sucking and piercing. Their larvae, called maggots, hatch in rotting meat or fruit.

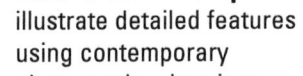 Grasshoppers have powerful back legs for jumping. Some grasshoppers can jump as far as two meters.

The praying mantis is a very large insect that eats other insects. Praying mantises have been known to eat small frogs. The praying mantis can turn its head. The female praying mantis eats the male after mating to provide nutrients for her developing eggs.

How to Use This Dictionary

What will you learn from your Dictionary? You will learn new words. You will learn what they mean, how to spell them, how to pronounce them, and how to use them. But that's only a small part of what there is to learn from a dictionary.

A dictionary is an important resource. Learning new words, with their meanings and histories, will help you learn more about the world. Being able to use the English language well will help you communicate better with people around the world.

The English language, with its wealth of words, is a wonderful tool for describing the world and for expressing thoughts and feelings. This dictionary will help you to experiment with and to explore unfamiliar words in your writing and speaking. When you learn new words, you feed your brain. You will become a better thinker and will be better able to convey your ideas clearly and effectively.

This dictionary is a snapshot of the English language as it is spoken in North America at the beginning of the twenty-first century. The vocabulary of English is like a treasure vault, a storehouse of riches that ordinary people have been adding to for over a thousand years.
To help you get at more of the treasure in this dictionary, we have provided a new word-finding tool, the Lexipedia Word Explorer. The word *lexipedia* combines the ancient Greek words *lex*, which means *word*, and *paideia*, which means *education*. This word was chosen because it emphasizes that discovering links between words is a powerful way to help you learn.

This dictionary contains many words and meanings. When you hear or read a new word, you can usually find its meaning by looking it up alphabetically in the dictionary. But what if you have an idea you want to express but don't know what word can be used for that meaning? The best thing to do is to find a group of words that are connected to your idea. Then you can explore their meanings until you find the best word. The Wordsmyth Lexipedia Word Explorer will help you in your search for the right word.

If you already know a word that is close to the idea you want to express, you can look it up in the Index of Keywords, which starts on page B52. There you may find some related words or meanings. If you don't know a word that is closely related to your idea, but you know the general topic you want to express, you can start with the Index of Topics. This section gives you some words you can start with in your exploration of related words. You can find out how to use the Index of Topics and the Index of Keywords by reading the "Guide to the Lexipedia Word Explorer," which starts on page B48. When you have learned to use all the parts of this dictionary, you will be rewarded with the keys to the storehouse of treasure that is English.

1. How to Look Up Words

a) Looking Up Words Alphabetically

From **aardvark** to **zucchini,** every entry in this dictionary has been put into alphabetical, or ABC, order. The alphabet song you learned in kindergarten is going to be useful. Believe it or not, it will help you for the rest of your life, whether you are ordering a pizza from the phone book or programming computers for NASA.

Looking up a word in the dictionary, however, is not as simple as just knowing the alphabet. There are over twelve thousand entry words in this dictionary, and only twenty-six letters in the alphabet. There are hundreds of words that start with the same letter. When there are fifty pages of words that begin with *a,* how do you begin to find the word **alligator**?

So that you can locate a particular word, this dictionary alphabetizes not only by the first letter, but by the whole word. **Alligator** and **apple** both start with the letter *a,* but the entry for **alligator** comes before the entry for **apple** because the second letter of alligator, *l,* comes before the second letter of apple, *p.* Often, even the second letter of two different words will be exactly the same, and you must then look at the third letter, and sometimes the fourth, fifth, and sixth. Can you tell which letter makes **antecedent** come before **antelope**?

alligator
apple
atom

antecedent
antelope
antenna

b) Using the Alphabet Strip and Guide Words

Let's try looking up **marvel**, a word for what you'll become once you've mastered your word-finding skills. The first letter of **marvel** is *m-,* so turn to the **M** section of the dictionary. An easy way of finding a letter is to use the *thumb-index tabs,* on the column of letters from **A** to **Z** along the side of each page. Find **M** on this column, hold your finger to the side of the page where **M** is, and close the book. Now see where your finger is on the edge of the closed pages and move it up or down within the lines where **M** was until you're touching the colored mark. Open the book where this colored mark is and you will be in the M section of the dictionary.

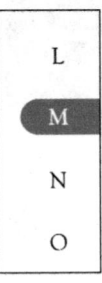

L
M
N
O

marshmallow – mason

Now that you are in the **M**'s, you need to get closer to the word you are trying to find. You do this by using the *guide words*. Guide words are the two words in the blue banner at the top of each page. They tell you the first and last entry word on each page. You will know you're on the right page when the word you are looking for comes after the first guide word and before the second guide word. To get to **marvel**, first find a page with **ma-** on it. There are fourteen pages of words that begin with **ma-**. Keep turning the pages, looking at the first three letters of the guidewords, until you find words that begin with **mar-** (**manuscript – maritime**). Now leaf through the pages, looking at the first four letters of each guideword. **Marvel** comes between the guide words **marshmallow** and **mason.** When you have found the page, start at the top of the first column and use your alphabetical skills to find out what you've become.

c) When Different Words Have the Same Spelling

*She shed a **tear** over the **tear** in her dress*

Occasionally you will need more than alphabetical order to find the word you are looking for. Sometimes two words have exactly the same spelling, even though they mean different things. These words are called homographs. In this dictionary, homographs always appear one after the other because they are in the same place alphabetically. You can tell them apart by the small raised number next to each of them: tear1 is a drop of salty liquid that falls from the eye, and tear2 means "to rip." When you look up a word and see that it is a homograph, read the definitions carefully to see which one fits the meaning you are looking for.

tear[1] 🔊 *noun* 1. a drop of salty liquid that comes from the eye. Tears clean the eye and keep it wet. 2. (plural) the expression of feeling through crying. *I could tell by her tears that she was glad to see me again.* {teer}
• **in tears**
crying. *He was in tears over the death of his pet.*

tear[2] *verb* (tore, torn, tearing, tears) 1. to pull apart or into pieces. *She tore the old clothes into rags.* 2. to cause or make by ripping. *He tore a hole in the knee of his pants.* 3. to disturb. *His life was torn by bad*

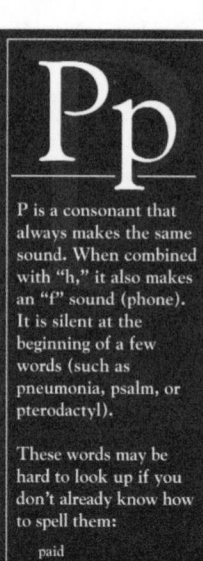

P is a consonant that always makes the same sound. When combined with "h," it also makes an "f" sound (phone). It is silent at the beginning of a few words (such as pneumonia, psalm, or pterodactyl).

These words may be hard to look up if you don't already know how to spell them:

paid
pamphlet
parallel
pastime
phenomenon
prophet
psychology
pursue

d) How to look up words you don't know how to spell

Sometimes there will be words you want to look up but aren't sure how to spell. English spelling is famous for being confusing. Its words are not always spelled the way they sound. You may hear the word "kwire" and want to look it up under *K* or *Q*, instead of *C* (for "choir"). The English alphabet has twenty-six letters and more than forty sounds, which means one letter can have several sounds. The letter c, for example, can have the "s", "k", or "sh" sound, as in "circle," "cottage," and "delicious." English also has silent letters, as in "bite," "doubt," "could," and "friend."

To help you look up words that you don't know how to spell, this dictionary provides a *Sound and Spelling Guide* on pages F28-F29 and *Look-Up Tips* at the beginning of each letter.

2. How to Read an Entry

a) Entry Word

When you have successfully looked up a word in the dictionary, you will be at the *entry word*. The pages in the A to Z section are divided into three columns. Entry words are printed in **bold** type along the left-hand side of each column. They hang over the column to make them more visible as you scan the page. The entry word combined with the information that follows is called an *entry*.

• Kinds of Entry Words

Most entry words are single words, such as **clever** and **barricade.** Some entry words are actually two or more words that have a particular meaning when used together: **horned lizard, primary color** or **cross reference.** A "beautiful lizard" is not a dictionary entry. A "horned lizard" is, because it is a species of lizard with this distinctive characteristic. These two-word and three-word entries are called *compound entries*. Compound entries are alphabetized in the same way as single-word entries.

Some entry words begin with a capital letter. These include geographical place names, such as cities, countries, states and provinces, rivers, and oceans; names of Greek and Roman mythological characters; and stars and constellations. These words begin with a capital letter because they are *proper nouns*. Words that name people, places, or things are called nouns. Words that are the name of one particular person, place, or thing are a special set of nouns called proper nouns. If you don't find a geographical name in the A to Z dictionary, you may find what you want in the **Reference Section** at the back of the book. All the world's nations and their capital cities are listed there, as well as states and provinces. The maps in the mini-atlas provide even more information.

• Information in the Entry Word

The entry word itself gives you information you need for writing the word correctly. It may begin with a capital letter (**Jamaica**), have a short hyphen (-) in the middle (**old-fashioned**), or an apostrophe (**Hallowe'en, it's**).

• Alternate Spellings

Sometimes there are two or three correct ways to spell the same word. For example, **bologna** (the sandwich meat) can be spelled into other ways. Alternate spellings are given after the entry word, such as: **bologna** or **boloney** or **baloney**. The first spelling given is the most common.

pa·go·da
of Asi
curved
lines a
its ma
stories
{pɔ **goł**
də}

paid *verb*
past te
ciple c

pail *noun*
steep s
bucket

b) Syllables

Most entry words can be broken into smaller sections according to where the different vowel sounds come, like this: dic-tion-ar-y. These sections are called syllables. Some words, like **stop**, have only one syllable. Others, like **autobiography**, have many: au-to-bi-o-graph-y. At times when you are writing, you will run out of space on a line before the end of a word. One way of dealing with this is to insert a hyphen (-) in the word and write the last part of the word on the next line. It is important to remember, however, that this hyphen may only go between syllables. To help you know where to break a word into syllables, your dictionary has small bullets (•) between each syllable of an entry word.

c) Part of Speech Labels: The Roles Words Play

The first piece of information you will find in an entry after the entry word and any alternate spellings is a part of speech label in *red italic type*. The part of speech label tells you the role that the word performs in a sentence. Let's look at the roles of each word in the following sentence:

> *The hungry cat begged loudly for food.*

- **cat** and **food** are nouns because they name things.
- **begged** is a verb because it shows an action.
- **hungry** is an adjective because it describes a noun (cat).
- **loudly** is an adverb because it describes a verb (begged).
- **for** is a preposition because it shows a connection between begged and food.

Most of the words in this dictionary are nouns, verbs, adjectives, adverbs, or prepositions. There are six other parts of speech. A complete list of the eleven parts of speech found in this dictionary appears below. If you look up **food**, **beg**, and **hungry** in this dictionary, you will find that each of these entry words only has one part of speech. **Food** must be used as a noun, **beg** as a verb, and **hungry** as an adjective. Otherwise, your writing will not make sense: The food cat hungried loudly for beg. Some words, however, do have more than one part of speech and can play different roles in a sentence. For example, the word **trick** can be a noun, verb, or adjective:

> noun—They played a mean **trick** on me.
> verb—They **tricked** him into going with them.
> adjective— They gave her a **trick** deck of cards.

In the entry for words like **trick** that have more than one part of speech, the definitions are grouped by part of speech. Each group of definitions starts with a red part of speech label. For example, if the first part of speech is a noun, the first thing you see after the entry word is the word "noun" in red italics. All the noun definitions for the entry word **trick** follow. After this, the second part of speech label appears in red italics, followed by all of its definitions, and so on.

This dictionary usually lists the most common part of speech of an entry word first. If you look up the entry for **sand**, for example, the noun definitions come before the verb definitions. The use of "sand" to mean the grains you find on a beach is more common than the verb "to sand," to smooth wood with sandpaper. The further down the entry you go, the more you will learn about a word, even a word you thought you knew.

trick *noun* 1. something done to fool or cheat someone. *His lie was a trick to get my money.* 2. a joke or prank. *My brother has played many tricks on me.* 3. an act of skill or magic. *He taught his monkey a new trick. / The gymnast did tricks on the high bar. adjective* 1. of or marked by deception or skill. *The football team used a trick play to score the goal.* 2. made for use in tricks. *The magician had a trick deck of cards. verb* (tricked, tricking, tricks) to cheat or fool someone. *They tricked me into paying twice what this dress is worth.* {trihk}

Parts of Speech in Your Wordsmyth Dictionary:

noun: a word that names a person, place, thing, or condition.

verb: a word that expresses a state of being or an action.

adjective: a word that describes or modifies a noun or pronoun.

adverb: a word that describes or modifies a verb, adjective, or other adverb.

preposition: a word that shows a connection or relation between a noun or pronoun and some other word.

interjection: a word or expression that shows strong feeling or exclamation.

conjunction: a word that connects other words, phrases, clauses, or sentences.

pronoun: a word that can take the place of a noun or noun phrase.

auxiliary verb: a verb used with other verbs to express certain tenses, aspects, or moods.

definite article: the article "the" in English grammar.

indefinite article: either of the articles "a" or "an" in English grammar.

d) Inflections: The Different Forms of Words

Following the part of speech label, there will often be words in parentheses in blue type: these are the inflected forms, or *inflections*, of the entry word. An inflection is a form of a word that is different from the simplest spelling of a word. You already know how to inflect words. The words "tables," "turned," and "faster" are inflected forms of "table," "turn," and "fast." We inflect a word (or change its form) when we want to show that there is more than one thing or person ("table" becomes "tables"), that an action happened in the past ("turn" becomes "turned), or that a quality described in an adjective is greater or more or most ("fast" becomes "faster" or "fastest"). This dictionary gives inflected forms for some nouns, some adjectives, some adverbs, and all verbs.

Noun Inflections

Most nouns can be made plural by adding "-s" or "-es" to the base word: "cat" becomes "cats", "dish" becomes "dishes" and "switch" becomes "switches."

Some words are *irregular* (not regular) *nouns* that do not follow this pattern. With irregular nouns, the spelling of the base word changes to form the plural. For example, in nouns that end in *y* ("sky," "penny," "factory"), the *y* changes to an *i* before the plural "–es" ending is added ("skies," "pennies," "factories"). Some irregular plurals follow no pattern at all. For example, the plural of "mouse" is "mice." The plural of "deer" is "deer."

pad·dy *noun* (paddies)

These irregular plurals are the ones you are most likely to need help with in spelling. This dictionary gives the plural form of nouns only when the plural does not follow the pattern of simply adding "-es" or "-es" to the base word. These plural forms appear in blue type after the part of speech label. If there is no plural inflection listed for a noun, it is regular and forms the plural by adding –s or -es to the base word.

Verb Inflections

Most English verbs change their form to show when the action takes place. The past can be shown by using the *past tense* form. This form is usually made by adding "-ed" to the base word: "he planted the garden." If a verb already ends in "e," then you need only add a "-d" to form the past. For example the past tense of taste is "tasted."

Sometimes you will want to use a helping verb to talk about an action that was completed in the past. This kind of sentence requires the *past participle* form of a verb, which is usually the same as the past tense: "He has planted the garden."

You may also want to use a helping verb to talk about an action happening in the present to show that it continues to happen. This is done by using the *present participle* verb form: "He is planting the garden." It is usually formed by adding "-ing" to the base word.

And when you want to talk about an action that happens in the present and is done by "he" "she" or "it" you must use the *third person singular present tense* form. This is formed by adding "-s" or "-es" to the base word: "He plants the garden."

grow *verb* (grew, grown, growing, grows)

This dictionary always lists the past tense, the present participle, and the third person singular present tense forms of all verbs. For example, in the entry for **walk**, the entry word is followed by the part of speech label and then these inflections, in parentheses: "walked, walking, walks."
The past participle form is also listed when it differs the past tense form, as is often the case with *irregular verbs*. Irregular verbs are those that require a different spelling of the base word to form any of the above inflections. For example, past tense of "grow" is not "growed" but "grew, " "The garden grew." The past participle of "grow" is "grown," "the garden has grown." In the entry for **grow**, the entry word and part of speech will be followed by these inflections in parentheses: "grew, grown, growing, grows."

Adjective and Adverb Inflections:

Adjectives and adverbs can show degree by using the *comparative* or *superlative* forms. This dictionary lists the comparative and superlative forms of adjectives and adverbs.

The *comparative form* is used to show that the quality being described by an adjective or adverb is greater or more. It is usually formed by adding "-er" to the base word. For example, you may be tall, but your father is taller (more tall); he may run fast, but she can run faster (more fast).

The *superlative form* is used to show that the quality being described by an adjective or adverb is greatest or most. It is usually formed by adding "-est" to the base word. For example, you may be smart, but he is the smartest (most smart); she may walk slower than you, but he walks the slowest (most slow).

Sometimes the spelling of the base word will change when you add "-er" or "-est." "Glad" becomes "gladder" and "gladdest"; "happy" becomes "happier" and "happiest."

Many inflections of adjectives and adverbs are irregular, and cannot form the comparative and superlatives simply by adding "-er" or "-est" to the base word. For example, you may be good, but they are better, and she is the best.

Often adjectives and adverbs with more than one syllable do not change form to show comparative or superlative. They require the words more or most to show degree: I am intelligent, but you are more intelligent, and your mother is the most intelligent person I know. If there are no inflections following the entry word for an adjective or adverb, the comparative is formed by using "more" and the superlative by using "most."

e) Definitions

Most of the time, you will use your dictionary to find definitions of words. A definition is a short description of the meaning of a word. The definition appears after the entry word, the part of speech, and any inflections.

Many of the words in this dictionary have more than one definition. Where there is more than one definition, the definitions are numbered. If the entry word has more than one part of speech, the numbers start at 1 for each part of speech.

The definitions within a part of speech are ordered in two ways. First, the more common and familiar meanings come first. Second, definitions of an entry word that are close in meaning usually come one after the other.

Take a look at the definitions for **tongue**. Definition 1 is probably the first meaning you think of when you hear the word "tongue." Definition 2, the tongue from an animal eaten as a food, is probably not what you first think of, but it is closely related to definition 1: both refer to the organ of taste in an animal's mouth. Definitions 3, 4, and 5 are less familiar meanings of "tongue." They are closely related to each other, in that all three have to do with speech and language. Definition 5 is the least common meaning of "tongue."

Expanded Definitions

Some of the definitions in this dictionary have a defining phrase followed by one or more longer sentences. These are called *expanded definitions*. The first part of the definition gives a quick definition of the entry word. Let's look at the definition for **armadillo**. We know right away that an armadillo is a mammal and that it has hard protective plates on its body just by reading the first defining phrase. But there are also three additional sentences that answer such questions as, Where does the armadillo live? How large does it get? What does it eat? You will find extended definitions for all the animals, as well as for entries that are not so easy to understand, such as **artificial intelligence.**

---

good *adjective* (better, best)

---

tongue 😊 😊 *noun* 1. the movable organ in the bottom of the mouth, used for licking, tasting, swallowing, and human speech. 2. this organ taken from a cow, ox, or other animal and used as food. 3. power or manner of speaking. *She spoke with a sharp tongue*. 4. the language or speech of a particular area. *She spoke in a foreign tongue*. 5. a flap of leather under the laces of a shoe or boot. {tuhng}

---

ar·ma·dil·lo *noun* (armadillos) a mammal whose body is protected by hard, bony plates. Armadillos live in Central and South America, and the southern United States. Some kinds of armadillos are only six inches long; other kinds grow up to four feet in length. They eat mostly insects and are related to sloths and anteaters. {ar mə dih loh}

man-of-war *noun* (men-of-war) 1. an old word for **war-ship**. 2. see **Portuguese man-of-war**. {<u>man</u> əv <u>wohr</u>}

Entry Word References: You will sometimes find a definition that refers you to another entry word for more information. Whenever you see a word in a definition printed in **bold**, this means you will get a fuller definition if you look up that word.

f) Example Sentences and Usage Notes

Knowing how to use a word in a sentence is as important as knowing how to define the word. Two features of this dictionary that show you how and when to use a particular word are the *example sentences* and the *usage notes*.

One of the most effective ways of learning the meaning of a word is to see or hear it used in *context*. Context is the language that appears around a word when it is used in a sentence. Many of the definitions in this dictionary are followed by an example sentence that shows how the word is used. Example sentences are useful whether you are using the dictionary to look up a word you have read or using it to look up a word you want to use in your own writing. An example sentence can help you better understand a hard definition. It can also show you how a word is typically used in a sentence. And finally, the example sentences can help you see the differences between closely related meanings.

In this dictionary, example sentences appear just after a definition in italic print. Two example sentences are given when the same meaning has a wider range of use than can be illustrated in one sentence. In the first definition of **short**, for example, which is "having little length; not long," there are two example sentences: *Her arms are too short to reach the steering wheel. / The book was short enough to read in one day.* Because the definition includes both a small amount of time and a small distance, two example sentences are given to show both uses of the word.

Usage notes are found in the definitions themselves. They appear in parentheses either between the definition number and the definition, or just after the definition. Usage notes provide specific information about how to use the word properly—when it is correct to capitalize "president" and "god," which prepositions can follow a verb, and when a noun must be plural. The example sentence following a definition with a usage note shows you what the usage note means.

The definition for **split**, verb 5, is "to divide into parts (often followed by "up")." The example sentence shows you what the usage note means: *Let's split up the pie.*

The definition for **stand**, noun 8, is "(plural) the seats at a playing field or stadium." The example sentence again illustrates the usage note: *Someone in the stands caught the baseball.*
When a usage note labels a definition as "informal," it suggests the kinds of situations in which it is appropriate to use the word. "Informal" language generally is not used in school essays, research papers, newspaper articles, or other kinds of formal writing.

beef *noun* (beeves) 1. *meat from a cow or steer. 2. (informal) a complaint. *Jack has a beef with Jill because she won't help him with chores.* {<u>beef</u>}

You probably would not read on the front page of the New York Times that the senator has a "beef" with the president; more likely the word "complaint" would be used. This sense of "beef" is marked as "informal."

It is important to remember that usage notes apply only to the definition they appear in.

g) Pronunciation

Do you know how to say the word "heir"? It may seem like it should begin with an "h" sound and have an "ee" sound in the middle, like "hear." Actually, the correct pronunciation of the word "heir" is exactly the same as the word "air."

Pronunciation is the way a word sounds when it is spoken. If English is your native language, you are already an expert in guessing pronunciation of new words. Once you know how to say "sail," you can probably figure out how to say "nail" and "bail," even if you don't know what the word means. On the other hand, if you come across the sentence "The white sow had piglets" while reading a story about a pig farm, you might know that "sow" means "female pig," but still not know whether it rhymes with "cow" or "low."

Sometimes it is difficult to figure out how a word is supposed to sound just by looking at its spelling. To help you with this, each entry in this dictionary gives a *pronunciation guide* for the entry word. The pronunciation guide appears in curly brackets after all the definitions and example sentences. The pronunciation guide appears near the end of the entry, in brackets, like this: **{nayl}.**

The pronunciation guide uses a special spelling system that is like a code for the sounds of the English language. For the key to this code, turn to the **Pronunciation Key** on page F28. The pronunciation guides also tell you which parts of the word are stressed.

Syllables and Stress in the Pronunciation Guides

In the pronunciation guides for words with more than one syllable, the syllables are separated by a space: {rih **layt**}.

Words with more than one syllable are often pronounced with greater stress on one syllable than on others. For example, in the word **meaning,** you give more stress to the first syllable, pronounced "mee-" than you give to "-ning."

The pronunciation guide for meaning looks like this: {**mee** ning}.
In words with more than one syllable:

- the syllable with the greatest stress is shown in **bold underlined** type.
- the syllable with secondary stress is in **bold** type, with no underline.
- syllables with no stress are shown in plain type.

Example: In the entry for **authentic,** you will see this at the end of the entry: {**aw thehn** tihk}

"Authentic" has three syllables. The second syllable is pronounced with the most stress, and is in bold underline. The first syllable is bold because it has some stress, but not as much as the second. The third syllable is in plain type and is pronounced with no stress.

In some entries, the pronunciation guide will have different syllable breaks than the entry word. This is because the rules for breaking up words into syllables in writing are supposed to make sure we can read the word easily when it is broken by a line end. Sound syllables show the way we actually say words.

Example: **cloth.ing** {kloh thing}

More than One Pronunciation

An entry word may have more than one pronunciation. Sometimes this is because people pronounce the word differently in different parts of the country. Sometimes this is because the word can be used as more than one part of speech: many words that can be used as nouns or verbs change their stress when their part of speech changes. Note that parts of speech in the example at right are abbreviated inside the curly brackets.

h) Derived Words

At the very end of an entry, after the pronunciation guide, you may find one or more additional words. These are words made up of the entry word plus an ending, or suffix. At the end of the entry for **smooth,** for example, the words "smoothly" and "smoothness" appear. Adding the ending to the entry word often changes the part of speech. Adding "ly" to an adjective is a way of turning it into an adverb. Each derived word is followed by a label that shows you its part of speech. The label is an abbreviation or short form: n. (noun), v. (verb), adj. (adjective), adv. (adverb).

---

garage to be built. {**kon** trakt, n., kən **trakt**, v.} contractible, adj.

---

make even or smooth. *He smoothed the wood with sandpaper.* 2. to remove difficulty or trouble. *The teacher smoothed our first day at school by showing us around.* {**smoohth**} smoothly, adv., smoothness, n.

air ✈ 🌀 🔥 💧 *noun* 1. the mixture of gases that surrounds the earth. Air is made up of oxygen, nitrogen, and other gases, and has no taste, odor, or color. 2. all that is above the ground; sky. *The kite flew high up in the air.* 3. movement of the atmosphere; breeze or wind. *We enjoyed the cool air coming in through the window.* 4. the way a thing or person appears to be. *The magician had an air of mystery. verb* (aired, airing, airs) 1. to open to the air or put outdoors. *We aired out the house on the first warm day.* 2. to speak about, usually in public. *He aired his problems.* {ayr}

• **into thin air**
out of sight. *She vanished into thin air.*

• **on [or] off the air**
broadcast on radio or television; not broadcast on radio or television. *The show was on the air last year. / Her favorite program went off the air because not many other people liked it.*

• **up in the air**
not decided, not settled, or not certain. *Our vacation plans are up in the air.*

ASPCA *abbreviation* a national organization whose purpose is to take care of lost or stray dogs, cats, and other small animals. This organization tries to find people to adopt these animals as pets. ASPCA is an abbreviation for "American Society for the Prevention of Cruelty to Animals."

---

ru·mour *noun or transitive verb* a spelling of **rumor** used in Canada and Britain. See **rumor.** {rooh mər}

---

i) Phrases

Sometimes the entry word you are looking for will actually be two or more words that have a special meaning beyond the meanings of the individual words together, such as **into thin air**. What does it mean for someone to vanish into thin air? Does it mean they really turn into air? Is the air really thin? These things are possible, but what people usually mean when they say "into thin air" is "out of sight." These words together as a phrase have taken on the meaning "out of sight." There are many such phrases in our language. **Go back on, take advantage of, and blow one's top** are a few entry words that are phrases. Find out what they mean by looking up the important word in each phrase.

Finding Phrases

To find a phrase in your dictionary, look under the entry for the most important word of that phrase. For example, to find the phrase "into thin air," you would look under the entry word **air.** "Into thin air" is printed in **bold** type with a small bullet before it as part of the entry for "air."

j) Special Entries

• **Abbreviations:** An *abbreviation* is a shortened form of a word or phrase used in writing. Abbreviations are useful when you want to save space in writing or speak quickly about a long name or group of words. There are two main kinds of abbreviations in this dictionary.

The first kind of abbreviation can be formed by shortening the letters of a single word and placing a period at the end. The letters used in such an abbreviation may be the first letters of a word as in **cont.** for "continue," the first letter of each part of a compound word as in **cm.** for "centimeter," or simply letters that seem to represent the sounds of a word as in **Mr.** for "Mister."

Tip: The definitions of this first kind of abbreviation include the entry word in bold type. Look up these words for more detailed information.

The second kind of abbreviation is formed by taking the first letter of each important word in a phrase, as in **ASPCA** for "American Society for the Prevention of Cruelty to Animals." Notice how the prepositions and articles of this phrase have not been included in the abbreviation. Often the letters of this kind of abbreviation will spell a new word themselves, as in **NASA** for "National Aeronautics and Space Administration." This is called an *acronym.* Acronyms are pronounced as spelled-out words.

Because abbreviations often represent words that are more than one part of speech, as in **SOS** for "save our ship," the word abbreviation has been printed in place of the part of speech label.

• **Contractions:** "Don't" and "he'll" are contractions. A contraction combines two words that are commonly used together and shortens the result by putting an apostrophe in the place of one or more of the letters. In "don't," an apostrophe takes the place of the letter o in the word "not." In "he'll," the apostrophe takes the place of the letters wi in "will." Some contractions can represent two combinations of words depending on their context. For example, the contraction "he'd" can mean either "he had" or "he would."

Because contractions also often represent words that are different parts of speech, the word *contraction* appears in place of the part of speech label.

• **Canadian Spellings:** Often there are differences between the way words are spelled in American English and Canadian English. **Rumor** in American English is spelled **rumour** in Canadian English. Canadian spellings appear as entry words in this dictionary. The definition does not give the meaning of the word, however. It tells you to look up the American spelling of the word for more detailed information.

• **Prefixes and Suffixes:** *Prefixes* and *suffixes* are word parts, not words. They have their own meanings. They are added to other words to make longer words that have different meanings. Many entry words in this dictionary have prefixes and suffixes. There are also entries for the prefixes and suffixes themselves.

•When the entry word is a prefix, it ends in a hyphen, as in **anti-** and **pre-,** to show that it cannot be used on its own. A prefix goes at the beginning of a word. The prefix "re-," meaning "again" or "anew" goes at the beginning of the word "write" to form "rewrite" (to write again).

When the entry word is a suffix, it begins with a hyphen, as in **–ness** and **-ability,** to show that it cannot be used on its own. A suffix goes at the end of a word. The suffix "-ness," meaning "condition" can be used to turn an adjective into a noun. "Happy" becomes "happiness."

Because prefixes and suffixes have no part of speech by themselves, the words prefix or suffix appear in place of the part of speech label.

3) Special Features

a) Lexipedia Word Explorer Icons

Occasionally, there will be an icon (a small picture) after an entry word. These icons are part of the **Word Explorer.** You will notice that the various icons appear at the bottom of every page in the dictionary. Each icon has a topic listed next to it. These topics refer you to the Index of Topics, the first part of the Word Explorer in the back of your book. When you see an icon next to an entry word, it means that this entry word is also a keyword in the **Index of Topics.** Let's see what we can learn about the entry word **car** using the **Word Explorer.**

Index of Topics

Look at the small icon next to the entry word **car,** and check the icon key at the bottom of the page. You will see that this icon stands for *everyday life.* You can now go to the *everyday life* section of your **Index of Topics** on page 50, where you will see a box with keywords that are related to **car.** Words like *airplane, boat, building,* and *city* are related to **car,** because they all fall under the topic *everyday life.* You can use this topic index when you want to brainstorm to find words that help you write about a certain topic. But the words in these boxes are also *keywords* that can be used to find further information in the **Index of Keywords,** the second part of your **Word Explorer.**

Index of Keywords

Perhaps, rather than find words that are related to the entry word **car,** you want to find words that tell you more *about* **car.** What are some kinds of cars? What are the parts of a car? Who uses a car? You can find answers to these questions in the **Index of Keywords.** The keywords in this index are arranged in alphabetical order in the same way entry words are arranged in the A through Z section of the dictionary. But instead of finding entries under the keywords, you will find phrases that organize information about the keyword. For example, under the keyword **car** the first phrase you will find is "Broader categories that include cars." Under this phrase you will find the words "transportation" and "vehicle." Under the next phrase, "Some kinds of cars," you will find *cab, compact, convertible, hatchback, racer, sedan,* and *taxicab.* Use this **Index of Keywords** when you want to find detailed information about a particular keyword.

For directions on how to use these two Indexes, go to the complete introduction to the **Lexipedia Word Explorer,** found in the back section of this book on pages B48-B49.

---

re- *prefix* 1. a prefix that means "again" or "anew." *To rewrite a paper is to write it again.* 2. a prefix that means "back" or "backwards." *To repay a debt is to pay back the debt.*

-ness *suffix* a suffix that means "condition." *When you are happy, you have a feeling of happiness.*

car ◐ *noun* 1. an automobile.

b) Synonym Notes

The English language has more words than any other language. This means that we have many words to choose from when we want to express a particular meaning. If we want to say that something is beautiful, we can say that it is fair, lovely, exquisite or even gorgeous. Words that mean the same thing are called synonyms. Synonyms can be found in three different places in this dictionary:

• **In definitions**: Your dictionary often uses synonyms in definitions to help you understand the meaning of entry words. These appear either as single word definitions, or as single words separated from the main definition by a semicolon (;). The definition for **calamity** is an example of this: "an event causing great harm, pain, or destruction; disaster." Perhaps you've never heard the word calamity before, but you know that disaster means "a sudden event causing much damage or suffering." If you know that calamity and disaster are synonyms, you will have a better idea of what calamity means, because you know that synonyms are two words that mean the same thing.

• **Synonym Notes:** Synonyms can also be useful when you are writing and find yourself using the same word over and over. It may sound dull to say, "I did my homework, did my exercises, and did my babysitting duties." It's more interesting and may be more precise to say "I completed my homework, performed my exercises, and fulfilled my babysitting duties." Synonyms help to add variety to your writing, which can keep both you and your reader interested in what you have to say. What's more, by considering other ways of saying what you have to say, your writing will end up being more precise. You will find out exactly what it is you want to say. The synonym boxes that follow some entries in this dictionary show you some of the choices you have when you write. When you look at a synonym box, notice that you are first told which which definition in the entry has these synonyms. The different meanings and the different parts of speech of a word may have different synonyms.

• **Extended Synonym Notes:** To help you learn about the different shades of meaning among synonyms and how they can be used, there are some extended synonym notes. Like the shorter synonym notes, these list synonyms for a particular definition in the entry above. But in these notes, each each synonym is also followed by a short explanation of how the synonym is used and then an example sentence in italics. Note: An easy way to find synonym notes quickly is to use your index in the back of the book.

c) Language Notes

The language notes alert you to common mistakes that writers and speakers make in the usage of particular words. For example, do you know when it is proper to use "among" and when it is proper to use "between"? Look at the language note on the page near the entry word to learn the answer.

d) Homophone Notes

The English language has many homophones because the vocabulary of English came from several different languages, each with its own ways of spelling a certain sound. Homophones can be fun. They can also be confusing when you try to look up a word based on its sound. You may end up at the wrong word. Let's say you are trying to find **eight** (the number), but you accidentally look up **ate** (the past tense of "eat"). This dictionary gives the homophones of entry words in a box at the end of the entry. After the entry for **ate**, the homophone note lets you know that there is a different spelling and meaning for a word with this sound.

e) Word Histories

Did you know that "accident" comes from a Latin word that means "to fall on?" Or that "stink" has not always meant a bad smell? The words we use did not come out of nowhere. Every word has a history of when it came into use in English and how its form and meaning have changed over time. The word histories that accompany many entries in this dictionary provide information about some of the more interesting word origins. When a word from a language other than modern English is used, it is in italic type. Take some time to look at the odd, old words in italics; their forms and their meanings are both like and unlike those of the modern English words.

A History of the English Language

This is the story of how English grew. How did the language of a few thousand people living on a small island become an international language, spoken by millions of people on every continent of the globe?

1. Celtic and Roman Britain

Let us begin our journey towards the present by traveling back in time more than two thousand years. We come to a large green island in northern Europe. People have been living here for hundreds of years. They live in villages and are mainly farmers. They have a rich tradition of storytelling and poetry. Their religion is based on reverence for Mother Earth, and they worship in sacred groves of oak and ash trees. Bards, traveling storytellers, wander from village to village, bringing news and reciting stories to the people. Their history, both distant and recent, is carried on only by word of mouth, for they have no written language. They do not read or write. There are no books and no paper. These ancient people were the Celts, and the large green island was Britain. Without a written language, how do we know about this ancient folk? The answer comes from across the water that separated their island from the mainland of Europe. It comes from people who were excellent writers, especially when writing about their own heroic deeds, the ancient Romans.

Over two thousand years ago, in 55 B.C.E., Julius Caesar made his first attempt to invade Britannia, the island we know as "Britain." Julius Caesar had recently invaded and conquered Gaul, the Roman name for France. Britannia was only about twenty miles across the water from Gaul, and it seemed a likely prize for the ambitious Romans. But Caesar's small army was no match for the fierce resistance of the British. And so the Romans left Britannia alone for about one hundred years. Then, in C.E. 43, Emperor Claudius sent a much larger invasion force to Britain. Within seven years, the Romans were firmly in control of Britannia. For the next few hundred years, the Romans kept their control of Britain. The Celtic tribes that had shown the most resistance to Roman rule were pushed farther and farther to the north and west of Britain, where their descendants, the Welsh and the Scottish, remain to this day. Many Celts moved off the island, west across the sea to Ireland.

The Celts who remained under Roman rule were slow to adapt to Roman ways. The Romans built houses of stone, while the Celts of Britain, or Britons, had lived in cottages of sticks, mud, and grass. The Romans had hot and cold running water and indoor plumbing. They had a sophisticated system of writing. In fact, the alphabet that we use today is the alphabet of the ancient Romans. Many Britons became part of the Roman government, and a few learned to read and write in the language of the Romans, Latin. The Romans brought with them a new religion, Christianity. But the words of the Roman church were Latin, strange to most of the Britons. Even after hundreds of years, most of the Britons kept their old language and their old ways.

By 410, three-and-a-half centuries after their conquest of Britain, the Romans were gone. They had been called back from Britain to defend their homeland from attacks by the Germanic tribes sweeping across Europe. Despite the later influence Latin was to have on the English language, the Romans left few traces in Britain aside from their great stone buildings. The Latin language did live on in many place names. The forts and outposts they built, which eventually became large towns and cities, have kept parts of their Latin names to this day. The Latin word for "encampment" was *castra*.

This word lives on in the many British place names that end in "-chester" or "-caster," such as Winchester and Lancaster. But the Roman tradition of reading and writing faded into the darkness.

2. The Dark Ages: Old English

Now, you might think that with the Romans gone, the Britons could finally live in peace. This was not to be. Without strong government, the Britons began to fight among themselves. Tribal chiefs tried to become powerful kings who ruled over larger and larger areas. One such person was Vortigern. It is said that he was so greedy for power, he invited two warlords from across the North Sea, Hengist and Horsa, to help him take over more of Britain. Hengist and Horsa arrived around 428 with their men from what is now Holland and northern Germany. To say that this plan backfired is an understatement. By 450, a full-scale invasion of Britain from northern Europe was underway. The invaders were from three main groups of Germanic people, the Angles, the Saxons, and the Jutes—the "Anglo-Saxons." After these invaders won territory in Britain, thousands of Anglo-Saxons began moving across the North Sea to Britain. Although the invasion was stopped for some years by the efforts of Britons united under Arthur Pendragon, or "King Arthur," the Anglo-Saxons finally proved unstoppable. By around 550, they were in control of most of the island. From this time, we can call the language of the Anglo-Saxons "Old English" and their country "England."

The Anglo-Saxons brought with them from Europe an ancient form of writing called the "futhorc" after its first six letters, or runes. Names and short sayings were carved into stone and wood in runes. Here are a few lines from *The Anglo-Saxon Rune Poem*. It is an alphabet poem, like "A is for Apple, B is for Banana," in Old English.

> *Thorn byth thearle scearp.* . . (Thorn is very sharp)
> *Haegl byth hwitust corna.* . . (Hail is the whitest corn)
> *Is byth oferceald.* . . (Ice is very cold)
> *Aesc byth oferheah.* . .(Ash tree is very high)

Although there were no books in runes, the Old English language flourished in its spoken form. People carried on their traditions of retelling old stories of great heroes, gods, and goddesses in rhythmic verse. The names of a few Anglo-Saxon gods and goddesses live on in some of our names for the days of the week. In fact, most of the words in the English of today have been with us from the time of the Anglo-Saxons. Most of the words in this sentence go back to Old English—all but "sentence," which is from Latin.

In 597, a second Roman "invasion" came to Britain, this time a peaceful one in the person of St. Augustine and other Catholic missionaries. St. Augustine brought with him not only the religion of Rome, but also the language of Rome. All around England, Anglo-Saxons converted to Christianity. Some attended church schools to learn Latin, the language of their new religion, and some joined the monasteries and became monks. England became known throughout Europe for its Latin scholars. As Anglo-Saxon monks learned to read and write in Latin, some of them began to use the Latin alphabet to write the words of their own language. It wasn't long before people began to learn to write in English before learning to write in Latin, because it was easier.

In the 700s, Britain again became the target of an invasion, this time not a peaceful one. The north and east coasts of the island were under attack by sea warriors, called

"Vikings" or "Norsemen," from Denmark and elsewhere in Scandinavia. Like the Anglo-Saxons, these Norsemen came to Britain with the plan of staying there. The Norsemen worked their way inland and threatened to take over all of England. They were finally stopped in 878, at the Battle of Ethadune by Alfred, king of Wessex. King Alfred negotiated a border with the Norsemen that allowed them to remain in England north of an old Roman road that ran between London and Chester. The Norse area became known as the "Danelaw." In the Danelaw, two languages lived side by side, Old English and Old Norse.

These two languages were very similar, and it wasn't hard for a speaker of one language to understand the other language. Many Old Norse words became part of the Old English vocabulary. Some of our most common, everyday words come from the Scandinavian languages: *egg*, *window*, *birth*, and *their*. Many English words that start with the "sk-" sound are borrowed from Old Norse, for example, *skin*, *scare*, *scalp*, and *skit*. It is interesting to note that the Norse word "skirt" and the English word "shirt" originally had the same meaning: "a short covering for the body." Because there were now two words for the same thing, "skirt" and "shirt" grew apart in meaning over many years. Another such pair of Norse-English words was "ship" and "skiff." Today, a ship is a large boat and a skiff is a small boat.

King Alfred knew that, without support from neighboring kingdoms, he and his subjects in Wessex could not keep the Norsemen from overrunning the rest of England. He rallied his people and those of neighboring kingdoms to unite against the Norsemen. He used their common language and traditions to unite them. He began to rebuild the monasteries that had been sacked by the Norsemen. He encouraged schools to teach writing and reading in English first, then Latin. King Alfred also started the writing of a record of current events in English. Known as *The Anglo-Saxon Chronicle*, this record was added to for about three hundred years, until the 1100s. You can see why King Alfred became known as "Alfred the Great."

Here is the *Chronicle* entry for 870. See if you can tell which words mean "king," "rode," "land," and "fought with." Are any words from the year 870 the same as they are today?:

> *Her rad se here over Mierce innan Eastengle and wintersetl*
> *namon aet Theodforda. And thy winter Eadmund cyning him*
> *withfeaht. And tha Deniscan sige namon and thone cyning*
> *ofslogon and thaet lond all geeodon.*
>
> (Here the [Norse] army rode over Mercia into East Anglia
> and took winter quarters at Thetford. And in this winter
> King Eadmund fought against [the army]. And the Danes
> took the victory and struck down the king and overran the
> whole land.)

3. The Middle Ages: Middle English

In the year 1066, a comet appeared in the sky. People who saw this comet believed it was a sign of danger and evil to come. The year 1066 certainly was fateful for the English. The peace between the English and the Norsemen began to fall apart. A new Danish king, Canute, began an invasion from across the North Sea. The English king Harold and his army went north to fight them. While the English army was fighting up north, the Normans, from northern France, invaded England from the south. Hearing of this, Harold and his army hurried south. By the time Harold and his army arrived in the south, however, the Normans, led by their king, William the Conqueror, had already set up a base in England and were ready to attack. The Normans defeated the English army at Hastings. Many of England's nobles died in this battle. King Harold himself died after being shot through the eye with an arrow. England would not have another English king for hundreds of years, and the Old English language was threatened.

William the Conqueror became King of England in 1066. Nobles from France took the places of the many English nobles who died at Hastings. William gave the French nobles great estates in England to persuade them to stay in England. French took the place of English as the official language of England. Now, while the people of England kept speaking English among themselves, they were forced to learn some French so that they could communicate with the local sheriff or tax collector. English people who had business at the court or with the local lord had to be able to get by in French. On the other hand, the French nobles needed to learn some English in order to communicate with the people around them. Buying and selling in the markets was done in English. The common people knew only English. Still, English was no longer taught in the monastery schools, only Latin.

After about two hundred years, things began to change. First, the King of France forced the French nobles to make a decision: They could serve the king in England or the king in France, but not both. Soon war broke out between the related kingdoms of England and France. This became known as the Hundred Years War, and it lasted from 1337 until 1454. England eventually lost this war. The second terrible event of this time was an outbreak of the plague. Between 1348 and 1351, almost one third of the people in England died of the plague.

Although the war and the terrible plague brought great sorrow to England and her people, they were good for the English language. With England and France fighting each other, it was considered patriotic for English people—nobles included—to speak English. There was no longer any advantage in speaking French in England. Also, with so many people dead of the plague, there were few people who knew how to read and write in any language, especially French and Latin. The government relied on trained clerks to keep court records, tax records, and the like. Now they had to hire clerks who could only write as they spoke, in English.

The English that was written at this time was quite different from the English of the Anglo-Saxons. We call this form of English "Middle English." Middle English kept the basic vocabulary of the Anglo-Saxons and added many French and Latin words. More and more English was written during the years 1200 through 1500. Not only were legal documents and historical records written in English, but there were also great works of poetry and fiction. The most popular form of fiction writing was the "verse romance." The verse romances were tales of adventure with knights and heroes. The old legends of ancient Britain, including tales of King Arthur and his knights, were written down at this time. Geoffrey Chaucer, an Englishman of French heritage, was one of the most famous Middle English writers. He is best known for *The Canterbury Tales*, a collection of stories narrated by a group of travelers on their way to Canterbury Cathedral. When you read these verses of Geoffrey Chaucer, can you tell which words come from French and which from Anglo-Saxon?

> A KNYGHT *ther was, and that a worthy man,*
> *That, fro the tyme that he first bigan*
> *To ridden out, he loved chivalrye,*
> *Trouthe and honour, fredom and curteisye.*

Chivalrye, trouthe, honour, fredom, and *curteisye* were all expected of a proper medieval knight. Three of these knightly characteristics are French: *chivalrye, honour,* and *curteisye.* Two of them are English: *trouthe* and *fredom.* All five of these words have stayed with English through the centuries: *chivalry, honor, courtesy, truth,* and *freedom.*

> A COOK *they hadde with hem for the nones*
> *To boille the chiknes with the marybones...*
> *He koude rooste and sethe and broille and frye,*
> *Maken mortreux and wel bake a pye.*
>
> ...
>
> *His yonge sone, that thre yeer was of age*
> *Unto hym seyde, Fader why do ye wepe?*
> *Whanne wol the gayler bryngen oure potage?*
> *Is ther no morsel breed that ye do kepe?*
> *I am so hungry that I may nat slepe.*

Look at the Middle English words that have to do with food and cooking in these verses. You can see how French gave words to English and how well they blended together, like the ingredients in a tasty stew, or *mortreux.* The cook can *sethe* and *boille.* Both of these words mean "boil," but *sethe* is English and *boille* is French. Present-day English still uses both of these words. *Sethe* is alive in English today as "seethe," which is a less common word for "boil." In the last verse, the little boy asks his father for a *morsel breed. Morsel* has a French origin and is with us today. *Breed* is Middle English for "bread." You can see how natural it was for speakers of Middle English to bring words from their two cultures together in one phrase.

4. The Renaissance
The next great change in the English language started around the year 1476. This is the year the first printing press was set up in England, by William Caxton of London. Until this time, books had to be copied by hand. Because this was expensive and took a long time, books were rare and precious. Most books were found in the monasteries, with a few in the libraries of rich nobles. These books were written on vellum, made from treated animal skin. Even a short book needed the skins of dozens of sheep or lambs. With paper now available, and with the printing press, many copies of a book could be produced much more quickly and cheaply. Common people in the towns and villages wanted books of their own. Because most people did not understand ancient Greek and Latin (these were still the languages of scholars), printers needed books written in English. But what kind of English? Because Caxton and other early printers set up shop in London, the English written in the books they printed reflects the English spoken in London. These books were read by people all over Britain, and readers from all over England became familiar with London English. In addition, the royal palace was near London, so London English came to be regarded as "good English" or "correct English."

5. Borrowings and New Coinages from the Classical Languages
Less than thirty years after Caxton set up his printing press in London, the first Europeans (since the Vikings) voyaged to America. It was beginning of the age of

exploration. During the age of exploration, England was ruled by a powerful queen, Elizabeth I, and became a great naval power. At home, the English people were full of confidence in themselves and their future. Literature and art flourished during the "Elizabethan Age." Perhaps the most famous writer from this time was William Shakespeare, the poet and playwright. Shakespeare wrote for the theater in London, and his plays have been in print since 1623. Shakespeare had a double gift, for drama and for language. Many words that are common today appear first in the works of Shakespeare and his contemporaries: *utopia, assassination, accommodation*, and *submerged*. But writers were not the only ones who contributed words to English.

During this time, students, scientists, and other learned people continued to speak and write Latin. Latin had been the language of teaching and learning in Britain and Europe since the days of the Romans. Scientists and scholars of Europe talked to each other and wrote books in Latin. Teaching and learning at high schools and universities was done in Latin. In this way, a scientist from Italy, say, could publish his findings and know that they would be read and understood in many different countries. Scientists drew on their knowledge of ancient Greek and Latin and gave new life to ancient words. They made up new words from Greek and Latin roots to describe their inventions and discoveries. Some of the words that came into English this way are names of scientific instruments such as *microscope, telescope, pendulum*, and *thermometer*. The names of bones and organs are for the most part borrowed from Latin, such as *antenna, patella, capillary, intestine, tonsil*, and *appendix*. Arabic culture led the way in mathematics, and the words *algebra* and *algorithm* were borrowed into English from Arabic. Many of our everyday words that have Greek or Latin roots were borrowed into English at this time. Here are a few: *anonymous, collapse, despicable, illegal, minimum, obvious, peninsula, demonstrate, stimulate, traction, accommodate, accumulate*. Even today, scientists use the ancient languages to name their latest discoveries—think of *megabyte, neutrino*, and *apatasaur*.

After Queen Elizabeth's death in 1603, King James of Scotland became the king of England as well. The islands of Britain and Ireland were now under the control of the English. The people of Ireland, Scotland, and Wales were forced to speak English. The year after he became king, James ordered that the Bible be translated into English. King James's translation was an act of defiance toward the Roman Catholic church. At the same time, he hoped that an English Bible would help unite the countries of England and Scotland. King James hired forty-seven translators, and they produced a clear and beautiful Bible in 1611. The writing of the "King James Bible" has had a strong influence on spoken and written English since that time. It helped to establish standards for English spelling, grammar, and usage. It also brought the language of London and south England to all English speakers throughout Britain and the world.

6. English Comes to America

From the 1600s, the British were establishing a worldwide empire. There would eventually be British colonies on every continent (except Antarctica) and on islands in every ocean. Sir Walter Raleigh, courtier of Queen Elizabeth and adventurer, made three attempts to start an English settlement, or colony, in the New World. He chose the coast of what is now Virginia for this settlement. None of these settlements lasted, and the settlers all died. But the lure of wealth kept pulling Europeans to the Americas. The pace of voyages picked up at the beginning of the 1600s, about four hundred years ago. Once again, the English tried to start a permanent settlement in Virginia, this time with greater success. During the next one hundred years, a flood of British people explored and settled what became the eastern United States and Canada. They often competed with people from other European countries for possession of the land. And, while there were some half-hearted tries to live side-by-side in peace with the Native Americans, the British considered it within their rights to claim the "New World" for themselves.

When English people came to North America, they brought their home language and customs with them. People from one part of England moved to America together, so that people living in one colony might talk like people from one part of England, while people in another colony might talk like people from another part of England. This is one reason why pronunciation varies from one region to another in North America.

Also during this time, Africans were brought to America as slaves for the first time. The slave trade, and the practice of slavery, was to continue for over two hundred years. The people who came from Africa spoke many languages. Their family and village groups were broken up after they arrived in America. In order to be able to communicate among themselves and with their white masters, the Africans had to learn English. Because they had no legal rights, these African Americans had no incentive to sound like the people who enslaved them. Enslaved African Americans were forbidden from learning to read and write, so their English did not follow the patterns of English as it was written in books and taught in schools. The English of the African Americans held on to traces of their home languages as they struggled to keep their culture and traditions alive.

7. American English
In 1776, the thirteen American colonies declared their independence from British rule. One way that the newly formed United States tried to show its independence was by breaking away from British English in its writing. In 1768, Benjamin Franklin proposed a new alphabet for American English. He wanted to get rid of the letters c, j, q, and x and add new letters for the sounds "th," "ng," and "ch" and "sh." Noah Webster, who had become well-known by publishing books on reading and writing, experimented with new ways of spelling, for example, "iz" for "is" and "proov" for "prove." But, when he published "An American Dictionary of the English Language" in 1828, he kept mostly to British spelling. The words that he spelled differently have kept their American spellings to the present day, such as "favor" instead of "favour," and "check" instead of "cheque." Because Canada has kept its close ties to Britain, Canadian spelling reflects British spelling, although it shows a strong influence from the United States.

The British were not the only Europeans to settle in North America centuries ago. Large parts of North America were held by France and Spain. French is one of the two official languages of Canada, and it is still spoken in parts of Louisiana. Many French place names in the United States show how far the *voyageurs* (French-speaking guides and traders) traveled in North America. English-speaking Canadians use some words from French where their U.S. cousins use an English word, for example, "serviette" for "napkin." In spite of strong laws in Quebec to limit the use of English, French-speaking Canadians use some words that show a strong English influence, for example *char* (related to an old French word for a horse-drawn carriage) is used for "car," while in France, the word for car is *voiture*. In some cases, Quebec has kept an older French form, where France has borrowed from English: *fin de semaine*, *week-end*.

The Spanish came to the Americas before the British, and they claimed much of the southern and southwestern part of what is now the United States. The Spanish language lives on not only in place names, but also in names for the earth formations in the Southwest: *mesa, arroyo, canyon,* and *sierra* are a few of these words. Also, many Native American words came into English through the Spanish, including *cigar, papaya, potato, puma, avocado, cannibal, canoe, chili, tomato, coyote, iguana,* and *hammock.* Many Americans are bilingual, speaking both Spanish and English. Spanish words continue to become part of the English language, including many names for foods: *salsa, taco, burrito,* and *tamale* are just a few. Maybe you have teased someone and called them "loco," or crazy. The expression "the whole enchilada," meaning "every bit" or "the whole thing" shows how much a part of our everyday speech some Spanish words have become.

8. Present-Day English Around the World

English grew and changed as it became a global language. In fact, there are now many "Englishes," each linked to a different part of the world. English picked up new words everywhere it went. From North America came many words from Native American languages. Animals and plants that did not exist in Europe often kept their native names: *raccoon, moose, skunk, hickory, terrapin, hominy, squash, pecan, tobacco.* Other words came from parts of Native American culture that did not have European counterparts. From the people of the far north come *parka, anorak, husky,* and *kayak.* Many place names in North America are Native American, including most of the U.S. state and Canadian province names. From the languages of India (a British colony until 1948) come *shampoo, bungalow, cashmere, cheetah, dungaree, dinghy, catamaran, jungle,* and *pajama.* From the aboriginal people of Australia come *boomerang* and *koala,* and many animal names. From the Maori of New Zealand comes *kiwi* (the bird and the fruit). From China comes *typhoon.* From Swahili in West Africa comes *jumbo.* From Tagalog, the language of the Philippines (formerly a U.S. territory), comes *boondocks.* Americans have contributed their own coinages to the English language: *gizmo, rock-and-roll, jazz, blues, skyscraper, jaywalk,* and *freeway.*

It is important to remember that English spread from a small island to countries around the world at the point of a sword. So why is it that when the British left their colonies, the English language stayed? There is no easy answer to this question. But, it is a fact that people grow up speaking English on every continent. Having one language has made global trade and communication easier. Just as Latin was used by scientists and philosophers all over Europe during the Middle Ages and Renaissance, so English is used today for global communication. After World War II, new technologies made it easier to spread the English language. At the same time, these technologies made it desirable for more and more people to know English. British and American radio and TV programs are broadcast around the globe. Movies from Hollywood are shown around the world. American and British popular music have a worldwide audience. Because the United States pioneered commercial air travel, English is the international language of air traffic controllers. The development of computers and computer software in English-speaking countries has made English the main language of the Internet. Astronauts from different countries speak English on the International Space Station. English is truly a world language.

Pronunciation Key

Below is the key to the symbols and letters that are used in this dictionary to show how to pronounce the entry words. Every entry word has a pronunciation guide in curly brackets { } following the entry's definitions and any example sentences.

Vowel Sounds

Pronunciation Symbol	Sound
ă	cat
ay	laid
ah	father
ar	star
aw	caught
eh	beg
ee	bee
ih	it
iy	lie
ŏ	hot
oh	flow
oi	toy
ow	down
uh	up
yoo	cute; few
ooh	blue; too
uu	book
uhr	germ, fur
ə	slogan; nickel, pencil, person, circus

Consonant Sounds

Pronunciation Symbol	Sound
b	big
ch	child
d	dare
f	fun; phone
g	got
h	hat
j	jam; germ
k	key; camp
ks	box
kw	quick
l	let
m	make
n	neat
ng	sing
p	pet
r	ring
s	see; city
sh	shoe
t	top
th	these
th	thump
v	van
w	win
y	yes
z	zebra
zh	treasure

The symbol "ə" represents "schwa," a vowel sound in an unstressed syllable.
In words with more than one syllable, the syllable with the greatest stress is shown in bold underlined type, the syllable with secondary stress is in bold type, and syllables with no stress are in plain type.

Sound and Spelling Guide

This chart shows different ways to spell each sound in English. Use it to figure out the spelling of unfamiliar words.

SOUND	SPELLING	EXAMPLE
ă	a	bat
	ai	plaid
	al	half
	au	laugh
ay	a	ate
	ae	aerospace
	ai	mail
	ay	say
	ea	steak
	ei	vein
	eig	reign
	eigh	eight
	ey	they
ah	a	father
	ah	ah
	al	palm
ar	ar	car
	ea	heart
aw	a	call
	al	talk
	au	caught; auto
	aw	saw
	oa	abroad
	ough	thought
b	b	bib
	pb	cupboard
ch	c	cello
	ch	children
	tch	watch
	ti	question
	tu	feature
d	d	did
	ed	mailed
	ld	would
eh	a	any
	ai	said
	ay	says
	e	pet
	ea	head
	ie	friend
ee	e	be
	ea	leap
	ee	feet
	ei	seize
	eo	people
	ey	key
	i	piano
	ie	believe
	y	very

SOUND	SPELLING	EXAMPLE
f	f	first
	gh	rough
	lf	calf
	ph	photo
g	g	got
	gg	egg
	gh	ghost
	gu	guest
	gue	catalogue
h	h	hat
	wh	who
ih	a	storage
	e	enough
	ee	been
	i	it
	ia	carriage
	u	business
	ui	building
	y	myth
iy	ai	aisle
	eigh	height
	ey	eye
	i	kite
	ie	tie
	igh	right
	is	island
	uy	buy
	y	my
	ye	dye
j	d	individual
	dg	judge
	di	soldier
	dj	adjust
	g	ginger
	ge	cage
	j	jam
k	c	catch
	ch	school
	ck	back
	k	keep
ks	x	box
kw	qu	quit
l	l	low
m	m	make
	mb	comb
	mn	hymn

n	gn	gnat
	kn	knee
	n	nice
	pn	pneumonia

ng	n	sink
	ng	sang
	ngue	tongue

ŏ	a	want
	o	hot

oh	eau	bureau
	ew	sew
	o	hole
	oa	goat
	oe	toe
	oh	oh
	ou	shoulder
	ough	though
	ow	slow
	owe	owe

oi	oi	noise
	oy	boy

ow	ou	our
	ough	bough
	ow	cow

p	p	pet

r	r	run
	rh	rhyme
	wr	write

s	c	city
	ps	psychology
	s	sell
	sc	science

sh	ce	ocean
	ch	machine
	ci	special
	s	sure
	sc	conscience
	sh	shell
	si	mansion
	ti	action

t	ed	poked
	ght	right
	t	tell

th	th	thin

th	th	there

uh	o	done
	oe	does
	oo	flood
	ou	trouble
	u	but

yoo	eau	beauty
	eu	feud
	ew	few
	iew	view
	u	cube
	ue	cue
	you	you
	yu	yule

ooh	eu	maneuver
	ew	blew
	ieu	lieutenant
	o	move
	oe	canoe
	oo	fool
	ou	soup
	ough	through
	u	flute
	ue	blue
	ui	fruit

uu	o	woman
	oo	wood
	ou	would
	u	put

uhr	er	germ
	ear	heard
	ir	stir
	ur	fur
	or	worse

v	f	of
	v	very

w	o	one
	w	wet
	wh	when

y	i	onion
	y	yes

z	s	was
	se	noise
	x	xylophone
	z	zero

zh	ge	garage
	s	treasure
	si	vision
	z	azure

ə	a	soda
	e	kitten
	i	pencil
	o	lemon
	u	circus
	ai	certain
	ea	sergeant
	ou	famous

Canadian Spellings

Some English words have more than one correct spelling. This is especially true of words spelled slightly differently in British English than in American English. People in Canada use British spellings more often than people living in the United States.

American spelling	Canadian spelling
amid	amidst
among	amongst
amphitheater	amphitheatre
anemia	anaemia
anesthesia	anaesthesia
analyze	analyse
appall	appal
arbor	arbour
armor	armour
armory	armoury
balk	baulk
behavior	behaviour
center	centre
check	cheque
color	colour
cozy	cosy
defense	defence
enclose	inclose
endeavor	endeavour
endorse	indorse
favor	favour
favorable	favourable
favorite	favourite
fiber	fibre
fiberglass	fibreglass
flavor	flavour
harbor	harbour
honor	honour
humor	humour
inquire	enquire
kilometer	kilometre
license	licence
maneuver	manoeuvre
meter	metre
molding	moulding
neighbor	neighbour
neighborhood	neighbourhood
neighborly	neighbourly
odor	odour
offense	offence
paralyze	paralyse
practice	practise
ruble	rouble
rumor	rumour
saber	sabre
story[2]	storey
theater	theatre
vapor	vapour
vigor	vigour

Aa

A is a vowel that makes several different sounds.

Tips to help you look up words starting with A:

Sometimes vowels sound similar to each other. If you can't find the word you're looking for under A, it may start with e, i, o, or u.

Also look under H for words that start with a silent h (such as heir).

These words may be hard to look up if you don't already know how to spell them:

accidental	allegiance
accommodate	almost
accurate	annual
ache	answer
acknowledge	anxiety
acquaint	appear
acquire	arctic
actual	arrangement
adjacent	ascend
aggravate	attendant
aisle	audience
all right	awkward

a or **A** *noun* (a's or A's) 1. the first letter of the English alphabet. 2. a grade given for excellent schoolwork. 3. the sixth note in the musical scale of C major. {**ay**}
• **from A to Z**
from beginning to end; completely; thoroughly.

a¹ *indefinite article* 1. any one of a group or kind. *A horse has hooves.* / *A man with a suitcase got on the bus.* 2. one (used before a noun that expresses an amount). *He dumped a cup of flour into the mixing bowl.* 3. any particular one. *The magician told her to pick a card.* {**uh** *or* **ay**}

a² *preposition* in every or in each; for every or for each. *I play tennis two times a week.* / *The fruit is one dollar a pound.* {**uh** *or* **ay**}

a-¹ *prefix* a prefix that means "on," "at," "into," or "to." *The word "aboard" means "on board."*

a-² *prefix* 1. a prefix that means "away," "from," or "off." *To avoid an angry crowd is to stay away from an angry crowd.* 2. a prefix that means "not" or "without." *The word "atypical" means "not typical."*

aard·vark *noun* a large mammal with a long snout, long ears, a long tail, and almost no hair. Aardvarks are active at night, when they use their powerful claws to dig open ant or termite nests. They catch their food with long, sticky tongues. Aardvarks live in southern and central Africa. Although they are sometimes called anteaters, aardvarks are not closely related to any other kind of mammal. {**ard** vark}

ab·a·cus *noun* (abacuses) a device used for counting or calculating. An abacus has beads or other counters that slide along rods or in grooves. {**ă** bə kəs}

ab·a·lo·ne *noun* (abalone) a large sea snail that has several shiny colors on the inside of its shell. Abalone are mollusks. People eat abalone meat and make decorations from the shells. {**ă** bə **loh** nee}

a·ban·don *verb* (abandoned, abandoning, abandons) 1. to leave behind with no plan to return; desert. *The frightened thieves abandoned the stolen car.* 2. to stop doing or pursuing; give up. *He abandoned his dream of being an actor.* / *She abandoned her chores and went fishing.* {ə **băn** dən} abandonment, n.

a·ban·doned *adjective* left forever; deserted. *They adopted the abandoned child.* / *No one dared enter the abandoned house.* {ə **băn** dənd}

a·bate *verb* (abated, abating, abates) 1. to become less in amount or intensity. *The wind died down as the storm abated.* / *The pain abated, and he fell asleep.* 2. to make less in amount or intensity. *The sight of his tears abated her anger.* {ə **bayt**}

ab·bey *noun* a religious place or building where monks or nuns live. {**ăb** ee}

ab·bre·vi·ate *verb* (abbreviated, abbreviating, abbreviates) 1. to shorten the time or length of. *When told he would have only fifteen minutes to speak, John abbreviated his speech.* 2. to shorten by using fewer let-

A B C D E F G H I J K L M N O P Q R S T U V W X Y Z

a

b
c
d
e
f
g
h
i
j
k
l
m
n
o
p
q
r
s
t
u
v
w
x
y
z

ters. *People usually abbreviate the word "Mister" and write "Mr."* {ə **bree** vee **ayt**}

ab·bre·vi·a·tion *noun* a shortened form of a word or phrase used in writing. *"Ave." is an abbreviation for the word "avenue." / "Tues." is an abbreviation for the word "Tuesday."* {ə **bree** vee **ay** shən}

ab·di·cate *verb* (abdicated, abdicating, abdicates) to officially give up a position of power or a right. *The dying king abdicated so that his daughter could become queen.* {**ăb** də **kayt**}

ab·do·men 🏃 ❶ *noun* 1. the part of the body between the chest and the hips. *The abdomen contains the stomach, intestines, and liver.* 2. the rear part of the body of an insect. {**ăb** də mən} abdominal, adj.

ab·duct *verb* (abducted, abducting, abducts) to carry off or lead away by force; kidnap. *During the night, the king's enemies abducted his son, the young prince.* {əb **duhkt**}

a·bide *verb* (abode [or] abided, abiding, abides) 1. to continue. *Although she is gone, his love for her abides.* 2. to live; dwell. *He abides in a cottage deep in the woods.* 3. to put up with; stand. *She cannot abide loud noises.* {ə **biyd**}
• **abide by**
to obey; agree to. *All swimmers must abide by the pool's rules.*

a·bil·i·ty *noun* (abilities) 1. the power to do something; the quality of being able. *Most birds have the ability to fly.* 2. skill or talent. *She has much ability as an ice skater.* {ə **bih** lih tee}

a·blaze *adjective* 1. on fire. *The farmer set the dead grass*

ablaze. 2. like fire in color. *The trees are ablaze with fall colors.* {ə **blayz**}

a·ble *adjective* (abler, ablest) 1. having the skill or power needed to do a thing. *He is proud of being able to read and write.* 2. having special skill or talent. *She is an able dancer.* {**ay** bəl}

-a·ble or **-ible** *suffix* 1. a suffix that means capable or worthy of being the object of a certain action. *If something is washable, that means it can be washed. / A likable person is a person who is worthy of being liked.* 2. a suffix that means "likely to." *A glass is breakable if it is likely to break when it is dropped on the floor.* 3. a suffix that means "having." *Humans are called reasonable animals because they have the power to reason.*

ab·nor·mal *adjective* not normal or usual. *The tree has an abnormal growth on its trunk.* {**ăb nohr** məl} abnormally, adv.

a·board *adverb* on or into a ship, bus, or plane; on board. *The luggage was brought aboard, and off we went.* *preposition* on; in; on board. *Right now, my brothers are aboard a ship headed for Alaska.* {ə **bohrd**}

a·bol·ish *verb* (abolished, abolishing, abolishes) to get rid of or do away with; end. *The United States abolished slavery in 1865.* {ə **bo** lihsh}

ab·o·li·tion *noun* 1. the act of abolishing. 2. (capitalized) the end of slavery in the United States. {ă bə **lih** shən}

ab·o·li·tion·ist *noun* a person who supported Abolition, or ending slavery, before the Civil War. {**ăb** oh **lih** shuhn ihst}

a·bom·i·na·ble *adjective* causing or deserving hate or disgust. *Kidnapping is an abominable crime.* {ə **bo** mih nə bəl} abominably, adv.

ab·o·rig·i·ne *noun* one of the first people to live in an area. *The Australian aborigines were the first inhabitants of western Australia.* {**ă** bə **rih** jə nee}

a·bound *verb* (abounded, abounding, abounds) to be found in large numbers or amounts. *Rabbits abound in these woods.* {ə **bownd**} aboundingly, adv.

a·bout *preposition* 1. concerning. *The library has some books about Hank Aaron.* 2. near to; almost. *We are about the same age.* 3. near; in the area of. *They are about the office somewhere.* 4. on each side of; around. *All about me was ocean, as far as the eye could see.* *adverb* 1. more or less; nearly. *It costs about ten dollars.* 2. on all sides; here and there. *Look about for the lost sock.* 3. in the same area; nearby. *They are somewhere about.* 4. to the opposite direction. *Turn the car about.* *adjective* moving around. *He was out and about early.* {ə **bowt**}
• **about to**
ready to; shortly going to. *I was about to leave when the phone rang.*

a·bove *adverb* at or to a higher place. *Hang one picture there and the other above.* *preposition* 1. at or to a higher place than. *The plane is flying above the clouds.* 2. higher in rank, level, or quality than. *He is in the grade above me.* 3. not willing or able to lower one's standards for. *She*

🏃 Human Body   ❓ Human Mind   👕 Everyday Life   🚩 History and Culture   📞 Communication

is above tattling to the teacher. {ə **buhv**}

a·bove·board *adverb or adjective* without tricks or lies; honest. *Ever since the company was caught cheating, they've had to operate aboveboard.* {ə **buhv bohrd**}

a·bra·sive *noun* something rough used to wear away or polish a surface. *Sandpaper is used as an abrasive on wood.* *adjective* scratchy, harsh, or irritating. *This cleanser is too abrasive to use on the china. / He has an abrasive laugh.* {ə **bray** sihv} abrasiveness, n.

a·breast *adverb* 1. side by side. *The two guards stood abreast, blocking the door.* 2. closely aware. *The radio station keeps listeners abreast of the news.* {ə **brehst**}

a·bridge *verb* (abridged, abridging, abridges) to make shorter. *Do not be surprised if the magazine abridges your story before publishing it.* {ə **brihj**}

a·broad *adverb* in or to a country that is not one's own. *The American traveled abroad to England and France.* {ə **brawd**}

ab·rupt *adjective* 1. sudden and not expected. *I lost my balance when the bus came to an abrupt stop.* 2. saying so little as to be rude or unpleasant. *I was abrupt with the salesman who called during dinner.* {ə **bruhpt**} abruptly, adv., abruptness, n.

ab·scess *noun* a sore that forms within the tissues of the body and is filled with pus. *Abscesses can be caused by an infection.* {**ăb** sehs} abscessed, adj.

ab·sence *noun* 1. the fact or condition of being away or not present. *After John's third absence, the teacher called his father. / An old proverb says, "Absence makes the heart grow fonder."* 2. a length of time of being away. *After an absence of two weeks, the neighbors returned from their beach trip.* 3. the state of not having; lack. *I noticed the absence of games and toys in the little girl's room.* {**ăb** səns}

ab·sent *adjective* not present; away from where one usually is. *Because of the class trip, we will be absent from school tomorrow.* {**ăb** sənt} absently, adv.

ab·sen·tee *noun* a person who is absent from work, school, or other duty. {**ăb** sən **tee**}

ab·sent-mind·ed *adjective* tending to not pay attention to a task or event because one is thinking about other things. *While his head was full of numbers, the absent-minded mathematician poured salt into his tea.* {**ăb** sənt **miyn** dihd} absent-mindedly, adv., absent-mindedness, n.

ab·so·lute *adjective* 1. complete; total. *The magician asked for absolute silence.* 2. without limits or restrictions. *If a king has absolute power, he can make whatever laws he wants and can break any laws he wants.* 3. sure; certain. *The police have absolute proof that she stole jewelry from the store.* {**ăb** sə **looht**}

ab·so·lute·ly *adverb* 1. precisely; exactly. *Her guess was absolutely right.* 2. totally; completely. *She was absolutely exhausted by the end of the day.* {**ăb** sə **looht** lee}

ab·sorb *verb* (absorbed, absorbing, absorbs) 1. to take in or soak up. *A paper towel will absorb the spilled milk.* 2.

to hold the full attention of. *Her new pet lizards absorbed her for weeks.* {əb **zohrb**}

ab·sorb·ent *adjective* able to soak up liquid or moisture. *Thick towels are very absorbent.* *noun* a material that soaks up liquid or moisture. *An absorbent was used to clean up the oil spill.* {əb **zohr** bənt}

ab·sorp·tion *noun* 1. the act of soaking up or absorbing. *A sponge is useful for the absorption of water.* 2. the state of having all of one's interest and attention taken up by one activity. *His absorption in the book was so complete that he forgot to eat.* {əb **zohrp** shən}

ab·stain *verb* (abstained, abstaining, abstains) 1. to choose not to do something. *He abstained from dessert because he had eaten too much already.* 2. to choose not to take part in a decision. *She abstained from voting in the election.* {əb **stayn**}

ab·stract *adjective* 1. formed only in the mind or in thought; not based on experience or the physical state of a thing. *The scientist's theory about how galaxies are formed is completely abstract.* 2. hard to understand, because not based on one's experience of the world. *The study of cell biology is too abstract for most third graders.* {**ăb** străkt *or* əb străkt}

ab·surd *adjective* silly; foolish; not true. *It is absurd to think the earth is flat.* {əb **suhrd**}

a·bun·dance *noun* a very large amount; plentiful supply. *There was an abundance of food at the Thanksgiving dinner.* {ə **buhn** dəns}

a·bun·dant *adjective* large in amount or number; more than enough. *The library has an abundant supply of books*

A
B
C
D
E
F
G
H
I
J
K
L
M
N
O
P
Q
R
S
T
U
V
W
X
Y
Z

a

b
c
d
e
f
g
h
i
j
k
l
m
n
o
p
q
r
s
t
u
v
w
x
y
z

and tapes. {ə **buhn** dənt} abun-dantly, adv.

a·buse 🏃 ❓ *verb* (abused, abusing, abuses) 1. to use in a way that is wrong or bad; misuse. *If you abuse your privileges, you will lose them. / She abuses alcohol.* 2. to hurt or harm by treating badly. *His father used to abuse him. / Smokers abuse their own lungs.* 3. to talk to or about in an insulting or unfair way. *As soon as he started to abuse my friends and my teachers, I walked away. noun* 1. bad or wrong use; misuse. *It is an abuse of power for the king to take money from poor people so that he can live in luxury.* 2. cruel or harmful treatment. *After two weeks of abuse, the new doll's head fell off.* 3. harsh or insulting words. *The enemies hurled abuse at each other.* {ə **byoos**} abuser, n.

a·byss *noun* a vast pit, too deep to be measured. {ə **bihs**}

ac·a·dem·ic *adjective* 1. having to do with a school. *Universities are academic institutions.* 2. having to do with learning or study. *She should spend more time on her academic work and less on sports. noun* a teacher or scholar at a college or university. {ă kə **deh** mihk}

a·cad·e·my 🟠 ⬜ *noun* (acade-mies) a private school or a school that offers special training. *He studied drawing at the art academy.* {ə **kă** də mee}

ac·cel·er·ate *verb* (accelerated, accelerating, accelerates) 1. to increase the speed or rate of. *The driver acceler-ated his sports car to see just how*

fast it could go. 2. to increase the speed or rate of some-thing. *She accelerated in order to pass the slower driver.* {ək **seh** lə **rayt**}

ac·cel·er·a·tion *noun* the act or process of accelerating or increasing speed. *This motor-cycle has faster acceleration than that one.* {ək **seh** lə **ray** shən}

ac·cent 🟣 *noun* 1. the stress a speaker gives to one syllable in a word. *The accent in the word "forget" is on "get."* 2. a mark (´ or `). Accents are used to show what parts of a word are to be said with more stress. 3. a way of speaking a language that is typical of people from a par-ticular area. *She has an English accent. verb* (accented, accenting, accents) 1. to give more stress to, when speaking. *To pronounce the verb form of the word "contest" correctly, you must accent the second syl-lable.* 2. to mark with an accent. *To understand the way the dictionary accents sylla-bles, read the introduction.* {**ăk** sehnt or ăk **sehnt**}

ac·cen·tu·ate *verb* (accentuated, accentuating, accentuates) to give more emphasis to; draw attention to. *His white T-shirt accentuated his suntan.* {ăk **sehn** chooh **ayt**}

ac·cept *verb* (accepted, accepting, accepts) 1. to take when given; receive will-ingly. *She would not accept the present. / I accepted his apology.* 2. to allow into a group. *The college accepted my brother in March.* 3. to think of as true or correct. *My parents accepted my explanation for why I was late.* 4. to say yes to. *I accepted the invitation.* {ək **sehpt**}

ac·cept·a·ble *adjective* good enough to be accepted or approved of. *My grades were acceptable to my parents.* {ək **sehp** tə bəl}

ac·cept·ance *noun* 1. the act of accepting something that is given. *His acceptance of my offer surprised me.* 2. the con-dition of being accepted or approved of. *The new law had the public's acceptance.* {ək **sehp** təns}

ac·cess *noun* 1. a way of approaching or coming to a place. *This path is the only access to the river.* 2. the right or ability to enter, look at, or use something. *The older stu-dents have access to the com-puters at school. verb* (accessed, accessing, accesses) 1. to get to; reach. *You can only access the base-ment from inside the house.* 2. to obtain or reach on a com-puter. *She could not access the Web site without a password.* {**ăk** sehs}

ac·ces·so·ry *noun* (accessories) 1. an item added on to something else to make it prettier, more complete, or more useful. *I bor-rowed her purse and earrings because I needed some acces-sories that matched my outfit. / The sun roof and stereo are accessories you have to pay extra for.* 2. a person who helps another person break the law but does not actually commit the crime. *He was an accessory in the bank robbery.* {ək **seh** sə ree}

ac·ci·dent 🏃 ⬜ *noun* 1. some-thing that happens without being planned. *We met by accident.* 2. a harmful event that happens by chance. *My*

uncle was hurt in a car accident. {**ăk** sih dənt}

Word History The word *accident* comes from a Latin word meaning "to fall upon" or "to happen." An accident is an event that seems to fall down on us instead of being within our control.

ac·ci·den·tal *adjective* happening by chance; not planned or expected. *Their meeting was accidental.* {ăk sih **dehn** təl} accidentally, adv.

ac·claim *verb* (acclaimed, acclaiming, acclaims) to show enthusiastic approval of. *Everyone acclaimed the President's decision. noun* enthusiastic praise or approval. *The returning astronauts were greeted with acclaim.* {ə **klaym**}

ac·com·mo·date *verb* (accommodated, accommodating, accommodates) 1. to have room for. *The motel accommodates one hundred people. / They accommodated the extra people by bringing in more chairs.* 2. to provide with meals or a place to sleep. *Our friends said they could accommodate us for a few days.* 3. to do a favor for; meet the needs of by changing one's own plans. *The teacher always accommodates us when we need more time.* {ə **ko** mə **dayt**}

ac·com·pa·ni·ment 🕑 *noun* 1. a part of a piece of music that supports or provides background for another, more important part. *The pianist played an accompaniment for the singer.* 2. something that is added to or goes along with something else. *She served fruit as an accompaniment to the cake.* {ə **kuhm** pə nee mənt}

ac·com·pa·ny *verb* (accompanied, accompanying, accom-panies) 1. to go with. *She will accompany us to the zoo.* 2. to be connected with; happen at the same time as; follow. *If the cough is accompanied by a fever, you may have the flu.* 3. to play or sing music as part of the performance of another. *Will you accompany me on the guitar?* {ə **kuhm** pə nee}

ac·com·plice *noun* a person who helps another person break the law or do something wrong. *The police are looking for the burglar's accomplice.* {ə **kŏm** plihs}

ac·com·plish *verb* (accomplished, accomplishing, accomplishes) to do or complete; carry out; achieve. *He accomplished his goal.* {ə **kŏm** plihsh}

ac·com·plish·ment *noun* 1. the act of accomplishing. *The accomplishment of our goals could take months.* 2. something that has been success-fully done or completed; an achievement. *His sailing trip around the world was a great accomplishment.* {ə **kŏm** plihsh mənt}

ac·cord *noun* 1. agreement; harmony. *In accord with tradition, the bride wore white.* 2. an agreement between or among countries. *One country refused to sign the peace accord. verb* (accorded, according, accords) 1. to give or grant. *I would like to thank the committee that has accorded me this honor.* 2. to agree or be in harmony (often followed by "with"). *His story does not accord with the facts.* {ə **kohrd**}

ac·cord·ance *noun* agreement. *The team played in accordance with the rules.* {ə **kohr** dəns}

ac·cor·di·on *noun* a musical instrument with a keyboard that is small enough to carry. An accordion is played by pressing the keys and squeezing the bellows to force air through metal reeds. {ə **kohr** dee ən}

ac·count *noun* 1. a story or report. *He gave an interesting account of their vacation. / The newspaper's account of the robbery was accurate.* 2. a record of money spent or received. *How much money does he have in his bank account?* 3. importance or worth. *Wealth is of little account to her. verb* (accounted, accounting, accounts) 1. to explain (usually followed by "for"). *No one could account for his disappearance.* 2. to give a count or record of money spent or received. *I can account for every dollar I spent.* 3. to be the cause of (usually followed by "for"). *Hard work accounts for his success.* {ə **kownt**}

• **on account of** because of. *The game was canceled on account of rain.*

• **take into account** to consider. *The judge took the boy's age into account before deciding on a punishment.*

ac·count·ant 🕑 *noun* a person who checks and takes care of business records or accounts. *The accountant spent all night working on the financial report.* {ə **kown** tənt}

ac·cu·mu·late *verb* (accumulated, accumulating, accumulates) 1. to pile up, collect, or gather. *The library accumulated many more books this year.* 2. to grow in amount or mass. *The snow accumulated overnight.* {ə **kyoo** myə **layt**}

ac·cu·mu·la·tion *noun* 1. the act of accumulating; piling up.

A
B
C
D
E
F
G
H
I
J
K
L
M
N
O
P
Q
R
S
T
U
V
W
X
Y
Z

a

b
c
d
e
f
g
h
i
j
k
l
m
n
o
p
q
r
s
t
u
v
w
x
y
z

The accumulation of snow on the road made driving difficult. 2. an amount that collects or piles up. *There was an accumulation of mail in our box when we returned.* {ə **kyoo** myə **lay** shən}

ac·cu·ra·cy *noun* (accuracies) the condition of being accurate. *Accuracy is important in keeping records.* {**ă** kyə rih see}

ac·cu·rate *adjective* 1. free of mistakes or error. *The radio gave an accurate report of the fire.* 2. careful and precise. *She was accurate in her measurements.* {**ă** kyə riht} accurately, adv.

ac·cu·sa·tion 💬 *noun* a statement that another person is guilty of a crime or error. *Be sure of the facts before you make this accusation.* {**ă** kyə **zay** shən}

ac·cuse *verb* (accused, accusing, accuses) to blame for or charge with a crime or something wrong. *The teacher accused her of cheating.* {ə **kyooz**} accuser, n., accusingly, adv.

ac·cus·tom *verb* (accustomed, accustoming, accustoms) to become used to or familiar with over time. *She accustomed herself to the loud music.* {ə **kuh** stəm}

ac·cus·tomed *adjective* 1. in the habit of (usually followed by "to"). *I am accustomed to sleeping late on Saturdays.* 2. normal; usual. *His mother was waiting for him at her accustomed spot by the gate.* {ə **kuh** stəmd}

ace *noun* 1. a playing card that has only one mark. 2. a person who is a master or expert at something. *He is an ace at math.* 3. a serve in tennis that wins a point because the other player cannot reach the ball. *The tennis player served four aces*

in a row and won the game. *verb* (aced, acing, aces) to get a grade of A on or for. *He aced his history course.* *adjective* excellent or expert. *The class president is an ace student.* {**ays**}

ache 🏃 *verb* (ached, aching, aches) 1. to hurt with a dull, constant pain. *The soccer player's legs ached after the long game.* 2. to want very much. *He is aching to go on vacation.* *noun* a dull, constant pain. *He has an ache in his knee from kneeling on the floor.* {**ayk**}

a·chieve *verb* (achieved, achieving, achieves) 1. to do or carry out successfully; accomplish. *He achieved everything he wanted to as president.* 2. to get by trying hard. *She achieved a good grade on her math test.* {ə **cheev**} achiever, n.

Synonyms

These words share a meaning with *achieve*, verb 1:

realize, perform, accomplish, attain, execute

---

a·chieve·ment *noun* 1. something achieved through hard work, courage, or skill. *Winning the race at his age was a great achievement.* 2. the act of achieving. *The achievement of their goals now seemed possible.* {ə **cheev** mənt}

ac·id 🏃🌎 *noun* a chemical substance that dissolves in water, has a sour taste, and turns blue litmus paper red. *adjective* 1. made of or containing an acid. *The acid solution smells bad.* 2. having a sour taste. *The acid taste of the vinegar made my mouth water.* 3. sharp or cutting in speech. *His acid remarks hurt my feelings.* {**ăs** ihd}

acid rain *noun* rain that contains acid from pollution.

The acid rain killed many plants. {**ă** sihd **rayn**}

ac·knowl·edge *verb* (acknowledged, acknowledging, acknowledges) 1. to admit the truth or existence of. *She would not acknowledge her mistake.* 2. to show thanks for. *Grandmother acknowledged my gift with a note of thanks.* 3. to reply to; say that one has received. *I called my friend and acknowledged her invitation.* {ək **no** lihj}

ac·knowl·edg·ment or **acknowledgement** *noun* 1. the act of acknowledging. *The jury was surprised by the accused man's acknowledgment of his guilt.* 2. something done to express thanks or show appreciation. *As an acknowledgment for her hard work, they presented her with flowers.* {ək **no** lihj mənt}

ac·ne *noun* a skin condition that makes pimples appear on the face, back, or chest. It happens when oil glands in the skin are blocked. *Washing one's face helps prevent acne.* {**ăk** nee}

a·corn *noun* the nut of an oak tree. *Squirrels and chipmunks eat acorns.* {**ay** kohrn}

a·cous·tic 🔊 *adjective* 1. having to do with sound or hearing. *The music hall has excellent acoustic equipment.* 2. able to make musical sounds without using electricity. *He plays acoustic guitar at his smaller concerts.* {ə **kooh** stihk}

a·cous·tics *noun* (acoustics) the aspects of a room or space that make sounds easy or difficult to hear (used with a plural verb). *The theater's acoustics were excellent.* {ə **kooh** stihks}

 Human Body   Human Mind   Everyday Life   History and Culture   Communication

ac·quaint *verb* (acquainted, acquainting, acquaints) to make known or make familiar (usually followed by "with"). *A guide acquainted us with the interesting wildlife of the area.* {ə **kwaynt**}

ac·quain·tance *noun* 1. a person one has met but does not know well. 2. knowledge of something that comes from personal experience. *I have an acquaintance with United States history.* {ə **kwayn** təns}

ac·quire *verb* (acquired, acquiring, acquires) to get or come to have as one's own. *He is acquiring some bad habits from his friends.* {ə **kwiyr**}

ac·quit *verb* (acquitted, acquitting, acquits) to free from a charge of breaking the law; declare not guilty. *The judge acquitted the old woman.* {ə **kwiht**}

a·cre *noun* a unit of area equal to 43,560 square feet, used to measure land. The acre is a standard unit of measurement in the United States and the United Kingdom. {**ay** kər}

Word History The word *acre* comes from the early English word *acer*. This word simply meant "a ploughed field." When the word "acre" was first used for an amount of land, it meant the amount of land that a pair of oxen could plough in one day. A three-acre field might differ in size from region to region. Later a law was passed in England that made an acre a standard unit of area.

a·cre·age *noun* the number of acres in an area of land. *What is the acreage of your farm?* {**ay** kə rəj}

ac·ro·bat *noun* a person who can do physical acts that take balance and skill. *We watched an acrobat walk on the tightrope at the circus.* {**ă** krə băt}

a·cro·bat·ic *adjective* having to do with acrobats or feats of balance and skill. {**ă** kroh **bă** tihk}

ac·ro·nym *noun* a word formed by putting together the first letters or parts of a series of words in a longer phrase. *"Scuba" is an acronym for "self-contained underwater breathing apparatus."* {**ă** krə nihm}

S.C.U.B.A.
Self-Contained
Underwater Breathing
Apparatus

a·cross *preposition* 1. from one side to the other of. *Someone hung streamers across the doorway.* 2. to or on the other side of. *I bought some candy at the store across the street.* 3. into contact with, especially by accident. *I came across him at the races.* *adverb* from one side to the other. *He came to a small stream and jumped across.* {ə **kraws**}

a·cryl·ic *noun* a kind of plastic used to make yarns, paint, and many other things. {ə **krih** lihk}

act ❷ 🗨 *noun* 1. a thing that is done; deed. *His act of bravery saved the child from drowning.* 2. the process of doing something. *He caught the puppy in the act of stealing the hamburger.* 3. a behavior of pretending to be or to feel something that is not true. *Her sadness was just an act.* 4. a short performance by a musician, comedian, or other entertainer. *The magician worked hard to improve his act.* 5. one of the main parts of a play or opera. *She sang a song in the third act of the play.* 6. a law. *The senators passed an act against drunk driving.* *verb* (acted, acting, acts) 1. to do something with purpose or energy. *He acted with great courage in battle.* 2. to be a performer in plays or movies; play a role. *She acted in the school play.* 3. to pretend to be. *He acted happy to see them.* {**ăkt**}
• **act up**
1. to behave in a bad or mischievous way; misbehave. 2. to happen again or return, as an illness or malfunction. *My allergies are acting up.*
• **clean up one's act** (informal) to improve one's performance or behavior.
• **get one's act together** (informal) to behave more responsibly.

ac·tion ❓ *noun* 1. something that is done or is happening. *What action are you going to take to stop him?* 2. (usually plural) a way of acting or behaving. *Her actions are not acceptable.* 3. the manner of a mechanism's moving or operating, or the mechanism itself. *The action of a clock fascinated the little boy.* 4. fighting that occurs during a war. *The new soldiers saw action soon after they arrived.* {**ăk** shən}

ac·tion verb *noun* a verb that shows its subject performing some action. "Run," "eat," "fly," and "sing" are examples of action verbs. {**ăk** shən **vuhrb**}

ac·ti·vate *verb* (activated, activating, activates) to cause action in or make active; start. *You will activate the alarm if you open the door.* {**ăk** tə **vayt**} activation, n.

ac·tive *adjective* 1. always doing something; busy; full of energy. *My grandmother is very active even though she is old.* 2. doing something or able to do something; working; functioning. *Is your*

a

b

c

d

e

f

g

h

i

j

k

l

m

n

o

p

q

r

s

t

u

v

w

x

y

z

library card still active? {**ăk** tihv} actively, adv.

ac·tiv·i·ty noun (activities) 1. the condition of being active or doing something; action; motion. *There was a lot of activity in the streets during the parade.* 2. a specific thing that is done. *My favorite activity after school is soccer.* {**ăk tih** vih tee}

ac·tor noun a person who acts a part in a play, a movie, or a radio or television program. {**ăk** tər}

ac·tress noun a woman or girl who plays a part in movies, television, plays, or radio. *She wants to be a famous actress in the movies.* {**ăk** trihs}

ac·tu·al adjective real; existing in fact. *My little sister believes that Peter Pan was an actual boy.* {**ăk** chooh əl}

ac·tu·al·ly adverb as a matter of fact; really. *Yes, I am actually going to do my homework before I watch television today.* {**ăk** chooh ə lee}

ac·u·punc·ture noun the practice of relieving pain or curing a disease by putting needles into certain parts of the body. Acupuncture is a traditional way to treat disease in China. {**ă** kyoo **puhngk** chər}

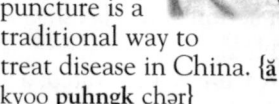

a·cute adjective 1. sharp; severe. *She was having acute pains in her stomach.* 2. sharp; quick; sensitive. *My dog has an acute sense of smell.* 3. very serious; very important; critical. *There was an acute shortage of medicine in the hospital during the war.* / *The school had many new students, and there was an acute need for more teachers.* 4. an angle of less than

ninety degrees. {ə **kyoot**} acutely, adv.

acute angle noun an angle of less than ninety degrees.

A.D. abbreviation after the birth of Jesus Christ. A.D. is an abbreviation for *anno domini*, which means "in the year of the Lord" in Latin. Something that happened in A.D. 50 happened fifty years after the birth of Christ.

ad noun advertisement. *The children asked their parents for the toys they had seen in television ads.* {**ăd**}

Homophone Note Are you looking for the word **add**? **Ad** and **add** sound alike but have different meanings.

ad·age noun an old familiar saying that shows the wisdom of a group of people; proverb. *One old adage is, "birds of a feather flock together."* {**ă** dəj}

a·dapt verb (adapted, adapting, adapts) 1. to change for a particular use. *They adapted the reading room for meetings.* 2. to become used to; adjust. *She adapted with ease to her new school.* {ə **dăpt**}

add verb (added, adding, adds) 1. to put on or with something else to make larger or better. *The soup tasted better after I added salt and pepper to it.* 2. to make larger or greater in size or amount; increase (followed by "to"). *The shouts from the street added to the noise outside.* 3. to find the sum of (often followed by "up"). *If you add up all the numbers, you will get the answer.* 4. to say or write more than what has been said or written. *I thanked them and then added that I had had a good time.* / *The teacher added a few sentences to the student's paper.*

5. to perform the mathematical operation of addition. *If you add 3 to 6 you get 9.* 6. to make the correct total or expected result (fol. by "up"). {**ăd**}

Homophone Note The words **add** and **ad** sound alike but have different meanings.

ad·dend noun a number or amount added to another to form a sum. *In the equation 4 + 3 = 7, the numbers 4 and 3 are addends.* {**ă** dehnd or ə **dehnd**}

ad·der noun a small, poisonous snake found in Europe and Asia. {**ăd** ər}

ad·dict noun 1. one who depends on something, such as a drug, that is usually bad for them and which they can't give up. 2. one who very much enjoys a hobby or interest and spends a lot of time and energy on it. *Ever since my parents bought a pool, I have been a swimming addict.* verb (addicted, addicting, addicts) to cause to depend on something that is hard to give up. *Having a candy bar every day addicted me to chocolate.* {**ă** dihkt, n., ə **dihkt**, v.}

ad·dic·tion noun the condition of being addicted, especially to something that is not good for one's health. *His addiction to coffee has caused his heart to race.* {ə **dihk** shən}

ad·di·tion noun 1. the act or process of adding. *The addition of cheese made the sandwich taste much better.* 2. the arithmetic operation of finding the total of two or more numbers. *Often the first example of addition that we learn is 1+1=2.* 3. anything that is added to something else. *The addition to our school will give us a new art room and*

 Human Body

 Human Mind

 Everyday Life

 History and Culture

 Communication

gym. / *This baby is an addition to our family.* {ə **dih** shən}

ad·di·tion·al *adjective* more; added. *I will need additional furniture for the living room.* {ə **dih** shə nəl}

ad·di·tive *noun* a substance added to another substance in small amounts to change or improve it. *Additives can keep food fresh.* {**ă** də tihv}

ad·dress *noun* 1. a formal speech or talk. *Many people watched the president's address on TV.* 2. the place where one lives or a business is located. *The address has the street name and number, city, and state or province. The address is 20 East Park Street, Washington, D.C.* 3. this information written or printed on things that are mailed. *It is hard to read the address on this envelope.* *verb* (addressed, addressing, addresses) 1. to speak or write to. *When he said that, he was addressing me, not you.* / *The mayor addressed the people of the town in a letter printed in the newspaper.* 2. to give attention to; deal with. *We addressed the problems right away.* 3. to write information on, telling where something can be delivered. *I addressed the letter to him in Paris.* {ə **drehs**}

ad·e·noid *noun* (usually plural) a mass of tissue that grows behind the nose in the upper part of the throat. When swollen, the adenoids can make breathing difficult. {**ă** də **noid**}

ad·ept *adjective* having great skill or ability. *My friends and I are adept at skiing.* {ə **dehpt**}

ad·e·quate *adjective* enough for the situation or need. *The coaches decided that the condition of the track was adequate for the race.* {**ă** də kwiht} adequately, adv.

ad·here *verb* (adhered, adhering, adheres) 1. to stick or cling firmly (usually followed by "to"). *The bandage adhered to her skin.* 2. to obey or follow (usually followed by "to"). *We adhered to the rules.* {ăd **heer**}

ad·he·sive *adjective* able or likely to stick to something; clinging. *The adhesive bandage kept my cut from getting dirty.* *noun* a sticky substance or material such as glue. *We'll need an adhesive to fix the broken dish.* {ăd **hee** sihv}

ad·i·os *interjection* a word that means "good-bye" in Spanish. *My Mexican friend speaks English but he still says "adios" when we say good-bye.* {ah dee **ohs**}

ad·ja·cent *adjective* near or next to. *The bank is adjacent to the post office.* {ə **jay** sənt}

ad·jec·tive ❷ *noun* a word that describes or modifies a noun or pronoun. In the sentence, "It was a hard test," the word "hard" is an adjective. {**ă** jək tihv}

> **Word History** The word *adjective* comes from a Latin word, *adjectiva*, which means "added." Adjectives add information to a noun.

ad·join *verb* (adjoined, adjoining, adjoins) to be next to; border on. *Our lawn adjoins the one next door.* {ə **join**}

ad·journ *verb* (adjourned, adjourning, adjourns) to end the work of a meeting or the like for a period of time. *The meeting adjourned until next week.* {ə **juhrn**}

ad·just *verb* (adjusted, adjusting, adjusts) 1. to bring to a better state or position; make fit. *I adjusted my seat belt.* 2. to change in order to fit in; get used to. *I'm still adjusting to the new school.* 3. to change or adapt. *He adjusted the rules so that the children could have more time for recess.* {ə **juhst**} adjustable, adj., adjuster, n.

ad·just·ment *noun* the act or process of changing or fixing something. *My teacher made an adjustment to my grade after I did some extra work.* {ə **juhst** mənt}

ad-lib *verb* (ad-libbed, ad-libbing, ad-libs) to make up as one goes along; say or do something without practice or planning. *He didn't know he would have to give a speech, so he ad-libbed.* / *In the middle of the play, I forgot my lines, so I ad-libbed.* *adjective* made up or said without practice; not rehearsed. *I sang a funny ad-libbed song.* {**ăd** lihb}

ad·min·is·ter *verb* (administered, administering, administers) 1. to manage, take care of, or be in charge of. *The Girl Scout leader administers the troop.* 2. to give or dispense. *He administered the correct amount of medicine.* 3. to serve or act in a helpful way; tend (usually followed by "to"). *A nurse is supposed to administer to the needs of her patients.* {əd **mih** nih stər}

ad·min·is·tra·tion *noun* 1. the act of being in charge of or managing something. *He is the president of a company, so he has experience in business administration.* 2. the people in charge of taking care of or managing something as a group. *The school administration had a meeting and listened to the teachers, parents, and*

🌲 Living World   🔬 Physical World   Natural Environment   〜 Economy   📖 Government and Law

a
b
c
d
e
f
g
h
i
j
k
l
m
n
o
p
q
r
s
t
u
v
w
x
y
z

students. 3. the executive officers of a government, or the term of office of such officers. *The president is the head of the administration of the United States. / None of us were alive during the administration of George Washington.* {əd **mih** nih <u>stray</u> shən}

ad·mi·ra·ble *adjective* very good; worthy of praise; deserving of being admired. *It was admirable of you to read to the sick children in the hospital.* {**ăd** mə rə bəl} admirably, adv.

ad·mi·ral *noun* an officer in the United States Navy of the highest rank; the commander of a fleet of ships or military unit. {**ăd** mə rəl}

ad·mi·ra·tion  *noun* a feeling of wonder, awe, or deep respect. *She was filled with admiration as she watched the doctor work with the sick children. / He had a deep admiration for his favorite baseball player.* {ăd mə <u>ray</u> shən}

ad·mire *verb* (admired, admiring, admires) 1. to have a high opinion of; respect. *I admire the hard work you do.* 2. to look at with delight, wonder, and approval. *Everyone was admiring my new bike.* {əd <u>miyr</u>} admirer, n., admiringly, adv.

ad·mis·sion *noun* 1. the act, process, or result of allowing to enter. *She was in charge of the admission of sick people to the hospital. / They were refused admission to the restaurant because they were barefoot.* 2. the price a person must pay to enter. *Admission to this movie is only two dollars.* 3. the act of telling the truth or confessing. *His admission of guilt did not come until after he found out that someone had seen him take the bike.* {əd **mih** shən}

ad·mit *verb* (admitted, admitting, admits) 1. to let in; allow to enter. *This movie ticket admits one. / The restaurant admitted us after a long wait.* 2. to tell the truth; confess. *Did he admit he broke the window?* {əd **miht**}

ad·mit·tance *noun* permission to enter; right of entry. *There will be no admittance for children under the age of thirteen.* {əd **mih** təns}

ad·mon·ish *verb* (admonished, admonishing, admonishes) 1. to warn or caution. *The teacher admonished the children to look more carefully when they crossed the street.* 2. to find fault with or correct in a mild but firm way. *He admonished us for speaking so loudly.* {əd **mo** nihsh}

a·do·be *noun* 1. a building material of clay mixed with straw that has been dried by the sun and made into bricks. 2. a building made of adobe bricks. {ə **doh** bee}

ad·o·les·cence *noun* the period in a person's life between childhood and adulthood. *In his adolescence, he was the junior high football star.* {ă də **leh** səns}

ad·o·les·cent *adjective* having to do with the period when a person is changing from a child to an adult. *The teens loved the adolescent movie, but the parents were bored by it.* *noun* a person who is changing from a child to an adult; teenager. *Adolescents often have a hard time talking with their parents.* {ă də **leh** sənt}

a·dopt *verb* (adopted, adopting, adopts) 1. to become a parent of by law. *My mom and dad adopted a little girl from China, so now I have a sister.* 2. to take on and use as one's own. *When did you adopt that attitude towards school? / She has adopted a weird laugh to get attention.* 3. to accept by voting for. *Congress adopted the law.* {ə **dŏpt**}

> **Language Note** *Adopt* and *adapt* are easy to confuse because they are close in spelling and pronunciation. Make sure you use the right word. If you *adopt* something, you take it as your own or become its legal parent. *Many people adopt pets from an animal shelter.* To *adapt* means to change so as to be useful or suitable. *Many animals adapt to their environment in surprising ways*

> **Word History** The English word *adopt* is from a Latin word *adoptare* that means "to choose for oneself" or "to choose as one's own." If you take away the prefix *ad-* from *adoptare*, the word *optare* is left. *Optare* means "to choose freely." Other English words that come from *optare* include "option" (a choice) and "opt" (choose).

a·dop·tion *noun* the act of adopting a child or being adopted by law. *The couple was happy when they found out the adoption was final. / My parents told me about my adoption when I was little.* {ə **dŏp** shən}

a·dor·a·ble *adjective* very cute; lovable; deserving of being loved. *My sister has an adorable new puppy.* {ə **dohr** ə bəl}

a·dore *verb* (adored, adoring, adores) 1. to honor and worship for being divine. *I adore God, and my Muslim friend adores Allah.* 2. to love and honor deeply. *He adores his grandmother and often brings her flowers.* 3. (informal) to like very much. *I adore that new song, don't you?* {ə **dohr**} adoringly, adv.

 Human Body    Human Mind    Everyday Life   History and Culture    Communication

a·dorn *verb* (adorned, adorning, adorns) to add beauty to; decorate. *We adorn our house with lights during Christmas to make it look pretty.* / *She adorned herself with jewelry.* {ə **dohrn**}

a·drift *adjective* moving or floating without being steered; drifting; not anchored. *Our raft was adrift in the sea.* / *When the string broke, the kite was adrift in the sky.* *adverb* without anchor; floating freely; drifting. *The ship was set adrift by the storm.* / *The balloon was set adrift by a blast of wind.* {ə **drihft**}

a·dult ⊕ ▲ *adjective* 1. having grown up; mature. *The adult dog was much bigger than the puppy.* 2. of or having to do with adults. *My parents and their friends were having an adult conversation at the dinner table.* *noun* 1. a person who is fully grown and mature; grown-up. *When I am an adult, I will be able to decide for myself.* / *The adults talked while the children played in the water.* 2. an animal or plant that is fully grown and mature. *The farmer put the plants into two groups: seedlings and adults.* {ə **duhlt**}

a·dult·hood *noun* the part of life when a person is grown up; the adult years. *When he reached adulthood, he left his parents' home.* {ə **duhlt** huud}

ad·vance *verb* (advanced, advancing, advances) 1. to move or send forward. *The quarterback advanced the ball ten yards.* 2. to come or move forward. *The car advanced ten feet.* 3. to offer or suggest. *She advanced her plan for a new youth center.* 4. to raise in rank or position. *They will advance him to captain.* 5. to make progress or grow. *His piano teacher says he is advancing nicely.* *noun* 1. a forward movement in space. *The runner made a quick advance to the finish line.* 2. progress or improvement. *The twentieth century saw great advances in the field of medicine.* 3. money paid before work is finished. *She asked for an advance on her allowance so that she could pay for her ticket.* {əd **văns**}

• **in advance**
before or early. *Please call in advance.*

ad·vanced *adjective* 1. beyond an early or beginning level; in a very developed state. *I'm a good swimmer and am in the advanced class.* / *The equipment was too advanced for me to use.* / *The small country was quite advanced in education.* 2. quite old. *My grandmother is advanced in years.* {əd **vănst**}

ad·vance·ment ♀ *noun* 1. a moving forward or being moved forward; progress. *Have you made any advancement in your job hunt?* / *There was quite an advancement in the building of the new store.* 2. a move to a higher or better position or rank. *My advancement to president of our club was a big surprise.* {əd **văns** mənt}

ad·van·tage *noun* 1. a better chance or position; upper hand. *When we raced, she had the advantage because she had been training.* / *He has an advantage in the class election because everyone knows and likes him.* 2. the good or benefit that is gained from something. *What are the advantages of leaving so early?* {əd **văn** tihj}

• **take advantage of**
1. to use for your own benefit; treat selfishly. *When I offered to let my friend use my bike one day, he took advantage of me by keeping it for a week.* 2. to use in order to help oneself; benefit by. *She took advantage of the chance to go to college.* / *He took advantage of the sale by buying the books he needed.*

ad·van·ta·geous *adjective* giving a benefit or advantage; helpful; useful. *Taking the bus was advantageous because it saved time.* {ăd vən **tay** jihs or ăd văn **tay** jihs}

ad·ven·ture *noun* 1. a journey or activity that is dangerous or exciting. *Sailing around the world alone would be quite an adventure.* / *The first time I rode a horse was a big adventure.* 2. taking part in such activities. *Let me tell you about my exciting adventures.* {əd **vehn** chər}

ad·ven·tur·ous *adjective* 1. willing to take risks in order to find excitement; daring. *Her parents worried about her because she had an adventurous spirit.* 2. exciting; full of risks. *He came across an angry elephant and several lions on his adventurous trip to Africa.* {əd **vehn** chə rihs}

ad·verb ❷ *noun* a word that describes or modifies a verb, adjective, or other adverb. {ăd vərb}

ad·ver·sar·y *noun* (adversaries) a person, group, or thing that is against another; opponent; enemy. *The two countries were adversaries and fought against each other during the war.* {ăd vər **sayr** ee}

ad·verse *adjective* 1. not helpful to one's wishes or interests. *The adverse weather made it hard to set up camp.* 2. causing

A
B
C
D
E
F
G
H
I
J
K
L
M
N
O
P
Q
R
S
T
U
V
W
X
Y
Z

harm or injury; bad; damaging. *The movie was too scary for children and had an adverse effect on the little girl. / Her skin had an adverse reaction to the cream.* {**ăd** vərs or əd **vərs**} adversely, adv.

ad·ver·si·ty *noun* (adversities) a condition of trouble or difficulty. *Times were bad, and the town was filled with adversity. / She lost her home in the flood but faced this adversity with courage.* {əd **vər** sih tee}

ad·ver·tise *verb* (advertised, advertising, advertises) 1. to present as good or favorable in order to win people's business or support. *The stores start advertising Halloween candy in September.* 2. to call attention to. *He advertises his wealth by wearing flashy gold jewelry.* 3. to try to find something by placing a notice or advertisement in a public place (usually followed by "for"). *She advertised for a babysitter in the newspaper.* {**ăd** vər **tiyz**} advertiser, n.

ad·ver·tise·ment *noun* a public notice that tells people about products, services, or things that are happening. *There was an advertisement on television for a new cereal. / Did you see the advertisement in the newspaper for the school play?* {**ăd** vər **tiyz** mənt}

ad·vice *noun* an idea or opinion offered as help in making a choice or a decision. *My father gave me good advice about how to make friends.* {əd **viys**}

ad·vis·a·ble *adjective* being good and wise advice; sensible; recommended. *It is advisable to start thinking about college now rather than later.* {əd **viy** zə bəl}

ad·vise *verb* (advised, advising, advises) 1. to give advice to; recommend. *My parents advised me about what to take on my trip.* 2. to tell; inform; notify. *I am waiting for the letter that will advise me that I made the team.* {əd **viyz**}

ad·vis·er or **advisor** *noun* a person who gives advice. *My school adviser is always there when I need to talk with someone.* {əd **viy** zər}

ad·vo·cate *verb* (advocated, advocating, advocates) to speak or act in favor of. *He advocates buying fruits and vegetables grown on local farms.* *noun* one who speaks or acts in favor of something. *I am an advocate for better care of our forests.* {**ăd** və kət, n., **ăd** və **kayt**, v.}

aer·i·al *adjective* 1. of or happening in the air or atmosphere. *The people who jumped out of the plane joined hands to form an aerial circle before they landed on the ground safely.* 2. having to do with or done by means of flying. *My house looked so small in the aerial photograph of my neighborhood.* *noun* a radio or television antenna. {**ayr** ee əl}

aer·o·bic *adjective* able to work the heart and lungs to help the body use oxygen better. *Running is an aerobic exercise.* {ayr **oh** bihk}

aer·o·bics *noun* (aerobics) (used with a singular or plural verb) a form of exercise that works the heart and lungs to help the body use oxygen better. Running, swimming, biking, or dance are forms of aerobics. *Aerobics should be done at least a few days a week.* {ayr **oh** bihks}

aer·o·dy·nam·ic *adjective* having a smooth, even shape that offers the least possible resistance to air currents or movement. *That new sports car has an aerodynamic design.* {ayr oh diy **năm** ihk}

aer·o·nau·tics *noun* (used with a singular verb) a science that deals with making and flying aircraft. {ayr ə **naw** tihks} aeronautic, adj.

aer·o·sol *noun* 1. liquid or solid particles suspended in a gas. 2. a liquid that is in a container under pressure and comes out in a fine spray. *Deodorants and paint can be bought in aerosol.* {**ayr** ə sawl}

aer·o·space *noun* the earth's atmosphere and the space beyond it. *Airplanes and spacecraft fly in aerospace.* {**ayr** oh **spays**}

aes·thet·ic or **esthetic** *adjective* having to do with beauty or art, including literature, dance, music, painting, drawing, and sculpture. *She filled her bedroom with aesthetic objects.* {ehs **theh** tihk}

a·far *adverb* at, to, or from a distance; far off. *He travelled afar, searching everywhere for the magic ring he had lost.* {ə **far**}

af·fa·ble *adjective* pleasant to talk to and be with; friendly; likeable. *The new girl in my class is affable, and everyone likes her.* {**ăf** ə bəl}

af·fair *noun* 1. an event, matter, or happening. *It was a sad affair when the widow Welby's wedding ring was stolen.* 2. (plural) public or business matters. *As mayor, he is busy with the affairs of the city.* 3. private matter; something that relates to or concerns only oneself. *How much money my father makes is my affair, not yours.* {ə **fayr**}

 Human Body    Human Mind    Everyday Life    History and Culture   Communication

af·fect[1] *verb* (affected, affecting, affects) 1. to cause a change in; influence. *When the sun came out, it affected my plans to stay inside and read.* 2. to cause to feel sad or sorry; move; touch. *The picture of the puppy with its sad eyes affected him deeply.* {ə **fehkt**}

af·fect[2] *verb* (affected, affecting, affects) to imitate or pretend to have. *He affected sadness, but in truth he was very happy to see the person leave.* {ə **fehkt**}

af·fec·tion ℗ *noun* a friendly feeling of liking or loving someone or something. *I have very strong affection for my grandparents.* {ə **fehk** shən}

af·fec·tion·ate *adjective* feeling or showing love or affection. *My affectionate mom always gives me a kiss and hug when I leave.* {ə **fehk** shə niht} affectionately, adv.

af·fil·i·ate *verb* (affiliated, affiliating, affiliates) 1. to join as a member or smaller branch of (usually followed by "with"). *Our school's science club affiliated itself with the national science club.* 2. to be closely joined or connected. *The reading club is affiliated with the library.* *noun* a person or group that is connected with another similar, larger group. *My Boy Scout troop is an affiliate of Boys Scouts of America.* {ə **fih** lee ət, n., ə **fih** lee ayt, v.} affiliation, n.

af·firm *verb* (affirmed, affirming, affirms) to state or declare as true. *I affirmed that I had washed my hands before sitting down to eat.* {ə **fərm**}

af·firm·a·tive *adjective* saying yes; affirming. *It was a cold day, so when he asked if I needed a ride, I gave an affirmative answer.* {ə **fər** mə tihv} affirmatively, adv.

affirmative action *noun* a policy to make sure certain groups of people are given a fair chance for jobs and education. In particular, this policy is for minority groups and women who were not given these opportunities in the past. Regulations made by the U.S. government support affirmative action. *The United States government believes in affirmative action.* {ə **fər** mə tihv **ăk** shən}

af·fix *verb* (affixed, affixing, affixes) to attach or join physically (usually used with "to"). *She affixed a poster to the wall.* *noun* an element of meaning that is added to a word to change its meaning or function; prefix or suffix.The prefix "pre-" and the suffix "-ness" are both affixes. {**ăf** ihks, n., ə **fihks**, v.}

af·flict *verb* (afflicted, afflicting, afflicts) to cause pain or suffering to. *The flu afflicts many people every year.* {ə **flihkt**}

af·flic·tion *noun* a condition of pain or suffering, or the cause of such a state. *She has a hard time walking because of her back affliction. / I looked at my freckles as an affliction.* {ə **flihk** shən}

af·flu·ent *adjective* having a lot of money; rich; wealthy. *The big houses on my street are owned by affluent families.* {**ăf** looh ənt}

af·ford *verb* (afforded, affording, affords) 1. to have enough money to buy; be able to pay for. *I can't afford a fancy television.* 2. to be able to do without fear of harm. *We can afford to waste time this morning because there is no school.* 3. to give; provide. *Travel affords the chance to see different parts of the world.* {ə **fohrd**} affordable, adj.

af·front *noun* something that is said or done on purpose to be rude or mean. *It was an affront when he called me a baby.* *verb* (affronted, affronting, affronts) to say or do something mean to on purpose. *The boy affronted the girl by pulling her hair.* {ə **fruhnt**}

Af·ghan *noun* 1. a person who was born in or who is a citizen of Afghanistan. 2. (lower case) a soft blanket that is knitted or crocheted. Afghans often have stripes or patterns. *My grandmother made me a blue and yellow afghan for my bed.* {**ăf** găn}

Af·ghan·i·stan *noun* a country in south central Asia. Kabul is the capital of Afghanistan. {**ăf** găn ə **stăn**} Afghan, n., adj.

a·field *adverb* 1. off the right track or course. *He went afield of the law and got into trouble.* 2. away from one's home. *He goes far afield to find unusual birds.* {ə **feeld**}

a·fire *adjective* 1. burning; on fire. *The house was afire, and smoke filled the sky.* 2. very interested. *I'm afire to know whether our team won the game or not!* {ə **fiyr**}

a·float *adverb or adjective* on the water; floating. *She was surprised that she could stay afloat.* {ə **floht**}

a·foot *adverb or adjective* on foot; walking. {ə **fuut**}

a·fraid ℗ *adjective* 1. feeling fear. *I am afraid of snakes.* 2. feeling sorry or unhappy about something. *I'm afraid I can't go to the party with you.* {ə **frayd**}

a
b
c
d
e
f
g
h
i
j
k
l
m
n
o
p
q
r
s
t
u
v
w
x
y
z

a·fresh *adverb* once again; anew. *The flowers will bloom afresh this summer.* {ə **frehsh**}

Af·ri·ca *noun* the second largest continent. Africa is south of Europe and between the Atlantic and Indian Oceans. It is in the Eastern Hemisphere. {**ăf** rə kə}

Af·ri·can *adjective* of or having to do with Africa, or its people or languages. *noun* a person who was born in or is a citizen of a country in Africa. {**ăf** rə kən}

Af·ri·can A·mer·i·can or **African-American** *adjective* of or having to do with American blacks, their African heritage, or their history or culture. *noun* an American of African descent. {**ăf** rə kən ə **mehr** ih kən}

Af·ro A·mer·i·can *adjective* See **African American**. {**ăf** roh ə **meh** rih kən}

af·ter *preposition* 1. later in time than, or behind in order. *After school, I had a snack. / The first house after the white one is mine.* 2. as a result of. *After what happened yesterday, she may never go back there.* 3. with the same name as. *The baby was named after me.* 4. looking for or in search of. *The dog chased after the squirrel. adverb* 1. at the rear; behind. *A bridesmaid walked down the aisle and the bride walked after.* 2. after some time; later. *She leaves the house at nine, and he leaves not long after. conjunction* following a certain event or time. *It happened after she left.* {**ăf** tər}

af·ter·noon *noun* the period between noon and evening. *School usually gets out in the afternoon. adjective* having to do with the period between noon and evening. *Every*

Sunday, I like to take an afternoon nap. {**ăf** tər **noohn**}

af·ter·ward *adverb* at a later time. *He painted the steps and afterward went out for pizza.* {**ăf** tər wərd} afterwards, adv.

Ag symbol of the chemical element silver.

a·gain *adverb* 1. one more time; over again. *Please say that again.* 2. once more; as before. *He was poor for a while, but now he's rich again.* {ə **gehn**}

• **again and again** many times. *She warned him against speeding again and again.*

a·gainst *preposition* 1. in the opposite direction to. *They were walking against the wind.* 2. in opposition to. *What you did was against the rules.* 3. in contact with. *Waves crashed against the shore.* 4. on or touching, so as to be supported by. *I'll lean the ladder against this tree.* {ə **gehnst**}

ag·ate *noun* 1. a type of quartz that has forms or bands of different colors that look like clouds. 2. a playing marble that is made of or looks like this stone. {**ăg** iht}

age  *noun* 1. the length of time that a person or thing has existed. *He said his age was twelve. / What is the age of this building?* 2. a particular time or stage in life. *He is at the age when children stop listening to their parents.* 3. the later years of life; old age. *It is age that is making him forget things.* 4. a period of history. *We live in the modern age.* 5. a very long time. *I waited for what seemed like an age. verb* (aged, aging, ages) 1. to show the signs of old age. *My grandfather has aged a lot since we last saw him.* 2. to become mature; ripen. *Wine ages in these casks.* 3. to make or

cause to grow old; mature. *We age cheese before eating it. / Her troubles have aged her.* {**ayj**}

a·ged or **aged** *adjective* 1. being old or having lived many years. *She does the housework for her aged grandfather.* 2. having or being the age of. *She had a sister aged three and a brother aged twelve. noun* old people as a group. *The aged wish for peace.* {**ay** jihd, n., **ayjd**, adj.}

age·ism *noun* the act of having a bad opinion of, or not treating in a fair way, a person or group of people based on age. This kind of discrimination is often against older people. *When the girls decided right off that the speaker would be boring because she is old, they were showing ageism.* {**ay** jih zəm}

a·gen·cy *noun* (agencies) 1. a company or organization that does business in support of other companies or people. *There is a large job agency that supplies workers for several companies in the area. / The job agency also helps people find work.* 2. an agent's place of business. *Our insurance agent works at this agency.* 3. a government department that manages laws and rules. *The hospital has to follow the rules set up by the national health agency.* {**ay** jən see}

a·gen·da *noun* a list of things to be done or talked about. *Washing his bike was on his agenda for the day. / Deciding where to camp this summer was on the agenda for the club meeting.* {ə **jehn** də}

a·gent *noun* 1. a person who has been given the power to do certain actions for another person. *The author's agent called to discuss his fees for*

 Human Body   Human Mind   Everyday Life    History and Culture   Communication

speaking at the school. 2. a force or means that brings about certain results; cause. *Whenever he was around, it seemed like bad things happened, so we called him the agent of doom. / We're going to have to use a very strong cleaning agent to get out that dirt.* {**ay** jənt}

ag·gra·vate *verb* (aggravated, aggravating, aggravates) 1. to make worse. *She aggravated the pain in her knee by walking too soon after she got hurt.* 2. (informal) to bother or annoy. *All of the noise on the playground aggravated me when I tried to read.* {**ăg** rə **vayt**}

ag·gres·sion ❓ *noun* 1. an attack or war against a country started without good cause by another country. *The aggression began when the large country's government decided they wanted to take over the small country.* 2. any mean or unfriendly act against another. *Punching someone is an act of aggression.* {ə **greh** shən}

ag·gres·sive *adjective* 1. mean and unfriendly in one's actions; ready to argue or start fights. *He has a hard time getting along with others because of his aggressive nature.* 2. very bold; acting as if full of power and authority; forceful. *The more aggressive kids pushed to the front of the line.* {ə **greh** sihv} aggressively, adv., aggressiveness, n.

a·ghast *adjective* filled with alarm or horror; shocked. *We were aghast when we saw that the fire was spreading towards the hospital.* {ə **găst**}

ag·ile *adjective* 1. moving quickly and gracefully. *Gymnasts are very agile.* 2. quick in mind; sharp; alert. *He has an agile*

mind and can quickly solve your riddle. {**ă** jəl} agility, n.

a·gil·i·ty ❓ *noun* the ability to move or think easily and quickly. *A tennis player must have agility.* {ă **jihl** ih tee}

ag·i·tate ❓ *verb* (agitated, agitating, agitates) 1. to cause to move in a quick, tumbling motion or with force; shake. *A washing machine works by agitating the clothes. / The wind blowing through the open window agitated the curtains.* 2. to upset or excite. *Our questions about the missing necklace agitated the babysitter.* 3. to try to stir up public support (often followed by "for" or "against"). *The parents are agitating for more teachers and smaller classes.* {**ă** jə **tayt**}

a·glow *adjective* 1. shining with a soft light; glowing; bright. *The sky was aglow with the light from millions of stars.* 2. looking happy and excited. *He was aglow from the trip to the lake.* {ə **gloh**}

a·go *adjective* before now. *I lost my jacket three days ago.* *adverb* in the past. *He lived long ago.* {ə **goh**}

ag·o·ny ❓ ❓ *noun* (agonies) great or intense pain and suffering in the mind or body, usually over a long period of time. *I was in agony when my dog died. / It was hard to see the patient in so much agony.* {**ă** gə nee}

Word History The word *agony* comes from a Greek word that means "a contest or struggle."

a·gree *verb* (agreed, agreeing, agrees) 1. to have the same opinion or feel the same way

(often followed by "with"). *I agree with my friend about most things.* 2. to say yes; consent. *He agreed to do the job for us.* 3. to come to an understanding or a shared decision. *They finally agreed on a solution to the problem.* 4. to be right for; fit. *That color agrees with her complexion.* 5. to be alike; match. *Do our answers agree?* {ə **gree**}

a·gree·a·ble *adjective* 1. pleasant, nice, or likable. *My doctor is an agreeable person.* 2. ready to say yes or give permission. *Was the teacher agreeable when you asked for no homework this weekend?* {ə **gree** ə bəl}

a·gree·ment ❓ *noun* 1. the act of coming to a common understanding or of agreeing. *My parents and I reached an agreement about how much time I must practice piano every day.* 2. an understanding between people or groups that states what kind of action is to be taken. *My parents asked me to sign an agreement that said I would clean my room at least once a week.* 3. common understanding; harmony; accord. *My friends and I were in agreement about renting a movie instead of watching TV.* {ə **gree** mənt}

a·gri·cul·tur·al *adjective* having to do with agriculture or farming. *I live in an agricultural area of the state.* {ăg rə **kuhl** chər əl}

ag·ri·cul·ture ❶ ❓ *noun* the science and work of raising crops and farm animals; farming. {ăg rə **kuhl** chər}

ah *interjection* a word used to express surprise, joy, pain, understanding, dislike, and other feelings. *Ah! I didn't see you there! / Ah, yes, now I see what you mean.* {**ah**}

a·ha *interjection* a word used to express feelings like surprise, success, discovery, or satisfaction. *Aha, I knew I'd find you there!* {ə **hah**}

a·head *adverb* 1. before; in front. *Call ahead if you want to get a hotel room.* 2. forward; toward a further time or position. *This line is not moving ahead.* 3. in the future. *Trouble lies ahead.* {ə **hehd**}

a·hoy *interjection* a word used as a greeting to attract the attention of sailors on a ship. *The sailors yelled "Ahoy there!" to the crew of a passing ship.* {ə **hoi**}

aid *verb* (aided, aiding, aids) to give help to or assist. *The doctor aided the accident victims.* *noun* 1. help or assistance that is given to someone in need. *The old lady was glad to have the aid of her neighbors.* 2. a person or thing that helps or assists. *He needs a hearing aid.* / *She was an aid to him when he was sick.* {**ayd**}

Homophone Note The words **aid** and **aide** sound alike but have slightly different meanings. A person who helps is called an "aide," not an "aid."

aide *noun* any assistant or person who gives support. *The teacher's aide helped me learn to read.* {**ayd**}

Homophone Note The words **aide** and **aid** sound alike but have slightly different meanings.

AIDS *abbreviation* a disease caused by a virus that stops the body from being able to protect itself from other diseases, usually leading to death. AIDS stands for "acquired immune deficiency syndrome." {**aydz**}

ail ● *verb* (ailed, ailing, ails) 1. to trouble or cause pain to. *His bad knees are ailing him.* / *I heard you moaning and want to know what ails you.* 2. to be ill or feel sick. *She has been ailing ever since the accident.* {**ayl**}

Homophone Note Are you looking for the word **ale** (an alcoholic drink)? **Ail** and **ale** sound alike but have different meanings.

ail·ment *noun* a sickness or disorder; illness. *She was not in school for a month because of an ailment.* {**ayl** mənt}

aim *verb* (aimed, aiming, aims) 1. to point carefully with the hope of hitting something or someone. *He carefully aimed the gun at the target.* 2. to point or position. *She aimed the camera toward the movie star and snapped a picture.* 3. to direct toward or intend for. *He aimed his remarks at me.* 4. to intend or try (often followed by "to" or "at"). *We aim to finish our book reports tomorrow.* *noun* 1. the act of aiming. *Her aim is perfect every time she shoots the arrow.* 2. intention; purpose; goal. *My aim this month is to finish planting my garden.* {**aym**}

aim·less *adjective* having no purpose or goal. *We took an aimless drive through the town on Sunday.* {**aym** lihs} aimlessly, adv., aimlessness, n.

ain't (informal) a contraction of "am not," "is not," "are not," "have not," or "has not."

Language Note *Ain't* is not correct English. So why is it in a dictionary? For one thing, it is part of American English. You may have heard people use "ain't," especially in everyday conversation. You may even use it yourself. This does not mean it is correct. In fact, "ain't" will make you sound uneducated, even ignorant, to some people. Use "am not" or "isn't" or "aren't," instead, especially in writing. Sometimes an author will write "ain't" on purpose, in order to show how a character talks. But authors probably don't talk that way themselves.

air ●●●●● *noun* 1. the mixture of gases that surrounds the earth. Air is made up of oxygen, nitrogen, and other gases, and has no taste, odor, or color. 2. all that is above the ground; sky. *The kite flew high up in the air.* 3. movement of the atmosphere; breeze or wind. *We enjoyed the cool air coming in through the window.* 4. the way a thing or person appears to be. *The magician had an air of mystery.* *verb* (aired, airing, airs) 1. to open to the air or put outdoors. *We aired out the house on the first warm day.* 2. to speak about, usually in public. *He aired his problems.* {**ayr**}

• **into thin air**
out of sight. *She vanished into thin air.*

• **on [or] off the air**
broadcast on radio or television; not broadcast on radio or television. *The show was on the air last year.* / *Her favorite program went off the air because not many other people liked it.*

• **up in the air**
not decided, not settled, or

 Human Body    Human Mind   Everyday Life   History and Culture   Communication

not certain. *Our vacation plans are up in the air.*

Homophone Note The words *air*, *ere*, and *heir* sound alike, but each has a different meaning.

air bag *noun* a bag in the front of some cars that blows up with air instantly in a crash to stop the passengers from being thrown forward. {<u>ayr</u> băg}

air con·di·tion·er *noun* a machine that cools the air in a room or car. An air conditioner also takes the dust and dampness out of the air. {<u>ayr</u> kən **dih** shən ər}

air conditioning *noun* a system that cools air and takes dust and dampness out of it. Air conditioning is used inside buildings and cars. {<u>ayr</u> kən **dih** shə ning}

air·craft *noun* (aircraft) any machine that can fly through the air, such as an airplane, helicopter, glider, or balloon. {<u>ayr</u> krăft}

aircraft carrier *noun* a very large ship with a flat deck on which airplanes can take off and land. {<u>ayr</u> krăft kayr ee ər}

air force *noun* the branch of a nation's armed forces that trains and fights using aircraft. {<u>ayr</u> fohrs}

air·line *noun* a business that offers the service of taking passengers or freight by airplane from one place to another. *Which airline will you take when you fly to your grandmother's house?* {<u>ayr</u> liyn}

air·lin·er *noun* a large airplane used to fly people from one place to another. {<u>ayr</u> liy nər}

air·mail *adjective* of or having to do with mail sent by air. *My airmail letter was sent last week and arrived in France yesterday.* *noun* 1. mail carried by airplane. *The airmail arrived in California an hour ago and has already been taken off the airplane and loaded onto the trucks.* 2. the sending of mail by airplane. *The package was sent by airmail.* *adverb* by way of air. *The letter came airmail.* *verb* (airmailed, airmailing, airmails) to send by air rather than by land or sea. *I will airmail my letter to you in Europe just as soon as I finish it.* {<u>ayr</u> mayl}

air·plane ⊙ *noun* a machine that can fly because of the force of air upon its wings; plane. An airplane is driven by propellers or a jet engine. {<u>ayr</u> playn}

air·port *noun* a large area of level land where airplanes can land and take off. *The airplane loaded passengers, cargo, and fuel at the airport.* {<u>ayr</u> pohrt}

air pressure *noun* the force of air on things. Air pressure has to do with how much force air has when it has been compressed into a space like a tire. It is also the pressure of the earth's atmosphere. {<u>ayr</u> preh shər}

air·ship *noun* an aircraft that is lighter than air and can be steered. An airship has an engine and is filled with gas. *Blimps are one kind of airship.* {<u>ayr</u> shihp}

air·sick *adjective* feeling sick or dizzy because of air travel; feeling ill due to flying. *I become airsick every time I fly in an airplane.* {<u>ayr</u> sihk}

air·strip *noun* a landing strip or cleared area where aircraft land or take off; runway. An airstrip usually is not paved and does not have the workers or equipment of an airport. {<u>ayr</u> strihp}

air·tight *adjective* 1. keeping air in or out. *Please put whatever you don't eat in an airtight container so that it will still be fresh tomorrow.* 2. having no weak points that could be open to attack. *I knew I had an airtight excuse for not doing my homework when I showed my teacher the note from the hospital.* {<u>ayr</u> tiyt} airtightness, n.

air·y *adjective* (airier, airiest) 1. open to the flow of air. *It felt nice to sit in the airy room on such a hot day.* 2. having a light, delicate look. *The thin curtains were made from an airy material.* {<u>ayr</u> ee}

aisle *noun* an open space for passing between rows or sections of seats or shelves. *I found the can of soup in one of the last aisles in the grocery store.* / *He walked slowly down the aisle of the church.* {<u>iy</u> əl}

Homophone Note The words *aisle*, *isle*, and the contraction *I'll*, sound alike, but each has a different meaning.

a·jar *adverb or adjective* partly opened. *The back door is ajar, so please make sure the dog doesn't get out.* {ə <u>jar</u>}

AK *abbreviation* an abbreviation for **Alaska**.

a·kim·bo *adverb or adjective* with hand on hip and elbow pointed away from the body. *I watched with my arms akimbo as the parade passed by.* {ə <u>kihm</u> boh}

a·kin *adjective* 1. belonging to the same family; related; kin. *My brother and I are akin.* / *My grandmother, my aunt, and I are akin.* 2. similar in kind or spirit; alike. *Smiles and laughter are akin.* {ə <u>kihn</u>}

Al symbol of the chemical element aluminum.

a
b
c
d
e
f
g
h
i
j
k
l
m
n
o
p
q
r
s
t
u
v
w
x
y
z

AL or **Ala.** *abbreviation* an abbreviation for **Alabama**.

-al[1] or **-ial** *suffix* a suffix that means "of" or "having to do with." *A historical novel is a novel having to do with history.*

-al[2] *suffix* a suffix that means "the action of." *Snow removal is the action of removing snow from roads and sidewalks.*

Al·a·bam·a *noun* a state in the southeastern United States. Its capital is Montgomery. (abbreviated: AL) {ă lə **bă** mə} Alabaman, n., adj., Alabamian, n., adj.

Word History *Alabama* was named after an Indian people in the region. The word "Alabama" may mean "people who gather plants."

al·a·bas·ter *noun* a hard, white stone that is often translucent. Alabaster is often carved to make statues and ornaments. *adjective* smooth and pale in appearance. *She has to be careful to keep her alabaster skin out of the sun. / It was an alabaster moon.* {**ă** lə bă stər}

a·larm *noun* 1. sudden fear caused by possible danger. *The report of a tornado filled us with alarm.* 2. a bell, buzzer, or siren that warns of some danger. *Smoke from the toaster set off the fire alarm.* 3. the bell or buzzer of an alarm clock. *I didn't hear my clock's alarm this morning. verb* (alarmed, alarming, alarms) to make afraid. *The dog's bark alarmed him.* {ə **larm**}

alarm clock *noun* a clock with a bell or buzzer that can be set to sound at a particular time. *The alarm clock woke me up in the morning.* {ə **larm** klŏk}

a·las *interjection* a word used to express sadness or disappointment. *Alas, we won't be seeing you during the holidays.* {ə **lăs**}

A·las·ka *noun* a state of the United States on the northwestern coast of North America. Its capital is Juneau. (abbreviated: AK) {ə **lă** skə} Alaskan, n., adj.

Word History *Alaska* is the English spelling of an Aleut word that means "great land."

Al·ba·ni·a *noun* a country in southeastern Europe. Albania is also called the People's Republic of Albania. Tirane is the capital of Albania. {ăl **bay** nee ə *or* ăl **bayn** yə} Albanian, n., adj.

Al·ber·ta *noun* a Canadian province located between Saskatchewan and British Columbia. Its capital is Edmonton. {ăl **buhr** tə}

Word History *Alberta* was named in honor of the British Princess Louise Caroline Alberta in 1882, when Canada divided the Northwest Territories into four parts.

al·bi·no *noun* (albinos) a human or animal that is born without normal coloring. Albinos have very pale skin and hair and pink eyes. Plants can also be albinos. {ăl **biy** noh}

al·bum ❷ *noun* 1. a book with blank pages or empty pockets in which a collection can be placed. An album can hold photographs, stamps, or mementos. 2. a musical recording that is made up of a few or several pieces of music. {ăl bəm}

al·co·hol ❷ *noun* 1. a clear liquid that burns easily and can be made from certain grains and fruits. Alcohol is present in such drinks as beer, wine, and whiskey. It is also used in making medicines and chemicals. 2. drinks that contain alcohol. *This restaurant does not serve alcohol.* {**ăl** kə **hawl** *or* **ăl** kə hŏl}

al·co·hol·ic *adjective* 1. containing alcohol. *They did not serve alcoholic drinks at the wedding.* 2. suffering from alcoholism. *My uncle divorced my aunt because she is alcoholic.* {**ăl** kə **haw** lihk *or* **ăl** kə **ho** lihk}

al·co·hol·ism *noun* a disease caused by the habit of drinking too much alcohol. Alcoholism is characterized by a strong desire to drink alcohol, difficulties in behaving properly, and troubling effects when alcohol use is stopped. {**ăl** kə hə lih zəm}

al·cove *noun* a partly enclosed area of a room. *We keep our telephone in an alcove off of the kitchen.* {**ăl** kohv}

al·der *noun* a tree or shrub of the birch family that grows in mostly cool, damp areas and drops its leaves every year. {**awl** dər}

ale *noun* an alcoholic drink that is like beer but more bitter. {**ayl**}

Homophone Note Are you looking for the word *ail* (to trouble or cause pain)? *Ale* and *ail* sound alike but have different meanings.

a·lert *adjective* watching carefully; quick to notice and act. *The alert driver avoided a hole in the road. noun* a warning of possible danger or the time during which such a warning lasts. *We stayed in the basement until the tornado alert*

 Human Body   Human Mind    Everyday Life   History and Culture   Communication

was over. *verb* (alerted, alerting, alerts) to warn or make aware. *The police alerted the town that a tiger had escaped from the zoo.* {ə **luhrt**} alertness, n.

Word History The English word *alert* comes from *a l'erte*, an early French phrase that means "on guard" or "on the watch." This French phrase came from an Italian military phrase, *all'erta*. *Erta* means "a high or raised place," such as a hilltop or tower soldiers might use to see the enemy coming from a distance. *All'erta* meant "standing on the high tower."

Al·e·ut or **Aleut** *noun* a member of a native people of the Aleutian Islands in Alaska. {**ăl** yoot *or* ə **looht** *or* ă **looht**}

Al·ex·an·dri·a *noun* a city in Egypt on the Mediterranean Sea at the tip of the Nile delta. Alexandria was founded by Alexander the Great. {ă ləg **zăn** dree ə}

al·fal·fa *noun* a plant with purple flowers that is grown as food for cattle and horses. Alfalfa is a member of the legume family of plants. {ăl **făl** fə}

Word History *Alfalfa* comes from an Arabic word meaning "the best kind of fodder (or animal feed)."

al·ga *noun* (algae) singular of **algae**. {**ăl** gə}

al·gae 🌐 *noun* organisms that live mainly in the water and make their food through photosynthesis. Algae are different from plants in that they have no true leaves,

roots, or stems. Seaweeds are algae. "Algae" is a plural noun; the singular form is "alga." {**ăl** jee}

al·ge·bra 🌐 *noun* a form of mathematics used to solve problems in which some of the numbers are not known. In an algebra problem, letters stand for the unknown numbers. {**ăl** jə brə}

Al·ge·ri·a *noun* a country in northern Africa. Algiers is the capital of Algeria. {**ăl jeer** ee ə} Algerian, [adj.], n.

a·li·as *noun* a false name used to hide one's real name. *adverb* otherwise known as; also named. *The police reported that Don Smith, alias John White, was arrested after a long car chase.* {**ay** lee əs}

a·li·bi *noun* (alibis) 1. a way of defending oneself against criminal charges by showing that one was not at the scene of the crime when it happened. *The accused woman had no alibi, for she could not prove she was at work at the time the murder took place.* 2. (informal) an excuse. *He gives his boss a new alibi every time he is late for work.* {**ă** lə biy}

Word History *Alibi* is a Latin word for "elsewhere." In the 1700s, English lawyers began using this word in court. A lawyer might say, "The prisoner has proved himself alibi"—in other words, the prisoner has proved he was not at the scene of the crime. By the late 1800s, *alibi* was being used as the name for this kind of proof.

al·ien 🌐 💬 *noun* 1. someone who lives in a country who is not a citizen of that country. 2. a living being from another planet; extraterrestrial. There is no evidence that aliens exist, but many

people believe there is life on other planets. *adjective* 1. belonging to another country; foreign. *Pineapple plants are alien to Canada.* 2. from another planet than Earth; extraterrestrial. 3. strange or odd because unfamiliar. *It seems alien to me that my British cousin drives on the left side of the road.* {**ay** lee ən **ayl** yən}

Word History The English word *alien* comes from a Latin word *alienus* that means "belonging to another place or person." In the English spoken in the 1300s, "alien" took on the meaning of "foreigner." Six hundred years later, in the 1900s, "alien" began to be used as a word for beings from another planet.

a·light[1] *verb* (alighted or alit, alighting, alights) 1. to step down or get off. *She alighted from the bus.* 2. to come to rest. *His greedy eyes alighted on her bracelet. / The fly alit on her arm.* {ə **liyt**}

a·light[2] *adverb or adjective* 1. lighted up. 2. in flames. {ə **liyt**}

a·lign or **aline** *verb* (aligned, aligning, aligns) to place or arrange in a straight line. *He aligned the books on the shelf.* {ə **liyn**}

a·like *adverb* in the same way; similarly or equally. *They dress alike. adjective* like one another; similar. *He and his brother are exactly alike.* {ə **liyk**}

alimentary canal *noun* the tube in the body through which food travels as it is digested. The alimentary canal goes from the mouth to the anus, and includes the esophagus, the stomach, and the small and large intestines. {ă lə **mehn** tə ree kə **năl**}

al·i·mo·ny *noun* (alimonies) money that a court orders one member of a divorced couple to pay to the other. *The alimony she receives from her husband every month is not enough to support her whole family.* {ă lə **moh** nee}

a·live *adjective* 1. having life; living. *Animals need air to stay alive.* 2. full of energy. *She felt alive again after her long illness.* 3. going on; not ended; active. *Our hopes for an end to the war are still alive.* {ə **liyv**}

all *adjective* 1. the whole of or every one of. *I waited all week for her call. / All men are created equal.* 2. any. *They gave up all hope of getting there in time. pronoun* 1. each of the people or things being talked about. *The boat they were on sank, but all were saved.* 2. everything. *All is quiet tonight. noun* everything a person has to give. *The soldiers gave it their all but lost the battle. adverb* 1. completely. *She is all wrong.* 2. each. *The score was two all.* {**awl**}

• **at all**
in the smallest amount; in any way. *I'm not worried at all.*

Synonyms
These words share a meaning with **all**, adjective 1:
every, whole, full, complete, total, entire

Homophone Note Are you looking for the word **awl** (a tool for making holes)? **All** and **awl** sound alike but have different meanings.

all- *prefix* a prefix that means in a complete or total way. *The word "all-American" means completely made up of Americans.* {**awl**}

Al·lah *noun* the name of the supreme deity in the Muslim religion. {ah lə}

all-A·mer·i·can *adjective* 1. chosen as one of the best players in the United States in a particular sport. *She was all-American in tennis last year.* 2. made up only of Americans or of parts made in America. *His daughter goes to an all-American school in Japan. / We buy only all-American cars.* {awl ə **meh** rih kən}

all-a·round *adjective* able to do many different things. *Many colleges want all-around students, not just ones with good grades.* {awl ə **rownd**}

al·lege *verb* (alleged, alleging, alleges) to say or claim to be true without having proof. *The police alleged that he had robbed the bank.* {ə **lehj**}

al·le·giance  *noun* loyalty or dedication to a person, country, or belief. *The soldiers gave their allegiance to the king. / We pledge allegiance to the flag every morning at school.* {ə **lee** jəns}

al·le·go·ry  *noun* (allegories) 1. a tool in art or literature that uses concrete characters, events, or things to represent ideas or beliefs. 2. a story that is written or told to represent an idea or belief. {ă lə **gohr** ee}

al·ler·gic *adjective* 1. caused by or relating to an allergy. *He had an allergic reaction to the peanuts.* 2. having an allergy. *Because she is allergic to cat hair, she will not enter their house.* {ə **lər** jihk}

al·ler·gy  *noun* (allergies) a condition in which a person's body has an unusual reaction to certain things. An allergy can cause itching, coughing, sneezing, or trouble breathing. Allergies to animal hair, pollen, and certain foods are among the most common. {ă lər jee}

al·ley *noun* (alleys) 1. a narrow street or path between or behind buildings. *She hid in the alley until her mother stopped calling her.* 2. a bowling lane. {ă lee}

al·li·ance  *noun* a group of people, countries, or groups that share certain goals and agree to work together. *Students formed an alliance against the school bullies. / The three countries formed an alliance during the war.* {ə **liy** əns}

al·lied *adjective* 1. related or alike in nature. *Doctors and nurses are in allied professions.* 2. joined by an alliance. *The allied nations agreed to fight together against their enemy.* {ə **liyd** or ă **liyd**}

al·li·ga·tor *noun* a large reptile with short legs, a long body and tail, and a long, wide snout. Alligators are protected by thick skin with many hard bumps. They live in rivers, lakes, swamps, and other bodies of water in the southeast United States and in China. They usually eat insects, fish, turtles, snakes, birds, and other water animals, but have been known to attack small land mammals. They are closely related to crocodiles. Chinese alligators are endangered because their habitat is being changed by people. {ă lih gay tər}

al·lit·er·a·tion *noun* the repetition of the same sound at the beginning of words in a phrase or sentence. *"She shears sheep" is an example of alliteration.* {ə lih tə **ray** shən}

al·lot *verb* (allotted, allotting, allots) 1. to set apart for a particular purpose; assign. *The teacher allotted an hour for*

Human Body   Human Mind   Everyday Life   History and Culture   Communication

the test. 2. to give out as portions. *The government allotted the land among the farmers.* {ə **lŏt**}

al·low *verb* (allowed, allowing, allows) 1. to let; permit. *We allowed him to go.* 2. to give or set aside. *Her mother allowed her ten dollars a week for spending money.* {ə **low**}

al·low·ance *noun* a sum of money given on a regular basis or allowed for a particular purpose. *His parents give him his allowance on Saturday. / The salesmen get a travel allowance each month.* {ə **low** əns}

al·loy ❶ *noun* a substance made by mixing two or more metals or a metal and another substance. *Brass is an alloy of zinc and copper.* {ă **loi**}

all-pur·pose *adjective* used in many different ways. *They used an all-purpose cleanser to clean the sink, shower, and floor of the bathroom.* {awl **puhr** pihs}

all right *adverb* in a satisfactory but not outstanding way; well enough. *He did all right on the test but could have done better.* *adjective* 1. not harmed or damaged; safe. *The car was wrecked, but the driver was all right.* 2. good enough; satisfactory. *The food is all right at school, but he prefers the lunches his mother makes.* *interjection* "okay"; "yes"; "as you wish." *All right, since you really want me to, I'll go.* {awl **riyt**}

all-round *adverb or adjective* all-around. *She is an all-round athlete.* {awl **rownd**}

all-star *adjective* made up entirely of the best players or performers. *The director wants an all-star cast for his next movie.* {awl **star**}

al·lude *verb* (alluded, alluding, alludes) to mention (usually followed by "to"). *She is always alluding to books we have not read.* {ə **loohd**}

Homophone Note Are you looking for the word *elude* (to escape)? *Allude* and *elude* sound and look almost alike and are often confused.

al·ly *verb* (allied, allying, allies) to join or unite for a particular purpose (usually followed by "to" or "with"). *Russia allied itself to France.* *noun* (allies) a person, group, or country that has joined with another for a particular purpose. *Great Britain, France, and the United States were allies in World War II. / She knew she could stand up to the bully if she had an ally.* {ə **liy** or ă **liy**}

al·ma·nac *noun* 1. a book of interesting and useful facts about many different subjects. 2. a book published every year that predicts the weather for each day and gives facts about the tides, the time the sun will rise and set, and other useful information. {awl mə **năk**}

al·might·y *adjective* having complete power or the most power. *The almighty lion rules the jungle.* *noun* (capitalized) God (used with "the"). *We prayed to the Almighty.* {awl **miy** tee} almightily, adv., almightiness, n.

al·mond *noun* 1. a small tree related to the cherry tree that grows in warm areas and produces seeds that can be eaten. 2. the hard oval seed of this tree that is like a nut and eaten as food. 3. a light tan color like the inner part of the seed of the almond. {**ah** mənd or **ahl** mənd}

al·most *adverb* not quite all; nearly. *The apples are almost gone.* {**awl** mohst or awl **mohst**}

a·loft *adverb* high above the ground. *He threw the ball aloft.* {ə **lawft** or ə **lŏft**}

a·lo·ha *noun* a Hawaiian word used for saying either "hello" or "goodbye." *"Aloha," we said to our friends as they left.* {ə **loh** hah or ah **loh** hah}

a·lone *adjective* 1. apart from everyone or everything else. *He was alone on the island.* 2. without anyone or anything else. *You alone will decide your future.* *adverb* without anything or anyone else. *She works alone.* {ə **lohn**} aloneness, n.
• **leave alone**
1. to let alone; not disturb. *She was angry, so we left her alone.* 2. not to bother; not interfere with. *Leave that cake alone!*

a·long *preposition* 1. by or through the length of; next to. *We ran along the path. / We walked along the cliff's edge.* 2. at some place on. *We will stop for supper along the way.* *adverb* 1. as a companion. *Walk along with me.* 2. toward what is ahead; forward. *Let's move along.* {ə **lawng**}
• **all along**
from the beginning; the whole time. *He knew all along that he would be famous.*

a·long·side *adverb* along, near, or by the side of. *She rode her bicycle and he jogged alongside.* *preposition* by the side of; next to; beside. *She swam*

a
b
c
d
e
f
g
h
i
j
k
l
m
n
o
p
q
r
s
t
u
v
w
x
y
z

alongside the boat. {ə **lawng siyd**}

a·loof *adjective* showing little interest or emotion around other people; not involved. *I don't care for my math teacher because she is aloof.* {ə **loohf**} aloofness, n.

a·loud *adverb* in a voice that can be heard; not in a whisper. *Please read aloud to the class.* {ə **lowd**}

al·pac·a *noun* (alpaca or alpacas) an animal with long legs and a long neck. Alpacas live in the mountains of South America. They are mammals closely related to llamas and to camels. Alpacas are raised for their long, soft wool. {ăl **pă** kə}

al·pha *noun* the name of the first letter of the Greek alphabet. {**ăl** fə}

al·pha·bet ○ *noun* the letters of a written language, given in proper order. *The English alphabet goes from a to z.* {**ăl** fə **beht**}

al·pha·bet·i·cal *adjective* arranged in the order of the alphabet. *I arranged the books in alphabetical order by their titles.* {ăl fə **beh** tih kəl} alphabetically, adv.

al·pha·bet·ize *verb* (alphabetized, alphabetizing, alphabetizes) to arrange in the order of the alphabet. *She alphabetized the guest list for the wedding.* {**ăl** fə bə **tiyz**}

Alps *plural noun* a high mountain range that goes from southern France through Switzerland, Italy, Germany, and Austria and into Yugoslavia and Albania. {**ălps**}

al·read·y *adverb* 1. by this or that time. *When I arrived at the station, the train had already left.* 2. so soon. *Has she arrived already?* {awl **reh** dee}

al·so *adverb* besides; in addition; too. *My sister has a motorcycle and also drives a truck.* {awl soh}

al·tar *noun* a raised table or platform used for religious ceremonies. *That church has a beautiful marble altar.* {**awl** tər}

Homophone Note Are you looking for the word *alter* (to change)? *Altar* and *alter* sound alike but have different meanings.

al·ter *verb* (altered, altering, alters) 1. to make different in some way; change. *He altered the dress to make it shorter.* 2. to become different; change. *The animal's hair color alters with the seasons.* {**awl** tər}

Homophone Note The words *alter* and *altar* sound alike but have different meanings.

al·ter·nate *verb* (alternated, alternating, alternates) 1. to take turns (usually followed by "with"). *She alternates with her sister in babysitting their younger brother.* 2. to move back and forth between two or more places, actions, or conditions (usually followed by "between"). *Before the big game, his feelings alternated between fear and excitement. / They alternate between living in New York and in Florida.* 3. to use in turn, one after another; switch between. *She alternated chocolate and vanilla layers on the cake.* *adjective* 1. following each other in turns, first one then the other. *My shirt has alternate red and white stripes.* 2. the second of every two; every other. *The class meets on alternate Wednesdays.* 3. substitute; a person or thing that takes the place of another. *He took an alternate route to work because the main highway*

was closed for repairs. *noun* a person who acts in place of another when needed; substitute. *When the president is ill, the vice-president may act as his alternate.* {**awl** tər nət, n., **awl** tər nət, adj., **awl** tər **nayt**, v.} alternately, adv., alternatingly, adv.

al·ter·na·tive *noun* 1. one of two or more choices. *As usual, he chose the easier alternative.* 2. the choice of one or more options. *You have the alternatives of bringing your lunch or buying it at school.* *adjective* offering or allowing a choice. *The salesman offered the couple alternative ways of paying for the car.* {awl **tuhr** nə tihv} alternatively, adv.

al·though *conjunction* in spite of the fact that; even though; though. *Although it snowed last night, we will go for a walk.* {awl **thoh**}

al·tim·e·ter *noun* a device that measures distance above the earth's surface. *The altimeter tells how high the airplane is flying.* {ăl **tih** mih tər}

al·ti·tude ○ *noun* the height of a thing above earth or above sea level. *The pilot flew at a higher altitude than usual to avoid the clouds.* {ăl tih **toohd**}

al·to ○ *noun* (altos) 1. the vocal range between tenor and soprano. Alto is the lowest range for the female voice and highest for the male. *My sister sings alto in the school choir.* 2. a singer with such a range. *They are altos in the community chorus.* 3. a musical instrument having the second highest range in its family of instruments. *That saxophone player is performing on the alto tonight.* *adjective* belonging to the range between tenor and soprano. *My father plays the alto clarinet.* {**ăl** toh}

 Human Body   Human Mind  Everyday Life   History and Culture Communication

al·to·geth·er *adverb* 1. completely; entirely. *His situation is altogether terrible.* 2. if everything is counted or included; overall. *Altogether, he has ruined three of my sweaters.* 3. if everything is considered; on the whole. *Altogether, she's better off now than before.* {<u>awl</u> tə <u>geh</u> thər or <u>awl</u> tə <u>geh</u> thər}

al·u·mi·num *noun* a strong, light, silvery metal that does not easily rust. Aluminum is a chemical element. (symbol: Al) {ə <u>looh</u> mih nəm}

al·ways *adverb* 1. at all times; without stopping; forever. *She always gets what she wants. / The stars are always in the sky. / I will always remember him.* 2. every time. *He always gets here early.* {<u>awl</u> wihz or <u>awl</u> wayz}

Synonyms
These words share a meaning with *always*, adverb 1:
ever, forever, continuously, continually, perpetually, incessantly

A.M. *abbreviation* the time between midnight and noon. A.M. is an abbreviation for "ante meridiem," which means "before noon" in Latin. *I set my alarm for 7:00 A.M.*

am *verb* A form of the verb "be" that is present tense and used with the pronoun I. *I am at home. / I am looking forward to seeing you again.* {<u>ăm</u>}

a·ma·teur *noun* 1. one who does something only for enjoyment rather than for money. *Her father wants her to be a professional musician, but she is happy being an amateur.* 2. one who is not skilled in a given area or activity. *The chef refuses to let amateurs help him in the kitchen. adjective* of or relating to an amateur or amateurs; not professional. *Our town's amateur theater puts on ten plays a year.* {<u>ă</u> mə chər}

Word History *Amateur* is a French word that means "lover of."

a·maze *verb* (amazed, amazing, amazes) to surprise greatly or fill with wonder; astonish. *The little girl's musical talent amazed the audience.* {ə <u>mayz</u>} amazing, adj., amazingly, adv.

a·maze·ment *noun* wonder; great surprise. *We watched in amazement as the puppies were born.* {ə <u>mayz</u> mənt}

Am·a·zon *noun* 1. the longest river in South America. It flows from the Andes mountains in Peru across northern Brazil to the Atlantic Ocean. 2. a member of a race of tall, strong, and fierce female warriors who are written about in Greek myth. {<u>ă</u> mə <u>zŏn</u>} Amazonian, adj.

am·bas·sa·dor ⊕ *noun* 1. a person who is sent by the government of one country to be its official representative in another country. *The Japanese ambassador to the United States met with the President in the White House.* 2. anyone who is sent as a representative or messenger. *A group of writers and artists were sent to Korea as cultural ambassadors.* {ăm <u>bă</u> sə dər}

am·ber *noun* 1. a hard, yellow or brown material that is used to make jewelry. It is a fossil that

comes from the resin of pine trees. 2. a yellowish brown color. {<u>ăm</u> bər}

am·bi·dex·trous *adjective* able to use both the left and right hands with equal skill. *Someone who is ambidextrous can write with either hand.* {ăm bih <u>dehk</u> strəs}

am·big·u·ous *adjective* unclear or uncertain because of having more than one possible meaning. *The politician's ambiguous answers left the reporters confused about what had really happened.* {ăm <u>bihg</u> yoo ihs}

am·bi·tion *noun* 1. a strong desire to become famous, rich, or to reach a goal. *His ambition is to earn a million dollars before he is thirty.* 2. the aim or goal of such a desire. *Winning first place was his ambition.* {ăm <u>bih</u> shən}

am·bi·tious *adjective* 1. having or showing a strong desire to succeed; having ambition. *Her friends all agree that Susan is ambitious.* 2. requiring great effort to be done successfully. *He has an ambitious plan to lose twenty pounds in two months.* {ăm <u>bih</u> shəs} ambitiously, adv.

Word History The word *ambitious* is from a Latin word that means "to go about" or "walk around." In Roman times, this Latin word, *ambitio*, came to have a special meaning. It was used for a man who went around town for a particular reason: to persuade people to vote for him. Today, we would still say that someone who enters an election is ambitious, but the English word now has a wider meaning.

am·ble *verb* (ambled, ambling, ambles) to walk at a slow, easy pace. *We amble through*

A
B
C
D
E
F
G
H
I
J
K
L
M
N
O
P
Q
R
S
T
U
V
W
X
Y
Z

a
b
c
d
e
f
g
h
i
j
k
l
m
n
o
p
q
r
s
t
u
v
w
x
y
z

the fields on summer days. {ăm bəl}

am·bu·lance *noun* a vehicle used to carry ill or injured people to a hospital. *When he fell off the roof, she called an ambulance.* {ăm byə ləns}

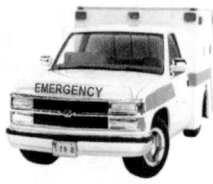

> **Word History** The English word **ambulance** was formed from *hôpital ambulant*, French words that mean "walking hospital." It was first used in the 1800s as a name for the carts that carried soldiers injured in the Crimean War. In the Crimean War, France and England were allies and fought against Russia.

am·bush *noun* 1. a surprise attack made from a hidden place. *The soldiers stopped the enemy with an ambush at dawn.* 2. a hiding place from which a surprise attack is made. *We waited in ambush behind some trees.* *verb* (ambushed, ambushing, ambushes) to make a surprise attack from a hidden place. *The soldiers ambushed the enemy near the edge of the forest.* {ăm buush}

a·me·ba *noun* (amebas [or] amebae) another spelling of **amoeba.** {ə mee bə}

a·men *interjection* a word used at the end of a prayer or statement to mean "may it be so." *When the doctor said to me, "I hope you will feel better soon," my father said, "Amen."* {ah mehn *or* ay mehn}

a·mend *verb* (amended, amending, amends) to change or add to a law, contract, or other document. *Congress will amend a section of the new crime bill that many people think is unfair.* {ə mehnd}

a·mend·ment ⬤ *noun* an official change made to a bill, law, or other document. *In 1865, an amendment to the Constitution banned slavery in the United States.* {ə mehnd mənt}

a·mends *noun* (amends) (used with a singular or plural verb) something given or paid to make up for a wrong done to a person or group. *She offered to do chores for her neighbor as amends for breaking his window.* {ə mehndz}

• **make amends**
to try to make up for harm done to someone. *They are sorry for what they have done and wish to make amends.*

A·mer·i·ca *noun* 1. the United States. *America's Statue of Liberty has welcomed millions of people here.* 2. either North America, Central America, or South America, or all three; the Americas. *The Americas include dozens of separate countries.* {ə meh rih kə}

A·mer·i·can *adjective* 1. of or having to do with the United States, or its people or language. 2. of or having to do with North, Central, or South America, or its people or languages. *noun* 1. a person who was born in or is a citizen of the United States. 2. a person who was born in or is a citizen of North, Central, or South America. 3. the language of the United States. {ə meh rih kən}

American English *noun* the English language as spoken and written in the United States. {ə meh rih kən ing glihsh}

American Indian *noun* a member of any of the native peoples of North America, Central America, South America, or the West Indies, except for Eskimos. American Indians are also called Native Americans. {ə meh rih kən ihn dee ən}

American Revolution *noun* the war of 1775-83 in which the American colonies won their independence from Great Britain. {ə meh rih kən reh və looh shən}

am·e·thyst *noun* a purple gem used in jewelry. Amethyst is a kind of quartz. {ă məh thihst}

a·mi·a·ble *adjective* having or showing a friendly manner. *She is so amiable that everybody loves being with her.* {ay mee ə bəl} amiably, adv.

a·mid *preposition* among or surrounded by. *The town is set amid the hills. / He is not shy amid his friends.* {ə mihd}

a·midst *preposition* in the middle of; among; amid. *There amidst the pine trees stood a house.* {ə mihtst}

a·mi·go *noun* (amigos) a Spanish word for "friend." {ə mee goh}

a·miss *adverb* in the wrong way. *I'm sorry if I spoke amiss.* *adjective* out of place or not right; wrong. *Is something amiss?* {ə mihs}

am·mo·ni·a *noun* 1. the gas with a strong smell that is formed by combining nitrogen and hydrogen. Ammonia is used to make refrigerators cold and in making fertilizers. 2. the liquid made from mixing ammonia gas with water. Certain cleaners are made with ammonia. {ə mohn yə}

am·mu·ni·tion ⬤ *noun* 1. the objects fired from any weapon, or material that can be exploded. Bullets, bombs, and gunpowder are types of ammunition. 2. any means

 Human Body   Human Mind   Everyday Life   History and Culture   Communication

used in a disagreement to attack or defend an opinion. *The candidate's mistake was ammunition for his opponent during their debate.* {ăm yə **nih** shən}

am·ne·sia *noun* partial or complete loss of memory as a result of an injury to the brain, illness, or shock. *Because of amnesia, she did not know her own children.* {ăm **nee** zhə}

a·moe·ba ❶ *noun* (amoebas or amoebae) a tiny living thing made of only one cell. Amoebas move by changing their shape. They eat by wrapping their bodies around their food. Amoebas live in fresh and salt water, soil, and in animals. Most kinds of amoebas can only be seen through a microscope. {ə **mee** bə}

Word History *Amoeba* is a Latin word that scientists began using in the mid-1800s. The Latin word came from a Greek word that means "a change."

a·mong *preposition* 1. in the middle of or included with. *We walked among the trees. / There were some shells among the stones.* 2. as a part of; in the company of. *He worked among friends.* 3. with a share for each. *Bread was shared among ten people.* 4. with all or most of. *He is liked among his classmates.* 5. in the group or class of. *Swimming and hiking are among the things we do at camp.* {ə **muhng**}

a·mongst *preposition* among. {ə **muhngst**}

a·mount ❶ *noun* 1. measure; quantity. *This amount of snow isn't enough for skiing.* 2. the sum of two or more quantities; total. *This is the amount of money you owe them. verb* (amounted, amounting,

amounts) to be equal to; to be the same as. *The bill amounts to more than I can pay. / Her stealing amounts to a request for help.* {ə **mownt**}

Language Note *Amount* or *number*? Which word is right for your sentence? Use *amount* when you are telling how much there is of something that cannot be counted in numbers. *A large amount of lava shot out of the volcano.*
Use *number* when you are telling how many there are of something that can be counted. *A great number of rocks tumbled down the mountain.*
Remember, the word *quantity* may be used both with things that can be counted and with things that cannot be counted. *Antarctica is covered by a great quantity of ice. A large quantity of penguins live in that frigid land.*

Word History *Amount* comes from *amonter*, an early French word that means "to go up" or "rise." The French word is from a Latin phrase that means "to the mountain."

am·per·sand *noun* a sign (&). It is used in place of the word "and." {ăm pər **sănd**}

am·phib·i·an ❶ *noun* 1. a small animal that spends part of its life cycle in water and part of its life cycle on land. Amphibians hatch in water and breathe with gills. Then they develop lungs so the adults can breathe air. Amphibians are cold-blooded animals with skeletons inside their bodies. Frogs, toads, and salamanders are amphibians. 2. a vehicle that can travel or operate on both land and water. Some tanks, boats, and airplanes are amphibians. {ăm **fih** bee ən}

am·phib·i·ous *adjective* 1. able to live both on land and in water. *Most frogs are amphibious.* 2. able to travel or operate on both land and water. *The army bought amphibious tanks and planes.* {ăm **fih** bee əs}

am·phi·the·a·ter ❶ *noun* an oval or round building with seats rising in rows from an open, central area. Amphitheaters are used for sports and other public events. {ăm fə **thee** ə tər}

am·phi·the·a·tre *noun* a spelling of **amphitheater** used in Canada and Britain. See **amphitheater** for more information. {ăm fə **thee** ə tər}

am·ple *adjective* (ampler, amplest) large in size, amount, or space; as much or more than is needed. *There was ample room in her closet for her huge collection of clothes. / We bought ample food for the picnic.* {ăm pəl}

am·pli·fi·er *noun* an electronic device used to make sound louder. {ăm plə **fiy** ər}

am·pli·fy *verb* (amplified, amplifying, amplifies) 1. to make larger or greater. *The speakers amplified the sound of the music.* 2. to explain further or make clearer by adding details. *May I amplify my answer to that question?* {ăm plə **fiy**}

am·pu·tate *verb* (amputated, amputating, amputates) to cut off, especially by surgery. *The doctor amputated the soldier's badly injured leg.* {ămp yə **tayt**} amputation, n.

Am·ster·dam *noun* the official capital city of the Netherlands. Most of the government of the Netherlands is located in another city, The Hague. {ăm stər dăm}

Amphibians

Ancient amphibians were the first animals with skeletons inside the body to live on land. Modern amphibians include frogs, toads, and salamanders. All amphibians lay eggs in water. Most amphibians live all or part of their adult lives on land.

Frogs and toads go through complete metamorphosis. The female lays jelly-covered eggs in water. The eggs hatch into larvae called tadpoles. Tadpoles eat plants and breathe through gills. As they change into their adult form, they grow long legs and lose their tails. They develop lungs so they can breathe air.

True frogs are usually green with moist skin. They spend a lot of time in or near water. Their long back legs are good for jumping, and their webbed back feet are good for swimming. They mostly eat insects.

Toads have shorter legs and live on land. They have bumpy brown or gray skin. Some toads have poisonous skin to keep predators away, but touching a toad will not give you warts.

Most tree frogs can change their skin color to match their surroundings. Some South American tree frogs are very poisonous. Their bright colors warn predators not to eat them.

Salamanders have long tails and short legs. They have smooth skin and no claws. Some salamanders have no back legs, and some have no legs at all. Many salamanders have poisonous skin to keep predators from eating them.

amt. *abbreviation* an abbreviation for **amount**.

a·muse *verb* (amused, amusing, amuses) 1. to hold the interest of in a pleasant way; entertain. *They amused the baby with a rattle.* 2. to cause to smile or laugh. *His jokes amused us.* {ə **myooz**}

a·muse·ment *noun* 1. something that amuses or entertains; fun. *My family's favorite amusement is singing.* 2. the condition of being amused or entertained. *The clown's antics caused amusement in the audience.* {ə **myooz** mənt}

amusement park *noun* an outdoor place with games, rides, and other forms of entertainment. {ə **myooz** mənt **park**}

an *indefinite article* another word for **a**. It is used before words that start with a, e, i, o, or u, or before words that begin with vowel sounds. *There is an apple for you and an orange for me. / Basil is an herb.* {**ăn**}

-an or **-ean** or **-ian** *suffix* 1. a suffix that means "from," "belongs to," or "lives in." *European cheese is cheese that comes from Europe. / An Asian language is a language of Asia. / The African elephant lives in Africa.* 2. a suffix that means one who works in or knows a great deal about. *A librarian works in a library. / A historian knows a lot about history.*

an·a·con·da *noun* a very large snake found in South America. Anacondas are not poisonous but kill other animals by squeezing them until they cannot breathe. Anacondas can grow to over twenty feet long. {ă nə **kŏn** də}

a·nae·mi·a *noun* another spelling of **anemia**. {ə **nee** mee ə}

an·a·log *adjective* representing information by physical measurements. *An analog watch shows the time by the position of the hour and minute hands; a digital watch shows the time in numerals only.* {ăn uh lawg}

an·a·lyse *verb* a spelling of **analyze** used in Canada and Britain. See **analyze** for more information. {ăn ə liyz}

a·nal·y·sis *noun* (analyses) 1. a careful study of the parts of something in order to understand more about the whole. *Her analysis of the painting helped us understand why it is considered a masterpiece.* 2. the process of separating something into parts in order to study it. *The chemist's analysis of the city's water showed that it was safe to drink.* {ə **nă** lə sihs}

an·a·lyze ⊕ *verb* (analyzed, analyzing, analyzes) to separate into parts for close study; examine and explain. *If we analyze the problem, perhaps we can solve it.* {ă nə **liyz**}

an·ar·chist *noun* 1. a person who believes in, desires, or tries to realize a society or state without a government. 2. a person who encourages disobedience toward any or all established governments. {ă nər kihst}

an·ar·chy ⊕ *noun* (anarchies) 1. a complete lack of government or law within a country or society. *There was anarchy after the royal family was kidnapped.* 2. a state of confusion or disorder. *The loss of electricity caused anarchy in the city.* {ă nər kee} anarchist, n.

an·a·tom·i·cal *adjective* of or relating to the structure of a plant or animal. {ă nə **to** mih kəl} anatomically, adv.

a·nat·o·my ⊕ ⊕ *noun* (anatomies) 1. the parts of a living thing and how they fit together. *We studied the anatomy of worms in science class.* 2. the science that studies the parts and structures of plants or animals. *All medical students take courses in human anatomy.* {ə **nă** tə mee}

an·ces·tor *noun* a person from whom one is descended and who lived several generations ago. *Her ancestors came to America from Africa.* {**ăn** sehs stər *or* **ăn** səs stər} ancestral, adj.

Word History The word *ancestor* comes from a Latin word that means "to go before."

an·chor *noun* 1. a heavy object that is dropped from a boat or ship by a cable to keep the vessel from moving. 2. something that keeps something else stable or in place. *Our love for one another is our family's anchor.* *verb* (anchored, anchoring, anchors) 1. to make secure or hold steady. *She anchored the tent to the ground with ropes and stakes.* 2. to keep a boat in place with an anchor. *They anchored close to the island.* {**ăng** kər}

an·cho·vy *noun* (anchovies) a small fish that is related to the herring and is used for food. Anchovies are found mostly in warm ocean waters. {**ăn** choh vee}

an·cient ⊖ *adjective* 1. very old; existing for many years. *Rome is an ancient city, with ancient buildings.* 2. of or relating to times long ago. *We compared ancient Greece to modern Greece in history class.* {**ayn** chənt} ancientness, n.

and *conjunction* 1. with; also; along with; as well as. *We had cake and ice cream for dessert.* 2. added to; plus. *Six and six make twelve.* 3. then, as a

A B C D E F G H I J K L M N O P Q R S T U V W X Y Z

a

result. *Have a glass of water and you will feel better.* {ănd}

• **and so forth** [or] **and so on**
1. with more of the same type. *We bought bananas, oranges, apples, and so on.* 2. followed by what one would expect. *Count one, two, three, and so forth.*

An·de·an *adjective* of, located in, or resembling the Andes. {ăn dee ən}

An·des *plural noun* a high mountain range that stretches along the entire west coast of South America. {ăn deez}

and·i·ron *noun* one of a pair of metal structures that holds logs in a fireplace. {ăn diy ərn}

an·droid *noun* a robot or machine having human characteristics. {ăn droid}

an·ec·dote *noun* a short tale about a funny or interesting event. *He told us anecdotes about his youth.* {ă nək doht}

a·ne·mi·a  or **anaemia** *noun* a medical condition caused by having too few red blood cells or red blood cells that are not working properly. People with anemia may be pale, feel tired and weak, and have difficulty breathing. {ə nee mee ə} anemic, adj.

an·e·mom·e·ter *noun* an instrument that measures the speed and force of the wind. {ă nə mo mih tər}

a·nem·o·ne *noun* a type of plant related to the buttercup that has large white, blue, or red flowers. {ə neh mə nee}

an·es·the·sia  or **anaesthesia** *noun* loss of consciousness or feeling in the body produced by drugs. *She will be under anesthesia during the operation.* {ă nihs thee zhə}

an·es·thet·ic or **anaesthetic** *noun* a drug that causes

numbness in the body or loss of consciousness. *The dentist gave her an anesthetic before pulling her tooth.* {ă nihs theh tihk}

an·es·the·tist or **anaesthetist** *noun* a person, usually a doctor or nurse, trained to give gas or drugs that cause lack of sensation or loss of consciousness. {ə nehs thə tihst}

a·new *adverb* once more; again. *After not speaking for years, they began their friendship anew.* {ə nooh}

an·gel *noun* 1. a spiritual being who acts as a servant or messenger of God. Angels are often represented as human figures with wings and a halo. 2. a person who has great goodness and kindness. *She was an angel for helping me with my homework.* {ayn jəl}

an·ger  *noun* a strong emotion brought on by a person or thing that causes one great pain or trouble. *His cruelty filled me with anger.* *verb* (angered, angering, angers.) 1. to cause anger in; make angry. *The speaker's words angered the crowd.* 2. to become angry. *He doesn't anger easily.* {ăng gər}

Word History The word *anger* comes from an early Icelandic word meaning "grief."

an·gle *noun* 1. the figure made by two lines or rays coming from a single point. *Every triangle has three angles.* 2. the space between such lines, measured in degrees. *Each angle in a square measures 90 degrees.* 3. a sharp corner. *The building seems made up entirely of angles and lines.* 4. a position or point of view. *The sculpture looks better from this angle.* *verb* (angled, angling, angles) to move at an angle.

The skier angled left to avoid hitting the tree. {ăng gəl}

An·go·la *noun* a country on the western coast of Africa. Luanda is the capital of Angola. {ăn goh lə} Angolan, n., adj.

An·go·ra *noun* 1. any of various animals that have long silky hair, such as a cat, rabbit, or goat. 2. (often lower case) the soft, silky hair of the Angora rabbit or Angora goat. 3. (often lower case) yarn or cloth made from either of these kinds of hair. Angora is used to make sweaters and other articles of clothing. {ăng gohr ə}

an·gry *adjective* (angrier, angriest) 1. feeling or showing anger (often followed by "at" or "with"). *Liz was angry at George for calling her names.* 2. as if showing anger, as a storm. *The ship set sail on the angry sea.* 3. inflamed, as a skin sore or rash. *He bandaged the angry sore.* {ăng gree} angrily, adv.

Synonyms
These words share a meaning with *angry*, adjective 1:

mad, sore, furious, indignant, livid, irate

an·guish *noun* terrible pain or suffering of the mind or body. *He felt anguish at not having been able to save the animals from the fire.* {ăng gwihsh} anguished, adj.

an·gu·lar *adjective* 1. made up of, having, or forming one or more angles. *He built a very angular sculpture.* 2. having a bony structure, as a person's body. *The thin boy has an angular build.* {ăng gyə lər} angularly, adv.

an·i·mal    *noun* 1. one of a large group of living things that can move around by themselves to find food. Ani-

 Human Body    Human Mind   Everyday Life   History and Culture    Communication

mals eat plants, fungi, or other animals. Birds, reptiles, fish, amphibians, mammals, insects, snails, and worms are some of the major kinds of animals. 2. such a creature other than humans. {ăn ə məl} animallike, adj.

Word History *Animal* comes from a Latin word that means "a breathing thing."

an·i·mal rights *plural noun* a movement that works for the rights of animals. People in favor of animal rights believe that animals should not be hurt or killed just to make the lives of humans easier. {ăn ih mŏl **riyts**}

an·i·mate *verb* (animated, animating, animates) 1. to bring to life. *A magic hat animated Frosty the snowman.* 2. to give zest or spirit to. *An African band animated the gathering.* 3. to inspire to move or act; prompt. *The union speaker animated the workers to strike.* 4. to give the illusion of movement. *The artist animated the cartoon characters.* *adjective* 1. alive; living. *Rocks are not animate objects.* 2. lively; full of energy. *The singer was very pleased to find such an animate audience.* {ăn ə mət, adj., ăn ə mayt, v.} animately, adv., animateness, n.

animated cartoon *noun* a motion picture made by photographing a series of drawings showing stages of movement. The motion seems real when the drawings are shown quickly one after another. {ăn ə **may** təd **kar** toohn}

an·i·mos·i·ty *noun* (animosities) strong dislike or behavior that shows strong dislike. *It is true that dogs and cats show animosity toward each other.* {ăn ə **mo** sih tee}

Word History The Latin word for "breath" or "spirit" was *anima*. Another Latin word, *animositatem*, was formed from *anima* and meant "full of spirit" or "lively." The English word **animosity** comes from these words. In the English spoken in the 1400s, "animosity" meant "liveliness, strength, or courage." Since then, its meaning has changed. "Animosity" is now a word for ill will or strong dislike.

an·kle *noun* the joint between the leg and the foot; the part of the leg just above the foot. {**ăng** kəl}

an·klet *noun* a short sock that reaches just above the ankle. {**ăng** kliht}

an·nex *verb* (annexed, annexing, annexes) 1. to add or attach to something larger. *He annexed his opinion to the letter his wife wrote.* 2. to make part of an existing nation or city. *Germany annexed Austria in 1938.* *noun* a building added to an existing building. An annex may be attached to or separate from the main building. {ə **nehks** or ăn əks} annexation, n.

an·ni·hi·late *verb* (annihilated, annihilating, annihilates) to destroy completely. *The fire annihilated the church.* {ə **niy** ə layt} annihilation, n., annihilator, n.

an·ni·ver·sa·ry *noun* (anniversaries) 1. the date each year that is the same date on which a wedding or other important event happened. 2. the celebration of such an event. *Hundreds of people attended the town's fiftieth anniversary.* {ăn ih **vuhr** sə ree}

an·nounce *verb* (announced, announcing, announces) to make known; declare. *They proudly announced the birth of their first baby.* {ə **nowns**}

an·nounce·ment *noun* 1. a public or formal statement. *The newspaper prints wedding announcements once a week.* 2. the act of announcing. *The announcement of the winners was followed by applause.* {ə **nowns** mənt}

an·nounc·er *noun* a person who presents programs or reads advertisements on radio or television. {ə **nown** sər}

an·noy *verb* (annoyed, annoying, annoys) to bother or disturb with irritating behavior. *Their loud music annoyed the neighbors.* {ə **noi**} annoyer, n.

an·noy·ance *noun* 1. the act of disturbing or irritating. *The neighbors are upset about your constant annoyance of their daughter.* 2. someone or something that bothers or irritates. *The loud music from next door is an annoyance.* 3. the feeling of being bothered or irritated. *She was in such a state of annoyance that she slammed the door.* {ə **noi** əns}

an·nu·al *adjective* 1. happening once every year. *The county's annual fair is a popular event.* 2. of or relating to a year; yearly. *She earns an annual salary of twenty thousand dollars.* *noun* a plant that grows for only one year or one season. *Corn and lettuce are*

A
B
C
D
E
F
G
H
I
J
K
L
M
N
O
P
Q
R
S
T
U
V
W
X
Y
Z

a

annuals. {**ăn** yoo əl} annually, adv.

an·nu·al·ly *adverb* once a year; yearly. *I pay for this magazine annually.* {**ăn** yoo əl ee}

an·nu·al ring *noun* one of the rings of wood on the inside of a tree that can be seen when the tree is cut into logs. Each ring represents a year of growth. {**ăn** yoo əl **ring**}

a·noint *verb* (anointed, anointing, anoints) to honor or make holy by applying oil as part of a religious ceremony. {ə **noint**}

a·non·y·mous *adjective* having an unknown name or identity. *An anonymous witness reported the crime.* {ə **no** nə mihs} anonymously, adv.

an·oth·er *adjective* 1. being one more just like the others; an additional. *May I have another piece of bread?* 2. of a different kind; not the same. *She lives in another country.* *pronoun* 1. a different or additional one. *Since that dish is broken, I'll buy another.* 2. one that is just the same. *Would you like another pancake?* {ə **nuh** thər}

an·swer   *noun* 1. a reply. *I want an answer to my question.* 2. an action in response. *His answer was to walk out the door.* 3. the solution to a problem. *You will find the right answer if you think about it.* *verb* (answered, answering, answers) 1. to reply in words or with an action. *Tina answered, but no one heard her.* 2. to be responsible; take responsibility (usually followed by for or to). *I will answer for my son's actions.* 3. to fit; agree with or match (usually followed by "to"). *He answers to that description.* 4. to respond or reply to.

Why won't someone answer me? {**ăn** sər}

ant *noun* an insect that lives in large, organized groups called colonies. Most kinds of ants live in or on the ground. Ants are related to bees and wasps. {**ănt**} antlike, adj.

-ant *suffix* 1. a suffix that means causing or doing an action. *A person who is hesitant will hesitate about doing something.* 2. a suffix that means someone or something that performs an action. *An informant is one who informs.* / *An irritant is something that irritates.* 3. a suffix that means being part of an action. *A contestant is a person who takes part in a contest.*

Homophone Note Are you looking for the word *aunt* (the sister of one's parent)? Some people say *ant* and *aunt* in exactly the same way, but these two words have different meanings.

ant·a·cid *noun* a substance people take to settle an upset stomach. Antacids work by reducing the strength of the acids that cause the upset. {**ănt ăs** ihd}

an·tag·o·nism *noun* a state of being enemies, or a strong feeling against someone or something. *Their antagonism made the rest of the group uncomfortable.* {**ăn tă** gə nih zəm}

an·tag·o·nist *noun* 1. a person who fights against another; an enemy or competitor. 2. a character who works against the hero of a story. *In "Snow White," the antagonist is the jealous queen.* {**ăn tă** gə nihst}

an·tag·o·nize *verb* (antagonized, antagonizing, antagonizes) to make an enemy of. *He antagonized the other*

players by cheating. {**ăn tă** gə niyz}

ant·arc·tic *adjective* of or having to do with the South Pole. *The antarctic waters are freezing cold and filled with ice.* {**ănt ark** tihk}

Ant·arc·tic *noun* the land or seas at or near the South Pole; Antarctica or the Antarctic Ocean (used with "the"). {**ănt ark** tihk}

Ant·arc·ti·ca *noun* the continent that surrounds the South Pole. {**ănt ark** tih kə}

Antarctic Ocean *noun* the waters surrounding Antarctica where the southern parts of the Pacific, Atlantic, and Indian Oceans meet. {**ănt ark** tihk **oh** shən}

ant·eat·er *noun* a mammal that uses its long, sticky tongue to eat ants and termites. True anteaters have no teeth, are furry, and live in Central or South America. They are related to armadillos and sloths. Other kinds of mammals that eat ants are also sometimes called anteaters, but they are not related to American anteaters. {**ănt** ee tər}

an·te·ced·ent *noun* the word or group of words that a pronoun refers to. In "The girls ate their dessert first," "girls" is the antecedent of "their." {**ăn** tə **see** dənt}

an·te·lope *noun* (antelope or antelopes) 1. an animal with horns, a long neck, long legs, and hooves. Antelopes are known for their fast running. Antelopes are mammals that eat plants and chew their cud. The smallest kind of antelope is only one foot tall; the largest antelope is six feet tall at the shoulder. Gazelles, gnus, and impalas are all antelopes. Most antelopes live in Africa; some

 Human Body   Human Mind   Everyday Life    History and Culture   Communication

also live in Asia. 2. the American pronghorn, an animal that looks like some of the true antelopes but is not closely related. {ăn tə **lohp**}

an·ten·na ● *noun* (antennas or antennae) 1. a metal device that sends or receives radio or television signals. *We need an antenna to get a clear picture on our television.* 2. one of a pair of long, thin body parts on the head of insects, crabs, and other animals. Antennae are used to feel and smell. {ăn **teh** nə}

Word History The word *antenna* is a Latin word for a long pole that sticks up from a ship's sail. "Antenna" entered the English language as a word for the feelers of insects in the 1300s.

an·them *noun* 1. a song of praise or patriotism. *The U.S. national anthem, "The Star-Spangled Banner," was written during the War of 1812.* 2. a religious song including words from the Bible. {ăn thəm}

an·ther *noun* the part of a flower's stamen that bears pollen. {ăn thər}

ant·hill *noun* a pile of earth made by ants as they dig their underground nest. Anthills are found near the nest entrance. {ănt hihl}

an·thol·o·gy ● *noun* (anthologies) a collection of written works, such as poems or stories. An anthology can be written by one or by several authors. *His favorite book was an anthology of French poetry.* {ăn **tho** lə jee} anthologist, n.

an·thra·cite *noun* a hard, shiny coal that burns with little flame or smoke. {ăn thrə siyt}

an·thrax *noun* (anthraces) an infectious, often fatal dis-

ease. Anthrax usually infects sheep or cattle, but can infect humans as well. {ăn **thrăks**}

an·thro·pol·o·gy ● *noun* the scientific study of human-kind. People who study anthropology learn about the origins and development of human beings and their societies and customs. {ăn thrə **po** lə jee} anthropological, adj.

an·ti- or **ant-** *prefix* 1. a prefix that means "against" or "opposed to." *Someone who is anti-war is against war.* 2. a prefix that means "preventing." *Antifreeze is something that prevents freezing.*

an·ti·bi·ot·ic ● *noun* substance derived from fungi or other organisms and used to destroy or prevent the growth of bacteria or other disease-causing organisms. {ăn tee **biy o** tihk} antibiotically, adv.

an·ti·bod·y *noun* (antibodies) a protein in blood that reacts to particular toxic substances by neutralizing or destroying them. Antibodies provide immunity against these toxic substances. {ăn tee **bo** dee}

an·tic·i·pate *verb* (anticipated, anticipating, anticipates) 1. to look forward to; expect. *I anticipate a fine vacation.* 2. to prevent by knowing in advance. *We anticipated their attack.* {ăn **tih** sə **payt**}

an·tic·i·pa·tion *noun* 1. the act or process of anticipating. *In anticipation of the hero's arrival, the people tied ribbons around the trees.* 2. the condition of expecting or hoping. *The fans were filled with anticipation as the teams took their positions.* {ăn tih sə **pay** shən}

an·ti·dote *noun* a substance that stops poison from working or cures a disease. {ăn tih **doht**}

an·ti·freeze *noun* a substance that lowers the freezing point of a liquid such as water. *Antifreeze is used in car radiators to keep the engine from freezing.* {ăn tee **freez**}

an·tique ● *adjective* from or made in a time long ago. *The museum has a collection of antique pots.* *noun* an object, such as a piece of furniture, made many years in the past. *This table is a valuable antique.* {ăn **teek**}

an·ti·sep·tic ● *noun* a substance or drug that kills germs that cause disease or decay. *The doctor put an antiseptic on the wound.* {ăn tih **sehp** tihk} antiseptically, adv.

an·ti·tox·in *noun* an antibody formed in the body to act against a specific poison. {ăn tee **tŏk** sən} antitoxic, adj.

ant·ler ● *noun* one of a pair of bony growths on the head of most kinds of deer. Male elk, moose, and white-tailed deer all grow antlers with branches or prongs. Deer grow new antlers every year. Caribou and rein-deer are the only deer that have antlers on both the males and the females. {ănt lər} antlered, adj.

an·to·nym ● *noun* a word that has the opposite meaning of another word. *"Late" is an antonym of "early."* {ăn tə **nihm**}

an·vil *noun* a heavy metal block with a flat top on which heated metal objects are hammered into shapes. {ăn vihl}

anx·i·e·ty ● *noun* (anxieties) a feeling of being worried, nervous, or afraid that some-

a

thing will happen. {ăng **ziy** ih tee}

anx·ious *adjective* 1. feeling worried, nervous, or afraid about something uncertain. *She was anxious as she waited to see the doctor.* 2. having a strong wish; eager. *He was anxious to return home and see his children.* {**ăngk** shəs} anxiously, adv.

an·y *adjective* 1. one or some, no matter which or how many. *You may sit at any table.* / *Did you have any cookies?* 2. one or another; each and every. *Draw a picture of any dog.* / *Any child can learn.* 3. even a very small amount of (used after "not"). *I do not want any trouble. pronoun* an amount of something; a number of. *Did you spend any of your allowance?* / *There aren't any in these drawers. adverb* at all; to a degree *Is he any better now?* {**ehn** ee}

an·y·bod·y *pronoun* any person; anyone. *Does anybody want to go to the movies?* {**ehn** ee **buh** dee *or* **ehn** ee **bo** dee}

an·y·how *adverb* 1. in any way at all. *I'll get home for the holidays anyhow I can.* 2. in any case; anyway. *We don't have a map, but let's go anyhow.* {**ehn** ee **how**}

an·y·more *adverb* 1. any longer. *After she moves to the city, we won't see her anymore.* 2. at the present time; these days. *People don't drive carriages much anymore.* {**ehn** ee **mohr**}

an·y·one *pronoun* any person; anybody. *Does anyone know where my book is?* {**ehn** ee **wuhn**}

an·y·place *adverb* in or to any place; anywhere. *She must* not go anyplace until she is well. {**ehn** ee **plays**}

an·y·thing *pronoun* any thing, happening, or subject whatever. *Is there anything you have not told me? noun* a thing at all or of any kind. *Do you know anything about the subject? adverb* in any way; at all. *He isn't anything like his father.* {**ehn** ee **thing**}

an·y·time *adverb* at any moment, hour, or day; whenever. *Anytime you want to talk, just call.* {**ehn** ee **tiym**}

an·y·way *adverb* in any case; anyhow; no matter what happens. *She was ill but went to school anyway.* {**ehn** ee **way**}

an·y·where *adverb* to or in any place or direction; at any place. *She liked adventure and was not afraid to go anywhere.* {**ehn** ee **wayr**}

a·or·ta *noun* (aortas) the main artery of the body. The aorta carries blood from the left side of the heart to all parts of the body except the lungs. {ay **ohr** tə}

A·pach·e *noun* (Apache or Apaches) a member of a North American Indian people living mostly in the southwestern United States and northern Mexico. {ə **păch** ee}

a·part *adverb* 1. away from each other in time or space; at or to a distance; separated. *We keep our cat and dog apart.* / *Jim and his sister are three years apart.* 2. into pieces. *The cake fell apart when he tried to cut it.* {ə **part**}
• **take apart**
to separate into its pieces or parts. *He took apart my bike but did not put it back together.*
• **tell apart**
to see what is different between. *I can't tell the twins apart.*

a·part·heid *noun* a policy of keeping people of different races separate and unequal in a society. *Under apartheid in South Africa, black people had less freedom and power than white people.* {ə **part** hayd *or* ə **part** hiyd}

a·part·ment ○ *noun* a room or set of rooms used as living space. {ə **part** mənt}

ap·a·thy *noun* lack of interest or feeling. *His bad grades were a result of his apathy.* {**ăp** ə thee}

a·pat·o·saur *noun* another name for **brontosaur**. {ə **păt** ə sohr}

ape *noun* a mammal in the group of primates, which includes chimpanzees, gibbons, gorillas, and orangutans. Apes do not have tails. They have very flexible hands and feet. Apes range in size from three to six feet tall, and they can weigh up to 450 pounds. Apes live in the forests in Africa and Asia. *verb* (aped, aping, apes) to imitate or copy. *She aped her big sister's way of walking.* {**ayp**} apelike, adj.

ap·er·ture *noun* 1. a narrow opening. *An aperture in the wall allowed us to peek into the room.* 2. an opening that controls the amount of light that reaches the lens on a camera. {**ă** pər chər}

 Human Body  Human Mind   Everyday Life   History and Culture  Communication

a·pex *noun* (apexes) the highest point; tip. *The wind swirled around the apex of the mountain.* {**ay** pehks}

a·phid *noun* a small insect that eats by sucking the juices of plants. Aphids have soft bodies and move slowly. {**ay** fihd *or* ă fihd}

Aph·ro·di·te *noun* the goddess of love and beauty in Greek myth. In Roman myth, Aphrodite is called Venus. {ă frə **diy** tee}

a·piece *adverb* for or from each one; each. *The apples cost a dollar apiece.* {ə **pees**}

A·pol·lo *noun* the god of light, music, poetry, and healing in Greek and Roman myth. Apollo was also the god of prophecy. People travelled to his shrine at Delphi to ask questions about future events. {ə **po** loh}

a·pol·o·get·ic *adjective* expressing or wanting to express regret, as for an error or an offense. {ə po lə **jeh** tihk} apologetically, adv.

a·pol·o·gize *verb* (apologized, apologizing, apologizes) to say that one is sorry. *I apologized for being late to class.* {ə **po** lə jiyz} apologizer, n.

a·pol·o·gy *noun* (apologies) a statement that one is sorry for something. *I accept your apology for breaking the window.* {ə **po** lə jee}

a·pos·tle *noun* (sometimes capitalized) one of the first twelve disciples of Jesus Christ. {ə **po** səl}

a·pos·tro·phe 🌐 *noun* 1. a punctuation mark ('). It is used to show where one or more letters or numbers have been left out. "Wouldn't" for "would not" and "'87" for "1987" use apostrophes this way. 2. this mark used to show possession. "Susan's clothes" and "citizens' rights" use apostrophes this way. 3. this mark used in plurals of letters or numbers. An example of this use is "You forgot to cross your t's." {ə **po** strə fee}

ap·pal *verb* (appalled, appalling, appals) another spelling of **appall**. {ə **pawl**}

Ap·pa·la·chi·a *noun* a region in the United States that stretches from southwestern Pennsylvania to northwestern Georgia and includes the southern Appalachian Mountains. {ăp ə **lay** chee ə}

Ap·pa·la·chi·an Moun·tains *noun* a mountain range in eastern North America that stretches from the southeastern part of Canada to central Alabama in the United States; Appalachians. {ăp ə **lay** chee ən **mown** təns}

ap·pall *verb* (appalled, appalling, appalls) to cause to feel shock or horror. *The shooting appalled the whole town.* {ə **pawl**}

ap·pa·ra·tus *noun* (apparatus or apparatuses) tools or equipment made for a particular task. *A camera is an apparatus for taking pictures.* {ă pə **ră** tihs}

ap·par·el 🌐 *noun* clothing. *This store is known for its fine men's apparel.* {ə **par** əl}

ap·par·ent *adjective* 1. easily seen or plain. *It is apparent that you didn't make the bed.* 2. clear to one's understanding; obvious. *It is apparent that Rachel likes you very much.* 3. seeming to be so at first, but not necessarily so. *The apparent winner of the race was later disqualified.* {ə **par** ənt *or* ə **payr** ənt} apparently, adv.

ap·peal *noun* 1. an earnest request for help. *The famous actor made an appeal for money to fight cancer.* 2. the ability to attract interest and attention. *He shops at that store because of its great appeal.* 3. a request that a higher court hear a case. An appeal is made after one has lost a case in a lower court. *verb* (appealed, appealing, appeals) 1. to make an earnest request. *The mayor appealed to the people for their support.* 2. to have attraction or interest. *Going to bed early during the summer does not appeal to me.* 3. to request a review of to a higher court. *The lawyer appealed the case all the way to the Supreme Court.* {ə **peel**}

ap·pear *verb* (appeared, appearing, appears) 1. to come into view; become visible. *He appeared out of nowhere.* 2. to seem. *Jared appears to be smart.* 3. to come before the public. *My favorite singer will appear on television tonight.* {ə **peer**}

ap·pear·ance 🌐 *noun* 1. the act or an instance of coming into view or appearing. *Everyone welcomed the appearance of the sun after days of rain.* 2. outward show or aspect; seeming. *His appearance of happiness fooled everyone.* 3. (plural) outward signs. *By all appearances, he's an honest man.* 4. the way in which someone is dressed or groomed. *Don't judge her by*

A
B
C
D
E
F
G
H
I
J
K
L
M
N
O
P
Q
R
S
T
U
V
W
X
Y
Z

a
b
c
d
e
f
g
h
i
j
k
l
m
n
o
p
q
r
s
t
u
v
w
x
y
z

her sloppy appearance. {ə **peer** əns}

ap·pease *verb* (appeased, appeasing, appeases) 1. to cause to become calmer by meeting demands. *She appeased the crying child with a new toy.* 2. to satisfy. *He appeased his sweet tooth with a piece of cake.* {ə **peez**}

ap·pen·di·ci·tis *noun* a painful infection of the appendix. {ə pehn də **siy** tihs}

ap·pen·dix *noun* (appendixes or appendices) 1. a section at the end of a book or magazine article that gives more information. 2. a short, closed tube of tissue that grows out of the large intestine. The appendix is on the right side of the lower abdomen. {ə **pehn** dihks}

appendix

ap·pe·tite *noun* 1. a desire to eat. *I lose my appetite when I am sad.* 2. a strong desire for anything. *She has an appetite for money.* {**ă** pə **tiyt**}

ap·pe·tiz·er *noun* a small amount of food or drink served before a meal. {**ă** pə **tiy** zər}

ap·pe·tiz·ing *adjective* pleasing to the appetite. *That pizza looks appetizing.* {**ă** pə **tiy** zing}

ap·plaud *verb* (applauded, applauding, applauds) 1. to clap the hands in approval. *The audience applauded when the play ended.* 2. to give approval to; praise. *I applaud you for all your hard work.* {ə **plawd**}

ap·plause *noun* 1. the clapping of hands in approval. *The sound of applause filled the the-*

ater. 2. approval or praise. *Her teacher's applause made her proud.* {ə **plawz**}

ap·ple *noun* 1. a firm, round fruit with juicy white flesh and red, green, or yellow skin. 2. the tree on which this fruit grows. {**ăp** əl}

ap·ple·sauce *noun* a sweet sauce made by cooking apples until they are soft. {**ăp** əl **saws**}

ap·pli·ance   *noun* a device used for a particular purpose. Stoves and refrigerators are appliances used in the home. {ə **pliy** əns}

ap·pli·ca·ble *adjective* relevant or appropriate to a given situation; capable of being applied. {**ă** plih kə bəl} applicability, n.

ap·pli·cant *noun* a person who applies for something, such as a job. *The applicant is waiting for his interview.* {**ă** plih kənt}

ap·pli·ca·tion *noun* 1. the act of putting to use. *The application of her math skills has helped her in her job.* 2. a way of being used. *Electricity has many applications in modern life.* 3. the act of putting something on. *After the first application of paint, he stepped back to look at his work.* 4. a request. *Today I filled out ten applications for summer work.* {**ă** plih **kay** shən}

ap·ply *verb* (applied, applying, applies) 1. to make use of or put to use. *Jane applied her knowledge of computers in solving the problem.* 2. to lay on. *He applied glue to the paper.* 3. to use with much effort. *They are really applying themselves to the job.* 4. to be related or to matter. *The book*

applies to what the class is studying. 5. to make a request. *Mr. Kane is applying for jobs across the country.* {ə **pliy**}

ap·point *verb* (appointed, appointing, appoints) 1. to name to a particular office or duty. *The president appointed a new secretary of state.* 2. to set or decide on. *Let's appoint a regular meeting time.* {ə **point**}

ap·point·ment *noun* 1. the act of choosing or naming for an office or duty. *The appointment of the new judge was made public today.* 2. a position held by one who is appointed. *Her appointment to the president's staff lasted four years.* 3. an arrangement to meet or to do something. *Tom has an appointment with the dentist.* {ə **point** mənt}

ap·praise *verb* (appraised, appraising, appraises) 1. to judge the quality or nature of. *The critic appraised the dancer's performance.* 2. to determine the value of; set a price for. *The jeweler appraised the diamond necklace at ten thousand dollars.* {ə **prayz**} appraiser, n.

ap·pre·ci·ate *verb* (appreciated, appreciating, appreciates) 1. to be grateful for or to. *Mrs. Lund appreciated the neighbors' help.* 2. to understand and accept the worth of; value. *We appreciate spring after the cold winter.* 3. to be well aware of. *I appreciate how hard your situation is.* 4. to grow in value. *Your investment will appreciate over time.* {ə **pree** shee **ayt**}

ap·pre·ci·a·tion *noun* 1. a feeling of thanks. *I told her of my appreciation for the cookies she baked.* 2. the act of judging worth or quality. 3. a rise in value. *The appreciation of that investment was a*

 Human Body  Human Mind  Everyday Life  History and Culture Communication

welcome surprise. {ə **pree** shee **ay** shən}

ap·pre·hend *verb* (apprehended, apprehending, apprehends) 1. to catch and place under arrest. *The police apprehended the thief.* 2. to understand the meaning of. *Do you apprehend what is happening to you?* {ă prih **hehnd**}

ap·pre·hen·sion *noun* 1. fear about what may happen. *The thought of meeting the bully on the playground filled him with apprehension.* 2. the act of understanding without studying. *He has little apprehension of how plants grow.* 3. the act of catching and arresting. *The apprehension of the suspect took place this morning.* {ă prə **hehn** shən}

ap·pre·hen·sive *adjective* feeling fearful about future events. *The storm warning made her apprehensive.* {ă prə **hehn** sihv} apprehensively, adv.

ap·pren·tice *noun* someone who works for somebody else to learn that person's skill or trade. *He was a carpenter's apprentice for three years before starting his own business.* *verb* (apprenticed, apprenticing, apprentices) to place as an apprentice to. *The cooking school apprenticed her to a famous chef.* {ə **prehn** tihs} apprenticeship, n.

ap·proach *verb* (approached, approaching, approaches) 1. to come or go near to. *The child approached the dog carefully.* 2. to go to with a request. *He approached his father about borrowing the car.* 3. to begin to work on; pre-

pare to do. *How do we approach this task?* *noun* 1. the act of coming near. *The approach of a fox woke the chickens.* 2. a way of entering or coming near. *The only approach to the woods was a small path.* 3. a way of dealing with something. *Her approach to studying for tests seems to work.* {ə **prohch**}

ap·proach·a·ble *adjective* friendly to others; easily approached. *The new principal is a very approachable person.* {ə **proh** chə bəl} approachability, n.

ap·pro·pri·ate *adjective* right for the purpose; proper. *Jeans and a T-shirt are not appropriate for a formal wedding.* *verb* (appropriated, appropriating, appropriates) to set aside for a particular purpose. *The town appropriated money for the senior center.* {ə **proh** pree ət, adj., ə **proh** pree ayt, v.} appropriately, adv., appropriateness, n.

ap·prov·al *noun* 1. the act of approving. *After getting the teacher's approval, the student went ahead with his project.* 2. good opinion; favorable thoughts. *The new mayor worked hard to win the approval of the people.* {ə **prooh** vəl}

ap·prove *verb* (approved, approving, approves) 1. to show approval or think well of something or someone. *He does not approve of people who smoke.* 2. to consider good or right. *If your mother approves it, you may stay up past your bedtime tonight.* 3. to accept and allow officially. *The town council approved a new building plan.* {ə **proohv**} approvingly, adv.

ap·prox·i·mate *adjective* almost exact; close to what is needed or expected. *He told*

us an approximate price to repair the bike. *verb* (approximated, approximating, approximates) to be quite like; come close to. *This synthetic fabric approximates the feel of silk.* {ə **prŏk** sə mət, adj., ə **prŏk** sə **mayt**, v.} approximately, adv.

ap·prox·i·mate·ly *adverb* about; almost exactly. *I'll arrive in approximately two hours.* {ə **prŏk** sə miht lee}

Apr. *abbreviation* an abbreviation for **April**.

ap·ri·cot *noun* 1. a soft round fruit with fuzzy, pale orange skin. 2. the tree that bears this fruit. {ăp rə kŏt or ay prə kŏt}

A·pril *noun* the fourth month of the year. April has thirty days. {**ay** prəl}

> **Word History** *April* comes from *Aprilis*, the month in the Roman calendar that was dedicated to Venus, a goddess of Roman mythology.

April Fools' Day *noun* the first day of April, when friendly tricks and jokes are played on people. {ay prəl **foohlz** day}

a·pron *noun* a garment that covers all or part of the front of the body. An apron is worn to protect the clothing underneath. {**ay** prən}

apt *adjective* 1. right for a particular situation; appropriate or suitable. *Since we were both hungry, sharing the sandwich was an apt solution.* 2. able to learn quickly. *She is an apt math student.* 3. likely. *We are apt to lose again.* {**ăpt**}

apt. *abbreviation* an abbreviation for **apartment**.

A
B
C
D
E
F
G
H
I
J
K
L
M
N
O
P
Q
R
S
T
U
V
W
X
Y
Z

ap·ti·tude *noun* 1. ability to learn quickly. *He shows great aptitude in class.* 2. a natural ability; talent. *Some people have an aptitude for drawing.* {**ăp** tə **toohd**}

aq·ua *noun* (aquas) the color that comes from mixing blue, green, and a small amount of white paint. {**ă** kwə *or* **ah** kwə}

aq·ua·cul·ture *noun* the farming of plants and animals that live in water. {**ă** kwə **kuhl** chər *or* **ah** kwə **kuhl** chər}

Aq·ua-Lung *noun* trademark for an underwater breathing device. {**ă** kwə **luhng** *or* **ah** kwə **luhng**}

a·quar·i·um ❶ *noun* (aquariums) 1. a tank or other container filled with water in which water animals and plants are kept. *The cat sat before an aquarium filled with tiny, colorful fish.* 2. A building where water animals and plants are kept and displayed. *Many families visit the aquarium on weekends.* {ə **kwayr** ee əm} aquarian, adj.

A·quar·i·us *noun* 1. a constellation located between Capricorn and Pisces. Aquarius is also called the Water Bearer. 2. the eleventh sign of the zodiac, the Water Bearer, which the sun enters about January 21. 3. a person born under this sign, between January 21 and February 20. {ə **kwayr** ee əs}

a·quat·ic ❶ *adjective* 1. of or taking place on the water. *She enjoys aquatic sports in the summer.* 2. living or growing in or on water. *Seaweed is an aquatic plant.* {ə **kwă** tihk}

aq·ue·duct *noun* 1. a channel or pipe built to carry water over a long distance. 2. a structure like a bridge for carrying a waterway or pipe across a river or valley. *The ancient Romans built enormous stone aqueducts.* {**ăk** wə **duhkt**}

a·qui·fer *noun* a layer of rock, sand, or gravel that contains water from which wells and springs are supplied. {**ăk** wih fər}

AR or **Ark.** *abbreviation* an abbreviation for **Arkansas**.

-ar *suffix* 1. a suffix that means "of" or "relating to." *A polar bear is a bear of the North Pole.* 2. a suffix that means "like" or "being." *A circular object is in the shape of a circle.*

Ar·ab *noun* 1. a member of a southwest Asian people that makes up most of the population of Arabia and other parts of the Middle East. 2. a person who was born in or is a citizen of an Arabian country. *adjective* 1. of or having to do with the Arabian countries. *Millions of people live in Arab countries.* 2. see Arabian. {**ar** əb}

A·ra·bi·a *noun* a peninsula in southwest Asia between the Red Sea and the Persian Gulf. {ə **ray** bee ə}

A·ra·bi·an *adjective* 1. of, having to do with, or characteristic of Arabia or its desert climate. *Arabian weather is hot and dry.* 2. of or relating to Arabs. *noun* a person who was born in or is a citizen of Arabia; Arab. *Many Arabians live in the desert.* {ə **ray** bee ən}

Ar·a·bic *adjective* of or having to do with Arabia or Arabs; Arabian. *There is a lot of detail in Arabic art.* *noun* the language of the Arabs. {**ar** ə bihk}

Arabic numeral *noun* any of the symbols for the numbers zero through nine; 0, 1, 2, 3, 4, 5, 6, 7, 8, 9. {**ar** ə bihk **nooh** mə rəl}

ar·a·ble *adjective* capable of being farmed. *There is no arable land in Antarctica.* {**ar** ə bəl}

ar·bi·trar·y *adjective* resulting from personal opinions, wishes, or feelings instead of from a rule or reason. *The jury's decision seemed unfair and arbitrary.* {**ar** bih **trayr** ee} arbitrarily, adv.

ar·bi·trate *verb* (arbitrated, arbitrating, arbitrates) 1. to make a decision about or settle. *The judge arbitrated an end to the disagreement.* 2. to have someone else settle; submit to arbitration. *The rival companies finally arbitrated their dispute.* {**ar** bih **trayt**}

ar·bor *noun* a shady area made by arranging trees and bushes or by growing vines on a frame. {**ar** bər}

ar·bour *noun* a spelling of **arbor** used in Canada and Britain. See **arbor** for more information. {**ar** bər}

arc *noun* any curved line; anything shaped like a bow or curve. *The rainbow formed an arc across the sky.* {**ark**}

Homophone Note Are you looking for the word *ark* (a large boat)? *Arc* and *ark* sound alike but have different meanings.

ar·cade *noun* 1. a row of arches connected to form a passageway. 2. a similar covered passageway that has shops or places to play video games along the sides. {**ar** **kayd**}

arch *noun* 1. a curved structure made out of stone or brick and used to span an open space such as a door. *The ancient Romans introduced the use of arches in buildings and other structures.* 2. anything that looks like such a struc-

 Human Body
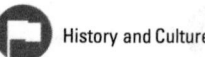 Human Mind
Everyday Life
 History and Culture
Communication

ture. *Good shoes support the arches of the feet.* *verb* (arched, arching, arches) 1. to form an arch or curve in. *The cat arched its back.* 2. to form an arch. *The bridge arched over the river.* {**arch**}

arch- or **archi-** *prefix* a prefix that means "main" or "most important." *An archbishop is a bishop of the highest rank.*

ar·chae·ol·o·gy ⭘ or **archeology** *noun* the study of past human life. An archaeologist digs up and then studies objects such as pottery, tools, and buildings. {**ar** kee **o** lih jee} archaeologist, n.

arch·bish·op *noun* a bishop of the highest rank. {**arch bih** shəp}

ar·che·ol·o·gy *noun* another spelling for archaeology. {**ar** kee **o** lə jee}

ar·cher *noun* a person who uses a bow and arrow. *The archer aimed carefully at the target.* {**ar** chər}

ar·cher·y *noun* the sport or practice of shooting with a bow and arrow. {**ar** chə ree}

ar·chi·pel·a·go *noun* (archipelagos [or] archipelagoes) a group of islands. *Indonesia is made up of over thirteen thousand islands in three main archipelagoes.* {**ar** kə **peh** lə goh}

ar·chi·tect *noun* a person who designs buildings and directs their construction. {**ar** kə **tehkt**}

ar·chi·tec·ture ⭘ ⭘ *noun* 1. the act or process of designing buildings, or the profession of an architect. 2. the style or way of building. *Ancient Greek architecture uses three styles of columns.* {**ar** kə **tehk** chər} architectural, adj., architecturally, adv.

arc·tic ⭘ ⭘ *adjective* 1. (often capitalized) of or having to do with the region around the North Pole. *The arctic wilderness may be opened someday for oil drilling.* 2. freezing or very cold weather as in the Arctic. *The city of Winnipeg has arctic weather in January.* *noun* (often capitalized) the region around the North Pole and inside the Arctic Circle. {**ark** tihk}

Arctic Circle *noun* an imaginary line drawn around the earth parallel to the equator which marks the boundary of the Arctic. North of this line there are periods of continuous night in the winter and continuous day in the summer. {**ark** tihk **sər** kəl}

Arctic Ocean *noun* the ocean that surrounds the North Pole. {**ark** tihk **oh** shən}

-ard or **-art** *suffix* a suffix that means one who does something too much or too often. *A drunkard is a person who drinks too much.*

ar·dent *adjective* having or showing very strong feelings such as passion, loyalty, or desire. *My brother is an ardent fan of rap music.* {**ar** dənt} ardently, adv.

are *verb* a form of the verb "be" that is present tense and used with the pronouns "you," "we," or "they." It is also used with plural nouns. {**ar**}

ar·e·a *noun* 1. a place or region. *They have never visited that area of the country.* 2. a field of study. *The doctor's area of medicine is heart disease.* 3. the amount of surface within a certain space. *The area of the room is two hundred square feet.* {**ayr** ee ə}

area code *noun* a set of three numbers given to different areas of the United States and Canada for telephone service. An area code must be dialed before the telephone number when calling someone outside a local area. {**ayr** ee ə **kohd**}

a·re·na ⭘ ⭘ *noun* 1. a stage, ring, or other enclosed area where shows or sports events are held. 2. a building that has an arena. *A large parking lot surrounded the arena.* 3. an area of activity or conflict. *There are many opinions in the arena of politics.* {ə **ree** nə}

aren't shortened form of "are not" and of "am not." *Aren't we leaving soon? / I'm right, aren't I?* {**arnt** or **ar** ənt}

Ar·es *noun* the god of war in Greek myth. In Roman myth, Ares is called Mars. {**ayr** eez}

Ar·gen·ti·na *noun* a country in southern South America. Buenos Aires is the capital of Argentina. {**ar** jən **tee** nə} Argentinean, n., adj.

ar·gue ⭘ *verb* (argued, arguing, argues) 1. to give reasons for or against something. *Some of the parents argued against school uniforms.* 2. to express disagreement; quarrel. *The children argued over which video to rent.* {**arg** yoo} arguer, n.

ar·gu·ment *noun* 1. a discussion by people who disagree. *They had an argument about whose turn it was to wash the dishes.* 2. a reason in favor of or against something. *Her father's argument against giving her a higher allowance was that she did not save her money.* {**arg** yə mənt}

ar·id *adjective* extremely dry, especially from lack of rainfall. *The camels went without water in the arid desert.* {**ar** ihd}

a
b
c
d
e
f
g
h
i
j
k
l
m
n
o
p
q
r
s
t
u
v
w
x
y
z

aridity, n., aridly, adv., aridness, n.

Ar·ies *noun* 1. a constellation located between Pisces and Taurus. Aries is also called the Ram. 2. the first sign of the zodiac, the Ram, which the sun enters about March 21. 3. a person born under this sign, between March 21 and April 20. {<u>ayr</u> eez}

a·rise *verb* (arose, arisen, arising, arises) 1. to appear; come into being. *Several good ideas arose during the discussion.* 2. to move upward. *Steam arose from the boiling water.* 3. to get up from sitting or sleep. *He arose before sunrise.* {ə <u>riyz</u>}

ar·is·toc·ra·cy *noun* (aristocracies) 1. a class of people who have a high social position because of the family they are born into. Members of the aristocracy are usually richer and have more privileges than other members of society. 2. any group or set of people thought to be superior to others. *The aristocracy of research scientists met to discuss world environmental problems.* {ar ih <u>sto</u> krə see}

a·ris·to·crat *noun* a member of the aristocracy; noble. {ə <u>rih</u> stə krăt}

a·rith·me·tic ❷ *noun* the method and process of using whole numbers to add, subtract, multiply, and divide. {ə <u>rihth</u> mə tihk} arithmetical, adj., arithmetically, adv.

Ar·i·zo·na *noun* a state in the southwestern United States. Its capital is Phoenix. (abbreviated: AZ) {ar ih <u>zoh</u> nə} Arizonan, n., adj., Arizonian, n., adj.

Word History *Arizona* is the Spanish spelling of a Papago or Pima word that means "place of the little stream."

ark *noun* 1. (sometimes capitalized) in the Bible, the large boat built by Noah to save his family and two of every animal from a flood sent by God. 2. in the Bible, a chest carried by the ancient Hebrews. The ark contained the two stone tablets on which the Ten Commandments were written. {<u>ark</u>}

Homophone Note The words *ark* and *arc* sound alike but have different meanings.

Ar·kan·sas *noun* a state in the south central United States. Its capital is Little Rock. (abbreviated: AR) {<u>ar</u> kən saw} Arkansan, n., adj., Arkansian, n., adj.

Word History *Arkansas* is the French spelling of *ugakhpah* or *quapaw*, a Native American nation from the region. It means "people who live downstream."

arm¹ 🟢 *noun* 1. the part of the human body between the shoulder and the wrist. 2. any part that looks like or is used like an arm. *Do not sit on the arm of that chair.* {<u>arm</u>} armless, n.

arm² 🟢 *noun* (usually plural) weapons. Guns, knives, and bombs are arms. *verb* (armed, arming, arms) 1. to give weapons to. *The leader armed his troops.* 2. to protect or make stronger. *The king armed the castle with three dozen knights. / The candidate armed herself with the latest facts before the debate.* {<u>arm</u>}

ar·ma·da *noun* a large group of ships armed for battle. *In 1588, Spain sent an armada of one hundred and thirty ships against England.* {ar <u>mah</u> də}

ar·ma·dil·lo *noun* (armadillos) a mammal whose body

is protected by hard, bony plates. Armadillos live in Central and South America, and the southern United States. Some kinds of armadillos are only six inches long; other kinds grow up to four feet in length. They eat mostly insects and are related to sloths and anteaters. {ar mə <u>dih</u> loh}

ar·ma·ment *noun* (usually plural) the total military power of a country, including weapons and supplies. *The small country felt threatened by the armaments of its powerful neighbor.* {<u>ar</u> mə mənt}

arm·chair *noun* a chair having supports at the sides for resting one's arms. {<u>arm</u> chayr}

armed forces *plural noun* all the military services of a country. {<u>armd</u> <u>fohr</u> sihz}

Ar·me·ni·a *noun* a country in southwestern Asia. Yerevan is the capital of Armenia. {ar <u>mee</u> nee ə} Armenian, n., adj.

ar·mi·stice *noun* an agreement by groups of people or countries at war to stop fighting; truce. {<u>ar</u> mə stihs}

ar·mor *noun* 1. a suit made of leather, metal, or other strong material, worn to protect the body during battle. *Both the knight and his horse wore armor.* 2. a covering placed on ships and vehicles that protects against weapons. *The shells could not damage the tank's armor.* 3. the covering on certain animals that protects them against attack. *The turtle wears its armor on its back.* *verb* (armored, armoring, armors) to outfit or cover with armor.

 Human Body
 Human Mind
 Everyday Life
 History and Culture
Communication

The soldiers armored the jeep with steel plates. {**ar** mər}

ar·mored *adjective* wearing or being covered by armor. *An armored car transports money.* {**ar** mərd}

ar·mor·y *noun* (armories) a place where weapons and other military equipment are made or stored. {**ar** mə ree}

ar·mour *noun* a spelling of **armor** used in Canada and Britain. See **armor** for more information. {**ar** mər}

ar·mour·y *noun* a spelling of **armory** used in Canada and Britain. See **armory** for more information. {**ar** mər ee}

arm·pit *noun* the hollow formed beneath the arm at the shoulder. {**arm piht**}

ar·my ⬤ *noun* (armies) 1. a large group of soldiers trained to use weapons to fight on land. 2. a great number of people or things. *The movie star has an army of fans.* 3. a large group that works together for a cause. *The mayor led an army of workers in cleaning up after the fire.* {**ar** mee}

a·ro·ma *noun* a pleasant smell; fragrance. *The kitchen had an aroma of freshly baked bread.* {ə **roh** mə}

Word History *Aroma* may come from a Greek word that means "to plow." Perhaps the good smell of plowed earth explains how a word for plowing became the origin of a word for fragrance.

a·rose *verb* past tense of **arise**. {ə **rohz**}

a·round *adverb* 1. in a circle. *The car spun around.* 2. in all directions or to all sides. *He looked around.* 3. measured along the outside edge; in circumference. *The tree trunk was eighteen inches around.* 4. (informal) about; nearby. *I'll be around if you need me.* 5. in or to the opposite direction. *The car turned around.* 6. through an area. *Will you show me around?* *preposition* 1. on all sides of. *There are bushes around the park.* 2. near to. *John had to stay around the house.* 3. in or to places within an area; here and there. *They drove around the country.* 4. so as to surround or go around. *Tie a string around your finger.* 5. so as to move in a circle. *Do you want to drive around the lake?* 6. somewhere near; about. *Come around noon.* {ə **rownd**}

a·rouse *verb* (aroused, arousing, arouses) 1. to awaken from sleep. *The alarm aroused me from my bed.* 2. to stir up; excite *The king's injustice aroused the people's anger.* {ə **rowz**} arousal, n.

ar·range *verb* (arranged, arranging, arranges) 1. to put in an order. *She arranged the cans according to size.* 2. to make plans for; prepare. *They arranged a surprise party for their friend.* 3. to change so as to fit a particular type of musical performance. *She arranged the violin piece for the piano.* {ə **raynj**} arranger, n.

ar·range·ment *noun* 1. the act of putting things in order. *The arrangement of the library books took days.* 2. the group of things that have been put in order. *The flower arrangements were beautiful.* 3. (usually plural) plans or preparations. *Max made the arrangements for his grandfather's retirement party.* 4. a piece of music that has been changed to fit a particular type of performance. *The band played an arrangement of standard songs.* {ə **raynj** mənt}

ar·ray *verb* (arrayed, arraying, arrays) 1. to put in order or position; organize or arrange. *The general arrayed the troops for a battle.* 2. to dress or clothe. *She arrayed herself in her best clothes for the party.* *noun* 1. a correct or proper arrangement. *Mae keeps her videotapes in a neat array on a shelf.* 2. a large and impressive set of things; display. *Her eyes widened when she saw the array of desserts on the table.* 3. beautiful or fine clothing. *The royal array was of satin and fur.* {ə **ray**}

ar·rest ⬤ *verb* (arrested, arresting, arrests) 1. to slow down; block; stop. *The storm arrested our hike up the mountain.* 2. to seize and hold or imprison for breaking the law. *The police arrested the robber as he ran out of the bank.* 3. to attract and keep hold of. *The teacher's story arrested the children's attention.* *noun* the act of seizing or the condition of being seized by the authority of the law. *The story of the thief's arrest appeared on the front page of the paper.* {ə **rehst**}

ar·ri·val *noun* 1. the act of reaching a certain place or goal. *The fans cheered her arrival at the finish line.* 2. a person or thing that has arrived. *We welcomed the new arrivals.* {ə **riy** vəl}

ar·rive *verb* (arrived, arriving, arrives) to reach a certain place or goal. *After driving all day, we arrived at the ocean.* {ə **riyv**}

ar·ro·gance *noun* 1. the condition or quality of being arrogant; belief in one's superiority, or excessive pride. 2. disagreeable behavior resulting from this condition. *He was asked to leave because his arrogance was offending everyone.* {**ar** ə gəns} arrogancy, n.

ar·ro·gant *adjective* having or showing too much pride; behaving as though one is more important than others. *Success makes some people arrogant.* {**ar** ə gənt} arrogantly, adv.

ar·row *noun* 1. a thin pointed rod that is shot from a bow. 2. a sign shaped like an arrow. An arrow is used to point out a place or show which way to go. *Follow the arrows to the park entrance.* {**ar** oh}

ar·row·head *noun* the sharp, pointed part on the end of an arrow. *The boys found some old arrowheads in the forest.* {**ar** oh hehd}

ar·roy·o *noun* (arroyos) a steep ditch carved in a plain or desert by the force of running water. Arroyos are usually dry except after a heavy rainfall. {ə **roi** oh}

ar·se·nal *noun* a building used for storing weapons and ammunition. {**ar** sə nəl}

ar·se·nic *noun* a poisonous substance that is one of the chemical elements. It can be either grayish white, yellow, or black. (symbol: As) {**ar** sə nihk}

ar·son *noun* the crime of burning buildings on purpose. {**ar** sən} arsonist, n.

art 🔵🔵 *noun* 1. the creation of things whose purpose is to be beautiful or full of meaning. 2. the works produced by painters, writers, musicians, sculptors, film directors, and other kinds of artists. *Poems, paintings, and ballets are all examples of art.* 3. a fine skill that has resulted from natural ability, practice, or study. *She has perfected the art of making fine pastries. / This*

poem shows great art. 4. the field of visual works such as painting and drawing. {art}

ar·te·fact *noun* another spelling of **artifact**. {**ar** tə făkt}

ar·ter·y 🔵 *noun* (arteries) 1. a blood vessel that carries blood away from the heart. 2. a major road or route. *The new highway will be a main artery for travel between the two cities.* {**ar** tə ree}

ar·thri·tis *noun* a disease of the joints in which they swell and become painful. {ar **thriy** tihs} arthritic, [adj.], n., arthritically, adv.

ar·thro·pod 🔵 *noun* a large group of animals with hard shells on the outsides of their bodies, legs with joints, and no bones inside their bodies. Insects, spiders, centipedes, and crabs are arthropods. {**ar** thrə pŏd}

ar·ti·choke *noun* a plant like a tall thistle with a flower head made up of thick leaves. The head of the artichoke is eaten as a vegetable. {**ar** tih **chohk**}

ar·ti·cle 🔵🔵 *noun* 1. a single thing; one item out of a group of similar objects. *She put several articles of clothing into her suitcase.* 2. a piece of writing on a particular subject that appears in a newspaper, magazine, or book. *The local newspaper had an article about the missing jewels.* 3. the words "a," "an," and "the." They are used with nouns and limit the way nouns can be used. 4. a specific section in a document such as a contract or a constitution. *The lawyer read us*

the article in the contract that explained our rights as consumers. {ar tih kəl}

ar·tic·u·late *adjective* able to speak or express oneself in a clear way. *He was articulate in asking for help.* *verb* (articulated, articulating, articulates) to speak or express in a clear way. *She articulated the words with great feeling.* {ar **tihk** yə **layt**} articulately, adv.

ar·ti·fact 🔵 *noun* any object made by human beings. *The museum had an exhibit of ancient Mexican artifacts.* {**ar** tih **făkt**}

ar·ti·fi·cial *adjective* 1. made by human beings; not natural. *The artificial flowers actually looked real.* 2. not true or sincere; pretended. *Her apology sounded artificial.* {ar tih **fih** shəl} artificiality, n., artificially, adv.

artificial intelligence *noun* an area of computer science that explores the ability of computers to think or have intelligence. Artificial intelligence is concerned with developing computer programs or computers that seem to use reason and make decisions. {ar tih **fih** shəl ihn **teh** lih jəns}

artificial respiration *noun* the forcing of air into and out of the lungs of a person who has stopped breathing. {ar tih **fih** shəl reh spə **ray** shən}

ar·til·ler·y *noun* 1. large weapons used in land battles, such as cannons or rockets. Artillery is too heavy for a person to carry and is sometimes mounted on wheels. 2. the branch of an army that uses these weapons. *He joined the artillery.* {ar **tih** lə ree} artilleryman, n.

ar·ti·san 🔵🔵 *noun* a person skilled in making things. People who make furniture,

 Human Body    Human Mind    Everyday Life    History and Culture   Communication

quilts, or other crafts are arti-sans. {**ar** tih zən} artisanship, n.

art·ist 🔵 🔵 *noun* 1. a person who is good at painting, music, writing, or any other art. 2. a person who does something with a great deal of skill or talent. *Wanda is a trapeze artist at the circus.* {**ar** tihst}

ar·tis·tic *adjective* 1. having to do with art or artists. *That girl shows real artistic talent.* 2. showing skill and imagination in creating. *We admired the artistic flower arrangement.* {ar **tih** stihk} artistically, *adv.*

As symbol of the chemical element arsenic.

as *adverb* 1. in equal measure; to the same extent. 2. for example; for instance. *Some sports, as baseball, require the use of a bat.* *conjunction* 1. in the same way or manner that; to the same degree. *She reads a lot, as does he.* 2. at the moment; when. *Tom stopped as Jerry started.* 3. though. *Wicked as he is, we love him still.* 4. because. *As I was tired, I went to bed.* *preposition* in the role of. *He has a job as a newspaper carrier.* {**ăz**}

• **as if**
how it would be if. *He looked as if he had been struck by lightning.*

• **as of**
beginning on; from. *As of my next birthday, I will be old enough to drive a car.*

ASAP *abbreviation* an abbreviation for "as soon as possible."

as·bes·tos *noun* a mineral that separates into fibers and does not catch fire or conduct electricity. Asbestos is used to make fireproof materials and insulation. *The ship was insulated with asbestos.* {**ăs** behs təs or ăz **behs** təs}

as·cend *verb* (ascended, ascending, ascends) 1. to go upward; climb; rise. *The airplane ascended above the clouds.* 2. to go up on or along; climb or rise on. *He ascended the staircase.* / *The pianist ascended the musical scale.* {ə **sehnd**}

as·cent *noun* 1. the act of going up; climb; rise. *Our ascent of the mountain took four hours.* 2. a way leading up; upward slope. *The explorers found a new ascent to the top of the ridge.* {ə **sehnt**}

Homophone Note The words *ascent* and *assent* sound alike but have different meanings.

as·cer·tain *verb* (ascertained, ascertaining, ascertains) to learn without question; determine. *The doctor ascertained the cause of her illness.* {ă sər **tayn**}

ash[1] *noun* the soft gray powder that is left after something has been burned. *The house burned to ashes.* {**ăsh**}

ash[2] *noun* 1. a tree that is related to the olive tree. It has seeds that look like wings and leaves of more than one part. 2. the wood of such a tree. *Baseball bats are often made of ash.* {**ăsh**}

a·shamed *adjective* 1. feeling shame or guilt for doing something wrong or foolish. *She was ashamed of herself for cheating on a test.* 2. not wanting to do something because of a fear of feeling shame or being embarrassed. *He didn't invite friends to visit because he was ashamed of his house.* {ə **shaymd**} ashamedly, *adv.*

a·shore *adverb* 1. to or onto the shore. *Row the boat ashore.* 2. on land. *During our cruise, we went ashore for a day.* {ə **shohr**}

A·sia *noun* the largest continent. Asia is surrounded by the Pacific, Indian, and Arctic Oceans, the Red Sea, and eastern Europe. It is in the Eastern Hemisphere. {**ay** zhə}

A·sian *adjective* of or having to do with Asia, or its people or languages. *noun* a person who was born in or is a citizen of a country in Asia. {**ay** zhən}

A·sian A·mer·i·can *adjective* of or having to do with American people of Asian origin, or their history or culture. *noun* An American person of Asian origin. {**ay** zhən ə **mehr** ih kən}

a·side *adverb* 1. on or toward the side. *He stood aside while the others talked.* / *As we approached each other, she stepped aside.* 2. out of one's thoughts. *Put your fear aside and try out for the team.* 3. set apart for future use or need. *It's wise to lay money aside.* {ə **siyd**}

• **aside from**
except for; besides. *Aside from one or two holes, this sweater is all right.*

ask *verb* (asked, asking, asks) 1. to put a question to. *He asked me if I had any money.* 2. to seek an answer to; inquire. *She asked about the new animals at the zoo.* 3. to make a request of. *The teacher asked him to close the window.* 4. to invite. *She asked Ben to the movies.* {**ăsk**}

a
b
c
d
e
f
g
h
i
j
k
l
m
n
o
p
q
r
s
t
u
v
w
x
y
z

a·skew *adverb or adjective* not straight. *Her hat was askew. / The crooked arrow flew askew.* {ə **skyoo**}

a·sleep *adjective* 1. sleeping. *Please be quiet while the baby is asleep.* 2. without feeling; numb. *She suddenly noticed that her leg was asleep.* *adverb* into a condition of sleep. *I fell asleep on the couch while reading.* {ə **sleep**}

as·par·a·gus *noun* a plant related to the lily, whose young shoots are cooked and eaten as a vegetable. The shoots are shaped like spears with scaly leaves at the tip. {ə **spar** ə gihs}

ASPCA *abbreviation* a national organization whose purpose is to take care of lost or stray dogs, cats, and other small animals. This organization tries to find people to adopt these animals as pets. ASPCA is an abbreviation for "American Society for the Prevention of Cruelty to Animals."

as·pect *noun* 1. a part or element. *Our assignment was to write about one interesting aspect of space travel, so I chose the training of astronauts.* 2. side or view. *Riding in the cart, we had a good view of the horse's rear aspect.* 3. a way in which something can be seen or considered. *From this aspect, the tree looks easy to climb.* 4. expression on the face. *Grandfather's grim aspect told me he already knew about the broken window.* {ă **spehkt**}

as·pen *noun* a kind of poplar tree with leaves that shake in the slightest breeze. {**ăs** pən}

as·phalt *noun* 1. a sticky black substance like tar. Asphalt is found naturally or obtained when oil is refined. It is used for making roads and roofs and for making things waterproof. 2. a mixture of this substance with gravel or sand, used to pave roads. {**ăs fawlt**}

as·pi·ra·tion *noun* a goal, aim, or ambition. *Her aspiration is to become a pilot.* {ă spə **ray** shən}

as·pire *verb* (aspired, aspiring, aspires) to want strongly; have as an aim (usually followed by to or after). *He aspires to power and fame.* {ə **spiyr**}

as·pi·rin *noun* (aspirin or aspirins) 1. a drug used to take away pain and bring down fever. 2. a tablet or pill that contains this drug. {**ă** spə rən}

ass *noun* 1. a mammal with long legs and hooves that is closely related to the horse. A donkey is a domestic ass. Asses look like horses but are smaller and have longer ears. Wild asses live in Africa and Asia and are in danger of becoming extinct. 2. a person who acts or appears stupid or silly. {**ăs**}

as·sas·sin *noun* a person who murders for money or for political reasons. {ə **să** sən}

as·sas·si·nate *verb* (assassinated, assassinating, assassinates) to murder for pay or for political reasons. *John Wilkes Booth assassinated President Lincoln at Ford's Theatre in 1865.* {ə **să** sih **nayt**} assassination, n., assassinator, n.

as·sault *noun* 1. a violent physical or verbal attack. *The candidate made an assault on* his opponent's character. 2. an attack made by armed forces, that often ends in close fighting. 3. the crime of attempting or threatening to hurt another person. *verb* (assaulted, assaulting, assaults) to make an assault on; attack. *The soldiers assaulted the fort.* {ə **sawlt**}

as·sem·ble *verb* (assembled, assembling, assembles) 1. to gather into a group. *Mr. Perez assembled the staff for a meeting.* 2. to put together; join the parts of. *The mechanic assembled the parts of the car engine.* 3. to come together in one group. *We assembled for my mother's birthday.* {ə **sehm** bəl} assembler, n.

as·sem·bly 🌐 *noun* (assemblies) 1. a group of people gathered together, usually for a specific purpose. *We have an assembly in the auditorium every Monday morning.* 2. a collection of parts put together to form a whole, as in a machine. *They discovered a problem in the wing assembly before the plane took off.* 3. the process of joining persons or things to form a whole. *Assembly of the bicycle took all afternoon.* 4. (often capitalized) a legislative body. *The Assembly is the lower branch of the state legislature.* {ə **sehm** blee}

assembly line *noun* a way of putting together a product in a factory by moving it along a line of workers. Each worker adds or adjusts a part until the product is finished. {ə **sehm** blee **liyn**} assembly-line, adj.

as·sent *verb* (assented, assenting, assents) to agree (usually followed by "to"). *Her boss assented to her request for a day off.* *noun*

 Human Body   Human Mind   Everyday Life  History and Culture   Communication

agreement, approval, or consent. *The class finally reached assent about a gift for their teacher.* {ə **sehnt**}

Homophone Note Are you looking for the word *ascent* (a climb)? *Assent* and *ascent* sound alike but have different meanings.

as·sert *verb* (asserted, asserting, asserts) 1. to state with force or confidence. *He asserted his innocence.* 2. to put forward strongly. *Once he started asserting himself more, he gained respect from others.* {ə **suhrt**}

as·ser·tive *adjective* forward or aggressive in speech or action. *You have to be assertive to get a good deal when you're buying a car.* {ə **suhr** tihv} assertively, adv., assertiveness, n.

as·sess *verb* (assessed, assessing, assesses) 1. to set or try to find the importance or value of; evaluate; estimate. *They assessed the damage to his car.* 2. to rate the value of something for taxation; value. *The city assessed their house at eighty thousand dollars.* 3. to set or establish the amount of. *The judge assessed a fine of fifty dollars for the parking violation.* {ə **sehs**}

as·set ☁ *noun* 1. something useful or valuable. *It's an asset to have good eyesight.* 2. (plural) property that can be exchanged for cash. *Her assets include a car and a sailboat.* {ă **seht**}

as·sign *verb* (assigned, assigning, assigns.) 1. to set apart or give out for a particular use. *The coach assigned hockey equipment to each of the team members.* 2. to choose or appoint, as for a duty. *His father assigned him to wash the dishes.* 3. to give as a

task. *The teacher assigned homework.* {ə **siyn**}

as·sign·ment *noun* 1. an assigned task, such as a job or lesson. *The history assignment was difficult.* 2. a position for which one is chosen. *My assignment is to clean the horse's stall.* 3. the act of assigning. *The coach is responsible for the assignment of positions.* {ə **siyn** mənt}

as·sist *verb* (assisted, assisting, assists) to give aid or support to. *May I assist you with your homework?* *noun* a play that helps another team member complete a play, such as a goal in soccer. {ə **sihst**}

as·sis·tance *noun* 1. the act of giving aid or support. *Her assistance in the project was very helpful.* 2. the aid or support given. *The charity sent assistance to the victims of the famine.* {ə **sihs** təns}

as·sis·tant *noun* a person who gives help, aid, or assistance. *The office assistant answered the telephone.* {ə **sihs** tənt}

as·so·ci·ate *verb* (associated, associating, associates) 1. to connect with something else in one's mind. *I associate fall with going back to school.* 2. to come together as friends, business partners, or companions (often followed by "with"). *Ms. Black associates with them only at the office.* *noun* 1. a person who is active in running a business enterprise; partner. *He received an e-mail from his associate.* 2. a friend, companion, or mate. *She met her associates at the café.* *adjective* 1. joined together or connected; having practically equal status. *All the associate judges agreed on the case before the court.* 2. having a position with less power, rank, or status. *She is an associate*

member of the club. {ə **soh** see iht *or* ə **soh** shee iht, n., adj., ə **soh** see ayt *or* ə **soh** shee ayt, v.}

as·so·ci·a·tion ☁ *noun* 1. a group of people joined together for a common purpose or by a shared interest. *You can join the association if you pay the dues.* 2. the connection of one idea, feeling, or emotion with another. *This school has some happy associations for me.* 3. the state of being associated. *Her association with that neighborhood ended when she moved away.* 4. friendship or companionship. *Our association began in grade school.* {ə **soh** see **ay** shən *or* ə **soh** shee **ay** shən}

as·so·cia·tive prop·er·ty *noun* in addition and multiplication, the characteristic that allows you to add or multiply a group of numbers in any order and get the same answer. For example, in multiplication, (5 x 2) x 7 is equal to (7 x 2) x 5. {ə **soh** shee **ay** tihv **prŏp** ər tee}

as·sort·ed *adjective* of different kinds or sorts, collected together; variety. *Fill the basket with assorted fruits.* {ə **sohr** tihd}

as·sort·ment *noun* a collection of different sorts of things; variety. *This shop sells an assortment of sandwiches.* {ə **sohrt** mənt}

as·sume *verb* (assumed, assuming, assumes) 1. to suppose to be a fact; take for granted. *He assumed school would be closed during the blizzard.* 2. to take on as one's own duty, job, or appearance; adopt. *She assumed the post of*

a
b
c
d
e
f
g
h
i
j
k
l
m
n
o
p
q
r
s
t
u
v
w
x
y
z

mayor one month after the election. 3. to put on in a false way; pretend. *She was nervous, but she assumed a relaxed manner.* {ə **soohm**}

as·sump·tion *noun* 1. something that is supposed or taken for granted. For example, if you ask someone whether she is allowed to watch TV during dinner, you have made an assumption that there is a TV in her house. Assumptions are ideas people have that are not based on proven facts. An assumption can be correct or incorrect. 2. a taking on of a duty, role, or position. *The whole kingdom celebrated the new queen's assumption of power.* {ə **suhmp** shən}

as·sur·ance *noun* 1. a statement meant to give confidence. *The nurse's assurances calmed the patient.* 2. a condition of being sure or sure of oneself. *There is no assurance that the criminal will be caught.* {ə **shoohr** əns}

as·sure *verb* (assured, assuring, assures) 1. to say to with force or conviction. *He assured me that he would come soon.* 2. to cause to feel certain or secure. *Hearing Bobby's voice on the phone assured his family that he was alive and well.* 3. to make certain; guarantee. *Signing up early will assure a place for you on the bus.* {ə **shoohr**}

as·ter *noun* a plant with white, pink, blue, or purple flowers. The flowers are made up of many narrow petals around a yellow center. {**ăs** tər}

as·ter·isk *noun* a sign (*). It is used to show that there is other information on the page that

explains the information where the sign is placed. *The asterisk led me to to a note at the bottom of the page.* {**ăs** tə rihsk}

as·ter·oid *noun* a small planet that circles the sun mostly between the orbits of Jupiter and Mars. The size of an asteroid can range from less than one mile to five hundred miles across. {**ăs** tə **roid**} asteroidal, adj.

asth·ma *noun* a disease of the lungs that makes it difficult to breathe. Asthma is often caused by an allergy. {**ăz** mə} asthmatoid, adj.

a·stir *adjective* in action; moving. *Under the rock, the soil was astir with beetles.* {ə **stuhr**}

as·ton·ish *verb* (astonished, astonishing, astonishes) to fill with great surprise or amazement. *The news that we had won free tickets astonished us.* {ə **sto** nihsh} astonishedly, adv., astonishingly, adv., astonishment, n.

as·ton·ish·ment *noun* great surprise or amazement. *The sight of the Grand Canyon filled me with astonishment.* {ə **sto** nihsh mənt}

as·tound *verb* (astounded, astounding, astounds) to cause surprise or wonder; amaze. *The sight of the tornado astounded her.* {ə **stownd**} astoundingly, adv.

a·stray *adverb or adjective* off the right or known path or course. *This little lamb is astray. / They must have gone astray at the second turn.* {ə **stray**}

a·stride *preposition* over or upon and with a leg on each side of. *They saw two people riding astride donkeys into the canyon.* adverb or adjective with a leg on each side. *He*

climbed up and sat astride. {ə **striyd**}

as·trol·o·gy 🌍 *noun* the study of the influence that the stars and planets may have on people's lives. {ə **stro** lih jee} astrologer, n., astrological, adj.

as·tro·naut 🌍 *noun* a person trained to take part in space flight. {**ă** strə **nawt**}

as·tron·o·mer *noun* a scientist who studies the universe beyond the earth. {ə **stro** nə mər}

as·tro·nom·i·cal *adjective* 1. having to do with astronomy. *This page of astronomical information gives the size of certain stars.* 2. enormous; immense. *He paid an astronomical price for his computer.* {ă strə **no** mih kəl} astronomically, adv.

as·tron·o·my 💬 🌍 *noun* the branch of science that studies the universe beyond the earth. {ə **stro** nə mee}

> **Word History** The word *astronomy* comes from *astronomos*, a Greek word that means "one who arranges the stars."

a·sy·lum *noun* 1. a place that offers safety. *He turned his home into an asylum for Jews during World War II.* 2. a place for the care of those who are not able to care for themselves, such as children without parents, people with mental illness, or the very old. 3. protection that is given by one country to refugees from another. *That country gave asylum to the refugee family.* {ə **siy** ləm}

at *preposition* 1. on or in the location of. *We played volleyball at the beach.* 2. on or upon the occurrence of; during the time of. *She moved to the city at the end of the*

44

year. 3. in the direction of; toward. *Look at the moon.* 4. engaged in the action of. *Don't disturb him when he's at work.* 5. concerning; about. *They're angry at him.* {**ăt**}

ate *verb* past tense of **eat**. {**āyt**}

-ate *suffix* 1. a suffix that means to become or cause to become or have. *To activate something is to make it become active.* 2. a suffix that means "to act upon" or "treat with." *To vaccinate is to treat with a vaccine.* 3. a suffix that means "having" or "showing." *An affectionate person is someone who shows affection.*

Homophone Note Are you looking for the word *eight* (the number)? *Ate* and *eight* sound alike but have different meanings.

a·the·ist *noun* a person who believes that there is no God or gods. {**āy** *thee* ihst} atheistic, adj.

A·the·na *noun* the goddess of wisdom, the arts, and warfare, in Greek myth. Athena was born out of the head of Zeus, ruler of the gods. In Roman myth, Athena is called Minerva. {ə **thee** nə}

Ath·ens *noun* the capital city of Greece, in modern and ancient times. {**ă** thənz}

ath·lete 🌳 🔬 *noun* a person who participates in sports or other physical activities. {**ăth** leet}

athlete's foot *noun* a common foot infection caused by fungi. Athlete's foot makes the skin itch and look scaly. {**ăth** leets fuut}

ath·let·ic *adjective* 1. having to do with sports and other physical activities. *That athletic equipment is in poor condition.* 2. talented or active in sports and other physical activities. *She remained athletic until she broke her leg.* {**ăth leh** tihk} athletically, adv.

ath·let·ics *noun* (athletics) (usually used with a plural verb) sports and physical activities. {**ăth leh** tihks}

At·lan·ta *noun* the capital city of the U.S. state of Georgia. {ăt **lăn** tə}

At·lan·tic *noun* an ocean bordered by Europe and Africa on the east and North and South America on the west; Atlantic Ocean. {ăt **lăn** tihk}

At·las *noun* 1. a giant in Greek myth who had to support the heavens on his shoulders. 2. (lower case) a book of maps, tables, or charts. {**ăt** lihs}

Word History Greek mythology tells of a giant whose punishment was to hold up the universe on his shoulders. This giant's name was *Atlas*. Artists drew pictures of Atlas holding up a globe that was meant to be the heavens. In the 1600s, a mapmaker named Mercator used such a picture on the cover of his book of maps. A collection of maps became known as an "atlas."

ATM *noun* an abbreviation for automated teller machine, a computerized machine used for banking.

at·mos·phere 🌍 *noun* 1. the gases surrounding the earth or another planet. 2. the air of a particular place. *The atmosphere is stuffy in the basement.* 3. a feeling or mood created by a particular place or a work of art. *The party decorations gave the room a cheerful atmosphere.* {**ăt** məs feer}

at·mos·pher·ic *adjective* of, relating to, or made of the gases that surround the earth. *The atmospheric conditions kept us from sailing on Saturday.* {ăt məs **feh** rihk *or* ăt məs **feer** ihk} atmospherically, adv.

at·oll *noun* an island or reef that surrounds a lagoon. An atoll is shaped like a ring. {**ă** tawl *or* **ă** tohl *or* ə **tohl**}

at·om 🔬 *noun* 1. the smallest possible unit of a chemical element. The major parts of atoms contain protons, neutrons, and electrons. They are the basis of all matter in the universe. 2. anything extremely small; tiny bit. *There was not an atom of food in the house after they left.* {**ă** təm}

Word History *Atom* is from an ancient Greek word that means "not able to be cut or divided."

a·tom·ic *adjective* 1. having to do with atoms or energy made from atoms. *Atomic energy is efficient but expensive.* 2. of, relating to, or resulting from an atomic bomb. *Their equipment can detect an atomic explosion thousands of miles away.* {ə **to** mihk}

atomic bomb *noun* a very destructive bomb; atom bomb. Its power comes from the great amount of energy released when atoms are split. {ə **to** mihk **bŏm**}

atomic energy *noun* 1. the energy that is released by atoms in nuclear reactions. 2. a source of power based on this energy; nuclear energy. {ə **to** mihk **eh** nər jee}

a·tone *verb* (atoned, atoning, atones) to make up for; make amends. *She atoned for her crime by paying a fine.* {ə **tohn**}

A B C D E F G H I J K L M N O P Q R S T U V W X Y Z

a·top *preposition* at or on the highest point of. *She sat atop the flagpole for three hours.* {ə **tŏp**}

a·tri·um *noun* (atria or atriums) 1. a courtyard inside a building, either open to the sky or with a glass ceiling. 2. either of the two upper compartments of the heart; auricle. Blood returning from the body flows into the atria, which pump the blood to the ventricles, the lower compartments of the heart. {**ay** tree əm} atrial, adj.

a·tro·cious *adjective* 1. very evil, cruel, or brutal. *He was punished for the atrocious crime.* 2. (informal) very bad; awful. *That dinner was atrocious.* {ə **troh** shihs} atrociously, adv.

at·tach *verb* (attached, attaching, attaches) 1. to join, fasten, or connect. *He attached the telephone wire to the wall.* 2. to hold the love or friendship of. *She is very attached to her pets.* 3. to consider as belonging to; lend or assign. *He attached great importance to our conversation.* {ə **tăch**}

at·tach·ment *noun* 1. the act or process of attaching. *With the attachment of the last solar panels, the space station was completed.* 2. a strong feeling of friendship or loyalty to a person, place, thing, or idea. *She has a strong attachment to her brother.* 3. something that can be attached to another thing. *The vacuum cleaner has several attachments.* / *She sent me the photograph as an e-mail attachment.* {ə **tăch** mənt}

at·tack ✪ 💬 *verb* (attacked, attacking, attacks) 1. to begin to cause harm to. *The cat attacked the mouse.* 2. to speak or write against; oppose. *The reporter attacked the town's spending plan.* 3. to start working on with energy and determination; tackle. *Let's attack this job and finish it.* *noun* 1. an act meant to hurt or destroy. *The army carried out a surprise attack.* 2. a sudden beginning of a disease or illness. *He had an attack of the flu.* {ə **tăk**} attacker, n.

at·tain *verb* (attained, attaining, attains) 1. to gain or achieve through work. *I will attain my goal of becoming a doctor.* 2. to arrive at or reach. *He will soon attain the age of twenty.* / *The climbers attained the summit.* {ə **tayn**} attainable, adj.

at·tempt *verb* (attempted, attempting, attempts) to try or seek. *He attempted to balance a ball on his nose.* *noun* 1. an effort to do or accomplish something. *This attempt to read every book in the library will not succeed.* 2. an act of violence. *An attempt was made on his life.* {ə **tehmpt**}

at·tend *verb* (attended, attending, attends) 1. to be present at. *Did you attend the funeral?* 2. to take care of; tend. *Nurses attend sick people.* 3. to go along with; accompany. *Several guards attended the king.* 4. to pay attention. *Please attend to what I am saying.* {ə **tehnd**}

at·ten·dance *noun* 1. the act of being present at an event. *Your attendance made the dinner special.* 2. the number of people present. *Attendance at the concert was low.* {ə **tehn** dəns}

at·ten·dant *noun* a person who serves another person. *The pool attendant handed us towels.* {ə **tehn** dənt}

at·ten·tion ✪ 💬 *noun* 1. the concentration of one's mind on something. *The movie held our attention for three hours.* / *The teacher could not get the children's attention.* 2. careful thought or notice. *The teacher will give my report his attention.* 3. (usually plural) acts of respect, care, or politeness. *We enjoyed the attentions of the waiter at the restaurant.* 4. a way in which a person stands in the military, with the body straight, the legs and feet together, and the eyes looking forward. *The soldier stood at attention.* {ə **tehn** shən}

at·ten·tive *adjective* 1. paying close attention. *The children were attentive while the story was read to them.* 2. paying attention to the needs or comfort of others. *The attentive waiter refilled our glasses without being asked.* {ə **tehn** tihv} attentively, adv., attentiveness, n.

at·test *verb* (attested, attesting, attests) 1. to show or prove the truth of. *His signature attested the legal document.* 2. to offer evidence or give proof (often followed by "to"). *In court, he attested to his friend's good character.* {ə **tehst**}

at·tic *noun* the space in a house directly beneath the roof. {**ă** tihk}

Word History An *attic* gets its name from the Attic peninsula of Greece, where a particular style of elegant architecture was used on the upper part of buildings.

at·tire ✪ *verb* (attired, attiring, attires) to dress up in fancy clothes. *I attired myself in party clothes.* *noun* clothing, especially fancy clothes. *Your*

 Human Body
 Human Mind
 Everyday Life
 History and Culture
 Communication

Halloween attire looks scary. {ə **tiyr**}

at·ti·tude 🌿 🔬 *noun* 1. a way of feeling or thinking about something or someone. *She has a bad attitude toward homework.* 2. position of the body. *The frightened boy stood with a stiff attitude.* {ă tih **toohd**}

at·tor·ney 📖 *noun* (attorneys) a person whose job is to give legal advice and to speak for people in court; lawyer. {ə **tuhr** nee}

at·tract *verb* (attracted, attracting, attracts) 1. to cause to come near. *The color red attracts hummingbirds.* 2. to gain the attention or admiration of. *Her strange clothing attracted us.* {ə **trăkt**}

at·trac·tion *noun* 1. the act or power of attracting. *They learned about magnetic attraction in class.* 2. a thing or quality that attracts. *The beach is one of this town's many attractions.* 3. a movie, concert, or other event that many people want to see. *The newspaper listed the attractions coming to the theater.* {ə **trăk** shən}

at·trac·tive *adjective* having qualities that attract people. *He is attractive enough to be a movie star.* {ə **trăk** tihv} attractively, adv., attractiveness, n.

at·tri·bute *verb* (attributed, attributing, attributes) 1. to view as the result of. *She attributed the bad weather to air pollution.* 2. to view as a quality belonging to. *She attributed understanding to her mother.* *noun* a characteristic or quality. *Sharp taste is an attribute of cheddar cheese.* {ă trih **byoot**, n., ə **trihb** yoot, v.} attributable, adj., attribution, n.

Au symbol of the chemical element gold.

au·burn *noun* the color that comes from mixing brown and red paint. {aw bərn}

auc·tion *noun* a public sale at which things are sold to the people who offer the most money. *verb* (auctioned, auctioning, auctions) to sell at an auction (often followed by "off"). *Before we moved, we auctioned off a lot of our furniture.* {**awk** shən}

au·di·ble *adjective* heard or able to be heard. *With this sore throat, my voice is barely audible.* {**aw** də bəl} audibly, adv.

au·di·ence 🔬 *noun* 1. a group of people gathered to see or hear something. *The audience was silent during his speech.* 2. the people reached by television, radio, newspapers, or magazines. *That television show has an audience of millions.* 3. a chance to be heard by someone in power. *The queen granted her an audience.* {**aw** dee əns}

au·di·o *adjective* 1. having to do with or using sound. *We listened for an audio signal.* 2. having to do with or used in recording or broadcasting sound. *The audio equipment at the studio was excellent.* {**aw** dee oh}

au·di·o- or **audi-** *prefix* a prefix that means "sound" or "hearing." *An audiobook is a book recorded on tape so that it can be heard instead of read.*

au·di·o·vis·u·al *adjective* having both sound and a picture. *Some teachers use audiovisual materials, such as films and computer software.* {aw dee oh **vih** zhooh əl}

au·di·tion *noun* a performance that tests the ability of an actor, musician, or dancer. *The actor had an audition for a part in the play.* *verb* (auditioned, auditioning, audi-tions) 1. to test by an audition. *He auditioned the singers who wanted to join the choir.* 2. to try out for a role or position by performing. *My sister auditioned for the part of Cinderella.* {aw **dih** shən}

au·di·to·ri·um 📖 🔬 *noun* (auditoriums) a large room or building where people gather for a performance or speech. {aw dih **tohr** ee əm}

au·di·to·ry *adjective* having to do with or referring to hearing or the sense of hearing. *My dog's auditory sense lets him hear cars before he can see them.* {aw dih **tohr** ee}

Aug. *abbreviation* an abbreviation for **August**.

au·ger *noun* a tool used by carpenters to make holes in wood. {**aw** gər}

aug·ment *verb* (augmented, augmenting, augments) to make greater in size or amount; increase. *She augmented her problems by not asking for help.* {awg **mehnt**}

Au·gust *noun* the eighth month of the year. August has thirty-one days. {**aw** gəst}

Word History In 8 B.C., the Roman Senate named this month *Augustus* in honor of the first emperor of Rome, Augustus Caesar.

auk *noun* a sea bird with webbed feet and short wings that lives in colder parts of the Northern Hemisphere. Auks are good at swimming and diving. {awk}

A
B
C
D
E
F
G
H
I
J
K
L
M
N
O
P
Q
R
S
T
U
V
W
X
Y
Z

a
b
c
d
e
f
g
h
i
j
k
l
m
n
o
p
q
r
s
t
u
v
w
x
y
z

aunt *noun* 1. the sister of one's mother or father. 2. the wife of one's uncle. {ănt *or* ahnt}

Homophone Note Some people say the words *aunt* and *ant* in exactly the same way, but these two words have different meanings.

au·ri·cle *noun* 1. the part of the ear that can be seen. 2. part of the heart. See **atrium**. {aw rih kəl}

aurora australis *noun* bands of light that appear in the skies at night near the South Pole; southern lights. {ə **rohr** ə aw **stray** lihs}

aurora borealis *noun* bands of light that appear in the skies at night near the North Pole; northern lights. {ə **roh** rə **bohr** ee ă lihs}

aus·tere *adjective* 1. being or looking very stern and serious. *The usually austere minister laughed loudly.* 2. having only what is needed; very simple or plain. *The austere room had little furniture.* {aw **steer**} austerely, adv.

aus·ter·i·ty *noun* (austerities) the condition or quality of being very stern and serious. *The teacher's austerity made it difficult for the students to enjoy school.* {aw **steh** rih tee}

Aus·tral·ia *noun* 1. the smallest continent. Australia is southeast of Asia, between the Indian and Pacific Oceans. It is in the Eastern Hemisphere. 2. a country made up of this continent. Australia is also called the Commonwealth of Australia. Canberra is the capital of Australia. {aw **stray** lee ə}

Aus·tral·ian *adjective* of or having to do with Australia, or its people or languages. *noun* a person who was born in or is a citizen of Australia. {aw **strayl** yən}

Aus·tri·a *noun* a country in central Europe. Vienna is the capital of Austria. {aw stree ə} Austrian, adj., n.

au·then·tic *adjective* real, genuine, or true. *He proved that his autograph of Abraham Lincoln was authentic.* {aw **thehn** tihk} authentically, adv.

au·thor  *noun* the writer of a book, play, story, or other written work. {aw thər}

au·thor·i·ta·tive *adjective* 1. having or showing authority. *If you speak in an authoritative voice, people will listen.* 2. accepted as correct and true; reliable as a source of information because said or written by an expert or authority. *The librarian gave me several authoritative books on ballet.* {ə **thohr** ih **tay** tihv *or* ə **thohr** ih **tay** tihv} authoritatively, adv., authoritativeness, n.

au·thor·i·ty   *noun* (authorities) 1. the right or power to give orders, make decisions, or control people. *Our teacher has all the authority in our classroom.* 2. (usually plural) people who have this right or power by law. *Even the authorities could not find the robbers.* 3. a source of expert information or opinion. *Mr. Larson is an authority on old coins.* {ə **thohr** ih tee}

au·thor·ize *verb* (authorized, authorizing, authorizes) 1. to give authority to. *My mother authorized the doctor to treat my brother's broken arm.* 2. to give official permission to; allow or approve. *The mayor authorized a parade through downtown.* {aw thə riyz}

au·to *noun* see **automobile**. {aw toh}

au·to- *prefix* a prefix that means done by oneself or itself. *An automobile is a vehicle that moves by itself, without being pulled by animals.*

au·to·bi·og·ra·phy *noun* (autobiographies) the story of a person's life written or told by that person. *"The Narrative of the Life of Frederick Douglass"* is a famous American autobiography. {aw toh biy **o** grə fee} autobiographer, n., autobiographical, adj.

au·to·graph *noun* the name of a person, especially a famous person, written in his or her own handwriting. *I was thrilled to get Sammy Sosa's autograph.* *verb* (autographed, autographing, autographs) to write one's name on. *The singer autographed his picture for many fans.* {aw tə **grăf**}

au·to·mat·ed tel·ler ma·chine *noun* a computerized machine used for banking. {aw tə **may** təd **teh** lər mə **sheen**}

au·to·mat·ic *adjective* 1. working or operating by itself. *This house has an automatic heating system.* 2. done without having to think about it. *Breathing and digestion are automatic actions.* {aw tə **mă** tihk} automatically, adv.

au·to·ma·tion *noun* the use of machines rather than people to do work. *The automation of the factory helped the business to make more money.* {aw tə **may** shən} automative, adj.

au·to·mo·bile   *noun* a vehicle with four wheels that is powered by a motor that uses gasoline or other fuel; car. An automobile is used on roads to carry people. {aw tə moh **beel** *or* aw tə moh **beel**}

au·top·sy *noun* (autopsies) a medical examination of a dead body to find the cause of death. {aw **tŏp** see}

 Human Body    Human Mind    Everyday Life    History and Culture    Communication

au·tumn *noun* the season of the year between summer and winter; fall. {<u>aw</u> təm}

aux·il·ia·ry *adjective* serving as an extra means of support; additional. *The hospital has an auxiliary power generator.* *noun* (auxiliaries) 1. a person or thing that helps, assists, or supports. *The fire department auxiliary helps out at large building fires.* 2. see auxiliary verb. {awg <u>zihl</u> yə ree *or* awg <u>zih</u> lə ree, n., awg <u>zihl</u> yə ree *or* awg <u>zih</u> lə ree, adj.}

auxiliary verb *noun* a verb used with other verbs to express certain tenses, aspects, or moods. Some examples of auxiliary verbs are "have" in "I have escaped" and "should" in "You should go." {awg <u>zihl</u> yə ree <u>vuhrb</u> *or* awg <u>zih</u> lə ree <u>vuhrb</u>}

a·vail·a·bil·i·ty *noun* the condition of being available. {ə <u>vay</u> lə <u>bih</u> lih tee}

a·vail·a·ble *adjective* able to be used or possible to get. *The baseball field is now available for the next two teams. / That style of shoe is no longer available.* {ə <u>vayl</u> ə bəl} availableness, n., availably, adv.

av·a·lanche *noun* 1. the sudden rush of a large amount of snow, ice, or rocks down a mountain. *An avalanche buried the mountain village.* 2. anything that comes suddenly and in large amounts. *The principal received an avalanche of complaints about the new dress code.* {<u>ăv</u> ə lănch}

Ave. *abbreviation* an abbreviation for **Avenue**.

av·e·nue *noun* a wide street. {<u>ăv</u> ə nooh}

av·er·age *noun* 1. a usual amount or kind; something that is not outside the ordinary. *The temperature this winter was the average for our area.* 2. the number gotten by adding two or more quantities, and then dividing that result by the number of quantities added. *The average of four, six, and two is four.* *adjective* 1. usual or typical; of the ordinary kind. *The average person in this country does not exercise enough.* 2. found by figuring out an average. *The average daily rainfall in April was one inch.* *verb* (averaged, averaging, averages) 1. to find the average of. *To arrive at our final grade, the teacher will average our test scores.* 2. to do or have as an average amount. *The runner averaged six miles a day.* {<u>ăv</u> ə rihj *or* <u>ăv</u> rihj, n., adj., v.}

• **average out**
1. to amount to an arithmetic average (usually followed by "to"). *My bowling scores for this month average out to 116.* 2. to reach a middle state or level, especially after a period of changes or extremity. *After all those hot and cold days earlier this summer, the weather has averaged out to be pleasant.*

• **on the average**
usually; generally. *On the average, we go to the movies twice a month.*

a·vert *verb* (averted, averting, averts) 1. to turn away or aside. *She averted her eyes from the horrible sight.* 2. to keep from happening; prevent. *The pilot's skillful handling of the ship averted an accident.* {ə <u>vuhrt</u>}

a·vi·a·tion ⊙ *noun* the act, practice, or science of flying airplanes. {ay vee <u>ay</u> shən}

a·vi·a·tor *noun* a person who flies an aircraft; pilot. {<u>ay</u> vee ay tər}

av·id *adjective* 1. having an eager desire for; greedy. *The kindergarten students are avid for learning.* 2. having or showing great enthusiasm. *They are avid baseball fans.* {<u>ă</u> vihd} avidly, adv.

av·o·ca·do *noun* (avocados) a tropical American fruit shaped like a pear. It has a green or black skin and a yellowish green pulp. {<u>o</u> və <u>kah</u> doh *or* <u>ă</u> və <u>kah</u> doh}

a·void *verb* (avoided, avoiding, avoids) to keep away from. *He avoided the other car by swerving.* {ə <u>void</u>} avoidable, adj., avoidably, adv., avoider, n.

a·wait *verb* (awaited, awaiting, awaits) 1. to wait for; look forward to. *We eagerly awaited our grandparents' visit.* 2. to be ready for; be in store for. *Many adventures awaited them on their journey.* {ə <u>wayt</u>}

a·wake *verb* (awoke or awaked, awaking, awakes) 1. to wake from sleep. *Please awake me in the morning before you go.* 2. to cause to become aware of. *He awoke my love of classical music.* *adjective* 1. not sleeping. *She is awake, so you don't have to whisper.* 2. very aware; alert. *We are awake to the problems in the school cafeteria.* {ə <u>wayk</u>}

a·wak·en *verb* (awakened, awakening, awakens) 1. to wake from sleep. *The song of birds awakened her.* 2. to make sharply aware. *The hike awakened us to the beauty of nature.* {ə <u>way</u> kən} awakener, n.

a·ward *verb* (awarded, awarding, awards) 1. to give as a prize or honor. *The college awards scholarships to students with high grades.* 2. to give as a result of a legal decision. *The judge awarded a large sum of money to those who*

A
B
C
D
E
F
G
H
I
J
K
L
M
N
O
P
Q
R
S
T
U
V
W
X
Y
Z

were hurt in the train crash. *noun* a prize given for a special achievement; honor. *The mayor presented her with an award for her volunteer work.* {ə **wohrd**} awardable, adj.

a·ware *adjective* knowing or careful (usually followed by "of"). *I am aware of the hole in my shirt.* {ə **wayr**} awareness, n.

a·way *adverb* 1. in or to another direction. *He walked away.* 2. out of being or existence. *The clouds are fading away.* 3. from a person's keeping or possession. *She gave away my secret. / Latoya wants to give away all her toys.* 4. without stopping. *He worked away into the night.* *adjective* 1. in another place; not present. *She went away for a week.* 2. in the distance. *He was ten miles away.* {ə **way**}
 • **do away with**
1. to get rid of or stop; no longer continue. *I hope the teacher will do away with that rule.* 2. to kill. *The detective figured out who did away with the old man.*
 • **right away**
at this moment; now; immediately. *Tell your brother to come home right away.*

awe *noun* a very strong feeling of wonder mixed with respect or fear. *We were in awe of the sunrise.* *verb* (awed, awing, awes) to cause to feel awe. *The size of the elephant awed the little boy.* {**aw**}

awe·some *adjective* causing awe. *The wizard had awesome power.* {**aw** səm} awesomely, adv., awesomeness, n.

aw·ful *adjective* 1. very bad; terrible; of poor quality. *She did an awful job on her report.* 2. terrible; horrible; very unpleasant. *There was an awful storm last night.* {**aw** fəl} awfulness, n.

Synonyms
These words share a meaning with *awful*, adjective 1:
poor, terrible, dreadful

aw·ful·ly *adverb* 1. very; extremely. *That was an awfully nice thing to do.* 2. terribly. *He sang so awfully that the neighbor's dog howled.* {**aw** fə lee *or* **awf** lee}

a·while *adverb* for a short time. *Let's talk awhile before class starts.* {ə **wiyl**}

awk·ward *adjective* 1. without physical skill or grace; clumsy. *My brother is an awkward dancer.* 2. difficult to use or deal with. *Some people find it awkward to eat with chopsticks.* 3. embarrassed or embarrassing. *It was an awkward moment when Paula asked us when our party was.* {**awk** wərd} awkwardly, adv., awkwardness, n.

awl *noun* a tool used to make holes in leather or wood. Awls are small and have a sharp point. {**awl**}

Homophone Note The words *awl* and *all* sound alike but have different meanings.

awn·ing *noun* a cover made of canvas or other material that is placed over a door or window. An awning keeps out sun and rain. {**aw** ning}

a·woke *verb* past tense of **awake**. {ə **wohk**}

a·wo·ken *verb* a past participle of **awake**. {ə **woh** kən}

ax *or* **axe** *noun* (axes) a tool with a blade attached to the end of a long handle. An ax is used for chopping wood. {**ăks**}

ax·is *noun* (axes) 1. a real or imaginary line through the center of an object, around which the object turns. *Earth makes a complete turn on its axis every twenty-four hours.* 2. (capitalized) the name for the union of Germany, Italy, Japan, and other countries during the Second World War. *The Axis powers were defeated in 1945.* {**ăk** sihs}

ax·le *noun* a bar or shaft on which a wheel or wheels turn. {**ăk** səl}

aye *or* **ay** *adverb* yes. *All in favor, say "aye."* *noun* a vote of yes, or a voter who votes yes. *The ayes have it.* {**iy**}

Homophone Note The words *aye*, *eye*, and *I* sound alike, but each has a different meaning.

AZ *abbreviation* an abbreviation for **Arizona**.

a·zal·ea *noun* a shrub with dark green leaves and brightly colored flowers. {ə **zayl** yə}

Az·tec *noun* a member of an Indian people who had an advanced civilization in central Mexico before Spain conquered it in 1519. {**ăz** tehk} Aztecan, adj.

az·ure *noun* the color of a clear blue sky. {**ă** zhuhr}

a b c d e f g h i j k l m n o p q r s t u v w x y z

50

 Human Body   Human Mind   Everyday Life   History and Culture    Communication

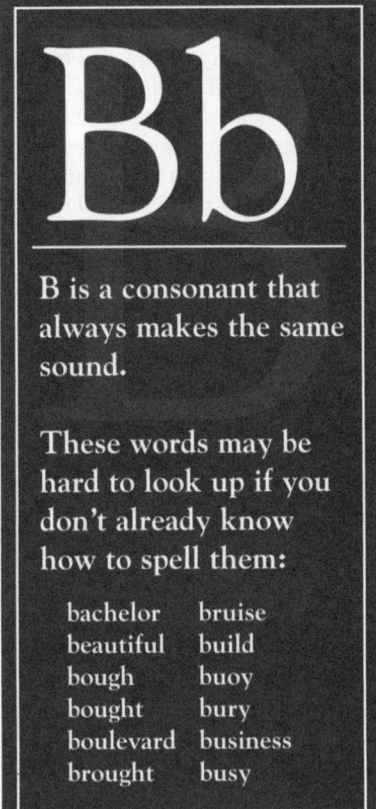

Bb

B is a consonant that always makes the same sound.

These words may be hard to look up if you don't already know how to spell them:

bachelor	bruise
beautiful	build
bough	buoy
bought	bury
boulevard	business
brought	busy

b or **B** *noun* (b's or B's) 1. the bsecond letter of the English alphabet. 2. a grade given for good, but not excellent, schoolwork. 3. the seventh note in the musical scale of C major. {**bee**}

B symbol of the chemical element boron.

B.A. *abbreviation* a college degree earned after four years of study. B.A. is an abbreviation for Bachelor of Arts.

Ba symbol of the chemical element barium.

baa *verb* (baaed, baaing, baas) to make the sound of a sheep; bleat. *noun* the cry of a sheep; bleat. {**bah** *or* **bă**, n., **bah** *or* **bă**, v.}

bab·ble *verb* (babbled, babbling, babbles) 1. to speak without making sense. *Babies babble before they learn to talk.* 2. to talk foolishly or for no reason; chatter. *She babbled on and on about her travels.* 3. to make a soft, bubbling sound. *The stream babbled.* *noun* 1. spoken words that cannot be heard or understood clearly. *When he speaks Italian, it sounds like babble to me.* 2. speech that is foolish or has no point; chatter. *We're tired of listening to your babble!* {**bă** bəl}

babe *noun* a baby. *Meg cradled the babe in her arms.* {**bayb**}

ba·boon *noun* a large monkey that has a long snout like a dog's. Baboons live on the ground in large groups in Africa and Arabia. They can be powerful fighters. {**bă boohn**}

ba·by ⊕ *noun* (babies) 1. a very young girl or boy; infant. 2. the youngest person in a family or group. *My father is the baby of his family.* 3. a person who behaves in a childish or immature way. *What a baby you are!* *adjective* 1. very young. *Many families came to the zoo to see the baby elephant.* 2. for or used by a baby. *This store sells baby clothes.* *verb* (babied, babying, babies) to treat like a baby or child; spoil. *My parents baby my brother, even though he is eight.* {**bay** bee} babyish, adj.

baby boom *noun* the great increase in the population of the United States that took place between 1946 and 1960. {**bay** bee **boohm**}

ba·by-sit *verb* (baby-sat, baby-sitting, baby-sits) to take care of children while their parents are away. *He missed the party because he was baby-sitting for his cousins.* {**bay** bee **siht**} baby-sitter, n.

ba·by tooth *noun* one of the first set of teeth in human babies and other mammals. Baby teeth fall out early in life to be replaced by adult teeth. {**bay** bee tuu*th*}

bach·e·lor *noun* a man who has not married. {**bă** chə lər *or* **băch** lər} bachelorhood, n.

back[1] ⊕ *noun* 1. the part of the body of a human or animal that is on the opposite side from the chest and between the neck and hips. 2. the backbone; spine. *Straighten your back!* 3. the opposite side from the front. *She found the blanket in the back of the car. / Put your name on the back of this paper.* *verb* (backed, backing, backs) 1. to cause to move backward. *He backed the car into the garage.* 2. to give support to; commit to helping. *The gov-*

ernor hopes the President will back him in the next election. *adjective* 1. in the rear part; behind the front part. *The children rode in the back seat of the car.* 2. old; from the past. *The library had the back issues of the newspaper I needed for my report.* {**băk**}

• **back and forth**
going backward then forward. *He was rocking back and forth on a chair.*

• **back out of**
to fail to do something that

A
B
C
D
E
F
G
H
I
J
K
L
M
N
O
P
Q
R
S
T
U
V
W
X
Y
Z

a
b
c
d
e
f
g
h
i
j
k
l
m
n
o
p
q
r
s
t
u
v
w
x
y
z

was agreed upon. *She backed out of our lunch date.*
• **behind one's back** when one is not present; secretly. *They planned the surprise party behind my back.*
• **turn one's back on** to pay no attention to the needs of; abandon. *He turned his back on me when I was in trouble.*

back[2] *adverb* 1. in the direction that is opposite from forward; backward; away. *The elephant moved back from the edge of the cliff.* 2. to a starting point or to an earlier time. *Think back to your childhood. / He went back home.* 3. in return or in reply. *Joe hit Bob, and Bob hit back. / I didn't call back.* {băk}
• **back and forth** from side to side. *The cat swayed back and forth while watching the mouse.*

back·board *noun* the board to which a basketball hoop is attached. {băk bohrd}

back·bone 🌐 ❶ *noun* 1. the row of bones that runs along the center of the back; spine. 2. courage under pressure; the quality of not giving in. *She showed real backbone in standing up to the bully.* {băk bohn}

back·fire *verb* (backfired, backfiring, backfires) 1. to give off a loud explosive noise that means the engine of a car or other vehicle is not working properly. 2. to have results that are the opposite of what one wanted. *Her plans to become president of the company backfired, and she lost her job.* *noun* a noisy explosion that occurs in a gasoline engine that is not working properly. {băk fiyr}

back·gam·mon *noun* a board game played by two people. The players throw dice and move their pieces around and then off the board. {băk gă mən}

back·ground *noun* 1. the part of a picture or scene that is towards the back or seems to be furthest away. *The artist painted a castle with mountains in the background.* 2. all of a person's experience, education, and origins. *His background in the law prepared him for his career as a judge.* {băk grownd}

back·hand *noun* a tennis stroke that involves a forward movement of the arm with the back of the hand outward. {băk hănd}

back·hoe *noun* a machine that is used for digging. It has a large metal bucket that scoops something up and toward the machine. {băk hoh}

back·pack *noun* a pack used to carry objects on one's back while hiking or walking. *Many students carry their books in a backpack.* *verb* (backpacked, backpacking, backpacks) to go camping or hiking using a backpack. *We backpacked to our camp.* {băk păk} backpacker, n., backpacking, n.

back·stroke *noun* the arm motion of a swimmer moving along on his or her back. {băk strohk}

back·ward *adverb* 1. in the direction of or toward the back. *I pulled the swing backward and then let it go.* 2. with the back part or back side first or leading. *If you walk backward, be careful not to*

trip. 3. in reverse order; in a way that is the opposite of that which is usual. *If I had my way, I'd eat dinner backward, with dessert before the main course.* *adjective* moving or facing toward the back, rear, or past. *They left the desert without a backward look.* {băk wərd} backwards, adv.
• **backward and forward** in depth; completely; thoroughly. *She knows the rules of checkers backward and forward.*
• **bend [or] lean over backward** to work extremely and unusually hard. *I have bent over backward trying to make you happy.*

ba·con *noun* salted and smoked meat taken from the back and side of the pig. {bay kən}

bac·te·ri·a 🌐 ❶ 🔵 *noun* microscopic organisms that have one cell. Various kinds of bacteria have different shapes. Bacteria live in all parts of the earth including oceans, deserts, glaciers, hot springs, and in the bodies of most living things. Some kinds of bacteria cause diseases in plants and animals, but most kinds are useful in helping animals digest food, as medicines, in making soil, and in many other natural processes. {băk teer ee ə}

bac·te·ri·um *noun* (bacteria) singular form of bacteria. {băk teer ee əm} bacterial, adj

bad *adjective* (worse, worst) 1. of low quality; cheap. *That picture was taken with a bad camera.* 2. not good; naughty. *Please don't be bad while the guests are here.* 3. in pain or poor health. *Max stayed home from school because he felt bad.* 4. terrible or serious. *This is bad weather.* 5. sorry; guilty.

 Human Body   Human Mind    Everyday Life    History and Culture   Communication

He felt bad about his cheating. 6. not pleasant; not positive. *It is hard to like a person who has a bad attitude.* 7. not healthy; harmful. *Sugar is bad for your teeth.* 8. wicked; evil. *He has done some mean things, but he is not a bad person.* 9. rotten; spoiled. *The meat went bad.* {bằd}

badge *noun* a pin, patch, or ribbon people wear to show that they belong to a group, have a particular job, or have done something special. *My brother's Boy Scout uniform is covered with badges.* {băj}

badg·er *noun* a mammal with short legs and a long body. Badgers have white fur with black stripes on their heads, light fur on their backs, and dark fur on their bellies. They eat worms, rodents, rabbits, and plants. Different kinds of badgers live in Europe, Asia, and North America. They are related to skunks, otters, and other kinds of weasels. *verb* (badgered, badgering, badgers) to bother in a stubborn or persistent way; harass. *I need to finish the plans for the picnic so my friends will stop badgering me about it.* {bă jər}

bad·ly *adverb* (worse, worst) 1. not well; in a bad way. *The baby bird flew badly.* 2. very much. *I want a new car badly.* 3. not in a nice way. *She talks badly about him.* {băd lee}

bad·min·ton *noun* a sport in which players use rackets to hit a small rubber object back and forth across a high net. {băd mihn tən}

bad·mouth *verb* (badmouthed, badmouthing, badmouths) (informal) to speak of in a way that is not kind or fair. *She doesn't have many friends because she badmouths everyone she meets.* {băd mowth}

baf·fle *verb* (baffled, baffling, baffles) to confuse; puzzle. *I was baffled by his explanation.* {bă fəl} bafflement, n., baffler, n., baffling, adj., bafflingly, adv.

bag *noun* 1. a soft container made of cloth, paper, or leather, used to hold things; sack; pouch. *The bag of flour split open.* 2. a purse, suitcase, or other luggage carried by hand. *You left your bag on the bus.* 3. the amount that a bag holds. *She ate a bag of popcorn.* *verb* (bagged, bagging, bags) to fill a bag with; put in a bag. *I bagged the food I bought at the market.* {băg}

ba·gel *noun* a kind of bread roll that is shaped like a ring. Bagel dough is boiled in water before it is baked. {bay gəl}

bag·gage *noun* suitcases, bags, or trunks used to carry things during travel; luggage. {băg əj}

bag·gy *adjective* (baggier, baggiest) hanging in a loose way; puffed out. *His baggy pants got caught in the bicycle chain.* {băg ee} bagginess, n.

Bagh·dad *noun* the capital city of Iraq. {băg dăd *or* bahg dahd}

bag·pipe *noun* a wind instrument made of a leather bag and pipes. It is played by blowing air into the bag and squeezing the bag to force air through pipes that produce musical tones. *Bagpipes are often played in Scotland and Ireland.* {băg piyp}

Ba·ha·mas *noun* 1. (used with a plural verb) a chain of islands southeast of Florida. 2. a country made up of these islands. The Bahamas are also called the Commonwealth of the Bahamas. Nassau is the capital of the Bahamas. {bə hah məz} Bahamian, n., adj.

bail[1] *noun* money left with a court to make sure that a person who is set free after arrest will return for trial. *The judge set bail at three hundred dollars.* *verb* (bailed, bailing, bails) 1. to pay for the release of (often followed by "out"). *There was no one around to bail him out of jail, so he had to spend the night there.* 2. (informal) to help out of a difficult situation (often followed by "out"). *I bailed him out by offering to tutor him in history.* {bayl}

bail[2] *verb* (bailed, bailing, bails) to remove water from a boat by scooping. {bayl}
  • **bail out** (informal) to jump from an airplane with a parachute. *The pilot bailed out when the plane's wing caught on fire.*

Homophone Note Are you looking for the word *bale* (a bundle)? *Bail* and *bale* sound alike but have different meanings.

bait ❶ *noun* 1. food used to attract and catch fish or animals. *We used worms as bait on our fishing trip.* 2. something that attracts; attraction; lure. *The shop used free coffee as bait to attract customers.* *verb* (baited, baiting, baits) 1. to put bait on or in for the purposes of trapping

a
b
c
d
e
f
g
h
i
j
k
l
m
n
o
p
q
r
s
t
u
v
w
x
y
z

or catching. My *father baited my hook for me*. 2. to try to anger by teasing or nagging. *My brother baited me into an argument.* {**bayt**}

bake ○ *verb* (baked, baking, bakes) 1. to cook using dry heat. *I baked a birthday cake.* 2. to become baked. *The bread is baking now.* 3. to make hard with heat. *The sun baked the desert sand.* {**bayk**}

bak·er *noun* a person who bakes. {**bay** kər}

bak·er·y *noun* (bakeries) a store in which baked goods, such as bread, cake, and pastry, are made or sold. {**bay** kə ree}

baking powder *noun* a powder that is used to raise dough or batter during baking. {**bay** king **pow** dər}

baking soda *noun* a white powder used to raise dough or batter during baking. It is also used to settle an upset stomach. {**bay** king **soh** də}

bal·ance ○ ○ ○ *noun* 1. an instrument for weighing objects that has two flat pans hanging from or resting on a bar; scales. 2. a state in which opposite forces are equal. *Try to have a balance between work and play in your life.* 3. the state of being steady in body or mind. *The dancer kept his balance while standing on one toe.* 4. that which remains or is left over. *Mr. Morse was glad to see a large balance in his bank account.* *verb* (balanced, balancing, balances) 1. to hold steady. *The seal balanced a ball on its nose.* 2. to be in or come into a state of balance.

The gymnast balanced on the beam. {**bă** ləns}

• **keep one's balance**
to stay steady and upright. *It's hard to keep your balance on a tightrope.*

• **lose one's balance**
to become unsteady or fall. *The librarian lost her balance while reaching for a book on the top shelf.*

Word History *Balance* is from an early French word that means "having two plates or scales."

bal·co·ny *noun* (balconies) 1. a platform with a low wall or railing that extends from the outside of a building. *Romeo visited Juliet on the balcony outside of her bedroom.* 2. an upper floor with rows of seats that juts out into a theater or auditorium. *We sat in the balcony of the opera house.* {**băl** kə nee}

bald *adjective* 1. having little or no hair on the head. 2. not covered by a natural growth. *The bald side of the mountain was swept by the wind.* {**bawld**}

bald eagle *noun* a large eagle of the United States and Canada that is dark brown with a white head and tail. Bald eagles have a wing-span of about seven feet. {**bawld** **ee** gəl}

bale *noun* a large, tightly packed bundle tied together with cord or wire. *Bales of hay were stacked in the barn.* {**bayl**} baler, n.

Homophone Note Are you looking for the word *bail*? *Bale* and *bail* sound alike but have different meanings.

ba·leen *noun* the bony, flexible strips in the upper jaws of whales that feed by filtering food from ocean water. These whales use baleen to strain large amounts of small food such as shrimp from the water. {bə **leen**}

balk *verb* (balked, balking, balks) 1. to stop suddenly and refuse to go on. *The horse balked before the gate.* 2. to refuse to do some act (usually followed by "at"). *Emma balked at her chores.* 3. to block the progress of; stop. *An injury balked the racer's hope of winning.* {**bawk**}

ball¹ ○ *noun* 1. a round or nearly round object. *They made a ball of snow.* 2. a round or nearly round object used in sports and games. 3. a game played with a ball, especially baseball. *They played ball all afternoon.* {**bawl**}

• **on the ball**
1. acting in a quick and able way. 2. paying attention; aware.

ball² *noun* 1. a large party where there is formal dancing. *Cinderella went to the ball.* 2. (informal) a very good time or experience. *We're having a ball on the bumper cars!* {**bawl**}

Homophone Note Are you looking for the word *bawl* (to cry loudly)? *Ball* and *bawl* sound alike but have different meanings.

bal·lad ○ *noun* a poem or song that tells a story. *He sang a sad ballad about an old man who died.* {**băl** əd}

bal·last *noun* 1. heavy material placed in a boat or ship to make it more stable. 2. heavy material placed in the car of a balloon to make it more stable. *Sand bags were used as ballast for the balloon.* {**băl** ihst}

  Human Body   (?) Human Mind   Everyday Life   History and Culture   Communication

ball bearing *noun* a machine part made of a groove in the shape of a circle with metal balls that roll in it. A ball bearing lets an axle or other part move easily. *Andy greased all the ball bearings in his skateboard to make the wheels spin faster.* {<u>bawl</u> <u>bayr</u> ing}

bal·le·ri·na *noun* a female ballet dancer. {băl ə <u>rih</u> nə}

bal·let ❷ *noun* 1. a form of dance that uses exact, graceful movements. 2. a performance of such dance, with music, for an audience. {băl <u>ay</u>}

ball·game *noun* a game played with a ball on a field. *We watched the ballgame on TV last night.* {<u>bawl</u> gaym}

bal·loon *noun* 1. a bag made of thin material that is filled with a gas which causes it to rise. 2. such a bag used to carry passengers or equipment. *They will try to travel around the world in a balloon.* 3. a bag made of rubber that is filled with air and used as a toy. *verb* (ballooned, ballooning, balloons) to swell like a balloon. *His neck ballooned when he was sick with the mumps.* {bə <u>loohn</u>}

bal·lot *noun* 1. a piece of paper on which people who are voting enter their choices. *Some people thought that the ballot was hard to read.* 2. the act or way of voting. *The issue will be decided by ballot.* *verb* (balloted, balloting, bal-lots) to vote by using ballots. *We balloted to choose our new mayor.* {<u>băl</u> iht}

ball·point *noun* a pen that has a small ball in its tip. The ball moves the ink from the pen to the paper. {<u>bawl</u> point}

ball·room *noun* a large room used for dancing. {<u>bawl</u> roohm}

bal·sa *noun* 1. a tree of tropical America, whose wood is very light in weight. 2. the wood of this tree, used for rafts and model airplanes. {<u>bawl</u> sə}

balsam fir *noun* a tree of the pine family, native to Canada and the northeastern United States. It is an evergreen tree and is cut for lumber and Christmas trees. {<u>bawl</u> səm <u>fuhr</u>}

bam·boo *noun* (bamboos) 1. a tropical grass plant that has hard, woody, hollow stems. Many kinds of bamboo grow as high as a tree. 2. the stems of such a plant, used for making furniture. {băm <u>booh</u>}

ban *verb* (banned, banning, bans) to forbid or have an official rule against; prohibit. *The law bans drunk driving.* *noun* a law or rule that prohibits. *Many people want a ban on smoking in public places.* {<u>băn</u>}

ba·nan·a *noun* a long, curved fruit that has a thick yellow skin. It grows in bunches on a tall tropical plant. {bə <u>nă</u> nə}

band¹ ❷ ❶ *noun* 1. a group of people, animals, or objects acting together. *There's a band of dogs in the neighborhood.* 2. a group formed to play music. *Jo plays drums in the band.* *verb* (banded, banding, bands) to come together into a group. *We always band together in emergencies.* {<u>bănd</u>}

band² *noun* 1. a thin strip of material that holds several objects together. *She put a rubber band around the pencils.* 2. a stripe or strip that contrasts with its surroundings in color or material. *That kind of snake is brown with yellow bands.* *verb* (banded, banding, bands) to tie with a strip of material in order to tell apart or bundle together; put a band on. *The scientists banded the birds to learn more about their habits.* {<u>bănd</u>}

band·age ❷ *noun* a strip of cloth used to protect or cover a wound or other injury. *I put a bandage on the cut.* *verb* (bandaged, bandaging, bandages) to cover with a bandage. *The doctor bandaged my leg.* {<u>băn</u> dəj}

Band-Aid *noun* 1. (Trademark) A Band-Aid brand bandage is a strip of tape that holds a gauze pad. It is used to cover small wounds. 2. (lower case) any bandage that is similar. 3. (lower case) a solution for a serious problem that is used for a short amount of time. *After the fire, the small gifts of money were only a band-aid for the family's loss.* {<u>băn</u> dayd}

ban·dan·na or **bandana** *noun* a large handkerchief with a brightly colored design that is worn on the head or neck. {băn <u>dăn</u> ə}

B and B *abbreviation* an abbreviation for bed and breakfast; a small inn.

ban·dit *noun* (bandits or banditti) a robber who is often a

A
B
C
D
E
F
G
H
I
J
K
L
M
N
O
P
Q
R
S
T
U
V
W
X
Y
Z

a
b
c
d
e
f
g
h
i
j
k
l
m
n
o
p
q
r
s
t
u
v
w
x
y
z

member of a gang that robs people while they are travelling. {**băn** diht}

bang *noun* 1. a sudden, loud, explosive sound. *The balloon burst with a bang.* 2. a sudden or hard hit or blow. *The falling branch gave me a bang on the shoulder.* *verb* (banged, banging, bangs) 1. to hit loudly or violently. *Tom banged the drum.* 2. to shut loudly; slam. *He banged the door when he left.* 3. to make a sudden explosive sound. *The gun banged.* {**băng**}
  • **bang up**
to damage or injure, as in a collision. *He banged up the car.*

Ban·gla·desh *noun* a country in central, southern Asia. Dhaka is the capital of Bangladesh. {**băng** glə **dehsh** or **bahng** glə **dehsh**} Bangladeshi, n., adj.

ban·gle *noun* a bracelet in the form of a solid ring. {**băng** gəl}

bangs *noun* (usually plural) a fringe of hair cut straight across the forehead. *My sister's bangs cover her eyebrows.* {**băng**}

ban·ish *verb* (banished, banishing, banishes) 1. to cast out of a country by official action. *The king banished the rebels.* 2. to force out or away. *She banished all thoughts of failure from her mind.* {**băn** ihsh} banishment, n.

ban·is·ter *noun* 1. the rail of a staircase; railing. 2. one of the posts that support such a rail. 3. the posts and rail together. {**bă** nə stər}

ban·jo *noun* (banjos) a musical instrument with a circular body, a long neck, and four or five strings that are plucked or

strummed. {**băn** joh} banjoist, n.

bank[1] 🌐 *noun* 1. a pile of something that is higher than the surrounding area. *The enormous cloud bank told us a storm was coming.* 2. the ground at the edge of a river or stream. *verb* (banked, banking, banks) to form into a pile. *She banked the sand into a little hill.* {**băngk**}

bank[2] 🌐 *noun* 1. a business for holding, borrowing, or exchanging money. 2. a supply or store. *The donated blood was sent to the city's blood bank.* *verb* (banked, banking, banks) to do business at a bank. *Where do you bank?* {**băngk**}
  • **bank on**
(informal) to count on. *You can bank on their winning the game.*

bank·rupt 🌐 *adjective* not able to pay money owed and free by law from having to pay. *Mr. Black went bankrupt after losing his job.* *verb* (bankrupted, bankrupting, bankrupts) to cause to become a bankrupt. *His gambling soon bankrupted him.* {**băng** krəpt}

bank·rupt·cy *noun* (bankruptcies) 1. the legal inability to pay debts. *Her business declared bankruptcy and closed down.* 2. a condition of utter failure, ruin, or lack. *Many societies have crumbled from moral bankruptcy.* {**băng** krəp see}

ban·ner *noun* a small flag with designs or writing on it that represents a team, club, or other group. *My brother carried the Boy Scouts' banner in the parade.* *adjective* more successful than usual; outstanding. *The charity had a banner year for gifts.* {**băn** ər}

ban·quet *noun* a fancy, formal dinner. *My sister's wedding*

was followed by a banquet for all the guests. {**băng** kwət} banqueter, n.

ban·shee *noun* a female spirit in Irish folk stories. Banshees wail to predict someone's death. {**băn** shee}

ban·ter *noun* joking, clever conversation. *There was lots of banter between the characters in the play.* *verb* (bantered, bantering, banters) to carry on banter. *Our parents bantered with us throughout our long plane trip.* {**băn** tər}

bap·tism 🔵 *noun* a Christian ceremony in which someone who wishes to join the church is sprinkled with water or dipped in water. {**băp** tih zəm}

bap·tize *verb* (baptized, baptizing, baptizes) 1. to perform the Christian ceremony of dipping in or sprinkling with water as a symbol of becoming a member of the church. 2. to give a Christian name to by means of this ceremony. *The baby was baptized John, after the prophet.* {**băp** tiyz}

bar 🔵 🔲 *noun* 1. a mass of solid material in the shape of a block or cylinder. *There were two bars of soap in the bathtub.* 2. anything that acts as a block or barrier. *Rita's height was a bar to her becoming a ballerina.* 3. a stripe or narrow marking. *The owl has bars on its chest.* 4. a place where drinks and sometimes food are served. 5. the legal profession; lawyers as a group. *Lawyers must pass an exam before they are admitted to the bar.* 6. a vertical line that marks the beginning or end of a measure of music, or the music between two of these lines. *verb* (barred, barring, bars) 1. to keep out. *The police barred anyone from crossing that*

 Human Body   Human Mind  Everyday Life   History and Culture Communication

street. 2. to place a bar across. *Bar your door for safety.* {**bar**}

• **behind bars**
in jail or prison. *Put every drunk driver behind bars!*

barb *noun* a small, sharp point that sticks out in the opposite direction of the main point or hook, as on an arrow or fishhook. {**barb**}

bar·bar·i·an *noun* 1. a person in a culture that is believed by others to be savage, primitive, or not civilized. *The Roman Empire was attacked by barbarians.* 2. a rough, crude person. {**bar** **bayr** ee ən}

bar·be·cue *noun* 1. an outdoor party at which meat and vegetables are cooked over an open fire. 2. the grill or stove that is used to cook a meal outdoors. 3. the food cooked in this way, often having a special sauce. *verb* (barbecued, barbecuing, barbecues) to roast over an open fire, often using a special sauce. {**bar** bə kyoo}

Word History *Barbecue* comes from *barbacoa*, a Spanish word for a frame used to roast meat or fish. The Spanish word may come from the language of the Taino people, who once lived on the islands between North and South America.

barbed wire *noun* wire with barbs. Barbed wire is used to make fences. {barbd **wiyr**}

bar·ber *noun* a person whose job is to shave, trim, or style hair and beards. {**bar** bər}

bar code *noun* a set of black bars on a white background printed on the labels of goods and mail. A bar code is scanned by a computer that reads information such as price. {**bar** kohd}

bare *adjective* (barer, barest) 1. wearing no clothing or covering; naked. *It's too cold to go outside with bare legs.* 2. not filled, covered, or decorated; empty. *The walls are bare.* 3. plain; simple. *Just give me the bare facts.* 4. only just enough; mere. *He had the bare essentials for living.* *verb* (bared, baring, bares) to uncover; show. *She bared the cut on her arm for the doctor to treat.* {**bayr**} bareness, n.

Homophone Note Are you looking for the word *bear*? *Bare* and *bear* sound alike but have different meanings.

Before getting out of the shower, the **bare bear** checked carefully to make sure no one was looking.

bare·back *adverb or adjective* on the back of a horse or donkey without a saddle. *He is a bareback rider.* / *He is riding bareback.* {**bayr** băk *or* **bayr** băkt}

bare·foot *adverb or adjective* with nothing on the feet. *The barefoot child stepped on a bee.* / *We ran barefoot through the grass.* {**bayr** fuut} barefooted, [adj.], adv.

bare·ly *adverb* only just; hardly. *Please speak louder; I can barely hear you.* {**bayr** lee}

bar·gain 🌐 *noun* 1. an agreement that contains the terms of a transaction or exchange. *Mr. Snow struck a bargain with the car dealer for a new van.* 2. something that is sold or bought at a good price, especially if it is worth more than what was given in exchange. *We got a great bargain on plane tickets.* *verb* (bargained, bargaining, bargains) to talk over the terms of a sale, purchase, or exchange; negotiate. *My mother bargained for a lower price on the furniture we wanted.* {**bar** gən}

barge *noun* a large, long boat with a flat bottom used for carrying freight. *The old canal barge was pulled by a mule.* {**barj**}

• **barge in**
to enter or interrupt in a rude or clumsy way. *He barged into my room without knocking.*

bar graph *noun* a graph that uses bars of different lengths to show information. {**bar** grăf}

bar·i·tone *noun* 1. the range of the male voice that is between tenor and bass. 2. a singer whose voice is in this range. *adjective* having the range of a baritone. *I play a baritone recorder.* {**bar** ih tohn}

bar·i·um *noun* a chemical element. Barium is usually found in compounds with other elements. (symbol: Ba) {**bayr** ee əm}

A
B
C
D
E
F
G
H
I
J
K
L
M
N
O
P
Q
R
S
T
U
V
W
X
Y
Z

a
b
c
d
e
f
g
h
i
j
k
l
m
n
o
p
q
r
s
t
u
v
w
x
y
z

bark[1] ❶ *noun* the harsh sound made by a dog. *verb* (barked, barking, barks) 1. to utter a bark or barks. 2. to say in a harsh or sharp manner. *The commander barked orders at the troops.* {<u>bark</u>}

bark[2] ❶ *noun* the outside covering of the trunks, branches, and roots of woody plants. *The paper birch has white bark.* *verb* (barked, barking, barks) to rub or scrape the skin from. *Be careful not to bark your knees on the sidewalk.* {<u>bark</u>}

A silly dog **barks** at some **bark**.

bar·ley *noun* 1. a plant that is like grass and whose grains are used to make food. 2. the grain of this plant. Barley is used to make food and beer. {<u>bar</u> lee}

bar mitzvah or **bar mizvah** *noun* a Jewish ceremony that celebrates a boy becoming an adult and the beginning of his religious duties. The bar mitzvah usually takes place when the boy is thirteen years old. {bar <u>mihts</u> və}

barn ❷ *noun* a large farm building used to shelter animals or store equipment or crops. {<u>barn</u>}

bar·na·cle *noun* a small sea animal that attaches its shell to rocks, the bottom of ships, docks, and other objects in shallow parts of the ocean. Barnacles float freely in the ocean when they are young. They develop shells with sharp edges as adults. Barnacles are kinds of crustaceans. {<u>bar</u> nə kəl}

barn·yard *noun* a yard or fenced area next to a barn. *We saw three cows and a bull in the barnyard.* {<u>barn</u> yard}

ba·rom·e·ter *noun* an instrument that measures the pressure of the atmosphere and is used to predict the weather. {bə <u>ro</u> mə tər} barometric, *adj.*

bar·on *noun* a nobleman by birth of a particular rank. {<u>bar</u> ən}

Homophone Note Are you looking for the word *barren* (not fruitful or useful)? *Baron* and *barren* sound alike but have different meanings.

bar·on·ess *noun* a noblewoman of a particular rank by birth or by marriage. {<u>bar</u> ə nihs}

bar·rack *noun* (usually plural) a building where soldiers live for a short amount of time. *The army houses soldiers in barracks during their basic training.* {<u>bar</u> ək}

bar·ra·cu·da *noun* (barracuda or barracudas) a fish that lives in warm ocean water and has a long body. Barracuda are fierce hunters. {bar ə <u>kooh</u> də}

bar·rage *noun* a great number of things coming one after another very quickly. *The barrage of gunfire from the roof kept the soldiers away from the building.* {bə <u>rözh</u>}

bar·rel *noun* 1. a round container with a flat top and bottom and bulging sides, often made of wood boards and metal hoops. 2. the amount that such a container can hold. *We'll need a barrel of water for the trip down the Amazon.* 3. any cylindrical part, such as the shaft of a gun. {<u>bar</u> əl}

• **over a barrel**
unable to refuse because of circumstances. *When she asked for a raise, I was really over a barrel.*

bar·ren *adjective* 1. not able to produce or support growth. *No crops grow in the barren desert.* 2. incapable of conceiving and bearing young; sterile. {<u>bar</u> ən} barrenness, *n.*

Homophone Note The words *barren* and *baron* sound alike but have different meanings.

bar·rette *noun* a small clip used for holding hair in place. {bə <u>reht</u>}

bar·ri·cade *noun* a structure that is put up quickly for protection or to block the way. *verb* (barricaded, barricading, barricades) to block off with a barricade. *The police barricaded the road so the parade could pass.* {<u>bar</u> ə kayd}

bar·ri·er *noun* 1. something that blocks the way such as a fence or wall. *We built a barrier to keep our dog from running into the street.* 2. anything that gets in the way of action or progress. *His youth was not a barrier in his search for a job.* {<u>bar</u> ee ər}

bar·ri·er island *noun* a long narrow island that is parallel to the mainland. A barrier island helps protect the shore from being worn away by the action of the ocean's waves. {<u>bar</u> ee ər <u>iy</u> lənd}

bar·ri·o *noun* (barrios) 1. one of the districts of a town in a Spanish-speaking country. 2. (informal) a section of a U.S. city inhabited mostly by Spanish speakers or persons of Hispanic origin. {<u>bahr</u> ee oh}

  Human Body Human Mind Everyday Life History and Culture Communication

bar·row *noun* a flat frame used for carrying a load. A barrow has two handles at each end or handles at one end and a wheel at the other; wheelbarrow. {<u>bar</u> oh}

bar·ter *verb* (bartered, bartering, barters) 1. to trade services or things for other services or things without using money. *Neither of them had any money, so they agreed to barter.* 2. to trade or exchange without the use of money. *Jack bartered his only cow for a handful of beans.* *noun* the act or practice of trading goods or services without using money. *This barter gave us both what we wanted.* {<u>bar</u> tər}

ba·salt *noun* a dark, heavy rock that is created by lava flowing from volcanoes. {bə <u>sawlt</u>} basaltic, adj.

base[1] 🌐🔬 *noun* 1. that on which something stands or rests; foundation. *The Statue of Liberty has a large base.* 2. the bottom part of something. *They chopped at the base of the tree.* 3. a central place; headquarters. *The military base has barracks, offices, stores, and an airport.* 4. one of the four corners of the infield in baseball or softball, or the bag marking any of these points. 5. a chemical compound that creates salts and water when mixed with acids. *Baking soda is a common base.* *verb* (based, basing, bases) 1. to make or provide a base for. *They based their company in Houston.* 2. to serve as a basis; establish. *The novel is based on her own life story.* {<u>bays</u>}
• **get to first base** to complete the first step towards reaching a goal; begin to succeed. *The salesman couldn't get to first*

base in selling his product.
• **off base** wrong; mistaken *His opinion was way off base.*

Homophone Note Are you looking for the word *bass*? *Base* and *bass[1]* sound alike but have different meanings.

base[2] *adjective* (baser, basest) 1. of little value when compared to something else. *The king lived in a splendid palace, while the peasants lived in base cottages.* 2. not brave, noble or honorable; selfish. *He was ashamed of his base actions.* {<u>bays</u>}

base·ball 🌐 *noun* 1. a game played with a bat and ball by two teams of nine players each, the object being to score runs by advancing runners around four bases. *Baseball is played mostly in the summer.* 2. the ball used in this game. *Babe Ruth signed that baseball.* {<u>bays</u> bawl}

base·ment *noun* the space in a building that is underground or partly underground. {<u>bays</u> mənt}

bash·ful *adjective* shy with people; timid. *Don't be bashful; come and give your Aunt Lucy a big kiss!* {<u>băsh</u> fəl}

ba·sic 🌐🔬 *adjective* of, forming, or at the basis; main; fundamental. *The basic idea of bowling is to knock over as many pins as you can.* *noun* (often plural) the basic knowledge or skills required to do something. *She doesn't even know the basics of cooking.* {<u>bay</u> sihk} basically, adv.

BASIC 🌐🔬 *noun* a beginning computer language. BASIC stands for "beginner's all-purpose symbolic instruction code." {<u>bay</u> sihk}

ba·sin *noun* 1. an open, shallow bowl used to hold water for washing. 2. a large area of land drained by a river. *The Amazon basin is in South America.* {<u>bay</u> sihn}

ba·sis *noun* (bases) something that supports and is needed by all the other parts; starting point or foundation. *Trust is the basis of friendship.* {<u>bay</u> sihs}

bask *verb* (basked, basking, basks) to lie in a warm, calm place. *We basked in the sun.* {<u>băsk</u>}

bas·ket *noun* 1. a container made of materials such as wood strips, grass, or straw that are woven or laced together. 2. the contents of such a container. *We picked a basket of peas from the garden.* 3. the open metal hoop and net through which the ball is shot to score points in basketball, or such an act of scoring. *She scored three baskets in last night's game.* {<u>băs</u> kiht}

bas·ket·ball 🌐 *noun* 1. a game played on a court by two teams of five players each. Points are scored by shooting the ball through a high metal hoop and net at the opponent's end of the court. 2. the ball used in this game. {<u>băs</u> kiht bawl}

bass[1] 🌐 *noun* 1. the lowest range of the male voice. 2. a large musical instrument with strings and low, deep tones. *adjective* in the

lowest musical range. *He plays the bass guitar.* {<u>bays</u>}

Homophone Note The words ***bass*** [1] and ***base*** sound alike but have different meanings. To find out why a bass player would not like to be called a base player, look up ***base*** [2].

bass [2] *noun* (bass or basses) any of several freshwater or saltwater food fishes with spiny fins. {<u>băs</u>}

bass drum *noun* a large drum that makes a low, booming sound. {<u>bays druhm</u>}

bas·soon *noun* a large woodwind instrument. The bassoon has a long wooden body attached to a curved, metal tube with a mouthpiece at its end. {bə <u>soohn</u>} bassoonist, n.

bass viol *noun* see double bass. {<u>bays viy</u> əl}

baste [1] *verb* (basted, basting, bastes) to sew with long, loose stitches. Basting lets one put together the pieces of a garment to see how it fits before the final sewing. *It was a good thing the tailor basted the coat first; he found that it was too big.* {<u>bayst</u>}

baste [2] *verb* (basted, basting, bastes) to keep moist with a liquid during cooking. *It's time to baste the turkey again.* {<u>bayst</u>} baster, n.

bat [1] *noun* a heavy club used to hit the ball in baseball, softball, or cricket. *verb* (batted, batting, bats) 1. to hit with a bat. *Bat the ball back to me.* 2. to take one's turn in baseball as a batter. *Bobby will bat next.* {<u>băt</u>}

• **right off the bat**

at once; immediately. *He recognized the artist right off the bat.*

bat [2] *noun* a small mammal that flies. Bats have small bodies and large wings covered with skin. Most bats eat at night, when they use sound to find and catch flying insects. Bats are found in most parts of the world. There are around one thousand kinds of bats. Their wingspans range from less than two inches to more than five feet. Some kinds of bats live in large colonies that roost in caves or in a section of forest. {<u>băt</u>}

• **blind as a bat**

barely able to see. *He needs new glasses because he's as blind as a bat.*

batch *noun* 1. an amount of

Our home team, the **Bats**, has a **batter** that hit 75 home runs the season he used his baseball **bat** with the wings of a **bat**.

something or a number of similar things grouped or considered as a whole. *Every fall there is a new batch of stu-*

dents. 2. an amount used or produced at one time. *The construction workers mixed a batch of cement.* {<u>băch</u>}

bath *noun* 1. the act of washing or soaking something in order to clean, refresh, or heal. 2. water or other liquid used for washing. *That was a cold bath.* 3. a bathroom. {<u>băth</u>}

bathe 🏃 👕 *verb* (bathed, bathing, bathes) 1. to give a bath to; wash. 2. to take a bath. 3. to go swimming. *We bathed in the creek behind my house.* 4. to cover or surround. *The lake was bathed in moonlight.* {<u>bayth</u>} bather, n., bathing, n.

bathing suit *noun* a garment worn for swimming. {<u>bay</u> thing sooht}

bath·robe *noun* a loose garment worn before or after bathing, over pajamas, or for relaxing in the home. {<u>băth</u> rohb}

bath·room 👕 *noun* a room with a toilet and often a sink or bathtub. {<u>băth</u> roohm}

bath·tub *noun* a large tub in which a person can wash. {<u>băth</u> tuhb}

bat mitzvah *noun* a Jewish ceremony that celebrates a girl becoming an adult and the beginning of her religious duties. The bat mitzvah usually takes place when the girl is thirteen years old. {<u>bŏt mihts</u> və, bŏs <u>meets</u> və}

ba·ton *noun* 1. a thin rod or stick used by a conductor in leading an orchestra. 2. a rod or staff of hollow metal that is carried or spun by a drum major or majorette. 3. a hollow cylinder that is carried and passed from one runner to the next in a relay race. {bə <u>tŏn</u>}

 Human Body   Human Mind   Everyday Life   History and Culture   Communication

bat·tal·ion *noun* a large group of soldiers, made up of several companies. {bə **tăl** yən}

bat·ter[1] *verb* (battered, battering, batters) 1. to beat hard again and again, or to damage by beating. *The young boxer battered the older fighter.* 2. to wear down by constant pressure or use. *Constant fear battered his confidence.* {**băt** ər}

bat·ter[2] *noun* a thick mixture of liquid, flour, eggs, and other ingredients, often baked into bread or cake. {**băt** ər}

bat·ter[3] *noun* the person who stands in to bat the ball in baseball, softball, or cricket. {**băt** ər}

battering ram *noun* a heavy beam once used in war to break through doors, walls, or gates. {**băt** ə ring **răm**}

bat·ter·y ❶ ⬤ *noun* (batteries) 1. a device that makes electricity by using chemical reactions. Batteries are used to power many things, including cars, flashlights, toys, and watches. *The car wouldn't start because its battery was dead.* 2. the act of battering. *The man was arrested for battery.* 3. a set of related things, usually used together. *My doctor gave me a battery of tests.* {**băt** ə ree}

bat·tle ⬤ *noun* 1. a fight between two armed persons or forces during a war. *The Battle of the Bulge took place during the end of 1944.* 2. a contest or competition. *The race was a battle between two excellent runners.* *verb* (battled, battling, battles) 1. to fight or struggle. *The ship's crew battled against the terrible storm.* 2. to fight or struggle

against. *I am battling a cold.* {**băt** əl}

bat·tle·field *noun* the area in which a battle takes place. {**băt** əl feeld}

bat·tle·ground *noun* a battlefield. {**băt** əl grownd}

bat·tle·ment *noun* (often plural) a wall along the top of a castle, fort, or tower that has openings for people to shoot through. {**băt** əl mənt}

bat·tle·ship *noun* a large military ship that has heavy armor and large guns. {**băt** əl shihp}

bawl *verb* (bawled, bawling, bawls) to cry loudly or strongly; wail. *He bawled about losing his toy.* *noun* a loud cry or shout. *I heard the baby's bawl from the next room.* {**bawl**}

• **bawl out** (informal) to scold loudly. *The coach bawled her out for skipping practice.*

Homophone Note The words *bawl* and *ball* sound alike but have different meanings.

bay ⬤ *noun* a part of a sea or lake that cuts into a coastline and is partly surrounded by land. {**bay**}

bay·o·net *noun* a weapon like a knife attached to the front end of a rifle for use in close fighting. {bay ə **neht**}

bay·ou *noun* (bayous) a stream that moves slowly through a swamp or marsh. Bayous are found in the southern United States. {**biy** ooh}

ba·zaar *noun* 1. an outdoor street market made up of rows of little shops or stalls where people buy and sell

things. *My parents bought a beautiful rug at a bazaar in Turkey.* 2. a sale of many different things for the purpose of raising money for an organization or charity. *Our school bazaar raised nine thousand dollars for new computers.* {bə **zar**}

B.C. *abbreviation* 1. an abbreviation for "before Christ." These letters are placed after a date that is earlier than the birth of Christ. *If something happened in 300 B.C., it happened 300 years before the birth of Christ.* 2. an abbreviation for British Columbia.

be *verb* (was, were; been; being; am, are, is) 1. to live or exist. *There once was a railroad here.* 2. to take place or happen. *The game is today.* 3. to occupy a certain place or position. *They are across the street.* 4. used to connect the subject of a sentence to a noun or adjective that describes it. *She is a doctor. / He is thin.* 5. used to introduce a command or a question. *Be quiet. / Is she here yet?* *auxiliary verb* (was, were; been; being; am, are, is) 1. used with a present participle to show a continuing action. *It is raining.* 2. used with the present participle or infinitive of a verb to show a future action that is required or intended. *They are seeing me tomorrow. / He is to go straight home.* 3. used with the past participle of another verb to connect the subject of the sentence to actions done to it. *We were pushed and shoved on the subway.* {**bee**}

Homophone Note Are you looking for the word *bee* (a flying insect)? *Be* and *bee* sound alike but have different meanings.

A
B
C
D
E
F
G
H
I
J
K
L
M
N
O
P
Q
R
S
T
U
V
W
X
Y
Z

a
b
c
d
e
f
g
h
i
j
k
l
m
n
o
p
q
r
s
t
u
v
w
x
y
z

Be *symbol of the* chemical element beryllium.

be- *prefix* 1. a prefix that means "to cause to be." *To say "she befriended the dog" is to say "she and the dog have become friends."* 2. a prefix that means "over," "on," or "around." *The word "beside" means "on the side."*

beach 🌐 *noun* the land at the edge of a lake, ocean, or other body of water. A beach slopes gently toward the water and usually has sand or pebbles. *verb* (beached, beaching, beaches) to pull or drive from the water onto the beach and cause to be stuck there. *The hurricane beached many boats.* {<u>beech</u>}

Homophone Note Are you looking for the word **beech** (a kind of tree)? **Beach** and **beech** sound alike but have different meanings.

bea·con *noun* a signal of light or radio waves that guides or warns ships or aircraft. {<u>bee</u> kən}

bead *noun*
1. a small, round object made of glass, wood, metal, or plastic. A bead has a small hole through its center so it can be put on a string to make necklaces or to decorate clothing. 2. any small, round object, such as a drop of liquid or a gas bubble. *Beads of rain covered the window.* *verb* (beaded, beading, beads) to decorate with beads. *She beaded the shirt with Native American designs.* {<u>beed</u>}

bea·gle *noun* a breed of dog. Beagles are small dogs with short legs, drooping ears, and smooth fur that is usually black, tan, and white. {<u>bee</u> gəl}

beak *noun* the hard, curved mouth part of a bird; bill. {<u>beek</u>} beaked, adj.

beak·er *noun* an open glass container with a flat bottom and a pouring spout. Beakers are used by chemists and other scientists. {<u>bee</u> kər}

beam ❓ 👕 *noun* 1. a long, strong piece of wood or metal used to support floors, ceilings or roofs. *Skyscrapers are built with steel beams.* 2. a narrow ray of light. *A beam of sunlight shone through the clouds.* *verb* (beamed, beaming, beams) 1. to shine brightly. *The hot sun beamed down on the farmer.* 2. to smile widely or happily. *Maria beamed when she won the prize.* 3. to send out or transmit. *The radio station beams its signal to a large area.* {<u>beem</u>}

bean ⬆ *noun* 1. the seed or seed pod of certain plants. Many kinds of beans are eaten as a vegetable. 2. any plant which grows beans. *The farmer planted a large crop of soy beans.* 3. anything that is like a bean. *She loves jelly beans.* *verb* (beaned, beaning, beans) To hit on the head with a ball or other thrown object. *The pitcher beaned the batter by accident.* {<u>been</u>}

• **full of beans**
1. (informal) full of energy; very active. *He was full of beans again only three days after he broke his leg.* 2. (informal) wrong; not giving correct information. *That coach is full of beans if she thinks her team can beat ours.*

• **spill the beans**
to tell a secret by accident or on purpose. *He spilled the beans about the party and ruined the surprise.*

Word History The phrase **full of beans** was first used in the 1800s. Racehorses were fed beans to make them more lively.

bear[1] *verb* (bore, borne or born, bearing, bears) 1. to carry. *The servants will bear the gift to the king.* 2. to hold up or support. *These beams bear the weight of tons of stone.* 3. to put up with; endure. *Pip could not bear being poor.* 4. to give birth to. *She bore a son and named him after his father.* 5. to produce by growth. *Apple trees bear fruit in the fall.* 6. to have or accept as a duty. *Who bears the blame for this?* 7. to go in a certain direction; turn. *Bear left at the traffic light.* {<u>behr</u>}

• **bear up**
to work through something difficult without giving up; endure. *He can make a lot of money at this job if he can bear up under the stress.*

• **bear with**
be patient with. *Please bear with me while I try to find that information for you.*

Homophone Note Are you looking for the word **bare** (without clothes)? **Bear** and **bare** sound alike but have different meanings.

bear[2] ⬆ *noun* a large furry mammal with a short tail. Bears are omnivorous; they may eat plants, honey, insects, fish, and small mam-

 Human Body   Human Mind   Everyday Life   History and Culture   Communication

mals. There are several kinds of bears, including black bears, brown bears, grizzly bears, and polar bears. {behr}

Homophone Note Are you looking for the word *bare*? *Bear* and *bare* (without clothes) sound alike but have different meanings.

beard *noun* 1. the hair growing on a man's face. *The sailor's beard grew long during the voyage.* 2. hair on an animal that looks likes a man's beard. *The goat has a white beard.* {beerd}

bear·ing *noun* 1. the way a person acts, behaves, stands, or walks. *The king had a proud bearing.* 2. relation or connection (usually followed by on). *The facts had no bearing on his decision.* 3. a machine part that holds another, moving part and allows it to move with less friction. Bearings are often used to help wheels turn. 4. (often plural) position in relation to other things; sense of direction. *We lost our bearings in the blizzard.* {beh ring}

beast *noun* 1. any mammal with four legs. *The beasts of the far North have thick fur.* 2. a part of human nature which is rude, cruel, or like a wild animal. *War can bring out the beast in people.* {beest}

beat ● *verb* (beat, beaten, beating, beats) 1. to hit again and again. *He beat the drum with his new drumsticks.* 2. to win against; defeat. *Mai beat her brother at tennis.* 3. to stir rapidly. *Beat the eggs.* 4. to pound; thump. *I was so scared that I could hear my heart*

beating. *noun* 1. a hit or blow, often in a series. *He gave the nail one last beat with his hammer.* 2. a thump. *The doctor listened carefully to the beat of my heart.* 3. musical rhythm. *We danced to the beat of the music.* 4. a person's regular route on the job. *The policeman walked his beat every day.* *adjective* (informal) very tired; exhausted. *Kim was beat after skiing all day.* {beet}

• **beat around the bush** to avoid or delay speaking about the most important matter. *Stop beating around the bush and just tell me why you're late.*

Homophone Note Are you looking for the word *beet* (a dark red vegetable)? *Beat* and *beet* sound alike but have different meanings.

beat·en *adjective* 1. used by many people; much traveled. *The hikers followed a beaten path through the woods.* 2. not able to keep going; discouraged. *They felt beaten after they lost their leader.* 3. hammered into a new shape, often flat. *The platter was made of beaten gold.* {bee tən}

• **off the beaten path** in a place that is hard to reach or not visited often. *That museum is off the beaten path, but it is worth seeing.*

beau·ti·ful *adjective* delightful to see, hear, or experience; lovely to the senses; having beauty. *The sunset was beautiful.* {byoo tih fəl} beautifully, adv.

Synonyms
These words share a meaning with *beautiful*, adjective 1:
fair, lovely, exquisite, gorgeous

beau·ti·fy *verb* (beautified, beautifying, beautifies) to make beautiful. *Planting tulips*

along the sidewalk beautified the entrance. {byoo tih fiy} beautification, n.

beau·ty ● ● *noun* (beauties) 1. the quality of being pleasant to the senses or beautiful; loveliness. *The beauty of the music delighted us.* 2. a person or thing with much beauty. *Her new sailboat is really a beauty.* {byoo tee}

bea·ver *noun* a large rodent, up to four feet long, with thick brown fur and a wide flat tail. Beavers use their long front teeth to cut down trees for food and to build dams and lodges (beaver houses). They use the dams to keep water around their lodges. Beavers live in North America, Europe, and Asia. {bee vər}

be·came *verb* past tense of **become**. {bə kaym}

be·cause *conjunction* for the reason that. *He passed the test because he had studied hard.* {bə kuhz or bə kawz}

beck·on *verb* (beckoned, beckoning, beckons) to signal to come using a motion of the head or hands. *Our host beckoned us into the dining room.* {beh kən}

be·come *verb* (became, become, becoming, becomes) 1. to grow or come to be. *Liz became ill after eating a poisonous mushroom. / This tadpole will become a frog.* 2. to look good with; suit well. *That jacket becomes you.* 3. to be correct for; fit or suit. *Respect for adults becomes a young child.* {bə kuhm}

• **become of** to happen to; to be the result

A
B
C
D
E
F
G
H
I
J
K
L
M
N
O
P
Q
R
S
T
U
V
W
X
Y
Z

a
b
c
d
e
f
g
h
i
j
k
l
m
n
o
p
q
r
s
t
u
v
w
x
y
z

of. *What became of your plan to travel?*

be·com·ing *adjective* pleasant or attractive looking. *That shirt is becoming on you.* {bə **kuh** ming}

bed  *noun* 1. a piece of furniture used for resting or sleeping. 2. an area of ground used for planting, or the plants themselves. *The cat dug up the flower bed.* 3. the bottom of a body of water. *Divers searched the ocean bed for lost treasure.* 4. a supporting base or layer. *The bricks are lying on a bed of gravel.* *verb* (bedded, bedding, beds) to give a resting or sleeping place to. *The old woman bedded the children near the fireplace.* {**behd**}
• **get up on the wrong side of the bed**
to be in a bad mood from early in the day.

Word History A Latin word that meant "to dig or burrow" was the origin of the English word **bed**.

bed·ding *noun* 1. blankets, sheets, pillows, and other coverings for a bed. 2. material such as straw or wood chips used as a bed for animals. *Lee changes her hamster's bedding every week.* {**beh** ding}

bed·pan *noun* a shallow pan used as a toilet by a person who cannot get out of bed. {**behd** păn}

be·drag·gled *adjective* 1. dirty, wet, or limp from having wandered or been dragged through mud and water. *Tai's hair looked bedraggled after walking home in the rain.* 2. in a messy or shabby state. *The puppy was bedraggled and hungry when we found him.* {bə **dră** gəld}

bed·rock *noun* the solid layer of rock in the earth's surface, found beneath soil, sand, or gravel. *It is a good idea to build a house on bedrock.* {**behd** rŏk}

bed·room *noun* a room used for sleeping. {**behd** roohm}

bed·side *noun* the space beside a bed, especially of a sick person. *The nurse stayed at his bedside until dawn.* *adjective* beside or near a bed. *An alarm clock sits on my bedside table.* {**behd** siyd}

bed·spread *noun* a covering for a bed. {**behd** sprehd}

bed·time *noun* the usual time when a person goes to bed. {**behd** tiym}

bee *noun* an insect with a hairy body, four wings, and sometimes a stinger. Some kinds of bees live in social groups, and some live alone. Many bees drink nectar from flowers. {**bee**}
• **have a bee in one's bonnet**
to think constantly of one idea or goal. *She had a bee in her bonnet about getting the house painted.*

Homophone Note The words **bee** and **be** sound alike but have different meanings.

beech *noun* a tree that has smooth, gray bark and nuts that people can eat. {**beech**}

Homophone Note Are you looking for the word **beach** (a sandy place)? **Beech** and **beach** sound alike but have different meanings.

beef *noun* (beeves) 1. meat from a cow or steer. 2. (informal) a complaint. *Jack has a beef with Jill because she won't help him with chores.* {**beef**}

beef·steak *noun* a slice of beef for frying or broiling. {**beef** stayk}

bee·hive *noun* 1. a shelter in which bees live. 2. a place of great activity. *Grand Central Station is a beehive during rush hour.* {**bee** hiyv}

been *verb* past participle of **be**. {**bihn** or **behn**}

Homophone Note Are you looking for the word **bin** (a large container)? Most Americans pronounce the words **been** and **bin** in exactly the same way.

beep *noun* a short, high sound that serves as a signal. A beep is made by an electronic device or a car horn. *verb* (beeped, beeping, beeps) 1. to give off a short, high sound as a signal. *The microwave oven beeps when the food is ready.* 2. to cause to give off a short, high sound as a signal. *The driver beeped his horn at the dog in the road.* {**beep**}

beer *noun* 1. an alcoholic drink made of hops and malt. 2. a drink without alcohol made from the roots of plants such as ginger or birch. {**beer**}

bees·wax *noun* the wax made by bees in building their honeycombs. {**beez** wăks}

beet *noun* a plant whose leaves and fleshy dark red root can be eaten. {**beet**}

Homophone Note Are you looking for the word **beat** (to hit or whip, or a musical rhythm)? **Beet** and **beat** sound alike but have different meanings.

bee·tle *noun* an insect with a pair of hard front wings that covers a pair of thin wings.

  Human Body Human Mind Everyday Life History and Culture  Communication

There are many different kinds of beetles. Japanese beetles, ladybugs, and fireflies are beetles. {**bee** təl}

> **Word History** *Beetle* comes from a word in early English that means "little biter."

be·fall *verb* (befell, befallen, befalling, befalls) 1. to take place; happen. *We were afraid of what might befall during our walk through the dark forest.* 2. to happen to. *Bad things befell him after he ran away from home.* {bə **fawl**}

be·fore *adverb* at an earlier time; in the past. *Sam thought he had read this book before.* *preposition* 1. in front of; ahead of. *She stood before the door and knocked.* 2. earlier than; previous to. *Cinderella forgot to leave before midnight.* 3. in the presence of; within view of. *The students performed the play before their families.* *conjunction* 1. earlier than the time when. *They planned their trip before they left.* 2. rather than. *He would go hungry before he would eat worms and grubs.* {bə **fohr**}

be·fore·hand *adverb* ahead of time; at an earlier time. *We went to the movie but ate dinner beforehand.* {bə **fohr** hănd}

be·friend *verb* (befriended, befriending, befriends) to be or act as a friend to. *He befriended his new neighbors.* {bə **frehnd**}

beg *verb* (begged, begging, begs) 1. to ask a favor of; to plead for. *I beg you to help.* 2. to ask for in a polite or in a desperate way. *He begged for mercy.* 3. to ask for charity or gifts. *She was forced to beg when she lost her job and home.* {**behg**}

be·gan *verb* past tense of **begin**. {bə **găn**}

beg·gar *noun* a person who begs as a way to meet basic needs such as food and clothing. {**behg** ər}

be·gin *verb* (began, begun, beginning, begins) 1. to do the first step in a process; start. *If you have your test, you may begin.* 2. to come into being. *North of the equator, summer begins in June.* 3. to perform the first step of (something); start. *She began her story by introducing the main characters.* {bə **gihn**}

be·gon·ia *noun* a tropical plant with bright flowers in many colors. The leaves are often streaked or spotted. {bih **gohn** yə}

be·gun *verb* past participle of **begin**. {bə **guhn**}

be·half *noun* 1. support; aid (used with "in" or "on" and followed by "of"). *They raised money on behalf of the poor.* 2. representing someone who is not present (used with "on" and followed by "of"). *Mr. Kelly greeted the new workers on behalf of the owner.* {bə **hăf**}

be·have *verb* (behaved, behaving, behaves) 1. to act or function in a certain way. *The young children behaved well at the restaurant.* 2. to act in a proper manner. *Will you please behave?* {bə **hayv**}

be·hav·ior ❓ *noun* 1. the way a person acts or behaves. *Miss Cole's behavior at lunch was shocking.* 2. the typical actions of a person, animal, thing, or group, either in general or in certain situations. *Crying when sad is a normal part of human behavior.* / *Atoms change their behavior when heated.* {bə **hayv** yər}

be·hav·iour *noun* a spelling of **behavior** used in Canada and Britain. See **behavior** for more information. {bee **hayv** yər}

be·head *verb* (beheaded, beheading, beheads) to cut off the head of. *Louis XVI, the King of France, was beheaded during the French Revolution.* {bə **hehd**}

be·held *verb* past tense and past participle of **behold**. {bə **hehld**}

be·hind *preposition* 1. in or at the back of; on the other side of. *Who is standing behind this door?* 2. at a stage or position less advanced than. *He's behind his brother in school.* 3. at a time later than. *The second train arrived five minutes behind the first.* 4. supporting; backing. *The people are behind the mayor's plan to build more parking lots.* *adverb* 1. at or toward the back; in the rear. *The dog trotted behind.* 2. in a place, time, or condition that has passed. *I left my suitcase behind.* 3. slower than expected or required; not keeping to the usual or necessary schedule. *I am behind in my work.* / *She is behind in her rent.* {bə **hiynd**}

be·hold *verb* (beheld, beholding, beholds) to see or observe. *We beheld the beautiful sunset.* *interjection* "look at" or "observe" (used as a command or exclamation). *Behold the Queen in all her beauty!* {bə **hohld**} beholder, n.

A B C D E F G H I J K L M N O P Q R S T U V W X Y Z

a
b
c
d
e
f
g
h
i
j
k
l
m
n
o
p
q
r
s
t
u
v
w
x
y
z

beige *noun* the color that comes from mixing tan and gray paint. {**bayzh**}

Bei·jing *noun* the capital city of China. The city is also called Peking. {bay **jing**}

be·ing *noun* 1. the state or fact of living or existing. *The first plants came into being in the ocean.* 2. any living creature. *Dolphins are intelligent beings.* {**bee** ing}

be·lat·ed *adjective* too late; tardy. *We gave her a belated birthday card.* {bə **lay** tihd}

belch *verb* (belched, belching, belches) 1. to release gas from the stomach through the mouth in a noisy burst; burp. *It's not polite to belch at the table.* 2. to throw out violently; spout. *The factory belched pollution into the air.* *noun* the act or an instance of belching. *He gave a belch and sighed.* {**behlch**}

bel·fry *noun* (belfries) a tower of a church or other building in which a bell is hung; bell tower. {**behl** free}

Bel·gium *noun* a country in northwestern Europe. Brussels is the capital of Belgium. {**behl** jəm} Belgian, n., adj.

Bel·grade *noun* the capital city of Yugoslavia. {behl **grayd** or **behl** grayd}

be·lief 🙂 😐 *noun* 1. a strong opinion. *My teacher has a strong belief that all children can learn.* 2. trust in a person, thing, or idea; confidence. *The coach's belief in me helped me to succeed.* 3. an idea accepted as true; something that is believed. *Some religions hold the belief that the human soul lives on after the body dies.* {bə **leef**}

be·lieve *verb* (believed, believing, believes) 1. to accept as honest or true. *Can you believe his crazy story?* 2.

to have some confidence in; suppose. *I believe they will arrive before noon.* {bə **leev**} believable, adj., believably, adv., believer, n.

• **believe in**
1. to be completely certain that something is true or right. *Do you believe in God?* 2. to be sure of the ability or value of. *The Prime Minister asked the people to believe in him.*

bell 🔔 *noun* 1. a hollow metal cup that makes a ringing sound when struck. 2. the opening of a brass or wind instrument where the sound comes out. *She held her hand over the bell of the trumpet to change its sound.* {**behl**} bell-like, adj.

• **ring a bell**
to sound familiar; to cause a person to remember something. *Her name doesn't ring a bell.*

bel·lig·er·ent *adjective* 1. having a fighting character; aggressive. *The boxer looked belligerent as he stepped into the ring.* 2. having to do with war or to people or countries at war. *The two belligerent countries refused to discuss peace.* {bə **lih** jə rənt}

bel·low *verb* (bellowed, bellowing, bellows) 1. to make the deep, loud cry of a bull. 2. to shout loudly and with a deep tone. *Our father bellowed at us to stop fighting.* 3. to say loudly and powerfully. *He bellowed his annoyance.* *noun* an act or sound of bellowing. *The yak's bellow scared us.* {**behl** oh}

bel·lows *plural noun* (used with a singular or plural verb) a bag that can be expanded to draw air in and squeezed to force air out. Bellows are

used to blow air on a fire or produce sound on a musical instrument. *That organ uses a bellows to blow air through its pipes.* {**behl** ohz}

bel·ly *noun* (bellies) the front of a person or underside of an animal; stomach. *Our dog loves having us rub his belly.* {**behl** ee}

bel·ly·but·ton *noun* (informal) the navel. {**behl** ih buh tən}

be·long *verb* (belonged, belonging, belongs) 1. to have a proper or appropriate location. *This painting belongs in a museum.* 2. to be accepted as part of a group; fit in. *I feel as if I belong.* {bə **lawng**}

• **belong to**
1. to be owned by. *This shirt belongs to my brother.* 2. to be a member of; to be part of. *Vicky belongs to the karate club.*

be·long·ing *noun* 1. the condition of being comfortable and friendly with others. *I had a feeling of belonging at summer camp.* 2. (plural) things that are owned by a person; possessions. *Nell packed all of her belongings and moved to London.* {bə **lawng** ing}

be·low *adverb* in or to a lower place; beneath. *Let's go below.* *preposition* 1. under; beneath. *His apartment is on the floor below mine.* 2. lower than in rank or value. *He placed below his brother in the race.* {bə **loh**}

belt *noun* 1. a strip of cloth, leather, or other material worn around the waist. 2. a continuous band of heavy, flexible material used to

 Human Body   Human Mind  Everyday Life  History and Culture  Communication

drive a machine or carry materials. *That car needs a new fan belt.* 3. a region or area that is known for something or used for a special purpose. *The country's farm belt grows most of our food.* {**behlt**}

• **below the belt**
not fair. *Her angry words hit below the belt.*

bench 🌳 ⚖ *noun* 1. a long seat, often without a back. 2. a table for working on, often with space for tools.

3. the position or job of being a judge. *Thurgood Marshall was appointed to the bench in 1967. verb* (benched, benching, benches) to remove from or prevent from playing in a sports contest. *The coach benched Cheryl because she missed practice.* {**behnch**}

bend *verb* (bent, bending, bends) 1. to cause to take on a curved or angled form, or a different form. *He bent the nail by mistake.* 2. to take on a curved or angled form. *The fishing rod bent under the weight of the fish. / The arm bends at the elbow.* 3. to lean one's upper body from the waist (often followed by "over," "forward," or "back"). *I bent over to pick up the litter.* 4. to change direction in a curving way. *The road bends sharply just in front of my house. noun* a curved thing, part, or area; curve. *The car crashed just before the bend in the road.* {**behnd**} bendable, adj.

• **around the bend**
(informal) crazy; insane. *The*

noise from the power tools was driving us around the bend.

• **bend over backward [or] backwards**
to try very hard; make a great effort. *He bent over backwards to please them.*

be·neath *adverb* in a lower place; below. *The sandwich has jelly on top and peanut butter beneath. preposition* 1. under; lower than; below. *The flowers planted beneath the tree didn't get enough light.* 2. not good enough for. *The millionaire thought eating in a diner was beneath him.* {bə **neeth**}

ben·e·fi·cial *adjective* having a good or favorable effect; helpful. *The dry weather was beneficial to my cough.* {beh nə **fih** shəl} beneficially, adv.

ben·e·fit *noun* 1. an object, action, or sum of money that improves someone's life; aid. *The company gives its workers benefits such as health insurance and vacation days.* 2. anything that does someone good or gives an advantage. *It is to your benefit to get a college education. verb* (benefited, benefiting, benefits) 1. to be helpful to; have good results for. *I hope these gifts will benefit you.* 2. to gain something good (usually followed by "from"). *The sailors benefited from the captain's advice.* {beh nə **fiht**}

bent *adjective* 1. not straight; curved or crooked. *We hung a swing from the bent branch of the tree.* 2. determined or insisting (usually followed by "on"). *He is bent on going with us. verb* past tense and past participle of **bend**. {**behnt**}

be·ret *noun* a soft, round, flat cap with a snug headband. A beret

does not have a visor. {bə **ray**}

Ber·lin *noun* the capital city of Germany. Between 1945 and 1990 the city was divided into East Berlin and West Berlin. For most of that time the Berlin Wall, a concrete and wire barrier, separated East and West Berlin. {bər **lihn** or behr **leen**}

ber·ry 🌳 *noun* (berries) any of several small, juicy fruits that do not have a pit, such as the strawberry, raspberry, or blueberry. *verb* (berried, berrying, berries) to seek or gather berries. {**beh** ree}

Homophone Note Are you looking for the word **bury**? Some people say **berry** and **bury** in exactly the same way, but these two words have different meanings.

berth *noun* 1. a shelf or bunk for sleeping on a ship or train. 2. a space for a ship to dock or anchor. *This ship has been at berth for two weeks.* {**buhrth**}

Homophone Note The words **berth** and **birth** sound alike but have different meanings. **Birth** is the thing you celebrate on your birthday.

be·ryl·li·um *noun* a hard, light, gray substance that is one of the chemical elements. Beryllium is sometimes combined with other elements to form an alloy. It is also used in building rockets. (symbol: Be) {bə **rih** lee əm}

be·seech *verb* (besought [or] beseeched, beseeching, beseeches) to make an important or urgent request; beg. *The queen beseeched the knight to kill the dragon.* {bə **seech**} beseecher, n.

be·set *verb* (beset, besetting, besets) to attack from all

A
B
C
D
E
F
G
H
I
J
K
L
M
N
O
P
Q
R
S
T
U
V
W
X
Y
Z

sides; besiege. *The wolves beset the moose.* {bə **seht**}

be·side *preposition* 1. next to; at the side of. *The dog is walking beside its master.* 2. compared with. *The bush looks small beside that tree.* {bə **siyd**}
• **beside oneself**
very upset or excited. *He was beside himself with worry.*

be·sides *adverb* also; in addition. *I want you to come; besides, you will have a good time.* *preposition* in addition to. *Besides the tigers, there are three big cats at the zoo.* {bə **siydz**}

be·siege *verb* (besieged, besieging, besieges) 1. to surround with soldiers in order to attack or capture. *The army besieged the city.* 2. to surround or attack from all sides with questions or doubts. *Fears besieged him when he stood up to give his speech.* {bə **seej**}

best *adjective* 1. superlative of good. 2. better than all others in quality or ability. *Orion was the best hunter. adverb* 1. superlative of well. 2. with the most success or effect. *She works best by herself. noun* 1. a thing or person better than all others. *Of all the runners, Robin is the best.* 2. a person's finest effort, performance, or behavior. *He did his best, but he lost anyway.* {**behst**}

Synonyms
These words share a meaning with ***best***, adjective 2:
first, top, excellent, super, foremost, first-class, first-rate, superlative

be·stow *verb* (bestowed, bestowing, bestows) to give as a gift or award (usually followed by "on"). *The President bestowed an award on the famous scientist.* {bə **stoh**} bestowal, n.

bet *verb* (bet or betted, betting, bets) to agree to pay if one's guess about some future event is wrong. *I bet you it will snow tomorrow. noun* 1. an instance of betting. *He lost the bet and had to give up his allowance.* 2. the amount of money or the item at stake when betting. *Jack didn't lose much money, because his bet was small.* {**beht**}
• **you bet**
(informal) to be sure; of course. *You bet I like ice cream!*

be·ta *noun* the name of the second letter of the Greek alphabet. {**bay** tə}

be·tray *verb* (betrayed, betraying, betrays) 1. to help the enemy of; commit treason. *The spy betrayed his country.* 2. to not be loyal or faithful to. *She betrayed her friend by telling his secret.* {bə **tray**} betrayal, n.

bet·ter *adjective* 1. comparative of good. 2. more excellent; of a higher quality. *This is a better restaurant because of its fine service.* 3. more useful; having more desirable results. *These shoes are better for walking than those sandals.* 4. healthier; no longer sick or injured. *Is she better after the operation?* 5. larger. *The house took the better part of a year to build. adverb* 1. comparative of well. 2. with more success or excellence. *The plants will grow better in the sun.* 3. more; greater; longer. *He drove better than ten miles to get here. verb* (bettered, bettering, betters) 1. to improve. *Abe bettered himself through education.* 2. to do better than; to top or outdo. *She bettered the school record in that race. noun* the greater or more excellent one. *This school is the better of the two.* {**beh** tər}
• **better off**
in a happier or improved condition or situation. *I'll be better off when the weather is warmer.*

Synonyms
These words share a meaning with ***better***, adjective 2:
greater, finer

be·tween *preposition* 1. in the area that separates. *Bob stood in line between Joe and Kate.* 2. joining, dividing, or involving. *There was an argument between the neighbors. / The wall between the rooms is thin.* 3. by the shared effort of two people. *Between them, John and Ann were able to paint the whole house.* 4. when comparing. *There are not many differences between my bike and yours.* 5. during a set time period. *Come for lunch between noon and one.* {bə **tween**}

Language Note The prepositions ***between*** and ***among*** are close in meaning, but there is an important difference in how they are used. Use ***between*** when you are talking or writing about two people or things. Use ***among*** when you are talking or writing about three or more people or things. *Eli and Jack discussed the problem between themselves. Soon an argument broke out among the entire class.*

bev·er·age ⊙ *noun* any liquid for drinking, except water or medicine. {**behv** rihj}

be·ware *verb* to be careful or wary (usually used imperatively). *Beware of the dog!* {bə **wayr**}

 Human Body
 Human Mind
 Everyday Life
 History and Culture
 Communication

be·wil·der *verb* (bewildered, bewildering, bewilders) to confuse or puzzle. *Having too many choices bewilders me.* {bə **wihl** dər} bewilderingly, adv., bewilderment, n.

be·witch *verb* (bewitched, bewitching, bewitches) 1. to enchant or cast a spell over with magic or as if with magic. *The evil fairy bewitched the princess.* 2. to charm or fascinate. *The many colors of her garden bewitched her guests.* {bə **wihch**}

be·yond *preposition* 1. past the farthest side of; farther on than; later than. *The cows are in the field beyond the barn. / Don't stay at the party beyond midnight.* 2. outside the ability or limits of. *A new car is beyond our budget.* {bih **yŏnd**}

bi- *prefix* 1. a prefix that means "two" or "both." *A bicycle has two wheels.* 2. a prefix that means "once every two." *A biennial event happens once every two years.*

bi·as *noun* 1. a line diagonal to the grain of a woven cloth. *Cut the fabric on the bias.* 2. an opinion or liking that does not let one be fair; prejudice. *The teacher did not show bias to either of the fighting students.* *verb* (biased, biasing, biases) to make biased. *His good manners biased the boss in his favor.* {biy ihs} biasedly, adv.

bib *noun* 1. a piece of cloth tied under the chin. A bib is worn by babies to protect the clothing during a meal. 2. the upper part of an apron that protects the clothing. {bihb}

Bi·ble *noun* 1. the main sacred writings of Judaism and Christianity. The writings of Judaism are made up of the Old Testament, while those of Christianity are made up of both the Old and New Testaments. 2. any collection of writings considered sacred to a religion. 3. (l.c.) any book or text that is considered authoritative or official. *He bought the Fisherman's Bible to learn how to catch more fish.* {biy bəl}

Bib·li·cal *adjective* (often lower case) of or in the Bible. *Andrew read the biblical story of Noah's ark.* {bih blih kəl} Biblically, adv.

bib·li·og·ra·phy *noun* (bibliographies) 1. a list of titles about a certain subject. *Include a bibliography with your report on Mali.* 2. a list of the works by one author. {bih blee **o** grə fee}

bi·ceps *noun* (biceps) the large muscle at the front of the upper arm that bends the elbow. {biy sehps}

bick·er *verb* (bickered, bickering, bickers) to quarrel about something that does not matter. *The two sisters bickered about which movie to watch.* {bihk ər}

bi·cus·pid *noun* a tooth ending in two points. {biy **kuh** spihd}

bi·cy·cle ⊙ *noun* a light vehicle with two wheels, one behind the other, a small seat, and handlebars for steering. Pedals make the wheels move. *verb* (bicycled, bicycling, bicycles) to ride on a bicycle. {**biy** sih kəl} bicycler, n., bicyclist, n.

> **Word History** *Bicycle* is a word that was borrowed from the French in the mid-1800s. It was made up of a Latin word and a Greek word. *Bi-* is a Latin prefix that means "two." "Cycle" comes from *kyklos,* a Greek word that means "circle."

bid *verb* (bade or bid, bidden or bid, bidding, bids) 1. to say to. *He bid her good morning.* 2. to direct; command. *She bade him enter the room.* 3. to offer. *He bid ten dollars for the table.* *noun* an act of bidding. *Your bid for this rare antique is too low.* {bihd} bidder, n.

bi·en·ni·al *adjective* 1. happening every second year. *This company holds a biennial meeting.* 2. lasting two years. *He's in a biennial program to learn French.* 3. having a life cycle of two years. *These biennial flowers will not bloom until next year.* *noun* 1. an event that happens once every two years. *The biennial will be held in Dallas.* 2. a plant with a life cycle of two years. {biy **eh** nee əl} biennially, adv.

big *adjective* (bigger, biggest) 1. large in size, number, or weight. *Elephants are big animals.* 2. important or of great concern. *Deciding where to live is a big question.* 3. older; more grown-up. *My big brother is learning how to drive a car.* {bihg} bigness, n.

• **big on** excited about; having a

Living World

Physical World

Natural Environment

Economy

Government and Law

A B C D E F G H I J K L M N O P Q R S T U V W X Y Z

liking for. *West High School is big on sports.*

Synonyms

These words share a meaning with **big**, adjective 1:

great Great means very big. *The explorers saw a great mountain in the distance.*

large Large means bigger than average. *For this many people, we will need to buy a large pizza.*

considerable Considerable means big enough to be worth noticing or mentioning. *I had to walk a considerable distance to find a pay phone.*

grand When something is grand, it is big in an impressive way. *Rich people often live in grand houses.*

Big Dipper *noun* the constellation Ursa Major. The stars that make up this constellation form a shape that looks like a ladle or dipper. {<u>bihg</u> <u>dih</u> pər}

big·horn *noun* (bighorn or bighorns) a wild sheep found in the Rocky Mountains of North America. The male has large, curved horns; the female has short, straight horns. They are also called Rocky Mountain sheep. {<u>bihg</u> hohrn}

bike *noun* (informal) a short form of bicycle or motorcycle. *verb* (biked, biking, bikes) to ride a bicycle or motorcycle. {<u>biyk</u>} biker, n.

bile *noun* 1. a bitter, yellowish liquid made in the liver. Bile helps to digest fats. 2. ill temper or anger. *Miss Kaplan's bile rose when she saw the broken window.* {<u>biyl</u>}

bi·lin·gual *adjective* 1. able to speak two languages well. *In Montreal there are many bilingual people who speak both French and English.* 2. written or spoken in two languages. *We use a bilingual dictionary to help with our Spanish homework.* {biy <u>ling</u> gwəl}

bill[1] ✏ 💻 *noun* 1. a written list showing the cost of items bought or services provided. *The carpenter sent a bill for fixing the stairs.* 2. a piece of paper money. *Mrs. Perez paid with a ten-dollar bill.* 3. a proposed law that has not yet been voted on. *The Senate debated an education bill.* *verb* (billed, billing, bills) to send a written list of costs to. *The electric company bills us every month.* {<u>bihl</u>}

Returning north after the winter, the Canada goose carries in its **bill** the **bill** for six months of travelling expenses.

bill[2] ⬤ *noun* the parts of a bird's jaw that form the beak. {<u>bihl</u>}

bill·board *noun* a large board for displaying outdoor advertisements, often seen next to highways. {<u>bihl</u> bohrd}

bill·fold *noun* a small folding case that holds paper money and fits in a pocket; wallet. {<u>bihl</u> fohld}

bil·liards *noun* (billiards) a game played with long sticks and hard balls on a special table covered with cloth. Players use a stick to hit the balls against each other and into pockets along the edges of the table. {<u>bihl</u> yərdz} billiardist, n.

bil·lion *noun* 1. the number that is equal to one thousand times one million; 1,000,000,000. 2. a very large number that is not named exactly. *There are billions of ants living in the rain forest.* *adjective* 1. being one billion in number. *The government spent over a billion dollars on education.* 2. being a very large number that is not named exactly. *We could see at least a billion stars.* {<u>bihl</u> yən}

bil·low *noun* a large wave in the ocean; swell. *Billows formed as the storm grew stronger.* *verb* (billowed, billowing, billows) to move in billows; rise and swell. *Smoke billowed from the chimney.* {<u>bihl</u> oh}

bin *noun* a container or space for storing things such as wood, potatoes, or coal. {<u>bihn</u>}

Homophone Note Are you looking for the word **been** (a form of "to be")? Most Americans say **bin** and **been** in exactly the same way.

bi·na·ry *adjective* 1. having two parts or components. *A binary star is really two stars that revolve around a center point.* 2. pertaining to a numbering system with a base of two. *In binary numbers, the number five is written as "101."* {<u>biy</u> nayr ee}

bi·na·ry sys·tem *noun* a numbering system with a base of

 Human Body   Human Mind   Everyday Life History and Culture Communication

two. In binary numbers, any number can be expressed by 1, 0, or a combination of these. The number five is written as "101" in the binary system. {**biy** nə ree **sihs** təm}

bind *verb* (bound, binding, binds) 1. to tie together or fasten tightly with a rope or cord. *He will bind the newspapers with string.* 2. to wrap or cover with a bandage. *The doctor bound her sprained arm.* 3. to force to do something by law or a sense of duty. *We will bind you with a promise.* / *He felt bound to attend the wedding.* *noun* a bad or difficult situation. *By not showing up, you put us in a real bind.* {**biynd**}

bin·go *noun* (bingos) a game in which players try to match numbers on a card with numbers read out by a caller. Each player has a card with numbered squares. The player who is the first to cover a whole row of squares is the winner. {**bing** goh}

bin·oc·u·lar *noun* (usually plural) a device that uses lenses and mirrors to make objects look larger. Binoculars are used with both eyes at once. *I could see the bird in the top of the tree through my binoculars.* {bih **nŏk** yə lər}

bi·o·de·grad·a·ble *adjective* able to be broken down by the action of living organisms such as bacteria. *Paper is biodegradable waste, but aluminum is not.* {**biy** oh də **gray** də bəl}

bi·og·ra·phy *noun* (biographies) the written story of the facts and events of a person's life. {**biy** o̲ grə fee}

bi·ol·o·gy ⊕ ❶ *noun* the science that studies the growth and life processes of living things. {**biy** o̲ lə jee}

bi·o·lu·mi·nes·cence *noun* light given off naturally by certain kinds of insects, fish, or bacteria. *The bioluminescence of fireflies allows them to blink on and off in the dark.* {biy oh **looh** mə **nehs** əns}

bi·o·mass *noun* the total amount of living things in a particular environment, measured by mass per unit of area or volume. *The scientist counted the fish, reptiles, mammals, and plants of the lake when figuring out its biomass.* {**biy** oh măs}

bi·on·ic *adjective* an electronic or mechanical device that replaces or helps something natural. An artificial leg is one kind of bionic device. {**biy** o̲ nihk}

birch *noun* a tree or shrub with hard wood and smooth bark that can be peeled off. {**buhrch**}

bird ❶ *noun* an animal with two wings, two feet, and a body covered with feathers. Most birds can fly. Birds are warm-blooded animals with skeletons inside their bodies. Birds lay eggs with hard shells. Robins, eagles, chickens, and ostriches are a few of the many kinds of birds. {**buhrd**} birdlike, adj.
- **birds of a feather** a group of people who have similar interests, values, opinions, or backgrounds. (from the expression "Birds of a feather flock together.") *People who like model trains are birds of a feather.*
- **kill two birds with one stone** to meet two goals with one action. *We killed two birds with one stone by eating lunch at the store where we bought the groceries.*

birth ⊕ ❶ *noun* 1. the act or fact of being born. 2. the act of bearing a child. *My mother has given birth to three boys.* 3. beginning; origin. *The birth of a new company brought more business to the city.* {**buhrth**}

Homophone Note Are you looking for the word **berth**? **Birth** and **berth** sound alike but have different meanings. A **berth** is something found on a ship or train.

birth·day ❷ *noun* the yearly celebration of the day of someone's birth. {**buhrth** day}

birth·mark *noun* a mark or mole on the skin present from birth. {**buhrth** mark}

birth·place *noun* the place of birth or origin of a person, idea, or movement. *Her grandmother's birthplace was a small village in Poland.* / *Greece is the birthplace of democracy.* {**buhrth** plays}

birth·right *noun* a right, privilege, or property to which one is entitled by birth. *Liberty is the birthright of every American.* {**buhrth** riyt}

bis·cuit *noun* (biscuits or biscuit) 1. a small bread made with baking powder or baking soda instead of yeast. 2. the British word for cookie or cracker. {**bihs** kiht}

Word History *Biscuit* comes from *bescuit*, an early French word that means "twice-cooked." In the English spoken in Great Britain, the word *biscuit* means cracker or cookie. Something that is cooked twice is hard and crisp, as crackers are.

A B C D E F G H I J K L M N O P Q R S T U V W X Y Z

a
b
c
d
e
f
g
h
i
j
k
l
m
n
o
p
q
r
s
t
u
v
w
x
y
z

Birds

hummingbird

wood duck

sacred ibis

great blue heron

house finch

kestrel

wild turkey

american goldfinch

bald eagle

bi·sect *verb* (bisected, bisecting, bisects) 1. to cut or split into two equal parts. *We learned how to bisect an angle in math class.* 2. to cut across or intersect. *The bike path bisected the park.* {biy **sehkt**}

bish·op *noun* 1. a clergyman who holds a high position in certain Christian churches. A bishop is often in charge of a group of churches. 2. a piece that can be moved diagonally across squares in the game of chess. {**bihsh** əp}

bi·son *noun* (bison) 1. a very large mammal with a large head, humped shoulders, and short curved horns. Bison used to roam the plains of North America in large herds, but they were hunted until they were almost extinct. North American bison are also called buffalo, but they are not related to the true buffalo of Africa and Asia. Bison have hooves and are closely related to cattle. Bison eat only plants and chew their cud. 2. a similar animal that lives in Europe. Both kinds of bison are closely related. {**biy** sən}

bit[1] *noun* 1. the metal part of a bridle that is placed in the mouth of a horse and used to control it. 2. the part of a drill that is pointed and makes holes. {**biht**}

bit[2] *noun* 1. a small amount; little piece. *The dog chewed the napkin to bits.* 2. a very short time; moment. *John said he would be home in a bit.* {**biht**}

bit[3] *noun* the smallest unit of information in a computer. {**biht**}

 Human Body   Human Mind   Everyday Life   History and Culture  Communication

bit[4] *verb* past tense and a past participle of **bite**. {<u>biht</u>}

bite ⊕ ⊙ *verb* (bit, bitten or bit, biting, bites) 1. to cut or pierce with the teeth. *She bit the apple.* 2. to grip with the teeth or with something like teeth. *The trap bit the fox's leg.* 3. to cause to sting or smart. *The cold wind bites my fingers and nose.* 4. to take or swallow bait. *These fish bite best in the evening.* *noun* 1. the act of biting. *A raccoon's bite can give rabies.* 2. a wound or injury from being bitten. *This mosquito bite stings.* 3. that which is bitten off; a mouthful. *He took a huge bite of pie.* 4. a stinging or smarting feeling. *Meg wore a heavy jacket against the bite of the cold.* 5. a quick meal; snack. *Let's grab a bite before we leave.* {<u>biyt</u>}

> **Homophone Note** Are you looking for the word *byte* (a computer term)? *Bite* and *byte* sound alike but have different meanings.

bit·ten *verb* a past participle of **bite**. {<u>biht</u> ən}

bit·ter *adjective* (bitterer, bitterest) 1. having a sharp, bad taste that is neither sour nor salty. *Some vegetables have a bitter taste.* 2. full of or causing anger, hatred, or sadness. *She cried bitter tears when her dog bit her.* / *They are good friends now but were once bitter enemies.* 3. uncomfortably cold or harsh. *We expect bitter weather in February.* {<u>biht</u> ər} bitterly, adv., bitterness, n.

black *noun* 1. the color of the night sky; the darkest color. 2. (sometimes capitalized) a person whose ancestors came from Africa and who has dark skin, eyes, and hair; African American. *Many American blacks fought for justice during the civil rights movement.* *adjective* (blacker, blackest) 1. having the color black. *This pen writes with black ink.* 2. (often capitalized) relating to people whose ancestors came from Africa and who have dark skin, eyes, and hair; African American. *In 1973, Detroit became the first U.S. city to elect a black mayor.* 3. angry, unhappy, or evil. *The thief sat in his jail cell, thinking black thoughts.* 4. very dark; without light. *It was a black night, with no moon or stars to light the way.* 5. taken without cream or milk. *Jan drinks her coffee black.* {<u>blăk</u>} blackness, n.

• **black out**
to faint or pass out. *Jim blacked out for a few seconds when he was hit in the head with a baseball.*

black bear *noun* 1. a medium-sized bear, usually with thick black or reddish brown fur. They are the most common bears in North America and live in forests and mountain areas. 2. an Asian bear with dark brown fur. {<u>blăk</u> **bayr**}

black·ber·ry *noun* (blackberries) 1. a dark purple or black berry that is made up of many large seeds. 2. the prickly bush that bears this fruit. {<u>blăk</u> **beh** ree}

black·bird *noun* a common songbird, the males of which are black or mostly black. Crows and grackles are blackbirds. {<u>blăk</u> bərd}

black·board ⊙ *noun* a smooth, hard panel for writing on with chalk; chalkboard. Blackboards are often made of slate and have a dark color. {<u>blăk</u> bohrd}

black·en *verb* (blackened, blackening, blackens) 1. to make black; make dark. *This artist blackens the paper before adding other colors.* 2. to harm; soil. *His lies blackened her reputation.* 3. to become black. *The walls blackened from the fire.* {<u>blă</u> kihn} blackener, n.

black eye *noun* bruised skin around the eye, often caused by being hit. {<u>blăk</u> <u>iy</u>}

black hole *noun* a region or body in space with gravity so strong that neither light nor matter can escape it. Scientists believe that black holes form when very large stars collapse. {<u>blăk</u> <u>hohl</u>}

black·mail *noun* 1. money obtained from someone by threatening to give out information that would harm that person. 2. the act of getting such money or of trying to get it. *verb* (blackmailed, blackmailing, blackmails) to obtain or try to obtain blackmail from. *The butler tried to blackmail Mrs. Potter after he found out that she poisoned her husband.* {<u>blăk</u> mayl} blackmailer, n.

black·out *noun* 1. the loss or hiding of all the lights of a city or region. Cities may have blackouts because of power failures. 2. loss of being conscious. *An old head injury causes him to suffer blackouts from time to time.* {<u>blăk</u> owt or blăk <u>owt</u>}

Black Sea *noun* a sea that lies between Europe and Asia. It is surrounded by Russia, Ukraine, Georgia, Turkey, Bulgaria, and Romania. {<u>blăk</u> see}

black·smith *noun* a person who forges and shapes iron. Blacksmiths soften the iron

A
B
C
D
E
F
G
H
I
J
K
L
M
N
O
P
Q
R
S
T
U
V
W
X
Y
Z

a
b
c
d
e
f
g
h
i
j
k
l
m
n
o
p
q
r
s
t
u
v
w
x
y
z

with heat and use hammers and anvils to form it into various items. {blăk smihth}

black·top *noun* a substance such as asphalt, used as pavement. *verb* (blacktopped, blacktopping, blacktops) to pave with blacktop. *The road crew blacktopped this street last week.* {blăk tŏp}

black widow *noun* a small spider of North and South America. The female has a shiny, black body with a red mark on her underside and a poisonous bite. {blăk wih doh}

blad·der 🔵 *noun* an organ inside the body that collects urine. The bladder gets larger when it fills and smaller when it becomes empty. {blăd ər}

blade *noun* 1. the cutting part of a knife, sword, scissors, or saw. 2. the metal runner on an ice skate. 3. a plant leaf. *Blades of grass tickled my bare feet.* 4. a thin, flat part, as of an oar or an electric fan. {blayd} bladed, adj.

blame *verb* (blamed, blaming, blames) 1. to place responsibility on for a mistake or fault. *Ms. Black blamed me for spilling the paint.* 2. to find fault with; criticize sharply. *Don't blame him because he's only a baby.* *noun* responsibility. *I took the blame for the mistake.* {blaym}
• **to blame**
in error or at fault. *No one is to blame for the accident.*

blank *adjective* 1. without marks or writing. *The teacher gave us each a blank sheet of paper.* 2. with spaces left empty to be filled in. *Take a blank test form and begin work.* 3. without expression, interest, or feeling. *His face went blank*

upon hearing the terrible news. *noun* 1. a place or space where something is left out or missing. *Fill in the blanks on this form.* 2. a printed form with spaces to be filled in. *You need to fill out this blank to apply for the job.* 3. a gun cartridge without a bullet. *The actors shoot blanks on TV shows and in the movies.* {blăngk} blankly, adv., blankness, n.
• **draw a blank**
1. to be unable to remember or recognize. *I drew a blank when I saw her and had to ask her name again.* 2. to be unable to produce an idea, solution, or answer. *He drew a blank on question five and failed the test.*

blan·ket 🔵 *noun* 1. a thick piece of material used on a bed for warmth or worn as clothing. 2. a layer of something, such as snow, clouds, or flowers, that covers a thing or area. *A blanket of mist covered the lake.* *verb* (blanketed, blanketing, blankets) to cover with a blanket or layer. *Blanket the garden with leaves for the winter.* {blăng kiht}

blare *verb* (blared, blaring, blares) to sound loudly and harshly. *The car horns blared.* *noun* a loud, harsh noise. *The blare of the police siren sent the thieves running down the street.* {blayr}

blast *noun* 1. a powerful and sudden gust or stream. *A blast of wind shook the trees.* 2. a loud and startling sound. *I woke to the blast of my alarm clock.* 3. an explosion. *Dynamite caused the blast.* *verb* (blasted, blasting, blasts) 1. to make a loud and startling sound with. *The patrol car blasted its siren.* 2. to ruin. *An injury*

blasted his hopes of playing in the big game. 3. to open up with an explosion. *They are blasting a tunnel for the railway.* {blăst} blaster, n.
• **at full blast**
(informal) at maximum speed, volume, or power. *The radio was playing at full blast.*

blast·off *noun* the launching of a spacecraft or missile. *The blastoff of the space shuttle was shown on television.* {blăst awf}

blaze¹ *noun* 1. a bright flame or light. *The blaze of the noon sun hurt my eyes.* 2. a strong outburst of fire or emotion. *Lightning started the blaze in the forest. / I felt a blaze of anger when I saw the bully trip that little boy.* 3. an intense display of color. *Tourists go to New England to see the blaze of autumn leaves.* *verb* (blazed, blazing, blazes) to burn or shine with or as though with fire. *Her eyes blazed with hate.* {blayz}

blaze² *noun* 1. a spot or mark on a tree to show a trail. 2. a white or light mark on the face of a cow or horse. *verb* (blazed, blazing, blazes) to mark or to show by marking. *We blazed a trail.* {blayz}

bleach *verb* (bleached, bleaching, bleaches) 1. to make white or lighter in color by using a chemical or sunlight. *He bleaches his socks*

 Human Body Human Mind Everyday Life History and Culture Communication

to get the stains out of them. 2. to become white or lighter in color. *The maps bleached in the sunlight. noun* a substance used to make something white or lighter in color. *Some people add bleach to their wash water to keep their white sheets looking fresh.* {**bleech**}

bleach·er *noun* (usually plural) a group of benches in rows that are placed one above another. Bleachers are used to seat  people at indoor and outdoor sports events. {**blee** chər}

bleak *adjective* (bleaker, bleakest) 1. bare, cold, or not protected from the weather. *The prairie is bleak in winter.* 2. hopeless; without cheer. *The widow lived in a bleak apartment.* {**bleek**} bleakness, n.

bleat *noun* 1. the sound made by a goat, sheep, or calf. 2. any sound that is similar to the cry of a goat, sheep, or calf. *The sleeping child let out a bleat when her mother picked her up. verb* (bleated, bleating, bleats) 1. to make a bleating sound. 2. to say in the same way as a bleat; whine. *The child bleated his complaints.* {**bleet**}

bleed 🌐 *verb* (bled, bleeding, bleeds) 1. to lose blood. *Matt's finger bled from a paper cut.* 2. to leak sap. *When the maple trees bleed, we can make maple syrup.* 3. to feel grief, sympathy, or sorrow. *My heart bleeds when I think about the loss of her parents.* {**bleed**}

blem·ish *verb* (blemished, blemishing, blemishes) to damage or spoil the perfection of. *You'll blemish the silk if you*

touch it with your dirty hands. *noun* 1. a mark that spoils the perfection of something; flaw. *The blemish on the sofa will come out with soap and water.* 2. a pimple or other flaw on the skin. *I like to think of it as a beauty mark, not a blemish.* {**blehm** ihsh}

blend *verb* (blended or blent, blending, blends) 1. to mix enough so that there no longer seem to be separate parts or ingredients. *We blend flour, eggs, and milk to make cake batter.* 2. to go together well. *This shade of red does not blend with my hair color.* 3. to become mixed together. *The sounds of music and voices blended gently in the summer night. noun* a mixture or combination made by blending. *The chef added a tasty blend of spices to the soup.* {**blehnd**}

bless *verb* (blessed or blest, blessing, blesses) 1. to make holy by religious ritual. *The priest blessed their marriage.* 2. to ask for favor from God. *Bless this gathering.* 3. to give something good to. *She is blessed with musical talent.* {**blehs**}

bless·ing *noun* 1. an act of one who blesses, or the words spoken as part of such an act. 2. a special favor or gift. *Your help during our troubles was a blessing.* 3. favor; approval. *He wanted his parents' blessing before he changed jobs.* {**blehs** ing}

blew *verb* past tense of **blow²**. {**blooh**}

Homophone Note Are you looking for the word *blue* (a color)? *Blew* and *blue* sound alike but have different meanings.

blight *noun* 1. a plant disease that destroys parts or all of a plant. *Potato blight caused a*

great famine in Ireland in the mid-1800s. 2. anything that spoils or destroys. *The gang is a blight on our community. verb* (blighted, blighting, blights) to spoil, ruin, or destroy. *Lack of money blighted his plans for the future.* {**bliyt**}

blimp *noun* an aircraft that holds its shape and flies because it is filled with a gas that is lighter than air; dirigible. {**blihmp**}

blind *adjective* (blinder, blindest) 1. not able to see; having no sight. *A large dog led the blind man across the street.* 2. not willing or able to recognize or understand. *He is blind to the truth about his father.* 3. out of sight; hidden. *A sign warned of the blind driveways on the street. verb* (blinded, blinding, blinds) 1. to cause to lose sight for a short time or permanently. *The car headlights blinded the deer.* 2. to make unable to judge well or think sensibly. *Love blinded him to her faults. noun* (plural) a window shade made of cloth or metal strips. *adverb* (blinder, blindest) without being able to see or understand. *The pilot flew the airplane blind.* {**bliynd**} blindness, n.

blind·fold *verb* (blindfolded, blindfolding, blindfolds) to cover the eyes with a strip of cloth or bandage. *noun* a bandage or cloth tied over the eyes to prevent seeing. {**bliynd fohld**}

blink *verb* (blinked, blinking, blinks) 1. to close and open the eyes very quickly. 2. to flicker; twinkle. *The lights of the airplane blinked across the night sky.* {**blingk**}
• **on the blink** broken; needing repair. *Our*

A
B
C
D
E
F
G
H
I
J
K
L
M
N
O
P
Q
R
S
T
U
V
W
X
Y
Z

refrigerator is on the blink again.

bliss *noun* very great happiness. *The thought of eating all that ice cream filled Ben with bliss.* {<u>blihs</u>} blissful, adj., blissfully, adv.

blis·ter *noun* 1. a swollen area of skin that is filled with liquid. A blister is caused by a burn or other injury. 2. a raised bubble in paint or a similar coating. *verb* (blistered, blistering, blisters) 1. to raise a blister on. *Ali blistered his finger by touching the hot pan.* 2. to break out in a blister. *Her skin blistered from the sunburn.* {<u>blihs</u> tər} blistery, adj.

bliz·zard *noun* a heavy snowstorm that lasts for a long time. {<u>blihz</u> ərd}

bloat *verb* (bloated, bloating, bloats) to make swollen or too full of air, water, or food. *The large meal bloated his stomach.* {<u>bloht</u>}

blob *noun* a soft mass that does not have a fixed or solid shape. *A blob of mustard fell out of the sandwich onto his shirt.* {<u>blŏb</u>}

block ❓ 👕 *noun* 1. a solid piece of hard material, such as wood or concrete, with flat sides. *The mason built a wall out of stone blocks.* 2. a small cube made out of wood or plastic and used as a child's building toy. 3. an area in a city or town surrounded by four connecting streets. The distance of one of the sides is also called a block. *Let's take a walk around the block. / He lives only one block from the store.* 4. the case that holds a pulley. 5. a group of people or things considered as a single unit. *They saved us a block of seats for the basketball game.* 6. something that slows down or obstructs. *The stalled car is a block to traffic.* 7. the use of

the body to stop the movement of another player in football and other sports. *That block of his opponent helped to win the game.* *verb* (blocked, blocking, blocks) 1. to get in the way of movement or stop progress. *The Senator tried to block discussion of the bill.* 2. to close off or obstruct by putting something in the way. *The stalled truck blocked the road.* {<u>blŏk</u>}

block·ade *noun* the shutting off of traffic into and out of a place. Military forces do this to seaports or cities during wars. *verb* (blockaded, blockading, blockades) to shut off with a blockade. {blo <u>kayd</u>}

block·house *noun* 1. a fort or building with openings for weapons to fire through, formerly built of heavy wood boards. 2. a structure used to protect people who are working on or watching a rocket launch or weapons test. {<u>blŏk</u> hows}

blond *adjective* (blonder, blondest) 1. having light yellow hair. 2. having a light yellow color. *Maple is a blond wood.* *noun* a person who is blond. *My brother is the blond over there.* {<u>blŏnd</u>}

blood 🏃 👕 *noun* 1. the red liquid containing oxygen and nutrients that pumps through the veins and arteries of humans and many other animals. 2. family line or ancestors. *Brothers and sisters are related by blood.* {<u>bluhd</u>}

• **in cold blood** with a definite intention to harm. *She shot him in cold blood.*

• **make one's blood boil** to make angry. *His insults made my blood boil.*

• **make one's blood run cold** to make one terrified. A

screeching sound from the old barn made Lydia's blood run cold.

blood bank *noun* a place where blood is collected and stored for later use by people who have lost too much blood. {<u>bluhd</u> băngk}

blood·hound *noun* a breed of dog. Bloodhounds are large dogs with baggy skin and long, drooping ears. They have an excellent sense of smell and are used to track people or animals. {<u>bluhd</u> hownd}

blood·shed *noun* the spilling of blood through injury or violence. *Wars result in much bloodshed.* {<u>bluhd</u> shehd}

blood·shot *adjective* red and irritated because of enlarged blood vessels. *Jane's eyes were bloodshot from staring at the computer screen all afternoon.* {<u>bluhd</u> shŏt}

blood·stream *noun* the blood flowing in a living thing. *Oxygen is brought to different parts of the body through the bloodstream.* {<u>bluhd</u> streem}

blood·thirst·y *adjective* eager to cause or interested in acts of bloodshed; cruel. *The bloodthirsty king sent his troops out to wage war.* {<u>bluhd</u> **th**uhr stee} bloodthirstily, adv., bloodthirstiness, n.

blood vessel *noun* any of the tubes in the body through which the blood moves. Arteries, veins, and capillaries are types of blood vessel. {<u>bluhd</u> veh səl}

blood·y *adjective* (bloodier, bloodiest) 1. covered with or leaking blood. *The nurse changed the bloody bandage.* 2. cruel; vicious. *Roman citizens were lucky to survive the bloody reign of Emperor Caligula.* *verb* (bloodied, bloodying, bloodies) to cover

🏃 Human Body   ❓ Human Mind   👕 Everyday Life   🏳 History and Culture   📞 Communication

or smear with blood. *The child bloodied her jeans when she scraped her knee.* {**bluh** dee} bloodiness, n.

bloom *noun* 1. a flower; blossom. 2. the state or time of being in blossom. *Many flowers are in bloom during the spring.* *verb* (bloomed, blooming, blooms) to produce flowers. *The tulips bloom after the daffodils.* {**bloohm**}

blos·som ❶ *noun* 1. the flower of a plant which forms a seed or fruit. 2. the condition of bearing flowers (usually preceded by "in"). *Cherry trees in blossom provide color in early spring.* *verb* (blossomed, blossoming, blossoms) 1. to produce flowers. *The apple trees blossom before they grow fruit.* 2. to grow in a strong, healthy way. *The child blossomed in the warmth of her family's love.* {**blo** səm} blossomer, n., blossomless, adj.

blot *noun* 1. a spot or stain. *There is a blot of ink on the paper where the pen leaked.* 2. something that spoils or is ugly. *The rotting garbage is a blot on the neighborhood.* *verb* (blotted, blotting, blots) 1. to make a stain or spot upon. *The dripping paintbrush blotted my jeans.* 2. to soak up or dry with something that absorbs liquid. *She blotted her eyes with a tissue.* {**blŏt**} blotty, adj.

blotch *noun* 1. a large stain or blot. *There is a blotch on his shirt where the ketchup spilled.* 2. a flaw on the skin. *Andy woke up with a red blotch on his face.* {**blŏch**}

blot·ter *noun* a piece of paper used to soak up ink or to protect a writing surface. {**blo** tər}

blouse *noun* a piece of clothing worn on the upper body. A blouse is worn with either a skirt or pants. {**blows**}

blow¹ *noun* 1. a quick, hard hit by the fist or by a hard object. *A hammer blow shattered the car's window.* 2. a sudden disappointment or disaster. *Her brother's nasty remark was a blow to her confidence.* {**bloh**}
  • **come to blows**
  to start to fight. *Tom and Jesse came to blows over who could use the computer first.*

blow² *verb* (blew, blown, blowing, blows) 1. to be in swift motion. *The wind blew all night.* 2. to be carried along by the wind. *My cap blew into the water.* 3. to move or force along by means of an air current. *The wind blew the raked leaves into the street.* 4. to force air out of the mouth. *She blew on the baby's fingers to warm them.* 5. to make a sound by forcing air through an instrument. *The whistle blew.* 6. to cause to make a sound by forcing air through. *Blow your horn, and I'll play my drums.* 7. to burst or stop working from being filled or used too much. *My tire blew yesterday. / I hope the lights don't blow during this storm.* {**bloh**}
  • **blow over**
  to let up; lessen or subside. *Let's wait for the storm to blow over.*
  • **blow up**
  1. to destroy or be destroyed through an explosion. *In many action movies, cars blow up all the time.* 2. to fill with air or gas. *Let's blow up the balloons.* 3. (informal) to lose

one's temper. *When he broke his promise to her, she blew up.*

blow·hole *noun* 1. a nostril in the top of the head of a whale, dolphin, or porpoise. The blowhole is used to breathe. 2. a hole in ice that covers a body of water. Whales and other sea mammals come to blowholes to breathe. 3. a vent to let out air or gases. *It is important to have a blowhole in an underground tunnel.* {**bloh** hohl}

blown *adjective* 1. swollen or bloated; inflated. *The blown balloons floated to the ceiling.* 2. made by blowing. *This blown glass vase is over a hundred years old.* *verb* past participle of **blow²**. {**blohn**}

blow·torch *noun* a small device that makes a very hot, small flame for melting or cutting metal. {**bloh** tohrch}

BLT *abbreviation* (BLTs) an abbreviation for bacon, lettuce, and tomato, or the sandwich made with these fillings.

blub·ber *noun* the layer of fat beneath the skin of whales, seals, and other large sea mammals. *verb* (blubbered, blubbering, blubbers) to cry loudly and without control. *Don't blubber like a baby!* {**bluh** bər}

blue *noun* the color of a clear sky; the color between green and violet on the color spectrum. *adjective* (bluer, bluest) 1. having the color blue. *The police officer wore a blue uniform.* 2. sad; unhappy. *He was blue about losing his pet.* {**blooh**}
  • **blue in the face**
  exhausted from too much effort or activity. *The lawyer talked until he was blue in the face.*
  • **out of the blue**
  without warning; suddenly.

A
B
C
D
E
F
G
H
I
J
K
L
M
N
O
P
Q
R
S
T
U
V
W
X
Y
Z

Then, out of the blue, my brother gave me a gift.

• the blue
1. the sky. *The plane took off and disappeared into the blue.* 2. the ocean or sea. *The boat sank to the bottom of the blue.*

Homophone Note The words *blue* and *blew* (past tense of "blow") sound alike but have different meanings.

blue·ber·ry *noun* (blueberries) 1. a small round berry that is blue in color and can be eaten. 2. the bush that produces this berry. {**blooh** beh ree}

blue·bird *noun* a small, blue, North American songbird. Males usually have a reddish breast. {**blooh** buhrd}

blue·fish *noun* (bluefish or bluefishes) a fish that lives in mild Atlantic waters of the North and South American coast. Bluefish are blue and are caught for sport or food. {**blooh** fihsh}

blue·grass *noun* 1. a grass with a blue-green color that is grown in pastures and on lawns. Kentucky is famous for bluegrass. 2. country music of the southern United States played on instruments that have strings, such as the banjo, fiddle, and mandolin. {**blooh** grăs}

blue jay *noun* a common jay bird of eastern North America. A blue jay has a crest on its head and a bright blue upper body with white and black markings on its wings and tail. {**blooh** jay}

blue·print *noun* 1. a print of a drawing that shows a building plan. Blueprints usually have white lines on a blue background. 2. a detailed plan or outline. *Igor's blueprint for the experiment was a success.* {**blooh** prihnt}

blues ❓ 🔵 *noun* 1. (used with a plural verb) a state of sadness. *I've had the blues since my dog died.* 2. (used with a singular or plural verb) a style of sad-sounding music with roots in African American folk music. Jazz and rock music developed from the blues. {**bloohz**}

blue whale *noun* a mammal that lives in the ocean. Blue whales are the largest kind of animal that has ever lived. They can grow up to 100 feet long and weigh up to 150 tons. Their large mouths have baleen instead of teeth. Blue whales use baleen to filter lots of very small food such as shrimp from ocean water. {**blooh** wayl}

bluff[1] *noun* a hill or shore with steep sides. {**bluhf**}

bluff[2] *verb* (bluffed, bluffing, bluffs) 1. to lead other people to believe that the cards in one's hand are better or worse than they really are. Bluffing is a strategy used in the game of poker. 2. to try to fool a person by pretending something is true when it is not. *That kid was bluffing when he said he had climbed Mount Everest.* *noun* an act of bluffing. *Mary said she would jump off the roof, but it was only a bluff.* {**bluhf**}

blun·der *noun* a silly or careless mistake. *It was a blunder to forget my host's name.* *verb* (blundered, blundering, blunders) 1. to act or move in an awkward way or without clear purpose. *We blundered about in the fog.* 2. to make a silly, careless, or stupid mistake. *He blundered at the party by shouting, "This food is terrible!"* {**bluhn** dər}

blunt *adjective* 1. having a dull edge or point; not sharp. *The knife was too blunt to cut the bread.* 2. direct in manner; abrupt and frank. *His blunt questions sometimes make people angry.* *verb* (blunted, blunting, blunts) to make dull. *He blunted the axe by hitting its blade on a stone.* {**bluhnt**} bluntly, adv., bluntness, n.

blur *verb* (blurred, blurring, blurs) 1. to cause to run together or become confused. *Spilled water blurred the ink on the page.* / *This paragraph blurs several different points.* 2. to make dim; dull the senses of. *That cold medicine blurs my vision.* 3. to become less clear or harder to see. *The landscape blurred as we sped past.* *noun* 1. a smudge or unclear mark. *That blur on the page was caused by dirt in the printer.* 2. the state of being blurred. *My mind was in a blur after I woke up from my nap.* {**bluhr**} blurriness, n., blurry, adj.

blurt *verb* (blurted, blurting, blurts) to say suddenly and without thought (usually followed by "out"). *She blurted out the name of the winner.* {**bluhrt**}

blush *verb* (blushed, blushing, blushes) to become red in the face because of shame or embarrassment. *He blushed when the teacher asked him to introduce himself.* *noun* 1. the act of becoming red in the face from shame or embarrassment. *A blush spread over her cheeks when she tripped on*

 Human Body   Human Mind    Everyday Life    History and Culture   Communication

stage. 2. a pink or red color. {bluhsh}

Word History The word *blush* comes from a word in early English that meant "to become red" or "glow." William Shakespeare was the first to use "blush" for a reddening of the face.

blus·ter *verb* (blustered, blustering, blusters) 1. to blow in a strong and noisy way. *The windows shook as the wind blustered outside*. 2. to act in a loud way. *The angry customer blustered about having to wait in line*. *noun* noisy threats that are without meaning. *His bluster didn't scare anyone*. {bluh stər}

Blvd. *abbreviation* an abbreviation for **Boulevard**.

boa constrictor *noun* a large snake that lives in the tropical areas of Central and South America. Boa constrictors are pale brown with darker marks and are not poisonous. They kill their prey by winding around it and squeezing it until it cannot breathe. {boh ə kən strihk tər}

boar *noun* 1. a male pig used for breeding. 2. a wild pig that lives in Europe, Asia, and Africa. Boars that have escaped from farms are now common in the southeastern mountains of the United States. {bohr}

Homophone Note Are you looking for the word *bore*? *Boar* and *bore* sound alike but have different meanings.

board *noun* 1. a flat, cut piece of wood; plank. 2. a flat piece of wood, cardboard, or other stiff material, used for a specific purpose. *John brought out the game board*. 3. a group of people who manage or direct something; committee; council. *The board of education will choose a new principal*. 4. meals served daily, usually for pay. *Now that he is eighteen, he pays his parents for room and board*. *verb* (boarded, boarding, boards) 1. to close or cover using boards (often followed by "up"). *They boarded up the old building to keep out trespassers*. 2. to give daily meals to, usually for pay. *We'll board Miss Jones in our house for a month*. 3. to get into or on. *It's time to board the airplane*. {bohrd}

Homophone Note Are you looking for the word *bored* (feeling tired or restless)? *Board* and *bored* sound alike but have different meanings.

boarding school *noun* a school at which students live as well as take classes. {bohr ding skoohl}

boast *verb* (boasted, boasting, boasts) 1. to talk with too much pride; brag. *She boasts about her musical talent whenever she has a chance*. 2. to be proud to own. *This zoo boasts the largest collection of reptiles in the world*. *noun* an act of boasting. *We were not pleased with her boast of having the best score on the test*. {bohst} boaster, n., boastingly, adv.

boat ● *noun* 1. a small, open vehicle for traveling on water. 2. a ship. *verb* (boated, boating, boats) to travel in a boat. *We boated down the river for more supplies*. {boht}

• **in the same boat** in the same situation, often difficult or dangerous. *Every one in this class is in the same boat*.

boat·house *noun* a small building or shed built near or partly over the water's edge and used to store boats. {boht hows}

bob¹ *verb* (bobbed, bobbing, bobs) to make a quick or jerky movement up and down. *The cork bobbed on the waves*. {bŏb}

bob² *noun* 1. a style of short haircut for women and children. 2. a cork or other floating object used in fishing. *verb* (bobbed, bobbing, bobs) 1. to cut very short. *They bobbed the horse's tail for the show*. 2. to try to take hold of floating or hanging objects with the mouth as part of a game. *We bobbed for apples at the party*. {bŏb}

Becky **bobbed** her hair so that it wouldn't get wet when she **bobbed** for apples with **Bob**.

bob·bin *noun* a spool on which thread or yarn is wound for use in sewing or weaving. {bŏb ihn}

bob·cat *noun* (bobcats or bobcat) a wild cat with red-brown fur, tufted ears, and a short tail. Bobcats are about twice the size of a house cat. They are a kind of lynx and live in southern

A
B
C
D
E
F
G
H
I
J
K
L
M
N
O
P
Q
R
S
T
U
V
W
X
Y
Z

Canada, the United States, and Mexico. Bobcats are carnivorous mammals. {**bŏb** kăt}

bob·o·link *noun* a black, yellow, and white North American songbird that is named for its cry. Bobolinks move from one region to another during certain times of the year. {**bŏb** ə leengk}

bob·sled *noun* a long racing sled with two separate sets of runners, a steering wheel, and brakes. *verb* (bobsledded, bobsledding, bobsleds) to ride or race in a bobsled. {**bŏb** slehd} bobsledder, n.

bob·white *noun* a brown and white North American bird that is named for its call. Bobwhites are a kind of quail. {**bŏb** **wiyt**}

bode[1] *verb* (boded, boding, bodes) to serve as a sign about the future; show ahead of time. *The early frost does not bode well for the fruit crop.* {**bohd**}

bode[2] *verb* a past tense of **bide**. {**bohd**}

bod·i·ly *adjective* of or relating to the human body. *Parents want to keep their children from bodily harm.* {**bŏd** ih lee}

bod·y *noun* (bodies) 1. all the physical material that makes up a person or animal, including limbs, organs, tissue, and other parts. 2. the main part of a person or animal, not including the head, arms, and legs. *A lizard has a long body and short legs.* 3. the main part of anything. *The body of the rocket will remain in orbit.* 4. a group of people or things thought of as a whole. *The student body elected her president.* 5. a separate mass of land, water, or other matter. *The Dead Sea is a large body of water between Israel and Jordan.* {**bŏd** ee}

bod·y·guard *noun* a person whose job is to protect another person or a group of people from harm. {**bŏd** ee gard}

bog *noun* an area of soft, wet earth; marsh. *verb* (bogged, bogging, bogs) to become or cause to be stuck as in a bog (usually followed by "down"). *Studying for exams bogged Anne down for the weekend.* {**bŏg** or **bawg**, n., **bŏg** or **bawg**, v.}

boil[1] 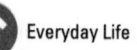 *verb* (boiled, boiling, boils) 1. to change from a liquid to a gas by heating. 2. to heat to boiling. *You must boil the water before pouring it over the tea leaves.* 3. to cook by boiling. *I like to boil eggs for breakfast.* 4. to be very angry. *She boiled at the news that she did not make the team. noun* the state or act of boiling. *When the water reaches a boil, add the noodles.* {**boil**}

• **boil down**
1. to decrease something by boiling. *Maple syrup is made by boiling down sap.* 2. to make into a smaller form. *The whole argument boils down to two points.*

• **boil over**
to boil until the liquid flows out of a container. *Turn off the soup before it boils over!*

boil[2] *noun* a swollen, painful sore that is filled with pus. A boil is an infection caused by bacteria. {**boil**}

boil·er *noun* a tank used to heat and store a supply of water. {**boi** lər}

boiling point *noun* 1. the temperature at which a liquid starts to boil. 2. (informal) the point at which one loses control of one's temper. *After being teased all evening, she reached her boiling point and punched her brother.* {**boi** ling point}

bold *adjective* (bolder, boldest) 1. brave; daring. *The bold man jumped into the river to save the drowning child.* 2. imaginative; creative. *Einstein was one of the boldest thinkers of the twentieth century.* 3. easy to notice; attracting attention. *The artist painted a bold design on the wall.* 4. not polite; rude. *His bold manner cost him his job.* 5. set in heavy type that stands out. *The word **bold** is in bold print.* {**bohld**} boldly, adv., boldness, n.

Bo·liv·i·a *noun* a country in western South America. La Paz is the capital of Bolivia. {bə **lihv** ee ə or boh **lihv** ee ə} Bolivian, n., adj.

boll *noun* the seed pod of plants, such as cotton. {**bohl**}

Homophone Note The words **boll** and **bowl** sound alike but have different meanings.

boll weevil *noun* a small beetle with a gray body and a long snout. It lays eggs in the seed pods of the cotton plant where they hatch and cause much damage to crops. {**bohl** **wee** vəl}

bo·lo·gna or **baloney** or **boloney** *noun* a sausage made of several meats and spices. {bə **loh** nee}

bol·ster *noun* a pillow shaped like a cylinder. *verb* (bolstered, bolstering, bolsters) to give support to. *Her smile bolstered me when I was feeling sad.* {**bohl** stər}

bolt *noun* 1. a metal or wooden bar on a door that slides into an opening in the frame of the door. It keeps the door

 Human Body  Human Mind Everyday Life History and Culture Communication

closed. 2. a metal screw with a flat end rather than a point. A bolt screws into a matching nut. 3. a sudden movement away from or toward something; dash. *There was a bolt for the ticket counter when the airline announced that the flight had been canceled.* 4. a large roll of cloth. 5. a stroke of lightning. *verb* (bolted, bolting, bolts) 1. to close or attach with a bolt or with something like a bolt. *I always bolt the door at night.* 2. to eat or drink in a hurry without chewing or tasting. *The hungry dog bolted the meat.* 3. to make a sudden dash or move to escape. *The horse bolted at the sound of the gun.* {**bohlt**}

• **bolt upright**
in a stiff, highly alert position. *Joe sat bolt upright when he heard the principal call his name.*

Frightened by the saw, the **bolt** **bolted** from the job.

bomb ⊕ *noun* 1. a metal shell filled with explosives. A bomb destroys a target after being thrown at or dropped on it. 2. (informal) a failure. *The play was a such a bomb that it closed after one performance.* *verb* (bombed, bombing, bombs) 1. to attack or destroy with a bomb. *Japan bombed Pearl Harbor on December 7, 1941.*

2. (informal) to fail. *The movie bombed in theaters all over the country.* {**bŏm**}

bom·bard *verb* (bombarded, bombarding, bombards) 1. to attack with bombs, cannon fire, or artillery. *The air force bombarded the city for weeks.* 2. to attack with many questions. *The angry customer bombarded the waiter with complaints.* {bŏm **bard**} bombardment, n.

Bom·bay *noun* the former name of a capital city of a state in India, on the west central coast. Bombay is now called Mumbai. {bŏm **bay**}

bomb·er *noun* 1. a plane used in war to carry and drop bombs. 2. a person who bombs people and places. {**bŏm** ər}

bond 🌐 ⬜ *noun* 1. something that joins, ties, or fastens together. *This glue creates a powerful bond. / She untied the bonds on my ankles, and I was free.* 2. a feeling or shared interest that brings people together. *Friendship is a special bond.* 3. a piece of paper that a government or business gives when it borrows money. A bond promises to repay the sum of money along with interest. {**bŏnd**}

bond·age *noun* the condition of being forced to serve another; slavery. *After many years of bondage, the slaves were freed.* {**bŏn** dəj}

bone 🌐 ❶ *noun* the hard tissue that forms the skeleton of a person or animal. *verb* (boned, boning, bones) to remove the bones from. *The butcher boned the chicken.* {**bohn**}

• **have a bone to pick**
to have reason for an argument or difference of opinion. *I have a bone to pick*

with Mr. Platt about my history grade.

bon·fire *noun* a large fire built outside for celebration or warmth. {**bŏn fiyr**}

Word History In the English spoken in the 1400s, a *bone-fire* was a fire that used bones for fuel rather than wood. This early English word is where our word **bonfire** came from.

bon·go[1] *noun* (bongos or bongo) an African antelope that is reddish brown with white stripes and has spiral-shaped horns. {**bŏng** goh *or* **bawng** goh}

bon·go[2] *noun* (bongos or bongoes) a small drum played with the fingers. Bongos come in connected pairs. {**bŏng** goh *or* **bawng** goh}

bon·net *noun* a cloth hat that is fastened beneath the chin with ribbons. Bonnets were once worn by women but are now worn mainly by babies. {**bŏn** iht}

bo·nus *noun* (bonuses) a payment added to a person's regular pay as a reward for hard work. *The successful company paid all its employees a bonus this year.* {**boh** nəs}

bon·y *adjective* (bonier, boniest) 1. having to do with or looking like bone. 2. full of bones. *The bony fish was difficult to eat.* 3. having bones that can be seen; thin. *The stray cat looked bony.* {**boh** nee} boniness, n.

boo *interjection* 1. a word used to express dislike. *The angry crowd yelled "Boo!" when the referee made a bad call.* 2. a word used to frighten or dis-

A
B
C
D
E
F
G
H
I
J
K
L
M
N
O
P
Q
R
S
T
U
V
W
X
Y
Z

Body Systems

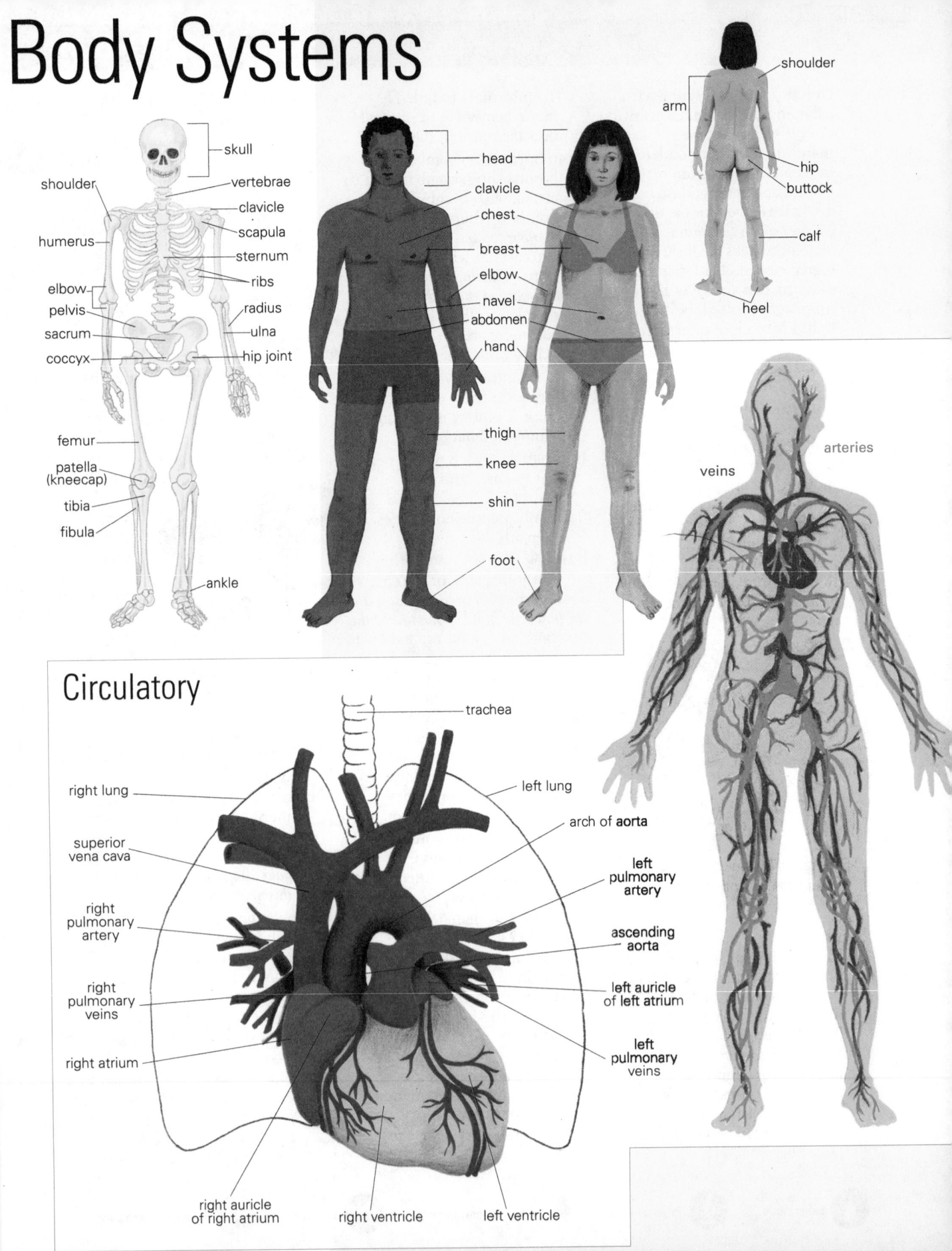

skull

shoulder

vertebrae

clavicle

humerus

scapula

sternum

elbow

ribs

pelvis

radius

sacrum

ulna

coccyx

hip joint

femur

patella
(kneecap)

tibia

fibula

ankle

head

clavicle

chest

breast

elbow

navel

abdomen

hand

thigh

knee

shin

foot

shoulder

arm

hip

buttock

calf

heel

veins

arteries

Circulatory

trachea

right lung

left lung

superior
vena cava

arch of **aorta**

left
pulmonary
artery

right
pulmonary
artery

ascending
aorta

right
pulmonary
veins

left auricle
of left atrium

right atrium

left
pulmonary
veins

right auricle
of right atrium

right ventricle

left ventricle

Digestive

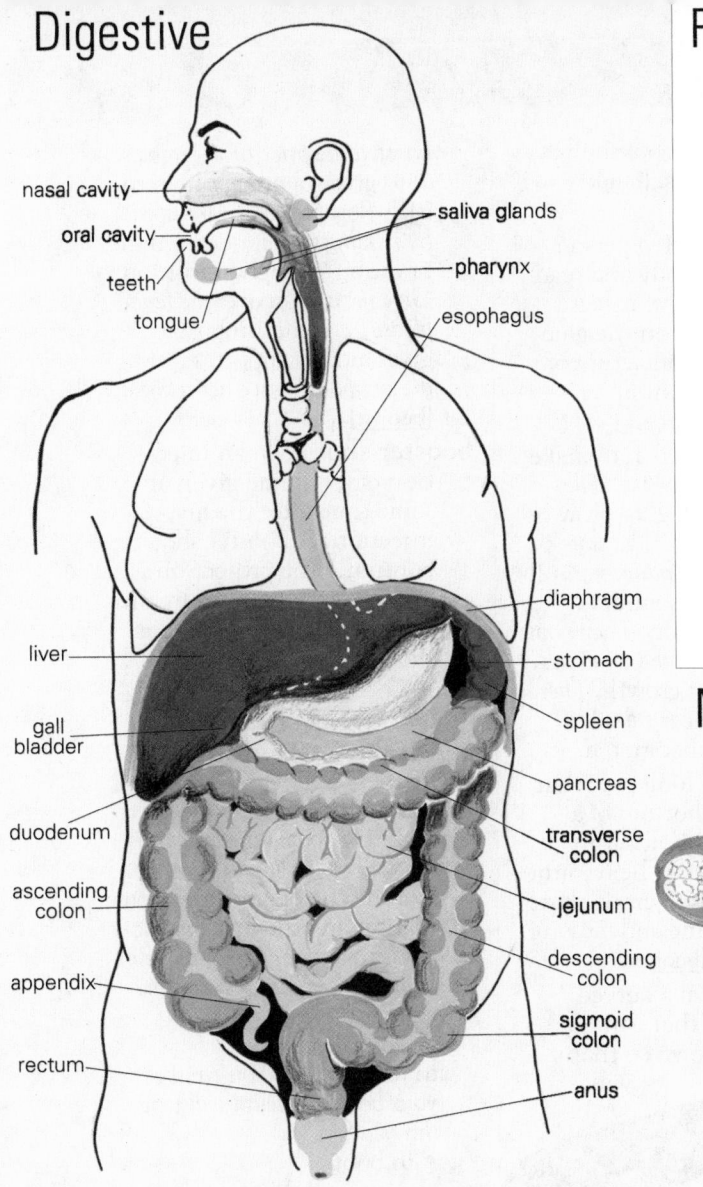

nasal cavity
oral cavity
teeth
tongue
saliva glands
pharynx
esophagus

liver
diaphragm
stomach
spleen
pancreas
gall bladder
duodenum
transverse colon
ascending colon
jejunum
appendix
descending colon
rectum
sigmoid colon
anus

Respiratory

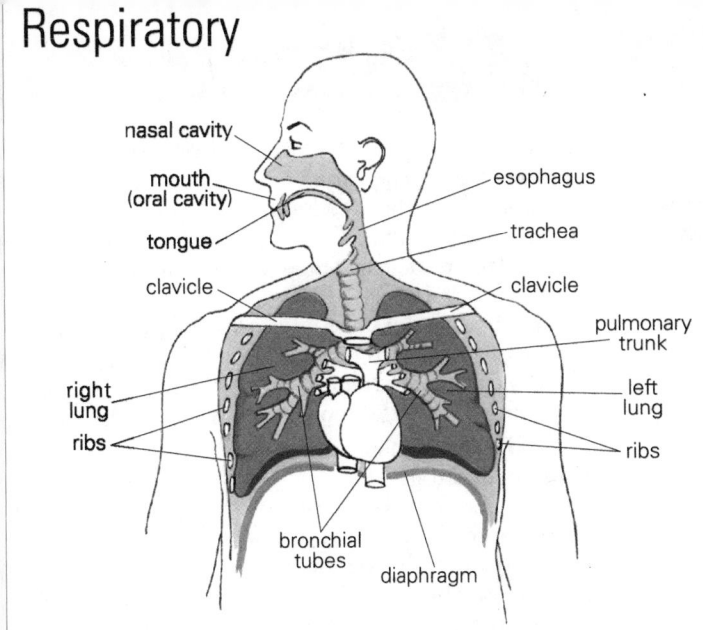

nasal cavity
mouth (oral cavity)
tongue
clavicle
right lung
ribs
esophagus
trachea
clavicle
pulmonary trunk
left lung
ribs
bronchial tubes
diaphragm

Nervous

Urinary

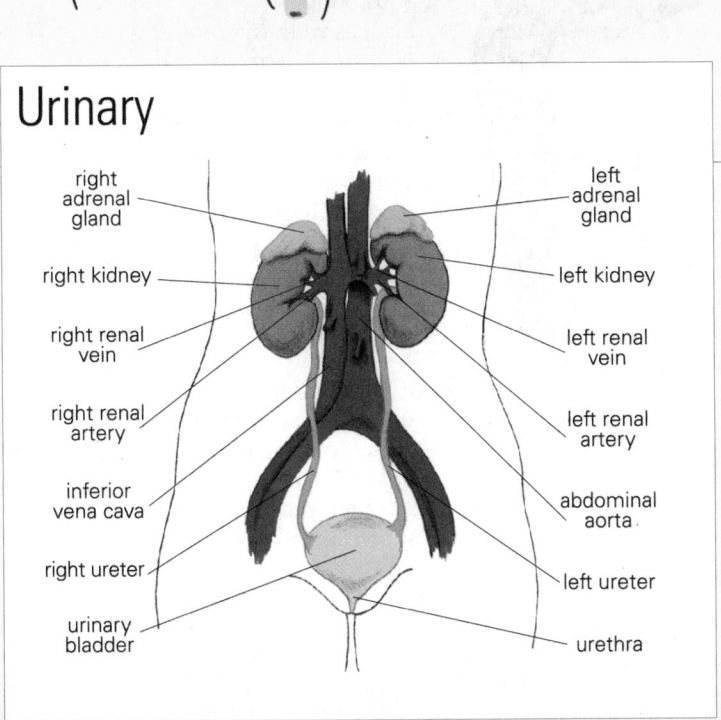

right adrenal gland
right kidney
right renal vein
right renal artery
inferior vena cava
right ureter
urinary bladder
left adrenal gland
left kidney
left renal vein
left renal artery
abdominal aorta
left ureter
urethra

Reproductive

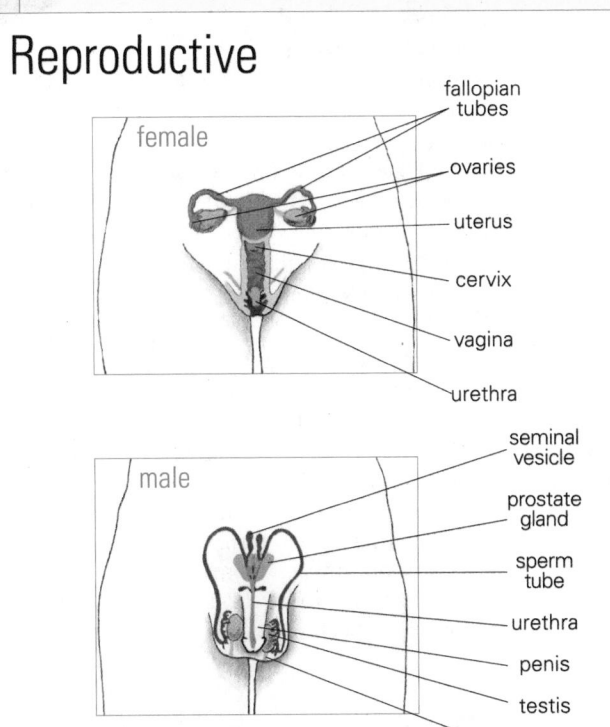

female
fallopian tubes
ovaries
uterus
cervix
vagina
urethra

male
seminal vesicle
prostate gland
sperm tube
urethra
penis
testis
scrotum

turb someone. *I yelled "Boo!" when my friend came around the corner.* noun (boos) a loud expression of dislike. *The crowd's boos made the young actor cry.* verb (booed, booing, boos) to express loud dislike of by shouting "boo." *The crowd booed the clumsy magician off the stage.* {booh}

book noun 1. sheets of paper bound together between two covers. These pages can be blank or can have writing, printing, or pictures on them. 2. a work of literature, such as a novel or a volume of poetry. verb (booked, booking, books) to arrange ahead of time, or to make an appointment for. *I booked a table at your favorite restaurant.* {buuk}
• **by the book** according to the rules; in the correct way. *She likes to do things by the book.*
• **like a book** completely; thoroughly. *She knows me like a book.*

book·case noun a set of shelves for holding books. {buuk kays}

book·kee·per noun the person who keeps the financial records for a business. {buuk kee pər}

book·keep·ing noun the practice of keeping records of the money taken in and paid out by a business. {buuk kee ping}

book·let noun a small book with paper covers; pamphlet. {buuk liht}

book·mark noun a strip of leather, ribbon, or paper placed between pages to mark a place in a book. {buuk mark}

book·mo·bile noun a library located in a bus or van. A bookmobile travels from place to place to lend books. {buuk moh beel}

book·shelf noun (bookshelves) a shelf for books. {buuk shehlf}

book·worm noun 1. a person who loves to study and read books. 2. a kind of insect larva that feeds on the glue used in the manufacture of books. {buuk wuhrm}

boom[1] verb (boomed, booming, booms) 1. to make a deep, hollow noise. *The cannon boomed.* 2. to grow or increase quickly. *The state's population is booming.* noun 1. a deep, hollow sound, as from an explosion. *The boom of thunder shook the windows.* 2. a time of fast growth. *There was a boom in car sales last year.* {boohm} boomer, n.

boom[2] noun 1. a long pole that stretches the bottom of a boat's sail and holds it in place. 2. the long, heavy arm on some kinds of crane that is used for lifting and moving heavy loads. {boohm}

boom·er·ang noun a curved wooden stick that can be thrown so that it will return to the thrower. Boomerangs are used as hunting weapons by Australian aborigines. {booh mə răng}

boon noun something that is a help or benefit. *Moving closer to school was a boon, because she no longer had to take the bus.* {boohn}

boost verb (boosted, boosting, boosts) 1. to raise to a higher position by pushing from below. *He boosted the child up so that she could see over the counter.* 2. to make greater or higher; increase. *The store boosted the price of vegetables.* 3. to give support or help to. *Miss Rogers boosted my spirits by reading to me.* noun 1. a lift or push to a higher position. *Give me a boost over the fence, please.* 2. something that gives aid or support. *Hearing the symphony gave her a boost.* {boohst}

booster shot noun an injection of a vaccine given at some time after the first injection. A booster shot continues the protection against disease begun by the earlier injection. {booh stər shŏt}

boot noun a covering for the foot and all or some of the leg. Boots are usually made of leather or rubber. verb (booted, booting, boots) 1. to kick. *He booted the ball into the goal.* 2. to start up by loading the operating system of or giving the first instructions to a computer. *You must boot the computer every time you use it.* {booht}
• **bet your boots** to feel certain. *You can bet your boots the team will win this year.*
• **to boot** also; as well. *My brother got a bike for his birthday, and hockey skates to boot!*

boo·tee or **bootie** noun a baby's soft sock. *My grandmother knit booties for my baby brother.* {booh tee}

Homophone Note The words ***bootee*** and ***booty*** (riches) sound alike but have different meanings.

booth noun 1. a closed place or stall that has room for one person or a small group. *We'll call her from a telephone booth.* 2. a temporary stall for showing and selling things or

 Human Body
 Human Mind
 Everyday Life
 History and Culture
 Communication

giving out information. {booth}

boo·ty *noun* (booties) 1. riches or goods stolen or taken from people in war; loot 2. any treasure or prize. *What booty did you receive for winning the race?* {booh tee}

Homophone Note The words *booty* and *bootee* sound alike but have different meanings. To find out why bootee does not interest a pirate, see the entry for bootee.

bor·der *noun* 1. edge; boundary. *There is a fence along the border of our yard.* 2. the line between two countries. *Show your passport at the border.* 3. the strip around the edge of something. *A border is used as a decoration on fabric or crafts.* 4. a strip of earth planted with flowers or bushes. *The garden has a border of marigolds.* *verb* (bordered, bordering, borders) to lie on the edge or boundary of. *Canada borders the United States.* {bohr dər}
 • **border on**
 to almost be. *The movie borders on trash.*

bore[1] *verb* (bored, boring, bores) 1. to make a hole in with a tool such as a drill. *He bored the metal so it could be nailed to the wall.* 2. to make by drilling. *She bored three holes in the board.* 3. to make by cutting or digging through. *They bored a tunnel through the mountain.* {bohr}

bore[2] *verb* (bored, boring, bores) to make tired by being dull. *He bores us by telling the same jokes over and over.* *noun* a person or thing that is dull.

The movie about rocks was a real bore. {bohr}

Homophone Note Are you looking for the word *boar* (a kind of pig)? *Bore* and *boar* sound alike but have different meanings.

bore[3] *verb* past tense of bear[1]. {bohr}

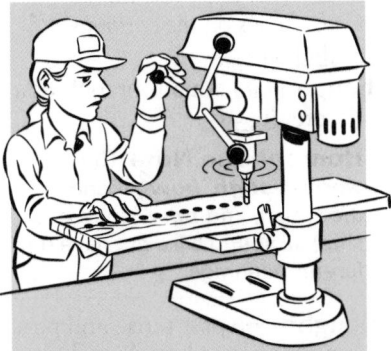

Boring the one thousandth hole of the day can be a real **bore**!

bored *adjective* feeling tired or restless because of having to do something that is not interesting. *I'm always so bored when my brother starts telling his long stories.* {bohrd}

bore·dom *noun* the state of being bored or of not feeling interested. *Boredom with the movie on TV made me want to go outside and play.* {bohr dəm}

born *adjective* 1. brought into life by birth. *This baby, born in Paris, is a French citizen.* 2. since birth; from natural talent rather than practice or education. *She is a born leader.* {bohrn}
 • **born yesterday**
 without experience and easily tricked. *The salesman tried to charge me too much, but I told him I wasn't born yesterday.*

Homophone Note The words *born* and *borne* sound alike but have different meanings.

borne *verb* a past participle of bear[1]. {bohrn}

Homophone Note The words *borne* and *born* sound alike but have different meanings.

bor·ough *noun* 1. a town that governs itself. 2. one of the five divisions of New York City: Manhattan, Brooklyn, Richmond (Staten Island), Queens, and the Bronx. {buur oh}

Homophone Note The words *borough*, *burro* and *burrow* sound alike, but each has a different meaning.

bor·row ⊛ *verb* (borrowed, borrowing, borrows) 1. to take with the promise to return or replace. *May I borrow your book for a few days?* 2. to take and use as one's own. *She borrowed her older sister's style of dressing.* {bar oh *or* baw roh} borrower, n.

Bosnia and Herzegovina *noun* a country in southeastern Europe. Sarajevo is the capital of Bosnia and Herzegovina. Bosnia and Herzegovina used to be part of Yugoslavia. {bŏz nee ə ənd hehrts ə goh vee nə} Bosnian, adj., n.

bos·om *noun* the breasts or chest of a human. *My mom held me close to her bosom while I cried.* *adjective* very close; intimate. *My friend and I are bosom buddies.* {buuz əm}

boss *noun* a person who gives directions to workers and watches over their work. *verb* (bossed, bossing, bosses) to act like the boss of; order or tell what to do. *Lisa bosses her brother around.* {baws}

boss·y *adjective* (bossier, bossiest) (informal) tending to tell others what to do. *My friend can be very bossy when*

a
b
c
d
e
f
g
h
i
j
k
l
m
n
o
p
q
r
s
t
u
v
w
x
y
z

something needs to get done. {**baw** see} bossily, adv., bossiness, n.

bot·a·ny ❶ noun (botanies) the science that studies plants. Botany is a branch of biology. {**bŏt** ə nee}

both adjective the two together; one and the other. Both students got high grades. pronoun the one in addition to the other. Bill couldn't decide between vanilla and chocolate ice cream, so he got both. conjunction used with "and" to show that two things are being included. Both girls and boys can play basketball. {**bohth**}

both·er verb (bothered, bothering, bothers) 1. to annoy or give trouble to. The loud noise is bothering us. 2. to make puzzled or worried. It bothers me that he looks so unhappy. 3. to make an effort; take the trouble. Tanya never bothers to clean her room. noun a person or thing that annoys or causes trouble. It is a bother to make dinner every day. {**bo** thər}

Bot·swa·na noun a country in central, southern Africa. Gaborone is the capital of Botswana. {**bŏt swah** nə} Botswanan, n.

bot·tle noun 1. a container with a narrow neck and no handle used to hold or pour liquids. A bottle is usually made of glass or plastic. 2. the amount such a container will hold. Doug drank a bottle of juice. verb (bottled, bottling, bottles) to put or seal in a bottle. This factory bottles soda. {**bŏt** əl} bottler, n.
• **bottle up**
to control or hold in; not express. He bottled up his anger.

bot·tom noun 1. the lowest or deepest part of something.

There are crumbs in the bottom of my backpack. 2. the area under; underside. The bottoms of your shoes are dirty. 3. the cause or most important part. Let's get to the bottom of the problem. 4. the solid part under a body of water. The boat sank to the bottom of the lake. adjective of or having to do with the bottom. She put the books on the bottom shelf. {**bŏt** əm}

bough noun a main branch of a tree. {**bow**}

Homophone Note The words **bough**, **bow**[1] (bend at the waist), and **bow**[3] (part of a ship) all sound alike but have different meanings.

bought verb past tense and past participle of **buy**. {**bawt**}

boul·der noun a large, rounded rock. {**bohl** dər}

boul·e·vard noun a wide city street, often with trees planted along its sides. {**buul** ih **vard**}

bounce verb (bounced, bouncing, bounces) 1. to spring back or up after hitting something, or to do so several times in a row. The ball bounced down the stairs. 2. to walk with a spring in one's step. The child bounced along the sidewalk. 3. to cause to hit against something and spring back. He bounced the tennis ball against the wall. noun a sudden spring or jump. With one bounce, the kangaroo was over the fence. {**bowns**} bounceable, adj.
• **bounce back**
to return to a normal condition quickly or completely. She has bounced back from her illness and is ready to work again.

-bound suffix 1. a suffix that means "going toward," or "planning to go to." On the

highway, the northbound lane is for traffic going north, and the southbound lane is for traffic going south. 2. a suffix that means "held back by" or "kept in." If people are housebound because of illness, it means that the illness is keeping them in. {**bownd**}

bound[1] adjective 1. held by ties or fastened by bands; tied. The prisoner was bound by his hands and feet. 2. having a cover or binding. Our library is filled with bound books of many shapes and sizes. 3. held to by law or duty. He is bound by his promise. 4. certain; sure. She is bound to be angry after what you did. {**bownd**}

bound[2] verb (bounded, bounding, bounds) to leap; spring. The deer bounded across the field. noun a leap. The cat jumped onto the table with a single bound. {**bownd**}

bound[3] noun 1. a line not to be crossed; limit; restriction. The princess crossed the bound into the Forbidden Forest. / That joke went beyond the bounds of good taste. 2. (usually plural) the area within or near a boundary or limit of something; border. We had to stay inside the bounds of the park. verb (bounded, bounding, bounds) to set the border of; limit. That fence bounds our yard. {**bownd**}
• **out of bounds**
beyond a boundary or a set limit. The ball went out of bounds four times during that period.

bound[4] adjective on the way to; headed (usually followed by "for"). We are bound for home after a hard day at school. {**bownd**}

bound·a·ry noun (boundaries) something that marks the edge or limit. The fence is the boundary of our neighbor's

 Human Body   Human Mind   Everyday Life  History and Culture Communication

property. {**bown** də ree *or* **bown** dree}

boun·ti·ful *adjective* 1. willing to give plenty; generous. *Her parents are in a bountiful mood during the holiday season.* 2. as much or more than is needed; abundant. *There was a bountiful supply of vegetables in the garden this summer.* {**bown** tih fəl} bountifully, adv., bountifulness, n.

boun·ty *noun* (bounties) 1. the quality of being willing to give plenty; generosity. *We are grateful for the bounty of nature.* 2. a reward or payment for catching outlaws or killing certain kinds of wild animals. *I've come to collect my bounty, Sheriff Tate.* {**bown** tee}

bou·quet *noun* a bunch of flowers. {booh **kay**}

bout *noun* 1. a match or fight between two people in wrestling or boxing. 2. a period or attack of sickness. *A bout of the flu kept her in bed for a week.* {**bowt**}

bow[1] *verb* (bowed, bowing, bows) 1. to bend the head or upper body forward in order to greet or take notice of someone. 2. to give up to or submit. *They finally bowed to the pressure from their friends.* *noun* the act of bending the head or upper body forward to greet or take notice of someone. *He made a deep bow when he finished his performance.* {**bow**}

• **bow and scrape**
to behave with too much politeness. *The king was pleased when his subjects bowed and scraped before him.*
• **bow out**
to stop taking part in an activity; leave or resign. *One candidate bowed out of the race for mayor.*
• **take a bow**

to come forward or stand up to receive applause, recognition, or praise. *The audience cheered as the ballerina took a bow.*

Frank **bows** over the edge of the dock to get a better look at the ship's **bow.**

bow[2] *noun* 1. a weapon used for shooting arrows. A bow is made of a curved strip of wood or other material with a cord stretched tight between the two ends. 2. a long, thin, straight piece of wood with hairs from horses stretched between the ends. It is used for playing the violin and other stringed instruments. 3. a knot that is easy to loosen. Bows have two or more loops and are used to tie shoes and wrap gifts. *verb* (bowed, bowing, bows) to play with a bow. *He bowed his fiddle with great energy.* {**boh**} bowedness, n.

bow[3] *noun* the front part of a ship or boat. {**bow**}

Homophone Note Are you looking for the word ***bough***? ***Bow***[1], ***bow***[3], and ***bough*** sound alike, but have different meanings.

bow·el *noun* (usually plural) the long tube below the stomach that forms part of the diges-

tive system; intestine. {**bow** əl *or* **bowl**}

Word History ***Bowel*** is from a Latin word that means "sausage." Look up the definition for ***sausage*** to find out why.

bowl[1] *noun* 1. a deep, rounded dish used for holding food or liquid. 2. the amount a bowl holds. *Perry ate a bowl of cereal.* 3. a rounded part of something. *You can scrub the sink bowl; I'll scrub the toilet bowl.* 4. a round stadium or outdoor theater. *The concert was held at the bowl.* 5. a football game played at the end of the season by winning teams. *The National Football League's championship game is called the Super Bowl.* {**bohl**}

At the Silly Things **Bowl**, Martin **bowls** a strike with a ceramic **bowl.**

bowl[2] *verb* (bowled, bowling, bowls) 1. to play the game of bowling. 2. to roll the ball in bowling, or pitch the ball in the sport of cricket. {**bohl**}
• **bowl over**
to overwhelm with surprise; astonish. *She was bowled over by his praise.*

Homophone Note Are you looking for the word ***boll*** (a seed pod)? ***Bowl*** and ***boll*** sound alike but have different meanings.

A
B
C
D
E
F
G
H
I
J
K
L
M
N
O
P
Q
R
S
T
U
V
W
X
Y
Z

bow·leg·ged *adjective* having legs that curve outward around or below the knees. {**boh** lehg gayd}

bowl·ing *noun* a game in which a heavy ball is rolled along a wooden alley toward wooden pins that stand at the far end. {**boh** ling}

box[1] *noun* 1. a container made of stiff material that usually has four rectangular sides, a bottom, and a lid. 2. the amount held in a box. *That dog ate the whole box of chocolates.* 3. the section of a courtroom where the jury sits. *The twelve jurors took their seats in the jury box.* 4. a section of a theater in which a small group of people sit to watch the show. *We sat in a box at the opera house.* *verb* (boxed, boxing, boxes) to place or pack in a box. *I'll box the gifts for mailing.* {**bŏks**}

box[2] *noun* a hit or blow struck with the hand or fist. *The fighter knocked him out with a box to the jaw.* *verb* (boxed, boxing, boxes) 1. to hit with a hand or fist. *The cruel master boxed the serving girl's ears.* 2. to fight as a sport or as a way of earning a living. *Kyle boxes at the community center.* {**bŏks**}

box·car *noun* a railroad car that is enclosed on all sides. It is used for carrying freight. {**bŏks kar**}

box·er *noun* 1. a person who fights with the fists as a sport or as a career. 2. a breed of dog. Boxers have short hair, a square jaw, and a brown coat. {**bŏk** sər}

box·ing *noun* the sport or style of fighting with the fists. {**bŏk** sing}

Box·ing Day *noun* a holiday in England, Canada, and some other countries, celebrated on the first weekday after Christmas. {**bŏk** sing day}

boy *noun* a male child or teenager. *interjection* used to express surprise. *Boy, that is hard to believe!* {**boi**}

Homophone Note Are you looking for the word **buoy** (a float)? **Boy** and **buoy** sound alike but they have different meanings. **Buoy** can be pronounced with or without the long u sound.

boy·cott *verb* (boycotted, boycotting, boycotts) to refuse to buy, use, or go to, in order to make a protest or bring about a change. *Customers are boycotting the supermarket to protest high meat prices.* *noun* the act of boycotting. *The Montgomery bus boycott began in 1955.* {**boi** kŏt} boy·cotter, n.

boy·friend *noun* (informal) a favorite male friend or companion. *Juliet was sad when her boyfriend had to leave town.* {**boi** frehnd}

boy·hood *noun* the state or period of life when one is a boy. *Josh lived on a farm during his boyhood.* {**boi** huud}

boy·ish *adjective* having to do with or like a boy. *His boyish face makes him look younger than he really is.* {**boi** ihsh} boyishly, adv., boyishness, n.

Boy Scout *noun* a member of a worldwide youth organization for boys called the Boy Scouts. {**boi** skowt}

Boy Scouts of A·mer·i·ca *noun* an American organization for boys, which teaches them outdoor skills, good citizenship, and physical fitness. {**boi** skowts uhv ə **mehr** ih kə}

Br symbol of the chemical element bromine.

brace *noun* 1. something that holds things in position. *The carpenter uses a brace to hold pieces of wood in place while he works.* 2. something that steadies or gives support to. *Julie wore a knee brace after her injury.* 3. (often plural) metal wires and bands attached to the teeth to straighten them and bring them into proper position. 4. a tool used for holding and turning bits that bore holes in wood. 5. a pair. *We spotted a brace of pheasants in the meadow this morning.* *verb* (braced, bracing, braces) 1. to support, hold steady, or provide strength with or as if with a brace. *Brace this chair against the door to keep it closed.* 2. to prepare and steady for a shock, disappointment, or force. *Brace yourself for some bad news.* 3. to give energy to. *The chill autumn air braced him.* {**brays**}

brace·let *noun* a band or chain worn around the wrist or arm as an ornament. {**brays** liht}

brack·et *noun* 1. a support shaped liked an L that is attached to a wall or other upright surface. *We'll need two brackets to hold up this shelf.* 2. one of a pair of punctuation marks ([ ]). They are used to enclose words or numbers. 3. a group of people who share something in common. *He is in the 18- to 25-year-old age bracket.* *verb* (bracketed, bracketing, brackets) 1. to enclose or set apart with brackets. *In math, bracket the part of the equation that you work with first.* 2. to group together. *That school brackets children according to their skills.* {**brăk** iht}

brad *noun* a thin nail with a small head. {**brăd**}

 Human Body Human Mind  Everyday Life  History and Culture  Communication

brag *verb* (bragged, bragging, brags) to speak with too much pride about oneself, or about anything or anyone that one knows; boast. *He bragged for two weeks about hitting the winning run for his team.* {brăg} bragger, n., braggingly, adv.

braid *verb* (braided, braiding, braids) 1. to weave together three or more pieces of material or strands of hair to form one length that looks like a rope. 2. to make by braiding. *Mrs. Cole braided a rag rug.* *noun* a narrow length of hair or material made by braiding. *The admiral's uniform is decorated with gold braid.* {brayd} braider, n.

Braille *noun* (often lowercase) a writing and printing system for blind people, in which patterns of raised dots are used to represent letters. Blind people touch the dots with their fingers to read. {brayl}

Word History In 1829, Louis *Braille*, who was blind, invented a system of letters that could be read by the sense of touch.

brain 🌳❓ *noun* 1. the organ inside the skull of humans and animals. The brain is the main part of the central nervous system. It controls the body's movements and activities, and is the center of thought, memory, and feelings. 2. (usually plural) intelligence. *He was the brains of the group.* {brayn}

brain·storm *noun* a bright idea or sudden inspiration.

Your brainstorm will help us solve the mystery. *verb* (brainstormed, brainstorming, brainstorms) to find ways of solving problems by having members of a group talk freely about their ideas. {brayn stohrm}

brake 🔵 *noun* a device used to slow or stop the motion of a vehicle or machine. *verb* (braked, braking, brakes) to cause to slow down or stop by using a brake. *I braked my bicycle when I saw the stop sign.* {brayk}

Homophone Note Are you looking for the word *break*? *Brake* and *break* sound alike but have different meanings.

bram·ble *noun* a kind of berry bush with thorns on its stems. Raspberry and blackberry plants are brambles. {brăm bəl}

bran *noun* the outer layer of wheat and other cereal grains. Bran is left after the grain is ground and the flour or meal is sifted out. {brăn}

branch 🔵 *noun* 1. a woody part of a tree or bush that grows out from the trunk; limb. 2. a part or division of the main part of something. *We chose a savings bank that has a branch near our house. / Geometry is an ancient branch of mathematics.* 3. a stream or creek. *This stream is a branch of the Mississippi river.* *verb* (branched, branching, branches) to separate into two or more paths, roads, or directions. *Green Street branches at the third traffic light.* {brănch}

cingulate gyrus
involved in survival behavior

parietal lobe
perceives touch, pressure, pain and temperature

cerebrum

frontal lobe

hippocampus
memory storage

occipital lobe
detects and interprets visual images

hypothalmus
control of automatic body process

cerebellum
plays role in precise movement, balance, posture and speech

pituitary gland

temporal lobe
recognition of tones, loudness; memory storage

brain stem

thalmus

• **branch out** to try new activities, interests, or pursuits. *This artist branched out into photography.*

brand *noun* 1. a kind of product made by one particular company. *Which brand of peanut butter do you prefer?* 2. a burn mark made on cattle or other animals with a hot iron to show who the owner is. *verb* (branded, branding, brands) 1. to mark with a hot iron. *The ranchers branded their cattle.* 2. to mark with disgrace or shame. *His classmates branded him a liar.* {brănd}

brand-new *adjective* 1. having never been used before; completely new. *We drove our brand-new car home from the car dealer.* 2. having come into being a very short time ago, or having just been bought. *The Hoopers brought their brand-new baby home from the hospital.* {brănd nooh}

bran·dy *noun* (brandies) a strong alcoholic drink that is made with fermented fruit juice or wine. {brăn dee}

brass 🔵 *noun* 1. a yellow metal made from melting copper and zinc together. 2. (often plural) a wind instrument made of brass. *The brass played well, but the strings were off-key.* {brăs}

brat *noun* a child who is spoiled or does not behave. {brăt} brattish, adj., bratty, adj.

brave ❓ *adjective* (braver, bravest) ready to face pain or danger; courageous. *The brave pilot flew alone through the storm.* *noun* a Native American warrior. *Many braves were killed by the early settlers.* *verb* (braved, braving, braves) to face or bear with courage. *The ship's crew braved the rough seas.*

A
B
C
D
E
F
G
H
I
J
K
L
M
N
O
P
Q
R
S
T
U
V
W
X
Y
Z

{**brayv**} bravely, adv., brave-ness, n.

Synonyms
These words share a meaning with **brave**, adjective 1:
game, bold, courageous, fearless

brav·er·y noun (braveries) the condition of being brave or of not feeling fear; courage. *Firefighters often show great bravery.* {**bray** və ree or **brayv** ree}

bra·vo interjection "good!"; "well done!" *The audience shouted "Bravo" when the tenor finished singing.* {**brah** voh}

bray noun the loud harsh sound that a donkey makes. verb (brayed, braying, brays) to make the sound of a donkey. {**bray**}

Bra·zil noun a country in eastern South America. Brasilia is the capital of Brazil. {brə **zihl**} Brazilian, adj., n.

breach noun 1. an act of breaking a law or promise. *It is a breach of trust to tell a lie.* 2. an opening or gap made by breaking through something. *The soldiers passed through the breach in the wall of the fort.* verb (breached, breaching, breaches) 1. to make an opening or breach in; break through. *The water breached the dam and flooded the town.* 2. to break or violate. *He breached the agreement he had made with his lawyer.* {**breech**}

bread noun 1. a food made by baking a dough of flour or meal. 2. the things a person needs to live. *She got a job to earn her*

bread. {**brehd**}

Homophone Note Are you looking for the word **bred** (past tense of "breed")? **Bread** and **bred** sound alike but have different meanings.

breadth noun the distance measured from one side to the other side of something; width. {**brehdth**}

bread·win·ner noun a member of a family or household who earns money to support the other members. {**brehd** wih nər}

break ⊕ verb (broke, broken, breaking, breaks) 1. to cause to come apart into pieces; smash. *She broke the nutshell with a hammer.* 2. to damage or make no longer usable. *She fell and broke her arm. / We have no music because you broke the radio.* 3. to tame or overcome the strength of by using force. *It took him two weeks to break the wild horse.* 4. to bring an end to; interrupt. *Brenda broke her smoking habit. / One brave student broke the silence.* 5. to make known. *Who will break the bad news to her?* 6. to fail to obey or be faithful to. *They broke the law. / He never breaks a promise.* 7. to soften the effect of. *The bushes broke his fall.* 8. to go beyond. *She may break the world record.* 9. to come apart into pieces; shatter. *His favorite cup broke into pieces.* 10. to become ruined or no longer usable. *My watch broke.* 11. to burst or collapse. *Water pipes can break when the temperature drops below freezing.* 12. to stop or disappear suddenly. *The fever has finally broken.* 13. to become known to the public. *The story broke, and he is now a celebrity.*

14. to move away suddenly and rapidly. *Seeing the rabbit, the dog broke from its owner.* noun 1. the act or result of breaking or coming apart into pieces. *The break in her leg healed in three weeks.* 2. a sudden, fast movement away; escape. *The robber made a break for the rear of the bank.* 3. a period of time when something stops; interruption. *We took a break from our work to eat dinner.* 4. a lucky chance; opportunity. *Getting a part in the film was a big break for her.* 5. a sudden change. *We hoped for a break in the hot, humid weather.* {**brayk**} breakable, adj.

• **break down**
1. to stop or stop working. *My computer broke down.* 2. to separate into smaller parts *He broke the job down into many steps.*

• **break in**
1. to enter by force and illegally. *Someone broke into the car and stole the radio.* 2. to train, or to prepare for use. *You should break in your new boots before the long hike.*

Homophone Note Are you looking for the word **brake** (a stopping device)? **Break** and **brake** sound alike but have different meanings.

break·down noun 1. a failure to work or run correctly. *The breakdown of the bus caused all the children to be late to school.* 2. a collapse or failure of a person's mind or body. *The singer had a breakdown halfway through his world tour.* {**brayk** down}

break·er noun a heavy ocean wave that breaks into foam on the shore or at sea. {**bray** kər}

break·fast noun the first meal of the day, eaten in the

 Human Body Human Mind Everyday Life  History and Culture 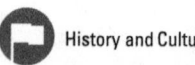 Communication

morning. *verb* (breakfasted, breakfasting, breakfasts) to eat breakfast. *We breakfast at nine on Sundays.* {<u>brehk</u> fəst}

Word History The English word ***breakfast*** is made of two words, "break" and "fast." A "fast" is a time when one goes without food. At breakfast, one breaks or ends a period of going without food. The word ***breakfast*** was first used in the 1400s.

breast 🌐 *noun* 1. the front part of the body between the neck and the stomach; chest. 2. either of the two glands on the human chest, usually bigger on women than on men. Babies get milk from female breasts. {<u>brehst</u>}

breast·bone *noun* the flat bone located in the center of the chest. A person's ribs on both sides of the chest are joined to the breastbone. {<u>brehst</u> bohn}

breath *noun* 1. the air that flows into and out of the lungs during breathing. 2. the act of taking in and letting out air. *Take a deep breath before you dive under.* 3. a slight movement of the air. *There isn't a breath of wind.* {<u>brehth</u>}
  • **hold one's breath** to wait with hope and expectation. *Don't hold your breath; he may never call.*
  • **take one's breath away** to fill suddenly with great surprise; startle. *The sight of wild horses took my breath away.*

breathe 🌐 *verb* (breathed, breathing, breathes) 1. to draw air into the lungs and let it out. *People breathe faster when they run.* 2. to whisper. *Don't breathe a word of this to anyone.* {<u>breeth</u>} breathable, adj.

breath·less *adjective* 1. breathing hard following a

lot of exercise or physical effort. *He was breathless after the race.* 2. holding one's breath for a moment because of excitement, amazement, or fear. *The scary movie left us breathless.* {<u>brehth</u> lihs} breathlessly, adv.

bred *verb* past tense and past participle of **breed**. {<u>brehd</u>}

Homophone Note Are you looking for the word ***bread*** (a kind of food)? ***Bred*** and ***bread*** sound alike but have different meanings.

breech·es *noun* (used with a plural verb) pants that reach to or just below the knee. {<u>brih</u> chihz}

breed ➊ *verb* (bred, breeding, breeds) 1. to keep for mating and reproduction. *My family breeds collies.* 2. to give birth to or produce offspring. *Birds usually breed in their nests.* 3. to cause; give rise to. *Anger breeds violence.* *noun* a particular type or kind of animal or plant. *My favorite breed of dog is the golden retriever.* {<u>breed</u>}

breed·ing *noun* 1. the act or process of producing offspring. 2. the way one is raised or trained. *Her good manners were a mark of excellent breeding.* {<u>bree</u> ding}

breeze 🌐 *noun* 1. a light or gentle wind. 2. (informal) a simple or quickly finished task. *Her math homework was a breeze.* *verb* (breezed, breezing, breezes) (informal) to progress or finish something quickly or with little effort. *She breezed down the hallway.* / *He breezed through the test.* {<u>breez</u>}

breve *noun* a mark (˘). A breve is placed over a vowel to indicate that the vowel is short. {<u>breev</u> or <u>brehv</u>}

brew *verb* (brewed, brewing, brews) 1. to make by soaking in boiling water. *He brewed a pot of coffee.* 2. to develop or plan (sometimes followed by "up"). *They brewed up a clever scheme.* 3. to begin to form or develop. *The teacher sensed that mischief was brewing in the back of the classroom.* / *A storm is brewing on the horizon.* *noun* a drink made by brewing. *Don't drink the witch's brew!* {<u>brooh</u>}

bri·ar *noun* a pipe made from the root of a brier. {<u>briy</u> ər}

bribe *noun* something promised or given to a person as a way of getting that person to do a certain thing. *If the babysitter offers you five dollars for not telling your parents that she left you alone for an hour, the babysitter is offering you a bribe.* *verb* (bribed, bribing, bribes) to give or offer a bribe to. *She bribed me with candy so that I would walk to the store with her.* {<u>briyb</u>} bribable (bribeable), adj., briber, n.

brick *noun* 1. a hard block of dried or baked clay used as a building material. 2. many of these blocks used for building. *All the houses on this street are made of brick.* {<u>brihk</u>}

bride *noun* a woman who is about to be married or was just married. {<u>briyd</u>}

bride·groom *noun* a man who is about to be married or was just married. {<u>briyd</u> groohm}

bridge *noun* 1. a structure built over a river, railroad, or other obstacle, that allows people to travel across. 2. the bony upper part of the human nose. 3. a high platform on a ship. The

 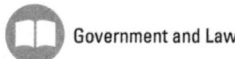
A B C D E F G H I J K L M N O P Q R S T U V W X Y Z

a
b
c
d
e
f
g
h
i
j
k
l
m
n
o
p
q
r
s
t
u
v
w
x
y
z

captain guides or controls the ship from the bridge. *verb* (bridged, bridging, bridges) to connect the two sides of; build a bridge over. *We bridged the stream with a log.* {**brihj**}

bri·dle *noun* the part of a horse harness that fits the head and is used to guide or control. *verb* (bridled, bridling, bridles) 1. to fit a bridle onto. *You must bridle the horse before you can ride her.* 2. to control or put limits on. *We couldn't bridle our excitement.* {**briy** dəl}

brief *adjective* (briefer, briefest) 1. short in length of time. *We had a brief conversation because he was in a hurry.* 2. using the smallest number of words needed. *Please be brief and get to the point.* 3. short or small in length. *She wore a brief skirt to the dance. noun* (plural) short, tight underpants with no legs. *verb* (briefed, briefing, briefs) to share or tell by means of a short explanation. *I will brief you on what happened in the meeting this morning.* {**breef**} briefly, adv., briefness, n.

bri·er[1] or **briar** *noun* 1. a kind of thorny plant or bush. 2. a thorny branch or stem. {**briy** ər}

bri·er[2] or **briar** *noun* a shrub of southern Europe. The brier's woody root is used in making tobacco pipes. {**briy** ər}

brig *noun* 1. a sailing ship with two masts and square sails. *The pirates sailed their brig around Cape Horn.* 2. a prison on board a ship. *The sailor was thrown into the brig for not following the captain's orders.* {**brihg**}

bri·gade *noun* 1. a part of the army, made up of more than one battalion. 2. a group of people gathered or organized

for a particular purpose. *The fire brigade arrived quickly at the burning building.* {brih **gayd**}

bright *adjective* (brighter, brightest) 1. giving much light; shining. *The sun is bright in the desert.* 2. strong or clear in color or shine. *The house is bright yellow.* 3. quick to learn; smart. *There are bright children in any neighborhood.* 4. lively; cheerful. *His bright face told me he had good news. adverb* (brighter, brightest) in a glowing or shining way; brightly. *In the country, the stars shine bright.* {**briyt**} brightly, adv.

Synonyms

These words share a meaning with **bright**, adjective 1:

shiny If something is shiny, it is often clean and new. *My uncle drove us to the city in his shiny new car.*

brilliant Brilliant is used to describe something intensely bright. *Brilliant fireworks lit the night sky.*

radiant Radiant can mean something is sending out heat as well as light. *The radiant sun warmed the hikers' backs.*

glittering Glittering is used to describe something that is bright with sparkling reflected light. *She admired the glittering diamond necklace.*

illuminated Illuminated is used to describe things that are bright with artificial light. *They walked along the illuminated streets.*

bril·liant ❷ *adjective* 1. very shiny or bright; glittering. *The brilliant stars lit up the night sky.* 2. having a very smart, sharp, and quick mind. *My sister is a brilliant thinker.* 3. wonderful or outstanding. *You wrote a brilliant book.* {**brihl** yihnt} brilliantly, adv.

brim *noun* 1. the top edge of a hollow object such as a cup; rim. 2. a flat edge that sticks out. *The brim of the cowboy's hat kept the sun from shining in his face. verb* (brimmed, brimming, brims) to be full to the brim. *The kitchen sink brimmed with water.* {**brihm**} brimming, adj.

brine *noun* 1. salt water. 2. salted water used for pickling foods. {**briyn**}

bring *verb* (brought, bringing, brings) 1. to take, lead, or carry toward the speaker speaking, or from one place to another. *Bring your game over to our house.* 2. to cause to happen or change. *Autumn brings cool weather. / She thinks a rabbit's foot brings her good luck.* 3. to sell for. *The old car brought several thousand dollars.* {**bring**}

brink *noun* 1. the edge or brim of a slope or cliff. *From the brink of the canyon, the river looked like a silver ribbon.* 2. the point just before a major change happens. *That country is on the brink of war.* {**bringk**}

brisk *adjective* (brisker, briskest) 1. active or full of energy; lively; quick. *He took a brisk walk around the town.* 2. refreshing or crisp; stimulating. *It was a brisk, cool morning.* {**brihsk**} briskly, adv., briskness, n.

bris·tle *noun* 1. a short, stiff hair on an animal. 2. something that is made of or looks like such a hair. *My hair brush is made of nylon bristles. verb* (bristled, bristling, bristles) 1. to make the bristles stand up straight in fright or anger. *The porcupine bristled when it saw the cat.* 2. to become stiff or tense with anger. *He bristled at my remarks.* {**brih** səl} bristly, adj.

 Human Body   Human Mind    Everyday Life    History and Culture   Communication

Brit *noun* (informal) a person from Great Britain. {**briht**}

Brit·ain *noun* see Great Britain. {**brih** tən}

Brit·ish *adjective* of or having to do with Great Britain or its people or language. *We studied British history.* *noun* 1. the people of Great Britain. 2. the language of Great Britain. {**brih** tihsh}

British Columbia *noun* a province in Canada on the Pacific coast. Its capital is Victoria. {**brih** tihsh kə **luhm** bee ə}

Word History American explorer Robert Gray named the Columbia River after his ship in 1792. The entire area around the river was then called "Columbia." When the United States and Canada drew a boundary through Columbia in 1846, the Canadian part became known as ***British Columbia***. British Columbia became a Canadian Province in 1871.

brit·tle *adjective* (brittler, brittlest) easily broken. *The freezing cold made the rubber brittle.* *noun* a candy made in sheets containing sugar and nuts. {**briht** əl} brittleness, n.

broad *adjective* (broader, broadest) 1. wide; large; full of space. *Many cars are able to travel on such a broad avenue.* 2. general; not limited. *The band's songs appeal to a broad audience.* 3. clear, full, or open. *The crime happened in broad daylight.* {**brawd**} broadly, adv., broadness, n.

broad·cast *verb* (broadcast or broadcasted, broadcasting, broadcasts) 1. to send over television or radio. *The radio station broadcasts the news at seven o'clock.* 2. to spread over a large area. *The news was rapidly broadcast by the neighbors.* *noun* anything that is sent over television or radio. *The television broadcast is watched by millions of people.* {**brawd** kăst} broadcaster, n.

broad·en *verb* (broadened, broadening, broadens) to make or become broad or broader. *The road crew will broaden the highway this summer. / Travel has broadened his mind.* {**braw** dən}

bro·cade *noun* a cloth woven with a raised pattern. {**broh** kayd}

broc·co·li *noun* a plant whose green flower buds and stalk are used for food. Broccoli is related to the cabbage plant. {**brŏk** ə lee}

broil O *verb* (broiled, broiling, broils) 1. to cook by direct heat. *We broiled the meat on an open fire.* 2. to subject to high heat; burn. *The sun broiled his pale skin.* {**broil**}

broil·er *noun* a pan, grill, or part of a stove used to broil food. {**broi** lər}

broke *verb* past tense of **break**. *adjective* having no money to spend or to live on. *He spent the money and is now broke.* {**brohk**}

bro·ken *adjective* 1. smashed into pieces or no longer working. *She asked me to fix her broken toy so she could play.* 2. cracked or fractured. *His broken leg hurts.* 3. not kept or carried out; violated. *His broken promise left me sad.* 4. not perfectly spoken. *The German man speaks broken Spanish.* *verb* past participle of **break**. *She has broken her glasses.* {**broh** kihn}

bro·mine *noun* a poisonous, dark reddish brown liquid that is one of the chemical elements. It evaporates quickly and combines easily with other elements. (symbol: Br) {**broh** meen *or* **broh** mihn}

bronchial tube *noun* one of the tubes that lead into the lungs from the windpipe. {**brŏng** kee əl **toohb**}

bron·chi·tis *noun* a swelling and soreness of the bronchial tubes. Bronchitis causes a bad cough. {**brŏng kiy** tihs}

bron·co *noun* (broncos) a wild or partly tamed horse or pony of the western United States. {**brŏng** koh}

bron·to·saur *or* **brontosaurus** *noun* a huge dinosaur that only ate plants. Brontosaurs had heavy bodies and very long necks and tails. They lived over 100 million years ago. Brontosaurs are now called apatosaurs by scientists who study dinosaurs. {**brŏn** tə **sohr, brŏn** tə **sohr** ihs}

bronze *noun* 1. a mixture of copper and tin. 2. a reddish brown color like that of the metal. {**brŏnz**}

brooch *noun* a piece of jewelry attached to clothing with a pin or clasp. *The diamond brooch Mary wears once belonged to her grandmother.* {**brohch**}

brood *noun* 1. a group of young birds or other animals hatched or born at the same time to one mother. 2. (informal) the children that belong to one family. *Aunt Mary is coming over with her noisy brood.* *verb* (brooded, brooding, broods) 1. to sit on eggs in order to hatch them. 2. to think or worry a lot about a single subject (usu-

a
b
c
d
e
f
g
h
i
j
k
l
m
n
o
p
q
r
s
t
u
v
w
x
y
z

ally followed by "on" or "over"). *She brooded over the problem all night.* {broohd} broodless, adj.

brook noun a small stream. {bruuk}

broom noun a device for sweeping. A broom has a bundle of straw or a brush attached to the end of a long handle. {broohm}

broth noun water in which meat, fish, grain, or vegetables have been boiled. Broth is often used as a base for soup. {brawth}

broth·er noun 1. a male person having the same mother or father as another person. *My uncle is my father's brother.* 2. a man who is connected to another man through shared interests, goals, or loyalty to the same group. *The strangers he met at camp became his brothers by the end of the summer.* {bruh thər}

broth·er·hood noun 1. a warm and close feeling between brothers or between people who feel like they are family. 2. a group of men who share interests or work. {bruh thər huud}

broth·er-in-law noun (brothers-in-law) 1. the brother of one's husband or wife. 2. the husband of one's sister. {bruh thər ihn law}

brought verb past tense and past participle of **bring**. *She brought her books to class.* {brawt}

brow noun 1. the ridge of bone above the eye, or the hair growing on it; eyebrow. 2. the entire forehead. {brow}

brown noun the color that comes from mixing red, yellow, and black paint. *adjective* (browner, brownest) having the color brown. *Brown leaves fell from the tree.* *verb* (browned, browning, browns) to make or become brown in cooking. *I browned the fish in the frying pan.* {brown}

brown bear noun a bear that is mainly brown in color, found in western North America and northern Europe and Asia. Brown bears vary in size from the small Syrian variety to the giant Kodiak bear and include the North American grizzlies. They are found in more parts of the world than any other kind of bear. {brown behr}

brown·ie noun 1. a small fairy or elf who is believed to do good things around the house in secret at night. 2. a small square of chocolate cake that is rich and chewy. 3. (capital) a member of the junior division of the Girl Scouts. {brow nee}

brown·out noun a cut or reduction of electrical power in a neighborhood or city. {brown owt}

browse verb (browsed, browsing, browses) 1. to examine things in a slow and casual way. *I'm just browsing, not shopping.* 2. to graze or feed on growing plants. *The cows browsed in the field all day.* {browz}

Word History *Browse* comes from a French word that means "a bud or sprout." In the 1400s, the English word "browse" meant "to graze." Grazing animals tend to nibble at the young, more tender parts of plants. *Browse* was first used to mean "look through a book casually or slowly" in the 1800s. When one browses through a book, it is as though one is slowly eating or nibbling lightly.

bruise verb (bruised, bruising, bruises) 1. to wound or damage without causing a break. *He fell and bruised his knee.* 2. to have or develop a physical bruise. *I bruise easily.* noun an injury that does not break the skin but leaves a black and blue mark on it. {broohz}

bru·nette adjective having a dark brown color. *Her hair and eyes are brunette.* noun a person with dark brown hair. *My sister is a brunette.* {brooh neht}

brush[1] noun 1.a tool made of stiff hairs or bristles that have been fastened to a handle. A brush is used for grooming, painting, or scrubbing. 2. the act of using a brush. *Your hair needs one last brush before you have your picture taken.* 3. a quick, light touch or short encounter. *She felt the brush of a moth against her cheek. / We had a brush with danger.* verb (brushed, brushing, brushes) 1. to use a brush on. *I brush my hair and my teeth every night.* 2. to lightly touch or move across. *When I crawled under the house, cobwebs brushed my face.* 3. to remove with a light movement as if using a brush. *I brushed the dirt off my pants.* {bruhsh}

• **brush up on** to bring up to date or review. *I must brush up on my French for the test.*

brush[2] noun 1. a thick group of small trees, shrubs, or bushes growing together. 2. land covered by thick growth of plants or trees. *He got lost in the brush.* {bruhsh}

 Human Body   Human Mind   Everyday Life  History and Culture Communication

Brus·sels *noun* the capital city of Belgium. {**bruh** səlz}

Brussels sprouts *plural noun* the small green buds that grow on the stem of a plant that is a type of cabbage. Brussels sprouts are eaten as vegetables. {**bruh** səl **sprowts**}

bru·tal *adjective* cruel or savage. *The brutal attack on the woman was reported in the newspapers the next morning.* {**brooht** əl} brutally, adv.

brute *noun* 1. any animal that is not human. 2. a cruel or unkind person. *That brute at my school always starts fights during lunch.* {**brooht**} brute-like, adj.

B.S. *abbreviation* a college degree earned in a science, such as biology or chemistry, after four years of study. B.S. is an abbreviation for Bachelor of Science.

bu. *abbreviation* an abbreviation for **bushel** or bushels.

bub·ble *noun* 1. a small, round volume of gas surrounded by a liquid or a solid. *Bubbles formed in the boiling water.* 2. a small round body of gas surrounded by a thin liquid film. *Bubbles can be made from soap and water.* *verb* (bubbled, bubbling, bubbles) 1. to make or form bubbles. *The boiling water is bubbling.* 2. to move along while making a sound like that of bubbles breaking. *The stream bubbled down the hill.* {**buhb** əl}

buck[1] *noun* an adult male deer, goat, or rabbit. Adult males of some similar animals are also called bucks. {**buhk**}

buck[2] *verb* (bucked, bucking, bucks) 1. to try to throw off a rider by leaping off the ground and coming down with stiff front legs. *The horse bucked, and the cowboy went flying.* 2. to go forward in a series of jerks. *The car was bucking wildly.* 3. to oppose strongly or force one's way against. *The boat bucked the whipping waves.* {**buhk**}

buck·et *noun* an open container with round sides, a flat bottom, and a curved handle attached to the top; pail. {**buhk** iht}
• **a drop in the bucket** a small amount compared to what is needed. *His donation, though generous, was but a drop in the bucket.*

buck·le *noun* 1.a fastener that is used to join two ends. *The belt buckle is made of silver.* 2. a bend or bulge. *The buckles in the pavement made it hard to ride my bike.* *verb* (buckled, buckling, buckles) 1. to join or fasten with a buckle. *Buckle your seat belt.* 2. to set oneself with will and a sense of purpose (usually followed by "down"). *She should buckle down to her studies.* 3. to bend or fall apart. *The bridge buckled in the wind.* / *His knees buckled from the force of the blow.* {**buhk** əl}

buck·skin *noun* 1. the skin of a deer. 2. a strong, tan leather made from the skin of a deer or a sheep. {**buhk** skihn}

buck·tooth *noun* (buckteeth) an upper front tooth that sticks out. {**buhk** toohth} bucktoothed, adj.

buck·wheat *noun* 1. a plant with seeds that are often ground into flour or used as food for farm animals. 2. the seeds of any of these plants, or flour made from the seeds. {**buhk** weet}

bud ❶ *noun* 1. a swelling on a plant that can grow into new parts, such as leaves or a flower. 2. a small, round part, such as a taste bud. *verb* (budded, budding, buds) to grow or form buds. *The rose bush is budding!* {**buhd**}
• **nip in the bud** to keep from growing or happening; stop at an early stage. *Our dreams of a lazy weekend were nipped in the bud when our teacher gave us a lot of homework.*

Word History *Bud* is from an early English word that means "to swell."

Bud·dha *noun* the title of the Indian religious leader and teacher who founded Buddhism. {**boohd** ə}

Bud·dhism *noun* a religion from Asia, founded in the sixth century B.C. by Buddha. Buddhism teaches freedom from the self and from one's wants. {**boohd** ihz əm} Buddhist, n., adj.

bud·dy *noun* (buddies) 1. (informal) a friend; pal. *His buddies like to go fishing together every other weekend.* 2. a name used when the real name of a male is not known.

A
B
C
D
E
F
G
H
I
J
K
L
M
N
O
P
Q
R
S
T
U
V
W
X
Y
Z

a
b
c
d
e
f
g
h
i
j
k
l
m
n
o
p
q
r
s
t
u
v
w
x
y
z

Hey, buddy, get your dog off my lawn! {**buh** dee}

budge *verb* (budged, budging, budges) 1. to change or begin to change position slightly. *The horse was tired and would not budge an inch.* 2. to cause to change or begin to change position slightly. *The two of us could not budge the boulder.* {**buhj**}

budg·et *noun* 1. a plan for how much money will be spent and earned during a certain period. *The school makes a new budget every year.* 2. the amount of money free to be spent for a certain period or purpose. *Our food budget is usually higher during the winter months.* *verb* (budgeted, budgeting, budgets) to plan the use or spending of. *He budgets his time well during the week so that he is able to play soccer on the weekends.* {**buh** jiht} budgetary, adj., budgeter, n.

buff *noun* 1. a soft, thick, yellow leather made from the skin of a buffalo or ox. 2. a stick or wheel covered with a soft cloth or piece of leather, used for cleaning or shining. 3. a yellowish brown color. *verb* (buffed, buffing, buffs) to clean or polish with a buff. *My dad buffs his shoes every Sunday to make them look nice for the week.* {**buhf**}

buf·fa·lo *noun* (buffaloes or buffalos or buffalo) a large mammal that has long legs, hooves, and horns, and that is closely related to cattle. Different kinds of buffaloes live in Africa or Asia. The North American bison is sometimes called a buffalo, but is not a true buffalo. {**buhf** ə loh}

buf·fet *noun* 1. a piece of furniture with a flat top and shelves or drawers to store table linens, dishes, and silverware. 2. a meal at which people help themselves to food laid out on a large table or buffet. {bə **fay**}

bug ⊙ *noun* 1. an insect with front wings that are thick at the base and thin at the tip. There are many kinds of bugs. All have mouths made for sucking, and most feed on plants. 2. any insect or crawling animal. *Spiders and ants are often called bugs.* 3. (informal) a germ that causes disease or sickness. *She did not come to school all week because she had a flu bug.* 4. (informal) a mistake or fault that keeps something from working properly. *Sometimes it is hard to fix bugs in a computer program.* 5. (informal) a tiny microphone hidden for the purpose of listening to and recording voices secretly. *The police put a bug in the suspect's kitchen in order to find out important information.* *verb* (bugged, bugging, bugs) to bother or annoy. *Please don't bug me while I'm trying to read.* {**buhg**}

bug·gy *noun* a small carriage with four wheels that is pulled by a single horse. {**buhg** ee}

bu·gle *noun* a horn shaped like a trumpet, usually without keys or valves. {**byoo** gəl} bugler, n.

build *verb* (built, building, builds) 1. to make by joining together different parts and materials; construct. 2. to make stronger or larger. *Success built her confidence.* / *They are building an excellent team.* 3. to grow in size, amount, or intensity. *Listen to the music build.* *noun* a particular type of body; figure. *Football players often have a large build.* {**bihld**}

• **build up** 1. to grow in size, amount, or intensity. *The pressure is building up.* 2. to enlarge, strengthen, or develop in stages. *She built up a resistance to disease.*

Synonyms
These words share a meaning with *build*, verb 3:
develop, swell, intensify

build·ing ⊙ *noun* 1. a large structure built for people to live in or do things in. Houses, schools, stores, and offices are buildings. 2. the act or job of making such structures. *Building on the new addition will continue until the end of the summer.* {**bihl** ding}

Human Body   Human Mind   Everyday Life   History and Culture   Communication

built-in *adjective* built as a permanent part of something larger; not able to be moved. *Our living room has built-in shelves on two walls.* {bihlt ihn}

bulb ① ② *noun* 1. a plant bud that begins to grow underground. Tulips and crocuses grow from bulbs. 2. any bulging or round part. *The bulb of a thermometer holds the mercury.* 3. a device made of rounded glass used to create electric light. *The bulb burned out.* {buhlb}

Bul·gar·i·a *noun* a country in southeastern Europe. Sofia is the capital of Bulgaria. {buhl **gayr** ee ə *or* buul **gayr** ee ə} Bulgarian, n., adj.

bulge *noun* a rounded or swollen part caused by pressure from below or within. *My camera makes a bulge in my handbag.* *verb* (bulged, bulging, bulges) to swell outward. *His stomach bulged over his belt.* {buhlj} bulgy, adj.

bulk *noun* 1. a large size or mass. *The crate's bulk made it hard to move.* 2. the larger part of something; most. *She finished the bulk of her work.* {buhlk}

bull *noun* an adult male of several kinds of mammals, such as cattle and elephants. {buul} bull-like, adj.
• **take the bull by the horns** to handle a difficult problem in a direct manner, even if one is afraid. *Jean took the bull by the horns and fixed her bike herself.*

bull·dog *noun* a breed of dog. Bulldogs are powerful dogs with short legs, short hair, and very strong, square jaws. {boohl dawg}

bull·doz·er *noun* a tractor with a large blade attached to the front that pushes or lifts soil or rocks. {buul doh zər}

bul·let 🔵 *noun* a small rounded or pointed metal object shot from a gun or rifle. {buul iht}

bul·le·tin *noun* 1. an announcement or report of the latest events or things of current interest. *Did you hear the news bulletin this evening about the big snow storm?* 2. a magazine or small newspaper published at regular times. *The university sends students a bulletin every month that lists new courses.* {buul ə tihn}

bull·fight *noun* a public show held in an arena in which performers first tease and tire out a bull, and then one person using a cape to draw the bull near tries to kill it with a sword. Bullfighting is popular in Spain and Mexico. {buul fiyt} bullfighter, n., bullfighting, n.

bull·frog *noun* a large frog found in North America that has a loud, deep croak. {buul frawg}

bull's-eye *noun* (bull's-eyes) 1. the center of a round target, usually marked with a small circle. 2. something that strikes the center of a target, such as a shot, or the act of striking the center of a target. *The champion archer shot twelve bull's-eyes.* {buulz iy}

bul·ly *noun* (bullies) someone who harasses and frightens others. *The bully in my school always steals my lunch money.* *verb* (bullied, bullying, bullies) to frighten or hurt. *That girl bullies all the other girls in her class.* {buul ee}

bum *noun* (informal) a poor person with no home and no job; tramp. *verb* (bummed, bumming, bums) (informal) to ask for and get, with no plan to pay back or return. *I tried to bum a few dollars from my brother for some lunch downtown.* *adjective* (bummer, bummest) (informal) bad or wrong. *You gave me bum advice about that test.* {buhm}

Word History *Bum* probably comes from a German word *Bummeln,* meaning "to be lazy" or "to hang loosely."

bum·ble·bee *noun* a large, furry bee, often with black and yellow stripes. Bumblebees make a loud humming or buzzing noise when they fly. {buhm bəl bee}

bump *verb* (bumped, bumping, bumps) 1. to knock against or hit, often by accident. *Our car bumped the car parked in front of it.* 2. to knock out of place. *She tripped and bumped the statue off its pedestal.* 3. to move along with jerks or jolts. *The wheelbarrow bumped along across the field.* *noun* 1. a knock or blow. *He received a nasty bump on the head.* 2. a small swelling or raised area. *The bump on her arm was a mosquito bite.* / *Watch out for the bump in the road!* {buhmp}
• **bump into** (informal) to meet by accident or chance. *What a surprise to bump into you here!*

bump·er *noun* the heavy bar on the front and back of cars and trucks that protects the vehicle from damage if it hits something. *adjective* very large. *Our farm had a bumper*

A
B
C
D
E
F
G
H
I
J
K
L
M
N
O
P
Q
R
S
T
U
V
W
X
Y
Z

crop of apples this year. {**buhm** pər}

bun *noun* 1. a loaf of bread small enough for a single serving; roll. 2. a hair style shaped like a bun. The hair is gathered at the back or top of the head. {**buhn**}

bunch *noun* 1. a number of things of the same kind that are attached together. *Please buy one bunch of bananas and one bunch of grapes.* 2. (informal) any group or collection. *She went to the movie with a bunch of her friends.* *verb* (bunched, bunching, bunches) 1. to collect into a bunch; bundle. *They bunched the crayons by color.* 2. to become a bunch; gather together. *The cows bunched together by the gate.* {**buhnch**}

bun·dle *noun* 1. a number of things that have been tied or packed together. *Bundles of hay lay about the field.* 2. a package wrapped to make it easier to carry. *He received a bundle from China.* *verb* (bundled, bundling, bundles) to put into a bundle. *He bundled the pipes for transport.* {**buhn** dəl}

• **bundle up**
to dress in warm, thick clothing. *We bundled up before going to the pond to skate.*

bun·ga·low *noun* a small, cozy house; cottage. {**buhng** gə loh}

> **Word History** *Bangla* is a word in the Hindi language for a style of one-story house found in Bengal, a part of India. From this Hindi word came the English word *bungalow*, which was first used in the 1600s.

bunk *noun* a small, single bed attached to a wall. *verb* (bunked, bunking, bunks) (informal) to sleep. *I'll bunk on the couch tonight.* {**buhngk**}

> **Word History** *Bunk* comes from the name of a county in North Carolina where a congressman named Felix Walker gave a long and boring speech.

bun·ny *noun* (bunnies) (informal) an animal with long ears, a short tail, and soft fur; a young rabbit. {**buhn** ee}

Bunsen burner *noun* a burner that has holes at the bottom where air enters, mixes with gas, and makes a hot blue flame. Bunsen burners are used in laboratory experiments. {**buhn** sən **buhr** nər}

bunt *verb* (bunted, bunting, bunts) to tap with a baseball or softball bat so that the ball lands close by. *noun* the act of bunting in baseball or softball. {**buhnt**}

bu·oy *noun* 1. a float attached by line to the bottom of a body of water to mark a location. 2. a float used to prevent someone from drowning. *verb* (buoyed, buoying, buoys) to cause to float (often followed by "up"). *A piece of wood buoyed him up in* the water. {**booh** ee *or* **bohee**, n., **booh** ee *or* **bohee**, v.}

> **Homophone Note** The words *buoy* and *boy* can sound alike but they have different meanings.

bur *noun* 1. the prickly and sharp covering for the seed of some plants. 2. any plant with burs. {**buhr**}

bur·den *noun* something that is carried or difficult to bear. *The pack was a heavy burden. / Her ill health is a burden on both of us.* *verb* (burdened, burdening, burdens) to place a burden on; give a heavy load to. *The teacher burdened us with a lot of homework for the weekend.* {**buhr** dən}

bu·reau 🖥 💻 *noun* (bureaus) 1. a chest of drawers. *I keep all of my shirts and pants in one bureau.* 2. a department in a government. *The Federal Bureau of Investigation (FBI) is one department of the United States government.* 3. an office or department that is responsible for certain jobs. *The news bureau gives important information to the people.* {**byuu** roh}

> **Word History** The word *bureau* comes from an early French word for a coarse woolen cloth used to cover a desk. *Bureau* became the word for desk, and then for the office in which the desk stood.

bur·glar *noun* someone who breaks into a building in order to steal something. {**buhr** glər}

bur·i·al *noun* the act of putting a dead body underground or in the sea. {**beh** ree əl}

 Human Body 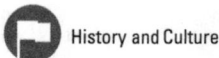 Human Mind Everyday Life  History and Culture Communication

bur·lap *noun* a rough cloth made from strong hemp or jute plant fibers. Burlap is used to make large packing bags and other things. {**buhr** lăp}

bur·ly *adjective* (burlier, burliest) having a large, husky, and strong body. *Many football players are big and burly.* {**buhr** lee} burliness, n.

Bur·ma *noun* a country in southeastern Asia. Burma became known as Myanmar in 1989. Rangoon (or Yangon) is the capital of Burma. {**buhr** mə} Burmese, n., adj.

burn ○ ○ *verb* (burned or burnt, burning, burns) 1. to be in flames; be on fire. *The forest burned for three days.* 2. to cause to be set on fire. *He burned his trash in the back yard.* 3. to sting or hurt sharply. *This bee sting burns.* 4. to hurt or damage by too much heat. *The pot burned my hand.* 5. to be cooked too much. *The popcorn is burning.* 6. to receive too much sun on the skin. *She burns easily in the sun.* 7. to be very hot. *His face was burning with fever.* *noun* an injury caused by heat. *She got a burn from touching a hot pan.* {**buhrn**}
• **burn down** to destroy by burning. *A forest fire burned down the forest.*
• **burn out** 1. to stop functioning because of a technical mistake or lack of fuel. *The light bulb burned out.* 2. to become extremely tired. *She burnt out after years of working overtime.*

burn·er *noun* the part of a furnace or stove that gives off heat or flame. {**buhr** nər}

burnt *verb* a past tense and past participle of **burn**. {**buhrnt**}

burp *noun* (informal) the act of letting gas out from the mouth in a loud manner; belch. *verb* (burped, burping, burps) 1. (informal) to let gas out from the mouth in a loud manner. *He said, "Excuse me," after he burped.* 2. (informal) to cause to let gas out from the mouth. *After feeding him, the mother burped her baby by patting him on the back.* {**buhrp**}

bur·ri·to *noun* (burritos) a Mexican food made of a flour tortilla stuffed with meat, cheese, beans, and other foods. {boohr **ee** toh}

bur·ro *noun* (burros) a small donkey used to carry supplies. {**buur** oh *or* **boohr** oh}

Homophone Note The words **burro**, **borough**, and **burrow** all sound alike but each has a different meaning.

bur·row ○ ○ *noun* a hole or tunnel dug by certain animals for use as a hiding place or home. *verb* (burrowed, burrowing, burrows) 1. to dig into or in the earth. *The rabbit burrowed in the garden.* 2. to move as if digging a burrow. *She burrowed her way through the snow drifts.* {**buhr** oh}

Homophone Note The words **burrow**, **borough**, and **burro** all sound alike, but each has a different meaning.

burst *verb* (burst, bursting, bursts) 1. to break, open up, or explode suddenly. *The balloon burst.* 2. to be full and seem ready to break open or explode. *The stadium was bursting with fans.* 3. to arrive or come out suddenly. *He burst into view.* 4. to suddenly express feelings or emotion. *We burst into laughter at his joke. / He burst into tears.* 5.

to cause to suddenly break or open up. *He blows up paper bags and bursts them.* *noun* 1. an act of bursting; explosion. 2. a sudden motion, event, or expression of feeling. *With a burst of speed, the race car whizzed over the finish line. / A burst of laughter came from the back of the room.* {**buhrst**}

bur·y *verb* (buried, burying, buries) 1. to cover in the ground with dirt. *He buried his money in the back yard.* 2. to put in a grave or tomb, or in the sea. *After he died, we buried our dog next to his favorite tree.* {**beh** ree}
• **bury one's head in the sand** to avoid the truth. *It won't do you any good to bury your head in the sand and pretend it never happened.*

Homophone Note Are you looking for the word **berry** (a fruit)? Some people say **bury** and **berry** in exactly the same way, but these two words have different meanings.

bus ○ *noun* (buses or busses) a long motor vehicle with many rows of seats used to carry large numbers of people. Buses usually travel along a regular route. *verb* (bused or bussed, busing or bussing, buses or busses) 1. to carry by bus. *Many children are bused to school.* 2. to ride in a bus. *They bus to work.* {**buhs**}

Word History **Bus** is a shortened form of the word *omnibus*, which was used by the French for a vehicle that could be used by all social classes. *Omnibus* is a Latin word meaning "for all."

bush ○ *noun* a low plant with many woody branches; shrub. {**buush**}

A
B
C
D
E
F
G
H
I
J
K
L
M
N
O
P
Q
R
S
T
U
V
W
X
Y
Z

a
b
c
d
e
f
g
h
i
j
k
l
m
n
o
p
q
r
s
t
u
v
w
x
y
z

bush·el *noun* a unit of measure equal to 4 pecks or 32 quarts, used for measuring grain and other dry products. {<u>buush</u> əl}

bush·y *adjective* (bushier, bushiest) looking like a bush; thick and shaggy. *My dad has a bushy beard.* {<u>buush</u> ee} bushiness, n.

busi·ness 🌐 *noun* 1. the work a person does to earn money; job or trade. *What business are you in?* 2. a company or other group that buys and sells goods or services in order to make money. *She owns two businesses, a card shop and a restaurant.* 3. a duty, concern, or interest. *It's my business to see that the work gets done.* 4. a particular matter, process, or event. *His disappearance was a strange business.* {<u>bihz</u> nihs}
   • **mean business**
   to be serious about doing something. *I could tell from the look on his face that he meant business.*

busi·ness·man *noun* (businessmen) a man who works in business. {<u>bihz</u> nihs **măn**}

busi·ness·wom·an *noun* (businesswomen) a woman who works in business. {<u>bihz</u> nihs **wuum** ən}

bust[1] 🌐 🌐 *noun* a sculpture or statue that shows the upper part of the human body from the head to the shoulders or chest. {<u>buhst</u>}

bust[2] *verb* (busted, busting, busts) 1. (informal) to break or burst. *The balloon will bust if you squeeze it.* 2. (informal) to break. *He busted my radio by knocking it off the table.* 3. (informal) to arrest. *The cop busted him for selling drugs.* *noun* (informal) a failure or flop. {<u>buhst</u>}
   • **bust up**
   to break up. *The police busted up the loud party.*

bus·y *adjective* (busier, busiest) 1. doing something or working on something; active. *The mechanic is busy putting the engine back together.* / *I will be too busy tomorrow to have lunch with you.* 2. full of work or activity. *Monday will be a busy day for you.* 3. being used; not available. *All the telephone lines were busy.* *verb* (busied, busying, busies) to keep busy or occupied. *She busied herself with homework.* {<u>bih</u> zee} busily, adv.

bus·y·bod·y *noun* (busybodies) someone who always pries into other people's lives and affairs. {<u>bih</u> zee bŏd ee}

but *conjunction* 1. in contrast; on the other hand. *She tried but failed.* 2. except that; only. *They wanted to play baseball, but it rained.* 3. except. *We did nothing but talk all night.* *preposition* with the exception of; except. *No one went but me.* *adverb* no more than; only; merely. *I caught but a few fish.* {<u>buht</u>}

Homophone Note The words **but** and **butt** sound alike but have different meanings.

butch·er *noun* 1. someone in the business of selling meat. 2. someone who kills or cuts up meat to make ready for sale. *verb* (butchered, butchering, butchers) to kill or cut meat to make ready for sale. *The farmer butchered the pig.* {<u>buuch</u> ər}

but·ler *noun* a man who works in a household as head servant. {<u>buht</u> lər}

butt[1] *noun* 1. the larger or stronger end of something. *I hit the tent stake with the butt of the knife.* 2. the end of something that remains after the rest has been eaten or broken off. *People should not throw cigarette butts on the ground.* {<u>buht</u>}

butt[2] *noun* a person, group, or thing that is made fun of. *I hate when I am the butt of my big sister's jokes.* {<u>buht</u>}

butt[3] *verb* (butted, butting, butts) to hit or push with the head or horns. *The goat butted the fence to try to escape.* {<u>buht</u>}

Homophone Note The words **butt** and **but** sound alike but have different meanings.

butte *noun* a steep hill or mountain with a flat top that stands alone on flat land. {<u>byoot</u>}

but·ter *noun* 1. a solid white or yellow fat made by churning cream and used for cooking and spreading on bread. 2. a food like butter in texture and used as a spread. *She put peanut butter on her sandwich.* *verb* (buttered, buttering, butters) to spread butter on. *Please don't butter my toast.* {<u>buht</u> ər}
   • **butter up**
   (informal) to be nice to or praise in the hope of gaining something from the person. *He buttered up the teacher in hopes of a better grade.*

but·ter·cup *noun* a plant with shiny yellow flowers shaped like cups. {<u>buht</u> ər kuhp}

but·ter·fat *noun* the fat of milk, from which butter is made. {<u>buht</u> ər făt}

but·ter·fly ❶ *noun* (butterflies) an insect with four large wings that flies mostly in the daytime. Butterflies are closely related to moths but have thinner

---

 Human Body   Human Mind   Everyday Life   History and Culture    Communication

bodies and are usually more brightly colored. {**buht** ər **fliy**}

but·ter·milk *noun* a sour liquid left after making butter from milk. Buttermilk is used as a drink or in cooking. {**buht** ər **mihlk**}

but·ter·nut *noun* 1. a tree of North America with leaves that drop every year. The butternut is related to the walnut. 2. the nut of this tree that can be eaten as food. {**buht** ər **nuht**}

but·ter·scotch *noun* a candy made from butter and brown sugar. {**buht** ər **skŏch**}

but·tock *noun* (usually plural) the rounded, fleshy part of the human body behind the hips; rear end. {**buht** ək}

but·ton
noun

1. a small round flat disk that fastens clothing by fitting through a slit or loop. 2. something that looks like a button, such as a round badge. 3. a small object that is pressed to make something happen. *He pushed the power button on his computer.* *verb* (buttoned, buttoning, buttons) 1. to fasten with buttons. *Will you please button your shirt?* 2. to be able to be buttoned. *This coat buttons rather than zips.* {**buht** ən}

but·ton·hole *noun* a small slit in a piece of clothing through which a button can be fastened. *verb* (buttonholed, buttonholing, buttonholes) to stop and force one's conversation upon. *My friend often buttonholes me to talk about herself.* {**buht** ən **hohl**}

but·tress *noun* a structure built to give support to the outside of a building or a wall. *verb* (buttressed, buttressing, buttresses) to give support to with a buttress. *The architect designed the wall to be buttressed with steal beams.* {**buht** rihs}

buy 🔵 *verb* (bought, buying, buys) 1. to get in return for paying money; purchase. *She saved her allowance and bought a bicycle.* 2. (informal) to accept as true; believe. *I won't buy that excuse.* *noun* something bought or intended for buying. *The car was a good buy.* {**biy**} buyer, n.

Homophone Note The words **buy** and **by** sound alike but have different meanings.

buzz *noun* 1. a soft, low hum. *The buzz of bees filled the air.* 2. (informal) a call on the telephone. *Give me a buzz next week.* *verb* (buzzed, buzzing, buzzes) 1. to make a soft, low humming sound. 2. to fly over very low in an aircraft. *The pilot buzzed the beach, frightening the swimmers.* {**buhz**}

buz·zard *noun* a very large bird with a hooked bill and sharp claws; American vulture. {**buhz** ərd}

buzz·er *noun* an electrical device that signals by buzzing. *Did you hear the door buzzer sound?* {**buhz** ər}

by *preposition* 1. next to; near. *The trees by the path are over a hundred years old.* 2. through the means of; on. *We travel by train.* 3. beyond; past. *The bus went by the station without stopping.* 4. made or created through the work of. *Our class read a play by Shaw.* 5. at or before a certain time. *Get here by tomorrow.* 6. through the action of. *He was hit by a car.* 7. in agreement with; according to. *Play by the rules.* 8. during. *We will work by day.* *adverb* 1. on hand; nearby. *There is a hospital close by.* 2. past. *A train sped by.* {**biy**}
• **by and by** before long; soon. *I will get there by and by.*
• **by and large** in general; mostly. *By and large, he is healthy.*

Homophone Note Are you looking for the word **buy** (to purchase)? **By** and **buy** sound alike but have different meanings.

by·gone *adjective* gone by; former; past. *The movie brought to life the bygone days when people rode in carriages.* {**biy** gawn}
• **let bygones be bygones** to forgive and forget past fights. *Why don't you just apologize and let bygones be bygones?*

by·pass *noun* a road that is built to go around a busy area or to avoid something in the way. *verb* (bypassed, bypassing, bypasses) to go around or avoid. *He bypassed the city by driving on back roads.* {**biy** păs}

by-prod·uct *noun* some thing or result that comes from an action intended for some other purpose. *Dog food is often made from the by-products of food made for humans.* {**biy** pro dəkt}

 Living World  Physical World  Natural Environment  Economy 🔵 Government and Law

a
b
c
d
e
f
g
h
i
j
k
l
m
n
o
p
q
r
s
t
u
v
w
x
y
z

by·stand·er *noun* someone who happens to be present when something takes place but does not take part in it. *A bystander who saw the crime take place had to testify in court.* {<u>biy</u> stăn dər}

byte *noun* a basic unit of information in computers. A byte is usually equal to eight binary digits or bits. {<u>biyt</u>}

Homophone Note Are you looking for the word *bite* (to cut with the teeth)? *Byte* and *bite* sound alike but have different meanings.

 Human Body

 Human Mind

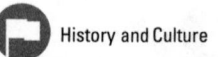 Everyday Life

 History and Culture

Communication

Cc

C is a consonant that usually makes the "k" sound. C also makes the "s" sound when it comes just before the letters e or i. When followed by the letter h, c usually makes the "chuh" sound (as in chalk).
C sometimes also makes the "sh" sound (as in chef or conscience or ocean).

Tips to help you look up words starting with c:
Also look under K for words starting with the "k" sound and under S for words starting with the "s" sound.

These words may be hard to look up if you don't already know how to spell them:

calf	concede
castle	conscience
caught	correspond
cello	cough
character	could
chasm	country
chauffeur	cousin
chief	cried
chlorophyll	cruel
choir	cruise
Christmas	curiosity
chrysalis	cylinder
collapse	cymbal
committee	

c or **C** *noun* (c's or C's) 1. the third letter of the English alphabet. 2. a grade given for average or moderately good schoolwork. 3. the first note in the musical scale of C major. {<u>see</u>}

C symbol of the chemical element carbon.

C *abbreviation* an abbreviation for **Celsius**, or **Centigrade**.

Ca symbol of the chemical element calcium.

CA or **Cal.** or **Calif.** *abbreviation* an abbreviation for **California**.

cab *noun* 1. a car that carries people who need a ride and pay a fare for this; taxicab. 2. the enclosed part of a truck or big machine where the driver or operator sits. 3. a carriage pulled by a horse that carries people for a fare. {<u>kăb</u>}

cab·bage *noun* a vegetable with large green or purple leaves that form a round head. {<u>kăb</u> ihj}

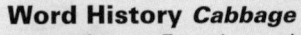

Word History *Cabbage* comes from a French word that means "head."

cab·in ◐ *noun* 1. a small house, usually built in a simple or rough way. 2. a room or compartment in a ship or airplane. *There are more than three hundred seats in the cabin of that jet.* {<u>kăb</u> ihn}

cab·i·net ◐ ◑ *noun* 1. a piece of furniture with shelves or drawers. Cabinets are used to store or hold objects. 2. (often capitalized) a group of officials who give advice to the head of a government. *The Cabinet met with the president to discuss the plan.* {<u>kăb</u> ə niht}

ca·ble *noun* 1. a thick, strong rope made of steel or fiber. *Bridges often hang from heavy cables.* 2. a bundle of insulated wires used to carry electric current. *We lost electricity when the cable broke in the storm.* 3. a message sent under the ocean by cable. *My father sent a cable from England.* 4. a form of television in which the sound and picture signals are sent by cable rather than through the air; cable television. *verb* (cabled, cabling, cables) to send a cable message to. *I cabled her with the news.* {<u>kay</u> bəl}

cable car *noun* an enclosed vehicle either on rails or hanging from a cable that is pulled back and forth by a moving cable. A cable car carries people up and down a steep slope or across a chasm. {<u>kay</u> bəl **kar**}

ca·boose *noun* a car at the rear of a freight train, used by the train's crew as a place for eating, sleeping, and observation of the tracks. *Most modern trains no longer have a caboose.* {kə <u>boohs</u>}

ca·ca·o *noun* (cacaos) 1. a South American tree with yellowish flowers and reddish brown seeds. 2. the seed of this tree, used in making chocolate and cocoa. {kə <u>kah</u> oh}

A
B
C
D
E
F
G
H
I
J
K
L
M
N
O
P
Q
R
S
T
U
V
W
X
Y
Z

 Living World
 Physical World
 Natural Environment
 Economy
 Government and Law
103

cack·le *verb* (cackled, cackling, cackles) 1. to make the sharp, broken cry of a hen. 2. to laugh or speak with such a sound. *Grandmother cackled with delight when she won the card game.* *noun* 1. the shrill, broken noise that a hen makes, especially after laying an egg. 2. sharp, broken laughter. *The actor on the stage heard cackles from the audience.* {kăk əl}

cac·tus ● *noun* (cacti or cactuses) a thick-stemmed, often prickly plant without conventional leaves that grows in hot, dry areas of America. {kăk tihs}

ca·det *noun* a student in a military school; person training to be a military officer. {kə **deht**}

caf·e·te·ri·a ● *noun* a dining hall or restaurant in which customers choose or are served their food at a counter. The customers then carry the food on trays to their tables. {kăf ə **teer** ee ə}

caf·feine *noun* a bitter substance found in coffee, tea, chocolate, and some sodas. Caffeine stimulates the heart and nervous system and can cause a person to stay awake and alert. {**kăf** een} caffeinate, v.

cage ● *noun* 1. a box or space closed in by wire or bars, used to keep and display animals or birds. 2. a similar structure that carries or protects people, such as an elevator car or a bank cashier's cage. 3. a movable screen used for batting practice in baseball or softball. *verb* (caged, caging, cages) to put into or keep in a cage or something like a cage. *She cages her cat when taking it to the veterinarian.* {kayj}

cai·man or **cayman** *noun* (caimans or caymans) a large reptile that is related to the crocodile and alligator. Caimans live in tropical areas of North and South America. {**kay** mən}

Cai·ro *noun* the capital city of Egypt, on the Nile River. {**kiyr** oh}

Ca·jun *noun* 1. a person of French Canadian descent, now usually native to Louisiana. 2. a form of the French language spoken by some Cajuns. {**kay** jən}

cake *noun* 1. a sweet, baked food made of flour, eggs, sugar, and flavoring. Cakes can be made in the form of a loaf or layers. 2. a flat, round portion of food that is baked or fried. *We had fish cakes for lunch.* 3. a hard, shaped mass of some substance. *Buy three cakes of soap.* *verb* (caked, caking, cakes) to become a hard mass. *Clean your boots before the mud cakes on them.* {kayk}

Cal. *abbreviation* 1. an abbreviation for **California**. 2. an abbreviation for **large calorie**, or large calories; the amount of energy needed to raise the temperature of one kilogram of water one degree Celsius.

ca·lam·i·ty *noun* (calamities) an event causing great harm, pain, or destruction; disaster. *The tornado was a calamity for the town.* {kə **lăm** ih tee} calamitous, n., adj.

Synonyms
These words share a meaning with *calamity*, noun 1:
disaster, tragedy, catastrophe

cal·ci·um ● ● *noun* a soft, silver-white substance that is one of the chemical elements. Calcium is found in many kinds of rocks. It is used by the body for building healthy bones and teeth. (symbol: Ca) {kăl see əm}

cal·cu·late *verb* (calculated, calculating, calculates) 1. to find out by using arithmetic; compute. *He calculated the cost of a dozen oranges at twenty-nine cents each.* 2. to determine; estimate. *She calculated how much gas we needed for our trip.* 3. to intend; design. *Her kind words were calculated to cheer us up.* {**kăl** kyə **layt**} calculation, n.

cal·cu·la·tor ● *noun* a machine used in calculating or computing numbers. {**kăl** kyə **lay** tər}

Cal·cut·ta *noun* the capital city of a state in India. Calcutta is on the eastern coast. {kăl **kuh** tə}

cal·en·dar *noun* 1. a chart of the days, weeks, and months of one or more years. 2. a list of important events arranged in the order in which they happen; schedule. *The library posts a calendar of special events on the Web.* {**kăl** ən dər}

calf[1] ● *noun* (calves) 1. a young cow or bull. A young whale, seal, or elephant is also known as a calf. 2. leather made from the skin of a calf. {kăf}

calf[2] ● *noun* (calves) the rounded back part of a

 Human Body Human Mind  Everyday Life  History and Culture  Communication

human's leg below the knee. {kăf}

Word History *Calf*[1] is from an early Scandinavian word for a young cow. It came to be used for the lower leg of a person because the swelling of the calf (of the leg) looks like the calf before it has left the cow.

cal·i·co *noun* (calicoes or calicos) a woven cotton cloth with a bright printed pattern. *adjective* 1. made of calico. *There are calico curtains in the baby's bedroom.* 2. having many colors; spotted. *Our calico cat has spots of brown and black.* {kăl ih koh}

Cal·i·for·nia *noun* a state in the western United States on the Pacific Coast. Its capital is Sacramento. (abbreviated: CA) {kă lih **fohrn** yə} Californian, n., adj.

Word History *California* got its name from Spanish explorers who, in the 1500s, began calling it the name of a wonderful imaginary land in Spanish literature.

cal·iph or **calif** *noun* in Islam, a spiritual and political leader in some Muslim countries. {**kay** lihf *or* kă lihf *or* ko **leef**}

cal·iph·ate *noun* the area ruled, length of rule, or office of a caliph. {kă lih **fayt** *or* kă lih fiht}

call *verb* (called, calling, calls) 1. to say in a loud voice or shout out. *She called his name, but nobody answered.* 2. to tell to come. *The bell called us to dinner.* 3. to telephone. *Call me next week.* 4. to name. *She called her story "The Missing Monkey."* 5. to make a visit. *Call on us when you are in town. noun* 1. a shout or loud cry. *We didn't hear his call for help.* 2. the sound made by a bird or animal. *The bullfrog's call sounds like a loose banjo*

string. 3. an act of telephoning. *We got her call early this morning.* 4. a short visit. *He paid her a call.* {kawl}

• **call for**
1. to stop by for; fetch. *You can call for the package at the post office.* 2. to require; demand. *The recipe calls for two eggs.*

• **call off**
to decide not to do or have; cancel. *We called off the picnic because of the storm.*

call num·ber *noun* a series of numbers or numbers and letters used to locate a book in a library. *You will find a copy of the book by J.R.R. Tolkien, call number PR6039.O32 L6 1986, in the general stacks.* {kawl nuhm bər}

cal·lous *adjective* 1. not having kindness; not sensitive; having a hard heart. *My friend was callous about my pain and told me to stop complaining.* 2. having an area of hard, thick skin; rough and hardened. *He has callous feet from walking barefoot all summer.* {kăl əs}

cal·lus *noun* a thickened, toughened area of skin or other tissue, such as bone or bark. {kăl əs}

calm *adjective* (calmer, calmest) 1. not moving; still. *The sea is calm today.* 2. not disturbed or excited. *A good nurse stays calm at the sight of blood. noun* 1. a condition of freedom from disturbance; peace and quiet. *There was calm in the house while they were gone.* 2. a lack of movement; stillness. *I like the calm of a forest before the wind comes up. verb* (calmed, calming, calms) 1. to reduce excitement; make quieter. *The speaker calmed the angry crowd.* 2. to become calm (usually followed by "down"). *I'll calm down when*

I know that she is safe. {kahm} calmly, adv.

Synonyms
These words share a meaning with *calm*, adjective 1:

still This sense of still is used to describe something that is undisturbed. *They sat by the still waters and watched the sun set.*

motionless Motionless is used to describe things that are sometimes active but are now not moving. *The scared rabbit hid motionless in the grass.*

stationary Stationary is a more formal or technical word used to say that something is not moving. *The police report noted that the truck had hit a stationary vehicle.*

cal·o·rie *noun* a unit for measuring the amount of energy that a food can produce when taken into the body. The more calories something has, the more energy it can provide for the body. (abbreviated: Cal.) {kă lə ree}

calves *noun* plural of **calf**. {kăvz}

Cam·bo·di·a *noun* a country in southeastern Asia. Phnom Penh is the capital of Cambodia. {kăm **boh** dee ə} Cambodian, n., adj.

cam·cord·er *noun* a portable video recording device that includes a camera and a videocassette recorder in one unit. {kăm kohr dər}

came *verb* past tense of **come**. {kaym}

cam·el *noun* a large animal with long legs and a long neck. Camels are domesticated mammals; people use camels for riding and for carrying loads across deserts. Camels from the deserts of Central Asia have two humps. Camels from northern Africa

A B C D E F G H I J K L M N O P Q R S T U V W X Y Z

and the Middle East have one hump. {kăm əl}

cam·er·a ● *noun* a device for taking photographs. A camera is a closed box with a small hole that allows light to reach the film inside. The light makes images on the film. {kăm rə *or* kăm ər ə}

Cam·e·roon *noun* a country in West Africa. Yaounde is the capital of Cameroon. {kăm ər oohn} Cameroonian, n., adj.

cam·ou·flage *noun* a way of hiding something by covering or coloring it so that it looks like its surroundings. The military uses camouflage to hide people, buildings, or vehicles from the enemy. *The coats of many animals are natural camouflage. verb* (camouflaged, camouflaging, camouflages) to hide by coloring or covering to look like the surroundings. *When it snows, the soldiers camouflage themselves by wearing white. / A chameleon can camouflage itself by changing the color of its skin.* {kăm ə flahzh}

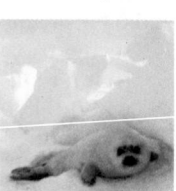

camp *noun* 1. an outdoor area where tents or shelters are set up to live or sleep in for a time. 2. the people in such tents or shelters. *Howling wolves kept the whole camp awake last night. verb* (camped, camping, camps) 1. to set up a camp. *Let's stop here and camp by the river.* 2. to live in a camp (usually followed by "out"). *Last summer we camped out in the mountains for three weeks.* {kămp}

Word History *Camp* is from *campus,* a Latin word that means "field where an army might stay."

cam·paign *noun* a series of planned actions carried out in order to reach a particular goal. *The scouts are having a car wash and bake sale as part of their campaign to raise money. / We are helping with the campaign for her election as governor. verb* (campaigned, campaigning, campaigns) to take an active part in a campaign. *I campaigned for him in the race for class president.* {kăm payn}

camp·er *noun* 1. a person who stays at a camp or goes camping. 2. a motor vehicle that is used as a living space while camping. *Some campers have a kitchen and bathroom.* {kămp ər}

camp·fire *noun* an outdoor fire used for cooking or warmth while camping. {kămp fiyr}

camp·ground *noun* an area for camping, such as a park. {kămp grownd}

cam·phor *noun* a white substance with a very strong smell that is taken from the camphor tree. A form of camphor can also be made by people. Camphor is used in making some kinds of medicine and plastic. {kăm fər}

cam·pus *noun* (campuses) the grounds of a school, college, or university. {kăm pəs}

can[1] *auxiliary verb* 1. to be able to; have the ability to. *She can speak French.* 2. to have the power or right to. *In some countries, women still cannot vote.* 3. to have permission to. *We can change the rules, if it is not fair. (See may.)* {kăn}

Language Note Can you tell the difference between *can* and *may*? *Can* means "to be able to do something," while *may* means "to have permission or be allowed to do something." *Maria can jump off the roof without getting hurt. Still, her parents say she may not do this.*

can[2] *noun* 1. a metal container for food or other products, made in the shape of a cylinder. 2. the amount such a container holds. *Jesse drank two cans of soda at the picnic. verb* (canned, canning, cans) to put in a sealed jar to keep fresh for future use. *We can tomatoes from our garden every summer.* {kăn}

Can·a·da *noun* a country in northern North America. Ottawa is the capital of Canada. {kăn ə də} Canadian, adj., n.

Canada Day *noun* a Canadian holiday on July 1. It celebrates the day in 1867 when Canada was formed by four provinces joining together. {kăn ə də day}

ca·nal *noun* 1. a channel of water used by boats. Canals also carry water to crops. 2. a part of an animal or plant body that is like a tube. Some canals carry air, and others carry liquids. {kə năl}

ca·nar·y *noun* (canaries) 1. a small yellow or greenish bird often kept as a pet. Canaries are native to the Canary Islands and are a kind of finch. 2. a pale to medium yellow color. {kə nayr ee}

can·cel *verb* (canceled, canceling, cancels) 1. to do away

 Human Body   Human Mind   Everyday Life   History and Culture  Communication

with; decide against; call off. *They canceled tonight's game because of rain. / I canceled my subscription to the magazine.* 2. to mark, cross out, or change to keep from being used again. *She canceled the check with a big stamp.* {kăn səl}

can·cer *noun* 1. a disease in which certain cells divide and grow much faster than they normally do. 2. (capitalized) a constellation located between Gemini and Leo. Cancer is also called the Crab. 3. (capitalized) the fourth sign of the zodiac, the Crab, which the sun enters about June 21. 4. (capitalized) a person born under this sign, between June 21 and July 20. {kăn sər} cancerous, adj.

can·di·date ⊙ *noun* a person who seeks to be elected or appointed to a certain position. *The candidates for mayor will speak on TV tonight.* {kăn dih **dayt** or kăn dih diht}

can·dle *noun* a stick of wax with a wick running through the middle that is burned to give light. {kăn dəl}
• **not hold a candle to** to not do nearly as well as. *In math, he does not hold a candle to his sister.*

can·dle·stick *noun* a holder for one or more candles. {kăn dəl **stihk**}

can·dy *noun* (candies) a sweet food made of sugar and flavorings such as chocolate or peppermint. *verb* (candied, candying, candies) to cook in sugar syrup in order to cover with sugar crystals or a glaze. *The chef candied cherries for dessert.* {kăn dee}

cane *noun* 1. a wooden or metal stick that helps someone walk. 2. the long, hard stem of the bamboo plant and

other large grass plants. 3. sugar cane. {kayn}

ca·nine ⊙ *adjective* having to do with dogs or animals related to dogs, such as wolves, foxes, and coyotes. *noun* 1. an animal of the dog family. 2. a pointed tooth between the front teeth and molars of many mammals. {kay niyn}

Canis Major *noun* a constellation in the northern sky that contains Sirius, the brightest of all stars. Canis Major means "Big Dog" in Latin. {kay nihs **may** jər}

Canis Minor *noun* a constellation in the northern sky. Canis Minor means "Little Dog" in Latin. {kay nihs **miy** nər}

can·ni·bal *noun* a person who eats human flesh. {kăn ə bəl} cannibalism, n.

can·non *noun* (cannon or cannons) a large gun that is set on wheels or some other base. Cannons fire heavy shells. {kăn ən}

can·not *verb* a form of can not. {kăn aht or kăn naht or kăn nŏt}

ca·noe ⊙ *noun* a narrow boat with pointed ends that is moved along by using a paddle. *verb* (canoed, canoeing, canoes) to ride in or paddle a canoe. {kə **nooh**}

can·o·py *noun* (canopies) a covering made of cloth and

hung over a bed or dining area. {kăn ə pee}

can't shortened form of "cannot." *Why can't I go to the movies?* {kănt or **kahnt**}

can·ta·loupe or **cantaloup** *noun* a round melon with a hard, rough skin and orange flesh. {kănt ə lohp}

can·teen *noun* 1. a small container for carrying water; flask. 2. a small store that sells food, drink, and some personal supplies. Canteens are found in schools, factories, and military bases. {kăn **teen**}

can·ter *noun* a horse's gait between a trot and a gallop. *verb* (cantered, cantering, canters) to go or cause to go at a canter. *We cantered across the meadow.* {kănt ər}

Homophone Note Are you looking for the word *cantor* (a song or prayer leader)? *Canter* and *cantor* sound alike but have two different meanings.

Word History *Canter* comes from the gait of the horses ridden by pilgrims on their way to the Canterbury cathedral, a famous church in England. Pilgrims made a yearly journey at an easy pace called "the Canterbury gallop."

can·tor *noun* the singer who leads the prayers in a synagogue. {kăn tər}

Homophone Note The words *cantor* and *canter* (a horse's gait) sound alike but have two different meanings.

A
B
C
D
E
F
G
H
I
J
K
L
M
N
O
P
Q
R
S
T
U
V
W
X
Y
Z

 Living World    Physical World   Natural Environment   Economy   Government and Law

can·vas 🔵 *noun* 1. heavy, strong cloth made of cotton, linen, or hemp. Canvas is used for making sails, tents, and covers for boats. 2. a piece of this material used as the surface for an oil painting. *The artist set up her canvas and began to paint.* {**kăn** vihs}

can·yon 🔵 *noun* a deep valley with steep sides. {**kăn** yən}

cap¹ *noun* 1. a soft hat with a peak or visor but no brim. 2. anything shaped like a cap that is used to cover an opening, such as a top for a bottle or tube. 3. a dot of explosive powder contained in paper for use in a toy pistol. *verb* (capped, capping, caps) to cover with a cap. {**kăp**} capless, adj.

• **cap in hand**
with meekness and respect; in a humble manner. *Cap in hand, he asked for a second chance.*

cap² *noun* a capital letter. {**kăp**}

ca·pa·bil·i·ty *noun* (capabilities) the quality of being skilled or able; ability. *She is very talented and has many capabilities.* {kay pə **bih** lih tee}

ca·pa·ble *adjective* 1. having the skill or power to do what is needed. *I know a capable mechanic who can fix your car.* 2. able to; ready for (usually followed by "of"). *I am capable of staying up all night.* {**kay** pə bəl} capably, adv.

Synonyms
These words share a meaning with **capable**, adjective 2:
able, open, ready, prepared

ca·pac·i·ty *noun* (capacities) 1. the amount that can be held in a particular space. *This pitcher has a capacity of one gallon. / The room has a seating capacity of one hundred.* 2. power or ability. *He has the capacity to be a great*

dancer. 3. a job or position. *In her capacity as mayor, she invited people to visit the city.* {kə **păs** ih tee}

cape¹ *noun* a garment without sleeves that hangs loosely over the back and shoulders. {**kayp**}

cape² *noun* a point of land that sticks out into a large body of water. {**kayp**}

ca·per *verb* (capered, capering, capers) to leap, hop, or skip about in a playful way; frolic. *The puppy capered in the yard.* *noun* 1. a playful bound or leap. *The fawn cleared the creek with a graceful caper.* 2. a playful trick or adventure; silly act. *They laughed at the children's crazy capers.* {**kay** pər}

cap·il·lar·y *noun* (capillaries) a tiny blood vessel joining the end of an artery to the beginning of a vein. {**kăp** ə layr ee}

cap·i·tal¹ 🔵 🔵 *noun* 1. the city where the government of a country, state, or province is located. *The capital of Peru is Lima. / The capital of Ontario is Toronto.* 2. a large form of a letter of the alphabet. *The first word in an English sentence should begin with a capital.* 3. money or other resources owned by a business. 4. money that is used to produce more money, as by starting a business or investing. *They have enough capital to buy the house.* *adjective* 1. of high quality; excellent; first rate. *That is a capital plan!* 2. having to do with the location of a state or national government. *We*

live outside the capital city. 3. in the large form of an alphabet letter. *In English, the first letter of your name must be written as a capital letter.* 4. able to be punished by death. *Murder is a capital crime in some states.* {**kăp** ih təl}

cap·i·tal² *noun* the top part of a column or pillar. {**kăp** ih təl}

Homophone Note
Are you looking for the word **capitol** (a building where state leaders meet)? **Capital** and **capitol** sound alike but have different meanings.

cap·i·tal·ism *noun* an economic system in which land, factories, and other resources are owned by individuals instead of the government. In this system, goods are sold for the purpose of making money. {**kăp** iht əl ihz əm}

cap·i·tal·ize *verb* (capitalized, capitalizing, capitalizes) to write or print in capital letters or with a capital letter at the beginning. *Names are always capitalized.* {**kăp** ih təl iyz}

cap·i·tol *noun* 1. the building in which the lawmakers of a state meet. 2. (capitalized) the building in which the U.S. Congress meets. {**kăp** ih təl}

Homophone Note
The words **capitol** and **capital** sound alike but have different meanings.

Cap·ri·corn *noun* 1. a constellation between Sagittarius and Aquarius. Capricorn is also called the Goat. 2. the tenth sign of the zodiac, the Goat, which the sun enters about December 22. 3. a person born under this sign, between December 22 and January 20. {**kăp** rə **kohrn**}

a
b
c
d
e
f
g
h
i
j
k
l
m
n
o
p
q
r
s
t
u
v
w
x
y
z

 Human Body
 Human Mind
 Everyday Life
 History and Culture
 Communication

cap·size *verb* (capsized, capsizing, capsizes) to turn over; upset. *A large ship does not capsize easily.* {kăp siyz}

cap·sule *noun* 1. a tiny case that holds one dose of medicine. Capsules are made of gelatin and dissolve when swallowed. 2. the area in a spacecraft that holds the crew and instruments. {kăp soohl}

cap·tain *noun* 1. a leader. *The president of that company is known as a captain of industry.* 2. the chief officer of a merchant ship or an airplane. 3. an officer of the U.S. Army, Air Force, or Marines, holding the rank just below major. 4. an officer of the U.S. Navy, holding the rank just below admiral. 5. the field leader of a sports team. *verb* (captained, captaining, captains) to lead as captain. *He captained the ship.* {kăp tihn}

Word History The word *captain* comes from a Latin word that means "head."

cap·tion *noun* the words that describe a picture or graph in a magazine, book, or newspaper. *Most photographs in magazines have captions underneath them.* {kăp shən}

cap·tive *noun* one who is captured and held prisoner. *The captive had no way to escape.* *adjective* held as prisoner. *The captive wolf howled all night.* {kăp tihv}

cap·ture *verb* (captured, capturing, captures) 1. to take hold of by force or the use of tricks. *They captured the escaped dog by using meat as bait.* 2. to put into a lasting form; preserve. *He captured his daughter's soccer game on film.* *noun* the act of capturing or being captured. *The animal avoided capture by hiding.* {kăp chər}

car ○ *noun* 1. an automobile. 2. a vehicle that runs along rails, such as a railroad car or cable car. 3. an enclosure for carrying people, such as an elevator car. {kar}

Word History The word *car* comes from a word used by ancient Romans long before the automobile was invented. A *carra* was a two-wheeled wagon used for carrying loads.

Ca·ra·cas *noun* the capital city of Venezuela. {kə rahk əs *or* kă rah kahs}

car·a·mel *noun* 1. sugar that is heated until it melts and turns brown. Caramel is used to color and flavor foods. 2. a soft candy with the color and flavor of burnt sugar. {kar ə məl *or* kahr mehl}

car·at *noun* a unit of weight for diamonds and other gems, equal to one-fifth of a gram. {kar ət}

Homophone Note The words *carat*, *caret*, and *carrot* all sound alike but have different meanings.

car·a·van *noun* 1. a band of people traveling together. Caravans are often formed for safety when crossing a remote area like a desert. 2. a group of vehicles or riding animals traveling together in a single line. *The police officer stopped us to let a caravan of trucks go by.* {kar ə văn}

car·bo·hy·drate *noun* a compound made of carbon, hydrogen, and oxygen. It is formed by plants and is rich in energy. Sugars and starches are carbohydrates. {kar boh hiy drayt}

car·bon *noun* a chemical element found in all living things. Pure carbon occurs as diamond or graphite. It is also often found in compounds with other elements. (symbol: C) {kar bən}

carbon dioxide ○ ○ *noun* a gas without color or odor that is made up of carbon and oxygen. Carbon dioxide is in the air and is used in soft drinks. Frozen carbon dioxide is called dry ice. {kar bən diy ŏks iyd}

carbon monoxide *noun* a poisonous gas with no color or smell. Carbon monoxide forms when a material made of carbon, like gasoline, is not fully burned because of too little air. {kar bən mə nŏks iyd}

car·bu·re·tor *noun* the part of an engine that makes a mixture of air and gasoline that is burned by the engine when it runs. {kar bə ray tər}

car·cass *noun* the body of a dead animal. {kar kəs}

card *noun* 1. a small piece of cardboard, plastic, or thick paper printed with information about a person. A card is used to identify the person whose name is on it. 2. one of a pack of small pieces of thick paper used for playing games like old maid or poker. These cards have numbers and designs printed on them. 3. (plural) any of the games played with such a pack. *Let's play cards.* 4. a small, thick piece of paper used for messages, such as a greeting card, or postcard. *He sent us a card from Florida.* {kard}

A
B
C
D
E
F
G
H
I
J
K
L
M
N
O
P
Q
R
S
T
U
V
W
X
Y
Z

 Living World   Physical World    Natural Environment   Economy    Government and Law   109

a
b
c
d
e
f
g
h
i
j
k
l
m
n
o
p
q
r
s
t
u
v
w
x
y
z

• **play one's cards** to make and carry out good choices. *If you play your cards right, you might win the contest.*

card·board *noun* a stiff material made of layers of paper and used to make things like boxes and signs. {<u>kard</u> bohrd}

car·di·nal *noun* 1. an official of the Roman Catholic Church who is chosen by the pope and is second in rank to him. 2. a North American songbird with a crest of feathers on its head. Male cardinals have bright red feathers and a black face and throat. *adjective* very important. *It is a cardinal rule that everyone be quiet in the library.* {<u>kard</u> ə nəl}

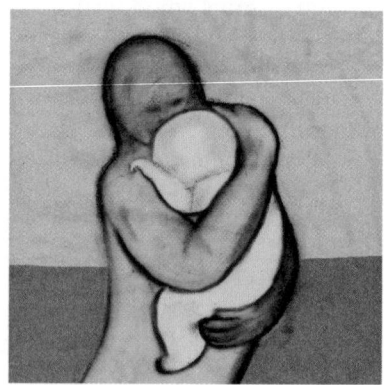

cardinal number *noun* any number used to indicate how many. One, three, and fifteen are cardinal numbers. {<u>kar</u> də nəl <u>nuhm</u> bər}

care *noun* 1. serious attention. *Do this important job with care.* 2. worry or concern. *She frowns all the time because she has so many cares.* 3. the act of watching over or tending; protection. *The sick man should be under the care of a doctor.* *verb* (cared, caring, cares) 1. to be concerned. *He didn't care what other people said about him.* 2. to feel a liking or attraction (usually followed by "for"). *Sam doesn't care for spinach.* 3. to watch over or tend to the needs of (usually followed by "for"). *Aunt Jane cared for me while I was sick.* 4. to want or wish (usually followed by an infinitive of another verb). *Would you care to go with us?* {<u>kayr</u>}

• **take care of** 1. to look after, watch over, or protect. *The clinic takes care of sick people.* / *His grandmother takes care of him while I am gone.* 2. to attend to; take action on. *Don't worry, I'll take care of the problem tomorrow.*

Word History *Care* comes from an Old English word that means "grief," "sorrow," or "anxiety." Since the 1700s, it has lost intensity and is much more likely to mean concerned attention.

ca·reer 🌀 *noun* the work a person chooses to do through life. *She wants to have a career as a scientist.* {kə <u>reer</u>}

care·free *adjective* having nothing to worry about; free of cares or serious thoughts; cheerful. *When school is out for the summer, we'll be carefree.* {<u>kayr</u> free or kayr <u>free</u>}

care·ful *adjective* 1. taking care in one's actions; cautious. *He is a careful driver.* 2. done with care and effort. *He did a careful job trimming the bushes.* {<u>kayr</u> fəl} carefully, adv., carefulness, n.

care·less *adjective* 1. not paying close attention; not careful or watchful. *A careless driver didn't see the light turn red.* 2. showing a lack of planning, thought, or interest. *He made many careless mistakes on his test.* {<u>kayr</u> lihs} carelessly, adv., carelessness, n.

ca·ress *noun* a soft or gentle touch that shows love or affection. *The little girl missed her father's caresses.* *verb* (caressed, caressing, caresses) to touch or stroke gently with love or affection. *The father took the crying boy in his arms and caressed him.* {kə <u>rehs</u>}

car·et *noun* a mark (^). It is used to show where an insertion is to be made in a text. {<u>kar</u> iht}

Homophone Note The words *caret*, *carat*, and *carrot* all sound alike but have different meanings.

care·tak·er *noun* 1. a person who takes care of a building or other property. *A caretaker was hired to look after the millionaire's estate.* 2. a person who takes care of another person who is ill or elderly. *We hired a caretaker for our father after his heart attack.* {<u>kayr</u> tayk ər}

car·fare *noun* the money that is paid for a ride in a taxi, bus, or subway. *He gave me carfare to go to the city.* {<u>kar</u> fayr}

car·go *noun* (cargoes or cargos) the goods carried by a ship, airplane, or other vehicle; freight. *This truck carries a cargo of fruit.* {<u>kar</u> goh}

Car·ib·be·an *noun* an extension of the Atlantic Ocean bor-

 Human Body   Human Mind   Everyday Life History and Culture Communication

dered by the West Indies and Central and South America. *adjective* of or relating to the islands and countries in the Caribbean Sea, or their peoples, languages, and cultures. {kə **rihb** ee ən *or* kar ə **bee** ən, n., kə **rihb** ee ən *or* kar ə **bee** ən, adj.}

car·i·bou *noun* (caribou or caribous) an animal with long legs and a long neck. Caribou are mammals with antlers and hooves. They live in the northern North America. Caribou are closely related to moose and other kinds of deer. Both male and female caribou have antlers. {**kar** ə booh}

car·ies *noun* (caries) bone or tooth decay. {**kayr** eez}

car·na·tion *noun* a flower with a pleasant smell and fringed petals. Carnations grow in many colors, including red, white, or pink. {kar **nay** shən}

car·ni·val *noun* a fair that travels from place to place and offers rides, games, and shows. {**kar** nə vəl}

Word History *Carnival* comes from Latin and means "to stop eating meat." In the 1500s, "carnival" time was the last three days before the Christian season of Lent. It was the last chance to eat meat until Easter.

car·ni·vore ● *noun* an animal that eats the flesh of other animals. {**kar** nih **vohr**}

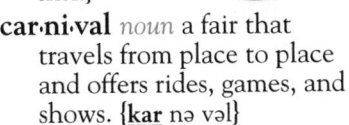

car·niv·o·rous *adjective* eating the flesh of ani-

mals. *Lions and tigers are carnivorous mammals.* {**kar** **nihv** ə rəs}

car·ob *noun* 1. a tree of the Mediterranean that has long, flat pods with a sweet pulp and hard seeds. 2. the pod of this tree, used to make drinks and candy that taste like chocolate. {**kar** əb}

car·ol *noun* a song of joy, especially a Christmas song. *verb* (caroled, caroling, carols) 1. to sing a carol or song joyfully. 2. to sing Christmas songs in a group. *We went from door to door, caroling.* {**kar** əl} caroler, n.

car·pen·ter *noun* a person who builds or repairs houses and other things made of wood. {**kar** pən tər}

car·pet *noun* 1. a heavy fabric covering for floors. 2. a covering like a carpet. *In the spring, a carpet of wildflowers covers this hill.* *verb* (carpeted, carpeting, carpets) to cover with a carpet or with something like a carpet. *The blizzard carpeted the hills with snow.* {**kar** piht}

car·pool *noun* an agreement among a group of automobile drivers who work together, or whose children go to the same school. Each driver takes turns driving the others. {**kar** poohl}

car·riage *noun* 1. a vehicle with wheels that is covered or enclosed and is used for carrying people. *She put my sister in the baby carriage.* / *Before cars were invented, many people travelled in horse-drawn carriages.* 2. a movable part of a machine that changes the position of another part. *Typewriters and printers have carriages.* 3. the way a person stands or walks; posture. *She*

walked with the carriage of a queen. {**kar** ihj}

car·ri·er *noun* 1. a person who carries or brings something. *She works as a mail carrier.* / *He was the carrier of good news.* 2. a company whose business is to carry or bring things to a particular place. *Which carrier brought your new computer?* {**kar** ee ər}

car·rot *noun* 1. a plant that produces an orange root that is eaten as a vegetable. 2. the long, thick, orange root of this plant. {**kar** ət}

Homophone Note The words *carrot*, *carat*, and *caret* all sound alike but have different meanings.

car·ry *verb* (carried, carrying, carries) 1. to take from one place to another; bear or support while moving; transport. *She carried my suitcase up the stairs.* / *The gas line carries fuel to your home.* 2. to hold oneself in a certain way. *He carries himself proudly.* 3. to have in stock; sell. *The store carries many different products.* 4. to be moved forward or conveyed. *He has a voice that carries.* {**kar** ee}

• **carry away**
to cause a strong reaction or emotions in. *She was carried away by her work.* / *We were carried away by the music.*

• **carry off**
1. to do with success. *He carried off the tightrope walk.* 2. to cause to die. *He was carried off by cancer.*

• **carry on**
1. to continue to do or go on as before. *After her husband's death, she carried on.* 2. to behave, especially verbally, in a foolish or silly way. *The*

A B C D E F G H I J K L M N O P Q R S T U V W X Y Z

teacher scolded him for carrying on in class.

• **carry out**
1. to do; bring to completion. *Tomorrow we must carry out our secret plan.* 2. to obey; follow. *The scouts carried out the leader's instructions.*

car·sick *adjective* having a sick feeling while riding in a car, bus, or train. {**kar** sihk}

cart *noun* 1. a large wagon with two or four wheels pulled by animals and used to carry a heavy load. 2. a small, light vehicle moved by hand and used to carry things. *Most large grocery stores have shopping carts for their customers to use.* *verb* (carted, carting, carts) 1. to carry in a cart or in something like a cart. *We loaded up the car with boxes and carted them off to the dump.* 2. to carry away with force or great effort (usually followed by "off"). *He carted off a great pile of laundry. / They carted the prisoner off to jail.* {**kart**}

• **put the cart before the horse**
to do or place things in a way that is not their logical order. *You're putting the cart before the horse if you spend money before you have it.*

car·ti·lage *noun* a tough, white tissue that forms part of the skeleton of humans and other animals. Cartilage is not as stiff as bone. Cartilage is found in the ear, nose, and joints. {**kar** tə ləj} cartilaginous, adj.

car·ton *noun* a box made of cardboard, paper, or plastic. *Milk, cereal, and eggs come in cartons.* {**kar** tən}

car·toon ● *noun* 1. a drawing or series of drawings that make people laugh or think; comic strip. Cartoons often have words to show what a character is thinking or saying or to help explain what is happening. 2. a motion picture made by filming a series of drawings; animated cartoon. {**kar** toohn}

car·tridge *noun* 1. a case shaped like a tube that holds gunpowder and a bullet. 2. a small case that holds some material or a piece of equipment. A cartridge is put into a larger device to help make it work. *My pen does not work without the ink cartridge.* 3. a special container made to hold film so that it is easy to load into a camera. {**kar** trihj}

cart·wheel *noun* 1. a sideways somersault with the arms and legs held out straight like the spokes of a wheel. 2. the wheel of a cart. {**kart** weel or **kart** hweel}

carve *verb* (carved, carving, carves) 1. to form or write by cutting. *She carves horses out of wood. / He carved his name in the table.* 2. to slice or cut into pieces. *Who will carve the roast beef?* {**karv**}

carv·ing *noun* the work or result of cutting and shaping wood, stone, or other material. *Carving is an art. / He makes beautiful carvings of birds.* {**karv** ing}

cas·cade *noun* a steep waterfall or series of small waterfalls.

verb (cascaded, cascading, cascades) to fall from one level to the next; flow down like a waterfall. *After the storm, water was cascading into the canyon.* {kăs **kayd**}

case¹ *noun* 1. an instance or example of something. *After the fifth case of theft in our office, we decided to take action.* 2. the real facts; what is true or actual. *It is not the case that Jack hit the other boy first.* 3. a matter that needs to be investigated by the police or other authorities. *When someone disappears for several days, that is a case for the police.* 4. a charge or complaint against someone that is investigated in a court of law; a lawsuit. *There is a case against him in court for not paying his bill.* 5. someone who is injured or sick; a patient. *The doctor has five new cases this week.* {**kays**}

• **in case**
if it happens that; if. *Take this umbrella in case it rains.*

case² *noun* a container for holding, carrying, or keeping safe. {**kays**}

cash ● *noun* money in the form of bills, coins, or checks; payment in such form. *He paid for the car with cash. / Will this be cash or charge?* *verb* (cashed, cashing, cashes) to give or get cash for; exchange for money. *I cashed my paycheck at the bank.* {**kăsh**}

cash·ew *noun* 1. a tropical American evergreen tree. A gum used in medicine is obtained from the bark. 2. a curved nut of this tree, which is eaten after roasting. {**kăsh** ooh}

 Human Body Human Mind Everyday Life  History and Culture  Communication

cash·ier *noun* 1. a person whose job is to take the money when a customer pays for something. *I paid the cashier for the sodas.* 2. a person whose job is to handle the money in a bank. *The cashier opened a savings account for me.* {kă **sheer**}

cash ma·chine *noun* a bank machine used for dispensing cash and other transactions. *I need to stop at a cash machine to get money for the movie.* {**kăsh** muh sheen}

cask *noun* a large, strong barrel used for holding wine or other liquids {**kăsk**}

cas·ket *noun* a box in which a dead person is buried; coffin. {**kăs** kiht}

cas·se·role *noun* 1. a dish, often deep and covered, in which food can be baked and served. *After making the potato mixture, put it into a casserole and bake it for half an hour.* 2. the food baked in such a dish. *He brought a casserole to the party.* {**kăs** ə **rohl**}

cas·sette *noun* a case with film, audio tape, or video tape inside. *Cassettes make it easy to load a camera or recorder.* {kə **seht**}

cast *verb* (cast, casting, casts) 1. to throw or fling. *The princess cast the ring out the window.* 2. to turn towards. *I was almost to my seat when the teacher cast his eyes on me.* 3. to give forth; direct or project. *The tree cast a long shadow on the grass. / This book casts light on the history of our nation.* 4. in fishing, to throw out into the air. *He cast his fishing line into the river.* 5. to choose for a part in a play or film. *They cast him as the king in the play.* 6. to form into a hard object by pouring or setting material into a mold. *The artist will cast a statue of a lion for the zoo entrance.* 7. to give, in a formal vote. *We each cast a vote for the class president.* *noun* 1. the act of throwing or casting. *His cast of the fishing line was too short to reach the deep part of the stream.* 2. an object shaped by a mold; casting. 3. a thick, stiff covering for a broken bone, made of cloth and fiberglass or plaster. 4. a group of people acting in a play or film. {**kăst**}

cas·ta·net *noun* one of a pair of wooden or ivory instruments that are partly hollowed out. They are held in the hand and clicked together to the rhythms of Spanish dance music. {kăs tə **neht**}

cast iron *noun* a mixture of iron and carbon, with other materials added to make it either hard and brittle or soft and strong. *Cast iron is made into pots for cooking.* {**kăst iy** ərn}

cas·tle *noun* 1. a large, strong building where a noble lived with his family and servants in the Middle Ages. Castles were built to defend those inside against attacks. 2. one of two game pieces in chess that may be moved forward, backward, or sideways over any squares not blocked; rook. {kă səl}

cas·u·al *adjective* 1. happening by chance; not planned. *On our way back from the park, we paid our friend a casual visit.* 2. done without much attention, planning, or thought; offhand. *The boss made only casual checks of my work.* 3. not formal in style or appearance. *We can wear casual clothes in this restaurant.* {kă zhooh əl} casually, adv.

cas·u·al·ty *noun* (casualties) 1. a person in the armed forces who is killed, wounded, or missing in action. *Her son was a casualty of war.* 2. a person who is hurt or killed in an accident. *There was a train accident, but there were no casualities.* {**kăz** hooh əl tee}

cat ❶ *noun* 1. a small, furry mammal with whiskers, short ears, and a long tail. Cats, also called house cats, are often kept as pets or to catch mice and rats. 2. any of the larger wild animals related to the kind of cat kept as a pet. Tigers, lions, and bobcats are all cats. Cats are carnivorous mammals. {**kăt**} catlike, adj .
• **let the cat out of the bag**
to reveal a secret. *I wanted the gift to be a surprise, but I let the cat out of the bag.*

cat·a·logue *noun* 1. an organized list of books, goods for sale, or other items. Catalogues usually give a short description of each item on the list.

A B C D E F G H I J K L M N O P Q R S T U V W X Y Z

2. the printed or electronic form of such a list. *We found the title we were looking for in the library's computer catalogue. / We ordered a tent and sleeping bag from the camping goods catalogue.* {kăt ə lŏg *or* kăt ə lawg}

cat·a·ma·ran *noun* a boat with two hulls joined side by side. {kăt ə mə **răn**}

cat·a·pult *noun* 1. an ancient weapon used to throw objects, such as large stones or arrows, at an enemy. 2. a machine for launching planes from the deck of a ship. *verb* (catapulted, catapulting, catapults) 1. pushed or thrown with force; thrust by or as though by a catapult. *One hit song catapulted him to success.* 2. to spring up or forward as though thrown by a catapult; leap. *She catapulted over the fence.* {kăt ə **puult**}

cat·a·ract *noun* 1. a large waterfall. 2. a clouding of the lens of the eye, blocking out light and making it difficult or impossible to see. {kăt ə răkt}

ca·tas·tro·phe *noun* an event that brings great harm, suffering, or loss to a large area or many people; terrible disaster. *The earthquake was a catastrophe that destroyed many cities.* {kə **tă** strə fee} catastrophic, adj.

Word History *Catastrophe* is from a Greek word that means "overturning" or complete change. It referred to the ending of a play, or the outcome of certain events. The ending could be either happy or tragic. "Catastrophe" is now mostly used for a tragic event.

cat·bird *noun* a dark gray North American songbird. One of its calls is like the sound a cat makes. {kăt **buhrd**}

catch *verb* (caught, catching, catches) 1. to take hold of or grab something or someone that is moving. *She caught the ball. / Catch me if you can.* 2. to discover and surprise suddenly. *The park ranger caught us littering.* 3. to get aboard in time to ride. *I caught the last bus home.* 4. to become ill with. *My father caught the flu.* 5. to get the attention of; attract. *This hat will catch his eye.* 6. to become gripped, fastened, or trapped. *His coat caught in the door.* 7. to begin to burn. *They waited for the wood to catch on fire.* 8. to play the position of catcher in baseball or softball. *noun* 1. an act of catching. *The ball was hit hard, but the fielder made the catch.* 2. a thing or the amount that is caught. *The lucky fisherman brought in a big catch.* 3. a thing that takes hold of something and slows or stops its motion; latch. *The catch was broken and the door would not close.* 4. a hidden trick or flaw in something. *When someone offers you a free car, there must be a catch.* {kăch}

• **catch up**
1. to reach or come up to from behind and next to (usually followed by "to" or "with"). *Stop running and let me catch up with you.* 2. to finish something, but later than planned (usually followed by "on" or "with"). *It's important to catch up on homework if you have been absent from school.*

catch·er *noun* the player who is behind the batter at home plate in baseball or softball. The catcher catches balls thrown by the pitcher. {kăch ər}

catch·ing *adjective* likely to infect or be passed on to another. *That disease is not catching.* {kăch ing}

catch·up *noun* another spelling of **ketchup**. {kăch əp *or* kehch əp}

cat·e·go·ry *noun* (categories) a particular section of a main group; class. *The books in the library are divided into many categories.* {kăt ə gohr ee}

ca·ter *verb* (catered, catering, caters) 1. to supply food or service for. *The company catered a wedding luncheon.* 2. to supply food or other service. *His business caters for children's parties.* 3. to supply anything needed or wanted (usually followed by "to"). *This music store caters to young people.* {kay tər}

cat·er·pil·lar *noun* the larva, or middle life stage, of a moth or butterfly. Caterpillars are round and long like worms, but have six legs. They may be brightly colored. {kă tər pihl ər}

cat·fish *noun* (catfish or catfishes) a fish with no scales and a large head, found mostly in fresh water. Catfish have long feelers around the mouth that look like a cat's whiskers. {kăt fihsh}

ca·the·dral *noun* 1. the main church of a bishop's dis-

 Human Body   Human Mind   Everyday Life   History and Culture   Communication

trict. 2. any large or important church. {kə **thee** drəl}

cath·o·lic *adjective* (capitalized) having to do with the Roman Catholic Church. *The pope is the head of the Catholic Church. noun* (capitalized) a member of the Roman Catholic Church. {**kăth** ə lihk *or* **kăth** lihk, n., **kăth** ə lihk˘ *or* **kăth** lihk, adj.}

CAT scan *noun* an image of an area of the body that is formed from a grouping of x-rays on a computer. CAT scans are used to make a diagnosis in medical treatment. CAT stands for computerized axial tomography. {**kăt** skăn}

cat·sup *noun* another spelling of **ketchup**. {**kăts** əp *or* **kăch** əp *or* **kehch** əp}

cat·tail *noun* a tall plant with long, flat leaves that grows in wet places. Cattails have long, brown, fuzzy flower spikes. {**kăt** tayl}

cat·tle ❶ *plural noun* large mammals raised on farms or ranches for their milk or meat. Female cattle are called cows. Male cattle are called bulls. Young cattle are called calves. The ox and the yak are kinds of cattle. {**kăt** əl}

cat·tle·man *noun* (cattlemen) a person who takes care of, feeds, or raises cattle on a ranch. {**kăt** əl mən}

caught *verb* past tense and past participle of **catch**. {**kawt**}

cau·li·flow·er *noun* a plant that bears a large head of firm white flowers that can be eaten. Cauliflower is related to the cabbage plant. {**kaw** lee **flow** ər}

caulk or **calk** *verb* (caulked or calked, caulking or calking, caulks or calks) to fill in cracks with putty or tar to keep air or water from leaking through. *He caulks the boat every spring before putting it in the water.* {**kawk**}

cause *noun* 1. something or someone that brings about a result or effect. *Smoking is one cause of lung cancer. / A cigarette was the cause of the fire.* 2. good reason or enough of a reason. *There is no cause for worry. / He slapped me without cause.* 3. an idea or goal that many are interested in. *They are working for the cause of world peace. verb* (caused, causing, causes) to make happen; be the cause of. *The rain caused flooding.* {**kawz**} causeless, adj.

cause·way *noun* a raised road or path across water or land that is wet. {**kawz** way}

cau·tion *noun* 1. close attention and care; the act of being careful and alert. *Please use caution when riding a bike on busy streets.* 2. a warning. *Pay attention to the signs of caution on the trail through the canyon. verb* (cautioned, cautioning, cautions) to give a warning to. *We cautioned him not to drink the hot chocolate until it had cooled down.* {**kaw** shən}

cau·tious *adjective* taking care to avoid danger or trouble; careful. *The children were cautious as they entered the haunted house.* {**kaw** shihs} cautiously, adv.

cav·al·ry *noun* (cavalries) soldiers who fight on horseback or from tanks or helicopters. {**kăv** əl ree} cavalryman, n.

cave 🜨 *noun* a natural hole or hollow in the earth. Many caves have openings in a hillside or cliff. {**kayv**}

• **cave in**
1. to fall in or sink in. *The walls of the old shed caved in.* 2. (informal) to give in or not resist. *He caved in to his friend's demands.*

cave dwell·er *noun* a human being who lives or lived in a cave. *Primitive cave dwellers often made crude drawings on the walls of their caves.* {**kayv** dwehl ər}

cave-in *noun* (cave-ins) a falling inward; collapse. *There was a cave-in at the underground mine.* {**kayv** ihn}

cave man *noun* a human being who lived in a cave thousands of years ago; cave dweller. {**kayv** măn}

cav·ern *noun* a large cave. {**kăv** ərn}

cav·i·ty *noun* (cavities) a hollow place or hole. *He hid money in a cavity of the old tree. / The dentist found three cavities in my teeth.* {**kăv** ih tee}

caw *noun* the cry of the crow or raven, or any harsh call that sounds like this. *verb* (cawed, cawing, caws) to make the sound of a crow or raven. {**kaw**}

CD *abbreviation* an abbreviation for **compact disk**.

cease *verb* (ceased, ceasing, ceases) 1. to stop or come to an end. *Will this snow never cease?* 2. to stop or bring to an end. *Cease that noise now! / The band ceased playing.* {**sees**}

ce·dar *noun* 1. an evergreen tree of the pine family that bears cones. Cedars have strong wood with a sweet smell. 2. the wood of these trees. {**see** dər}

ce·dil·la *noun* a mark (¸). It is placed under certain letters to change that letter's pronunciation in French, where

A
B
C
D
E
F
G
H
I
J
K
L
M
N
O
P
Q
R
S
T
U
V
W
X
Y
Z

 Living World    Physical World   Natural Environment   Economy   Government and Law   115

"ç" has the sound of "s." {sə **dihl** ə}

ceil·ing *noun* 1. the top inside surface of a room. 2. something that looks like or acts like such a surface. *The airplane was hidden from view by a ceiling of clouds.* 3. an upper limit. *Max's father put a ceiling on how much money he could spend for the bicycle.* {see ling}

Homophone Note The words *ceiling* and *sealing*, a form of the verb "to seal," sound alike but have different meanings.

cel·e·brate *verb* (celebrated, celebrating, celebrates) 1. to make special or honor with gifts, parties, or activities. *The town is celebrating the holiday with a parade.* 2. to perform as part of public worship. *The priest celebrates Mass every Sunday.* {sehl ə **brayt**} celebrator, n.

cel·e·bra·tion ○ *noun* 1. the act of honoring or celebrating. *We spent the evening in celebration of the new year.* 2. anything that is planned or done in order to honor something. *There will be a celebration for her eightieth birthday.* {sehl ə **bray** shən}

ce·leb·ri·ty *noun* (celebrities) a person who is famous. *Some actors are celebrities.* {sə **lehb** rih tee}

cel·er·y *noun* a plant with crisp, pale green stalks that are eaten as a vegetable. Celery leaves and seeds are used as seasoning. {sehl ə ree *or* sehl ree}

cell ○ ○ ○ *noun* 1. a tiny unit of plant or animal life, having a nucleus and surrounded by a very thin membrane. *Living things are made of cells.* 2. a very small room for a prisoner, nun, or monk. 3. any small, hollow space within a larger group of hollow spaces. *Bees build a honeycomb with many cells.* 4. a device that makes electricity by chemical means. *A car battery has several cells.* {**sehl**}

Homophone Note The words *cell* and *sell* sound alike but have different meanings.

Word History *Cell* comes from *celare*, a Latin word that means "to hide." By the 1300s, "cell" meant "small monastery" or "small room." In the late 1300s, it was used for the compartments that the brain was thought to be separated into. The current use of the word "cell" in biology first occurred in 1845.

cel·lar *noun* a room or rooms built underground, usually beneath a building. {sehl ər}

cel·lo *noun* (cellos) a large musical instrument with four strings. The cello is in the violin family but has a deeper tone than the violin. {**cheh** loh} cellist, n.

cel·lo·phane *noun* a thin, clear material made from cellulose. Cellophane is used to wrap food and other things. {sehl ə **fayn**}

cel·lu·loid *noun* a plastic that burns easily. Celluloid is used for motion picture film. {sehl yə **loid**}

cel·lu·lose *noun* the main element of plant tissue, used in making paper, cellophane, and fabrics. *The woody parts of trees and plants are made of cellulose.* {sehl yə lohs}

Cel·si·us *adjective* relating to a temperature scale on which water freezes at zero degrees and boils at one hundred degrees; centigrade. (abbreviated: C) *U.S. weather reports often do not use the Celsius temperature scale.* {sehl see əs}

ce·ment *noun* 1. a powder made of clay and limestone that becomes hard when water is added. Cement is used as a building material. 2. a sticky material, such as paste or glue, that gets hard when it dries. *verb* (cemented, cementing, cements) to glue or fasten with cement. *I cemented the broken bowl back together.* {sə **mehnt**}

Language Note The nouns *cement* and *concrete* are often confused. *Cement* is a powder made of crushed rock and minerals. It is an ingredient of concrete. *Concrete* is a hard, strong building material made of cement and sand or gravel mixed with water. Cement is often mixed into concrete in large trucks at a building site.

cem·e·ter·y *noun* (cemeteries) a place where the dead are buried; graveyard. {sehm ə tehr ee}

Word History *Cemetery* comes from *koimeterion*, a Greek word for "sleeping room." The Greek noun comes from the verb *koiman*, which means "to put to sleep."

cen·sor *noun* 1. an official who decides what art, movies, or books may be published. A censor works for a government, religion, or other organization, and promotes its ideas. *During the war, military*

 Human Body    Human Mind   Everyday Life   History and Culture    Communication

censors didn't allow news reporters to publish anything that might hurt the war effort. 2. anyone who exercises control over information or ideas. *The office manager became a censor when he told us we couldn't send personal e-mail.* *verb* (censored, censoring, censors) to examine and control the content of. *Although she believes in freedom of speech, my teacher censors our student newspaper.* {<u>sehn</u> sər} censorable, adj.

cen·sus 🔵 *noun* (censuses) an official count of the people who live in a country or other area. A census is also used to collect information about these people, such as their job, age, or sex. *In the United States, a national census is taken every ten years.* {<u>sehn</u> sihs}

cent *noun* a coin of many countries, including the United States and Canada. A cent is equal to a hundredth part of the standard national currency. {<u>sehnt</u>}

Homophone Note The words **cent**, **scent**, and **sent** sound alike, but each has a different meaning.

cen·taur *noun* a creature in Greek mythology that has the head, arms, and chest of a man and the trunk and legs of a horse. {<u>sehn</u> tohr}

cen·ten·ni·al *adjective* having to do with a one hundredth anniversary. *The town was planning a centennial parade to celebrate its founding.* *noun* a one hundredth anniversary. *In 1876, the United States celebrated its centennial.* {<u>sehn tehn</u> ee əl}

cen·ter *noun* 1. the point that is the same distance from all points on the outside line or surface of something; exact middle. 2. the middle of anything; core. *There is a nut in the center of this candy.* 3. a place, person, or thing that is the main object of attention or interest. *Mali was a center of commerce and learning in the middle ages.* 4. a player who is in a middle position on a playing field or court. *verb* (centered, centering, centers) 1. to place at a center. *Please center the title on the page.* 2. to focus or concentrate. *We centered our thoughts on finding ways to help the people in need.* {<u>sehn</u> tər}

cen·ti- or **cent-** *prefix* 1. a prefix that means "one hundredth." *There are one hundred centimeters in one meter.* 2. a prefix that means "one hundred." *There are one hundred years in a century.*

cen·ti·grade *adjective* see **Celsius**. {<u>sehn</u> tə grayd}

cen·ti·me·ter *noun* a unit of length equal to one hundredth of a meter or 0.3937 inch. (abbreviated: cm) {<u>sehn</u> tih **mee** tər}

cen·ti·pede *noun* a small animal with a narrow body like a worm. A centipede's body is divided into many segments, each having a pair of legs. The front legs have poison claws. Centipedes are a kind of arthropod and are active at night. {<u>sehn</u> tə peed}

cen·tral *adjective* 1. in the center or being the center. *The library is in the central part of town.* 2. main or principal; most important. *Harry is the central character in the book.* {<u>sehn</u> trəl} centrally, adv.

Central African Republic *noun* a country in central Africa. Bangui is the capital of the Central African Republic. {<u>sehn</u> trəl <u>ăf</u> rə kən rə <u>puh</u> blihk} Central African, n., adj.

Central America *noun* the piece of land that connects North America with South America. Central America has six countries. {<u>sehn</u> trəl ə <u>meh</u> rih kə} Central American, [n.], adj.

cen·tre *noun or verb* a spelling of **center** used in Canada and Britain. See **center** for more information. {<u>sehn</u> tər}

cen·tu·ry 🔵 *noun* (centuries) 1. a unit of time equal to one hundred years. *Some giant tortoises live for more than a century.* 2. one of the hundred-year periods into which human history is divided. Centuries are usually counted forward or backward from the beginning of the Christian era. *The twenty-first century began in the year 2001 and will end in 2100.* {<u>sehn</u> chə ree}

ce·ram·ic *adjective* of or having to do with objects made of baked clay. *She makes ceramic bowls and cups.* {sə <u>răm</u> ihk}

A
B
C
D
E
F
G
H
I
J
K
L
M
N
O
P
Q
R
S
T
U
V
W
X
Y
Z

a
b
c
d
e
f
g
h
i
j
k
l
m
n
o
p
q
r
s
t
u
v
w
x
y
z

ce·re·al ○ ● *noun* 1. any plant whose grains are used for food, such as wheat, oats, rice, or rye. 2. food made from grain and eaten for breakfast. {<u>seer</u> ee əl}

Homophone Note The words *cereal* and *serial* (in a series) sound alike but have different meanings.

Word History *Cereal* is from *Ceres*, goddess of the harvest in Roman mythology.

cer·e·mo·ny ○ *noun* (ceremonies) 1. a formal act or series of acts done in a particular way to honor a special occasion. *My mother cried during the graduation ceremony.* 2. very polite

behavior, often more formal than is needed. *He opened the door for us with great ceremony.* {<u>sehr</u> ə moh nee}

Ce·res *noun* the goddess of farming in Roman mythology. In Greek mythology, Ceres is called Demeter. {<u>seer</u> eez}

cer·tain *adjective* 1. sure; positive; having no doubt. *I'm certain she is still alive.* 2. known to be true without any doubt; definite. *It is certain that Earth is round and not flat.* 3. specific; fixed. *The club admits a certain number of people every year.* 4. used to mention a particular person or thing without naming it. *A certain person has been asking about you.* {<u>suhr</u> tən}
• **for certain**
without question; definitely.

The doctor can tell us for certain whether you have the mumps.

cer·tain·ly *adverb* 1. without doubt or question. *I'll certainly do my best.* 2. yes, indeed; of course. *Certainly, you may have some.* {<u>suhr</u> tən lee}

cer·tain·ty *noun* (certainties) 1. the state of being sure or confident. *I've been in the house all day, and I can say with certainty that no one has called.* 2. a fact that cannot be argued with. *It is a certainty that she will win the prize.* {<u>suhr</u> tən tee}

cer·tif·i·cate *noun* a statement on paper that shows or proves that certain facts are true. *He didn't believe my age, so he asked to see my birth certificate.* {sər <u>tih</u> fə kiht}

ce·ta·cean ● *noun* a kind of mammal that lives in the water and has front limbs that look like paddles and back limbs that do not show. Whales, porpoises, and dolphins are all cetaceans. {sə <u>tay</u> shən}

Chad *noun* a country in central Africa. N'djamena is the capital of Chad. {<u>chăd</u>} Chadian, n., adj.

chain *noun* 1. a row of links, usually made of metal, that are joined together and used to pull, hold, or fasten something. *The workers used chains to drag the logs up the hill. / The boy tied his dog with a chain. / The door is locked with a chain.* 2. a series of

things or events that are connected to each other. *A chain of mountains stretched across the state. / There has been a chain of robberies in the city.* 3. a series of businesses of the same kind, owned by one person or company. *My uncle owns a hotel chain.* *verb* (chained, chaining, chains) 1. to hold or fasten with a chain. *I chained the door shut.* 2. to hold or keep in place with a chain. *He chained the dog to keep it from running away.* {<u>chayn</u>}

chair ○ *noun* 1. a piece of furniture for one person to sit on. A chair has four legs, a back, and sometimes arms. 2. a short form of **chairman** or **chairperson**. {<u>chayr</u>}

chair·lift *noun* a line of chairs hanging from a moving cable, used to carry people up or down a mountain. A chairlift is used at a ski slope. {<u>chayr</u> lihft}

chair·man *noun* (chairmen) a man who is in charge of a meeting or committee. *They elected him chairman of the dance committee.* {<u>chayr</u> mən} chairmanship, n.

chair·per·son *noun* a person who is in charge of a meeting or committee. *We chose a chairperson, a secretary, and a treasurer for our games club.* {<u>chayr</u> puhr sən}

chalk ○ ● *noun* 1. a soft, white limestone that comes mostly from tiny sea shells. 2. a piece of chalk or something like chalk, used for marking a blackboard. *verb* (chalked, chalking, chalks) to write down or draw with chalk. *We chalked pictures on the sidewalk.* {<u>chawk</u>}
• **chalk up**
1. to score; earn. *The team chalked up another win.* 2. to regard as the result of;

 Human Body   Human Mind   Everyday Life   ◼ History and Culture   ☎ Communication

attribute. *Chalk up his sleepiness to the party last night.*

chalk·board *noun* a smooth, dark board to be written on with chalk; blackboard. *The teacher wrote the sentence on the chalkboard.* {**chawk** bohrd}

chal·lenge *noun* 1. an invitation to enter into a fight or other contest of skill. *The cowboy heard the bandit's challenge and turned to face him.* 2. an interesting or difficult problem or task. *Learning all the state capitals was a challenge.* 3. a calling into question; request for an explanation or proof. *When they announced the class president, there was a challenge because there were some missing votes.* *verb* (challenged, challenging, challenges) 1. to invite to enter into a fight or contest of skill; dare. *She challenged him to another tennis match.* 2. to question the right of. *The Queen challenged Sir John's claim to the throne.* 3. to stir up or make more active; stimulate. *This book will challenge your thinking.* {**chǎl** ihnj} challenger, n.

cham·ber *noun* 1. a room. *The mysterious old man never left his tiny chamber.* 2. a large room or meeting hall used by people in government to make and discuss laws. *The town meeting was held in the council chamber.* 3. (plural) a judge's office, where people can discuss matters not to be heard in open court. *Part of the hearing was held in chambers to protect the children's privacy.* 4. a compartment or cavity. *The human heart has four chambers.* 5. the compartment of a gun that holds the shell or cartridge. *The police officer loaded bullets into the chamber.* {**chaym** bər}

cha·me·le·on *noun* a lizard that is able to change its skin color to match its environment. {kə **meel** ee ən}

cham·pagne *noun* a white wine with bubbles originally made in the Champagne region of France. {shǎm **payn**}

cham·pi·on *noun* 1. a person or animal that has taken first place in a contest or game; winner. 2. someone who speaks or acts in favor of a person or cause. *He was a champion of the poor.* *verb* (championed, championing,

champions) to fight for or defend; act in favor of. *The senator championed higher pay for teachers.* {**chǎm** pee ən}

cham·pi·on·ship *noun* 1. (sometimes plural) one or more contests held to decide the champion. *The chess championships begin next week.* 2. the position or title of champion. *We did not expect our team to win the championship.* {**chǎm** pee ən **shihp**}

chance *noun* 1. the quality of happening by accident and without being planned or predicted. *It was chance that led the lost boy to a house in the woods.* 2. luck; fortune. *It was by chance that you won in that card game.* 3. a measure of how likely it is that a thing will happen; probability. *What is your chance of winning the lottery?* 4. opportu-

nity. *I would like the chance to travel someday.* 5. an action that could have bad results; risk. *He took a chance and tried out for the school play.* *verb* (chanced, chancing, chances) 1. to happen by accident. *I chanced to see Mr. Sanchez on the bus.* 2. (informal) to take the risk of (often followed by "it"). *The boat may sink, but we'll have to chance it if we want to escape.* *adjective* happening when not expected or planned; caused by accident. *He had a chance meeting with an old friend.* {**chǎns**}

• **on the off chance** with the very slight possibility; against the slight hope. *Let's go to the airport now on the off chance that the plane will arrive on time.*

chan·cel·lor *noun* 1. the head of state in Austria or Germany. 2. the chief official of a university. {**chǎn** sə lər *or* **chǎn** slər}

change *verb* (changed, changing, changes) 1. to make different; alter the content or form of. *He changed his story when he told it to us.* 2. to cause to have a completely different form (usually followed by "to" or "into"). *The witch changed him into a toad.* 3. to put another in place of; exchange. *I change schools next fall.* 4. to become different. *You have changed since the last time I saw you. / The leaves change in the fall.* 5. to put on other clothing. *I want to change before the party.* *noun* 1. the act of changing; the fact of being changed. *There are two changes in the class schedule today. / The artist made some changes to his sketch.* 2. money given in smaller bills or coins in

A B C D E F G H I J K L M N O P Q R S T U V W X Y Z

a
b
c
d
e
f
g
h
i
j
k
l
m
n
o
p
q
r
s
t
u
v
w
x
y
z

exchange for a larger bill or coin. *May I have four quarters as change for a dollar?* 3. coins. *Some change fell out through a hole in his pocket.* 4. anything exchanged for or put in place of something else. *I was staying overnight, so I brought a change of clothes.* {**chaynj**}

chan·nel *noun* 1. a long, narrow body of water that joins two larger bodies of water. 2. the deepest part of a body of water. *The chart shows how deep the channel of the river is.* 3. a frequency band used by radio or television stations. *Many people use a remote control to change TV channels.* *verb* (channeled,

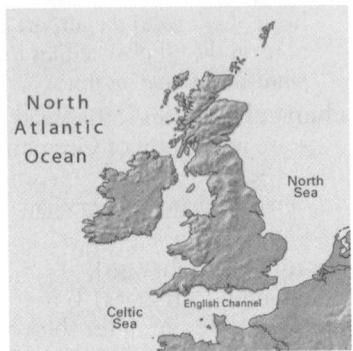

channeling, channels) to make a channel in. *They channeled the land and let it fill with water.* {**chăn** əl}

chant *noun* 1. a song that is sung on the same note or the same few notes throughout. 2. words spoken in rhythm over and over on a single pitch. *The team gave a victory chant after the game.* *verb* (chanted, chanting, chants) 1. to sing in a chanting style. 2. to read or speak in a chant. *The students chanted the poem they had learned by heart.* {**chănt**}

Cha·nu·kah *noun* see **Hanukkah.** {**hah** nə kə *or* **khah** nuu kah}

cha·os *noun* a state, condition, or place of complete confusion or disorder. *The class was in chaos on the last day of school.* {**kay** ŏs}

chap[1] *verb* (chapped, chapping, chaps) to crack, dry, or make red. *Washing dishes every day can chap the hands.* {**chăp**}

chap[2] *noun* (informal) a man or boy; fellow. {**chăp**}

chap·el *noun* a small building or a room in a larger building used for worship. *The hospital has its own chapel for private services.* {**chăp** əl}

chap·lain *noun* a member of the clergy who leads religious services and does counselling for a military unit, a hospital, or other group. {**chăp** lihn}

chaps *plural noun* leather clothing worn over pants, especially by cowboys, to protect the legs while riding horseback. {**chăps**}

chap·ter *noun* 1. one of the main parts of a book. Chapters are usually numbered or given a title. 2. a local branch of a club or organization. *Our chapter has over a hundred members.* {**chăp** tər}

char·ac·ter ❓ 🔧 *noun* 1. all those things that make a person, place, or thing different from others. *This neighborhood has a friendly character. / He has an honest character.* 2. strong moral qualities. *We expect character in our leaders.* 3. a person in a story, play, or movie. *Many actors have played the character of Hamlet in Shakespeare's play.* 4. a letter or symbol used in an alphabet or in mathematics. *"B," "z," and "5" are all characters.* 5. (informal) someone who is considered odd or peculiar. *What a character!* 6. a person, in relation to certain qualities. *He is a strange character,*

smiling one minute and angry the next. {**kar** ək tər}

char·ac·ter·is·tic *adjective* having to do with a typical or special quality of a person, group, action, or thing. *He has a characteristic way of walking. / Exciting plots are a characteristic of this author's books.* *noun* something that makes a person or thing different from others. *Tails that can grasp things are a characteristic of monkeys.* {**kar** ək tə **rihs** tihk} characteristically, adv.

char·ac·ter·ize *verb* (characterized, characterizing, characterizes) 1. to describe the particular character or qualities of; give certain characteristics to. *The press characterized him as a criminal.* 2. to be a special quality of. *His music is characterized by its loud beat.* {**kar** ək tə **riyz**}

char·coal *noun* 1. the solid, black form of carbon made by burning wood or other matter in a space with very little oxygen. 2. a piece of charcoal or a pencil that contains charcoal, used for drawing. {**char** kohl}

charge 🏃 💬 📞 *verb* (charged, charging, charges) 1. to give a responsibility or duty to. *I charged him with the care of my pets while I was away.* 2. to blame for a crime; accuse (often followed by "with"). *She was charged with theft.* 3. to supply with power or energy. *He charged the battery.* 4. to demand or ask as a price. *The cafe charges a dollar for a cup of coffee.* 5. to put off payment for until a later date; pay for with a credit card. *He charged his purchases instead of paying cash.* 6. to rush ahead. *They charged into battle.* 7. to demand payment. *The pizza shop charges for*

 Human Body   Human Mind  Everyday Life  History and Culture Communication

delivery. *noun* 1. a price asked for; fee. *The charge for our meal was more than we expected.* 2. care or protection. *She put her son in our charge when she became too sick to take care of him.* 3. a claim that a person has done something wrong; accusation. *He was arrested on a robbery charge.* 4. the amount of electricity in an object. Charge causes electrical energy to flow in a current. The movement of electrical energy from one point to another is caused by a difference between the charges at the two points. An electrical charge can be positive or negative. 5. a military attack. *The soldiers stood strong against the charge of the opposing army.* {**charj**}

char·i·ot *noun* a vehicle with two wheels used in ancient times. A chariot was pulled by horses and driven from a standing position. It was used in wars, races, and other public events. {**chayr** ee iht}

char·i·ty *noun* (charities) 1. something given to a person or persons in need. *It is hard for some people to accept charity.* 2. a group or organization that helps people in need. *This charity raises money to help find a cure for cancer.* 3. not willing to judge others in a harsh way; good will. *He shows charity towards others.* {**char** ih tee}

charm *noun* 1. the ability to attract, delight, and please. *Movies have great charm for people everywhere.* 2. any small object to be worn on a chain as a decoration. 3. an

object, act, or word believed to have magic powers. *verb* (charmed, charming, charms) to attract or delight. *The baby charms everyone with his cute smile.* {**charm**} charmer, n.

charm·ing *adjective* full of charm; pleasant; attractive. *Aunt Ellen has charming manners.* {**charm** ing} charmingly, adv.

chart *noun* 1. a sheet that gives information in the form of a graph or table. 2. a map used to guide a ship across water or an airplane through the skies. *verb* (charted, charting, charts) 1. to make a map of; measure. *The captain charted a course around the islands.* 2. to show on a table or graph. *On this page the author charts changes in temperature.* {**chart**}

char·ter *noun* 1. an official document given by a government or ruler to a business or other group. The charter explains the group's rights and responsibilities. 2. a contract to hire a bus, airplane, or ship for the use of a group or a person. *verb* (chartered, chartering, charters) 1. to give a charter to or be chartered. *The city chartered a company to start a bus service.* 2. to hire for a short time. *The school chartered a bus for our field trip to the museum.* {**char** tər} charterer, n.

chase *verb* (chased, chasing, chases) 1. to follow with the goal of catching; run after. *The police chased the suspect down the street.* 2. to force to go in a certain direction; drive away. *Ms. Cohen chased the dog out of the shop.* noun the act of chasing; pursuit. *The rider, in chase of her horse, ran across the field.* {**chays**}

chasm *noun* a deep crack in the earth's surface. {**kăz** əm}

chas·sis *noun* (chassis) the frame that supports the body and engine in a vehicle. {**chăs** ee or **shăs** ee}

chat *verb* (chatted, chatting, chats) to talk in a friendly or easy manner. *My friend and I like to chat on the phone after school.* noun a friendly conversation. *We had a long chat about the movie we saw last night.* {**chăt**}

chat·ter *verb* (chattered, chattering, chatters) 1. to speak rapidly and without saying anything important. *She chattered on and on about the shoe sale at the mall.* 2. to make a series of quick, short sounds. *The squirrels chattered to each other in the trees.* 3. to make a series of clicking sounds by knocking together. *Her teeth were chattering from the cold.* noun 1. quick, foolish speech. *His grandmother doesn't understand his chatter about video games.* 2. a series of quick sounds, as of certain birds and animals. {**chăt** ər}

chauf·feur *noun* a person whose job is to drive an automobile. {**shohf** ər or **shoh fuhr**}

cheap *adjective* (cheaper, cheapest) 1. having a low price. *Vegetables are cheap at the farmer's market.* 2. charging low prices. *This is a cheap grocery store.* 3. of poor quality. *Cheap clothing wears out quickly.* 4. not willing to spend much money; stingy. *Andy was too cheap to buy a birthday gift for his friend.* {**cheep**} cheaply, adv.

Homophone Note Are you looking for the word *cheep* (a chirping sound)? *Cheap* and *cheep* sound alike but have different meanings.

cheat *noun* a person who acts in a dishonest way in order to

a
b
c
d
e
f
g
h
i
j
k
l
m
n
o
p
q
r
s
t
u
v
w
x
y
z

gain something. *verb* (cheated, cheating, cheats) 1. to act in a dishonest way in order to get something from someone. *He cheated the woman by telling her the fake diamonds he sold her were genuine.* 2. to break the rules in a dishonest way. *They cheated during the test by whispering the answers to each other.* {**cheet**} cheater, n.

check ● *noun* 1. a test or search to make sure that something is correct or in order. *The stage crew ran a check of the sound system before the concert started.* 2. a written order to a bank to pay money from an account. *I pay my bills by check.* 3. a bill for food and drink at a bar or restaurant. 4. a design or pattern made up of small squares. *She wore a dress of red and black checks.* 5. something that controls, holds back, or limits. *The rule against loud noise in the neighborhood put a check on band practice.* 6. the situation in chess in which the king is under attack by an opponent's piece. *verb* (checked, checking, checks) 1. to look over to make sure of correctness; examine carefully. *Would you check my paper to see if I have made any spelling mistakes?* 2. to put under someone's care for a short time. *We checked our bags at the desk while we walked around the train station.* 3. to cause to stop suddenly. *The rider checked his galloping horse.* 4. to put a mark next to in order to show that something is correct or has been done (often followed by "off"). *Please check off the*

items on the grocery list after you have found them. {**chehk**}

Homophone Note The words **check** and **Czech** sound alike but have different meanings.

check·er *noun* (plural but used with a singular verb) a game played by two people. Each player has twelve pieces to move over a board divided into sixty-four squares of two alternating colors. {**chehk** ər}

check·er·board *noun* a surface marked into sixty-four squares of two alternating colors. It is used as a game board for checkers or chess. {**cheh kər bohrd**}

check·up ● *noun* any examination of a person or thing. Having a doctor look closely at a body to make sure that a person is healthy is one kind of checkup. Having a mechanic look at a car to make sure it is running properly is another kind of checkup. {**chehk uhp**}

cheek *noun* 1. either side of the face between the nose and the ear. 2. bold or rude behavior. *She scolded him for having the cheek to talk back to his teacher.* {**cheek**}

cheep *verb* (cheeped, cheeping, cheeps) to make a peeping sound; chirp. *The little bird cheeped in its cage.* *noun* a chirp or peep. {**cheep**}

Homophone Note Are you looking for the word **cheap** (low in price)? **Cheep** and **cheap** sound alike but have different meanings.

cheer ● *noun* 1. glad feelings; happiness. *We are filled with*

cheer during the holidays. 2. a shout of encouragement, happiness, or praise. *The crowd let out a cheer when their favorite team scored a goal.* *verb* (cheered, cheering, cheers) 1. to comfort or make happy (sometimes followed by "up"). *The good news cheered them up.* 2. to become happier or less glum (usually followed by "up"). *As the rain stopped, we began to cheer up.* 3. to give a shout of encouragement, happiness, or praise to. *They cheered the winners wildly.* {**cheer**} cheery, adj.

cheer·ful *adjective* 1. full of cheer; happy. *She is always cheerful when I get home from school.* 2. bright or pleasant; bringing a feeling of good cheer. *I love a cheerful fire on a rainy night.* {**cheer** fəl} cheerfully, adv., cheerfulness, n.

cheese *noun* a food made by pressing together a mass of soft, thick soured milk solids. {**cheez**} cheesey, adj.

chee·tah *noun* a large wild cat of Africa and southern Asia that has solid black spots on its fur. Cheetahs have long legs and are the fastest animal on land. Sometimes they are trained for hunting game. {**cheet** ə}

chef ● *noun* a cook in charge of a hotel or restaurant kitchen. {**shehf**}

chem·i·cal ● *adjective* 1. of or having to do with the science of chemistry. *He works in a chemical lab.* 2. made by or being like chemicals. *The science teacher showed us two kinds of chemical reactions*

 Human Body   Human Mind   Everyday Life   History and Culture   Communication

today. *noun* a substance used in or produced by a chemical process. *A substance made from chemicals is used to make some drinks taste sweet.* {**kehm** ih kəl} chemically, adv.

chem·ist *noun* one who is active or expert in the field of chemistry. {**kehm** ihst}

chem·is·try 🌀 *noun* (chemistries) 1. the science that studies the form and function of basic elements and their compounds. 2. chemical properties and phenomena. {**kehm** ih stree}

chem·o·ther·a·py *noun* the science or practice of treating disease by using chemicals. {kee moh **thehr** ə pee *or* keh moh **thehr** ə pee}

cheque *noun* a spelling of **check** used in Canada and Britain. This spelling is only used when the meaning is "a form of payment." See **check** for more information. {**chehk**}

cher·ish *verb* (cherished, cherishing, cherishes) to value with great love and care. *She cherishes their friendship.* {**chehr** ihsh}

Cher·o·kee *noun* (Cherokees or Cherokee) a member of a Native American people that used to live in the southeastern United States. The Cherokee now live mostly in Oklahoma and also in North Carolina. {**chehr** ə kee}

cher·ry *noun* (cherries) 1. a small, round fruit that grows on a tree. It is red, yellow, or purple in color and has a hard pit in the center. 2. a kind of tree or shrub of the rose family grown for its showy flowers, its sweet or sour fruit, and for lumber. 3. the wood of the cherry tree. *Our dining room*

table is made of cherry. 4. a bright red color. {**chehr** ee}

chess *noun* a board game played by two people in which each player has sixteen pieces, and the object is to trap the opponent's king. {**chehs**}

chest 🌀 🌀 *noun* 1. the upper front part of the body between the neck and waist. 2. a large, strong box with a lid, used for holding things. *The chest that I brought to summer camp was filled with clothes, sheets, and blankets.* {**chehst**}

chest·nut *noun* 1. a nut that grows inside a prickly shell. It has a sweet taste. 2. a kind of tree that produces this nut. 3. the wood of the chestnut tree. 4. a reddish brown color. {**chehst** nuht}

chew 🌀 *verb* (chewed, chewing, chews) to tear or grind between the teeth. *Chew the pizza before you swallow it.* {**chooh**} chewable, adj.
  • **chew out**
to scold (informal). *The librarian chewed him out when he forgot to return the book.*

chewing gum *noun* a sweet and flavored gum for chewing. {**chooh** ing guhm}

Chey·enne *noun* 1. a member of a Native American people that now lives in Montana and Oklahoma. 2. the capital city of the U.S. state of Wyoming. {**shiy** **ehn**}

Word History *Cheyenne* is a Dakota Indian word that means "to speak red." The Dakota word *shaia* means "to speak strangely" or "to speak red." The Dakota considered their own speech "white" and ridiculed the speech of the Cheyenne people by calling it "red."

Chi·ca·go *noun* a city in the U.S. state of Illinois. It is near the southern tip of Lake Michigan. {shə **kah** goh}

Chi·ca·na *noun* a woman or girl of Mexican descent who lives in or is a citizen of the United States. {chih **kah** nah}

Chi·ca·no *noun* (Chicanos) a person of Mexican descent who lives in or is a citizen of the United States. {chih **kah** noh *or* chih **kă** noh}

chick *noun* a bird that has just hatched or a young bird, especially a young chicken. {**chihk**}

chick·a·dee *noun* a small North American bird with a gray body and black head and throat. {**chihk** ə dee}

chick·en 🌀 *noun* 1. a common farm bird that is raised for its meat and eggs. 2. the meat of a chicken used for food. 3. (informal) a person who is scared of doing something; a coward. *She called him a chicken because he didn't want to fight.* *verb* (chickened, chickening, chickens) (informal) to become scared of doing something after saying that one would do it; back out (usually followed by "out"). *He had planned to go skiing but chickened out after seeing the mountain.* {**chihk** ən}

chicken pox *noun* a disease that produces a fever and a rash. It is caused by a virus passed from person to person. {**chihk** ən pŏks}

A
B
C
D
E
F
G
H
I
J
K
L
M
N
O
P
Q
R
S
T
U
V
W
X
Y
Z

 Living World
 Physical World
 Natural Environment
 Economy
 Government and Law

a
b
c
d
e
f
g
h
i
j
k
l
m
n
o
p
q
r
s
t
u
v
w
x
y
z

chief *noun* the most powerful or important person in a group; leader. *The chief of the tribe was strong and wise.* *adjective* 1. having the highest position. *My aunt is the chief operating officer of a big company.* 2. most important; main. *Potatoes are the chief crop of Idaho.* {<u>cheef</u>}

chief·ly *adverb* 1. especially. *She is chiefly interested in basketball.* 2. mainly; mostly. *The yard is chiefly grass.* {<u>cheef</u> lee}

chief·tain *noun* a leader of a clan or tribe. {<u>cheef</u> tihn}

chig·ger *noun* the tiny larva of a mite that lives in the skin of animals and causes great itching. It is usually not dangerous but can sometimes spread disease. {<u>chihg</u> ər}

child ⊕ *noun* (children) 1. a young human; baby. 2. a son or daughter. {<u>chiyld</u>} childless, adj.
• **with child** pregnant.

child·birth *noun* the act of giving birth to a child. {<u>chihld</u> buhr*th*}

child·hood *noun* the period or state of being a child. {<u>chiyld</u> huud}

child·ish *adjective* 1. typical of or fit for a child. *Old maid is a childish card game, but poker is played by adults.* 2. marked by weak, foolish, or immature behavior. *Crying when you don't get your way seems childish.* {<u>chiyl</u> dihsh} childishly, adv., childishness, n.

child·like *adjective* of or like a child; innocent; simple. *My father had a sudden, childlike wish to run and play in the park.* {<u>chiyld</u> liyk}

chil·dren *noun* plural of **child**. {<u>chihl</u> drən}

chil·e *noun* see **chili**. {<u>chih</u> lee}

> **Homophone Note** The words *Chile*, *chilly*, and *chili* sound alike, but each has a different meaning.

Chil·e *noun* a country in southern South America. Santiago is the capital of Chile. {<u>chih</u> lee *or* <u>chee</u> lay} Chilean, n., adj.

chil·i or **chile** or **chilli** *noun* (chilies or chiles or chillies) 1. the pod of a tropical pepper plant. Chili has a strong, sharp flavor. 2. a spice or food made from this dried pod. *I like nothing better than a big bowl of spicy chili on a cold winter day.* {<u>chih</u> lee}

> **Homophone Note** The words *chili*, *chilly*, and *Chile* sound alike but have different meanings.

An unusual cold spell in Mexico left the **chili** underdressed and very **chilly**.

chill *noun* 1. a mild but uncomfortable coldness. *There is a chill in the damp basement.* 2. a feeling of cold and shivering caused by lowered temperature. *She got a chill when she walked out the door without her coat on.* 3. a sudden, cold feeling caused by fear or dread. *That scary movie gave her the chills.* *adjective* (chiller, chillest) having physical or emotional coolness. *There is a chill breeze this morning.* / *She gave him a chill greeting.* *verb* (chilled, chilling, chills) 1. to cause to become cooler or cold. *She chilled the bottles of water.* 2. to become colder. *His hands chilled from holding the icy can of soda.* {<u>chihl</u>} chillingly, adv.

chill·y *adjective* (chillier, chilliest) 1. causing a cool feeling that is uncomfortable. *It is a chilly day for swimming.* 2. feeling coolness or cold. *Without a coat, she was chilly.* 3. not warm; unfriendly. *He gave me a chilly welcome.* {<u>chihl</u> ee} chillily, adv., chilliness, n.

> **Homophone Note** The words *chilly*, *Chile*, and *chili* sound alike but have different meanings.

chime *noun* 1. (usually plural) a set of tuned bells or other hollow objects that produce musical sounds when struck. 2. a bell, or the sound of a bell. *He heard the chimes in the clock tower.* *verb* (chimed, chiming, chimes) to ring out. *The school bell chimed, letting us know that it was time to go to class.* {<u>chiym</u>}
• **chime in** to interrupt suddenly; add one's opinion. *My little brother chimed in to say that he wanted Mom and Dad to buy the red car.*

chim·ney *noun* (chimneys) a hollow, upright structure above a fireplace or furnace that carries smoke upward

 Human Body   Human Mind   Everyday Life    History and Culture   Communication

and to the outside. {**chihm** nee}

chimp *noun* a short form of **chimpanzee**. {**chihmp**}

chim·pan·zee *noun* a mammal that lives in African rain forests. Chimpanzees are in the group of primate mammals called apes. They are related to, but smaller than, gorillas. Chimpanzees are very intelligent and sometimes use tools to get food. {**chihm** păn **zee**}

chin *noun* the part of the face below the mouth and above the neck; the center of the lower jaw. *verb* (chinned, chinning, chins) to pull up from a hanging position to an overhead bar until the chin is level with the bar. *Children with strong arms and shoulders can chin themselves several times.* {**chihn**}
  • **keep one's chin up** to stay hopeful; not lose hope. *I told my friend to keep her chin up after she lost her dog.*

chi·na *noun* 1. delicate ceramic material; porcelain. 2. plates, dishes, and cups. *Please clear the china from the table.* {**chiy** nə}

Chi·na *noun* a country in eastern Asia. China is also called the People's Republic of China. Beijing is the capital of China. {**chiy** nə}

China Sea *noun* a large body of water in southeast Asia. {**chiy** nə **see**}

chin·chil·la *noun* a small mammal from the mountains of South America. Chinchillas are rodents closely related to guinea pigs. They have very soft fur and live in tunnels called burrows. Sometimes they are kept as pets. {**chihn** **chihl** ə}

Chi·nese *noun* (Chinese) 1. a person who was born in or is a citizen of China. 2. the main language of China. *adjective* of or having to do with China, or its people or languages. {**chiy** **neez**}

chink[1] *noun* a narrow crack. *Light shone through a chink between two boards in the floor.* {**chingk**}

chink[2] *verb* (chinked, chinking, chinks) to make or cause to make a sharp sound like a chime. *The grownups chinked their wine glasses together in celebration of my aunt's wedding.* {**chingk**}

chip *noun* 1. a small piece broken, cut, or chopped off of a hard material. *A chip flew off the stone when I hit it with a hammer.* 2. a dent or flaw caused by breaking off a small piece. *The rim of the plate has a chip.* 3. a microchip. *verb* to lose small pieces from the edge or surface. *This china chips easily.* {**chihp**}
  • **chip in** 1. to give money or effort. *The whole class chipped in and bought her a gift.* 2. to add to a discussion or to interrupt with. *When the teacher asked for ideas for our class trip, several students chipped in.*
  • **chip off the old block**

someone who is very much like one of his or her parents.
  • **chip on one's shoulder** a bitter or unhappy feeling that lasts for a long time; grudge. *After all these years, he still has a chip on his shoulder about our argument.*

chip·munk *noun* a small brown squirrel with a striped back and a flat, bushy tail. Chipmunks eat nuts, seeds, berries, and insects. They make underground burrows for sleeping and for storing food. Chipmunks live in North America and Asia. {**chihp** mungk}

chirp *verb* (chirped, chirping, chirps) to make a short sound with a high pitch. *The birds outside my window chirp at sunrise.* *noun* the sound made by chirping. *At the sight of a squirrel, the bird gave a loud chirp and flew off.* {**churp**}

chis·el *noun* a metal tool with a sharp edge, used for cutting stone, wood, or metal. *verb* (chiseled, chiseling, chisels) to cut or shape with a chisel. *He chiseled the stone to make a statue.* {**chih** zəl}

chiv·al·ry *noun* the qualities expected of an ideal knight during the Middle Ages in Europe. These included courage, honor, politeness, and being prepared to help those in need. {**shihv** əl ree}

chlo·rine *noun* a substance that is one of the chemical elements. It combines with sodium to form table salt. It is also used in making bleach. Chlorine is poisonous in its pure gas form. (symbol: Cl) {**klohr** een}

A B **C** D E F G H I J K L M N O P Q R S T U V W X Y Z

a
b
c
d
e
f
g
h
i
j
k
l
m
n
o
p
q
r
s
t
u
v
w
x
y
z

chlorinity, n., chlorinous, adj.

chlo·ro·phyll ➊ *noun* the green matter in the leaves and stems of plants that is necessary to produce food for plants from sunlight. {<u>klohr</u> ə fihl}

choc·o·late *noun* 1. a food made from ground cacao seeds. *Chocolate is native to the Americas.* 2. a candy or syrup made of ground cacao with added sugar. 3. a drink made by mixing sweet chocolate with water or milk. *We drank a cup of hot chocolate to warm up after playing in the snow.* 4. a dark brown color. *adjective* made with chocolate. *My mom won't let me eat chocolate cake for breakfast.* {<u>chŏk</u> liht} chocolaty, adj.

choice *noun* 1. the act of picking or choosing; selection. *It was hard to make the right choice.* 2. the thing or person chosen. *Jack was the choice for the role of king in our play.* 3. the right or chance to choose. *She gave us a choice between doing our homework during recess or at home.* 4. one of a number of things that can be chosen. *That shop offers a large choice of ice cream flavors. adjective* (choicer, choicest) of very good quality; excellent. *We cooked a choice piece of meat for dinner.* {<u>chois</u>}

choir *noun* a group of people who sing together; chorus. {<u>kwiyr</u>}

choke *verb* (choked, choking, chokes) 1. to stop or prevent the breathing of by squeezing or blocking the windpipe. *Loosen that rope around the dog's neck before it chokes him.* 2. to have a hard time breathing, speaking, or swallowing. *He choked on a chicken bone. / She was laughing so hard that she could only choke out a greeting to us.* 3. to clog or block. *A ball of hair is choking the pipe. noun* a device that controls the amount of air in an engine carburetor. {<u>chohk</u>}

• **choke up**
1. to become unable to speak because of strong emotion or stress. *He became all choked up when he saw the gift that his children had made.* 2. to move one's hands up from the bottom end of a baseball bat.

cho·les·ter·ol *noun* a white substance, found in the tissues of all animals, which acts to clean the bloodstream and surrounds certain nerves. {kə <u>lehs</u> tə rŏl}

choose *verb* (chose, chosen, choosing, chooses) 1. to pick one or more from a group. *Paul chose three books from the library.* 2. to decide (often followed by "to"). *We chose to go to a movie instead of a concert.* {<u>choohz</u>}

chop *verb* (chopped, chopping, chops) 1. to cut by using of a sharp tool. *She chopped the log into three pieces with an ax.* 2. to cut into many small pieces (often followed by "up"). *The chef chopped up an onion for the soup. noun* 1. an act or instance of chopping. *It took only one chop to split the board in two.* 2. a thick slice of meat with a rib left in it. *Would you like lamb chops for dinner?* {<u>chŏp</u>}

chop·stick *noun* one of a pair of thin sticks used for eating, especially in Asian countries. {<u>chŏp</u> stihk}

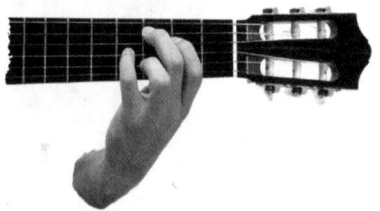

chord[1] *noun* a line that connects two points on a circle. *A diameter is a chord that passes through the center of a circle.* {<u>kohrd</u>}

chord[2] *noun* three or more musical notes played at the same time. {<u>kohrd</u>}

Homophone Note Are you looking for the word *cord*? *Chord* and *cord* sound alike but have different meanings.

chore *noun* 1. a routine task around the house or yard. *Taking out the garbage is her least favorite chore.* 2. an unpleasant or difficult task. *Gardening is a hobby for some people, but a chore for others.* {<u>chohr</u>}

cho·rus ➋ *noun* (choruses) 1. a group of people who sing together. 2. a group of people who sing and dance together in shows. 3. a part of a song that is repeated after every verse. {<u>kohr</u> ihs}

• **in chorus**
all together; at the same time. *When Mom walks into the room, I want everyone to shout "happy birthday!" in chorus.*

chose *verb* past tense of **choose**. {<u>chohz</u>}

cho·sen *verb* past participle of **choose**. {<u>choh</u> zən}

 Human Body   Human Mind   Everyday Life   History and Culture Communication

chow[1] *noun* (informal) food. {**chow**}

chow[2] *noun* a Chinese breed of dog. Chows are sturdy dogs of medium size with a thick red or black coat, a black tongue, and a tail that curls over the back. {**chow**}

A Chinese chow enjoys some puppy chow.

chow·der *noun* a thick soup in which clams, fish, or corn are added to potatoes and onions in a milk or tomato base. {**chow** dər}

Christ *noun* See **Jesus Christ**. {**kriyst**} Christlike, adj.

chris·ten *verb* (christened, christening, christens) 1. to give a name to at baptism. 2. to give a name to or dedicate. *He christened the sailboat "Little Joe" after his son.* {**krih** sən}

Chris·tian *adjective* 1. of, or coming from the person, actions, or words of Jesus Christ, or the religion based on his life. 2. being a member of or following this religion. *noun* 1. a member of a Christian church. 2. one who believes in the divine nature of Jesus Christ and follows his words and teachings. {**krihs** chən}

Chris·ti·an·i·ty *noun* 1. the Christian religion, including its many separate branches. 2. the religion based on the teachings of Jesus Christ. {**krihs** tee **ăn** ih tee *or* **krihs** chee **ăn** ih tee}

Christ·mas *noun* 1. December 25, a Christian holiday that celebrates the birth of Jesus Christ. 2. this day as a holiday according to the law. It is a time for sending greetings and giving gifts. {**krihs** məs}

Christmas tree *noun* a real or fake evergreen tree, usually placed indoors and decorated with lights and ornaments at Christmas. {**krihs** məs **tree**}

chro·mat·ic *adjective* 1. having to do with color or colors. *This painting by Van Gogh has a bold chromatic approach.* 2. having to do with a musical scale, where the difference between each note is one half step. *The composer J.S. Bach is famous for his "Chromatic Fantasy."* {krə **măt** ihk}

chromatic scale *noun* a musical scale of half steps. {krə **măt** ihk **skayl**}

chro·mi·um *noun* a shiny, silver-gray metal that is one of the chemical elements. Chromium does not rust easily. It is used on surfaces, such as the metal trim on cars, because it stays shiny. It can be combined with other metals to form alloys. (symbol: Cr) {**kroh** mee əm}

chro·mo·some 🌿 📖 *noun* a part found in the cells of all plants and animals. Chromosomes contain genes which pass on physical characteristics from parent to offspring. {**kroh** mə **sohm**}

chron·ic *adjective* 1. done for a long time or by habit. *His chronic stealing was a serious problem.* 2. happening often and lasting a long time. *She suffers from chronic back problems.* {**krŏn** ihk} chronically, adv.

chron·o·log·i·cal *adjective* arranged according to the order in which things happen. *He wrote a chronological family history.* {**krŏn** ə **lŏj** ih kəl} chronologic, adj., chronologically, adv.

chrys·a·lis *noun* (chrysalises) the hard outside covering on a moth or butterfly while it is a pupa, the stage before it becomes an adult with wings. Many kinds of moths and butterflies make a chrysalis instead of a cocoon. Chrysalis is also sometimes used as another name for the pupa itself. {**krihs** ə lihs}

chry·san·the·mum *noun* 1. a type of plant grown for its flowers that bloom in autumn. Some species are grown for a compound that kills insects on crop plants. 2. the flower of this plant. {krih **săn** thə məm}

chub·by *adjective* (chubbier, chubbiest) plump and round. *What a cute, chubby face your baby sister has!* {**chuhb** ee} chubbiness, n.

chuck *verb* (chucked, chucking, chucks) 1. to touch or pat lightly with affection. *My uncle always chucks me under the chin when he sees me.* 2. to throw or toss. *He chucked a shoe at the cat to make her stop clawing the curtain.* 3. (informal) to throw away; to get rid of. *She chucked her old sneakers into the trash.* *noun* 1. a light tap, especially under the chin. 2. a throw or toss. {**chuhk**}

chuck·le *verb* (chuckled, chuckling, chuckles) to

A
B
C
D
E
F
G
H
I
J
K
L
M
N
O
P
Q
R
S
T
U
V
W
X
Y
Z

a
b
c
d
e
f
g
h
i
j
k
l
m
n
o
p
q
r
s
t
u
v
w
x
y
z

laugh softly or in a quiet manner. *The old man chuckled at her joke.* noun a soft or quiet laugh. {chuhk əl}

chug noun a short, steady sound. *We heard the chug of the old train as it approached the station.* verb (chugged, chugging, chugs) to move while making a chugging sound. *The train chugged up the mountain.* {chuhg}

chum noun a close friend; pal. {chuhm}

chunk noun a thick lump or piece of any material. *She gave him a chunk of chocolate to nibble on.* {chungk}

church ○ ○ noun 1. a building used for public Christian religious services. 2. Christian religious services. *Church is on Sunday mornings and usually lasts for one hour.* 3. (often capitalized) a group of Christian people who have the same beliefs; denomination. *King Henry the Eighth founded the Church of England.* {church}

churn noun a container in which cream or milk is beaten or shaken to form butter. verb (churned, churning, churns) 1. to beat or shake in a churn to make butter. 2. to move or stir powerfully. *Rough seas churned the seaweed up onto the beach.* 3. to move or stir with great force. *Storm clouds churned in the dark sky.* {churn}

chute noun a passage down which things may slide in order to be moved from one area to another. *This hotel has a laundry chute on each floor.* {shooht}

Homophone Note The words *chute* and *shoot* sound alike but have different meanings.

ci·ca·da noun (cicadas or cicadae) a large insect with a stout body and two pairs of thin, clear wings. The male cicada makes a loud, shrill noise. {sih **kay** də or sih **kah** də}

ci·der noun the juice pressed out of apples, used for drinking. {**siy** dər}

ci·gar noun a thin, tight roll of tobacco leaves prepared for smoking. {sih **gar**}

cig·a·rette noun a short, narrow tube of thin paper that contains cut tobacco for smoking. {sihg ə **reht** or **sihg** ə reht}

cin·der noun a small piece of partly burned wood or coal that can continue to burn but without a flame. {**sihn** dər} cinderlike, adj.

cin·e·ma ○ noun 1. the art or business of making movies. *He is writing a book on the history of cinema.* 2. a movie theater. {**sihn** ə mə} cinematic, adj.

cin·na·mon noun 1. a spice made from the dried bark of a tropical Asian tree. 2. a tree that bears this bark. {**sihn** ə mən}

cir·cle noun 1. a closed curve made up of points that are all the same distance from a fixed center point. 2. anything that is shaped like a circle. *The children sat in a circle at story time.* 3. a group of people who are related by blood or have the same interests. *Our family circle comes together for holidays.* verb (circled, circling, circles) 1. to make a circle around. *The shark circled its prey before attacking.* 2. to move around in a circle. *The dancers circled the stage.* {**suhr** kəl}

cir·cuit ○ noun 1. a line or route around an area. *We walked the outer circuit of the park.* 2. an act of moving or turning around. *The earth makes a circuit around the sun.* 3. the area that someone travels regularly to carry out their work. *We know our mailman because our neighborhood has been part of his circuit for many years.* 4. the closed path followed by an electric current. {**suhr** kiht}

circuit breaker noun a switch or other device that automatically breaks an electric circuit when too much electricity flows through it. {**suhr** kiht **bray** kər}

cir·cu·lar adjective 1. having the shape of a circle; round. 2. moving in the form of a circle. *The bird flew in a circular path.* noun a piece of printed matter, usually an advertisement, sent or given to many people. {**suhr** kyə lər} circularly, adv.

cir·cu·late verb (circulated, circulating, circulates) 1. to move or flow along a closed path or system. *Blood circulates through the body.* / *Water circulates in the fish tank.* 2. to move around from person to person or from place to place. *He is circulating among the guests at the party.* / *Jokes circulate rapidly among children.* {**suhr** kyə **layt**} circulatory, adj.

cir·cu·la·tion noun 1. the movement or passage of something, such as money or news, from person to person or place to place. *The new stamps are now in circulation.* / *That wild story has been in circulation for too long.* 2. the movement of blood through the arteries and veins of the body. *Grandmother's hands get*

 Human Body
 Human Mind
 Everyday Life
 History and Culture
Communication

cold easily because she has poor circulation. 3. the number of copies of a newspaper or magazine that are sold at a given time, or the selling itself. *Our town newspaper has a circulation of twenty thousand.* {**suhr** kyə **lay** shən}

cir·cu·la·tor·y sys·tem *noun* a system in the body made up of the heart, blood vessels, blood, and lymph vessels that carries blood and lymph around the body. *Circulatory system health problems include strokes, anemia, and heart attacks.* {**sər** kooh lo tohr ee sihs təm}

cir·cum·fer·ence *noun* 1. the line that forms the outside edge of a circle or other round figure or area. *We walked around the circumference of the camp.* 2. the length of such a line; distance around something. *The circumference of the ball is ten inches.* {sər **kuhm** fər əns *or* sər **kuhm** frəns}

cir·cum·stance *noun* a condition or fact connected with or having an effect on an event or situation. *Bad weather was a circumstance we didn't think about when planning the picnic.* {**suhr** kəm **stǎns**}

• **under no circumstances** in no instance; never. *Under no circumstances would his parents let him quit school to help out on the farm.*

• **under the circumstances** given the facts as they are. *Under the circumstances, I would feel better if you walked home with a friend.*

cir·cus *noun* (circuses) 1. a traveling show with clowns, trained animals, acrobats, and other acts. 2. a large, outdoor stadium in ancient Rome used for public events and games. *The ancient*

Romans held chariot races in the circus. {**suhr** kəs}

cir·rus *noun* (cirrus or cirri) a type of cloud that usually appears in the form of strings or threads. {**seer** əs}

cite *verb* (cited, citing, cites) to use the words of someone else; quote. *Max cited a history book and a Web page in his report on civil rights.* {**siyt**}

Homophone Note The words *cite*, *sight*, and *site* all sound alike but have different meanings.

cit·i·zen *noun* 1. a person who is a member of a country either because of being born there or being declared a member by law. 2. a person who lives in and has the rights given by a town or city. *As citizens of the town, we can vote in the election for the office of mayor.* {**siht** ə sən *or* **siht** ə zən}

cit·i·zen·ship *noun* 1. the state of being a citizen. 2. the act of being a citizen. *Citizenship for me means taking part in town meetings and helping to make our town better.* {**siht** ə sən shihp *or* **siht** ə zən shihp}

cit·rus *noun* (citruses or citrus) a group of trees grown for their juicy fruit, such as the orange, lemon, and grapefruit. *adjective* of or related to

the fruit of such trees. *The restaurant served a fresh citrus drink of lemon and lime.* {**sih** trihs}

cit·y *noun* (cities) 1. a large and important town where many people live and work. 2. all of the people who live in a city. *The city is angry at the company for polluting the water.* {**siht** ee}

civ·ic *adjective* 1. of or having to do with a city. *Paying taxes is a civic duty.* 2. of or having to do with citizens or citizenship. *We have civic rights and responsibilities.* {**sihv** ihk}

civ·ics *noun* the study of the rights and duties of citizens in relation to how the government works. {**sihv** ihks}

civ·il *adjective* 1. having to do with citizens or the general population. *As a citizen, do you know your civil duties?* 2. of the daily activities of citizens as opposed to those of religious or military groups. *My parents were married in a civil ceremony at the courthouse.* 3. using good manners; polite. *She behaves in a civil way toward everyone.* {**sihv** əl} civilly, adv.

ci·vil·ian *noun* a person who is not serving in the armed forces or the police. *The soldiers were sent to rescue a group of civilians who were being held by the enemy. adjective* of civil life or civilians; not of the military or police. *Before leaving work, my father changes out of his policeman's uniform into his civilian clothes.* {sə **vihl** yən}

civ·i·li·za·tion *noun* 1. the achievements of an advanced society, including art, government, and technology. 2. the culture of a given time, place, or

A
B
C
D
E
F
G
H
I
J
K
L
M
N
O
P
Q
R
S
T
U
V
W
X
Y
Z

a
b
c
d
e
f
g
h
i
j
k
l
m
n
o
p
q
r
s
t
u
v
w
x
y
z

group of people. *We studied the civilizations of ancient Mexico.* {sihv ə lih **zay** shən}

civ·i·lize *verb* (civilized, civilizing, civilizes) to bring education and training to, especially in the arts, science, and government. {**sihv** ə liyz}

civil rights *plural noun* 1. the rights given by a nation's government to all its citizens. 2. in the United States, certain rights, such as the right to vote, own property, and have a fair trial. These rights are guaranteed by the Constitution and Acts of Congress. *Martin Luther King was a leader in the fight for civil rights for African Americans.* {**sihv** əl **riyts**}

civil service *noun* any branch of government that is not part of the legislature, court system, or the military. {**sihv** əl **suhr** vihs} civil-service, *adj.*

civil war *noun* a war within a country between different groups or areas. {**sihv** əl **wohr**}

Cl symbol of the chemical element chlorine

clad[1] *verb* a past tense and past participle of **clothe**. {**klăd**}

clad[2] *verb* (cladded, cladding, clads) to join a metal to another metal in order to make it stronger or protect it. {**klăd**}

claim *verb* (claimed, claiming, claims) 1. to state or demand as one's right. *She claimed the first seat on the bus.* 2. to state as true. *He claimed that his father was seven feet tall.* 3. to need or call for. *The children claimed her attention.* *noun* 1. a demand for something as one's right. *These people say they have a claim on the old farm.* 2. a statement of something as true. *The king ques-*

tioned the nobles' claim of loyalty. {**klaym**}

clam *noun* an animal with a soft body and a hard shell made of two hinged pieces that open and close. Many kinds of clams live in the ocean and in fresh water. People eat some kinds of clams. Clams are mollusks. *verb* (clammed, clamming, clams) 1. to search or dig for clams. *We went clamming at the beach.* 2. (informal) to refuse to speak (often followed by "up"). *He clammed up when the teacher entered the room.* {**klăm**}

clam·bake *noun* a picnic or party on the beach at which clams and other foods are cooked. The food is usually baked or steamed on heated rocks covered with a layer of seaweed. {**klăm** bayk}

clam·ber *verb* (clambered, clambering, clambers) to climb with effort using both hands and feet. *The scouts clambered up the steep, rocky slope.* {**klăm** bər}

clam·or *noun* 1. a loud noise that goes on for sometime. *The neighborhood was kept awake by the clamor from the party next door.* 2. a strong public protest. *There was a clamor against the new shopping mall.* *verb* (clamored, clamoring, clamors) to produce a clamor. *At the end of the concert, the crowd clamored for more songs.* {**klăm** ər}

clamp *noun* a device used to fasten, support, or press together two or more objects or pieces. *My reading lamp has a*

clamp that attaches to the shelf over my bed. *verb* (clamped, clamping, clamps) to fasten or support with a clamp. *The carpenter clamped the board to the bench while he worked.* {**klămp**}

clan *noun* 1. a group among the Scottish people that is made up of families with a common ancestor. 2. a group of people from the same family. *The Smith clan got together at the beach last summer.* {**klăn**}

clang *verb* (clanged, clanging, clangs) to make a clear, loud sound or ring, such as that made when two heavy metal objects are struck together. *When the lunch bell clangs, there is a rush to the cafeteria.* *noun* a clanging sound. *At midnight, a clang of bells rang in the new year.* {**klăng**}

clank *noun* a short sound, as of metal being struck, that does not ring. *The iron bar fell with a clank.* *verb* (clanked, clanking, clanks) 1. to make a clanking sound. *The gate clanked when it shut.* 2. to move with a clanking sound. *Soldiers in armor clanked across the bridge.* 3. to cause to make a sharp or clanking sound. *The prisoners clanked their leg irons and demanded food.* {**klăngk**}

clap *verb* (clapped, clapping, claps) 1. to strike together, making a sharp, short sound. *Garth clapped his book shut.* 2. to strike one's open hands together again and again as a way of showing approval. *Everyone clapped when the show was over.* 3. to strike lightly with an open hand and in a friendly manner. *The coach clapped us on our backs after we won the game.* *noun* 1. a slap or blow. *He gave her a*

 Human Body   Human Mind   Everyday Life   History and Culture  Communication

clap on the back when he saw that she was choking. 2. a sudden, loud sound. *A sudden clap of thunder frightened the dog.* {**klăp**}

clar·i·fy *verb* (clarified, clarifying, clarifies) to make easier to understand; make clear. *She drew a map to clarify the directions.* {**klar** ih **fiy**} clarification, n., clarifier, n.

clar·i·net *noun* a woodwind instrument with a reed mouthpiece attached to a long tube with finger holes and keys along its length. {**klar** ih **neht**} clarinetist (clarinettist), n.

Word History *Clarinet* is borrowed from *clarinette*, an early French word that means "bell," which comes from an earlier French word that means "clear."

clar·i·ty *noun* 1. the state or condition of being clear or being understood. *The clarity of the teacher's lessons makes learning easy.* 2. the state or condition of being clear or pure. *We saw many colorful fish because of the clarity of the sea water.* {**klar** ih tee}

clash *verb* (clashed, clashing, clashes) 1. to strike together with force, making a loud noise. *The knights' swords clashed in battle.* 2. to disagree sharply. *They clashed over who should be the leader.* 3. to not match or work together in color, tone, or time. *Your red shirt clashes with those orange shorts.* / *The time of our club meeting clashes with my hockey game.* *noun* 1. a harsh, loud sound. *There was a clash of metal against metal when one car backed into the other.* 2. a fight, battle, or disagreement.

The two hockey teams had a clash on the ice. {**klăsh**}

clasp *noun* 1. a device with two parts that fit together, used to fasten something. *The clasp broke and I lost my bracelet.* 2. a grasping or gripping with a hand or arm, or as if with a hand or arm. *He would not loosen his tight clasp on her diary.* / *Fear had him in its clasp!* *verb* (clasped, clasping, clasps) 1. to fasten with a clasp. *She clasped the string of pearls around her neck.* 2. to grasp or grip with a hand or arm, or something like a hand or arm. *She clasped my hand in hers.* {**klăsp**}

class 🌳 🏭 🌀 *noun* 1. a group of people or things that are similar in certain ways. *Of all the classes of books, my favorite is fantasy.* 2. a group or division that is based on quality. *That dealer sells a better class of cars.* 3. a group of people who have a similar way of life and position in society. *Many members of the upper class live in large, fancy houses.* 4. all of the students who graduate in the same year. *My brother was in the class of 1997.* 5. a group of students who meet together to learn in school. *Everyone in Frank's English class took a test today.* 6. the time during which a group of students meets. *History class is at one o'clock every day.* 7. a large grouping or division of living beings in biology. *Tigers and sloths belong to the class of mammals.* *verb* (classed, classing, classes) to group into a class; classify. *Our librarian classed the books by author.* {**klăs**}

clas·sic 🔲 🌀 *adjective* 1. something that remains popular over a long period of time. *"Treasure Island" is a classic work of fiction.* 2. typical of a class or category; serving as an example against which others are judged. *My aunt owns a classic Mustang.* *noun* 1. a work of art or literature that is considered to be one of the best. A classic is an example against which other works are judged. *Shakespeare's "Hamlet" is a classic.* 2. (plural) the literature of ancient Greece or Rome. {**klăs** ihk}

clas·si·cal *adjective* 1. having to do with ancient Greek and Roman culture. *This museum has many examples of classical art.* 2. having to do with the complex music of the European tradition that is neither folk nor popular music. *Mozart composed classical music.* {**klăs** ih kəl} classically, adv.

clas·si·fy *verb* (classified, classifying, classifies) to group or order in classes. *He classified his coin collection according to type and age.* {**klăs** ih **fiy**} classifiable, adj.

class·mate *noun* a person in the same class as another at a college or school. {**klăs** mayt}

class·room *noun* a room in a school or college where classes are held. {**klăs** roohm}

clat·ter *verb* (clattered, clattering, clatters) to make a loud rattling noise. *The old engine clattered as he drove up the hill.* / *The children clattered down the stairs wearing their dress shoes.* *noun* a loud rattling noise. *A loud clatter could be heard coming from the attic at midnight.* {**klăt** ər} clattery, adj.

clause *noun* 1. a group of words that has a subject and a verb.

a
b
c
d
e
f
g
h
i
j
k
l
m
n
o
p
q
r
s
t
u
v
w
x
y
z

Clauses can be part or all of a sentence. 2. a section, article, or provision of a legal document or of other documents. *The senators added a clause to the new law.* {**klawz**}

claw 🏃❓ *noun* 1. a thin, sharp, curved nail on the foot of an animal. 2. the grasping part on the leg of a crustacean or insect. *Look out, or the crab's claw will pinch your toe!* 3. any object that looks or acts like a claw. *Use the claw of the hammer to pull out the nails.* *verb* (clawed, clawing, claws) to scratch, tear, dig, or pull with or as if with claws. *The cat clawed his leg. / I clawed my way up the slippery hillside.* {**klaw**}

clay 🌍 *noun* moist, stiff earth that is used for making brick, pottery, and tile. {**klay**}

clean *adjective* (cleaner, cleanest) 1. not dirty or stained. *I got a clean dish from the shelf.* 2. pure; free from pollution. *Everyone should have clean air to breathe.* 3. done or made without difficulty or mistake. *The soldiers made a clean escape from the prison camp.* 4. fair. *It was a clean fight.* *adverb* completely. *The runaway horse jumped clean over the fence.* *verb* (cleaned, cleaning, cleans) to remove dirt or stains from; make clean. *Clean your shoes on the mat.* {**kleen**} cleanliness, n.

• **come clean**
(informal) to admit the truth. *He came clean about his past crimes.*

clean·er *noun* 1. a person or thing that cleans. *We'll need to use a strong cleaner on this dirty kitchen floor.* 2. (plural) a business that dry-cleans clothing. *Please drop these shirts off at the cleaners.* {**kleen** ər}

clean·ing *noun* clothing that is taken to a dry-cleaning store instead of being washed at home. *He will pick up the cleaning on the way home from work.* {**kleen** ing}

clean·li·ness *noun* the condition of being clean, or not dirty; the habit of always keeping clean. *Cats are well known for their cleanliness.* {**kleen** lee nihs}

cleanse *verb* (cleansed, cleansing, cleanses) to make clean; remove dirt from. *I cleanse my face with soap and water every night before I go to bed.* {**klehnz**}

clean·ser *noun* a liquid or powder used for cleaning. {**klehn** zər}

clear *adjective* (clearer, clearest) 1. free of darkness, clouds, or haze. *It was a clear, sunny day.* 2. free of defects or flaws. *The diamond was clear and perfect.* 3. free of confusion. *The professor gave me a clear explanation.* 4. unable to be mistaken for something else; obvious. *This is a clear case of murder.* 5. free from guilt; innocent. *My conscience is clear.* 6. not blocked; open. *There was a clear path through the woods.* *adverb* (clearer, clearest) in a clear way; clearly. *I can hear you loud and clear.* *verb* (cleared, clearing, clears) 1. to make free of confusion or doubt. *We did not understand the homework assignment at first, but he cleared it up for us.* 2. to make free of anything in the way; make open. *Workers cleared the path of fallen branches.* 3. to pass by or near without touching. *The horse cleared the fence.* 4. to give permission to for an action. *The control tower cleared the plane for takeoff.* 5. to become clear. *After a week of rain, the sky finally cleared.* {**kleer**}

• **in the clear**
free from danger or charges of guilt. *The police let him go when he was found to be in the clear.*

clear·ance *noun* 1. the space between things that keeps them from striking against each other. *The car had enough clearance to fit in the parking space.* 2. the act of clearing. *The clearance of the building during a fire drill takes fifteen minutes.* {**kleer** əns}

clear·ing *noun* an open piece of land that has no trees or bushes. *They built a log cabin in a clearing in the forest.* {**kleer** ing}

clear·ly *adverb* 1. in a clear manner. *She told the story clearly.* 2. without a doubt. *She is clearly right for the job.* {**kleer** lee}

cleav·er *noun* a heavy tool with a wide blade used especially by butchers for cutting meat. {**klee** vər}

clef *noun* one of four signs placed on a musical staff. They show in what range the notes are to be played. *This symphony is written in the bass, treble, alto, and tenor clefs.* {**klehf**}

cleft *adjective* split; divided. *I recognized Juan by his cleft chin.* *noun* an opening made by or as if by a split. *We hid the box in a cleft in the tree.* {**klehft**}

clench *verb* (clenched, clenching, clenches) 1. to close tightly shut. *He clenched his fists in anger. / She clenched her teeth as the doctor set the broken bone.* 2. to hold in a tight grip. *The child clenched a doll in her hand.* {**klehnch**}

 Human Body   Human Mind   Everyday Life   History and Culture    Communication

cler·gy *noun* (clergies) the group of people who have the authority to lead religious services, such as ministers, priests, and rabbis. {<u>kluhr</u> jee}

cler·gy·man *noun* (clergymen) a member of the clergy. {<u>kluhr</u> jee mən}

clerk *noun* 1. a person who does office work, such as keeping records and typing letters. 2. a person who sells goods to customers in a store; salesperson. {<u>kluhrk</u>}

cle·ver ❓ *adjective* 1. having a bright, sharp, and quick mind; intelligent. *She is a clever student who asks interesting questions.* 2. showing original or creative thought. *His clever invention was successful where many others had failed.* {<u>klehv</u> ər} cleverly, adv., cleverness, n.

click *noun* 1. a slight, sharp sound. *Her high heel shoes clicked on the sidewalk.* 2. a sound that is made in some African languages by breathing in and clicking the tongue. *verb* (clicked, clicking, clicks) 1. to make a slight, sharp sound. *The door clicked shut behind him.* 2. (informal) to fit together well in friendship; agree. *We clicked as soon as we met and were friends for many years.* 3. to cause to make a clicking noise. *She clicked her heels together and made a wish.* {<u>klihk</u>} clicker, n.

cli·ent *noun* one who pays for the services of another. *The lawyer met with her client to talk about their first day in court.* {<u>kliy</u> ənt}

cliff 🌐 *noun* a high, steep face of rock or earth. *It is dangerous to stand near the edge of a cliff.* {<u>klihf</u>}

cli·mate 🌐 *noun* the usual weather conditions in a place. *Antarctica has a cold climate.* {<u>kliy</u> miht} climatic, adj.

Word History *Climate* is from an ancient Greek word that means "slope of the earth" or "region of the earth." The Greeks believed that the earth sloped from the equator to the north and south poles. They divided the earth into zones, and each zone was called a *klima*. By the 1600s, "climate" was being used in English for weather conditions.

cli·max *noun* 1. the most exciting or interesting point in a series of events. *The climax of his life as a swimmer was setting a world record.* 2. the point at which a conflict reaches a crisis in a work of literature. *At the story's climax, the boy must either help his friend or let him down.* {<u>kliy</u> mäks}

climb *verb* (climbed, climbing, climbs) 1. to go up by foot. *Let's climb the hill.* 2. to move upward; go towards the top; rise. *He climbed for an hour until he reached the top of the hill. / The airplane climbed sharply after it took off.* 3. to grow upward on a tall support. *The ivy climbed to the roof of the house.* *noun* 1. the act of climbing. *The family made several mountain climbs during their vacation.* 2. something to be climbed. *That cliff is a difficult climb.* {<u>kliym</u>} climber, n.

clinch *verb* (clinched, clinching, clinches) to make certain or final; settle. *The runner moved ahead and clinched the race for first place.* {<u>klihnch</u>}

cling *verb* (clung, clinging, clings) 1. to stick closely. *Excuse me, but a strand of spaghetti is clinging to your chin!* 2. to hold onto someone or each other tightly. *Lost in the snowy woods, they clung together for warmth.* {<u>kling</u>} clinginess, n., clingy, adj.

clin·ic *noun* a place that gives medical treatment to people who do not need to stay in a hospital overnight. {<u>klihn</u> ihk}

clink *verb* (clinked, clinking, clinks) to make or cause to make a short, sharp, ringing sound. *They clinked their glasses together in celebration.* *noun* a clinking sound. *The pirate loved to hear the clink of gold coins.* {<u>klingk</u>}

clip[1] *verb* (clipped, clipping, clips) 1. to cut off, cut out, or trim with scissors or shears. *He clipped an article from a magazine. / She clipped her fingernails.* 2. (informal) to hit sharply. *He clipped me on the ear.* *noun* 1. the act of clipping, or a single such cut. *Give those bushes by the driveway a clip.* 2. (informal) a quick, sharp blow. *The boxer took a clip on the chin.* 3. a fast rate of speed. *The bike raced down the hill at a frightening clip.* {<u>klihp</u>}

She **clipped clips** at a good **clip**.

clip[2] *noun* 1. a device that holds or fastens. *Tanya used a paper*

clip to hold the pages of her report together. 2. a device holding several bullets that is put into a gun. *verb* (clipped, clipping, clips) to hold together or join by means of a clip. {<u>klihp</u>}

clip·per *noun* 1. (often plural) a tool for clipping or cutting. *Use the nail clippers to trim your fingernails.* 2. a fast type of sailing ship. {<u>klihp</u> ər}

clip·ping *noun* a piece cut off or from. *We can use a clipping from this plant to grow a new one. / They collect magazine clippings about famous people.* {<u>klihp</u> ing}

cloak *noun* 1. a long, loose, outer garment without sleeves. 2. something that hides or covers. *A cloak of fog settled on the lake. verb* (cloaked, cloaking, cloaks) to hide or cover with or as if with a cloak. *They cloaked themselves against the cold wind. / He cloaked his thoughts in silence.* {<u>klohk</u>}

clob·ber *verb* (clobbered, clobbering, clobbers) (informal) to strike hard; beat up. *The two boxers clobbered each other.* {<u>klob</u> ər}

clock *noun* a device, other than a watch, for measuring and showing the time. *verb* (clocked, clocking, clocks) to find out the time or speed of, using a clock or watch. *We clocked the horse at thirty miles per hour.* {<u>klŏk</u>}
• **around the clock** through all twenty-four hours; without stopping. *She sat by his bedside around the clock.*

Word History *Clock* is from a Celtic word meaning "bell." In the 1300s, the time was announced with the sounding of a bell.

clock·wise *adverb or adjective* in or turning in the direction in which a clock's hands turn. *He gave the knob on the radio a clockwise turn. / He turned the knob clockwise.* {<u>klŏk</u> wiyz}

clod *noun* 1. a lump of earth or clay. 2. a dull, stupid person. *Unkind people called him a clod, when he was only shy.* {<u>klŏd</u>}

clog *verb* (clogged, clogging, clogs) 1. to block passage along or through. *Traffic clogs the city streets. / The pipe was clogged with dirt.* 2. to become blocked with sticky matter. *The sink drain has clogged again. noun* a shoe with a thick wooden sole. {<u>klŏg</u> *or* <u>klawg</u>, n., <u>klŏg</u> *or* <u>klawg</u>, v.}

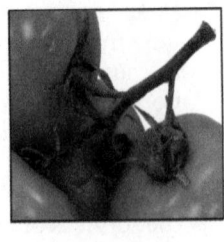

clois·ter *noun* 1. a place such as a monastery or convent where people live quiet, spiritual lives. 2. a covered walk around the inside of a building that faces an open central courtyard. {<u>klois</u> tər}

clop *noun* a sharp, hollow sound. *I could hear the clop of horses as they paraded by. verb* (clopped, clopping, clops) to make such a sound, or walk making such a sound. *She clopped down the stairs in her wooden shoes.* {<u>klŏp</u>}

close *verb* (closed, closing, closes) 1. to stop up; shut. *Close the door.* 2. to block; obstruct. *The police closed the street.* 3. to end; finish. *She closed the speech with a funny story.* 4. to draw together; join. *Close the curtains.* 5. to become closed or shut. *The elevator doors closed.* 6. to end. *The show will close tomorrow.* 7. to stop working; become no longer available

for business. *The restaurant will close in an hour. adjective* (closer, closest) 1. near in space or time. *It is close to the end of the movie.* 2. near in relation or association. *My sister is my closest relative.* 3. tight, confining, or shut in. *It was difficult to live in such close quarters.* 4. narrow; nearly decided another way. *The race was close, but he finally won.* 5. careful or thorough. *Pay close attention. / I gave the story a close reading. adverb* (closer, closest) in a close manner; near. *The comet passed very close to the earth. noun* an end. *We will leave at the close of the day.* {<u>klohz</u>, n., <u>klohs</u>, adj., <u>klohs</u>, adv., <u>klohz</u>, v.} closely, adv., closeness, n.
• **close in on** to come near to or surround in order to capture. *The police closed in on the criminal hiding in the woods.*

Homophone Note The words *close* and *clothes* have similar sounds. To choose the right spelling, remember that clothes are made out of cloth.

clos·et *noun* a small room for storing things such as clothes or supplies. {<u>klŏz</u> iht}

close-up *noun* a picture taken very close to someone or something to show details. Close-ups are taken in still photographs and films for television and movies. *The close-up showed every freckle on her face.* {<u>klohs</u> <u>uhp</u>}

clot *noun* a thick lump or mass of liquid, such as blood. *verb*

 Human Body  Human Mind 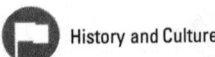 Everyday Life  History and Culture Communication

(clotted, clotting, clots) to make a clot or clots. *His blood won't clot.* {**klŏt**}

cloth *noun* 1. material made by weaving threads of cotton, wool, nylon, or other fibers; fabric. 2. a piece of woven material used for a particular purpose. *She used a cloth to wash off the table.* {**klawth**}

clothe *verb* (clothed or clad, clothing, clothes) to put clothing on; dress. *He clothed the baby after giving her a bath.* {**klohth**}

clothes ○ *plural noun* things worn on the body, such as pants, shirts, and dresses; clothing; garments. {**klohz** or **klohthz**}

clothes·pin *noun* a clip or forked peg of wood or plastic, used to hold clothes on a line for drying. {**klohz pihn**}

cloth·ing *noun* things worn to cover the body; clothes. *Her clothing was plain.* {**klohth** ing}

cloud *noun* 1. a white or gray mass of fine drops of water or ice high in the earth's atmosphere. 2. something like a cloud, such as dust or smoke. *His boots kicked up a cloud of dust as he walked into the store.* 3. something that threatens or makes dark and gloomy. *Everyone in the city lived under a cloud of fear.* *verb* (clouded, clouding, clouds) 1. to cover with clouds. *Smoke from the burning building clouded the neighborhood.* 2. to become cloudy (often followed by "up"). *The sky clouded up before the storm began.* {**klowd**} cloudless, adj., cloudlike, adj.

Word History *Cloud* is from *clud*, an Old English word that means "rock or hill," and from *clouden* which means "to dim or darken."

cloud·burst *noun* a sudden, heavy rainfall. *The cloudburst put an end to our picnic.* {**klowd buhrst**}

cloud·y *adjective* (cloudier, cloudiest) 1. covered by or filled with clouds. *Will there ever be an end to these cloudy skies?* 2. not clear; muddy. *The water is too cloudy to see the fish.* {**klow** dee} cloudiness, n.

clove[1] *noun* the dried flower bud of an East Indian tree, used to flavor food or drink. {**klohv**}

clove[2] *noun* one of the small plant bulbs formed from the main bulb. *This soup recipe needs four cloves of garlic.* {**klohv**}

clo·ver
noun a common plant that has leaves in groups of three and small, rounded flowers. Clover is often grown in fields to help enrich the soil. {**kloh** vər}

clown *noun* 1. an actor who wears odd clothes and makeup to make people laugh. Clowns act out jokes and do tricks in circuses, at parties, and at other events. 2. a person who acts in a silly manner. *The class clown is often in trouble with the teacher.* *verb* (clowned, clowning, clowns) to act as a clown or to try to get attention by acting silly (sometimes

followed by "around"). *Stop clowning around and get back to work.* {**klown**} clownish, adj.

club *noun* 1. a heavy wooden stick that is used as a weapon. 2. a group of people who meet for a special, shared purpose. *My friend belongs to a book club.* 3. the place where a club meets. *Mr. Perez goes to a health club every Thursday.* 4. a long stick used to hit the ball in golf. 5. a black figure in the shape of a clover that can be found on a playing card; a card marked with this figure. *The three of clubs is considered bad luck in some card games.* *verb* (clubbed, clubbing, clubs) to hit or strike with a club or as if with a club. *Some people were clubbed by the police during the riot.* {**kluhb**}

cluck *verb* (clucked, clucking, clucks) to make the noise of a hen calling chicks. *noun* the sound of a hen. {**kluhk**}

clue *noun* a hint that helps solve a puzzle, problem, or mystery. *The detective found many clues at the scene of the crime.* {**klooh**}
  • **clue in**
  to provide with information or make aware. *Clue me in to the situation here, will you?*

clump *noun* 1. a group of things close together. *We are going to build a barn near that clump of trees.* 2. a thick lump or mass. *Nate scraped clumps of dirt off his boots before going into the house.* 3. a heavy, dull sound; thump. *The clump of boots in the hall woke me up.* *verb* (clumped, clumping, clumps) to walk with heavy, dull noises. *The monster clumped down the stairs.* {**kluhmp**}

 Living World    Physical World   Natural Environment   Economy   Government and Law

clum·sy *adjective* (clumsier, clumsiest) 1. without physical grace or control; awkward. *That clumsy child is always dropping things.* 2. difficult to handle or use. *It took a long time to set up the large, clumsy tent.* 3. without social skills. *His clumsy effort to tell a joke was met by silence.* {**kluhm** zee} clumsily, *adv.*, clumsiness, *n.*

clung *verb* past tense and past participle of **cling**. {**kluhng**}

clus·ter *noun* a small, close group of things that are alike. *In spring, these trees will have clusters of pink flowers.* *verb* (clustered, clustering, clusters) to grow or gather together in close groups. *These berries are easy to pick because they cluster on the bush. / We clustered around the wood stove to get warm.* {**kluhs** tər}

clutch *verb* (clutched, clutching, clutches) 1. to keep in a firm grasp; hold tightly; grip. *She clutched the teddy bear with both hands.* 2. to try to grab (usually followed by "at"). *When his foot slipped, he clutched at a branch of the tree.* *noun* 1. a firm grasp or grip. *Her clutch on the glass slipped, and it crashed to the floor.* 2. a device for working the gears of an engine, as in a car. {**kluhch**}

clut·ter *verb* (cluttered, cluttering, clutters) to fill or litter with a messy collection of things. *His old car parts are cluttering the garage. / Don't clutter your mind with useless facts.* *noun* a collection of things that is messy. *I picked up the clutter in my room.* {**kluht** ər}

cm *abbreviation* an abbreviation for **centimeter** or centimeters.

Co symbol of the chemical element cobalt.

CO *abbreviation* an abbreviation for **Colorado**.

Co. *abbreviation* 1. company. 2. county.

c/o *abbreviation* used to show that something is being sent to one person at another person's address. C/o is an abbreviation for "care of."

co- *prefix* a prefix that means "together" or "with." *To cooperate is to operate or work together.*

coach *noun* 1. a person who trains and teaches athletes. 2. a person who trains or teaches a student in a special area, such as singing, acting, or a school subject. 3. a section of seats on an airplane or train. Tickets for this section are less expensive than first class. *The food in coach is not as fancy as the food in first class.* 4. a closed carriage that is pulled by horses. A coach has four wheels, and an outside seat for the driver. *Before there were cars, many people rode in coaches.* 5. a public bus. *verb* (coached, coaching, coaches) to train, teach, or prepare. *She is coaching the soccer team. / My lawyer coached me on what to say in court.* {**kohch**}

coal ❶ *noun* 1. a hard black or dark brown substance that is found in the earth and burned as fuel. 2. a piece of burning or glowing coal or wood. *We cooked potatoes over the hot coals of the campfire.* {**kohl**}

coarse *adjective* (coarser, coarsest) 1. having large grains or pieces, or a rough surface. *The truck dumped a load of coarse gravel for the new driveway. / This coarse wool cloth scratches my skin.* 2. without social skills; crude; vulgar. *His coarse way of speaking doesn't win him many friends.* {**kohrs**} coarsely, *adv.*, coarseness, *n.*

> **Homophone Note** Are you looking for the word *course*? *Coarse* and *course* sound alike but have different meanings.

coast ❶ 🌎 *noun* the land next to the ocean; seashore. *verb* (coasted, coasting, coasts) 1. to slide down a hill. *The children coasted in the park on their new sleds.* 2. to move without effort or energy. *When the car ran out of gas, we coasted to the nearest gas station.* {**kohst**}

coast·al *adjective* of, at, or near a coast. *She lives in a coastal town and likes to walk on the beach. / The coastal storm sank several ships in the harbor.* {**koh** stəl}

coast guard *noun* (capitalized) a U.S. military service that patrols and protects the nation's coasts. {**kohst** gard}

coast·line *noun* the outline or shape of a coast. *Florida has a long coastline.* {**kohst** liyn}

coat *noun* 1. a piece of outer clothing with long sleeves, usually worn to keep warm. 2. the jacket that one wears with a suit. 3. the fur or body hair of an animal. *I found a cat with a shiny, gray coat.* 4. a covering or layer. *These walls need a new coat of paint.* *verb* (coated, coating, coats) to cover with a layer. *The bread was coated with melted cheese.* {**koht**}

coat·ing *noun* a layer that covers the surface of something; coat. *There was a coating of snow on the ground.* {**koh** ting}

 Human Body 　 Human Mind 　  Everyday Life 　  History and Culture 　 Communication

coat of arms *noun* the symbol of a family, country, or organization. It shows designs and figures on and around a shield. {**koht** əv **armz**}

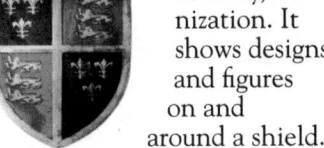

coax *verb* (coaxed, coaxing, coaxes) to get someone to do something by gentle urging. *He coaxed his daughter out of her room with the promise of a trip to the circus.* {**kohks**}

cob *noun* the hard center of an ear of corn; corncob. {**kŏb**}

co·balt *noun* a brittle silver-white metal that is one of the chemical elements. Cobalt is sometimes added to other metals in alloys to make them harder. It is also used in making some kinds of paint. (symbol: Co) {**koh bawlt**}

cob·bler *noun* 1. a person who makes or fixes shoes or boots. 2. a fruit dessert with a thick top crust that is baked in a deep dish. {**kŏb** lər}

cob·ble·stone *noun* a naturally rounded stone about the size of a fist, at one time used to pave streets. {**kŏb** əl **stohn**}

co·bra *noun* a poisonous snake found in Asia and Africa. When excited, cobras are known to rear up and spread the skin of their necks into a shape like a hood. {**koh** brə}

cob·web *noun* 1. a web spun by a spider, or a single piece of this web. 2. (plural) mental confusion. *He tried to clear the cobwebs and think about his problem.* {**kŏb** wehb}

cock[1] *noun* 1. an adult male chicken or the male of other closely related birds, such as turkeys or pheasants; rooster. 2. a device like a faucet used to control the flow of a liquid or gas. *verb* (cocked, cocking, cocks) to set the hammer of so as to be ready to fire. *Annie cocked her gun before aiming at the target.* {**kŏk**}

cock[2] *verb* (cocked, cocking, cocks) to tip to one side or turn up; tilt. *The actor cocked his hat to the audience as he crossed the stage. / The dog cocked his ears at the sound of the door opening.* {**kŏk**}

cock·a·too *noun* (cockatoos) a crested parrot that is mostly white. There are several kinds of cockatoos. They are found in Australia and in some South Pacific islands. {**kŏk** ə **tooh**}

cocker spaniel *noun* a breed of dog. Cocker spaniels are small dogs with short legs, a long, soft coat, and long ears. {**kŏk** ər **spăn** yəl}

cock·le *noun* a small animal with a soft body and a hard shell shaped like a heart. Cockles are mollusks with two hinged shells that open and close. They are kinds of clams. People sometimes eat cockles. {**kŏk** əl}

cock·pit *noun* 1. the area from which the pilot and crew control an airplane. 2. a low, open area

near the stern of a boat with space for the person steering, the crew, and passengers. {**kŏk** piht}

cock·roach *noun* an insect with a flat body and long antennae that lives in most parts of the world. Some kinds of cock-roaches are pests that live in homes and other build-ings. All cock-roaches are active at night. {**kŏk** rohch}

cock·tail *noun* 1. a drink made with alcohol and juice, soda, or other beverages. 2. an item of food or drink served before a meal, such as juice, mixed chopped fruit, or cold sea-food with a sauce. *We ate a shrimp cocktail before dinner.* {**kŏk** tayl}

cock·y *adjective* (cockier, cock-iest) sure of oneself in a rude way; arrogant. *The other team members got tired of his cocky talk before the game.* {**kŏk** ee} cockiness, n.

co·coa *noun* 1. a powder made by grinding the dried seeds of the cacao tree and removing the fat. 2. a drink made by mixing this powder with milk or water and sugar. 3. a brown or reddish brown color. {**koh** koh}

co·co·nut *noun* 1. a tropical palm tree that bears large seeds that can be eaten; coconut tree; coconut palm. 2. the seed of the coconut tree, which contains hard flesh and milky liquid that can be used for food. {**koh** kə **nuht**}

A B C D E F G H I J K L M N O P Q R S T U V W X Y Z

co·coon *noun* a covering made by young insects and some other arthropods to protect themselves while they change from a pupa into an adult. Some spiders make cocoons to hide their eggs. {kə **koohn**}

c.o.d. *abbreviation* an abbreviation for "collect on delivery," or "cash on delivery." Ordering an item c.o.d. means that payment is not required until the goods arrive.

cod *noun* (cod or cods) a large fish found in the ocean. Cod are used for food. {kŏd}

code 🔵 🟢 ⬜ *noun* 1. a set of rules or laws. *The dress code at school does not allow us to wear shorts or jeans.* 2. a system of symbols or signals used in place of letters and numbers for sending messages. *verb* (coded, coding, codes) to put into a system of symbols for sending messages. *The spy coded the message so the enemy could not read it.* {kohd}

co·ed·u·ca·tion *noun* the education of males and females at the same school and in the same classes. {koh ehj ə **kay** shən} coeducational, adj.

cof·fee 🔵 *noun* 1. a tropical plant that produces beans. These beans are used to make a dark brown drink. *Coffee is grown on large farms in Africa, Asia, and the Americas.* 2. the beans of this plant, or the drink made from the roasted and ground beans. *I went to the store to buy some coffee. / More adults than children drink coffee.* {**kaw** fee}

Word History *Coffee* comes from a Turkish word *kahveh*, which originally meant "wine."

cof·fin *noun* a box in which a dead person is buried; casket. {**kaw** fihn}

cog *noun* one of a series of teeth on a gear. {kŏg}

co·her·ence *noun* the condition of being logical and easy to understand. *The teacher's coherence helped her students learn their lessons.* {koh **heer** əns}

coil *verb* (coiled, coiling, coils) to wind into circles. *The firefighters coiled the hose. noun* something that has been wound into circles. *Bring me that coil of rope.* {koil}

coin 🔵 *noun* a piece of metal money that is small, flat, and round. *Pennies, nickels, dimes, and quarters are all coins. verb* (coined, coining, coins) 1. to make money by stamping metal. *They coin thousands of pennies every week.* 2. to invent or make up. *People coined the word "smog" by combining the words "smoke" and "fog."* {koin}

co·in·cide *verb* (coincided, coinciding, coincides) 1. to be in the same place or happen at the same time. *Our lunch breaks coincide, so we get to eat together.* 2. to be the same in some respect; agree. *What you made for supper coincides with what I wanted to eat.* {koh ihn **siyd**}

co·in·ci·dence *noun* the chance happening of two events at the same time. *What a coincidence that you came in just as I was thinking of you.* {koh **ihn** sih dəns}

coke *noun* the carbon substance that is left after coal has been heated without air. Coke is used as a fuel for doing certain kinds of work in a factory. {**kohk**}

cold *adjective* (colder, coldest) 1. without heat or warmth. *This room is so cold.* 2. having a body temperature below normal. *After I waited outside in the snow, my fingers and toes were cold.* 3. not kind or friendly. *He gave me a cold stare and wouldn't speak to me.* 4. feeling a lack of warmth in an unpleasant way; feeling chilled. *I'm so cold that I need an extra blanket.* 5. chilled by a refrigerator; served cool. *Dad poured me a glass of cold milk. noun* 1. weather marked by low temperature. *The cold was awful when I walked to school.* 2. a common sickness that causes sneezing, coughing, and a runny nose. Colds are caused by a virus. {**kohld**} coldly, adv., coldness, n.

cold-blood·ed 🔵 *adjective* 1. having blood whose temperature changes with the temperature of the air or water. Animals such as fishes, snakes, and lizards are cold-blooded. 2. done without kindness or other feelings; cruel. *He went to prison for cold-blooded murder.* {**kohld bluhd** ihd} cold-bloodedly, adv.

  Human Body   ❓ Human Mind   👕 Everyday Life   🚩 History and Culture   📞 Communication

cole·slaw *noun* a salad made of shredded cabbage and a dressing. {**kohl** slaw}

col·i·se·um or **colosseum** *noun* a large building or theater used for entertainment events and sports. *We went to the coliseum to see my favorite singing group in concert.* {kŏl ih **see** əm}

col·lab·o·rate *verb* (collaborated, collaborating, collaborates) to work with someone else on a project. *They collaborated on planning the party.* {kə **lăb** ə **rayt**}

col·lage *noun* a type of art work in which different kinds of materials are pasted onto a surface to make a picture. These materials can be anything from paper and photographs, to cloth and buttons. {kə **lahzh** or koh **lahzh**}

Word History *Collage* is a French word that means "gluing." When French artists such as Picasso began making the first "collages" around 1912, the word entered English as a name for this type of artwork.

col·lapse *verb* (collapsed, collapsing, collapses) 1. to fall down; give way; cave in. *The bridge collapsed because of heavy traffic.* 2. to stop working or end suddenly; fail. *After the new attack, the peace talks collapsed.* 3. to have a construction which permits folding. *This is a kind of chair that collapses.* 4. to suddenly lose strength or health because of disease or exhaustion. *She collapsed from a heart attack.* *noun* a sudden falling down or in. *Seven workers were hurt in the mine collapse.* {kə **lăps**}

col·lar *noun* 1. the part of a piece of clothing that goes around the neck. It is sometimes folded over. *My jacket has a fur collar. / The boys had to wear a shirt with a collar and a tie.* 2. anything that fits around the neck. *The first thing I did when I got my new dog was to put a collar on him. / The princess was wearing a collar of jewels.* *verb* (collared, collaring, collars) (informal) to arrest or capture. *The police collared the thief and brought him to jail.* {**kŏl** ər}
• **hot under the collar** (informal) very angry or upset. *Her dad got hot under the collar about the telephone bill.*

col·lar·bone *noun* either of two bones joining the breastbone and the shoulder blades. {**kŏl** ər bohn}

col·lard *noun* 1. a type of vegetable like cabbage that is grown for food. 2. (plural) collard leaves as a food. {**kŏl** ərd}

col·league *noun* a person who has the same job or employer as another. *I met my mother's colleagues at the post office.* {**kŏl** eeg}

col·lect *verb* (collected, collecting, collects) 1. to gather together. *I collected the papers that had fallen on the floor.* 2. to gather things as a hobby; make a collection of. *He has been collecting stamps since he was five years old.* 3. to get payment for. *The landlord collected the rent.* 4. to make oneself calm, especially after being upset or disturbed. *After the accident, she collected herself quickly.* *adverb* or *adjective* paid by the person who receives the message. *I made a collect phone call to my sister in Alaska. / I called her collect.* {kə **lehkt**}

col·lec·tion *noun* 1. the act of collecting. *Garbage collection happens every Monday morning.* 2. a gathering of a group of things of the same type. *We saw a coin collection at the museum.* 3. the gathering of money from members of a group. *Our class took up a collection for new library books.* {kə **lehk** shən}

col·lege *noun* a school of higher learning that one attends after high school. Most college programs require four years of study. *I went to college to study history.* {**kŏl** ihj}

col·lide *verb* (collided, colliding, collides) 1. to strike or bump into one another with force. *The cars collided in the icy parking lot.* 2. to disagree strongly. *They collided over who would win the election.* {kə **liyd**}

col·lie *noun* a Scottish breed of dog. Collies are large dogs with long, narrow heads and long hair. They were once raised to herd sheep. {**kŏl** ee}

col·li·sion *noun* an act or instance of coming together with force; crash. *While waiting to cross the street, I saw a collision between two cars.* {kə **lihzh** ən}

Co·lom·bi·a *noun* a country in northern South America. Bogota is the capital of Colombia. {kə **luhm** bee ə} Colombian, n., adj.

co·lon[1] *noun* 1. a punctuation mark (:). It is used to introduce a series, quotation, or explanation. 2. This mark, used to separate the hour and minute in writing times of

day, as in "2:43 in the after-noon." {**koh** lən}

co·lon² *noun* (colons) the largest part of the large intestine. {koh lən}

colo·nel *noun* an officer in the U.S. Army, Air Force, and Marines who ranks above lieutenant colonel and below general. {**kuhr** nəl}

Homophone Note The words *colonel* and *kernel* sound alike but have different meanings. If you read the definition for *colonel* you will understand why a colonel would not like to be confused with a kernel.

co·lo·ni·al *adjective* 1. of or related to a colony or colonies. *India and South Africa were once part of the British colonial empire.* 2. of or related to the thirteen British colonies that became the United States, or to the period before they became independent. *We learned about American colonial history in class.* {kə **loh** nee əl}

col·o·nist *noun* 1. a person who lives in or is a member of a colony. 2. a member of a group setting up a colony. {**kŏl** ə nihst}

col·o·nize *verb* (colonized, colonizing, colonizes) to start or form a colony on; settle. *They colonized several small islands.* {**koh** lə **niyz**} colonization, n., colonizer, n.

col·on·nade *noun* a series of columns that holds up a roof or beam. {koh lə **nayd**}

col·o·ny ❶ ⊕ *noun* (colonies) 1. a place where a group of people come to settle which is under the control of their home country. *America was a colony of England before it became independent.* 2. a group of people who come from the same country, or animals of the same type living closely together. *There is a colony of Japanese people living in Brazil. / I built an ant farm so I could study a colony of ants at work.* {**ko** lə nee}

col·or ❷ *noun* 1. a quality of light as our eyes see it. Light is made up of waves, which hit objects and are reflected from their surfaces. The colors we see depend on how these light waves are reflected. Objects of different colors reflect different kinds of light waves. 2. something used to give color, such as dye or paint. *I put color in the cake batter to turn it pink.* 3. the complexion of the skin, especially of the face. *He has better color now that his fever has passed.* 4. skin color that is not white. *I am a person of color.* *verb* (colored, coloring, colors) to give color to. *I colored the picture with crayons.* {**kuhl** ər}

Col·o·rad·o *noun* 1. a state in the western United States. Its capital is Denver. (abbreviated: CO) 2. a river that flows southwest from this state to the Pacific Ocean. {kŏl ə **răd** oh *or* kŏl ə **rah** doh}

Word History *Colorado* means "colored red" in Spanish. Early Spanish explorers named the area for its red rocks.

col·or-blind *adjective* 1. partly or completely unable to see color or a difference between colors. *He is so color-blind that red and green look the same to*

him. 2. treating others alike, without thinking about their skin color. *Justice should be color-blind.* {**kuhl** ər **bliynd**}

col·or·ful *adjective* 1. having many colors; bright in color. *He wore a colorful scarf with his black coat.* 2. lively; interesting. *My uncle is a colorful character. / She used colorful language to describe her trip to Mexico.* {**kuhl** ər fəl} colorfully, adv., colorfulness, n.

col·or·ing *noun* 1. something used to give color to. *We will dye the Easter eggs with food coloring.* 2. the color of the skin. *My sister's coloring is darker than mine.* {**kuhl** ə ring}

col·our *noun or verb* a spelling of **color** used in Canada and Britain. See **color** for more information. {**kuhl** ər}

colt *noun* a young male horse, donkey, zebra, or related animal, usually one that is less than four years old. {**kohlt**}

col·um·bine *noun* a plant related to the buttercup whose flowers have five long petals. {**kohl** əm **biyn**}

col·umn *noun* 1. an upright structure that looks like a post. A column helps support a building. 2. an article or other piece of writing in a newspaper or magazine that appears on a regular schedule. *My sister and my father like to read the sports column at breakfast every morning.* 3. one of two or more sections of print divided on the page by white space. *There are three columns on that page of the magazine.* 4. a vertical list or row. *I added*

 Human Body   Human Mind   Everyday Life    History and Culture   Communication

up the column of numbers. {**kŏl** əm}

co·ma *noun* a long, deep state of being unconscious, caused by disease or injury. *After the car accident, he was in a coma for three weeks.* {**koh** mə}

comb  *noun* 1. a thin piece of plastic or other material that has teeth along one side. It is used to smooth, arrange, or hold hair in place. 2. any tool that is used as a comb. 3. the fleshy crest on the head of chickens and other birds. It is easiest to notice on male birds, such as roosters. *verb* (combed, combing, combs) 1. to remove the knots from, arrange, or smooth with a comb. *My mother combs my hair every morning.* 2. to search thoroughly. *I combed the room for my lost home-work.* {**kohm**}

com·bat *verb* (combated or combatted, combating or combatting, combats) to fight against. *Doctors combat disease. / She combated the desire to cry.* *noun* a fight or battle. *The brave soldier won a medal for his behavior in combat.* {**kŏm** băt, n., kəm **băt**, v.}

com·bi·na·tion *noun* 1. the result of an act of combining; things that are brought together or combined. *The soup was a combination of chicken and vegetables.* 2. a series of numbers used to open a lock. {**kŏm** bə **nay** shən}

com·bine *verb* (combined, com-bining, combines) to bring or join together into a whole. *He combined dirt and water to make mud.* *noun* a machine used to harvest crops. A combine cuts and cleans the grain. {**kŏm** biyn, n., kəm **biyn**, v.}

com·bus·tion *noun* the act or process of burning. *Most automobiles have an engine which creates energy by the combustion of gasoline.* {kəm **buhs** chən}

come *verb* (came, come, coming, comes) 1. to move or travel toward the speaker; approach. *Some friends are coming here for dinner tonight.* 2. to arrive or enter. *Here she comes now! / I came into the room when I heard the shouts.* 3. to be in a certain place, position, or order among others. *Dessert usually comes after dinner.* 4. to be from; to originate (usually followed by "from"). *She comes from Japan.* {**kuhm**}

• **come across**
1. to discover or find by chance. *I came across a new recipe in that magazine.* 2. to make or give an impression; seem. *He comes across as a shy person.*

co·me·di·an *noun* a person who entertains by telling jokes and acting in a way that makes people laugh. {kə **mee** dee ən}

com·e·dy  *noun* (comedies) a play, film, story, or television show that is funny. {**kŏm** ih dee} comedic, adj.

com·et *noun* an object in space that travels around the sun. A comet is made up of dust and gas, and some-times forms a long, bright tail. {**kŏm** iht}

com·fort *verb* (com-forted, comforting, comforts)

to give relief from a painful or difficult situation; soothe. *My mother comforted me when I lost my favorite toy.* *noun* 1. a pleasant condition that comes from not having worry, pain, or a difficult life. *The rich family lived in great comfort.* 2. a person or thing that gives relief and strength. *When I was sick, holding my favorite toy bear was a com-fort.* {**kuhm** fərt}

Word History *Comfort* comes from *confortare*, a Latin word meaning "to strengthen much."

com·fort·a·ble *adjective* 1. feeling at ease. *After a month, I felt comfortable at my new school.* 2. giving ease or com-fort to the body. *When I wear comfortable shoes, my feet don't hurt.* {**kuhmf** tər bəl or **kuhm** fər tə bəl} comfortably, adv.

com·ic *adjective* amusing or funny. *It was a comic situation when we found out that we had bought each other the same thing for Christmas.* *noun* 1. a person who is paid to make people laugh; comedian. 2. (plural) one or more series of cartoons, or a book, maga-zine, or newspaper section that contains such series. *I like to read the Sunday comics in the paper.* {**kŏm** ihk}

com·i·cal *adjective* funny; amusing. *He wore a comical costume to the party.* {**kŏm** ih kəl} comically, adv.

comic strip *noun* a series of car-toons in a newspaper that tells a funny story. {**kŏm** ihk **strihp**}

com·ma *noun* a punctuation mark (,). It is used to sepa-rate words, phrases, or other parts of a sentence or list, or to show a pause in speech. It is used when writing num-

A
B
C
D
E
F
G
H
I
J
K
L
M
N
O
P
Q
R
S
T
U
V
W
X
Y
Z

Living World Physical World Natural Environment Economy Government and Law

a
b
c
d
e
f
g
h
i
j
k
l
m
n
o
p
q
r
s
t
u
v
w
x
y
z

bers of one thousand or greater to mark off groups of three digits. *He won $1,000,000 in the lottery.* {**kŏm** ə}

com·mand ⊘ *verb* (commanded, commanding, commands) 1. to order or instruct. *She commanded him to leave the building.* 2. to lead and control. *The general commands his troops.* 3. to draw out or call for; to capture. *Her bravery commands our respect. / His loud voice commanded our attention. noun* 1. the act of commanding. *You will be under his command.* 2. an instruction meant to be obeyed; order. *She won't follow his commands.* 3. the ability to use or control. *He has a good command of Spanish.* 4. an instruction given to a computer using the keyboard. {kə **mănd**}

com·mand·er *noun* 1. a person who leads and controls. *Our coach is the commander of the team.* 2. an officer who is the leader of a military unit. *The commander gave the order to march.* 3. the rank directly below captain in the U.S. Navy. {kə **măn** dər}

com·mand·ment *noun* 1. an order or law. *The monk lived by a commandment never to eat meat.* 2. in the Jewish or Christian Bible, one of the Ten Commandments or laws given to Moses by God. {kə **mănd** mənt}

com·mem·o·rate *verb* (commemorated, commemorating, commemorates) to honor the memory of. *Postage stamps have commemorated presidents and movie stars.* {kə **mehm** ə **rayt**}

com·mence *verb* (commenced, commencing, commences) to begin or start. *The meeting commenced.* {kə **mehns**}

com·mence·ment *noun* 1. the day or ceremony of graduation from a school or college. *We will get our diplomas at commencement.* 2. the act or time of beginning. *Before the commencement of the game, players must stay at their end of the field.* {kə **mehns** mənt}

com·mend *verb* (commended, commending, commends) to speak of with praise for some act or service. *He commended him for helping other students.* {kə **mehnd**} commendable, adj., commendably, adv.

com·ment *noun* a written or spoken statement of opinion. *Her comments on my written work were helpful. verb* (commented, commenting, comments) to give a spoken or written opinion. *He always comments on her hairstyle.* {**kŏm** ehnt}

com·men·ta·tor *noun* a person who comments on something. Commentators often appear on radio or television shows to give opinions or explanations of news and events. *The radio commentator said that the new shopping mall is not necessary.* {**ko** mən **tay** tər}

com·merce *noun* the buying and selling of goods or services; trade; business. *The United States has increased its commerce with Mexico. / Cities are centers of commerce.* {**kŏm** ərs}

com·mer·cial ⊘ ◠ *adjective* 1. having to do with trade or business. *The commercial part of town has many shops and businesses.* 2. having to do with making money. *His books were good, but not a commercial success. noun* an advertisement on television or radio. *The commercials for that automobile are silly.* {kə **muhr** shəl} commercially, adv.

com·mis·sion *noun* 1. the act of doing, performing, or committing. *There were fewer commissions of theft in the city last year.* 2. an order giving permission to perform a certain task. *The author received a commission to write a biography of the film star.* 3. a group of people chosen to perform a certain task. *A commission was formed to study the need for a new school.* 4. money given to a salesperson as a reward for selling something. *She gets a commission for every car she sells.* 5. the order that gives a rank to an officer in the military. *He received a commission as a captain during the war. verb* (commissioned, commissioning, commissions) 1. to give the power to perform a certain task. *The queen commissioned a young artist to paint her portrait.* 2. to put into active service. *The admiral commissioned the ship.* {kə **mihsh** ən}

• **out of commission** not in working condition. *This car is out of commission.*

com·mis·sion·er *noun* 1. the head of a government department. *He is the commissioner of health.* 2. a member of a commission. *The commissioners of education will have a meeting.* {kə **mihsh** ə nər}

com·mit *verb* (committed, committing, commits) 1. to do; perform. *He committed a crime.* 2. to dedicate, devote or pledge. *She committed herself to helping the poor.* 3. to put under the care or control of a person or institution, such as a prison or mental hospital. *They committed him to the mental hospital.* {kə **miht**}

 Human Body    Human Mind   ◉ Everyday Life   ▢ History and Culture    Communication

com·mit·tee *noun* a group of persons chosen to give attention to a particular matter. *The class formed a committee to discuss the problem of teasing.* {kə **mih** tee}

com·mod·i·ty *noun* (commodities) something that can be bought and sold. *Corn is an important commodity in this part of the country.* {kə **mŏd** ih tee}

com·mon *adjective* (commoner, commonest) 1. belonging equally to all members of a group. *My friends and I have a common interest in football.* 2. shared and used by all. *The library has a common room where people from all over town come to read.* 3. usual; easily found; happening often. *Pigeons are common in our part of the country. / Snow is common in winter.* *noun* (often plural) an area of land that can be used by everybody. *People come to Boston Common to relax, play sports, and picnic.* {kŏm ən}

• **in common**
owned or used together; shared. *My brother and I have several friends in common.*

common cold *noun* a common sickness that causes sneezing, sore throat, coughing, and a stuffy nose; cold. *There is no cure for the common cold.* {kŏm ən **kohld**}

common denominator *noun* a number into which the denominators of two or more fractions can all be evenly divided. *The fractions 5/12, 1/4, and 2/3 have a common denominator of 12.* {kŏm ən də **nŏm** ə nay tər}

common noun *noun* a noun that indicates a class of things or a general member of a class of things, people, or places. Common nouns usually have articles. (see proper noun.) *The word "cat" is a common noun.* {**ko** mən **nown**}

com·mon·place *adjective* 1. ordinary; not special. *It is becoming commonplace to see a computer in someone's home.* 2. not new or original; dull. *His ideas are commonplace.* {**kŏm** ən **plays**}

common sense *noun* ordinary good judgment in everyday matters. Common sense is learned through experience and not through education. *It is common sense to wear a jacket when it is cold outside.* {**kŏm** ən **sehns**} commonsense, adj.

com·mon·wealth  *noun* 1. a state or nation governed by the people. 2. the official title of certain U.S. states and Puerto Rico. *The state of Massachusetts is a commonwealth.* {**kŏm** ən **wehlth**}

com·mo·tion *noun* a noisy confusion; disorder. *There was a commotion when someone yelled "Fire!"* {kə **moh** shən}

com·mu·ni·ca·ble *adjective* capable of being spread or passed on; contagious. *Measles is a communicable disease.* {kə **myoo** nih kə bəl}

com·mu·ni·cate *verb* (communicated, communicating, communicates) 1. to make known. *I communicated the message to him.* 2. to pass along or carry to another. *She communicated the flu to her brother.* 3. to exchange thoughts, ideas, or information. *Since my best friend moved away, we communicate by telephone.* 4. to express one's thoughts and feelings easily and well. *She really knows how to communicate.* {kə **myoo** nih **kayt**} communicator, n.

com·mu·ni·ca·tion *noun* 1. the sharing or exchange of messages, information, or ideas. *Sign language is a form of communication used by deaf people.* 2. a message. *Her communication said she would arrive by tonight.* 3. (plural) means of sending messages, such as telephone, radio, and television. *The storm shut down all communications.* {kə myoo nih **kay** shən}

com·mun·ion *noun* 1. a sharing of feelings or thoughts. *There was communion between him and his father.* 2. (capitalized) the part of a Christian service that honors the last supper of Jesus and his apostles. {kə **myoon** yən}

com·mun·ism  *noun* (sometimes capitalized) a system of government in which all factories, farms, and natural resources are owned in common. {**kŏm** yə nihz əm}

com·mun·ist *noun* 1. one who believes in or supports communism. 2. (capitalized) one who belongs to the Communist party. {**kŏm** yə nihst} communistic, adj.

Communist party *noun* a political party that supports communism. {**kŏm** yə nihst **par** tee}

com·mu·ni·ty *noun* (communities) 1. a particular area where a group of people live. *A new store opened next to the school in my community.* 2. a group of people who live close together or have shared interests. *The scientific community was excited about the new discovery.* 3. all the plants and animals that live together in the same area. *The animals in a forest community need trees for food and shelter.* {kə **myoo** nih tee}

com·mute *verb* (commuted, commuting, commutes) to ride or drive a long distance to and from work or school. *Since we moved out of the city,*

A
B
C
D
E
F
G
H
I
J
K
L
M
N
O
P
Q
R
S
T
U
V
W
X
Y
Z

a
b
c
d
e
f
g
h
i
j
k
l
m
n
o
p
q
r
s
t
u
v
w
x
y
z

my father commutes. noun regular travel to or from work or school. *My commute takes fifty minutes.* {kə **myoot**} commutable, adj.

com·pact[1] *adjective* 1. firmly packed together; dense. *The soil was very compact where many people had walked over it.* 2. taking up a small amount of space. *They bought a compact dishwasher because their apartment was small.* 3. shortened, but still containing what is most important. *I'm reading a compact history of modern art. verb* (compacted, compacting, compacts) to pack closely and tightly together. *The machine compacts soda cans before they are recycled. noun* 1. a small case that contains face powder and a mirror. 2. a small automobile. {**kŏm** păkt, n., kəm **păkt** or **kŏm** păkt, adj., kəm **păkt** or **kŏm** păkt, v.} compactly, adv. compactness, n.

com·pact[2] *noun* an agreement or contract between people or groups. *The two kingdoms entered into a compact not to make war on each other.* {**kŏm** păkt}

compact disk *noun* a small disk on which music or information is stored. A compact disk is played on a machine that uses a laser to read it. {**kŏm** păkt **dihsk**}

com·pan·ion *noun* 1. one who spends time with another or others. *She was my childhood companion.* 2. a match or mate in a pair. *I found one shoe, but where is its companion?* {kəm **păn** yən}

com·pan·ion·ship ● *noun* the relationship between or among companions; friendship. *I miss your companionship.* {kəm **păn** yən **shihp**}

com·pa·ny *noun* (companies) 1. a business firm or organization. *The company hired many new workers this year.* 2. a group of people gathered together for a common purpose. *The dance company is giving a concert at our school.* 3. a guest or guests. *We had company for dinner last night.* 4. the presence of another person; companionship. *I enjoy your company.* 5. a group of soldiers. *The company says "Yes, sir" when the captain gives an order.* {**kuhm** pə nee}

• **part company** to end a friendship or relationship. *They parted company at the end of the school year.*

Word History *Company* is from a Latin word that means "the sharing of bread with another."

com·par·a·tive *adjective* 1. of or involving comparison. *He took a class in comparative literature to learn about stories from many cultures.* 2. measured or estimated by comparison; relative. *The new worker in the office is a comparative child.* 3. of or describing the form of adjectives and adverbs that indicate that one is talking about a greater degree of some quality. *"Newer" and "more patiently" are the comparative forms of "new" and "patiently." noun* the comparative degree, or a form or word of this degree. (see positive, superlative.) {kəm **par** ə tihv} comparatively, adv.

com·pare *verb* (compared, comparing, compares) 1. to note or describe the similarities or differences of. *His mother often compares his bedroom to a pigsty.* 2. to bring together for the purpose of discov-ering similarities and differences. *I compared the two brands of soup and decided this one tastes better.* 3. to be considered similar. *Even a great painting cannot compare with the beauty of the sunset.* {kəm **payr**}

Language Note Do you mean **compare** or **contrast**? These two words are sometimes confused with each other. When you **compare** two things, you show how they are similar or different. When you **contrast** two things, you show only how they are different. *Jay's report compared animals of the temperate rain forest with animals of the tropical rain forest. In it, he contrasted the climate in Oregon with the climate in Brazil.*

com·par·i·son *noun* 1. the act of comparing or the result of being compared. *A comparison of the two pictures shows how important the right light is in photography.* 2. a likeness that allows two things to be compared. *There is no comparison between our Little League team and the Yankees.* {kəm **par** ih sən}

com·part·ment *noun* a part or area of something that is divided off as a section of the whole. *The jewelry box has eight compartments.* {kəm **part** mənt}

com·pass *noun* 1. an instrument for showing direction. A typical compass has a moving magnetic needle that points north. *Many sailors use a compass to find their way across the ocean.* 2. (often plural) an instrument with two hinged legs that is used for drawing circles. One leg ends in a point and the other holds a

 Human Body   Human Mind   Everyday Life   History and Culture   Communication

pencil. *Last night I used a compass for my math homework.* {**kŏm** pəs}

com·pas·sion ❓ *noun* a feeling of sharing another's suffering that leads to a desire to help. *He was a leader with great compassion for the people of his country.* {kəm **păsh** ən}

Word History *Compassion* comes from a Latin word that means "to suffer with another."

com·pel *verb* (compelled, compelling, compels) to force or drive to do something. *His violent actions compelled the teacher to call the police.* {kəm **pehl**}

com·pen·sate *verb* (compensated, compensating, compensates) 1. to take the place of or make up for something (usually followed by "for"). *Her experience compensates for her lack of education.* 2. to pay or repay. *I compensated him for the dinner he gave us.* {**kŏm** pən **sayt**}

com·pen·sa·tion *noun* something given in return for or to make up for something else. *The compensation for painting my house will be one thousand dollars.* / *Debra received compensation for the injury she got while at work.* {kŏm pən **say** shən}

com·pete *verb* (competed, competing, competes) 1. to try to win or get something that others are also trying to get. *The two friends competed for the starring role in the play.* 2. to take part in a contest or game. *Do you think she will compete in the next Olympic games?* {kəm **peet**}

com·pe·tent *adjective* having the skill to do something; capable. *Only competent drivers get licenses.* {**kŏm** pə tənt} competently, adv.

com·pe·ti·tion 🌐 *noun* 1. the process or act of trying to win. *Those two boys are in competition for first place.* 2. a contest or game. *The diving competition will be held tomorrow.* {kŏm pə **tih** shən}

com·pet·i·tive *adjective* 1. having to do with or decided by competition. *A competitive exam will decide who gets the scholarship money.* 2. having a strong desire to win or do better than others in almost every situation. *She is a very competitive person.* {kəm **peh** tih tihv} competitively, adv., competitiveness, n.

com·pet·i·tor *noun* a person, group, or thing that competes. *My sister and I were competitors in the race.* {kəm **peht** ih tər}

com·pile *verb* (compiled, compiling, compiles) to gather information together to form one written work. *They are compiling a dictionary.* {kəm **piyl**}

com·pla·cent *adjective* too satisfied with oneself or one's situation. *Complacent people do not try to make the world a better place.* {kəm **play** sənt}

com·plain *verb* (complained, complaining, complains) 1. to express pain, sadness, or unhappy feelings about something. *He complained of a headache.* / *She complained about the cold weather.* 2. to make a formal charge against someone or something. *They complained to the police about the noise from the house next door.* {kəm **playn**}

com·plaint *noun* 1. an act of complaining. *My complaint about the food upset the cook.* 2. something that one has found fault with. *I have no complaints about the work you have been doing.* 3. a formal charge or accusation. *I made a complaint to the police after I was robbed.* {kəm **playnt**}

com·ple·ment *noun* something that goes well with a thing or makes a perfect addition to it. *Fruit would be a good complement to this meal.* *verb* (complemented, complementing, complements) to go well with, complete, or perfect. *These lights complement her art work.* {**kŏm** plə mənt}

Homophone Note Are you looking for the word *compliment* (a flattering comment)? *Complement* and *compliment* sound alike, but they have different meanings.

com·plete *adjective* (completer, completest) 1. having all of the necessary parts; whole. *I have a complete set of kitchen knives.* 2. finished; ended. *I handed my complete report to my teacher.* 3. perfect or thorough; total. *I have complete faith in the weather report.* 4. a forward pass in football that has been caught by a player of the same team. *verb* (completed, completing, completes) 1. to finish. *He completed the test in one hour.* 2. to make whole or perfect. *The rare stamp from France completed his collection.* {kəm **pleet**} completely, adv.

com·ple·tion *noun* 1. the act or process of finishing or completing. *The completion of this job will take two weeks.* 2. the condition of being finished or made whole. *I will bring the report to completion by tomorrow.* {kəm **plee** shən}

com·plex *adjective* 1. difficult to understand. *This math homework is complex.* 2. having many connected parts. *A spider's web is complex and beautiful.* {kəm **plehks** or **kŏm** plehks}

A
B
C
D
E
F
G
H
I
J
K
L
M
N
O
P
Q
R
S
T
U
V
W
X
Y
Z

a
b
c
d
e
f
g
h
i
j
k
l
m
n
o
p
q
r
s
t
u
v
w
x
y
z

com·plex·ion *noun* the natural color and and condition of the skin, especially of the face. *She has a dark complexion.* {kəm **plehk** shən}

com·plex·i·ty *noun* (complexities) the state or condition of being complex or complicated. *The story is interesting because of its complexity.* {kəm **plehk** sih tee}

complex sentence *noun* a sentence made of a main or independent clause and one or more dependent or subordinate clauses. An example of a complex sentence is, "I went to the theater, which was very crowded with people." {kŏm plehks **sehn** təns}

com·pli·cate *verb* (complicated, complicating, complicates) to make more difficult to do or understand. *The bad weather complicated our vacation plans.* {kŏm plih **kayt**}

Word History *Complicate* is from a Latin word that means "to fold or weave together."

com·pli·cat·ed *adjective* hard to understand; difficult to do or to deal with. *Our teacher gave us a complicated problem to work on.* {kŏm plih **kay** tihd}

com·pli·ca·tion *noun* something that makes a situation more difficult or complicated. *The bad weather has caused a complication in our travel plans.* {kŏm plih **kay** shən}

com·pli·ment *noun* 1. an expression of praise, admiration, or approval. *He gave her a compliment on her speech.* 2. (plural) a polite greeting. *Please give my compliments to your family.* *verb* (complimented, complimenting, compliments) to give a compliment to. *The principal com-*

plimented us on our work. {kŏm plə mənt}

Homophone Note Are you looking for the word **complement** (something that completes or perfects)? **Compliment** and **complement** sound alike and look almost the same, but they have different meanings.

com·pli·men·ta·ry *adjective* 1. expressing or giving praise. *She had complimentary things to say about my book.* 2. free of charge. *The newspaper critic received complimentary tickets to the play.* {kŏm plə **mehn** tə ree}

com·ply *verb* (complied, complying, complies) to do what is asked or demanded; act in agreement with a rule (sometimes followed by "with"). *I complied with my teacher's request that I get permission from my parents.* / *Please comply with the campground's rule against littering.* {kəm **pliy**}

com·po·nent *noun* a part of something. *One of the components of the engine is missing.* / *Vegetables are a component of a healthy diet.* {kəm **poh** nənt}

com·pose *verb* (composed, composing, composes) 1. to be the parts of; make up. *These twenty people compose the class.* 2. to create or write. *She has composed several poems.* 3. to make calm or quiet. *I must compose myself before I go on stage.* {kəm **pohz**}

com·pos·er *noun* someone who composes something, especially music. *Mozart was a famous composer.* {kəm **poh** zər}

com·pos·ite *adjective* made up of several parts. *The picture was a composite of many small photographs.* {kəm **pŏz** iht}

com·po·si·tion *noun* 1. the act of composing. *The composition of this opera took most of his life.* 2. the way the parts of something are put together; order or structure. *The team sent a submarine to study the composition of the sea bottom.* 3. a particular written or musical work. *She has written many beautiful compositions.* 4. a material or substance that is made up of other materials or substances. *The green paint we used was a composition of blue and yellow paint.* 5. a short piece written as a school assignment. *Write a composition on water pollution.* {kŏm pə **zih** shən}

com·post *noun* a mixture of decaying leaves, vegetables, or manure that is used to improve garden soil. {kŏm **pohst**}

com·po·sure *noun* calmness in thinking or acting; self-control. *Her composure helped to end the fight.* {kəm **poh** zhər}

com·pound *adjective* having to do with a word made up of two or more parts, or a sentence made up of two or more main clauses. *"Housefly" is a compound word, made of the words "house" and "fly."* *noun* 1. something made up of two or more parts or elements. *Tears are a compound of salt and water.* 2. a substance formed by combining two or more chemical elements. *Water is a compound of hydrogen and oxygen.* *verb* (compounded, compounding, compounds) 1. to mix or combine. *The artist compounded two paints to make a new color.* 2. to make greater or worse by adding to. *Yelling only compounds the problem.* {kŏm pownd, n., **kŏm** pownd, adj., kəm **pownd**, v.}

 Human Body   Human Mind   Everyday Life  History and Culture Communication

compound sentence *noun* a sentence made of two or more independent clauses. The sentences are joined by a conjunction or semicolon. "The sky darkened, and the wind howled" is a compound sentence. {<u>kŏm</u> pownd <u>sehn</u> təns}

com·pre·hend *verb* (comprehended, comprehending, comprehends) to understand or grasp the meaning of. *Do you comprehend what the teacher said?* {kŏm prə <u>hehnd</u>} comprehensible, adj.

com·pre·hen·sion *noun* the act, process, or result of comprehending; understanding. *His comprehension of mathematics is good. / I read the paragraph several times, but had no comprehension of what it was about.* {kŏm prə <u>hehn</u> shən}

com·pre·hen·sive *adjective* including everything or almost everything; wide in range. *It took him many years to write a comprehensive history of rock music.* {kŏm prə <u>hehn</u> sihv} comprehensively, adv.

com·press *verb* (compressed, compressing, compresses) 1. to press into less space; squeeze closely together. *I compressed the clothes so that they would fit into the suitcase. / She compressed a long story into a few words.* 2. to form into a solid mass by pressing together. *I compressed the soil around the plant roots.* *noun* a soft pad of cloth, used to put pressure, cold, heat, or medicine on some part of the body. {<u>kŏm</u> prehs, n., kəm <u>prehs</u>, v.} compressibility, n., compressible, adj.

com·prise *verb* (comprised, comprising, comprises) 1. to include. *The United States once comprised thirteen states.* 2. to be made up of; consist of. *It's a list that comprises all the men who died in the war.* {kəm <u>priyz</u>}

com·pro·mise *noun* a settlement of a disagreement in which each side gives up something, or the result of such a settlement. *We were both happy with the compromise we made.* *verb* (compromised, compromising, compromises) 1. to make a compromise. *She wanted to go see a movie, and I wanted to stay home, so we compromised by renting a video.* 2. to endanger the character or reputation of. *You have compromised yourself by lying so much.* {<u>kŏm</u> prə <u>miyz</u>} compromiser, n.

com·pul·so·ry *adjective* required or demanded. *This test is compulsory for graduation.* {kəm <u>puhl</u> sə ree}

com·pute *verb* (computed, computing, computes) 1. to figure out or calculate by using arithmetic. *Compute the score to see who won the game.* 2. to figure out or determine by using a computer. *My father computed the monthly bills.* {kəm <u>pyoot</u>}

com·put·er ⚙ ⚙ ⚙ *noun* an electronic device that is used to store and sort information and work with data at a high speed. {kəm <u>pyoot</u> ər}

com·pu·ter graph·ics *noun* images produced by a computer than can be displayed on the screen or printed. *She mainly uses computer graphics in her design business.* {kəm <u>pyoot</u> ər grăf ihks}

com·pu·ter lan·guage *noun* a system of words and symbols that is used to program a computer; code. There are hundreds of computer languages, such as C, Cheetah, and JavaScript. *If you want to be a video game creator, you must learn computer languages.* {kəm <u>pyoot</u> ər lăng gwihj}

com·put·er sci·ence *noun* the science and study of computers, including how they are made and how they work. *Many people study computer science in high school and college.* {kəm <u>pyoot</u> ər <u>siy</u> əns}

computer virus *noun* a code added to a computer program that can attach itself to and seriously damage other programs. {kəm <u>pyoot</u> ər <u>viy</u> rəs}

com·rade *noun* a close friend who shares one's main interests. *My comrades and I went skateboarding after school.* {<u>kŏm</u> răd} comradeship, n.

con- *prefix* a prefix that means "with" or "together." *A conference is a group of people meeting together to discuss something.*

con·cave *adjective* curved inward like the inside of a bowl. (see convex.) *I made a concave shape with my hands and scooped up some water.* {kŏn <u>kayv</u> or <u>kŏn</u> kayv}

con·ceal *verb* (concealed, concealing, conceals) to hide or keep hidden from sight. *He concealed the birthday gift so that it would be a surprise.* {kən <u>seel</u>} concealable, adj., concealer, n., concealment, n.

con·cede *verb* (conceded, conceding, concedes) 1. to admit the truth or justice of. *I concede that he is stronger than me. / She finally conceded that she should apologize.* 2. to admit one has lost; yield. *He conceded before the votes were counted.* {kən <u>seed</u>}

con·ceit·ed *adjective* having too high an opinion of oneself; vain. *He is so conceited that he thinks any girl would be happy to go out with him.* {kən <u>see</u> tihd} conceitedly, adv.

A
B
C
D
E
F
G
H
I
J
K
L
M
N
O
P
Q
R
S
T
U
V
W
X
Y
Z

a
b
c
d
e
f
g
h
i
j
k
l
m
n
o
p
q
r
s
t
u
v
w
x
y
z

con·ceive ❓ *verb* (conceived, conceiving, conceives) 1. to give shape to in the mind. *She conceived a clever story.* 2. to be able to think of. *I cannot conceive how our house will look painted purple.* 3. to form an idea or concept (usually followed by "of"). *Can you conceive of a world without computers?* 4. to become pregnant with. *She conceived her second child this year.* {kən **seev**}

con·cen·trate *verb* (concentrated, concentrating, concentrates) 1. to bring together; focus. *Concentrate your attention on this problem.* 2. to gather; come together. *The crowd of people concentrated in the center of the room.* 3. to focus attention or thought (sometimes followed by "on"). *Concentrate on what I'm saying.* 4. to make stronger or more pure. *Boiling concentrates thin maple sap into syrup.* *noun* something in concentrated form, such as juice or flavoring. *Add some orange concentrate to the other ingredients.* {**kŏn** sən **trayt**}

con·cen·tra·tion ❓ *noun* 1. the act or process of concentrating, or the state of being concentrated. *The concentration of animals around the watering hole allowed the explorers to see many different kinds of animals at once.* 2. close attention; focused mental energy. *This problem is difficult and demands your concentration.* {kŏn sən **tray** shən}

con·cept ❓ *noun* a general idea or thought. *What is your con-*

cept of love? {**kŏn** sehpt} conceptual, n., adj.

con·cep·tion *noun* 1. the forming of concepts or ideas, or the power to do so. *His conception of what the new building should look like is different from mine.* 2. the fertilizing of an egg by a sperm; beginning of pregnancy. {kən **sehp** shən}

con·cern ❓ *verb* (concerned, concerning, concerns) 1. to have to do with; be about; affect. *This matter does not concern you.* 2. to make worried or troubled. *Her careless attitude concerns me.* *noun* 1. a matter that is important to someone. *Getting that homework done is my concern.* 2. worry or anxiety. *He has so much concern for his family.* {kən **suhrn**}

con·cern·ing *preposition* having to do with; about; in regard to. *He spoke to us concerning our weekend plans.* {kən **suhrn** ing}

con·cert ❓ *noun* a musical or dance performance before an audience; recital. *We are going to a jazz concert this weekend.* {**kŏn** sərt}

con·cer·to *noun* (concertos or concerti) a piece of music for one or more solo instruments and an orchestra. {kən **chayr** toh}

con·ces·sion *noun* 1. an act or instance of yielding or conceding. *The teacher's concession was to let him turn in the homework one day late.* 2. something yielded or conceded, such as a right or a point in an argument. *I made a concession and agreed to work for one more hour.* 3. a grant of land given by a government or other authority for a specific purpose. *The government granted many mining concessions.* 4. the

renting or lending of space within a building or other property for a specific purpose. *We were given a concession to sell pizza during the fair.* {kən **seh** shən}

conch *noun* (conchs or conches) 1. a sea animal with a soft body and a large, spiral shell. Conches are carnivorous mollusks that eat smaller mollusks such as clams. Several kinds of conches live in warm parts of the ocean all around the world. Conches are closely related to snails. 2. the shell of the conch animal. People often make decorations from conches. {**kŏngk** or **kŏnch**}

con·cise *adjective* saying much in a few words; short and to the point. *He read the book and wrote a concise report.* {kən **siys**} concisely, adv.

con·clude *verb* (concluded, concluding, concludes) 1. to bring to an end; finish or complete. *We concluded the meeting and went out for lunch.* 2. to think about carefully and form an opinion. *The principal concluded that he had done nothing wrong.* {kən **kloohd**}

con·clu·sion *noun* 1. an ending, result, or outcome. *The conclusion of the book was a surprise.* 2. an opinion reached after careful thinking. *What is your conclusion about my ideas?* {kən **klooh** zhən}

con·coct *verb* (concocted, concocting, concocts) 1. to make by putting together a number of parts or ingredients. *He concocted a fancy dessert.* 2. to make up out of one's imagination; invent. *She concocted*

 Human Body   Human Mind   Everyday Life   History and Culture   Communication

an excuse for not being on time. {kən **kŏkt**}

con·crete *adjective* 1. able to be seen and touched; real. *Trees are concrete objects.* 2. made of concrete. *They are making a concrete driveway.* *noun* a hard, strong building material made by mixing sand, gravel, cement, and water. {kŏn **kreet** or **kŏn** kreet, n., kŏn **kreet** or **kŏn** kreet, adj.} concretely, adv., concreteness, n.

con·cur *verb* (concurred, concurring, concurs) to share the same opinion; agree. *The second doctor didn't concur with the first, so we're still not sure what to do.* {kən **kuhr**}

con·cus·sion *noun* 1. a violent shaking or heavy blow; shock. *The concussion of the earthquake cracked the sidewalk.* 2. an injury to the brain caused by a heavy blow, fall, or shock. *He fell from the ladder and got a concussion.* {kən **kuh** shən} concussive, adj.

con·demn *verb* (condemned, condemning, condemns) 1. to call wrong, evil, or inadequate; strongly disapprove of. *In his speech, the mayor condemned the acts of violence that had recently occurred.* 2. to declare not safe or fit for use. *The fire chief condemned the old school building.* 3. to order punishment to be given to; sentence or convict. *The judge condemned her to prison.* {kən **dehm**} condemnable, adj.

con·den·sa·tion *noun* 1. the act or process of changing from a gas to a liquid. *The condensation of steam from the boiling tea kettle made the window fog up.* 2. something condensed. *I wrote a condensation of the story.* {kŏn dən **say** shən}

con·dense *verb* (condensed, condensing, condenses) 1. to make smaller or less in volume; make more closely packed together; concentrate. *She condensed the fruit juice by boiling it for a long time.* 2. to make shorter or put in fewer words. *He condensed his report from ten pages to five.* 3. to cause to change from a gas to a liquid or solid through cooling. *Coldness in an object condenses steam into drops of water on its surface.* 4. to change from a gas to a liquid or solid. *The steam from my breath condensed on the window.* {kən **dehns**}

con·di·tion *noun* 1. the state of being of someone or something. *He has been in bad condition since his pet died.* 2. a state of health or of being fit for use. *Her teeth are in good condition from frequent brushing. / The car is in bad condition and needs a new engine.* 3. something that must happen before another event or thing can occur. *Being over sixteen years old is a condition for getting a driver's license.* 4. a sickness or an unhealthy state of the body. *My mother has a back condition that makes it difficult for her to walk.* *verb* (conditioned, conditioning, conditions) 1. to make fit, healthy, or ready to use. *I conditioned myself for the big race by running five miles every day.* 2. to cause to become used to; accustom. *Living in the desert conditioned her to extreme heat.* 3. to respond in a certain way to things; to develop a habit of. *She was conditioned to smile and say "How are you?" when adults said "Hello" to her.* {kən **dih** shən}

con·do·min·i·um ❂ *noun* an apartment building in which each apartment is owned by the persons living in it. Each of these apartments is also called a condominium. {kŏn də **mih** nee əm}

con·dor *noun* one of two kinds of vultures that are the largest flying birds of the Western Hemisphere. They have a bald head and neck, dark feathers, and can measure twelve feet across when they spread their wings. {kŏn **dohr** or kŏn dər}

con·duct ❓❷❸ *noun* the way one acts; behavior. *His conduct during our meeting was very polite.* *verb* (conducted, conducting, conducts) 1. to behave or manage. *She conducts herself well.* 2. to lead or guide. *She conducted a tour of the museum.* 3. to carry or allow passage through or along. *Those wires conduct electricity to our house.* 4. to direct in a performance. *He will conduct the chorus.* {kŏn duhkt, n., kən **duhkt**, v.}

con·duc·tor *noun* 1. the leader of a musical group. *The conductor led the orchestra during the concert.* 2. anything that carries or allows passage of heat, electricity, or sound. *Metal is a good conductor of heat.* 3. the person on a train or bus who collects payment. *The conductor called for them to board the train.* {kən **duhk** tər}

cone *noun* 1. a solid figure with a flat base in the shape of a circle and one curved face that narrows into a point. 2. anything shaped like a cone. *I had an ice cream cone for dessert.* 3. the fruit of many evergreen

A
B
C
D
E
F
G
H
I
J
K
L
M
N
O
P
Q
R
S
T
U
V
W
X
Y
Z

trees that has the shape of a cone and bears seeds. *Many pine cones fall off of the pine tree outside my house.* {kohn}

con·fed·er·a·cy *noun* (confederacies) 1. an alliance or union of people, groups, states, or nations. 2. (capitalized) the eleven southern states that seceded from the United States in 1860 and 1861. {kən **fehd** ər ə see}

con·fed·er·ate *adjective* 1. joined or united in a confederacy; allied. *The confederate nations made a treaty to reduce their armies.* 2. (capitalized) having to do with the eleven southern states that separated from the United States in 1860 and 1861. *His ancestor was a Confederate soldier. noun* 1. a member of a group or confederacy; ally. *The confederates announced their alliance at a press conference.* 2. (capitalized) a person or state allied with the Confederacy during the U.S. Civil War. {kən **fehd** ə riht}

con·fed·er·a·tion *noun* 1. the act or process of confederating or allying. *The confederation of the five neighboring nations brought peace among the Iroquois.* 2. a confederated group, as of countries; league; alliance. *The nations formed a confederation to prevent war.* {kən fehd ə **ray** shən}

con·fer *verb* (conferred, conferring, confers) 1. to give or award. *They conferred the Medal of Honor upon him.* 2. to meet for discussion; hold a conference. *The judges conferred to decide who should be the winner.* {kən **fuhr**}

con·fer·ence *noun* a meeting to discuss a particular matter. *The school held a conference with teachers, students, and parents to plan the new play-*

ground. {**kŏn** fər əns *or* **kŏn** frəns}

con·fess *verb* (confessed, confessing, confesses) 1. to admit as true. *Sarah confessed that she ate the last cookie.* / *I confess my ignorance about computers.* 2. to admit to a priest. *David confessed his mistake before going to Mass.* 3. to admit guilt. *She confessed to the theft and was punished.* {kən **fehs**}

con·fet·ti *plural noun* (used with a singular verb) small pieces of colored paper thrown into the air during parades, parties, and other festivities. *It's fun to throw confetti at weddings.* {kən **feht** ee}

con·fide *verb* (confided, confiding, confides) to share secrets or personal information (usually followed by "in"). *I can always confide in my brother.* {kən **fiyd**}

con·fi·dence *noun* 1. a sense of trust or faith in a person or thing, or in oneself. *She has confidence in the work I do.* / *He writes with great confidence.* 2. a secret. *Matt and Bill shared confidences with each other.* 3. trust that another will keep a secret. *She told me her plans in confidence.* {**kŏn** fih dəns}

con·fi·dent *adjective* 1. having trust or faith; satisfied and sure. *We are confident that our team will win.* 2. sure about one's own abilities. *Lara was shy, but new friends have made her more confident.* {**kŏn** fih dənt} confidently, adv.

con·fi·den·tial *adjective* secret. *The information in this letter is confidential.* {**kŏn** fih **dehn** shəl} confidentiality, n., confidentially, adv.

con·fine *verb* (confined, confining, confines) 1. to keep within limits; restrict. *The storm confined me to the*

house. / *She confined her advice to his most serious problem.* 2. to shut in; put in prison. *The king confined the thief for thirty days. noun* (usually plural.) border or limit. *We kept Rover within the confines of our yard.* {kən **fiyn**}

con·firm *verb* (confirmed, confirming, confirms) 1. to prove, become certain of, or show to be true. *She confirmed the story about the escaped tiger.* 2. to make certain or definite; approve. *I called the airline to confirm my seat on the flight.* / *The Senate confirmed the tax plan.* {kən **fuhrm**} confirmable, adj.

con·fir·ma·tion *noun* 1. the act or process of confirming or proving. *The editor told the reporter that the story needed confirmation before it could be published.* 2. something that confirms or proves. *The success of the experiment was a confirmation of our theory.* 3. a ceremony that makes a person a member of a church or other religious organization. {**kŏn** fər **may** shən}

con·fis·cate *verb* (confiscated, confiscating, confiscates) to take by the power of authority. *The teacher confiscated the paper airplanes.* / *The army confiscated the rebels' guns.* {**kŏn** fih **skayt**} confiscation, n.

con·flict *verb* (conflicted, conflicting, conflicts) to disagree strongly; differ. *My plans for a vacation conflicted with his. noun* 1. a strong disagreement or difference of opinion. *The conflict of opinions led to arguments about the best way to build our clubhouse.* 2. a fight, battle or war. *The conflict between England and France lasted for*

 Human Body    Human Mind    Everyday Life    History and Culture   Communication

many years. {**kŏn** flihkt, n., kən **flihkt**, v.}

con·form *verb* (conformed, conforming, conforms) to act in a way that agrees with a rule or standard. *We have to conform to our school's dress code.* {kən **fohrm**} conformist, n.

con·front *verb* (confronted, confronting, confronts) to meet, face, or stand up to boldly. *Hannah confronted her friend about the missing money.* {kən **fruhnt**} confrontation, n., confrontational, adj.

con·fuse *verb* (confused, confusing, confuses) 1. to fail to see the difference between or among. *He was so tired that he confused the sofa with his bed.* 2. to mix up or bewilder. *The loud noises and bright lights confused me.* {kən **fyooz**} confusedly, adv.

con·fu·sion *noun* the act of confusing or state of being confused. *There was confusion in the computer lab when the power went out.* {kən **fyoo** zhən}

con·ga *noun* 1. a dance from Cuba performed by people following a leader around the dance area in single file. 2. a tall drum played with the hands. {**kŏng** gə}

con·geal *verb* (congealed, congealing, congeals) to make thick or hard, especially by cooling or freezing. *The cold weather congealed the pine sap into a solid lump.* {kən **jeel**}

Con·go *noun* 1. Democratic Republic of the Congo, formerly called Zaire, and before that known as the Belgian Congo; a country in Central Africa, north of Angola and south of the Republic of the Congo. Kin-

shasha is the capital of the Democratic Republic of the Congo. 2. Republic of the Congo, formerly known as the French Congo; a country in Central Africa, south of Gabon and north of the Democratic Republic of the Congo. Brazzaville is the capital of the Republic of the Congo. {**kŏng** goh}

con·grat·u·late *verb* (congratulated, congratulating, congratulates) to praise and express pleasure at the achievement or good luck of. *The losing team congratulated the winners.* {kən **grăch** ə layt} congratulator, n., congratulatory, adj.

con·grat·u·la·tion *noun* 1. the act of congratulating. *There were shouts of congratulation from the audience.* 2. (plural) used as an expression of good wishes or praise. *You got an A? Congratulations!* {kən **grăch** ə **lay** shən}

con·gre·gate *verb* (congregated, congregating, congregates) to bring or come together to form a group; gather. *The tourists congregated around the statue.* {**kŏng** grə **gayt**}

con·gre·ga·tion *noun* 1. a crowd of people; assembly. *There was a congregation around the street musician.* 2. the members of a church or other religious organization. *The minister spoke to the congregation.* {**kŏng** grə **gay** shən}

con·gress ⊙ *noun* 1. the branch of a national government that makes laws. 2. (capitalized) the branch of the U.S. government that is elected to make laws. Congress is made up of the Senate and the House of Representatives. {**kŏng** grihs} congressional, adj.

con·gress·man *noun* (congressmen) (often capitalized)

a male member of the U.S. House of Representatives. {**kŏng** grihs mən}

con·gress·wom·an *noun* (congresswomen) (often capitalized) a female member of the U.S. House of Representatives. {**kŏng** grihs **wuum** ən}

con·gru·ent *adjective* exactly the same in shape and size. {**kŏng** grooh ənt *or* kən **grooh** ənt} congruence, n.

con·i·fer *noun* a tree with cones and narrow leaves called needles. Pines and firs are conifers. Most conifers are evergreen. {**kŏn** ih fər}

con·junc·tion *noun* a word that connects other words, phrases, clauses, or sentences. "And," "while," and "because" are some conjunctions. {kən **jungk** shən} conjunctional, adj., conjunctionally, adv.

con·nect *verb* (connected, connecting, connects) 1. to join together; link. *I connected the plug to an extension cord.* 2. to become joined or linked. *The trains connected at the freight yard.* 3. to think of as related; associate. *He connects elephants with the circus.* {kə **nehkt**} connectible (connectable), adj., connector (connecter), n.

Con·nec·ti·cut *noun* a state in the northeastern United States. Its capital is Hartford. (abbreviated: CT) {kə **neht** tih kət}

Word History *Connecticut* means "at the long tidal river" in the Mohegan (Mohican) language. The state was named for the Connecticut River.

con·nec·tion *noun* 1. something that connects. *I lost my telephone connection in last night's storm.* 2. the act of

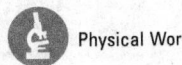 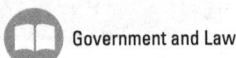

A B C D E F G H I J K L M N O P Q R S T U V W X Y Z

Conservation

Our natural resources have limits. Bad things happen when too many trees are cut down or when too many cattle graze an area. Without plants rooted in the soil, severe erosion occurs. The ruined land can no longer support life.

It is important to conserve unique ecosystems, such as old-growth forests, deserts, and grasslands. Without them, many plants and animals have no habitat. As a result, they are in danger of becoming extinct.

The danger of pesticides used on farms was discovered in the 1960s and 1970s. Rain and snow wash toxic pesticides from farms into streams and rivers. These poisons spread through the food chain and endangered many birds.

A new challenge faces us as we look at our oceans and rivers. Many kinds of fish are threatened with extinction because of overfishing, acid rain, and pollution from industry and oil spills. It is important for people to understand that even the vast oceans have their limits.

You can help conserve our natural world by remembering the three R's: reduce, reuse, recycle. Reduce means 'to decrease or lower.' Can you think of a way to decrease the amount of water you use and the amount of trash you create? Reuse means 'use again'. Do you reuse plastic forks and spoons after a picnic? Recycle means 'make ready for reuse'. Do you recycle cans and paper?

People use natural resources for energy. Some resources, such as coal and oil, are nonrenewable. They can never be replaced. Conservation means creating energy from sources that will always be available, like the sun and wind.

Through the efforts of conservationists, some birds of prey, such as the peregrine falcon and bald eagle, are increasing in number and are no longer endangered in many areas. National parks and preserves around the world are important to help diverse plant and animal species survive. These large areas of land have been set aside to protect the animals that live there. Countries are working together to end destruction of the rain forests and other ecosystems.

connecting. *The traffic engineer is planning a connection between the new road and the main highway.* 3. the fact of being related; relationship or association. *There is a connection between drugs and crime.* {kə **nehk** shən}

con·quer *verb* (conquered, conquering, conquers) 1. to get or overcome by force. *Alexander the Great conquered Persia.* 2. to gain control of through great effort. *It was a difficult climb, but we conquered the mountain.* 3. to master or overcome by strength of mind or character. *He conquered his fear of spiders.* {**kŏng** kər} conquerable, adj.

con·quer·or *noun* one who defeats another. *The conquerors marched into the capital city.* {**kŏng** kə rər}

con·quest *noun* 1. the act or process of conquering. *Their conquest of our country left many towns in ruins.* 2. something gained by conquering, such as land or riches. *Their conquest included gold and jewels.* {**kŏn** kwehst or **kŏng** kwehst}

con·science *noun* the sense that allows a person to decide between right and wrong actions. *Did it bother your conscience to skip the meeting?* {**kŏn** shəns}

con·sci·en·tious *adjective* careful; precise. *He does conscientious work in school.* {kŏn shee **ehn** shəs} conscientiously, adv., conscientiousness, n.

con·scious *adjective* 1. awake; able to feel, think, hear, and see. *Dave fell down the stairs, but was still conscious.* 2. sensitive to; knowing; aware (often followed by "of"). *I was conscious of someone standing behind me.* 3. done

on purpose; deliberate. *Did she make a conscious choice to turn in her work late?* {**kŏn** shəs} consciously, adv.

con·scious·ness *noun* 1. the physical condition of being awake and aware. *Mike lost consciousness after being hit in the head by a rock.* 2. all the ideas and feelings of a person or of a group of people. *The desire for freedom is part of our national consciousness.* 3. the state of being aware or informed; awareness. *Consciousness of our past mistakes will help us to not repeat them.* {**kŏn** shəs nihs}

con·sec·u·tive *adjective* following one after another without a break. *It rained for eight consecutive days.* {kən **sehk** yə tihv} consecutively, adv.

con·sent *verb* (consented, consenting, consents) to give permission or approval; agree (often followed by "to"). *They consented to her going on a trip with her friends.* *noun* permission or approval of another's plan or action. *Pat had his parents' consent to drive their car.* {kən **sehnt**}

con·se·quence *noun* 1. that which follows; result. *Her stomach pain was a consequence of eating too much.* 2. importance or significance. *She asked a question of some consequence.* {**kŏn** sə **kwehns** or **kŏn** sə kwəns}

con·se·quent·ly *adverb* as a result; therefore. *I went to bed late and consequently was tired today.* {**kŏn** sə kwənt lee}

con·ser·va·tion  *noun* 1. the act of keeping and protecting from waste, loss, or destruction. *The mayor offered a plan for the conservation of old buildings.* 2. the protection of natural resources, such as soil, water,

or forests, from loss, pollution, or waste. *Our town council supports conservation.* {kŏn sər **vay** shən}

con·serv·a·tive *adjective* 1. wanting things to stay as they are; not favoring change. *The conservative teachers opposed the idea of getting rid of the school's dress code.* 2. old-fashioned; showing a liking for what has always been. *He wears conservative clothes to work.* 3. not willing to take chances or risks; safe; not too extreme. *She lives a conservative life. / He sold the car at a conservative price.* 4. (capitalized) having to do with the U.S. or British Conservative party. *noun* 1. a person who wants things to stay as they are and is against change. *He is a conservative in how he runs his business.* 2. (capitalized) a member of a conservative party. {kən **suhr** və tihv} conservatively, adj.

con·serve *verb* (conserved, conserving, conserves) to keep safe from loss, destruction, or waste. *We are conserving our supply of water.* {kən **suhrv**}

con·sid·er *verb* (considered, considering, considers) 1. to think carefully about; reflect on. *She is considering moving to Alaska.* 2. to think of as. *I consider Shakespeare a great writer.* 3. to keep in mind; take into account. *My teacher considers test grades, homework, and class participation when she writes report cards.* {kən **sih** dər}

Word History *Consider* is from a Latin word *sidus,* which was combined with the prefix "con-" to mean "to observe, contemplate, or examine the stars."

 Human Body Human Mind  Everyday Life History and Culture  Communication

con·sid·er·a·ble *adjective* large in size or amount. *I walked a considerable distance.* {kən **sihd** ə rə bəl} considerably, adv.

con·sid·er·ate *adjective* thoughtful of the feelings and needs of others. *It was considerate of you to help us paint the house.* {kən **sihd** ə riht} considerately, adv.

con·sid·er·a·tion *noun* 1. careful attention or thought. *The class must give consideration to the problem of bullying.* 2. something that must be taken into account in making a decision. *He wants to buy a car, but the cost is a consideration.* 3. respect or concern for the needs of others. *Please show each other some consideration.* {kən **sihd** ə **ray** shən}

con·sist *verb* (consisted, consisting, consists) to be made up or formed (usually followed by "of"). *The United States consists of fifty states.* {kən **sihst**}

con·sist·en·cy *noun* (consistencies) 1. agreement or similarity between or among different things. *It is hard to tell what she will do because there is no consistency in her actions.* 2. the thickness, firmness, stiffness, or density. *Add more milk to the pudding mixture to get the right consistency.* {kən **sih** stən see}

con·sist·ent *adjective* 1. having a regular style or pattern; not changing. *He has a consistent way of throwing the ball.* 2. in agreement. *Her words are consistent with her actions.* {kən **sihs** tənt} consistently, adv.

con·sole[1] *verb* (consoled, consoling, consoles) to give comfort in time of loss or suffering; make less sad. *She consoled* him after his grandmother died. / *He lost the game and could not be consoled.* {kən **sohl**} consolable, adj., consolingly, adv.

con·sole[2] *noun* a cabinet for a television set, CD player, or radio. {**kŏn** sohl}

con·sol·i·date *verb* (consolidated, consolidating, consolidates) to join together into a whole; combine. *They consolidated their businesses into one company.* {kən **sŏl** ih **dayt**}

con·so·nant *noun* 1. any of the letters of the English alphabet except "a," "e," "i," "o," and "u." 2. any of the sounds represented by the consonant letters. Consonants are made by stopping or restricting the flow of air through the mouth with the tongue, teeth, or lips. {**kŏn** sə nənt}

consonants
bcdfghjklmn
pqrstvwxyz

con·spic·u·ous *adjective* easily seen; obvious. *His purple hair is conspicuous.* {kən **spihk** yoo əs} conspicuously, adv., conspicuousness, n.

con·spir·a·cy *noun* (conspiracies) a secret agreement among two or more people to do something wrong or illegal; plot. *The queen discovered a conspiracy to end her rule.* {kən **speer** ih see} conspiratorial, adj., conspiratorially, adv.

con·spire *verb* (conspired, conspiring, conspires) to plan secretly to do something wrong or illegal with another person or people. *They conspired to give false information to the police.* {kən **spiyr**} conspirator, n.

con·sta·ble *noun* a police officer in a small town or village. {**kŏn** stə bəl}

con·stant *adjective* 1. going on without a pause; persistent. *The child's constant crying annoyed the neighbors.* 2. loyal; faithful. *She has been my most constant friend.* {**kŏn** stənt} constantly, adv.

con·stel·la·tion 🌢 *noun* a group of stars in the sky that is thought to look like, and is named after, an animal, object, or person. *The Big Dipper, Orion, and the Southern Cross are all constellations.* {**kŏn** stə **lay** shən}

con·stit·u·ent *adjective* forming a part of something. *Hydrogen is a constituent element of water.* noun 1. a necessary part of something. *Iron is a constituent of steel.* 2. someone who gives another the power to represent him or her. *The senator's constituents complained to her about the increase in taxes.* {kən **stih** chooh ənt}

con·sti·tute *verb* (constituted, constituting, constitutes) 1. to form or make up. *Seven days constitute a week.* 2. to set up; create; establish. *The money she received will constitute the means for her education.* 3. to elect or appoint to a position or office. *She is constituting him as her assistant.* {**kŏn** stih **tooht**}

con·sti·tu·tion 🏛 *noun* 1. the system of basic laws by which a nation, state, or other organization is governed. *The country's constitution is over five hundred years old.* 2. (sometimes capitalized) the written record of such a system. *Have you read the Constitution of the United States?* 3. the physical makeup of a person. *He has a*

A
B
C
D
E
F
G
H
I
J
K
L
M
N
O
P
Q
R
S
T
U
V
W
X
Y
Z

 Living World   Physical World    Natural Environment   Economy   Government and Law   155

Constellations of the Northern Hemisphere

We have always been star-gazers, finding pictures in the night sky and telling stories about them. People all around the world have named the constellations after animals, things, or characters in their favorite stories.

Astronomers gave many constellations Latin names of characters in Greek mythology: Hercules; Aries; the winged horse Pegasus; and the beautiful princess Andromeda and her parents, King Cepheus and Queen Cassiopeia of Ethiopia. Other constellations are named after a toucan, a chameleon, a giraffe, and a dragon. Can you find them?

20. The Milky Way is not a constellation, but a bright band of stars that stretches across the entire night sky. The Aztec Indians called this part of the sky Centzoni (which means many, many) because there are too many stars to count.

1. Northern Pisces
(Fish)

2. Cetus
(Whale)

3. Aries
(Ram)

4. Triangulum
(Triangle)

5. Andromeda
(Andromeda)

6. Pegasus
(Winged Horse)

7. Equuleus
(Little Horse)

8. Delphinus
(Dolphin)

9. Auila
(Eagle)

10. Sagitta
(Arrow)

11. Cygnus
(Swan)

12. Lacerta
(Lizard)

13. Cepheus
(King)

14. Cassiopeia
(Lady in the Chair)

15. Camelopardus
(Giraffe)

16. Perseus
(Perseus)

17. Auriga
(Charioteer)

18. Taurus
(Bull)

19. Orion
(Hunter)

20. The Milky Way

21. Gemini
(Twins)

22. Lynx
(Lynx)

23. Polaris
(North Star)

24. Ursa Minor
(Little Bear/
Little Dipper)

25. Draco
(Dragon)

26. Lyra
(Lyre)

27. Hercules
(Hercules)

28. Ophiuchus
(Serpent Bearer)

29. Serpens
(Serpent)

30. Corona Borealis
(Northern Crown)

31. Bootes
(Herdsman)

32. Coma Berenices
(Berenice's Hair)

33. Canes Venatici
(Hunting Dogs)

34. Ursa Major
(Great Bear/
Big Dipper)

35. Leo Minor
(Little Lion)

36. Cancer
(Crab)

37. Canis Minor
(Little Dog)

38. Hydra
(Water Snake)

39. Leo
(Lion)

40. Virgo
(Virgin)

Constellations of the Southern Hemisphere

For thousands of years, sailors have used the constellations to guide them while sailing at night. Polynesian sailors used constellations such as the Southern Cross to explore the Pacific Ocean.

As Earth moves around the Sun during the year, we face different parts of the sky at night. People living near the Equator can see each constellation during some part of the year. People living north of the Equator never see constellations such as the Southern Cross or the Chameleon. People living south of the Equator never see constellations such as Ursa Minor, which includes the North Star. What constellations can you see from where you live?

1. Cetus (Whale)	8. Eridanus (River Eridanus)	15. Tucana (Toucan)	22. Ara (Altar)	29. Columba (Dove)	36. Centaurus (Centaur)
2. Aquarius (Water Bearer)	9. Orion (Hunter)	16. Pavo (Peacock)	23. Triangulum Australe (Southern Triangle)	30. Canis Major (Great Dog)	37. Ophiuchus (Serpent Bearer)
3. Capricornus (Goat)	10. Lepus (Hare)	17. Indus (Indian)	24. Apus (Bird of Paradise)	31. Puppis (Shipís Stern)	38. Libra (Scales)
4. Piscis Austrinus (Southern Fish)	11. Caelum (Chisel)	18. Corona Australis (Southern Crown)	25. Musca (Fly)	32. Pyxis (Shipís Compass)	39. Hydra (Water Snake)
5. Grus (Crane)	12. Dorado (Swordfish)	19. Sagittarius (Archer)	26. Chamaeleon (Chameleon)	33. Carina Shipís Keel	40. Corvus (Crow)
6. Phoenix (Phoenix)	13. Reticulum (Net)	20. Serpens (Serpent)	27. Volans (Flying Fish)	34. Vela (Shipís Sails)	41. Virgo (Virgin)
7. Formax (Furnace)	14. Hydrus (Sea-Serpent)	21. Scorpius (Scorpion)	28. Pictor (Painterís Easel)	35. Crux (Southern Cross)	42. Crater (Cup)

a
b
c
d
e
f
g
h
i
j
k
l
m
n
o
p
q
r
s
t
u
v
w
x
y
z

strong, healthy constitution. {kŏn stih **tooh** shən}

con·sti·tu·tion·al *adjective* having to do with a constitution. *Free speech is a constitutional right in the United States.* *noun* a walk taken for one's health. *I'll take the dog on my constitutional.* {kŏn stih **tooh** shih nəl} constitutionally, adv.

con·strict *verb* (constricted, constricting, constricts) to pull or squeeze in; make smaller or more narrow; tighten. *She wore tight belts to constrict her waist.* {kən **strihkt**} constrictive, adj.

con·stric·tor *noun* a snake that kills its prey by winding around it and squeezing it until it can not breathe. Pythons, boa constrictors, and anacondas are constrictors. {kən **strihk** tər}

con·struct *verb* (constructed, constructing, constructs) to build; put together. *They constructed the garage in three days.* {kən **struhkt**} constructor (constructer), n.

con·struc·tion *noun* 1.the act or process of building or construction. *Construction of the new park will begin next year.* 2. something that is put together or built; building or structure. *That construction is the tallest in the city.* 3. the job or business of constructing buildings, roads, or other structures. *My parents work in construction.* {kən **struhk** shən}

con·struc·tive *adjective* serving to make better or more clear; helpful. *Her constructive criticism helped me to improve my story.* {kən **struhk** tihv}

con·sul *noun* a government official who lives in a foreign city. A consul looks after the interests of his or her nation's citizens who live or travel there. {kŏn səl}

con·sult *verb* (consulted, consulting, consults) to look to for advice or information. *Ms. Schwartz consulted a doctor about her stomach pain.* {kən **suhlt**}

con·sult·ant *noun* someone whose job it is to give advice to others on a particular subject; expert. *The school hired a consultant to design their new gym.* {kən **suhl** tənt}

con·sume *verb* (consumed, consuming, consumes) 1. to eat; devour. *He consumed enough food for two people.* 2. to destroy. *Fire consumed the house.* 3. to use up. *A car's engine consumes fuel.* {kən **soohm**} consumable, adj.

con·sum·er ❶ ✆ *noun* someone who buys goods or services. *Consumers spend a lot of money during the holidays.* {kən **sooh** mər}

con·sump·tion *noun* the act or process of using up or consuming. *Consumption of fuel for heating goes up during the cold winter months.* {kən **suhmp** shən}

cont. *abbreviation* an abbreviation for **continued**.

con·tact *noun* 1. the touching of two things or people. *The child fell when her foot came in contact with the slippery ice.* 2. communication. *I am finally in contact with my cousin again after all these years.* *verb* (contacted, contacting, contacts) to be in communication with. *I contacted my friend about our weekend plans.* {kŏn **tăkt**}

contact lens *noun* a thin, plastic lens that is worn on the eyeball to correct vision or change the color of the eyes. {kŏn **tăkt** lehnz}

con·ta·gious *adjective* able to be spread from person to person. *Measles is a contagious disease.* {kən **tay** jihs} contagiously, adv., contagions, n.

con·tain *verb* (contained, containing, contains) 1. to hold or have within. *Many foods contain sugar.* 2. to be able to hold or have within. *A tablespoon contains three teaspoons.* 3. to hold back; set limits on. *He wanted to start a fight but contained his anger.* {kən **tayn**}

con·tain·er *noun* something, such as a box, barrel, or can, that contains or can contain something else. {kən **tay** nər}

con·tam·i·nate *verb* (contaminated, contaminating, contaminates) to make dirty, polluted, or not usable by touching or by adding something to. *Chemicals are contaminating the town's water supply. / Put a bandage on that cut to keep it from being contaminated with germs.* {kən **tăm** ih **nayt**} contaminable, adj., contaminator, n.

con·tem·plate ❓ *verb* (contemplated, contemplating, contemplates) 1. to look at carefully for a long time. *He contemplated the painting.* 2. to think about deeply and seriously. *She contemplated the problem and finally solved it.* {kŏn təm **playt**} contemplative, adj.

con·tem·po·rar·y ❓❓ *adjective* 1. happening in or belonging to the same period of time. *The telephone and the automobile were contemporary inventions.* 2. of or belonging to

 Human Body Human Mind Everyday Life History and Culture  Communication

the present time; current; modern. *He doesn't like contemporary art.* noun (contemporaries) an object or person belonging to the same period of time as another or others. *William Shakespeare and Queen Elizabeth were contemporaries.* {kən **tehm** pə **ray** ree} contemporaneous, adj.

con·tempt *noun* 1. the feeling or expression of angry disgust at something wicked, mean, or not worthy. *His teacher has contempt for people who cheat.* 2. the state of being scorned or despised; disgrace. *The rich nobles held the poor in contempt.* {kən **tehmpt**}

con·tend *verb* (contended, contending, contends) 1. to struggle; fight against difficulties or opposition. *The ship contended with the high waves. / She has to contend with heavy traffic on her way to work.* 2. to compete. *The athletes are contending for first place.* 3. to argue; dispute; debate. *They contended over which book was best.* {kən **tehnd**}

con·tent[1] *noun* 1. (usually plural) whatever is held or contained in a container or receptacle. *He showed me the contents of his pockets.* 2. (usually plural) the information or chapters in a book or other written work. *The names of the book's chapters are listed in the table of contents. / The contents of this letter are top secret.* {**kŏn** tehnt}

con·tent[2] *adjective* wanting no more than what one has; satisfied. *She is content with her life.* verb (contented, contenting, contents) to make content or satisfied; appease. *The hungry child was contented with an apple.* {kən **tehnt**} contentedly, adv.

con·tent·ed *adjective* satisfied with things as they are; content. *She is a very contented person.* {kən **tehn** tihd} contentedly, adv., contentedness, n.

con·test *noun* 1. a fight or struggle to win or to be better. *A contest between the gods is a theme of ancient tales.* 2. a race or game that people try to win to get a prize; competition. *My cousin won first prize in the math contest.* *verb* (contested, contesting, contests) 1. to fight or struggle for. *The armies contested the fort.* 2. to argue against; challenge. *He is contesting the grade he got on his science project.* {**kŏn** tehst, n., kən **tehst**, v.} contestable, adj.

con·test·ant *noun* someone who takes part in a contest; competitor. *Both of them are contestants in the swimming competition.* {kən **tehs** tənt}

con·text *noun* the setting of a word or phrase in speaking or writing that determines or affects its meaning. Context can be pictures, sounds, other words, or physical surroundings. *The meaning of "crash" depends on its context. / Do not use the word "ain't" in a formal context.* {**kŏn** tehkst}

con·ti·nent *noun* one of the earth's seven major areas of land. The continents are Africa, Antarctica, Asia, Australia, Europe, North America, and South America. {**kŏn** tih nənt}

continental shelf *noun* the edge of a continent that is below water. Just beyond the continental shelf lies a steep slope leading down to the ocean floor. {**kŏn** tih **nehn** təl **shehlf**}

con·tin·u·al *adjective* going on without stopping. *The rain has been continual this week.* {kən **tihn** yoo əl} continually, adv.

con·tin·ue *verb* (continued, continuing, continues) 1. to keep happening or being; to last for a long time. *The snow continued to fall. / The party continued.* 2. to start again after stopping or taking a break. *The game will continue after half time.* 3. to go on with; persist in. *The police will continue the search until they find the thief.* 4. to begin again after a break or pause. *The runner fell, but he got back up and continued the race.* {kən **tihn** yoo}

con·tin·u·ous *adjective* going on without pausing or stopping; not broken. *The continuous noise of construction work on my street is very annoying. / There is a continuous flow of water from the spring.* {kən **tihn** yoo əs} continuously, adv.

con·tour *noun* the outline of a figure or surface; shape. *A plane's wing has a curved contour to give it lifting power.* {**kŏn** toohr}

con·tract *noun* 1. an agreement that is supported by the law. *Marriage is a contract.* 2. the piece of paper or document that shows this agreement. *Sign your name at the bottom of the contract.* *verb* (contracted, contracting, contracts) 1. to make smaller by drawing together; shrink or make

 Living World    Physical World    Natural Environment    Economy    Government and Law

tighter. *The earthworm contracted its body when I touched it.* 2. to become smaller; shrink. *Ice contracts as it melts.* 3. to get or acquire. *I contracted a cold from my friend.* 4. to make a formal agreement or contract. *She contracted for a garage to be built.* {kŏn trăkt, n., kən **trăkt**, v.} contractible, adj.

con·trac·tion *noun* (contractions) 1. an act of contracting. *Muscle contractions can cause pain.* 2. a shortened form of a word or words. *"Don't" is a contraction of "do not."* {kən **trăk** shən}

con·tra·dict *verb* (contradicted, contradicting, contradicts) to say the opposite of; deny the truth of. *The TV reporter contradicted the story that we heard on the street. / The facts contradict what you are telling me.* {kŏn trə **dihkt**}

con·tra·dic·to·ry *adjective* 1. The two suspects told contradictory stories about their activities at the time of the robbery. *His words and his actions are contradictory.* 2. likely to oppose or argue. *She has a contradictory attitude toward her teachers.* {kŏn trə **dihk** tə ree}

con·tra·ry *adjective* 1. completely different; opposite. *You and I hold contrary opinions. / The two boys took off in contrary directions.* 2. stubborn; willful. *He is so contrary about everything I ask him to do.* *noun* (contraries) something opposite or completely different from something else. *The weather was the contrary of what we expected for our vacation.* {kŏn trayr ee} contrarily, adv., contrariness, n.

• **on the contrary** not agreeing with something already said. *I had nothing to do with what happened; on the contrary, I was not even there.*

con·trast *verb* (contrasted, contrasting, contrasts) 1. to compare in order to make differences clear. *The book contrasted women's lives a hundred years ago with the lives of women today.* 2. to show or reveal differences when compared. *A job as a firefighter contrasts with a job at a desk in terms of danger.* *noun* 1. the act or result of contrasting; difference. *What a contrast between your sour mood yesterday and your good cheer today!* 2. a person or thing that shows a strong difference compared to something else. *He's quite a contrast to his brother.* {kŏn trăst, n., kən **trăst**, v.}

con·trib·ute *verb* (contributed, contributing, contributes) 1. to give for a purpose. *She contributed time and money to the rescue work.* 2. to write for publication. *She contributed an article about unusual pets to the magazine.* {kən **trihb** yoot} contributor, n.

con·tri·bu·tion *noun* 1. the act of contributing. *Your contribution of money will help the family whose house burned down.* 2. something that is contributed. *They have made many contributions to a group that gives food to the poor.* {kŏn trih **byoo** shən}

con·trive *verb* (contrived, contriving, contrives) to plan in a clever way; invent. *I contrived a surprise birthday party for both of my friends. / He contrived a story about what he saw on the way home.* {kən **triyv**}

con·trol *verb* (controlled, controlling, controls) 1. to use power to manage or command. *The king and queen control their country.* 2. to

hold back or restrain. *My friend tries to control her quick temper.* 3. to stop the spread or growth of. *It is hard to control insects in our garden.* *noun* 1. the power or authority to control someone or something. *Pirates have control over that island. / Our teacher keeps control over our class.* 2. the condition of being directed or controlled. *The prisoners were under the total control of the warden. / The car went out of control.* 3. (often plural) something used to guide or operate a vehicle or other type of machine. *The pilot used the controls to land the airplane safely.* {kən **trohl**} controllable, adj., controllably, adv.

control tower *noun* a tower at an airport. Air traffic is directed by radios in the control tower. {kən **trohl** tow ər}

con·tro·ver·sial *adjective* causing arguments. *His controversial ideas will prevent him from being elected.* {kŏn trə **vuhr** shəl}

con·tro·ver·sy *noun* (controversies) a disagreement; debate. *There was a major controversy about cutting down old trees to make the road wider.* {kŏn trə **vuhr** see}

con·vec·tion *noun* the movement or transfer of heat through a liquid or gas because of the natural rising of the heated parts and sinking of the cooled parts. {kən **vehk** shən}

con·vene *verb* (convened, convening, convenes) to gather or come together for a meeting. *The children convened to plan a surprise for their parents.* {kən **veen**}

con·ven·ience *noun* 1. the quality of being useful or handy for someone's purpose or need. *I like the convenience*

 Human Body   Human Mind   Everyday Life    History and Culture   Communication

of having a grocery store next door. 2. something that adds to comfort or ease. *Compared to washing clothes by hand, a washing machine is a convenience.* {kən **veen** yəns}

con·ven·ient *adjective* easily used for someone's needs, purposes, or comfort; useful. *A vacuum cleaner is a convenient machine for cleaning the house.* {kən **veen** yənt} conveniently, adv.

con·vent *noun* 1. a group of nuns living together and devoted to a religious life. 2. the buildings lived in by such a group. {**kŏn** vehnt *or* **kŏn** vənt}

con·ven·tion *noun* 1. a formal meeting or gathering where people discuss shared interests. *There is a convention for motorcycle owners this weekend.* 2. a practice or way of doing something that is accepted by most people; custom. *It is a convention to begin a letter with the word "dear."* {kən **vehn** shən}

con·ven·tion·al *adjective* put in place by custom or use; traditional. *Shaking hands is a conventional way of greeting another.* {kən **vehn** shə nəl} conventionally, adv.

con·ver·sa·tion 🌐 *noun* talk between people. *There is little time for conversation at work.* {**kŏn** vər **say** shən}

con·verse *verb* (conversed, conversing, converses) to have a talk. *I conversed with my parents about the movie we had just seen.* {kən **vuhrs**}

con·ver·sion *noun* 1. the act or process of changing. *The conversion of the basement into an apartment will bring in extra money.* 2. the changing of a person's religious beliefs. *Her family was surprised to hear about her conversion to Hinduism.* {kən **vuhr** zhən}

con·vert *verb* (converted, converting, converts) 1. to change into another form or state. *He converted the sofa into a bed.* 2. to cause to accept different beliefs or ideas. *The salesman tried to convert us into thinking that his product is the best.* 3. to become converted. *He converted to Christianity because his parents asked him to.* *noun* a person who has been converted or who has adopted new beliefs. *He is a recent convert to Islam.* {**kŏn** vərt, n., kən **vuhrt**, v.}

con·vert·i·ble *adjective* able to be changed. *A convertible sofa can become a bed.* *noun* a car or boat with a top that can be folded down. {kən **vuhr** tə bəl}

con·vex *adjective* having a surface or edge that curves outward like the outside of a ball. *The convex lens helps me see small objects.* {**kŏn** vehks *or* kŏn **vehks**}

con·vey *verb* (conveyed, conveying, conveys) 1. to carry from one place or person to another. *Please convey this letter to the principal.* 2. to make known; express. *The picture conveys a feeling of joy.* {kən **vay**} conveyable, adj.

con·vey·or belt *noun* a mechanical moving strap that carries things from one place to another. *I watched the conveyor belt carry my tray from the dining room to the kitchen of the school cafeteria.* {kŏn **vay** ohr **behlt**}

con·vict *verb* (convicted, convicting, convicts) to find guilty of a crime. *After a long trial, the jury convicted the company of polluting the water.* *noun* a person who is serving time in jail or prison. *The convict was sorry for what he* had done. {**kŏn** vihkt, n., kən **vihkt**, v.}

con·vic·tion 🌐 💬 *noun* 1. the act or process of finding a person guilty of a crime. *The help of a surprise witness led to the thief's conviction.* 2. the state of having been proved guilty. *His conviction will make it hard for him to find a job when he gets out of prison.* 3. a belief or opinion that is strongly held. *It is his conviction that taking bribes is always wrong.* {kən **vihk** shən}

con·vince *verb* (convinced, convincing, convinces) to cause to believe or accept (often followed by "of"). *She convinced the judge of her innocence. / I can't convince him that he needs to eat vegetables.* {kən **vihns**} convincing, adj., convincingly, adv.

con·vulse *verb* (convulsed, convulsing, convulses) to cause to shake without control. *She was convulsed by his jokes. / The city was convulsed by the earthquake.* {kən **vuhls**} convulsive, adj.

con·vul·sion *noun* 1. a violent, involuntary contraction of the muscles. *The wrong medicine caused convulsions in the patient.* 2. a fit of shaking from laughter or fear. *That play was so funny that I went into convulsions of laughter.* {kən **vuhl** shən}

cook 🌐 *verb* (cooked, cooking, cooks) 1. to prepare food for eating by using heat. *She cooked the green beans in boiling water.* 2. to prepare food or meals. *I cooked dinner for my whole family.* 3. to be cooked. *The rice needs to cook for thirty minutes.* *noun* a person who cooks. *The cook prepared a picnic for us.* {**kuuk**}

• **cook up** (informal) to make up or invent a story; devise. *I had*

A
B
C
D
E
F
G
H
I
J
K
L
M
N
O
P
Q
R
S
T
U
V
W
X
Y
Z

a
b
c
d
e
f
g
h
i
j
k
l
m
n
o
p
q
r
s
t
u
v
w
x
y
z

to cook up an excuse for being late again.

cook·book *noun* a book of recipes, directions for cooking, and other information about food. {**kuuk** buuk}

cook·ie *noun* a small, sweet, flat cake baked from stiff dough. {**kuuk** ee}

cook·out *noun* a social gathering at which a meal is cooked and eaten outdoors. {**kuuk** owt}

cool *adjective* (cooler, coolest) 1.

somewhat cold; not warm. *It was a cool spring day.* 2. giving relief from heat. *You should wear cool clothing because it will be hot outside today.* 3. calm and controlled. *He stays cool in an emergency.* 4. not having warmth or enthusiasm; unfriendly. *I could not understand why they were so cool toward me.* 5. (informal) great; admirable. *This game is really cool. noun* something that is cool or somewhat cold. *We shivered in the cool of early morning. verb* (cooled, cooling, cools) 1. to become cool or less warm. *Dinner cooled as we waited.* 2. to lower in temperature; make less warm. *The fan cooled the room.* 3. to become less; decrease. *His passion for his work cooled over the years.* {**koohl**} coolly, adv., coolness, n.

• **cool off** (informal) to become calmer

or less upset. *It took him a long time to cool off after the fight.*

coop *noun* a cage or pen for small animals. *It's time to clean the chicken coop. verb* (cooped, cooping, coops) to shut up in or as though in a coop (often followed by "up"). *They cooped themselves up in the house until the storm was over.* {**koohp**}

co·op·er·ate *verb* (cooperated, cooperating, cooperates) to work with others. *The two writers cooperated on the history book.* {koh **ŏp** ə **rayt**}

co·op·er·a·tion *noun* the act of working together. *With your cooperation, we can finish planting the flowers today.* {koh ŏp ər **ay** shən}

co·op·er·a·tive *adjective* 1. willing to work together or cooperate. *If you'd be more cooperative, we could finish this job sooner.* 2. achieved through cooperation. *Cleaning the garage was a cooperative effort. noun* a project that is owned and run by several people. *This cooperative sells many interesting books.* {koh **ŏp** ər ə tihv or koh **ŏp** rə tihv, n., koh **ŏp** ər ə tihv or koh **ŏp** rə tihv, adj.} cooperatively, adv.

co·or·di·nate or **co-ordinate** *noun* (plural) a pair of numbers that identifies a point on a graph or grid; ordered pair. *The coordinates of that point are written (1,5). verb* (coordinated or co-ordinated, coordinating or co-ordinating, coordinates or co-ordinates) 1. to arrange to work well together. *He tries to coordinate the colors of his jeans and shirts.* 2. to order according to a common goal. *It's time to coordinate plans for the summer festival.* {koh **ohr** də niht, n., koh **ohr** də nayt, v.} coordinator, n.

co·or·di·na·tion 🔊 or **co-ordination** *noun* 1. the act of coordinating or the state of being coordinated. *She'll take care of all the coordination necessary for the party. / I would like to thank those responsible for the coordination of tonight's event.* 2. the working together of different muscles to carry out a complicated movement. *Athletes usually have good coordination.* {koh **ohr** dih **nay** shən}

cope *verb* (coped, coping, copes) to handle or deal with in a successful way (often followed by "with"). *I can't cope with all that information.* {**kohp**}

Co·pen·ha·gen *noun* the capital city of Denmark, on the eastern coast. {koh pən **hay** gən or koh pən **hah** gən or **kohp** ən **hah** gən}

cop·per *noun* 1. a reddish brown metal that is one of the chemical elements. Copper is used to make pipes, because it does not easily rust. It is used to make wires, because it is an excellent conductor of electricity. It can be combined with other metals to make alloys such as brass and bronze. (symbol: Cu) 2. the reddish brown color of copper. *Copper is one of the colors in my box of crayons. adjective* 1. made of or having to do with copper. *There is a copper pipe under the sink.* 2. having the color of copper. *His copper hair shined in the sunlight.* {**kŏp** ər} coppery, adj.

 Human Body   Human Mind   Everyday Life    History and Culture    Communication

cop·per·head *noun* a poisonous snake that has a copper-colored body with darker bands. Copperheads are found in the southeastern United States. {kŏp ər hehd}

cop·y *noun* (copies) 1. something that looks exactly like another. *That picture is a copy of the original painting.* 2. one of a number of books, magazines, photographs, or scores of music that were printed at the same time. *I have a copy of that book.* *verb* (copied, copying, copies) 1. to make a copy of. *I copied the spelling list in my best handwriting.* 2. to do something in the same way as another; imitate. *Lisa copied her friend's style of dress.* 3. to be copied. *Photographs do not copy well on that machine.* {kŏp ee}

cor·al *noun* 1. the hard skeleton of tiny sea animals that are also called corals. Most kinds of coral live in warm tropical oceans, where the skeletons of thousands of corals form reefs and atolls. 2. a yellowish red or pink color. *adjective* made of coral. *I bought my sister a coral necklace.* {kohr əl}

coral snake *noun* a small, poisonous snake that has red, yellow, and black bands around its body. It is found in the southwestern part of the United States and in Central and South America. {kohr əl snayk}

cord *noun* 1. a thick string. 2. a covered wire used to supply power from an electrical outlet to an appliance such as a toaster or lamp. 3. any part of the body that looks like a cord, such as the spinal cord or the umbilical cord. 4. an amount of wood cut for fuel that equals 128 cubic feet. A cord of wood is arranged in a pile measuring 4 feet wide, 4 feet high, and 8 feet long. {kohrd}

Homophone Note Are you looking for the word *chord*? *Cord* and *chord* sound alike but have different meanings.

cor·dial *adjective* warm and friendly; courteous. *She was very cordial to us while we stayed in her house.* {kohr jəl} cordially, adv.

cor·du·roy *noun* 1. cloth that has lengthwise ribs. 2. (plural) pants made of corduroy. {kohr də roi}

core ❶ ⓔ *noun* 1. the hard center part of certain fruits. *The seeds are protected in the core of an apple.* 2. the most important part of something. *The core of his theory is that pets are good for people.* *verb* (cored, coring, cores) to remove the core of a fruit. *His grandmother cored the apples and sliced them to make a pie.* {kohr}

• **to the core** through and through; completely. *He's rotten to the core.*

Homophone Note Are you looking for the word *corps* (a military branch)? *Core* and *corps* sound alike but have different meanings.

cork *noun* 1. a kind of oak that has a thick, soft bark. Corks grow near the Mediterranean Sea. 2. the bark of this tree used to make objects such as floats and bottle stoppers. Cork is light and resists water. 3. a bottle stopper or other object made of this bark. *verb* (corked, corking, corks) to fit or seal with a cork. *Cork the bottle and put it back in the refrigerator.* {kohrk}

cork·screw *noun* a tool shaped like a spiral that is used to remove corks from bottles. *adjective* looking like a corkscrew; tightly spiraled. *She made corkscrew pasta for supper.* {kohrk skrooh}

corn *noun* 1. a tall plant that has ears with rows of yellow or white seeds that can be eaten. Corn is a grain that is used for food. 2. the seed of this plant. *Many birds like to eat corn.* {kohrn}

corn·cob *noun* the woody center of an ear of corn. The corncob holds the kernels. {kohrn kŏb}

cor·ne·a *noun* the clear part of the eyeball's outer coating. The cornea covers the iris and pupil. {kohr nee ə}

cor·ner *noun* 1. the place where two lines or surfaces meet to form an angle. *Stand in the corner of the room.* / *Someone tore off the corners of the pages in this library book.* 2. the place where two paths, roads, or streets meet. *The bank is on the corner of Madison Street and Washington Avenue.* 3. a position from which escape is difficult. *Telling all those lies really put him in a corner.* 4. a far away or little known place or region. *She has gone*

A B C D E F G H I J K L M N O P Q R S T U V W X Y Z

away to a far corner of the earth. **verb** (cornered, cornering, corners) to put in an uncomfortable or difficult position. *She cornered him to find out who had said those mean things about her. / The campers were cornered by a bear.* {**kohr** nər}

cor·net *noun* a brass wind instrument that is like a trumpet but smaller. {**kohr neht**}

corn·meal *noun* corn that has been ground into a rough powder. {**kohrn meel**}

cor·nu·co·pi·a *noun* 1. the mythical horn of a goat that had an endless supply of food; horn of plenty. *The cornucopia is used as a symbol of having plenty to eat.* 2. an overflowing supply of something; abundance. *We had a cornucopia of food on the table for the feast.* {**kohr** nə **koh** pee ə}

cor·o·na·tion *noun* the ceremony at which a king or queen is crowned. *We watched the queen's coronation on television.* {**kohr** ə **nay** shən}

cor·po·ral *noun* an officer in the U.S. Army, Air Force, or Marine Corps who is ranked below sergeant and above private first class. {**kohr** pər əl *or* **kohr** prəl}

cor·po·ra·tion *noun* a group of people allowed by law to do certain things as if they were one person. *My brother and I formed a corporation and bought a bank in Nevada.* {**kohr** pə **ray** shən}

corps *noun* (corps) 1. a branch of the military that does a special kind of work. *After graduating, he joined the medical corps and practiced medicine all over the world.* 2. a group of people who do an activity together. *This will be* his third season as the best dancer in the ballet corps. {**kohr**}

Homophone Note The words ***corps*** and ***core*** sound alike but have different meanings.

corpse *noun* a dead human body. {**kohrps**}

cor·pus·cle *noun* a cell that moves freely in the blood. Red and white blood cells are corpuscles. {**kohr** pə səl *or* **kohr** puhs əl}

cor·ral *noun* an area with a fence around it. Corrals are used to keep horses and cattle from wandering away. *verb* (corralled, corralling, corrals) to drive into or keep in or as if in a corral. *The cowboys corralled the horses.* {kə **răl**}

cor·rect *verb* (corrected, correcting, corrects) 1. to fix the mistakes in; change to make right. *The student corrected the answers on her test after the teacher graded it.* 2. to show the mistakes of; scold; punish. *My mother corrected him for his bad manners.* 3. to make agree with a standard. *She will need glasses to correct her eyesight.* *adjective* 1. with no mistakes; accurate. *The teacher smiled when the student gave the correct answer.* 2. agreeing with a rule or accepted way of doing things; proper. *We were careful to use correct manners at the ball.* {kə **rehkt**} correctly, adv., correctness, n.

Word History ***Correct*** comes from a Latin word that means "to make straight."

cor·rec·tion *noun* 1. the act of making something correct. *The correction of your vision means getting eyeglasses.* 2. something right put in place of something wrong. *The teacher made corrections to my essay.* 3. punishment in order to improve. *Prison is a place of correction for people who have broken the law.* {kə **rehk** shən} correctional, adj.

cor·re·spond *verb* (corresponded, corresponding, corresponds) 1. to agree; match (often followed by "with" or "to"). *Your story corresponds with your neighbor's.* 2. to be the same; be equal (usually followed by "to"). *His job as president corresponds to hers as prime minister.* 3. to write letters. *I correspond with a pen pal in India.* {kohr ə **spŏnd**}

cor·re·spond·ence *noun* 1. agreement or similarity between or among things. *The detective noticed the correspondences between the two crimes and suspected that they were the work of one man.* 2. the writing of letters, or the letters themselves. *My correspondence with my pen pal lasted for ten years. / I bought a book of my favorite writer's correspondence.* {kohr ə **spŏn** dəns}

cor·re·spond·ent *noun* 1. a person who writes letters to another, especially over a period of time. 2. a person who reports news or contributes articles regularly to a newspaper, magazine, TV network, or the like, from a distant area. {kohr ə **spŏn** dənt}

cor·ri·dor *noun* a hall or passageway. *They had to walk down a long corridor to get to their hotel rooms.* {**kohr** ə dər}

cor·rode *verb* (corroded, corroding, corrodes) to cause to wear away

 Human Body   Human Mind    Everyday Life    History and Culture    Communication

slowly. *Rust had corroded the car.* {kə **rohd**}

cor·ro·sion *noun* 1. the act or condition of being worn or eaten away slowly. *Many years of bad weather caused the corrosion of the paint on the car.* 2. a result of this process. Rust is an example of corrosion. *He patched the corrosion on my car.* {kə **roh** zhən}

cor·rupt *adjective* 1. not honest; wicked. *The judge sent those corrupt men to prison.* 2. able to be bribed. *They found that the police officer was not corrupt.* *verb* (corrupted, corrupting, corrupts) 1. to cause to become dishonest or wicked. *A group of bad friends corrupted her.* 2. to bribe. *The honest police officer could not be corrupted with offers of money.* {kə **ruhpt**}

cor·sage *noun* a small bunch of flowers worn by a woman at the shoulder, waist, or on the wrist. {kohr **sahzh**} .

cos·met·ic 🌐 *noun* a preparation used on the face or body to make the person wearing it look more attractive. Lipstick, nail polish, and powder are cosmetics. {kŏz **meh** tihk} cosmetically, adv.

cos·mic 🌐 *adjective* of or relating to the universe. {**kŏz** mihk} cosmically, adv.

cos·mo·naut *noun* an astronaut from Russia or the former Soviet Union. {**kŏz** mə nawt}

cosmos *noun* the universe considered as a whole. {**kŏz** mohs}

cost 🌐 *noun* 1. the amount of money charged or paid for something. *The cost of cereal is higher than it used to be.* 2. the amount of money needed

to make or produce something. *Production costs for computers are falling.* 3. something lost or sacrificed. *The cost of war was the destruction of many homes.* *verb* (cost, costing, costs) 1. to have the price of. *The shoes cost forty dollars.* 2. to cause to lose. *His absence cost us the game.* {**kawst**}

• **at all costs**
without considering the amount of work or effort needed. *The police want to catch the thief at all costs.*

Costa Rica *noun* a country in Central America. San José is the capital of Costa Rica. {kŏs tə **ree** kə}

cost·ly *adjective* (costlier, costliest) of high cost or value. *Diamonds are costly.* {**kawst** lee} costliness, n.

cos·tume *noun* 1. the type of clothing worn in a particular place or time or by members of a particular group. *The kilt is part of the traditional costume of Scotland.* 2. clothing worn to make one look like some other person, animal, or thing. *Dylan wore a pirate costume on Halloween.* {**kŏs** toohm or **kŏs** tyoom}

cosy *adjective* (cosier, cosiest) another spelling of **cozy.**

cot *noun* a small bed that folds up. {**kŏt**}

cot·tage ⚙ *noun* a small house. *Grandmother lived in a cottage on the edge of the forest.* {**kŏt** ihj}

cottage cheese *noun* a soft, white cheese made of slightly soured skim milk. {**kŏt** ihj **cheez**}

cot·ton *noun* 1. a plant that makes soft, white fibers. These fibers are used to make thread or cloth. 2. the soft, white fiber of this plant. *The cotton was spun and dyed in a*

factory. 3. thread or cloth made from cotton fibers. *I wore a cotton shirt and wool trousers.* {**kŏt** ən}

cot·ton·mouth *noun* a poisonous North American snake that lives in swamps; water moccasin. {**kŏt** ən **mowth**}

cot·ton·tail *noun* a kind of rabbit that has brown or gray fur and a fluffy white tail. Cottontails live in North and South America. {**kŏt** ən **tayl**}

cot·ton·wood *noun* 1. a North American tree of the poplar family. Cottonwoods grow quickly and bear seeds surrounded by fiber that looks like cotton. 2. the wood of this tree. {**kŏt** ən **wuud**}

couch *noun* a large piece of furniture made for several people to sit on at the same time; sofa. {**kowch**}

cougar *noun* a common name for a puma, a large wild cat with tan fur. Cougars live in many parts of North and South America. They are carnivorous mammals. They are also

called mountain lions or panthers. {**kooh** gər}

cough 🌐 *verb* (coughed, coughing, coughs) 1. to release air noisily from the lungs. A cough results from illness or from breathing in foreign matter. *Smoke from the flaming toaster made her cough.* 2. to bring up or eject by means of coughing. *The*

A
B
C
D
E
F
G
H
I
J
K
L
M
N
O
P
Q
R
S
T
U
V
W
X
Y
Z

cat coughed up a piece of yarn. noun 1. an instance of coughing. *Brian could tell by his cough that he was getting sick.* 2. an illness that causes a person to cough. *My goodness, you've got a terrible cough.* {<u>kawf</u>}

could *auxiliary verb* past tense of **can**[1]. {<u>kuud</u>}

could·n't shortened form of "could not." *I couldn't see you in the crowded room.* {<u>kuud</u> ənt}

coun·cil *noun* a group of persons gathered together to discuss or make decisions about public matters. For example, a city council may make laws for or give advice on how to run a city. {<u>kown</u> səl}

Homophone Note Are you looking for the word *counsel* (advice or an attorney)? *Council* and *counsel* sound alike but have different meanings.

counsel *noun* 1. help or advice given by an authority or wise person. *My parents' counsel helped me to do better in school.* 2. a lawyer or group of lawyers hired to give legal advice or to speak for one in court. *verb* (counseled or counselled, counseling or counselling, counsels) to give advice or counsel to. *Ms. Diaz has counseled many middle-school students.* {<u>kown</u> səl}

Homophone Note The words *counsel* and *council* (a decision-making group) sound alike but have different meanings.

coun·se·lor *noun* 1. a person who gives advice. 2. a person who watches over and helps children at a camp. 3. a lawyer; attorney. {<u>kown</u> sə lər or <u>kown</u> slər}

count[1] *verb* (counted, counting, counts) 1. to list or name one by one in order to find the total. *Hasani counted the people in his class.* 2. to list or name numbers in order. *I taught my little brother to count from one to ten.* 3. to add up; calculate. *Count your money and see if you have enough to buy a ticket.* 4. to take into account; include. *There are six of us if you count John.* 5. to consider to be; regard. *I count myself lucky to have lived through the car accident.* 6. to have worth or be important; matter. *In her mind, he does not really count.* noun 1. the act of counting. *A count of the books showed that there was one missing.* 2. the total number reached by counting. *The count of the people going on the trip is fifteen.* {<u>kownt</u>} countable, adj.

• **count on**
1. to depend or rely on. *Can I count on you to keep a secret?* 2. to look forward to; hope for. *He is counting on taking a vacation this year.*

count[2] *noun* a European nobleman of a particular rank. {<u>kownt</u>}

count·down *noun* the act of counting down to zero from a higher number to prepare for the start of an event. *The countdown for the rocket launch began at exactly twelve noon.* {<u>kownt</u> down}

count·er[1] *noun* 1. a long, high table. People sit on stools or stand at a counter to eat, prepare food, or do business. 2. an object used for counting in a game. Counters are usually a small piece of wood or metal and are used to help keep score. {<u>kown</u> tər}

coun·ter[2] *adverb* in an opposite direction or manner. *He ran on the side of the road counter to the traffic.* *verb* (countered, countering, counters) to go against; oppose. *When I suggested bike riding, he countered by saying that it was going to rain.* {<u>kown</u> tər}

coun·ter- *prefix* 1. a prefix that means "opposite to." *To move counterclockwise is to move opposite to clockwise.* 2. a prefix that means "similar in function or purpose." *My counterpart at work is a person who does the same kind of work as I do.* {<u>kown</u> tər}

coun·ter·clock·wise *adverb* or *adjective* opposite to the direction in which the hands of a clock move. *He gave the knob on the radio a counterclockwise turn. / Loosen the screw by turning it counterclockwise.* {<u>kown</u> tər <u>klŏk</u> wiyz}

coun·ter·feit *adjective* made to look like something real in order to cheat people. *It is against the law to use counterfeit money.* noun something made to look real in order to cheat people. *This painting is a counterfeit, but it fooled the people who bought it.* *verb* (counterfeited, counterfeiting, counterfeits) to make a copy of in order to cheat people. *The criminal counterfeited ten-dollar bills.* {<u>kown</u> tər fiht} counterfeiter, n.

coun·ter·part *noun* 1. someone or something that is just like or similar to another. *That lamp by the window is the counterpart of the one sitting on the table.* 2. a person who has a rank or who does a job that is similar to that of

 Human Body
 Human Mind
 Everyday Life
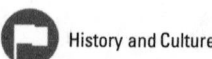 History and Culture
Communication

another person. *This secretary is the counterpart of that assistant.* {**kown** tər **part**}

coun·tess *noun* 1. a woman married to a count or earl. 2. a European noblewoman who has the rank of count or earl. {**kown** tihs}

count·less *adjective* very great in number; not able to be counted. *There were countless people marching in the parade.* {**kownt** lihs}

coun·try  *noun* (countries) 1. a large area of land where people live under the same government or have the same culture; nation. *Laos is a country in Asia.* 2. the land that belongs to a nation or state. *That country has many mountains and rivers.* 3. the people of a state or nation. *The whole country speaks the same language.* 4. the land a person is born in or is a citizen of. *We had to leave our country because of war.* 5. the land outside of towns and cities. *The Millers live in the country on a farm.* {**kuhn** tree}

coun·try·man *noun* (countrymen) 1. a person who lives in or was born in the same country as oneself. 2. a person who lives in the country. {**kuhn** tree mən}

coun·try mu·sic *noun* a type of popular music, based on the traditional music of the rural South and the cowboy music of the West. Country music often expresses sad personal emotions. {**kuhn** tree **myoo** zihk}

coun·try·wom·an *noun* (countrywomen) 1. a woman from the same country as oneself. 2. a woman who lives in the country. {**kuhn** tree **wuum** ən}

coun·ty *noun* (counties) 1. one of several sections into which a U.S. state is divided. *New Jersey has twenty-one*

counties. 2. a section into which some countries are divided for local government. *Cork is a county of Ireland.* 3. all of the people who live in a county. *Most of the county turned out to vote.* {**kown** tee}

cou·ple *noun* 1. two things or people that are related or that go together in some way. *We received a couple of glasses as a gift. / A couple from our school was chosen to greet the governor.* 2. a few; several. *Amanda said she would be back in a couple of minutes.* 3. two people who are together by marriage or by being in a romantic relationship. *I met a nice couple at the party.* *verb* (coupled, coupling, couples) to bring or join together in pairs; connect. *They coupled the box car to the train engine.* {**kuhp** əl}

cou·pon *noun* a small, printed slip of paper that gives someone a discount, admission to a performance, or a chance to win a prize. *This coupon is for twenty cents off the price of two cans of soup. / I couldn't get back into the play because I had lost the coupon from my ticket.* {**kooh** pŏn}

cour·age *noun* the ability to face fear or danger; bravery. *It takes courage to stand up for what you believe in.* {**kuhr** ihj}

cou·ra·geous *adjective* brave. *The courageous firefighters rescued the people who were trapped in the burning building.* {kə **ray** jəs} courageously, adv.

course *noun* 1. progress from one point to another; movement. *Will you go to Mexico in*

the course of your travels? 2. the direction or route along which something moves. *The course of the river takes many twists and turns.* 3. passage through time. *Brian has done many good things in the course of his life.* 4. a series of lessons in a subject. *I took a course in painting.* 5. an area of land or water set aside for sport. *Let's go to the golf course.* 6. a part of a meal. *The second course was soup.* *verb* (coursed, coursing, courses) to move or run swiftly; race. *The lion coursed swiftly after the zebra.* {**kohrs**}

• of course
1. certainly. *Of course I want to come with you!* 2. naturally. *We'll do our homework before we watch TV, of course.*

Synonyms
These words share a meaning with *course*, noun 1:
way, road, progress, passage

Homophone Note Are you looking for the word *coarse* (rough)? *Course* and *coarse* sound alike but have different meanings.

court *noun* 1. an open space surrounded by buildings or walls; courtyard. *She waited for me in the court by the garden.* 2. a place where legal cases are heard. *The judge kept order in the court.* 3. the judges or other people who hear and decide legal cases. *The Supreme Court hears many important cases.* 4. the place where a king, queen, or other important ruler lives and works. *The royal council met at court.* 5. a short street with a dead end. *The court that I live on has only four houses.* *verb* (courted, courting, courts) 1. to try to gain the favor or love of. *John*

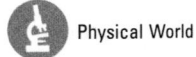 

courted Jane for one year until they agreed to marry. 2. to act in a way that brings on or ends in. *He is courting disaster by walking across the frozen lake.* {**kohrt**}

cour·te·ous *adjective* being polite or showing good manners. *A courteous person says "please" and "thank you."* {**kuhr** tee əs} courteously, adv.

cour·te·sy *noun* (courtesies) 1. good manners or politeness. *She had the courtesy to open the door for her grandmother.* 2. a kindness or favor. *We got a lower price on the new car by courtesy of the manager.* {**kuhr** tih see}

court·house *noun* a building where courts of law and other government offices are located. {**kohrt** hows}

court·room *noun* a room in which legal cases are heard before a judge. {**kohrt** roohm}

court·yard *noun* a yard surrounded by buildings or walls. *Ari and Tanya were married in the courtyard of the church.* {**kohrt** yard}

cous·in *noun* the son or daughter of an aunt or uncle. {**kuhz** ən}

cove *noun* a small bay. *Bob kept his boat in the cove until the storm had passed.* {**kohv**}

cov·er *verb* (covered, covering, covers) 1. to put or spread something over or on. *Cover your bicycle so it doesn't get rained on.* 2. to lie on the surface of. *Snow covers the ground.* 3. to take into account; include. *The book on magic didn't cover wizards.* 4. to pass over a certain distance; travel. *We covered a thousand miles in the car last summer. noun* 1. something laid over or on something else to shelter, protect, or hide. *Put the cover back on the*

can of paint. / *The cover of a book helps keep the pages from being torn.* 2. something that hides or protects someone or something. *The hikers looked for cover during the storm.* {**kuhv** ər}

• **take cover**
to seek protection or a hiding place. *The mouse took cover from the attacking hawk.*

• **under cover**
hidden; in secret. *The spies carried out their mission under cover.*

covered wagon *noun* a large wagon with a high, curved, canvas cover.

American pioneers rode west in covered wagons. {**kuh** vərd **wă** gən}

cov·er·ing *noun* something that covers or hides. *A tablecloth is a covering for a table.* / *Don't remove the covering from the statue until it's time for the ceremony.* {**kuhv** ər ing}

cov·et *verb* (coveted, coveting, covets) to wish to have very much; envy. *He coveted his friend's new computer.* {**kuhv** iht}

cow ❶ *noun*
1. the adult female of cattle. 2. the female of other

large mammals such as buffalo, elephants, and whales. {**kow**}

cow·ard *noun* a person who does not have the courage to face danger, pain, or some-

thing difficult. *I'm a coward about speaking in front of an audience.* {**kow** ərd}

> **Word History** *Coward* is from an early French word that means "tail." Today we say that a frightened animal or person may "turn tail" and run.

cow·ard·ice *noun* a lack of bravery to work through danger, pain, or other difficult things. *He shows his cowardice by running away from every spider he sees.* {**kow** ər dihs}

cow·ard·ly *adjective* 1. of or like a coward. *The profession of astronaut is not suited to cowardly people.* 2. having or showing no courage. *She was cowardly and decided to let someone else try to catch the bat. adverb* like a coward. *In the face of danger, he behaved cowardly.* {**kow** ərd lee} cowardliness, n.

cow·boy *noun* a man who herds and takes care of cattle. *Cowboys work on ranches and often ride horses.* {**kow** boi}

cow·girl *noun* a woman who herds and takes care of cattle. *Cowgirls work on ranches and often ride horses.* {**kow** guhrl}

cow·hand *noun* a person who works on a cattle ranch; cowboy or cowgirl. {**kow** hănd}

cow·hide *noun* the skin and hair of a cow, or leather made from the skin of a cow. {**kow** hiyd}

co·work·er *noun* one of two or more people who work together; fellow worker. *Mary and her coworkers treated themselves to lunch after finishing the huge project.* {**koh** wuhr kər}

coy·ote *noun* (coyote or coyotes) a North American

168

 Human Body   Human Mind   Everyday Life   History and Culture  Communication

mammal that is closely related to dogs, foxes, and wolves. Coyotes have a pointed nose and ears and a bushy tail. They hunt small animals, and they also sometimes eat plants. {<u>kiy</u> oht *or* kiy <u>oh</u> tee}

co·zy *or* **cosy** *adjective* (cozier or cosier, coziest or cosiest) warm and snug in a comfortable way. *I feel safe when I fall asleep in my cozy bed.* {<u>koh</u> zee} cozily, adv., coziness, n.

CPR *abbreviation* a method of reviving heart attack victims by breathing into the mouth and strong, rhythmic pressing down on the chest. CPR is an abbreviation for "cardiopulmonary resuscitation."

Cr symbol of the chemical element chromium.

crab *noun* an animal with a wide, flat body covered by a hard shell. Crabs have ten legs, including a pair of claws, eyes on short stalks, and antennae. Most kinds of crabs live in the ocean and eat many kinds of food. Crabs are crustaceans, which are a kind of arthropod. The biggest crabs are larger than any other arthropod. {<u>krăb</u>}

crab apple *noun* 1. a small, hard, sour apple used for making jelly. 2. a tree that bears such fruit. {<u>krăb</u> ăp əl}

crack *verb* (cracked, cracking, cracks) 1. to break apart with a snapping sound. *The old tree branch cracked under the weight of the child.* 2. to break or snap but not into separate pieces. *The plate cracked, but it's still useful.* 3. to make a sharp sound. *The rifle cracked loudly in the quiet forest.* 4. to hit and break, but not into separate pieces; cause to snap. *A stone cracked the car windshield.* 5. to cause to make a sudden sharp noise. *The lion tamer cracked the whip.* 6. to figure out; find a

solution to. *They cracked the secret code.* *noun* 1. a sharp sound. *The loud crack of thunder frightened him.* 2. a break in something. *There is a crack in the wall.* 3. a narrow opening. *Daylight came through a crack in the curtains.* {<u>krăk</u>}

• **crack down on** to treat more harshly or strictly. *Our teacher cracked down on us by giving us more homework.* / *The mayor wants to crack down on crime in this city.*

• **crack up** (informal) to break into laughter. *Eli's parents cracked up when they saw his Halloween costume.*

crack·er *noun* a thin, hard biscuit. {<u>krăk</u> ər}

crack·le *verb* (crackled, crackling, crackles) 1. to make a series of small snapping noises. *The flames crackled softly.* 2. to cause something to make a crackling sound. *He crackled the thin plastic sheet by shaking it.* *noun* the sound of crackling. *The crackle of candy wrappers during a movie distracts me.* {<u>krăk</u> əl}

cra·dle *noun* 1. a baby's bed set on rockers. 2. the beginning place of an event or idea. *We visited a country that is said to be the cradle of civilization.* 3. anything that looks like or works like a cradle. Phones have cradles. *verb* (cradled, cradling, cradles) to hold or rock in or as in a cradle. *She cradled the child in her arms.* {<u>kray</u> dəl}

craft ● *noun* (crafts or craft) 1. skill or talent in making things by hand or in the arts. *The poet is known for his craft with words.* 2. skill at fooling or tricking. *The fox used its craft to escape the hunting dogs.* 3. a trade or occupation that requires skill with the hands. *Sue has learned the carpenter's craft.* 4. a boat, ship, airplane, or space vehicle, or any group of these together. *We took a small craft across the bay.* / *The craft of that airline are all jets.* {<u>krăft</u>}

-craft *suffix* a suffix that means "skill or practice in the use of." *If a woodcarving shows excellent handicraft, it shows great skill in the use of the hands.* {<u>krăft</u>}

crafts·man *noun* (craftsmen) a person who works at a craft or skilled trade; artisan. {<u>krăfs</u> mən} craftsmanship, n.

craft·y *adjective* (craftier, craftiest) sly or cunning. *The crafty witch pretended to be the boy's mother.* {<u>krăf</u> tee} craftily, adv., craftiness, n.

cram *verb* (crammed, cramming, crams) 1. to fill with more than can be easily held. *Hundreds of people crammed the hall.* 2. to force into a space that is too small; stuff.

A B C D E F G H I J K L M N O P Q R S T U V W X Y Z

a
b
c
d
e
f
g
h
i
j
k
l
m
n
o
p
q
r
s
t
u
v
w
x
y
z

(usually followed by "inside," "into," or "down.") *If you cram any more of that sandwich into your mouth, your cheeks will explode.* 3. to study hard at the last minute for an examination. *We crammed all night before the final exam.* {**krăm**}

cramp[1] *noun* 1. (sometimes plural) a sharp pain in a muscle that suddenly becomes tight. *The cramp in his hand was so bad that he could barely let go of the pen. / Leg cramps kept her from finishing the race.* 2. (usually plural) strong pains in the abdomen. *He was sick with cramps.* *verb* (cramped, cramping, cramps) to tighten suddenly and cause pain. *As he was running, his calf muscle cramped.* {**krămp**}

cramp[2] *verb* (cramped, cramping, cramps) to limit the freedom of by closely confining. *His teacher's rules cramped his sense of humor.* {**krămp**}

cran·ber·ry *noun* (cranberries) a shrub that bears a sour, red berry, or the berry itself. Cranberries grow in wet ground in North America. {**krăn behr** ee}

crane *noun* 1. a tall wading bird with long legs and a long neck and bill. A whooping crane is one kind of crane. 2. a machine with a tall arm that can move up and down or around in a circle to lift and move heavy objects. *The workers used a crane to lift cement blocks onto the truck.* *verb* (craned, craning, cranes) to stretch up or out in order to see something. *I craned my neck to see over the crowd.* {**krayn**}

crank *noun* 1. a device that moves things in a circle. Cranks have a lever attached at a right angle to the end of an arm that moves in a circle. Cranks are turned by hand or by another arm that connects to the lever. 2. (informal) a person who has odd ideas or interests. *The crank spent all weekend in his garage building a television combined with a refrigerator.* 3. (informal) a person who is always grouchy or in a bad mood. *verb* (cranked, cranking, cranks) to turn by using of a crank, or start by using a crank or other device. *Tim cranked the lid open. / Her grandfather cranked the old car until it started.* {**krăngk**}

• **crank out**
to make in great numbers in a mechanical way. *That author cranks out a new book every few months.*

crank·y *adjective* (crankier, crankiest) in a bad mood; grouchy. *The baby is cranky when he is hungry.* {**krăng** kee} crankily, adv., crankiness, n.

crash *verb* (crashed, crashing, crashes) 1. to smash or destroy with great force and loud noise. *He crashed his new car.* 2. to drive or push with great power and noise (usually followed by "through," "in," "into," or "past"). *Superman crashed through the brick wall.* 3. (informal) to enter without being invited or allowed. *I am afraid that they will crash my party.* 4. to strike violently against something while riding or moving. *The car crashed during the blizzard.* 5. to make a loud noise as if being smashed. *Thunder crashed all around us.* *noun* 1. a loud noise of things breaking or

colliding. *There was a huge crash when the shelf fell down.* 2. a violent impact or collision. *Luckily, no one was hurt in the car crash.* {**krăsh**} crasher, n.

crate *noun* a box for packing and shipping made of wood or other material. *verb* (crated, crating, crates) to pack in a crate. *We crated all our dishes before we moved.* {**krayt**}

cra·ter *noun* a hollow area shaped like the inside of a bowl. The mouth of a volcano is a crater, and the moon has many craters on its surface. {**kray** tər}

crave *verb* (craved, craving, craves) to need or desire very much. *After hiking in the sun all day, Rhona craved a drink of water.* {**krayv**}

craw·fish *noun* (crawfish or crawfishes) another form of **crayfish**. {**kraw** fihsh}

crawl *verb* (crawled, crawling, crawls) 1. to move slowly along the ground on the hands and knees; creep. *The baby crawled over to his mother.* 2. to move very slowly or stop many times along the way. *The car crawled through the heavy traffic on the highway.* 3. to be or feel as if covered with crawling things. *The ground crawled with ants. / My skin crawled with fear.* *noun* 1. the act of crawling; creeping action. *It was a long crawl to the end of the tunnel.* 2. a very slow movement. *Traffic slowed to a crawl on Thanksgiving day.* 3. a swimming stroke. The swimmer keeps his face in the water while the feet kick without stop-

 Human Body   Human Mind   Everyday Life   History and Culture   Communication

ping and the arms reach in front of the head one at a time. {<u>krawl</u>}

cray·fish or **crawfish** *noun* (crayfish or crayfishes) a small animal with a hard, jointed shell that lives in fresh water. Crayfish are crustaceans and are closely related to lobsters. {<u>kray</u> fihsh, <u>kraw</u> fihsh}

cray·on ⬤ ⬤ *noun* a colored stick or pencil made of wax. A crayon is used for drawing and coloring. *verb* (crayoned, crayoning, crayons) to color or draw with crayon. {<u>kray</u> ŏn}

cra·zy ⬤ *adjective* (crazier, craziest) 1. having a mental illness; insane. *The crazy person was being cared for by a doctor.* 2. not reasonable or practical; silly; foolish. *They had a crazy plan to win a million dollars.* 3. (informal) very enthusiastic; excited. *Jane is crazy about dancing.* 4. (informal) acting in a way that is not easy to predict; odd. *We have been having crazy weather, freezing cold one day and warm the next.* {<u>kray</u> zee} crazily, adv., craziness, n.

• **like crazy** (informal) to a very great or extreme degree; wildly. *They loved each other like crazy. / The crowd cheered like crazy when the home team won.*

creak *verb* (creaked, creaking, creaks) to make or move with a grinding or squeaking noise. *The chair creaked when he sat down in it. / Her bones creak when the weather is cold and damp.* *noun* a grinding or squeaking sound. *The rusty* gate moved with a creak. {<u>kreek</u>}

Homophone Note Are you looking for the word *creek* (a small stream)? In many parts of the US, *creak* and *creek* are said in exactly the same way.

cream *noun* 1. the part of whole milk that contains fat. Butter is made from cream. 2. a thick liquid or lotion used on the skin. *My sister puts cream on her face at night.* 3. a yellowish white color. 4. a food that is like cream or is made with cream. 5. the best part of something. *The cream of this year's class will go to college.* *verb* (creamed, creaming, creams) to beat something until it is as smooth as cream. *Cream the butter and sugar, then add the eggs.* {<u>kreem</u>}

cream·y *adjective* (creamier, creamiest) 1. having the taste, color, or texture of cream. *Joan has a creamy complexion.* 2. having a large amount of cream. *Mark felt ill after eating too much of the creamy dessert.* {<u>kree</u> mee} creaminess, n.

crease *noun* a fold or dent made by heat or pressure. *I ironed a crease into my best pants.* *verb* (creased, creasing, creases) to make a dent, fold, or wrinkle in or on. *He creased the sleeve with an iron. / She creased her forehead and frowned.* {<u>krees</u>}

cre·ate *verb* (created, creating, creates) 1. to bring into being. *The chef created a new dish. / Beethoven created nine symphonies.* 2. to cause; pro- duce. *Poor planning creates problems.* {kree <u>ayt</u>}

Synonyms
These words share a meaning with *create*, verb 1:
found, form, develop, invent, originate, initiate

cre·a·tion *noun* 1. the act of creating or of causing something to exist. *The creation of the famous painting took two years.* 2. the product of such an act of creation. *She stepped back to look at her creation.* 3. the universe or the creatures in it. *They enjoyed seeing creation as they walked in the forest.* {kree <u>ay</u> shən}

cre·a·tive ⬤ ⬤ *adjective* able to make or do something new or with imagination. *Lucas is a creative chess player. / That creative inventor designed a new kind of wheelchair.* {kree <u>ay</u> tihv} creatively, adv., creativity, n.

cre·a·tor *noun* 1. a person who creates. *The creator of that building was a famous architect.* 2. (capitalized) God (used with "the"). {kree <u>ay</u> tər}

crea·ture *noun* a living person or animal. *When I was young, I thought that there was a creature underneath my bed. / Owls and bats are creatures of the night.* {<u>kree</u> chər}

cred·it ⬤ *noun* 1. the condition of being able to be believed or trusted. *If someone else saw him hit you first, that will lend credit to your story.* 2. a source of honor. *This kind and helpful young man is a credit to his family.* 3. the right to buy things at the present time and not pay until later. Having credit often depends on one's reputation for paying one's debt. *Marcy has good credit at the clothing store.* 4. approval or praise given to

A
B
C
D
E
F
G
H
I
J
K
L
M
N
O
P
Q
R
S
T
U
V
W
X
Y
Z

 Living World   Physical World  Natural Environment  Economy ⬤ Government and Law

a person or group for something that has been done; recognition. *I give him credit for trying so hard. / She got all the credit for my great idea.* 5. the amount of money in an account or an amount added to an account. *verb* (credited, crediting, credits) 1. to take as a fact; believe. *We did not credit the news report because we saw what really happened.* 2. to add to a person's account. *When you make a deposit, the bank will credit your account.* {**kreh** diht}

credit card *noun* a card from a bank or store that lets a person buy things and pay for them later. {**kreh** diht **kard**}

cred·i·tor *noun* someone to whom money is owed. *I will send another payment to my creditor this month.* {**kreh** dih tər}

creed *noun* a set of beliefs held by a person or group. {**kreed**}

creek 🌐 *noun* a stream that is smaller than a river; brook. {**kreek**}

Homophone Note In many parts of the US, the words **creek** and **creak** (squeak) are said in exactly the same way. However, these two words have different meanings.

Creek *noun* (Creek [or] Creeks) a member of a group of American Indian peoples formed from groups who lived in Alabama and Georgia, but are now mostly in Oklahoma. {**kreek**}

creep *verb* (crept, creeping, creeps) 1. to move with the body close to the ground; crawl. *The baby crept across the carpet on her hands and knees.* 2. to move slowly. *The traffic was*

creeping along. 3. to grow along a surface like a vine or the roots of certain plants. *The ivy crept over the windows.* 4. to feel uneasy. *Watching that big spider makes my skin creep. noun* 1. the act or process of creeping. *Weighed down by the boxes, her walk slowed to a creep.* 2. (informal, usually plural) a feeling as if something were crawling over the skin (used with "the"). *Horror movies give me the creeps.* {**kreep**}

crepe *noun* 1. a thin cloth with a wrinkled surface. 2. **crepe paper**. 3. a thin pancake served with a filling or topping. {**krayp** *or* **krehp**}

crepe paper *noun* thin paper with wrinkles. Crepe paper is used for decoration. {**krayp pay** pər}

crept *verb* past tense and past participle of **creep**. {**krehpt**}

cre·scen·do *noun* (crescendos) an increase in loudness or force in a piece of music. *This song starts quietly and builds to a crescendo.* {krə **shehn** doh}

cres·cent *noun* 1. the shape of the moon when it looks like a curved line with a point at each end. The moon appears as a crescent in its first and last quarters. 2. any shape, sign, or object that looks like a crescent moon. *The wizard's hat was decorated with crescents and stars. adjective* shaped like the moon in its first or last quarter. *The host served crescent rolls with dinner.* {**krehs** ənt}

crest *noun* 1. a tuft of feathers, bone, or fur on an animal's head, or something that looks like this. The comb of a rooster is one kind of crest. 2. a decoration dis-

played above the shield on a coat of arms. *This dragon is the traditional crest of their family.* 3. the peak of a mountain or wave. 4. the highest level. *The crest of her career as a dancer has passed.* {**krehst**} crested, adj.

crew *noun* 1. a group of people who work together. *The road crew finished putting a new surface on the highway.* 2. all of the people who work on a ship or an airplane. {**krooh**}

crib *noun* 1. a bed with high sides for a baby or young child. 2. a box from which cattle eat. 3. a storage bin or building for corn. {**krihb**}

crick·et[1] *noun* an insect that is related to a grasshopper. It has long antennae and strong hind legs for jumping. The male makes a chirping noise by rubbing his front wings together. {**krihk** iht}

Word History *Cricket*[1] comes from *criquer*, an early French word that means "to creak."

crick·et[2] *noun* an English game played outdoors with a ball and bat by two teams of eleven members each. {**krihk** iht} cricketer, n.

cried *verb* past tense and past participle of **cry**. {**kriyd**}

crime 💬 *noun* 1. something done against the law. *Driving while drunk is a crime.* 2. something done that is wrong. *It is a crime that children are allowed to go hungry.* {**kriym**}

crim·i·nal *adjective* 1. of or having to do with crime. *Criminal activity in our neighborhood has gone down since the city put up more street lights.* 2. guilty of crime. *She was punished for her criminal*

🏃 Human Body　　❓ Human Mind　　👕 Everyday Life　　🚩 History and Culture　　📞 Communication

behavior. *noun* a person who is guilty of a crime. *The criminal went to prison for four years.* {<u>krihm</u> ih nəl}

crim·son *noun* the color that comes from mixing red and a small amount of purple paint. {<u>krihm</u> sən}

crin·kle *verb* (crinkled, crinkling, crinkles) 1. to make small ripples or wrinkles in. *I crinkled my paper by holding it too tightly.* 2. to make small crackling sounds. *We crinkled the dry leaves under out boots.* *noun* 1. a small ripple or wrinkle. *He has crinkles around his eyes when he smiles.* 2. a small crackling sound. *The crinkle of paper distracted me during the play.* {<u>kring</u> kəl}

crip·ple *noun* a person or animal that cannot use a part of its body because of a disease or injury. *verb* (crippled, crippling, cripples) 1. to cause a serious injury in. *The car accident crippled him for life.* 2. to damage or cause not to work well. *Power shortages crippled the city.* {<u>krihp</u> əl}

cri·sis *noun* (crises) 1. the point or moment just before a very important change. *Having to choose between staying in town or moving across the country was a crisis for the whole family.* 2. a situation that is not stable or certain. *The murder of the president threw the country into a crisis.* {<u>kriy</u> sihs}

crisp *adjective* (crisper, crispest) 1. firm but breaking easily into pieces. *The crisp crackers broke into crumbs all over the floor.* 2. clear and cool; brisk. *He enjoyed a run in the crisp breeze.* 3. short and to the point. *It would be good to make this a crisp speech.* {<u>krihsp</u>} crispy, adj., crisply, adv., crispness, n.

criss·cross *adjective* with two or more lines crossing each other. *That crisscross pattern will look great on your sofa.* *noun* a mark or pattern of two or more lines crossing each other. *He filled the page with crisscrosses.* *verb* (crisscrossed, crisscrossing, crisscrosses) 1. to mark or make with crossing lines. *Tire tracks crisscrossed one another in the mud.* 2. to move or cause to move back and forth. *I crisscrossed the parking lot looking for my dropped glove.* {<u>krihs</u> kraws}

crit·ic 🌐📖 *noun* 1. a person whose work is to judge and write opinions about music, plays, art, and literature. 2. a person who often looks for and points out something wrong. *Jill's piano teacher is a harsh critic.* {<u>kriht</u> ihk}

crit·i·cal *adjective* 1. likely to find fault. *She is always critical of the cafeteria food.* 2. of the nature of a crisis; serious or dangerous. *He was rushed to the hospital with a critical illness.* 3. very important. *It is critical that you understand my point.* {<u>kriht</u> ih kəl} critically, adv.

crit·i·cism *noun* 1. the act of judging what is good or bad in something. *The coach's criticism helped us learn to be better players.* 2. the act of finding problems or mistakes in something. *Kim's criticism of his classmates made him unpopular.* {<u>kriht</u> ə sihz əm}

crit·i·cize *verb* (criticized, criticizing, criticizes) 1. to judge what is good or bad in. *The writer did a good job criticizing the new play.* 2. to find problems or mistakes in. *He criticizes everything that I say.* {<u>kriht</u> ə siyz}

cri·tique *noun* 1. a written evaluation of a work of art or literature. 2. a discussion about what is good or bad in something. *In class, we did critiques of each other's writing.* *verb* (critiqued, critiquing, critiques) to discuss or write about what is good or bad in. *The speaker critiqued a play by William Shakespeare.* {krih <u>teek</u>}

croak *verb* (croaked, croaking, croaks) to make a low, hoarse sound with the voice. *The bullfrogs croaked by the pond.* *noun* a low, hoarse sound like that of a frog. {<u>krohk</u>}

cro·chet *noun* needlework made with a hooked needle that pulls the thread or yarn in a pattern of connected loops. *verb* (crocheted, crocheting, crochets) to form by looping thread in a pattern of connected stitches. *Aunt Rose crocheted a tablecloth for their wedding gift.* {kroh <u>shay</u>}

croc·o·dile *noun* a large reptile that is found in tropical swamps. It has a thick, tough skin, a long tail, and a long, pointed snout. {<u>krŏk</u> ə diyl}

croc·o·dil·i·an *noun* a reptile of the group that includes the crocodile. Alligators and caimans are crocodilians. {kro kə <u>dihl</u> ee ən}

cro·cus *noun* (crocuses or croci) a small plant that blooms in early spring with one colorful flower. {<u>kroh</u> kəs}

crook *noun* 1. something bent, curved, or hooked. *The deer jumped over the crook in the stream.* 2. a hooked tool. *The shepherd used his crook to rescue a sheep that had fallen in the pond.* 3. a thief. *The police caught the crook in the act of stealing.* *verb* (crooked, crooking, crooks) to bend, curve, or hook. *When it was*

 Living World Physical World Natural Environment Economy  Government and Law

a
b
c
d
e
f
g
h
i
j
k
l
m
n
o
p
q
r
s
t
u
v
w
x
y
z

time to leave, she crooked a finger at me. {**kruuk**}

crook·ed *adjective* 1. bent, curved, or twisting. *We walked on the crooked path.* 2. not honest. *The crooked prime minister tricked most of the people into voting for him.* {**kruuk** ihd} crookedly, adv., crookedness, n.

crop 🔺 *noun* 1. plants grown on a farm. *Corn is an important crop.* 2. the harvest of one or more farm products in a year or a season. *The potato crop was small this year.* 3. any group that appears within a short time. *A new crop of students graduated this year.* 4. a whip handle, or the short riding whip used on horses. 5. a pouch in the digestive system of a bird, between its mouth and stomach. *The crop stores food and prepares it for digestion.* *verb* (cropped, cropping, crops) 1. to cut off the top or ends of. *He cropped the bushes along the path.* 2. to trim. *She cropped the photo before she put it in a frame.* {**krŏp**}
 • **cream of the crop** the best one. *We have many fine dogs, but this puppy is the cream of the crop.*
 • **crop up** to appear or happen as a surprise. *A visitor cropped up at our house.*

cro·quet *noun* a lawn game in which mallets are used to hit wooden balls through wire hoops toward a goal. {**kroh** **kay**}

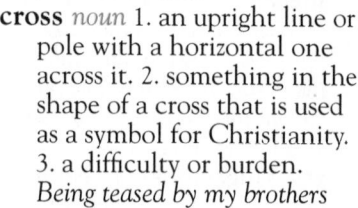

cross *noun* 1. an upright line or pole with a horizontal one across it. 2. something in the shape of a cross that is used as a symbol for Christianity. 3. a difficulty or burden. *Being teased by my brothers*

was my cross to bear while I was growing up. 4. a mixture of two kinds of animals or plants that has characteristics of both parents; hybrid. *A mule is a cross between a horse and a donkey.* *verb* (crossed, crossing, crosses) 1. to move across. *Let's cross the street.* 2. to place in a crossed position. *I crossed my arms across my chest.* 3. to pass across or intersect. *The bridge crossed the stream.* 4. to mark off or scratch out from a list (usually followed by "out" or "off"). *We crossed out the names of the people who were not coming to the party.* 5. to work against; oppose. *If you cross Miss Chen, she will be very angry.* *adjective* (crosser, crossest) in a bad mood. *He's very cross today, so don't bother him.* {**kraws**}

cross·bow *noun* a bow on a wooden stock. Crossbows shoot arrows when someone pulls a trigger. {**kraws** boh}

cross-eye *noun* a condition in which one or both eyes turn toward each other. {**kraws** iy} cross-eyed, adj.

cross·ing *noun* 1. a place where two roads, routes, or railroad tracks cross each other. 2. a place where a street or river can be crossed. *We got on the ferry at the crossing.* {**kraw** sing}

cross reference *noun* a reference from one part of a book, index, or file to another part that contains additional or related information. *I checked the cross reference to find more ideas on the topic.* {**kraws** **reh** frəns or **kraws** **reh** fə rəns}

cross-ref·er·ence *verb* (cross-referenced, cross-referencing, cross-references) to give a reference to in a book

or other written work. *In this dictionary, the entry word "hippo" cross-references the headword "hippopotamus."* {**kraws** **reh** frəns or **kraws** **rehf** ə rəns} cross-reference, n.

cross·road *noun* the place where two roads cross one another; intersection. {**kraws** rohd}

cross section *noun* 1. a part of something made visible by cutting straight through it. *Our science book had a picture of a cross section of a brain.* 2. a sample of typical parts that show what the whole is like. *The cross section of the population shows that most people own televisions.* {**kraws** sehk shən}

cross·walk *noun* a lane or path in a road that is marked off for people to cross on foot. *It is safest to cross the street in the crosswalk.* {**kraws** wŏk}

crossword puzzle *noun* a puzzle in which a person must guess words from clues and enter them in a pattern of squares, one letter per square. {**kraws** wuhrd **puhz** əl}

crotch *noun* the place where two long, straight parts, such as legs or tree branches, come together. *She fixed the seam in the crotch of the pants.* {**krŏch**}

crouch *verb* (crouched, crouching, crouches) to lower the body close to the ground by bending the legs. *A cat about to pounce crouches, as does a person getting ready to run in a race.* *noun* a lowering of the body by crouching. *Minh hid under the table in a crouch.* {**krowch**}

croup *noun* a disease in children that causes coughing

 Human Body  Human Mind  Everyday Life  History and Culture Communication

and difficult breathing. {**kroohp**}

crow[1] *noun* a shiny black bird known for its shrill, harsh cry. Crows are often seen looking for food. {**kroh**}

crow[2] *verb* (crowed, crowing, crows) 1. to make the harsh cry of a rooster. 2. to make sounds of happiness without using words. *The baby crowed with delight.* *noun* the harsh cry of a rooster. {**kroh**}

crow·bar *noun* a heavy, metal bar or rod with a flattened and bent end. A crowbar is used to lift or pry things. {**kroh** bar}

crowd *noun* 1. a large number of people gathered together. *There was a crowd at the baseball game.* 2. people in general. *It's not always best to follow the crowd.* *verb* (crowded, crowding, crowds) 1. to gather together in a crowd. *People crowded to see the circus.* 2. to press, push, or pack tightly together. *He crowded cardboard boxes into the tiny closet.* 3. to fill up completely. *We crowded the room.* {**krowd**}

crown *noun* 1. a covering for the head made of jewels and gold or silver. Kings and queens wear crowns. 2. (sometimes capitalized) the government that a king or queen heads. *The enemy's army put the Crown in danger.* 3. the highest part of something. *Jack hurt his crown when he fell on his head. / We climbed to the crown of the mountain.* *verb* (crowned, crowning, crowns) to place a crown or wreath on the head of. *The bishop crowned the new queen.* {**krown**}

crow's-nest *noun* a small platform near the top of a ship's mast. A person stands in the crow's-nest to see what is happening on and around the ship. {**krohz** nehst}

cru·cial *adjective* very important; deciding the success or failure of something. *It is crucial that you follow directions during a fire drill. / The surgeon had reached a crucial moment during the operation.* {**krooh** shəl} crucially, adv.

crude *adjective* (cruder, crudest) 1. natural; raw. *The pile of crude fiber will be made into yarn.* 2. not having skill, intelligence, or manners. *Nobody wanted to see the crude paintings. / He told a crude joke.* 3. done in a rough way. *She quickly drew a crude map of the area.* {**kroohd**} crudely, adv., crudeness, n.

cru·el *adjective* (crueler, cruelest) 1. willing to cause pain or suffering; showing no mercy. *The country's cruel leader did nothing to prevent the people from starving.* 2. causing pain or suffering. *The cruel wind blew through the cracks of the cottage walls.* {**kroohl** or **krooh** əl} cruelly, adv.

cru·el·ty *noun* (cruelties) 1. the state or characteristic of being cruel. *The cruelty of the wicked witch was known throughout the land.* 2. a cruel action or comment. *She will be punished for her cruelty to animals.* {**kroohl** tee or **krooh** əl tee}

cruise *verb* (cruised, cruising, cruises) 1. to travel for pleasure in a ship. *My grandparents cruised around the world.* 2. to travel at the same speed for a while. *He was cruising along when a deer ran in front of his car.* *noun* a pleasure trip on a ship. *We took a cruise to the islands of the Caribbean.* {**kroohz**}

cruis·er *noun* 1. a fast ship of medium size. Cruisers are used in wars. 2. a large boat to live in; cabin cruiser. *The Keegans lived in a cruiser in the Florida Keys after they retired.* 3. a police car. *The cruiser came up behind the speeding car.* {**krooh** zər}

crumb *noun* a tiny piece that breaks or falls from baked goods. *We cleaned cake crumbs off the floor after the birthday party.* {**kruhm**}

crum·ble *verb* (crumbled, crumbling, crumbles) 1. to break or crush into bits or crumbs. *He crumbled the cracker into his soup.* 2. to fall into small bits; decay. *That castle crumbled a long time ago.* {**kruhm** bəl}

crum·ple *verb* (crumpled, crumpling, crumples) 1. to press or crush and cause wrinkles. *She crumpled the paper in her fist.* 2. to fall down or collapse. *He crumpled in a faint from the heat.* {**kruhm** pəl} crumply, adj.

crunch *verb* (crunched, crunching, crunches) 1. to chew with a crackling noise; crush by biting. *The dog crunched the bone.* 2. to break in a loud way by grinding or crushing. *She crunched the glass under her heel.* *noun* a crunching sound or act of crunching. *The crunch of popcorn echoed in the movie theater.* {**kruhnch**}

cru·sade *noun* 1. (often capitalized) any of the wars between European Catholics and Middle Eastern Muslims between 1095 and 1291. During these wars, the Catholics tried to take territory away from the Muslims. 2. a fight against something considered evil. *The police organized a crusade against drugs.* *verb* (crusaded, crusading,

A B C D E F G H I J K L M N O P Q R S T U V W X Y Z

Living World Physical World Natural Environment Economy Government and Law

crusades) to take part in a crusade. *Many women crusaded to be allowed to vote.* {krooh **sayd**} crusader, n.

crush *verb* (crushed, crushing, crushes) 1. to cause to lose shape or become flat by pressing or squeezing very hard. *I crushed a cardboard box. / Chris crushed her belongings into the suitcase.* 2. to put down or defeat without question. *The army crushed the rebels. / Pete crushed his opponent in the tennis match.* *noun* 1. great pressure from pressing or squeezing. *The crush of his shoe squashed the bug.* 2. a strong but temporary romantic attraction to a person, or the person who is the object of the attraction. *He has a crush on a girl in his class. / I'll introduce you to her latest crush.* {**kruhsh**} crushable, adj.

crust *noun* 1. the hard, brown dough on the outside of baked goods. 2. any hard or crisp outer layer. *Bert fell through the snow's crust.* 3. the outer layer of Earth, another planet, or a moon. *Earth's crust is divided into several sections.* *verb* (crusted, crusting, crusts) 1. to coat with a hard or crisp covering. *Ice crusted the lake by the middle of January.* 2. to get a hard or crisp cover. *The corners of my eyes crusted because of the infection.* {**kruhst**}

Word History *Crust* is from a Latin word that means "rind" or "shell." "Crustacean" comes from the same root.

crus·ta·cean ❶ *noun* an animal with a hard, jointed shell. Crustaceans live in fresh or salt water. There are

many kinds of crustaceans, including crabs, crayfish, lobsters, and shrimps. Crustaceans are kinds of arthropods. {kruh **stay** shən}

crutch *noun* a support used to help injured people walk. A crutch is a pole with a padded top that rests under the arm. {**kruhch**}

cry 🏃 ❓ *verb* (cried, crying, cries) 1. to make a loud shout or yell (sometimes followed by "out"). *Cry out if you need help.* 2. to shed tears as the result of pain or strong feelings; weep. *The baby cried when he lost his toy.* 3. to make a sound or call characteristic of an animal. *The hawk cried as it dove from the sky.* *noun* (cries) 1. a loud shout or yell. *I let out a cry when I hurt my toe.* 2. a short period of weeping. *You'll feel better after you have a good cry.* 3. the call of an animal. *The cry of the wolf is a lonely sound.* {**kriy**}

• **a far cry**
a long way; quite different. *That house is nice, but it's a far cry from being a mansion.*
• **cry over spilled milk**
to worry about something that cannot be changed. *There's no use crying over spilled milk.*

Synonyms
These words share a meaning with *cry*, verb 1:
shout, yell, holler

crys·tal *noun* 1. a clear kind of rock that has a regular shape. Diamonds, quartz, and grains of salt are crystals. 2. glass of very high quality. *That beautiful vase is made of crystal.* 3. the clear cover on the face of a watch. *This crystal is so scratched he can*

hardly read the time. *adjective* 1. made of or like crystal. *Blanche served the fruit in a crystal bowl.* 2. clear; not clouded. *The crystal stream provided water for many thirsty animals.* {**krihs** təl} crystalline, n, adj.

Word History *Crystal* comes from a Greek word that means "clear ice."

crys·tal·lize *verb* (crystallized, crystallizing, crystallizes) to change into or cause to become crystals. {**krihs** tə liyz} crystallization, n.

CT or **Conn.** *abbreviation* an abbreviation for **Connecticut.**

cu. *abbreviation* an abbreviation for **cubic.**

cub *noun* the young offspring of some carnivorous mammals, such as the bear, lion, and wolf. *The mother tiger protected her cub fiercely.* {**kuhb**}

Cu·ba *noun* a country on the largest island in the West Indies in the Caribbean Sea. Havana is the capital of Cuba. {**kyoo** bə} Cuban, n., adj.

cube *noun* 1. a solid figure with six square faces all the same size, or any similar solid figure. *I dropped a cube of ice in my drink.* 2. The product of a number multiplied by itself twice. *Eight is the cube of two (2x2x2=8).* *verb* (cubed, cubing, cubes) 1. to cut into cubes. *We cubed the melon for our fruit salad.* 2. to multiply by itself twice. *If you cube three, the product is twenty-seven (3x3x3=27).* {**kyoob**}

cu·bic *adjective* 1. having form in three dimensions. *The volume of that can is forty cubic centimeters.* 2. shaped like a cube. *The cubic chair would not match his other furniture.* 3. having the volume

 Human Body  Human Mind  Everyday Life  History and Culture Communication

of a cube whose edge is a certain length. *I need a cubic meter of space to store this box.* {**kyoo** bihk}

Cub Scout *noun* a member of the junior section of the Boy Scouts of America. Boys between ages eight and eleven can be Cub Scouts. {**kuhb skowt**}

cuck·oo *noun* (cuckoos) a bird of Europe and America with a slim body and a long tail. A cuckoo's color can range from gray to brown. Some cuckoos have a call that sounds like their name. *adjective* (slang) crazy or foolish. *Sometimes my brother makes faces and does cuckoo things.* {**kooh** kooh}

cu·cum·ber *noun* a long fruit shaped like a cylinder with hard green skin and white flesh. Cucumbers are grown as food and are eaten raw. {**kyoo** kuhm bər}

cud *noun* food that certain animals such as cows bring up from the first stomach to chew again. {**kuhd**}

cud·dle *verb* (cuddled, cuddling, cuddles) to hold and hug in a tender and loving way. *I cuddled my baby in my arms.* {**kuhd** əl} cuddly, adj.

cue[1] *noun* 1. anything done or said during a play that is a signal for an actor to say or do something. *When he dropped the book it was my cue to laugh.* 2. anything that tells someone when to do something. *The bell was our cue to come to dinner.* *verb* (cued, cuing, cues) to give a sign or cue to. *The director cued the actor to enter from stage left.* {**kyoo**}

cue[2] *noun* a long, thin stick with a narrow tip, used to hit the ball in the game of pool or billiards. {**kyoo**}

cuff[1] *noun* 1. a band of material at the end of a shirt sleeve or pants leg that is folded over. A cuff is often sewn in place. 2. a short form of **handcuff**. {**kuhf**}

• **off the cuff**
(informal) done without planning or thinking ahead. *His oral report was off the cuff.*

cuff[2] *verb* (cuffed, cuffing, cuffs) to hit or slap with an open hand. *I cuffed my brother for taking my diary.* *noun* a hit or slap with an open hand. *My brother gave me a cuff on the ear in return.* {**kuhf**}

cul·prit *noun* a person who is charged with or is guilty of doing something wrong. *Which one of you is the culprit who stole my lunch money?* {**kuhl** priht}

cul·ti·vate ⚙ *verb* (cultivated, cultivating, cultivates) 1. to make fit for growing plants by plowing, weeding, or adding fertilizer. *We worked hard to cultivate the soil for our new garden.* 2. to plant and help grow. *The Mays family cultivates wheat and oats on their farm.* 3. to help grow and develop. *She is a rich person who cultivates the arts.* / *I am cultivating her friendship.* {**kuhl** tih **vayt**}

cul·ti·va·tion *noun* 1. the act of preparing and improving. *The cultivation of children's minds will help them to think for themselves.* / *We bought fifty acres of vacant farm land and now must begin its cultivation.* 2. the state of being cultivated. *The farmer has one hundred acres of land under cultivation.* / *Smithers was well known for his great learning and cultivation.* {**kuhl** tih **vay** shən}

cul·ti·va·tor *noun* a machine or hand tool that prepares soil for planting by loosening the

soil and removing weeds. {**kuhl** tih vay tər}

cul·tur·al *adjective* of or relating to culture. *We studied the cultural differences between Japan and the United States.* {**kuhl** chə rəl} culturally, adv.

cul·ture 🗨 ⟳ *noun* 1. the language, customs, ideas, and art of a particular group of people. *Respect for Mother Earth is an important part of Iroquois culture.* 2. the quality of knowing and caring about art, literature, good manners, and what goes on in the world. *She became a woman of culture at college.* 3. the raising of plants or animals. *He is an expert on the culture of tomato plants.* 4. bacteria or other microorganisms that are grown by scientists or doctors for use in tests and experiments. *Doctors take throat cultures to test for infection.* {**kuhl** chər}

cum·ber·some *adjective* difficult to hold or carry because of size, shape, or weight. *Please help me with these cumbersome packages!* {**kuhm** bər səm} cumbersomely, adv.

cu·mu·lus *noun* (cumuli) a large, fluffy, white cloud with a flat bottom. {**kyoom** yə lihs}

cun·ning *noun* skill used in a sly or tricky way. *The cat showed cunning by trapping the mouse in a corner.* *adjective* skilled at tricking others. *The cunning fox escaped the hounds.* {**kuhn** ing} cunningly, adv.

cup *noun* (cups) 1. a small container used for drinking. 2. what a cup holds. *Would you like a cup of tea?* 3. a unit of measure equal to eight fluid ounces or one half pint. (abbreviated: c) *The recipe called for two cups of milk.* 4. a fancy metal cup that is given to the winner of a contest or game. *The soccer team won a*

a
b
c
d
e
f
g
h
i
j
k
l
m
n
o
p
q
r
s
t
u
v
w
x
y
z

silver cup. *verb* (cupped, cupping, cups) to shape into the form of a cup. *She cupped her hands.* {**kuhp**}

cup·board *noun* a cabinet with shelves for food, dishes, or other items. {**kuhb** ərd}

cup·cake *noun* a little cake for one person. Cupcakes are baked in a mold that has the size and shape of a cup. {**kuhp** kayk}

cup·ful *noun* (cupfuls) the amount that fills one cup; cup. *I added a cupful of sugar to the cookie dough.* {**kuhp** fəl}

Cu·pid *noun* the god of love in Roman mythology. {**kyoo** pihd}

curb *noun* 1. a raised rim where a street meets the edge of the sidewalk. *The young driver drove the car up onto the curb.* 2. anything that controls or holds something back. *John's broken leg put a curb on our fun.* *verb* (curbed, curbing, curbs) to control or hold back. *I am trying hard to curb my anger.* {**kuhrb**}

curd *noun* (sometimes plural) a soft, thick substance taken from milk. Curds can be eaten or made into cheese. {**kuhrd**}

cur·dle *verb* (curdled, curdling, curdles) to turn into curd. *They curdled the milk to make cheese.* {**kuhr** dəl}

cure *noun* 1. something that makes a sick person healthy or well. *Scientists are searching for a cure for cancer.* 2. the process of making a sick person healthy or well. *The cure of my sore throat took several days.* *verb* (cured, curing, cures) 1. to cause to become completely free of a disease or other unhealthy condition. *Antibiotics cure many people who have infections.* 2. to preserve by salting,

smoking, or drying. *The farmer cured a dozen hams this year.* {**kyoor**}

cur·few *noun* a rule or law that sets a time after which everyone must be off the street and inside for the night. Curfews sometimes apply only to a particular group, such as young people. {**kuhr** fyoo}

Word History *Curfew* comes from *curfu*, an early English word for a bell rung at a set time in the evening. The early English word came from an early French word that meant "to cover fire." People were required to cover their fires at night to prevent them from burning out of control. As this usage disappeared, the word came to be used for the time when residents of a city must keep off the streets.

cu·ri·os·i·ty *noun* (curiosities) 1. the desire to learn or know. *He read his great-grandmother's diary with great curiosity.* 2. an unusual or odd thing. *To many women today, a hat with a veil is just a curiosity.* {**kyoor** ee **ŏs** ih tee}

cu·ri·ous *adjective* 1. eager to learn or know. *She was curious about how stars were formed.* 2. interesting because unusual or strange. *I wonder why Greg has that curious look on his face.* {**kyoor** ee əs} curiously, adv.

curl *verb* (curled, curling, curls) 1. to make into coils or rings. *Terry curled the ribbon on the present.* 2. to take on the shape of a coil or ring. *My hair curls whenever it rains.* 3. to become curved at an edge. *Wet paper curls when it dries.* 4. to move in a curving way. *Smoke curled up from the fire.* *noun* 1. an individual ring of hair. *I just love your baby's curls!* 2. anything shaped like a coil or ring. *Curls of smoke*

rose from his pipe. {**kuhrl**}

• **curl up**
to get into a comfortable sitting or lying position. *The cat curled up on the rug.* / *We curled up together on the couch.*

curl·y *adjective* having curls or likely to curl *Sam has curly hair.* {**kuhr** lee}

cur·rant *noun* 1. a small raisin with no seeds. 2. the sour berry of a bush related to the gooseberry. Currants are used in making buns, pies, and jelly. {**kuhr** ənt}

Homophone Note Are you looking for the word *current* (of the present time)? *Currant* and *current* sound alike but have different meanings.

cur·ren·cy *noun* (currencies) 1. the money that is used in a country. *The dollar is the basic unit of U.S. currency.* 2. the condition of being used or accepted by many people. *Her ideas about how girls should act no longer have currency.* {**kuhr** ən see}

cur·rent *adjective* 1. of or happening in the present time. *My current number is in the phone book.* 2. used or known by many. *He wears styles that are no longer current.* *noun* 1. a part of a mass of liquid or air that flows in one direction. *The kite rose on a current of air.* / *It is hard to swim against the current.* 2. the flow of electricity in a wire or other conductor. {**kuhr** ənt}

Homophone Note The words *current* and *currant* (a berry or raisin) sound alike but have different meanings.

curse *noun* 1. a statement of a wish that something bad will happen to someone or something. *"May it always rain on your birthday!"* was the curse

 Human Body   Human Mind   Everyday Life   History and Culture Communication

that he shouted at me. 2. a word or words used to swear. *We heard a loud crash and then curses from Uncle Joe's workshop*. 3. something that brings harm or suffering. *Millions live with the curse of not having enough to eat*. *verb* (cursed, cursing, curses) 1. to make a statement that wishes harm on. *He cursed his enemy to bring him bad luck*. 2. to swear at. *She cursed the dog for digging up her flowers*. 3. to cause to suffer. *She was cursed with a desire to have what she could not have*. {**kuhrs**}

cur·sor *noun* a movable marker on a computer screen. The cursor shows where to click on an icon or where letters or numbers can be typed in. {**kuhr** sər}

curt *adjective* (curter, curtest) rudely short or brief in speech. *Her curt reply made me wonder what was wrong*. {**kuhrt**} curtly, adv., curtness, n.

cur·tain *noun* 1. a piece of cloth hung in a window or other opening to shut out light or to cover something. 2. anything that acts as a screen or cover. *The house was hidden from the road by a curtain of trees*. 3. the curtain used to hide the stage in a theater. *The scenery was changed while the curtain was closed*. *verb* (curtained, curtaining, curtains) to hide or block off with or as if with a curtain. *From the mountain, his view of the town was curtained by fog*. {**kuhr** tən}

curt·sy or **curtsey** *noun* (curtsies or curtseys) a bow that shows respect, made by bending the knees and lowering the body

slightly. A curtsy is usually made by women and girls. *verb* (curtsied or curtseyed, curtsying or curtseying, curtsies or curtseys) to make a curtsy. *The dancers curtsied at the end of the show*. {**kuhrt** see}

curve *noun* 1. a line that bends smoothly in one direction without any straight parts or angles. 2. a bend in a road, path, or river. *Drive slowly around the curve*. 3. a baseball pitch in which the ball curves toward the opposite side from which it was thrown; curve ball. *verb* (curved, curving, curves) 1. to cause to curve; give a curve to. *The carpenter curved the corners of the table top with a plane*. 2. to take the shape of a curve; bend. *The river curves around the rocks*. {**kuhrv**}

cush·ion *noun* 1. a pillow or pad that one sits on or leans on for comfort. Some cushions are used for decoration. 2. something that softens a blow or protects against damage. *When a car hits something, its bumper acts as a cushion*. *verb* (cushioned, cushioning, cushions) 1. to make less hard or damaging; soften. *My heavy jacket cushioned the fall*. 2. to place on, supply with, or hold up with a cushion. *She cushioned the baby on the park bench*. {**kuush** ən}

cus·tard *noun* a cooked dessert made with eggs, milk, and sugar. {**kuhs** tərd}

cus·to·di·an *noun* 1. a person who is responsible for taking care of someone or something. *Parents are usually the legal custodians of their children*. / *The custodian at an art museum makes sure that valuable paintings are safe*. 2. a person who cleans, makes

repairs, and does odd jobs in a building; janitor. {kə **stoh** dee ən}

cus·to·dy *noun* (custodies) 1. the legal right to take care of and control someone or something. *The father has custody of his child*. 2. kept in prison by the police. *The thief is now in custody*. {**kuhs** tih dee}

cus·tom *noun* 1. a way of acting that is usual or accepted for a person or a social group. *Shaking hands when you meet someone is a common custom in the United States*. 2. (plural but used with a singular verb) a tax collected on products brought into a country from another country. *adjective* made exactly as ordered by a particular person. *My rich uncle drives a custom car*. {**kuhs** təm}

cus·tom·ar·y *adjective* done as a custom; usual. *In Greece, it is customary to close shops during the hottest part of the day*. {**kuh** stə **mayr** ee} customarily, adv.

cus·tom·er *noun* a person who buys products or services. *The store held a special sale for its regular customers*. {**kuh** stə mər}

cut *verb* (cut, cutting, cuts) 1. to pierce, slice, open, or form with a sharp tool such as a knife, ax, saw, or scissors. *The barber cut my hair*. / *She cut her name into the wood with a knife*. 2. to divide with something sharp. *Cut the cake so that we can all have some*. 3. to allow cutting or being cut. *A dull knife doesn't cut well*. / *This tender meat cuts easily*. 4. to make shorter or less; diminish. *He cut his speech to ten minutes*. / *The store cut its prices during the sale*. 5. to grow through the gum. *The baby is cutting a new tooth*. 6.

to be absent from on purpose. *He cut all his classes today.* 7. to make a quick shift from one thing to another. *The film cut to another scene.* 8. to go across or through something (usually followed by "through" or "across"). *Matt cut across his neighbor's yard on his way home.* / *The path cuts through the woods.* *noun* 1. the act or result of cutting. *I got a cut on my hand while chopping vegetables.* 2. the way in which something is cut. *The cut of your clothes is very elegant.* 3. a decrease. *The toy store is advertising a cut in prices.* 4. something left out or taken away. *The editor made several cuts in the article.* {**kuht**}

cute *adjective* (cuter, cutest) (informal) pretty, charming, or adorable. *She looks cute in pigtails.* {**kyoot**} cutely, adv., cuteness, n.

cu·ti·cle *noun* the tough, dead skin along the bottom edge and sides of the fingernails and toenails. {**kyoo** tih kəl}

cut·lass *noun* a short, thick sword with one cutting edge and a curved blade. {**kuht** ləs}

cut·ter *noun* 1. something that cuts, or someone whose job it is to cut things. *Trim the hedge with this cutter.* / *He started in the movie business as a film cutter.* 2. a sailing ship with one mast. {**kuht** ər}

cut·ting *noun* something that has been cut from something else. *Cara planted the cuttings from her rose bushes.* / *Bill collects newspaper cuttings about his famous uncle.* *adjective* 1. able to cut. *He used the cutting edge of the knife.* 2. hurting someone's feelings; mean. *She made a cutting comment about my soccer skills.* {**kuht** ing}

cyb·er- *prefix* a prefix that means of, relating to, made by, or existing only on computers. *A chat room is a place where people get together and talk in cyberspace.* {**siy** bər}

cy·cle *noun* 1. an event or series of events that is repeated at regular intervals. *Summer follows spring in the cycle of seasons.* 2. a bicycle or motorcycle. *verb* (cycled, cycling, cycles) to travel by bicycle or motorcycle. *We cycled around the park.* {**siy** kəl}

cy·clone *noun* a storm with very strong winds that turn around a center of low pressure in the atmosphere. {**siy** klohn} cyclonic, adj.

Cy·clops *noun* (Cyclopes) a giant in Greek mythology who has only one eye, in the middle of his forehead. {**siy** klŏps}

cyg·net *noun* a young swan. {**sihg** niht}

cyl·in·der *noun* a solid figure that is shaped like a can. It has parallel circular faces joined by a curved face. {**sihl** ən dər}

cy·lin·dri·cal *adjective* in the shape of a cylinder. {sə **lihn** drih kəl}

cym·bal *noun* a percussion instrument that is round and made of metal. Cymbals are played by striking a pair of them together or hitting one with a drumstick or brushes. {**sihm** bəl}

Homophone Note The words *cymbal* and *symbol* (a thing that represents) sound alike but have different meanings.

cy·press *noun* an evergreen tree that has tiny leaves like scales. {**siy** prəs}

Homophone Note The words *cypress* and *Cyprus* sound alike but have different meanings.

Cy·prus *noun* a country on an island in the Mediterranean Sea near the coast of Turkey. Nicosia is the capital of Cyprus. {**siy** prəs} Cypriot, n., adj.

Homophone Note The words *Cyprus* and *cypress* (an evergreen tree) sound alike but have different meanings.

cyst *noun* a small pouch within body tissue that is filled with fluid. Cysts are usually abnormal. {**sihst**}

cy·to·plasm *noun* the thick liquid substance that holds all the parts that are inside a cell. {**siyt** oh plăz əm}

czar *noun* the title of male Russian rulers before 1917. {**zar**}

cza·ri·na *noun* the wife of a czar. {zar **ee** nə}

Czech·o·slo·va·ki·a *noun* a country in Central Europe until 1993. Czechoslovakia is now divided into two countries, the Czech Republic and Slovakia. {cheh kə slə **vah** kee ə} Czechoslovakian, n., adj.

Czech Re·pub·lic *noun* a country in Central Europe. The Czech Republic was part of Czechoslovakia until 1993. Prague is the capital of the Czech Republic. {**chehk** rih **puh** blihk} Czech, n., adj.

Homophone Note The words *Czech* and *check* sound alike but have different meanings.

Human Body   Human Mind   Everyday Life   History and Culture   Communication

Dd

D is a consonant that always makes the same sound.

Tips to help you look up words starting with d: Words that start with the "duh" sound may be spelled "do" or "dou" as well as "du."

double
dove
dozen

These words may be hard to look up if you don't already know how to spell them:

dangerous
dead
deaf
debt
deceive
December
decide
description

didn't
discussion
doesn't
don't
doubt
during
dynamite

d or **D** *noun* (d's or D's) 1. the fourth letter of the English alphabet. 2. a grade given for poor, or below average school work. 3. the second note in the musical scale of C major. {<u>dee</u>}

dab *verb* (dabbed, dabbing, dabs) 1. to pat or press lightly. *I dabbed the stain with a sponge.* 2. to put on with light patting touches. *She dabbed some perfume behind her ears. noun* 1. a light pressing or patting stroke. *The kitten gave my face a dab with its paw.* 2. a small moist bit. *A dab of paint fell on the rug.* 3. a small amount. *Put a dab of salt in the soup.* {<u>dăb</u>}

dab·ble *verb* (dabbled, dabbling, dabbles) 1. to wet by splashing or dipping. *The child dabbled his toes in the pool.* 2. to work at something in a way that is not serious or steady. *He dabbles in all the arts but doesn't have the patience to become skilled in any of them.* {<u>dă</u> bəl}

dachs·hund *noun* a German breed of dog. Dachshunds have long bodies, very short legs, and drooping ears. {<u>dahk</u> suund}

dad *noun* (informal) father. {<u>dăd</u>}

dad·dy *noun* (daddies) (informal) father. {<u>dă</u> dee}

dad·dy-long·legs *noun* (used with a singular or plural verb) a small animal that resembles a spider. Daddy-longlegs are arachnids and have a small, rounded body with eight very long, thin legs. {<u>dă</u> dee <u>lawng</u> lehgz}

daf·fo·dil *noun* a plant with tall stems and bright yellow or white flowers shaped like bells. Daffodils grow from bulbs and appear in the spring. {<u>dă</u> fə dihl}

dag·ger *noun* a short, pointed weapon like a sword, with two sharp edges. {<u>dă</u> gər}

dai·ly *adjective* happening or done every day. *She is taking her daily walk in the garden. noun* (dailies) a newspaper that is printed every day or every day except Sunday. *adverb* each day; day by day. *I read the comics daily.* {<u>day</u> lee}

dain·ty *adjective* (dantier, daintiest) small, pretty, and delicate. *Be careful with that dainty china cup.* {<u>dayn</u> tee}

dair·y ❶ ❷ *noun* (dairies) 1. a place where milk is stored and butter and cheese are made. 2. a business that sells milk, butter, and cheese. 3. a farm where cows are raised for their milk; dairy farm. {<u>dayr</u> ee}

da·is *noun* a raised platform for speakers or the seating of special guests. {<u>days</u> or <u>day</u> əs or <u>diy</u> əs}

dai·sy *noun* (daisies) a plant that has flowers with white, pink, or yellow petals around a yellow center. {<u>day</u> zee}

Word History *Daisy* comes from an Old English word that means "day's eye." The English daisy opens in the morning and closes at night.

dale *noun* a valley. {<u>dayl</u>}

Dal·ma·tian *noun* a breed of dog. Dalmatians are large dogs that have short white hair with black or brown spots. {<u>dahl</u> <u>may</u> shən}

dam *noun* a wall built across a river or stream to keep the water from flowing and to raise the water level behind it. *verb* (dammed, damming, dams) to build a dam on, in,

A B C D E F G H I J K L M N O P Q R S T U V W X Y Z

or across; to block with a dam. *A family of beavers dammed the river with mud and branches.* {dăm}

dam·age *noun* harm or injury that makes something less useful or valuable. *We paid for the damage we did to our neighbor's vegetable garden.* *verb* (damaged, damaging, damages) to harm or injure. *The movers damaged some furniture. / Insects damaged the crops.* {dă mihj}

dame *noun* (capitalized) a title of honor given by a British king or queen to a woman who has done something important. {daym}

damp *adjective* (damper, dampest) slightly wet; moist. *The towel was still damp.* *noun* moisture in the air or on a surface. *Come in out of the damp and cold. / Our basement floor is rotting from damp.* {dămp} dampness, n.

damp·en *verb* (dampened, dampening, dampens) 1. to make moist or slightly wet. *She dampens the clothes before ironing them.* 2. to weaken or dull. *The news dampened our hopes.* {dăm pihn}

dance 🏃 💬 📞 *verb* (danced, dancing, dances) 1. to move the feet and body in a rhythmic way, usually to music. *Everyone got up and danced when the band started playing.* 2. to jump or skip along in excitement. *She was so happy she danced down the hall.* 3. to move quickly and lightly in a way that suggests dancing. *The treetops danced in the wind.* *noun* 1. a set pattern of steps or movements usually done to music. *The waltz was a popular dance in the 1800s.* 2. The art of dancing. *She is studying music and dance.* 3. a party or gath-

ering where people come to dance. *The school dance is on Saturday night.* 4. an act of dancing; one turn of dancing. *He chose a partner for the last dance of the evening.* {dăns}

danc·er *noun* someone who is dancing or whose profession is dancing. *The dancers leapt across the stage.* {dăn sər}

dan·de·li·on *noun* a common plant with bright yellow flowers and leaves with points along the edges. Dandelion leaves can be eaten raw or cooked as vegetables, and wine is sometimes made from the flowers. {dăn də liy ən}

dan·druff *noun* a thin white crust of dead skin that forms on the scalp and is shed in flakes. {dăn drəf}

dan·dy *adjective* (dandier, dandiest) (informal) very fine; pleasing; excellent. *Going on a picnic is a dandy idea.* {dăn dee}

Dane *noun* a person who was born in or is a citizen of Denmark. {dayn}

dan·ger *noun* 1. a chance or likelihood that something bad or harmful may happen; peril; risk. *The old shed is in danger of falling down.* 2. something that causes harm or injury. *Firemen face many dangers in their work.* {dayn jər}

dan·ger·ous *adjective* likely to cause harm; not safe. *The path along the edge of the cliff is dangerous.* {dayn jə rəs} dangerously, adv.

dan·gle *verb* (dangled, dangling, dangles) 1. to hang or swing loosely. *The baby's legs dangled from the chair.* 2. to let something hang or swing loosely. *I dangled a string in front of the kitten.* {dăng gəl} dangler, n.

Dan·ish *adjective* of or having to do with Denmark, or its people or language. *noun* the language of Denmark. {day nəsh}

dare *verb* (dared, daring, dares) 1. to be brave enough or careless enough to do something. *He did not dare to climb the tall tree.* 2. to challenge someone to do something as a test of courage. *I dared her to eat a grasshopper.* *noun* an act of daring or challenging. *He accepted our dare and rode his bike down the steepest hill of all.* {dayr}

dare·dev·il *noun* a person who puts himself or herself in danger by doing daring or dangerous things. *Only a daredevil would try to climb a skyscraper.* *adjective* daring or reckless. *She does daredevil tricks on her bicycle.* {dayr deh vəl}

dar·ing *noun* the quality of being bold and willing to take risks; courage. *That pilot is known for his daring.* *adjective* willing to take risks; bold; adventurous. *Only a daring person would try to climb that cliff.* {dayr ing} daringly, adv.

dark *adjective* (darker, darkest) 1. having little or no light. *It was a dark, moonless night.* 2. not light or pale in color. *Black and brown are two of the darkest colors.* 3. gloomy, evil,

 Human Body   Human Mind   Everyday Life    History and Culture   Communication

or mysterious. *Sometimes Beethoven's music is dark and sometimes it is full of joy. / The witch cast a dark spell.* *noun* 1. lack of light. *He lied about his fear of the dark.* 2. night. *She told him to be home before dark.* {**dark**}

• **in the dark**
knowing nothing; uncertain. *He kept us in the dark about his plans.*

> **Word History** *Dark* comes from an early German word that means "to hide something," particularly in a dark place.

dark·en *verb* (darkened, darkening, darkens) 1. to cause to be dark or darker. *Clouds darkened the summer sky.* 2. to become dark. *The room darkened when the sun went behind a cloud. / Her face darkened with disappointment.* {**dar** kən}

dark·ness *noun* 1. lack of light. *We were soon lost in the total darkness of the cave.* 2. gloomy sadness or evil. *Everyone noticed the darkness of the king's mood as they prepared to go into battle.* {**dark** nihs}

dar·ling *noun* a person who is loved very much by the person speaking. *Darling, will you help me with this?* *adjective* deeply loved. *My darling daughter gave me this bracelet.* {**dar** ling}

darn *verb* (darned, darning, darns) to mend by weaving thread or yarn over a hole in cloth. *I need to darn the elbows of my sweater.* {**darn**}

dart *noun* 1. a short arrow thrown with the hand or shot from a gun. 2. (plural, but used with a singular verb) a game in which these objects are thrown at a target. *Let's play darts.* *verb* (darted, darting, darts) 1. to move quickly;

dash. *The lizard darted out of sight.* 2. to shoot out or send out suddenly. *A snake darts its tongue out. / She darted a quick look at the boy she liked.* {**dart**}

dash *verb* (dashed, dashing, dashes) 1. to throw or toss with great force so as to break. *The storm dashed the boat against the rocks.* 2. to do or carry out in a hurry (usually followed by "off"). *She dashed off her homework in ten minutes so she would have more time to play.* 3. to hit with great force; smash. *The waves dashed against the cliffs.* 4. to make hopeless; ruin. *An injury dashed his hopes of being an Olympic skater.* 5. to move swiftly; run rapidly; rush. *He dashed across the street before the light changed.* *noun* 1. a short run at top speed; a short track race. *He ran a one hundred-meter dash in twelve seconds.* 2. a small amount of an ingredient. *The cook added a dash of pepper to the soup.* 3. a punctuation mark (--). It is used to show a break in speech or thought. {**dăsh**}

dash·board *noun* a panel below the windshield in a car or other vehicle. Dashboards have dials, controls, and spaces for keeping things. {**dăsh** bohrd}

da·ta *noun* facts, figures, or other pieces of information that can be used in different ways. The word "data" is the plural form of "datum," but is usually used with a singular verb. *Data about the U.S. population is collected every ten years.* {**dă** tə or **day** tə}

da·ta·base or **data base** *noun* a large collection of information in a computer. In a database, information is arranged so that it can be quickly changed or searched

through. *The librarian searched the computer database to find books on my topic.* {**dă** tə bays or **day** tə bays}

data processing ❶ *noun* the storing and use of information by computers. *My brother works in the data processing department of the bank.* {**dă** tə **pro** seh sing or **day** tə **pro** seh sing}

date[1] *noun* 1. a particular day or point in time. *What is today's date?* 2. an appointment to meet for a social event. *We made a date to have dinner.* *verb* (dated, dating, dates) 1. to write or print the date on. *Date your paper before you turn it in.* 2. to find out the date of. *The scientists tried to date the ancient pottery they dug up.* 3. to meet with socially at particular times. *How long have you been dating her?* 4. to be of a particular time. *These toy soldiers date from the 1950s.* {**dayt**}

• **out of date**
not modern or in fashion. *My father's clothes are out of date.*

date[2] *noun* the sweet fruit of the date palm tree, which grows in the Middle East. {**dayt**}

dat·ed *adjective* 1. having a date. *If the form is signed and dated, please hand it in.* 2. not modern or in fashion. *What is in style today will look dated five years from now.* {**day** tihd}

daub *verb* (daubed, daubing, daubs) to smear or cover with something soft and sticky, such as paint. *The toddler daubed peanut butter on the wall.* *noun* something daubed on; a single stroke of this. *You have a*

daub of paint on your nose. {**dawb**}

daugh·ter *noun* a person's female child. {**daw** tər}

daugh·ter-in-law *noun* (daughters-in-law) the wife of one's son. {**daw** tər ihn **law**}

daw·dle *verb* (dawdled, dawdling, dawdles) to waste time; be slow. *She dawdled over her chores.* {**daw** dəl} dawdler, n.

dawn *noun* 1. the first daylight that appears in the morning; daybreak. *He was up at dawn.* 2. the very beginning of something. *The dawn of a new century is an exciting time. verb* (dawned, dawning, dawns) 1. to start to become light in the morning. *The day dawned bright and clear.* 2. to start to grow; begin to develop. *A new age dawned with the invention of the printing press.* 3. to start to be understood (usually followed by "on"). *It finally dawned on me that my watch was wrong.* {**dawn**}

day *noun* 1. the period between sunrise and sunset. *He spent the whole day at the beach.* 2. a unit of time equal to the twenty-four hours included in one day and night. *Our vacation lasted ten days.* 3. (often plural) a particular period of time. *In the days of the Old West, buffalo roamed free.* {**day**}
• **call it a day**
to finish working. *It's time to call it a day and rest.*

day·break *noun* the first daylight in the morning; dawn. {**day** brayk}

day care *noun* care during the day in a home or day-care center for children too young for school or older children after school or during vacation. Day care may also offer care for elderly or disabled

people. {**day** kayr} day-care, adj.

day·dream *noun* a pleasant or exciting story or event that someone who is awake imagines is happening to them. *All during class, I had daydreams about summer vacation. verb* (daydreamed, daydreaming, daydreams) to have daydreams. *We daydream about meeting our heros.* {**day** dreem} daydreamer, n.

day·light *noun* the light of the day. *She woke before daylight.* {**day** liyt}

day·time *noun* the time between dawn and evening. *More crimes take place at night than in the daytime.* {**day** tiym}

daze *verb* (dazed, dazing, dazes) to stun by a blow or shock. *The punch dazed him, but he stayed on his feet. noun* a state of being shocked or confused. *He walked around in a daze after the bad news.* {**dayz**}

daz·zle *verb* (dazzled, dazzling, dazzles) 1. to make almost blind with too much bright light. *Outside the cave, the sunlight dazzled us.* 2. to amaze or impress. *The cyclist's quick movements dazzled us.* {**dă** zəl}

DC *abbreviation* 1. an abbreviation for **District of Columbia**. 2. an abbreviation for **direct current**.

DE or **Del.** *abbreviation* an abbreviation for **Delaware**.

de- *prefix* 1. a prefix that means "from," "away from," or "off." *The word "deplane" means "to get off an airplane."* 2. a prefix that means "down" or "lower." *To descend the stairs is to go down the stairs.* 3. a prefix that means to undo or reverse an action. *To deflate a tire is to take out the air that has been pumped into it.*

dea·con *noun* 1. a clergyman in certain Christian churches. 2. a member of certain Christian churches who has a set of church duties but is not a member of the clergy. {**dee** kən}

dead *adjective* (deader, deadest) 1. no longer alive. *The dead tree was gray and leafless.* 2. seeming like death. *She fell down in a dead faint.* 3. useless or without activity. *I tried to make a call, but the telephone was dead.* 4. without spirit, excitement, or movement. *The party was dead at first, but soon it became more fun.* 5. exact; precise. *The arrow hit the dead center of the target. noun* 1. those who are dead. *The dead live on in our memories.* 2. the darkest or coldest period. *It was the dead of winter. adverb* (deader, deadest) completely; exactly. *He was dead wrong. / I was dead tired after the game.* {**dehd**}

dead·en *verb* (deadened, deadening, deadens) to make less painful or intense. *This pill will deaden the pain.* {**deh** dən}

dead end *noun* a street that is closed at one end, allowing no way through. {**dehd ehnd**}

dead·line *noun* a date or time by which something must be done. *I am not going to finish*

a b c d e f g h i j k l m n o p q r s t u v w x y z

 Human Body   Human Mind   Everyday Life  History and Culture  Communication

this report by tomorrow's deadline. {**dehd** liyn}

dead·ly ⊕ *adjective* (deadlier, deadliest) 1. able to cause death. *The scorpion's poison can be deadly. / A gun is a deadly weapon.* 2. aiming to destroy or kill. *They were deadly enemies.* 3. very boring. *Aunt Marsha's tea parties are deadly.* {**dehd** lee}

Dead Sea *noun* a large salt lake between the countries of Israel and Jordan. *The Dead Sea lies at about 1300 feet below sea level, which makes it the lowest known place on the surface of the earth.* {**dehd** **see**}

deaf *adjective* 1. not able to hear, or not able to hear well. *The deaf student taught us some sign language.* 2. not willing to listen to the ideas or advice of others. *He is deaf to our warnings.* {**dehf**} deafness, n.

deaf·en *verb* (deafened, deafening, deafens) 1. to cause to become deaf. *As a child, he had been deafened by an illness.* 2. to overcome with loud noise. *The loud music deafened us.* {**deh** fən}

deal ❍ *verb* (dealt, dealing, deals) 1. to be concerned or to handle (usually followed by "with" or "in"). *We must deal with this subject carefully.* 2. to act or behave (usually followed by "with"). *She is honest in the way she deals with people.* 3. to do business; trade. *My uncle deals in antiques.* 4. to give out cards in a card game. *I'll shuffle, and you can deal.* *noun* 1. an agreement or bargain. *We made a deal to share the money*

equally. 2. amount (usually used with "good" or "great"). *She tended her plants with a great deal of care.* {**deel**}

deal·er ❍ ⚙ *noun* 1. a person whose job is to buy and sell. *We bought our car from a used-car dealer.* 2. the one who gives out cards to players in a card game. *Who wants to be the dealer this time?* {**dee** lər}

dealt *verb* past tense and past participle of **deal**¹. {**dehlt**}

dear *adjective* (dearer, dearest) 1. much loved. *My dear friend Janet is coming to visit.* 2. (capitalized) used as a greeting that begins a letter. *"Dear Carlos," the letter began.* 3. costing a lot of or too much money. *A ring with a real diamond will be dear.* *noun* a person who is liked or loved by the person speaking. *What would you like, dear?* *interjection* used to express surprise, disappointment, or dismay. *Oh dear, I've lost my key.* {**deer**} dearly, adv.

Homophone Note Are you looking for the word *deer* (an animal)? *Dear* and *deer* sound alike but have different meanings.

---

death ⊕ ⚑ *noun* 1. the end of life in any living thing. *Her death came after a long illness.* 2. destruction or end of anything. *This injury could mean the death of his basketball career.* {**dehth**}

de·bate ❓ ❍ *noun* a discussion between two people or groups who disagree on an important subject. A debate usually takes place in a formal meeting or gathering. *The debate in Congress lasted two days.* *verb* (debated, debating, debates) 1. to discuss the different sides of a

subject or issue. *We debated whether it was fair to make students take swimming lessons.* 2. to consider; think over. *I am debating whether to go or not.* {dih **bayt**} debater, n.

deb·it *noun* an amount of money taken out of or owed on an account, or the record of that amount. *My bank account shows a debit of ten dollars for the check I wrote.* *verb* (debited, debiting, debits) to subtract or charge with an amount owed. *The bank debited my savings account twenty dollars.* {**deh** biht}

de·bris *noun* scattered pieces left after something has been destroyed. *A pile of debris was all that remained after the fire.* {də **bree** or **day** bree}

debt ⚙ *noun* 1. something owed to another person. *I paid all my debts except the five dollars I owe my sister.* 2. a condition of owing more than one can pay back. *Borrowing the money to buy a new car put my parents in debt.* {**deht**}

debt·or *noun* a person who owes a debt to another. *When you get a loan from a bank, you become the bank's debtor.* {**deh** tər}

de·bug *verb* (debugged, debugging, debugs) 1. (informal) to find and remove mistakes or flaws from. *A computer programmer writes, tests, and debugs computer programs.* 2. to remove secret microphones from. *Special agents debugged the room before the top secret meeting took place.* {dee **buhg**}

a
b
c
d
e
f
g
h
i
j
k
l
m
n
o
p
q
r
s
t
u
v
w
x
y
z

de·but *noun* a person's first appearance on stage, in concert, or on film. *Tonight is her singing debut.* *verb* (debuted, debuting, debuts) to present to an audience for the first time. *The singing sisters will debut their new songs tonight.* {də **byoo**}

Dec. *abbreviation* an abbreviation for **December**.

dec·ade *noun* a unit of time equal to ten years. *A man who is ninety has been alive for nine decades.* / *During the decade of the 1930s, many families listened to radio shows in the evening.* {**deh** kayd}

dec·a·gon *noun* a figure with ten sides and ten angles. {**deh** kə gŏn}

de·cal *noun* a design or picture on specially prepared paper. Decals can be transferred from the paper to glass, metal, or other hard surfaces. *My brother has sports decals all over his locker.* {**dee** kăl *or* dih **kăl**}

de·cant·er *noun* a pretty glass bottle with a stopper. A decanter is usually used to serve wine or liquor. {dih **kăn** tər}

de·cath·lon *noun* an athletic contest made up of ten different track and field events. Each athlete takes part in all ten events, over a period of two days. {dih **kăth lahn**}

de·cay *verb* (decayed, decaying, decays) 1. to rot or become rotted. *The floor of the forest is covered with leaves that are decaying.* 2. to lose health, strength, or excellence. *Her health has decayed over the past year.* *noun* 1. a process of slowly losing quality, strength, or health. *The old house is in decay because no one takes care of it.* 2. the process of rotting or condition of being rotted. *Daily brushing helps prevent tooth decay.* {dih **kay**}

de·ceased *adjective* no longer alive; dead. *Three of my four grandparents are deceased.* *noun* a particular dead person or persons (usually used with "the"). *The minister spoke highly of the deceased at her funeral.* {dih **seest**}

de·ceit *noun* 1. the act of lying or cheating. *She used deceit to get what she wanted.* 2. the quality that makes someone tell lies or hide the truth. *Nobody liked her because she was full of deceit.* {dih **seet**}

de·ceive *verb* (deceived, deceiving, deceives) to cause to believe something that is not true; trick or fool. *He deceived us about his age.* / *The store deceived its customers into thinking its fish was fresh.* {dih **seev**} deceiver, n.

De·cem·ber *noun* the twelfth month of the year. December has thirty-one days. Winter begins in December for people who live north of the equator. {dih **sehm** bər}

Word History *December* comes from *decem*, the Latin word for "ten." December was the tenth month in the Roman calendar.

de·cent *adjective* 1. proper or suitable. *In some parts of the world, it is not decent for a woman to show her hair in public.* 2. fairly good; satisfactory. *She is a decent cook but will never be a chef.* 3. kind and thoughtful. *It was decent of him to help me carry the groceries.* {**dee** sənt} decently, adv.

de·cep·tion *noun* the act of causing someone to believe something that is not true. *He used deception to get money from strangers.* {dih **sehp** shən}

dec·i·bel ● *noun* a unit used to measure the loudness of sound. (abbreviated: dB) {**deh** sih behl *or* **deh** sih bəl}

de·cide ● *verb* (decided, deciding, decides) 1. to make up one's mind about something; make a choice to do something. *He decided not to run away from home.* 2. to settle, choose, or solve. *In a boxing match, judges decide the winner.* / *We asked the teacher to decide our dispute.* 3. to bring to an end. *The game was decided by a shot in the final second.* {dih **siyd**}

Word History *Decide* is from a Latin word that means "to cut off" or "to end."

de·cid·u·ous ● *adjective* having leaves that drop off each year. *Oaks and maples are deciduous trees, but pines keep their needles.* {dih **sih** jooh əs} deciduously, adv.

dec·i·mal *adjective* based on the number ten. *Our everyday way of naming and writing numbers is a decimal system.* *noun* 1. a fraction with a denominator that is a multiple of ten. *The number "forty-seven hundredths" is a decimal.* 2. a number in the base ten system written with a decimal point. Money

 Human Body   Human Mind   Everyday Life   History and Culture    Communication

amounts are written as decimals. {**deh** sə məl}

dec·i·mal point *noun* a period placed between the units and the tenths in decimal numbers. It is used when writing money amounts to separate dollars and cents. {**deh** sə məl **point**}

de·ci·pher *verb* (deciphered, deciphering, deciphers) 1. to change from a code into ordinary language. *An expert deciphered the messages written in code.* 2. to figure out the meaning of, when the handwriting is bad or the use of words is not clear. *Your handwriting is so tiny I can't decipher it.* {dih **siy** fər}

de·ci·sion *noun* the act or result of making up one's mind. *I have made the decision not to go to camp this summer.* {dih **sih** zhən}

de·ci·sive *adjective* 1. able to make firm decisions or end arguments. *Leaders should be decisive.* 2. definite; clear. *The soccer team had a decisive win last night: the score was 6-0.* {dih **siy** sihv}

deck *noun* 1. the floor on a ship or boat. Sometimes a ship has several decks at different levels. *All the sailors were called to the main deck.* 2. an outdoor floor or platform that looks like the deck of a ship. *The restaurant has a deck for dining outdoors.* 3. a pack of playing cards. *verb* (decked, decking, decks) to dress or decorate in a fancy way for a special event or celebration. *He was decked out in his best suit.* / *Deck the halls with boughs of holly.* {**dehk**}

• **on deck**
next in line to bat in a baseball game.

dec·la·ra·tion *noun* the act of declaring or making something known. *His declaration of love came as a surprise.* / *The country made a declaration of war.* {deh klə **ray** shən}

Declaration of Independence *noun* the public document by which the thirteen American colonies declared their independence from England in 1776. {**deh** klə **ray** shən əv **ihn** də **pehn** dəns}

de·clar·a·tive sen·tence *noun* a sentence that makes a statement. There are many examples of declarative sentences, such as, "It is raining outside." {dih **klar** ə tihv **sehn** təns}

de·clare *verb* (declared, declaring, declares) 1. to announce in a formal way. *Congress declared war.* 2. to say strongly or firmly. *She declared she would never speak to him again.* 3. to reveal or make known. *He declared his love to me.* {dih **klayr**}

de·cline *verb* (declined, declining, declines) 1. to refuse to do, in a polite way. *The mayor declined to appear.* 2. to grow weaker or smaller gradually. *My health is declining.* / *The show's popularity has declined since one of the stars left.* 3. to slope or slant downward. *The road declines sharply here.* *noun* a drop or loss. *Last year, there was a decline in the number of crimes.* {dih **kliyn**}

de·code *verb* (decoded, decoding, decodes) to change from code into ordinary language. *I finally decoded the secret message.* {dee **kohd**} decoder, n.

de·com·pose *verb* (decomposed, decomposing, decomposes) to decay. *After our garbage decomposes, we spread*

it in the garden. {dee kəm **pohz**} decomposition, n.

dec·o·rate *verb* (decorated, decorating, decorates) 1. to make more beautiful by adding decorations or designs. *We decorated the Christmas tree with blue lights.* 2. to give a medal or other badge of honor to. *The army decorates its bravest soldiers.* {**deh** kə **rayt**}

dec·o·ra·tion ○ *noun* 1. an act of decorating. *I gave careful thought to the decoration of my bedroom.* 2. something used to decorate or to make something else more beautiful. *For decorations, I will have posters and velvet pillows.* 3. a medal, badge, or ribbon given as a sign of honor. *The soldier wore his decorations proudly.* {deh kə **ray** shən}

de·coy *noun* something used to attract animals or people into danger. Wooden decoys in the shape of birds or animals are often used by hunters to lead animals into a trap. *verb* (decoyed, decoying, decoys) to trap or lure into danger. *We caught the cat by decoying him with a toy mouse.* {dee **koi**}

de·crease *verb* (decreased, decreasing, decreases) 1. to become less or smaller. *The price of gas decreased.* / *Her interest in television has decreased since she started reading.* 2. to cause to

A
B
C
D
E
F
G
H
I
J
K
L
M
N
O
P
Q
R
S
T
U
V
W
X
Y
Z

become less. *She decreased her spending at expensive stores.* noun 1. the act of becoming less or smaller. *We are hoping for a decrease in gas prices.* 2. the amount by which something becomes less. *The store offered a ten percent decrease in prices.* {**dee** krees, n., dih **krees**, v.} decreasingly, adv.

de·cree ⬤ *noun* an official order or decision by a ruler or government. *The king's decree ordered all young men into the army.* verb (decreed, decreeing, decrees) to order or decide officially. *The government decreed a national holiday.* {dih **kree**}

ded·i·cate *verb* (dedicated, dedicating, dedicates) 1. to set apart for a special use or purpose. *The mayor dedicated the new library building.* 2. to devote to a particular person, cause, or course of action. *I will dedicate myself to my studies. / She has dedicated her life to helping others.* {**deh** də **kayt**}

ded·i·ca·tion *noun* 1. the ceremony of opening something newly built, such as a building, a park, or a ship. *The dedication of the new ship will take place tomorrow.* 2. the condition of being faithful or devoted to something. *We admire your dedication to your work.* {**deh** də **kay** shən}

de·duct *verb* (deducted, deducting, deducts) to subtract from another amount or sum. *My father deducted the cost of the broken window from my allowance.* {dih **duhkt**}

de·duc·tion *noun* 1. something that is subtracted or deducted. *Because the skirt had a hole in it, the store gave us a deduction of ten dollars.* 2. the process of finding an answer by using what is already known to be true. *If you see footprints in the snow, and you know that the snow started falling after dark, deduction will tell you that somebody was here last night.* 3. an opinion or solution reached by this process. *His missing jacket led me to the deduction that he had left.* {dih **duhk** shən} deductive, adj.

deed ⬤ *noun* 1. an act or action. *I try to do at least one good deed daily.* 2. a piece of paper that shows who by law owns a piece of property. *When he bought the house, the bank gave him a deed.* {**deed**}

deep ⬤ ⬤ *adjective* (deeper, deepest) 1. having great space below or behind a certain point; reaching far down or back; not shallow. *The lake is very deep in the middle. / His cut was deep and needed stitches.* 2. hard to understand; profound. *I liked the book, but much of it was too deep for me.* 3. intensely felt. *I felt deep sorrow when my friend moved away.* 4. low in pitch. *He has a deep voice.* noun 1. a very deep place in the ocean or other body of water. *Strange fish live in the deep.* 2. the most intense period. *I woke up in the deep of night. / It was the deep of winter, and the forest was covered in snow.* adverb (deeper, deepest) to or at a great depth. *The submarine sank deep into the ocean.* {**deep**} deeply, adv.

deep·en *verb* (deepened, deepening, deepens) to make or become deep or deeper. *We need to deepen the hole to plant the bush. / The pool deepens here.* {**dee** pən}

deer *noun* (deer) an animal with long legs and a long neck. Deer are mammals with hooves. All kinds of deer run very fast. The males of most kinds of deer grow and shed antlers every year. Deer are herbivores that chew their cud. Caribou, elk, moose, reindeer, and white-tailed deer are all kinds of deer. {**deer**}

Homophone Note Are you looking for the word *dear*? *Deer* and *dear* sound alike but have different meanings.

de·face *verb* (defaced, defacing, defaces) to damage the surface or appearance of. *Some teenagers defaced the wall by drawing on it.* {dih **fays**}

de·feat ⬤ *verb* (defeated, defeating, defeats) 1. to win a victory over; beat in a game or battle. *He defeated me in tennis.* 2. to cause to fail; keep from success. *The weather defeated our plans.* noun 1. the act or fact of defeating. *We read of the hero's defeat of the giant.* 2. the fact of being defeated; loss; failure. *After we'd tried so hard, our defeat was hard to bear.* {dih **feet**}

de·fect *noun* a weakness, flaw, or bad quality. *Laziness is his worst defect. / Even a beautiful painting can have defects.* {dih **fehkt** or **dee** fehkt}

de·fec·tive *adjective* having a flaw or defect; not perfect. *We returned the defective television to the store.* {dih **fehk** təv}

de·fence *noun* a spelling of **defense** used in Canada and Britain. See **defense** for more information. {dih **fehns**}

de·fend ⬤ ⬤ ⬤ *verb* (defended, defending, defends) 1. to pro-

 Human Body Human Mind Everyday Life  History and Culture ☎ Communication

tect from harm; guard. *He defended his brother from the angry dog.* 2. to speak, write, or act in support of. *He defended his beliefs when I made fun of them.* {dih **fehnd**} defender, n.

de·fense *noun* 1. the act of protecting or guarding. *The government spends billions of dollars each year on national defense.* 2. something that protects or guards. *The castle's defenses included high walls and a moat.* 3. an explanation or excuse for something done or believed in. *His defense was that he had picked up her wallet by mistake.* {dih **fehns**} defenseless, adj.

de·fen·sive *adjective* used as a defense. *A defensive wall was built around the fort.* {dee **fehn** sihv}

de·fer[1] *verb* (deferred, deferring, defers) to not do until later; put off; delay. *We deferred our trip until Mom felt better.* {dih **fuhr**}

de·fer[2] *verb* (deferred, deferring, defers) to give in to what someone else wants or thinks. *Our parents taught us to defer to the wishes of adults.* {dih **fuhr**}

de·fi·ance *noun* bold disobedience and lack of respect for authority. *Sticking out your tongue at someone is a sign of defiance.* {dih **fiy** əns}

de·fi·ant *adjective* showing no respect for authority; refusing to obey. *Defiant students will be sent to the office. / The band's defiant songs made them famous.* {dih **fiy** ənt} defiantly, adv.

de·fi·cien·cy *noun* (deficiencies) the condition or quality of not having something that is needed or required. *A vitamin deficiency has made her ill.* {dih **fih** shən see}

de·fi·cient *adjective* 1. lacking something needed. *His diet is deficient in fruits and vegetables.* 2. not enough or not good enough. *Your math skills are deficient.* {dih **fih** shənt}

def·i·cit *noun* The amount by which something is less than what is needed. *A deficit of money is caused by spending more than has been taken in. Some areas of our country face a deficit of teachers. / The new restaurant showed a deficit of earnings during its first three months of business.* {**deh** fə siht}

de·fine *verb* (defined, defining, defines) 1. to explain or state the meaning of. *The teacher asked me to define the word "demolish."* 2. to describe the nature of. *Is the ability to think what defines human beings?* {dih **fiyn**}

def·i·nite *adjective* 1. clear or exact. *I have no definite plans for Friday night.* 2. known without a doubt; certain; sure. *You have no definite proof that she stole your lunch.* {**deh** fə niht}

definite article *noun* the article "the" in English grammar. The definite article is used with a noun when one is referring to something that is already known or has already been talked about. {**deh** fə niht **ar** tə kəl}

def·i·ni·tion *noun* the statement of the meaning of a word or phrase. *This dictionary gives two definitions for the word "deed."* {**deh** fə **nih** shən}

de·flate *verb* (deflated, deflating, deflates) 1. to cause to shrink or collapse by letting out air or gas. *They deflated the hot-air balloon when the*

tourists returned from their ride. 2. to lessen the spirit or confidence of. *His anger deflated her good mood.* 3. to become shrunken or smaller. *The balloon deflated until it looked like a wrinkled puddle of plastic.* {dih **flayt**}

de·flect *verb* (deflected, deflecting, deflects) to turn aside. *This shield will deflect arrows.* {dih **flehkt**}

de·for·es·ta·tion *noun* the act or process of cutting down the trees of a forest. *Deforestation drives out animals and insects that live in and among the trees.* {dee fohr ehs **tay** shuhn}

de·form *verb* (deformed, deforming, deforms) 1. to damage the shape or form. *Being pulled this way and that had deformed the doll.* 2. to spoil the appearance of; make ugly. *He took a black pen and deformed the walls of his bedroom.* {dih **fohrm**}

de·frost *verb* (defrosted, defrosting, defrosts) 1. to remove frost or ice from. *My mother hates defrosting the refrigerator.* 2. to become free of frost or ice. *When the car windows have defrosted, we can go.* {dih **frawst**}

deft *adjective* skillful, quick, and clever in action. *Her deft fingers flew as she knitted.* {**dehft**} deftly, adv.

de·fy *verb* (defied, defying, defies) 1. to refuse to obey. *I defied my father and went to the movie.* 2. to resist efforts at. *That puzzle defies solving.* 3. to challenge or dare to do something very difficult or impossible. *He defied them to prove he wasn't brave.* {dih **fiy**}

 Living World  Physical World Natural Environment  Economy  Government and Law

a
b
c
d
e
f
g
h
i
j
k
l
m
n
o
p
q
r
s
t
u
v
w
x
y
z

de·grade *verb* (degraded, degrading, degrades) 1. to bring down from a higher to a lower rank or degree by taking away a position or title. *They degraded the soldier to private because of his drinking.* 2. to lower in the opinion of others or in self-respect. *She has degraded herself by becoming friends with the girls who lie and steal.* 3. to reduce in value, amount, or strength. *Too much farming of this field has degraded its soil.* {dih **grayd**}

de·gree 🌐 *noun* 1. a stage or step in a course of action. *I am learning to play the guitar by degrees.* 2. measure or amount. *Skiing takes a high degree of skill.* 3. a unit for measuring temperature. *The temperature today is 82 degrees.* 4. a title given by a university or college to a student who has completed a program of study. *He has degrees in business and law.* {dih **gree**}
 • **by degrees**
 by steps or stages; gradually. *She and I are getting to know each other by degrees.*
 • **to a degree**
 somewhat. *To a degree, I think you're right about that.*

de·hy·drate *verb* (dehydrated, dehydrating, dehydrates) 1. to remove water from in order to preserve. *Grapes are dehydrated to make raisins.* 2. to lose water; dry out. *The body dehydrates quickly during exercise in hot weather.* {dee **hiy** drayt} dehydration, n.

de·i·ty *noun* (deities) 1. a god or goddess. *Venus was the Roman deity of love.* 2. (capital) God. *They sang hymns to their Deity.* {dee ə tee}

de·ject·ed *adjective* in low spirits; sad. *My dog looked dejected when I left without*

her. {dih **jehk** təd} dejectedly, adv., dejectedness, n.

Del·a·ware *noun* (Delaware) a state in the eastern United States. Its capital is Dover. (abbreviated: DE) {**deh** lə **wayr**}

> **Word History** *Delaware* gets its name from Delaware Bay, which was named in honor of Lord De La Warr, governor of the English colony of Virginia.

de·lay *verb* (delayed, delaying, delays) 1. to put off until a later time. *We delayed our vacation until we had saved more money.* 2. to cause to be late. *Rain delayed the start of the baseball game. / I wonder what has delayed him.* 3. to linger or cause delay. *If you delay another minute, you are going to be late for class.* *noun* 1. the act of putting off until a later time. *We asked what the reason was for the delay.* 2. the amount of time by which someone or something is delayed. *There was a one-hour delay before the plane took off.* {də **lay**}

del·e·gate ⬤ *noun* a person who is chosen to speak or act for others. *The class chose me as its delegate to the student government.* *verb* (delegated, delegating, delegates) 1. to give or pass on to another; make the responsibility of someone else. *Before she went away, my mother delegated the dusting and vacuuming to me.* 2. to choose or send as an agent or representative. *The college delegated one student to attend a national meeting on the environment.* {**deh** lə gət, n., **deh** lə gayt, v.}

del·e·ga·tion *noun* a group of people chosen to speak or act

for others. *A delegation of students complained to the principal about the bus schedules.* {deh lə **gay** shən}

de·lete *verb* (deleted, deleting, deletes) to remove from a written work. *A computer can delete a mistake with a click of the mouse.* {dih **leet**}

del·i *noun* (delis) (informal) short form of **delicatessen**. {**deh** lee}

de·lib·er·ate ❓ *adjective* 1. said or done on purpose. *I may have hurt your feelings, but it wasn't deliberate.* 2. thought out ahead of time; carefully considered. *The president's words were deliberate as he tried to get the two countries at war to end their differences.* *verb* (deliberated, deliberating, deliberates) to think about an issue or question in a careful and thorough way, sometimes by discussing them with others. *The jury deliberated for five hours before reaching their decision.* {də **lih** briht or də **lih** bə riht, adj., dih **lih** bə **rayt**, v.} deliberately, adv.

del·i·cate *adjective* 1. pleasing to the senses in a light, soft, or mild way. *She enjoyed the delicate color and smell of the flowers.* 2. easy to break or hurt. *I handled the delicate vase as gently as I could.* 3. requiring care and gentle handling. *Her weight is a delicate topic.* 4. very fine; intricate; skilfully made. *The dress was trimmed with delicate lace.* 5. in a way that is considerate and gentle. *He was delicate in his handling of*

 Human Body   Human Mind   Everyday Life    History and Culture    Communication

the embarrassing situation. {**deh** lə kət} delicately, adv.

del·i·ca·tes·sen *noun* a shop that sells cheese, cooked meats, and other food that is ready to eat. {**deh** lə kə **teh** sən}

de·li·cious *adjective* having a pleasing taste or smell. *The apple pie is delicious.* {də **lih** shəs}

de·light *noun* 1. great pleasure or joy. *I take great delight in teasing my little brother.* 2. a source of great pleasure or joy. *That child is such a delight!* *verb* (delighted, delighting, delights) 1. to give great pleasure or joy. *He delighted us with his wild stories.* 2. to take or find pleasure (usually followed by "in"). *He delights in a good book.* {də **liyt**}

de·light·ful *adjective* very pleasing; causing joy. *My grandmother tells delightful stories about when she was young.* {də **liyt** fəl} delightfully, adv., delightfulness, n.

de·lir·i·ous *adjective* 1. confused from a fever or other cause. *Delirious from the high fever, he began to see things that weren't there.* 2. wildly excited. *He was delirious with joy when she agreed to marry him.* {də **lih** ree əs} deliriously, adv.

de·liv·er *verb* (delivered, delivering, delivers) 1. to send or bring to a particular person or place. *The dairy delivers fresh milk to the supermarket every day.* 2. to speak or read aloud. *He was very nervous when he delivered the speech.* 3. to set free or save. *They prayed that their god would deliver them from danger.* 4. to direct or throw. *Then the*

boxer delivered a punch that ended the match. {də **lih** vər} deliverer, n.

de·liv·er·y *noun* (deliveries) 1. an act of bringing or sending something to a particular person or place. *The supermarket makes deliveries to its customers' homes.* 2. the way in which speech is said or a song is sung. *The actor's delivery was so powerful that it made me cry.* {də **lih** və ree or də **lihv** ree}

del·ta *noun* 1. the name of the fourth letter of the Greek alphabet. 2. a triangle of sand and soil deposited at the mouth of some large rivers. {**dehl** tə}

del·uge *noun* 1. a flood caused by a great amount of water. *In the Bible, Noah escaped the deluge in an ark.* 2. a huge amount. *We received a deluge of answers to our ad.* *verb* (deluged, deluging, deluges) 1. to flood with water. *The dam broke and deluged the entire town.* 2. to flood with a large amount of something. *News reporters deluged my father with phone calls when he won the lottery.* {**dehl** yooj}

de·lu·sion *noun* 1. the act of causing someone to believe in something false or not real, or the belief in something false or not real. *He had given himself delusions of greatness when he was just an ordinary painter.* 2. a false belief that continues even when it has been shown to be false. *Delusions may be caused by certain mental illnesses. The man's illness gave him the delusion that he was God.* {dih **looh** zhən}

de·mand ◔ *verb* (demanded, demanding, demand) 1. to ask for forcefully; order. *I demand that you sit down and*

listen to me. / She demanded her money back. 2. to need or require. *Babies demand a lot of attention.* *noun* 1. the act of commanding forcefully; order. *His demand that everyone on the team work harder was met with groans and heavy sighs.* 2. that which is demanded. *Equality and justice are the demands of the people.* 3. something that must be done; claim. *There are just too many demands on my time.* 4. the desire for goods or services. *There is now a big demand for fruit grown without pesticides.* {dih **mănd**}

de·mand·ing *adjective* 1. giving many, or too many, orders. *Her boss was so demanding that she quit her job.* 2. requiring great attention or effort. *Planning a wedding is a demanding task.* {dih **măn** ding}

de·mer·it *noun* a mark made on a person's record because of some fault or failure. *She had so many demerits for lateness that she feared being fired from her job.* {dih **meh** riht}

De·me·ter *noun* the goddess of farming, marriage, and childbirth in Greek mythology. In Roman mythology, Demeter is called Ceres. {dih **mee** tər}

de·moc·ra·cy ◔ *noun* (democracies) 1. a form of government in which power rests with the people, either directly or through elected representatives. 2. a state or government that is a democracy. {dih **mo** krə see}

Word History *Democracy* comes from two Greek words that together mean "rule of the common people."

A B C D E F G H I J K L M N O P Q R S T U V W X Y Z

dem·o·crat *noun* 1. a person who believes that government should be run by the people or that all people are equal. 2. (capitalized) a member of the Democratic Party of the United States. {**deh** mə **krăt**}

dem·o·crat·ic *adjective* 1. believing that all people should be treated as equals. *We try to be democratic at club meetings by asking every member to vote.* 2. of or relating to a democracy. *Our democratic form of government gives everyone an equal vote.* 3. (cap.) of or relating to the Democratic Party of the United States. *The Democratic and Republican Parties are the largest U.S. political parties.* {**deh** mə **krǎ** tihk}

Democratic Party *noun* one of the two major U.S. political parties. {**deh** mə **krǎ** tihk **par** tee}

de·mol·ish *verb* (demolished, demolishing, demolishes) to tear down or destroy. *We demolished the old barn and built a new one. / The car was demolished in the accident.* {dih **mo** ləsh}

de·mon *noun* 1. an evil spirit; devil. 2. a person who has a great amount of energy and enthusiasm. *She is a demon for exercise.* {**dee** mən}

Word History *Demon* comes from *daimon*, a Greek word that means "a less important god" or "a good or bad spirit."

dem·on·strate *verb* (demonstrated, demonstrating, demonstrates) 1. to explain or describe in detail, using many examples. *The dance teacher demonstrated the jumps she wanted us to learn.* 2. to show evidence of; prove. *By the end of the trial, the lawyer had demonstrated my inno-*

cence. 3. to reveal; show. *This painting demonstrates his talent as an artist.* 4. to take part in a public activity to show support for or against a cause. *The workers demonstrated for better pay and a safer place to work.* {**deh** mən **strayt**}

dem·on·stra·tion *noun* 1. an activity that shows how something works or how it is made. *He gave us a demonstration of how to hang wallpaper.* 2. a rally or other public activity in support of or against a particular cause. *We attended the big demonstration against a cut in teachers' pay.* {**deh** mən **stray** shən} demonstrational, adj.

de·mon·stra·tive *adjective* showing love and affection in an open way. *She is not a demonstrative person but she does love you.* {də **mǒn** strə tihv}

den  *noun* 1. the resting place of wolves, lions, and other wild animals. *The wolf carried her cub back to the den.* 2. a comfortable, cozy room used for reading, watching TV, and other enjoyable activities. {**dehn**}

de·ni·al *noun* 1. a statement that something is false. *His denial of the charges against him did not convince anyone that he was innocent.* 2. the act of refusing to honor a request.

The bank's denial of his request for a loan meant he could not buy a car. {dih **niy** əl}

de·nim *noun* 1. a strong cotton cloth used in clothing. 2. (plural) pants or overalls made of this cloth. {**deh** nəm}

Word History *Denim* comes from a French term, *de Nimes* ("from Nimes"). Nimes is the name of a town in France where this fabric was made.

Den·mark *noun* a country in northern Europe. Copenhagen is the capital of Denmark. {**dehn** mark}

de·nom·i·na·tion *noun* 1. a religious group or division. *Protestants can choose from the Baptist, Methodist, and many other denominations.* 2. any one in a series of values, weights, or other systems. *The denominations of U.S. coins include the penny, nickel, dime, and quarter.* {dih **no** mih **nay** shən}

de·nom·i·na·tor *noun* the number in a fraction that is below the division line. It shows the number of equal parts into which the whole set is divided. *In the fractions 1/8 and 7/8, 8 is the denominator.* {dih **no** mih **nay** tər}

de·note *verb* (denoted, denoting, denotes) 1. to be a mark or sign of. *A flashing red light denotes a danger.* 2. to be a name for; mean. *The word "mother" denotes a woman who has one or more children.* {dih **noht**}

de·nounce *verb* (denounced, denouncing, denounces) 1. to speak out against. *Frederick Douglas denounced slavery in his speeches.* 2. to accuse. *The king denounced his younger brother for planning to steal the throne from him.* {dih **nowns**}

 Human Body   Human Mind   Everyday Life   History and Culture   Communication

dense *adjective* (denser, densest) having parts very close together with little space between. *The forest was so dense that it blocked out all the sunlight.* {**dehns**}

den·si·ty *noun* (densities) the state or condition of having parts very close together with little space between. *The density of houses in the city makes some people feel that they have no privacy.* {**dehn** sih tee}

dent *noun* a small hollow made in a surface by or as if by pressure or a blow. *There is a small dent in the car where I backed into a shopping cart.* *verb* (dented, denting, dents) to make a dent on or in. *I dropped the hammer and dented the table top.* {**dehnt**}
 • **make a dent in**
 1. to make progress on a task by getting some of it done. *Can you make a dent in this pile of work?* 2. to make less or weaker. *Buying the new car made a big dent in my savings.*

den·tal *adjective* 1. of or related to the teeth. *For good dental health, you need to brush your teeth often.* 2. of or related to dentists or dental medicine. *Our dentist uses only the best dental equipment.* {**dehn** təl}

dental floss *noun* a strong thread, covered with wax, used for removing food from between the teeth. {**dehn** təl flaws}

den·tine or **dentin** *noun* the bony material underneath the enamel of a tooth that forms the main part of the tooth. *Dentine is sensitive to heat, cold, and touch.* {**dehn** tihn}

den·tist *noun* a doctor who takes care of the teeth and mouth. {**dehn** tihst}

de·ny *verb* (denied, denying, denies) 1. to say that some-thing is not true; refuse to agree with. *I denied that I had broken the lamp.* / *He said she was clumsy, and she denied it.* 2. to refuse to give or provide. *My parents denied my request for a larger allowance.* {dih **niy**}

de·o·dor·ant *noun* a substance for stopping or covering up unpleasant odors. {dee **oh** də rihnt}

de·part *verb* (departed, departing, departs) to leave; go away. *The bus will depart in about five minutes.* {dih **part**}

de·part·ment 🌐 ⚖ *noun* a separate part of a large organiza-tion, such as a government, school, or business. *The camera department is on the third floor of the store.* / *He teaches in the history depart-ment at the college.* {dih **part** mənt}

department store *noun* a large store with separate depart-ments, each selling a certain type of goods. *The toy depart-ment is on the third level of the department store.* {dih **part** mənt **stohr**}

de·pend *verb* (depended, depending, depends) 1. to trust or rely (usually followed by "on" or "upon"). *I can always depend on my best friend to cheer me up when I am sad.* 2. to be decided by or subject to (usually fol-lowed by "on"). *Whether I can go to the park depends on how quickly I can finish my work.* {dih **pehnd**}

de·pend·a·ble *adjective* deserving trust or confidence; able to be counted on. *I felt proud when Mom told me how dependable I am.* {dih **pehn** də bəl} dependability, n.

de·pend·ence or **dependance** *noun* the condition of relying on another for help, or to provide what one needs. *Teenagers grow tired of their dependence on their parents and look forward to becoming adults themselves.* {dih **pehn** dihns}

de·pend·ent or **dependant** *adjec-tive* 1. relying on another for help or to provide what one needs. *Children are dependent on their parents for food and shelter.* 2. controlled by how something else turns out. *How much water I'll need to drink is dependent on how far I run.* *noun* one requiring the help of another in order to survive. *My parents have two dependents to take care of: myself and my brother.* {dih **pehn** dihnt}

de·pict *verb* (depicted, depicting, depicts) to show, describe, or portray in a painting, sculpture, or written work. *The author depicts life a hundred years in the future.* {dih **pihkt**} depic-tion, n.

de·port *verb* (deported, deporting, deports) to make a person leave a country. *The government deported the crimi-nals after their trial.* {dih **pohrt**}

de·pos·it 🌐 ⚖ *verb* (deposited, depositing, deposits) 1. to hand over to a bank or other safe place. *I deposited all my birthday money at the bank.* 2. to put down or place. *The ocean waves deposit shells on the beach.* / *He deposited his change on the table.* 3. to place in the coin slot of a machine. *You need to deposit*

A
B
C
D
E
F
G
H
I
J
K
L
M
N
O
P
Q
R
S
T
U
V
W
X
Y
Z

a
b
c
d
e
f
g
h
i
j
k
l
m
n
o
p
q
r
s
t
u
v
w
x
y
z

three quarters to get a soda from the machine. *noun* 1. money that has been put in a bank or anything that has been deposited. *I made a deposit of fifty dollars in my savings account. / The snow-plow left a huge deposit of snow by the garage.* 2. a large amount of a natural substance found beneath the ground. *Large deposits of oil were discovered in Alaska.* 3. a partial payment. *They put a deposit on the house they wanted to buy.* {dih **po** ziht}

de·pot *noun* 1. a bus or train station. 2. a place for storing and giving out military supplies or other goods. {**dee** poh or **deh** poh}

de·press *verb* (depressed, depressing, depresses) to cause to be unhappy or in low spirits. *His failure depressed him.* {dih **prehs**}

de·pres·sion ❓ ⬗ *noun* 1. a mood of unhappiness and low spirits that can last a long time and cannot always be explained. *His depression about losing his job lasted for weeks.* 2. a low spot or hollow. *My bike rode roughly over a depression in the road.* 3. an economic state in which business is very bad and many people are out of work and poor. 4. (capitalized) an economic depression that affected the United States and other countries from 1929 to 1939. {dih **preh** shən}

de·prive *verb* (deprived, depriving, deprives) to take away from; not allow to have. *A bad storm deprived the city of electric power. / When Gilbert didn't do his chores, he was deprived of his allowance.* {dih **priyv**}

depth *noun* 1. the condition or quality of being deep. *The depth of my love for you cannot be measured.* 2. the distance from top to bottom or from front to back. *The lake has a depth of 3,000 feet. / She measured the depth of the window frame.* {**dehpth**}

• **in depth**
in a thorough way. *She understands the subject in depth.*

dep·u·ty *noun* (deputies) a person appointed to assist and sometimes act in the place of someone else. *Our school is so large the principal has a deputy to help her.* {**dehp** yə tee}

der·by *noun* (derbies) 1. a horse race run every year and limited to three-year-old horses. *The Kentucky Derby is famous all over the world.* 2. a hard hat made of felt with a round top and a curved, narrow brim. {**duhr** bee}

de·rive *verb* (derived, deriving, derives) 1. to obtain from a particular source (usually followed by "from"). *Many medicines have ingredients derived from plants.* 2. to come from a particular source; originate (usually followed by "from"). *The English word "virtue" derives from Latin.* {də **riyv**}

der·rick *noun* 1. a machine for lifting and moving heavy loads. It has a center beam that does not move and a long arm that turns around the base. 2. a tower built over an oil well or other drill hole. It is used to support and move equipment. {**deh** rihk}

des·cend *verb* (descended, descending, descends) 1. to move downward or to a lower position. *The sun is descending. / An angel descended from the heavens.* 2. to be passed along from one generation to the next. *Red hair has descended in their family for centuries.* 3. to be related by blood through several generations. *He descends from African kings.* 4. to move to a lower position on or by means of. *He descended the stairs.* {dih **sehnd**}

de·scend·ant *noun* one who comes from a given ancestor or ancestors. *I am a descendant of Irish farmers and English sailors.* {dih **sehn** dihnt}

de·scent *noun* 1. the act or process of going downward. *The parachutist's descent to the ground took only a few minutes.* 2. a path or passage that slopes downward. *She made her way down a steep, narrow descent, not knowing where she would end up.* {dih **sehnt**}

Homophone Note The words **descent** and **dissent** sound alike but have different meanings.

de·scribe *verb* (described, describing, describes) to tell or write about; create a picture of in words. *He described the costumes worn in the movie to all of his friends.* {dih **skriyb**}

de·scrip·tion *noun* 1. the act of using words to tell others what something is or was like. *His description of the fire made us cry.* 2. a spoken or

 Human Body   ❓ Human Mind   👕 Everyday Life   🏳 History and Culture   ☎ Communication

written account of something. *Her description of her first day at school is very funny.* 3. kind; sort; variety. *The fair offered foods of every description.* {dih **skrihp** shən}

de·scrip·tive *adjective* using or full of description. *The writer gave a descriptive account of life in Alaska.* {dih **skrihp** tihv} descriptively, adv., descriptiveness, n.

de·seg·re·gate *verb* (desegregated, desegregating, desegregates) to stop the practice of having separate schools and other facilities for people of different races. *The courts desegregated the city's schools.* {dee **seh** grih **gayt**}

de·sert[1] *noun* a very dry, sandy area with few or no plants growing in it. {**deh** zərt}

de·sert[2] *verb* (deserted, deserting, deserts) to leave behind even though it is one's duty to stay; abandon. *He deserted his children. / The sailor deserted his ship.* {dih **zuhrt**}

> **Homophone Note** Are you looking for the word *dessert* (a sweet food)? *Desert*[2] when used as a verb (to leave behind) and *dessert* sound alike but have different meanings.

de·serve *verb* (deserved, deserving, deserves) to be worthy of or have a right to. *He deserves a medal for saving the child from the fire.* {dih **zuhrv**}

de·sign *verb* (designed, designing, designs) 1. to make or draw plans for the structure or form of. *She designed the costumes for the movie. / He designed his house himself.* 2. to plan for a certain goal or purpose. *They designed that playground for very young children.* *noun* 1. a plan or outline showing how something is to be built or carried out. *The architect showed us his designs for the new office building.* 2. pattern. *The pillow cases have a floral design on them.* {dih **ziyn**}

des·ig·nate *verb* (designated, designating, designates) 1. to point out or name. *Yellow paint designates the trees that are to be cut down.* 2. to stand for or mean. *A white flag designates surrender.* 3. to choose for a particular job or purpose. *The king designated her the messenger because she ran so swiftly.* {**deh** zihg **nayt**}

designated hitter *noun* a member of an American League baseball team who is chosen at the beginning of a game to bat in place of the pitcher. {**deh** zihg **nay** tihd **hih** tər}

de·sir·a·ble *adjective* 1. having pleasing or attractive qualities. *My brother thinks he's the most desirable boy in his class.* 2. worth having or doing. *It is desirable that all students learn to type.* {dih **ziyr** ə bəl} desirability, n.

de·sire *verb* (desired, desiring, desires) to want or wish for. *A new bicycle was what she desired.* *noun* 1. a strong wish or longing. *She has a great desire to be a doctor.* 2. someone or something desired or wished for. *Her greatest desire was to be an actress.* {dih **ziyr**}

> **Word History** *Desire* comes from *desiderare*, a Latin word that means "to await what the stars will bring." The Latin word *siderus* means "star or heavenly body." Sometimes people wish upon a star for what they most desire.

desk *noun* a piece of furniture with drawers and a flat sur-

face used for reading and writing. {dehsk}

desk·top *noun* the flat, upper working surface of a desk. *The marble desktop was the most handsome feature of the president's office.* *adjective* of or intended for use on a desktop. *Most office workers use a desktop computer.* {**dehsk** tŏp}

desk·top pub·lish·ing *noun* the creation and preparation of text and graphics for publishing using small computers. *The new restaurant used desktop publishing to make its menu. / Even long books can be made ready for printing by using desktop publishing.* {**dehsk** tŏp **puhb** lihsh ing}

des·o·late *adjective* 1. without the things that are necessary or desirable for life. *The ship sank at sea, leaving the passengers stranded on a desolate island.* 2. having no people; lonely. *With the rest of my family away, the house seems desolate.* 3. very lonely or without hope. *I was desolate when everyone was invited but me.* {**deh** sə liht *or* **deh** zə liht}

de·spair *noun* the complete lack of hope. *I am in despair over our lost puppy.* *verb* (despaired, despairing, despairs) to lose all hope (often followed by "of"). *They despaired of ever finding their way home.* {dih **spayr**}

des·per·ate *adjective* 1. not caring about danger because of great need. *She made a desperate attempt to enter the burning house and save the children.* 2. almost hopeless; very serious. *The people trapped in the cave were in a desperate situation.* 3. having a great need or desire. *She was desperate to have a friend.* {**deh** spə riht *or* **deh** spriht} desperately, adv.

A B C D E F G H I J K L M N O P Q R S T U V W X Y Z

a
b
c
d
e
f
g
h
i
j
k
l
m
n
o
p
q
r
s
t
u
v
w
x
y
z

des·per·a·tion *noun* the feeling or condition of being desperate or without hope. *Out of desperation, she asked a complete stranger for money.* {deh spə **ray** shən}

de·spise *verb* (despised, despising, despises) to hate or scorn. *I despise anyone who is mean to animals.* {dih **spiyz**} despiser, n.

de·spite *preposition* in spite of; regardless of. *Despite the snowstorm, he kept driving.* {dih **spiyt**}

des·sert *noun* a sweet, fruit, or other food served at the end of a meal. *We had apple pie and ice cream for dessert.* {dih **zuhrt**}

Homophone Note The words *dessert* and *desert*² (to leave behind) sound alike but have different meanings.

des·ti·na·tion *noun* the place to which a person is going or goods or baggage are sent. *After a five-hour flight, the tourists reached their destination.* {deh stih **nay** shən}

des·tine *verb* (destined, destining, destines) to set aside for a particular end or purpose. *I am destined to be famous.* {deh stihn}

des·ti·ny *noun* (destinies) that which has happened or must happen to someone because of fate or luck. *Mom and Dad said that it was their destiny to marry one another.* {deh stih nee}

des·ti·tute *adjective* having no money or other means of living. *When she lost her job, she feared she would become destitute.* {deh stih **tooht**}

de·stroy *verb* (destroyed, destroying, destroys) to ruin completely. *Their barn was destroyed by a fire.* {dih **stroi**}

de·stroy·er *noun* a small, fast warship. {dih **stroi** ər}

de·struc·tion *noun* 1. the act of ruining completely or destroying. *We watched the destruction of the buildings.* 2. the state of being completely ruined or destroyed. *The tornado left behind a trail of destruction.* {dih **struhk** shən}

de·struc·tive *adjective* causing complete ruin or destruction. *Tornados can be very destructive.* / *Hatred is a destructive emotion.* {dih **struhk** tihv}

de·tach *verb* (detached, detaching, detaches) to separate from a whole. *Who detached the doll's arms and legs?* / *We have to detach the trailer from the car.* {dih **tăch**} detachable, adj.

de·tail *noun* 1. a small item; a particular. *I told Mom every detail about the dance.* 2. all the particulars of something considered together. *If you get the details right, the model plane will be perfect.* *verb* (detailed, detailing, details) to describe or tell with all the particulars. *She detailed everything that happened on her trip.* {**dee** tayl or dee **tayl**, n., dih **tayl** or dee **tayl**, v.}
• **in detail**
including all the particulars. *The mechanic explained in detail how an engine works.*

de·tain *verb* (detained, detaining, detains) 1. to keep from going on; stop or delay. *Heavy traffic detained me.* 2. to force to stay or keep in prison. *The police detained the suspect for twelve hours.* {dih **tayn**} detainment, n.

de·tect *verb* (detected, detecting, detects) to discover or notice. *I detected anger in her voice.* / *I detected the smell of smoke and discovered the pie was burning.* {dih **tehkt**} detectable, adj.

Synonyms
These words share a meaning with *detect*, verb 1:
find, discover, reveal, perceive, uncover

de·tec·tive *noun* a person, often a police officer, whose job is to find information that will solve crimes. {dih **tehk** tihv}

de·tec·tor *noun* a device that finds or detects something, such as changes in temperature or pressure. *A smoke detector warns people of fires.* / *A metal detector finds coins buried in the ground.* {dih **tehk** tər}

de·ten·tion *noun* the detaining of someone for a short time, either as punishment or until a trial can be held. *He was given detention for starting a fight during recess.* / *The drunk driver is in detention.* {dih **tehn** shən}

de·ter *verb* (deterred, deterring, deters) to stop or discourage from some action by creating doubt or fear. *Her parents tried to deter her from becoming a painter by telling her most artists are poor.* {dih **tuhr**} determent, n.

de·ter·gent *noun* a chemical substance in the form of a liquid or powder used for washing things. {dih **tuhr** jihnt}

de·te·ri·o·rate *verb* (deteriorated, deteriorating, deteriorates) to make or become less in value or quality. *Since she started smoking, her health has deteriorated.* / *Rust deteriorates metal.* {dih **teer** ee ə **rayt**} deterioration, n.

de·ter·mi·na·tion *noun* 1. the quality of having a firm goal

 Human Body
 Human Mind
Everyday Life
 History and Culture
Communication

or being determined. *People admire his determination to improve at sports.* 2. the act of coming to a decision or settling something. *The determination of the guest list took a long time.* {dih **tuhr** mih **nay** shən}

de·ter·mine *verb* (determined, determining, determines) 1. to decide or settle finally and without question. *We determined a date for the wedding.* 2. to conclude after studying or watching. *Some scientists have determined the age of the dinosaur teeth.* 3. to bring about; cause. *The colors you choose will determine the mood of the picture.* {dih **tuhr** mihn}

de·ter·mined *adjective* showing determination. *The determined kids said they would wait in line all night to get tickets to the concert.* {dih **tuhr** mihnd} determinedly, adv., determinedness, n.

de·test *verb* (detested, detesting, detests) to have a strong dislike for; hate. *I detest people who whine all the time.* {dih **tehst**}

det·o·nate *verb* (detonated, detonating, detonates) to explode or cause to explode. *The police removed the bomb before it detonated.* {**deh** tə **nayt**} detonation, n.

de·tour *noun* a temporary route made to avoid a road repair or other problem, or some other way that is longer than the direct route. *They were late because they had to take a detour.* *verb* (detoured, detouring, detours) 1. to travel by way of a detour. *We detoured on back roads to avoid the crowded highway.* 2. to cause to travel by way of a detour. *Traffic was detoured because of a car accident.* {**dee** toohr}

de·tract *verb* (detracted, detracting, detracts) to lessen or take away (often followed by "from"). *A flaw in the diamond detracted from its value.* / *The person kicking my seat detracted from my enjoyment of the film.* {dih **trăkt**}

det·ri·men·tal *adjective* causing harm. *Her poor eating habits are detrimental to her health.* {**deh** trə **mehn** təl} detrimentally, adv.

dev·as·tate *verb* (devastated, devastating, devastates) 1. to destroy or ruin. *An earthquake devastated the village.* 2. to upset greatly. *The news of his death devastated our family.* {**deh** və **stayt**} devastating, adj., devastatingly, adv.

de·vel·op  *verb* (developed, developing, develops) 1. to bring out the potential of; advance to a more complete or more effective condition. *Try to develop your best qualities.* 2. to cause to gain strength; cause to grow. *He tried to develop his muscles by lifting weights.* 3. to become stronger; grow. *Teenagers develop at a rapid pace.* 4. to bring into being or operation; generate. *Scientists are developing a new kind of plastic.* 5. to come into being or operation. *The tadpoles will develop into frogs.* 6. to treat with chemicals so as to create a photographic image. *He develops his own film.* {dih **veh** ləp}

de·vel·op·ment *noun* 1. the act of developing or bringing to a completed state. *The development of the new shopping mall took several years.* 2. an important event or happening. *The president spoke of the latest development in the war.* 3. a group of houses or other buildings built by the

same person or company. *All of the houses in the development looked very much alike.* {dih **veh** ləp mənt} developmental, adj.

de·vi·ate *verb* (deviated, deviating, deviates) 1. to turn away from a direct course or one that has already been set. *The rocket deviated from its path.* 2. to stray from normal or accepted behavior. *This restaurant deviates from the typical breakfast menu.* {**dee** vee **ayt**}

de·vice  *noun* 1. an invention or machine used to perform simple tasks or something else made for a specific purpose. *She gave me a small device that can quickly remove the core from an apple.* / *The computer is a device that has changed the way people work.* 2. a trick or scheme. *She used the device of fainting to get his attention.* {dih **viys**}

dev·il *noun* 1. (often capitalized) the chief spirit of evil in Christianity. The Devil is the master of Hell and enemy of God; Satan. 2. a bad, cruel, or wicked person; villain. *Jeff is friendly and kind, but his brother is a devil.* 3. an especially mischievous, clever, or energetic person. *What a little devil that child is!* {**deh** vəl}

de·vi·ous *adjective* not open or honest. *Cheating is a devious way to win.* {**dee** vee əs} deviously, adv., deviousness, n.

de·vise *verb* (devised, devising, devises) to invent or think out. *She devised a plan to earn money.* {dih **viyz**} deviser, n.

de·vote *verb* (devoted, devoting, devotes) 1. to give to a purpose; dedicate. *They devoted their time and energy to helping others.* 2. to set apart for a special purpose.

A
B
C
D
E
F
G
H
I
J
K
L
M
N
O
P
Q
R
S
T
U
V
W
X
Y
Z

Let's devote this room to quiet reading. {dih **voht**}

de·vot·ed *adjective* true or loyal. *He is a devoted husband and father. / She is a devoted football fan.* {dih **voh** tihd} devotedly, adv., devotedness, n.

de·vo·tion 🔊 💬 *noun* strong affection or loyalty. *They show great devotion to their children.* {dih **voh** shən}

de·vour *verb* (devoured, devouring, devours) 1. to eat or swallow in a greedy way. *Our hike made us so hungry we devoured our lunch.* 2. to swallow up or consume as if by eating quickly. *The fire devoured thousands of trees.* 3. to take in with the mind or senses in a greedy way. *She devours books.* {dih **vowr**} devourer, n.

de·vout *adjective* 1. devoted to religion. *She tries to be a devout Christian.* 2. truly felt; sincere. *He gave the bride and groom his devout wishes for their happiness.* {dih **vowt**} devoutly, adv., devoutness, n.

dew *noun* little drops of water that collect at night on grass, plants, and other cool surfaces. {**dooh**}

Homophone Note The words *dew*, *do*[1], and *due* sound alike in American English, but have different meanings.

dew·lap *noun* a loose fold of skin below the neck of cattle, dogs, and certain other animals. {**dooh** lăp}

dex·ter·i·ty *noun* grace and easy quickness in using the hands or body; skill. *He played the piano with amazing dexterity.* {dehk **steh** rih tee}

di·a·be·tes *noun* a disease in which there is too much blood sugar. People with diabetes are treated with insulin, which the body needs to use sugar properly. {**diy** ə **bee** teez *or* **diy** ə **bee** tees *or* **diy** ə **bee** tihs}

di·a·bet·ic *adjective* of or resulting from diabetes. *noun* a person who has diabetes. {**diy** ə **beh** tihk}

di·a·bol·ic *adjective* very evil; devilish. *He had a diabolic plan to take over the world.* {**diy** ə **bŏl** ihk}

di·ag·no·sis 🔊 *noun* (diagnoses) 1. the act or process of finding out the nature of an illness or injury by examining its signs and symptoms. *Doctors learn the skill of diagnosis in medical school.* 2. the conclusion reached by this process. *The doctor's diagnosis was that I have broken ribs.* {**diy** əg **noh** sihs}

di·ag·o·nal *adjective* 1. joining one corner to the opposite corner of a square, rectangle, or other flat shape with straight sides. 2. having slanting lines or markings. *This skirt is made of a fabric with diagonal stripes.* {**diy** **ă** gə nəl} diagonally, adv.

di·a·gram *noun* a drawing or plan that shows the parts of something or how the parts work together. *He drew a diagram to show me how my computer works.* *verb* (diagramed or diagrammed, diagraming or diagramming, diagrams) to show by a diagram. *She diagramed the steps in building a bench.* {**diy** ə **grăm**} diagrammable, adj.

Word History *Diagram* comes from a Greek word that means "something marked out by lines."

di·al *noun* 1. a disk that has numbers and a moving pointer that shows time, weight, or some other measure. 2. the face of a clock or watch. 3. a disk or knob on a television or radio for tuning to different channels. 4. the disk with numbered finger holes on some telephones. A telephone dial allows the caller to select the numbers being called by turning the disk. *verb* (dialed, dialing, dials) 1. to choose or tune to by using a radio or television dial. *She dialed her favorite radio station.* 2. to call on a telephone by using a dial or buttons. *I dialed the wrong number.* {**diy** əl} dialer, n.

di·a·lect 💬 *noun* a form of a language that is spoken in a specific region or by a specific group of people. {**diy** ə **lehkt**}

di·a·logue *noun* a talk between two or more people or between characters in a play, film, or novel. *We practiced until we knew our dialogue by heart.* {**diy** ə **lŏg** *or* **diy** ə **lawg**}

dial tone *noun* the steady hum or buzzing sound in a telephone receiver showing that the line is open and a number may be dialed or entered. {**diy** əl **tohn**}

di·am·e·ter *noun* 1. a straight line from one side of a circle or sphere to the other that passes through the center. 2. the length of this line. 3. the width of a circle, sphere, or cylinder. {**diy** **ă** mih tər}

di·a·mond 🏃 💬 *noun* 1. a clear mineral that is a crystal form of pure carbon. Diamonds are the hardest natural substance known. They are used in making jewelry and as

 Human Body   Human Mind   Everyday Life    History and Culture   Communication

tools for cutting hard materials. 2. a figure shaped like this with four straight, equal sides and four angles. 3. the red figure designating one suit in a deck of playing cards, or anything else with this shape. 4. a playing card of the diamond suit. 5. the part of a baseball field that is marked by the four bases and the paths connecting them. {**diy** mənd} diamondlike, adj.

dia·per *noun* a baby's underwear of soft cloth or paper folded between the legs and fastened at the waist. {**diy** pər}

di·a·phragm *noun* 1. a wall of muscle that separates the chest and abdomen in humans and certain animals. 2. a thin disk in electronic tools such as microphones, speakers, and telephones. In a microphone, the diaphragm changes sound vibrations into electrical signals. In a speaker, it changes electrical signals into sound vibrations. {**diy** ə **frăm**}

di·ar·rhe·a *or* **diarrhoea** *noun* a condition marked by frequent and watery bowel movements. {**diy** ə **ree** ə}

di·a·ry *noun* (diaries) 1. a daily record of a person's experiences and thoughts. *I keep a diary of my dreams.* 2. a book for recording such events. *My diary is private.* {**diy** ə ree} diarist, n.

dice *plural noun* small cubes with dots on each side num-

bering one to six. Dice are often used in pairs for board games and games of chance. *verb* (diced, dicing, dices) to cut into small cubes. *He diced the potatoes for the stew.* {**diys**}

dic·tate *verb* (dictated, dictating, dictates) 1. to say or read aloud for someone to write down or for a machine to record. *She dictated several letters to her secretary.* 2. to state or order with authority. *The company owners dictate what the workers are allowed to do. noun* (often plural) a rule or requirement that guides or controls what one does. *If you follow the dictates of common sense, you will not make so many mistakes.* {**dihk** tayt *or* dihk **tayt**}

dic·ta·tor *noun* a ruler who has total authority. *Many dictators use their power in a cruel or selfish way.* {**dihk** tay tər}

dic·tion·ar·y *noun* (dictionaries) a book that lists the words of a language in alphabetical order, along with information about their meaning, spelling, and pronunciation. {**dihk** shə **nayr** ee}

did *verb* past tense of **do**[1]. {**dihd**}

did·n't shortened form of "did not." *I didn't get to bed until late.* {**dih** dənt}

die[1] *verb* (died, dying, dies) 1. to stop living; become dead. *The plant died because he never watered it.* 2. to lose force or stop working. *The car's engine died.* 3. to need or want very much. *I am dying for a glass of water.* 4. to fade away; gradually disappear (usually followed by "away," "down," or "out"). *The sounds of the parade died away.* {**diy**}

die[2] *noun* singular of **dice**. {**diy**}

Homophone Note Are you looking for the word **dye** (a color or stain)? **Die** and **dye** sound alike but have different meanings.

diesel engine *noun* a type of engine that burns fuel oil. Diesel engines are different from most car engines, which use an electric spark to ignite the fuel. In a diesel engine, the fuel is sprayed into a chamber and set on fire by the heat of air that has been put under high pressure. Big trucks have diesel engines. {**dee** zəl **ehn** jihn}

di·et *noun* 1. the food and drink usually eaten and drunk by a person or animal. *The diet of a newborn baby is usually his mother's milk.* 2. a special selection of food and drink to improve one's health or to correct physical problems. *The doctor put him on a diet that is low in salt. verb* (dieted, dieting, diets) to eat less food or choose certain foods to improve health or lose weight. {**diy** iht} dieter, n.

Word History *Diet* comes from *diaeta*, a Latin word that means "a recommended way of life." This Latin word came from a Greek word that meant "to select food and drink."

di·e·ti·tian *noun* a person who is trained to plan healthful meals for both ill and healthy people. {**diy** ə **tih** shən}

dif·fer *verb* (differed, differing, differs) 1. to be not the same as; be unlike. *The twins look alike but differ in most other ways.* 2. to have a different opinion; disagree. *You and I differ on this point.* {**dih** fər}

A B C D E F G H I J K L M N O P Q R S T U V W X Y Z

a
b
c
d
e
f
g
h
i
j
k
l
m
n
o
p
q
r
s
t
u
v
w
x
y
z

dif·fer·ence *noun* 1. the condition of being different from or not like. *She could not tell the difference between right and wrong.* 2. a particular instance of differing. *The teacher told us to list the differences between frogs and toads.* 3. a disagreement or argument. *We have had our differences from time to time, but we are still good friends.* 4. the amount by which one thing or number differs from another. *Two is the difference between five and seven.* {<u>dih</u> fə rəns *or* <u>dih</u> frəns}

dif·fer·ent *adjective* 1. not the same; not alike. *The twins wore different shirts so the teacher could tell them apart.* 2. separate; not the same. *There are two different routes you can take to the library.* {<u>dih</u> fə rənt *or* <u>dih</u> frənt} differently, adv.

Language Note There is no firm rule to tell you when to use **different from** and when to use **different than**. Most of the time, **different from** comes before a noun phrase. **Different than** usually comes before a clause. (A clause is a sentence part with a noun and a verb.) *The shoes Cinderella wore to the ball were different from her everyday ones. After midnight, she looked different than she did at the ball.*

dif·fi·cult *adjective* 1. hard to do or understand. *He enjoys difficult homework assignments.* / *The president has to make many difficult decisions.* 2. hard to deal with or please. *Her parents say she has always been a difficult child.* {<u>dih</u> fə kəlt}

dif·fi·cul·ty *noun* (difficulties) 1. the condition of being hard to do. *The astronauts were prepared for the difficulty of walking in space.* 2. something

that causes worry or trouble; problem. *I have had nothing but difficulties with this computer.* {<u>dih</u> fə **kuhl** tee}

dig *verb* (dug, digging, digs) 1. to make a hole by removing dirt, sand, or the like. *Pirates dig for buried treasure.* 2. to make by digging. *The ditch digger dug a ditch.* 3. to turn over or remove with a shovel or other tool. *She dug dirt from the garden for potting some plants.* 4. to find by searching (often followed by "out"). *He went to the library to dig out the information he needed for class.* 5. to shove or poke. *He dug his elbow in my side.* noun 1. a thrust or poke. *He gave me a dig with his finger.* 2. a research project that involves digging for artifacts or bones. *The archaeologist is on a dig in Egypt.* {dihg}

di·gest *verb* (digested, digesting, digests) 1. to break down into materials that can be absorbed and used by the body. *Your body digests food more slowly at night.* 2. to think about; ponder. *I read that book slowly in order to digest it.* noun a collection of stories, news articles, or other written works. The items in a digest are often shortened so that more of them can fit in one book or magazine. {<u>diy</u> jehst, n., dih <u>jehst</u> *or* <u>diy</u> jehst, v.}

di·ges·tion *noun* the process by which the stomach and intestines change food into a form that the body can use as energy. {dih <u>jehs</u> chən *or* <u>diy</u> <u>jehs</u> chən}

di·ges·tive *adjective* of or relating to digestion. *The body's digestive system includes the mouth, the stomach, and the intestines.*

{dih <u>jeh</u> stihv *or* diy <u>jeh</u> stihv}

di·ges·tive sys·tem *noun* the parts of the body that work together to break down food so that it can be used by the body as energy. The human digestive system includes the mouth, esophagus, stomach, and intestines. *Good diet is important to keep a digestive system healthy.* {diy <u>jehs</u> tihv <u>sihs</u> təm}

dig·it *noun* 1. a finger or toe. *Counting fingers and toes, we have twenty digits.* 2. any of the whole numbers from zero through nine. {<u>dih</u> jiht}

dig·it·al *adjective* showing information by a row of numerical digits rather than by numbers on a dial. *I wear a digital watch because it's easy to read.* {<u>dih</u> jih təl} digitally, adv.

dig·ni·fied *adjective* having or showing dignity. *Grandfather's white hair and straight posture give him a dignified appearance.* {dihg nih fiyd}

dig·ni·ty *noun* (dignities) one's sense of worth; pride or self-respect as shown in one's appearance or behavior. *She showed her dignity in the way she handled her troubles.* {<u>dihg</u> nih tee}

dike *noun* a dam or high wall built to prevent flooding. *verb* (diked, diking, dikes) to furnish, enclose, or protect with a dike. *They diked the farm land to keep out flood waters.* {diyk}

di·lap·i·dat·ed *adjective* fallen into ruin or decay. *The town finally tore down the dilapidated old school building.* {dih <u>lăp</u> ih **day** tihd}

 Human Body  Human Mind Everyday Life Flag History and Culture Phone Communication

di·lem·ma *noun* a situation that requires a choice between two actions, neither of which will be a good solution. *He found himself in a dilemma: Either he tells on his friend and loses a friend, or he keeps quiet and lets the wrong person take the blame.* {dih **lehm** ə}

dil·i·gent *adjective* trying hard and steadily to achieve a goal. *I am diligent about getting to school on time every day.* {**dihl** ə jənt} diligently, adv.

di·lute *verb* (diluted, diluting, dilutes) to make thinner or weaker by adding a liquid. *I diluted the orange juice by adding some water.* {dih **looht** or **diy looht**}

dim *adjective* (dimmer, dimmest) 1. not well lighted; dark. *It's hard to read in that dim corner.* 2. faint or dull. *The surface of the old mirror was scratched and dim.* / *The star gave off a dim light.* 3. not clear to the senses or mind. *I could see only dim shapes in the fog.* / *We had only a dim idea of how to build the shed.* 4. not able to see or understand clearly. *Old age has made his eyes dim. verb* (dimmed, dimming, dims) to make dim. *I dimmed the lights in the room.* {**dihm**} dimly, adv., dimness, n.

dime *noun* a coin of the United States and Canada equal to ten cents. {**diym**}
  • **a dime a dozen** (informal) plentiful and easy to get; common; cheap.
  • **on a dime** (informal) with great quickness or accuracy. *The bike has such good brakes that it could stop on a dime.*

di·men·sion *noun* 1. size as measured in length, width, or depth. *The dimensions of the box are two feet long, one foot wide, and six inches deep.* 2. (usually plural) importance or size. *The dimensions of their family problems slowly became clear.* {dih **mehn** shən}

di·min·ish *verb* (diminished, diminishing, diminishes) 1. to make smaller or cause to appear smaller in size or importance. *My younger brother's A+ in math diminished my achievements.* 2. to decrease. *The pain diminished after he took aspirin.* {dih **mihn** ihsh} diminishment, n.

di·min·u·tive *adjective* very small; tiny. *The baby wiggled its diminutive toes.* {dih **mihn** yə tihv}

dim·mer *noun* a device that controls the brightness of an electric light. *They used a dimmer to lower the light in the dining room.* {**dihm** ər}

dim·ple *noun* 1. a small natural dent or hollow that forms in the cheeks during a smile. *The baby's dimples made her especially cute.* 2. any small dent or hollow. *I wouldn't even try to guess how many dimples there are on a golf ball! verb* (dimpled, dimpling, dimples) to form or cause to form dimples in. *A grin dimpled her face.* {**dihm** pəl} dimply, adj.

din *noun* a loud, steady noise. *The din of the machines hurt the workers' ears. verb* (dinned, dinning, dins) to repeat over and over in a loud voice. *He dinned the truth into me.* {**dihn**}

dine *verb* (dined, dining, dines) to eat dinner. *We usually dine at six o'clock.* {**diyn**}
  • **dine out** to eat dinner away from one's home. *Our family dines out about once a month.*

din·er *noun* 1. one who eats a meal. *This restaurant seats one hundred diners.* 2. a roadside restaurant that serves inexpensive meals at a long counter or booths. {**diy** nər}

di·nette *noun* a small room or section of a room used for eating meals. {**diy neht**}

din·ghy *noun* (dinghies) a small boat used as a lifeboat or for short trips to shore and back. {**ding** ee}

din·go *noun* (dingoes) a kind of wild dog found only in Australia. Dingoes have long legs, pointed ears, and yellowish brown or reddish brown fur. They hunt small mammals, but have learned to hunt sheep and cattle brought to Australia by European settlers. {**ding** goh}

din·gy *adjective* (dingier, dingiest) 1. dirty or not cared for well. *We spent a day cleaning and painting the dingy apartment.* 2. dull in color; not bright. *My white socks are dingy because they were washed with new blue jeans.* {**dihn** jee} dinginess, n.

dining room *noun* a room in a home or hotel where meals are eaten. {**diy** ning **roohm** or **diy** ning **ruum**}

din·ner ● *noun* 1. the main meal of the day. *He has to be home for dinner by six o'clock.* 2. a formal meal in honor of a person or event. *We had Thanksgiving dinner with our grandparents.* {**dihn** ər}

di·no·saur ● *noun* one of a group of extinct animals. Some kinds of dinosaurs were the largest animals that

A
B
C
D
E
F
G
H
I
J
K
L
M
N
O
P
Q
R
S
T
U
V
W
X
Y
Z

Dinosaurs

What did dinosaurs really look like? What kind of world did they live in? How can we know? The science that attempts t answer these questions is called **paleontology**. A paleontologist s fossils, or the remains of living things th been preserved in rocks and soil over mi years, to learn what these living things may h like. By piecing together a dinosaur's skeleton we basic shape and size of its body. Then, by comparing the its bones to those of modern animals with similar structur reconstruct models of the soft tissues that fleshed its body surprisingly accurate picture of how these creatures looked. Fu fossils of plants and the composition of stones can teach us what kind of envir dinosaurs lived in. There are three basic periods during which dinosaurs lived. the **Triassic,** a time of desert-like climates and little vegetation, when the e recovering from the greatest mass extinction in its history. The next is the **Ju** which saw the largest dinosaurs ever to walk the face of the earth. Last i **Cretaceous,** which ended in violent volcanic eruptions and, some beli catastrophic meteor collision that sent the earth into a deep freeze and dinosaurs into extinction. Some questions, however, are still unanswerable. For example, because the chemicals that produce color are not preserved in fossils, we can only guess the skin colors of various dinosaurs.

coelophysis

fossils

ceratos

triceratops

protoceratops

minm

archeopteryx

velociraptor

tyrannosaurus

225 - 205	205 - 135	135 - 65 million years ago
Triassic	Jurassic	Cretaceous

Did you know that the first dinosaurs are believed to have lived on a huge super-continent that stretched from pole to pole? Comparisons of fossil records found on various modern continents suggest that Africa, Australia, Antarctica, and North and South America once fit together like puzzle pieces to form a giant continent named Pangaea.

stegosaurus

ever lived on land. Other dinosaurs were as small as chickens. The first kinds of dinosaurs developed over two hundred million years ago. The last kinds became extinct about sixty-five million years ago. {**dıy** nə **sohr**}

Word History *Dinosaur* is formed from two Greek words that together mean "terrible lizard."

di·o·cese *noun* a group of churches or a district under the authority of a bishop. {**dıy** ə sees *or* **dıy** ə sihs}

di·ox·ide *noun* a compound containing two atoms of oxygen bound to a single atom of another element. {dıy **ŏk** siyd}

dip *verb* (dipped, dipping, dips) 1. to put into a liquid briefly. *He dipped his toes into the water.* 2. to take out with a scoop. *He dipped some ice cream out of the carton.* 3. to lower quickly. *He dipped his head just as the ball flew by.* 4. to slope downward or seem to sink. *The road dips beyond that tree.* / *The sun dipped below the horizon.* *noun* 1. the act or process of dipping. *A dip in the pool cooled us off right away.* 2. the amount that is taken up by dipping. *I'll have two dips of lime sherbet, please.* 3. a sauce or soft mixture for dipping small pieces of food. *She served chips and onion dip at the start of her party.* 4. a downward slope in a road. *My bike bounced over the dip in the road.* {**dihp**}

di·plo·ma *noun* an official piece of paper stating that a student has earned a degree or finished a course of study. High schools, col-

leges, and universities give out diplomas. {dih **ploh** mə}

dip·lo·mat ● *noun* 1. a person whose job is to handle relations with the governments of other countries. 2. a person who is skilled in dealing with people. *My mother is a diplomat and often settles the arguments I have with my brother.* {dih plə **măt**}

dip·lo·mat·ic *adjective* 1. of or relating to diplomats. *My uncle worked in England as a member of the diplomatic service.* 2. careful not to anger people or hurt their feelings. *It was diplomatic of him to call my mistake "unfortunate" rather than "stupid."* {dih plə **mă** tihk} diplomatically, adv.

dip·per *noun* 1. a cup with a long handle used to lift liquids. 2. see **Big Dipper** and **Little Dipper**. {**dihp** ər}

dire *adjective* (direr, direst) 1. causing or involving horror, fear or suffering. *The fire was a dire event for the families whose homes burned.* 2. terrible or urgent. *After the earthquake, many people were in dire need of medical care.* {**dıyr**}

di·rect ● ● *verb* (directed, directing, directs) 1. to manage or control. *The chief of police directs the police force.* 2. to control by giving orders; command. *We directed the movers to put the sofa by the window.* 3. to tell how to get to a place. *Can you direct me to the nearest phone?* 4. to aim what one

says or writes towards a particular person or group. *I directed my letter of complaint to the head of the company.* / *One reporter directed his question to the first lady, not to the president.* 5. to send or aim towards a place. *He directed the beam of light at the back of the closet.* *adjective* 1. going in a straight line or on a straight course. *I'll show you the most direct route to my house.* 2. truthful and open. *He was direct but kind when he pointed out my mistakes.* *adverb* in a straight line without stopping. *We will fly direct to Tokyo.* {də **rehkt**} directness, n.

direct current *noun* an electric current that flows in one direction. {də **rehkt kuh** rihnt}

di·rec·tion *noun* 1. control or guidance. *He practiced the piano under the direction of his instructor.* 2. (usually plural) information on which way to go or how to do something. *A stranger asked us for directions to the fair.* / *Directions for making the cake are in the cookbook.* 3. an order or command. *Soldiers must follow directions.* 4. the way in which one may face or travel. *Which direction did they go in?* / *All the houses on this street face in one direction.* {də **rehk** shən}

di·rect·ly *adverb* 1. in a direct line or way; straight. *This road runs directly south.* 2. exactly. *The store is directly across from the post office.* 3. without space or action in between. *I have to go directly home after school.* {də **rehkt** lee}

 Human Body Human Mind  Everyday Life  History and Culture Communication

direct object *noun* the part of a sentence that shows the object, goal, or receiver of the action of a verb. "The ball" in "She kicked the ball" is a direct object. {də **rehkt** **ŏb** jehkt}

di·rec·tor  *noun* 1. a person who guides the affairs of a business or other organization. 2. a person who guides the actors and directs the performance of the script for a play or movie. {də **rehk** tər}

di·rec·to·ry *noun* (directories) a list of names and addresses of people or businesses. *I found his phone number in the telephone directory. / The mall directory helps shoppers find the stores they want.* {də **rehk** tə ree}

dir·i·gi·ble *noun* an airship that can be steered or guided, such as a blimp. {**deer** ih jə bəl}

dirt *noun* 1. loose earth or soil. *The dog is digging a hole in the dirt.* 2. any dirty material such as mud or dust. *His clothes were covered in dirt after the game.* {**duhrt**}

dirt·y *adjective* (dirtier, dirtiest) 1. not clean; soiled. *The windows were so dirty you could hardly see out of them.* 2. not honest; unfair. *We stopped playing cards with him because he was a dirty player.* 3. not pleasant to do. *Give someone else the dirty work.* 4. nasty; mean. *She gave me a dirty look.* *verb* (dirtied, dirtying, dirties) 1. to make dirty; soil. *Put an apron on so you don't dirty your shirt.* 2. to become dirty or stained. *White clothes dirty easily.* {**duhr** tee} dirtiness, n.

dis- *prefix* 1. a prefix that means "not" or "lack of." *A dishonest person is someone who is not honest. / The word "disorder" means "lacking order."* 2. a prefix that means "away" or "apart." *To discourage a person is to take away his or her courage.*

dis·a·ble *verb* (disabled, disabling, disables) 1. to take away a person's ability. *She had to quit her job after the injury disabled her.* 2. to make useless or unable to work. *The burglar disabled the alarm on the door before he broke in.* {dihs **ay** bəl}

dis·a·bled *adjective* 1. not working. *My car has been disabled ever since the engine caught on fire.* 2. unable to do certain things because of a medical condition or an accident. *This disabled person cannot walk without a cane.* {dihs **ay** bəld}

dis·ad·van·tage *noun* 1. a condition or situation that makes it more difficult to succeed. *Despite the disadvantage of being poor, he became very successful.* 2. something that causes a condition that is not favorable; drawback. *One disadvantage of this car is its small size.* {dihs əd **văn** tihj}

dis·a·gree *verb* (disagreed, disagreeing, disagrees) 1. to differ in opinion. *He thinks that it will take two weeks to finish the job, but I disagree.* 2. to argue or quarrel. *They disagreed about who had won the contest.* 3. to have a harmful effect (usually followed by "with"). *Cow's milk disagrees with the baby.* {dihs ə **gree**}

dis·a·gree·able *adjective* 1. causing dislike; not pleasant. *I find cleaning the bathroom a disagreeable task.* 2. grumpy, unpleasant, or difficult to get along with. *She is disagreeable when she has a headache.* {dihs ə **gree** ə bəl}

dis·a·gree·ment *noun* 1. a difference of opinion. *They were in disagreement about which color* to paint the house. 2. an argument or quarrel. *They had a loud disagreement about whose turn it was to take out the trash.* {dihs ə **gree** mənt}

dis·ap·pear *verb* (disappeared, disappearing, disappears) 1. to be no longer seen. *The plane disappeared in the clouds.* 2. to exist no longer. *The clouds will soon disappear. / Her smile disappeared.* {dihs ə **peer**}

dis·ap·pear·ance *noun* the act of disappearing or the fact of having disappeared. *There were stories about her disappearance in all of the newspapers.* {dihs ə **peer** əns}

dis·ap·point *verb* (disappointed, disappointing, disappoints) to fail to do or give something expected or hoped for. *His poor grades disappointed his parents.* {dihs ə **point**} disappointingly, adv.

> **Word History** *Disappoint*
> comes from an early French word that means "to dismiss from an appointment or job."

dis·ap·point·ment *noun* 1. the act of disappointing. *This will mean the disappointment of all his hopes.* 2. the fact or feeling of being disappointed. *I tried to hide my disappointment at not getting into ballet school.* 3. someone or something that disappoints. *The movie was a disappointment.* {dihs ə **point** mənt}

dis·ap·prove *verb* (disapproved, disapproving, disapproves) to have a low opinion of someone or something; not approve (often followed by "of"). *Her parents disapproved of her new friends.* {dihs ə **proohv**} disapprovingly, adv.

dis·as·ter *noun* 1. a sudden event causing much damage or suffering. *The volcanic eruption was a disaster for the*

A B C D E F G H I J K L M N O P Q R S T U V W X Y Z

 Living World    Physical World    Natural Environment    Economy   Government and Law

a
b
c
d
e
f
g
h
i
j
k
l
m
n
o
p
q
r
s
t
u
v
w
x
y
z

town. 2. a complete failure. *The first meal I tried to cook was a disaster.* {dih z**ă** stər}

Word History *Disaster*
comes from *disastro,* an Italian word that means "without the stars." In former times, it was thought that the stars influenced human events. Terrible events were believed to have been caused by an unlucky position of the stars.

dis·be·lief *noun* a condition of being unable or not willing to believe. *We stared in disbelief as a purple dog ran down the street.* {dihs bə **leef**}

disc *noun* another spelling of **disk.** {dihsk}

dis·card *verb* (discarded, discarding, discards) to throw out or away; cast off. *We discarded some old clothing.* {dih **skard**}

dis·charge *verb* (discharged, discharging, discharges) 1. to shoot or fire off. *They discharged a cannon at the fort.* 2. to unload, empty, or release. *The ship discharged its catch of fish. / The factory discharged smoke into the air.* 3. to fire or dismiss. *He was discharged from his job at the bank.* 4. to release from a place, such as a prison or hospital. *You may not leave until you are discharged.* *noun* 1. the act of firing a weapon. *He heard the discharge of a gun.* 2. the release from duty. *She got a discharge from the army.* {dihs charj or dihs **charj,** n., **dihs** charj or dihs **charj,** v.}

dis·ci·ple *noun* 1. one who follows a leader or teacher; pupil. 2. one of the twelve original followers of Jesus Christ; apostle. {dih **siy** pəl}

dis·ci·pline 🌑 🌑 *noun* 1. training of the body or mind according to rules. *Miss Cole believes in strict discipline.* 2.

punishment for the sake of training or changing behavior. *He was given severe discipline for breaking the rules.* 3. an area of study or learning. *Astronomy and biology are scientific disciplines.* *verb* (disciplined, disciplining, disciplines) 1. to train according to rules. *Practice helped to discipline the team. / I disciplined myself to snack on fruit instead of candy.* 2. to punish for the sake of training or changing behavior. *He had to discipline his dog for jumping on people.* {dih sə plihn}

disc jockey or **disk jockey** *noun* a person whose job is to play recorded music on the radio or for an event such as a dance. {dihsk jo kee}

dis·close *verb* (disclosed, disclosing, discloses) 1. to make known; tell. *She would not disclose her name.* 2. to uncover; open to view. *He pulled back the curtain and disclosed a secret door.* {dihs **klohz**}

dis·co *noun* (discos) 1. a place for dancing to recorded music. 2. a style of popular dance music with a heavy, steady beat. {**dihs** koh}

dis·com·fort *noun* a condition of being uneasy or in pain. *He felt discomfort for weeks after the surgery. / I noticed her discomfort at being asked to talk in class.* {dihs **kuhm** fərt}

dis·con·nect *verb* (disconnected, disconnecting, disconnects) 1. to break off or stop the connection of or between. *The plumber disconnected the hose from the faucet.* 2. to break the flow of electric current to; separate from the power source. *Please dis-*

connect the toaster before you clean it. {dihs kə **nehkt**}

dis·con·tent·ed *adjective* not satisfied or content; unhappy. *Mr. Ruiz is discontented with his job.* {dihs kən **tehn** tihd} discontentedly, adv.

dis·con·tin·ue *verb* (discontinued, discontinuing, discontinues) to stop or put an end to. *The newspaper has discontinued my favorite comic strip.* {dihs kən **tihn** yoo}

dis·cord *noun* 1. lack of agreement or harmony among people or things; conflict. *The city's plan to build a skateboard park is causing discord in the community.* 2. a combination of musical sounds that is harsh or unpleasant. {**dihs** kohrd}

dis·count *verb* (discounted, discounting, discounts) 1. to take away from a cost or price. *The store owner discounted ten percent from the packages of broken cookies.* 2. to pay little or no attention to. *I discounted the rumors about my best friend.* *noun* an amount taken away from the full or regular price or cost. *Tina got a discount on the dress because the hem was torn.* {**dihs** kownt or dih **skownt**}

dis·cour·age *verb* (discouraged, discouraging, discourages) 1. to cause to lose hope or confidence. *His bad test grade discouraged him.* 2. to try to prevent or persuade not to do. *Her parents discouraged her from going skydiving.* {dihs **kuh** ihj} discouraging, adj.

dis·cour·te·ous *adjective* not having or showing good manners; not polite; rude. *Her mother scolded her for being discourteous to the*

 Human Body  Human Mind 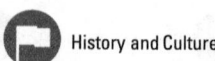 Everyday Life  History and Culture Communication

guests. {dihs **kuhr** tee ihs} dis-courteously, adv.

dis·cov·er *verb* (discovered, discovering, discovers) 1. to find or see before anyone else. *The scientist discovered a cure for the disease. / He discovered oil on his property.* 2. to learn or find out about through study or by observing. *We discovered that the game was easy to play if you know the rules.* {dihs **kuh** vər} discoverer, n.

Synonyms
These words share a meaning with *discover*, verb 1:
find, detect, stumble on

dis·cov·er·y *noun* (discoveries) 1. the act of discovering. *The discovery of antibiotics saved many people's lives.* 2. something that has been discovered. *The mammoth bones are an important discovery.* {dihs **kuh** və ree *or* dihs **kuhv** ree}

dis·crim·i·nate *verb* (discriminated, discriminating, discriminates) 1. to judge or treat someone unfairly because he or she belongs to a particular group or category of people (usually followed by "against"). *Some people discriminate against immigrants.* 2. to see a clear difference; make a distinction. *He could not discriminate between the two brands of cola.* {dihs **krih** mih **nayt**}

Word History *Discriminate*
comes from a Latin word that means "to divide, separate, or distinguish." It was first used for the separation of people of different colors or races in the mid-1800s.

dis·crim·i·na·tion *noun* 1. the act of seeing differences or distinguishing. *He makes no discrimination between students who are lazy and those who are slow learners.* 2. the

act of treating some people unfairly because of prejudice. *The civil rights movement fought to bring an end to discrimination in this country.* {dihs **krih** mih **nay** shən}

dis·cus *noun* (discuses) 1. a disk made of wood with a metal rim, thrown for distance by some track and field athletes. 2. the sports event in which this disk is thrown. *He won a gold medal in the discus.* {**dihs** kəs}

dis·cuss *verb* (discussed, discussing, discusses) 1. to talk together about. *We met to discuss plans for the party.* 2. to consider in writing or speech. *In this article, the writer discusses the alternatives to war.* {dihs **kuhs**}

Word History *Discuss*
comes from a Latin word that means "to shake apart" or "break up."

dis·cus·sion *noun* the act or an instance of talking or writing about something. *I had an interesting discussion with my father about the importance of friends.* {dihs **kuh** shən}

dis·ease *noun* a condition that causes harm to a person's health; illness; sickness. {dih **zeez**}

dis·fa·vor *noun* an opinion that is not favorable; dislike or disapproval. *The boys looked with disfavor at the girls playing football.* {dihs **fay** vər}

dis·fig·ure *verb* (disfigured, disfiguring, disfigures) to damage the appearance or shape of. *The accident disfigured his face.* {dihs **fihg** yər}

dis·grace *noun* 1. loss of respect, honor, or favor; shame. *The team was in disgrace with its fans after losing three games in a row.* 2. that which has or causes shame. *He is a disgrace*

to his family. *verb* (disgraced, disgracing, disgraces) to bring shame to. *He disgraced the team by cheating.* {dihs **grays**}

dis·guise *verb* (disguised, disguising, disguises) 1. to change or hide the looks of in order to prevent recognition. *She disguised herself with a wig.* 2. to cover or hide so as to hide the truth. *He disguised his plans very well. / She disguised the scratch on the table with a brown pen.* *noun* 1. something worn, such as a costume,

mask, or the like, to hide one's identity. *He wore a great disguise for Halloween.* 2. the act of disguising or state of being disguised. *Nobody knew who the man in disguise was.* {dihs **giyz**}

dis·gust *verb* (disgusted, disgusting, disgusts) to cause strong dislike or illness in. *The sight of the dead animal in the road disgusted her.* *noun* a strong dislike caused by something that offends. *We were filled with disgust when we saw how the animals in the pet store were treated.* {dihs **guhst** *or* dihs **kuhst**} disgustedly, adv.

dis·gust·ing *adjective* causing disgust. *Rotten fish has a disgusting smell.* {dihs **guhs** ting *or* dihs **kuh** sting}

dish *noun* 1. a container for serving or holding food, such as a plate, cup, or bowl. *We cleared the table and washed the dinner dishes.* 2. the amount of food held in a plate or bowl. *He ate a large dish of spaghetti.* 3. a certain

A B C D E F G H I J K L M N O P Q R S T U V W X Y Z

a
b
c
d
e
f
g
h
i
j
k
l
m
n
o
p
q
r
s
t
u
v
w
x
y
z

kind of prepared food. *Tamales are a Mexican dish.* *verb* (dished, dishing, dishes) to serve in a dish. *He dished up the ice cream after dinner.* {**dihsh**}

• **dish it out**
to deliver criticism or cruel treatment with force. *He can dish it out, but he can't take it.*

• **dish out**
to give out; supply. *Most people dish out candy on Halloween.*

di·shev·eled *adjective* not neat; messy. *His clothing was disheveled after he ran home from work.* {dih **sheh** vəld}

dis·hon·est *adjective* tending to lie, steal, or cheat; not honest. *Some students are dishonest about how much time they spend on their homework.* {**dihs** o nihst} dishonestly, adv.

dis·hon·or *noun* loss of honor or reputation. *He felt the pain of dishonor when he was caught cheating.* *verb* (dishonored, dishonoring, dishonors) to cause to lose honor or reputation; disgrace; shame. *The policeman has dishonored the police force by taking a bribe.* {dihs **o** nər}

dish·wash·er *noun* 1. a person who washes dishes as a job. 2. a machine that washes dishes, pans, and the like. {**dihsh** wo shər} dishwashing, n.

dis·il·lu·sion *verb* (disillusioned, disillusioning, disillusions) to take away false beliefs or hopes; remove the illusions of. *Many people were*

disillusioned by the assassination of President Kennedy. {dihs ih **looh** zhən} disillusionment, n.

dis·in·fect *verb* (disinfected, disinfecting, disinfects) to clean in order to kill or remove germs. *He disinfected the cut on his arm.* {dihs ihn **fehkt**} disinfection, n.

dis·in·fect·ant *noun* something that kills germs. *This bathroom cleanser contains a disinfectant.* {dihs ihn **fehk** tənt}

dis·in·te·grate *verb* (disintegrated, disintegrating, disintegrates) 1. to come apart; break down into parts or pieces. *The old log disintegrated when he picked it up.* 2. to break down into parts or pieces. *Acid from the battery disintegrated the tips of my gloves.* {dih **sihn** tə grayt} disintegration, n.

dis·in·ter·est·ed *adjective* not having a personal interest in or opinion about something. *She was a disinterested witness at the trial.* {dihs **ihn** trih stihd}

disk or **disc** *noun* 1. any thin, flat, round object, or one that appears flat and round. *Tiddlywinks is played with a set of small disks.* 2. a phonograph record. 3. a thin, round plate used to record data entered on a computer. {**dihsk**}

disk·ette *noun* see **floppy disk**. {dih **skeht**}

dis·like *verb* (disliked, disliking, dislikes) to have a feeling of not liking; have objections to. *She doesn't come by often because she dislikes my dog.* *noun* a feeling of not liking. *He has a strong dislike for people who brag.* {dihs **liyk**} dislikable (dislikeable), adj.

dis·lo·cate *verb* (dislocated, dislocating, dislocates) to put out of proper place. *The football player dislocated his knee and had to sit out of the game.* {dihs lə **kayt**}

dis·lodge *verb* (dislodged, dislodging, dislodges) to remove or force out of a fixed position. *He dislodged the thorn from the lion's paw. / We dislodged their team from first place.* {dihs **lŏj**}

dis·mal *adjective* full of gloom; sad. *It was a dismal day when we sold the house I grew up in.* {**dihz** məl} dismally, adv., dismalness, n.

> **Word History** *Dismal* is from *dies male*, a Latin phrase that means "evil days." In medieval Britain, two days in each month were marked on the calendar as unlucky days.

dis·man·tle *verb* (dismantled, dismantling, dismantles) to tear down; take apart. *They dismantled the circus tent in under two hours.* {dihs **măn** təl}

dis·may *verb* (dismayed, dismaying, dismays) 1. to trouble or upset the hopes of. *It dismayed her to see her best friend making fun of her.* 2. to frighten or discourage. *The doctor was dismayed by the sight of so many wounded people in need of his help.* *noun* 1. alarm, confusion, or mental distress. *We listened with dismay to the news of the flood.* 2. sudden or total loss of courage or confidence. *The losing team walked off the court in dismay.* {dihs **may**}

dis·miss *verb* (dismissed, dismissing, dismisses) 1. to send away or allow to go away. *You*

 Human Body   Human Mind   Everyday Life   History and Culture  Communication

must stay in your seats until the teacher dismisses class. 2. to remove from a job; fire. *The company dismissed twenty workers.* 3. to reject as not worth considering. *I wish she would not always dismiss my worries. / He dismissed the idea that fish could walk.* {dihs **mihs**}

dis·mount *verb* (dismounted, dismounting, dismounts) to get down from a horse or vehicle. *Jill dismounted from her bike and began pushing it up the hill.* {dihs **mownt**}

dis·o·be·di·ent *adjective* refusing to obey; naughty. *The disobedient child was punished for breaking the rules.* {dihs oh **bee** dee ihnt} disobediently, adv.

dis·o·bey *verb* (disobeyed, disobeying, disobeys) to fail or refuse to obey. *Calvin disobeyed his mother and went fishing instead of cleaning his room.* {dihs oh **bay**}

dis·or·der *noun* 1. lack of order or arrangement. *Our house is in disorder because we're moving next week.* 2. a physical or mental sickness or ailment. *She has a heart disorder that won't allow her to exercise.* *verb* (disordered, disordering, disorders) to disturb the order of. *Don't disorder the papers on the table.* {dihs **ohr** dər}

dis·or·der·ly *adjective* 1. not orderly or neat. *Books lay in disorderly piles on the desk.* 2. out of control. *Who could learn in such a disorderly class?* {dihs **ohr** dər lee} disorderliness, n.

dis·own *verb* (disowned, disowning, disowns) to refuse to have any relationship with; deny one's ownership of. *She was afraid her family would disown her if she ran away from home. / The senator dis-*

owned a speech he had given ten years before. {dihs **ohn**}

dis·patch *verb* (dispatched, dispatching, dispatches) to send off to a particular place or for a particular purpose. *He was dispatched to the gym to get a soccer ball.* *noun* a message sent with speed, such as a news bulletin. *Our commander has just received a dispatch from the general.* {dihs **păch**}

dis·pel *verb* (dispelled, dispelling, dispels) to scatter or drive away in all directions. *A brisk wind dispelled the fog.* {dihs **pehl**}

dis·pense *verb* (dispensed, dispensing, dispenses) 1. to give out in portions; distribute. *This machine dispenses candy.* 2. to carry out or put into operation. *Courts dispense justice.* {dihs **pehns**}

• **dispense with**
to do without or do away with. *Let's dispense with practice and play the game.*

dis·perse *verb* (dispersed, dispersing, disperses) 1. to drive away in all directions; scatter. *A gunshot dispersed the flock of geese.* 2. to break up and scatter. *The crowd dispersed as soon as the police arrived.* 3. to spread or distribute in a wide area. *My job was to disperse leaflets about the sale. / Birds help trees disperse their seeds.* {dihs **puhrs**}

dis·place *verb* (displaced, displacing, displaces) 1. to force out of a home territory or particular place. *They were displaced by the flood.* 2. to move out of the usual or proper place. *Did you displace the papers on my desk?* 3. to take the place of. *Computers have displaced typewriters in most offices.* {dihs **plays**}

dis·play *verb* (displayed, displaying, displays) 1. to cause

to be seen; show. *Artists display their paintings along the sidewalks of New York City.* 2. to make known; disclose. *He displayed no interest in my new invention.* *noun* 1. an act or instance of displaying. *We had never seen such a display of anger from him.* 2. anything displayed or brought forth to be seen. *We looked over the display of fine jewelry.* 3. in computers, the screen on which information is shown, or the information itself. *Please follow the instructions you see on the display.* {dihs **play**}

dis·please *verb* (displeased, displeasing, displeases) to fail to please; annoy; offend. *It displeases your father when you forget your chores. / Marlene was displeased with the photographs she took.* {dihs **pleez**} displeasingly, adv.

dis·pos·a·ble *adjective* meant to be thrown out after use. *She used disposable cups and plates for the birthday party.* {dih **spoh** zə bəl}

dis·pos·al *noun* 1. a giving away or a getting rid of something. *Safe disposal of chemicals is important for the environment.* 2. the power to control or direct someone or something. *We are at your disposal if you need us to do anything.* 3. a device for grinding garbage so that it goes down the drain. {dih **spoh** zəl}

dis·pose *verb* (disposed, disposing, disposes) to place or arrange. *She disposed the vases of flowers about the room.* {dih **spohz**}

• **dispose of**
1. to deal with; take care of. *He disposed of his homework and went out to play.* 2. to give away or get rid of. *We need to dispose of these bags of leaves.*

dis·po·si·tion ⊘ *noun* 1. a person's usual mood or attitude. *She has a sunny disposition.* 2. a tendency. *She has a disposition to argue.* {**dih** spə **zih** shən}

dis·prove *verb* (disproved, disproving, disproves) to prove to be not true or valid. *I can disprove her claim that she saw us letting the air out of her tires.* {**dihs proohv**} disprovable, adj.

dis·pute *verb* (disputed, disputing, disputes) 1. to argue or debate about. *They disputed who would get the last piece of cake.* 2. to question the value or truth of. *The player disputed the referee's call.* 3. to argue over; compete for. *The two countries have disputed this border for years.* *noun* an argument or debate. *There is some dispute among scientists about the causes of global warming.* {dihs **pyoot**}

dis·qual·i·fy *verb* (disqualified, disqualifying, disqualifies) to make not fit or qualified. *The coach disqualified her from the team for smoking.* {dihs **kwo** lih **fiy**}

dis·re·gard *verb* (disregarded, disregarding, disregards) to pay no attention to; ignore. *He disregarded his mother's advice, and look what happened.* *noun* lack of attention or respect. *She shows a complete disregard for other people's feelings.* {dihs rih **gard**}

dis·rep·u·ta·ble *adjective* having a bad reputation; not having the respect or trust of others. *That auto mechanic is said to be disreputable.* {dihs **rehp** yə tə bəl}

dis·re·spect *noun* lack of respect; rudeness. *He treats his teachers with disrespect.* *verb* (disrespected, disrespecting, disrespects) to con- sider or treat with a lack of respect. *Some of the workers disrespect the boss.* {dihs rih **spehkt**}

dis·rupt *verb* (disrupted, disrupting, disrupts) 1. to disturb or cause confusion in. *A wasp disrupted class.* 2. to interrupt or break off. *The storm disrupted our telephone service.* {dihs **ruhpt**}

Word History *Disrupt* comes from *disruptus*, a Latin word that means "break apart or split." In Latin, there is a root (or word part), *rupt*, which means "break." The English words *erupt*, which means "to break out or burst," and *rupture*, which means "to break open," also contain this root.

dis·sat·is·fac·tion *noun* the state or condition of not being satisfied, or a cause of this condition. *The crowd booed to show their dissatisfaction with the score.* {dih **să** tihs **făk** shən}

dis·sat·is·fied *adjective* not pleased; disappointed. *He was dissatisfied with his painting.* {dih **să** tihs **fiyd**}

dis·sect *verb* (dissected, dissecting, dissects) 1. to cut open or apart in order to examine. *They dissected a frog in science class.* 2. to examine closely; analyze. *The newspapers dissected the president's speech.* {diy **sehkt**}

dis·sent *verb* (dissented, dissenting, dissents) to disagree with an opinion or belief held by many others. *Six of the judges agreed she should win the contest, and two dissented.* *noun* a difference of opinion; disagreement. *There is dissent in the community over how late the nightclub should be allowed to stay open.* {dih **sehnt**}

Homophone Note Are you looking for the word *descent* (the act of going down)? *Dissent* and *descent* sound alike but have different meanings.

dis·si·dent *adjective* not agreeing with or opposed to the opinions of others or the power of some group or organization. *A group of dissident workers went on strike outside the factory.* *noun* one who disagrees or dissents. *The governments of some countries treat dissidents as criminals.* {**dihs** ə dihnt} dissidently, adv.

dis·solve *verb* (dissolved, dissolving, dissolves) 1. to mix completely with liquid. *He dissolved the medicine in water.* 2. to melt or become liquid. *The salt dissolved in the stew.* 3. to disintegrate or scatter so as to vanish. *The clouds dissolved, leaving a clear blue sky.* / 4. to end or do away with. *The musicians dissolved their rock band because they could not agree on anything.* *noun* in films and videotapes, a change of scene by having one fade while the next appears dimly and gradually grows clearer and replaces the first. {dih **zŏlv**} dissolvable, adj.

dis·tance *noun* 1. the measure of space between things, places, or points in time. *The distance from our house to the street is one hundred feet.* / *The shortest distance between two points is a straight line.* 2. an amount of space. *They walked a distance across the field and then stopped.* 3. a place far away. *We spotted a ship in the distance.* {**dihs** tihns}

 Human Body Human Mind Everyday Life History and Culture  Communication

• **keep one's distance** to stay far away or avoid getting involved. *He keeps his distance and won't speak to us.*

dis·tant *adjective* 1. far away in time or space. *My brother moved to a distant country. / In the distant past, Native Americans lived where these houses now stand.* 2. not friendly; cold. *She seemed distant when we talked.* 3. not closely related. *Lou is a distant cousin of mine.* {**dihs** tihnt} distantly, adv.

dis·taste·ful *adjective* not to one's liking; unpleasant. *I find his jokes about poor people distasteful.* {dihs **tayst** fəl} distastefully, adv.

dis·tem·per *noun* a disease that infects mostly dogs, but also cats and horses. Distemper causes fever, loss of appetite, and breathing difficulties. {dihs **tehm** pər}

dis·tinct *adjective* 1. different or set apart; separate (sometimes followed by "from"). *Her laugh is distinct from everyone else in the audience. / She divided the class into three distinct groups.* 2. clearly seen, heard, or understood; evident. *On a clear day, the mountains are distinct. / There was a distinct change in her mood.* 3. very likely. *There is a distinct possibility that she won't like him.* {dih **stingkt**} distinctness, n.

dis·tinc·tion *noun* 1. a mark or feature that makes someone or something different. *He has the distinction of being the first in his family to go to college.* 2. recognition of differences. *He makes fine distinctions in his writing.* 3. honor; excellence. *She performed with distinction. / She has written one essay of distinction and two*

that are ordinary. {dih **stingk** shən}

dis·tinc·tive *adjective* serving to set apart or mark as distinct or unusual. *The actor, John Wayne, had a distinctive way of walking.* {dih **stingk** tihv} distinctively, adv., distinctiveness, n.

dis·tin·guish *verb* (distinguished, distinguishing, distinguishes) 1. to tell apart by seeing differences (often followed by "from"). *People who are color blind often cannot distinguish red from green.* 2. to understand or point out differences (usually followed by "between"). *This historian distinguishes between just wars and unjust wars.* 3. to see or hear in a clear way. *I could not distinguish his face in the dark.* 4. to act in a way that draws special recognition or distinction. *She has distinguished herself as the best runner on the team.* {dih **sting** gwihsh} distinguishable, adj.

dis·tin·guished *adjective* 1. known for excellence; admired. *His courage and wisdom made him a distinguished leader.* 2. having a dignified appearance or manner. *The black robes make judges look distinguished.* {dihs **ting** gwihsht}

dis·tort *verb* (distorted, distorting, distorts) 1. to twist out of shape; change the way a thing looks or acts. *The ripples in the pond distorted his reflection.* 2. to make false or change the meaning of. *A good newspaper article does not distort the news. / Exaggerating and lying are two ways of distorting the truth.* {dihs **tohrt**}

dis·tract *verb* (distracted, distracting, distracts) 1. to draw away the attention of. *The radio distracted him from his work.* 2. to disturb or upset. *The sad news distracted her, and she couldn't enjoy the party.* {dihs **trăkt**}

dis·tress *noun* 1. worry, pain, or suffering, or anything that causes suffering. *Jim felt distress after his dog ran away.* 2. a state of great need or trouble. *A ship in distress radioed the coast guard.* *verb* (distressed, distressing, distresses) to cause great worry or pain to; trouble greatly. *The news that their son needed surgery distressed them.* {dihs **trehs**} distressingly, adv.

dis·trib·ute *verb* (distributed, distributing, distributes) 1. to divide into parts and give out to each of several people or groups. *The teacher distributed the tests to her students.* 2. to spread over an area; scatter. *The farmer distributed the seeds over the field.* {dih **strih** byoot}

dis·tri·bu·tion 🌎 🌐 *noun* 1. the act of distributing. *We took over distribution of the newspaper in our neighborhood.* 2. way of distributing or being distributed. *She counted the number of children in order to make an equal distribution of the cake.* {dihs trih **byoo** shən}

dis·trib·u·tive prop·er·ty *noun* in mathematics, a characteristic of numbers that allows you to multiply a group of numbers and get the same answer you would get if you multiplied each member of the group and then combined the answers. For example, 4 x (8 + 1 + 5) is equal to (4 x 8) + (4 x 1) + (4 x 5). {dih **strihb** ooh tihv **prŏp** ər tee}

a
b
c
d
e
f
g
h
i
j
k
l
m
n
o
p
q
r
s
t
u
v
w
x
y
z

dis·trict *noun* 1. an area of a country, city, or other place used for a particular purpose. *We went shopping in the business district of the city.* 2. an area that is divided so as to be controlled or managed. *We moved so that we could be in the same school district as our cousins.* {**dihs** trihkt}

District of Columbia *noun* an area on the Maryland side of the Potomac River that contains only the U.S. capital city of Washington. (abbreviation: DC) {**dihs** trihkt əv kə **luhm** bee ə}

dis·trust *verb* (distrusted, distrusting, distrusts) to lack faith or confidence in; to doubt. *We started to distrust him after he lied to us.* *noun* lack of faith or confidence; doubt or suspicion. *She has a distrust of doctors.* {dihs **truhst**}

dis·turb *verb* (disturbed, disturbing, disturbs) 1. to interrupt, especially by making noise. *The party next door disturbed our sleep.* 2. to upset or put in disorder. *The wind disturbed the surface of the pond. / The cat disturbed my papers.* 3. to make nervous or uneasy; to trouble. *It disturbed him to see his mother lying in the hospital.* {dih **stuhrb**}

dis·turb·ance *noun* 1. an act or instance of disturbing. *The police came because someone reported a disturbance.* 2. something that disturbs. *The teacher says talking in class is a disturbance she will not allow.* {dih **stuhr** bihns}

ditch *noun* a long narrow opening in the ground used to drain away or supply water. *verb* (ditched, ditching, ditches) to make an emergency landing on water. *The pilot had to ditch his plane when he ran out of fuel.* {dihch}

dit·to *noun* (dittos) the same as said or written before. *He'll have a cheese sandwich, and ditto for me.* {**diht** oh}

Word History *Ditto* is from *detto*, an Italian word that means "said before."

dive *verb* (dived or dove, diving, dives) 1. to plunge or fall downward rapidly, usually head or front first. *I dived into the pool. / The falcon dove from the sky.* 2. to plunge into an opening. *A mouse will dive into its hole if it is frightened. / His hand dived into my bag of popcorn.* 3. to practice a sport or hobby such as acrobatic diving, scuba diving, or skydiving. *I dive in the bay on weekends.* *noun* 1. a fall or plunge, usually head or front first. *His dive from the cliff into the lake was impressive.* 2. an act of sport or hobby diving. *We saw an octopus on our dive.* {diyv}

div·er *noun* 1. a person who dives into water from a board or platform. 2. a person who works under water, using special clothing and equipment for breathing. *The police sent divers to search for the missing sailors.* {**diy** vər}

di·verse *adjective* 1. made up of different kinds or sorts. *We have a diverse group of students in our class.* 2. of a different kind. *People came from diverse parts of the country to take part in the rally.* {dih **vuhrs**} diversely, adv.

di·ver·sion *noun* 1. an act or instance of turning aside. *There was a diversion of traffic because of construction on the bridge.* 2. something that turns the mind or attention away from serious matters. *Playing pinball is his favorite diversion.* {dih **vuhr** zhən}

di·ver·si·ty *noun* (diversities) 1. the state or condition of being diverse. *Because the college values diversity, it wants students of all races to apply.* 2. a variety. *We observed the diversity of plant life in the forest.* {dih **vuhr** sə tee}

di·vert *verb* (diverted, diverting, diverts) 1. to turn aside or away from something. *The police are diverting traffic because of the parade.* 2. to draw away from; distract. *A loud crash diverted my attention.* 3. to draw away from serious matters; amuse. *While his mother was gone, we diverted the baby with his favorite toys.* {dih **vuhrt**}

di·vide ❶ *verb* (divided, dividing, divides) 1. to separate into parts. *Divide this piece of paper into thirds. / The argument divided the class.* 2. to become separated into two or more parts. *The river divides into two smaller streams. / Cells reproduce by dividing.* 3. to share in equal parts. *Let's divide the pie among all of us.* 4. to separate a number into equal sets of another number by using division. *Can you divide six by two?* *noun* a ridge of land that separates two areas. *Rivers on the west of the continental divide flow into the Pacific Ocean.* {dih **viyd**}

div·i·dend *noun* 1. the number to be divided by another number in math equations. *In the equation ten divided by two equals five, ten is the dividend.* 2. a share of profits paid to those who own stock in a company or who are insur-

 Human Body   Human Mind   Everyday Life    History and Culture   Communication

ance policy owners. {**dih** və **dehnd**}

di·vine *adjective* 1. of, from, or having to do with a god or gods. *He claims to have divine wisdom. / The sailors believed that divine mercy kept the ship from going under.* 2. coming from a god or gods; holy. 3. like God or a god in power, beauty, or excellence. *Divine music flowed from her violin.* {dih **viyn**} divinely, adv.

diving board *noun* a springy board that is fixed to a stand and reaches out over water, used for diving. {**diy** ving **bohrd**}

di·vis·i·ble *adjective* able to be divided into equal parts without anything left over. *Ten is divisible by five or two.* {dih **vih** zə bəl}

di·vi·sion *noun* 1. the act of dividing or separating into parts. *The division of the country into three parts will not help keep the peace.* 2. the condition of being divided. 3. a part of a whole. *We each received a division of the money.* 4. something that separates or marks a separation. *The yellow line serves as a division between the two lanes of traffic.* 5. the arithmetic operation that finds how many times one number contains another. *We used division to find out how many nickels are in seven dollars.* 6. a unit in government, business, the military, schools, sports, and other institutions. *The company has one division for sales and one for research. / The New York Rangers are in the Atlantic Division of the National Hockey League.* {dih **vih** zhən} divisional, adj.

di·vi·sor *noun* the number in an arithmetic problem by which another number is to be divided. *In the equation fifteen divided by three equals five, three is the divisor.* {dih **viy** zər}

di·vorce *noun* the ending of a marriage as recognized by law. *verb* (divorced, divorcing, divorces) to end a marriage by law. *He wants to divorce his wife.* {dih **vohrs**}

> **Word History** *Divorce* is from a Latin word that means "to separate," "leave one's husband," or "turn aside."

diz·zy *adjective* (dizzier, dizziest) 1. having a feeling of spinning around and being about to lose one's balance. *The carnival ride made him dizzy.* 2. confused or overwhelmed. *I was dizzy with excitement.* 3. causing a giddy or confused feeling. 4. (informal) foolish or silly. *He is having another one of his dizzy ideas.* {dih zee} dizzily, adv., dizziness, n.

DJ *abbreviation* an abbreviation for **disc jockey**.

DMV *abbreviation* the government office of each state that issues drivers' licenses and makes driving regulations. DMV is an abbreviation for Department of Motor Vehicles.

DNA 🌐 *noun* a substance found in cells that contains information about the characteristics of a living thing. DNA plays a part in the passing on of characteristics from parent to offspring. DNA is an abbreviation for "deoxyribonucleic acid." {dee ehn **ay**}

do[1] *verb* (did, done, doing, does) 1. to carry out; perform. *The clown did jumping jacks. / I have already done my homework.* 2. to cause or bring about. *He did no harm.* 3. to work at. *Yesterday we did the rugs and today we'll do the windows.* 4. to form or shape. *She does sculpture.* 5. to behave or act. *Mae does exactly as she pleases.* 6. to get along. *He is doing well at school.* 7. to be good enough. *Will this shirt do, or should I put on something nicer?* *auxiliary verb* 1. used to stress the main verb. *I did knock first.* 2. used to introduce a question. *Do you want to go to the movies?* 3. used to avoid repeating a main verb. *My brother says whatever I do.* {**dooh**}

• **do away with**
1. to get rid of. *The congressman wants to do away with the speed limit in his district.* 2. to kill. *The mean old man did away with the cat.*

> **Synonyms**
> These words share a meaning with **do**, verb 1:
> complete, perform, accomplish, fulfill, execute

> **Homophone Note** The words **do**[1], **dew**, and **due** sound alike in American English but have different meanings.

do[2] *noun* (dos) the syllable that indicates the first or last tone of a musical scale. {**doh**}

Doberman pinscher *noun* a breed of dog. Doberman pinschers have short, smooth, black hair with tan markings and are used as guard dogs. {**doh** bər mən **pihn** shər}

doc·ile *adjective* obedient and easy to manage. *For my first lesson, I was given a docile pony to ride.* {**dŏs** əl} docility, n.

dock *noun* 1. a raised platform that is built out into the water, or the water between

A
B
C
D
E
F
G
H
I
J
K
L
M
N
O
P
Q
R
S
T
U
V
W
X
Y
Z

a
b
c
d
e
f
g
h
i
j
k
l
m
n
o
p
q
r
s
t
u
v
w
x
y
z

two such platforms. *The boats are tied up at the dock. / The boat floated into the dock.* 2. (often plural) a general landing area for ships. *The docks were filled with ships unloading their cargo.* 3. a raised platform used to load and unload trucks or trains. *The boxes on the dock will be loaded onto the truck. verb* (docked, docking, docks) 1. to bring to a dock or landing area. *He docked the boat and began to unload.* 2. to link with another spacecraft while out in space. *In 1975, a Russian spacecraft and an American spacecraft docked while in orbit.* {dŏk}

doc·tor 😊 ❓ *noun* 1. a person trained and licensed to treat sick people or animals. 2. a person who has received the highest degree at a college or university. {dŏk tər}

doc·trine *noun* a belief or set of beliefs held by a religion, government, or other group. *This book compares Christian doctrine with Hindu doctrine.* {dŏk trihn} doctrinal, adj.

doc·u·ment *noun* a written or printed paper that gives factual information or proof of something. Birth certificates, marriage licenses, and passports are kinds of documents. *verb* (documented, documenting, documents) to provide evidence for. *The scientist did not document his experiments, so no one believed his results.* {dŏk yə mənt}

doc·u·men·ta·ry *adjective* based on written information or evidence from an authority. *He had documentary proof that a crime was committed. noun* (documentaries) a film based on real facts and events that often has pictures of the events as they happened. {dŏk yə **mehn** tə ree}

dodge *verb* (dodged, dodging, dodges) 1. to avoid something by moving quickly aside or changing direction. *The speeding taxi dodged around the slowly moving cars.* 2. to avoid by a quick shift of position or direction. *My father taught me how to dodge a punch.* 3. to avoid by being clever or by tricking. *She dodged her chores by pretending to be ill. / The politician dodged the reporter's tough questions. noun* 1. a sudden movement or change of direction. *He made a quick dodge to the side to avoid the slap.* 2. a trick or plan to avoid having to do something difficult or to fool someone. *Pretending to be sick is a common dodge to get out of taking a test.* {dŏj}

do·do *noun* (dodoes or dodos) a large bird, now extinct, with wings so small that it could not fly. Dodos were once found on islands in the Indian Ocean. {doh doh}

doe *noun* (doe or does) an adult female deer, goat, or rabbit. Adult females of some similar animals are also called does. {doh}

Homophone Note Are you looking for the word *dough* (a mixture for making bread)? *Doe* and *dough* sound alike but have different meanings.

does *verb* a present tense of **do**[1]. *He does the dishes after dinner.* {duhz}

does·n't shortened form of "does not." *Playing ball in the house doesn't seem like a good idea.* {duh zənt}

dog 🌀 *noun* a furry animal with four legs, a pointed nose, and a tail. Their sharp teeth and claws are good for hunting small animals as food, but they also sometimes eat plants as food. Dogs are mammals, closely related to coyotes, foxes, and wolves. There are many kinds or breeds of dogs, with a wide range of sizes and appearances. Some dogs are bred for special jobs, such as herding sheep. Dogs are often kept as pets. *verb* (dogged, dogging, dogs) to follow closely or track. *My brother did not stop dogging me until I agreed to play ball with him.* {dawg}

• **lead a dog's life** to have a life that is unhappy and filled with trouble.

Dog Star *noun* the brightest star in the sky. The Dog Star is in the constellation Canis Major and is also called Sirius. {dawg star}

dog·wood *noun* a tree that has groups of small flowers surrounded by pink or white leaves that look like petals. {dawg wuud}

doi·ly *noun* (doilies) a small mat, often made of embroidered cloth, lace, or paper that looks like lace. Doilies are used to decorate or protect furniture and dishes. {doi lee}

do-it-your·self *adjective* for use by people without particular skills in building or repair. *He used a do-it-yourself book to figure out how to install cabinets.* {dooh iht yər **sehlf**}

doll *noun* a toy made to look like

 Human Body    Human Mind   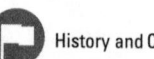 Everyday Life   History and Culture    Communication

a baby, child, or other person. {**dŏl**} dollish, adj., dollishly, adv.

Word History *Doll*, a shortened form of the name Dorothy, came to be used as a general term of affection for a person or female pet in the 1500s. By the 1700s, "doll" was used for a child's toy.

dol·lar ● *noun* 1. the main unit of money in the United States, Canada, and several other countries. One dollar is equal to one hundred cents. *This bike isn't worth five dollars.* 2. a coin or paper money worth one hundred cents. *She tore my dollar in half.* {**dŏl** ər}

dol·phin *noun* a mammal that lives in the water. Dolphins look like large fish but they breathe air. They have teeth and a snout that looks like a beak. Most kinds of dolphins live in the ocean. A few kinds live in large rivers in Asia and South America. Dolphins are closely related to porpoises and other toothed whales. {**dŏl** fihn}

do·main *noun* 1. the land owned by or under the control of a single ruler or government. *During the Second World War, Germany tried to increase its domain by invading Russia.* 2. an area of knowledge, interest, or activity. *World geography is my domain, but I do know something about history.* {doh **mayn**}

dome *noun* a rounded roof or ceiling on a room or building. {**dohm**}

do·mes·tic ● ● *adjective* 1. of or related to the home or family. *After work, he enjoys a nice, quiet domestic life.* 2. used to living with humans; tame. *Cows are domestic animals.* 3. of the country one is in; not imported. *He prefers domestic cars.* {də **meh** stihk} domestically, adv.

Word History *Domestic* comes from *domus*, the Latin word for "house." It was first used to mean "of one's own country" in 1545. The English word *dome* also comes from *domus*.

do·mes·ti·cate *verb* (domesticated, domesticating, domesticates) to tame. *It took a lot of work to domesticate the wild horse. / Cats were first domesticated thousands of years ago.* {də **meh** stə **kayt**} domestication, n.

dom·i·nant *adjective* 1. most powerful; ruling or controlling. *The British navy was dominant in the 1800s.* 2. main; primary. *Space travel was our dominant topic of discussion.* {**dŏm** ə nənt} dominantly, adv.

dom·i·nate *verb* (dominated, dominating, dominates) 1. to control by the use of power; rule. *The large country dominates the small countries that are next to it. / My older sister tries to dominate me.* 2. to rise above; tower over. *The surrounding hills dominate our city.* {**dŏm** ə **nayt**} dominator, n.

Dominican Republic *noun* a country on an island in the West Indies in the Caribbean Sea. Santo Domingo is the capital of the Dominican Republic. The Dominican Republic shares the island with the country of Haiti. {də **mih** nə kən rə **puh** blihk} Dominican, n., adj.

do·min·ion *noun* 1. the power or authority to rule or control. *At one time, the British and French fought for dominion over parts of Canada.* 2. the area that a single ruler or government controls. *Canada's dominion now extends from coast to coast.* {də **mihn** yən}

Dominion Day *noun* see **Canada Day.** {də **mihn** yən day}

dom·i·no *noun* (dominoes or dominos) 1. one of a set of small, flat game pieces shaped like rectangles, each having a different number of dots on its face. 2. (plural, but used with a singular verb) a game played with such pieces. {**dŏm** ih noh}

don *verb* (donned, donning, dons) to put on; dress oneself in. *They donned their best clothes for the wedding.* {**dŏn**}

do·nate *verb* (donated, donating, donates) to give in order to help a charity or other group. *We donated cans of food to a charity for the homeless.* {**doh** nayt or doh **nayt**} donator, n.

do·na·tion *noun* 1. the act or an instance of giving or donating. *This library depends on the donation of books.* 2. the gift or contribution thus made. *The charity received many donations this year.* {də **nay** shən}

done *verb* past participle of do[1]. *adjective* 1. cooked enough and ready to eat. *When the vegetables are done, we will have dinner.* 2. acceptable as behavior; proper; polite. *Coming to a dinner party*

A B C D E F G H I J K L M N O P Q R S T U V W X Y Z

 Living World Physical World Natural Environment Economy Government and Law

without an invitation is simply not done. {**duhn**}

• **done for**
(informal) dying or dead; near death. *When the car went off the road, she thought she was done for.*

• **done in**
(informal) very tired; worn out. *After six hours of cleaning and scrubbing, I was done in.*

don·key *noun* (donkeys) a mammal with hooves that is closely related to the horse. Donkeys are domestic asses. They are sturdy animals used for riding and carrying loads. In Mexico and the southwestern United States, they are called burros. {**dŏng** kee}

do·nor *noun* 1. one who gives, contributes, or donates something. *The charity sent a letter of thanks to each donor.* 2. one who contributes blood, tissue, or an organ for medical purposes. *The doctors have found a kidney donor for my uncle.* {**doh** nər}

don't shortened form of "do not." *I don't like fish.* {**dohnt**}

do·nut *noun* another spelling of **doughnut.** {**doh** nuht}

doo·dle *verb* (doodled, doodling, doodles) to draw or scribble without purpose. *He doodles in class when he should be taking notes.* *noun* a drawing, sketch, or scribble made without a purpose. {**dooh** dəl} doodler, n.

doom *noun* an event or end that one cannot escape; fate; destiny. *The sailors thought the storm would be their doom.*

verb (doomed, dooming, dooms) to set on a fixed course to an unhappy or bad end. *Some scientists think that a change in climate doomed the dinosaurs.* {**doohm**}

door 🔾 *noun* 1. an opening through which one enters or leaves a room or building. *He appeared at my door and said hello.* 2. the movable object that covers an entrance to a room or building. *A wreath hangs on his front door during the holidays.* 3. a way of reaching the inside of a vehicle or other closed object. *Did you close the refrigerator door?* {**dohr**}

• **out of doors**
outside of a building; in the open air. *The concert was held out of doors.*

door·bell *noun* a bell on an outside door that is rung by a person who wants to be let inside. {**dohr** behl}

door·knob *noun* a rounded handle or knob used to open and close a door. {**dohr** nŏb}

door·step *noun* a step or series of steps leading up to an outside door. {**dohr** stehp}

door·way *noun* the way of entrance into a room or building. *She walked through the doorway into the kitchen.* {**dohr** way}

dope *noun* 1. a product that is used to protect and strengthen fabric or paper, as on balloons or model airplane wings. 2. (informal) a narcotic or drug. 3. (informal) a slow, stupid person. *I felt like a dope when I noticed I'd put my socks on over my shoes.* *verb* (doped, doping, dopes) (informal) to give drugs or narcotics to. *They doped me before putting*

my dislocated shoulder back in place. {**dohp**}

dor·mant *adjective* 1. asleep or appearing to be asleep. *Bears are dormant in the winter.* 2. not active; at rest. *A dormant volcano is one that has not erupted for years.* {**dohr** mənt} dormancy, n.

dor·mi·to·ry 🔾 *noun* (dormitories) a building with many bedrooms. Many colleges have dormitories for students. {**dohr** mə tohr ee}

dor·mouse *noun* (dormice) a small mammal that sleeps during the day. Dormice are rodents that live in Europe, Asia, and Africa. Many kinds of dormice look like small squirrels. {**dohr** mows}

do·ry[1] *noun* (dories) a small, narrow boat with a flat bottom, high sides, and a sharply pointed bow. {**doh** ree}

do·ry[2] *noun* (dories) either of two fishes of the Atlantic Ocean that have narrow, flattened bodies and fins like spines. {**doh** ree}

dose *noun* an amount of medicine to be taken at one time or at certain times. *He took a dose of cold medicine before going to bed.* {**dohs**}

dot *noun* 1. a little mark or spot; speck. *His shirt has purple dots on it.* 2. a small mark made by a pencil, pen, or other pointed object. *He never remembers to put a dot over the letter "j."* 3. a decimal point or a multiplication sign. *verb* (dotted, dotting, dots) 1. to mark with a dot or dots. *He dotted the "j" of his first name.* 2. to cover with dots or something like dots. *Stars dotted the sky.*

 Human Body   Human Mind   Everyday Life   History and Culture  Communication

{dŏt}
• **on the dot**
(informal) exactly on time; punctually. *Make sure you're there at 6 o'clock on the dot.*

dote *verb* (doted, doting, dotes) to have or show too much love or affection (usually followed by "on" or "upon"). *It is silly the way she dotes on that cat.* {doht}

dou·ble *adverb* in two; in a pair. *I saw double for a minute after I hit my head.* *adjective* 1. two times as much; twice the amount or number. *I got double pay for working on Sunday. / He made a double batch of cookies.* 2. made or meant for two. *My parents have a double bed.* 3. having two equal parts. *The double doors opened onto the yard.* *noun* 1. one the same as, or nearly the same as, another. *You are your sister's double. / This car is the double of mine.* 2. anything made twice as much in size or amount. *Eight is the double of four.* 3. a hit in baseball that allows the batter to reach second base. *verb* (doubled, doubling, doubles) 1. to become twice as large. *The town's population doubles every ten years.* 2. to make twice as much or twice as great. *I doubled the recipe.* 3. to bend or to fold in two (often followed by "over"). *He doubled over the blanket before putting it away.* 4. to bend or fold (often followed by "over"). *We held our bellies and doubled over with laughter.* 5. to stand in for or replace something or someone. *Can you double for me at work next Tuesday?* 6. to hit the ball so as to reach second base safely in baseball or softball. {duh bəl}
• **on the double**
(informal) right away; imme-

diately. *Get over here on the double!*

dou·ble-cross *verb* (double-crossed, double-crossing, double-crosses) (informal) to fool or cheat by doing the opposite of what one has agreed to do. *She double-crossed me by stealing the presents she had promised to deliver to my friend.* {duh bəl kraws} double-crosser, n.

dou·ble-head·er *noun* two games held one after the other on the same day. *The Mets-Cubs double-header lasted nearly seven hours.* {duh buhl hehd ər}

doubt *verb* (doubted, doubting, doubts) 1. to not know for sure; be uncertain about the truth of. *He doubts that he passed the exam. / She began to doubt that a stork brought her baby brother.* 2. to lack trust in. *Do you doubt that he will do what he promised?* *noun* 1. a feeling of not being certain or sure. *He was filled with doubt about his ability to perform in front of an audience.* 2. a feeling of being suspicious. *His words filled her with doubt.* 3. a condition of being unsure or uncertain. *The future of the old drugstore is in doubt because few people shop there anymore.* {dowt} doubter, n., doubtingly, adv.
• **beyond the shadow of a doubt**
with complete certainty; indeed. *The lawyer proved his case beyond the shadow of a doubt.*
• **no doubt**
certainly. *He will no doubt attend the party.*

doubt·ful *adjective* 1. having or causing doubt. *He was doubtful that he would finish the race. / The evidence is doubtful.* 2. not likely; not probable. *It is doubtful that we*

will have rain today. 3. of uncertain result. *The night before the presidential election, some states were still doubtful.* {dowt fəl} doubtfully, adv., doubtfulness, n.

doubt·less *adverb* certainly. *He will doubtless graduate from college.* {dowt lihs} doubtlessly, adv.

dough *noun* 1. a thick mixture of flour or meal and a liquid such as water or milk that is prepared for baking into bread, cake, or the like. 2. (slang) money. *I want to go to the movies, but I don't have any dough.* {doh}

Homophone Note The words *dough* and *doe* (a female deer) sound alike but have different meanings.

dough·nut or **donut** *noun* a small, sweet cake shaped like a ring, that has been fried in deep fat. {doh nuht}

dove[1] *noun* 1. a type of small pigeon, or a bird like a pigeon. 2. a symbol of peace. {duhv}

dove[2] *verb* a past tense of **dive**. {dohv}

down[1] *adverb* 1. from a higher to a lower position; toward or into a lower position. *The rain came down in buckets. / She reached down to pick up the cat.* 2. to or at a lower or worse level. *Turn down the radio. / His grades have gone down.* 3. to or in a lying or sitting position. *He sat down on the couch. / Lie down and go to sleep.* 4. from a past time. *That story has been handed down in my family for generations.* 5. in writing. *It is*

a
b
c
d
e
f
g
h
i
j
k
l
m
n
o
p
q
r
s
t
u
v
w
x
y
z

wise to put your ideas down on paper. *preposition* 1. to a lower position or level. *They walked down the stairs.* 2. along; through. *We ran down the path.* *adjective* 1. unhappy; sad; discouraged. *He has been feeling down since he broke his leg.* 2. sick. *The whole family is down with the flu.* *noun* a bad period. *We have had our ups and downs.* *verb* (downed, downing, downs) 1. to knock over; cause to fall. *The wind downed a telephone pole.* 2. (informal) to beat; defeat. *Our team downed their team six to nothing.* 3. to drink quickly; gulp. *She downed a glass of juice before running to catch the bus.* {down}

down² *noun* fine, soft, fuzzy feathers. Down covers young birds. Down is also found underneath the outside feathers of some adult birds. {down}

down·cast *adjective* 1. looking downward. *The servant kept his eyes downcast when the prince spoke to him.* 2. unhappy or sad. *When the cat disappeared, the children were downcast.* {down kăst}

down·load *noun* a computer file that is sent from one computer to another. *She keeps all of her downloads in one folder.* *verb* (downloaded, downloading, downloads) to cause to send information, such as a computer file, from one computer to another. *We download songs from the Internet.* {down lohd}

down·pour *noun* a very heavy rain. *We got caught in a downpour.* {down pohr}

down·right *adjective* complete; absolute. *It's a downright shame that you have to go so soon.* *adverb* extremely; completely. *She's not just grumpy;* she's downright mean! {down riyt}

down·size *verb* (downsized, downsizing, downsizes) to reduce the size of a company or cut down the number of its workers. *My father lost his job when the company he worked for downsized.* {down siyz}

down·stairs *adverb* at, to, or on a lower floor. *I couldn't find my screwdriver in the kitchen, so I went downstairs to look in the basement.* *adjective* of a lower floor. *On Saturday we cleaned all of the downstairs rooms.* *noun* (used with a singular verb) the lower floor or floors. *The downstairs doesn't have any heat yet.* {down stayrz}

down·stream *adverb* in the direction that a stream or current is flowing. *We rowed our boat downstream.* *adjective* having to do with the part of a stream lying in the direction of the current's flow. *The hut is five miles further downstream.* {down streem}

down·town *adverb* at, to, or toward the lower part or the business area of a town or city. *We went downtown to shop for clothes.* *adjective* of or located in the lower part or the business area of a town or city. *We do most of our shopping in downtown stores.* {down town}

down·ward *adverb* toward a lower place or condition. *The ball rolled downward into the creek.* *adjective* moving or headed toward a lower place or condition. *We climbed to the top of a hill then followed a downward path to the end of the trail. / Her grades are showing a downward trend.* {down wərd} downwards, adj., adv.

dow·ry *noun* (dowries) the money or other property brought by a woman to her husband at marriage. *The bride's father offered a house, a thousand dollars, and his fattest pig as dowry.* {dowr ee}

doz. *abbreviation* an abbreviation for **dozen**, or dozens.

doze *verb* (dozed, dozing, dozes) 1. to sleep lightly or for a short time. *He dozed in the car on the ride home.* 2. to fall into a light sleep (often followed by "off"). *She was so tired that she dozed off in class.* *noun* a short, light sleep. *He took a doze on the couch.* {dohz} dozer, n.

doz·en *noun* (dozen or dozens) a group of twelve. *The dinner rolls are sold by the dozen.* *adjective* twelve. *She bought a dozen eggs.* {duh zən}

Dr. *abbreviation* 1. an abbreviation for **Doctor**. *Dr. Gibbon is my favorite doctor.* 2. an abbreviation for **Drive**.

drab *adjective* (drabber, drabbest) not bright; dull. *My gloves seem drab next to your bright ski jacket.* {drăb} drably, adv., drabness, n.

draft 🏃 👕 *noun* 1. a rough piece of writing that needs more work; sketch. *He has written a draft of his book report.* 2. a drawing, design, or plan of something to be built. *The drafts for the new building have been made.* 3. the choosing of one or more people for military duty or or for certain sports teams. *A draft has not been held in the United States since the Vietnam War.* 4. a current of air in a closed space such as a room, chimney, or stove. *The fire roared to life once we got a draft going. / The draft in this*

 Human Body   Human Mind   Everyday Life   History and Culture Communication

room is making me chilly. 5. a device that controls the flow of air in a stove or furnace. Fires need the oxygen in air in order to burn. *To start a fire, open the draft on the stove so that there is plenty of oxygen.* verb (drafted, drafting, drafts) 1. to make a sketch or rough version of. *He drafted a letter to his senator and asked me what I thought of it.* 2. to choose by draft from a group for military service or a sports team. *When the army drafted him, he reported for duty. / She was drafted by the Baltimore Comets.* adjective used for pulling heavy loads. *The cart was pulled by a draft horse.* {**drăft**}

drag verb (dragged, dragging, drags) 1. to pull along with effort; haul. *We dragged the logs up the hill.* 2. to trail behind or on the ground. *Please tie your shoelaces so they won't drag.* 3. to go or pass slowly. *Traffic often drags at this time of day. / His speech dragged on and on.* 4. to fall behind; lag. *The lame horse dragged behind the rest of the herd.* 5. to search the bottom of. *We dragged the pond for the missing bicycle.* {**drăg**}

Synonyms
These words share a meaning with *drag*, verb 3:
inch, crawl, creep

drag·on ○ noun an imaginary monster that looks like a giant lizard with wings, claws, and a long tail. In stories or pictures, dragons breathe fire and often guard a

place or treasure. {**dră** gən}

Word History *Dragon* comes from a Greek word that means "the one with the deadly glance."

drag·on·fly noun (dragonflies) a brightly colored insect with a long, narrow body. It has four long, clear wings that are held out from the body. Dragonflies live near fresh water and eat mosquitoes and other insects. {**dră** gən **fliy**}

drain verb (drained, draining, drains) 1. to remove a liquid from by means of flow through a pipe. *Should I drain the bathtub?* 2. to remove from gradually by pouring or letting flow. *She drained the antifreeze from her car radiator.* 3. to make empty by drinking the contents of. *He drained his glass in one swallow.* 4. to cause to be used up. *The exercise drained his strength.* noun 1. a device, such as a pipe, through which a liquid is drained. 2. something that slowly uses up energy, money, or some other resource. *Doctors' bills are a drain on our savings.* {**drayn**} drainer, n.
• **down the drain**
to no good purpose; wasted. *Buying this lousy bicycle was money down the drain.*

drain·age noun the act or method of draining. *The baseball field has good drainage.* {**dray** nihj}

drain·pipe noun a pipe used to drain liquids. {**drayn** piyp}

drake noun an adult male duck. {**drayk**}

dra·ma ○ noun 1. a story written so that it can be acted out for an audience; play. *We have tickets for the new drama at the children's*

theater. 2. an event or series of events that raises strong emotions or is very interesting to watch. *The night my sister ran away was filled with drama.* {**drah** mə}

dra·mat·ic adjective 1. of or having to do with drama. *The school gave a dramatic performance of the Thanksgiving story.* 2. out of the ordinary; exciting. *Spring brought a dramatic change in the weather.* {drə **mă** tihk} dramatically, adv.

dram·a·tize verb (dramatized, dramatizing, dramatizes) 1. to show or present in the form of a drama. *The play dramatized the life of George Washington.* 2. to make exciting or dramatic, sometimes by exaggerating. *She dramatizes her problems.* {**dră** mə **tiyz**}

drank verb past tense of **drink**. {**drăngk**}

drape verb (draped, draping, drapes) 1. to decorate or cover with a cloth that hangs in folds. *The tailor draped his customer with the dress material.* 2. to put down or hang in a careless or casual way. *He draped his coat over the back of the chair. / She draped her arm over the edge of the bed.* noun (often plural) a long, heavy curtain or set of curtains. *She closed the drapes to keep out the sun.* {**drayp**}

dra·per·y noun (draperies) 1. a long, heavy curtain or set of curtains. *She is hiding in the living room behind the drapery.* 2. clothing or other cloth that hangs in loose folds. *The artist laid silk drapery over his model.* {**dray** pə ree} draperied, adj.

dras·tic adjective harsh; extreme. *Quitting his job with no warning was a drastic*

A B C D E F G H I J K L M N O P Q R S T U V W X Y Z

a
b
c
d
e
f
g
h
i
j
k
l
m
n
o
p
q
r
s
t
u
v
w
x
y
z

action. {**drăs** tihk} drastically, adv.

Word History *Drastic* comes from an ancient Greek word that means "effective," or "thing to be done." In the 1600s, a strong medicine that acted with force on the body was called a "drastic." "Drastic" was first used to mean "extreme" or "severe" in the early 1800s.

draw ⊙ *verb* (drew, drawn, drawing, draws) 1. to make a picture of with a pen, pencil, or other writing tool. *She drew her house on the chalkboard.* 2. to move by pulling or dragging. *We drew the sleeping dog across the floor on a blanket.* 3. to take out or remove. *Who will draw the winning ticket from the bowl? / She drew water from the well.* 4. to cause to come near; attract. *The rock star always draws a large crowd.* 5. to move slowly in a certain direction (often followed by "near," "away," "out," "into," or "toward"). *We waved goodbye as the train drew away.* 6. to breathe in; inhale. *She drew a deep breath before diving into the pool.* 7. to pick or be dealt. *I drew three cards. noun* a game or contest that ends with both sides having the same score; tie. *The chess match was a draw.* {**draw**}

• **draw a blank**
to not be able to remember something. *I drew a blank when I tried to remember the capital of Wyoming.*

• **draw out**
to make last longer. *Our grandmother drew out the story until we all fell asleep.*

• **draw the line**
to set a limit. *He was willing to help but drew the line at cooking dinner for twelve people.*

• **draw up**
1. to prepare by putting into writing. *She drew up her will. / The architect will draw up plans for the addition.* 2. to come to a stop. *The car drew up at the hotel.*

draw·back *noun* a thing that keeps something from being good or successful; flaw. *The one drawback to having a little sister is that I can't have my own room.* {**draw** băk}

draw·bridge *noun* a bridge built so that it can be raised to allow tall ships to pass beneath or keep people from crossing over. {**draw** brihj}

draw·er *noun* a box that slides in and out of a desk, dresser, or other piece of furniture. *Desk drawers hold pens and paper, and bureau drawers hold clothes.* {**drohr**}

draw·ing *noun* 1. the act of making pictures or designs with a pen, pencil, or other writing tool. *Drawing and painting are his favorite things to do.* 2. a picture or design made by drawing. *She made a drawing in art class.* 3. the choosing of the winning ticket in a raffle, lottery, or contest. *The lottery drawing will be held on Saturday.* {**draw** ing}

drawl *verb* (drawled, drawling, drawls) to speak slowly with vowel sounds drawn out. *The southern man drawled his sentences. noun* the sounds or speech of one who drawls. *Our new neighbors speak with a Texan drawl.* {**drawl**} drawler, n, drawlingly, adv.

drawn *verb* past participle of **draw**. {**drawn**}

draw·string *noun* a cord or string that is drawn through fabric and pulled to

tighten or close an opening, as of pants, a bag, or the like. {**draw** string}

dread ❓ *verb* (dreaded, dreading, dreads) 1. to be very afraid of. *Some people dread flying.* 2. to look ahead to with worry or dislike. *She dreads the end of summer vacation. noun* great fear. *Dread of the dentist keeps me from eating sweets. adjective* causing great fear; terrifying. *Polio used to be a dread disease.* {**drehd**}

dread·ful *adjective* 1. causing great fear; terrible. *A dreadful wind last night blew over several trees.* 2. very bad; awful; no good. *That dreadful music is giving me a headache.* {**drehd** fəl} dreadfully, adv.

dread·locks *plural noun* a hairstyle in which the hair is worn in long, twisted strands. {**drehd** lŏks}

dream ❓ *noun* 1. a series of pictures or visions that a sleeping person experiences. *Last night I had a dream about flying like a bird.* 2. a strong hope or goal. *Her dream is to become a doctor.* 3. a person who is attractive or very nice. *I think her brother is a real dream. verb* (dreamed (dreamt), dreaming, dreams) 1. to have a dream or vision during sleep. *I dreamt about a magical castle last night.* 2. to imagine or think of (usually followed by "of"). *He dreamed of fame.* 3. to pass or spend by daydreaming (often followed by "away"). *He dreamed away the whole morning.* {**dreem**} dreamer,

 Human Body   Human Mind   Everyday Life History and Culture  Communication

n., dreamless, adj.

• **dream up**
to use one's imagination to create ideas or solutions. *He is always dreaming up ways to get rich.*

dreamt *verb* a past tense and past participle of **dream**. {**drehmt**}

drear·y *adjective* (drearier, dreariest) gloomy, sad, or dull. *Yesterday was a dreary winter day.* {**dreer** ee} drearily, adv., dreariness, n.

> **Word History** *Dreary* comes from an Old English word that originally meant "gory or bloody." In time, "dreary" came to mean "horrid." By the 1600s, its meaning had softened to "gloomy."

dredge *noun* a piece of equipment used to clear solid matter from the bottom of a body of water. *verb* (dredged, dredging, dredges) to gather or remove using a dredge. *They dredge the river every year.* {**drehj**}

dregs *plural noun* 1. solid matter that sinks to the bottom of drinks such as wine or coffee. 2. the part of anything that is left over or that has the least value or use. *Some people think beggars are the dregs of society.* {**drehgz**}

drench *verb* (drenched, drenching, drenches) to soak, or wet completely. *The rain drenched me before I got inside.* {**dre·hnch**}

dress ○ *noun* 1. a piece of clothing usually worn by girls or women. A dress has a top or blouse connected to a skirt. 2. clothing in general.

The performers wore the traditional dress of their country. *verb* (dressed, dressing, dresses) 1. to put clothing on. *He dresses his cat in baby clothes.* 2. to put clothes on oneself. *She dressed nicely for dinner.* 3. to decorate. *We dressed the windows with lace curtains.* 4. to clean or put a bandage on; treat. *He dressed the cut on his horse's leg.* 5. to prepare for cooking. *He dressed the turkey before roasting it.* {**drehs**}

• **dress up**
to dress in fancy or formal clothes. *Are you going to dress up for the party?*

dress·er *noun* a piece of furniture with drawers or shelves for holding clothing or other items. {**dreh** sər}

dress·ing *noun* 1. a sauce for certain foods. *He makes salad dressing out of oil and vinegar.* 2. stuffing for poultry or fish. *Mother filled the turkey with dressing.* 3. a bandage or medicine used to cover a wound. *The dressing on his burn came loose.* {**dreh** sing}

dress rehearsal *noun* the last full rehearsal of a play or other production before performance, done in full costume. {**drehs** rə **huhr** səl}

drew *verb* past tense of **draw**. {**drooh**}

drib·ble *verb* (dribbled, dribbling, dribbles) 1. to drip or flow slowly in drops. *He dribbled paint from his brush.* 2. to move along in repeated bounces, kicks, or pushes. *The basketball player dribbled the ball and then shot.* *noun* a slow flow of liquid; drip. *The water leaked from the faucet in little*

dribbles. {**drihb** əl} dribbler, n.

dried *verb* past tense and past participle of **dry**. {**driyd**}

dri·er *adjective* a comparative of **dry**. *The soil keeps getting drier and drier because we've had no rain.* {**driy** ər}

drift *noun* 1. the act of drifting. *They tied ropes to the dock to stop the drift of the boat.* 2. a mass or bank made up of drifting matter such as snow. *Our car got stuck in a snow drift.* *verb* (drifted, drifting, drifts) 1. to be carried along by an outside force, such as wind or water. *The boat drifted in the current.* 2. to wander without purpose. *He drifted from town to town.* 3. to be moved into piles. *The snow drifted in our yard.* {**drihft**}

drift·wood *noun* wood that has been left upon a beach by water or is floating on water. {**drihft wuud**}

drill *noun* 1. a tool with a shaft that has sharp cutting edges and is turned at a high speed to make holes in wood, metal, and other materials. 2. a learning or training method in which an action or item is repeated over and over. *Our class practiced multiplication drills.* *verb* (drilled, drilling, drills) 1. to produce using a drill. *The carpenter drilled a hole in the wall.* 2. to teach or train by means of having a person repeat something over and over. *His father drilled him in spelling.* {**drihl**} drillable, adj., driller, n.

A
B
C
D
E
F
G
H
I
J
K
L
M
N
O
P
Q
R
S
T
U
V
W
X
Y
Z

a
b
c
d
e
f
g
h
i
j
k
l
m
n
o
p
q
r
s
t
u
v
w
x
y
z

drink ○ *verb* (drank, drunk, drinking, drinks) 1. to take into the mouth and swallow. *I drink orange juice every morning.* 2. to swallow a liquid. *Eat, drink, and be merry.* 3. to drink alcoholic beverages. *It is dangerous to drink and then drive a car.* *noun* 1. a liquid for swallowing; a certain quantity of liquid to be swallowed. *Apple juice is my favorite drink. / Take a drink of water with that pill.* 2. an alcoholic beverage. *The neighbors invited my parents over for drinks.* {**dringk**}

drip *verb* (dripped, dripping, drips) 1. to flow downward in drops. *Water is dripping from the faucet.* 2. to let drops flow downward. *This faucet drips.* *noun* 1. the action of dripping. *The plumber fixed the drip.* 2. liquid that flows downward in drops. *A drip of white paint landed on my boot.* {**drihp**}

drive ○ *verb* (drove, driven, driving, drives) 1. to cause to move by force; push. *She drove a spike into the ground with a hammer. / The golfer drove the ball three hundred yards.* 2. to operate a car, truck, or other vehicle. *She learned to drive a truck.* 3. to travel in a car, truck or other vehicle. *We drove to the beach.* 4. to take or carry in a vehicle. *I will drive her to the theater.* 5. to cause to be in a certain condition. *He drives me crazy with his silly jokes.* *noun* 1. a trip in a car or other vehicle. *We took a drive around the lake.* 2. a forceful push. *With one last drive of the battering ram, they broke down the door of the fort.* 3. a road designed for cars and other vehicles to travel on. *Rodeo Drive in Los Angeles is famous for its expensive stores.* 4. a

strong desire; ambition. *She is talented but does not have the drive to succeed.* 5. a group effort to reach a goal, such as to raise money. *We had a drive to raise money for the field trip.* {**driyv**} drivable (driveable), *adj.*

drive-in *noun* (drive-ins) any business that serves people who drive up and are seated in their cars. *We had dinner at a drive-in restaurant. / It's convenient to go to a drive-in bank instead of getting out of the car.* {**driyv ihn**}

driv·er *noun* someone who drives. *He is a truck driver.* {**driy** vər}

drive·way *noun* a private road that leads from a street to a building such as a house or garage. {**driyv way**}

driz·zle *verb* (drizzled, drizzling, drizzles) to rain in light drops. *It is still drizzling outside but the rainstorm is over.* *noun* a light, steady rain. *It won't hurt us to walk to school in a drizzle.* {**drih** zəl} drizzly, *adj.*

drom·e·dar·y *noun* (dromedaries) a camel from northern Africa and the Middle East. Dromedaries have one hump. {**drŏm** ə **deh** ree}

drone[1] *noun* a male honeybee or other male bee whose only known function is to mate with the queen bee. {**drohn**}

drone[2] *verb* (droned, droning, drones) 1. to make a low, steady hum. *We heard the drone of the helicopter before we spotted it.* 2. to talk in a boring voice without changing one's tone. *She droned on and on about what she feeds her canary.* *noun* a low, steady hum, as of a bee or a musical instrument such

as a bagpipe. {**drohn**} droningly, *adv.*

drool *verb* (drooled, drooling, drools) to let saliva run from the mouth. *The dog drools when he is waiting to be fed.* {**droohl**}

droop *verb* (drooped, drooping, droops) to hang or sink down; bend in a limp manner. *The plant drooped for lack of water.* {**droohp**}

drop *noun* 1. a small amount of liquid, usually with a round shape. *Dew forms drops on the grass.* 2. a very small amount of anything. *I like a drop of milk in my tea.* 3. a sudden fall. *We were shaken up when the plane took a drop. / There was a drop in temperature before the storm.* 4. the distance from the top to the bottom of something. *There is a drop of twenty feet from the bridge.* 5. a decrease in amount. *The restaurant owner expects a drop in business after the holiday season.* *verb* (dropped, dropping, drops) 1. to let fall. *I dropped the plate of spaghetti. / She dropped an ice cube in her glass.* 2. to fall to a lower level. *The book will drop off the shelf if you don't move it.* 3. to fall in amount, volume or quality. *Their voices dropped when the teacher came in. / The temperature drops after sunset.* 4. to visit when not expected (followed by

222

 Human Body   Human Mind   Everyday Life   History and Culture   Communication

"in" or "by"). *We dropped by my grandparents' house.* 5. to give up or leave out. *I had to drop band practice to make time for studying.* {<u>drŏp</u>}
• **at the drop of a hat**
without much cause; easily. *My grandfather laughs at the drop of a hat.*
• **drop off**
to fall asleep.
• **drop out**
to quit; stop participating. *She dropped out of the chorus.*

drought *noun* a long period with little or no rain. *The crops were ruined by drought.* {<u>drowt</u> or <u>drowth</u>}

drove[1] *verb* past tense of **drive**. {<u>drohv</u>}

drove[2] *noun* 1. a group of animals gathered into a herd or flock and made to move along together. *The cowboys finally got the drove of cattle into the corral.* 2. (usually plural) a large number of people going or coming for a similar purpose or in a similar manner. *Droves of shoppers came to the sale.* {<u>drohv</u>}

drown *verb* (drowned, drowning, drowns) 1. to die from lack of air as the result of being under water. *A rat can swim for days before it will drown.* 2. to kill by drowning. *My sister drowned a spider by putting it in a glass of water.* {<u>drown</u>}
• **drown out**
to cover up the sound of with a louder sound. *The screams of the audience almost drowned out the music.*

drow·sy *adjective* (drowsier, drowsiest) nearly asleep; very sleepy. *He felt*

drowsy after dinner. {<u>drow</u> zee}
drowsily, adv., drowsiness, n.

Word History *Drowsy*
comes from an Old English word that means "to sink" or "become low or slow."

drudg·er·y *noun* (drudgeries) hard, boring, and unpleasant work. *My father thinks that mowing the lawn is drudgery.* {<u>druh</u> jə ree}

drug *noun* 1. a substance used to cure or heal; medicine. *The doctor gave him a special drug to help his digestion.* 2. a substance that causes a chemical change in the body and may cause addiction; narcotic. *He is trying to break his addiction to drugs.* *verb* (drugged, drugging, drugs) to give a drug to. *The veterinarian drugged the cat to lessen the pain of the operation.* {<u>druhg</u>}

drug·gist *noun* a person who has a license to prepare and sell medicine; pharmacist. {<u>druhg</u> ihst}

drug·store *noun* a store that sells medicine. Drugstores often also sell candy, cosmetics, magazines, and other things. {<u>druhg</u> stohr}

drum *noun* 1. a percussion instrument shaped like a cylinder. A drum has a hollow body covered at one or both ends by a tight material. It is played by beating with sticks or the hands. 2. a container shaped like a cylinder, such as a barrel or a machine part. *We bought a fifty-gallon drum of oil.* *verb* (drummed, drumming, drums) 1. to strike a drum. *We drummed for hours at the music festival.* 2. to hit

or tap a surface again and again. *She drums on her desk when she is nervous.* 3. to force a person to learn something by repeating it over and over. *He drummed the answers into my head.* {<u>druhm</u>}

drum major *noun* the leader of a marching band who beats time and often twirls a baton. {<u>druhm</u> may jər}

drum majorette *noun* a woman or girl who leads a marching band and often twirls a baton. {<u>druhm may</u> jə <u>reht</u>}

drum·mer *noun* a musician who plays drums. {<u>druhm</u> ər}

drum·stick *noun* 1. a stick used to play a drum. 2. the lower leg of a bird, when thought of as food. *I always ask for the drumstick when we have turkey for dinner.* {<u>druhm</u> stihk}

drunk *adjective* (drunker, drunkest) having had too much alcohol to drink; intoxicated. *It is against the law to drive when you are drunk.* *noun* a person who often drinks too much alcohol. *He can't keep a job*

A
B
C
D
E
F
G
H
I
J
K
L
M
N
O
P
Q
R
S
T
U
V
W
X
Y
Z

because he's a drunk. *verb* past participle of **drink**. {drungk}

dry *adjective* (drier or dryer, driest or dryest) 1. not wet, damp, or moist. *The clothes are dry after hanging in the sun.* 2. having little or no rain. *This year we had a dry summer.* 3. not in or under water or other liquid. *Most snakes live on dry land.* 4. thirsty. *We were very dry after the long walk.* 5. not interesting; boring. *Our history book was very dry. verb* (dried, drying, dries) 1. to make or cause to be dry. *Be sure to dry your hair before you go outdoors.* 2. to become dry. *We dried off in the sun after swimming. / This fabric dries quickly.* {driy}

dry cell *noun* an electric battery cell in which the chemicals are stored as a paste that will not spill. {driy sehl}

dry-clean *verb* (dry-cleaned, dry-cleaning, dry-cleans) to clean using chemicals other than water. *This suit must be dry-cleaned because water will ruin the material.* {driy kleen} dry cleaner, n.

dry·er 🌐 ⊙ *noun* a machine used for drying something. *Mom put my wet laundry into the dryer. / I always use a hair dryer after I wash my hair.* {driy ər}

du·al *adjective* of or having two parts; double. *Brushing your teeth has the dual purpose of cleaning your teeth and freshening your breath.* {doohl or dooh əl} duality, n., dually, adv.

Homophone Note The words *dual* and *duel* sound alike but have different meanings. To find out what these two words have in common, look up *duel.*

duch·ess *noun* 1. a woman who is married to or the widow of a duke. 2. a woman who has title and power equal to those of a duke. {duhch ihs}

duck[1] *noun* 1. a bird that lives in or near water and has webbed feet for swimming and a large flat bill. 2. a female duck. The male is often called a drake. {duhk}

During hunting season the smart **duck** knows just when to **duck**.

duck[2] *verb* (ducked, ducking, ducks) 1. to lower the head or whole body quickly to avoid something. *I ducked, and the snowball missed me. / He ducked behind a bush so that no one would see him.* 2. to lower into water quickly and for a short time. *She ducked her dog in the pond.* 3. to avoid something. *Josie never ducked her chores even when she wanted to.* {duhk}

duck·ling *noun* a young duck. {duhk ling}

duct *noun* a pipe or tube that carries air or liquid. *Hot air flows through heating ducts to warm the building.* {duhkt}

dud *noun* (informal) something that does not work well or fails in some way. *Try the pen*

before you pay for it so that you don't get a dud. {duhd}

Word History *Dud* comes from *dudde*, an early English word that means "cloak" or "mantle." How did the word's meaning change from "cloak" to "something that does not work well"? By the 1500s, "dud" had the meaning "ragged clothing." In the 1800s, it was used for "a person in ragged clothing." Then, in the early 1900s, people began to use "dud" as a word for a useless person or thing. During World War One, a shell that did not explode was a "dud." Since then, its meaning has widened to include any bad item in a batch.

dude *noun* 1. a person visiting a western U.S. ranch who is from the city or does not know much about ranch life. 2. (slang) any man or boy. *Hey, dude, let's go to the movies.* {doohd}

due *adjective* 1. owed as a debt. *The payment for your new bike is due.* 2. supposed to arrive; expected. *He is due here any minute. / Her baby is due in January. / The assignment is due tomorrow.* 3. deserved; proper. *They helped the old man to his seat with due care. noun* 1. that which is expected, deserved or owed. *Give him his due for all his help.* 2. (plural) the fee paid by a member of a club. *He hasn't paid his dues. adverb* straight; directly. *The ship sailed due north.* {dooh}

Homophone Note The words *due, do*[1], and *dew* sound alike in American English but have different meanings.

du·el *noun* a formal, arranged fight between two people using guns or swords. *verb* (dueled, dueling, duels) to fight a duel. {doohl or dooh əl,

 Human Body 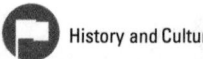 Human Mind Everyday Life  History and Culture Communication

n., <u>doohl</u> or <u>dooh</u> əl, v.} dueler, n.

Homophone Note The words *duel* and *dual* (double) sound alike but have different meanings.

du·et *noun* a piece of music written for or performed by two players or singers. {dooh <u>eht</u>}

dug *verb* past tense and past participle of **dig**. {<u>duhg</u>}

dug·out *noun* 1. a hole in the ground used as a shelter for protection from storms or bombs. 2. an area with benches on which baseball players can sit during a game when they are not on the playing field. 3. a boat or canoe made by hollowing out a tree trunk. {<u>duhg</u> owt}

duke *noun* a nobleman with the highest rank below a prince. {<u>doohk</u>}

dull *adjective* (duller, dullest) 1. not having a sharp cutting edge. *You cannot slice a tomato with a dull knife.* 2. not interesting or lively; boring. *She fell asleep halfway through the principal's dull speech.* 3. not smart; slow to learn. *He expects all athletes to be dull.* 4. not felt in a sharp way. *The nurse asked whether the pain in his side was dull or sharp.* *verb* (dulled, dulling, dulls) to become or cause to become dull. *He dulled the knife by cutting wood with it.* {<u>duhl</u>} dullness, n.

dumb *adjective* (dumber, dumbest) 1. not having the power of speech; without a voice. *Helen Keller became blind, deaf, and dumb after a childhood illness. / Animals are dumb creatures.* 2. not smart; stupid. *It was a dumb idea to cut your own hair.* 3. silent because of fear or shock. *When he realized he was on*

television, *he was struck dumb.* {<u>duhm</u>}

dumb·bell *noun* a short bar with a heavy weight at each end. Dumbbells are used to develop muscles. {<u>duhm</u> behl}

dum·my *noun* (dummies) 1. an object made to look like another object. *The baby plays with a rubber dummy of a hammer.* 2. such an object representing a human body. *They tackle a dummy in football practice.* 3. (informal) a stupid person. *I know he's not a dummy because he does well in school.* {<u>duhm</u> ee}

dump *verb* (dumped, dumping, dumps) 1. to drop in one big load. *He dumped the newspapers in the recycling can.* 2. to empty or unload by tipping or turning over. *Please dump the spoiled milk down the drain.* *noun* a place for unloading trash and garbage. *We took our trash to the town dump.* {<u>duhmp</u>}

dunce *noun* a stupid, foolish, or ignorant person. *I felt like a dunce for getting that easy question wrong on the test.* {<u>duhns</u>}

dune ● *noun* a mound or hill of sand built up by the action of wind. {<u>doohn</u>}

dung *noun* the manure of animals. {<u>dung</u>}

dun·ga·ree *noun* 1. a heavy cotton fabric; blue denim. 2. (plural) pants made of this

cloth; blue jeans. {<u>dung</u> gə <u>ree</u>}

Word History *Dungaree* comes from a Hindi word that means "coarse cotton cloth."

dun·geon *noun* a dark, damp, underground jail. *The king ordered that his enemies be thrown into the dungeon of the palace.* {<u>duhn</u> jən}

dunk *verb* (dunked, dunking, dunks) 1. to dip in a liquid. *She dunks her cookies in milk.* 2. to push forcefully through a basketball hoop from above. *He dunked the ball and won the game.* {<u>dungk</u>}

du·pli·cate *noun* something that is an exact copy of something else. *Make me a duplicate of that letter for our office records.* *verb* (duplicated, duplicating, duplicates) 1. to copy exactly. *He duplicated the dancer's steps.* 2. to do again in the same way; repeat. *I'll bet you can't duplicate your first dive.* *adjective* made exactly alike. *They wore duplicate shirts.* {<u>dooh</u> plə kiht, n., <u>dooh</u> plə kiht, adj., <u>dooh</u> plə **kayt**, v.}

• in duplicate in two exact copies. *Fill out this form in duplicate.*

du·ra·ble *adjective* not easily broken or worn out; lasting; sturdy. *He bought durable furniture for the kids' room. / Tires are made of a durable material.* {<u>doohr</u> ə bəl} durability, n.

du·ra·tion *noun* the length of time during which something goes on. *We stayed for the duration of the concert.* {də <u>ray</u> shən}

dur·ing *preposition* 1. throughout the entire time of. *During the summer she does not go to school.* 2. at some time in the course of. *She*

A
B
C
D
E
F
G
H
I
J
K
L
M
N
O
P
Q
R
S
T
U
V
W
X
Y
Z

a
b
c
d
e
f
g
h
i
j
k
l
m
n
o
p
q
r
s
t
u
v
w
x
y
z

arrived during the night. {<u>doohr</u> ing}

dusk *noun* the time of day just before night; last moments of twilight. *The park closes at dusk.* {<u>duhsk</u>}

dust *noun* tiny, dry pieces of soil, dirt, or other material. *The dust collected in the corners of the room. verb* (dusted, dusting, dusts) 1. to clean or wipe dust from. *Please dust the shelves.* 2. to cover with dust or powder. *We dusted the cake with sugar. / The gymnast dusted her hands with chalk.* {<u>duhst</u>}

dust·y *adjective* (dustier, dustiest) 1. full of or covered with dust. *Every corner of the old house was dusty.* 2. like dust; powdery. *The soil gets dry and dusty in the summer.* {<u>duh</u> stee} dustiness, n.

Dutch *adjective* of or having to do with the Netherlands, or its people or language. *noun* 1. (used with a plural verb) the people of the Netherlands. 2. the language of the Netherlands. {<u>duhch</u>}
• **go Dutch** (informal) to go on an outing or order a meal, with each person paying his or her own share.

du·ti·ful *adjective* doing what is expected or required. *Dutiful children go to bed without a lot of fuss when they are asked to.* {<u>dooh</u> tih fəl} dutifully, adv.

du·ty ⊕ ◉ *noun* (duties) 1. something that a person should do because it is right or fair; responsibility. *It is his duty to tell the judge the whole truth.* 2. the things a person must do in a particular job or position. *His duties as class president include making a speech.* 3. a tax on goods brought into or taken out of a country. {<u>dooh</u> tee}

dwarf *noun* (dwarfs or dwarves) 1. a person who is much smaller than usual. 2. a plant or animal that is much smaller than usual. 3. a small, ugly, and oddly shaped little man in fairy tales and legends. Dwarfs have magical powers. *verb* (dwarfed, dwarfing, dwarfs) to cause to appear small by being huge in comparison. *The new skyscraper dwarfed the buildings around it.* {<u>dwohrf</u>}

dwell *verb* (dwelt or dwelled, dwelling, dwells) 1. to have one's home in; live or stay in. *He dwells in the mountains.* 2. to think, write, or speak about over and over again for a long time (often followed by "on" or "upon"). *He dwelled upon his mother's death. / You must not dwell upon your mistakes.* {<u>dwehl</u>} dweller, n.

dwell·ing *noun* a place where a person lives; home; house. *This tiny cottage has been their dwelling for years.* {<u>dweh</u> ling}

dwin·dle *verb* (dwindled, dwindling, dwindles) to become or cause to become gradually smaller or less until almost nothing remains; shrink. *The crowd dwindled. / Our savings dwindled away.* {<u>dwihn</u> dəl}

dye *noun* a substance that is used to give color to cloth, hair, or other materials. *verb* (dyed, dyeing, dyes) to color or stain by soaking in dye. *She dyed her hair red.* {<u>diy</u>}

Homophone Note The words *dye* and *die* sound alike but have different meanings.

dy·ing *adjective* close to death; losing life. *A dying bird lay beneath the tree.* {<u>diy</u> ing}

dy·nam·ic *adjective* full of energy and strength; lively; active.

He is a dynamic actor. {<u>diy</u> <u>năm</u> ihk} dynamically, adv.

Word History *Dynamic* comes from *dynamikos*, an ancient Greek word that means "powerful."

dy·na·mite *noun* a strong explosive. Dynamite has many uses, including blasting through rock to make roads, tunnels, and mines. *Dynamite was invented by Alfred Nobel. verb* (dynamited, dynamiting, dynamites) to blow up, blast holes in, or destroy by using dynamite. *They dynamited a tunnel through the mountain. adjective* (informal) wonderful; outstanding. {<u>diy</u> nə <u>miyt</u>}

dy·na·mo *noun* (dynamos) a machine that produces electric current. {<u>diy</u> nə <u>moh</u>}

dy·nas·ty *noun* (dynasties) a series of rulers from the same family or group. {<u>diy</u> nə stee} dynastic, adj.

 Human Body   Human Mind   ⊕ Everyday Life   ⊡ History and Culture   Communication

Ee

E is a vowel that makes several different sounds.

Tips to help you look up words starting with e: Sometimes vowels sound similar to each other. If you can't find the word you're looking for under E, it may start with a, i, o, or u.

Also look under H for words (such as herb) that start with a silent h.

Some words that start with the "ee" sound are spelled "ea," such as "each" or "easel."

These words may be hard to look up if you don't already know how to spell them:

earn	exhaustion
eight	exhibition
enough	eye

e or **E** *noun* (e's or E's) 1. the fifth letter of the English alphabet. 2. the third note in the musical scale of C major. {<u>ee</u>}

E *abbreviation* an abbreviation for **east**.

e- *prefix* a prefix that means "from," or "out of." *To eject a tape is to push it out of a tape recorder.*

each *adjective* every one of two or more. *The clown had a ball in each hand. pronoun* every one of a group considered as individuals. *Many children came to the party, and each brought a gift. adverb* for, to, or from each one; apiece. *They gave us a dollar each.* {<u>eech</u>}

ea·ger *adjective* wanting very much. *We were eager for the game to start.* {<u>ee</u> gər} eagerly, adv., eagerness, n.

ea·gle *noun* a large bird with a strong, curved beak and very good eyesight. Eagles hunt and eat small animals and fish. They are related to hawks but are usually larger. {<u>ee</u> gəl}

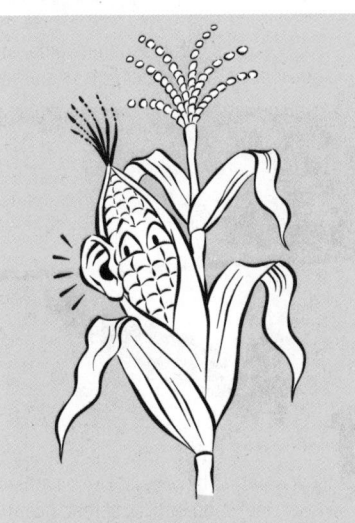

A very sensitive **ear** of corn can hear the farmer coming from a mile away.

ear[1] 🔊 *noun* 1. the organ of hearing in people and some other animals. 2. sense of hearing. *When her shouts reached our ears, we ran in the direction of the sound.* 3. an ability to hear sounds clearly and accurately. *He has a good ear for music.* {<u>eer</u>}

• **in one ear and out the other**
heard, but with little or no attention paid. *He made the same mistakes over again, as if everything I told him went in one ear and out the other.*

ear[2] 🔊 *noun* the part of the corn plant and certain other plants that bears seeds. {<u>eer</u>}

ear·ache *noun* a pain inside the ear. {<u>eer</u> ayk}

ear·drum *noun* the part of the middle ear that receives sounds. The eardrum vibrates when sound waves reach it. {<u>eer</u> druhm}

earl *noun* a British nobleman of a particular rank. {<u>uhrl</u>}

ear·lobe *noun* the soft lower part of the ear. {<u>eer</u> lohb}

ear·ly *adverb* (earlier, earliest) 1. in the first part of something; near the beginning of something. *To be back by noon, we should start our hike early in the morning.* 2. before the usual or expected time. *She arrived early to school, so she had time to clean out her locker before class. adjective* (earlier, earliest) 1. of or happening in the first part of. *Crocuses appear in early spring.* 2. before the usual or expected time. *We had an early dinner on Sunday.* {<u>uhr</u> lee}

ear·muffs *plural noun* a pair of coverings worn over the ears to protect against cold. {<u>eer</u> muhfs}

earn *verb* (earned, earning, earns) 1. to receive as pay for work done. *We earn fifty cents an hour for babysitting.* 2. to get or deserve because of hard work or good behavior.

A B C D E F G H I J K L M N O P Q R S T U V W X Y Z

 Living World   Physical World Natural Environment  Economy   Government and Law

a
b
c
d
e
f
g
h
i
j
k
l
m
n
o
p
q
r
s
t
u
v
w
x
y
z

They must earn his respect. {**uhrn**}

Homophone Note The words *earn* and *urn* (a vase or pot) sound alike but have different meanings.

ear·nest *adjective* having or showing a serious manner. *The President is always earnest when giving a speech.* {**uhr** nihst} earnestly, adv.

earn·ing *noun* 1. (plural) money received as pay; wages. *His earnings doubled at his new job.* 2. (plural) the profits from a business. *The earnings from his bicycle repair business were higher than he expected.* {**uhr** ning}

ear·phone *noun* a small speaker that fits on or in the ear for listening to sound from a radio, tape player, telephone, or other electronic machine. {**eer** fohn}

ear·ring *noun* a piece of jewelry worn on the earlobe. {**eer** ring}

earth 🜨 🌍 *noun* 1. (often capitalized) the fifth largest planet in our solar system and the third in distance from the sun. 2. all of the people who live on Earth. *Earth hopes for peace.* 3. the outer layer of the planet; ground. *When the wind stopped, the kite fell to the earth.* 4. soil or dirt. *The mole left a pile of earth by his hole.* {**uhrth**}

earth·en *adjective* 1. made up of earth, soil, or dirt. *My great-grandmother grew up in a house with an earthen floor.* 2. made of clay. *They found an earthen pot in the ruins of the ancient city.* {**uhr** thən}

earth·ly *adjective* (earthlier, earthliest) 1. having to do with the earth; of this world. *We earthly creatures like to imagine the world of fairies and*

Earth and Its Natural Disasters

ozone layer | stratosphere
— crust
mantle
core

Earthquakes occur where Earth's plates move past, under, or away from each other in a process called "plate tectonics".

Volcanos erupt when magma, or molten rock, pushes up from under Earth's surface.

Floods are caused by very heavy rain or exceptionally high tides. Human actions have added to their number and size.

Forest fires are caused by lightning, but some are started by people. Dry weather and strong wind can make forest fires spread over thousand of acres.

Tornados, hurricanes, and squalls can destroy buildings and cause floods and landslides.

 Human Body
 Human Mind
 Everyday Life
 History and Culture
 Communication

elves. 2. possible; that can be imagined. *There is no earthly reason why he should fail.* {<u>uhrth</u> lee}

earth·quake 🌐 *noun* a shaking or other movement of part of the earth's surface. It is caused by movement deep within the earth. Earthquakes can cause the ground to split. {<u>uhrth</u> kwayk}

earth·worm *noun* a long worm made up of many segments that loosens the soil by making tunnels. {<u>uhrth</u> wuhrm}

ease *noun* 1. freedom from pain, worry, or hard work. *She is having a month of ease after working so hard.* 2. skill that makes something seem not difficult. *He speaks Spanish with ease.* *verb* (eased, easing, eases) 1. to free from pain, worry, or trouble. *Her phone call eased my mind.* 2. to move carefully and slowly. *He eased himself into his seat.* {<u>eez</u>}

• **at ease**
a standing position in the military. When at ease, soldiers may relax but must stay in place and cannot talk.

ea·sel *noun* a stand for holding an artist's canvas, blackboard, or sign. {<u>ee</u> zəl}

eas·i·ly *adverb* 1. without effort, pain, or trouble. *He is moving more easily now that his ankle has healed.* / *We work easily together.* 2. without doubt; certainly. *He is easily the best dancer.* {<u>ee</u> zə lee}

east *noun* 1. the direction in front of a person facing the rising sun. 2. one of the four major points of direction on the compass. The east is directly opposite the west. 3. (often capital) the eastern part of a country or area. *He's from the East.* 4. (capital) the Orient; the Near East; the Far East. *These spices come from the East.* *adjective* 1. from, of, or in the east. *There's an east wind blowing.* 2. toward or facing the east. *I walked in the east gate.* *adverb* from, in, or toward the east. *I've been driving east.* {<u>eest</u>}

East·er *noun* a Christian holiday to celebrate that Jesus Christ returned to life after he died. Easter is held every spring on the Sunday after the first full moon between March 21 and April 25. {<u>eest</u> ər}

east·er·ly *adverb or adjective* 1. of or toward the east. *He headed off in an easterly direction.* / *The path runs easterly for five miles.* 2. blowing from the east. *The captain says we need a strong easterly wind to reach our destination.* *noun* (easterlies) a storm or wind from the east. *They almost lost their ship in the easterly.* {<u>eest</u> ər lee}

east·ern *adjective* 1. in, to, from, or having to do with the east. *We travelled in the eastern part of Europe.* 2. (capitalized) Asian. *He is studying Eastern religions.* {<u>eest</u> ərn}

east·ern·er *noun* (often capitalized) a person living in an eastern area or region. *People who live on the east coast of the United States are Easterners.* {<u>eest</u> ər nər}

Eastern Hemisphere *noun* the half of the earth that contains Europe, Africa, Asia, and Australia. {<u>eest</u> ərn <u>hehm</u> ihs <u>feer</u>}

East Germany *noun* a country in north central Europe from 1949 until 1990. East Germany and West Germany are now one country again, officially called the Federal Republic of Germany. East Germany was also called the German Democratic Republic. {<u>eest</u> <u>juhr</u> mə nee} East German, [n.], adj.

East Indies *noun* a group of islands southeast of Asia that includes Indonesia; East India. {<u>eest</u> <u>ihn</u> deez} East Indian, n., adj.

east·ward *adverb* toward the east. *We traveled eastward.* *adjective* in, at, facing, or moving toward the east. *Take the eastward path.* {<u>eest</u> wərd} eastwards, adv.

eas·y *adjective* (easier, easiest) 1. not hard or difficult. *The lazy girl wanted an easy job.* / *She helped her younger brother find an easy book.* 2. without trouble or worry. *He leads an easy life.* 3. not harsh or strict. *Many students like the easy teachers best.* 4. not in a hurry; not rushed. *The horse trotted at an easy pace.* {<u>ee</u> zee}

eat ⏱ 🍎 *verb* (ate, eaten, eating, eats) 1. to put into the mouth, chew, and swallow. *We will eat soup and sandwiches for lunch.* 2. to destroy through wearing away. *Rust eats metal.* 3. to use up. *One trip to the comic book store ate his entire allowance.* 4. to bother or disturb. *What's eating them?* {<u>eet</u>} eater, n.

• **eat one's words**
to take back what one has said. *I will eat my words if I turn out to be wrong.*

eave *noun* (usually plural) the lower part of a roof that hangs out beyond the wall of a building. {<u>eev</u>}

eaves·drop *verb* (eavesdropped, eavesdropping, eavesdrops)

a
b
c
d
e
f
g
h
i
j
k
l
m
n
o
p
q
r
s
t
u
v
w
x
y
z

to listen to other people talk without letting them know. *I eavesdropped from behind the door and heard what she said about me.* {**eevz** drŏp} eavesdropper, n.

Word History *Eavesdrop* comes from an Old English word that means "the area around a house where water drops from the eaves (the lower part of the roof)." A person who stands in such a spot is close enough to the house to listen to what is being said inside.

ebb *noun* the flowing of the tide away from the land to the sea; ebb tide. *Many shells were exposed on the beach by the ebb of the tide. verb* (ebbed, ebbing, ebbs) 1. to flow away from land; recede. *The tide ebbed under the setting sun.* 2. to weaken or become less; decay. *As a person grows old, strength gradually ebbs.* {**ehb**}

eb·on·y *noun* (ebonies) 1. a hard black wood that comes from tropical Asian trees. 2. a tree that produces this wood. 3. a deep shiny black color. {**ehb** ə nee}

ec·cen·tric ❓ *adjective* not behaving or thinking in an ordinary or accepted way; odd; peculiar. *They called her eccentric for having her five poodles dyed the colors of the rainbow. noun* a person having or showing odd behavior, ideas, or interests. *My uncle was an eccentric who decorated his front yard with large sculptures of penguins.* {**ehk** **sehn** trihk}

ech·o *noun* (echoes) the repeating of a sound caused by the bouncing of sound waves from a surface. *I heard the echo of my footsteps in the empty hallway. verb* (echoed, echoing, echoes) 1. to pro-

duce an echo. *The sound of running horses echoed in the canyon.* 2. to be filled with echoes. *The canyon echoed with the sound of tourists.* 3. to repeat or imitate. *She echoes whatever he says.* {**ehk** oh}

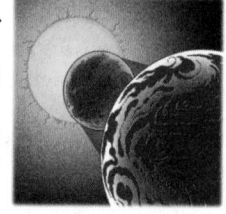

e·clipse ☀ *noun* the blocking from view of the sun, a moon, or a planet by another heavenly body. In an eclipse of the sun, the sun is hidden from earth's view by the moon passing between the sun and the earth. *verb* (eclipsed, eclipsing, eclipses) 1. to bring about a darkening or an eclipse of. *The moon eclipsed the sun.* 2. to cause to be less important; surpass. *The new hockey star has eclipsed the other players.* {ih **klihps**}

Word History *Eclipse* comes from *ekleipsis,* a Greek word that means "to leave its usual place."

e·col·o·gy 🌐 *noun* the scientific study of the relationships between living things and their environments. {ih **kŏl** ə jee} ecological, adj., ecologically, adv., ecologist, n.

e·co·nom·ic *adjective* having to do with a money system. *The board met to discuss the school's economic situation.* {eek ə **nŏm** ihk *or* ehk ə **nŏm** ihk}

e·co·nom·i·cal *adjective* using only a small amount; without waste; frugal. *This house is very economical and uses little fuel to heat it.* {eek ə **nŏm** ih kəl *or* ehk ə **nŏm** ih kəl}

e·co·nom·ics *noun* (used with a singular verb) the study of how goods and services are produced and distributed. {eek ə **nŏm** ihks *or* ehk ə **nŏm** ihks}

e·con·o·mize *verb* (economized, economizing, economizes) to spend less money; lower expenses; be economical. *If we economize this winter, we can afford to take a vacation next summer.* {ih **kŏn** ə **miyz**}

e·con·o·my *noun* (economies) 1. the careful use of money, resources, and means of production. *She praised his economy in running the business.* 2. the way a certain place or region uses and distributes its money. *The American economy hasn't been stable this year.* {ih **kŏn** ə mee}

ec·o·sys·tem 🌐 *noun* a community of living things, together with their environment. *A pond is an interesting ecosystem to study.* {**ehk** oh sihs təm}

ec·ru *noun* a pale yellowish or grayish tan color. Ecru is the color of old lace. {**eh** krooh *or* **ay** krooh}

ec·sta·sy *noun* (ecstasies) a feeling of great pleasure or joy. *He was in ecstasy at the wonderful concert.* {**ehk** stə see}

Ec·ua·dor *noun* a country in western South America on the Pacific coast. Quito is the capital of Ecuador. {**ehk** wə dohr} Ecuadoran, n., adj., Ecuadorian, adj., n.

-ed *suffix* 1. a suffix used to form the past tense of regular verbs. *"He jumped" means*

 Human Body   Human Mind   Everyday Life   History and Culture    Communication

that he made a jump in the past but he is not jumping now. 2. a suffix used to form adjectives that relate to a particular verb. *Parked cars are cars that people have parked.*

ed·dy *noun* (eddies) a small current of water, air, fog, or dust that spins against the main current. *The toy sailboat became caught in an eddy in the stream. verb* (eddied, eddying, eddies) to move or turn in circles or eddies. *The river water eddied behind the fallen log.* {**eh** dee}

E·den *noun* 1. the garden where the first humans lived, according to the Old Testament in the Bible; Garden of Eden. 2. any delightful place or condition; paradise. {**ee** dən}

edge *noun* 1. a line where two surfaces meet. *Be sure to paint all the way to the edges of the box. / A cube has twelve edges.* 2. the border or outside line. *We saw a deer at the edge of the forest.* 3. the cutting side of a knife blade or other sharp tool. *We keep the edges of the scissors sharp.* 4. lead; advantage. *He has an edge on me in this game. verb* (edged, edging, edges) 1. to put trim or a border on. *She edged the skirt with ribbon.* 2. to move forward slowly or with care. *The children edged toward the clowns.* {**ehj**}
• **on edge**
nervous or anxious; full of worry. *The movie was so scary we were on edge the whole time.*

edge·wise *adverb* 1. with the edge forward or outward. *A dollar bill fits edgewise through the slot of a soda machine.* 2. with the side of the body forward; sideways. *We had to move edgewise through the* narrow opening. {**ehj** wiyz} edgeways, adv.

edg·y *adjective* (edgier, edgiest) nervous or impatient; on edge. *He is edgy about giving a speech tonight.* {**ehj** ee}

ed·i·ble *adjective* able to be eaten as food; safe. *Those wild plants are edible.* {**ehd** ə bəl}

ed·it *verb* (edited, editing, edits) to correct, cut, add to, or change with the goal of producing a finished piece of writing or a film. *I need to edit my essay before it is ready to hand in. / The actor worried that the film editor would edit his scenes out of the movie.* {**ehd** iht}

e·di·tion *noun* 1. one of a series of printings of the same published work. *This second edition of this book is much better than the first.* 2. the form in which a particular work or set of works is printed. *I gave my grandfather the large-print edition of the book.* {ə **dih** shən}

ed·i·tor *noun* 1. a person who reads and corrects materials for publication. *The editor made few changes in the author's new book.* 2. a person who writes editorials for a newspaper or magazine. *In his weekly column, the editor praised the mayor for her actions.* {**ehd** ih tər}

ed·i·to·ri·al *noun* an article in a newspaper, or a statement on television, that gives an opinion or point of view. *The editorial found fault with the new law. adjective* having to do with an editor or what an editor does. *I would like to do editorial work for an art magazine.* {eh dih **tohr** ee əl}

ed·u·cate *verb* (educated, educating, educates) to provide knowledge, training, and guidance to. *The coach educated us on the rules of soccer.* {**ehj** ə kayt}

ed·u·ca·tion *noun* 1. the act or work of learning or training. *Reading is an important part of education.* 2. the knowledge a person gets through learning. *A high school education is needed for most jobs.* {ehj ə **kay** shən}

ed·u·ca·tion·al *adjective* 1. having to do with education. *There was a meeting to discuss the educational system of the city.* 2. giving knowledge or skill. *They are going on an educational trip to Washington.* {ehj ə **kay** shə nəl}

eel *noun* (eel or eels) a long fish that looks like a snake. Eels live in fresh water or salt water. {**eel**}

ee·rie *adjective* (eerier, eeriest) mysterious and frightening; weird. *He heard eerie laughter in the dark forest.* {**eer** ee} eeri-ness, n.

ef·fect *noun* 1. something produced by a cause. *The effect of the snow storm was a day off from school.* 2. ability to bring about a result. *A day at the beach has the effect of calming me.* 3. the state of being in force. *The new rules go into effect tomorrow. verb* (effected, effecting, effects) to bring into operation; cause to happen. *He worked to effect change in local government.* {ih **fehkt**}
• **in effect**
in active operation. *That law is no longer in effect.*
• **take effect**
to start operating; start to work. *The new fee on late books takes effect today.*

ef·fec·tive *adjective* 1. able to make happen or change something. *That was an effective way to get the work done.* 2. in operation. *This rule is effective immediately.* {ih **fehk** tihv} effectively, adv., effectiveness, n.

A B C D E F G H I J K L M N O P Q R S T U V W X Y Z

a
b
c
d
e
f
g
h
i
j
k
l
m
n
o
p
q
r
s
t
u
v
w
x
y
z

ef·fi·cient *adjective* operating or working in a way that gets results, with little wasted effort. *He is an efficient worker.* {ih **fihsh** ənt} efficiently, adv.

ef·flu·ent *noun* sewage or other liquid waste that flows into a body of water such as a river or lake. *Many fish and plants in the lake were killed by the effluent that spilled from the broken sewage pipes.* {**ehf** looh ihnt}

ef·fort *noun* 1. the action of physical or mental energy. *It took great effort to move all that furniture.* 2. a hard try; attempt. *Let's make an effort to finish painting the house this week.* {**ehf** ərt}

Word History *Effort* comes from an early French word that means "to force oneself."

egg¹ 🌐 🥚 ⭕ *noun* 1. a cell in a female animal or in some kinds of plants that can develop into a new individual after it is fertilized. 2. a round or oval object that contains a young bird, reptile, insect, or other animal. Each egg includes food to help the developing animal grow. Bird and reptile eggs have shells. Some kinds of eggs are used as food by people and other animals. {**ehg**}

Egging on his rival to cross the road, the **egg** shouted, "What are you, a chicken?"

egg² *verb* (egged, egging, eggs) to urge or encourage to act (usually followed by "on"). *He climbed the tree while his friends egged him on.* {**ehg**}

egg·plant *noun* a plant grown for its dark purple, oval fruit. Eggplant is eaten as a vegetable. {**ehg** plănt}

e·go·cen·tric *adjective* concerned with oneself. *It's egocentric to never think of others.* {ee goh **sehn** trihk}

e·gret *noun* a kind of heron that is usually white and grows a long plume of feathers in breeding season. There are several kinds of egrets. {**ee** griht}

E·gypt *noun* a country in North Africa on the Mediterranean and Red Seas. Egypt is also called the Arab Republic of Egypt. Cairo is the capital of Egypt. {**ee** jihpt}

E·gyp·tian *adjective* of or having to do with Egypt or its people. *They wrote an article on Egyptian history.* *noun* 1. a person who was born in or is a citizen of Egypt. 2. the language of ancient Egypt. {ih **jihp** shən}

eight *noun* the number that comes after 7 and before 9 in the sequence of cardinal numbers; 8. *adjective* being eight in number. *There are eight rooms in that building.* {**ayt**}

Homophone Note The words *eight* and *ate* (past tense of "eat") sound alike but have different meanings.

eight·een *noun* the number that comes after 17 and before 19

in the sequence of cardinal numbers; 18. *adjective* being eighteen in number. *My sister has eighteen pairs of shoes.* {**ay** teen}

eight·eenth *adjective* coming next after the seventeenth in a series. *The eighteenth point won the football game.* *noun* 1. one of eighteen equal parts of a whole; 1/18. *Only an eighteenth of the people in town voted for him.* 2. the number, person, or thing that comes next after the seventeenth in a series. *The eighteenth was the best book in the series.* {**ay** teenth}

eighth *adjective* coming next after the seventh in a series. *My house is the eighth one down from the corner.* *noun* 1. one of eight equal parts of a whole; 1/8. *There's an eighth of a tank of fuel left in the plane.* 2. the number, person, or thing that comes next after the seventh in a series. *I think the eighth is the prettiest kitten I've seen.* {**aytth** or **ayth**, n., **aytth** or **ayth**, adj.}

eight·i·eth *adjective* coming next after the seventy-ninth in a series. *She won the basketball game by scoring the eightieth point.* *noun* 1. one of eighty equal parts of a whole; 1/80. *If each student does an eightieth of the work, we'll have it done in no time.* 2. the number, person, or thing that comes next after the seventy-ninth in a series. *There was no better birthday than her eightieth.* {**ay** tee ihth}

eight·y *noun* (eighties) the number that is equal to eight times ten; 80. *adjective* being eighty in number. *I have a collection of eighty records.* {**ay** tee}

ei·ther *adjective* 1. one or the other of two. *You may choose either the pie or the cake.* 2.

 Human Body   ❓ Human Mind   👕 Everyday Life   🚩 History and Culture   📞 Communication

A B C D **E** F G H I J K L M N O P Q R S T U V W X Y Z

each of two. *There are pillows on either side of the bed.* *pronoun* one or the other. *I don't want either.* *conjunction* used to show a choice (followed by "or"). *You can either go or stay.* *adverb* also; likewise. *If you don't want dessert, I don't either.* {ee thər}

e·ject *verb* (ejected, ejecting, ejects) 1. to throw out with force. *He ejected the noisy kids from the library.* 2. to throw or propel oneself out of a plane in an emergency. *The pilot ejected from the fighter plane when the engine failed.* {ih **jehkt**}

e·lab·o·rate *adjective* planned or carried out with great care and attention to details. *He made up an elaborate game for us to play.* *verb* (elaborated, elaborating, elaborates) to add details to something; explain more fully (often followed by "on" or "upon"). *Elaborate on your ideas for building a new library.* {ih **lăb** ə **rayt**} elaborately, adv.

e·lapse *verb* (elapsed, elapsing, elapses) to go or slip by; pass or come to an end. *Weeks elapsed before we heard from her.* {ih **lăps**}

e·las·tic *adjective* able to return to its original form after being stretched or squeezed. *Rubber bands are elastic.* *noun* a fabric that can be stretched but will go back to its original shape. {ih **lă** stihk}

el·bow *noun* 1. the bend or joint between the upper arm and the lower arm. 2. anything shaped or bent like this joint. *There is an elbow in the river.* / *She used an elbow to connect the two pipes.* *verb* (elbowed, elbowing, elbows) to push at or away, with or as with one's elbow. *He elbowed me aside and walked past.* {**ehl** boh}
• **rub elbows with**

mingle or mix with. *We rubbed elbows with movie stars at the award ceremony.*

Word History *Elbow* was formed from two Old English words: *ell* means "length of the forearm" and *boga* means "to bend."

eld·er *adjective* born earlier; older. *The elder sister slept on the top bunk, and the younger on the bottom.* *noun* an older person. *She was taught to respect her elders.* {**ehl** dər}

eld·er·ly *adjective* old or aging. *Elderly people often enjoy visiting their grandchildren.* {**ehl** dər lee}

eld·est *adjective* born first; oldest. *She is the eldest child of three.* {**ehl** dihst}

e·lect *verb* (elected, electing, elects) 1. to choose by means of voting. *They elected her as president.* 2. to choose or decide. *He elected to speak rather than to stay silent.* {ih **lehkt**}

e·lec·tion 🌐 *noun* the process of choosing a person for office by voting. *In the United States, the election of the President takes place every four years.* {ih **lehk** shən}

e·lec·tric *adjective* 1. of or having to do with electricity. *From cars to computers, we use electric current to make our lives easier.* 2. working by or giving off electricity. *I like playing with my electric train set.* / *Electric eels are fish that give mild shocks.* 3. exciting; thrilling. *The singer's performance was electric.* {ih **lehk** trihk}

e·lec·tri·cal *adjective* having to do with electricity; electric. *The television, refrigerator,*

and microwave oven are three electrical devices in my house. {ih **lehk** trih kəl} electrically, adv.

e·lec·tri·cian *noun* one whose job is to install or repair electrical equipment. *An electrician will wire your new house for electricity.* {ih lehk **trih** shən}

e·lec·tric·i·ty 🌐 *noun* 1. energy caused by the movement of electrons through matter. *Lightning is a natural form of electricity.* 2. electrical current. *The television needs electricity in order to work.* 3. a state of tension or excitement. *When the game became tied you could feel the electricity in the crowd.* {ih **lehk** **trih** sih tee}

Word History *Electricity* is from an ancient Greek word that means "produced by amber." The Greek word was in existence many centuries before electricity was discovered. Why did the discoverers of electricity choose such an old word for something so new? Amber is tree resin that has hardened over centuries. When it is rubbed, amber produces static electricity and attracts light objects. The ancient Greeks observed this characteristic of amber and had a word for it, without knowing what caused it.

e·lec·tro·cute *verb* (electrocuted, electrocuting, electrocutes) to kill by electricity. *The prisoner was electrocuted for committing murder.* / *She was electrocuted by lightning while walking during a storm.* {ih **lehk** trə **kyoot**} electrocution, n.

e·lec·trode *noun* a part of an electric or electronic device. *An electrode allows electric current to enter or leave a device such as a battery.* {ih **lehk** trohd}

a
b
c
d
e
f
g
h
i
j
k
l
m
n
o
p
q
r
s
t
u
v
w
x
y
z

e·lec·tro·mag·net *noun* an iron or steel core with wire wound around it. It becomes magnetic when an electric current is passed through the wire. {ih lehk troh **măg** nət}

e·lec·tron *noun* a very small particle that moves outside the nucleus of an atom. Electrons have a negative charge. {ih **ehk** trŏn}

e·lec·tron·ic *adjective* 1. having to do with electronics. *I am reading an electronic book.* 2. having to do with electrons. *The physicist is studying electronic motion.* {ih lehk **tro** nihk} electronically, adv.

electronic mail *noun* a written message sent between people from a computer in one location to a computer in another location; e-mail. {ih lehk tro nihk **mayl**}

e·lec·tron·ics *noun* (used with a singular verb) the science that is concerned with the flow of electrons and their uses. {ih lehk **tro** nihks}

el·e·gant *adjective* fine or rich in quality. *They stayed at an elegant hotel.* {ehl ə gənt} elegantly, adv.

el·e·ment *noun* 1. a part of any whole. *One element of this recipe is missing.* 2. a comfortable or natural position to be in. *When he paints, he is in his element.* 3. (plural) the weather; forces of nature. *He survived the elements during his winter camping trip.* 4. any of the 107 substances that cannot be separated into simpler substances by using chemistry. Lead, gold, and oxygen are examples of elements. {**ehl** ə mənt}

el·e·men·ta·ry *adjective* having to do with the most basic or simplest parts of something. *Learning the alphabet is an elementary step to reading and writing.* {ehl ə **mehn** tə ree *or* ehl ə **mehn** tree}

elementary school *noun* a school for the first six to eight years of a child's education. {ehl ə **mehn** tə ree skoohl *or* ehl lə **mehn** tree skoohl}

el·e·phant *noun* an enormous mammal with a very long nose called a trunk. Elephants have curved tusks, huge, floppy ears, and four long, thick legs. Elephants use their trunks to pick up food, drink water, or lift things. They use their tusks to dig roots. Elephants travel in herds, eating tons of plants every day. African elephants are the largest mammals that live on land. Indian elephants are smaller and can be trained to work with people. {ehl ə fənt}

Word History *Elephant* comes from a Greek word that means "ivory beast."

el·e·vate *verb* (elevated, elevating, elevates) to raise or lift up to a higher physical position. *Members of the team elevated their star player onto their shoulders.* {ehl ə **vayt**}

el·e·va·tion *noun* 1. the height to which something rises or is raised, or its height above sea level or ground level. *Those houses would be safe during a flood, because they are at a high elevation.* 2. the act of raising, or the condition of being raised. *The elevation of the roof for the new house took three days.* {ehl ə **vay** shən}

el·e·va·tor *noun* 1. a platform or small room used to raise and lower people or goods from one level or floor to another in a building. 2. a grain storage building used to lift and pour out grain; grain elevator. {ehl ə **vay** tər}

e·lev·en *noun* the number that comes after 10 and before 12 in the sequence of cardinal numbers; 11. *adjective* being eleven in number. *There are eleven students in my art club.* {ih **leh** vən}

e·lev·enth *adjective* coming next after the tenth in a series. *We won the eleventh game of the season. noun* 1. one of eleven equal parts of a whole; 1/11. *There's only an eleventh of the formula left in the bottle.* 2. the number, person, or thing that comes next after the tenth in a series. *What do you have planned for the eleventh?* {ih **leh** vənth}

elf *noun* (elves) an imaginary, small creature that looks like a human and has magical powers. {**ehlf**}

el·i·gi·ble *adjective* qualified for something; in a position to be chosen. *Only kids under twelve years old are eligible to enter the contest.* {**eh** lih jə bəl}

e·lim·i·nate *verb* (eliminated, eliminating, eliminates) 1. to get rid of or destroy. *He is trying to eliminate weeds from his garden.* 2. to decide to leave out; remove from the set of choices. *Because he cheated, the judges eliminated him from the contest.* {ə **lih** mih nayt}

 Human Body   Human Mind  Everyday Life History and Culture  Communication

elk *noun* (elks or elk) 1. a large deer found in northern Europe and Asia. It has large antlers shaped like a palm with spread fingers. In North America the same kind of animal is called a moose. 2. a large deer found in North America that has large, spreading antlers. This kind of deer is sometimes called American elk or wapiti. {**ehlk**}

el·lipse *noun* a shape that looks like a flattened circle; oval. {ih **lihps**}

elm *noun* a large shade tree with spreading branches. {**ehlm**}

e·lope *verb* (eloped, eloping, elopes) to run away and marry in secret. *They eloped because their parents did not approve of their marriage.* {ih **lohp**}

el·o·quent *adjective* using words well, in a way that others enjoy hearing or reading. *The crowd applauded loudly after her eloquent speech.* {**ehl** ə kwihnt} eloquently, adv.

El Salvador *noun* a country in Central America on the Pacific coast. San Salvador is the capital of El Salvador. {ehl **săl** və dohr} Salvadoran, n., adj.

else *adjective* 1. different; other. *Talk to someone else, not to me.* 2. in addition; more; further. *Can you do anything else today?* *adverb* 1. in another place, time, or way; in addition. *Tell me where else you would like to go. / How else would I know if you didn't tell me?* 2. otherwise; if not. *Hurry up or else you will be late.* {**ehls**}

• **or else** or you will be sorry. *Give me what you stole, or else.*

else·where *adverb* in or to another place; somewhere else. *I'll go elsewhere so I won't disturb you while you work.* {**ehls** wayr}

e·lude *verb* (eluded, eluding, eludes) to get away from or avoid by speed or skill. *I tried to catch the dog, but he eluded me.* {ih **loohd**}

> **Homophone Note** Are you looking for the word *allude* (to mention)? *Elude* and *allude* sound alike but have different meanings.

e·lu·sive *adjective* hard to find or catch. *For seven weeks, the sheriff searched the hills for the elusive outlaw.* {ih **looh** sihv}

elves *noun* plural of **elf**. {**ehlvz**}

e·mail or **email** 🌐 🌐 *noun* 1. the practice of sending written messages from one computer to another; electronic mail. 2. a written message sent from one computer to another; electronic mail. *verb* (e-mailed, e-mailing, e-mails) 1. to send a message to by computer. *I e-mailed my friend to let her know that I was coming for a visit.* 2. to send by computer. *Jane and John e-mailed pictures of their new baby to everyone in the family.* {ee **mayl**}

e·man·ci·pate *verb* (emancipated, emancipating, emancipates) to free from slavery or other control. *The prisoner was emancipated when they found he was not guilty.* {ə **măn** sə payt} emancipative, adj., emancipator, n.

em·bank·ment *noun* a mound of earth or stone made to support a road or protect an area from water. {ehm **băngk** mənt}

em·bar·go *noun* (embargoes) 1. a government order that restricts trade or the shipment of goods. *An embargo was placed on the buying and selling of products made from elephant tusks.* 2. a government order that forbids ships to move in or out of its ports. *The embargo prevented us from sailing to their country.* {ehm **bar** goh}

em·bark *verb* (embarked, embarking, embarks) 1. to board a ship when beginning a trip. *We embarked from New York Harbor.* 2. to set out on or begin something (usually followed by "on"). *We embarked on a trip down the Amazon.* {ehm **bark**}

em·bar·rass *verb* (embarrassed, embarrassing, embarrasses) to make uncomfortable or ill at ease. *My silly behavior embarrassed my sister.* {ehm **bar** ihs}

em·bar·rass·ment 💬 *noun* 1. the condition of being made uncomfortable or ashamed. *It was an embarrassment to have forgotten her birthday gift.* 2. something that causes shame, shyness, or discomfort. *His loud friends are an embarrassment to him.* {ehm **bar** ihs mənt}

em·bas·sy 🌐 *noun* (embassies) 1. an ambassador and his or her staff. 2. the building where an ambassador lives and works. {**ehm** bə see}

em·bed or **imbed** *verb* (embedded or imbedded, embedding or imbedding, embeds or imbeds) to set firmly in some surrounding

A
B
C
D
E
F
G
H
I
J
K
L
M
N
O
P
Q
R
S
T
U
V
W
X
Y
Z

Periodic Table of the Elements

The periodic table shows all of the chemical elements.
Each element has its own box in the periodic table.
The following information about each element is given in its box:

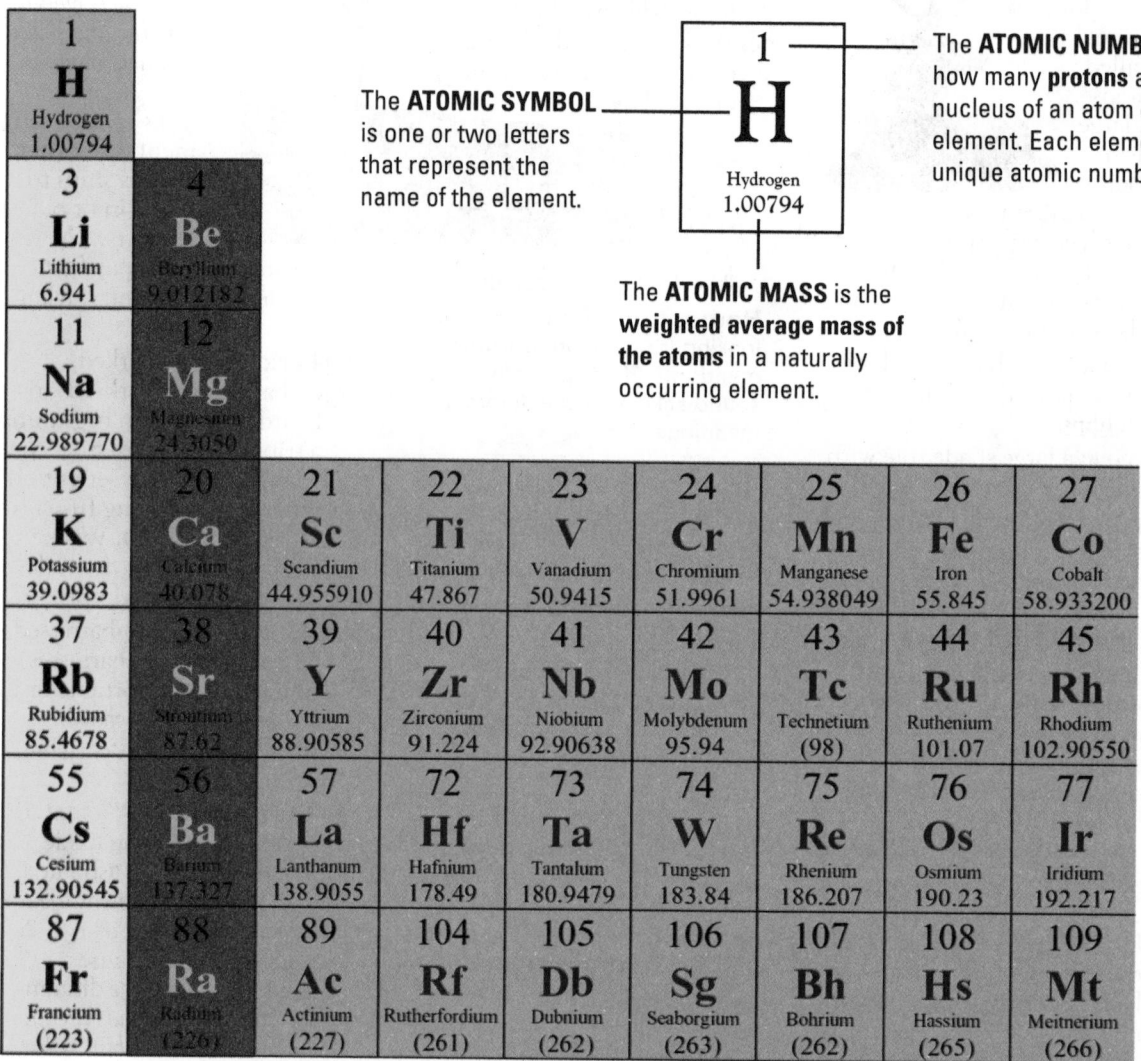

The **ATOMIC SYMBOL** is one or two letters that represent the name of the element.

The **ATOMIC NUMBER** shows how many **protons** are in the nucleus of an atom of this element. Each element has a unique atomic number.

The **ATOMIC MASS** is the **weighted average mass of the atoms** in a naturally occurring element.

1 H Hydrogen 1.00794								
3 Li Lithium 6.941	4 Be Beryllium 9.012182							
11 Na Sodium 22.989770	12 Mg Magnesium 24.3050							
19 K Potassium 39.0983	20 Ca Calcium 40.078	21 Sc Scandium 44.955910	22 Ti Titanium 47.867	23 V Vanadium 50.9415	24 Cr Chromium 51.9961	25 Mn Manganese 54.938049	26 Fe Iron 55.845	27 Co Cobalt 58.933200
37 Rb Rubidium 85.4678	38 Sr Strontium 87.62	39 Y Yttrium 88.90585	40 Zr Zirconium 91.224	41 Nb Niobium 92.90638	42 Mo Molybdenum 95.94	43 Tc Technetium (98)	44 Ru Ruthenium 101.07	45 Rh Rhodium 102.90550
55 Cs Cesium 132.90545	56 Ba Barium 137.327	57 La Lanthanum 138.9055	72 Hf Hafnium 178.49	73 Ta Tantalum 180.9479	74 W Tungsten 183.84	75 Re Rhenium 186.207	76 Os Osmium 190.23	77 Ir Iridium 192.217
87 Fr Francium (223)	88 Ra Radium (226)	89 Ac Actinium (227)	104 Rf Rutherfordium (261)	105 Db Dubnium (262)	106 Sg Seaborgium (263)	107 Bh Bohrium (262)	108 Hs Hassium (265)	109 Mt Meitnerium (266)

Elements 58 to 71 (**lanthanides**) are the **rare earth elements**.

Elements 90 to 103 (**actinides**) are **radioactive rare earth elements**.

58 Ce Cerium 140.116	59 Pr Praseodymium 140.90765	60 Nd Neodymium 144.24	61 Pm Promethium (145)	62 Sm Samarium 150.36
90 Th Thorium 232.0381	91 Pa Protactinium 231.03588	92 U Uranium 238.0289	93 Np Neptunium (237)	94 Pu Plutonium (244)

The elements are arranged in order of increasing atomic number. The element with the lowest atomic number (hydrogen) is in the upper left, and the element with the highest atomic number (Lawrencium) is in the lower right. The horizontal rows of the periodic chart are called "periods."

The elements are arranged in such a way that **similar elements are grouped together.** The groupings are based on how the elements react with other elements. The groupings are shown as vertical columns. For example, the column on the far right contains the "noble gases." The elements in this group all occur naturally as gases, and they do not combine easily with other elements. The largest group of elements is the metals. All metals have these characteristics in common: they conduct electricity, they can be pulled into wire or hammered into thin sheets (ductility and malleability), and they have a shiny appearance.

						2 **He** Helium 4.003
5 **B** Boron 10.811	6 **C** Carbon 12.0107	7 **N** Nitrogen 14.00674	8 **O** Oxygen 15.9994	9 **F** Fluorine 18.9984032		10 **Ne** Neon 20.1797
13 **Al** Aluminum 26.981538	14 **Si** Silicon 28.0855	15 **P** Phosphorus 30.973761	16 **S** Sulfur 32.066	17 **Cl** Chlorine 35.4527		18 **Ar** Argon 39.948

28 **Ni** Nickel 58.6934	29 **Cu** Copper 63.546	30 **Zn** Zinc 65.39	31 **Ga** Gallium 69.723	32 **Ge** Germanium 72.61	33 **As** Arsenic 74.92160	34 **Se** Selenium 78.96	35 **Br** Bromine 79.904	36 **Kr** Krypton 83.80
46 **Pd** Palladium 106.42	47 **Ag** Silver 107.8682	48 **Cd** Cadmium 112.411	49 **In** Indium 114.818	50 **Sn** Tin 118.710	51 **Sb** Antimony 121.760	52 **Te** Tellurium 127.60	53 **I** Iodine 126.90447	54 **Xe** Xenon 131.29
78 **Pt** Platinum 195.078	79 **Au** Gold 196.96655	80 **Hg** Mercury 200.59	81 **Tl** Thallium 204.3833	82 **Pb** Lead 207.2	83 **Bi** Bismuth 208.98038	84 **Po** Polonium (209)	85 **At** Astatine (210)	86 **Rn** Radon (222)

63 **Eu** Europium 151.964	64 **Gd** Gadolinium 157.25	65 **Tb** Terbium 158.92534	66 **Dy** Dysprosium 162.50	67 **Ho** Holmium 164.93032	68 **Er** Erbium 167.26	69 **Tm** Thulium 168.93421	70 **Yb** Ytterbium 173.04	71 **Lu** Lutetium 174.967
95 **Am** Americium (243)	96 **Cm** Curium (247)	97 **Bk** Berkelium (247)	98 **Cf** Californium (251)	99 **Es** Einsteinium (252)	100 **Fm** Fermium (257)	101 **Md** Mendelevium (258)	102 **No** Nobelium (259)	103 **Lr** Lawrencium (262)

The first periodic chart was made by Dimitri Mendeleev, a Russian scientist, in 1869. It was later revised by Henry Moseley, a British scientist.

material. *We embedded the new plants in the soil.* {ehm **behd**}

em·ber *noun* a small piece of glowing wood or coal in a dying fire. {ehm bər}

em·bez·zle *verb* (embezzled, embezzling, embezzles) to steal what was put in one's care. *The vice-president embezzled the money from the bank and left the country.* {ehm **behz** zl} embezzlement, n., embezzler, n.

em·blem *noun* an object that stands for something; symbol. *A heart is an emblem of love.* {ehm bləm}

em·bod·y *verb* (embodied, embodying, embodies) to put in a form that can be seen; make real. *Her book embodies ideas about freedom and truth.* {ehm **bo** dee}

em·boss *verb* (embossed, embossing, embosses) 1. to raise or represent in relief (a surface design). 2. to decorate the surface of with a raised design. *They embossed the ring with gold flowers.* {ehm **baws**}

em·brace *verb* (embraced, embracing, embraces) 1. to hold closely in one's arms; hug. *I embraced my father before I got on the bus.* 2. to take up or accept easily. *I embraced the chance to go to Europe.* *noun* an act or instance of holding someone closely in one's arms; hug. *His embrace comforted me.* {ehm **brays**}

em·broi·der *verb* (embroidered, embroidering, embroiders) 1. to make or decorate with needlework. *Mother embroidered the sleeves of my wedding gown.* 2. to add made up details to a story. *He embroi-*

dered the story of his trip to Alaska. {ehm **broi** dər}

em·broi·der·y *noun* (embroideries) the art or result of sewing designs on cloth; needlework. {ehm **broi** də ree}

em·bry·o 🏃⚡ *noun* (embryos) an animal or plant that is just starting to develop. An embryo grows inside an egg, a seed, or its mother. {ehm bree yoh}

em·er·ald *noun* 1. a clear green stone that is used in jewelry. 2. a rich dark or yellowish green color. {ehm rəld *or* **eh** mər əld}

e·merge *verb* (emerged, emerging, emerges) 1. to rise up from or come into view. *A shape emerged from the mist.* 2. to become known or clear. *Eventually the truth about the stolen money will emerge.* {ih **muhrj**}

e·mer·gen·cy 🏃❓ *noun* (emergencies) a serious situation or sudden crisis that calls for fast action. *The flooding created an emergency for many families living along the river.* {ih **muhr** jən see}

em·er·y *noun* a powder made from a hard mineral. It is used for grinding and polishing. {ehm ə ree}

em·i·grant *noun* one who leaves a country to live in another. *My grandparents were emigrants from eastern Europe.* {ehm ə grənt}

em·i·grate *verb* (emigrated, emigrating, emigrates) to leave one country or region in order to settle in another.

Her parents emigrated from Germany to escape from the Nazis. {ehm ə grayt}

em·i·nent *adjective* standing above others in fame or achievement; outstanding. *She is an eminent scientist.* {ehm ə nənt}

e·mit *verb* (emitted, emitting, emits) 1. to send out or give off. *The freshly baked loaves emitted warmth.* 2. to give voice to. *He emitted a yelp of surprise when I dropped ice down the back of his shirt.* {ih **miht**}

e·mot·i·con *noun* (from emotion icon) a small icon made of punctuation characters and letters that is placed in an e-mail; smiley. *An emoticon shows the mood of the writer, such as :-(and :-D* {ih **moh** tih kŏn}

e·mo·tion ❓ *noun* 1. a strong feeling such as joy, hatred, sorrow, or fear. Emotion includes physical changes such as an increase in pulse, crying, or trembling. 2. a state or condition that is marked by such a feeling or response. *The story of how her parents met always filled her with emotion.* {ih **moh** shən}

Word History *Emotion* is from *exmovere*, a Latin word that means "to move out from" or "stir up." When a person's feelings are stirred up, the feelings seem to move out from inside them. The expression of emotion through sounds, movements, or words, is a way that feelings move from our insides to the outside.

e·mo·tion·al *adjective* 1. having to do with strong feeling or emotion. *Caring for a pet can have emotional benefits.* 2. easily moved to feel; tending to experience emotion. *She was an emotional girl, who*

🏃 Human Body   ❓ Human Mind   👕 Everyday Life   🚩 History and Culture   📞 Communication

often cried during the sad parts of movies. 3. able to stir emotions. *It was an emotional film.* {ih **moh** shə nəl} emotionally, adv.

em·per·or *noun* the male ruler of an empire. {**ehm** pə rər}

em·pha·sis *noun* (emphases) 1. special importance attached to something. *She puts so much emphasis on the way her clothes look.* 2. attention given to a particular word, phrase, or idea. *The president's speech put emphasis on world peace.* {**ehm** fə sihs}

em·pha·size *verb* (emphasized, emphasizing, emphasizes) to give particular attention to; stress. *Your essay emphasizes only the bad side of having a little brother.* {**ehm** fə **siyz**}

em·pire *noun* a group of nations or peoples under one ruler or government. *The Roman empire included lands throughout the Mediterranean world.* {**ehm piyr**}

em·ploy *verb* (employed, employing, employs) 1. to make use of; use. *She employed a drill to make the hole.* 2. to provide work for or get services from in exchange for payment; hire. *We employed a plumber to fix the drain.* {ehm **ploi**}

em·ploy·ee ☁ *noun* someone who works for a person or business in return for pay. {ehm **ploi** ee *or* ehm ploi **ee**}

em·ploy·er *noun* a person or business that pays others to work. *Her employer owns stores around the country.* {ehm **ploi** ər}

em·ploy·ment *noun* 1. an instance or act of employing. *Employment of more workers will allow us*

to finish the job on time. 2. the condition of being employed. *His employment at that store lasted six years.* 3. work done for pay; job. *Her employment as an engineer was interesting.* {ehm **ploi** mənt}

em·press *noun* 1. the female ruler of an empire. 2. the wife of an emperor. {**ehm** prihs}

emp·ty *adjective* (emptier, emptiest) 1. holding or containing nothing; without the usual contents. *Please recycle the empty boxes.* 2. not occupied or used by people; vacant. *The house will be empty while we are on vacation.* 3. without purpose, activity, or meaning. *His life seemed empty after he retired.* *verb* (emptied, emptying, empties) 1. to remove what is inside of; make empty. *Empty the garbage can.* 2. to move or transfer. *Please empty the bowl of peas into the pan.* 3. to become empty. *The classroom emptied as soon as the bell rang.* 4. to flow or pour (often followed by "out", "into", or "onto"). *The river empties into the lake.* {**ehmp** tee} emptiness, n.

Word History *Empty* is from *aemetig,* an Old English word that means "rest" or "leisure." When truly at rest, you are emptied of worry or concern.

e·mu *noun* a large bird with long legs that runs very fast but cannot fly. Emus live in Australia. {**ee** myoo}

en·a·ble *verb* (enabled, enabling, enables) to give means or power to; make able; allow. *The light enables*

me to see better. / *This ticket enables you to swim here.* {eh **nay** bəl}

en·act *verb* (enacted, enacting, enacts) 1. to make into a law. *Congress enacted a bill to protect the water supply.* 2. to act out or act the part of in a play. *They will enact a scene from a famous play.* {eh **năkt**}

e·nam·el *noun* 1. a smooth, shiny coating baked onto metal, glass, or pottery. Enamel is used for protection or decoration. 2. paint, polish, or varnish that makes a smooth, shiny surface. 3. the hard, shiny covering of a tooth. *verb* (enameled, enameling, enamels) to coat with enamel; apply enamel to. *He enameled the ceramic pot so that it could hold water.* {ih **năm** əl}

-ence *suffix* 1. a suffix that means "condition" or "quality." *A country that has won its independence is an independent country.* / *A person who has confidence is confident.* 2. a suffix that means "an action" or "result of an action." *Violence happens when a person is acting violent.*

en·chant *verb* (enchanted, enchanting, enchants) 1. to put under a magic spell; bewitch. *The magician enchanted the prince and turned him into a frog.* 2. to charm and delight. *His music enchants us.* {ehn **chănt**}

en·chant·ing *adjective* very likeable; charming; enjoyable. *We had an enchanting weekend at the lake.* {ehn **chăn** ting}

en·chant·ment *noun* a magic charm or spell; an instance of casting a spell. *The enchantment of the princess was sup-*

A B C D E F G H I J K L M N O P Q R S T U V W X Y Z

a b c d **e** f g h i j k l m n o p q r s t u v w x y z

posed to last one hundred years. {ehn **chănt** mənt}

en·cir·cle *verb* (encircled, encircling, encircles) to form a circle around; surround. *Houses encircle the lake.* {ehn **suhr** kəl}

en·close *verb* (enclosed, enclosing, encloses) 1. to close in or shut in with walls or a container. *They enclosed their back yard with a fence.* 2. to include inside or with. *She enclosed a letter in the package.* {ehn **klohz**}

Synonyms
These words share a meaning with *enclose*, verb 1:
confine, encompass, envelop

en·clo·sure *noun* 1. a space that is surrounded, or something that surrounds. *They keep their dogs in an enclosure. / The carpenters are making an enclosure for the yard.* 2. something sent in an envelope along with a letter. *He sent an enclosure of money along with the letter to his family.* {ehn **kloh** zhər}

en·com·pass *verb* (encompassed, encompassing, encompasses) 1. to surround or enclose. *The football field is encompassed by a stadium.* 2. to include all of. *This book encompasses all you need to know for the test.* {ehn **kuhm** pihs}

en·core *interjection* "Once more!"; "Again!" *When the audience shouted, "Encore! Encore!" the singer sang one more song.* *noun* 1. a request by an audience that a performance continue. *The band responded to our encore by playing two more songs.* 2. something added to a performance after the audience asks for more. *The musician played three encores before leaving the stage.* {**ahn kohr**}

en·coun·ter *verb* (encountered, encountering, encounters) 1. to meet or come upon suddenly or by chance. *I encountered a bear in the woods. / I encountered him at the zoo.* 2. to meet with, or come up against. *We encountered bad weather on our trip.* 3. to meet in battle or conflict. *The football teams encountered each other for the third time this season.* *noun* a brief, chance meeting. *The encounter with a snake frightened me.* {ehn **kown** tər}

en·cour·age *verb* (encouraged, encouraging, encourages) 1. to give hope or courage to; give confidence to. *Her praise encouraged me to continue playing the violin.* 2. to give help, support, or approval to; urge. *His uncle encouraged him to study law.* {ehn **kuh** rihj}

en·cour·age·ment *noun* 1. the act of encouraging or condition of being encouraged. *I couldn't have finished writing the book without your encouragement.* 2. someone or something that encourages. *She was a great encouragement to me.* {ehn **kuh** rihj mənt}

en·cy·clo·pe·di·a ❷ or **encyclo-paedia** *noun* a book or set of books that has information on a wide variety of subjects, or on many aspects of one subject. *Encyclopedias are arranged in alphabetical order.* {ehn siy klə **pee** dee ə}

end *noun* 1. the point at which anything that has length starts or stops. *Please tie a knot at the end of the string. / There will be a stop sign at the end of the road.* 2. a point in time at which something stops or finishes; conclusion. *I look forward to going home at the end of the day.* 3. the last part. *I cried at the end of the*

show. 4. goal, purpose, or aim. *I am working hard toward a good end.* *verb* (ended, ending, ends) 1. to cause to stop; finish; conclude. *The fire in the building ended the school day earlier than expected.* 2. to reach a finish or conclusion; stop. *The class will end around 3:30pm.* 3. to arrive at the final result; wind up (usually followed by "up"). *He ended up staying at home.* {**ehnd**}

• **at loose ends**
without clear plans or things to do; not sure what to do with oneself; uneasy. *I'm at loose ends about my future.*

• **make ends meet** or **make both ends meet**
to make enough money to pay for needed things. *She works hard just to make ends meet.*

en·dan·ger *verb* (endangered, endangering, endangers) to put in a dangerous situation. *She endangered all of us with her reckless driving.* {ehn **dayn** jər} endangerment, n.

endangered species ❶ *noun* a species of plant or animal that is in danger of becoming extinct. *The giant panda is one of hundreds of endangered species.* {ehn **dayn** jərd **spee** sheez or ehn **dayn** jərd **spee** seez}

en·deav·or *verb* (endeavored, endeavoring, endeavors) to make an effort; try; strive. *We should endeavor to finish painting the house before dark.* *noun* a serious attempt. *I'm happy with my endeavor to finish reading this very long book.* {ehn **deh** vər}

 Human Body   Human Mind   Everyday Life   History and Culture   Communication

end·ing *noun* the last part; conclusion. *The book had a terrible ending.* {**ehn** ding}

end·less *adjective* 1. having or seeming to have no end; without limits; infinite. *We traveled endless highways on our trip last summer.* / *The possibilities for the future are endless.* / *The sky over the desert looks endless.* 2. unbroken; continuous. *A rubber band is endless.* {**ehnd** lihs} endlessly, adv., endlessness, n.

en·dorse *verb* (endorsed, endorsing, endorses) 1. to give support to; approve of. *He endorsed her for governor.* 2. to sign one's name on the back of a check. *Endorse the check and the teller will cash it.* {ehn **dohrs**}

en·dow *verb* (endowed, endowing, endows) 1. to give money or property to. *She endowed a building for the homeless.* 2. to provide with some ability or quality. *He was endowed with a good sense of humor.* {ehn **dow**}

en·dur·ance *noun* the ability to go on under pain or hardship. *Great endurance is needed to run a marathon.* {ehn **doohr** ihns}

en·dure *verb* (endured, enduring, endures) 1. to bear up under or function in spite of. *We endured the desert heat until the sun set.* 2. to continue through time; last. *Boats don't last, but the oceans endure.* {ehn **doohr**}

en·e·my 🟢 💬 *noun* (enemies) 1. one who hates or wants to harm another. *The wicked king made many enemies among his people.* 2. a state or power that hates or fights another. *During World War II, Germany and Japan were the enemies of the United States.* 3. something likely to cause harm or injury. *Hungry insects can be an enemy to growing vegetables.* {**ehn** ə mee}

en·er·get·ic *adjective* full of energy; active. *He is energetic when he's had enough sleep.* {**ehn** ər **jeh** tihk} energetically, adv.

en·er·gy 💬 🔵 *noun* (energies) 1. the power or ability to make something work or be active. *Plants use the energy of the sun to grow.* 2. the amount of such power needed to do something. *He has no energy to continue the job.* 3. eager interest; liveliness. *He spoke with energy on the subject of boat building.* {**ehn** ər jee}

Synonyms
These words share a meaning with *energy*, noun 1:
might, power, force

Word History *Energy* is from *energos*, a Greek word that means "active or working." The word "energy" was first used in the scientific sense of mechanical or electrical energy in the 1800s.

en·force 💬 *verb* (enforced, enforcing, enforces) to put in force; make people obey. *He enforces the rules.* {ehn **fohrs**}

Eng. *abbreviation* an abbreviation for **England**, or **English**.

en·gage *verb* (engaged, engaging, engages) 1. to get or use the service of; hire. *We engaged a cook for the party.* 2. to get or hold the interest of; occupy. *The story engaged their attention.* 3. to battle with. *Our troops engaged the enemy.* 4. to take part in; involve oneself. *She engaged in the relief effort after the hurricane.* {ehn **gayj**}

en·gaged *adjective* keeping a promise and plan of marriage. *They were engaged for one year before they were married.* {ehn **gayjd**}

en·gage·ment *noun* 1. the act of engaging or state of being engaged. *He arranged for the engagement of a lawyer.* 2. a meeting with someone at a certain time; appointment. *I have an engagement at two o'clock.* 3. a promise to marry; a period of time before the marriage. *Their engagement lasted a year before they were married.* {ehn **gayj** mənt}

en·gine 🔵 🟠 *noun* 1. a machine that uses energy from fuel or electricity to do work, such as to move. 2. a railroad locomotive; train. {ehn jihn}

en·gi·neer *noun* 1. one who is trained in the use or design of machines or engines, or in other technologies. *My brother is an electrical engineer.* 2. one who runs an engine or locomotive. *The engineer slowed the train as it neared the station.* {ehn jih **neer**}

en·gi·neer·ing 🟠 *noun* the study and practice of using scientific and mathematical knowledge to do practical things. Knowledge of engineering is needed to design and build roads, bridges, tools, and machines. {ehn jih **neer** ing}

Eng·land *noun* the largest country on the island of Great Britain. {**ing** glihnd}

Eng·lish 🟠 *adjective* 1. of or having to do with England, or its people. *English weather can be damp.* 2. of or having to do with the language of England, and other countries such as Australia, New Zealand, Canada, and the United States. *English students usually study Shakespeare.* *noun* 1. (used with a plural verb) the people of England (usually used with "the"). *The English enjoy*

a
b
c
d
e
f
g
h
i
j
k
l
m
n
o
p
q
r
s
t
u
v
w
x
y
z

talking about the weather. 2. the language of this country or a manner of speaking that language. English is also standard in various other countries such as the United States. {ing glihsh}

English horn *noun* a wood-wind instrument that looks like the oboe but is larger and lower in tone. {ing glihsh **hohrn**}

Eng·lish·man *noun* (Englishmen) a man who was born in or is a citizen of England. {ing glihsh mən}

Eng·lish·wom·an *noun* (Englishwomen) a woman who was born in or is a cit-izen of England. {ing glihsh **wuum** ən}

en·grave *verb* (engraved, engraving, engraves) 1. to cut a design or lettering into. *He engraved their names in the marble.* 2. to use an engraved surface to print. *She engraved the invitations for our party.* {ehn **grayv**} engraver, n.

en·grav·ing *noun* 1. the act, art, or procedure of carving into a surface or engraving. *I took a class in stone engraving.* 2. an image printed by using an engraved surface. {ehn **gray** ving}

en·gross *verb* (engrossed, engrossing, engrosses) to take all the attention of; interest fully. *Reading a good book will engross me for hours.* {ehn **grohs**}

en·gulf *verb* (engulfed, engulfing, engulfs) to cover entirely, as if by a flood. *The old house was engulfed in flames.* {ehn **guhlf**}

en·hance *verb* (enhanced, enhancing, enhances) to make greater in price; add to the quality or attractiveness of. *Putting in a swimming pool will enhance the value of the*

property. / *The flowers in the park enhanced my enjoyment of the day.* {ehn **hăns**}

en·joy ⑦ *verb* (enjoyed, enjoying, enjoys) 1. to find pleasure or joy in. *I enjoy skating.* 2. to do well because of; have the use of. *The stu-dents enjoyed the library's large choice of books.* 3. to experi-ence pleasure or happiness for (followed by "oneself"). *She enjoyed herself at the party.* {ehn **joi**}

en·joy·a·ble *adjective* pleasant; giving joy. *That was an enjoy-able trip to the city.* {ehn **joi** ə bəl} enjoyably, adv.

en·joy·ment *noun* the state or act of enjoying; pleasure. *I get enjoyment from going to see movies with my friends.* {ehn **joi** mənt}

en·large *verb* (enlarged, enlarging, enlarges) 1. to make larger. *She enlarged her collection of dolls.* 2. to become bigger. *The pupils of the eyes enlarge when it is dark.* {ehn **larj**} enlarger, n.

en·large·ment *noun* 1. the act or result of making larger; expansion. *The enlargement of the house will give us two extra rooms.* 2. anything that is made larger than the orig-inal. *He made an enlargement of the photograph.* {ehn **larj** mənt}

en·light·en ⑦ *verb* (enlight-ened, enlightening, enlightens) to give informa-tion or knowledge to. *She enlightened us about the lack of food in other countries.* {ehn **liyt** ən}

en·list *verb* (enlisted, enlisting, enlists) 1. to sign up to serve in the military or in some cause. *He will enlist in the army.* 2. to get the services of. *They enlisted our help to finish the job.* {ehn **lihst**}

e·nor·mous *adjective* very large in size or amount; huge. *The Atlantic Ocean contains an enormous amount of water.* / *The Empire State building is an enormous building.* {ih **nohr** məs} enormously, adv.

e·nough *adjective* as much or as many as needed or required. *I have enough money.* *noun* an amount needed. *Do you have enough to finish the job?* *adverb* in a way or to a degree that is needed or required. *The job pays well enough.* {ih **nuhf**}

en·quire *verb* (enquired, enquiring, enquires) another spelling of **inquire**. {ihn **kwiyr**}

en·rage ⑦ *verb* (enraged, enraging, enrages) to make very angry or furious; put into a rage. *Waving the red flag at the bull enraged it.* {ehn **rayj**}

en·rich *verb* (enriched, enriching, enriches) 1. to make wealthier or richer. *Selling this property will enrich us.* 2. to provide with more of any valuable or desirable thing or quality. *The teacher enriched the students' under-standing of the book.* / *The cook enriched the sauce with cream.* {ehn **rihch**} enrich-ment, n.

en·roll or **enrol** *verb* (enrolled or enroled, enrolling or enroling, enrolls or enrols) to enlist or sign up officially. *Will you enroll me in your class?* {ehn **rohl**}

en·roll·ment or **enrolment** *noun* 1. the act or process of enlisting or becoming a member. *He wants to begin enrollment of new members.* 2. the number of people enrolled. *We need to increase the club's enrollment.* {ehn **rohl** mənt}

en route *adverb* during the journey; on or along the way.

 Human Body   Human Mind   Everyday Life    History and Culture    Communication

We stopped to pick her up en route to the picnic. {ahn **rooht**}

en·sign *noun* 1. a flag, banner, or badge. *The students waved the ensign of the school at the football game.* 2. the lowest rank of an officer in the U.S. Coast Guard or Navy. {**ehn** sihn}

en·sure *verb* (ensured, ensuring, ensures) 1. to make sure or certain. *Those dark clouds ensure rain.* 2. to protect or make safe. *She ensures her good health by eating right and exercising.* {ehn **shoohr**}

en·tan·gle *verb* (entangled, entangling, entangles) 1. to cause to be snarled or tangled. *The spider web entangled the fly.* 2. to cause to get involved in a difficult situation. *He entangled me in his problems.* {ehn **tăng** gəl}

en·ter *verb* (entered, entering, enters) 1. to come or go into. *I entered the house.* 2. to come or go in. *We entered through the big doors on the side of the building.* 3. to begin; start (usually followed by "upon"). *They entered upon a new adventure.* 4. to pass through; pierce; penetrate. *The nail entered the wood as he hit it with a hammer.* 5. to be admitted to; enroll. *He was young when he entered college.* 6. to take part in or compete in. *We entered the race.* 7. to write on a list; type into a computer. *I entered my name on the sheet of paper.* {ehn tər}

en·ter·prise *noun* 1. a plan or project that is risky, bold, or difficult to carry out; undertaking. *The expedition to the south pole was a complicated enterprise.* 2. a business organization. *Their software enterprise made huge profits last year.* {ehn tər **priyz**}

en·ter·pris·ing *adjective* willing to do things that require energy and imagination. *My enterprising father built a tree house from scrap wood.* {ehn tər **priy** zing}

en·ter·tain ❓ ➋ *verb* (entertained, entertaining, entertains) 1. to amuse; keep interested. *She entertained me with stories about the people she met on her travels.* 2. to have as a guest. *We entertained four guests at dinner last night.* 3. to have in mind; consider. *I have entertained thoughts of selling my bicycle.* {ehn tər **tayn**}

en·ter·tain·er *noun* one who entertains by performance, such as an actress, musician, or comedian. {ehn tər **tay** nər}

en·ter·tain·ment *noun* 1. something that amuses or interests. *The entertainment at today's school assembly will be a musical.* 2. the act of entertaining. *The entertainment of my little sister is my responsibility when my mom needs a nap.* {ehn tər **tayn** mənt}

en·thrall *verb* (enthralled, enthralling, enthralls) to hold the complete attention of; fascinate. *That mystery story enthralled me.* {ehn **thrawl**}

en·thu·si·asm *noun* 1. a strong interest in something. *He has more enthusiasm for playing sports than for doing anything else.* 2. something that causes such great interest in an activity. *Reading is her only enthusiasm.* {ehn **thooh** zee ă zəm}

Word History *Enthusiasm* comes from an ancient Greek word that means "to be god-inspired."

en·thu·si·as·tic *adjective* having or showing great interest. *Her book report got an enthusiastic response from the teacher.* {ehn **thooh** zee ă stihk} enthusiastically, adv.

en·tire *adjective* 1. having all the parts; whole. *We'll need the entire set of tools to do the job right.* 2. whole; every one of. *The entire class is unhappy about how hard the math test was.* {ehn **tiyr**}

en·tire·ly *adverb* completely; in every way. *You are entirely correct.* {ehn **tiyr** lee}

en·ti·tle *verb* (entitled, entitling, entitles) 1. to give a right or legal claim to. *We are entitled to freedom of speech. / You are entitled to half the money from the sale.* 2. to give a title to; name. *She entitled the poem, "Worm trip."* {ehn **tiy** təl}

en·trance¹ *noun* 1. the act of entering. *The children were excited by the entrance of the story teller.* 2. a doorway or other place through which one enters. *The main entrance to the building faces the street.* 3. The right or permission to enter. *Were you given entrance to the school tonight?* {ehn trihns}

en·trance² *verb* (entranced, entrancing, entrances) to put into a trance or a state of delight; charm. *His magic tricks entranced the audience.* {ehn **trăns**}

en·trant *noun* one who enters or takes part in a contest. *The sailboat race has thirty entrants.* {ehn trənt}

en·treat *verb* (entreated, entreating, entreats) to beg for something, or to do something. *I entreated him not to tell anyone my secret.* {ehn **treet**}

a
b
c
d
e
f
g
h
i
j
k
l
m
n
o
p
q
r
s
t
u
v
w
x
y
z

en·trust *verb* (entrusted, entrusting, entrusts) 1. to hand over to for the care or protection of. *We entrusted the pets to our neighbors while we were on vacation.* 2. to hand over something or give some task to as a responsibility. *I entrusted him with the key to the office safe.* {ehn **truhst**}

en·try *noun* (entries) 1. an act or instance of entering; entrance. *His entry drew a lot of attention at the party. / Her entry in the race was a surprise.* 2. an area for entering. *The entry into the building was blocked by a crowd of people.* 3. something that is added to a written list or record. *He made an entry in his notebook.* 4. a word or phrase listed and defined in a dictionary. {ehn tree}

e·nun·ci·ate *verb* (enunciated, enunciating, enunciates) to speak or pronounce in a clear voice. *Enunciate these words carefully so we can understand you.* {ih **nuhn** see **ayt**} enunciation, n.

en·vel·op *verb* (enveloped, enveloping, envelops) to cover, wrap, enclose, or surround. *Fog enveloped the river. / Mom enveloped me in her arms.* {ehn **vehl** əp}

en·ve·lope *noun* a folded paper covering or container usually used to mail letters. {**ahn** və lohp *or* **ehn** və lohp}

en·vi·a·ble *adjective* worthy of being wanted or envied. *Doctors earn an enviable amount of money.* {ehn vee ə bəl}

en·vi·ous *adjective* showing or feeling envy or desire for what another has. *I am envious of her new red shoes.* {**ehn** vee əs} enviously, adv.

en·vi·ron·ment 🌐 *noun* 1. the objects and conditions that make a place what it is. *My favorite restaurant is known for its friendly environment.* 2. everything that surrounds a living thing and affects its growth and health. *Many tropical birds thrive in the environment of a rain forest.* {ehn **viy** ərn mənt *or* ehn **viyr** ən mənt} environmental, adj., environmentally, adv.

en·vy *noun* (envies) 1. a feeling of wanting what someone else has. *He looked at her new car with envy.* 2. something someone has that other people wish they had. *His new jacket was the envy of everyone.* *verb* (envied, envying, envies) to look upon with envy. *I envied her success.* {**ehn** vee}

en·zyme *noun* a protein that helps a chemical reaction take place within a living thing. *Enzymes in saliva help digest food.* {**ehn** ziym}

e·on 🌐 *noun* a very long period of time. *That fossil was formed eons ago.* {**ee** ŏn *or* **ee** ən}

ep·ic 🌐 📖 *adjective* 1. having to do with a long poem that tells the story of a hero or heroine. *He read an epic poem about a Greek goddess.* 2. on a grand scale. *He told of an epic battle.* *noun* a long poem, novel, or film. {**eh** pihk}

ep·i·cen·ter *noun* the point on the earth's surface directly above the central source of an earthquake. {**ehp** ə **sehn** tər}

ep·i·dem·ic 🌐 *noun* an outbreak of disease that spreads rapidly to many people. *The school had an epidemic of measles.* {**ehp** ə **deh** mihk}

ep·i·lep·sy *noun* a nervous system disorder that causes convulsions and unconsciousness. {**ehp** ə lehp see}

ep·i·sode *noun* one event in a series of events in a person's life or a story. *Let's read the next episode in the story.* {**ehp** ə sohd}

ep·och 🌐 *noun* an important period in human history. *The invention of the personal computer started a new epoch in information technology.* {**ehp** ək}

e·qual *adjective* 1. having the same value, measure, or amount as something else. *The two sisters are of equal height.* 2. the same for everyone. *We all have an equal chance to win the game.* *noun* a person or thing that is the same as or equal to another. *He is my equal at playing sports.* *verb* (equaled, equaling, equals) to be the same as or equal to. *The load I'm carrying equals yours.* {**ee** kwəl}

e·qual·i·ty 🌐 📖 *noun* (equalities) the condition, fact, or quality of being equal. *We asked for equality in our pay.* {ih **kwŏl** ih tee}

e·qua·tion 🌐 *noun* a statement in arithmetic that uses an equal sign to show the equality of two quantities. *3 + 3 = 6 is an equation.* {ih **kway** zhən *or* ee **kway** zhən}

e·qua·tor *noun* the imaginary circle around the earth that is halfway between the North and South Poles. {ih **kway** tər *or* ee **kway** tər}

 Human Body  Human Mind 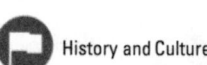 Everyday Life History and Culture Communication

e·qua·to·ri·al *adjective* 1. from, near, or on any equator. *She studies equatorial plants.* 2. like or having to do with conditions near the earth's equator. *We had equatorial heat last summer.* {ee kwə **tohr** ee əl *or* eh kwə **tohr** ee əl}

e·ques·tri·an *adjective* of or relating to horseback riding. *Equestrian events show the skill of both horse and rider.* *noun* a person who is a trained horseback rider. *His skill in riding shows he is a true equestrian.* {ih **kwehs** tree ən}

e·qui·lat·er·al *adjective* having all the sides or faces equal. *Draw an equilateral triangle.* {ee kwə **lăt** ər əl *or* eh kwə **lă** tə rəl}

e·qui·lib·ri·um *noun* a state of balance between two or more forces. *When two people are sitting on a seesaw and the seesaw is level, their weights are in equilibrium.* {ee kwə **lih** bree əm *or* eh kwə **lihb** ree əm}

e·qui·nox *noun* either of the two times during the year when the sun's rays are perpendicular to the earth's equator, occurring in March and September. During the equinox, day and night are both 12 hours long all over the world. {ee kwə **nŏks** *or* eh kwə **nŏks**}

e·quip *verb* (equipped, equipping, equips) to provide with what is needed to complete a task. *She equipped herself for the camping trip with a backpack and sleeping bag.* {ih **kwihp**}

e·quip·ment *noun* 1. anything made or to be used for a particular use. *Ice skates, footballs, and golf clubs are different kinds of sporting equipment.* 2. the act of equipping. *Desks and books will be needed for the equipment of the school.* {ih **kwihp** mənt}

e·quiv·a·lent *adjective* the same as or equal to another in force, value, measure, or meaning. *Three feet is equivalent to one yard.* *noun* something that is the same or equal. *One dollar is the equivalent of one hundred pennies.* {ih **kwih** və lihnt}

-er[1] *or* **-or** *or* **-r** *suffix* 1. a suffix that means "one who performs an action." *A catcher is someone who catches.* / *A sailor is someone who sails.* 2. a suffix that means "one born or living in." *A Southerner is a person who is born or living in the southern part of the United States.*

-er[2] *or* **-r** *suffix* a suffix used to change the form of short adjectives and adverbs to make them express the idea of more when compared. *If someone is stronger than I am, they have greater strength.* / *If something is heavier than something else, it weighs more.*

e·ra ⊖ *noun* a period of time in history. An era often begins or ends with an important event. *My grandfather knows a lot about the industrial era, when machines and factories first came into wide use.* {eh rə *or* **eer** ə}

e·rad·i·cate *verb* (eradicated, eradicating, eradicates) to do away with completely; wipe out. *They eradicated the ants from the kitchen.* {ih **ră** də kayt} eradication, n.

e·rase *verb* (erased, erasing, erases) 1. to remove by rubbing, wiping, or scraping away. *He erased the wrong answer and wrote the correct answer.* 2. to rub, wipe, or scrape off marks or writing from. *The teacher erased the blackboard.* {ih **rays**} erasable, adj.

e·ras·er *noun* an object used to erase or rub out writing or marks. {ih **ray** sər}

ere *conjunction or preposition* before. This word is used in poems and stories written long ago. *The sky grew dark ere his death.* / *He was gone ere I could speak.* {**ayr**}

Homophone Note The words *ere*, *air*, and *heir* sound alike but have different meanings.

e·rect *adjective* 1. upright in posture or position. *The soldiers stood erect in a line.* 2. pointing up stiffly. *The dog held his ears erect at the sound.* *verb* (erected, erecting, erects) 1. to build from the ground up. *They are erecting a house.* 2. to raise into an upright position. *They erected the large sign with a crane.* {ih **rehkt**}

E·rie *noun* 1. Lake Erie, the most southern of the Great Lakes. It lies between the United States and Canada. 2. a member of an Native American people that lived in the region south of this lake. {**eer** ee}

er·mine *noun* a weasel that has white fur in the winter. Ermines live in very cold regions of North America, Europe, and Asia. {**uhr** mihn}

e·rode *verb* (eroded, eroding, erodes) to wear away or eat into. *Pounding waves eroded the beach.* {ih **rohd**}

e·ro·sion ⊙ *noun* wearing away of the earth's surface by wind or water. *Heavy rains cause erosion of the river bank.* {ih **roh** zhən}

A B C D **E** F G H I J K L M N O P Q R S T U V W X Y Z

er·rand *noun* 1. a quick trip taken for a particular purpose. *He went on errands to the bank, the post office, and the grocery store.* 2. the purpose for taking a short journey. *His errand was to bring the teacher a message.* {**ehr** ənd}

er·rat·ic *adjective* 1. not expected or predicted; not regular. *The farmer was surprised by the erratic weather.* 2. not usual or accepted. *We were confused by his erratic ideas.* {ih **ră** tihk} erratically, adv.

er·ror *noun* a mistake in thought or action; something that is wrong. *I corrected the errors on my math test.* {**ehr** ər}

e·rupt *verb* (erupted, erupting, erupts) to break or burst out suddenly. *Lava erupts from a volcano. / A fight erupted on the playground.* {ih **ruhpt**}

e·rup·tion *noun* the act or process of erupting. {ih **ruhp** shən}

es·ca·la·tor *noun* a set of stairs that moves by means of a belt drive. An escalator carries people between floors of large buildings, such as department stores, airports, or train stations. {**ehs** kə lay tər}

es·cape *verb* (escaped, escaping, escapes) 1. to get free. *The prisoner escaped from jail.* 2. to get away; avoid being caught or harmed. *The dog escaped before we could catch him.* 3. to leak out. *Gas escaped from the stove and filled the room with an awful smell.* noun 1. the act or an instance of escaping. *Escape was impossible. / The prisoner's escape from jail was not successful.* 2. a way of getting away from something that will harm. *Most apartment buildings have at least one fire escape.* {ih **skayp**}

es·cort *noun* 1. a group of people who travel with someone for protection or to show respect. *The President always travels with an escort.* 2. a person who goes with or brings another person to a party. *Harry was my escort at the banquet.* verb (escorted, escorting, escorts) to act as an escort for. *My cousin escorted me to the movie.* {**ehs** kohrt}

Es·ki·mo *noun* (Eskimo or Eskimos) a member of any of the native peoples of northern Canada, Alaska, Greenland, and northeastern Russia. Some Eskimo peoples are now called Inuit. {**ehs** kə moh}

e·soph·a·gus *noun* (esophagi) a tube that moves food from the mouth to the stomach of an animal. {ih **sŏf** ə gihs}

es·pe·cial·ly *adverb* 1. more than usually; to a great degree. *The chicken is especially good at this restaurant.* 2. in particular. *The trip will be expensive, especially if we go by plane.* 3. specially; mainly. *I bought this bracelet especially for you.* {ih **spehsh** ə lee}

es·pi·o·nage *noun* the act of spying to collect information. *The company used espio-*nage to find out the secret formula. {**ehs** pee ə **nŏzh**}

es·say *noun* a short piece of writing that gives the writer's ideas, feelings, and opinions on a particular subject. {**ehs** ay}

es·sence *noun* 1. that which makes something what it is; central nature. *Kindness is the essence of friendship.* 2. a concentrated substance taken from a plant that keeps its scent, flavor, or other special traits. *Perfume is made with the essence of flowers.* {**ehs** ihns}

es·sen·tial *adjective* necessary, needed. *Flour is an essential part of bread.* noun 1. something that is absolutely necessary. *Food and water are essentials of life.* 2. an important or basic thing. *A strong voice is an essential for actors.* {ih **sehn** shəl} essentially, adv.

-est or **-st** *suffix* a suffix used to change the form of many adjectives and adverbs to make them express the idea of "most." *We say that the Nile is the longest river in the world because it is the river that is greatest in length.*

es·tab·lish *verb* (established, establishing, establishes) 1. to bring into being; to found. *He established a new club.* 2. to prove or show to be true. *The lawyer established the suspect's guilt.* {ih **stă** blihsh}

es·tab·lish·ment *noun* 1. the act of establishing. *We celebrated the establishment of a new school in our town.* 2. (often capitalized) the people in control of society or government. *In the 1960s, many*

 Human Body   Human Mind   Everyday Life   History and Culture   Communication

young people in America and Europe were opposed to the values of the Establishment. 3. a business, or a place of business. *We always get our hair cut at that establishment.* {eh **stă** blihsh mənt}

es·tate *noun* 1. a piece of land with a large house on it. *Her family owned a huge estate in Italy.* 2. all the property of a person or family; the property left by someone when they die. *After my grandfather died, his estate went to my mother and my uncle.* {eh **stayt**}

es·teem *verb* (esteemed, esteeming, esteems) to have a high opinion of; respect; honor. *I esteem friendship more than money.* *noun* high opinion; respect. *We gave the winner a medal to show our esteem for her.* {eh **steem**}

> **Word History** *Esteem* is from a Latin word that means "to fix the price or value of." The meaning "respect for a person" was first used in the 1500s.

es·ti·mate *verb* (estimated, estimating, estimates) 1. to make a careful guess about the amount, size, or worth of. *We estimated our grocery bill before we got to the cashier.* 2. to make an estimate. *We estimated that two thousand people were at the soccer game.* *noun* a careful guess as to the amount, size, or value of something. *My estimate of the total was off by only a few dollars.* {eh stih **mayt**}

> **Synonyms**
> These words share a meaning with *estimate*, verb 1:
> figure, reckon, calculate, compute

es·ti·ma·tion *noun* a careful guess or opinion based on experience and information.

Our estimation is that the project will take three weeks to complete. {ehs tih **may** shən}

es·tu·ar·y *noun* (estuaries) the wide part of a river's lower end, where it meets the sea. *The ship waited in the estuary for the tide to go out before it sailed out to sea.* {ehs chooh **ayr** ee}

etc. *abbreviation* an abbreviation for **et cetera**.

et cetera and others of the same kind; and the like; and so forth. "Et cetera" is Latin for "and others." (abbreviated: etc.) {eht **seh** tə rə}

etch *verb* (etched, etching, etches) to create a picture, design or lettering on a hard surface such as glass or metal by removing parts of the surface with acid. *The artist etched a picture of a tree.* {ehch}

etch·ing *noun* a print made by using an etched metal plate. {**ehch** ing}

e·ter·nal *adjective* 1. having no beginning or end; lasting always and forever. *Many people believe that God is eternal.* 2. seeming to have no end or to go on forever. *We hoped the twins would stop their eternal fighting.* {ih **tuhr** nəl} eternally, adv.

e·ter·ni·ty *noun* (eternities) 1. time without beginning or end; all of the past, present, and future. *Scientists believe the universe will be in motion for eternity.* 2. a period of time that seems to last forever. *The lecture lasted an eternity.* {ih **tuhr** nə tee}

e·ther *noun* a liquid that makes a person unable to think,

feel, or move. Ether burns easily, has a strong smell, and was once used in medicine to make people unconscious during surgery. {**ee** thər}

E·thi·o·pi·a *noun* a country in eastern Africa near the Red Sea. Addis Ababa is the capital of Ethiopia. {ee thee **oh** pee ə} Ethiopian, n., adj.

eth·nic *adjective* of or relating to a group of people with its own language, history, or culture. *Our class celebrates many ethnic holidays.* {**ehth** nihk} ethnically, adv.

et·i·quette ❓ *noun* rules for good behavior and manners. *You must follow special etiquette when you meet the Queen.* {**eht** ə kiht}

et·y·mol·o·gy *noun* (etymologies) an account of the roots and history of a word and its meanings. {eh tə **mŏl** ih jee} etymologist, n.

eu·ca·lyp·tus *noun* (eucalyptuses or eucalypti) a kind of tall evergreen tree native to Australia. The eucalyptus has leaves that give off a strong smelling oil that is used in medicines. {yoo kə **lihp** təs}

Eu·phra·tes *noun* a river in southwest Asia. It flows from eastern Turkey south through Iraq. It joins the Tigris River in a valley where some of the most ancient civilizations were located. {yoo **fray** teez}

Eu·ro *noun* the currency unit of twelve countries in the European Union. The Euro was introduced in 1999 to replace local currency by 2002

A
B
C
D
E
F
G
H
I
J
K
L
M
N
O
P
Q
R
S
T
U
V
W
X
Y
Z

 Living World   Physical World   Natural Environment    Economy    Government and Law

a
b
c
d
e
f
g
h
i
j
k
l
m
n
o
p
q
r
s
t
u
v
w
x
y
z

in participating countries. {**yoor** oh}

Eu·rope *noun* a continent that is between Asia and the Atlantic Ocean and is north of the Mediterranean Sea. Europe is in the Eastern Hemisphere. {**yuh** rəp}

Eu·ro·pe·an *adjective* of or having to do with Europe, or its peoples or languages. *noun* a person who was born in or is a citizen of a country in Europe. {yuh rə **pee** ən}

e·vac·u·ate *verb* (evacuated, evacuating, evacuates) 1. to move or take away from a dangerous place. *The police are evacuating people from the flood area.* 2. to leave or to empty of people for safety reasons. *The area was evacuated before the attack.* {ih **văk** yoo ayt}

e·vade *verb* (evaded, evading, evades) 1. to get away from by using skill or tricks. *The fox evaded the hunters.* 2. to avoid or fail to obey. *The mayor evaded the difficult questions. / It is a crime to evade paying taxes.* {ih **vayd**}

e·val·u·ate *verb* (evaluated, evaluating, evaluates) to judge or set the worth of. *Teachers give tests to evaluate what their students have learned. / In its report, the magazine evaluated ten new cars.* {ih **văl** yoo ayt} evaluation, n.

e·vap·o·rate *verb* (evaporated, evaporating, evaporates) 1. to turn from liquid into gas; pass away in the form of vapor. *When water evaporates, it becomes water vapor.* 2. to disappear as if vaporized. *The team's early lead evaporated in the second half.* {ih **vă** pə **rayt**} evaporation, n.

eve *noun* (sometimes cap.) the evening or day before a holiday or other special day. *Our parents let us stay awake until midnight on New Year's Eve.* {**eev**}

e·ven *adjective* 1. smooth, level, or flat. *The children liked to play ball at the park because the ground was nice and even.* 2. at the same level or height; parallel. *The snow is even with the tops of my boots.* 3. steady; calm. *Ms. Smyth has an even temper and does not get angry easily.* 4. no more or less in amount or measure; equal in amount. *My brother and I have even amounts of milk in our glasses.* 5. the same amount all over. *The painter put an even coat of paint on the walls.* 6. able to be divided exactly by two. *Six is an even number, but five is not.* *adverb* 1. used to show something surprising or not expected. *Even Paul, who is usually shy, stayed for the party.* 2. used for emphasis when comparing things. *Kit runs fast, but her sister runs even faster.* 3. used to add more emphasis or force before "though" and "if." *Even though I'm not tired, my mother is making me go to bed. / I won't go even if you beg me.* 4. at the same moment. *It started to rain even as I walked out the front door.* *verb* (evened, evening, evens) 1. to cause to be level, flat, smooth, or regular. *We evened the surface of the path by filling in some holes.* 2. to become even. *The paint evened as it dried.* {**ee** vihn} evenly, adj.

• **get even**
to pay another back for harm or mischief done; get revenge. *I got even with my brother for putting the frog in my bed by hiding all of his clothes.*

eve·ning *noun* the period between late afternoon and nightfall. *I like to go out dancing in the evening.* *adjective* relating to or taking place during the early hours of night. *We sat down for the evening meal.* {**eev** ning}

e·vent 🔵 *noun* 1. anything that happens. An event is usually a special or important happening. *Scoring the winning goal was the greatest event of my life.* 2. one contest in a series of sports contests. *The athlete ran in three events at the track meet.* {ih **vehnt**}

• **in any event**
no matter what happens; in any case. *It might rain, but in any event the game will take place.*

e·ven·tu·al *adjective* sure to happen at some time in the future. *The clouds gathered, and we feared the eventual storm.* {ih **vehn** chooh əl}

e·ven·tu·al·ly *adverb* at a future time; in the end; finally. *Cut flowers will eventually die.* {ih **vehn** chooh ə lee}

ev·er *adverb* 1. at some time; at any time. *If I ever see him, I'll tell him.* 2. at all times; always. *Ever since the accident, we are more careful. / He is ever playing the part of a clown.* 3. in any way; at all. *How can we ever know the truth?* {**ehv** ər}

ev·er·glade 🌐 *noun* a very large swamp in a warm climate. Rivers or streams flow slowly through an everglade, and tall, thick grass grows throughout. *We visited the everglades of Florida on our vacation.* {**ehv** ər **glayd**}

ev·er·green *adjective* having green leaves that stay on a plant throughout the year. *Pine trees are evergreen plants. noun* a

  Human Body    Human Mind    Everyday Life    History and Culture    Communication

tree, bush, or other plant with leaves that remain green throughout the year. *Redwood trees are very tall evergreens.* {<u>ehv</u> ər green}

ev·er·last·ing *adjective* going on forever; never ending. *People have always hoped for everlasting peace.* {<u>ehv</u> ər <u>lă</u> sting}

eve·ry *adjective* 1. each and all parts of a group of people or things. *Every person turned toward the door. / Every seat in the theater was taken.* 2. the greatest degree of; all possible. *They showed me every kindness.* {<u>ehv</u> ree}
  • **every once in a while, every so often, [or] every now and then**
  from time to time; upon occasion. *Every once in a while, we will visit my aunt who lives in Florida.*
  • **every other**
  every second or every alternate. *I go swimming every other day.*

eve·ry·bod·y *pronoun* each and all persons; every person. *Everybody needs to bring a pencil for the test. / Everybody who likes chocolate, please raise your hands.* {<u>ehv</u> ree **buh** dee}

eve·ry·day *adjective* 1. happening daily; routine. *Washing the dishes is an everyday chore.* 2. ordinary; common. *You should not wear your everyday clothes when you visit the Queen.* {<u>ehv</u> ree **day**}

eve·ry·one *pronoun* each and every person; everybody. *Everyone in my family has red hair.* {<u>ehv</u> ree **wuhn**}

eve·ry·thing *pronoun* 1. every part; all. *I ate everything on my plate. / Everything was ruined by the storm.* 2. all that is important. *Her work is everything to her.* {<u>ehv</u> ree thing}

eve·ry·where *adverb* in every place; in all places. *I looked everywhere for the keys.* {<u>ehv</u> ree **wayr**}

e·vict *verb* (evicted, evicting, evicts) to legally force to leave a rented property. *The landlord evicted the man from his apartment because he could not pay the rent.* {ih **vihkt**} eviction, n.

ev·i·dence *noun* something that gives proof or a reason to believe. *Scientists have not yet found evidence of life on Mars.* {<u>ehv</u> ə dihns}

ev·i·dent *adjective* easily seen; clear. *Her happiness was evident to all.* {<u>ehv</u> ə dihnt}

e·vil *adjective* bad or wicked. *Leaving the old people with nowhere to live was an evil thing to do.* *noun* 1. anything wrong or bad; wickedness. *Fortunately, there is more good than evil in the world.* 2. an act or condition that causes suffering or harm. *Cancer is an evil we must continue to fight.* {ee vəl} evilly, adv., evilness, n.

e·vo·lu·tion *noun* 1. the process of changing and adapting to an environment over time. *Due to evolution, desert plants do not need much water to survive in dry climates.* 2. the theory that describes how all life forms developed from simpler life forms by changes that took millions of years. 3. changes that take place over time and often show an improvement. *We were amazed by the evolution in basketball shoes over the last twenty years.* {eh və <u>looh</u> shən}

e·volve *verb* (evolved, evolving, evolves) 1. to develop, change, or improve by steps. *Some scientists believe that birds evolved from dinosaurs.* 2. to develop gradually; come into being. *The plans evolved*

after weeks of discussion. {ih <u>vŏlv</u>}

ewe *noun* an adult female sheep. {<u>yoo</u>}

Homophone Note The words *ewe*, *yew*, and *you* sound alike but have different meanings.

ex- *prefix* 1. a prefix that means "out of" or "from." *To exit the building is to go out of the building. / Exhaust from an automobile comes out of the pipe.* 2. a prefix that means "earlier" or "previous." *An ex-president is someone who was president at an earlier time.*

ex·act *adjective* having no mistakes; correct. *You may check a dictionary to find the exact spelling of a word.* *verb* (exacted, exacting, exacts) to demand or cause to be given up by using a threat of force. *The witch exacted a promise from the poor fisherman.* {ehg <u>zăkt</u>}

ex·act·ing *adjective* 1. strict in making demands. *An exacting teacher will make you do homework every night.* 2. needing great attention to detail. *Proofreading is an exacting job.* {ehg <u>zăk</u> ting}

ex·act·ly *adverb* 1. in a correct or accurate way. *To make a good cake, you need to measure the flour exactly.* 2. in every respect; just. *He does exactly what he wants.* 3. that is correct. *Exactly! I couldn't agree more.* {ehg <u>zăkt</u> lee}

ex·ag·ger·ate *verb* (exaggerated, exaggerating, exaggerates) 1. to present as larger, more important, or more valuable. *She exaggerated the size of the snake she found.* 2. to make seem larger or greater. *The*

A
B
C
D
E
F
G
H
I
J
K
L
M
N
O
P
Q
R
S
T
U
V
W
X
Y
Z

a
b
c
d
e
f
g
h
i
j
k
l
m
n
o
p
q
r
s
t
u
v
w
x
y
z

tall hat exaggerates his height. {ehg **ză** jə **rayt**}

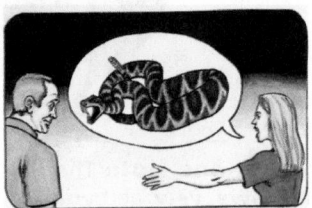

ex·am 🏃 💬 *noun* (informal) an examination, such as a test given at school or a physical checkup by a doctor. *We will have a math exam tomorrow. / You must pass a health exam before you can play football.* {ehg **zăm**}

ex·am·i·na·tion *noun* 1. the act of examining; inspection. *The mechanic's examination of my car showed that it needed new tires.* 2. a test of skill used to see how much a person knows or can do. *Before you can become a lawyer, you must pass a legal examination.* {ehg **zăm** ih **nay** shən}

ex·am·ine ❓ *verb* (examined, examining, examines) 1. to look at closely and carefully. *We examined an insect with a magnifying glass.* 2. to test by asking questions. *The teacher examined the students in history.* {ehg **zăm** ihn} examiner, n.

ex·am·ple *noun* 1. something that shows what a group of things is like. *An apple is an example of a fruit.* 2. a model that should be either copied or avoided. *His big brother set a good example by helping around the house. / She set a bad example for her sister by driving too fast.* 3. a punishment meant to serve as a warning to others. *The teacher made an example of the lazy student by calling on him often.* 4. a math problem used to show how similar math

problems can be solved. *The examples on the blackboard really helped me to understand multiplication.* {ehg **zăm** pəl}

• **for example**
as an example or examples. *We have many kinds of white flowers; for example, there are these roses and daisies.*

ex·as·per·ate *verb* (exasperated, exasperating, exasperates) to bother or annoy to the point of causing anger. *The trumpet player exasperated his neighbors by playing so loudly.* {ehg **zăs** pər **ayt**}

ex·ca·vate *verb* (excavated, excavating, excavates) 1. to make a hole or hollow place in by digging. *The builders are excavating the ground where the new house will be.* 2. to uncover by digging.

Archaeologists excavated the ancient city. {ehk skə **vayt**}

ex·ceed *verb* (exceeded, exceeding, exceeds) 1. to go beyond or do more than. *Don't exceed the speed limit. / She exceeded the record for high jumps.* 2. to be or do better than. *This student has exceeded our expectations.* {ehk **seed**}

ex·ceed·ing·ly *adverb* in a way that exceeds the usual; very; extremely. *Gordon talks exceedingly fast.* {ehk **see** ding lee}

ex·cel *verb* (excelled, excelling, excels) to do or perform better than others. *The Brazilian national team excels at soccer.* {ehk **sehl**}

ex·cel·lence *noun* the condition of being very good or out-

standing. *Her excellence as a guitar player was well known.* {ehk sə lihns}

ex·cel·lent *adjective* very good or much better than others. *He is doing well in math this year because he has an excellent teacher.* {ehk sə lihnt} excellently, adv.

ex·cept *preposition* apart from; not including; but. *Everyone except Mary went to the seashore.* *conjunction* 1. if it were not that; only; but. *We would have gone except it rained.* 2. unless; otherwise than. *He never stopped talking except to take a drink of water.* {ehk **sehpt**}

Language Note *Except* is easy to confuse with *accept* because these two words sound alike. *Accept* is a verb that means "to receive or agree to." *Except* is a preposition that means "not including." *Mrs. Mulligan could not accept Jesse's excuse for being late. She believed his whole story, except the part about the aliens.*

ex·cep·tion *noun* 1. the act or fact of leaving out. *Everyone pitched in, with the exception of Suzy.* 2. something left out or different from others in a group. *Most boys do not like ballet, but Joe is an exception.* {ehk **sehp** shən}

ex·cep·tion·al *adjective* 1. different, unusual, or out of the ordinary. *Snow is exceptional in this part of the world.* 2. excellent or outstanding. *She gave an exceptional performance on her violin.* {ehk **sehp** sha nəl} exceptionally, adv.

ex·cerpt *noun* a short section taken from a play, film, or written work. *Excerpts from the winning movies were shown at the award ceremony.* *verb* (excerpted, excerpting, excerpts) to select and use

 Human Body  Human Mind  Everyday Life  History and Culture Communication

part of a book, a film, or other work. *Every month, the magazine excerpts the first chapter of a new book.* {ehk **sərpt**}

ex·cess *noun* an amount that is more than what is needed. *We bought an excess of food for the party, so please take some home with you.* *adjective* more than is needed or usual; extra. *There were excess brownies at the picnic because everyone brought some.* {ehk **sehs**}

ex·ces·sive *adjective* more than is needed or considered fair; not reasonable. *Five dollars for a hamburger seemed like an excessive price.* {ehk **seh** sihv}

ex·change ⊕ *verb* (exchanged, exchanging, exchanges) 1. to give in return for something else; trade. *I exchanged my old car for a new one.* 2. to give up for another of the same kind. *We exchanged phone numbers, but she has not called me yet.* *noun* 1. the act of giving or getting one thing in return for another; trade. *The exchange of rings is a part of some wedding ceremonies.* 2. a place where things are bought, sold, or traded. *My mother buys and sells shares at the stock exchange.* {ehks **chaynj**}

ex·cite *verb* (excited, exciting, excites) to stir up the feelings of; arouse. *The start of the play excited the audience. / The first snow of the year always excites children.* {ehk **siyt**}

ex·cite·ment *noun* 1. the state of being excited. *Their excitement about summer vacation made it difficult to pay attention in class.* 2. something that stimulates or causes much interest. *Going to the*

zoo was a big excitement for my little sister. {ehk **siyt** mənt}

ex·cit·ing *adjective* causing excitement. *The most exciting part of the movie happens when the monster leaps out of the closet.* {ehk **siy** ting}

ex·claim *verb* (exclaimed, exclaiming, exclaims) 1. to speak suddenly and with strong feeling. *She exclaimed loudly when we told her the exciting news.* 2. to say loudly and with strong feeling. "Bingo!" *exclaimed the woman.* {ehk **sklaym**} exclaimer, n.

ex·cla·ma·tion *noun* 1. the act of exclaiming. *She gave an exclamation of joy when she heard the good news.* 2. a single word or phrase that is said when a person has strong feelings. "Wow!" *is an exclamation that people use when they are surprised or amazed.* "Oh dear!" *is an exclamation that people use when something disappoints or worries them.* {ehk sklə **may** shən}

ex·cla·ma·tion mark *noun* a punctuation mark (!). It is used after a word or words that express strong feeling; exclamation point. {ehk sklə **may** shən **mark**}

ex·cla·ma·tion point *noun* a punctuation mark (!) used after an exclamation, interjection, or command. {**ehks** kleh **may** shuhn **point**}

ex·clude *verb* (excluded, excluding, excludes) to leave out; keep out. *Did you mean to exclude Kate from your list of guests? / The club she wants to join excludes boys.* {ehk **skloohd**}

ex·clu·sive *adjective* 1. keeping out all others. *At four o'clock, the teachers have exclusive rights to the computer room.* 2. giving attention or service only to a certain type of person. *This exclusive club allows only rich people to join and play golf on its course.* {ehk **sklooh** sihv} exclusively, adv.

ex·crete 🌎 *verb* (excreted, excreting, excretes) to get rid of from the body. *Some animals excrete sweat through pores in the skin.* {ehk **skreet**}

ex·cru·ci·at·ing *adjective* very painful; causing agony. *The pain was excruciating when the large rock fell on my toe.* {ehk **skrooh** shee ay ting} excruciatingly, adv.

ex·cur·sion *noun* 1. a short trip made for some purpose. *Mom made a two-day excursion to California for business.* 2. a group tour taken for pleasure, often at a lower fare. *My grandmother went on an excursion to Las Vegas.* {ehk **skuhr** zhən}

ex·cuse *verb* (excused, excusing, excuses) 1. to forgive or pardon. *Please excuse me for stepping on your foot.* 2. to be the reason or cause for; serve as an explanation for. *The fact that my sister is just a baby excuses her pulling the dog's tail.* 3. to let go from duty or obligation. *The government excused him from the army.* *noun* 1. a reason offered to explain, or ask for pardon for, a fault. *My excuse for being late is that I missed the bus.* 2. a reason or explanation used to escape blame. *She is always making up excuses for not doing her homework.* {ehk **skyoos**, n., ehk **skyooz**, v.} excusable, adj.

ex·e·cute *verb* (executed, executing, executes) 1. to put into action; carry out. *The*

A
B
C
D
E
F
G
H
I
J
K
L
M
N
O
P
Q
R
S
T
U
V
W
X
Y
Z

inventor had a thousand good ideas but never executed them. / The gymnast executed her routine perfectly. 2. to make by following a plan. *The carpenters executed the designs of the architect.* 3. to put to death by law. *The murderer was executed.* {**ehk** sih **kyoot**}

ex·e·cu·tion *noun* 1. the act of executing or carrying out. *The execution of the plan will require everyone's help.* 2. the following through of a death sentence. *The governor stopped the execution of the prisoner.* 3. the manner or quality of an action; technique. *The pianist was praised for her skillful execution of a very difficult piece.* {**ehk** sih **kyoo** shən}

ex·ec·u·tive *noun* 1. a person who has a managing or directing role in a business or government. *The company's top executives met to discuss how to increase sales.* 2. the branch of government that manages the business of the country and makes sure that laws are carried out. *adjective* 1. having the ability or authority to carry out plans or ideas. *In our company, the boss has all the executive power.* 2. having to do with the carrying out of laws. *The executive branch of the U.S. government includes the president and his cabinet.* {ehg **zeh** kyə tihv}

ex·empt *verb* (exempted, exempting, exempts) to free from something that others are always required to do; excuse. *My brother was exempted from physical education class because he plays on the football team.* *adjective* excused from something that others are required to do. *The team captain is exempt from*

carrying the water bottles. {ehg **zehmpt**}

ex·er·cise   *noun* 1. activity done to keep the body or mind strong or to make them stronger. *Swimming is good exercise.* / *Reading is great mental exercise.* 2. an act of putting into practice; use. *When teaching young children, the exercise of patience is important.* 3. (often plural) a ceremony. *We cheered for Melissa at her graduation exercises.* *verb* (exercised, exercising, exercises) 1. to put into practice or make use of. *He failed to exercise his right to vote.* 2. to do physical exercise or activity. *I exercise in the gym every morning.* {**ehk** sər **siyz**}

> **Word History** *Exercise* is from a Latin word that means "to keep busy" or "drive on." In the English spoken in the early 1300s, "exercise" referred to mental effort. By the late 1300s, its meaning had broadened to include physical activity.

ex·ert *verb* (exerted, exerting, exerts) 1. to use or put into action; apply. *The senator exerted her influence to help pass the new law.* 2. to push into effort or action; strain. *Don't exert yourself if you're feeling sick.* {ehg **zuhrt**}

ex·hale *verb* (exhaled, exhaling, exhales) to breathe out; give out breath or vapor. *When the swimmer finally came up from underwater, he exhaled deeply.* {ehks **hayl**}

ex·haust *verb* (exhausted, exhausting, exhausts) 1. to make tired; wear out. *The long day at school exhausted her.* 2. to use all of; use up. *The campers exhausted their supply of food and had to catch fish.* *noun* 1. the smoke or gas given off by an engine. 2. the

part of an engine through which gas or steam pass out. {ehg **zawst**}

ex·haus·tion *noun* 1. the act of using up completely or the condition of being used up completely. *Our group is trying to stop the exhaustion of our state's natural resources.* 2. complete loss of energy; extreme fatigue. *Exhaustion kept the singer from finishing her world tour.* {ehg **zaws** chən}

ex·hib·it *verb* (exhibited, exhibiting, exhibits) to show or display. *She exhibits her paintings at the art gallery.* *noun* something that is shown or exhibited to many people. *We went to see the exhibit of ancient Egyptian art at the museum.* {ehg **zih** biht} exhibitor (exhibiter), n.

ex·hi·bi·tion *noun* 1. an act of exhibiting, or something that is exhibited. *Your exhibition of bad manners spoiled the dinner party.* 2. a public showing of art, crafts, products, or skills. *We went to see the exhibition of farm animals at the state fair.* {ehk sih **bih** shən}

ex·hil·a·rate *verb* (exhilarated, exhilarating, exhilarates) 1. to fill with energy. *The cold air and bright snow exhilarated us.* 2. to make very cheerful. *Winning the tournament exhilarated the team.* {ehk **sih** lə **rayt**}

ex·ile *noun* 1. the condition of being sent away from one's country and not allowed to return as a punishment. *The government sent the spy into exile for ten years.* 2. a person

 Human Body   Human Mind   Everyday Life   History and Culture   Communication

who is separated from his or her country or home. *Many Cuban exiles live in the United States.* verb (exiled, exiling, exiles) to send away from one's country or home as a punishment. *The king exiled the traitor.* {**ehg** ziyl or **ehk** siyl, n., **ehg** ziyl or **ehk** siyl, v.}

ex·ist verb (existed, existing, exists) 1. to be real; have being. *She does not believe that monsters exist.* 2. to stay alive; live. *He existed on berries and insects until he was rescued.* 3. to be alive; live. *Fish cannot exist out of water.* {ehg **zihst**}

Word History *Exist* comes from a Latin word that means "to stand forth" or "to emerge."

ex·ist·ence noun 1. the condition of being alive or real. *Dinosaurs are no longer in existence. / She does not believe in the existence of unicorns.* 2. continued being or life. *Humans are putting the existence of tigers in danger.* 3. a way of life. *The pioneers led a difficult existence on the prairies.* {ehg **zih** stihns}

ex·it noun 1. a way out. *She left the theater through the rear exit.* 2. the act of going out; leaving. *Bela made a sudden exit from the party.* verb (exited, exiting, exits) to go out; leave. *He exited through the back door.* {**ehk** siht}

ex·o·dus noun the leaving of large numbers of people. *The lack of jobs in the south caused an exodus to the north.* {**ehk** səd ihs}

ex·o·tic adjective 1. from a foreign place. *The zoo in Chicago has exotic birds from Africa.* 2. very unusual and interesting. *Her exotic outfits make people stare.* {ehg **zŏt** ihk}

ex·pand verb (expanded, expanding, expands) 1. to make larger or wider. *The*

school made a plan to expand its playground. 2. to become larger or wider. *The stomach expands when a person eats.* {ehk **spănd**} expandable (expandible), adj.

ex·panse noun a wide and open area or land. *The oceans are great expanses of water.* {ehk **spăns**}

ex·pan·sion noun 1. the act or process of expanding, or the condition of being expanded. *The expansion of the supermarket will take four weeks.* 2. something made larger by being expanded. *The writer's novel is an expansion of a short story he once wrote.* {ehk **spăn** shən}

ex·pect verb (expected, expecting, expects) 1. to hope for or look forward to. *They expected a letter from their son to arrive soon.* 2. (informal) to guess or suppose. *I expect you'd like a drink of water after your run.* {ehk **spehkt**}

ex·pec·ta·tion noun 1. the act of waiting for or looking forward to. *The dog sits by the door at the same time each day in expectation of its owner's return from work.* 2. a belief that something is likely to happen. *They brought umbrellas because of their expectation of rain.* {ehk spehk **tay** shən}

ex·pe·di·tion noun a journey taken for a reason, or a group taking such a trip. *The scientists made an expedition to the rain forest. / The expedition ran into trouble when its boat*

sprang a leak. {ehk spih **dih** shən}

Word History *Expedition* comes from a Latin word that means "to free the feet." "Ped," which forms part of the word "expedition," means "foot" or "feet" in Latin. Other English words which contain "ped" and come from Latin include **pedal** and **quadruped**.

ex·pel verb (expelled, expelling, expels) 1. to force out or drive out. *He coughed to expel the dust from his lungs.* 2. to send away or dismiss. *They expelled the player from the game for fighting.* {ehk **spehl**}

ex·pend·i·ture noun 1. the act of paying or expending. *The space program requires the expenditure of huge amounts of money.* 2. something which is paid out or spent. *The government's expenditures rose last year.* {ehk **spehn** dih chər}

ex·pense ⬤ noun 1. money needed to buy or do something; cost. *His parents work hard to afford the expense of new school clothes.* 2. a cause of spending money or paying out. *Buying a new car is a big expense.* {ehk **spehns**}

ex·pen·sive adjective costing a lot of money; having a high price. *She wanted the most expensive sneakers in the store. / New cars are expensive.* {ehk **spehn** sihv}

ex·pe·ri·ence noun 1. something that a person has done or lived through. *The war was a terrible experience for everyone.* 2. everything done or lived through in a person's life. *I've learned so much from my grandmother's experience.* 3. understanding or skills gained from repeated prac-

A
B
C
D
E
F
G
H
I
J
K
L
M
N
O
P
Q
R
S
T
U
V
W
X
Y
Z

a
b
c
d
e
f
g
h
i
j
k
l
m
n
o
p
q
r
s
t
u
v
w
x
y
z

tice or activity. *We need a worker with two years of computer experience. / Captain Black has a lot of experience with that kind of boat.* *verb* (experienced, experiencing, experiences) to go through; feel or know. *He experienced defeat for the first time. / She experienced pain after the accident.* {ehk <u>speer</u> ee ihns}

Word History *Experience* is from a Latin word that means "to try out or test."

ex·pe·ri·enced *adjective* knowing a lot about something as a result of practice or experience. *My grandfather was an experienced fisherman with little patience for beginners like me.* {ehk <u>speer</u> ee ihnst}

ex·per·i·ment ❶ *noun* a carefully planned test used to discover something unknown. *The science class did an experiment to see what happens when water and oil are mixed.* *verb* (experimented, experimenting, experiments) to perform an experiment; to explore by trying different things. *The cook experimented until he found the right spices for his dish.* {ehk <u>spehr</u> ə mənt} experimenter, n.

ex·per·i·men·tal *adjective* 1. having to do with testing or experiments. *The scientists talked about the experimental results.* 2. being an experiment or like an experiment. *The experimental rocket crashed right after lift off.* {ehk <u>spehr</u> ə <u>mehn</u> təl}

ex·pert *noun* someone who knows a great deal about a particular thing. *He is an expert on the history of the American West.* *adjective* 1.

having a great deal of skill or knowledge. *Sasha is an expert chess player.* 2. having to do with special skills or knowledge. *We need expert advice on which skis to buy.* {ehk spərt}

ex·pi·ra·tion *noun* 1. a coming to an end or close. *I must get a new driver's license before the expiration of my old one.* 2. the act of breathing out. *The pig's expirations were noisy.* {ehk spə <u>ray</u> shən}

ex·pire *verb* (expired, expiring, expires) 1. to come to an end. *Your magazine subscription will expire next October.* 2. to breathe out. *The air we expire contains more carbon dioxide than the air we breathe in.* 3. to die. *The old horse expired after a short illness.* {ehk <u>spiyr</u>}

ex·plain *verb* (explained, explaining, explains) 1. to make clear in speech or writing; show in detail. *The carpenter explained how he had made the cabinets.* 2. to give reasons for. *Please explain why you were not in class this morning.* 3. to show the meaning of. *The museum guide explained the painting to us.* {ehk <u>splayn</u>}

• **explain away** to make less important by explaining. *Gary tried to explain away the hurtful thing he had done.*

ex·pla·na·tion *noun* the act or process of making clear in speech or writing. *Her explanation of the story helped me to understand it.* {ehk splə <u>nay</u> shən}

ex·plic·it *adjective* said or written in a clear and direct way. *We gave you explicit instructions not to use the computer.* {ehk <u>splihs</u> iht} explicitly, adv.

ex·plode *verb* (exploded, exploding, explodes) 1. to

burst because of too much pressure inside. *If you blow too much air into a balloon, it will explode.* 2. to burst out suddenly into laughter, crying, or shouting. *The little boy exploded into tears after he fell off his bike.* 3. to cause to burst with great force. *He was arrested after exploding a bomb in his yard.* {ehk <u>splohd</u>}

Word History *Explode* comes from a Latin word that means "to drive off the stage by clapping," the Roman version of booing. In English, "explode" first had the meaning "to drive away with a loud noise." During the 1700s it came to be used for something that goes off with a loud noise, such as a bomb.

ex·ploit[1] *noun* a deed of daring or courage. *The exploits of Alexander the Great continue to amaze us today.* {ehk <u>sploit</u>}

ex·ploit[2] *verb* (exploited, exploiting, exploits) 1. to make full use of and gain from. *A country should exploit its resources with care.* 2. to use for one's own advantage and in a way that is unfair to the thing or person being used. *Children are exploited as cheap workers in some countries.* {ehk <u>sploit</u>}

ex·plo·ra·tion *noun* 1. the act of investigating or examining. *The book is an exploration of life in Japan during the 1800s.* 2. the act of exploring new or unknown places. *Their exploration of Antarctica was filled with danger.* {ehk splə <u>ray</u> shən}

ex·plore *verb* (explored, exploring, explores) 1. to travel across or through in order to discover or search for something. *We explored the jungle in hope of finding the ancient city.* 2. to try to understand by examining

 Human Body   Human Mind   Everyday Life   History and Culture  Communication

xploration

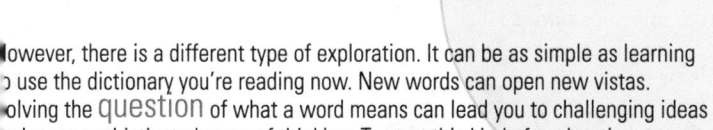

The traditional image of an explorer is someone on a voyage to an unknown shore or on an overland trip into some remote territory. One day soon we will enter into a new era with the possibility of trips to distant planets.

However, there is a different type of exploration. It can be as simple as learning to use the dictionary you're reading now. New words can open new vistas. Solving the question of what a word means can lead you to challenging ideas and more sophisticated ways of thinking. To start this kind of exploration, try out the Word Explorer section in the back of this dictionary.

In exploring the globe, the compass was probably the greatest single invention. It allowed a ship to maintain an accurate course across open ocean. Travelers could use a compass to penetrate unknown regions and return to the place they started from.

Language is the key to thinking and learning. Understanding words and how to use them can be a compass on your journey through life.

carefully. *Let us explore this idea.* {ehk <u>splohr</u>}

Word History *Explore* is from a Latin word that means "to investigate" or "search out." This Latin word may have originally meant "to make a loud cry," particularly the cry made by hunters to scare an animal out of its hiding place.

ex·plor·er *noun* a person who explores an area that is not known. {ehk <u>splohr</u> ər}

ex·plo·sion *noun* 1. the act of bursting or the noise made by bursting. *They heard the explosion of fireworks in the distance.* 2. a laugh, cry, or yell that is sudden and loud. *We heard an explosion of laughter coming from the circus tent.* {ehk <u>sploh</u> zhən}

ex·plo·sive *adjective* 1. able to cause an explosion. *Gasoline and fire make an explosive combination.* 2. having to do with or like an explosion. *The symphony has an explosive ending.* *noun* a substance that is able to cause an explosion. *Dynamite is an explosive.* {ehk <u>sploh</u> sihv}

ex·port 🌐 *verb* (exported, exporting, exports) to send to another country to sell. *Japan exports cars to many countries around the world.* *noun* the act of sending goods to another country to sell. *The export of fruits is important to the Mexican economy.* {<u>ehk</u> spohrt *or* <u>ehk</u> spohrt *or* ehk <u>spohrt</u>} exporter, n.

ex·pose *verb* (exposed, exposing, exposes) 1. to uncover or reveal. *We exposed our skin to the sun.* / *The gardener exposed a colony* of ants with his spade. 2. to put in danger by not protecting. *Walking barefoot exposes your feet to sharp objects.* 3. to allow light to reach in order to make a photographic image. *A camera exposes the film to light to make a photograph.* {ehk <u>spohz</u>}

ex·po·si·tion *noun* 1. a statement with many details that is used to explain something. *The lawyer wrote an exposition of the new law.* 2. a public display of tools or goods; exhibition. *There were many new trucks at the exposition.* {ehk spə <u>zih</u> shən}

ex·po·sure *noun* 1. the act or process of exposing. *The news reporter won an award for his exposure of crime in city hall.* 2. the condition of being exposed to wind, cold, heat, rain, or other forces of nature. *The exposure of your skin to the sun can cause it to burn.* 3. the act of exposing film to light, or the amount of time that film is exposed to light. *Your pictures will come out well if you use the right exposure.* 4. position in relation to the sun, wind, or compass direction. *The porch has a northern exposure.* {ehk <u>spoh</u> zhər}

ex·press 🔵 ❓ 👕 *verb* (expressed, expressing, expresses) 1. to make thoughts or feelings known by saying or writing. *The president's speech expresses the idea that good schools are needed to make the country stronger.* 2. to show thoughts or feelings of. *I expressed my happiness by smiling.* *adjective* stated in full; clear. *I went to the town court for the express purpose of proving my innocence.* *noun* any fast means of transporting people, goods, or messages. *We took the* express into the city and got there in only an hour. {ehk <u>sprehs</u>}

ex·pres·sion *noun* 1. the act of telling or showing thoughts or feelings. *His gift was an expression of his love.* 2. an action of the face or body that is able to make feelings known. *She has tears in her eyes and a sad expression on her face.* 3. a tone of voice or position of the body or face that shows a feeling. *The teacher read the story with lots of expression.* 4. a common saying. *My brother uses the expression, "It takes one to know one."* {ehk <u>spreh</u> shən} expressionless, adj., expressionlessly, adv.

ex·pres·sive *adjective* full of feeling or meaning. *Sojourner Truth was an expressive speaker.* {ehk <u>spreh</u> sihv}

ex·press·way *noun* a highway with many lanes and few stops that lets traffic move quickly. {ehk <u>sprehs</u> way}

ex·qui·site *adjective* very beautiful; made in a lovely or delicate way. *The duchess wore an exquisite diamond necklace.* {ehk <u>skwih</u> ziht} exquisitely, adv.

ex·tend *verb* (extended, extending, extends) 1. to make longer in size; make last longer. *We extended the ladder so that it would reach the top of the tree.* / *The teacher extended recess by fifteen minutes.* 2. to stretch out. *He extended his hand in greeting.* 3. to give or offer. *We would*

 Human Body    Human Mind    Everyday Life   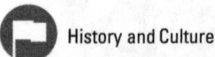 History and Culture    Communication

like to extend our help to you. {ehk **stehnd**}

ex·ten·sion *noun* 1. the act of extending or condition of being extended. *We were all happy about the teacher's extension of the deadline.* 2. something that extends another thing; an addition. *They are building an extension to the old school building.* 3. an extra telephone line connected to the main line. *Dial the number for the office and ask for Mr. Swan's extension.* {ehk **stehn** shən}

ex·ten·sive *adjective* 1. reaching or extending very far. *The forest fire did extensive damage.* / *The United States has extensive power around the world.* 2. very large in size or quality. *The university library has an extensive collection of antique books.* {ehk **stehn** sihv}

ex·tent *noun* 1. the area or amount to which something extends; reach or range. *This map shows the extent of the journey made by Lewis and Clark.* / *The extent of his knowledge is amazing.* 2. the limit of something's reach. *I'm sorry, but that is the extent of what I know about the accident.* {ehk **stehnt**}

ex·te·ri·or *adjective* on or having to do with the outside; outer. *The exterior walls of our house are painted green.* *noun* 1. the outside or outer part. *The exterior of the car has a lot of dents and scratches.* 2. the way a person or thing looks on the surface; appearance. *She has a happy exterior even though her life is full of trouble.* {ehk **steer** ee ər}

ex·ter·mi·nate *verb* (exterminated, exterminating, exterminates) to get rid of by destroying; wipe out. *They hired someone to exterminate the insects in their house.* {ehk **stuhr** mih **nayt**} extermination, n., exterminator, n.

ex·ter·nal *adjective* of the outside or outer part. *He cleaned only the external surfaces of the oven.* / *Cold-blooded animals need warmth from external sources like the sun.* {ehk **stuhr** nəl} externally, adv.

ex·tinct *adjective* 1. no longer existing. *Dinosaurs have been extinct for millions of years.* 2. no longer active or burning. *An extinct volcano will not erupt again.* {ehk **stingkt**}

ex·tinc·tion 🌲 🔬 *noun* the act or process of becoming or making extinct. *What caused the extinction of the dodo bird?* {ehk **stingk** shən}

ex·tin·guish *verb* (extinguished, extinguishing, extinguishes) 1. to put out; stop the burning of. *The fire department extinguished the fire and saved the house.* / *Please extinguish the lights before you go to bed.* 2. to put an end to. *The thunder and lightning extinguished all hope of a walk on the beach.* {ehk **sting** gwihsh}

ex·tra *adjective* more than is expected or usual. *I asked for extra time to finish the test.* *noun* 1. an added and often better thing. *The new house has many extras, including a swimming pool.* 2. an edition of a newspaper that is added to a regular publication schedule. *Many newspapers printed an extra when President Kennedy was killed.* *adverb* to a higher degree; more than is usual. *The fabric of those jeans is extra heavy.* {ehk **strə**}

ex·tra- or **extro-** *prefix* a prefix that means "beyond" or "outside." An extraordinary musical skill is a skill that is beyond the ordinary. / *The word "extraterrestrial" means "from someplace outside the planet Earth."*

ex·tract *verb* (extracted, extracting, extracts) to take out by using force; remove. *The dentist extracted my tooth.* *noun* a strong, concentrated form of a substance. *We used vanilla extract to flavor the cake batter.* {ehk străkt, n., ehk **străkt**, v.}

ex·traor·di·nar·y *adjective* 1. very unusual; far beyond the ordinary. *We marveled at the extraordinary paintings in the museum.* 2. wonderful; remarkable. *Our teacher told us we did extraordinary work last week.* {ehk **strohr** dih **nayr** ee} extraordinarily, adv.

ex·tra·ter·res·tri·al *adjective* existing or coming from a place outside planet Earth. *Meteorites are extraterrestrial rocks.* {ehk strə tə **rehs** tree əl}

ex·trav·a·gance *noun* 1. the act of spending too much money or spending money in a foolish way. *Marla shows her extravagance when she buys expensive clothes that she doesn't need.* 2. something done or bought at a very high cost. *Renting out a fancy restaurant for the baby's first birthday party was an extravagance.* {ehk **străv** ə gəns}

ex·trav·a·gant *adjective* 1. spending too much; spending in a foolish or careless way. *Her extravagant parents buy a new car every year.* 2. more than is reasonable in price; too expensive. *Jenny wore an extravagant dress to the school dance.* {ehk **străv** ə gənt} extravagantly, adv.

ex·treme *adjective* 1. at or to the farthest point of something. *Their cottage was at the*

a
b
c
d
e
f
g
h
i
j
k
l
m
n
o
p
q
r
s
t
u
v
w
x
y
z

extreme end of the mainland. 2. far beyond what is usual or reasonable. *Snowboarding is an extreme sport. / I do not agree with your extreme ideas.* 3. very great; to the highest degree. *She is in extreme pain. noun* the farthest point or greatest degree. *I live at one extreme of the island, and she lives at the other. / His moods go from one extreme to the other.* {ehk **streem**}

ex·treme·ly *adverb* very; to an extreme degree. *I did extremely well on that last quiz. / It was an extremely hot July day.* {ehk **streem** lee}

ex·trem·i·ty *noun* (extremities) 1. the farthest point or reach of something. *The extremities of the field were marked by a fence.* 2. the greatest extreme. *She felt the extremity of joy when she won the championship.* 3. (usually plural) the parts of the body at the ends of the limbs; hands and feet. 4. a condition of great danger or urgent need. *He didn't understand the extremity of his situation until night came and he was still lost in the forest.* {ihk **streh** mih tee}

ex·tro·vert *noun* a person who is outgoing and likes to be with other people. *Extroverts enjoy parties more than shy people do.* {**ehk** strə **vuhrt**} extroverted (extraverted), adj.

eye 🌐 *noun* 1. the organ of the body that gives humans and other animals sight, and the area close around it, including the lids, lashes, and brow. 2. skill in being able to observe. *You certainly have an eye for color.* 3. the center of a storm. *The eye of*

the hurricane passed right over our county. 4. any of a number of things that look like an eye. *Thread passes through the eye of a needle. verb* (eyed, eyeing, eyes) to look at in a fixed way, or with doubt. *My teacher eyed me when I walked into class late.* {**iy**}

eyelash
cornea
pupil
iris
lens
eyelash
retina
optic nerve

• **catch someone's eye** to get the attention of. *The chocolate cream pie caught his eye as soon as he walked into the bakery.*

• **keep an eye on** to watch or tend with care. *She will keep an eye on the house while we are on vacation.*

• **keep an eye out** to watch closely. *Keep your eye out for the black cat with white paws.*

• **keep up with** to go at the same speed or pace as. *The little boy can't keep up with his older brothers.*

• **see eye to eye** to agree exactly. *My mother and I don't see eye to eye on everything.*

Homophone Note The words *eye*, *aye*, and *I* sound alike but have different meanings.

eye·ball *noun* the part of the eye that is shaped like a ball. The eyeball sits in the eye socket. {**iy** bawl}

eye·brow *noun* 1. the ridge of bone above each eye. 2. the line of short hairs growing along the ridge of bone above the eye. {**iy** brow}

eye·drop·per *noun* a small glass or plastic tube used to apply drops of medicine, especially to the eyes. {**iy drŏp** ər}

eye·glass *noun* (plural) two lenses in a frame that rests on the nose and ears, worn to help a person see better; glasses. {**iy glăs**}

eye·lash *noun* the short, fine hairs that grow on the edge of the upper or lower eyelid; a single one of these hairs. {**iy lăsh**}

eye·let *noun* a small hole in cloth or leather with bound or covered edges. An eyelet is used to pass cord or thread through, fasten hooks into, or serve as decoration. *My new shoes have ten eyelets, five on each side of the tongue.* {**iy** liht}

Homophone Note The words *eyelet* and *islet* sound alike but have different meanings. To find out why an islet could never fit through an eyelet, look up *islet*.

eye·lid *noun* a fold of skin that can be opened or shut over the eyeball. {**iy** lihd}

eye·lin·er *noun* makeup used to draw a thin line on the edges of the eyelids. {**iy liyn** ər}

eye·sight *noun* 1. the ability to see; vision. *It is important for airplane pilots to have excellent eyesight.* 2. the distance the eye can see; view. *I watched until the bird was out of eyesight.* {**iy** siyt}

eye·tooth *noun* (eyeteeth) a pointed tooth in the upper jaw, located beneath the eye. The eyeteeth are also called "canines." {**iy** tooth}

eye·wit·ness *noun* a person who has seen something happen with his or her own eyes. *The eyewitness to the crime was called on to tell her story in court.* {**iy wiht** nihs}

 Human Body
 Human Mind
 Everyday Life
 History and Culture
🌐 Communication

Ff

F is a consonant that always makes the same sound.

Tips to help you look up words starting with f: Also look under P for some words that start with the "f" sound. Another way to spell the "f" sound is "ph" (as in photograph).

These words may be hard to look up if you don't already know how to spell them:

facsimile	foreign
February	forty
field	forward
fight	freight
folks	friend

f or **F** *noun* (f's or F's) 1. the sixth letter of the English alphabet. 2. a grade given for failing schoolwork. 3. the fourth note in the musical scale of C major. {**ehf**}

F symbol of the chemical element fluorine.

F *abbreviation* an abbreviation for **Fahrenheit**.

fa *noun* the syllable that indicates the fourth tone of a musical scale. {**fah**}

fa·ble ◗ ◑ *noun* 1. a short tale that teaches a lesson. The characters in fables are often animals who speak and act like people. *"The Fox and the Grapes" is a well-known fable by Aesop.* 2. a false story; lie. *He told us a fable about his father being a jet pilot.* {**fay** bəl}

fab·ric *noun* cloth that is woven or knitted; material. *The shirt is made of a very soft fabric.* {**făb** rihk}

Word History The words *fabric* and *fabricate* both come from a Latin word that means "something made or constructed."

fab·u·lous *adjective* 1. almost impossible to believe; amazing. *He told us about the fabulous birds he had seen in South America.* 2. (informal) wonderful; excellent. *It was a fabulous party.* {**făb** yə ləs} fabulously, adv.

face ◑ *noun* 1. the front part of the head from the forehead to the chin and from ear to ear. 2. a look or expression on the face that shows feelings. *Why do you have such a sad face?* 3. the way something looks; outward look or appearance. *On the face of it, the team seems likely to lose.* 4. one's honor or self-respect. *He saved face by saying he was sorry.* 5. a front part or surface. *We climbed the face of the cliff. / A cube has six faces.* *verb* (faced, facing, faces) 1. to look or turn toward. *Please face me when you speak.* 2. to turn or be placed so that the front is to a particular direction (usually followed by "on" or "toward"). *That house faces toward the road.* 3. to stand before or deal with in a brave way. *Ed climbed that mountain to face his fear of heights.* {**fays**}

• **face to face**
very close to; right up to; in person. *I will explain it to you when we can talk face to face. / Firefighters come face to face with danger.*

• **face up to**
to meet bravely. *She faced up to the bully when he tried to grab her lunch.*

• **in the face of**
when faced with. *It is sometimes hard to stay calm in the face of an emergency.*

fac·et *noun* one of the small, flat, polished surfaces of a cut gem. *The many facets of this diamond make it sparkle in the light.* {**fă** siht} faceted (facetted), adj.

fa·cial *adjective* of or relating to the face. *Many men shave their facial hair.* {**fay** shəl}

fa·cil·i·tate *verb* (facilitated, facilitating, facilitates) to make less difficult; help in the doing of. *The ramp facilitates entry for people who use wheelchairs.* {fə **sihl** ih **tayt**} facilitator, n.

fa·cil·i·ty ◗ *noun* (facilities) 1. a building made or used for a particular activity. *The new sports facility will offer evening basketball.* 2. ease; skill. *She has an amazing facility with languages.* {fə **sihl** ih tee}

fac·sim·i·le *noun* 1. an exact copy or duplicate of something printed or of a picture. 2. an electronic method of sending images, or an image sent by this means. {făk **sih** mə lee}

fact *noun* 1. something said or known to be true. *It is a fact that water covers most of the earth's surface.* 2. something

that is real or that happened or is happening. *It is a fact that it is raining at this very moment.* {**făkt**}

• **in fact**
in reality; really; indeed. *In fact, I don't like loud music.*

Word History *Fact* is from a Latin word that means "event" or "deed."

fac·tor *noun* 1. one of the causes of something; something that makes a difference in a result. *Gasoline fumes from cars are a factor in air pollution.* 2. any one of two or more numbers that are multiplied together to give a product. *The factors of twelve are one, two, three, four, six, and twelve.* *verb* (factored, factoring, factors) to show as a product of factors. *We learned how to factor whole numbers in fifth grade.* {**făk** tər}

fac·to·ry ⚪ *noun* (factories) a building or set of buildings where products are made by machines. {**făk** tə ree}

fac·tu·al *adjective* containing facts; true. *It turned out that the story was not factual. / I have to write a factual essay about dinosaurs.* {**făk** chooh əl}

fac·ul·ty ⚪⚪⚪ *noun* (faculties) 1. an ability or talent for doing a particular thing. *She has a faculty for making learning fun.* 2. one of the abilities of the human mind. Memory, reasoning, and perception are all faculties. *My great-grandfather has started to lose his faculties.* 3. the group of teachers in a school or college. *A new teacher is joining the faculty.* {**făk** əl tee}

fad *noun* something that is liked by many people for a short amount of time. *Swal-* lowing goldfish was a fad in the 1920s. / Disco music was a fad in the 1970s.* {**făd**}

fade *verb* (faded, fading, fades) 1. to lose color. *Her black jeans faded after they were washed.* 2. to cause to fade. *The sun has faded the blue curtains.* 3. to gradually disappear (sometimes followed by "out" or "away"). *The sound of the train faded away into the distance.* 4. to lose strength. *Her enthusiasm is fading.* {**făyd**}

Fahr·en·heit *adjective* relating to a temperature scale on which water freezes at 32 degrees and boils at 212 degrees. (abbreviated: F) {**fehr** ən hiyt}

fail *verb* (failed, failing, fails) 1. to not do or not succeed in doing; be unable. *Rick failed at the task.* 2. to lose force or stamina. *The runner's strength began to fail after the fifteenth mile.* 3. to stop working. *The engine failed, so we walked home.* 4. to not meet the hopes of; disappoint. *You fail your friends when you lie to them.* 5. to receive a grade below passing in. *Sue failed her driving test.* 6. to give a grade below passing. *No teacher likes to fail a student.* {**făyl**}

fail·ure *noun* 1. the act of not succeeding or not doing. *His failure to win did not stop him from trying again.* 2. a person or thing that fails or does not succeed. *The scientist's experiment was a failure.* 3. the condition of not being enough. *The heavy rain caused a crop failure.* 4. a stopping of normal performance; breakdown. *Engine failure caused the plane crash.* {**făyl** yər}

faint *adjective* (fainter, faintest) 1. weak or slight. *There is still a faint odor of fish in here. /* We heard a faint whisper. 2. very tired, dizzy, or about to become unconscious. *She felt faint after gym class. verb* (fainted, fainting, faints) to become unconscious for a short time; pass out. *Paul faints at the sight of blood. noun* a condition in which a person becomes unconscious for a short time. *She fell in a faint.* {**făynt**}

Homophone Note The words *faint* and *feint* sound alike but have different meanings. To find out why a basketball player would rather feint than faint on the court, look up *feint*.

Word History *Faint* comes from an early French word that means "cowardly" and "lacking in spirit."

fair¹ *adjective* (fairer, fairest) 1. without showing favor; just. *The principal was being fair when she punished both of you.* 2. according to the rules. *It was a fair fight.* 3. pleasing to the eye; lovely. *The fair princess has saved the kingdom.* 4. free from rain, snow, and storms; clear. *We enjoyed fair weather while we were in New Mexico.* 5. average; acceptable. *A fair number of people were at the concert.* 6. of a light tone. *Her fair skin burns easily. adverb* (fairer, fairest) in a just manner; fairly. *Why won't you play fair?* {**fayr**} fairness, n.

fair² *noun* 1. a gathering at which farm animals and farm produce are shown and judged. A fair is usually held over several days and includes games and amusements. 2. a gathering to show products to people interested in buying. *We spent the day*

 Human Body    Human Mind   Everyday Life    History and Culture    Communication

looking through books at the book fair. {fayr}

Homophone Note Are you looking for the word *fare*? *Fair* and *fare* sound alike but have different meanings.

fair·ground *noun* (often plural) an open, flat space where fairs are held. {fayr grownd}

fair·ly *adverb* 1. in a just or honest way. *The judge decided fairly.* 2. somewhat; moderately. *She is doing fairly well in school.* 3. by the rules; honestly. *He did not win the game fairly.* {fayr lee}

fair·y *noun* (fairies) an imaginary tiny creature in human form, thought to have magic powers. {fayr ee}

Homophone Note The words *fairy* and *ferry* are similar in sound but have different meanings. To find out why you are more likely to ride on a ferry than on a fairy, look up the word *ferry*.

faith 🙂 💬 *noun* 1. trust or confidence. *He has faith that the minister knows best.* 2. belief or trust in something that has never been proved. *I have faith that there is life after death.* 3. any particular religion and its teachings. *He is of the Jewish faith, and she is Muslim.* {fayth}

faith·ful *adjective* 1. able to be trusted or relied on. *She is a faithful friend.* 2. staying close to fact; truthful or accurate. *She gave a faithful account of the accident.* {fayth fəl} faithfully, adv., faithfulness, n.

fake *verb* (faked, faking, fakes) 1. to make a false copy of. *She faked her mother's handwriting on the note.* 2. to pretend. *Mark faked surprise at the party.* noun* 1. anything that is not real or genuine. *Those diamonds are fakes.* 2. a person who pretends to feel or be something. *He claimed to be a real magician, but he was just a fake. adjective* not real or genuine; made to look like something that it is not. *We were almost fooled by the fake money.* {fayk}

fal·con *noun* a bird with long, powerful wings and a hooked beak. Falcons are related to hawks. They hunt other animals for food during the day. {fawl kən *or* făl kən}

fall *verb* (fell, fallen, falling, falls) 1. to drop downward from a higher place; descend. *At the end of the play, the curtain fell. / He fell from the top of the tree.* 2. to become less; go down in amount, volume, or degree. *The price of gasoline fell last month. / The students' voices fell to a whisper when the teacher walked in.* 3. to hang down. *His hair fell in curls over his forehead.* 4. to be taken over by force; be defeated or overthrown. *After three days of battle, our city fell to the attackers.* 5. to happen; occur. *Night fell and the children got ready for bed.* 6. to become; pass into a particular condition or position. *She fell ill. / He fell behind in his work. noun* 1. the act or condition of falling to a lower place. *The climber had a bad fall. / We watched the fall of the leaves.* 2. (usually plural) a sudden drop in a river or stream that causes water to fall; waterfall. *The Niagara Falls drop about one hundred and sixty feet.* 3. a defeat or capture by force. *The fall of King Rufus led to civil war.* 4. autumn. *Fall is the harvest season in this part of the country.* {fawl}

• **fall back on** to have another choice if something does not work out; resort to. *If I don't get the job at the park, I can fall back on my old job at the store.*

• **fall behind** to not keep up with; lag behind. *She fell behind the group and could not walk fast enough to catch up.*

• **fall under** to be put or classed in a group as; included in. *Lacrosse falls under the category of sports.*

fall·en *verb* past participle of **fall**. *adjective* 1. having dropped or come down. *The fallen leaves covered the ground in a blanket of red and gold.* 2. dead. *There was a moment of silence for the fallen soldiers.* {faw lən}

fall·out *noun* the radioactive particles that fall from a nuclear explosion. {fawl owt}

fal·low *adjective* plowed but not planted with seeds. *The field was left fallow for two years so the soil could recover. noun* land on a farm that has been plowed but not planted for one or more seasons. {fă loh}

false *adjective* (falser, falsest) 1. not true or not correct. *"The world is flat" is a false statement.* 2. purposely not true or honest. *The bully tells false stories to make himself look tough.* 3. not real; fake or artificial. *George Washington had false teeth made of wood.* {fawls}

A B C D E F G H I J K L M N O P Q R S T U V W X Y Z

 Living World Physical World  Natural Environment  Economy 🔵 Government and Law

a
b
c
d
e
f
g
h
i
j
k
l
m
n
o
p
q
r
s
t
u
v
w
x
y
z

false·hood *noun* a lie. *She told a falsehood to protect her mother.* {<u>fawls</u> huud}

fal·ter *verb* (faltered, faltering, falters) 1. to move, speak, or act in a way that is not sure or not steady; stumble. *She faltered over the words she did not know.* 2. to hesitate because of being confused or not sure. *I will never falter in my quest for the truth.* {<u>fawl</u> tər}

fame *noun* the condition of being well known or respected by a great number of people. *Joe found fame and fortune as an actor.* {<u>faym</u>}

fa·mil·iar *adjective* 1. known by many people; easily recognized. *The audience sang along with the familiar song.* 2. having some knowledge of. *She is familiar with that part of town.* 3. close; friendly. *I am on familiar terms with my teacher.* {fə <u>mihl</u> yər}

fam·i·ly ❶ ❷ *noun* (families) 1. a group made up of a parent or parents and their children. *My dad came from a large family.* 2. all those related by blood. *He could trace his family back over two hundred years. / We will visit family on Thanksgiving.* 3. any group living together as if they were related by blood. *At college, my friends became my family.* 4. any group of things related in what they look like, do, or where they come from. *French, Spanish, and Italian are all part of the same family of languages.* {<u>făm</u> ih lee or <u>făm</u> lee}

Synonyms
These words share a meaning with *family*, noun 2:
people, relations, kin

family room *noun* a large room in which a family gets together to relax, talk, or play games. {<u>făm</u> lee roohm}

fam·ine *noun* a great lack of food over a wide area. *Many people in Ireland starved to death during the famine.* {<u>făm</u> ihn}

fa·mous *adjective* recognized or liked by the public. *"The Four Seasons" is a famous piece of music.* {<u>fay</u> məs}

fan¹ ⊙ *noun* 1. a machine that makes air move by means of spinning blades. It is usually driven by an electric motor. 2. a device that is waved back and forth with the hand to cool the face or body. *verb* (fanned, fanning, fans) to stir or move with or as with a fan. *He fanned the coals to make the fire burn hotter.* {<u>făn</u>}

fan² ⊙ *noun* a person who is very interested in a sport or a performing art, or in a person who does that activity. *The football fan painted his face in the team colors.* {<u>făn</u>}

During the heat wave, Roberta was a big **fan** of electric **fans**.

fa·nat·ic *noun* a person who is enthusiastic about something in a way that is extreme or not reasonable.

adjective interested or enthusiastic to an extreme point. *The fanatic soccer players practice several hours every day.* {fə <u>năt</u> ihk} fanatical, adj., fanaticism, n.

Word History *Fanatic* comes from a Latin word that means "temple." In early English, a "fanatic" was a person who was thought to be possessed by a god. Later, the word "fanatic" was used for a person overly enthusiastic about religious matters.

fan·cy *noun* (fancies) 1. something pictured in the mind or wished for that may not be based on reason or real life. *She has a fancy that she will marry a prince.* 2. imagination. *Flying cows are animals of fancy.* 3. a liking for something, or the object that is liked. *Emma has a fancy for horses. / Chocolate is my fancy.* *adjective* (fancier, fanciest) 1. splendid; grander than the average. *She wore a fancy gown to the ball.* 2. special; excellent; very skilled. *The skater got everyone's attention with her fancy moves.* *verb* (fancied, fancying, fancies) 1. to imagine or picture. *Can you fancy me as a cowboy?* 2. to like or be fond of. *I fancy your red hair.* {<u>făn</u> see}

fang ⊙ *noun* a long pointed tooth. Some animals use their fangs to hold and tear prey. Some snakes have hollow fangs through which they inject poison. {<u>făng</u>} fanged, adj.

fan·tas·tic *adjective* 1. wildly imaginative and incredible. *Her brother told a fantastic story about being kidnapped by wolves.* 2. strange or unusual.

 Human Body  Human Mind Everyday Life History and Culture  Communication

We read about the fantastic life forms on the ocean floor. 3. (informal) excellent or superb. *She was a fantastic singer when she was young.* {**făn tăs** tihk} fantastically, adv.

fan·ta·sy *noun* (fantasies) 1. imagination or something imagined. *In fantasy, anything can happen.* 2. a kind of story that is very imaginative and contains strange characters, places, or events. *In that fantasy, the characters find a doorway to another world.* {**făn** tə see}

far *adverb* (farther or further, farthest or furthest) 1. at or to a long distance in space or time. *We traveled far.* / *Far in the past, people lived in caves.* 2. very much. *My cold is far worse today.* adjective (farther or further, farthest or furthest) 1. distant in space or time. *Polar bears live in the far north.* 2. more distant; farther. *We parked in the far parking lot.* {**far**}
• **by far**
without a doubt; indeed. *She was by far the best runner on the team.*
• **far and wide**
over a great distance; everywhere. *We searched far and wide for blue shoes to match my dress.*

• **so far so good**
no problems yet. *So far so good with the new puppy!*

far·a·way *adjective* 1. distant or remote. *She dreamed of a faraway island where it would always be sunny and warm.* 2. not paying attention, as if one's mind were on distant subjects. *He sat in class with a faraway look in his eyes.* {**far** ə way}

fare *noun* the price paid to ride on a bus, train, taxi, or airplane, or a passenger who pays this price. *The bus fare is only fifty cents for children.* / *The taxi driver picked up seven fares this afternoon.* verb (fared, faring, fares) to get along or be treated. *How is she faring in her new job?* {**fayr**}

Homophone Note Are you looking for the word *fair*? *Fare* and *fair* sound alike but have different meanings.

Word History *Fare* comes from an Old English word that means "a journey."

fare·well *interjection* "may you fare well"; "good-bye and good wishes." *"Farewell!" said the princess as she left the castle.* noun an expression of good wishes that is said when people part. *They said their farewells and left for the airport.* {**fayr wehl**}

farm *noun* 1. an area of land and the buildings on it used to grow vegetables or raise animals for food or clothing. 2. an area of land or water used to raise certain kinds of crops or animals. *Those trout come from a fish farm.* verb (farmed, farming, farms) 1. to cultivate or raise. *My grandfather had to drain a swamp before he could farm the land.* / *For years he farmed pigs.* 2. to raise

crops or animals. *Many families farm for a living.* {**farm**}

farm·er *noun* a person who owns or runs a farm. {**far** mər}

farm·ing 🌐 *noun* the business or practice of raising crops and livestock. *That family has been in farming for almost a hundred years.* {**farm** ing}

far·sight·ed *adjective* 1. able to see objects well in the distance, but not so well if they are close. *He needs to wear reading glasses because he is farsighted.* 2. wise about guessing or knowing what will happen in the future. *They were farsighted enough to buy that car before the price went up.* {**far siy** tihd} farsightedly, adv., farsightedness, n.

far·ther *adverb* to or at a greater distance. "Farther" is a comparative form of the adjective **far.** *Jim can jump farther than Kevin can.* adjective more distant; covering a greater distance. "Farther" is a comparative form of the adverb **far.** *We set sail for the farther shore.* {**far** thər}

far·thest *adjective* most far or distant. "Farthest" is a superlative of "far." *Pluto is the farthest planet from the sun.* adverb to or at the greatest distance. *I threw the ball farthest.* {**far** thəst}

fas·ci·nate *verb* (fascinated, fascinating, fascinates) to attract and hold the attention and interest of. *The northern lights fascinate me.* {**făs** ih **nayt**}

fash·ion *noun* 1. the style of clothes or way of acting that is popular. *What's the fashion in skirts these days?* 2. the manner or way of something. *He behaved in an odd fashion last night.* verb (fashioned, fashioning, fashions) to make, shape, or form. *He*

A B C D E F G H I J K L M N O P Q R S T U V W X Y Z

fashioned a rabbit out of clay. {**făsh** ən}

fast[1] *adjective* (faster, fastest) 1. moving or operating with speed. *He's a fast runner. / She drives a fast car.* 2. done in a short time. *She prepared a fast meal.* 3. true and loyal. *Meg and I are fast friends.* 4. fixed or firmly attached. *I tried to shake him off, but he had a fast grip on my arm.* 5. ahead of the correct time. *That clock is five minutes fast.* 6. not easily faded; fixed firmly. *The blue in this shirt won't wash out because the color is fast.* *adverb* (faster, fastest) 1. with speed; quickly. *He came fast when his mother called him for dinner.* 2. tightly; firmly. *She held fast to her child's hand.* 3. deeply; soundly. *We fell fast asleep.* {**făst**}

Synonyms
These words share a meaning with *fast*, adjective 1:
quick, rapid

fast[2] *verb* (fasted, fasting, fasts) 1. to eat no food. *She had to fast for twelve hours before the operation* 2. to eat very little or no food for religious or political reasons. *Muslims fast from sunrise to sunset during the month of Ramadan.* *noun* a period when one does not eat any food. *His fast lasted three days.* {**făst**}

fas·ten *verb* (fastened, fastening, fastens) 1. to join or attach firmly to something else or in place. *The policeman fastened the badge to his uniform.* 2. to close firmly or cause to stay closed with a lock, buttons, or other fastener. *Mother fastened the suitcase. / Fasten the door after we go out.* 3. to direct at in a fixed or focused way. *The dog fastened its eyes on the hamburger.* {**fă** sən} fastener, n.

fas·ten·er *noun* a device that joins together or fastens. *Buttons, snaps, and clips are kinds of fasteners.* {**fă** sən ər}

fast-food *adjective* selling food that is quickly made and served. *We bought lunch at a fast-food restaurant.* {**făst foohd**}

fat 🏃 ⚫ *adjective* (fatter, fattest) 1. having a lot of extra flesh that is not muscle; plump; overweight. *That cat is so fat that he can hardly jump.* 2. thick. *How many pages does that fat book have?* *noun* 1. a white or yellow oily substance found in some parts of animals or plants. Fat is made of carbon, hydrogen, and oxygen. 2. animal or plant tissue that contains such a substance. *Butter and lard are fats. / His fat hung over his belt.* {**făt**}

• **fat chance**
slight or no chance. *That other team is so good, we've got a fat chance of winning.*

fa·tal *adjective* 1. causing or able to cause death. *He died in a fatal accident.* 2. leading to trouble, ruin, or destruction. *The thief made the fatal mistake of boasting of his crime in a public place.* {**fay** təl}

fate *noun* 1. the power that is often believed to decide what will happen in human life or history. *Fate was on her side when she won the contest.* 2. an ending or outcome that had to happen because of this power; destiny. *It was his fate to become successful in business.* {**fayt**}

Word History *Fate* is from a Latin word that means "thing spoken by the gods."

fa·ther *noun* 1. a male parent. 2. a person who founds, begins, or invents something. *Who is the father of modern medicine?* 3. a priest. {**fah** thər}

fa·ther-in-law *noun* (fathers-in-law) the father of a person's wife or husband. {**fah** thər ihn **law**}

fath·om *noun* (fathom or fathoms) a unit of length equal to six feet, used to measure the depth of water or mines. *verb* (fathomed, fathoming, fathoms) to get to the bottom of or understand completely. *I'll never fathom how to use this kind of computer.* {**făth** əm}

fa·tigue *noun* the condition of being tired in body or mind. *The hospital nurses are suffering from fatigue.* *verb* (fatigued, fatiguing, fatigues) to tire out or make weary. *A long day of hiking fatigued the campers.* {**fə teeg**}

fat·ten *verb* (fattened, fattening, fattens) 1. to make fat. *The farmer fattens his animals with corn.* 2. to become plump or fat. *The bear fattened on berries before the long winter.* {**făt** ən}

fau·cet *noun* a device for turning on and off the flow of liquid from a pipe or container; tap. {**faw** siht}

fault *noun* 1. something wrong with a thing or person that causes problems for someone or something else. *Nick's fault is talking too much. / The car makes loud noises because of a fault in the engine.* 2. a mistake; error. *Her job at the factory is to find faults in the finished products.* 3. responsibility for a mistake or error. *Whose fault is it that the work didn't get done?* {**fawlt**}

• **at fault**

 Human Body    Human Mind   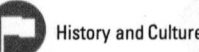 Everyday Life   History and Culture    Communication

responsible for mistakes or errors. *Who is at fault for breaking the vase?*

• **to a fault**

to a degree or amount that is almost too good. *His kindly uncle was generous to a fault.*

fa·vor *noun* 1. a kind or helpful act. *Would you please do me a favor and set the table?* 2. high respect; liking; approval. *He was a good player and won the favor of the coach.* 3. a special liking; leaning; preference. *That teacher shows favor to the student who gets the highest grades.* 4. a gift given to each person at a social event. *Adam gave out kazoos as favors at his birthday party.* *verb* (favored, favoring, favors) 1. to have good feelings about; support; approve of. *I favor the rule about wearing bicycle helmets.* 2. to give special treatment to; prefer. *It's not fair when a parent favors one child over another.* {**fay** vər}

• **in favor of**

in support of. *Most senators voted in favor of the new civil rights law.*

fa·vor·a·ble *adjective* 1. giving a benefit or advantage; helpful. *The favorable winds made it a good day to fly a kite.* 2. pleasing; causing approval. *He makes a favorable impression.* 3. showing the promise of something good. *A favorable weather report meant the parade would go on.* {**fay** vər ə bəl} favorably, adv.

fa·vor·ite *noun* 1. a person or thing treated with special favor. *Scary movies are my favorites.* 2. a person or animal thought to be the most likely winner of a game or sport. *Out of the horses in the race, that one is the favorite.* *adjective* liked over all others. *Oranges are my favorite fruit.* {**fay** vər iht *or* **fayv** riht, n., **fay** vər iht *or* **fayv** riht, adj.}

fa·vour *noun or verb* a spelling of **favor** used in Canada and Britain. See **favor**. {**fay** vər}

fa·vour·a·ble *adjective* a spelling of **favorable** used in Canada and Britain. See **favorable**. {**fay** vər o behl}

fa·vour·ite *noun or adjective* a spelling of **favorite** used in Canada and Britain. See **favorite**. {**fay** vər iht}

fawn *noun* a young deer, especially one that is still drinking its mother's milk. {**fawn**}

fax *noun* 1. a machine for sending and receiving pages that are transmitted electronically over telephone lines to or from another such machine. "Fax" is short for "facsimile." *To get this form in on time, we will have to send it by fax.* 2. a paper copy that is produced by a fax machine. *Have you read the fax from Ms. Marx?* *verb* (faxed, faxing, faxes) to send by fax. *Please fill out the form and fax it to us.* {**fäks**}

FBI *abbreviation* the U.S. government agency responsible for investigating crimes against national laws. FBI is an abbreviation for "Federal Bureau of Investigation."

Fe symbol of the chemical element iron.

fear ⊙ *noun* 1. a strong feeling one gets when one expects danger or pain. *Her fear of fire is based on a bad experience.* 2. something that causes such an emotion. *His greatest fear is of losing his parents.* *verb* (feared, fearing, fears) 1. to be frightened of. *I*

fear high places. 2. to be worried or in doubt about. *Kyle feared that he was being lied to.* {**feer**}

Word History *Fear* comes from *fere*, an Old English word. Its earliest meaning, in the 700s, was "danger or peril." It was not used for the feeling of fear until the 1300s.

fear·ful *adjective* 1. feeling fear; afraid. *She was fearful of traveling by airplane.* 2. causing or likely to cause fear. *A fearful storm is coming.* {**feer** fəl} fearfully, adv., fearfulness, n.

fear·less *adjective* without fear; brave. *The fearless firefighter ran into the burning house.* {**feer** lihs} fearlessly, adv., fearlessness, n.

feast *noun* any large and elaborate meal. *verb* (feasted, feasting, feasts) to eat a lot of food at a large, special meal. *The family feasted on roast turkey and apple pie.* {**feest**}

feat *noun* an act or achievement that shows courage, strength, or skill. *Rafting down the raging river was quite a feat.* {**feet**}

Homophone Note Are you looking for the word *feet* (plural of foot)? *Feat* and *feet* sound alike but have different meanings.

 Living World   Physical World  Natural Environment Economy  Government and Law

feath·er ❶ *noun* one of the soft and light parts of a bird that grows from the skin and covers the body. *verb* (feathered, feathering, feathers) to put feathers on or in. *My mom feathered the inside of my pillow to make it softer.* {**feh** thər}

fea·ture *noun* 1. a part of the face such as the eyes, nose, or chin. *A baby has tiny features.* 2. a part or quality of something. *The best feature of that house is its sunny porch.* 3. the main film in a movie theater. *There were two cartoons before the feature.* *verb* (featured, featuring, features) to give special importance to. *Today's newspaper features an article about the Olympic games.* {**fee** chər}

Feb. *abbreviation* an abbreviation for **February**.

Feb·ru·ar·y *noun* (Februaries) the second month of the year. February usually has twenty-eight days, but it has twenty-nine days in a leap year. {**feh** brooh **ayr** ee}

Word History *February* comes from a Latin name for the month, *februarius mensis*, which means "month of the Februa festival." *Februa* was a Roman festival of purification celebrated in February. In English, the month has been called "February" since 1200. Before that, February was called by an Old English name that meant "mud month."

fed *verb* past tense and past participle of **feed**. {**fehd**}
• **fed up**
bored, disgusted, or irritated. *She is fed up with her job.*

fed·er·al ⬤ *adjective* 1. having to do with a system of government that unites several states under a central government. The states have their own governments, yet they recognize the rule of the central government as well. 2. having to do with the central government of a country. *The United States has local, state, and federal courts.* {**fehd** ə rəl *or* **fehd** rəl} federally, adv.

fed·er·a·tion *noun* a government or league formed by the union of several states, clubs, or other groups. *The American Federation of Labor was formed when several trade unions came together in 1886.* {**fehd** ə **ray** shən}

fee *noun* 1. an amount of money requested or paid for a service. *Doctors and lawyers often charge high fees.* 2. an amount paid for a right to do something. *We paid a fee to park our car in the closest lot.* {**fee**}

fee·ble *adjective* (feebler, feeblest) without strength; weak in body or mind. *Although he is feeble, the old man walks a mile every day.* {**fee** bəl} feebleness, n.

Word History *Feeble* comes from *flebeles*, a Latin word that means "to be wept over."

feed ❶ ⬤ *verb* (fed, feeding, feeds) 1. to provide food for or give food to. *The mission feeds homeless people.* / *Did you feed the dog this morning?* 2. to build up; support; add to the strength of. *Caring for a horse at the stable feeds his dream of having his own.* 3. to put something into; supply. *Lisa fed the fire with sticks she found.* / *The river feeds the lake.* 4. to eat food. *Deer feed on grass.* *noun* food for birds and animals, such as seeds, grain, or hay. *Tim bought feed for his hamster at the pet store.* {**feed**}

feel ⬤ ⬤ *verb* (felt, feeling, feels) 1. to find out about or perceive by the sense of touch. *Can you feel this bump on my head?* 2. to sense or be aware of. *She felt a headache starting.* 3. to have or be moved by a strong emotion of. *We felt great sadness at the loss of life from the earthquake.* 4. to have a belief or opinion. *They feel it would be dangerous for so many of us to go in one car.* *noun* the quality of something to the touch. *I like the feel of this cool, hard stone.* {**feel**}
• **feel like**
to have a desire for or interest in. *I feel like going for a swim.*
• **feel up to**
(informal) to be able to. *Do you feel up to coming over tonight?*

feel·er *noun* a part of an animal's body that is used for touching and feeling. The long, thin feelers that grow on the heads of many insects are called antennae. {**fee** lər}

feel·ing ⬤ *noun* 1. the ability to sense things by touch. *After the accident he lost all feeling in his right hand.* 2. the condition of being aware. *A feeling of hunger came over Jim as we walked past the bakery.* 3. an emotion. *Love, anger, joy, and fear are human feelings.* {**feel** ing}

feet ⬤ ❶ *noun* plural of **foot**. {**feet**}

Homophone Note Are you looking for the word *feat* (a courageous act)? *Feet* and *feat* sound alike but have different meanings.

feign *verb* (feigned, feigning, feigns) to pretend or fake; put on a false show

 Human Body   Human Mind   Everyday Life  History and Culture  Communication

of. *She feigned sleep when her mother looked into the room.* {**fayn**}

feint *noun* a false movement that is meant to trick an opponent by taking attention away from the real target. *A feint with his right hand fooled the other boxer.* *verb* (feinted, feinting, feints) to move or attack in a way that takes attention away from the real target. *She feinted to the left and then kicked the ball to the right.* {**faynt**}

Homophone Note The words *faint* and *feint* sound alike but have different meanings.

fe·line ◐ *adjective* 1. having to do with cats, both house cats and cats that live in the wild. *The veterinarian studied feline medicine.* 2. looking or acting like a cat, such as moving in a silent or graceful way. *The dancer was known for her feline movements.* *noun* a closely related group of animals that includes both large cats like lions and tigers and small cats such as house cats and bobcats. Most cats have flat noses, small ears, and long tails. Felines are carnivorous mammals. They use their sharp teeth and claws for hunting other animals as food. {**fee liyn**}

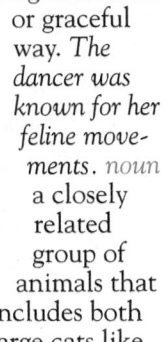

fell[1] *verb* past tense of **fall**. {**fehl**}
fell[2] *verb* (felled, felling, fells) 1. to cut or strike down. *He is felling trees for firewood.* 2. to strike down or kill in a fight or battle. *His mighty sword felled many enemies that day.* {**fehl**}

fel·low *noun* 1. a man or boy. *He's a good fellow.* 2. a partner; companion. *The fellows met for a game of golf.* *adjective* belonging to the same group, having the same job, or sharing the same interests. *The president began his speech with "My fellow countrymen." / Scott and his fellow classmates raised money for the refugees.* {**fehl** oh}

Word History The earliest meaning of *fellow* in English was "partner." The word "fellow" comes from an early Norse word that meant "fee layer," or a person who lays down money for some enterprise. Those who put their money or property together were partners, or "fellows." In Iceland, the word was also used for a husband or wife.

fel·low·ship *noun* 1. the condition of being companions; company or friendship. *He enjoyed the fellowship of many old friends.* 2. a group of people who share common interests. *Nina is part of the fellowship of chess players.* {**fehl** oh shihp}

felt[1] *verb* past tense and past participle of **feel**. {**fehlt**}

felt[2] *noun* a cloth made of wool or other animal fibers that have been pressed instead of woven together. {**fehlt**}

fe·male *noun* 1. any person or animal of the sex that produces eggs or gives birth to young. 2. a woman or girl. *A female was seen leaving the scene of the crime.* *adjective* 1. being a member of the sex that produces and takes care of young. *We saw a female bird sitting on her nest.* 2.

having to do with women or girls or with the way women or girls often act. {**fee mayl**}

fem·i·nine *adjective* of or having to do with a woman or girl; of the female sex. *"Jane" is a feminine name, and "John" is a masculine name.* {**fehm** ə nihn}

fence *noun* a structure used to mark off an area or to keep animals or people in or out. *verb* (fenced, fencing, fences) 1. to place a fence around (often followed by "in," "off," or "out"). *They fenced off their share of the property.* 2. to take part in the sport of fencing. *The two competitors fenced well in the match.* {**fehns**} fencer, n.

fenc·ing *noun* the art, sport, or practice of fighting with swords. {**fehn** sing}

fend·er *noun* 1. a metal guard over the wheel of a truck, car, or bicycle. 2. a low metal guard in front of a fireplace. {**fehn** dər}

fer·ment *noun* 1. a substance that causes the chemical change of fermentation. *Yeast is used as a ferment when making beer.* 2. a state of upset or fast change. *The country was in a ferment when rebels tried to take over the government.* *verb* (fermented, fermenting, ferments) 1. to undergo the chemical change of fermentation. *The fruit juice is fermenting in the jar.* 2. to cause to ferment. *We fermented the grapes to make wine.* {**fuhr** mehnt, n., fər **mehnt**, v.}

fer·men·ta·tion ◐ *noun* 1. the chemical change of a sugar into alcohol. Fermentation

a
b
c
d
e
f
g
h
i
j
k
l
m
n
o
p
q
r
s
t
u
v
w
x
y
z

produces gas bubbles. *It is fermentation that changes grape juice into wine.* 2. excitement, upset, or unrest; ferment. *The country was in a state of fermentation before the revolution.* {**fuhr** mehn **tay** shən}

fern *noun* a family of plants with large green leaves shaped like feathers. Ferns do not make flowers or seeds. {**fuhrn**}

fe·ro·cious *adjective* fierce; savage. *Mother bears can become ferocious if their cubs are hurt.* {fə **roh** shəs} ferociously, adv., ferociousness, n.

fer·ret *noun* 1. a European polecat that has been domesticated for use in hunting rabbits and rodents. 2. a small mammal with light fur and black feet. Ferrets are a kind of weasel. They live in the plains of North America, where they eat prairie dogs. The North American ferret is closely related to the European ferret or polecat. *verb* (ferreted, ferreting, ferrets) 1. to use ferrets to hunt for small burrowing animals such as rabbits or rodents. 2. to search for lost or hidden items or information. *The detective tried to ferret out a clue to find the missing woman.* {**fehr** ət}

Ferris wheel *noun* a ride at a carnival or amusement park made of a very large upright wheel with seats hanging from the

rim. A motor turns the wheel while people sit in the seats. {**fehr** ihs **weel**}

fer·ry *noun* (ferries) a boat or ship that carries people or freight back and forth across a river or other body of water. *verb* (ferried, ferrying, ferries) to carry by boat or airplane a short distance, often across water. *A small plane ferried tourists to the island.* {**fehr** ee}

> **Homophone Note** Are you looking for the word *fairy* (an imaginary creature)? *Ferry* and *fairy* sound alike but have different meanings.

fer·tile *adjective* 1. producing or able to produce farm crops or other plant life. *The soil in river valleys is fertile.* 2. producing or able to produce young, seeds, fruit, eggs, or other offspring. *The most fertile cows give birth to calves every year.* 3. producing in large amounts or without stopping; creative. *That painter has a fertile imagination.* {**fuhr** tihl}

fer·ti·lize ✦ ◉ *verb* (fertilized, fertilizing, fertilizes) 1. to cause the fertilization of. *Bees fertilize the flowers.* 2. to apply fertilizer to. *He fertilizes his lawn.* {**fuhr** tə **liyz**}

fer·ti·liz·er *noun* a natural or chemical substance added to soil to make it better for growing plants. *Some gardeners use bone meal as a fertilizer.* {**fuhr** tə **liy** zər}

fes·ti·val ◉ *noun* 1. a day or more of celebration in honor of a special event, such as a religious holiday. *The city holds a festival to celebrate the New Year.* 2. a series of shows, exhibits, or special activities. Festivals are often planned around a theme such as a type of food, a

season, or a kind of art or music. *Our teacher took us to the jazz festival.* {**fehs** tih vəl}

fes·tive *adjective* 1. of, relating to, or intended for a feast or celebration. *The Halloween decorations made the room look festive.* 2. merry and joyful. *It's always a festive occasion when their son comes home from college.* {**fehs** tihv}

fes·tiv·i·ty *noun* (festivities) 1. a celebration; festival. *Mrs. Costa is planning a big festivity for her husband's sixtieth birthday.* 2. (plural) the events or activities planned for or happening at a celebration. *Jerry was eager to join in the holiday festivities.* {**fehs** **tih** vih tee}

fetch *verb* (fetched, fetching, fetches) to bring back or cause to come; get. *Go and fetch your tools.* {**fehch**}

feud *noun* anger, unfriendliness, or fighting between families or other related groups that lasts for a long time. *No one remembers what started the feud, but the two cousins haven't spoken to each other in years.* *verb* (feuded, feuding, feuds) to carry on a feud. *The two families have been feuding for fifty years.* {**fyood**}

feu·dal·ism ◍ ▢ *noun* a political and economic system in Europe and Japan during the Middle Ages. Royal or noble families owned the land and allowed people to live on and farm the land in return for a share of the crops and their service in war. {**fyood** ə lihz əm} feudalist, adj., n., feudalistic, adj.

 Human Body   ❓ Human Mind   Everyday Life   🏳 History and Culture   📞 Communication

fe·ver *noun* 1. a body temperature higher than normal that is usually caused by illness. *He stayed home in bed with a fever.* 2. a state of intense excitement or activity. *The kids were in a fever about the latest action movie.* {**fee** vər}

few *adjective* (fewer, fewest) only a small number of. *Few people become millionaires.* / *There are a few seats left.* *noun* a very small number (used with a plural verb). *A few of the pencils fell to the floor.* *pronoun* a small number of people or things (used with a plural verb). *Few understand his poetry.* {**fyoo**}

• **few and far between** not often happening; seldom seen. *In this town, sunny days are few and far between.*

• **quite a few** a rather large number of people or things. *Quite a few were absent from school yesterday.*

fib *noun* a lie about something that is not important. *For telling only a fib, he got a very harsh punishment.* *verb* (fibbed, fibbing, fibs) to tell a fib. *She fibs about her age.* {**fihb**} fibber, n.

fi·ber 🌐 🔵 ⭕ *noun* 1. a small, thin part of a plant, animal, or mineral that is shaped like a thread. *My jacket is made from cotton and wool fibers.* / *It is dangerous to breathe in asbestos fibers.* 2. a plant material found in food that is hard to digest. *Whole wheat bread is high in fiber.* {**fiy** bər}

fi·ber·glass *noun* fine threads of glass made into a building material. Fiberglass can be made into insulation for buildings, or it can be molded into a strong solid used in making parts of boats, cars, furniture, and other things. {**fiy** bər **glăs**}

fi·bre *noun* a spelling of **fiber** used in Canada and Britain. See **fiber**. {**fiy** bər}

fi·bre·glass *noun* a spelling of **fiberglass** used in Canada and Britain. See **fiberglass**. {**fiy** bər glăs}

fic·tion 🌐 *noun* 1. writing that tells a story made up in a writer's imagination. Fiction is usually written in prose, not poetry. Novels, short stories, and tales are pieces of fiction. 2. something made up or not true. *His reason for not doing his homework was pure fiction.* {**fihk** shən}

fid·dle *noun* (informal) a violin or similar instrument. *verb* (fiddled, fiddling, fiddles) 1. (informal) to play on a violin. *Three musicians fiddled at the square dance.* 2. to move the fingers or hands without purpose or in a nervous way to fix or adjust something. *He fiddled with the zipper on his backpack.* 3. to waste time (often followed by "around"). *Stop fiddling around and get to work!* {**fihd** əl} fiddler, n.

fidg·et *verb* (fidgeted, fidgeting, fidgets) 1. to move in a nervous or restless way. *Tom fidgeted in his seat as his teacher handed out papers.* 2. to handle or touch restlessly or without purpose; fiddle (often followed by "with"). *Stop fidgeting with your food.* {**fihj** iht} fidgety, adj.

field 🌐 ⭕ *noun* 1. a wide area of open land. *That field is planted with soybeans.* 2. any wide, open area. *From the plane, he looked down on a field of ice.* 3. an open area where sports events take place. *My school has football and soccer fields.* 4. an area of special activity or interest. *Liz works in the field of medicine.* *verb* (fielded, fielding, fields) to catch or stop in a game of baseball, softball, or cricket. *The pitcher fielded the ball and threw it to first base.* {**feeld**}

field·er *noun* a player in the field in baseball, softball, or cricket. {**feel** dər}

field glass *noun* (usually plural) a pair of binoculars used outdoors. {**feeld** glăs}

field trip *noun* a trip away from class by a group of students to learn or gain experience. {**feeld** trihp}

fierce *adjective* (fiercer, fiercest) 1. wild and dangerous; ferocious. *Beware! A fierce tiger is on the loose.* 2. extremely strong or violent. *A fierce storm knocked down many trees last night.* {**feers**} fiercely, adv., fierceness, n.

fier·y *adjective* (fierier, fieriest) 1. on fire or containing fire; flaming. *He rescued the dog from the fiery house.* 2. like fire; very hot or red. *That restaurant serves a fiery chili.* 3. with strong feeling or emotion, or quick to anger. *They had a fiery argument.* / *He has a fiery temper.* {**fiy** ər ee}

fi·es·ta *noun* a festival or religious celebration in nations where Spanish is spoken. {**fee** **ehs** tə}

fife *noun* a small wind instrument that looks like a flute and has a high pitch. The fife usually plays along with drums in marching music. {**fiyf**} fifer, n.

 Living World Physical World  Natural Environment  Economy Government and Law

a
b
c
d
e
f
g
h
i
j
k
l
m
n
o
p
q
r
s
t
u
v
w
x
y
z

fif·teen *noun* the number that comes after 14 and before 16 in the sequence of cardinal numbers; 15. *adjective* being fifteen in number. *There are fifteen kids on the track team.* {**fihf** <u>teen</u>}

fif·teenth *adjective* coming next after the fourteenth in a series. *On the fifteenth day of school, we learned how to identify the leaves of different trees.* *noun* 1. one of fifteen equal parts of a whole; 1/15. *Human hairs are about a fifteenth of a millimeter thick.* 2. the number, person, or thing that comes next after the fourteenth in a series. *The fifteenth is the fastest computer in the lab.* {**fihf** <u>teenth</u>}

fifth *adjective* coming next after the fourth in a series. *My locker is the fifth one down from the library door.* *noun* 1. one of five equal parts of a whole; 1/5. *Each month I pay off a fifth of the money I owe.* 2. the number, person, or thing that comes next after the fourth in a series. *She was the fifth to join the writing club.* {**fihfth**}

fif·ti·eth *adjective* coming next after the forty-ninth in a series. *She celebrated her fiftieth birthday by going out to a big dinner with close friends.* *noun* 1. one of fifty equal parts of a whole; 1/50. *Each state has a fiftieth of the power in the U.S. Senate.* 2. the number, person, or thing that comes next after the forty-ninth in a series. *The last star to be added to the U.S. flag was the fiftieth.* {**fihf** tee əth}

fif·ty *noun* (fifties) the number that is equal to five times ten; 50. *adjective* being fifty in number. *There are fifty states in the United States of America.* {**fihf** tee}

fig *noun* a soft fruit, with many small seeds, that grows on a tree native to the Mediterranean, or the tree on which the fruit grows. {**fihg**}

fight *noun* 1. the use of weapons, bodies, or words to struggle with someone or something; battle; quarrel. *The fight between the two armies began at dawn. / My brother and I had a fight over whose turn it was to wash the dishes.* 2. a boxing match. *My dad likes to watch the fights on television.* *verb* (fought, fighting, fights) 1. to do battle; take part in a struggle. *The ducks fought over the bread we tossed to them.* 2. to battle or struggle against. *The swimmer fought the strong current to reach the other shore.* 3. to box against. *He fought the champion and won.* {**fiyt**}

fight·er *noun* 1. a boxer. *The two fighters started off in opposite corners of the ring.* 2. one who has the strength or courage to fight back or resist. *He recovered from the injury because he was a real fighter.* {**fiy** tər}

fig·ure 🏃❓ *noun* 1. a number or other written symbol that is not a letter of the alphabet. *3, 7, and 8 are figures.* 2. a value or amount given in numbers. *He gave me the figure of $27.50 as the cost of supplies.* 3. the form or outline of something; shape of something not able to be identified. *All they could see was a figure in the darkness.* 4. the shape of a human body. *His figure hasn't changed in twenty years.* 5. a person of note. *Since she wrote that book, Ms. Howe has become a public figure.* 6. (plural) arithmetic. *Are you good at figures?* *verb* (figured, figuring, figures) 1. to find an answer to by using numbers; calculate. *I figured the cost of the party by adding up how much I spent on food and drinks.* 2. (informal) to believe or conclude. *He figured it was time to go home because it was getting dark.* 3. to play a part, be related, or appear. *Rain and fog both figured in the car accident.* {**fihg** yər}

fig·ure·head *noun* 1. a carved figure on the prow, or front, of a ship. 2. a person whose title sounds important but who has no real power. *Although she is the executive director of the company, she does little and is really just a figurehead.* {**fihg** yər **hehd**}

figure of speech *noun* words used in an unusual way to produce a certain effect. Metaphors and similes are figures of speech. *The sentence, "The unfairness of it all made her blood boil," uses a figure of speech.* {**fihg** yər əv <u>speech</u>}

fil·a·ment *noun* 1. a fine thread, wire, or fiber. 2. a fine wire that lights or heats up when electric current is passed through it. *Electricity makes the filament inside a light bulb glow.* {**fihl** ə mənt}

file[1] *noun* 1. a holder for keeping papers or other objects safe and in order. 2. the papers or other objects that are so kept. *Schools keep files on all their students.* 3. a line of things or people standing in order. *We walked down the hall in single file.* *verb* (filed, filing, files) 1. to store in a file. *The secretary filed the reports in alphabetical order.* 2. to present, hand in,

 Human Body   Human Mind  Everyday Life  History and Culture 📞 Communication

or send. *The lawyer filed a notice at the courthouse. / Have you filed your tax return yet?* 3. to march in a line. *The parade filed through downtown.* {fiyl}

file² *noun* a long, thin steel tool with ridges on its surface. A file is used to shape, smooth, or grind down wood, metal, plastic, or other hard material. *verb* (filed, filing, files) to shape, smooth, or grind down with a file or other tool. *Lisa filed her fingernails.* {fiyl}

file·name *noun* the name of a file on a computer. Every file on a computer must have a unique name. *The documents in that folder are arranged alphabetically by filename.* {fiyl naym}

fi·let *verb or noun* another spelling of the word **fillet**. {fih lay}

fil·ings *plural noun* small pieces removed by grinding with a file. {fiy lingz}

fill *verb* (filled, filling, fills) 1. to cause to become full; put as much as possible into. *He filled the bag with leaves.* 2. to become full. *The room filled with guests from all over the world.* 3. to take up all or most of the space in. *Rabbits filled the cage.* 4. to work or perform in. *He fills the role of teacher very well.* 5. to close up or plug. *The dentist filled a cavity in the boy's tooth.* 6. to prepare or make up. *The pharmacist filled my prescription for cough medicine.* *noun* an amount that is enough to make full or satify. *He ate his fill of peanuts.* {fihl}

• **fill in**
1. to give or write down information. *I have to fill in my friend on what happened at school while he was absent. / On the test, you must fill in the*

blanks. 2. to be a substitute (often followed by "for"). *Can you fill in for me at work?*

• **fill out**
to complete by giving missing information. *Kai had to fill out a form to get his library card.*

fil·let or **filet** *noun* a piece of meat or fish that has no bones. *verb* (filleted, filleting, fillets) to remove the bones from; cut into fillets. *The cook filleted the salmon.* {fih lay}

fill·ing *noun* 1. material used to fill a cavity in a tooth. *My dentist uses gold fillings.* 2. a mixture of food used to fill certain kinds of food dishes. *The chef made tacos with a chicken filling.* {fihl ing}

fil·ly *noun* (fillies) a young female horse, usually one that is five years old or younger. {fihl ee}

film 🌀 *noun* 1. a thin layer or coating. *There was a film of dust on the desk.* 2. a thin strip of material covered with a substance that changes in the light. Film is used to make photographs and movies. 3. a motion picture; movie. *What film did you see last night?* *verb* (filmed, filming, films) 1. to photograph with a movie camera or tape with a video recorder. *She filmed her sister's wedding.* 2. to become covered with a thin layer or coating. *The illness made his eyes film over.* {fihlm}

fil·ter *noun* 1. a device used to remove dirt or other solids from liquids or gases. A filter can be made of paper, charcoal, or other material with tiny holes in it. *The paper in a tea bag is a kind of filter.* 2. a device that controls or changes the brightness of light or character of a sound.

The special lens filter on that camera makes a sunny day look like evening. *verb* (filtered, filtering, filters) 1. to remove dirt from by using a filter. *The campers filtered the stream water before drinking it.* 2. to separate out by the use of a filter. *She filters her e-mail messages before she reads them.* 3. to go through or as if through a filter. *Sunshine filtered through the fog.* {fihl tər}

Word History *Filter* is from a Latin word that means "felt," a fabric once used to filter liquids.

filth *noun* material that is dirty, disgusting, or foul. *The bottom of the garbage can was covered with a layer of filth.* {fihlth}

filth·y *adjective* (filthier, filthiest) very dirty or foul; nasty. *The explorers were filthy from hiking through the swamp.* {fihlth ee}

fin 🌀🌀 *noun* 1. a thin, flat body part of fish and other animals that live in the water which is used for swimming or balance. 2. anything that looks or works like a fin. Fins are often found on airplanes, boats, or cars. 3. a rubber flipper worn on the feet by an underwater swimmer. {fihn}

Homophone Note The words *fin* and *Finn* sound alike but have different meanings. To find out why a fish has little use for a Finn, look up *Finn*.

fi·nal *adjective* 1. happening at or being the end of something; last. *The mystery was not solved until the final chapter of the book.* 2. not to be

A B C D E F G H I J K L M N O P Q R S T U V W X Y Z

a b c d e **f** g h i j k l m n o p q r s t u v w x y z

changed; decisive. *The decision of the court was final.* *noun* 1. (often plural) the last sports contest in a series, played by the two best teams or players. *Their track team made it to the state finals.* 2. (often plural) the test of a school subject that covers all the material taught in the course. *He studied hard for his French finals.* {**fiy** nəl}

fi·nal·e 🔊 *noun* 1. the last part of a piece of music. *The concert ended with a stirring finale.* 2. the last part of a play or course of events. *For his finale, the magician made an elephant disappear.* {fih **năl** ee}

fi·nal·ist *noun* a person or team chosen to take part in the final game or contest of a series. *He was a finalist in the school spelling bee.* {**fiy** ə lihst}

fi·nal·ly *adverb* at the final moment; at last. *After driving around for an hour, they finally found the house.* {**fiy** nəl ee}

fi·nance 🔊 *noun* 1. the management of money or other resources. *People who work for a bank must know about finance.* 2. (plural) the money owned by a person, bank, government, or other institution; funds. *Mr. Burr's finances were in bad shape after he lost his job.* *verb* (financed, financing, finances) to provide money for. *Tax money financed the new highway.* {**fiy năns**}

fi·nan·cial *adjective* having to do with money or those who deal in finance. *The company is having financial problems.* {fə **năn** shəl} financially, adv.

finch *noun* a small bird with a bill that is excellent at cracking seeds. Sparrows and cardinals are kinds of finches. {**fihnch**}

find *verb* (found, finding, finds) 1. to come upon or meet by accident. *I found some money in my pocket.* 2. to come upon after losing or searching for. *Alex found a lost watch under the sink.* 3. to discover. *The explorers found a pass through the mountains.* 4. to consider or regard. *She found the poem hard to understand.* 5. to come to a decision in a court of law. *The man was found guilty by the jury.* *noun* something pleasant, valuable, or rare that is discovered. *That colorful shell from the beach is quite a find!* {**fiynd**}

• **find out**
to discover; learn. *Did you find out what time the movie starts?*

Synonyms
These words share a meaning with ***find***, verb 1:
happen upon, encounter

fine¹ *adjective* (finer, finest) 1. very good; excellent. *That was a fine meal.* 2. made up of extremely small particles. *These plants need very fine soil.* 3. very thin. *The baby has such fine hair.* *adverb* (finer, finest) very well. *I was doing fine juggling those eggs until the phone rang!* {**fiyn**}

fine² *noun* a sum of money charged as a punishment for a crime or offense. *verb* (fined, fining, fines) to require a sum of money from, as punishment for a crime or offense. *The judge fined him fifty dollars for skateboarding.* {**fiyn**}

fin·ger 🔊 *noun* 1. one of the five jointed parts at the end of the hand. Sometimes the thumb is not counted as a finger. 2. the part of a glove that covers a finger. *verb* (fingered, fingering, fingers) to touch lightly with the fin-

gers. *Lily fingers her necklace when she's nervous.* {**fing** gər}

• **keep one's fingers crossed**
to hope for a good ending or result. *I don't know if he'll win, but I'm keeping my fingers crossed.*

• **lift a finger**
to make an effort to help or do work. *Mr. Jones does all the work, and Mrs. Jones never lifts a finger.*

fin·ger·nail *noun* a hard, clear piece that grows at the end of the finger. {**fing** gər **nayl**}

fin·ger·print *noun* a mark made by the tip of a finger on an object that it has touched. Police and hospital records keep fingerprints made by a finger dipped in ink. These are used for identification, because no two people have the same fingerprint. *verb* (fingerprinted, fingerprinting, fingerprints) to take the fingerprints of. *The police fingerprinted the suspect at the station.* {**fing** gər **prihnt**}

fin·ish *verb* (finished, finishing, finishes) 1. to reach or cause the end of; complete. *Let's take a swim when we finish our school today. / Did you finish that book?* 2. to completely use up or eat (often followed by "up" or "off"). *Someone finished off the last of the cake.* 3. to put a polish on or coat the surface of. *She finished the old oak floors to protect them.* *noun* 1. the end or last part of something. *It was a long movie, but we watched it to the finish.* 2. the coating on or texture of a hard surface. *The car's finish is badly scratched.* {**fihn** ihsh}

Homophone Note Are you looking for the word ***Finnish*** (a language or nationality)? ***Finish*** and ***Finnish*** sound alike but have different meanings.

 Human Body  Human Mind  Everyday Life  History and Culture Communication

Fin·land *noun* a country on the Scandinavian Peninsula in northern Europe. Helsinki is the capital of Finland. {**fihn** lənd}

Finn *noun* a person who was born in or is a citizen of Finland. {**fihn**}

Homophone Note Are you looking for the word *fin* (a part of a fish)? *Finn* and *fin* sound alike but have different meanings.

Finn·ish *noun* the main language of Finland. *adjective* of or having to do with Finland, or its people or language. {**fihn** ihsh}

Homophone Note The words *Finnish* and *finish* (to complete) sound alike but have different meanings.

fiord *noun* another spelling of fjord. {**fyohrd**}

fir *noun* a type of evergreen tree. Fir trees bear cones and are related to the pines. There are many different kinds of firs. {**fuhr**}

Homophone Note Are you looking for the word *fur* (the hair on an animal)? *Fir* and *fur* sound alike but have different meanings.

fire ❶ *noun* 1. the heat, light, and flames produced by burning. 2. a particular burning, as in a stove or furnace. *Mrs. Brown lit a fire in the fireplace.* 3. an instance of burning that harms or destroys. *There was a fire at the library last night.* 4. excitement or passion; strong emotion. *You could see the fire in his eyes when he talked about sailing.* 5. the shooting of a weapon or weapons. *The fire of guns marked the start of the parade.* *verb* (fired, firing, fires) 1. to shoot. *Don't fire*

that rifle! 2. to use extreme heat on; bake in a kiln. *He fired the clay pots to make them hard.* 3. to make full of energy; excite (sometimes followed by "up"). *The coach fired up his team before the game.* 4. to let go or dismiss from a job. *The boss fired him for being late to work.* 5. to shoot a gun. *He fired at the target.* {**fiyr**}

• **catch fire**
to start to burn. *He lit a match and the paper caught fire.*

• **play with fire**
to bring about danger by doing something in a reckless way. *You are playing with fire when you throw those knives around like that.*

• **set fire to**
to cause to start burning; ignite. *He set fire to the pile of dead leaves.*

fire·arm *noun* a small gun, such as a pistol or rifle. {**fiyr** arm}

fire·crack·er *noun* a small paper tube filled with gunpowder, which explodes and makes a loud noise when its fuse is lit. Firecrackers are sometimes used during celebrations. {**fiyr** krăk ər}

fire department *noun* a part of a city or town government that works to prevent and put out fires, or the people who work for it. {**fiyr** dih **part** mənt}

fire engine *noun* a large truck that carries firefighters and their tools to a fire. Fire engines usually have a ladder and a pump for spraying

water or chemicals used to put out fires. {**fiyr** ehn jən}

fire escape *noun* a metal stair or ladder used as an emergency exit in case of fire. Fire escapes are usually on the outside of buildings. {**fiyr** ə skayp}

fire extin·guisher *noun* a container for chemicals that can be sprayed on a fire to put it out. {**fiyr** ihk **sting** gwə shər}

fire·fight·er *noun* someone who fights fires, either for pay or as a volunteer. {**fiyr** fiyt ər} firefighting, n.

fire·fly *noun* (fireflies) an insect whose lower body flashes with light at night. A firefly is a kind of beetle. {**fiyr** fliy}

fire·house *noun* a building in which equipment for fighting fires is kept and where firefighters meet; fire station. {**fiyr** hows}

fire·man *noun* (firemen) a male firefighter. {**fiyr** mən}

fire·place *noun* a brick or stone space in a room for making fires. A fireplace has a chimney, which keeps smoke from building up inside the room. {**fiyr** plays}

fire·proof *adjective* difficult or impossible to set on fire or to damage or destroy with fire. *Firefighters wear fireproof suits to protect them from the flames.* {**fiyr** proohf}

fire·side *noun* the area near a fireplace. *We sat by the fireside and drank hot cocoa.* {**fiyr** siyd}

fire·wood *noun* wood that is burned for cooking or heating. {**fiyr** wuud}

A
B
C
D
E
F
G
H
I
J
K
L
M
N
O
P
Q
R
S
T
U
V
W
X
Y
Z

 Living World  Physical World   Natural Environment  Economy  Government and Law

a
b
c
d
e
f
g
h
i
j
k
l
m
n
o
p
q
r
s
t
u
v
w
x
y
z

fire·works *plural noun* 1. devices that burn or explode to make noise, bright lights, or brilliant colors. 2. a show of fireworks. *People in England celebrate Guy Fawkes Day with fireworks.* {**fiyr wuhrks**}

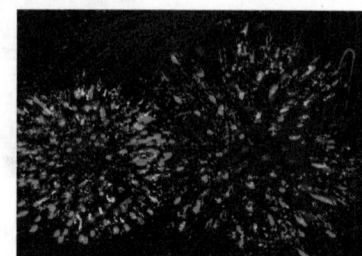

firm[1] *adjective* (firmer, firmest) 1. hard or solid when pressed; not soft. *I would rather sleep on a firm mattress.* 2. not easily changed by outside forces or pressures; steady. *She has very firm opinions on government.* {**fuhrm**} firmly, adv., firmness, n.

firm[2] *noun* a business started by two or more people. {**fuhrm**}

first *adjective* before all others in time, importance, or quality. *He was the first person to climb that mountain. / She won first prize. adverb* 1. in the position before all others. *He finished first in the race.* 2. to begin with; firstly. *We should read the directions first. noun* 1. the number, person, or thing that comes before all others in a series. *He was the first of many great jazz musicians.* 2. beginning. *We were in trouble from the first.* {**fuhrst**}

• **first off**
at once; immediately. *First off, let's finish our work.*

first aid ☺ *noun* emergency medical help given to a hurt or sick person while waiting for a doctor. *The ambulance driver gave the patient first aid.* {**fuhrst ayd**} first-aid, adj.

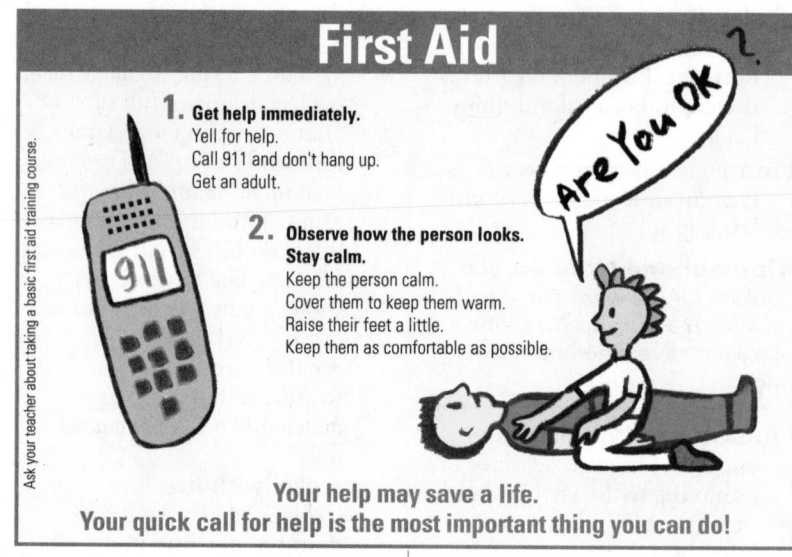

First Aid

1. Get help immediately.
Yell for help.
Call 911 and don't hang up.
Get an adult.

2. Observe how the person looks. Stay calm.
Keep the person calm.
Cover them to keep them warm.
Raise their feet a little.
Keep them as comfortable as possible.

Are You OK ?

Ask your teacher about taking a basic first aid training course.

Your help may save a life.
Your quick call for help is the most important thing you can do!

first-class *adjective* of the highest in quality; best. *That was a first-class show. adverb* by the most expensive way to mail, travel, or dine. *The businesswoman has enough money to fly first-class.* {**fuhrst klăs**}

first·hand *adverb* from the source; directly. *The reporter got her information firsthand from the police officer. adjective* from or having to do with the first source; direct. *The soldier gave a firsthand account of the battle.* {**fuhrst hănd**}

first-rate *adjective* of the highest quality; excellent. *Not many people have heard of her, but she is a first-rate writer.* {**fuhrst rayt**}

fish ❶ *noun* (fish or fishes) 1. an animal that lives in water and has fins for swimming and gills for breathing. Fish are cold-blooded animals with skeletons inside their bodies. Most fish have scales on their skin. There are many kinds of fish, including salmon, goldfish, tuna, and sharks. 2. the flesh of fish eaten as food. *verb* (fished, fishing, fishes) 1. to catch or try to catch fish. *Cara goes*

fishing almost every weekend with her father. 2. to pull or draw out (often followed by "up" or "out"). *He fished a sock out of the drawer.* 3. to search for or try to find out about something, often in a way that is not direct. *He's always fishing around for new ideas. / She fished in her purse for some coins.* {**fihsh**}

• **fish out of water**
someone in a place or situation where he or she does not feel comfortable. *When she moved to the city, she felt like a fish out of water.*

fish·er·man *noun* (fishermen) a man who catches fish either as a sport or as a way to make a living. {**fihsh** ər mən}

fish·er·y *noun* (fisheries) 1. a business that catches or sells fish and other seafood. 2. a place where fish are hatched to be used for study or to be released into larger bodies of water. {**fihsh** ə ree}

fish·hook *noun* a metal hook with a barb and sharp tip, used to catch fish. {**fihsh huuk**}

fishing rod *noun* a long thin pole with a line, hook, and

274

 Human Body   Human Mind   Everyday Life    History and Culture   Communication

often a reel that is used for catching fish. {**fihsh** ing rŏd}

fish·y *adjective* (fishier, fishiest) 1. like a fish in taste or smell. *After catching a trout, my hands smelled fishy.* 2. cold and without life or feeling. *The exhausted man had a fishy look in his eye.* 3. (informal) seeming not to be true or likely. *His story about the alien sounded fishy.* {**fihsh** ee}

fis·sion *noun* the splitting of the nucleus of an atom into two or more nuclei. This makes more atoms of lighter elements and gives off large amounts of energy. {**fih** shən *or* **fih** zhən}

fist *noun* the hand, when the fingers are curled tightly into the palm. {**fihst**}

fit[1] ● ● *adjective* (fitter, fittest) 1. proper or acceptable; right. *This video is fit for children.* 2. in good bodily condition; healthy. *Cora is very fit because she exercises daily.* *verb* (fitted or fit, fitting, fits) 1. to be the right shape and size for. *Does the shirt fit him?* 2. to be proper for. *I like the song, but it doesn't fit the occasion.* 3. to change or prepare until appropriate. *The suit is a bit big, but the tailor will fit it for you.* *noun* the way in which something fits. *These shoes are a perfect fit.* {**fiht**} fitness, n.

fit[2] ● *noun* 1. a sudden attack, outbreak, or convulsion related to an illness. *She had a coughing fit.* 2. a sudden pouring out of strong feelings. *Jeff had a fit when someone stole his skates.* {**fiht**}

five *noun* the number that comes after 4 and before 6 in the sequence of cardinal numbers; 5. *adjective* being five in number. *They have five children.* {**fiyv**}

fix *verb* (fixed, fixing, fixes) 1. to make stable or steady; fasten firmly; attach. *He fixed the wooden sign to his tree house.* 2. to decide on or set; bring into a final state that cannot be changed. *We fixed a date for the party.* 3. to hold steady or direct. *The teacher asked us to fix our attention on the map.* 4. to mend or repair. *Do you think you can fix my bike chain?* 5. to make or prepare. *The cook fixed a delicious meal.* 6. (informal) to set up through cheating so as to get what one wants. *He fixed the card game by using marked cards.* *noun* a difficult situation; trouble. *I'm in a fix because I lost my lunch money.* {**fihks**}

fix·ture *noun* something fixed into place as a permanent part. *Bathroom fixtures include a tub, sink, and toilet.* {**fihks** chər}

fjord or **fiord** *noun* a long, narrow ocean inlet that passes between high and rocky banks or steep cliffs. {**fyohrd**}

FL or **Fla.** *abbreviation* an abbreviation for **Florida**.

flag *noun* a piece of cloth, in the shape of a rectangle or triangle, with colors and designs. Flags are used for signaling or as symbols of a country or organization. *verb* (flagged, flagging, flags) to signal, using a flag or as if using a flag (sometimes followed by "down"). *She flagged down the police car.* {**flăg**}

flag·pole *noun* a pole on which to hang or fly a flag. {**flăg** pohl}

flail *noun* a farm tool used to separate seeds from grain. A flail has a long handle with a short, swinging bar on one end. *verb* (flailed, flailing, flails) 1. to beat with a flail, whip, or the fists. *The angry man threatened to flail the person who broke his window.* 2. to cause to move wildly. *He flailed his arms to get the helicopter pilot's attention.* 3. to move or wave wildly. *The beginning swimmer flailed about in the pool.* {**flayl**}

flair *noun* a natural ability; talent. *She has a flair for acting.* {**flayr**}

Homophone Note Are you looking for the word **flare** (a bright light)? **Flair** and **flare** sound alike but have different meanings.

flake *noun* 1. a small, thin piece that has split off from or peeled off of a surface. *Flakes of paint fell from the walls of the old house.* 2. any small or light piece. *Flakes of snow fell through the air.* 3. (slang) an odd or strange person. *Some people think Fred is a flake because of the way he dresses.* *verb* (flaked, flaking, flakes) to peel or split off from a surface in flakes. *The paint on the wall is flaking.* {**flayk**}

flame ● *noun* 1. the mixture of burning gas and vapor that rises from an object that is on fire. Flame is seen as brightly colored, flickering light. 2. (often plural) the state of something that is burning. *The building is in flames.* *verb* (flamed, flaming, flames) 1. to burst into or produce flames; burn. *The*

pool of gasoline *flamed* when he dropped a lit match in it. 2. to experience any strong emotion. *She flamed with anger.* {flaym}

fla·min·go *noun* (flamingos) a large, tropical, wading bird with very long legs, a long neck, and bright pink or red feathers. {flə **ming** goh}

flam·ma·ble *adjective* able to catch on fire easily. *Dry leaves are flammable.* {flăm ə bəl}

Language Note *Flammable* and *inflammable* sound like they are antonyms, or opposites. In fact, they are synonyms, words that have the same meaning. Both *flammable* and *inflammable* mean "quick to catch fire and burn." You might see either word printed on a warning sign on a tank truck. If you want to describe something that is slow or not able to catch fire and burn, try "not flammable" or "fire-resistant."

flank *noun* 1. the area between the hip and the ribs on either side of the body. *Nora rubbed the horse's flank.* 2. the left or right side of something. *The soldier marched in the right flank of his unit.* *verb* (flanked, flanking, flanks) to be at the side of something. *The two boys flanked their grandmother at the table.* {flăngk}

flan·nel *noun* a soft material made of wool or cotton. Flannel is used for warm clothing and bed covers, among other things. {flăn əl}

flap *verb* (flapped, flapping, flaps) 1. to move or beat quickly up and down. *The bird flapped its wings.* 2. to swing or wave back and forth with a slapping sound. *The flags flapped in the wind.* *noun* 1. a thin or flat piece that is attached only at one edge

and hangs loose. *He tied the tent flap open.* 2. the act or an instance of flapping. *Hours of flapping caused the boat's sail to tear.* 3. the sound made by flapping. *The flapping of the broken screen kept us awake all night.* {flăp}

flap·jack *noun* a flat cake made of batter and cooked in a pan; pancake. {flăp jăk}

flare *verb* (flared, flaring, flares) 1. to begin to burn brightly (often followed by "up"). *She blew on the coals, and the fire flared up.* 2. to come into being suddenly or become stronger and more intense (often followed by "up"). *Tempers flared when the game was called off.* / *His health problems flare up every winter.* 3. to become wider along a length. *Sailors wear pants that flare at the bottom.* *noun* 1. a sudden bright light. *The flare we saw in the night sky was a meteor.* 2. a bright light used

to signal or give light. *The police set up flares around the accident scene to warn drivers.* {flayr}

Homophone Note Are you looking for the word *flair* (a special talent)? *Flare* and *flair* sound alike but have different meanings.

flash *noun* 1. a sudden, bright light that shines, then quickly disappears. *The flash of lightning was followed by a clap of thunder.* 2. a sudden

show of feelings, talent, or understanding. *A flash of disappointment crossed the coach's face when Paul missed the catch.* / *The solution to the problem came to her in a flash.* 3. a very short amount of time; an instant. *I'll be there in a flash.* *verb* (flashed, flashing, flashes) 1. to give off a sudden, bright light that quickly disappears or that blinks on and off. *Shop signs flash to attract attention.* 2. to come, move, or happen suddenly; pass quickly. *An image of her flashed into his mind.* 3. to shine brightly; gleam. *The diamond ring flashed in the sun.* *adjective* happening suddenly and without warning. *The flash flood ruined many homes.* {flăsh} flasher, n., flashingly, adv.

flash·light *noun* a small lamp or light that is held in the hand and powered by batteries. {flăsh liyt}

flask *noun* a rounded bottle with a narrow neck. *The chemist poured the acid into a flask.* {flăsk}

flat *adjective* (flatter, flattest) 1. having a surface that is straight and even; level. *When it snows and I have to shovel, I am always glad our driveway is flat.* 2. having a surface that does not have higher and lower places; smooth; even. *It is important that a football field be flat.* 3. having little or no air; deflated. *Will this flat tire make us late for the game?* 4. lying pressed against a level surface. *The rug is not flat.* / *His hair was flat when he came out of the pool.* 5. having little interest, energy, or flavor; dull. *His weekends have been*

 Human Body   Human Mind   Everyday Life   History and Culture   Communication

flat since his friend moved away. / Ms. Burns spoke in a flat voice. *noun* 1. (sometimes plural) something flat or having a long level space, such as an area of land. *Most of the factories were built on the flats outside of town.* 2. a musical tone that is a half step lower than another. *adverb* (flatter, flattest) 1. in a position that is level to the ground. *He fell flat on his back.* 2. absolutely; completely. *Jon can't go to the movie because he is flat broke.* 3. absolutely; without question. *When she said that elephants are little, she was flat wrong.* 4. lower than the correct pitch. *He sang flat on that song.* {flăt}

flat·car *noun* a railroad car with a flat platform and no walls or roof. {flăt kar}

flat·fish *noun* (flatfish or flatfishes) a kind of fish that lives in salt water and has a flat body with both eyes on the top side. Sole, halibut, and flounder are flatfish. {flăt fihsh}

flat·ten *verb* (flattened, flattening, flattens) to make flat. *The car ran over the toy and flattened it.* {flăt ən}

flat·ter *verb* (flattered, flattering, flatters) 1. to give too much or false praise; try to please by praising. *He flattered his mother to get her in a better mood.* 2. to make look attractive or better. *Your blue sweater really flatters you. / The school photo flatters him.* {flăt ər}

Word History *Flatter* comes from an early French word that means "to caress."

flat·ter·y *noun* (flatteries) too much praise; praise that is often not meant. *Jamal's flattery didn't make Tonya feel*

better about her horrible new haircut. {flăt ə ree}

fla·vor *noun* 1. the particular way something tastes. *Salt brings out the flavor of some foods.* 2. a particular quality that is noticed about a thing. *His letter had an angry flavor.* *verb* (flavored, flavoring, flavors) to give a flavor to. *The chef flavored the stew with garlic and onion.* {flay vər} flavorless, adj.

fla·vor·ing *noun* something added that gives a particular flavor. *He likes his milk with chocolate flavoring.* {flay vər ing}

fla·vour *noun or verb* a spelling of **flavor** used in Canada and Britain. See **flavor**. {flay vər}

flaw *noun* 1. a fault or defect. *His worst flaw is his short temper. / The flaw in the car's finish was caused by a paint bubble.* 2. a crack or break. *The mechanic found a flaw in a part of the jet engine.* *verb* (flawed, flawing, flaws) to make a flaw in. *When his hand slipped, he flawed his drawing.* {flaw} flawless, adj.

flax *noun* 1. a plant with tiny blue flowers and with seeds from which an oil is pressed. 2. a fiber made from the stem of this plant. The fiber is spun into thread. *Linen is made from flax.* {flăks}

flea *noun* a tiny insect that does not have wings but can jump far. Fleas feed on the blood of the animals they bite. {flee}

Homophone Note Are you looking for the word *flee* (to run)? *Flea* and *flee* sound alike but have different meanings.

fled *verb* past tense and past participle of **flee**. {flehd}

flee *verb* (fled, fleeing, flees) 1. to run away or escape. *The burglar fled when he heard the dog bark.* 2. to escape from by leaving quickly; run away from. *Hundreds of people fled the country during the war.* {flee}

Homophone Note Are you looking for the word *flea* (a tiny insect)? *Flee* and *flea* sound alike but have different meanings.

fleece *noun* 1. the wool of an animal, usually a sheep. 2. material with a deep, soft pile. *My fleece cap keeps me warm all winter.* *verb* (fleeced, fleecing) to cut the wool from. {flees}

fleet[1] *noun* 1. a group of navy ships under one command. *The fleet set sail for the Pacific.* 2. a group of ships, planes, trucks, or cars that work together or belong to one company. {fleet}

fleet[2] *adjective* fast and graceful. *The fleet gazelle escaped the lion.* {fleet}

fleet·ing *adjective* passing quickly; very brief; lasting only a moment. *I got a fleeting look at the eagle.* {fleet ing}

flesh 🌐⭕ *noun* 1. the soft tissue, including muscle and fat, that lies between the skin and the bones. 2. this part of an animal used as food. 3. the soft or juicy part beneath the skin of a fruit or vegetable. {flehsh}

flesh·y *adjective* (fleshier, fleshiest) having a lot of flesh or fat. *He squeezed his fleshy body into the chair.* {flehsh ee}

A
B
C
D
E
F
G
H
I
J
K
L
M
N
O
P
Q
R
S
T
U
V
W
X
Y
Z

 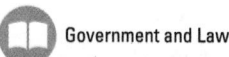

a
b
c
d
e
f
g
h
i
j
k
l
m
n
o
p
q
r
s
t
u
v
w
x
y
z

flew *verb* a past tense of **fly**[1]. {flooh}

Homophone Note The words *flew*, *flu*, and *flue* sound alike but have different meanings.

flex *verb* (flexed, flexing, flexes) 1. to bend again and again. *Tony flexed the straw until it broke.* 2. to make harder or tighter. *The athlete flexed his muscles.* {flehks}

flex·i·ble *adjective* 1. easily bent without breaking. *Give the baby some flexible toys.* 2. able to change or meet new situations. *They had a flexible plan for the day's activities.* {flehk sə bəl} flexibility, n.

flick *noun* 1. a sharp, light snap or blow. *With a flick of his finger, he sent the coin flying across the room. / The flick of the whip made the camel move faster.* 2. a swift, jerky movement. *The puppy watched the back-and-forth flick of the cat's tail. verb* (flicked, flicking, flicks) 1. to hit or get rid of with a sharp, light blow. *She flicked the spider off her notebook.* 2. to move with a sharp or jerky motion. *The deer flicked its ears. / She flicked the television off.* {flihk}

flick·er[1] *verb* (flickered, flickering, flickers) 1. to burn or shine in an unsteady way. *The candle flickered and went out. / The picture on the TV keeps flickering.* 2. to move quickly back and forth; flutter. *Shadows flickered on the wall. noun* 1. a quick, unsteady light or movement. *The flicker from the campfire*

made shadows on the trees. 2. a look or feeling that comes and goes very quickly. *I saw a flicker of a smile on the solemn man's face when he heard the joke.* {flihk ər} flickery, adj.

flick·er[2] *noun* a large North American woodpecker. It is mostly brown and white and has either yellow or red under its wings and tail. {flih kər}

flied *verb* a past tense and past participle of **fly**[1], *verb* 6. *The batter flied out to right field.* {fliyd}

fli·er or **flyer** *noun* 1. something or someone that flies. 2. a printed sheet with information about people or events that is handed out to the public. *The grocery store sends out sale fliers every week.* {fliy ər}

flight[1] *noun* 1. an act of passing through air or space by flying. *There are few things as beautiful as a bird in flight.* 2. a trip on a plane from one place to another. *His flight to New York leaves in two hours.* 3. the time or distance covered by an airplane or other flying object. *It is a four-hour flight to Vancouver.* 4. a series of stairs between two floors or landings. *The movers carried the furniture up three flights.* {fliyt}

flight[2] *noun* an act or instance of fleeing. *The story is about the flight of escaped slaves.* {fliyt}

flight attendant *noun* a person who works on an airplane helping the passengers during a flight. *The flight attendant brought our dinners.* {fliyt ə tehn dənt}

flim·sy *adjective* (flimsier, flimsiest) not solid or strong; weak. *His shoes were too flimsy for the rocky trail. / No*

one believed her flimsy excuse. {flihm zee} flimsiness, n.

flinch *verb* (flinched, flinching, flinches) to draw away suddenly in pain or fear. *Josh flinched when the dog growled at him.* {flihnch}

fling *verb* (flung, flinging, flings) to throw hard or with force. *After missing the ball, the catcher flung his mitt to the ground in frustration. noun* 1. the act of flinging. *She sent the stone flying with a fling.* 2. a short period of fun and play with no cares. *This trip will be his last fling before going back to school.* {fling}

flint·lock *noun* 1. a part of an old-fashioned gun no longer in use. This part makes a spark that sets the powder inside on fire. 2. a gun that has this device. *The pirate pointed his flintlock at the sailor and told him to walk the plank.* {flihnt lŏk}

flip *verb* (flipped, flipping, flips) 1. to throw in such a way as to cause to turn over or spin. *He flipped the coin to see who would get the seat by the window.* 2. to toss with a quick, sharp movement. *Bill flipped the car keys to Sally.* 3. to turn or turn over quickly and easily. *She flipped the pages until she found the map she was looking for. / He flipped the turtle on its back.* 4. to do a somersault in the air. *The circus dog jumped and flipped. noun* 1. an act or instance of flipping. *With a flip of the light switch, the darkness was gone.* 2. a somersault in the air. *He did an amazing back flip.* {flihp}

• **flip one's lid** (slang) to lose control of yourself. *When my brother broke my favorite toy, I flipped my lid.*

Human Body   Human Mind   Everyday Life   History and Culture   Communication

flip·per ❶ *noun* 1. a wide, flat limb on a whale, turtle, or other animal that is used for swimming. 2. one of a pair of flat, rubber shoes shaped like a frog's foot and used for swimming or underwater diving. {**flihp** ər}

flirt *verb* (flirted, flirting, flirts) to play at love; act in a romantic way that is not serious. *They flirted with each other at the party.* *noun* a person who is likely to flirt or who flirts often. {**fluhrt**}

flit *verb* (flitted, flitting, flits) to fly or move in a quick or light way. *The cook flitted about the kitchen while preparing the meal.* {**fliht**}

float *verb* (floated, floating, floats) 1. to rest on the surface of a liquid without sinking, or drift in a gas such as air without falling. *The girl floated on her back in the water. / The balloon floated in the breeze.* 2. to move in a light and airy way. *The dancer floated across the stage.* *noun* 1. any object that floats on water. A float is often used to hold up something else on or in the water. *The fisherman attached a float to his line.* 2. a platform with decorations and displays that is usually on wheels and is used in a parade. *The mayor rode on a float in the parade.* {**floht**}

flock ❶ *noun* 1. a group of animals or birds of one kind that stay or are kept together, such as geese or sheep. *The shepherd watched over his flock of sheep.* 2. a large group of people or things. *A flock of reporters gathered around the actor.* *verb* (flocked, flocking, flocks) to gather or travel in a crowd, group, or flock. *People flocked to the new museum on opening day.* {**flŏk**}

floe *noun* a large sheet of floating ice. *That part of the Arctic Ocean is filled with ice floes.* {**floh**}

Homophone Note Are you looking for the word *flow*? *Floe* and *flow* sound alike but have different meanings.

flood ❻ *noun* 1. an overflow of water onto land that is not normally under water. *Our house was destroyed in the flood.* 2. a great pouring out or flow. *There was a flood of anger when they closed the youth center.* *verb* (flooded, flooding, floods) 1. to cover or fill with a flow of water. *The rains flooded the fields.* 2. to fill or overwhelm with too much of something. *Local radio stations were flooded with telephone calls.* 3. to rise, pour, or overflow in a flood or as if in a flood. *The river has flooded twice this year. / Students flooded into the hall.* {**fluhd**}

flood·light *noun* an electric lamp that shines a bright beam of light over a wide area. {**fluhd liyt**}

floor *noun* 1. the lowest surface in a room; the surface on which one stands in a room. 2. the lowest surface of any structure. *The floor of our old car is rusted.* 3. the ground surface. *The divers went to the ocean floor.* 4. a level of a building. *Her office is on the tenth floor.* *verb* (floored, flooring, floors) 1. to cover with or provide with a floor or floor covering. *The workers floored the new apartment with carpet.* 2. to throw into great confusion; to greatly puzzle. *Dad was floored when I told him I was getting married.* {**flohr**}

flop *verb* (flopped, flopping, flops) 1. to fall down or over in a limp or heavy manner. *She flopped on the bed and cried.* 2. (informal) to fail completely. *She'll flop as an architect if she doesn't work harder.* *noun* 1. the act or sound of flopping. *She heard a flop when the book fell off the bookcase.* 2. something that has failed completely. *The play was a flop.* {**flŏp**}

flop·py *adjective* (floppier, floppiest) hanging or flapping in a loose way. *Kyle's pet rabbit has floppy ears.* *noun* (floppies) a floppy disk. {**flŏp ee**}

floppy disk *noun* a thin plastic disk with a special coating, on which computer information can be stored; diskette. {**flŏp ee dihsk**}

flo·ral *adjective* of, having to do with, or made up of flowers. *He placed the floral arrangement in the center of the table. / She chose a scarf with a floral design.* {**flohr əl**}

Flor·i·da *noun* a state in the southeastern United States on the Atlantic Coast. Its capital is Tallahassee. (abbreviated: FL) {**flohr ih də**}

Word History *Florida* is a Spanish word that means "land of flowers." Spanish explorer Juan Ponce de León chose the name in 1513, when he claimed the land for Spain.

flo·rist *noun* a person who works at growing, keeping, or arranging flowers and plants in order to sell them. {**flaw** rihst or **flar** ihst}

floss *noun* 1. soft, silky thread used for sewing and embroidery. 2. soft thread used for cleaning between the teeth; dental floss. *verb* (flossed, flossing, flosses) 1. to clean between teeth with dental floss. *She flosses after every meal.* 2. to use dental floss to

A
B
C
D
E
F
G
H
I
J
K
L
M
N
O
P
Q
R
S
T
U
V
W
X
Y
Z

clean. *The dental assistant will floss your teeth.* {**flaws**}

floun·der[1] *verb* (floundered, floundering, flounders) 1. to move forward in a clumsy way, often losing balance. *They floundered through the deep snow.* 2. to act in a confused or clumsy way. *He floundered to find the right words.* {**flown** dər}

Confused and bewildered, the lost **flounder** found itself **floundering** near the shoreline.

floun·der[2] *noun* (flounder or flounders) a flatfish that lives in the ocean. Flounder are used for food. {**flown** der}

flour ⊙ *noun* the fine, ground meal or powder of wheat or other grain. Flour is used to make bread, pasta, and other foods. *verb* (floured, flouring, flours) to sprinkle or coat with flour. *Flour the chicken before frying it.* {**flowr**}

flour·ish *verb* (flourished, flourishing, flourishes) 1. to grow in a strong, healthy way. *Plants flourish in this rich soil.* 2. to do well; succeed. *Joan flourished in her new school.* 3. to wave about in a bold or dramatic way. *The children flourished cardboard swords in the school play. noun* 1. the act of moving or waving about in a showy way. *The magician performed his trick with a flourish of his magic wand.* 2. an added decoration. *He*

signed his name with a flourish. {**fluh** rihsh}

flow *verb* (flowed, flowing, flows) 1. to move in a smooth, steady stream. *The river flows to the sea.* / *Sand flowed through her fingers.* 2. to move in a smooth and easy way. *Thoughts flowed through his mind as he listened to the music. noun* 1. the act of flowing. *They stopped the flow of water by building a dam.* 2. a series of things, ideas, or events that continue in a steady stream. *The car moved with the flow of traffic.* {**floh**}

Homophone Note The words *flow* and *floe* sound alike but have different meanings. To find out why a floe might flow on a hot summer day, look up *floe*.

flow chart *noun* a chart or diagram that shows step-by-step how something grows, develops, or is made. {**floh** chart}

flow·er ↑ *noun* 1. the part of a plant that has petals and that makes fruit or seeds; blossom. Flowers often have a pleasant smell. *Her hobby is arranging flowers.* 2. a plant that puts forth blossoms and that is grown for its beauty. *Has anyone watered the flowers lately? verb* (flowered, flowering, flowers) to blossom or produce flowers; bloom. *Cherry trees flower every spring.* {**flow** er}

flown *verb* a past participle of **fly**[1]. {**flohn**}

flu *noun* a short form of the word **influenza**. {**flooh**}

Homophone Note The words *flu, flew,* and *flue* sound alike but have different meanings.

flue *noun* a hollow pipe inside a chimney that lets hot or cold air, smoke, or steam escape to the outside. {**flooh**}

Homophone Note The words *flue, flew,* and *flu* sound alike but have different meanings.

flu·ent *adjective* able to speak or write easily and naturally. *She is fluent in several languages.* {**flooh** ənt} fluency, n., fluently, adv.

fluff *noun* a soft, light material, or a mass of such a material. *Dandelion fluff floated above the field. verb* (fluffed, fluffing, fluffs) to shake, pat, or puff into a lighter or less dense mass. *She fluffed the sofa cushions before the guests arrived.* {**fluhf**}

fluff·y *adjective* (fluffier, fluffiest) 1. of, made of, or covered with fluff. *She loves her soft, fluffy slippers the best.* 2. soft, light, or airy like fluff. *The sky is full of fluffy clouds.* {**fluhf** ee}

flu·id ⊙ ⊙ *noun* a liquid or gas. A fluid flows easily and takes the shape of the container that holds it. Water and air are fluids. *adjective* capable of flowing; like a fluid. *Water remains fluid at room temperature.* {**flooh** ihd}

Language Note *Liquid* and *fluid* are close in meaning, but they are not synonyms. Both words refer to a state of matter. A liquid is matter in a form that flows easily and is neither a solid nor a gas. *Milk and blood are liquids. Mercury is the only metal that is a liquid at room temperature.* A fluid is matter in a form that flows easily and is not a solid. *Water and air are fluids.*

fluke *noun* something that is accidental good luck. *Finding*

 Human Body   Human Mind Everyday Life  History and Culture Communication

ten dollars on the sidewalk was a fluke. {**floohk**}

flung *verb* past tense and past participle of **fling**. {**fluhng**}

flu·o·res·cent *adjective* able to give off visible light after being exposed to a source of heat, light, or other form of energy. *I can find my fluorescent key ring easily in the dark. / The office has fluorescent lighting.* {floohr **eh** sənt}

fluor·i·date *verb* (fluoridated, fluoridating, fluoridates) to add a fluoride to, in order to keep teeth healthy. *The town argued about whether to fluoridate the local water supply.* {**flohr** ih **dayt**}

flu·o·ride 🌐 🔬 *noun* a chemical compound that contains fluorine as one of its elements. *Fluoride is a common toothpaste ingredient.* {**flohr** iyd *or* **floohr** iyd}

flu·o·rine *noun* a substance that is a chemical element. Fluorine combines easily with other elements to form compounds. Some of these compounds are used to prevent tooth decay. Fluorine is poisonous in its pure gas form. (symbol: F) {**floohr** een *or* **flohr** een}

flur·ry *noun* (flurries) 1. a light fall of snow that ends quickly. 2. a sudden, short spell of activity or excitement. *He got a flurry of phone calls before he left work.* {**fluhr** ee}

flush[1] *noun* 1. a brief, heavy flow of water or other liquid. *A flush of water from the reservoir washed the fish downstream.* 2. a red color or glow in the face or skin. *Fever brought a flush to her cheeks.* 3. a sudden burst of feeling. *Mr. Lim felt a flush of joy when he opened the gift.* *verb* (flushed, flushing, flushes) 1. to wash out, clean, or empty with a

Flowers

stamen
anther
filament

corolla
(petals)

pistil
stigma
style
ovary

ovule

top left:
tulip, fritillaria, cyclamen
cactus, monarda, coreopsis
daisy, aster, iris
clematis, impatiens, tulip

petal
leaf
trumpet
bulb
root hairs

A B C D E F G H I J K L M N O P Q R S T U V W X Y Z

rush of water. *City workers flushed the water main.* / *I flushed the toilet.* 2. to flow in a quick, heavy manner. *Water flushed from the pump.* 3. to blush or turn red. *She flushed when the teacher called on her.* 4. to cause to turn red or blush. *Her face was flushed after she ran five miles in the heat.* {**fluhsh**}

flush² *adjective* (flusher, flushest) 1. even or level with another surface or line. *The top of the table is flush with the window sill.* 2. right next to or up against. *The bookcase is flush with the wall.* {**fluhsh**}

flus·ter *verb* (flustered, flustering, flusters) to cause to become nervous, confused, or upset. *The questions flustered him.* *noun* a state of nervous confusion. *Maya was in a fluster over her weekend plans.* {**fluh** stər}

flute *noun* a woodwind instrument with a high pitch. It is a long tube with finger holes or keys along it and is played by blowing into a hole near one end. {**flooht**}

flut·ter *verb* (fluttered, fluttering, flutters) 1. to wave rapidly back and forth or up and down. *The tail of the kite fluttered in the wind.* 2. to fly with quick, light wing movements. *A bird fluttered to the roof.* 3. to beat lightly and quickly. *Jason's heart fluttered when he heard the good news.* *noun* 1. a quick, light, flapping movement. *We listened to the flutter of the sails in the breeze.* 2. a state of excitement or fluster. *The town was in a flutter during the queen's visit.* {**fluht** ər}

fly¹ ⊙ *verb* (flew or flied, flown, flying, flies) 1. to move through the air by means of

wings. *The birds flew over the house.* 2. to travel in or pilot an aircraft. *They will fly to Tokyo next week.* 3. to pass by or move quickly. *She flew from the room when she heard her mother calling.* 4. to wave or float in the air. *The flag flew from the top of the pole.* 5. to cause to wave or float in the air. *They were flying a kite.* 6. to hit a baseball or softball in the air. (This is the only meaning of "fly" for which "flied" is the correct past tense.) *He flied to center field.* *noun* (flies) 1. a strip of material along the edge of a piece of clothing that hides buttons or a zipper. Flies are usually found on the front of pants. 2. a batted baseball or softball that rises high in the air; fly ball. {**fliy**} flyer, n.

• **fly off the handle**
to become suddenly very angry. *Alice's parents flew off the handle when she came home after midnight.*

fly² ⊙ *noun* (flies) an insect with two wings. Most flies are active in the daytime, and many have large eyes. Mosquitoes and houseflies are among the thousands of types of flies. {**fliy**}

fly·catch·er *noun* a bird that lives in Europe and America and eats insects that it catches in the air. There are many different kinds of flycatchers. {**fliy** kăch ər}

flying fish *noun* a fish that lives in the ocean and has fins that look like wings. Flying fish can glide in the air after jumping from the water. {**fliy** ing fihsh}

flying saucer *noun* a bright, flying object shaped like a disk that some people

believe is a spacecraft from another world; UFO. {**fliy** ing **saw** sər}

foal *noun* a young horse, donkey, or related animal, usually one that is less than a year old. *verb* (foaled, foaling, foals) to give birth to a foal. *The mare foaled with the help of a veterinarian.* {**fohl**}

foam *noun* 1. a mass of small bubbles. 2. bubbly sweat on the skin of or saliva at the mouth of a horse or other animal after heavy exercise. *verb* (foamed, foaming, foams) to make foam; froth. *The waves foamed in the storm.* {**fohm**}

foam rubber *noun* a firm, light rubber that feels like sponge. Foam rubber is often used to make seats and mattresses. {**fohm ruhb** ər}

fo·cus *noun* (focuses or foci) 1. the point at which rays of light or heat come together or from which they seem to move away. 2. the area of greatest attention or activity. *Volcanoes of the Pacific were the focus of the report.* 3. An adjustment that gives a clear image of things viewed through a lens. *The focus on the microscope allowed her to see every detail of the cell.* *verb* (focused, focusing, focuses) 1. to adjust to make a clear image. *Lee focused the camera lens.* 2. to direct or devote to a central point or task. *His thoughts were focused on his homework.* 3. to become

 Human Body   Human Mind   Everyday Life  History and Culture Communication

focused. *She focused on getting her work done.* {**foh** kəs}

Word History In Latin, *focus* means "hearth" or "fireplace." It entered English in the 1600s as a word for the point where rays of light meet. The meaning "center of activity or energy" came into use in the 1700s. Because the hearth was for centuries the center of home life, it is not surprising that, today, several of the meanings of "focus" have something to do with a center or meeting point.

fod·der *noun* feed for farm animals, such as stalks of corn cut and mixed with hay. {**fŏd** ər}

foe *noun* one who wishes ill on another; personal enemy. *His foes made a vow to capture him.* {**foh**}

fog *noun* 1. a thick mass, like a cloud, made up of tiny water drops floating in the air near the ground; mist. 2. a condition of mental confusion or lack of certainty. *He was in a fog all day and couldn't get any work done. verb* (fogged, fogging, fogs) 1. to cover with or as if with a fog. *The child fogged the window with her breath.* 2. to be or become covered with or as if with a fog. *The bathroom mirror fogged during my shower.* {**fŏg** *or* **fawg**, n., **fŏg** *or* **fawg**, v.}

fog·gy *adjective* (foggier, foggiest) 1. full of or covered by fog. *The accident happened on a foggy stretch of the road.* 2. fuzzy; mixed up. *His mind was foggy with sleep.* {**fŏg** ee *or* **fawg** ee} foggily, adv., fogginess, n.

fog·horn *noun* a loud, deep horn on a ship or on the shore, used in fog or at night to give warning signals. {**fŏg** hohrn *or* **fawg** hohrn}

foil *noun* a very thin, flexible sheet of a metal, such as aluminum. {**foil**}

-fold *suffix* 1. a suffix that means "multiplied by" or "times." *Sevenfold means multiplied by seven.* 2. a suffix that means having that number of parts. *Twofold means having two parts.*

fold[1] *verb* (folded, folding, folds) 1. to bend over upon itself so that one section lies on or against another section. *She folded the letter before putting it in the envelope.* 2. to bring together by crossing or twining together. *He folded his arms and leaned against the wall.* 3. to bring in toward the body from a stretched position. *The hawk landed on a branch and folded its wings.* 4. to hold close; clasp or twine together. *He folded her in his arms.* 5. to wrap, place in a case, or enclose. *She folded the jewel in a piece of gold cloth.* 6. to be or be able to be folded. *These chairs fold for storage. noun* 1. a section that has been bent back over another; pleat. *There was mud in the fold of his pants.* 2. the line, crease, or bend made by folding. *She cut the paper along the fold.* {**fohld**}

fold[2] *noun* an area within a fence or wall where sheep or other animals are kept. {**fohld**}

fold·er *noun* 1. a piece of paper or cardboard folded at the center. A folder can hold papers or letters. 2. A sheet or sheets of paper folded to make a small book. {**fohl** dər}

fo·li·age ● *noun* 1. leaves on a tree or other plant. *Many trees have thick foliage.*

2. the leaves on many trees together. *We enjoyed the fall foliage on our walk through the woods.* {**foh** lee ihj}

folk ● ● *noun* (folk or folks) 1. a group of people who come from the same country and share the same kind of life. *City folk are known for their busy lives.* 2. people in general. *Some folks say the weather will get worse.* 3. a person's parents or whole family. *My folks helped me plant a garden. adjective* 1. coming from common people. *Plants are often used in folk medicine.* 2. having to do with the art forms of a people's traditions or culture. *They enjoyed an evening of folk music.* {**fohk**}

folk dance *noun* 1. A dance made up and handed down by the common people of a region or country. 2. music for such a dance. *The teacher played a folk dance on the piano.* {**fohk** dăns}

folk·lore *noun* the stories and ways of a group of people from a certain place or country. Such stories and traditions are handed down through the years from one generation to the next. {**fohk** lohr}

folk music *noun* music made up and played by the common people of a region or country. Such music is often simple, with parts that are played over and over. {**fohk** myoo zihk}

folk sing·er *noun* a singer of folk songs. {**fohk** sing ər}

folk song *noun* a piece of folk music meant for singing. {**fohk** sawng}

folk tale *noun* a story that has been handed down for generations among the common people of a region. {**fohk** tayl}

A
B
C
D
E
F
G
H
I
J
K
L
M
N
O
P
Q
R
S
T
U
V
W
X
Y
Z

fol·low *verb* (followed, following, follows) 1. to come or go after or behind. *He followed me down the street.* 2. to move forward on or along. *Follow this road until you reach the city.* 3. to take place after. *A party will follow the wedding.* 4. to understand or comprehend. *Did you follow the story he told?* 5. to pay attention to closely. *He follows the news.* 6. to happen as a result of something else. *If there are no stores in town, it follows that people will have to shop somewhere else.* {**fŏl** oh}

• **follow up**
to act further to keep something from being forgotten. *Miss Perez followed up her letter to the mayor with a phone call.*

fol·low·er *noun* a person who believes in, studies, or supports the ideas of a teacher or other leader. *Johannes Brahms was a follower of Beethoven.* {**fŏl** oh ər}

fol·low·ing *noun* 1. a group of followers or supporters. *The young star already has a large following.* 2. something that comes next in a talk or piece of writing (always used with "the"). *For more information, see the following.* *adjective* 1. occurring next or after. *I got a letter from Marla and wrote back to her the following day.* 2. about to be named or listed (used to introduce a group of things or people). *The following students will remain after school: Jennifer, Emily, and Luisa.* {**fŏl** oh ing}

fol·ly *noun* (follies) a lack of good sense or judgment. *It is folly to think that money grows on trees.* {**fŏl** ee}

fond *adjective* 1. having or expressing tender or loving feelings. *He has fond memories of his grandparents.* 2. having an affection or taste for. *I am fond of chocolate.* {**fŏnd**}

Word History When you say you are **fond** of someone, you mean that like or have tender feelings toward that person. But the word "fond" comes from a early English word that means "to be foolish." In the 1500s, it could also mean "foolishly tender." What do being fond and being foolish have to do with each other?

fon·dle *verb* (fondled, fondling, fondles) to touch or stroke in a tender way. *She fondled her toy rabbit.* {**fŏn** dəl}

font[1] *noun* an open container that holds holy water for baptism. {**fŏnt**}

font[2] *noun* a complete set of type, all of the same size, style, or face. {**fŏnt**}

food 🔽 ⊙ *noun* anything that contains nutrients and is eaten by living creatures in order to maintain life, health, and growth. {**foohd**}

• **food for thought**
something to be thought about or pondered. *Your questions are food for thought.*

Synonyms
These words share a meaning with **food**, noun 1:
nourishment, nutrient

food chain *noun* a series of living beings in which each serves as food for the next. *Bats eat insects, and so are above them in the food chain.* {**foohd** chayn}

food processor *noun* an electric kitchen appliance that has a container and different kinds of blades. It is used to grind, grate, chop, slice, or otherwise prepare food. {**foohd** pro seh sər}

food web *noun* the interlocking food chains within an ecological community. {**foohd** wəb}

fool *noun* 1. a person who does not have good sense or judgment. *Max was a fool to think he could get up late and make it to school on time.* 2. a person who has been or is likely to be tricked or made to look silly. *I felt like a fool when I slipped and fell in the cafeteria.* 3. a person whose job was to entertain people by acting in a funny or foolish way for a king or noble; jester. *verb* (fooled, fooling, fools) 1. to trick into believing something that is not true; deceive. *He fooled his mother with a card trick.* 2. to pretend; tease. *He said he was a nuclear rocket scientist, but he was only fooling.* 3. to act without serious purpose or in a silly way (usually followed by "around"). *They were fooling around when they should have been working.* {**foohl**}

Word History *Fool* comes from *follis*, a Latin word that means "bellows" or "leather bag." Later, it came to be used for an empty-headed person.

fool·ish *adjective* not having good sense; silly. *It was foolish to go out in the rain without a coat.* {**foohl** ihsh} foolishly, adv., foolishness, n.

foot ⊙ *noun* (feet) 1. the end part of the leg of humans and other animals, on which the body stands and walks. 2. a unit of length equal to twelve inches or 30.48 centimeters. (abbreviated: ft.) 3. the part of something that is lowest or opposite the head. *They set up camp at the foot of*

 Human Body ❓ Human Mind 👕 Everyday Life History and Culture ☎ Communication the mountain. / *His cat sleeps at the foot of his bed.* {**fuut**}

• **on foot**
by walking. *Zach went to school on foot because he missed the bus.*

foot·ball ⭘ *noun* 1. a game played in the United States and Canada by two teams on a long field. Each team tries to score points by passing or carrying the ball to the other team's end of the playing area. 2. the oval leather ball used in this game. 3. in other countries, the game of soccer. {**fuut** bawl}

foot·hill *noun* a lower hill near the base of a mountain or group of mountains. {**fuut** hihl}

foot·ing *noun* 1. a firm base on which one can stand, build, or grow. *She started school on a strong footing.* 2. the safe or firm placing of the feet while moving. *He lost his footing on the rocky path.* 3. position or relationship. *It is important to be on a good footing with one's neighbors. / Tom and Jack entered the contest on equal footing.* {**fuut** ing}

foot·note *noun* a note at the bottom of a page or the end of a chapter that explains a part of the main text. {**fuut** noht}

foot·print *noun* a mark pressed by a foot onto a surface, such as a step in wet sand or a print left by a muddy shoe. {**fuut** prihnt}

foot·step *noun* 1. a single step with the foot, or the sound it makes. 2. the mark left by a step; footprint. {**fuut** stehp}

• **follow in the footsteps of**
to have the same job or lead the same kind of life as

someone else. *She followed in her father's footsteps by becoming a pilot.*

foot·stool *noun* a low stool on which to rest the feet while seated. {**fuut** stoohl}

for *preposition* 1. used to show the purpose or aim of an action. *They are working for peace. / He was heading for the door.* 2. used to show who is to receive something or how it is to be used. *The gift is for Julie. / I put some money aside for a bike.* 3. as the result of. *Jesse won a prize for his drawing.* 4. used to show a length of time. *We walked for an hour.* 5. with respect to. *It is too cold for June.* 6. in order to do or get. *We are going for lunch.* 7. in place of. *Who will speak for me when I'm not there?* 8. in favor of. *They voted for the new law.* 9. in exchange for. *He paid three dollars for that pen.* 10. by reason of; because of. *They clapped for joy.* 11. used as a sign of; indicating. *A dove is the symbol for peace.* *conjunction* since; because. *He won't go, for he's not feeling well.* {**fohr**}

Homophone Note The words **for**, **four**, and the prefix **fore-** sound alike but have different meanings. "Fore-" is a prefix meaning "in front." You do not have a forhead you have a forehead.

for·age *noun* food for animals such as horses or cattle. *verb* (foraged, foraging, forages) 1. to search for food or supplies. *Bees foraged among the flowers.* 2. to look through or search for what what one needs or wants. *She foraged through her closet for her*

favorite shoes. {**fohr** ihj} for·ager, n.

for·bade or **forbad** *verb* a past tense of **forbid**. {fohr **băd**}

for·bid *verb* (forbade or forbad, forbidden or forbid, forbidding, forbids) to give orders that prevent or prohibit. *They have forbidden swimming here.* {fər **bihd**}

force ⭘ *noun* 1. power, energy, or physical strength. *The force of the wind knocked down the trees.* 2. the use of such power, energy, or strength. *It took force to open the jar.* 3. someone or something with the power to influence or cause change. *She was the main force behind the city's smoking ban.* 4. a group of people with a common goal or activity. *She is a member of the police force.* *verb* (forced, forcing, forces) 1. to make or cause to do something by using strength or power. *Ivan forced her to tell the truth.* 2. to make happen by being stronger or having more power than. *She had to force the lock to open the door.* {**fohrs**}

Word History *Force* comes from *fortis*, a Latin word that means "strong." This Latin word is also the source of our words *fort* and *fortify*.

force·ful *adjective* having power, force, or effectiveness. *Sojourner Truth was a forceful speaker. / One forceful blow broke down the door.* {**fohrs** fəl} forcefully, adv.

for·ceps *noun* (forceps) a tool, shaped like a pair of tongs or tweezers, used to grasp and pull. Dentists and medical doctors use forceps. {fohr səps}

ford *noun* a shallow place in a river or other body of water that can be crossed without a

 Living World Physical World  Natural Environment  Economy Government and Law

boat or raft. *verb* (forded, fording, fords) to cross at a ford. *They forded the stream without getting their clothes wet.* {**fohrd**}

fore- *prefix* 1. a prefix that means "before" or "coming before." A *"forefather"* is an ancestor, a father who has come before the fathers now living. / To *"forewarn"* a person of danger is to warn her before the dangerous thing happens. 2. a prefix that means "front," or "in front." The word *"forehead"* means "the front of the head." / A *"foreleg"* is an animal's front leg.

Homophone Note The prefix *fore-* sounds just like *for* and *four*, but these words each have a different meaning.

fore·arm *noun* the lower arm in humans, between the elbow and wrist. {**fohr** arm}

fore·cast *verb* (forecast or forecasted, forecasting, forecasts) to state as likely to happen; predict. *The weather report forecasts rain for this afternoon. noun* a guess or estimate about something that will happen in the future. *Stay tuned for the weekend weather forecast.* {**fohr** **kăst**} forecaster, n.

fore·fa·ther *noun* a male ancestor. {**fohr** fah thər}

fore·fin·ger *noun* the finger next to the thumb; index finger. {**fohr** fing gər}

fore·foot *noun* (forefeet) one of the front feet of an animal that has four or more legs. {**fohr** fuut}

fore·gone *adjective* having been decided ahead of time; certain. *It was a foregone conclusion that the package would arrive late.* {**fohr** **gawn**}

fore·ground *noun* the part of a picture or view that appears to be nearest to the person looking at it. *This painting shows a tree in the foreground and mountains in the background.* {**fohr** grownd}

fore·head *noun* 1. the part of the human face above the eyes and below the hair; brow. 2. the part above the eyes on the face of any animal. {**fohr** hehd}

for·eign *adjective* 1. in, from, or having to do with a country that is not one's own. *For people who live in Brazil, English is a foreign language.* 2. strange or not familiar. *City life was foreign to Anna who grew up on a farm.* {**fohr** ihn}

for·eign·er *noun* a person who is born in or is from a foreign country. {**fŏrh** ihn ər}

fore·leg *noun* one of the two front legs of an animal that has four or more legs. {**fohr** lehg}

fore·man *noun* (foremen) 1. the leader of a group of workers in a factory, shop, or other workplace. 2. the person who speaks for a jury. *The foreman read the verdict to the judge.* {**fohr** mən}

fore·most *adverb or adjective* first in time, place, importance, or rank. *He is the foremost physicist at the university.* / *First and foremost, you must decide what to do.* {**fohr** mohst or **fohr** məst, adj., adv.}

fore·run·ner *noun* 1. a person or thing that came before another; ancestor; predecessor. *The new governor is smarter than her forerunner.* / *The phonograph was a forerunner of the CD player.* 2. something that signals or gives notice of what is to come; omen. *Dark clouds and high winds are often forerunners of a storm.* {**fohr** ruhn ər}

fore·saw *verb* past tense of **foresee**. {**fohr** **saw**}

fore·see *verb* (foresaw, foreseen, foreseeing, foresees) to see in advance as likely to happen; predict. *Cassie had foreseen the fall of the kingdom.* {**fohr** **see**} foreseeable, adj.

fore·seen *verb* past participle of **foresee**. {**fohr** **seen**}

fore·sight *noun* concern and planning for future needs and events; prudence. *The farmer had the foresight to plan for dry weather.* {**fohr** siyt}

for·est 🌐 *noun* a large area of land covered with many trees and other plants. {**fohr** ihst}

fore·tell *verb* (foretold, foretelling, foretells) to tell of as likely or certain to happen; forecast; predict. *The wise man foretold a future of peace and plenty.* {**fohr** **tehl**}

fore·told *verb* past tense and past participle of **foretell**. {**fohr** **tohld**}

for·ev·er *adverb* 1. for all time; eternally. *Dinosaurs are gone forever.* 2. always; constantly. *He's forever talking to his*

 Human Body   Human Mind   Everyday Life   History and Culture    Communication

friends on the phone. {fə **rehv** ər}

fore·word *noun* a statement at the beginning of a written text, such as a book; introduction or preface. {**fohr wuhrd**}

for·feit *noun* something demanded or given up as a penalty for not acting as required by law, contract, or rules. *verb* (forfeited, forfeiting, forfeits) 1. to be made to give up as a penalty or fine. *She forfeited her driver's licence because she was caught speeding three times.* 2. to lose or give up because of not following a rule, law, or contract. *Our team forfeited the game because we arrived too late.* {**fohr** fiht}

for·gave *verb* the past tense of **forgive.** {fər **gayv**}

forge¹ *noun* 1. a furnace or hearth where metal is heated to be worked or shaped. 2. the building in which such work is done. *verb* (forged, forging, forges) 1. to form or shape by heating and hammering. *The blacksmith forged shoes for the horse.* 2. to form or shape by any means. *The general forged a plan of attack.* 3. to invent or imitate in order to deceive. *He forged many checks before he was caught by the police.* {**fohrj**}

forge² *verb* (forged, forging, forges) to move forward gradually but with strength of purpose (often followed by "ahead"). *Although many people opposed it, we forged ahead with our plan.* {**fohrj**}

for·get *verb* (forgot, forgotten or forgot, forgetting, forgets) 1. to fail to remember. *I keep forgetting his name.* 2. to fail to do because of not remembering (usually followed by an infinitive verb). *Sam forgot to go to the store.* 3. to

leave behind without meaning to. *Did you forget your lunch money again?* {fər **geht**}

for·get·ful *adjective* likely to forget. *Mrs. Park becomes forgetful when she's worried.* {fər **geht** fəl}

for·get-me-not *noun* a kind of plant with clusters of blue flowers. The flowers are considered to be symbols of faithfulness in friendship or love. {fər **geht** mee nŏt}

for·give *verb* (forgave, forgiven, forgiving, forgives) 1. to give up or let go of anger against. *Mrs. Petrov forgave the child who broke her window.* 2. to excuse or pardon. *The teacher forgave his lateness. / Please forgive her; it was an accident.* {fər **gihv**}

for·give·ness *noun* 1. the act of forgiving. *The robber asked for his victim's forgiveness.* 2. the state of being likely or willing to forgive. *The good king was known for his forgiveness.* {fər **gihv** nihs}

for·got *verb* past tense and a past participle of **forget.** {fər **gŏt**}

for·got·ten *verb* a past participle of **forget.** {fər **gŏt** ən}

fork *noun* 1. a tool with a handle and two or more points. Small forks are used for eating. Large forks are used for digging and pitching hay. 2. the point where something divides into two or more branches, or one of the branches. *Go to the fork in the highway and stay in the middle lane. / Take the left fork.* *verb* (forked, forking, forks) 1. to pierce, dig, lift, or carry with a fork. *He is forking hay into the horse's stall. / She forked the meat*

from the grill to the plate. 2. to separate into branches. *The river forks about a mile from here.* {**fohrk**}

• **fork over, out,** or **up** (informal) to hand over, without being completely willing. *She forked out fifty dollars for that hat!*

form *noun* 1. structure or shape. *That piece of music has a classical form. / His plans had no form.* 2. the body or outward shape of an animal or person; figure. *It was hard to make out the bear's form in the dark.* 3. a document with empty spaces for writing in information. *She filled out a form to apply for a driver's license.* 4. type or kind. *This is a rare form of plant life.* 5. the state of being fit in body or mind for sports or other activities. *She was in good form on the tennis court today.* *verb* (formed, forming, forms) 1. to make, build, or create. *He formed the clay into a pot.* 2. to be one, many, or all of the parts of; constitute. *Those three students form the executive committee of the club.* 3. to come into being; develop; arise. *A group formed to fight crime in the neighborhood.* {**fohrm**}

for·mal *adjective* 1. following accepted rules of behavior; proper, legal, or official. *He made a formal request for help with his project.* 2. with ceremony; according to custom or tradition. *Jim bought a new suit for the formal wedding.* 3. proper to the point of being cold; stiff. *Her parents were so formal that they made their guests feel uncomfortable.* *noun* 1. a dance or other social event to which formal clothing is worn. *Are you going to the winter formal?* 2. an evening dress or gown.

A
B
C
D
E
F
G
H
I
J
K
L
M
N
O
P
Q
R
S
T
U
V
W
X
Y
Z

a
b
c
d
e
f
g
h
i
j
k
l
m
n
o
p
q
r
s
t
u
v
w
x
y
z

She wore a formal to the ball. {**fohr** məl} formally, adj.

for·ma·tion *noun* 1. the act of forming or the state of being formed. *Ten people took part in the formation of the new science club.* 2. the way in which a thing is formed. *The drawing compared the formation of a bird's wing and a bat's wing.* 3. something that has been formed. *She hiked out to get a better view of the rock formation.* 4. a particular arrangement of people. *The soldiers waited in formation before boarding the ship. / The basketball players got into a defensive formation.* {**fohr may** shən}

for·mer *adjective* 1. happening in or having to do with the past; previous. *He was a great baseball player in his former career.* 2. being the first of two, or the first mentioned of two. *She preferred the former suggestion to the latter.* 3. having once been. *The senator is a former history professor.* {**fohr** mər}

for·mer·ly *adverb* in the past; in a time before now. *New York was formerly called New Amsterdam.* {**fohr** mər lee}

for·mu·la ① *noun* (formulas or formulae) 1. a routine group of words or symbols used in a procedure. *Use the formula "one-half base times height," or "bh/2" to find the area of a triangle.* 2. a conventional model for doing something. *The author used an old formula in his latest mystery.* 3. a list of ingredients or steps; recipe. *Do you know any formulas for* $E=mc^2$ *making soap bubbles?* 4. a set of symbols used to name the elements of a chemical compound. *The formula for carbon*

dioxide is CO_2. 5. a liquid food for feeding babies; artificial milk. {**fohrm** yə lə}

for·sake *verb* (forsook, forsaken, forsaking, forsakes) 1. to leave or desert. *Forsaking his friends, Ron left the playground.* 2. to give up or turn away from. *He tried hard to forsake smoking.* {**fohr sayk** or fər **sayk**}

for·sa·ken *verb* past participle of **forsake.** *adjective* deserted; abandoned; desolate. *This forsaken desert is actually home to a surprising number of lizards.* {**fohr say** kən or fər **say** kən, v., **fohr say** kən or fər **say** kən, adj.}

for·sook *verb* past tense of **forsake.** {**fohr suuk**}

for·syth·i·a *noun* a bush that has bright yellow flowers along its long, thin branches. *Forsythias bloom in early spring.* {**fohr sih** thee ə or fər **sih** thee ə}

fort *noun* a strong building used during battles for protection and defense. {**fohrt**}

forth *adverb* 1. forward; onward in time or location. *They stayed friends from that day forth.* 2. out; into view. *The wolf come forth from its den.* {**fohrth**}

> **Homophone Note** Are you looking for the word ***fourth*** (coming after the third)? ***Forth*** and ***fourth*** sound alike but have different meanings.

for·ti·eth *adjective* coming next after the thirty-ninth in a series. *This is the fortieth year this store has been in business.* *noun* 1. one of forty equal parts of a whole; 1/40. *Each member's vote counted as a fortieth of the club's decision.* 2. the number, person, or thing that comes next after the thirty-ninth in a series. *They held a surprise party for her fortieth birthday.* {**fohr** tee ihth}

for·ti·fi·ca·tion *noun* 1. the act of adding strength or fortifying. *Steel beams were used in the fortification of the concrete wall.* 2. something that adds strength or fortifies. *The castle's fortifications included thick stone walls.* {**fohr** tə fih **kay** shən}

for·ti·fy *verb* (fortified, fortifying, fortifies) to give more strength, resistance, or energy to; reinforce. *The carpenter fortified the walls of the old barn. / The warm drink fortified me.* {**fohr** tih **fiy**}

for·tress *noun* a large, fortified building or area, often around a town or settlement. {**fohr** trihs}

for·tu·nate *adjective* 1. having good fortune; lucky; blessed. *You are fortunate to receive such a good education.* 2. bringing or brought by good fortune. *It was fortunate that the police got there in time to stop the fight.* {**fohr** chə niht} fortunately, adv.

for·tune *noun* 1. a large amount of money or wealth. *She made her fortune buying and selling land.* 2. luck, whether good or bad. *He had the good fortune to win the raffle.* 3. a person's destiny, or the results of experiences during a person's life. *Some say it was her fortune to become a great leader.* {**fohr** chən}

for·tune·tell·er *noun* a person who claims to have the ability to see and tell about events that will happen in the future. {**fohr** chən teh lər} fortunetelling, n.

for·ty *noun* (forties) the number that is equal to four times ten; 40. *adjective* being forty

 Human Body    Human Mind   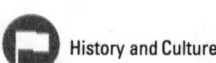 Everyday Life    History and Culture   Communication

in number. *He baked a batch of forty cookies.* {**fohr** tee}

fo·rum *noun* (forums) 1. the central place in ancient Roman cities where people gathered for business and public meetings. 2. a public meeting to discuss some problem of public or general interest. *The university held a forum on race relations.* {**fohr** əm}

for·ward *adverb* 1. toward a place or time that is further on; ahead. *She looked forward to a long vacation. / The line for tickets finally moved forward.* 2. closer or into view. *If you want to help, please step forward. adjective* 1. at or toward the front. *They found seats in the forward part of the train.* 2. too bold. *He was forward about asking for more money. noun* a player in or near the front of the team in basketball, hockey, or certain other games. *verb* (forwarded, forwarding, forwards) to send on to a new address. *The post office forwarded our mail to our new home.* {**fohr** wərd} forwards, adv.

fos·sil 🌐 ⊙ *noun* the remains or trace of a living animal or plant from a long time ago. Fossils are found embedded in earth or rock. {**fŏs** əl}

Word History *Fossil* is from a Latin word that means "dug up."

fos·sil fuel *noun* any carbon-containing fuel formed from the remains of prehistoric plants and animals. Coal, petroleum, and natural gas are examples of fossil fuel. {**fŏs** ihl **fyoohl**}

fos·ter *verb* (fostered, fostering, fosters) to aid and encourage the growth or development of. *They fostered trust in their family by always being honest. adjective* giving or receiving care in a family not related by birth or adoption. *This foster family has two foster children.* {**fŏs** tər}

fought *verb* past tense and past participle of **fight**. {**fawt**}

foul *adjective* (fouler, foulest) 1. very unpleasant to taste, smell, or look at. *What is that foul odor?* 2. very dirty or muddy. *They found the old woman living in a foul apartment.* 3. cloudy, rainy, or otherwise unpleasant. *The weather has been really foul lately.* 4. very bad; not fair; evil. *Kicking the puppy was a foul act.* 5. falling outside of the lines that mark an area for fair play in a sport. *He hit a foul ball. noun* 1. a failure to play by the rules of a game or sport. *The referee said that pushing is a foul.* 2. a ball hit outside of the lines that mark the area for fair play in baseball or softball; foul ball. *verb* (fouled, fouling, fouls) 1. to make dirty or put dirt in or on. *He fouled his jeans in the mud.* 2. to entangle or catch. *She fouled her hair in the telephone cord.* 3. to commit a foul against in a game or sport. *He fouled me when I tried to shoot a basket.* 4. to hit a foul ball in baseball or softball. *He fouled three times before he finally hit a fair ball.* {**fowl**}

• **foul up** (informal) to make serious mistakes, or cause someone else to do so. *He really fouled up his driving test.*

Homophone Note Are you looking for the word *fowl* (a bird). *Foul* and *fowl* sound alike but have different meanings.

foul line *noun* 1. either of the lines on a baseball field drawn from home plate through first and third bases to the outfield. Foul lines mark the area within which fair play takes place. 2. a line on a basketball court drawn fifteen feet from the backboard. A player may shoot freely from this line when the other team commits a foul. {**fowl** liyn}

found¹ *verb* past tense and past participle of **find**. {**fownd**}

found² *verb* (founded, founding, founds) to set up or create; establish. *In 1857, Dr. Elizabeth Blackwell founded a hospital run by women.* {**fownd**}

foun·da·tion *noun* 1. the basis of something such as an action, substance, structure, or opinion. *He has enough money to give his business a good foundation. / Your ideas about her are completely without foundation.* 2. the act of beginning or establishing. *Denise's family helped with the foundation of this school.* 3. the stone or concrete structure that holds up a building from beneath. *A house built on a strong foundation will last many years.* 4. an organization started with gifts of money. Foundations give money to individuals or groups in need. {**fown day** shən}

found·ry *noun* (foundries) a place where metal is formed into different objects. {**fown** dree}

A
B
C
D
E
F
G
H
I
J
K
L
M
N
O
P
Q
R
S
T
U
V
W
X
Y
Z

a
b
c
d
e
f
g
h
i
j
k
l
m
n
o
p
q
r
s
t
u
v
w
x
y
z

foun·tain *noun* 1. a spray of water created by a machine, or the structure from which the water flows. *There is a drinking fountain right outside the classroom. / The garden fountain attracts many birds.* 2. a source or origin. *My grandmother is a fountain of wisdom.* {<u>fown</u> tən}

fountain pen *noun* a pen that holds a small supply of ink, which is drawn to the pen's point. {<u>fown</u> tən **pehn**}

four *noun* the number that comes after 3 and before 5 in the sequence of cardinal numbers; 4. *adjective* being four in number. *I own four red shirts.* {<u>fohr</u>}

Homophone Note The words *four*, *for*, and the prefix *fore-* sound alike but have different meanings.

Four·-H club *noun* an organization in the U.S. that teaches young people about farming and how to take care of a home. Four-H clubs are so named because they are meant to improve the heads, hearts, hands, and health of their members. {fohr <u>aych</u> kluhb}

four·square *adjective* 1. having four equal sides that meet in four right angles; square. 2. firm and clear. *They gave the candidate foursquare praise.* 3. direct and blunt. *He spoke his mind like the foursquare fellow that he is.* *adverb* in a direct and clear way. {fohr <u>skwayr</u>}

four·teen *noun* the number that comes after 13 and before 15 in the sequence of cardinal numbers; 14. *adjective* being fourteen in number. *My* house is fourteen blocks away from school. {fohr <u>teen</u>}

four·teenth *adjective* coming next after the thirteenth in a series. *It's been raining for the fourteenth day in a row.* *noun* 1. one of fourteen equal parts of a whole; 1/14. *That school is so competitive, it only accepts a fourteenth of the applicants.* 2. the number, person, or thing that comes next after the thirteenth in a series. *I sit in the fourteenth desk from the front.* {fohr <u>teenth</u>}

fourth *adjective* coming next after the third in a series. *She was the fourth member elected to the student council.* *noun* 1. one of four equal parts of a whole; one quarter; 1/4. *Each child took a fourth of the profits of the lemonade business.* 2. the number, person, or thing that comes next after the third in a series. *I was fourth in line to see the movie.* {<u>fohrth</u>}

Homophone Note Are you looking for the word *forth* (forward)? *Fourth* and *forth* sound alike but have different meanings.

Fourth of July *noun* Independence Day in the United States. {<u>fohrth</u> əv jə <u>liy</u>}

fowl *noun* 1. a bird such as a chicken that is raised for its eggs or meat. Ducks, geese, and turkeys are also domestic fowl. 2. a wild bird, such as a duck, goose, pheasant, or quail, that is hunted for its meat. {<u>fowl</u>}

Homophone Note Are you looking for the word *foul*? *Fowl* and *foul* sound alike but have different meanings.

fox *noun* (foxes) 1. a wild mammal that has a pointed nose, pointed ears, and a bushy tail. Foxes are closely related to coyotes, dogs, and wolves. Foxes hunt insects, birds, and other small animals but will sometimes eat plants, especially fruit. 2. the fur of such an animal. 3. a person who acts with slyness or cunning. *You were a real fox to fool them with that trick.* {<u>fŏks</u>}

fox·hound *noun* a breed of dog. Foxhounds are dogs of medium size with short hair and are bred and trained to hunt foxes. {<u>fŏks</u> hownd}

frac·tion *noun* 1. a part or very small part of a whole. *I found only a fraction of my lost money.* 2. a number written as one number divided by another (separated by a hypen). *The fraction "two-fourths" (2/4) is the same as "two divided by four."* {<u>frăk</u> shən}

Word History *Fraction* comes from a Latin word that means "a breaking into pieces." In the English spoken in the 1400s, a bone fracture was called a "fraction."

frac·ture *noun* a break or crack. *He has a fracture in one of his leg bones.* *verb* (fractured, fracturing, fractures) 1. to break or cause a break in. *She fractured her arm when she fell on the sidewalk.* 2. to break or crack. *The ice began to fracture as she stepped on it.* {<u>frăk</u> chər}

 Human Body   Human Mind   Everyday Life  History and Culture  Communication

frag·ile *adjective* easily broken; delicate. *The fragile chair cracked when he sat on it.* {**frǎ** jihl *or* **frǎ** jiyl} fragilely, adv., fragileness, n., fragility, n.

frag·ment *noun* a broken-off or incomplete part. *Mike cut his foot on a fragment of glass. / She remembered only a fragment of the song.* {**frǎg** mənt}

fra·grance *noun* a pleasant smell. *The fragrance of roses filled the room.* {**fray** grəns}

fra·grant *adjective* having a pleasant smell. *The cook added fragrant spices to the stew.* {**fray** grənt} fragrantly, adv., fragrantness, n.

frail *adjective* 1. weak or sickly. *The frail old woman walked with a cane.* 2. easily broken or damaged. *The frail crystal vase shattered when she dropped it.* {**frayl**} frailly, adv., frailness, n.

frame *noun* 1. a structure made of parts that are joined together and that supports a larger object. *The body of the car was damaged, but its frame was still good.* 2. a rim or border that fits around something. *The new window frames are made of aluminum.* 3. the build of a person's body; form. *Mr. George has a large frame.* *verb* (framed, framing, frames) 1. to express in a particular way or for a particular purpose. *She framed the question in simple words for the child.* 2. to enclose within a rim or border. *Curly dark hair framed his face. / Lisa framed her college diploma.* {**fraym**}

frame·work *noun* a structure that supports something built on or around it. *The carpenter nailed siding to the framework of the house.* {**fraym** wuhrk}

franc *noun* the unit of money once used by France, Belgium, and several other countries. {**frǎngk**}

Homophone Note The words *franc* and *frank* sound alike but have different meanings.

France *noun* a country in western Europe. Paris is the capital of France. {**frǎns**}

frank[1] *adjective* (franker, frankest) honest, direct, and open. *The author asked for a frank opinion about her latest book.* {**frǎngk**} frankness, n.

frank[2] *noun* (informal) frankfurter; hot dog. *They had franks and beans for lunch today.* {**frǎngk**}

Homophone Note Are you looking for the word *franc* (a French unit of money)? *Frank* and *franc* sound alike but have different meanings.

frank·furt·er *noun* a thin, smoked sausage that is usually made from beef or a mixture of beef and pork. {**frǎngk** fuhrt ər}

Word History *Frankfurter* comes from the city of *Frankfurt* in Germany, where a sausage similar to a hot dog was made.

fran·tic *adjective* very excited by worry or fear; frenzied. *The child became frantic when he couldn't find his parents in the crowded mall.* {**frǎnt** ihk} frantically, adv.

fraud *noun* 1. the use of lies or tricks to cheat or take advantage of in a way that is often against the law. *The dishonest salesman went to jail for committing fraud.* 2. a person who uses tricks or lies to get something; fake. *The woman who says she can tell your future is really a fraud.* {**frawd**}

fray *verb* (frayed, fraying, frays) 1. to wear or rub thin. *Constant use frays a shirt collar.* 2. to become worn thin. *This fine fabric frays easily.* {**fray**}

freak *noun* 1. a person or animal that is very different from what is considered normal, or that has a surprising defect. *A calf born with two heads is a freak.* 2. something that seems very unusual and without cause. *The summer blizzard was a freak of nature.* *adjective* very unusual or seeming to have no cause. *The rescue workers were not prepared for the freak accident.* {**freek**}

freck·le *noun* a light brown dot or mark in the skin, often brought out by exposure to sunlight. *He gets freckles all over his face in the summer.* {**frehk** əl}

free *adjective* (freer, freest) 1. not held back or confined; not enslaved and not in prison. *The prisoner forgot what it was like to be free.* 2. having a type of government that is controlled by all the people and that gives rights to all the people. *The people of Canada live in a free nation.* 3. not under the control of another; independent. *You are free to do as you please. / A free press does not fear the government.* 4. not troubled by or worried about (usually followed by "of" or "from"). *We were on vacation and free of cares.* 5. not blocked. *The drain is now free.* 6. without cost. *That store gives a free balloon to every child.* 7. empty; not in use. *Is this seat free?* *adverb* (freer, freest) without cost. *Children ride free on this bus.* *verb* (freed, freeing, frees) 1. to set loose;

make free. *Jeremy freed the animal from the cage.* 2. to clear or untangle. *Sarah freed the kite from the tree.* {**free**} freely, adv. freeness, n.

free·dom *noun* 1. the condition of being free or freed; liberty. *After years of being forced to work for no pay, the slaves at last gained their freedom.* 2. the state of being free to act or move as one wishes. *The children enjoy the freedom they have to run and scream at recess.* 3. a specific right. *Freedom of speech is a right enjoyed by all Americans.* {**free** dəm}

free fall *noun* the first stage of a parachute jump, before the parachute opens. {**free** fawl} free-fall, v.

free·ware *noun* software that is given away for no charge by its author. People may use the software but not sell it. *Many games are available as freeware on the Internet.* {**free** wayr}

free·way *noun* a highway with more than two lanes and no stop signs or traffic lights, allowing traffic to move at high speeds. {**free** way}

freeze *verb* (froze, frozen, freezing, freezes) 1. to harden into ice or become solid from cold temperatures. *Water freezes at 32 degrees Fahrenheit.* 2. to become blocked by or filled with ice. *The water pipes froze this winter.* 3. to suddenly stop moving or become still. *The policeman shouted "Freeze!" / I froze in my tracks when I heard footsteps behind me.* 4. to feel very cold. *She said she was freezing and went back inside.* noun 1. the act of freezing or state of being frozen. *Skaters are dis-*

appointed that there has been no lake freeze yet this year. 2. a period of very cold weather. *The long freeze was bad for the plants.* {**freez**} freezable, adj.

freez·er *noun* a very cold refrigerator that freezes foods or stores frozen foods. {**free** zər}

freight *noun* goods shipped by boat, plane, train, or truck. *The truck is carrying hundreds of pounds of freight.* {**frayt**} freightless, adj.

freight·er *noun* a ship for taking goods from one place to another. {**fray** tər}

French *adjective* of or having to do with France, or its people or language. *noun* 1. (used with a plural verb) the people of France (usually used with "the"). 2. the language of France and several other countries. {**frehnch**}

Bienvenue à la maison

French fries *plural noun* (often lower case) potatoes cut into long strips and fried in fat. {**fre-hnch friyz**}

French Guiana *noun* a territory of France in northern South America, on the Atlantic coast. Cayenne is the capital city of French Guiana. {**frehnch** gee ă nə *or* **frehnch** gee ah nə}

French horn *noun* a brass wind instrument. It is a long coiled tube that ends in a wide bell shape. {**frehnch hohrn**}

French·man *noun* a man who was born in or is a citizen of France. {**frehnch** măn}

French·wo·man *noun* a woman who was born in or is a cit-

izen of France. {**frehnch** wuu mən}

fren·zy *noun* (frenzies) a state of wild excitement or anger. *By the end of the bullfight, the crowd was in a frenzy.* {**frehn** zee}

fre·quen·cy ❶ *noun* (frequencies) 1. the condition of happening often or being frequent. *She got headaches with such frequency, that she decided to see a doctor.* 2. the number of times something happens within a certain period of time. *This computer program calculates the frequency of any word in a text.* 3. the number of energy waves that pass a certain point in a certain time period. Frequency is used to measure radio waves and other kinds of radiation. *Some radiation has a frequency that allows us to see it as color.* {**free** kwən see}

fre·quent *adjective* happening often or repeated often. *We make frequent trips to the store for milk.* {**free** kwənt} frequenter, n., frequentness, n.

fresh *adjective* (fresher, freshest) 1. newly made, gotten, or experienced. *They enjoyed a fresh cup of tea. / Please put on a fresh T-shirt.* 2. still good to eat or drink; not spoiled. *The milk is not fresh.* 3. not preserved by freezing or canning. *We like fresh fish.* 4. feeling new and alive. *Ezra came to work feeling fresh again after his vacation.* 5. not salty. *We drank fresh water from the mountain stream.* 6. cool, refreshing, and pure. *We enjoyed the fresh sea air.* 7. (informal) rude; sassy. *His father scolded the boy for being so fresh.* {**frehsh**} freshly, adv., freshness, n.

 Human Body   Human Mind  Everyday Life  History and Culture 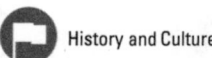 Communication

fresh·en *verb* (freshened, freshening, freshens) 1. to cause to be fresh; renew. *The waiter freshened our water glasses.* 2. to become fresh or renewed. *The air has freshened in here.* {**frehsh** ən}
• **freshen up**
to make oneself feel more comfortable or attractive, as by cleaning oneself. *She freshened up after her workout.*

fresh·man *noun* (freshmen) a student in the first year of high school, college, or university. {**frehsh** mən}

fresh·wa·ter *adjective* of, having to do with or living in water that is not salty. *The rainbow trout is a freshwater fish.* {**frehsh** waw tər}

fret[1] *verb* (fretted, fretting, frets) to feel troubled or uneasy. *She fretted when her daughter was late getting home.* {**freht**}

fret[2] *noun* one of the ridges set across the neck of a stringed instrument such as a guitar or lute to mark where the fingers should press the strings for each note. {**freht**}

Fri. *abbreviation* an abbreviation for **Friday**.

fri·ar *noun* a man who is a member of a Roman Catholic order; monk. {**friy** ər}

fric·tion *noun* 1. the rubbing of objects against each other. *If you don't have gloves, you can warm your hands with friction.* 2. the resistance of a surface to motion, as of an object sliding or rolling over it. *On a rainy day, there may not be enough friction to stop your car quickly.* 3. disagreement between people or groups of people; conflict. *It bothers me that there is so much friction in our family.* {**frihk** shən} frictionless, adj.

Fri·day *noun* the sixth day of the week. Friday comes between Thursday and Saturday. The word Friday comes from an Old English word meaning "Frigg's day." Frigg was the name of a pagan goddess of heaven and family life. {**friy** day}

Word History *Friday* was once called "Frigga's day." Frigga was a goddess of heaven and love in the ancient mythology of Scandinavia.

fried *adjective* cooked in oil, butter, or some other fat. *Would you like your potatoes baked or fried? verb* past tense and past participle of **fry**. {**friyd**}

friend ⊙ *noun* 1. a person whom you know well and like and who likes you. *Sheila and I have been friends since kindergarten.* 2. a person who supports a group or a cause with money. *The friends of the library raised money to buy books.* {**frehnd**} friendless, adj.

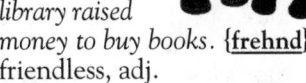

friend·ly *adjective* (friendlier, friendliest) 1. welcoming and pleasant toward others. *I try to be friendly toward people I don't like. / Our town is a friendly place.* 2. kind and helpful. *The friendly waiter made our meal enjoyable.* {**frehnd** lee} friendliness, n.

friend·ship *noun* 1. the state or condition of being a friend. *Their friendship has lasted for many years.* 2. friendly feeling. *The President greeted the Prime Minister with friendship.* {**frehnd** shihp}

fright ⊙ *noun* 1. strong fear caused by sudden danger. *In her fright, she dropped her basket and ran.* 2. something or someone that causes such fear. *It was quite a fright when you walked in with blood all over your shirt.* {**friyt**}

fright·en *verb* (frightened, frightening, frightens) 1. to cause fear in; scare. *The growling dog frightened the children.* 2. to cause to move away suddenly by causing fear (usually followed by "away" or "off"). *The scarecrow will frighten away the crows.* {**friyt** ən} frighteningly, adv.

fright·ful *adjective* 1. terrible or frightening. *The vampire smiled, revealing his frightful fangs.* 2. awful or shocking. *The nurse made a frightful mistake and gave Mrs. Jones the wrong baby.* {**friyt** fəl} frightfully, adv., frightfulness, n.

frig·id ⊛ *adjective* 1. very cold; freezing. *The air is frigid in February.* 2. unfriendly or without emotion; emotionally cold. *He eyed us with a frigid stare.* {**frihj** ihd} frigidity, n., frigidly, adv.

fringe *noun* 1. an edge of hanging threads, yarn, or strips of leather used to decorate clothing or drapes. 2. anything that looks like such an edge. *A fringe of hair fell in Fukiko's eyes.* {**frihnj**} fringeless, adj., fringelike, adj.

Fris·bee *noun* a trade name for a thin plastic disk that is thrown and caught in outdoor games. {**frihz** bee}

frisk *verb* (frisked, frisking, frisks) 1. to leap or skip in a

---

 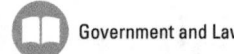

lively and happy way. *The deer frisked about in the field.* 2. to search for something hidden by passing one's hands over a person's clothing. *The police frisked everyone entering the prison.* {**frihsk**} frisker, n., friskingly, adv.

friv·o·lous *adjective* likely to be too silly; lacking sense. *Such a frivolous boy cannot be trusted to watch his baby sister.* {**frihv** ə ləs} frivolously, adv.

frog *noun* 1. a small, jumping animal with smooth, moist skin, long back legs, webbed feet, and no tail. Frogs are amphibians; they live in water during the first part of their lives and on land as adults. 2. a hoarse human sound caused by mucus on the vocal cords. *You have a frog in your throat.* {**frŏg** or **frawg**}

frog·man *noun* (frogmen) a swimmer who works underwater. *Frogmen were sent to repair the underneath of the ship.* {**frŏg măn** or **frawg măn**}

frol·ic *verb* (frolicked, frolicking, frolics) to act in a playful way by romping about, making merry, or playing jokes. *The children frolicked in the pool.* {**frŏ** lihk} frolicker, n.

from *preposition* 1. used to show a starting point in place or time. *We ran from his house to mine. / We are meeting her one hour from now.* 2. used to identify the origin or source. *Don got a postcard from his* friend. / *Joe is from Kentucky. / Wood comes from trees.* 3. used to show difference. *The farmer can tell one chick from another.* 4. used to show distance or separation. *The school is eight miles from here.* 5. used to show cause. *They were tired out from sledding.* {**fruhm**}

frond *noun* a long leaf with many small divisions. Ferns and palm trees have fronds. {**frŏnd**}

front *noun* 1. the most forward part or side of something.

The entrance is at the front of the building. 2. the position or place at the head or beginning. *He went to the front of the line.* 3. the area where fighting takes place in a war. *All was quiet on the western front.* 4. the forward edge of a mass of cold or warm air. *It started to rain as the cold front came closer.* *adjective* having to do with or located in the front. *The story was on the front page of the newspaper.* *verb* (fronted, fronting, fronts) to face or look out on. *The hotel fronts the ocean.* {**fruhnt**}

fron·tier *noun* 1. a border between two countries, or the area nearby on either side. *There is fighting on the frontier between India and Pakistan.* 2. (sometimes plural) the part of a settlement, exploration, or field of study which is being newly discovered. *These scientists are working on the frontiers of cancer research. / Outer space is the final frontier.* {**fruhn teer**}

frost *noun* 1. a light, white covering of dew or water vapor frozen into ice crystals. *This morning, the grass is covered with frost.* 2. the condition produced when the air temperature falls below the freezing point of water, or the temperature at which this happens. *There will be a frost tonight.* *verb* (frosted, frosting, frosts) 1. to develop or get a covering of frost or like frost. *The car windows are frosting over.* 2. to cover with frost. *Snow frosted the rooftops.* 3. to put frosting on a cake or other baked goods; ice. *Who wants to frost the cupcakes?* {**frawst** or **frŏst**, n., **frawst** or **frŏst**, v.} frostless, adj., frostlike, adj.

frost·bite *noun* damage to the skin or body by freezing. *If you don't wear your gloves, you might get frostbite.* *verb* (frostbit, frostbitten, frostbiting, frostbites) to damage by freezing. *The cold wind frostbit my ears.* {**frawst biyt** or **frŏst biyt**, n., **frawst biyt** or **frŏst biyt**, v.}

frost·ing *noun* a sweet covering or filling for baked goods, often made of sugar, butter, and flavoring; icing. {**frawst** ing or **frŏst** ing}

frost·y *adjective* (frostier, frostiest) 1. causing or marked by frost; freezing. *On frosty mornings, we walked quickly to school.* 2. made of or covered with frost or with something that looks like frost. *She drank a nice frosty mug of lemonade.* {**frawst** ee or **frŏst** ee} frostily, adv., frostiness, n.

 Human Body    Human Mind   Everyday Life   History and Culture   Communication

froth *noun* any collection of bubbles formed on a liquid. *Grandfather would blow the froth off his beer before he drank it.* *verb* (frothed, frothing, froths) to produce froth; foam. *The sick dog frothed at the mouth.* {**frawth** or **frŏth**, n., **frawth** or **frŏth**, v.}

frown ❶ ❷ *verb* (frowned, frowning, frowns) 1. to wrinkle the forehead to show anger, unhappiness, or confusion. *Why are you frowning?* 2. to disapprove (usually followed by "on" or "upon"). *She frowned upon his rude behavior.* *noun* a wrinkling of the face that shows anger, unhappiness, or confusion ; scowl. *I could tell by his frown that he didn't like the peas.* {**frown**} frowner, n., frowningly, adv.

froze *verb* past tense of **freeze**. {**frohz**}

fro·zen *verb* past participle of **freeze**. *adjective* 1. changed into a solid or made hard by freezing. *Ice is frozen water.* 2. covered or surrounded by ice. *The frozen river was perfect for skating.* 3. fixed in place or made unable to move or change. *He was frozen with fear when he saw the cobra.* {**froh** zən}

fru·gal *adjective* 1. likely to try to save money; careful with spending. *Frugal shoppers like discount stores.* 2. small in amount or cost; meager. *The poor man ate a frugal dinner.* {**frooh** gəl} frugality, n., frugally, adv.

fruit ❶ ❷ *noun* (fruit or fruits) the part of a plant that has seeds and flesh, such as apple or strawberry. Most fruits are sweet and can be eaten raw. {**frooht**}

> **Word History** *Fruit* comes from a Latin word that means "to have the use of" and "enjoy."

frus·trate *verb* (frustrated, frustrating, frustrates) 1. to prevent from happening or being done. *Bad weather frustrated our plans for a picnic.* 2. to disappoint or puzzle. *It frustrates me that she doesn't listen.* {**fruh strayt**}

fry ❶ *verb* (fried, frying, fries) to cook in hot butter, oil, or other fat. *Would you like to fry these vegetables or steam them?* *noun* (fries) (usually plural) long pieces of potato that have been fried. *She ordered a hamburger with fries.* {**friy**}

Ft. *abbreviation* an abbreviation for **Fort**, when writing a proper name. *"Fort McHenry" can be abbreviated "Ft. McHenry."*

ft. *abbreviation* an abbreviation for **foot** or **feet**.

fudge *noun* a soft candy or frosting made by cooking sugar with butter and other ingredients, such as chocolate and nuts. {**fuhj**}

fu·el ❶ ❷ *noun* anything such as wood or gasoline that is burned as a source of energy. {**fyool**} fueler, n.

fu·gi·tive *noun* a person who is escaping or running away. *The police finally caught the fugitive.* {**fyoo** jə tihv}

-ful *suffix* 1. a suffix that means "full of" or "having the character of." *A cheerful face is a face that looks full of cheer.* / *A peaceful classroom has the character of peace.* 2. a suffix that means "able" or "likely to." *A helpful person is a person who is likely to help.* 3. a suffix that means "an amount that will fill." *A mouthful of food is the amount of food that will fill a mouth.*

ful·crum *noun* (fulcrums) the point of support on which a lever turns. {**fuul** krəm}

ful·fill *verb* (fulfilled, fulfilling, fulfills) 1. to do or carry out as expected or required. *He fulfilled his duty of caring for the child.* 2. to meet or satisfy. *He has fulfilled the physical education requirement.* {**fuul fihl**}

full *adjective* (fuller, fullest) 1. not able to hold or contain any more. *The trunk is full, so put your suitcase in the back seat.* 2. having a large number or amount. *Your spelling test was full of mistakes.* 3. whole; complete. *Grandpa has a full life these days.* *adverb* (fuller, fullest) completely; exactly. *Dad hugged me full around the middle.* {**fuul**} fullness, n.

• **in full**
in the complete or required amount. *We have paid for our car in full.*

full moon *noun* 1. the moon when it is on the side of Earth that is opposite the sun and looks from Earth like a complete

A
B
C
D
E
F
G
H
I
J
K
L
M
N
O
P
Q
R
S
T
U
V
W
X
Y
Z

circle. 2. the time of the month when the moon is in this position. *What date is the full moon this month?* {**fuul moohn**}

ful·ly *adverb* 1. in a way that is complete, entire, or thorough; totally. *The hotel is fully booked.* 2. at least. *We arrived fully an hour ahead of time.* {**fuu** lee}

fum·ble *verb* (fumbled, fumbling, fumbles) 1. to search or feel about for something in a nervous or clumsy way. *He fumbled for his eyeglasses in the dark. / During the speech he fumbled for words.* 2. to handle in a clumsy way; make a mess of. *He fumbled the business deal because of his stupid jokes.* 3. to lose one's grip or control of in a sporting event. *The quarterback fumbled the football.* *noun* the act of fumbling. *The other team got the ball after our fumble.* {**fuhm** bəl} fumbler, n., fumblingly, adv.

fume *noun* (often plural) a vapor, smoke, or odor that is not pleasant or healthy. *You can't sleep in a room full of paint fumes.* *verb* (fumed, fuming, fumes) to show anger or unhappiness. *She fumed whenever her mistake was mentioned.* {**fyoom**}

fun ❷ ❶ *noun* something that amuses or entertains. *Flying the kite was a lot of fun.* *adjective* providing enjoyment or amusement. *I want to play a fun game.* {**fuhn**}
• **make fun of** to laugh at; mock. *He made fun of me because I wear glasses.*

func·tion *noun* 1. the purpose or role for which an object or a person is used. *The function of a firefighter is to put out fires. / The function of a screw is to fasten.* 2. a formal social gathering or ceremony. *She and her husband will attend the function.* *verb* (functioned, functioning, functions) to run or operate in a particular way; act. *The city cannot function without electricity.* {**fuhngk** shən} functionless, adj.

fund *noun* 1. a supply of money or other resources that is held for a particular purpose. *She is saving for her retirement fund.* 2. supply; stock. *Our teacher has a fund of good books on history.* 3. (plural) money available or on hand. *My funds are running low since I had to pay for the car repairs.* {**fuhnd**}

fun·da·men·tal *adjective* basic; central; serving as a foundation. *You have to know the fundamental rules of grammar to write for the school paper.* *noun* a basic principle or necessary part. *Good attitude is a fundamental in any group sport.* {**fuhn** də **mehn** təl} fundamentally, adv.

fu·ner·al *noun* a ceremony for a dead person. {**fyoo** nə rəl}

fun·gi *plural noun* a plural form of fungus. {**fung** giy}

fun·gus ❶ *noun* (fungi or funguses) one of a large group of living things that get their food from plants, animals, or other living things. Mushrooms, yeasts, and molds are fungi. Fungi help decompose dead plants and animals.

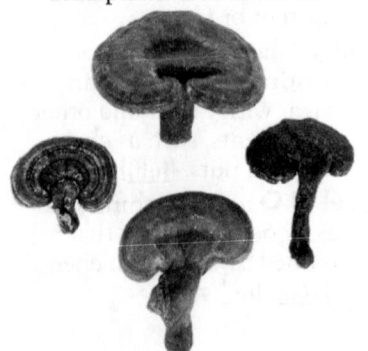

{**fung** gəs} fungal, adj., fungus-like, adj.

fun·nel *noun* 1. a tool shaped like a cone with a narrow tube at the small end. Funnels are used for pouring something into a small opening. 2. a smokestack on a ship or locomotive. {**fuhn** əl}

fun·ny *adjective* (funnier, funniest) 1. causing laughter or amusement. *My uncle's jokes are funnier than my father's.* 2. strange or odd; unusual. *There was a funny smell in the attic.* {**fuhn** ee}

fur ❷ ❶ *noun* 1. the soft thick hair that covers the bodies of certain animals such as the mink or fox. 2. the skin of an animal that has such hair, used in the making of clothing or other items. *These hats are made of fur.* 3. clothing made of fur. *People who live in cold climates often wear furs.* {**fuhr**} furless, adj.

Homophone Note Are you looking for the word *fir* (a kind of tree)? *Fur* and *fir* sound alike but have different meanings.

fu·ri·ous *adjective* 1. full of anger; wild with fury. *She was furious that he had cheated her out of money.* 2. very violent; fierce. *There was a furious storm last night.* {**fyoor** ee əs} furiously, adv., furiousness, n.

fur·lough *noun* a vacation for a person in the military. *My aunt came while she was on furlough.* {**fuhr** loh}

fur·nace *noun* anything in which heat is made for a specific purpose by burning fuel. A furnace can be used to heat a building or to melt metal. {**fuhr** nihs}

 Human Body   Human Mind   Everyday Life History and Culture   Communication

fur·nish *verb* (furnished, furnishing, furnishes) 1. to supply with furniture. *They still have not furnished their apartment.* 2. to supply or provide (often followed by "with"). *She furnished me with the information I needed.* {**fuhr** nihsh} furnisher, n.

fur·ni·ture ⊙ *noun* movable objects such as chairs, tables, and beds used to make a room fit for living in. *My grandmother bought beautiful new furniture for my bedroom.* {**fuhr** nih chər}

fur·row *noun* 1. a long narrow ditch made in the ground for planting seeds. 2. any narrow groove in a surface. *The furrows in his forehead showed he was concentrating.* *verb* (furrowed, furrowing, furrows) to make furrows in. *Ice can furrow rock. / Worry furrowed his face.* {**fuhr** oh}

fur·ry *adjective* (furrier, furriest) 1. having a coat of fur. *The raccoon is a furry animal.* 2. like fur. *She walked barefoot across the furry rug.* {**fuhr** ee} furrily, adv., furriness, n.

fur·ther *adverb* at or to a greater distance or extent; farther. "Further" is a comparative form of the adverb **far**. *Buses travel further than taxi cabs.* *adjective* 1. more distant or extended. "Further" is a comparative form of the adjective **far**. *My house is further from town than yours.* 2. more. *The judge asked if there were further comments to be made.* *verb* (furthered, furthering, furthers) to move forward or help make progress. *Hard work furthered his career.* {**fuhr** thər}

fur·ther·more *adverb* besides; in addition; moreover. *Candy costs money; furthermore, it's bad for you.* {**fuhr** thər **mohr**}

fur·thest *adjective* to or at the greatest point or extent. "Furthest" is a superlative form of the adjective **far**. *Of all my friends, Joanne has gone out of her way the furthest to help me.* *adverb* most distant in time or space. "Furthest" is a superlative form of the adverb **far**. *We've all been to far away places, but my sister has traveled the furthest.* {**fuhr** thihst}

fu·ry ⊙ *noun* (furies) 1. very wild anger; rage; frenzy. *She was overcome by fury when she discovered someone had taken her place.* 2. violent action. *The fury of a storm can be measured by the speed of the wind.* {**fyoor** ee}

fuse[1] *noun* any device used to set off an explosion. {**fyooz**}

fuse[2] *verb* (fused, fusing, fuses) 1. to cause to become liquid by using heat; melt. *Iron workers use extreme heat to fuse the iron ore.* 2. to become liquid after being heated; melt. *Some synthetic fabrics fuse if the iron is too hot.* 3. to cause to combine by melting together or as if by melting together. *The foundry fuses zinc and copper to make brass. / They fused their ideas to come up with a plan.* *noun* an electrical device with a connection that melts if there is too much heat. *Fuses protect buildings by breaking a circuit before a fire can start.* {**fyooz**}

fu·se·lage *noun* the body of an airplane. The engines, wings, and tail are attached to the fuselage. The passengers, cargo, and crew ride in the fuselage. {**fyoo** sə **lŏzh** or **fyoo** sə lihj}

fu·sion *noun* 1. the act of fusing or joining together. *The fusion of iron and carbon makes steel. / The band's fusion of rock and classical music surprised the audience.* 2. the state of being fused or melted together. *The two metals were joined in a fusion.* 3. the result of an act of fusing. *Brass is a fusion of copper and zinc.* 4. a reaction that combines the nuclei of atoms to form heavier nuclei. A huge amount of energy is released during nuclear fusion. {**fyoo** zhən}

fuss *noun* activity or attention that is not necessary. *Why make a fuss over such a small thing?* *verb* (fussed, fussing, fusses) 1. to pay too much attention to things that are not important. *She fusses over her hair for an hour every morning.* 2. to complain about things that are not important. *He fussed about the price of toothbrushes.* {**fuhs**} fusser, n.

fu·ture *noun* 1. time that is yet to come. *He hopes to become a teacher in the future.* 2. a verb tense that indicates action in a time yet to come. *adjective* of or taking place in the time yet to come. *All future e-mails should be sent to our new e-mail address.* {**fyoo** chər} futureless, adj.

fu·ture tense *noun* a form of a verb that shows that something will happen or a condition will exist in the future. In the sentence "We will go to the zoo," "will go" is in the future tense. {**fyoo** chər **tehns**}

fuzz *noun* (fuzz) loose, light, fluffy matter such as fibers or hairs. *My sweater collects a lot*

A B C D E F G H I J K L M N O P Q R S T U V W X Y Z

a
b
c
d
e
f
g
h
i
j
k
l
m
n
o
p
q
r
s
t
u
v
w
x
y
z

of fuzz. / The newborn kittens are covered in fuzz. {<u>fuhz</u>}

Word History *Fuzz* comes from an old word of uncertain origins. This word may be a shortened form of **fusball**, which means puffball, a kind of fungus that gives off a cloud of tiny spores.

fuz·zy *adjective* (fuzzier, fuzziest) 1. covered with fuzz. *Emma ate a fuzzy peach.* 2. not clear; blurry. *The picture was too fuzzy to see who was in it.* {<u>fuh</u> zee} fuzzily, adv., fuzziness, n.

 Human Body    Human Mind    Everyday Life    History and Culture   Communication

Gg

G is a consonant that usually makes a hard "guh" sound, especially when it comes before the letters a, o, or u. G sometimes makes a softer "jih" sound, especially when it comes before the letters e or i (as in George or ginger).

Tips to help you look up words starting with g: Also look under J for more words that start with the "jih" sound.

Sometimes "g" is followed by a silent letter, such as "h" (as in ghost) or "u" (as in guard, guest or guilt).

These words may be hard to look up if you don't already know how to spell them:

gaiety	glove
gauge	great
genius	guarantee
genus	guess
ghetto	guide

g or **G** *noun* (g's or G's) 1. the seventh letter of the English alphabet. 2. the fifth note in the musical scale of C major. {**jee**}

g *abbreviation* an abbreviation for **gram** or grams.

GA or **Ga.** *abbreviation* an abbreviation for **Georgia**.

ga·ble *noun* the part of an outside wall that is shaped like a triangle because it fills the space between two sloping ends of a roof. {**gay** bəl}

Ga·bon *noun* a country in west Africa on the Atlantic coast. Libreville is the capital of Gabon. {gə **bohn**} Gabonese, n., adj.

gadg·et ○ *noun* a small tool or device with a clever design or unusual use. *This gadget cuts vegetables into fancy shapes.* {**găj** iht}

gag[1] *verb* (gagged, gagging, gags) 1. to prevent from speaking or crying out by putting something across or inside the mouth. *They gagged the prisoner, so that he could not call for help.* 2. to choke or vomit. *The smell of broccoli makes me gag.* *noun* something put across or into a person's mouth to prevent speaking or other sound. {**găg**}

gag[2] *noun* (informal) a joke or prank. *As a gag, they gave him a rubber chicken for his birthday.* {**găg**}

gai·e·ty *noun* (gaieties) the state of being happy and cheerful. *The family reunion brought gaiety to our quiet home.* {**gay** ə tee}

gai·ly *adverb* in a cheerful or happy way. *They skipped gaily through the park.* {**gay** lee}

gain *verb* (gained, gaining, gains) 1. to get. *He worked hard to gain respect.* 2. to win or get by winning. *She gained* the title of "Most Valuable Player." 3. to arrive at or reach. *We finally gained the entrance to the cave.* 4. to take on as an increase. *The doctor is glad that I'm gaining weight.* 5. to get closer or move nearer (usually followed by "on"). *"Faster! He's gaining on us!" panted Billy. noun* 1. something gotten or gained; benefit. *Where is the gain in hurting your brother?* 2. an improvement or increase. *The baby's gain this month was two pounds.* {**gayn**}

gait *noun* a way of walking or running. *The Arabian horse has a graceful gait.* {**gayt**}

Homophone Note Are you looking for the word *gate* (a part of a fence)? *Gait* and *gate* sound alike but have different meanings.

gal. *abbreviation* an abbreviation for **gallon**, or gallons.

ga·la *noun* a happy celebration, especially a large, elaborate one. *We welcomed the returning soldiers with an elegant gala.* {**gayl** ə or **gă** lə}

gal·ax·y ○ *noun* (galaxies) a collection of billions of stars and other matter held together by gravity. Earth and the sun belong to the Milky Way galaxy. They are

only tiny parts of this galaxy. {găl ǝk see}

gale *noun* 1. a strong wind of about thirty to sixty miles per hour. 2. a loud outburst. *Gales of laughter swept the audience.* {gayl}

gal·lant *adjective* brave and dashing. *The gallant knight was admired throughout the land.* {găl ǝnt} gallantly, adv.

gal·ler·y *noun* (galleries) 1. an upper floor which opens over a theater or large hall; balcony. 2. a building used to display or sell art. {găl ǝ ree}

gal·ley *noun* (galleys) 1. a large, low ship of ancient and medieval times that was moved by oars and sometimes by sails. 2. the kitchen of a ship, boat, or airplane. {găl ee}

gal·lon *noun* a unit of measure equal to 4 quarts or 3.7854 liters. (abbreviated: gal.) {găl ǝn}

gal·lop *verb* (galloped, galloping, gallops) 1. to ride a horse at full speed. *The cowboy galloped alongside the herd of cattle.* 2. to move or run forward rapidly; go fast. *Wild horses galloped freely across the range.* *noun* the fastest pace of a horse or other animal that has four legs. During a gallop, all four feet are off the ground at one point during each stride. {găl ǝp}

gal·lows *noun* (gallows or gallowses) a high wooden frame to which one or more ropes for hanging criminals are attached. Only three states in the United States still use hanging as a form of execution. {găl ohz}

gam·ble *verb* (gambled, gambling, gambles) 1. to bet money or other things on the way a game, race, or other event will end. *She gambled on the turtle race and lost five dollars.* 2. to put down as a bet. *I gambled two dollars on the state basketball finals.* 3. to take a risk, hoping for a good result. *We are gambling that the weather will be good on the day of the barbecue.* *noun* a risky action; something of uncertain result. *Buying an old used car is always a gamble.* {găm bǝl} gambler, n.

game 🏃 👕 *noun* 1. something done for fun or amusement; play. *I made a game of waving to the baby.* 2. a form of play or sport having certain rules and equipment for play. *We enjoyed a game of chess. / My whole family went to the football game.* 3. wild animals hunted for sport or food. *The men went to the mountains to hunt game.* *adjective* (gamer, gamest) 1. daring in spirit; brave. *The game tourists went into the jungle without a guide.* 2. (informal) ready or willing to take part in. *Are you game for a hike?* {gaym}

gan·der *noun* an adult male goose. {găn dǝr}

gang *noun* 1. a group of people who come together to cooperate in some activity. These activities may be just for fun, or they may involve crime. *Bill and his gang go bowling every Thursday night. / Gangs are responsible for a lot of crime in the city.* 2. a group of workers who do some common task; team. *We passed a gang of workers who were cleaning the park.* {găng}

• **gang up on**
(informal) to blame or attack as a group. *She was really hurt when they all ganged up on her.*

Gan·ges *noun* a river in India. It flows through northern India and central Bangladesh into the Indian Ocean. {găn jeez}

gang·plank *noun* a board or other movable walkway used for getting on or off a ship; gangway. {găng plăngk}

gang·ster *noun* a person who belongs to a criminal gang. {găng stǝr}

gang·way *noun* 1. a path into, out of, around, or through something; passageway. *There is a narrow gangway into the attic.* 2. an opening in the side of a ship that is above the deck. A gangway is used for getting on or off the ship. 3. a ramp that reaches from a ship to the shore; gangplank. *The passengers walked up the gangway of the cruise ship.* *interjection* "Get out of the way!"; "Make way!" "Gangway! We're carrying heavy boxes!" {găng way}

gap *noun* 1. a space or opening made by or as if by breaking or separating. *I have a gap between my two front teeth. / She will fix the gap in the fence tomorrow.* 2. a space or blank in something that is otherwise connected or complete. *There are gaps in my diary where I didn't feel like writing anything.* {găp}

ga·rage 👕 *noun* 1. a building or part of a building built to shelter cars, trucks, or other vehicles. 2. a business for

 Human Body ❓ Human Mind 👕 Everyday Life 🚩 History and Culture 📞 Communication

repairing cars, trucks, or other vehicles. *Our old car is at the garage again.* {gər **ahzh**}

> **Word History** *Garage* is from an early French word that means "to shelter or dock ships." The French word came from a German word that meant "to take care."

gar·bage ○ *noun* food or other things that are thrown away; waste. {**gar** bihj}

gar·den ○ *noun* an area of land used for growing flowers or vegetables. *verb* (gardened, gardening, gardens) to plant or take care of a garden. *My family gardens in the summer.* {**gar** dən}

gar·den·er *noun* 1. a person whose job is taking care of plants, lawns, and the like. 2. a person who gardens for pleasure. {**gar** də nər}

gar·de·nia *noun* 1. a type of shrub from Asia that is grown for its large flowers that have a pleasant smell. 2. the flower of this plant. {**gar dee** nee ə}

gar·gle *verb* (gargled, gargling, gargles) to tip the head back and breathe out through a liquid held at the back of the throat. *He gargled saltwater to soothe his sore throat.* noun a liquid used for gargling. {**gar** gəl}

> **Word History** *Gargle* comes from *gargouille,* an early French word that means "throat." *Gargoyle* comes from the same French word. The open mouths of gargoyles were often made into water spouts.

gar·goyle *noun* 1. a sculpture of an odd or ugly animal or person carved as a decoration on a building. 2. a pipe or spout for rain in the shape of such an ornament. {**gar** goil}

gar·land *noun* a wreath, chain, or string worn for celebration or decoration. Garlands are made of flowers, leaves, or vines. {**gar** lənd}

gar·lic *noun* a strong smelling plant related to the onion. Its bulbs are used for seasoning. {**gar** lihk}

gar·ment ○ *noun* any piece of clothing. {**gar** mənt}

gar·net *noun* a common type of hard mineral that can have a variety of colors and includes the dark red stone often used in jewelry. {**gar** niht}

> **Word History** *Garnet* is from an early French word that means "red like a pomegranate."

gar·nish *verb* (garnished, garnishing, garnishes) to decorate with something that adds another flavor, color, or texture. *The chef garnished the plate with parsley.* noun anything used to garnish food. *Lemon slices are often used as a garnish for seafood.* {**gar** nihsh}

gar·ri·son *noun* 1. a military force that is located in a fort, village, or similar place. 2. a military fort. *verb* (garrisoned, garrisoning, garrisons) 1. to establish a military position in. *The army garrisoned the small village.* 2. to place in a garrison. *The soldiers were garrisoned in the small town.* {**gar** ih sən}

gar·ter *noun* an elastic band used to hold up a stocking or shirt sleeve. {**gar** tər}

garter snake *noun* a small snake with stripes that does not harm people. It is common in North America. {**gar** tər **snayk**}

gas ○ ○ *noun* (gases or gasses) 1. a form of matter that is neither liquid nor solid. A gas rapidly spreads out when it is warmed and contracts when it is cooled. 2. a fuel in the form of a gas that is burned for heat, light, or cooking. 3. a short form of gasoline. {**găs**}

gas·e·ous *adjective* in the form of gas. *There was a gaseous leak coming from the pipes.* {**găsh** əs or **găs** ee əs}

gas mask *noun* a mask worn on the face to protect from dangerous gases or fumes. {**găs măsk**}

gas·o·line ○ ○ *noun* a liquid that burns, used mainly as fuel for engines. Gasoline is made from petroleum. *Most automobiles run on gasoline.* {**găs** ə **leen**}

> **Word History** The word *gasoline* is a combination of the word "gas" and a form of the word "oil," and was first used in 1871. "Gas'" comes from *chaos,* an ancient Greek word that means "empty space."

gasp *noun* a sudden, brief taking in of air through the mouth, because of surprise or difficulty breathing. *There was a gasp of horror from the audi-*

ence as the monster appeared on screen. *verb* (gasped, gasping, gasps) 1. to breathe in gasps; struggle for breath; pant. *The runners gasped as they crossed the finish line.* 2. to say while or as if gasping. *"The barn's on fire!" he gasped.* {g**ă**sp}

gas station *noun* a place where gas, oil, and other supplies for running a car can be bought; filling station; service station. {g**ă**s stay sh**ə**n}

gate *noun* 1. a part of a fence or wall that swings to open and close. 2. an opening for entering or leaving a building or walled area. *We left the stadium through the main gate.* {g**ayt**}

Homophone Note The words *gate* and *gait* (a way of walking) sound alike but have different meanings.

gate·way *noun* 1. an opening that may be closed with a gate. *The gateway to the palace is always guarded.* 2. a place or point that lets one into something. *Education is the gateway to success.* {g**ayt** way}

gath·er *verb* (gathered, gathering, gathers) 1. to bring together into one place or collection. *The boy gathered his marbles and put them in a bag.* 2. to collect from different sources; bring together. *The reporter gathered information for her story.* 3. to slowly collect or build up. *The car gathered speed.* 4. to come to an understanding based on evidence; conclude. *He gathered from the smile on her face that she liked the gift.* 5. to come together; assemble. *The crowd gathered to hear the poetry reading.* {g**ăth** **ə**r} gatherer, n.

gath·er·ing *noun* 1. a meeting. *We had a gathering to plan the*

school celebration. 2. anything that is gathered or collected. *That is a beautiful gathering of flowers.* {g**ă** th**ə** ring}

gaud·y *adjective* (gaudier, gaudiest) decorated with too much bright color or pattern; showy. *His gaudy suits attract laughter.* {g**aw** dee}

gauge *verb* (gauged, gauging, gauges) 1. to make an estimate of; judge. *The students tried to gauge how hard the substitute teacher would be.* 2. to measure exactly the size or contents of. *The weatherman gauged the amount of snow that had fallen.* *noun* 1. an accepted scale for measuring. *European post offices use the metric system as a gauge for weighing letters and packages.* 2. a tool used to measure. *A pressure gauge will tell you how much air the tire needs.* 3. a rule or procedure for making a judgment. *Whether you like someone is not a good gauge of their ability.* 4. a standard of measuring, as for the distance between railroad tracks or the thickness of wire. *What gauge of strings do you use on your guitar?* {g**ayj**}

gaunt *adjective* very thin and bony. *He's been eating well but he still looks gaunt.* {g**awnt**}

gauze *noun* 1. a thin cloth that one can see through or other material with a loose or open weave. 2. thin cotton cloth used to cover a wound. {g**awz**}

gave *verb* past tense of **give**. {g**ayv**}

gav·el *noun* a small wooden hammer. It is used by a judge or someone in charge of a meeting or auction to get attention, call for order, or signal a sale. {g**ăv** **ə**l}

gay *adjective* (gayer, gayest) 1. of or in a happy mood; merry. *The peasants celebrated the harvest with gay songs.* 2. bright or colorful. *The room was decorated with gay flowers.* {g**ay**}

Gaza Strip *noun* a coastal region along the eastern Mediterranean Sea that was taken over by Israel in 1967. {g**ah** z**ə** **strihp**}

gaze *verb* (gazed, gazing, gazes) to look steadily. *He gazed into my eyes.* *noun* a steady look that doesn't blink. {g**ayz**}

ga·zelle *noun* a kind of antelope found in Africa and Asia. Gazelles are mammals with hooves and long legs. They are graceful runners. Their horns are slightly curved and have dark rings. {g**ə** **zehl**}

gear *noun* 1. a part of a machine that causes another part to move because of teeth which connect the two moving parts. 2. a particular arrangement of gears, especially in a vehicle. *I ride my bike up hills in a low gear.* 3. any equipment, clothes, or tools used for some particular purpose. *The scouts packed their camping gear and set out on a hike.* *verb* (geared, gearing, gears) to prepare or adjust to fit particular people or conditions. *She geared the story to teenagers.* {g**eer**}

• **gear up**
to make preparations; get

Human Body   Human Mind   Everyday Life   History and Culture   Communication

a b c d e f g h i j k l m n o p q r s t u v w x y z

ready for. *The hotel geared up for the tourist season.*

gear·shift *noun* a lever used to change gears in a car, truck, or other motor vehicle. {<u>geer</u> shihft}

geck·o *noun* (geckos or geckoes) a small lizard with soft skin that eats insects. The gecko has a short body and large head and can climb walls and trees. It is found in tropical areas. {<u>geh</u> koh}

geese *noun* plural of goose. {<u>gees</u>}

Gei·ger coun·ter *noun* an instrument used to find and measure radioactivity. {<u>giy</u> gər kown tər}

gel *noun* a chemical mixture that does not separate and that looks and feels like jelly. *Use this gel to style your hair.* *verb* (gelled, gelling, gels) to change into a gel. *The fat rose to the top and gelled on the chicken soup after it cooled.* {<u>jehl</u>}

gel·a·tin *noun* 1. an animal protein that is used in glue, on film, and for making things like jelly. 2. a dessert made with gelatin, water, fruit juice or flavoring, and sugar. {<u>jeh</u> lə tihn}

gem 🌐 *noun* 1. a precious stone that has been cut and polished, or a pearl of high quality; jewel. 2. anything or anyone that is very valuable. *My cousin is a real gem.* {<u>jehm</u>}

Gem·i·ni *noun* 1. a constellation located between Taurus and Cancer. Gemini is also called the Twins. 2. the third sign of the zodiac, the Twins, which the

sun enters about May 21. 3. a person born under this sign, between May 21 and June 20. {<u>jeh</u> mih <u>niy</u>}

gene 🌐 ⬤ *noun* a tiny section of a chromosome. A gene causes a particular characteristic, such as eye color or hair color, to be passed on from parent to offspring. {<u>jeen</u>}

gen·er·a *noun* a plural of **genus**. {<u>jehn</u> ə rə}

gen·er·al *adjective* 1. relating to or including the whole. *The general public is invited to the meeting.* 2. not detailed; not specific. *He gave us a general idea of what the new building would look like.* 3. common, customary, or widespread. *The general opinion is that he should win.* *noun* an officer of high military rank in the U.S. and other armed forces. {<u>jehn</u> ər əl or <u>jehn</u> rəl, n., <u>jehn</u> ər əl or <u>jehn</u> rəl, adj.}

gen·er·al·ize *verb* (generalized, generalizing, generalizes) 1. to come to a broad idea or rule about something after considering particular facts. *At the end of his report, Tom generalized that most lizards live in warm climates.* 2. to make useful to a wide range of situations or ideas. *The teacher generalized some rules for behavior at school.* 3. to think or speak using ideas or language that is not specific. *When he generalizes like that, it's hard to figure out what he really means.* {<u>jehn</u> ər ə <u>liyz</u> or <u>jehn</u> rə <u>liyz</u>}

gen·er·al·ly *adverb* 1. for the most part. *The doctor said my grandmother was generally healthy but needed to keep up her weight.* 2. usually; ordinarily. *Professor Dewey's lectures are generally boring.* {<u>jehn</u> ə rə lee or <u>jehn</u> rə lee}

gen·er·ate *verb* (generated, generating, generates) to bring into being or to produce. *The human body generates heat.* {<u>jehn</u> ə rayt}

gen·er·a·tion 🌐 *noun* 1. the entire group of people who were born around the same time. *People of grandmother's generation did not have television when they were kids.* 2. the period of time between the birth of parents and the birth of their children. *Technology has changed a lot in one generation.* 3. the act or process of generating or creating. *With the help of a microscope, it is possible to see the generation of new cells.* {<u>jehn</u> ər <u>ay</u> shən}

gen·er·a·tor *noun* a machine or device that produces electricity or other energy. *The hospital has its own generator so that it will have electricity even during a blackout.* {<u>jehn</u> ər ay tər}

ge·ner·ic *adjective* 1. applying to all members of a particular group. *"Fruit" is a generic term for apples, oranges, and pears.* 2. produced or sold without a brand name. *The generic cereal costs less but doesn't come with a fun prize.* {jə <u>neh</u> rihk}

gen·er·os·i·ty *noun* (generosities) the condition of being willing and ready to give. *We thanked the volunteers for their generosity.* {jehn ər <u>ŏs</u> ih tee}

gen·er·ous *adjective* 1. willing to give or share; not selfish. *She was generous and let her sister borrow the new CD.* 2. larger than average; abundant. *I ate a generous slice of pie.* {<u>jehn</u> ər əs} generously, adv.

ge·net·ics *noun* (used with a singular verb) the science that studies how characteristics are passed on from parent to offspring. Genetics is con-

A B C D E F **G** H I J K L M N O P Q R S T U V W X Y Z

cerned with the influence of genes on the appearance, development, and evolution of plants and animals. {jə **neht** ihks}

gen·ial *adjective* 1. cheerful and friendly. *We were always happy to see our genial uncle.* 2. mild, pleasant, or comfortable. *We live in a genial climate, neither too hot nor too cold.* {<u>jee</u> nee əl *or* <u>jeen</u> yəl}

ge·nie *noun* a spirit, often in human form, that will grant one's wishes. There are many genies in Arabian literature. {<u>jee</u> nee}

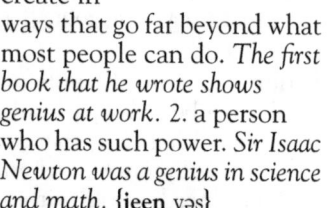

gen·ius *noun* (geniuses) 1. an unusual ability to think or create in ways that go far beyond what most people can do. *The first book that he wrote shows genius at work.* 2. a person who has such power. *Sir Isaac Newton was a genius in science and math.* {<u>jeen</u> yəs}

Word History *Genius* comes from a Latin word, *gignere*, which means "to produce or bring into being."

gen·tile *noun* (sometimes capitalized) a person who is not Jewish. {<u>jehn</u> **tiyl**}

gen·tle *adjective* (gentler, gentlest) 1. kind; generous; mild. *We love him for his gentle ways.* 2. soft; mild; not harsh or violent. *A gentle breeze blew through the leaves.* 3. gradual or mild; not steep or sudden. *The gentle slope was easy to hike.* 4. easy to manage or control. *He gave her a gentle horse to ride.* {<u>jehn</u>

təl} gentleness, n., gently, adv.

Word History *Gentle* comes from a Latin word that means "of the same family or race." The present use of "gentle" first occurred in the 1200s.

gen·tle·man *noun* (gentlemen) 1. a polite and honorable man. *If you were a gentleman, you would have apologized for that.* 2. a man of noble birth or high social position. 3. a polite word for "man." *I believe this gentleman was next in line.* {<u>jehn</u> təl mən}

gen·tle·wom·an *noun* (gentlewomen) 1. a polite and honorable woman. 2. a woman of noble birth or high social position. {<u>jehn</u> təl **wuum** ən}

gen·u·ine *adjective* 1. true to what is claimed; real. *That watch is made of genuine gold.* 2. honest; sincere. *Her interest in the students was genuine.* {<u>jehn</u> yoo ihn} genuinely, adv.

Word History *Genuine* comes from a Latin word that means "natural or native."

ge·nus ❶ *noun* (genera or genuses) a large group of different but closely related plants and animals. A genus contains more organisms than a species but fewer than a family. *Dogs and wolves are different species but belong to the same genus.* {<u>jee</u> nəs}

ge·og·ra·phy ❻ *noun* (geographies) 1. the science of the earth's surface and all life on it. When studying geography, one learns about the different countries and people of the earth, its climate, its natural resources, and its oceans, rivers, and mountains. 2. the physical features of an area on the earth's surface. *Deserts are part of the*

geography of the southwestern United States. {jee <u>o</u> grə fee}

Word History *Geography* comes from a Latin word that means "a written description of the earth."

ge·ol·o·gy ❶ ❻ *noun* (geologies) 1. the study of the physical structure of the earth and how it has changed over time. Geologists gain this knowledge by studying rocks. Some geologists study other planets. 2. the parts of a particular place or planet that have to do with geology. *We will study the geology of the Rocky Mountains.* {jee <u>o</u> lə jee} geological, adj., geologic, adj., geologist, n.

ge·o·met·ric *adjective* 1. having to do with geometry. *A square is one geometric shape; a triangle is another.* 2. made up of lines or shapes like those of geometry. *The quilt, with its pattern of squares and circles, has a geometric design.* {jee ə **meh** trihk} geometrical, adj.

ge·om·e·try ❶ *noun* (geometries) 1. the area of mathematics concerned with the study of shapes and objects. Geometry deals with the measurement and relation of angles, points, lines, planes, and solid figures. 2. the shape, arrangement, or design of an object. *He studied the geometry of the snowflake that fell on his jacket.* {jee <u>o</u> mə tree}

Geor·gia *noun* 1. a state in the southeastern United States on the Atlantic coast. Atlanta is the capital of Georgia. (abbreviated: GA) 2. a country in southwestern Asia. Georgia used to be a republic of the Union of Soviet Socialist Republics. Tbilisi is the capital of

 Human Body    Human Mind   Everyday Life   History and Culture    Communication

Georgia. {**johr** jə} Georgian, n., adj.

ge·o·ther·mal *adjective* having to do with the heat produced inside the earth. *Steam rose from the geothermal geyser in the park.* {jee ə **thuhr** məl}

ge·ra·ni·um *noun* a garden plant with red, pink, or white flowers that grow in bunches. {jə **ray** nee əm}

ger·bil *noun* a very small rodent that looks like a mouse with a furry tail. Gerbils live in burrows in the deserts of Africa and Asia. They are often kept as pets. {**juhr** bəl}

germ ◉ ◉ *noun* 1. a microscopic organism that causes illness. Bacteria and viruses that cause diseases are called germs. 2. a basic part of a living organism, such as the inside of a seed or the embryo of an egg, from which other parts grow. {**juhrm**}

Ger·man *adjective* of or having to do with Germany, or its people or language. *noun* 1. a person who was born in or is a citizen of Germany. 2. the language of Germany, Austria, and parts of Switzerland. {**juhr** mən}

Wilkommen bei mir daheim

Ger·man·ic *adjective* of or having to do with the language group that includes German, Dutch, English, and some other European languages. {jər **măn** ihk}

German shepherd *noun* a breed of dog. German shepherds are large dogs that resemble wolves and have a thick brown or black coat. They are used as guard dogs and as guide dogs for blind people. {**juhr** mən **shehp** ərd}

Ger·ma·ny *noun* a country in central, northern Europe. Germany was divided into East and West Germany from 1949 to 1990. Berlin is the capital of Germany. {**juhr** mə nee}

ger·mi·nate *verb* (germinated, germinating, germinates) to start or cause to start growth; sprout. *The seed will germinate if it gets enough water and sunlight.* {**juhr** mih **nayt**} germination, n.

ges·ture ◉ ◉ *noun* 1. a movement of one's body or face that shows feeling or thought. *Raising your hand in class is a gesture that shows you wish to speak.* 2. an action meant to show feeling or that is done for effect. *His bringing flowers was a kind gesture.* *verb* (gestured, gesturing, gestures) to make a gesture or gestures. *He gestured wildly with his arms.* {**jehs** chər}

get *verb* (got, gotten or got, getting, gets) 1. to receive; come to have; gain; acquire. *I got a new bicycle for my birthday.* 2. to go after and bring back; fetch. *Get your coat.* 3. to come under the power of; catch. *She is getting a cold.* 4. to cause to be or cause to be done. *Dave got his suitcase packed.* 5. to understand. *Do you get the meaning of this story?* 6. to convince; persuade. *I will get Phil to stop teasing you.* 7. to arrive. *You will get home one way or another.* 8. to become. *She is getting mad.* {**geht**}

• **get across**
to make or become clear; to explain or to become understood. *He got his point across. / The joke finally got across to her.*

• **get along**
1. to survive or manage. *He is getting along well in his new job.* 2. to be friendly; have a relationship without conflict. *My mother gets along with my stepmother.*

• **get away with**
to do without being noticed, caught, or punished. *She got away with being late to class.*

• **get in**
1. to go in; enter. *We couldn't get in without tickets.* 2. to arrive. *The bus won't get in until noon.*

• **get out**
1. to leave or be let out (often followed by of). *We got out of school late today.* 2. to become known. *She hoped the secret wouldn't get out.*

• **get over**
to recover from. *I'm getting over the flu.*

• **get up**
1. to stand up or sit up. *He got up from the sofa and left.* 2. to rise from bed. *I'll get up early tomorrow.*

get·a·way *noun* an escape, especially from the police. *The thief made a quick getaway through an open window.* {**geht** ə way}

gey·ser *noun* a spring that shoots a stream of hot water, steam, or mud into the air from time to time. {**giy** zər}

Gha·na *noun* a country in western Africa on the Atlantic coast. Accra is the capital of Ghana. {**gah** nə} Ghanaian, n., adj., Ghanian, n., adj.

a
b
c
d
e
f
g
h
i
j
k
l
m
n
o
p
q
r
s
t
u
v
w
x
y
z

ghast·ly *adjective* (ghastlier, ghastliest) 1. causing great fear or terror. *She had a ghastly nightmare.* 2. very pale. *He looked ghastly during his illness.* {<u>găst</u> lee}

ghet·to *noun* (ghettos or ghettoes) 1. a part of a town or city in which people of a particular race or religion are forced by law to live. 2. such an area where people live, not by law, but because they are poor or are discriminated against. {<u>geh</u> toh}

ghost *noun* 1. the spirit of a person who has died, especially one that is believed to haunt a place or living people. 2. a slight possibility or tiny amount. *There is only a ghost of a chance of winning the lottery.* {<u>gohst</u>}

ghost·ly *adjective* (ghostlier, ghostliest) like a ghost; pale or eerie. *A ghostly figure flitted through the room.* {<u>gohst</u> lee}

ghost town *noun* a town that has been deserted, especially one in the American West where gold or silver mines have closed. {<u>gohst</u> town}

ghoul *noun* an evil spirit that is believed to eat people and dead bodies. {<u>goohl</u>} ghoulish, adj.

gi·ant *noun* 1. an imaginary being who looks like a person but has enormous size and strength. 2. a person or thing of very great size, strength, power, or importance. *Ludwig van Beethoven was a giant among composers.* *adjective* very great in size, strength, or importance. *She took a giant leap across the brook.* {<u>jiy</u> ənt}

gib·bon *noun* a kind of primate that lives in Asian rain forests. Gibbons are small apes that can weigh up to twenty-five pounds. They have long arms and can swing quickly through trees. All kinds of gibbons are endangered. {<u>gihb</u> ən}

gid·dy *adjective* (giddier, giddiest) 1. faint or dizzy. *Spinning around made her feel giddy.* 2. not serious; silly. *Fred is too giddy to babysit his younger sister.* {<u>gihd</u> ee} giddiness, n.

gift *noun* 1. something a person gives without wanting anything in return; a present. 2. a special talent, quality, or ability. *He has a gift for writing songs.* {<u>gihft</u>}

gift·ed *adjective* having a special talent or ability. *She is a gifted painter.* {<u>gihf</u> tihd}

gig·a·byte *noun* 1,073,741,824 bytes. The capacity of a computer's hard drive is often measured in gigabytes. The abbreviation for gigabyte is G or GB. *Our new computer has a 30-gigabyte hard drive.* {<u>gih</u> geh biyt}

gi·gan·tic *adjective* like a giant; huge. *We climbed a gigantic mountain. / He has gigantic feet.* {jiy <u>găn</u> tihk}

gig·gle *verb* (giggled, giggling, giggles) to laugh in a silly or nervous way. *The children giggled when the teacher's chalk flew out of her hand.* *noun* a silly or nervous laugh. *I heard giggles from the closet.* {<u>gihg</u> gəl}

Gila monster *noun* a large, poisonous reptile that lives in the southwestern part of the United States and in Mexico. This lizard has a short tail and scales in patterns of black with orange, yellow, or pink. {<u>hee</u> lə <u>mŏn</u> stər}

gild *verb* (gilded or gilt, gilding, gilds) to cover or coat with gold. *The artist gilded the king's throne.* {gihld}

Homophone Note Are you looking for the word *guild* (a group of workers)? *Gild* and *guild* sound alike but have different meanings.

gill ❶ *noun* the organ used for breathing by fish and other animals that live in water. {<u>gihl</u>}

gilt *verb* a past tense and past participle of **gild**. *adjective* covered with a thin layer of gold or gold paint; gilded. *We have a gilt mirror frame.* *noun* a thin layer of gold or gold paint used for gilding. *He applied gilt to the picture frame.* {<u>gihlt</u>}

Homophone Note Are you looking for the word *guilt*? *Gilt* and *guilt* sound alike but have different meanings.

gim·mick *noun* a clever device or idea whose only purpose is to get a customer's attention. *The car dealer's gimmick was to give away free ice cream cones to people who visited his lot.* {<u>gih</u> mihk}

gin[1] *noun* an alcoholic drink made from grain flavored with juniper berries. {<u>jihn</u>}

gin[2] *noun* a machine for removing the seeds from raw cotton; cotton gin. {<u>jihn</u>}

gin·ger *noun* 1. the root of a tropical plant, used as a spice to flavor food. 2. the plant that produces this root. {<u>jihn</u> jər}

gin·ger·bread *noun* a type of cake or cookie flavored with ginger and molasses. {<u>jihn</u> jər brehd}

 Human Body
 Human Mind
 Everyday Life
 History and Culture
 Communication

ging·ham *noun* a strong cotton cloth that often has a pattern, such as checks or stripes. {**ging** əm}

gi·raffe *noun* a mammal with a very long neck, long legs, and hooves. Giraffes have short horns covered with fur. They live in Africa and eat the tops of trees. Male giraffes can be up to eighteen feet tall. They are the tallest animal that lives on land. {jə **răf**}

gird·er *noun* a heavy beam made of steel or wood used to support the floor or framework of a bridge or building. *Thousands of steel girders were used in building that skyscraper.* {**guhr** dər}

girl *noun* 1. a female child or teenager. 2. a close female friend; girlfriend. {**guhrl**}

Word History *Girl* comes from an early English word that was used for a young person of either sex.

girl·friend *noun* 1. a favorite female friend or companion. *He gave flowers to his girlfriend.* 2. a friend who is female. *Mona and her girlfriends went to the movies.* {**guhrl** frehnd}

girl·hood *noun* the state or time of being a girl. *Sara loved school during her girlhood.* {**guhrl** huud}

Girl Scout *noun* a member of a U.S. youth organization for girls called the Girl Scouts. {**guhrl** skowt}

girth *noun* the length around something. *The girth of an elephant is about sixteen feet. / The mason laid a brick wall* around the girth of the building. {**guhrth**}

give *verb* (gave, given, giving, gives) 1. to present. *The teacher gave the students their report cards.* 2. to hand over in return for something. *I gave him a dollar for the ticket.* 3. to put into the hands of. *Give him the butter.* 4. to produce. *Cows give milk.* 5. to do by movement, act, or sound. *Give a push to my car. / The baby gave a cry.* 6. to break under pressure. *The kids jumped up and down on the board until it gave.* *noun* the quality of being able to move or bend easily. *This mattress doesn't have much give.* {**gihv**}
  • **give away** 1. to give for free instead of selling; give as a gift. *He gave away all his furniture.* 2. to tell or reveal. *Don't give away the answer.*
  • **give up** 1. to surrender; yield. *She gave up the stolen money to the police.* 2. to stop. *He gave up playing football after breaking his hand.* 3. to stop trying to do something. *Don't give up just because it's difficult.*

giv·en *verb* past participle of **give**. *adjective* because of; based on; due to. *Given the cold weather, I'll wear my winter coat.* *noun* something already known, proven, or assumed to be true. *It is a given that he will be late.* {**gihv** ən}

gla·cier  *noun* a large mass of ice formed in cold regions from compacted snow, often slowly moving downhill. {**glay** shər}

glad  *adjective* (gladder, gladdest) 1. happy; delighted; pleased or relieved. *Mona was glad she brought a sweater. / I am so glad it's Christmas.* 2. very willing. *We'll be glad to help.* {**glăd**} gladly, adv., gladness, n.

Synonyms
These words share a meaning with *glad*, adjective 1:
happy, pleased, delighted, gratified

Word History *Glad* comes from an Old English word that means "shining" or "bright."

glad·i·a·tor *noun* a man in ancient Rome who fought other men or animals, often to the death, to entertain an audience. {**glă** dee **ay** tər}

glad·i·o·lus *noun* (gladioli or gladioluses) a garden plant that has long leaves and colorful flowers growing on tall stems. It is a member of the iris family. {**glă** dee **oh** lihs}

glam·our *noun* the quality of being exciting, charming, and very attractive. *That movie star is known for her glamour.* {**glăm** ər}

glance *verb* (glanced, glancing, glances) 1. to take a quick look. *He glanced at the clock to see if he was late.* 2. to hit something at a slant and move off at an angle. *The rock glanced off the wall.* *noun* a quick look. *One glance at her told me she was angry.* {**glăns**}

gland  *noun* a group of cells or an organ that produces fluids that are released into the body or pass out of the body. *Sweat is produced by sweat glands.* {**glănd**}

a
b
c
d
e
f
g
h
i
j
k
l
m
n
o
p
q
r
s
t
u
v
w
x
y
z

glare *noun* 1. a light so strong and bright that it hurts the eyes or makes seeing difficult. *I could barely see because of the glare of the sun.* 2. an angry look or stare. *My mother's glare told me that I was in big trouble.* *verb* (glared, glaring, glares) 1. to give off a very bright light or glare. *The sunlight glared off the cars on the expressway.* 2. to stare steadily or angrily. *The teacher glared at the noisy students.* {**glayr**}

glar·ing *adjective* 1. extremely bright. *The glaring sun made it almost impossible to see out the window of the car.* 2. very easily noticed; obvious. *I'm embarrassed about the glaring mistakes I made in my essay.* 3. staring in an angry or hostile way. *The glaring cat arched its back and hissed.* {**glayr** ing}

glass ○ *noun* 1. a hard, clear material that breaks easily. Glass is used to make windows, bottles, mirrors, and the like. 2. a container used for drinking, usually made of glass. 3. (plural) a pair of lenses set in frames that help a person to see better; eyeglasses. {**glăs**}

glaze *verb* (glazed, glazing, glazes) 1. to give a shiny coating to during cooking or baking. *The baker glazed the doughnuts with sugar.* 2. to fit glass in. *We glazed the window on the front door.* *noun* a shiny coating on pottery. {**glayz**}

gleam *noun* 1. a small or brief flash or beam of light. *We saw a gleam of light in the window of the old house.* 2. a sudden or quick feeling. *He felt a gleam of pride when he passed the test.* *verb* (gleamed, gleaming, gleams) to give out a flash or beam of light. *The candle gleamed in the dark room. / The wolf's teeth gleamed in the moonlight.* {**gleem**}

glee *noun* a feeling of delight or joy. *Lupe opened her birthday presents with glee.* {**glee**}

glen *noun* a small, narrow valley. *We hiked through the glen.* {**glehn**}

glide *verb* (glided, gliding, glides) to move smoothly and without effort. *The hawk glided through the air. / The skaters glided around the rink.* *noun* the act of gliding. {**gliyd**}

glid·er *noun* a light aircraft without a motor that flies on air currents. {**gliy** dər}

glim·mer *noun* 1. a dim or unsteady light; flicker. *We saw the glimmer of a lantern through the trees and knew we were close to camp.* 2. a small sign; hint; trace. *There was a glimmer of hope that the team would win the game.* *verb* (glimmered, glimmering, glimmers) to give off a dim or unsteady light. *The stars glimmered in the sky.* {**glihm** ər}

glimpse *noun* a quick look. *I caught a glimpse of him before he vanished in the crowd.* *verb* (glimpsed, glimpsing, glimpses) to get a quick look at. *I glimpsed the presents in the closet before she closed the door.* {**glihmps**}

glint *noun* 1. a brief flash or flicker of reflected light. *The sheriff spotted the glint of guns in the desert sun.* 2. a brief or faint showing; trace. *There was a glint of happiness in her eyes.* *verb* (glinted, glinting, glints) to give off small flashes of reflected light. *Sun-light glinted on the lake.* {**glihnt**}

glis·ten *verb* (glistened, glis-tening, glistens) to shine or sparkle with reflected light. *The brass candlesticks glis-tened after being polished.* {**glih** sən}

glitch *noun* (informal) a small problem or defect. *He couldn't finish his work because of a computer glitch.* {**glihch**}

glit·ter *verb* (glittered, glit-tering, glitters) to shine brightly; sparkle. *The dia-mond necklace glittered.* *noun* 1. sparkling reflected light. *There was a glitter of coins in the fountain.* 2. small bits of material that sparkle, used for decoration. *They put glitter in their hair just for fun.* {**gliht** ər} glittery, adj.

gloat *verb* (gloated, gloating, gloats) to feel or show great pride or satisfaction, often when someone else does badly or fails. *She gloated when her brother fell on the ice, and for once she stayed up.* {**gloht**}

glob·al ⓖ *adjective* 1. having to do with the whole earth. *The pollution of the oceans is a global concern.* 2. in the shape of a globe. {**gloh** bəl} globally, adv.

glo·bal warm·ing *noun* an increase in the world's tem-peratures, which many scien-tists believe is caused in part by the greenhouse effect. {**gloh** buhl **wohrm** ing}

globe *noun* 1. the world; planet Earth. *She travelled around the globe.* 2. a round ball with a map of the earth on it, or

 Human Body

 Human Mind

Everyday Life

 History and Culture

Communication

anything shaped like a ball. {**glohb**}

glock·en·spiel *noun* a percussion instrument composed of a set of metal bars that are struck with hammers. {**glahkk** ən **speel** *or* **glawk** ən **shpeel**}

gloom *noun* 1. lack of light; darkness. *I stumbled in the gloom of the basement.* 2. a mood or air of sadness or sorrow. *When my cat ran away, I was filled with gloom.* {**gloohm**}

gloom·y *adjective* (gloomier, gloomiest) 1. dim or dark. *The sky looks gloomy today.* 2. showing or filled with sadness. *He has a gloomy expression on his face.* 3. causing a sad or dreary feeling. *That new movie was gloomy.* {**glooh** mee} gloomily, adv., gloominess, n.

glo·ri·fy *verb* (glorified, glorifying, glorifies) 1. to praise, honor, or worship. *The town gathered to glorify the soldiers who fought in the war.* 2. to cause to appear better or more important than is actually the case. *In his speech, he glorified his college years.* {**glohr** ə **fiy**}

glo·ry *noun* (glories) 1. great honor, praise, or fame. *Beowulf earned glory after slaying a monster.* 2. great beauty. *I still remember the glory of the view from the top of Mount Kilimanjaro.* 3. a thing that is worthy of praise. *The glory of the city was its medieval city hall.* *verb* (gloried, glorying, glories) to be filled with joy and a sense of pride. *The coach gloried in the team's success.* {**glohr** ee}

gloss *noun* a shine on a surface. *He admired the gloss of polished wood in the new house.* {**glaws** *or* **glŏs**}

glos·sa·ry 🔊 *noun* (glossaries) a list of unusual or difficult words and their meanings. A glossary is usually placed at the end of a book. {**glŏs** ə ree *or* **glaws** ə ree}

glove *noun* 1. a covering for the hand that has separate parts for each finger and the thumb. 2. a large, padded leather glove used by baseball or softball players in the field. Unlike most gloves, the fingers on a baseball or softball glove are laced together. 3. a large padded mitt worn by a boxer; boxing glove. {**gluhv**}

glow *noun* 1. a steady light, especially the light given off by something very hot. *The lantern's glow lit the path.* 2. brightness of color, especially redness. *The glow of the clouds made a beautiful sunset.* 3. a warm and rosy look on the face or body. *We knew they had worked hard by the glow on their faces.* *verb* (glowed, glowing, glows) 1. to shine with bright light, as something very hot but flameless does. *The coals were so hot they glowed.* 2. to have a bright, usually reddish color. *Our cheeks glowed after we ran home.* 3. to show strong, good feelings; be radiant. *He glowed with excitement.* {**gloh**}

glow·worm *noun* a worm-shaped insect that can give off light from its body. The larvae and the females of the firefly are kinds of glowworm. {**gloh** wuhrm}

glue 🔊 *noun* a thick, sticky liquid used to join things together. *verb* (glued, gluing, glues) to fasten or hold with or as if with glue. *I glued the broken pieces back together.* /

His eyes were glued to the television. {**glooh**}

glum *adjective* (glummer, glummest) in low spirits; sad or gloomy. *He felt glum when his best friend moved away.* {**gluhm**} glumly, adv.

gnarled *adjective* 1. bent and twisted; crooked. *There is a gnarled old apple tree in our yard.* 2. having a rough and worn appearance because of age or hard work. *The carpenter's hands were gnarled from years of work.* {**narld**}

gnat *noun* a small flying insect with two wings. Some gnats bite people or animals. {**năt**}

gnaw *verb* (gnawed, gnawing, gnaws) to bite or chew on again and again. *The dog gnawed all the meat off the bone.* {**naw**}

gnome *noun* a creature in fairy tales that lives inside the earth and guards precious treasure. Gnomes are often portrayed as little old men with beards. {**nohm**}

gnu *noun* (gnu or gnus) a large mammal with a large head and long, curving horns. Gnus live in Africa and are a kind of antelope. They have a beard, a mane, and a long tail. {**nooh**}

Homophone Note The words *gnu*, *new*, and *knew* sound alike but have different meanings.

Word History *Gnu* is a word from the language of the Cape Bush people of South Africa.

a
b
c
d
e
f
g
h
i
j
k
l
m
n
o
p
q
r
s
t
u
v
w
x
y
z

go *verb* (went, gone, going, goes) 1. to move; travel. *I go to school by bus. / We went to the beach on Saturday.* 2. to move away from a place; leave. *We will miss her when she goes.* 3. to reach from one point to another. *The driveway goes from the house to the road.* 4. to be moving or working properly. *My electric train will not go.* 5. to pass. *How fast the days go!* 6. to belong with something else. *This blouse goes with that skirt.* 7. to be used up. *Money goes fast.* 8. to make a certain sound. *"Vroom! Vroom!" went the engine.* 9. to belong or fit. *The forks don't go in that drawer.* 10. to become. *The milk has gone sour.* 11. to come to be in a certain state; become. *The whole class went quiet.* 12. (informal) to say. *I go, "Why?" and he goes, "Because."* *noun* (goes) 1. a try; an attempt. *She had a go at tennis.* 2. energy and spirit. *The old horse still has a lot of go left in her.* *interjection* "begin the race." *On your mark, get set, go!* {goh}

• **go back on**
to take back. *I'm mad at my sister, because she went back on her promise to take me swimming.*

goal *noun* 1. a result or end that a person wants and works for; aim or purpose. *Her goal is to become an animal doctor.* 2. the structure or area in certain sports into which a player must get a ball or puck in order to score. 3. the points scored by getting a ball or puck into the goal. *Dustin scored two goals in the first period of the game.* {gohl}

goal·ie *noun* a short form of **goalkeeper**. {goh lee}

goal·keep·er *noun* the player who defends the team's goal in sports such as soccer or hockey. {gohl kee pər} goalkeeping, n.

goat ● *noun* an animal with hooves, hollow horns, and rough hair. Goats are mammals that are raised for their milk, wool, and meat. They are closely related to sheep. {goht}

goat·ee *noun* a small pointed beard on a man's chin that looks like the beard of a goat. {goh tee}

gob·ble[1] *verb* (gobbled, gobbling, gobbles) to eat in a fast, greedy, and sometimes noisy way. *He gobbled up the pie and asked for more.* {gŏb əl}

gob·ble[2] *verb* (gobbled, gobbling, gobbles) to make a sound like that of a turkey. *The turkey gobbled when the farmer grabbed him.* *noun* the sound that a turkey makes. {gŏb əl}

gob·let *noun* a drinking glass with a stem and base, used mainly for wine. {gŏb liht}

gob·lin *noun* an ugly creature in fairy tales that does evil or mischief to humans. {gŏb lihn}

god ● *noun* 1. a being that is worshipped and believed to have special powers over nature or life. The ancient Greeks and Romans believed in the existence of many gods and goddesses. 2. (capitalized) the supreme being that is worshipped by Christians, Jews, and Muslims as the maker and ruler of the universe. {gŏd}

god·dess *noun* a female god. {gŏd ihs}

god·fa·ther *noun* a male godparent. {gŏd fahth ər}

god·moth·er *noun* a female godparent. {gŏd muhth ər}

god·par·ent *noun* an adult who promises at a child's baptism to take on certain responsibilities for the child. {gŏd par ənt}

goes *verb* the present tense of **go**. {gohz}

gog·gle *noun* (plural) a pair of special glasses worn to protect the eyes from dust, wind, water, or harsh light. *Chemists wear safety goggles in the lab. / Skiers' goggles shield against blowing snow.* {gŏg əl}

gold ● *noun* 1. a soft, heavy, yellow metal that is one of the chemical elements. It is often combined with other metals to make it harder and stronger. Gold is very valuable. (symbol: Au) 2. a mixture of metals that contains gold and is used to make coins, jewelry, and decorations. 3. something that is like gold in its beauty, goodness, or worth. *He has a heart of gold.* 4. a yellow color like that of gold. *Gold is the color of her long hair.* *adjective* 1. something that is like gold, contains gold, or is plated with gold. *The pirates buried a chest filled with gold coins.* 2. having the color of gold. *He drives a gold sports car.* 3. having sold more than a specific number of copies, usu-

 Human Body　 Human Mind　 Everyday Life　 History and Culture　🕿 Communication

ally one million. *The pop singer hung his first gold record on the wall in his living room.* {**gohld**}

gold·en *adjective* 1. having a shiny, deep yellow color. *Sunflowers have golden petals.* 2. made of gold. *The queen wore a golden crown.* 3. very special or excellent. *Silence is golden.* {**gohl** dən}

gold·en·rod *noun* a plant with small, yellow flowers on top of tall, stiff stems. It blooms in late summer or early fall. {**gohl** dən **rŏd**}

gold·finch *noun* a small finch with yellow and black markings, found in North America, Europe, and Asia. {**gohld** fihnch}

gold·fish *noun* (goldfish or goldfishes) a small fish that lives in fresh water. Goldfish are usually yellow or orange and are often kept in ponds or aquariums. {**gohld fihsh**}

golf *noun* a game played on a large outdoor course with small holes in the ground, spaced far apart. Players use special clubs to hit a small white ball into each of the series of holes. There are nine or eighteen holes in a golf course. The object of the game is to get the ball into each hole using as few strokes as possible. *verb* (golfed, golfing, golfs) to play golf. *She golfs every Sunday.* {**gŏlf** or **gawlf**, n., **gŏlf** or **gawlf**, v.} golfer, n.

gon·do·la *noun* 1. a long, narrow boat with a flat bottom and high curved ends, propelled by a person standing at the stern using a long pole. Gondolas are used for carrying passengers on the canals of Venice, Italy. 2. a basket, car, or sling that hangs below a balloon or blimp, used for carrying passengers or instru-

ments. {**gŏn** də lə or gŏn **doh** lə}

gone *verb* past participle of go. *adjective* 1. no longer at a particular place. *The bird I saw outside is gone.* 2. used up; finished. *The candy is gone.* {**gahn** or **gŏn**, v., **gahn** or **gŏn**, adj.}

gong *noun* a large piece of metal shaped like a plate that makes a loud sound when struck with a stick or hammer. {**gŏng** or **gawng**}

goo *noun* (informal) a thick, wet, or sticky substance. *There's some kind of goo stuck to the bottom of my sneaker.* {**gooh**}

good *adjective* (better, best) 1. having qualities that are desired. *That was a good movie. / She makes good soup.* 2. doing what is right. *A good person helps others.* 3. better than the average. *He always got good grades.* 4. pleasant. *We had a good time at the park.* 5. sound; in good condition; able to be relied on. *She was in good health. / He gave us good advice.* 6. behaving in the proper way. *Spot is a good dog.* 7. kind. *He has a good heart. noun* 1. that which is good. *You have to take the good with the bad.* 2. benefit; advantage. *The new laws were for the good of all the people.* 3. kindness; virtue. *She has a lot of good in her heart. adverb* (better, best) well. *I feel good today.* {**guud**}
• **for good**

forever; permanently. *He has moved to New York for good.*

Synonyms
These words share a meaning with **good**, adjective 1:

positive Positive is used to describe things that are helpful, useful, or constructive. *The coach said positive things about how the team was playing.*

desirable Desirable is used to describe something that is good because it is wanted or in demand. *Typing is a desirable skill for all students to learn.*

beneficial Beneficial is used to describe something that has a good effect or result. *The lemon tea was beneficial to my cough.*

good-bye or **good-by** or **goodbye** *interjection* a word used by or to someone who is leaving or ending a telephone call; farewell. *noun* (good-byes or good-byes) a farewell. *We said our good-byes and went home.* {**guud biy**}

Word History *Good-bye* comes from the early English word *godbwye*. This word was a shortened form of "god be with ye," a way of wishing a person well when parting.

Good Friday *noun* a Christian holiday on the Friday before Easter Sunday that marks the death of Jesus Christ. {**guud friy** day}

good-heart·ed *adjective* having a kind and generous nature. *Our good-hearted neighbor takes care of stray animals.* {**guud har** tihd} good-heartedly, adv., good-heartedness, n.

good-na·tured *adjective* having or showing a pleasant, cheerful, or friendly character or mood. *She is a good-natured girl who smiles a lot.* {**guud nay** chərd} good-naturedly, adv., good-naturedness, n.

good·ness *noun* the quality or condition of being good. *Alex is known for his sweet temper and goodness.* *interjection* a word used to express surprise or alarm. *Goodness! You've had all your hair shaved off!* {<u>guud</u> nihs}

good night *noun* used to say good-bye at night. {<u>guud</u> <u>niyt</u>}

goods ✆ *plural noun* 1. things that belong to someone; possessions; belongings. *They managed to rescue their household goods from the flood.* 2. things that are sold; merchandise; wares. *That shop is known for its baked goods.* {<u>guudz</u>}

good will or **goodwill** *noun* 1. a friendly or kindly feeling. *Show good will to others, whether rich or poor.* 2. cheerful agreement. *They accepted the new boss with good will.* {<u>guud</u> <u>wihl</u>}

goose *noun* (geese) 1. a water bird that looks like a duck but is usually larger, with a longer neck and legs and a more pointed bill. Some geese are raised by farmers, and some are found in the wild. 2. the female of this bird. The male is called a gander. 3. the meat of a goose, used as food. *We had goose for dinner.* 4. (informal) a silly or stupid person. *I felt like a goose when I spilled the paint.* {<u>goohs</u>}

goose bump *noun* roughness of the skin that looks like the skin of a plucked goose. Goose bumps last only for a short while and are caused by cold or fear. *Watching that scary movie gave me goose bumps.* {<u>goohs</u> buhmp}

goose flesh *noun* roughness of the skin that looks like the skin of a plucked goose. Goose flesh lasts only for a short while and is caused by cold or fear. *I heard a creak on the stairs and broke out into goose flesh.* {<u>goohs</u> flehsh}

goose pim·ple *noun* a small bump on the skin caused by cold or fear. {<u>goohs</u> pihm pəl}

go·pher *noun* a small rodent with gray or brown fur and a short tail. Gophers live in burrows and tunnel underground to look for food. They are also called pocket gophers, because they have pouches outside their cheeks where they carry food and nesting material. Gophers live in Central and North America. {<u>goh</u> fər}

gorge *noun* a narrow space between rocky cliffs. *We walked along the stream at the bottom of the gorge.* *verb* (gorged, gorging, gorges) to fill with too much food; stuff. *Lucy gorged herself with birthday cake.* {<u>gohrj</u>}

gor·geous *adjective* very beautiful; splendid. *What gorgeous feathers the peacock has!* {<u>gohr</u> jəs}

go·ril·la *noun* a very large ape that lives in African forests. Gorillas are the largest of the primates. Male gorillas living in zoos can weigh as much as six hundred pounds. All gorillas living in the wild are in danger of extinction. {gə <u>rihl</u> ə}

Homophone Note The words *gorilla* and *guerilla* sound alike but have different meanings. To find out why it might be dangerous to call a guerilla a gorilla, look up **guerilla**.

gos·ling *noun* a very young goose. {<u>gohz</u> ling}

gos·pel *noun* 1. (often capitalized) the lessons taught by Jesus Christ and his apostles. 2. (capitalized) any of the four accounts of Jesus Christ's life, death, and teachings in the New Testament books of Matthew, Mark, Luke, and John. 3. anything that is held on faith to be completely true or of great importance. *Many people take what they see on the news as gospel.* {<u>gŏs</u> pəl}

Word History *Gospel* comes from two early English words that together mean "a good story."

gos·sip ✆ *noun* 1. tales or talk about the personal lives and secrets of others when they are not present. *Don't believe what Pete told you, as it's only gossip.* 2. a person who often takes part in the telling of gossip. *Be careful what you tell her; she's a gossip.* *verb* (gossiped, gossiping, gossips) to take part in the telling of gossip. *The people in that office like to gossip about their boss when he is not around.* {<u>gŏs</u> ihp}

Word History *Gossip* comes from *godsibb*, an early English word for a godparent. Over time, "gossip" came to mean any close friend. By the late 1500s, the word was being used for someone who chatters about things of no importance. Today, most people would not like to be known as a "gossip."

got *verb* past tense and a past participle of get. {<u>gŏt</u>}

got·ten *verb* a past participle of get. {<u>gŏt</u> ən}

gouge *noun* 1. a type of chisel with a blade shaped like a scoop, used to carve wood. 2.

 Human Body Human Mind  Everyday Life 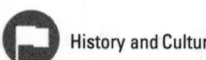 History and Culture  Communication

a cut or hole made with something sharp. *There is a gouge in the floor from when we moved the bookcase.* verb (gouged, gouging, gouges) to cut or carve with, or as if with a gouge. *We gouged a face in the pumpkin to make our jack-o'-lantern.* {gowj}

gourd ● noun the rounded fruit of a plant related to the squash. Certain kinds of gourds are dried and then used to make containers or decorations. {gohrd}

gour·met noun a person who loves and knows much about good food and fine wine. {goohr **may**}

Gov. abbreviation an abbreviation for **governor**.

gov·ern verb (governed, governing, governs) 1. to rule or lead. *The sheikh and his family governed the country.* 2. to control or hold back. *She governs her anger well.* {**guhv** ərn}

Word History *Govern* comes from a Greek word that meant "to steer or pilot (a ship)." From the Greek came the Latin word *gubernare*, meaning "to direct, rule, or guide."

gov·ern·ment ◌ noun 1. the political direction and control of people living in a community, state, or nation. *Government is challenging in a country where the people speak different languages.* 2. the group of people that give this direction and have this control. *The city government decided to build a public skate park.* 3. the type of system by which a community, state, or nation is governed. *Ancient Athens had the first democratic*

government. {**guhv** ərn mənt or **guhv** ər mənt} governmental, adj.

gov·er·nor noun a person who leads a government, especially that of a state of the United States. {**guhv** ər nər or **guhv** ə nər}

govt. abbreviation an abbreviation for **government**.

gown noun 1. a dress worn on special occasions. *The hostess wore a silk and satin gown.* 2. a long, loose piece of clothing, such as a nightgown or the robe worn by a judge or minister. {**gown**}

grab verb (grabbed, grabbing, grabs) to take hold of suddenly or with force; snatch. *The man grabbed his hat and rushed out.* noun an act of grabbing. *She made a grab for the balloon.* {**grăb**}
• **up for grabs** (informal) able to be taken by anyone; not yet decided. *The award for best actress is up for grabs this year.*

grace noun 1. beauty or charm in form, style, or motion. *She danced with the grace of a ballerina.* 2. the tendency to do what is kind, right, or polite; manners. *Martha had the grace not to point out his mistake.* 3. a prayer said before, or sometimes after, eating. *We bowed our heads and said grace.* verb (graced, gracing, graces) to add beauty or charm to. *A beautiful fountain graced the garden.* {**grays**}
• **in someone's good [or] bad graces** being liked and cared for, or being disliked and not cared

for by someone. *She tried to get back in her sister's good graces by doing her chores for her.* / *John has been in my bad graces since he broke my computer.*

grace·ful adjective marked by grace or beauty of movement or manner. *Fred and Alice are graceful skaters.* {**grays** fəl} gracefully, adv., gracefulness, n.

gra·cious adjective likely to do what is polite, kind, or right. *Our gracious host gave us a tour of downtown.* {**gray** shəs} graciously, adv., graciousness, n.

grack·le noun a North American blackbird with a long tail and shiny black feathers. {**grăk** əl}

grade noun 1. a level, degree, or rank in a scale. *These are the top grade of eggs.* 2. a division made by age to group school children for instruction, or the children who belong to such a division. *Chris is in second grade.* / *The sixth grade went to the museum yesterday.* 3. a number or letter given on schoolwork to show quality or correctness. *What grade did you get on your book report?* 4. the slope of a road or railroad. *The locomotive chugged up the steep grade.* verb (graded, grading, grades) 1. to give a grade to; evaluate. *The teacher graded the papers.* 2. to organize or sort by steps or degrees; classify. *Beef is graded by the amount of fat it contains.* 3. to make

A B C D E F G H I J K L M N O P Q R S T U V W X Y Z

a
b
c
d
e
f
g
h
i
j
k
l
m
n
o
p
q
r
s
t
u
v
w
x
y
z

level or even. *The crew graded the road.* {gra̱yd}

Word History The word *grade* comes from a Latin word that means "a step" or "a degree."

grade school *noun* see elementary school. {gra̱yd skoohl}

grad·u·al *adjective* happening by degrees that are small and even. *There was a gradual change in the weather. / The tree showed gradual growth.* {gra̱j ooh əl} **gradually**, *adv.*

grad·u·ate *noun* a person who has finished studying at a high school or college. *A diploma is given to a graduate to show that all the necessary work has been done.* *verb* (graduated, graduating, graduates) to be given a diploma upon finishing studies at a school or college. *She will graduate from high school this spring.* {gra̱j ooh iht, n., gra̱ jooh ayt, v.}

grad·u·a·tion *noun* 1. the act or process of graduating. *Everyone must pass this class for graduation.* 2. the ceremony at which a diploma is given or received. *My family will be at my college graduation.* {gra̱j ooh a̱y shən}

graf·fi·ti *noun* (graffiti) something written, scratched, or drawn on subway cars, buses, or walls in public places. {grə fe̱e tee}

graft *noun* 1. a part of a plant that is taken off and placed into a slit on another plant so that the two parts will grow together and become

one plant. 2. a living material, such as skin, that is removed and placed on another body or on another part of the same body. *verb* (grafted, grafting, grafts) to attach as a graft. *The surgeon grafted skin from the burn victim's thigh onto his face.* {gra̱ft}

gra·ham *noun* a flour made from the entire wheat grain. {gra̱y əm *or* gra̱m}

grain ❶ *noun* 1. the small hard seeds of cereal plants such as wheat or rice. Grains are used for food and often ground into flour. 2. any tiny, hard piece of something. *The ant carried away a grain of sugar.* 3. the pattern made by fibers that runs through wood, cloth, or other material. *By looking at the grain, he can tell which kind of wood the table is made of.* {gra̱yn}

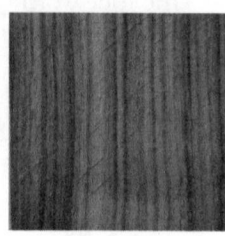

gram *noun* the basic unit of weight in the metric system, equal to one thousandth of a kilogram or 0.0353 ounce. (abbreviated: g) {gra̱m}

gram·mar ❷ *noun* 1. the rules for forming the words and sentences of a language. Some of these rules have to be learned. Other rules are already in the head of a native speaker. For example, a native English speaker would not say, "I a cat bitten by was," because the grammar does not make sense. When one learns a new language, most of the rules of its grammar have to be learned. *I found Latin grammar hard to master.* 2. the use of these language rules in

speaking and writing. *She is smart but she uses bad grammar.* {gra̱m ər}

grammar school *noun* see elementary school. {gra̱m ər skoohl}

gram·mat·i·cal *adjective* 1. of or having to do with grammar. *Pete's paper had several grammatical errors in it.* 2. following the rules of grammar. *I am learning to write grammatical sentences.* {grə ma̱t ih kəl}

grand *adjective* (grander, grandest) 1. splendid in size or appearance. *Rich people often live in grand houses.* 2. of the highest rank; very important. *The grand prize was a new car.* 3. complete; including everything. *What is the grand total of the repair bill?* *noun* (informal) an amount of one thousand dollars. *This boat cost me six grand!* {gra̱nd}

grand- *prefix* a prefix that means "one generation away." *Bill's grandfather is the father of Bill's mother, who is one generation away from Bill. / A granddaughter is one generation away from her father's parents.* {gra̱nd}

Grand Canyon *noun* a long, deep valley with steep, rocky walls formed by the Colorado River. The Grand Canyon is in northwestern Arizona. {gra̱nd ka̱n yən}

grand·child *noun* (grandchildren) a child of one's son or daughter. {gra̱nd chiyld}

grand·daugh·ter *noun* a female child of one's son or daughter. {gra̱n daw tər}

grand·fa·ther *noun* the father of a person's mother or father. {gra̱nd fahth ər}

grand·fa·ther clock *noun* a pendulum clock that is in a tall, narrow cabinet. {gra̱nd fah thər klŏk}

 Human Body   Human Mind  Everyday Life  History and Culture  Communication

grand·moth·er *noun* the mother of a person's father or mother. {**grănd** muh*th* ər}

grand·par·ent *noun* the father or mother of one's parent; a grandmother or grandfather. {**grănd** par ənt}

grand·son *noun* the male child of one's son or daughter. {**grănd** suhn}

grand·stand *noun* the rows of seats where people watch a sports event or parade. The seats are often covered by a roof. {**grănd** stănd}

gran·ite *noun* a hard stone made by the activity of volcanoes. It is used for making buildings, monuments, and sculptures. {**grăn** iht}

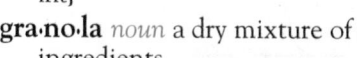

gra·no·la *noun* a dry mixture of ingredients such as grains, raisins, nuts, and honey. It is eaten as a snack or breakfast cereal. {grə **noh** lə}

grant *verb* (granted, granting, grants) 1. to present or give what is asked for or wanted. *The genie granted the girl three wishes.* 2. to admit or accept. *I grant that your idea will probably work better than mine.* *noun* that which is given; a gift. *The scientist got a grant of ten thousand dollars to study sharks.* {**grănt**}

grape *noun* a small juicy fruit, like a berry, with a smooth skin that is either green, red, or purple.

Grapes grow in bunches on woody vines. {**grayp**}

grape·fruit *noun* a large, juicy fruit with yellow skin and yellow or pink pulp which is often sour. The grapefruit is a citrus fruit like the orange or lemon. {**grayp frooht**}

grape·vine *noun* 1. a vine on which grapes grow. 2. an informal way of passing information and gossip about other people from person to person. *I heard through the grapevine that those two are engaged.* {**grayp** viyn}

graph 🌿 ⚛ *noun* a diagram that shows a relationship between two or more changing things by lines, bars, dots, or portions of a circle. *This graph shows how the world population has grown in the past fifty years.* *verb* (graphed, graphing, graphs) to represent or express by means of a graph. *The students graphed the results of their experiment.* {**grăf**}

-graph *suffix* 1. a suffix that means "something drawn or written." *An autograph is a written name.* 2. a suffix that means "something for writing, drawing, recording, or sending." *A telegraph is a machine that was used to send messages.* / *A phonograph is a machine that was used to play recorded music.*

graph·ic 🌿 *adjective* 1. of or related to pictures or writing such as photography, painting, and printing. *He is responsible for the graphic design of the magazine.* 2. described clearly and vividly. *The soldier gave a graphic account of the battle.* *noun* a picture, diagram, or other image used as an illustration. {**grăf** ihk} graphically, adv.

graph·ics *noun* 1. (used with a plural verb) the charts, maps, drawings, and other images used in printed works such as books and magazines. *Our science book has a lot of graphics.* 2. (used with a singular or plural verb) the process of making drawings, charts, and other images on a computer screen. *This computer has great software for graphics.* {**grăf** ihks}

graph·ite *noun* a soft black or gray form of carbon. It is the writing material in pencils, and it has many uses in industry. {**gră** fiyt}

grasp *verb* (grasped, grasping, grasps) 1. to take hold of with a hand. *He grasped the suitcase by its handle.* 2. to get the meaning of; understand. *The detective suddenly grasped the importance of the clue.* *noun* 1. an act of grabbing or taking hold. *The puppy escaped from his grasp and ran away.* 2. the power of holding, understanding, or controlling. *She has a good grasp of mathematics.* / *The actor held the audience in his grasp.* {**grăsp**}

grass ⚛ *noun* 1. a green plant with narrow pointed leaves and stems with joints. Grass often covers lawns and meadows. 2. an area planted with many such plants. *Please don't ride your bicycle on the grass.* {**grăs**}

grass·hop·per *noun* an insect with long, powerful hind legs for jumping and two pairs of wings. Grasshoppers eat plants. {**grăs** hŏp ər}

 Living World   Physical World   Natural Environment    Economy    Government and Law

grass·land *noun* a large area of land covered by grass. *Herds of antelope roam the grasslands of Africa.* {grăs lănd}

grate[1] *noun* 1. a frame of metal bars used as a covering or guard for a window or door. 2. a frame of metal bars that holds the fuel in a furnace, stove, or fireplace. {grayt}

grate[2] *verb* (grated, grating, grates) 1. to rub against a rough surface to make into small pieces. *She grated the block of cheese to use as a pizza topping.* 2. to make a sharp grinding noise. *The rusty gate grated on its hinges as it swung open.* 3. to scrape or rub in a harsh way. *The boat grated against a rock.* 4. to irritate or annoy. *Her loud voice grates on me.* {grayt} grater, n.

Homophone Note Are you looking for the word **great** (very large or important)? **Grate** and **great** sound alike but have different meanings.

grate·ful *adjective* feeling thankful or showing thanks for kindness or something pleasing. *We were grateful for your help fixing the tire.* {grayt fəl} gratefully, adv., gratefulness, n.

grat·i·fy *verb* (gratified, gratifying, gratifies) to please; satisfy. *Her good behavior gratified her parents.* {grăt ə fiy}

grat·ing *noun* a frame of bars that covers an opening; grate. {grayt ing}

grat·i·tude *noun* the feeling of being thankful; gratefulness. *Gemma expressed her gratitude to her guests by writing them thank-you notes.* {grăt ih toohd}

grave[1] *noun* a hole dug in the ground where a dead body is buried. {grayv}

grave[2] *adjective* (graver, gravest) 1. very serious or important; causing deep concern. *The Civil War was a grave period in the nation's history.* 2. likely to cause harm. *Driving fast on the icy road placed him in grave danger.* 3. serious; somber. *The doctor greeted us with a grave expression on her face.* {grayv} gravely, adv., graveness, n.

grav·el *noun* a loose mixture of small stones, pebbles, and sometimes sand. {grăv əl}

grave·yard *noun* an area of ground where dead people are buried; cemetery. {grayv yard}

grav·i·ta·tion *noun* the force that pulls planets, stars, or particles toward one another. *Gravitation holds people and other objects to the surface of the earth.* {grăv ə tay shən} gravitational, adj.

grav·i·ty  *noun* (gravities) 1. the force by which all objects in the universe are attracted to each other. *On Earth, objects fall to the ground because of gravity's pull.* 2. very serious nature or manner. *She needed an operation because of the gravity of her injuries. / He spoke with gravity.* {grăv ə tee}

Word History The word **gravity** comes from a Latin word that means "heavy." Its first meaning in English was "seriousness and dignity." It was first used as a scientific term for the force that causes objects to have weight in 1641. A year later, Sir Isaac Newton was born, and Galileo died.

gra·vy *noun* (gravies) a sauce made from the juice that drips from cooking meat. {gray vee}

gray or **grey** *noun* the color of the sky before it rains; the color between black and white. *adjective* (grayer or greyer, grayest or greyest) 1. having the color gray. *My grandfather has gray hair.* 2. gloomy. *It was another gray day.* 3. having gray hair. *My grandmother used to be blond, but now she is gray.* {gray} grayish (greyish), adj.

graze[1] *verb* (grazed, grazing, grazes) 1. to feed on growing grass. *The cattle grazed in the pasture.* 2. to put out to feed on growing grass. *The cowboys grazed their horses near the river.* {grayz}

When walking through the pasture, Odd Tom likes to **graze** against the **grazing** cattle.

graze[2] *verb* (grazed, grazing, grazes) 1. to touch or brush lightly in passing. *He grazed her arm as he ran past her.* 2. to scrape. *She grazed her knee when she fell off of the bicycle.* *noun* 1. a light touching, brushing, or scraping action. *He felt the graze of the cat against his leg.* 2. a slight scrape. *The wound was only a graze.* {grayz}

grease *noun* 1. melted or soft animal fat. *Bacon leaves a lot of grease in a pan after it has been cooked.* 2. a thick, oily

 Human Body Human Mind 👕 Everyday Life 🚩 History and Culture  Communication

material used on machine parts, such as those in a car engine. Grease lets the parts rub against one another smoothly while the machine is working. *verb* (greased, greasing, greases) 1. to coat with grease; lubricate. *He greased his bicycle chain.* 2. to put butter, margarine, or some other kind of grease on. *He greased the pan while she mixed the batter.* {grees}

Homophone Note The words *grease* and *Greece* sound alike but have different meanings. To find out why someone who is dieting would rather eat food made in Greece than food made in grease, look up *Greece*.

greas·y *adjective* (greasier, greasiest) 1. covered with grease. *The mechanic's hands were greasy from working on the car.* 2. full of grease. *Those fries are too greasy.* 3. slippery or oily. *This skin lotion is greasy.* {gree see *or* gree zee} greasiness, n.

great *adjective* (greater, greatest) 1. very large in size or number. *A great crowd came to see the parade.* 2. unusual in degree or amount. *He showed great courage in saving the drowning child.* 3. very important or distinguished; major. *Shakespeare was a great writer who lived hundreds of years ago.* 4. (informal) very good. *This is great ice cream.* *adverb* (greater, greatest) (informal) very well. *He is doing great at work.* *noun* a person famous for excellence in a particular field; star. *She is one of soccer's greats.* {grayt} greatness, n.

Synonyms
These words share a meaning with *great*, adjective 1:
huge, vast, enormous, tremendous, immense

Homophone Note Are you looking for the word *grate* (a frame of bars or a sharp sound)? *Great* and *grate* sound alike but have different meanings.

great- *prefix* a prefix that means "one generation away." A person's great-aunt is the aunt of that person's mother or father. {grayt}

Great Britain *noun* the main island of the United Kingdom. Great Britain is located off the coast of France and includes England, Scotland, and Wales. {grayt briht ən}

Great Dane *noun* a breed of dog. Great Danes are very large, powerful dogs with short hair, long legs, and a square muzzle. {grayt dayn}

great-grand·child *noun* (great-grandchildren) a child of one's grandson or granddaughter. {grayt grănd chiyld}

great-·gran·df·ather *noun* the grandfather of a person's mother or father. {grayt grănd fah thər}

great-·gran·dm·other *noun* the grandmother of a person's mother or father. {grayt grănd muhth ər}

great-grand·par·ent *noun* a parent of one's grandmother or grandfather. {grayt grănd par ənt}

Great Lakes *plural noun* five large, connected freshwater lakes of North America. They lie on the border between the United States and Canada; Lakes Superior, Michigan, Huron, Erie, and Ontario. {grayt layks}

great·ly *adverb* very much. *He enjoyed himself greatly at the party.* {grayt lee}

Greece *noun* a country in southern Europe on the Mediterranean Sea. Athens is the capital of Greece. {grees}

Homophone Note The words *Greece* and *grease* sound alike but have different meanings.

greed *noun* a great desire for more wealth and possessions than one needs or deserves. *Scrooge was known and disliked for his greed.* {greed}

greed·y *adjective* (greedier, greediest) 1. having a very strong desire for ever more money or things. 2. wanting to eat very large amounts of food. *The greedy child took her brother's piece of cake and stuffed it in her mouth.* {gree dee} greedily, adv., greediness, n.

Greek *adjective* of or having to do with Greece, or its people or language. *noun* 1. a person who was born in or is a citizen of Greece. 2. the language of the Greeks. {greek}

green *noun* 1. the color of grass or of young, growing leaves; the color between yellow and blue on the color spectrum. 2. an area with plenty of grass. *We had a picnic on the green.* 3. (plural) leaves of lettuce or other plants; vegetables. *She loves to eat turnip greens but not turnips.* *adjective* (greener, greenest) 1. having the color green. *She caught a green frog.* 2. full of or covered with living plants, trees, or grass. *The hills are green at this time of year.* 3. not completely grown; not ripe. *Eating green bananas can give you an upset stomach.* 4. without experience; in need of training. *William was very green when he began his job, but now he has experience.* 5.

A
B
C
D
E
F
G
H
I
J
K
L
M
N
O
P
Q
R
S
T
U
V
W
X
Y
Z

a b c d e f g h i j k l m n o p q r s t u v w x y z

sick looking; pale. *You looked a little green after eating that big meal.* {**green**} greenish, adj.

green·house *noun* a building used to grow plants all year long. A greenhouse usually has a glass roof and walls. {**green** hows}

greenhouse effect *noun* the warming of the earth's surface that takes place when heat from the sun is held in by the earth's atmosphere. The greenhouse effect can be caused by too much carbon dioxide being released into the air from the burning of fossil fuels. {**green** hows ə fehkt}

Green·land *noun* the largest island in the world, located in the north Atlantic Ocean. Greenland is a part of North America. It belongs to the country of Denmark. Nuuk is the capital of Greenland. {**green** lənd} Greenlander, n.

green thumb *noun* a special skill to make plants grow well. *She made a lovely garden with that green thumb of hers.* {**green** **thuhm**}

greet *verb* (greeted, greeting, greets) 1. to speak to with friendly or polite words upon meeting or when starting a letter. *The Porters greeted their dinner guests at the door.* 2. to respond to or receive in a certain way. *He greeted the news with a frown.* 3. to make itself seen or heard by. *A beautiful sunrise greeted me this morning.* {**greet**} greeter, n.

greet·ing *noun* 1. words or actions used to greet others. *She waved a friendly greeting as she got off the bus.* 2. (plural) a message of friendliness or respect. *Please give my greetings to your family when you see them.* {**greet** ing}

gre·nade *noun* a small bomb that is thrown by hand or shot from a rifle after its fuse is set. {grə **nayd**}

grew *verb* past tense of **grow**. {**grooh**}

grey *adjective* another spelling of **gray**. {**gray**}

grey·hound or **grayhound** *noun* a breed of dog. Greyhounds have a narrow body and head and long legs. They can run very fast. {**gray** hownd}

grid *noun* 1. a frame of crossing or parallel bars; grating. 2. parallel horizontal and vertical lines that cross each other to form squares of equal size. Grids are used to locate points on a map or to make diagrams. *Graph paper is printed with a grid.* {**grihd**}

grid·dle *noun* a flat pan or flat heated surface used in cooking. *We made pancakes on the griddle.* {**grihd** əl}

grid·i·ron *noun* 1. a flat frame of metal bars or wires, used for cooking foods. 2. a football field. {**grihd** iy ərn}

grid·lock *noun* a traffic jam in which no vehicles can move in any direction because key streets are blocked by traffic. *It took many hours to drive across town because of the gridlock.* {**grihd** lŏk}

grief ⊘ *noun* great sadness. *Her grief over her friend's death lasted many months.* {**greef**}

grieve *verb* (grieved, grieving, grieves) 1. to feel great sadness; mourn. *Grandmother grieved over the loss of her husband.* 2. to cause to feel great sadness. *It grieves me to tell you this bad news.* {**greev**}

grill ⊘ *noun* 1. a frame of metal bars used to hold foods for cooking over flames; gridiron. 2. a restaurant where grilled foods are served. *verb* (grilled, grilling, grills) 1. to cook on a grill. *We grilled hamburgers for dinner.* 2. (informal) to ask many questions of in a harsh way for a long time. *The police grilled the suspect until he broke down and confessed to the crime.* {**grihl**}

grim *adjective* (grimmer, grimmest) having a hard look or manner; stern; harsh. *The sheriff's face looked grim as he rode out to find the cattle thieves.* {**grihm**} grimly, adv., grimness, n.

grim·ace *noun* a twisting of the face to show pain, disgust, or anger. *He took a sip of the medicine with a grimace.* *verb* (grimaced, grimacing, grimaces) to make a grimace. *She grimaced as I pulled the splinter from her finger.* {**grih** məs}

grime *noun* dirt clinging to or rubbed into a surface. *Roll up your sleeves, because cleaning the grime off this stove is going to take hours.* {**griym**}

grin *verb* (grinned, grinning, grins) to smile broadly, so

 Human Body   Human Mind   Everyday Life   ▭ History and Culture   ☏ Communication

that the teeth are showing. *She grinned when she heard the good news.* *noun* a wide smile that shows the teeth. *Emil's grin told us he liked the gift.* {**grihn**}

grind *verb* (ground, grinding, grinds) 1. to crush or make by crushing into very small pieces or a powder. *He ground the nuts to make peanut butter.* 2. to make sharp or smooth by rubbing against. *He ground the edge of the knife on a stone.* 3. to rub together in a harsh way. *He ground his teeth in anger.* {**griynd**}

grind·stone *noun* a stone wheel that is turned to sharpen knives and tools, grind grain, or sand and shape items by rubbing or scraping. {**griynd stohn**}

grip *noun* 1. a firm grasp. *I felt the grip of his hand on my wrist.* 2. the act of grasping or holding firmly. *Get a grip on that dog!* 3. a good understanding of something. *She has a good grip on these math problems.* 4. a part that can be held; handle. *The tool has a rubber grip.* *verb* (gripped, gripping, grips) 1. to grasp or hold firmly. *She gripped the child's arm when he tried to run into the street.* 2. to hold the attention of. *The children were gripped by the scary movie.* {**grihp**} gripper, n.

grit *noun* 1. tiny rough bits of sand or stone. *He was covered with grit after working outside all day.* 2. toughness of character; courage. *Firefighters show grit each time they rush into a burning building.* *verb* (gritted, gritting, grits) to bite down and grind

together. *She gritted her teeth in pain when the doctor set her broken arm.* {**griht**}

grits *plural noun* ground white corn. Grits are a kind of cereal that is cooked before eating. {**grihts**}

griz·zled *adjective* gray or somewhat gray. *The man's beard became grizzled as he grew older.* {**grihz** əld}

grizzly bear *noun* a large bear found in the northwestern United States and western Canada. The fur of the grizzly bear can be grayish or brown. {**grihz** lee **bayr**}

groan *noun* a deep sound made to show pain, grief, or sadness. *The groans of the wounded soldiers filled the hospital.* *verb* (groaned, groaning, groans) to make a groaning sound. *The class groaned when the teacher gave them extra homework.* {**grohn**}

Homophone Note Are you looking for the word *grown* (past participle of "grow")? *Groan* and *grown* sound alike but have different meanings.

gro·cer *noun* a person who sells food and other supplies for household use. {**groh** sər}

gro·cer·y ○ *noun* (groceries) 1. a store where food and other household supplies are sold; grocery store. *My parents run a small grocery.* 2. (usually plural: groceries) the food and other things sold in such a store. *We need to pick up some groceries on the way home.* {**groh** sə ree *or* **groh** shə ree *or* **grohs** ree}

grog·gy *adjective* (groggier, groggiest) confused, dizzy, or sleepy. *She was groggy after*

getting hit in the head with a baseball. {**gro** gee} grogginess, n.

groom *noun* 1. a man who is about to be or has just been married. 2. a person whose job is to take care of horses or a stable. *verb* (groomed, grooming, grooms) 1. to make clean and neat in appearance. *He went upstairs to groom himself before dinner.* 2. to wipe down, brush, and care for. *He groomed the horse after it had been ridden.* {**groohm**} groomer, n.

groove *noun* a long narrow cut or dent in a surface. *Their skates left grooves in the ice.* *verb* (grooved, grooving, grooves) to cut a groove into. *The carpenter grooved the wood.* {**groohv**}

grope *verb* (groped, groping, gropes) 1. to feel about or feel one's way with the hands. *She groped in the dark for the light switch.* 2. to search for in an uncertain or blind way. *She groped for the right words to say.* {**grohp**}

gross *adjective* (grosser, grossest) 1. before anything is taken out; total. *Your gross pay for the week will be eight hundred dollars.* 2. easily seen; completely obvious. *The mayor made a gross mistake by telling the police chief he didn't know how to do his job.* 3. rude or disgusting. *Please don't use such gross language.* *noun* (gross or grosses) 1. twelve dozen or 144. *The order is for a gross of light bulbs.* 2. a total amount or whole before any-

A B C D E F G H I J K L M N O P Q R S T U V W X Y Z

thing is taken out. *Your gross is five hundred dollars.* {grohs}

gro·tesque *adjective* ugly or badly shaped in character or appearance. *My Halloween mask was so grotesque, it even scared me!* {groh <u>tehsk</u>}

> **Word History** *Grotesque* comes from *grotta*, an early Italian word for "cave." English speakers first used the word "grotesque" to describe the weird paintings of humans and animals found on the basement walls of Roman ruins.

grouch *verb* (grouched, grouching, grouches) to complain; grumble. *He grouched about having to stay inside on a rainy day.* *noun* a person who is often in a bad mood or who often complains. *She is such a grouch, so nobody was surprised to hear that she did not enjoy her vacation.* {<u>growch</u>} grouchiness, n.

grouch·y *adjective* (grouchier, grouchiest) likely to be cross and complaining. *I am grouchy in the morning if I wake up too early.* {<u>grow</u> chee} grouchily, adv., grouchiness, n.

ground[1] 🧠 🏠 *noun* 1. the earth's solid surface; land. 2. (often plural) a piece of land that has a special purpose. *There are several gardens on the grounds of the estate.* 3. (sometimes plural) the reason or basis for saying or doing something. *What are the grounds for your argument?* 4. (always plural: grounds) tiny bits that settle at the bottom of a liquid. *There were coffee grounds in the bottom of the cup.* *verb* (grounded, grounding, grounds) 1. to make the basis for; establish. *He grounded his argument in facts.* 2. to run against the ground. *We*

grounded the boat on the beach. 3. to connect to an electrical ground. *The farmer grounded his barn with a lightning rod to protect it from fire.* 4. to keep from flying. *Bad weather grounded the airplane.* {<u>grownd</u>}

ground[2] 🧠 🏠 *verb* past tense and past participle of **grind**.

Farmer Ted gets up early each morning to dig dirt out of the **ground** for his famous fresh-**ground** mud pies.

adjective 1. made into very small particles by grinding. *The cook added ground nuts to the cookie dough.* 2. having been through the action of grinding. *Kay made ground meat from the leftover roast.* {<u>grownd</u>}

ground·hog *noun* another name for a woodchuck. {<u>grownd</u> hŏg *or* <u>grownd</u> hawg}

group *noun* 1. a collection of people, things, or ideas that are in one place or are related by characteristics; cluster. *A large group of people met to discuss the plan.* 2. a small musical band, especially one that plays pop or jazz music. *verb* (grouped, grouping, groups)

1. to put with other items that are similar; classify. *The librarian grouped the books by topic.* 2. to bring together into a group; gather. *The teacher grouped the students in a circle.* {<u>groohp</u>}

> **Synonyms**
> These words share a meaning with *group*, noun 1:
> body, set, collection, bunch, cluster, assortment, congregation

grouse *noun* (grouse or grouses) a plump game bird with dull, spotted feathers. The male does a complicated dance or call for the female. {<u>grows</u>}

grove *noun* a small group of trees. *The children hid from their mother in the grove.* {<u>grohv</u>}

grow 🧠 ⬆️ *verb* (grew, grown, growing, grows) 1. to become larger by natural development; increase. *She grew an inch over the summer.* 2. to be able to live. *This plant doesn't grow in the shade.* 3. to become. *The weather grew warmer.* 4. to come from or develop from. *Sandy's ideas about children grew from her experiences as a teacher.* 5. to make grow. *The farmer grows corn and beans.* {<u>groh</u>}

• **grow up** to become an adult; to mature. *I plan to be a computer scientist when I grow up.*

growl ⬆️ *verb* (growled, growling, growls) 1. to make a deep, rumbling sound to express anger or hostility. *The dog will growl if you try to take away his bone.* 2. to make a deep rumbling

 Human Body   Human Mind    Everyday Life    History and Culture    Communication

sound like a growl. *His stomach is growling.* noun the act or sound of growling. *She was awaked by the growl of a bear outside her tent.* {**growl**}

grown *adjective* having reached adulthood. *Now that she is grown, she has opinions of her own.* verb past participle of grow. {**grohn**}

Homophone Note Are you looking for the word ***groan*** (a deep sound)? ***Grown*** and ***groan*** sound alike but have different meanings.

grown-up *adjective* 1. having become an adult. *Now that my sister is grown-up, she has an apartment of her own.* 2. of or meant for adults. *The grown-up talk at my parents' dinner party was boring.* {grohn **uhp**}

growth 🌿 📖 *noun* 1. the process of growing. *Teenagers experience rapid growth. / That town had a large growth in population during the 1990s.* 2. that which has grown. *A growth of weeds is taking over the garden.* 3. an area of tissue that is not normal. *The doctor removed a growth from my arm.* {**grohth**}

grub *noun* the larva of some beetles and other insects. Grubs are a young stage in the growth of the insect. They look like short, fat worms. *verb* (grubbed, grubbing, grubs) 1. to dig up, especially to take out rocks or roots. *We grubbed the soil before planting a garden.* 2. to dig in the soil; to look for something as if by digging. *Lou grubbed in the garden all morning. / The raccoons grubbed through our garbage.* {**gruhb**}

grub·by *adjective* (grubbier, grubbiest) dirty or messy. *Please change out of those* grubby clothes before you sit down to dinner. {**gruh** bee}

grudge *noun* anger that is held onto for a long time. *She has a grudge against him that goes back six years.* verb (grudged, grudging, grudges) to not want to give or allow. *My older brother grudged me the use of the phone.* {**gruhj**}

gru·el·ing *adjective* very tiring or difficult. *The soldiers did grueling exercises as part of their training.* {**grooh** ling}

grue·some *adjective* frightening in a disgusting way; horrible. *The town still talks about the gruesome crime that took place more than fifty years ago.* {**grooh** səm}

gruff *adjective* 1. low and harsh. *The substitute teacher's gruff voice frightened the children.* 2. rough and not polite. *The gruff ticket agent took our money and slammed the window shut.* {**gruhf**} gruffly, adv., gruffness, n.

grum·ble *verb* (grumbled, grumbling, grumbles) 1. to complain in a low voice. *Jean grumbled to herself about the flat tire as she searched for a jack.* 2. to make deep, muffled sounds; rumble. *His stomach grumbled in hunger.* noun 1. a muttered complaint. *There were grumbles from the students who had to stay after school.* 2. a series of deep, low sounds; rumble. *We heard the grumble of thunder before the storm hit.* {**gruhm** bəl}

grump·y *adjective* (grumpier, grumpiest) in a bad mood; cross. *Missing the school bus made her grumpy.* {**gruhm** pee} grumpily, adv., grumpiness, n.

grunt *verb* (grunted, grunting, grunts) 1. to make a short deep sound like a hog. *The movers grunted as they picked up the piano.* 2. to express

using a sound like a grunt. *With his mouth full, he grunted, "This pie is great!"* noun a short, deep sound like that made by a hog. {**gruhnt**}

guar·an·tee *noun* 1. a promise, in writing, that something one has bought will work properly. If it does not, the seller or maker must either repair or replace it. *There is a two-year guarantee on my new computer.* 2. a promise to make sure that some duty or responsibility will be met. *The babysitter gave us her guarantee that she would be here every afternoon at three o'clock.* verb (guaranteed, guaranteeing, guarantees) 1. to serve as a guarantee for. *My job guarantees the money needed to buy a new car.* 2. to make certain or promise. *The salesman guaranteed my satisfaction with the new van.* {gar ən **tee**}

guard *verb* (guarded, guarding, guards) 1. to protect from danger or harm. *The dog guarded the sheep.* 2. to watch over to prevent escape. *Please guard the prisoners.* 3. to do what is necessary to prevent (followed by "against"). *The farmers in the valley need to guard against floods in the rainy season.* noun 1. a person who watches out for danger or protects property. *The museum had guards at every exit.* 2. A person who watches over another person to prevent escape. *There are guards in the prison day and night.* 3. a device used to prevent harm to something. *Soccer players wear shin guards.* {**gard**}

• **off guard** not ready; careless. *They succeeded in their attack by catching the enemy off guard.*

 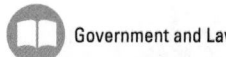

a
b
c
d
e
f
g
h
i
j
k
l
m
n
o
p
q
r
s
t
u
v
w
x
y
z

• **on guard**
alert and prepared. *Be on guard for leeches when you go swimming in that lake.*

guard·i·an *noun* 1. a person who guards or protects. *The police are the guardians of our neighborhood.* 2. an adult chosen by law to be responsible for the care and protection of a child or a person who cannot care for himself or herself. {**gar** dee ən}

Gua·te·ma·la *noun* a country in Central America. Guatemala City is the capital of Guatemala. {gwah tə **mah** lə} Guatemalan, n., adj.

gua·va *noun* 1. a tropical American tree that bears white flowers and fruit that can be eaten. 2. the fruit of the guava tree. A guava is yellow and shaped like a pear. {**gwah** və}

guer·ril·la or **guerilla** *noun* one of a group of soldiers who do not work as part of an official army. Guerillas make surprise attacks against an enemy. {gə **rih** lə}

guess *verb* (guessed, guessing, guesses) 1. to form an opinion without enough information to be certain. *He tried to guess the reason for her laughter.* 2. to figure out correctly without knowing for certain. *Can you guess the answer?* 3. to think or believe; suppose. *I guess she will be here soon.* *noun* an opinion, estimate, or answer based on little or no information. *My guess wasn't even close.* {**gehs**}

guest *noun* 1. a person who is a visitor in another's home. *Please offer our guest another helping of potatoes.* 2. a customer at a hotel or restaurant. {**gehst**}

guid·ance *noun* 1. the act of guiding. *With my grand-*

mother's guidance, I learned how to quilt. 2. advice. *The school counselor gave me guidance about what courses to take in high school.* {**giyd** əns}

guide *verb* (guided, guiding, guides) 1. to direct or lead along a way that is not familiar. *The librarian guided us to the books about Asian snakes.* 2. to offer advice to; counsel. *My father guided me through the job application.* 3. to influence or control. *The prime minister guided the country through a time of crisis.* *noun* 1. a person who points out the way or leads others. *The guide led us up the mountain.* 2. a handbook or manual. {**giyd**}

guided missile *noun* a missile that can be guided throughout its flight until it reaches its target. {**giyd** ihd **mih** səl}

guide word *noun* one or two words printed at the top of the page in a reference book to help the reader find the right page. In this dictionary, the guide words at the top of each page show what the first and last entries on that page are. {**giyd** wuhrd}

guild *noun* 1. a group of people who work together on a common interest or hobby. *The hospital guild is looking for donations from the public.* 2. a group of people in the Middle Ages in Europe who were in the same trade and who joined together to protect their common interests. Guilds were concerned with the prices and quality of their products. {**gihld**}

Homophone Note Are you looking for the word *gild* (to cover with gold)? *Guild* and *gild* sound alike but have different meanings.

guil·lo·tine *noun* a device having a sharp blade that is dropped between two guide posts to execute a person by chopping off his or her head. *verb* (guillotined, guillotining, guillotines) to chop off the head of with a guillotine. *The king ordered that the murderer be guillotined.* {**gihl** ə teen *or* gee ə **teen**, n., **gihl** ə teen *or* gee ə **teen**, v.}

Word History In 1789, a French physician, Joseph Guillotin, came up with a new means of execution. The first *guillotine* was built two years later. It was used to execute many people during the French Revolution (1789-1799).

guilt *noun* 1. the fact of having done something wrong or having broken a law. *The police used fingerprints as evidence of his guilt.* 2. a feeling of being sorry or responsible for having done something wrong. *You could see the guilt on her face after she broke her neighbor's window.* {**gihlt**}

Homophone Note Are you looking for the word *gilt* (a past tense and past participle of "gild")? *Guilt* and *gilt* sound alike but have different meanings.

guilt·y *adjective* (guiltier, guiltiest) 1. feeling or showing guilt. *My lunch money was nowhere to be found, and then I noticed the guilty look on his face.* 2. responsible for breaking a law or doing something wrong. *The judge sent the guilty man to prison.* {**gihl** tee}

Guin·ea *noun* a country in western Africa on the Atlantic coast. Conakry is the capital of Guinea. {**gih** nee} Guinean, n., adj.

guinea pig *noun* 1. a small mammal with short legs and

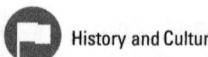 Human Body

? Human Mind

Everyday Life

History and Culture

 Communication

no tail. Guinea pigs are rodents closely related to chinchillas and porcupines. Some science laboratories use guinea pigs for research and to test new medicines. Wild guinea pigs live in South America. 2. a person who is used to test new products or procedures. *I was the guinea pig for Mom's new recipe.* {**gih** nee **pihg**}

guitar *noun* a stringed instrument with a long neck and five, six, or twelve strings that are strummed or plucked. {gih **tar**}

gulch *noun* a rocky valley with steep sides. A gulch sometimes has a stream running through it. {**guhlch**}

gulf *noun* 1. a large area of ocean partly surrounded by land. 2. a deep crack in the earth's surface. 3. a large difference. *There is a gulf between what I think of as a clean room and what my mother thinks of as a clean room.* {**guhlf**}

gull *noun* a water bird that has webbed feet, gray and white feathers, and long, pointed wings. They are graceful and powerful in flight. {**guhl**}

gul·li·ble *adjective* believing almost anything; easily tricked. *Did you know that "gullible" isn't in the dictionary?* {**guhl** ih bəl}

gul·ly *noun* (gullies) a deep cut or ditch in the land made by running water. {**guhl** ee}

gulp *verb* (gulped, gulping, gulps) 1. to quickly draw in a breath; to gasp. *She gulped when she saw the price tag on the dress.* 2. to take large swallows of; drink or eat

eagerly or rapidly (often followed by "down"). *Rosa gulped down the juice and poured another glass. / He gulped down his food and ran out the door.* *noun* 1. the act of gulping. *The baby drank his milk in loud gulps.* 2. a large mouthful or swallow. *She took such a gulp of water, she coughed it up.* {**guhlp**}

gum[1] *noun* 1. a sticky substance that is given off by certain plants. 2. a glue made from this substance. 3. chewing gum. *verb* (gummed, gumming, gums) 1. to smear or stick together with gum. *She gummed the envelope and sealed it.* 2. to clog (often followed by "up"). *Putting food down the drain will gum up the pipes.* {**guhm**}

gum[2] *noun* (often plural) the flesh inside the mouth around the base of the teeth. {**guhm**}

gum·drop *noun* a small candy that is like a firm jelly and coated with sugar. {**guhm** drŏp}

gun ⬭ *noun* 1. a weapon with a tube made of metal from which bullets, shells, or other missiles are fired. Guns include pistols, rifles, and cannons. 2. a tool that shoots small objects or liquids out through a tube or nozzle. *We used a spray gun to paint the house. / The carpenter's work went faster when he used a nail gun.* *verb* (gunned, gunning, guns) to shoot using a rifle or gun (often followed by "down"). *The police gunned down the fugitive.* {**guhn**}

gun·fire *noun* the firing of a gun. {**guhn** fiyr}

gun·ner *noun* a soldier or sailor who fires or helps to fire a large gun or cannon. {**guhn** ər}

gun·pow·der *noun* a black powder that explodes when touched with fire. Gunpowder is used in firing guns. {**guhn** pow dər}

gun·wale *noun* the upper edge of the side of a boat or ship. {**guhn** əl}

gup·py *noun* (guppies) a small fish that lives in fresh water in South America and the West Indies. Guppies have bright colors and are often kept in aquariums. {**guhp** ee}

gur·gle *verb* (gurgled, gurgling, gurgles) 1. to flow with a noisy, bubbling sound. *The creek gurgled as the water flowed over the rocks.* 2. to make a noise like a bubbling flow of liquid. *The baby gurgled happily.* *noun* the act or sound of gurgling. *We could hear the gurgle of the water as it went down the drain.* {**guhr** gəl}

gush *verb* (gushed, gushing, gushes) 1. to flood out in large amounts and with great force; spurt. *Water gushed from the hose when I turned on the faucet.* 2. to speak with too much emotion or enthusiasm. *Nora frowned when Aunt Ellie gushed about how grown-up she looked.* *noun* a sudden or heavy flow that happens with great force. *The plumber knew how to stop the gush of water from the pipe.* {**guhsh**}

gust *noun* 1. a sudden rush or blast of wind. *The gust carried his kite even higher.* 2. a sudden burst of emotion. *As the audience watched the funny play, a gust of laughter filled the theater.* {**guhst**}

gut *noun* 1. the stomach or intestines. 2. strips of a strong material taken from the intestines of an animal. Gut is used to make strings for musical instruments and to

A B C D E F **G** H I J K L M N O P Q R S T U V W X Y Z

sew up wounds. 3. (usually plural) the inner parts of something that make it work. *He opened the lid and examined the guts of the computer.* 4. (plural; informal) courage or nerve. *Jumping off the high dive took a lot of guts.* *verb* (gutted, gutting, guts) to destroy the inside of. *Fire gutted the building.* {**guht**}

gut·ter *noun* a ditch along the edge of a road, or a pipe under the lower edge of a roof for carrying off water. {**guht** ər}

guy[1] *noun* 1. (informal) a boy or man; fellow. 2. (plural) people, including males and females. *Why don't you guys come with us?* {**giy**}

Word History In London, in 1605, Guy Fawkes was arrested for planning to blow up the Houses of Parliament. His failure is still celebrated every year on the fifth of November, which is known in England as "Guy Fawkes Day." On this day, "guys," made by stuffing an old suit with straw, are wheeled around town and then tossed into bonfires. The word *guy* came to be used for a poorly dressed person in the 1800s. Soon after that, it began to be used in a more general way for a man or fellow.

guy[2] *noun* a rope or wire used to guide something or hold something in place. *The tent was held in place by stakes at its corners and guys attached to nearby trees.* {**giy**}

Gu·ya·na *noun* a country in northern South America on the Atlantic coast. Guyana was known as British Guiana until its independence from the United Kingdom in 1966. Georgetown is the capital of Guyana. {giy **ăn** ə} Guyanese, n., adj.

gym *noun* 1. (informal) a short form of gymnasium. 2. physical education. *We have gym twice a week.* {**jihm**}

gym·na·si·um *noun* (gymnasiums) a building or large room that has equipment for physical education, sports, and games. {jihm **nay** zee əm}

gym·nast *noun* a person who is skilled in gymnastics. {**jihm** nəst}

gym·nas·tics *noun* 1. (used with a plural verb) physical exercises used to develop and show strength, control, and agility. Gymnastics are often done with the aid of special equipment, such as bars and ropes. 2. (used with a singular verb) the competitive sports based on such exercises. *Gymnastics is popular around the world.* {jihm **nă** stihks}

Word History *Gymnastics* is from a Greek word that means "to train or exercise naked."

Gyp·sy or **Gipsy** *noun* (Gypsies or Gipsies) 1. a member of a group of wandering people who came from India long ago. Gypsies are now found throughout the world. 2. (lower case) one thought of as acting like a Gypsy. *She lives like a gypsy because her job requires so much travelling.* {**jihp** see}

Word History Wandering people in Britain who were believed to come from Egypt were called *Gypsies*. They were actually the Romany people from northwestern India.

gy·ro·scope *noun* an instrument with a turning wheel, mounted on an axis that can turn in any direction. When the axis turns, the wheel stays level. Gyroscopes are used to help keep ships and airplanes on course. {**jiyr** ə **skohp**}

 Human Body   Human Mind   Everyday Life    History and Culture   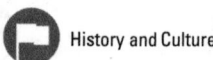 Communication

Hh

H is a consonant that always makes the same sound.

Tips to help you look up words starting with h: Also look under W for words that start with the "h" sound but are spelled with a silent "w" (such as who or whole).

These words may be hard to look up if you don't already know how to spell them:

half	high
handkerchief	hospital
haughty	huge
health	humor
heaven	hygiene
height	hypocrite

h or **H** *noun* (h's or H's) the eighth letter of the English alphabet. {<u>aych</u>}

ha or **hah** *interjection* a word used to show triumph, surprise, discovery, amazement, or annoyance. *Ha! Look what I found!* {<u>hah</u>}

hab·it  *noun* 1. a regular action; routine. *He is in the habit of washing the dishes right after dinner.* 2. a fixed, repeated action, often done without meaning to or wanting to. *She has an annoying habit of tapping her toes.* 3. clothes worn for a specific purpose or role. *It is no longer common for nuns to wear habits. / People who ride horses in the English style often wear a riding habit.* {<u>hă</u> biht}

hab·i·tat *noun* the natural environment of an animal or plant. *An animal may suffer if it is removed from its natural habitat. / What kind of habitat does a palm tree need?* {<u>hă</u> bih tăt}

ha·bit·u·al *adjective* 1. done by habit. *She has her habitual cup of coffee at the start of each day.* 2. in keeping with habit; regular. *I always keep a pack of gum handy because I'm a habitual gum chewer.* {hə <u>bih</u> chooh əl} habitually, adv., habitualness, n.

ha·ci·en·da *noun* a large estate used as a farm or ranch. Haciendas can be found in many countries where the people speak Spanish or in the southwestern United States. {hah see <u>ehn</u> də}

hack *verb* (hacked, hacking, hacks) 1. to cut or chop with heavy blows. *He hacked the wood into pieces.* 2. to clear by chopping out anything that blocks the way. *We hacked a path through the tall weeds.* 3. to give out short, harsh coughs. *He has the flu and hacked all night.* {<u>hăk</u>}

hack·er  *noun* 1. (informal) someone who is expert at correcting computer programs and is seen as a person interested only in computers. *The hackers at school spend all their free time in the computer lab.* 2. someone who is able to use a computer to get into carefully protected computer systems owned by a government, business, or individual. *A hacker broke into the teacher's computer files and stole the answers to the history exam.* {<u>hă</u> kər}

had *verb* past tense and past participle of **have.** {<u>hăd</u>}

Ha·des *noun* the underworld of Greek mythology, ruled by the god Pluto. {<u>hay</u> deez} Hadean, adj.

had·n't shortened form of "had not." *He explained why he hadn't done his homework.* {<u>hă</u> dənt}

hag·gard *adjective* having a very tired, worried, or wasted look. *The woman got lost in the mountains and looked haggard when she was found two days later.* {<u>hă</u> gərd} haggardly, adv., haggardness, n.

hai·ku *noun* a Japanese verse form made of three lines, or any poem written in this form. The first line has five syllables, followed by a line of seven syllables, then another line of five. {<u>hiy</u> kooh}

> Raindrops turn to snow
> mittened fingers, hats on heads
> tear-wet faces smile
> — G. Tavares

hail¹ *verb* (hailed, hailing, hails) 1. to welcome or greet. *He hailed me at the door.* 2. to attract the attention of by calling out or waving. *The girl hailed the bus, but it did not stop.* noun a cry or shout to greet or attract the attention of someone. *The prince was met with loud hails from his faithful men.* interjection used to express a greeting or acclamation. *Hail! hail! the gang's all here!* {<u>hayl</u>}

• **hail from**
to have as one's place of birth or residence; come

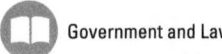

a
b
c
d
e
f
g
h
i
j
k
l
m
n
o
p
q
r
s
t
u
v
w
x
y
z

from. My grandparents hail *from a small village in Italy.*

Fred is pelted by **hail** as he tries to **hail** a taxi cab home.

hail² 🔊 *noun* 1. round pieces of frozen rain or a storm of this frozen rain. 2. something that comes in large numbers or with force. *After his speech there was a hail of questions from the audience.* / *I knocked over a jar and caused a hail of sugar to spill all over the floor.* *verb* (hailed, hailing, hails) 1. to fall or pour down in icy rain. *It is getting colder and may hail tomorrow if it doesn't rain.* 2. to fall down or strike like hail. *Dust and plaster hailed down on us during the earthquake.* {**hayl**}

hair 🔊 🔊 *noun* 1. a thin, thread-like strand that grows from the skin of humans and other mammals. *We looked at a hair under the microscope.* 2. a mass of such strands growing on a person's head or on the skin of a mammal. *Her hair is messy.* 3. a tiny amount. *This sauce needs a hair more salt.* {**hayr**} hairlike, adj.
• **make one's hair stand on end**
to make very frightened. *The sudden howl of a wolf made our hair stand on end.*

Homophone Note Are you looking for the word *hare* (a rabbit)? *Hair* and *hare* sound alike but have different meanings.

hair·cut *noun* 1. the act or process of cutting hair. *Mom saved a lock of hair from my first haircut.* / *Don't bother the barber when he's in the middle of a haircut!* 2. the style or shape in which hair is cut. *She has a new, short haircut.* {**hayr** kuht} haircutting, n.

hair·do *noun* (hairdos) the style or shape in which hair is arranged. *I love my new hairdo because it makes me look older.* {**hayr** dooh}

hair·pin *noun* a metal pin in the shape of a U, used to keep hair in place or to attach something to the hair. *adjective* sharply curved. *The mountain road had many hairpin turns.* {**hayr** pihn}

hair·y *adjective* (hairier, hairiest) covered with or having a lot of hair. *My dog is so hairy that you can't see his eyes.* {**hayr** ee} hairiness, n.

Hai·ti *noun* a country on an island in the West Indies in the Caribbean Sea. Port-au-Prince is the capital of Haiti. Haiti shares the island with the Dominican Republic. {**hay** tee} Haitian, n., adj.

half *noun* (halves) one of two equal parts of a whole. *Two is half of four.* *adjective* 1. being one of two equal parts of a whole. *We like to buy juice by the half gallon.* 2. having just one parent in common with someone. *He is my half brother.* *adverb* 1. to the extent of half or approximately half. *The dish was half*

empty. 2. not completely; partially. *I was only half awake.* {**hăf**}

half brother *noun* a male who is a brother through one parent only. *My half brother and I have the same mother but different fathers.* {**hăf** **bruh** thər}

half·heart·ed *adjective* done with or showing little interest or enthusiasm. *His blankets were still messy after his halfhearted effort to make his bed.* {**hăf** har tihd} half-heartedly, adv., halfheartedness, n.

half-mast *noun* a point halfway down a flagpole. A flag is flown at half-mast as a sign of respect or sorrow when someone has died or, on a ship, as a signal of great need or trouble. {**hăf** **măst**}

half sister *noun* a female who is a sister through one parent only. *My half sister and I have the same father but different mothers.* {**hăf** **sih** stər}

half step *noun* an interval in music that is halfway between two notes. {**hăf** stehp}

half time *noun* the rest period between the two halves of football and basketball games and certain other sports events. {**hăf** tiym}

half·way *adverb* 1. to or at the middle point between two ends or conditions. *We are halfway towards our goal.* 2. not completely; nearly. *I halfway agreed with him.* *adjective* 1. half the way between two ends or points. *Several of the marathon runners dropped out at the*

 Human Body   Human Mind   Everyday Life    History and Culture    Communication

halfway point. **2.** including only half or a part of what is possible or necessary. *Mending the chair with string is only a halfway solution.* {hăf way}

hal·i·but *noun* (halibut or halibuts) a flatfish that lives in the northern Atlantic and Pacific Oceans. Halibut are used for food. {hăl ə biht}

Word History *Halibut* comes from two early English words. *Butte* meant "flatfish." *Haly* meant "holy" and was combined with *butte* because fish was eaten on holy days.

hall *noun* **1.** a narrow passageway in a building; corridor. *This hall goes to the bedrooms.* **2.** a large room or public building for meetings or social gatherings. *The dance will be at the community hall. / The meeting will be at City Hall.* **3.** the room or entrance area just inside the main door of a building; lobby. *Please leave your boots in the hall before you come in.* {hawl}

Homophone Note Are you looking for the word *haul* (to transport)? *Hall* and *haul* sound alike but have different meanings.

hal·le·lu·jah *interjection* a word used to express joy or praise to God. *Hallelujah! We have arrived safely! noun* a cry of joy or praise. *They sang hymns and shouted hallelujahs.* {hă lə looh yə}

Hal·low·een ⊙ or **Hallowe'en** *noun* October 31. Halloween is celebrated by children who dress up in costumes

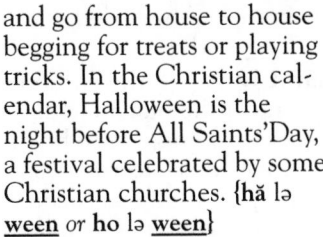

and go from house to house begging for treats or playing tricks. In the Christian calendar, Halloween is the night before All Saints' Day, a festival celebrated by some Christian churches. {hă lə ween *or* ho lə ween}

hall·way *noun* a narrow passage in a house or building; corridor. {hawl way}

ha·lo *noun* (halos or haloes) **1.** a circle of light shining around the head of God, an angel, or a saint in a picture. **2.** any circle or band of light that appears around a source of light, such as the sun or moon. {hay loh}

Word History *Halo* comes from an ancient Greek word that means "a disk around the sun or moon."

halt *verb* (halted, halting, halts) **1.** to stop or pause. *Schoolwork halted while everyone ate their lunch.* **2.** to cause to stop. *The crossing guard halted the cars so the children could cross. noun* a stop or pause in activity. *Dancing came to a halt while the band took a break. interjection* used as a command to stop. *"Halt!" is often used to direct marching troops or to stop a person from going into a particular area. Halt! About face! Forward march! / Halt! This area is off limits.* {hawlt}

hal·ter *noun* **1.** a rope or strap that is set on the head or neck of a horse, ox, or other animal to tie or guide it. **2.** a woman's blouse that covers the chest and ties around the neck and back but leaves the rest of the upper body bare. {hawl tər}

halve *verb* (halved, halving, halves) to divide into two equal parts. *If we halve this*

tomato, we both will eat the same amount. {hăv}

Homophone Note The words *halve* and *have* sound alike but have different meanings.

halves *noun* plural of **half**. *Two halves equal a whole.* {hăvz}

ham[1] *noun* **1.** the meat from the rear leg of a hog. *She served ham for the holiday meal.* **2.** the back of the human thigh. *My hams are sore after climbing the mountain.* {hăm}

ham[2] *noun* **1.** an actor who exaggerates his emotions and movements on stage. *For such a quiet man, he is a real ham on stage.* **2.** an amateur radio operator. {hăm}

ham·burg·er *noun* ground beef, or a patty of ground beef cooked and served as a sandwich. *My father bought two pounds of hamburger at the market. / We ordered hamburgers for lunch.* {hăm buhr gər, hăm buhrg}

ham·let *noun* a small village or settlement. {hăm liht}

Ham·let *noun* the title character in one of Shakespeare's tragedies. Hamlet is a prince who avenges his father's death by slaying the murderer, his own uncle. {hăm liht}

ham·mer *noun* **1.** a hand tool with a solid, heavy head on a handle. It is used to pound or to beat something into shape or place. **2.** anything that is used like a hammer to produce a sound. *The hammers inside a piano strike the strings.*

A
B
C
D
E
F
G
H
I
J
K
L
M
N
O
P
Q
R
S
T
U
V
W
X
Y
Z

verb (hammered, hammering, hammers) 1. to hit or strike with a hammer; pound. *He hammered nails into the wood.* 2. to shape by pounding with a hammer. *She hammered the metal into the shape of a leaf.* 3. to pound like a hammer. *His heart hammered against his ribs.* {**hăm** ər} hammerer, n., hammerlike, adj.

ham·mock *noun* a swinging bed made of canvas or netting that is hung between two trees or poles. {**hăm** ək}

ham·per[1] *verb* (hampered, hampering, hampers) to get in the way of. *Bad weather hampered our climb up the mountain.* {**hăm** pər} hamperer, n.

ham·per[2] *noun* a large basket or container with a cover, used to hold picnic supplies or dirty laundry. *She packed the hamper with sandwiches and cookies.* {**hăm** pər}

ham·ster *noun* a very small mammal with a round body, short tail, and large pouches in its cheeks. Hamsters are rodents that live in burrows and come out at night to find food. They are often kept as pets or used in scientific experiments. Different kinds of wild hamsters live in

Europe, Africa, and Asia. {**hăm** stər}

hand *noun* 1. the part on the end of the human arm. It is used for grasping or holding. 2. a worker. *He worked on the farm as a hired hand.* 3. the pointer of a clock or dial. *The short hand on this watch is pointing toward four.* 4. handwriting. *The letter was written in a large hand.* 5. the cards given out to each player in a card game. *My good hand won me the game.* 6. help. *We gave her a hand with the chores.* 7. a promise of marriage. *He asked for her hand over a romantic dinner.* 8. a part or share in controlling or directing something. *He had a hand in starting the new business.* 9. side or direction. *You will sit at my right hand at dinner.* 10. a round of applause. *After he sang we all gave him a hand.* *verb* (handed, handing, hands) to give or pass to with the hand. *Please hand me an apple.* {**hănd**}

• **hand down** to give to one's children or from one generation to another. *These books were handed down from my grandfather.*

• **hand out** to give to each person; pass out; distribute. *We handed out candy on Halloween.*

• **on hand** ready right there. *We made lunch from the food we had on hand.*

• **to hand over** to give up control of; surrender. *We handed over the car to the new owners.*

hand- *prefix* a prefix that means "for or by the hand." *A handrail is a rail that is for the hand to hold onto. / A handmade quilt is a quilt made by hand.* {**hănd**}

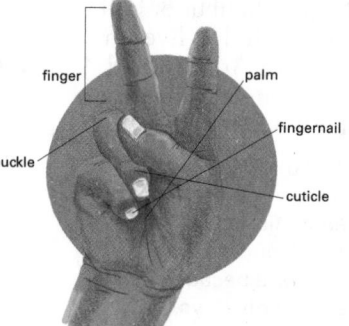

finger, palm, fingernail, cuticle, knuckle

hand·bag *noun* a bag or case used to carry small personal articles; purse. *She keeps her wallet in her handbag.* {**hănd** băg}

hand·ball *noun* 1. a game in which a ball is batted against a wall or walls with the hand. Handball can be played by two or four players. 2. the small rubber ball used in this game. *The handball bounced away from me.* {**hănd** bawl} handballer, n.

hand·book *noun* a book that gives information on a specific subject; manual. {**hănd** buuk}

hand·cuff *noun* one of two metal rings that are joined to each other by a short chain or bar. Handcuffs are locked around a prisoner's wrists. *verb* (handcuffed, handcuffing, handcuffs) to put handcuffs on. *The police caught and handcuffed the robber.* {**hănd** kuhf}

hand·ful *noun* 1. the amount that can be held in a single hand. *She put a handful of dirt in the flower pot.* 2. a small number or amount. *The audience asked only a handful of questions.* 3. (informal) a person or thing that is diffi-

 Human Body   Human Mind Everyday Life History and Culture   Communication

cult to deal with or control *The new puppy is really a handful!* {**hănd** fəl}

hand·i·cap *noun* 1. anything that makes things harder or keeps one from doing better. *Despite the handicap of being blind, she graduated from college. / His greatest handicap is not believing in himself.* 2. an advantage or disadvantage placed on a team or player in a race or contest. This is done to give everyone an equal chance to win. *Runners over the age of sixty were given a head start as a handicap.* *verb* (handicapped, handicapping, handicaps) to put at a disadvantage; hinder. *His fear of speaking up handicapped him in class.* {**hăn** dee kăp}

hand·i·capped *adjective* 1. having a physical or mental condition that makes success harder. *She was handicapped by her problems in reading.* 2. having been given an advantage or disadvantage in a race or contest. *The slower runners were handicapped to give them a better chance in the race.* {**hăn** dee kăpt}

hand·i·craft *noun* 1. skill at making things by hand. *She needs handicraft to be good at her job as an artist.* 2. work that requires skill at making things by hand or the products of such work. *Weaving, pottery, and carving are all handicrafts. / That handmade rug is a beautiful handicraft.* {**hăn** dee krăft}

hand·ker·chief *noun* a small piece of thin cloth used to wipe the nose or face, or worn as decoration in a pocket. {**hăng** kər chihf}

han·dle *noun* the part of an object made to be held in order to lift or hold the

object. *Use the handles to open the drawer.* *verb* (handled, handling, handles) 1. to deal with; manage. *He handled the arrival of extra guests very well.* 2. to touch or examine with the hands. *Please handle the flowers gently.* 3. to behave or operate in a certain way when used. *My new bicycle handles hills well.* {**hăn** dəl}

• **fly off the handle**
to become very angry; lose one's temper [an informal use]. *He flew off the handle when he discovered the dish was broken.*

han·dle·bar *noun* (usually plural) a curved bar with handles used for steering a bicycle, scooter, or other vehicle with two wheels. {**hăn** dəl bar}

hand·made *adjective* made by hand or with hand tools, rather than by machine. *I like handmade gifts better than those made by machines.* {**hănd** mayd}

hand·out *noun* 1. a gift of money, food, or something else to the poor. 2. a piece of printed matter or something else given out free. {**hănd** owt}

hand·rail *noun* a narrow rail that a person grips by the hand for support or protection. *When you go down the stairs, make sure you use the handrail.* {**hănd** rayl}

hand·shake *noun* the gripping and shaking of hands between two people when they meet or say good-bye. *I will always remember my handshake with the President.* {**hănd** shayk}

hand·some *adjective* (handsomer, handsomest) 1. having a pleasing and healthy appearance; nice to look at. *He is a handsome man.* 2. large or generous in

amount. *She was given a handsome reward.* {**hăn** səm} handsomely, adv., handsomeness, n.

Word History The word ***handsome*** comes from an early English word that means "easy to handle." The meaning of "handsome" changed, to "good-looking," about five hundred years ago in the 1500s.

hand·spring *noun* a complete somersault in which a person flips onto the hands and then springs off the hands back to a standing position. {**hănd** spring}

hand·writ·ing *noun* 1. words written by hand with a pen or pencil. *Because of his bad handwriting, my brother uses a computer to write letters.* 2. the way a particular person's writing looks. *He has crooked handwriting.* {**hănd** riy ting} handwritten, adj.

hand·y *adjective* (handier, handiest) 1. nearby; easy to reach and use. *Do you have a pencil handy?* 2. useful. *The hammer is a handy tool.* 3. good at doing things with one's hands; skillful. *He's handy in the kitchen and in the garden.* {**hăn** dee}

hang *verb* (hung or hanged, hanging, hangs) 1. to attach to a point above without support from below. *She hung a pair of curtains.* 2. to be attached to a point above without support from below. *The swing hung from a big branch on the old tree.* 3. to kill by fastening a rope tied around the neck to a point above and removing all support. *The town hanged the outlaw for murder.* 4. to put up or fasten. *Let's hang this picture on the wall.* *noun* (informal) the idea of how to do something; knack. *He's*

A
B
C
D
E
F
G
H
I
J
K
L
M
N
O
P
Q
R
S
T
U
V
W
X
Y
Z

finally got the hang of horse-back riding. {**hăng**}

• **hang up**
1. to put the telephone receiver back in its cradle. *When you finish talking, please hang up the telephone.* 2. to put on a hook or hanger. *Hang up your coat, please.*

hang·ar *noun* a shelter for aircraft. {**hăng** ər}

Homophone Note Are you looking for the word *hanger*? *Hangar* and *hanger* sound alike but have different meanings.

hang·er *noun* 1. a frame with a hook at the top, made of wire, wood, or plastic, and shaped so that one may hang clothes over it. *I put my coat on a hanger in the closet.* 2. any device used to hang something. *I need to buy a plant hanger.* {**hăng** ər}

hang glider *noun* a glider that looks like a large kite and is used for sailing in the air. {**hăng** gliy dər} hang gliding, n.

hang·nail *noun* a small, loose piece of skin at the side or bottom of the fingernail. {**hăng** nayl}

han·ker *verb* (hankered, hankering, hankers) to wish or long for something (often followed by "for" or "after"). *I am hankering for an ice cream cone. / He has been hankering after fame and fortune as long as I've known him.* {**hăng** kər}

Ha·noi *noun* the capital city of Vietnam. {hah **noi**}

Ha·nuk·kah *noun* a Jewish festival that runs for eight days in December in which a special candle is lit each night. Hanukkah celebrates the anniversary of the dedication of the temple at Jerusalem and the miracle of the lamp. {hah nə kə *or* **khah** nuu kah}

hap·haz·ard *adjective* having no order; without aim or purpose. *The locker was filled with a haphazard pile of papers and books. adverb* by chance; without order. *As he undressed, he threw his clothes haphazard on the floor.* {hăp **hă** zərd} haphazardness, n.

hap·pen *verb* (happened, happening, happens) 1. to take place; occur. *The wedding will happen next summer. / Small earthquakes happen often in Japan.* 2. to occur or take place by chance. *They both happened to arrive at the same time.* 3. to encounter by chance (usually followed by "on" or "upon"). *The detective happened on a clue that helped him solve the crime.* {**hăp** ən}

hap·pen·ing *noun* something that happens; event; occurrence. *The strange happenings in the old house made us believe in ghosts.* {**hă** pə ning}

hap·pi·ly *adverb* 1. in a happy way. *She smiled happily.* 2. luckily. *Happily, we found him before he left.* {**hă** pih lee}

hap·pi·ness *noun* the fact or condition of being happy or glad. {**hă** pee nihs}

hap·py *adjective* (happier, happiest) 1. feeling joy or pleasure; being glad or content. *She was very happy with her birthday gifts.* 2. lucky or fortunate. *It was a happy coincidence that we were both there at the same time.* {**hă** pee}

Synonyms
These words share a meaning with *happy*, adjective 1:
pleased, glad

hap·py-go-luck·y *adjective* free of cares or serious thoughts; leaving everything to luck. *Joe's boss doesn't like Joe's happy-go-lucky attitude at work.* {**hă** pee **goh** **luh** kee}

har·ass *verb* (harassed, harassing, harasses) to trouble or bother again and again. *My mother asked me to stop harassing her while she was trying to work. / Some of the girls were harassed after being allowed to join the boys' football team.* {hə **răs** *or* **har** əs} harassingly, adv., harassment, n.

Word History *Harass* may come from an early French word that means "to excite the hunting dogs."

har·bor   *noun* 1. a sheltered area of water where boats can be anchored. 2. any shelter or safe place. *My home and my family have always been my safe harbors. verb* (harbored, harboring, harbors) 1. to provide shelter or safety for. *That old inn harbored slaves who were escaping north.* 2. to hide or conceal. *They harbored the slaves in the cellar.* 3. to have in the mind. *She harbors bad thoughts about him.* {**har** bər} harborer, n., harborless, adj.

hard *adjective* (harder, hardest) 1. not soft; solid; firm; tough. *It hurt when I fell on the hard ground.* 2. difficult. *Learning to ice skate is hard for some people.* 3. not easy to deal with. *I had to think for a while before I answered that hard question.* 4. full of energy; giving a strong effort. *We were happy to have a hard worker on our team.* 5. without kindness or softness. *The witch had hard eyes.* 6. asking for a great effort; strict; demanding. *We think she is a hard teacher because she gives so much homework. adverb* (harder, hardest) 1. with much effort; diligently. *He worked hard in the fields. / I thought hard about the problem.* 2. in a harsh or

 Human Body   Human Mind   Everyday Life    History and Culture   Communication

severe way. *She looked at me hard before turning away.* 3. with great force or strength. *It rained hard last night.* / *He hit me hard.* {**hard**}

Synonyms

These words share a meaning with **hard**, adjective 6:

severe Severe is used to describe very hard discipline or punishment. *The judge gave him a severe sentence.*

harsh To be harsh is to be hard in a cruel way. *The prison rules seemed harsh to the new prisoner.*

strict Strict describes someone or something that is hard because it must be obeyed. *Her strict parents never let her out of their sight.*

demanding When someone or something is demanding, it is hard because it asks much or too much from people. *Her boss was so demanding that she quit her job.*

hard-boiled *adjective* 1. an egg that is boiled in the shell until firm all the way through. 2. (informal) not moved by feelings; tough. *He was a hard-boiled detective.* / *Although she seems hard-boiled, deep down she cares a lot.* {**hard boild**}

hard drive *noun* a device for storing information on a computer's hard disk. A hard drive can be built into a computer or can sit outside the computer and be connected to it by a cable. *You will need a lot of room on your hard drive to install this computer game.* {**hard driyv**}

hard·en *verb* (hardened, hardening, hardens) 1. to make hard. *She hardened the clay bowl by baking it.* 2. to become hard or harder. *The*

paste hardened. 3. to make tough or uncaring. *Spending a year in jail hardened his heart.* {**har** dən}

hard·ly *adverb* 1. almost not at all; barely. *I can hardly hear the radio.* 2. not likely; surely not. *We can hardly go camping without a tent.* {**hard** lee}

hard·ship *noun* 1. a condition of great want, suffering, or difficulty. *It was a poor country and the people faced many hardships.* 2. a particular instance or cause of such a condition. *The fire was a hardship that cost them their home.* {**hard** shihp}

hard·ware *noun* 1. tools and equipment used for making and fixing things. Hardware is usually made of metal. 2. computer parts and equipment; all the mechanical and electronic parts of a computer. {**hard wayr**}

hard·wood *noun* 1. any of several types of trees with strong, hard wood and broad leaves. Oak, cherry, and mahogany are all hardwoods. 2. the wood from such a tree. Hardwood is used by carpenters to make things. {**hard wuud**}

hard·y *adjective* (hardier, hardiest) 1. able to stand hardship; tough; brave. *My mother was a hardy woman who liked to go camping alone.* 2. able to stand or live through harsh weather or bad conditions; not easily killed. *That plant is so hardy it keeps growing even if I leave it out in the cold or forget to water it.* {**har** dee}

hare *noun* (hare or hares) a small mammal with long ears. Hares are large rabbits with very strong back legs

used for jumping. Various kinds of hares live in Europe, Asia, Africa, and North and Central America. {**hayr**}

Homophone Note Are you looking for the word **hair** (something that grows on mammals)? **Hare** and **hair** sound alike but have different meanings.

harm *noun* 1. injury or hurt. *Although he fell a long way, no harm came to the child.* 2. wrong or evil. *He did great harm by lying to us.* *verb* (harmed, harming, harms) to hurt or damage. *Too much sun can harm the skin.* {**harm**}

harm·ful *adjective* causing or likely to cause harm; dangerous. *Smoking is harmful to your health.* {**harm** fəl} harmfully, adv., harmfulness, n.

har·mon·i·ca *noun* a small wind instrument in the shape of a rectangle. It is held in the hands and played by blowing and inhaling air over a set of metal reeds; mouth organ. {**har mŏn** ih kə}

har·mo·ny 🔊 🔊 *noun* (harmonies) 1. being in agreement; unity. *There was great peace and harmony in their happy marriage.* 2. a pleasant or organized relation among the parts of something. *There was a certain harmony to the way she had decorated the room.* 3. musical notes played at the same time that make a pleasant sound. *He sang harmony with her.* {**har** mə nee}

har·ness *noun* 1. a set of straps by which a work animal is attached to a cart, carriage, or plow. The harness is used to control and guide the animal. 2. something that looks or

A
B
C
D
E
F
G
H
I
J
K
L
M
N
O
P
Q
R
S
T
U
V
W
X
Y
Z

acts like such a set of straps. *If you parachute, make sure your harness is in perfect shape.* verb (harnessed, harnessing, harnesses) 1. to put a harness on. *The farmer harnessed the horse to the plow.* 2. to bring under control and make ready for use. *The city will harness the river to produce electricity.* {<u>har</u> nihs} harnesser, n.

harp *noun* a large musical instrument with an upright triangular frame. Harps have forty-six strings and are played by plucking the strings with the fingers. {<u>harp</u>} harper, n.

har·poon *noun* a weapon that is like a spear with a barbed head and a rope at the tail end. Harpoons are used in hunting whales and large fish. *verb* (harpooned, harpooning, harpoons) to strike or spear with a harpoon, or as though with a harpoon. *The sailor yelled in surprise when he found he had harpooned a giant piece of rubber instead of a whale.* {<u>har</u> <u>poohn</u>}

harp·si·chord *noun* a musical instrument with one or two keyboards. It is like a piano except that its strings are plucked when the keys are pressed. {<u>harp</u> sih <u>kohrd</u>} harpsichordist, n.

har·row *noun* a farm tool used to break up and level ground that has been plowed. A harrow has spikes or upright disks mounted on a heavy frame. *verb* (harrowed, harrowing, harrows) 1. to go over or break up with a harrow. *The farmer spent several days harrowing his fields.* 2. to cause to suffer or worry a great deal. *The fire at the school harrowed the whole town.* {<u>har</u> oh} harrowing, adj.

harsh *adjective* (harsher, harshest) 1. rough or not pleasing to the eyes, ears, or other senses. *The harsh music hurt my ears.* 2. rough and not pleasing in action or result. *She had a harsh manner.* 3. severe or strict. *The mayor wants harsher punishments for drug dealers.* {<u>harsh</u>} harshly, adv., harshness, n.

har·vest ❶ ❻ *noun* the gathering of ripe crops, the crops or the amount gathered, or the season in which they are gathered. *It is time to begin the harvest. / They had a very good harvest of apples. / We met at harvest.* *verb* (harvested, harvesting, harvests) to gather in a crop. *We harvested tomatoes and beans from our garden.* {<u>har</u> vihst}

har·ves·ter *noun* 1. one who gathers ripe crops. *The harvesters had a party because it had been a good year.* 2. a machine used to gather ripe crops. *The farmer is getting the harvester ready for the corn field.* {<u>har</u> vih stər}

has *verb* the present tense of **have**, used with "he," "she," or "it," or with singular nouns. *He has two sisters. / The horse has a long tail.* {<u>hăz</u>}

hash *noun* 1. a dish of chopped meat and vegetables that have already been cooked. Hash is fried or heated again in gravy. 2. a mess or jumble. *He is hoping to get his school project in order because right now it's such a hash.* {<u>hăsh</u>}

has·n't shortened form of "has not." *She hasn't been to college yet.* {<u>hă</u> zənt}

has·sle *noun* something that bothers or troubles someone in a small way. *Planning the party was a hassle because no one would help me.* verb (hassled, hassling, hassles) (informal) to bother or cause trouble for. *I hate the way my parents hassle me about homework.* {<u>hăs</u> əl}

haste *noun* 1. speed or hurry. *Please take this message and deliver it with haste to Miss Carson.* 2. hurrying too fast or in a careless way. *Haste makes waste.* {<u>hayst</u>}

has·ten *verb* (hastened, hastening, hastens) 1. to move or act with speed; hurry. *She hastened to catch the bus. / Realizing he had hurt her feelings, he hastened to say he was sorry.* 2. to cause or encourage to act or move quickly. *She hastened him out the door.* 3. to make happen sooner or faster. *When he struck out, it hastened the end of the inning.* {<u>hay</u> sən} hastener, n.

hast·y *adjective* (hastier, hastiest) 1. fast or quick; hurried. *Seeing he was in the wrong room, he made a hasty exit.* 2. too quick or careless. *He did a hasty job on his homework and made several mistakes.* {<u>hay</u> stee} hastily, adv., hastiness, n.

hat ⭕ *noun* a covering for the head worn for warmth, protection, or decoration. {<u>hăt</u>}

 Human Body Human Mind  Everyday Life  History and Culture Communication

hatch[1] *verb* (hatched, hatching, hatches) 1. to help young animals develop inside their eggs and then to break out or be born. Birds, reptiles, and certain kinds of fish hatch eggs. *Ducks hatch their eggs by keeping their nest warm.* 2. to produce or create. *They hatched a plan to surprise him.* 3. to come out of an egg; to be born from an egg. *The ducklings all hatched the same afternoon.* {**hăch**} hatchability, n., hatchable, adj., hatcher, n.

hatch[2] *noun* 1. an opening in the floor, roof, or side of a building or vehicle. Hatches are often found on ships and allow passengers or cargo to pass through. 2. a cover or door for such an opening. {**hăch**}

hatch·back *noun* a kind of car in which a back panel is lifted up to open the rear storage area. {**hăch** băk}

hatch·er·y *noun* (hatcheries) a place where the eggs of fish, chickens, or other animals are hatched. {**hăch** ə ree}

hatch·et *noun* a small ax with a short handle that can be used with one hand. {**hăch** iht} hatchetlike, adj.
• **bury the hatchet** to make peace; forget past conflicts. *My friend and I didn't speak for two months, but then we decided it was time to bury the hatchet.*

hate ⓦ *verb* (hated, hating, hates) to dislike very strongly; detest. *The people hated the cruel king for allowing their children to die of starvation.* {**hayt**}

hate·ful *adjective* 1. causing hatred. *The city was shocked by the hateful crime.* 2. full of

hate; showing hate. *The teacher listened calmly to the angry student's hateful words.* {**hayt** fəl} hatefully, adj., hatefulness, n.

hat·red *noun* a feeling of hate or strong dislike. *Hatred has led to many wars.* {**hay** trihd}

haugh·ty *adjective* (haughtier, haughtiest) proud in a way that shows a low opinion of others; thinking of others as beneath oneself. *That haughty girl thinks she's better than everyone else.* {**haw** tee} haughtily, adv., haughtiness, n.

haul *verb* (hauled, hauling, hauls) 1. to pull or drag with force. *We hauled the garbage can out to the street.* 2. to carry from one place to another in a vehicle; transport. *My dad hauls freight for a living.* *noun* 1. an act or instance of pulling or tugging. *She gave the rope a good haul.* 2. an act or instance of carrying from one place to another in a vehicle, or the distance something is carried. *Everything went very well during the haul.* / *Moving was just a short haul across town.* 3. (informal) an amount that is received at one time. *My friend and I got a good haul of candy on Halloween.* {**hawl**}

Homophone Note The words *haul* and *hall* (a walkway) sound alike but have different meanings.

haunch *noun* 1. the area of the body that includes the hip, buttocks, and upper thigh. 2. the same area on an animal. {**hawnch**}

haunt *verb* (haunted, haunting, haunts) 1. to live in or visit as a ghost. *It is said that ghosts haunt that old, empty house.* 2. to go to often. *My friends and I haunt the mall every Sat-*

urday. 3. to come very often to the mind or memory of. *The memory of that day still haunts her.* {**hawnt**}

Ha·van·a *noun* the capital city of Cuba. Havana is a seaport on the Gulf of Mexico. {hə **vă** nə}

have *verb* (had, having, has) 1. to own; possess. *I have five dollars.* 2. to experience; feel. *We always have a good time at recess.* 3. to include or contain. *Our team will have ten members.* 4. to be obliged to; must. *I have to go to school.* 5. to think about or hold in mind. *I have a great idea.* 6. to give birth to. *Mother is having a baby in the hospital.* 7. to get or receive. *Let's have a cup of tea.* 8. to cause to happen. *I need to have my hair cut.* *auxiliary verb* (had, having, has) used with a past participle to express a completed action. *They have gone.* / *He has finished the sandwich.* / *We had just arrived home when the phone rang.* {**hăv**}

Homophone Note The words *have* and *halve* (to cut in half) sound alike but have different meanings.

ha·ven *noun* 1. the place where a ship anchors; harbor or port. *The haven is filled with boats every weekend.* 2. a place of safety, shelter, or comfort. *Dad's lap was a haven during the scary movie.* / *In a storm even an old cabin is a haven.* / *The tree was my haven after a sad day.* {**hay** vən}

have·n't shortened form of "have not." *I haven't read that book.* {**hă** vənt}

Ha·wai·i *noun* 1. an island state of the United States in the Pacific Ocean. Its capital is Honolulu. (abbreviated: HI)

 Living World    Physical World   Natural Environment   Economy   Government and Law

A B C D E F G **H** I J K L M N O P Q R S T U V W X Y Z

a
b
c
d
e
f
g
h
i
j
k
l
m
n
o
p
q
r
s
t
u
v
w
x
y
z

2. the largest island in this state. {hə **wiy** ee *or* hə **wah** yee}

Word History *Hawaii* (also spelled Hawai'i) comes from the Polynesian name for the original settlers' homeland, *Hawaiki*.

hawk[1] *noun* a bird with a short hooked beak and curved claws. Hawks catch and eat small animals. {**hawk**} hawklike, adj.

hawk[2] *verb* (hawked, hawking, hawks) to offer for sale by calling out or going from place to place. *She hawked her fresh muffins from* door to door. {**hawk**}

haw·thorn *noun* a shrub or small tree with long thorns that has white or pink flowers and small red berries. {**haw** thohrn}

hay ◐ *noun* grass, clover, or alfalfa that is cut, dried, and stored for animal food. *verb* (hayed, haying, hays) to make grass or other plants into hay. *We hayed the fields in late summer.* {**hay**}

Homophone Note The words *hay* and *hey* sound alike but have different meanings.

hay fever *noun* a condition marked by a runny nose, sneezing, and headache that is caused by an allergy to plant pollen. {**hay** fee vər}

hay·loft *noun* the upper part of a barn or stable, used for storing hay. {**hay** lawft *or* **hay** lŏft}

hay·stack *noun* a large pile of hay stacked outdoors. {**hay** stăk}

haz·ard *noun* 1. danger or risk. *There were many hazards on the steep mountain trail.* 2. something that causes a danger or risk. *Smoking is a hazard to your health.* *verb* (hazarded, hazarding, hazards) 1. to put in danger or at risk. *You are hazarding my life with your careless driving!* 2. to risk or chance. *Let me hazard a guess as to why you are late.* {**hă** zərd}

Word History *Hazard* comes from an Arabic word that means "one of the dice." When "hazard" entered the English language in the Middle Ages, it meant "risk" or "venture."

haz·ard·ous *adjective* full of danger; having great or many risks. *Science has shown that*  *smoking is hazardous to one's health.* {**hăz** ər dəs} hazardously, adv., hazardousness, n.

haze *noun* mist, smoke, or dust in the air, making it hard to see. *There was a haze over the lake, so we couldn't see the other side.* {**hayz**}

ha·zel *noun* 1. a shrub or small tree that bears brown nuts that can be eaten. 2. the wood or nut of such a shrub or tree. 3. a light brown color. *Hazel is the color of her eyes.* *adjective* 1. of or relating to the hazel. *I have a beautiful box made of hazel and oak woods.* 2. of or relating to the color hazel. *My eyes are hazel but my sister's are blue.* {**hay** zəl}

ha·zy *adjective* (hazier, haziest) 1. marked or clouded by haze; misty. *The mountains in the distance are hazy.* / *There was a hazy blue sky over Los Angeles.* 2. not clear; fuzzy or confused. *I only have a hazy memory of my grandmother who died when I was little.* {**hay** zee} hazily, adv., haziness, n.

H-bomb *noun* a very powerful bomb that releases energy by nuclear fusion. "H-bomb" is short for **hydrogen bomb**. {**aych** bŏm}

He symbol of the chemical element helium.

he *pronoun* 1. the male human being or animal that is being discussed or was recently referred to. *Where is your brother? He is at school.* 2. a human being or animal whose sex is not specified; whoever. *He who laughs last, laughs best.* *noun* a male human being; man. *I am a he and you are a she.* {**hee**}

head ◉ ◐ *noun* 1. the top part of a human or animal body which contains the brain and has eyes, ears, a nose and a mouth. 2. mind; intellect; understanding. *She has a good head for business.* 3. a position of leadership or authority, or the person in such a position. *She is the head of the agency.* 4. the part of anything regarded as the top or most prominent part. *He hit the nail on the head.* 5. one person or animal of a group, especially when they are being counted. *She*

 Human Body   Human Mind   Everyday Life   History and Culture   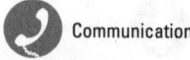 Communication

counted five head of cattle. / The firehouse is charging ten dollars per head for the spaghetti dinner. 6. the side of a coin that shows the main design. *President Lincoln is on the head of a penny.* *adjective* of the highest rank or position; superior; leading; primary. *He is the head chef. / I am the head waiter.* *verb* (headed, heading, heads) 1. to be the director or head of; lead. *He heads the children's reading program.* 2. to have the lead or top position or status. *Chocolate heads our list of popular flavors.* 3. to move toward a certain goal or in a certain direction. *He is heading for trouble. / I am heading for the nearest diner.* {hehd}

• **head off** to stop or interfere with the progress of; intercept. *He headed off his opponent with a quick move.*

• **over one's head** beyond one's ability to understand. *His older sister's math textbook was over his head.*

Word History In Old English, the word for *head* was *heafod*. The modern spelling appeared first in 1420. At that time, the word "head" rhymed with "bead."

head·ache *noun* 1. a pain in the head. 2. (informal) a person or thing that causes trouble or worry. *My younger brother can be such a headache when he misbehaves.* {hehd ayk}

head·band *noun* a band worn around the head. Headbands are used to hold back the hair or to soak up wetness. *The runners wore headbands to keep sweat out of their eyes.* {hehd bǎnd}

head·dress *noun* a covering or decoration for the head. *She wore a beautiful Native American headdress for the ceremony.* {hehd drehs}

head·first *adverb* with the head in front of the body. *Let's dive headfirst into the water!* {hehd fuhrst}

head·ing *noun* a word or group of words at the top or front of a piece of writing; title. {hehd ing}

head·land *noun* a high piece of land that sticks out into a body of water. {hehd lənd}

head·light *noun* a bright light on the front of a vehicle. {hehd liyt}

head·line *noun* the title to a newspaper article that tells what the article is about. *The headline for the most important news is in the largest type on the front page of the paper.* *verb* (headlined, headlining, headlines) to be the most important as a performer at; be the main attraction of. *Of the four bands that were going to play, the most popular one headlined the event.* {hehd liyn} headliner, n.

head·long *adverb* 1. with the head first. *He jumped on the sled and went flying headlong down the hill.* 2. suddenly or quickly; without proper thought ahead of time. *We rushed headlong into a bad business deal.* *adjective* 1. falling or done with the head first. *She took a headlong fall down the icy steps.* 2. sudden

or quick. *We made a headlong dash for the car through the rain.* {hehd lawng}

head·on *adjective* meeting with the front part or head first. *The two cars were wrecked in a head-on collision.* *adverb* with the head or front part leading; in a direct way. *The car crashed head-on into a tree. / We attacked the problem head-on.* {hehd ŏn}

head·phone *noun* (usually plural) a sound receiver for a radio or stereo system that is held over one or both ears by a band; earphones. {hehd fohn}

head·quar·ters *noun* (headquarters) 1. (used with a singular or plural verb) the main office of any organization. *The company's headquarters is in Chicago.* 2. the place or center of command of a military unit or police force. {hehd kwohr tərz}

head·rest *noun* a rest or support for the head. Many chairs or seats in motor vehicles have headrests. {hehd rehst}

head start *noun* an early start in a race, or an advantage in any other activity. *Kit won the race even though Lon had a head start.* {hehd start}

head·stone *noun* a stone set at the head of a person's grave; tombstone.

Headstones honor that person's memory and usually have writing carved into them. {hehd stohn}

A B C D E F G **H** I J K L M N O P Q R S T U V W X Y Z

a
b
c
d
e
f
g
h
i
j
k
l
m
n
o
p
q
r
s
t
u
v
w
x
y
z

head·strong *adjective* determined to have one's own way; stubborn; willful. *My puppy is so headstrong he'll need special training to learn how to obey.* {<u>hehd</u> strawng} headstrongness, n.

head·wa·ters *plural noun* the streams that form the beginning of a river. {<u>hehd</u> waw tərz}

head·way *noun* 1. forward movement; progress. *Our boat could make little headway against the strong current.* 2. progress toward some goal. *He is making some headway in cleaning his room.* {<u>hehd</u> way}

heal 🔁 *verb* (healed, healing, heals) 1. to make whole or healthy again; cure. *When I got hurt I was surprised at how quickly my body healed itself.* 2. to become healthy or whole again. *I'm glad to see that your cut is healing.* {<u>heel</u>} healer, n.

> **Homophone Note** The words *heal* and *heel*, and the contraction *he'll* (he will), sound alike but have different meanings.

health 🔁 ❶ *noun* 1. the condition of one's body or mind. *She was in bad health from years of smoking.* 2. the condition of being without sickness or pain; fit *You should eat well and exercise often to keep your health.* {<u>hehlth</u>}

health food *noun* food believed to be good for one's health. Health food is grown without chemicals and contains no additional substances. {<u>hehlth</u> foohd}

health·ful *adjective* good for the health. *Exercise and good foods are healthful.* {<u>hehlth</u> fəl} healthfully, adv., healthfulness, n.

health·y *adjective* (healthier, healthiest) 1. being free from sickness; well; fit. *Will you be healthy enough to play in the game tomorrow?* 2. having to do with a good mind and body. *Eating well every day is a healthy way to live.* 3. showing good mental or physical condition. *She has a healthy appetite for fruits and vegetables.* {<u>hehl</u> thee} healthily, adv., healthiness, n.

heap *noun* many things lying on top of each other; pile. *As she dumped her purse, all kinds of things fell out, landing in a heap on the table.* *verb* (heaped, heaping, heaps) 1. to put or form in a heap; pile up (often followed by "up" or "on"). *He heaped all his books on the desk.* 2. to be piled up; to be in one or more heaps (often followed by "up"). *The snow heaped up behind the fence.* 3. to give or fill in large amounts (usually followed by "on" or "upon"). *The teacher heaped praise upon her students. / I heaped up my plate with spaghetti.* 4. to fill or fill with too much. *He heaped the laundry basket with dirty clothes.* {<u>heep</u>}

hear 🔁 *verb* (heard, hearing, hears) 1. to receive sound with the ears. *Did you hear that noise?* 2. to receive a letter, phone call, or other information from another. *He heard from his sister yesterday.* 3. to be told about; learn. *I heard he was coming back to town.* 4. to listen carefully. *Please hear what I have to say.* {<u>heer</u>} hearer, n.

> **Homophone Note** Are you looking for the word *here* (in this place)? *Hear* and *here* sound alike but have different meanings.

heard *verb* past tense and past participle of **hear.** {<u>huhrd</u>}

hear·ing *noun* 1. the ability to hear or sense sound. *My grandfather's hearing is very bad, so I have to speak loudly to him.* 2. the chance to be heard. *He would not give me a hearing.* 3. a session in which arguments are presented, as in a court of law. *The judge agreed to give the woman a hearing in court.* 4. the distance over which one can hear or be heard. *He ran away and was soon out of hearing.* {<u>heer</u> ing}

hearing aid *noun* a small electronic device that makes sound louder and is worn to make poor hearing better. {<u>heer</u> ing ayd}

hear·say *noun* information heard from another person but not proved. *Do you know for a fact that she ran away from home, or is that just hearsay?* {<u>heer</u> say}

heart 🔁 *noun* 1. the organ that pumps blood through the body of a person or animal. 2. a person's truest feelings or personality. *In his heart he realized he was wrong.* 3. love or sympathy. *My grandmother has a big heart.* 4. the center of a place or thing. *Her office is in the heart of the city.* 5. energy and courage; spirit. *My pet dog has a lot of heart.* 6. anything shaped like the hearts on playing cards. *Her shirt was printed with red and green*

 Human Body   Human Mind  Everyday Life 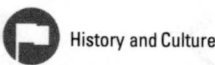 History and Culture  Communication

hearts. {**hart**}

• **by heart**

by memory. *She knows the song by heart.*

heart·beat *noun* a single complete pumping motion of a heart. {**hart** beet}

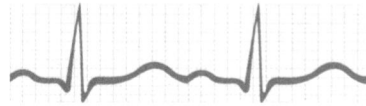

heart·bro·ken *adjective* filled with deep and sometimes lasting sorrow or grief. *She was heartbroken when her grandfather died.* {**hart** broh kən} heartbrokenly, adv.

hearth *noun* 1. the floor of a fireplace, or the stone or brick area in front of it. 2. the home, as a place of warmth. *My hearth was comfortable and cozy.* {**harth**}

heart·less *adjective* having or showing no kindness or sympathy; not sharing another's pain. *When I fell off my bike, my heartless brother told me to stop crying.* {**hart** lihs} heartlessly, adv., heartlessness, n.

heart·y *adjective* (heartier, heartiest) 1. full of warmth and enthusiasm; friendly. *His hearty welcome made us glad we had decided to visit.* 2. showing energy and enthusiasm. *When the play ended, the auditorium was filled with hearty applause. / Full of joy and energy, she let out a hearty yell.* 3. strong; sturdy. *She is a hearty woman who walks three miles every morning.* 4. large and filling; nourishing. *Before the hike, I ate a hearty breakfast.* {**har** tee}

heat 🌲🔬🌋 *noun* 1. a form of energy, or the state of being very warm; hotness; warmth. *We were warmed by the heat of the fire. / We like the heat of a summer day.* 2. depth of

feeling; passion. *I felt the heat of her anger after I broke her doll.* *verb* (heated, heating, heats) 1. to cause to become warm or hot (often followed by "up"). *We heated up the soup on the stove. / We heat our house with wood during the winter.* 2. to become warm or hot (often followed by "up"). *The room heated up after we turned on the furnace.* {**heet**}

heat·er *noun* a device that gives heat. Heaters are used to make water or the air in a building warmer. {**hee** tər}

heath *noun* an area of wild, flat land where only heather and other low plants grow. {**heeth**}

hea·then *noun* (heathens or heathen) someone who does not believe in the God of Christians, Jews, or Muslims. {**hee** thən} heathenish, adj., heathenism, n.

heath·er *noun* an evergreen plant that has tiny pink or purple flowers that are shaped like bells. {**hehth** ər}

heave *verb* (heaved, heaving, heaves) 1. to push up or out with great effort. *She heaved the heavy book onto the top shelf.* 2. to throw with great force. *The boy heaved the stone as hard as he could.* 3. to let out loudly or with difficulty. *She heaved a big sigh when the baby finally stopped crying.* 4. to throw up from one's stomach. *After eating grass, the dog heaved it up.* 5. to rise and fall heavily. *His chest heaved as he tried to catch his breath. / The boat heaved in the rough waves.* *noun* an act or instance of pulling hard. *Let's give one more heave to lift the box.* {**heev**}

heav·en *noun* 1. (usually plural) the sky, including the stars, sun, moon, and planets as seen from the earth. *It was a perfect night for gazing at the*

heavens. 2. the place where God or the gods live, in some religions. 3. a state or condition of great happiness. *It is heaven to see you again.* 4. (plural) an expression of surprise. *Heavens no, I don't want that one!* {**hehv** ən}

heav·en·ly *adjective* 1. having to do with heaven as in religion or the space above the earth. *I believe that angels are heavenly beings. / The stars, sun, and moon are heavenly bodies.* 2. wonderful or beautiful. *What heavenly weather!* {**hehv** ən lee}

heav·i·ly *adverb* 1. as if with a heavy weight. *The large man moves slowly and heavily.* 2. deeply or terribly. *Our team lost heavily in the last football season.* 3. in great amounts. *It snowed heavily last night.* 4. in a dense way; thickly. *The forest is heavily wooded.* {**hehv** ih lee}

heav·y *adjective* (heavier, heaviest) 1. having much weight or hard to lift. *We tried to lift the heavy box.* 2. of great size or amount. *There was a flood after the heavy rain.* 3. causing great concern; very serious. *We had to face a heavy problem.* 4. very sad; weighed down. *I went to bed with a heavy heart after my dog died.* {**hehv** ee}

He·brew *noun* 1. a member of the group of people who descend from the Jewish tribes written about in the Old Testament of the Bible. 2. the language of the ancient Hebrews, now the official language of Israel. *adjective* of the Hebrews. {**hee** brooh}

בָּרוּכִים הַבָּאִים לְבֵיתִי

 Living World   Physical World    Natural Environment   Economy   Government and Law

heck·le *verb* (heckled, heckling, heckles) to bother a public speaker or performer by saying rude things or asking annoying questions. *The mayor did not seem angry when the man in the audience heckled him by shouting during his speech.* {<u>hehk</u> əl} heckler, n.

hec·tare *noun* a unit of area equal to 10,000 square meters or 2.471 acres, used to measure land. {<u>hehk</u> tər}

hec·tic *adjective* marked by hurry, confusion, and too much activity. *We had a very hectic day getting ready for the big party.* {<u>hehk</u> tihk} hectically, adv., hecticness, n.

he'd shortened form of "he had" or "he would." *He'd already eaten. / He'd like to come with us.* {heed}

Homophone Note Are you looking for the word *heed* (to pay attention to)? *He'd* and *heed* sound alike but have different meanings.

hedge *noun* a solid row of bushes, used as a kind of fence. *verb* (hedged, hedging, hedges) 1. to close in or mark off with a hedge; border (usually followed by "in"). *Tall weeds hedged in the playing field on three sides.* 2. to avoid saying what one thinks or will do by not answering directly. *I hedged when he invited me to join the team by saying that I'd have to ask my parents.* {hehj}

hedge·hog *noun* 1. a very small animal with a pointed nose and a very short tail. Hedgehogs have brown and yellow fur with spines that stick out and protect them when they roll into a ball. They make tunnels in rows of bushes called hedges. Hedgehogs are insectivores; they are mammals that eat insects. Different kinds of hedgehogs live in Europe, Asia, and Africa. 2. another name for the American porcupine, a kind of rodent. {<u>hehj</u> hŏg or <u>hehj</u> hawg}

heed *verb* (heeded, heeding, heeds) to give one's attention to; listen to; take notice of. *I was glad he heeded my warning that the plate was hot and didn't burn himself.* *noun* careful notice or attention. *I paid heed to the weather report and wore shorts.* {heed} heeder, n., heedful, adj., heedfully, adv., heedfulness, n.

Homophone Note Are you looking for *he'd* (contraction of he had or he would)? *Heed* and *he'd* sound alike but have different meanings.

heel *noun* 1. the rounded, back part of the human foot, or a part like it in an animal. 2. the part of a shoe that supports the back part of a human foot. 3. the end piece of something. *I cut off the heel of the loaf of bread.* *verb* (heeled, heeling, heels) 1. to provide with heels. *The man at the shoe repair shop heeled my old boots.* 2. to follow closely behind. *The dog heeled at its owner's command.* {heel}

• **at one's heels** following closely. *John was at my heels for most of the race.*

• **kick up one's heels** to have a merry time. *We really kicked up our heels at the party last night.*

Homophone Note The words *heel*, *heal*, and the contraction *he'll*, sound alike, but each has a different meaning.

heif·er *noun* a young cow that has not had a calf. {<u>hehf</u> ər}

height *noun* 1. the distance from the bottom to the top. *The height of that pine tree is fifteen feet.* 2. how tall a person is. *My height right now is five feet.* 3. the peak or highest point. *At its height, that building seems to touch the clouds.* 4. the highest point or degree. *She's at the height of her success. / At the height of the sale, there were hundreds of people shopping.* 5. (often plural) a high place from which one can look out. *From the heights of that hill one can see the whole town. / I looked down at the street below from the heights of the skyscraper.* {hiyt}

height·en *verb* (heightened, heightening, heightens) 1. to make higher. *I heightened the basketball hoop by raising the pole.* 2. to make stronger or more intense; add to. *A drum roll heightened the excitement as we waited for the acrobats to do their most daring trick.* 3. to become stronger or greater in degree. *The more he thought about how unfair his parents*

had been, the more his anger heightened. {**hiy** tən}

Heim·lich ma·neu·ver *noun* an emergency technique used to save a person choking on something, such as food. One must stand behind the person choking and wrap one's arms around the person, just below the rib cage. One then presses hard in an upward movement to force air from the lungs. The rush of air should eject the object. {**hiym** lihk mo **nooh** vər}

heir *noun* a person who receives or has the right to receive another person's property or title after that person's death. *I am the heir to my grand-mother's house. / As the king's heir, the prince knew that he would one day be king.* {**ayr**} heirless, adj.

Homophone Note The words *heir*, *air*, and *ere* sound alike but have different meanings.

heir·ess *noun* a female who has the right to or has received the money or property of a person who has died. *She was the heiress to a large fortune and lived in a very fancy house.* {**ayr** ihs}

heir·loom *noun* an object passed down through gener-ations of a family. *This teapot is an heirloom passed down from my great grand-mother.* {**ayr** loohm}

held *verb* past tense and past participle of **hold**. {**hehld**}

hel·i·cop·ter *noun* a type of aircraft that is held in the air and moved

along by spinning blades attached to its top side. {**hehl** ə **kŏp** tər}

he·li·um *noun* a gas that is one of the chemical elements. It is used to fill balloons and blimps because it is lighter than air. (symbol: He) {**heel** ee əm}

he'll shortened form of "he will." *He'll do the dishes tonight.* {**heel**}

Homophone Note The con-traction *he'll*, and the words *heal* and *heel* sound alike, but each has a different meaning.

hell *noun* 1. the place where evil spirits live and where wicked people are punished after death, according to the Bible. 2. a condition or place of great pain and suffering. *He went through hell as a pris-oner of war.* {**hehl**}

Word History *Hell* comes from an Old English word that means "place of the dead."

hel·lo *interjection* a word used as a greeting, statement of sur-prise, or call for attention. *Hello! It's great to see you!* *noun* (hellos) the word "hello" used in greeting. *I gave her a hello as we passed in the street.* {heh **loh** or hə **loh**, intj., heh **loh** or hə **loh**, n.}

helm *noun* a wheel or lever used for steering a ship. *When the captain let me stand at the ship's helm, I asked if I could steer.* {**hehlm**}

hel·met *noun* a hard covering worn to protect the head. {**hehl** miht} hel-meted, adj., hel-metlike, adj.

help *verb* (helped, helping, helps) 1. to aid or assist. *I helped my mother set the table.* 2. to avoid or keep from (usually used with

"can" or "cannot"). *I could not help noticing that his socks didn't match. / Don't walk those streets at night if you can help it.* 3. to take for oneself. *Help yourself to the pie. noun* 1. the act of giving assis-tance. *When they had a lot of planting to do, she offered her help.* 2. one who gives assis-tance. *She is a big help to her mother.* 3. a worker or group of workers. The word "help" is often used for maids, cooks, and servants. *He gave the help a day off. interjection* used to express trouble; a signal for rescue. *Help! I'm drowning!* {**hehlp**}

Synonyms
These words share a meaning with *help*, noun 1:
service, aid, assistance

help·ful *adjective* giving help or aid. *I wish you would be more helpful around the house.* {**hehlp** fəl} helpfully, adv., helpfulness, n.

help·ing *noun* a normal amount of food served to a person at one meal. *You've had your helping of ice cream tonight.* {**hehl** ping}

help·ing verb *noun* another name for **auxiliary verb**. {**hehlp** əng vərb}

help·less *adjective* 1. unable to take care of oneself. *My baby sister is helpless and can't feed or change herself.* 2. without power or control. *We knew we were helpless in our small boat during the big storm.* {**hehlp** lihs} helplessly, adv., helplessness, n.

Hel·sin·ki *noun* the capital city of Finland. Helsinki is a sea-port city. {**hehl** **sing** kee}

hem *verb* (hemmed, hemming, hems) to fold and sew down the edge of. *I hemmed my pants because they were too long. noun* an edge of a dress,

a
b
c
d
e
f
g
h
i
j
k
l
m
n
o
p
q
r
s
t
u
v
w
x
y
z

curtain, or something else made of cloth, when it has been folded back and sewn down. *I tore the hem of my skirt when I fell.* {<u>hehm</u>} hemmer, n.

hem·i·sphere *noun* 1. either of two halves of the earth. A hemisphere is formed by dividing the earth into the Northern and Southern Hemispheres at the equator, or into the Eastern and Western Hemispheres at a meridian. *North and South America are in the Western Hemisphere.* 2. a half of any sphere. *If you cut that ball in half, you will have two hemispheres.* {<u>hehm</u> ihs **feer**}

hem·lock *noun* 1. an evergreen tree of North America that has short needles and small cones, or the wood of this tree. 2. a poisonous plant that has a hollow stem and small white flowers. {<u>hehm</u> lŏk}

hemp *noun* 1. a tall plant first found in Asia. Hemp is an important source of fiber for rope and coarse cloth. 2. the fiber made from the stem of this plant. {<u>hehmp</u>} hemplike, adj.

hen *noun* an adult female chicken or the female of other closely related birds, such as turkeys, pheasants, and peacocks. {<u>hehn</u>} hen-like, adj.

hence *adverb* 1. from this moment; from now. *Two years hence they will meet again.* 2. for this reason; therefore; thus. *He exercises and eats well and hence is healthy.* {<u>hehns</u>}

her *pronoun* 1. the female person or animal already talked about (a form of "she" used after an object of a verb or preposition). *Please don't tell her what I said. / I went with her to the store.* 2. belonging to or having to do with a female person or animal already talked about. *Her story made me cry.* {<u>huhr</u>}

He·ra *noun* the goddess of marriage in Greek mythology. Hera was the wife and sister of Zeus, ruler of the gods. In Roman mythology, Hera is called Juno. {<u>hehr</u> ə}

herb ❶ *noun* 1. a flowering plant whose stem is soft rather than woody and that dies at the end of a growing season. 2. any of these plants that have value as medicine, as an aroma, or as a way to add flavor to food. {<u>uhrb</u> *or* <u>huhrb</u>}

her·bi·vore ❶ *noun* an animal that only feeds on plants. {<u>huhr</u> bih **vohr** *or* <u>uhr</u> bih **vohr**}

her·biv·o·rous *adjective* eating only plants; feeding on plants. *Cows, horses, and rabbits are all herbivorous mammals.* {hər <u>**bih**</u> və rəs *or* ər <u>**bih**</u> və rəs} herbivorously, adv.

Her·cu·les *noun* a hero in Greek and Roman mythology. Hercules was half man and half god and known for his amazing strength. {<u>huhr</u> kyə **leez**}

herd ❶ *noun* 1. any group of cattle or wild animals that feed and travel together. *We waited for the herd of cows to cross the road.* 2. the common people; most people. The expression "He (or she) follows the herd" means that a person tends to do what everybody else does, like a cow in a herd, and does not think for himself or herself.

verb (herded, herding, herds) 1. to gather or come together as a herd. *The children herded into the cafeteria.* 2. to drive or lead a herd of. *He herded the cattle into the pasture.* {<u>huhrd</u>}

Homophone Note Are you looking for the word **heard**? **Herd** and **heard** sound alike but have different meanings.

here *adverb* 1. in, at, or to this specific place or location. *The guests are here. / Will you please come here so that I can talk to you?* 2. at this point in time; now. *Here he laughed.* *noun* this place or moment. *Here in my room is where I feel most at home. / Here is where the video ends.* *interjection* used to get attention or offer help. *Here, let me take your coat. / Here, kitty, kitty.* {<u>heer</u>}

Homophone Note Are you looking for the word **hear** (to receive sound)? **Here** and **hear** sound alike but have different meanings.

here·af·ter *adverb* after this; from this point on. *I am too old for that silly name and, hereafter, please don't call me that!* {<u>heer</u> **ăf** tər}

here·by *adverb* by this means; at this moment. *As he placed a pin on my shirt, the president of the club said, "I hereby make you a member."* {<u>heer</u> **biy**}

 Human Body   Human Mind   Everyday Life  History and Culture  Communication

he·red·i·tar·y *adjective* 1. having to do with characteristics that are passed or could be passed from parent to offspring. *My red hair and blue eyes are hereditary. / Doctors like to know your family history because some illnesses are hereditary.* 2. having to do with money, property, or title that is inherited by law. *He spent all of his hereditary wealth and had to get a job.* {hə **reh** dih **tayr** ee} hereditarily, adv.

he·red·i·ty *noun* (heredities) 1. the passing of characteristics from parent to offspring. *It is because of heredity that the boy looks like his father.* 2. the characteristics passed on in this way. *The boy's pointed nose and green eyes are part of his heredity from his mother.* {hə **reh** dih tee}

here's shortened form of "here is." *Here's the key to my house.* {heerz}

her·it·age *noun* something that one believes, thinks, or does that comes from one's family or ethnic background; tradition. *I think my love of freedom is part of my African heritage.* {**hehr** ih tihj}

Her·mes *noun* the messenger of the gods, in Greek mythology. Hermes was also the god of travelers, of trade, of theft, and of skill in speaking. He is often shown with wings on his hat and shoes. In Roman mythology, Hermes is called Mercury. {**huhr** meez}

her·mit *noun* a person who lives alone and away from others. Often a person becomes a hermit in order to lead a religious life. {**huhr** miht} hermitic, adj.

he·ro *noun* (heroes) 1. a person who is brave, good, and often looked up to by others. *After climbing the tree to save his neighbor's cat, the boy was called a hero.* 2. the main male character of a play, poem, story, or book. *The Harry Potter books are about my favorite hero.* {**heer** oh}

he·ro·ic *adjective* 1. of or having to do with a hero or heroes. *The firefighter had a heroic life.* 2. like a hero; noble and courageous. *Jumping into the river to save the boy was a heroic deed.* 3. having to do with literature about a hero. *He liked to read heroic poems.* {hə **roh** ihk} heroically, adv.

her·o·in *noun* a drug made from a substance found in certain plants. Heroin is addictive and harmful. It is against the law to make, use, or possess heroin in the United States. {**hehr** oh ihn}

her·o·ine *noun* 1. a woman who is looked up to for her good character or fine actions. *The woman who set up the food kitchen for the poor was a heroine.* 2. the main female character in a play, poem, story, or book. *In this book, the heroine fights the dragon and saves the prince.* {**hehr** oh ihn}

her·on *noun* a wading bird with long legs, a long neck, and a long pointed bill. An egret is a kind of heron. {**hehr** ən}

her·ring *noun* (herring or herrings) a small fish that lives in northern waters. Herring are used for food. {**hayr** ing}

hers *pronoun* that or those belonging to her. "Hers" is a possessive form of "she." *You should use hers, not mine. / My flowers are nice, but hers are nicer.* {**huhrz**}

her·self *pronoun* 1. her own self (used to show that an action is done to the same female who carries out the action). *She watched herself in the mirror.* 2. the same female person. *She herself did all the chores.* 3. in her normal, healthy, or usual condition. *She is not herself today.* {hər **sehlf**}

he's shortened form of "he is" or "he has." *He's my best friend. / He's seen that movie three times!* {**heez**}

hes·i·tant *adjective* not feeling sure; in doubt. *I want to go to the party, but I'm hesitant because I won't know anyone there.* {**hehz** ih tənt} hesitantly, adv.

hes·i·tate *verb* (hesitated, hesitating, hesitates) 1. to stop or pause because of not feeling sure. *My dog hesitated when I gave him a command he did not know.* 2. to be slow to act because of not feeling very sure or willing. *He hesitated to try out for the football team because he had heard how much they practice.* {**hehz** ih **tayt**} hesitatingly, adv.

Word History *Hesitate* is from a Latin word that means "to stick, cling, or hold back."

hes·i·ta·tion *noun* the action of hesitating. *I noticed the shy boy's hesitation to join in the fun.* {**hehz** ih **tay** shən}

A B C D E F G H I J K L M N O P Q R S T U V W X Y Z

a
b
c
d
e
f
g
h
i
j
k
l
m
n
o
p
q
r
s
t
u
v
w
x
y
z

hex·a·gon *noun* a flat, closed figure with six straight sides. {**hehks** ə gŏn}

hey *interjection* a word used to draw attention or to show surprise, mild delight, or anger. *Hey! I'm right over here. / Hey! What are you doing in my room?* {**hay**}

Homophone Note Are you looking for the word *hay* (animal food)? *Hey* and *hay* sound alike but have different meanings.

Hg symbol of the chemical element mercury.

hi *interjection* (informal) "Hello!" *Hi! It's so nice to see you!* {**hiy**}

Homophone Note Are you looking for the word *high*? *Hi* and *high* sound alike but have different meanings.

HI *abbreviation* an abbreviation for **Hawaii.**

hi·ber·nate *verb* (hibernated, hibernating, hibernates) to sleep through the winter in a den or burrow to save energy. Bears, snakes, and certain other animals hibernate. *When the bear hibernates, does he wake up hungry?* {**hiy** bər **nayt**} hibernation, n., hibernator, n.

hic·cup or **hiccough** *noun* 1. a sudden, quick taking in of breath that is not done on purpose. A hiccup is caused when the muscles used to breathe tighten up. 2. (plural) the state of having one hiccup after another. *He gets the hiccups whenever he drinks soda.* *verb* (hiccupped or hiccoughed, hiccupping or hiccoughing, hiccups or hiccoughs) to make a hiccup or the sound of one. *She hiccupped so loud everyone turned to look.* {**hihk** uhp}

hick·o·ry *noun* (hickories) 1. a tree of the walnut family, found mostly in North America. The hickory has nuts that can be eaten and wood that is hard and useful. 2. the wood of a hickory tree, or a rod made of this wood for use as a walking stick or whip. {**hihk** ə ree}

hid *verb* past tense and a past participle of **hide.** {**hihd**}

hide[1] *verb* (hid, hidden or hid, hiding, hides) 1. to put or hold out of sight; keep from view. *Did you hide the present under the bed?* 2. to keep as a secret. *He hid the truth from his parents.* 3. to make or keep oneself out of view. *The child hid from his father.* {**hiyd**}

hide[2] *noun* the skin of one of the larger animals such as a buffalo or cow. {**hiyd**}

hide-and-seek *noun* a children's game in which one player tries to find the others, who are hiding. {**hiyd** ənd **seek**}

hid·e·ous *adjective* looking very ugly or frightening; disgusting. *In the book, a hideous monster hid under the bridge. / Mom bought me a hideous dress.* {**hih** dee əs} hideously, adv., hideousness, n.

hide·out *noun* a place where a person can hide from the police or other people. *The policeman found the bank robbers in their hideout.* {**hiyd** owt}

hi·er·o·gly·ph·ic *adjective* having to do with writing that uses pictures and symbols to stand for words or sounds. *noun* a picture or symbol that stands for a word or sound; single

hieroglyphic symbol. *Hieroglyphics were used by the ancient Egyptians.* {**hiy** ər oh **glihf** ihk} hieroglyphical, adj., hieroglyphically, adv.

high *adjective* (higher, highest) 1. reaching up a great distance; tall. *We had a great view from the top of the high cliff.* 2. at a given distance from the ground. *That branch is fifteen feet high.* 3. above what is usual. *The train traveled at a high speed.* 4. raised in pitch. *He has a high voice. / It is hard for me to sing the high notes.* 5. important, serious, or dignified in nature. *Our teacher holds us to high standards of behavior. / My brother is a person of high ideals.* *adverb* (higher, highest) in or to a high position or place. *The bird flew high in the sky.* *noun* something that is high, such as an amount or a person's spirits. *Gas prices reached a new high this summer. / My brother is on a high because he got all A's and B's this year.* {**hiy**}

Homophone Note The words *high* and *hi* (a greeting) sound alike but have different meanings.

high jump *noun* a contest in which each person jumps over a bar which is raised after each successful jump. {**hiy** juhmp} high jumper, n.

high·land *noun* 1. land that is higher than the area around it. 2. (plural) a part or region of a country that has many hills or mountains. *We climbed several mountains on our visit to the Scottish highlands.* {**hiy** lənd}

high·ly *adverb* 1. in a way that shows praise or respect. *He speaks highly of his math teacher.* 2. to a great degree. *Firefighting is a highly dan-*

 Human Body
 Human Mind
Everyday Life
 History and Culture
Communication

gerous job. 3. at a high cost. *Many doctors are highly paid.* {<u>hiy</u> lee}

high·ness *noun* (capital) a title of honor used when speaking to or about a royal person. (usually preceded by "His", "Her", or "Your"). *We are pleased to serve you, your Highness.* {<u>hiy</u> nihs}

high-rise *noun* a tall building that has many stories. {<u>hiyr</u> iyz}

high school *noun* a school that begins with grades nine or ten and ends with grade twelve. {<u>hiy</u> skoohl} high-school, adj.

high seas *noun* the area of a sea or ocean outside the control of any country. {<u>hiy</u> <u>seez</u>} high-sea, adj.

high-strung *adjective* very nervous; easily upset; usually tense. *It's not a good idea to choose a high-strung horse when you are first learning to ride.* {<u>hiy</u> strung}

high tide *noun* the highest point reached by a tide, or the time of day when this happens. *The ship sets sail at high tide, when the water in the bay is deepest.* {<u>hiy</u> tiyd}

high·way ◐ *noun* any main road where one can travel at a high speed. {<u>hiy</u> way}

high·way·man *noun* (highwaymen) someone who robbed people travelling on roads in the 1700s and 1800s. Highwaymen usually rode horses and held up people riding in coaches. {<u>hiy</u> way mən *or* <u>hiy</u> way măn}

hi·jack *verb* (hijacked, hijacking, hijacks) to take control of an airplane or other vehicle by force. People who hijack airplanes often demand things in return for returning the vehicle and letting the

people on it go free. {<u>hiy</u> jăk} hijacker, n.

hike *verb* (hiked, hiking, hikes) to take a long walk in the country for fun, exercise, or training. *We hiked in the forest near our house.* *noun* a long walk in the country for fun, exercise, or training. *We took a hike along the lake.* {<u>hiyk</u>} hiker, n.

• **take a hike**
(slang) to leave because one is not wanted.

hi·lar·i·ous *adjective* very funny. *We all laughed at the hilarity story.* {hihl <u>ayr</u> ee əs} hilariously, adv., hilariousness, n.

hill *noun* 1. a raised area of land smaller than a mountain. *We live on the other side of that hill.* 2. a small pile or heap. *Look at all of those ant hills in the yard.* {<u>hihl</u>}

hill·side *noun* the side of a hill. {<u>hihl</u> siyd}

hill·top *noun* the highest part of a hill. {<u>hihl</u> tŏp}

hilt *noun* the handle of a sword or knife. {<u>hihlt</u>}

• **to the hilt**
as much as possible; completely. *I will defend you to the hilt.*

him *pronoun* the male person or animal already talked about (a form of "he" used after an object of a verb or preposition). *Can we see him?* / *Please walk with him to the car.* {<u>hihm</u>}

Homophone Note Are you looking for the word *hymn* (a song)? *Him* and *hymn* sound alike but have different meanings.

Him·a·la·yas *plural noun* the highest mountain range in the world, located between India and Tibet. {hihm ə <u>lay</u> əz}

him·self *pronoun* 1. his own self (used to show that an action is done to the same male who does that action). *He shot himself by accident.* 2. the same male person. *He himself finished all of the chores.* 3. in his normal, healthy, or usual condition. *Since he got sick, he just hasn't been himself.* {hihm <u>sehlf</u>}

hind *adjective* at or near the back; rear. *The poodle stood on its hind paws and begged.* {<u>hiy</u>nd}

hin·der *verb* (hindered, hindering, hinders) to hold back or stop the progress of. *Heavy chains hindered the elephant's movements.* {<u>hihn</u> dər}

Hin·di *noun* the official language of India. {<u>hihn</u> dee}

hin·drance *noun* someone or something that slows or stops progress. *His lack of effort was a hindrance to our plans.* {<u>hihn</u> drəns}

Hin·du·ism *noun* the main religion of India, which has many gods that are part of the same supreme being. Hinduism has a strict system of social classes and a belief that the soul can be born again after death into a different body. {<u>hihn</u> dooh ih zəm}

hinge *noun* a device on a door, window, or lid made of two pieces connected so that one piece can open, close, or swing upon the other. *verb* (hinged, hinging, hinges) 1. to supply or join with a

A B C D E F G H I J K L M N O P Q R S T U V W X Y Z

a
b
c
d
e
f
g
h
i
j
k
l
m
n
o
p
q
r
s
t
u
v
w
x
y
z

hinge. *He hinged the door to the door frame.* 2. to depend (usually followed by "on" or "upon"). *Our success hinges upon our hard work.* {**hihnj**} hingelike, adj.

hint *noun* a sign or suggestion that is not made in a direct way. *Give me a hint of where to look.* *verb* (hinted, hinting, hints) to mention or suggest in a way that is not direct. *She hinted that she wanted a new pair of shoes.* {**hihnt**} hintingly, adv.

hip *noun* the part on either side of the body between the waist and the thigh. {**hihp**} hipless, adj., hiplike, adj.

hip·bone *noun* the three joined bones that form one side of the skeleton from the upper thigh to the waist. {**hihp bohn**}

hip·po *noun* (hippos) a short form of hippopotamus. {**hih poh**}

hip·po·pot·a·mus *noun* (hippopotamuses or hippopotami) a very large, round mammal that has short legs with hooves and thick skin with almost no hair. Hippopotamuses live in or near rivers and lakes of tropical Africa. They eat plants. {**hihp** ə **pŏt** ə məs}

Word History *Hippopotamus* comes from the ancient Greek word for this animal, which means "horse of the river."

hire *verb* (hired, hiring, hires) 1. to take on as a worker for money or other reward. *We hired a crew to paint the house.* 2. to have the use of in return for a payment of money. *We hired the concert hall for the*

evening. *noun* the fact or condition of being hired. *We paid for the hire of a car for the weekend.* {**hiyr**} hirable (hireable), adj., hirer, n.

• **for hire**
available for service or use in return for a payment of money. *There are boats for hire at the dock.*

his *pronoun* that or those which belong to him. *The shirt is his. / His idea was the best.* {**hihz**}

His·pan·ic *adjective* 1. Spanish or of Spanish descent or origin. 2. Latin American. *noun* a person of Latin American or Spanish origin who lives in the United States. {**hih spăn** ihk}

hiss *verb* (hissed, hissing, hisses) 1. to make a sound as if holding an "s" for a long time. *The snakes hiss. / Air hissed from the tire.* 2. to show dislike by hissing. *We hissed at the other team.* 3. to say or express disapproval of with a hiss. *The crowd hissed its anger. / The audience hissed the actor.* *noun* a sound like an "s" held for a long time. *We knew there was a snake in the room when we heard a hiss.* {**hihs**} hisser, n., hissingly, adv.

his·to·ri·an *noun* one who writes about or is an expert on history. {**hih stohr** ee ən}

his·tor·ic *adjective* important in history. *We still talk about the historic election of 2000.* {**hih stohr** ihk}

his·tor·i·cal *adjective* 1. of or having to do with history. *We wrote an historical report on the Civil War.* 2. based upon history. *We watched a historical play about the Salem witch hunt.* {**hih stohr** ih kəl} historically, adv., historicalness, n.

his·to·ry ● *noun* (histories) 1. everything that has happened in the past to someone

or something. *He wrote a history of the Vietnam War.* 2. the field of knowledge that is concerned with past events. *History is my favorite subject in school.* 3. the written record of things that happened in the past. *Abraham Lincoln was a famous president in United States history.* 4. an interesting record of past events, especially having to do with a person, place, thing, or family. *Their family farm has quite a history.* {**hihs** tə ree *or* **hih** stree}

Word History *History* comes from a Latin word for "story," "tale," or "account."

hit *verb* (hit, hitting, hits) 1. to give a blow or stroke to; strike. *He hit the ground with a stick.* 2. to come in contact with. *The stone hit the window.* 3. to drive or send by striking. *He hit the golf ball with the club.* 4. to reach or get to. *The car hit its top speed.* 5. to find, meet with, or discover. *I hit some trouble in that math problem.* 6. to have a strong effect on. *Her leaving town hit me hard.* *noun* 1. a blow or stroke. *The boxer took three hits to the stomach.* 2. someone or something that is very popular. *The young piano player was a hit with the audience. / The movie was a big hit.* 3. the batter's successful contact with the ball so as to reach a base in a baseball game. *He got a base hit.* {**hiht**} hitless, adj., hitter, n.

hitch *verb* (hitched, hitching, hitches) 1. to join or fasten with a rope or straps. *The farmer hitched the ox to the plow.* 2. to pull with a quick jerk (usually followed by "up"). *He hitched up his bathing trunks.* 3. to be caught, fastened, or tangled

 Human Body Human Mind Everyday Life  History and Culture   Communication

in. My *sleeve hitched on the nail.* noun 1. any of several knots used for hitching. *The scouts learned to tie a clove hitch and a half hitch.* 2. a delay or obstacle; catch. *The party went on without a hitch.* 3. a jerk or pull, especially upward. *He gave his pants a hitch.* {<u>hihch</u>}

hitch·hike verb (hitchhiked, hitchhiking, hitchhikes) to try to get, or to get, a free ride in a vehicle. *We hitchhiked to get home after our car broke down.* {<u>hihch</u> hiyk} hitchhiker, n.

hive noun 1. something built for or by bees to live in. *We gathered honey from the hive.* 2. the colony of bees that lives in such a thing. *The hive began to swarm out of the old tree.* {<u>hiyv</u>}

hives plural noun (used with a singular or plural verb) a mild disease that causes small bumps on the skin that itch. Hives are often the result of an allergy. {<u>hiyvz</u>}

hoard noun a collection or supply of something that is hidden or stored in order to have it available in the future. *Our family keeps a hoard of food in the basement in case of disaster.* verb (hoarded, hoarding, hoards) to collect or save up as a hoard. *A squirrel hoards nuts to eat in winter.* {<u>hohrd</u>} hoarder, n.

Homophone Note Are you looking for the word **horde** (large number)? **Hoard** and **horde** sound alike but have different meanings.

hoarse adjective (hoarser, hoarsest) 1. having a rough and weak sound because of illness or too much use. *His voice was hoarse after giving a long speech.* 2. having such a voice. *He was hoarse after yelling for the dog.* {<u>hohrs</u>} hoarsely, adv., hoarseness, n.

Homophone Note The words **hoarse** and **horse** (an animal) sound alike but have different meanings.

hoax noun 1. an act meant to trick or deceive. *He used a hoax to make us feel sorry for him.* 2. something false or fake presented as true or real. *The photograph of giant footprints was a hoax that many people believed was real.* {<u>hohks</u>} hoaxer, n.

hob·ble verb (hobbled, hobbling, hobbles) 1. to walk with trouble or in an awkward manner; limp. *He hobbled after breaking his leg.* 2. to cause to limp; make lame. *A pulled muscle hobbled the runner.* 3. to control by tying a rope or strap around two legs of. *We hobbled the horses to stop them from running away.* noun 1. a walk that is not smooth and steady; limp. *I walked with a hobble because of my sprained ankle.* 2. a rope or strap used to hobble an animal. {<u>hŏb</u> əl} hobbler, n., hobblingly, adv.

hob·by noun (hobbies) an interest or activity that one does for pleasure in one's spare time. *His favorite hobby is taking pictures with an old camera.* {<u>hŏb</u> ee} hobbyist, n.

Ho Chi Minh City noun the largest city in Vietnam. Ho Chi Minh City used to be called Saigon. Saigon was formerly the capital of South Vietnam. {hoh chee mihn <u>sih</u> tee}

hock·ey ⊙ noun 1. a sport played on ice, with two teams of six skating players; ice hockey. Each team tries to

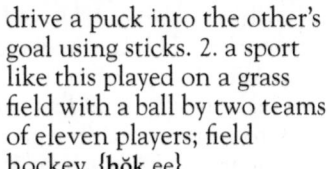

drive a puck into the other's goal using sticks. 2. a sport like this played on a grass field with a ball by two teams of eleven players; field hockey. {<u>hŏk</u> ee}

hoe noun a garden tool with a thin, flat blade at the end of a long handle. It is used for breaking up the soil and removing weeds. verb (hoed, hoeing, hoes) to use a hoe on; dig or weed. {<u>hoh</u>} hoer, n.

hog noun 1. an adult pig raised for meat. Hogs weigh well over 100 pounds. 2. any member of the pig family, such as the wild boar. 3. a person who is greedy or dirty. verb (hogged, hogging, hogs) to take more of than is fair; to take too much of. *He hogged all the butter.* {<u>hŏg</u> or <u>hawg</u>, n., <u>hŏg</u> or <u>hawg</u>, v.} hoglike, adj.

• **go whole hog** (informal) to do something as completely as possible, without holding back.

• **live high on the hog** to live in a way that shows that you spend a lot of money. *Our neighbors lived high on the hog after they won the lottery.*

ho·gan noun a type of house built by the Navajo and other Native American people. A hogan is made of earth walls supported by logs. {<u>hoh</u> gən}

hoist verb (hoisted, hoisting, hoists) to lift or haul up using a mechanical device. *He hoisted the flag to the top of the pole.* noun ropes and pulleys, or an elevator, used for lifting heavy or large loads. *We used a hoist to lift the bathtub to the second floor.* {<u>hoist</u>} hoister, n.

hold[1] verb (held, holding, holds) 1. to have or contain

A
B
C
D
E
F
G
H
I
J
K
L
M
N
O
P
Q
R
S
T
U
V
W
X
Y
Z

 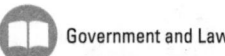

within one's hand. *I picked up a cricket and held it gently.* 2. to keep for a certain time. *Hold this letter until I return.* 3. to contain within a particular area. *The theater holds two hundred people.* 4. to keep by using force. *The pirates held the sailors as prisoners.* 5. to organize and carry on; have; conduct. *Let's hold a meeting.* 6. to exercise control over. *She held her temper even though she was mad at her brother.* 7. to have in one's mind; to believe. *He holds odd ideas.* 8. to keep the interest of. *Her speech held the audience.* 9. to keep to a particular position, condition, or course. *Hold still until I tell you to move. / Hold to the main road.* 10. to remain in force. *That rule about parking holds on weekends only.* *noun* 1. the act of taking or carrying with the hand; grasp; grip. *I dropped the table because I couldn't get a good hold on it.* 2. something to grasp, such as a handle or other support. *When you climb a cliff, you must find holds for your hands and your feet.* 3. the power to keep control over. *She has a hold on me.* {hohld}

• **hold out**
1. to stand firm and not give in; resist. *The union held out for higher pay.* 2. to continue; last; endure. *Our water will hold out for two days. / We cannot hold out for long in the desert without more water.*

• **hold up**
1. to keep from falling; support. *Your neck holds up your head.* 2. to stop or delay. *The passing of a long train held up traffic.* 3. to last or continue. *The tires on the car did not hold up well.* 4. to rob using a gun. *A gang of men held up the jewelry store.*

hold² *noun* the space inside a ship used to store things. *The hold was filled with several tons of coal.* {hohld}

hold·er *noun* 1. an object used for holding. *This new car has five drink holders.* 2. one who owns or has the use of something. *He is the holder of a college diploma.* {hohl dər}

hold·up *noun* 1. a stop or delay in the progress of something. *There was a traffic holdup during rush hour.* 2. a robbery by someone using a gun. *The police arrested a man for the holdup at the store.* {hohld uhp}

hole *noun* 1. an opening or hollow cavity in something. *We dug a small hole for the seeds.* 2. an animal's burrow. *Some snakes live in holes in the ground.* 3. a mistake or weak point; fault. *There is a hole in his theory about what the moon is made of.* {hohl}

Homophone Note The words *hole* and *whole* (entire) sound alike but have different meanings.

hol·i·day *noun* a day on which most people do not work in honor or celebration of some person or event. *Thanksgiving and New Year's Day are two holidays.* {hŏl ih day}

hol·land *noun* linen or cotton cloth, often glazed, used to make window shades, upholstery, and clothing. {hahl ənd}

Hol·land *noun* see Netherlands. {hahl ənd}

hol·ler *verb* (hollered, hollering, hollers) (informal) to cry out, yell, or shout. *His mother hollered at him to come home for dinner.* *noun* (informal) a loud cry, yell, or shout. *We gave a holler to the people on the shore when the boat tipped over.* {hahl ər}

hol·low *adjective* (hollower, hollowest) 1. having an empty space on the inside; not solid within. *That kind of flower has a hollow stem.* 2. curving in or down; concave. *We hid in a hollow place in the ground. / The hungry child has hollow cheeks.* 3. dull or deep in tone. *I heard a hollow sound when I banged on the door.* *noun* 1. an empty space inside something; hole; cavity; gap. *We hid a dollar in a hollow in the wall.* 2. a low area of land; a small valley. *Our home was in the hollow, surrounded by hills.* *verb* (hollowed, hollowing, hollows) 1. to make hollow (often followed by "out"). *We hollowed out a tree trunk to use as a boat.* 2. to shape or form by making a material hollow (often followed by "out"). *He hollowed a figure of a dog out of a block of wood.* {hahl oh} hollowly, adv., hollowness, n.

hol·ly *noun* (hollies) 1. a type of bush or tree with small white flowers, red berries, and shiny green leaves with sharp, pointed edges. 2. the leaves and berries of this plant used for Christmas decorations. {hahl ee}

hol·ly·hock *noun* a common garden plant that has tall stalks covered with bright flowers. {hahl ee hŏk}

hol·o·caust *noun* 1. a great destruction by fire. *During the cold war, many people feared a nuclear holocaust.* 2. (capitalized) the killing of millions of Jews by Nazis during the Second World War. *The Holocaust is remembered as one of history's most terrible crimes against humanity.* {hahl

 Human Body   Human Mind   Everyday Life    History and Culture   Communication

ə **kawst** or **hoh** lə **kawst**} holo-caustal, adj., holocaustic, adj.

Word History *Holocaust* comes from an ancient Greek word meaning "burnt whole." The English word *caustic* also has Greek beginnings. A caustic chemical is one that causes a burning feeling on the skin. Compare the words "caustic" and "holocaust," and you may be able to guess which part of the word "holocaust" comes from the ancient Greek word for "burnt."

hol·ster *noun* a case for a gun or pistol that can be attached to a belt and is made of leather or other material. {**hohl** stər} holstered, adj.

ho·ly ❓ 💬 *adjective* (holier, holiest) 1. sacred according to a particular religion. *We read from the holy scriptures each night.* 2. devoted to the church, to God, or to religion. *The priest is a holy man.* 3. of the character of a saint. *That holy woman spent her life helping poor children.* {**hoh** lee}

Homophone Note Are you looking for the word *wholly* (entirely)? *Holy* and *wholly* sound alike but have different meanings.

home 🔄 *noun* 1. the place where a person or animal lives. *I got home and went to bed. / The forest is home to many animals.* 2. the house, apartment, or other building in which a person lives. *Her home has three rooms.* 3. the center of a person's family life. *He comes from an unhappy home. / Home is where the heart is.* 4. the

country, town, or other area where a person lives or grew up. *Although I lived in Japan for ten years, Canada will always be my home.* 5. a place where people who cannot take care of themselves live and are cared for. *Our town has a group home for children who have no parents.* 6. home plate in baseball or softball. *adjective* having to do with one's home. *His home life is happy. adverb* 1. to or toward home; homeward. *I take the bus home after school.* 2. in the direction pointed to or aimed at. *Robin's arrow struck home.* {**hohm**}

home·land *noun* one's native country or region. *I was born in Paris, the capital of my homeland, France.* {**hohm** lănd}

home·less *adjective* having no home. *We found a homeless cat and brought it to the animal shelter. noun* those people who have no home and usually live on the street (usually used with "the"). *Many of the homeless eat at soup kitchens.* {**hohm** lihs} homelessly, adv., homelessness, n.

home·ly *adjective* (homelier, homeliest) 1. not pretty or handsome; plain. *The homely girl was shy about her looks.* 2. not fancy or special; simple. *She wore a homely dress to work every day.* 3. simple, direct. *We felt comfortable with their homely manners.* {**hohm** lee} homeliness, n.

home·made *adjective* made at home rather than bought. *We love the taste of homemade ice cream.* {**hohm** **mayd**}

home page *noun* (home pages) the main page of a Web site. A home page often has a table of contents and links to other parts of the Web page. *Our school's home page has a*

photograph of the school and links to each of the classes. {**hohm** **payj**}

home plate *noun* a flat slab of hard rubber at which the batter stands in a baseball game. The base runner must touch home plate in order to score a run. {**hohm** **playt**}

Ho·mer *noun* a Greek poet who is thought to have lived around the eighth century B.C. {**hoh** mər}

hom·er *noun* a home run in baseball or softball. *When Joe hit a homer he ran the bases with pride, knowing he'd won the game.* {**hohm** ər}

home·room *noun* a classroom where students meet at the beginning of the school day for attendance and announcements. {**hohm** roohm}

home run *noun* a hit that allows the batter in a baseball game to touch all four bases and score a run. {**hohm** **ruhn**}

home·sick *adjective* longing for one's home. *Sometimes children who go away to camp feel homesick.* {**hohm** **sihk**} homesickness, n.

home·spun *adjective* 1. made into cloth or spun into yarn at home. *Their shirts were made of homespun wool.* 2. plain, simple. *We enjoyed their homespun humor. noun* a plain cloth made at home or

A B C D E F G H I J K L M N O P Q R S T U V W X Y Z

of wool spun into yarn at home. *All of the farm family's clothes were made of home-spun.* {hohm spuhn}

home·stead *noun* 1. a house and the land and buildings that are around it; a farm. 2. a piece of land that was given by the United States government to someone who promised to live on it and farm it. {hohm stehd}

home·ward *adverb* to or toward home. *adjective* moving or headed toward home. *Our homeward journey was filled with excitement.* {hohm wərd} homewards, adv.

home·work ⚙ *noun* school-work that is to be done at home rather than at school. *You're not allowed to watch TV until you finish your homework.* {hohm wuhrk}

hom·i·ny *noun* a food made of kernels of dried corn that are ground and then cooked with water. *We enjoy hominy with butter for breakfast.* {hŏm ə nee}

ho·mog·e·nize *verb* (homogenized, homogenizing, homogenizes) to break up and blend the particles of fat in. *The dairy farmers homogenized the raw milk.* {hə mŏj ə niyz} homogenization, n., homogenized, adj., homogenizer, n.

hom·o·graph *noun* a word that has the same spelling as another but a different meaning and history. Homographs are often pronounced differently from each other. In the sentence, "She shed a tear over the tear in her dress," the two words spelled

"t-e-a-r" are homographs. {hŏm ə grăf *or* hoh mə grăf}

Language Note *Homograph*, **homonym**, or *homophone*?

Homographs (from ancient Greek words for "same writing") are two or more words that are spelled the same but have different, unrelated meanings.
• *punch* (the drink), *punch* (the blow)
• *lead* (the heavy metal), *lead* (guide)
• *wind* (moving air), *wind* (turn or coil)
• *pen* (the writing tool), *pen* (a pig's place)

Homonyms (from ancient Greek for "same name") are two or more words that sound the same, but have different meanings.
• *hare* (like a rabbit), *hair* (on your head)
• *rank* (a place in line), *rank* (smelly)

Homophones (from ancient Greek for "same sound") are two or more words that sound the same but are spelled differently.
• *time* (on a clock), *thyme* (an herb)
• *size* (how big), *sighs* (breath)
• *flu* (influenza), *flew* (past tense of fly), *flue* (in a chimney)
• *carat* (weight of a diamond), *caret* (proof-reading mark), *karat* (purity of gold), *carrot* (orange vegetable)

In some parts of the United States, there are words that are pronounced as homophones, but in other parts of the country, those same words are not. Do you think these words are homophones? *marry, merry, Mary; pore, pour, poor; berry, bury; din, den.*

hom·o·nym *noun* a word that is pronounced and often spelled the same as another word, but has a different meaning. In the sentence, "She was mean to me, but she didn't mean it," the two instances of "mean" are homonyms. {hŏm ə nihm}

homonymic, adj., homonymity, n.

hom·o·phone *noun* a word that sounds the same as another but has a different meaning and often a different spelling. In the sentence, "I've been feeling weak for almost a week," the words, "weak" and "week" are homophones. {hŏm ə fohn *or* hoh mə fohn}

Hon·du·ras *noun* a country in Central America. Tegucigalpa is the capital of Honduras. {hahn doohr əs} Honduran, n., adj.

hon·est ⚙ *adjective* 1. truthful, real or sincere. *She made an honest attempt to answer their questions.* 2. not lying or cheating in one's friendships or business relations. *I trust her because she has always been honest with me.* 3. not meant to trick or mislead. *I assure you, I'm telling the honest truth.* 4. earned in a fair way. *He makes an honest wage as a carpenter.* {ŏn ihst}

hon·est·ly *adverb* in an honest way. *She lives honestly and never lies.* *interjection* used to express surprise or mild shock. *Honestly! Why do you act so silly?* {ŏn ihst lee}

hon·es·ty *noun* the fact or condition of being honest; integrity; truthfulness. *He was able to answer the questions with complete honesty.* {ŏ nih stee}

hon·ey *noun* (honeys) 1. a thick, sweet liquid made from flower nectar by bees. It is yellow or brown. 2. sweet one; dear. *Honey, you mean so much to me.* {huhn ee} honeylike, adj.

hon·ey·bee *noun* a bee that makes honey from the nectar of flowers. Honeybees are often kept in beehives. {huhn ee bee}

 Human Body   Human Mind   Everyday Life    History and Culture   Communication

hon·ey·comb *noun* 1. a group of many small cells made of wax in which bees store their honey. Each cell has thin walls and six sides. 2. something that looks or feels like a honey-comb. *The porch was fitted with a honeycomb of lattice.* *verb* (honeycombed, honeycombing, honeycombs) to fill with holes or pockets. *The ants honeycombed the log.* {**huhn** ee **kohm**}

honeydew melon *noun* a melon with a smooth rind that is light green in color and that has sweet, green flesh. {**huhn** ee **dooh meh** lən}

hon·ey·moon *noun* a vacation or trip taken by a couple to celebrate their marriage. *Their honeymoon lasted for two weeks.* *verb* (honeymooned, honeymooning, honeymoons) to spend the time of a honeymoon (usually followed by "in" or "on"). *The couple will honeymoon in Paris.* {**huhn** ee **moohn**} honeymooner, n.

hon·ey·suck·le *noun* a bush or vine with white, yellow, or pink flowers that have a sweet smell and taste. {**huhn** ee **suh** kəl}

Hong Kong *noun* a region off the southern coast of China. Hong Kong was once a British colony but was returned to Chinese rule in 1997. {**hŏng kŏng** *or* **hawng kawng**}

honk *noun* 1. the loud, harsh sound made by a goose. 2. any sound like this, such as the sound of an automobile horn. *verb* (honked, honking, honks) 1. to make the sound of a honk. *The cars honked in the busy street.* 2. to cause to make a loud, harsh sound. *I honked the horn at a boy who had run into the street.* 3. to cause an automobile horn to sound. *I honked at the dog in the road.* {**hŏngk**} honker, n.

hon·or *noun* 1. high public value or respect. *The mayor holds a place of honor in our community.* 2. the state of having a good character and honest behavior. *A person of honor will not cheat her friends.* 3. a special award. *The soldiers who fought in that battle received honors from the general.* 4. the privilege of meeting with famous, noble, or otherwise special people. *It is an honor to meet you, Sir Charles.* 5. a source of pride or credit. *That doctor is an honor to her profession.* *verb* (honored, honoring, honors) 1. to show respect or admiration for. *We honored our mother on Mother's Day.* 2. to give a special award or recognition to. *The world champions were honored by the President.* {**ŏn** ər} honorless, adj.

hon·or·a·ble *adjective* worthy of respect or honor. *Farming is honorable work.* {**ŏn** ə rə bəl}

hon·or·ar·y *adjective* given as an honor or as an award for achievement, but not earned in the ordinary way. *The movie actor received an honorary degree from the college.* {**ŏn** ə **ray** ree}

ho·nour *noun or verb* a spelling of **honor** used in Canada and Britain. See **honor**. {**ŏn** ər, n., **on** ər, v.}

-hood *suffix* 1. a suffix that means "state" or "condition." *Childhood is the time of life when you are a child.* / *The likelihood of rain means that it is likely there will be rainy weather conditions.* 2. a suffix that means "a group of people." *A neighborhood is a group of people who are neighbors.*

hood *noun* 1. a covering for the head and neck, often attached to a coat, jacket, or robe. 2. something that resembles such a covering, such as the parts of some flowers or the skin around the neck of a cobra snake. 3. the metal lid that covers a car's engine. {**huud**} hoodless, adj., hoodlike, adj.

hood·lum *noun* 1. a person who commits criminal acts. *A hoodlum robbed the bank.* 2. a rough young man who gets into trouble. *The windows were broken by hoodlums.* {**huud** ləm}

hoof ❶ *noun* (hoofs or hooves) 1. the hard, tough covering on the feet of certain mammals such as horses, pigs, and deer. 2. the entire foot of such mammals. {**huuf**} hooflike, adj.

hook *noun* 1. a curved piece of metal or plastic that is used for holding, hanging, or pulling things. *We put a hook into the wall to hold the new painting.* 2. a fishhook. 3. a sharp bend or curve in something, such as a river, a road, or a piece of land next to water. *The current of the river is dangerous near the hook.* 4. the curve of a ball in the direction opposite to the throwing or striking hand. 5. a short swinging blow or punch, made by a boxer with

A B C D E F G H I J K L M N O P Q R S T U V W X Y Z

a bent arm. *verb* (hooked, hooking, hooks) 1. to hold, hang, or pull with a hook. 2. to catch with a fishhook. 3. to bend or curve sharply. *The road hooks to the right.* 4. to become held, connected, or fastened with a hook. *My sweater hooked on a nail.* 5. to curve away from the thrower or striker. *The ball hooked to the left.* {**huuk**} hookless, adj., hooklike, adj.
  • **by hook or by crook** in any possible way, using any possible means. *I will get to Paris by hook or by crook.*
  • **hook, line, and sinker** (informal) without any question or hesitation; completely. *She swallowed the lies hook, line, and sinker.*

hooked *adjective* curved or shaped like a hook. *That bird has a hooked beak.* {**huukt**} hookedness, n.

hoop *noun* 1. a large ring of wood, plastic, or metal, used as a child's toy. 2. a round band of metal used to hold together the strips that form the sides of a barrel. 3. (informal) the basket used in basketball. {**hoohp**} hooplike, adj.

Homophone Note The words *hoop* and *whoop* sound alike but have different meanings.

hoo·ray *interjection or noun or verb* another spelling of **hurrah**. {hoohr **ay** or hə **ray**, intj., hoohr **ay** or hə **ray**, n., hoohr **ay** or hə **ray**, v.}

hoot *verb* (hooted, hooting, hoots) 1. to give a loud shout or cry to show scorn. *The crowd hooted at the visiting team.* 2. to make the sound an owl makes. *The owl hooted and we hooted back at it.* 3. to drive out, off, or away with shouts or cries. *They hooted*

the actor off the stage. *noun* 1. the sound an owl makes. 2. a sound like an owl's cry, such as the sound of a car horn. 3. a shout or cry of scorn. {**hooht**} hooter, n.
  • **not give a hoot** (informal) to not care at all. *I don't give a hoot whether you stay or go.*

hooves *noun* a plural of **hoof**. {**huuvz** or **hoohvz**}

hop¹ *verb* (hopped, hopping, hops) 1. to make a short, quick leap or leaps. *The rabbit hopped across the yard and then disappeared.* 2. to jump or leap over with a short, quick motion. *He hopped the fence.* 3. to jump or skip on one foot only. *Do you think you could hop all the way to school? noun* a short, quick leap or jump, especially on one foot. *The frog took a few hops and landed in the water.* {**hŏp**}

hop² *noun* 1. a tall, climbing vine that bears green cone-shaped flowers. 2. (plural) the dried flowers of this plant, used to make beer. {**hŏp**}

hope *noun* 1. a feeling or chance that something will happen the way one wants it to. *I have hope that she will get well. / Is there any hope you will get home before the sun sets?* 2. a wish for something that one thinks could come true; desire. *It is my hope to play on the high school baseball team someday.* 3. a thing or a person that will help one get what is wished or desired. *This batter is our last hope. verb* (hoped, hoping, hopes) 1. to look ahead to with a

good feeling, with confidence. *I hope I get a good score on the test.* 2. to want events to turn out well. *I hope we can visit again soon. / I hope you won't think I'm silly.* {**hohp**}

hope·ful *adjective* 1. showing or feeling hope. *She had hopeful thoughts about passing the test.* 2. showing that something hoped for will happen. *Melting snow is a hopeful sign of spring coming soon.* {**hohp** fəl} hopefulness, n.

hope·less *adjective* 1. beyond hope. *Doctors tried to find a cure for the hopeless disease.* 2. without hope; in despair. *The hurricane left many people in a hopeless situation.* {**hohp** lihs} hopelessly, adv., hopelessness, n.

Ho·pi *noun* (Hopis [or] Hopi) a member of a tribe of Pueblo American Indians of northeastern Arizona. {**hoh** pee}

hop·per *noun* 1. someone or something that hops. 2. a bin or container that can be opened from the bottom and that is shaped like a funnel. A hopper is used to store grain, coal, or other loose materials. {**hŏp** ər}

hop·scotch *noun* a children's game in which players toss a stone onto a pattern of numbered squares drawn on the ground. The players then hop or jump from square to square, picking up the stone as they move. {**hŏp** skŏch}

Word History The word *hop-scotch* was first used in English about 200 years ago. It was formed from the English words "hop" and "scotch." "Scotch" means "to cut a line into."

horde *noun* a large number, group, or crowd. *There was a*

 Human Body   Human Mind Everyday Life History and Culture   Communication

horde of flies in the barn. {**hohrd**}

Homophone Note Are you looking for the word **hoard** (a collection or supply)? **Horde** and **hoard** sound alike but have different meanings.

ho·ri·zon *noun* 1. the line where the earth and the sky appear to meet. *The ship seemed to disappear over the horizon.* 2. the outer limit of vision or knowledge. *Reading books will stretch your horizons.* {hə **riy** zən}

hor·i·zon·tal *adjective* parallel to the surface of the earth or to the horizon. *Most people sleep in a horizontal position.* {**har** ə **zŏn** təl *or* **hohr** ə **zŏn** təl} horizontally, adv.

hor·mone *noun* a substance made by certain cells in the body. Hormones move around the body in the blood and have effects on certain organs and cells. Hormones help control body processes such as growth. {**hohr mohn**} hormonal, adj., hormonally, adv.

horn *noun* 1. a hard, hollow growth on the head of certain mammals. Deer, cows, and sheep are some animals that have horns. Horns usually grow in pairs. 2. a musical instrument usually

made of brass. Horns are played by blowing into their narrow end. *I play the horn in the school band.* 3. a device used to make a loud warning sound. *Dad blew the horn on his car to warn the dog away.* {**hohrn**} hornless, adj., horn-like, adj.

horned lizard *noun* a lizard with a short tail and short legs that eats insects; horned toad. It lives in the western part of the United States and in Mexico. The horned lizard has spines that look like horns on its head and rough scales and spines on its body. {**hohrnd lih** zərd}

horned toad *noun* another name for horned lizard. {**hohrnd tohd**}

hor·net *noun* a large, stinging insect that is a kind of wasp. Hornets live together in groups called colonies. They build large, round nests from a material that looks like paper. {**hohr niht**}

horn·y *adjective* (hornier, horniest) 1. having horns or horn-like projections. *Some toads are very horny.* 2. made of or similar to horns. *The goat had two horny little bumps starting on its head.* 3. hardened, or calloused. *You have horny feet from all that running you do.* {**hohr nee**} hornily, adv., horniness, n.

hor·ri·ble *adjective* 1. causing a feeling of fear, horror; dreadful. *She had a horrible nightmare.* 2. not pleasant; very ugly or bad. *Did you make this horrible mess in the*

kitchen? {**hohr** ih bəl *or* **har** ih bəl} horribly, adv.

Word History *Horrible* comes from a Latin word that means "bristly or savage looking."

hor·rid *adjective* 1. causing a feeling of horror; dreadful; frightening. *The book had a scary picture of a horrid monster.* 2. very bad; not pleasant. *Some people think the Arctic has a horrid climate.* {**hohr** ihd *or* **har** ihd} horridly, adv., horridness, n.

hor·ri·fy *verb* (horrified, horrifying, horrifies) to cause feelings of horror in; frighten, shock. *The sight of the dead animal horrified us.* {**hohr** ih fiy *or* **har** ih fiy} horrifyingly, adv.

hor·ror *noun* 1. a great and painful feeling of fear or shock. *I jumped in horror when I heard the loud scream.* 2. someone or something that causes horror. *The huge dragon was a horror to the people of the village.* 3. a strong dislike. *I have a horror of snakes.* {**hohr** ər *or* **har** ər}

horse *noun* 1. a large mammal with long legs and hooves. A horse has a long neck with a mane, short hair, and a long tail. In the wild, horses live in herds and eat grass and other plants. For thousands of years, people have used horses for riding and for pulling or carrying loads. 2. a

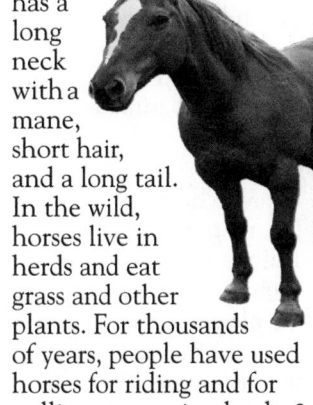

A B C D E F G H I J K L M N O P Q R S T U V W X Y Z

a
b
c
d
e
f
g
h
i
j
k
l
m
n
o
p
q
r
s
t
u
v
w
x
y
z

frame with legs, used for holding or supporting things. *We used saw horses to hold the boards.* 3. a large padded block on legs used for gymnastic activities. *We used a ramp to help us jump over the horse.* {hohrs}

• **hold one's horses**
to wait more calmly; be patient. *Hold your horses until I say it's time to go outside!*

• **horse around**
to play in a silly or foolish way; to be very active. *Please do not horse around in the library.*

• **look a gift horse in the mouth**
not to be grateful for a gift; to criticize something received as a gift. *Don't look a gift horse in the mouth: a lot of people would be glad to have this old car your parents gave you.*

Homophone Note The words *horse* and *hoarse* sound alike but have different meanings. To find out why the talkative horse sometimes gets hoarse, look up *hoarse*.

horse·back *noun* the back of a horse. *adverb* on the back of a horse. *We rode horseback through the mountains.* {hohrs băk}

horse·fly *noun* (horseflies) a large fly that is sometimes found in large numbers around horses, cows, or other animals. Female horseflies bite and feed on the blood of people and animals. {hohrs fliy}

horse·man *noun* (horsemen) 1. a man who rides on a horse. 2. a man who has skill in riding or caring for horses. {hohrs mən}

horse·play *noun* rough or noisy play. *We don't allow horseplay in school.* {hohrs play}

horse·pow·er *noun* a unit of energy equal to 746 watts or the energy needed to lift 550 pounds in one second, used in measuring the power of engines. (abbreviated: hp) {hohrs pow ər}

horse·shoe *noun* 1. a narrow, flat piece of iron shaped like a U that is fitted and nailed to a horse's hoof. 2. (plural but used with a singular verb) a game in which players toss horseshoes at a stake some distance away. {hohrs shooh} horseshoer, n.

horse·wom·an *noun* (horse-women) 1. a woman who rides on a horse. 2. a woman who has skill in riding or caring for horses. {hohrs wuum ən} horsewomanship, n.

hose *noun* (hose or hoses) 1. a flexible tube of rubber or plastic through which a liquid can pass. 2. (used with a plural verb) socks or stockings. *I need new hose because mine have holes in the toes.* *verb* (hosed, hosing, hoses) (usually followed by down) to water, spray, soak, or wash with a hose. *Because it was hot, we hosed each other down.* {hohz}

ho·sier·y *noun* socks or stockings as a group. *My dresser has one drawer just for hosiery.* {hoh zhə ree}

hos·pi·ta·ble *adjective* friendly, giving, and warm to guests. *We ate in a cozy restaurant in that hospitable town.* {hŏs pih

tə bəl *or* ho spiht ə bəl} hospitableness, n., hospitably, adv.

hos·pi·tal 🏃 ❓ *noun* a place where sick or hurt people go to find care or help. {hŏs pih təl}

Word History The words *hospital* and *hospitality* both come from a Latin word for "guest-house." During the Middle Ages in England, houses of shelter for the poor and needy were called "hospitals." "Hospital" did not mean "a place for sick people" until 1549.

hos·pi·tal·i·ty *noun* (hospitalities) the friendly, warm, and generous treatment of guests or strangers. {hŏs pih tăl ih tee}

hos·pi·tal·ize *verb* (hospitalized, hospitalizing, hospitalizes) to place in a hospital for medical treatment. *The doctor hospitalized my son after he broke his arm.* {hŏs pih tə liyz}

host¹ *noun* 1. a person who entertains guests. *Our host served pizza, soda, and birthday cake at his party.* 2. a plant or animal that has a parasite living on or in it. A parasite gets its food and energy from the host organism. *verb* (hosted, hosting, hosts) to be or serve as a host at. *Her parents are hosting the wedding.* {hohst}

host² *noun* a very large number of people or things. *He has a host of troubles. / A host of knights rode up to the castle.* {hohst}

hos·tage *noun* someone held prisoner by a person or group trying to force another person or group to meet certain demands. {hŏs tihj}

hos·tel *noun* a place that offers shelter at a low cost for

 Human Body Human Mind  Everyday Life 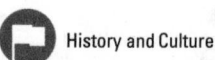 History and Culture  Communication

young people who are traveling. *We stayed in youth hostels during our bicycle tour of Massachusetts.* {hŏs təl}

Homophone Note Are you looking for the word **hostile** (unfriendly)? **Hostel** and **hostile** sound alike but have different meanings.

hos·tess *noun* 1. a woman who entertains guests. *Our hostess served pizza, soda, and birthday cake at the party.* 2. a woman whose job is to greet customers. {hohs tihs}

hos·tile *adjective* 1. feeling or showing dislike; unfriendly. *Mary gave me a hostile look that hurt my feelings.* 2. hard to bear; harsh. *Antarctica has a hostile climate.* {hŏs tihl or hŏs tiyl} hostilely, adv.

Homophone Note The words **hostile** and **hostel** sound alike but have different meanings. To find out why you'd never want to stay in a hostel whose owners were hostile, look up **hostel**.

hos·til·i·ty *noun* (hostilities) 1. the state of being unfriendly or full of hate. *He felt hostility toward her after she hit him.* 2. (plural) acts of war. *We were sad to hear of new hostilities between the two countries.* {ho stihl ih tee}

hot 🔵 🔵 🔵 *adjective* (hotter, hottest) 1. holding or giving off great heat. *The hot soup was delicious.* 2. causing the physical feeling of great heat. *It's a hot summer day.* 3. causing a burning feeling in the mouth. *I like to put hot pepper on my spaghetti.* 4. showing or feeling anger or other strong emotion. *He tries hard to control his hot temper.* 5. completely new or fresh. *The

newspaper is hot off the press.* {hŏt} hotly, adv., hotness, n.
• **in hot water** (informal) in a bad situation; in trouble. *Jack and Jill were in hot water after breaking their pail.*

Synonyms
These words share a meaning with **hot**, adjective 4:
fiery, inflamed

hot dog *noun* a hot, cooked sausage or frankfurter eaten in a long, soft roll. *interjection* (informal) used to express excitement or delight. *Hot dog! We won the game!* {hŏt dawg or hŏt dŏg, intj., hŏt dawg or hŏt dŏg, n.}

ho·tel *noun* a place with many rooms and beds where people pay money to sleep, eat meals, or buy other services. {hoh tehl}

hot·house *noun* a heated glass building used to grow plants. {hŏt hows}

hot spring *noun* a natural spring that has water warmer than body temperature. {hŏt spring}

hound *noun* 1. any of several breeds of dogs. Hounds have short hair, a deep voice, and long, drooping ears. They are used for hunting. 2. a dog of any kind. *verb* (hounded, hounding, hounds) to nag or urge without stopping. *The boy is hounding his parents for a new computer.* {hownd} hounder, n.

hour *noun* 1. a unit of time equal to sixty minutes. *I spent two hours on my homework last night.* 2. one of the twenty-four such periods in a day. *The siren sounds every day at the noon hour.* 3. a time

of the day connected with certain types of activity. *I like to take a walk during my lunch hour.* 4. the distance that can be traveled in one hour. *We live two hours from our grandparents' house.* {owr}

Homophone Note The words **hour** and **our** (belonging to us) sound alike but have different meanings.

hour·glass *noun* an instrument used to measure time that sends sand through a narrow opening between two larger glass bulbs. It takes exactly one hour for the sand to pass from one bulb to the other. {owr glăs}

hour·ly *adjective* 1. done or happening every hour. *I take an hourly break when I have a lot of homework.* 2. by the hour. *The workers are paid an hourly wage.* *adverb* each hour. *We check the children hourly.* {owr lee}

house 🔵 🔵 *noun* 1. a building in which people live. *This neighborhood has houses and shops.* 2. the people who live in such a building; household. *Our house has five people.* 3. a building that is used for a particular purpose. *We visit our house of worship every week. / We went to the coffee house to meet our friends.* 4. a group or assembly that meets to write, discuss, and pass laws. *The house is in session for six months a year.* 5. the audience at a public event. *There was a large house

A B C D E F G H I J K L M N O P Q R S T U V W X Y Z

for the film. **verb** (housed, housing, houses) to provide room and board or living quarters for. *That school houses students on campus. / The animals are housed in a barn.* {hows}

• **on the house**
free, as a gift from a business. *Soft drinks are on the house if you order a large pizza.*

Synonyms
These words share a meaning with **house**, noun 1:
home, residence, dwelling

house·boat *noun* a large boat that has been made for use as a home. {hows boht}

house·fly *noun* (houseflies) an insect with two wings that is found in and around houses and other places where people live. It does not bite people, but it can spread a number of diseases. {hows

fliy}

house·hold *noun* the group of people, such as a family, that lives in a particular house. *adjective* of or relating to a household. *We have three household pets.* {hows hohld}

house·keep·er *noun* a person who is hired to take care of a home. {hows kee pər}

House of Commons *noun* one of the houses of the British and Canadian parliaments.

Members are elected by the people. {hows əv ko mənz}

House of Lords *noun* one of the houses of the British parliament, made up of nobles and certain religious leaders. Members are not elected. {hows əv lohrdz}

House of Representatives *noun* the lower legislative house in many governments, including the United States, most U.S. states, and countries such as Mexico and Japan. {hows əv reh prə zehn tə tihvz}

house·plant *noun* a plant grown indoors, especially as decoration. {hows plănt}

house·wife *noun* (housewives) a married woman whose main work is taking care of the cooking, cleaning, and other duties of her family's household. {hows wiyf}

house·work *noun* the work of taking care of a household, such as cooking and cleaning. {hows wuhrk}

hous·ing *noun* 1. a shelter or place to live. *The college helps its students find housing.* 2. houses or living places as a group. *Her goal is to improve the quality of housing in the United States.* 3. a case that covers or protects. *We had to fix the cracked motor housing.* {how zing}

hov·el *noun* a small, uncomfortable, dirty house or hut. {huhv əl *or* hŏv əl}

hov·er *verb* (hovered, hovering, hovers) 1. to stay hanging in the air, often by quick flapping or spinning. *The helicopter hovered over-*

head. 2. to stay very near and watch closely. *He hovers over his children for fear they will get lost.* {huhv ər} hoverer, n., hoveringly, adv.

how *adverb* 1. by what manner or means. *How is it made?* 2. in what way, state, or condition. *How are you feeling?* 3. to what amount or degree. *How big is he?* 4. for what purpose or reason. *How are you going to use this?* 5. used to give emphasis to what follows. *How he loves to dance!* *conjunction* 1. the way in which. *I don't know how to do it.* 2. about the way or manner in which. *Be careful how you talk to him.* {how}

• **how about**
what is your wish about having or doing. *How about dinner tonight?*

• **how come**
(informal) why is it that. *How come you don't want to go?*

how'd shortened form of "how did" or "how would." *How'd you do on the test? / How'd you like to come swimming with us?* {howd}

how·dy *interjection* "Hello"; "How are you?" *Howdy! It's good to see you.* {how dee}

how·ev·er *adverb* 1. in whatever way. *Finish the race however you can.* 2. no matter what or how. *However you do, I will be proud.* *conjunction* in spite of that; yet. *It is raining; however, it is not cold.* {how ehv ər}

howl *verb* (howled, howling, howls) 1. to utter or make a long, loud, sad sound like that of a wolf or dog. *The wolf howled at the moon. / The angry baby screamed and howled for twenty minutes.* 2. (informal) to laugh very loudly and with much energy. *They howled at*

  Human Body Human Mind Everyday Life  History and Culture 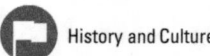 Communication

his jokes. 3. to express by howling. *The crowd howled its anger at the mayor.* *noun* a long, loud, sad cry or sound, such as that of a wolf or dog. *We heard the howl of an old coyote.* {**howl**}

hr. *abbreviation* an abbreviation for **hour** or hours.

ht. *abbreviation* an abbreviation for **height**.

html or **HTML** *abbreviation* abbreviation for "hypertext markup language," a computer language used to create documents on the World Wide Web. *If you want to create a really great Web page, you should learn html.*

hub *noun* 1. the turning center part of a wheel to which spokes and other parts are connected. 2. a central location around which activity happens. *The kitchen is the hub of our household.* {**huhb**}

hub·bub *noun* a confusing mix of loud sounds such as voices; uproar. *The sound of the doorbell was lost in the hubbub.* {**huh buhb**}

hub·cap *noun* a round metal cover over the hub of a car wheel. {**huhb kăp**}

huck·le·ber·ry *noun* (huckleberries) 1. a low berry bush common in North America. The huckleberry is related to the blueberry. 2. the dark blue fruit of this plant. {**huhk əl behr ee**}

hud·dle *verb* (huddled, huddling, huddles) 1. to gather in a small, close group. *He huddled his family in the doorway out of the rain.* 2. to move close together or push in against one another when sharing something such as heat. *They huddled together in the tent during the storm.* 3. to meet in a small, close group to discuss. *Let's huddle for five* minutes and work out a solution. *noun* 1. a small group of people or animals pushed or drawn together. *One penguin was not allowed to join the huddle.* 2. a gathering of a football team's players to get instructions for the next

play. {**huhd əl**}

hue 🌐 *noun* a particular color, such as sky blue; shade. *I want paint of a slightly darker hue.* {**hyoo**}

huff *noun* a state of bad temper; an angry mood. *She walked off in a huff over an insult.* *verb* (huffed, huffing, huffs) to breathe hard; to blow or puff. *He was huffing when he reached the top of the stairs.* {**huhf**}

hug *verb* (hugged, hugging, hugs) 1. to hold or squeeze with the arms in a loving way; embrace. 2. to stay close to while moving beside or on. *We hugged the wall as we walked through the hallway.* 3. to hold one another in an embrace. *They hugged and then went their own ways.* *noun* a hold using the arms, often showing love or friend- ship; embrace. *I gave my mother a hug.* {**huhg**} huggable, adj., hugger, n., huggingly, adv.

Word History *Hug* comes from a Norse word that means "to comfort." When "hug" entered the English language in the 1500s, it meant "to embrace," as it does today. In 1617, "hug" began to be used as a noun, as in, "Give me a hug." At that time, however, the noun form was used only for a wrestling squeeze.

huge *adjective* (huger, hugest) of very large weight, size, or amount. *He is a huge man. / That is a huge piece of wood.* {**hyooj**} hugely, adv., hugeness, n.

hulk *noun* 1. an old ship that no longer is in use. *The rusty hulk sat for years at the dock.* 2. a large, clumsy person. *I was startled by the hulk standing at the front door.* {**huhlk**}

hull[1] 🔴 🟢 *noun* 1. the outer shell or covering of fruits, nuts, and seeds. 2. the outer covering of the flower buds of certain fruits, such as the strawberry. *verb* (hulled, hulling, hulls) to strip or break the outer layers from vegetables or seeds. *We hulled the peas from our garden.* {**huhl**} huller, n.

hull[2] *noun* the rigid frame and outer shell of a ship. *The hull of the ship is made of steel.* {**huhl**}

hum *verb* (hummed, humming, hums) 1. to vibrate with a continuous low sound. *The computer hums when it is running.* 2. to make the sound of a song without opening the lips. *She hummed to music on the radio.* 3. to be busy and productive. *The owners were happy to see that their business*

a
b
c
d
e
f
g
h
i
j
k
l
m
n
o
p
q
r
s
t
u
v
w
x
y
z

was humming. noun the sound or act of humming. *I cannot hear the hum of the refrigerator from my bedroom.* {**huhm**} hummer, n.

hu·man 🏃❓ *adjective* having to do with or being a part of people. *There are many human beings living on this planet. noun* a person; human being. *Humans are part of the group of mammals called primates.* {**hyoo** mən} human-like, adj., humanness, n.

hu·man be·ing *noun* a human; person. {**hooh** măn **bee** əng}

hu·mane *adjective* showing kindness or mercy. *We try hard to give humane care to our house pets.* {hyoo **mayn**} humanely, adv., humaneness, n.

hu·man·i·ty *noun* (humanities) 1. the race of human beings; people. *All of humanity has the same needs for food, water, and clean air.* 2. sympathy, concern, or compassion. *The leader showed his humanity by taking care of the poor.* 3. (plural) studies that deal with human thoughts and human culture. The humanities include music, art, history, and literature, but do not include the sciences. {hyə **măn** ih tee}

hu·man·kind *noun* the group of all humans; the human race or species. {**hyoo** mən **kiynd**}

hum·ble *adjective* (humbler, humblest) 1. not proud; modest. *Although he was rich and powerful, he remained a humble man.* 2. low in cost, rank, or position; simple. *Our humble home is small and cozy. / Even a humble job is important to the community. verb* (humbled, humbling, humbles) to bring down; make humble. *The proud coach was humbled by his team's loss.* {**huhm** bəl} hum-

bleness, n., humbler, n., humblingly, adv., humbly, adv.

> **Word History** The words *humble* and *human* both go back to *humus,* the Latin word for "earth" or "soil."

hu·mid *adjective* having a high amount of water vapor; damp; moist. *The climate of a rain forest is very humid.* {**hyoo** mihd} humidly, adv., humidness, n.

hu·mid·i·ty *noun* water vapor or moisture in the air. {**hyoo** **mihd** ih tee}

hu·mil·i·ate *verb* (humiliated, humiliating, humiliates) to cause to lose pride or feel ashamed; embarrass. *The teasing by his friends humiliated John.* {hyoo **mih** lee **ayt**} humiliatingly, adv., humiliator, n.

hum·ming·bird *noun* a tiny, brightly colored bird with a long, slender bill and narrow wings that beat very rapidly. {**huhm** ing **buhrd**}

hu·mor ❓ *noun* 1. a quality that makes people laugh or feel amused. *The story was filled with humor.* 2. the ability to express or understand what is funny or amusing. *She has a good sense of humor.* 3. a mood or state of mind. *I'm in a bad humor today, so leave me alone. verb* (humored, humoring, humors) to give in to the wishes or mood of. *Let's humor him today.* {**hyoo** mər} humorless, adj., humorlessness, n.

hu·mor·ous *adjective* having the character or quality of humor; funny. *We found ourselves in a humorous situation.*

{**hyoo** mə rəs} humorously, adv., humorousness, n.

hu·mour *noun or verb* a spelling of **humor** used in Canada and Britain. See **humor.** {**hooh** mər}

hump *noun* a rounded lump of flesh, as is found on the back of a camel. {**huhmp**}

hu·mus *noun* a material that is made up of partly decayed leaves and plants. Humus adds nutrients to soil and helps it hold water. {**hyoo** məs}

hunch *verb* (hunched, hunching, hunches) to lift up or arch into a hump. *He hunched over the table to write a letter. noun* a feeling that something is going to happen; a guess. *I had a hunch that he would be late.* {**huhnch**}

hun·dred *noun* (hundreds [or] hundred) 1. the number that is equal to ten times ten; 100. 2. (plural) the numbers from 100 through 999. *adjective* being one hundred in number. *There are one hundred years in a century.* {**huhn** drihd}

hun·dredth *adjective* coming next after the ninety-ninth in a series. *The magazine included a special article and pictures for its hundredth anniversary issue. noun* 1. one of one hundred equal parts of a whole; 0.01 or 1/100. *Lisa made a slight adjustment to the*

 Human Body    Human Mind    Everyday Life    History and Culture    Communication

position of the telescope by moving it nine hundredths of a degree. 2. the number, person, or thing that comes next after the ninety-ninth in a series. *She knew all the cows were safe in the pasture after she counted the hundredth.* {**huhn** drihtth}

hung *verb* a past tense and past participle of **hang**. *My dad hung the lights on the Christmas tree.* {**hung**}

Hun·ga·ry *noun* a country in central Europe. Budapest is the capital of Hungary. {**hung** gə ree} Hungarian, n., adj.

hun·ger *noun* 1. the need or desire for food. *After skipping lunch he felt hunger in the afternoon.* 2. the feelings and conditions created by such need, such as weakness or discomfort. *Children who suffer from hunger often do not grow well.* 3. a strong desire. *His hunger for knowledge led him to read many books.* verb (hungered, hungering, hungers) 1. to experience a need or desire for food; be hungry. 2. to experience a strong desire. *She hungered for revenge.* {**hung** gər} hungeringly, adv.

hun·gry *adjective* (hungrier, hungriest) 1. feeling a need or desire for food. *I'm hungry because I didn't eat breakfast this morning.* 2. having a strong wish or desire. *I am hungry to start working on my new project.* {**hung** gree} hungrily, adv., hungriness, n.

hunk *noun* a large piece; chunk. *We ate the whole hunk of cheese at lunch.* {**hungk**}

hunt *verb* (hunted, hunting, hunts) 1. to set out to find and kill for food or sport. *They needed to hunt deer in order to stay alive.* 2. to try to find; search (often followed by "for", "up", or "down").

He hunted for the lost gloves. *noun* 1. an act or instance of finding and killing wild animals. *The men left at dawn to begin the deer hunt.* 2. a search to find something. *I always look forward to the easter egg hunt every year.* {**huhnt**}

hunt·er *noun* 1. one who hunts. 2. a dog or horse trained to help in hunting wild animals. *We always bring our dog hunting because he is an excellent hunter.* {**huhn** tər}

hur·dle *noun* 1. a barrier over which a runner or horse must leap in the course of certain races. 2. (plural but used with a singular verb) a type of race in which the runners must leap over such barriers. 3. something that one must overcome in order to progress. *The championship game was our final hurdle of the season.* verb (hurdled, hurdling, hurdles) to leap over in a race. *The horse hurdled five fences in the competition.* {**huhr** dəl} hurdler, n.

hurl *verb* (hurled, hurling, hurls) to throw with force. *He hurled the ball at the wall.* {**huhrl**} hurler, n.

Hu·ron *noun* 1. Lake Huron, one of the Great Lakes. It lies between the U.S. state of Michigan and the Canadian province of Ontario. 2. a member of one of the Native American peoples that once lived near this lake. {**hyoor** ŏn}

hur·rah or **hooray** or **hurray** *interjection* a word used to express joy, approval, victory, or encouragement. *Hurrah! We're winning!* noun a shout of "hurrah". *The stadium was filled with hurrahs after the game.* {hə **rah,** hə **ray**}

hur·ri·cane *noun* a powerful storm with heavy rains and winds that blow in a circle at

73 miles per hour or more. Hurricanes usually form in the West Indian region of the Atlantic Ocean. {**huhr** ih **kayn**}

Word History *Hurricane* came into English from the Spanish word *huracan*. The Spanish word came from *hurakan*, which meant "an evil spirit of the sea" in the Taino language once spoken in the West Indies.

hur·ried *adjective* 1. moving or acting quickly; forced to hurry. *Please don't make me feel so hurried; I'm moving as fast as I can.* 2. done quickly; rushed. *That was a hurried job, so you may have to do it again.* {**huhr** eed} hurriedly, adv., hurriedness, n.

hur·ry *verb* (hurried, hurrying, hurries) 1. to move or act with speed; to rush (sometimes followed by "up"). *If we don't hurry up we'll miss the train.* 2. to move or push to do quickly or too quickly. *The bus hurried them to work. / He hurried her into marriage before she was ready.* noun (hurries) a state or condition of acting or moving very quickly. *I can't talk now because I'm in a hurry.* {**huhr** ee}

hurt ⊕ ⊕ *verb* (hurt, hurting, hurts) 1. to cause pain, harm, or suffering to. *Did you hurt*

A B C D E F G H I J K L M N O P Q R S T U V W X Y Z

a
b
c
d
e
f
g
h
i
j
k
l
m
n
o
p
q
r
s
t
u
v
w
x
y
z

yourself when you fell off the bike? 2. to cause painful feelings in. *You really hurt her with your mean words.* 3. to feel pain or suffering. *My head hurts.* 4. to harm or damage. *The low test score hurt his grade in the class. noun* a pain or injury. *Did the hurt go away when you took aspirin? adjective* having pain or suffering. *My hurt finger took two weeks to heal. / My mom tried to comfort my hurt feelings.* {**huhrt**}

Synonyms
These words share a meaning with *hurt*, verb 1:
damage, wound, injure

hur·tle *verb* (hurtled, hurtling, hurtles) 1. to move with great speed and often with great noise. *The comet hurtled through space.* 2. to throw or launch with great force. *The powerful engine hurtled the rocket into space.* {**huhr** təl}

hus·band *noun* a man who is married; the man to whom a woman is married. {**huhz** bənd}

hush *interjection* "Be quiet." *Hush! I can't hear the movie. verb* (hushed, hushing, hushes) 1. to become quiet; stop all noise. *The crowd hushed when the president began to speak.* 2. to cause to be quiet. *The mother hushed her children when they started to argue.* 3. to keep from public knowledge (often followed by "up"). *The government tried to hush up the truth about what happened. noun* a calm or silence after noise stops. *We enjoyed the hush of evening after a difficult day at work.* {**huhsh**} hushedly, adv., hushful, adj., hushfully, adv.

husk *noun* the dry outer covering of some seeds and fruits. *We learned to make*

dolls out of corn husks. *verb* (husked, husking, husks) to strip the husk from. *He husked the corn before cooking it.* {**huhsk**} husker, n., husklike, adj.

Word History *Husk* comes from a Dutch word that means "little house."

I've been feeding Max four meals a day and now he's one **husky** Siberian **husky**.

husk·y[1] *adjective* (huskier, huskiest) 1. big and strong. *Our football team is made up of husky young men.* 2. somewhat rough or gruff sounding. *My dog obeys when I use a husky voice.* {**huhs** kee} huskily, adv., huskiness, n.

husk·y[2] *noun* (huskies) (often capitalized) a breed of dog. Huskies are strong, have thick fur, and are often raised to pull sleds in arctic regions. {**huhs** kee}

hus·tle *verb* (hustled, hustling, hustles) 1. to work or go swiftly. *They hustled to finish the assignment on time.* 2. to push or shove in a crowd. *We hustled our way to the front row.* 3. to force or help to move rapidly from, into, through, or toward a place. *The owner hustled the children out the door. noun* fast or busy activity. *We felt lost in the hustle of the market.* {**huh** səl}

Word History *Hustle* comes from a Dutch word that means "to shake back and forth."

hut *noun* a small house or shelter made of grass, mud, or logs. {**huht**}

hutch *noun* 1. a pen or shelter for small animals such as rabbits. 2. a piece of furniture that has drawers below and open shelves above, usually used for storing dishes. {**huhch**}

hy·a·cinth *noun* a plant that bears tall stalks of colorful flowers that have a sweet smell. The hyacinth grows from a bulb and is related to the lily. {**hiy** ə **sihn**th} hyacinthine, adj.

hy·brid ❶ *noun* the offspring of two plants or animals that are of different species or breeds. *The mule is a hybrid of a horse and a donkey.* {**hiy** brihd} hybridism, n.

hy·drant *noun* an upright pipe with a valve from which water can be drawn from a water main. *It is*

 Human Body   Human Mind   Everyday Life    History and Culture    Communication

against the law to park in front of a fire hydrant. {**hiy** drənt}

Word History *Hydrant* comes from a Greek word, *hydor* that means "water." A number of other English words contain the letters *hydr-* and they all have something to do with water. *Hydrogen* is a word invented by a French scientist in the 1700s. It means "producing water," because hydrogen forms water when it is mixed with oxygen.

hy·dro·e·lec·tric *adjective* having to do with producing electricity by means of the energy created by moving water. *A hydroelectric dam was built near the waterfall to provide electricity for our city.* {**hiy** droh ih **lehk** trihk} hydroelectricity, n.

hy·dro·gen 🌐 🔬 *noun* a very light gas that burns easily and is one of the chemical elements. Hydrogen is the most abundant element in the universe. It combines with oxygen to make water, and it is found in all living things. Hydrogen combines with many substances and has many uses. (symbol: H) {**hiy** drə jən}

hydrogen bomb *noun* a very powerful type of bomb. When its hydrogen atoms are forced together under great heat and pressure, they release energy in a huge explosion. {**hiy** drə jən **bŏm**}

hy·e·na *noun* a mammal with very long front legs and shorter back legs. Hyenas look like dogs, but are more

closely related to cats. They have a cry that sounds like strange human laughter. Most kinds of hyena are nocturnal and eat the remains of dead animals. Hyenas are found in Africa and Asia. {**hiy** <u>ee</u> nə}

hy·giene 🌐 *noun* the practice of keeping clean to stay healthy and prevent disease. *Brushing one's teeth often is an important part of good hygiene.* {**hiy** jeen}

hy·gien·ist *noun* a person skilled in the areas of hygiene, such as a dentist's assistant. {**hiy** <u>jeh</u> nihst *or* **hiy** <u>jee</u> nihst}

hymn 🔈 🌐 *noun* a song or poem written in praise of God or a country. *We sang a hymn of thanksgiving.* {**hihm**} hymnlike, adj.

Homophone Note The words **hymn** and **him** (a form of he) sound alike but have different meanings.

hym·nal *noun* a book of church hymns. {**hihm** nəl}

hype *verb* (hyped, hyping, hypes) to create interest in by making exaggerated claims. *The company is hyping this medicine as a new miracle drug. noun* an instance or practice of creating interest in by exaggeration. *We are tired of reading all the hype about movie stars' lives.* {**hiyp**}

hy·per·ac·tive *adjective* very active or stimulated beyond what is normal. *A hyperactive child often has trouble sitting quietly in school.* {**hiy** pər <u>ăk</u> tihv} hyperactivity, n.

hy·per·text mark·up lan·guage *noun* a computer language used to create documents on the World Wide Web; html. {**hiy** pər tehkst **mar** kuhp **lăn** gwihj}

hy·phen *noun* a punctuation mark (-). It is used to join the parts of a compound word. It is also used at the end of a line to divide a word between syllables. {**hiy** fən}

hy·phen·ate *verb* (hyphenated, hyphenating, hyphenates) to write, join, or divide with a hyphen. *You should hyphenate the word "hard-hearted."* {**hiy** fə **nayt**} hyphenation, n.

hyp·no·sis *noun* (hypnoses) a condition like sleep that is caused by the direction of another person. People under hypnosis may do or say things as directed or suggested by the person who has put them in this condition. {hihp <u>noh</u> sihs}

hyp·no·tize *verb* (hypnotized, hypnotizing, hypnotizes) to put into a state of hypnosis. {**hihp** nə tiyz} hypnotizability, n., hypnotizable, adj.

hy·po·crite *noun* a person who pretends to be different or better than he or she really is. Someone who does not act according to his or her stated beliefs is a hypocrite. *We thought he was a hypocrite because he told us cheating was bad, even though he has cheated on several tests.* {**hihp** ə **kriht**} hypocritical, adj., hypocritically, adv.

Word History Our word *hypocrite* comes from an ancient Greek word that means "actor" or "pretender."

hy·pot·e·nuse *noun* the side opposite the right angle in a right triangle; the longest side of a right triangle. {**hiy** po tə **noohs**}

A B C D E F G **H** I J K L M N O P Q R S T U V W X Y Z

a
b
c
d
e
f
g
h
i
j
k
l
m
n
o
p
q
r
s
t
u
v
w
x
y
z

hy·po·ther·mi·a *noun* a condi-tion of very low body tem-perature. {hiy poh **thuhr** mee ə}

hy·poth·e·sis *noun* (hypotheses) a prediction or educated guess that can be tested and can be used to guide further study. *This chapter explains scientists' new hypothesis about the birth of stars.* {hiy **po** thə sihs}

hys·ter·i·cal  *adjective* 1. having or likely to have fits of wild behavior such as laughing or crying. *She was hysterical after her dog was hit by a car.* 2. causing much laughter; wildly funny. *That comic act was hysterical!* {hih **steh** rih kəl} hysterically, adv.

 Human Body
 Human Mind
 Everyday Life
 History and Culture
Communication

I i

I is a vowel that makes several different sounds.

Tips to help you look up words starting with i: Sometimes vowels sound similar to each other. If you can't find the word you're looking for under I, it may start with a or e (such as aisle or eye).

These words may be hard to look up if you don't already know how to spell them:

immediate	innocence
inauguration	inoculate
indict	insist
influence	irrelevant
ingenious	island
initiative	isle

i or **I** *noun* (i's or I's) the ninth letter of the English alphabet. {**iy**}

I symbol of the chemical element iodine.

I *pronoun* the one who is speaking or writing. *I left yesterday. / I am the farmer's son.* {**iy**}

Homophone Note The words *I*, *eye*, and *aye* sound alike but have different meanings.

IA *abbreviation* an abbreviation for **Iowa**.

-ic *suffix* 1. a suffix that means "like" or "having to do with." *A historic figure is a person who is important in history.* 2. a suffix that means "related to" or "made of." *A metallic object is made out of metal.* 3. a suffix that means "causing" or "producing." *A terrific clap of thunder is one that causes some people to feel terror.*

-i·cal *suffix* 1. a suffix that means "related to" or "like." *A historical fact is a fact related to history.* 2. a suffix that means "made up of." *A comical story is a story that has much comedy in it.*

ice 🌳 🔬 💧 *noun* 1. water in a frozen, solid state. 2. a body of frozen surface water on a lake, pond, sea or river. 3. a dessert made of sweetened crushed ice. *verb* (iced, icing, ices) 1. to make very cold, especially through contact with ice; chill. *He iced the bottles of soda for the party.* 2. to coat or decorate with icing. *She iced the cupcakes with chocolate.* 3. to become coated with ice (often followed by "up" or "over"). *The pond ices over in January.* {**iys**}

• **break the ice**
to relieve social tensions caused by formal conventions or awkwardness. *The counselor led a game that broke the ice on the first day of summer camp.*

ice age *noun* a long period of time when glaciers covered large parts of the earth. *Our part of the country was covered with ice and snow during the last ice age, over ten thousand years ago.* {**iys** ayj}

ice·berg *noun* a large floating mass of ice that has broken from a glacier. {**iys** buhrg}

Word History *Iceberg* comes from a Dutch word that means "ice mountain."

ice·box *noun* 1. a refrigerator. 2. a box that contains ice and is used for keeping food cold. {**iys** bŏks}

ice·break·er *noun* 1. a ship that can break a passage through thick ice. 2. something that breaks the tension in a formal or awkward social situation. *His jokes served as an icebreaker at the party.* {**iys** brayk ər}

ice·cap *noun* a large, thick sheet of ice that spreads out over the land in all directions from the center. *The North Pole is covered by an ice cap.* {**iys** kăp}

ice cream 💧 *noun* a rich, sweet, frozen food made by mixing cream and milk products. Ice cream is made in many different flavors. {**iys** kreem}

ice hockey *noun* see **hockey**. {**iys** ho kee}

Ice·land *noun* an island country in northern Europe. Iceland is in the North Atlantic. Reykjavik is the capital of Iceland. {**iys** lənd} Icelander, n.

ice-skate *verb* (ice-skated, ice-skating, ice-skates) to skate on ice. *She will ice-skate on the frozen pond.* {**iys** skayt}

A B C D E F G H I J K L M N O P Q R S T U V W X Y Z

a
b
c
d
e
f
g
h
i
j
k
l
m
n
o
p
q
r
s
t
u
v
w
x
y
z

i·ci·cle *noun* a spike of ice formed by the freezing of dripping water. {**iy** sih kəl}

ic·ing *noun* a sweet substance used for covering or decorating cakes, cookies, or other baked goods; frosting. {**iy** sing}

i·con *noun* 1. an image, likeness, or symbol. 2. an image or picture of a religious figure which is itself seen as holy by some Christian churches. {**iy** kŏn}

i·cy *adjective* (icier, iciest) 1. made of, covered with, or looking like ice. *Drive slowly on icy roads!* 2. very cold. *Penguins swim in icy water.* 3. without warmth or feeling; unfriendly in manner. *He spoke to me in an icy tone of voice.* {**iy** see}

I'd shortened form of "I would" or "I had." *I'd love to go with you. / I'd already eaten dinner when you called.* {**iyd**}

ID *abbreviation* 1. an abbreviation for **Idaho**. 2. an abbreviation for **identification**.

I·da·ho *noun* a state in the northwestern United States. Its capital is Boise. (abbreviated: ID) {**iy** də hoh} Idahoan, n., adj.

Word History The name *Idaho* was invented in 1860 by George Willing, a spokesman for western mining companies. He suggested "Idaho" as a name for what became Colorado because it sounded like an Indian word and Indian place names were popular then. He said Idaho meant "gem of the mountains." Congress rejected "Idaho" as a name for the Colorado Territory, but approved it for the Idaho Territory in 1863.

i·de·a *noun* 1. any thought, belief, picture, or image that is formed in the mind. *What ideas do you have for your next painting?* 2. an opinion, theory, or conviction. *His ideas about the death sentence are different from mine.* 3. a plan, purpose, or goal. *He has ideas of becoming a movie star.* 4. a general impression or meaning of a concept, action or situation. *Give me an idea of what your trip to India was like.* {**iy** dee ə}

Synonyms
These words share a meaning with *idea*, noun 2:

view, theory, opinion, belief, judgment, conviction

i·de·al *noun* 1. an idea of something in its perfect form. *A community without violence is an ideal worth working for.* 2. a belief or aim considered to be worthy of honor or respect. *He has high ideals.* 3. something or someone that is seen as perfect. *The famous singer was her ideal.* *adjective* 1. of or having to do with being an ideal. *In an ideal school, both teachers and children would be eager to learn what interests them.* 2. seen as a model of being perfect. *Teaching is the ideal job for Mark.* 3. seen or understood as the best of its kind or the best under certain conditions. *That is an ideal restaurant for a party.* {**iy** deel}

i·den·ti·cal *adjective* 1. the same. *We met in that identical spot at the park.* 2. alike in every way. *No two snowflakes are*

identical. {**iy** **dehn** tə kəl *or* ih **dehn** tə kəl}

i·den·ti·fi·ca·tion *noun* 1. the act of showing who a person is or what a thing is. *They went for a walk in the woods and took a book on the identification of birds.* 2. something that proves who a person is, such as a driver's license or passport. *The spy had to show her identification before the guards would let her into the secret cave.* {**iy** dehn tə fih **kay** shən}

i·den·ti·fy *verb* (identified, identifying, identifies) 1. to figure out or show who someone is or what something is. *She identified him as the criminal. / The scientist identified the bird as a rare kind of parrot.* 2. to connect in feeling or action (usually followed by "with"). *I identify that author with exciting adventure stories.* 3. to feel oneself to be in the position or situation of another. *She identified with him when he lost his job.* {**iy** **dehn** tih fiy}

i·den·ti·ty *noun* (identities) 1. all of those things by which a person or thing is known to be himself, herself, or itself. *When he is on stage, an actor loses his identity* 2. the condition of being exactly the same as another person or thing. *Even though they look the same, the twins do not have the same identity.* {**iy** **dehn** tih tee}

Word History *Identity* comes from a Latin word that means "over and over again."

id·i·om *noun* a phrase that cannot be understood by understanding the meanings of each of its words. The phrase "fall out," meaning "have a disagreement," is an idiom. {**ihd** ee əm}

 Human Body   Human Mind   Everyday Life    History and Culture   Communication

id·i·ot *noun* a stupid person; fool. {ih dee iht}

Word History *Idiot* comes from an ancient Greek word that means "private person" or "peculiar person." The word was used for someone who did not hold public office and was not educated. For the Greeks, to call someone a private person was an insult.

i·dle *adjective* (idler, idlest) 1. not active or in use; not working. *The factory sat idle after the company went out of business.* 2. wanting to avoid work; lazy. *The idle students never finished their work.* 3. having little or no use or value. *For some people, video games are an idle activity.* 4. having no basis in fact; not true. *An idle rumor spread through the school.* *verb* (idled, idling, idles) 1. to pass time in not working or in avoiding work. *She idled away the weekend.* 2. to run an engine out of gear without causing motion. *The car idled in the driveway.* {iy dəl} idleness, n., idly, adv.

Homophone Note The words *idle* and *idol* (a statue) sound alike but have different meanings.

i·dol *noun* 1. a statue or image of a god that is used as an object of worship. 2. one who is loved and respected to a great degree; hero. {iy dəl}

Homophone Note Are you looking for the word *idle* (not moving)? *Idol* and *idle* sound alike but have different meanings.

if *conjunction* 1. on the condition that; in the event that. *If I pay, will you go to the movies with me?* 2. though it may be true that. *If the car won't start, can't we find* another way to go? 3. whether. *I don't know if he wants to go to the zoo.* 4. I really wish that. *If he could see me dancing!* {ihf}

ig·loo *noun* (igloos) an Inuit hut, shaped like a dome and made of blocks of ice or hard snow. {ihg looh}

Word History *Igloo* is an Inuit (Eskimo) word for "house." To the Inuit people, it may seem that *house* is the English word for "igloo."

ig·ne·ous *adjective* having to do with rocks formed by a volcano or other source of great heat. {ihg nee əs}

ig·nite *verb* (ignited, igniting, ignites) 1. to cause to begin burning; set on fire. *He ignited the paper with a match.* 2. to subject to great heat; cause to glow with heat. *The hot coals ignited the logs.* {ihg niyt}

ig·ni·tion *noun* 1. the act of starting to burn or being set on fire. *It is exciting to see the ignition of a rocket engine as it takes off.* 2. a device for getting something to burn by means of a spark or friction. In a car or other vehicle, the ignition is the device or system that ignites the fuel to start the engine. {ihg nih shən}

ig·no·rance *noun* lack of education or information. *Ignorance of the laws can get a person into trouble. / He failed the test out of ignorance, not because he is stupid.* {ihg nə rəns}

ig·no·rant *adjective* 1. without knowledge or education. *Some people are ignorant because they do not know how to read.* 2. not aware; not informed. *He is ignorant of his true feelings. / We are ignorant* about other countries. {ihg nə rənt}

ig·nore *verb* (ignored, ignoring, ignores) to refuse to recognize or fail to take notice of; pay no attention to. *She ignored me at the dance.* {ihg nohr}

Word History *Ignore* comes from a Latin word that means "to not know."

i·gua·na *noun* a large lizard found mostly in the warmer parts of Central and South America. Many iguanas have a ridge of spines down the middle of the back. Unlike other lizards, iguanas eat only plants. {ih gwah nə}

IL or **Ill.** *abbreviation* an abbreviation for **Illinois**.

il- *prefix* a prefix that means "not" or "without." It is used before words that start with the letter L. *The word "illegal" means "not legal." / An illogical idea is an idea that is not logical.*

I'll shortened form of "I will." *I'll get some milk from the store.* {iyl}

Homophone Note The contraction *I'll*, and the words *aisle* and *isle* sound alike but have different meanings.

ill *adjective* (worse, worst) 1. not healthy; sick. *He became ill with fever.* 2. evil; harmful; bad. *She felt the ill effects of eating too much dessert.* 3. not kind; unfriendly. *There were ill feelings between them after the fight.* *noun* evil or harm; trouble. *A bad law leads to many ills. / I don't wish them ill.* *adverb* 1. in an unfriendly, unkind, or evil way. *He spoke ill of everyone.* 2. not prop-

A B C D E F G H I J K L M N O P Q R S T U V W X Y Z

erly; badly. *Her visit was ill-planned.* {ihl}

• **ill at ease**
causing uncomfortable feelings; uneasy. *She felt ill at ease in her new school.*

il·le·gal *adjective* against the law or rules; not lawful. *Stealing is illegal.* {ih **lee** gəl} illegally, adv.

il·leg·i·ble *adjective* difficult or impossible to read. *He wrote down some directions, but they were illegible.* {ih **leh** jə bəl} illegibly, adv.

Il·li·nois *noun* a state in the midwestern United States. Its capital is Springfield. (abbreviated: IL) {ihl ə **noi**} Illinoisan, n., adj., Illinoisian, n., adj.

Word History *Illinois* is the French spelling of *illini*, an Algonquin name for the group of six Indian nations living in the area. *Illini* means "warriors" or "superior people."

il·lit·er·ate *adjective* not able to read or write. *Because he is illiterate, his daughter reads his mail to him.* {ih **lih** tə riht}

ill·ness *noun* 1. the condition of being ill; sickness. *Because of her illness, she missed two days of school.* 2. an instance of being ill. *He has a serious illness.* {ihl nihs}

il·log·i·cal *adjective* not logical or reasonable. *It is illogical to think you can drive from New York to California in one day.* {ih **lo** jih kəl}

il·lu·mi·nate *verb* (illuminated, illuminating, illuminates) 1. to light up; make bright with light. *Lights illuminated the stage.* 2. to make clear or easier to understand; explain. *The teacher's example illu-*

minated the math problem. 3. to give knowledge to; enlighten. *This book has illuminated many people on the importance of fighting against prejudice.* 4. to become lit up. *The sky illuminated with millions of stars.* {ih **looh** mə **nayt**}

il·lu·sion *noun* 1. a false or misleading idea or fantasy. *He was under the illusion that he didn't have to work on Saturday night.* 2. a state of seeing, hearing, or otherwise sensing things in a false way. *The magician created the illusion that he was sawing a woman in half.* {ih **looh** zhən}

il·lus·trate *verb* (illustrated, illustrating, illustrates) 1. to explain or make clear by giving examples. *By using a prism, she illustrated how rainbows are formed.* 2. to draw pictures to go along with a book or other written material. *He illustrated the children's book with pictures of dinosaurs.* {ihl ə **strayt**}

Word History *Illustrate* comes from a Latin word that means "light up." The words "luster" and "lustrous" come from related Latin words.

il·lus·tra·tion *noun* 1. a picture or drawing used to explain or decorate a book or other written material. 2. something that explains or makes clear; example. *The teacher gave an illustration of how gravity works.* {ihl ə **stray** shən}

il·lus·tra·tor *noun* an artist who makes illustrations for books

or other written works. {ihl ə **stray** tər}

ill will *noun* unfriendly feelings; dislike. *There has been ill will between the two brothers for many years.* {ihl **wihl**}

I'm shortened form of "I am." *I'm the tallest girl in class.* {**iym**}

im-[1] *prefix* a prefix that means "in," "into," or "on." It is used before words beginning with the letters P, B, or M. *The word "imprison" means "to be put in prison."*

im-[2] *prefix* a prefix that means "not" or "without." It is used before words that begin with the letters P, B, or M. *An impatient person is a person who is without patience.* / *An imperfect jewel is a jewel that is not perfect.*

im·age ❓ ❓ *noun* 1. a picture or some other likeness of a person or thing. *The dollar bill has an image of George Washington on one side of it.* 2. a picture of something formed by a mirror; reflection. *I saw my own image in the mirror.* 3. a person or thing that looks very similar to or exactly like someone or something else. *She is the image of her father.* {**ihm** ihj}

im·age·ry *noun* (imageries) images that are created in the mind while reading or looking at art. *The book is full of jungle imagery.* {**ihm** ihj ree}

im·ag·i·nar·y *adjective* existing only in the imagination. *My mother told me that the monster under my bed is imaginary.* {ə **măj** ih **nayr** ee}

im·ag·i·na·tion ❓ *noun* the act or power of the mind to form a thought, picture, or image of something or someone that is not present to

 Human Body   Human Mind   Everyday Life   History and Culture Communication

the senses. *She uses her imagination to write stories.* {ə **măj** ih **nay** shən}

im·ag·i·na·tive *adjective* having or showing an active or good imagination. *He is an imaginative child. / He wrote imaginative books about animals who talk to children.* {ə **măj** ih nə tihv}

im·ag·ine *verb* (imagined, imagining, imagines) 1. to form in the mind a thought, picture, or image of. *Imagine living on the planet Mars.* 2. to guess; suppose. *I imagine he will be here by the end of the week.* {ə **mă** jihn}

Word History *Imagine*
comes from *imaginari*, a Latin word that means "to form an image in one's own mind."

im·i·tate *verb* (imitated, imitating, imitates) 1. to copy the actions of; try to be like. *Small children often imitate their parents.* 2. to make a copy of; reproduce. *He imitates real gold jewelry using cheap metal.* {**ihm** ə **tayt**} imitator, n.

im·i·ta·tion *noun* 1. the act of imitating or copying. *Grandfather does a great imitation of an opera singer.* 2. a copy of something else; likeness. *She bought an imitation of one of Picasso's paintings.* *adjective* meant to look like something better. *The old woman's coat was made of imitation fur.* {ihm ə **tay** shən}

im·mac·u·late *adjective* not dirty; completely clean. *She wore an immaculate dress to church.* {əm **măk** yə liht}

Word History *Immaculate*
comes from a Latin word that means "without any spots or stains."

im·ma·ture *adjective* 1. not completely grown or developed; not mature. *The immature apples taste sour.* 2. without the wisdom or good sense of an adult; childish or foolish. *It was immature of him not to apologize for breaking the doll.* {ihm mə **choohr**} immaturity, n.

im·meas·ur·a·ble *adjective* impossible to measure; very great. *Her love for her daughter was immeasurable.* {ihm **meh** zhə rə bəl}

im·me·di·ate *adjective* 1. happening right away; instant. *When she asked him to explain his absence, he gave her an immediate answer.* 2. next in order; without anything between. *He sat on her immediate left.* 3. close in space or time; near. *All her friends live in the immediate neighborhood. / The immediate past is easier to remember than the distant past.* {ə **mee** dee iht}

im·me·di·ate·ly *adverb* right away; at once. *If he doesn't leave immediately, he'll be late for the meeting.* {ə **mee** dee iht lee}

im·mense *adjective* very large; huge. *An immense wave pulled the boat under water.* {ihm **mehns**} immensely, adv.

im·merse *verb* (immersed, immersing, immerses) 1. to almost cover or cover completely with liquid. *The spoon was immersed in the sauce.* 2. to involve deeply; hold all one's attention; absorb. *Dan was immersed in his video game and did not hear his mother call him for dinner.* {ihm **muhrs**}

im·mi·grant *noun* a person who moves to another country from his or her native land. *They were immigrants to the United States from Israel.* {**ihm** ə grənt}

im·mi·grate *verb* (immigrated, immigrating, immigrates) to come to live in a country where one was not born. *My parents immigrated to the United States from Mexico.* {**ihm** ə grayt}

Language Note *Immigrate* and *emigrate* are verbs that are related and that sound almost alike. *Immigrate* means to come to live in a country where one was not born. *Emigrate* means to leave one country to settle in another. *Andrea immigrated to the United States from Bosnia. Her family emigrated because of the war.*

im·mi·gra·tion *noun* the act of coming to live in a new country. *About one hundred and twenty years ago, the U.S. government first approved the immigration of Koreans.* {ih mə **gray** shən}

im·mi·nent *adjective* about to happen or likely to happen soon. *My mother's imminent arrival means that I must clean my apartment.* {**ihm** ə nənt} imminently, adv.

im·mor·al *adjective* bad; evil; not moral. *Cheating on a test is immoral.* {ih **mohr** əl} immorally, adv.

im·mor·tal *adjective* 1. never dying; living forever. *In that* story, *all the vampires were immortal.* 2. lasting forever in memory or in fame. *Shakespeare's poetry is immortal.* {ih **mohr** təl}

im·mune *adjective* 1. protected from a disease, either naturally or by getting a vaccine. *Now that you've had the mumps, you are immune. / Humans are immune to many diseases that affect cats and dogs.* 2. not influenced by something that does affect others; protected. *In a democratic country, no one should be immune from the law.* {ih **myoon**}

im·mu·ni·ty *noun* (immunities) the condition of being able to resist a disease. *I had to prove immunity to several diseases before my trip to Africa.* {ih **myoo** nih tee}

im·mu·nize *verb* (immunized, immunizing, immunizes) to make immune. *A nurse gave the students vaccines to immunize them against measles.* {**ihm** yə **niyz**} immunization, n.

im·pact *noun* 1. the coming together of objects with great force; crash; collision. *The impact of the bus hitting the tree cracked the windshield.* 2. a strong and powerful effect. *The senator's speech on gun control had a great impact on voters.* {**ihm** păkt}

im·pair *verb* (impaired, impairing, impairs) to lessen the strength or ability of; damage. *Old age impaired his vision and hearing.* {ihm **payr**} impairment, n.

im·pal·a *noun* (impala or impalas) an African antelope with long legs and reddish brown fur. Male impalas have long, curved horns. Impalas can jump up to ten feet in the air, higher than any other kind of antelope. {ihm **păl** ə *or* ihm **pah** lə}

Word History *Impala* is a word from the Zulu language first used in English around 1875.

im·par·tial *adjective* not favoring one more than another; not prejudiced; fair. *Judges are supposed to be impartial.* {ihm **par** shəl}

im·pa·tience *noun* the quality or condition of being unable to wait calmly or bear annoyances. *Jane's impatience for summer vacation to begin was keeping her from finishing her homework.* {ihm **pay** shəns}

im·pa·tient *adjective* 1. not patient; not willing or able to wait calmly. *After waiting in line for twenty minutes, he became impatient.* 2. showing a lack of patience. *She is very impatient with students who don't do their homework.* {ihm **pay** shənt} impatiently, adv.

im·peach *verb* (impeached, impeaching, impeaches) to accuse a person in public office of wrong or improper conduct. *Only two U.S. presidents have been impeached.* {ihm **peech**} impeacher, n.

im·per·a·tive *adjective* 1. very important; urgent. *It is imperative that you return today.* 2. of or describing the mood of the verb used to make demands or give orders. *In the sentence, "Come here!" the verb "come" is imperative.* {ihm **pehr** ə tihv}

im·per·a·tive sen·tence *noun* a sentence that tells someone to do something or makes a request. *An example of an imperative sentence is "Tie your shoes."* {ihm **pehr** ə tihv **sehn** təns}

im·per·fect *adjective* not perfect or complete; having mistakes or faults. *Because its diamond is imperfect, the ring was less expensive.* {ihm **puhr** fihkt} imperfectly, adv.

im·pe·ri·al *adjective* 1. having to do with an empire or an emperor. *The imperial palace was large and beautiful.* 2. having to do with one country's control over other countries. *The saying, "The sun never sets on the British Empire" comes from a time when England had imperial rule over large parts of the world.* {ihm **peer** ee əl}

Word History *Imperial* and *imperative* come from *imperare*, a Latin word that means "to command."

im·per·son·al *adjective* 1. not having to do with a particular person; general. *The principal spoke in an impersonal way about the students' behavior in the cafeteria.* 2. without warm feelings towards others. *Her impersonal stare hurt my feelings.* {ihm **puhr** sə nəl}

im·per·son·ate *verb* (impersonated, impersonating, impersonates) to copy the appearance and actions of; pretend to be. *He has a talent for impersonating famous singers. / It is against the law to impersonate a police officer.* {ihm **puhr** sə **nayt**} impersonation, n., impersonator, n.

im·per·ti·nent *adjective* rude or too bold. *He thinks it is impertinent to ask old people their age.* {ihm **puhr** tə nənt}

 Human Body   Human Mind   Everyday Life  History and Culture  Communication

a b c d e f g h i j k l m n o p q r s t u v w x y z

im·pet·u·ous *adjective* done suddenly and without much thought; impulsive. *She made an impetuous decision to cut off all her hair.* {ihm **pehch** ooh əs}

im·plant *verb* (implanted, implanting, implants) to plant or set firmly in something. *The gardener implanted stakes in the soil.* *noun* something placed in the body by surgery. {ihm **plănt**}

im·ple·ment *noun* something used to do a particular job; tool or device. *A hoe is a gardening implement. / A pen is a writing implement.* *verb* (implemented, implementing, implements) to carry out or put into action. *The government is finally implementing the new laws on industrial pollution.* {**ihm** plə mənt} implemental, adj., implementation, n., implementer, n.

im·pli·ca·tion *noun* something hinted at or suggested, but not said directly. *When he asked me if I had his watch, the implication was that I had stolen it.* {ihm plə **kay** shən}

im·ply *verb* (implied, implying, implies) to hint or suggest without saying directly. *When she said that the floor was dirty, she was implying that I should mop it.* {ihm **pliy**}

im·po·lite *adjective* not polite; rude. *It is impolite to leave without saying goodbye.* {ihm pə **liyt**} impolitely, adv., impoliteness, n.

im·port *verb* (imported, importing, imports) to bring in from another country. *The United States imports tomatoes from Israel.* *noun* something that is imported from another country. *Most tea that Americans drink is an* import from China or India. {ihm **pohrt** or ihm **pohrt**} importer, n.

Language Note *Import* and **export** are verbs that have the same meaning but in opposite directions. **Import** means to bring in from another country. **Export** means to send to another country. *Many countries import wheat from Canada. Canada exports wheat to many countries around the world.*

---

im·por·tance *noun* the quality or condition of being important. *The doctor talked about the importance of a healthy diet.* {ihm **pohr** təns}

im·por·tant *adjective* 1. having great meaning or value. *Buddha's teachings have been important to many people.* 2. powerful or having great influence. *The mayor of our city is an important woman.* {ihm **pohr** tənt} importantly, adv.

Synonyms
These words share a meaning with **important**, adjective 2:

major Major suggests that a person or thing is ranked among the most important. *Robert Frost is considered a major poet in American literature.*

prominent If someone is prominent, he or she is well known. *Since she was elected, she has become a prominent person.*

influential Influential is used to describe those that have the ability to affect others. *Those students were influential in getting the school to set up a recycling program.*

eminent Eminent is often used to describe those who have achieved great things. *She is an eminent scientist.*

---

im·pose *verb* (imposed, imposing, imposes) to set as something that needs to be followed, done, or obeyed. *The state imposed taxes on cigarettes.* {ihm **pohz**}
• **impose on** [or] **upon** to make demands of without being invited or at a bad time. *Bill imposes on us by coming to our house right at dinner time.*

Synonyms
These words share a meaning with **impose**, verb 1:
set, establish, institute

---

im·pos·si·ble *adjective* 1. not able to happen, or be done; not possible. *It is impossible to walk across the ocean.* 2. very difficult; not easy to deal with. *You are impossible! / He has gotten himself into an impossible situation.* {ihm **pŏs** ə bəl}

im·pos·tor *noun* a person who cheats or tricks others by pretending to be another person. *The man who was thought of as a famous baseball player turned out to be an impostor.* {ihm **pŏs** tər}

im·prac·ti·cal *adjective* 1. not useful or wise to do; not practical. *Going to Alaska in the middle of winter is impractical.* 2. not able to deal with everyday, practical things; foolish. *It was impractical to spend one month's salary on a dress.* {ihm **prăk** tih kəl}

im·press *verb* (impressed, impressing, impresses) to have a strong effect on the mind or feelings of. *His test score of 100 percent impressed the teacher.* {ihm **prehs**}

im·pres·sion 🄌 *noun* 1. a strong feeling or idea that comes from experience. *My impression of my teacher got better as the year went on.* 2. a belief or a feeling that is created at the beginning of an experience. *Paul had the impression that Sal liked him, but he was wrong.* 3. a mark made by pressing. *Our feet made impressions in the wet sand.* {ihm **prehsh** ən}

im·pres·sive *adjective* having a lasting effect on the mind or feelings; making a strong impression. *The new skyscraper is an impressive building.* / *His poetry is impressive.* {ihm **prehs** ihv}

im·print *noun* 1. a mark or design made by pressing or printing on a surface. *Our feet made imprints in the wet sand.* 2. a lasting effect. *She left her imprint on history by creating a new antibiotic.* *verb* (imprinted, imprinting, imprints) 1. to mark by pressing or stamping. *Be sure to imprint the date of payment on every bill.* 2. to fix firmly in the mind, memory, or feelings. *His unusual photograph is imprinted in my memory.* {ihm **prihnt** or ihm **prihnt** or **ihm prihnt**}

im·pris·on *verb* (imprisoned, imprisoning, imprisons) to put or keep in a prison. *He was imprisoned for forty years.* {ihm **prihz** ən} imprisonment, n.

im·prop·er *adjective* 1. not correct. *The machine was ruined by improper use.* 2. showing bad manners; not acceptable. *He made improper remarks about the boy who stutters.* {ihm **prŏp** ər} improperly, adv.

improper fraction *noun* a fraction in which the denominator is smaller than the numerator. *The numbers 9/5 and 11/8 are improper fractions.* {ihm **prŏp** ər **frăk** shən}

im·prove *verb* (improved, improving, improves) 1. to make better. *Salt and pepper improved the sauce.* 2. to become better. *She has improved as an artist.* / *Dick improved slowly after the accident.* {ihm **proohv**}

im·prove·ment *noun* 1. the act of improving or the condition of being improved. *The teacher noticed an improvement in his handwriting.* 2. a change that makes something better than it was. *Cutting your hair was an improvement.* {ihm **proohv** mənt}

im·pro·vise *verb* (improvised, improvising, improvises) 1. to make up while one is performing; perform without planning or practice. *The piano player was improvising that beautiful music.* 2. to make from whatever materials are around. *We improvised a fort out of chairs and blankets.* {ihm prə **viyz**}

Word History *Improvise* comes from *improvviso*, an Italian word that means "not prepared" or "not known in advance."

im·pu·dent *adjective* not showing respect; bold and rude. *The impudent child poked his mother's nose and told her she was stupid.* {ihm pyə dənt}

im·pulse *noun* 1. a sudden wish or desire that makes a person want to do something. *She had an impulse to break the plate.* 2. a force that causes motion. *The windmill is turned by the wind's impulse.* {ihm **puhls**}

im·pul·sive *adjective* 1. acting without thinking or planning. *He is impulsive when he shops and buys more than he needs.* 2. done as a result of a sudden desire, without thinking or planning. *The leather jacket was an impulsive buy.* {ihm **puhl** sihv} impulsiveness, n.

im·pure *adjective* mixed with something that is harmful; polluted or not pure. *Coal miners get sick from breathing impure air.* / *The metals in an impure diamond may give it a yellow color.* {ihm **pyoor**}

in *preposition* 1. surrounded or contained by; living or located at. *They were caught in the rain.* / *The sandwich is in the refrigerator.* / *He lives in the city.* 2. during a period of time that is less than or equal to. *He finished the work in ten minutes.* 3. to or toward the inside of. *He got in his car.* 4. using; by the means of. *She spoke in a loud voice.* 5. used to indicate change from one state or condition to another. *The boat split in two.* *adverb* 1. to, toward, or into a place. *Let's drive in.* 2. within a particular place. *Let's stay in today.* {**ihn**}

Homophone Note The words *in* and *inn* (a small hotel) sound alike but have different meanings.

IN or **Ind.** *abbreviation* an abbreviation for **Indiana**.

in-¹ *prefix* a prefix that means "in," "on," or "into." *The word "indoors" means "in a house or building."* / *When a person is infuriated, he or she is in a state of fury.* / *When skin is inflamed, it has become hot and red, as though it were on fire.*

in-² *prefix* a prefix that means "not" or "without." *The word "incomplete" means "not complete."* / *The word "inequality" means "without equality."*

🏃 Human Body ❓ Human Mind 👕 Everyday Life 🚩 History and Culture 📞 Communication

in·a·bil·i·ty *noun* lack of ability or power to do something. *Her inability to read kept her from getting a good job.* {ihn ə **bih** lih tee}

in·ac·cu·rate *adjective* not correct, true, or exact. *What they are saying about Ed is inaccurate. / The clock is inaccurate.* {ihn **ăk** yər iht}

in·ad·e·quate *adjective* not enough; not good enough. *She brought an inadequate amount of food to the picnic. / He failed the test because his answers were inadequate.* {ihn **ăd** ə kwiht}

in·ap·pro·pri·ate *adjective* not right or proper for the time or place; not appropriate. *Is a black dress inappropriate for a wedding?* {ihn ə **proh** pree iht} inappropriately, adv.

in·au·di·ble *adjective* impossible to hear. *The music was inaudible with the vacuum cleaner running.* {ihn **awd** ih bəl}

in·au·gu·rate *verb* (inaugurated, inaugurating, inaugurates) 1. to put in office with an official ceremony. *They inaugurated the new president.* 2. to start or cause to start formally. *The Pathfinder's landing on Mars inaugurated a new era of space exploration.* {ihn **awg** yə **rayt**}

Word History *Inaugurate* comes from *inaugurare*, a Latin word that means "to act as a fortuneteller." In ancient Rome, the fortuneteller looked for omens of the future in the flights of birds. Based on what he saw, he would decide whether or not it was a favorable time for an important ceremony, such as the crowning of a king.

i·naug·u·ra·tion *noun* a formal beginning or start. *We celebrated the inauguration of her new job as a writer.* {ih **nawg** yoo **ray** shuhn}

in·born *adjective* in a person at birth; not learned. *He had an inborn talent for painting.* {ihn **bohrn**}

In·ca *noun* (Inca or Incas) a member of one of the Indian peoples that ruled Peru before being conquered by Spain in the sixteenth century. {**ing** kə} Incan, n., adj.

in·can·des·cent *adjective* giving off light as a result of being heated. *The common lightbulb is a kind of incandescent lamp.* {ihn kən **deh** sənt *or* ihn kăn **deh** sənt}

in·ca·pa·ble *adjective* 1. not having the ability or power that is needed; not able. *With an injured foot, he is incapable of climbing the mountain. / I am incapable of doing five things at once.* 2. without skill; poor. *He is a completely incapable actor.* {ihn **kay** pə bəl}

in·cense¹ *noun* a substance that has a pleasant smell when burned. *He lit incense to mask the smell of fish cooking.* {ihn **sehns**}

in·cense² *verb* (incensed, incensing, incenses) to make very angry. *I was incensed when someone stole my wallet.* {ihn **sehns**}

in·cen·tive *noun* something that makes a person want to work or do something. *Free food was an incentive to join the club.* {ihn **sehn** tihv}

in·ces·sant *adjective* never stopping; constant. *The incessant noise of truck traffic kept me awake all night.* {ihn **seh** sənt} incessantly, adv.

inch *noun* 1. a unit of length equal to one twelfth of a foot or 2.54 centimeters. (abbreviated: in.) 2. a small amount. *He hasn't moved an inch in the last hour.* *verb* (inched, inching, inches) to move by very small degrees or amounts. *The dog inched over to the piece of meat.* {ihnch}

inch·worm *noun* a moth larva that arches and stretches its body over and over again in order to move forward. *Inchworms are thin and look like worms.* {ihnch **wuhrm**}

in·ci·dent *noun* something that happens; a single event. *Several incidents led them to believe she was a thief.* {ihn sə dənt}

in·ci·den·tal·ly *adverb* apart from the main subject; by the way. *Incidentally, did you read her last book?* {ihn sə **dehn** tə lee *or* ihn sə **dehnt** lee}

in·ci·sion *noun* a cut made during surgery. *The surgeon made an incision on her right knee.* {ihn **sih** zhən}

in·cite *verb* (incited, inciting, incites) 1. to bring about, especially by angering or upsetting. *The managers' decision to lower wages incited a protest at the factory.* 2. to urge to action by stirring up emotions. *Her speech incited the workers to go on strike.* {ihn **siyt**}

in·cli·na·tion *noun* 1. a natural tendency towards. *Her inclination to tell lies left her with few friends.* 2. a liking or preference. *My inclination is to buy a new dress rather than repair this old one.* 3. a slope; slant. *The steep inclination of the hill prevented them from climbing it.* {ihn klə **nay** shən}

in·cline *verb* (inclined, inclining, inclines) 1. to slope or slant. *The road up the mountain inclines sharply.* 2. to cause to bend or move in a particular way. *He inclined his head to hear what his youngest daughter said.* *noun* a surface that slopes. *The old bus couldn't make it up the hill's*

a
b
c
d
e
f
g
h
i
j
k
l
m
n
o
p
q
r
s
t
u
v
w
x
y
z

steep incline. {**ihn** kliyn, n., ihn **kliyn**, v.}

in·close *verb* (inclosed, inclosing, incloses) another spelling of **enclose**. {ihn **klohz**}

in·clude *verb* (included, including, includes) 1. to have or contain as a part. *The new clock includes batteries.* 2. to put in a group or class. *She included all her friends on the list of people invited to the birthday party.* {ihn **kloohd**}

in·co·her·ent *adjective* not logical or clear; hard to understand. *He was so nervous that he gave an incoherent speech.* {ihn koh **heer** ənt} incoherently, adv.

in·come 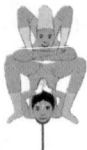 *noun* the money received for work or from property that is owned. *The lawyer has an income of $100,000. / The landlord is raising the rent to increase her income.* {ihn **kuhm**}

income tax *noun* a tax on the income of a person or business. *In the United States, the amount of money paid in income tax goes up as one's pay increases.* {ihn **kuhm tăks**}

in·com·pat·i·ble *adjective* 1. not able to be together in a peaceful or happy way. *When Mike's parents realized they were incompatible, they got a divorce.* 2. not matching; not consistent. *Your story is incompatible with what I heard from Miguel.* {ihn kəm **păt** ə bəl}

in·com·pe·tent *adjective* without the skills or knowledge needed to do something well. *Incompetent players won't make the basketball team.* {ihn **kŏm** pə tənt} incompetently, adv.

in·com·plete *adjective* not complete; not finished. *Caroline*

received a C for her incomplete essay. {ihn kəm **pleet**} incompletely, adv.

in·com·pre·hen·si·ble *adjective* impossible to understand. *It was incomprehensible to me that my best friend would steal my bicycle. / His handwriting is incomprehensible.* {ihn **kŏm** prə **hehn** sə bəl}

in·con·ceiv·a·ble *adjective* impossible to imagine, understand, or think about. *Being blind is inconceivable to me.* {ihn kən **see** və bəl}

in·con·clu·sive *adjective* 1. not proving something completely. *The judge dismissed the case because the evidence was inconclusive.* 2. not leading to a clear outcome or ending. *The war has been inconclusive.* {ihn kən **klooh** sihv}

in·con·sid·er·ate *adjective* not thinking of other people's feelings; thoughtless or rude. *After all the help you gave Melanie, it was inconsiderate of her not to thank you.* {ihn kən **sihd** ə riht} inconsiderately, adv., inconsiderateness, n.

in·con·spic·u·ous *adjective* not likely to be seen or noticed. *The color of its skin makes the snake inconspicuous in the woods.* {ihn kən **spihk** yoo əs}

in·con·ven·ience *noun* 1. the quality of causing bother or making things difficult. *She complained about the inconvenience of her long drive to work each day.* 2. a thing or situation that causes trouble or makes things difficult. *Not having a computer room at school is an inconvenience. verb* (inconvenienced, inconveniencing, inconveniences) to cause trouble or extra effort for. *Would it inconvenience you to drive me home?* {ihn kən **veen** yəns}

in·con·ven·ient *adjective* causing trouble or extra effort; not convenient. *The new supermarket is in an inconvenient location for people who do not have cars.* {ihn kən **veen** yənt} inconveniently, adv.

in·cor·po·rate *verb* (incorporated, incorporating, incorporates) 1. to include as part of a larger thing; blend. *If you no longer want your books, I'll incorporate them into my collection. / She incorporated all the food from last night's dinner into a stew.* 2. to make into a legal corporation. *The owners of the bicycle shop incorporated their growing business.* {ihn **kohr** pə **rayt**} incorporation, n.

in·cor·rect *adjective* not correct; wrong. *He had many incorrect answers on his test.* {ihn kə **rehkt**} incorrectly, adv., incorrectness, n.

in·crease *verb* (increased, increasing, increases) 1. to make larger or greater; add to. *I asked my mom to increase my allowance on my birthday.* 2. to become greater in amount, number, or size. *The population of our town is increasing. noun* the amount by which something is made larger. *There was an increase in the number of violent crimes last year.* {**ihn** krees or ihn **krees**} increasingly, adv.

Synonyms

These words share a meaning with *increase*, verb 1:

build, add to, jack up, expand, multiply, enlarge, boost, augment

in·cred·i·ble *adjective* 1. difficult or impossible to believe. *Her story about a monster under her bed was*

 Human Body  Human Mind Everyday Life  History and Culture  Communication

incredible. 2. amazing; astonishing. *What incredible luck!* {ihn **krehd** ə bəl} incredibly, adv.

in·cred·u·lous *adjective* not able to believe something. *Dave was incredulous when he heard that he had won the lottery.* {ihn **krehj** ə ləs}

in·crim·i·nate *verb* (incriminated, incriminating, incriminates) to show involvement in a crime. *The evidence in the criminal's house incriminated him.* {ihn **krihm** ə **nayt**}

in·cu·bate *verb* (incubated, incubating, incubates) to keep warm until time to hatch. *A hen incubates her eggs by sitting on them.* {**ing** kyə **bayt**}

Word History *Incubate* comes from *incubare*, a Latin word that means "to lie on." A hen lies on its eggs to keep them warm enough for growth and life to continue.

in·cu·ba·tor *noun* 1. a warm container that protects and helps babies that are sick or born too early. An incubator allows doctors to control the temperature, amount of oxygen, and other conditions that affect a baby's health. 2. a machine that uses heat to hatch eggs. {**ing** kyə **bayt** ər}

in·cur·a·ble *adjective* not capable of being cured. *She has an incurable disease.* {ihn **kyoor** ə bəl *or* ihn **kyuhr** ə bəl}

in·debt·ed *adjective* owing money, thanks, or a favor to another person. *I was indebted to him for getting my*

cat out of the tree. {ihn **deht** ihd}

in·de·cent *adjective* improper, crude, or causing offense. *It was indecent of her to use foul language at the children's party.* {ihn **dee** sənt} indecently, adv.

in·deed *adverb* without any question or doubt; truly. *I do indeed like the new plaid pants you bought for me.* *interjection* used to express strong agreement, surprise, or doubt. *Indeed! We'll see about that!* {ihn **deed**}

in·def·i·nite *adjective* not certain, not clear, or not having fixed limits. *My plans for this summer are still indefinite.* / *She will be in Florida for an indefinite amount of time.* {ihn **dehf** ə niht} indefinitely, adv.

indefinite article *noun* either of the articles "a" or "an" in English grammar. These articles do not restrict the noun to a particular person, place or thing. In the sentence, "A dog ran into my yard," the indefinite article "a" is used to show that it could have been any dog, and that a particular dog is not being named. {ihn dehf ə niht **ar** tih kəl}

in·dent *verb* (indented, indenting, indents) to begin to write or type farther from the left margin than the other lines. *Indent the first line of a new paragraph.* {ihn **dehnt**}

in·de·pend·ence *noun* 1. the state or condition of being independent. *I celebrate my country's independence on July fourth.* 2. freedom from outside control. *The American Revolution was fought for independence from England.* {ihn dih **pehn** dəns}

Independence Day *noun* a U.S. national holiday celebrated on July 4 to remember

the signing of the Declaration of Independence from England in 1776; Fourth of July. {ihn dih **pehn** dəns **day**}

in·de·pend·ent *adjective* 1. not ruled by another; ruling oneself. *France is an independent nation.* 2. separate or without connection. *This telephone line is independent from the others in the building.* 3. not needing the support or advice of another; self-sufficient. *She makes enough money to be an independent person.* {ihn dih **pehn** dənt} independently, adv.

in·dex ➋ *noun* (indexes) an alphabetical list of subjects, names, or other information in a book, with page numbers given for each item. *verb* (indexed, indexing, indexes) to make an index for. *The author indexed the book's most important information.* {ihn **dehks**}

Word History *Index* was a Latin word that came from another Latin word, *indicare*, which means "to point out" or "indicate." In Latin, "index" could mean "forefinger," "pointer," "list," or anything that points to something else. The index of a book points you to the places in the book you are interested in.

In·di·a *noun* a country in southern Asia surrounded on three sides by the Indian Ocean. New Delhi is the capital of India. {ihn **dee** ə}

In·di·an *noun* 1. a person who was born in or is a citizen of India. 2. a member of one of the native peoples of the Western Hemisphere, except the Eskimos, Aleuts, and Inuits; American Indian; Native American. *adjective* 1. of or having to do with India, or its people or languages. 2. of or having to do

A
B
C
D
E
F
G
H
I
J
K
L
M
N
O
P
Q
R
S
T
U
V
W
X
Y
Z

a
b
c
d
e
f
g
h
i
j
k
l
m
n
o
p
q
r
s
t
u
v
w
x
y
z

with American Indians, or their languages. {**ihn** dee ən}

In·di·an·a *noun* a state in the midwestern United States. Its capital is Indianapolis. (abbreviated: IN) {**ihn** dee **ăn** ə} Indianian, n., adj.

> **Word History** *Indiana* means "land of the Indians."

Indian corn *noun* a grain that grows on the ears of a tall plant; maize. *Indian corn was used for decoration at our Thanksgiving dinner.* {**ihn** dee ən **kohrn**}

Indian Ocean *noun* an ocean south of Asia. It reaches from Africa to Australia. {**ihn** dee ən **oh** shən}

in·di·cate *verb* (indicated, indicating, indicates) 1. to show or point out. *Indicate the books you enjoyed most.* 2. to signal or serve as a sign, token, or index. *Those dark clouds indicate that it will rain.* 3. to state or express briefly. *Please indicate that you have finished the exam by raising your hand.* {**ihn** dih **kayt**}

in·di·ca·tion *noun* anything that indicates, such as a sign. *He gave no indication that he wanted to come to the party.* {**ihn** dih **kay** shən}

in·dict *verb* (indicted, indicting, indicts) to bring a legal charge against. *The police indicted the suspect for stealing.* {**ihn** **diyt**}

In·dies *noun* 1. see East Indies, West Indies. 2. India and the East Indies. {**ihn** deez}

in·dif·fer·ent *adjective* without interest or concern; not caring. *He was indifferent to his daughter's need for a warm coat.* {**ihn** **dihf** ər ənt *or* ihn **dih** frənt} indifferently, adv.

in·di·ges·tion *noun* 1. difficulty in digesting food. *Eating when you are upset can cause indigestion.* 2. an instance of discomfort caused by this difficulty. *She had indigestion after eating too much spicy food.* {**ihn** dih **jehs** chən}

in·dig·nant *adjective* feeling or showing anger about something considered to be unfair or without value. *When asked if she was lying, she gave an indignant reply.* {**ihn** **dihg** nənt} indignantly, adv.

in·di·go *noun* (indigos or indigoes) 1. a dark blue dye that comes from plants or is made by people. 2. a plant with red or purple flowers from which this dye comes. 3. a deep blue violet color; the color between blue and violet on the color spectrum. {**ihn** dih goh}

in·di·rect *adjective* 1. not in a straight line, course, or route. *I took an indirect route home so that I could stop and see the foal.* 2. caused by something, but not directly. *There were some indirect benefits from the accident.* 3. not direct; to avoid stating the truth. *When I asked Mira why she was late, she gave me an indirect reply.* {**ihn** də **rehkt**} indirectly, adv.

indirect object *noun* the part of a sentence that indicates a person or thing that is indirectly affected by the action of the verb. In the sentence, "I made him some tea," "him" is the indirect object. {**ihn** də **rehkt ŏb jehkt**}

in·dis·pen·sa·ble *adjective* absolutely necessary; essential. *A calculator is indispensable for this math class.* {**ihn** dih **spehn** sə bəl}

in·di·vid·u·al *adjective* 1. single, separate, or distinct. *Do I really have to water each individual plant? / Use commas to separate individual items in a series.* 2. referring to one person. *At the assembly, students will be honored for their individual achievements.* 3. having characteristics that show that something is different from others. *Stella has her own, individual style of telling a story.* *noun* 1. a single human being; person. *Each individual in this country has the right to vote.* 2. a single person as different from a group. *Do not expect the army to treat you as an individual.* {**ihn** dih **vihj** ooh əl} .

> **Word History** *Individual* comes from *individuus*, a Latin word that means "indivisible (not able to be divided)."

in·di·vid·u·al·i·ty 🔊 *noun* the qualities and characteristics of a person that make them different from all others. *She has a lot of individuality.* {**ihn** dih **vihj** ooh **ăl** ih tee}

in·di·vid·u·al·ly *adverb* 1. in an individual and separate way. *In this class, each child is taught how to read individually.* 2. one by one; one at a time. *The people stood in line to have their questions answered individually.* {**ihn** dih **vihj** ooh ə lee}

in·di·vis·i·ble *adjective* not able to be divided or separated. *Since the Civil War, the United States has been indivisible.* {**ihn** dih **vihz** ə bəl}

In·do·ne·sia *noun* a country in southeastern Asia made up of a group of islands

 Human Body   Human Mind   Everyday Life   History and Culture   Communication

stretching from the Indian Ocean into the Pacific Ocean. Jakarta is the capital of Indonesia. {ihn də **nee** zhə} Indonesian, n., adj.

in·door *adjective* located or happening inside a house or building. *They are wealthy enough to have an indoor tennis court.* {ihn **dohr**}

in·doors *adverb* in or into a building. *They went indoors when it started to rain.* {ihn **dohrz**}

in·dorse *verb* (indorsed, indorsing, indorses) another spelling of **endorse** {ihn **dohrs**}

in·dulge *verb* (indulged, indulging, indulges) 1. to give in to or gratify a desire, appetite, or whim. *The weather was so hot that we indulged in some ice cream.* 2. to give in to or gratify. *She indulged her desire for chocolate.* {ihn **duhlj**}

in·dus·tri·al *adjective* 1. having to do with the making of goods and services by industry. *She works at the first building in the industrial park.* 2. having a very current system of industries. *The industrial nations of the world are the most prosperous.* {ihn **duhs** tree əl}

in·dus·tri·al·ize *verb* (industrialized, industrializing, industrializes) to bring industry into; make industrial. *At the turn of the century, many American cities were industrialized.* {ihn **duhs** tree ə liyz} industrialization, n.

in·dus·tri·ous *adjective* working hard; producing in an active way. *Some very industrious students are helping with the school carnival.* {ihn **duh** stree əs}

in·dus·try ◐ *noun* (industries) 1. a manufacturing business. 2. a number of companies making a particular product. *The automobile industry employs thousands of people.* 3. the tendency to work hard. *The student showed much industry and earned an A.* {ihn dəs tree}

in·ed·i·ble *adjective* not safe to be eaten. *The food that we left out last night is inedible.* {ihn **ehd** ə bəl}

in·ef·fi·cient *adjective* taking too much time or supplies to produce or reach results. *The use of separate cars for travel to work is an inefficient use of energy compared to travelling by bus or subway.* {ihn ə **fihsh** ənt} inefficiently, adv.

in·e·qual·i·ty *noun* (inequalities) the condition of not being equal. *The civil rights movement fought against racial inequality.* {ihn ee **kwŏl** ih tee}

in·ert *adjective* not being able to move, act, or resist. *She took sleeping pills and is lying inert on the couch.* {ih **nuhrt**}

in·er·tia *noun* 1. the tendency of an object that is not moving to remain still, or of an object that is moving to continue to move, unless something else moves or stops the object. *Inertia kept the truck from stopping in time for the intersection.* 2. lack of willingness to move; motionlessness. *People are angry about the inertia of Congress on this important issue.* {ih **nuhr** shə}

in·ev·i·ta·ble *adjective* certain to happen; not able to be avoided. *It is inevitable that you will have to go to school on Monday morning.* {ihn **ehv** ih tə bəl} inevitably, adv.

in·ex·pen·sive *adjective* low or moderate in cost. *I bought two pairs of shoes, because they were so inexpensive.* {ihn ehk **spehn** sihv}

in·ex·per·i·enced *adjective* without the knowlege or skill that comes from practice or long life; not experienced. *The pilot is too inexperienced to fly in this storm.* {**ihn** ehk **speer** ee ənst}

in·fant ◉ *noun* a child in the first months of life. *adjective* 1. of, for, or having to do with infants. *Infant death rates decreased last year.* 2. young or early; still growing or developing. *He puts a lot of time into his infant business.* {ihn fənt}

Word History *Infant* comes from a Latin word that means "not able to speak."

in·fan·try ◐ *noun* (infantries) soldiers on foot, or the branch of the military to which they belong. {ihn fən tree}

in·fat·u·at·ed *adjective* unable to make good decisions because of a foolish attraction to someone or something. *He is so infatuated with video games that he isn't getting his home-*

A
B
C
D
E
F
G
H
I
J
K
L
M
N
O
P
Q
R
S
T
U
V
W
X
Y
Z

a
b
c
d
e
f
g
h
i
j
k
l
m
n
o
p
q
r
s
t
u
v
w
x
y
z

work done. {ihn **făch** ooh **ay** tihd}

in·fect *verb* (infected, infecting, infects) to spread germs or disease to. *If you cover your mouth when you cough, you won't infect others with your cold.* {ihn **fehkt**}

in·fec·tion 🔵 *noun* 1. the act of infecting or an instance or condition of being infected. *Infection can result from drinking lake water. / An infection is keeping him home from school this week.* 2. a germ or sickness that causes something to be infected. *Everyone in school is sick from an infection.* {ihn **fehk** shən}

in·fec·tious *adjective* 1. able to be given to others by infection. *We had to keep the cat by itself for six weeks because its disease was infectious.* 2. spreading easily as though by infection. *He has such an infectious smile!* {ihn **fehk** shəs}

in·fer *verb* (inferred, inferring, infers) to make a guess based on facts and observations; conclude. *I inferred from the books on his shelf that he enjoyed reading adventure stories.* {ihn **fuhr**}

in·fe·ri·or *adjective* 1. lower in rank, position, or degree. *He is an inferior officer in the army.* 2. of less value, importance, or quality. *The apples from the grocery store are inferior to the ones we picked ourselves.* {ihn **feer** ee ər} inferiority, n.

in·fer·tile *adjective* 1. not able to produce crops. *The farmer could not grow anything on the infertile land.* 2. not able to reproduce. *They wanted to have children, but he was infertile.* {ihn **fuhr** təl} infertility, n.

in·field *noun* a baseball diamond, the positions at the four corners of the diamond,

or the people playing those positions as a group. {ihn **feeld**}

in·fil·trate *verb* (infiltrated, infiltrating, infiltrates) to enter into in secret. *Spies infiltrated government buildings.* {ihn fihl **trayt**} infiltrator, n.

in·fi·nite *adjective* having no limits or end; without measure. *Your imagination is infinite. / Astronauts traveled into infinite space.* {ihn fə niht} infinitely, adv.

in·fin·i·tive *noun* the simple form of a verb that has no subject and does not show past, present or future tense. It is usually formed by the word "to" followed by the base form of a verb. In the sentence, "I want to leave now," "to leave" is an infinitive. {ihn **fihn** ih tihv}

in·firm *adjective* weak or ill, as from old age. *My grandfather came to live with us when he became infirm.* {ihn **fuhrm**}

in·flame *verb* (inflamed, inflaming, inflames) 1. to stir up or intensify. *The lack of food inflamed the people's anger.* 2. to become emotionally excited. *The mob inflamed at the sight of police officers.* 3. to cause or produce redness and swelling in. *An infection inflamed the wound on his knee.* {ihn **flaym**}

in·flam·ma·ble *adjective* able to catch fire and burn, or easy to set on fire and burn; flammable. *Gasoline is highly inflammable.* {ihn **flăm** ə bəl}

in·flam·ma·tion *noun* a small area of tissue that is hot, red, swollen, and sore because of infection or injury. {ihn flə **may** shən}

in·flate *verb* (inflated, inflating, inflates) 1. to make larger or expand. *Inflate the balloon by blowing into the open end.* 2. to become inflated. *The rubber raft inflates in three minutes.* {ihn **flayt**} inflatable, adj.

in·fla·tion 🔵 *noun* 1. an increase in the average price level. *They can't afford to buy a car this year because of inflation.* 2. the act of inflating or the condition or character of being inflated. *This tire needs inflation.* {ihn **flay** shən}

in·flex·i·ble *adjective* 1. not able to be bent, or not easy to bend; stiff. *Concrete is inflexible and breaks during earthquakes.* 2. not able to compromise or accommodate; not able to change. *The teacher was very inflexible about his rules.* 3. not likely to change under pressure or influence; stubborn. *She gets her work done with inflexible determination.* {ihn **flehk** sə bəl}

in·flict *verb* (inflicted, inflicting, inflicts) 1. to strike by physical attack. *They inflicted a heavy blow on their enemies.* 2. to impose. *The neighbor upstairs inflicted his loud music on us.* {ihn **flihkt**}

in·flu·ence *noun* 1. the ability of one thing or person to affect another. *He had a lot of influence on her decision to go to college.* 2. a thing or person that has such an ability. *He was a big influence on her piano style.* *verb* (influenced, influencing, influences) to have influence on; affect.

 Human Body   Human Mind   Everyday Life    History and Culture   Communication

Your ideas have influenced my thinking. {**ihn** flooh əns}

Word History The words *influence* and *influenza* both had their beginnings in a Latin word that meant "to flow in." In Roman times, the Latin word was often used for the effects the stars had on human affairs. The belief that the position of the stars could bring about good or evil events continued into the Renaissance period in Britain and western Europe. The flu was thought to be caused by a bad influence from the stars.

in·flu·en·tial *adjective* having power or influence. *She is a very influential person in this town.* {**ihn** flooh **ehn** shəl}

in·flu·en·za *noun* a disease caused by a virus in humans and some animals; flu. Influenza causes fever, indigestion, coughing and muscle pain. {**ihn** flooh **ehn** zə}

in·fo *noun* shortened form of **information.** {**ihn** foh}

in·fo·mer·cial *noun* a long commercial in the form of a television program. {**ihn** foh mər shuhl}

in·form 🔊 *verb* (informed, informing, informs) 1. to give knowledge to; tell. *They informed me that today is your birthday.* 2. to provide information about someone that shows that person has done something wrong. *Bill's classmates were angry that he informed on them.* {ihn **fohrm**}

in·for·mal *adjective* 1. casual; without ceremony. *They would not allow him into the ball in informal dress.* 2. used often and correctly in everyday conversation or casual writing. *He told the class not to use informal language in their essays.* {ihn **fohr** məl} informally, adv.

in·for·ma·tion 🔊 🔊 *noun* 1. knowledge or facts that come from a source. *The newspaper is full of information.* / *I have some information about Josh that you might be interested in.* 2. a telephone service that can tell the caller the phone number of a person or business. *Harry called information to get the phone number for Porky's Pizza Palace.* {ihn fər **may** shən}

in·fre·quent *adjective* not happening often. *Kansas City experiences infrequent earthquakes.* {ihn **free** kwənt} infrequently, adv.

in·fu·ri·ate *verb* (infuriated, infuriating, infuriates) to cause great anger in; enrage. *The heavy traffic infuriated the drivers.* {ihn **fyoor** ee **ayt**}

-ing[1] *suffix* a suffix used to form the present participle of verbs. *"I am thinking about you"* shows the present participle of the verb "think."

-ing[2] *suffix* a suffix used to turn a verb into a noun. *"Singing" comes from the verb "sing" and is used to name an activity, as in "her beautiful singing."*

in·gen·ious *adjective* clever or creative in setting up or working through problems. *He is ingenious at living on very little money.* {ihn **jeen** yəs}

in·ge·nu·i·ty *noun* (ingenuities) the quality of, or an instance of being ingenious; cleverness. *He used his ingenuity to invent new gadgets.* {ihn jə **nooh** ih tee}

in·got *noun* an amount of metal made into a shape that makes it easy to hold or store. {**ing** gət}

in·gre·di·ent *noun* one of the parts of a mixture. *What ingredients do you need to make fudge?* {ihn **gree** dee ənt}

in·hab·it *verb* (inhabited, inhabiting, inhabits) to live in; use as a dwelling. *Would you like to inhabit a cave?* {ihn **hăb** iht}

in·hab·it·ant *noun* someone or something that lives in a place; resident. {ihn **hăb** ih tənt}

in·hab·it·ed *adjective* lived in; populated. *This house was inhabited by a famous artist.* {ihn **hăb** ih tihd}

in·hale 🔊 *verb* (inhaled, inhaling, inhales) to take in by breathing; breathe in. *During the fire, she inhaled so much smoke that it made her ill.* {ihn **hayl**}

in·her·it *verb* (inherited, inheriting, inherits) 1. to receive from a person who has died; be heir to. *I inherited an accordion from my grandfather.* 2. to receive through a parent's genes. *She inherited those blue eyes from her father.* {ihn **hehr** iht}

in·her·it·ance *noun* 1. money, property, or position that is or may be inherited legally. *My grandmother left me a huge inheritance.* 2. the process of passing characteristics to later generations by genes or the characteristics passed in this way. *When I saw her father, it was obvious where the inheritance of red hair came from.* {ihn **hehr** ih təns}

in·hu·man *adjective* without human feelings such as warmth, mercy, or sympathy; cruel, brutal, or not caring. *As prisoners of war, the soldiers were given inhuman treatment.* {ihn **hyoo** mən} inhumanly, adv., inhumanness, n.

in·i·tial *adjective* of the beginning; first. *My initial impression of him is that he is as boring as wet cardboard.* *noun* (usually plural) the first letters in a person's name. *The*

A
B
C
D
E
F
G
H
I
J
K
L
M
N
O
P
Q
R
S
T
U
V
W
X
Y
Z

artist put her initials in the corner of her painting. *verb* (initialed, initialing, initials) to mark with one's initials. *Please initial each paragraph to show that you have read and understood it.* {ih **nih** shəl} initially, adv.

in·i·ti·ate *verb* (initiated, initiating, initiates) 1. to cause to begin; start; originate. *Our teacher initiated a rule of no eating in the classroom.* 2. to welcome as a member of a club or society by holding a formal ceremony or ritual. *They had a tea party to initiate her into the sewing club.* {ih **nihsh** ee **ayt**}

in·i·ti·a·tive *noun* 1. the power, energy, or ability to organize or accomplish something. *She will succeed as president because of her initiative.* 2. the first or leading action in a process. *When they asked for volunteers, he took the initiative.* {ih **nihsh** ee ə tihv *or* ih **nihsh** ə tihv}

in·ject *verb* (injected, injecting, injects) 1. to introduce into by force or pressure with a needle. *The doctor injected the antibiotics.* 2. to bring or introduce into a discussion, presentation, or situation. *He injected a little humor into the conversation.* {ihn **jehkt**}

in·jec·tion *noun* 1. a measured dose of liquid medicine that is injected into the body. *The doctor gave me an injection of antibiotics.* 2. the act of injecting. *I always wince during an injection,*

because it might hurt. {ihn **jehk** shən}

in·jure *verb* (injured, injuring, injures) to harm; damage; wound. *He injured his leg in the car accident.* {ihn jər}

in·ju·ry 🌐 *noun* (injuries) any damage or wrong that causes pain or difficulty. *It took almost a month for him to get over his injuries.* {ihn jə ree}

in·jus·tice *noun* 1. the lack of justice or fairness. *We must fight against injustice.* 2. an act that is not just, not legal or not moral; a wrong. *It's an injustice to punish an innocent person.* {ihn **juh** stihs}

ink *noun* a liquid or paste, usually black or colored, that is used to write or print. *verb* (inked, inking, inks) to mark or color with ink. *She inked the poster with colorful birds.* {**ingk**}

Word History *Ink* comes from a Greek word that means "to burn in."

ink·ling *noun* a blurry or partial idea or understanding. *He had only an inkling of what the book was about.* {**ingk** ling}

in·land *adjective* in the part of a country that is away from the coast or border. *We traveled to the inland mountains and lakes.* *adverb* away from the coast or border and toward the center of a country. *The explorer led his team inland.* {ihn lănd}

in·let 🌐 *noun* a bay, stream, or other narrow body of water that leads inland from a shore. {ihn liht}

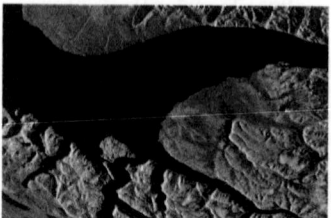

inn *noun* a small hotel for people who are travelling. {ihn}

Homophone Note The words *inn* and *in* sound alike but have different meanings.

in·ner *adjective* 1. located inside. *We walked to the inner parts of the cave.* 2. having to do with the spirit or mind. *The stories she writes come from her inner life.* {ihn ər}

in·ning *noun* the unit of a baseball of softball game during which each side has a turn at bat. {ih ning}

inn·keep·er *noun* the owner or manager of an inn. {ihn kee pər}

in·no·cence *noun* 1. the condition of being innocent. 2. freedom from guilt, blame, or fault. *You think that I ate Ann's birthday cake, but I can prove my innocence.* {ihn ə səns}

in·no·cent *adjective* 1. free from evil or knowledge of evil. *There is nothing more innocent than a newborn baby.* 2. free from guilt or blame. *Everyone knew that the girl was innocent.* 3. causing no harm. *Rough games may seem innocent, but someone might get hurt.* {ihn ə sənt} innocently, adv.

Word History *Innocent* comes from a Latin word that means "not capable of doing harm."

in·no·va·tion *noun* a new idea, product, or way to do something. *Thanks to innovations in technology, many people can now make use of a computer.* {ihn ə **vay** shən}

in·oc·u·late *verb* (inoculated, inoculating, inoculates) to inject with a very small amount of a disease to help resist that disease in the

 Human Body   Human Mind   Everyday Life  History and Culture   Communication

future. *They inoculated me with the flu so I wouldn't be sick with it this winter.* {ihn **ŏk** yə **layt**}

Word History *Inoculate* is from a Latin word that means "to put a bud into," which is how the grafting of a tree was done. In grafting, a bud from one tree is planted into another tree, so that the two parts will grow together into one, superior plant. An innoculation puts germs into the body to grow, so that the body will develop immunity to diseases.

in·put *noun* 1. information that is put into a computer. *My computer is large enough to store a lot of input.* 2. an opinion, advice, or help. *I've written a paper and would like your input.* *verb* (inputted or input, inputting, inputs) to put or cause to be put into a computer; enter. *The secretary input the data yesterday.* {ihn **puut**}

in·quire *verb* (inquired, inquiring, inquires) to ask to find out or learn. *He inquired about my parents.* {ihn **kwiyr**}

in·quir·y *noun* (inquiries) 1. a process of looking for truth or correct information. *The newspaper reporter's inquiry made the governor nervous.* 2. a question or request for information. *I sent an inquiry about available jobs.* {ihn **kwiyr** ee *or* ihn **kwiy** ə **ree**}

in·quis·i·tive ❓ *adjective* given to asking and inquiring; eager to learn. *My inquisitive nephew wanted to find the Caribbean islands.* {ihn **kwihz** ə tihv}

in·sane ❓ *adjective* 1. having a disease of the mind; crazy; mad. *The insane woman shouts at imaginary people as she walks down the street.* 2. for, or used by, insane persons. *They put their aunt in a home for the insane.* 3. very foolish or silly. *He could always make us laugh with his insane jokes.* {ihn **sayn**} insanely, adv.

in·san·i·ty *noun* (insanities) the condition of having a disease in the mind. *He's had so much hardship that it drove him to insanity.* {ihn **săn** ih tee}

in·scribe *verb* (inscribed, inscribing, inscribes) to write by carving. *They inscribed her name on the tombstone.* {ihn **skriyb**}

Word History *Inscribe* is from a Latin word that means "to write in." *Scribble*, *scribe*, and *script* have the same origins.

in·sect ❶ *noun* 1. a small animal with a hard covering over its body. Most kinds of insects have a body that is divided into three parts. Most insects also have three pairs of legs and one or two pairs of wings. Insects are arthropods. Bees, ants, butterflies, beetles, and flies are kinds of insects. 2. a tiny animal similar to true insects, such as a spider or centipede. {ihn **sehkt**}

in·sec·ti·cide *noun* a poison used to kill insects. {ihn **sehk** tə siyd} insecticidal, adj.

in·sec·ti·vore ❶ *noun* 1. an animal that eats insects or a plant that traps insects. 2. a small mammal in a group of animals that eat insects. Moles, shrews, and hedgehogs are insectivores. {ihn **sehk** tə vohr}

in·se·cure *adjective* 1. without enough protection; not safe or secure. *That apartment is too insecure to be safe from robbers.* 2. not firmly built or established; unstable. *The insecure beach house was washed away by the storm.* 3. not sure of oneself; filled with doubt. *She was so insecure that she felt nervous even around friends.* {ihn sə **kyoor** *or* ihn sə **kyuhr**} insecurely, adv.

in·sen·si·tive *adjective* without concern for or understanding of the feelings of others. *She was upset by the teacher's insensitive remark.* {ihn **sehn** sə tihv}

in·sert *verb* (inserted, inserting, inserts) to put or cause to be put in, into, or within. *If you insert a quarter in this machine, you will get some bubble gum.* *noun* that which is placed in, into, or within. *Advertising inserts in magazines are annoying.* {ihn **suhrt**}

in·side *preposition* in the inner part of; within. *It's not much to look at, but inside the house it is very cozy.* *adverb* into or in the inner part. *She went inside when it started to rain.* *noun* 1. the inner part or side. *The inside of this jacket is made of silk.* 2. (plural) the inner organs of the body. *My insides hurt after I ate four pieces of cake.* *adjective* 1. being on or in the inner side. *The inside doors in our house have no locks.* 2. taken from a private source. *He has inside information about the crime.* {ihn **siyd**}

• **inside out**
1. having the inner surface facing out. *I was embarrassed to see that I had put my shirt on inside out.* 2. completely; thoroughly. *He knows this building inside out.*

A
B
C
D
E
F
G
H
I
J
K
L
M
N
O
P
Q
R
S
T
U
V
W
X
Y
Z

a
b
c
d
e
f
g
h
i
j
k
l
m
n
o
p
q
r
s
t
u
v
w
x
y
z

in·sight *noun* 1. the power to understand a meaning or truth. *We admired the professor's insight into the causes of war.* 2. an instance of this power. *Her article was full of insights about human nature.* {**ihn** siyt}

in·sig·ni·a *noun* (insignia or insignias) a badge, button, medal, or mark that indicates membership in a certain group. *He proudly wore the insignia of the U.S. Army.* {ihn **seeg** nee ə}

in·sig·nif·i·cant *adjective* having no value, importance, or significance; trivial. *All the work he had done was considered insignificant.* {**ihn** sihg **nihf** ih kənt} insignificance, n.

in·sin·cere *adjective* showing false or dishonest feelings or opinions; hypocritical. *I don't believe he is really sorry for what he did, because his apology seemed insincere.* {ihn sihn **seer**} insincerely, adv.

in·sist *verb* (insisted, insisting, insists) 1. to be firm about something; refuse to give up. *He insists on being the first one in the lunch line.* 2. to emphasize something in a firm way (usually followed by "on"). {ihn **sihst**}

in·so·lent *adjective* rude, arrogant, or not showing respect in speech or behavior. *The child shocked everyone by speaking in an insolent way to the teacher.* {ihn sə lənt}

in·som·ni·a *noun* difficulty in getting to sleep. *If I seem tired, it's because I've had insomnia for the last two weeks.* {ihn **sŏm** nee ə}

Insects

Insects make up the largest group of animals in the world. There are about a million different kinds of insects, and scientists find and identify more kinds every year.

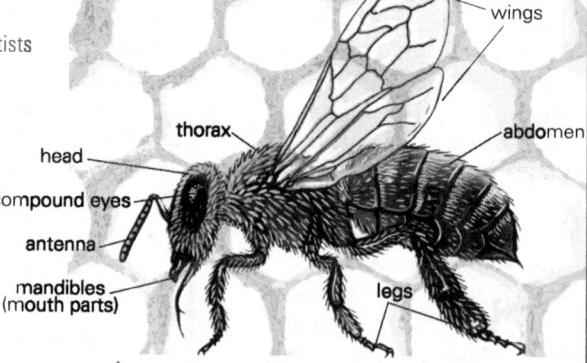

wings

thorax

head

abdomen

compound eyes

antenna

mandibles (mouth parts)

legs

The monarch butterfly is a champion flyer. In the fall, large numbers of monarchs travel from Canada and the United States to Mexico. The monarchs mate and lay their eggs in Mexico. When the eggs hatch in the spring, the young butterflies journey north to Canada and the United States.

Some bees build nests called "hives". They make thousands of connected chambers out of wax where the queen lays her eggs. Each tiny chamber is in the shape of a six-sided hexagon.
Some wasps build large nests out of paper. They make their own paper by chewing wood into pulp.

A female mosquito must feed on the blood of a mammal before her eggs can develop. The male sucks juice out of fruits. Mosquitos spread many serious diseases.

Most flies have only one pair of wings. They have mouth parts for sucking and piercing. Their larvae, called maggots, hatch in rotting meat or fruit.

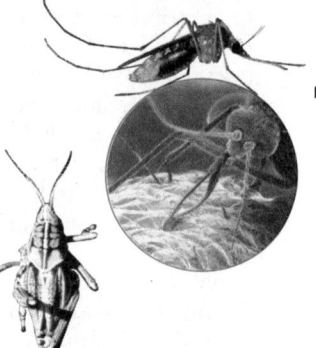

The praying mantis is a very large insect that eats other insects. Praying mantises have been known to eat small frogs. The praying mantis can turn its head. The female praying mantis eats the male after mating to provide nutrients for her developing eggs.

Grasshoppers have powerful back legs for jumping. Some grasshoppers can jump as far as two meters.

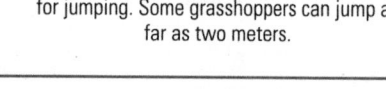 Human Body  Human Mind Everyday Life 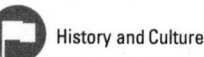 History and Culture  Communication

in·spect *verb* (inspected, inspecting, inspects) 1. to look at very carefully to find any problems. *He inspected the dress for stains.* 2. to look at in a critical and formal way to make sure that standards are kept. *The captain inspects his crew every morning to make sure they're ready for action.* {ihn **spehkt**}

in·spec·tion *noun* 1. the act or an instance of inspecting. *I had to bring my car into the garage for an inspection.* 2. an official review or examination. *Every morning, the troops line up for the sergeant's inspection.* {ihn **spehk** shən}

in·spec·tor *noun* 1. one who inspects, often in an official capacity. *After we wired the house, an inspector came to make sure everything was done correctly.* 2. an officer in a police or fire department. *The fire inspector found what caused the house to burn down.* {ihn **spehk** tər}

in·spi·ra·tion ❓ *noun* 1. an action, thought, person, or other influence that inspires. *Your poems have been a great inspiration for me to start writing.* 2. something that is inspired or inspiring, such as an idea. *Your idea to have a party for the old folks was an inspiration.* {ihn spə **ray** shən}

in·spire *verb* (inspired, inspiring, inspires) 1. to cause confident feelings in. *The captain's bravery inspired the crew to face the storm without fear.* 2. to cause, urge, stimulate or influence to do. *My mother's kindness inspired me to write a book about her.* 3. to cause to happen. *His speech inspired a revolt.* {ihn **spiyr**}

in·stall *verb* (installed, installing, installs) 1. to put into position and make ready for use. *The mechanic installed a new engine in my car.* 2. to put in an office, position, or rank. He was installed as head of the company.* {ihn **stawl**}

in·stall·ment[1] or **instalment** *noun* one of the parts in which something is paid, written, or supplied at regular times. *He paid his debt in monthly installments. / The next installment of her story will appear in tomorrow's paper.* {ihn **stawl** mənt}

in·stall·ment[2] or **instalment** *noun* the act of installing or condition of being installed. {ihn **stawl** mənt}

in·stance *noun* a case, example or occasion. *In this instance, I will excuse you.* {ihn **stəns**}
• **for instance**
as an example; for example. *I've lived in many cities, for instance, New York, Boston, and Chicago.*

in·stant *noun* 1. a very short space of time; moment. *He disappeared in an instant.* 2. a particular point in time. *The instant they left home, she arrived. adjective* 1. happening right away; without delay; immediate. *The teacher gave me an instant answer to my question.* 2. needing only water, milk, or the like to be ready to eat or drink; capable of being prepared quickly. *Sometimes I eat instant oatmeal in the morning because it does not take long to make.* {ihn **stənt**}

in·stant·ly *adverb* at once; without delay; immediately.

My father knew the answer instantly. {**ihn** stənt lee}

in·stead *adverb* in place of; rather. *I don't care for the mountains, so let's go to the beach instead.* {ihn **stehd**}
• **instead of**
in place of. *I would like water instead of milk with dinner.*

in·step *noun* 1. the curved middle section of the foot between the heel and the toes. 2. the part of a shoe or sock that covers this part of the foot. {**ihn** stehp}

in·still *verb* (instilled, instilling, instills) to put gradually into someone's mind or feelings. *They instilled a love for learning in their children.* {ihn **stihl**}

in·stinct ❓ *noun* 1. the cause of natural behavior that is not learned in any species. *Instinct makes the geese fly south.* 2. a strong natural tendency or ability. *Mozart had an instinct for composing music.* {**ihn** steengkt}

in·stinc·tive *adjective* 1. having to do with instinct. *It is instinctive behavior for beavers to build dams.* 2. caused by, or as if by, instinct; impulsive. *He had an instinctive understanding of how to be a good parent.* {ihn **steengk** tihv} instinctively, adv.

in·sti·tute *verb* (instituted, instituting, institutes) 1. to bring into being or set in operation. *He instituted a way to get the work done more quickly.* 2. to begin or initiate. *I'd like to institute a dinosaur club at school. noun* 1. an organization set up to provide a service or support a cause. *My mother is an active member of an institute for women's rights.* 2. a college teaching a special subject matter, such as art or technology. *He is a ballet student*

at an institute of fine arts. {**ihn** stih **tooht**}

in·sti·tu·tion *noun* 1. an organization set up for a specific purpose. Hospitals, churches, prisons, and schools can be institutions. 2. an established custom or law in a society. *Is there any culture that does not have the institution of marriage?* {**ihn** stih **tooh** shən}

in·struct ❓⭕ *verb* (instructed, instructing, instructs) 1. to teach; educate; tell. *My boss instructed me in how to work on a computer.* 2. to order or direct; command. *The police instructed her to leave the building immediately.* {ihn **struhkt**}

Word History *Instruct* is from a Latin word that means "to equip or furnish with information."

in·struc·tion *noun* 1. the act of giving knowledge; teaching. *I went to a class to receive instruction in African dance.* 2. (often plural) directions or orders. *The instructions say to pull the plug on the toaster before taking it apart.* {ihn **struhk** shən} instructional, adj.

in·struc·tor *noun* one who teaches or instructs; a teacher. {ihn **struhk** tər}

in·stru·ment 🌍⭕ *noun* 1. a tool or mechanical device used for special work. *The dentist has a special instrument for cleaning teeth.* 2. any of various devices for making music, such as a trumpet or piano. {ihn strə mənt}

in·suf·fi·cient *adjective* not enough in number, degree, amount, or quality; not suffi-

cient. *I have insufficient money to go to London at this time.* {**ihn** sə **fihsh** ənt} insufficiently, adv.

in·su·late *verb* (insulated, insulating, insulates) to cover, line, or surround with a material that reduces or stops the movement of heat, electricity, or sound. *We insulated our house to save money on our heating bill. / The wire gave off sparks because it was not properly insulated.* {**ihn** sə **layt**}

Word History The word *insulate* comes from *insulare*, a Latin word that means "to make something like an island."

in·su·la·tion *noun* 1. material used to insulate. 2. the act of insulating or the condition of being insulated. *We hired workers for the insulation of our attic.* {**ihn** sə **lay** shən}

in·su·lin *noun* 1. a hormone of the pancreas that controls and regulates the body's use of sugars and starches. 2. any of the common substitutes for this hormone, taken from an animal pancreas and used to treat diabetes. {**ihn** sə lihn}

in·sult *verb* (insulted, insulting, insults) to speak to or treat without respect or in a way that hurts feelings. *His comments about her clothes insulted her.* *noun* a rude statement or action that hurts someone's feelings. *Not attending her sister's wedding was an insult to the family.* {**ihn** suhlt, n., ihn **suhlt**, v.}

Word History *Insult* comes from a Latin word that means "to leap at" or "leap upon." By the 1600s, it had come to mean "to treat with scorn and abuse." Today, an insult is an assault that uses words, not the body.

in·sur·ance *noun* 1. a protection against certain accidents that is provided by a company in return for payment of a fee. *After the fire, the insurance made it possible for us to build a new house.* 2. businesses that provide such protection. {ihn **shoohr** əns or ihn **shuh** rəns}

in·sure *verb* (insured, insuring, insures) to guarantee against loss or harm with an insurance policy. *When you buy a house, you must insure it.* {ihn **shoohr** or ihn **shuhr**}

in·tact *adjective* staying complete, whole, or without damage; not changed or harmed. *The car was intact after the accident.* {ihn **tăkt**}

in·take *noun* 1. the place at which a liquid or gas is taken into something. *The car would not run properly, because the intake was plugged and would not allow gas to flow to the engine.* 2. the act or process of taking in. *It is important that your intake of food is balanced by the amount of energy your body uses in a day.* {**ihn** tayk}

in·te·ger *noun* a positive or negative whole number or zero. *The integers greater than -3 and less than 4 are -2, -1, 0, 1, 2, and 3.* {**ihn** tə jər}

in·te·grate *verb* (integrated, integrating, integrates) 1. to bring together and mix into a whole. *Comic strips integrate two art forms: drawing and writing.* 2. to make open to all cultures and races. *Many schools were integrated during the civil rights movement.* {**ihn** tə grayt}

in·te·gra·tion *noun* 1. the process of bringing all parts together into a whole. 2. the end of the separation of races. *Integration was an important step toward equality*

 Human Body
 Human Mind
 Everyday Life
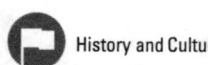 History and Culture
 Communication

in the United States. {ihn tə **gray** shən}

in·teg·ri·ty *noun* a strong sense of honesty; firmness of moral character. *He showed great integrity when he refused to lie for his employer.* {ihn **teh** grih tee}

in·tel·lect 🌐 *noun* the ability to reason and understand. *My philosophy teacher has a powerful intellect.* {**ihn** tə lehkt}

in·tel·lec·tu·al *adjective* 1. of or having to do with the intellect. *I had a good intellectual discussion with my brilliant friends.* 2. being very smart. *The intellectual students are starting a reading and discussion group.* *noun* a person of great intellect, often considered to be one of a group or class of such people. *He comes from a family of intellectuals who love learning.* {ihn tə **lehk** chooh əl} intellectually, adv.

in·tel·li·gence *noun* 1. the ability to learn, reason, and understand. *Those math problems are easy for him, because of his high intelligence.* 2. the branch of government or the military that collects and analyzes information about other governments. *The president got information from intelligence before he made any decisions.* 3. knowledge or information, or the collecting of such knowledge or information. *The general received intelligence of a secret attack.* {ihn **teh** lə jəns}

in·tel·li·gent *adjective* having a great ability to reason and understand. *The teacher was very pleased with the work of her intelligent class.* {ihn **tehl** ə jənt} intelligently, adv.

in·tel·li·gi·ble *adjective* able to be easily understood; easy to comprehend. *Her writing is*

barely intelligible. {ihn **teh** lih jə bəl}

in·tend *verb* (intended, intending, intends) 1. to have in mind as something to do. *I intend to leave at daybreak.* 2. to plan for a specific purpose. *He intended the books for his sister.* {ihn **tehnd**}

in·tense *adjective* 1. having a very great degree of something, such as heat, or being in a very great degree or state. *The intense heat from the burning building made it impossible for the fire fighters to go in.* 2. strong or very deep. *He has intense feelings of love for her.* {ihn **tehns**} intensely, adv.

in·ten·si·fy *verb* (intensified, intensifying, intensifies) 1. to make stronger, more acute, or more intense. *His disturbing speech intensified the anger of the crowd.* 2. to become stronger, more acute, or more intense. *Each day the pain in his back intensified.* {ihn **tehn** sih **fiy**}

in·ten·si·ty *noun* (intensities) 1. the quality of being intense. *The intensity of the workout made me very sore and tired.* 2. strength or energy of thought or action. *He practiced on the guitar with great intensity.* {ihn **tehn** sih tee}

in·tent[1] *noun* 1. plan; aim; intention. *My intent is to become rich.* 2. meaning; significance. *Did you understand the intent of the essay?* {ihn **tehnt**}

in·tent[2] *adjective* 1. very concentrated in attention; focused. *An intent stare from a lion means you are about to be its dinner.* 2. decided; determined. *He was intent on winning the race.* {ihn **tehnt**} intently, adv.

in·ten·tion *noun* a decided course of action; plan. *He*

went to college with the intention of getting a degree. {ihn **tehn** shən}

in·ten·tion·al *adjective* done on purpose; deliberate. *He was very sorry for bumping into my bike and said it was not intentional.* {ihn **tehn** sh nəl} intentionally, adv.

in·ter·act *verb* (interacted, interacting, interacts) 1. to respond to one another in a social situation. *We were pleased to see how our parents were interacting.* 2. to have an effect on or change one another. *It is important to know how the drugs interact.* {ihn tər **ăkt**} interactive, adj.

in·ter·ac·tion *noun* action of one upon another or others; action in response to others; influence, or effect. *The group's awkward social interaction showed that they were strangers.* {ihn tər **ăk** shən}

in·ter·ac·tive *adjective* 1. allowing two-way communication between a computer and a person. *Most computer games are highly interactive.* 2. acting or able to act upon one another. *We enjoyed the interactive concert because we could take part in the music making.* {ihn tər **ăk** tihv}

in·ter·cept *verb* (intercepted, intercepting, intercepts) to stop or take hold of; interrupt the movement or progress of. *He intercepted the*

A
B
C
D
E
F
G
H
I
J
K
L
M
N
O
P
Q
R
S
T
U
V
W
X
Y
Z

a
b
c
d
e
f
g
h
i
j
k
l
m
n
o
p
q
r
s
t
u
v
w
x
y
z

thieves as they tried to escape. {**ihn** tər <u>sehpt</u>}

in·ter·change·a·ble *adjective* able to be put or used in place of each other. *After tasting the strange, sweet stew, the cook decided that salt and sugar are not interchangeable.* {**ihn** tər <u>chayn</u> jə bəl} interchangeably, *adv.*

in·ter·com *noun* a system or device that allows communication from room to room. *The secretary used the intercom to tell his boss that there was a client to see her.* {**ihn** tər <u>kŏm</u>}

in·ter·est ❓ ⬤ *noun* 1. the desire to learn, know, or take part in something. *The professor took an interest in his student's work.* 2. someone or something that causes such a desire. *Plato is one of my interests.* 3. the power to cause such a desire. *Video games have no interest for me anymore.* 4. a rate that is paid for the use of another person's money. *The bank will pay us 7.9 percent interest on the money we keep there.* 5. a right or share in something. *My sisters and I have equal interest in our family's company.* 6. concern for one's own self or benefit. *It is in your best interest to finish that report.* *verb* (interested, interesting, interests) 1. to convince to take part in; tempt. *Can I interest you in a cup of tea?* 2. to cause to have the desire to learn or know about something. *Math has interested me for many years.* {**ihn** tər ihst}

in·ter·est·ing *adjective* causing attention to, concern about, or interest in. *I've read all her books, because she is an interesting author. / She found Japanese culture interesting and difficult to understand.* {**ihn**

trihst ing *or* **ihn** tər ihst ing} interestingly, *adv.*

> **Synonyms**
> This word shares a meaning with *interesting*, adjective 1:
> stimulating

in·ter·face *noun* the equipment or programs used to communicate between different computer systems or programs. *I used my computer as an interface to search the college library.* {**ihn** tər **fays**}

in·ter·fere *verb* (interfered, interfering, interferes) 1. to be or get in the way (usually followed by "with"). *Noise from the party next door interefered with her sleep.* 2. to show too much interest in the lives of others without having been asked; meddle (usually followed by "with" or "in"). *He asked his parents not to interfere with how he arranged his bedroom.* {**ihn** tər <u>feer</u>}

> **Word History** *Interfere*
> comes from an early French word that means "to strike or knock together." The French word referred to the horseshoe striking the lower part of a horse's leg, which would interfere with the horse's gait.

in·ter·fer·ence *noun* 1. the act or an instance of interfering. *The teacher was not pleased with the boy's rude interference in her class.* 2. illegally getting in the way of a ball or opposing player in a sporting event. *The referee charged him with interference when he pushed the receiver who was trying to catch the ball.* 3. static that makes a radio or TV signal not clear. *There was too much interference for us to hear our favorite program.* {**ihn** tər <u>feer</u> əns}

in·ter·ga·lac·tic *adjective* of, having to do with, or located in the space between galaxies. *The scientists designed an intergalactic probe to explore other galaxies.* {**ihn** tər gə <u>lăk</u> tihk}

in·te·ri·or *adjective* 1. being inside or within. *The outside of the house was beautiful, but the interior decorations were awful.* 2. of the inside or inner part. *Blue paint was chosen for the interior walls of our school.* *noun* 1. the inside area of a house, building, or car. *Mr. Adams's new car has a leather interior.* 2. the part of a country or area that is away from the coast or borders with other countries or areas. *We lived on the coast for years and then moved to the interior.* {**ihn** <u>teer</u> ee ər}

in·ter·jec·tion *noun* a word or expression that shows strong feeling; exclamation. "Oh no!" and "Oops!" are examples of interjections. {**ihn** tər <u>jehk</u> shən}

in·ter·me·di·ate *adjective* being or happening between two things, stages, positions, or persons; being in the middle. *I've reached the intermediate level in my swimming class, which means I can swim in the deep section, but I can't use the diving board yet.* {**ihn** tər <u>mee</u> dee iht}

in·ter·mis·sion *noun* a pause or stop between times of activity; recess. *During the play's intermission, we got snacks and used the bathroom.* {**ihn** tər <u>mihsh</u> ən}

in·tern *noun* a doctor who recently graduated and is working with more experienced doctors to finish training. *verb* (interned, interning, interns) to be an intern. *My uncle interned for three years before he started his*

 Human Body    Human Mind   Everyday Life   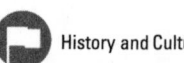 History and Culture    Communication

own medical practice. {**ihn tuhrn**, n., ihn **tuhrn**, v.}

in·ter·nal *adjective* 1. located on the inside; inner. *He looked fine but had some internal bleeding from the fall.* 2. having to do with what happens inside a country. *The president is working on internal matters, such as education and better housing.* {ihn **tuhr** nəl} internally, adv.

in·ter·na·tion·al 🔵 *adjective* of or having to do with what happens between two or more countries. *An international meeting was held for the leaders of many countries to discuss the need for medicine and food in Afghanistan.* {ihn tər **nă** shən əl} internationally, adv.

In·ter·net 🟢🔵 or **internet** *noun* the world's largest computer network, which is made of millions of computers that are linked together. Some parts of the Internet are the World Wide Web, electronic mail, and chat rooms. *Our computer is connected to the Internet by a cable modem.* {**ihn** tər neht}

in·ter·plan·e·tar·y *adjective* being, happening, or working between planets. *In the future, interplanetary travel to Mars may be as easy as an overseas vacation.* {ihn tər **plăn** ə tayr ee}

in·ter·pret ❓🔵 *verb* (interpreted, interpreting, interprets) 1. to decide on or explain the meaning of. *How do you interpret his latest book?* 2. to understand in a particular way. *Dan interpreted his father's frown as a refusal.* 3. to perform in a way that

shows new meaning. *The pianist interpreted Mozart in a way I had never heard.* 4. to change or translate from one language into another. *I understand French, but don't know how to interpret it into English.* {ihn **tuhr** priht} interpreter, n.

in·ter·pre·ta·tion *noun* 1. the act or process of explaining or making clear the meaning of something. *Her interpretation of the novel helped the class to recognize the greatness of the author's imagination.* 2. showing the meaning of music, drama, or something similar through performance. *Their performance was a beautiful interpretation of a ballet I'd seen many times.* {ihn **tuhr** prə **tay** shən}

in·ter·ro·gate *verb* (interrogated, interrogating, interrogates) to question at length and in a thorough way, often for an official purpose. *The police interrogated the suspect for several hours.* {ihn **tehr** ə gayt}

in·ter·rog·a·tive *adjective* having to do with, forming, or being a question. "Why don't you take a walk?" is an example of an interrogative sentence. *noun* a word, phrase, or other expression that is often used to ask a question. "When" is an interrogative in the sentence, "When will they arrive?" {ihn tə **rŏg** ə tihv}

in·ter·rog·a·tive sen·tence *noun* a sentence that asks a question. "Have you read this book?" is an example of an interrogative sentence. {ihn tə **rŏg** ə tihv **sehn** təns}

in·ter·rupt *verb* (interrupted, interrupting, interrupts) 1. to cause to stop; break off. *Loud banging on the door interrupted the conversation.* 2. to begin to speak over, in the middle of, in a way that breaks off. *Never interrupt the president while he is giving a speech.* {ihn tə **ruhpt**}

in·ter·rup·tion *noun* 1. the act of interrupting or the state of being interrupted. *The teacher does not allow interruptions while she is speaking.* 2. that which interrupts. *Everyone in the class was curious about the interruption in the hallway.* {ihn tə **ruhp** shən}

in·ter·sect *verb* (intersected, intersecting, intersects) 1. to cut across or pass through; cross. *This road intersects the state highway.* 2. to meet or cross at a point. *These railroad lines intersect at the station.* {ihn tər **sehkt**}

in·ter·sec·tion *noun* the point or place where two or more lines, roads, or other straight things meet. *Be careful when crossing a busy intersection.* {ihn tər **sehk** shən}

in·ter·state *adjective* having to do with or connecting two or more states. *They stayed mainly on interstate highways when they traveled.* {**ihn** tər **stayt**}

in·ter·val *noun* 1. the period of time between two events or situations. *There will be a five minute interval between classes.* 2. a space between objects or measured points. *There must be an exact interval between railroad ties.* {ihn tər vəl}

A
B
C
D
E
F
G
H
I
J
K
L
M
N
O
P
Q
R
S
T
U
V
W
X
Y
Z

International Currency

International travel can make you hungry.
Do you know how to pay for lunch in Nairobi, Sydney, or Hamburg?
Make sure you have the right kind of
currency in your wallet before you order!

Britain
3.5 pounds

China
42 yuan

Australia
10 dollars

Mexico
50 pesos

USA
5 dollars

Europe
7.5 euros

Canada
8 dollars

India
250 rupees

Italy

Kenya
400 shilingis

in·ter·view *noun* 1. a meeting between a person who has applied for a job and the person who is offering the job. During such an interview, job requirements, qualifications, and pay are discussed. *She applied for six jobs and got three interviews.* 2. a conversation between a reporter and a person who will be the subject of the report, or the report itself. *There was an interview of the mayor on the radio. verb* (interviewed, interviewing, interviews) to have an interview with or of. *He interviewed several people who had escaped from the concentration camps.* {ihn tər vyoo} interviewee, n., interviewer, n.

in·tes·tine *noun* (usually plural) the lower part of the digestive system, below the stomach. The intestine is a long, coiled tube. It is divided into the small intestine and the large intestine. {ihn **teh** stihn} intestinal, adj.

Word History *Intestine* comes from *intestina*, a Latin word that means "internal" or what is within.

in·ti·mate *adjective* 1. very warm, friendly, or close. *I have only a few intimate friends that I trust with my secrets.* 2. very personal or private. *In the story, he revealed intimate information about his family.* {ihn tə **miht**} intimately, adv.

in·to *preposition* 1. to the inside of. *Go into the room.* 2. to a point or moment in. *An hour into the movie, Carla began to feel sick.* 3. against. *The clowns bumped into each other.* 4. in the direction of. *Let's head into the city.* 5. to the state, condition, or form of. *The rain turned into snow during the night.* {ihn tooh}

in·tol·er·a·ble *adjective* too difficult or unpleasant to be near or to bear. *The way she sings off key is intolerable.* {ihn **tŏl** ə rə bəl} intolerably, adv.

in·tol·er·ant *adjective* not able or not willing to accept different opinions, beliefs, customs, or people; not tolerant. *Her parents can be very intolerant.* {ihn **tŏl** ər ənt}

in·tox·i·cate *verb* (intoxicated, intoxicating, intoxicates) 1. to cause to be less rational by means of alcohol or drugs. *It is against the law to intoxicate a minor.* 2. to make excited, stimulated, or exhilarated. *The beautiful sounds of the violin intoxicated me.* {ihn **tŏk** sih **kayt**}

in·trans·i·tive verb *noun* a verb that cannot have a direct object. In the sentence, "I ran for an hour," "ran" is an intransitive verb. {ihn **trŏn** sih tihv **vuhrb**}

in·tra·ve·nous *adjective* being in or entering through a vein or veins. *The doctor gave the baby intravenous antibiotics to fight the infection.* {ihn trə **vee** nəs} intravenously, adv.

in·tri·cate *adjective* having many complex parts, angles, or aspects; involved; elaborate. *If you take the time, there is a lot to see in his intricate drawings.* {ihn trə kiht} intricately, adv., intricateness, n.

in·trigue *verb* (intrigued, intriguing, intrigues) to draw the strong interest of; puzzle; fascinate. *The odd fairy tale intrigued the children. noun* a secret plot or scheme. *There were many intrigues against the king.* {ihn treeg, n., ihn **treeg**, v.}

in·tro·duce *verb* (introduced, introducing, introduces) 1. to present to another person. *Please don't introduce me to all your friends.* 2. to bring to one's notice or into one's experience. *She introduced music to me when I was very young.* 3. to begin. *The first chapter introduces the book.* 4. to bring to public notice. *Congress introduced a new bill to fight crime.* {ihn trə **doohs**}

Word History *Introduce* is from a Latin word that means "to lead or bring within." *Intro-* is a prefix that means "into." *Duc-* is a Latin word part (or root) that appears in many English words. It means "to lead." *Duke*, *conduct*, and *duct* are all formed from this Latin root.

in·tro·duc·tion 🔊 *noun* 1. the act or process of introducing. *She began the meeting with a brief introduction.* 2. the preface to a book or other work. *He read the introduction to see if the book interested him.* {ihn trə **duhk** shən}

in·tro·duc·to·ry *adjective* serving to introduce. *He kept his introductory speech brief, because we were all more interested in the main speaker.* {ihn trə **duhk** tə ree}

in·trude *verb* (intruded, intruding, intrudes) to enter or thrust oneself in when not invited or welcome. *The salesman intruded on their dinner with his phone call.* {ihn **troohd**} intruder, n.

in·tu·i·tion *noun* the power to know or understand something without thinking it through in a logical way. *He never learned the rules of*

a
b
c
d
e
f
g
h
i
j
k
l
m
n
o
p
q
r
s
t
u
v
w
x
y
z

grammar, but he writes well by intuition. {ihn tooh **ih** shən}

In·u·it noun 1. a member of a group of native people living in areas from Greenland to Canada and Alaska. 2. the preferred term for Eskimo people who speak the Inuit language, especially in Canada. {**ihn** ooh iht}

in·vade verb (invaded, invading, invades) 1. to enter as an enemy, by force, in order to free, conquer, or plunder. In 1944, the Allied Forces invaded France to free it from German occupation. 2. to disturb or break into without being asked or wanted; intrude on; violate. He invaded her privacy by walking into the room without knocking. {ihn **vayd**} invader, n.

in·va·lid[1] noun a person who is ill or disabled. {**ihn** və lihd}

in·val·id[2] adjective no longer legal or in effect; void; not valid. He got a ticket for driving with an invalid license. {**ihn văl** ihd}

in·val·u·a·ble adjective having value too great to guess or measure; priceless. He gave invaluable help during her illness. / This ring from my grandmother is invaluable to me. {**ihn văl** yoo ə bəl or **ihn văl** yə bəl}

in·va·sion noun 1. an act or instance of invading by an enemy or hostile army. 2. an act of intruding into another's life. Reading her diary was an invasion of her privacy. {ihn **vay** zhən}

in·vent verb (invented, inventing, invents) 1. to think of, come up with, or create something new. The man who invented the steam engine must have been very intelligent. 2. to think up or make up. She invented an

excuse for not washing the dishes. {ihn **vehnt**}

Word History *Invent* is from a Latin word that means "to come upon" or "find."

in·ven·tion ⊙ noun 1. the act or process of inventing. The invention of the automobile changed the world. 2. something that is invented. His invention can peel apples automatically. 3. something imagined or made up, such as a story or a falsehood. I didn't believe her invention about the groundhog climbing a tree. {ihn **vehn** shən}

in·ven·tive adjective good at thinking up new ideas or at devising new objects or methods; imaginative. His inventive ideas are helping the business to grow. {ihn **vehn** tihv} inventiveness, n.

in·ven·tor noun one who invents. He wants to be the inventor of a car that drives itself. {ihn **vehn** tər}

in·ven·to·ry ⊙ noun (inventories) 1. a complete list of things on hand or in a particular place. All of the toys on the shelves and in the back room are on the inventory. 2. the goods or materials on such a list. The store had sold so much of its inventory that many of the shelves were empty. {**ihn** vən **tohr** ee}

in·vert verb (inverted, inverting, inverts) 1. to reverse the order, position, or direction of. If you invert the letters of the word "part," you get "trap." 2. to turn upside down. If you invert that glass

of water, the floor will get wet. {ihn **vuhrt**}

in·ver·te·brate ⊙ adjective without a backbone. A slug is an invertebrate animal. noun an animal that does not have a backbone or skeleton inside its body. Insects, spiders, worms, snails, clams, crabs, and squids are some kinds of invertebrates. {ihn **vuhr** tə **brayt** or ihn **vuhr** tə briht, n., ihn **vuhr** tə **brayt** or ihn **vuhr** tə briht, adj.}

in·vest ⊙ verb (invested, investing, invests) 1. to put into use for the purpose of making money. He invested his money in a new company and hoped to get back twice as much. 2. to spend. She invested a lot of time in dance lessons. {ihn **vehst**}

in·ves·ti·gate ⊙ ⊙ verb (investigated, investigating, investigates) to look into carefully and closely so as to learn the facts; examine. The police are investigating the crime. {ihn **veh** stih **gayt**} investigator, n.

in·ves·ti·ga·tion noun the act of investigating. My friends and I enjoyed our investigation of the old ship. {ihn veh stih **gay** shən}

in·vest·ment noun 1. the act or process of investing. Mr. Thomas lost money on his investment. 2. that which is invested. I made a five-dollar investment in some candy that I sold for fifteen dollars. 3. something into which money, time, or effort is invested. Buying that house was an investment that didn't pay off. {ihn **vehst** mənt}

in·ves·tor noun a person or company that invests or puts

 Human Body

 Human Mind

 Everyday Life

 History and Culture

Communication

money into use for the purpose of making more money. {ihn **vehs** tohr}

in·vis·i·ble *adjective* not able to be seen; not visible. *He was invisible through the heavy fog.* {ihn **vihz** ə bəl}

in·vi·ta·tion *noun* the act of inviting. *I said, "Yes!" to her invitation to come for dinner.* {ihn vih **tay** shən} invitational, adj.

in·vite *verb* (invited, inviting, invites) 1. to ask in a polite way to come somewhere or do something. *Dora's friend invited her to spend the night.* 2. to welcome or ask for. *The farmer invited questions from the children about the animals on his farm.* 3. to bring about by doing or saying; to risk causing. *He invited an accident by talking on the phone while driving on the busy highway.* {ihn **viyt**}

in·vol·un·tar·y *adjective* 1. not caused or decided by one's own choice, will, or wish. *During a war, military duty is often involuntary.* 2. not on purpose; without conscious control; automatic. *Breathing is an involuntary action.* {ihn **vŏl** ən **tayr** ee}

in·volve *verb* (involved, involving, involves) 1. to have as a necessary part or result; include. *Baseball involves throwing, catching, and batting a ball. / Police work involves some danger.* 2. to bring into a situation. *He involved me*

in a fight with his friend. 3. to give full attention to or be busy with. *She was involved in learning her part for the school play.* {ihn **vŏlv**} involvement, n.

in·ward *adverb* in or toward the inside or center. *The museum guide led the crowd inward.* *adjective* moving or pointed toward the inside or center. *The crowd moved with an inward rush into the stadium.* {ihn wərd} inwards, adv.

in·ward·ly *adverb* 1. on, in, or toward the inside. *That door opens inwardly.* 2. within one's own self; in private. *She laughed with the others, but inwardly she was crying.* {ihn wərd lee}

i·o·dine *noun* 1. a substance that is one of the chemical elements. Iodine combines easily with other elements. It is found in salt water and seaweed. Iodine is poisonous in its pure crystal form. (symbol: I) 2. a mixture of iodine, compounds of iodine, and alcohol, which can be put on cuts to kill germs and stop infections. {**iy** ə **diyn** *or* **iy** ə dihn}

i·on *noun* an atom or group of atoms that has an electrical charge. {**iy** ŏn *or* **iy** ən}

-ion *suffix* 1. a suffix that means "an act" or "a process." *Celebration is the act of celebrating.* 2. a suffix that means "condition" or "state of being." *The word "adoption" means "the state of being adopted."*

I·o·wa *noun* a state in the midwestern United States. Its capital is Des Moines. (abbreviated: IA) {**iy** ə wə *or* **iy** ə **way**}

Word History *Iowa* was named after the Pahoja nation, which was called *ioways* by the Dakota Sioux.

I·ran *noun* a country in southwestern Asia. Tehran is the capital of Iran. {ih **răn** *or* ee **rahn** *or* **iy răn**} Iranian, n., adj.

I·raq *noun* a country in southwestern Asia. Baghdad is the capital of Iraq. {ih **răk** *or* ih **rahk**} Iraqi, n., adj.

i·rate *adjective* very angry. *My mother was irate when I arrived home after ten o'clock.* {iy **rayt**}

Ire·land *noun* 1. an island in western Europe. Ireland is in the northern Atlantic Ocean, west of Great Britain. 2. a country on most of this island, not including the northern end. This country is also called the Republic of Ireland. Dublin is the capital of Ireland. {**iyr** lənd} Irelander, n.

ir·i·des·cent *adjective* 1. emitting or reflecting a lustrous play of colors covering the spectrum, like a rainbow. *Most hummingbirds have iridescent plumage.* 2. shiny, lustrous, or brightly colored. *The toothpaste ad promises you an iridescent smile.* {**eer** ih **deh** sənt} iridescence, n., iridescently, adv.

i·ris *noun* (irises) 1. the colored circle around the pupil of the eye. *A person with blue eyes has blue irises.* 2. a plant that has leaves shaped like swords and large, showy flowers. {**iy** rihs}

Word History *Iris* is an ancient Greek word. In ancient Greece, it was a word for a kind of lily and for the colored ring on the surface of the eye. In English, it still has these meanings. In Greek mythology, Iris was the name of a female messenger of the gods. She appeared to mortals as the rainbow. Our word *iridescent* comes from the word "iris."

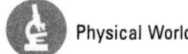 

a
b
c
d
e
f
g
h
i
j
k
l
m
n
o
p
q
r
s
t
u
v
w
x
y
z

I·rish *adjective* of or having to do with Ireland, or its people or language. *noun* 1. (used with a plural verb) the people of Ireland (usually used with "the"). 2. the language of Ireland. {**iy** rihsh}

Irish setter *noun* a breed of dog. Irish setters have long red hair and a silky coat. {**iy** rihsh **seht** ər}

i·ron 🏃 👕 *noun* 1. a heavy gray metal that is one of the chemical elements. Iron rusts easily and can be magnetized. It is found in many minerals in the earth's crust and is also found in blood. Iron is often combined with other metals to form alloys such as steel. (symbol: Fe) 2. any alloy of iron with carbon and other elements which can be used to make a variety of tools, containers, and other objects. 3. a heavy appliance with a flat surface that is heated and used to press wrinkles out of cloth. 4. (plural) chains used to hold a prisoner. *adjective* 1. made of iron metal or a mixture of iron and other metals. *The jail had iron bars on its windows.* 2. strong or firm as iron. *She has an iron will.* 3. stern or cruel; hard. *The old king has an iron heart.* *verb* (ironed, ironing, irons) 1. to press out the wrinkles of, using a heated iron. *I ironed some shirts and a tablecloth.* 2. to use a heated iron to press out wrinkles in clothing or other items made out of fabric. *She ironed all morning.* {**iy** ərn}
• **iron out** to clear up or smooth out. *We ironed out our problems by talking about them calmly.*
• **strike while the iron is hot** to take advantage of an opportunity without waiting. *We had to strike while the iron was hot if we wanted to buy that house.*

i·ro·ny *noun* spoken or written words that mean the opposite of their usual meaning. *It was an irony when the sick person said he felt "just great."* {**iy** ər nee *or* **iy** rə nee}

Ir·o·quois *noun* (Iroquois) a member of a large, united group of American Indian peoples of New York State. The Iroquois confederacy is made up of six different Indian nations. {**eer** ə **kwhoi**}

ir·ra·tion·al ❓ *adjective* without reason or sense. *Because of her irrational fear of insects, she searches her bed every night before she goes to sleep.* {ihr **răsh** ə nəl} irrationally, adv.

ir·reg·u·lar *adjective* 1. uneven in shape, arrangement, surface, or some other way. *The road up the mountain was very irregular.* 2. uneven in how often or for how long something happens. *There was an irregular beep coming from the smoke detector.* 3. not fitting into a standard law, method, or custom. *In our country, it is highly irregular to serve dessert before dinner.* 4. being an exception to the general rules of grammar or spelling. *It can be difficult for a learner of English to use an irregular verb correctly.* {ihr **rehg** yə lər} irregularly, adv.

ir·reg·u·lar·i·ty *noun* (irregularities) 1. the quality of being irregular. *The irregularity of the store's hours made it hard for the customers to know when it would be open.* 2. a failure to follow rules, customs, or usual ways. *To wear your pajamas to school would be an irregularity.* {ihr **rehg** yə **lar** ih tee}

ir·rel·e·vant *adjective* not having anything to do with the matter being considered or talked about. *The question of who won last night's game would be irrelevant on a history test.* {ihr **rehl** ə vənt}

ir·re·sist·i·ble *adjective* impossible not to give in to or resist. *Chocolate cream pie is an irresistible treat.* / *When he ripped his pants, she had an irresistible urge to laugh.* {ihr rə **zih** stə bəl} irresistibly, adv.

ir·re·spon·si·ble *adjective* not having or showing responsibility; not able to be counted on or trusted. *He was irresponsible about feeding and walking the dog.* / *It was irresponsible to hit the ball so close to the window.* {ihr rə **spŏn** sih bəl} irresponsibly, adv.

ir·re·vers·i·ble *adjective* impossible to reverse, turn back, or change. *No matter how much we begged, going to bed at eight o'clock was an irreversible rule.* {ihr rə **vuhr** sə bəl}

ir·ri·gate 💧 *verb* (irrigated, irrigating, irrigates) to supply with water by artificial means from a natural source of water. *The farmer irrigated the dry land so he could grow corn.* {**ihr** ih **gayt**} irrigator, n.

ir·ri·ga·tion *noun* the supplying of water to land by manmade means. *Some home owners use irrigation to grow grass in Arizona.* / *The farmer uses irrigation to get water to his dry land.* {**ihr** ih **gay** shən}

ir·ri·ta·ble *adjective* easily bothered or angered. *My teacher*

 Human Body    Human Mind    Everyday Life    History and Culture   Communication

was irritable as usual. {**ihr** rih tə bəl} irritably, adv.

ir·ri·tate *verb* (irritated, irritating, irritates) 1. to anger or bother. *When you chew your gum noisily, it irritates me.* 2. to make sore, red, or raw; inflame. *The smoke irritated my eyes.* {**ihr** rih **tayt**}

is *verb* a form of the verb "be" which is used with "he," "she," "it," and with singular nouns. *She is happy.* {**ihz**}

-ish *suffix* 1. a suffix that means "of" or "from." *Irish music comes from Ireland.* 2. a suffix that means "like." *A childish person is a person who acts like a child.* 3. a suffix that means "somewhat" or "almost." *Reddish brown hair is brown hair that is somewhat red.*

Is·lam *noun* 1. a religion founded by Muhammad. Its holy book is called the Koran. 2. all the people who believe in this religion. 3. all the countries in which Islam is the main religion. {**ihs** ləm *or* **ihz** ləm *or* **ihs** lahm *or* **ihz** lahm} Islamic, adj.

Word History *Islam* is from an Arabic word that means "to surrender (to God)."

Is·lam·a·bad *noun* the capital city of Pakistan. {ihs **lahm** ə **bahd**}

is·land *noun* 1. an area of land smaller than a continent and surrounded by water on all sides. *Hawaii is a group of islands that many people like to visit.* 2. something that looks like such a body of land, in being different than the other things around it. *There was an island of trees in the middle of the open field.* {**iy** lənd}

is·land·er *noun* a person who was born on or lives on an island. {**iy** lən dər}

isle *noun* an island. {**iyl**}

Homophone Note The words *isle*, *aisle*, and the contraction *I'll*, sound alike but have different meanings.

is·let *noun* a tiny island. {**iy** liht}

Homophone Note The words *islet* and *eyelet* sound alike but have different meanings.

is·n't shortened form of "is not." *Isn't it time you went to bed?* {**ih** zənt}

i·so·late *verb* (isolated, isolating, isolates) to set apart or separate so as to be alone. *The mother isolated the angry child. / His house is isolated in the woods.* {**iy** sə **layt**}

isosceles triangle *noun* a triangle with two sides that are equal in length. {iy **sŏs** ə **leez triy** ăng gəl}

Is·ra·el *noun* 1. a country in southwestern Asia on the Mediterranean Sea. Israel was formed as a Jewish state in 1948. Jerusalem is the capital of Israel. 2. a name for the Jewish people as a whole, according to Jewish scriptures. {**ihz** ree əl *or* **ihz** ray əl}

Is·ra·e·li *noun* a person who was born in or is a citizen of Israel. *adjective* of or having to do with Israel or its people. *The Israeli people have had a difficult history.* {ihz **ray** lee}

is·sue *noun* 1. something that is made, sent out, or published. *Did you get the June issue of this magazine?* 2. a point or subject in question or being talked about. *The students talked about the issue of saving energy.* *verb* (issued, issuing, issues) 1. to make, give out, or publish. *The officer issued parking tickets. / The government issues money.* 2. to give out to members of the mili-

tary. *The soldiers were issued food and supplies.* {**ihsh** ooh} issuer, n.

-ist *suffix* 1. a suffix that means a person who does or makes. *An artist is a person who makes art. / A pianist is a person who plays the piano.* 2. a suffix used for someone who is skilled in or works at. *A chemist is a person who has studied chemistry and who works with chemicals.* 3. a suffix that means a person who believes in or follows certain teachings. *A Buddhist is a person who follows the teachings of Buddha.*

Is·tan·bul *noun* a city in Turkey at the entrance to the Black Sea. {ihs tahn **boohl** *or* ihs tăn **buul**}

isth·mus *noun* (isthmuses) a narrow strip of land that joins two larger pieces of land. An isthmus has water on its long sides. *There is an isthmus between North and South America.* {**ihs** məs}

it *pronoun* 1. the thing, animal, person, or object that has been or will be talked about. *Have you read it yet? / I gave it to the mailman. / Don't let it bite you.* 2. the action or condition that has been or will be talked about. *Flying may be a fast way to travel, but I don't like it.* 3. used as the subject of the verb "be." *It is sunny today. / It was he who found the mistake.* *noun* the general situation. *How is it with your friend today?* {**iht**}

I·tal·ian *adjective* of or having to do with Italy, or its people or language. *noun* 1. a person who was born in or is a citizen of Italy. 2. the language of Italy. {ih **tăl** yən}

i·tal·ic *adjective* of or having to do with a style of type whose letters slope to the right. *Italic type is often used to call*

A
B
C
D
E
F
G
H
I
J
K
L
M
N
O
P
Q
R
S
T
U
V
W
X
Y
Z

a
b
c
d
e
f
g
h
i
j
k
l
m
n
o
p
q
r
s
t
u
v
w
x
y
z

attention to certain words or ideas. *noun* (often plural) a type style whose letters slope to the right. *This sentence is printed in italics.* {ih **tă** lihk}

i·tal·i·cize *verb* (italicized, italicizing, italicizes) to print in italic type. *You should italicize a book's title.* {ih **tă** lih **siyz**}

It·a·ly *noun* a country in southern Europe. Rome is the capital of Italy. {**iht** ə lee}

itch *verb* (itched, itching, itches) 1. to have a tingling feeling on the skin that causes a desire to scratch. *The insect bite on my arm itches.* 2. to cause such a feeling or sensation. *I got sand down my shirt and it itches.* 3. to have a restless desire for something or to do something. *Everyone was itching for spring.* / *He was itching to pick up a baseball bat. noun* 1. a tingling feeling on the skin or skin disorder that causes the desire to scratch. *Beth asked me to scratch the itch on her back.* 2. a restless, continuing desire. *She has an itch to travel to Spain.* {**ihch**}

i·tem *noun* 1. a single, particular thing in a group or list. *My mom gave me a list of six items to buy at the store.* 2. a particular bit of information or news. *There was an item in the newspaper about the forest fires in New Mexico.* {**iy** təm}

i·tem·ize *verb* (itemized, itemizing, itemizes) to say or write each item of. *He itemized all the equipment needed to build his race car.* {**iy** tə **miyz**}

it'll shortened form of "it will." *It'll be a long time before this storm stops.* {**iht** əll}

it's shortened form of "it is" or "it has." *It's cold in here!* / *It's*

been snowing for three days. {**ihts**}

> **Homophone Note** The contraction ***it's*** and the word ***its*** sound alike but have different meanings.

its *pronoun* belonging to or having to do with the one already mentioned. *What is its color?* {**ihts**}

> **Homophone Note** The word ***its*** and the contraction ***it's*** sound alike but have different meanings.

it·self *pronoun* 1. its own self (used to show that an action is done to the same thing that does that action). *The cat cleaned itself.* 2. used to make very clear; emphasize. *The neighborhood was fine, but the house itself was a problem.* 3. a normal, healthy, or usual condition. *The cat is not itself today.* {iht **sehlf**}

-i·ty or **-ty** *suffix* a suffix that means "condition" or "quality." *Anxiety is a condition of being anxious.* / *Loyalty is the quality of a loyal person.*

IV *abbreviation* (IVs) an apparatus for giving medicine or nutrients through the veins. IV is an abbreviation for **intravenous**.

I've shortened form of "I have." *I've been working on this for hours.* {**iyv**}

-ive *suffix* a suffix that means likely to do something, connected with, or performing an action. *Doctors who practice preventive medicine are trying to prevent disease.* / *An inventive person is likely to invent things or have new ideas.*

i·vo·ry *noun* (ivories) 1. the hard, white material that forms the tusks of elephants and other animals. 2. a pale yellowish white color. *adjec-*

tive made of ivory. *He was selling an ivory statue.* {**iy** və ree *or* **iyv** ree, n., **iy** və ree *or* **iyv** ree, adj.}

Ivory Coast *noun* a country in western Africa on the Atlantic Ocean. *Yamoussoukro is the capital of the Ivory Coast. The Ivory Coast is now more commonly called Côte d'Ivoire.* {**iy** və ree **kohst** *or* **iyv** ree **kohst**} **Ivory Coaster**, n.

i·vy *noun* (ivies) 1. a woody vine that has shiny evergreen leaves, and black berries, and often climbs walls or buildings. 2. any of several plants like this, that climb or grow along the ground. *Stay away from the poison ivy!* {**iy** vee}

 Human Body   Human Mind   Everyday Life   History and Culture    Communication

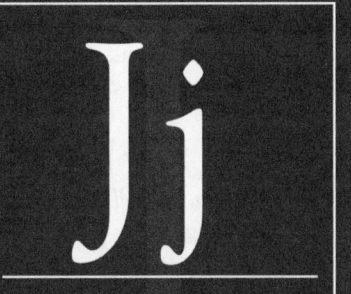

Jj

J is a consonant that always makes the same sound.

Tips to help you look up words starting with j: Also look under G for some words starting with the "jih" sound that are spelled with "g" (such as ginger).

These words may be hard to look up if you don't already know how to spell them:

> January
> jealous
> jewelry
> judgment

j or **J** *noun* (j's or J's) the tenth letter of the English alphabet. {**jay**}

jab *verb* (jabbed, jabbing, jabs) 1. to poke with a pointed object. *He jabbed me in the ribs with his pencil.* 2. to hit with a quick, hard blow or a weapon. *The boxers jabbed each other in the ring.* *noun* the act or an instance of jabbing; poke or short punch. *She gave me a jab with the point of her umbrella.* {**jăb**}

jack *noun* 1. a device for lifting a heavy object a short distance by means of a lever. *She used a jack to raise her car so that she could change the tire.* 2. the face card with the lowest value in a deck of cards. The jack is pictured as a young man in uniform. 3. (plural but used with a singular verb) a children's game in which one bounces a ball and picks up as many small, star-shaped metal pieces as one can before the ball lands. *verb* (jacked, jacking, jacks) 1. to lift using a jack (usually followed by "up"). *The mechanic jacked up the truck.* 2. to raise or increase (usually followed by "up"). *The theater jacked up the price of a ticket.* {**jăk**}

jack·al *noun* a mammal that is closely related to wolves and dogs. Jackals eat the remains of dead animals and hunt for small or weak animals. Several kinds of jackals are found in Asia and Africa. {**jăk** əl}

jack·et ⊙ *noun* 1. a short coat used as a piece of outer clothing. 2. a covering made to protect or keep warm what is inside. *The title of the book is printed on its jacket.* {**jăk** iht}

Word History In the 1300s, "Jacques" was a nickname for any French peasant. A peasant's short coat was also called a *Jacque*, which is the origin of the English word **jacket**.

jack-in-the-box *noun* (jack-in-the-boxes) a toy that is made up of a box with a puppet inside. The puppet springs out when the lid of the box is opened. {**jăk** ihn thə **bŏks**}

jack·knife *noun* (jack-knives) 1. a large pocketknife whose blade can be folded into the handle. 2. a kind of dive in which a person bends in the air, touches his feet, and straightens out before reaching the water. {**jăk** niyf}

jack-o'-lan·tern *noun* (jack-o'-lanterns) a pumpkin that is hollowed out and has a face carved into it and a candle in the bottom. Jack-o'-lanterns are used at Halloween as lamps or decorations. {**jăk** ə lăn tərn}

jack·pot *noun* the largest or final prize in a game or contest. {**jăk** pŏt}
• **hit the jackpot** (informal) to have sudden good luck or success; to win a jackpot. *After a long search for a cheap car, I finally hit the*

A
B
C
D
E
F
G
H
I
J
K
L
M
N
O
P
Q
R
S
T
U
V
W
X
Y
Z

jackpot. / Mrs. Cohen hit the jackpot in bingo.

jack rabbit *noun* a large hare of the western United States. Jack rabbits have long ears and very long, strong back legs. {jăk răb iht}

Ja·cuz·zi *noun* trademark for a type of bath that has underwater jets. The jets shoot air into the water, making it whirl around. {jə kooh zee}

jade *noun* a hard green stone or the jewelry or works of art made from it. {jayd}

jag·ged *adjective* having points that are sharp and uneven. *The broken window had jagged edges.* {jăg ihd}

jag·uar *noun* a large mammal with short yellow fur and black rings. Jaguars are carnivores that hunt or fish for food. They live in the southern United States and Central and South America. Jaguars are closely related to lions, tigers, and other big cats. They are sometimes called panthers. {jăg war}

Word History *Jaguar* was the name for all carnivorous (or meat-eating) animals in *Tupi*, one of Brazil's native languages.

jail *noun* a building in which a government keeps people who are waiting for a trial or who have been found guilty of breaking the law. *verb* (jailed, jailing, jails) to place in a jail. *The judge jailed the man for thirty days.* {jayl}

jail·bird *noun* (informal) a person who is or who has been locked up in jail; convict. {jayl buhrd}

jam¹ *verb* (jammed, jamming, jams) 1. to force or pack tightly into a small space. *He jammed a peg in the hole. / She jammed the books in a box.* 2. to push suddenly and with force. *He jammed his foot on the brake pedal.* 3. to fill up or block. *Ice jammed the stream.* 4. to hurt by strong, sudden pressure. *Cheryl jammed her finger playing basketball.* 5. to be blocked or not work properly. *The window jammed shut.* 6. to play or improvise jazz or rock-'n'-roll music with others. *The musicians jammed at the club for hours.* *noun* 1. a large gathering or mass that slows or stops movement. *The stream was blocked by an ice jam. / We were stuck in a traffic jam.* 2. (informal) a difficult or embarrassing situation; trouble. *Peter was in a jam at work.* {jăm}

jam² *noun* a sweet spread made by cooking crushed fruit and sugar. {jăm}

Ja·mai·ca *noun* an island country in the West Indies, in the Caribbean Sea. Kingston is the capital of Jamaica. {jə may kə} Jamaican, n., adj.

Jan. *abbreviation* an abbreviation for **January**.

jan·gle *verb* (jangled, jangling, jangles) 1. to make a harsh, clashing sound. *The keys jangled as he shook the key ring.* 2. to cause to make a harsh, clashing sound. *The ghost jangled his chains and moaned.* 3. to bother or upset very much. *The loud music jangled our nerves.* *noun* a harsh, clashing sound. *The jangle of the old church bells hurt my head.* {jăng gəl}

Synonyms
These words share a meaning with **jangle**, verb 3:
upset, disturb, rattle

jan·i·tor *noun* a person whose work is to clean and take care of a building. *The janitor keeps our school looking nice and clean.* {jăn ih tər} janitorial, adj.

Word History There were *janitors* in ancient Rome, but the word "janitor" meant something different then. It meant "doorkeeper." When it entered the English language in the 1500s, "janitor" still meant "doorkeeper." Its meaning changed over the next 200 years, and by the 1700s was a word for the caretaker of a building.

Jan·u·ar·y *noun* (Januaries) the first month of the year. January has thirty-one days. {jăn yoo ayr ee}

Word History The word *January* was formed from the Latin word *Janus*, the name of a Roman god of gates and beginnings. In Roman art, Janus has two faces, one looking back and one looking forward. The month of January is like Janus; it looks back at the old year and forward to the year to come.

Ja·pan *noun* a country in eastern Asia made up of islands in the Pacific Ocean. Tokyo is the capital of Japan. {jə păn}

Jap·a·nese *adjective* of or having to do with Japan, or its people or language. *noun* (Japanese) 1. a person who

 Human Body Human Mind Everyday Life 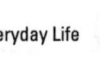 History and Culture 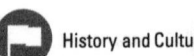 Communication

was born in or is a citizen of Japan. 2. the language of Japan. {jă pə **neez** or jă pə **nees**, n., jă pə **neez** or jă pə **nees**, adj.}

ようこそ いらっしゃいました

Japanese beetle *noun* a shiny green and brown insect that came to the United States from Asia. It eats the leaves, fruits, flowers, and roots of plants and can cause a lot of damage. {jă pə **neez** <u>bee</u> təl or jă pə **nees** <u>bee</u> təl}

jar¹ *noun* 1. a round container with a wide mouth, usually made of glass or pottery, and often having a lid. 2. the amount that such a container will hold. *Would you please get me a jar of water?* {<u>jar</u>}

jar² *verb* (jarred, jarring, jars) 1. to crash into or bump so as to cause movement; jolt. 2. to crash into or bump against. *The shopping cart jarred the cart in front of it.* 3. to have a bad effect on; upset. *The sound of the steam hammer is jarring my nerves.* *noun* a crash or shock that causes something to shake or vibrate; jolt. *The jar of the landing made my teeth rattle.* {<u>jar</u>}

jar·gon *noun* special words or language used by a particular group or to describe a particular interest. *To be a good lawyer you have to know all the*

legal jargon. / "A can of corn" is baseball jargon for "a fly ball that is easy to catch." {<u>jar</u> gən}

jaun·dice *noun* a condition of the liver that causes the eyes and skin to become yellow. {<u>jawn</u> dihs}

jaun·diced *adjective* having or looking as if one had jaundice. *Her jaundiced skin looked unhealthy.* {<u>jawn</u> dihst}

jaunt *noun* a short trip made for fun and pleasure. *We took a little jaunt to the beach.* {<u>jawnt</u>}

jaun·ty *adjective* (jauntier, jauntiest) having a light manner; lively and confident. *His jaunty walk showed that he was happy.* {<u>jawn</u> tee}

jav·e·lin *noun* 1. a light spear thrown as a weapon. 2. a pointed pole that looks like a spear. A javelin is thrown in an athletic contest. 3. a field event in which a javelin is thrown for distance as a test of strength and skill. {<u>jăv</u> ə lihn}

jaw 🌐 *noun* 1. either or both of the two bones that frame the mouth and hold the teeth. 2. the mouth and the parts that frame it. *He was hit in the jaw.* 3. either of two parts of a tool that close or grip like jaws, as on pliers. *Clara held a nut in the jaws of the nutcracker.* {<u>jaw</u>}

jaw·bone *noun* any of the bones that are part of the jaw, especially the lower one. {<u>jaw</u> bohn}

jay *noun* a brightly colored, noisy bird that belongs to the crow family. A blue jay is one kind of jay. {<u>jay</u>}

jay·walk *verb* (jaywalked, jaywalking, jaywalks) to walk across a street in a place or at a time that is against traffic laws. *If you cross the street in the middle of the block, you are*

jaywalking. {<u>jay</u> wŏk} jaywalker, n.

jazz *noun* a form of music with strong, complex rhythms that started with African Americans in the late 1800s. Jazz musicians often add notes or make up parts as they play. {<u>jăz</u>}

jeal·ous *adjective* 1. afraid of losing someone's love or attention to another person. *She became jealous when her parents spent so much time with the new baby.* 2. feeling envy of what another person has or can do. *He was jealous of his friend's new bike.* {<u>jeh</u> ləs} jealously, adv., jealousness, n.

jeal·ous·y 🌐 *noun* (jealousies) a feeling of envy towards another person and what he or she has or can do. *He couldn't hide his jealousy when his friend won first prize.* {<u>jeh</u> lə see}

jeans *noun* pants made from a heavy, often blue, cotton cloth. {<u>jeen</u>}

Homophone Note The words *jean* and *gene* sound alike but have different meanings.

jeep *noun* 1. (Trademark) A Jeep is a brand of sturdy, powerful car made for driving off roads on rough ground. It was first made for military use. 2. a small, powerful automobile that can be used on land and rough roads. {<u>jeep</u>}

A B C D E F G H I J K L M N O P Q R S T U V W X Y Z

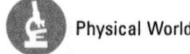 

a
b
c
d
e
f
g
h
i
j
k
l
m
n
o
p
q
r
s
t
u
v
w
x
y
z

jel·ly *noun* a soft, firm food that is usually spread on bread or toast. Jelly is often sweet, made from fruit juice and sugar. {**jeh** lee}

jel·ly·fish *noun* (jellyfish or jellyfishes) a water animal with a soft body shaped like a bell. Jellyfish have many tentacles hanging down from their bodies. Most kinds of jellyfish live in the ocean. {**jehl** lee fihsh}

jeop·ard·y *noun* danger of harm, death, or loss; at risk. *A dog crossing a busy road is in jeopardy. / The team's perfect record was in jeopardy when its star player got sick.* {**jeh** pər dee}

jerk *noun* 1. any sudden, sharp movement that is not expected or planned. *Nick awoke from his bad dream with a jerk.* 2. a sudden, sharp pull or twist. *The fish gave a jerk on the line.* 3. (slang) a person who is thought of as stupid or difficult to get along with. *When he threw water on me, I called him a jerk. verb* (jerked, jerking, jerks) 1. to pull or twist suddenly; yank. *She jerked the rug out from under the leg of the table.* 2. to make a sudden movement that is not expected or planned. *He jerked when the needle poked him.* {**juhrk**}

jerk·y[1] *adjective* (jerkier, jerkiest) having sudden starts and stops or other quick movements that are not expected. *Her neck is sore from that jerky ride at the fair.* {**juhr** kee}

jer·ky[2] *noun* beef or deer meat that has been cut into long pieces and dried. Drying the meat preserves it so that it can be eaten at a later time. {**juhr** kee}

jer·sey *noun* (jerseys) 1. a knitted shirt that is often worn by people who play sports. A jersey is pulled on over the head. 2. the material from which such a shirt is made. {**juhr** zee}

Je·ru·sa·lem *noun* the capital city of Israel. {jə **rooh** sə ləm}

jest *noun* a funny saying or action; joke. *He added a jest or two to his speech. verb* (jested, jesting, jests) to act or speak in a funny, playful way; joke. *He was jesting when he said there was a spider on my back.* {**jehst**}

jest·er *noun* someone hired to tell jokes in royal courts during the Middle Ages in Europe. Jesters often made fun of court life. {**jehs** tər}

Je·sus Christ *noun* the teacher and prophet who founded the Christian faith. He is considered by Christians to be the son of God and the Christ or savior. Jesus lived from about 4 B.C. to 29 A.D. {**jee** səs **kriyst**}

jet[1] *noun* 1. a stream of liquid or gas shooting from an opening, usually with great pressure. *There are jets in the pool that circulate the water.* 2. an airplane that is moved by engines that give off a backward flow of heated gases to cause forward movement. *verb* (jetted, jetting, jets) to shoot forth; spurt in a stream. *Water jetted into the road when the pipe broke.* {**jeht**}

jet[2] *noun* a deep, shiny black color. {**jeht**}

jet engine *noun* an engine that causes forward movement by the power of a stream of gases being forced out under pressure in the opposite direction. Jet engines are often used in aircraft. {**jeht** ehn jihn}

jet lag *noun* a feeling of being very tired or not well after traveling by airplane across different time zones. *When she flew from Los Angeles to Beijing, she had jet lag for a few days.* {**jeht** lăg}

jet-pro·pelled *adjective* using the power of a jet engine or engines. *Everyone watched as the jet-propelled rocket was launched.* {**jeht** prə **pehld**}

jet propulsion *noun* a way of giving aircraft and some small ships the power to move forward. Jet propulsion forces air and hot gases under high pressure to go through a jet nozzle. {**jeht** prə **puhl** shən}

jet stream *noun* a narrow band of strong, fast wind several miles above the earth's surface. The jet stream usually flows from west to east. {**jeht** streem}

jet·ti·son *verb* (jettisoned, jettisoning, jettisons) 1. to throw from a ship or airplane to make it lighter or more stable. *The crew jettisoned the cargo as the ship began to toss about in the storm.* 2. to throw away or call off. *She jettisoned her old magazines. / I jettisoned my*

 Human Body Human Mind Everyday Life History and Culture Communication

plans to wash the car when it started raining. {**jeht** ih sən or **jeht** ih zən}

jet·ty *noun* (jetties) 1. a group of rocks or wooden beams built out into a body of water. Jetties are used to control the flow of water and protect the shore from strong waves. 2. a platform built where ships can dock; wharf. {**jeht** ee}

Jew *noun* 1. a person whose ancestors were the Biblical Hebrews. 2. a person whose religion is Judaism. {**jooh**}

jew·el *noun* 1. a special stone that has been cut and made smooth; gem. Jewels are used to make jewelry and ornaments. 2. any object or person that is thought of as a treasure or having great value. *That new chemistry teacher is a jewel.* {**joohl** or **jooh** əl}

Word History *Jewel* comes from a early French word that means "game or play."

jew·el·er *noun* a person who makes, fixes, or sells gems or jewelry. {**jooh** lər or **jooh** ə lər}

jew·el·ry ⊙ *noun* rings, watches, necklaces, or other ornaments; jewels. {**joohl** ree or **jooh** əl ree}

Jew·ish *adjective* of or having to do with Jews, their culture, traditions, or religion. *Passover is a Jewish holiday.* {**jooh** ihsh}

jib *noun* a sail that is shaped like a triangle and used in the front of a sailing boat. {**jihb**}

jif·fy *noun* (jiffies) (informal) a very short time; instant. *I'll*

be done in a jiffy. {**jihf** ee} jiff, n.

jig *noun* 1. a fast, lively dance. *He was so happy, he did a jig.* 2. music written or played for such a dance. *Mary learned a jig on her fiddle.* *verb* (jigged, jigging, jigs) 1. to dance a jig. 2. to move up and down quickly and sharply; bob. *The kite jigged in the wind.* {**jihg**}

jig·saw *noun* a saw that can be used to cut sharp corners or curved designs. Jigsaws are usually powered by electricity. {**jihg** saw}

jigsaw puzzle *noun* a puzzle that is made of a picture that has been cut into many small uneven pieces. The pieces must be put together to form the picture again. {**jihg** saw puh zəl}

jin·gle *verb* (jingled, jingling, jingles) 1. to make a sound like light metal objects hitting against each other again and again. *The sleigh bells jingled.* 2. to cause to make a jingling sound. *He jingled the coins in his pocket.* *noun* 1. a jingling sound. *We heard the jingle of the wind chimes on the porch.* 2. a light, lively song or poem that is easy to remember. Jingles are often used to help sell products on radio and television. {**jing** gəl}

jinx *noun* someone or something that is believed to cause bad luck. *The losing team thought their new uniforms were a jinx.* *verb* (jinxed, jinxing, jinxes) to cause to have bad luck or turn out badly. *He thinks his sister jinxed him by telling everyone he'd lose the game.* {**jingks**}

job ⊙ ⊛ *noun* 1. a particular task or piece of work. *The job*

of cleaning the windows took two hours. 2. a regular position for which a person is paid to do particular duties. *Does your job require you to wear a suit every day?* 3. a duty or responsibility. *It's his job to mow the lawn.* {**jŏb**}

jock·ey *noun* (jockeys) a person whose work is riding horses in races. {**jŏk** ee}

jog *verb* (jogged, jogging, jogs) 1. to give a little push or shake; nudge. *By accident I jogged her arm while she was writing.* 2. to cause to remember something or become stirred up. *Hearing that song jogged his memories of childhood.* 3. to run at a slow, steady pace for exercise. *noun* a slow, steady running pace. *She ran the first mile fast and the second mile at a jog.* {**jŏg**} jogger, n.

join *verb* (joined, joining, joins) 1. to put, bring, or fasten together. *Let's join hands and sing songs.* 2. to come together; be in contact; meet. *The trail joins with the main road just past your house.* 3. to become a member of. *Will you join the Girl Scouts this year?* 4. to come into the company of, or go along with. *Will you be joining us for dinner?* 5. to take part in with others (often followed by

A
B
C
D
E
F
G
H
I
J
K
L
M
N
O
P
Q
R
S
T
U
V
W
X
Y
Z

"in"). *If you want to play, you can join in anytime.* {join}

Synonyms
These words share a meaning with *join*, verb 1:
couple, fix, link, connect, fasten

joint 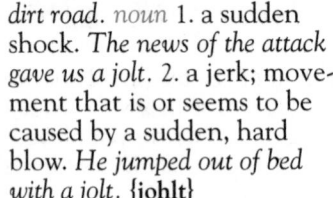 *noun* a place or point where two or more parts come together or are connected. *A person's hand and arm come together at the wrist joint. / We had to glue the joint where the leg meets the table.* *adjective* done or shared by two or more people or groups acting together. *They were joint owners of the property.* {joint}

• **out of joint** not joined in a proper or usual manner. *His hip is out of joint.*

joke *noun* a short story, usually with a funny ending, that is told to make people laugh. *verb* (joked, joking, jokes) 1. to talk or act so as to make people laugh; jest. *Please don't joke around in class.* 2. to talk in a way that is not serious. *He didn't mean it -- he was only joking.* {johk} jokingly, adv.

Word History *Joke* is from a Latin word that originally meant "a game of words."

jol·ly *adjective* (jollier, jolliest) cheerful, full of fun, and merry. *He has a jolly smile.* {jŏl ee}

jolt *verb* (jolted, jolting, jolts) 1. to shake up or cause to move with a jerk. *The clap of thunder jolted her out of her chair.* 2. to move in a rough, jerky way. *The wagon jolted along the*

dirt road. *noun* 1. a sudden shock. *The news of the attack gave us a jolt.* 2. a jerk; movement that is or seems to be caused by a sudden, hard blow. *He jumped out of bed with a jolt.* {johlt}

jon·quil *noun* a white or yellow flower with a pleasant smell. *The jonquil is much like the daffodil.* {jŏng kwihl *or* jŏn kwihl}

Jor·dan *noun* 1. a country in southwestern Asia. It lies east of Israel. Amman is the capital of Jordan. 2. a river in southwestern Asia. It flows from Lebanon, along the border of Israel and Jordan, and into the Dead Sea. {johr dən} Jordanian, [n.], adj.

jos·tle *verb* (jostled, jostling, jostles) to push, crowd, or bump into on purpose. *The children jostled each other as they waited in line. noun* the action or an instance of jostling; bump. *He gave me a jostle that made me drop my books.* {jŏs əl}

jot *verb* (jotted, jotting, jots) to write in a quick and simple way (usually followed by "down"). *Let me jot down the directions to your house.* {jŏt}

Word History The word *jot* comes from the word *iota*, which is the smallest letter in the Greek alphabet.

jour·nal  *noun* 1. a record of a person's experiences, thoughts, or daily events; diary. 2. a newspaper or magazine. *He read about the new treatment in a medical journal.* {juhr nəl}

jour·nal·ism *noun* the work of collecting news and information and giving it out to the public through newspapers, magazines, radio, television, or other media. {juhr nə lihz əm}

jour·nal·ist *noun* a person whose work is journalism. {juhr nə lihst}

jour·ney *noun* (journeys) a long trip from one place to another. *verb* (journeyed, journeying, journeys) to go on a trip; travel. *She journeyed to the Arctic in search of adventure.* {juhr nee}

joust *noun* a real or pretend fight between two knights on horseback. Each knight tries to knock the other off his horse with a lance. *verb* (jousted, jousting, jousts) to fight a joust. *The knights jousted to win the favor of the princess.* {jowst}

jo·vi·al *adjective* very cheerful, friendly, and merry; jolly. *His jovial way won him many friends.* {joh vee əl}

Word History *Jovial* comes from the name of the king of the Roman gods, Jupiter. Jupiter was also called "Jove." He was believed to be the source of joy and happiness.

jowl *noun* skin or flesh that hangs down from the lower jaw. *When the fat man shook his*

 Human Body   Human Mind   Everyday Life   History and Culture   Communication

head, his jowls shook, too. {**jowl**}

joy ⓘ *noun* 1. a great feeling of happiness or pleasure; delight. *Knowing you has given me joy.* 2. something that causes good feelings or happiness. *The baby is a joy to its parents.* {**joi**}

joy·ful *adjective* feeling, showing, or causing great happiness; glad; happy. *He gave her a joyful smile. / She laughed when she heard the joyful news.* {**joi** fəl} joyfully, adv., joyfulness, n.

joy·ous *adjective* full of joy; happy. *Have a joyous holiday!* {**joi** əs} joyously, adv., joyousness, n.

joy·stick *noun* (informal) the control stick for an airplane, computer, or game. {**joi** stihk}

ju·bi·lant *adjective* having or showing great joy; having a happy feeling of success. *The jubilant team hugged each other after their win.* {**jooh** bə lənt}

Synonyms
These words share a meaning with ***jubilant***, adjective 1:
joyful, overjoyed, joyous, rapturous

Ju·da·ism *noun* the religion of the Jewish people. It is based on the belief in one God and on two holy books, the Old Testament of the Bible and the Talmud. {**jooh** dee ihz əm *or* **jooh** day ihz əm}

judge ⓘ ⓘ *noun* 1. a person trained to hear and decide cases brought before a court of law. 2. a person who decides the winner in a contest or competition. 3. a

person who knows enough about something to give an opinion or suggestion. *You are a good judge of character.* *verb* (judged, judging, judges) 1. to hear and decide cases brought before a court of law. *The court judged the case in our favor.* 2. to decide or select the winner of. *The sheriff judged the pies at the county fair.* 3. to form an opinion of or about. *Don't judge a book by its cover.* {**juhj**}

judg·ment or **judgement** *noun* 1. an opinion formed after carefully studying all of the information. *In the mayor's judgment, a new city hall is needed.* 2. a decision made by someone in power; an official decision; verdict. *The court handed down a judgment in favor of the person who was hurt by a drunk driver.* {**juhj** mənt} judgmental, adj.

ju·di·cial *adjective* 1. having to do with judges, law courts, or their activities. *The judge wore her judicial robe in court. / The U.S. Supreme Court is part of the judicial branch of the federal government.* 2. decided in or coming from a court of law. *He must pay the fine according to a judicial order.* {**jooh dih** shəl}

ju·do *noun* a sport or way of fighting without weapons. Judo does not allow blows or throws that harm. {**jooh** doh}

Word History *Judo* is a Japanese word that means "the art of gentleness."

jug *noun* 1. a container for holding liquids. A jug usually has a handle and a narrow spout or opening. 2. the amount that such a container is able to hold; jugful.

I'm so thirsty, I could drink a jug of water. {**juhg**}

jug·ger·naut *noun* any large, powerful force, group, or object that can overcome or crush anything around it. *Our football team is a real juggernaut this year. / The tornado was a juggernaut that destroyed the town.* {**juhg** ər nawt}

jug·gle *verb* (juggled, juggling, juggles) 1. to do tricks that take great skill with the hands. A common juggling trick is to throw and catch three or more objects, one at a time. 2. to keep in motion in the air while tossing and catching. *The clown juggled three shiny balls.* 3. to do or cope with at the same time. *She juggles the work of mother and professional engineer.* {**juhg** əl}

juice ⓘ *noun* the natural liquid from plants or meats. The liquid from fruits is used for drinking. {**joohs**}

juic·y *adjective* (juicier, juiciest) having a great amount of juice. *Watermelon is a juicy fruit.* {**jooh** see} juiciness, n.

juke·box *noun* a machine that holds many different records or CDs and plays music when

A
B
C
D
E
F
G
H
I
J
K
L
M
N
O
P
Q
R
S
T
U
V
W
X
Y
Z

money is put in. By pushing a button, a person chooses which song will play. {**joohk bŏks**}

Ju·ly *noun* (Julies) the seventh month of the year. July has thirty-one days. {jə **liy**}

jum·ble *verb* (jumbled, jumbling, jumbles) 1. to put or throw together in a confused pile. *She jumbled her clothes in the suitcase and forced it shut.* 2. to mix up; confuse. *He jumbled the directions so badly that he got lost.* *noun* 1. a mess; a pile that is not tidy. *The dirty laundry is in a jumble on the floor.* 2. a state of confusion. *My mind was in a jumble after trying to learn so many facts.* {**juhm** bəl}

jum·bo *adjective* very large. *Would you like a regular or a jumbo hamburger?* {**juhm** boh}

jump *verb* (jumped, jumping, jumps) 1. to leap into the air. *She jumped for joy.* 2. to rise quickly to a standing position (often followed by "up"). *I jumped from my seat when I heard the doorbell.* 3. to move or jerk suddenly; start. *Tom jumped when he heard the loud clap of thunder.* 4. to respond quickly and eagerly. *He jumped at the chance to take a vacation.* 5. to increase suddenly in amount. *The price of a new car jumped last year.* 6. to leap over. *The fox jumped the fence.* *noun* 1. the act of jumping. *Her jump was measured at twelve feet.* 2. a sudden leap or shift from one amount to another or one subject to another. *There was a large jump in the price of apples. / There was a jump in our discussion from baseball to ice hockey.* 3. a sudden move or jerk; a start. *She gave a jump when she saw the tree blow over.* 4. a fence or other barrier to be jumped over. *The horse easily made the first two jumps.* 5. a space or level, as in a game. *I am two jumps ahead of him.* {**juhmp**}

   • **jump at**
to take or accept quickly and eagerly. *She jumped at the chance to go to the beach.*

jum·per *noun* 1. a dress without sleeves worn over a shirt or blouse. 2. (often plural) a piece of child's clothing that has pants attached to a bib. {**juhm** pər}

jump rope *noun* a rope held at each end and swung under the feet and over the head as a person jumps. Jump ropes are used for exercise or as a game. {**juhmp** rohp}

jump suit *noun*
1. a piece of clothing that covers the arms, legs, and body and is worn by people who parachute. 2. a piece of clothing that is like the suits worn by people who parachute. {**juhmp** sooht}

junc·tion *noun* 1. a point or place where things are joined together. *There was a small leak at the junction of the two pipes.* 2. a place where two or more roads, railways, or rivers meet or join each other. *There was a car acci-*

dent at the junction of State and Main Streets. {**jungk** shən}

June *noun* the sixth month of the year. June has thirty days. Summer begins in June for people who live north of the equator. {**joohn**}

jun·gle ⊛ *noun* land covered with many trees, vines, and bushes; a tropical rain forest. {**jung** gəl}

jungle gym *noun* an outdoor structure of pipes and bars for children to play on. {**jung** gəl jihm}

jun·ior *adjective* 1. younger. (Used in this sense, "junior" is usually shortened to "Jr." and used after one's name, when one has the same first and last name as one's father.) *John Smith's son is named John Smith, Jr.* 2. of a lower position or rank. *This company's junior executive started work last month.* 3. of the class above sophomore and below senior in U.S. colleges and high schools; third year. *noun* 1. one who is younger than another. *Nate is my junior by five years.* 2. a student in the third year of study at a U.S. high school or college. {**joohn** yər}

junior high school *noun* a school between elementary school and high school; middle school. Junior high school usually includes grades seven, eight, and nine. {**joohn** yər **hiy** skoohl}

ju·ni·per *noun* an evergreen shrub or small tree with

🏃 Human Body   ❓ Human Mind   👕 Everyday Life   🚩 History and Culture   📞 Communication

cones that produce berries. {**jooh** nih pər}

junk[1] *noun* things having little worth; trash. *The garage is filled with junk.* *verb* (junked, junking, junks) to throw away because no longer working or valuable. *Tim junked his rusty old bicycle.* {**jungk**}

Synonyms

These words share a meaning with *junk*, noun 1:

garbage, trash, refuse, rubbish

Word History No one is sure where the word *junk* came from. We do know that it was first used for old cable or rope found on a sailing ship. In the 1800s, "junk" came to be used for any discarded items from a ship, and then for old things of any kind. The term "junk food" was first used in 1973.

junk[2] *noun* a boat found in China with a high stern and flat bottom, driven by square sails. {**jungk**}

junk food *noun* snack food that does not give the body many nutrients. Junk food usually contains a great deal of fat or sugar. {**jungk foohd**}

junk mail *noun* mail that is not wanted or asked for. Letters asking for money or trying to sell products are usually considered junk mail. {**jungk mayl**}

junk·yard *noun* a yard or lot in which junk is collected, kept, and sold. Old metal and cars are often found in a junkyard. {**jungk yard**}

Ju·no *noun* the goddess of marriage in Roman mythology. Juno was the wife and sister of Jupiter. In Greek mythology, Juno is called Hera. {**jooh** noh}

Ju·pi·ter *noun* 1. the ruler of the gods in Roman mythology. Jupiter controlled the weather and protected the government and its laws. In Greek mythology, Jupiter is called Zeus. 2. the largest planet in the solar system and fifth in distance from the sun. Jupiter has sixteen moons and is more than one thousand times larger than Earth. {**jooh** pih tər}

ju·ror *noun* a person who is a member of a jury. {**joohr** ər}

ju·ry *noun* (juries) 1. a group of people called to a court of law who listen to the facts of a case and decide its outcome. *The jury found the accused person not guilty.* 2. a group of people formed to judge a contest or competition. *Each band had to play before the jury to see who would win the prize.* {**joohr** ee}

Word History *Jury* is from an early French word that means "to swear." At the beginning of a trial, the jury members swear to seek the truth and make a fair verdict.

just *adjective* 1. fair and honest. *We accepted our parents' just rules.* 2. having a fair and honest character. *The just judge was known for making good decisions.* 3. deserved or earned. *Punishment was the criminal's just reward.* *adverb* 1. a very short time ago. *He just left.* 2. only. *He ate just a few bites of cake.* / *It's just a scratch.* 3. by a very small margin; barely. *Kim just missed the bus.* 4. exactly. *That's just the point I meant to make.* {**juhst**}

• **just about** practically; almost; nearly. *That's just about right.*

jus·tice *noun* 1. the upholding of what is fair, just, and right. *The innocent prisoner was freed in the interest of justice.* 2. the giving out of something that is deserved; reward or punishment. *After many years, the wrongly accused man finally received justice.* 3. a person whose job is to decide questions brought before a court; judge. *Sandra Day O'Connor was the first female justice of the U.S. Supreme Court.* {**juhs** tihs}

jus·ti·fy *verb* (justified, justifying, justifies) 1. to show to be true or right; prove. *The photograph justified his claim that he had met the president.* 2. to show good reasons or cause for. *I justified eating the last piece of pie by saying that it would be thrown away otherwise.* {**juhs** tih **fiy**}

jut *verb* (jutted, jutting, juts) to project or stick out sharply (often followed by "out"). *His long nose jutted out from his face.* / *The balcony juts out from the side of the building.* {**juht**}

jute *noun* 1. a thick, strong fiber taken from a plant and used to make rope and rough cloth. 2. one of the plants from which this fiber is taken. Jute is grown in Asia. {**jooht**}

ju·ve·nile *adjective* 1. young; not grown up. *The juvenile dalmations played on the ice.* 2. of or like a young person; right for a young person. *"The Secret Garden" is a*

A B C D E F G H I J K L M N O P Q R S T U V W X Y Z

a
b
c
d
e
f
g
h
i
j
k
l
m
n
o
p
q
r
s
t
u
v
w
x
y
z

classic of juvenile literature. 3. foolish and silly; childish; not mature. *The two men got into a juvenile fight over the television control.* *noun* one who is not yet grown up; young person; adolescent. *As a juvenile, he was not allowed to see certain movies.* {<u>jooh</u> və **niyl**}

 Human Body   Human Mind    Everyday Life   History and Culture    Communication

Kk

K is a consonant that always makes the same sound.

Tips to help you look up words starting with k: Also look under C or Q for words starting with the "k" sound. Some words spelled with "ch" (such as character or chronic) make a "k" sound because the "h" is silent. Most words that start with the "kw" sound are spelled with "qu" (such as quote).

These words may be hard to look up if you don't already know how to spell them:

key
khaki
kindergarten
knew
knowledge

k or **K** *noun* (k's or K's) the eleventh letter of the English alphabet. {**kay**}

K symbol of the chemical element potassium.

Ka·bul *noun* the capital city of Afghanistan. {**kah** bəl}

ka·lei·do·scope *noun* a tube with small bits of colored glass and mirrors inside. The tube is held to the eye and turned to see changing forms. {kə **liyd** ə skohp}

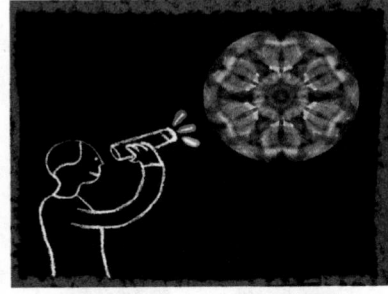

kan·ga·roo *noun* (kangaroos or kangaroo) a mammal with long pointed ears, short front legs, and big, powerful back legs. Kangaroos use their large tails for balance when hopping. Kangaroos are marsupials that live in Australia and New Guinea. The females

have a pouch in their belly, where they carry their baby for a few months after it is born. Some kinds of kangaroos are as small as rabbits; other kinds are as large as grown humans. {kăng gə **rooh**}

Kan·sas *noun* a state in the midwestern United States. Its capital is Topeka. (abbreviated: KS) {kăn zihs} Kansan, n., adj.

Word History *Kansas* means "people of the south wind." The state was named for the Kansas Sioux people.

ka·ra·o·ke *noun* a kind of music entertainment system that plays the music of popular songs, but leaves out the vocals. This allows a person to sing along with the music. Karaoke was invented in Japan. {**keh** ro oh kee}

kar·at *noun* a unit of measure for the purity of gold equal to one twenty-fourth part of pure gold. {**kar** iht}

ka·ra·te *noun* a way to protect and guard oneself without weapons. Karate uses hard blows with the elbows or the edges of the hands or feet. {kə **rah** tee}

Word History *Karate* is a Japanese word that means "empty or bare hand."

ka·ty·did *noun* a large, green insect that is related to the grasshopper. Katydids live in trees and are often heard calling on summer nights. The male makes a noise that sounds like "katydid" by rubbing its wings together. {**kay** tee **dihd**}

kay·ak *noun* 1. a boat, used by the Inuit people, that is slim with a light frame and is pointed at both ends. Kayaks are covered

A
B
C
D
E
F
G
H
I
J
K
L
M
N
O
P
Q
R
S
T
U
V
W
X
Y
Z

with a waterproof skin that may be pulled tight around the waist of the person inside. 2. a boat that looks like this and is used in sports and for fun. {kiy ăk}

Word History *Kayak* comes from *kajakka*, an Inuit (or Eskimo) word that means "a small boat of skins."

keel *noun* a long piece of wood or metal that runs down the length of the bottom of a boat or ship. The keel makes a boat or ship stable in the water. {keel}
• **keel over**
to fall over suddenly; faint. *It was so hot outside that he keeled over from the heat.*
• **on an even keel**
in balance or stable. *She's not feeling on an even keel today.*

keen ⊙ *adjective* (keener, keenest) 1. very sharp; able to cut easily into thin, exact pieces. *That knife has a keen blade.* 2. quickly able to sense or understand; sharp. *Dogs have keen hearing. / Erin has a keen mind.* 3. felt strongly; eager; intense. *She has a keen interest in sports.* {keen} keenly, adv.

keep *verb* (kept, keeping, keeps) 1. to hold or continue to hold. *The bank will keep your money for you.* 2. to manage, attend to, or take care of. *He keeps tropical fish.* 3. to put or store. *She keeps her notes in a locked drawer.* 4. to cause to remain in a certain state or position. *Please keep the baby quiet. / Keep the dog outside for a few minutes.* 5. to continue being responsible for; be faithful to. *Peter kept his promise to Wendy.* 6. to continue; persist. *Keep going along this road until you get to Main Street.* 7. to stop or hold back. *He can't keep from*

lying. *noun* means of support; living. *How do you earn your keep?* {keep}

Synonyms
These words share a meaning with **keep**, verb 1:
have, hold, possess, retain

keep·ing *noun* 1. harmony or agreement. *Her behavior was in keeping with the rules.* 2. care or custody. *His dog will be in good keeping while he is on vacation.* {keep ing}

keg *noun* a small barrel holding less than ten gallons. {kehg}

kelp *noun* 1. a coarse brown seaweed. 2. the ashes of this seaweed used to add flavor or nutrients to food. {kehlp}

Kel·vin *noun* 1. a temperature scale having intervals that correspond to those of the Celsius scale. On the Kelvin scale, zero degrees (zero Kelvins)is equal to -273.15 degrees Celsius. 2. (lower case) one unit of the Kelvin scale. *adjective* relating to the Kelvin scale of temperature or a unit of this scale. {kehl vihn}

ken·nel *noun* (often plural) a place where dogs are raised and trained, or cared for while their owners are away. {kehn əl}

Ken·tuck·y *noun* a state in the east central United States. Its capital is Frankfort.

(abbreviated: KY) {kihn **tuh** kee} Kentuckian, n., adj.

Word History *Kentucky* is the English spelling of an Iroquois word *kentake*, which means "meadow land" or "land of tomorrow." The name was chosen when three western Virginia counties formed a new state in 1792.

Ken·ya *noun* a country in eastern Africa on the Indian Ocean. Nairobi is the capital of Kenya. {**kehn** yə or **keen** yə} Kenyan, n., adj.

kept *verb* past tense and past participle of **keep**. {kehpt}

ker·chief *noun* a square cloth that is tied over the head or around the neck. {**kuhr** chihf}

Word History *Kerchief* comes from *couvrechief*, an early French word that means "cover the head."

ker·nel *noun* 1. the seed inside a nut or a fruit pit. 2. a grain of wheat or corn. 3. the most basic part of something; the heart of the matter; core. *We had to admit there was a kernel of truth in what she said.* {**kuhr** nəl}

Homophone Note Are you looking for the word **colonel** (a military officer)? **Kernel** and **colonel** sound alike but have different meanings.

ker·o·sene *noun* a thin liquid fuel. Kerosene is usually made from petroleum, but can also be made from oil, coal shale, or tar. {**kehr** ih seen or keh rih **seen**}

ketch·up or **catchup** or **catsup** *noun* a thick red sauce for meat or potatoes made with tomatoes and spices. {kehch əp or **kăch** əp or **kăts** əp}

ket·tle *noun* 1. a wide, deep pot used for boiling liquids, such as water or soup. 2. a kettle

 Human Body   Human Mind  Everyday Life  History and Culture 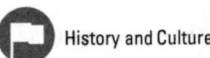 Communication

with a spout used to make and then pour tea or other hot drinks. {keht əl}

ket·tle·drum *noun* a large, deep drum that is shaped like a bowl and played with soft mallets. {keht əl druhm}

key[1] 🔵 🔵 *noun* 1. a metal object cut in a special way to open or close locks. 2. something that leads to or helps someone get something. *Hard work is the key to success.* 3. a list that gives an explanation of codes or symbols. *We read a key to understand a map.* 4. a button or part of a machine or musical instrument that makes it work when pressed. *This computer has twelve function keys. / The piano has eighty-eight keys.* 5. the main tone of the scale in a musical work. *This song is written in the key of* C. *adjective* main; central. *He made the key point in the discussion.* {kee}

• **key up**
to bring to a state of strong feeling or excitement. *The actor was keyed up before the show.*

key[2] 🔵 *noun* a low island near shore. *We took a trip to the Florida Keys last winter.* {kee}

Homophone Note Are you looking for the word *quay* (a pier or wharf)? *Key* and *quay* sound alike but have different meanings.

key·board 🔵 🔵 *noun* a row or rows of keys. Pianos, typewriters, and computers have keyboards. {kee bohrd} keyboarder, n., keyboardist, n.

key·hole *noun* a hole in a lock into which a key is put to lock and unlock it. {kee hohl}

key·pad *noun* a small panel with keys or buttons. Keypads are used to send a signal to an electronic device. Computers, telephones, calculators, and remote controls all have keypads. *Many computer keyboards have a small keypad for numbers and math symbols.* {kee păd}

key ring *noun* a metal ring for holding keys. {kee ring}

key·stone *noun* 1. the central stone at the top of an arch. 2. something upon which other things depend; necessary and very important part. *His sense of humor was the keystone of his success as an author.* {kee stohn}

kg *abbreviation* an abbreviation for **kilogram**, or kilograms.

khak·i *noun* (khakis) 1. a dull yellowish brown color. 2. a sturdy cloth of this color, used for military uniforms and work clothes. 3. (often plural) pants or uni-

forms made of this material. {khăk ee}

Word History *Khaki* is a word in the Urdu language that means "dusty." Urdu is the language of Pakistan and is spoken by many Muslims in India. In the 1800s, "khaki" was first used in English as a name for the uniforms made of dust-colored fabric worn by the British cavalry in India.

kick *verb* (kicked, kicking, kicks) 1. to strike with the foot. *She kicked him in the shin.* 2. to set in motion using a blow with the foot. *Julie kicked the can down the road.* 3. to move back suddenly and with force. *The rifle kicked hard and bruised his shoulder.* *noun* 1. the act or an instance of kicking; blow delivered with the foot. *His kick sent the ball down the field.* 2. a strong, sudden backward thrust. *That rifle has quite a kick.* 3. (informal) a feeling of excitement; thrill. *He gets a kick out of sky diving.* {kihk}

kick·off *noun* 1. a kick in football that puts the ball into action and signals the beginning or continuing of the game. *In the National Football League, a kickoff must travel ten yards or be touched by the receiving team.* 2. (informal) the beginning of something. *Max had a party to celebrate the kickoff of the new hockey season.* {kihk awf or kihk awf}

kid[1] 🔵 🔵 *noun* 1. a young goat. 2. leather from the skin of a young goat, used for making gloves or other products.

3. (informal) a child or young person. {**kihd**}

kid² verb (kidded, kidding, kids) 1. (informal) to joke or tease. *Please don't kid me about my new haircut.* 2. (informal) to tell a lie to or fool. *Were you kidding me when you said your mother gave you ice cream for dinner?* {**kihd**} kidder, n., kiddingly, adv.

kid·nap verb (kidnapped or kidnaped, kidnapping or kidnaping, kidnaps) to take by force and hold against a person's will in order to get money or some other valuable thing. {**kihd** năp} kidnapper (kidnaper), n.

kid·ney noun 1. one of a pair of organs in the body which remove water and waste products from the blood. The waste products go from the kidneys to the bladder in the form of urine. The kidneys are found high in the abdomen near the spine. 2. the kidney of certain animals, used as food. {**kihd** nee}

Ki·ev noun the capital city of Ukraine. {**kee** **ehv** or **kee** **ehf** or **kee** ehv}

kill verb (killed, killing, kills) 1. to cause to die. *The hunter killed a deer.* 2. to put an end to; destroy. *The boring teacher killed the girl's interest in history.* 3. to make pass; use up. *She killed time in school playing with her pencil.* 4. to cause great pain to. *My tooth was killing me so I went to the dentist.* noun 1. the act or process of killing. *The tiger closed in for the kill.* 2. animals that have been killed in a hunt. *The hunters hauled the kill back to camp.* {**kihl**} killer, n.

kill·deer noun (killdeer or killdeers) a bird that is a kind of plover, with two black bands on a white breast. Killdeers

are native to inland waters and fields of North America and have a loud, shrill cry that sounds like their name. {**kihl** deer}

killer whale noun a black and white, toothed whale. Killer whales kill and eat seals and large fish. {**kihl** ər **wayl**}

kiln noun an oven for burning, baking, and drying. A kiln is used to make pottery and bricks or to dry wood. *The potter fired the bowl in the kiln after glazing it.* {**kihln**}

kil·o noun (kilos) see **kilogram**. {**kee** loh}

kil·o- prefix a prefix that means "one thousand." *A kilogram of salt is one thousand grams of salt.* {**kih** lə}

kil·o·byte noun a unit of measurement equal to 1,024 bytes. Kilobytes are used to measure the amount of electronic information that can be stored by a computer. (abbreviated: k) {**kih** lə **biyt**}

kil·o·gram noun a unit of weight equal to one thousand grams or 2.205 pounds. (abbreviated: kg) {**kih** lə **grăm**}

kil·o·hertz noun (kilohertz) a unit that measures the frequency of radio waves. One kilohertz is equal to one thousand cycles per second. (abbreviated: kHz) {**kihl** ə **huhrtz**}

kil·om·e·ter noun a unit of length equal to one thousand meters or 0.621 mile. (abbreviated: km) {kə **lŏm** ih tər or **kihl** ə mee tər} kilometric, adj.

kil·o·me·tre noun a spelling of **kilometer** used in Canada and Britain. See **kilometer**. {**kihl** ə mee tər}

kil·o·watt noun a unit of electrical power equal to one thousand watts. (abbreviated: kw, kW) {**kihl** ə **wŏt**}

kilt noun a plaid wool skirt that has pleats. Kilts are worn by men in Scotland. {**kihlt**}

ki·mo·no noun (kimonos) a long, loose Japanese robe that has wide sleeves and a broad sash. {kih **moh** noh}

kin noun (kin) the members of an extended family together; relatives. *All his kin gathered at the reunion.* {**kihn**}

kind¹ adjective (kinder, kindest) 1. helpful; friendly; good. *You were so kind to help that old woman down the stairs.* 2. showing understanding or sympathy. *Your kind words made him feel better.* {**kiynd**}

> **Synonyms**
> These words share a meaning with ***kind***, adjective 1:
> good, gentle, decent, good-hearted

kind² noun 1. a group of things, people, or animals that are thought of together because of like characteristics. *They were not familiar with our kind.* 2. type; sort. *What kind of hat is that?* {**kiynd**}
  • **kind of** (informal) somewhat; rather. *He's actually kind of nice.*

kin·der·gar·ten noun a program for very young children. Kindergarten teaches some of the activities that are done in school. {**kihn** dər **gar** tən}

kin·dle verb (kindled, kindling, kindles) 1. to build or start. *The campers used twigs and matches to kindle a fire.* 2. to start to burn; catch fire. *The crumpled paper kindled.* 3. to make excited; to inspire. *That book kindled his interest in poetry.* {**kihn** dəl}

kin·dling noun dry material that burns easily and is used to start a fire. {**kihnd** ling}

kind·ly adjective (kindlier, kindliest) showing or having kindness. *That kindly man*

Human Body   Human Mind   Everyday Life   History and Culture     Communication

often helps his neighbors. *adverb* (kindlier, kindliest) 1. in a friendly or kind way. *She acted kindly toward the stranger.* 2. please. *Would you kindly help me?* {**kiynd** lee}

kind·ness *noun* 1. the quality of being kind. *The veterinarian is known for his kindness toward animals.* 2. a generous act or favor. *What do we owe you for this kindness?* {**kiynd** nihs}

king ⊕ *noun* 1. a male head of a royal family who rules a country for life. 2. a person, animal, or thing that is the most powerful, important, or admired among others of its kind. *The lion is the king of beasts.* 3. the most important piece in the game of chess. 4. a playing card with a picture of a king. {**king**}

king·dom *noun* 1. a country that is ruled by a king or queen. 2. one of the large divisions of living things, such as the plant kingdom, the animal kingdom, and the fungus kingdom. {**king** dəm}

king·fish·er *noun* a brightly colored bird with a large head, strong beak, and small feet. Kingfishers' heads are often crested. They often live around streams and rivers and eat fish or insects. {**king** fihsh ər}

king-size *adjective* 1. larger than the usual size. *A king-size box of cereal will last all month.* 2. having a mattress and frame more than six feet long and six feet wide. *That hotel has a king-size bed in every room.* {**king** siyz} king-sized, adj.

kink *noun* 1. a tight curl or twist. *Her hair has kinks in it. / The wire has a kink where it was held by the pliers.* 2. a sore muscle that feels like it is in a knot. *He got a kink in his neck while exercising.* 3. a small problem that does not allow something to work well. *The rain put a kink in our picnic plans.* *verb* (kinked, kinking, kinks) to cause to be curled or twisted. *Todd kinked the hose and the water stopped.* {**kingk**}

kiss *verb* (kissed, kissing, kisses) to touch or press with the lips as a sign of love, friendship, passion, or respect. *I kissed my mother good night.* *noun* 1. an act or instance of kissing. *She gave her friend a kiss.* 2. a small piece of candy, often chocolate. {**kihs**} kisser, n.

kit *noun* 1. a collection of items for a particular use. *She took a bandage out of the first-aid kit.* 2. a case for a collection of items. *They put all of their tools in a metal kit.* 3. a group of parts and materials used to make something. *The children read the instructions for the model airplane kit.* {**kiht**}

kitch·en ⊙ *noun* a room where food is stored and cooked. {**kihch** ihn}

kitch·en·ette *noun* a very small kitchen. {**kihch** ih **neht**}

kite *noun* 1. a light frame covered with paper, plastic, or cloth that is flown in the air at the end of a long string. 2. a bird like a hawk that has pointed wings and a forked tail. {**kiyt**}

kit·ten *noun* a young cat. {**kih** tihn}

kit·ty[1] *noun* (kitties) a kitten or cat. {**kih** tee}

kit·ty[2] *noun* (kitties) money collected from people for a particular purpose. *Is there enough money in the kitty to buy a snack for the next club meeting?* {**kih** tee}

ki·wi *noun* (kiwis) 1. a bird of New Zealand that has gray-brown feathers, a long, thin bill, and small, weak wings that can not be used for flying. 2. a small oval fruit that is good to eat. Kiwis have brown skin and green flesh. {**kee** wee *or* **kee** wee}

klutz *noun* a clumsy person. klutziness, n., klutzy, adj. {**kluts**}

km *abbreviation* an abbreviation for **kilometer** or kilometers.

knack *noun* a natural talent; ability with ease. *She has a knack for training horses.* {**năk**}

knap·sack *noun* a bag worn on the back to carry things. A knapsack is often made of leather, canvas, or nylon. {**năp** săk}

Word History A *knapsack* is where a soldier carried his food, which might have to be eaten quickly. "Knapsack" meant "eating bag" in the English spoken in the 1600s. *Knap* comes from a German word that means "a bite" or "snap."

A B C D E F G H I J **K** L M N O P Q R S T U V W X Y Z

knead *verb* (kneaded, kneading, kneads) 1. to mix by pressing, folding, and pulling. *He kneaded the bread dough with his hands.* 2. to press, rub, or squeeze with the hands; massage. *She kneaded his shoulders to relax his sore muscles.* {<u>need</u>}

Homophone Note The words **knead** and **need** sound alike but have different meanings.

knee *noun* 1. the joint between the upper and lower parts of a human leg. 2. something that looks like a bent knee. *The carpenter joined the boards in a knee.* *verb* (kneed, kneeing, knees) to hit, push, or touch with the knee. *He kneed me in the back during class to get my attention.* {<u>nee</u>}

knee·cap *noun* the flat, round bone in front of the knee. {<u>nee</u> kăp}

kneel *verb* (knelt or kneeled, kneeling, kneels) to rest on the knee or knees. *She liked to kneel on the ground and watch ants carry food.* {<u>neel</u>}

knelt *verb* past tense and past participle of **kneel**. {<u>nehlt</u>}

knew *verb* past tense of **know**. {<u>nooh</u>}

Homophone Note The words **knew**, **gnu**, and **new** sound alike but have different meanings.

knick·knack *noun* a small object used to decorate. *Her shelves are filled with knickknacks that she bought while on vacation.* {<u>nihk</u> năk}

knife ⊙ *noun* (knives) a tool with a handle and a thin, sharp blade, used for cutting. *Lisa makes gnomes with her wood-carving knife.* *verb* (knifed, knifing,

After a hard day's jousting every **knight** wants a good **night**'s sleep.

knifes) to cut or stab with a knife. {<u>niyf</u>}

knight *noun* 1. a soldier on horseback in the Middle Ages. A knight had to serve as an apprentice and follow many rules. 2. a man given a rank of honor by a king or queen for service to his country. *The general was made a knight after the war.* 3. a chess piece in the shape of a horse's head. *verb* (knighted, knighting, knights) to give the title of knight to. *The queen knighted the writer for his outstanding books.* {<u>niyt</u>}

Homophone Note The words **knight**, and **night** (the opposite of day) sound alike but have different meanings.

knight·hood *noun* the position held by a knight. *The king bestowed a knighthood on the brilliant scientist.* {<u>niyt</u> huud}

knit *verb* (knit or knitted, knitting, knits) 1. to make by joining together loops of yarn by hand with long nee-

dles or by machine. *She knit a sweater.* 2. to bring into a whole; unite. *He knit his friends into a tight group.* 3. to join together and make secure. *The broken table leg was knitted with glue.* 4. to move closely together and form wrinkles. *She knit her brow and thought about the problem.* {<u>niht</u>}

knives *noun* plural of **knife**. {<u>niyvz</u>}

knob *noun* a rounded piece on a door or drawer; a switch on a machine. *Lee turned a knob on the radio to change the station.* {<u>nŏb</u>}

knock *verb* (knocked, knocking, knocks) 1. to strike or hit something, such as a door, so as to get permission to enter. *Please knock before you enter the room.* 2. to bump or crash. *He knocked into the wall.* 3. to make a pounding or beating sound. *The car's engine knocks.* 4. to give a sharp blow to; strike; hit. *The boxers knocked each other in the head several times.* *noun* 1. the act or an instance of knocking. *Your knock on the door woke me up.* 2. a sound made by a bad engine. *When did you first hear the knock in your car?* {<u>nŏk</u>}

knock·er *noun* a metal piece with a hinge that is attached to the outside of a door. A knocker is used to call for those inside. {<u>nŏk</u> ər}

knoll *noun* a small rounded rise of land; hill. {<u>nohl</u>}

knot *noun* 1. a tying together of material such as rope, string, or yarn that is used to fasten. *She tied her shoelaces in a tight knot.* 2. the place where a branch grows out of the trunk of a tree. When wood is cut into boards, the

 Human Body   Human Mind   Everyday Life   History and Culture    Communication

knot looks like a dark spot. 3. a tight group. *A knot of tourists formed around the statue.* 4. a measure of speed used for sea travel. A knot is about 6,080 feet per hour. *We were sailing at ten knots when the storm hit.* *verb* (knotted, knotting, knots) 1. to form into a knot, or to tie knots in. *I knotted the ribbon around my hair.* 2. to fasten with one or more knots. *The captain knotted the line to the mast of the boat.* {**nŏt**}

Homophone Note The words *knot* and *not* sound alike but have different meanings.

knot·hole *noun* a hole in a piece of lumber from which a knot has come out. {**nŏt** hohl}

knot·ty *adjective* (knottier, knottiest) 1. having knots. *The table is made out of knotty pine.* 2. difficult to understand; complex. *The knotty problem took hours to solve.* {**nŏt** ee}

know *verb* (knew, known, knowing, knows) 1. to understand, perceive, or experience directly. *Do you know what I'm doing?* 2. to have the skill to be able to (usually followed by "how"). *Do you know how to ski?* 3. to be sure of; be aware of. *He knows your name.* / *She knows all the multiplication facts.* 4. to be acquainted with. *She knows some famous people.* / *He knows the plays of Shakespeare.* {**noh**}
  • **know of**
  to be aware of; have heard about. *I know of a place we can hide.*

Homophone Note The words *know* and *no* sound alike but have different meanings.

know-how *noun* the knowledge needed to do a certain task. *He has the know-how to run a successful business.* {**noh** how}

knowl·edge ⊙ *noun* 1. understanding; awareness. *Alice left home without her parents' knowledge.* 2. a particular form of understanding or skill. *Working in a restaurant gave Jim a good knowledge of cooking.* 3. learning; education. *Reading books will increase your knowledge.* {**nŏl** ihj}

knowl·edge·a·ble *adjective* having information or knowledge; familiar. *The professor is knowledgeable about Islamic art.* {**nŏl** ih jə bəl}

known *verb* past participle of **know.** {**nohn**}

knuck·le *noun* a joint of a finger. *The ring cannot fit over his knuckle.* {**nuhk** əl}
  • **knuckle down**
  to start working in a serious manner. *It's time to knuckle down and finish your homework!*

ko·a·la *noun* a mammal with gray fur, round ears, and a short black nose. Koalas are marsupials and live in trees. The female has a pouch in her belly where she carries her baby. Koalas are only found in Australia. They are sometimes called "koala bears," but they are not related to true bears. {koh **ah** lə or kə **ah** lə}

kook *noun* (slang) a person considered to be strange or crazy. kooky, adj.

Ko·ran *noun* the sacred book of Islam that is the basis of Muslim religion. Muslims believe that Allah gave the words of the Koran to the prophet Muhammad. The Koran is written in Arabic. {koh **răn** or koh **rahn**} Koranic, adj.

Ko·re·a *noun* see North Korea, South Korea. {kə **ree** ə}

Ko·re·an *adjective* of or having to do with the people or language of North and South Korea. *noun* the language of North and South Korea. {kə **ree** ihn}

ko·sher *adjective* 1. prepared according to Jewish laws of food preparation. *Dairy products and meat are not eaten at the same time during a kosher meal.* 2. following Jewish laws of food preparation. *Kosher hot dogs are made with kosher beef.* {**koh** shər}

Kr symbol of the chemical element krypton.

kryp·ton *noun* a gas that is a chemical element. Krypton does not combine easily with other elements. (symbol: Kr) {**krihp** tŏn}

KS or **Kan.** *abbreviation* an abbreviation for **Kansas.**

Ku·wait *noun* a country in southwestern Asia at the northern end of the Persian Gulf. Kuwait City is the capital of Kuwait. The capital is also called Al Kuwait. {kooh **wayt**} Kuwaiti, n., adj.

A B C D E F G H I J K L M N O P Q R S T U V W X Y Z

a
b
c
d
e
f
g
h
i
j
k
l
m
n
o
p
q
r
s
t
u
v
w
x
y
z

kwan·za or **kwanzaa** *noun* (kwanza or kwanzas) 1. the main unit of money in Angola. 2. (capitalized) an African American holiday that celebrates family, community, and culture. Kwanza lasts from December 26 to January 1. {<u>kwahn</u> zah}

KY or **Ky.** *abbreviation* an abbreviation for **Kentucky**.

 Human Body   Human Mind   Everyday Life   History and Culture   Communication

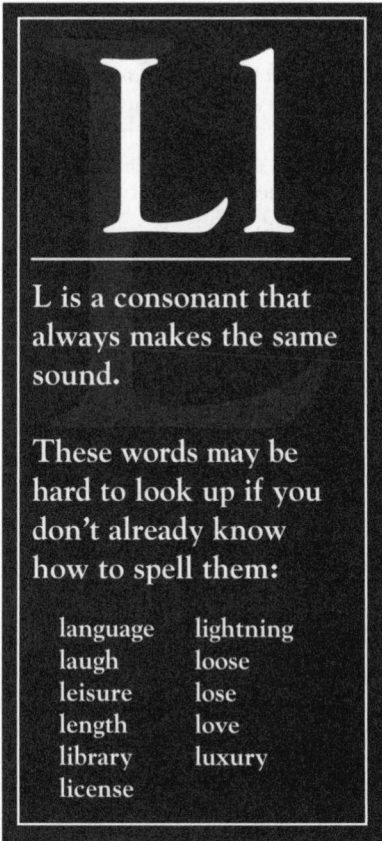

L l

L is a consonant that always makes the same sound.

These words may be hard to look up if you don't already know how to spell them:

language	lightning
laugh	loose
leisure	lose
length	love
library	luxury
license	

l or **L** *noun* (l's or L's) the twelfth letter of the English alphabet. {**ehl**}

l *abbreviation* an abbreviation for **liter** or liters.

LA or **La.** *abbreviation* an abbreviation for **Louisiana**.

la *noun* the syllable that indicates the sixth tone of a musical scale. {**lǒ**}

lab *noun* a short form of **laboratory**. {**lăb**}

la·bel *noun* 1. a piece of paper or cloth that is attached to an object. A label gives information about what the object contains, how to use it, or who owns it. 2. a term or phrase used to describe a person or thing. *My teachers gave him the label "bookworm" because he reads a lot.* *verb* (labeled, labeling, labels) 1. to put a label on. *My father labels his suitcase with a tag*

before he travels. 2. to mark with a label. *She labeled her clothes before she went to camp.* {**lay** bəl}

la·bor *noun* 1. hard work or effort. *The workers did hours of labor to finish the building.* 2. a group of workers. *The neighbors next door hired labor to build their garage.* 3. childbirth. *She went into labor at five and had the baby before midnight.* *verb* (labored, laboring, labors) 1. to do hard work. *They labored on the house until it was done.* 2. to go with difficulty; struggle. *The old car labored up the hill.* {**lay** bər}

lab·o·ra·to·ry 🌐 *noun* (laboratories) 1. a place used for scientific experiments. *In the laboratory, scientists test food for safety.* 2. a place where new products are made. *Drugs and other chemicals are made at a laboratory.* {**lă** brə **tohr** ee *or* **lăb** ər ə **tohr** ee *or* lə **boh** rə **tohr** ee}

Labor Day *noun* a holiday in the United States and Canada to honor the labor of working people. Labor Day is the first Monday in September. {**lay** bər **day**}

labor union *noun* a group of workers that help and protect each other's interests. Labor unions ask employers to improve wages and working conditions. *Some janitors belong to a labor union that makes sure they get paid a*

fair amount of money. {**lay** bər **yoon** yən}

Lab·ra·dor *noun* a very large peninsula in eastern Canada that contains portions of the province of Quebec and the province of Newfoundland & Labrador. {**lă** brih **dohr**}

lace *noun* 1. a fabric made of fine threads that has holes in it as part of the design. *Grandmother's collar is made of lace.* 2. a string used to hold together two edges; shoelace. *verb* (laced, lacing, laces) to tie together with a string passed through holes in two edges. *The salesperson will lace the shoes for you.* {**lays**}

lack *noun* the condition of being without. *She had to cancel her vacation because of a lack of money.* *verb* (lacked, lacking, lacks) to be without. *He lacked the strength to climb the rope.* {**lăk**}

lac·quer *noun* a liquid used on wood or metal to protect and make it shiny. *verb* (lacquered, lacquering, lacquers) to coat with lacquer. *They will lacquer the table twice for a shiny finish.* {**lă** kər}

la·crosse 🌐 *noun* a game played on a field. The players use sticks with a net on one end to carry the ball and throw it

A B C D E F G H I J K **L** M N O P Q R S T U V W X Y Z

into the other team's goal. {lə **kraws**}

lad *noun* a boy or young man. {**lăd**}

lad·der *noun* a pair of side pieces joined with horizontal bars called rungs, used for climbing. {**lăd** ər}

lad·en *adjective* filled with a great weight. *The wheelbarrow was laden with sticks and logs.* {**lay** dən}

la·dle *noun* a spoon with a long handle and a deep bowl used for serving liquids such as soup or punch. *verb* (ladled, ladling, ladles) to serve with a ladle. *The host ladled punch into our drinking glasses.* {**lay** dəl}

lady *noun* (ladies) 1. a polite word for a woman or girl. 2. a woman of high social position or good manners. *That's not how a lady behaves.* 3. a title for a noblewoman. *The lady of the castle is in her room.* {**lay** dee}

la·dy·bug *noun* a small, round beetle that is red or orange with black spots. Ladybugs

eat aphids and other insects that are harmful to plants. {**lay** dee **buhg**}

lag *verb* (lagged, lagging, lags) 1. to fall behind an expected pace. *The store lagged in stocking new products.* 2. to fail or become weaker. *Her energy lagged toward the end of the race.* *noun* 1. the act or condition of lagging. *After an eight hour flight, she felt a severe lag.* 2. the duration of falling behind an expected pace; delay. *Our company had a two-month lag in production.* {**lăg**}

la·goon *noun* 1. a shallow body of salt water by the sea. A lagoon is separated from the sea by sandbars, coral reefs, or islands. *The lagoons near the ocean have many sea animals in them.* 2. a body of fresh water that connects to a larger lake or river. {lə **goohn**}

laid *verb* past tense and past participle of **lay**[1]. {**layd**}

lain *verb* past participle of **lie**[2]. {**layn**}

lair *noun* a wild animal's shelter; den. {**layr**}

lake *noun* a large body of fresh or salt water that is surrounded on all sides by land. {**layk**}

lamb *noun* a young sheep, or its meat used as food. {**lăm**}

lame *adjective* (lamer, lamest) 1. not able to walk well; disabled. *The horse has a lame leg after racing*

for too many years. 2. sore and difficult to move. *The woman had a lame back after lying in bed for a week.* 3. not adequate; poor. *I gave my parents a lame apology for not helping with the chores.* *verb* (lamed, laming, lames) to cause to be unable to walk well. *Pulling too much weight will lame a horse.* {**laym**} lamely, adv., lameness, n.

lamp *noun* a device that gives off light. {**lămp**}

lance *noun* a weapon with a long pole and pointed metal head. *The knight on horseback used a lance in battle.* *verb* (lanced, lancing, lances) to cut open with a sharp tool. *The doctor lanced the swelling on my foot.* {**lăns**}

land *noun* 1. the solid part of the earth's surface. *Fish live in the sea, and tigers live on land.* 2. a country or nation. *We visited many lands on our vacation.* 3. soil that has a particular use or condition (often used in combination). *Some people think the desert is a wasteland.* *verb* (landed, landing, lands) 1. to cause to touch down upon a surface. *She landed the plane.* 2. to cause to end up in a certain situation or condition. *A serious disease landed him in the hospital.* 3. to arrive upon the ground or other surface. *The plane landed on time.* 4. to come to the shore. *We landed on the north beach.* 5. to end up in some place or condition. *He landed in jail soon after the trial.* {**lănd**}

land·ing *noun* 1. the act of one that lands. *The bird made a*

beautiful landing on the pond. 2. a point where goods are loaded and passengers get on or off, as on or from a ship or airplane. 3. the floor at the top or bottom of a flight of stairs. {**lăn** ding}

land·la·dy *noun* (landladies) a woman who rents property to others. {**lănd** lay dee}

land·lord *noun* a man or woman who rents property to others. {**lănd** lohrd}

land·mark *noun* 1. a point in a landscape that is used as a reference or marks a boundary. *The large red house on the corner is the landmark for our street.* 2. an historic building. *The Eiffel Tower is a famous landmark in Paris, France.* 3. an event that marks an important change. *The college's decision to allow women to attend was a landmark in education.* {**lănd** mark}

land·scape 🌳 🌍 *noun* 1. the area that can be seen from one point; view. *There is a spectacular view of the landscape from the top floor of their house.* 2. a picture that shows a view of an area. *He gave me a beautiful landscape to hang on the wall.* *verb* (landscaped, landscaping, landscapes) to change a piece of land by planting trees, shrubs or other plants. *They will landscape the yard by taking out the small hill and planting flowers.* {**lănd** skayp}

land·slide *noun* 1. the falling of earth down a steep slope. *The landslide destroyed many trees on the mountain.* 2. a great victory in a contest. *She was very popular and won the election by a landslide.* {**lănd** sliyd}

lane 🔊 *noun* 1. a narrow passage, as between hedges, walls, or buildings. 2. a narrow country road or city street. 3. a marked route for traffic going in one direction, as for a line of cars on a highway or for a single swimmer or runner in a race. *The four lane road turned into two lanes as we came closer to town.* 4. a wooden path along which a bowling ball is rolled; alley. {**layn**}

Homophone Note The words *lane* and *lain* sound alike but have different meanings.

lan·guage 🔊 *noun* 1. the system of spoken or written words with which people communicate thoughts, ideas, or feelings. *Language is a way of sharing our ideas with one another.* 2. a particular system used by people of the same nation, region, or group to communicate with one another. *The English language is hard for some people to learn.* 3. a way to communicate without using words. *Her body language says she is tired.* {**lăng** gwihj}

Word History *Language* comes from *lingua*, a Latin word that means "the tongue."

lank·y *adjective* (lankier, lankiest) tall, thin, and awkward. *A lanky boy may grow into a graceful man.* {**lăng** kee}

lan·tern *noun* a case or container that is made of a material through which a light can shine and be protected. *He uses a kerosene lantern when he is camping.* {**lăn** tərn}

La·os *noun* a country in southeastern Asia. Vientiane is the capital of Laos. Laos is also called Lao People's Democratic Republic. {**lah** ohs *or* **lows**} Laotian, n., adj.

lap¹ *noun* the front of the human body, from the waist to the knees, in a sitting position. The part of clothing that covers this part of the body is also called the lap. {**lăp**}

lap² *verb* (lapped, lapping, laps) 1. to lay or fold over so as to cover another; overlap. *The carpenter lapped the shingles on the roof to prevent leaks.* 2. to lie over part of something; overlap. *noun* one part of a passage, such as around a race course. *Four laps on the track equal one mile.* {**lăp**}

lap³ *verb* (lapped, lapping, laps) 1. to gently splash or slap against. *The waves lapped the shore with a peaceful sound.* 2. to lick up with the tongue, as drink or food (often followed by "up"). *The cat was lapping up the milk. noun* the act or sound of licking up something. *We heard the lap of our dog as he drank from his bowl.* {**lăp**}

la·pel *noun* a front part of a coat or jacket that goes down the chest from the collar and is folded back. {lə **pehl**}

lapse *noun* 1. a slight failure to meet some accepted standard. *Not saying "thank you" was a lapse of good manners.* 2. an amount of time that has passed or is passing. *After a lapse of ten years the artist started painting again.* 3. a decline or fall that happens a little at a time or slowly. *A lapse into poor health will follow if you do not exercise. verb* (lapsed, lapsing, lapses) 1. to fall below or fail to meet an accepted standard. *The old house lapsed into bad condition.* 2. to come to an end

A B C D E F G H I J K L M N O P Q R S T U V W X Y Z

People from around the world send you a greeting — *Welcome!*

All written languages probably began as pictures representing spoken words. In Chinese, Japanese, and Korean, a writing symbol often stands for a whole word or idea. The other writing systems shown here use only letters that represent sounds.

Hindi

आप क

स्वागत

है !

Many Islamic cultures base their writing on the Arabic alphabet. South Asian languages such as Hindi are based on the Sanskrit alphabet.

Hebrew

Egyptian

Thai

Japanese

The written form of some Asian languages are based on ancient Chinese characters.

Chinese

Welcome!

English

Vietnamese

VUi MÙNG

KÍNH MỜI

Добро пожаловать! Russian

Many of these greetings, including English and Russian, are written in alphabets based on letters from ancient Mediterranean cultures.

Wilkommen bei mir daheim

German

Italian

Benvenuto!

Ewe

Wiedzɔ fe ŋye Apfeme

Creole

Byen vini

Creoles often evolve from pidgins, a very simple form of a language used by groups of people who need to communicate but who speak different languages.

Anggaplah seperti

di rumah sendiri.

Indonesian

Bienvenido a mi casa! Spanish

after a certain period of time. *The insurance policy lapsed at the end of last year.* {lăps}

lap·top com·pu·ter *noun* a small computer that is easy to carry; notebook computer. *Laptop computers are usually more expensive than desktop computers.* {lăp tŏp kuhm **pooh** tər}

larch *noun* 1. A kind of tree that has cones and looks like an evergreen but has needles that turn yellow and are shed in the fall. 2. the wood of this tree. It is durable and used for docks and other things built in water. {larch}

lard *noun* the fat of pigs that has been melted down, used in cooking. {lard}

lar·der *noun* a place or room for keeping or storing food, or the supply of food stored there. {lar dər}

large *adjective* (larger, largest) of a size, or amount bigger than normal or average; not small. *We will need to buy a large pizza for this many people.* {larj} largeness, n.

Synonyms
These words share a meaning with *large*, adjective 1:
big, considerable

large intestine *noun* the large, lower part of the intestines. The large intestine absorbs water from digested food and forms solid waste matter. {larj ihn **teh** stihn}

large·ly *adverb* in large part; mostly; mainly. *The delicious dessert was largely made of sugar.* {larj lee}

lar·i·at *noun* a long rope with a sliding loop at one end. It is used to catch running animals such as cattle or horses. {layr ee iht}

lark[1] *noun* a songbird with a long hind claw and a musical song. There are many kinds of larks. {lark}

lark[2] *noun* a happy adventure. *Mother and I had a lark together this afternoon.* {lark}

lark·spur *noun* a plant with bright blue, pink, or white flowers on a tall stalk. The flowers have a long projection called a spur. {lark spuhr}

lar·va ❶ *noun* (larvae) 1. an insect after it hatches from an egg and before it changes into its adult form. Larvae do not have wings and look like worms. Most kinds of insects spend part of their lives as larvae. Caterpillars are a type of larva. 2. the young form of other animals without backbones that change their shape in different stages of their lives. {lar və} larval, adj.

Word History *Larva* is a Latin word that means "mask" or "ghost." The Swedish botanist Linnaeus gave this Latin word a scientific sense in 1768. He chose this word because, in its larva stage, the true, adult form of the insect is masked.

lar·yn·gi·tis *noun* an inflammation of the part of the throat called the larynx. A person with laryngitis might not be able to speak louder than a whisper. {lar ihn **jiy** tihs}

lar·ynx *noun* (larynxes) the structure at the top of the windpipe that contains the vocal cords, which produce the human voice; voice box. {lar ingks}

la·sa·gna *noun* long, wide, flat noodles, or a dish made of these noodles that is baked with sauce, cheese and ground meat or vegetables. {lə **zahn** yə *or* lah **sahn** yŏ}

la·ser *noun* a device that makes a strong, narrow beam of light by stimulating the atoms in a gas or crystal. {lay zər}

lash[1] *noun* 1. a whip or the striking part of a whip. 2. a stroke, sweep, or blow by a whip. *The lash of the whip made the horse run faster.* 3. a beating, as though with a whip. *The lash of the waves against the shore washed the sand away.* 4. an eyelash. *verb* (lashed, lashing, lashes) 1. to strike with, or as if with, a whip. *He lashed the prisoner to punish him.* 2. to beat or beat against. *Rain lashed the window.* 3. to attack someone or something with words (often followed by "out"). *I lashed out at him when I was angry.* 4. to move suddenly or with force; whip. *The tiger's tail lashed back and forth.* {lăsh}

lash[2] *verb* (lashed, lashing, lashes) to tie down with a rope, cord, or chain. *My father lashed the luggage to the top of the car.* {lăsh}

lass *noun* a girl or young woman. {lăs}

las·so *noun* (lassos or lassoes) a long rope with a sliding loop on one end; lariat. It is used to catch running animals such as cattle or horses. *verb* (lassoed, lassoing, lassos or lassoes) to catch with a lasso. *The cowboy lassoed the calf.* {lă sooh *or* lăs oh *or* lă **sooh**, n., lă sooh *or* lăs oh *or* lă **sooh**, v.}

last[1] *adjective* 1. coming after or finishing behind all others. *Ours is the last house on our block.* 2. coming just before the present time; the most recent; latest. *Last night I saw a shooting star.* 3. being the

A B C D E F G H I J K L M N O P Q R S T U V W X Y Z

only one left. *This is your last chance.* *adverb* 1. after all others. *His name appeared last on the program.* 2. most recently in time. *When did you last see him?* *noun* 1. a person or thing that is last. *I was last in line for the movie.* 2. the final mention or sight. *You haven't seen the last of me.* {lăst}

• **at last**
after a long time or wait; finally. *Spring has arrived at last.*

last² *verb* (lasted, lasting, lasts) 1. to go on through time; continue. *The movie lasted for two hours.* 2. to stay in good condition. *My car lasted for a long time, but it finally broke down.* 3. to remain in good supply. *My Halloween candy lasted until December.* {lăst}

last·ing *adjective* continuing for a long time, not ending. *We all hoped for a lasting peace.* {lăst ing}

latch *noun* a device that fastens or locks with a bar or bolt that goes into a notch or hole. *Latches fasten doors, windows, and gates.* *verb* (latched, latching, latches) to lock or fasten with a latch. *Please latch the gate so the dog does not get out.* {lăch}

late *adjective* (later, latest) 1. happening after the usual or expected time. *I was later for work, because I missed the bus.* 2. happening toward the end of the night or evening. *It's late, so I think I'll go to bed.* 3. happening not long ago; recent. *Did you hear the latest news?* 4. having recently died. *We all loved the late Mr. Smith.* *adverb* (later, latest) 1. after the usual or expected time. *The bus arrived late.* 2. at or to a time or period near

the end. *Success came to him late in life.* {layt} lateness, n.

> **Word History** *Late* comes from an early English word that meant "slow," "lazy," or "sluggish." It was first used in its present meaning ("not on time") in the 1200s. Today, it is possible to be late without being lazy.

late·ly *adverb* of late; recently. *She has not called lately.* {layt lee}

lat·er·al *adjective* about, from, or toward a side or sides; sideways. *The dancer moved in a lateral direction on stage.* *noun* a sideways or backward football pass to another player. *The receiver caught the lateral and then ran for a first down.* {lăt ər əl} laterally, adv.

lathe *noun* a machine for shaping a piece of wood, metal, or other hard material. The lathe holds and spins the material while another cutting tool is held against it. {layth}

lath·er *noun* 1. foam made by soap or detergent mixed in water. 2. foamlike sweat on a horse or other animal during heavy work or exercise. *verb* (lathered, lathering, lathers) 1. to form a lather. *The new shampoo lathers well.* 2. to coat or cover with lather. *He lathered his face before he shaved.* {lă thər} lathery, adj.

Lat·in *noun* 1. the language of ancient Rome. The Romance languages are derived from Latin. 2. a member of any of the peoples who speak any of the Romance languages. *adjective* of or having to do with

the Romance languages, the peoples who speak them, or the countries in which they are spoken. {lă tən}

Lat·i·na *noun* a woman or girl who was born in or is a citizen of a country in Latin America, or an American woman or girl of Hispanic origin. *adjective* of or having to do with Latinas. {lo tee nŏ}

Latin America *noun* all the countries in the Western Hemisphere south of the United States where the main language spoken is a Romance language. {lă tən ə mehr ih kə}

Lat·in A·mer·i·can *adjective* of or having to do with Latin America, or its people or languages. *noun* a person who was born in or is a citizen of a country in Latin America. {lă tən ə mehr ih kən}

La·ti·no *noun* (Latinos) a person who was born in or is a citizen of a country in Latin America, or an American of Hispanic origin. *adjective* of or having to do with Latinos. {lă tee noh}

lat·i·tude *noun* the distance between the equator and a point north or south on the earth's surface. This distance is measured in degrees. {lăt ih toohd} latitudinal, adj.

lat·ter *adjective* 1. the second of two things mentioned. *Of the two songs we heard, I like the latter one best.* 2. near the end. *Her hair turned gray in the latter part of her life.* {lăt ər}

lat·tice *noun* a flat framework made with strips of wood or other material. The strips cross each other and have open spaces in between. A lattice is often used as a screen on a porch or in a garden. {lăt ihs}

 Human Body Human Mind Everyday Life ⚑ History and Culture 👂 Communication

laugh ? *verb* (laughed, laughing, laughs) to express happiness, amusement, ridicule, or other feelings, by making sounds with the mouth and changing the face to an expression like a smile. *The class laughed at the teacher's jokes. noun* 1. the act of laughing. *His laugh made us all feel better.* 2. the sound of laughing. *He recognized her deep laugh.* {lăf}

laugh·a·ble *adjective* causing laughter or ridicule. *In the play, she had the part of a laughable character.* {lăf ə bəl}

laugh·ter *noun* the act or sound of laughing. *I could hear laughter in the next room.* {lăf tər}

launch[1] *verb* (launched, launching, launches) 1. to put in motion with force. *He launched the paper airplane.* 2. to put in the water. *They launched the new boat today.* 3. to start. *She launched her campaign for president.* 4. to start forth. *The rocket launched into space. noun* the act of launching or an instance of launching.

The launch of the space shuttle is planned for tomorrow. {lawnch}

launch[2] *noun* a large open boat with a motor for power. {lawnch}

launch pad *noun* the platform or base from which a rocket or missile is launched. {lawnch păd}

laun·der *verb* (laundered, laundering, launders) to wash, or wash and iron. *The dry cleaners laundered his shirts.* {lawn dər}

Laun·dro·mat *noun* (Trademark.) a place where people pay to use washing machines and clothes dryers. {lawn drə măt}

laun·dry ? *noun* (laundries) 1. clothing, sheets, and other things that are cleaned by washing or that are washed and ironed. 2. a room or business where such cleaning is done. {lawn dree}

lau·rel *noun* 1. an evergreen tree or shrub that has large, shiny leaves and yellow flowers. 2. a tree or shrub that is like a laurel, such as the mountain laurel. 3. (plural) honor or distinction. The ancient Greeks gave crowns of laurel leaves to their heroes. {law rəl}

• **rest on one's laurels** to be content with what one has done in the past and not interested in trying to achieve more. *After winning the award, he stopped writing novels and rested on his laurels.*

la·va *noun* 1. hot, melted rock that erupts from a volcano. 2. the rock formed when this hot, melted rock cools and gets hard. {lah və}

lav·a·to·ry ? *noun* (lavatories) 1. a room with sinks and toilets. 2. a sink or basin for washing or bathing. It usually has running water. {lăv ə tohr ee}

lav·en·der *noun* 1. a plant of the mint family with pale purple flowers. 2. the dried flowers, leaves, and stems of this plant that are used for their

scent. 3. a pale purple color. {lăv ən dər}

lav·ish *adjective* 1. generous in using or spending. *She was lavish in her praise of his performance.* 2. being large in amount or expensive; more than enough. *The movie star had lavish parties. verb* (lavished, lavishing, lavishes) to give or spend a large amount or without limit. *He lavished attention on his children.* {lăv ihsh} lavishly, adv., lavishness, n.

> **Word History** *Lavish* comes from *lavache,* an early French word for a torrent (or very heavy fall of rain). The French word came from a Latin word meaning "to wash."

law ? *noun* 1. the set of rules that people in a society must follow. *Each country has its own system of law.* 2. any one rule that must be observed or obeyed. *According to the law, you must be eighteen years of age to vote.* 3. a force or principle that something is based on. *"What goes up must come down" is a law of nature.* 4. the science, study, or profession dealing with legal matters. *One must go to school for many years in order to have a career in law.* 5. the people or groups who enforce the rules in a society (used with "the"). *He's in trouble with the law again.* {law}

law·ful *adjective* allowed by law; legal. *Driving faster than the speed limit is not lawful.* {law fəl} lawfully, adv.

lawn *noun* an area of ground planted with grass and usually mown short. {lawn}

lawn mower *noun* a machine with a turning blade that cuts the grass of a lawn. {lawn moh ər}

A B C D E F G H I J K **L** M N O P Q R S T U V W X Y Z

law·suit *noun* a case brought before a court of law. {**law** sooht}

law·yer 🔊 *noun* one whose job is to help people with legal matters and represent them in court; attorney. {**loi** ər}

lay[1] *verb* (laid, laying, lays) 1. to place, put, or set down. *He laid the pencil on the table.* 2. to place or put down in a flattened position. *She will lay the carpet herself.* 3. to give or put. *He lays the blame for the accident on me.* 4. to think of or come up with. *The generals laid their plans for the next attack.* 5. to produce an egg. *The hen laid an egg. noun* the way in which land is arranged or formed. *He hiked around for a week to become familiar with the lay of the park.* {**lay**}

Language Note *Lay* and *lie* are confusing. These two words are close in meaning, and their various forms are similar. "Lay" means "place or set down." It should always be used with a direct object. "Lie" means "be in a flat, resting position." It should never used with a direct object. *Lay down your weapons! He is laying the sword on the table now. He laid the lance on the ground last night. He has laid the spear on the table already. Lie down and go to sleep! She is lying in bed now. She lay in bed last night, too. She has lain in bed since yesterday, because she has the flu.*

lay[2] *verb* past tense of **lie**[2]. {**lay**}

Homophone Note Are you looking for the word *lei* (a garland of flowers)? *Lay* and *lei* sound alike but have different meanings.

lay·er *noun* 1. a thickness of something that is spread over a surface. *All the furniture had a thin layer of dust on it.* 2. a section of something that alternates with a different material from top to bottom. *The cake had two layers with decorations between them.* 3. a chicken that lays eggs. *These hens are good layers.* {**lay** ər}

lay·off *noun* the act of putting a person or group of people out of work. {**lay** awf *or* lay **awf**}

la·zy *adjective* (lazier, laziest) 1. not willing to give much effort or work to. *Please don't be so lazy about cleaning your room.* 2. slow to move or react. *They walked through the park at a lazy pace.* {**lay** zee} lazily, adv., laziness, n.

lb. *abbreviation* an abbreviation for **pound** or pounds.

lead[1] 🔊 *verb* (led, leading, leads) 1. to give direction to; show the way to; guide. *He led us through the woods.* 2. to command or direct; take charge of. *The president led the nation during a difficult time.* 3. to experience. *She leads an interesting and active life.* 4. to cause. *New information led me to change plans.* 5. to be first among others. *That horse leads in the race.* 6. to set a course to a place. *That river leads to the sea.* 7. to tend toward a particular result (usually followed by "to"). *Hard work often leads to success. noun* 1. the first or front position. *She took the lead early in the race.* 2. the amount by which something is ahead of others. *The visiting team had a lead of ten points.* 3. the main part played by an actor in a play, movie, or other show. 4. a hint or clue. *The police have no leads in the case.* 5. a short introduction that begins a news story.

adjective first or most important. *The lead story in today's paper was about our school.* {**leed**}

lead[2] 🔊 *noun* 1. a heavy, soft gray metal that is one of the chemical elements. Because it is very heavy and dense, lead is useful for making things such as weights, shot, and shields that protect against radiation. (symbol: Pb) 2. a rod of graphite that makes marks. It is used in pencils. {**lehd**}

Homophone Note The words *lead*[2] and *led* sound alike but have different meanings.

lead·er 🔊 *noun* one that leads or guides. *Who will be the leader on our walk today?* {**lee** dər}

lead·er·ship *noun* 1. ability or skill as a leader. *She showed leadership when asked to take over the meeting.* 2. the actions of a leader. *Because of his leadership, our team won the game.* 3. all leaders of a group considered together. *The city leadership passed a law against littering.* {**lee** dər **shihp**}

leaf 🔊 *noun* (leaves) 1. one of the usually green, flat parts of a plant or tree that grows from the stem or branch. *Many leaves fell from the tree during the wind storm.* 2. a sheet of paper, usually bound in a book. *Each side of a leaf is a page.* 3. the part of a table top, door, or the like that can be removed or is hinged. *We will need to add a leaf to the dining room table. verb* (leafed, leafing, leafs) 1. to bear or sprout leaves. *Has the*

 Human Body Human Mind Everyday Life History and Culture  Communication

tree you planted last year begun to leaf yet? 2. to quickly turn the pages of a book, magazine, or the like (usually followed by "through"). *She had time to leaf through the book, but not to read it.* {**leef**} leafless, adj.

• **turn over a new leaf** to change one's behavior for the better; make a new start. *He decided to turn over a new leaf and stop smoking.*

leaf·let *noun* 1. a printed piece of paper that is usually given to people free of charge. It contains information or advertisements and is often folded. 2. any of the small parts that form a leaf. {**leef** liht}

league[1] *noun* 1. a number of countries, groups, or people joined together for a common cause. *The League of Nations was formed after World War I.* 2. a group of sports teams that compete with one another. *Our baseball team joined a league.* {**leeg**}

league[2] *noun* a unit of length equal to about 3 miles or 4.8 kilometers. {**leeg**}

leak *noun* 1. an opening or crack that lets something pass out or in by accident. *There was a leak in the water pipe.* 2. the release of secret or private information without permission. *Because of a leak in the White House, the President's secrets were reported on the news.* *verb* (leaked, leaking, leaks) 1. to allow something to pass through an opening or crack in a way that was not intended. *Because the ceiling leaks, we keep a bucket on the floor to catch drops of water.* 2.

to pass or escape through an opening of this sort. *The water is leaking through a crack in the roof.* 3. to become known by many people because information was told without permission (usually followed by "out"). *News of the crime had already leaked out.* {**leek**}

Homophone Note Are you looking for the word *leek*? *Leak* and *leek* sound alike but have different meanings.

lean[1] *verb* (leaned, leaning, leans) 1. to bend or slant. *He leaned backwards.* 2. to rest against something or be supported by it. *He leaned against the fence while waiting for the bus.* 3. to favor (often followed by "toward"). *She leans toward plain jewelry.* 4. to depend. *I lean on her for many things.* {**leen**}

lean[2] *adjective* (leaner, leanest) 1. having little flesh. *That animal looks very lean.* 2. having little fat. *My mother buys the leanest meat that she can find.* {**leen**}

leap *verb* (leaped or leapt, leaping, leaps) 1. to spring into the air, moving straight up or to another position. *The frog leaped onto the bank.* 2. to move or act suddenly or quickly with, or as though with, a leap. *He leapt to the side to avoid an accident.* / *She leapt at the chance to go to music camp.* *noun* an act or instance of leaping; quick jump. *The frog made a long leap to the rock.* {**leep**}

• **by leaps and bounds** very quickly. *She is learning to play the guitar by leaps and bounds.*

Synonyms
These words share a meaning with *leap*, verb 1:
spring, jump, bound

leap·frog *noun* a game in which one player bends over while the other players take turns jumping over. {**leep** frŏg or **leep** frawg}

leapt *verb* a past tense and past participle of **leap**. {**lehpt** or **leept**}

leap year *noun* a year that has 366 days, which happens every four years. The extra day is February 29. {**leep** yeer}

learn ⓘ *verb* (learned or learnt, learning, learns) 1. to get to know or gain knowledge of through study or experience. *She learned the craft of weaving from her grandmother.* 2. to find out about; become aware or informed of. *Did you ever learn how the accident happened?* 3. to fix in the mind; memorize. *I learned the poem for my English class.* {**luhrn**} learner, n.

Word History *Learn* is from an early German word that means "to follow along a track."

learn·ed *adjective* having or showing knowledge or learning. *My grandfather is a learned man.* {**luhr** nihd}

learn·ing *noun* knowledge gained through careful study or experience. *A person of learning knows a lot about a particular subject.* {**luhr** ning}

learnt *verb* a past tense and a past participle of **learn**.

 Living World    Physical World   Natural Environment    Economy    Government and Law

a
b
c
d
e
f
g
h
i
j
k
l
m
n
o
p
q
r
s
t
u
v
w
x
y
z

lease 🌀 *noun* an agreement for living in or using another person's property in exchange for money or something else of value. *They have a one year lease on the apartment.* *verb* (leased, leasing, leases) 1. to make an agreement for the use of property for a certain period of time; rent. *I leased a new car instead of buying.* 2. to live in or have use of by lease. *The family wanted to lease the house until May.* {lees}

leash *noun* a length of leather, chain, or rope attached to the collar of an animal to keep it under control. *verb* (leashed, leashing, leashes) to control, hold back, or tie with a leash. *She leashed the dog on her walk through the park.* {leesh}

least *adjective* 1. superlative of little. *Aren't you the least bit happy?* 2. smallest in size, amount, or degree. *She has the least worry about her oldest child.* *noun* that which is the smallest in size, amount, or degree. *The least I could do is help you.* *adverb* 1. superlative of **little**. *My dog was the least active of all the animals.* 2. in or to the smallest amount or degree. *I like him least.* {leest}
• **at least**
1. at the lowest amount; not less than. *They will invite at least fifty guests.* 2. in any case; at any rate. *We may not have much, but at least we have each other.*
• **in the least**
at all. *I don't mind your singing in the least.*

leath·er 🌀 *noun* material made from the skin of an animal by removing the hair and tanning. Leather is used for making shoes, jackets, luggage, and many other things. *adjective* made of or like leather. *She bought a pair of leather boots.* {leh thər}

leave[1] *verb* (left, leaving, leaves) 1. to go away from or depart. *I'll leave the city soon.* 2. to let remain. *Leave the book there.* 3. to let stay without bothering. *Leave me alone.* 4. to let stay for action or for later decision. *Leave the problem until tomorrow.* 5. to give into the care or possession of as a result of one's death. *He left his money to his sons.* {leev}
• **leave off**
to stop or cease. *He left off raking and rested for awhile.*
• **leave out**
not to put in or not include; omit. *She made a cake but left out the sugar by mistake.*

leave[2] *noun* 1. permission. *When he asked if he could stay up late, his mother gave him leave.* 2. a permitted period of vacation or absence. *The soldier received two weeks' leave to be with his family.* {leev}

leaves *noun* plural of **leaf**. {leevz}

Leb·a·non *noun* a country in southwestern Asia on the Mediterranean coast, north of Israel. Beirut is the capital of Lebanon. {lehb ə nahn} Lebanese, n., adj.

lec·ture *noun* 1. a talk given in front of an audience. *The professor gave a lecture to his class.* 2. a long speech given to warn another. *He gave the boy a lecture about his poor table manners.* *verb* (lectured, lecturing, lectures) 1. to present a lecture. *The artist lectured about his work.* 2. to warn or scold. *Dad really lectured me after I left his tools in the rain.* {lehk chər}

led *verb* past tense and past participle of **lead**[1]. {lehd}

Homophone Note Are you looking for the word **lead**[2] (the metal)? **Led** and **lead**[2] sound alike but have different meanings.

ledge *noun* 1. a narrow part like a shelf that comes out of a wall. *The cat sat on the window ledge in the sunshine.* 2. a shelf of rock coming out from a wall or cliff. *They walked on the narrow ledge of the mountain.* {lehj}

lee *noun* the side that faces away from the wind. *We were told to go to the lee of the ship during the storm.* *adjective* of, relating to, on, or toward the side that is protected from the wind. *They stood on the lee side of the mountain to protect themselves from the heavy wind.* {lee}

leech *noun* a kind of worm that lives in water or mud and sucks blood from animals. Leeches were once used in medicine to draw blood from people. Leeches are still sometimes used to prevent blood from clotting when reattaching fingers and toes that have been cut off. {leech}

leek *noun* a plant related to the onion. It has wide, green leaves and a long white bulb. {leek}

Homophone Note The words **leek** and **leak** sound alike but have different meanings.

left[1] *adjective* of or relating to the west side when one is facing north; opposite of right. *We planted bushes on the left side of our house.* *noun* the left side. *He looked to the*

418

left and right before crossing the street. {**lehft**}

left² *verb* past tense and past participle of **leave¹**. {**lehft**}

left-hand *adjective* 1. on or toward the left. *In some countries people drive on the left-hand side of the road.* 2. of or for the left hand. *I found a left-hand glove in the snow.* {**lehft** **hănd**}

left·hand·ed *adjective* 1. using the left hand more easily than the right. 2. made to be worn on or used by the left hand. *He needs a pair of left-handed scissors.* 3. done with the left hand. *She made a left-handed catch.* {**lehft** **hăn** dihd} left-handedness, n.

left·o·ver *noun* a part of something that was not used. *She served leftovers from yesterday's dinner.* {**lehft** oh vər}

leg ⊕ *noun* 1. one of the body parts of an animal or human that is used for standing and walking. 2. something similar to a leg in appearance and use. *One of the table's legs is bent.* 3. the part of a pair of pants that covers the leg. *The dog tore a hole in the leg of the boy's pants.* 4. a specific distance in a journey or race. *I fell in the last leg of the race.* {**lehg**}

• **on one's last legs** having very little energy, strength, hope, or ability to go on; likely to collapse or die. *This old car is on its last legs.*

leg·a·cy *noun* (legacies) 1. money, property, or other goods left to someone in a will. *Part of her legacy was her grandmother's jewelry.* 2. anything that is passed down from ancestors or someone who came before. *Honesty between a wife and husband will be a useful legacy for their children.* {**lehg** ə see}

le·gal *adjective* 1. of or having to do with law. *A lawyer is a member of the legal profession.* 2. allowed by law. *I am the legal owner of the car.* {**lee** gəl} legally, adv.

leg·end *noun* 1. a story that has been handed down from an earlier time. Many people know these stories, but they cannot be proven true. *The coyote is a central figure in Native American legend.* 2. a person about whom such stories are told. *Johnny Appleseed was an American legend.* 3. a table that explains the symbols used on a map, chart, or other illustration. {**leh** jənd}

leg·end·ar·y *adjective* having to do with or like a legend. *John Henry is a legendary figure.* {**leh** jən **dayr** ee}

leg·ging *noun* (often plural) a covering for the lower leg or for the whole leg. Leggings may be made of strong cloth or leather. {**lehg** ing}

leg·i·ble *adjective* able to be understood or read. *His handwriting is small, but very legible.* {**lehj** ih bəl} legibly, adv.

le·gion *noun* 1. an army unit in ancient Rome that was made up of soldiers on foot and on horseback. *The emperor sent his legions into battle.* 2. any large group of people or things. *Legions of people gathered to hear the president speak.* {**lee** jən}

leg·is·la·tion *noun* 1. a law made by a body of government. *Congress passed new legislation to protect the natural environment.* 2. the act or process of passing laws. *The senator worked hard at legislation concerning the environment.* {**lehj** ihs **lay** shən}

leg·is·la·tive *adjective* 1. having to do with the branch of government that has the power

to pass laws. *The Senate is part of the legislative branch of government in the United States.* 2. having to do with legislation or a legislature. *Changing the law required legislative action.* {**lehj** ihs **lay** tihv}

leg·is·la·ture ⊕ *noun* a group of people within a government that has the power to make or change laws. *The legislature is voting on the proposal to change the tax laws.* {**lehj** ihs **lay** chər}

le·git·i·mate *adjective* 1. allowed by the law; legal. *We checked to make sure it was a legitimate business.* 2. according to what is accepted or right. *He had a legitimate excuse for not being in school.* {**lə** **jiht** ə miht} legitimately, adv.

leg·ume ⊕ *noun* 1. any of the family of plants that grow their seeds and fruit in pods. Beans and peas are legumes. 2. the pods, seeds, or fruits of such a plant that can be eaten. {**leh** gyoom}

lei *noun* (leis) a wreath of flowers, usually worn around the neck in Hawaii. {**lay**}

Homophone Note The words *lei* and *lay* sound alike but have different meanings.

lei·sure ⊕ *noun* freedom from work or other duties that take time and effort; free time. *She does not have much leisure since she started her new job.* {**lee** zhər}

lem·ming *noun* a very small mammal that looks like a mouse with a short tail. Lemmings are rodents that live in the far northern parts of Europe, Asia, and North America. Some kinds of lem-

A
B
C
D
E
F
G
H
I
J
K
L
M
N
O
P
Q
R
S
T
U
V
W
X
Y
Z

 Living World   Physical World  Natural Environment Economy Government and Law 419

mings migrate in groups if their population gets very large. Migrating lemmings may drown in bodies of water. {**lehm** ing}

lem·on *noun* 1. a small citrus fruit with yellow skin and sour juice. 2. the tree on which this fruit grows. It has thorns and evergreen leaves. 3. (informal) something that does not work well; dud. *The car was such a lemon that the factory replaced it.* {**lehm** ən}

lem·on·ade *noun* a drink made from lemon juice, sugar, and water. {**lehm** ə **nayd**}

lend *verb* (lent, lending, lends) 1. to give with the understanding that what has been given will be returned. *He lent me the car for a week.* 2. to give someone money that must be paid back. Usually there is also a payment of interest. *The bank will lend her money to pay for college.* 3. to give in a helpful way. *Please lend your support to the cause.* {**lehnd**} lender, n.

length *noun* 1. the distance from the beginning to the end. *The bench is twenty-four inches in length.* 2. the entire amount of such distance. *We walked the length of the street.* 3. a part of the entire extent of something. *Here is a length of rope to tie the dog to the tree.* 4. an amount of time. *The baby didn't cry for the entire length of the film.* 5. an amount of effort. *They went to great lengths to succeed.* {**length**}
 • **at length**
 1. for a long time; in great detail. *She talked at length about her trip to Japan.*
 2. at last; finally. *At length, we stopped working and ate supper.*

length·en *verb* (lengthened, lengthening, lengthens) to make or become longer. *She lengthened the rope by tying two pieces together.* / *Daylight lengthens in the summer months.* {**leng** thən}

length·wise *adverb or adjective* in the direction of the longer or longest side. *She folded the blanket lengthwise.* / *What is the lengthwise measurement of the box?* {**length** wiyz}

le·ni·ent *adjective* not strict with rules; tolerant. *Our teacher is lenient about being late for class during bad weather.* {**leen** yənt}

lens *noun* (lenses) 1. a piece of clear material such as glass that bends light rays passing through it. The surface of a lens is curved to bend light rays toward or away from a central point. 2. a number of such pieces connected together in a camera or telescope. 3. a clear part of the eye that brings together the rays of light needed for sight. The lens focuses rays of light so that they form an image inside the eye on the retina. {**lehnz**}

lent *verb* past tense and past participle of **lend**. {**lehnt**}

Lent *noun* the forty weekdays from Ash Wednesday to Easter, observed by Christians as a time to fast, pray, and be sorry for having done wrong. {**lehnt**}

len·til *noun* 1. a round, flat seed produced by the lentil plant. It is used as food. 2. a plant that produces such seeds. The lentil plant is a legume, related to the pea. {**lehn** təl}

leop·ard *noun* a large mammal with short yellow or gray fur and black spots. Leopards with very dark fur are called black leopards or panthers. They live in southern Asia and Africa but are threatened or endangered in all their habitats. Leopards are carnivores and are closely related to lions, tigers, and other big cats that roar. {**leh** pərd}

Word History *Leopard* comes from a combination of two ancient Greek words that mean "lion" and "male panther." The ancient Greeks thought a leopard was the offspring of a lion and a panther.

le·o·tard *noun* a garment worn by dancers, gymnasts, and others. It is made of one piece and covers the body while it stretches to allow freedom of movement. {**lee** ə tard}

Word History *Leotard* comes from the name of a French trapeze artist, Jules Leotard, who wore this garment when he performed in the 1800s.

lep·re·chaun *noun* an elf in Irish folklore who knows about secret treasure. He must tell the location of the treasure to whoever can catch him. {**lehp** rə **kŏn**}

Word History *Leprechaun* comes from a Gaelic (native Irish) word that means "small body."

lep·ro·sy *noun* a disease of the skin and nerves caused by infection. People with leprosy have sores on their skin and lose feeling in their

Human Body   Human Mind   Everyday Life   History and Culture   Communication

bodies. They sometimes lose fingers and toes. {leh prə see}

less *adverb* 1. comparative of **little**. *I work less than she does at school.* 2. to a smaller degree or amount. *He is less patient than I am.* *adjective* 1. comparative of **little**. *I have less money than she has.* 2. smaller in degree or amount. *He has less patience than I.* *noun* a smaller amount. *I have less than you.* *preposition* made smaller by; minus. *Three less one is two.* {lehs}

Language Note *Less* or *fewer*? Which word is right for your sentence? Use *fewer* with things you can count. *There are fewer pencils than pens in my desk.* Use *less* with things that can't be counted. *There is less time to finish this assignment than I thought.*

-less *suffix* a suffix that means "not having." *A fearless person is a person who has no fear.*

less·en *verb* (lessened, lessening, lessens) to become or make smaller in amount or size. *The wind lessened as the storm ended.* {lehs ən}

Homophone Note Are you looking for the word *lesson*? *Lessen* and *lesson* sound alike but have different meanings.

less·er *adjective* 1. comparative of **less**. *She chose a math book of lesser difficulty.* 2. smaller in amount, size, degree, or importance. *Work of a lesser quality will get a lower grade.* {lehs ər}

les·son *noun* 1. something to be learned or studied. *I have a piano lesson every Monday afternoon.* 2. any experience that leads to a gain of knowl-

edge. *Getting a speeding ticket was a lesson to him.* {lehs ən}

Homophone Note The words *lesson* and *lessen* sound alike but have different meanings.

let *verb* (let, letting, lets) 1. to allow; permit. *He let the children pet his dog.* 2. to make or cause. *Let it be known that there will be a meeting tomorrow.* 3. to rent or lease. *I'm letting an apartment downtown.* 4. to allow to come or go. *He let the dog in the house.* {leht}

• **let down** to fail to satisfy; disappoint. *The team was let down by the loss of the game.*

• **let go** 1. to stop holding; set free. *I caught a fish but I let it go.* 2. to take away the job of; fire. *They let him go because he was always late for work.*

• **let off** to release from punishment or something unpleasant; excuse. *He was let off from having to do the dishes.*

• **let out** to allow to be known. *I let out the secret that I had a little sister on the way.*

• **let up** to stop or become lesser. *Finally the rain let up.*

-let *suffix* a suffix that means "small." *A droplet is a small drop. / A piglet is a baby pig.*

let's shortened form of "let us." *Let's go out and play!* {lehts}

let·ter ✏ *noun* 1. a written mark that stands for a speech sound; specific character of an alphabet. *"A" and "Z" are the first and last letters of our alphabet.* 2. a written message. *My parents sent me a special letter on my birthday.* *verb* (lettered, lettering, letters) to draw, copy, or write

with letters. *She carefully lettered her name on the drawing.* {leht ər}

letter carrier *noun* someone who delivers mail. {leh tər kar ee ər}

let·ter·ing *noun* 1. the act or art of printing or writing letters. *Lettering is a skill.* 2. letters on a sign or poster. *He liked the style of lettering on the sign.* {leht ər ing}

let·tuce *noun* 1. a plant with large, crisp leaves that can be eaten. 2. leaves of this plant used as food in salad or sandwiches. {leht əs}

Word History *Lettuce* is from a Latin word that means "milk." Lettuce has a milky juice.

leu·ke·mi·a *noun* a disease that is a type of cancer inside the bones. With this disease the body makes too many white blood cells. {looh kee mee ə}

lev·ee *noun* 1. an embankment built to keep river water from flooding the land. 2. a place along a river where boats land. {leh vee}

Homophone Note Are you looking for the word *levy* (a collection)? *Levee* and *levy* sound alike but have different meanings.

lev·el *adjective* 1. having a flat, even surface. *The ground here is level and easy to walk on.* 2. being on a line with the horizon or parallel to the ground. *The marbles rolled to the floor because the table was not level.* 3. being of the same height or position as another. *My eyes were just level with the bottom of the window.* 4. calm, even, and steady. *He is very level and does not anger easily.*

A B C D E F G H I J K L M N O P Q R S T U V W X Y Z

Living World   Physical World   Natural Environment   Economy   Government and Law

noun 1. position in height, stage, or rank. *People have different levels of ability at math. / The level of the water in the river was high after the flood.* 2. a flat surface. *We took the elevator to the top level of the building.* 3. a tool used by carpenters to see if a surface is parallel to the ground. *verb* (leveled, leveling, levels) 1. to make flat or even. *The bulldozer leveled the bumpy ground.* 2. to tear down or destroy. *The bombs leveled the town during the war.* 3. to aim or direct. *He leveled his rifle at the deer. / She leveled her eyes at me.* {**lehv** əl}

lev·er *noun* 1. a basic tool used to lift or pry things open. A crowbar is one type of lever. 2. a handle used to control or set the position of a part in a machine. {**lehv** ər *or* **leev** ər}

Word History *Lever* comes from *levare*, a Latin word that means "to raise," which comes from *levis*, which means "light in weight." The simple machine we call a "lever" allows us to lift a heavy weight as easily as we could a much lighter one.

lev·y *noun* (levies) 1. the collection by a government of money, property, or troops. *The levy of taxes will take place at the end of the year.* 2. that which is collected in this way. *The king counted the levy.* *verb* (levied, levying, levies) to carry out the levy of; col-

lect. *The city levied a tax on property owners.* {**lehv** ee}

Homophone Note The words *levy* and *levee* (an embankment) sound alike but have different meanings.

li·a·ble *adjective* 1. held responsible by law. *You will be liable for any damage to the car.* 2. likely to happen. *Flooding is liable during this heavy rain.* {**liy** ə bəl *or* **liy** bəl}

li·ar *noun* a person who tells lies instead of the truth. {**liy** ər}

Homophone Note The words *liar* and *lyre* sound alike but have different meanings. To find out why a music teacher would rather have a lyre in class than a liar, look up *lyre*.

lib·er·al *adjective* 1. generous. *The cook used a liberal amount of salt and pepper in this meal.* 2. respectful of differences; tolerant. *He had a liberal attitude toward new ideas.* 3. (often capitalized) favoring progress and change in government. *She was the leader of a liberal organization.* *noun* a person who wants a certain kind of government. That government would support social change and the freedom of people to make their own choices. *The liberals on the committee think that the government should do more to help poor people.* {**lihb** ə rəl *or* **lihb** rəl, n., **lihb** ə rəl *or* **lihb** rəl, adj.} liberally, adv.

lib·er·ate *verb* (liberated, liberating, liberates) to free or let out. *We liberated the hawk from its cage.* {**lihb** ə **rayt**} liberation, n., liberator, n.

Li·be·ri·a *noun* a country in western Africa. Monrovia is the capital of Liberia. {**liy beer** ee ə} Liberian, n., adj.

lib·er·ty *noun* (liberties) 1. freedom from being con-

fined or controlled. *The slaves dreamed of liberty.* 2. freedom from control by another government. *The American colonies fought for liberty from England.* 3. the right or power to act and choose freely. *She had the liberty to vote for anyone she wanted.* {**lihb** ər tee}

• at liberty
1. free from being confined. *The prisoner is at liberty.* 2. allowed. *I am not at liberty to tell you what she said to me.*

Li·bra *noun* 1. a constellation located between Virgo and Scorpio. Libra is also called the Scales. 2. the seventh sign of the zodiac, the Scales, which the sun enters about September 23. 3. a person born under this sign, between September 23 and October 23. {**liy** brə *or* **lee** brə}

li·brar·i·an *noun* a person trained to work in a library, or who takes care of a particular collection of books. {liy **brayr** ee ən}

li·brar·y 🔵 🔵 *noun* (libraries) 1. a place where books, records, and other materials are kept and from which they may be borrowed. 2. a specific collection of such materials. *My grandfather has a valuable library of materials about World War II.* {**liy** brayr ee}

Lib·y·a *noun* a country in northern Africa. Tripoli is the capital of Libya. {**lihb** ee ə} Libyan, n., adj.

lice *noun* plural of **louse**. {**liys**}

li·cence *noun* a spelling of **license** used in Canada and Britain. This spelling is used only for the noun. See **license**. {**liy** sihns}

li·cense *noun* a paper or card showing legal or official permission to do something. *My brother got his driver's license today.* *verb* (licensed,

 Human Body   Human Mind   Everyday Life   History and Culture   Communication

licensing, licenses) to give a license to or for. *The pilot was licensed to fly the airplane.* {**liy** sihns}

li·chen *noun* a living thing that is a fungus and a form of algae or special bacteria living together. The algae or the bacteria use photosynthesis to make food for the fungus. There are many kinds of lichens with different colors, such as green, gray, black, or red. They can look like scales, crusts, or branches. Lichens live on rocks and other places where there is no soil. {**liy** kən}

lick *verb* (licked, licking, licks) 1. to pass the tongue over or along the surface of. *A cat cleans itself by licking its foot and then rubbing over its body.* 2. to eat or drink by licking. *She licked her ice cream cone. / The dog licked up the water.* 3. to reach toward or pass lightly over. *The flames licked the edges of the wood. / The waves licked the shore.* 4. (informal) to do better than or defeat. *She licked her opponent easily. noun* 1. the act or process of licking with the tongue. *The dog gave my face a lick.* 2. See **salt lick**. 3. (informal) even a small amount. *He hasn't done a lick of work.* {**lihk**}

lic·o·rice *noun* 1. a plant of the legume family that has a strong, sweet smell and flavor. 2. a flavoring made from the root of this plant. 3. a candy flavored with licorice. {**lihk** ə rihs *or* **lihk** ə rihsh *or* **lihk** rihsh}

lid *noun* 1. a cover for a container that can be opened or removed. *I cut my finger on the lid of the can.* 2. a fold of skin and muscle that can be closed over the eye; eyelid. *The dust made the lids of my eyes itch.* {**lihd**}

lie¹ 🛈 *noun* an untrue statement made on purpose. *I told Mom a lie because I was afraid to tell her the truth. verb* (lied, lying, lies) to make a false statement on purpose. *Misha lied when he said the dog ate his homework.* {**liy**}

lie² *verb* (lay, lain, lying, lies) 1. to be in or place oneself in a flat or resting position. *I spent all morning lying in bed.* 2. to rest or remain, as, on, or under a surface. *Several books lay open on the table.* 3. to be located. *The road lies to the west.* 4. to be placed; exist (followed by "on," "with," or "upon"). *The responsibility lies with him.* {**liy**}

> **Homophone Note** Are you looking for the word *lye* (a harsh substance)? *Lie* and *lye* sound alike but have different meanings.

lieu·ten·ant *noun* a military officer of low rank. *The lieutenant reported to the captain.* {looh **tehn** ənt}

> **Word History** *Lieutenant* entered the English language in 1378. It comes from an early French word meaning "one who holds the place of another." Originally, a lieutenant was someone who could be called on to substitute for the king or officer he served.

life 🛈 *noun* (lives) 1. the state of being that sets animals and plants apart from rocks, minerals, and other things that are not alive. Things that have life grow, reproduce, and use energy. 2. something that is alive, or all alive things. *Ten lives were lost at sea yesterday. / Pollution has affected the plant life in the area.* 3. the time between birth and death. *He has had a long life.* 4. the period during which something lasts or works. *These tires should last for the life of my car.* 5. way of being. *Graham leads an active life.* 6. energy, movement, or spirit. *He is full of life.* 7. a biography or story of someone's life. *I have just finished reading a life of Gandhi.* {**liyf**}

life·boat *noun* a boat made for quick rescue of people. It can be carried on a larger boat, or it can be used from shore. {**liyf** boht}

life cycle 🌐 *noun* the sequence of changes that a living thing goes through as it grows and develops. Birth, growth, reproduction, aging, and death are all stages in the life cycle of an animal. {**liyf** **siy** kəl}

life·guard *noun* a person hired to watch over a swimming area and rescue anyone who might be drowning. {**liyf** gard}

life jacket *noun* a life preserver in the form of a vest or jacket with no sleeves. {**liyf** jăk iht}

life·less *adjective* 1. having or appearing to have no life; unconscious. *The policeman discovered the lifeless body.* 2. not lively; dull. *She had a lifeless expression on her face.* {**liyf** lihs}

life·like *adjective* looking like something in real life. *She drew a lifelike picture of the house in the woods.* {**liyf** liyk}

life·long *adjective* going on throughout the whole of a person's life. *They shared a lifelong friendship.* {**liyf** lŏng}

life preserver *noun* a device used to help a person float in water and not drown. A life preserver is usually made in the shape of a ring, belt, or vest. {**liyf** prə **zuhr** vər}

life span *noun* the length of time that a human, animal, or plant lives or can be expected to live. {**liyf span**}

life·time *noun* 1. the time during which a person's life goes on. *She hoped to do many things during her lifetime.* 2. the length of time something is expected to work well. *The battery has a lifetime of four years.* {**liyf** tiym}

lift *verb* (lifted, lifting, lifts) 1. to bring upward; raise. *He lifted his hand to salute.* 2. to rise. *The hot air balloon slowly lifted into the air.* 3. to pick up. *We lifted the canoe from the water.* 4. to bring higher in position or condition; raise. *The song lifted their spirits.* 5. to end, cancel, or take back. *The city lifted the law against smoking in restaurants.* 6. to disappear or move away because of an upward force. *The fog lifted.* *noun* 1. the act of lifting. *He gave her a lift onto the horse.* 2. a machine used for raising or carrying. *They went up the mountain on the ski lift.* 3. a ride given to a person who is traveling on foot. *I saw that she was tired, so I gave her a lift in my car.* 4. a happier feeling; rise in spirits. *The good news gave us a lift.* {**lihft**}

lift·off *noun* the moment of launching a missile or rocket, or the movement of the rocket itself. *People gathered to watch the liftoff.* {**lihft awf**}

lig·a·ment *noun* a band of tough tissue that connects bones or supports muscles or organs. {**lihg** ə mənt}

light[1] *noun* 1. the form of energy that makes it possible for the eye to see. The sun produces light. 2. something that gives off light, or the brightness produced by it. *Turn off the light when you go to bed.* 3. dawn or daytime. *We woke up at first light.* 4. something that makes clear or gives understanding. *The biologist cast light on the subject of water pollution.* 5. the way in which something is seen or thought of. *I now see her in a new light.* *adjective* (lighter, lightest) 1. being bright or illuminated. *This room isn't light enough to read in.* 2. pale in color. *He has very light hair.* *verb* (lighted or lit, lighting, lights) 1. to cause to catch on fire. *After I light the candles, we can sing "Happy Birthday."* 2. to catch fire. *The wet logs would not light.* 3. to make brighter; provide with light; illuminate. *The street lamps lit the empty road.* 4. to be made bright (often followed by "up"). *The fireworks lighted up the sky. / Her face lit up when she saw the presents.* {**liyt**}

light[2] *adjective* (lighter, lightest) 1. not heavy, full, intense, or powerful. *My backpack was light enough to carry all day. / The light rain barely made the grass wet. / He woke up from a light sleep.* 2. not serious or important. *She did some light reading before going to bed.* 3. happy or cheerful; spirited. *My heart was light when I thought about the long summer vacation ahead.* {**liyt**}

• **make light of** to treat as or consider silly or not important. *He laughed and made light of my problem.*

light·en[1] *verb* (lightened, lightening, lightens) 1. to become brighter or lighter in color. *We watched the sky lighten at sunrise.* 2. to make more pale in color. *The painter lightened the dark walls with a coat of yellow paint.* {**liy** tən}

light·en[2] *verb* (lightened, lightening, lightens) 1. to reduce the weight of. *I had to lighten the load in my backpack.* 2. to become less worried or sad. *Lamin's mood lightened when he saw the new puppy.* {**liy** tən}

light·heart·ed *adjective* cheerful or gay; carefree. *Kiki is a lighthearted girl who sings as she plays.* {**liyt har** tihd} lightheartedly, adv., lightheartedness, n.

light·house *noun* a tower with a flashing light for guiding ships and warning them of dangers in the water. {**liyt** hows}

light·ing *noun* the type and arrangement of lights in an area. *The teacher asked for better lighting in her dark classroom.* {**liy** ting}

light·ly *adverb* 1. with little weight or force. *Feathers fall lightly.* 2. to a small or slight degree. *She put on her lipstick lightly.* 3. without serious thought. *He took my request for help too lightly.* {**liyt** lee}

light·ning *noun* natural electricity produced in thunderclouds. Lightning appears as a bright flash or streak of light in the sky. *adjective* like lightning, especially in regard to movement. *Kyle moves with lightning speed on the tennis court.* {**liyt** ning}

 Human Body   Human Mind   Everyday Life    History and Culture   Communication

lightning bug *noun* another name for **firefly**. {**liyt** ning buhg}

light pen *noun* an electronic device that can detect light and dark areas on a computer screen. It is used to select objects on the screen. *Some people use a light pen instead of a mouse for data input on their computer.* {**liyt** pən}

light-year *noun* (light-years) a unit of distance equal to the distance light can travel in one year, about six trillion miles. {**liyt yeer**}

lik·a·ble *or* **likeable** *adjective* liked by others, or easy to like. *He is a likable guy.* {**liy** kə bəl}

-like *suffix* a suffix that means "similar to" or "like." *A cat-like jump is a jump like a jump that a cat would make.*

like[1] *adjective* having close resemblance. *After hearing her story, he told of a like experience while travelling in Spain.* *preposition* 1. the same as or similar to. *He is like his father.* 2. in the character of; in the same manner of. *She runs like her mother.* 3. open to; wishing for or leaning toward. *I feel like going home.* 4. tending to; inclined to (usually used with "feel"). *It feels like rain today.* {**liyk**}

Language Note *Like* is a preposition that means "in the manner of" or "similar to." *Joe tries to act like his big brother.* *As* is a conjunction that means "in the same way or manner that." It is usually followed by a noun or pronoun and a verb. *Do as I say, not as I do.* When you are listing things that are examples of similar things, use "such as" (not "like" or "such like"): *She can identify different kinds of evergreen trees, such as pine, spruce, fir, and cedar.*

like[2] *verb* (liked, liking, likes) 1. to find pleasure in; enjoy. *Annette likes going to the movies.* 2. to have affection or regard for. *I really like her a lot.* 3. to feel a desire or want. *We can go swimming if you like.* *noun* (usually plural) the things a person enjoys or prefers. *What are his likes and dislikes?* {**liyk**}

Synonyms

These words share a meaning with *like*, verb 1:

love, enjoy, relish

like·li·hood *noun* the state of being likely. *The likelihood of his winning the race is great.* {**liyk** lee **huud**}

like·ly *adjective* (likelier, likeliest) 1. to be expected; probable. *It is likely that she will pass the test.* 2. apparently true; able to be believed. *His winning the lottery was not a likely story.* 3. fitting or appropriate. *Mr. Dill is a likely candidate for the job.* *adverb* probably. *He will likely be here tomorrow.* {**liyk** lee}

like·ness *noun* 1. the condition of looking like or being similar to someone or something else; similarity. *There was a strong likeness between the two brothers.* 2. a picture or portrait. *She drew a likeness of President Kennedy.* {**liyk** nihs}

like·wise *adverb* 1. as well; also. *He thanked his sister, and likewise, his brother.* 2. in the same way; the same; similarly. *She works hard and wants her children to do likewise.* {**liyk** wiyz}

lik·ing *noun* a feeling of preferring, enjoying, or being fond of. *He has a strong liking for chocolate.* {**liyk** ing}

li·lac *noun* 1. a shrub that has large clusters of purple, white, or pink flowers. 2. the flower of this shrub. 3. a pale purple color. {**liy** lăk *or* **liy** lahk}

lil·y *noun* (lilies) 1. a plant that grows from a bulb and has large flowers shaped like bells or trumpets. 2. the flower of this plant. 3. any of several similar plants or flowers, such as the day lily. {**lihl** ee}

lily of the valley *noun* (lilies of the valley) a plant of the lily family that has small, white flowers shaped like bells. The flowers have a pleasant smell and are grown by many people. {**lihl** ee əv thə **văl** ee}

lima bean *noun* 1. a plant that bears wide pods that have large green or white seeds inside them. 2. the seed of this plant, used for food. Lima beans are cooked before being eaten. {**liy** mə **been**}

limb ✿ ▲ *noun* 1. a main branch of a tree. 2. a part of the body that can move and bend. Arms, legs, and wings are limbs. {**lihm**}

lime[1] *noun* a white powder made of calcium oxide. Lime is used in cement, in making steel and paper, and in making some soils better for growing plants. {**liym**}

lime[2] *noun* 1. a small green citrus fruit. 2. a tree that bears this fruit. {**liym**}

lim·er·ick *noun* a humorous poem that has five lines, with the first two lines rhyming with the last, and the third and fourth lines rhyming with each other. {**lihm** ə rihk}

lime·stone *noun* a rock formed mostly from shells and other animal remains. Limestone is

A B C D E F G H I J K L M N O P Q R S T U V W X Y Z

used in building and in making cement, lime, and carbon dioxide. {**liym** stohn}

lim·it *noun* 1. the point at which something ends; a boundary or border. *The limit of our yard is that line of trees.* 2. something that holds back or restrains. *Can't you put a limit on your rude behavior?* *verb* (limited, limiting, limits) to put boundaries on or around; restrict. *We limited our game to two hours.* {**lihm** iht}

limp[1] *verb* (limped, limping, limps) to walk in an uneven, difficult way because of a lame or injured leg or foot. *He limped for days after twisting his ankle.* *noun* an uneven, lame way of walking. *She walked with a limp after hurting her foot.* {**lihmp**}

limp[2] *adjective* (limper, limpest) not stiff or firm. *The noodles were limp after I cooked them.* {**lihmp**} limply, adv., limpness, n.

Lin·coln's Birth·day *noun* a holiday on February 12, the day on which President Abraham Lincoln's birthday is cele-brated.  {**ling** kuhnz **buhrth** day}

line[1] *noun* 1. a long, thin mark. *I drew a line in the dust with a stick.* 2. a boundary or limit; point at which something must stop. *We drove across the state line.* / *Jamie, your behavior has crossed the line!* 3. a string, rope, or wire. *Put the wet clothes out on the line to dry.* 4. a row of people or things. *The line for tickets went all the way around the block.* 5. a transportation system, or a particular path taken by vehicles in the system. *To get to the shopping mall, you have to change to another bus line.* 6. a wire or set of wires that carries electricity or electronic signals. *The telephone line on our street was knocked down in the storm.* 7. a very short written message; letter. *Drop me a line and let me know when you will be in town.* *verb* (lined, lining, lines) 1. to take a place in a line (usually followed by "up"). *We lined up in front of the booth to get cotton candy.* 2. to cause to form into a line or row. *The teacher lined the children up by height, with the shortest one first.* 3. to mark with a line or lines. *I used a ruler to line my paper.* {**liyn**}

line[2] *verb* (lined, lining, lines) 1. to cover the inside of. *The tailor lined the jacket with silk.* 2. to fill. *She lined her purse with money.* {**liyn**}

lin·e·ar *adjective* 1. having to do with a line; straight. *The fence poles were in a linear arrangement.* 2. measured in one dimension; having to do with length. *The runner ran five linear miles.* {**lihn** ee ər}

lin·en *noun* 1. cloth, yarn, or thread made from flax. 2. (often plural) things for the house made of linen or a material like it. Sheets, napkins, and towels are linens. {**lihn** ən}

lin·er[1] *noun* a commercial ship or airplane that carries passengers on a regular route. {**liy** nər}

lin·er[2] *noun* something that lines the inside or covers the outside of something. It is usually for protection and can often be removed. {**liy** nər}

lin·ger *verb* (lingered, lingering, lingers) to remain or be slow to leave. *One student lingered after class to talk to the teacher.* {**ling** gər}

lin·ing *noun* a layer of tissue or other material covering the inside of something. *The lining of the nose makes mucus.* / *I tore the lining of my coat.* {**liyn** ing}

link *noun* 1. one of the separate closed pieces of a chain. *My chain bracelet fell off my arm because a link broke.* 2. anything that joins or connects; bond. *I feel a powerful link to my grandparents.* *verb* (linked, linking, links) to join or unite by a link or connection. *We are linked by our love of music.* {**lingk**}

linking verb *noun* a verb that connects a subject to the words that tell about the subject. In the sentence, "I was very tired," "was" is a linking verb. {**lingk** ing **vuhrb**}

li·no·le·um *noun* a floor covering that is not easily worn out. Linoleum is made by pressing linseed oil and ground-up wood products onto a canvas backing. {lih **noh** lee əm}

linseed oil *noun* a yellowish oil that comes from the seed of flax plants. It is used in making oil paints, ink, and linoleum. {**lihn** seed oil}

li·on *noun* a large, very strong mammal with short tan fur.

 Human Body   Human Mind   Everyday Life   History and Culture 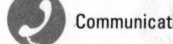 Communication

Male lions have a mane of longer hair around the neck and head. Lions live in parts of Africa and Asia. They are carnivores and are closely related to tigers, leopards, and other big cats that roar. {**liy** ən}

li·on·ess *noun* a female lion. {**liy** ə nihs}

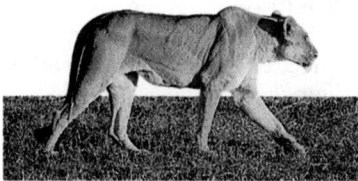

lip 🌐 *noun* 1. either of the upper or lower edges of flesh that circle the mouth and are used in speech. 2. the edge of a container such as a cup; rim. *Milk dripped from the lip of the cup.* 3. the edge of any hole or opening. *He stood on the lip of the canyon.* {**lihp**}

lip-read *verb* (lip-read, lip-reading, lip-reads) to understand by looking at a speaker's lips instead of by hearing the words. *My cousin is deaf, but he lip-reads the news on television.* {**lihp** reed} lip-reader, n.

lip·stick *noun* a cosmetic for coloring the lips. It usually comes in stick form inside a tube. {**lihp** stihk}

liq·uid 🌐 *adjective* in a form that flows easily and is neither a solid nor a gas. *Her mother poured the liquid medicine into a cup for her to drink.* *noun* a form of matter that flows easily and is neither a solid nor a gas. Liquid can take on the shape of any container it is poured into. *Water that is neither vapor nor ice is a liquid.* {**lih** kwihd}

liq·uor *noun* a type of strong alcoholic drink. {**lih** kər}

li·ra *noun* (lire or liras) the main unit of money of Italy, San Marino, and Vatican City. {**leer** ə}

Lis·bon *noun* the capital city of Portugal. {**lihz** bən}

lisp *noun* a speech problem in which "s" is pronounced like the "th" sound in "thick" and "z" is pronounced like the "th" sound in "this." *verb* (lisped, lisping, lisps) to speak with a lisp. *He lisps words such as "sad" or "season."* {**lihsp**}

list[1] *noun* a series of names, numbers, or things placed one after another in a written form. *She made a list of friends to invite to the party.* *verb* (listed, listing, lists) to put into a list. *He listed his favorite books on a piece of paper.* {**lihst**}

list[2] *noun* a leaning to one side, as of a boat or ship; tilt. *The list of our boat made a dip in the water.* *verb* (listed, listing, lists) (used to describe ships or boats) to lean to one side. *She fell into the water when the sailboat listed.* {**lihst**}

lis·ten 🌐 *verb* (listened, listening, listens) 1. to try to hear. *I listened for the sound of my mother's car in the driveway.* 2. to pay attention to. *Listen to the rushing stream, the bird's song, and the wind in the trees.* {**lih** sən} listener, n.

lit *verb* a past tense and past participle of **light**[1]. {**liht**}

li·ter *noun* the basic unit of capacity of the metric system, equal to 1.056 liquid quarts or 0.908 dry quarts. (abbreviated: l) {**lee** tər}

lit·er·a·cy 🌐 🌐 *noun* the state of being able to read or write. *The literacy rate is very high in the United States and Canada.* {**liht** ər ə see}

lit·er·al·ly *adverb* 1. word for word. *She translated the poem from Japanese to English literally.* 2. in fact; really. *The farmer literally worked from morning until night.* {**liht** ər ə lee}

Language Note *Literally* means "in fact, exactly, or really." *Figuratively* means the opposite. When you speak figuratively, you compare a real situation with a made-up, usually exaggerated situation. Sometimes people say "literally" when they mean "figuratively," as in "It was so hot, I was literally melting from the heat." Literally, that's not a pretty picture. If you're not sure which one of these words to use, be safe and don't use either. "I stopped dead in my tracks" is better than "I literally stopped dead in my tracks."

lit·er·ar·y *adjective* 1. having to do with literature or those who write or read literature. *Her poem was published in a literary magazine.* 2. having knowledge about literature. *She is a literary person.* {**lih** tə rayr ee}

lit·er·ate *adjective* 1. able to read and write. *Most of the adults in the United States are literate.* 2. very educated or showing knowledge. *My French teacher is a literate person.* {**liht** ər iht}

lit·er·a·ture 🌐 🌐 *noun* 1. writings that have lasting value. Literature includes stories, poems, plays, and essays. *She studied literature before she became an English teacher.* 2. any printed matter. *The man running for the office of mayor*

A
B
C
D
E
F
G
H
I
J
K
L
M
N
O
P
Q
R
S
T
U
V
W
X
Y
Z

handed us some literature about himself. {**liht** ər ə chər}

Word History *Literature* comes from *literatura*, a Latin word that means "writing" or "forming letters."

litmus paper *noun* a small strip of treated paper used in chemistry. Litmus paper turns red in an acid and blue in a base. {**liht** məs **pay** pər}

Word History The word "litmus" comes from early Scandinavian words that mean "drip" and "moss." Litmus is a blue dye obtained from lichen. The term *litmus paper* was first used in 1803.

lit·ter 🔊 *noun* 1. a mess of waste materials or other objects scattered about. *We cleaned up the litter along the side of the road.* 2. a group of young animals, such as puppies, born to one mother at one time. 3. a device for carrying a sick or injured person. *The soldier who had been wounded in battle was placed on a litter and carried to safety.* *verb* (littered, littering, litters) 1. to make messy by scattering rubbish or other objects. *He littered the floor with bits of paper.* 2. to scatter refuse or other objects about. *It is not good manners to litter.* {**liht** ər}

Word History *Litter* comes from an early French word for "bed." "Bed" was the first meaning of the word in English, and all of its modern meanings have something to do with a bed.

lit·tle *adjective* (littler or less or lesser, littlest or least) 1. small in size. *The kittens are still little, but they are growing fast.* 2. not much. *We have very little money. / There is little time left to practice before the game.* 3. of a certain

amount; some (used with "a"). *I had a little trouble starting the car. / Give him a little ice cream.* 4. short in time. *I'll be there in a little while. adverb* (less, least) 1. hardly at all. *It matters little to him whether or not we go.* 2. not very often; rarely; seldom. *He thinks of her very little. noun* 1. a small or not important amount. *We got little done today.* 2. a small distance. *His house is a little down the road.* {**liht** əl}

• **little by little**
in small amounts; gradually. *Little by little, she saved her money.*

Synonyms
These words share a meaning with *little*, adverb 1:
just, hardly, barely, scarcely

Little Dipper *noun* the constellation Ursa Minor. The stars that make up this constellation form a pattern that looks like a dipper. {**liht** əl **dihp** ər}

live¹ *verb* (lived, living, lives) 1. to have life; be in an active state. *We live in a very interesting time in history.* 2. to support oneself in life. *I can live on very little money.* 3. to stay or reside (often followed by "in" or "at"). *He lives in a cabin in the mountains.* 4. to continue to be in existence or be present to the memory. *Even though she's gone, her memory lives in her children.* {**lihv**}

Synonyms
These words share a meaning with *live*, verb 3:
stay, dwell, abide, reside

live² *adjective* (liver, livest) 1. being alive; having life. *We saw live baby chicks at the farm.* 2. carrying electric current. *The electricians were*

careful to step around the live wires. 3. being broadcast on television or radio at the same moment that the action is taking place. *The TV program was a live broadcast. adverb* of radio and television programs, during performance. *This program comes live from Chicago.* {**liyv**}

live·li·hood *noun* means of earning or getting what is needed to live. *Farming is his livelihood.* {**liyv** lee **huud**}

live·ly *adjective* (livelier, liveliest) 1. full of life or energy. *She is a very lively person.* 2. gay or exciting. *This is a lively party.* 3. striking. *The painter Vincent van Gogh used colors to create a lively effect. adverb* (livelier, liveliest) with quick movements or lots of energy. *The gym teacher told us to move lively.* {**liyv** lee} liveliness, n.

liv·er 🔊 *noun* 1. a large, reddish brown organ in the body that has many functions. The liver cleans the blood, stores energy and nutrients, makes bile, and helps the body digest fats. It is found at the top of the abdomen. 2. the liver of certain animals, used as food. {**lih** vər}

liv·er·y *noun* (liveries) 1. a uniform worn by a male servant such as a butler or chauffeur. *The doorman always wore gloves as part of his livery.* 2. a stable where horses and vehicles pulled by horses are kept and rented out; livery stable. *We hired a horse and carriage at*

 Human Body Human Mind Everyday Life  History and Culture  Communication

the livery. {**lihv** ə ree *or* **lihv** ree}

lives *noun* plural of **life**. *The people in our small town enjoy their quiet lives.* {**liyvz**}

live·stock *noun* (used with a singular or plural verb) cows, horses, sheep, or other animals raised or kept on a farm or ranch. {**liyv** stŏk}

liv·id *adjective* 1. dark grayish or purplish blue from a bruise. *The day after I fell, my arm was livid.* 2. very angry; furious. *His face was livid with anger.* {**lihv** ihd}

liv·ing *adjective* 1. having life. *All living things need water.* 2. alive at this time. *The author of that book is still living.* 3. still in use. *She wants to study a living language rather than one that is no longer spoken.* *noun* 1. the action of one that lives. *He sees living as an adventure.* 2. the way in which one manages one's life. *Healthy living is important if you want to have a long life.* 3. the way in which a person earns money; occupation. *She makes her living as an artist.* {**lihv** ing}

living room ⟳ *noun* a room in a home in which people can relax or gather together. The living room usually has a couch and comfortable chairs. {**lihv** ing **roohm** *or* **lihv** ing **ruum**}

liz·ard *noun* a reptile with rough, scaly skin, four legs,

and a long tapering tail. {**lih** zərd}

lla·ma *noun* an animal with long legs and a long neck. Llamas are mammals that live in the mountains of South America. They are closely related to camels, but are smaller. Llamas are raised for their meat, milk, and wool. {**lah** mə}

load *noun* 1. an amount of something carried. *The train carried a load of logs.* 2. the usual amount carried. *This basket can hold two loads of laundry.* 3. a heavy burden or responsibility, or a large amount of work to be done. *Not being able to tell him the truth was a load on her mind.* / *I have a load of homework to do tonight.* *verb* (loaded, loading, loads) 1. to put on or in something in order to carry. *Every morning, I load my books in my backpack and walk to school.* 2. to put into a device. *Did you load the camera with film?* / *The policeman loaded his gun.* {**lohd**}

Homophone Note Are you looking for the word *lode* (a mineral deposit)? *Load* and *lode* sound alike but have different meanings.

loaf[1] *noun* (loaves) 1. a mass of bread or cake baked in one piece. 2. a shaped mass of some other food, such as ground meat. *We had meat loaf and mashed potatoes for dinner.* {**lohf**}

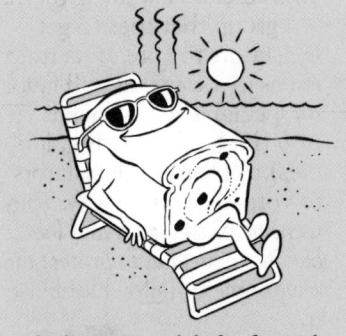

A cinnamon raisin **loaf** tans its crust **loafing** in the sun all day.

loaf[2] *verb* (loafed, loafing, loafs) to spend time in a lazy way. *They loafed at the pool all afternoon.* {**lohf**}

loan ⟳ *noun* 1. something that is lent or borrowed. *He got a loan from the bank to help pay the bills.* 2. the act of lending. *Do you need the loan of a car to get home?* *verb* (loaned, loaning, loans) 1. to give with the understanding that what is given will be returned. *Will you loan me a suitcase for my trip?* 2. to lend money that must be repaid with interest. *The bank loaned money to her family.* {**lohn**}

Homophone Note Are you looking for the word *lone* (without others)? *Loan* and *lone* sound alike but have different meanings.

loathe *verb* (loathed, loathing, loathes) to dislike very much; hate. *I loathe the sound of his voice.* {**lohth**}

loath·some *adjective* extremely unpleasant; disgusting. *A*

A B C D E F G H I J K L M N O P Q R S T U V W X Y Z

a
b
c
d
e
f
g
h
i
j
k
l
m
n
o
p
q
r
s
t
u
v
w
x
y
z

loathsome smell was coming from the pile of garbage. {**lohth** səm *or* **lohth** səm}

lob·by ❂ ⬤ *noun* (lobbies) 1. a hall or open room inside the entrance of a hotel, theater, or other large building. It is often used as a waiting room. 2. a group that tries to get legislators to vote on certain issues in a way that will favor its special wants or needs. *verb* (lobbied, lobbying, lobbies) to try to get legislators to vote in a certain way. *They went to Washington and lobbied for new laws to protect the environment.* {**lŏb** ee} lobbyist, n.

lob·ster *noun* (lobster or lobsters) 1. an animal with a hard, jointed shell that lives in the ocean. Lobsters have four pairs of legs and a pair of large claws. They are a kind of crustacean. 2. the flesh of the lobster when cooked and eaten. {**lŏb** stər}

lo·cal *adjective* 1. having to do with a particular place such as a neighborhood or town. *They called the local police for help.* 2. making repeated stops. *It took longer to get here because we rode the local train.* 3. having to do with a certain area in the body. *The doctor gave me a local anesthetic before he treated my broken finger.* *noun* 1. a local vehicle of transport such as a bus. *To get there you have to ride the local, because the express will skip that stop.* 2. one who lives in the local area. *The locals don't trust people who*

are just passing through town. {**loh** kəl}

lo·cal·i·ty *noun* (localities) a particular neighborhood, place, or region. *This locality is known for its hot and spicy food.* {loh **kăl** ih tee}

lo·cate *verb* (located, locating, locates) 1. to find the position or place of. *Have you located his house?* 2. to put or set in a certain place. *He located his business in the city.* {**loh** kayt}

lo·ca·tion *noun* 1. place or position. *I marked the location of my house on the map.* 2. the act of locating. *Your location of the missing puzzle piece was very helpful.* {loh **kay** shən}

lock[1] ❂ *noun* 1. a mechanical device for keeping others from opening a door, window, or a safe. Locks are usually opened with a key or a combination. 2. part of a canal that is closed off with gates in order to change the level of water in an area. A lock lets a ship move safely from one level of water to another. *verb* (locked, locking, locks) 1. to keep closed by means of a lock. *We locked all of the doors and windows of our house when we left for vacation.* 2. to jail or keep in prison (usually followed by "up" or "in"). *The sheriff locked up the prisoner.* 3. to hold together by joining or linking together. *The people at the protest locked arms when the police came.* {**lŏk**}

lock[2] ❂ *noun* 1. a curl or piece of hair. *Mom saved a lock of hair from my first haircut.* 2. (plural) the hair of the head.

Goldilocks got her name from her yellow locks. {**lŏk**}

lock·er *noun* a chest or cabinet that can be locked. *There are rows of metal lockers along the walls at school.* {**lŏk** ər}

lock·et *noun* a small metal case that holds a picture or a lock of hair. It is usually worn on a chain around the neck. {**lŏk** iht}

lock·jaw *noun* a disease that causes the muscles of the jaw to first become tight and then close the jaw shut. Lockjaw is a type of tetanus. {**lŏk** jaw}

lock·smith *noun* a person who makes or fixes locks. {**lŏk** smihth}

lo·co·mo·tion *noun* the act of moving or the power to move from one place to another. *Trains and airplanes are used for locomotion.* {**loh** kə **moh** shən}

lo·co·mo·tive *noun* an engine that moves by its own power. It is used to pull or push railroad cars. {**loh** kə **moh** tihv}

Word History *Locomotive* entered English from French in 1612, long before trains existed. Its first meaning was "able to move from place to place." It became a word for a railroad engine in the 1800s.

lo·cust *noun* 1. an insect that travels in large groups called swarms. They damage crops and other plants in their path by eating them. They are a type of grasshopper.

  Human Body Human Mind Everyday Life History and Culture  Communication

2. an insect that is a type of cicada. These insects spend many years living in the ground as larvae and then come out of the ground in large groups and become adults. 3. a North American tree in the legume family that has leaves with many parts and white flowers that hang in clusters. {<u>loh</u> kəst}

lode *noun* a deposit of a mineral that fills a crack in an area of rock. *The mine workers discovered a lode of copper ore.* {lohd}

Homophone Note The words *lode* and *load* sound alike but have different meanings.

lode·stone *noun* a rock that acts as a magnet and attracts iron. {<u>lohd</u> stohn}

lodge *noun* 1. a cabin, hut, or other shelter meant to be used by people doing outdoor activities. *The men stayed in a lodge during their hunting trip.* 2. a small house on the grounds of a larger house or estate. *We stayed in the guest lodge at the family estate.* 3. a local branch of certain organizations, or the place they meet. *The meeting was held at the Elks lodge.* *verb* (lodged, lodging, lodges) 1. to live in a place for a short time. *They lodged with friends while the house was being repaired.* 2. to provide with a place to live for a short time. *She lodges college students in her spare rooms.* 3. to be or become caught or stuck in a certain position. *The kite lodged in the tree.* 4. to file in court or bring before another authority. *We lodged a complaint against our neighbor because of his barking dog.* {lŏj}

lodg·er *noun* a person who rents a furnished room or rooms.

The widow took in lodgers to make extra money after her husband died. {<u>lŏj</u> ər}

lodg·ing *noun* 1. a place to live in for a short time; dwelling. *They found lodging for their summer in the mountains.* 2. (often plural) a room or rooms rented to live in. *My neighbor has lodgings for rent.* {<u>lŏj</u> ing}

loft *noun* 1. an open space or room just under the roof; attic. *The farmer stored hay in the loft of the barn.* / *The children slept in the loft of the cabin.* 2. a balcony in a church or other public building. *At our church the choir sits in the loft.* 3. the top floor of a warehouse or factory. It is usually a large, open space. *The lofts of the factories in this part of town have been transformed into fancy apartments.* {lŏft}

loft·y *adjective* (loftier, loftiest) 1. of great height; high. *We walked through a forest of lofty trees.* 2. noble or superior. *The professor had lofty thoughts that she shared with her students.* 3. showing a belief that one is better than other people; proud. *The lofty manner of the new boss made him very unpopular with the workers.* {<u>lŏf</u> tee}

log *noun* 1. a large, thick piece of a tree that has been cut

down and is ready for sawing, burning, or building. *Frank sawed logs to burn in the fireplace.* 2. a daily record of a trip by a ship or plane. A log keeps records of speed, distance traveled, and any important events. *The plane's log showed that we had traveled three hundred miles.* *verb* (logged, logging, logs) 1. to cut down the trees from. *The lumber crew has been logging those hills for about three months.* 2. to record in the log of a ship or airplane, or in a similar record. *A sailor logs the distance the ship has travelled each day.* 3. to cut down and transport trees for lumber or firewood. *The lumberjack logged in the forest near the sawmill.* {lŏg}

• **log on**
to enter a computer system with a password. *Log on, and we'll send her a message.*

lo·gan·ber·ry *noun* (loganberries) 1. a prickly plant grown for its berries. 2. the large, dark red fruit of the loganberry plant. It is somewhat like the blackberry. {<u>loh</u> gən beh ree}

log·ger *noun* a person who works in logging; lumberjack. {<u>lo</u> gər}

log·ic Ⓣ *noun* a way of solving a problem that uses careful thought and reasoning. *The detective used logic to figure out who stole the diamonds.* {<u>lŏj</u> ihk}

log·i·cal *adjective* 1. in accord with the rules of logic. *A computer is programmed using logical languages.* 2. resulting from clear thinking; sound. *He made some logical arguments at the debate.* 3. following with logic or reason from events or statements that have come before. *It's only logical that he would reject*

A
B
C
D
E
F
G
H
I
J
K
L
M
N
O
P
Q
R
S
T
U
V
W
X
Y
Z

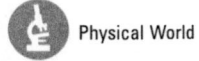 

a
b
c
d
e
f
g
h
i
j
k
l
m
n
o
p
q
r
s
t
u
v
w
x
y
z

such an action after having done so before. {lŏj ih kəl} logically, adv.

-log·i·cal *suffix* a suffix that means "related to the study of." "Zoo" is short for "zoological garden," a garden devoted to zoology, which is the study of animals.

lo·go *noun* a company's name, trademark, or symbol. {loh goh}

-l·o·gy or **-ology** *suffix* a suffix that means "the science or study of." *Biology is the study of living things.*

loin *noun* 1. the part of the body on either side of the spine between the ribs and the hip. 2. a cut of meat taken from this part of an animal. {loin}

loi·ter *verb* (loitered, loitering, loiters) to stand around idly. *Teenagers loitered outside the movie theater.* {loi tər} loiterer, n.

loll *verb* (lolled, lolling, lolls) 1. to stand, sit, or lie in a lazy or relaxed manner; lounge. *She lolled on the sofa and watched television.* 2. to hang down loosely; dangle. *The dog's tongue was lolling from its mouth.* {lŏl}

lol·li·pop *noun* a piece of hard candy attached to the end of a small stick. {lŏl ee pŏp}

Lon·don *noun* the capital city of England and the United Kingdom. {luhn dən}

lone *adjective* 1. without others; alone. *One lone man walked along the empty beach.* 2. without others of its kind; only; single. *The lone grocery store in that area was always busy.* 3. set off by itself; iso-

lated. *We discovered a lone cabin in the woods.* {lohn}

Homophone Note The words **lone** and **loan** sound alike but have different meanings.

lone·ly *adjective* (lonelier, loneliest) 1. without company; alone. *There was a lonely hill on the horizon. / She is content with her lonely life.* 2. empty of humans; deserted; lonesome. *He walked for miles through lonely woods.* 3. unhappy because alone; lonesome. *I felt lonely for my family while I was away at camp.* {lohn lee} loneliness, n.

lone·some *adjective* 1. sad because of being alone. *I was lonesome after my best friend moved away.* 2. having no people around; deserted. *At night the park became a lonesome place.* {lohn səm}

long[1] *adjective* (longer, longest) 1. having greater than usual length in distance or time. *There is a long driveway leading to our house. / The runners were very tired after the long race.* 2. of a particular length in time or size. *The test was two hours long. / Our porch is thirty feet long.* *noun* a great period of time. *I've got the motor running, so I can't stay here for long.* *adverb* (longer, longest) 1. for or during a long period of time. *Moving to the beach was a change that he had long wanted.* 2. at a time far in the past. *It happened long ago.* 3. throughout a particular period. *She sang all night long.* {lŏng}

long[2] *verb* (longed, longing, longs) to want very much (often followed by "for"). *I long for a vacation.* {lŏng}

long distance *noun* telephone service that is not local. *He*

used long distance to call his grandmother who lives in another state.* {lŏng dihs təns} long-distance, adj.

long·hand *noun* writing done by hand in which words are written out in full. {lŏng hănd}

long·horn *noun* a breed of cattle with very long horns. Longhorns were once raised in the southwestern United States for their meat but are now rare. {lŏng hohrn}

long·ing *noun* a strong and lasting desire. *Since childhood, he has had a longing to travel to Africa.* {lŏng ing} longingly, adv.

lon·gi·tude *noun* distance on the earth's surface east or west of an imaginary line on the globe that goes from the north pole to the south pole and passes through Greenwich, England. Longitude is usually measured in degrees. {lŏn jih toohd}

look *verb* (looked, looking, looks) 1. to use the eyes to see. *I feel happy when I look at my puppy.* 2. to turn one's glance or attention. *He looked to me for help.* 3. to seem or appear. *My new haircut looks awful.* 4. to face a certain direction. *The house looked north.* 5. to try to find; search (usually followed by "for"). *She looked for the lost keys.* 6. to inspect or examine quickly (usually followed by "over"). *He looked over the photos without much interest.* *noun* 1. the act of looking; glance. *My father's angry look scared me.* 2. way of appearing. *My new dress has a nice look.* 3. a search. *Have a look for my gloves, will you?* 4. (plural) personal appearance. *Good looks are not everything.* {luuk}

• **look after**

 Human Body    Human Mind    Everyday Life   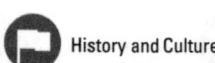 History and Culture    Communication

to take care of. My *best friend looked after my kitten while I was away.*

• **look down one's nose at** to feel that one is better than or superior to. *The boss looks down his nose at office workers.*

• **look forward to** to wait for eagerly. *She is looking forward to her birthday party.*

• **look up** to search for in a book. *I looked up the names of all the U.S. Presidents in a history book.*

• **look up to** to respect; admire. *She looks up to her mother.*

looking glass *noun* a mirror made of glass. {<u>luuk</u> ing **glăs**}

look·out *noun* 1. the act of keeping watch or searching. *Keep a lookout for the missing puppy while you are out walking.* 2. a high place from which someone can observe a wide area. *The tower is used as a lookout for forest fires.* 3. someone whose job is to keep watch. *The lookout on the ship watched for dangers in the water.* {<u>luuk</u> owt}

loom[1] *noun* a device or machine for weaving cloth. {<u>loohm</u>}

Bill often feared that one day a giant **loom** would **loom** over him.

loom[2] *verb* (loomed, looming, looms) 1. to appear or come into view, often as a very large, dim, or twisted shape. *The monster loomed in the heavy mist of the dark forest.* 2. to appear to the mind as something very difficult or dangerous. *The exam loomed for weeks before he took it.* {<u>loohm</u>}

loon *noun* a large black and white water bird with a call that sounds like a loud laugh. {<u>loohn</u>}

loop *noun* 1. the rounded shape made when a piece of string, ribbon, or rope is folded back on itself. 2. something that has this shape. *He drew loops on the paper. / We came to a loop in the path.* 3. a movement in which an airplane is flown in this shape. *The stunt pilot performed some amazing loops.* 4. a set of instructions that a computer program repeats over and over again. *verb* (looped, looping, loops) to make or shape into a loop or loops. *She looped her shoelaces and tied them into a bow.* {<u>loohp</u>}

loose *adjective* (looser, loosest) 1. not joined or attached tightly; free. *There is a loose button on your shirt.* 2. not held back; free. *When school was over, we were loose for the summer.* 3. not tight. *I wear loose clothes in hot weather.* *adverb* (looser, loosest) to a condition of freedom of movement. *Turn the dogs loose.* *verb* (loosed, loosing, looses) 1. to set free; let loose. *The children loosed the dog at the park.* 2. to make less tight; unfasten. *He loosed his belt after the big meal.* {<u>loohs</u>} loosely, adv., looseness, n.

loose-leaf *adjective* made to hold sheets of paper that can be removed. *She got new* loose-leaf notebooks for school. {<u>loohs</u> **leef**}

loos·en *verb* (loosened, loosening, loosens) 1. to undo or release. *He loosened the latch on the cage.* 2. to make loose; relax. *She loosened her hold on the dog when it stopped barking.* {<u>looh</u> sən}

loot *noun* 1. valuables taken by force in a war; spoils. *Before sinking the enemy ship, they took all the loot they could carry.* 2. goods taken by stealing or other dishonest means. *The stolen loot was found in the trunk of a car.* 3. (informal) a number of things bought or gifts received. *He came home from the shopping trip with plenty of loot.* *verb* (looted, looting, loots) to take valuables from by force; plunder. *The enemy soldiers looted the village.* {<u>looht</u>} looter, n.

Homophone Note The words **loot** and **lute** sound alike but have different meanings. To find out why a musical thief would be happy to find a lute among his loot, look up **lute**.

lope *verb* (loped, loping, lopes) to trot or run gracefully and easily with long steps; to ride a horse at this gait. *The horse loped across the field.* *noun* a way of running or cantering that is graceful and easy. *The pony ran home at a lope.* {<u>lohp</u>}

lop·sid·ed *adjective* having one side that is larger or heavier than the other; uneven. *She baked a lopsided cake.* {<u>lŏp</u> <u>siy</u> dihd}

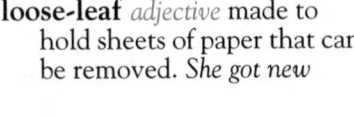 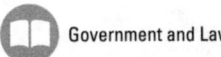
A B C D E F G H I J K L M N O P Q R S T U V W X Y Z

a b c d e f g h i j k **l** m n o p q r s t u v w x y z

lord *noun* 1. a person who rules. *The most powerful lord ruled the largest section of the country.* 2. a title for a nobleman. *The lord and his lady lived in a handsome castle.* 3. (capital) God or Jesus Christ. {lohrd}

Word History *Lord* comes from an Old English word that means "keeper of the bread."

Los Angeles *noun* a city in the U.S. state of California, on the Pacific Ocean. {lŏs **ăn** jə lees *or* lŏs **ăn** jə ləs *or* lŏs **ăng** gə leez}

lose *verb* (lost, losing, loses) 1. to no longer have; be unable to find; misplace. *I lost my shoes.* 2. to fail to keep. *I just lost a quarter in this candy machine.* 3. to fail to win. *They lost the contest.* 4. to fail to use; waste. *They lost time when the plane was grounded because of the storm.* {loohz}

loss *noun* 1. a failure to keep or continue. *The loss of his friendship made me very sad.* 2. a decrease in size or amount. *The loss of ten pounds made him look very thin.* 3. that which is lost; someone or something that can not be found or is taken away. *After the fire, the business was a loss.* 4. the harm caused by losing or having something taken away. *He felt a great loss when his friend died.* 5. a defeat or failure to win. *The team was unhappy about their loss.* {laws *or* lŏs}

lost *adjective* 1. no longer possessed; not able to be found. *They finally found their lost puppy.* 2. not won. *The basketball team was unhappy about the lost games this season.* 3. not held on to or kept in existence. *He thought of his year in prison as lost time.* 4. not aware of where one is. *We left the path and were lost in the woods.* 5. ruined or destroyed. *They were afraid the ship would be lost in the storm.* 6. not used; wasted. *If he doesn't go to camp, it will be a lost opportunity.* *verb* past tense and past participle of **lose**. {lawst *or* lŏst, v., lawst *or* lŏst, adj.}

lot *noun* 1. a large amount or number. *We bought a lot of food for the party.* 2. a group of people or objects of the same type. *My mother liked the lot of old dishes that were being sold at the auction.* 3. one of a set of objects used to decide something by chance. *They drew lots to see who would go first.* 4. a piece of land. *My brother hopes to build a house on the new lot that he just bought.* 5. a person's fate or situation in life. *Is it my lot to be poor all my life?* {lŏt}

lo·tion *noun* a thick liquid for rubbing on the skin. Lotions are used to moisten, heal, or protect the skin. {loh shən}

lot·ter·y *noun* (lotteries) a game of chance in which people buy or are given tickets with numbers on them and the winning number is chosen at random. {lŏt ə ree}

lo·tus *noun* 1. a kind of flowering plant that lives in the water. Some waterlilies are lotuses. 2. a plant in an ancient Greek legend. It was believed that those who ate the fruit of this plant happily forgot their troubles. {loh təs}

loud *adjective* (louder, loudest) 1. having a large amount of sound; easily heard. *The dish made a loud crash when it fell to the floor.* 2. tastelessly bright in color; gaudy. *He wore a loud jacket to the dance.* *adverb* (louder, loudest) in a loud way; loudly. *You'll have to speak loud to be heard over* the noisy crowd. {lowd} loudly, adv., loudness, n.

Synonyms
This word shares a meaning with *loud*, adjective 1:
noisy

loud·speak·er *noun* an electronic device that makes sound louder and broadcasts it in one area, such as a room or a stadium. {lowd spee kər}

Lou·i·si·an·a *noun* a state in the southern United States. Its capital is Baton Rouge. (abbreviated: LA) {looh **ee** zee **ăn** ə *or* looh ee zee **ăn** ə} Louisianan, n., adj., Louisianian, n., adj.

Word History *Louisiana* was named in honor of France's King Louis the Fourteenth in 1682, when Sieur de la Salle claimed the Mississippi River valley for France.

lounge ○ *verb* (lounged, lounging, lounges) to lie down, sit, or walk in a lazy or very relaxed way (often followed by "around" or "along"). *After a big meal, the leopard lounged in the tree.* *noun* 1. a room or area where people can relax or wait. *We waited in the hotel lounge until our room was ready.* 2. a long seat or couch. Some lounges have no back or arms. Other lounges have one end that is raised or a headrest. {lownj}

louse *noun* (lice or louses) a very small insect without wings that lives on the bodies of people, birds, and other ani-

 Human Body    Human Mind   Everyday Life   History and Culture   Communication

mals. Lice suck blood from animals, and some kinds can spread disease. {**lows**}

lous·y *adjective* (lousier, lousiest) 1. covered with lice. 2. (informal) nasty or mean. *Tripping your brother was a lousy thing to do.* 3. (informal) very bad; without value. *No one can read her lousy handwriting.* {**low** zee} lousily, adv., lousiness, n.

lov·a·ble *adjective* having a nature that attracts love. *Mary is so lovable!* {**luh** və bəl}

love 🔊 *noun* 1. strong feelings of affection for another person. *She has a deep love for her childhood friend.* 2. strong interest in or liking for something. *He has a great love for music.* 3. a person, activity, or object for which one has great affection or strong liking. *She was his first love. / Sailing is one of her loves.* *verb* (loved, loving, loves) 1. to have strong and tender affection for. *I think I love my puppy as much as her own mother does.* 2. to enjoy or have a strong interest in. *I love fishing and swimming.* {**luhv**}

love·ly *adjective* (lovelier, loveliest) 1. charming or beautiful in appearance. *Mom looked lovely in her new dress.* 2. having a beauty that relates to character rather than to appearance. *My grandmother has a lovely spirit.* {**luhv** lee} loveliness, n.

lov·ing *adjective* feeling or showing love. *He is a loving father. / She has a loving smile.* {**luhv** ing} lovingly, adv.

low *adjective* (lower, lowest) 1. close to the ground or bottom; not high. *The wall is low enough for us to step over it.* 2. below the normal level. *The water in the lake was too low for sailing.* 3. unhappy or weak. *She was in a low mood because of her poor grade in math.* 4. not loud. *I heard the low sound of a train in the distance.* 5. below average in quality. *His history grade is low.* 6. nearly used up or empty. *We have to stop for gas because the tank is low.* *adverb* (lower, lowest) 1. in or to a lower position or level. *The birds flew low over the lake.* 2. in or to a state of being empty. *The gas in the car is running low.* 3. at a somewhat quiet level. *She sang the lullaby low.* *noun* something that is low, such as an amount, an action, or a person's spirits. *Gas prices have hit a low. / Today is one of her lows.* {**loh**}

low·er *verb* (lowered, lowering, lowers) 1. to cause to move to a position below; let down. *Lower the boat into the water.* 2. to come down, grow less, or descend. *The price of milk lowered during the sale.* 3. to make less in amount or quantity. *The shop lowered the price of flowers before Mother's Day.* 4. to make less loud. *Please lower your voice in the library.* *adjective* 1. comparative of **low**. *The oak trees were planted lower on the hill than the pine trees.* 2. not as high in position, rank, or value. *The private is lower in rank than the sergeant.* {**loh** ər}

lower case *noun* Letters that are not capitals. In printing, the tray that holds these let-

ters is called the lower case. {**loh** ər **kays**}

low tide *noun* the tide at its lowest water level, or the time when this happens. {**loh** tiyd}

loy·al *adjective* showing devotion and faithfulness to someone or something. *Few friends are more loyal than a dog. / He was a loyal member of the organization.* {**loi** əl} loyally, adv.

loy·al·ty *noun* (loyalties) the condition of being faithful or loyal. *The soldiers showed great loyalty to their country during the war.* {**loi** əl tee}

loz·enge *noun* a small piece of hard candy that contains medicine. A lozenge is held in the mouth and sucked to ease a sore throat or cough. {**lo** zihnj}

lu·bri·cate *verb* (lubricated, lubricating, lubricates) to coat or supply with grease, oil, or another slippery sub-

A B C D E F G H I J K **L** M N O P Q R S T U V W X Y Z

stance. *He lubricated his bicycle chain before the race.* {**looh** brih **kayt**} **lubrication,** n.

luck *noun* 1. the force believed to guide things which seem to happen to a person by chance. *It was luck that brought them to that place at the same time. / He's had terrible luck with his new business and will soon have to close.* 2. good fortune; success. *Have you had luck in your search for the lost kitten?* {**luhk**}

luck·i·ly *adverb* by good fortune. *Luckily, the plan worked.* {**luhk** ih lee}

luck·y *adjective* (luckier, luckiest) resulting from or having good fortune. *My father is a lucky man to have a job that he loves.* {**luhk** ee}

Synonyms
These words share a meaning with *lucky*, adjective 1:
happy, fortunate

lug *verb* (lugged, lugging, lugs) to pull, lift, or carry with a great effort. *He lugged the heavy boxes out to the truck.* {**luhg**}

lug·gage *noun* suitcases, boxes, and bags for carrying one's things on trips; baggage. {**luhg** ihj}

Word History The word *luggage* was first used around 1600. It was formed from the word "lug," which means "to drag or carry." "Lug" comes from a Scandinavian word that means "to pull or drag by the hair."

luke·warm *adjective* 1. only slightly warm; tepid. *He washed the baby in lukewarm water.* 2. showing little interest or enthusiasm. *He gave a lukewarm answer when I asked if he liked my new haircut.* {**loohk wohrm**}

lull *verb* (lulled, lulling, lulls) to calm or cause to sleep. *My baby brother is quickly lulled to sleep when Mom rocks him in her arms.* *noun* a calm, quiet period. *We ran home during a lull in the storm.* {**luhl**}

lull·a·by *noun* (lullabies) a song sung to put a child to sleep. {**luhl** ə biy}

lum·ber[1] 🔄 *noun* logs cut into boards or beams for use in building. *The carpenter brought a truckload of lumber to build the barn.* {**luhm** bər}

An exhausted plank of **lumber lumbers** home at the end of the day.

lum·ber[2] *verb* (lumbered, lumbering, lumbers) to move in a heavy, clumsy way. *A bear lumbered through the forest.* {**luhm** bər}

lum·ber·jack *noun* a person whose work is to cut down trees and deliver them to a lumber mill. {**luhm** bər **jăk**}

lu·mi·nous *adjective* giving off light; glowing. *The stars were luminous in the night sky.* {**looh** mih nəs}

lump *noun* 1. a small mass or pile with no special shape; hunk. *He took a lump of clay and made it into a vase.* 2. a bump or swelling. *I had a lump on my forehead from running into a tree.* *verb* (lumped, lumping, lumps) 1. to gather into or consider as a single whole (often followed by "together"). *He lumps girls together as if they were all the same.* 2. to come to have or be formed into a lump or lumps. *If you don't stir the oatmeal while you cook it, it will lump.* {**luhmp**}

lu·nar *adjective* of or having to do with the moon. *The spacecraft made a lunar landing.* {**looh** nər}

lunch 🔄 *noun* a meal eaten in the middle of the day, or any light meal during the day. *Many people each lunch around noon.* *verb* (lunched, lunching, lunches) to eat lunch. *We lunched on the boat.* {**luhnch**}

lunch·eon *noun* a special meal served at lunch time. *The students prepared a birthday luncheon for their teacher.* {**luhn** chən}

lung 🔄 *noun* one of two organs in the chest that are used in breathing. Lungs are found in mammals, birds, reptiles, and some other animals. They bring oxygen to the body and get rid of carbon dioxide. {**luhng**}

lunge *noun* a sudden movement toward something; thrust, leap, or dive. *Bill made a lunge for the escaping puppy.* *verb* (lunged, lunging, lunges) to move with a

 Human Body   Human Mind   Everyday Life   History and Culture 🔄 Communication

sudden forward motion, such as a dive, thrust, or leap. *He lunged for the ball and caught it. / She lunged at the dragon with her sword.* {luhnj}

lurch *noun* 1. a sudden sideways motion, as of a boat. *The boat lurched and he dropped his oar.* 2. a sudden, unsteady movement; stagger. *He stepped back with a lurch when he saw the snake.* *verb* (lurched, lurching, lurches) to make a sudden movement sideways or move with a stagger. *He lost his balance when the boat lurched.* {luhrch}

lure *noun* 1. something that attracts or tempts by promising some reward. *The flashing sign of the ice cream store was a lure for hungry kids.* 2. something used to attract and catch fish or other animals; bait. *He caught three fish with his new lure.* *verb* (lured, luring, lures) to attract with the promise of a reward. *They lured the dog back to the house with a bowl of food.* {loohr}

lurk *verb* (lurked, lurking, lurks) 1. to be hidden; lie in wait. *Joe lurked behind a tree, waiting to scare his friends.* 2. to sneak about; prowl. *A cat lurked in the shadows.* {luhrk}

lus·cious *adjective* delicious to taste or smell. *She took a bite of the luscious pear.* {luh shəs}

lush *adjective* 1. growing thick and healthy. *She entered a lush garden of colorful flowers.* 2. rich, abundant, or fancy. *The palace was filled with lush furniture.* {luhsh}

lust *noun* a strong desire for something (usually followed by "for"). *He could not control his lust for chocolate.* *verb* (lusted, lusting, lusts) to want or like very much (often followed by "for" or

"after"). *She lusted for a dress she saw in the shop window.* {luhst}

lus·ter *noun* the shine of a surface that softly reflects light; glow. *Moonlight gave a luster to the snow.* {luhs tər}

lute *noun* a stringed instrument that has a bent neck and a body shaped like a pear. {looht}

Homophone Note The words *lute* and *loot* sound alike but have different meanings.

Lux·em·bourg *noun* a country in western Europe between Germany, Belgium, and France. Luxembourg City is the capital of Luxembourg. {luhk səm burg} Luxembourger, n.

lux·u·ri·ant *adjective* 1. growing thickly and in great numbers; lush. *The crab apple tree was luxuriant with blossoms.* 2. fancy or having much decoration. *The prince wore a luxuriant cloak.* {luhg zhur ee ənt *or* luhk shur ee ənt}

lux·u·ri·ous *adjective* giving great comfort or pleasure. *He enjoyed a long, luxurious afternoon with no work.* {luhg zhur ee əs *or* luhk shuh ree əs}

lux·u·ry *noun* (luxuries) 1. something very pleasant but not necessary. *It was a luxury to be served breakfast in bed.* 2. a way of living that is full of great pleasure and comfort. *Does everyone dream of living in luxury?* {luhk shə ree *or* luhg zhə ree}

-ly *suffix* 1. a suffix that means in a certain way. *To write neatly is to write in a neat way.* 2. a suffix that means like or having the character of. *A saintly person is*

like a saint. / A cowardly person is like a coward. 3. a suffix that means happening or done at regular times. *A monthly magazine is a magazine that comes out once a month.*

lye *noun* a strong substance used in making soap. It was once made from wood ashes. {liy}

Homophone Note The words *lye* and *lie* sound alike but have different meanings.

ly·ing[1] *noun* the telling of lies. *He was punished for lying.* *adjective* not telling the truth on purpose; not honest; false. *Don't believe that lying man.* *verb* present participle of **lie**[1]. {liy ing}

ly·ing[2] *verb* present participle of **lie**[2]. {liy ing}

lymph *noun* a slightly yellowish liquid produced by body tissues. It contains many white blood cells. {lihmf}

lynx *noun* a mammal with soft, spotted fur, tufted ears, and a short tail. Several kinds of lynx live in Europe, North America, and Asia. They are carnivores and are related to other wild cats. Lynx are about twice the size of house cats. {lingks}

lyre *noun* a stringed instrument of ancient Greece that is like a harp. {liyr}

A
B
C
D
E
F
G
H
I
J
K
L
M
N
O
P
Q
R
S
T
U
V
W
X
Y
Z

a
b
c
d
e
f
g
h
i
j
k
l
m
n
o
p
q
r
s
t
u
v
w
x
y
z

lyr·ic *adjective* relating to poetry that has a musical rhythm and often expresses private feelings and thoughts. *She wrote a lyric poem about her love of nature.* *noun* 1. a lyric poem. *He wrote a lyric in English class.* 2. (often plural) the words to a song. *When my sister and I write songs together, she writes the music, and I write the lyrics.* {<u>leer</u> ihk}

lyr·i·cal *adjective* showing deep feeling. *He wrote a lyrical love song.* {<u>leer</u> ihk əl}

 Human Body   Human Mind 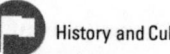 Everyday Life  History and Culture Communication

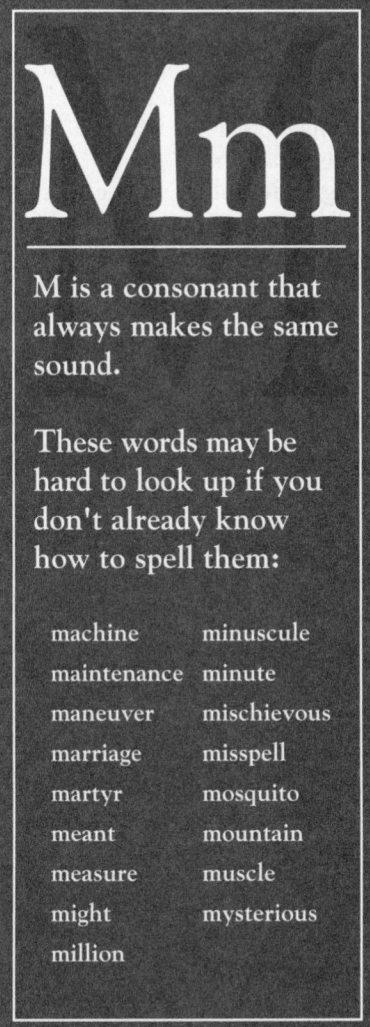

Mm

M is a consonant that always makes the same sound.

These words may be hard to look up if you don't already know how to spell them:

machine	minuscule
maintenance	minute
maneuver	mischievous
marriage	misspell
martyr	mosquito
meant	mountain
measure	muscle
might	mysterious
million	

m or **M** *noun* (m's or M's) the thirteenth letter of the English alphabet. {**ehm**}

m. *abbreviation* an abbreviation for **meter**, or meters.

M.A. *abbreviation* a degree earned in particular fields after one or two years of additional study following college. M.A. is an abbreviation for "Master of Arts."

ma *noun* (informal) **mother**.

MA or **Mass.** *abbreviation* an abbreviation for **Massachusetts**.

ma'am *noun* (informal; often capitalized) madam. *Thank you, ma'am, for helping me.* {**məm**}

mac·a·ro·ni *noun* (macaroni) dried noodles made from flour and water, often shaped into curved, hollow tubes. {măk ə **roh** nee}

Mac·e·do·ni·a *noun* a country in southeastern Europe north of Greece. Macedonia is also called the Former Yugoslav Republic of Macedonia. Skopje is the capital of Macedonia. {mă sih **doh** nee ə *or* mă sih **dohn** yə} Macedonian, adj., n.

ma·chine 🔧 ⚙ *noun* a device with a system of parts that work together to perform a task. Cars, computers, hair dryers, and vacuum cleaners are all examples of machines. {mə **sheen**} machinelike, adj.

machine gun *noun* an automatic gun that fires bullets one right after the other as long as its trigger is pressed. {mə **sheen** guhn}

ma·chin·er·y *noun* (machineries) 1. machines in general. *Workers are repairing the street with noisy machinery.* 2. the working parts of a machine. *The mechanics will repair the oil-drilling machinery.* 3. a combination of people and actions that makes something work; system. *Our country's leaders try to keep the machinery of government running smoothly.* {mə **sheen** ər ee}

ma·chin·ist *noun* a person who has skill in using, repairing, or building machines. {mə **sheen** ihst}

mack·er·el *noun* (mackerel or mackerels) a fish that has dark marks that look like waves on its back and a silver underside.

Mackerel live in the Atlantic Ocean and are used for food. {**măk** ə rəl *or* **măk** rəl}

ma·cron *noun* a mark (¯). It is placed over a vowel to show that the vowel is long. {**may** krŏn *or* mă krŏn}

mad 🔊 *adjective* (madder, maddest) 1. crazy; insane. *He went mad after months of being imprisoned in a tiny cell.* 2. angry. *My mother was mad at me when I didn't do my chores.* 3. suffering from rabies. *A mad animal may act strangely and foam at the mouth.* 4. wild, confused, or frantic. *The thief made a mad rush for the exit.* 5. very fond of. *My parents are mad about opera.* 6. not wise or practical; foolish. *The officer at the bank thought that my uncle's plan for making money was mad.* {**măd**}

• **like mad** (informal) with great speed or enthusiasm. *The football player ran like mad for the goal line.*

Synonyms
These words share a meaning with **mad**, adjective 1:
crazy, insane, irrational

Mad·a·gas·car *noun* an island country in the Indian Ocean off the coast of southern Africa. Antananarivo is the capital of Madagascar. {măd ə **găs** kər} Madagascan, n., adj.

mad·am *noun* (mesdames or madams) (sometimes capitalized) a polite word to use when talking to a woman. *Would you like some tea, madam?* {**măd** əm}

mad·ame *noun* (mesdames) a formal or polite way to address a married woman. (abbreviation: Mme.) *May I help you, madame?* {**mă** dəm *or* mə **dăm** *or* mə **dahm** *or* mo **dŏm**}

A
B
C
D
E
F
G
H
I
J
K
L
M
N
O
P
Q
R
S
T
U
V
W
X
Y
Z

a
b
c
d
e
f
g
h
i
j
k
l
m
n
o
p
q
r
s
t
u
v
w
x
y
z

made *verb* past tense and past participle of **make**. {mayd}

Homophone Note Are you looking for the word **maid** (a female servant)? **Made** and **maid** sound alike but have different meanings.

mad·e·moi·selle *noun* a French title for a girl or woman who is not married. The abbreviation is Mlle. *Excuse me, Mademoiselle, but is this your purse?* {mă də mə **zehl** or măd mwə **zehl**}

made-up *adjective* 1. not real or true; invented. *She gave her parents a made-up excuse for being late.* 2. wearing makeup. *Her made-up face made her look older than she really was.* {mayd **uhp**}

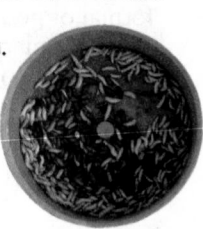

Ma·drid *noun* the capital city of Spain. {mə **drihd**}

mag·a·zine 🔊 *noun* 1. a printed collection of stories, pictures, articles, and advertisements. Magazines come out weekly, monthly, or at some other regular period of time. 2. the part of a gun that holds the bullets. {mă gə zeen}

Word History *Magazine* comes from an Arabic word that means "storehouse."

ma·gen·ta *noun* the color that comes from mixing red and purple paint. {mə **jehn** tə}

mag·got *noun* the larva of flies and certain other insects. Maggots do not have legs or wings. {mă gət}

mag·ic *noun* 1. mysterious control of physical forces or events through spells or special ceremonies. *Some say that witches use magic to turn people into frogs.* 2. tricks used to entertain by suggesting such mysterious control. *He did magic to entertain the children.* *adjective* 1. of, concerning, or used in the practice of magic. *The witch flew through the air on her magic broom.* 2. produced by magic or as if by magic. *The wizard put her to sleep with a magic potion.* {mă jihk}

mag·i·cal *adjective* of or made by magic. *The witch gave magical shoes to Dorothy.* {mă jih kəl}

ma·gi·cian *noun* a person who has skill in magic and entertains people with magic tricks. {mə **jih** shən}

mag·ma *noun* hot, liquid matter beneath the Earth's surface that cools to form igneous rock. Magma that reaches the Earth's surface, as when a volcano erupts, is called lava. {mă mə}

mag·ne·si·um 🔊 *noun* a light, silver-white metal that is a chemical element. It burns brightly when heated and is used for making fireworks. (symbol: Mg) {mă **nee** zee əm or mă **nee** zhəm}

mag·net *noun* an object that has the power to pull items made of iron toward itself. {mă niht}

mag·net·ic *adjective* 1. having to do with magnets and the way they work. *Certain stones have magnetic properties.* 2. having the power to attract and keep people's attention. *The new governor is a magnetic speaker.* {măg **neh** tihk}

magnetic field *noun* the space around a magnet in which a magnetic force is active. {măg **neh** tihk **feeld**}

magnetic pole *noun* 1. either of the two points of a magnet where the lines of magnetic force meet and are strongest. 2. either of two areas on the earth's surface, one near the geographic north pole and one near the geographic south pole, where the earth's magnetic fields are strongest. *A compass needle points to the magnetic north pole.* {măg **neh** tihk **pohl**}

magnetic tape *noun* a thin plastic ribbon with a magnetic coating, used to record sound and images. Magnetic tape is found in audio cassettes and videocassettes. {măg **neh** tihk **tayp**}

mag·net·ism *noun* 1. the power of a magnet to attract. 2. the power of someone or something to attract people. *Leaders are often chosen because of their magnetism.* {măg nə tih zəm}

mag·net·ize 🔊 *verb* (magnetized, magnetizing, magnetizes) to cause to become a magnet. *Electricity can magnetize steel.* {măg nə tiyz}

mag·nif·i·cence *noun* the quality of being grand or splendid. *The magnificence of the sunset filled them with wonder.* {măg **nih** fə səns}

mag·nif·i·cent *adjective* very grand in size or splendid in beauty. *The princess lived in a magnificent palace.* {măg **nih** fə sənt}

mag·ni·fy *verb* (magnified, magnifying, magnifies) 1. to cause to appear larger. *A telescope magnifies the stars.* 2. to cause to seem more impor-

 Human Body   Human Mind  Everyday Life  History and Culture Communication

tant than it is. *She magnifies her troubles to get her parents' attention.* {**măg** nih **fīy**} magnifiable, adj., magnifier, n.

magnifying glass
noun a lens that makes objects seen through it appear larger. {**măg** nih **fīy** ing **glăs**}

mag·ni·tude *noun* 1. size or extent. *The magnitude of the universe can make us feel small.* 2. greatness or importance. *The first moon landing was an event of great magnitude.* {**măg** nih **toohd**}

mag·no·li·a *noun* 1. a tree or shrub with large pink, white, or purple flowers. In many species blooms appear before the leaves. 2. the flower of such a plant. {**măg noh** lee ə *or* **măg nohl** yə}

mag·pie *noun* a large black and white bird with a long tail and a noisy, chattering call. {**măg** pīy}

ma·hog·a·ny *noun* (mahoganies) 1. an evergreen tree that grows in tropical North and South America. It has hard, reddish brown wood. 2. the wood of this tree, which is used to make furniture. *Our dining room table is made of mahogony.* 3. a rich, reddish brown color. {mə **hŏg** ə nee}

maid *noun* 1. a girl or woman who is paid to do housework. 2. a girl or young woman who is not married; maiden. {**mayd**}

Homophone Note The words *maid* and *made* sound alike but have different meanings.

maid·en *noun* a young woman or girl who is not married. *adjective* first. *The Titanic sank on its maiden voyage.* {**may** dihn}

maiden name *noun* the last name of a woman before she marries and takes her husband's last name. *Mrs. Smith's maiden name is González.* {**may** dihn **naym**}

maid of honor *noun* (maids of honor) an unmarried woman who is the most important attendant of a bride at her wedding. {**mayd** əv **o** nər}

mail¹ ● *noun* 1. the system set up to send and deliver letters, packages, and other items; postal system. *She sent the package in the mail.* 2. material sent through the postal system. *Our town's post office handles thousands of pieces of mail every day.* 3. a delivery of such material. *Has the morning mail arrived yet?* *verb* (mailed, mailing, mails) to send by means of the postal service. *I mailed a birthday card to my cousin.* {**mayl**}

mail² ● *noun* flexible armor made of connected metal rings. *The knights wore mail into battle.* {**mayl**}

Homophone Note Are you looking for the word *male* (the opposite of female)? *Mail* and *male* sound alike but have different meanings.

mail·box *noun* 1. a public box in which people place letters to be sent by mail. 2. a box for receiving the mail delivered to one particular address. {**mayl** bŏks}

mail carrier *noun* a person whose job is to deliver mail. {**mayl** kar ee ər}

mail·man *noun* (mailmen) a man whose job is to deliver mail; postman. {**mayl** măn}

maim *verb* (maimed, maiming, maims) to hurt badly by destroying a part of the body or making it useless. *Many soldiers were maimed in the war.* {**maym**}

main *adjective* most important; chief; primary. *She gave us a list of the main chapters to study for the final exam.* / *The main entrance to the building is on the other side.* *noun* a large pipe for distributing water or gas to homes or other buildings. *A leak in the water main caused the village to be without water for days.* {**mayn**}

Homophone Note The words *main*, *Maine*, and *mane* sound alike but have different meanings.

Maine *noun* a state in the northeastern United States on the Atlantic Coast. Its capital is Augusta. (abbreviated: ME) {**mayn**} Mainer, n.

Homophone Note The words *Maine*, *main*, and *mane* sound alike but have different meanings.

Word History *Maine* may have its name because English settlers living on the Atlantic coast and on islands in the Atlantic Ocean referred to the mainland as "The Maine." Or, they may have named it after "Maine," a province in France owned by the Queen of England.

main·frame *noun* a computer that is much bigger and more powerful than ordinary computers. Mainframes are used chiefly by large companies and other organizations. A mainframe can be connected to a number of computer terminals and used by many people at the same time. {**mayn** fraym}

main·land *noun* the main land mass of a country or conti-

 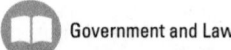

A B C D E F G H I J K L **M** N O P Q R S T U V W X Y Z

nent, not including nearby islands. *It's a long trip from the U.S. mainland to Hawaii.* {**mayn** lănd *or* **mayn** lənd}

main·ly *adverb* for the most part; mostly. *The movie was mainly about monkeys that had escaped from a zoo.* {**mayn** lee}

main·stay *noun* 1. a strong rope or cable that holds and steadies the mast of a sailing ship. 2. the main support of something. *Bread is the main-stay of many people's diet.* {**mayn** stay}

main·tain *verb* (maintained, maintaining, maintains) 1. to continue; keep in existence. *The children of the neighbor-hood maintained their friend-ships for many years.* 2. to take care of; keep in good condition. *Many gardeners are needed to maintain the park.* 3. to state in a firm and sure way. *He maintains that he did not break the window.* {**mayn tayn**}

main·te·nance *noun* 1. the act of maintaining. *Maintenance of the kitchen is the cook's responsibility.* 2. money and things needed to live. *He worked hard to provide his own maintenance.* {**mayn** tə nəns}

maize *noun* see **Indian corn**. {**mayz**}

Homophone Note The words *maize* and *maze* (a com-plicated path) sound alike but have different meanings.

ma·jes·tic *adjective* having maj-esty; grand; splendid; noble. *The Taj Mahal is a majestic building.* / *The people cheered their majestic king.* {mə **jehs** tihk} majestically, *adv.*

maj·es·ty *noun* (majes-ties) 1. the great-ness, dignity, or power of a royal person. 2. (capitalized) a title used when speaking to or about a royal person, such as a king or queen. *I have come with gifts of gold, Your Majesty.* {**măj** ih stee}

ma·jor *noun* the military rank above captain and below lieutenant colonel. *adjective* 1. greater in size or number. *The congressman played a major part in getting the seat-belt laws passed.* 2. great in importance, position, or rep-utation. *He wants to play in the major leagues.* / *Robert Frost is considered a major poet in American literature.* {**may** jər}

ma·jor·ette *noun* see **drum majorette**. {may jə **reht**}

ma·jor·i·ty *noun* (majorities) 1. the greater number or amount; a number or amount greater than half. *The majority of students in our class like vanilla ice cream better than chocolate.* 2. the number of votes over half of the votes cast. *She was elected president by a small majority of votes.* 3. the age at which a person becomes an adult according to the law. {mə **jôr** ih tee}

major scale *noun* a musical scale of whole steps, with two half-steps that occur between the third and fourth steps and the seventh and eighth steps. {**may** jər **skayl**}

make *verb* (made, making, makes) 1. to bring into being by building from separate parts. *Tammy made a model airplane.* 2. to create or pro-duce. *Stop making so much noise!* 3. to cause to be. *The news that his friend was moving made him sad.* 4. to force to. *The teacher made him stop pulling her hair.* 5. to add up to. *Two and six make eight.* 6. to put in order; prepare. *I will make the bed if you'll do the dishes.* / *He makes dinner for us every night.* 7. to earn. *Mr. Marks makes a lot of money.* 8. to arrive at or in time for. *Did you make the bus?* 9. (informal) to be accepted as a member. *Did you make the tennis team?* *noun* the kind, type, or brand of something. *What make of car is that?* {**mayk**}

• **make believe**
to pretend or imagine. *We made believe that we were a king and a queen.*

• **make it**
to do well; succeed. *She made it as a writer.*

• **make up**
1. to form or be the parts of. *My family is made up of my parents, my brother, and me.* 2. to pay back. *I made up for being mean to Mom by washing the dishes without being asked.* 3. to become friends again after a quarrel. *I made up with my friend the day after our fight.*

Synonyms

These words share a meaning with *make*, verb 1:

form To form is to shape or give structure to something that has no definite shape. *He formed the clay into a human figure.*

build To build is to make from various materials. *American pio-neers built houses from mate-rials that were readily available.*

prepare Prepare is often used when speaking of food being made from various ingredients. *He prepared the soup from the meat and vegetables he had bought.*

construct Construct is often used to speak of making things on a larger scale. *The bridge was constructed last summer.*

assemble To assemble is to make something by putting together parts that were made to fit with each other. *She assem-bled the motor by following the instructions.*

Human Body   Human Mind   Everyday Life   History and Culture   Communication

make·be·lieve *noun* pretending; imagination. *He said he saw a ghost in the attic, but that was just make-believe.* *adjective* not real; imaginary. *My little brother has a make-believe friend.* {mayk bə leev}

make·shift *noun* something used for a short time or in place of the usual thing. *When the table broke, we used a box as a makeshift. adjective* made to meet a need; not meant to last. *They built a makeshift tent out of blankets.* {mayk shihft}

make·up *noun* 1. lipstick, powder, and other cosmetics put on the face to change the way it looks or to make it look better. *On Halloween she put on makeup to make herself look like a tiger.* 2. the way the parts of something are put together. *The makeup of Congress was half Democrat and half Republican.* 3. the basic character of a person. *It was not in his makeup to be mean to others.* {may kuhp *or* mayk uhp}

ma·lar·i·a *noun* a disease carried by mosquitoes that causes chills, fever, and sweating. {mə layr ee ə} malarial, adj., malarian, adj., malarious, adj.

Word History *Malaria* comes from Italian words that mean "bad air." The disease was thought to come from the damp air around swamps.

Ma·la·wi *noun* a country in southeastern Africa. Lilongwe is the capital of Malawi. {mə lah wee} Malawian, n., adj.

Ma·lay·sia *noun* a country in southeastern Asia. Kuala Lumpur is the capital of Malaysia. {mə lay zhə *or* mə lay shə} Malaysian, n., adj.

male *adjective* of or having to do with men or boys. *noun* a person or animal of the masculine sex; one that fathers rather than bears offspring. {mayl}

Homophone Note Are you looking for the word *mail*? *Male* and *mail* sound alike but have different meanings.

Ma·li *noun* a country in western Africa. Bamako is the capital of Mali. {mah lee} Malian, n., adj.

mal·ice *noun* the wish to harm others; ill will. *Gossip is sometimes an act of malice.* {mǎl ihs}

ma·li·cious *adjective* caused by or showing a wish to harm. *That is a malicious lie!* {mə lihsh əs} maliciousness, n.

ma·lign *verb* (maligned, maligning, maligns) to speak badly of or tell harmful lies about. *Some students maligned the speaker because they didn't like his ideas.* {mə liyn}

ma·lig·nant *adjective* 1. meant to cause harm; evil. *She lost her job because of his malignant lies.* 2. likely to cause death. *The doctor removed the malignant growth from the man's back.* {mə lihg nənt}

mall *noun* 1. an open space covered with grass and lined with shade trees. A mall is used for walking and enjoyment. *After a busy day at work, we enjoyed a quiet stroll on the mall.* 2. a large indoor area that contains shops and restaurants; shopping center. A mall can also be an outdoor shopping area that is closed off to traffic. {mawl}

Homophone Note Are you looking for the word *maul* (a heavy hammer)? *Mall* and *maul* sound alike but have different meanings.

mal·lard *noun* (mallard or mallards) a common wild duck. The male has a shiny dark green head and neck. {mǎl ərd}

mal·let *noun* 1. a hammer with a short handle and a wooden head, used as a tool. 2. a similar tool with a long handle, used to drive a ball in croquet or polo. 3. a light hammer with a round head, used to strike notes on a musical instrument. *A musician uses mallets to play the xylophone.* {mǎ liht}

mal·nu·tri·tion *noun* the condition of not having enough food or not having the right kind of food for good health. *In some countries, malnutrition is a leading cause of death.* {mǎl nooh trih shən}

malt *noun* barley that is allowed to sprout, then used to make beer and ale. {mawlt}

malted milk *noun* a drink made of milk and dried malt mixed with ice cream. {mawl tihd mihlk}

ma·ma *or* **mamma** *noun* (informal) mother. {mah mə}

mam·mal ❶ *noun* a warm-blooded animal with fur or hair on its skin and a skeleton inside its body. Mammal mothers produce milk to feed their babies. Most mammals have four legs or two arms and two legs. Dogs, cows, elephants, mice, whales, and humans are all mammals. {mǎm əl}

mam·moth *noun* a very large extinct mammal closely

 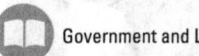
A B C D E F G H I J K L **M** N O P Q R S T U V W X Y Z

Mammals

All mammals have furry skin for at least part of their life cycle. We humans call our fur "hair". Even whales have a few hairs on their skin.

Mammals feed their young milk. Marsupials such as kangaroos and opossums have pouches where very young babies drink milk while being carried safely by their mothers.

bison

human

dolphin

sheep

kangaroo

horse

monkey

lion

lemur

zebra

rhinoceros

dog

pig

elephant

related to elephants. Mammoths were much bigger than elephants and had shaggy black fur and long tusks that curved upward. Several kinds of mammoths lived in the Northern Hemisphere until the end of the last Ice Age. They were hunted by Old Stone Age humans, who may have caused their extinction over ten thousand years ago. *adjective* enormous; huge; gigantic. {**măm** əth}

man *noun* (men) 1. an adult male human being. 2. human beings in general; the human race. *Man cannot live without air and water.* 3. a playing piece used in board games. *I beat him in checkers by jumping his last man.* *verb* (manned, manning, mans) to supply with people to do a job. *More sailors were needed to man the ship.* {**măn**}

man·age *verb* (managed, managing, manages) 1. to direct or control. *She manages a bookstore.* / *He managed the lively horse with calming words.* 2. to succeed in doing in spite of problems. *Anna finally managed to escape.* 3. to handle or use. *Police officers are taught how to manage guns in a safe way.* {**măn** ihj}

Word History *Manage* is from an Italian word that means "to handle or direct (a horse)."

man·age·ment *noun* 1. the act or process of managing. *The school runs smoothly under the principal's management.* 2. the person or persons in charge of a business or other group. *A raise in pay was announced by the management.* {**măn** ihj mənt}

man·ag·er ● *noun* the person who controls a business or acts as the leader of a plan or project. *My father is the manager of a dry-cleaning business.* / *Sally is the manager of the junior high's science fair.* {**măn** ih jər}

man·a·tee *noun* a mammal that lives in the ocean and has flippers for front legs. Manatees eat sea plants and are very gentle. Different kinds of manatees live near the shores or in coastal rivers of Florida, the West Indies, Central America, South America, and West Africa. They are also called sea cows. {**măn** ə tee}

man·da·rin *noun* 1. a public official, or a person of high rank or influence in imperial China. 2. (capitalized) the dialect spoken in Beijing, China. Standard Chinese is based on Mandarin. 3. a small, somewhat flattened citrus fruit with a loose skin and flesh of yellow to reddish orange; mandarin orange. {**măn** də rihn}

man·date *noun* 1. the command or message given to an elected official by the votes of the people. *The mayor received a mandate to build a new city park.* 2. an order or command given by a person or group that has authority. *The prince refused to obey the king's mandate.* *verb* (mandated, mandating, mandates) to require by law or because of a vote of the people. *The voters mandated that the polluted lake be cleaned up.* {**măn** dayt}

man·do·lin *noun* a musical instrument in the lute family with four or five pairs of strings that are usually strummed. {**măn** də lihn *or* măn də **lihn**} mandolinist, n.

mane ● *noun* the long hair on the back and sides of the neck of horses, lions, and other animals. {**mayn**}

Homophone Note The words *mane*, *main*, and *Maine* sound alike but have different meanings.

ma·neu·ver *noun* 1. a planned movement of soldiers, ships, or tanks. *The general ordered that the maneuver take place at dawn.* 2. a movement or change in direction that requires skill. *The boxer's maneuvers took our breath away.* 3. a clever or sly plan. *She won the chess match with a brilliant maneuver.* *verb* (maneuvered, maneuvering, maneuvers) 1. to make a careful change in the position of. *The captain maneuvered the ship into the harbor.* 2. to change position or location as part of a plan. *The other people in line were angry when we maneuvered in front of them.* {mə **nooh** vər} maneuverability, n., maneuverable, adj.

Word History *Maneuver* is from two Latin words that mean "hand" and "to do work."

man·ga·nese *noun* a dense, hard, grayish white metal that is one of the chemical elements. It is used in making steel and is also used to color glass purple. (symbol: Mn) {**măng** gə nees *or* **măng** gə neez}

man·ger *noun* a box or trough from which farm animals eat. {**mayn** jər}

man·gle *verb* (mangled, mangling, mangles) to damage badly by cutting, crushing, or tearing apart. *A huge truck backed into their car and mangled its front end.* / *Try not to mangle the milk carton when you open it.* {**măng** gəl} mangler, n.

A B C D E F G H I J K L **M** N O P Q R S T U V W X Y Z

a
b
c
d
e
f
g
h
i
j
k
l
m
n
o
p
q
r
s
t
u
v
w
x
y
z

man·go *noun* (mangoes or mangos) a sweet, juicy fruit with a long shape and smooth yellow-orange skin. {**măng** goh}

man·hole *noun* an opening in a street large enough for a person to climb into to make repairs underneath the street. A manhole is usually covered by a lid. *A worker climbed down into the manhole to repair a broken water pipe.* {**măn** hohl}

man·hood *noun* the condition of being an adult male. *When he reached manhood, his parents bought him a car.* {**măn** huud}

ma·ni·ac *noun* 1. a person who is insane. 2. a wild, violent person who is a danger to others. 3. a person who has a very strong desire or enthusiasm for something. *She is a maniac about bicycle racing. / I am a maniac for Mexican food.* {**may** nee ăk}

man·i·cure *noun* a treatment for the fingernails that includes trimming, shaping, and sometimes polishing. *verb* (manicured, manicuring, manicures) to give a manicure to. *Who manicures your nails?* {**măn** ih kyoor}

Man·i·to·ba *noun* a Canadian province between Ontario and Saskatchewan. Its capital is Winnipeg. {**măn** ih **toh** bə} Manitoban, n.

Word History *Manitoba* probably comes from the Cree words *manitou bou,* which mean "the narrows of the Great Spirit." The province was named after Lake Manitoba, which becomes very narrow near its center where the waves make loud noises on the rocks. The Cree believe the sounds come from a huge drum beaten by the spirit *Manitou.*

man·kind *noun* the whole human race. *It is up to mankind to make the world a safe place to live.* {**măn kiynd** or **măn kiynd**}

man-made *adjective* made or formed by human beings; not natural. *Nylon is a man-made material.* {**măn mayd**}

man·ner *noun* 1. a way of doing something; style. *She arranged the books in a careful manner.* 2. a way of behaving or acting. *The teacher yelled at him for his lazy manner.* 3. (plural) correct behavior. *The children were instructed in manners before their audience with the king.* {**măn** ər}

Homophone Note Are you looking for the word *manor* (an estate)? *Manner* and *manor* sound alike but have different meanings.

man·oeu·vre *noun or verb* a spelling of **maneuver** used in Canada and Britain. See **maneuver.** {mə **nooh** vər}

man-of-war *noun* (men-of-war) 1. an old word for **warship.** 2. see **Portuguese man-of-war.** {**măn** əv **wohr**}

man·or *noun* a large estate and its main house or mansion. *The manor has several flower gardens.* {**măn** ər}

Homophone Note The words *manor* and *manner* sound alike but have different meanings.

man·sion *noun* a large, grand, expensive home. {**măn** shən}

man·slaugh·ter *noun* the crime of killing a person without

planning or meaning to do so. *The driver was charged with manslaughter after the car accident that killed two people.* {**măn** slaw tər}

man·tel *noun* 1. a frame around the sides and top of a fireplace. 2. a shelf at the top of a fireplace; mantelpiece. {**măn** təl}

Homophone Note The words *mantel* and *mantle* sound alike but have different meanings. To learn why it's safer to have a mantel over the fire than a mantle, look up *mantle.*

man·tle ⏺ *noun* 1. a full, sleeveless cloak. 2. the layer of the earth that lies between the crust and the core. {**măn** təl}

Homophone Note The words *mantle* and *mantel* sound alike but have different meanings.

man·u·al ⏺ *adjective* 1. having to do with use of the hands. *Long ago, people used only manual skills to make clothing.* 2. worked by hand. *He used a manual switch to turn on the machine.* *noun* a book of instructions. *Maggie read the manual to learn how to use the new software.* {**măn** yoo əl} manually, adv.

man·u·fac·ture *verb* (manufactured, manufacturing, manufactures) 1. to make by machine in a large quantity. *This factory manufactures car parts.* 2. to invent; make up. *We had to manufacture a good excuse for being late.* *noun* the making of goods on a large scale. *Switzerland is famous for the manufacture of chocolate.* {**măn** yə **făk** chər} manufacturer, n.

ma·nure *noun* the waste matter of animals, such as cows and horses, used to fertilize the

 Human Body   Human Mind    Everyday Life    History and Culture   Communication

soil and help plants grow. {mə **noohr**}

man·u·script ⊘ *noun* a piece of writing prepared by the author before it becomes a printed article or book. *He put his manuscript in an envelope and mailed it to the magazine editor.* {**mă** nyə **skrihpt**}

man·y *adjective* (more, most) a large number of. *At the animal shelter, there were many kittens that needed homes.* *noun* a large number of persons or things. *Many in the group could not go on the trip because they became ill.* *pronoun* a great number of people or things. *Although the firefighters worked hard to save the animals, many died.* {**mehn** ee}

Synonyms
These words share a meaning with *many*, noun 1:
plenty

map ⊙ *noun* a picture of a particular area of the earth or sky drawn or printed to scale on a flat surface. *The students located the Niger river on a map of Africa.* *verb* (mapped, mapping, maps) 1. to make a map of. *That company maps forest areas.* 2. to lay out carefully (often followed by "out"). *We mapped out a plan for winning the contest.* {**măp**}

ma·ple *noun* 1. a tree with notched leaves and hard wood, grown for its beauty, wood, or sweet sap. *The maple in our yard gives us shade from the sun.* 2. the wood of maple trees. *Maple is used to build fine furniture.* {**may** pəl}

maple syrup *noun* a thick, sweet liquid made by boiling the sap of maple trees. {**may** pəl **sih** rəp}

Mar. *abbreviation* an abbreviation for **March**.

mar·a·thon *noun* 1. a race in which participants run 26.2 miles. 2. any contest or activity that requires great effort over a long period of time. *Their climb up the mountain was a real marathon.* {**mar** ə **thŏn**}

mar·ble *noun* 1. a kind of stone that can be cut and polished to a hard, shiny surface. There are many kinds and colors of marble. 2. a very small ball made of colored glass, used in children's games. {**mar** bəl}

March *noun* the third month of the year. March has thirty-one days. Spring begins in March for people who live north of the equator. {**march**}

Word History *March* comes from *Mars*, the name of the god of war in Roman mythology.

march *verb* (marched, marching, marches) 1. to walk with steady, regular steps together with others. *Several school bands marched in the Flag Day parade.* 2. to walk in a way that shows strength and determination. *I marched into his office and demanded some answers.* *noun* 1. the act or an instance of marching. *Thousands of people took part in a march for civil rights.* 2. a piece of music suited for marching to. *The brass band played a march by John Philip Sousa.* {**march**}

Word History The word *march* comes from an early French word that means "to trample."

mare *noun* an adult female horse, donkey, zebra, or related animal. {**mayr**}

mar·ga·rine *noun* a food used in place of butter. Margarine is made of vegetable oil, milk, coloring, and other ingredients. {**mar** jə rihn}

mar·gin *noun* 1. an edge or the area near it; border. *Wildflowers were planted at the margin of the woods. / It is not safe to drive along the margin of a highway.* 2. the blank space between written or printed matter and the edge of a page. *The teacher asked us to leave a wide margin on our papers.* 3. an extra amount allowed in case more than expected is necessary. *Leave a margin of time when driving in stormy weather.* {**mar** jihn}

mar·i·gold *noun* a garden plant that bears yellow, orange, or red and yellow blossoms. {**mar** ih gohld}

ma·ri·na ⊙ *noun* a harbor that has docks, services, and supplies for pleasure boats. {mə **ree** nə}

ma·rine *adjective* 1. having to do with the sea; living in or caused by the sea. *Marine charts will help us plan our trip across the ocean. / All marine snakes are poisonous.* 2. having to do with ships. *They picked up marine supplies at the dock.* *noun* (sometimes capitalized) a member of the U.S. Marine Corps. {mə **reen**}

Marine Corps *noun* a branch of the U.S. armed forces, trained for combat on land, at sea, and in the air. {mə **reen** kohr}

mar·i·on·ette *noun* a puppet whose arms and legs are worked with strings or wires. {mar ee ə **neht**}

mar·i·time *adjective* 1. of or relating to sea ships or navi-

gation of the sea. *Ships and boats must obey maritime laws.* 2. living or located in or near the sea. *Norway and Denmark are maritime countries.* {mar ih **tiym**}

mark[1] *noun* 1. something, such as a spot or scar, that can be seen on a surface. *The wet glass left a mark on the table.* 2. a symbol or sign. *Did you remember to put a question mark at the end of that sentence?* 3. a goal or target. *His work didn't come up to the mark.* 4. a grade on a school paper or test. *I am proud of my high marks in school.* *verb* (marked, marking, marks) 1. to put a mark on. *Barb's muddy fingers marked the front door.* 2. to label or be a feature of. *His graceful movements marked him as a dancer.* 3. to show limits (often followed by "off"). *This line marks off our property.* 4. to give a grade to. *Mr. Frank marks our homework before he returns it.* 5. to pay attention to; mind. *Mark well what I am saying.* {**mark**}

mark[2] *noun* a unit of money in Germany. {**mark**}

mar·ket *noun* 1. a place where goods are sold. *Fruits and vegetables are sold at the farmers' market.* 2. the desire for a type of good or service. *There is a big market for skis* in areas that get a lot of snow. *verb* (marketed, marketing, markets) 1. to buy in a market; shop. *The women of the village marketed every Saturday morning.* 2. to sell or offer for sale. *That company*

markets camping goods on-line. {**mar** kiht} marketer, n.

mar·ket·place *noun* an area, either outside or inside, where goods are sold. *She sold baskets in the marketplace.* {**mar** kiht **plays**}

mark·ing *noun* 1. a mark or marks. *The trees had markings to show which ones should be cut down.* 2. a pattern of marks or coloring on a plant or animal. *The raccoon has interesting markings on its face and tail.* {**mar** king}

mar·ma·lade *noun* a jam that contains bits of fruit and peel. {**mar** mə **layd**}

ma·roon[1] *adjective* having a dark brownish-red color. {mə **roohn**}

ma·roon[2] *verb* (marooned, marooning, maroons) to leave on an island or coast, far from other people; abandon. *The pirates marooned the children on a desert island.* {mə **roohn**}

> **Word History** *Maroon*[1] and *maroon*[2] are homographs; they are spelled the same but have different meanings and different origins. *Maroon*[1] comes from a French word that means "a chestnut" (a deep red-brown nut). *Maroon*[2] comes from an early Spanish word that meant "a mountain-top." Five hundred years ago, in the West Indies, a "maroon" was an escaped slave who had fled to the mountains to escape Spanish rulers. The word "maroon" later came to mean "to abandon someone in a wild and isolated place."

mar·quee *noun* a canopy or a covering like a roof over the entrance to a building. The marquee over a theater shows the title of the current play or film and sometimes the names of the actors. {**mar** kee}

mar·quis *noun* (marquises or marquis) a nobleman whose rank is above an earl or count and below a duke. {**mar** kee or **mar** kwihs}

mar·quise *noun* 1. the wife or widow of a marquis. 2. a woman who holds a title equivalent to that of a marquis. {**mar** keez}

mar·riage ○ *noun* 1. the state of being joined as husband and wife. *Their marriage lasted for fifty years.* 2. the ceremony in which a man and a woman are joined as husband and wife; wedding. *After the marriage, guests were invited to dance and eat wedding cake.* {**mar** ihj}

mar·row *noun* the soft tissue that fills the hollow centers of most bones. One type of marrow makes new blood cells. {**mar** oh}

mar·ry *verb* (married, marrying, marries) 1. to take in marriage; take as one's husband or wife. *John is going to marry Tina on Saturday.* 2. to join as husband and wife. *The priest married them in a garden behind the church.* {**mar** ee}

Mars *noun* 1. the god of war in Roman mythology. In Greek mythology, Mars is called Ares. 2. the seventh largest planet in the solar system and fourth in distance from the sun. Mars is known as "the red planet" because of its unusual color. {**marz**}

marsh *noun* a low, wet area, often thick with tall grasses; bog. *My brother and I hunted for frogs in the marsh.* {**marsh**}

mar·shal *noun* 1. in the United States, an officer of a federal court whose duties are like

 Human Body   ? Human Mind   Everyday Life   History and Culture   Communication

a b c d e f g h i j k l **m** n o p q r s t u v w x y z

those of a sheriff. 2. a person who is in charge of a parade or ceremony. *verb* (marshaled, marshaling, marshals) to arrange in proper order. *He marshaled his facts before presenting the case.* {<u>mar</u> shəl} marshalcy, n., marshaler, n., marshalship, n.

Homophone Note The words *marshal* and *martial* sound alike but have different meanings.

marsh·mal·low *noun* a soft, spongy candy. {<u>marsh</u> mehl oh *or* <u>marsh</u> măl oh}

mar·su·pi·al ● *noun* an animal in a group of mammals that includes kangaroos and opossums. Female marsupials have a pouch outside their belly where the mother carries her young after they are born. Most marsupials live in Australia. {<u>mar</u> <u>sooh</u> pee əl}

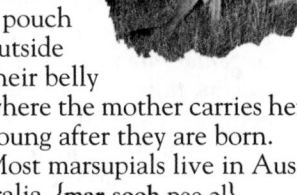

mar·tial *adjective* having to do with war or military activities. *During the war, the city was under martial law.* {<u>mar</u> shəl} martialism, n., martialist, n., martially, adv.

Homophone Note Are you looking for the word *martial* (concerning war)? *Martial* and *marshal* sound alike but have different meanings.

Word History *Martial* comes from *Mars*, the Roman God of war.

mar·tin *noun* a bird of the swallow family. Martins eat insects while in flight. {<u>mar</u> tihn}

Martin Luther King Day *noun* a holiday observed in honor of the birthday of Martin Luther King, Jr., an important black leader of the civil rights movement. Martin Luther King Day is the third Monday of January. {<u>mar</u> tihn <u>looh</u> thər <u>king</u> day}

mar·tyr *noun* 1. a person who chooses to die or be killed rather than give up his or her religion. 2. a person who suffers or is killed for defending some belief or cause. *Martin Luther King was a martyr in the cause of justice.* {<u>mar</u> tər}

mar·vel *noun* a thing, person, or event that causes wonder or amazement. *His invention is a mechanical marvel.* *verb* (marveled, marveling, marvels) to be filled with wonder or amazement. *Sara marveled at the sound of the ocean inside the shell.* {<u>mar</u> vəl}

mar·vel·ous *adjective* 1. causing wonder or amazement. *It was a marvelous sight to see the space shuttle take off.* 2. of the highest quality; splendid. *You have done a marvelous job and should be very proud.* {<u>mar</u> və ləs} marvelously, adv.

Mar·y·land *noun* a state in the eastern United States. Maryland lies on the Atlantic Coast between Delaware and Virginia. Its capital is Annapolis. (abbreviated: MD) {<u>mar</u> ih lənd} Marylander, n.

Word History King Charles I of England named *Maryland* in honor of his wife, Henrietta Maria, when it was founded as a colony in 1632.

mas·car·a *noun* a paste put on the eyelashes to make them look darker. {mə <u>skar</u> ə}

mas·cot *noun* an animal, person, or thing that is considered to bring good luck. Mascots are sometimes kept by a sports team. {mă <u>skŏt</u> *or* mă skət}

mas·cu·line *adjective* 1. having to do with men or boys; male. *"John" is a masculine name.* 2. having qualities considered to be typical of men or boys. *My father has a deep, masculine voice.* {<u>măs</u> kyə lihn} masculineness, n.

mash *noun* 1. a mixture of grain or meal and hot water that is fed to farm animals. 2. any soft, mushy mixture. *She crushed the turnips into a mash.* *verb* (mashed, mashing, mashes) 1. to crush or smash. *The closing door mashed her finger.* 2. to make into a soft mass by grinding or crushing. *This tool will mash potatoes.* {<u>măsh</u>}

mask *noun* 1. a covering that hides all or part of the face. *Latisha and Bill wore monster masks for Halloween.* 2. anything that hides or covers up. *He hid his sad feelings behind the mask of a smile.* *verb* (masked, masking, masks) 1. to cover up or hide. *They masked the ugly wall with many colorful posters.* / *She masked her true feelings.* 2. to cover with a mask. *The children masked their faces for the costume party.* {<u>măsk</u>}

ma·son *noun* a person whose work is building with stone, brick, or cement. {<u>mă</u> sən}

A
B
C
D
E
F
G
H
I
J
K
L
M
N
O
P
Q
R
S
T
U
V
W
X
Y
Z

ma·son·ry *noun* (masonries) something built by a mason with stone, brick, or cement. {**may** sən ree}

mas·quer·ade *noun* 1. a party or ball at which the guests wear costumes and masks. 2. a false or pretended appearance. *Her masquerade of confidence fooled everyone.* *verb* (masqueraded, masquerading, masquerades) 1. to try to be or look like another person. *She was masquerading as a member of the royal family.* 2. to wear a costume. *The children masqueraded as ghosts and monsters.* {mă skə **rayd**} masquerader, n.

mass *noun* 1. a large amount or number. *A mass of people walked into the hall.* 2. a body of matter that has no form. *He took a mass of wet clay and began to shape it.* 3. the greater part of anything. *The mass of the students wanted more lunch choices in the cafeteria.* 4. weight, size, or bulk. *The mass of this brick is greater than the mass of that book.* 5. (plural) the total body of common people (usually with "the"). *The royal family listened to the will of the masses.* *adjective* having to do with the masses or large numbers of people. *TV is a form of mass communication.* *verb* (massed, massing, masses) to come together to form a mass. *The people massed in front of the governor's door.* {măs}

Mass *noun* a religious ceremony in the Roman Catholic and certain other churches. At a Mass, people seek communion with God. {măs}

Mas·sa·chu·setts *noun* a state in the northeastern United States on the Atlantic Coast. Its capital is Boston. (abbreviated: MA) {mă sə **chooh** sihts}

> **Word History** *Massachusetts* means "at the Great Hill" in an Algonquin language. English settlers named the Massachusetts Bay Colony after the Massachusetts Algonquins who were living there.

mas·sa·cre *noun* the killing of a large number of people or animals in a cruel and violent manner. *The emperor ordered the massacre of the villagers.* *verb* (massacred, massacring, massacres) to kill in great numbers in a cruel manner. *Many Native Americans were massacred by U.S. soldiers.* {mă sə kər}

mas·sage ⚫ *noun* a treatment of the body that involves rubbing and kneading to help the blood circulate better and to relax muscles. *verb* (massaged, massaging, massages) to treat by rubbing the body; give a massage to. *She massaged my back.* {mə **sahzh** or mə **sahj**, n., mə **sahzh** or mə **sahj**, v.} massager, n.

mas·sive *adjective* 1. having a very large amount of matter; big and heavy; solid. *The wrestler has a massive chest.* / *They used a crane to move the massive rock.* 2. making a strong impression because of great size or strength. *Visitors gazed up at the fort's massive stone walls.* {**măs** ihv} massively, adv., massiveness, n.

mass media *plural noun* those ways of communicating that reach large numbers of people, such as newspapers, magazines, television, and radio. {**măs** **mee** dee ə}

mass production *noun* the making of goods in large numbers by means of machines or assembly lines. {**măs** prə **duhk** shən}

mass trans·it *noun* a system of public transportation that carries people from place to place within a city by bus and train. {**măs** **trăns** iht}

mast *noun* 1. a long upright pole that rises from the bottom of a sailboat or ship to support the sails and lines. 2. a tall, upright pole, such as those on which flags are flown. {măst}

mas·ter *noun* 1. a person with power or control. *The captain is the master of the ship.* 2. a person who owns a slave or animal. 3. a person who is very skilled or expert. *Those carpenters are masters at building furniture.* *adjective* being very skilled or expert. *Our neighbor is a master carpenter.* *verb* (mastered, mastering, masters) 1. to become skilled in or expert at. *He mastered chess quickly.* 2. to control; overcome. *You must learn to master your anger.* {**măs** tər} masterless, adj.

mas·ter·ful *adjective* having or showing the skill of a master or expert. *The violinist gave a masterful performance.* {**măs** tər fəl} masterfully, adv., masterfulness, n.

mas·ter·ly *adjective* showing the ability or skill of a master; expert. *He did a masterly job of painting the house.* {**măs** tər lee} masterliness, n.

mas·ter·piece ⚫ *noun* 1. a work of art of the highest quality. *Beethoven's Fifth and Ninth symphonies are masterpieces.* 2. a person's finest piece of work. *The artist considers this*

 Human Body   Human Mind   Everyday Life    History and Culture   Communication

painting to be her masterpiece. {**măs** tər pees}

mas·to·don *noun* a very large extinct mammal. Several kinds of mastodons lived in Africa, Europe, Asia, and North America tens of thousands of years ago. The last kind of mastodon became extinct at the end of the last Ice Age. Mammoths and modern elephants may have developed from earlier mastodons. {**măs** tə **dŏn**} mastodonic, adj.

mat 🔵 *noun* 1. a piece of material that is used as a covering to protect a floor or other surface. 2. a small piece of material that is placed under a vase or dish, used to protect a surface or as a decoration. 3. a pad that is placed on the floor to protect people who are practicing gymnastics, wrestling, or other sports. 4. a thick mass of tangled hair or fur. *verb* (matted, matting, mats) 1. to cover with or turn into a tangled mass. *A large growth of weeds matted the garden.* 2. to become a tangled mass. *Her hair mats easily.* {**măt**}

match¹ 🔵 *noun* a thin strip of wood or cardboard with a material on the end that burns when it is struck against something. {**măch**}

To win the scavenger hunt you must find four **matching matches**.

match² 🔵 *noun* 1. a person or thing that is very like another. *This chair is a match of the one in your living room.* 2. a person able to equal another in a contest or other activity. *He was no match for her in the spelling bee.* 3. a contest or game. *We won the tennis match because we practiced hard.* *verb* (matched, matching, matches) 1. to be the same as or equal to. *His skill as a baseball player does not match hers.* 2. to bring together because of being equal or alike. *The object of the game is to match pairs of cards.* 3. to be similar in size, color, or other qualities. *Your socks don't match.* {**măch**}

mate *noun* 1. a marriage partner; husband or wife. *My parents say that they are mates for life.* 2. one of two matched things. *Where is the mate to this shoe?* 3. one of a pair of animals that live or have offspring together. *The dog helped his mate take care of their puppies.* 4. a close friend or companion. *My brother and his mates love spending time together.* 5. an officer on a ship who ranks directly below the captain; first mate. *verb* (mated, mating, mates) to come together to have offspring. *The dogs mated and had ten puppies.* {**mayt**} mateless, adj.

ma·te·ri·al *noun* 1. anything used for building or making something else. *The materials for the tree house included wood, metal, and rope.* 2. cloth or fabric. *Karin wears clothes made only of cotton material.* 3. any group of ideas or information that can be used to create a larger work. *The writer used the diaries of her grandfather and great-grandfather as material for a*

novel. adjective of or relating to matter; physical. *The material world is filled with the wonders of nature.* {mə **teer** ee əl}

ma·ter·nal *adjective* 1. of, having to do with, or like a mother. *She showered her children with maternal love.* 2. related on the mother's side of the family. *I went to see my maternal grandfather.* {mə **tuhr** nəl}

math *noun* short for **mathematics.** {**măth**}

math·e·mat·i·cal *adjective* of or having to do with mathematics. *He enjoys working on mathematical problems.* {măth ə **măt** ih kəl} mathematic, adj., mathematically, adv.

math·e·ma·ti·cian *noun* a person who works in mathematics. {măth ə mə **tih** shən *or* măth mə **tih** shən}

math·e·mat·ics 🔵 *noun* (used with a singular verb) the study of numbers, amounts, shapes, and the relationship between them, using symbols to represent these things. Arithmetic, algebra, and geometry are some branches of mathematics. {măth ə **măt** ihks *or* măth **măt** ihks}

Word History *Mathematics* comes from *mathema*, an ancient Greek word that means "learning or knowledge."

mat·i·nee *or* **matinée** *noun* a morning or afternoon performance of a play, film, or the like. {măt ih **nay**}

mat·ter 🔵 *noun* 1. all substances that contain atoms and take up space. *Matter includes solids, liquids, and gases.* 2. a topic of concern or interest. *I want to discuss the matter of my allowance.* 3. difficulty or trouble. *What's the matter?* 4. something written or printed. *I have lots of*

A
B
C
D
E
F
G
H
I
J
K
L
M
N
O
P
Q
R
S
T
U
V
W
X
Y
Z

a
b
c
d
e
f
g
h
i
j
k
l
m
n
o
p
q
r
s
t
u
v
w
x
y
z

reading matter about U.S. history. *verb* (mattered, mattering, matters) to be of importance. *It does not matter to me.* {**măt** ər}

mat·tress *noun* a large pad made of a strong cloth filled with soft material such as cotton, hair, straw, or foam rubber, and used as a cushion to sleep on. {**măt** rihs}

ma·ture ⊕ ⊙ *adjective* 1. fully grown. *A mature oak tree is very tall.* 2. fully developed in mental or physical qualities. *It was very mature of you to let your brother have the front seat.* *verb* (matured, maturing, matures) 1. to cause to become ripe or fully developed. *Plenty of sun and water matured the apples.* 2. to come to full or complete physical development. *She matured more rapidly than her friends.* {mə **choohr** or mə **toohr**, adj., mə **choohr** or mə **toohr**, v.} maturely, adv., matureness, n.

maul *noun* a heavy hammer, sometimes with a wooden head, used to drive stakes, piles, or the like. *verb* (mauled, mauling, mauls) to hurt by beating or through other rough treatment. *The police were afraid of getting mauled by the angry crowd.* {**mawl**} mauler, n.

Homophone Note The words **maul** and **mall** sound alike but have different meanings.

Mau·ri·tan·i·a *noun* a country in western Africa. Nouakchott is the capital of Mauritania. {**mŏr** ih **tayn** ee ə or **mŏr** ih **tayn** yə} Mauritanian, n., adj.

mauve *noun* the color that comes from mixing blue, purple, and white paint. {**mohv**}

max·i·mum *noun* (maximums) the largest possible amount or number. *A maximum of two people are allowed on the swing.* *adjective* being or having the largest amount or number possible. *What is the maximum weight this elevator can hold?* {**măk** sih məm}

may *auxiliary verb* 1. to be allowed to. *You may not run in the halls at school.* (See *can¹*.) 2. to be likely to (used to express possibility or probability). *Don't forget your umbrella. It may rain this afternoon.* 3. used to express a sincere wish or desire. *May all your dreams come true.* {**may**}

May *noun* the fifth month of the year. May has thirty-one days. {**may**}

Word History *May* was probably named after *Maia*, a goddess in Roman mythology.

Ma·ya *noun* (Maya or Mayas) 1. a member of an ancient Indian civilization of Mexico and Central America that was discovered and destroyed by Europeans in the 1500s. 2. a member of a modern Indian people who are descendants of this civilization. {**mah** yə} Mayan, n., adj.

may·be *adverb* perhaps; possibly. *Maybe the sun will come out today.* {**may** bee}

may·fly *noun* (mayflies) 1. a delicate insect with two pairs of wings. The mayfly larva may live for several years in a stream, lake, or river. Once it turns into an adult, it lives for only a few hours. 2. a fishing lure made to look like the adult form of this insect. {**may** fliy}

may·on·naise *noun* a thick dressing of oil, vinegar or lemon juice, seasonings, and egg yolks. Mayonnaise is used in salads, sandwiches, and other dishes. {**may** ə nayz or **may** ə **nayz** or **may** nayz}

may·or *noun* the head of government in a village, town, or city. {**may** ər or **mayr**}

May·pole *noun* a high pole decorated with flowers and ribbons, around which people dance to celebrate May Day. {**may** pohl}

The great attraction of this year's state fair was the 100 acre **maze** built entirely within walls of **maize**.

maze *noun* a complicated network of paths or passages between high walls or thick hedges which are often designed to confuse those who travel through them. {**mayz**}

Homophone Note Are you looking for the word **maize** (Indian corn)? **Maze** and **maize** sound alike but have different meanings.

  Human Body ? Human Mind 👕 Everyday Life ⚑ History and Culture ☎ Communication

mb *abbreviation* an abbreviation for **megabyte**, or megabytes.

M.B.A. *abbreviation* a degree earned in accounting or other areas of business after one or two years of additional courses following college. M.B.A. is an abbreviation for "Master of Business Administration."

M.D. *abbreviation* Doctor of Medicine. M.D. is the abbreviation for the Latin words "medicinae doctor."

MD or **Md.** *abbreviation* an abbreviation for **Maryland**.

me *pronoun* the form of I that is used as the object of a verb or preposition. *The dress fits me well. / Will you let me talk now?* {<u>mee</u>}

ME or **Me.** *abbreviation* an abbreviation for **Maine**.

mead·ow *noun* an open field of grass that is growing wild or is used for pasture or to grow hay. *The sheep grazed in the meadow.* {<u>meh</u> doh}

mead·ow·lark *noun* one of two kinds of North American songbirds that nest in open fields and have a sweet, musical song. A meadowlark has a yellow breast marked with black. {<u>meh</u> doh <u>lark</u>}

mea·ger *adjective* low in amount, strength, or value; poor. *The family lives on meager resources.* {<u>mee</u> gər}

meal[1] 🔵 *noun* 1. an occasion when food is prepared and eaten at a specific time. *Twenty people were at our house for our Thanksgiving meal.* 2. the food itself. *A healthy meal includes vegetables.* {<u>meel</u>}

meal[2] 🔵 *noun* corn, oats, or other grain that has been ground. *She made taco shells from the meal.* {<u>meel</u>}

mean[1] 🔵 *verb* (meant, meaning, means) 1. to have as a goal or purpose; intend. *I mean to leave soon.* 2. to have intentions or have in mind. *Carl means well, even though his actions don't show it.* 3. to intend to express. *What do you mean?* 4. to have a particular sense. *The word "tomorrow" means "the day after today."* 5. to cause as a result. *The teacher's arrival means recess is over.* 6. to have a certain degree of importance. *She means a great deal to her friends.* {<u>meen</u>}

mean[2] 🔵 *adjective* (meaner, meanest) 1. not nice; nasty or cruel. *The mean wizard turned the children into toads.* 2. low in quality or poor in appearance. *The peasants lived in mean cottages far from the castle.* {<u>meen</u>}

mean[3] 🔵 *noun* 1. something halfway between two extremes. *Can't we find a mean between getting rid of the TV and watching TV five hours a day?* 2. the value that is found by dividing the sum of a set of numbers by the number of items added; average. *The mean of 3, 4, and 8 is 5.* *adjective* being between extremes or in the middle. *At five feet tall, Jane is above the mean height for girls in fifth grade.* {<u>meen</u>}

me·an·der *verb* (meandered, meandering, meanders) 1. to wind back and forth. *The stream meanders through the*

hillside. 2. to wander in speech or movement without a goal or direction. *The lost puppy meandered through the streets.* {mee <u>ăn</u> dər}

mean·ing *noun* 1. what is meant by a word; definition. *What is the meaning of "centipede"?* 2. importance or value. *What he said had no meaning for me.* {<u>mee</u> ning}

meant *verb* past tense and past participle of **mean**[1]. {<u>mehnt</u>}

mean·time *noun* the time that is in between. *You go ahead, and in the meantime I will wait for the others to arrive.* {<u>meen</u> tiym}

mean·while *adverb* at the same time; during or in the time between. *I drove all night to get home; meanwhile my family was waiting up for me.* {<u>meen</u> wiyl}

mea·sles *noun* (used with a singular or plural verb) a very contagious disease that causes a fever and red spots on the skin. Measles usually affects children and does not last a long time. {<u>mee</u> zəlz}

meas·ure 🔵🔵 *noun* 1. exact length, weight, or amount of something. *The measure of the box was three feet in length and one foot in width.* 2. an instrument or system for making exact measurements. *A ruler is a measure that is marked off in inches or centimeters.* 3. (usually plural) something done to get a particular result. *The police force is taking serious measures to stop speeding downtown.* 4. limit. *There was no measure to his kindness.* 5. a unit of rhythm in music; bar. *The first melody lasts for sixteen measures and then is repeated.* *verb* (measured, measuring, measures) 1. to make exact measurements. *He measured the room before*

A
B
C
D
E
F
G
H
I
J
K
L
M
N
O
P
Q
R
S
T
U
V
W
X
Y
Z

 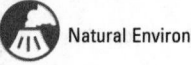

buying a rug. 2. to mark off and separate from the whole (often followed by "out"). *Jan measured out two cups of sugar.* 3. to have as a measurement. *This board measures three feet in length.* {<u>meh</u> zhər}

meas·ure·ment ❶ *noun* 1. the act or process of measuring. *The tailor's measurements were all wrong.* 2. the specific size of something that is determined by measuring. *The measurements of the room are 10 feet by 20 feet.* {<u>meh</u> zhər mənt}

meat ❷ ❶ *noun* 1. the flesh of animals when used as food. 2. the inner part, which can be eaten, in contrast to the shell or skin. *She peeled the orange to get to its meat.* 3. the most important part of a speech or written work. *The meat of the story was in the fourth chapter, where things really got interesting.* {<u>meet</u>}

Homophone Note Are you looking for the word **meet**? **Meat** and **meet** sound alike but have different meanings.

meat·ball *noun* chopped or ground meat that is seasoned, shaped into a small ball, and cooked, often in a sauce. {<u>meet</u> bawl}

me·chan·ic *noun* a worker who is skilled in making, using, and repairing tools, machines, and motors. {mə <u>kăn</u> ihk}

me·chan·i·cal *adjective* 1. made of or having to do with machines. *Cars have many mechanical parts.* 2. produced or run by a machine or machines. *He did not need*

batteries for his mechanical toy. 3. without spirit or energy; like a machine. *The telephone operator did his job in a mechanical way.* {mə <u>kăn</u> ih kəl} mechanically, adv.

mech·an·ism *noun* 1. the whole or parts of a machine, mechanical system, or device. *When the clock stopped, he wound the mechanism.* 2. the working or moving part or process that causes a result. *Enzyme action is the mechanism by which food is digested.* {<u>mehk</u> ə nihz əm}

med·al *noun* a flat, small piece of metal that has a design or words stamped on it, used as an honor or reward. *She won a gold metal in the long jump.* {<u>mehd</u> əl}

Homophone Note Are you looking for the word **meddle** (to interfere)? **Medal** and **meddle** sound alike but have different meanings.

med·dle *verb* (meddled, meddling, meddles) to take part in matters that concern someone else, without being asked; interfere. *Don't meddle with my plans for the weekend.* {<u>mehd</u> əl} meddler, n.

Homophone Note The words **meddle** and **medal** (an award) sound alike but have different meanings.

me·di·a ❸ *noun* 1. a plural of **medium**. *This sculptor works in several media, including clay, marble, and bronze.* 2. the means of distributing information to large numbers of people, through newspapers, magazines, radio, and television; mass media. *The media gave much attention to Princess Diana's death.* {<u>mee</u> dee ə}

Word History *Media* comes from a Latin word for "middle."

me·di·ae·val *adjective* another spelling of **medieval**. {<u>mee</u> dee ee vəl or meh <u>dee</u> vəl}

me·di·an *noun* 1. the middle value in a series of numbers. *Five is the median of the set of numbers 1, 3, 5, 7, 9.* 2. a strip of land that divides two lanes of traffic going in opposite directions on a highway. {<u>mee</u> dee ən}

med·ic *noun* a medical doctor, intern, or student. {<u>mehd</u> ihk}

med·i·cal *adjective* of or having to do with the study or practice of medicine. *After years of medical school, he finally became a doctor.* {<u>mehd</u> ih kəl} medically, adv.

med·i·cine ❸ *noun* 1. a drug or other substance used to treat a disease, injury, pain, or other symptoms. *She took medicine every day for her cough.* 2. the science of identifying and treating disease or injury. *Ms. Smyth has a job in the field of medicine.* {<u>mehd</u> ih sən}

medicine man *noun* a person who heals, or is thought to have spiritual powers, among North American Indians and some other peoples. {<u>mehd</u> ih sən măn}

me·di·e·val or **mediaeval** *adjective* of, or having to do with the Middle Ages. *Charlemagne was a great ruler of medieval Europe.* {<u>mee</u> dee ee vəl or mih <u>dee</u> vəl}

med·i·tate *verb* (meditated, meditating, meditates) to think calmly, deeply, and at length (sometimes followed by "on" or "upon"). *He meditated on the choice between dropping out of school and*

working at the gas station. {**mehd** ə **tayt**}

Med·i·ter·ra·ne·an *noun* see **Mediterranean Sea.** {**mehd** ih tə **ray** nee ən}

Mediterranean Sea *noun* a large sea connected to the Atlantic Ocean. It is bordered by Europe on the north, Asia on the east, and Africa on the south. {**mehd** ih tə **ray** nee ən **see**}

me·di·um *noun* (media or mediums) 1. a substance that is a means of passing on a force or an effect. *Copper wire is a medium for conducting electricity.* 2. a means or tool. *Money is a medium of exchange.* 3. a middle thing or condition. *There must be a happy medium.* 4. a way or method of communicating or expressing, such as painting, music, or language. *Ansel Adams is an artist whose medium is photography.* 5. the natural or social environment in which one lives. *Bread is an excellent medium for growing mold.* / *Water is a lobster's medium.* *adjective* middle or average in size or amount. *He has a medium build.* / *The medium soda is smaller than it used to be.* {**mee** dee əm}

med·ley *noun* (medleys) 1. a musical piece that uses the melodies from several different pieces of music. 2. a mixture of things that are not usually placed together. *He used a medley of foods to make the soup.* {**mehd** lee}

meek *adjective* 1. doing what others want; not standing up for oneself; tame. *The meek child always did as he was told.* 2. patient and mild; not easily angered or upset, even when treated unfairly. *The Bible says, "the meek shall inherit the earth."* {**meek**}

meet *verb* (met, meeting, meets) 1. to come face to face with; encounter. *Mel met Ann while he was waiting for the bus.* 2. to be introduced to. *My parents will meet my teachers tonight.* 3. to satisfy. *The trip met all of their hopes for a wonderful vacation.* 4. to gather together for a meeting. *The chess club will meet next Tuesday.* 5. to come together; join. *Look for a sign where the two roads meet.* *noun* a gathering of athletes for a contest. *Jefferson High School won the track meet.* {**meet**}

Homophone Note Are you looking for the word *meat* (the flesh of animals)? *Meet* and *meat* sound alike but have different meanings.

meet·ing *noun* 1. the act of coming face to face; encounter. *Our meeting at the library was a pleasant surprise.* 2. an assembly of persons for a particular purpose. *The Acme tool company has weekly staff meetings.* 3. a coming together or joining. *A large rock marked the meeting of two paths.* {**mee** ting}

meg·a·byte *noun* a unit of measurement equal to 1,048,576 bytes. Megabytes are used to measure the amount of electronic information that can be stored by a computer. {**mehg** ə **biyt**}

meg·a·phone *noun* a device shaped like a cone that is held by a person and used to direct the sound of a voice and make it louder. {**mehg** ə **fohn**}

mel·an·chol·y ❷ *noun* a feeling of sadness or depression. *Sam was overcome with melancholy when his grandmother died.* *adjective* 1. suffering from or likely to suffer from sadness or depression. *She is a melancholy girl who spends a lot of time by herself.* 2. causing such feelings. *The loss of our pet cat was a melancholy event.* {**meh** lən **ko** lee}

mel·low *adjective* (mellower, mellowest) 1. soft, juicy, and full of flavor, because it is ripe. *The peaches have turned mellow.* 2. rich and not bitter from being aged. *The chef added mellow cheese to the potatoes.* 3. soft in tone. *He played a mellow song on the guitar.* / *There was a mellow light from the candles.* 4. having the knowledge and sympathy that often comes with experience and age; being without anger. *Our father has gotten mellow over the years and doesn't get upset easily.* *verb* (mellowed, mellowing, mellows) to make or become mellow. *Many fine wines mellow with age.* {**mehl** oh} mellowness, n.

me·lo·di·ous *adjective* 1. having a pleasant melody. *I was awakened by the melodious song of birds.* 2. having melody. *You have a melodious voice.* {mə **loh** dee əs}

mel·o·dy ❷ *noun* (melodies) 1. musical sounds in a pleasant order and arrangement. 2. a musical phrase or theme made up of a sequence of single tones. {**mehl** ə dee}

mel·on *noun* a fruit that grows on vines and has a hard outer layer and thick, juicy flesh. {**meh** lən}

melt *verb* (melted, melting, melts) 1. to change from a solid to a liquid state through heat or pressure. *The wax*

A B C D E F G H I J K L **M** N O P Q R S T U V W X Y Z

melted as the candle burned. 2. to fade or mix, as from one state to another (often followed by "away," "in," or "into"). *Our fortune is melting away. / He melted into the crowd.* 3. to experience a sudden feeling of love or affection. *Her smile made him melt.* 4. to cause to gradually blend into solution. *He melted the butter before putting it on the popcorn.* {**mehlt**}

mem·ber *noun* 1. one of the people or things in a particular group. 2. a part, such as a leg or arm, of a human or other animal. {**mehm** bər}

mem·ber·ship *noun* 1. the state of being a member. *He pays for a membership at the health club.* 2. the number of people in a particular group. *The book club has a large membership.* {**mehm** bər **shihp**}

mem·brane 🟢🔵 *noun* a thin layer of tissue found in living things. Some kinds of membranes cover the outside or inside of organs. Other membranes separate or connect different parts of the body. *The toes of frogs are connected by membranes.* {**mehm** brayn}

me·men·to *noun* (mementos or) something, such as a small object, that reminds a person of a past event, period of time, or relationship. *He kept the rock as a memento of his visit to the mountains.* {mə **mehn** toh}

mem·o *noun* (memos) a short form of **memorandum**. {**mehm** oh}

mem·o·ra·ble *adjective* worth remembering because special. *It was a memorable day when the First Lady visited our town.* {**mehm** ə rə bəl} memorably, adv.

mem·o·ran·dum *noun* (memorandums or memoranda) 1. a short written note to help a person remember something. 2. a written message between two workers or groups of workers in the same business or other organization. {**mehm** ə **răn** dəm}

me·mo·ri·al 🟢🔵 *noun* a ceremony, custom, building, or statue to honor a dead person or past event. *The town held a memorial for the soldiers who died in the Vietnam war.* {mə **mohr** ee əl}

Memorial Day *noun* a U.S. holiday to honor dead soldiers, usually held on the last Monday in May. {mə **mohr** ee əl **day**}

mem·o·rize *verb* (memorized, memorizing, memorizes) to learn completely so as to hold in the memory. *He didn't need to read the words of the song because he had memorized them.* {**mehm** ə **riyz**} memorization, n.

mem·o·ry 🟢 *noun* (memories) 1. the ability to remember an experience. *My memory is very good when it comes to the events in my childhood.* 2. an experience, person, or thing that one remembers. *I have happy memories of my visit with you.* 3. the length of time that is remembered. *Nothing in memory was as thrilling as the first time men walked on the moon.* 4. the part of a computer that stores information. {**mehm** ə ree}

men *noun* plural of **man**. {**mehn**}

men·ace *noun* that which presents a danger or threat. *That thief is a menace to society.* *verb* (menaced, menacing, menaces) to direct a threat against. *He was menaced by a bully after*

school. {**mehn** ihs} menacingly, adv.

> **Word History** *Menace* comes from a Latin word that means both "threats" and "points that stick out."

mend *verb* (mended, mending, mends) 1. to repair or fix. *The carpenter mended the hole in the fence.* 2. to correct or make better. *Mend your ways or you will be in trouble.* 3. to get back one's health; improve or heal. *It took him a long time to mend from the flu.* *noun* the act or result of mending; repair. *The mend in his shirt can hardly be seen.* {**mehnd**} mendable, adj.
• **on the mend**
getting better after an injury. *The basketball player's broken leg is on the mend.*

me·no·rah *noun* a candlestick with seven or nine branches, used in Jewish worship. {mə **nohr** ə}

-ment *suffix* 1. a suffix that shows an action or process. *Management is the act of managing.* 2. a suffix that means the result of an action. *When something is measured, the result is a measurement.*

men·tal *adjective* 1. of or having to do with the operation of the mind. *The very old man still had all his mental powers.* 2. done by or present in the mind. *He did some mental arithmetic and realized it would take him a year to save up for a motorcycle.* 3. of, or having to

Human Body   ? Human Mind   Everyday Life   History and Culture   Communication

do with an illness of the mind. *She had to stay in a mental hospital for a month.* {**mehn** təl}

men·tion *verb* (mentioned, mentioning, mentions) to speak of briefly or in passing. *Sam mentioned that he is going away for the weekend.* *noun* a brief, casual statement, said in passing. *She made a mention of next week's concert.* {**mehn** shən} mentionable, adj.

men·tor *noun* someone who is a guide and teacher to another person. {**mehn** tər}

men·u *noun* a list of foods served at a restaurant. {**mehn** yoo}

me·ow *noun* the sound made by a cat. *verb* (meowed, meowing, meows) to make the sound of a cat. {mee **ow** or **myow**, n., mee **ow** or **myow**, v.}

mer·chan·dise ☁ *noun* goods for buying and selling. *He looked at the merchandise at the clothing store.* {**muhr** chən diyz or **muhr** chən **diys**} merchandiser, n.

mer·chant *noun* 1. one who buys goods and sells them for a profit. 2. an owner of a shop. *The jewelry merchant on the corner is closing his shop.* *adjective* having to do with trade or business. *Our office is in the merchant building.* {**muhr** chənt}

merchant marine *noun* 1. the ships of a country that are used in business or trade. 2. the people who work on such ships. {**muhr** chənt mə **reen**}

mer·cu·ry *noun* (mercuries) 1. a heavy, silver-white metal that is one of the chemical elements. Mercury is liquid at room temperature. It is used in thermometers and barometers. (symbol: Hg) 2. (capitalized) the messenger of the gods in Roman mythology. In Greek mythology, Mercury is called Hermes. 3. (capitalized) the planet of the solar system that is nearest to the sun. Mercury is the second smallest planet. {**muhr** kyə ree}

mer·cy *noun* (mercies) 1. kind treatment by someone who has some power over another. *The principal showed mercy to the students who broke the window.* 2. something to be thankful for. *The early arrival of spring was a mercy we did not expect.* {**muhr** see}

• **at the mercy of** completely in the power of. *The prisoners are at the mercy of the warden.*

Word History *Mercy* comes from a Latin word that means "reward or wages."

mere *adjective* (merest) being neither more nor better than what is spoken of. *She is a mere beginner. / He is a mere fool.* {**meer**}

merge *verb* (merged, merging, merges) 1. to cause to be combined or joined. *The two airlines merged into one larger company.* 2. to come together or mix into a single unit or whole. *The sea and sky merged on the horizon.* {**muhrj**}

merg·er *noun* the combining of two or more companies into one, or the transfer of the property of one company to another. {**muhr** jər}

me·rid·i·an *noun* 1. an imaginary circle around the earth that passes through the North and the South Pole, or either half of such a circle from one pole to the other. 2. the highest point or peak; zenith. {mə **rih** dee ən}

mer·it *noun* 1. worth or high quality. *That idea has merit.* 2. (plural) the facts of a legal matter, apart from personal feelings or issues related to procedure. *He won the case on its merits.* *verb* (merited, meriting, merits) to be worthy of or deserve. *Such good work merits praise.* {**mehr** iht}

mer·maid *noun* an imaginary sea creature with the head and upper body of a woman and the lower body and tail of a fish. {**muhr** mayd}

mer·ry ❓ *adjective* (merrier, merriest) cheerful and happy, or likely to be so. *She is always such a merry person.* {**mehr** ee}

mer·ry-go-round *noun* a round platform that turns by the power of a machine and has seats in the form of animals that go up and down on poles. People pay for rides on a merry-go-round. {**mehr** ee goh **rownd**}

mer·ry·mak·ing *noun* the act of laughing and having fun. *The last day of school was a time for parties and merrymaking.* {**mehr** ee **may** king}

a
b
c
d
e
f
g
h
i
j
k
l

m

n
o
p
q
r
s
t
u
v
w
x
y
z

me·sa *noun* a high piece of land with a flat top and steep sides, found in Mexico and the southwest area of the United States. {<u>may</u> sə}

Word History *Mesa* is a Spanish word that means "table."

mesh *noun* 1. a material or article made of fiber woven to form open spaces, as in a net. *She wore stockings made of mesh.* 2. any of the open spaces in a net or wire screen. *verb* (meshed, meshing, meshes) 1. to work or cause to work by connecting. *When you pedal your bike, the chain meshes the teeth on the gears to drive the wheels forward.* 2. to fit together or be coordinated with. *Martha's plans meshed with the rest of the family's.* {<u>mehsh</u>}

mess *noun* 1. a state of being dirty or not neat. *I had to agree that my room was a mess.* 2. a state of confusion or trouble. *The office was a mess after the secretary quit.* 3. a meal eaten by a group, or the room in which this meal is eaten. *Soldiers eat their meals in the mess.* *verb* (messed, messing, messes) 1. to make dirty or not tidy (often followed by "up"). *The dogs messed up the garden by digging up the plants.* 2. to spoil or confuse (often followed by "up"). *Losing my ticket messed up my plan to go to the concert.* {<u>mehs</u>}

• **mess around** (informal) to spend time without any purpose. *The boys in the neighborhood like to mess around after school.*

Word History The word *mess* comes from an early French word that means "an amount of food put out at a meal."

mes·sage *noun* 1. spoken or written information, sent from one person or group to another. A message is usually delivered by someone or something other than the person who wants to communicate. *I found a message on the table saying that my parents would be home late.* / *There are three messages on the answering machine.* 2. a public speech or other official communication. *The mayor gave his yearly message in front of City Hall.* {<u>mehs</u> ihj}

mes·sen·ger *noun* a person who carries and delivers messages and packages. {<u>meh</u> sən jər}

mess·y *adjective* (messier, messiest) 1. dirty or not tidy. *Please clean your messy room!* 2. difficult, embarrassing, or unpleasant. *They are having a very messy argument.* {<u>mehs</u> ee} messiness, n.

met *verb* past tense and past participle of **meet**[1]. {<u>meht</u>}

me·tab·o·lism 🔵 *noun* the processes in plants and animals by which food is changed into energy or used to make cells and tissues. *Mice have a high rate of metabolism.* {mə <u>tăb</u> ə lihz əm} metabolic, adj.

met·al 🔵 *noun* a group of elements that exhibit similar characteristics such as the ability to conduct heat or electricity. Most metals may be shaped under heat or pressure. Iron, silver, copper, and gold are metals. *Most of the chemical elements are metals.* {<u>meht</u> əl} metallike, adj.

Word History *Metal* is from an ancient Greek word that means "mine."

me·tal·lic *adjective* 1. made of or containing metal. *He dug up a metallic rock.* 2. of or like metal. *She painted the model airplane with sparkling metallic paint.* {mə <u>tăl</u> ihk}

met·a·mor·phic *adjective* 1. having to do with a change in form. *To become a butterfly, a caterpillar goes through a metamorphic stage.* 2. showing or related to changes in the structure of rock. *Marble is one type of metamorphic rock.* {meh tə <u>mohr</u> fihk}

met·a·mor·pho·sis 🔵 *noun* (metamorphoses) 1. the changes in form of some living things as they grow. The change from caterpillar to butterfly or from tadpole to frog are examples of metamorphoses. 2. a complete change of form, parts, or character. *The vacant lot went through a metamorphosis as the new playground was built.* {meh tə <u>mohr</u> fə sihs}

met·a·phor *noun* a statement in which a word or phrase is used to compare one thing with another so that they appear to be similar. *"Life is a bowl of cherries"* is an example of a metaphor, in which life is compared to something sweet and pleasing. {<u>meh</u> tə fohr} metaphorical, adj., metaphorically, adv.

Word History The word *metaphor* comes from an ancient Greek word that meant "to transfer or carry over to something else." When you use a metaphor, it is as though you are taking the word for one thing and transferring it to another thing that you perceive to be like the first thing.

me·te·or *noun* A piece of matter traveling through space. Upon entering a planet's

 Human Body    Human Mind    Everyday Life   History and Culture   Communication

atmosphere, a meteor can be seen as a bright streak in the sky and is called a meteorite or shooting star. {<u>mee</u> tee ər *or* <u>mee</u> tee **ohr**}

me·te·o·rite *noun* a mass of stone or metal from a meteor that has landed on earth. {<u>mee</u> tee ər **iyt**}

me·te·or·ol·o·gy 🜨 *noun* the science that studies the earth's weather and atmosphere. {mee tee ə <u>rŏl</u> ə jee}

-me·ter *suffix* a suffix that means "measure," or "a device for measuring." *Diameter is a measure across the widest part of a circle. / A speedometer is a device for measuring speed.*

me·ter[1] *noun* the basic unit of length of the metric system, equal to one hundred centimeters or 3.28 feet. {<u>mee</u> tər}

me·ter[2] *noun* 1. a particular rhythmic pattern or the rhythmic pattern of units or feet of poetry. *Renaissance poets wrote poems in strict meter.* 2. the rhythmic measure in music provided by the division of notes into equal units or bars. *There are four beats to a measure in this meter.* 3. the time value and number of beats for each note in a musical composition. {<u>mee</u> tər}

me·ter[3] *noun* a device that measures or records distance, speed, time, quantity, or degree. *Many homes have gas and electricity meters.* {<u>mee</u> tər}

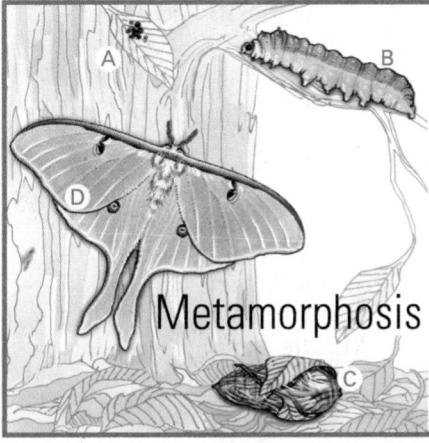

meth·ane *noun* a gas made of carbon and hydrogen atoms that is stored in and collected from the earth. Methane is used for heating and cooking in the form of natural gas. {<u>meth</u> **ayn**}

meth·od *noun* 1. a way of doing something. *He has his own method of working.* 2. system or order in one's actions. *There was no method to how she planted the garden.* {<u>mehth</u> əd}

me·tre *noun* a spelling of **meter**[1] (unit of measure) and **meter**[2] (musical time) used in Canada and Britain. See **meter**. {<u>mee</u> tər}

met·ric *adjective* having to do with the metric or international system of measurement. *The book weighed one kilogram on a metric scale.* {<u>meh</u> trihk}

metric system *noun* a system of weights and measures that is based on the number ten. *The metric system uses the meter to measure length, the gram for weight, and the liter for volume.* {<u>meh</u> trihk **sihs** təm}

met·ro·nome *noun* a device that marks a regular period of time with a clicking sound. A metronome can be set at different speeds and is used by musicians to keep time during practice. {<u>meht</u> rə **nohm**}

me·trop·o·lis *noun* a large city. *New York City is a metropolis.* {mə <u>trŏp</u> ə lihs}

met·ro·pol·i·tan *adjective* having to do with a large city and the communities around it. *The metropolitan area of Miami was warned about the hurricane.* {meh trə <u>pŏl</u> ih tən}

mew *noun* a small cry made by a cat. *verb* (mewed, mewing, mews) to make a small cry like that of a cat. *The just born baby mewed in her arms.* {**myoo**}

Mex·i·can *adjective* of or having to do with Mexico or its people. *noun* a person who was born in or is a citizen of Mexico. {<u>mehks</u> ih kən}

Mex·i·co *noun* a country in North America south of the

The life cycle of the luna moth shows complete metamorphosis. The adult moth lays her eggs on a leaf A. The eggs hatch into caterpillars B. The caterpillar is the moth larva. It feeds on leaves and grows larger. Once the caterpillar is fully grown, it spins a cocoon of silk around itself in the leaves under the tree C. Inside the cocoon it becomes a pupa. The pupa does not move or eat. Its body is changing form. It develops a hard outer skeleton and it grows wings. After several months, an adult moth emerges from the cocoon D. The adult moth has no mouth and does not eat. Its only function is to mate, and its life is very short. The adult female lays her eggs, and the life cycle begins again.

Metamorphosis

United States. Mexico City is the capital of Mexico. {**mehks** ih koh}

Mexico City *noun* the capital city of Mexico. {**mehks** ih koh **sih** tee}

mg *abbreviation* an abbreviation for **milligram**, or milligrams.

Mg symbol of the chemical element **magnesium**.

MI or **Mich.** *abbreviation* an abbreviation for **Michigan**.

mi *noun* the syllable that indicates the third tone of a musical scale. {**mee**}

mi. *abbreviation* an abbreviation for **mile**, or miles.

MIA *abbreviation* an abbreviation for "missing in action," used to describe members of the armed forces who became missing during a war.

mice *noun* plural of **mouse**. {**miys**}

Mich·i·gan *noun* 1. a state of the north central United States. Its capital is Lansing. (abbreviated: MI) 2. Lake Michigan, one of the Great Lakes. It lies between this state and Wisconsin. {**mihsh** ə gən} Michigander, n.

Word History *Michigan* is the French spelling of *michigama*, the Chippewa word for "large lake." The state was named after Lake Michigan.

mi·crobe *noun* a life form that can only be seen with a microscope. Many microbes are germs that cause disease. {**miy** krohb}

mi·cro·chip *noun* a tiny plate of silicon that holds many electronic parts. Microchips are used to run computers and other devices. {**miy** kroh chihp}

mi·cro·com·put·er *noun* a small computer that is designed for use by a single person. Microcomputers are used by

small business and in homes. They are also known as personal computers. {**miy** kroh kəm **pyoo** tər}

mi·cro·or·gan·ism ❶ *noun* any life form so small that it can only be seen with a microscope. Microorganisms include bacteria, viruses, and many protozoans. {**miy** kroh **ohr** gə nih zəm}

mi·cro·phone *noun* a device that changes sound waves into electronic signals. Microphones are used to make sounds louder or to broadcast or record them. {**miy** krə **fohn**}

Word History The word *microphone* was formed from two ancient Greek words: *mikros* (small) and *phone* (sound). A microphone makes little sounds bigger.

mi·cro·scope ❶ ❷ *noun* an instrument that uses a lens to make very small objects larger so that they can be seen by the eye. *We looked at a drop of pond water with a microscope.* {**miy** krə skohp}

mi·cro·scop·ic *adjective* 1. too small to be seen with the eye. *Viruses are microscopic.* 2. having to do with a microscope. *The doctor did a microscopic study of my blood.* {**miy** krə **skŏp** ihk} microscopically, adv.

mi·cro·wave *noun* a type of radio wave with a high frequency. Microwaves are used to send messages over long distances and in special ovens to heat food and liquids. {**miy** kroh **wayv**}

mi·cro·wave ov·en *noun* an oven that cooks or heats food or beverages quickly

using high-frequency radiation. {**miy** kroh wayv **uhv** ən}

mid *preposition* amid or among. {**mihd**}

mid- *prefix* a prefix that means "middle." *Midnight is the middle of the night.*

Mi·das *noun* a king in Greek mythology who was given the power to turn everything he touched into gold. {**miy** dəs}

mid·day *noun* the middle part of the day. *Lunch is usually served at midday.* {**mihd** day}

mid·dle *adjective* halfway between two things, places, or points. *He is the middle child. / I sleep in the middle bed.* *noun* the middle location, point, or position. *The boat is in the middle of the lake.* {**mihd** əl}

middle age *noun* the period of human life between youth and old age, or the years between forty and sixty-five. *What will you do when you reach middle age?* {**mihd** əl **ayj**}

mid·dle-aged *adjective* having to do with the period of human life between youth and old age, or the years between forty and sixty-five. *Are your parents middle-aged?* {**mihd** əl ayjd}

Middle Ages *plural noun* the period of European history between ancient times and the Renaissance, from A.D. 500 to A.D. 1500. *The great castles of Europe were built during the Middle Ages.* {**mihd** əl **ay** jihz}

middle class *noun* the class of people between the rich and the poor. *Most of the people in my home town were in the middle class.* {**mihd** əl **klăs**} middle-class, adj.

Middle East *noun* the region along the southeastern and eastern border of the Medi-

 Human Body  Human Mind   Everyday Life  History and Culture Communication

terranean Sea, from Libya in North Africa to Afghanistan in Asia. {mihd əl eest} Middle Eastern, adj.

Middle English *noun* the English language as it was spoken and written between the years 1100 and 1500. *Middle English was the language of the great poet, Geoffrey Chaucer.* {mihd əl ing glihsh}

Middle West *noun* see **Midwest**. {mihd əl wehst}

midg·et *noun* a very small person with the same body proportions as a normal adult; dwarf. {mihj iht}

mid·land *noun* the interior part of a region or country. *We traveled from the midland to the coast of England on our vacation. adjective* having to do with an interior land area. *Ithaca is a midland city of New York State.* {mihd lənd}

mid·night *noun* twelve o'clock at night. {mihd niyt}
• **burn the midnight oil** to stay awake very late for work or study. *She burned the midnight oil the night before the test.*

midst *noun* 1. the middle of a situation or event. *In the midst of the confusion, he lost his wallet.* 2. the middle of a large gathering. *We spotted him in the midst of the crowd.* {mihdst}

mid·way *adverb or adjective* halfway between; in the middle. *The two boats met at the midway point of the river. / We had driven midway when the car ran out of gas. noun* the area or strip where food stands, shows, and games are found at fairs, circuses, and carnivals {mihd way}

Mid·west *noun* the north central part of the United States from the Rocky Mountains through Ohio, Kansas, and Missouri; Middle West. {mihd wehst}

might[1] *auxiliary verb* 1. used to show that something is possible. *She might not want cream in her coffee, so you had better ask her.* 2. past tense of **may**. {miyt}

might[2] *noun* great force or power; ability. *He lifted the rock with all his might.* {miyt}

> **Homophone Note** The words *might* and *mite* sound alike but have different meanings. To learn why a sled dog would rather have great might than mites, look up *mite*.

might·y *adjective* (mightier, mightiest) 1. having or showing great power or strength. *The lion gave a mighty roar.* 2. very large in size or power; huge. *A mighty fortress stood on the hill.* {miy tee} mightiness, n.

mi·grant *adjective* moving from place to place. *At one time, some Native Americans were migrant people. noun* 1. a person who travels from place to place to find work. *Migrants harvest grapes, apples, lettuce, and other farm crops.* 2. an animal that travels according to the seasons from one region to another. *The robin is a migrant that flies south in the winter.* {miy grənt}

mi·grate *verb* (migrated, migrating, migrates) 1. to move from one region into another. *Their grandparents migrated from Ohio to Florida.* 2. to change habitat or location. *Geese migrate to the south when the weather gets cold. / Many Mexicans migrate north to the United States to find work.* {miy grayt}

mild *adjective* (milder, mildest) 1. gentle or calm. *She is a mild girl, compared to her wild sister.* 2. not harsh; not extreme. *We had a mild winter.* 3. not harsh in taste. *These are mild peppers.* {miyld} mildly, adv., mildness, n.

mil·dew *noun* a fungus that grows on plants and materials made from living things. *Mildews often look like powder.* {mihl dooh} mildewy, adj.

mile *noun* 1. a unit of length equal to 5,280 feet or 1.609 kilometers. (abbreviated: mi.) 2. a very great length or distance. *Sam hit the ball a mile.* {miyl}

mile·age *noun* 1. distance in miles. *What is the mileage from your house to your cousin's house?* 2. the number of miles that a vehicle can travel per unit of fuel. *Our new car gets better mileage than our old one.* {miy lihj}

mile·stone *noun* 1. a stone or mark that shows the distance in miles to a specific place. *The milestone showed the bicyclists how far they had gone.* 2. an important event or turning point in history or in a person's life. *The discovery of electricity was a milestone in the history of science.* {miyl stohn}

mil·i·tar·y ⬤ *adjective* 1. having to do with war. *Some countries depend on the military power of the United States.* 2. having to do with soldiers or armies. *Dan wore a military uniform. noun* the armed forces. *Did you serve in the military?* {mihl ə tayr ee} militarily, adv.

mi·li·tia *noun* a group of trained citizens who are not soldiers but can serve as members of the military in an emergency. *The National Guard is a militia in the United States.* {mə lih shə} militiaman, n.

a

b

c

d

e

f

g

h

i

j

k

l

m

n

o

p

q

r

s

t

u

v

w

x

y

z

milk 🏃❓ *noun* 1. a white liquid produced by female mammals as food for their young. 2. this liquid produced by cows or female goats and collected for people to drink. 3. a white liquid or juice produced by certain plants. *This recipe calls for coconut milk.* *verb* (milked, milking, milks) 1. to get milk from a female mammal. *Helen milked the cows.* 2. to drain of energy, information, or money in a way that is not fair. *They milked him for every cent he had.* {**mihlk**}

Milky Way *noun* the galaxy that contains the earth, the sun, and the solar system. It can be seen in the night sky as a long, cloudy group of stars. {**mihl** kee **way**}

mill *noun* 1. a building where raw materials are changed into basic products such as steel or lumber. 2. a machine that grinds or crushes whole or solid substances. *Please grind these coffee beans in the coffee mill.* *verb* (milled, milling, mills) 1. to grind or crush in a mill. *They milled the grain into flour.* 2. to move about without any purpose (often followed by "around" or "about"). *The crowd milled around near the entrance.* {**mihl**} millable, adj.

mil·len·ni·um *noun* (millenniums or millennia) a unit of time equal to one thousand years. {mə **lehn** ee əm}

mil·ler *noun* a person who owns or works in a mill. {**mihl** ər}

mil·li- *prefix* a prefix that means "one thousandth." *A meter contains one thousand millimeters.*

mil·li·gram *noun* a unit of weight equal to one thousandth of a gram. (abbreviated: mg) {**mihl** ə **grăm**}

mil·li·me·ter *noun* a unit of length equal to one thousandth of a meter or 0.03937 inch. (abbreviated: mm) {**mihl** ə **mee** tər}

mil·lion *noun* (millions [or] million) 1. the number that is equal to one thousand times one thousand; 1,000,000. 2. a very large number that is not named exactly. *Millions of people came to the Olympic Games.* *adjective* 1. being one million in number. *He won a million dollars in the lottery.* 2. being a very large number that is not named exactly. *There must be a million mosquitoes in the swamp.* {**mihl** yən} millionth, [adj.], n.

mil·lion·aire *noun* a person whose money and property amount to at least a million dollars. {**mihl** yə **nayr**}

mil·li·pede or **millepede** *noun* a small animal that has a narrow body like a worm, with a hard outer layer. The body of the millipede is divided into many segments, and most segments have two pairs of legs. The millipede is a kind of arthropod. {**mihl** ə **peed**}

mim·e·o·graph *noun* a machine that makes copies of written material using an ink printing process. *Ms. Lamb used a mimeograph to copy our test.* {**mihm** ee ə **grăf**}

mim·ic *verb* (mimicked, mimicking, mimics) 1. to copy or imitate the actions, expression or speech of another person. *The chimp mimicked our movements.* 2. to make fun of a person by imitation. *My sister gets angry when I mimic her.* *noun* a person who imitates others. *The mimic got lots of laughs from the audience.* {**mihm** ihk}

min. *abbreviation* an abbreviation for **minute**, or minutes.

min·a·ret *noun* a tall, thin tower on a mosque. A minaret has a platform near the top from which a person calls Muslims to prayer. {mihn ə **reht**}

mince *verb* (minced, mincing, minces) to cut into very small, fine pieces. *The cook minced the onion before adding it to the sauce.* {**mihns**}

mince·meat *noun* a mixture of chopped apples, raisins, currants, orange peel, and sometimes meat, that is used as a filling for pies. {**mihns meet**}

mind ❓ *noun* 1. the part of a person that thinks, understands, remembers, directs, and feels. *My mind is full of names and dates from history class.* 2. memory or awareness. *Please keep Arnie's request in mind.* 3. desire or opinion. *I have a mind to travel.* *verb* (minded, minding, minds) 1. to take care of. *Are you minding the children?* 2. to not like or object to. *I don't mind your coming with me.* 3. to pay attention to and obey. *Children should mind their parents and teachers.* {**miynd**}

• **make up one's mind** to decide. *Michelle made up her mind to move to Florida.*

mine[1] *pronoun* the one or ones that belong to me. *That book is mine.* {**miyn**}

mine[2] *noun* 1. a deep hole or area of holes made in the earth. Minerals such as gold, coal, or precious stones are dug out of mines. 2. a large supply or good source. *He is a mine of information.* 3. a kind of bomb hidden in the ground or in water. A mine is set off by putting pressure on it or by lighting its fuse. *verb*

🏃 Human Body   ❓ Human Mind   👕 Everyday Life   🏳 History and Culture   📞 Communication

(mined, mining, mines) 1. to dig in the earth for minerals such as gold or coal; work in a mine. *He mines in the mountains all day, hoping to strike it rich.* 2. to lay bombs under. *The enemy mined the field.* {**miyn**}

min·er *noun* a person whose job is to obtain coal or other minerals from a mine. {**miy** nər}

Homophone Note Are you looking for the word *minor*? *Miner* and *minor* sound alike but have different meanings.

min·er·al ❶ *noun* a substance formed in the earth that is not of an animal or a plant. *Gold, silver, iron, and salt are minerals.* *adjective* having to do with or full of minerals. *Do you drink mineral water? / The land is rich with mineral deposits.* {**mihn** ər əl}

Mi·ner·va *noun* the goddess of wisdom and art in Roman myth. In Greek myth, Minerva is called Athena. {mih **nuhr** və}

min·gle *verb* (mingled, mingling, mingles) 1. to come together or join with other people. *He's usually too shy to mingle at parties.* 2. to bring together; mix. *Mr. Carr likes to mingle work with play.* {**ming** gəl}

min·i·a·ture *noun* 1. a very small copy or model of something. *He bought a miniature of his favorite car.* 2. something that is smaller than other members of the same class. *That poodle is a miniature.* *adjective* on a very small scale. *She has a min-*

iature tea set. {**mihn** ee ə chər}

min·i·mize *verb* (minimized, minimizing, minimizes) 1. to make as small as possible. *He wore a shirt to minimize the chance of getting a sunburn.* 2. to make seem less important or less valuable. *The senator minimized the need for better housing downtown.* {**mihn** ə miyz} minimization, n., minimizer, n.

min·i·mum *noun* (minimums) 1. the smallest or least possible amount, degree, or number. *There is an age minimum for this movie.* 2. the smallest or lowest amount or degree reached. *The temperature dropped to a minimum of ten degrees last month.* *adjective* the smallest or least in amount, number, or degree. *We had to pay the minimum parking fee.* {**mihn** ə məm}

min·ing *noun* the act or business of digging up coal, ore, or other minerals in a mine. *He father is in mining.* {**miy** ning}

min·is·ter *noun* 1. a person authorized to perform or help at the religious services of some religions. *He is the minister at our church.* 2. (often capitalized) a person who is the head of a government department. *The Minister of Education will now give a speech.* 3. a person who represents a government in a foreign country. *verb* (ministered, ministering, ministers) to care for; attend to. *Nurses minister to those who are sick or hurt.* {**mihn** ih stər}

mink *noun* (mink or minks) 1. a small mammal with dark brown fur, a long body, short legs, and a bushy tail. Mink live near water, where they hunt water animals. One kind of mink lives in Europe and Asia; another kind lives

in North America. Mink are closely related to polecats, ferrets, and other weasels. 2. the fur of this animal. Mink fur is valuable because it is very soft. {**mingk**}

Min·ne·so·ta *noun* a state in the midwestern United States. Its capital is St. Paul. (abbreviated: MN) {**mihn** ih **soh** tə} Minnesotan, n., adj.

Word History *Minnesota* means "water that reflects the sky" in the Dakota Sioux language. The state was named after the Minnesota River.

min·now *noun* (minnow or minnows) a small fish that lives in fresh water. {**mihn** oh}

mi·nor *adjective* 1. less important or serious than others of the same kind. *My problem is a minor one compared to yours.* 2. under the age of an adult as recognized by law. *Minor children are not allowed to see this film.* *noun* a person under the age of an adult as recognized by law. *Minors cannot vote.* {**miy** nər}

Homophone Note The words *minor* and *miner* (one who mines something) sound alike but have different meanings.

mi·nor·i·ty *noun* (minorities) 1. a part or amount that is less than half the total. *A minority of students protested the new rules.* 2. a group of people whose race, religion, or politics is different from the larger population group. *Many countries have laws that protect minorities.* {mih **nor** ih tee *or* miy **nor** ih tee}

minor scale *noun* any musical scale in which there is a half-step between the second and third tones and seventh and eighth tones. {**miy** nər **skayl**}

min·strel *noun* 1. a musician and poet who traveled from place to place to entertain people during the Middle Ages. 2. a singer, musician, or poet. *We went to see the minstrels in the park.* {**mihn** strəl}

mint[1] *noun* 1. a plant with a strong, pleasant smell whose leaves are used as a flavoring. Peppermint and spearmint are members of the mint family. 2. a candy that is flavored with mint. *She offered mints after dinner.* {**mihnt**}

mint[2] *noun* 1. a factory where money is manufactured by the government. 2. a large amount of money. *He earned a mint working in Alaska.* *adjective* new or like new; not damaged. *That car is in mint condition.* *verb* (minted, minting, mints) to make by stamping metal. *New quarters were minted by the government this year.* {**mihnt**}

min·u·end *noun* a number from which another number is subtracted. *In the equation "10-5=5," "10" is the minuend.* {**mihn** yoo ənd}

mi·nus *preposition* 1. made less by subtracting. *Ten minus three is seven.* 2. missing or without. *That bicycle is minus a pedal.* *adjective* less than zero; negative. *The temperature was minus ten degrees this morning.* *noun* 1. the math sign used to show subtraction (–); minus sign 2. a fault or lack; shortcoming. *His short temper was a minus for his career.* {**miy** nəs}

min·ute[1] *noun* 1. a unit of time equal to sixty seconds or one sixtieth of an hour. (abbreviated: min.) 2. a very short period of time. *Would you please come inside for a minute?* 3. (plural) the written record of a meeting. *The clerk read the minutes of* the last council meeting. 4. a distance that a person can walk or drive in one minute. *Our new apartment is only ten minutes from school.* {**mihn** iht}

mi·nute[2] *adjective* (minuter, minutest) 1. very small in size or amount; tiny. *Grandmother is ill and will eat only a minute amount of food.* 2. with attention to fine details. *He makes minute drawings of city life.* {mih **nooht** or mih **nyoot**}

min·ute·man *noun* (minutemen) an American soldier of the Revolutionary War, who was ready to fight on a minute's notice. {**mihn** iht **măn**}

mir·a·cle *noun* 1. an event that cannot be explained by the known laws of nature and is thought to be caused by a power not of the earth. *An earthquake was once thought to be a miracle.* 2. a wonderful or amazing event or thing. *We learned about the miracles of modern science.* {**meer** ə kəl}

Word History *Miracle* comes from a Latin word that means "to look at with astonishment."

mi·rac·u·lous *adjective* 1. of the nature of a miracle. *Saints are said to have done miraculous things.* 2. amazing, incredible. *He made a miraculous escape from the cave.* {mə **răk** yə ləs}

mi·rage *noun* an illusion in which something is seen in the distance but is not really there. A mirage often occurs in the desert or on hot pavement, creating the illusion of water. A mirage is caused when light is reflected by air masses of different temperatures. {mih **rahzh**}

mir·ror ❶ ❷ *noun* a smooth surface that reflects an image of whatever is in front of it. A mirror is usually made of glass with a coat of shiny metal on the back. *verb* (mirrored, mirroring, mirrors) to reflect or show in or as if in a mirror. *The surface of the pond mirrored the trees.* {**meer** ər}

Word History *Mirror* comes from a Latin word that means "to look at or admire."

mis- *prefix* a prefix that means "bad" or "wrong." *Misfortune means bad fortune.*

mis·be·have *verb* (misbehaved, misbehaving, misbehaves) to act or behave badly. *The children misbehaved in the restaurant.* {mihs bə **hayv**}

mis·cal·cu·late *verb* (miscalculated, miscalculating, miscalculates) to calculate or judge incorrectly. *He miscalculated the distance from the stop sign to the corner.* {mihs **kălk** yə layt} miscalculation, n., miscalculator, n.

mis·cel·la·ne·ous *adjective* made up of many different kinds. *There is a pile of miscellaneous junk in the garage.* {mihs ə **lay** nee əs} miscellaneously, adv.

mis·chief *noun* 1. behavior such as teasing that is playful but can be annoying or dangerous to others. 2. the quality that leads to such behavior. *Those boys have mischief in them.* {**mihs** chihf}

mis·chie·vous *adjective* 1. tending to behave in an annoying or mildly harmful

 Human Body   Human Mind  Everyday Life  History and Culture  Communication

way. *He is a mischievous child.* 2. teasing or sly. *She gave her mother a mischievous look.* {mihs chə vəs} mischievously, adv., mischievousness, n.

mis·con·duct *noun* wrong behavior or conduct. *He was punished for his misconduct.* {mihs **kŏn** duhkt}

mis·count *verb* (miscounted, miscounting, miscounts) to count incorrectly. *The coach miscounted the number of players on his team.* *noun* an incorrect count. *There was a miscount of votes in the last election.* {mihs **kownt**, n., mihs **kownt**, v.}

mi·ser *noun* a greedy, stingy person who lives in a poor way in order to save money. {**miy** zər}

Word History The English word *miser* comes from the Latin word *miser*, which means "miserable."

mis·er·a·ble ⊙ *adjective* 1. very unhappy; wretched. *He's miserable about losing his job.* 2. having or causing discomfort or unhappiness. *She suffered through a miserable illness.* / *We are all tired of this miserable weather.* 3. having little value; poor. *He did a miserable job of cleaning his room.* {**mihz** ə rə bəl *or* **mihz** rə bəl} miserableness, n., miserably, adv.

mis·er·y *noun* (miseries) 1. a condition in which one is very unhappy or suffers very much. *She was in misery when her house burned down.* 2. a state of need and suffering caused by being poor, sick, or in trouble. *He is living in misery.* {**mih** zə ree}

mis·for·tune *noun* 1. an instance of bad luck. *One misfortune after another ruined our camping trip.* 2. bad luck, often over a long period of

time. *His family has suffered from the misfortunes of war.* {mihs **fohr** chən}

mis·giv·ing *noun* a feeling of worry, doubt, or fear. *I have no misgivings about traveling alone.* {mihs **gihv** ing}

mis·guid·ed *adjective* led into making mistakes or doing the wrong thing. *The misguided girl skipped school with her friends.* {mihs **giyd** ihd}

mis·hap *noun* an unlucky event; accident. *He had several mishaps while painting the house.* {**mihs** hăp}

mis·lay *verb* (mislaid, mislaying, mislays) to put somewhere and forget where; lose. *I have mislaid my keys.* {mihs **lay**}

mis·lead *verb* (misled, misleading, misleads) 1. to guide in a wrong direction. *We were misled by the guide and got lost in the woods.* 2. to cause to think or act in a wrong manner. *The flashy advertisement misled them into thinking the game was exciting.* {mihs **leed**} misleading, adj.

mis·place *verb* (misplaced, misplacing, misplaces) to put in a wrong place; lose. *He misplaced his baseball glove.* {mihs **plays**}

mis·print *noun* a mistake in printing. *The newspaper had several misprints today.* {**mihs prihnt**}

mis·pro·nounce *verb* (mispronounced, mispronouncing, mispronounces) to pronounce the wrong way. *Goethe's name is often mispronounced.* {mihs prə **nowns**} mispronunciation, n.

mis·read *verb* (misread, misreading, misreads) to read or understand incorrectly. *I mis-*

read the sign and went north instead of south. / *She misread his expression.* {mihs **reed**}

miss[1] *verb* (missed, missing, misses) 1. to fail to hit, catch, reach, cross, or touch. *He missed the ball.* / *I missed the plane.* 2. to fail to see, hear, or understand. *He missed what I said.* 3. to fail to perform, attend, or otherwise experience. *I missed the concert.* 4. to fail to do or get. *They missed a good chance of winning the game.* 5. to avoid or escape. *The car missed the tree.* 6. to feel sad or lonely without. *She missed her friend.* *noun* 1. a failure to hit or catch something. *She made five baskets in a row before a miss.* 2. any failure or thing that is left out. *Our plan turned out to be a miss.* {mihs}

miss[2] *noun* 1. (capitalized) the title used before the name of a girl or woman who is not married. "Miss" is sometimes replaced by "Ms." *The name of our teacher is Miss Jones.* 2. a form of address used in speaking to a young woman. *Pardon me, miss, but could you give me directions to State Street?* {mihs}

mis·shap·en *adjective* badly formed or shaped. *He won't let the city cut down that old, misshapen apple tree in his yard.* {mihs **shay** pən}

mis·sile *noun* 1. an object or weapon that is thrown or shot at a target that is far away. *A bullet fired from a gun is a missile.* 2. a powerful weapon shot at a target in a rocket that has its own controls. {mihs əl}

miss·ing *adjective* 1. not where it should be; absent. *He's had a missing finger since birth.* 2. lost; not to be found. *If I don't find that missing book,*

A
B
C
D
E
F
G
H
I
J
K
L
M
N
O
P
Q
R
S
T
U
V
W
X
Y
Z

a b c d e f g h i j k l **m** n o p q r s t u v w x y z

I'll have to pay for it. {<u>mihs</u> ing}

mis·sion *noun* 1. a special job or task given to a person or group of people. The task may be government or religious work. *The spy was on a secret mission for the president.* 2. the buildings and land used by such a group. *The monks live in a mission outside the city.* 3. a particular task or duty done with strong belief. *His mission was to help the poor.* 4. any task that one is sent to do. *Bob was sent on a mission to the grocery store by his mother.* {<u>mihsh</u> ən}

mis·sion·ar·y *noun* (missionaries) a person who is sent by a church or religious order to a foreign country to teach, convert, heal, or serve. *The missionary set up a clinic in the jungle.* {<u>mih</u> shə **nayr** ee}

Mis·sis·sip·pi *noun* 1. a state in the southern United States. Its capital is Jackson. (abbreviated: MS) 2. the longest river in the United States. It flows from Minnesota to the Gulf of Mexico. {**mihs** ih <u>sih</u> pee}

Word History *Mississippi* means "great river" in the Chippewa language. The state was named after the Mississippi River.

Mis·sour·i *noun* 1. a state in the midwestern United States. Its capital is Jefferson City. (abbreviated: MO) 2. a river of the central United States. It flows from Montana southeast through several states to Missouri, where it joins the Mississippi River. {mih <u>zoohr</u> ee *or* mih <u>zoohr</u> ə} Missourian, n.

Word History *Missouri* means "people of the big canoes" in an Algonquin language. The state was named after the Missouri River.

mis·spell *verb* (misspelled or misspelt, misspelling, misspells) to spell in an incorrect way. *He misspelled two words in his book report.* {mihs <u>spehl</u>}

mist *noun* a mass or cloud of tiny water drops in the air. *There was mist on the mountain.* *verb* (misted, misting, mists) 1. to become covered with mist. *The car windows misted in the fog.* 2. to rain in fine drops. *It is misting outside, so put on your jackets.* 3. to cover or hide with or as if with mist. *A heavy fog misted the lake.* {<u>mihst</u>}

mis·take *noun* a thought or action that is not correct; error. *The teacher noticed his mistake on the test.* *verb* (mistook, mistaken, mistaking, mistakes) 1. to understand incorrectly. *Ms. North mistook what I said.* 2. to take for another; confuse with another. *I mistook him for his brother.* {mih <u>stayk</u>}

mis·tak·en *adjective* 1. being an error. *She had a mistaken idea about when the movie started.* 2. in error; wrong. *He thought it was a costume party, but he was mistaken.* {mih <u>stā</u> kən} mistakenly, adv., mistakenness, n.

Mis·ter *noun* a title placed before a man's last name. It is usually abbreviated as "Mr." *Our teacher's name is Mr. Smith.* {<u>mihs</u> tər}

mis·tle·toe *noun* 1. a poisonous, evergreen plant that has white berries and small, yellow flowers. Mistletoe is a parasite that grows on trees. 2. a sprig of this plant used as a Christmas decoration. *It is a custom to kiss the person who stands under the mistletoe.* {<u>mihs</u> əl toh}

mis·took *verb* past tense of **mistake.** {mihs <u>tuuk</u>}

mis·treat *verb* (mistreated, mistreating, mistreats) to treat badly. *He mistreated his dog until it bit him.* {mihs <u>treet</u>} mistreatment, n.

mis·tress *noun* a woman in charge of something. *My mother is the mistress of our household.* {<u>mihs</u> trəs}

mis·trust *noun* lack of confidence or trust; doubt. *Mistrust broke up their friendship.* *verb* (mistrusted, mistrusting, mistrusts) to have no trust in; to be suspicious of. *I mistrust people who lie to me.* {mihs <u>truhst</u>}

mist·y *adjective* (mistier, mistiest) 1. made up of mist or looking like mist. *The surface of the lake is misty in the morning.* 2. covered as if by mist. *Jean has only a misty memory of her childhood.* {<u>mihst</u> ee}

mis·un·der·stand *verb* (misunderstood, misunderstanding, misunderstands) to fail to understand correctly; give the wrong meaning to. *He misunderstood the teacher's directions.* {mihs uhn dər <u>stănd</u>}

mis·un·der·stand·ing *noun* 1. a failure to understand correctly. *Our misunderstanding of the rules caused us to lose the game.* 2. a quarrel. *My friend and I had a misunderstanding about who was stronger.* {mihs uhn dər **stăn** ding}

mis·un·der·stood *adjective* 1. not understood correctly. *That is an often misunderstood poem.* 2. not thought well of. *Jeff is a misunderstood boy who was wrongly accused of breaking the window.* {mihs uhn dər **stuud**}

mis·use *noun* a wrong or incorrect use. *Misuse of a saw could be dangerous. verb* (misused, misusing, misuses) 1. to use in a wrong or incorrect way. *He misused his study time and failed the test.* 2. to treat badly; abuse. *He misused the bicycle, and now it doesn't work.* {mihs **yoos**, n., mihs **yooz**, v.}

mite[1] *noun* a tiny animal that is related to the spider. Most mites are parasites and live on other animals or plants. {**miyt**}

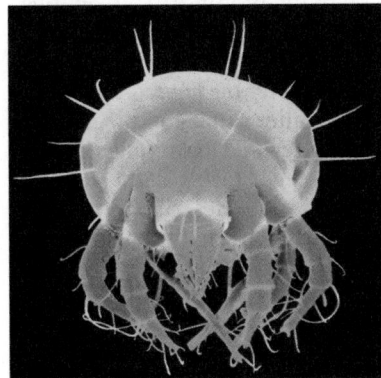

mite[2] *noun* a tiny amount of something, such as money. {**miyt**}

Homophone Note Are you looking for the word *might*? *Mite* and *might* sound alike but have different meanings.

mitt *noun* 1. a baseball glove. 2. a mitten. {**miht**}

mit·ten *noun* a covering for the hand, worn for warmth. Mittens have one section for the thumb and one section for the four fingers. {**mih** tən}

Word History *Mitten* is from a Latin word that means "the middle," "center," or "a half." A mitten is halved between the fingers and thumb.

mix *verb* (mixed, mixing, mixes) 1. to put different things together so that the parts become one. *If you mix yellow and blue you will have green.* 2. to put together in a confused way (often followed by "up"). *Their hats and coats were all mixed up.* 3. to meet and greet other people. *I mixed with many interesting people at the party last night. noun* something that is made of parts or substances meant to be mixed with liquid. *We will need to add milk to the cake mix.* {**mihks**}

mixed number *noun* a number made up of a whole number and a fraction. *Two and three fourths, or 2-3/4, is a mixed number.* {**mihkst nuhm** bər}

mix·er *noun* a device used for mixing different things together. *We used the mixer to make cookie dough. / He drives a cement mixer.* {**mihk** sər}

mix·ture *noun* something that is made by two or more things that are mixed together. *A mixture of flour and water made a paste.* {**mihks** chər}

mix-up *noun* a confused situation. *There was a mix-up about who would give us a ride home from the mall.* {**mihks uhp**}

ml *abbreviation* an abbreviation for **milliliter**, or milliliters.

mm *abbreviation* an abbreviation for **millimeter**, or millimeters.

Mn symbol of the chemical element **manganese**.

MN or **Minn.** *abbreviation* an abbreviation for **Minnesota**.

MO or **Mo.** *abbreviation* an abbreviation for **Missouri**.

mo. *abbreviation* an abbreviation for **month**.

moan *noun* a long, low sound of pain, grief, or sorrow. *Moans came from the sick man's room. verb* (moaned, moaning, moans) 1. to make a moan or a similar sound. *The dog moaned outside the door.* 2. to express unhappiness; complain. *He moaned about his bad luck.* {**mohn**}

Homophone Note The words *moan* and *mown* (past participle of "mow") sound alike but have different meanings.

moat *noun* a deep ditch dug around a castle, fort or town for protection against enemies. Moats are usually filled with water. {**moht**}

mob *noun* 1. a large crowd of angry or excited people. *A mob gathered outside the jail.* 2. (informal) an organized group of people who break the law. *Police arrested members of the mob. verb* (mobbed, mobbing, mobs) to crowd around, when angry or

excited. *The people mobbed the president after his speech.* {mŏb}

mo·bile *adjective* able to move or be moved easily from one place or position to another. *I have a mobile phone.* *noun* a work of art made of pieces that are hung and connected by wire or string. A mobile moves when touched by a breeze. {<u>moh</u> beel, n., <u>moh</u> bəl, adj.}

mobile home *noun* a house or trailer that can be moved but is often placed in one location for a long time. {<u>moh</u> bəl <u>hohm</u>}

moc·ca·sin *noun* a soft leather shoe or slipper without a heel. Moccasins were first made and worn by American Indians. {<u>mŏk</u> ə sən}

mock *verb* (mocked, mocking, mocks) 1. to make fun of in a mean way. *The other kids mocked him when he fell off his scooter.* 2. to make fun of by imitation. *She mocks the way her mother speaks.* *adjective* not real or true. *Her bag is made of mock alligator skin.* {mŏk}

Word History *Mock* comes from a Latin word that means "to wipe the nose." This gesture was seen as a sign of scorn.

mock·ing·bird *noun* a gray and white North American songbird. It has many different calls and can also copy the sounds that other birds make. {<u>mo</u> king buhrd}

mode *noun* a way of doing something. *Cars, buses, and trains are popular modes of transportation.* {mohd}

mod·el ⊘ *noun* 1. an example that should be copied or an ideal that others are compared to. *Mr. Magnus, the millionaire, is my model of success.* 2. a small copy of something, often used as a guide to making the thing in full size. 3. a particular type or style of a product. *The salesman showed us a newer model of car.* 4. a person who poses for a painter, photographer, or other artist. 5. a person whose job is to display new clothing by wearing it for customers or posing for photographs. *adjective* 1. serving as an example or ideal that should be copied. *Carmen has always been a model citizen who works to help the community.* 2. being a model. *His hobby is building model airplanes.* *verb* (modeled, modeling, models) 1. to plan or form according to a model. *She modeled herself after her mother.* 2. to form or shape. *He modeled the clay.* 3. to work as a fashion model or an artist's model. {<u>mo</u> dəl}

mo·dem ⊘ ❶ *noun* an electronic device that allows information to be sent from or to a computer using telephone lines or other lines of communication. {<u>moh</u> dehm}

mod·er·ate *adjective* not too much or too little; within limits. *He paid a moderate price for the book. / There was a moderate change in the temperature last night.* *verb* (moderated, moderating, moderates) 1. to make less strong or extreme. *The workers have moderated their demands for more money.* 2. to direct, guide, or preside over a discussion or meeting. *She was asked to moderate the meeting.* 3. to become less strong. *The storm has moderated.* {<u>mŏd</u> ər iht, adj., <u>mŏd</u> ər ayt, v.} moderately, adv.

mod·ern ⊘ ❶ *adjective* 1. having to do with the present or current times. *We live in the modern age.* 2. of or having to do with the latest styles or ideas. *Our school just bought a modern sound system.* {<u>mŏd</u> ərn}

mod·ern·ize *verb* (modernized, modernizing, modernizes) 1. to make modern; bring up to date. *We modernized our kitchen.* 2. to become modern. *The nation is trying to modernize.* {<u>mŏd</u> ər niyz}

mod·est *adjective* 1. not thinking too highly of oneself; humble. *Ann was modest about getting the highest grade on the test.* 2. simple or humble in appearance. *They found a modest little house to buy in the country.* 3. moderate in amount, size, or value. *The boat cost a modest amount of money.* {<u>mŏd</u> ihst} modestly, adv.

mod·i·fy *verb* (modified, modifying, modifies) 1. to change in some way; alter. *To save money, they modified their plans for the house.* 2. to make smaller or less; reduce; moderate. *The restaurant staff modified their request for more pay.* 3. to describe or limit the meaning of; qualify. *"Noisy" modifies "car" in the phrase "a noisy car."* {<u>mŏd</u> ih fiy}

mod·ule *noun* 1. a part of a device or machine that can be separated from the main section. 2. a section of a spacecraft that is used to carry out a particular task. {<u>mŏ</u> joohl or <u>mŏd</u> yool}

Mo·hawk *noun* (Mohawks or Mohawk) 1. an important river of New York State. It

 Human Body   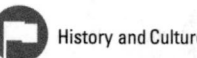 Human Mind   Everyday Life   History and Culture    Communication

flows east from central New York toward the Atlantic. 2. a member of a Native American people who once lived along this river, and now lives in northern New York and Canada. The Mohawk belong to the Iroquois confederation of Six Nations. {moh hawk}

moist *adjective* somewhat wet; damp. *I used a moist towel to clean the bicycle.* {moist}

mois·ten *verb* (moistened, moistening, moistens) to make or become slightly wet. *She moistened the rag and washed the car.* {moi sən} moistener, n.

mois·ture *noun* a small amount of liquid in the air or on a surface. *The light rain left moisture on the ground.* {mois chər}

mo·lar *noun* a large tooth located in the back of the mouth, with a broad surface used for grinding food. {moh lər}

mo·las·ses *noun* a thick, sweet dark brown syrup made from sugar cane. {mə lă sihz}

mold¹ ❶ *noun* a hollow form used to give a particular shape to a soft or liquid substance that is poured into it. The material becomes hard and takes the shape of the mold. *The workers poured cement into a mold for the curb.* *verb* (molded, molding, molds) 1. to work into a certain shape or form. *She molded the clay into a human head.* 2. to influence the growth or character of. *His father's ideas molded him.* {mohld} moldability, n., moldable, adj.

mold² ❶ *noun* a fungus that grows on the surface of plant or animal materials such as food or leather. Some kinds of mold are fuzzy or fluffy. Penicillin is a kind of mold. {mohld}

mold·ing *noun* 1. the act of shaping or forming something. *He made a molding of the fossil.* 2. a strip of wood, stone, or other material used to frame or finish a door, window or wall. Moldings are often used for decoration in a home. *Grandmother's old house has molding along the ceiling in the living room.* {mohld ing}

mole¹ *noun* a small, permanent spot on the skin. Moles are usually brown and sometimes slightly raised. {mohl}

mole² *noun* 1. a small animal with tiny eyes and very soft fur that lives underground in tunnels. Moles are insectivores; they are mammals that eat insects. Different kinds of moles are found in Europe, Asia, and North America. 2. a person who spies for one country by getting a job working for the government of another country. {mohl}

mol·e·cule ❷ *noun* the smallest unit of a substance that has all the properties of that substance. A molecule is made up of a single atom or group of atoms. *Each molecule of water has two hydrogen and one oxygen atoms.* {mŏl ə kyool}

Word History *Molecule*
comes from *moles*, a Latin word that means "mass." "Molecule" is a French word for "tiny mass."

mol·lusk ❶ *noun* an animal in a large group of invertebrates or animals without backbones. Most kinds of mollusks live in the ocean and have soft bodies covered by a shell. Snails, clams, squid, and octopuses are examples of mollusks. {mŏl əsk} molluskan, adj., n., mollusklike, adj.

molt *verb* (molted, molting, molts) to shed or cast off skin, feathers, fur, or horns, and grow a new covering. *Snakes molt as they grow.* {mohlt} molter, n.

mol·ten *adjective* made liquid by very high heat. *Magma is molten rock.* {mohl tən} moltenly, adv.

mom *noun* (informal) **mother**. {mŏm}

mo·ment *noun* 1. a very short amount of time. *May I talk with you for a moment after class?* 2. a particular point in time. *The moment he got home, the phone rang.* {moh mənt}

mo·men·tar·y *adjective* lasting only a moment. *There was a momentary break in the game when the ball went over the fence.* {moh mən tayr ee}

mo·men·tous *adjective* very important. *The Battle of Hastings was a momentous event in British history.* {moh mehn təs} momentously, adv., momentousness, n.

mo·men·tum *noun* (momenta [or] momentums) strength of movement. *He leapt, and the momentum carried him across the stream.* {moh mehn təm}

Mon. *abbreviation* an abbreviation for **Monday**.

mon·arch *noun* 1. a ruler such as a king, queen, or emperor. *Queen Elizabeth is the monarch of the United Kingdom and its dominions.* 2. a large orange, black, and white butterfly. Mon-

 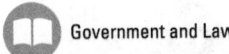

a
b
c
d
e
f
g
h
i
j
k
l
m
n
o
p
q
r
s
t
u
v
w
x
y
z

archs migrate over great distances in the fall and spring. {**mŏn** ark} monarchal, adj., monarchally, adv., monarchial, adj.

mon·ar·chy ○ noun (monarchies) a nation or government ruled by or in the name of a monarch. A monarch's power is either unlimited or limited by a constitution. {**mŏn** ər kee or **mŏn** ar kee}

> **Word History** *Monarchy* is from two ancient Greek words that mean "to rule" and "alone."

mon·as·ter·y noun (monasteries) a community of monks, or the buildings used by such a community. {**mŏn** ə **stayr** ee}

Mon·day noun the second day of the week. Monday comes between Sunday and Tuesday. {**muhn** day}

> **Word History** *Monday* comes from an early English word that means "the day of the moon."

mon·e·tar·y adjective having to do with currency or money. *We made a monetary decision not to go to the movies.* {**mŏn** ih **tayr** ee} monetarily, adv.

mon·ey ● noun (moneys or monies) the coins or paper notes of a country used to buy things or pay for services. {**muh** nee} moneyless, adj.

> **Word History** The Romans made coins at the temple of the goddess Juno. The word *money* comes from one of Juno's titles, *Juno Moneta.*

Mon·gol noun 1. a person who was born in or is a citizen of Mongolia. 2. any language of

Mongolia. *adjective* of or having to do with Mongolia, or its people or languages. *Mongol armies conquered much of East and Central Asia in the eleventh century.* {**mŏng** gəl or **mŏng** gohl or **mŏn** gəl or **mŏn** gohl, n., **mŏng** gəl or **mŏng** gohl or **mŏn** gəl or **mŏn** gohl, adj.}

Mon·go·li·a noun 1. a country in eastern Asia. Mongolia is also called the Republic of Mongolia. Ulaanbaatar, also called Ulan Bator, is the capital of Mongolia. 2. a region that includes this country and part of China. {**mŏng goh** lee ə or **mŏn goh** lee ə}

mon·goose noun a mammal related to the ferret, known for its ability to kill poisonous snakes. {**mŏng goohs** or **mŏn goohs**}

mon·grel noun a plant or animal that is a mix of two or more breeds or kinds. *The veterinarian said that mongrels make good pets.* {**mŏng** grəl or **mŏn** grəl}

mon·i·tor noun 1. a student given the task of helping to keep order within a school. *Nita is a hallway monitor.* 2. a device for collecting information about the use, operation, or condition of something. *James was attached to a heart monitor while he was in the hospital.* 3. a screen for a computer that shows information. 4. a large lizard found in Southeast Asia, Australia, and Africa. Some monitor lizards are fierce predators. *verb* (monitored, monitoring, monitors) to observe in order to check on. *We monitored the progress of the space mission.* {**mo** nih tər}

monk noun a man who has joined other men in a religious community and taken

vows to live a simple life. {**muhngk**}

mon·key ❶ noun (monkeys) 1. a small mammal that is one of the primates. Monkeys have very flexible hands and feet. Some kinds of monkeys have tails which they use to hang from trees. Different kinds of monkeys live in Central and South America, Africa, and Asia. 2. one who acts like a monkey, being playful and mischievous. *verb* (monkeyed, monkeying, monkeys) to play in a careless or mischievous way (often followed by "with" or "around"). *Don't monkey with the new computer!* {**muhng** kee}

monkey wrench noun a tool with a jaw that can be adjusted to grip different sizes of nuts and bolts. *The plumber used a monkey wrench to fix the leaking pipe.* {**muhng** kee **rehnch**}

mon·o·gram noun a design made from two or more initials. A monogram is used to mark or decorate things such as a person's clothing or writing paper. *verb* (monogrammed, monogramming, monograms) to mark with a design made of two or more initials. *The shop monogrammed Bill O. Washington's shirt with "BOW."* {**mŏn** ə **grăm**}

> **Word History** *Monogram* is formed from two ancient Greek words. *Mono-* means "one" or "single." *Gramma* means "letter."

mon·o·logue noun 1. a long speech or reading given by a

 Human Body   Human Mind    Everyday Life   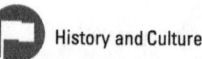 History and Culture    Communication

single speaker. 2. a speech in a play given by an actor alone or as if alone on the stage. *Shakespeare's plays are famous for their monologues.* {**mŏn** ə **lawg** or **mŏn** ə **lohg**} monologuist (monologist), n.

mo·nop·o·lize *verb* (monopolized, monopolizing, monopolizes) to get or keep sole control of; have for oneself alone; take over. *At the party, one man monopolized the conversation. / My brother is monopolizing the television.* {mə **nŏp** ə **liyz**}

mo·nop·o·ly 🌐 *noun* (monopolies) 1. complete control over a service or product within a given area. *Dennis had a monopoly on cutting grass in his neighborhood.* 2. a company that has such control. *The government has laws to break up monopolies.* {mə **nŏp** ə lee}

mon·o·rail *noun* a railroad whose cars run along a single rail, or the rail itself. {**mŏn** oh **rayl**}

mon·o·tone *noun* speech with little or no change in tone. *Though the topic was interesting, the speaker's monotone almost put the audience to sleep.* {**mŏn** ə **tohn**}

mon·ot·o·nous *adjective* not interesting because of having to do the same thing over and over. *It is a monotonous task to copy spelling words over and over.* {mə **nŏt** ə nəs} monotonously, adv.

mon·sieur *noun* (messieurs) the French title for a man meaning "Mister" or "Sir." *Would you like to see a menu, monsieur?* {mə **syuhr**}

mon·soon *noun* a wind system of the Indian Ocean that blows from the southwest in the summer and the northeast in the winter. The

southwest monsoon brings with it a season of heavy rain. {mŏn **soohn**}

mon·ster *noun* 1. a large, frightening imaginary creature. *He likes books about monsters.* 2. anything that is large enough to be shocking. *That twenty-pound trout is a real monster.* 3. a person who is mean or cruel. *Only a monster would beat his dog.* 4. any being that is not normal in appearance or shape. *A snake born with two heads is a monster.* {**mŏn** stər} monsterlike, adj.

Word History *Monster* comes from a Latin word that means "omen" or "warning." Watch out.

mon·strous *adjective* 1. so ugly that it is scary. *The monstrous creatures in that movie frightened Beth.* 2. horrible or shocking. *That man was put in prison for life because of his monstrous crime.* 3. huge; unusually large. *We ate a monstrous sundae that had thirty scoops of ice cream.* {**mŏn** strəs}

Mon·tan·a *noun* a state in the northwestern United States. Its capital is Helena. (abbreviated: MT) {**mŏn tăn** ə} Montanan, n.

Word History *Montana* means "mountainous" in Spanish. The name was first used officially when the Montana Territory was formed in 1864.

month *noun* one of the twelve parts of a year. {**muhnth**}

Word History *Month* comes from an Old English word that means "moon."

month·ly *adjective* 1. showing up or happening once a month. *Our monthly meetings take place on the second*

Tuesday. 2. lasting for a month. *The class must read four books as part of their monthly reading project.* noun (monthlies) a magazine or journal that is published once a month. *My soccer magazine is a monthly, but my baseball magazine comes out only four times a year.* adverb each month; once a month. *We take a spelling test monthly.* {**muhnth** lee}

mon·u·ment *noun* 1. something built in memory of a person, event, or special deed. *The monument in front of the hospital honored the doctor who had saved so many lives.* 2. a special or great example; an example worth special attention. *Beethoven's symphonies are a monument in the history of music.* {**mŏn** yə mənt}

moo *verb* (mooed, mooing, moos) to make the long, low sound of a cow. *The cow moos when it is hungry.* noun (moos) the long, low sound that cows make. {**mooh**}

mood 😊 *noun* the way a person feels at a certain time. *Overwork has put him in a bad mood.* {**moohd**}

mood·y *adjective* (moodier, moodiest) 1. having moods that change often or without a pattern. *That moody Sam was laughing one minute and crying the next.* 2. usually feeling angry or sad. *Moody Alice never wants to play with us.* {**mooh** dee} moodiness, n.

moon 🌙 *noun* 1. the earth's natural satellite. It revolves around the earth from west to east in about 28 days. The moon joins the earth in its orbit around the sun. The moon does not give off light. Instead, its

Living World

Physical World

Natural Environment

Economy

Government and Law

shine comes from the light it reflects from the sun. 2. any planet's natural satellite. *Jupiter has 16 moons.* {moohn}

moon·beam *noun* a ray of light from the moon. {moohn beem}

moon·light *noun* the light of the moon. {moohn liyt}

moor[1] *noun* an area of land that is open and wet. Heather and other plants that need acid soil grow on moors. {moohr}

moor[2] *verb* (moored, mooring, moors) 1. to make a boat or ship stay in place; anchor. *We moored and stepped ashore.* 2. to fix in place with cables or lines. *We moored the boat with rope.* {moohr}

moose *noun* (moose) the largest kind of deer. Male moose have very large antlers that are shaped like a hand with spread fingers. Moose are mammals with hooves. They live in the northern United States and in Canada. Moose also live in northern Europe and Asia, where they are called elk. {moohs}

mop *noun* 1. a tool with rags, a sponge, or yarn attached to one end of a long handle. A mop is used to wash floors or decks. 2. a thick or tangled mass. *It was hard to get a comb through her mop of hair.* *verb* (mopped, mopping, mops) to wipe or rub as if with a mop; clean with a mop. *The runner mopped the sweat from her forehead. / He mops the kitchen floor at least once a week.* {mŏp}

mope ❓ *verb* (moped, moping, mopes) 1. to act dull and sad; sulk; pout. *Kai always mopes when it's time to do homework.* 2. to move slowly and without spirit or purpose. *When it rained, the children moped around the house.* {mohp}

mo·ped *noun* a heavy bicycle fitted with a motor that does not have much power. {moh pehd}

mor·al *adjective* 1. having to do with what is right and what is wrong in how a person acts. 2. following rules of right or fair behavior. *He is not friendly but he is moral.* *noun* 1. the lesson about right and wrong learned from a story or event. *The moral of the story is, "What comes around, goes around," or how you treat someone will come back to you.* 2. (plural) ideas or habits of behavior that relate to what is right and what is wrong. *A person with morals will not cheat or steal.* {mohr əl or mŏr əl, n., mohr əl or mŏr əl, adj.}

mo·rale *noun* the state of mind of a person or group; spirit. *The team's morale was high for their first home game.* {mə răl}

more *adjective* 1. in greater number, amount, or degree. *He has read more books than the rest of us.* 2. extra; additional. *I'd like more spaghetti, please.* *noun* 1. an additional or greater amount or degree. *I want more than I have.* 2. something better. *I expected more from the President.* *adverb* 1. in or to a greater amount or degree. *The dress cost more than I wanted to pay.* 2. again; further. *She ate more. / Will you swim more?* {mohr}

• **more or less**
1. in some ways; somewhat. *John was more or less happy with the birthday gift.* 2. nearly. *The tickets cost thirteen dollars, more or less.*

Synonyms
These words share a meaning with **more**, adjective 1:
greater, larger, bigger

---

more·o·ver *adverb* beyond what has already been said; in addition; also. *She is smart; moreover, she is always cheerful.* {mohr oh vər}

Mor·mon *noun* a member of the Church of Jesus Christ of Latter-day Saints. *adjective* having to do with the Mormons or their church or beliefs. {mohr mən} Mormonism, n.

morn·ing *noun* 1. the early part of the day, beginning when the sun rises and ending about noon. 2. the time between midnight and noon. *At three o'clock in the morning the town is very quiet.* {mohr ning}

morning glory *noun* a climbing vine with flowers that open in the morning and close by evening. Morning glory flowers are shaped like a trumpet and come in several colors. {mohr ning glohr ee or mohr ning glohr ee}

Mo·roc·co *noun* a country in northern Africa. Rabat is the capital of Morocco. {mə rŏk oh} Moroccan, adj., n.

mo·ron *noun* a very foolish or stupid person. {mohr ŏn} moronic, adj.

mor·sel *noun* a small piece that is the right size for one bite; bit. *The mouse ate a morsel of cheese.* {mohr səl}

mor·tal *adjective* 1. not living forever; having to die some day. *All animals are mortal.* 2. having to do with human beings; human. *Atoms can*

 Human Body
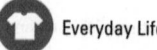 Human Mind
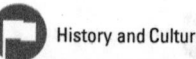 Everyday Life
 History and Culture
Communication

not be see with our mortal eyes. 3. causing or likely to cause death; fatal. *The knight raised his sword and gave the dragon a mortal blow.* 4. great and very intense; terrible and continuing. *Some people have a mortal fear of spiders.* noun a human being. *The movie was about an alien who wanted to be a mortal.* {**mohr** təl}

mor·tar[1] *noun* a heavy bowl in which things are ground or pounded into powder with a tool called a pestle. {**mohr** tər}

mor·tar[2] *noun* a material made from lime, sand, and water and used to hold bricks or stones in place. {**mohr** tər}

mo·sa·ic *noun* a picture or design made with many small colored pieces of glass, tile, or stone. These pieces are fitted together and cemented into place. {moh **zay** ihk}

Mos·cow *noun* the capital city of Russia. {**mŏs** koh *or* **mŏs** kow}

Mos·lem *adjective or noun* another spelling for **Muslim.** {**mŏz** ləm *or* **mŏs** ləm, n., **mŏz** ləm *or* **mŏs** ləm, adj.}

mosque *noun* a Muslim place of worship. {**mŏsk**}

mos·qui·to *noun* (mosquitoes or mosquitos) an insect with a thin body and two wings. The females bite and suck the blood of animals and people. Some mosquitoes spread disease. {mə **skee** toh}

moss ❶ *noun* a small, green plant without flowers that grows in soft, thick clumps.

Moss grows in mats on rocks, trees, and wet ground. {**maws**}

most *adjective* 1. greatest in number, amount, or degree. *This is the most fun I've ever had.* 2. the majority of. *Most birds can fly.* noun 1. the greatest number, amount, or degree. *He has most of the money.* 2. the majority of people. *Most do not like the new building on the corner.* 3. the best. *This is the most you can ask for.* adverb in the greatest extent or degree. *He was most foolish at the party.* {**mohst**}

• **for the most part**
to a great degree; usually. *For the most part she is a hard worker.*

most·ly *adverb* for the most part; mainly. *The weather report said that today will be mostly sunny.* {**mohst** lee}

mo·tel *noun* a hotel with parking spaces near the bedrooms for those who travel by car. {**moh** **tehl**}

moth *noun* 1. an insect that has broad wings and flies mostly at night. Moths look like butterflies, but they usually have thicker bodies and bushy antennae and are less colorful. 2. an insect called the clothes moth. It lays its eggs in wool or other fabric or fur. When the eggs hatch, the larvae feed on the fabric and damage it. {**mawth** *or* **mŏth**}

moth·er *noun* 1. a female parent. 2. the origin or source of something. *Greece was the mother of democracy.* adjective 1. being a female parent. *We*

could see the mother bear with her cubs. 2. relating to or like a mother. *He gives his roses mother love.* verb (mothered, mothering, mothers) to take care of and protect. *She mothered her new puppy.* {**muhth** ər} motherless, adj.

moth·er-in-law *noun* (mothers-in-law) the mother of a person's husband or wife. {**muhth** ər ihn **law**}

moth·er·ly *adjective* of or like a mother. *The teacher had a motherly interest in her students.* {**muhth** ər lee}

mo·tion *noun* 1. the act or particular way of changing place; movement. *With one jumping motion, the rabbit was gone. / The car's motion made me sick.* 2. a movement of the body used to express meaning. *The clown's silly motions made us laugh.* 3. the process of getting to work on something or making things happen; state of being in action. *She decided what to do, then set her plan in motion.* 4. a formal suggestion made to a government group or other meeting. *The teacher would not accept our class president's motion to allow pets at school.* verb (motioned, motioning, motions) to signal by a movement of the body. *The crossing guard motioned the children to wait at the corner.* {**moh** shən} motionless, adj.

motion picture *noun* 1. a series of pictures or photographs shown one after the other on a screen. The pictures or photographs appear so quickly that they seem to be moving. 2. a story that is told by means of filmed pictures and recorded sound; film or movie. {**moh** shən **pihk** chər} motion-picture, adj.

A B C D E F G H I J K L **M** N O P Q R S T U V W X Y Z

a
b
c
d
e
f
g
h
i
j
k
l
m
n
o
p
q
r
s
t
u
v
w
x
y
z

mo·tive *noun* an idea, need, desire, or impulse that causes a person to act in a particular way or do a particular thing; reason. *His motive for robbing the bank was not clear.* {**moh** tihv}

mo·tor ○ ● *noun* a machine that causes motion or power. *The mechanic put a new motor in the car. adjective* 1. having to do with a motor or a thing driven by a motor. *The car has run out of motor oil.* 2. having to do with the action of muscles and nerves. *Yanking your hand away from a flame is a motor reflex. verb* (motored, motoring, motors) to drive or ride in a motor vehicle. *He is motoring around the Irish countryside this summer.* {**moh** tər}

mo·tor·boat *noun* a boat that works by means of a motor. {**moh** tər boht}

mo·tor·cy·cle *noun* a vehicle with two wheels, a heavy frame, and an engine. {**moh** tər **siy** kəl} motorcyclist, n.

mot·to *noun* (mottoes or mottos) a short saying used as a reminder of a belief or rules of behavior. *The Boy Scout motto is, "Be prepared."* {**mŏt** oh}

mould·ing *noun* a spelling of **molding** used in Canada and Britain. See **molding**. {**mohld** ing}

mound *noun* 1. a raised pile; heap. *The children shoveled sand into a big mound.* 2. a slightly raised hill of dirt in the center of a baseball field. The pitcher throws from this mound. *verb* (mounded, mounding, mounds) to form into a pile or heap. *They mounded the*

leaves into a huge pile and jumped in. {mownd}

mount¹ *verb* (mounted, mounting, mounts) 1. to climb. *Be careful as you mount the ladder.* 2. to place oneself on top of. *She mounted her horse and galloped away.* 3. to set firmly into position on a surface for study or display; attach or set in place. *The teacher mounted the skeleton for her students. / He mounted his butterfly collection and hung it on the wall.* 4. to move upward; rise. *Smoke from the forest fire mounted in the sky.* 5. to become greater; increase. *The price of oil has mounted this year. noun* 1. a horse or other animal that one rides on. *The princess's mount had a golden mane.* 2. a stand, frame, or surface that holds something for display. *We bought a new mount for the picture at the frame store.* {**mownt**}

mount² *noun* a mountain or high hill. {**mownt**}

moun·tain ● *noun* 1. a land mass with great height and steep sides that is higher than a hill. *The Rocky Mountains are in the United States.* 2. a big pile or large amount. *He looked at the mountain of bills and sighed.* {**mown** tən}

moun·tain·eer *noun* 1. a person who climbs mountains for sport. 2. a person who was born or who lives in the mountains. {**mown** tə **neer**}

mountain lion *noun* a common name for a puma, a large wild cat with tan fur. Mountain lions live in many parts of North and South America. They are carnivorous mammals. Mountain lions are also called cougars or panthers. {**mown** tən **liy** ən}

moun·tain·ous *adjective* 1. having many mountains. *There are many ski slopes in the mountainous areas of northeastern United States.* 2. very large or high; huge. *She served me a mountainous bowl of ice cream for dessert.* {**mown** tə nəs}

mountain range *noun* a group of connected mountains that were formed during the same time period. *The Himalayas are a mountain range in Asia.* {**mown** tən **raynj**}

mourn *verb* (mourned, mourning, mourns) 1. to feel or act very sad because of a death or great loss; grieve. *The city mourned for the people who had died in the explosion.* 2. to feel very sad or be sorry for. *Mr. Diaz mourned the loss of his job.* {**mohrn**}

mourn·ing *noun* 1. acts or feelings that express great sadness. *We were in mourning for weeks after our friend died.* 2. black clothing or some other item worn to show great sadness at a death. *The widow was dressed in mourning from head to toe.* {**mohr** ning}

mouse ● ● *noun* (mice) 1. a very small mammal with gray or brown fur. Mice are rodents. They have pointed faces, round ears, and long tails with no fur. Different kinds of mice are found in many parts of the world. 2. a small tool used with personal computers. The person using the computer moves the mouse to select and move items on the computer screen. Most mice are connected to the computer by a cord that looks

 Human Body   Human Mind   Everyday Life    History and Culture   Communication

like a mouse's tail. {mows} mouselike, adj.

mous·tache *noun* another spelling of **mustache**. {məs tăsh or muhs tăsh}

mouth 🌍❶🌿 *noun* 1. the opening in the face through which one eats, breathes, and makes sounds. 2. a natural opening into or from a cave or other hole. 3. the place where a river runs into a larger body of water. *verb* (mouthed, mouthing, mouths) 1. to say in a false way. *He is only mouthing his apologies.* 2. to form silently with the mouth. *My mother mouthed the words, "Stop talking so loudly."* {mowth}

mouth·ful *noun* the amount taken into the mouth at one time; bite or sip. {mowth fəl}

mouth organ *noun* another name for **harmonica**. {mowth ohr gən}

mouth·piece *noun* 1. a part of an object that is put into or near the mouth. Mouthpieces may be used to help pass speech and other sounds from one person to another or to make music. *She blew into the trumpet mouthpiece.* 2. a rubber or plastic object worn inside the mouth to protect the teeth. *It's important for football players to wear a mouthpiece.* {mowth pees}

mov·a·ble *adjective* 1. able to be moved; not stuck in place. *This doll has movable arms and legs.* 2. happening on a different date each year. *Easter and Hanukkah are movable holidays.* {moohv ə bəl} movability, n.

move 🌍❶ *verb* (moved, moving, moves) 1. to change position or place. *Let's move to better seats up front.* 2. to go ahead or progress. *Work on the new bridge is moving slowly.* 3. to change the loca-

tion of one's home or business. *They are moving to California next month.* 4. to make a request at a meeting. *The mayor moved that the law be passed.* 5. to change the position or location of. *I moved my bed to the other side of the room.* 6. to put or keep in motion. *The wind moved the sailboat.* 7. to cause to have tender or powerful feelings. *We were moved to tears by his story.* *noun* 1. the act or an instance of moving. *The dog made a move toward the cat.* 2. an action planned to bring about something. *He thought about what would help the situation before he made a move.* 3. in checkers and other board games, the act of making a play. *In one move, I jumped three of his men.* {moohv}

• **move on** to change to a new place, position, or subject. *Now that this job is done, let's move on.*

• **move over** to change position to make room for another. *Please move over so I can sit on the sofa, too.*

move·ment *noun* 1. the act or manner of moving; motion. *There was hurried movement toward the door when the bell rang.* 2. a group or groups of people acting as one. *Many people joined the peace movement because they wanted the war to end.* 3. a main section in a musical piece. *That symphony has four movements.* {moohv mənt}

mov·er *noun* (sometimes plural) a person or company whose business is to move furniture from one home or business to another. {mooh vər}

mov·ie 🌍 *noun* 1. a motion picture; film. 2. (plural) a theater where motion pictures

are shown. *Let's go to the movies.* {mooh vee}

mov·ing *adjective* 1. that changes place or position. *I saw a moving car out of the corner of my eye.* 2. producing or causing motion. *Wind is a moving force.* 3. causing a strong feeling. *He read some moving poems.* {mooh ving}

mow *verb* (mowed, mowed or mown, mowing, mows) 1. to cut down with a blade or machine. *He mowed grass to earn some money.* 2. to cut down the plant growth on. *The farmer mowed the field to make hay.* {moh}

mow·er *noun* a machine for mowing grass or a person who mows. *He got a job as a mower at the golf course.* {moh ər}

mown *verb* a past participle of **mow**. {mohn}

Homophone Note The words *mown* and *moan* sound alike but have different meanings.

Mo·zam·bique *noun* a country in southeastern Africa. Maputo is the capital of Mozambique. {moh zăm beek} Mozambican, n., adj.

M.P. *abbreviation* an abbreviation for "Member of Parliament."

mpg *abbreviation* an abbreviation for "miles per gallon."

mph *abbreviation* an abbreviation for "miles per hour."

Mr. *abbreviation* (Messrs.) an abbreviation for **Mister**, which is used before a man's name. {mih stər}

Mrs. *abbreviation* (Mmes.) an abbreviation for **Mistress**, which is used before a married woman's name. {mih sihz}

MS *abbreviation* an abbreviation for **Mississippi**.

a
b
c
d
e
f
g
h
i
j
k
l
m
n
o
p
q
r
s
t
u
v
w
x
y
z

Ms. *abbreviation* a title of respect often used before a woman's last name.

MT or **Mont.** *abbreviation* an abbreviation for **Montana**.

Mt. *abbreviation* an abbreviation for **mount**, or **mountain**.

much *adjective* (more, most) great in degree, number, or amount. *You don't have much time to finish your homework. / There isn't much time before the sun goes down.* *noun* a great amount or number. *Much work is needed to finish the new highway.* *adverb* (more, most) 1. to a great degree. *The others don't like him much. / Do you go to the movies much?* 2. nearly. *She and I are much the same.* {<u>muhch</u>}

Language Note *Much* or *many*? Which word is right for your sentence? Use *many* with things you can count. The answer to the question "how many?" will include a number. *Many fish are in the aquarium. How many fish? Fourteen fish.* Use *much* with things that cannot be counted. The answer to the question "how much?" will include an amount. *So much snow fell last night. How much snow? A lot of snow.*

mu·ci·lage *noun* a sticky substance used as glue. {<u>myoo</u> sə lihj}

mu·cus *noun* a slimy, slightly sticky material that coats and protects certain parts of the body, such as the inside of the nose and throat. {<u>myoo</u> kəs}

mud  *noun* wet earth that has been turned soft and sticky. {<u>muhd</u>}

mud·dle *verb* (muddled, muddling, muddles) 1. to cause to be confused; mix up. *The new teacher muddled the names of her students.* 2. to do badly; to make a mess of. *Because he rushed, he muddled the drawing.* 3. to think or act in a confused way. *After getting only three hours of sleep, Tom just muddled about all morning.* *noun* a confused state; mess. *Sue's first day of middle school was a muddle. / Looking for his sweater, he made a muddle of the closet.* {<u>muhd</u> əl}

Word History The word *muddle* originally meant "to stir up mud."

mud·dy *adjective* (muddier, muddiest) covered with or full of mud. *verb* (muddied, muddying, muddies) to cover with mud; make muddy. *We will muddy our boots if we walk through this wet field.* {<u>muh</u> dee} muddiness, n.

muff *noun* a tube made of warm, heavy cloth or fur. People hold their hands inside the muff to keep them warm. {<u>muhf</u>}

muf·fin *noun* a small bread that is shaped like a cupcake. Muffins are a single serving and are often eaten warm or toasted. {<u>muhf</u> fhn}

muf·fle *verb* (muffled, muffling, muffles) 1. to wrap or cover so as to protect or keep warm (often followed by "up"). *Sarah muffled up the baby in a thick blanket.* 2. to make quieter by using a covering of some sort. *The thick carpet muffled the sound of my footsteps.* {<u>muhf</u> əl}

muf·fler *noun* 1. clothing that is wrapped around the neck for warmth; scarf. 2. a device used to make the sound of a car's engine quieter. {<u>muhf</u> lər}

mug *noun* 1. a drinking cup with a handle. Mugs are made of glass, plastic, metal, or pottery. 2. the amount that such a cup holds. *I like to drink a mug of hot chocolate on a cold day.* *verb* (mugged, mugging, mugs) to attack and try to rob on the street or in some other public place. *A young criminal mugged Ms. Jones last night.* {<u>muhg</u>}

mug·gy *adjective* (muggier, muggiest) warm and damp so as to make breathing difficult. *It was hard to work on such a muggy day.* {<u>muhg</u> ee} mugginess, n.

Mu·ham·mad or **Mohammed** *noun* an Arab religious leader and the person who started Islam. He lived from A.D. 570 to A.D. 632. {mooh <u>hăm</u> əd}

mul·ber·ry *noun* (mulberries) 1. any of several shade trees that have broad leaves and berrylike fruits. 2. the fruit of such a tree. 3. a dark reddish purple color. {<u>muhl</u> behr ee}

mule *noun* 1. the offspring of a male donkey and a female horse. Mules are as large as horses, with the longer ears of a donkey. Mules can not produce young. People breed mules to use for riding or for pulling loads. 2. a person who is like a mule in some way, such as being strong or stubborn. {<u>myool</u>}

mul·ti·me·di·a or **multi-media** *adjective* the combination of sound, still pictures, and video. *Her slide show on whales shows a great use of multimedia.* *noun* the combination of sound, still pictures, and video. {<u>muhl</u> tiy mee dee uh}

 Human Body   Human Mind   Everyday Life History and Culture Communication

mul·ti·ple *adjective* having or made of more than one part; many. *The old house had multiple stories and multiple rooms. / He had multiple prints made of his favorite picture.* *noun* a number into which another number may be divided without remainder. *Six is a multiple of two.* {**muhl** tih pəl}

mul·ti·pli·cand *noun* a number that is to be multiplied by another. {**muhl** tə plih **kănd**}

mul·ti·pli·ca·tion *noun* 1. an arithmetic operation that combines two numbers to give one number, called a product. *Four times three in multiplication means combining four groups of three to give twelve in all.* 2. the act or process of increasing rapidly or multiplying. *The multiplication of geese in the park is becoming a problem.* {**muhl** tə plih **kay** shən} multiplicational, adj.

mul·ti·pli·er *noun* a number by which another number is multiplied. {**muhl** tə **pliy** ər}

mul·ti·ply ❶ ❷ *verb* (multiplied, multiplying, multiplies) 1. to increase the number, degree, or amount of. *Sam multiplied her problems when she parked in a "No Parking" area on the wrong side of the street.* 2. to grow in number, degree, or amount. *The number of new students multiplied when an apartment house was built in the neighborhood.* 3. to find the product of by doing multiplication. *You get twelve when you multiply four by three.* 4. to perform arithmetic multiplication. *Multiply to find out what 8 percent of $5.99 is.* 5. to produce offspring; reproduce. *Rabbits multiply very quickly.* {**muhl** tih **pliy**}

mul·ti·tude *noun* a large number of people, animals, or things. *A multitude gathered to watch the fireworks.* {**muhl** tih **toohd**}

mul·ti·vi·ta·min *noun* a compound or combination of several vitamins in a single pill, tablet, or dose. {**muhl** tee **viy** tə mən}

mum·ble *verb* (mumbled, mumbling, mumbles) 1. to speak low and in a way that is not easy to understand; mutter. *If you mumble, I won't be able to hear you.* 2. to say in a low voice that is not clear. *She mumbled her answers.* *noun* words that are said quietly and in a way that is not easy to understand. *His mumble made it hard for me to catch his name.* {**muhm** bəl}

mum·my *noun* (mummies) a dead body that has been preserved with special chemicals and wrapped in cloth. *The ancient Egyptians are famous for their mummies.* {**muhm** ee}

mumps *noun* (used with a singular or plural verb) a disease that children get that causes the glands to swell. {**muhmps**}

munch *verb* (munched, munching, munches) to chew in a noisy way, making a crunching sound. *He munched popcorn as he watched the movie.* {**muhnch**}

mu·nic·i·pal *adjective* of or having to do with a local government or unit of government. *The state police came to help the municipal police solve the crime.* {myoo **nih** sih pəl}

mu·ral *noun* a large picture painted on or made a part of a wall or ceiling. *The artist painted a huge mural of a garden on the wall of the restaurant.* {**myoor** əl}

> **Word History** *Mural* is from a Latin word that means "a wall."

mur·der ● *noun* the deliberate and unlawful killing of a person. *verb* (murdered, murdering, murders) to kill a person in a way that is deliberate or cruel. *He murdered three people and will be in prison for the rest of his life.* {**muhr** dər} murderer, n., murderess, n.

murk·y *adjective* (murkier, murkiest) 1. dark or gloomy. *There were scary noises coming from the murky cellar.* 2. cloudy or difficult to understand; obscure. *He had only a murky idea of what the book was about.* {**muhr** kee} murkiness, n.

mur·mur *noun* a sound that is soft, muffled, and ongoing, like the sound made by quiet conversation. *verb* (murmured, murmuring, murmurs) to make a soft, muffled, continuous sound. *We heard the brook murmur in the distance.* {**muhr** mər} murmuring, adj.

mus·cle ● *noun* 1. tissue in the body of animals and humans that moves parts of the body. Muscle is made up of bundles of fibers that move the body by tightening and relaxing. 2. a mass of such tissue that moves a particular part of the body. *The biceps is a muscle at the front of the upper arm that bends the elbow.* 3. physical strength. *It took a lot of muscle for them to lift the log.* {**muhs** əl}

> **Homophone Note** The words *muscle* and *mussel* (a mollusk) sound alike but have different meanings.

 Living World   Physical World  Natural Environment Economy  Government and Law

Musical Instruments

gong

drumsticks

maracas

African marimba

Percussion

snare drum

dumbek

bongos

djembe

electronic d

spike fiddle

electric guitar

banjo

violin

acoustic guitar

bass

harp

String

Word History *Muscle* comes from a Latin word that means "little mouse." Some muscles in the arm and leg look like a mouse moving under the skin.

mus·cu·lar *adjective* 1. having to do with muscle. *In science class we learned about muscular diseases.* 2. having muscles that are large or strong. *Tennis players have muscular arms.* {**muhs** kyə lər} muscularity, n.

muse ❓ *verb* (mused, musing, muses) to think about something silently or for a long time. *My father looked through the photographs and mused about the old days.* {**myooz**}

Muse 🔵 *noun* 1. any of the nine Greek goddesses of the arts and sciences. 2. (lower case) the source of creative ideas for an artist or scientist. {**myooz**}

mu·se·um 🔵🔵 *noun* a building where collections of objects that are important to history, art, or science are kept and shown to the public. {myoo **zee** əm}

Word History *Museum* comes from an ancient Greek word that meant "place of the Muses."

mush *noun* 1. a thick, soft cereal that is made of corn meal boiled in water or milk. 2. any mass that is like this cereal in texture. *Eat your ice cream before it turns into mush!* {**muhsh**}

mush·room 🔽 *noun* a fungus with a stalk and a cap that looks like a small umbrella. Some kinds of mushrooms can be eaten; other kinds are poisonous. Mushrooms live in damp places and are the fruiting bodies of certain kinds of fungi. *adjective* of or containing mushrooms. *This mushroom soup is delicious.* *verb* (mushroomed, mushrooming, mushrooms) to appear, grow, spread, or develop quickly, like a mushroom. *The number of video stores has mushroomed in the past few years.* {**muhsh** roohm}

mush·y *adjective* (mushier, mushiest) soft and thick, like mush. *The mud felt mushy between his toes.* {**muhsh** ee} mushiness, n.

mu·sic 🔵🔵 *noun* 1. sound with tones and rhythm that can be listened to and enjoyed. Music can be made by voices or instruments. *When the music started, people clapped their hands and tapped their feet.* 2. the art of taking different tones and rhythms and making them into a piece that can be played or sung; the art of creating a musical composition. *We learned about the history of music in the United States by listening to CDs.* 3. a work of art that can be played or sung. It is made by combining tones and rhythms into a complete musical piece. *Do you like this music by my favorite composer?* 4. the written or printed signs for a musical piece; the written form of a musical composition; score. *I bought the music for some of my favorite songs so I could play them on the piano.* {**myoo** zihk}

mu·si·cal *adjective* 1. of, like, or having to do with music. *The robin's song was very musical.* / *The piano is a musical instrument.* 2. good at or fond of music. *Bob was a musical child who started playing the flute when he was only three.* 3. having or using music; with music. *Andrew Lloyd Webber wrote musical plays, including "Cats," and "Phantom of the Opera."* {**myoo** zih kəl}

music box *noun* a box containing a mechanical device that plays music. The music plays by winding a knob, lifting the lid of the box, or some other action. {**myoo** zihk **bŏks**}

mu·si·cian *noun* a person skilled at playing, singing, or writing music. *She practiced the piano for years before she thought of herself as a musician.* {myoo **zih** shən}

musk *noun* 1. a substance with a strong smell made by the gland of a certain kind of male deer. Musk is used in making some perfumes. 2. an artificial substance that smells like the natural deer substance. This kind of musk is also used in making perfume. {**muhsk**}

mus·ket *noun* a heavy gun with a long barrel. Muskets were carried on the shoulder. They were used over three hundred years ago, before rifles were invented. {**muh** skiht}

mus·ket·eer *noun* a soldier who carried and used a musket. {muhs kə **teer**}

musk·mel·on *noun* a round melon with juicy, sweet flesh that ranges in color from almost white to light orange or green. A cantaloupe is a kind of muskmelon. {**muhsk** meh lən}

musk ox *noun* a large mammal with long, dark fur and wide horns. Musk oxen live in the northern regions of North America and Greenland. They have wide hooves for walking on snow. Musk oxen are closely related to cattle. {**muhsk** ŏks}

 Human Body   Human Mind   Everyday Life    History and Culture   Communication

musk·rat *noun* (muskrat or muskrats) a North American rodent that lives in and near water. Muskrats are about one foot long with brown fur and a long tail. They make burrows in the banks of streams or build reed huts in marshes and ponds. {<u>muhsk</u> răt}

Mus·lim *adjective* dealing with the religion of Islam. *noun* one who follows the religion of Islam. {<u>mŏz</u> ləm *or* <u>mŏs</u> ləm}

mus·lin *noun* a sturdy cotton cloth used for sheets and clothing. {<u>muhz</u> lihn}

muss *verb* (mussed, mussing, musses) to make a mess of; put into disorder (often followed by "up"). *Someone has mussed up my desk.* {muhs}

mus·sel *noun* an animal with a soft body and a hard shell made of two hinged pieces that open and close. Many kinds of mussels live in the ocean and in fresh water. Mussels are mollusks and are closely related to clams and oysters. People eat some kinds of mussels. {<u>muh</u> səl}

Homophone Note The words *mussel* and *muscle* (a body part) sound alike but have different meanings.

Working out underwater six days a week, the **mussel** strutted on the beach to show off his new **muscles**.

must *auxiliary verb* 1. to be forced to; have to or need to. *We must breathe in order to live.* 2. to be required to; ought to; should. *Children must attend school.* 3. used to command or suggest. *You must not pull the cat's tail!* 4. to be likely to. *The road is wet, so it must have rained.* {muhst}

mus·tache or **moustache** *noun* the hair that grows above a human's upper lip. This hair is often allowed to grow and then is cut or trimmed into shape. *My uncle's mustache is so long that he must comb it.* {<u>muhs</u> tăsh *or* mə <u>stăsh</u>}

mus·tang *noun* a wild horse of the western plains of North America. {<u>muhs</u> tăng}

mus·tard *noun* 1. a group of plants native to Europe and Asia. Mustard plants have yellow flowers and seeds that grow in pods. 2. a powder or paste with a strong taste made from the ground seeds of the mustard plant. Mustard is used to flavor food or spread on the skin as medicine. 3. a dark yellow color that looks like this paste. {<u>muhs</u> tərd}

mus·ter *verb* (mustered, mustering, musters) 1. to cause to come together; assemble. *The mayor mustered two dozen people to pick up litter along the highway.* 2. to come together or gather for a purpose. *The team mustered in the gym to get their uniforms.* 3. to gather up or call forth from within oneself (often followed by "up"). *He mustered up all his courage and told the man he had broken the window.* *noun* a group brought together or assembled, such as a military unit. *A muster of sailors stood at attention on the deck.* {<u>muh</u> stər}

must·n't shortened form of "must not." *You mustn't use such rude language.* {muhs ənt}

must·y *adjective* (mustier, mustiest) having a taste or smell of mold; damp or stale. *After being closed up all winter, the attic smelled musty.* {<u>muhs</u> tee} mustiness, n.

mu·tant *noun* a life form whose genes are different from those of its parents. A mutant has new traits or characteristics that it can pass on to its offspring. {<u>myoo</u> tənt}

mute *adjective* (muter, mutest) 1. not able or willing to speak; silent. *He was mute in the presence of the king.* 2. not having the power of speech. *The man was both deaf and mute.* 3. not pronounced. *The letter "b" in the word "comb" is mute.* *noun* 1. a person who cannot speak. 2. a device used to soften the sound of a musical instrument. *He put a mute on his trumpet so as not to disturb the neighbors while he practiced.* *verb* (muted, muting, mutes) to decrease the sound or force of. *He muted the television during the commercials.* {<u>myoot</u>} muteness, n.

mu·ti·late *verb* (mutilated, mutilating, mutilates) 1. to destroy by cutting or tearing off a necessary part. *The tiger mutilated its prey.* 2. to harm or damage by taking off or destroying parts. *The angry child mutilated the doll by pulling off its arms.* {<u>myoot</u> ə <u>layt</u>} mutilation, n., mutilator, n.

mu·ti·neer *noun* one who openly goes against the person or group in charge; one who takes part in a mutiny. {myoo tih <u>neer</u>}

mu·ti·ny *noun* (mutinies) open disobeying or fighting against

A
B
C
D
E
F
G
H
I
J
K
L
M
N
O
P
Q
R
S
T
U
V
W
X
Y
Z

 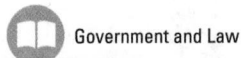

a
b
c
d
e
f
g
h
i
j
k
l
m
n
o
p
q
r
s
t
u
v
w
x
y
z

the leaders in charge; open rebellion against lawful authority. *verb* (mutinied, mutinying, mutinies) to openly disobey or fight the leaders in charge or a lawful authority. *The sailors mutinied against their cruel captain.* {**myoot** ih nee}

mutt *noun* a dog of mixed or unknown breed; mongrel. *Spot may be a mutt, but he's still a good dog.* {**muht**}

mut·ter *verb* (muttered, muttering, mutters) to speak in a low tone that is hard to understand; mumble. *Casey muttered to herself when she failed to catch the ball. noun* quiet complaining speech that is hard to understand or not clear. *A mutter of disgust went through the crowd as the player struck out.* {**muht** ər}

mut·ton *noun* the meat of an adult sheep. {**muht** ən}

mu·tu·al *adjective* 1. felt, said, or done by each for the other; shared by two or more people; given and received. *Karen and Ralph have a mutual love for each other. / We made a mutual promise to write one another.* 2. having the same relationship toward each other or one another. *Cats and dogs are mutual enemies.* {**myoo** chooh əl} mutually, adv.

muz·zle *noun* 1. the part of the head of some animals that contains the nose, jaws, and mouth. *Some dogs have a long muzzle and others, like boxers, do not.* 2. a device made of leather or wire mesh that is placed over this part of the head to keep the animal from biting, eating, or barking. 3. the open end of the barrel of a gun. A bullet is shot out of a gun through the muzzle. Old rifles were loaded through the muzzle. 4.

something that holds back or stops free expression. *In some countries, the government puts a muzzle on news reporters. verb* (muzzled, muzzling, muzzles) 1. to cover the jaws and mouth to stop from biting, barking, or eating. *Our neighbor muzzled his dog after it tried to bite someone.* 2. to stop from speaking freely in public. *The harsh government muzzled anyone who complained about the new laws.* {**muhz** əl}

my *pronoun* of or belonging to the speaker (a possessive form of "I"). *Have you seen my jacket?* {**miy**}

My·an·mar *noun* a country in southeastern Asia. Myanmar was called Burma until 1989. Rangoon (or Yangon) is the capital of Myanmar. {**mee** ən mar}

myr·tle *noun* 1. a kind of shrub that has evergreen leaves and bears pink or white flowers and fragrant dark blue berries. Myrtle is found in the Mediterranean region and western Asia. 2. a kind of plant found in the United States that grows close to the ground and has shiny evergreen leaves and blue flowers. {**muhr** təl}

my·self *pronoun* (ourselves) 1. used to emphasize "me" or "I." *I myself am not fond of chocolate.* 2. my own self (used to show that the action is done by and to the speaker's own self). *Today I will take myself out to dinner.* 3. my normal or customary condition or way of being. *I am not myself today.* {**miy sehlf**}

mys·te·ri·ous *adjective* 1. full of or relating to mystery. *"I have a secret," she said, in a mysterious whisper.* 2. not known and not able to be explained;

puzzling. *Astronomers became interested in the mysterious flashes of light in the sky.* {mih **steer** ee əs} mysteriously, adv.

mys·ter·y ❷ ⬭ *noun* (mysteries) 1. a matter that is secret or that cannot be known or explained. *Nobody fully understands the mystery of how the human brain works.* 2. a book, play, or other piece of fiction about a crime that is puzzling. *Sir Arthur Conan Doyle wrote many mysteries about the detective Sherlock Holmes.* {**mihs** tə ree}

mys·ti·fy *verb* (mystified, mystifying, mystifies) to confuse or puzzle, often on purpose. *The last math problem mystified me.* {**mihs** tih **fiy**} mystification, n.

myth ⬭ *noun* 1. a story or group of stories that form part of the traditional knowledge of a society. Myths often use imaginative plots and characters to explain how the world began and why nature and people behave the way they do. *An old Egyptian myth tells why the Nile River floods every year.* 2. a story, person, or thing that has been made up or imagined and is not real. *Her story about seeing an alien spacecraft is a myth.* {**mihth**}

myth·i·cal *adjective* 1. having to do with or appearing in a myth. *Many constellations have mythical names.* 2. not real; not existing in fact; imaginary. *We found out that her rich father and her mansion were entirely mythical.* {**mihth** ih kəl} mythic, adj.

my·thol·o·gy *noun* (mythologies) a collection of myths. *Niagwahe is a fearful beast of Iroquois mythology.* {mih **thŏl** ə jee}

 Human Body ❓ Human Mind  Everyday Life 🚩 History and Culture  Communication

Nn

N is a consonant that always makes the same sound.

Tips to help you look up words starting with n: A few words are spelled with a silent letter before the "n." Also look under G, K, or P for words such as gnash, gnome, knew, knight, or pneumonia.

These words may be hard to look up if you don't already know how to spell them:

necessary	night
negotiate	ninety
neighbor	none
neither	November
nestle	nuclear
nickel	nuisance

n or **N** *noun* (n's or N's) the fourteenth letter of the English alphabet. {**ehn**}

N symbol of the chemical element nitrogen.

Na symbol of the chemical element sodium.

NAACP *abbreviation* an organization that works for equal rights for African Americans. NAACP is the abbreviation for "National Association for the Advancement of Colored People."

nab *verb* (nabbed, nabbing, nabs) 1. (informal) to catch or seize; arrest. *After a long chase, the police officer nabbed the bank robber.* 2. to grab or snatch. *The thief nabbed her purse.* {**năb**}

nag[1] *verb* (nagged, nagging, nags) 1. to bother by complaining or asking for something again and again; pester. *The children nagged their mother for ice cream all afternoon.* 2. to trouble, bother, or make uncomfortable for a long time. *This cough is nagging me.* *noun* a person who nags. *My sister can be a nag when she wants something badly.* {**năg**}

nag[2] *noun* a horse that has little value and cannot be used for hard work. *The old nag can pull a small cart, but she can no longer pull a plow.* {**năg**}

nail  *noun* 1. a slim, pointed metal rod with a flat top. A nail is hammered into pieces of wood or other material in order to fasten them together. 2. a hard growth at the end of a finger or toe. *I clipped my nails so it would be easier to play the piano.* *verb* (nailed, nailing, nails) to fasten or strengthen with a nail or nails. *Dad nailed the basketball hoop to the side of the garage.* {**nayl**}

na·ked *adjective* 1. wearing no clothing; bare. *The naked baby splashed in the bathtub.* 2. without the usual covering. *In winter we can see the* squirrel nests high in the naked tree branches. 3. without the help of any lenses to make the sight better. *Most cells are too small to be seen by the naked eye.* {**nay** kihd} naked-ness, n.

name *noun* 1. a word or group of words by which something or someone is known. *What is the name of that kind of snake?* / *The name of the thirteenth president of the United States is Millard Fillmore.* 2. reputation. *She has established a good name for herself.* *verb* (named, naming, names) 1. to give a name to. *I named my kitten Fluffy, because she has fluffy fur.* 2. to call or mention by name. *The teacher named those who had to stay after school.* 3. to choose for a particular office or duty. *The mayor named him chief of police.* {**naym**}

name·ly *adverb* that is to say; in other words. Used before stating more exactly who or what one is talking about. *She was happy to have met those fine young men, namely, Bill, Bob, and Ben.* {**naym** lee}

nan·ny *noun* (nannies) a person who is hired to take care of another person's children. *A nanny watches Andy and his sister while their parents are at work.* {**năn** ee}

nap[1] *verb* to sleep for a short time during daylight hours. *The baby naps at two o'clock every afternoon.* *noun* a short period of sleep during daylight hours. *My grandfather takes a quick nap every afternoon.* {**năp**}

nap[2] *noun* the soft, fuzzy, or furry surface on cloth or leather. *This carpet has a thick nap.* / *Velvet has a soft nap.* {**năp**}

nap·kin *noun* a piece of cloth or paper used to protect the

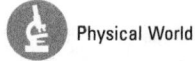 Living World    Physical World   Natural Environment   Economy    Government and Law

a
b
c
d
e
f
g
h
i
j
k
l
m
n
o
p
q
r
s
t
u
v
w
x
y
z

clothing and to wipe the mouth and hands while eating. {**năp** kihn}

nar·cis·sus *noun* (narcissuses) 1. a kind of plant that has yellow or white flowers and long, thin leaves. The narcissus grows from a bulb planted in the soil. Its flowers are shaped like a tube. 2. the flower of this plant. 3. (capital) in Greek mythology, a young man who fell in love with his own reflection and, when he perished from unfulfilled love, was transformed into a flower. {nar **sihs** əs}

nar·cot·ic *noun* a drug that causes a person to become sleepy or unconscious and that may be used as a medicine to dull pain or cause sleep. Narcotics can be dangerous when not used as a medicine and can become hard to give up. {nar **kŏt** ihk}

nar·rate  *verb* (narrated, narrating, narrates) to tell the tale or give an account of; relate. *Frederick Douglass narrates the events of his life in a famous book.* {nar **ayt**}

nar·ra·tive *noun* a story, description, or account of events. *Novels are long narratives.* {**nar** ə tihv}

nar·ra·tor *noun* a person or character who tells a story. *In this book, the narrator is a teenager.* {nă **ray** tər}

nar·row *adjective* (narrower, narrowest) 1. not wide or broad. *The bus could not pass through that narrow alley.* 2. being fixed in ideas or opinions. *People with narrow minds don't often trust new ideas.* 3. barely enough; close. *We had a narrow escape when the tornado passed two blocks from our house.* *verb* (narrowed, narrowing, narrows) 1. to become narrower. *The*

road narrows here, so drive carefully. 2. to make narrower. *The police narrowed the area of their search for the lost child.* *noun* (plural, but used with a singular or plural verb) a narrow part of a river or other body of water. *The bridge spanned the narrows.* {**nar** oh} narrowly, adv., narrowness, n.

NASA *abbreviation* an American organization that conducts space travel and research. NASA stands for "National Aeronautics and Space Administration." {**năs** ə}

na·sal *adjective* 1. of the nose. *This cold medicine will clear your nasal passages.* 2. sounding as if spoken by pushing air up through the nose instead of the mouth. *That singer has a nasal voice. / The French language has many nasal sounds.* {**nay** zəl}

na·stur·ti·um *noun* a kind of garden plant that grows close to the ground and has bright yellow, orange, or red flowers. Nasturtium leaves and flowers can be eaten. {nă **stuhr** shəm *or* nə **stuhr** shəm}

nas·ty *adjective* (nastier, nastiest) 1. disgusting to sight, smell, or taste; foul or filthy. *Rotten eggs have a nasty smell.* 2. rude, mean, or hateful; not nice or decent. *Jill had to apologize for playing a nasty trick on Jack.* 3. causing harm, troubles, or danger. *He took a nasty fall.* {**năs** tee}

na·tion *noun* 1. a people living in the same region of the world and having a common history, language, and culture. *Mexico is a nation in North America.* 2. a people living under its own independent government. *Our nation elects a president*

every four years. {**nay** shən} nationhood, n.

na·tion·al *adjective* 1. of or having to do with an entire nation. *Public education is a national concern.* 2. specific to or characteristic of one particular nation. *Baseball is the national pastime of the United States.* {**năsh** ə nəl} nationally, adv.

na·tion·al·ism *noun* devotion to one's own nation; desire for one's nation to be successful or independent; patriotism. *A wave of nationalism swept the country after the attacks of September 11, 2001.* {**năsh** ə nə lihz əm}

na·tion·al·i·ty *noun* (nationalities) 1. the condition of belonging to a particular nation by having been born there or by becoming a citizen. *Our guest's nationality is Egyptian.* 2. a people living in the same region of the world and having a common history, language, and culture. *People of many nationalities visit the United Kingdom.* {**năsh** ə **năl** ih tee}

na·tive *adjective* 1. being the place of birth or origin. *He was lonely for his native land.* 2. beginning with a person at birth; natural. *Leila has a native talent for music.* 3. belonging to a person or persons because of their place of birth. *Spanish is his native language.* *noun* 1. an original resident of a given place, such as the Inuit people of Alaska and northern Canada. *This river has been fished by natives for thousands of years.* 2. a person born or raised in a given place. *Thomas Jefferson was a native of Virginia.* 3. an animal or plant found naturally in a given place. *Lions are natives of Africa.* {**nay** tihv}

 Human Body    Human Mind   Everyday Life    History and Culture   Communication

Native American *noun* a member of any of the peoples who were living in North America, South America, or Central America, before the Europeans arrived. {**nay** tihv ə **meh** rih kən}

NATO *abbreviation* a group of nations that have promised to defend each other in times of need. NATO stands for "North Atlantic Treaty Organization." The United States, Canada, Turkey, and many European nations are members of NATO. {**nay** toh}

nat·u·ral *adjective* 1. of or produced by nature; not made by humans. *She uses only natural ingredients in her cooking.* 2. according to or resulting from human nature. *Human beings have a natural desire for companionship.* 3. not pretended or forced. *Your smile in this school photo doesn't look natural.* 4. expected; ordinary. *It is natural for teenagers to be confused about life.* 5. having to do with the sciences that study and describe nature. *He started out as a physicist, but soon took an interest in the natural sciences.* *noun* a person who is considered to be gifted or just right for a particular activity. *He's a natural for the part of King Arthur.* {**nǎch** ər əl *or* **nǎch** rəl, n., **nǎch** ər əl *or* **nǎch** rəl, adj.} naturalness, n.

natural gas *noun* a mixture of gases found in the earth's crust. Natural gas is burned as cooking and heating fuel. {**nǎch** ər əl **gǎs** *or* **nǎch** rəl **gǎs**}

natural history *noun* the study of plants, animals, rocks, land forms, and other objects in nature or the physical world. {**nǎch** ər əl **hihs** tə ree}

nat·u·ral·ist *noun* a person who studies the natural world, especially plants and animals. {**nǎch** ə rə lihst *or* **nǎch** rə lihst}

nat·u·ral·ize *verb* (naturalized, naturalizing, naturalizes) to make a citizen of; grant the rights of a citizen to. *In a special ceremony, the judge naturalized a large group of people who had moved to Canada from other countries.* {**nǎch** ə rə liyz *or* **nǎch** rə liyz}

nat·u·ral·ly *adverb* 1. in a natural way; in a normal manner. *I tried to speak naturally when I gave my report, even though my knees were shaking.* 2. by nature. *She is a naturally curious child.* / *Dogs wag their tails naturally.* 3. of course; surely; without a doubt. *Naturally I will pass the test.* {**nǎch** ə rə lee *or* **nǎch** rə lee}

natural resources 🌐 *noun* materials that are found in nature and that can be used by people in many ways. Fresh water, soil, coal, and forests are all examples of natural resources. {**nǎ** chər əl **ree sohr** sihz}

na·ture ❓🌐 *noun* 1. basic character and qualities of a person or thing. *It's not in her nature to be mean.* / *He doesn't understand the nature of our business.* 2. the physical world and living things in their natural state; all things that are not made by people. *A camping trip is a good way to experience nature.* 3. kind; variety. *He likes action films, adventure books, and things of that nature.* {**nay** chər}

naught *or* **nought** *noun* 1. the number zero. *Naught plus two equals two.* 2. nothing. *Our weeks of planning for a picnic came to naught because of a bad storm.* {**nawt**}

naugh·ty *adjective* (naughtier, naughtiest) not behaving or obeying; mischievous. *That naughty girl hit her sister.* / *Hiding grandfather's slippers was a naughty thing to do.* {**naw** tee} naughtily, adv., naughtiness, n.

> **Word History** *Naughty* comes from an early English word that meant "having naught (nothing)," "needy," or "evil." By 1600, "naughty" was no longer a strong enough word to describe an evil person. Around this time, the word was being used for behavior that was disobedient, or for things of poor quality, such as "naughty apples."

nau·se·a *noun* a sick feeling in the stomach with the need to vomit. *Riding a roller coaster causes nausea in some people.* {**naw** see ə *or* **naw** shə *or* **naw** zee ə *or* **naw** zhə}

> **Word History** *Nausea* is a Latin word that means "seasickness." The English word "nautical" (having to do with sailors) is related to this word.

nau·ti·cal *adjective* having to do with the sea, sailing, or sailors. *The seafood restaurant had nautical decorations.* {**naw** tih kəl} nautically, adv.

nautical mile *noun* a unit of length equal to 1.852 kilometers or 6,076.1 feet, used to measure the distance traveled by sea and air. {**naw** tih kəl **miyl**}

Nav·a·jo *or* **Navaho** *noun* (Navajo or Navajos) a member of a Native American people whose homeland lies in parts of Arizona, New

A B C D E F G H I J K L M **N** O P Q R S T U V W X Y Z

 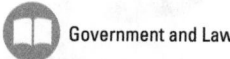

Native Americans

When Columbus landed in America in 1492, both North and South America were already home to a great number of Native American cultures. These cultures were as diverse as the climates and terrains they inhabited, from the tip of South America to the Arctic Circle. Columbus called the Americans he first encountered "Indians" because he thought he was in India.

We still know little about the early history of the first Americans. We know much more about how the arrival of Europeans in the 1500s changed their history. Spain, England, and France saw great opportunities in the "New World" of the Americas. The first Spanish explorers were hungry for the precious metals and jewels they had heard were in South America. The French were more interested in fishing, hunting, and the fur trade. The English wanted to acquire land and develop it for farming on a large scale. Unfortunately, these opportunities were often seized at the expense of the freedom, lives, and property of the Native Americans.

Sacajawea

Sacajawea was a young Shoshone woman who, with her infant son, accompanied Lewis and Clark on their expedition to the Pacific Ocean in 1804. Sacajawea had been sold into slavery by another tribe and forced to marry a French Canadian man. On the journey with Lewis and Clark, Sacajawea played an important role as a translator.

Joseph Brant

Chief Joseph Brant (1743-1808) was a Mohawk leader. In the more peaceful periods, he tried to unite the tribes of the northeast. He thought that together they could protect their homeland from being taken over by the new Americans.

Jim Thorpe

Jim Thorpe is considered one of the greatest athletes of the twentieth century. He was a member of the Sauk and Fox tribes. His prowess as an all-around athlete led him to the 1912 Olympic Games. He won medals for both the decathlon and the pentathlon. He was also an outstanding professional football player and baseball player.

Geronimo

Geronimo was an Apache leader, the last and most important leader of the Apache Wars. Geronimo had a fierce ability in warfare; he also had fantastic luck. This combination led people to regard him as a medicine man as well as a warrior.

Sitting Bull

Sitting Bull was one of the main leaders of the Sioux people. Sitting Bull was more a political leader than a war leader, although his courage was legendary. The Sioux and their allies had much power in the northern Plains. In the struggle to keep control over the riches of their lands, Sitting Bull led the Sioux into the battle at Little Big Horn in 1876. The Sioux destroyed Custer's army. He led what was left of the Sioux nation into Canada.

Squanto

05, Squanto sailed to England, where he learned glish. He returned to the New World, where he s kidnapped by an English captain and sold into slavery. Squanto finally managed to return to erica once again, only to find his tribe and family been wiped out by smallpox. A man without a try, he devoted the rest of his life to teaching the ms the crafts and skills they needed for survival.

Sequoia

a, a Cherokee genius, is famous for developing ly written Indian language. Before this event, the tribe's history, stories, and legends were ed on by the spoken word. After Sequoia, the tribe published newspapers!

Tecumseh

Tecumseh, a Shawnee, also tried to unite tribes from all over the continent. He was driven by his conviction that all of the American land was owned by all of the tribes and that no tribe could sell a part of this common heritage. He had some success in uniting the tribes, but war continued and he died fighting the new Americans in October, 1813.

Mexico, and Utah. {**năv** ə hoh or **nah** və hoh}

na·val *adjective* 1. having to do with a navy or its ships. *The naval officers stood on the deck of the patrol boat.* 2. having a navy. *For hundreds of years, England was a great naval power.* {**nay** vəl} navally, adv.

Homophone Note Are you looking for the word *navel* (a scar on the abdomen)? *Naval* and *navel* sound alike but have different meanings.

na·vel *noun* a round scar or hollow just below a person's waist. The navel is the spot where the umbilical cord was attached before the person's birth. {**nay** vəl}

Homophone Note The words *navel* and *naval* (of ships) sound alike but have different meanings.

nav·i·gate *verb* (navigated, navigating, navigates) 1. to plan, manage, or control the course of. *The astronauts navigated the space shuttle to and from the space station.* 2. to sail, fly, or travel across, along, or through. *The captain navigated the Panama Canal.* {**năv** ih gayt}

nav·i·ga·tion *noun* the act of setting a course for or controlling a ship or aircraft. *Navigation is difficult in bad weather. / My grandfather is teaching me how to navigate by the stars.* {**năv** ih **gay** shən}

nav·i·ga·tor *noun* a person who charts, sets, and steers the course of a ship or aircraft. {**năv** ih **gay** tər}

na·vy ⊕ *noun* (navies) 1. (often capitalized) the part of a nation's military organization that conducts war on or over the sea. *My grandfather served in the Navy during World War Two.* 2. all of a

country's warships together with their crews, officers, bases and supplies. *Countries with seacoasts often have a navy.* 3. a dark blue color. *Navy is a good choice for a business suit.* {**nay** vee}

nay *adverb* no. The word "nay" used to be part of common speech but now is only used to say "no" in voting. *The congresswoman voted nay on the tax bill.* *noun* a vote against. *Out of all the votes cast, there were only two nays.* {**nay**}

Homophone Note Are you looking for the word *neigh* (the sound of a horse)? The words *nay* and *neigh* sound alike but have different meanings.

Na·zi *noun* (Nazis) a member of the political party that held power in Germany from 1933 to 1945. This political party was led by Adolf Hitler. The word "Nazi" is a short form of the German name for "National Socialist German Workers' Party." {**naht** see} Nazism (Naziism), n.

NC or **N.C.** *abbreviation* an abbreviation for **North Carolina**.

NC17 *abbreviation* a movie rating that means persons seventeen years old and younger will not be admitted. NC17 stands for "No Children 17 or Under."

ND or **N. Dak.** *abbreviation* an abbreviation for **North Dakota**.

NE *abbreviation* 1. an abbreviation for **Nebraska**. 2. an abbreviation for **northeast**. 3. an abbreviation for **New England**.

Ne symbol of the chemical element neon.

near *adverb* (nearer, nearest) 1. to, at, or within a short dis-

tance from a person or thing. *I recognized his face as he came near.* 2. close in time, state, or condition. *Your birthday draws near.* 3. almost; nearly. *We walked near five miles on our hike.* *adjective* (nearer, nearest) 1. not far; close. *I look forward to seeing you in the near future.* 2. closely related, connected, or associated. *They are near relations.* 3. happening by a small amount; almost not happening. *We've had several near misses with deer on this road at night.* *preposition* at or close to. *He bought a house near the ocean.* *verb* (neared, nearing, nears) to move close or closer to. *The train neared the station.* {**neer**} nearness, n.

Synonyms
These words share a meaning with *near*, adverb 1:

about About is a less formal way of saying a person or thing is in the same general area as another. *They are somewhere about.*

around Around means in the same general area as something else. *If you go outside, stay around the house.*

close Close is almost exactly synonymous with near. *The comet passed very close to the earth.*

nearby Nearby often implies being ready to offer aid or comfort. *Stay nearby in case we need you to help.*

near·by *adjective* located close at hand; not far away. *Tanya works at a nearby supermarket.* *adverb* in an area or position close by. *Stay nearby in case we need your help.* {**neer** **biy**}

near·ly *adverb* almost; just about but not quite. *We are nearly there.* {**neer** lee}

near·sight·ed *adjective* able to see objects clearly only when

 Human Body Human Mind Everyday Life History and Culture Communication

they are near. *After she got glasses, the nearsighted girl could see the chalkboard from the back of the room.* {**neer siyt** ihd} nearsightedness, n.

neat *adjective* (neater, neatest) 1. clean and in proper order, or liking to keep things that way; tidy. *I keep my room neat. / Luke is a neat person and always cleans up after himself.* 2. careful and exact; organized and simple. *Sharif found a neat way to solve that math problem.* 3. clever. *He came up with the neat idea of shoveling sidewalks to earn money.* {**neet**} neatly, adv., neatness, n.

Synonyms
These words share a meaning with **neat**, adjective 1:
orderly, trim, tidy

Neb. *abbreviation* an abbreviation for **Nebraska**.

Ne·bras·ka *noun* a state in the midwestern United States. Its capital is Lincoln. (abbreviated: NE) {nə **brăs** kə}

Word History *Nebraska* means "flat water," and was based on the Oto name for the Platte River.

neb·u·la *noun* (nebulae or nebulas) a cloud of dust or gas found between the stars. A nebula may seem either bright or dark, depending on how it reacts with light. *On a clear winter night, you can see a bright nebula in the constellation Orion.* {**nehb** yə lə} nebular, adj.

Word History *Nebula* is a Latin word that means "cloud or mist." It entered the English language in the 1500s as a term for the clouding of the eye we now call a "cataract." In the 1700s, "nebula" became a term in astronomy.

nec·es·sar·i·ly *adverb* certain to be. *Rich people are not necessarily happy.* {nehs ə **sayr** ih lee}

nec·es·sar·y *adjective* 1. needed; not able to be put aside. *My brother does not have the cash necessary to buy a car. / A strong goalie is a necessary part of a soccer team.* 2. expected or needed under given circumstances. *He made the necessary arrangements for his guests.* {**nehs** ə **sayr** ee}

ne·ces·si·ty *noun* (necessities) 1. a person or thing that is needed. *Eight hours of sleep every night is a necessity for me.* 2. the state or condition of being needed. *We understood the necessity of seeing a dentist for a toothache.* {nə **sehs** ih tee}

neck 🌐 *noun* 1. the part of the body of both human beings and animals that connects the head with the body. 2. the part of an article of clothing that fits around the neck. *She wore a gold pin just below the neck of her blouse.* 3. the narrow top section of something. *The neck of the bottle was too small for the coins to fit through. / The neck of the guitar was made of maple.* {**nehk**}

 • **neck and neck**
in almost the same position; nearly even. *The horses were racing neck and neck.*

neck·er·chief *noun* a square of cloth folded and tied about the neck. *A neckerchief is part of the scout uniform.* {**neh** kər chihf}

neck·lace *noun* jewelry worn around the neck. A necklace can be made of beads, precious stones,

metals, or other materials. {**nehk** lihs}

neck·tie *noun* a strip of cloth worn around the neck, usually by men. A necktie is tucked under the collar of a shirt and knotted at the throat. {**nehk tiy**}

nec·tar *noun* the sweet liquid a plant makes that attracts insects and birds. *Bees use nectar to make honey.* {**nehk** tər}

nec·tar·ine *noun* a type of peach with a smooth skin. {**nehk** tə **reen** or **nehk** tə reen}

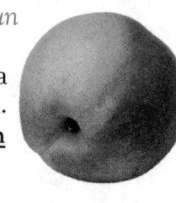

need *noun* 1. something that one wants or must have. *I have a need to be with my family.* 2. the lack of something that is necessary or essential. *The crops are in need of rain. / There is a need for skilled workers.* 3. a state of want; poverty. *It is a shame that many people live in need.* *verb* (needed, needing, needs) to have a requirement for. *Humans need water to live.* *auxiliary verb* (needed, needing, needs) to have to do because necessary or promised. *You need not go to the meeting.* {**need**}

Synonyms
These words share a meaning with **need**, noun 2:
want, lack, shortage, deficiency

Homophone Note Are you looking for the word **knead** (to press or rub)? **Need** and **knead** sound alike but have different meanings.

nee·dle 🔵 🟠 *noun* 1. a thin instrument made of steel with a hole at one end for thread and a sharp point at the other. A needle is used

A B C D E F G H I J K L M **N** O P Q R S T U V W X Y Z

for sewing cloth or closing wounds. 2. a long, slender rod used for knitting or crocheting, and made of steel, wood, plastic, or some other material. 3. a very thin metal tube with a sharp point, used to put medicine into the body. 4. a long, thin pointer on a clock, meter, or dial. *The needle on a compass points north.* 5. a leaf of an evergreen tree that looks like a needle. *The floor of the pine grove was covered with pine needles.* verb (needled, needling, needles) (informal) to tease, annoy or make angry. *They needled Harry about his broken glasses.* {**nee** dəl}

need·less *adjective* of no use; not wanted. *Another chair would be a needless piece of furniture in this tiny room.* {**need** lihs} needlessly, adv.

nee·dle·work *noun* work done with a needle and thread as decoration; embroidery. *We admired the fine needlework on my grandmother's wedding dress.* {**nee** dəl **wuhrk**}

need·n't shortened form of need not.

need·y *adjective* (needier, neediest) needing things such as food, money, family, or love. *The needy family received a gift of food for the holidays. / The needy child wanted to be held all the time.* {**nee** dee} neediness, n.

neg·a·tive *adjective* 1. saying or meaning "no." *He gave a negative answer to the question.* 2. not helpful or constructive. *She made negative comments about my singing.* 3. being a number or quantity less than zero. *The temperature is negative ten degrees.* noun 1. a state-

ment, action, or gesture showing that one refuses or is against something. *His answer was a negative.* 2. a photographic image on which light areas of the original subject appear dark and dark areas appear light. 3. a number or quantity less than zero. *Adding a negative to a positive is the same as subtracting.* {**nehg** ə tihv} negatively, adv., negativeness, n., negativity, n.

ne·glect *verb* (neglected, neglecting, neglects) 1. to pay too little or no attention to. *Claude was so busy with work that he neglected his friends. / Don't neglect your studies.* 2. to fail to take proper care of. *Dan neglected his goldfish, and some of them died.* 3. to fail to do or perform. *Do not neglect your duty.* noun 1. an act, instance, or result of neglecting. *The starving cats were victims of neglect.* 2. the condition of being neglected. *The vacant house lay in neglect.* {nə **glehkt**}

Word History The origin of the word **neglect** is *neglectus*, a Latin word that means "to not pick up or select."

neg·li·gent *adjective* not showing proper concern; careless. *The negligent cook forgot to add sugar to the cookie dough.* {**nehg** lih jənt}

ne·go·ti·ate *verb* (negotiated, negotiating, negotiates) to bargain or come to an agreement with another person. *If the price is too high, try negotiating with the seller.* {nə **goh** shee ayt} negotiator, n.

ne·go·ti·a·tion *noun* (often plural) discussions meant to help people agree on something. *Negotiations between*

the two countries led to a peace treaty. {nə **goh** shee **ay** shən}

Ne·gro *noun* (Negroes) a former term for **black** or **African American**. *adjective* relating to a Negro or Negroes; Black. {**nee** groh}

neigh *verb* (neighed, neighing, neighs) to make the sound of a horse; whinny. *noun* the sound made by a horse; whinny. {**nay**}

Homophone Note The words **neigh** and **nay** (no) sound alike but have different meanings.

neigh·bor *noun* 1. a person who lives close to someone else. *New neighbors just moved into the house across the street.* 2. a fellow human. *Treat your neighbors with respect.* verb (neighbored, neighboring, neighbors) to border on; live near to. *His property neighbors a public park.* {**nay** bər}

neigh·bor·hood *noun* 1. a small area or district in a city or town that is set off from other areas because it is a community or has a special character. *Most of the dogs are friendly in my neighborhood. / Toronto is known for its ethnic neighborhoods.* 2. the entire group of people who live in such an area. *Our neighborhood gets together for a Labor Day picnic every year.* {**nay** bər **huud**}

• **in the neighborhood of** (informal) about; approximately. *The opera tickets cost in the neighborhood of a hundred dollars each.*

neigh·bor·ing *adjective* located close by or next to something. *The race starts in a neighboring town and will finish here.* {**nay** bər ing}

neigh·bor·ly *adjective* like a kind neighbor; friendly or helpful. *It was neighborly of*

 Human Body  Human Mind  Everyday Life 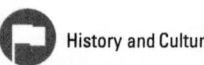 History and Culture  Communication

him to water my plants while I was away. {**nay** bər lee}

neigh·bour *noun* a spelling of **neighbor** used in Canada and Britain. See **neighbor**. {**nay** bər}

neigh·bour·hood *noun or adjective* a spelling of **neighborhood** used in Canada and Britain. See **neighborhood**. {**nay** bər huud}

neigh·bour·ly *adjective* a spelling of **neighborly** used in Canada and Britain. See **neighborly**. {**nay** bər lee}

nei·ther *conjunction* not one or the other of two; not either (usually paired with "nor" in a sentence). *Neither the cat nor the dog came into the house.* *adjective* not either; not one or the other. *Neither plan has worked.* *pronoun* not either; not one person or thing or the other. *She asked two different people for directions, but neither could help her.* {**nee** thər}

ne·on ❶ *noun* a gas that is one of the chemical elements. Neon is used in making electric signs, because it glows orange when an electric current passes through it. (symbol: Ne) *adjective* containing or using neon. *The store had a bright neon sign over its doorway.* {**nee** ŏn}

Word History *Neon* is an ancient Greek word that means "new." British scientists in 1898 chose this name for the glowing gas they had just discovered.

Ne·pal *noun* a country in southern Asia. Kathmandu is the capital of Nepal. {nə **pahl** or nay **pahl**} Nepalese, n., adj.

neph·ew *noun* the son of one's brother or sister; the son of one's brother-in-law or sister-in-law. {**nehf** yoo}

Nep·tune *noun* 1. the god of the sea in Roman mythology.

Neptune had control of the tides. In Greek mythology, Neptune is called Poseidon. 2. the fourth largest planet in the solar system and eighth in distance from the sun. {**nehp toohn**}

nerd *noun* a person who chooses to spend a lot of time doing one activity, often in a technical field such as computers, math, or science. *Heather is such a math nerd that she takes her calculator everywhere.* {**nuhrd**} nerdy, adj.

nerve ❷ ❸ *noun* 1. any of the fibers that carry messages to and from the brain and other parts of the body. Nerves are bundled together into a complicated system that connects all parts of the body to the spinal cord and brain. *The injured nerves in his hand made it difficult for him to feel heat or cold.* 2. courage, strength, or patience. *It took a lot of nerve for him to jump off the high diving board.* 3. (informal) boldness without shame or respect. *She has a lot of nerve to say mean things about me.* {**nuhrv**}

ner·vous *adjective* 1. of or having to do with the nerves. *We studied the central nervous system in science class.* 2. having a very anxious or fearful nature. *Kathy fidgets and bites her nails because she's a nervous person.* 3. being fearful or anxious in a specific situation. *That big dog is making me nervous.* {**nuhr** vəs} nervously, adj., nervousness, n.

nervous system *noun* the system of nerves and nerve centers in most animals with more than one cell. {**nuhr** vəs **sihs** təm}

-ness *suffix* a suffix that means "condition." *When you are happy, you have a feeling of happiness.*

nest ❶ *noun* 1. a structure used by a bird to lay eggs and rear young. Nests are built in trees and other protected places using materials such as twigs and mud. 2. any place made or used by an animal to lay eggs or rear young. *Sea turtles make nests in the sand on ocean beaches.* 3. a number of animals living in a single nest. *Dad got rid of the hornets' nest in our attic.* 4. a comfortable place for rest or being alone. *The puppies lay on a warm nest of blankets.* *verb* (nested, nesting, nests) to build or live in a nest and rear young. *Birds nested in the old barn every spring.* {**nehst**} nester, n.

nes·tle *verb* (nestled, nestling, nestles) 1. to lie close or curled next to. *The lamb nestled against its mother.* 2. to place or press in a snug or loving way. *The cat nestled its head against my foot.* {**neh** səl}

Word History *Nestle* comes from an Old English word that means "to build a nest."

net[1] *noun* 1. a fabric woven or knotted together to leave open spaces of even size. 2. something made of such a fabric. *The ball skimmed the top of the tennis net.* 3. some-

thing made of such a fabric and used for catching fish, butterflies, and other animals. *The fisherman pulled the trout out of the water with his net.* verb (netted, netting, nets) to catch with a net. *He netted a butterfly, then set it free.* {**neht**}

net² adjective 1. relating to what money is left after subtracting taxes and other costs. *The company's net income was small last year because its expenses were high.* 2. what remains after a certain amount is subtracted. *To find the net weight of a can of soup, you must subtract the weight of the can from the weight of the soup and the can combined.* verb (netted, netting, nets) to result in or get as net profit. *That horror movie netted millions of dollars.* {**neht**}

Neth·er·lands noun a country in northern Europe on the North Sea; Holland. Amsterdam is the capital of the Netherlands. However, the government is located in another city, called The Hague. {**nehth** ər ləndz}

net·tle noun a plant whose leaves and stems are covered with hairs that sting the skin when touched. {**neht** əl}

net·work noun 1. a system that involves a number of persons or groups. *The Underground Railroad was a network of people and safe houses, not a railroad with tracks and trains.* 2. a group of radio or television stations, or a company that controls such a group. 3. any system of roads or lines connected to each other like a net. *A vast network of highways crosses our country.* 4. a system of computers that are connected to one or more other computers. *The Internet is a huge computer network.* verb (networked, networking, networks) to create a network in or for. *The technician networked all the computers in the office.* {**neht** wuhrk}

neu·rot·ic adjective suffering from needless fears and worries. *To a neurotic person, small worries can seem enormous.* {nə **rŏt** ihk}

neu·tral adjective 1. not taking any side in an argument or contest. *When her friends had a quarrel, she remained neutral. / Sweden is a neutral country.* 2. matching most other colors well. *Gray is a neutral color.* 3. neither an acid nor a base in chemistry. *Water is a neutral liquid.* noun a position of gears where they are not engaged in an engine. *She put the car in neutral and let it coast down the hill.* {**nooh** trəl} neutrally, adv.

Word History *Neutral* comes from *neutralis*, a Latin word that means "not either."

neu·tral·ize verb (neutralized, neutralizing, neutralizes) 1. to cause to have no effect or become useless. *The alien neutralized the human's puny weapons.* 2. to cause to be neutral. *Antacid tablets neutralize stomach acid.* {**nooh** trə liyz} neutralizer, n.

neu·tron noun a small particle present in the nucleus of all atoms except the hydrogen atom. Neutrons have no electrical charge. The mass of a neutron is about equal to the mass of a proton. {**nooh** trŏn}

Ne·va·da noun a state in the western United States. Its capital is Carson City. (abbreviated: NV) {nə **vah** də or nə **vă** də} Nevadan, n.

Word History *Nevada* means "snow-capped" in Spanish. Nevada has many mountain ranges, including part of the Sierra Nevada.

nev·er adverb 1. not on any occasion; not at any time. *It almost never snows in Florida.* 2. not in any way; not at all. *I never knew you were his brother.* {**nehv** ər}

nev·er·the·less adverb however; still. *He forgot to study; nevertheless, he must take the exam.* {**nehv** ər thə **lehs** or nehv ər thə **lehs**}

new adjective (newer, newest) 1. having recently arrived, been produced, or come into being. *The band's new CD is now in the stores.* 2. not known; strange. *He had a desire to see new places.* 3. not used. *Start your essay on a new sheet of paper.* 4. beginning or repeating as part of a cycle. *We began the new year with a big party.* {**nooh**} newness, n.

Homophone Note The words *new*, *gnu*, and *knew* sound alike but have different meanings.

new·bie noun (informal) someone who is learning to use the Internet. *That newbie has just figured out how to e-mail his friends!* {**nooh** bee}

new·born adjective 1. just born. *Our cat surprised us with five newborn kittens.* 2. as if just begun or begun again. *The runner found newborn strength when the finish line came into sight.* noun a baby that has just been born. *The mother gazed at her sleeping newborn.* {**nooh** bohrn}

New Brunswick noun a province in southeastern Canada.

 Human Body　　 Human Mind　　Everyday Life　　 History and Culture　　Communication

Its capital is Fredericton. {nooh **bruhnz** wihk}

Word History *New Brunswick* was named for King George the Third of England, whose family name was "Brunswick."

new·com·er *noun* one who arrived not long ago. *Mr. Miller is a newcomer to the neighborhood.* {**nooh** kuh mər}

New England *noun* the six states in the northeastern corner of the United States; Connecticut, Rhode Island, Massachusetts, New Hampshire, Vermont, and Maine. {nooh **ing** glənd}

new·fan·gled *adjective* new and different, but not always better. *People laughed at his newfangled ideas.* {nooh **făng** gəld} newfangledness, n.

New·found·land *noun* an eastern province of Canada, including the island of Newfoundland in the Atlantic Ocean. The full name of the province is Newfoundland & Labrador. Its capital is St. John's. {**nooh** fənd lənd *or* **nooh** fənd **lănd** *or* nooh **fownd** lənd} Newfoundlander, n.

Word History Italian explorer John Cabot named the island of *Newfoundland* "new founde isle" in 1497. By 1502, English maps showed the area as "New found launde."

New Hampshire *noun* a state in the northeastern United States. Its capital is Concord. (abbreviated: NH) {nooh **hămp** shər} New Hampshirite, n.

Word History *New Hampshire* was named in 1629, by Captain John Mason, after his home in Hampshire County, England.

New Jersey *noun* a state in the eastern United States on the Atlantic Coast. Its capital is Trenton. (abbreviated: NJ) {nooh **juhr** zee} New Jerseyite, n.

Word History *New Jersey* was named after the Isle of Jersey, an island in the English Channel.

new·ly *adverb* not long ago. *It was exciting to see pictures of a newly discovered dinosaur nesting ground.* {**nooh** lee}

New Mexico *noun* a state in the southwestern United States. Its capital is Santa Fe. (abbreviated: NM) {**nooh** **mehks** ih koh} New Mexican, n.

Word History *Mexico* comes from an Aztec word meaning "place of Mexitli," an Aztec god. Spanish explorers called the area *Nuevo Mexico. Nuevo* means "new" in Spanish.

new moon *noun* the phase of the moon when it cannot be seen because it passes directly between the sun and the earth. {**nooh** **moohn**}

news *noun* (used with a singular verb) a report of recent important events, read out on the television or radio, or printed in a newspaper, magazine, or Web site. {**noohz**}

news·cast *noun* a program on television or radio that presents the news. {**noohz** kăst} newscaster, n.

news·group *noun* a discussion group on a computer network such as the Internet in which people leave messages for each other on topics they are all interested in. {**noohz** groohp}

news·pa·per 🌐 *noun* a publication made of several large sheets of folded paper printed with news, opinions, advertisements, and other information. Most newspapers come out either every day or once a week. {**noohz** pay pər}

news·stand *noun* a booth or other place where newspapers and magazines are sold. {**noohz** stănd}

newt *noun* a small animal with a long, slender body and tail, and four legs. Newts have smooth, moist skin. They are a kind of small salamander and are amphibians. They spend part of their lives in water and part on land. {**nooht**}

New Testament *noun* the books of the Christian Bible that tell of the life and works of Jesus Christ and his apostles. {nooh **tehs** tə mənt}

New World *noun* the Western Hemisphere. North and South America make up the New World. {nooh **wuhrld**}

New Year's Day *noun* the first day of the new year, January 1. {nooh yeerz **day**}

New York *noun* 1. a state in the eastern United States. Its capital is Albany. (abbreviated: NY) 2. a city in the southeast corner of this state; New York City. {nooh **yohrk**} New Yorker, n.

Word History *New York* was named for the English Duke of York in 1664, when the English sent a fleet of ships to capture the colony from the Dutch.

New York Cit·y *noun* a metropolis in the southeast corner of New York State. {nooh **yohrk** **siht** ee}

New Zealand *noun* a country on two large islands and a number of small islands in the South Pacific, southeast of Australia. Wellington is

A B C D E F G H I J K L M N O P Q R S T U V W X Y Z

a
b
c
d
e
f
g
h
i
j
k
l
m
n
o
p
q
r
s
t
u
v
w
x
y
z

the capital of New Zealand. {**nooh** <u>**zee**</u> lənd} New Zealander, n.

next *adjective* 1. coming immediately after; following. *I'll see you next week. / The first question on the test was easy, but the next one was hard.* 2. closest in position. *My best friend lives in the next house.* *adverb* 1. in the time, place, or position that is nearest or that follows immediately after. *The chief of police sat next to the mayor.* 2. on the occasion that follows immediately after the present. *When next you come to visit, bring your children.* {<u>**nehkst**</u>}
  • **next door to** in the house closest to. *We live next door to an elderly couple.*
  • **next to** nearly; almost. *He was next to exhausted.*

next-door *adjective* in or at the closest building, house, or apartment. *We had dinner with our next-door neighbors.* {nayks <u>dohr</u> *or* nehkst <u>dohr</u>}

NH or **N.H.** *abbreviation* an abbreviation for **New Hampshire.**

Ni symbol of the chemical element nickel.

nib·ble *verb* (nibbled, nibbling, nibbles) 1. to eat in small bites. *She nibbled on the carrot like a rabbit.* 2. to eat or bite off in small amounts or bites. *The cat nibbled her food.* 3. to bite gently (often followed by "at"). *It didn't hurt when the puppy nibbled at my finger.* 4. to bite gently again and again. *The fish nibbled the bait, but never took it.* *noun* 1. a small bite or bit of food. *Nate gave her a nibble of his cookie.* 2. an act of nibbling. *She ate the cracker with little nibbles.* 3. a small bite on bait by a fish. *I got a few nibbles on*

my line but didn't catch anything. {<u>nihb</u> əl}

Nic·a·ra·gua *noun* a country in Central America. Managua is the capital of Nicaragua. {nih kə <u>rah</u> gwə} Nicaraguan, n., adj.

nice *adjective* (nicer, nicest) 1. pleasant; attractive. *He has a nice face. / Your room is nice.* 2. having good manners; polite. *Theo has some nice friends.* 3. showing a high degree of skill or craftsmanship. *Nice shoes are expensive.* {<u>niys</u>} nicely, adv., niceness, n.

Synonyms
These words share a meaning with *nice*, adjective 2:
polite, gracious, courteous, well-mannered

Word History *Nice* is from a Latin word that means "not to know." Before the 1300s, it meant "ignorant," and in early English, "timid, fussy, or dainty." By the the 1500s, it meant "precise or careful," but not until 1830 did it come to mean "kind or thoughtful." Who knows what "nice" will mean a hundred years from now?

niche *noun* 1. a hollow place set into a wall to hold a statue or some other object. *She placed a vase in the niche.* 2. a job or activity that seems just right for a particular person. *She knew she had found her niche the first time she picked up a saxophone.* {<u>nihch</u> *or* <u>neech</u> *or* neesh}

Word History *Niche* comes from *nicchia*, an Italian word that means "nook." This Italian word was formed from an earlier word, *nicchio*, which means "seashell."

nick *noun* a shallow cut or chip in a surface. *His knife made a nick in the table.* *verb* (nicked,

nicking, nicks) to make a shallow cut or chip in a surface. *She nicked her finger while cutting celery.* {<u>nihk</u>}
  • **in the nick of time** at the last possible moment to produce some result. *We got to the train station in the nick of time.*

nick·el *noun* 1. a dense, hard, silver-white metal that is one of the chemical elements. It is sometimes combined with other metals to make alloys such as stainless steel. (symbol: Ni). 2. a coin of the United States and Canada worth five cents. {<u>nihk</u> əl}

nick·name *noun* 1. a name given to a person, place, or thing in place of the real name. *New York City's nickname is "The Big Apple."* 2. a familiar or short form of a proper name, such as "Bob" for "Robert." *verb* (nicknamed, nicknaming, nicknames) to give a nickname to. *Wilt Chamberlain was nicknamed "Wilt the Stilt" because he was so tall.* {<u>nihk</u> naym}

Word History "Nick-" in the word *nickname* comes from *an eke*, an early English term that means "another."

nic·o·tine *noun* a poisonous substance found in the tobacco plant. Nicotine is what causes people to become addicted to cigarettes. {<u>nihk</u> ə teen *or* nihk ə <u>teen</u>}

niece *noun* a daughter of one's brother or sister; a daughter of one's brother-in-law or sister-in-law. {<u>nees</u>}

Ni·ger *noun* 1. a country in north central Africa. Niamey is the capital of Niger. 2. a river of west Africa. It flows from Guinea through Mali, Niger, and Nigeria into the

 Human Body  Human Mind Everyday Life History and Culture  Communication

Atlantic Ocean. {**niy** jər} Nigerien, n., adj.

Ni·ger·i·a *noun* a country in western Africa on the Atlantic Ocean. Abuja is the capital of Nigeria. {niy **jeer** ee ə} Nigerian, n., adj.

night *noun* 1. the hours of darkness between sunset and dawn. *Snow had fallen during the night.* 2. the time when night begins; nightfall. *In the winter, night comes earlier.* 3. the darkness during night. *The bus disappeared into the night.* {**niyt**}

• **night and day** without rest or interruption; seeming to have no end. *She works night and day.*

Homophone Note The words **night** and **knight** sound alike but have different meanings. To learn why the princess is scared of the night, but loves her knight, look up **knight**.

night·fall *noun* the time when day ends and night begins. *We waited until nightfall to light the lamps.* {**niyt** fawl}

night·gown *noun* a long loose gown that is worn in bed. {**niyt** gown}

night·in·gale *noun* a small bird that lives in Europe and is known for its beautiful song. A nightingale is a kind of thrush. {**niy** tən **gayl** *or* **niy** ting **gayl**}

night·ly *adjective* happening or done every night. *She enjoyed her nightly snack of cheese and crackers.* *adverb* on every night. *Concerts in the park took place nightly.* {**niyt** lee}

night·mare *noun* 1. a frightening dream. *Alice was awakened by a terrible nightmare.* 2. an experience or state of mind that is like a terrible dream. *Taking the test was a*

nightmare. {**niyt** mayr} nightmarish, adj.

Word History *Nightmare* comes from two early English words that together mean "night goblin."

night·time *noun* the time between sunset and dawn. {**niyt** tiym}

Ni·ke *noun* the goddess of victory in Greek mythology. {**niy** kee}

Nile *noun* the longest river in the world. It flows north from Uganda in East Africa through Sudan and Egypt into the Mediterranean Sea. {**niyl**}

nim·ble *adjective* (nimbler, nimblest) quick and light in movement. *The dog was old but nimble.* {**nihm** bəl} nimbleness, n.

nine *noun* the number that comes after 8 and before 10 in the sequence of cardinal numbers; 9. *adjective* being nine in number. *I ate nine cookies before I had had enough.* {**niyn**}

nine·teen *noun* the number that comes after 18 and before 20 in the sequence of cardinal numbers; 19. *adjective* being nineteen in number. *There are nineteen days left of school.* {niyn **teen**}

nine·teenth *adjective* coming next after the eighteenth in a series. *You will be staying in the nineteenth cabin at summer camp.* *noun* 1. one of nineteen equal parts of a whole; 1/19. *The image flashes on the screen for one nineteenth of a second.* 2. the number, person, or thing that comes next after the eighteenth in a series. *After selling the nineteenth in only an hour, she knew her book would do well.* {niyn **teenth**}

nine·ti·eth *adjective* coming next after the eighty-ninth in a series. *He hit a home run to win the ninetieth game of the season.* *noun* 1. one of ninety equal parts of a whole; 1/90. *Our car broke down after getting only about a ninetieth of the way there.* 2. the number, person, or thing that comes next after the eigthy-ninth in a series. *The race car driver took one last victory lap after the ninetieth.* {**niyn** tee ih*th*}

nine·ty *noun* (nineties) the number that is equal to nine times ten; 90. *adjective* being ninety in number. *The movie runs about ninety minutes.* {**niyn** tee}

nin·ja *noun* (ninja or ninjas) a medieval Japanese warrior specially trained as a spy or assassin. {**nihn** jə}

ninth *adjective* coming next after the eighth in a series. *My classroom is the ninth door down on the right.* *noun* 1. one of nine equal parts of a whole; 1/9. *We're finished with all but a ninth of the project.* 2. a number, person, or thing that comes next after the eighth in a series. *The ninth was the best applicant for the babysitting job.* {**niynth**}

nip *verb* (nipped, nipping, nips) 1. to press sharply between two points; bite or pinch. *The parrot nipped the bars of its cage.* 2. to cut or pinch off. *I nipped dead blossoms off the plants.* 3. to cause to sting sharply with cold. *The icy air nipped their noses.* 4. to stop the growth of. *Frost nipped the buds on our apple tree.* *noun* 1. the act of nipping; a pinch or small bite. *The puppy gave my finger a nip.* 2. a sharp feeling of cold. *There is a nip in the air when the sun goes down.* {**nihp**}

A
B
C
D
E
F
G
H
I
J
K
L
M
N
O
P
Q
R
S
T
U
V
W
X
Y
Z

Living World   Physical World   Natural Environment   Economy   Government and Law   495

a
b
c
d
e
f
g
h
i
j
k
l
m
n
o
p
q
r
s
t
u
v
w
x
y
z

nip·ple *noun* 1. the rounded tip at the center of a mammal's breast. *The baby sucks milk from its mother's nipple.* 2. a rubber cap on a baby's bottle. {**nihp** əl}

ni·tro·gen 🌐 🔬 *noun* a gas with no color or smell that is one of the chemical elements. Nitrogen makes up about eighty percent of the earth's atmosphere, and it is also found in all living things. (symbol: N) {**niy** trə jən}

NJ or **N.J.** *abbreviation* an abbreviation for **New Jersey**.

NM or **N.M.** *abbreviation* an abbreviation for **New Mexico**.

no[1] *adverb* 1. not so. *No, I don't want to go.* 2. not at all; not any (used with the comparative form of an adjective). *I did a poor job painting the room, but at least it looked no worse than it did before.* *noun* (noes or nos) 1. a use, in speech or writing, of the word "no." *The teacher answered our request to go home early with a no.* 2. a vote against or a person who votes against. *The noes are in the minority.* {**noh**}

no[2] *adjective* 1. not any. *We have no bananas here.* 2. not at all; not close to being. *I would be careful about letting Mike work on your car because he is no expert.* {**noh**}

Homophone Note Are you looking for the word *know*? *No* and *know* sound alike but have different meanings.

no. *abbreviation* an abbreviation of **number**.

no·bil·i·ty *noun* (nobilities) 1. a class of people of noble rank. *The French Revolution tried to do away with the nobility in France.* 2. the condition of being noble in rank, birth, or character. *He led a life of kind-*

ness and nobility. {noh **bih** lih tee}

no·ble *adjective* (nobler, noblest) 1. belonging to a class of people with a high rank or title. *When she married a duke, she became part of a noble family.* 2. of or showing a strong or excellent mind or character. *Putting yourself at risk to help another is a noble act.* 3. having a strong effect; grand or splendid. *They made a noble effort to put out the fire. / A noble statue of Lincoln stands in the park.* *noun* a person of high rank or title. *Only nobles were invited to the ball.* {**noh** bəl} nobleness, n., nobly, adv.

no·ble·man *noun* (noblemen) a man of high rank or title. {**noh** bəl mən}

no·ble·wom·an *noun* (noblewomen) a woman of high rank or title. {**noh** bəl **wuum** ən}

no·bod·y *pronoun* no one; no person; not anybody. *Nobody likes to fail.* *noun* (nobodies) (informal) a person of no value or importance. *The kids at Barb's new school treated her like a nobody.* {**noh** bo dee}

noc·tur·nal
❶ *adjective* 1. happening in the night. *A raccoon made a nocturnal visit*

to our garbage can. 2. active at night. *Owls are nocturnal animals.* {nŏk **tuhr** nəl} nocturnally, adv.

nod *verb* (nodded, nodding, nods) 1. to move the head up and down as to show greeting or approval. *She nodded and said hello. / When the boy asked if he could go, his mother nodded.* 2. to express

by lowering and raising the head. *She nodded her agreement.* 3. to drop the head in sleep for a short time. *When he nodded in class, his friend poked him.* *noun* an up and down movement of the head. *The teacher gave Hannah a nod when it was her turn to answer.* {nŏd}

noise *noun* 1. sound or a sound. *Strange noises came from the locked basement.* 2. loud, harsh, or unpleasant sound. *What is music to one person may be noise to another.* {noiz}

nois·y *adjective* (noisier, noisiest) 1. making a lot of noise. *A noisy dog kept the whole neighborhood awake last night.* 2. full of noise. *The library is not a noisy place.* {**noi** zee} noisily, adv., noisiness, n.

no·mad *noun* 1. a member of a group or tribe that has no fixed home and moves from place to place. *Nomads often live in tents because they are easy to pack up and move.* 2. a person or animal that moves from place to place without a fixed home. *That kind of duck is rare in this part of the country because it is a nomad.* {**noh** măd}

no·mad·ic
adjective living like a nomad. *His nomadic life takes him to*

many places around the world. {noh **măd** ihk}

nom·i·nate *verb* (nominated, nominating, nominates) 1. to choose as a candidate for election. *The students nominated three people for the position of class president.* 2. to choose for an office; to name for an honor. *The committee nominated Mr. Brown for the*

 Human Body   Human Mind Everyday Life History and Culture  Communication

school board. / We nominated her project as the best at the science fair. {**nŏm** ə **nayt**} nominator, n.

nom·i·na·tion *noun* the act of choosing a person to run for office. *Nominations for president take place every four years.* {**nŏm** ə **nay** shən}

nom·i·nee *noun* a person or thing that has been nominated for an office or honor. *He is our nominee for mayor. / This painting is a nominee for first prize.* {**nŏm** ih **nee**}

non- *prefix* a prefix that means "not," "not having," or "failure to." *A nondairy drink is a drink that has no dairy in it. / Nonsense poetry is poetry that fails to make sense.*

none *pronoun* 1. no person or thing; not one. *None of the cookies are left.* 2. (used with a plural verb) no persons or things; no one. *Several tried, but none were able to reach the top of the mountain.* 3. not any. *Bad food is better than none. adverb* in no way; not at all. *The guests arrived none too soon.* {**nuhn**}

Homophone Note The words **none** and **nun** (a religious woman) sound alike but have different meanings.

non·fic·tion ◐ *noun* written works that are not fiction. Textbooks, biographies, and essays are examples of nonfiction. {**nŏn** **fihk** shən} nonfictional, adj.

non·sense *noun* 1. words or actions that have no meaning or make no sense. *Stop talking nonsense!* 2. rude or silly behavior. *The student's nonsense angered the teacher.* {**nŏn** sehns}

non·stop *adverb or adjective* without any stops. *We will take a nonstop train to Chi-*

cago. / *The plane flew nonstop to Vancouver.* {**nŏn** **stŏp**}

noo·dle *noun* a flat, narrow strip of dough that has been dried. Noodles are boiled in water to make them soft for eating. {**nooh** dəl}

nook *noun* a corner of a room or a small area set off from a main room. *She kept her toys in a nook under the window.* {**nuuk**}

noon *noun* twelve o'clock in the daytime; midday. *It is usually hottest at noon.* {**noohn**}

Word History *Noon* is from an Old English word, *non*, which means "ninth." Until some time during the 1100s, noon was the ninth hour of daylight, which was three o'clock in the afternoon.

no one *pronoun* no person; nobody. *The house was dark and no one was home.* {**noh** wuhn}

noon·time *noun* midday; noon. *We ate our lunch at noontime.* {**noohn** tiym}

noose *noun* a loop that passes through a knot in the end of a rope or other line. When the rope is pulled, the loop becomes smaller. *The rodeo cowboy threw his noose neatly around the mustang's neck.* {**noohs**}

nor *conjunction* 1. used to introduce a negative statement, especially after a phrase using "neither." *He is neither honest nor clever.* 2. used to continue or expand a negative statement. *They never visit, nor do I care.* {**nohr**}

nor·mal *adjective* 1. close to what is usual, average, or standard. *My height is normal for my age.* 2. having a

healthy mind; without mental or emotional illness. *A normal person does not enjoy making animals suffer.* 3. physically healthy; usual according to the laws of nature. *The doctor said my heart sounds normal. noun* the average or expected form, condition, level, or amount; standard. *The temperature was below normal last month.* {**nohr** məl} normality, n.

Word History The word *normal* comes from a Latin word that means "a carpenter's square."

Norse *adjective* of or having to do with ancient Scandinavia, or its people or languages; Scandinavian. {**nohrs**}

north *noun* 1. the direction to the left of a person facing the rising sun. 2. one of the four major points of direction on the compass. The north is directly opposite the south. 3. (often capital) the northern part of a country or area. *During the Civil War, many slaves escaped to the North. adjective* 1. from, of, or in the north. *There's a north wind blowing.* 2. toward or facing the north. *We walked along the north wall. adverb* from, in, or toward the north. *We sailed north to get to Alaska.* {**nohrth**}

North America *noun* the third largest continent. North America is between the Atlantic and Pacific Oceans. It is in the Western Hemisphere. {**nohrth** ə **meh** rih kə}

North A·mer·i·can *adjective* of or having to do with North America, or its people or languages. *noun* a person who was born in or is a citizen of a country in North America. {**nohrth** ə **mehr** ih kən}

A B C D E F G H I J K L M **N** O P Q R S T U V W X Y Z

a
b
c
d
e
f
g
h
i
j
k
l
m
n
o
p
q
r
s
t
u
v
w
x
y
z

North Carolina *noun* a state in the southeastern United States on the Atlantic Coast. Its capital is Raleigh. (abbreviated: NC) {**nohrth** kar ə **liy** nə} North Carolinian, n.

Word History *Carolina* means "the land of Charles" in Latin, after King Charles I of England, who established the first permanent European colony in the area. Carolina was divided into the colonies of North Carolina and South Carolina in 1710.

North Dakota *noun* a state in the north central United States. Its capital is Bismarck. (abbreviated: ND) {**nohrth** də **koh** tə} North Dakotan, n.

Word History *Dakota* means "allies" or "friends" in a Sioux language. The Dakota Territory was named after the Dakota Sioux, one of several Indian nations from the area. The Dakota Territory was divided into North Dakota and South Dakota when they became states in 1889.

north·east *noun* 1. a point on the compass halfway between north and east. 2. a region in the direction of northeast. *Their main office is in the northeast of the state.* *adverb or adjective* 1. located in or near the northeast. *I live in the northeast state of New Hampshire. / He lives northeast of us.* 2. from, toward, or facing the northeast. *We looked out the northeast window. / We traveled northeast to get from Toronto to Ottawa.* {**nohrth** **eest**}

north·east·ern *adjective* of, located in, or coming from the northeast. {**nohrth** **ees** tərn}

north·er·ly *adverb or adjective* 1. of or toward the north. *This animal lives in a northerly climate. / The path runs northerly for five miles.* 2. blowing from the north. *The northerly winds blew across the prairie. / The breeze blew northerly.* *noun* (northerlies) a storm or wind from the north. *The captain says a northerly is on its way.* {**nohrth** ər lee}

north·ern *adjective* in, to, from, or having to do with the north. *The Sahara Desert is in the northern part of Africa. / A cold northern wind was blowing.* {**nohr** thərn}

north·ern·er *noun* (often capitalized) a person born or living in the northern part of a region. {**nohr** thər nər}

Northern Hemisphere *noun* the half of the earth that is north of the equator. {**nohr** thərn **hehm** ih sfeer}

Northern Ireland *noun* a division of the United Kingdom, in the northeastern part of the island of Ireland. Belfast is the capital of Northern Ireland. {**nohr** thərn **iy** ər lənd}

northern lights *plural noun* see **aurora borealis**. {**nohr** thərn **liyts**}

North Korea *noun* a country on the eastern coast of Asia. North Korea is also called the Democratic People's Republic of Korea. P'Yongyang is the capital of North Korea. {**nohrth** kə **ree** ə} North Korean, n., adj.

North Pole *noun* the point on the earth's surface that is farthest north. The North Pole is intersected by the northern end of the earth's axis. {**nohrth** **pohl**}

North Sea *noun* a sea that is part of the Atlantic Ocean. It lies between Great Britain, Scandinavia, and the north coast of the European mainland. {**nohrth** **see**}

North Star *noun* a bright star in the constellation Ursa Minor; Polaris. {**nohrth** **star**}

north·ward *adverb* toward the north. *They travelled northward across the Arctic.* *adjective* in, at, facing, or moving toward the north. *The northward lane of the highway is open.* {**nohrth** **wərd**} northwards, adv.

north·west *noun* 1. a point on the compass halfway between north and west. 2. a region in the direction of northwest. *Washington State is located in the northwest of the United States.* *adverb or adjective* 1. located in or near the northwest. *I live in the northwest state of Oregon. / He lives northwest of us.* 2. from, toward, or facing the northwest. *We looked out the northwest window. / We traveled northwest to get from Rome to Paris.* {**nohrth** **wehst**}

north·west·ern *adjective* of, located in, or coming from the northwest. {**nohrth** **wehs** tərn}

Northwest Territories *plural noun* a northern Canadian territory east of the Yukon. Its capital is Yellowknife. {**nohrth** wehst **tehr** ih tohr eez}

Word History In 1870, Britain gave Canada control of Rupert's Land and the area north and west of Rupert's Land, which Britain called "the North West Territory." Canada combined the two areas into the ***Northwest Territories***. In 1999, the Northwest Territories were divided into Nunavut and a smaller Northwest Territories.

Nor·way *noun* a country on the Scandinavian Peninsula in northern Europe. Oslo is the capital of Norway. {**nohr** way}

Nor·we·gian *adjective* of or having to do with Norway, or

Human Body   Human Mind   Everyday Life    History and Culture    Communication

its people or language. *noun* 1. a person who was born in or is a citizen of Norway. 2. any of the languages of Norway. {nohr **wee** jən}

nose *noun* 1. the part of the face on people and certain animals through which they breathe and smell. 2. the sense of smell. *My cat has a good nose for fish and cheese.* 3. the front part of something that sticks out. *The plane's nose pointed upwards as it took off.* *verb* (nosed, nosing, noses) 1. to notice by smell. *The raccoon nosed the dead fish in the garbage.* 2. to move forward slowly or carefully. *We nosed our way up to the stage.* 3. to meddle; snoop (often followed by "about," "around," or "into"). *He's always nosing into someone else's business.* {**nohz**}

Homophone Note The words *nose* and *knows* (a form of "know") sound alike but have different meanings.

nose·bleed *noun* bleeding from the nose. {**nohz** bleed}

nose cone *noun* the front part of a rocket that is shaped like a cone. {**nohz** kohn}

nos·tal·gia *noun* a longing for the past. *Seeing my old school again filled me with nostalgia.* {nə **stăl** jə} nostalgic, adj.

nos·tril *noun* one of the two outside openings in the nose. {**no** strəl}

Word History *Nostril* is from *nosthryl*, an Old English word that means "nose hole."

nos·y or **nosey** *adjective* (nosier, nosiest) showing too much interest in other people's activities. *I refuse to answer your nosy questions.* {**noh** zee} nosily, adv., nosiness, n.

not *adverb* in no way; to no degree; at no time. *You must not open that door. / That's not what I meant. / It did not snow last month.* {**nŏt**}

Homophone Note Are you looking for the word *knot* (a tying together)? *Not* and *knot* sound alike but have different meanings.

no·ta·ble *adjective* worthy of special attention; remarkable. *She has a notable talent for playing the piano.* *noun* a very important person. *The author was one of many notables at the party.* {**noh** tə bəl} notably, adv.

no·ta·tion *noun* 1. a system of signs used to stand for numbers, words, or musical notes. *He is able to read musical notation.* 2. a quick note to help a person remember something. *She made a notation of the meeting time in her date book.* {noh **tay** shən}

notch *noun* 1. a cut shaped like a V in an edge or object. 2. (informal) a little bit. *Please turn the radio down a notch.* *verb* (notched, notching, notches) to cut a notch in something. *He notched the sticks so they would fit together.* {**nŏch**}

note *noun* 1. a short letter. *We got caught passing notes in class.* 2. (plural) a short written explanation or comment on something. *I took notes on the book to help me study for the test.* 3. a single musical tone. *The guitarist missed a note at the beginning of the song.* 4. a hint of something. *There was a note of anger in his voice.* 5. importance. *Many people of note gave money to the emergency fund.* *verb* (noted, noting, notes) 1. to pay close attention to. *That morning, the manager carefully noted the time of each employee's arrival.*

2. to write down. *I noted the homework for tomorrow's class.* 3. to mention or observe. *She noted that she liked the wallpaper.* {noht}
• **take note of**
to observe carefully so as to remember. *Please take note of the new speed limit on this road.*

note·book *noun* a book of blank pages to keep notes in. *I have one notebook for math and another for social studies.* {**noht** buuk}

note·book com·pu·ter *noun* a very small, light computer that is easy to carry; laptop computer. *Mary carries a notebook computer in her backpack.* {**noht** buuk kuhm **pyoot** ər}

not·ed *adjective* well known; famous. *A noted scientist spoke at our school.* {**noh** tihd} notedly, adv.

noth·ing *noun* 1. not anything; no thing. *There is nothing for you here.* 2. something or someone of no importance. *He is nothing to me now.* 3. zero. *The score was two to nothing, and our team was losing.* *adverb* in no respect or degree; not at all. *The show was nothing like what we had expected.* {**nuhth** ing}
• **nothing doing**
1. indeed not. *"Nothing doing!" replied Mom when we asked to go to a movie at midnight.* 2. no important activity. *There was nothing doing last night.*

no·tice *noun* 1. warning, news, or sign of something, especially in written or printed form. *There is a notice on wine bottles about the dangers of alcohol.* 2. attention; observation. *The new building escaped my notice.* *verb* (noticed, noticing, notices) to be aware of; observe. *I*

a
b
c
d
e
f
g
h
i
j
k
l
m
n
o
p
q
r
s
t
u
v
w
x
y
z

noticed that you weren't in school today. {**noh** tihs}

no·tice·a·ble *adjective* easily noticed. *The man walked with a noticeable limp.* {**noh** tih sə bəl}

no·ti·fy *verb* (notified, notifying, notifies) to tell about; give notice of. *The contest judges notified the winners by mail.* {**noh** tih **fiy**} notifier, n.

no·tion *noun* 1. an idea, opinion, or view. *I have no notion of what you mean.* 2. a sudden idea or desire. *He had a notion for mashed potatoes. / I had a notion to swim across the lake.* {**noh** shən}

no·to·ri·ous *adjective* known for something bad. *The thief was notorious for stealing diamonds.* {nə **tohr** ee əs}

noun *noun* a word that names a person, place, thing, or condition. A noun may be the subject of a sentence or the object of a verb or preposition. In the sentence, "Mary likes to eat popcorn at the movies," "Mary," "popcorn," and "movies" are nouns. {**nown**}

nour·ish *verb* (nourished, nourishing, nourishes) 1. to supply with food needed for life and growth. *Mammals nourish their babies with milk. / The sun helps to nourish plants.* 2. to help to grow or improve in some way. *Good books nourish the mind.* {**nuhr** ihsh}

nour·ish·ment  *noun* something needed for life and growth; food. *Music is nourishment for the soul. / Growing children need plenty of nourishment.* {**nuhr** ihsh mənt}

Nov. *abbreviation* an abbreviation for **November**.

Nova Scotia *noun* a province in southeastern Canada on the Atlantic coast. Its capital is Halifax. {**noh** və **skoh** shə}

Word History *Nova Scotia* means "new Scotland" in Latin. The British colony was founded by settlers from Scotland in 1629.

nov·el[1] *noun* a long work of fiction, usually having a plot and characters. {**nŏv** əl}

Word History The word *novel* comes from the Italian word *novella,* which meant "new story."

nov·el[2] *adjective* new and unusual. *The inventor found a novel use for old tires.* {**nŏv** əl}

nov·el·ty *noun* (novelties) 1. the quality of being new or unusual. *Washing cars was fun until the novelty wore off.* 2. something new or different. *One hundred years ago, automobiles were a novelty.* 3. a little toy or decoration. *I bought hats and balloons and other novelties for the party.* {**nŏv** əl tee}

No·vem·ber *noun* the eleventh month of the year. November has thirty days. {noh **vehm** bər}

Word History *November* comes from *novem,* the Latin word for "nine." November was the ninth month in the Roman calendar.

nov·ice *noun* 1. a person with little or no experience at a particular job or activity. *I am still a novice at using computers.* 2. A person who is training to be a member of a religious order. *Teresa was a novice before she became a nun.* {**nŏv** ihs}

now *adverb* 1. at this time or in these times. *If we leave now we won't be late for school. / More women work outside the home now.* 2. directly; imme-

diately. *Come here now.* 3. at the point of time being talked or written about; by this time. *Now it was getting dark.* 4. a short time ago or in the near future (usually used with "just" or "only"). *She called home just now. / We are leaving just now.* 5. because of what has happened or is happening; as matters stand. *Now they won't want to go.* *conjunction* because of the fact; since. *We can talk out loud, now that she's gone.* *noun* the present moment or time. *It was easy until now.* {now}

• **now and again** [or] **now and then** sometimes; every once and a while. *We meet at the cafe now and again.*

now·a·days *adverb* during these present times. *Nowadays machines do much of the work that used to be done by hand.* {**now** ə dayz}

no·where *adverb* 1. not anywhere; in no place. *My favorite jacket was nowhere to be found.* 2. at or to no place. *All my hard work got me nowhere.* *noun* 1. the state of really or apparently not existing. *They came out of nowhere.* 2. a place that is far off or not well known. *Some people say that our town is in the middle of nowhere.* 3. failure or the state of not being known. *He came from nowhere to become a famous singer.* {**noh** wayr}

noz·zle *noun* a narrow spout fitted to the end of a hose or pipe. A nozzle is used to control the flow or spray of a liquid or gas. {**nŏz** əl}

nu·cle·ar  *adjective* 1. of, or having to do with, or being the nucleus of an atom or a cell. *A proton is a nuclear particle. / The nuclear membrane*

 Human Body  Human Mind 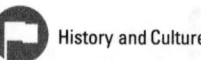 Everyday Life 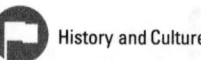 History and Culture  Communication

surrounds the nucleus of a cell. 2. using the nuclei of atoms. *He is in the field of nuclear physics. / There was a protest against building a nuclear power plant.* 3. of or having atomic or hydrogen bombs. *The United States is a nuclear power.* {**nooh** klee ər}

nuclear energy *noun* energy released from the nuclei of atoms, either by splitting or by fusing them. *Nuclear energy can be used to produce electricity.* {**nooh** klee ər **ehn** ər jee}

nu·cle·i *noun* plural of **nucleus**. {**nooh** klee **iy**}

nu·cle·us *noun* (nuclei or nucleuses) 1. the central, essential, or most active part around which other parts are grouped. *Main Street is the nucleus of the town.* 2. the part of a cell that contains chromosomes, which control growth and reproduction in most living things. 3. the central part of an atom, which has a positive charge. {**nooh** klee əs}

nude *adjective* 1. not wearing clothes. *The nude baby splashed in the tub.* 2. not covered; bare. *We covered the nude walls with posters. noun* a naked person in works of art. *Michelangelo's famous statue of David is a nude.* {**noohd**}

nudge *verb* (nudged, nudging, nudges) to push gently or touch with the elbow to attract attention. *Kim nudged me to make me stop talking. noun* a slight or gentle push. *He gave her a nudge so she would walk faster.* {**nuhj**}

nug·get *noun* a small, solid lump. *The gold nugget sparkled in the river bed.* {**nuhg** iht}

nui·sance *noun* a person or thing that is annoying. *The barking dog was a nuisance to the neighbors.* {**nooh** səns}

numb *adjective* 1. not able to feel; lacking in feeling or movement. *After swimming in the cold lake, my body felt numb.* 2. not able to act or feel in a normal way. *He was numb for weeks after his dog died. verb* (numbed, numbing, numbs) to cause to become numb, or to become numb. *The dentist numbed the area around my tooth before starting to drill. / My tooth numbed after the shot.* {**nuhm**} numbness, n.

num·ber *noun* 1. a unit in math with a fixed value that is used in counting or to tell the position of something in a series. *Four, four tenths, and four hundred are all numbers. Numbers can also be written in numerals: 4, 0.4, 400.* 2. a number or numeral used to label or name something. *Write down my telephone number. / Football players wear numbers on their shirts.* 3. total amount; sum. *The number of people in this room is eight.* 4. a large quantity. *A number of icicles formed on the roof.* 5. one piece of a musical program. *The pianist played a lively number. verb* (numbered, numbering, numbers) 1. to set apart or label with a number. *Please number your pages.* 2. to limit in number or amount. *The sheriff told the outlaw that his days of stealing horses were numbered.* 3. to amount to a total of. *Guests at the party numbered twenty.* 4. to be included. *I am numbered among the students on the honor roll.* {**nuhm** bər}

nu·mer·al *noun* one or more words, symbols, or marks used to express or represent a number. *The numeral "2" stands for two.* {**nooh** mər əl}

nu·mer·a·tor *noun* the number in a fraction that is above the division line, over the denominator. *In the fraction 5/6, 5 is the numerator.* {**nooh** mə **ray** tər}

nu·mer·i·cal *adjective* of or having to do with numbers. *He is an expert at working with numerical data.* {nooh **meh** rih kəl} numeric, adj., numerically, adv.

nu·mer·ous *adjective* 1. being in great number; many. *I have numerous uncles, aunts, and cousins.* 2. made up of a great number. *China has a numerous population.* {**nooh** mər əs}

nun *noun* a woman who is a member of a religious order. *Nuns promise to live simply, not marry, and obey God. Many nuns live in convents.* {**nuhn**}

Homophone Note The words *nun* and *none* (no person or thing) sound alike but have different meanings.

Nu·na·vut *noun* a territory in northern Canada. Its capital is Iqaluit. {**nooh** nə **vooht**}

Word History *Nunavut* means "our land" in Inuktitut, the language of the Inuit people who live there. Nunavut became a separate territory of Canada in 1999.

nurse  *noun* 1. a person who is trained to care for sick and injured people. *I went to see the school nurse when I scraped my knee.* 2. a person who is paid to look after a child or several children. *A nurse takes care of the baby while her parents work. verb* (nursed, nursing, nurses) 1. to give medical care to. *She nursed the sick kitten.* 2. to feed from a breast. *My mother*

A B C D E F G H I J K L M **N** O P Q R S T U V W X Y Z

a b c d e f g h i j k l m **n** o p q r s t u v w x y z

Number Systems (or "how to count your allowance")

Hindu-Arabic 0 1 2 3 4 5 6 7 8 9

The number system we use today began in India over two thousand years ago. It was refined and spread by Arab mathematicians. This number system makes it easy to write large numbers and do arithmetic.

Roman I II III IV V VI VII VIII IX X

The ancient Romans began using letters for numbers over two thousand years ago. This number system was widely used in Europe until the Renaissance. It's hard to write very large numbers in Roman numerals.

Binary 1 10 11 100 101 110 111 1000 1001 1010

The binary, or base-two, number system is the foundation of all computer languages. Think of 0 as an "off" switch and 1 as an "on" switch (look at the power button on a computer).

Hindu-Arabic	Roman	Binary
11	XI	1011
38	XXXVIII	100110
547	DXLVII	1000100011

nurses my baby brother. {**nuhrs**}

nurs·er·y *noun* (nurseries) 1. a room where babies or young children sleep or play. 2. a place where plants or trees are grown for sale. 3. a place where babies and young children are taken care of while their parents are working or in school; nursery school. {**nuhr** sə ree}

nursery school *noun* a school for children before they go to kindergarten. {**nuhr** sə ree skoohl *or* **nuhrs** ree skoohl}

nut ❶ *noun* 1. a dry seed or fruit made up of a kernel or meat contained in a hard, tough shell. The kernel or meat of nuts is often used as food. 2. the kernel or meat without the shell. *We made trail mix with oats, raisins, and nuts.* 3. a piece of metal or other material in the shape of a square or hexagon. A nut has a hole in it into which a bolt is screwed. 4. (slang) a foolish or crazy person. {**nuht**}

nut·crack·er *noun* a tool for cracking the shell of a nut. {**nuht** krăk ər}

nut·hatch *noun* a small bird with a short tail and a long, narrow beak. It climbs about on trees in search of insects,

moving down the trunk head first. {**nuht** hăch}

nut·meat *noun* the part of a nut that can be eaten. {**nuht** meet}

nut·meg *noun* the seed of an evergreen tree of East India. Nutmeg is made into a powder and used as a spice. {**nuht** mehg}

nu·tri·a *noun* a small mammal with thick brown fur and a long thin tail. Nutrias are rodents closely related to guinea pigs and porcupines. They build burrows near wet areas such as swamps. Nutrias used to only live in South America, but they have spread to much of the United States and Europe. {**nooh** tree ə}

nu·tri·ent ❂ ❂ *noun* something in food that helps people, animals, and plants live and grow. *If you don't get enough nutrients, you may become sick.* {**nooh** tree ənt}

nu·tri·tion ❂ *noun* 1. the act or process of eating and using the nutrients in food for living and growing. *The veterinarian is an expert in the nutrition of pigs.* 2. food; nourishment. *Poor nutrition can cause illness.* {**nooh** **trih** shən} nutritional, adj.

nu·tri·tious *adjective* having a large amount of vitamins, minerals, or other nutrients. *Cotton candy is not very nutritious.* {nooh **trih** shəs} nutritiousness, n.

nut·shell *noun* the hard cover of a nut. {**nuht** shehl}

nuz·zle *verb* (nuzzled, nuzzling, nuzzles) to touch, push, or rub the nose against. *The horse nuzzled her foal until it stood on its own.* {**nuhz** əl}

NV or **Nev.** *abbreviation* an abbreviation for **Nevada**.

NW *abbreviation* an abbreviation for **northwest**.

NY or **N.Y.** *abbreviation* an abbreviation for **New York**.

ny·lon *noun* 1. a strong, artificial material used to make yarn, cloth, plastic, and many other products. 2. cloth or yarn made of this material. *His backpack is made of nylon.* {**niy** lŏn}

nymph *noun* 1. one of the goddesses in Greek or Roman mythology who live in rivers, mountains, or trees. 2. an insect in an early stage of life. *A nymph looks like a small adult.* {**nihmf**}

 Human Body Human Mind Everyday Life  History and Culture  Communication

Oo

O is a vowel that makes several different sounds.

Tips to help you look up words starting with o: Sometimes vowels sound similar to each other. If you can't find the word you're looking for under O, it may start with a, u, or especially with "au" (such as author or autumn).

Also look under H for words that are spelled with a silent "h" at the beginning (such as honest, honor or hour).

These words may be hard to look up if you don't already know how to spell them:

ocean
of
off
onion
orchestra
ought

o or **O** *noun* (o's or O's) the fifteenth letter of the English alphabet. {oh}

O symbol of the chemical element oxygen.

oak  *noun* 1. a tree that belongs to the beech family and bears acorns. 2. the tough, lasting wood of such a tree. {ohk} oaken, adj.

oar *noun* a long pole that is wide and flat at one end. Oars are used to row or steer a boat. {ohr} oarless, adj., oar-like, adj.

Homophone Note The words *oar*, *or*, and *ore* sound alike but have different meanings.

o·a·sis *noun* (oases) an area in a desert where plants can grow. The plants are fed by water from a spring or well. {oh **ay** sihs}

oat *noun* 1. (usually plural; used with a singular or plural verb) a grain plant that is grown in cool regions. 2. the seed of this plant, which is used as food for people and animals. {oht}

oath *noun* 1. a serious promise. *He made an oath to tell the truth in court. / Boy Scouts repeat the Boy Scout oath at every meeting.* 2. a rude word; curse. {oh**th**}

oat·meal *noun* 1. meal made by grinding or rolling oats. 2. a cooked food made from this meal. {oht meel}

o·be·di·ent *adjective* likely or willing to obey rules or orders. *He isn't obedient when his father is away.* {oh **bee** dee ənt} obediently, adv.

o·bese *adjective* very fat. *The children made fun of the obese man.* {oh bees}

o·bey *verb* (obeyed, obeying, obeys) 1. to follow or carry out the command, instruction, or wishes of. *She obeyed her mother and cleaned her room.* 2. to observe or carry out as instructed. *The first-grade students tried hard to obey the teacher's rules.* 3. to move or act in agreement with; respond to. *Falling objects obey the law of gravity.* {oh **bay**}

Word History The word *obey* comes from an early French word that means "give ear to" or "pay attention to."

o·bi *noun* (obis) a wide sash worn at the waist over a Japanese kimono. {**oh** bee}

ob·ject *noun* 1. anything that has shape or form and can be seen or touched. *The only object in the room was a chair.* 2. any thing or person to which a thought or action is directed. *I sent a Valentine to the object of my affection.* 3. the purpose or goal of a particular activity. *The object of the game is to get rid of all your cards.* 4. a noun or noun phrase that receives the action of a verb in a sentence. *In the sentence, "I forgot my bag," the noun "bag" is the object.* *verb* (objected, objecting, objects) 1. to present reasons against something; protest or oppose. *Some parents object to the city's plan to build a skateboard park.* 2. to dislike or be against something; show disapproval. *The store owner*

A
B
C
D
E
F
G
H
I
J
K
L
M
N
O
P
Q
R
S
T
U
V
W
X
Y
Z

objected when we walked in without our shoes. {**ŏb** jehkt, n., əb **jehkt**, v.} objector, n.

ob·jec·tion *noun* 1. a statement of not liking or not agreeing with something. *Ling's objections to the law were printed in today's paper.* 2. a cause or reason for not liking or agreeing with something. *She didn't understand her mother's objection to her wearing makeup.* {əb **jehk** shən}

ob·jec·tion·a·ble *adjective* causing someone to object or disagree; offensive. *Spitting is objectionable behavior.* / *Picky Paul finds something objectionable in every idea.* {əb **jehk** shə nə bəl} objectionably, adv.

ob·jec·tive *noun* a goal or purpose that a person works to achieve; aim. *My objective is to become a teacher.* *adjective* not influenced by personal feelings or opinions. *The teacher thought about her student's problem in an objective way.* {əb **jehk** tihv} objectively, adv.

ob·li·gate *verb* (obligated, obligating, obligates) to make someone do something because of a law or moral principle. *The law obligates us to drive slowly through town.* / *His knowledge of right and wrong obligated him to return the wallet he had found.* {**o** blih gayt}

ob·li·ga·tion *noun* 1. something that someone should or should not do because of a law or moral principle. *In some countries, military service is an obligation.* 2. the condition of having to do something because of a law or moral principle. *The dishonest man felt no obligation to return the wallet he had found.* {**o** blih **gay** shən}

o·blige *verb* (obliged, obliging, obliges) 1. to make a person

do something. *Their friendship obliged them to help each other.* 2. to cause to be grateful. *His towing our car out of the ditch obliged us to the mechanic.* 3. to do a kind act or service. *I eagerly obliged when he asked me to help him build a boat.* {ə **bliyj**}

o·blig·ing *adjective* ready to help or do favors. *Because Janice is an obliging person, she gladly helped her cousin move into the new house.* {ə **bliy** jing} obligingly, adv.

oblique angle *noun* an angle that is not a right angle. {oh **bleek** ăng gəl}

ob·long *adjective* longer than it is wide. *This shoe box is oblong to fit the boots.* *noun* an object or figure that is longer than it is wide. *I drew some oblongs, mostly rectangles and ellipses, to try out my new pen.* {**ŏb** lawng}

ob·nox·ious *adjective* offensive or not pleasant. *Two obnoxious children screamed during our trip to the museum.* / *Skunks give off an obnoxious smell.* {əb **nŏk** shəs} obnoxiously, adv.

o·boe *noun* a woodwind instrument with a high tone. It has a long, thin body with finger holes or keys, and is played by blowing into a mouthpiece. {**oh** boh}

ob·scene *adjective* offensive and not decent. *Some people thought the painting at the museum was obscene.* {əb **seen**} obscenely, adv.

ob·scure *adjective* (obscurer, obscurest) 1. hard to see or not distinct. *The obscure figure in the fog might have been a dog.* 2. not famous or little known. *Although he was an obscure author, he wrote beautiful poetry.* / *We like to vacation in obscure areas.* 3. not clear in meaning or

expression. *Her obscure style of writing makes her poems difficult to understand.* *verb* (obscured, obscuring, obscures) to dim or conceal. *Clouds obscured our view of the stars last night.* {əb **skyuhr**} obscurely, adv.

ob·ser·va·tion *noun* 1. the act or an instance of perceiving the environment through one of the senses. *A good artist must be skilled at close observation.* 2. the state of being seen or noticed. *The doctor wanted to keep the patient under observation.* 3. a comment; remark. *Her guest made the observation that the dinner table looked beautiful.* {ŏb zər **vay** shən}

ob·serv·a·tory ❶ *noun* (observatories) a building that has equipment for studying the sun, moon, planets, and stars. {əb **zuhr** və **tohr** ee}

ob·serve *verb* (observed, observing, observes) 1. to notice or see. *The parents observed that their child enjoyed music.* 2. to watch closely; make a careful observation of. *The cat observed the bird with hungry interest.* 3. to say in a casual way; mention; remark. *Our teacher observed that we were getting better at solving problems.* 4. to act in keeping with; follow. *She observed all the rules of the game.* 5. to celebrate; keep. *The nation observes several holidays.* {əb **zuhrv**}

ob·so·lete *adjective* no longer in use. *Some of the words you use now will one day be obsolete.* / *Covered wagons are obsolete.* {ŏb sə **leet** or ŏb sə **leet**}

ob·sta·cle *noun* something that stops forward movement or progress. *That high fence is an obstacle.* / *His path to success was filled with obstacles.* {**ŏb** stə kəl}

Human Body   Human Mind   Everyday Life   History and Culture   Communication

ob·sti·nate *adjective* not willing to change one's ideas; stubborn. *James was obstinate about not eating vegetables.* {**ŏb** stə niht}

ob·struct *verb* (obstructed, obstructing, obstructs) 1. to block or clog. *Large rocks obstruct the path.* 2. to prevent or delay the passage or progress of. *Large rocks obstructed our climb. / The new law obstructs further building.* 3. to get in the way of seeing; block from view. *Their large hats obstructed the movie screen.* {əb **struhkt**}

ob·struc·tion *noun* 1. something that blocks the way or prevents progress. *The mountains were an obstruction for travelers until airplanes were invented.* 2. an act or instance of obstructing, or the condition of being obstructed. *Eating too much fat can lead to obstruction of blood vessels.* {əb **struhk** shən}

ob·tain *verb* (obtained, obtaining, obtains) to get; gain. *He obtained his college degree in just three years.* {əb **tayn**} obtainable, adj.

ob·tuse an·gle *noun* an angle greater than 90 degrees and less than 180 degrees. {ŏb **toohs** ăng gəl}

ob·vi·ous *adjective* easily seen or understood; clear. *It was obvious how much he liked her.* {**ŏb** vee əs} obviously, adv.

oc·ca·sion *noun* 1. an event or the time at which it happens. *He has been late on several occasions.* 2. a special event; celebration. *A party at the governor's mansion is always an occasion.* 3. a good time for something; opportunity. *Let's use this occasion to reflect on our past mistakes.* {ə **kay** zhən}

• **on occasion** now and then; irregularly. *I travel to other countries on occasion.*

oc·ca·sion·al *adjective* happening now and then or not too often. *She gives me occasional tennis lessons.* {ə **kay** zhə nəl}

oc·cu·pant *noun* someone who lives or works in a place or fills a position. *The occupants of the office building stood outside during the fire drill. / Is the queen the present occupant of the throne?* {**ŏk** yə pənt}

oc·cu·pa·tion 🌐 *noun* 1. the work a person does to earn a living; profession. *Teaching is the occupation of most members of her family.* 2. the act or process of being in or taking over an area. *Germany's occupation of France took place in 1940. / The cat's occupation of the dog's bed made everyone laugh.* 3. the condition of being taken over or occupied. *Algeria's occupation by France lasted for over a hundred years.* {**ŏk** yə **pay** shən}

oc·cu·py *verb* (occupied, occupying, occupies) 1. to take and control. *Germany occupied Poland during World War II.* 2. to take up; fill. *Tables and chairs are occupying the space you want for your game. / How do you occupy your free hours?* 3. to live in. *My grandparents have occupied their house for forty years.* 4. to serve in or hold. *U.S. presidents occupy that position for four years at a time.* {**ŏk** yə **piy**}

oc·cur *verb* (occurred, occurring, occurs) 1. to take place; happen. *While we were exploring the old house, something occurred that I shall never forget.* 2. to be found; appear. *Some colors never occur in nature.* 3. to appear in one's thoughts (usually followed by "to"). *It never occurred to me to invite her to the party until you suggested it.* {ə **kuhr**}

oc·cur·rence *noun* 1. the process or fact of taking place or happening. *If you are involved in another occurrence of bullying, you will be suspended.* 2. an event that takes place; incident. *Jon wanted to report the strange occurrences to the police.* {ə **kuh** rəns}

o·cean 🌐 *noun* 1. the vast body of salt water covering about three quarters of the earth's surface. 2. any of the major divisions of this body of water. *The Atlantic, Pacific, Indian, and Arctic are the names of the four oceans.* {**oh** shən}

> **Word History** *Ocean* is from an ancient Greek word that means "great river surrounding the earth." *Okeanos* was the Greek god of the ocean.

o·cea·nog·ra·phy *noun* the science that studies the oceans and the animals and plants that live in oceans. {oh shə **no** grə fee} oceanographer, n.

o·ce·lot *noun* a wild cat with yellow or brown fur and black spots or stripes. Ocelots look like leopards but are smaller. They live in South and Central America, sometimes as far north as Texas. They are carnivorous mammals that eat birds, snakes, and small mammals. {**o** sə **lŏt**}

> **Word History** The word *ocelot* is from an Aztec word that means "field jaguar."

o'clock *adverb* of or according to the clock. *Our train leaves at five o'clock.* {ə **klŏk**}

A
B
C
D
E
F
G
H
I
J
K
L
M
N
O
P
Q
R
S
T
U
V
W
X
Y
Z

Oct. *abbreviation* an abbreviation for **October**.

oct- *prefix* see **octo-**.

oc·ta·gon *noun* a flat closed figure with eight straight sides. *In North America, stop signs are in the shape of an octagon.* {ŏk tə gŏn}

oc·tave *noun* 1. a musical tone with the same name as another, higher or lower tone. When a tone is played with its octave, the tones blend together and sound almost like a single note. The higher of the tones in an octave always has twice as many vibrations per second as the lower note. 2. the interval between these two tones, or the tones or keys of an instrument within this interval. {ŏk tihv *or* ŏk tayv}

oc·to- *or* **oct-** *or* **octa-** *prefix* a prefix that means "eight." *An octopus has eight legs.*

Oc·to·ber *noun* the tenth month of the year. October has thirty-one days. {ŏk toh bər}

Word History *October*
comes from *octo*, the Latin word for "eight." October was the eighth month in the Roman calendar.

oc·to·pus *noun* (octopuses or octopi) a sea animal with a soft, rounded body and eight long tentacles. Octopuses are carnivores that eat crabs, lobsters, and other small sea animals. They are mollusks and are closely related to

squids. {ŏk tə pəs}

Word History *Octopus*
comes from *oktopous*, an ancient Greek word that means "having eight feet"

odd *adjective* (odder, oddest) 1. different from what is expected or usual; strange. *Joe looked odd in his striped pants, green shoes, and flowered hat.* 2. being the only one of a set or pair. *That drawer is full of odd socks.* 3. left over; remaining. *My mother used odd scraps of cloth to make a beautiful quilt.* 4. not able to be divided exactly by two. *Three is an odd number. (See even.)* {ŏd} oddly, adj., oddness, n.

odd·i·ty *noun* (oddities) 1. a strange or unusual thing, person, or event. *Having one blue eye and one brown eye is an oddity.* 2. the state or characteristic of being strange. *The oddity of Joe's clothes made people stare.* {o dih tee}

odds *plural noun* 1. the probability that one thing is more likely to happen than another. *The odds are against that team's winning. / Studying will increase your odds of passing the test.* 2. numbers that express how likely this is. *The odds are two to one that the home team will win.* {ŏdz}
• **at odds**
not agreeing. *Katie is often at odds with her parents.*

odds and ends *plural noun* a group of different kinds of items; bits and pieces; scraps. *I bought some odds and ends for the house during the sale.* {ŏdz ənd ehndz}

o·dor *noun* smell or scent. *A strange odor filled the kitchen. / Honeysuckle flowers have a sweet odor.* {oh dər} odorless, adj.

o·dour *noun* a spelling of **odor** used in Canada and Britain. See **odor**. {oh dər}

of *preposition* 1. used to show distance or separation from. *I was within a foot of the door when the phone stopped ringing. / They were cheated of their money.* 2. used to indicate cause or explanation. *He died of heart failure.* 3. made from. *I wear clothes of a light material when the weather is hot.* 4. containing. *The dog knocked over the pail of water.* 5. having as an important quality. *Our mayor is a man of honor.* 6. belonging to. *After school I sometimes visit the home of my friend.* 7. relating to; about. *We had a discussion of our vacation plans.* {uhv}

off *adverb* 1. away from a point or position. *The dog ran off.* 2. so as not to be on or connected. *She got on her bike, but soon fell off. / Turn off the lights before you go to bed.* 3. away from a job or duty. *She took a year off when she had a baby.* *preposition* 1. so as to be separated or away from. *Please take your feet off the table!* 2. away from. *The park off the main street is my favorite place to sit and relax.* *adjective* 1. of low quality; spoiled. *The meat smells a little off.* 2. free from work. *My father likes to read in his off hours.* 3. not accurate; not correct. *My guess was off about how many people would come to the picnic.* 4. slight; not likely. *For actors, there is only the off chance that they will become famous.* 5. not taking place. *The parade is off because it is raining.* 6. in a certain condition. *In matters of money she is well off.* *interjection* "away"; "gone." *Get off! / Be off!* {awf}

 Human Body    Human Mind   Everyday Life   History and Culture   Communication

of·fence *noun* a spelling of **offense** used in Canada and Britain. See **offense**. {<u>aw</u> fehns}

of·fend 🌐 💻 *verb* (offended, offending, offends) to cause to be angry, annoyed, or insulted. *Cruelty to animals offends most people. / I was offended when he called me a liar.* {ə <u>fehnd</u>} offender, n.

of·fense *noun* 1. the act of breaking a law or rule or doing something wrong; crime; sin. *After the drunk driver's third offense, the judge sent him to jail.* 2. something that causes anger or a feeling of not being respected. *The five rusty cars on his front lawn are an offense to the neighborhood.* 3. the players or sports team that drives forward, generally with the ball. *Our football team lost because the offense didn't play well.* {ə <u>fehns</u>}

of·fen·sive *adjective* 1. not pleasant; disagreeable. *Wet animals can have an offensive smell.* 2. causing anger or hurt feelings. *His rude comments were offensive to everyone.* 3. of or made for attack. *The general ordered the soldiers into an offensive position.* *noun* an attitude or position of attack; attacking side of an army or sports team. *Several army divisions were sent to take the offensive.* {ə <u>fehn</u> sihv} offensively, adv.

of·fer *verb* (offered, offering, offers) 1. to present to be accepted or refused. *I offered a toy to the baby.* 2. to present for discussion; suggest. *She offered ideas about how we could save money.* 3. to show a desire to do or give something. *Evan offered to help paint the house.* 4. to put up. *My mother offered strong reasons against moving to the city.*

noun 1. the act of offering. *I accepted Yvette's offer to help with the cleaning.* 2. that which is offered. *We made an offer of nine hundred dollars for the boat.* {<u>aw</u> fər}

off·hand *adjective* done without thinking or preparing ahead of time. *I'm sorry that my offhand remarks hurt your feelings.* {<u>awf</u> <u>hănd</u>} offhanded, adj.

of·fice 🌐 💻 *noun* 1. a place where business or professional work is done. *Tom works in an office with twenty other people.* 2. those who work in such a place. *The office was happy about the new manager.* 3. a position of trust or responsibility. *Karen holds the office of treasurer.* {<u>aw</u> fihs}

of·fic·er *noun* 1. a person holding a position of trust and responsibility in a business, organization, or government agency. 2. a person who has the power to command and lead others in the armed forces. 3. a policeman or policewoman. {<u>aw</u> fih sər}

of·fi·cial *noun* a person who holds an office in a business organization or a government. *The city officials met to discuss the building of a new highway.* *adjective* 1. of or having to do with an office or position of responsibility or authority. *The ambassador's official duties included meetings with leaders from other countries.* 2. named by or acting for an organization or government. *An ambassador is a nation's official representative in another country.* 3. approved by an authority; formal and public. *There was an official celebration of the town's two hundredth birthday.* {ə <u>fih</u> shəl} officially, adv.

off-road *adjective* of a type of vehicle used away from

streets and highways. *Snowmobiles are off-road vehicles.* {<u>awf</u> <u>rohd</u>}

off·set *verb* (offset, offsetting, offsets) to make up for or balance. *The delicious dessert helped offset the horrible stew.* {<u>awf</u> <u>seht</u>}

off·shoot *noun* 1. a branch or shoot from the main stem of a plant. 2. a branch or something else that comes from a source. *This business is an offshoot of a much larger company.* {<u>awf</u> shooht}

off·shore *adverb* away from the shore. *He works offshore on an oil rig.* *adjective* 1. turned or moving away from the shore. *It was an offshore storm until it moved toward the island yesterday.* 2. located or taking place at a distance from the shore. *The guide took us to the best offshore fishing spot.* {<u>awf</u> <u>shohr</u>}

off·spring *noun* (offspring) the child or young of a particular human, animal, or plant. *This lamb is the offspring of our prize ewe.* {<u>awf</u> spring}

of·ten *adverb* at many times; frequently. *How often do you go swimming?* {<u>aw</u> fən or <u>awf</u> tən}

o·gre *noun* 1. an ugly giant or monster in folk tales and children's stories. Ogres are said to eat people. 2. a very evil, ugly, or cruel person. *The football coach can be an ogre when his team loses.* {<u>oh</u> gər}

oh *interjection* a word used to express surprise, pain, or

A B C D E F G H I J K L M N O P Q R S T U V W X Y Z

other feelings. *Oh! I can't believe you did that!* {<u>oh</u>}

Homophone Note The words *oh* and *owe* (to be in debt to) sound alike but have different meanings.

OH or **O.** *abbreviation* an abbreviation for **Ohio**.

O·hi·o *noun* 1. a state in the midwestern United States. Its capital is Columbus. (abbreviated: OH) 2. a river of the eastern and central United States. It flows from Pennsylvania into the Mississippi River. {oh <u>hiy</u> oh} Ohioan, n.

Word History *Ohio* means "great river" or "beautiful water" in an Iroquois language. The state was named for the Ohio River.

oil 🔵🔵 *noun* 1. any one of the greasy liquids that come from minerals, animals, plants or chemicals. Oil can be dissolved in alcohol, but not water. *Olive oil is used for cooking, while pine oil is used to make cleaners.* 2. a liquid found beneath the earth's surface, or the products made from this liquid and used for fuel or lubrication; petroleum. 3. artists' paint that uses oil as its base. *The painting class is using oils this month and watercolors next month.* {<u>oil</u>}

oil well *noun* a well from which petroleum is drawn or pumped. {<u>oil</u> wehl}

oil·y *adjective* (oilier, oiliest) 1. of or like oil. *She used an oily spray to keep the door from creaking.* 2. containing a lot of oil, or covered with oil; greasy. *The food was too oily. / Their bikes slid on the oily road surface.* {<u>oi</u> lee} oiliness, n.

oint·ment *noun* a soft, oily substance made to be rubbed into the skin. Ointment may be used as medicine or to soften the skin. {<u>oint</u> mənt}

O·jib·wa *noun* (Ojibwa) a member of an American Indian people living around Lake Superior in the United States and Canada. {oh <u>jihb</u> way *or* oh <u>jihb</u> wə}

OK or **O.K.** or **okay** *adjective* (informal) all right; satisfactory. *That restaurant is OK, but this one is excellent. / She felt sick yesterday, but she is OK now.* *adverb* (informal) acceptably; all right. *He did OK on the history test.* *interjection* "all right"; "yes." *OK, I'll do it.* *noun* (OK's or okays) (informal) a sign of approval or acceptance. *My parents gave their OK for the party.* *verb* (OK'd or okayed, OK'ing or okaying, OK's or okays) (informal) to agree to; approve. *Did your teacher OK your idea for the science project?* {oh <u>kay</u>}

OK or **Okla.** *abbreviation* an abbreviation for **Oklahoma**.

o·kay *verb or adjective or adverb or noun or interjection* another spelling of **OK**. {oh <u>kay</u>}

O·kla·ho·ma *noun* a state in the southwestern United States. Its capital is Oklahoma City. (abbreviated: OK) {oh klə <u>hoh</u> mə} Oklahoman, n.

Word History *Oklahoma* comes from the Choctaw words *okla*, meaning "people," and *humma*, meaning "red." The name was applied to the area after the Choctaw and other Native Americans were forced to migrate there between 1820 and 1842.

o·kra *noun* 1. a green vegetable that is shaped like a tube. Okra becomes sticky when cooked and is used in soups or fried. 2. the plant on which this vegetable grows as seed pods. {<u>oh</u> krə}

old *adjective* (older, oldest) 1. having lived for many years; not young. *My grandparents are old, but they are healthy.* 2. having existed for many years; not new. *There is a lot of old furniture in our house.* 3. worn by use or age. *She likes the comfort of her old shoes.* 4. of a time past; former. *My mother showed me her old neighborhood.* 5. known for a long time. *Larry and I are old friends.* {<u>ohld</u>} oldness, n.

Synonyms
These words share a meaning with *old*, adjective 4:

past Past is the most common way of referring to time that has gone by. *In past times, many people died of diseases that today we can cure.*

former Former describes something or someone that was but is no more. *He was a great baseball player in former years.*

previous Previous means before the present. *In previous years, very few people had computers.*

bygone Bygone suggests a feeling of nostalgia or longing for the past. *The movie brought to life the bygone days when people rode in carriages.*

old·en *adjective* of or having to do with ancient times. *In olden days, walking was the main way to travel.* {<u>ohl</u> dən}

 Human Body   Human Mind   Everyday Life   History and Culture   Communication

Old English *noun* the English language as it was spoken from about 450 to about 1400. {ohld ing glihsh}

old-fash·ioned *adjective* 1. looking or being like past styles, manners, or ways of behaving. *That dress looks old-fashioned because of the lace on the sleeves.* 2. sharing or liking the values or manners of the past. *My old-fashioned teacher does not let us wear hats indoors.* {ohld fǎ shənd} old-fashionedly, adv., old-fashionedness, n.

Old Testament *noun* the Christian name for the writings that make up the first major part of the Bible. *The Old Testament is also part of the Hebrew scriptures.* {ohld teh stə mənt}

Old World *noun* the Eastern Hemisphere, which includes Europe, Asia, Australia, and Africa. {ohld wuhrld}

o·le·o·mar·ga·rine *noun* a food like butter made from vegetable oil instead of milk; margarine. {oh lee oh mar jə rihn}

ol·ive *noun* 1. a small green or black fruit with a pit. Olives are eaten raw or used to make olive oil. 2. the evergreen tree that bears such fruit. Olives grow in warm areas around the Mediterranean Sea. 3. a dull yellowish green color. *adjective* of or having to do with the color olive. *That olive shirt looks good on you.* {o lihv}

olive oil *noun* oil pressed from ripe olives. *Olive oil is used for cooking.* {o lihv oil}

O·lym·pus *noun* a mountain in northern Greece, believed in ancient times to be the place where the gods lived; Mount Olympus. {ə lihm pəs}

om·e·let or **omelette** *noun* a food made from beaten eggs that are cooked into a single sheet and often folded over a filling of vegetables, meat, or cheese. {o mə lət or ǒm lət}

o·men *noun* something that is believed to be a sign of future good or evil. *They assumed that sunny weather on their wedding day was a good omen. / Gary thought stepping on a crack in the sidewalk was a bad omen.* {oh mən}

om·i·nous *adjective* giving a sign of future evil or trouble. *The black clouds looked ominous, so we decided to go to the lake some other day.* {o mə nəs} ominously, adv.

o·mit *verb* (omitted, omitting, omits) to leave out; not include. *She omitted the second page from the speech.* {oh miht}

om·ni·vore ⬥ *noun* an animal that lives on a diet of both plant and animal food. {ǒm nih vohr}

om·niv·or·ous *adjective* living on a diet of both plant and animal food. *Human beings are omnivorous.* {ǒm nih və rəs}

on *preposition* 1. above and supported by. *There is a grammar book on the shelf.* 2. in contact with; touching. *He put his hand on her shoulder. / She put paint on the brush.* 3. located near. *Their house is on the lake.* 4. supported by or hanging from. *Emma put paintings on the wall.* 5. into, onto, or in the direction of. *He got on the train. / Her house is on the right.* 6. at the time of; at the moment of. *We moved into our new apartment on Wednesday. / He smiled on hearing the joke.* 7. with regard to; about; concerning. *We agreed on a plan. / Leslie wrote an article on* cooking. 8. associated with for service or work. *Jake is on the student council.* 9. in a state or process of. *The thieves were on the run. / The house was on fire.* 10. near to, as in an encounter. *Suddenly they came on a graveyard.* 11. by means of. *We were speaking on the phone.* 12. toward; at. *He looked on the servants with disgust.* *adverb* 1. into contact with or into the proper position. *He put his glasses on.* 2. into operation or process. *Turn the lights on.* 3. forward through time or space. *He walked on. / I talked on.* 4. firmly; with a tight hold. *Hold on to the rail.* 5. towards something or someone. *Our boss looked on as we worked.* *adjective* 1. running or in process. *The stove is on.* 2. happening or about to happen; scheduled. *The meeting is on for tomorrow.* 3. (informal) performing with much skill or energy. *The guitar player was really on last night.* {ǒn}

• **be on to** (informal) to have inside information about. *"I'm on to you," said the policeman to the crook.*

• **on and on** for too long a time. *He talked on and on until everyone had fallen asleep.*

once *adverb* 1. at one time in the past; formerly. *She was once a teacher, but that was a long time ago.* 2. only one time. *Dad gets his hair cut once a month.* *conjunction* if ever; whenever; when. *Once you've told me, I won't forget.* *noun* a single instance; one time. *When it comes to riding ponies, once is never enough.* {wuhns}

• **at once** 1. at the same time. *Everyone arrived at once.* 2. now; imme-

diately; without any delay. *We must leave at once.*

on·com·ing *adjective* coming toward or near; approaching. *We saw the lights of an oncoming car.* {**ŏn kuh** ming}

one *adjective* 1. being a single thing or person. *Each of you may have one candy.* 2. united; not divided. *They all shared one purpose.* 3. at some future time, not named. *Let's go to the movies one day next week.* *noun* 1. the number that comes after zero and before two in the sequence of cardinal numbers; 1. 2. a single thing or person. *Sean is the best one on his team. pronoun* 1. a person or object that is not named but is part of a group. *One of the girls on our team was named best player.* 2. any person; a person not named, often referring to the person speaking. *One can't be right all the time.* {**wuhn**}

Homophone Note The words *one* and *won* (past tense of "win") sound alike but have different meanings.

one·self *pronoun* a person's own self (used to show that an action is done to the same person who does that action). *One should take care of oneself to stay healthy.* {wuhn **sehlf**}

one-si·ded *adjective* 1. giving only one side or position. *She told a one-sided story about the street fight.* 2. being not even or not equal. *Our swimming team took little joy in their one-sided win.* {**wuhn siy** dihd} one-sidedly, adv., one-sidedness, n.

one-way *adjective* moving or allowing to move in a single direction. *She drove the wrong way on a one-way street.* {**wuhn way**}

on·go·ing *adjective* continuing from sometime in the past into the future. *They have an ongoing discussion about whether they should buy a larger house.* {**ŏn goh** ing}

on·ion *noun* 1. a round bulb with a sharp taste and smell. Onions are used in cooking and as a flavoring. 2. the plant that grows these bulbs. Onions are members of the lily family. {**uhn** yən}

Word History The word *onion* comes from *unionem*, a Latin word that means both "onion" and "a large pearl."

on-line or **online** *adjective* connected to or reached through a computer or computer network. *Many library catalogs are now on-line. adverb* while under the direct control of another computer, or while connected to a computer network. *She can work on-line from her computer at home.* {**ŏn liyn**}

on·ly *adverb* 1. as the single instance. *Only you understand me.* 2. at least; just. *If he would only listen to me, he would be much better off. adjective* 1. alone or single; being without others. *The pilot was the only person alive after the plane crash.* 2. without a brother or sister. *Both my parents were only children. conjunction* except that; but. *I would have gone, only my father didn't want me to.* {**ohn** lee}

on·set *noun* 1. the early stage; beginning. *At the onset of my cold, I went right to bed.* 2. an attack. *They could not protect themselves against the onset of the enemy.* {**ŏn seht**}

On·tar·i·o *noun* 1. a south central province of Canada that lies on the north shore of the Great Lakes. Its capital is Toronto. 2. Lake Ontario, the smallest of the Great Lakes. It lies between the state of New York and the province of Ontario. {**ŏn tayr** ee oh}

Word History *Ontario* may mean "large lake" or "sparkling water." It comes from the Iroquois name for the area. It may refer to Lake Ontario, one of the Great Lakes, or to Niagara Falls.

on·to *preposition* 1. to a position on or on top of. *They walked onto the stage.* 2. aware of another's hidden reasons for doing something. *I have a feeling she is onto our plan for her surprise party.* {**ŏn** tooh}

on·ward *adverb* toward a point or position ahead in space or time. *After a short rest, the army marched onward. adjective* moving toward a point ahead; advancing. *The onward march of the army continued into the night.* {**ŏn** wərd} onwards, adv.

ooze *verb* (oozed, oozing, oozes) to leak out slowly. Liquids, gases, and sounds may ooze. *Tears oozed from under her eyelids. / Weird music oozed from the haunted house.* {**oohz**}

o·pal *noun* a mineral that is white, black, blue, or yellow. Opals are used as gems. {**oh** pəl}

o·paque *adjective* 1. not letting light pass through. *Opaque window shades darken the room.* 2. having a flat, dull surface. *I like the opaque vase*

 Human Body  Human Mind  Everyday Life   History and Culture   Communication

better than the shiny one. {oh **payk**} opaqueness, n.

OPEC *abbreviation* an association made up of several Arab nations that sell the oil they produce to other countries. OPEC is an abbreviation for "Organization of Petroleum Exporting Countries." {**oh** pehk}

o·pen *adjective* 1. allowing entry; not shut or closed. *A cool breeze came through the open window.* 2. having no trees or structures. *We rode our horses through the open field.* 3. that may be attended or taken part in by all; public. *Our town held an open meeting to introduce the new mayor.* 4. available. *My school has open positions for two teachers.* 5. behaving or speaking in an honest or direct way. *Maria is open about her problems in school. / Frankie told an open lie.* 6. prepared to do business. *That supermarket is open twenty-four hours a day.* 7. able to accept new ideas or beliefs. *Our teacher is open to our ideas about the class trip.* *verb* (opened, opening, opens) 1. to change from being shut or closed. *I opened the door to let in the dog.* 2. to become open. *The flowers opened after I put them in water.* 3. to free from obstacles to allow passage. *They opened the path by removing the fallen trees.* 4. to begin. *She opened the meeting with a short speech.* 5. to start or begin. *The play opens with a speech by a young girl.* 6. to spread out or expand. *The bird opened its wings and flew away.* 7. to become spread out (often followed by "out"). *My umbrella opens when the button on its handle is pushed.* *noun* 1. the outdoors (preceded by "the"). *They* went out in the open for some cool air. 2. the condition of being without secrecy or not being hidden (usually used with "the"). *Let's bring the truth into the open.* {oh pən} openly, adv., openness, n.

o·pen·er *noun* 1. someone or something that opens. *You can be the opener of this gift. / Do you have my letter opener?* 2. a tool that opens bottles and cans. *We didn't eat the canned tuna because I forgot to bring an opener.* 3. the first in a series of events. *The weather was perfect for the opener of the football season.* {**oh** pə nər}

o·pen·ing *noun* 1. the act, process, or result of making open or causing to become open. *Everyone gathered around for the opening of birthday presents.* 2. a gap, hole, or empty space. *The actors waved at me through an opening in the curtain.* 3. a beginning of a book, play, concert, movie, or game. *The opening of the story caught her interest.* 4. the first performance or showing of a play or film. *We had a big party after the opening of the play.* 5. a job or position that has not yet been filled. *There is an opening for a nurse at the hospital.* {oh pə ning}

o·pen-mind·ed *adjective* not having made opinions or decisions ahead of time; willing to consider new ideas. *The older man was open-minded and interested in learning everything he could.* {oh pən **miyn** dihd} open-mindedness, n.

op·er·a  *noun* a play in which all or most of the words are sung and the music is played by an orchestra. {**ŏp** ə rə *or* **ŏp** rə}

op·er·ate *verb* (operated, operating, operates) 1. to work or run. *This new sewing machine operates for several hours on batteries.* 2. to perform surgery (usually followed by "on"). *The doctor operated on the patient's heart for six hours.* 3. to control the running of. *My smart little sister operates the computer very well.* {**ŏp** ə rayt}

op·er·a·tion *noun* 1. the act or process of working or running. *The operation of a computer was hard for her to learn.* 2. a particular set of activities that make up the running of something. *The operation of that large store requires hundreds of workers.* 3. a surgery. *Thanks to an eye operation, his grandfather can see well again.* 4. a number process in mathematics such as adding, subtracting, multiplying, and dividing. {**ŏp** ə **ray** shən}

op·er·a·tor *noun* 1. someone who controls the working of a machine or the activities of a business. *He is a bulldozer operator. / The operator of that restaurant started out as a waiter.* 2. someone who connects telephones through a central system and gives information and other help to people using telephones. *I called the operator to see if I could get Aunt Lucy's telephone number.* {**ŏp** ə **ray** tər}

op·er·et·ta *noun* a short, funny opera, with words that are spoken as well as sung. {**ŏp** ə **reh** tə}

oph·thal·mol·o·gist *noun* a doctor who works in the branch of medicine that studies and treats diseases of the eye. {ŏp thəl **mŏl** oh jihst}

oph·thal·mol·o·gy *noun* the branch of medicine that studies and treats diseases of the eye. {ŏf thəl **mo** lə jee *or* ŏp thəl **mo** lə jee *or* ŏf thə **mo** lə jee *or* ŏp thə **mo** lə jee}

o·pin·ion *noun* 1. what one thinks about something or somebody; viewpoint. An opinion is not necessarily based on facts. Feelings and experiences usually help a person form an opinion. *In my opinion, our math teacher is the best teacher in the school.* 2. a person's judgment of another's character or qualities. *What is your opinion of John?* 3. advice or a judgment by an expert or professional, such as a doctor, lawyer, or judge. *He went to several doctors for opinions on his illness.* {ə **pihn** yən}

o·pos·sum *noun* (opossum or opossums) 1. a small mammal with gray fur, a pointed nose, and a long tail, which it uses to hang from tree branches. The common opossum is the only marsupial that lives in North America. Several other kinds of opossums live in Central and South America. The female opossum carries her young in a pouch in her belly. 2. a group of Australian marsupials similar to the opossums that live in North, Central, and South America. {ə **po** səm}

op·po·nent *noun* one who fights, plays, or takes a position against another. *I never win at tennis when he is my opponent.* {ə **poh** nənt}

op·por·tu·ni·ty *noun* (opportunities) 1. a chance for a better situation. *The new job is a wonderful opportunity.* 2. a good chance or favorable situation. *Her trip to Asia was an opportunity to learn about different cultures.* {o pər **tooh** nih tee *or* o pər **tyoo** nih tee}

op·pose *verb* (opposed, opposing, opposes) 1. to think, act, or be against; resist. *The students oppose the idea of a longer school day.* 2. to balance; be in contrast to. *Her desire to be alone opposes her wish to join the drama club.* {ə **pohz**} opposer, n.

op·po·site *adjective* 1. located at or on the sides across from each other; facing. *I moved my bed to the opposite side of the room.* 2. as different as possible. *He and his father always seem to have opposite opinions.* *noun* a person or thing that is completely different from another. *My sister and I are opposites in looks, tastes, and interests.* / *Up and down are opposites.* *preposition* across from; facing. *They are building their house opposite mine.* {**ŏp** ə siht} oppositeness, n.

op·po·si·tion *noun* 1. the act or state of being against, or the state of having someone against another. *I am in opposition to my parents' plans to move.* / *Mattie's parents were in opposition to her efforts to become a dancer.* 2. one or more persons who are against someone or something. *The opposition wrote letters to the newspapers to complain about the mayor's plan for new taxes.* 3. a political party that is not in power. *The opposition has received a lot of money for their candidate in this election.* {ŏp ə **zih** shən} oppositional, adj.

op·press *verb* (oppressed, oppressing, oppresses) 1. to treat in a way that is cruel or not fair. *Many dictators have oppressed the citizens of their countries.* 2. to trouble or burden. *The thought of all that homework oppresses me.* / *The terrible heat oppressed us.* {ə **prehs**} oppressor, n.

opt *verb* (opted, opting, opts) to decide; choose (usually followed by "for" or an infinitive). *She opted for the red car.* / *We are opting to stay at home this summer.* {ŏpt}

op·ti·cal *adjective* 1. of or having to do with the sense of sight or the eye. *Optical tests tell you whether or not you need glasses.* 2. meant to make vision better. *Glasses are optical devices made to correct a problem with seeing.* {ŏp tih kəl} optically, adv.

op·ti·cian *noun* a person who makes or sells eyeglasses and contact lenses. {ŏp **tih** shən}

op·ti·mis·tic *adjective* likely to be hopeful that things will work out well. *She is optimistic about her success in school.* {ŏp tə **mih** stihk} optimistically, adv.

op·tion *noun* 1. the right, power, or freedom to choose. *Americans have the option to speak for or against public officials.* 2. something that is or may be chosen. *You have three options for dessert: fruit salad, apple pie, and peach ice.* {**ŏp** shən}

op·tion·al *adjective* left to someone's choice; not required. *Sports are optional at my school.* {**ŏp** shə nəl} optionally, adv.

op·tom·e·trist *noun* a person who is trained to examine people's eyes and to fit them with eyeglasses or contact lenses. {ŏp **to** mə trihst}

or *conjunction* 1. used to indicate alternatives. *Open the door or the window.* / *Either you go or I will.* 2. used to indicate similar things or alternative ways of referring to such things. *You may call them stars or suns.* 3. used to indicate a lack of certainty. *I'll be there in three or four hours.* {**ohr**}

Homophone Note The words *or*, *oar*, and *ore* sound alike but have different meanings.

 Human Body   Human Mind   Everyday Life  History and Culture Communication

OR *abbreviation* 1. an abbreviation for **Oregon**. 2. an abbreviation for "operating room."

-or *suffix* See **-er**[1]

o·ral *adjective* 1. spoken, rather than written; carried out by speaking. *The assignment is to give an oral report.* 2. of, taken by, or having to do with the mouth. *He got oral cancer from smoking. / The doctor gave her oral medicine that tastes terrible.* {**ohr** əl} orally, adv.

or·ange *noun* 1. a round fruit with a reddish yellow peel. It is sweet and juicy on the inside. 2. a citrus tree that bears such a fruit. 3. the color of this fruit when ripe; the color between red and yellow on the color spectrum. *adjective* having the color orange. *She carried an orange bag for Halloween.* {**ohr** ənj *or* **ar** ənj *or* **ohrnj** *or* **arnj**, n., **ohr** ənj *or* **ar** ənj *or* **ohrnj** *or* **arnj**, adj.} orangish, adj.

or·ange·ade *noun* a soft drink made with orange juice or orange flavoring. {**ohr** ənj **ayd** *or* **ar** ənj **ayd** *or* **ohrnj ayd** *or* **arnj ayd**}

o·rang·u·tan *or* **orangoutang** *noun* a large ape that lives in the rain forests of a few south Asian islands. Orangutans have long, red-brown fur and long arms. They spend most of their time in trees. They are a kind of primate. Orangutans are endangered. {ə **răng** ə tăn *or* ə **răng** ə

tăng *or* ə **răng** gə tăn *or* ə **răng** gə **tăng**}

Word History *Orangutan* comes from Malaysian words that mean "man of the woods."

or·bit *noun* 1. the curved path in which a planet, satellite, or spacecraft moves in a circle around another body. *They steered the spacecraft to cross the orbit of the satellite.* 2. one complete trip along this path. *The earth makes one orbit around the sun each year.* *verb* (orbited, orbiting, orbits) to move in a circle around. *Several moons orbit Jupiter.* {**ohr** biht} orbital, adj.

Word History *Orbit* comes from an early French word that means "the track of a wheel."

or·chard 🌳 *noun* a piece of land planted with fruit or nut trees. {**ohr** chərd}

or·ches·tra 🎵 *noun* 1. a group of musicians who play different kinds of instruments and perform together. 2. the space in front of and below the stage in a theater. The orchestra is where a group of musicians plays during an opera or play. 3. the section of seats in the front of a theater's main floor. {**ohr** kə strə} orchestral, adj.

Word History *Orchestra* is an ancient Greek word for the area in a theater where the dancers performed.

or·chid *noun* 1. a plant that bears showy flowers. Most orchids are found in the tropics. 2. the flower of this plant. The flowers come in many colors and sizes. 3. a light reddish or

bluish purple color. {**ohr** kihd}

or·dain *verb* (ordained, ordaining, ordains) 1. to admit to the clergy as a priest, minister, or rabbi in a formal ceremony. *The council will ordain ten new ministers.* 2. to order or decide by law or authority. *The principal ordained that school would be closed because of snow.* {**ohr dayn**}

or·deal ❓ *noun* a painful, difficult experience, or test of one's character. *My parents' divorce was an ordeal for them and for me.* {**ohr deel**}

or·der ❓ ⬤ 💬 *noun* 1. a direction or command. *The sailor was punished for not following the captain's order.* 2. a request for goods to be made or delivered, or the goods themselves. *She placed an order for new carpet. / If this is our order, where are the French fries?* 3. the way something is set up or arranged in space or time. *Please write your spelling words in alphabetical order.* 4. the working condition of something. *If a phone has no dial tone, it is out of order.* 5. the condition in which the rules and laws of a society are obeyed; social or civil peace. *Sometimes the police are needed to keep order in the streets.* 6. a related group of living things. *Snakes and turtles both belong to the reptile order.* 7. a group of persons with common interests. *Grandfather belongs to a men's club called the Order of Moose.* *verb* (ordered, ordering, orders) 1. to tell to do in a firm way; give a command to. *The lifeguard ordered everyone to leave the water.* 2. to ask to be delivered or made. *She ordered a game from the catalogue. / Excuse me, but I*

A
B
C
D
E
F
G
H
I
J
K
L
M
N
O
P
Q
R
S
T
U
V
W
X
Y
Z

ordered chicken, not ham. 3. to put in order; organize. *He ordered the books on the shelf by topic.* {ohr dər} ordered-ness, n., orderless, adj.

• **in order to**

for the purpose of; so that. *In order to complete the job today, we must begin now.*

Synonyms

These words share a meaning with ***order***, noun 1:

direction, command, instruction

or·der·ly *adjective* 1. arranged in a neat way; in order. *The librarian keeps the books very orderly.* 2. behaving well or in keeping with rules or a system. *Everyone was glad of the crowd's orderly behavior at the game. noun* (orderlies) 1. a soldier who does certain tasks for one or more officers. 2. someone who cleans and does other basic work in a hospital. {ohr dər lee} orderli-ness, n.

ordinal number *noun* any number that indicates a position in a numbered order. "First," "third," "fifteenth," and "thousandth" are ordinal numbers. {ohr də nəl **nuhm** bər}

or·di·nar·i·ly *adverb* as a rule; usually. *His mother and grand-mother ordinarily eat lunch together every Tuesday.* {ohr də **nayr** ih lee}

or·di·nar·y *adjective* 1. usual or normal. *His ordinary way of doing things is to be slow and careful.* 2. without special qualities; usual or common. *He was a won-derful athlete but had just an ordi-nary mind. noun* (ordinaries) the usual or common degree or condi-tion. *Her singing is*

out of the ordinary. {ohr də **nayr** ee}

Synonyms

These words share a meaning with ***ordinary***, adjective 1:

normal, usual, standard, customary

ore 🌐 *noun* a rock or mineral from which a metal or other useful substance can be removed. {ohr}

Homophone Note The words ***ore***, ***oar***, and ***or*** sound alike but have different mean-ings.

Ore. *abbreviation* an abbrevia-tion for **Oregon**.

Or·e·gon *noun* a state in the northwestwrn United States on the Pacific Coast. Its cap-ital is Salem. (abbreviated: OR) {ohr ə gən *or* **ŏr** ə gən *or* ohr ə gŏn *or* **ŏr** ə gŏn} Orego-nian, n.

Word History No one is sure where the word ***Oregon*** came from. It may be based on *ouragon*, the French version of a Native American name for the Columbia River. Or it may come from *ouisconsink*, a Native American name for the Wis-consin River. The name "Oregon" became popular around 1843, when white set-tlers began using the Oregon Trail to reach the northwest.

or·gan 🌀 🕐 *noun* 1. a musical instrument with a keyboard. It is played by pressing keys attached to a device that forces air through pipes. 2. a part of plants or animals that performs a particular task. The heart, the lungs, the

skin, and the eyes are all organs of animals. {ohr gən}

or·gan·ic *adjective* having to do with or coming from living things. *Protein is an organic substance.* {ohr **gă** nihk}

or·gan·ism ❶ *noun* an indi-vidual living thing, such as a plant, an animal, or a bacte-rium. {ohr gə nih zəm}

or·gan·i·za·tion ⊙ *noun* 1. the act or process of organizing. *She was in charge of the organi-zation of the spelling contest.* 2. the state of being organized. *My calendar shows the organi-zation of my daily schedule.* 3. a body of persons acting together for some purpose. *That organization helps people during emergencies.* {ohr gə nih **zay** shən} organizational, adj.

or·gan·ize *verb* (organized, orga-nizing, organizes) 1. to set in order; arrange in an orderly way. *I organized my loose-leaf notes by subject.* 2. to build a union of workers. *Our city's waiters have organized a union.* 3. to join together into a group or movement. *The neighborhood organized to clean up the park.* {ohr gə **niyz**} organizable, adj.

o·ri·ent *noun* (capitalized) the countries east and southeast of Europe; Asia; the Far East. *verb* (oriented, orienting, ori-ents) to help to make familiar or comfortable. *A tour of the neighborhood ori-ented the children to their new home.* {ohr ee ehnt}

Word History ***Orient*** comes from a Latin word that means "the part of the sky in which the sun rises."

o·ri·en·tal *adjective* (often capi-talized) of or having to do with the countries east and southeast of Europe. *People used to call any Asian food "Oriental," even if it came*

 Human Body   Human Mind    Everyday Life    History and Culture    Communication

from places as different as Japan and Indonesia. *noun* (often capitalized) a person who was born of a native population of a country east or southeast of Europe. *Years ago, Europeans and Americans called anyone who came from an Asian country an "Oriental."* {ohr ee **ehn** təl}

o·ri·en·ta·tion *noun* the act or process of preparing oneself or others for a new situation. *The orientation for new employees was a helpful introduction to my job.* {ohr ee ehn **tay** shən}

o·ri·ga·mi *noun* the Japanese art or technique of folding paper into pleasing figures. *He used origami to make a paper crane.* {ohr ə **gah** mee}

o·ri·gin *noun* 1. the point or place from which something comes; source. *The explorers searched for the origin of the River Nile.* 2. parents or ancestors. *Nicole's family is of African origin.* {ohr ə jihn *or* **ŏr** ə jihn}

o·rig·i·nal *adjective* 1. first; earliest. *The original owner of our car had it for ten years.* / *Of all the Frankenstein movies, I like the original one best.* 2. new or fresh. *She has an original idea for a book.* 3. able to think of new ideas. *He has good grammar and spelling, but when it comes to writing stories, he is not very original.* 4. first; not a copy; real. *Our library has an original letter signed by Abraham Lincoln.* *noun* 1. that from which a copy or translation can be made. *I left the original in the copy machine.* 2. the real work as opposed to a copy. *The art expert proved that the* painting was an original, painted by Picasso himself. {ə **rih** jə nəl}

o·rig·i·nal·i·ty *noun* (originalities) 1. the ability to think or act in a new way or as an individual. *The way he uses words in poetry shows originality.* 2. the quality or condition of being new or fresh. *The originality of the way that artist uses color has made her paintings famous.* {ə **rih** jə **nă** lih tee}

o·rig·i·nal·ly *adverb* at first. *He originally wanted to be a veterinarian.* {ə **rih** jə nə lee}

o·rig·i·nate *verb* (originated, originating, originates) 1. to start or come into being. *His novel originated from stories about his own family.* 2. to give being to or create. *He originated the idea of labor unions.* {ə **rih** jə **nayt**} origination, n., originator, n.

o·ri·ole *noun* a songbird that can be found in many parts of the world. Males have black and bright yellow or orange feathers. There are two main groups of birds that are considered orioles. There are several different kinds of orioles in each group. {**ohr** ee əl *or* **ohr** ee **ohl**}

O·ri·on *noun* 1. a hunter and giant in Greek myth. 2. a large winter constellation in the northern sky. {ə **riy** ən}

or·na·ment *noun* something that is added to make something more beautiful to look at; decoration. *We made ornaments to hang on the Christmas tree.* *verb* (ornamented, ornamenting, ornaments) to add ornaments to. *They ornamented the party tent with bright lights and streamers.* {**ohr** nə mənt}

or·nate *adjective* having a lot of decoration; fancy. *She wore* an ornate dress covered with lace and pearls. {ohr **nayt**}

or·ner·y *adjective* mean; stubborn. *That ornery boy hits other children.* / *The dog is ornery about getting in the car.* {ohr nə ree}

or·ni·thol·o·gy *noun* the study of birds. {ohr nih **tho** lə jee} ornithologist, n.

or·phan *noun* a child whose parents have died. *verb* (orphaned, orphaning, orphans) to cause to become an orphan. *The war has orphaned hundreds of children.* {**ohr** fən}

or·phan·age *noun* a place where orphans live and are cared for. {**ohr** fə nihj}

or·tho·don·tics *plural noun* (used with a singular verb) the branch of dental medicine that deals with the straightening of teeth. {ohr thə **dŏn** tihks}

> **Word History** The word **orthodontics** was coined in 1909. It was formed from *orthos* and *odontos,* two ancient Greek words that mean "straight" and "tooth."

or·tho·don·tist *noun* a dentist who works in the branch of dental medicine that deals with the straightening of teeth. {**ohr** thoh **dŏn** tihst}

or·tho·dox *adjective* of, having to do with, or following what is believed or practiced by most other people. *She educated her children at home because she doesn't agree with the orthodox view of education.* {ohr thə **dŏks**}

Os·lo *noun* the capital city of Norway. {**ŏz** loh *or* **ŏs** loh}

os·mo·sis *noun* the passage of a liquid through a membrane until the concentration is the same on both sides of the

A B C D E F G H I J K L M N O P Q R S T U V W X Y Z

membrane. {ŏz **moh** sihs or ŏs **moh** sihs}

os·trich *noun* (ostrich or ostriches) a large, powerful African bird that can run very fast but cannot fly. It has two toes on each foot and no feathers on its long legs and neck. {**aw** strihch or ŏ strihch}

oth·er *adjective* 1. different from the one or ones mentioned. *No, I want the other dress.* 2. the one remaining out of two or more. *Since I am busy, maybe some other person can help.* 3. additional or more. *I saw other hats I liked better than this one.* 4. not long ago. *The other day I forgot to take lunch money to school.* *pronoun* 1. the additional one. *There are others in the cupboard.* 2. the remaining one. *May I have the other?* 3. (usually plural) those aside from oneself. *The others stayed at the party after I left.* *adverb* in another way; otherwise (usually followed by "than"). *We could not do anything other than wait.* {**uh** thər}

• **every other** every second one. *I have singing lessons every other day.*

oth·er·wise *adverb* 1. in a different manner or other way. *Others said that it was a good movie, but I saw it and think otherwise.* 2. under other conditions; in other circumstances. *I'm feeling sick; otherwise I would love to go to the party with you.* 3. in other respects. *He forgot his lines once, but otherwise did fine in the play.* {**uh** thər **wiyz**}

Ot·ta·wa *noun* (Ottawas or Ottawa) 1. the capital city of Canada. Ottawa is in the province of Ontario. 2. a member of a Canadian Indian people that lived near the upper Great Lakes. {ŏ tə wə}

ot·ter *noun* (otter or otters) a mammal with brown fur, a long body, short legs, and webbed feet. Otters live in the water where they eat fish, frogs, and other water animals. Different kinds of otters are found in most parts of the world. They live in groups and are very playful. Otters are related to skunks, badgers, and other kinds of weasels. {ŏ tər}

ouch *interjection* a word used to express sudden pain. *Ouch! That hurts!* {owch}

ought *auxiliary verb* 1. used to express the need to do something because of duty or responsibility. *With all that money, he felt that he ought to help the poor.* 2. used to express what is expected or likely. *The moon ought to rise soon.* 3. used to express what is wise or appropriate. *You ought to get some sleep.* {awt}

ounce *noun* 1. a unit of weight equal to one sixteenth of a pound or 28.350 grams. (abbreviated: oz.) 2. a unit of capacity equal to one sixteenth of a pint or 29.57 milliliters; fluid ounce. 3. any very small amount. *He does not have an ounce of common sense.* {owns}

our *pronoun* of, having to do with, or belonging to us (possessive form of "we"). *Our house is white with a green roof.* {owr or ow ər}

Homophone Note Are you looking for the word *hour* (a unit of time)? *Our* and *hour* sound alike but have different meanings.

ours *pronoun* the one or ones that belong to us. *Which car is ours?* {owrs}

our·selves *plural pronoun* 1. our own selves (used to show that an action is done to the same people who are doing the action). *We bought ourselves a new car.* 2. used to put the emphasis on "we" or "us." *We did the work ourselves.* 3. our normal selves. *We were not ourselves the day our dog died.* {**ar** sehlvz or **owr** sehlvz or **ow** ər sehlvz}

-ous *suffix* a suffix that means "having much" or "full of." *A poisonous plant is full of poison. / A person who is famous is a person who has gained much fame.*

oust *verb* (ousted, ousting, ousts) to force out; expel. *The principal ousted him for starting a fight.* {owst}

out *adverb* 1. beyond; away from. *The dog ran out the door.* 2. outdoors. *She shut off the TV and told us to go out and play.* 3. not included. *He was left out of the game.* 4. not operating; off. *Turn the lights out.* 5. into public notice. *The film finally came out.* 6. in a state of not having. *Time is running out.* 7. from a material. *The chimney is made out of stone.* *adjective* 1. beyond certain limits. *The ball was out.* 2. not present. *Mrs. Ferguson is out; may I take a message?* 3. not having; being without (usually followed by "of"). *We are out of sugar.* 4. removed from play in baseball or softball. *The batter is out.* *preposition* through. *My advice to you goes in one ear and out the other.* *noun* any play in baseball that removes a player from the possibility of scoring. *The team has two outs.* {owt}

 Human Body   Human Mind   Everyday Life   History and Culture   Communication

- **out of** as a result of. *He helped me out of kindness.*

out- *prefix* 1. a prefix that means "out," "outside," or "outward." *When the cat is outdoors, it is outside the house. / An outflow of water from a pipe is water that is flowing out of a pipe.* 2. a prefix that means "beyond," "better," or "more." *A dessert that outdid the salad is a dessert that was better than the salad. / If he outruns you, it means he has run beyond you.*

outboard motor *noun* a small gasoline engine with a propeller, which is attached to the stern of a boat. {owt bohrd moh tər}

out·break 🌐 *noun* 1. a sudden breaking out. *Everyone fears an outbreak of war.* 2. a sudden breaking out or increase in activity of disease. *There was an outbreak of flu last month.* {owt brayk}

out·burst 🌐 *noun* a sudden coming forth of strong feeling. *There was an outburst of laughter in the audience when a barking dog ran across the stage.* {owt buhrst}

out·cast *noun* one who is driven out or rejected by society or a group. *She was an outcast in her family for not going to church.* {owt kăst}

out·come *noun* a result of something. *I'm pleased with the outcome of your work.* {owt kuhm}

out·cry *noun* (outcries) 1. a loud cry, shout, or uproar. *We heard an outcry from the street.* 2. a strong public protest. *There was an outcry about the sale of animal furs.* {owt kriy}

out·dat·ed *adjective* not in fashion or no longer in use. *Grandmother never threw away outdated clothes, saying that old styles often come back.* {owt day tihd}

out·did *verb* past tense of **outdo**. *Rebecca outdid the best swimmer on the team.* {owt dihd}

out·do *verb* (outdid, outdone, outdoing, outdoes) to do more or better than. {owt dooh}

out·done *verb* past participle of **outdo**. {owt duhn}

out·door *adjective* used or happening in the open air. *They are building an outdoor pool. / Harry likes outdoor sports.* {owt dohr}

out·doors *adverb* in the open air; outside. *The weather was perfect for holding our party outdoors. noun* (used with a singular verb) the open air, outside houses or other buildings. *They like to drive to the country and spend time in the outdoors.* {owt dohrz}

out·er *adjective* of or having to do with the part most distant from the center. *Many families choose to live in the outer areas of the city. / The rain drenched our outer clothes.* {ow tər}

outer space *noun* region beyond the atmosphere of the earth. *The spacecraft will fly into outer space to explore the moon.* {ow tər spays}

out·field *noun* 1. the area of a baseball or softball field beyond the infield. 2. the playing positions in this area, or all of the players in that area. *He plays outfield.* {owt feeld}

out·fit *noun* 1. a set of equipment for a particular activity. *Greg has a new diving outfit.* 2. a complete set of clothes. *Gretta bought a new summer outfit.* 3. a group of people who work together to carry out a particular activity. *Gail belongs to our army outfit. verb* (outfitted, outfitting, outfits) to supply with equipment needed; equip. *The outdoor store outfitted us with camping gear.* {owt fiht} outfitter, n.

out·go·ing *adjective* 1. going out or leaving. *The outgoing ship was held up by the storm.* 2. liking to talk to and interested in others. *Holly has an outgoing manner.* {owt goh ing}

out·grew *verb* past tense of **outgrow**.

out·grow *verb* (outgrew, outgrown, outgrowing, outgrows) 1. to grow too big or old for. *Kevin outgrew his clothes quickly. / She is outgrowing those baby toys.* 2. to give up or lose as one grows older or changes. *Jermaine has outgrown the bad habit of biting his nails.* 3. to grow greater than. *Michael outgrew his father in height.* {owt groh}

out·grown *verb* past participle of **outgrow**.

out·house *noun* a small shed used for an outdoor toilet. {owt hows}

out·ing *noun* a trip away from home or school for pleasure; field trip. {ow ting}

out·law *noun* a person who often breaks the law; criminal. *The outlaw is being hunted by a posse. verb* (outlawed, outlawing, outlaws) to make illegal or prohibit.

A B C D E F G H I J K L M N O P Q R S T U V W X Y Z

a
b
c
d
e
f
g
h
i
j
k
l
m
n
o
p
q
r
s
t
u
v
w
x
y
z

Hunting is outlawed in the city. {**owt** law}

out·let ○ *noun* 1. an opening through which something is let out or allowed to escape; vent. 2. a market for services or goods. *I went to the shoe outlet for a bargain.* 3. a means of expressing oneself; way to get rid of something. *Writing stories is an outlet for her imagination.* 4. the point in an electrical system where the cord is plugged into the current. {**owt** liht}

out·line ○ *noun* 1. a line or shape showing the outside edge of a figure or object. *Draw an outline of your own house.* 2. a short, written plan of the main ideas of a book, speech, or report. *verb* (outlined, outlining, outlines) 1. to draw the outline of. *She outlined the figures before she began to paint.* 2. to give the main ideas or topics of. *He quickly outlined his speech for us.* {**owt** liyn}

out·look *noun* 1. what may come in the future. *The outlook for tomorrow's weather is good.* 2. a way of thinking. *He has a grim outlook on life.* {**owt** luuk}

out·ly·ing *adjective* away from the center of something; distant. *He lives in an outlying suburb of the city.* {**owt** liy ing}

out·num·ber *verb* (outnumbered, outnumbering, outnumbers) to be larger in number than. *The no votes outnumbered the yes votes.* {owt **nuhm** bər}

out-of-date *adjective* old-fashioned or no longer in use. *Black-and-white television is out-of-date.* {**owt** əv **dayt**}

out·pa·tient *noun* a person who is being treated at a hospital or clinic but who is not kept there overnight. {**owt** pay shənt}

out·post *noun* a military post at some distance from a main station. {**owt** pohst}

out·put *noun* 1. the amount produced in a given time period. *That writer's output is five pages a day.* 2. the information stored in a computer when it is transmitted to a screen or printer. {**owt** puut}

out·rage ? *noun* 1. an act that causes a strong feeling of anger because of its violence or cruelty. *Beating children is an outrage.* 2. the anger or fury caused by such an act. *The pollution of our drinking water filled us with outrage.* *verb* (outraged, outraging, outrages) to cause anger and shock in. *He outraged me with his cruel words.* {**owt** rayj}

out·ra·geous *adjective* 1. extremely wrong or harmful. *Kicking the dog was an outrageous thing to do.* 2. shocking in behavior or speech. *It's outrageous to call her stupid in front of the whole class.* {owt **ray** jəs} outrageously, adv.

out·ran *verb* past tense of **outrun**.

out·rig·ger *noun* a frame attached to one side of a boat to make it more stable. {**owt** rih gər}

out·right *adjective* complete or total. *The fire was an outright disaster.* *adverb* 1. entirely; completely. *I believed him outright.* 2. in a frank and honest way. *Luke told me outright what had happened.* 3. immediately or all at once. *The buyer offered me the money outright.* {**owt** **riyt**}

out·run *verb* (outran, outrun, outrunning, outruns) to run faster, farther, or longer than. *The deer outran the hunters.* {**owt** **ruhn**}

out·set *noun* the start; first stage; beginning. *He hasn't* been happy with that school from the outset. {**owt** seht}

out·side *noun* 1. the outer side or surface. *Please write your name on the outside of your notebook.* 2. any space not inside. *We stood on the outside of the building.* *adjective* 1. of or relating to the outer side or surface. *The cake has an outside layer of chocolate.* 2. not likely; slight. *He has only an outside chance of winning.* *adverb* in or to the outdoors. *We played outside on the porch.* *preposition* on, in, or to the outer space of. *The cat watched the bird outside the house.* {owt **siyd** or **owt** siyd, n., owt **siyd** or **owt** siyd, adj., owt **siyd** or **owt** siyd, adv., owt **siyd** or **owt** siyd, prep.}

out·sid·er *noun* a person who does not belong to a particular group. *She feels like an outsider in her new school.* {owt **siy** dər or **owt** siy dər}

out·skirts *plural noun* the edges or outlying areas of a city or town. *His family has a farm on the outskirts of the village.* {**owt** skuhrts}

out·smart *verb* (outsmarted, outsmarting, outsmarts) to get the better of by being clever; outwit. *She outsmarted me in that game.* {owt **smart**}

out·spo·ken *adjective* speaking in an honest and open way. *He is very outspoken about his opinions on the prison system.* {owt **spoh** kən} outspokenness, n.

out·stand·ing *adjective* 1. standing out from others because of high quality; excellent. *He is an outstanding friend.* 2. not paid; yet to be settled. *My new salary will help me take care of my outstanding bills.* {owt **stăn** ding}

out·ward *adjective* 1. on or moving toward the outside

 Human Body  Human Mind  Everyday Life  History and Culture Communication

or surface of. *The outward appearance of the house was cheerful.* 2. of or relating to the surface or outside only. *His face showed no outward sign of fear.* adverb toward the outside. *The door swung outward.* {<u>owt</u> wərd} **outwards,** adv.

out·wit *verb* (outwitted, outwitting, outwits) to get the better of by using one's wits or by being more clever. *Can he outwit the other players?* {owt <u>wiht</u>}

o·val *adjective* having the general shape of an egg; ellipse. *She gave me an oval mirror.* *noun* something shaped like an egg or ellipse. {<u>oh</u> vəl}

o·va·ry 🌐 *noun* (ovaries) 1. the organ in a female animal that produces eggs and certain hormones. 2. the part of a flower that contains the seeds and grows into a fruit. {<u>oh</u> və ree}

ov·en 🌐 *noun* a compartment that can be heated for baking or roasting food. A kitchen stove usually has an oven. {<u>uhv</u> ən}

o·ver *preposition* 1. above in position; higher than. *Robin held the umbrella over our heads.* 2. across to the other side of. *Danny leaped over the fence.* 3. on top of, so as to cover. *I pulled the blanket over my head.* 4. throughout; across. *We traveled all over Canada.* 5. in the time of; during. *The snow has really piled up over the last few days.* 6. on the subject of. *We argued over whose turn it was to wash the dishes.* adverb 1. across a space. *We will sail over to England.* 2. so as to cover. *Snow fell all over.* 3. to this or that place. *I went over to see her.* 4. to the side. *Move over.* 5. across the edge of and down. *The water is boiling*

over. 6. about; concerning. *They fought over ideas.* 7. once again; again. *Please do the job over.* 8. down and to the side; down. *She bent over.* / *He fell over.* adjective 1. more than. *My father is over six feet tall.* 2. finished; done. *The story is over.* {<u>oh</u> vər}

• **all over with** completed; finished. *Sadly, he knew their friendship was all over with.*

• **over and above** in addition to; besides. *I did work around the house over and above my regular chores.*

o·ver- *prefix* 1. a prefix that means "too much." *When you overdo something, you have done it too much.* 2. a prefix that means "above," "across," or "superior." *An overhead light is a light above your head.* / *Overseas travel is to travel across the sea.* / *An overlord is a ruler who is superior to other lords or rulers.*

o·ver·all *adverb or adjective* including nearly all; general. *Their overall goal for the day was to enjoy themselves.* *noun* (plural) work pants made of denim, with a bib that covers the chest. {<u>oh</u> vər awl}

o·ver·board *adverb* over the side of a boat into the water. *She threw the anchor overboard.* {<u>oh</u> vər bohrd}

• **go overboard** to do far too much, or with too much energy. *Sometimes he goes overboard at the office and works late into the night.*

o·ver·came *verb* past tense of **overcome**.

o·ver·cast *adjective* cloudy. *There's been a week of overcast*

skies. {<u>oh</u> vər <u>kăst</u> *or* oh vər <u>kăst</u>}

o·ver·coat 🌐 *noun* an outer coat worn in rainy or cold weather. {<u>oh</u> vər koht}

o·ver·come *verb* (overcame, overcome, overcoming, overcomes) 1. to win against or defeat; to get over or past. *She overcame all her opponents in the tennis tournament.* / *He overcame many problems.* 2. to cause to be weak or no longer conscious. *The medicine quickly overcame him, and he fell asleep.* 3. to catch up to and then go beyond. *I overcame his lead on the last turn of the race.* {oh vər <u>kuhm</u>}

o·ver·did *verb* past tense of **overdo.**

o·ver·do *verb* (overdid, overdone, overdoing, overdoes) 1. to do too much or go too far. *Don't overdo the praise; a simple "thank you" is enough.* 2. to cook too long or at too high a temperature. *The turkey was tough because I overdid it.* 3. to get tired; wear out. *I overdid working in the yard and had to go to bed early.* {oh vər <u>dooh</u>}

o·ver·done *verb* past participle of **overdo.**

o·ver·dose *noun* too high a dose of medicine or drugs. *Be careful not to take an overdose of the cough syrup.* {<u>oh</u> vər dohs}

o·ver·dress *verb* (overdressed, overdressing, overdresses) to dress in a way that is too formal, or too warm for the occasion. *He overdressed because he thought she said "tea party," not "beach party."* {oh vər <u>drehs</u>}

A B C D E F G H I J K L M N O P Q R S T U V W X Y Z

o·ver·due *adjective* 1. not paid, delivered, or returned by the due date. *These library books are overdue.* 2. expected or needed for a long time. *This vacation is overdue.* {oh vər **dooh**}

o·ver·eat *verb* (overate, overeaten, overeating, overeats) to eat more than a comfortable, proper, or healthy amount. *I overate, and now I feel awful.* {oh vər **eet**}

o·ver·flow *verb* (overflowed, overflowing, overflows) 1. to flow over the top edge of something. *The river overflows each spring.* 2. to flood over or across. *The brook overflowed its banks and the nearby fields.* 3. to be so full that the contents spill over the top edge. *The blocked sink overflowed.* 4. to spill from one space into another. *The crowd overflowed into the hallway.* *noun* that which flows over because the container is too full. *He caught the overflow in a bucket.* {oh vər **floh**, n., oh vər **floh**, v.}

o·ver·grew *verb* past tense of **overgrow**.

o·ver·grow *verb* (overgrew, overgrown, overgrowing, overgrows) to grow over with a thick cover of leaves. *Ivy had overgrown the old well.* {oh vər **groh** or oh vər groh}

o·ver·grown *verb* past participle of **overgrow**.

o·ver·hand *adverb* with forearm and elbow raised. *She always throws overhand.* *adjective* done with forearm and elbow raised. *He threw an overhand volleyball serve.* {oh vər **hănd**} overhanded, adv., adj.

o·ver·haul *verb* (overhauled, overhauling, overhauls) 1. to go over carefully, taking apart as necessary and making all needed repairs. *He overhauled the furnace in* time for winter. 2. to catch up to; overtake in a race. *We overhauled their boat and won the race.* *noun* a complete examination and repair. *The mechanic did an engine overhaul.* {oh vər **hawl** or oh vər hawl, n., oh vər **hawl** or oh vər hawl, v.}

o·ver·head 🔊 *adverb* at any height directly or generally above the head. *A flock of geese flew overhead.* *adjective* located or installed above head level. *An overhead skylight let sunshine pour into my bedroom.* *noun* the general expenses of a business. Money spent for heat, rent, electricity, or taxes is part of the overhead of running a business. *The owner of the shop wanted to reduce his overhead, so he installed a more efficient furnace.* {oh vər **hehd**, n., oh vər hehd, adj., oh vər **hehd**, adv.}

o·ver·hear *verb* (overheard, overhearing, overhears) to hear without the speaker's knowledge. *While waiting in the hall, I overheard their argument.* {oh vər **heer**}

o·ver·heard *verb* past tense and past participle of **overhear**.

o·ver·joyed *adjective* filled with joy; extremely happy. *I am overjoyed that I scored 100 on the science exam.* {oh vər **joid**}

o·ver·lap *verb* (overlapped, overlapping, overlaps) to cover or go over part of. *The shingles on the roof overlap each other.* {oh vər **lăp**}

o·ver·load *verb* (overloaded, overloading, overloads) to put too heavy or great a load in or on. *I think that teacher overloads her students with homework.* {oh vər **lohd**}

o·ver·look *verb* (overlooked, overlooking, overlooks) 1. to fail to see or notice. *He overlooked the possibility that the weather could change, so he got caught in the rain.* 2. to pay no attention to; ignore. *I overlooked his lies because I wanted to believe him.* 3. to excuse; pardon. *She wouldn't overlook his careless behavior.* 4. to allow a view over. *His home overlooks the beach.* {oh vər **luuk**}

o·ver·night *adverb* 1. for a single night. *We will stay here overnight and then drive the rest of the way home tomorrow.* 2. suddenly. *Success usually doesn't come overnight.* *adjective* 1. lasting or staying one night. *My cousin came for an overnight visit.* 2. for use on trips that are short or for a single night. *I packed an overnight bag.* 3. sudden. *Her song brought her overnight fame.* {oh vər **niyt**, adj., oh vər **niyt**, adv.}

o·ver·pass *noun* a bridge or road that crosses over another road or railroad. {oh vər **păs**}

o·ver·pow·er *verb* (overpowered, overpowering, overpowers) 1. to beat or overcome by greater force. *The robber overpowered the bank guard.* 2. to weaken or make helpless; overwhelm. *The fumes from the fire nearly overpowered us.* {oh vər **pow** ər}

o·ver·ran *verb* past tense of **overrun**.

o·ver·rule *verb* (overruled, overruling, overrules) 1. to rule or decide against. *She overruled any further discussion about going out for ice cream.* 2. to make a judgment against. *The judge overruled the mayor and the council.* {oh vər **roohl**}

o·ver·run *verb* (overran, overrun, overrunning, overruns) 1. to spread over,

 Human Body   Human Mind  Everyday Life   History and Culture  Communication

taking hold. *Weeds have overrun the garden.* 2. to run past; go beyond. *The batter overran first base.* 3. to flow over; flood. *The creek overran its banks.* {oh vər <u>ruhn</u>}

o·ver·seas *adverb* across any of the oceans; abroad. *My uncle was working overseas during the holidays, but sent presents from England and France.* *adjective* 1. having to do with people or places that are located abroad. *We visited overseas countries.* 2. having to do with passage across an ocean. *My father took us on an overseas flight.* {oh vər <u>seez</u>, adj., oh vər <u>seez</u>, adv.}

o·ver·shoe *noun* a rubber or plastic boot worn over other shoes in order to protect them from water or snow. {oh vər <u>shooh</u>}

o·ver·sight *noun* 1. a lack of attention. *It was an oversight that you were not invited.* 2. careful direction or guidance of what someone is doing. *The teacher's oversight of the children's work is appreciated.* {oh vər <u>siyt</u>}

o·ver·sleep *verb* (overslept, oversleeping, oversleeps) to sleep beyond the time one meant to get up. *Casey overslept and was late for the game.* {oh vər <u>sleep</u>}

o·ver·slept *verb* past tense and past participle of **oversleep**.

o·ver·take *verb* (overtook, overtaken, overtaking, overtakes) 1. to catch up or come even with. *The cat overtook the mouse and pounced.* 2. to pass by after catching up with. *She overtook me and won the race.* 3. to come upon suddenly. *The storm overtook us before we got back to camp.* {oh vər <u>tayk</u>}

o·ver·ta·ken *verb* past participle of **overtake**.

o·ver·threw *verb* past tense of **overthrow**.

o·ver·throw *verb* (overthrew, overthrown, overthrowing, overthrows) to remove from power by force. *The knights overthrew the king.* *noun* the act of overthrowing or the state of being overthrown. *The people cheered the overthrow of the dictator.* {oh vər <u>throh</u>, n., oh vər <u>throh</u>, v.}

o·ver·thrown *verb* past participle of **overthrow**.

o·ver·time *noun* 1. time worked beyond the regular working hours in a day or week. *The overtime on this job is usually about six hours a week.* 2. money paid for such time. *Do you want to earn overtime?* *adverb* more than the normal amount of time. *My parents worked overtime to make the house ready for grandmother's visit.* {oh vər <u>tiym</u>}

o·ver·took *verb* past tense of **overtake**.

o·ver·ture *noun* 1. an opening move to begin something. *She refused all overtures of friendship.* 2. a musical composition that begins a longer work. {oh vər <u>chər</u>}

o·ver·turn *verb* (overturned, overturning, overturns) 1. to cause to tip over; upset. *The donkey overturned the apple cart.* 2. to do away with or abolish. *The court overturned last year's ruling.* {oh vər <u>tuhrn</u>}

o·ver·weight *adjective* having too much weight; too heavy. *The veterinarian said that my dog is ten pounds overweight.* {oh vər <u>wayt</u>}

o·ver·whelm *verb* (overwhelmed, overwhelming, overwhelms) 1. to beat or defeat by greater force; destroy. *The troops overwhelmed the city.* 2. to load or burden with too much of something. *The TV station was overwhelmed with letters about the new program.* {oh vər <u>wehlm</u>}

o·ver·work *verb* (overworked, overworking, overworks) 1. to cause to work too many hours; tire completely with work. *The mine owners overworked the miners.* 2. to work more than is reasonable or healthy. *She overworked and was exhausted.* *noun* work beyond a fair or healthy amount. *Overwork made him grumpy.* {oh vər <u>wuhrk</u>}

owe *verb* (owed, owing, owes) 1. to have to pay or repay; be in debt to. *I owe ten dollars to my sister. / He owes her for many favors.* 2. to feel the need to do or to give to. *I owe my little brother some attention.* {oh}

Homophone Note The words *owe* and *oh* sound alike but have different meanings.

owl *noun* a bird with large eyes set in front of a large head, a strong, hooked beak, and strong, sharp claws. Owls are most active at night and hunt other animals for food. There are many different kinds of owls. {owl}

own *adjective* belonging to oneself or itself alone. *I bought this hat with my own money.* *noun* one's property, inheritance, fate, or what is felt to be one's due or potential. *When he turned sixteen, he came into his own as both an athlete and a student.* *verb* (owned, owning, owns) 1. to have possession of, especially

A B C D E F G H I J K L M N O P Q R S T U V W X Y Z

 Living World Physical World  Natural Environment Economy Government and Law

a
b
c
d
e
f
g
h
i
j
k
l
m
n

o

p
q
r
s
t
u
v
w
x
y
z

by some right or law. *We own our house and the two acres of land around it.* 2. to admit or confess to (usually followed by "up to" or "to"). *He owned up to his mistake after they questioned him.* {**ohn**}

own·er *noun* a person who owns. *The store owner enjoyed the children who stopped in for a snack after school.* {**oh** nər}

ox *noun* (oxen) one of a breed of large cattle used on farms to pull heavy loads. {**ŏks**}

ox·bow *noun* a wooden collar in the shape of a U that goes around the neck of an ox. It is fastened to a yoke. {**ŏks boh**}

ox·en *noun* plural of **ox.** {**ŏk** sən}

oxeye daisy *noun* a daisy that has a bright yellow center with white petals around it. {**ŏks** iy **day** zee}

ox·ford *noun* a sturdy, plain shoe that laces over the top of the foot. {**ŏks** fərd}

ox·ide *noun* a compound that includes oxygen. *Carbon dioxide is an oxide.* {**ŏk** siyd}

ox·i·dize *verb* (oxidized, oxidizing, oxidizes) 1. to combine with oxygen. *Iron rusts when water oxidizes it.* 2. to become oxidized. *Tin oxidizes when left in water.* {**ŏk** sih **diyz**}

ox·y·gen 🏃 ❓ *noun* a gas with no color or smell that is one of the chemical elements. Oxygen combines with hydrogen to make water. It also makes up about twenty percent of the earth's atmo-sphere. Most living things need oxygen. (symbol: O) {**ŏk** sə jən}

oys·ter *noun* a small animal with a soft body and a hard shell in two pieces. Oysters have a rough shell with a very shiny inside, where pearls sometimes grow. Oysters live in shallow ocean water. They are mollusks and are closely related to clams and mussels. People eat some kinds of oysters. {**oi** stər}

oz. *abbreviation* an abbreviation for **ounce** or ounces.

o·zone *noun* a form of oxygen that occurs when oxygen is exposed to an electrical charge, like lightning. It is found naturally in Earth's atmosphere. {**oh** zohn}

o·zone hole *noun* an area in the ozone layer where the ozone becomes thin. There is a large ozone hole over Antarctica and a smaller one over the North Pole. Scientists warn us this is dangerous. {**oh** zohn **hohl**}

ozone layer *noun* an atmospheric layer between ten and twenty miles above the earth that contains a large amount of ozone, which absorbs certain types of harmful radiation from space. {**oh** zohn **lay** ər}

🏃 Human Body   ❓ Human Mind   👕 Everyday Life   🚩 History and Culture   Communication

Pp

P is a consonant that always makes the same sound. When combined with "h," it also makes an "f" sound (phone). It is silent at the beginning of a few words (such as pneumonia, psalm, or pterodactyl).

These words may be hard to look up if you don't already know how to spell them:

paid
pamphlet
parallel
pastime
phenomenon
prophet
psychology
pursue

p or P *noun* (p's or P's) 1. the sixteenth letter of the English alphabet. 2. a grade given for passing or satisfactory school work. {**pee**}
• **mind** or **watch one's p's and q's**
to be careful of what one does and says. *He forgot to mind his p's and q's in front of the principal.*
P symbol of the chemical element **phosphorus**.

p. *abbreviation* **page.**
PA *abbreviation* an abbbreviation for **Pennsylvania.**
pace *noun* 1. the length of one step; stride. *The proper military pace is thirty inches.* 2. the step or stride itself. *She moved forward two paces.* 3. rate of movement. *The pace of the game was slow. / We walked at a fast pace.* 4. the forward movement of a horse as it raises both hooves on the same side at once. *The trainer is working on the horse's pace for the parade.* *verb* (paced, pacing, paces) 1. to set the rate or speed of. *The coach paced the runners.* 2. to control the energy loss of. *The runner paced himself well.* 3. to move across with paces or steps. *He was so worried that he paced the floor.* 4. to measure by paces or steps. *Pace the size of this room.* {**pays**}
• **put one through one's paces**
to cause one to show skill or ability. *The teacher put the piano student through his paces.*
pace·mak·er *noun* a small electronic device put under the skin to control the heart rate in people with heart problems. {**pays** may kər}
Pa·cif·ic *noun* the largest ocean in the world. It lies between North America and Asia in the north, and South America and Australia in the south; Pacific Ocean. {pə **sih** fihk}

Word History *Pacific* comes from a Latin word that means "peaceful." Magellan named this ocean "the Pacific Ocean" because he found it free of violent storms on his voyage to the Philippines.

pac·i·fy *verb* (pacified, pacifying, pacifies) to calm or bring back peace of mind to. *The speaker pacified the angry crowd. / Talking about the problem pacified her.* {**pă** sih fiy}
-pack *suffix* a suffix that means a package containing that number of items. *A six-pack contains six cans of soda.*
pack *noun* 1. a group of things arranged together in a container; package. *There are eight greeting cards in each pack.* 2. a container for carrying things on the back. *She carries her books and papers in a pack.* 3. a group of animals that are alike. *Wolves often travel in packs.* *verb* (packed, packing, packs) 1. to put in a container for carrying or storing. *The farmer packed the fruit into wooden crates.*

2. to fill up with things; stuff. *I packed a suitcase for my trip.* 3. to form into a thick or solid mass. *Jimmy packed the snow into a snowball.* 4. to crowd together in. *One hundred people packed the room.* *adjective* used in carrying goods. *The explorers used pack horses to carry their supplies.* {**păk**} packable, adj.
pack·age *noun* 1. an object or bundle that is packed, wrapped, or boxed; bundle. *I bought a package of cake mix at the store.* 2. a container used for storing or transporting something. *The post office had thousands of packages to deliver before Christmas.* *verb* (packaged, packaging, packages) to place in a container

A
B
C
D
E
F
G
H
I
J
K
L
M
N
O
P
Q
R
S
T
U
V
W
X
Y
Z

or in wrapping. *She packaged the gift in a red box.* {păk kihj}

pack·et *noun* a small bundle or parcel. *I bought her a packet of gum.* {păk iht}

pact *noun* 1. an agreement or a sworn promise. *We made a pact never to tell.* 2. a written agreement between or among countries; treaty. *The three countries signed a trade pact.* {păkt}

pad ⊙ *noun* 1. a piece of soft material used as cushioning for protection or comfort. *Football players wear shoulder pads. / I need a pad for this hard seat.* 2. a block of paper sheets glued together at one edge. *I bought a drawing pad.* 3. a cushion used for holding ink for rubber stamps. 4. a flat platform for landing or taking off. *The astronauts waited on the rocket pad.* 5. the small cushion of flesh on the bottom of the toes or feet of some animals. *verb* (padded, padding, pads) 1. to fill or protect by stuffing or to cover with soft material. *Grandmother padded her old chairs.* 2. to make longer or thicker by adding things that are not important. *She padded the report with useless information.* {păd}

pad·dle *noun* 1. a short oar with a wide blade. A paddle is used with both arms for moving a small boat through the water. 2. a similar, smaller device used to hit the ball in table tennis. *verb* (paddled, paddling, paddles) 1. to use a paddle to move a canoe. *We paddled down the river to our camp.* 2. to hit or spank with

a paddle or hand. *The boy cried when his father paddled him.* {păd əl}

paddle wheel *noun* a wheel that has boards or paddles fixed at right angles around it. A paddle wheel is used to move a river steamboat. {pă dəl weel}

pad·dock *noun* 1. a field surrounded by a fence, near a barn. Animals graze or exercise in a paddock. 2. an area near a race track where horses are kept before the race. {păd ək}

pad·dy *noun* (paddies) a flooded field for growing rice. {păd ee}

pad·lock *noun* a lock with a bar shaped like a U used to fasten doors, boxes, or cables. One end of the bar moves on a hinge. The other end of the bar is slipped through a ring before being snapped into the body of the lock. *verb* (padlocked, padlocking, padlocks) to fasten with a padlock. *Be sure to padlock your locker.* {păd lŏk}

pa·gan *noun* 1. a person who practices a religion that worships many gods. 2. a person outside of accepted Western religions; one who is not a Christian, Jew, or Muslim; heathen. {pay gən}

Word History *Pagan* comes from a Latin word that means "a villager." In later Latin it also meant "heathen." After Christianity became an established religion, those who continued to practice the old religions were usually from country villages.

page¹ *noun* one side of a sheet of printed or written paper. *verb* (paged, paging, pages) to turn pages (often fol-

lowed by "through"). *The librarian paged through the new book.* {payj}

page² *noun* 1. a young person who worked as a servant for a person such as a king. 2. a young person who carries messages and does other errands. *She was a page in the United States Senate.* *verb* (paged, paging, pages) to call out a person's name in a public place. *They paged us at the airport.* {payj}

pag·eant *noun* a public show about events in history or legend. {pă jənt}

pa·go·da *noun* a religious temple of Asia that has curved roof lines at each of its many stories. {pə goh də}

paid *verb* past tense and past participle of **pay.** {payd}

pail *noun* 1. a container with steep sides and a handle; bucket. *The pail is old and rusty.* 2. an amount that will fill a pail. *How many pails of water do you need?* {payl}

Homophone Note Are you looking for the word *pale* (light in color)? *Pail* and *pale* sound alike but have different meanings.

pain ⊕ ⊙ *noun* 1. physical hurt or discomfort that is usually caused by injury or illness. Pain is the nervous system's way of telling the brain that something is wrong. *The pill helped to lessen the pain in her back.* 2. hurt feelings; mental or emotional suffering; sorrow. *Her mother's death caused her great pain.* 3. (plural) great care or effort. *She took pains to make every-*

 Human Body  Human Mind  Everyday Life History and Culture   Communication

thing perfect for her daughter's wedding. *verb* (pained, paining, pains) to cause distress in; anger; hurt. *It pains me to see him unhappy.* {**payn**}

Homophone Note The words **pain** and **pane** (a sheet of glass) sound alike but have different meanings.

pain·ful *adjective* 1. causing pain. *The injury was so painful that I cried.* 2. hard to accept or do. *It was painful for him to move away from his friends.* {**payn** fəl} painfully, adv.

paint ○ *noun* 1. a mixture of liquid and pigments that is used to cover the surface of something. *She used blue paint for her bedroom.* 2. coloring material used in the art of painting pictures. *Mom used oil paints to do a picture of the horse.* *verb* (painted, painting, paints) 1. to cover with paint. *Who painted the walls of my room orange?* 2. to make a picture or design using paint. *A local artist painted a picture of the barn.* {**paynt**}

paint·er *noun* 1. one who paints pictures. *Picasso was a famous painter.* 2. a worker who covers the surfaces of buildings with paint. *The painter put a coat of paint on the living room walls.* {**payn** tər}

paint·ing ○ ○ *noun* 1. a specific picture done by a painter. *Her painting won second prize at the art show.* 2. the field of art that deals with pictures made using paints. *I want to study painting in college.* 3. the act or occupation of covering building surfaces with paint. *He owns a house painting business.* {**payn** ting}

pair *noun* (pairs or pair) 1. two things that are alike and meant to be used together. *I*

bought a new pair of shoes yesterday. 2. a single object made up of two parts joined together. *He brought five pairs of shorts to camp.* 3. two persons who are married, engaged, or living together, or who like the same things. *Those two friends are a happy pair.* 4. two animals brought together to mate or to work. *A pair of horses pulled the hay wagon.* *verb* (paired, pairing, pairs) to put into groups of two; make a pair or pairs of.

The teacher paired the students before we entering the museum. {**payr**}

Homophone Note The words **pair**, **pare**, and **pear** sound alike but have different meanings.

pa·jam·as *plural noun* a loose jacket and pants worn for sleeping. {pə **jăh** məz *or* pə **jăm** əz}

Word History *Pajama* comes from a Hindi word that means "leg clothing."

Pa·ki·stan *noun* a country in southern Asia. Pakistan is also called the Islamic Republic of Pakistan. Islamabad is the capital of Pakistan. {**păk** ə **stăn** *or* **păh** kə **stahn**} Pakistani, n., adj.

pal *noun* (informal) a fairly close friend. *I like to sit next to my pal on the bus.* {**păl**}

pal·ace *noun* the official home of a king or queen or other

persons of high rank or authority. {**păl** ihs}

Word History *Palace* comes from *Palatium*, the Latin name for the grand house of the emperor Augustus Caesar, which sat on the Palatine Hill in Rome.

pal·ate *noun* 1. the roof of the mouth. The palate is made up of a bony front section and a soft back section. 2. the sense of taste. *What food would please your palate?* {**păl** liht}

Homophone Note Are you looking for the word **palette** (a board for holding paints)? **Palate** and **palette** sound alike but have different meanings.

pale *adjective* (paler, palest) 1. light in color. *The sky is pale this morning.* 2. of a color that is lighter than usual because of sickness or emotion. *The illness left her with pale skin.* *verb* (paled, paling, pales) to become pale. *He paled when he saw the blood.* {**payl**} paleness, n.

Homophone Note Are you looking for the word **pail** (a bucket)? **Pale** and **pail** sound alike but have different meanings.

pa·le·on·tol·o·gy *noun* the science that studies animal and plant fossils for information about life in the past. {pay lee ŏn **to** lə jee *or* pă lee ŏn **to** lə jee} paleontologist, n.

Pa·le·o·zo·ic *adjective* of, relating to, or belonging to the era in the earth's history from about 540 million years ago to about 250 million years ago. During this time, the first fishes, amphibians, reptiles, insects, and land plants appeared. {pay lee ə **zoh** ihk *or* pă lee ə **zoh** ihk}

A B C D E F G H I J K L M N O P Q R S T U V W X Y Z

a
b
c
d
e
f
g
h
i
j
k
l
m
n
o
p
q
r
s
t
u
v
w
x
y
z

Pal·es·tine *noun* a region in southwestern Asia on the Mediterranean that was the country of the Jews in Biblical times. Palestine is now occupied by Arabs and Jews. {**păl** ih stiyn}

pal·ette *noun* a thin, oval board, with a thumb hole, on which a painter holds and mixes colors. {**păl** iht}

Homophone Note The words *palette* and *palate* (the roof of the mouth) sound alike but have different meanings.

pal·i·sade *noun* 1. a tall strong fence of pointed stakes. 2. (plural) a long line of steep cliffs, along a river or coastline. {**păl** ih **sayd** *or* **păl** ih **sayd**}

pal·let *noun* a small or temporary bed, or mattress stuffed with straw. Pallets are sometimes used during emergencies. {**păl** iht}

palm[1] *noun* the inner surface of the hand, between the wrist and the base of the fingers. *verb* (palmed, palming, palms) to hide something in the hand. *The magician palmed the quarter to make it disappear.* {**pahm**}

• **palm off** to sell or get rid of by tricking someone. *The police arrested them for palming off fake gold watches.*

palm[2] *noun* any of a group of tropical plants. Most palms are trees without branches that are topped by crowns of large leaves shaped like feathers. {**pahm**}

pal·met·to *noun* (palmettos or palmettoes) a small palm that has leaves shaped like a fan. {**păl meh** toh}

pal·o·mi·no *noun* (palominos) one of a breed of horses that

has a golden or tan coat and a yellowish white mane and tail. {**păl** ə **mee** noh}

pam·per *verb* (pampered, pampering, pampers) to treat or please with too much care or attention; spoil. *The woman who lives upstairs pampers her dog with expensive meat.* {**păm** pər}

pam·phlet *noun* a thin book that has a paper cover, written to give information on some topic. {**păm** fliht}

pan ✪ *noun* 1. an open, shallow metal container for cooking or baking. *The cook used the large frying pan to cook the eggs.* 2. any object that looks like or acts like such a container. *The mechanic took the oil pan off the car. verb* (panned, panning, pans) 1. (informal) to be critical of. *All the newspapers in town panned the play.* 2. to wash gravel or sand in a pan to remove gold or other precious metals. *They panned for gold in the mountain stream.* {**păn**}

Pan *noun* the god of woods and fields in Greek mythology, who protects shepherds and sheep. Pan has the legs and sometimes the horns and ears of a goat. {**păn**}

Pan·a·ma *noun* 1. a country in Central America on the border of South America. Panama City is the capital of Panama. 2. Isthmus of Panama, the narrow body of land that connects Central America to South America. {**păn** ə mə *or* **pă** nə **maw** *or* **păn** ə **mah**} Panamanian, n., adj.

pan·cake *noun* a flat round cake of batter fried on both sides in a frying pan or a griddle. {**păn** kayk}

pan·cre·as *noun* a large gland near the stomach. The pancreas makes digestive juices

and insulin. {**păn** kree əs *or* **păng** kree əs} pancreatic, adj.

pan·da *noun* 1. a large black-and-white mammal that is related to bears. They live in the mountains of western China and eat only bamboo plants. They are also called giant pandas. 2. a mammal that has red-brown fur and a long, bushy tail with rings on it. They are closely related to giant pandas, but are smaller and look more like a raccoon. They are also called red pandas or lesser pandas, and they live in southern Asia. {**păn** də}

Pan·dor·a *noun* the first woman, according to Greek mythology. Pandora opened the lid of a box out of curiosity and let all the evils fly out into the world. {**păn dohr** ə}

pane *noun* a sheet of glass in a window or door. {**payn**}

Homophone Note Are you looking for the word *pain* (hurt)? *Pane* and *pain* sound alike but have different meanings.

pan·el *noun* 1. the part of a door or wall that is set apart from the area around it by being raised, sunken, or decorated. 2. the part of a machine where the controls and dials are located. *The pilot showed me the instrument panel of his airplane.* 3. a group of persons gathered together for a particular purpose. *The dancers were graded by a panel of judges. verb* (paneled, paneling, panels) to cover or decorate with panels. *They*

 Human Body   Human Mind   Everyday Life   History and Culture    Communication

paneled the walls with pine. {**păn** əl}

pang *noun* 1. a sudden, sharp pain. *I skipped lunch and have pangs of hunger.* 2. a sharp feeling. *Mike felt a pang of fear when his dog ran out into the street.* {**păng**}

pan·ic *noun* a sudden terror that often causes wild behavior and spreads to many other individuals. *The fire caused a panic in the building.* *verb* (panicked, panicking, panics) to feel or be overcome by panic. *She panics whenever she has to give a speech.* {**păn** ihk}

Word History Our word *panic* comes from *Pan*, the name of the Greek god of woods and shepherds. Pan was believed to be the cause of sudden, wild fear that could not otherwise be explained.

pan·o·ram·a *noun* a full, wide view of a large area. *There is a beautiful panorama from the top of the mountain.* {**păn** ə **ră** mə *or* **păn** ə **rah** mə} panoramic, adj.

pan·sy *noun* (pansies) a garden flower that has flat, rounded petals that feel like velvet. Pansies grow in many colors. {**păn** zee}

pant *verb* (panted, panting, pants) 1. to breathe in quick, short breaths; gasp. *The runners were panting at the end of the race.* 2. to speak in a gasping way. *He panted a hello as he ran past us.* {**pănt**}

pan·ther *noun* 1. a leopard, especially a black one with no spots that show. Leopards live in Africa and Asia. They are carnivorous mammals and are closely related to lions, tigers, and other large cats that roar. 2. a common name for a puma, a large wild cat with tan fur. Pumas live in many parts of North and South America. They are also called cougars or mountain lions. {**păn** thər}

pan·to·mime *noun* 1. a type of play in which stories are told by gestures and facial expressions. Talking is not allowed in pantomime. 2. telling something by the use of gesture, without words. *She did a pantomime to let us know she would be off the phone in a minute.* *verb* (pantomimed, pantomiming, pantomimes) to tell by gestures, and without words. *The actor pantomimed a man eating.* {**păn** tə **miym**}

pan·try *noun* (pantries) a small room near a kitchen, for keeping food, dishes, and other supplies. *She stored the pies in the pantry.* {**păn** tree}

pants ⊙ *plural noun* an article of clothing that covers the area below the waist, reaching down as far as the feet and covering each leg separately; trousers. {**pănts**}

pa·pa *or* **poppa** *noun* (informal) **father; dad.** {**pah** pə *or* pə **pah**}

pa·pa·ya *noun* the yellow fruit of a tropical American tree, or the tree itself. {pə **piy** ə}

pa·per ⊙ ⊙ *noun* 1. a thin material made from wood, rags, or grasses. Paper is used for writing, wrapping, and covering walls. *He wrapped the presents with red paper.* 2. a single piece or sheet of this material. *Write your names on this paper.* 3. any written or printed document. *Birth records and other important papers are often kept in a safe.* 4. a newspaper. *The boy delivers the paper every morning.* *verb* (papered, papering, papers) to cover with wallpaper. *She papered the kitchen in blue.* {**pay** pər}

Word History The word *paper* comes from the Latin word *papyrus*. See the entry for *papyrus* to find out why.

pa·per·back *noun* a book having a soft paper cover. {**pay** pər **băk**}

paper clip *noun* a piece of wire bent back on itself that holds papers together. {**pay** pər **klihp**}

pa·poose *noun* a North American Indian baby or young child. {pə **poohs**}

pap·ri·ka *noun* a red powder made from dried sweet red peppers. Paprika is used to add spice to food. {**pah** **pree** kə *or* pə **pree** kə *or* **păp** rih kə}

Papua New Guinea *noun* a country on the eastern part of the island of New Guinea in the Pacific Ocean. Port Moresby is the capital of Papua New Guinea. {**păp** yoo ə **nooh** **gih** nee *or* **pah** pooh ə **nooh** **gih** nee} Papua New Guinean, n., adj.

pa·py·rus *noun* (papyruses or papyri) 1. a tall water plant of the Nile valley in Egypt grown as an ornamental plant and once used to make a material like paper. 2. a kind of paper that was made in ancient Egypt from the crushed and pressed stems of this plant. {pə **piyr** əs}

a b c d e f g h i j k l m n o **p** q r s t u v w x y z

par *noun* 1. normal or average in amount or degree; standard. *His health is par for a person his age.* 2. an equal amount, degree, or quality; level. *Her soccer skills are on a par with the rest of the team.* {par}

par·a·ble *noun* a very short story told to teach a moral or religious lesson. {par ə bəl}

Word History The word *parable* comes from Latin and ancient Greek words that mean "a comparison." One learns most from a parable when one understands that the story is supposed to be compared with something else. What that "something else" is, the reader must discover.

par·a·chute *noun* a large device made of strong, thin cloth that opens up like an umbrella. A parachute slows the fall of a person who jumps from an airplane. It can also be used in the same way for something that is dropped from an airplane. *verb* (parachuted, parachuting, parachutes) 1. to drop or deliver by parachute. *The Air Force parachuted medical supplies to the troops.* 2. to come down by using a parachute. *The pilot parachuted from the small airplane.* {par ə shooht} parachuter, n.

Word History The word *parachute* combines a French word, *chute*, which means "fall," with the prefix, "para-," which means "defense against."

pa·rade 🔊 *noun* a public procession of people, marching bands, or vehicles in front of spectators as part of a celebration or ceremony. *Our town has a big parade every Fourth of July. verb* (paraded, parading, parades) 1. to show off or display. *She paraded her knowledge of insects for the*

class. 2. to march or participate in a public procession. *The class paraded down the aisle for the graduation ceremony.* {pə **rayd**} parader, n.

par·a·dise *noun* 1. (sometimes capitalized) a place where good people go after death; heaven. 2. a state or place of great beauty, delight, or joy. *Spending a week on the island was paradise.* {par ə diys}

par·af·fin *noun* a white substance like wax, that is made from petroleum. It is used for candles, sealing materials, and waxed paper. {par ə fihn}

par·a·graph *noun* a part of something written that is made up of one or more sentences that develop a certain idea. A paragraph begins on a new line which is usually indented from the other lines. *Our teacher told us to write three paragraphs about an interesting person.* {par ə grăf}

Par·a·guay *noun* a country in central South America. Asunción is the capital of Paraguay. {par ə gway *or* pahr ə gwiy} Paraguayan, n., adj.

par·a·keet *noun* a small parrot with a long, pointed tail and brightly colored feathers. {par ə keet}

par·al·lel *adjective* 1. lying or moving in the same direction and being the same distance apart at every point. Parallel lines never meet or cross each other. *Your notebook paper has parallel lines.* 2. alike in certain ways; similar. *We live in different countries but have parallel interests. noun* 1. a plane or line that is the same distance at every corresponding point from another. *The floor and ceiling are parallel to each other.* 2. a

comparison showing the ways in which different things are alike. *Are there any parallels between the lives of humans and animals?* 3. any of the imaginary lines that circle the earth in the same direction as the equator. Parallels mark degrees of latitude. *verb* (paralleled, paralleling, parallels) 1. to make a parallel to; equal. *This street parallels the main highway.* 2. to be or move on a course similar to. *Her life parallels her mother's life.* {par ə lehl}

par·al·lel·o·gram *noun* a flat closed figure with four straight sides. The opposite sides are parallel and equal to each other. {par ə **leh** lə **grăm**}

par·a·lyse *verb* a spelling of **paralyze** used in Canada and Britain. See **paralyze**. {**pehr** o liyz}

pa·ral·y·sis *noun* (paralyses) a loss of feeling in or the ability to move a body part. Paralysis is caused by injury or disease of the nervous system. {pə **răl** ə sihs}

par·a·lyze *verb* (paralyzed, paralyzing, paralyzes) 1. to take away the ability to move or feel in a part or parts of the body. *The disease paralyzed his arms.* 2. to cause to be helpless or unable to move. *The shock of her husband's death paralyzed her. / The airline strike will paralyze travellers.* {par ə liyz}

par·a·me·ci·um *noun* (paramecia) a living thing made of one cell that lives in fresh water. Paramecia can only be seen through a microscope. Paramecia are protozoans, tiny organisms that are similar to animals. {par ə **mee** see əm *or* par ə **mee** shee əm}

par·a·mount *adjective* most important; chief; highest.

🏃 Human Body   ❓ Human Mind   👕 Everyday Life   🚩 History and Culture   📞 Communication

The doctor's paramount concern was for his patients' health. {par ə mownt}

par·a·site *noun* a plant, animal, or fungus that lives on or in another living thing, called the host. A parasite gets its food and energy from the host organism. {par ə siyt}

Word History *Parasite* comes from an ancient Greek word for someone who earned free meals at the table of another by flattering the host during dinner.

par·a·sol *noun* a light umbrella used to protect against the sun. {par ə sŏl}

par·a·troop·er *noun* a soldier trained to parachute from an airplane into an area where there is fighting. {par ə trooh pər}

par·cel *noun* 1. something wrapped or packed for carrying or shipping; **package.** *Please mail this parcel for me.* 2. a piece of land that is a part of a larger piece. *The large piece of land was divided into parcels.* *verb* (parceled, parceling, parcels) to divide into parts to be given out or sold (usually followed by "out"). *Grandfather parceled out the land to his children.* {par səl}

parch *verb* (parched, parching, parches) 1. to make very dry by heating. *The sun parched all the crops.* 2. to make thirsty or dry. *The desert sun parched the riders and their horses.* {parch}

parch·ment *noun* 1. a material like paper made of the skins of sheep or goats. 2. paper that is like this material. {parch mənt}

par·don *noun* 1. forgiveness for a small disturbance. *I beg your pardon, I didn't mean to startle you.* 2. an official act that frees a person from punishment for a crime. *The president sometimes grants pardons.* *verb* (pardoned, pardoning, pardons) 1. to free from punishment for a crime. *The judge pardoned the hungry thief.* 2. to forgive or excuse. *Pardon me for arriving late.* {par dən} pardonable, adj.

pare *verb* (pared, paring, pares) 1. to cut off the outside layer or ends from. *She pared the potatoes.* 2. to make less, little by little; cut down. *He lost weight by paring the amount of food he eats at meals.* {payr} parer, n.

Homophone Note The words **pare**, **pair**, and **pear** sound alike but have different meanings.

par·ent  *noun* a mother or a father. {payr ənt *or* par ənt} parenthood, n.

pa·ren·the·sis  *noun* (parentheses) either of a pair of punctuation marks ( ). They are used to enclose information that is not part of the main sentence. They are also used to set apart mathematical quantities to be treated as a unit. {pə rehn thə sihs}

Par·is *noun* the capital city of France. {Par ihs}

par·ish *noun* a district of a Christian religion that has its own church and priest or minister. {par ihsh}

Homophone Note Some Americans pronounce **parish** and **perish** in exactly the same way, but they have different meanings.

park  *noun* 1. an area of public land, as in a city, that is set aside for rest and enjoyment. *The town park has a playground, a swimming pool, and a picnic area.* 2. a field or stadium used for sports. *The batter hit the baseball out of the park.* *verb* (parked, parking, parks) to put a car or other vehicle temporarily in a particular place. *The driver parked the bus in front of the school.* {park}

par·ka *noun* a warm jacket with a hood. *My parka has a fur lining.* {par kə}

Word History *Parka* is an Inuit and Russian word that means "pelt" or "a jacket made from pelt."

park·way *noun* a divided road or highway with trees, grass, or bushes along the sides or on the center strip. {park way}

par·lia·ment  *noun* 1. a group of people who make the laws for a country. 2. (capitalized) this group of people in the United Kingdom, and some other countries. Parliament is made up of the House of Commons and House of Lords. {par lə mənt}

par·lor *noun* 1. a room in a house, hotel, restaurant, or the like for conversation or for entertaining guests. 2. a room or business used for a particular activity or service. *My grandmother goes to the beauty parlor once a week.* {par lər}

Word History *Parlor* comes from an early French word that means "chat room."

pa·ro·chi·al *adjective* having to do with or in a church parish. *The parochial school is across the street from the public school.* {pə roh kee əl}

pa·role *noun* the release of a prisoner before the time of punishment is finished. Prisoners who are given parole have behaved well in prison. When on parole, they must obey certain rules. *He was*

given parole after one year in prison. *verb* (paroled, paroling, paroles) to free a person from prison according to the rules of parole. *They paroled three prisoners.* {pə **rohl**}

par·rot *noun* a tropical bird with a short, hooked bill and brightly colored feathers. Parrots can often imitate spoken words and other sounds. *verb* (parroted, parroting, parrots) to repeat the words or actions of another person, usually without understanding them. *The child parroted the long words used by his father.* {**par** ət}

pars·ley *noun* a garden herb used to season or decorate food. {**par** slee}

pars·nip *noun* 1. a plant like a carrot. The parsnip has yellow flowers and a large, pale root that can be eaten. 2. the root of the parsnip, eaten as a vegetable. {**par** snihp}

par·son *noun* a pastor in a Protestant church; minister. {**par** sən}

part *noun* 1. a separate piece or section of a whole. *We couldn't finish the puzzle because it was missing two parts.* 2. an important basic characteristic or quality. *Hard work was part of the reason she was a success.* 3. role. *I was excited about having the lead part in the play.* 4. share; duty. *He will do his part to finish the job.* 5. a section of a work of literature or other written work. *That part of the book was the most interesting.* 6. one of two or more equal portions that make up a whole. *The directions called for two parts of water to four parts of salt.* 7. the line in the hair made by a comb. *I wear my part on the right side.* *verb* (parted, parting, parts) 1. to cause to be apart; separate. *I parted the dog and cat because they were fighting.* 2. to separate one from another. *The men fought but parted as friends.* 3. to comb in a certain way. *I parted my hair down the middle.* *adverb* in part; partly. *I am part Irish and part German.* {**part**}

• **for the most part** to a large degree; usually. *For the most part he is a good worker.*

• **take someone's part** to join with or support someone. *She always takes his part in an argument.*

Synonyms
These words share a meaning with *part*, noun 1:
piece, section, portion

par·tial *adjective* 1. not complete. *There is a partial list of the toys he wants for his birthday.* 2. showing more favor to one than another. *The teacher was partial to the smarter students.* 3. being very fond of. *She is partial to chocolate.* {**par** shəl} partially, adv.

par·tic·i·pant *noun* a person who takes part. *I will not be a participant in this silly argument.* {par **tih** sə pənt}

par·tic·i·pate *verb* (participated, participating, participates) to take part; share (usually followed by "in"). *All the children participated in making the cookies.* {par **tih** sə payt} participation, n.

par·ti·ci·ple *noun* a form of a verb that may function as an adjective, a noun, a preposition, or part of a verb. {**par** tih sih pəl}

par·ti·cle *noun* a tiny amount or small piece; speck; trace. *There's a particle of dirt on your glasses.* {**par** tih kəl}

par·tic·u·lar *adjective* 1. of or having to do with a single person, thing, or event; not general. *I have a particular dress in mind to wear tonight.* 2. special; unusual. *Mothers have a particular talent for guessing what their children are thinking.* 3. being distinct and apart from others; specific. *This particular house is the one I would like to live in.* 4. concerned too much with details; hard to please. *My neighbor is very particular about his yard.* *noun* (plural) details or specific information. *Give me the particulars of your situation at school.* {pər **tihk** yə lər}

par·ti·tion *noun* a wall or partial wall that separates or divides space. *Partitions were set up in the gym.* *verb* (partitioned, partitioning, partitions) 1. to divide into parts or sections. *The farmer partitioned the field into several small gardens.* 2. to separate into parts using dividing walls. *They partitioned the basement to make three rooms.* {par **tih** shən}

part·ly *adverb* in some degree or measure; in part. *The accident was partly my fault.* {**part** lee}

part·ner *noun* 1. someone who owns and runs a business with another person. *My father and uncle are partners in business.* 2. one of two people dancing with each other. *He asked her to be his partner for the dance.* 3. a person who plays with another on the same side or team. *She could not play because her tennis partner was ill.* {**part** nər}

 Human Body Human Mind Everyday Life History and Culture  Communication

a b c d e f g h i j k l m n o p q r s t u v w x y z

part·ner·ship *noun* a business that is owned by two or more persons. *Our lawn care business is a partnership.* {**part** nər shihp}

part of speech ❷ *noun* one of the major categories into which words are often grouped, according to their function. Adjectives, adverbs, conjunctions, interjections, nouns, prepositions, pronouns, and verbs are parts of speech in English. {**part** əv **speech**}

par·tridge *noun* (partridge or partridges) a plump game bird with brown or gray feathers that make a whirring sound when the bird is rising to fly. The grouse and bobwhite are kinds of partridges. {**par** trihj}

part-time *adverb or adjective* less than full time. *He has a part-time job. / She works part-time at a flower shop.* {**part tiym** or **part tiym** or **part tiym**}

par·ty ❷ ❷ *noun* (parties) 1. a gathering of people to celebrate or have fun. *My parents had a big party for their anniversary.* 2. a group brought together for a particular purpose. *The search party finally found the missing child.* 3. a group of people who share the same political opinions and beliefs. *Political parties try to spread their ideas and gain new members.* 4. a specific person. *Are you the party who owns this car?* {**par** tee}

Word History The word *party* comes from an early French word that means "divided" or "something divided or shared." "Party" was first used as a word for a social gathering in 1716.

pass *verb* (passed, passing, passes) 1. to go past; move beyond. *The red car passed the blue one.* 2. to complete with success. *She passed the math test.* 3. to hand or move to someone else. *Please pass the milk* 4. to cause to move. *She passed the thread through the eye of the needle.* 5. to live through; spend. *She passed her vacation at the shore.* 6. to approve or make into law. *The legislature passed a new law against drunk driving.* 7. to throw, hit, or otherwise move a ball or other object to another player in some sports. *He passed the basketball to another player.* 8. to move ahead; go. *The week is passing slowly.* 9. to spend or use time. *Time passes quickly when I'm enjoying myself.* 10. to stop living; die. *He passed during the night.* 11. to end. *The storm finally passed.* *noun* 1. a road or other means of passage through which one can travel. *The storm made it impossible to go through the mountain pass.* 2. a free ticket allowing one to enter, come, or go at will. *He won a pass to the movie theater for two months.* 3. an act of passing in some sports. *The quarterback threw an excellent pass.* {**păs**}

• **pass out** to faint. *I almost passed out from the heat.*

pas·sage *noun* 1. a way through which something can pass; corridor; channel. *This mountain has an underground passage.* 2. a part of a written or musical work. *In this book, the author wrote a moving passage about his father's death.* 3. a journey by water. *The ship had a difficult passage through the storm.* 4. official approval. *The NAACP worked for the passage of the Civil Rights Act.* {**păs** ihj}

pas·sage·way *noun* a hall or other way along which people or things may pass. *There are secret passageways under the castle.* {**păs** ihj **way**}

pas·sen·ger ❷ *noun* a person who is not driving, but travels in an automobile, bus, train, or other vehicle. {**păs** ən jər}

pass·ing *adjective* 1. going by, in position or time. *We stood on the sidewalk to watch the passing parade. / He grows taller with each passing year.* 2. lasting a short time; involving little or brief attention; temporary. *She had only a passing interest in tennis.* 3. showing that one has passed a test, assignment, or course. *The students were happy to get passing grades on the math test.* *noun* the act of one that passes. *We sat on the shore and watched the passing of the boats.* {**păs** ing} passingly, adv.

pas·sion *noun* 1. any strong feeling or emotion. *The mayor spoke with passion about poverty in the city.* 2. a strong liking for something, or the object of such liking. *Swimming is his passion.* {**pă** shən}

pas·sion·ate *adjective* having or showing strong emotions. *She made a passionate speech against cutting down more trees.* {**pă** shə niht} passionately, adv.

pas·sive *adjective* 1. receiving an action without acting in return. *The spectators were passive at the game tonight.* 2. offering no resistance. *He is*

A
B
C
D
E
F
G
H
I
J
K
L
M
N
O
P
Q
R
S
T
U
V
W
X
Y
Z

so passive that people take advantage of him. {pă sihv} passively, adv., passiveness, n., passivity, n.

Pass·o·ver *noun* a Jewish holiday that celebrates the escape of the ancient Hebrews from Egypt. {păs oh vər}

pass·port *noun* an official document that shows that the holder is a citizen of a country. A passport gives one the right to travel in other countries and return to one's own country. {păs pohrt}

Word History *Passport* comes from French words that mean "pass through the port." One passed through a port to enter or leave a country.

pass·word *noun* a secret word or phrase that allows one to enter a place, or get information that is given only to those who use the password. *I forgot the password for my e-mail.* {păs wuhrd}

past ● *adjective* 1. gone by in time; ended. *The excitement of the project is past.* 2. having happened at an earlier time; former. *In past times, many people died young.* 3. just ended; happened recently. *During the past hour, the phone has rung ten times.* *noun* 1. the time that has gone by. *We can learn from the mistakes of the past.* 2. history of a nation. *In this class, you will be studying America's past.* 3. a former time in a person's life. *When I think of my past, I realize how lucky I have been.* 4. the past tense of a verb. *"Had" is the past of "have."* *adverb* so as to go by or move beyond. *He ran past and didn't stop to talk.* *preposition* 1. beyond in time; after. *It's five minutes past the hour.* 2. beyond in space. *The shed is

past the barn.* 3. beyond the number, amount, or degree of. *She is past fifty.* {păst}

Homophone Note The words **past** and **passed** sound alike but have different meanings. **Passed** is the past tense form of the verb **pass**, while **past** means "a time before now" (noun) or "in a time before now (adjective)."

pas·ta *noun* a food made from flour, eggs, and water and dried in various forms, such as macaroni or spaghetti. {pah stə}

paste *noun* 1. a mixture used to stick paper or other light materials together. Paste is usually made of water and flour. 2. any soft, thick, moist substance or mixture. *One of the ingredients in this recipe is tomato paste.* *verb* (pasted, pasting, pastes) 1. to cause to stick by means of paste. *She pasted the photos into an album.* 2. to cover with some material that has paste on it. *He pasted the walls of his room with posters of his favorite singers.* {payst}

pas·tel *noun* 1. a pale, soft color. *She decorated the room in pastels of blue and yellow.* 2. a crayon that is like chalk, used in drawing. *The artist used pastels to draw this picture.* 3. the art of drawing with such crayons, or a picture made by using them. *The art students hung their pastels in the halls of the school.* *adjective* 1. pale and soft in color. *She wore a pastel blue dress.* 2. drawn using pastels. *The museum has a pastel drawing of the lake.* {pă stehl}

pas·teur·ize *verb* (pasteurized, pasteurizing, pasteurizes) to heat for a certain length of time. Food and drinks are pasteurized in order to kill

most of the harmful bacteria. *This dairy pasteurizes its milk.* {păs chə riyz}

Word History The French chemist Louis Pasteur invented the process of pasteurization.

pas·time *noun* an activity that makes the time pass in a pleasant way. *Drawing is my favorite pastime.* {păs tiym}

pas·tor *noun* a minister or priest in charge of a church or congregation. {pă stər}

past participle *noun* a participle that either indicates a completed action or past state, such as "broken" in "I have broken my arm," or serves as an adjective, as "broken" in "a broken toy." {păst par tih sih pəl}

pas·try *noun* (pastries) 1. a dough of flour, shortening, and water that is baked and used for pie crusts. 2. sweet baked goods, made with such dough. *There were pies, tarts, and other kinds of pastry for sale.* {pay stree}

past tense *noun* a form of a verb that shows that something happened in the past or that a condition existed in the past. In the sentence, "We baked a cake," "baked" is in the past tense. {păst tehns}

pas·ture ● *noun* 1. a piece of land on which animals are put to graze. *The sheep were eating grass in the pasture.* 2. grass or other plants that grazing animals feed on. *The farmer chose the land with the best pasture for his cows.* *verb* (pastured, pasturing, pastures) to feed by putting in a pasture to graze. *We pastured the sheep early each morning.* {păs chər}

pat *verb* (patted, patting, pats) 1. to strike or tap softly with something flat, such as the open palm or fingers. *He

Human Body   Human Mind   Everyday Life   History and Culture   Communication

patted the clay to make it flat. 2. to tap gently with the hand to show feelings of warmth or affection. *I patted the dog's head.* noun 1. a light tap or stroke with the open hand or a flat object. *He gave the sand castle one last pat.* 2. a small flat piece of some substance. *I need a pat of butter for my toast.* {**păt**}

• **pat someone on the back** (informal) to show praise or thanks by words or actions. *He gave his son a pat on the back for mowing the lawn.*

patch *noun* 1. a small piece of material used to cover a hole or tear or to make a weak place stronger. *I have elbow patches on my jacket.* 2. a small pad or other covering used to protect an injury. *He had to wear a patch after he scratched his eye.* 3. a fairly small piece of land on which a particular crop grows. *There was a vegetable patch behind the house.* 4. an area that is part of a larger area but is different from it in color or some other way. *There is a patch of skin on my arm that itches.* *verb* (patched, patching, patches) 1. to repair or make stronger with one or more patches. *My mother patched the elbow of my torn sweater.* 2. to put together or repair in a quick or careless way. *The children patched together a club house out of some old boards and crates.* / *He patched the broken tennis racket with some tape.* {**păch**}

patch·work *noun* pieces of cloth or leather sewn together in a pattern. *My mother makes*

quilts of patchwork. {**păch wuhrk**}

pat·ent *noun* a government grant that gives someone the right to make, use, or sell an invention. A patent is given for a certain number of years. *He got a patent for the toy he designed.* *verb* (patented, patenting, patents) to get a patent on. *The engineer patented her invention.* {**pă** tənt or **pay** tənt, n., **pă** tənt or **pay** tənt, v.}

patent leather *noun* leather that has a hard, shiny finish. *He has shoes of black patent leather.* {**pă** tənt **leh** thər}

pa·ter·nal *adjective* 1. having to do with or typical of a father. *Since our father died, my oldest brother has taken on the paternal role in our family.* 2. related through one's father. *Your father's mother is your paternal grandmother.* {pə **tuhr** nəl}

path *noun* 1. a track beaten by the feet of people or animals. *We walked along a path through the woods.* 2. a narrow road or way. *The town will make a bicycle path around the park.* 3. a course along which someone or something travels. *The city lay in the path of a hurricane.* {**păth**}

pa·thet·ic *adjective* causing feelings of pity or sorrow. *The limping dog was a pathetic sight.* {pə **theh** tihk}

pa·tience *noun* 1. the ability to calmly put up with pain or trouble without getting upset or angry. *He showed a lot of patience when his son scratched the new car.* 2. the ability to

stay calm when there is a delay. *He waited for the bus with patience.* {**pay** shəns}

Homophone Note The words *patience* and *patients* sound alike but have different meanings. The word "patients" is the plural form of "patient," someone in the care of a doctor.

pa·tient *noun* a person or animal that is getting treatment from a doctor. *My father was a patient in the hospital.* *adjective* 1. able to stand trouble or pain without complaining. *The barber was patient with the squirming child.* 2. able to wait without complaining or becoming upset. *How could she be so patient when he kept her waiting for an hour?* {**pay** shənt} patiently, adv.

pa·ti·o *noun* (patios) a paved area next to a house that is used for dining or relaxing outdoors. {**păt** ee oh}

pa·tri·arch *noun* 1. a man who is the leader of a family or tribe. 2. an old man who is respected and honored; or some other living thing that is like a patriarch. *The town patriarch knows a lot about the history of the area.* / *We call that big, old tree the "patriarch of the woods."* {**pay** tree **ark**} patriarchal, adj.

pa·tri·ot *noun* one who loves, supports, and defends his or her country. {**pay** tree ət}

pa·tri·ot·ic *adjective* feeling or showing love for and loyalty to one's country. *Saying "The Pledge of Allegiance" or singing "The Star Spangled Banner" are patriotic acts.* {**pay** tree **o** tihk} patriotically, adv.

pa·tri·ot·ism *noun* love for and loyalty to one's country. *Both fighting in a war and protesting against a war can be acts of patriotism.* {**pay** tree ə tih zəm}

A B C D E F G H I J K L M N O P Q R S T U V W X Y Z

pa·trol *verb* (patrolled, patrolling, patrols) to guard by making regular trips along or through. *Two police officers patrol the neighborhood every night.* *noun* 1. the act of guarding in this way. *The police go out on patrol every three hours.* 2. a person or group, on foot or in vehicles, that guards in this way. *The patrol is made up of two officers who ride in a police car.* {pə **trohl**} patroller, n.

pa·tron *noun* 1. a regular customer of a shop, restaurant, or some other business. 2. a person who gives money or other support to an artist, a group, or a cause. *As patron of stray animals, he is giving money for the new animal shelter.* {**pay** trən}

pa·tron·ize *verb* (patronized, patronizing, patronizes) 1. to shop at or use the services of regularly. *Business is good because many people patronize the store.* 2. to serve as one who supports with money or in other ways. *She has long patronized the local theater group.* {**pay** trə **niyz** or **pă** trə **niyz**} patronizer, n.

pat·tern *noun* 1. an arrangement of shapes, lines, letters, numbers, or colors that can be repeated or used again and again. *My new wallpaper has a dinosaur pattern.* / *Beth drew a pattern of squares and triangles.* / *The cups and saucers have a floral pattern.* 2. a guide; model. *Using a pattern, it was easy to make the dress.* 3. the typical activities and qualities of a group, person, or thing. *The veterinarian asked about changes in the dog's eating patterns.* *verb* (patterned, patterning, patterns) to make or behave according to a pattern. *He patterns his way of speaking after his favorite actor.* {**păt** ərn}

pat·ty *noun* (patties) 1. a small, flat, round cake of ground meat or other food. 2. a piece of candy shaped like a small, flat round cake. {**păt** ee}

pau·per *noun* a very poor person who must live on public money. {**paw** pər}

pause *noun* a short stop. *I took a pause from my homework to eat a snack.* *verb* (paused, pausing, pauses) to stop for a short time. *While sweeping the floor, the custodian paused to let the children pass.* {**pawz**}

pave *verb* (paved, paving, paves) to cover with concrete, asphalt, stones, or some other material to make a hard flat surface. *The town finally paved the old dirt road.* {**payv**}

pave·ment *noun* 1. a hard surface for a road, driveway, or sidewalk. *The children like to roller skate on the pavement in front of the school.* 2. the material making up such a surface. *The workers are pouring the pavement for the new bicycle path.* {**payv** mənt}

pa·vil·ion *noun* 1. a light building with open sides used for shelter or recreation. *We held our class picnic at the pavilion in the park.* 2. one of a group of buildings that form a complex such as of a hospital or school. *The high school held its art show in the new arts pavilion.* {pə **vihl** yən}

paw ⊕ *noun* the foot of an animal with four legs and claws. *verb* (pawed, pawing, paws) 1. to hit, dig at, or scrape with claws or feet. *The dog pawed the ground where he had buried his bone.* 2. to handle in a rough or awkward way. *The children pawed the frightened kitten.* {**paw**}

pawn[1] *verb* (pawned, pawning, pawns) to leave with a lender of money to get a loan. In order to get the item back, the loan must be paid back. *After being out of work for several months, she had to pawn her valuable jewelry.* {**pawn**}

pawn[2] *noun* 1. one of the eight pieces in the game of chess. The pawn has the lowest value and is placed in the front rank at the beginning of a game. 2. a person, group, or thing used by a powerful person, nation, or the like to gain an advantage. *The kidnapped child was used as a pawn by the criminals to get a large sum of money.* {**pawn**}

Word History *Pawn* comes from a Latin word that means "foot soldier."

pay ☁ *verb* (paid, paying, pays) 1. to give money to. *Dad paid me five dollars for washing the car.* 2. to settle by giving money. *He paid his bill at the restaurant.* 3. to visit or call. *We paid our grandparents a visit yesterday.* 4. to be worth doing or good for one. *It pays to work hard.* 5. to experience revenge or punishment. *The outlaw said that he would make the sheriff pay for putting him in jail.* *noun* money or something else of value that is given for work. *The workers get their pay every two weeks.* *adjective* needing payment of money to work. *I used the pay phone at the store.* {**pay**}

• **pay back**
to return what is owed or borrowed; repay. *I paid her back for the books she bought me.*

• **pay off**

 Human Body   Human Mind   Everyday Life   History and Culture   Communication

to finish payments on. *He finally paid off his college loan.*

Word History The word *pay* goes back to a Latin word that means "to keep peaceful or satisfied." By the Middle Ages, "pay" meant "satisfy someone to whom you owe money."

pay·ment *noun* 1. the act or an instance of giving money in return for something. *He made payments every month for a year to buy the car.* 2. an amount that is paid. *We made three payments of $200 each for our new sofa.* {**pay** mənt}

pay·roll *noun* 1. a list of those who are to be paid by an employer and the amount of money due to each. *That large company has hundreds of people on its payroll.* 2. the total amount of money paid to employees. {**payr** ohl}

Pb symbol of the chemical element **lead**.

pe *noun* the name of the seventeenth letter of the Hebrew alphabet. {**pay**}

pea *noun* 1. a small, round green seed that grows in a pod on a climbing plant. Peas are eaten as a vegetable. 2. the plant that bears such seeds. {**pee**}

peace ⬜ *noun* 1. a state of freedom from war or conflict. *The people longed for peace after years of war.* 2. a state of quiet or calm. *There is an air of gentle peace about this town.* 3. civil order and safety; law and order. *It's the job of the police to keep the peace in the city.* {**pees**}

Homophone Note Are you looking for the word *piece*? *Peace* and *piece* sound alike but have different meanings.

peace·ful *adjective* 1. quiet; calm. *The sleeping baby looked peaceful.* 2. free from war or

conflict. *The people had only five peaceful years before war broke out again.* {**pees** fəl} peacefully, adj., peacefulness, n.

peace pipe *noun* a long pipe smoked by some Native American peoples as a sign of peace or friendship. {**pees** piyp}

peach *noun* 1. a fruit that has yellow or reddish skin covered with a soft fuzz. It has sweet, juicy flesh and a large, rough pit. 2. the tree that bears this fruit. 3. a yellowish pink color. {**peech**}

pea·cock *noun* 1. a male peafowl. It has a long, colorful tail, which it can raise and spread like a fan. 2. any peafowl, either male or female. {**pee** kŏk}

pea·fowl *noun* (peafowl or peafowls) a large Asian pheasant. The males have long colorful tails, which they can raise and spread like a fan. {**pee** fowl}

peak *noun* 1. the top part of a mountain that rises to a point, or such a mountain itself. 2. the front part of a cap that sticks out. *He wrote his name on the peak of his cap.* 3. the highest point or degree. *The price of houses reached a new peak this month.* {**peek**}

Homophone Note Are you looking for the word *peek* (a quick look)? *Peak* and *peek* sound alike but have different meanings.

peal *noun* 1. a loud ringing of bells of different tones. *I heard the peal of church bells.* 2. a long, loud noise. *The audience broke into peals of*

laughter at his joke. / *The silence was broken by a peal of thunder.* *verb* (pealed, pealing, peals) to make a long, loud noise; resound; ring. *The church bells pealed in honor of their wedding.* {**peel**}

Homophone Note Are you looking for the word *peel* (to pull or tear away)? *Peal* and *peel* sound alike but have different meanings.

pea·nut *noun* a seed like a nut that grows in a dry pod under the ground. Peanuts can be prepared and eaten in many ways. *I ate a bowl of peanuts as I watched TV. / A stew of peanuts is eaten in eastern Africa.* {**pee** nuht}

peanut butter *noun* a paste made by grinding roasted peanuts. It is used in cooking or as a spread on sandwiches or crackers. {**pee** nuht **buh** tər}

pear *noun* 1. a sweet, juicy fruit that is shaped like a bell. 2. the tree, related to apples and roses, that bears this fruit. {**payr**}

Homophone Note The words *pear*, *pair*, and *pare* sound alike but have different meanings.

pearl *noun* a smooth, round gem that is formed inside the shells of oysters. A pearl forms to cover something, such as a grain of sand, that gets stuck in an oyster and irritates it. {**puhrl**}

peas·ant *noun* a member of the class of farm workers and small farmers in Europe and Asia. {**peh** zənt}

peat *noun* soil from a wet area that is made up of decayed plants. Peat can be used as a fuel or fertilizer. {peet}

peb·ble 🌐 *noun* a small, smooth rock rounded by the action of water. {**pehb** əl}

pe·can *noun* 1. a nut that has a thin, smooth, oval shell. 2. the tree that bears this nut. The pecan is related to hickories and walnuts and grows in the southern United States. {pih **kahn** or pih **kăn** or **pee** kăn}

Word History *Pecan* is a word borrowed from the Algonquin family of languages.

pec·ca·ry *noun* (peccaries) a mammal that looks like a pig. Peccaries are smaller than true pigs, but have tusks and large heads. Wild peccaries are the only pig relative native to North and South America. Peccaries are omnivores that eat many kinds of foods. They live in many habitats, from deserts to rain forests. {**pehk** ə ree}

peck[1] *noun* 1. a unit of measurement of grains and other dry things. A peck is equal to eight quarts, one fourth of a bushel, or 8.81 liters. 2. (informal) a large amount. *I got into a peck of trouble for picking the neighbor's flowers.* {**pehk**}

peck[2] *verb* (pecked, pecking, pecks) 1. to strike, or pick up quickly with the beak. *The chickens pecked at their feed.* 2. to make by striking with or as if with a beak. *The bird pecked a large hole in the tree for its home.* 3. (informal) to kiss quickly and lightly. *She pecked him on the cheek.* *noun* 1. a stroke or blow with or as with a beak. *The baby cried when the bird gave her a peck on the head.* 2. (informal) a quick light kiss. *Her first kiss from him was just a peck on the cheek.* {**pehk**}

pe·cu·liar *adjective* 1. odd, strange, or unusual. *It is peculiar that you like peanut butter and onion sandwiches.* 2. belonging only to a particular person, group, thing, or place. *That style of writing is peculiar to her. / Their way of praying is peculiar to their religion. / That plant is peculiar to Africa.* {pih **kyool** yər}

pe·cu·li·ar·i·ty *noun* (peculiarities) 1. the state or fact of being odd or strange. *His peculiarities in dress and speech were quickly noticed.* 2. a quality that is unusual or not common. *This murder case has several peculiarities.* {pih **kyoo** lee **ayr** ih tee}

ped·al *noun* a lever pushed by the foot to run or control a machine. *The first sewing machines were run by pedals.* *verb* (pedaled, pedaling, pedals) to work the pedal or pedals of. *I will pedal my bike around the park.* {**pehd** əl}

Homophone Note Are you looking for the word *peddle* (to sell)? *Pedal* and *peddle* sound alike but have different meanings.

ped·dle *verb* (peddled, peddling, peddles) to offer for sale on the street or from door to door. *That man peddles magazines in our neighborhood twice a year.* {**pehd** əl}

Homophone Note The words *peddle* and *pedal* (a foot operated lever) sound alike but have different meanings.

ped·es·tal *noun* a support or base for a column, statue, or some other object. {**pehd** ə stəl}

pe·des·tri·an *noun* a person who is walking. *In a city, pedestrians should use the sidewalks, not walk in the streets.* {pə **deh** stree ən}

pe·di·a·tri·cian *noun* a doctor who takes care of babies and children. {pee dee ə **trih** shən}

ped·i·gree ⊖ *noun* a list or table of the ancestors of an animal or person. *These cats have a very fine pedigree.* {**pehd** ih gree}

peek *verb* (peeked, peeking, peeks) to look quickly or secretly. *I peeked through the keyhole to see who was in the room.* *noun* a quick or secret look. *He took a peek at the newspaper before dinner. / She got a peek at her present before her mother wrapped it.* {**peek**}

Homophone Note The words *peek* and *peak* (the top of something) sound alike but have different meanings.

peel ❶ *verb* (peeled, peeling, peels) 1. to pull, tear, or cut the outer covering from. *He always peels his apple before eating it.* 2. to strip off or remove. *She peeled the bandage off her arm.* 3. to come off in patches or strips. *Weathered paint often peels.* 4. to lose skin or some outer layer. *Sunburned skin will peel after a few days.* *noun* the outer layer or skin of some fruits and vegetables. *You must remove the peel before you can eat your banana.* {**peel**} peeler, n.

Homophone Note Are you looking for the word *peal* (a loud ringing)? *Peel* and *peal* sound alike but have different meanings.

 Human Body   Human Mind   Everyday Life   History and Culture   Communication

peep[1] *verb* (peeped, peeping, peeps) 1. to look quickly or secretly through a narrow opening or from a hiding place. *The little girl peeped out from behind the curtain.* 2. to appear for a short time or to a slight degree. *The sun peeped through the dark clouds. / Her slip peeped from under her skirt.* *noun* a quick or secret look; peek. *The baker took a peep at the cake to see if it was done. / I sneaked a peep at my sister's diary.* {**peep**}

peep[2] *noun* 1. a weak, sharp, short sound of a young bird. *There were tiny peeps coming from the nest in the tree.* 2. any weak, sharp, short sound. *One more peep out of you and I'll be angry!* *verb* (peeped, peeping, peeps) to make a weak, sharp, short cry. *The birds peeped for their mother.* {**peep**}

peer[1] *noun* 1. a person of the same rank, age group, or ability as another person; equal. *He had no peer as a singer. / He hasn't found any friends among his peers.* 2. a duke, baron, or some other member of the British noble class. {**peer**}

peer[2] *verb* (peered, peering, peers) 1. to look hard or closely to see something better. *The sailor peered into the thick fog, looking for the shore.* 2. to appear to a slight degree; peep. *The moon peered through the thick trees.* {**peer**}

Homophone Note Are you looking for the word *pier* (a structure for docking boats)? *Peer* and *pier* sound alike but have different meanings.

peg *noun* 1. a small piece of wood or other material used to hold things together, fill a hole, or mark a place. 2. a pin in the neck of a musical instrument that may be turned to change the tension of a string. *verb* (pegged, pegging, pegs) to fasten, plug, or mark with a peg or pegs. *She pegged the tent to the ground.* {**pehg**}

• **take someone down a peg** to make humbler. *When she bawled him out, it really took him down a peg.*

Pe·king *noun* the capital city of China, known as Beijing. {**pee king**}

Pe·king·ese *noun* (Pekingese) a small breed of dog with short legs and long, silky, light brown hair. Pekingese were first bred in China. {**pee king eez** or **pee kə neez**}

pel·i·can *noun* a large water bird that lives in warm areas. It has a pouch in the lower half of its long bill for catching and holding fish. {**pehl** ə kən}

pel·let *noun* 1. a small bullet or small piece of shot. 2. a small rounded mass of food, medicine, or some other substance. *Use these pellets to feed the fish. / Take one of these pellets every four hours for your sore throat.* {**pehl** iht}

pell-mell *adverb* in a quick, confused, jumbled manner. *He yelled "Fire!," and everyone rushed pell-mell to get outside.* {**pehl mehl**}

pelt[1] *verb* (pelted, pelting, pelts) 1. to attack by throwing things or by repeated blows. *The kids pelted each other with snow balls. / The boxers pelted each other.* 2. to hit again and again. *Hard rain pelted me as I ran to the car.* {**pehlt**}

pelt[2] *noun* the skin or hide of an animal. *The hunter used a beaver pelt to make a hat.* {**pehlt**}

pen[1] 🔾 🔾 *noun* a long, thin tool used for writing or drawing in ink. {**pehn**}

Word History The English word **pen** comes from *penna*, the Latin word for "feather." Writing was done with a feather pen for over a thousand years. The "penknife" is so called because it was used to sharpen the point of a feather pen.

pen[2] 🔾 *noun* 1. a small, fenced area for animals. *The pig pen held three sows and their many babies.* 2. any small enclosed area, such as a child's playpen. *verb* (penned or pent, penning, pens) to put in or as if in a pen. *The farmer penned the sheep near the barn. / All this extra work will pen me in my office for the weekend.* {**pehn**}

pe·nal·ize *verb* (penalized, penalizing, penalizes) to give penalty or punishment to. *The referee penalized our football team.* {**pee** nə **liyz**}

pen·al·ty *noun* (penalties) 1. a punishment given for breaking a law, rule, or agreement. *The penalty for robbery is usually jail.* 2. a punishment or disadvantage given in sports to a player or team that breaks a rule. *Our football team was given a penalty of five yards for an illegal move.* {**pehn** əl tee}

pen·cil 🔾 🔾 *noun* a long, thin tool used for writing or drawing. Pencils are made of a narrow stick of graphite held within a case of wood. *My friend gave me a new set of drawing pencils for my birthday.* *verb* (penciled, penciling, pencils) to mark, write, or draw by pencil. *He penciled some dates into his calendar.* {**pehn** sihl}

pen·dant *noun* something hanging as an ornament on a

A B C D E F G H I J K L M N O **P** Q R S T U V W X Y Z

chain around the neck or on an earring. {pehn dənt}

pen·du·lum *noun* a weight hung on a long cord, wire, or lever so that it swings back and forth. Pendulums are used to control the movements of some clocks. {pehn jə ləm *or* pehn də ləm}

pen·e·trate *verb* (penetrated, penetrating, penetrates) 1. to pierce or go into or through. *The dart penetrated his skin. / The explorers penetrated the jungle.* 2. to see through or understand. *His eyes couldn't penetrate the fog. / Scientists penetrated the secrets of the atom.* {peh nə trayt}

pen·guin *noun* a large water bird with webbed feet that lives in colder regions of the Southern Hemisphere. Penguins do not fly, but use their wings like flippers for swimming. {pehn gwihn}

pen·i·cil·lin *noun* a kind of mold that is used to make medicines. Penicillin kills some kinds of bacteria that cause diseases. {pehn ə sih lən}

pen·in·su·la *noun* a piece of land surrounded on nearly all sides by water. It is connected to a larger body of land by a narrow strip of land. Florida and Michigan are peninsulas. {pə nihn sə lə}

pe·nis *noun* (penises [or] penes) The male sex organ through which sperm is transferred to a female. The penis is also used to dispose of urine. {pee nihs}

pen·i·ten·tia·ry *noun* (penitentiaries) a prison for people who have been found guilty of serious crimes. {pehn ih tehn shə ree}

pen·knife *noun* (penknives) a small folding knife. {pehn niyf}

pen·man·ship *noun* the art, skill, or manner of handwriting. *The class has lessons in penmanship three times a week. / Her penmanship is very graceful.* {pehn mən shihp}

pen name *noun* a name used by authors in place of their real names. {pehn naym}

pen·nant *noun* a long flag shaped like a triangle. Pennants are used on ships for signaling or as a sign for a school, team, or some other group. *The crowd waved school pennants to cheer on the players at the big game.* {pehn ənt}

pen·ni·less *adjective* having no money at all; very poor. *He became nearly penniless when he lost his job.* {pehn ee lihs *or* peh nih lihs}

Penn·syl·va·ni·a *noun* a state in the eastern United States. Its capital is Harrisburg. (abbreviated: PA) {pehn səl vayn yə}

> **Word History** *Pennsylvania* means "Penn's Woods" in Latin. The English colony was founded by William Penn in 1681 and named for his father, Sir William Penn.

pen·ny *noun* (pennies) 1. a coin of the United States and Canada equal to one cent. 2. The smaller unit of money in the United Kingdom and Ireland. {pehn ee}

pen·sion *noun* money paid at regular times by a former employer to a person who has retired, or by the government to a person who is not able to work. *Grandmother gets a monthly pension of one thousand dollars.* {pehn shən}

pen·ta·gon *noun* 1. a flat closed figure with five straight sides. 2. (capitalized) the building that houses the main offices for the armed services of the United States, or the military people who work in this building. The Pentagon is a building with five sides. {pehn tə gŏn}

pent·house *noun* an apartment or house built on the top floor or roof of a tall building. {pehnt hows}

pe·o·ny *noun* (peonies) 1. a garden plant with large pink, red, or white flowers. 2. the flower of this plant. {pee ə nee}

peo·ple *noun* (people or peoples) 1. all persons who belong to the same community, country, religion, or race. *The people of this country come from all over the world.* 2. family; relatives. *My people came from Scotland.* 3. the mass of ordinary persons (often used with "the"). *The president looked to the people for support.* *verb* (peopled, peopling, peoples) to come to live in or settle. *Native Americans were the first to people the country we now call the United States.* {pee pəl}

> **Synonyms**
> These words share a meaning with *people*, noun 1:
>
> **community** A community is a small group of people that live together or share common interests. *The scientific community was excited about the new discovery.*
>
> **nation** Nation is used to refer to a large group of people living in the same geographical region under the same government. *Mexico is a nation in North America.*
>
> **race** Race is used to refer to people that share common physical features. *There are many different races of people living in the United States.*
>
> **tribe** Tribe is often used when speaking of native peoples. *Her family left their tribe in Africa.*

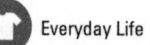 Human Body   Human Mind 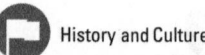 Everyday Life  History and Culture Communication

pep *noun* (informal) lively energy or spirit. *He has a lot of pep for his age. verb* (pepped, pepping, peps) (informal) to fill with lively energy or spirit (followed by "up"). *The fresh air pepped them up.* {**pehp**}

pep·per ⬤⬤ *noun* 1. a spice that comes from the dried berries of tropical vines in southeast Asia. *I like salt and pepper on my potatoes.* 2. a hollow fruit that varies in size, shape, and color. Peppers can have either a hot or sweet taste. They are eaten as a vegetable or used to season other foods. *verb* (peppered, peppering, peppers) 1. to season or dot with pepper. *The cook peppered the stew until it was just right.* 2. to hit with small objects. *The gardener peppered the ground with grass seed.* {**pehp** ər}

pep·per·mint *noun* 1. a kind of mint plant that has small pink or white flowers and is grown for its oil. Peppermint is used in medicine and as a flavoring for toothpaste, gum, and candy. 2. the oil from this type of mint, or a flavoring made from this oil. *This cookie recipe calls for a few drops of peppermint.* 3. a candy flavored with this oil. {**pehp** ər **mihnt**}

per *preposition* for each. *The babysitting job pays three dollars per hour.* {**puhr**}

Homophone Note The words *per* and *purr* (the sound a cat makes) sound alike but have different meanings.

per- *prefix* a prefix that means "through." *To perforate paper is to put holes through it.*

per·ceive ⬤ *verb* (perceived, perceiving, perceives) 1. to become aware of through the senses. *He perceived smoke*

coming from the kitchen and called the fire department. 2. to understand. *She read the paragraph over and over until she perceived what it meant.* {pər **seev**}

per·cent or **per cent** *noun* one part or unit of each hundred. *Ten percent of one hundred is ten. / Only eighty percent of the tickets were sold.* {pər **sehnt**}

per·cent·age *noun* 1. some part of a whole based on a total of one hundred parts. *If one out of ten children in the class is at home with the flu today, what percentage are missing school?* 2. part of a whole. *A large percentage of the people who live in that apartment building are poor.* {pər **sehn** tihj}

per·cep·tion *noun* 1. the ability to become aware of or know through the senses. *Her poor perception of sounds is helped by a hearing aid.* 2. understanding that is based on the senses. *My perception of what he said is different from yours.* {pər **sehp** shən} perceptional, adj.

perch¹ *noun* 1. a branch or bar on which birds sit. 2. a small place to sit or rest up high. *verb* (perched, perching, perches) to rest or come to rest on a branch or bar. *The sparrows perched on the clothes line.* {**puhrch**}

Yellow Bird figured he could cross the lake more quickly **perched** on the back of a **perch**.

perch² *noun* (perch or perches) a fish that lives in fresh water and has fins with spines. Perch are used for food. {**puhrch**}

per·cus·sion ⬤ *noun* 1. the striking of one hard object against another with force so that sound is produced. *The percussion of steel against steel hurt my ears.* 2. drums, cymbals, and the other musical instruments that produce sound when struck. {pər **kuh** shən}

percussion instrument *noun* a musical instrument that is sounded when some part of it is struck. Pianos, drums, cymbals, and xylophones are percussion instruments. {pər **kuh** shən **ihn** strə mənt}

per·en·ni·al *adjective* 1. lasting throughout the year or for many years. *The story "Cinderella" is a perennial favorite.* 2. continuing to happen. *He seems to have a perennial problem with keeping a job.* 3. having a life cycle of more than two years as a plant. *Roses are one of the most beautiful perennial plants. noun* a plant that lives longer than two years. *We planted only perennials in our flower garden.* {pə **rehn** ee əl}

per·fect *adjective* 1. free from mistakes or faults. *I would like my homework to be perfect. / Nobody's perfect!* 2. exact. *A perfect circle can be drawn with a compass.* 3. completely enjoyable; most excellent. *It was a perfect day for a picnic. verb* (perfected, perfecting, perfects) to make perfect. *Practice has perfected her drawing skills.* {**puhr** fihkt, adj., pər **fehkt**, v.}

per·fec·tion *noun* the state or condition of being without a fault or mistake. *We practiced the play every day for two*

A B C D E F G H I J K L M N O P Q R S T U V W X Y Z

a
b
c
d
e
f
g
h
i
j
k
l
m
n
o
p
q
r
s
t
u
v
w
x
y
z

months, trying to reach perfection. {pər **fehk** shən}

per·fect·ly *adverb* 1. in a manner that is without a fault or mistake. *The children behaved perfectly at the restaurant. / I practiced my song until I could sing it perfectly.* 2. totally; completely. *The weather was perfectly beautiful.* {**puhr** fihkt lee}

per·fo·rate *verb* (perforated, perforating, perforates) 1. to make a hole in. *The nail perforated his foot.* 2. to make a series of small holes in to make tearing easier. *Perforating the pages in this spiral-bound notebook made them easier to tear out.* {**puhr** fə **rayt**}

per·form ● *verb* (performed, performing, performs) 1. to carry out; do. *She performed the lab experiment with care. / The mayor is not performing his duties.* 2. to do or present for the entertainment of an audience. *He performed the role of the king. / The school chorus will perform songs from popular musicals.* {pər **fohrm**}

per·for·mance *noun* 1. a particular entertainment presented before an audience. *The auditorium was filled for the final performance of the play.* 2. the act of performing. *He practiced the dance so often that his performance was perfect.* 3. way of working or operating. *He's unhappy with his car's performance.* {pər **fohr** məns}

per·for·mer *noun* a person who sings, acts, or does some form of entertainment for an audience; one who performs. *My sister loves to dance and wants to be a performer.* {pər **fohr** mər}

per·fume *noun* 1. a liquid, made from flowers, herbs, or other substances that has a pleasant smell. Perfume is put on the body. 2. a pleasant

odor. *The perfume of roses filled the room.* *verb* (perfumed, perfuming, perfumes) to give a sweet or pleasing odor to. *The flowers perfumed the air.* {**puhr** fyoom *or* pər **fyoom**, n., **puhr** fyoom *or* pər **fyoom**, v.}

per·haps *adverb* maybe; possibly. *Perhaps I will see you tomorrow.* {pər **hăps**}

per·il *noun* 1. the condition of being in danger or at risk. *If you drink and drive you put lives in peril.* 2. something that creates a danger or risk. *Falling rocks are a peril to be aware of when climbing this mountain.* {**peh** rihl}

pe·rim·e·ter *noun* 1. the boundary or border of a figure or area. *The farmers built a fence along the perimeter of the pasture.* 2. the length of this boundary or border, equal to the sum of the lengths of its sides. *The bedroom rug has a perimeter of ten meters.* {pə **rih** mə tər} perimetric, adj.

pe·ri·od ● ● *noun* 1. a section of time with a set beginning and end. *We will be on vacation for a period of three weeks.* 2. a section of time in history. *Read the chapter about the Renaissance period in Europe.* 3. a section of a school day. *She takes English during fourth period.* 4. a punctuation mark (.). It is used at the end of a sentence or after an abbreviation. {**peer** ee əd}

pe·ri·od·ic *adjective* happening or appearing at regular times. *We make periodic visits to the doctor to make sure we're healthy. / The full moon is a*

periodic sight in the night sky. {**peer** ee **o** dihk}

pe·ri·od·i·cal *noun* a magazine that is printed every week, month, or at some other regular time. {**peer** ee **o** dih kəl}

per·i·scope *noun* an instrument on a submarine that is made up of a long tube with mirrors and prisms that allow one to see ships and other things above the surface of the water. {**pehr** ih **skohp**}

per·ish *verb* (perished, perishing, perishes) to die or be destroyed by violence or in some other way that is not natural. *Many people perished in the earthquake.* {**pehr** ihsh}

Homophone Note Are you looking for the word *parish* (a Christian district)? *Perish* and *parish* sound alike but have different meanings.

per·ish·a·ble *adjective* likely to spoil or rot in a short time. *Put the meat and other perishable food in the refrigerator right away.* {**pehr** ih shə bəl} perishability, n.

per·ju·ry *noun* (perjuries) the crime of telling a lie in a court after promising under oath to tell the truth. {**puhr** jə ree}

per·ma·nent *adjective* lasting or meant to last for a very long time; everlasting. *The new porch is a nice, permanent addition to the house.* *noun* a hairdo of curls or waves that lasts for several months. {**puhr** mə nənt} permanently, adv.

per·mis·sion *noun* 1. the act of permitting. *With your permission, I'd love to take your dog for a walk.* 2. consent from an authority to do something. *I asked the teacher for permission to hand in my homework late.* {pər **mih** shən}

 Human Body   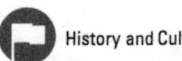 Human Mind   Everyday Life   History and Culture    Communication

per·mit *verb* (permitted, permitting, permits) 1. to allow; let. *Will you permit me to go to the dance?* 2. to give the opportunity for or to. *An extra traffic lane would permit the faster drivers to pass.* *noun* a written statement that officially allows someone to do something; license. *He got a building permit for the new porch. / The officer asked to see his fishing permit.* {pər **miht** or **puhr** miht}

per·pen·dic·u·lar *adjective* 1. at a right angle to. *This red bar is perpendicular to the blue bar.* 2. straight up and down. *That cliff is a dangerous, perpendicular climb.* {**puhr** pən **dihk** yə lər}

per·pet·u·al *adjective* 1. lasting forever. *A number of religions believe in a perpetual life after death.* 2. lasting or meant to last for a very long time. *The money his father left gives him a perpetual income.* 3. happening or continuing without stopping. *That active baby seems to be in perpetual motion.* {pər **peh** chooh əl} perpetually, adv.

per·pet·u·ate *verb* (perpetuated, perpetuating, perpetuates) to cause to last or be remembered. *Smoking perpetuates his lung problem. / My grandmother's kindness perpetuated her in our hearts.* {pər **peh** chooh **ayt**}

per·se·cute *verb* (persecuted, persecuting, persecutes) to continually treat in a cruel or harsh way because of race, religion, political ideas, or some other difference. *Adolf Hitler persecuted the Jewish people.* {**puhr** sə **kyoot**} persecutor, n.

per·se·cu·tion *noun* the act of continually treating others in a cruel way because of race, religion, politics, or some other difference; or the condition of being treated in this way. *Many people came to America to escape religious persecution.* {**puhr** sə **kyoo** shən}

Per·sia *noun* 1. an ancient empire in southwestern Asia, centered in what is now Iran; Persian Empire. 2. the former name of Iran. {**puhr** zhə}

Per·sian *adjective* of or having to do with Iran or Persia, or its people or language. *noun* 1. a person who was born in or is a citizen of Iran. 2. the language of Iran. 3. a native of ancient Persia. {**puhr** zhən}

Persian Gulf *noun* a part of the Arabian Sea. It lies between Iran and the Arabian Peninsula. {**puhr** zhən **guhlf**}

per·sim·mon *noun* a sweet, juicy, orange or yellow fruit whose skin and pulp is like that of a plum. {pər **sih** mən}

per·sist *verb* (persisted, persisting, persists) 1. to continue in a firm, steady way. *Freezing weather persisted for several weeks.* 2. to continue in a course of action or hold on to a belief in a firm, steady way. *Mother persisted in refusing to allow me to go. / She persists in believing in creatures from outer space.* {pər **sihst**}

per·sist·ent *adjective* 1. continuing, lasting, or holding on in a firm, steady way. *A persistent salesman, he could sell ice to an Eskimo.* 2. lasting a long time. *I can't seem to get rid of this persistent cough.* {pər **sih** stənt} persistently, adv.

per·son *noun* 1. a human being. *Each person who lives in this country should obey its laws.* 2. the qualities a particular person has; personality; self. *He's a good doctor, but I don't like his person.* 3. one of three groups of personal pronouns that show who the subject of the verb is. The first person, ("I" or "we") is used for the person who speaks or writes. The second person, ("you") is used for the person who reads or listens. The third person ("he," "she," "it," or "they") is used for the person or thing the speaker is talking about. *He writes all his stories in the first person.* {**puhr** sən}

• **in person** being actually present, rather than on the phone or radio, in pictures, or in the movies. *I met him in person after I saw him in the movie.*

> **Synonyms**
> These words share a meaning with *person*, noun 1:
> human, individual, soul

per·son·al *adjective* 1. of or relating to a person; private. *He writes personal thoughts and feelings in his diary.* 2. of or relating to the body. *My personal health habits include eating right and exercising every day.* 3. done in person. *The famous singer made a personal visit to the sick child.* {**puhr** sə nəl}

personal computer *noun* a small computer used by one person or a few people; microcomputer. {**puhr** sə nəl kəm **pyoo** tər}

per·son·al·i·ty ⊘ *noun* (personalities) 1. all of the qualities of a person that make that person different from others. *One twin has a cheerful personality, while the other is more serious.* 2. a famous person. *There were many personalities*

in the audience at the movie awards event. {**puhr** sə **nă** lih tee}

per·son·al·ly *adverb* 1. in person; without the aid of others. *He delivered the flowers personally.* 2. as a person or individual. *I like my boss personally, but he can be difficult to work for.* 3. as if meant for one as a person or individual. *Please don't take my bad mood personally.* {**puhr** sə nə lee}

per·son·nel *noun* all of the people who work for a business or other organization. *The boss thanked his personnel for their hard work.* {**puhr** sə **nehl**}

per·spec·tive *noun* 1. a way of showing objects on the flat surface of a picture so that they seem the correct size and distance from one another. 2. the way things are seen from a particular point of view. *The perspective from the airplane made everything below look tiny.* 3. the ability to understand the relationships between things and to judge the importance of each. *I was so angry that I lost all perspective.* {pər **spehk** tihv}

per·spi·ra·tion *noun* 1. the act or process of giving off moisture through the pores of the skin; sweating. Perspiration is the body's way of cooling off when it gets too hot. 2. the moisture given off in this process; sweat. {**puhr** spə **ray** shən}

per·spire ⊕ *verb* (perspired, perspiring, perspires) to give off moisture through the pores of the skin; sweat. *I perspired so much during my run that my shirt was all wet.* {pər **spiyr**}

per·suade ⊕ *verb* (persuaded, persuading, persuades) 1. to cause to do something by using reason or argument. *The lawyer persuaded the judge that he was not the thief.* 2. to cause to believe something. *She persuaded her mother that singing lessons are a good idea.* {pər **swayd**}

per·sua·sion *noun* 1. the act of convincing someone to believe something or do something. *It was his parents' persuasion that changed his mind.* / *Her offer to serve us dinner was a powerful persuasion for us to stay longer.* 2. the ability to convince someone to believe something or do something. *The salesman's persuasion succeeded in getting her to buy the car.* {pər **sway** zhən}

per·tain *verb* (pertained, pertaining, pertains) 1. to relate to or have to do with something. *The captain knew everything pertaining to the ship.* 2. to be a part of or belong to something. *A bat and ball are two things that pertain to baseball.* {pər **tayn**}

per·ti·nent *adjective* having to do with or connected to a subject; relevant. *Sailing is not pertinent to a discussion about the desert.* {**puhr** tə nənt} pertinence, n.

Pe·ru *noun* a country in western South America. Lima is the capital of Peru. {pə **rooh**} Peruvian, adj., n.

pe·so *noun* (pesos) the main unit of money of Mexico, Cuba, and several other countries. {**pay** soh}

pes·si·mis·tic *adjective* feeling in a negative way about things; expecting the worst to happen. *She is pessimistic about her chances for making the swim team.* {pehs ə **mih** stihk} pessimistically, adv.

pest ❶ *noun* someone or something that annoys or bothers; nuisance. *Mosquitos are pests.* {**pehst**}

pes·ter *verb* (pestered, pestering, pesters) to bother again and again. *I already said no, so stop pestering me about going!* {**pehs** tər}

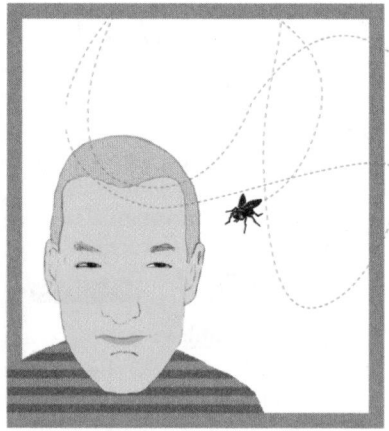

pes·ti·cide *noun* a chemical substance used to kill insects that harm plants and crops. {**peh** stih **siyd**} pesticidal, adj.

pes·tle *noun* a tool used for grinding or pounding substances into powder in a bowl called a mortar. {**peh** səl or **peh** stəl}

pet ❷ ❸ *noun* 1. a tame animal people keep in their homes as a companion or for plea-

Pet your puppy every day and your **pet** will make your bad moods go away.

 Human Body   Human Mind   Everyday Life  History and Culture  Communication

sure. *Mary's house is full of pets.* 2. a person who is treated better than others or with special kindness; favorite. *She is her father's pet.* *adjective* kept or treated as a pet. *My uncle has a pet turtle.* *verb* (petted, petting, pets) to pat or stroke; touch or treat as a pet. *My sister was petting all the cats at the animal shelter.* {peht}

pet·al 🛈 *noun* one of the separate leaves that form the outer part of a flower head. Petals are usually a different color from the plant's other leaves. {peht əl}

pe·ti·tion *noun* a formal, written request by many people that is made to a person in authority. *Many parents signed the petition asking the school board to lower taxes.* *verb* (petitioned, petitioning, petitions) to make a formal request to. *Many citizens have petitioned the city council to fix up the park.* {pə tih shən} petitioner, n.

pet·ri·fy *verb* (petrified, petrifying, petrifies) 1. to turn into stone. Minerals left behind by water petrify wood by replacing woods cells when they die. 2. to make unable to act or move from terror. *That monster movie really petrified me.* {peh trə fiy}

pe·tro·le·um *noun* a thick oil found by drilling beneath the earth's surface. Petroleum is made into gasoline, heating oil, and other products. {pə troh lee əm}

pet·ti·coat *noun* a skirt worn under an outer skirt; slip. {peh tee koht}

pet·ty *adjective* (pettier, pettiest) 1. of little importance or interest. *Most of the arguments I have with my friend are over petty matters.* 2. mean, or having a narrow mind. *It was petty of him to refuse to help her.* {peht ee} pettiness, n.

pe·tu·ni·a *noun* a common garden plant that has flowers shaped like trumpets. {pə toohn yə}

pew *noun* a church bench with a back and arms at the ends. Pews are arranged in rows facing the front of the church. {pyoo}

pew·ter *noun* a metal made from tin, copper, and other metals. Pewter looks like silver and is used to make plates, candlesticks, and other objects that are both useful and beautiful. {pyoo tər}

pg. *abbreviation* an abbreviation for **page**.

phan·tom *noun* a ghost or something else that seems real, but is not real. *The sailor told a story about the phantom of a pirate ship that appears on dark, stormy nights.* {făn təm}

Phar·aoh *noun* (sometimes lower case) the title of each of the kings of ancient Egypt. {far oh}

phar·ma·cist *noun* a person who is trained to prepare and sell drugs and medicine in keeping with the orders of a doctor. {far mə sihst}

phar·ma·cy *noun* (pharmacies) a store in which drugs are prepared and sold; drugstore. {far mə see}

phase *noun* 1. a particular stage in a cycle of development or process of change. *The "terrible twos" are a phase when children say no a lot. / We're in the planning phase of building a new house.* 2. one of the stages of the moon or smaller planets as they change their relation to the sun. A phase is shown by how much of the moon's or planet's lighted area can be seen. *In its full phase, the moon is completely round and very bright.* {fayz}

Ph.D. *abbreviation* a degree that is earned following college after several years of additional study and the completion of a major research project. Ph.D. is an abbreviation for Latin words which mean Doctor of Philosophy.

pheas·ant *noun* (pheasant or pheasants) a large bird with a long tail and bright feathers. {feh zənt}

phe·nom·e·non *noun* (phenomena or phenomenons) 1. a happening or fact that can be seen or known through the senses. *The aurora borealis is a visual phenomenon in the skies over Alaska.* 2. an unusual or remarkable person or event. *It's a phenomenon that she can read when only three years old. / Jack's beanstalk, which grew to its full height overnight, was a phenomenon.* {fə no mə nən or fə no mə nŏn}

Phil·ip·pines *plural noun* an island country in the Pacific Ocean, off the coast of southeastern Asia. Manila is the capital of the Philippines. {fihl ə peenz or fihl ə peenz} Filipino, n., Philippine, adj.

phil·o·den·dron *noun* (philodendrons or philodendra) a tropical American climbing

A B C D E F G H I J K L M N O P Q R S T U V W X Y Z

a
b
c
d
e
f
g
h
i
j
k
l
m
n
o
p
q
r
s
t
u
v
w
x
y
z

plant, grown indoors. {fee lə **dehn** drən}

phi·los·o·pher *noun* one who studies the nature of life, truth, knowledge, and other important human matters. {fih **lo** sə fər}

Word History The word *philosopher* comes from an ancient Greek word that means "a lover of wisdom."

phi·los·o·phy ❓ ⬤ *noun* (philosophies) 1. the study of the nature of life, truth, knowledge, and other important human matters. 2. the personal values and rules that guide one in life. *His philosophy is that people should always help others in need.* {fih **lo** sə fee}

phlox *noun* (phlox or phloxes) 1. a North American plant that bears groups of white, purple, or red flowers. 2. the flower of this plant. {**flŏks**}

Phoe·nix *noun* the capital of Arizona. {**fee** nihks}

phoe·nix *noun* (sometimes cap.) a beautiful bird in Egyptian mythology that lives for five hundred years, then sets itself on fire and rises alive again from the ashes. The phoenix is a symbol of immortality. {**fee** nihks}

-phone *suffix* 1. a suffix that means "sound." *A homophone is a word that has the same sound as another.* 2. a suffix that means an instrument used to receive or send sound. *A telephone is an instrument that sends and receives sound.*

phone *noun* a short form for **telephone**. *verb* (phoned, phoning, phones) to call on the telephone. *The doctor will phone him tomorrow.* {**fohn**}

pho·net·ic *adjective* 1. relating to the method of representing speech sounds by symbols. *The phonetic system of reading has the reader sound out each letter.* 2. characteristic of the speech sounds of human language. *Phonetic symbols, such as ^ above o, help readers make the letter's sound.* {fə **neht** ihk} phonetically, adv.

pho·no·graph *noun* a machine that reproduces sound that has been recorded in the grooves of a disk; record player. {**foh** nə **grăf**}

phos·pho·rus 🔬 *noun* a substance that is a chemical element. One of the common forms of phosphorus is a poisonous yellow solid that glows in moist air. Phosphorus is important to living things. It is used in fertilizers to help plants grow. (symbol: P) {**fŏs** fə rəs}

pho·to *noun* (photos) (informal) a short form for **photograph**. {**foh** toh}

pho·to- *prefix* a prefix that means "light." *A photograph is a picture created with light.* / *Photosynthesis is the process of plants making energy for themselves through the use of sunlight.*

pho·to·graph ⬆ ⬤ *noun* a picture made by using a camera that records an image on a surface that is sensitive to light. *verb* (photographed, photographing, photographs) to take a photograph of. *Mother photographs the family when we get together during the holidays.* {**foh** tə **grăf**}

pho·tog·ra·pher *noun* a person whose job is to take photographs. {fə **tŏg** rə fər}

pho·tog·ra·phy *noun* the art or practice of taking and making photographs. {fə **tŏg** rə fee}

pho·to·syn·the·sis ⬤ *noun* the process by which a green plant uses sunlight to change water and carbon dioxide into food for itself. {foh toh **sihn** thə sihs} photosynthetic, adj.

phrase ⬤ *noun* 1. a group of words that has meaning and grammatical order but does not have both a subject and a verb. 2. a short unit or passage of music. *They played that phrase very well.* *verb* (phrased, phrasing, phrases) to express or say in a particular way. *How should I phrase this introduction?* {**frayz**}

phys·i·cal ⬤ 👕 *adjective* 1. of the body. *He did hard physical training to prepare for the race.* 2. of the material world. *My physical surroundings consist of a small room with a bed, chair, and desk.* / *Two physical features of this area are hills and lakes.* *noun* an examination of the body given by a doctor. *I get a yearly physical to make sure I stay healthy.* {**fih** zih kəl} physically, adv.

phy·si·cian *noun* a doctor of medicine, who is licensed to treat illness and injury. {fih **zih** shən}

phys·i·cist *noun* a scientist who works in physics. {**fih** zih sihst}

phys·ics ⬤ *plural noun* (used with a singular verb) the science that deals with matter and energy, their qualities, and the relationships between them. Physics includes the study of light, heat, sound, electricity, and force. {**fih** zihks}

🏃 Human Body ❓ Human Mind 👕 Everyday Life ⬛ History and Culture 💬 Communication

pi *noun* a number equal to the ratio of the circumference of a circle to its diameter. The value of pi is approximately 3.1416 or 22/7. {piy}

Homophone Note The words *pi* and *pie* (a dessert) sound alike but have different meanings.

pi·an·ist *noun* a person who plays the piano. {pee ə nihst *or* pee ăn ihst}

pi·an·o *noun* (pianos) a musical instrument with a key-board and many wire strings. A piano is played by pressing keys that cause small hammers to strike the strings. {pee ăn oh}

Word History *Piano* is a shortened form of the word *pianoforte*, an Italian word that means "soft and loud." The full name of the piano refers to its difference from earlier keyboard instruments, such as the harpsichord.

pic·co·lo *noun* (piccolos) a small flute with a pitch that is an octave higher than that of the standard flute. {pihk ə loh}

pick[1] *verb* (picked, picking, picks) 1. to choose from a group. *From five flavors of ice cream, I picked chocolate.* 2. to gather by pulling off or out; pluck. *She picked cat hair off her sweater.* 3. to cause to happen. *He picked a quarrel with his father.* 4. to open with a sharp instrument and often for the purpose of stealing. *The thief picked the lock.* 5. to steal from someone's pocket or purse. *Someone picked Dad's pocket at the mall.* *noun* 1. the best part. *That bright yellow banana is the pick of the bunch.* 2. an act of choosing; choice. *Take your pick of these tomatoes.* 3. something or someone chosen. *What is your pick for the best movie of the year?* 4. a small piece of plastic or other material used to pluck the strings of a musical instrument. *The musician uses a pick to play her guitar.* {pihk}

• **pick on**
(informal) to treat someone in a mean way, either with words or in a physical way. *He's a big bully who picks on smaller children.*

• **pick out**
to choose. *She picked out the prettiest flowers.*

• **pick up**
1. to lift up by hand. *The nurse picked up the baby when he began to cry.* 2. to make neat by putting objects in order. *I picked up my room, which was an awful mess.* 3. to learn or master. *The student from France picked up English quickly.*

pick[2] *noun* a sharp, pointed tool used for digging or breaking up rocks or other hard substances. *The fishermen used an ice pick to cut a hole in the ice.* {pihk}

pick·ax or **pickaxe** *noun* a pick that has one pointed end and a blade that is shaped liked a chisel on the other end. {pihk ăks}

pick·er·el *noun* (pickerel or pickerels) a fish that is related to pike. Pickerel are used for food or sport. {pihk ə rəl}

pick·et *noun* 1. a pointed post fixed into the ground, used to make a fence or hold something in place. 2. a person or group of people who stand or walk in front of a business or building to protest or demand something. *The pickets outside the factory are protesting against the dangerous working conditions.* *verb* (picketed, picketing, pickets) to protest against as a picket during a strike or at other times. *The steel workers are picketing.* {pihk iht} picketer, n.

pick·le *noun* a cucumber or another vegetable or fruit that has been preserved in salt water, vinegar, and seasonings. *verb* (pickled, pickling, pickles) to preserve in salt water, vinegar, and seasonings. *We pickled cucumbers and beets from our garden.* {pihk əl}

pick·pock·et *noun* a person who steals from pockets or purses in crowded or public places. {pihk po kiht}

pick·up *noun* 1. the act of taking something onto or into a vehicle. *The garbage pickup is every Tuesday.* 2. a small truck with a flat bed and low sides. *I rented a pickup to move my furniture to my new apartment.* {pihk uhp *or* pihk uhp}

pic·nic *noun* 1. a social gathering at which food is eaten outdoors. *Everyone enjoyed the picnic by the lake.* 2. (informal) anything that is easy or enjoyable. *That exam was no picnic.* *verb* (picnicked, picnicking, picnics) to attend or hold a picnic. *We landed the canoe and picnicked by the stream.* {pihk nihk}

pic·ture ○ ◐ *noun* 1. a painting, drawing, or photograph. *The hall was lined with pictures of the Presidents.* 2. a description or mental image. *My grandparents try to give us a picture of what life was like when they were young.* 3. a

A B C D E F G H I J K L M N O P Q R S T U V W X Y Z

motion picture; movie; film. *The local theater is showing a really good picture.* 4. a good example. *My mother is the very picture of energy and good health.* *verb* (pictured, picturing, pictures) 1. to create an image of in one's mind; imagine. *It's hard to picture your parents as children.* 2. to make a drawing, painting, or photograph of. *The artist pictured a young boy holding a puppy.* 3. to describe. *My uncle's letter colorfully pictured the cities he was visiting in Europe.* {**pihk** chər}

pic·tur·esque *adjective* something that is as pleasing or interesting to look at as a picture or painting. *We stayed in a picturesque cabin by the lake.* {pihk chə **rehsk**}

pie *noun* a pastry shell filled with fruit, meat, or other filling, and baked. {**piy**}

Homophone Note The words *pie* and *pi* (a mathematical value) sound alike but have different meanings.

piece *noun* 1. a section or part separated from the whole. *Only three pieces of pie were sold at the bake sale.* 2. an item that belongs to a group of such items. *There are so many pieces to this puzzle.* 3. a work of art, literature, or music. *The pianist practiced the piano piece until he could play it perfectly.* 4. a coin. *A nickel is a five cent piece.* *verb* (pieced, piecing, pieces) to join in order to mend or make a whole (often followed by "together"). *The detective pieced together what had really happened.* {**pees**}

Homophone Note Are you looking for the word *peace* (freedom from war)? *Piece* and *peace* sound alike but have different meanings.

pier *noun* 1. a long, flat structure built out from land over water that is used for landing boats; dock. 2. a heavy post or pillar used to support a bridge or building. {**peer**}

Homophone Note Are you looking for the word *peer*? *Pier* and *peer* sound alike but have different meanings.

pierce *verb* (pierced, piercing, pierces) 1. to pass or go through with or as if with something sharp; penetrate. *Pierce the potato before baking.* / *A scream pierced the air.* 2. to make a hole in. *The arrow pierced the target.* {**peers**}

pig *noun* 1. an animal with a wide, flat nose, four short legs, a thick body, and a short, curly tail. Pigs are mammals with hooves. Wild pigs often have tusks. Domestic pigs are raised for their meat, which is called pork. Adult pigs are also called hogs. 2. a person who is very messy, greedy, or rude. *I was so hungry I ate like a pig.* / *She had the table manners of a pig.* {**pihg**}

pi·geon *noun* a bird with a plump body, small head, and short legs. Some kinds of pigeons are also called rock doves. {**pih** jən}

pig·gy·back *adverb or adjective* upon the shoulders or back. *She rides piggyback on my shoulders.* / *He gave his little sister a piggyback ride.* {**pihg** ee băk}

piggy bank *noun* a small bank in which coins are put through a slot and saved.

Piggy banks are often in the shape of a pig. {**pihg** ee băngk}

pig·ment ❷ *noun* 1. anything that is used to or serves to provide color. *Pigment makes our skin whatever color it is.* / *The green leaves of plants get their color from a pigment.* 2. a powder that is mixed with oil or water to make paint, ink, or another coloring material. {**pihg** mənt}

pig·pen *noun* a yard or cage where pigs are kept. {**pihg** pehn}

pig·sty *noun* (pigsties) 1. an enclosed area or cage where pigs are kept; pigpen. 2. a very sloppy or dirty place. *Mom said that my room is a pigsty and I had better clean it up.* {**pihg** stiy}

pig·tail *noun* a braid of hair that hangs from the head. {**pihg** tayl}

pike *noun* (pike or pikes) a fish that lives in fresh water and has a long, flat snout. Pike are used for food or sport. {**piyk**}

pile[1] *noun* 1. a number of things on top of each other; heap; stack. *There is a huge pile of laundry to do.* 2. (informal) a large amount of anything. *As a popular movie star, she earns a pile of money.* *verb* (piled, piling, piles) 1. to place in a pile or form a pile from (often followed by "up"). *He piled up the wood by the side of the house.* 2. to cover with a pile; stack. *She piled her desk with books and papers.* 3. to become greater in number or size (usually followed by "up"). *The dishes piled up in the sink.* 4. to move as a group, in a disorderly way. *We all piled into the taxi.* {**piyl**}

 Human Body Human Mind  Everyday Life  History and Culture 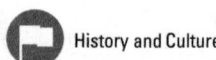 Communication

pile[2] *noun* a large post of steel, wood, or concrete that is forced or pounded into the ground to support something. Piles are used to hold up bridges, walls, buildings, and other structures. *A huge machine drove the piles into the ground.* {**piyl**}

pile[3] *noun* the thick, soft fiber on the surface of a rug or a piece of cloth. Pile is made of loops of yarn or other material that are sometimes cut. *Rugs with a deep pile sometimes look shaggy.* {**piyl**}

pil·grim *noun* 1. someone who takes a trip to a holy place for a religious purpose. 2. (capitalized) one of the English people who founded the Plymouth colony in Massachusetts in 1620. {**pihl** grəm}

pill ○ *noun* a small tablet of medicine that is taken by mouth. {**pihl**}

pil·lar *noun* a tall column shaped like a cylinder that is used to support a structure or to serve as a decoration or monument. *The porch is held up by pillars. / That pillar is a monument to all the soldiers from our town.* {**pihl** ər}

pill bug *noun* a small animal that resembles an insect, but with more legs. Pill bugs have segmented bodies that they can curl into a ball. {**pihl buhg**}

pil·lo·ry *noun* (pillories) a wooden structure that had holes for holding a person's head and hands. Pillories were used in early America to punish people who had broken the law by having them displayed in this way and be laughed at by the public. {**pihl** ə ree}

pil·low *noun* a soft pad filled with stuffing and used for resting the head on while sleeping. {**pihl** oh}

pil·low·case *noun* a cloth cover for a pillow that can be removed for cleaning. {**pihl** oh **kays**}

pi·lot ○ *noun* 1. the operator of an aircraft. 2. a person who guides a ship into or out of a harbor, or through otherwise difficult waters. *The captain of the huge freighter needed a pilot to help him dock.* *verb* (piloted, piloting, pilots) to steer or operate. *He piloted the ship through dangerous waters.* {**piy** lət}

pim·ple *noun* a small, painful swelling of the skin that is filled with pus. {**pihm** pəl}

pin *noun* 1. a small, stiff wire with a sharp point and usually a flat head. Pins are used to fasten or attach cloth, paper, or other materials. 2. a button, or piece of jewelry that fastens to clothing by using such a pointed piece of wire. 3. a wooden or metal peg used for connecting or holding parts together. *On older bicycles, the pedal is held to the crank by a steel pin.* 4. any of the ten wooden clubs that are shaped like bottles at which the ball is rolled in bowling. *verb* (pinned, pinning, pins) 1. to hold together with pins. *She pinned together the pieces of the dress before she actually sewed them.* 2. to hold firmly, so as to prevent motion. *He pinned his brother to the ground.* {**pihn**}

pinball machine *noun* a game machine played by using levers to drive a metal ball up a slanted surface. The object is to keep the ball in play to score points by hitting particular bars and pins. {**pihn bawl** mə **sheen**}

pinch *verb* (pinched, pinching, pinches) 1. to press hard between two surfaces, such as the finger and thumb. *He pinched my cheek. / The door closed on my thumb and pinched it.* 2. to press too tightly on. *The helmet was so small it pinched her ears.* 3. to cause to look pale or troubled *Sadness pinched his face.* 4. (informal) to take into police custody; arrest. *The police pinched the robber as she ran from the bank.* *noun* 1. the action or an instance of squeezing between two fingers or two other surfaces. *She woke up her brother with a pinch.* 2. an amount that can be picked up between the thumb and a finger. *This soup needs a pinch of salt.* 3. an instance or condition of great need or emergency. *When he was in a pinch and needed money, she helped him out.* {**pihnch**}

pin·cush·ion *noun* a small padded cushion used to store pins and needles that are stuck into it. {**pihn kuu** shən}

pine ○ ○ *noun* 1. an evergreen tree with cones and leaves shaped like needles. 2. the soft wood of such a tree. Pine is often used as a building material and in making furniture, paper, and paint thinner. {**piyn**}

pine·ap·ple *noun* 1. a large, juicy fruit, shaped like an egg, with sweet yellow flesh. The pineapple grows on a tropical plant. 2. the tropical plant that bears this fruit. The pineapple plant has

Living World

Physical World

Natural Environment

Economy

Government and Law

swordlike leaves and grows low to the ground. {**piyn** ă pəl}

Ping-Pong *noun* the trademark name for the game of table tennis. {**ping** pawng *or* **ping** pŏng}

pink *noun* 1. the color that comes from mixing white and red paint. 2. a plant that has a sweet scent and bears pink, red, white, or yellow flowers. 3. the highest degree. *He was in the pink of health after his vacation.* *adjective* (pinker, pinkest) having the color pink. *She wore a pink dress to the dance.* {**pingk**} pinkish, adj., pinkness, n.

pink·eye *noun* a condition of the inner part of the eyelids that causes red, sore eyes. Pinkeye is easily passed from one person to another. {**pingk** iy}

pin·ni·ped *noun* a mammal with front and back limbs that look like fins. Pinnipeds have a round head and a round body that gets thinner towards the end. They spend much of their life in the ocean, but raise their young on land. Walruses, sea lions, and seals are kinds of pinnipeds. {**pihn** ə pehd}

pin·point *noun* a point on a map, a spot of ink, or something else that is very small. *verb* (pinpointed, pinpointing, pinpoints) to find or explain exactly. *We pinpointed the location of the lake on a map. / The mechanic pinpointed the car's problem.* {**pihn** point}

pint *noun* a unit of measure equal to sixteen fluid ounces or one half quart. (abbreviated: pt.) {**piynt**}

pin·to *noun* (pintos) a horse or pony with spots of two or more colors. {**pihn** toh}

pin·wheel *noun* a plastic or paper toy, similar to a windmill, that is pinned to a stick and has a wheel that is spun by the wind or someone's breath. {**pihn** weel}

pi·o·neer *noun* 1. someone who is one of the first in a culture to explore or live in a place. *During the 19th century, American pioneers traveled to the West in covered wagons.* 2. a person or organization that is the first to do something. *The United States and Russia were pioneers in space travel.* *verb* (pioneered, pioneering, pioneers) to be the first one to explore an area of activity or research; to open the way for others. *Susan B. Anthony pioneered in the fight for women's rights.* {**piy** ə **neer**}

pi·ous *adjective* 1. showing love for a god or gods in thought and action; religious. *A pious man, he thinks of everyone as a child of God.* 2. having a religious content. *The church library has a large collection of pious books.* {**piy** əs}

pipe ⬤ ⬤ ⬤ *noun* 1. a tube of metal, plastic, or other material, through which a gas or liquid may flow. 2. a tube made up of a bowl and a hollow stem and used for smoking. *My grandfather has a collection of pipes that he carved himself.* 3. (sometimes plural) a musical instrument made up of one or several tubes that make notes when air is blown through them. 4. a single tube of such an instrument. *The organ at our church has more than a hundred pipes.* *verb* (piped, piping, pipes) 1.

to make music or give a signal with a pipe. *The organ piped throughout the hall.* 2. to cause to flow through a pipe or as if through a pipe. *The town piped water from the lake.* {**piyp**}

pipe·line *noun* a long line of pipes for moving gas or oil from where it is produced to where it is used or sold. {**piyp** liyn}

pi·ra·cy *noun* (piracies) 1. robbery or attack at sea. 2. the act of breaking the law or doing wrong by copying or using another's writing, music, or ideas. *Those singers say that another group practiced piracy by copying their songs.* {**piyr** ə see}

pi·rate *noun* 1. someone who attacks or robs ships at sea. 2. someone who breaks the law or does wrong by copying or using another's writing, music, or ideas. *verb* (pirated, pirating, pirates) to copy or use in a way that breaks the law or is wrong. *That store owner was arrested for pirating videos and selling them.* {**piyr** ət}

Pis·ces *noun* 1. a constellation located between Aquarius and Aries. Pisces is also called the Fish. 2. the twelfth sign of the zodiac, the Fish, which the sun enters about February 21. 3. a person born under this sign, between February 21 and March 20. {**piy** seez}

pis·ta·chi·o *noun* (pistachios) 1. a green nut with a tan shell that is sometimes dyed red.

Pistachios have a sweet taste. 2. an Asian and European tree, related to the cashew and mango, that bears this nut. {pihs tă shee oh}

pis·til ❶ *noun* the portion of a flower where seeds grow. It is the female part of a flower. {**pihs** tihl}

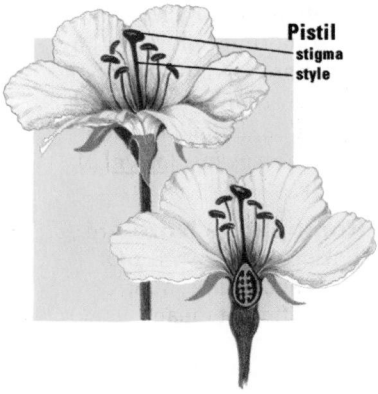

Pistil
stigma
style

Homophone Note Are you looking for the word *pistol* (a gun)? *Pistil* and *pistol* sound alike but have different meanings.

---

pis·tol ❶ ⬛ *noun* a small gun that is held and fired with one hand. {**pihs** təl}

Homophone Note The words *pistol* and *pistil* sound alike but have different meanings. To learn why a bank robber would never try to hold up a bank using a pistil, look up *pistil*.

---

pis·ton *noun* a part of an engine or some other machine that moves up and down within a tight sleeve in order to make the machine work. {**pihs** tən}

pit[1] ⬤ *noun* 1. a wide, deep hole that either is dug or already in the ground. *A pit was dug to bury the dead animals.* 2. a small hole in a surface. 3. (plural; slang) the worst or most terrible (used with

"the"). *I think cleaning the bathroom is the pits.* *verb* (pitted, pitting, pits) 1. to cause to have holes. *A brief, heavy rain pitted the soft soil.* 2. to set against one another. *The war pitted Japan against Russia.* {**piht**}

pit[2] ❶ *noun* the hard seed at the center of a cherry, plum, or certain other fruits. *verb* (pitted, pitting, pits) to take out the pit of a fruit. *The plums are being pitted for the plum pudding.* {**piht**}

pitch[1] *verb* (pitched, pitching, pitches) 1. to throw or toss. *He pitched the ball to his father.* 2. to set up or anchor. *He pitched camp near the river. / The campers pitched their tent on level ground.* 3. to throw toward the batter in baseball or softball. *He pitched three strikes in a row.* 4. to serve as a baseball or softball pitcher. *My brother pitched three games in five days.* 5. to rock or move suddenly from one side or end to the other. *The ship pitched hard in the storm.* *noun* 1. the throw of a baseball by the pitcher toward the batter, who tries to hit it. *She threw three perfect pitches and struck out the batter.* 2. the rise or slope. *The pitch of the road makes speeding dangerous.* 3. the highest degree or pace. *The children were in a pitch of excitement before the party.* 4. the high or low quality of a sound or musical note. *The high pitch of the cat's cries hurt my ears.* {**pihch**}

• **pitch in** (informal) to help others do

something. *Everyone pitched in to clean the house.*

pitch[2] *noun* a thick, black, sticky material made from coal or wood tar. Pitch is used for paving roads and covering roofs to protect them from water. *He bought five gallons of pitch for the new roof.* {**pihch**}

pitch·er[1] *noun* a container with a handle and spout, used to hold and pour milk, juice, or other liquids. {**pih** chər}

pitch·er[2] *noun* the baseball or softball player who throws the ball to the batter. {**pih** chər}

pitch·fork *noun* a long, sharp tool that is shaped like a fork and is used to move hay or straw. {**pihch** fohrk}

pith *noun* the soft central part of certain plant stems and feathers or other animal parts. {**pihth**}

pit·i·ful *adjective* 1. causing pity or sympathy. *The cries of the lost child were pitiful.* 2. causing scorn or angry disgust. *He gave a pitiful excuse for not doing his homework.* {**pih** tee fəl} pitifully, adv., pitifulness, n.

pit·y *noun* (pities) 1. sympathy or sorrow caused by another's pain, bad luck, or suffering. *She has such pity for her sick friend.* 2. that which is a cause for sorrow or regret. *It's a pity that he lost his job.* *verb* (pitied, pitying, pities) to feel or show sympathy for. *I pity those people who do not have a warm place to sleep at night.* {**pih** tee}

piv·ot *noun* a rod or pin upon which another part rotates, swings, or moves back and forth. *Bike wheels turn on pivots.* *verb* (pivoted, pivoting, pivots) 1. to rotate,

A
B
C
D
E
F
G
H
I
J
K
L
M
N
O
P
Q
R
S
T
U
V
W
X
Y
Z

a
b
c
d
e
f
g
h
i
j
k
l
m
n
o
p
q
r
s
t
u
v
w
x
y
z

swing, or move back and forth on or as if on a pivot. *The door pivots on hinges.* / *The dancer pivoted on her right foot.* 2. to cause to rotate, swing, or move back and forth on or as if on a pivot. *The soldier pivoted the gun on the tank toward the target.* {**pih** vət}

pix·el *noun* one of the tiny dots of light that make up an image on a computer or television screen. A pixel is the smallest unit of a video image. The word "pixel" is a shortened form of the phrase "picture element". {**pihk** səl}

pix·y or **pixie** *noun* (pixies) a fairy or elf who is playful or full of mischief. {**pihk** see}

piz·za *noun* an Italian food made of a flat crust covered with tomato sauce, cheese, and often meat or vegetables and then baked. {**peet** sə}

pl. *abbreviation* an abbreviation for **plural**.

place *noun* 1. a certain area of space that is taken up by something. *She cleared a place on the shelf for her books.* 2. a space used for a specific purpose. *Here is a place to work on your art projects.* 3. a duty or job. *It's the photographer's place to take pictures of the wedding.* 4. a particular point in a written work. *I lost my place in the book.* 5. situation or position. *Wouldn't you hate to be in her place?* 6. one's home. *Let's meet at your place tomorrow.* 7. a point in a series. *He finished in third place in the race.* 8. a proper position. *Is there a place for me in this community?* *verb* (placed, placing, places) 1. to put in a certain spot or position. *He placed a spider in my shoe.* 2. to recognize from the past. *I couldn't place him at first, but now I remember him.*

3. to put in a rank or order. *She loved her work, and placed it above everything.* 4. to finish a race or contest in a particular position. *The magician placed second in the talent contest.* {**plays**}

• **take place**
to happen. *The picnic took place at the lake.*

Synonyms
These words share a meaning with ***place***, noun 2:
position, spot, station

plac·id *adjective* calm, smooth, or peaceful. *The lake is so placid that it looks like a sheet of glass.* / *He is a quiet, placid child who loves to read.* {**plă** sihd}

plague *noun* 1. a deadly disease, sudden invasion of harmful insects, or any terrible thing that harms many people. 2. a disease that spread quickly and killed many people in former times. *verb* (plagued, plaguing, plagues) 1. to bother or annoy. *She plagued her older sister with questions.* 2. to cause to suffer from or as if from a plague. *War plagued the country.* {**playg**}

plaid *noun* 1. a cloth with a pattern of stripes of different widths and colors, crossing at right angles. 2. the pattern itself. *adjective* having a pattern like that of a plaid. *The girls wear plaid skirts as a part of their school uniform.* {**plăd**}

plain *adjective* (plainer, plainest) 1. easily seen or heard; clear; visible. *The tower on the hill is in plain view of everyone in town.* 2. clear and understood; obvious. *Our principal is known for his*

plain speaking. / *It was plain to everyone that she was angry.* 3. not complicated or fancy; without anything extra; simple. *The manager wore a plain suit today.* 4. not beautiful; common looking. *He is tall and rather plain.* *adverb* without question or doubt. *The belief that the earth is flat was just plain wrong.* *noun* (sometimes plural) a large, flat area of land without trees. *Many years ago, thousands of buffalo lived on the western plains.* {**playn**} plainly, adv.

Homophone Note Are you looking for the word ***plane***? ***Plain*** and ***plane*** sound alike but have different meanings.

plan *noun* 1. an action one intends to take; aim. *Her plan is to travel in Europe after she graduates.* 2. a way something is to be done that is thought out ahead of time. *If you want the surprise party to be a success, you must have a good plan.* 3. a drawing that shows how something is to be built. *The architect showed the builders her plans for the new planetarium.* *verb* (planned, planning, plans) to develop or design a plan for. *The children planned the best way to ask their mother if they could have a puppy.* {**plăn**}

plane[1] *noun* 1. a flat or level surface. *The floor and ceiling form horizontal planes.* 2. a short form of the word "airplane." 3. a flat surface on which any two points can be joined by a straight line. *Joining three points on a plane will form a triangle.* *adjective* flat or level. *Squares and circles are plane figures.* {**playn**}

plane[2] *noun* a hand tool with a blade, used to make the surface of wood smooth or even.

 Human Body   Human Mind   Everyday Life   History and Culture   Communication

verb (planed, planing, planes) to make smooth with a plane. *The carpenter planed the top of the door so that it would shut.* {playn}

Homophone Note The words *plane* and *plain* (ordinary or easy to understand) sound alike but have different meanings.

plan·et ● *noun* a large body in outer space that circles around the sun or another star. Mercury, Venus, Earth, Mars, Jupiter, Saturn, Uranus, Neptune, and Pluto are all planets in our solar system. {plăn iht}

Word History The word *planet* entered English eight hundred years ago, during the Middle Ages. "Planet" comes from the ancient Greek term *asteres planetai* or "wandering stars." In 1640, astronomers began using the word "planet" in its modern sense of a body that circles a star (the sun).

plan·e·tar·ium *noun* (planetariums or planetaria) 1. a device that projects images of the sun, moon, stars, and planets on a ceiling that is shaped like a dome. 2. a museum, building, or room in which such a device is located. {plăn ə tayr ee əm}

plank *noun* a length of wood thicker than a board. {plăngk}

plank·ton ● *noun* a mixture of very small plants and animals floating in fresh or salt water. Most kinds of plankton are microscopic. Plankton is an important food source for many animals that live in water. {plăngk tən}

plant ● 🔬 ☁ *noun* 1. one of a large group of living things that usually contain green parts used to make their own food. Most plants have leaves, stems, roots and either flowers or cones. Plants use a green pigment called chlorophyll to absorb energy from sunlight. Grasses, trees, vines, vegetables, cactuses, ferns and mosses are plants. 2. a building or group of buildings that have machinery and equipment for making things; factory. *The fifth grade class went on a tour of the automobile plant.* *verb* (planted, planting, plants) 1. to put into the ground to grow. *We planted a vegetable garden behind our house.* 2. to put into the mind. *Don't plant any crazy ideas in his head.* 3. to place firmly or with force. *He planted his feet and would not move.* {plănt}

plan·tain *noun* a fruit similar to the banana, but larger, firmer, and less sweet. Plantains have a lot of starch and are eaten as a cooked vegetable. {plăn tihn *or* plăn tayn}

plan·ta·tion *noun* a large farm or estate used for growing rubber, cotton, or other crops to sell. {plăn tay shən}

plaque *noun* 1. a flat plate or tablet, with writing or decoration on it, that is hung on a wall. 2. a film of bacteria and saliva that forms on teeth. {plăk}

plas·ma 🌐 *noun* the clear, liquid part of blood. Blood cells are suspended in the plasma. {plăz mə} plasm, n., plasmic, adj.

plas·ter *noun* a paste of sand, lime, and water that becomes hard when it dries. Plaster is used to cover walls and ceilings. *verb* (plastered, plas-tering, plasters) 1. to cover with plaster or a substance like plaster. *The workmen plastered the new walls before painting them.* 2. to paste on. *They plastered movie posters on the walls of the room.* {plăs tər}

plas·tic *noun* an artificial substance made from certain kinds of chemicals that can be easily shaped when soft. Plastic is formed into many materials and products. *adjective* 1. made of plastic. *A plastic cup will not break as easily as a glass one.* 2. able to be easily shaped or molded. *The clay had been left out to dry, and was no longer plastic.* 3. not honest or genuine in character; fake. *The computer salesman gave me a plastic smile.* {plăs tihk}

Word History *Plastic* comes from *plastikos*, an ancient Greek word that means "able to be molded." This was its meaning for about three hundred years, until the development of materials called "plastics" in the early 1900s.

plate ● *noun* 1. a flat, round dish from which food is served or eaten; the food on such a dish. *I couldn't finish everything on my plate. / I ordered the special plate for lunch at the diner.* 2. a thin sheet of metal. *The battleship has steel plates to protect it.* 3. a drawing or picture in a book, often in color and covering an entire page. *I cut out several plates from my art book and hung them on the wall.* 4. a flat piece of metal or other material that is engraved and used to make printed copies; the copy or picture made from this. *The printers carefully arranged the plates to make copies of the print.* *verb* (plated, plating, plates) to

A B C D E F G H I J K L M N O P Q R S T U V W X Y Z

 Living World   🔬 Physical World    Natural Environment   Economy   Government and Law

a
b
c
d
e
f
g
h
i
j
k
l
m
n
o
p
q
r
s
t
u
v
w
x
y
z

cover with a thin layer of gold, silver, or some other metal. *The jeweler plated an iron ring with gold so it would look shiny and beautiful.* {**playt**}

pla·teau *noun* (plateaus) a high, level area of land. {**plă toh**}

plate tectonics ❶ *noun* (used with a singular verb) a theory that scientists use to explain the movement of continents, the eruption of volcanoes, and other changes or events in the earth's geology. The theory of plate tectonics says that the earth's crust is made up of separate sections that are like very large plates. These sections move around constantly because they float on melted rock. The movement of these sections of the crust causes earthquakes. {**playt** tehk **to** nihks}

plat·form *noun* 1. a raised, level surface used as a stage. *The school had a special platform built for our talent show.* 2. any raised surface used as a place to stand. *The railroad platform was crowded with people waiting for the next train.* 3. the stated ideas and goals of a political party or person running for public office. *The people who agree with Ms. Smith's platform will vote for her in the election.* {**plăt fohrm**}

plat·i·num *noun* a soft, heavy, silver-white metal that is one of the chemical elements. Platinum is very valuable and is used in making jewelry. It can be combined with

other metals to form alloys. (symbol: Pt) {**plă** tə nəm}

pla·toon *noun* a military unit of two or more squads that is led by a lieutenant and has its own headquarters. {plə **toohn**}

plat·ter *noun* a large shallow dish used for serving food. {**plăt** ər}

plat·y·pus *noun* (platypuses) a mammal with a wide bill, a long, flat tail, and webbed feet for swimming. Platypuses live near streams in Australia. They are one of only two kinds of mammals that lay eggs. They are sometimes called duck-billed platypuses. {**plăt** ih pəs}

play ❓ ❷ *noun* 1. activity that is meant to relax or amuse. *The parents watched their children at play.* 2. a story written to be acted on a stage; drama. *Our class put on a play for the whole school.* 3. a specific action in a game. *He made a daring play in the last quarter of the football game.* *verb* (played, playing, plays) 1. to act the part of in a drama. *She will play Cinderella in the school production.* 2. to be in a game or contest. *Let's play soccer.* 3. to make music with. *She loves playing piano.* 4. to have fun. *The children played all day in the yard.* 5. to behave in a certain way. *Watch out because he doesn't play fair.* {**play**}

play·er *noun* 1. someone who takes part in a game or sport. *My brother is the best player on our baseball team.* 2. someone who plays a musical instrument. *She is the piano player for the choir.* 3. an actor in a drama. *All of the players took a bow at the end of the play.* {**play** ər}

play·ful *adjective* 1. cheerful and having a lot of energy. *The children were in a playful mood.* 2. with gentle humor; not serious. *The tone of her voice was playful when she called him a "bad boy."* {**play** fəl} playfully, adv., playfulness, n.

play·ground ❸ *noun* an outdoor area where children can play. Many playgrounds have equipment such as swings and slides. {**play** grownd}

playing card *noun* one of a set of fifty-two cards that are divided into four suits of spades, clubs, hearts, and diamonds. Playing cards are used in playing different games. {**play** ing **kard**}

play·mate *noun* a child who plays with another child. {**play** mayt}

play·pen *noun* a small pen where a baby or young child can play safely. {**play** pehn}

play·thing *noun* something that is played with; toy. {**play** thing}

play·wright *noun* one who writes plays. {**playr** iyt}

pla·za *noun* 1. a public square or open space in the center of a town. *The elderly couple sat on a bench in the plaza and watched people go by.* 2. a shopping area. *The plaza was filled with shoppers.* {**plah** zə or **plă** zə}

plea ❹ *noun* 1. a serious or sincere call for help; appeal. *Everyone ignored the teacher's plea for silence.* 2. a statement given in a court of law by someone charged with breaking the law. *The man gave a plea of not guilty to the judge.* {**plee**}

 Human Body   Human Mind   Everyday Life   History and Culture   Communication

plead *verb* (pleaded or pled, pleading, pleads) 1. to ask in a sincere or serious way. *The student pleaded with the teacher to open the window.* 2. to answer to a specific charge of having broken a law. *She stood before the judge and pled guilty.* {<u>pleed</u>}

pleas·ant *adjective* 1. nice; pleasing. *It was such a pleasant day that we decided to have a picnic in the park.* 2. having a friendly manner. *The new girl in the neighborhood is so pleasant that everyone wants to be her friend.* {<u>pleh</u> zənt}

please *verb* (pleased, pleasing, pleases) 1. to make content or give pleasure to; make happy. *His thoughtful answers pleased the teacher.* 2. to be willing to; be agreeable to (used with polite requests). *Please take this form to the office.* 3. to wish or like. *She does what she pleases.* {<u>pleez</u>}

pleas·ure *noun* 1. a feeling of happiness, delight, or joy. *Walking the dog gives her pleasure.* 2. something that gives a feeling of joy or happiness. *Seeing friends is always a pleasure.* 3. a desire or preference. *Which of these two flowers is your pleasure?* {<u>pleh</u> zhər}

pleat *noun* a flat, even fold that is sewn or pressed in cloth. *She bought a fancy dress with many pleats.* *verb* (pleated, pleating, pleats) to make pleats in. *Grandmother pleated the curtains for the living room windows.* {<u>pleet</u>}

pled *verb* a past tense and past participle of **plead**. {<u>plehd</u>}

pledge *noun* 1. a serious promise; vow. *She made a pledge to keep her friend's secret.* 2. an amount of money promised as a gift to a group in need. *Many people gave pledges for the families* who were affected by the fire. 3. something given to make sure that an agreement is met. *I gave the store five dollars as a pledge that I would return to buy the coat.* 4. a person allowed into a private club or group but not yet having the full rights of members. *He is a pledge in a group at his college.* *verb* (pledged, pledging, pledges) 1. to hold by a serious promise. *He pledged her to secrecy.* 2. to promise or affirm. *He pledged his aid to the cause.* 3. to give as a pledge. *He pledged his car for a loan from the bank.* 4. to become a new member of a club or group. *He pledged with the Boy Scouts.* 5. to make or give a promise; vow. *She pledged to clean up her room.* {<u>plehj</u>}

plen·ti·ful *adjective* large in amount; more than enough. *The cook had a plentiful supply of fish.* {<u>plehn</u> tih fəl}

plen·ty *noun* a full amount or

supply. *There was plenty of food in the kitchen for a picnic lunch.* {<u>plehn</u> tee}

ple·si·o·saur *noun* an extinct marine reptile with limbs like paddles, a large flattened body, and a short tail. *The plesiosaur lived millions of years ago.* {<u>plee</u> see ə sohr}

pli·ers *plural noun* a tool that has a pair of jaws connected to handles and is used for holding, bending, or cutting things. {<u>pliy</u> ərz}

plod *verb* (plodded, plodding, plods) 1. to move in a slow, tired, or heavy way. *She plodded up the stairs to bed.* 2. to work slowly and steadily on a boring task. *He plodded through all of his homework.* {<u>plŏd</u>}

plop *verb* (plopped, plopping, plops) 1. to drop in a heavy manner or with force. *She plopped the toys on the floor.* 2. to drop or fall in a heavy manner. *The tired boy plopped down on the bench.* *noun* the sound or motion that a heavy object makes when falling into water. *The plop of the rock in the pond startled the frog.* {<u>plŏp</u>}

plot[1] *noun* 1. the story line or order of events in a book, play, or movie. *The plot of the film was long and complicated.* 2. a secret plan that has an illegal or dangerous purpose. *The robbers formed a plot to steal the painting.* *verb* (plotted, plotting, plots) 1. to make secret plans for a bad or illegal purpose. *The men plotted to take over the government.* 2. to make a map or chart of a route being traveled. *We plotted the group's progress as they climbed the mountain.* {<u>plŏt</u>}

plot[2] *noun* a small piece of land. *There is a garden plot behind the house.* {<u>plŏt</u>}

plo·ver *noun* (plover or plovers) a bird with a rounded body, a short tail, and a short bill. Plovers run along the sea shore in short starts and stops, looking for food. The killdeer is one of the many different kinds of plovers. {<u>pluhv</u> ər *or* <u>plohv</u> ər}

plow *noun* 1. a heavy farm tool that has a wide blade and is pulled by a tractor or strong animal. Plows are used for turning over and cutting

A B C D E F G H I J K L M N O **P** Q R S T U V W X Y Z

a b c d e f g h i j k l m n o **p** q r s t u v w x y z

through soil. 2. any similar heavy tools or machines, such as a machine to clear away snow. *verb* (plowed, plowing, plows) 1. to cut or turn over by using a plow. *The farmer plowed his fields.* 2. to cut with a plow or to cut as if with a plow (sometimes followed by "up"). *She plowed up the yard for a new garden. / The ship plowed the waves.* 3. to go ahead in a strong way, but with difficulty, into or through something. *The teacher plowed through the pile of tests that she needed to grade.* {<u>plow</u>}

pluck *verb* (plucked, plucking, plucks) 1. to grab with the fingers and pull off; pick. *She plucked an apple from the tree.* 2. to remove the feathers of. *The farmer plucked the goose before cooking it.* 3. to play on by pulling and letting go. *He plucked the guitar strings as he sang.* 4. to grab and remove quickly. *He plucked a hair from his soup. noun* 1. the act of tugging or grabbing. *With a quick pluck, she untied her shoelace.* 2. strong courage or spirit. *It takes pluck to jump out of an airplane.* {<u>pluhk</u>}

plug *noun* 1. an object made of cork, rubber, or other material used to block an opening. *When he pulled the plug, the water in the bathtub went down the drain.* 2. a device with two or three prongs on the end of an electrical cord. It is put into an outlet to make a connection with an electric circuit. *verb* (plugged, plugging, plugs) 1. to close or stop up with a plug. *They plugged the hole in the boat with a rag.* 2. to work in a slow and steady way (often followed by "away" or "along"). *The writer plugged away at her novel.* {<u>pluhg</u>}

• **plug in** to connect an electronic device to a power source. *Will you please plug in the lamp?*

plum *noun* a type of fruit that has smooth red, purple, green, or yellow skin. It has sweet, juicy flesh and a small, smooth pit. {<u>pluhm</u>}

Homophone Note The words *plum* and *plumb* sound alike but have different meanings. There is a silent 'B' at the end of *plumb*.

plum·age *noun* the feathers of a bird. *The canary has yellow plumage.* {<u>plooh</u> mihj}

plumb *noun* a small weight tied to a line. A plumb is used to measure the depth of water or to test if something is straight up and down. *adjective* straight up and down. *The carpenter checked to make sure the wall was plumb. verb* (plumbed, plumbing, plumbs) 1. to test with a plumb. *He plumbed the lake before he dove into the water.* 2. to examine closely. *The detective plumbed the mystery of the missing jewels.* 3. to fit with pipes and tubes used in plumbing. *They hired someone to plumb the cabin.* {<u>pluhm</u>}

Homophone Note The words *plumb* and *plum* sound alike but have different meanings. To learn why a plum tastes much better than a plumb, look up *plum*.

plumb·er *noun* a person who fits and works on water pipes in buildings. {<u>pluhm</u> ər}

Word History *Plumber* comes from *plumbarius*, a Latin word that means "worker in lead." Water pipes are often made of lead.

plumb·ing 🜨 *noun* 1. the system of pipes in a building that brings water in and removes water and waste. *The old plumbing in that building has many leaks.* 2. the work or business of a plumber. {<u>pluhm</u> ing}

plume *noun* a large, fluffy, colorful feather. *He has a plume in his hat.* {<u>ploohm</u>}

plump *adjective* (plumper, plumpest) full and round in shape; chubby. *The baby was plump and happy. verb* (plumped, plumping, plumps) to make something rounder; fill out (often followed by "up" or "out"). *Could you plump up those cushions?* {<u>pluhmp</u>} plumpness, n.

plun·der *verb* (plundered, plundering, plunders) to steal from by force. *The pirates plundered the island village. noun* stolen goods. *The robbers grabbed their plunder and ran off.* {<u>pluhn</u> dər}

plunge *verb* (plunged, plunging, plunges) 1. to thrust into something soft or liquid. *She plunged her hand into the muck and felt for her ring.* 2. to dive or jump. *The swimmer plunged into the cold pool.* 3. to move suddenly forward or downward. *The temperature plunged. noun* the act of diving. *She took a plunge in the ocean.* {<u>pluhnj</u>}

plu·ral *adjective* having to do with or naming the form of a word that signals more than

Human Body | Human Mind | Everyday Life | History and Culture | Communication one. *The word "kittens" is a plural noun.* noun the form of a word that names or refers to more than one thing. *The plural of "dog" is "dogs."* {**pluh** rəl}

plus *preposition* 1. added to; made greater by adding. *Three plus five equals eight.* 2. in addition to; along with. *She has four birds plus a cat.* *adjective* having to do with or showing addition. *Pay attention to the plus and minus signs in these problems.* noun (pluses or plusses) 1. the math sign that shows addition (+); plus sign. 2. something done or added that gives a positive or extra value. *Being left-handed is a real plus in fencing.* {**pluhs**}

plush *noun* a type of cloth having long, soft, thick fibers. *She has two stuffed bears, one made of corduroy and the other of plush.* *adjective* (plusher, plushest) 1. having a soft, fuzzy surface. *That plush wool coat is warm in the winter.* 2. full of comfort and luxury. *The millionaire lives in a plush house.* {**pluhsh**}

Plu·to *noun* 1. the god of wealth and of the underworld in Greek mythology. 2. the smallest planet in the solar system and the farthest from the sun. {**plooh** toh}

plu·to·ni·um 🔵 *noun* a radioactive chemical element. Plutonium is used to produce nuclear energy. (symbol: Pu) {plooh **toh** nee əm}

ply·wood *noun* a strong board made from thin layers of wood pressed and glued together. {**pliy** wuud}

P.M. *abbreviation* 1. the time between noon and midnight. P.M. is the abbreviation for *post meridiem,* meaning "after noon" in Latin. *We ate lunch*

at one P.M. 2. an abbreviation for **Prime Minister**.

pneu·mo·nia *noun* a serious disease in which the lungs become swollen and painful and fill with liquid. Pneumonia is caused by viruses or bacteria. {nə **mohn** yə *or* nə **moh** nee ə}

P.O. *abbreviation* an abbreviation for **post office**.

pock·et *noun* 1. a small piece of material, open at the top and sewn onto clothing. A pocket forms a bag for keeping small objects. *Ben keeps his house key in his pants pocket.* 2. a space in the earth that contains ore. *The miners found a pocket of silver near the river.* *adjective* small enough in size or amount to carry in a pocket. *My grandfather carries a pocket watch.* *verb* (pocketed, pocketing, pockets) to put into one's pocket. *She pocketed the change.* {**pŏk** iht}
• **in one's pocket** under one's control. *The little girl has her grandfather in her pocket.*

pock·et·book *noun* a small handbag used to carry money and personal things; purse. {**pŏk** iht **buuk**}

pock·et·knife *noun* (pocketknives) a small knife with a blade or blades that fold into the handle. {**pŏk** iht **niyf**}

pod *noun* a long, thin, firm pouch that contains the seeds of a pea or bean plant. {**pŏd**}

po·em *noun* a piece of writing, often with words that rhyme and have a particular rhythm. Poems usually have imaginative language that expresses strong feeling. {**poh** əm}

poet *noun* a person who writes poetry. {**poh** iht}

po·et·ic *adjective* 1. like poetry in style or character. *The president made a poetic speech.* 2. of or having to do with a poet or poetry. *We admire the poetic craft of Maya Angelou.* {poh **eh** tihk}

po·et·ry 💬 🌐 *noun* 1. poems as a group. *We study poetry in English class.* 2. the art of writing poetry, or the work of a poet. *Robert Frost's poetry is known and loved by many.* {**poh** ih tree}

poin·set·ti·a *noun* a plant native to Mexico and Central America that has small yellow flowers surrounded by large red, white, or pink leaves that look like flower petals. {**poin seh** tee ə *or* poin **seh** tə}

point *noun* 1. the sharp end of something. *The pencil point broke when he pressed on it.* 2. a piece of land that stretches out into the water. *We had a picnic on the point.* 3. a position or degree on a scale. *Do you know the freezing point of water?* 4. a particular moment in time. *She was at the point of eating dinner when the phone rang.* 5. the meaning or purpose of a statement or action. *What's the point of that joke?* 6. a special quality. *This horse has many good points.* 7. one of the thirty-two directions as marked on a compass. 8. a punctuation mark (.). It is also called a period. 9. a unit used for keeping score in certain sports. *She scored sixteen points in the basketball game.* *verb* (pointed, pointing,

points) 1. to aim or direct at something. *The captain pointed the sailboat into the wind.* 2. to call attention to by signalling (usually followed by "out"). *The guide pointed out many interesting buildings.* 3. to show direction or location by indicating with one's finger. *I pointed to the path the dog had taken.* {**point**}

• **beside the point**

not important to the main object of interest or discussion. *Your wanting to drive is beside the point, because you are only ten years old.*

• **to the point**

having to do with the main subject of interest or discussion. *The article on volcanoes was well written and to the point.*

point·er *noun* 1. a device, such as a stick or laser, used to show points on a map or other display. 2. a hand or needle on a measuring device such as a watch or compass. 3. a word of advice; suggestion. *She gave me a few pointers on how to get a job.* 4. any of several breeds of dogs. Pointers are dogs that are trained to hunt birds by pointing with the nose and body toward the animal being hunted. {**poin** tər}

point of view 🔵 *noun* a way of thinking about or looking at something. *The coach did not agree with the referee's point of view.* {**point** əv **vyoo**}

poise *noun* 1. the ability to act in a calm and confident manner. *The speaker faced the audience with great poise.* 2. a state or position of balance. *She sat on the trotting horse with perfect poise.* *verb*

(poised, poising, poises) 1. to be in a balanced state. *The boy poised on one leg while he tied his shoe.* 2. to be in position and at rest before action. *The cat poised in the corner, ready to pounce on the mouse.* {**poiz**}

poi·son *noun* 1. a substance that can kill or seriously harm living beings if it is swallowed, breathed, or otherwise taken in. *Parents should keep bug sprays and other poisons where children cannot reach them.* 2. something that destroys or injures pleasure, happiness, or other good things. *Her bad temper was a poison to the family gathering.* *verb* (poisoned, poisoning, poisons) 1. to give poison to; use poison to hurt or kill. *The jealous queen hated Snow White and tried to poison her.* 2. to add poison to. *The queen poisoned an apple and gave it to Snow White.* 3. to harm or pollute; corrupt. *Some people think that watching violent shows on TV poisons children's minds.* {**poi** zən}

poison ivy *noun* 1. a North American plant with shiny leaves in groups of three and white berries. If it touches the skin, poison ivy can cause an itchy rash. 2. the skin rash caused by touching any part of this plant. *She got poison ivy while hiking in the woods.* {**poi** zən **iy** vee}

poi·son·ous 🔵 *adjective* 1. filled with or containing poison. *The scorpion has a poisonous sting.* 2. likely to cause serious harm or death; deadly. *Some berries are poisonous to humans but not to birds.* 3. full of ill will or evil feelings. *She wrote a poisonous letter but decided not to send it.* {**poi** zə nəs}

poke *verb* (poked, poking, pokes) 1. to push or jab with a thin or sharp object. *The farmer poked the goat with a stick to make it walk up the hill.* 2. to cause or make by jabbing or pushing. *He poked a hole in the balloon with a pencil.* 3. to stick out suddenly; thrust. *The rabbit poked its head out of the hole.* 4. to move slowly. *The turtle poked along toward the lake.* 5. to explore or examine something in a manner that is not hurried. *They spent hours poking around the barn looking for old tools.* *noun* a quick pushing motion; jab. *I gave him a poke to wake him up.* {**pohk**}

• **poke fun at**

to tease. *My sister likes to poke fun at me.*

pok·er[1] *noun* a pointed metal rod for stirring up a fire. {**poh** kər}

pok·er[2] *noun* a card game in which players bet on the value of the cards in their hands. {**poh** kər}

Po·land *noun* a country in central Europe. Warsaw is the capital of Poland. {**poh** lənd}

po·lar *adjective* of or having to do with the North Pole or South Pole of the earth. *The polar expedition studied rare life forms.* {**poh** lər}

polar bear *noun* a large bear with thick white fur that lives in arctic areas. {**poh** lər **bayr**}

 Human Body   Human Mind    Everyday Life   History and Culture   Communication

Po·lar·is *noun* a bright star in the constellation Ursa Minor; North Star. {poh **lar** ihs or pə **lar** ihs}

Pole *noun* a person who was born in or is a citizen of Poland. {**pohl**}

pole[1] *noun* a long, round post or rod made of metal, wood, or some other material. *The flag flew from the top of the pole. / Tom went fishing with a bamboo pole.* {**pohl**}

pole[2] *noun* 1. either end of a planet's, moon's, or star's axis. *The earth is coldest at the north and south poles.* 2. either of the opposite ends of a magnet, or either of the charged ends of an electric battery. *Opposite poles on a magnet attract each other. / She attached a wire to each pole of the battery.* {**pohl**}

Homophone Note The words *pole* and *poll* (as in voting) sound alike but have different meanings.

pole·cat *noun* 1. a small mammal with dark fur, a long body, and short legs. Polecats are a kind of weasel. They live in Europe, northern Africa, and North America. Domesticated polecats are called ferrets. In North America, a kind of wild polecat is also called a ferret. 2. another name for a skunk. Skunks are closely related to true polecats and other weasels. {**pohl** kăt}

pole·star *noun* a bright star in the constellation Ursa Minor; Polaris; North Star. {**pohl** star}

pole vault *noun* an athletic event in which a person uses a long pole to leap over a bar set high above the ground. {**pohl** vawlt}

po·lice 🟢 🔵 *noun* 1. a department of a town, city, or state government that has the power to enforce laws, investigate crimes, and keep order. *She called the police when she saw someone break into the bank.* 2. the members of such a department. *The police taught us about bicycle safety.* *verb* (policed, policing, polices) to control, keep safe, or cause to obey the law. *Security guards policed the grounds of the White House.* {pə **lees**}

po·lice·man *noun* (policemen) a man who is a member of a police force. {pə **lees** mən}

police officer *noun* a person who is a member of a police force. {pə **lees** aw fə sər}

po·lice·wom·an *noun* (policewomen) a woman who is a member of a police force. {pə **lees** wuum ən}

pol·i·cy[1] *noun* (policies) a set of rules or a plan that is used as a guide for action. *The library policy lets people borrow books for two weeks at a time.* {**po** lə see}

pol·i·cy[2] *noun* (policies) a written contract that contains the terms of an agreement between an insurance company and the person being insured. {**po** lə see}

po·li·o *noun* a short form of **poliomyelitis**. {**poh** lee oh}

po·li·o·my·e·li·tis *noun* a disease caused by a virus that attacks the spinal cord and damages the nervous system. Poliomyelitis affects mainly children and can lead to paralysis or deformed limbs. Jonas Salk invented a vaccine that prevents poliomyelitis. {**poh** lee oh miy ə **liy** tihs}

pol·ish *verb* (polished, polishing, polishes) 1. to give a shiny surface to. *We polished the furniture before the guests arrived.* 2. to cause to become finished or more perfect. *She is polishing her acting skills in a summer theater.* *noun* 1. a substance used to make something smooth or shiny. *The silver polish removed the black stains from our forks.* 2. a sleek surface. *I can see myself in this polish!* {**pŏl** ihsh} polisher, n.

• **polish off** (informal) to complete or get rid of. *He is polishing off his chores. / She polished off a quart of milk.*

Po·lish *adjective* of or having to do with Poland, or its people or language. *noun* the language of Poland. {**poh** lihsh}

po·lite *adjective* showing good manners or being thoughtful of others; courteous. *She didn't like the food that was served to her, but she ate it to be polite.* {pə **liyt**} politely, adv., politeness, n.

po·lit·i·cal *adjective* having to do with the study or practice of politics, politicians, or government. *He is not interested in political issues and never votes. / The United States has a democratic political system.* {pə **lih** tih kəl} politically, adv.

pol·i·ti·cian *noun* 1. a person involved in party politics. *Politicians are very busy at election time.* 2. a person who holds a government office. *The politician said he would support a bill to clean up the environment.* {po lih tih shən}

pol·i·tics 🔵 *noun* (politics) 1. the work or study of government. *He volunteered as a campaign worker to learn more about politics.* 2. the activities or practice of leaders in government. *Most people who run for president have been in politics for years.* 3. opinions or ideas having to do with how government operates. *She has strong politics when it*

A
B
C
D
E
F
G
H
I
J
K
L
M
N
O
P
Q
R
S
T
U
V
W
X
Y
Z

 Living World  Physical World  Natural Environment Economy  Government and Law

comes to raising taxes. {**pŏl** ih **tihks**}

pol·ka *noun* 1. a lively dance from central Europe that is done by pairs of people. 2. music for this dance. *The band played a polka.* {**pohl** kə *or* **poh** kə}

polka dot *noun* 1. one of many small round dots in a pattern. *She wore a green blouse with yellow polka dots.* 2. a pattern or design made up of small dots. {**poh** kə **dŏt**}

poll *noun* 1. the collection and counting of votes in an election. 2. the number of ballots cast in an election. 3. (plural) the place where people go to vote in an election. 4. a set of questions given to large numbers of people. Polls are used to gather information about what the public thinks. *The food company's poll showed that most people like ketchup better than mustard.* *verb* (polled, polling, polls) 1. to get a certain number of votes in an election. *The mayor polled only a thousand votes.* 2. to question people in order to gather facts or opinions about something. *The school polled the students about what they liked best for lunch.* {**pohl**}

Homophone Note Are you looking for the word *pole*? *Poll* and *pole* sound alike but have different meanings.

pol·len 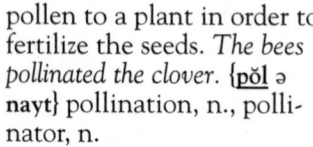 *noun* the fine, yellow powder made by a flowering plant. When pollen is carried by the wind or by an insect to another plant of the same kind, it fertilizes that plant's seeds. {**pŏl** ən}

pol·li·nate *verb* (pollinated, pollinating, pollinates) to move or carry pollen to a plant in order to fertilize the seeds. *The bees pollinated the clover.* {**pŏl** ə **nayt**} pollination, n., pollinator, n.

pol·lute *verb* (polluted, polluting, pollutes) to make dirty or harmful to health by mixing in or adding waste material. *The company polluted the river by dumping oil in the water.* {pə **looht**} polluter, n.

pol·lu·tion *noun* 1. an act or instance of polluting. *The company paid a fine for its pollution of the soil near the factory.* 2. poisons, wastes, or other materials that pollute. *Pollution in the lake is killing the fish.* {pə **looh** shən}

Word History *Pollution* comes from a Latin word that means "to make filthy." The Latin word for mud is *lutum.*

po·lo *noun* a game played on horseback by two teams of three or four members each. The players use mallets with long handles to hit a small wooden ball into the opponent's goal. {**poh** loh}

pol·y·gon *noun* a flat, closed figure with three or more sides bounded by straight lines. *Triangles and rectangles are polygons.* {**pŏl** ee gŏn}

Word History *Polygon* comes from two Greek words. *Poly-* means "many," and *gonia* means "angle."

pol·yp *noun* a small water animal with a soft body and a mouth surrounded by tentacles. Polyps attach themselves to rocks or other underwater objects. Corals, sea anemones, and jellyfish spend part of their lives as polyps and part of their lives floating freely. {**pŏl** ihp}

pome·gran·ate *noun* 1. a red fruit with a tough rind and many seeds. The seeds are in a juicy pulp and can be eaten. 2. the tree that bears this fruit. {**pŏm** grăn iht *or* **pŏm** ih grăn iht}

pomp *noun* a splendid display; magnificence. *The president was greeted with pomp when he visited Russia.* {**pŏmp**}

pon·cho *noun* (ponchos) a cloak that is like a blanket with a hole in the center for a person's head. {**pŏn** choh}

pond *noun* a small body of still water. {**pŏnd**}

pon·der *verb* (pondered, pondering, ponders) to think about something deeply and carefully. *She pondered what to do when she realized her cat was missing.* {**pŏn** dər}

po·ny *noun* (ponies) a kind of small horse. {**poh** nee}

pony express *noun* a system of delivering the mail using riders on horseback. The pony express ran between St. Louis, Missouri and Sacramento, California during 1860 and 1861. {**poh** nee ihk **sprehs**}

po·ny·tail *noun* a hair style in which all the hair is drawn up and tied at the back so that the ends hang free. {**poh** nee **tayl**}

poo·dle *noun* a breed of dog. Poodles range in size from very small to large and have thick, curly hair that can be cut in a fancy way. {**pooh** dəl}

pool *noun* 1. any small area of liquid that has collected on a surface; puddle; pond. A

pool formed in the basement after the heavy rain. 2. a deep place in a stream or river. *The water in the pool is colder than the water near the banks.* 3. a large hole that is filled with water and used for swimming; swimming pool. *verb* (pooled, pooling, pools) to collect into a pool of liquid. *The spilled milk pooled in the center of the table.* {<u>poohl</u>}

poor *adjective* (poorer, poorest) 1. without money, possessions, or other basic needs. *The community center serves free meals to poor people.* 2. wanting; lacking. *The land was so poor that nothing could grow there.* 3. below standard. *She got a poor grade on the test.* 4. having bad fortune or bad luck. *The poor woman's husband died.* *noun* (used with a plural verb) poor people considered as a group (usually used with "the"). *There are many community programs to help the poor.* {<u>poohr</u>}

Homophone Note The words *poor*, *pore*, and *pour* sound alike but have different meanings.

pop[1] ⚪ *verb* (popped, popping, pops) 1. to make a short, sharp sound. *The cork popped as it shot out of the bottle.* 2. to burst open or explode with such a sound. *The balloon popped when the dog put his paw on it.* 3. to burst apart with a short, sharp sound. *He popped the balloon with a pin.* 4. to move or appear quickly or as a surprise. *The neighbors popped in for a visit.* 5. to stretch or open wide in surprise. *His eyes popped when he saw his new bike.* 6. to put quickly. *She popped a piece of gum into her mouth.* 7. to hit very high up in the air. *The*

batter popped the ball into left field. *noun* 1. a short, sharp sound. *We heard the pop of the balloon all the way across the room.* 2. a soft drink; soda pop. {<u>pŏp</u>}

• **pop the question** (informal) to ask to marry. *They got married six months after he popped the question.*

pop[2] ⚪ *adjective* (informal) relating to or performing popular music. The word "pop" is a short form of **popular**. *His first pop record sold over one million copies.* {<u>pŏp</u>}

pop[3] ⚪ *noun* (informal) father. {<u>pŏp</u>}

pop·corn *noun* 1. a kind of corn whose kernels pop open into puffs when heated. 2. the popped kernels of corn that are eaten as a snack food. {<u>pŏp</u> kohrn}

pope *noun* (often capitalized) the head of the Roman Catholic Church. {<u>pohp</u>}

pop·lar *noun* 1. a tall tree that grows rapidly and has wide leaves. Aspen and cottonwood are members of the poplar family. 2. the soft wood of this tree. {<u>pŏp</u> lər}

pop·o·ver *noun* a light, puffed, hollow muffin made with flour, eggs, and milk. {<u>pŏp</u> oh vər}

pop·py *noun* (poppies) a plant with brightly colored flowers that is grown in mild climates. {<u>pŏp</u> ee}

pop·u·lar *adjective* 1. liked or enjoyed by many people. *She is popular at school. / That is a popular book.* 2. having to do with or coming from the common people. *U.S. senators are elected by popular vote.* {<u>pŏp</u> yə lər}

pop·u·lar·i·ty *noun* the condition of being popular. *The popularity of the movie could*

be seen by the long line to buy tickets. {<u>pŏp</u> yə <u>layr</u> ih tee}

pop·u·late *verb* (populated, populating, populates) 1. to live in; inhabit. *Thousands of birds populate the jungle.* 2. to supply with residents or inhabitants. *The king decided to populate the island with prisoners who could build houses and work the soil.* {<u>pŏp</u> yə <u>layt</u>}

pop·u·la·tion ⚪ *noun* 1. the people who live in an area, considered as a group. *The population was told to prepare for a hurricane.* 2. the total number of people living in a country, city, or other area. *New York City has a population of more than eight million.* {<u>pŏp</u> yə <u>lay</u> shən}

pop·u·lous *adjective* having a large population. *Beijing is a populous city.* {<u>pŏp</u> yə ləs}

por·ce·lain *noun* a hard, white, shiny pottery; china. {<u>pohr</u> sə lihn or <u>pohr</u> slihn}

porch *noun* 1. an open platform with a roof that serves as the back or front entrance of a house. 2. a structure, either open or having windows or screens, that is attached to the outside of a house; sun porch; veranda. *We sat on our front porch and watched the sunset.* {<u>pohrch</u>}

por·cu·pine *noun* a small mammal with bristles or spines in its fur. Porcupines are rodents closely related to guinea pigs, but much larger. Some porcupines have quills with barbs that hurt any animal that attacks them. Different kinds of porcupines live in North and South America, Europe, Africa, and Asia. {<u>pohrk</u> yə piyn}

pore[1] *verb* (pored, poring, pores) to study or read carefully. *The student pored over his books before the test.* {<u>pohr</u>}

A B C D E F G H I J K L M N O P Q R S T U V W X Y Z

pore[2] *noun* a tiny opening in the skin of an animal or outer surface of a plant through which air, water, or sweat may pass. {**pohr**}

Homophone Note The words *pore*, *poor*, and *pour* sound alike but have different meanings.

pork *noun* meat from a pig or hog. {**pohrk**}

po·rous *adjective* having many pores. *Sponges have porous bodies.* {**pohr** əs} porousness, n.

por·poise *noun* (porpoise or porpoises) 1. a mammal that lives in the ocean. Porpoises look like large fish, but they breathe air. Some kinds of porpoises have a triangular fin on their back. Porpoises are closely related to dolphins and other whales with teeth. Porpoises have a round head with a blunt snout. 2. in North America, a name sometimes used for dolphins. {**pohr** pəs}

Word History *Porpoise* comes from a French word that means "pig fish."

por·ridge *noun* a food made of cereal grains such as oatmeal that are boiled in water or milk. {**pohr** ihj}

port[1] *noun* 1. a place where ships load and unload, and its nearby town or city. *The ship came into port with a load of fish.* 2. a place where ships can anchor and take shelter; harbor. *The sailors looked for a port where they could wait out the storm.* {**pohrt**}

port[2] *noun* the left side of a ship or airplane when facing forward. {**pohrt**}

port·a·ble *adjective* able to be carried or easily moved. *We brought a portable radio to the picnic.* {**pohr** tə bəl} portability, n.

por·ter *noun* 1. a person whose job is to carry baggage at a train station, airport, or hotel. 2. a person who serves passengers aboard a train. {**pohr** tər}

port·hole *noun* a small opening or window in the side of a ship or airplane. {**pohrt** hohl}

por·ti·co *noun* (porticoes or porticos) a covered walk or porch with a roof that is held up by columns. *That church has a large portico at the main entrance.* {**pohr** tih koh}

por·tion *noun* 1. a part of a whole. *He read a portion of the book.* 2. a serving or helping of food that is enough for one person. *verb* (portioned, portioning, portions) to divide or to give out parts of something. *We portioned the pizza so that everyone got a slice.* {**pohr** shən}

por·trait ◑ *noun* 1. a painting, drawing, photograph or sculpture of a person. *A portrait of Abraham Lincoln hangs on the wall.* 2. a written description of a person or thing. *The author's portrait of village life was fun to read.* {**pohr** triht *or* **pohr** trayt}

por·tray *verb* (portrayed, portraying, portrays) 1. to make a picture of in images or words. *The reporter portrayed the firefighter as a hero.* 2. to play the part of in a play or movie. *He portrays the bad guy in the new film.* {**pohr** **tray**}

Por·tu·gal *noun* a country in southwestern Europe. Lisbon is the capital of Portugal. {**pohr** chə gəl}

Por·tu·guese *adjective* of or having to do with Portugal, or its people or language. *noun* (Portuguese) 1. a person who was born in or is a citizen of Portugal. 2. the main language of Portugal and Brazil. {**pohr** chə **geez** *or* **pohr** chə **gees** *or* **pohr** chə geez *or* **pohr** chə gees, n., **pohr** chə **geez** *or* pohr chə **gees** *or* **pohr** chə geez *or* **pohr** chə gees, adj.}

Portuguese man-of-war *noun* a kind of jellyfish that lives in warm oceans. Each man-of-war is a colony or group of animals that live together. The colony has many long stinging tentacles that can hurt people or other animals. {**pohr** chə geez măn əv **wohr** *or* **pohr** chə gees măn əv **wohr**}

pose ◑ *verb* (posed, posing, poses) 1. to take or hold a position. *We posed for a photograph at the park.* 2. to pretend to be what one is not. *The detective posed as a criminal to solve the case.* 3. to present or offer. *The teacher posed a question to the class.* *noun* 1. a fixed position of the body. *The model held her pose for the photographer.* 2. a way of acting in order to fool people. *That woman may look rich, but it is only a pose.* {**pohz**}

Po·sei·don *noun* the god of the sea in Greek mythology. In Roman mythology, Poseidon is called Neptune. {pə **siy** dən}

po·si·tion *noun* 1. the location of a person or thing. *The control tower asked the pilot to give the position of his airplane.* 2. the proper location of a person or thing. *The librarian was upset because the books on the shelf were out of position.* 3. the way something is placed or arranged. *We learned the right positions for the dance.* 4. a person's rank or status within a group. *The prime minister has a position of authority in Canada.* 5. point of view; opinion. *Sarah's parents took the same position on her going to*

 Human Body   Human Mind    Everyday Life   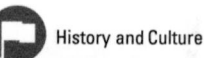 History and Culture   Communication

the party. 6. an appointed job. *My cousin has a new position as chief of police. verb* (positioned, positioning, positions) to put in a particular place or arrange in a particular way. *I positioned the lamp to give me good light for reading.* {pə **zih** shən}

pos·i·tive *adjective* 1. certain; sure. *I am positive that she lives on this street.* 2. saying or meaning yes. *My mother gave a positive answer when we asked for some money.* 3. favorable or helpful. *The coach said positive things about how the team was playing.* 4. having to do with an amount greater than zero. *Ten and eleven are positive numbers. / Jane keeps a positive balance in her bank account. noun* 1. something that is good or helpful. *Having a college education is a big positive in life.* 2. a number greater than zero. *After a week of freezing weather, the temperature climbed back into the positives.* {**pŏz** ih tihv}

pos·se *noun* a group of people gathered by a sheriff to help pursue and bring in a criminal. *A posse searched the woods for the bank robbers.* {**pŏs** ee}

pos·sess *verb* (possessed, possessing, possesses) 1. to own or have. *I now possess a new bicycle. / She possesses good writing skills.* 2. to have as a part of one's character. *That author possesses a great sense of humor.* 3. to control the actions of. *The desire to be class president possessed him.* {pə **zehs**}

pos·ses·sion *noun* 1. the act or condition of having or owning something. *The soccer players struggled for possession of the ball.* 2. something that is owned. *I have many possessions besides my car.* 3. an area ruled by a state or country. *Guam became a possession of the United States after the Spanish-American War.* {pə **zeh** shən}

pos·ses·sive *adjective* 1. having a strong desire to own and keep things. *He is too possessive about his books to let me borrow one.* 2. wanting to control friends or relatives and to stop them from having other friends because of jealousy. *Her possessive boyfriend always asks her where she's been.* 3. showing ownership through grammar. *"His" is a possessive pronoun, and "John's" is a possessive noun.* {pə **zeh** sihv} possessively, adv., possessiveness, n.

pos·si·bil·i·ty *noun* (possibilities) 1. the fact or state of being possible. *The possibility of rain kept us inside all day.* 2. something that might happen. *Sending humans to Mars is a possibility.* {pŏs ə **bih** lih tee}

pos·si·ble *adjective* 1. capable of being, happening, being done, or being used. *It is not possible to draw a round square. / Riding a bike is one possible way to get to school.* 2. capable of being true; somewhat likely. *If he didn't answer, it's possible that he didn't hear you.* {**pŏs** ih bəl}

pos·si·bly *adverb* 1. maybe; perhaps. *She is possibly the tallest girl in the fourth grade.* 2. by any possibility. *Could you possibly give me a ride to the mall?* {**pŏs** ih blee}

pos·sum *noun* a short form of **opossum**. {**pŏs** əm}

• **play possum** to pretend to be asleep or dead; keep very still to avoid being noticed. Opossums do this so predators will ignore them. *We played possum when our mother checked to see what that noise in the attic was.*

post¹ *noun* a pole or stake placed upright in the ground to mark or support something. *The stop sign is attached to a metal post. verb* (posted, posting, posts) 1. to attach to a wall or other surface. *We posted signs for our yard sale on a few telephone poles.* 2. to announce with a sign or poster. *The director will post the cast list tomorrow.* {**pohst**}

post² *noun* 1. a job or duty to which a person is assigned. *She has a post at the State Department.* 2. a military base. 3. a place where someone is assigned or put to work. *The guard did not leave his post until dawn. verb* (posted, posting, posts) to place in or at a post. *The queen posted a guard at the castle gate.* {**pohst**}

post³ *noun* the system for delivering mail, or a mail delivery. *A letter sent by post usually takes only a few days to arrive. / There was a package for me in today's post.* {**pohst**}

post- *prefix* a prefix that means "after" or "later than." *A postscript is a few words or sentences added after the end of a letter. / When mail is postpaid it is paid for after it is mailed.*

post·age *noun* the amount of money charged for sending a letter or package by mail. {**pohs** tihj}

postage stamp *noun* a small, printed label that is put on a piece of mail to show that the postage has been paid. Postage stamps often have pictures on them. {**poh** stihj stămp}

post·al *adjective* having to do with the mail service. *Some postal workers sort letters and packages.* {**pohs** təl}

post·card *noun* a small card that can be mailed without an envelope. Postcards often have a picture on one side

A
B
C
D
E
F
G
H
I
J
K
L
M
N
O
P
Q
R
S
T
U
V
W
X
Y
Z

Living World · Physical World · Natural Environment · Economy · Government and Law

and space for a message, address, and stamp on the other. {pohst kard}

post·er 🌐 *noun* a sign made of paper or cardboard that is hung in a public place for advertising. {pohs tər}

post·man *noun* (postmen) a person who delivers mail. {pohst mən}

post·mark *noun* a mark stamped on mail by the post office. A postmark cancels the stamp on a piece of mail and shows the date and place of mailing. *verb* (postmarked, postmarking, postmarks) to mark with a postmark. *This machine postmarks thousands of letters every day.* {pohst mark}

post·mas·ter *noun* the person in charge of a post office. {pohst măs tər} postmastership, n.

post office 🌐 *noun* 1. a department or branch of a government responsible for handling mail. 2. an office or building where mail is received and sorted and where stamps are sold. {pohst aw fihs}

post·pone *verb* (postponed, postponing, postpones) to put off until later. *The umpire postponed the baseball game because of rain.* {pohst pohn or pohs pohn} postponement, n.

post·script *noun* a note or message added at the end of a letter following the writer's signature. *I added a postscript to my letter that said, "P.S., I miss you."* {pohst skrihpt}

pos·ture *noun* the general position of or manner of holding the body. *Her poor posture makes her seem like she is tired.* {pŏs chər}

post·war *adjective* having to do with the period of time after a war. *Many new houses were built during the postwar years.* {pohst war}

pot 🌐 *noun* 1. a deep round container made of metal, used for cooking and serving food. 2. the contents of such a container. *We ate a pot of stew for dinner.* *verb* (potted, potting, pots) to put into a pot. *The gardener dug up the plants and potted them.* {pŏt}

po·tas·si·um 🌐 *noun* a soft, silver-white metal that is one of the chemical elements. Potassium is used in making fertilizer, soap, glass, and explosives. It occurs in nature only in compounds with other elements. (symbol: K) {pə tă see əm}

po·ta·to *noun* (potatoes) a kind of thick, underground plant stem that is eaten as a vegetable. Potatoes have pale flesh and thin skin that is usually brown, yellow, or red. {pə tay toh}

> **Word History** *Potato* comes from *batata*, the Haitian word for "sweet potato."

po·ten·tial *adjective* able to come into being; possible. *That broken stair is a potential danger.* *noun* a certain skill that may be developed. *He has the potential to be a great dancer.* {pə tehn shəl}

po·tion *noun* a mixture for drinking that is supposed to have special powers. A potion may heal, do magic, or be a poison. *The witch used a potion to make the princess fall asleep.* {poh shən}

Po·to·mac *noun* a river of the eastern United States. It flows from West Virginia along the border of Washington, D.C., and into the Atlantic Ocean. {pə toh mək}

pot·ter *noun* a person who makes pottery. {pŏt ər}

pot·ter·y *noun* (potteries) plates, bowls, pots, and other items made of clay. {pŏt ə ree}

pouch *noun* 1. a sturdy bag or sack of any size that is used to carry things. *Nellie keeps her marbles in a leather pouch.* 2. a natural pocket of skin in some female animals that is used to hold and carry young. *The kangaroo has a pouch.* {powch}

poul·try 🌐 *noun* chickens, turkeys, and other birds that are raised for their meat and eggs. {pohl tree}

pounce *verb* (pounced, pouncing, pounces) to jump or swoop down in order to grab or take something. *The basketball player pounced on the ball.* *noun* the act of pouncing on something. *With one pounce, the cat caught the mouse.* {powns}

> **Word History** *Pounce* comes from *pownse*, an early English word that means "the talon or claw of a bird of prey."

pound[1] *verb* (pounded, pounding, pounds) 1. to strike over and over with heavy blows. *The carpenter pounded the nails with a hammer.* 2. to put into someone's mind by repeating over and over. *He won't remember to do it unless you pound it into him.* 3. to throb or beat. *My heart was pounding after the race.* *noun* the act of pounding. *Barry gave the tent stake a good pound with a rock.* {pownd}

pound[2] *noun* 1. a unit of weight equal to 16 ounces or 453.592 grams. (abbrevi-

 Human Body    Human Mind    Everyday Life   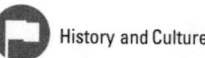 History and Culture   Communication

ated: lb.) 2. the main unit of money of the United

In Britain, dog catchers are paid ten **pounds** for every **pound** of stray animal returned to the **pound**.

Kingdom and Ireland. {**pownd**}

pound³ *noun* a shelter for keeping stray animals. {**pownd**}

pour *verb* (poured, pouring, pours) 1. to cause to flow in a steady stream. *Calvin poured milk into his cereal bowl.* 2. to rain hard. {**pohr**}

Homophone Note The words *pour*, *poor*, and *pore* sound alike but have different meanings.

pout *verb* (pouted, pouting, pouts) to show unhappy feelings with an expression of the face. When children pout, they often push out their lips. *Madeline pouted when she couldn't have more candy.* {**powt**}

pov·er·ty *noun* the condition of being poor; a lack of money. *Too many people live in poverty.* {**pŏv** ər tee}

pow *interjection* a word used to suggest the loud sound of a shot, blow, or explosion. *Pow! the thunder cracked.* *noun* the loud sound of a

shot, blow, or explosion. *Lucas jumped at the pow of a firecracker.* {**pow**}

POW *abbreviation* a person who has been taken prisoner by the enemy during a war. POW is an abbreviation for "prisoner of war."

pow·der *noun* 1. a mass of fine, loose grains that are made when a solid material has been ground or crushed. *This foot powder is made of crushed talc.* 2. something that is produced in the form of very fine grains. *Add a teaspoon of baking powder to the batter.* *verb* (powdered, powdering, powders) 1. to dust or sprinkle with powder. *She powdered her face.* 2. to crush or grind into a powder. *We powdered the dog's pill and mixed it into his food.* {**pow** dər}

pow·er 🌐 💬 *noun* 1. the ability to act, cause, or function. *That movie has the power to make people cry.* 2. the ability to control others. *The peasants feared the king's power.* 3. a person, group, or nation that has control or influence over others. *The United States is one of the world's great powers.* 4. the right of a government or other organization to do something. *The government has the power to tax its citizens.* 5. energy that can do work. *Electric power changed the way people live.* 6. the number of times another number is multiplied by itself. Three to the fourth power is equal to 3 x 3 x 3 x 3, or 81. *verb* (powered, powering, powers) to supply with energy or force. *Gasoline powers most car engines.* {**pow** ər}

Word History *Power* comes from an early French word that means "to be able."

pow·er·ful *adjective* having or able to use power or force. *The race car has a powerful engine. / The principal is in a powerful position.* {**pow** ər fəl} powerfully, adv., powerfulness, n.

pp. *abbreviation* an abbreviation for **pages**.

PR *abbreviation* an abbreviation for **Puerto Rico**.

prac·ti·cal *adjective* 1. having to do with real life and experience. *We did not expect to get any practical information from a book about wizards.* 2. able to be used or put into practice; useful. *They needed a practical solution to the problem of how to get the kite out of the tree.* 3. given to useful activities. *The company wants to hire a person who is both imaginative and practical.* {**prăk** tih kəl} practicality, n.

practical joke *noun* a trick or prank played on someone. *Denise's favorite practical joke was to put salt in her brother's glass of milk.* {**prăk** tih kəl **johk**}

prac·ti·cal·ly *adverb* almost; nearly. *The wind practically knocked me over.* {**prăk** tih klee}

prac·tice *noun* 1. the doing of some activity many times to become skilled at it. *Leila spends a few hours every day on violin practice.* 2. an activity that is the usual way of doing something; rule; habit. *It is our family's practice to go to church on Sunday mornings.* 3. the act or process of doing a thing. *It seemed like a good idea to shampoo the cat, but in prac-*

a
b
c
d
e
f
g
h
i
j
k
l
m
n
o
p
q
r
s
t
u
v
w
x
y
z

tice it was a failure. 4. the work of an occupation or profession. *Three of my cousins are in the practice of medicine.* *verb* (practiced, practicing, practices) 1. to do as a habit. *The spry woman practices yoga.* 2. to do many times in order to become skilled. *I practiced the poem until I could recite it from memory.* 3. to work at an occupation. *She practices criminal law.* {**prăk** tihs} practicer, n.

Synonyms
These words share a meaning with *practice*, noun 1:
exercise, drill, repetition

prac·tise *noun* a spelling of **practice** used in Canada and Britain. See **practice.** {**prăk** tihs}

Prague *noun* the capital city of the Czech Republic. {**prahg**}

prai·rie *noun* a large area of land covered with grass. {**prayr** ee}

prairie dog *noun* a small rodent with light brown fur. Prairie dogs make burrows and live in large colonies called "towns." Several kinds of prairie dogs live in Mexico and the United States. Prairie dogs are not related to true dogs, but have a cry that sounds like a dog's bark. {**prayr** ee dawg}

prairie schooner *noun* a large covered wagon used by American pioneers to cross the prairies. {**prayr** ee skooh nər}

praise *noun* words that show admiration or respect. *The dog received praise for doing a trick.* *verb* (praised, praising, praises) 1. to speak well of.

The coach praised the players for their hard work. 2. to honor with words or song. *The congregation praised God.* {**prayz**}

prance *verb* (pranced, prancing, prances) 1. to raise the front legs and spring forward with the rear legs. *The pony pranced around the ring at the circus.* 2. to move or walk in a lively, happy manner. *Mike pranced around the soccer field after scoring a goal.* {**prăns**}

prank *noun* a teasing trick; stunt. *Sam put a frog in his brother's lunch box as a prank.* {**prăngk**}

pray *verb* (prayed, praying, prays) 1. to thank, ask, or speak to God or some other spiritual being. *Devout Muslims pray five times a day.* 2. to ask for something in a serious or sincere manner. *"I pray you will treat this rare book with care," said the librarian.* {**pray**}

Homophone Note Are you looking for the word *prey* (as in hunting)? *Pray* and *prey* sound alike but have different meanings.

prayer 🔵 *noun* 1. the act of asking God or another spiritual being to use his or her power. *The parents made a prayer for their baby's recovery.* 2. a form of group worship that praises or gives thanks to God or some other holy thing. *The people in church recited prayers and sang hymns.* 3. a serious request. *Peter said a prayer for a blizzard so school would be cancelled.* {**prayr**}

praying mantis
noun a long, slender insect that eats other insects and can turn its head from side to

side. A praying mantis has a large, bright green body and holds its strong front legs up in a way that looks like hands folded in prayer. {**pray** ing **măn** tihs}

pre- *prefix* 1. a prefix that means "before." *A premature baby is a baby that is born before he or she is mature.* 2. a prefix that means "in front of." *A prefix is attached to the beginning of a word.*

preach *verb* (preached, preaching, preaches) 1. to give a talk on religion that is used to teach; give a sermon. *Our minister preaches on Sunday mornings and evenings.* 2. to give advice to the public; tell or encourage others to accept. *She preached tolerance to the assembly.* {**preech**}

preach·er *noun* a person who gives talks on religion, such as a minister or priest. *The preacher gave a sermon about honesty.* {**pree** chər}

pre·cau·tion *noun* something done beforehand to avoid or prevent a danger or harm; something done to make sure everything goes well. *The trapeze artist always used a net as a precaution.* {prə **kaw** shən}

pre·cede *verb* (preceded, preceding, precedes) to come before in time. *The movie was preceded by several ads for other movies.* {prə **seed**}

prec·e·dent *noun* an action that may serve as an example for future acts of the same nature. *Amelia Earhart's flight across the Atlantic Ocean set a precedent for other female pilots.* {**prehs** ə dənt}

pre·cinct *noun* an area in a town or city that forms a separate district for voting or that is looked after by one police unit. {**pree** singkt}

 Human Body   Human Mind   Everyday Life   History and Culture  Communication

pre·cious *adjective* 1. of great worth or value. *Gold is a precious metal.* 2. loved or dear to a person. *Miss Marker's pet poodle is very precious to her.* {**preh** shəs} preciously, adv., preciousness, n.

pre·cip·i·tate *verb* (precipitated, precipitating, precipitates) 1. to make something happen sooner than planned or wanted. *The brothers' fighting precipitated their going to bed early.* 2. to change from water vapor and fall to the ground as rain, snow, or sleet. {prə **sih** pə **tayt**} precipitately, adv.

pre·cip·i·ta·tion ❂ *noun* 1. the act of water falling in the form of rain, snow, sleet, or hail. *The weather report predicted precipitation today.* 2. snow, sleet, rain, or hail that falls to the surface of the earth, or the amount of it that falls in a given period of time. *We got two inches of precipitation in the last hour.* {prə **sih** pə **tay** shən}

pre·cise *adjective* 1. clearly said or communicated. *Thanks to the precise directions, we were able to find our way easily.* 2. no more or no less; exact. *I will need a precise count of the people in the room.* {prih **siys**} precisely, adv

pre·ci·sion *noun* 1. the state of being accurate or exact. *The student's precision on his math test earned him a good grade. / Candy thermometers must have a high degree of precision.* 2. physical exactness. {prih **sih** zhən}

pre·co·cious *adjective* having the skills or knowledge of a much older person. *My little sister is a precocious girl who knows more about math than some of my college friends.* {prih **koh** shəs}

pred·a·tor ❶ *noun* an animal that hunts other animals for food. {**preh** də tər}

pred·e·ces·sor *noun* a person who holds a position or job before another person. *At work, my predecessor trained me before he left the company.* {**pree** dih **seh** sər *or* **preh** dih **seh** sər}

pre·dic·a·ment *noun* a difficult or dangerous situation with a solution that may be hard to find. *Cornered by an angry bear, the campers found themselves in a predicament.* {prə **dih** kə mənt}

pred·i·cate *noun* the part of a sentence that tells what the subject does, or what is done to the subject. It is made of the verb and all the words that describe the verb or that the verb affects. {**preh** də kiht}

pre·dict *verb* (predicted, predicting, predicts) to tell in advance that something will happen. *The general predicted an easy victory.* {prə **dihkt**} predictability, n., predictable, adj., predictably, adv.

pre·dic·tion *noun* 1. a statement that something might happen or is expected to happen. *Jean's prediction was that the coin would land heads up.* 2. an event that is told about before it happens. *The wizard made a prediction that the treasure would be found in seven years.* {prə **dihk** shən}

pref·ace *noun* 1. an introduction to a book or other written material that gives information about the author or work. 2. a short introduction to a speech. *verb* (prefaced, prefacing, prefaces) to begin a book or speech with a short introduction. *The professor prefaced her speech with a quote from Thomas Jefferson.* {**prehf** ihs}

pre·fer *verb* (preferred, preferring, prefers) to choose above all others as the best liked or most wanted. *He prefers carrots to all other vegetables.* {prə **fuhr**}

pref·er·ence *noun* 1. a person or thing that is liked better. *Dan has a preference for action movies.* 2. something good or helpful given to one over others. *She was given preference because she had waited longer.* 3. the act of preferring or the state of being preferred. *He played basketball in preference to anything else.* {**preh** fə rəns *or* **prehf** rəns}

pre·fix ❷ *noun* a word part with its own meaning that is added to the beginning of a word to make a new word that has a different meaning. "Re-" in "reform" is a prefix. {**pree** fihks}

preg·nant *adjective* having one or more young growing within the body of a woman or other female mammal. {**prehg** nənt}

pre·his·tor·ic ❸ *adjective* belonging to a period in a time before written history. *Dinosaurs were prehistoric beasts that roamed the earth.* {**pree** hih **stohr** ihk} prehistorical, adj.

prej·u·dice ❹ *noun* 1. an opinion that is formed without knowing or understanding all the facts. *She has a prejudice against eating seafood.* 2. hatred or unfair treatment toward a person or group without cause or

A
B
C
D
E
F
G
H
I
J
K
L
M
N
O
P
Q
R
S
T
U
V
W
X
Y
Z

reason. Prejudice is often directed toward people of a certain race or religion. *There are laws that protect people against acts of prejudice.* *verb* (prejudiced, prejudicing, prejudices) to change the way a person feels about someone or something. *Getting bitten when she was young prejudiced Cathy against all dogs.* {**preh** jə dihs}

pre·lim·i·nar·y *adjective* coming before, so as to prepare for something else. *A preliminary exam will show you what you need to study for the final exam.* {prə **lih** mə **nayr** ee}

pre·ma·ture *adjective* done, happening, or born before the expected time; too soon. *The premature announcement of the team's win was embarrassing when the videotape showed that they lost. / The premature baby weighed only four pounds.* {**pree** mə **chuhr** or **pree** mə **toohr**} prematurely, adv., prematureness, n., prematurity, n.

pre·mier *noun* the prime minister of a government. *The president honored the visiting premier with a special banquet.* *adjective* first in importance; leading. *That chocolate company claims to make the premier candy in the world.* {prə **meer** or prə **myeer**, n., prə **meer** or prə **myeer**, adj.}

pre·mise *noun* 1. a statement that forms the basis of an argument and that is usually accepted. *The premise of the U.S. Constitution is that all men are created equal.* 2. (plural) a piece of land and the buildings on it. *The store owner told the bullies to get off his premises, or he would call the police.* {**prehm** ihs}

prep·a·ra·tion *noun* 1. the act of getting something ready. *Giving a large party requires a*

lot of preparation 2. a state of being ready. *Gifts rested under the tree in preparation for Christmas.* 3. a mixture used as a medicine. *I rubbed the preparation on my gums to make them stop hurting.* {prehp ə **ray** shən}

pre·pare *verb* (prepared, preparing, prepares) 1. to make ready. *He prepared his house for guests by cleaning.* 2. to make or put together from different parts. *The chef cut up the meat and vegetables that he needed to prepare the stew.* 3. to make things or oneself ready. *With a hurricane approaching, the town prepared for the worst.* {prih **payr**} preparer, n.

pre·po·si·tion 🔊 *noun* a word that shows a connection or relation between a noun or pronoun and some other word. In the sentence, "We went to the market and talked about the weather," "to" and "about" are prepositions. {prehp ə **zih** shən} prepositional, adj.

pre·scribe *verb* (prescribed, prescribing, prescribes) to order or suggest as a medicine. *The doctor prescribed a cream for his rash.* {prih **skriyb**} prescriber, n.

pre·scrip·tion *noun* 1. an order written by a doctor for medicine to treat a patient. *Nadia's doctor gave her a prescription for cough medicine.* 2. the act of prescribing or the thing prescribed. *She picked up her prescription at the pharmacy.* {prih **skrihp** shən}

pres·ence *noun* 1. the state or condition of being in a place at a certain time. *The snake made its presence known by rattling its tail.* 2. the condition of being near in time and space. *The police officers talked with the suspect in the*

presence of his lawyer. {**preh** zəns}

Homophone Note The words ***presence*** and ***presents*** sound alike but have different meanings. "Presents" is the plural form of ***present*** (a gift).

pres·ent[1] *adjective* 1. existing at this time; current. *The present head of the company has been in charge for two years.* 2. being with others or another in a specific place. *All of the students were present in class today.* 3. having to do with the tense of a verb that describes action or existence now. "Is," "possess," and "throws" are examples of verbs in the present tense. *noun* the period of time between the past and future; present time. *The troubles you have in the present will soon be over.* {**preh** zənt}

• **at present**
right now. *We have no work for you at present.*

• **for the present**
at least at this moment, though perhaps not afterwards. *We will leave things as they are for the present.*

pres·ent[2] *verb* (presented, presenting, presents) 1. to give or provide with a gift or award. *The judges presented a blue ribbon to the winner.* 2. to show. *The theater presented a play by Shaw. / He presented his driver's license to the police officer.* 3. to introduce in a formal way. *May I present Mr. Bascomb?* 4. to show up at a place. *You must present yourself at the office on Tuesday for an inter-*

 Human Body   Human Mind   Everyday Life  History and Culture  Communication

view. {prih **zehnt**}

Homophone Note Are you looking for the word *presence*? The plural of *present* ("presents") sounds like *presence*.

pres·en·ta·tion *noun* the act of presenting. *I watched the presentation of movie awards on television.* / *There was a great presentation on wolves at school.* {**preh** zən **tay** shən}

pres·ent·ly *adverb* 1. in a little while; very soon. *Be patient, for we will eat presently.* 2. at the present time. *The doctor is presently with another person and cannot see you now.* {**preh** zənt lee}

present participle *noun* a form of a verb ending in "-ing" that either shows action going on, that an action is taking place, or that action will happen in the future. {**preh** zənt **par** tə sih pəl}

pre·sent tense *noun* a form of a verb that shows that something is happening now or that a condition exists in the present time. In the sentence, "The sky is blue," "is" is in the present tense.

pre·ser·va·tion *noun* protection from loss or damage; the act of preserving. *The preservation of water is necessary for all life to continue.* {**preh** zər **vay** shuhn}

pre·serv·a·tive *noun* a substance used to keep foods from going bad or spoiling. *Salt can be used as a preservative on meat.* {prih **zuhr** və tihv}

pre·serve *verb* (preserved, preserving, preserves) 1. to protect from being hurt or harmed. *The man preserved the car by always parking it in a garage.* 2. to keep safe from loss. *The court will preserve the right to freedom of speech.* 3. to

prepare for future use. *We preserved the ham by salting and smoking it.* *noun* 1. (usually plural) fruit or vegetables that are cooked with sugar to last a long time. *Joan spread strawberry preserves on her toast.* 2. an area of land or water set aside for the protection of fish and animals. *Kenya is known for its wildlife preserves.* {prih **zuhrv**} preserver, n.

pre·side *verb* (presided, presiding, presides) to act as the one in charge. *Ms. Hawkes presides over all the staff meetings.* {prih **ziyd**}

pres·i·den·cy *noun* (presidencies) the office, length of service, and jobs of a president. *Millard Fillmore's presidency lasted from 1850 to 1853.* {**prehz** ih dən see}

pres·i·dent  *noun* 1. an officer elected to lead a group or organization. *I worked hard as president of our book club.* 2. (often capitalized) the head of a republican form of government, especially that of the United States. *George W. Bush became president in January, 2001.* {**prehz** ih dənt}

pres·i·dent-e·lect *noun* a person who has been elected president but has not yet taken office. {**prehz** ih dənt ih **lehkt**}

press *verb* (pressed, pressing, presses) 1. to bear down. *I pressed hard on the suitcase while trying to fasten it.* 2. to make flat or smooth. *He pressed his shirts with an iron.* 3. to hold or hug closely. *The woman pressed her baby close to shield him from the rain.* 4. to keep asking in such a way as to make uncomfortable. *My father is pressing me to make a decision.* 5. to move forward; continue to move ahead (often followed by "on" or "forward"). *The hikers*

pressed on in spite of the heat. *noun* 1. newspapers and magazines and the people who work for them. *The press followed the movie star wherever he went.* 2. the act of putting weight or pressure on something. *With the press of a button, you can lock all four doors of the car.* 3. any of certain machines that act by pressing. *The invention of the printing press changed human history.* / *The farmer loaded a bushel of apples into the cider press.* {**prehs**}

pres·sure *noun* 1. a steady force upon a surface. *Put pressure on a cut to make it stop bleeding.* 2. a strong influence or burden on the mind or emotions. *I feel a lot of pressure to do well in school.* *verb* (pressured, pressuring, pressures) to force into an action by strong influence or urging. *My friend pressured me to try out for the soccer team.* {**preh** shər}

pres·tige *noun* high respect from others because of work well done. *Albert Einstein's work brought him fame and prestige.* {**preh steej** or **preh steezh**}

pres·to *adverb* quickly or suddenly. *Get this job done presto.* *interjection* used by magicians to express wonder or amazement. *Presto! The rabbit disappeared!* {**prehs** toh}

pre·sume *verb* (presumed, presuming, presumes) 1. to take for granted. *I presumed you would wait for me even if I was late.* 2. to act without power or invitation. *He presumed his job was to seat guests at the luncheon.* 3. to take something as fact without anything showing that it really is true. *I presume you're the one who ate the last cookie.* {prih zoohm} presumedly, adv., presumption, n.

pre·tend *verb* (pretended, pretending, pretends) 1. to claim or act in a false way in order to trick. *The bird pretended to be hurt to lure the fox away from the nest.* 2. to imagine or make believe. *Let's pretend that we're exploring the moon.* {prih **tehnd**}

pret·ty ❓ *adjective* (prettier, prettiest) pleasing or attractive to the eyes or ears. *What a pretty dress! / That's a pretty song.* *adverb* 1. somewhat or fairly. *I am finding school pretty hard this year.* 2. very; quite. *It snowed pretty hard.* {**prih** tee}

pret·zel *noun* a thin, crisp food that is like a cracker. *A pretzel is shaped into a knot or stick, and then baked and salted.* {**preht** səl}

pre·vent *verb* (prevented, preventing, prevents) to keep or stop from happening. *The iron gate prevented cars from entering.* {prih **vehnt**}

pre·ven·tive *adjective* 1. made to get in the way of or to block something. *Locking the doors of one's car is a preventive action against thieves.* 2. protecting against disease or illness. *Eating healthy foods is part of preventive medicine.* *noun* a medicine that keeps disease or sickness away. *A flu shot is given as a preventive.* {prih **vehn** tihv}

pre·view *noun* a showing of a film, play, or work of art for a chosen audience before the public sees it. *Several famous people went to the preview of the great director's new movie.* *verb* (previewed, previewing, previews) to show or see ahead of time. *The teacher previewed the film before showing it to the class.* {**pree** vyoo}

pre·vi·ous *adjective* 1. coming just before another. *His previous car was pink.* 2. earlier. *In previous years, this information was not available on the Internet.* {**pree** vee əs} previously, adv.

prey ❶ 🌐 *noun* 1. an animal being hunted, caught, and eaten by another animal. *Rabbits are a favorite prey of coyotes.* 2. a person that becomes a victim. *He was the prey of a scheme to steal his money.* 3. the habit or typical action of preying. *Eagles are birds of prey.* *verb* (preyed, preying, preys) 1. to hunt, catch, and eat another animal. *Some bats prey on insects.* 2. to cheat or harm someone; to take advantage of another person. *The bully preyed on smaller classmates.* 3. to bother or distress. *Guilt preyed on her mind.* {**pray**}

Homophone Note The words **prey** and **pray** (to speak to God) sound alike but have different meanings.

price *noun* 1. the sum of money needed to buy an item or service. *The price of that shirt is too high.* 2. the cost of a particular result or gain. *The price of victory was many lives lost.* *verb* (priced, pricing, prices) 1. to mark with a price. *The store clerk priced the goods with stickers.* 2. to set a price for. *We thought the dealer had priced the car too high.* 3. to find out the price of. *Michele priced the books before buying them.* {**priys**} pricer, n.

price·less *adjective* having a worth greater than any price or amount of money. *That ancient statue is priceless. / The love of one's family is priceless.* {**priys** lihs} pricelessness, n.

prick *noun* a small mark or hole made by something with a sharp or pointed end. *I have a prick in my finger where the nurse took some blood.* *verb* (pricked, pricking, pricks) to mark, put a hole in, or cause pain with a small, sharp object. *Prick the potato before baking it. / I pricked my finger on the thorn of a rose.* {**prihk**}

prick·ly *adjective* (pricklier, prickliest) 1. full of small, sharp points. *Don't touch the prickly cactus.* 2. stinging. *I had a prickly feeling on my skin after brushing against the nettles.* {**prihk** lee}

prickly pear *noun* a cactus that is known for its bright flowers. *Some kinds of prickly pear bear a fruit that can be eaten.* {**prihk** lee **payr**}

pride *noun* 1. an inborn feeling of self-worth. *Despite being homeless, she carried herself with pride.* 2. a sense of personal value that comes from what one has or can do. *He takes pride in his work.* 3. a sense of one's own value that is too high. *Roger's pride made him hard to like.* *verb* (prided, priding, prides) to have a deep feeling of pride (usually followed by "on" or "upon"). *I pride myself on being a good listener.* {**priyd**} prideful, adj., pridefully, adv.
  • **pride and joy** something or someone highly valued or loved. *The grandchildren are her pride and joy.*

priest *noun* a person who is authorized by a church to

 Human Body   Human Mind   Everyday Life   History and Culture   Communication

lead prayers and religious services. *A priest performed their marriage ceremony.* {**preest**}

prim *adjective* (primmer, primmest) correct and proper beyond what is needed. *Janet felt uncomfortable in her prim clothes at the picnic.* {**prihm**}

pri·ma·ry *adjective* 1. main; chief. *He played a primary role in our success. / Beethoven's pieces for piano helped make the piano the primary keyboard instrument.* 2. first in time or order. *The caterpillar is the primary growth stage of the butterfly.* *noun* (primaries) an early election in the United States, where members of each political party vote for a candidate to run for office in the general election. {**priy** mayr ee}

pri·mar·y col·or *noun* any one of the three basic colors of the spectrum from which all other colors can be made by blending. In paint, they are red, yellow, and blue. {**priy** mər ee **kuhl** ohr}

primary school *noun* a school that has the first three or four grades and sometimes kindergarten. {**priy** mayr ee skoohl}

pri·mate ❶ *noun* any animal in the category of mammals that includes humans, monkeys, apes, and some smaller, simpler animals. Most primates have large brains and flexible hands. {**priy** mayt}

prime *adjective* 1. first in importance. *Sugar was the prime export of Hawaii for many years.* 2. first in choice or value. *We had prime seats in the front row.* 3. not possible to be divided evenly by any whole number except itself and one. *Seven is a prime number.* *noun* the time in a life or career when a person is at his or her best. *Many athletes are past their prime when they reach the age of thirty.* *verb* (primed, priming, primes) to make ready or prepare. *He primed the pump by forcing the air out of it.* {**priym**}

prime minister *noun* the chief minister and head of a government with a parliament. *Both England and Canada have a prime minister.* {**priym mihn** ih stər}

prime number *noun* a number that can be evenly divided only by itself or by one. Two and eleven are prime numbers. {**priym nuhm** bər}

prim·i·tive *adjective* 1. having to do with an early stage or a condition that is not developed. *Primitive humans learned how to use fire. / I have only a primitive understanding of how computers work.* 2. simple or not developed. *The holy man lived in a primitive house made of mud and grass.* *noun* a human being of a primitive society. {**prihm** ih tihv} primitively, adv., primitiveness, n.

Word History *Primitive* comes from a Latin word that means "first or earliest of its kind."

prim·rose *noun* a plant that grows tube-shaped flowers in many colors. Primroses have large leaves at the base of the flower stalk. {**prihm** rohz}

prince *noun* the son or grandson of a king or queen. {**prihns**}

Prince Edward Island *noun* a province of Canada on an island off the eastern coast. Its capital is Charlottetown. {**prihns ehd** wərd **iy** lənd}

Word History *Prince Edward Island* was named in honor of Prince Edward, the father of Queen Victoria of England. In 1604, French explorers named it *Île de Saint Jean* (Isle of Saint John). The British called it St. John's Island until they changed its name to honor Prince Edward in 1799.

prin·cess *noun* 1. a daughter or granddaughter of a king or queen. 2. the wife of a prince. {**prihn** sehs or **prihn** sihs}

prin·ci·pal *adjective* greatest or first in importance. *The principal job of the police is to keep the peace.* *noun* 1. the person who is head of a school. *No student wants to be sent to the principal's office.* 2. the main person who leads or plays an important part in an activity. *At the end of the meeting, the principals shook hands to show they had reached an agreement.* {**prihn** sə pəl}

Homophone Note *Principal* and *principle* sound alike but have different meanings.

prin·ci·ple *noun* 1. a basic law or truth on which action or behavior is based. *Our country's laws are based on the principles of liberty and justice.* 2. (plural) a set of personal rules for behavior. *He is a man of high principles.* {**prihn** sih pəl}

Homophone Note The words *principle* and *principal* sound alike but have different meanings.

print ❷ *verb* (printed, printing, prints) 1. to copy by transferring ink to a surface using mechanical pressure. *Those stamps are so valuable because only few of them were ever printed.* 2. to write in letters

A B C D E F G H I J K L M N O **P** Q R S T U V W X Y Z

like those of printed type. *The girl printed her name carefully at the bottom of her drawing.* 3. to publish. *All of the newspapers in the state printed the story about the terrible fire.* 4. to transfer a photograph to paper by means of light sent through a negative image. *The photography lab printed copies of the wedding pictures.* noun 1. printed letters. *The print was so small it was hard to read.* 2. a shape marked or pressed onto a surface. *Her feet left prints in the wet sand.* 3. a photograph copied on paper. *They made prints of the family photo for all the grandparents.* 4. a cloth or article of clothing covered with a pattern, or the pattern itself. *My favorite dress has a print of flowers and leaves on it.* {**prihnt**}

• **print out**
to produce a copy on paper, by means of a computer printer. *Dave typed his report and then printed it out.*

print·er *noun* 1. a person whose job or trade is printing. 2. a machine that makes printed copies from a computer. *Please load more paper into the printer.* {**prihn** tər}

print·ing *noun* 1. the business or art of making printed materials. 2. writing in which the characters are like printed type. {**prihn** ting}

printing press *noun* a machine for printing letters or pictures on paper or other material with ink. {**prihn** ting prehs}

print·out *noun* a printed paper copy from a computer. *The teacher asked for a printout of my essay.* {**prihnt** owt or **prihnt** owt}

prism *noun* 1. a solid glass or crystal object that light can pass through. It has three sides that are rectangles and two ends shaped like triangles. A prism splits a ray of light into the colors of the rainbow. 2. a solid figure that has parallel bases that are the same size and shape and faces that are parallelograms. *The shape of most boxes is a prism.* {**prihz** əm}

pris·on ● *noun* a building for holding and punishing people who have broken the law. *People who sell drugs will be sent to prison.* {**prih** zən}

pris·on·er *noun* 1. a person who is held in a jail or prison while on trial or after being sentenced for a crime. 2. a person who is controlled by someone or something. *Tim is a prisoner to his own fears.* {**prih** zə nər or **prihz** nər}

pri·va·cy *noun* the condition of being alone or away from the view of other people. *Please respect my privacy.* {**priv** və see}

pri·vate *adjective* 1. personal and not to be shared. *I write my private thoughts in a diary.* 2. allowing only certain people to take part in or to know about. *They held a private meeting to discuss how the money should be spent.* 3. out of the attention of the public. *She returned to private life after serving as mayor for four years.* 4. owned by a person or group rather than by the government. *This private beach is not open to the public.* 5. tending not to talk about personal things or feelings. *My father is a very private person.* noun a soldier of the lowest rank. {**priv** viht} privately, adv.

• **in private**
with no one else near; pri-

vately or secretly. *My teacher spoke to me in private about my poor grades.*

priv·i·lege *noun* a right or benefit that is given only to a certain person, group, or social class. *The high school seniors have the privilege of leaving campus.* {**prih** və lihj or **prihv** lihj}

prize *noun* 1. a reward given to the winner of a contest or game. *Mrs. Higgins won a prize for her roses at the state fair.* 2. anything worked or aimed for; something that is worth a great effort. *Freedom is a prize many have fought and died for.* adjective having won a prize. *My uncle used to be a prize boxer.* verb (prized, prizing, prizes) to hold in high honor; value. *The cowboy prized his palomino horse.* {**priyz**}

pro¹ *noun* (pros) a reason in favor of something. *We wrote down the pros and cons of moving to the city.* {**proh**}

pro² *noun* (pros) (informal) a short form of **professional**, or someone as skilled as a professional. *He's a real pro when it comes to cooking.* {**proh**}

pro- *prefix* 1. a prefix that means "forward." *To make progress is to move forward.* 2. a prefix that means "in front of" or "before." *To proclaim something is to announce it in front of an audience.*

prob·a·bil·i·ty *noun* (probabilities) 1. the condition or fact that something might happen. *Since you studied, there is a high probability that you will pass the test.* 2. a likely event or condition. *Snow tonight is a probability.* 3. a number that expresses how likely something is to happen. *What is the probability that you will pick the win-*

 Human Body   Human Mind  Everyday Life  History and Culture  Communication

ning lottery numbers? {prŏb ə **bih** lih tee}

prob·a·ble *adjective* likely to happen or be true. *Because we left early, it is probable that we will get good seats.* {**prŏb** ə bəl}

prob·a·bly *adverb* quite likely; almost certainly. *If it snows a lot tonight we probably won't have school tomorrow.* {**prŏb** ə blee}

pro·ba·tion *noun* a period of time for testing a person's ability, character, or behavior. *The club has accepted me on a three-month probation.* {proh **bay** shən} probational, adj., probationary, adj.

probe *verb* (probed, probing, probes) 1. to look deeply into. *The detective probed the case for clues.* 2. to examine or explore with a probe. *The doctor probed my ear.* *noun* 1. an instrument or tool used to explore the shape, condition, or depth of something that cannot be seen directly. *The doctor used a probe to look inside my throat.* 2. the act of looking for facts showing a crime was committed or a law was broken. *The lawyer asked for a probe of the mayor's actions.* {**prohb**}

prob·lem *noun* 1. a question or condition that is difficult to understand or to deal with. *Poverty is still a problem that faces our nation.* 2. a question, puzzle, or statement that is to be discussed or solved. *I spent an hour working on math problems last night.* *adjective* difficult to manage. *His boss thinks he is a problem worker.* {**prŏb** ləm}

pro·ce·dure *noun* a series of steps that must be taken in order to do something. *The*

procedure for making pancakes starts with mixing the batter. {prə **see** jər}

pro·ceed *verb* (proceeded, proceeding, proceeds) 1. to move forward after a stop. *After you say your name, you may proceed to the front of the line.* 2. to continue doing or speaking. *The student proceeded to answer the question.* {prə **seed**}

pro·ceeds *plural noun* the amount of money raised from a sale or other activity. *All the bake sale proceeds went to the marching band.* {**proh** seedz}

proc·ess *noun* 1. a series of actions used to produce something or reach a goal. *We are learning the process of milking cows.* 2. a series of changes or acts that happen one after another. *The process of growing up takes many years.* *verb* (processed, processing, processes) to handle, treat, or change something by following a procedure. *The new computer processes data at very high speeds.* {**pro** sehs} processor (processer), n.

pro·ces·sion *noun* 1. the act of moving forward in a formal, orderly way. *At seven o'clock, the procession of people into the theater began.* 2. a line or group of people or vehicles moving forward in a formal, orderly way. *The wedding procession made its way down the aisle.* {prə **seh** shən}

pro·claim *verb* (proclaimed, proclaiming, proclaims) to say or state for the public to

know. *The king proclaimed a public holiday.* {prə **klaym**} proclaimer, n.

proc·la·ma·tion *noun* the act of announcing to the public, or something that is said for the public to hear. *The mayor's proclamation was published in this morning's newspaper.* {pro klə **may** shən}

pro·cras·ti·nate *verb* (procrastinated, procrastinating, procrastinates) to put off doing something; delay. *Jim procrastinates and is behind in his work.* {prə **kră** stih **nayt**} procrastination, n., procrastinator, n.

prod *verb* (prodded, prodding, prods) 1. to poke with, or as though with, a pointed rod or instrument. *The cowhand prodded the cattle to move them along.* 2. to move or incite to action as though by poking. *The reporter prodded the governor to answer.* *noun* any pointed instrument used for prodding. {**prŏd**} prodder, n.

pro·duce ➋➊ *verb* (produced, producing, produces) 1. to bring into being. *Our chickens produce eggs for market.* 2. to make or manufacture. *This factory produces towels.* 3. to present; bring forward into view. *The lawyer produced new evidence at the trial.* 4. to put together and present for the public to enjoy. *The class produced a play about forest life.* *noun* something made or grown. *That farmer's produce is the best in the county.* {pro doohs or **proh** doohs, n., prə **doohs**, v.}

a
b
c
d
e
f
g
h
i
j
k
l
m
n
o
p
q
r
s
t
u
v
w
x
y
z

pro·duc·er *noun* a person or company that makes something. *That company is a producer of computer chips.* {prə **dooh** sər}

prod·uct 🌐 ♻ *noun* 1. something made by means of either human work or that of a machine. *This store sells all kinds of paper products.* 2. a result or outcome. *Her good grades are the product of hard work.* 3. the result of multiplying two or more numbers. *Five multiplied by two gives a product of ten.* {pro **duhkt**}

pro·duc·tion *noun* 1. the act or process of making or producing. *That factory began production of automobiles eighty years ago.* 2. a thing or amount that is made. *A new kind of seed has increased the farm's production of corn.* {prə **duhk** shən}

pro·duc·tive *adjective* 1. making or producing easily or in large amounts. *The most productive cows on their farm give over ten tons of milk in a year.* 2. having or producing results that are helpful or useful. *I spent a productive day at work.* {prə **duhk** tihv} productivity, n.

pro·fess *verb* (professed, professing, professes) 1. to claim or state as true. *She professed sadness but felt none.* 2. to make known out in the open. *The bride and groom professed their love for each other.* {prə **fehs**}

pro·fes·sion ♻ *noun* 1. a job or type of work that needs special training or study. *He entered the legal profession after finishing law school.* 2. the act of saying something out loud; declaration. *A profession of faith is part of some church services.* {prə **feh** shən}

pro·fes·sion·al *adjective* 1. of or having to do with a certain job or work. *The doctor gave me her professional advice.* 2. doing a job as a way of earning money. *He works as a professional dancer.* *noun* 1. a person working in a job that needs special training or education. *Let a professional repair your car.* 2. a person paid to perform in an activity such as art or sports. {prə **feh** shə nəl} professionally, adv.

pro·fes·sor *noun* a teacher with a high rank at a college or university. {prə **feh** sər} professorial, adj.

pro·file *noun* 1. an outline or view of something from the side. *Her face has a delicate profile.* 2. a short story or report about someone that gives only the most important facts. *Profiles of the candidates were printed in the newspaper.* {**proh** fiyl}

prof·it ♻ *noun* 1. the amount of money made by a business that is more than the amount put in at the start. *The oil company reported a large profit this year.* 2. a benefit or advantage that comes from doing something. *What profit is there in continuing to smoke?* *verb* (profited, profiting, profits) to gain something from an experience. *He profited from his extra hours of piano practice.* {**prŏf** iht} profiter, n., profitless, adj.

Homophone Note Are you looking for the word **prophet** (a person who predicts the future)? **Profit** and **prophet** sound alike but have different meanings.

prof·it·a·ble *adjective* 1. bringing earnings or a good outcome. *Mr. Hughes's business is profitable and well run.* / *Studying in Japan was a profitable experience.* 2. useful or helpful. *Moving to San Diego will be profitable if you like good weather.* {**pro** fih tə bəl} profitability, n.

pro·found *adjective* 1. coming from or going to a great depth. *She felt profound sadness after the death of her father.* 2. having a deep, thorough understanding. *The travel agent had a profound knowledge of West Africa.* {prə **fownd** or proh **fownd**} profoundly, adv., profoundness, n.

pro·fuse *adjective* 1. great in amount or number. *The flowers in the bouquet were profuse.* 2. given in a generous way. *The grandparents were profuse in their love of their grandchildren.* / {prə **fyoos**} profusely, adv.

pro·gram *noun* 1. a plan of what will be done; schedule. *The library has a weekly program for young readers.* 2. a public presentation, such as a play. *The middle school program was held in the auditorium.* 3. a description or list of information about a performance or presentation. *The opera program included a list of the cast.* 4. a television or radio show. *My favorite TV programs are the Saturday morning cartoons.* 5. a plan for solving a problem. *The government has programs to help people find jobs.* *verb* (programmed or programed, programming or programing, programs) to make a computer program for. *My brother programmed our computer to keep track of the money he spends each month.* {**proh** grăm} programmable (programable), adj.

pro·gram·mer or **programer** *noun* a person who writes

 Human Body   Human Mind   👕 Everyday Life   🏳 History and Culture   📞 Communication

programs for a computer. {**proh**·grǎ mər}

prog·ress *noun* 1. forward movement toward an end. *Are you making any progress with your work?* 2. forward movement in time or space. *The hikers made slow progress through the snow.* *verb* (progressed, progressing, progresses) 1. to move forward in time or space. *The ship progressed across the ocean. / Work on the project is progressing.* 2. to develop in a good way or grow. *She has progressed nicely after a year of French horn lessons.* {**pro** grehs}

• **in progress**
in the process of happening; taking place; occurring. *Please be quiet while the meeting is in progress.*

pro·gres·sive *adjective* 1. moving steadily forward. *Her return to health was slow but progressive.* 2. going forward in regular or ordered steps. *Elementary school, middle school, and high school are progressive levels of education.* 3. in favor of social progress or change. *His progressive ideas about the economy helped him get elected.* *noun* a person who follows and believes in social movements. {prə **greh** sihv} progressively, adv., progressiveness, n.

pro·hib·it *verb* (prohibited, prohibiting, prohibits) 1. to not allow by law. *State law prohibits smoking on buses.* 2. to forbid from taking a particular action. *Our parents prohibit us from jumping on the furniture.* 3. to make impossible or prevent from going forward. *Icy roads prohibited further travel.* {prə **hih** biht or proh **hih** biht}

pro·ject *noun* 1. any activity that takes great effort or planning. *The building project*

will take five years to complete. 2. a large group of homes, usually built with public money. *My grandparents are moving into a housing project for older people.* *verb* (projected, projecting, projects) 1. to throw or cast forward or outward. *He projects the image of a hero.* 2. to figure or develop in one's imagination. *Can you project the cost of building the house?* 3. to cause to appear on a surface. *In movie theaters, a machine is used to project film images onto a large screen.* 4. to extend outward or stick out. *A balcony projected from the side of the building.* {**pro** jehkt, n., prə **jehkt**, v.}

pro·jec·tile *noun* any object that is thrown, fired, or shot by an outside force or weapon. *The American Revolution was fought with bullets, arrows, and other projectiles.* {prə **jehk** tiyl or prə **jehk** tihl}

pro·jec·tion *noun* 1. the act of pushing or throwing outward. *With a quick projection of its tongue, the frog zapped a fly.* 2. a thing or part that sticks out. *The climber grabbed hold of a projection on the rock face.* 3. a plan for a course of action. *The library presented its projection for adding more books to its collection.* 4. a guess of a future situation based on looking at the present situation. *His projection turned out to be true: Danny married Liz, and Donny married Jane.* 5. the way a film's picture is shown on a screen. *The projection of the movie was interrupted when the film broke.* {prə **jehk** shən}

pro·long *verb* (prolonged, prolonging, prolongs) to add length to or make last longer. *One way to prolong a pet's life*

is to feed it well. {prə **lawng** or prə **lŏng**} prolonged, adj.

prom·i·nent *adjective* 1. easy to see or notice because of some difference. *That rose is prominent because of its odd color.* 2. sticking out beyond a surface. *We identified him by his prominent nose.* 3. well known or important. *He was a prominent judge before he retired.* {**prŏm** ih nənt} prominently, adv.

prom·ise *noun* 1. a statement that something absolutely will happen or be done. *She made a promise that she would call.* 2. cause for hope of success or excellence; potential. *Dad says that I show promise in music and art.* 3. a sign of a likely future condition or event. *Warm winds held the promise of spring.* *verb* (promised, promising, promises) 1. to give one's word or assure (usually followed by an infinitive or clause). *We promise to be home before dark.* 2. to give reason for expecting. *His hard work promises success in the future.* {**prŏm** ihs}

prom·on·to·ry *noun* (promontories) a high cliff that sticks out into a large body of water or that rises above an area of lower land. *The divers jumped from the promontory into the ocean.* {**pro** mən **tohr** ee}

pro·mote *verb* (promoted, promoting, promotes) 1. to support the growth of or help move forward. *Eating well promotes health.* 2. to move to a higher position. *The boss promoted my father to a better job.* 3. to help in pushing the purchase of. *The supermarket is promoting Italian foods this week.* {prə **moht**}

pro·mo·tion *noun* 1. a raise to a higher grade or position. *The private received a promotion to corporal.* 2. active support;

A
B
C
D
E
F
G
H
I
J
K
L
M
N
O
P
Q
R
S
T
U
V
W
X
Y
Z

a
b
c
d
e
f
g
h
i
j
k
l
m
n
o
p
q
r
s
t
u
v
w
x
y
z

backing. *The DJ's promotion of our restaurant brought in many new customers.* 3. the act of advancing or encouraging. *The promotion of growth by using hormones should only be considered as a last resort.* {prə **moh** shən} promotional, adj.

prompt *adjective* (prompter, promptest) 1. done immediately and without pause. *This snack bar is known for its prompt service.* 2. swift to answer. *The fire department was prompt in getting to the burning building.* *verb* (prompted, prompting, prompts) 1. to cause to act. *He prompted the dog to jump through the hoop.* 2. to assist by providing forgotten words in theater, radio, and television. *The stage manager prompted the star when she forgot her line.* {**prŏmpt**} promptly, adv., promptness, n.

prone *adjective* 1. having the habit of; being likely to. *She is prone to arrive late to school.* 2. lying or turned face down. *The girl was prone on the floor, asleep.* *adverb* face down or downward. *Ed was stretched out prone on his bed.* {**prohn**}

prong *noun* 1. a thin, sharply pointed part of a tool. *The tool for picking up litter was a pole with a prong on one end.* 2. a pointed end of a deer antler. *verb* (pronged, pronging, prongs) to pierce or hold with a sharp object. *She pronged the potato and lifted it out of the oven.* {**prŏng**}

pro·noun *noun* a word that can take the place of a noun or noun phrase. In the sentence, "He gave it to someone," "he," "it," and "someone" are examples of pronouns. {**proh** nown}

pro·nounce *verb* (pronounced, pronouncing, pronounces) 1. to make the sound of or express with the voice in a specific way. *He pronounced the long words very slowly.* 2. to state something officially. *I now pronounce you husband and wife.* {prə **nowns**}

pro·nun·ci·a·tion 🔊 *noun* 1. the act, manner, or result of saying words. *The pronunciation of the wedding vows made me cry.* 2. an accepted way of saying words. *There are two pronunciations for the word "Caribbean."* {prə **nuhn** see **ay** shən}

proof *noun* 1. any material that proves something is true or real. *Scientists are searching for proof of life on other planets.* 2. a test for truth or quality. *We will put those men to the proof to find out which is the real prince.* 3. a trial piece of printed material used for finding and correcting mistakes before the final printing. *The author checked the proofs of her novel.* *adjective* protecting against or resisting damage. *My new boots are proof against snow and rain.* *verb* (proofed, proofing, proofs) 1. to check or test. *The baker proofed the yeast before he made the bread.* 2. to improve so as to protect against or resist weather damage. *We proofed our tent before the camping trip.* 3. to proofread. *I always proof my homework before I hand it in.* {**proohf**}

-proof *suffix* a suffix that means "able to resist" or "able to protect against." *A waterproof jacket is able to resist water.*

proof·read *verb* (proofread, proofreading, proofreads) to examine for mistakes and make corrections. *I asked a friend to proofread my report.* {**proohr** eed} proofreader, n.

prop[1] *verb* (propped, propping, props) 1. to support so as to hold in place. *Prop the door open with a broom.* 2. to rest or lean on for support. *He propped his chin on his hands.* *noun* a physical object used to support and hold in place. *We used a stick as a prop to hold the window open.* {**prŏp**}

prop[2] *noun* a piece of furniture or other movable article used in the presentation of a play; stage property. *One job of a stage manager is to keep track of the props.* {**prŏp**}

prop·a·gan·da *noun* information or opinions that are made public to promote or attack a movement, cause, or person. *The government spread propaganda to boost support for the war.* {prŏp ə **găn** də}

pro·pel *verb* (propelled, propelling, propels) to cause to move forward; thrust, push, or drive. *The paddle propelled the canoe through the water.* {prə **pehl**}

pro·pel·ler *noun* a device used to make an airplane or ship move forward. A propeller is made of tilted blades

 Human Body   Human Mind  Everyday Life History and Culture Communication

that are attached to and spin around a hub. *Small airplanes often have propellers, not jet engines.* {prə **peh** lər}

prop·er *adjective* 1. correct for a certain purpose. *Shorts and a T-shirt are not the proper clothing for a wedding.* 2. according to ideas or rules that have been accepted as correct. *To make a proper cup of tea, warm the teapot before pouring boiling water over the tea leaves.* 3. in the most firm sense of the word. *I live in New York City, or should I say, Manhattan proper.* {**prŏp** ər}

prop·er·ly *adverb* 1. in the appropriate way. *Aunt Agatha showed me how to set the table properly.* 2. correctly. *Some words are hard to spell properly.* 3. with appropriate behavior. *Those children do not know how to sit properly in a restaurant.* {**prŏp** ər lee}

proper noun *noun* a capitalized noun that names a particular person, place, or thing. In the sentence, "I am from Russia," "Russia" is the proper noun. {**prŏp** ər **nown**}

prop·er·ty *noun* (properties) 1. anything that is owned; all of one's possessions taken as a whole. *The poor man's property included some clothing and little else.* 2. a piece of land or real estate. *We plan to build a summer house on our property by the lake.* 3. a quality that something is known by; characteristic. *A tour of the plant showed us the useful properties of steel.* {**prŏp** ər tee}

proph·e·cy *noun* (prophecies) 1. a prediction or warning of future events. *Hundreds of years ago, Mother Shipton made a prophecy that machines would fly.* 2. an act of seeing into the future, or the ability to see into the future. *That*

old woman claims to have the gift of prophecy. {**prŏf** ih see}

proph·et *noun* a person who predicts the future. *In Greek mythology, Cassandra was a prophet whose fate was to be believed by nobody.* {**prŏf** iht}

Homophone Note The words **prophet** and **profit** (money or benefit) sound alike but have different meanings.

Word History *Prophet* comes from an ancient Greek word that means "interpreter" or "one who speaks for the gods."

pro·por·tion *noun* 1. a part of a whole. *A large proportion of the forest will be cut down.* 2. the relationship in number or size of two things or sets of things; ratio. *The proportion of girls to boys in our class is eleven to twelve.* 3. (plural) size. *The millionaire built a house of enormous proportions.* {prə **pohr** shən}

pro·pos·al *noun* 1. a suggested plan. *The architect showed us a proposal for a new building.* 2. an offer of marriage. *She said yes to his proposal.* {prə **poh** zəl}

pro·pose *verb* (proposed, proposing, proposes) 1. to present or suggest as an idea to be considered. *The council proposed a new bike path around the lake.* 2. to intend or plan. *She proposed saving money for a trip around the world.* 3. to present an offer of marriage. *He proposed to his girlfriend.* {prə **pohz**} pro-poser, n.

prop·o·si·tion *noun* 1. a suggested plan of action. *I like Gabby's proposition that we put up posters to advertise our babysitting services.* 2. anything offered for the purpose of discussion or thought. *The*

author's proposition is that Americans care too much about money and possessions. {prŏp ə **zih** shən}

pro·pul·sion *noun* the act of causing forward movement, or the condition of being moved forward. *A sailboat relies on the wind for its propulsion through the waves.* {prə **puhl** shən}

prose *noun* writing or speech in its usual form of a series of sentences. Most language that is not poetry can be described as prose. Novels, short stories, essays, and letters are examples of writing done in prose. {**prohz**}

pros·e·cute ⬤ *verb* (prosecuted, prosecuting, prosecutes) to begin or carry on a court action against in order to enforce the law. *The lawyer prosecuted the man for breaking into a house.* {**pro** sə **kyoot**}

pros·pect *noun* 1. something that is looked forward to. *Going to college is an exciting prospect.* 2. a likelihood of success. *The prospects look good for the new store in town.* 3. a possible customer or employee. *He is a good prospect for the job.* *verb* (prospected, prospecting, prospects) to search for precious minerals and metals. *Thousands of people prospected the rivers of California for gold in the 1850s.* {**prŏs** pehkt}

pros·pec·tor *noun* a person who prospects, or searches, for precious minerals and metals. {**prŏs** pehk tər}

pros·per *verb* (prospered, prospering, prospers) to be successful or have good luck; thrive. *The computer industry prospered in the 1990s.* {**prŏs** pər}

pros·per·i·ty *noun* (prosperities) the state of being

 🌲 Living World   🔬 Physical World   🏭 Natural Environment   〰️ Economy   📖 Government and Law

a
b
c
d
e
f
g
h
i
j
k
l
m
n
o
p
q
r
s
t
u
v
w
x
y
z

wealthy and successful. *The Great Depression was not a time of prosperity for most people.* {prŏs **peh** rih tee}

pros·per·ous *adjective* having wealth, success, or good fortune. *The prosperous business paid its workers large bonuses.* {prŏs pə rəs}

pro·tect 🔴 🔵 *verb* (protected, protecting, protects) to defend or keep safe; shield from danger or harm. *A fence protects us from our neighbor's vicious dog.* {prə **tehkt**}

pro·tec·tion *noun* 1. the act of keeping something safe from harm or the condition of being protected. *We lock the doors at night for protection.* 2. a person or thing that protects. *Use sunscreen as protection against sunburn.* {prə **tehk** shən}

pro·tec·tive *adjective* protecting or made to protect. *She wears protective clothing in the rain.* / *The mother bear is protective of her cub.* {prə **tehk** tihv}

pro·tein 🔵 *noun* a substance that is made up of nitrogen, carbon, oxygen, hydrogen, and possibly other elements. Proteins are found in all living things and are a necessary part of life processes. *Eggs, meat, and beans are good sources of protein.* {proh teen}

pro·test *noun* an objection or complaint. *The teacher ignored his protests about having too much homework.* *verb* (protested, protesting, protests) 1. to make a protest; object to. *Many people protested against the plan to pave over the ball fields.* 2. to express objection to or disagreement with, in a planned, organized way. *Thousands of citizens protested the Vietnam war during the 1960s.* {proh tehst, n., prə **tehst**, v.} protester, n.

Prot·es·tant *noun* a Christian who belongs to a church other than the Catholic Church or an Eastern Orthodox church. {prŏ tə stənt}

pro·ton 🔵 *noun* a tiny particle in the nucleus of an atom. A proton has a positive electrical charge. {proh tŏn}

pro·to·plasm 🔵 *noun* a substance that is like a jelly and is a necessary part of plant and animal cells. {proh tə **plă** zəm}

pro·to·zo·an *noun* (protozoans or protozoa) a tiny living thing that is similar to an animal but has only one cell or lives as a colony of single cells. Protozoans include amoebas and paramecia. {proh tə **zoh** ən} protozoic, adj.

pro·trude *verb* (protruded, protruding, protrudes) to push or stick out. *The turtle's head protrudes from its shell.* {proh **troohd**}

proud *adjective* 1. feeling pleased, satisfied, and worthy because of something one owns or has done. *He is proud of his new car.* / *I am proud of my good grades.* 2. having respect for one's own independence and worth. *The proud old man did not like to accept help from anyone.* 3. having too high an opinion of one's self. *The proud millionaire refused to ride the bus.* {prowd} proudly, adv., proudness, n.

Synonyms
These words share a meaning with **proud**, adjective 3:

vain, conceited, cocky, smug, complacent

prove *verb* (proved or proven, proving, proves) 1. to show to be true or correct. *The evidence failed to prove the guilt of the prisoner.* 2. to show to be worthy. *Young drivers must prove themselves before they get a driver's license.* 3. to be found or shown in the end. *His guess that we would win the game proved true.* {proohv} provability, n., provable, adj.

pro·ven *verb* a past participle of **prove**. *adjective* a past participle of **prove**. {proohv vən}

prov·erb *noun* a short, often-used saying that expresses something wise or true. *"Actions speak louder than words" is a proverb.* {prŏ vərb}

pro·vide *verb* (provided providing, provides) 1. to give what is needed; supply. *The math teacher provided books, rulers, and paper.* 2. to set as a rule; arrange as a condition. *The law provides that people who litter will be fined.* 3. to supply necessary items such as money (often followed by "for"). *She provides for her children.* {prə **viyd**} provider, n.

pro·vid·ed *conjunction* on the condition that; only if. *He will work, provided they pay him.* {prə **viy** dihd}

Prov·i·dence *noun* the capital of Rhode Island. {prŏv ih dəns}

prov·ince *noun* 1. one of the divisions of some countries, each with its own government. *Canada is made up of ten provinces.* 2. (plural) the parts of a country outside of its main cities (usually used with "the"). *We go to the provinces for vacation.* 3. an area of knowledge, authority, or activity. *Prescribing medi-*

 Human Body   Human Mind   Everyday Life   History and Culture   Communication

cine falls under the province of a doctor. {**prŏv** ihns}

pro·vin·cial *adjective* of or having to do with a province. *The provincial government of Manitoba is located in Winnipeg.* {prə **vihn** shəl}

pro·vi·sion *noun* 1. the act of giving something needed; providing. *The teacher was responsible for the provision of books, pencils, and paper to her students.* 2. the act of preparing and planning ahead for future needs. *We made provisions against a blizzard.* 3. (plural) a supply of food. *The campers loaded up their backpacks with provisions.* *verb* (provisioned, provisioning, provisions) to supply with food and other supplies. *He was in charge of provisioning the family for the picnic.* {prə **vih** zhən} provisioner, n.

pro·voke *verb* (provoked, provoking, provokes) 1. to make angry, annoyed, or emotional; bring to action. *Her fiery speech provoked the audience.* 2. to arouse or bring out. *The poem provoked feelings of joy.* 3. to stir up; excite. *The unfair law provoked protest.* {prə **vohk**} provoker, n.

prow *noun* the front, pointed part of a ship or boat; bow. {**prow**}

prowl *verb* (prowled, prowling, prowls) 1. to move around slowly and secretly, like an animal looking for prey. *The burglars prowled around the house.* 2. to move or roam quietly and secretly, searching for something. *The police were prowling the area for the suspect.* *noun* the act of roaming in a secret, quiet

way. *The cat was on the prowl.* {**prowl**}

pru·dence *noun* good judgement and caution; sensibleness. *She showed prudence in always looking both ways before crossing the street.* {**prooh** dəns}

pru·dent *adjective* showing good judgment and caution; sensible. *My parents gave me prudent advice about saving money.* {**prooh** dənt} prudently, adv.

prune[1] *noun* a plum that has been dried. {**proohn**}

prune[2] *verb* (pruned, pruning, prunes) to cut off or remove branches, twigs, or other parts from; trim. *They pruned the apple trees.* {**proohn**}

pry[1] *verb* (pried, prying, pries) 1. to be too curious about another person's private life. *This is none of your business, so please don't pry.* 2. to look closely or curiously in a sly way. *Someone has been prying into the secret files.* {**priy**}

pry[2] *verb* (pried, prying, pries) 1. to move, lift, or open with something that acts as a lever. *We pried the door open with a crowbar.* 2. to get by trying hard. *He could not pry the secret out of her.* {**priy**}

P.S. *abbreviation* written to introduce a note added to a letter that is below the writer's signature. P.S. is an abbreviation for **postscript**. *At the end of the letter, she wrote "P.S. I'll call you next week."*

psalm *noun* a sacred or holy song or poem; hymn. *There are many psalms in the Old Testament.* {**sahm**}

psy·chi·a·trist *noun* a medical doctor who treats people with mental and emotional illnesses. {sih **kiy** ə trihst *or* siy **kiy** ə trihst}

psy·chi·a·try ❓ *noun* the branch of medicine that deals with mental and emotional illness. {sih **kiy** ə tree *or* siy **kiy** ə tree} psychiatric, adj.

psy·cho·log·i·cal *adjective* 1. of or having to do with psychology. *School counselors use psychological tests to find out the cause of learning problems.* 2. of or having to do with the mind or emotions. *The parents worried about their daughter's psychological condition.* {**siy** kə **lo** jih kəl} psychologically, adv.

psy·chol·o·gist *noun* a person who is trained in and works in psychology. {**siy ko** lə jihst}

psy·chol·o·gy ❓ *noun* (psychologies) the study or science of the mind and of the ways that people feel and act. {**siy ko** lə jee}

pt. *abbreviation* 1. an abbreviation for **point**. 2. an abbreviation for **pint** or pints.

pter·o·dac·tyl *noun* a flying reptile that lived at the same time as dinosaurs. Pterodactyls had wings covered with skin. Some were huge and glided over the oceans and caught fish. They became extinct over sixty-five million years ago. {**teh** rə **dăk** tihl}

Pu symbol of the chemical element plutonium.

pub·lic ⭕ 💬 *adjective* 1. of, for, or having to do with all members of a community; not private. *Our town's most beautiful public building is the new library.* 2. connected with or serving the people or government. *My father is thinking of running for public office.* 3. shared by or open to all. *The author gave a free public reading from her latest book.* *noun* a community of people as a whole. *That beach is not open to the public.* {**puhb** lihk}

A
B
C
D
E
F
G
H
I
J
K
L
M
N
O
P
Q
R
S
T
U
V
W
X
Y
Z

 Living World    Physical World   Natural Environment   Economy   Government and Law

• in public where other people are present, especially in large numbers. *They never fight in public.*

pub·li·ca·tion *noun* 1. the act of publishing printed material. *She was excited about the publication of her first novel.* 2. a magazine, book, newspaper, or other thing that is published. *This newspaper is a daily publication.* {puhb lih **kay** shən}

pub·lic·i·ty *noun* 1. information given out through the media that gets the attention of the public. *The royal wedding got a lot of publicity.* 2. the process of getting the attention of the public. *The governor has people to help her with publicity.* {pə **blih** sih tee}

public school *noun* an elementary, middle, or high school in the United States that is free and supported by people's taxes. {**puhb** lihk **skoohl**}

pub·lish *verb* (published, publishing, publishes) to prepare and bring out for sale for the public to read. *This company publishes mainly textbooks.* {**puhb** lihsh}

puck *noun* the hard rubber disk that is used in ice hockey. Players try to hit the puck into the net to score a goal. {puhk}

puck·er *verb* (puckered, puckering, puckers) to gather or draw up into small folds or wrinkles. *He puckered his lips.* {puhk ər}

pud·ding *noun* a soft, creamy, cooked dessert that is made with milk, flour, eggs, sugar, and flavoring. {puud ing}

pud·dle *noun* 1. a small, shallow pool of water. *The children splashed in the puddles on the sidewalk.* 2. a small, shallow pool of any liquid. *There was a puddle of juice on the kitchen floor.* {puhd əl}

pudg·y *adjective* (pudgier, pudgiest) fat and short. *The baby has pudgy legs.* {puhj ee} pudginess, n.

pueb·lo *noun* (pueblos) 1. a house made of adobe or stone built by Native Americans in the southwest United States. Pueblos are shared by the community and are usually several stories high. 2. (capitalized) a member of any of the Native American peoples who live in this type of house. {pweh bloh}

Puerto Rico *noun* an island in the Caribbean Sea associated with the United States. Puerto Rico is in the West Indies. San Juan is the capital of Puerto Rico. {pwehr tə **ree** koh *or* pohr tə **ree** koh} Puerto Rican, n., adj.

puff *noun* 1. a short, strong burst of breath, air, smoke, or steam. *The locomotive gave off a puff of steam.* 2. a light pastry filled with a sweet, creamy mixture. *We had cream puffs for dessert.* 3. a small, soft pad for putting makeup on the face or body. *She applies powder with a powder puff after her shower.* *verb* (puffed, puffing, puffs) 1. to blow in short, strong breaths or bursts. *The smokestack puffed a thick, black cloud of smoke into the air.* 2. to breathe fast and hard; pant. *The runner was puffing after the first mile.* 3. to

cause to swell. *She took a deep breath and puffed her chest out.* 4. to become swollen; swell. *She has an allergy that makes her eyes puff up.* 5. to fill with too much pride. *The newspaper article puffed her up after she won the election.* {puhf}

puf·fin *noun* a northern sea bird with black and white feathers and a large, flat, colorful bill. {puhf ihn}

pull *verb* (pulled, pulling, pulls) 1. to bring closer by using force upon. *She pulled the door shut.* 2. to draw after oneself or itself by attaching and moving forward. *The tow truck pulled the car.* 3. to remove with force from a fixed position. *The carpenter pulled the nail from the board.* 4. to tear in a specific way. *She pulled the cooked chicken apart to make chicken salad.* 5. to hurt by stretching. *The skater pulled a thigh muscle.* 6. to move. *The car pulled into the driveway.* *noun* 1. the act or process of pulling. *The dog barked when the baby gave a pull on its ear.* 2. the force used in pulling or working against pulling. *She couldn't fight the pull of the waves.* {puul}

• pull through to continue to live in spite of a particular danger or difficulty. *Everyone hoped that she would pull through after the heart operation.*

pul·ley *noun* (pulleys) a wheel or set of wheels with grooves around them that a rope or chain can be pulled over. A pulley is a simple machine that is used for lifting. {**puul** ee}

pull·o·ver *noun* a sweater or shirt that is put on and taken off by being pulled over the head. {**puul** oh vər}

 Human Body   Human Mind 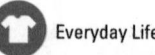 Everyday Life  History and Culture  Communication

pulp *noun* 1. the soft, juicy part of a fruit. 2. any soft, wet mass of material. *Paper is made from wood pulp.* 3. the soft, center part of a tooth. It contains nerves and blood vessels. {**puhlp**}

pul·pit *noun* the raised platform in a house of worship where a member of the clergy stands to speak to the gathered people. {**puhl** piht}

pulse *noun* 1. the regular beating of the arteries that is caused by the beating of the heart. The pulse can be felt in the wrist or neck. 2. any regular beat. *We danced to the pulse of the music.* *verb* (pulsed, pulsing, pulses) to vibrate or beat; throb. *My heart pulsed quickly when I heard the noise coming from the attic.* {**puhls**}

pu·ma *noun* a large wild cat with tan or gray fur and no spots. Pumas live in many parts of North and South America. Pumas are carnivorous mammals. They are also called cougars, mountain lions, or panthers. {**pyoo** mə or **pooh** mə}

pump *noun* a machine for moving a liquid or gas from one place to another. *I pulled up my car to the gas pump.* *verb* (pumped, pumping, pumps) 1. to move using a pump or as if using a pump. *We pumped water from the flooded basement.* 2. to take away a fluid from by using a pump (often followed by "out"). *We pumped out the tank.* 3. to cause to fill with gas or air by using a pump (often followed by "up"). *She pumped up her bicycle tire.* 4. to move with quick motions up and down or back and forth. *He pumped the brake pedal to test the car's brakes.* 5. to try hard to get informa-

tion from someone. *Ted pumped me for information about Tina.* {**puhmp**}

pump·kin *noun* a large, round, orange fruit that has a thick inside pulp that can be eaten. Pumpkins grow on vines. {**puhmp** kihn}

pun *noun* a humorous play on words based on two words that are close in sound but different in meaning. *Here is a joke that has a pun: There was a mushroom who couldn't understand why nobody invited him to their parties. He thought he was such a fungi!* *verb* (punned, punning, puns) to use or make a pun or puns. {**puhn**}

punch[1] *noun* 1. a hard, quick blow with the fist. *She gave her pillow a punch.* 2. a push of a switch on a machine. *He gave the elevator button a punch.* *verb* (punched, punching, punches) 1. to hit with the fist. *My brother punched someone in the face.* 2. to push or press. *The clerk punched a button on the cash register to open the cash drawer.* {**puhnch**}

punch[2] *noun* a tool or machine for making small holes or for pressing a design onto a surface. *verb* (punched, punching, punches) to make a small hole in or press a design onto by using a punch. *The conductor punched our train tickets.* {**puhnch**}

punch[3] *noun* a sweet drink made by mixing spices with fruit juices, soda, or other liquids. {**puhnch**}

punc·tu·al *adjective* on time; prompt. *It is important to be*

punctual for a job interview. {**pungk** chooh əl} punctuality, n., punctually, adv., punctualness, n.

punc·tu·ate *verb* (punctuated, punctuating, punctuates) to place punctuation marks in. *Jean punctuated this sentence correctly.* {**pungk** chooh **ayt**}

punc·tu·a·tion 🔊 *noun* 1. the use of question marks, commas, periods, and other marks in writing to help make the meaning clear. 2. one or more punctuation marks. *Please check your spelling and punctuation before you turn in your essay.* {**pungk** chooh **ay** shən}

punctuation mark *noun* any of a group of marks that are used to help make the meaning of written material clear. Commas, question marks, and periods are examples of punctuation marks. {**pungk** chooh **ay** shən **mark**}

punc·ture *noun* a small hole caused by a sharp object. *There is a puncture in the tire.* *verb* (punctured, puncturing, punctures) to make or pierce with a sharp object. *Which of you punctured my tire? / She punctured a hole in the wall with a pen.* {**pungk** chər}

pun·gent *adjective* sharp and strong in taste or smell. *That pungent cheese is delicious.* {**puhn** jənt} pungency, n.

pun·ish *verb* (punished, punishing, punishes) 1. to cause to suffer for doing something wrong. *The principal punished Tyler for skipping class.* 2. to harm or treat in a rough way; injure. *Running the long race punished my legs.* {**puhn** ihsh} punisher, n.

pun·ish·ment *noun* 1. a penalty for doing something wrong. *The punishment for littering is a fine.* 2. the act of punishing. *Punishment of criminals is the*

A B C D E F G H I J K L M N O **P** Q R S T U V W X Y Z

a
b
c
d
e
f
g
h
i
j
k
l
m
n
o
p
q
r
s
t
u
v
w
x
y
z

responsibility of the judge. {**puhn** ihsh mənt}

pu·ny *adjective* (punier, puniest) very small or weak; feeble. *I chose a puny kitten from the litter.* {**pyoo** nee} puniness, n.

pup *noun* 1. a young dog; puppy. 2. the young of foxes, wolves, seals, whales, and some other mammals. {**puhp**}

pu·pa *noun* (pupae or pupas) an insect in a middle stage of its development, after it is a larva. Pupas do not eat or move; they are changing into their adult form. Many kinds of insects, including butter-flies, spend their time as a pupa inside a cocoon. {**pyoo** pə}

pu·pil[1] *noun* a person who is taught by a teacher. {**pyoo** pəl}

pu·pil[2] *noun* the small, dark opening in the center of the eye. Light passes through the pupil into the eye. {**pyoo** pəl}

Word History The word *pupil* comes from a Latin word that means "girl," "doll," or "puppet." The pupil of someone else's eye is like a mirror where one can see a tiny image of one-self.

pup·pet *noun* a doll that looks like a person or an animal. Some puppets move by being placed over a hand, and others move by strings held from above. {**puhp** iht}

pup·py *noun* (puppies) a young dog,

usually less than one year old {**puhp** ee} puppy-hood, n., puppyish, adj.

pur·chase

⊘ *verb* (pur-chased, pur-chasing, purchases) to get by paying money for; buy. *noun* 1. something that is bought. *The clerk helped me carry my purchases to my car.* 2. the act of purchasing. *My sister helped me save enough money for the purchase of a new video game.* {**puhr** chəs} purchaser, n.

pure *adjective* (purer, purest) 1. not mixed with anything else; made of only one sub-stance. *She's wearing a jacket made of pure wool.* 2. clean; not dirty. *The pure drinking water came from a spring.* 3. without evil; innocent. *The hero had a pure heart.* 4. nothing but. *It was pure good fortune to win the lottery.* {**pyoor**} pureness, n.

pure·bred *adjective* having ancestors that are all the same breed of animal. *That cat is a purebred Persian. noun* an animal that is purebred. A *purebred usually costs more than a mutt.* {**pyoor brehd**}

pu·ri·fy *verb* (purified, purifying, purifies) to make clean or pure. *Use a filter to purify water before you drink it.* {**pyuhr** ih **fiy**} purification, n., purifier, n.

Pu·ri·tan *noun* a member of a group of Protestants in England in the 1500s and 1600s. The Puritans believed in simpler forms of worship and strict morals. Some Puri-tans came to live in what is now Massachusetts. {**pyuhr** ih tən}

pur·ple *noun* the color that comes from mixing red and blue paint. *adjective* having the color purple. {**puhr** pəl} purplish, adj.

Word History *Purple* comes from *porphura,* an ancient Greek name for a shellfish from which purple dye is made.

pur·pose *noun* 1. a reason or plan that guides an action; design or goal. *The purpose of wearing boots is to keep your feet warm and dry.* 2. determi-nation or will. *He practices violin with a great sense of pur-pose.* 3. the reason for which something exists. *My father says the purpose of cats is to clear the world of mice.* {**puhr** pəs}

• **on purpose**
not by accident; deliber-ately. *He broke his sister's doll on purpose.*

pur·pose·ful *adjective* 1. having a purpose. *He walked to work in a purposeful way.* 2. having or showing determination. *She made a purposeful effort to do well in school.* {**puhr** pəs fəl} purposefully, adv., purpose-fulness, n.

pur·pose·ly *adverb* on purpose; deliberately. *Ellen purposely ignored me after our fight.* {**puhr** pə slee}

purr *verb* (purred, purring, purrs) to make a soft, low, rumbling sound, like the one made by a happy cat. *noun* a soft, low, rumbling sound made by, or like the sound made by, a happy cat. *The purr of the new car's engine excited the driver.* {**puhr**}

Homophone Note The words *purr* and *per* (for each) sound alike but have different meanings.

purse *noun* 1. a pouch or bag made of leather, cloth, or a

similar material, used for carrying money and other personal items; handbag. 2. a smaller container for coins or other small objects. *I keep my lunch money in a change purse.* 3. money given as a prize or present. *The horse race had a purse of one million dollars.* *verb* (pursed, pursing, purses) to draw together tightly; pucker. *Mrs. Skillet purses her lips when she is angry.* {**puhrs**}

pur·sue *verb* (pursued, pursuing, pursues) 1. to follow in order to reach or catch; chase. *The police officer pursued the thief on foot.* 2. to spend time doing; work at; practice. *The stamp collector pursued her hobby for twenty years. / He pursued a career in engineering.* {pər **sooh**} pursuer, n.

pur·suit *noun* 1. the act of pursuing. *The cat is in pursuit of the mouse.* 2. any hobby or activity to which one gives time and energy. *Collecting baseball cards is one of my pursuits.* {pər **sooht**}

pus *noun* a thick, white or yellow liquid that forms around infections and that contains white blood cells. {**puhs**}

push *verb* (pushed, pushing, pushes) 1. to use pressure against in order to move. *I pushed my bed under the window.* 2. to move ahead by shoving. *They pushed their way through the crowd.* 3. to urge strongly toward a particular action or way of thinking. *Jeff pushed his friends to make him team captain.* 4. to use pressure against something. *He pushed against the gate to open it.* *noun* 1. a shove. *She gave the door a push.* 2. a strong effort. *Dan made a real push to get his homework done by eight o'clock.* {**puush**}

push-up *noun* an exercise in which a person lies face down and raises and lowers the body by straightening and bending the arms. {**puush uhp**}

pussy willow *noun* a small willow with furry, gray flowers that grow in clusters along its branches. {**puus** ee **wih** loh}

put *verb* (put, putting, puts) 1. to move to a particular position or place. *The cashier put the groceries in a bag.* 2. to cause to be in a particular state, situation, or relationship. *We put him in a private school. / The doctor put the patient on bed rest.* 3. to impose. *She put the blame on me. / They put a tax on gasoline.* 4. to express; state. *Put it in your own words.* 5. to make use of; apply. *He put his ideas to work.* {**puut**}

• **put down**
1. to write down. *I put down my thoughts on paper.* 2. to treat as not important or ridiculous. *Stop putting down all of my suggestions.*

• **put on**
1. to dress in. *Sophie put on her mother's hat.* 2. to stage or perform. *We put on a play we had written ourselves.*

putt *verb* (putted, putting, putts) to hit with a gentle stroke that rolls a golf ball into or near the hole. *noun* a gentle stroke in golf that rolls the ball into or near the hole. {**puht**}

put·ter[1] *verb* (puttered, puttering, putters) to move about or work randomly and without much effort. *He puttered about the house all weekend.* {**puht** ər}

put·ter[2] *noun* 1. a short golf club that is used in putting. 2. a person who putts or is putting. {**puht** ər}

put·ty *noun* (putties) a soft mixture that is like clay. It is used to hold panes of glass in windows and to fill small holes and cracks. {**puht** ee}

puz·zle *noun* 1. a toy or problem that is solved by using thought or by rearranging letters, words, numbers, or objects. *The local newspaper publishes a crossword puzzle every day. / It took us a few weeks to finish that jigsaw puzzle.* 2. anything that confuses. *Car engines are a puzzle to some people.* *verb* (puzzled, puzzling, puzzles) 1. to confuse. *The book's ending puzzled me.* 2. to think about something that is confusing or is hard to understand. *John puzzled for days over the meaning of her letter.* {**puh** zəl} puzzledly, adv., puzzlingly, adv.

• **puzzle out**
to work out a solution to.

A B C D E F G H I J K L M N O P Q R S T U V W X Y Z

a
b
c
d
e
f
g
h
i
j
k
l
m
n
o
p
q
r
s
t
u
v
w
x
y
z

The team puzzled out a way to increase sales.

pyr·a·mid *noun* 1. a solid figure whose sides are triangles that meet at a single point. The base of a pyramid can be any flat shape with straight sides, such as a triangle or square. 2. anything shaped like this. *The circus acrobats formed themselves into a pyramid.* 3. a huge stone structure that is shaped like a pyramid. Pyramids were built long ago as tombs in Egypt and as temples in Mexico. {**pihr** ə mihd}

py·thon *noun* a snake that is not poisonous and lives in Africa, Asia, and Australia. Pythons kill by winding around their prey and squeezing it until it can not breathe. {**piy thŏn** *or* **piy** *th*ən}

582

 Human Body    Human Mind   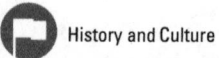 Everyday Life    History and Culture   Communication

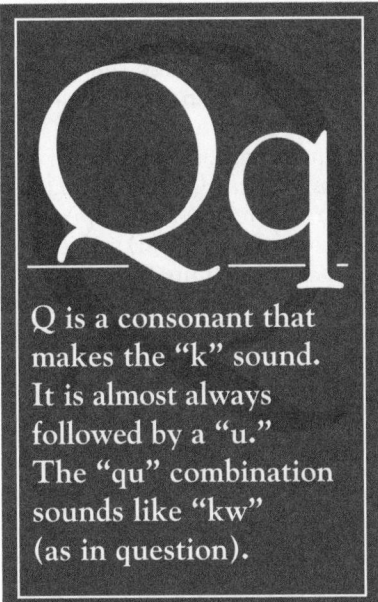

Q is a consonant that makes the "k" sound. It is almost always followed by a "u." The "qu" combination sounds like "kw" (as in question).

q or **Q** *noun* (q's or Q's) the seventeenth letter of the English alphabet. {**kyoo**}

qt. *abbreviation* an abbreviation for **quart**, or quarts.

quack¹ *noun* the sound that a duck makes. *I heard a quack coming from the pond. verb* (quacked, quacking, quacks) to make the sound that a duck makes. *The duck quacked all morning and gave me a headache.* {**kwăk**}

quack² *noun* 1. a person who pretends do be a doctor, but doesn't have proper training or skill. *That quack promised that eating fast food would cure my stomach flu.* 2. anyone who pretends to be an expert; a fraud. *That quack claimed that he was a lawyer, though he never finished law school. adjective* like or relating to a quack. *She follows quack advice about dieting, but it never helps her lose weight.* {**kwăk**}

quad·ri·lat·er·al *noun* any flat closed figure with four straight sides, such as a square or parallelogram. {**kwŏd** rə **lăt** ər əl}

quad·ru·ped *noun* an animal with four feet. {**kwŏd** rə **pehd**}

quad·ru·ple *adjective* multiplied by four. *He bought a quadruple order of fries. verb* (quadrupled, quadrupling, quadruples) to multiply or be multiplied by four. *The population of the country quadrupled in fifteen years.* {**kwŏ drooh** pəl}

quad·ru·plet *noun* one of four children or animals born to the same mother at the same time. {**kwŏ druh** pliht *or* **kwŏ drooh** pliht}

qua·hog *noun* a small, round clam that lives in the ocean along the eastern coast of North America. Quahogs are mollusks with a soft body and a hard shell. Quahogs are eaten by people. {kwaw **hŏg** *or* **kwaw** hawg *or* kwə **hŏg** *or* kwə **hawg**}

> **Word History** *Quahog* is a form of a Pequot Algonquin word that means "hard clam."

quail *noun* (quail or quails) a bird related to the chicken that lives on the ground and is often hunted for sport and food. {**kwayl**}

quaint *adjective* pleasant in an old-fashioned way. *We walked along the cobblestone streets of the quaint village.* {**kwaynt**}

quake 🌀 *verb* (quaked, quaking, quakes) 1. to tremble, shake, or shiver. *Jack quaked with fright when he heard the giant roar.* 2. to shake or tremble. *The buildings and ground quaked, causing a lot of damage in the city. noun* an earthquake. *There was a huge quake in California three years ago.* {**kwayk**}

Quak·er *noun* a member of a Christian religious group founded in England about 1650, called the Society of Friends. {**kway** kər}

qual·i·fi·ca·tion *noun* 1. something that makes a person fit for an activity or job. *The ability to type quickly is one of the qualifications for the job of a secretary.* 2. something that limits or restricts. *I love my family without qualification.* {**kwŏl** ih fə **kay** shən}

qual·i·fied *adjective* 1. having the qualities or skills that are needed. *She is not qualified for the job of an accountant, because she has no training.* 2. with limits; with reservation. *She gave us qualified approval to watch television on a weekday.* {**kwŏl** ih **fiyd**}

qual·i·fy *verb* (qualified, qualifying, qualifies) 1. to make or be fit for a job or activity. *Her training qualified her to be a lifeguard.* 2. to limit the meaning of; modify. *Adjectives qualify nouns.* 3. to limit or make less strong; to moderate. *He qualified his praise by saying that she sometimes sings out of key.* {**kwŏl** ih **fiy**}

> **Synonyms**
> These words share a meaning with *qualify*, verb 1:
> train, prepare, license

qual·i·ty *noun* (qualities) 1. a feature that makes a person or thing what it is. *She has interesting qualities. / One of the qualities of velvet is smoothness.* 2. degree of value or

A B C D E F G H I J K L M N O P Q R S T U V W X Y Z

a b c d e f g h i j k l m n o p q r s t u v w x y z

excellence. *He bought a winter coat of high quality.* *adjective* being of high quality. *We ate dinner at a quality restaurant, and the food was excellent.* {kwŏl ih tee}

Word History *Quality* comes from a Latin word that means "what sort of thing is it?"

qualm *noun* 1. a feeling of guilt or doubt. *She had no qualms about stealing the money.* 2. a sudden uneasy or sick feeling. *I had qualms about getting a shot at the doctor's office.* {kwŏm or kwahm}

quan·ti·ty *noun* (quantities) 1. amount or number. *What quantity of apples do you need for the pie?* 2. a large amount or number. *This factory makes pencils in quantity.* {kwŏn tih tee}

quar·an·tine *noun* the keeping of a person, animal, or thing away from others to stop a disease from spreading. *The child with chicken pox was put in quarantine.* *verb* (quarantined, quarantining, quarantines) to put a person or thing in quarantine. *The doctor quarantined the patients with malaria in a separate part of the hospital.* {kwar ən teen or kwar ən

teen, n., kwar ən teen or kwar ən teen, v.}

Word History *Quarantine* comes from the Italian word for "forty." In the early 1600s, "quarantine" was the forty days that a woman could remain in her husband's house after he died. In the late 1600s, a ship that was suspected of carrying disease was kept in the port for forty days. This period was also called "quarantine."

quar·rel *noun* an angry argument or disagreement. *They had a quarrel about whose turn it was to clean the room.* *verb* (quarreled, quarreling, quarrels) 1. to argue or disagree in an angry way. *We quarreled about who should do the dishes.* 2. to find fault; complain. *I won't quarrel with your decision.* {kwaw rəl or kwar əl, n., kwaw rəl or kwar əl, v.}

quar·ry *noun* (quarries) a large open hole or pit dug for mining stone, marble, gravel, or the like. *verb* (quarried, quarrying, quarries) to take, blast, or cut (stone, marble, or the like) from or as if from a quarry. {kwŏr ee or kwar ee, n., kwŏr ee or kwar ee, v.}

quart *noun* a unit of measure equal to two pints or a quarter of a gallon. A quart is a little less than a liter. (abbreviated: qt.) {kwŏrt}

quar·ter *noun* 1. an amount equal to one fourth of a whole. *I was so hungry that I ate a quarter of the pizza in ten minutes.* 2. a coin of the United States and Canada equal to twenty-five cents. 3. one fourth of an hour. *She leaves for work every morning at quarter past seven.* 4. one

fourth of the time, or seven days, that it takes the moon to revolve around the earth. *The moon is in its first quarter.* 5. an section of a town or city; neighborhood. *We admired the historic buildings in the French quarter of New Orleans.* 6. (plural) a place to stay for a limited time. *The maids had separate quarters from the main house.* 7. one of four parts of a sports contest. *Our football team scored three touchdowns in the fourth quarter.* *verb* (quartered, quartering, quarters) 1. to divide into four equal parts. *We quartered the apple so each of us had a piece.* 2. to give a place to stay. *They quartered the soldiers in tents.* {kwŏr tər}

quar·ter·back *noun* the football player who calls the plays and handles the ball in most plays. {kwŏr tər băk}

quar·ter·ly *adjective* happening or appearing four times a year, often once every three months. *She makes quarterly payments on her motorcycle.* *adverb* once every three months, or four times a year. *The fishing magazine is published quarterly.* {kwŏr tər lee}

quar·tet *noun* 1. four musicians or singers who perform together as a group. *The string quartet played wonderfully.* 2. a piece of music written for four musicians or singers. *The singers sang a quartet at the concert.* 3. any group of four objects or people. *A quartet of friends went to the movies.* {kwŏr teht}

quartz *noun* a common, hard mineral that is usually found as glass-like crystals. {kwŏrts}

584

 Human Body    Human Mind   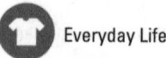 Everyday Life   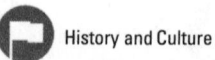 History and Culture    Communication

qua·sar *noun* a heavenly object like a star. Quasars are far away from the earth and send out powerful radio waves. {<u>kway</u> zar}

quay *noun* a pier, wharf, or other landing place for loading and unloading boats or ships. {<u>kee</u>}

Homophone Note The words *quay* and *key* sound alike but have different meanings.

quea·sy *adjective* (queasier, queasiest) 1. feeling sick to one's stomach. *He felt queasy on the airplane.* 2. uneasy or worried. *I'm queasy about the final exam.* {<u>kwee</u> zee} queasiness, n.

Que·bec *noun* a province in eastern Canada on the U.S. border between New Brunswick and Ontario. Its capital is Quebec City. {kwih <u>behk</u> or keh <u>behk</u>} Quebecer or Quebecker, n.

Word History *Quebec* is the French spelling of the Micmac word *gepèg*, which means "narrow passage." *Gepèg* refers to the place where the St. Lawrence River narrows.

queen 🔵 *noun* 1. a female ruler of a kingdom. 2. the wife or widow of a king. 3. a woman, place, or thing of excellent qualities. *My family calls my grandmother the Queen of Kindness.* 4. a playing card having the picture of a queen. {<u>kween</u>}

queer *adjective* strange, unusual, or not expected; odd; peculiar. *Don't you think it's queer that he likes fried eggs with his ice cream?* {<u>kweer</u>}

quench *verb* (quenched, quenching, quenches) 1. to satisfy. *The ice cold water quenched my thirst.* 2. to extinguish or put out. A bucket of water quenched the fire. {<u>kwehnch</u>} quencher, n.

que·ry *noun* (queries) a question. *Did you answer her queries about the job?* *verb* (queried, querying, queries) 1. to ask about. *She queried my reason for walking to work in the rain.* 2. to question; to ask. *I queried him about his new friend.* {<u>kweer</u> ee}

quest *noun* a search or pursuit. *He went on a quest for a hidden treasure.* *verb* (quested, questing, quests) to search or hunt; seek (often followed by "for" or "after"). *She quested after happiness.* {<u>kwehst</u>}

ques·tion 🔵 *noun* 1. a sentence that asks for a reply. *Did you ask me a question?* 2. a matter to be discussed. *Our town is looking at the question of whether to build a new school.* 3. a matter that is in doubt or not certain; problem. *The question of when the war will end is on everyone's mind.* *verb* (questioned, questioning, questions) 1. to ask a question of. *She questioned him about his life with his family.* 2. to express doubt about. *I question your decision to leave home.* {<u>kwehs</u> chən} questioner, n.

• **beyond question** without any doubt. *It is beyond question that I love my parents very much.*
• **in question** that is being considered or argued about. *Our move to New York is in question.*
• **out of the question** impossible. *Since we have no money, going to the movie is out of the question.*

Word History The words *question* and *quest* both come from a Latin word that means "to seek or ask."

question mark 🔵 *noun* a punctuation mark (?). It is used at the end of a sentence that asks a question. {<u>kwehs</u> chən **mark**}

ques·tion·naire *noun* a list of questions used for gathering useful information from people. {kwehs chə <u>nayr</u>}

quet·zal *noun* (quetzals) a large bird of Central and South America that has bright red and green feathers. {keht <u>sahl</u>}

quick *adjective* (quicker, quickest) 1. done in a short time; fast. *I got a quick answer to my letter.* 2. moving with speed. *She is a very quick runner.* 3. thinking, acting, or learning with speed. *She has a quick mind.* *adverb* (quicker, quickest) with speed or quickly. *Come quick!* {<u>kwihk</u>} quickness, n.

quick·ly *adverb* in a short time; rapidly. *Get ready quickly so that we'll get to the movie on time.* {<u>kwih</u> klee}

quick·sand *noun* a deep, wet, mixture of sand and water. Quicksand pulls down and swallows up a person or thing that stands on it. {<u>kwihk</u> sănd}

Word History The word *quicksand* is the modern form of an early English word, *quysond*, which means "living sand."

a
b
c
d
e
f
g
h
i
j
k
l
m
n
o
p
q
r
s
t
u
v
w
x
y
z

qui·et *adjective* (quieter, quietest) 1. making no sound or noise. *He was a quiet baby.* 2. free from trouble or much activity. *They had some quiet days in their vacation home.* 3. peaceful and calm. *The neighborhood is quiet tonight.* 4. showing little or no movement. *The wind was finally quiet.* *verb* (quieted, quieting, quiets) 1. to make quiet. *Will you quiet your dog?* 2. to become quiet (often followed by "down"). *The baby quieted down when I sang to him.* *noun* freedom from noise. *We love going to the lake because of the quiet there.* {**kwiy** iht} quietly, adv., quietness, n.

quill *noun* 1. a large, stiff feather. 2. a pen made from the hollow stem of a feather. 3. one of the sharp hollow spines of a porcupine or other mammal. {**kwihl**}

quilt *noun* a bed covering made of two layers of material that are filled with feathers, wool, cotton, or other soft materials. The layers are stitched together so that the stitches make patterns on the cloth. *verb* (quilted, quilting, quilts) 1. to make a quilt. *My aunt quilted the scraps of fabric.* 2. to make quilts or clothes by stitching with a soft lining or padding. *Kathryn's grandmother has been quilting for years.* {**kwihlt**} quilter, n.

quin·tu·plet *noun* 1. one of five children or animals born to a mother at a single birth. 2. a group of five. {kwihn **tuh** pliht or kwihn **tooh** pliht}

quit *verb* (quit or quitted, quitting, quits) 1. to stop; give up; refuse to take further part in. *She quit her job as a teacher to become a truck driver.* 2. to stop. *He quit eating when he was full.* 3. to go away from; leave. *He quit the city for the country.* {**kwiht**}

quite *adverb* 1. to the greatest degree; completely; entirely. *Bart is not quite finished with his book report.* 2. to a large degree; somewhat; rather. *I thought that I did quite well cleaning my room.* 3. actually; really. *Are you quite sure he said that?* {**kwiyt**}

quiv·er[1] *verb* (quivered, quivering, quivers) to shake or tremble slightly; shiver. *Her chin quivered as the tears came down.* *noun* a slight shake or shiver. *There was a quiver in his voice as he gave his speech in front of a big audience.* {**kwih** vər}

quiv·er[2] *noun* a case designed to hold and transport arrows, often strapped to the back or waist. {**kwih** vər}

quiz *verb* (quizzed, quizzing, quizzes) 1. to question in order to test knowledge. *The teacher quizzed the class on their spelling.* 2. to examine or ask questions of. *My mother quizzed me when I came home after my curfew.* *noun* a short or informal test. {**kwihz**}

quo·ta *noun* 1. the part or share of something that is due to a person or group. *Each soldier is given his or her daily quota of meat and bread.* 2. an amount of something that is required or expected from a person or group. *The company set a production quota for its employees.* {**kwoh** tə}

quo·ta·tion 🔊 *noun* 1. the act of quoting. 2. a quoted passage from a book or the like. {kwoh **tay** shən}

quotation mark *noun* either of a pair of punctuation marks (" "). Quotation marks are used at the beginning and end of a quotation. {kwoh **tay** shən **mark**}

quote *verb* (quoted, quoting, quotes) to repeat a passage or information from. *He quoted Shakespeare.* *noun* something that is quoted; quotation. {**kwoht**}

quo·tient *noun* the number that is obtained by dividing one number into another. *In the equation "ten divided by two equals five," "five" is the quotient.* {**kwoh** shənt}

Word History *Quotient*
comes from *quotiens*, a Latin word that means "how many times?"

 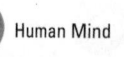 Human Body    Human Mind    Everyday Life    History and Culture   Communication

Rr

R is a consonant that always makes the same sound.

Tips to help you look up words starting with r: Also look under W for words (such as write) that start with a silent "w." Sometimes "r" is followed by a silent "h" (as in rhyme).

These words may be hard to look up if you don't already know how to spell them:

ranger	restaurant
ready	rhythm
really	ridiculous
receive	right
relevant	rough

r or **R** *noun* (r's or R's) the eighteenth letter of the English alphabet. {**ar**}

Ra symbol of the chemical element radium.

rab·bi *noun* (rabbis) a teacher of the Jewish religion who is usually the leader of a Jewish congregation. {**răb** iy}

rab·bit *noun* (rabbits or rabbit) a small mammal with long ears and long back legs for running or jumping. Rabbits have soft fur and a short tail. They are herbivores with long front teeth. Some kinds of rabbits make tunnels or burrows in the ground. Cottontails and hares are kinds of rabbits. {**răb** iht}

ra·bies *noun* a disease that is caused by a virus and can kill people, dogs, and other mammals. Symptoms of rabies are foaming at the mouth and violent or strange behavior. A person can get rabies if scratched or bitten by an animal that has the disease. {**ray** beez *or* **ray** bee eez}

rac·coon *noun* (raccoon or raccoons) a small mammal with brown and gray fur, a long tail with black rings, and a pointed face with black markings that look like a mask. Raccoons eat plants and small animals such as insects and frogs. In towns and cities, they eat garbage. Several kinds of raccoons live in North and South America and on Caribbean islands. {**ră koohn** *or* rə **koohn**}

Word History Raccoon comes from *arahkun*, an Algonquin word that means "he scratches with his hands."

race[1] ◯ *noun* 1. a sport or contest of speed. *My brother cried when he came in last in the race.* 2. any process in which the goal is to do something sooner or more quickly than others; competition. *Russia beat the United States in the race to put the first person in outer space.* 3. the political contest before an election. *Most of the neighborhood supported Mr. Ruiz in his race for mayor. verb* (raced, racing, races) 1. to take part in a contest of speed. *Our favorite horse is injured and will not race today.* 2. to move at high speed. *I raced to school so that I would get there before the last bell.* 3. to run or compete against. "*I'll race you to the road and back,*" *said Tina.* 4. to cause to run or move at high speed. *The ambulance raced her to the hospital after the accident. / The drivers raced their engines at the starting line.* {**rays**}

race[2] *noun* 1. a human population sharing certain common physical characteristics that have been passed down from one generation to the next. *People of many different races live in the United States.* 2. all human beings; humankind. *The future of the race lies with the children.* {**rays**}

rac·er *noun* 1. a person who takes part in races. *She was a racer in high school.* 2. an automobile, boat, or horse that competes in races. *That car is a fast racer.* 3. a kind of slender North American snake. {**ray** sər}

race·track *noun* a track or course used for racing. *We went to the racetrack to see the horse race.* {**rays** trăk}

ra·cial *adjective* 1. having to do with a race of people. *Skin color is considered a racial characteristic.* 2. having to do with relationships or connections between races of people living in the same

A	
B	
C	
D	
E	
F	
G	
H	
I	
J	
K	
L	
M	
N	
O	
P	
Q	
R	
S	
T	
U	
V	
W	
X	
Y	
Z	

a
b
c
d
e
f
g
h
i
j
k
l
m
n
o
p
q
r
s
t
u
v
w
x
y
z

country, city, or neighbor-hood. *This neighborhood is known for its racial diversity.* {**ray** shəl} racially, adv.

rac·ism 🔵 *noun* 1. the opinion or belief that one's own race is better than another race or races. 2. unfair treatment of people based on the opinion that one race is better than another race or races. *The civil rights movement fought to end racism in America.* {**ray** sih zəm} racist, n.

rack *noun* a frame or stand used to hold, hang, or show things. *This wine rack holds twenty bottles.* / *The dresses on this rack don't come in my size.* *verb* (racked, racking, racks) 1. to cause great suffering or pain to; torture. *Pain racked his body.* 2. to cause stress or strain to. *She racked her brains trying to remember.* {**răk**}

rack·et[1] 🔵 *noun* 1. a loud, confusing noise. *The bus driver told us to stop making such a racket.* 2. (sometimes plural) dishonest activities by a group of people whose aim is to cheat others of their money. {**răk** iht}

Word History *Racket* comes from an early French word that means "palm of hand." In the 1300s, people played an early form of tennis called *raket*, in which players hit the ball with the palm of the hand.

rack·et[2] or **racquet** *noun* an object used to hit the ball in tennis and similar sports. It is made of a round or oval frame with a net-work of tightly laced strings and a long handle. {**răk** iht}

rac·quet·ball *noun* a game played by two or four players in a small court with four walls. The players use rackets to hit a rubber ball against the walls. {**răk** iht **bawl**}

radar *noun* 1. the use of radio waves to track the location, distance, and speed of far-away objects. Waves are sent out and then picked up again when they bounce back after hitting some object. 2. the equipment used for this method of tracking. {**ray** dar}

ra·di·ant *adjective* 1. sending out heat or rays of light; shining brightly. *The radiant sun warmed our backs.* 2. showing joy, happiness, or other good feelings; glowing or beaming. *She greeted her grandmother with a radiant smile.* {**ray** dee ənt}

ra·di·ate *verb* (radiated, radiating, radiates) 1. to send out rays. *Light radiates from the sun.* 2. to send out. *The fire radiated warmth.* 3. to spread out in many directions from a center. *The spokes radiate from the center of a bicycle wheel.* 4. to have a quality or be in a mood that everyone notices or feels. *She radiated confidence.* {**ray** dee **ayt**}

ra·di·a·tion 🔵 *noun* the waves of energy sent out by sources of heat or light, or by radioactive material. *She wore a hat to protect her skin from the radiation of the sun.* / *Many people are concerned about radiation from nuclear waste.* {**ray** dee **ay** shən}

ra·di·a·tor *noun* 1. a device that uses steam or hot water passing through pipes in order to heat a room. 2. a device in a car that cools the engine. It is made up of metal tubes that hold and cool water and other liquids. {**ray** dee **ay** tər}

rad·i·cal *adjective* 1. having to do with the root or source; basic; fundamental. *There are radical differences between your idea of happiness and mine.* 2. very great or complete; extreme. *Moving from public school to private school made a radical difference in her life.* 3. in favor of extreme changes in politics or society. *She was a member of a radical political party.* *noun* a person who supports extreme social and political changes. {**răd** ih kəl} radically, adv.

ra·di·i *noun* a plural of **radius**. {**ray** dee **iy**}

ra·di·o 🔵 🔵 *noun* (radios) 1. a way of sending signals made of waves that travel through the air. These radio waves are picked up and translated into sounds by electronic devices. 2. a device that picks up radio signals; receiver. *verb* (radioed, radioing, radios) to send by means of radio. *The pilot radioed her location to the airport.* {**ray** dee oh}

ra·di·o·ac·tive *adjective* giving off energy as a result of the decay of unstable atoms. *Nuclear waste is dangerous because it is highly radioactive.* {**ray** dee oh **ăk** tihv}

ra·di·o·ac·tiv·i·ty 🔵 *noun* the giving off of energy as a result of the decay of unstable atoms. *Uranium has a high level of radioactivity.* {**ray** dee oh **ăk** tih vih tee}

rad·ish *noun* 1. a plant that has a crisp and strong-tasting root. 2. the root of this plant, usually eaten raw as a relish or in salads. {**ră** dihsh}

ra·di·um *noun* a silver-white, radioactive metal that is one

 Human Body
 Human Mind
 Everyday Life
 History and Culture
Communication

of the chemical elements. Radium glows in the dark. It is used to treat cancer. (symbol: Ra) {**ray** dee əm}

ra·di·us *noun* (radii or radiuses) 1. a straight line from the center to the edge of a circle or sphere. 2. a circular area measured by the length of its radius. *There are no stores within a mile radius of my house.* {**ray** dee əs}

ra·don *noun* a radioactive gas that is one of the chemical elements. It is found in small amounts in some soils and rocks. (symbol: Rn) {**ray** dŏn}

raf·fle *noun* a game in which the person who has bought the ticket that is drawn wins a prize. *She bought several tickets in the raffle for a new car.* *verb* (raffled, raffling, raffles) to offer or give as a prize in a raffle (often followed by "off"). *Our school raffled off a vacation to Florida.* {**răf** əl}

raft *noun* 1. a flat platform made of materials that can float, such as wood or barrels filled with air. Rafts are often used to carry people or goods. 2. a wide boat of rubber or similar material, with a flat bottom and tubes filled with air that serve as the front, back, and sides. *verb* (rafted, rafting, rafts) to float or travel on a raft. *We rafted down the Colorado River on our vacation.* {**răft**}

rag¹ *noun* 1. a scrap or small piece of cloth. *Use a rag to wipe the kitchen counter.* 2. (plural) old or worn pieces of clothing. *She was dressed in rags.* {**răg**}

rag² *verb* (ragged, ragging, rags) (informal) to tease or scold. *They ragged him about his clumsy way of walking.* {**răg**}

rage ⊙ *noun* 1. extreme anger; fury. *In her rage, she threw her favorite doll against the wall.* 2.

a fad; fashion. *Short hair is all the rage.* *verb* (raged, raging, rages) to act or talk violently or with intense anger. *She raged for an hour about the damage the dog had done to the furniture.* {**rayj**}

rag·ged *adjective* 1. worn down into rags; torn. *His ragged coat didn't keep him warm.* 2. wearing shabby and worn-down clothing. *The ragged stranger begged for food.* 3. having rough, uneven, or sharp edges or surfaces. *The waves threw themselves against the ragged rocks.* 4. harsh; rough sounding; grating. *Her ragged voice was not pleasant to listen to.* {**răg** ihd}

rag·weed *noun* a weed that produces a large amount of pollen in the fall. Many people are allergic to ragweed. {**răg** weed}

raid *noun* 1. a sudden, surprise attack. *The soldiers went on a raid at dawn.* 2. a surprise entry by police into private property to arrest someone or seize something. *The police planned a midnight raid of the robbery suspect's motel room.* *verb* (raided, raiding, raids) to make a raid on. *The police raided the thief's hideout. / The Vikings raided villages in England.* {**rayd**} raider, n.

rail *noun* 1. a bar of wood or metal that runs between two posts and serves as a fence or barrier. 2. one of the pair of metal bars along which a railway car travels. 3. the railroad. *They travel by rail.* {**rayl**}

rail·ing *noun* 1. a barrier or fence made of posts and rails. *We leaned over the railing and waved at the people below.* 2. a banister. *Hold onto the railing while you go down the stairs.* {**ray** ling}

rail·road *noun* 1. a road of steel rails upon which train cars travel. *The railroad once ran through the center of the town.* 2. the entire set of trains, tracks, workers, and equipment that make up a rail transportation system. *The first railroad to cross the North American continent was completed in 1869.* {**rayl** rohd}

rail·way *noun* 1. a railroad. 2. a set of tracks on which a train runs. {**rayl** way}

rain ⊙ *noun* 1. drops of water that form in the clouds and fall from the sky to the earth. *The heavy rain drowned many plants in our garden.* 2. a fast and steady fall of anything. *The soldier tried to protect himself from the rain of arrows.* *verb* (rained, raining, rains) 1. to come down as water from the clouds. 2. to fall in the manner of rain. *The soda machine broke, and coins rained out all over the floor.* 3. to pour forth or send down. *My mother rained affection on us.* {**rayn**}

• **rain cats and dogs** to rain very hard. *You can't walk home when it's raining cats and dogs!*

Homophone Note The words *rain*, *reign*, and *rein* sound alike but have different meanings. To find out why a wild horse prefers rain to reins, look up *rein*.

rain·bow ⊙ *noun* a curved arc of light of many colors across the sky. Rainbows are caused by the sun's shining through drops of water during or after a rain. {**rayn** boh}

A
B
C
D
E
F
G
H
I
J
K
L
M
N
O
P
Q
R
S
T
U
V
W
X
Y
Z

a
b
c
d
e
f
g
h
i
j
k
l
m
n
o
p
q

r

s
t
u
v
w
x
y
z

rain·coat *noun* a coat that repels water to keep a person dry when it is raining. {**rayn** koht}

rain·drop *noun* a drop of rain. {**rayn** drŏp}

rain·fall *noun* 1. a falling of rain. 2. the amount of rain that falls over a certain area during a certain period of time. *This area has a yearly rainfall of about twenty inches.* {**rayn** fawl}

rain forest 🌐 *noun* a dense evergreen forest, mostly found in a tropical areas, that receives a large amount of rain all year long. *Rain forests are home to a great variety of plants and animals.* {**rayn** fohr ihst *or* **rayn** far ihst}

rain·y *adjective* (rainier, rainiest) having much rain. *On rainy Saturdays, he stays in and reads.* {**ray** nee}

raise *verb* (raised, raising, raises) 1. to move to a higher position; lift. *I raised the window to let in the cool air.* 2. to build. *The farmer raised a barn on his property.* 3. to cause to grow. *My parents raised four children.* / *The farmers down the road raise beans and corn.* 4. to ask or bring up. *At dinner, I raised the topic of getting my own room.* 5. to stir up. *Accidents at the playground are raising fears about the safety of the equipment.* 6. to gather; collect. *The skating club raised over a hundred dollars from the bake sale.* *noun* an increase in rate of pay. *Dad got a big raise at work.* {**rayz**}

rai·sin *noun* a sweet grape that has been dried for eating. {**ray** zihn}

rake *noun* a tool that has a long handle and a row of teeth or prongs at one end. It is used to gather hay or fallen leaves or to smooth down soil. *verb* (raked, raking, rakes) 1. to collect, move, or clear away using a rake. *She raked the leaves into a big pile.* 2. to clear of ruins or trash, spread smoothly, or cultivate with a rake. *He raked the flower bed.* 3. to search completely through. *She raked the bedroom looking for the book.* {**rayk**}

ral·ly *verb* (rallied, rallying, rallies) 1. to unite again or raise the spirits of after a disappointment or failure. *The coach rallied his players at halftime.* 2. to call together for some common goal; assemble. *The politician rallied his supporters and asked for their vote.* 3. to recover quickly after being weak, ill, or hurt by loss. *After a week of fever, the patient rallied and began eating again.* 4. to come to someone's aid; take someone's side; give support (often followed by "behind"). *They rallied behind the president.* *noun* (rallies) a gathering of people for a common purpose; demonstration. *I attended a political rally.* {**ră** lee}

ram *noun* 1. an adult male sheep. 2. a tool or part of a machine used to drive, hammer, or crush something. *The soldiers broke through the castle gate with a battering ram.* 3. (usually capitalized) the constellation Aries. *verb* (rammed, ramming, rams) 1. to hit with great force. *The car rammed the tree.* 2. to force into a small or tight space; cram. *He rammed the last suitcase into the trunk of his car.* {**răm**}

RAM *abbreviation* the information a computer stores for a short time and can recall quickly. RAM stands for "random access memory." {**răm**}

Ram·a·dan *noun* 1. the ninth month of the Muslim calendar. 2. the daily fasting from sunrise to sunset during this month. {**rahm** ə **dahn** *or* **rahm** ə **dahn**}

Word History *Ramadan* is an Arabic word that means "the hot month."

ram·ble *verb* (rambled, rambling, rambles) 1. to wander or stroll without any particular goal; roam. *They rambled through the woods all afternoon.* 2. to talk or write without a clear purpose or point, wandering from thought to thought. *My friend rambled about the different movies he had seen.* *noun* a relaxed walk or stroll. *After dinner we took a ramble through the park.* {**răm** bəl}

ramp *noun* a sloping platform or other surface connecting two different levels. *We walked up the ramp and onto the airplane.* {**rămp**}

ram·rod *noun* a rod that fits inside the barrel of a gun. A ramrod is used for pushing gunpowder into the barrel or for cleaning the barrel of the gun. {**răm** rŏd}

ran *verb* past tense of **run.** {**răn**}

ranch *noun* a large farm where cattle, horses, or sheep are

590

 Human Body   Human Mind   Everyday Life    History and Culture   Communication

raised on the open range. There are many ranches in the plains of the United States and South America. *verb* (ranched, ranching, ranches) to own or work on a ranch. *His family ranches in Texas.* {**rănch**}

ran·dom *adjective* made or done without purpose or pattern; made or done by chance. *I made a random choice of five books from the library.* {**răn**dəm} randomly, adv.

rang *verb* past tense of **ring²**. {**răng**}

range *noun* 1. the extent or limits between which something can vary. *This shirt comes in a wide range of sizes and colors.* 2. the distance or area over which something can reach or function. *Dogs can hear sounds that are not in the range of human hearing. / A fifteen-mile run is outside my range as a runner.* 3. an area used for practice in shooting. *Police officers learn to shoot at a shooting range.* 4. a large, open area of land on which livestock graze and roam. *Cattle wander on the open range.* 5. a series of connected mountains. *The Himalayan mountain range is the highest on earth.* 6. a cooking stove with burners and an oven. *verb* (ranged, ranging, ranges) 1. to be within certain limits. *The ticket prices range from twenty to fifty dollars.* 2. to roam; wander. *He ranged all over Kentucky before settling down. / Our conversation ranged over many subjects.* {**raynj**}

rang·er *noun* 1. a person whose work is looking after or patrolling a park, forest, or other natural area. 2. a soldier trained for surprise attacks. {**rayn**jər}

rank¹ *noun* 1. a position in society. *The mayor is a person of rank in my community.* 2. an office or position. *She achieved the rank of general.* 3. (plural) the common soldiers of an army. *The soldier rose from the ranks to become an important military leader.* *verb* (ranked, ranking, ranks) 1. to place in order; classify. *Boxers are ranked by their weight.* 2. to hold a certain rank or position. *She ranks first in our math class.* {**răngk**}

rank² *adjective* (ranker, rankest) 1. having a strong and very bad smell or taste. *Skunks give off a rank odor.* 2. not decent; foul; disgusting. *Her rank behavior shocked her parents.* 3. total; complete. *It was clear that he was a rank beginner when he tried to stop the car by stepping on the gas pedal.* {**răngk**}

ran·som *noun* the payment demanded in return for setting a kidnapped person free, or the act of setting someone free by paying the price demanded. *The kidnappers demanded a ransom of one hundred thousand dollars. / They are holding a five-year-old child for ransom.* *verb* (ransomed, ransoming, ransoms) to set free by paying a ransom. *Our government agreed to ransom the reporters who were being held captive in another country.* {**răn**səm}

rap¹ *verb* (rapped, rapping, raps) to hit with a quick, hard stroke. *She rapped the door three times.* *noun* 1. a quick blow or sharp knock. *She gave him a rap on the head with her book.* 2. the sound made by a quick, sharp knock on a hard surface; tap. *We heard a rap on the door.* 3. (slang) blame or punishment. *Three years in prison isn't a bad rap for what he did.* {**răp**}

rap² *noun* a kind of popular music in which verses that rhyme are spoken and accompanied by a strong beat. {**răp**}

Homophone Note Are you looking for the word *wrap* (to cover)? *Rap* and *wrap* sound alike but have different meanings.

rap·id *adjective* 1. happening in a short or brief time. *When he turned thirteen, a rapid change took place in his appearance.* 2. very quick or swift; fast. *The horse galloped at a rapid pace during the race.* 3. marked or distinguished by speed. *His rapid speech made him difficult to understand.* *noun* (usually plural) a part of a river or stream where the water moves very quickly. *My father rafted down the rapids of the Colorado River.* {**răp**ihd} rapidly, adv.

Word History *Rapid* comes from a Latin word that means "to hurry away or carry off." If you fall into the river rapids, you are likely to be carried off.

rap·ture *noun* great happiness, joy, or ecstasy; bliss. *Watching the ballet filled us with rapture.* {**răp**chər} rapturous, adj.

rare¹ *adjective* (rarer, rarest) 1. not often found or seen; not common. *A cool day in the middle of July is rare.* 2. unusually great; excellent; admirable. *She has a rare talent for singing.* 3. worth a lot because of uncommonness. *The museum paid a high price for the collection of rare coins.* 4. not dense; thin. *The air is rare on the top of a high mountain.* {**rayr**}

rare² *adjective* (rarer, rarest) cooked for a short period of

A B C D E F G H I J K L M N O P Q R S T U V W X Y Z

time. *He likes his steak rare.* {**rayr**}

rare·ly *adverb* not often; seldom. *She rarely goes shopping for new clothes.* {**rayr** lee}

ras·cal *noun* 1. a dishonest person; scoundrel. *That rascal left town without paying his bills.* 2. a mischievous person. *My little brother is such a rascal.* {**răs** kəl}

rash[1] ❓ *adjective* (rasher, rashest) not careful; reckless or hasty. *He regretted his rash decision.* {**răsh**}

rash[2] ❓ *noun* 1. a condition in which red bumps or spots break out on the skin. *Allergies can cause a rash.* 2. a sudden burst of many of the same types of events happening in a short period of time. *There has been a rash of car thefts in that neighborhood.* {**răsh**}

rasp *verb* (rasped, rasping, rasps) to make a rough, grating sound. *The old gate rasped as it swung open.* *noun* a rough, grating sound. *Her cold and sore throat put a rasp in her voice.* {**răsp**}

rasp·ber·ry *noun* (raspberries) 1. a prickly plant. 2. the sweet, small fruit of this plant. 3. a deep pinkish red or reddish purple color. *I love the raspberry color of this sweater.* {**răz** beh ree}

rat *noun* 1. a small mammal with a pointed face and a very long tail. *Rats are rodents that look like mice, but are larger.* 2. (slang) a

mean person, especially one who betrays someone else; tattletale. *She called him a rat for telling her secret.* *verb* (ratted, ratting, rats) (slang) to report the bad behavior of friends; tattle. *My brother ratted to Mom that I broke the lamp.* {**răt**}

rate *noun* 1. a quantity measured with respect to another measured quantity. *He drives the race car at a rate of over two hundred miles per hour.* / *She is paid at a rate of ten dollars per hour.* 2. the condition, grade, or quality of something. *The baseball team was first rate.* 3. price or cost. *The electric rate is high in this part of the country.* *verb* (rated, rating, rates) 1. to regard. *He rated the book as excellent.* 2. to put in a certain rank or order. *The judges rated the skaters.* {**rayt**}

rath·er *adverb* 1. in a more willing way; sooner. *I'd rather swim than sit on the beach.* 2. in some measure or degree. *He sang rather well.* 3. more correctly or accurately. *She spoke loudly, or rather she screamed.* {**ră** thər}

rat·i·fy *verb* (ratified, ratifying, ratifies) to approve in an official way; confirm. *The Senate ratified the treaty.* {**răt** ih **fiy**} ratification, n.

ra·tio *noun* (ratios) 1. a relation or comparison between numbers or things based on amount or degree. *The school counts the number of male and female students to find the ratio of boys to girls in the school.* / *My mother remembers the ratio of sugar to flour in the recipe.* 2. the relation between two numbers seen as the number of times the second number can be divided into the first. *If there are 6 apples and 3 oranges in a fruit basket,*

the ratio of apples to oranges is 2 to 1. {**ray** shee oh}

ra·tion *noun* 1. a fixed share or portion. *During the war, each family received a ration of food.* 2. (plural) a fixed portion of food for each soldier in an army. *The soldier received daily rations.* *verb* (rationed, rationing, rations) 1. to limit the use or supply of. *The government rationed eggs during the war.* 2. to give out in portions. *The government rationed out food for the flood victims.* 3. to control the spending or amount of; budget. *He rationed his money so it wouldn't run out.* / *She rationed her strength by resting often.* {**ră** shən or **ray** shən, n., **ră** shən or **ray** shən, v.}

ra·tion·al ❓ *adjective* 1. based on reasoning or logic; sensible. *She made a rational decision to stay home when she wasn't feeling well.* 2. in control of one's mind; not insane or crazy. *He became so angry, he was no longer rational.* 3. able to think or think clearly and logically. *Humans are rational creatures.* {**ră** shə nəl} rationally, adv.

rat·tle *verb* (rattled, rattling, rattles) 1. to make a series of hard, short knocking sounds. *The windows rattled during the storm.* 2. to speak quickly, without thought or serious purpose. *He rattled on about the game long after it was over.* 3. to cause to rattle by shaking. *The prisoner rattled the bars of the prison cell.* 4. to confuse or upset. *The lawyer's rapid questions rattled the witness.* *noun* 1. a series of hard, short knocking sounds. *The rattle of windows awakened me.* 2. a baby's toy that makes a rattling noise when shaken. {**răt** əl}

• **rattle off**

 Human Body   Human Mind   Everyday Life  History and Culture Communication

to list or recite quickly from memory. *I rattled off the names of all of the players on my favorite football team.*

rat·tle·snake *noun* a poisonous snake found in North, Central, and South America. A rattlesnake has a structure at the end of its tail that makes a rattling sound when the snake shakes it. {**răt** əl **snayk**}

rave *verb* (raved, raving, raves) 1. to talk with much enthusiasm; praise. *The critics raved about the new book.* 2. to talk in a strange, irrational, or crazy way. *My brother's high fever made him rave.* {**rayv**}

rav·el *verb* (raveled, raveling, ravels) to separate into loose threads; unravel. *The old sock began to ravel.* {**răv** əl}

rav·en *noun* a large, shiny, black bird that looks like a crow. It makes a sound like a loud, sharp croak. *adjective* having a shiny black color. *She brushed her long, raven hair.* {**rayv** ən}

rav·en·ous *adjective* very hungry; starved. *I was ravenous after hiking in the woods all day.* {**ră** və nəs}

ra·vine *noun* a deep, narrow valley. Ravines are usually created by flowing water. {rə **veen**}

ra·vi·o·li *noun* (used with a singular or plural verb) small packets of pasta filled with ground meat, cheese, or other similar mixtures. *Ravioli are boiled and then served with sauce.* {**răv** ee **oh** lee *or* **rahv** ee **oh** lee}

raw *adjective* (rawer, rawest) 1. not cooked or changed by any process. *Raw carrots are one of my favorite snacks.* 2. with the skin rubbed off; sore. *His knees were raw after he fell off his skateboard. / My throat was so raw, it hurt to swallow.* 3. not trained; having no experience. *The soldier laughed at how the raw recruits struggled with the drills.* 4. damp and chilly. *We stayed in the house because it was so raw outside.* {**raw**}

raw·hide *noun* 1. cattle skin or hide that has not been tanned. *His belt is made of rawhide.* 2. a rope or whip made of such leather. {**raw hiyd**}

ray¹ *noun* 1. a thin beam of light or some other radiation. *We enjoyed the warmth of the sun's rays.* 2. a part of a line having a point at one end. *An angle is made of two rays.* 3. a very small amount. *She had a ray of hope that she would find her ring.* {**ray**}

ray² *noun* a fish with a flat body and a skeleton made of cartilage. Rays have broad fins and long, narrow tails. {**ray**}

ray·on *noun* 1. a thread made from cellulose. 2. fabric made from such thread. {**ray** ŏn}

ra·zor *noun* a tool with a very sharp blade that is used for shaving hair from the body or face. {**ray** zər}

RBI *abbreviation* the number of runs a baseball player has caused to be scored over a given time. RBI is an abbreviation for "runs batted in."

re- *prefix* 1. a prefix that means "again" or "anew." *To rewrite a paper is to write it again.* 2. a prefix that means "back" or "backwards." *To repay a debt is to pay back the debt.*

reach *verb* (reached, reaching, reaches) 1. to extend or stretch as far as. *Her hair reaches her shoulders.* 2. to touch or take hold of by extending part of the body. *Can you reach the glass on the top shelf?* 3. to get in touch with. *They can reach us by mail.* 4. to arrive at. *We reached the lake after a three-hour drive. / Has he reached a decision?* 5. to extend something such as the hand. *I reached into my closet for my shoes.* 6. to try to touch or get hold of something. *They reached for his hand in the dark.* 7. to extend in direction, length, or distance. *The curtains reached down to the floor.* *noun* 1. an act or process of reaching. *With a reach of my arm I got hold of the book on the top shelf.* 2. the extent or distance reached or able to be reached. *He was beyond the reach of her voice.* 3. the range of a person's understanding or ability to handle. *That physics problem is beyond the reach of most middle-school students.* 4. the extent or stretch of something. *We drove through an enormous reach of desert.* {**reech**}

re·act *verb* (reacted, reacting, reacts) 1. to act in response to something. *I reacted to the*

sad movie by crying. 2. to respond to anything. *She reacted well to the news.* 3. to undergo chemical change when combined. *Rust is formed when iron reacts with hydrogen and oxygen.* {ree **ăkt**}

re·ac·tion 🧠👤 *noun* an action or response to something that has happened or has been done. *My reaction to getting straight A's on my report card was to jump and shout.* {ree **ăk** shən}

re·ac·tor *noun* 1. a device in physics for starting and controlling a nuclear chain reaction; nuclear reactor. 2. any person or thing that reacts. *He is a reactor, not one who plans ahead.* {ree **ăk** tər}

read 🧠 *verb* (read, reading, reads) 1. to examine and understand the meaning of something written. *My little brother is learning to read.* 2. to speak aloud something written; recite. *The teacher reads one chapter of a book every afternoon after recess.* 3. to understand the nature or meaning of. *I could read the disappointment on her face. / He read my mind.* 4. to say or show. *The clock reads eight.* {**reed**}

Homophone Note Are you looking for the word **reed** (tall grass)? **Read** and **reed** sound alike but have different meanings. The past tense of **read** and the color **red** also sound alike but have different meanings.

read·er *noun* 1. a person who reads. 2. a textbook used in teaching writing or reading. 3. a person who reads or recites before an audience. *The reader held the audience's attention for almost an hour.* {**reed** ər}

read·i·ly *adverb* 1. promptly or easily. *Cereal was readily*

available at the supermarket. 2. willingly; without hesitation. *He readily does chores when asked.* {**rehd** ə lee}

read·ing *noun* 1. the action of one who reads. *We have to do a lot of reading for our social studies class.* 2. a spoken presentation of something written. *The poet gave a public reading of her latest poems.* 3. the point shown on an instrument of measurement. *The high reading on the thermometer convinced Mom that I was sick.* {**ree** ding}

read·y *adjective* (readier, readiest) 1. prepared. *I am ready to go home.* 2. able to work or perform; fit. *Are you ready for the game?* 3. quick to answer, understand, or communicate. *He has a ready sense of humor.* 4. willing. *She is always ready to help others.* 5. able to be used right away. *I have some ready cash in my wallet.* *verb* (readied, readying, readies) to cause to be ready or to make ready; prepare. *He readied his house for winter.* {**rehd** ee}

re·al *adjective* 1. not imagined; actually existing; true. *It's hard to believe that real dinosaurs once walked the earth.* 2. not a copy; genuine. *Her boots are made of real leather.* {**reel**}

• **for real**
(informal) real or really; actual or actually. *We could hardly believe that our dream house was for real.*

Homophone Note Are you looking for the word **reel**? **Real** and **reel** sound alike but have different meanings.

real estate *noun* an area of land, including the trees, water, and buildings on it. {**reel** ih **stayt**}

re·al·is·tic *adjective* 1. tending to see things as they really are; practical. *She needs to be realistic about how much money she can spend to buy a car.* 2. showing people and things as they really are. *She painted a realistic portrait of her mother.* {ree ə **lihs** tihk}

re·al·i·ty *noun* (realities) 1. the state or quality of being real. *She didn't believe in the reality of aliens in outer space.* 2. a person, thing, or event that is real. *Her dream of owning a car became a reality.* {ree **ăl** ih tee}

• **in reality**
in fact; actually. *In reality, she did look a lot like her mother.*

re·al·i·za·tion *noun* 1. the act of being made real; achievement. *Becoming a teacher was the realization of his dreams.* 2. something that has been suddenly understood; insight. *She came to the realization that she would never be a movie star.* {ree ə lih **zay** shən *or* ree liy **zay** shən}

re·al·ize *verb* (realized, realizing, realizes) 1. to understand completely. *Do you realize how big a redwood tree is?* 2. to make real or make happen. *She realized her dream of success.* {ree **liyz**}

re·al·ly *adverb* 1. in fact; actually. *We may not look alike, but we really are brothers. / I'm not really sure.* 2. certainly; truly. *You really have a nice house.* *interjection* used to show disgust, surprise, or doubt. *Really! Your behavior is shocking.* {**ree** lee}

realm *noun* 1. a royal kingdom. *Have you read about King Arthur's realm?* 2. an area or field of something. *The entire realm of science is very interesting to me.* {**rehlm**}

reap *verb* (reaped, reaping, reaps) 1. to cut down and

 Human Body    Human Mind   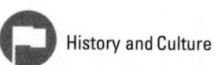 Everyday Life    History and Culture   Communication

gather. *The farmer reaped the grain from the field.* 2. to get in return for something. *The actor's excellent performance reaped applause from the audience.* {**ree**p}

re·ap·pear *verb* to come into view again; appear again. *The ship reappeared when the fog lifted.* {**ree** ə peer}

rear[1] *noun* 1. the back part of something. *The rear of the car was dented.* 2. a position behind or in back of something. *We sat in the rear of the theater.* 3. the part of a military unit or area that is farthest away from the enemy. *The soldier was part of the rear guard.* *adjective* having to do with or being at the back or the rear. *Go through the rear entrance.* {**ree**r}

rear[2] *verb* (reared, rearing, rears) 1. to raise to adulthood; bring up. *My uncle rears chickens on his farm.* 2. to raise upright. *The snake reared its head to strike.* 3. to rise on the hind legs. *The horse reared and ran away.* {**ree**r}

re·ar·range *verb* (rearranged, rearranging, rearranges) 1. to change the order of or arrange in a different way. *I rearranged the living room furniture.* 2. to arrange again. *She rearranged her papers after they fell to the floor.* {**ree** ə **raynj**}

rea·son ❷ *noun* 1. a cause or explanation for an action, opinion, or event. *He had a good reason for being late.* / *What's the reason for the party?* 2. the power to think clearly. *Human beings are creatures of reason.* *verb* (reasoned, reasoning, reasons) 1. to think clearly. *It's hard to reason when you're tired or angry.* 2. to think through (often followed by "through").

It took hours to reason through the difficult algebra problem. {**ree** zən}

rea·son·a·ble *adjective* 1. using good sense and clear thinking. *The judge made a reasonable decision after carefully listening to the case.* 2. not too much; fair. *The homework assignment was reasonable.* 3. showing good sense and clear thinking. *Her answer on the test was reasonable.* 4. not too expensive. *The price for the leather jacket was reasonable.* {**ree** zə nə bəl} reasonably, adv.

re·as·sure *verb* (reassured, reassuring, reassures) 1. to make less worried; give back confidence to. *My mother reassured me that everything would be fine.* 2. to assure again. *The coach reassured the team that the game would continue despite the rain.* {**ree** ə **shoohr** or **ree** ə **shuhr**} reassurance, n., reassuringly, adv.

re·bate *noun* a part of a payment that is returned. *The store offered rebates to customers who bought television sets.* *verb* (rebated, rebating, rebates) to give back as a rebate. *The company rebated part of our payment by check.* {**ree bayt**}

reb·el *noun* 1. one who fights against or does not obey authority. *That teenager is a rebel.* 2. a person who fights against or is not loyal to the government of his or her country. *The rebels tried to overthrow the emperor.* *adjective* having to do with those who are rebels. *The band of fighters waved their rebel flag in the air.* *verb* (rebelled, rebelling, rebels) 1. to fight against those in control or refuse to obey their rules; revolt. *During the Revolutionary War, the American colonies rebelled against English*

rule. 2. to show feelings of strong dislike or opposition. *My dog rebelled when I tried to make him beg for treats.* {**reh** bəl, n., **reh** bəl, adj., rih **behl**, v.}

Word History *Rebel* comes from *bellum*, the Latin word for "war." With the prefix "re-," it means "make war against."

re·bel·lion *noun* 1. an armed fight against one's government; uprising. *The rebellion was stopped by the army after three months of fighting.* 2. the act of disobeying rules or fighting against authority. *The students showed their rebellion by refusing to wear the school uniform.* {reh **behl** yən}

re·call ❷ *verb* (recalled, recalling, recalls) 1. to bring a past event into the mind; remember. *Do you recall the day we went to the zoo together?* 2. to cause to return; call back. *The lawyer recalled the witness to the stand.* 3. to have products returned to the factory where they were made. *Companies recall a product if it is found to be dangerous or damaged in some way. The factory recalled the defective bicycles.* *noun* the act of remembering. *I have very little recall of being three years old.* {rih **kawl** or **ree kawl**}

re·cap·ture *verb* (recaptured, recapturing, recaptures) 1. to take, catch, or capture again. *The team was able to recapture some of the points they had lost.* / *We recaptured our runaway kittens.* 2. to remember clearly. *When I smell gingerbread, I can recapture the memory of my grandmother's kitchen.* *noun* the act of capturing again or the condition of being captured again. *The*

 Living World   Physical World    Natural Environment   ⟨∿∿⟩ Economy   ▭ Government and Law

A B C D E F G H I J K L M N O P Q R S T U V W X Y Z

a
b
c
d
e
f
g
h
i
j
k
l
m
n
o
p
q
r
s
t
u
v
w
x
y
z

recapture of the escaped giraffe took the zookeepers many hours. {ree **kăp** chər}

re·cede *verb* (receded, receding, recedes) 1. to move back to the same low level or point as before. *The flood waters receded after the rain stopped.* 2. to move away or back; become more distant. *The hills appeared to recede as we drove away from them.* {ree **seed**}

re·ceipt 🔊 *noun* 1. the act or fact of receiving. *Upon the receipt of your payment, the company will send the books you ordered.* 2. a piece of paper showing that money or things were received. *The cashier at the store gave me my change and a receipt.* 3. (usually plural) an amount of money received from selling something. *The receipts from the team's car wash were over two hundred dollars.* {rih **seet**}

re·ceive *verb* (received, receiving, receives) 1. to get or take. *He received many gifts while he was in the hospital.* 2. to welcome or greet. *They receive guests often. / We received him as a member of our club.* 3. to experience. *She received a serious injury in the accident.* 4. to find out about. *We received the news yesterday.* 5. to pick up signals. *The radio signal they were receiving was very weak.* 6. to play football in the position of one whose job is to catch forward passes. *This season he will be receiving for the high school team.* {rih **seev**}

re·ceiv·er *noun* 1. a person who receives. 2. a device that receives electronic signals and changes them into something that can be seen, heard, or understood. Televisions, telephones, and radios all work by using receivers. 3.

a football player whose job is to catch a forward pass. *The receiver ran down the field ahead of the other players.* {rih **see** vər}

re·cent *adjective* 1. having to do with or happening in the very near past. *After the recent storm, many people are still without electricity.* 2. done, made, or appearing just before the present time; new. *I enjoy looking at magazines to see the recent fashions.* {**ree** sənt} recently, adv.

re·cep·ta·cle *noun* a container for receiving and keeping something. *Please do not put anything that can be recycled in the trash receptacle.* {rih **sehp** tə kəl}

re·cep·tion *noun* 1. the act or process of receiving. *This department handles the reception of mail.* 2. way of greeting or welcoming. *The singer was pleased with the warm reception he received.* 3. a party or gathering at which guests are received. *After the graduation ceremony, there was a reception for graduates and their parents.* 4. the receiving of radio or television signals or the quality of these signals. *We get very bad reception with our old television.* {rih **sehp** shən}

re·cess 🔊 *noun* 1. a relaxing break from an activity, such as school classes or trials in court. *Everyone went outside to the playground during recess. / The judge announced a recess of two hours.* 2. an area on a surface or edge that is hollow or bends inward. *The small recesses in the cliff gave the climber something to hold on to.* 3. (plural) hidden places. *She found the bracelet in the recesses of the sofa. / He hid in the deepest recesses of the cave.* *verb* (recessed,

recessing, recesses) to stop activity for a period of time; take a recess. *Court will recess for half an hour.* {ree sehs, n., rih **sehs**, v.}

rec·i·pe *noun* a list of ingredients and instructions for making a food dish. {**reh** sih pee}

re·cit·al 🔊 *noun* 1. a concert of music or dance that is meant to demonstrate the ability of the performers. *My piano teacher wants all her students to play in the recital.* 2. a detailed report or list. *He gave us a long recital of everything he had done that day.* {rih **siy** təl}

re·cite *verb* (recited, reciting, recites) 1. to speak the words of from memory and in front of others. *Edna recited her poems.* 2. to list in detail. *She recited the names of all of the presidents.* {rih **siyt**}

reck·less *adjective* paying no attention to danger; not at all careful. *She is a reckless driver and often goes much too fast.* {**rehk** lihs} recklessly, adv.

DANGER
STEEP CLIFF
KEEP OFF

reck·on *verb* (reckoned, reckoning, reckons) 1. to count

 Human Body   Human Mind   Everyday Life   History and Culture    Communication

or estimate; figure. *He reckoned how much he would need to save for a new skateboard.* 2. (informal) to expect or judge that. *I reckon my mom is the best cook in town.* {**reh** kən}

re·cline *verb* (reclined, reclining, reclines) 1. to lie down in a comfortable position. *The man reclined in his hammock for a nap.* 2. to cause to move into a leaning or tilted position. *The artist reclined the easel so that she could work more easily.* {rih **kliyn**}

rec·og·ni·tion *noun* 1. the act of realizing that one knows someone or something. *Whenever he saw his former owner, the dog wagged his tail in recognition.* 2. the condition of being recognized in this way. *He wore dark glasses to avoid recognition.* 3. notice or approval. *She received recognition from the school for her high grades.* 4. acceptance that something is true or real. *The prisoners demanded recognition of their rights.* {reh kəg **nih** shən}

rec·og·nize *verb* (recognized, recognizing, recognizes) 1. to identify from an earlier experience. *She recognized him as her former neighbor.* 2. to admit, understand, or accept as true. *He recognized his mistake and worked to correct it.* {**reh** kəg **niyz**} recognizable, adj.

rec·ol·lect *verb* (recollected, recollecting, recollects) to bring back from memory; remember; recall. *I can't recollect when I last saw him.* {reh kə **lehkt**}

rec·om·mend *verb* (recommended, recommending, recommends) 1. to speak or write of in a favorable way; support. *She recommends him highly for the job.* 2. to present

as worth doing; suggest; advise. *I recommend that we not disturb the hornets' nest.* 3. to cause to appear good. *He has no special skills to recommend him for the job.* {reh kə **mehnd**}

re·cord 🔊 *verb* (recorded, recording, records) 1. to put in writing. *The nurse recorded my height and weight in my health chart.* 2. to copy by use of a mechanical or electronic device for later hearing or viewing. *The popular group recorded hundreds of songs. / I recorded my favorite TV program so I could watch it later.* *noun* 1. a written account or other collection of information. *The historical record shows that Native Americans once owned this land. / A record of our tax payments is kept at city hall.* 2. a disk onto which recorded sounds have been copied. *She owns many rock-'n'-roll records.* 3. the greatest achievement in a particular field. *In 2001, Barry Bonds broke the record for the most home runs scored in a season.* 4. the written facts about one's past actions. *The student records are kept in the principal's office.* {**reh** kərd, n., rih **kohrd**, v.}

re·cord·er *noun* 1. a person whose job is to keep records. 2. a device that records sound or images. 3. a musical instrument made of wood or plastic that is like a flute. It has a mouthpiece like a whistle at one end. {rih **kohr** dər}

re·cord·ing *noun* 1. the act or process of making a record, compact disk, or cassette tape. *Recording the interview helped the reporter write an accurate*

article. 2. something that is recorded on a record, compact disk, or cassette tape. *My mother still has recordings she made of us talking when we were little.* {rih **kohr** ding}

re·cov·er *verb* (re-covered, re-covering, re-covers) to cover again. *The couch is worn and will have to be re-covered.* {ree **kuh** vər}

re·cov·er 🔊 *verb* (recovered, recovering, recovers) 1. to get back. *She recovered her lost wallet.* 2. to make up for. *Mike recovered lost hours of sleep by taking a nap.* 3. to return to a normal or healthy condition. *She is home from the hospital after recovering from her illness.* {rih **kuh** vər}

re·cov·er·y *noun* (recoveries) 1. the act of getting back something that had been lost or stolen. *The recovery of my missing wallet was a great relief to me.* 2. a return to a normal condition or to good health. *The forest's recovery from the fire took many years. / We wished her a quick recovery from her operation.* {rih **kuh** və ree}

rec·re·a·tion 🔊 *noun* activity that is relaxing or fun. *We go swimming every weekend for recreation.* {rehk ree **ay** shən}

re·cruit *noun* 1. a soldier who has just joined or been drafted into the armed forces. *The new recruits were given uniforms.* 2. a new member of a group or organization. *Our soccer team has some talented recruits this year.* *verb* (recruited, recruiting, recruits) to get to join. *The coach is trying to recruit new players for the tennis team.* {rih **krooht**} recruiter, n.

rec·tan·gle *noun* a flat, closed figure with four straight sides, four right angles, and oppo-

site sides parallel to each other. {**rehk** tăng gəl}

Word History *Rectangle* is a word made by combining *rectus*, the Latin word for "right," and "angle."

re·cu·per·ate *verb* (recuperated, recuperating, recuperates) to become healthy again after being ill. *He is still recuperating from the measles.* {rih **kooh** pə **rayt**}

re·cur *verb* (recurred, recurring, recurs) to happen again or over and over. *If the pain recurs, call the nurse. / The strange lights in the sky recurred every night for a week.* {rih **kuhr**}

re·cy·cle *verb* (recycled, recycling, recycles) to put through a process that allows used things to be reused. *The city recycles old tires for use in making new roads.* {ree **siy** kəl} recyclable, adj.

red *noun* the color of blood; the first color on the color spectrum. *adjective* (redder, reddest) having the color red. {**rehd**} reddish, adj., redness, n.

Homophone Note The words *red* and *read* (the past tense verb) sound alike but have different meanings.

red blood cell *noun* a cell in the blood that carries oxygen to the body's tissues. {**rehd** **bluhd** sehl}

red·coat *noun* a British soldier in colonial America during the American Revolution and other wars. {**rehd** koht}

Red Cross *noun* an international organization that gives medical care to people hurt during wars and natural disasters. {**rehd** **kraws**}

re·deem *verb* (redeemed, redeeming, redeems) 1. to exchange for cash, prizes, or other goods. *I redeemed my coupon for a free soda.* 2. to make up for; balance. *The player struck out, but he redeemed himself later when he hit a home run.* {rih **deem**}

red-hand·ed *adverb* or *adjective* in the act of doing something wrong or illegal. *The police caught him red-handed stealing the car.* {**rehd** **hăn** dihd}

Red Sea *noun* a part of the Indian Ocean. It lies between the Arabian Peninsula and East Africa. The Suez Canal connects it to the Mediterranean Sea. {**rehd** **see**}

re·duce *verb* (reduced, reducing, reduces) 1. to make less in amount or size. *The new roads reduced traffic jams.* 2. to bring to a low condition (often followed by "to"). *The fire reduced the house to ashes. / Her problems reduced her to tears.* {rih **doohs**}

re·duc·tion *noun* 1. the act of reducing or state of being reduced. *Exercise and the reduction of fat in the diet are two ways to improve health.* 2. the amount by which something is reduced. *The store is selling furniture at a ten-percent reduction off their usual price.* {rih **duhk** shən}

red·wood *noun* 1. a very tall evergreen tree found in northwestern North America. Redwoods live for a long time and are among the largest trees in the world. 2. the reddish brown wood of this tree. {**rehd** wuud}

reed *noun* 1. a tall grass with straight, jointed stalks that grows in low, wet areas. 2. a small strip of cane or metal set into the mouthpiece of some wind instruments. A player blows through the mouthpiece to make the reed vibrate and produce sound. {reed}

Homophone Note Are you looking for the word *read* (what one does with a book)? *Reed* and *read* sound alike but have different meanings.

reef *noun* a ridge of rock, sand, or coral at or near the surface of ocean waters. {**reef**}

reel[1] *noun* 1. a spool or other device on which fishing line, cord, tape, film, or other material can be wound. 2. the amount of material that is or can be wound on such a device. *The photographer's bag held many reels of film.* *verb* (reeled, reeling, reels) 1. to wind on a reel. *It took him a long time to reel the fishing line because it was tangled.* 2. to catch or get back by winding with a reel (often follwed by in). *She reeled in a large trout.* {**reel**}
• **reel off** say quickly and easily. *He reeled off a dozen excuses for being late.*

reel[2] *verb* (reeled, reeling, reels) 1. to sway, stagger, or lose one's balance. *The exhausted runner was reeling after the marathon.* 2. to turn in circles; whirl. *We danced so fast that the room seemed to reel around us.* {**reel**}

 Human Body Human Mind Everyday Life History and Culture  Communication

reel[3] *noun* a lively Scottish folk dance, or the music that it is danced to. {reel}

Homophone Note Are you looking for the word *real*? *Reel* and *real* sound alike but have different meanings.

re·e·lect *verb* to be chosen again by means of voting; to elect again. *The team reelected her as captain.* {ree ee lehkt}

re·en·try or **re-entry** *noun* (reentries or re-entries) 1. an act of entering again. *Upon the president's reentry into the room, everyone stood up again.* 2. the return of a spacecraft or rocket into the earth's atmosphere. *The spaceship is now preparing for reentry.* {ree **ehn** tree}

ref *noun* (informal) a referee.

re·fer *verb* (referred, referring, refers) 1. to send or direct to a source for help. *He referred me to a good doctor.* 2. to pass or hand over for advice or help. *We referred the problem to an expert.* 3. to speak of; mention. *She referred to his work in her speech.* {rih **fuhr**}

ref·er·ee *noun* a sports official who makes sure that players follow the rules of the game. *verb* (refereed, refereeing, referees) to act as a referee in. *The coach's assistant offered to referee the game.* {reh fə **ree**}

ref·er·ence *noun* 1. the act or fact of mentioning. *The newspaper made no reference to the bus accident.* 2. a source of information. *This dictionary is an excellent reference for writers.* 3. a person who speaks in support of another for a position or job. *My teacher said I could use her as a reference when I applied for a summer job.* {**reh** fə **rəns** *or* **reh** frəns}

ref·er·ence book *noun* a book that is a source of information. Dictionaries and encyclopedias are reference books. {**rehf** ər ihns **buuk**}

re·fill *verb* (refilled, refilling, refills) to fill again. *The thirsty runners refilled their water bottles halfway through the race. noun* something that refills or replaces. *I need a refill of ink for my printer. / She finished her soda and asked for a refill.* {**ree** fihl, n., ree **fihl**, v.}

re·fine *verb* (refined, refining, refines) to make pure or fine. *Raw cane juice is refined to make sugar.* {rih **fiyn**}

re·flect ❶ *verb* (reflected, reflecting, reflects) 1. to throw back from a surface. *Insulation reflects heat back into a building.* 2. to throw back an image of; mirror. *The ocean reflected the setting sun.* 3. to show as the result of; express. *These grades reflect your hard work.* 4. to give a particular view of a person's ability or character (usually followed by "on"). *Her rude comments will reflect badly on her.* 5. to think about; ponder. *He reflected on the problem.* {rih **flehkt**}

re·flec·tion ❶ *noun* 1. the act of reflecting or state of being reflected. *When we see colors, we see the reflection of light by objects.* 2. heat, light, or an image that bounces off an object or surface. *We looked at our reflections in the lake.* 3. the process of deep or serious thinking, or a particular thought that results from this process. *Upon careful reflection, I have decided not to go. / His book is filled with interesting reflections on how computers have changed people.* {rih **flehk** shən}

re·flec·tor *noun* a surface that throws back heat, light, or sound. *If you ride your bicycle at night, be sure it has reflectors.* {rih **flehk** tər}

re·flex ❓ *adjective* having to do with a response or reaction that is automatic and not controlled by conscious thought. *His leg moved in a reflex action when the doctor tapped his knee. noun* 1. a response or reaction of the body that is not chosen or controlled by conscious thought. A reflex occurs when the nervous system reacts to a stimulus. *Breathing is a human reflex.* 2. (plural) the ability to respond or react quickly. *Most tennis players have good reflexes.* {**ree** flehks}

re·for·est *verb* (reforested, reforesting, reforests) to plant new trees in. *The rangers decided to reforest an area of the park that had burned down.* {ree **far** ihst *or* ree **fohr** ihst} reforestation, n.

re·form *noun* the changing of wrong or bad conditions to make them better. *The corrupt city government is in need of reform. verb* (reformed, reforming, reforms) 1. to make better; improve. *The women's group worked to reform laws that were unfair to women.* 2. to give up bad

A B C D E F G H I J K L M N O P Q R S T U V W X Y Z

refrain – register

behavior. *He used to be a thief, but he has reformed.* {rih **fohrm**}

re·frain *noun* a phrase or melody that is repeated regularly during a song or poem. {rih **frayn**}

re·fresh *verb* (refreshed, refreshing, refreshes) 1. to bring back the energy or spirits of. *The meal at the inn refreshed the travellers.* 2. to bring back knowledge or memory to. *I have already studied, but I still need to refresh my memory before the exam.* {rih **frehsh**}

re·fresh·ment *noun* 1. (often plural) something that refreshes, such as food and drink. *There will be refreshments after the wedding.* 2. the act of refreshing or the condition of being refreshed. *We needed refreshment after a hot day, so we decided to have a swim.* {rih **frehsh** mənt}

re·frig·er·ate *verb* (refrigerated, refrigerating, refrigerates) to make cold or cool. *If you don't refrigerate the eggs, they will spoil.* {rə **frih** jə **rayt**}

re·frig·er·a·tor *noun* a room, box, or appliance where food is kept cold to prevent spoiling. {rə **frih** jə ray tər}

ref·uge ❶ *noun* 1. a place that protects from danger or difficulty. *We took refuge in the cave during the storm.* / *The wildlife refuge takes care of*

hurt and sick animals. 2. anything a person turns to for comfort or help. *My violin is my refuge.* {**rehf** yooj}

ref·u·gee *noun* a person forced to leave his or her home or country to seek safety or protection. {**rehf** yoo **jee**}

re·fund *verb* (refunded, refunding, refunds) to return or pay back. *The store will refund your money if you are not satisfied.* *noun* an amount of money returned. *I was given a refund of ten dollars.* {**ree** fuhnd, n., rih **fuhnd**, v.}

> **Word History** *Refund* comes from a Latin word that means "pour back," "give back," or "restore."

re·fuse¹ *verb* (refused, refusing, refuses) 1. to not accept or agree to; turn down. *I refused the stranger's offer of a ride.* / *The bank refused his request for a loan.* 2. to be unwilling to do. *I refuse to tell you my phone number.* 3. to say no; to not permit or agree to something. *I asked her if I could borrow her book, but she refused.* {rih **fyooz**}

re·fuse² *noun* something without any worth; garbage; trash. {**rehf** yoos}

re·gain *verb* (regained, regaining, regains) 1. to get back; recover. *He regained his balance on the tightrope.* / *After their mistake, the bank worked hard to regain my trust.* 2. to reach or get to again. *At long last, the ship regained the shore.* {rih **gayn**}

re·gard *verb* (regarded, regarding, regards) 1. to think of with a particular feeling or in a certain way; consider. *I regard her as one of my best friends.* 2. to look at. *The dog regarded me with suspicion from inside the fence.* 3. consider; pay attention to.

He did not regard the doctor's advice, and now he is sicker than ever. *noun* 1. respect; esteem. *The workers hold their boss in high regard.* 2. (plural) best wishes; respectful greetings. *Please give your family my regards.* {rih **gard**}

re·gard·ing *preposition* having to do with; about; concerning. *Let's make plans regarding your visit.* {rih **gar** ding}

re·gard·less *adjective* without concern or thought. *Regardless of her neighbor's stares, she went ahead and painted her house purple.* *adverb* without paying attention to warnings or dangers; anyway. *They say it is a difficult trail, but we are going to hike it regardless.* {rih **gard** lihs}

re·gime *noun* a system of rule or government. *We will pay higher taxes under the new regime.* {rə **zheem**}

reg·i·ment *noun* a troop of soldiers made up of two or more battalions. {**reh** jə mənt}

re·gion ❺ *noun* 1. a large space or area. *This region is famous for its apples.* 2. an area of the earth's surface that has certain features of land and climate. *I have traveled a lot in the Rocky Mountain region.* / *This tree only grows in tropical regions.* {**ree** jən}

reg·is·ter *noun* 1. a book used to record names, events, or other information. *The hotel kept a register of its guests.* 2. a cash register. 3. a grate or other opening that lets heated or cooled air pass into a room. 4. the range of notes that a musical instrument or voice can produce. *The singer chose a song with very high and low notes to show off her register.* *verb* (registered, registering, registers) 1. to write down or enter in a record book or register. *The clerk*

  Human Body Human Mind Everyday Life History and Culture Communication

asked me to register my license number. 2. to sign up for something by having one's name put on an official list. *Have you registered to vote yet?* / *He registered in the army.* 3. to show or express. *His face registered sadness.* 4. to show on a measuring device or scale. *The butcher piled bacon on the scale until it registered three pounds.* 5. to have officially recorded to prevent loss or theft. *I registered the package at the post office before mailing it.* {<u>reh</u> jih stər}

registered nurse *noun* a nurse who has completed training and who has a license to practice nursing. In order to receive a license, nurses must pass an examination given by a state government. {<u>reh</u> jih stərd <u>nuhrs</u>}

re·gret ❓ *verb* (regretted, regretting, regrets) to feel sorry or guilty for. *The prisoner regretted his mistakes.* *noun* 1. a feeling of sadness about something one has done; guilt. *She had no regrets about her decision.* 2. (plural) a polite apology for refusing an invitation. *I sent my regrets that I couldn't make the party.* {rih <u>greht</u>} regrettable, adj., regrettably, adv.

reg·u·lar *adjective* 1. normal or usual. *We'll meet at the regular place.* 2. following the same or standard ways of doing something. *He is very creative and doesn't do things in the regular way.* 3. even or steady. *She tapped a regular beat with her foot.* 4. happening at fixed points over a period of time. *She had to miss one of her regular Tuesday softball practices.* 5. having or following the most common rule in grammar. *The regular ending for verbs in the past tense is "-*

ed." For example, "*I baked a cake yesterday.*" 6. having equal angles, sides, or faces. *The shape of a stop sign is a regular octagon.* {<u>rehg</u> yə lər} regularity, n.

reg·u·late *verb* (regulated, regulating, regulates) 1. to control by rules or a method. *The government regulates the sale of guns.* / *Green plants help to regulate the amounts of different gases in the atmosphere.* 2. to make accurate by adjusting. *He regulated all of the clocks in our house.* {<u>rehg</u> yə layt}

reg·u·la·tion 🌐 💻 *noun* 1. a rule or law that controls or directs people's actions. *City regulations require buildings to have fire escapes.* 2. the act or process of regulating. *Is the government's regulation of pollution making the air and water cleaner?* *adjective* conforming to a rule or order. *All of the soldiers wear regulation uniforms.* {<u>rehg</u> yə <u>lay</u> shən}

re·hears·al *noun* the act or process of practicing for a play, concert, or other performance. *We have three more rehearsals before our performance.* {rih <u>huhr</u> səl}

re·hearse *verb* (rehearsed, rehearsing, rehearses) to practice for a show, play, concert, or other performance. *Let's rehearse those dance steps one more time.* {rih <u>huhrs</u>}

reign 💻 *noun* 1. rule by a king or queen. *The queen's reign was fair and just.* 2. the period of one monarch's rule. *Shakespeare wrote his plays during the reign of Queen Elizabeth.* *verb* (reigned, reigning, reigns) 1. to hold the

power of a monarch; rule. *The king reigned for many years.* 2. to have complete and widespread control or influence. *Terror reigned during the long years of war.* {<u>rayn</u>}

Homophone Note The words **reign**, **rain**, and **rein** sound alike but have different meanings.

rein *noun* 1. (usually plural) a set of leather straps attached to both ends of a horse's bridle bit. Using reins, a driver or rider can control the horse. 2. a means of controlling or guiding. *The boss holds the reins of power in this company.* / *In most classes the teacher holds the reins.* *verb* (reined, reining, reins) 1. to stop, guide, or hold back by using reins (often followed by "in"). *The rider reined in her horse.* 2. to guide or control (often followed by "in"). *I was very angry, but I reined in my temper.* {<u>rayn</u>}

Homophone Note The words **rein**, **rain**, and **reign** sound alike but have different meanings.

rein·deer *noun* (reindeer or reindeers) an animal with long legs and a long neck closely related to caribou. Reindeer are mammals with antlers and hooves. They are raised in the northern parts of Europe and Asia for their milk, meat, fur, and transportation. Reindeer are closely related to moose and other kinds of deer. Reindeer and caribou are the only deer that have ant-

A B C D E F G H I J K L M N O P Q R S T U V W X Y Z

lers on both males and females. {**rayn** deer}

re·in·force *verb* (reinforced, reinforcing, reinforces) to add strength to or increase the effect of. *They reinforced the fence with barbed wire.* {**ree** ihn **fohrs**}

re·ject *verb* (rejected, rejecting, rejects) to refuse to take, approve, or believe. *She rejected his offer. / To be an original thinker, you must often reject old ideas.* {rih **jehkt**} rejection, n.

re·joice *verb* (rejoiced, rejoicing, rejoices) to be full of joy or show great pleasure (sometimes followed by "in"). *We rejoiced in the coolness of the pool. / When she heard that her brother was safe, she rejoiced.* {rih **jois**}

re·lapse *verb* (relapsed, relapsing, relapses) to return to bad behavior or poor health after a period of improvement. *After many years without stealing anything, the thief relapsed into her old ways. noun* the act or result of relapsing. *He seemed to be recovering from his illness, but then he had a relapse.* {rih **lăps** or **ree lăps**}

re·late *verb* (related, relating, relates) 1. to tell the story of. *The traveler related his adventures in Alaska.* 2. to see or find connections between; link. *She related five o'clock with dinner time. / The speaker did not relate the snores he heard to his boring speech.* 3. to understand or get along with others. *She relates well to everyone in her class.* 4. to have a connection. *Her ques-*

tion did not relate to the topic we were discussing. {rih **layt**}

re·lat·ed *adjective* 1. having some connection. *The two robberies were related.* 2. connected by family ties. *I am related to a famous actor.* {rih **lay** tihd}

re·la·tion *noun* 1. (plural) the activities that go on between people, groups, or nations. *The two countries had friendly relations.* 2. connection. *Is there a relation between candy and tooth decay?* 3. a person who belongs to the same family; relative. *Some of her relations are coming for a visit.* {rih **lay** shən}

re·la·tion·ship ○ *noun* 1. the condition or fact of being related or connected. *There is a relationship between exercise and good health.* 2. a connection between people. *I have a good relationship with my parents.* {rih **lay** shən **shihp**}

rel·a·tive *noun* a person who belongs to the same family as someone else. *All our relatives, including my mother's aunt Gertrude, are coming to visit. adjective* having meaning or truth only in relation to something else. *How large an object appears is relative to how far away you stand from it.* {**reh** lə tihv}

re·lax *verb* (relaxed, relaxing, relaxes) 1. to make looser or less stiff. *Relax your leg so the doctor can test your reflexes.* 2. to become less tense or more at ease. *The workers relaxed during their lunch break.* 3. to make less harsh or strict. *The school decided to relax its dress code and allow blue jeans.* {rih **lăks**}

re·lay *noun* 1. a team in which people take turns doing a task or running part of a race. 2. a race in which each team member completes part of

the course and is then followed by another who does the same. *verb* (relayed, relaying, relays) to carry or pass on. *Will you relay my complaint to the manager?* {**ree** lay or rih **lay**}

relay race *noun* a race between two or more teams in which each runner completes part of the race and then is replaced or relieved by another team member. {**ree** lay rays}

re·lease *verb* (released, releasing, releases) 1. to set free. *We released the tadpoles into the pond. / The landlord would not release him from his contract.* 2. to let go of or loosen. *He released the handle.* 3. to allow to be shown, sold, or published. *The police department released photos of the suspects. / When was Elvis Presley's first record released? noun* the act or process of releasing. *His family celebrated his release from prison.* {rih **lees**}

re·lent *verb* (relented, relenting, relents) to become less harsh or less strict. *The bad weather finally relented. / My father finally relented and let me go outside instead of doing my chores.* {rih **lehnt**}

rel·e·vant *adjective* related to what is being discussed or is presently important. *His comment about cooking was not relevant to our discussion about sports.* {**rehl** ə vənt} relevance, n.

re·li·a·ble *adjective* capable of being trusted or relied on; dependable. *Her boss knows that she is an honest and reliable employee.* {rih **liy** ə bəl} reliably, adv.

rel·ic *noun* something that has survived from the past, such as an object or a

 Human Body   Human Mind    Everyday Life    History and Culture   Communication

custom. *The museum had a display of old weapons and other relics from the Revolutionary War.* {**rehl** ihk}

re·lief[1] *noun* 1. the feeling of being freed from pain, distress, or worry. *The aspirin gave me relief from my headache.* 2. a means of gaining such a feeling. *The good news was a great relief to me.* 3. help given to those in need. *Relief was promised to the victims of the flood.* 4. a person or persons taking over the work of others for a time. *After several hours of work, our relief finally arrived.* {rih **leef**}

re·lief[2] *noun* raised pictures or designs on a surface. *The map shows hills and mountains in relief. / The vase was decorated with designs carved in relief.* {rih **leef**}

relief map *noun* a map that shows the height or depth of different places in an area. Relief maps may use three dimensions, different colors, or different shadings to show hills, mountains, and valleys. {rih **leef** măp}

re·lieve *verb* (relieved, relieving, relieves) 1. to make less painful or troubling; ease. *Hot tea will relieve your sore throat. / She relieved my worries about the exam.* 2. to free from fear, worry, need, or poverty. *It relieves me to hear that you are all right.* 3. to take over the work of. *At noon, a new crew will relieve the morning workers.* {rih **leev**}

re·li·gion 🌐 ◖ *noun* 1. a set of beliefs about how the universe was made and what its purpose is. Religion usually involves worship of a god or gods, and the belief in certain ideas about right and wrong behavior. 2. the practice of one's religious beliefs. *He is very devout in his reli-*

gion. 3. anything that a person has an extreme devotion or commitment to. *Sports is his religion.* {rih **lih** jən}

> **Word History** *Religion*
> comes from a Latin word that means "to bind or tie strongly" or "to place an obligation on."

re·li·gious *adjective* 1. having to do with religion. *The Koran is a religious book.* 2. showing or having religious beliefs. 3. having high standards; very careful. *He is religious about being on time.* {rih **lih** jəs} religiously, adv.

rel·ish *noun* 1. a great enjoyment of something. *He always ate with relish.* 2. a spicy topping used to flavor food. Relish is often made out of chopped, pickled vegetables and served on hot dogs or hamburgers. *verb* (relished, relishing, relishes) to take great pleasure in; enjoy. *I would relish the chance to meet him.* {**reh** lihsh}

re·luc·tant *adjective* not willing or enthusiastic. *She was reluctant to go into the dark house.* {rih **luhk** tənt} reluctantly, adv.

re·ly *verb* (relied, relying, relies) to trust or depend (usually followed by "on" or "upon"). *I rely on your help to finish the job.* {rih **liy**}

re·main *verb* (remained, remaining, remains) 1. to go

on being; continue in a particular way without a change. *He remained quiet all afternoon. / After a week in the hospital, the patient remains very ill.* 2. to stay or be left in the same place after others have gone. *I will remain here while you go to the store.* 3. to be left. *Who will win remains to be seen. / There are some mistakes in your work that remain to be corrected.* {rih **mayn**}

re·main·der *noun* something that remains after other things have been taken away. *Jim spent some of his money and saved the remainder. / When you divide ten by six, you get one with a remainder of four.* {rih **mayn** dər}

re·mains *plural noun* 1. that which is left when parts have been taken away or destroyed. *The remains of this morning's breakfast were still on the table.* 2. a dead body; corpse. *His remains are buried in the town cemetery.* 3. ruins or traces of the past. *We visited the remains of the ancient temple.* {rih **maynz**}

re·mark *verb* (remarked, remarking, remarks) 1. to make a comment or statement. *"There is a bird outside the window," he remarked.* 2. to notice or see. *I remarked that it looked like it was going to snow. noun* a comment or short statement. *My friend made a remark about the clothes I was wearing.* {rih **mark**}

re·mark·a·ble *adjective* 1. unusual or exceptional. *That summer was remarkable for its lack of rain.* 2. worthy of being noticed or mentioned. *He is a remarkable tennis player.* {rih **mar** kə bəl} remarkably, adv.

A B C D E F G H I J K L M N O P Q R S T U V W X Y Z

a
b
c
d
e
f
g
h
i
j
k
l
m
n
o
p
q
r
s
t
u
v
w
x
y
z

rem·e·dy *noun* (remedies) 1. something used to take away pain or heal a disease. *Aspirin can be a good remedy for a headache.* 2. something that corrects or fixes a wrong. *They hope the new stop sign will be a remedy for speeding drivers in our neighborhood. / Is there a remedy for laziness?* *verb* (remedied, remedying, remedies) 1. to make better; heal. *This medicine will remedy that cough.* 2. to set right or fix. *Whenever she makes a mistake, she tries to remedy it. / The new principal hopes to remedy the noise in the hallways.* {**rehm** ih dee}

re·mem·ber ❓ *verb* (remembered, remembering, remembers) 1. to bring back into the mind from memory; recall. *I could not remember his name.* 2. to keep in the memory. *I will always remember my seventh birthday party.* 3. to send warm greetings from. *Remember me to her, will you?* {rih **mehm** bər}

re·mind *verb* (reminded, reminding, reminds) to cause to recall. *She reminded me to stop at the store on the way home.* {rih **miynd**} reminder, n.

re·mis·sion *noun* a lessening or stopping of the symptoms or progress of a disease. *His cancer was in remission.* {rih **mih** shən}

re·mod·el *verb* (remodeled, remodeling, remodels) to change the design or structure of. *We remodeled our home.* {ree **mo** dəl}

re·morse *noun* a feeling of guilt and real sorrow over having done something wrong. *The murderer felt no remorse for his crime.* {rih **mohrs**}

re·mote *adjective* (remoter, remotest) 1. at a far distance in space or time. *The moon is very remote from the earth. / In the remote past, dinosaurs walked the earth.* 2. far from towns or human settlement. *The lake is in a remote area.* 3. slight. *He has a remote chance of surviving.* {rih **moht**} remotely, adv.

remote control *noun* 1. the control of a machine or other object from a distance. *The airplane was being flown by remote control.* 2. a device held in the hand that is used to control a television set, a toy, or some other electronic object from a distance. {rih **moht** kən **trohl**}

re·mov·al *noun* the act or process of removing. *He works for a furniture removal company. / This cleaner is good for the removal of spots.* {rih **mooh** vəl}

re·move *verb* (removed, removing, remove) 1. to take away from a place or position. *She removed the empty boxes from the doorway. / He removed all the posters from the wall.* 2. to take off or shed. *He removed his sweater.* 3. to force to leave a job or position of responsibility; dismiss. *The dishonest governor was removed from office.* 4. to get rid of; take off or away. *He tried to remove the ink stains with soap and water.* {rih **moohv**} remover, n.

ren·ais·sance *noun* 1. a renewal or revival. 2. (capitalized) the revival of art, literature, and learning that began in Europe in the 1300s and lasted into the 1600s. During the Renaissance, scholars, writers, and artists took a great interest in the writings and ideas of classical culture. {rehn ə **sahns** or rehn ə **sahns**}

Word History *Renaissance* is a French word that means "rebirth."

ren·der *verb* (rendered, rendering, renders) 1. to cause to become; make. *His broken leg rendered him helpless.* 2. to give or offer. *They rendered aid to the needy.* {**rehn** dər}

ren·dez·vous *noun* (rendezvous) 1. a meeting that has been arranged ahead of time. *The rendezvous will take place in three days.* 2. the place chosen for such a meeting. *The old farmhouse will be our rendezvous.* *verb* (rendezvoused, rendezvousing, rendezvous) to meet at an arranged time or place. *We will rendezvous at ten o'clock.* {**rahn** də vooh or **rahn** day vooh, n., **rahn** də vooh or **rahn** day vooh, v.}

re·new *verb* (renewed, renewing, renews) 1. to make like new; restore. *They renewed the old house with a fresh coat of paint.* 2. to begin again. *We will renew our efforts after a break.* 3. to continue or extend for an additional period of time. *Do you want to renew your magazine subscription? / The two countries renewed their trade agreement.* {rih **nooh**} renewable, adj.

re·nowned *adjective* known and praised by many; famous. *The renowned musician had played in many countries around the world. / He was renowned for his skill in painting.* {rih **nownd**}

rent *noun* a regular payment made to an owner of property for the right to live in or use that property. *The rent for*

 Human Mind   Everyday Life    History and Culture   Communication

our house is $850 a month. *verb* (rented, renting, rents) 1. to live in or use in exchange for payment. *We rented a house on the lake for our summer vacation.* 2. to grant use of in exchange for payment. *My uncle rents out part of his land to a farmer from the next town.* 3. to be offered for rent. *The room rents for two hundred dollars a month.* {**rehnt**}

• **for rent**
available to live in or use in exchange for payment. *There is a new apartment for rent.*

re·pair *verb* (repaired, repairing, repairs) 1. to put in good condition again after damage has been done; fix. *I took my broken bicycle to the shop to be repaired.* 2. to make right; correct. *I will repair these mistakes.* *noun* 1. the act of repairing. *Our computer is in need of repair.* 2. (usually plural) work done to repair something. *The repairs on the car were expensive.* 3. the general condition that something is in. *The old shed is still in good repair.* {rih **payr**} repairer, n.

re·pay *verb* (repaid, repaying, repays) 1. to pay back. *He repaid the money that he had stolen.* 2. to pay money back to. *You must repay her for the loan she gave you.* 3. to do or give in return; reward. *How can I repay your kindness?* {rih **pay**} repayment, n.

re·peal *verb* (repealed, repealing, repeals) to do away with or cancel officially. *The state government*

voted to repeal the law. *noun* the act of repealing. *Most people were happy with the repeal of the tax.* {rih **peel**}

re·peat *verb* (repeated, repeating, repeats) 1. to state or say again. *The teacher repeated the question for the students who didn't hear it the first time.* 2. to recite; say over. *I repeated a joke that I heard from my sister.* 3. to tell to another. *You must promise never to repeat this secret.* 4. to do or experience again. *Nick had to repeat second grade.* *noun* something repeated. *I enjoy watching the repeats of my favorite TV shows.* {rih **peet**}

re·pel *verb* (repelled, repelling, repels) 1. to ward off or force back. *We will repel the attacking army.* / *This candle repels insects.* 2. to keep out; resist. *The raincoat repels water.* / *Oil and water repel each other.* 3. to cause to feel disgust. *I was repelled by the rotten food.* {rih **pehl**}

re·pel·lent *adjective* 1. causing disgust or dislike. *The smell of the garbage heap was repellent.* 2. having the effect of driving away. *We wore water-repellent clothes to keep us dry in the rain.* *noun* something that repels or drives away. *Put some insect repellent on before you go into the forest.* {rih **peh** lənt}

rep·e·ti·tion *noun* 1. the act or process of repeating. *Repetition is a good way to learn how to say difficult words.* 2. an act that is repeated. *Do ten repetitions of the exercise.* {reh pə **tih** shən}

re·place *verb* (replaced, replacing, replaces) 1. to put in place of. *The mechanic replaced the car's dead battery.* 2. to take the place of. *A new girl replaced the lead singer in*

the band. / *The CD has replaced the phonograph record.* 3. to put back in the same place as before. *When I finished raking the lawn, I replaced the rake and wheelbarrow in the garage.* {rih **plays**} replaceable, adj.

re·ply *verb* (replied, replying, replies) 1. to give an answer in words or writing. *Did you reply to your cousin's letter?* 2. to answer or respond in some way. *He replied with a shake of his head.* *noun* (replies) 1. an answer in words or writing. *I asked her a question, but she made no reply.* 2. an action or motion in response to something. *When the ship's crew saw the signal from the shore, they raised a flag in reply.* {rih **pliy**}

re·port *noun* a statement or account of something. *I enjoyed writing the book report.* *verb* (reported, reporting, reports) 1. to prepare and present an account or statement of. *The sheriff reported the results of his investigation.* 2. to make a charge against. *I reported the thief to the police.* 3. to tell; state. *I reported the good news to my friends.* 4. to present oneself. *She reported for work early.* {rih **pohrt**}

report card *noun* a written report of a student's progress in school that is usually sent to the student's home. {rih **pohrt** kard}

re·port·er *noun* a person whose job is to gather and report news for a newspaper or magazine, or for a television station or radio station. *The reporter wrote an interesting newspaper article about our school.* / *There is always a crowd of reporters outside the White House.* {rih **pohr** tər}

A
B
C
D
E
F
G
H
I
J
K
L
M
N
O
P
Q
R
S
T
U
V
W
X
Y
Z

 Living World
 Physical World
Natural Environment
 Economy
Government and Law

rep·re·sent *verb* (represented, representing, represents) 1. to stand for or be a sign of. *A skull and crossbones represents danger.* 2. to act or speak for. *The company asked me to represent them at the meeting.* 3. to show or picture in a work of art. *His drawing represents a forest scene.* 4. to speak or make decisions for in government. *The senator represents the people of the state of Idaho.* {**reh** prih **zehnt**}

rep·re·sent·a·tive ❶ *noun* 1. a person who speaks or acts for a group or community. *U.S. citizens vote for representatives in Congress.* 2. a typical example of something. *This hat is a good representative of the styles of the 1930s.* *adjective* 1. having to do with government by representatives. *The United States has a representative form of government.* 2. being a typical example of a certain group or kind. *This song is representative of the musician's work.* {**reh** prih **zehn** tə tihv}

re·pro·duce *verb* (reproduced, reproducing, reproduces) 1. to make a copy of. *The furniture maker reproduced a chair made hundreds of years ago.* 2. to make or produce again. *Can you reproduce that sound you just made?* 3. to have young or offspring. *Many animals reproduce once a year.* {ree prə **doohs**}

re·pro·duc·tion ❶ ❷ *noun* 1. the process of reproducing or being reproduced. *A tape recorder is a machine used for the reproduction of sounds.* 2. a copy of something. *I have a reproduction of the Mona Lisa in my room.* 3. the process by which living things create young or offspring. *Reproduction is necessary for a species to survive.* {ree prə **duhk** shən}

rep·tile ❶ *noun* a cold-blooded animal with a skeleton inside its body and dry scales or hard plates on its skin. Most reptiles lay eggs with soft, leathery shells. Some kinds of reptiles live in water, but use their noses to breathe air into their lungs. Lizards, turtles, snakes, and crocodiles are kinds of reptiles. Most reptiles have short legs, but snakes creep on the ground without legs. {**rehp** tiyl}

re·pub·lic ❶ *noun* 1. a nation in which those who make the laws and run the government are elected by the people. 2. a particular nation that is a republic. *We visited the Republic of Turkey.* {rih **puh** blihk}

Word History *Republic* comes from the Latin words, *res publica. Res* means "things" or "affairs." *Publica* means "public."

re·pub·li·can *adjective* 1. having the nature of a republic. *The United States has a republican government.* 2. (capitalized) having to do with the Republican Party of the United States. *The current mayor is Republican.* *noun* 1. someone who believes in or supports a republican form of government. 2. (capitalized) someone who is a member of the Republican Party of the United States. {rih **puh** blih kən}

Republican Party *noun* one of the two major political parties in the United States. The Republican Party was founded in 1854 as part of a movement against slavery. {rih **puh** blih kən **par** tee}

rep·u·ta·tion *noun* 1. the level of respect with which a person is thought of by others. *She has a good reputation because she is kind and talented.* 2. the condition of being known for something. *That restaurant has a reputation for fast service.* {rehp yə **tay** shən}

re·quest *noun* 1. the act of asking for something. *The teacher did not hear her request for help.* 2. something that is asked for. *The DJ played our request on the radio.* *verb* (requested, requesting, requests) to ask for politely. *We requested a bigger table at the restaurant.* {rih **kwehst**}

re·quire *verb* (required, requiring, requires) 1. to need. *Babies require a lot of attention.* 2. to order or demand. *The hotel requires that its guests check out before noon.* {rih **kwiyr**}

re·quire·ment *noun* 1. something that is needed or necessary. *Water is a requirement for all living things.* 2. something that is demanded or must be done; duty. *Gym class is a requirement at many schools.* {rih **kwiyr** mənt}

re·run *verb* (reran, rerun, rerunning, reruns) to run again or show once more. *They reran the race that had been cut short by rain.* / *This television special will be rerun next week.* *noun* 1. a film or television program that is shown again. 2. the act of running or showing again. {**ree** ruhn, n., ree **ruhn**, v.}

res·cue *verb* (rescued, rescuing, rescues) to free or save. *The firefighters rescued three people from the burning building.* *noun* the act of delivering from danger, harm, or other bad situations. *His rescue of the drowning puppy was shown on TV.* {**rehs** kyoo} rescuer, n.

re·search ❶ *noun* careful study of something in order to find

Reptiles

Reptiles were the first animals (other than insects and their relatives) that could lay their eggs on land. A few kinds of snakes give birth to live young instead of laying eggs. Baby reptiles look exactly like their parents, only smaller. Reptiles are NOT slimy! Most reptiles have skin covered with nice, dry scales.

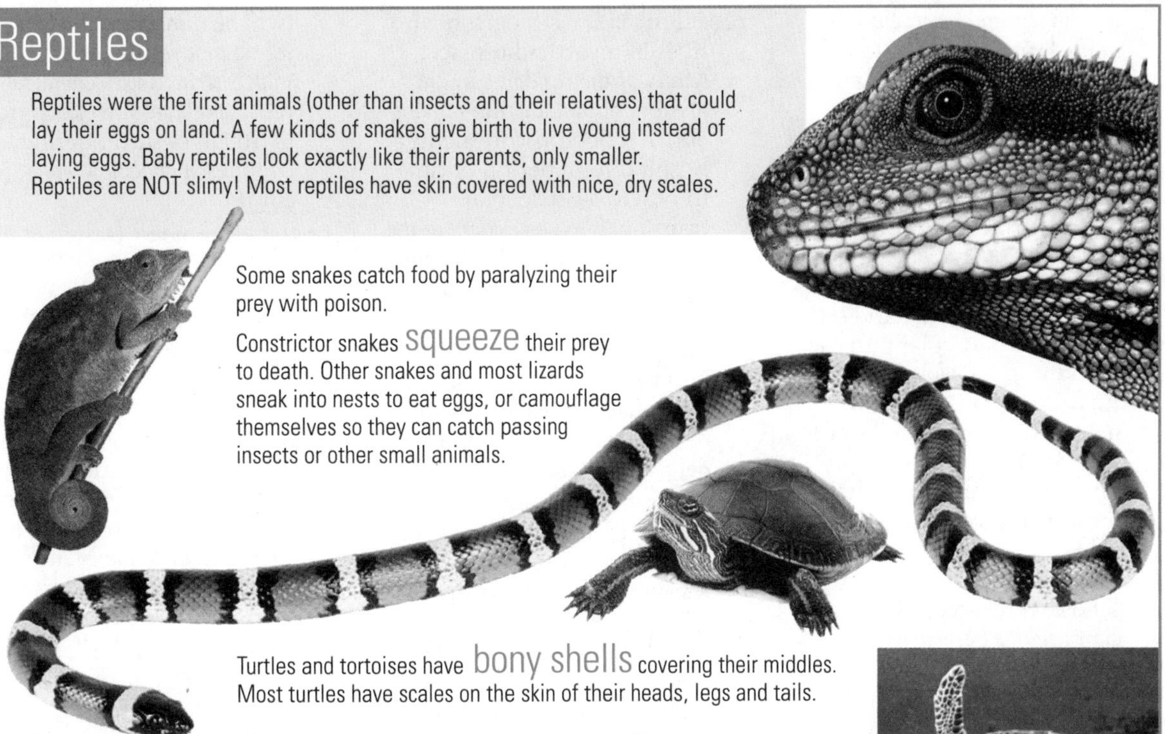

Some snakes catch food by paralyzing their prey with poison.

Constrictor snakes squeeze their prey to death. Other snakes and most lizards sneak into nests to eat eggs, or camouflage themselves so they can catch passing insects or other small animals.

Turtles and tortoises have bony shells covering their middles. Most turtles have scales on the skin of their heads, legs and tails.

Crocodiles and alligators are the largest reptiles. They spend most of their time in the water, but they come onto land to lay their eggs and sometimes to catch birds or small mammals.

A B C D E F G H I J K L M N O P Q **R** S T U V W X Y Z

out information about it. *Scientists are doing research on the effects of pollution.* *verb* (researched, researching, researches) to do research into. *I researched the American Civil War for my history class.* {rih **suhrch** or **ree suhrch**, n., rih **suhrch** or **ree suhrch**, v.} researcher, n.

re·sem·blance *noun* the condition of being or looking alike. *The twins have a strong resemblance to each other.* {rih **zehm** bləns}

re·sem·ble *verb* (resembled, resembling, resembles) to be similar to or to look like. *They both have brown eyes but do not otherwise resemble each other.* {rih **zehm** bəl}

re·sent *verb* (resented, resenting, resents) to feel anger or bitterness about or toward. *She resents being treated like a baby.* / *He resented the police officer for giving him a ticket.* {rih **zehnt**}

res·er·va·tion *noun* 1. something that keeps one from completely accepting or believing something; doubt. *I have reservations about lending others my bike.* 2. (often plural) an arrangement to have something saved for a particular person, such as a seat on a plane, a hotel room, or a table in a restaurant. *We made reservations for our flight.* 3. an area of land set aside by the U.S. Government for the use of Native Americans. {**rehz** ər **vay** shən}

re·serve *verb* (reserved, reserving, reserves) 1. to hold back or save for later use. *The scouts reserved half of their water for the hike back home.* 2. to save for a particular purpose or person. *Let's call the*

 Living World  Physical World Natural Environment  Economy  Government and Law

restaurant and reserve a table. *noun* **1.** something held back or kept for a particular purpose. *The squirrel dug up his reserve of acorns. / It is important for a country to have reserves of grain.* **2.** a formal and controlled way of acting or feeling. *His reserve keeps him from showing his feelings.* **3.** an area of public land set aside for a particular purpose. *Hunting is not allowed in the wildlife reserve.* **4.** (plural) members of the armed forces who are not on active duty but can be called in to help during emergencies. {rih **zuhrv**}

• **in reserve**
set aside; reserved. *The magician held his best trick in reserve.*

re·served *adjective* **1.** put aside or saved for a particular purpose. *These seats are reserved for us.* **2.** having a quiet, formal, or controlled way of acting or feeling. *She is nice, but very reserved.* {rih **zuhrvd**}

res·er·voir *noun* **1.** a place where water is collected and stored. *Towns and cities often have reservoirs for their water supply.* **2.** a large supply of anything. *The library is a reservoir of knowledge.* {**rehz** ər **vwar** or **rehz** ər **vohr**}

re·side *verb* (resided, residing, resides) to live in a place for a long time; dwell. *Where do your grandparents reside?* {rih **ziyd**}

res·i·dence *noun* **1.** a house or any other place where one lives; home. *His family lives in a grand old residence up on the hill.* **2.** the act or a period of living in a place. *I enjoyed my residence in Hawaii.* {**rehz** ih dəns}

res·i·dent *noun* **1.** a person who lives in a particular place. *Many of the residents in our apartment building are moving out.* **2.** a doctor working in a hospital for a period of time in order to get special training. *He is a resident at the county hospital.* {**rehz** ih dənt}

res·i·den·tial *adjective* **1.** having to do with residences. *She owns a residential construction business.* **2.** used for residence. *The speed limit is lower on residential streets.* {**reh** zih **dehn** shəl}

re·sign *verb* (resigned, resigning, resigns) **1.** to give up a job or other duty. *She resigned from the company.* **2.** to accept something one does not like or enjoy. *He resigned himself to sharing a room with his brother.* {rih **ziyn**}

res·ig·na·tion *noun* **1.** the act of giving up a job or other position, or a formal letter announcing this. *We were sorry to hear of the secretary's resignation. / She handed her boss her resignation.* **2.** a giving in to something without opposing it or complaining. *He accepted the extra work with resignation.* {**rehz** ihg **nay** shən}

res·in *noun* **1.** a sticky substance produced by fir trees and certain other plants. Resin is used to make plastics, medicines, paints, and other products. **2.** a similar substance made by people and used in plastics. {**rehz** ihn}

re·sist *verb* (resisted, resisting, resists) **1.** to fight against or oppose. *The workers are resisting the new rules.* **2.** to keep away or not be affected by. *The raincoat is made out of fabric that resists water. / The milk is treated with chemicals to resist spoiling.* **3.** to keep from giving in or surrendering to. *I can't resist chocolate cake.* {rih **zihst**}

re·sist·ance *noun* **1.** the act or process of resisting. *The proposal to tear down the library was met with resistance.* **2.** the opposing power of one force against another. *Vitamins help your body build resistance to disease.* **3.** (often capitalized) a secret organization formed to oppose an army that has taken over a country. *During World War II, the French Resistance fought against the German army that was occupying France.* {rih **zih** stəns}

res·o·lu·tion *noun* **1.** strong purpose or determination. *It takes resolution to get through medical school.* **2.** something officially decided upon by a group or organization. *The town council quickly passed a resolution to combat littering.* **3.** a solution or end to an argument or other conflict. *I was glad that we found a resolution to the problem.* {**rehz** ə **looh** shən}

re·solve *verb* (resolved, resolving, resolves) **1.** to deal with in a successful way; settle. *The problem was resolved quickly.* **2.** to decide firmly or reach a conclusion. *Nicholas approached his chores with resolve. noun* firmness of purpose; determination. *It takes resolve to exercise every day.* {rih **zŏlv**}

res·o·nant *adjective* **1.** echoing. *Our footsteps were resonant in*

 Human Body   Human Mind   Everyday Life    History and Culture   Communication

the empty room. 2. full and deep in sound. *The resonant sound of the foghorn could be heard for miles.* 3. causing sound to be louder or last longer. *The music hall was built to be resonant.* {<u>rehz</u> ə nənt}

re·sort *verb* (resorted, resorting, resorts) to go to or turn to for help, often as a last choice when everything else has been tried. *She resorted to eating berries when she ran out of food.* *noun* 1. a place where people go to relax and have fun while on vacation. *My family went to a ski resort this winter.* 2. a person or thing that is turned to for help. *Please help me; you are my last resort.* {rih <u>zohrt</u>}

re·sound *verb* (resounded, resounding, resounds) 1. to be full of sound. *When the play ended, the theater resounded with clapping.* 2. to make a loud or clearly heard sound. *Music resounded through the hall.* {rih <u>zownd</u>}

re·source *noun* 1. a source of help or support. *The library is a good resource for information.* 2. (plural) all of a country's wealth and its ways of producing wealth. *Oil is one of Iraq's most important natural resources.* 3. (usually plural) money or things that are available for a particular use. *We do not have the resources to go on vacation this year.* 4. (often plural) talents and skills. *She has the resources to succeed in difficult jobs.* {<u>ree</u> sohrs or rih <u>zohrs</u>}

re·spect ⊕ *noun* 1. the state or condition of being thought of with honor or admiration; such admiration itself. *My grandparents enjoy the respect and love of our entire family.* 2. a particular point or detail (usually used with "in"). *She*

is like her father in one respect. 3. regard; relation; reference. *The new worker has a few questions with respect to the rules.* 4. (plural) a polite expression of greeting or esteem. *Please give my respects to your family.* *verb* (respected, respecting, respects) 1. to express honor or esteem towards. *You should respect your mother.* 2. to show consideration for. *My mother respects the need I have to be by myself sometimes.* {rih <u>spehkt</u>}

Word History *Respect* comes from a Latin word that means "an act of looking back at."

re·spect·a·ble *adjective* 1. having a good reputation or being thought well of in one's community. *They are respectable people.* 2. good enough. *He does not get A's, but his grades are respectable.* 3. worthy of respect. *The teacher expects respectable behavior from the students.* {rih <u>spehk</u> tə bəl} respectably, adv.

re·spect·ful *adjective* having or showing respect; being polite. *It is not respectful to stick out your tongue.* {rih <u>spehk</u> fəl} respectfully, adv.

re·spec·tive *adjective* of or belonging to each one. *The brothers' respective ages are sixteen and twenty-three.* {rih <u>spehk</u> tihv}

re·spec·tive·ly *adverb* in the order that two or more people or things have been named. *If John and Mary are ages eight and fifteen respectively, then John is eight and Mary is fifteen.* {rih <u>spehk</u> tihv lee}

res·pi·ra·tion *noun* the act of breathing. *Respiration slows down during sleep.* {rehs pə <u>ray</u> shən}

res·pi·ra·to·ry *adjective* having to do with or used in the act of breathing. *The lungs are part of the respiratory system.* {<u>rehs</u> pə rə tohr ee}

res·pi·ra·tor·y sys·tem *noun* the system that brings oxygen to the body. It is made up of the lungs, diaphragm, windpipe, and nasal passages. {<u>rehs</u> pih ro tohr ee <u>sihs</u> təm}

re·spond ⊕ *verb* (responded, responding, responds) 1. to answer or give a reply, in words or otherwise. *I asked her a question, but she did not respond.* 2. to react. *The patient responded well to the treatment.* {rih <u>spŏnd</u>}

re·sponse *noun* 1. a written or spoken answer; reply. *I wrote to my senator and received a response.* 2. a reaction. *The doctor is pleased with the patient's response to the medicine.* {rih <u>spŏns</u>}

re·spon·si·bil·i·ty *noun* (responsibilities) 1. the condition or fact of being responsible. *Take responsibility for your actions.* 2. something for which a person is responsible; duty. *Cleaning the bathroom is my responsibility. / The puppy is your responsibility.* {rih <u>spŏn</u> sə <u>bih</u> lih tee}

re·spon·si·ble *adjective* 1. expected to take care of particular duties and jobs. *He is responsible for keeping track of our money.* 2. being the cause of something. *I am responsible for the accident.* 3. able to make the right decisions. *She is very responsible and can be trusted.* {rih <u>spŏn</u> sih bəl} responsibly, adv.

rest[1] ⊕ ⊕ *noun* 1. a state of feeling refreshed because of relaxing or sleeping. *A nap will give you the rest your body needs.* 2. a time of calm and quiet after work or activity; break. *I needed a rest after*

 Living World
 Physical World
 Natural Environment
Economy
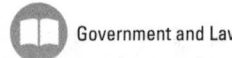 Government and Law

cleaning my room all afternoon. 3. relief from trouble of the body or mind. *Mom helped me put my problem to rest.* 4. something used as a support. *Dad's chair has a head rest.* 5. the ending or lack of motion. *The baby is so active that his body is at rest only when he's sleeping.* 6. a clear silence between musical notes, or the mark that shows it. *I carefully marked the rests in my music. verb* (rested, resting, rests) 1. to relax by sleeping or lying down. *I rested on the sofa.* 2. to end motion or activity. *After a hard race, she finally rested.* 3. to be without trouble or worry. *I couldn't rest until I knew the end of the story.* 4. to be supported. *He rested against the wall.* 5. to look at something for a long time. *Her eyes rested on the figure across the street.* 6. to give rest to. *He rested his horse after their long ride.* {**rehst**}

• **at rest**
not active, not moving, or sleeping. *Keep your voice down, the baby is at rest in the crib.*

rest² *noun* 1. a piece or part that is left. *Do you want the rest of the cake?* 2. all the others. *One is black but the rest are red. verb* (rested, resting, rests) to remain or continue to be. *You can rest assured that I will help.* {**rehst**}

Homophone Note Are you looking for the word **wrest** (to take away)? **Rest** and **wrest** sound alike but have different meanings. The w is silent in "wrest."

res·tau·rant *noun* a place where meals are prepared and sold

to the public. {**rehs** tər **ahnt** or **rehs** **trahnt**}

Word History *Restaurant* is a French word that originally meant "something that restores."

rest·ful *adjective* 1. giving rest. *I had a restful nap.* 2. peaceful and quiet. *My garden is a restful place.* {**rehst** fəl}

rest·less *adjective* 1. not able to relax, sit still, or stay quiet. *The children were restless after many hours in the car.* 2. always in motion. *The restless wind rattled the windows all day.* 3. giving no rest. *I spent a restless night tossing and turning in bed.* {**rehs** lihs}

re·store *verb* (restored, restoring, restores) 1. to bring back into use or existence. *The queen's wise rule restored peace in the land.* 2. to return to an earlier or normal condition. *It took many months to restore the old house. / Rest restored him to health.* 3. to give back after loss or theft. *The police restored the stolen wallet to its owner.* {rih **stohr**}

re·strain *verb* (restrained, restraining, restrains) 1. to hold back or control. *Try to restrain your anger.* 2. to take away the freedom of. *The police restrained the criminal with handcuffs.* {rih **strayn**}

re·strict *verb* (restricted, restricting, restricts) to keep within limits. *They restricted him to his room. / Can we restrict our discussion to one topic?* {rih **strihkt**}

re·stric·tion *noun* 1. something that limits or restricts. *There are restrictions on making campfires in the park.* 2. the act of restricting or condition of being restricted. *Restriction of dogs is the law in this city.* {rih **strihk** shən}

rest·room *noun* a public bathroom. {**rehst** roohm or **rehst** ruum}

re·sult *verb* (resulted, resulting, results) 1. to happen because of something. *The accident resulted from the driver's not paying attention.* 2. to end in a certain way. *His efforts resulted in success. noun* something happens because of something else. *We were surprised by the results of the contest.* {rih **zuhlt**}

re·sume *verb* (resumed, resuming, resumes) 1. to start again after stopping. *We resumed the game when it stopped raining.* 2. to take again; return to. *He resumed his place at the table after washing his hands.* {rih **zoohm**}

re·tail *noun* the sale of things in small amounts to customers who will use them. *adjective* having to do with the selling of goods directly to those who will use them. *A toy shop and a grocery store are retail stores.* {**ree** tayl} retailer, n.

re·tain *verb* (retained, retaining, retains) 1. to hold or keep. *The sidewalk retains heat from the sun. / Our team retained control of the ball for most of the game.* 2. to be able to remember. *She has retained everything she learned in science class last year.* 3. to have the services of; hire. *He retained a lawyer to defend him in court.* {rih **tayn**}

re·tard·ed *adjective* slower than most people in mental or emotional growth. {rih **tar** dihd}

ret·i·na *noun* (retinas) the part of the eye at the back of the inside of the eyeball. The retina has cells that sense light and color. Images are formed on the retina and sent to the brain. {**reht** ih nə}

 Human Body   Human Mind   Everyday Life  History and Culture Communication

re·tire *verb* (retired, retiring, retires) 1. to give up a job or career. *Many Americans retire when they turn sixty-five.* 2. to go away to be alone or find shelter. *He retired to his cabin in the woods.* 3. to go to bed. *I think I will retire for the night.* {rih **tiyr**}

re·tire·ment *noun* 1. the act of retiring. *After his retirement, he traveled around the world.* 2. the time of one's life during which one is retired. *He is saving money for his retirement.* {rih **tiyr** mənt}

re·treat *noun* 1. the act of moving back or away from a place or situation. *We made a careful retreat from the edge of the cliff.* 2. a quiet place for resting, thinking, or being alone. *The pond in the middle of the woods is my favorite retreat.* 3. the act of pulling back from battle. *The captain ordered a retreat from the attacking army.* *verb* (retreated, retreating, retreats) 1. to move back or away from danger or a challenge. *When I vacuum, the cat retreats to the closet.* 2. to move backwards. *We watched the waves come toward us and then retreat.* {rih **treet**}

re·trieve *verb* (retrieved, retrieving, retrieves) 1. to bring or get back; recover. *The lifeguard retrieved my glasses from the bottom of the pool.* 2. to find and bring back; fetch. *The hunter's dog was trained to retrieve ducks.* {rih **treev**}

re·triev·er *noun* one of several breeds of dog bred for their ability to retrieve wounded or killed game for hunters. {rih **tree** vər}

ret·ro·rock·et *noun* a small rocket attached to a spacecraft and used to help the spacecraft slow down or change direction. Retrorockets fire in the direction opposite to the direction the main rocket is going in. {**reh** troh rŏk iht}

re·turn *verb* (returned, returning, returns) 1. to go back or come back. *We returned home tired after our tennis game.* 2. to send, put, give, or take back to an earlier place. *I returned the book to the library. / Return the form after you have filled it out.* 3. to give in exchange for something similar. *He returned the favor.* 4. to report in an official way. *The jury returned a verdict of guilty.* *noun* 1. the act of coming or going back. *We look forward to the return of the loons every spring.* 2. the act of sending or receiving back. *There was a long line for returns at the store.* 3. (usually plural) a report on the counted ballots in an election. *The returns showed that he had won the election by just twenty votes.* *adjective* 1. of or relating to a coming back. *She promised to make a return visit next year.* 2. happening or done again. *The popular singer gave a return performance.* 3. providing a means for coming back. *The return route was longer than the road there.* {rih **tuhrn**}

• **in return**
a paying back or in exchange. *What can I give you in return for your kindness?*

re·un·ion *noun* a meeting of friends, family, or other people who have been apart from each other for a long time.

At my family reunion, I saw many cousins whom I had not seen in years. {ree **yoon** yən}

re·veal *verb* (revealed, revealing, reveals) 1. to make known; tell. *I won't reveal your secret.* 2. to show or uncover. *The stage curtain lifted to reveal the actors behind it.* {rih **veel**}

Synonyms
These words share a meaning with *reveal*, verb 1:
tell, uncover, disclose

rev·e·la·tion *noun* 1. the act of revealing. *When will the revelation of the winner's name take place?* 2. something that is revealed that was not known before. *The biography is filled with new revelations about the pop star.* {rehv ə **lay** shən}

re·venge *verb* (revenged, revenging, revenges) to get even for or pay back by causing injury or harm. *The musketeer vowed to revenge the death of his brother.* *noun* 1. the act of giving punishment in payment for a wrong that has been done. *His friends convinced him not to seek revenge on the school bully.* 2. harm or punishment done in payment for something. *Gina locked me out of the house as revenge for eating her candy.* 3. the desire to take revenge. *She tore up his favorite comic book out of revenge.* {rih **vehnj**}

rev·e·nue ⬡ *noun* 1. money gained from selling property or investing money. *We used the revenue from the sale of our house to start a new business.* 2. the money a government makes by collecting taxes.

A
B
C
D
E
F
G
H
I
J
K
L
M
N
O
P
Q
R
S
T
U
V
W
X
Y
Z

The government spends part of its revenue on national defense. {**rehv** ə nooh}

rev·er·ence *noun* a feeling of great respect mixed with love. *She held the ancient scrolls with reverence.* {**rehv** ə rəns}

re·verse *adjective* 1. opposite in direction, position, or movement; backward. *We lined up in reverse alphabetical order.* 2. causing backward movement. *The driver put the truck into reverse gear.* 3. facing away or to the back. *We found a message written on the reverse side of the painting.* *noun* 1. the opposite side. *The reverse of what he said is true.* 2. a change for the worse in one's luck or fortune. *The business suffered a reverse when one of the partners left town.* 3. the gear in a car that causes backward movement. *Put the car into reverse and back out of the parking spot.* *verb* (reversed, reversing, reverses) 1. to cause to move in an opposite direction. *Mom reversed the car into the road.* 2. to turn inside out or over. *I reversed my shirt before washing it.* 3. to turn in an opposite position or direction. *The hikers reversed their course because they were lost.* {rih **vuhrs**}

re·view 🌐 *noun* 1. an article in a newspaper or magazine that judges the worth of a recent book, film, play, or other work of art. *The movie got good reviews.* 2. a looking back over past events, memories, or facts. *This textbook has a review at the end of every chapter.* 3. an official inspection. *The soldiers lined up for the review.* *verb* (reviewed, reviewing, reviews) 1. to examine or look over again. *I reviewed my notes before the exam.* 2. to give a report on the strengths and weaknesses of. *She reviews books for the newspaper.* 3. to look back over; think back on. *The graduate reviewed his years in high school.* 4. to inspect in an official way. *The general reviewed the troops.* {rih **vyoo**}

re·vise *verb* (revised, revising, revises) 1. to change or make different. *We had to revise our plans because of the weather.* 2. to correct or edit so as to improve. *I revised my paper before turning it in.* {rih **viyz**}

re·viv·al *noun* 1. the act or process of renewing or reviving. *During the Renaissance, there was a revival of interest in science and art.* 2. a new showing or a new version of an old play. *The theater put on a revival of a musical that was popular in the 1950s.* 3. a lively religious meeting meant to revive religious feeling in people. *The Baptists in our community hold a revival every summer.* {rih **viy** vəl}

re·vive *verb* (revived, reviving, revives) 1. to bring back into use or popularity. *Fashion designers like to revive old styles.* 2. to give new health, strength, or life to. *The rain shower revived the crops.* 3. to wake up or make conscious again. *The nurse revived the patient who had fainted.* {rih **viyv**}

> **Word History** *Revive* comes from a Latin word that means "to live again."

re·voke *verb* (revoked, revoking, revokes) to take back, cancel, or make no longer valid. *The officer revoked his hunting license for hunting out of season.* {rih **vohk**}

re·volt *verb* (revolted, revolting, revolts) 1. to rise up and fight against the government or other authority; rebel. *When the laws became too harsh, the citizens revolted.* 2. to cause to feel disgust or shock. *Horror movies revolt me.* *noun* the act of rising up against the government or other authority; rebellion. *The army put an end to the revolt.* {rih **vohlt**}

rev·o·lu·tion *noun* 1. the overthrow of a political system or government by force, and the setting up of a new government in its place. *The colonists fought the British government during the American Revolution.* 2. a time of great change. *The invention of the printing press caused a revolution in learning.* 3. the action of turning or spinning on an axis. *The merry-go-round made one more revolution before stopping.* 4. motion in orbit around a point. *Day and night are caused by the earth's revolution around the sun.* {rehv ə **looh** shən}

rev·o·lu·tion·ar·y *adjective* 1. having to do with or marked by a desire for revolution. *The leaders of the group were arrested for revolutionary activity.* 2. creating or leading to great change. *The new invention was revolutionary.* *noun* (revolutionaries)

 Human Body Human Mind Everyday Life History and Culture  Communication

someone who takes part in a revolution against the government. {rehv ə **looh** shə **nayr** ee}

Revolutionary War *noun* see **American Revolution.** {rehv ə **looh** shə **nayr** ee **wohr**}

re·volve *verb* (revolved, revolving, revolves) 1. to turn or spin in place. *The baby watched as the spinning top revolved.* 2. to move in a circle around a fixed point. *The moon revolves around the earth.* 3. to mainly involve or be concerned with (followed by "around"). *Her life revolves around her piano playing.* {rih **vŏlv**}

re·volv·er *noun* a pistol with a revolving cylinder that holds bullets. A revolver can fire several shots without having to be loaded each time. {rih **vŏl** vər}

re·ward *noun* 1. something of value that is promised to someone for good work or a good deed. *We offered a fifty-dollar reward to the person who found our lost kitten.* 2. anything that satisfies or pleases, as a return for something done. *Seeing her smile was all the reward I needed.* *verb* (rewarded, rewarding, rewards) to give something to as a reward. *Mom rewarded us for our good grades by letting us stay up late.* {rih **wohrd**}

re·word *verb* (reworded, rewording, rewords) to write or say again using different words. *That sentence will sound better if you reword it.* {ree **wuhrd**}

Rhine *noun* a river of Central Europe. It flows from Switzerland through Germany and the Netherlands to the North Sea. {**riyn**}

rhi·noc·er·os *noun* (rhinoceros or rhinoceroses) a large mammal with hooves and very thick skin. Rhinoceroses have one or two horns on their noses. They eat plants. Wild rhinoceroses live in Africa and southern Asia. Four of the five kinds of rhinoceroses are in danger of becoming extinct. {**riy no** sə rəs}

Word History *Rhinoceros* comes from two ancient Greek words that mean "nose" and "horn."

Rhode Island *noun* a state in the northeastern United States on the Atlantic Coast. Its capital is Providence. (abbreviation: RI) {**rohd iy** lənd} Rhode Islander, n.

Word History The full name of *Rhode Island* is "Rhode Island and Providence Plantations." In 1663, a group of island and mainland communities formed an English colony with that name. The colony probably took its name from *Roodt Eylandt,* the Dutch words for "red island" chosen by Dutch explorer Adriaen Block in 1614. Almost one hundred years earlier, Italian explorer Giovanni Verrazano had named a coastal island "Rhodes Island," after the Mediterranean island, Rhodes.

rho·do·den·dron *noun* a shrub or small tree with flat evergreen leaves and

clusters of bright pink, red, purple, white, or yellow flowers. {roh də **dehn** drən}

rhom·bus *noun* (rhombuses or rhombi) a flat, closed figure in which all four sides are equal in length, and both pairs of opposite sides are parallel. {**rŏm** bəs}

rhu·barb *noun* a plant with long green or reddish stalks, which are often cooked with sugar and eaten in pies and other desserts. The leaves of rhubarb are poisonous. {**rooh** barb}

rhyme *noun* 1. a word that ends with the same or almost the same sound as another word. *"Skip" and "trip" are rhymes for "slip."* 2. a similarity or repetition in the sounds at the ends of lines of verse. *These lines use rhyme: "What a lovely walk we've taken! Let us dine on Beans and Bacon!"* 3. poetry or verse using words that rhyme at the ends of lines. *Do you know the nursery rhyme "Baa, Baa, Black Sheep"?* *verb* (rhymed, rhyming, rhymes) 1. to match with another word that ends with the same sound. *Can you rhyme "orange" with another word?* 2. to put into rhyme. *I rhymed a poem for an assignment.* {**riym**}
• **rhyme or reason** apparent sense or logic.

rhythm *noun* 1. movement marked by the regular repetition of sounds. *We clapped our hands to the rhythm of the drums.* 2. a particular type of such movement. *We danced to the rhythm of a waltz.* {**rihth** əm}

rhyth·mic *adjective* having a rhythm; relating to rhythm; rhythmical. *We clapped to the rhythmic pattern of the song.* {**rihth** mihk}

A B C D E F G H I J K L M N O P Q R S T U V W X Y Z

a
b
c
d
e
f
g
h
i
j
k
l
m
n
o
p
q
r
s
t
u
v
w
x
y
z

rhyth·mi·cal *adjective* 1. having to do with rhythm. *I like to write rhythmical poems.* 2. having a strong rhythm. *This song is rhythmical and is fun to dance to.* {**rihth** mih kəl} rhythmically, adv.

RI or **R.I.** *abbreviation* an abbreviation for **Rhode Island**.

rib *noun* 1. one of the bones that curve from the spine around the chest of a person or animal. 2. something that looks like a rib in shape or purpose, such as the wires that hold open an umbrella. {**rihb**}

rib·bon *noun* 1. a narrow strip or band of colorful material used to hold the hair or to tie up presents. 2. a long, narrow strip that looks like a ribbon, such as a measuring tape. 3. (plural) torn or tattered strips; shreds. *My old shirt was torn to ribbons by my cat.* {**rihb** ən}

rice ⬥ *noun* 1. a grass that is usually grown in warm, wet areas such as parts of India and China. 2. the seed of this grass, which is a very important food. *Rice is cooked and eaten by millions of people around the world.* {**riys**}

rich ⬥ *adjective* (richer, richest) 1. having a great amount of money or valuable property. *The rich man drives a fancy car.* 2. having many natural resources. *Crops grow well in our rich soil.* 3. having much; filled (usually followed by "in" or "with"). *Spinach is rich in important vitamins and minerals.* 4. having large amounts of butter, fats, eggs, or sugar. *We made a rich chocolate cake for dessert.* 5. full or round in tone. *The singer's*

rich voice thrilled the audience. *noun* (used with a plural verb) wealthy people as a group (usually used with "the"). *The rich usually live in beautiful homes.* {**rihch**} richness, n.

Synonyms
These words share a meaning with *rich*, adjective 1:
wealthy, prosperous, affluent, well-off

rich·es *plural noun* 1. a large amount of money and property. *The sultan has great riches.* 2. valuable or precious goods, or things that occur in nature in large quantities. *The ship carried riches across the Mediterranean.* / *People should not waste the riches of the rain forest.* {**rihch** ihz}

Rich·mond *noun* the capital of Virginia. {**rihch** mənd}

rick·et·y *adjective* 1. likely to fall over or fall apart; shaky. *Don't lean on that rickety fence.* 2. weak in the joints with age; tottering. *My grandmother is anything but a rickety old woman.* {**rihk** ih tee}

rid *verb* (rid or ridded, ridding, rids) to clear or free from something that is not wanted (usually followed by "of"). *I want to rid the garden of weeds.* {**rihd**}

rid·dle[1] *noun* 1. a puzzling, tricky, and often funny question asked as a game or as a test of one's thinking skills. *Here is a riddle: When is a door not a door? Answer: When it is ajar.* 2. any question, problem, person, or

thing that is difficult to figure out. *How our dog found us hundreds of miles from home is a riddle.* / *That shy boy is a riddle to me.* {**rihd** əl}

rid·dle[2] *verb* (riddled, riddling, riddles) to pierce with a large number of holes. *Bullets riddled the target.* {**rihd** əl}

ride ⬥ *verb* (rode, ridden, riding, rides) 1. to be carried by a vehicle or animal. *We all rode on the train.* / *She rode on a camel at the fair.* 2. to be held up or carried. *The boat rode down the river.* / *He was riding on a wave of success.* 3. to sit on the back and direct the movement of. *We rode the donkey up the mountain trail.* *noun* 1. an act of riding or a journey on an animal or in a vehicle. *We took a ride to the lake in our new car.* 2. a large device, such as a merry-go-round or roller coaster, that people ride for fun. *They went on all the rides at the fair.* {**riyd**}

rid·er *noun* a person who rides something. *Liz is an experienced horseback rider.* {**riy** dər}

ridge *noun* 1. a long, narrow, raised section at the top of something; crest. *From the ridge of the hill we had a beautiful view of the valley below.* 2. any narrow raised strip, as on cloth or in a plowed field. *The ridges of the field made a beautiful design when seen from an airplane.* 3. a range or chain of hills or mountains. *I began to feel sick as we drove across the ridge.* {**rihj**}

rid·i·cule *noun* talk or actions that make unkind fun of someone or something. *Rabbit's long ears left him open to ridicule from the other animals.* *verb* (ridiculed, ridiculing, ridicules) to make fun of or laugh at in an unkind way. *The bully ridiculed the*

 Human Body   Human Mind   Everyday Life   🚩 History and Culture   📞 Communication new kid because of his eyeglasses. {**rihd** ih **kyool**}

ri·dic·u·lous *adjective* silly; foolish; laughable. *He felt ridiculous dressed in a suit while the other kids were wearing jeans.* {rih **dihk** yə ləs} ridiculously, adv.

ri·fle *noun* a gun that has a long barrel and that is shot from the shoulder. {**riy** fəl}

rig *verb* (rigged, rigging, rigs) 1. to make ready for use by attaching sails, lines, and rope. *The crew rigged the boat.* 2. to put together from whatever materials are available in order to use for a short time (usually followed by "up"). *They rigged up a kitchen at the camp.* 3. to provide with equipment, gear, or clothing (usually followed by "out" or "up"). *The counselor rigged out the campers with supplies for the fishing trip.* *noun* 1. equipment or gear made for a special purpose. *We'll need the right rig for our climbing trip.* 2. the arrangement and number of masts and sails of a particular type of boat or ship. {**rihg**}

rig·ging *noun* 1. all the ropes, wires, and chains used on a boat or ship to hold up the masts and work the sails. 2. equipment used to lift, move, support, or work something, such as stage sets. {**rihg** ing}

right *adjective* (righter, rightest) 1. in keeping with what is fair and good. *Helping her was the right thing to do.* 2. in keeping with the rules of justice, law, or society. *It is not right to steal.* 3. in keeping with fact or reason; true; correct. *All her answers were right.* 4. facing out; outer; front. *The right side of the carpet shows the design.* 5. proper; appropriate. *His new job was just right for him.* 6. healthy in body or mind. *He was not in his right mind when he threatened her.* 7. of or relating to the side of the human body opposite the heart. *I do most things with my right hand rather than my left.* *noun* 1. that which is just, fair, or good. *I did right by returning the lost wallet.* 2. the side of the human body opposite the heart. *I will walk on your right.* 3. (sometimes plural) that which is due to a person from nature or law. *Free speech is one of the most important rights enjoyed by Americans.* 4. that which agrees with fact or reason. *I got all of the answers right on the history test.* 5. the quality or condition of being correct. *I have to admit you were right about her.* *adverb* 1. directly; straight. *He walked right toward me.* 2. without delay; immediately. *They went right home.* 3. to a large degree; completely. *The wind blew the roof right off.* 4. exactly. *Your keys are right where you left them.* 5. correctly. *This dress doesn't fit right.* / *You did not spell "crispy" right.* 6. properly or lawfully. *He was not dressed right for a job interview.* / *She got a ticket for not parking right.* 7. on or in the direction of the right. *We turned right at the stop sign.* *verb* (righted, righting, rights) 1. to place in or return to an upright position. *She righted her chair.* 2. to place in or return to the proper order, position, or condition. *He righted the papers.* 3. to correct or repair. *The knight's only goal was to right the wrong done to his lady.* {**riyt**}

• **right and left** in all places or directions; everywhere. *There were people right and left at the carnival.*

• **right away** [or] **right off** at once; immediately. *We left right away.*

Homophone Note Are you looking for the word **write**? **Right** and **write** sound alike but have different meanings. The 'W' is silent in the word **write**.

right angle *noun* the angle formed where two perpendicular lines meet. It measures ninety degrees. *Each corner of a square is a right angle.* {**riyt** ăng gəl} right-angled, adj.

right-hand·ed *adjective* 1. using the right hand more often or more easily than the left. 2. done with or made for the right hand. *Most school desks are right-handed.* *adverb* with the right hand. *He throws right-handed.* {**riyt** **hăn** dihd} right-handedly, adv., right-handedness, n.

right triangle *noun* a triangle with a right angle. {**riyt** **triy** ăng gəl}

rig·id *adjective* 1. difficult or impossible to bend; stiff. *We'll need a rigid pole to hold up the tent.* / *The muscles in her face were rigid with anger.* 2. firmly in place; not

changing. *She was bored by the rigid schedule of the summer camp.* {**rihj** ihd}

rim *noun* 1. the edge or border of something round or circular. *I cut myself on the broken rim of the glass.* 2. a metal ring or hoop from which a basketball net is hung. *The ball bounced off the rim and into the basket. verb* (rimmed, rimming, rims) to fit with a rim or serve as a rim for; border. *Stones rim the flower bed.* {**rihm**}

rind *noun* a thick, firm outer layer or covering. *Oranges, melons, and some cheeses have rinds.* {**riynd**}

ring[1] ○ *noun* 1. the outer edge of a circle. *There was a ring of dark clouds above the mountain.* 2. a small band of metal or other hard material in the shape of a circle. *Rings are worn on the finger for their beauty or as a symbol. My parents wear matching gold wedding rings.* 3. a band in the shape of a circle used to surround or hold something. *We use rings to hold the curtains open.* 4. an enclosed area for a sports event or circus performance. *Seven elephants danced around the ring. verb* (ringed, ringing, rings) 1. to put a ring around; circle. *We ringed the room with candles for the wedding.* 2. to shape into a ring or rings. *She ringed her hair into a crown of curls.* {**ring**}

ring[2] *verb* (rang, rung, ringing, rings) 1. to give out a clear, deep sound. *The doorbell and the telephone rang at the same time.* 2. to seem to be. *Her words rang true.* 3. to sound loudly and deeply (often followed by "out"). *Her voice rang out in the empty hall.* 4. to be filled with sound. *The classroom rang with the sound* of laughter. 5. to hear a humming sound or echo. *After the concert his ears were ringing.* 6. to cause to make a clear, deep sound. *All of the churches in town rang their bells at midnight.* 7. to sound by hitting a bell or by similar means. *I rang the doorbell. noun* 1. the sound of a ringing bell. *The ring of our telephone is hard to hear.* 2. a clear, deep sound like that of a bell. *My grandmother's voice has a sweet ring.* 3. a telephone call. *Give me a ring when you get home.* {**ring**}

• **ring up**
to record or add up on a cash register. *The waiter rang up our bill.*

> **Homophone Note** Are you looking for the word *wring* (to twist)? *Ring* and *wring* sound alike but have different meanings. The w is silent in the word *wring*.

rink *noun* 1. a smooth surface of ice used for ice skating or ice hockey. 2. a smooth wood surface used for roller skating. 3. a building that holds the surfaces for ice skating or roller skating. {**ringk**}

rinse *verb* (rinsed, rinsing, rinses) 1. to clean by dipping into or spraying with water. *Rinse that pot out before you cook soup in it.* 2. to wash off with water. *Be sure to rinse all the shampoo out of your hair. noun* an act or instance of rinsing. *Give your mouth a rinse after brushing your teeth.* {**rihns**}

Rio de Janeiro *noun* a city in southeastern Brazil on the Atlantic Ocean. {**ree** oh day zhə **nayr** oh}

ri·ot *noun* 1. a violent disturbance caused by a large number of people. 2. (informal) a person or thing that is wildly funny. *His stories are a riot. verb* (rioted, rioting, riots) to take part in a public riot. *An angry mob rioted in the city.* {**riy** ət}

• **run riot**
to move, act, or grow without control. *The children ran riot through the playground.*

R.I.P. *abbreviation* an abbreviation for Latin words that mean "rest in peace." R.I.P is used when a person dies and is often written on a person's gravestone.

rip *verb* (ripped, ripping, rips) 1. to cut open, off, or apart with force; tear. *The nail ripped my shirt.* 2. to be cut open or apart roughly; tear or split. *The curtain will rip if you pull too hard. noun* the result of ripping, or the place where it has happened; tear; cut. *He has a rip in the knee of his jeans.* {**rihp**}

• **rip into**
(informal) to attack with much energy. *Jenny's parents ripped into her for staying out past midnight.*

• **rip off**
1. (slang) to rob or steal. *Someone ripped off my bike last night.* 2. to cheat. *This company rips people off by selling flimsy products.*

ripe *adjective* (riper, ripest) fully grown and ready for harvest or eating. *The ripe peaches tasted wonderful.* {**riyp**} ripeness, n.

rip·en *verb* (ripened, ripening, ripens) to become or cause to become ripe or ready. *These tomatoes will ripen if you leave them in a paper bag for a couple of days.* {**riy** pən}

rip·ple *verb* (rippled, rippling, ripples) 1. to move or flow in small waves. *The stream rippled down the mountain.* 2. to

 Human Body   ? Human Mind   Everyday Life   History and Culture    Communication

make small waves in or on. *A breeze rippled the surface of the pond.* noun 1. a small wave. *I could see a ripple in the tall grass as the cat passed by me.* 2. something that looks, sounds, or seems like a ripple. *I felt a ripple of fear when I heard the creak on the stairs.* {**rihp** əl}

rise *verb* (rose, risen, rising, rises) 1. to stand after lying, kneeling, or sitting. *Everyone rose when the judge entered the courtroom.* 2. to get up from bed. *We rose at four o'clock in the morning for our fishing trip.* 3. to move upward. *The smoke from the fire rose above the trees.* 4. to rebel. *The people rose up against the cruel king.* 5. to become greater or higher. *The lake rose by four inches.* 6. to increase in number, value, or degree. *Prices rise when there aren't enough goods being made.* 7. to start or begin. *This stream rises deep in the mountains.* 8. to move upward in rank or importance. *She rose to the position of manager.* 9. to swell or become higher. *The bread dough rose fast in the warm, covered bowl.* noun 1. an instance or act of rising. *His rise from poverty to wealth is an amazing story.* 2. an increase in height or level. *The townspeople watched the rise of the river.* 3. the movement of the sun or planets above the horizon. *We watched the rise of the sun.* 4. an upward movement in rank or position. *Her rise to a top position in the company has been very fast.* 5. an angry reaction. *His teasing got a rise out of her.* 6. an increase in number, value, or degree. *There has been a steep rise in accidents on the interstate highway.* 7. an area of ground that slopes upward. *There is a beautiful view from the top of the rise.* {**riyz**}

risk *noun* a chance of getting hurt or losing something. *The pioneers faced many risks as they traveled across the plains.* *verb* (risked, risking, risks) 1. to put in danger. *She risked her life to climb the mountain.* 2. to take the risk of. *The soldier risked punishment by not following the order.* {**rihsk**}

rit·u·al 🔊 *noun* 1. a set form for going through the steps of a religious ceremony. *Some Christian rituals include prayer and reading from the Bible.* 2. a set of actions always done in the same way. *Paul's bedtime ritual ends with fluffing his pillow and turning out the light.* {**rihch** ooh əl} ritually, adv.

ri·val *noun* a person whom one tries to be better than; competitor. *Those two tennis players have been rivals for years.* *adjective* being, or able to be, a rival; competing. *The rival team will get the ball first.* *verb* (rivaled, rivaling, rivals) 1. to be as good as; equal. *The desserts at this diner rival those at a fancy restaurant.* 2. to try to do better than; compete with or against. *The team from Ohio rivals the Michigan team.* {**riv** vəl}

> **Word History** *Rival* comes from *rivus*, a Latin word that means "stream." *Rivalus*, the Latin word for "rival," originally meant "a person who uses the same stream as another."

riv·er 🔊 *noun* 1. a large natural stream of water flowing in a particular course toward a lake, ocean, or other body of water. 2. a pouring out; stream. *I cried a river of tears when my pet hamster died. / The rain turned the path into a river of mud.* {**rihv** ər}

riv·et *noun* a metal bolt that pins metal plates or other objects together. *The steel bridge is held together with rivets. / The pockets on those jeans are sewn and then strengthened with brass rivets.* *verb* (riveted, riveting, rivets) 1. to fasten with a rivet or rivets. *The worker riveted a connecting plate to the beam.* 2. to attract and hold firmly. *The burning building across the street riveted our attention.* {**rihv** iht} riveter, n.

Rn symbol of the chemical element radon.

roach *noun* a short form of cockroach. {**rohch**}

road 🔊 *noun* 1. a long, narrow course, with a smooth surface for vehicles and people to travel on from one place to another; street. *The town built a new road from the park to the lake.* 2. a way; course. *Many people feel that hard work is the road to success.* {**rohd**}

> **Homophone Note** The words *road* and *rode* (past tense of "ride") sound alike but have different meanings.

road map *noun* a map used by drivers that shows the streets, highways, and mileage in and between towns of an area. {**rohd** măp}

road·run·ner *noun* a fast North American bird that moves about on the ground instead of flying. The roadrunner has a long tail, a crest, and

A B C D E F G H I J K L M N O P Q R S T U V W X Y Z

streaked feathers. {**rohd** ruhn ər}

road·side *noun* the side or edge of a road. *We stood on the roadside waiting for the bus.* *adjective* at, on, or near the side or edge of the road. *We bought peaches at a roadside fruit stand.* {**rohd** siyd}

roam *verb* (roamed, roaming, roams) to move or travel around without a plan; wander. *Great herds of buffalo once roamed the plains.* {**rohm**} roamer, n.

Homophone Note The words *roam* and *Rome* (a city) sound alike but have different meanings.

roan *adjective* having a dark coat thickly sprinkled with white. *Her favorite was the roan colt.* *noun* a roan horse or other animal. *I will ride the gray mare, and you will ride the roan.* {**rohn**}

roar *verb* (roared, roaring, roars) 1. to make a deep, loud cry or shout, as in anger, pain, or excitement. *The angry crowd roared at the referee.* 2. to laugh loudly. *We roared at our cousin's silly jokes.* *noun* 1. a loud, deep cry or shout. *The roar of the lion scared the little child.* 2. a loud, steady noise made by things such as flames, surf, or machines. *The roar of the machines could be heard outside the building.* {**rohr**}

roast *verb* (roasted, roasting, roasts) 1. to cook or bake with dry heat in an oven or over an open fire. *We roasted a turkey for Thanksgiving dinner.* 2. to dry, parch, or brown by heat. *Let's roast some peanuts in the oven.* 3. to be uncomfortable from too much heat. *Beth was roasting after an hour of lying on the beach.* 4. to make too hot. *He*

took his jacket off because it was roasting him. *noun* 1. a cut of meat cooked by roasting or that can be used for roasting. *The butcher sold him three pounds of pork roast.* 2. an outdoor meal at which the main food is cooked by roasting. *We invited our friends to a corn roast.* {**rohst**}

rob *verb* (robbed, robbing, robs) 1. to steal from by using force or threats. *A thief broke into his house and robbed him.* 2. To take something away from. *Rain robbed her of a day at the beach.* {**rŏb**} robber, n.

Language Note *Rob* and *steal* are close in meaning. Both verbs mean "to take from by force, without permission." The object of *rob* is the person or place that something was taken from. The object of *steal* is the thing that was taken. *Help! Someone robbed the jewelry store. The thief stole thousands of dollars worth of gold and diamonds.*

rob·ber *noun* a person who robs or steals by using force. {**rŏb** ər}

rob·ber·y *noun* (robberies) the act of robbing. *There have been two robberies at that store.* {**rŏb** ə ree}

robe *noun* 1. a long, loose gown worn at certain ceremonies. *The students all wore black robes at their graduation.* 2. a loose gown worn as a covering; bathrobe. *She put on a robe to answer the door.* {**rohb**}

rob·in *noun* a large North American songbird that has a rusty red breast, a dark head and back, and a bright yellow bill. The North American robin is a type of thrush. {**rŏb** ihn}

ro·bot *noun* a machine that can perform some of the same

tasks as a human being. {**roh** bŏt} robotic, adj.

Word History *Robot* comes from a Czech word that means "forced labor." The word *robot* was first used in a play about mechanical men that were built to do all the hard physical labor of a society.

ro·bust *adjective* 1. strong, healthy, and full of energy. *The robust woman runs four miles every morning.* 2. full of high spirits; noisy. *He broke into robust laughter.* {roh **buhst**}

Word History The word *robust* has its roots in the Latin word *robus*, which means "oak tree" or "hard timber."

rock¹ *noun* 1. a solid mass made up of minerals. Rock forms much of the earth's outer layer, including cliffs and mountains. 2. a piece of such matter, such as a stone or pebble. *We cleared the soil of rocks before planting a garden.* 3. a person or thing that gives support or acts as a strong foundation. *Grandfather is the rock of the family.* {**rŏk**}

rock² *verb* (rocked, rocking, rocks) 1. to move strongly back and forth or from side to side. *The ship rocked in the storm.* 2. to move back and forth in a rocking chair. *Aunt Esther rocked as she knitted.* 3. to cause to move back and forth or from side to side. *I rocked the baby to sleep.* 4. to cause to shake hard. *Stop rocking my desk!* *noun* a form of popular music with a strong beat and usually played loudly on electronic instruments such as guitars; rock-'n'-roll. *adjective* of or relating to rock-'n'-roll. *Who is your favorite rock star?* {**rŏk**}

 Human Body   Human Mind   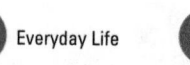 Everyday Life   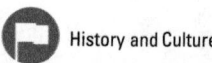 History and Culture    Communication

rock·er *noun* 1. one of the curved pieces on the bottom of a chair that allows it to have a rocking motion. 2. a chair with curved pieces attached to the bottom that allows a person to rock while sitting; rocking chair. 3. a person who plays, listens to, or dances to rock music. {rŏk ər}

rock·et *noun* a flying device, shaped like a tube, that is driven by hot gases released from engines in its rear. Rockets are used to launch fireworks, signals, weapons, and spacecraft. *Many U.S. rockets are launched from the Kennedy Space Center in Florida.* *verb* (rocketed, rocketing, rockets) 1. to move or rise as swiftly as a rocket. *Dorie's temperature rocketed when she got sick with the flu.* 2. to rise suddenly and without warning; sky-rocket. *The price of cucumbers has rocketed during the past month.* {rŏk iht}

rocking chair *noun* a chair mounted on rockers or springs that allow it to rock back and forth. {rŏk ing chayr}

rocking horse *noun* a toy horse built on springs or rockers that is large enough for a child to ride. {rŏk ing hohrs}

rock-'n'-roll or **rock-and-roll** *noun* a form of popular music with a strong beat; rock. *verb* (rock-'n'-rolled, rock-'n'-rolling, rock-'n'-rolls) to listen to, dance to, or play rock-'n'-roll. *We rock-'n'-rolled all night long.* {rŏk ən rohl} rock-'n'-roller, n.

rock·y¹ *adjective* (rockier, rockiest) having many rocks; full of rocks. *The rocky trail was difficult to climb.* {rŏk ee}

rock·y² *adjective* (rockier, rockiest) 1. likely or tending to rock; not steady; shaky. *The table was rocky because one leg was shorter than the others.* 2. marked by difficulties; not certain. *His poor grades seemed to promise a rocky future.* {rŏk ee}

Rocky Mountains *plural noun* a high mountain range in North America that stretches from Alaska to northern New Mexico; Rockies. {rŏk ee mown tənz}

rod *noun* 1. a straight, thin stick or bar. *I bought new curtain rods for the living room windows.* 2. see **fishing rod**. 3. a unit of length equal to 16.5 feet or 5.029 meters. 4. a stick or switch used for punishment by whipping. {rŏd}

rode *verb* past tense of **ride**. {rohd}

Homophone Note Are you looking for the word **road** (a street)? **Rode** and **road** sound alike but have different meanings.

ro·dent ❶ *noun* a small mammal with long front teeth used for gnawing. Many kinds of rodents are found all over the world. Rodents include rats, mice, hamsters, porcupines, chinchillas, guinea pigs, squirrels, prairie dogs, gophers, woodchucks, and beavers. {roh dənt}

Word History *Rodent* is from *rodere*, a Latin word that means "to gnaw." *Erode* and *corrode* come from the same Latin word.

ro·de·o *noun* (rodeos) a show or contest of cowboy skills such as riding wild horses or roping cattle. {rohd dee oh}

roe¹ *noun* fish eggs. {roh}

roe² *noun* (roe or roes) a small deer found in Europe and Asia. The male roe has antlers with three points. {roh}

Homophone Note The words **roe**, **row¹**, and **row²** sound alike but have different meanings.

rogue *noun* 1. a person who is dishonest or mean. *That rogue ran off with my wallet.* 2. a person who is naughty or full of mischief. *That little rogue is always playing tricks on people.* 3. an animal, often a male elephant, that lives apart from the rest of the herd because it is vicious. {rohg}

role *noun* 1. the character played by an actor. *The role of Hamlet is a challenge for any actor.* 2. a part played by a person or thing. *She was happy with her role as a mother. / A role of salt is to bring out the taste of food.* {rohl}

Homophone Note The words **role** and **roll** (to turn over) sound alike but have different meanings.

A B C D E F G H I J K L M N O P Q R S T U V W X Y Z

role model *noun* a person whose actions set an example or are copied by others. *Neil's father is his role model. / Eleanor Roosevelt was a role model for many Americans.* {**rohl** mŏd əl}

roll *verb* (rolled, rolling, rolls) 1. to move by turning over and over. *Jack and Jill rolled down the hill.* 2. to move or travel by wheels or as if by wheels. *The car rolled into the driveway.* 3. to rock from side to side. *The ship pitched and rolled on the stormy sea.* 4. to spread over an area as waves. *The flood rolled over the town.* 5. to move; pass. *The hours rolled by.* 6. to make a sound like thunder. *The drums rolled.* 7. to be made flat by a roller. *This dough rolls easily.* 8. to cause to move by turning over and over. *We rolled the tire into the garage.* 9. to wrap in something. *The baker rolled the balls of dough in coconut flakes.* *noun* 1. an act of rolling. *The roll of the boat made me sick.* 2. any material wound into the shape of a cylinder or tube. *There were hundreds of rolls of carpet in the warehouse.* 3. a cylinder around which certain material is wound; roller. *Please hand me the roll of tape.* 4. something with the shape of a cylinder or tube. *Four rolls of quarters are worth forty dollars.* 5. a thick, round type of bread. *I'd like a ham and cheese sandwich on a roll, please.* 6. a list of names of a group. *I am studying hard to make the honor roll.* 7. a gentle movement like that of waves. *The roll of the sea put me to sleep.* 8. a deep, rumbling sound. *Lisa was startled by the sudden roll of thunder.* 9. a quick series of beats. *The king entered the hall to the sound of a drum roll.* {rohl}

> **Homophone Note** Are you looking for the word **role** (a part in something)? **Roll** and **role** sound alike but have different meanings.

roll·er *noun* 1. a wheel attached to the bottom of a heavy object to make it easier to move. 2. an object shaped like a tube, around which something is rolled. *When I let go of the window shade, it spun around the roller.* 3. an object shaped like a tube used to flatten, spread, or crush something. *We painted the walls with a roller. / A steam roller flattened out the road.* 4. a small tube around which hair is rolled for setting. {**roh** lər}

roller coaster *noun* an amusement park ride in which a train of open cars rides up and down a winding track. {**roh** lər koh stər}

roller skate *noun* a shoe, or frame that fits over a shoe, with four small wheels made for skating on a hard surface. {**roh** lər skayt}

rolling pin *noun* a hard, smooth cylinder of wood or marble with handles at each end. It is used to roll out dough. {**roh** ling pihn}

ROM *abbreviation* computer memory that can only be read, not written to. ROM stands for "read-only memory." {rŏm}

Ro·man *adjective* 1. having to do with modern or ancient Rome or its people. 2. (usually lower case) relating to upright printing type or lettering. *The definitions in this dictionary are set in roman type.* *noun* 1. a person born or living in Rome. 2. (usually lower case) roman printing type. {**roh** mən}

Roman Catholic Church *noun* a Christian church that is headed by the pope, the bishop of Rome. {**roh** mən **kǎth** lihk **chuhrch**}

ro·mance 🔊 🔊 *noun* 1. a love relationship, either in life or in literature or film. *The couple celebrated their twenty-year romance.* 2. the spirit of adventure and love, either in life or in literature and film. *The young man dreamed of a life of romance.* 3. a tale of the adventures and deeds of knights or other heroes. *adjective* (capitalized) having to do with certain modern languages that came from Latin. {**roh** mǎns or roh **mǎns**, n., **roh** mǎns or roh **mǎns**, adj.}

Ro·mance lan·guage *noun* one of the modern languages that come from Latin. Italian, French, Spanish, and Portuguese are Romance languages. {**roh** mǎns lǎn gwihj}

Roman Empire *noun* the lands ruled by ancient Rome, stretching from Britain to North Africa and the Middle East. {**roh** mən **ehm** piyr}

Roman numeral *noun* a letter used as a number in the ancient Roman number system. The letter I equals 1, V equals 5, X equals 10, L equals 50, C equals 100, D equals 500, and M equals 1,000. In this system, a letter followed by one of equal or

 Human Body  Human Mind   Everyday Life  History and Culture Communication

lesser value means the two are added; seven is VII, or 5+1+1. A letter followed by one of greater value means that the first is subtracted from the second; four hundred is CD, or 500-100. *The Roman numeral for 15 is XV and for 4 is IV. / The United Nations was founded in 1945, or in Roman numerals, MCMXLV.* {<u>roh</u> mən <u>nooh</u> mə rəl}

ro·man·tic *adjective* 1. having to do with romance. *His head is full of romantic ideas.* 2. causing or showing thoughts and feelings of love. *She wrote a romantic letter.* 3. daring and heroic. *He loved to read the romantic tales of knights and dragons.* *noun* a person who is romantic or is too sentimental and not practical. *Harry was a romantic who daydreamed while he should have been studying.* {roh <u>măn</u> tihk}

Rome *noun* 1. the capital city of Italy. 2. the capital city of the Roman Empire. {<u>rohm</u>}

Homophone Note The words *Rome* and *roam* (to travel) sound alike but have different meanings.

romp *verb* (romped, romping, romps) to move about or play in a lively manner. *The dogs romped together in the park.* *noun* lively and merry play. *We sang songs on our romp through the woods.* {<u>rŏmp</u>}

roof *noun* 1. the surface or covering on the top of a building. *The roof of a house protects it from rain and snow.* 2. anything that resembles such a surface or structure. *I cut the roof of my mouth on a chicken bone.* {<u>roohf</u> or <u>ruuf</u>}
• **a roof over one's head** a place to live; home; shelter.

Where I live is not important, as long as I have a roof over my head.

rook *noun* a chess piece that can move over any number of empty squares sideways or forward and backward; castle. {<u>ruuk</u>}

rook·ie *noun* 1. a professional athlete in his or her first season on a team. 2. a member of a group who has not yet had training or experience. *My brother is a police officer, but he is still a rookie.* {<u>ruuk</u> ee}

room 🌐 *noun* 1. space that is used or available for use. *The school gym has plenty of room for dancing.* 2. an area of a building separated from similar areas by walls or doors. *Our house has ten rooms.* 3. the people present in a room of a building. *The eyes of the whole room were on me when I sang my song.* 4. place; possibility. *There is no room for lazy workers in this business.* *verb* (roomed, rooming, rooms) to live in a room or living quarters; stay. *I roomed with my best friend at camp last summer.* {<u>roohm</u> or <u>ruum</u>, n., <u>roohm</u> or <u>ruum</u>, v.}

Word History In Old English, the word *rum* meant "space" or "enough space."

room·y *adjective* (roomier, roomiest) having plenty of space; large. *This tent is roomy enough for two people.* {<u>rooh</u> mee}

roost *noun* a perch on which birds rest or sleep, or a place containing such perches. *That farm has a chicken roost.* *verb* (roosted, roosting, roosts) to land or rest on a roost. *Wild turkeys roost in trees at night.* {<u>roohst</u>}

roost·er *noun* an adult male chicken or the male of another closely related bird, such as the pheasant; cock. {<u>rooh</u> stər}

root[1] 🌐 *noun* 1. the part of a plant that usually grows underground. Roots take up water and nutrients, and hold the plant in the soil. 2. the part that attaches a hair, nail, or tooth to the body but cannot be seen. 3. the place from which something comes; source. *The root of his problem is that he does not believe in himself.* 4. (often plural) family or ethnic background. *I traveled to Vietnam to discover my roots.* 5. a number that when multiplied by itself yields a given number. *Two is the square root of four.* *verb* (rooted, rooting, roots) 1. to grow a new root or roots. *These plants will root if placed in water.* 2. to become fixed or set. *I am rooted to this chair and refuse to move until this TV show is over.* 3. to fix; plant. *The shock rooted him to the spot.* {<u>rooht</u>}
• **take root** 1. to send out new roots; begin to grow or become fixed in the ground. *The young tree we planted will soon take root.* 2. to become fixed, accepted, or established. *I felt comfortable speaking Spanish after my lessons took root.*

root[2] *verb* (rooted, rooting, roots) 1. to dig or turn over soil. *Our pig got loose and*

a
b
c
d
e
f
g
h
i
j
k
l
m
n
o
p
q
r
s
t
u
v
w
x
y
z

rooted in the garden. 2. to move things around while searching for something. *She rooted through the drawer for a pencil.* {**rooht**}

root[3] ❓ *verb* (rooted, rooting, roots) 1. to cheer for a team or a person in a contest. *The crowd rooted for the home team.* 2. to give support to another person. *We are rooting for him to get well soon.* {**rooht**}

Homophone Note Are you looking for the word **route** (a road or course)? Some people say **root** and **route** in exactly the same way, but these two words have different meanings.

rope *noun* 1. a strong cord of twisted or woven fiber, wire, or similar material. Ropes can be used to tie, pull, or lift. 2. several things strung or wound together, in the form of a heavy cord. *The Italian restaurant has ropes of garlic hanging in the kitchen.* *verb* (roped, roping, ropes) 1. to tie or tie up with a rope, or as if with a rope. *Elise roped her suitcase closed when the latch broke.* 2. to separate or mark off with a rope or ropes (often followed by "off"). *They roped off part of the seating area for special guests.* 3. to catch with a lasso, or as if with a lasso. *The cowboy roped the calf.* {**rohp**}

rose[1] *noun* 1. a flower that grows on a plant or vine that has thorns. Roses smell sweet and come in many different colors. 2. the bush or vine that bears such flowers. 3. a deep reddish pink color. *adjective* having the color, shape, or

smell of a rose. {**rohz**}

rose[2] *verb* past tense of **rise**. {**rohz**}

rose·bud *noun* the bud of a rose. {**rohz** buhd}

Rosh Hashanah *noun* a high holy day that celebrates the beginning of the New Year according to the Jewish calendar. Rosh Hashanah takes place on the first day or the first and second days of Tishri. {**rohsh** hə **shah** nə *or* **rohsh** hə **shaw** nə}

ros·y *adjective* (rosier, rosiest) 1. having a deep pink color. *She chose a rosy lipstick.* 2. filled with hope and promise. *Her new job promised her a rosy future.* {**roh** zee}

rot *verb* (rotted, rotting, rots) 1. to decompose or decay. *Our old Halloween pumpkin finally rotted.* 2. to decay or become useless (often followed by "away" or "through"). *The pier's supports had partly rotted through.* 3. to cause decay in. *Water in the basement rotted my books.* *noun* any of several diseases in plants and animals caused by decay. *Feather rot is a disease of tree trunks caused by a fungus.* {**rŏt**}

ro·ta·ry *adjective* 1. turning or able to turn on an axis. *My old telephone has a rotary dial.* 2. having a part or parts that turn on an axis. *I dialed her number on my old rotary telephone.* {**roh** tə ree}

ro·tate *verb* (rotated, rotating, rotates) 1. to cause to turn around on an axis. *I rotated the globe to find South America.* 2. to replace according to planned cycles.

The coach rotated the players to give everyone a chance to play. 3. to turn on or around a fixed point. *Spin the top to make it rotate.* 4. to change in a certain order; take turns. *The nurses on duty rotated every eight hours.* {**roh** tayt}

Language Note *Rotate* and *revolve* are often confused. Both of these words describe the motion of Earth and other planets, moons, and stars. *Rotate* means to spin around an axis. *Earth rotates completely in about 24 hours. Each rotation is one day.* *Revolve* means to travel in a curved path around a central object. *Earth revolves around the sun in about 365.25 days. Each revolution is one year.*

ro·tor *noun* 1. the part of a machine that turns or rotates. 2. a set of turning blades. Rotors lift helicopters off the ground and keep them in the air. {**roh** tər}

rot·ten *adjective* (rottener, rottenest) 1. in the state of being rotted; bad; spoiled. *We had to throw out several of the apples because they were rotten.* 2. very bad; not at all satisfactory. *No one dares tell her she is a rotten singer.* {**rŏt** ən}

rou·ble *noun* a spelling of **ruble** used in Canada and Britain. See **ruble**. {**rooh** bəl}

rouge *noun* red or pink cosmetics used to color the cheeks or lips. {**roohzh**}

rough *adjective* (rougher, roughest) 1. having an uneven surface; not smooth. *Our car shook as we drove over the rough road. / The rough cloth scratched my cheek.* 2. marked by difficult conditions. *The rough sea rocked the*

 Human Body　❓ Human Mind　👕 Everyday Life　🏳 History and Culture　☎ Communication ship. / *Lots of snow made for a rough winter.* 3. not polite or kind. *He was friends with a rough bunch of people.* 4. without the good things of ordinary daily life. *Poor people often have rough lives.* 5. not finished. *We had just a rough idea of what we wanted our new house to be like.* 6. needing physical strength. *Clearing the rocks from the field was rough work.* {**ruhf**} roughly, *adv.*, roughness, *n.*

• **rough it**
to live without the ordinary daily comforts. *They like to rough it when they go camping.*

Homophone Note Are you looking for the word *ruff* (a collar)? *Rough* and *ruff* sound alike but have different meanings.

round *adjective* (rounder, roundest) 1. shaped like a ball or circle. *Most cookies are round. / That is a round cheese.* 2. having a curved surface or outline that is close to the curve of a ball or circle. *Apples and plums are round.* 3. somewhat curved; without angles. *The plump baby has round cheeks. noun* 1. anything that is shaped like a ball or circle. 2. (often plural) a complete series of stops or visits. *The guard made his rounds every two hours.* 3. a completed game, series, or course. *He played two rounds of golf.* 4. a bursting out. *The singer received a round of applause.* 5. a single shot from a gun or larger weapon, or the ammunition for such a shot. *The soldiers fired dozens of rounds at the enemy. adverb* around. *She spun round to see who was behind her. preposition* around *He will leave round midnight. verb* (rounded, rounding, rounds) 1. to make round in

shape. *I rounded the dough into balls for making rolls.* 2. to become round or curved in shape. *The dough for the bread rounded as it rose.* 3. to go around; pass around. *We rounded the corner too fast.* 4. to express as a round or whole number (sometimes followed by "off"). *Would you round this number off to the nearest ten?* {**rownd**}

• **round out**
to make complete or perfect. *A class in music would round out his studies.*

• **round up**
to bring together; collect. *The bus will leave as soon as all the passengers are rounded up.*

round·a·bout *adjective* not direct. *We took a roundabout way through the woods and almost got lost.* {**rownd** ə **bowt**}

round·house *noun* a round building with a turntable inside where trains are repaired and stored. {**rownd hows**}

round num·ber *noun* a number given in terms of the nearest whole number, or given in the nearest tens, hundreds, or the like. *The number 50 is a round number for 47.* {**rownd nuhm** bər}

round trip *noun* a trip to a given place and then back to the starting point. *We made a round trip from Boston to New York and back to Boston again.* {**rownd trihp**} round-trip, *adj.*

round·up *noun* 1. the act of driving cattle together for branding or shipping to market. 2. a gathering together by the police of persons suspected of breaking the law. 3. a short account; report. *He gave us a roundup of his travel adventures.* {**rownd** uhp or rownd **uhp**}

rouse *verb* (roused, rousing, rouses) 1. to waken from

sleep. *The noise roused me from my sleep.* 2. to stir up the feelings of; excite. *Lively music roused the crowd.* 3. to wake up; get out of bed. *I roused early today.* 4. to be stirred from sleep or rest. {**rowz**}

rout[1] *noun* 1. a confused retreat of troops after they have been beaten. *The battle ended in a rout of the enemy.* 2. a total defeat. *Our team was discouraged after the rout. verb* (routed, routing, routs) 1. to cause to run away or retreat. *The government troops routed the rebels.* 2. to defeat completely. *The visitors routed the home team.* {**rowt**}

rout[2] *verb* (routed, routing, routs) 1. to root about with the snout. *The pigs routed in the mud.* 2. to poke or search around; rummage. *I routed through the attic until I found my old toys.* 3. to drive, force, or turn out. *The sheriff finally routed the outlaw from his hiding place. / My parents routed me out of bed to help with the chores.* {**rowt**}

Homophone Note Are you looking for the word *route* (a road or course)? Some people say *rout* and *route* in exactly the same way, but these two words have different meanings.

route *noun* 1. a road or course of travel from one place to another. *The bus travels a different route than it used to.* 2. the usual path travelled by a person who is selling or delivering something along the way. *A paper route often covers several city blocks. verb* (routed, routing, routes) to send or direct by a certain route. *The company routed our package through Dallas, so*

A
B
C
D
E
F
G
H
I
J
K
L
M
N
O
P
Q
R
S
T
U
V
W
X
Y
Z

it arrived late. {**rooht** or **rowt**, n., **rooht** or **rowt**, v.}

Homophone Note Some people say **route** and **root** (a part of a plant) in exactly the same way. Others say **route** so that it sounds just like **rout** (to drive out). Whichever way you say it, remember how it's spelled.

rou·tine noun 1. a regular course of action. *Brushing her teeth was part of her morning routine.* 2. a course of activity that never changes. *The same routine day after day can be boring.* adjective according to routine; regular. *We did routine exercises every morning.* {rooh **teen**} routinely, adv.

row¹ noun things or people arranged in a straight line. *She sits in the front row of the classroom.* {**roh**}

row² verb (rowed, rowing, rows) to cause a boat to move forward using oars. *They rowed to the shore.* noun a trip in a boat that is rowed. *He went for a row across the pond.* {**roh**} rower, n.

Homophone Note Are you looking for the word **roe** (fish eggs or a small deer)? **Row**¹, **row**², and **roe** sound alike but have different meanings.

row³ noun a loud quarrel or fight. *The kids had a row over whose turn it was.* {**row**}

row·boat noun a boat that is moved by oars. {**roh boht**}

roy·al adjective 1. of or having to do with a king or queen, or any members of their family. *The royal wedding was shown on*

TV. 2. having to do with a country led by a king or queen. *She studied at the Royal Academy of Music in England.* {**roi** əl}

roy·al·ty noun (royalties) 1. a member of a royal family; royal persons as a group. *In that country, the royalty live in palaces.* 2. the power or position of a royal person. *Royalty entitled him to special privileges.* 3. a share of money paid to authors or composers from the sale or performance of their work, or a share paid to inventors for the use of their work. {**roi** əl tee}

RR abbreviation 1. an abbreviation for **railroad**. 2. an abbreviation for "rural route."

rte. abbreviation an abbreviation for **route**.

rub verb (rubbed, rubbing, rubs) 1. to use pressure on with a back and forth motion. *He rubbed his sore arm.* 2. to spread against or onto another surface by means of pressure. *She's rubbing wax onto the floor.* 3. to take away by using pressure (often followed by "off" or "out"). *He rubbed the stain off his shirt with a wet cloth.* 4. to move or slide against. *Her shoulder rubbed against me as we went out the door.* noun the process or an instance of rubbing. *Give my back a rub.* {**ruhb**}

• **rub the wrong way** to bother or annoy. *Her tone of voice rubs me the wrong way.*

rub·ber noun 1. a stretchy substance made from the dried sap or liquid from certain tropical plants. 2. this substance made tougher through a chemical process. Rubber is used to make tires, erasers, rubber bands, and many other things. 3. (usually plural) an overshoe

made of rubber. *He put on his rubbers before walking in the rain.* {**ruhb** ər}

Word History The elastic substance obtained from tropical plants acquired the name **rubber** in the 1700s because it was used to make erasers, which the British call "rubbers." Before that, "rubber" meant simply "a thing that rubs."

rubber band noun a narrow loop of rubber used to hold objects together. {**ruhb** ər **bănd**}

rub·bish noun 1. material that is thrown away or useless; garbage. *Our rubbish is picked up once a week.* 2. foolish talk or writing; non-sense. *His claim to have traveled to Jupiter is pure rubbish.* {**ruhb** ihsh}

rub·ble noun pieces of broken rock, brick, or other material. *After the war, nothing was left of the town but rubble.* {**ruhb** əl}

ru·ble or **rouble** noun the main unit of money of Russia and other countries of the former Soviet Union. {**rooh** bəl}

ru·by noun (rubies) 1. a valuable, deep red stone used in making jewelry. 2. a color like

 Human Body   Human Mind   Everyday Life   History and Culture   Communication

that of a ruby. {**rooh** bee}

rud·der *noun* a movable blade at the rear end of a ship or airplane, used to control direction. {**ruhd** ər}

rude *adjective* (ruder, rudest) 1. showing poor manners; not polite. *It was rude to take the gift without saying "thank you."* 2. crude or simple. *We made a rude shelter out of tree branches.* {**roohd**} rudely, adv., rudeness, n.

Synonyms
These words share a meaning with *rude*, adjective 1:
crude, impolite, insolent, impudent, impertinent, discourteous

ruff *noun* 1. a high, round, stiff collar worn by men and women in the 1500s and 1600s. 2. a ring or collar of hair, fur, or feathers around the neck of an mammal or bird. {**ruhf**}

Homophone Note The words *ruff* and *rough* (not smooth) sound alike but have different meanings.

ruf·fle *verb* (ruffled, ruffling, ruffles) 1. to disturb a smooth, even surface. *Wind ruffled the surface of the pond.* 2. to bother or fluster. *While giving her book report, Marge was ruffled by the sight of the class clown making faces.* noun a strip of cloth, gathered along one edge in small folds. *My dress is trimmed with ruffles.* {**ruhf** əl}

rug *noun* a piece of thick material used to cover part of a floor. {**ruhg**}

rug·ged *adjective* 1. having a surface that is rough and broken. *They headed up the rugged trail.* 2. strong and rough looking. *The farmer has a rugged face.* 3. strong or sturdy. *The rugged ship made it*

through the storm. 4. causing hardship or strain; harsh. *His ancestors lived a rugged life in the highlands of Scotland.* {**ruhg** ihd} ruggedly, adv., ruggedness, n.

ru·in *noun* 1. complete destruction. *The earth's rain forests are facing ruin.* 2. (usually plural) the result or condition of such destruction. *After the flood, the house was in ruins.* 3. a complete breakdown of health or social standing. *Drug abuse led to the movie star's ruin.* 4. the cause of destruction or damage. *Greed was his ruin.* verb (ruined, ruining, ruins) 1. to bring to ruin; wreck. *An earthquake ruined the village.* 2. to bring ruin upon. *Stealing from friends ruined her.* {**rooh** ihn}

rule *noun* 1. a law or direction that guides behavior or action. *Baseball has many rules of play.* 2. what is usual or normal. *As a rule, we stay home on Sundays.* 3. a government or control. *The king's rule is just.* 4. a strip of wood or other material that is used to measure length; ruler. verb (ruled, ruling, rules) 1. to have authority over; govern. *The law rules the country.* 2. to mark with straight lines. *I ruled the sheet of paper with a red pen.* 3. to make a particular decision in a court of law. *The court ruled against them.* {**roohl**}

• **rule out**
to decide not to include in the set of choices. *We ruled out Bart as the cookie thief, because he can't reach the top shelf.*

rul·er *noun* 1. a person who rules or leads. *The sultan was a wise ruler.* 2. a tool for measuring the length of something. A ruler is marked off in inches, centimeters, or other units. {**rooh** lər}

rum *noun* an alcoholic beverage made from molasses or sugar cane. {**ruhm**}

rum·ble *verb* (rumbled, rumbling, rumbles) 1. to make a long, low, rolling sound. *My stomach rumbles when I'm hungry.* 2. to move with such a sound. *The huge truck rumbled down the street.* noun a low, heavy, rolling sound. *We heard a rumble of thunder in the distance.* {**ruhm** bəl}

rum·mage *verb* (rummaged, rummaging, rummages) 1. to make a thorough search by turning over and looking through the contents of. *I rummaged the drawer for my keys.* 2. to make a quick, vigorous search. *He rummaged through the closet to find his football.* {**ruhm** ihj}

ru·mor *noun* a piece of information or a story passed from one person to another without any proof that it is true. *It is only a rumor that the store is closing.* verb (rumored, rumoring, rumors) to tell or spread by rumor. *It is rumored that school will close early today.* {**rooh** mər}

ru·mour *noun or transitive verb* a spelling of **rumor** used in Canada and Britain. See **rumor.** {**rooh** mər}

rump *noun* 1. the back section of an animal. 2. a cut of meat from this area of an animal. {**ruhmp**}

a
b
c
d
e
f
g
h
i
j
k
l
m
n
o
p
q
r
s
t
u
v
w
x
y
z

run ⊙ *verb* (ran, run, running, runs) 1. to make oneself go forward by moving the legs very quickly. *I had to run to catch up with her.* 2. to move quickly; make a fast trip. *Please run over to the barn and grab my toolbox.* 3. to escape by moving away quickly. *If you don't keep the dog on a leash he will run away.* 4. to seek office in an election. *She ran for mayor three times.* 5. to work or operate. *This machine runs well.* 6. to flow or spread. *The river runs fast. / Paint is running down the wall.* 7. to move between places on a schedule. *The bus to town runs every two hours.* 8. to continue through time or space. *The movie ran for a week. / This road runs for thirty miles.* 9. to have stitches break. *Her stocking ran.* 10. to move quickly over or along. *He ran three miles.* 11. to cause to run. *Cowboys who run cattle work hard.* 12. to perform in by running. *She ran the race well.* 13. to operate. *He ran the pump to clear the basement of water.* 14. to manage or own. *He ran a shoe business.* 15. to print in a publication for advertising. *We ran an ad to sell our boat.* 16. to go quickly past or through. *It is against the law to run a stop sign.* 17. to put oneself in a particular place or condition. *She ran the risk of falling by skiing so fast.* 18. to push with force against, off, or into something. *They ran me off the road.* *noun* 1. the act of running. *He takes a long run every morning.* 2. a pace faster than a walk. *He circled the building at a run.* 3. a contest of running; race. *I finished the run in fifteen minutes.* 4. a quick trip. *Brian made a run to the store for milk and bread.* 5. the distance covered in a period of running. *I made a run of three miles this morning.* 6. freedom to move about in or use. *He has the run of the house.* 7. a period of time during which something continues to happen or the length of a single series of things. *He had a long run of good luck. / That run of railroad track is fifteen miles long.* 8. a single period of production in printing. *His first novel had a run of ten thousand copies.* 9. an enclosed outdoor space for animals. *They built a run for the dog behind the garage.* 10. a place where stitches have broken in a stocking or other knitted article. *My stocking got a run when I fell.* 11. a score in baseball or softball. *The home team scored three runs in the last inning.* 12. an effort to win office in an election. *Lots of people helped him in his run for mayor.* {<u>ruhn</u>}

• **in the long run**
at the end of a period of time; finally. *In the long run, he was glad he had moved to another state.*

• **run across**
to meet by chance. *I ran across my teacher at the mall.*

• **run down**
1. to look over; review. *She ran down the list of report topics.* 2. to chase until caught. *I finally ran down my busy neighbor to invite her over.*

• **run out of**
to use up the entire amount of. *We have run out of milk and juice.*

run·a·way *noun* a person or animal that has run away or escaped. *I hope they find the runaway soon.* *adjective* having run away or escaped. *The runaway teenager took a bus to the city.* {<u>ruhn</u> ə **way**}

run-down *adjective* 1. in poor condition. *The run-down house looked better after a fresh coat of paint.* 2. tired or weak. *The run-down girl recovered after a week at the beach.* 3. not in proper working order. *This run-down car needs new brakes, a radiator, and a muffler.* {<u>ruhn</u> **down**}

rung[1] *verb* past participle of **ring**[2]. {<u>rung</u>}

rung[2] *noun* a bar that forms the step of a ladder, or the piece between the legs of a chair. {<u>rung</u>}

Homophone Note Are you looking for the word *wrung* (past tense and past participle of "wring")? *Rung* and *wrung* sound alike but have different meanings.

run·ner *noun* 1. a person, animal, or thing that runs or races. *She is a faster runner than he is.* 2. one of the two long, narrow pieces on which a sled or sleigh slides; blade. 3. a long, narrow carpet or rug. *There is a runner on the stairs.* 4. a part of a plant that grows along the ground and sends roots into the ground. {<u>ruhn</u> ər}

run·ner-up *noun* (runners-up) the person or team that finishes in second place. {<u>ruhn</u> ər <u>uhp</u>}

running mate *noun* a candidate running for a less important office than the one for which the fellow candidate is running. *The candidate for vice president is the running mate of the candidate for president.* {<u>ruhn</u> ing <u>mayt</u>}

 Human Body  Human Mind Everyday Life 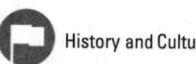 History and Culture  Communication

run·ny *adjective* (runnier, runniest) 1. soft and liquid; flowing. *I don't like runny eggs.* 2. flowing with mucus. *I stayed home from school with a runny nose.* {<u>ruhn</u> ee}

runt *noun* a dog, pig, or other animal that is the smallest of a litter. {<u>ruhnt</u>}

run·way *noun* 1. a smooth, level strip on which airplanes take off and land. 2. a narrow platform attached to a stage. Models and actors walk on runways to be closer to the audience.

{<u>ruhn</u> way}

rup·ture *noun* 1. the act of breaking open or breaking off. *The rupture of the dam caused a flood.* 2. a break in friendly connections between people or nations. *A rupture between the two countries started a war.* *verb* (ruptured, rupturing, ruptures) to break or tear open. *He ruptured a tendon in his leg.* {<u>ruhp</u> chər}

ru·ral *adjective* having to do with country life. *People in rural areas often live by farming.* {<u>ruur</u> əl}

rush¹ *verb* (rushed, rushing, rushes) 1. to act or go quickly; hurry. *We rushed to catch the bus.* 2. to cause to hurry or act too quickly. *Don't rush me; I'm coming.* 3. to carry or send quickly. *Rush him to the doctor.* *noun* 1. a quick and sudden forward movement. *There was a rush of water over the falls.* 2. a state of hurry. *I'm in a rush, so don't bother me.* 3. a quick movement by many people to a place. *There was a rush to the doors when the movie ended.* {<u>ruhsh</u>}

rush² *noun* a grass that grows in wet places. Rushes have thin, hollow stems, small green or brown flowers, and are used to make baskets and other items. {<u>ruhsh</u>}

rus·set *noun* 1. a reddish brown color. 2. an apple with rough, reddish skin. *adjective* of a russet color. *The leaves of some trees turn russet in autumn.* {<u>ruhs</u> iht}

Rus·sia *noun* a country in eastern Europe and northern Asia. Russia is also called the Russian Federation. Moscow is the capital of Russia. Russia used to be the largest republic of the Union of Soviet Socialist Republics. {<u>ruhsh</u> ə}

Rus·sian *adjective* of or having to do with Russia, or its people or language. *noun* 1. a person who was born in or

Добро пожаловать!

is a citizen of Russia. 2. the main language of Russia. {<u>ruhsh</u> ən}

rust *noun* 1. an orange or reddish brown coating that forms on metal that has been exposed to air and water. 2. a plant disease that causes reddish brown or black spots on leaves and stems. It is caused by a fungus. *verb* (rusted, rusting, rusts) to become rusty. *The fender of my bike is rusting.* {<u>ruhst</u>}

rus·tic *adjective* 1. living or happening in the country. *We chose rustic life over city life.* 2. relating to the country; crude; simple. *She taught us a rustic dance.* / *We stayed overnight in a rustic cottage.* {<u>ruhs</u> tihk}

rus·tle *verb* (rustled, rustling, rustles) 1. to make soft, hissing sounds like things rubbing together. *Her skirt rustled when she walked.* 2. to cause to make a soft, hissing sound. *Wind rustled the dry leaves.* 3. to steal livestock. *Movies about the Old West often show people rustling cattle.* *noun* a soft hissing sound. *I heard a rustle of voices in the next room.* {<u>ruhs</u> əl}

rust·ler *noun* a person who rustles or steals livestock. {<u>ruhst</u> lər}

rust·y *adjective* (rustier, rustiest) 1. covered with rust; not working well. *Tools left out in the rain become rusty.* / *My brain feels rusty today because I didn't sleep well last night.* 2. not as good as it once was; out of practice. *My piano playing is rusty.* {<u>ruhs</u> tee}

rut *noun* 1. a hollow track worn into the ground. *The wagon wheels made ruts in the dirt road.* 2. a boring routine or way of life. *Try new things to keep from falling into a rut.* *verb* (rutted, rutting, ruts) to make ruts in. *The*

a
b
c
d
e
f
g
h
i
j
k
l
m
n
o
p
q
r
s
t
u
v
w
x
y
z

tractor wheels rutted the field. {**ruht**}

ruth·less *adjective* having no mercy or sympathy; cruel. *Slaves in the South were often treated in a ruthless manner.* {**roohth** lihs} ruthlessly, adv.

rye ❶ *noun* 1. a grass grown for its grain. Rye seeds are used for cereal, flour, and other grain products. 2. the seeds of the rye plant. {**riv**}

 Human Body

 Human Mind

 Everyday Life

 History and Culture

Communication

Ss

S is a consonant. It always makes the "s" sound at the beginning of words. "S" makes the "sh" sound when it is combined with "h" (ship) or with "u" (sugar or sure).

Tips to help you look up words starting with s: Also look under C and P for words starting with the "s" sound. Many words start with the "s" sound if they are spelled with "ce" (certain) or "ci" (circle). Some words have a silent "p" in front of the "s" (psychology).

These words may be hard to look up if you don't already know how to spell them:

said	souvenir
schedule	special
school	sphinx
science	square
scissors	straight
should	strength
sign	surge
soften	sword
soldier	

s or **S** *noun* (s's or S's) 1. the nineteenth letter of the English alphabet. 2. a grade given for satisfactory school work. {**ehs**}

S *abbreviation* an abbreviation for **south**.

-'s[1] *suffix* a suffix used to form the possessive of most singular nouns, some plural nouns not ending in "s," and some pronouns. *The cat's tail is the tail of the cat. / The children's clothing is the clothing that belongs to the children.*

-'s[2] *suffix* 1. a suffix used as a shortened form of "is." *"It's hot" means "it is hot."* 2. a suffix used as a shortened form of "has." *"She's begun" means "she has begun."* 3. a suffix used as a shortened form of "does." *"What's that mean?" means "What does that mean?"*

-s[1] *suffix* a suffix used to form the third person singular present tense of all regular and most irregular verbs. *"He drives" is the third person singular present form of the verb "drive."*

-s[2] *suffix* a suffix used to form the regular plural of most nouns. *"Stars" is the plural of "star."*

Sab·bath *noun* 1. Saturday, the day of rest and worship for Jews and some Christians. 2. Sunday, the day of rest and worship for Christians. {**să** bəth}

sa·ber *noun* a heavy sword with one sharp edge. It is usually curved. {**say** bər}

saber-toothed tiger *noun* a large wild cat with very long teeth curving from its upper jaw. Saber-toothed tigers were carnivores that hunted the young of mammoths and other large animals. The last kinds of saber-toothed tigers became extinct over ten thousand years ago. Modern tigers are not related to saber-toothed tigers. {**say** bər **tooht**ht **tiv** gər}

sa·ble *noun* 1. a small mammal with very dark brown fur, a long body, and short legs. Sables live in Europe and Asia and are related to weasels. 2. the fur of this mammal. 3. a grayish brown or black color. *adjective* having the color of a sable; very dark in color; black. *Her sable hair shone in the sunlight.* {**say** bəl}

sab·o·tage *noun* damage done to property in secret in order to stop some activity. *Angry workers used sabotage to stop their company from using dangerous chemicals. verb* (sabotaged, sabotaging, sabotages) to attack or damage by sabotage. *The spy sabotaged the enemy's plan of attack.* {**să** bə **tŏzh** or să bə **tăzh**, n., **să** bə **tŏzh** or să bə **tăzh**, v.}

sa·bre *noun* a spelling of **saber** used in Canada and Britain. See **saber**. {**say** bər}

sac *noun* a plant or animal part shaped like a bag or pouch. *A spider's eggs are held in a sac.* {**săk**}

Homophone Note The words *sac* and *sack* sound alike but have different meanings.

SAC *abbreviation* Strategic Air Command. {**săk**}

sac·cha·rine *adjective* 1. having to do with sugar; extremely sweet. *This dessert is too saccharine for my taste.* 2. sweet in a false way. *Her saccharine words didn't fool me.* {**să** kə rihn or **să** kə **riyn**}

sack[1] *noun* *a large bag made of thick paper or other strong material and used for holding

 Living World Physical World  Natural Environment  Economy Government and Law

A
B
C
D
E
F
G
H
I
J
K
L
M
N
O
P
Q
R
S
T
U
V
W
X
Y
Z

things like grain or potatoes. *The farm workers loaded sacks of potatoes onto the truck.* *verb* (sacked, sacking, sacks) (slang) to fire a person from a position or job. *The boss sacked her because she missed too many days of work.* {s**ă**k}
• **hit the sack** or **sack out** (slang) to go to bed. *It's time to hit the sack. / The campers sacked out in their tents.*

sack[2] *verb* (sacked, sacking, sacks) to steal valuable things from, after capturing. *Thousands of years ago, a Greek army sacked the walled city of Troy.* *noun* the act of stealing from and destroying a place that has been captured. *Many great heroes died in the sack of Troy.* {s**ă**k}

Homophone Note The words *sack* and *sac* sound alike but have different meanings.

sa·cred ⊜ *adjective* 1. having to do with religion. *The choir sings sacred music in church.* 2. shown great respect. *Memories of my grandfather are sacred to me.* {s**ay** krihd}

sac·ri·fice *noun* 1. the act of giving up something of great value to show loyalty or deep affection. *Nick's parents made sacrifices so they could pay for his college education.* 2. the gift of something to a god as an act of worship. *The sacrifice of animals is not a common practice today.* 3. a person or thing offered as a sacrifice. *Odysseus laid the sacrifice to Athena on the altar.* 4. a hit in the game of baseball that lets

a player already on base move forward, even though the player hitting the ball is put out. *verb* (sacrificed, sacrificing, sacrifices) 1. to allow to be taken away for the sake of something or someone else. *She sacrificed her vacation to take care of her grandmother.* 2. to make an offering of to a god. *Abraham was ready to sacrifice his son, Isaac.* 3. to make a hit in the game of baseball that lets a player who is already on base move ahead, even though the player hitting is put out. {s**ă** krə **fiys**}

sad *adjective* (sadder, saddest) 1. unhappy or without joy. *Steve was so sad when his dog died.* 2. causing unhappiness. *The movie had a sad ending.* {s**ă**d} sadly, adv.

Word History The word *sad* has been part of the English language for many centuries but did not mean "unhappy" until the 1300s. In Old English, "sad" meant "satisfied." Later, it came to mean "tired or weary of."

sad·den *verb* (saddened, saddening, saddens) to make or become sad. *Losing the tennis match saddened her.* {s**ă**d ən}

sad·dle *noun* 1. a leather seat that is used on the back of a horse or other animal to carry a rider. 2. a seat on a bicycle, or something else like a saddle in shape and use. *verb* (saddled, saddling, saddles) 1. to put a saddle on. *She saddled her horse.* 2. to burden or load. *They saddled him with the job of cleaning up after the party.* 3. to climb

into a saddle (often followed by "up"). *The cowboys saddled up and rode off.* {s**ă**d əl}
• **in the saddle** having authority; in a position to direct. *After six months off to have a baby, she was back in the saddle as vice president of the company.*

sad·ness ⊙ *noun* the state or quality of being unhappy. *I feel terrible sadness over my parents' divorce. / There was sadness in her voice.* {s**ă**d nihs}

sa·fa·ri *noun* an expedition for watching or hunting large animals. *They took pictures of lions, giraffes, and elephants on their African safari.* {sə **far** ee}

Word History *Safari* means "journey or expedition" in the Swahili language.

safe *adjective* (safer, safest) 1. not in danger; free from harm. *We were safe at home when the storm hit.* 2. careful; cautious. *Nico is a safe driver.* *noun* a strong metal box with a lock, used for keeping money and valuable things secure. {s**ayf**} safely, adv.

safe·guard *noun* a person, thing, or action that gives protection; a way of making sure that something is safe. *Seat belts in cars are a safeguard against getting hurt in an accident.* *verb* (safeguarded, safeguarding, safeguards) to keep safe; guard; protect. *The fireman taught us how to safeguard our home.* {s**ayf** gard}

safe·ty *noun* (safeties) the condition of being safe from danger. *Sue wears a helmet for safety when she rides her bike.* {s**ayf** tee}

safety belt *noun* 1. a harness that fits across the lap and often the chest of a person riding in a car or airplane; seat belt. Safety belts are worn for protection. 2. a har-

Human Body   Human Mind   Everyday Life   History and Culture    Communication

ness to keep persons who work in high places from falling. *Workers who repair telephone lines wear safety belts.* {**sayf** tee **behlt**}

safety pin *noun* a pin folded back on itself to form a clasp. There is a spring at one end and a guard at the other end to cover the point. A safety pin is used to hold two pieces of cloth or other material together. {**sayf** tee **pihn**}

sag *verb* (sagged, sagging, sags) 1. to sink, hang, or bend downward in the middle. *The shelf sagged from the weight of too many books.* 2. to grow weak or become less firm. *His shoulders sagged under the heavy load. / Her spirits sagged when she failed the test.* {**săg**}

sage *noun* a very wise person. *The sage answered some puzzling questions for us.* *adjective* (sager, sagest) having or showing good judgment; wise. *The boy's father gave him sage advice.* {**sayj**}

sage·brush *noun* a bushy plant with silver leaves that have a pleasant smell. It has white or yellow flowers and grows in the dry plains of the western United States. {**sayj bruhsh**}

Sag·it·ta·ri·us *noun* 1. a constellation between Scorpio and Capricorn in the brightest part of the Milky Way. Sagittarius is also called the Archer. 2. the ninth sign of the zodiac, the Archer, which the sun enters about November 21. 3. a person born under this sign, between November 21 and December 21. {**să** jih **tayr** ee əs}

Sa·ha·ra *noun* a vast desert in northern Africa stretching from the Atlantic Ocean to the River Nile. {sə **hah** rə} Saharan, adj.

Sai·gon *noun* the former name of Ho Chi Minh City. {**siy gŏn** or siy **gŏn**}

sail ○ *noun* 1. a large piece of cloth that is attached to a boat. Sails move boats forward by catching the wind. 2. anything like a sail that is used to catch the force of the wind. *The part of a windmill that catches the wind is called a sail.* 3. a trip on a sailboat. *We had a beautiful sail around the lake.* *verb* (sailed, sailing, sails) 1. to move over the water. *The boat sailed across the lake.* 2. to travel on a sailboat. *We will sail down the coast for vacation this summer.* 3. to begin a trip on a boat. *The ship will sail at sunset.* 4. to operate a sailboat. *My aunt is teaching me to sail.* 5. to travel quickly or without difficulty. *The kite sailed through the air. / He sailed through his classes.* {**sayl**}

Homophone Note The words *sail* and *sale* (an instance of selling) sound alike but have different meanings.

sail·boat *noun* a boat pushed by wind blowing against its sails. {**sayl boht**}

sail·or *noun* 1. a member of the navy who works aboard a ship. 2. a person who works on a boat. {**say** lər}

saint *noun* 1. a person who has been recognized by the Roman Catholic Church as having lived a holy life. (abbreviation: St. or Ste.) 2. a person whom others consider very kind or good. *That man was a saint for stopping to help us when our car broke down.* {**saynt**}

sake *noun* 1. reason; purpose. *He got a new job for the sake of earning more money.* 2. advantage or benefit; good. *For your own sake, you should pay more attention in class.* {**sayk**}

sal·ad *noun* 1. a mixture of cold vegetables such as lettuce, tomato, and cucumber, served with a dressing. 2. a similar mixture made with meat, chicken, seafood, or fruit. {**săl** əd}

sal·a·man·der *noun* a small animal with a long, thin body, a long tail, and moist, smooth skin. Although salamanders look like lizards, they are amphibians closely related to frogs and toads. Young salamanders live in water. Most adult salamanders live in moist woodlands. {**săl** ə **măn** dər}

sa·la·mi *noun* a spicy sausage that is usually made with beef or pork. {sə **lah** mee}

sal·a·ry ○ *noun* (salaries) a fixed amount of money paid at regular times for the work a person has done. *My father is paid his salary every two weeks.* {**să** lə ree}

Word History *Salary* comes from a Latin word that means "an allowance given to soldiers to buy salt." Salt is essential to the human diet. For past civilizations, salt was often expensive and difficult to obtain.

sale *noun* 1. An exchange of goods for money. *We had a family meeting to talk about the sale of the farm.* 2. a selling of

goods for a lower price than usual. *The store is having a big sale on winter coats.* {**sayl**}

• **for sale**
available for purchase. *The house on the corner is for sale.*

Homophone Note The words *sale* and *sail* (as in a ship) sound alike but have different meanings.

sales·man *noun* (salesmen) a man whose job is to sell goods or services. {**saylz** mən}

sales·per·son *noun* (salespeople) a person whose job is to sell goods or services. {**saylz** puhr sən}

sales·wom·an *noun* (saleswomen) a woman whose job is to sell goods or services. {**saylz wuu** mən}

sa·li·va 🌐 *noun* a liquid produced by glands in the mouth that helps us to chew and digest food. Saliva has no color or taste. {sə **liy** və} salivary, adj.

salm·on *noun* (salmon or salmons) 1. a fish that lives in salt water but lays its eggs in fresh-water streams. Salmon have a color like silver and are used for food. Salmon are related to trout. 2. a light yellowish or orangish pink color. {**să** mən}

sa·lon *noun* 1. a pleasant room in a large house or apartment used for entertaining guests. 2. a business that offers a service or product related to grooming. *I had my hair trimmed at a beauty salon.* {sə **lahn** or **săl** ahn}

sal·sa *noun* a spicy sauce made with peppers, onions, and tomatoes. It is used in Latin American food dishes. {**sahl** sə}

salt 🌐 🌐 *noun* 1. a white substance that is found in sea water and in the earth. Salt is used for preserving and seasoning foods. 2. a chemical substance that is made by replacing an acid with a base. *verb* (salted, salting, salts) 1. to preserve or season with salt. *They salted the hams to keep them all winter.* 2. to sprinkle with salt as a seasoning. *I salted my French fries.* *adjective* preserved with salt. *We had salt pork with beans for dinner.* {**sawlt**}

• **with a grain of salt**
with some doubt. *I took his promises with a grain of salt.*

salt lick *noun* a natural deposit of salt that animals lick to obtain sodium. {**sawlt lihk**}

salt·wa·ter *adjective* full of salt water; living in salt water. *Have you ever gone swimming in a saltwater lake? / Tuna is a saltwater fish.* {**sawlt wo** tər}

salt·y *adjective* (saltier, saltiest) having the taste of salt. *I like salty potato chips. / This soup is too salty.* {**sawl** tee} saltiness, n.

sa·lute *verb* (saluted, saluting, salutes) 1. to show respect by raising the right hand to the forehead. *In school we salute the flag every morning.* 2. to greet with an expression of respect or good will. *We saluted our teacher by standing up when she entered the room.* *noun* the act of saluting. *We all gave a salute as the flag passed by.* {sə **looht**}

sal·vage *noun* the act of saving property from destruction. *The salvage of a burning ship was reported on the news tonight.* *verb* (salvaged, salvaging, salvages) to save or rescue something from harm or destruction. *We helped him salvage his books from the flooded basement.* {**săl** vihj}

salve *noun* a substance used to heal wounds or make them feel better. *My mother put salve on my cut finger before she bandaged it.* {**săv** or **sŏv** or **sălv**}

same *adjective* 1. not at all different; alike in every way. *He wore the same shoes every day. / Lenny has the same shoes as I do.* 2. similar in amount or size. *The radios were the same price, but one sounded better.* 3. not changed; being as before. *He's the same person he was last year.* {**saym**}

• **all the same**
1. however; in any case. *It's difficult, but it's fun all the same.* 2. of no importance; making no difference. *It's all the same to me if we go or stay.*

sam·ple *noun* 1. a small part of something that shows what the whole is like. *I brought home a sample of wallpaper to see how it will look in my room.* 2. a part of a group used for studying the characteristics of the whole group. *We surveyed a sample of sixth graders about the kinds of music they like.* *verb* (sampled, sampling, samples) to test a part of something. *Would you like to sample this pie?* {**săm** pəl}

sam·u·rai *noun* (samurai [or] samurais) a warrior in the service of a lord in medieval

 Human Body   Human Mind   Everyday Life    History and Culture   Communication

Japan. *The samurai had great skill with swords.* {să mə **riy**}

sanc·tion *noun* 1. permission for an action; approval. *The principal gave her sanction for our field trip.* 2. public support for an action. *The president's decision had the sanction of the people.* 3. something to make sure that a law is obeyed; a punishment for not obeying a law. *Refusing to trade with another country is one type of sanction.* *verb* (sanctioned, sanctioning, sanctions) to approve of; support. *I do not sanction such rude behavior.* {**săngk** shən}

sanc·tu·ar·y *noun* (sanctuaries) 1. a holy or sacred place. *The service will take place in the church sanctuary.* 2. a place that offers protection from arrest. *They escaped to a sanctuary where they would be safe.* 3. the protection given by such a place. *The spy found sanctuary in another country.* 4. a piece of land that has been set aside as a shelter for wild animals. {**săngk** chooh **ayr** ee}

sand 🌐 *noun* tiny, loose grains of ground rock found on beaches and in deserts. *verb* (sanded, sanding, sands) 1. to make smooth or polish with sandpaper. *Maura sanded the board before painting it.* 2. to cover with sand or something like sand. *In winter they sand the icy roads.* {**sănd**}

san·dal *noun* an open shoe made from a sole fastened to the foot with straps. {**săn** dəl}

sand·bar *noun* a ridge of sand in a river or near a shore. It is formed by the action of waves or currents. {**sănd** bar}

sand·pa·per *noun* paper covered on one side with sand or some other rough material. It is used to smooth wood and other surfaces. *verb* (sandpa-pered, sandpapering, sandpapers) to smooth with sandpaper. *We sandpapered the table to remove the old paint.* {**sănd** **pay** pər}

sand·stone *noun* rock that is formed mostly of sand and held together with a sub-stance that is like cement. {**sănd** stohn}

sand·wich *noun* slices of bread with other food between them such as meat, cheese, or jelly. *verb* (sandwiched, sandwiching, sandwiches) to fit or squeeze in between two things. *She sandwiched herself between two people in the crowded subway.* {**sănd** wihch or **săn** wihch, n., **sănd** wihch or **săn** wihch, v.}

Word History The *sandwich* was named after the English Earl of Sandwich, John Montagu, who liked to spend hours at a time at the gambling tables. Instead of stopping to have a meal, he had his food brought to him in an unusual fashion: meat in between slices of toast.

sand·y *adjective* (sandier, sand-iest) 1. made of or like sand. *Many plants won't grow in sandy soil.* 2. of the same color as sand; yellow with a red or gray shade. *She has sandy hair.* {**săn** dee}

sane 🌐 🌐 *adjective* (saner, sanest) 1. having a healthy mind. 2. sound; reasonable. *Jared made a sane decision* when he decided to leave the wild party. {**sayn**}

Homophone Note The words *sane* and *seine* (a fishing net) sound alike but have dif-ferent meanings.

San Francisco *noun* a city in the U.S. state of California on a peninsula between the Pacific Ocean and a large bay. {săn frən **sihs** koh}

sang *verb* past tense of **sing**. {**săng**}

san·i·ta·tion *noun* the practice of keeping the public healthy by providing clean living conditions. Sanitation includes removing garbage and keeping drinking water clean. {să nih **tay** shən}

san·i·ty 🌐 *noun* a healthy state of mind. {**să** nih tee}

Santo Domingo *noun* 1. the capital city of the Domin-ican Republic. 2. the former name of the Dominican Republic. {sahn toh doh **meeng** goh or **săn** toh doh **ming** goh}

sap *noun* the liquid that carries nutrients and water to all parts of a plant. {**săp**}

sap·ling *noun* a young tree. {**să** pling}

sar·casm *noun* 1. a scornfully ironic remark. 2. the use of scornful or mocking remarks. {**sar** kă zəm}

Word History The word *sar-casm* comes from an ancient Greek verb that means "to speak bitter words," "to tear flesh like a dog," and "to bite one's lips in anger." Sarcasm is an effective way to be mean to others, but the Greeks knew it could leave the user feeling a bit sore too.

sar·cas·tic *adjective* using harsh or bitter words that are meant to hurt or make fun of another person. *His sarcastic*

A B C D E F G H I J K L M N O P Q R S T U V W X Y Z

a
b
c
d
e
f
g
h
i
j
k
l
m
n
o
p
q
r
s
t
u
v
w
x
y
z

reply hurt the girl's feelings. {**sar kă** stihk} sarcastically, adv.

sar·dine noun a small fish that lives in the ocean and is used for food. Sardines are usually packed with oil or some other liquid in tin cans. {**sar deen**}

sa·ri noun (saris) a length of fine cloth which, when wrapped around the waist and over the shoulder, is the common dress of many women in India and Pakistan. {**sah ree**}

sash[1] noun a band of cloth worn around the waist or over the shoulder. The blue sash added a bright touch to her white dress. {**săsh**}

sash[2] noun the frame that holds the glass panes of windows or doors in place. {**săsh**}

Sas·katch·e·wan noun a south central Canadian province on the U.S. border between Alberta and Manitoba. Its capital is Regina. {**săs kăch ə wən**}

Word History
Saskatchewan is the English spelling of the Cree words, *kisiskatchewani sipi*, which mean "swift flowing river." It is the Cree name for the Saskatchewan River.

Sat. abbreviation an abbreviation for **Saturday**.

Sa·tan noun the supreme evil spirit in Christianity and Judaism. Satan is considered to be the enemy of humans, the rival of God, and the ruler of hell; the Devil. {**say** tən}

sat·el·lite 🌐🛰 noun 1. a heavenly body that moves around a planet or another larger body. The moon is a satellite of Earth. 2. a spacecraft that is sent into orbit around a planet or other heavenly body to gather or send back information. 3. a country that is controlled by another, more powerful country. {**săt** ə liyt}

Word History *Satellite* comes from a Latin word that means "someone who attends a person of importance." In the 1600s, the moons that revolve around planets were first referred to as "satellites."

sat·in noun a smooth fabric that is shiny on one side and dull on the other. {**săt** ihn} satiny, adj.

Word History The word *satin* may have come from an Arabic word that means "from Zaitun," a city in southern China where the fabric was made.

sat·is·fac·tion noun 1. a pleasant feeling that comes from completing something and doing it well. Building the model airplane gave me great satisfaction. 2. the act of satisfying. When I work, satisfaction is my goal. {săt ihs **făk** shən}

sat·is·fac·to·ry adjective good enough to meet a need or desire. My grade in English is satisfactory, but I had hoped to do better. {săt ihs **făk** tə ree or săt ihs **făk** tree} satisfactorily, adv.

sat·is·fy verb (satisfied, satisfying, satisfies) 1. to give what is wanted or needed. The small snack didn't satisfy her. 2. to drive away feelings of doubt; convince. Sam's excuse for being late satisfied his teacher. {**săt** ihs **fiy**}

sat·u·rate verb (saturated, saturating, saturates) to fill or soak completely. The heavy rain saturated his clothes. {**să** chə rayt}

Sat·ur·day noun the seventh day of the week. Saturday comes between Friday and Sunday. {**săt** ər **day**}

Word History *Saturday* comes from an early English word that means "day of Saturn." *Saturn* was the god of farming in Roman mythology.

Sat·urn noun 1. the second largest planet in the solar system and sixth in distance from the sun. Saturn is known for the icy rings that circle its middle. 2. the god of farming in Roman mythology. {**săt** ərn}

sauce noun 1. a liquid dressing or topping served with food. I like chocolate sauce over ice cream. 2. boiled or stewed fruit. We always have cranberry sauce with Thanksgiving dinner. {**saws**}

sauce·pan noun a fairly deep cooking pan with a long handle. {**saws** păn}

sau·cer noun a small, shallow dish used for holding a cup. {**saws** ər}

Saudi Arabia noun a country in southwestern Asia. Riyadh is the capital of Saudi Arabia. {**sow** dee ə **ray** bee ə or **saw** dee ə **ray** bee ə or sah **ooh** dee ə **ray** bee ə} Saudi Arabian, adj., n.

sau·sage noun a mixture of chopped meat and spices stuffed into a casing of animal intestine. {**saw** sihj}

sav·age adjective 1. fierce; cruel. The wolf rushed at the man in a savage attack. / The newspaper printed a savage attack on the mayor. 2. not tamed; wild. Savage beasts live in the jungle. 3. not civilized. Those children who live next door are savage, always running around naked, dirty, and out of control! noun 1. a member of a group of people who are not

 Human Body  Human Mind  Everyday Life 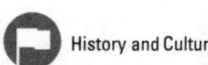 History and Culture  Communication

thought to be civilized. 2. a cruel or vicious person. {**săv** ihj}

sa·van·na 🌐 *noun* a flat plain covered with grass and few trees. Savannas are found in Africa and other tropical regions. {sə **vă** nə}

save[1] 🌐 *verb* (saved, saving, saves) 1. to rescue from harm or danger. *The lifeguard saved the girl who fell out of the boat.* 2. to keep or store for future use. *Jerome saved his Halloween candy. / They are saving money for college.* 3. to keep from being done or used in way that would be wasteful; spare. *Save your strength for the job ahead. / It will save me another trip to the store if you pick up milk on your way home.* *noun* a move by the goalkeeper that keeps a ball or puck from going into the goal. *Without the goaltender's saves, we would not have won the hockey game.* {**sayv**}

save[2] *preposition* except; with the exception of. *She ate all the cookies save one.* {**sayv**}

sav·ing *noun* 1. a lower price or cost. *We received a saving of thirty cents a box when we picked our own berries.* 2. (plural) money that has been collected over a period of time. *Over the past year I have added fifty dollars to my savings.* {**say** ving}

sav·ior *noun* 1. someone who rescues or saves people from danger or destruction. 2. (capitalized) Jesus Christ. {**sayv** yər}

saw[1] *noun* a tool with a thin metal blade that has sharp teeth along the edge. Saws are used for cutting hard materials such as wood or metal. *verb* (sawed, sawed or sawn, sawing, saws) to cut, separate, or shape with a saw

or a tool like a saw. *He sawed the wood for the new deck.* {**saw**}

saw[2] *verb* past tense of **see**[1]. {**saw**}

saw·dust *noun* the tiny bits that fall away when wood is sawed. {**saw** duhst}

saw·horse *noun* a frame with four legs used to support wood that is being sawed. {**saw** hohrs}

saw·mill *noun* a building in which logs are cut into lumber. {**saw** mihl}

sax·o·phone *noun* a wind instrument with a curved metal body and a mouthpiece with a single reed. {**săk** sə **fohn**} saxophonist, n.

Word History The *saxophone* was named after its inventor, the Belgian instrument maker, Adolphe Sax.

say *verb* (said, saying, says) 1. to speak in words. *Did you say something just now?* 2. to express in speech or written words. *I said how glad I was to see them. / In my letter, I said what was bothering me.* 3. to report. *Everyone says the story is true.* 4. to show on a clock. *My watch says it is three o'clock.* *noun* 1. a chance to express an opinion. *He wants his say in the matter.* 2. authority. *Teachers have the say in their classrooms.* {**say**}

say·ing *noun* a familiar statement that often contains advice or wisdom. *"Don't cry over spilled milk" is a saying.* {**say** ing}

SC or **S.C.** *abbreviation* an abbreviation for **South Carolina**.

scab *noun* 1. the crust that forms over a wound in the skin to protect it. 2. a person who works in place of another worker who is on strike, or who does not support the actions of a labor union. {**skăb**}

scab·bard *noun* a case for holding a sword or other weapon with a blade. {**skăb** ərd}

scaf·fold *noun* a platform above the ground where workers stand while they work on a building. {**skăf** əld or **skă** fohld}

scale[1] 🌐 *noun* 1. one of the many small, hard, thin plates that cover fish, reptiles, and certain other animals. 2. any thin, flat piece that flakes off skin or another surface. *When I scratched my arm, scales of skin fell off.* *verb* (scaled, scaling, scales) to remove the scales from. *We need to scale and clean the fish before we cook them.* {**skayl**}

The climber climbs a **scale** weighing tons of **scales**.

scale[2] 🌐 *noun* (often plural) a device used for weighing. {**skayl**}

scale[3] 🌐 🌐 *noun* 1. a set of numbered marks made at evenly spaced points along a

A
B
C
D
E
F
G
H
I
J
K
L
M
N
O
P
Q
R
S
T
U
V
W
X
Y
Z

a
b
c
d
e
f
g
h
i
j
k
l
m
n
o
p
q
r
s
t
u
v
w
x
y
z

ruler, thermometer, or other measuring device. *The scale of this measuring tape is in inches.* 2. the size of a model or map compared to the actual size of the thing it represents. *This map has a scale of one inch to ten miles.* 3. degree, extent, or level. *The movie director likes to do things on a large scale.* 4. a series of musical tones going up or down in pitch. *I need to practice my scales before my piano lesson. verb* (scaled, scaling, scales) 1. to climb up or on top of. *Jenny scaled a steep cliff.* 2. to change or adjust (sometimes followed by "down"). *Phil scaled his hopes to what was possible. / We have scaled down the cost of the new house.* {skayl}

scalene triangle *noun* a triangle that has three sides with different lengths. {skay leen triy ăng gəl}

scal·lop *noun* 1. a small animal that lives in the ocean and has two rounded, ribbed shells that protect its soft body. The hinged shells open and close with a large muscle. People sometimes eat this muscle. Scallops are mollusks and are closely related to clams and mussels. 2. the edible muscle from some kinds of scallops. 3. one of a series of curves in a border. *There are scallops around the collar of her dress. verb* (scalloped, scalloping, scallops) to cut or shape with scallops. *My mother scalloped the hem of my new dress.* {skŏ ləp or skă ləp, n., skŏ ləp or skă ləp, v.}

scalp *noun* 1. the skin on the top and back of the head and usually covered by hair. 2. a section of this skin with the attached hair. In the past, a scalp was sometimes taken from the head of an enemy as a trophy. *verb* (scalped, scalping, scalps) to remove the scalp from. {skălp}

scal·y *adjective* (scalier, scaliest) covered with scales. *Snakes have scaly skin. / Fish are scaly.* {skay lee}

scamp·er *verb* (scampered, scampering, scampers) to run quickly or playfully. *Squirrels scampered around the yard.* {skăm pər}

scan *verb* (scanned, scanning, scans) 1. to read or look over quickly. *I scanned the newspaper for weather reports.* 2. to look at or study carefully. *We scanned the clouds for signs of rain. noun* 1. the act of scanning. *I did a quick scan of the entire room.* 2. the use of a machine that scans something. Medical scanners make pictures of living tissue. Computer scanners copy pictures or writing from an object into a computer. 3. an image produced in this way. *Her bone scan was normal.* {skăn}

Scan·di·na·vi·a *noun* a region in northern Europe made up of Norway, Sweden, Denmark, and Finland. {skăn də nay vee ə}

Scan·di·na·vi·an *adjective* of or having to do with Scandinavia, or its peoples or languages. *noun* a person who was born in or is a citizen of a country in Scandinavia. {skăn də nay vee ən}

scan·ner *noun* a device that scans printed material and changes it into an electronic signal that can be read by a computer. {skăn ər}

scant *adjective* (scanter, scantest) 1. barely enough; very little. *After weeks of hiding in the hills from the sheriff, the outlaw's supply of food had become scant.* 2. just short of a certain measure. *I use a scant teaspoon of sugar in my tea.* {skănt}

scar 🌐 *noun* 1. the mark left when a wound has healed. *The burn left a scar on my arm.* 2. any mark left after physical or emotional damage. *The roller skate left a scar in the wood floor. / The evil clown in the movie scarred the little boy for life, making him forever afraid of clowns. verb* (scarred, scarring, scars) to mark with a scar. *The cat's claws scarred the table.* {skar}

scarce *adjective* (scarcer, scarcest) 1. in short supply. *Food was scarce during the war.* 2. difficult to find; not common. *That kind of bird is scarce in this part of the country.* {skayrs}

scarce·ly *adverb* 1. almost not; just barely. *I was so happy that I could scarcely speak.* 2. certainly not. *We can scarcely leave our favorite toys behind!* {skayrs lee}

scare ❓ *verb* (scared, scaring, scares) 1. to frighten. *Your screaming scared me.* 2. to become filled with fear. *My sister doesn't scare easily. noun* 1. a feeling of fear. *You gave us a bad scare when you ran away.* 2. a period or state of fear or panic. *School was closed because of a bomb scare.* {skayr}

Synonyms
These words share a meaning with *scare*, verb 1:
frighten, startle, spook

scare·crow *noun* a figure of a person made from stuffed clothes and placed in a field to scare birds away from crops. {skayr kroh}

scarf *noun* (scarfs or scarves) a long piece

 Human Body   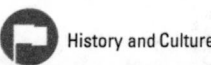 Human Mind   Everyday Life    History and Culture   Communication

of cloth or knitted material worn around the neck, head, or shoulders. {skarf}

scar·let *noun* a bright red or reddish orange color. *adjective* having the color scarlet. *I bought a pair of scarlet gloves.* {skar liht}

scar·y *adjective* (scarier, scariest) causing fear; frightening. *I don't like hearing scary stories at night.* {skayr ee} scariness, n.

scat·ter *verb* (scattered, scattering, scatters) 1. to cause to separate in all directions. *Strong winds scattered the clouds.* 2. to toss here and there. *The farmer scattered grain for the chickens.* 3. to separate and move quickly in different directions. *The crowd scattered at the sound of thunder.* {skăt ər}

scav·en·ger *noun* an animal that finds and eats dead animals or rotting plants; a person who finds things that others no longer want. *Hyenas are scavengers. / My grandfather is a real scavenger at yard sales.* {skăv ihn jər}

Word History In the 1300s, English towns began collecting a tax called "scavage" on goods sold by people who did not live in the town. The *scavenger* was the person who collected the tax. After this practice ended, the word was used for a person hired to remove trash from the streets.

scene ● *noun* 1. the place where any event takes place. *They rushed to the scene of the accident.* 2. a particular view in a painting or photograph. *The artist painted many street scenes of Paris.* 3. a part of an act in a movie or play. *The last scene in the movie was very sad.* 4. a show of strong feeling in front of other

people. *She made a scene when they told her she couldn't go to the party.* {seen}

• **behind the scenes** not in view or on display; in private; in secret. *Mr. Ruiz told Ms. Kramer what was going on behind the scenes at his office.*

Homophone Note The words *scene* and *seen* (past participle of "see") sound alike but have different meanings.

scen·er·y *noun* (sceneries) 1. the way the land looks in a particular place. *We enjoyed the scenery around the lake.* 2. the painted walls or objects that make up the set of a play or movie. *We helped build the scenery for our school play.* {see nə ree}

scent *noun* 1. a smell. *Roses have a lovely scent.* 2. the smell given off by a person or animal. *Dogs traced the scent of the lost child.* 3. a liquid that gives off a pleasant smell; perfume. *I like that scent my mother is wearing.* 4. the sense of smell. *Hunting dogs have a keen scent.* *verb* (scented, scenting, scents) to sense something by or as if by using the sense of smell. *The dogs scented the fox. / Do you scent trouble?* {sehnt}

Homophone Note The words *scents*, *cents*, and *sense* sound alike but have different meanings.

scep·ter *noun* a rod carried by a king or queen as a symbol of royal power. {sehp tər}

sched·ule *noun* 1. a list of times when certain events will

happen. *Do you have a schedule for the dog show?* 2. a list of times when public vehicles such as buses and trains arrive and depart. *I checked the bus schedule to find out when my cousin will arrive.* *verb* (scheduled, scheduling, schedules) 1. to include in a schedule. *Be sure to schedule a stop at the museum.* 2. to plan according to a schedule. *Our teacher scheduled the events for our talent show.* {skeh jooh əl or skeh joohl, n., skeh jooh əl or skeh joohl, v.}

scheme *noun* 1. a plan or plot. *The outlaw had a scheme to escape from jail and take revenge on the sheriff.* 2. a plan or program for doing something. *We thought of a scheme for making money this summer.* 3. the arrangement of parts seen as a whole; design. *Lyn is planning a new color scheme for her room.* *verb* (schemed, scheming, schemes) 1. to plan. *The lieutenant schemed a way to trap the enemy.* 2. to form a plan; plot. *The boys schemed to surprise their friend on his birthday.* {skeem} schemer, n.

schol·ar *noun* 1. a person who has much knowledge, usually acquired from research and study. *My aunt is a scholar of American history.* 2. any student. *These young scholars will graduate from high school in two years.* {skŏl lər}

schol·ar·ship *noun* 1. money given to students to help pay for their education. *Sally won a scholarship to the state university.* 2. the work of a scholar. *Eric has received many honors for his excellent scholarship.* {skŏl ər shihp}

school¹ ● ● *noun* 1. a place for teaching and learning. *Those girls go to my school.* 2. the time when students attend

A B C D E F G H I J K L M N O P Q R **S** T U V W X Y Z

school. *School starts in September.* / *Jerad is late for school today.* *verb* (schooled, schooling, schools) to train or teach. *Lettie has been schooled in car repair.* {**skoohl**}

Word History The word *school* comes from *schole*, an ancient Greek word that means "leisure time spent in learning."

school² ❶ *noun* a large group of the same kind of fish or sea animals. *Sharks sometimes swim in schools.* {**skoohl**}

school·house *noun* a building used as a school. {**skoohl hows**}

school·work *noun* study or practice done at school or as homework. *Her schoolwork is harder this year than it was last year.* {**skoohl wuhrk**}

schoon·er *noun* a sailing ship with at least two masts. The front mast is shorter than the other masts. {**skooh nər**}

schwa *noun* 1. a vowel sound that is spoken without any stress, such as the first "a" in "away." 2. a sign (ə) used for a vowel sound that is spoken without stress. {**shwah** *or* **shvah**}

sci·ence ❶ *noun* 1. a system of studying, testing, and experimenting on things in nature. Science is a search for general laws about how the world works. 2. a particular branch of this activity. *Physics and biology are two sciences.* {**siy** əns}

Word History *Science* comes from a Latin word that means "knowledge."

sci·en·tif·ic *adjective* having to do with science. *He found a scientific solution to the problem.* {**siy** ən tih fihk} scientifically, adv.

sci·en·tist *noun* a person who works in some branch of science. {**siy** ən tihst}

scis·sors *noun* (usually used with a plural verb) a tool used for cutting. Scissors are made up of two blades that are joined so that their edges may be opened and closed. *Use this pair of scissors to cut the cloth.* / *Where are the scissors?* {**sihz** ərz}

scold *verb* (scolded, scolding, scolds) to speak in a sharp or angry way. *The woman scolded her child for being mean to his brother.* *noun* a person who often scolds others. *No one liked him because he was such a scold.* {**skohld**}

Word History *Scold* probably comes from the early Norse word *skald*, which means "poet." Centuries ago, the wandering poets of Scandinavia were experts at mocking and scolding in a memorable way.

scoop *noun* 1. a tool with a short handle attached to a deep, curved bowl, used to take up food or grain. *The farmer used a scoop to feed corn to the chickens.* 2. a tool with a thick handle attached to a small round bowl; ladle. *Use this*

scoop to serve the ice cream. 3. the amount of food that fits in a scoop. *Do you want one or two scoops of ice cream?* *verb* (scooped, scooping, scoops) 1. to lift with a scoop, or as if with a scoop. *I scooped flour into the bowl.* 2. to remove with a scoop, or as if with a scoop; empty. *He scooped sand out of his shoes.* 3. to gather in or pick up swiftly. *Grandmother scooped the children into her arms.* {**skoohp**}

scoot *verb* (scooted, scooting, scoots) 1. to go with quick, sudden movements. *A mouse scooted across the floor.* 2. to move in a quick, sliding manner. *Would you please scoot over so I can sit down?* {**skooht**}

scoot·er *noun* a child's toy that has a steering handle attached to a low board with one wheel at each end. A scooter is ridden by standing with one foot on the board while using the other foot to push against the ground. {**skooh** tər}

scope *noun* the range or extent of one's view or thoughts. *Long division is beyond the scope of most first graders.* *verb* (scoped, scoping, scopes) (slang) to look over or check; examine (often followed by "out"). *Let's go scope out the new ice cream shop!* {**skohp**}

-scope *suffix* a suffix that means an instrument for seeing or observing. *A microscope is an instrument for seeing small things in a larger form.*

scorch *verb* (scorched, scorching, scorches) 1. to burn slightly. *She scorched her blouse with the iron.* 2. to dry out with heat. *The sun scorched a patch of grass in our lawn.* *noun* a slight burn, or a mark left by it. *I don't want to*

 Human Body   Human Mind   Everyday Life   History and Culture   Communication

wear the shirt with the scorch. {**skohrch**}

score 🔵🔵 *noun* 1. the record of the total points earned in a game or test. *I got a perfect score on the spelling test.* 2. the printed or written form of a musical piece. *A musical score shows all the parts that are played or sung.* 3. a group of twenty. *A score of musicians made up the band. / Mom was born two score years ago.* 4. the making of a goal, run, or basket in sports. *The forward had a score on that play. verb* (scored, scoring, scores) 1. to add up the points of a contest. *Our p.e. teacher scored the basketball game.* 2. to give a grade to. *The teacher scored our tests and returned them the next day.* 3. to make a point in a contest. *Omar scored one run in the baseball game.* 4. to achieve or win. *I scored a big win when I made the honor roll.* {**skohr**} scorer, n.

scorn *noun* a feeling of hatred for someone or something thought of as worthless or evil. *She looked with scorn upon the man who had told lies about her. verb* (scorned, scorning, scorns) 1. to treat as hateful or not proper. *They scorned the idea of dressing in silly costumes.* 2. to refuse. *She scorned all offers of help.* {**skohrn**}

Scor·pi·o *noun* 1. a constellation located between Libra and Sagittarius. Scorpio is also called the Scorpion. 2. the eighth sign of the zodiac, the

Scorpion, which the sun enters about October 24. 3. a person born under this sign, between October 24 and November 20. {**skohr** pee oh}

scor·pi·on *noun* a small animal related to the spider. It has a long narrow body and a tail with a poisonous tip. Scorpions live in many warm, dry areas of the world. {**skohr** pee ən}

Scot *noun* a person who was born in or is a citizen or Scotland. {**skŏt**}

Scotch *adjective* of or having to do with Scotland, or its people; Scottish. {**skŏch**}

Scot·land *noun* a country in Europe on the northern part of the island of Great Britain. Edinburgh is the capital of Scotland. {**skŏt** lənd}

Scot·tish *adjective* of or having to do with Scotland, or its people or language. *noun* 1. (used with a plural verb) the people of Scotland; Scots (usually used with "the"). 2. the variety of English spoken in Scotland. {**skŏt** ihsh}

scoun·drel *noun* a wicked person; villain. *That scoundrel ran off with my watch.* {**skown** drəl}

scour[1] *verb* (scoured, scouring, scours) 1. to clean by rubbing hard. *The cook scoured the copper pots.* 2. to remove by rubbing hard. *They had to scour the dirt from the old bathtub.* 3. to open up by making water pass through. *He scoured the blocked pipes until they were no longer blocked.* {**skowr**}

scour[2] *verb* (scoured, scouring, scours) to travel over an area while looking for something. *We scoured the beach for seashells.* {**skowr**}

scout *noun* 1. a person, ship, or plane sent to spy or gather information. *The scout returned with photographs of the enemy camp.* 2. a person who looks for new sports or entertainment talent. *The football scout noticed a talented college quarterback.* 3. a member of a Boy Scout or Girl Scout troop. *verb* (scouted, scouting, scouts) 1. to explore an area in order to bring back information. *We scouted around the forest, looking for the bears' den.* 2. (informal) to look for, or to find by searching for (usually followed by "up" or "out"). *The campers scouted up some dry wood for the fire.* {**skowt**}

scout·mas·ter *noun* the adult in charge of a Boy Scout troop. {**skowt** măs tər}

scowl *verb* (scowled, scowling, scowls) to make an angry frown. *He scowled at his son, who was being mean to the puppy. noun* an act or instance of frowning in an angry way. *Seeing Mom's scowl, I knew right away I'd done something wrong.* {**skowl**}

scram·ble *verb* (scrambled, scrambling, scrambles) 1. to move quickly using both the hands and feet. *We scrambled over the rocks and up the hill.* 2. to try hard to gain something, or to avoid failing. *He was scrambling to keep up with his friends in math class.* 3. to mix or throw together in a quick or random way. *She scrambled the pieces of the puzzle.* 4. to cook in an open pan while stirring. *Dad scrambled some eggs for breakfast.* 5. to mix up a signal or message so that it cannot be understood. *When the cable company scrambled that television channel, we couldn't watch our favorite program.*

A B C D E F G H I J K L M N O P Q R S T U V W X Y Z

noun 1. a fast climb or crawl over uneven ground. *I fell during my scramble up the rocky path.* 2. a struggle to gain something, or to avoid failing. *There was a scramble to finish assignments by the end of the year.* 3. any rushed or confused action to do something. *When the fire alarm went off there was a scramble for the exits.* {skrăm bəl}

scrap[1] *noun* 1. a small bit, such as a piece left over or thrown away. *I picked up a scrap of paper. / They tossed scraps of bread to the ducks.* 2. a collection of materials that have been thrown away but might be used again. *We took metal scrap to the recycling center.* *adjective* having to do with scrap or scraps. *Do you have a piece of scrap paper I can use?* *verb* (scrapped, scrapping, scraps) to throw away because useless or without value. *He scrapped the old computer that did not work anymore.* {skrăp}

scrap[2] *noun* (informal) a fight. *Two boys got into a scrap on the playground.* *verb* (scrapped, scrapping, scraps) (informal) to get into a fight; exchange blows. *They scrapped until one of them got hurt.* {skrăp}

scrap·book *noun* a book with blank pages for saving pictures, newspaper clippings, and other mementos. {skrăp boohk}

scrape *verb* (scraped, scraping, scrapes) 1. to rub with something sharp or rough. *I had to scrape the pan to remove the burned food.* 2. to remove from a surface by rubbing with something sharp or rough. *He scraped the old paint off the house.* 3. to hurt or damage by rubbing against something sharp or rough. *The boy scraped his knee on the pavement.* 4. to gather together or make with difficulty (usually followed by "together" or "up"). *She scraped together enough money to buy a car.* *noun* 1. the act or sound of scraping. *We heard the scrape of metal when one car ran into another.* 2. an injury or damage from scraping. *She had a scrape on her elbow.* 3. a quarrel or fight. *Two children got into a scrape.* 4. a difficult situation. *I was in a scrape when I forgot my wallet.* {skrayp}

scratch *verb* (scratched, scratching, scratches) 1. to scrape or damage with something sharp. *Carol scratched her eye when she broke her glasses.* 2. to relieve an itch by scraping or digging at with the nails or claws. *I scratched the mosquito bite on my arm.* 3. to strike out by drawing a line through or writing over (often followed by "out"). *I scratched out my name from the list.* *noun* 1. a mark or slight injury caused by rubbing against something sharp. *I have scratches on my arm from playing with the cat.* 2. the act or process of scratching. *I just have to give this itch a scratch.* 3. a scraping or grating sound. *The dog made scratches at the door to go out.* {skrăch}

• **from scratch**
from the very beginning. *Our house of cards fell, so we had to build it again from scratch.*

scrawl *verb* (scrawled, scrawling, scrawls) to write or draw in a quick or careless way. *The child scrawled his name on the blackboard.* *noun* something written or drawn in a quick or careless way. *I can't read this scrawl.* {skrawl}

scraw·ny *adjective* (scrawnier, scrawniest) very thin; skinny. *The newborn fawn's legs are weak and scrawny.* {skraw nee}

scream *verb* (screamed, screaming, screams) 1. to make a shrill, loud cry or sound. *The girl screamed in fear. / The wheels screamed on the pavement as the car sped away.* 2. to speak or shout in a shrill, harsh, or angry tone. *The mean boss is always screaming at the workers.* *noun* 1. a shrill, loud cry or sound. *I let out a scream when I saw the lion.* 2. (informal) someone or something that is very funny. *She is a scream at parties.* {skreem}

screech *verb* (screeched, screeching, screeches) to make a harsh, shrill cry or sound. *The car's brakes screeched.* *noun* a screeching sound. *We heard screeches coming from the monkey house at the zoo.* {skreech}

screen *noun* 1. a closely woven wire mesh. Screens can be used to filter liquid or grains, or to keep insects from entering through windows or doors. 2. anything that shields, hides, or protects. *The tall hedge acted as a screen around the yard.* 3. a large white surface on which movies, pictures, or other images can be shown. *verb* (screened, screening, screens) 1. to hide from view. *We hoped the trees would screen us from his view.* 2. to separate out. *She screens her*

 Human Body   Human Mind   Everyday Life    History and Culture   Communication

phone calls. 3. to project on a screen. *The theater is screening the movie three times a day.* {<u>skreen</u>}

screen sa·ver *noun* a small program that takes over a computer's screen if it has not been used for a set length of time. Screen savers were first used to prevent computer screens from being damaged, but now they are mainly used for decoration. *Many people use a series of their family photographs as a screen saver.* {<u>skreen</u> say vər}

screw *noun* 1. a metal fastener that is like a nail with grooves that wind around it. A screw can be driven into a surface by turning it while pressing down on the head. 2. the propeller on a ship. *verb* (screwed, screwing, screws) 1. to fasten or attach with a screw or screws. *She screwed the shelf onto the wall.* 2. to attach by turning (often followed by "on" or "in"). *He screwed in the light bulb. / I screwed the lid on the jar.* 3. to be attached by being turned. *The light bulb screws in clockwise.* {<u>skrooh</u>}

• **put the screws on** to make someone do something by exerting pressure or force. *The boss put the screws on him to get the job done quickly.*

screw·driv·er *noun* a tool for turning a screw. A screwdriver has a handle for turning and a long metal piece that fits the head of the screw. {<u>skrooh</u> **driy** vər}

scrib·ble *verb* (scribbled, scribbling, scribbles) to write quickly or carelessly; scrawl. *I scribbled the message on a scrap of paper. noun* a piece of drawing or writing that has little or no meaning. *There*

were scribbles around the edges of the paper. {<u>skrihb</u> əl}

scribe *noun* a person whose job is to copy letters, books, or other written materials by hand. {<u>skriyb</u>}

scrimp *verb* (scrimped, scrimping, scrimps) to save in every way possible; to spend very little. *Yoko scrimped and saved until she had enough money to buy a car.* {<u>skrihmp</u>}

script *noun* 1. the written text of a play, movie, or television show. 2. the characters used in handwriting; handwriting in which the letters are joined. *My uncle writes with a beautiful script.* {<u>skrihpt</u>}

Scrip·ture *noun* 1. (often plural) the Bible; Holy Scriptures. 2. (often lower case) a passage from the Bible. 3. (sometimes lower case) any sacred writing. {<u>skrihp</u> chər}

Word History *Scripture* comes from a Latin word that means "the product of writing."

scroll *noun* a roll of paper or parchment, usually with writing on it. *verb* (scrolled, scrolling, scrolls) to move the text up, down, or sideways on a computer screen so that new parts of it appear as other parts disappear. *I scrolled the story so I could read it from beginning to end.* {<u>skrohl</u>}

scrub *verb* (scrubbed, scrubbing, scrubs) to clean by rubbing hard. *He scrubbed the pots until they were shiny. noun* an act of scrubbing. *I gave the table a scrub.* {<u>skruhb</u>}

scruff *noun* the back of the neck. *The mother cat carried her kitten by the scruff of its neck.* {<u>skruhf</u>}

scru·ple *noun* a feeling of doubt about what is right or wrong that keeps someone from doing something. *His scruples did not allow him to accept payment from the man who had just lost his job.* {<u>skrooh</u> pəl}

Word History *Scruple* comes from a Latin word that means "small sharp stone or pebble."

scru·pu·lous *adjective* 1. always doing what is right; moral. *Judges must be scrupulous in how they treat people.* 2. extremely careful or exact. *They made a scrupulous count of the money.* {<u>skrooh</u> pyə ləs}

scru·ti·nize *verb* (scrutinized, scrutinizing, scrutinizes) to look at closely and carefully, with attention to detail. *The detectives scrutinized every inch of the crime scene.* {<u>skrooh</u> tih niyz}

scuba diving *noun* the act of swimming underwater while wearing special breathing equipment. {<u>skooh</u> bə **diy** ving} scuba diver, n.

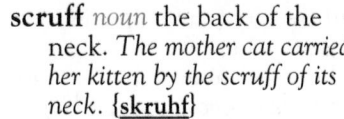

scuff *verb* (scuffed, scuffing, scuffs) to become damaged by scraping. *These soft shoes scuff easily. noun* damage caused by scuffing. *There are scuffs on your new boots.* {<u>skuhf</u>}

 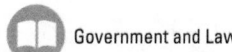

A
B
C
D
E
F
G
H
I
J
K
L
M
N
O
P
Q
R
S
T
U
V
W
X
Y
Z

scuf·fle *verb* (scuffled, scuffling, scuffles) to take part in a brief, confused fight. *Several people scuffled in the parking lot.* *noun* a brief, confused fight among a few people. *When some boys grabbed his book, he started a scuffle.* {<u>skuhf</u> əl}

sculpt *verb* (sculpted, sculpting, sculpts) to make by carving or molding. *She sculpted a statue out of clay.* {<u>skuhlpt</u>}

sculp·tor *noun* an artist who makes sculptures. {<u>skuhlp</u> tər}

sculp·ture 🔵 🔵 *noun* 1. the art or craft of making statues or other objects by carving, chiseling, or molding. 2. any object made in this way. *She carves sculptures out of blocks of marble.* *verb* (sculptured, sculpturing, sculptures) to make by carving, chiseling, or molding; sculpt. {<u>skuhlp</u> chər}

scum *noun* 1. a layer of waste matter that forms on the surface of a liquid. *We cleaned scum off the top of the pool.* 2. a person or persons considered to be low or bad. *Marta thinks that people who sell drugs are scum.* {<u>skuhm</u>}

scur·ry *verb* (scurried, scurrying, scurries) to move quickly or in a hurried way. *Mr. Roy scurried to clean the house before his guests arrived. / Mice scurried about in the walls.* {<u>skuhr</u> ee}

scur·vy *noun* a disease caused by not having enough vitamin C in the diet. *A person with scurvy is usually very weak and has bleeding gums.* {<u>skuhr</u> vee}

scythe *noun* a tool that has a long handle with a long, curved blade attached to the end at a right angle. It is used for cutting grass or harvesting grain by hand. {<u>siyth</u>}

SD or **S. Dak.** *abbreviation* an abbreviation for **South Dakota**.

SE *abbreviation* an abbreviation for **southeast**.

Se symbol of the chemical element selenium.

sea 🔵 🔵 *noun* 1. the salt water covering most of the earth; ocean. 2. a smaller body of fresh or salt water, completely or partly surrounded by land. 3. a particular area of water within an ocean. 4. a vast area or a great number. *The field was a sea of wheat stalks. / A sea of people gathered to hear the famous band.* {<u>see</u>}

• **at sea**
1. on the ocean waters. *The ship has been at sea for many months.* 2. confused; without understanding. *She was at sea about how to make the machine work.*

> **Homophone Note** The words *seas*, *sees*, and *seize* sound alike but have different meanings.

sea anemone *noun* a small sea animal with many tentacles. It looks like a flower. Sea anemones are related to jellyfish, but unlike jellyfish they spend their entire lives attached to underwater objects. {<u>see</u> ə <u>nehm</u> ə nee}

sea·board *noun* a region along the coast of a body of water. *Maine is on the Atlantic seaboard.* {<u>see</u> bohrd}

sea·coast *noun* land near or on the sea; seashore. {<u>see</u> kohst}

sea·far·ing *adjective* 1. traveling by sea. *A seafaring ship has to be sturdy.* 2. working or living at sea. *The captain enjoyed his seafaring life.* {<u>see</u> fayr eeng}

sea·food *noun* any sea animal that is served as food. {<u>see</u> foohd}

sea gull *noun* a gull that lives on or near the sea. {<u>see</u> guhl}

sea horse *noun* a small fish that swims with its head facing forward, but with its body and tail hanging down. Sea horses live in warm parts of the ocean. They use their curly tails to hang onto water plants. {<u>see</u> hohrs}

seal[1] *noun* 1. a design that is stamped on wax or other soft material. Seals are used to make a document authentic or official. *The letter carried the seal of the president.* 2. a material or object used to close something tightly. *Aspirin bottles have seals so that small children can't open them and harm themselves.* 3. a stamp or sticker used for decoration or to raise money for a cause. *We put seals with snowmen on our holiday cards.* *verb* (sealed, sealing, seals) 1. to close using a seal. *Seal the box with tape.* 2. to settle with an action that is a sign of agreement. *Joseph and Tom sealed their agreement by shaking hands.* {<u>seel</u>}

> **Homophone Note** Are you looking for the word *ceiling* (the top of a room)? *Sealing* and *ceiling* sound alike but have different meanings.

seal[2] *noun* a mammal that spends most of its life in the ocean. Seals are a kind of pinniped, or mammal with

 Human Body  Human Mind  Everyday Life  History and Culture Communication

flippers instead of feet. Various kinds of seals live in both warm and cold parts of the world's oceans. A few kinds live in fresh water. Seals are carnivores that eat fish and sea birds. They are closely related to sea lions and walruses. {see **seel**}

sea level *noun* the surface level of the sea, halfway between high and low tide. It is used as the starting point for measuring elevations and depths. *Our town is 1,000 feet above sea level.* {see **lehv** əl}

sea lion *noun* a mammal that spends most of its life in the ocean. Sea lions are a kind of pinniped, or mammal with flippers instead of feet. Various kinds of sea lions live on the coasts of the Pacific Ocean. Sea lions are carnivores that eat fish and squid. They are closely related to seals and walruses. {see **liy** ən}

seam *noun* 1. a line formed by sewing two pieces of fabric together. *A seam on your dress is coming apart.* 2. a line where two objects are joined. *We tried not to step on the seams in the sidewalk.* 3. a long narrow layer of ore in the earth. *They found a new seam of coal in the mine.* {see **seem**}

Homophone Note Are you looking for the word *seem* (to appear to be)? *Seam* and *seem* sound alike but have different meanings.

sea·plane *noun* an airplane that can land on and take off from water. {see **playn**}

sea·port *noun* a city, town, or harbor where ships that travel on the sea can dock, load, and unload. {see **pohrt**}

search *verb* (searched, searching, searches) to look through very carefully in order to find something. *I searched everywhere in my room for the missing book.* *noun* an act of searching. *The pirates went on a search for hidden treasure.* {see **suhrch**}

search·light *noun* a lamp that can direct a powerful beam of light in any direction. {see **suhrch liyt**}

sea·shell *noun* the shell of an oyster, clam, or other sea animal. Seashells are often found washed up on shore. {see **shehl**}

sea·shore *noun* land that borders on the ocean. {see **shohr**}

sea·sick *adjective* feeling sick and dizzy from the rolling motion of a boat. {see **sihk**}

sea·son *noun* 1. one of the four parts of the year; spring, summer, fall, and winter. 2. a certain part of the year that is marked by a particular condition or activity. *I can't wait until baseball season. / Our family will get together for the holiday season.* *verb* (seasoned, seasoning, seasons) 1. to improve the flavor of by adding salt, herbs, spices, or other flavorings. *The cook seasoned the dish with garlic and pepper.* 2. to cause to fully develop by going through certain conditions. *Covering the local politics seasoned her skills as a news reporter.* {see **zən**}

sea·son·al *adjective* having to do with the seasons or a particular season of the year. *Lifeguards at the beach have a seasonal job.* {see **zə nəl**} seasonally, adv.

sea·son·ing *noun* something that is added to food to make it taste better. Salt, herbs, and spices are seasonings. {see **zə ning**}

seat ⭕ *noun* 1. a chair, bench, or other object for sitting on. *We have six seats around our kitchen table.* 2. a space in which one may sit. *There were no seats left on the train.* 3. membership or position. *My mother has a seat on the library board of directors.* 4. the buttocks or the area of one's clothing that covers the buttocks. *The dog bit him in the seat of his pants.* 5. a space for someone in a theater or elsewhere. *This hall has seats for 200 people.* *verb* (seated, seating, seats) to assist to sit; provide with a place to sit. *They seated the guests of honor first.* {see **seet**}

seat belt *noun* a strap or belt that holds a person in the seat of a car, airplane, or other vehicle. Seat belts protect people against a sudden stop or crash. {see **seet behlt**}

sea urchin *noun* a small sea animal with a soft body inside a hard, round shell. Its shell is covered with long, thin spines. Sea urchins are related to starfish. {see **uhr chihn**}

sea·weed *noun* 1. a kind of alga that grows in salt water. 2. any plant that grows in the sea. {see **weed**}

A B C D E F G H I J K L M N O P Q R S T U V W X Y Z

a
b
c
d
e
f
g
h
i
j
k
l
m
n
o
p
q
r
s
t
u
v
w
x
y
z

sec. *abbreviation* an abbreviation for **second**, or seconds.

se·cede *verb* (seceded, seceding, secedes) to withdraw from a group or a political union. *Croatia seceded from Yugoslavia.* {sih **seed**}

se·clud·ed *adjective* 1. hidden away from view. *No one could see them in their secluded yard.* 2. set apart from other people; alone. *The very ill patient stayed in a secluded room in the hospital.* {sih **klooh** dihd}

sec·ond[1] *adjective* coming next after the first in a series. *My name was second on the recital program.* *noun* 1. the member of a series between first and third. *John is the second of their three sons.* 2. (plural) another helping of food. *The cake was so delicious that we all had seconds.* 3. (plural) items for sale that have minor flaws. *The socks were sold as seconds because their tops are crooked.* *verb* (seconded, seconding, seconds) to give support to. *She seconded the motion to end the meeting.* *adverb* in a position between first and third. *He finished second in the race.* {**sehk** ənd}

sec·ond[2] *noun* 1. a unit of time equal to one of the 60 equal parts of a minute. 2. a very short period of time. *I'll be there in a second.* {**sehk** ənd}

sec·ond·ar·y *adjective* not first in importance or value; less important. *For my sister, playing the piano is secondary to playing the violin. / The secondary roads were not plowed after the snowstorm.* {**sehk** ən **dayr** ee}

sec·ond·hand *adjective* 1. not from the original source. *The story in the newspaper came from secondhand information.* 2. not new; used. *Secondhand books do not cost as much as new ones.* 3. buying and selling used goods. *We bought some furniture at the secondhand store.* {**sehk** ənd **hănd**}

se·cre·cy *noun* (secrecies) 1. the condition of being secret. *He worked on his plans in secrecy.* 2. the habit of keeping things secret. *His secrecy worries me.* {**see** krə see}

se·cret *adjective* 1. kept from being seen or known by others; private. *When she was in her secret hiding place, no one could find her.* 2. kept from everybody except those involved. *We voted on whether to let David into our secret club.* *noun* 1. something hidden on purpose, such as knowledge or information. *The spy learned government secrets.* 2. something known to only a few people. *Can you keep a secret?* 3. a mystery. *Scientists try to discover the secrets of nature. / What is the secret of your success?* {**see** kriht} secretly, *adv.*

sec·re·tar·y *noun* (secretaries) 1. a person who writes letters, keeps records straight, and manages mail. A secretary might work for another person or for a business. 2. (often capitalized) an official who is the head of a government department. 3. a piece of furniture that has a desk top, drawers, and shelves for books. {**sehk** rə **tayr** ee}

se·crete 🌐 *verb* (secreted, secreting, secretes) to produce a fluid or other substance and release it into or out of the body. *Glands in the eye secrete tears.* {sih **kreet**}

sec·tion *noun*
1. a part that is separated from the whole. *I like living in this* 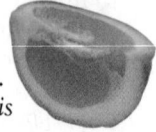 section of the city. / Put the book back in the top section of the bookcase. 2. a part of something written. *Please pass me the first section of the newspaper.* 3. the view of an object as if cut straight through. *We looked at a cross section of a plant stem under the microscope.* *verb* (sectioned, sectioning, sections) to divide into separate parts. *She sectioned the apples into quarters.* {**sehk** shən}

se·cure *adjective* 1. free from fear or danger. *I feel secure when my dog is with me.* 2. free from care or worry. *Steffi feels secure now that she has a steady job.* 3. able to be counted on; reliable. *These old steps don't feel secure.* 4. providing safety. *The basement can be a secure hiding place during a storm.* 5. tightly fastened. *The box has a secure lid.* *verb* (secured, securing, secures) 1. to get. *Vincent secured a good job.* 2. to make safe or free from harm. *We secured the money by putting it in a safe.* 3. to make fast or tight. *Secure the chain to the gate.* 4. to make a place safe from unwanted entrance or attack. *Police secured the building.* 5. to tie up. *He secured the trunk with rope.* {sih **kyoor**} securely, *adv.*

se·cu·ri·ty *noun* (securities) 1. freedom from fear or danger; safety. *Friends and family give me a feeling of security.* 2. something that gives protection. *A smoke alarm is a security that every home should have.* {sih **kyoor** ih tee}

se·dan *noun* an automobile with a hard roof and a front and a back seat. {sih **dăn**}

sed·i·ment 🌐 *noun* 1. solid material that settles to the bottom of a liquid. *There was sediment at the bottom of my*

Human Body ❓ Human Mind 👕 Everyday Life 🏴 History and Culture 📞 Communication

glass. 2. material deposited by water, wind, or ice. *The glacier left behind a sediment of rocks as it melted.* {sehd ə mənt}

sed·i·men·ta·ry *adjective* formed from sediment. *Limestone is one type of sedimentary rock.* {sehd ə **mehn** tə ree}

see 🌐 *verb* (saw, seen, seeing, sees) 1. to look at. *Let's go and see the animals at the zoo.* 2. to have or use the power of sight. *After the operation, he could see again.* 3. to understand; to know. *I don't see the point.* 4. to visit for social or other reasons. *I must see my lawyer.* 5. to find out. *Would you go see what the trouble is?* 6. to have experience of. *He saw combat in Africa.* 7. to make sure. *Will you see that the work is finished today?* {see}

Synonyms
These words share a meaning with *see*, verb 1:
look at, notice, view, sight, observe

Homophone Note The words *sees*, *seas*, and *seize* sound alike but have different meanings.

seed 🌐 *noun* (seeds or seed) 1. the small part of a flowering plant that grows into a new plant. *We planted seeds in the*

garden. 2. such parts as a group. *We planted grass seed on our new yard.* 3. a source or beginning of something. *The new leader planted seeds of hope with his first speech.* *verb* (seeded, seeding, seeds) 1. to sow with seed. *The farmer seeded the field with corn.* 2. to remove seeds from. *She seeded the melon before she ate it.* {seed} seedless, adj., seedlike, adj.

seed·ling *noun* a young tree or plant grown from a seed. {seed ling}

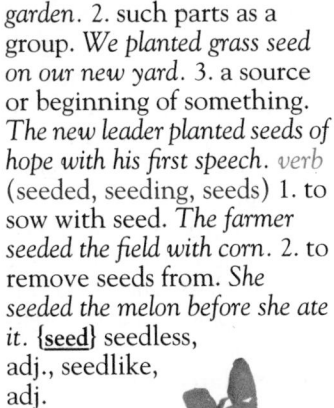

seek *verb* (sought, seeking, seeks) 1. to try to find; look for. *I am seeking a pair of shoes for my costume.* 2. to try to get or obtain. *He is seeking his fortune in Europe. / I will seek her help.* 3. to try (usually followed by an infinitive). *Juan sought to find the answer.* {seek} seeker, n.

seem *verb* (seemed, seeming, seems) 1. to appear to be or do. *He seems like a nice man.* 2. to appear to be real. *It seems you are right; our flight has been cancelled.* {seem}

Homophone Note Are you looking for the word *seam* (a line where two things join)? *Seem* and *seam* sound alike but have different meanings.

seep *verb* (seeped, seeping, seeps) to spread or flow through gradually. *An odor is seeping through the house.* {seep}

seethe *verb* (seethed, seething, seethes) 1. to boil or bubble. *The water seethed in the pot.* 2. to be very upset or angry.

Halle seethed when she saw the broken vase. {seeth} seethingly, adv.

seg·ment *noun* 1. one of the parts into which something is or can be separated. *She divided the orange into segments. / He wrote about one segment of our history.* 2. a part of a line bounded by a point at each end; line segment. {sehg mənt} segmentary, adj.

seg·re·ga·tion *noun* the practice of separating people according to groups, especially racial groups. *Black children could not go to school with white children when segregation was in practice in the United States.* {sehg rə **gay** shən} segregational, adj.

seine *noun* a net used for fishing that is held in the water with weights at the bottom and floats at the top. {sayn} seiner, n.

Homophone Note The words *seine* and *sane* (mentally healthy) sound alike but have different meanings.

Seine *noun* a river in northern France. It flows through Paris and into the English Channel. {sayn *or* sehn}

seis·mo·graph *noun* an instrument used to measure and record the strength of earthquakes. {siyz mə grăf} seismographer, n., seismographic, adj., seismographically, adv.

seize *verb* (seized, seizing, seizes) 1. to take hold of in a quick, forceful way; grab. *He seized a cookie from the plate.* 2. to capture. *The police seized the thief.* {seez}

sei·zure *noun* 1. a sudden attack caused by a disease such as epilepsy. *A nurse helped the boy who was having a seizure.* 2. any act of seizing. *The news*

A B C D E F G H I J K L M N O P Q R S T U V W X Y Z

tonight reported a large seizure of drugs. {**see** zhər}

sel·dom *adverb* not often; rarely. *He seldom comes to see us.* {**sehl** dəm}

se·lect *verb* (selected, selecting, selects) to choose; pick. *Please select the song you would like to play.* *adjective* preferred over others. *She was on the select team in soccer.* {sə **lehkt**} selectness, n., selector, n.

se·lec·tion *noun* 1. the act of selecting. *Please make a selection from the menu.* 2. something or someone selected. *Maya is our selection for class president.* 3. a group from which things or people may be selected. *The market offers a large selection of vegetables.* {sə **lehk** shən}

se·lec·tive *adjective* very careful in choosing. *She is selective about the clothes she buys.* {sə **lehk** tihv} selectively, adv., selectiveness, n.

self *noun* (selves) 1. one's own being, character, and nature. *He was sick and didn't seem like his old self.* 2. a single thing or person considered as separate and complete. *That girl is very independent and has a strong sense of her own self.* {**sehlf**}

self- *prefix* a prefix that means of, by, to, for, or in oneself or itself. *To exercise self-control is to keep control of oneself. / To have self-respect is to have respect for oneself.*

self-con·fi·dence *noun* faith in oneself and one's own abilities. *The gymnast's self-confidence helped her to perform well.* {**sehlf** kŏn fə dəns} self-confident, adj.

self-con·tained *adjective* having everything needed to survive or function. *The self-con-*

tained community grew all its own food. {**sehlf** kən **taynd**}

self-con·trol *noun* control of one's feelings or behavior. *It takes self-control for me not to yell when I'm angry.* {**sehlf** kən **trohl**}

self-es·teem *noun* confidence or pride in oneself; self-respect. *Low self-esteem keeps her from developing her talents.* {**sehlf** ih **steem**}

self-ex·plan·a·to·ry *adjective* needing no further explanation; clear. *The homework instructions should be self-explanatory.* {**sehlf** ihk **splǎ** nə **tohr** ee}

self·ish *adjective* concerned only with oneself and not concerned about others. *The selfish boy refused to share his toys with his brother.* {**sehl** fihsh} selfishly, adv., selfishness, n.

self-re·spect *noun* the proper regard for oneself and one's worth as a person. *He lost his self-respect when he lost his job.* {**sehlf** rih **spehkt**}

self-serv·ice *adjective* relating to a business in which customers serve themselves. *Gas stations and cafeterias are often set up as self-service businesses.* {**sehlf** **suhr** vihs}

self-suf·fi·cient *adjective* able to get along without any help from others. *Her children were self-sufficient at an early age.* {**sehlf** sə **fih** shənt}

sell ✆ *verb* (sold, selling, sells) 1. to exchange with another for money. *Robert decided to sell his baseball cards.* 2. to offer for sale. *I think I'm ready to sell my car and buy a new one.* 3. to cause or influence to buy. *The jeweler sold him on the diamond pin.* 4. to be part of selling anything. *In the Tiptop Trading Company, one department buys and another*

department sells. 5. to have a particular price (usually followed by "for"). *That T-shirt sells for twelve dollars.* {**sehl**} seller, n.

Homophone Note Are you looking for the word *cell*? *Sell* and *cell* sound alike but have different meanings.

se·mes·ter *noun* one half of a school or college year. *My brother will take an art class next semester.* {sə **meh** stər}

Word History *Semester* comes from two Latin words that mean "six months."

sem·i·cir·cle *noun* one half of a circle. {**sehm** ee **suhr** kəl *or* **sehm** iy **suhr** kəl}

sem·i·co·lon ✆ *noun* a punctuation mark (;). It is used to separate independent clauses in a sentence when there is no conjunction. {**sehm** ee **koh** lən *or* **sehm** iy **koh** lən}

sem·i·fi·nal *adjective* relating to the game or match that comes just before the last one. *Roger made it to the semifinal round of the spelling bee.* *noun* one of two games or matches in a sports tournament that come just before the last one. The winners of each semifinal play in the final to see who will become the champion. *Our soccer team made it to the semifinals.* {**sehm** ee **fiy** nəl *or* **sehm** iy **fiy** nəl, n., **sehm** ee **fiy** nəl *or* **sehm** iy **fiy** nəl, adj.}

sem·i·nar·y *noun* (seminaries) a school for training men and women for work as ministers, priests, or rabbis. {**sehm** ə **nayr** ee}

Sem·i·nole *noun* (Seminole or Seminoles) a member of a North American Indian

 Human Body
 Human Mind
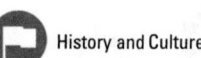 Everyday Life
 History and Culture
Communication

people that now live mostly in Florida and Oklahoma. {**sehm** ə **nohl**}

sem·i·trail·er *noun* a large trailer used for carrying freight. The trailer is attached at the front to the tractor cab that pulls it. {**sehm** ee **tray** lər *or* **sehm** iy **tray** lər}

sen·ate 🌐 *noun* 1. (capitalized) one of the two houses of the United States Congress, or a similar part of national government in other countries. *The United States Senate has two members from each state.* 2. a council with the power to make laws. *Most U.S. states have a senate as part of their government.* {**seh** niht}

Word History The English word *senate* comes from a Latin word that means "assembly of old men."

sen·a·tor *noun* a member of a senate. {**seh** nə tər}

send *verb* (sent, sending, sends) 1. to cause to be carried to another place; have delivered. *I will send you a letter. / He sent her flowers.* 2. to cause to go. *I sent him to pick up the papers.* 3. to direct or cause to move to a certain place or point. *He sent the ball over the fence.* {**sehnd**} sender, n.

sen·ior 🌐 *adjective* 1. being the older of two male relatives having the same name. The word "Senior," often written as "Sr.," is used after the name of a father whose son has the same name. *Mark T. Smith, Sr. is the father of Mark T. Smith, Jr.* 2. having served longer at a job or position. *Laurie is a senior member of* the club. 3. of higher rank. *Mr. Scott is a senior officer.* 4. relating to a person or class in the final year of high school or college. *Awards were given to members of the senior class. noun* 1. a person who is the older of two. *I am his senior by three years.* 2. a person who is higher in rank than someone else. *I am her senior at the factory because I have worked there longer.* 3. a student in the last year of high school or college. *The seniors will graduate in June.* {**seen** yər}

senior citizen *noun* an older person, especially one who is past the age of sixty-five and retired. {**seen** yər **sih** tə zihn *or* **seen** yər **sih** tə sihn}

sen·sa·tion *noun* 1. a condition of being aware of one of the senses. *She felt a sensation of cold when she stepped in the lake.* 2. the function of the senses. *He had almost no sensation in his right hand.* 3. a feeling of great interest or excitement. *The news caused a sensation in my neighborhood.* 4. the cause of such excitement. *The new song was a sensation.* {**sehn say** shən}

sen·sa·tion·al *adjective* 1. causing or meant to cause great excitement or interest. *We aren't fooled by sensational ads on TV.* 2. wonderful; terrific. *She looks sensational in that hat.* {**sehn say** shə nəl}

sense 🌐 *noun* 1. any of five ways to understand or experience one's surroundings. The senses are touch, smell, taste, sight, and hearing. 2. the use of any of these senses; a feeling. *Oddly, she had a sense of burning in her fingers after holding the ice cube.* 3. the power to reason; judgment. *He is a man with good sense* when it comes to business. 4. a particular ability to understand or judge. *She had no sense of what was needed to make kids happy.* 5. meaning of a word or passage. *Which sense of "sell" do you mean?* 6. purpose or intelligence; point. *There's no sense in paying for trumpet lessons if you don't like being in the band. verb* (sensed, sensing, senses) 1. to feel or experience by means of the senses. *Susan sensed the cold as soon as Rick opened the window.* 2. to understand. *Gabe sensed that what the party needed was a little music.* {**sehns**}

Homophone Note The words *sense*, *cents*, and *scents* sound alike but have different meanings.

sense organ *noun* a part of the body that takes in information and sends it to the brain. The eyes and the taste buds are sense organs. {**sehns ohr** gən}

sen·si·ble *adjective* having or showing good sense; wise. *It was sensible not to walk on the frozen pond.* {**sehn** sə bəl} sensibly, adv.

sen·si·tive *adjective* 1. able to smell, hear, taste, feel, or see very well. *A dog's nose is very sensitive to smell.* 2. highly aware or feeling things strongly. *Most artists are sensitive people. / My sister is sensitive about being teased.* 3. showing a strong response to chemicals or other things in the environment. *I am sensitive to cigarette smoke. / Camera film is sensitive to light.* {**sehn** sə tihv}

sen·sor *noun* a device that detects and responds to certain changes in the environment. Sensors respond to light, temperature, sound, or

A
B
C
D
E
F
G
H
I
J
K
L
M
N
O
P
Q
R
S
T
U
V
W
X
Y
Z

pressure and then send information to other instruments. {**sehn** sər}

sent *verb* past tense and past participle of **send**. {**sehnt**}

Homophone Note The words **sent**, **cent**, and **scent** sound alike but have different meanings.

sen·tence 🌐 💬 *noun* 1. a complete unit of words in either writing or speech with a clear beginning and a full stop. A sentence usually has a subject and a verb. Sentences can state things, ask questions, give commands, or be exclamations. 2. a punishment for a particular crime decided and declared in a court of law. *He received a sentence of thirty days in jail for stealing a purse.* *verb* (sentenced, sentencing, sentences) to pass a sentence on. *The judge sentenced him to thirty days in jail.* {**sehn** təns}

sen·ti·ment ❓ *noun* 1. a way of thinking or feeling about something. *The sentiment against him was very strong.* 2. feeling or emotion. *She talked about sentiments of love.* {**sehn** tə mənt}

sen·ti·men·tal *adjective* causing or showing tender feelings. *That radio station always plays sentimental music.* {**sehn** tə **mehn** təl} sentimentally, adv.

sen·try *noun* (sentries) a person who guards an entrance or keeps watch against dangers. *Sentries guard Buckingham Palace in London.* {**sehn** tree}

Se·oul *noun* the capital city of South Korea. {**sohl**}

se·pal *noun* a part of a plant, shaped like a leaf, that lies at the base of a flower. Sepals hold and protect developing flower buds. {**see** pəl}

sep·a·rate *verb* (separated, separating, separates) 1. to set apart or keep apart. *The teacher separated the two children who were talking during the lesson.* 2. to divide into parts. *She separated the paper into piles.* 3. to become disconnected. *The marching band separated into two lines.* 4. to sort; divide. *Let's separate into groups of three.* 5. to become divided. *Oil and water will separate after mixing.* 6. to no longer live together as a married couple. *Mr. and Mrs. Long separated, even though they still cared for each other.* *adjective* 1. not connected or not attached. *I keep my shirts and pants in separate drawers.* 2. standing alone; independent. *The house has a separate garage.* 3. individual. *Copy each separate number in the list.* {**sehp** ə riht or **seh** priht, adj., **sehp** ə rayt, v.} separately, adv.

sep·a·rate·ly *adverb* apart; not together; in a separate way. *My parents live separately.* / *We drove separately to the concert.* {**sehp** ar eht lee}

sep·a·ra·tion *noun* 1. the act of separating or condition of being separated. *The separation of books into groups took a long time.* / *The friends met after a long separation.* 2. a hole or space that separates; gap. *He has a separation between his two front teeth.* {**sehp** ər **ray** shən}

Sept. *abbreviation* an abbreviation for **September**.

sept- *prefix* a prefix that means "seven." *September was the seventh month in the ancient Roman calendar.*

Sep·tem·ber *noun* the ninth month of the year. September has thirty days. Autumn begins in September for people who live north of the equator. {**sehp** **tehm** bər}

Word History *September* comes from *septem*, the Latin word for "seven." September was the seventh month in the Roman calendar.

sep·tic *adjective* 1. infected with harmful bacteria. *The septic wound was treated by the doctor* 2. causing or able to cause infection. *Clean the area to guard against septic bacteria.* {**sehp** tihk}

se·quel 🌐 *noun* a book or movie that is complete in itself but continues a story begun in an earlier work. *Have you read the sequel yet?* {**see** kwəl}

se·quence *noun* 1. the order in which things follow one another. *Classes at our school follow the same sequence every day.* 2. a series of related or connected things. *Paula wrote a sequence of articles in the newspaper.* {**see** kwəns}

se·quin *noun* a very small shiny disk of plastic or metal. Sequins are sewn onto clothing as decoration. {**see** kwihn}

se·quoi·a *noun* a very large evergreen tree that grows in California; redwood or giant sequoia. {sih **kwoi** ə}

se·rene *adjective* free from trouble; calm. *I felt serene after talking to my friend.* / *The surface of the lake was smooth and serene.* {sə **reen**}

serf *noun* a person in earlier times who was like a slave. Serfs had to stay on the property where they worked and lived. If the land was sold, they were sold along with it. {**suhrf**}

Homophone Note The words **serf** and **surf** (as in ocean waves) sound alike but have different meanings.

Human Body ❓ Human Mind Everyday Life History and Culture Communication

ser·geant *noun* 1. a rank above corporal in the U.S. Army, Marine Corps, or Air Force. 2. a person holding such a rank. 3. a police officer whose position is below a captain, lieutenant, or inspector. {<u>sar</u> jənt}

se·ri·al *noun* a long story that is divided into parts and produced at regular times. *We enjoy watching our favorite serials on television. adjective* arranged in a series. *Many machines are stamped with serial numbers when they are made.* {<u>sih</u> ree əl} serially, adv.

Homophone Note Are you looking for the word *cereal* (as in grain)? *Serial* and *cereal* sound alike but have different meanings.

ser·ies *noun* (series) a group of related things that come one after another. *She read a series of articles in the newspaper. / He had a series of back injuries.* {<u>sih</u> reez}

ser·i·ous 🔊 *adjective* 1. marked by careful thinking or consideration. *He has a serious decision to make.* 2. not smiling or laughing; solemn; grave. *The policeman had a serious look on his face.* 3. important; needing careful thought. *Air pollution is a serious matter.* 4. dangerous; requiring attention right away. *He has a serious heart problem. / A serious storm is heading toward Buffalo.* {<u>seer</u> ee əs} seriously, adv., seriousness, n.

ser·mon *noun* 1. a talk given during a religious service. *The minister gave a sermon at church.* 2. a long speech that is intended to teach or scold; lecture. *My mother gave me a sermon about my manners.* {<u>suhr</u> mən}

ser·pent *noun* a snake. {<u>suhr</u> pənt}

se·rum *noun* (serums) 1. the thin, watery liquid that remains when the solid parts of blood have formed a clot. 2. the antidote given to a person or animal to protect from a disease or venom. It is taken from an animal that has been exposed to the same disease or venom. *It's a good thing the doctor had some rattlesnake serum on hand when Joe was bitten.* {<u>seer</u> əm}

ser·vant *noun* 1. a person, such as a maid or cook, who has a job working in someone else's home. 2. a person hired to provide services to others. *A policeman is a public servant.* {<u>suhr</u> vənt}

serve *verb* (served, serving, serves) 1. to give aid or help; be of use. *He served as a volunteer at the hospital.* 2. to work as a servant. *She served as a nanny for the busy family.* 3. to offer or provide food and drink to. *The waiter served us our dinner.* 4. to complete a period of service. *He served in the Army for ten years.* 5. to have a particular use. *This table serves as a desk.* 6. to hit the ball to begin a point in tennis and other games. *Cynthia serves first in this match.* 7. to provide with something; supply. *The pie will serve six people. noun* an instance of serving in tennis and other games, or the ability to serve in a particular way. *Claude has a powerful serve.* {suhrv}

serv·er *noun* 1. a person who serves food. *I am going to be the server at lunch today.* 2. a person who serves the ball in tennis and other games. *In our volleyball game we took turns being the server.* {<u>suhr</u> vər}

ser·vice 🌳 📖 *noun* 1. the act or an instance of helping. *He provides many services as a coach.* 2. the act of one who serves, such as a waiter, repair person, or government worker. *We needed the service of an auto mechanic.* 3. a government department. *I work for the foreign service in the State Department.* 4. any work done for another. *We offered our services to the neighborhood clean-up team.* 5. work done for the public. *He opened a clinic for health services.* 6. the armed forces; military. *He was in the service after high school.* 7. a religious ceremony. *We went to the evening service at our church.* 8. a set of items used for serving and eating food. *The china service was a gift from my grandmother. verb* (serviced, servicing, services) to repair and to keep in working order. *My father was able to service our washing machine.* {<u>suhr</u> vihs}

service station *noun* a place that sells gasoline and other things needed for cars, trucks, and other motor vehicles. Repairs are also made in some stations. {<u>suhr</u> vihs **stay** shən}

serv·ing *noun* one helping of food or drink. *I had two servings of oatmeal for breakfast.* {<u>suhr</u> ving}

ses·sion *noun* 1. a meeting or set of meetings of a court or a government council. *We visited a Senate session today.* 2. the period of time when such meetings happen. *This session of court will last for six weeks.*

A
B
C
D
E
F
G
H
I
J
K
L
M
N
O
P
Q
R
S
T
U
V
W
X
Y
Z

a
b
c
d
e
f
g
h
i
j
k
l
m
n
o
p
q
r
s
t
u
v
w
x
y
z

3. the period of time when a school is open for classes. *He took a course during summer session.* {**seh** shən}

set *verb* (set, setting, sets) 1. to put in a particular position or location. *Rebecca set the glass on the table.* 2. to put into a particular state. *They set the wild bird free.* 3. to be in a fixed state. *He was set in his ways.* 4. to put in order or arrange in order to make ready for use. *Please set the table for lunch.* 5. to fix. *The library set a limit on the number of books people can borrow.* 6. to assign to perform a particular task. *Dad set us to washing the dishes.* 7. to establish. *The manager set a goal for her workers.* 8. to position for proper operation. *Francis set the hands on the clock.* 9. to cause to be stiff or fixed in position. *He set his jaw in anger.* 10. to put back in place after being broken. *The doctor set Lee's broken leg and then put it in a cast.* 11. to go below the horizon; sink. *We will arrive before the sun sets.* 12. to become hard or solid. *This dessert will set when it is chilled.* *noun* 1. a group of related objects that are used together. *I bought a new set of tools.* 2. the scenery for a play or movie. *The set for our play included a castle with hills in the background.* 3. a radio or television receiver. *We gathered around the TV set for our favorite show.* 4. a series of games that is the principal unit of a match in tennis. *The player who wins the most sets wins the match.* 5. a group of points or numbers that are related to each other in some way. *The set of even numbers contains all whole numbers that can be divided by two.* *adjective* 1. already

decided; fixed. *We meet at a set time every day.* 2. not willing to change. *She is set in her ideas.* 3. prepared; ready. *Are you all set to leave?* {**seht**}
• **set in**
to begin or take effect. *Winter set in early this year.*

set·tle *verb* (settled, settling, settles) 1. to finally agree upon or decide. *We settled our argument.* 2. to come to a decision (often followed by "on" or "upon"). *We settled on the the green car instead of the red one.* 3. to find or make a home for. *He settled his family near the town.* 4. to become a resident of a place. *Their family settled in our town eight years ago.* 5. to make calm. *The music settled the crying baby.* 6. to become relaxed or calm. *As soon as the excitement ends, he will settle.* 7. to pay. *After years of having a car loan, he finally settled his debt with the bank.* 8. to stop moving. *The dust settled.* 9. to sink. *Our house has cracks in the foundation from where the ground has settled.* {**seht** əl}
• **settle down**
1. to adopt a quieter and more stable way of living. *After traveling for years, she settled down.* 2. to become calmer. *Miss Crumm told the children to settle down.*

set·tle·ment *noun* 1. the act of settling, or the condition of being settled. *The settlement of the American West was a time of difficulty as well as adventure.* 2. a place where people have recently settled; colony. *In the 1800s many settlements sprang up across the Great Plains.* 3. an agreement. *They reached a settlement that satisfied both of them.* {**seht** əl mənt}

set·tler *noun* a person who settles in a new area. *The settlers had to leave many things behind when they traveled to a new land.*
{**seht** ə lər *or* **sehtl** ər}

sev·en *noun* the number that comes after 6 and before 8 in the sequence of cardinal numbers; 7. *adjective* being seven in number. *There are seven days in a week.* {**sehv** ən}

sev·en·teen *noun* the number that comes after 16 and before 18 in the sequence of cardinal numbers; 17. *adjective* being seventeen in number. *We drove for seventeen miles to the country.* {**sehv** ən **teen**}

sev·en·teenth *adjective* coming next after the sixteenth in a series. *Mine is the seventeenth mailbox.* *noun* 1. one of seventeen equal parts of a whole; 1/17. *This bolt needs a nut that is one seventeenth of an inch wide.* 2. the number, person, or thing that comes next after the sixteenth in a series. *The seventeenth is the highest setting on this machine.* {**sehv** ən **teenth**}

sev·enth *adjective* coming next after the sixth in a series. *You are the seventh person to ask me that question.* *noun* 1. one of seven equal parts of a whole; 1/7. *This tiny bug is only a seventh of an inch long.* 2. the number, person, or thing that comes next after the sixth in a series. *I'm on the seventh of a twelve page paper.* {**sehv** ənth}

sev·en·ti·eth *adjective* coming next after the sixty-ninth in a series. *This is the seventieth time I've climbed this mountain.* *noun* 1. one of seventy equal parts of a whole; 1/70. *Each student raised one seventieth of the money we needed for our class trip.* 2. the

 Human Body   Human Mind   Everyday Life   History and Culture   Communication

number, person, or thing that comes next after the sixty-ninth in a series. *There were many pages missing in my book after the seventieth.* {**seh** vən tee i*th*}

se·ven·ty *noun* (seventies) the number that is equal to seven times ten; 70. *adjective* being seventy in number. *My grandfather blew out all seventy candles on his birthday cake.* {**seh** vən tee}

sev·er·al *adjective* being not many more than two in number. *There is a mall several miles from here.* *noun* a small number of things or people; some. *Several were chosen to join the team.* {**sehv** ər əl *or* **sehv** rəl, n., **sehv** ər əl *or* **sehv** rəl, adj.}

se·vere *adjective* (severer, severest) 1. very strict; harsh. *The prison had severe rules.* 2. very strong or intense. *A broken bone can cause severe pain.* / *The news reporter warned us of severe weather.* 3. very difficult. *Climbing the mountain was a severe test of strength.* {sə **veer**} severely, adv.

sew ○ *verb* (sewed, sewn or sewed, sewing, sews) to make or repair with a needle and thread. *Anna sews her own dresses.* / *Aaron sewed up the hole in his sock.* {**soh**}

• **sew up**
1. (informal) to bring to a close. *She finally managed to get the deal sewn up.* 2. to control the result of; be sure of winning. *The other team was so far ahead, they had the game sewn up.*

Homophone Note The words *sew*, *so*, and *sow*[1] sound alike but have different meanings.

sew·age *noun* water and waste material that is carried away in sewers. {**sooh** ihj}

sew·er ○ ⊕ *noun* a large underground pipe that carries off the liquid and solid waste of a town or city. {**sooh** ər}

sewing machine *noun* a machine for sewing clothes and other things. *My mother makes quilts on her sewing machine.* {**soh** ing mə **sheen**}

sex *noun* the fact of being either female or male. *Mammals of the female sex give birth to and make milk for their young.* / *Animals of the male sex produce sperm to fertilize the eggs made by the females.* {**sehks**}

sex- *prefix* a prefix that means "six." *A sextet is a group of six singers.*

sex·ist *adjective* the unfair treatment of a person because of his or her sex. *It is a sexist idea that girls aren't good at math.* {**sehk** sihst}

shab·by *adjective* (shabbier, shabbiest) 1. showing signs of wear. *She wore a shabby coat.* / *We hope to move out of our shabby apartment.* 2. of poor quality. *The painters did a shabby job.* 3. mean or selfish for no good reason; unfair. *There is no excuse for his shabby behavior.* {**shăb** ee}

shack ○ *noun* a small, poorly built building, used as a house or for storage. {**shăk**}

shade ○ *noun* 1. darkness caused by light rays being blocked. *On hot, sunny days, we like the shade of the old oak tree.* 2. an area that has such darkness. *The horses stood in the shade to cool off.* 3. an object or device on a lamp or window that blocks light or heat rays. *We need to buy a shade to soften the harsh light of this lamp.* / *Close the shade so it stays dark in here in the*

morning. 4. the degree of darkness of a color. *My set of crayons has three shades of green.* 5. a small difference or change. *This poem has many shades of meaning.* 6. (plural; informal) sunglasses. *That movie star never goes out without his shades on.* *verb* (shaded, shading, shades) 1. to hide or protect from light. *We shaded our eyes as we looked across the desert.* 2. to change by slight degrees. *She shaded the truth to make herself seem innocent.* {**shayd**}

shad·ow *noun* 1. the dark image cast on some surface by a person or thing blocking the light of the sun or another source of light. 2. an area of darkness. *We walked in the shadow of the forest.* 3. a trace; hint. *His face had the shadow of a frown.* *verb* (shadowed, shadowing, shadows) 1. to cast a shadow on or over; shade. *The road was shadowed by the mountain.* 2. to follow closely and in secret in order to watch; trail. *The girl had no privacy because her mother always shadowed her.* {**shăd** oh}

shad·y *adjective* (shadier, shadiest) 1. in the shade. *We sat at a shady picnic table.* 2. giving shade. *We rested near a shady stand of trees.* 3. not of good character; not to be trusted. *We refused to rent from the shady landlord.* / *The business deal seemed shady to me.* {**shay** dee}

shaft *noun* 1. an arrow or spear, or the long, straight part of one that is connected to the head. *He held the spear by the shaft as he threw it.* 2. a

A
B
C
D
E
F
G
H
I
J
K
L
M
N
O
P
Q
R
S
T
U
V
W
X
Y
Z

straight beam or ray. *Shafts of light broke through the clouds.* 3. a long, straight section or handle of something. *The shaft of the hoe was made of wood.* 4. a tall, straight pole or support. *The shaft of the flagpole at school is metal.* 5. a rod in a machine that turns and is often attached to gears. The shaft transfers power or motion from one part to another. *A drive shaft in a car carries power and motion from the engine to the wheels.* 6. a deep passage that goes straight down or at a slant. *An elevator moves up and down inside an elevator shaft. / A mine shaft is often built on a slant.* {**shăft**}

shag·gy *adjective* (shaggier, shaggiest) 1. having long, rough hair or something like hair. *The shaggy dog was hard to brush. / We have a shaggy carpet in the family room.* 2. long, tangled, and bushy. *The old man had shaggy eyebrows.* {**shăg** ee}

shake *verb* (shook, shaken, shaking, shakes) 1. to move back and forth or up and down with quick motions. *Shake the juice before you pour it.* 2. to tremble with cold; shiver. *She began to shake without her coat.* 3. to cause to tremble; vibrate. *The ground shook from the earthquake.* 4. to take the hand of another in greeting or congratulations. *In this country it is considered friendly to shake when you are introduced to someone.* 5. to take or grasp in greeting. *We said hello and shook hands.* 6. to remove by quick movements. *Gail shook the leaves from the branch.* 7. to upset; disturb. *The news of her accident shook him.* *noun* 1. the act or an instance of shaking or trembling. *The*

dog gave his tail a shake.* 2. a drink made by shaking its ingredients together. *Kids love milk shakes.* {**shayk**}

shak·y *adjective* (shakier, shakiest) 1. shaking; trembling. *Coffee makes him shaky.* 2. not steady or secure. *We crossed the river by a shaky bridge.* {**shay** kee}

shale *noun* a rock made of many thin layers that can easily be split into sheets. {**shayl**}

shall *auxiliary verb* 1. am going to, or expecting to; will. *We shall never forget her kindness.* 2. definitely will, as by order. *He shall repay me.* {**shăl**}

shal·low *adjective* (shallower, shallowest) 1. measuring little from top to bottom; not deep. *They crossed where the river was shallow.* 2. without deep thought or feeling. *I can only have shallow conversations with Peter.* *noun* (usually plural) a place where the water is not deep. *They waded in the shallows.* {**shăl** oh}

shame *noun* 1. a painful feeling brought about by the knowledge that one has done something wrong or not proper. *She felt shame after failing the test.* 2. the ability to feel this pain. *He is without shame.* 3. loss of honor; disgrace. *His arrest brought shame on his family.* 4. something to feel badly about; disappointment. *It's a shame you can't go on vacation. / What a shame!* *verb* (shamed, shaming, shames) 1. to make someone feel ashamed. *She shamed her family by lying.* 2. to cause loss of respect; bring embarrassment to. *He was shamed after he failed to finish his assignment.* 3. to force through guilt. *We shamed him into paying the money he owed us.* {**shaym**}

• **for shame!**
you should feel embarrassed or guilty about your action. *For shame! Teasing a baby like that!*

• **put to shame**
1. to cause to feel ashamed. *The punishment by his teacher put the boy to shame.* 2. to make a person or thing appear to be of less worth. *Your excellent cooking puts mine to shame.*

Synonyms
These words share a meaning with *shame*, verb 1:
disgrace, embarrass, humiliate

sham·poo *verb* (shampooed, shampooing, shampoos) to clean with a soap solution. *We will shampoo the rug with a special machine.* *noun* (shampoos) 1. a soap solution used to clean the hair. 2. a liquid cleanser used on rugs and the fabric part of furniture. 3. an act of shampooing. *I went to the barber for a shampoo and a trim.* {**shăm** **pooh**}

Word History English speakers did not use *shampoo* until the 1860s. The word itself entered English in the 1700s. It was an English version of a Hindi word meaning "to massage." The word did not have the present meanings of "wash the hair" and "soap for the hair" until the 1860s.

sham·rock *noun* a clover plant with leaves that have three parts. It is the national emblem of Ireland. {**shăm rŏk**}

shape ❶ *noun* 1. the appearance of an object as defined by its outer surface or outline; form. *Anne sorted the blocks*

 Human Body   Human Mind    Everyday Life    History and Culture   Communication

by shape, cubes on the left and cylinders on the right. 2. an ordered or organized form. *Writing often helps people to give shape to their ideas.* 3. physical condition. *The professional athlete is in top shape.* verb (shaped, shaping, shapes) 1. to give a certain form or shape to; mold. *We shaped the clay into a pot.* 2. to give a direction or character to. *He is shaping his life after his grandfather's.* 3. to happen in a particular way (usually followed by "up"). *If our project shapes up well, we will present it to the whole school.* {shayp}
• **take shape**
to come to have a more complete form. *After days of planning and work, our dinosaur project took shape.*

share noun 1. a part of a whole that one member of a group is given or owed. *We gave him his share of the money.* 2. one of the equal parts into which the stock of a business divided. *They own several shares of the company.* verb (shared, sharing, shares) 1. to divide and give out in shares. *I shared the money with her.* 2. to receive, use, or enjoy together with one or more others. *All the guests shared the delicious meal.* 3. to take part (often followed by "in"). *We shared in the building of the barn.* {shayr}

share·ware noun software that is delivered free of charge by its author. The user is asked to pay a small fee to the author if he or she continues to use the software. *You can download some great shareware off the Internet.* {shayr wayr}

shark[1] noun a fish that lives in the ocean and has tough skin and a skeleton made of cartilage. Most sharks eat other fish. {shark}

shark[2] noun a person who cheats or swindles others. *That shark took all of my money!* {shark}

sharp adjective (sharper, sharpest) 1. having a thin edge or a fine point for cutting or piercing. *I'll need a sharp knife to cut this pumpkin.* 2. quick and sudden. *Try not to take the sharp turn too fast.* 3. biting to the sense of taste or smell. *The sharp cheese brought tears to my eyes.* 4. harsh and causing hurt. *Her sharp words hurt her friends.* 5. easily seen; clear. *This camera makes a sharp image.* 6. intelligent; clever. *The sharp student knew the answers right away.* adverb (sharper, sharpest) 1. in a sharp or alert way. *Look sharp, or you will miss the bus.* 2. exactly. *Come to my office at three o'clock sharp.* noun a musical tone that is a half step higher than another. {sharp} sharply, adv., sharpness, n.

sharp·en verb (sharpened, sharpening, sharpens) to make or become sharp. *He sharpened the knife with a special stone.* {shar pən} sharpener, n.

shat·ter verb (shattered, shattering, shatters) 1. to break suddenly into small pieces. *The baseball shattered the window.* 2. to ruin completely. *Bad weather shattered our plans.* 3. to be broken into small pieces. *The mirror shattered.* {shăt ər}

shave verb (shaved, shaving, shaves) 1. to remove by cutting with a razor. *Should I shave my mustache?* 2. to cut off in thin slices. *The carpenter shaved the top of the door so it would fit.* noun the act of shaving hair off the face. *He had a shower and a shave.* {shayv}

shav·ing noun 1. a very thin slice or piece. *Wood shavings fell to the floor as he worked.* 2. the action of someone or something that shaves. *Shaving is part of his morning routine.* {shay ving}

shawl noun a piece of fabric that is worn over the shoulders or around the head and shoulders. It is larger and heavier than a scarf. *My grandmother wears a shawl instead of a sweater.* {shawl}

she pronoun the female person or animal that is being talked about. *My sister is only three, but she can already count.* noun a female animal or person. *Is this lizard a he or a she?* {shee}

shear verb (sheared, sheared or shorn, shearing, shears) 1. to cut off with scissors or a tool like scissors. *He sheared the ends of the branches.* 2. to trim the fleece or hair from. *The farmers are shearing their sheep.* {sheer} shearer, n.

Homophone Note Are you looking for the word *sheer*? *Shear* and *sheer* sound alike but have different meanings.

shears plural noun a tool that is like a large scissors. *Mr. Greene trimmed the bushes with a pair of shears.* {sheerz}

sheath noun a case for the blade of a sword or knife. {sheeth}

she'd shortened form of "she had" or "she would." *She'd been planning this trip for years. / She'd like to come with us.* {sheed}

a
b
c
d
e
f
g
h
i
j
k
l
m
n
o
p
q
r
s
t
u
v
w
x
y
z

shed[1] *noun* a small building used for storage or shelter. *My older brother turned our shed into a workshop.* {**shehd**}

shed[2] *verb* (shed, shedding, sheds) 1. to cast off, take off, or let fall. *He shed his clothes. / The maple sheds its leaves in autumn.* 2. to let something flow out. *She is shedding tears.* 3. to send out or give off. *The lamp sheds light on my book.* 4. to stop something from getting through. *A waterproof raincoat sheds water.* {**shehd**}

sheep *noun* (sheep) 1. an animal with hooves, hollow horns, and long, curly hair. Sheep are mammals that are raised for their wool; some people also use their milk and meat. They are closely related to goats. 2. a person who follows what others do without thinking. {**sheep**}

sheer *adjective* (sheerer, sheerest) 1. thin or fine enough to see through. *The scarf was made from a sheer fabric.* 2. pure and total. *The story filled her with sheer terror. / She won the prize by sheer hard work.* 3. straight up and down, or almost so. *He looked up at the sheer side of the canyon.* {**sheer**}

Homophone Note The words *sheer* and *shear* (to cut or trim) sound alike but have different meanings.

sheet *noun* 1. a large piece of cotton or linen cloth used to cover a bed. 2. a thin, broad surface. *The parking lot was covered with a sheet of ice.* 3. a single piece of paper. *I need ten sheets of paper for my art project.* {**sheet**}

sheik *noun* a leader of an Arab community or tribe. {**sheek** or **shayk**}

shelf ◯ *noun* (shelves) 1. a thin, flat piece of wood, metal, or other material that is attached to a wall or set into a piece of furniture. Shelves are used to hold books, dishes, and other things. *He put the cups and saucers on the shelf.* 2. something that is like a shelf, such as a rock ledge. *The submarine hit an underwater shelf and sank.* {**shehlf**}

• **on the shelf**
not in use at the present time; put aside until later. *The idea of going to the zoo was put on the shelf after I sprained my ankle.*

she'll shortened form of "she will." *She'll be living here for the next few years.* {**sheel**}

shell ◯ *noun* 1. a hard outer covering, as on a bird's egg, a nut, or an animal such as a snail, turtle, or clam. 2. any hard outer layer that is hollow or protects, such as the outer walls of a building. *Pour the mixture into the pie shell. / This canoe has an aluminum shell.* 3. a piece of ammunition used in a cannon or gun. *verb* (shelled, shelling, shells) 1. to remove the shell or shells of. *We shelled the crabs.* 2. to hit with shells fired from a cannon or gun. *They shelled the enemy position for hours.* {**shehl**}

shel·lac *noun* 1. thin sheets or flakes of a material produced by insects. It is used in making varnish and other products. 2. a liquid used to coat furniture and floors to protect them and make them shine. *verb* (shellacked, shellacking, shellacs) 1. to cover with shellac. *The living room floor glowed after we shellacked it.* 2. (slang) to defeat. *The team shellacked their opponent.* {**shə lǎk**}

shell·fish *noun* (shellfish or shellfishes) a small animal that lives in fresh or salt water and has a shell outside its body. Shellfish are not true fish. They are invertebrates, or animals with no backbone. People can eat many kinds of shellfish, including clams, oysters, shrimp, and lobsters. {**shehl fihsh**}

shel·ter ◯ *noun* 1. a place or structure that gives protection against weather or danger. *During the storm we used a little shack as our shelter.* 2. the protection given by such a place. *The cave offered shelter from the wind.* 3. the condition of being in a home or other place where one is safe and protected. *Everyone needs food, clothing, and shelter.* *verb* (sheltered, sheltering, shelters) to give cover, protection, or shelter to. *We sheltered the lost dog in our home.* {**shehl** tər}

shep·herd *noun* 1. a person who herds and watches over sheep. 2. a person who guides and protects. *The minister was the shepherd of his congregation.* *verb* (shepherded, shepherding, shepherds) to guide and protect. *The guard shepherded us through the dark hallways.* {**shehp** ərd}

sher·bet *noun* a frozen dessert made mainly of fruit juice, sugar, and gelatin. {**shuhr** biht}

sher·iff *noun* the main law officer of a county. {**shehr** ihf}

654

 Human Body   ? Human Mind   Everyday Life   History and Culture   Communication

she's shortened form of "she is" or "she has." *She's my best friend. / She's never been here before.* {**sheez**}

Shetland pony *noun* a breed of very small but strong pony native to the Shetland Islands of Scotland. {**sheht** lənd **poh** nee}

shield *noun* 1. a piece of armor worn or carried on the arm to protect against blows from weapons. 2. something shaped like this piece of armor. 3. something that gives protection. *The farmer planted trees as a shield against the wind.* 4. a person who gives protection. *The mother was a shield between her child and the barking dog.* *verb* (shielded, shielding, shields) to protect. *The man shielded his eyes from the sunlight.* {**sheeld**}

shift *verb* (shifted, shifting, shifts) 1. to move from one place to another; change position. *Our family shifted from town to town. / The boy shifted in his chair.* 2. to move; change the position of. *He shifted books from the top shelf to the bottom shelf.* 3. to change from one position to another. *She shifted seats so that she could see better.* *noun* 1. a change from one person, place, condition, or thing to another. *There was a shift in the wind. / The woman felt a shift in her health.* 2. a regular time period when people work. *He likes working during the night shift.* 3. the people who work during that period. *The morning shift was coming out of the factory.* 4. the act of changing gears when driving a car or truck. *The car jerked when he shifted gears.* {**shihft**}

shil·ling *noun* 1. the main unit of money of Kenya and several other African countries. A shilling is equal to one hundred cents. 2. a coin formerly in circulation in England and colonial America. {**shih** ling}

shim·mer *verb* (shimmered, shimmering, shimmers) to shine with a soft, flickering light. *The lake shimmered in the moonlight.* {**shihm** ər}

shin *noun* the front part of the leg between the knee and ankle. *verb* (shinned, shinning, shins) to climb by gripping with the knees and the hands or arms and pulling oneself up. *We shinned up the rope in gym class.* {**shihn**}

shin·bone *noun* the large bone in the lower half of a person's leg. {**shihn** bohn}

shine *verb* (shone or shined, shining, shines) 1. to give off or reflect light. *The moon shone on our house.* 2. to aim the light of. *Please shine the flashlight over here.* 3. to show or give off in a clear or intense way. *The little girl's eyes shone with excitement.* 4. to do very well. *Lizzie shines in math.* 5. to cause to shine; polish. *He shined the lamp.* *noun* 1. the act or an instance of shining. *The cowboy gave his boots a shine.* 2. the glow that comes from a source of light. *The fog dimmed the shine of the headlights.* 3. luster. *I admired the shine of the polished floors.* {**shiyn**}

shin·gle *noun* a thin, flat piece of wood or other building material. Shingles are attached in overlapping rows to cover the roof or sides of a building. *verb* (shingled, shingling, shingles) to cover with shingles. *The workers shingled the roof.* {**shing** gəl}

Shin·to *noun* a major religion in Japan. People of the Shinto religion worship nature and ancestors. {**shihn** toh} Shintoism, n., Shintoist, n., adj.

shin·y *adjective* (shinier, shiniest) 1. having a gloss; polished. *His shoes were nice and shiny.* 2. glowing with light; bright; shining. *The surface of the pond was shiny in the sun.* {**shiy** nee}

ship ○ *noun* 1. a large vessel built to carry people or goods long distances through deep water. *The ship took a week to cross the ocean.* 2. an airplane or other aircraft. *verb* (shipped, shipping, ships) to place on and send by ship, truck, or other vehicle. *We shipped a package to our friends across the country.* {**shihp**}

-ship *suffix* 1. a suffix that means "condition of," "character of," or "quality of." *"Friendship" means "the condition of being friends."* 2. a suffix that means "office" or "position." *When a person has an apprenticeship, he or she is in the position of an apprentice.* 3. a suffix that means "art," "craft," or "skill." *Penmanship is the skill of handwriting.*

ship·ment *noun* 1. the act of shipping goods. *The toys at the factory were put in boxes for shipment.* 2. goods shipped, or an amount of goods shipped at one time.

A B C D E F G H I J K L M N O P Q R S T U V W X Y Z

a
b
c
d
e
f
g
h
i
j
k
l
m
n
o
p
q
r
s
t
u
v
w
x
y
z

The shipment was damaged by rain. {shihp mənt}

ship·ping *noun* 1. the act or business of sending or transporting goods. *Shipping is a major industry in port cities.* 2. a group of ships that belong to a single industry or country. *The harbor is open to shipping from many countries.* {shih ping}

ship·wreck *noun* 1. the destruction or loss of a ship at sea. *The storm caused a terrible shipwreck.* 2. the remains of a ship that has been wrecked or sunk. *The shipwreck rested on the bottom of the ocean.* *verb* (shipwrecked, shipwrecking, shipwrecks) 1. to cause to be wrecked or sunk. *Those hidden rocks have shipwrecked many boats.* 2. to destroy or ruin. *The sudden loss of his business shipwrecked his plans.* {shihp rehck}

ship·yard *noun* a place where ships are built or repaired. {shihp yard}

shirk *verb* (shirked, shirking, shirks) to escape from or avoid doing. *She shirked her chores all day.* {shuhrk} shirker, n.

shirt  *noun* a piece of clothing for the upper part of the body. Shirts usually open at the front and have a collar and sleeves. {shuhrt}
• **in one's shirt sleeves** not wearing a coat. *The mayor spoke in his shirt sleeves.*
• **keep one's shirt on** (informal) to stop oneself from becoming angry or losing patience; hold one's temper. *Don't rush me; keep your shirt on.*
• **lose one's shirt** to lose all that one owns. *The businessman lost his shirt in the stock market.*

shiv·er *verb* (shivered, shivering, shivers) to tremble or

shake. *He shivered with cold.* *noun* a trembling or shaking motion. *The ghost story gave me the shivers.* {shihv ər}

shoal *noun* a shallow place in a river, ocean, or other body of water. {shohl}

shock[1] *noun* 1. a sudden and powerful scare; an upset of the mind or feelings. *News of the disaster came as a shock.* 2. a sudden, powerful blow or jar. *The shock of the explosion knocked down trees and buildings.* 3. the feeling caused by an electrical current passing through the body. *I got a shock when I touched the wire.* 4. a dangerous weakening of the body that can be caused by serious injury or illness. *The injured man started to go into shock.* *verb* (shocked, shocking, shocks) 1. to disturb suddenly, in a way that causes intense surprise, upset, or disgust. *She shocked us with the bad news.* 2. to give an electric shock to. *The electric fence shocked him when he touched it.* {shŏk}

shock[2] *noun* a bundle of stalks of corn or other grain standing upright against one another in a field. {shŏk}

shock[3] *noun* a thick mass of hair. *The boy had a shock of brown hair.* {shŏk}

shock·ing *adjective* causing surprise, disgust, or other emotional upset. *The book was banned at school for its shocking language.* {shŏk ing}

shoe 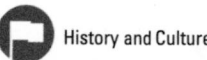 *noun* 1. a protective covering for the human foot, often made of leather or canvas. 2. a horseshoe. 3. (plural; informal) place or position, either good or bad. *I would love to be in your shoes.* *verb* (shod or shoed, shod or shoed or shodden, shoeing, shoes) to dress in or fit with a shoe or shoes. *The*

young rider knows how to shoe his own horses.* {shooh}

shoe·lace *noun* a string or cord used for fastening a shoe. {shooh lays}

shone *verb* a past tense and past participle of **shine**. {shohn}

> **Homophone Note** Are you looking for the word **shown** (a past participle of "show")? **Shone** and **shown** sound alike but have different meanings.

shook *verb* past tense of **shake**. {shuuk}

shoot *verb* (shot, shooting, shoots) 1. to hit, wound, destroy, or kill with a bullet, arrow, or similar object. *The hunter shot a deer.* 2. to cause a bullet, arrow, or other missile to fly forth from; to fire. *He shot his gun at the target.* 3. to cause to fly forth. *He shot three bullets from his rifle.* 4. to move with great speed (usually followed by "around," "by," or "out"). *The speeding car shot by us.* 5. to send with force towards a goal in sports. *The hockey player shot the puck into the goal.* 6. to cause to extend suddenly. *The goalie shot her leg out to block the ball.* 7. to put forth buds. *The oak tree usually shoots around the beginning of May.* *noun* 1. a shooting contest or a hunting expedition. *The hunting club held a turkey shoot.* 2. a bit of new growth. *New shoots on the trees appear every spring.* {shooht} shooter, n.

> **Homophone Note** Are you looking for the word **chute**? **Shoot** and **chute** sound alike but have different meanings.

shooting star *noun* a chunk of metal or rock from outer space that burns up as it enters the earth's atmo-

Human Body   ? Human Mind   Everyday Life   History and Culture   Communication

sphere; meteor. {<u>shooh</u> ting <u>star</u>}

shop *noun* 1. a small store. *There is a toy shop downtown.* 2. a place where a worker such as a mechanic or carpenter keeps tools and does work; workshop. *My car is in the shop.* *verb* (shopped, shopping, shops) to buy or look at the things in stores or shops. *My mother is shopping for new clothes.* {<u>shŏp</u>}

• **talk shop**
to discuss one's work or interests. *The two scientists were talking shop.*

shop·lift *verb* 1. to steal from a store. *His friends dared him to shoplift some candy, but he would not.* 2. to steal things from a store while it is open. *The store owner caught the kids shoplifting and called the police.* {<u>shŏp</u> lihft}

shop·lift·er *noun* a person who steals things from a store while pretending to be a customer. {<u>shŏp</u> lihf tər} shoplifting, n.

shopping center *noun* a group of stores that share a parking area and often include other businesses and restaurants. {<u>sho</u> ping <u>sehn</u> tər}

shore ⊕ *noun* 1. the land beside an ocean, sea, lake, or river. *We collected seashells along the shore.* 2. the land rather than the sea. *The sailors were eager to get back to shore.* {<u>shohr</u>}

short *adjective* (shorter, shortest) 1. having little length; not long. *Her arms are too short to reach the steering wheel.* / *The book was short enough to read in one day.* 2. having little height; not tall. *He was too short to reach the cupboard.* 3. lasting a small amount of time; brief. *The family went on a short vacation.* 4. having less than is needed; lacking. *We were two dollars short of what we needed.* *adverb* (shorter, shortest) 1. suddenly. *When the car stopped short, everyone was thrown forward.* 2. at a point or place before the goal is reached. *The water balloon fell short of its target.* *noun* 1. a break in an electrical circuit; short circuit. *A short in the wire caused the lights to go out.* 2. (plural) trousers that do not reach past the knee. *In the summer people often wear shorts.* 3. (plural) men's underwear. {<u>shohrt</u>}

• **for short**
as a shorter form. *We call Elizabeth "Liz" for short.*

short·age *noun* 1. an amount that is less than is needed; lack. *There is a shortage of food in many countries.* 2. a lack of a particular amount. *The cash register showed a shortage of four dollars.* {<u>shohr</u> tihj}

short·com·ing *noun* a fault or weakness in character, behavior, or ability. *Not being brave was his shortcoming.* {<u>shohrt</u> kuh ming}

short·cut *noun* 1. a quicker or more direct route. *I took a shortcut to the store and got there ten minutes faster.* 2. a quicker or easier way of doing something. *We learned some shortcuts in cooking class.* {<u>shohrt</u> kuht}

short·en *verb* (shortened, shortening, shortens) 1. to make shorter. *I shortened the dress by three inches.* 2. to become shorter. *As winter approaches, the days shorten.* {<u>shohr</u> tən}

short·en·ing *noun* a solid fat used in baking. *The recipe calls for a tablespoon of vegetable shortening.* {<u>shohr</u> tə ning}

short·hand *noun* a system of writing used to record speech quickly. Simple symbols are used to represent sounds, words, or phrases. *The secretary took notes in shorthand.* {<u>shohrt</u> hănd}

short-hand·ed *adjective* not having enough workers or helpers. *The restaurant was short-handed and had to close early.* {<u>shohrt</u> <u>hăn</u> dihd}

short·ly *adverb* in a short while; soon. *The bus will arrive shortly.* {<u>shohrt</u> lee}

short·sight·ed *adjective* 1. not looking ahead or thinking about what might happen in the future. *It was shortsighted of him to leave his papers outside on a windy day.* 2. not able to see objects clearly that are far away; nearsighted. *Because he was shortsighted, he wore glasses while driving.* {<u>shohrt</u> siy tihd}

short·stop *noun* the position between second and third base in baseball or softball, or the player in this position. {<u>shohrt</u> stŏp}

shot[1] *noun* (shots or shot) 1. an instance of shooting with a weapon. *Shots were fired, police said.* 2. the distance a gun or other weapon can be fired; range. *The men stayed out of rifle shot.* 3. a small metal ball that is fired from a gun, or a group of such balls. *The soldiers ran out of lead shot in the middle of the battle.* 4. one who shoots. *Annie is a*

A B C D E F G H I J K L M N O P Q R S T U V W X Y Z

a
b
c
d
e
f
g
h
i
j
k
l
m
n
o
p
q
r
s
t
u
v
w
x
y
z

good shot. 5. the act of trying to score by sending or throwing a ball toward a goal. *Her last shot won the basketball game.* 6. an injection with a needle. *Some people get flu shots every year.* {shŏt}

shot² *verb* past tense and past participle of **shoot.** *adjective* (informal) ruined or not usable. *My car is shot.* {shŏt}

shot put *noun* a sports event in which a heavy metal ball is thrown as far as possible. {shŏt puut} shot-putter, n.

should *auxiliary verb* 1. past tense of **shall.** *I thought I should never see him again.* 2. used to express what one is supposed to do. *You should do your homework.* 3. used to express what may happen or is expected. *They should be here soon.* 4. used to express a possible course of action (often used with "if"). *If she should refuse, we will have to ask somebody else.* {shuud}

shoul·der *noun* 1. the part of the human body between the neck and the upper arm. 2. a similar part of an animal's body. 3. the edge or border of a road where cars can stop. *The driver had to park on the shoulder of the road until the rain stopped.* *verb* (shouldered, shouldering, shoulders) 1. to place on one's shoulders. *They shouldered the canoe.* 2. to push roughly with the shoulder or shoulders. *The football players shouldered each other.* {shohl dər}

shoulder blade *noun* either of the two large, flat, triangular bones in the upper back that form the back parts of the shoulders. {shohl dər blayd}

should·n't shortened form of "should not." *You shouldn't*

ride your bike without a helmet. {shuu dənt}

shout *verb* (shouted, shouting, shouts) 1. to call out loudly; yell. *He shouted to his friend across the street.* 2. to yell or say very loudly. *I heard Leo shout my name. noun* a loud cry or call. *The sailor gave a shout of warning when he saw the huge wave.* {showt} shouter, n.

shove *verb* (shoved, shoving, shoves) 1. to push in a rough way or without care. *The boy shoved his brother out of the way.* 2. to push along with a steady pressure. *She shoved the heavy box across the floor. noun* an act of shoving. *Give the car door a shove to close it.* {shuhv}

shov·el *noun* 1. a large scoop with a long handle used for digging or lifting heavy material such as earth, snow, or coal. 2. a machine fitted with such a scoop, used for digging *The builders used a steam shovel to dig a basement.* 3. the amount of material that can be held in a shovel. *He threw a shovel of wood chips around the tree. verb* (shoveled, shoveling, shovels) 1. to lift and move with a shovel. *They shoveled the ground to find worms.* 2. to throw or move quickly, in large amounts. *She shoveled food into her mouth.* {shuh vəl}

show *verb* (showed, shown or showed, showing, shows) 1. to cause or allow to be seen. *Irene showed her report card to her parents.* 2. to become easily noticed, evident, or visible. *Your belly button is showing.* / *His hard work showed in his science project.* 3. to make clear by example; explain. *The teacher showed the answers on the blackboard.* 4. to direct. *Show him to his*

seat. 5. to provide an example of; reveal. *His yawn showed that he was tired.* 6. to display or exhibit. *She showed her photographs at the library. noun* 1. a public performance, display, or demonstration. *We won first prize in the talent show.* 2. a television or radio program. *I like to watch my favorite show after dinner.* 3. an act of making something clear. *Many people joined the picket as a show of support for the workers.* 4. something false or pretended. *His tears were nothing but a show.* {shoh}

• **get the show on the road** (slang) to begin; get started. *Let's get the show on the road.*

• **show off** to do something to impress others or to attract attention. *He shows off by talking too loudly.*

• **show up** to arrive at a place. *We waited, but he never showed up.*

show·er *noun* 1. a fall of rain that lasts a short time. *The shower lasted only a few minutes.* 2. a fall of many objects of the same kind. *A shower of leaves covered us when the wind blew.* 3. a large supply or flow. *The family had a shower of good fortune.* 4. a device that sprays water from an overhead nozzle, so that one can wash oneself. *I turned on the shower and washed my hair.* 5. an act of washing with such a device. *He takes a shower every morning. verb* (showered, showering, showers) 1. to wash oneself in a shower. *She showers every day after sports practice.* 2. to wet or spray with a shower of rain or water. *He showered the garden with water from the hose.* 3. to give in large amounts. *The boy's grand-*

 Human Body    Human Mind   Everyday Life   Everyday Life History and Culture   Communication

mother showered gifts on him. {<u>show</u> ər}

show-off *noun* someone who tries to get attention from others. *The show-off was always trying to get people to watch him do magic tricks.* {<u>shoh</u> awf}

show·y *adjective* (showier, showiest) 1. bright, colorful, or splendid in appearance. *Carnations are showy flowers.* 2. too colorful, bright, or fancy. *The bank does not allow its workers to wear showy neckties. / He has a showy way of playing the piano.* {<u>shoh</u> ee} showily, adv., showiness, n.

shrank *verb* a past tense of **shrink.** {<u>shrăngk</u>}

shred *noun* 1. a long strip that is torn or cut off, or almost torn off. *I can use a shred of cloth to tie up the curtain. / The dress was in shreds.* 2. a very tiny amount; scrap. *There was not a shred of truth in that story.* *verb* (shredded or shred, shredding, shreds) to cut or tear to shreds. *Please shred some lettuce for the salad.* {<u>shrehd</u>}

shrew *noun* a very small animal with a long, pointed nose and tiny eyes. Shrews are mammals that eat insects. Many kinds of shrews live in Europe, Asia, North America, and northern South America. Some shrews are smaller than any other kind of mammal. {<u>shrooh</u>}

shrewd *adjective* (shrewder, shrewdest) clever and careful. *A shrewd customer always looks for the best price before buying.* {<u>shroohd</u>} shrewdly, adv., shrewdness, n.

shriek *noun* a loud shrill cry of fear, joy, or surprise. *She let out a shriek when I jumped out from behind the door.*

verb (shrieked, shrieking, shrieks) to make a loud shrill cry. *The parrots shrieked at us from the trees.* {<u>shreek</u>}

shrill *adjective* having a high, sharp sound. *Please stop blowing that shrill whistle!* {<u>shrihl</u>}

shrimp *noun* (shrimp or shrimps) a small animal with a hard, jointed shell and five pairs of legs. Most kinds of shrimp live in the ocean, but a few kinds live in fresh water. Shrimp are crustaceans and are closely related to crabs and lobsters. Many people like to eat shrimp. *verb* (shrimped, shrimping, shrimps) to fish for shrimp. {<u>shrihmp</u>}

shrine *noun* 1. a sacred place or object that is devoted to some holy person or god. *The family worshipped at the shrine of their favorite saint.* 2. any place or object devoted to the honor and memory of some important person or event in history. *The Tomb of the Unknown Soldier is a national shrine.* {<u>shriyn</u>}

shrink *verb* (shrank or shrunk, shrunk or shrunken, shrinking, shrinks) 1. to become smaller. *Wool clothing shrinks in hot water.* 2. to avoid or draw back from something. *She shrank in fear from the growling wolf.* {<u>shringk</u>}

shriv·el *verb* (shriveled, shriveling, shrivels) to cause to wrinkle or become smaller. *The hot sun shriveled the tulips in the garden.* {<u>shrih</u> vəl}

shrub ❶ *noun* a plant with woody stems that branch out close to the ground; bush. A

shrub can be very short or as tall as a small tree. {<u>shruhb</u>}

shrug *verb* (shrugged, shrugging, shrugs) to raise the shoulders to show one does not know, does not care, or is not responsible. *noun* the motion of raising and drawing in the shoulders. *He didn't know the answer so he replied with a shrug.* {<u>shruhg</u>}

• **shrug off**
1. to act as if something does not matter. *The runner shrugged off his pain and continued on.* 2. to give up or get rid of. *She shrugged off her worries and went to a movie.* 3. to wiggle out of something worn on or over the shoulders. *The children shrugged off their jackets.*

shud·der *verb* (shuddered, shuddering, shudders) to tremble or give a sudden shiver. *The baby shuddered when she tasted a lemon.* *noun* a sudden, strong trembling. *A shudder of fear ran through me when I heard the howl.* {<u>shuhd</u> ər}

shuf·fle *verb* (shuffled, shuffling, shuffles) 1. to drag or scrape the feet along the floor while walking. *Holding their lunch trays, the children shuffled to their tables.* 2. to mix playing cards to change their order. *I shuffled the cards before dealing.* 3. to move or change the position of something in a quick, careless manner. *He shuffled the papers but did no real work.* *noun* an act of shuffling. *The dealer gave the cards a shuffle. / Grandfather walks with a shuffle.* {<u>sthuhf</u> əl}

• **lost in the shuffle**
forgotten, ignored, or lost in the general confusion. *I felt lost in the shuffle on my first day of middle school.*

shun *verb* (shunned, shunning, shuns) to keep away from or

a b c d e f g h i j k l m n o p q r **s** t u v w x y z

avoid on purpose. *He has shunned his brother for years. / She shuns foods that are not healthy.* {**shuhn**}

shut *verb* (shut, shutting, shuts) 1. to close by moving something that covers an opening. *Please shut the window.* 2. to close by folding the parts together. *Misha shut the book and looked up at me.* 3. to put in a place where movement is limited or difficult; confine or enclose. *Who shut the dog in the closet?* {**shuht**}

• **shut down**
to stop the operation of something. *The factory shut down for a month.*

• **shut off**
to stop the flow of. *Shut off the water when you are done washing the dishes.*

• **shut up**
to make or become quiet. *He shut up when I walked in.*

shut·ter *noun* 1. a wooden or metal cover that closes over the outside or inside of a window. 2. a device that opens and closes the lens of a camera. *The shutter opens to let light onto the film when a picture is taken.* {**shuht** ər}

shut·tle *noun* 1. a device used in weaving that carries thread back and forth through the threads on the loom. 2. a bus, airplane, train, or spacecraft that travels the same route back and forth. *verb* (shuttled, shuttling, shuttles) to move or cause to move back and forth. *The science teacher shuttled between the lab and the classroom.* {**shuht** əl}

shy *adjective* (shyer or shier, shyest or shiest) 1. not comfortable with other people. *The shy child did not talk to anyone in class.* 2. easily frightened. *A shy horse should not be ridden near traffic.* 3.

falling short of a necessary amount or number. *The team is shy a few players.* *verb* (shied, shying, shies) to draw back or away from in fear or lack of trust (often followed by "away"). *Their cat shies away from loud noises.* {**shiy**} shyly, adv., shyness, n.

Synonyms
These words share a meaning with *shy*, adjective 1:
reserved, timid, bashful

Siamese cat *noun* a breed of cat. Siamese cats are native to Thailand. They are known for their blue eyes and a pale gray or brown coat with darker ears, tail, and paws. {**siy** ə **meez** **kăt** *or* **siy** ə **mees** **kăt**}

Si·ber·i·a *noun* a region in northern Asia that goes from the Ural Mountains to the Pacific Ocean. Siberia is a part of Russia. {**siy** **beer** ee ə} Siberian, [adj.], n.

sick ⊕ *adjective* (sicker, sickest) 1. suffering from an illness; not well. *Phoebe was sick with a cold.* 2. suffering from a feeling of needing to throw up. *The carnival ride made him sick.* 3. tired, disgusted, or upset. *She is sick of practicing.* 4. having a mental illness. {**sihk**}

sick·le *noun* a tool with a long, sharp, curved blade and a short handle. It is used to cut grain and long grass. {**sihk** əl}

sick·ly *adjective* (sicklier, sickliest) 1. often sick; not strong or healthy. *The sickly child often had to stay in bed.* 2. having to do with or caused by sickness.

His skin had a sickly yellow color. {**sihk** lee}

sick·ness *noun* 1. the condition of being sick; illness. *There was a lot of sickness at school this month.* 2. a particular disease. *Measles is a sickness.* {**sihk** nihs}

side *noun* 1. one of the outer surfaces of an object, or one of the lines forming the border of a geometric shape. *I bumped the right side of your car while I was parking. / A triangle has three sides.* 2. the right or left half of a human or animal body. *He rolled over onto his side.* 3. an area or border that refers to a central point or space. *The boy moved to the side of the driveway to avoid the car.* 4. one of the ways a thing appears or is understood. *They each told a different side of the story.* 5. one of two opposing groups or opinions. *Are you on my side in this argument?* 6. one half of a family in relation to its history. *She is a cousin on my father's side.* *adjective* 1. at, on, towards, or from a side. *The people came in through the side doors.* 2. added to, or along with, the main part. *She ordered steak for supper and salad as a side dish. / Sleepiness is a side effect of some cold medicines.* *verb* (sided, siding, sides) to join one person or group of people that is against another person or group of people. *I sided with her because I thought she was right.* {**siyd**}

• **side by side**
next to each other. *They walked side by side.*

side·burns *plural noun* hair or whiskers growing along the

  Human Body 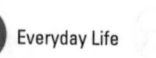 Human Mind  Everyday Life  History and Culture 📞 Communication

side of a man's face. {**siyd buhrnz**}

side·line *noun* 1. a line at the side of an area; the side boundary of a playing field. *The football player stepped over the sideline.* 2. a business or activity that a person carries out in his or her spare time. *His business was selling books, but he sold candles as a sideline.* {**siyd liyn**}

side·show *noun* a small, extra show connected to the main show. *We saw the sideshow at the circus.* {**siyd shoh**}

side·step *verb* (sidestepped, sidestepping, sidesteps) 1. to step aside or to one side. *I had to sidestep to avoid being hit by the bus.* 2. to avoid. *The witness sidestepped the question by changing the subject.* {**siyd stehp**}

side·walk *noun* a path for walking along the side of a street or road. Sidewalks are usually paved. {**siyd wŏk**}

side·ways *adverb* from, to, or toward the side. *He jumped sideways to avoid the charging bull.* *adjective* moving, facing, or angled toward one side. *Please turn that chair sideways so it faces forward like the others.* {**siyd wayz**}

• **look at someone sideways** to look at someone in a doubtful or suspicious way. *She looked at me sideways when I said I didn't care if anyone remembered my birthday.*

siege *noun* a military act of surrounding a city or base, attacking it, and cutting off supplies. The goal of a siege is to force the city or fort to surrender. {**seej**}

si·er·ra *noun* a chain of mountains with sharp peaks that look like the teeth of a saw. {**see ayr ə**}

sieve *noun* a tool used to separate solid from liquid or to separate smaller pieces of something from larger pieces. Sieves have small holes or wire mesh on the bottom. {**sihv**}

sift *verb* (sifted, sifting, sifts) 1. to spread or sprinkle using a sieve or as though using a sieve. *She sifted flour onto the dough.* / *The child sifted sand over her toes.* 2. to scatter or fall from a sieve or as though from a sieve. *Snow sifted through the tree branches onto the ground below.* {**sihft**} sifter, n.

sigh *verb* (sighed, sighing, sighs) 1. to breathe out with a long breath because of being sad, tired, or relieved. *The students sighed when the teacher gave them more homework.* 2. to make any sound like this. *The wind sighed in the trees.* *noun* the sound or act of sighing. *She gave a sigh of relief.* {**siy**}

sight *noun* 1. the ability to see; vision. *Pilots must have good sight.* 2. the act or an instance of seeing. *Do you believe in love at first sight?* 3. something that one sees. *The Grand Canyon is a beautiful sight.* 4. a range of view at a particular time. *A black cat came into sight from behind the building.* 5. a thing worth seeing; spectacle. *We saw the sights of the city.* 6. a device on a gun or telescope that is used to aim. *verb* (sighted, sighting, sights) to observe or suddenly see. *After two months at sea, we sighted land.* {**siyt**}

sight·less *adjective* not able to see; blind. *The sightless mole uses its whiskers to find its way in its burrow.* {**siyt lihs**}

sight·see·ing *noun* the act or hobby of visiting and seeing interesting places; touring. *Tanya made plans for sightseeing in Tokyo.* *adjective* having to do with, engaged in, or used for seeing sights. *The sightseeing tour took them to most of the interesting buildings in the city.* {**siyt see ing**} sightseer, n.

sign *noun* 1. something that shows or demonstrates a fact, event, or quality; indication. *Her smile was a sign that she agreed.* / *The bruise was a sign of injury.* 2. a mark or symbol that stands for a word or thing. *The sign "+" stands for addition.* 3. a printed direction, notice, or warning put on a surface or on an upright support. *I always obey stop signs.* / *Jane hung a for-sale sign on her car.* 4. something that relates to a future event or condition. *The return of robins is a sign of spring.* 5. a trace. *There were no signs of life in the cabin.* *verb* (signed,

A B C D E F G H I J K L M N O P Q R S T U V W X Y Z

a
b
c
d
e
f
g
h
i
j
k
l
m
n
o
p
q
r
s
t
u
v
w
x
y
z

signing, signs) 1. to write one's name on. *She signed the contract. / He signed the letter.* 2. to communicate with a sign or signal. *Many deaf people learn to sign with their hands.* {**siyn**}

• **sign up**
to join or cause to join a particular group, class, or activity; register. *We signed up for a dance class.*

sig·nal *noun* 1. a movement, action, or device used to give directions, warning, or other information. *We waited for the signal to cross the street. / She changed lanes without using her turn signal.* 2. an understood movement or other sign that is meant to start some action. *A raised flag was the signal to begin the race.* 3. electrical or sound waves that are sent or received. *The TV signal is weak in this area.* *adjective* acting as a signal. *The signal light is used to warn boats on the lake.* *verb* (signaled, signaling, signals) 1. to direct a signal to. *She signaled me to come closer.* 2. to make known or express with a signal. *The horn signaled the end of the game.* 3. to send a message by making a signal or signals. *The plane signaled that it was going to land.* {**sihg** nəl}

sig·na·ture *noun* 1. a person's written name, used to sign documents, letters, or checks. 2. a sign used to indicate the key or tempo of a piece of music. *Most waltzes are written in a 3/4 time signature.* {**sihg** nə chər}

sig·nif·i·cance *noun* 1. great value; importance. *This picture has significance for me.* 2. meaning. *The critic missed the significance of the entire play.* {sihg **nih** fə kəns}

si·lence *noun* 1. a lack of sound; quiet. *The teacher asked for silence.* 2. the fact or condition of not making sound or not speaking. *Her silence showed that she did not want to talk about it.* *verb* (silenced, silencing, silences) to make silent, calm, or still. *He silenced the dog with a bone.* {**siy** ləns}

si·lent *adjective* 1. making no sound. *The house was silent.* 2. not willing or wanting to speak. *She is a silent girl.* 3. unable to speak. *I was silent with rage.* 4. made known or expressed in ways other than speech. *He said a silent prayer.* 5. appearing as a letter in a word but not spoken when the word is said out loud. *There is a silent "h" in the word "honor."* {**siy** lənt} silently, adv.

sil·hou·ette *noun* 1. an outline or side view of a person's head that is filled with a dark, solid color. 2. any dark figure seen against a light background, so that details are hard to see. *The artist painted the silhouette of the city skyline at sunset.* *verb* (silhouetted, silhouetting, silhouettes) to outline or display in silhouette. *The sun silhouetted the trees against the sky.* {sih looh **eht**}

sil·i·con *noun* a hard, dark gray substance that is a chemical element. It is found in silica, a compound that makes up one fourth of the earth's crust. Silicon is used in making glass, concrete, bricks, and computer chips. (symbol: Si) {**sih** lih **kŏn** *or* **sih** lih kən}

silk *noun* 1. a fine, soft, shiny fiber produced by certain insects. *The silkworm makes silk as it spins its cocoon.* 2. thread, cloth, or clothing made of this material. *She bought a scarf made of silk.* 3. certain materials that are like threads of silk, such as the fine strands found on an ear of corn. *adjective* made of or having to do with silk. *You can't make a silk purse out of a sow's ear.* {**sihlk**}

silk·worm *noun* a caterpillar of a moth, originally from Asia. The caterpillar makes silk thread that it uses to spin its cocoon. People use the cocoons to make silk cloth. {**sihlk wuhrm**}

silk·y *adjective* (silkier, silkiest) of or like silk; smooth, delicate, or shiny. *He has silky black hair.* {**sihl** kee}

sill *noun* a horizontal strip or block serving as the bottom of a window or door frame. {**sihl**}

sil·ly *adjective* (sillier, silliest) without good sense; foolish. *He was silly enough to look in the refrigerator for his hat. / Silly ideas sometimes turn out to be good ideas.* {**sihl** ee}

Word History The meaning of *silly* has changed many times over the centuries. In the 1200s, it meant "happy, fortunate, or holy." It then came to mean "innocent," and then "helpless or weak." By the 1500s, it was used to mean "simple, ignorant, or foolish."

si·lo *noun* (silos) 1. a tall building that is used to store food for farm animals. Silos are often shaped like cylin-

 Human Body   Human Mind   Everyday Life   History and Culture    Communication

ders. 2. an underground place for storing and launching missiles. {**siy** loh}

silt *noun* fine particles of earth, clay, or sand that eventually settle out of water. {**sihlt**} silty, adj.

sil·ver ⬤ ⬤ *noun* 1. a shiny white metal that is soft and easy to shape. Silver is one of the chemical elements. It is used in making jewelry, coins, and table utensils. (symbol: Ag) 2. coins made of silver, used as money. *I like the jingle of silver in my pocket.* 3. knives, forks, spoons, and other table utensils made of or coated with silver; silverware. *We washed and dried the silver and then put it in the drawer.* 4. a color like that of silver. *adjective* 1. made of, coated with, or having silver. *The man paid his bill with a silver dollar.* 2. having the color or luster of silver. *Bob drives a silver car. / Barb has silver hair. verb* (silvered, silvering, silvers) to coat with a thin layer of silver. *The jeweler silvered the ring before setting a ruby in it.* {**sihl** vər}

sil·ver·smith *noun* a person who makes, plates, or fixes objects made of silver. {**sihl** vər **smih**th}

sil·ver·ware *noun* 1. knives, forks, and spoons. Silverware is used for eating and serving food. It can be made of or plated with silver or other metals. 2. other objects used for serving or eating food. Such silverware is also made of or plated with silver or other metals. {**sihl** vər **wayr**}

sim·i·lar *adjective* having resemblance or likeness. *Lee's handwriting is similar to mine.* {**sihm** ə lər} similarly, adv.

sim·i·lar·i·ty *noun* (similarities) 1. the state or quality of being similar; resemblance.

There was no similarity between this crime and the one last week. 2. a specific point or instance of likeness. *One similarity among mammals is that they are warm-blooded.* {**sihm** ə **lar** ih tee}

sim·i·le *noun* a figure of speech in which two different things are compared by using the words "like" or "as." "The cake was as light as a feather" is an example of a simile. {**sihm** ə lee}

sim·mer *verb* (simmered, simmering, simmers) to cook in a liquid that is kept near the boiling point. *I simmered the pasta for several minutes.* {**sihm** ər}

• **simmer down** to become calmer after some excitement. *It was difficult for us to simmer down after the fun at the amusement park.*

sim·ple *adjective* (simpler, simplest) 1. easy to do or understand; not complicated. *Last year I thought this simple math problem was difficult!* 2. made of only one part or thing. *A lever is a simple machine.* 3. ordinary or common. *It was a simple dress, not fancy.* {**sihm** pəl} simply, adv.

simple sentence *noun* a sentence that has only one clause. "We waited for the bus early in the morning" is an example of a simple sentence. {**sihm** pəl **sehn** təns}

sim·plic·i·ty *noun* (simplicities) 1. the condition or quality of being simple. *The simplicity of the instructions helped us assemble the bike quickly.* 2. the quality of being sincere and humble; natural. *The president spoke with honest simplicity.* {**sihm** **plih** sih tee}

sim·pli·fy *verb* (simplified, simplifying, simplifies) to make plainer, easier, or less complex. *I simplified the game so*

that my younger brother could play. {**sihm** plih **fiy**}

sim·ply *adverb* 1. in a simple, clear way. *I gave the directions simply so that everyone would understand.* 2. in a plain or honest way. *The farmer dressed simply. / She spoke simply of her love for the land.* 3. only; just. *I'm not sick, I'm simply tired.* 4. absolutely. *That new book is simply wonderful.* {**sihm** plee}

si·mul·ta·ne·ous *adjective* existing, happening, or done at the same time. *The gymnasts all did a simultaneous flip.* {**siy** məl **tay** nee əs}

sin *noun* an act of not obeying religious law. *According to the Bible, it is a sin to kill. verb* (sinned, sinning, sins) to disobey a religious law. *She believed she had sinned when she lied to her parents.* {**sihn**}

since *adverb* 1. from then until now (often follows the word "ever"). *He was in a school play and has been an actor ever since.* 2. at some time between a past time and now. *He left for college but has since returned. preposition* after a general or particular past time. *There have been many changes since then. conjunction* 1. in the time following the time when. *I have been hungry since I smelled the cookies baking.* 2. because. *Since we are late, we will have to hurry.* {**sihns**}

sin·cere *adjective* (sincerer, sincerest) genuine, true, and not pretended. *The mayor took a sincere interest in the people and their problems.* {**sihn** **seer**} sincerely, adv.

sin·ew *noun* a **tendon**. {**sihn** yoo}

sing ⬤ ⬤ *verb* (sang, sung, singing, sings) 1. to make musical sounds with the voice. *She sings in the shower.* 2. to perform as a singer. *The*

chorus sang during intermission. 3. to produce musical sound of particular beauty. *That trumpet really sings!* 4. to state or announce with great enthusiasm. *After the home-run, the coach was singing my praises.* {**sing**}

Sin·ga·pore *noun* 1. a country in southeastern Asia. 2. the capital city of the country of Singapore. {**sing** ə **pohr** *or* **sing** gə **pohr**}

sing·er *noun* 1. a person who sings as a job or hobby. 2. a bird, insect, or other animal that sings. {**sing** ər}

sin·gle *adjective* 1. only one. *He had only a single dime left in his bank.* 2. of or for one person. *He got a single room at the motel.* 3. considered as a separate or individual thing. *Every single person had a good time at the party.* 4. not married. *My aunt is single.* *verb* (singled, singling, singles) 1. to choose or pick from others (usually followed by "out"). *She singled out a dress to buy.* 2. to hit the ball in a baseball or softball game so as to reach first base. *After striking out three times, he finally singled.* *noun* 1. one person or thing. 2. a hit in baseball or softball with which the batter gets to first base. {**sing** gəL}

sin·gle-hand·ed *adjective* done without help. *His single-handed attempt to carry all the boxes ruined his back.* *adverb* alone and without help. *She moved the furniture single-handed.* {**sing** gəl **hăn** dihd} single-handedly, adv.

sin·gle-mind·ed *adjective* focused on a single goal or purpose. *My brother was single-minded in pursuit of his goal to swim across the English Channel.* {**sing** gəl **miyn** dihd}

sin·gu·lar *adjective* having to do with or designating the form of a word that indicates only one. *The word "kitten" is a singular noun.* *noun* the form of a word that names or refers to only one person or thing. *You used the plural, "dogs," when you should have used the singular, "dog."* {**sing** gyə lər}

sin·is·ter *adjective* threatening or suggesting evil, injury, or danger; ominous. *In the movie, the villain looked sinister.* {**sih** nih stər}

sink  *verb* (sank *or* sunk, sunk, sinking, sinks) 1. to fall or drop slowly to another level. *We watched the rock sink in the pond.* 2. to cause to fall or drop to a lower level. *The golfer sank the ball in the hole.* 3. to settle into or become covered by another substance (often followed by "in" or "into"). *The truck's wheels sank into the mud.* 4. to cause to become submerged in another substance. *They sank the boat in the lake.* 5. to become less strong. *His voice sank when he entered the library.* 6. to enter the mind gradually (usually followed by "in"). *The meaning of the riddle finally sank in.* 7. to bury or plant in the ground. *They sank the drill deep in the ground while looking for oil.* *noun* a fixed basin connected to a water supply and a drain. *Wash your hands in the sink.* {**singk**}

si·nus *noun* (sinuses) any of the hollow places in the skull that connect with the nose. {**siy** nəs}

Sioux *noun* (Sioux) a member of a group of American Indian peoples who are from the plains of the northern United States and southern Canada. {**sooh**}

> **Homophone Note** The words *Sioux* and *sue* (to start legal action) sound alike but have different meanings.

sip *verb* (sipped, sipping, sips) to drink slowly and a little at a time. *The toddler sipped the juice.* *noun* 1. the act or an instance of sipping. *Take small sips until your throat feels better.* 2. a quantity of liquid sipped. *I would like to try a sip of the cranberry juice.* {**sihp**}

si·phon *noun* a tube or pipe used to suck a liquid over the top of its container and into a lower one by means of air pressure. *We had to use a siphon to refill our gas tank when we were driving in the wilderness.* *verb* (siphoned, siphoning, siphons) to draw off or move with a siphon or as if with a siphon. *I siphon half of the water out of my fish tank every week and replace it with fresh water.* {**siy** fən}

sir *noun* 1. (often capitalized) a form of address for a man, usually used in place of his name. *Excuse me, sir, do you know the time?* 2. (capitalized) a title of honor for a knight used with his name. *Sir Walter Raleigh was made a knight by Queen Elizabeth I.* {**suhr**}

si·ren *noun* a warning device that makes a loud, piercing noise. Emergency vehicles and police cars have sirens. {**siyr** ən}

Sir·i·us *noun* the brightest star in the sky. Sirius is in the constellation Canis Major and is also called the Dog Star. {**seer** ee əs}

sis·sy *noun* (sissies) a coward. {**sih** see}

sis·ter *noun* 1. a female having the same parents as

 Human Body    Human Mind   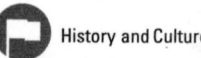 Everyday Life    History and Culture   Communication

another person. 2. a female who is bound to another or others by a common interest or through an organization. 3. a nun. {**sihs** tər}

sis·ter·hood *noun* 1. the relationship between or among sisters. *Sisterhood can be a strong and lasting bond.* 2. a group or organization of women. *She joined the sisterhood at her church.* {**sihs** tər **huud**}

sis·ter-in-law *noun* (sisters-in-law) 1. the sister of one's husband or wife. 2. the wife of one's brother. {**sihs** tər ihn **law**}

sit *verb* (sat, sitting, sits) 1. to be in a position in which one is resting on the buttocks and thighs. *She sat in a chair.* 2. to cause to be seated. *Nancy sat herself close to me.* 3. to be placed or located. *His ranch sits on top of the hill.* 4. to meet or hold a session. *This court will sit again in two weeks.* 5. to hold a position for an artist or photographer. *He sat for a portrait.* 6. to take care of a child while its parents are away; babysit. *When our parents go out, my aunt sits for us.* {**siht**}

site *noun* the location or proposed location of a town, city, building, or event. *The site on the mountain would be a good place for a ski area.* {**siyt**}

Homophone Note The words *site*, *cite*, and *sight* sound alike but have different meanings.

sit·u·a·tion *noun* state of affairs; circumstances. *The snowstorm put the drivers in a dangerous situation.* {**sih** chooh **ay** shən}

sit-up *noun* (sit-ups) an exercise for the stomach muscles. To do a sit-up, a person lies flat

on the back and sits up without bending the legs or using the arms. {**siht** uhp}

six *noun* the number that comes after 5 and before 7 in the sequence of cardinal numbers; 6. *adjective* being six in number. *I have six notebooks for school.* {**sihks**}

six·teen *noun* the number that comes after 15 and before 17 in the sequence of cardinal numbers; 16. *adjective* being sixteen in number. *My cat is sixteen months old.* {sihks **teen**}

six·teenth *adjective* coming next after the fifteenth in a series. *She took the elevator to the sixteenth floor.* *noun* 1. one of sixteen equal parts of a whole; 1/16. *She used a wrench that was one sixteenth of an inch wide.* 2. the number, person, or thing that comes next after the fifteenth in a series. *My car is the sixteenth from the edge of the parking lot.* {sihks **teenth**}

sixth *adjective* coming next after the fifth in a series. *They gave a prize to the sixth person to walk through the door.* *noun* 1. one of six equal parts of a whole; 1/6. *We divided the pie into sixths.* 2. the number, person, or thing that comes next after the fifth in a series. *I was the sixth to sign up for the basketball team.* {sihks **sth**}

six·ti·eth *adjective* coming next after the fifty-ninth in a series. *Today is my grandmother's sixtieth birthday.* *noun* 1. one of sixty equal parts of a whole; 1/60. *A minute is one sixtieth of an hour.* 2. the number, person, or thing that comes next after the fifty-ninth in a series. *I stopped counting sheep after the sixtieth.* {**sihks** tee ihth}

six·ty *noun* (sixties) the number that is equal to six times ten; 60. *adjective* being sixty in

number. *There are sixty minutes in an hour.* {**sihks** tee}

siz·a·ble *adjective* of large size or quantity; big. *She bought a sizable piece of land.* {**siyz** ə bəl}

size *noun* 1. the physical dimensions of anything. *The size of his ears was smaller than average.* 2. a measure of largeness or smallness according to a numbered scale. *What is your shirt size?* 3. amount, quantity, or dimension. *The size of her salary made her feel successful.* {**siyz**}

siz·zle *verb* (sizzled, sizzling, sizzles) to make the hissing or crackling sound of frying fat or oils. *When the grease sizzled, we knew the pan was hot.* {**sihz** əl}

skate[1] *noun* a shoe with either a blade or a set of small wheels attached to the bottom. Skates are used to move on ice or other hard surfaces. *I use a pair of ice skates in the winter and a pair of roller skates when there isn't any ice.* *verb* (skated, skating, skates) to move along on ice skates or roller skates, or as though on such skates; glide or skim. *I skate three times each week during January. / The boat skated over the water.* {**skayt**} skater, n.

skate[2] *noun* a kind of fish that has a skeleton of cartilage, a flat body, fins that look like wings, and a pointed snout. Skates live along the western coast of the United States. {**skayt**}

skate·board *noun* a flat, short, narrow board that has four wheels on the bottom. People stand to ride on a skateboard. {**skayt** bohrd} skateboarder, n.

skein *noun* a length of yarn or thread wound in a long, loose loop before it is knitted

A
B
C
D
E
F
G
H
I
J
K
L
M
N
O
P
Q
R
S
T
U
V
W
X
Y
Z

or woven. *The cat unwound an entire skein of yarn before we noticed.* {skayn}

skel·e·ton *noun* 1. the inner framework of bones and cartilage in vertebrate animals. Skeletons support the body and protect softer body parts. 2. a supporting framework. *The carpenters built the skeleton of the house out of rough lumber.* {skehl ə tən} skeletal, *adj.*

Word History *Skeleton* comes from *skeletos,* an ancient Greek word that means "dried up."

skep·ti·cal *adjective* having or showing doubt; questioning. *I was skeptical of the salesman and refused to buy the knives.* {skehp tih kəl}

sketch *noun* 1. a drawing or painting that was done in a hurry or without detail. Sketches are sometimes done to prepare for later work. *The artist made a sketch of the same bull several times to prepare for his greatest painting.* 2. a quick or rough design, outline, or draft for a written work. *The writer put together a rough sketch of how she wanted the novel to go.* 3. a brief story or other composition performed as part of a series in a theater. *My favorite sketch was the one about the clown.* *verb* (sketched, sketching, sketches) 1. to make a preliminary drawing, draft, or outline of. *This author always sketches the plot before she begins to write a book.* 2. to make a sketch or sketches. *The artist sketched all day at the dog show.* {skehch}

sketch·y *adjective* (sketchier, sketchiest) 1. giving only outlines or major points; like a sketch. *Here are some sketchy thoughts I've been working on for the report.* 2. slight, not complete, or not perfect. *Her sketchy understanding of the topic explains her terrible grade on the test.* {skehch ee}

ski 🔵 *noun* (skis) 1. one of a pair of long, narrow, smooth runners. Skis have curved front tips and are attached to boots and used to glide over snow. 2. see water ski. *verb* (skied, skiing, skis) to move over snow on skis. *They skied down the mountain together.* {skee}

skid *noun* a sudden, sideways sliding of a vehicle. *It was scary when the car went into a skid.* *verb* (skidded, skidding, skids) to slide suddenly sideways, as a vehicle that has lost traction. *The truck skidded into the restaurant during the blizzard.* {skihd}

skill *noun* 1. the power or ability to perform a task well, especially because of training or practice. *After taking this class, her writing skills have improved.* 2. a kind of work or craft that requires special care and training. *Painting is a skill.* {skihl}

skilled *adjective* 1. having skill. *We hired a skilled carpenter to build our new cabinets.* 2. requiring skill. *The factory is hiring for skilled jobs.* {skihld}

skil·let *noun* a shallow pan with a long handle, used for frying food; frying pan. {skihl iht}

skill·ful or **skilful** *adjective* having or using skill; adept. *He is a skillful mechanic and can fix any car.* {skihl fəl} skillfully (skilfully), *adv.*

skim *verb* (skimmed, skimming, skims) 1. to remove from the surface of a liquid, or to clear the surface of by removing fat or other floating matter. *She skimmed fat from the gravy. / He skimmed the soup.* 2. to fly or glide over in a light way. *Birds skimmed the waves.* 3. to glance through in a hurry or without attention. *I only skimmed the chapter but still did fine on the quiz.* 4. to throw so that a liquid surface is only touched in a brief or light way. *My friend can skim a stone halfway across the river.* {skihm}

skim milk *noun* milk from which the cream has been separated. {skihm mihlk}

skin 🔵 *noun* 1. the thin tissue covering the body of a person or animal. 2. the outer covering of some fruits and vegetables. *The skin of an apple can be red, green, or yellow.* 3. the skin and fur removed from an animal. *We have a rug made of bear skin in our living room.* *verb* (skinned, skinning, skins) 1. to remove the skin from. *He skinned the deer.* 2. to scrape skin from, by accident. *She skinned her arm when she fell.* {skihn}

• **have a thin skin** to be very easily offended. *She has a thin skin, so don't criticize her too harshly.*

skin diving *noun* swimming in which the swimmer uses flippers, a face mask, and an air tank to swim underwater quickly and easily. {skihn diy ving}

 Human Body Human Mind Everyday Life  History and Culture 🔵 Communication

skin·ny *adjective* (skinnier, skinniest) very thin and bony. *He became quite skinny while he was ill.* {<u>skihn</u> ee}

skip *verb* (skipped, skipping, skips) 1. to jump forward lightly by sliding and hopping on one foot and then the other. *The children skipped down the sidewalk.* 2. to jump or pass lightly over without touching or staying on. *She skipped every other step as she ran up the stairs.* 3. to jump about from one thing to another, ignoring or leaving out important details. *The speaker skipped from one idea to the next in her speech.* 4. to miss or leave out. *She skipped the fourth grade.* 5. to bounce lightly over or along a surface. *The boat skipped across the waves.* 6. to cause to skim across the surface of water. *The children like to skip stones across the river.* 7. to fail to attend. *Maura skipped hockey practice. / They skipped class but got caught.* *noun* a skipping step, or bounce. *He crossed the room in three skips.* {<u>skihp</u>}

skirt ⊙ *noun* 1. a piece of clothing that hangs from the waist and is worn by a woman or girl. *She wore a blouse and skirt.* 2. the part of a piece of clothing such as a dress or jacket that hangs down from the waist. *verb* (skirted, skirting, skirts) 1. to be located on the edge of. *Thick forests skirt the town.* 2. to go around rather than through or into. *The road skirts the city.* {<u>skuhrt</u>}

skit *noun* 1. a short, usually funny play. *We did skits about our group leaders at camp.* 2. a short, funny piece of literature. {<u>skiht</u>}

skit·tish *adjective* easily startled or excited. *The colt was skit-*tish until he became accustomed to the farm.* {<u>skiht</u> ihsh}

skull ⊕ *noun* the bony framework of the head and face that protects the brain. {<u>skuhl</u>}

skunk *noun* 1. a small mammal with black and white fur and a bushy tail. Skunks defend themselves with a spray that smells very bad. They are active at night, when they hunt rodents, insects, and eggs. Several kinds of skunks live in North and South America. They are related to badgers, otters, and other kinds of weasels. 2. a person who has done something mean or nasty. {<u>skungk</u>}

sky ⊕ *noun* (skies) 1. the air or space above the earth which appears to arch over it. *We saw a kite moving in the sky.* 2. (often plural) the way the air above looks with respect to the weather. *We will have blue skies this week.* {<u>skiy</u>}

sky diving *noun* the sport of jumping from an airplane and falling for a while before opening the parachute. {<u>skiy</u> diyv ing} sky diver, n.

sky·light *noun* a window in a roof or ceiling. Skylights let in light. {<u>skiy</u> liyt}

sky·line *noun* 1. the line formed by the apparent boundary between the earth and the sky; horizon. 2. the outline of natural or man-made structures against the sky. *The Space Needle is a unique feature of Seattle's skyline.* {<u>skiy</u> liyn}

sky·rock·et *noun* an explosive that shoots high in the air before exploding in a shower of bright, colored sparks. *verb* (skyrocketed, skyrocketing, skyrockets) to rise or cause to rise with the speed, suddenness, and height of a rocket. *His fame skyrocketed after his movie was released.* {<u>skiy</u> ro kiht}

sky·scrap·er *noun* a very tall building. *The world's tallest skyscraper is in Malaysia.* {<u>skiy</u> skray pər}

slab *noun* a flat, wide, and thick piece of some solid. Rocks and foods can be slabs. *Concrete slabs were the foundation of the road. / He took a big slab of meat from the barbeque.* {<u>slăb</u>}

slack *adjective* 1. not tight; hanging loose; drooping. *His slack jaw indicated surprise. / The slack sail showed that there was not enough wind.* 2. moving in a slow or lazy way. *The wide river has a slack current.* *noun* a thing or part that hangs loosely. *Pull the slack of the rope to turn on the light.* *verb* (slacked, slacking, slacks) to avoid or not do because one is lazy or does not care. *He slacked in his duty to take care of his dog.* {<u>slăk</u>} slacker, n.

slacks *plural noun* casual pants for men or women. *He needs a new pair of black slacks since he wore through the knees on his other pair.* {<u>slăks</u>}

slam *verb* (slammed, slamming, slams) 1. to shut with force and loud noise. *I slammed the door because I was furious.* 2. to hit, drop, or throw with a loud or forceful impact. *The driver slammed the truck into a tree. / She slammed the ball into left field.* 3. to hit, drop, or throw with force and noise. *He slammed into the wall with his bike.* *noun* a movement that makes a loud noise on impact, or the noise itself. *The slam of the ocean waves against the rocks kept us awake.* {<u>slăm</u>}

A B C D E F G H I J K L M N O P Q R S T U V W X Y Z

a
b
c
d
e
f
g
h
i
j
k
l
m
n
o
p
q
r
s
t
u
v
w
x
y
z

slan·der *noun* a false statement or statements made to hurt someone's reputation, or the act of making such statements. *I can't believe the newspaper published that slander.* *verb* (slandered, slandering, slanders) to make damaging statements about. *The mayor claimed the the council member slandered her.* {**slăn** dər}

slang 🌐 *noun* very informal speech that is made up of new words, or new meanings of old words. Slang is not appropriate for serious conversation or writing. *Try not to use slang when giving your speech at the governor's mansion.* {**slăng**}

slant *verb* (slanted, slanting, slants) to be at a leaning or tilting angle. *The roof of the shed slants to the ground. / My pencil slants when I hold it correctly.* *noun* a slope or incline. *The slant of the hill was too steep for the tractor.* {**slănt**}

slap *noun* 1. a sharp blow with an open hand that makes a cracking sound. *She pretended to give him a slap on the face.* 2. the sound of such a blow. *There was a loud slap when he batted the volleyball with his hand.* *verb* (slapped, slapping, slaps) 1. to hit with a flat surface. *She slapped the mosquito when it landed on her arm.* 2. to hit against something with the sound of a slap. *The waves slapped against the shore.* 3. to put or throw down with the sound of a slap. *She slapped her papers down on the desk.* {**slăp**}

slap·dash *adjective* done or made in a hurry and without attention. *The teacher was not pleased with his slapdash homework.* {**slăp** dăsh}

slash *verb* (slashed, slashing, slashes) 1. to cut or strike with a strong, sweeping motion. *The criminal slashed the tires of the cars.* 2. to sharply reduce; cut. *The new theater manager slashed the price of a ticket by two dollars.* *noun* 1. a cut, slit, or mark made with the stroke of a sharp instrument. *The slashes on that tree trunk look as if they'd been made by a bear.* 2. a sharp reduction. *We were able to buy a new car because of the slash in prices.* 3. a punctuation mark (/). It has the meaning of "or" as in "and/or" or "per" as in "miles/hour." This mark is also used to show division in math and to separate parts of an internet address. {**slăsh**} slasher, n.

slat *noun* a long, narrow strip of wood or metal. Slats can be used to make flat surfaces, such as mattress supports, window covers, and bench or chair backs. {**slăt**}

slate *noun* 1. a rock that tends to split in smooth layers. 2. a piece of this rock, or something made from it. Chalkboards and roof tiles can be made of slate. 3. a dark or bluish gray color. {**slayt**}

• **clean slate**
1. an honorable record. *The mayor started his term with a clean slate.* 2. a record cleared of any negative information. *Because the student's behavior improved, the principal decided to give him a clean slate.*

slaugh·ter *noun* 1. the killing and butchering of animals for food. *The rancher sent his cattle to slaughter.* 2. the brutal killing of large numbers of people or animals; massacre. *Many were grieved by the slaughter of so many soldiers in battle.* *verb* (slaugh-

tered, slaughtering, slaughters) 1. to kill and butcher for food. *We slaughtered a chicken for the feast.* 2. to kill brutally and in large numbers. {**slaw** tər}

slave *noun* 1. a person who is owned by and forced to work for another with no pay or rights. 2. a person who is under the control of some habit or other power. *He is a slave to television.* 3. a person who works very hard and without using the imagination. *He is a factory slave.* *verb* (slaved, slaving, slaves) to work like a slave. *She slaved all day without reward.* {**slayv**}

Word History The word *slave* comes from *Slav*, a word for the people who lived in east-central Europe in the Middle Ages. Great numbers of Slavs were bought and sold as slaves by conquering peoples from the West.

slav·er·y *noun* 1. the owning of people by other people; bondage. *Frederick Douglass called for an end to slavery.* 2. the state or condition of being a slave. *The Civil War resulted in the freeing of many black people from slavery.* 3. very hard work. {**slay** və ree *or* **slayv** ree}

slay *verb* (slew, slain, slaying, slays) to kill deliberately and violently. *The knight slayed the dragon.* {**slay**}

Homophone Note Are you looking for the word *sleigh* (a horse-drawn sled)? *Slay* and *sleigh* sound alike but have different meanings.

sled *noun* a low platform of wood or other material that slides on blades and is used to

 Human Body   Human Mind   Everyday Life   🚩 History and Culture   📞 Communication

travel over snow and ice. *verb* (sledded, sledding, sleds) to use a sled. *We sledded together down the hill.* {slehd}

sledge·ham·mer *noun* a large, heavy hammer that has a long handle. A sledgehammer is held with both hands and used for such tasks as driving posts into the ground. {slehj hăm ər}

sleek *adjective* (sleeker, sleekest) 1. smooth or shiny. *Muskrats have sleek fur that repels water.* 2. healthy and well fed. *The basketball players all looked sleek and fit.* {sleek}

sleep 🌐 ❓ *verb* (slept, sleeping, sleep) 1. to be in the state of rest for the body and mind in which the eyes are closed and one is not fully conscious. *I will sleep when I get tired.* 2. to be not active or not aware. *noun* 1. the condition of a person or animal that is sleeping. *I went to bed early to get plenty of sleep.* 2. any state of being completely without activity. *The hibernation of animals is sometimes called sleep.* {sleep}

sleeping bag *noun* a large bag with a warm lining and a zipper used to sleep in outdoors. {sleep ing băg}

sleep·y *adjective* (sleepier, sleepiest) 1. in need of or starting to sleep. *Reading a boring book makes me sleepy.* 2. not active; dull. *They lived in a sleepy little town.* {sleep ee} sleepily, adv., sleepiness, n.

sleet 🌐 *noun* freezing rain. *verb* (sleeted, sleeting, sleets) to fall as freezing rain. *It's sleeting, so drive carefully!* {sleet}

sleeve *noun* the part of a shirt, dress, or other garment that covers all or part of the arm. {sleev} sleeveless, adj.

• **up one's sleeve**

held secretly or in reserve. *I've got one more trick up my sleeve.*

sleigh *noun* a light cart on runners that is used to carry people over snow and ice. Horses pull sleighs. {slay}

Homophone Note The words *sleigh* and *slay* (to kill) sound alike but have different meanings.

slen·der *adjective* (slenderer, slenderest) 1. slim in an attractive way. *She looked slender in the black dress.* 2. small in width. *There is only enough room for a slender book on the shelf.* 3. of a limited measure or amount. *We won by a slender margin.* {slehn dər}

slice *noun* 1. a broad and flat piece of a larger object. Slices may also be shaped like wedges. *I'd like one slice of bread and two slices of pie for lunch.* 2. a part or segment of anything. *The employees demanded a slice of the company's profits.* *verb* (sliced, slicing, slices) 1. to divide into slices. *Will you slice the cake?* 2. to take from a larger portion by cutting (sometimes followed by "off," "from," or "away"). *He sliced some cheese off the block.* 3. to use a knife or something like a knife to cut into or across. *The surgeon sliced the skin.* 4. to move swiftly and in a straight line. *The speed boat sliced through the waves.* {sliys} slicer, n.

slick¹ *adjective* (slicker, slickest) having a smooth, shiny, or slippery surface. *The roads were slick with ice.* *noun* an area with a slippery surface, or the substance that makes it slippery. *The leak in the car left an oil slick on the driveway.* {slihk}

slick² *verb* (slicked, slicking, slicks) to give a smooth or slippery surface to. *He slicked down his hair with oil.* {slihk}

slide *verb* (slid, sliding, slides) 1. to move easily along a surface. *The children were sliding on the ice.* 2. to send slipping over a smooth surface. *Slide your car keys across the table.* 3. to slip or slip down by accident. *The car slid on the wet road. / The baby's diaper was sliding down.* 4. to fall from a running position and move along the ground toward a base in baseball or softball. *He slid into home and beat the throw.* 5. to move without being noticed. *No one saw her slide into the car.* 6. to give quietly so as to avoid being noticed. *She slid the coins into his hand. noun* 1. the act or movement of sliding. *We went for a slide down the hill on our sleds.* 2. a smooth, sloping track down which a person or thing can slide; chute. *There are slides and swings in the playground.* 3. a small piece of glass that holds an item so that it can be looked at under a microscope. 4. a piece of film on which there is a picture or diagram that may be shown on a screen. *We showed the slides from our vacation.* 5. a landslide, or the rocks and earth that move during one. {sliyd}

slight *adjective* (slighter, slightest) 1. small in amount or degree. *The slight wind ruffled her hair.* 2. not important; insignificant. *He made a slight error on the test but still got a good grade.* 3. thin; slender. *Most jockeys have a slight build.* *verb* (slighted, slighting, slights) to give little attention to. *She is slighting her work today.*

A B C D E F G H I J K L M N O P Q R **S** T U V W X Y Z

noun an act of ignoring another or treating with neglect; snub. *She didn't invite me to the party and I was confused by the slight.* {sli̱yt} **slightly,** *adv.*

slim *adjective* (slimmer, slimmest) 1. attractively thin in form; slender. *The slim boy looked fit in his uniform.* 2. of small size, amount, or value; slight. *The team had slim hopes for a victory. / My parents gave me a very slim allowance.* *verb* (slimmed, slimming, slims) to make or become slim or slimmer (usually followed by "down"). *It's hard to slim down when there are still Christmas cookies in the house.* {sli̱hm}

> **Word History** *Slim* comes from *slimp*, an early Dutch word that means "bad or crooked."

slime *noun* a slippery liquid, such as thin mud or the slippery substance on fish. *People often find slime disgusting.* {sli̱ym}

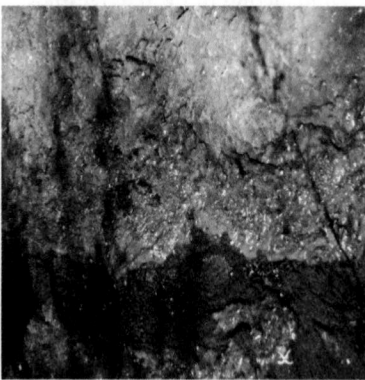

slim·y *adjective* (slimier, slimiest) 1. made of or like slime. *The seaweed felt slimy.* 2. evil or disgusting. *The actor played a slimy villain.* {sli̱y mee}

sling *noun* 1. a broad piece of cloth that is tied around the neck to support an injured arm or hand. *The ice skater wore a sling after falling and* breaking her wrist. 2. a leather loop used to throw a stone or other small object. *verb* (slung, slinging, slings) 1. to throw with force; hurl. *He slung the stone at the target. / I'll sling the rope over the branch for you to catch.* 2. to lift, support, or move with a sling. *They slung the cargo onto the barge.* {sli̱ng}

sling·shot *noun* a small weapon shaped like a Y with a piece of elastic attached to the branches of the Y. Slingshots are held in the hand and are used to shoot stones or other small objects. {sli̱ng shŏt}

slip[1] *verb* (slipped, slipping, slips) 1. to move smoothly or easily. *The cowboy slipped the rope around the calf's leg.* 2. to cause to move with an easy or sliding motion. *They slipped the canoe onto the sand.* 3. to move or leave without being noticed. *She slipped out of her seat.* 4. to slide suddenly, as on a slippery surface. *I slipped on the ice.* 5. to become worse or more weak. *Her health is slipping.* 6. to make a mistake. *He slipped on the math test.* 7. to pass or put quickly or quietly. *Grandma slipped a five-dollar bill into my pocket.* 8. to put on or take off quickly or casually. *The visitor slipped his coat off.* 9. to fail to be remembered by. *Her name slips my mind.* *noun* 1. the act or an instance of slipping. *One slip was all it took to break his hip.* 2. a mental mistake. *The bookkeeper added the numbers wrong but, luckily, he caught his slip.* 3. a slight mistake in speaking. *Saying, "I spent all my funny," is a slip of the tongue.* 4. an item of clothing worn under a dress or skirt. {sli̱hp}

• **give someone the slip**

to escape from. *The police looked for the crook but he gave them the slip.*

slip[2] *noun* 1. a small piece of paper on which messages or information may be written. *He found the slip with her phone number on it.* 2. a cutting from a plant. *verb* (slipped, slipping, slips) to make or take slips from. *She slipped her spider plant and put the cutting in water.* {sli̱hp}

slip·per *noun* any small, flat shoe that may be easily put on and taken off. Slippers are indoor shoes. {sli̱hp ər}

slip·per·y *adjective* (slipperier, slipperiest) 1. having a slick surface that is difficult to move upon without sliding. *These steps are slippery in winter.* 2. difficult to grasp because of a slick surface. *The slippery piece of soap was hard to hold in the shower.* 3. not to be trusted; dishonest. *The salesperson seemed like a slippery character.* {sli̱hp ə ree}

slip·shod *adjective* carelessly done or made. *The repairs were slipshod, and I had to have them done again.* {sli̱hp shŏd}

slit *verb* (slit, slitting, slits) to cut a long straight line into or through. *We'll slit the lime and squeeze out the juice.* *noun* a long straight cut or opening. *There's a slit in her skirt.* {sli̱ht}

slith·er *verb* (slithered, slithering, slithers) to move by twisting and sliding along a surface. *The snake slithered across the road.* {sli̱hth ər}

sliv·er *noun* a small, thin splinter of wood or glass that has broken off. *That rough wooden handle left slivers in my hand.* {sli̱hv ər}

slo·gan *noun* a short phrase used to state a principle or polit-

 Human Body   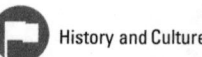 Human Mind   Everyday Life   History and Culture    Communication

ical message or to advertise a product; motto. *"I like Ike" was the campaign slogan for President Dwight Eisenhower.* {<u>sloh</u> gən}

Word History *Slogan* comes from *slogorne*, an early Scottish Gaelic word that meant "war cry."

sloop *noun* a sailboat that has one mast and sails that reach from one end of the boat to the other. {<u>sloohp</u>}

slop *verb* (slopped, slopping, slops) 1. to cause to spill or splash. *The baby slopped mashed peas in her hair.* 2. to splash or spill over. *The water slopped on the ground when we carried the full bucket. noun* (usually plural) a thin soup or food scraps fed to animals. *The farmer brought slops out to the pigs.* {<u>slŏp</u>}

slope *verb* (sloped, sloping, slopes) to slant up or down. *The trail slopes down to the pond. noun* 1. ground that is not level or flat; side of a hill. *We climbed up the grassy slope.* 2. the amount that something slants or slopes. *The road has a steep slope here.* 3. any surface that is set at an angle. *I sat on the slope of the roof and watched the stars.* {<u>slohp</u>}

slop·py *adjective* (sloppier, sloppiest) 1. wet or muddy. *The roads were sloppy when the snow started to melt.* 2. not maintained well; messy or not tidy. *My bedroom looks sloppy when I don't put my clothes away.* 3. careless or inferior. *That restaurant is known for its sloppy service. / My painting was a sloppy piece of work.* {<u>slŏp</u> ee} sloppiness, n.

slot *noun* a long, narrow notch or opening into which something may be put. *The mail goes in this slot. / The coin slot on the parking meter was jammed.* {<u>slŏt</u>}

sloth *noun* 1. laziness; not liking work or exercise. *Sloth caused me to watch TV when I should have been doing homework.* 2. a mammal that spends its entire life in trees, using its long claws to hang upside down. Sloths live in the tropical rain forests of Central and South America. They move very slowly, and their long fur turns green from algae growing in it. Sloths are related to armadillos and anteaters. {<u>slawth</u> or <u>slŏth</u>}

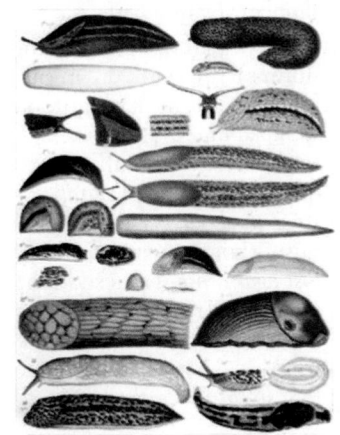

slouch *verb* (slouched, slouching, slouches) 1. to sit, stand, or move with a bent, careless posture. *He slouches instead of standing straight.* 2. to cause to droop or bend. *He slouched his back and put his head on the desk. noun* 1. a bent or drooping posture or movement. *Her slouch made her look tired.* 2. a person who is awkward, lazy, or without ability. *My friend is no slouch when it comes to riding horses.* {<u>slowch</u>}

slov·en·ly *adjective* careless or disgustingly dirty. *Her boss fired her for her slovenly work habits. / After a week in the wilderness, his appearance was becoming slovenly.* {<u>sluhv</u> ən lee}

slow *adjective* (slower, slowest) 1. not moving or not able to move quickly. *The slow swimmers did not get chosen for the team.* 2. taking a long time. *The patient is making slow progress.* 3. not smart; not quick to learn or understand. *He is great in English but slow in science.* 4. not quick to react. *Cheryl is slow to become angry.* 5. not having much business; not busy. *It was a slow day at the shop. adverb* in a slow manner. *Go slow and be careful. verb* (slowed, slowing, slows) 1. to make slow (often followed by "down" or "up"). *The engineer slowed down the train.* 2. to become slow or slower. *His bicycle slowed as he went up the hill.* {<u>sloh</u>} slowly, adv., slowness, n.

slow·poke *noun* (informal) a person who acts, works, or goes slowly. *Try to keep up with us and don't be a slowpoke!* {<u>sloh</u> pohk}

Word History *Slowpoke* comes from Australian English. It was formed by combining "slow" and "poke," which means "to walk at an easy pace."

slug[1] *noun* 1. a small land animal with a soft body and two tentacles with eyes. Slugs are mollusks closely related to snails, but they do not have a visible shell. They live in wet places and eat plants. 2. a small, round piece of metal, such as a bullet or a fake coin. {<u>sluhg</u>}

 Living World
 Physical World
 Natural Environment
 Economy
 Government and Law

A
B
C
D
E
F
G
H
I
J
K
L
M
N
O
P
Q
R
S
T
U
V
W
X
Y
Z

slug² *verb* (slugged, slugging, slugs) (informal) to hit heavily with a clenched fist. *He was thrown out of the game because he slugged another player.* {<u>sluhg</u>}

slug·gish *adjective* 1. moving slowly. *The river was sluggish in July.* / *The store experienced sluggish sales after it changed location.* 2. lazy or without energy. *After the big meal, I felt sluggish.* {<u>sluhg</u> ihsh}

sluice *noun* 1. a channel made by people through which water flows. Sluices have gates to control the amount of water that flows through the channel. 2. a sloping water channel made by people in order to move objects such as logs from place to place. *The sluice jammed during the busiest time of the logging season.* {<u>sloohs</u>}

slum *noun* (often plural) a crowded, run-down area of a city where poor people live. {<u>sluhm</u>}

slum·ber *verb* (slumbered, slumbering, slumbers) 1. to sleep lightly. *The cat slumbered in the sunlight.* 2. to be temporarily without activity. *The sky is blue, the wind is still, and the ocean is slumbering.* *noun* (sometimes plural) a state or period of sleep. *Some people need an alarm clock to awaken from slumber.* {<u>sluhm</u> bər}

slump *verb* (slumped, slumping, slumps) 1. to sink down or fall with all one's weight. *She slumped into the hammock.* 2. to deteriorate or fall off quickly. *Sales have slumped since the holidays.* / *His enthusiasm slumped when his team lost again.* *noun* 1. a sudden sinking or reduction, as in health, business activity, or interest. *Her health has been in a slump since she fell.* 2. a long period of losing or playing a sport poorly. *The team was in a slump, having lost five games in a row.* {<u>sluhmp</u>}

slurp *verb* (slurped, slurping, slurps) to make loud noises with the mouth while eating or drinking. *It is polite to slurp the soup if you are dining in Japan.* *noun* a noisy sucking of food or drink. *She drank the cider with a loud slurp.* {<u>sluhrp</u>}

slush *noun* snow that is partly melted. *I stomped in the slush and it sprayed everywhere.* {<u>sluhsh</u>}

sly *adjective* (slier or slyer, sliest or slyest) 1. devious or not to be trusted. *The guard had to be extra careful with the sly criminal.* 2. crafty in a funny way; full of mischief. *Her sly smile told me it was all a joke.* {<u>sliy</u>}

• **on the sly**
secretly; in a crafty way. *We bought the gift on the sly so she wouldn't see it.*

smack *verb* (smacked, smacking, smacks) 1. to hit noisily with an open hand; slap. *He smacked the horse to get it moving.* 2. to make a sharp noise by quickly closing and then opening. *Paul finished the pie and smacked his lips with enjoyment.* 3. to kiss loudly. *The grandmother smacked the child on the forehead.* *noun* 1. a loud kiss. *Carol gave Brian a smack on the cheek for Valentine's Day.* 2. a sharp, noisy slap. *She smacked her hands together loudly.* *adverb* directly. *Zoe hit the puck smack into the center of the goal.* {<u>smăk</u>}

small *adjective* (smaller, smallest) 1. little in size, number, or amount. *They live in a small house.* / *A small crowd gathered in front of the stage.* 2. not important. *Except for a small mistake, her work was fine.* 3. having little property or business. *The woman runs a small business out of her garage.* 4. very young. *The small child is learning how to walk.* 5. weak or soft. *I could hardly hear her small voice.* *noun* the narrow, lower part of the back. *He had a terrible ache in the small of his back.* {<u>smŏl</u>}

small intestine 🟢 *noun* the narrow part of the intestine which connects the stomach and the large intestine. The small intestine digests food and absorbs nutrients into the blood. {<u>smŏl</u> ihn <u>teh</u> stihn}

smart *adjective* (smarter, smartest) 1. clever; intelligent. *The smart boy taught himself how to read.* 2. of the latest fashion. *She came to work wearing a smart outfit.* 3. showing no respect; rude. *Our teacher will have no smart talk in class.* 4. active or quick. *We set off at a smart pace.* *verb* (smarted, smarting, smarts) 1. to cause or feel sharp but not serious pain. *That paper cut smarts.* / *His eyes smarted in the harsh wind.* 2. to be upset. *He still smarted from her insults.*

 Human Body  Human Mind 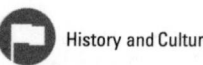 Everyday Life  History and Culture Communication

{**smart**} smartly, adv., smartness, n.

smash *verb* (smashed, smashing, smashes) 1. to break into small pieces by hitting, throwing, or dropping, often making a loud noise. *He smashed the mirror with a rock.* 2. to crack into pieces. *The windows smashed during the earthquake.* 3. to hit hard; batter. *The police smashed the door so they could get in.* 4. to hit with great force (usually followed by "against," "into," or "through"). *The frightened horse smashed through the fence.* 5. to spoil completely; ruin. *The long drought smashed their plans for the farm.* *noun* 1. the act or an instance of smashing. *The smash of the window was the result of a baseball.* 2. the sound produced by this. *The smash from the car accident woke us up in the middle of the night.* 3. a car wreck or collision. *It was a smash that involved several cars, but no one was hurt.* 4. (informal) something that is very popular; a complete success. *Their latest song is a real smash.* *adjective* (informal) of, having to do with, or being a popular success. *The song was a smash hit.* {**smăsh**}

smear *verb* (smeared, smearing, smears) 1. to spread or apply on or over a surface. *They smeared jelly on the bread.* 2. to coat or spread with something sticky, greasy, or oily. *She smeared her face with suntan lotion.* 3. to be or become spread or smudged on or over a surface. *Her* makeup smeared in the rain. 4. to damage the reputation or name of by using slander. *His opponent smeared him in the last election.* *noun* a mark or spot made by spreading a sticky or greasy substance over a surface; smudge. *I had to clean off the smear with a soapy rag.* {**smeer**}

smell *verb* (smelled or smelt, smelling, smells) 1. to sense the odor of by means of the nose. *I think there must be a fire, because I smell smoke.* 2. to have or give off an odor. *The garden smelled of flowers.* 3. to have or give off a bad odor; stink. *The rotten vegetables started to smell.* 4. to examine by using the sense of smell. *She smelled the soup to see if it was ready.* 5. to become aware of. *When the dog bared its teeth, I smelled a bad situation.* *noun* 1. the act or an instance of smelling. *He gave the fresh bread a smell.* 2. the sense through which scent is recognized. *My dog has a strong sense of smell.* 3. an odor or scent. *She likes the smell of coffee.* {**smehl**}

• **smell a rat**
to suspect that something is wrong. *Things seem strange around here, and I smell a rat.*

smelt[1] *verb* (smelted, smelting, smelts) to melt or fuse in order to separate and obtain the metal content. *You must smelt the copper ore before you can make things out of the copper.* {**smehlt**}

smelt[2] *noun* (smelt or smelts) a kind of small fish that lives in freshwater and coastal marine areas of Europe and North America. Smelt are safe to eat and have a silver color. {**smehlt**}

smelt[3] *verb* a past tense and past participle of **smell**. {**smehlt**}

smile *verb* (smiled, smiling, smiles) to have an expression on the face in which the corners of the mouth turn up and the eyes get brighter. A smile usually shows that a person is happy, amused, or friendly. *noun* the act or an instance of smiling. *She gave him a big smile.* {**smiyl**}

smi·ley *noun* a small icon made of punctuation characters and letters and placed in an e-mail; emoticon. A smiley shows the mood of the writer, such as :-o {**smiy** lee}

smith *noun* a person who works in metals (often used in combination). *The silversmith made a beautiful necklace.* {**smihth**}

smock *noun* a loose, light jacket, coat, or other similar garment, that is worn over clothing to protect it from soil, paint, or damage. {**smŏk**}

smog *noun* a mixture of smoke and fog that is caused by moist air and human pollution. *Smog is a problem in many large cities.* {**smŏg** or **smawg**} smoggy, adj., smogless, adj.

smoke *noun* 1. the visible black or gray particles given off into the air by something that is burning. *The smoke went up the chimney.* 2. something that is like this, such as a vapor or cloud. *Our science project produced some smoke.* 3. the act or an instance of smoking tobacco. *verb* (smoked, smoking, smokes) 1. to give off smoke or a vapor or gas that looks like smoke. *Although the fire was out, the forest still smoked.* 2. to breathe in and let out the smoke of. *It's bad for you to smoke a cigarette.* 3. to preserve, and give a flavor to by treating with the smoke of burning wood. *We smoked the*

ham with hickory wood. {**smohk**}

smoke detector *noun* a device that makes a loud noise to warn people of smoke or fire. {**smohk** dih **tehk** tər}

smoke·stack *noun* a chimney or pipe that is used to carry off smoke from a factory, ship, or any place that uses fire. {**smohk** stǎk}

smok·y *adjective* (smokier, smokiest) 1. giving off smoke in large amounts. *The smoky fire made us cough.* 2. filled, covered, or mixed with smoke. *The bowling alley was too smoky for us.* 3. like or looking like smoke. *A smoky fog settled on the valley in the early morning.* {**smohk** ee}

smol·der or **smoulder** *verb* (smoldered or smouldered, smoldering or smouldering, smolders or smoulders) 1. to burn slowly and with smoke, but with little or no flame. *The campfire smoldered all night.* 2. to be present or continue in a quiet or hidden way. *It is not healthy to let anger smolder for a long time.* {**smohl** dər}

smooth *adjective* (smoother, smoothest) 1. not rough; even. *The carpenter sanded the floor until it had a smooth surface.* 2. even in movement; without trouble. *This company runs a smooth operation.* 3. easily done; polished. *Dot has a smooth swing of the bat from all her practice.* 4. without lumps. *My mother stirred the sauce until it was smooth.* 5. delivered in a way that charms or fools. *Cal is a smooth talker, so don't believe everything he says.* *adverb* (smoother, smoothest) in a smooth way; smoothly. *The mechanic got the engine to run smooth.* *verb* (smoothed, smoothing, smoothes) 1. to make even or smooth. *He smoothed the wood with sandpaper.* 2. to remove difficulty or trouble. *The teacher smoothed our first day at school by showing us around.* {**smoohth**} smoothly, adv., smoothness, n.

smoth·er *verb* (smothered, smothering, smothers) 1. to kill by not allowing enough air; suffocate. *In the movie, the bad guy smothers his boss with a pillow.* 2. to be overcome or die from lack of air; suffocate. *She smothered in the smoke from the fire.* 3. to put out or extinguish by covering. *We smothered the campfire with moist soil.* 4. to cover completely and thickly. *Carla smothered her ice cream with chocolate syrup.* 5. to hide or cover up. *Gil smothered his tears and tried to smile.* {**smuh** thər}

smoul·der *verb or noun* another spelling of **smolder**. {**smohl** dər}

smudge *noun* a dirty mark or blot; stain. *It took bleach to remove the smudge from the quilt.* *verb* (smudged, smudging, smudges) 1. to make a dirty mark on or with; smear. *The pen smudged the paper with ink. / The children smudged chocolate on their clothes.* 2. to become stained or dirty; smear. *This fabric will not smudge.* {**smuhj**}

smug *adjective* (smugger, smuggest) confident of or satisfied with oneself to the point of annoying other people; complacent. *He was smug about his successes.* {**smuhg**}

smug·gle *verb* (smuggled, smuggling, smuggles) 1. to take in or out of a country illegally. *They were smuggling drugs.* 2. to bring in or take out in secret. *The officer caught her* smuggling a gun into the building. {**smuhg** əl} smuggler, n.

Sn symbol of the chemical element **tin**.

snack ⚪ *noun* a small meal eaten between meals. *verb* (snacked, snacking, snacks) to eat a quick, light meal between meals; have a snack. *If I snack too much after breakfast, I can't eat all my lunch.* {**snǎk**}

snail *noun* 1. a small animal with a soft body and a spiral shell. Many kinds of snails live on land, in fresh water, or in the ocean. They move slowly using their wide, strong foot. Snails are mollusks. 2. a person who moves or works very slowly. *She is a snail when it comes to doing her homework.* {**snayl**}

snake ⚪ *noun* 1. a long, narrow reptile that has scales but no legs. 2. a person who acts in a sly or evil way toward others. *verb* (snaked, snaking, snakes) to move or curve in the manner of a snake. *The path snakes through the woods.* {**snayk**}

snap *verb* (snapped, snapping, snaps) 1. to break suddenly with a cracking noise. *The branch snapped when I stepped on it.* 2. to cause to break suddenly, often with a cracking noise. *He snapped the sticks into smaller pieces to build a small fire.* 3. to make a sudden cracking noise. *The wood snapped as it burned in the fire.* 4. to cause to make a

 Human Body   Human Mind   Everyday Life History and Culture  Communication

cracking noise. *Ms. Arnold snapped her fingers to get our attention.* 5. to close or open with a sharp noise. *The bottle cap snaps on and off.* 6. to cause to close or open, often with a sharp noise. *He snapped the bottle shut.* 7. to grab or try to grab something suddenly with the teeth (usually followed by "at"). *The dog snapped at me.* 8. to take suddenly and without hesitation (usually followed by "up"). *The cat snapped up the fish from the tank.* 9. to speak in a short, sharp, or annoyed way (usually followed by "at"). *The grouchy clerk snapped at me.* *noun* 1. a sharp or cracking sound, or the movement that causes it; crack. *The fire gave off a hiss and a snap.* 2. a device that closes or opens something and often makes a sharp noise in so doing. *My shirt has snaps instead of buttons.* 3. a short period of cold weather. *We are going through a snap, but it should warm up soon.* 4. a quick and sudden try to grab or bite. *The snap of a turtle can be dangerous.* 5. a photograph taken with an ordinary camera; snapshot. *We have lots of snaps of our vacation.* *adjective* made or done quickly or without care. *It's important to think things through and not make a snap decision.* {snăp}

snap·drag·on *noun* a garden plant that has spikes of colorful flowers. {snăp drăg ən}

snap·shot *noun* a photograph taken with a small, ordinary camera. *I'd like a copy of your snapshot of the bear.* {snăp shŏt}

snare[1] *noun* a trap for catching small animals and birds. Snares usually have a noose. *verb* (snared, snaring, snares) to capture with a trap or snare. *We snared rabbits and released them away from our garden.* {snayr}

snare[2] *noun* a string or wire that is stretched over the bottom skin of a snare drum. {snayr}

snare drum *noun* a small drum fitted with snares or wires that make a rattling sound. {snayr druhm}

snarl[1] *verb* (snarled, snarling, snarls) 1. to growl and show teeth in a threatening or vicious way. *The bear snarled at the raccoon.* 2. to speak sharply with anger or menace. *She snarled at me when I asked the same question twice.* *noun* an angry or vicious growl. *Your dog's snarl sounds mean.* {snarl}

snarl[2] *noun* 1. a tangle or mat. *I had to cut the snarl out of my hair.* / *It will take an hour to remove the snarl in the fishing line.* 2. a confused or tangled situation. *The traffic was in a snarl because of road work.* *verb* (snarled, snarling, snarls) 1. to cause to become tangled or knotted. *The cat snarled my yarn.* 2. to make complicated; confuse (sometimes followed by "up"). *The accident snarled up traffic.* / *Too many details snarled up my book report.* {snarl}

snatch *verb* (snatched, snatching, snatches) to take quickly or suddenly; grab. *He snatched the book from my hands.* *noun* 1. the act or an instance of grabbing something quickly. *He grabbed my toy with a snatch and ran off to hide it.* 2. a small amount or piece; bit. *We heard only snatches of the conversation.* {snăch}

sneak *verb* (sneaked or snuck, sneaking, sneaks) 1. to move quietly and in a sly way. *The burglar was sneaking through the house.* 2. to move, put, bring, or take in a secret or sly manner. *They sneaked a peek at the papers on the desk.* / *He tried to sneak another piece of cake.* *noun* a person who is cowardly, dishonest, or sly; someone who is not worthy of being trusted. *That sneak broke a window and lied about it.* {sneek}

sneak·er *noun* a shoe that has a rubber sole. Sneakers are made of cloth or other flexible material and are worn to play sports. {sneek ər}

Word History Shoes with rubber soles were first called *sneakers* about a hundred years ago. Someone walking in such shoes could sneak around without being heard.

sneer *verb* (sneered, sneering, sneers) to smile or move one's mouth to show scorn. *The criminal sneered as the police questioned him.* *noun* a look on the face that expresses scorn or lack of respect. *She walked up to me with a sneer and pulled off my hat.* {sneer}

sneeze *verb* (sneezed, sneezing, sneezes) to let out a sudden, involuntary burst of air through the mouth and nose. *Angela sneezes whenever she is in a dusty room.* *noun* the act or an instance of sneezing. *A loud sneeze could be heard throughout the theater.* {sneez}

snick·er *verb* (snickered, snickering, snickers) to laugh in a sly and partly restrained way. *They were snickering because he had a sign on his back and didn't know it.* *noun* the act or an instance of snickering.

A B C D E F G H I J K L M N O P Q R **S** T U V W X Y Z

Their snickers disrupted the classroom. {**snihk** ər}

sniff *verb* (sniffed, sniffing, sniffs) 1. to take in short breaths of air through the nose that can be heard. *His cold made him sniff through the whole speech.* 2. to draw into the nose or smell with short breaths. *The cook sniffed the stew and was pleased.* 3. to smell an odor with short breaths through the nose. *The dog sniffed at the trail of the rabbit.* *noun* a short breath of air through the nose that can be heard. *One sniff told us the baby needed changing.* {**snihf**}

snif·fle *verb* (sniffled, sniffling, sniffles) to sniff continuously because of a cold or crying. *noun* the act or sound of repeated sniffing. *The movie was sad and you could hear sniffles in the theater.* {**snihf** əl}

snip *verb* (snipped, snipping, snips) to cut or clip with short, quick strokes of scissors. *I will snip the threads and let out the hem.* *noun* 1. the act of snipping or the sound produced by this. *Just a few more snips, and your haircut will be perfect.* 2. a small piece that has been cut off by snipping. *I brought a snip of fabric to the store so I could find shoes to match it.* {**snihp**}

snob *noun* 1. a person who admires and imitates people of a high social or intellectual class. Snobs act or feel superior to anyone of a lower class. 2. a person who is sure of or proud of his or her superiority in a field of knowledge. {**snŏb**}

snoop *verb* (snooped, snooping, snoops) to look into others' affairs or possessions in a secret way. *You'd better not snoop in my diary.* *noun* a person who snoops. *That snoop was trying to open my locker.* {**snoohp**}

> **Word History** *Snoop* comes from *snoepen,* a Dutch word that means "to eat in secret," "eat sweets," or "steal (food)."

snooze *verb* (snoozed, snoozing, snoozes) (informal) to sleep for a short period of time; nap. *I snoozed during math class.* *noun* (informal) a short sleep; nap. *You'll feel better after a snooze.* {**snoohz**}

snore *verb* (snored, snoring, snores) to breathe with loud, hoarse noises while sleeping. *My aunt sounds like a lawn mower when she snores.* *noun* the sound produced by snoring. *That's the loudest snore I've ever heard.* {**snohr**}

snor·kel *noun* a tube that is held in the mouth and extends above the surface of water. Snorkels allow swimmers to breathe while their faces are in the water. {**snohr** kəl}

snort *verb* (snorted, snorting, snorts) 1. to push air through the nose in a noisy, rough, and forceful way. *The horse snorted into the oats.* 2. to make a sudden, harsh sound to express annoyance, scorn, contempt, or other negative feelings. *She snorted in anger.* *noun* 1. a loud, rough sound produced by forcing air violently through the nose. *He let out a snort of disgust when he heard his team had lost.* 2. a sound that is similar to this. *We could hear the snort and sputter of the motor from inside the house.* {**snohrt**}

snout ❶ *noun* the front part of an animal's head that sticks out. The snout includes the nose, mouth, and jaws. {**snowt**}

snow ❷ *noun* 1. soft, white flakes of ice that fall from the sky to the earth. Snow is formed when water in the upper air freezes into crystals. 2. a layer of such flakes. *The snow on the mountain tops shone in the sun.* 3. a storm during which such flakes fall; snowstorm. *No one will ever forget the big snow of 1996.* *verb* (snowed, snowing, snows) 1. to fall as snow. *It snowed last night.* 2. to cover, close, or block with snow (usually followed by "in," "under," or "over"). *The blizzard snowed them in for two days.* {**snoh**}

snow·ball *noun* a mass of snow that has been packed together into a ball. Snowballs are used for play or games. *verb* (snowballed, snowballing, snowballs) to grow rapidly in size, importance, or intensity. *The crime problem has snowballed.* {**snoh bawl**}

snow·flake *noun* a single flake of snow. {**snoh flayk**}

snowman *noun* (snowmen) a figure made of packed snow that looks a little bit like a person. {**snoh măn**}

snow·mo·bile *noun* a small motor vehicle with two skis on the front for traveling on snow. {**snoh moh beel**}

snow·plow *noun* a machine or vehicle with a large shovel or blade for clearing snow from streets, highways, runways, or driveways. {**snoh plow**}

snow·shoe *noun* a light frame that is shaped like a racket and strung with netting. Snowshoes can be attached to a boot and used for

 Human Body   Human Mind   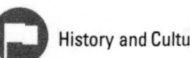 Everyday Life    History and Culture   Communication

walking on deep snow. {**snoh** shooh}

snow·storm *noun* a storm in which a lot of snow falls. Snowstorms have strong winds. {**snoh** stohrm}

snub *verb* (snubbed, snubbing, snubs) to ignore as a way to show dislike, dissatisfaction, or contempt. *The other students snubbed her because her clothes were not in fashion.* *noun* an act or instance of ignoring someone; insult. *I was hurt by his snub at the party.* {**snuhb**}

snug *adjective* (snugger, snuggest) 1. small and comfortable; cozy. *My grandmother lives in a snug apartment.* 2. having a close fit; slightly tight. *The pants are small and look snug on her.* {**snuhg**}

snug·gle *verb* (snuggled, snuggling, snuggles) to lie in a comfortable way next to someone or something; cuddle. *They were snuggling in front of the fire.* {**snuhg** əl}

so *adverb* 1. to the amount or degree expressed or understood. *She was so ill that she could not work.* 2. to a great degree; very. *I'm so happy the job is finished.* 3. also; too. *I ate lunch, and so did she.* 4. therefore; as a result. *He is tired, and so does not want to go running today.* 5. in the way that is shown or told. *Look, you need to hold the brush so.* 6. in that way. *He was painting lying down, and while he was so working, he fell asleep.* *conjunction* 1. in order that. *Please be on time, so we won't miss any of the party.* 2. with the result that. *You were late, so you missed the spelling*

test. *pronoun* 1. such as what has been suggested or said; the same. *Lizzie became a doctor and remained so.* 2. about; more or less. *Your share of the bill will be ten dollars or so.* *interjection* used as an expression of surprise, amazement, or understanding. *So! You really think you can run that fast?* *adjective* true; based on fact. *She wouldn't say it if it weren't so.* {**soh**}

• **so what?**
Who cares? What difference does it make?

Homophone Note The words *so*, *sew*, and *sow*[1] sound alike but have different meanings.

soak *verb* (soaked, soaking, soaks) 1. to lie in and become covered or completely wet with a liquid. *She soaked in a hot bath. / The skirt should soak in soapy water.* 2. to place in a liquid in order to make wet; saturate. *He soaked the linens in bleach.* 3. to pass through or penetrate something that has many small holes (often followed by "in," "into," or "through"). *The tea soaked into the carpet.* 4. to draw in or absorb (usually followed by "up"). *The sponge soaked up the excess water. / We soaked up as much information as possible.* 5. to be very wet; drenched. *His hair is soaked with perspiration.* 6. to make completely wet; drench. *We were soaked by the sudden storm.* *noun* the act or an instance of soaking, or the condition of being soaked. *These dirty cloths should be put into hot water for a good long soak.* {**sohk**}

soap ⊙ *noun* a cleaning substance that is made from fat or oil and comes in the form

of a bar, liquid, powder, or flakes. *verb* (soaped, soaping, soaps) to rub with soap. *He soaped the dog from head to tail.* {**sohp**}

soap·y *adjective* (soapier, soapiest) 1. containing, covered with, or filled with soap. *I washed the car with soapy water.* 2. characteristic of or like soap. *This milk has a soapy taste.* {**soh** pee}

soar *verb* (soared, soaring, soars) 1. to fly or glide in a swift, easy way and at a very great height. *The falcon soared over the fields and mountains.* 2. to grow rapidly in value or intensity; rise in a quick way. *The price of broccoli soared. / Her spirits were soaring after the good news.* {**sohr**}

Homophone Note Are you looking for the word *sore* (as in a wound)? *Soar* and *sore* sound alike but have different meanings.

sob *verb* (sobbed, sobbing, sobs) to cry with great emotion while making short gasps for breath. *She was sobbing when she broke her leg skiing.* *noun* an instance or sound of crying without control and while taking short breaths. *Many sobs were heard at the funeral.* {**sŏb**}

so·ber *adjective* 1. not drunk; not intoxicated. *When he was sober, he was nice to be with.* 2. serious or full of thought; solemn. *She had a sober atti-*

A
B
C
D
E
F
G
H
I
J
K
L
M
N
O
P
Q
R
S
T
U
V
W
X
Y
Z

tude toward work and family. verb (sobered, sobering, sobers) to make or become sober (often followed by "up"). *His war experience sobered him. / She sobered up after many years of drinking.* {soh bər} soberingly, adv., soberly, adv., soberness, n.

soc·cer *noun* a game in which two teams of eleven players try to move a ball into a goal by kicking or hitting it without using the hands or arms. {sŏk ər}

> **Word History** *Soccer* was officially called "Association Football" in England. The word comes from the abbreviation "assoc." with the suffix "-er" added to it.

so·cial *adjective* 1. living in groups or communities instead of alone. *Ants and bees are social animals.* 2. of or related to such a way of living. *Discrimination against immigrants is a social problem.* 3. friendly; enjoying the company of others. *He enjoys parties because he is very social.* 4. of or related to the highest levels of society or the upper class. *The charity ball was an important social event.* noun a gathering or party. *We are planning an ice cream social.* {soh shəl} socially, adv.

> **Word History** *Social* comes from *socialis*, a Latin word that means "united" or "living with others."

so·cial·ism *noun* a theory of government in which the whole community rather than individuals owns all of its property and resources. {soh shə lih zəm}

so·cial·ist *noun* a person who works in favor of or practices socialism. {soh shə lihst}

social studies ○ ○ *plural noun* a course of study including history, geography, civics, and other social sciences. This course is taught in elementary and secondary schools. {soh shəl stuh deez}

so·ci·e·ty *noun* (societies) 1. the members of a community or group considered together. *It is important for every society to agree on certain laws.* 2. all people considered together as they interact in groups. *He worked his whole life for the good of society.* 3. company; companionship. *His society is pleasant to me.* 4. a group of persons who get together for a particular purpose or activity. *He is a member of the local art society.* {sə siy ə tee}

sock *noun* (socks or sox) a covering for the foot made of a woven or knitted material. Socks reach to a point between the ankle and knee. {sŏk}

sock·et *noun* 1. an opening into which something fits or is put. *Put the electric plug into the socket in the wall.* 2. a hollow place in which a body part rests or turns. *A person's eyes are set in sockets.* {sŏk iht}

sod *noun* the layer of ground that contains the grass; turf. *verb* (sodded, sodding, sods) to lay with sod. *We decided to sod the front lawn, rather than seed it.* {sŏd}

so·da ○ *noun* 1. a drink made with a sweet flavoring and water that contains carbon dioxide. 2. water that contains carbon dioxide; soda water. 3. a cold drink made with soda water, a sweet syrup, and ice cream; ice cream soda. {soh də}

soda water *noun* water filled with carbon dioxide. It is used to mix and drink. {soh də wo tər}

so·di·um *noun* a soft, silver-white metal that is a chemical element. It combines easily with other elements, and is found in nature only in compounds with other elements. Sodium reacts with chlorine to form table salt. (symbol: Na) {soh dee əm}

so·fa ○ *noun* a long comfortable seat with arms and a back; couch. {soh fə}

> **Word History** *Sofa* comes from an Arabic word that means "bench."

soft *adjective* (softer, softest) 1. easy to bend or to shape; not firm or hard. *I like to sleep on a soft bed. / The metal became soft when we heated it.* 2. smooth; not rough. *She has soft hands from the special lotion she uses.* 3. not strong or bright. *This painter uses very soft colors.* 4. quiet or low in tone. *There was soft music playing as we ate dinner.* 5. not demanding; easy. *He is a soft teacher and never gives too much homework.* 6. not harsh; light. *He was lucky to receive such a soft punishment for his bad behavior.* 7. (informal) not difficult. *Mr. Silver has a soft position at the bank.* 8. in poor shape for physical activity. *She is soft after sitting on the couch all winter.* adverb (softer, softest) in a soft manner; gently. *He let me down soft.* {sŏft} softly, adv., softness, n.

soft·ball ○ *noun* 1. a type of baseball played on a smaller field with a larger, softer ball that is pitched underhand. 2. the ball that is used in this game. {sŏft bawl}

Human Body   Human Mind   Everyday Life   History and Culture   Communication

sof·ten *verb* (softened, softening, softens) to make or become soft or softer. *She softened her pillow before laying her head down. / Enzymes can soften the fibers in beef.* {**so** fən}

soft·ware *noun* any of the programs that are written to operate a computer. {**sŏft wayr**}

sog·gy *adjective* (soggier, soggiest) completely wet; heavy with moisture; saturated. *Walking on the wet ground made his shoes soggy.* {**sŏg** ee or **sawg** ee}

soil[1]  *noun* 1. the top layer of the earth's surface. *This soil is full of clay.* 2. region; land; country. *We will fight for our soil.* {**soil**}

soil[2] *verb* (soiled, soiling, soils) 1. to make dirty. *The baby soiled his bib with strawberry jam.* 2. to bring shame or disrespect to; disgrace. *Your rumors have soiled my reputation.* 3. to become dirty or stained. *White clothes soil easily.* {**soil**}

sol *noun* the syllable that indicates the fifth tone of a musical scale. {**sohl** or **soh**}

so·lar *adjective* 1. of, having to do with, or coming from the sun. *We watched the solar eclipse with special glasses. / The solar flare disrupted radio communication all over the world.* 2. powered by the sun's energy. *He has a solar calculator that never needs batteries.* {**soh** lər}

solar system *noun* a system that includes a star and all of the matter which orbits that star, including planets and their moons. {**soh** lər **sihs** təm}

sold *verb* past tense and past participle of **sell**. {**sohld**}

sol·der *noun* any mixture of metals that is melted and used to connect pieces of metal. *verb* (soldered, soldering, solders) to use a melted mixture of metals to connect. *The artist soldered the seams of his stained glass window.* {**sŏ** dər}

sol·dier *noun* a person who serves in the army and who is not an officer. *The soldiers guarded the entrance to the base.* {**sohl** jər}

sole[1] *adjective* 1. single and alone; not one among others; only. *He is the sole remaining blacksmith in the town.* 2. not shared; exclusive. *Patents give people the sole right to decide the fate of their inventions.* {**sohl**}

The latest fad in footwear is the Sole Sneaker with a the shape of a **sole** stamped into the **sole**.

sole[2] *noun* the bottom of something that comes in contact with the ground. Feet and shoes have soles. *verb* (soled, soling, soles) to provide with a sole. *The shoe repairer soled my boots with rubber.* {**sohl**}

sole[3] *noun* (sole or soles) any flatfish from the ocean that is used for food. {**sohl**}

Homophone Note Are you looking for the word *soul* (spirit)? *Sole* and *soul* sound alike but have different meanings.

sol·emn *adjective* 1. serious in appearance, sound, or occasion. *The solemn guests left the funeral. / She was always in a solemn mood when she was tired.* 2. deeply sincere because of religious character. *Martin made a solemn promise to become a monk if he survived the storm.* {**sŏl** əm} solemnly, adv.

sol·id *adjective* 1. having a firm shape or form that can be measured in length, width, and height; not like a liquid or a gas. *Cement becomes solid when it dries.* 2. not hollow. *A solid iron bar is very heavy.* 3. made entirely of a single material or thing. *The statue was solid silver.* 4. without a break; continuous. *Our house is lined by a solid row of trees.* 5. sturdy; strong. *The masons built a solid wall out of brick.* 6. uniform in color or some other trait. *Her dress is solid blue. noun* 1. a figure in geometry or some other object that has length, width, and height. *A cube is a solid.* 2. any thing or material that is neither a liquid nor a gas. *Wood and steel are solids.* {**sŏl** ihd} solidly, adv., solidness, n.

sol·i·tar·y *adjective* 1. being, traveling, or living without others; alone. *We found a solitary bear while we were climbing the mountain.* 2. happening or done without the company of others. *I enjoyed a solitary evening in front of the television. / Writing is a solitary pastime.* 3. single or only; lone. *The hot tub was his solitary refuge from the stress of his job.* {**sŏl** ə **tayr** ee}

sol·i·tude *noun* the condition of living or being by oneself. *The hermit lived in solitude in the mountains until she died.* {**sŏl** ə **toohd**}

A B C D E F G H I J K L M N O P Q R S T U V W X Y Z

 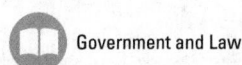

The Solar System

The majestic movement of heavenly bodies through our solar system and the mystery of the laws that guide them have inspired thinkers and dreamers throughout human history, from poets to philosophers, religious scholars to astrophysicists. The center of our solar system is a star we call the sun. Orbiting the sun are nine known planets, some of which are orbited by one or more moons, as your home planet, Earth, is. Earth is very small compared to the sun, and the sun is only one of billions of stars in our galaxy, the Milky Way, which itself is like a tiny speck in an unimaginably vast universe.

Jupiter

Mars

The Sun

Earth

Venus

Mercury

Saturn

Uranus

Neptune

Pluto

Galaxy NGC 3310

Do You Know...

The **Sun** is made of hot gases, including hydrogen and helium.

Mercury has craters like the Moon but no atmosphere.

Venus is the hottest planet and is closest to the Earth.

Three-fourths of **Earth's** surface is liquid water.

Mars is covered with rocks and dust made of iron, which give a red appearance.

The largest planet is **Jupiter,** which has a cloudy surface thousands of miles deep.

Saturn has rings made of ice, dust, and rock.

Uranus has eleven thin rings and a horizontal axis.

Neptune used to be the farthest planet from the Sun but traded places with Pluto in 1999.

The smallest, coldest planet is **Pluto.**

so·lo *noun* (solos) 1. a performance by one person. *The pianist had a solo in the middle of the concert.* 2. a piece of music for a single person. *adjective* done by one person alone and without help. *Her solo flight broke a record for distance. adverb* alone or without accompanying assistance. *He flew solo from New York to Paris. verb* (soloed, soloing, solos) to perform solo. *She soloed in the middle of my favorite song.* {<u>soh</u> loh}

sol·stice *noun* either of the two times in the year when the sun is furthest from the celestial equator, occurring in June and December. {<u>sohl</u> stihs *or* <u>sŏl</u> stihs}

> **Word History** *Solstice* is formed from two Latin words that together mean mean "the point at which the sun seems to stand still."

so·lu·tion *noun* 1. the act or process of solving a problem or question. *The solution to the puzzle took us several hours.* 2. an answer to or explanation of a problem. *Mary used multiplication to find the solution.* 3. the process in which one substance spreads evenly through another. *The salt mixed in a solution with the water.* 4. a mixture that contains two or more unlike substances combined evenly. *We made a solution of sugar and water to feed the hummingbirds.* {sə <u>looh</u> shən}

solve *verb* (solved, solving, solves) to find an answer to. *She solved all of the math problems. / He solved the crime.* {<u>sŏlv</u>}

som·ber *adjective* 1. of a dark shade or condition. *The child painted his room a somber brown.* 2. sad, dismal, or full of gloom. *My aunt's funeral was a very somber occasion.* {<u>sŏm</u> bər}

som·bre·ro *noun* (sombreros) a straw or felt hat that has a wide brim and high crown. *Sombreros are worn in Mexico.* {sŏm <u>breh</u> roh *or* səm <u>breh</u> roh}

> **Word History** *Sombrero* is a Spanish word that comes from a Latin word that means "shade."

some *adjective* 1. being an amount or number that is not stated. *He gave me some money.* 2. not known or named. *Some man stopped to ask about a job.* 3. being of a great but not stated number or amount. *It will take some time to finish this report. pronoun* certain people, things, or events that are not named or known. *I'm nervous around strange dogs because some are friendly and some are not. adverb* 1. about; approximately. *It cost some fifty dollars for those tickets.* 2. (informal) a bit; somewhat. *He reads some, but not much.* {<u>suhm</u>}

> **Homophone Note** The words *some* and *sum* (the result of adding) sound alike but have different meanings.

-some[1] *suffix* a suffix that means "to be" or "likely to cause." *A lonesome person is one who is alone. / A troublesome person is a person who is likely to cause trouble.*

-some[2] *suffix* a suffix that means the number in a group. *A foursome is a group of four.*

some·bod·y *pronoun* some person, not named or known; someone. *Somebody is ringing the doorbell. noun* (somebodies) an important or well-known person. *She is a somebody in the world of science.* {<u>suhm</u> bŏd ee}

some·day *adverb* at some time in the future. *Humans will walk on Mars someday.* {<u>suhm</u> day}

some·how *adverb* in a way not known or understood. *Our car is out of gas, but we'll manage to get home somehow. / Somehow the leopard escaped from its cage.* {<u>suhm</u> how}

some·one *pronoun* one who has not been identified or who is not known; somebody. *Someone forgot to take out the garbage.* {<u>suhm</u> wuhn}

som·er·sault *noun* a motion in which the body rolls all the way over backward or forward. *She did somersaults down the hill. verb* (somersaulted, somersaulting, somersaults) to tuck the body and roll head over heels either forward or backward. *The clown somersaulted into the stadium.* {<u>suhm</u> ər sŏlt}

some·thing *pronoun* a thing that is not known or named. *Something smells bad. / We have brought something for you to eat. adverb* in some amount or degree; somewhat; a little. *It tastes something like chicken.* {<u>suhm</u> thing}

some·time *adverb* 1. at a time not known or certain. *He disappeared sometime last week.* 2. at a time in the future. *Please come to visit sometime.* {<u>suhm</u> tiym}

some·times *adverb* now and then; at times; not always. *They go walking sometimes. / Sometimes she enjoys class.* {<u>suhm</u> tiymz}

some·what *adverb* in some measure, degree, or proportion; rather. *She is somewhat lazy.* {<u>suhm</u> wuht *or* <u>suhm</u> wŏt}

some·where *adverb* 1. at, to, or in a place or position that is not stated. *Lee went somewhere without saying goodbye.*

a
b
c
d
e
f
g
h
i
j
k
l
m
n
o
p
q
r
s
t
u
v
w
x
y
z

/ *My glasses must be around here somewhere.* 2. at some point in space. *Put your suitcase down somewhere and have a seat.* 3. at some point in time. *She lost her bookbag somewhere between this morning and this afternoon.* {<u>suhm</u> **wayr**}

son *noun* a person's male child. *They have two sons and a daughter.* {<u>suhn</u>}

Homophone Note Are you looking for the word *sun* (a star)? *Son* and *sun* sound alike but have different meanings.

so·nar *noun* 1. a way to find objects underwater by sending and reflecting sound waves. (The word is formed from "sound navigation and ranging.") 2. a device or apparatus used in this procedure. {<u>soh</u> **nar**}

song 🎵 *noun* 1. a short musical composition for singing. *He sang us a song about true love.* 2. the musical sounds made by certain animals. *The finch's song lasted exactly one minute before repeating.* {<u>sŏng</u>}

song·bird *noun* a bird that has a musical song or call. {<u>sŏng</u> **buhrd**}

son·ic *adjective* 1. of or related to audible sound or sound waves. 2. of, related to, or being a speed approaching or equal to that of sound in air, at the same distance above sea level. {<u>sŏn</u> ihk}

son·net *noun* a poem of fourteen lines that usually rhymes in set ways. {<u>sŏn</u> iht}

As we approach the end of ninety-nine,
I see that people look at life with fear.
These people always whimper and they whine
As we come to the ending of this year.

Some people have great fear of a new age,
A fear that this will make computers crash.
Some people look at this with eyes of rage,
And see the world explode in one bright flash.

As we approach the new millennium
And mayhem really does rule in our city,
As all the people stand around so glum,
They will end with nothing but my pity.

So as we journey to our new decade,
i will survive because I'm not afraid.

soon *adverb* (sooner, soonest) 1. in a short time; shortly. *Dinner will be ready soon.* 2. right away; quickly. *Please call as soon as you get home.* 3. done as a matter of choice. *I'd as soon stay home.* {<u>soohn</u>}

soot *noun* a fine, black powder made during burning. Soot collects in chimneys or is carried into the air in smoke. {<u>suut</u>}

soothe *verb* (soothed, soothing, soothes) 1. to make less angry, pained, or distressed; calm or comfort. *We soothed the cat by petting her and feeding her warm milk.* 2. to help take away; lessen; ease; relieve. *She soothed the pain of his sore muscles by giving him a massage.* {<u>soohth</u>} soother, n., soothingly, adv.

so·phis·ti·cat·ed *adjective* having or showing a lot of knowledge or experience; not ignorant or simple. *This author writes for a sophisticated audience.* {sə <u>fih</u> stə **kay** tihd}

soph·o·more *noun* a student in the second year of high school or college. {<u>sŏf</u> ə **mohr** or <u>sŏf</u> **mohr**}

so·pran·o 🎵 *noun* (sopranos) 1. the singing voice or part with the highest range. *I sing soprano in the chorus.* 2. a female or young male singer with such a voice. *The conductor told the sopranos to sing first.* *adjective* having the range of a soprano. *He plays the soprano saxophone.* {sə <u>prăn</u> oh or sə <u>prahn</u> oh, n.,

sə <u>prăn</u> oh or sə <u>prahn</u> oh, adj.}

sore 🌐 *adjective* (sorer, sorest) 1. painful. *She had a sore arm after playing tennis.* 2. feeling or suffering physical pain; hurting. *You will be sore after your first time on horseback.* 3. causing or likely to cause a person to be embarrassed or annoyed. *Grades are a sore topic with my older brother.* 4. (informal) angry or annoyed. *She was sore at him for not remembering her birthday.* *noun* a painful place on the body where the skin is broken; wound. *She had a sore on her leg.* {<u>sohr</u>} soreness, n.

Homophone Note Are you looking for the word *soar* (to fly)? *Sore* and *soar* sound alike but have different meanings.

sor·row *noun* 1. the suffering or distress that results from a loss, misfortune, or injury; grief. *He felt a lot of sorrow when his grandmother died.* 2. the cause of such suffering and distress. *It was a great sorrow when our cat ran away.* {<u>sar</u> oh or <u>sŏr</u> oh}

sor·ry *adjective* (sorrier, sorriest) 1. feeling regret, sympathy, or sadness. *We are sorry to have missed you. / I'm sorry that you lost the game. / She was sorry that her friend moved away.* 2. of low quality; terrible; poor. *He is a sorry excuse for a painter. / The old house was in a sorry state.* 3. without honor; low. *His lies will bring him to a sorry end someday.* *interjection* used as an expression of apology or regret. *Sorry! I didn't mean to step on your foot.* {<u>sar</u> ee or <u>sŏr</u> ee, intj., <u>sar</u> ee or <u>sŏr</u> ee, adj.}

• **be sorry**
to suffer for an action or a choice one has made. *You*

🏃 Human Body   ❓ Human Mind   👕 Everyday Life   🚩 History and Culture   📞 Communication

will be sorry if you don't obey me.

sort *noun* kind; type. *What sort of dog is that?* *verb* (sorted, sorting, sorts) to place or separate into groups or types. *Sort the clothes before you wash them.* {**sohrt**} sorter, n.

• **out of sorts**
1. in a bad temper. *The argument made him out of sorts.* 2. (informal) rather ill. *She was feeling out of sorts after the plane ride.*

SOS *noun* (SOS's) a call for help from a ship that is in trouble. SOS is an abbreviation for "save our ship." {**ehs oh ehs**}

sought *verb* past tense and past participle of **seek**. {**sawt**}

soul ⓔ *noun* 1. the part of human beings separate from the physical body that is thought of as the center of feeling, thought, and spirit. *Some religions teach that a person's soul goes to heaven when he or she dies.* 2. the central or most important part of something. *She is the soul of the team; without her, we would be nothing.* 3. a nearly perfect example of a quality. *He is the soul of honesty.* 4. a human being; person. *She is a kind soul.* {**sohl**}

Homophone Note The words **soul**, **sol**, and **sole** sound alike but have different meanings.

sound¹ ⓔⓔ *noun* 1. that which can be heard when vibrations are picked up by the ears. *He did not hear a sound.* 2. a particular noise. *I love the sound of the sea.* 3. the range in which something may be heard. *Are they within the sound of my voice?* 4. the impression given. *The sound of your idea worries me.* *verb* (sounded, sounding, sounds)

1. to make or send forth sound. *He sounds too loud when he sings.* 2. to cause to send forth sound. *He sounded the bell for lunch.* 3. to announce with or as if with a sound. *The officer sounded the alarm.* 4. to say aloud. *He sounds his words carefully.* 5. to express an impression. *That sounds very odd to me.* {**sownd**}

sound² ⓔ *adjective* (sounder, soundest) 1. free of damage; healthy or in good condition. *I felt sound after a good night's sleep.* 2. having a solid base. *The inspector said that the building was sound and would be standing for years to come.* 3. stable or secure. *He made a sound investment that helped to pay for his daughter's college tuition.* 4. continuous and deep. *The princess fell into a sound sleep for a hundred years.* {**sownd**} soundly, adv.

sound³ *verb* (sounded, sounding, sounds) 1. to measure the depth of with a pole or a weight attached to a line. *We sounded the lake before we jumped in.* 2. to dive deeply under water. *The whales sounded to the deepest parts of the ocean.* {**sownd**}

sound⁴ ⓔ *noun* 1. a body of water between two larger bodies of water or between an island and the mainland. *The ships pulled into Long Island sound.* 2. a sea inlet. {**sownd**}

sound bite *noun* a short statement taken from a video or audio tape that is to be included in a later broadcast. {**sownd biyt**}

soup *noun* a liquid food made with small pieces of vegetables, meat, fish, or grains cooked in water or broth. {**soohp**}

sour *adjective* (sourer, sourest) 1. having a tart or acid taste like lemon juice or vinegar. *The limes were sour enough to pucker my mouth.* 2. having become acid or spoiled. *We had to throw out the sour milk.* 3. bitter, unhappy, or otherwise in a bad mood. *Losing the kite put a sour expression on his face.* 4. not up to the usual standard; poor. *His bowling was sour last night.* 5. harshly off pitch. *She's not a terrible singer, but she does hit some sour notes now and then.* *verb* (soured, souring, sours) 1. to become or cause to become sour in taste or smell. *The milk soured quickly on the hot day.* 2. to become or cause to become bitter, unhappy, or uninterested. *Her mood soured whenever she thought about her taxes.* {**sowr**} sourness, n.

source *noun* the start or cause of something. *Peanuts are the source of peanut butter.* {**sohrs**}

south *noun* 1. the direction to the right of a person facing the rising sun. 2. one of the four major points of direction on the compass. The south is directly opposite the north. 3. (often capital) the southern part of a country or area. *You can tell by her drawl that she's from the South.* *adjective* 1. from, of, or in the south. *There's a south wind blowing.* 2. toward or facing the south. *We came in through the south entrance.* *adverb* from, in, or toward the south. *The bus took us south to Florida.* {**sowth**}

South Africa *noun* a country in southern Africa. South Africa has three capitals, one for each main branch of its government. The capitals are

A B C D E F G H I J K L M N O P Q R S T U V W X Y Z

Cape Town, Pretoria, and Bloemfontein. {**sowth** ăf rih kə} South African, [n.], adj.

South America *noun* the fourth largest continent. South America is between the Atlantic and Pacific Oceans. It is in the Western Hemisphere. {**sowth** ə **mehr** ih kə}

South A·mer·i·can *adjective* of or having to do with South America, or its people or languages. *noun* a person who was born in or is a citizen of a country in South America. {**sowth** ə **mehr** ih kən}

South Carolina *noun* a state in the southeastern United States on the Atlantic Coast. Its capital is Columbia. (abbreviation: SC) {**sowth** kar ə **liy** nə} South Carolinian, n.

> **Word History** *Carolina* means "the land of Charles" in Latin, after King Charles I of England, who established the first permanent European colony in the area. Carolina was divided into the colonies of South Carolina and North Carolina in 1710.

South Dakota *noun* a state in the midwestern United States. Its capital is Pierre. (abbreviation: SD) {**sowth** də **koh** tə} South Dakotan, n.

> **Word History** *Dakota* means "allies" or "friends" in a Sioux language. The Dakota Territory was named after the Dakota Sioux, one of several Native American nations from that area. The Dakota Territory was divided into South Dakota and North Dakota when they became states in 1889.

south·east *noun* 1. a point on the compass halfway between south and east. 2. a region in the direction of southeast. *I live in the southeast of town. adjective*
1. located in or near the southeast. *I live in the southeast state of Florida. / He lives southeast of us.* 2. from, toward, or facing the southeast. *We looked out the southeast window. / We traveled southeast to get from Oregon to Florida. adverb* from, in, or toward the southeast. {**sowth eest**}

south·east·ern *adjective* of, located in, or coming from the southeast. {**sowth ee** stərn *or* **sow ee** stərn}

south·er·ly *adverb or adjective* 1. of or toward the south. *This animal lives in a southerly climate. / The path runs southerly for five miles.* 2. blowing from the south. *A southerly storm threw our ship off course. noun* (southerlies) a storm or wind coming from the south. *The captain says we need a strong southerly to reach our destination.* {**suh** thər lee}

south·ern *adjective* in, to, from, or having to do with the south. *They travelled in the southern part of Europe. / Walk three miles in a southern direction.* {**suh** thərn}

south·ern·er *noun* (often capitalized) a person who was born or who lives in a southern area or region. {**suh** thər nər}

Southern Hemisphere *noun* the half of the earth that is south of the equator. {**suh** thərn **heh** mih **sfeer**}

South Korea *noun* a country on the eastern coast of Asia. South Korea is also called the Republic of Korea. Seoul is the capital of South Korea. {**sowth** kə **ree** ə} South Korean, [n.], adj.

South Pole *noun* the point on the earth's surface that is farthest south. The South Pole is intersected by the
southern end of the earth's axis. {**sowth pohl**}

south·ward *adverb* toward the south. *They travelled southward into Mexico. adjective* in, at, facing, or moving toward the south. *He walked off in a southward direction.* {**sowth** wərd *or* **suhth** ərd, adj., **sowth** wərd *or* **suhth** ərd, adv.} southwards, adv.

south·west *noun* 1. a point on the compass halfway between south and west. 2. a region in the direction of southwest. *She lives in the southwest of town. adverb or adjective* 1. located in or near the southwest. *I live in the southwest state of Texas. / He lives southwest of us.* 2. from, toward, or facing the southwest. *We looked out the southwest window. / We traveled southwest to get from New York to Texas.* {**sowth wehst** *or* **sow wehst**, n., **sowth wehst** *or* **sow wehst**, adj., **sowth wehst** *or* **sow wehst**, adv.}

south·west·ern *adjective* of, located in, or coming from the southwest. {**sowth weh** stərn *or* **sow weh** stərn}

sou·ve·nir *noun* something kept as a reminder of a place, event, or friendship; memento. *He bought a glass egg as a souvenir of the ostrich farm.* {**sooh** və **neer** *or* **sooh** və **neer**}

sov·er·eign *noun* a monarch or other royal ruler. *Japan has a long history of powerful sovereigns. adjective* 1. having the most political power or authority. *The tyrant was the sovereign ruler of his starving country.* 2. having independent government. *South Africa is a sovereign nation.* {**sŏv** rən *or* **sŏv** ə rihn, n., **sŏv** rən *or* **sŏv** ə rihn, adj.}

Soviet Union *noun* a country that no longer exists that was

 Human Body Human Mind   Everyday Life   History and Culture Communication

made up of fifteen republics in eastern Europe and northern Asia. It was also called the Union of Soviet Socialist Republics. Moscow was the capital of the Soviet Union. {<u>soh</u> vee **eht** <u>yoon</u> yən}

sow[1] *verb* (sowed, sown or sowed, sowing, sows) to plant or scatter in or over the ground. *She sows petunia seeds in her garden every year.* {<u>soh</u>} sowable, adj., sower, n.

Homophone Note The words ***sow***[1], ***sew***, and ***so*** sound alike but have different meanings.

sow[2] *noun* an adult female pig or hog. {<u>sow</u>}

soy·bean *noun* 1. a plant of the legume family. Soybeans are grown for their nutritious seeds, for soil improvement, and for food for farm animals. 2. the seed of this plant that is high in protein and very nutritious. {<u>soi</u> **been**}

spa *noun* 1. a mineral spring. 2. a resort area with such a spring or springs. 3. a hotel or resort that offers fitness and health programs. {<u>spah</u>}

space ● *noun* 1. the area that contains the entire material world and its events. 2. the area that contains the entire universe; outer space. *They sent a rocket into space.* 3. an empty area or place. *There is a space in the back row of the room.* 4. a period of time. *I got two phone calls in the space of five minutes.* 5. an area set aside for a particular use. *Your car is in my parking space.* 6. the empty place between printed words. *verb* (spaced, spacing, spaces) to arrange using spaces. *We spaced the books close together on the table.* {<u>spays</u>}

space·craft *noun* (spacecraft) a vehicle designed to travel in outer space. {<u>spays</u> **krăft**}

space shuttle *noun* a spacecraft designed to carry astronauts and their equipment back and forth between the earth and space. {<u>spays</u> **shuh** təl}

space station *noun* a large spacecraft in orbit for a long period of time. Space stations are used for scientific study and for launching other spacecraft. {<u>spays</u> **stay** shən}

space·suit *noun* a suit worn by astronauts that lets them breathe in outer space. {<u>spays</u> **sooht**}

space·walk *noun* the action of an astronaut moving about outside a spacecraft in outer space. {<u>spays</u> **wŏk**} space-walker, n.

spa·cious *adjective* having plenty of space. *My older sister picked the most spacious room in our new house.* {<u>spay</u> shəs} spaciousness, n.

spade[1] *noun* a tool shaped like a shovel and used for digging. A spade has a long handle and a flat blade that can be pushed into the ground with a foot. *verb* (spaded, spading, spades) to dig or cut with a spade. *He spades the ground to prepare it for planting.* {<u>spayd</u>}

spade[2] *noun* 1. a black figure shaped like a pointed leaf with a short stem, used on playing cards. 2. a playing card printed with one or more of these figures. 3. (plural, but used with a singular or plural verb) the suit of cards printed with these figures. {<u>spayd</u>}

spa·ghet·ti *noun* a form of pasta made in long, thin strings. Spaghetti is often served with a sauce that may con-tain meat or tomatoes. {spə **geh** tee}

Spain *noun* a country in southern Europe. Madrid is the capital of Spain. {<u>spayn</u>}

Spam *noun* 1. (Trademark) Spam is the brand name for a kind of canned meat made from pork pieces and seasoning. 2. (lower case) junk mail received by e-mail. Spam is usually advertising sent to a large group of people. *When I checked my e-mail, I saw that it was mostly spam.* *verb* (spammed, spamming, spams) (lower case) to send electronic junk mail. *People get angry when large companies spam them several times a week.* {<u>spăm</u>}

span *noun* 1. the stretch or reach between two points. *The span from one end of the city to the other is about twenty miles.* 2. the length of time. *He had a short life span.* 3. the section or distance between two supports. *The span of that bridge is the longest in the world.* *verb* (spanned, spanning, spans) to stretch or reach over or across. *The bridge spans the river.* / *Her life spanned eighty years.* {<u>spăn</u>}

span·gle *noun* a small, thin piece of shiny metal used for decoration on clothing. {<u>spăng</u> gəl}

span·iel *noun* any of several breeds of dogs. Spaniels are small to medium in size with short legs, long ears,

A
B
C
D
E
F
G
H
I
J
K
L
M
N
O
P
Q
R
S
T
U
V
W
X
Y
Z

a
b
c
d
e
f
g
h
i
j
k
l
m
n
o
p
q
r
s
t
u
v
w
x
y
z

and long, silky hair. {**spăn** yəl}

Word History *Spaniel* comes from an early French word that means "of Spain" or "Spanish."

Span·ish *adjective* of or having to do with Spain, or its people or language. *noun* 1. the language of Spain and Spanish America. 2. (used with a plural verb) the people of Spain (usually used with "the"). {**spăn** ihsh}

Bienvenido a mi casa!

spank *verb* (spanked, spanking, spanks) to hit with the open hand or a hard object as punishment. *My dad spanked me because I would not wash the dishes.* {**spăngk**}

spare *verb* (spared, sparing, spares) 1. to handle gently; to not hurt. *We spared his feelings by not talking about his mistakes.* 2. to save from having to do something. *He was spared having to wait.* 3. to keep from hurting or destroying. *We spared the bird that fell by putting it back in its nest.* 4. to use a little amount of. *Please try to spare the hot water.* 5. to allow; afford. *Please spare me a minute of your time.* 6. to keep from including or talking about. *Spare me the sad stories.* *adjective* (sparer, sparest) 1. kept for later use. *He has a spare battery in the garage.* 2. being more than needed. *I don't have any spare money to give.* 3. thin; lean. *He is such a spare boy from not eating enough.* 4. barely enough; small in amount. *The poor man sat down to eat a spare meal.* *noun* 1. an item that is put aside for future use. *We have a spare in case we get a flat tire.* 2. the knocking down of all pins with two

rolls of the ball in bowling. *He only got three pins with his first ball, but he picked up the spare with his second try.* {**spayr**}

spark *noun* 1. a hot and glowing material thrown off by burning wood. 2. a short, bright flash. *Sparks are made when electricity passes across a space.* 3. a small but important amount; a trace. *Her smile showed a spark of hope.* *verb* (sparked, sparking, sparks) 1. to produce or cause to produce sparks. *The fire sparked in the darkness.* 2. (informal) to set in motion; stir up. *The principal's decision sparked anger from some of the students.* {**spark**}

spar·kle *verb* (sparkled, sparkling, sparkles) 1. to throw off or reflect little flashes of light; glitter. *The rubies and diamonds sparkled.* 2. to give off gas bubbles; bubble. *Our soda pop sparkled.* 3. to be lively or full of energy. *She sparkled at the party.* *noun* a flash or gleam of light; glitter. *The sparkle of the stars in the night sky was beautiful.* {**spar** kəl}

spar·row *noun* a small, common songbird with brown or gray feathers. There are several kinds of sparrows and they can be found in many different areas. {**spar** oh}

sparse *adjective* (sparser, sparsest) not thick or dense; scattered in thin amounts. *There was a sparse crowd at the show last night.* {**spars**} sparsely, adv., sparseness, n., sparsity, n.

spat[1] *noun* a short, slight quarrel. {**spăt**}

spat[2] *verb* a past tense and past participle of **spit**[1]. {**spăt**}

spat·ter *verb* (spattered, spattering, spatters) 1. to splash or scatter in small bits or drops. *I spattered the canvas with blue paint.* 2. to splash or scatter bits or drops of a liquid on; spot. *The grease from the hamburger spattered the stove.* *noun* 1. the act or sound of spattering. *There was the spatter of rain on the roof.* 2. a bit, drop, or splash of something spattered. *There is a spatter of paint on the floor.* {**spăt** ər}

spat·u·la *noun* a cooking tool used for spreading or mixing. Spatulas have wide, flat blades that can bend easily. {**spă** chə lə}

spawn *noun* the large number of eggs produced by fish, frogs, and other water animals. *verb* (spawned, spawning, spawns) to produce a large number of eggs. *Salmon spawn in fresh water just before they die.* {**spawn**}

SPCA *abbreviation* an organization whose purpose is to take care of lost or stray dogs, cats, and other small animals. This organization tries to find people to adopt these animals as pets. SPCA is an abbreviation for "Society for the Prevention of Cruelty to Animals."

speak 🔊 *verb* (spoke, spoken, speaking, speaks) 1. to utter words in one's usual voice; talk. *Can you speak louder?* 2. to say in one's usual voice. *She spoke my name.* 3. to express a thought or idea using the voice. *I will speak to her about the party.* 4. to express. *They spoke the truth.* 5. to deliver a speech. *He will speak at our graduation.* 6. to take part in conversation. *He interrupted as we were*

 Human Body   ❓ Human Mind   👕 Everyday Life   🚩 History and Culture   📞 Communication

speaking. 7. to be able to speak in. *He speaks German and English.* {**speek**} speakable, adj.

speak·er *noun* 1. a person who speaks. *We had a visiting speaker in our class today.* 2. an electronic device that produces sound; loudspeaker. *My stereo system has two speakers.* 3. (sometimes capitalized) the leader of the U.S. House of Representatives or other legislative assembly. *In 1999, Dennis Hastert became the Speaker of the House of Representatives.* {**speek** ər}

spear[1] *noun* a weapon with a long wooden shaft and a sharp pointed tip. Spears are thrown or thrust with the hand. *verb* (speared, spearing, spears) to pierce or hold fast with or as if with a spear. *The fisherman speared the salmon. / The child speared the meat with her fork.* {**speer**}

spear[2] *noun* a pointed sprout or shoot of a plant. *Asparagus grow in spears.* {**speer**}

spear·mint *noun* a common mint plant. Spearmint leaves produce an oil that is used for flavoring. {**speer** mihnt}

spe·cial *adjective* 1. different from others; unique. *His father designed him a special kind of knee brace.* 2. out of the ordinary; better or more important than the usual. *Your birthday is a special occasion. / We're going to a special restaurant to celebrate.* 3. having a particular purpose or use. *The PTA had a special meeting to discuss violence in schools. / She uses a special needle to repair leather.* 4. valued and respected; dear; close. *He is a special friend of mine. noun* 1. a sale of certain things for lower prices. *The supermarket has a special on picnic supplies this week.* 2. a single television program that presents a particular event or topic. *We watched the comedy special.* {**speh** shəl} specially, adv.

spe·cial·ist *noun* a person who has a special interest or area of study. *She is a specialist in Chinese poetry.* {**speh** shə lihst}

spe·cial·ty *noun* (specialties) 1. a special skill or field of study. *Her specialty was French.* 2. an article or thing of particular value. *Wedding dresses are the specialty in that clothing store.* {**speh** shəl tee}

spe·cies ❶ *noun* (species) a group of living things that can mate with one another but not with those of other groups. *A hound and a poodle belong to the same species.* {**spee** sheez *or* **spee** seez}

spe·cif·ic *adjective* 1. certain and exact; particular. *There is a specific person at the party whom I want you to meet.* 2. special or unique to something. *That flower is specific to this part of the country.* {spə **sih** fihk} specifically, adv.

spec·i·men *noun* 1. a part or example used to represent a larger whole. *My grandfather tracks specimens of certain birds to learn their patterns of flight.* 2. a small amount of tissue or liquid from the body used for testing. *Doctors often use specimens of blood to find out why someone is sick.* {**speh** sə mən}

speck *noun* 1. a small mark or spot. *There are specks of mud on my white pants.* 2. a tiny bit or particle. *There is a speck of dirt in my eye.* {**spehk**} speckless, adj.

spec·ta·cle *noun* 1. an unusual or splendid sight or public show. *Yesterday's parade was a spectacle.* 2. (plural) a pair of eyeglasses. {**spehk** tə kəl}

• **make a spectacle of one-self**
to behave in a silly or foolish way in public. *He made a spectacle of himself at the party.*

Word History *Spectacle* comes from *spectare*, a Latin word that means "to view or watch."

spec·tac·u·lar *adjective* of or having to do with a spectacle; splendid; marvelous. *The fireworks were spectacular.* {spehk **tăk** yə lər}

spec·ta·tor *noun* one that watches or observes. *The spectators cheered loudly for their football team.* {**spehk** tay tər}

spec·trum *noun* (spectra or spectrums) a band of colors that is formed when light is passed through a prism, or in some other way. The six colors of a spectrum are red, orange, yellow, green, blue, and purple. *A rainbow is one kind of spectrum that is formed when sunlight passes through rain.* {**spehk** trəm}

spec·u·late *verb* (speculated, speculating, speculates) 1. to make guesses or wonder about something (often followed by "on" or "about"). *We can only speculate about her next move.* 2. to risk a loss of money or property with the promise or hope of making large amounts of money. *We speculated in a small business that turned out to be very successful.* {**spehk** yə **layt**}

speech ❷ *noun* 1. the power to speak, or the act of speaking. *His speech was soft when he talked to the children. / Speech separates humans from animals.* 2. spoken language. *He prefers speech to the written word.* 3. a talk given in front

A
B
C
D
E
F
G
H
I
J
K
L
M
N
O
P
Q
R
S
T
U
V
W
X
Y
Z

🌲 Living World   🔬 Physical World   ♨ Natural Environment   〰 Economy   📖 Government and Law   687

a
b
c
d
e
f
g
h
i
j
k
l
m
n
o
p
q
r
s
t
u
v
w
x
y
z

of an audience. *The mayor gave a speech at city hall.* 4. way of speaking. *His soft speech made it hard to understand what he said.* 5. the way of speaking of a particular country or region. *The Texan speech of the new girl made her the center of attention for a few days.* {speech}

speed *noun* 1. the act of moving rapidly or swiftly. *The bicycle picked up speed as he rode down the hill.* 2. rate of motion. *This jet can travel at the speed of sound. verb* (sped or speeded, speeding, speeds) 1. to go or cause to go faster (usually followed by "up"). *The driver sped up his car to win the race.* 2. to drive a vehicle faster than the law allows. *Because he was speeding, he got a ticket.* 3. to move rapidly or swiftly. *She speeded across the street.* 4. to act or perform at a fast pace (usually followed by "up"). *We will speed up our work on the project.* {speed}

spell[1] *verb* (spelled or spelt, spelling, spells) 1. to name or write the letters of in order. *He can spell Mississippi.* 2. to be the letters of. *C-A-T spells "cat."* 3. to mean. *Wealth does not spell happiness.* {spehl}

• **spell out**
to explain in detail so that no part is difficult to understand. *Do you understand, or shall I spell it out for you?*

spell[2] *noun* 1. a word or group of words used to work magic. *The witch cast a spell on us that made our heads invisible.* 2. a condition of being under someone's power because of magic. *We were helpless under her spell.* 3. any thing that greatly attracts or fascinates. *Caught by the spell of the harp's lovely sound, she forgot her*

unhappiness. {spehl} spell-like, adj.

spell[3] *noun* 1. a short period of time. *Let's rest a spell.* 2. a period that stands out because one kind of event or experience keeps happening. *The river was low after the dry spell. / Talk to him during one of his happy spells.* 3. a period of work or other activity; shift. *He did a spell in the factory. verb* (spelled, spelling, spells) to take the place of for a time. *The children spelled each other during the soccer game.* {spehl}

spell·bound *adjective* held in attention as if by a spell; amazed; fascinated. *We were spellbound by the beautiful music.* {spehl bownd}

spell·er *noun* 1. a person who spells words. *She is the best speller in the class.* 2. a book that teaches spelling; spelling book. {spehl ər}

spell·ing *noun* 1. the way one or more words are spelled. *The class studied spelling every day.* 2. the act of a person who spells. *He has good spelling.* {spehl ing}

spend *verb* (spent, spending, spends) 1. to pay out. *I will spend my money on a new book.* 2. to pass. *He should have spent more than a week training his monkey.* 3. to use up completely. *After the long rehearsal, her energy was spent.* {spehnd}

sperm *noun* (sperm or sperms) a cell made by male animals. These cells fertilize the eggs made by a female, so that the animal can reproduce. {spuhrm}

sperm whale *noun* a very large mammal that lives in the ocean. Sperm whales dive very deeply and can hold their breath for over an hour. They are related to por-

poises, dolphins, and other whales with teeth. Sperm whales are the largest toothed whale. {spuhrm wayl}

spew *verb* (spewed, spewing, spews) 1. to spurt out; vomit. *He spewed his dinner all over the table.* 2. to throw out with force, energy, or excitement. *The volcano spews lava.* 3. to be thrown out with force or in large amounts. *Words spewed out of her.* {spyoo}

sphere *noun* 1. a round, solid figure in which every point on the surface is an equal distance from the center. *Globes are made in the shape of a sphere.* 2. a field or area that someone or something has knowledge or power in. *She is a leader in her social sphere. / The mayor's sphere of influence reaches far beyond her city.* {sfeer}

sphinx *noun* (sphinxes) 1. a creature in Egyptian mythology that has a lion's body and the head of a human or animal. 2. (capitalized) the huge stone statue of such a creature that is located in Egypt. {sfingks}

spice ⊙ *noun* 1. a vegetable substance with a particular smell or taste. Spices are used to flavor food and drink. *Pepper and cinnamon are two common spices.* 2. that which adds excitement or interest. *Danger added spice to the adventure. verb* (spiced, spicing, spices) 1. to use spice in or on. *We spiced the soup with a bit of pepper.* 2. to add flavor or interest to. *She spiced up her dull outfit with a colorful hat.* {spiys}

spic·y *adjective* (spicier, spiciest) 1. made with or having strong spices. *She likes to cook and eat spicy food.* 2. having a strong flavor or smell. *The spicy plants in our garden help*

⊙ Human Body   ❓ Human Mind   ↻ Everyday Life   ⚑ History and Culture   ☏ Communication keep pests away. {**spiy** see} spiciness, n.

spi·der ❶ *noun* a small animal with eight legs and a body made up of two parts. Most spiders spin webs in which they nest and catch insects to eat. Spiders are related to mites, ticks, and scorpions. {**spiy** dər}

spike *noun* 1. a long, thick nail used to fasten or tie heavy logs or railroad tracks. 2. a sharply pointed object. *We couldn't climb over the fence spikes.* 3. (plural) such metal objects on the bottom of a sport shoe. *Baseball players usually wear spikes. verb* (spiked, spiking, spikes) to hit sharply downward across the net in volleyball. *Our team spiked the ball to win the first point of the game.* {**spiyk**}

spill *verb* (spilled or spilt, spilling, spills) 1. to cause or allow to flow or fall from a container. *She spilled the coffee all over her dress.* 2. to flow or fall out of a container. *The milk will spill if you aren't careful.* 3. to cause to fall off or out. *The wagon fell over and spilled us onto the road.* 4. to spread out in a rush or beyond some boundary. *People spilled from the theater when the fire started.* 5. (informal) to tell or reveal. *She spilled what she knew about his family. noun* 1. that which has spilled, or the amount spilled. *The spill we left on the floor made my mom angry.* 2. (informal) a fall. *She took a bad spill on the ice.* {**spihl**}

spin *verb* (spun, spinning, spins) 1. to draw out, twist, and wind, or to make by doing this. *She spins her own yarn.* 2. to make using thread that comes from the body. *The spider spun a web to catch flies.* 3. to cause to turn quickly on an axis or as if on an axis. *The boy was spinning a ball on his finger. / He spun me around.* 4. to turn or seem to whirl rapidly. *Her pinwheel was spinning in the wind. / My head was spinning with excitement.* 5. to form or develop from the imagination. *She spun a mystery for us. noun* 1. the act of spinning or causing something to spin. *He gave the toy a spin.* 2. a twirling motion or feeling. *He put spin on the ball as he threw it.* 3. a short drive or ride in an automobile, boat, or small airplane. *Let's go for a spin in my new car.* {**spihn**}

spin·ach *noun* a green plant with leaves, often eaten as a vegetable. {**spihn** ihch}

spi·nal *adjective* having to do with the spine or spinal cord. *The spinal column protects the spinal cord.* {**spiy** nəl}

spinal column *noun* the row of bones that runs along the center of the back; spine; backbone. The bones of the spinal column are called vertebrae. The spinal column protects the nerves in the spinal cord. {**spiy** nəl **ko** ləm}

spinal cord *noun* the thick cord of nerve tissue inside the spine that runs from the base of the brain to the end of the spine. {**spiy** nəl **kohrd**}

spin·dle *noun* a thin rod on which thread is twisted and wound as it is spun. {**spihn** dəl}

spine ❶ *noun* 1. the backbone; spinal column. 2. a sharp, pointed part that sticks out on certain plants or animals. *Cactus plants and porcupines both have spines.* 3. a stiff, hard back or ridge, such as the back part of a book or the narrow peak of a mountain. {**spiyn**}

spi·ral *noun* 1. a curve that circles around from a fixed point. A spiral gets bigger or smaller as it moves away from the fixed point. 2. something shaped like or moving like a spiral. *adjective* curved in the form of a spiral. *There is a spiral path to the center of the garden. verb* (spiraled, spiraling, spirals) to form or cause to form a spiral. *The staircase spiraled from the top floor to the floor below.* {**spiyr** əl}

spire *noun* a tall, narrow, upward structure shaped like a cone on the outside of a building; steeple. {**spiyr**}

spir·it *noun* 1. a force that is thought to be a part of human beings; soul. *Some people believe that when you die, your spirit lives on.* 2. a being that is not of this world, such as a devil, ghost, or fairy. *He told me that the old house is haunted by evil spirits.* 3. the way a person feels or thinks, as marked by qualities such as courage and energy. *He led the team with his courageous spirit.* 4. (plural) a feeling or mood. *He was in low spirits from the bad news.* 5. the meaning or intent of a thing. *The judge tried to stay true to the spirit of the law. verb* (spirited, spir-

A
B
C
D
E
F
G
H
I
J
K
L
M
N
O
P
Q
R
S
T
U
V
W
X
Y
Z

a
b
c
d
e
f
g
h
i
j
k
l
m
n
o
p
q
r
s
t
u
v
w
x
y
z

iting, spirits) to remove secretly (usually followed by "off" or "away"). *The thieves spirited away our car.* {**speer** iht}

Word History *Spirit* comes from *spiritus,* a Latin word that could mean either "breath" or "soul." In cultures even more ancient than the Roman or Greek, the breath and the soul were the same thing.

spir·it·ual *adjective* 1. of, having to do with, or made up of spirit, rather than the physical body or world. *Many people believe that ghosts visit us from a spiritual world.* 2. of or having to do with a church or religion. *He writes spiritual music. noun* a religious song of a kind that began among black people in the southern United States. {**speer** ih chooh əl} spiritually, adv., spiritualness, n.

spit[1] *verb* (spit or spat, spitting, spits) 1. to force saliva or something else from the mouth. *He spat in the sink.* 2. to make a spitting sound. *The fire sizzled and spat.* 3. to force from the mouth (often followed by "out"). *I spat out my gum.* 4. to force out as though by spitting. *The engine is spitting oil. noun* saliva that has come from the mouth. {**spiht**}

spit[2] *noun* 1. a thin, pointed rod on which meat is placed and turned while roasting. 2. a narrow, pointed piece of land that extends into a body of water. {**spiht**}

spite *noun* the wish to hurt, bother, or embarrass a person. *He told my secret out of spite. verb* (spited, spiting, spites) to act with spite toward. *To spite them, she did not show up at their party.* {**spiyt**}

• **in spite of** without being changed or prevented by; despite. *In spite of her best effort, she failed the test. / We set off on foot in spite of the rain.*

splash *verb* (splashed, splashing, splashes) 1. to dash or spray. *The car splashed mud all over me.* 2. to dash or spray a liquid, or be dashed or sprayed. *The waves splashed on the shore.* 3. to wet or soil by this means. *The truck splashed our car with mud.* 4. to fall or move with a dashing of liquid. *We splashed in the ocean. noun* 1. the act or sound of splashing. *At night I could hear the splash of waves.* 2. a spot made by a splash of water or by other means. *There was a splash of sunlight on the sidewalk.* {**splăsh**}

spleen *noun* an organ near the stomach that stores blood. The spleen gets rid of old red blood cells, and makes certain kinds of white blood cells. {**spleen**}

splen·did *adjective* 1. beautiful or grand; making a strong impression. *He wore a splendid robe of velvet with diamond trim.* 2. outstanding; excellent. *The painters did a splendid job on our house.* {**splehn** dihd} splendidly, adv.

splice *verb* (spliced, splicing, splices) 1. to join at the ends. *He spliced the movie film.* 2. to fasten together by weaving together strands. *We spliced the two pieces of rope to make a longer piece.* {**spliys**} splicer, n.

splint *noun* a thin piece of wood, metal, or plastic used to support and keep steady a broken bone. {**splihnt**}

splin·ter *noun* a small, sharp piece of material that is broken off from a larger piece. *My sister had to pull out*

a splinter of wood from my foot. verb (splintered, splintering, splinters) to break or break off into splinters. *The blow splintered the glass. / The glass splintered.* {**splihn** tər}

split *verb* (split, splitting, splits) 1. to divide along the length or in layers. *We split the wood for the fireplace.* 2. to divide, break up or off, or separate. *The road splits here. / The rock split into small pieces.* 3. to break up or separate by force or as though by force; tear apart. *Physicists split atoms. / He split a seam in his pants.* 4. to break or fall apart, as from pressure or disagreement. *The package split open. / The couple split in a very sad divorce.* 5. to divide into parts (often followed by "up"). *Let's split up the pie.* 6. to divide or separate into different groups or directions. *The class was split at lunch time. noun* 1. the act, product, or result of splitting. *There was a split in my shirt.* 2. a division between two or more people. *There was a split over who would be president of the club.* 3. (sometimes plural) a movement in gymnastics in which the legs are spread in opposite directions as the body sinks to the ground. *She is so flexible, she can do splits with ease. adjective* separated; divided. *The court handed down a split decision.* {**spliht**}

spoil *verb* (spoiled or spoilt, spoiling, spoils) 1. to damage or ruin; make unable to be used or enjoyed. *She spoiled her new dress. / The rain spoiled our camping trip.* 2. to harm the character of by giving too much freedom, too much money, or not enough punishment. *They spoiled their daughter.* 3. to go

 Human Body   Human Mind   Everyday Life   History and Culture   Communication

rotten; decay. *Meat spoils rapidly in hot weather.* *noun* (plural) material goods or other things gained by winning a victory. *The pirates laughed as they divided up the spoils.* {<u>spoil</u>}
• **be spoiling for** (informal) to be eager for. *She is spoiling for revenge.*

Synonyms
These words share a meaning with *spoil*, verb 1:
damage, ruin, wreck

spoke[1] *verb* past tense of **speak**. {<u>spohk</u>}

spoke[2] *noun* a rod or bar that goes from the center of a wheel to the rim. {<u>spohk</u>}

spo·ken 🔄 *verb* past participle of **speak**. *adjective* said by using words; oral. *Spoken words sometimes get more attention than written words.* {<u>spoh</u> kən}

sponge *noun* 1. a tiny sea animal that has a body with many holes. Thousands of kinds of sponges live in the ocean. Most kinds of sponges live in groups or colonies on coral reefs, rocks, shells, or other objects. 2. the light skeleton of some kinds of sponge colonies. People harvest sponges after the animals die and then dry the skeletons. People use sponges for cleaning and bathing. 3. an artificial material with many small holes that can soak up water easily. *verb* (sponged, sponging, sponges) 1. to wipe, clean, or make wet with a sponge. *My parents sponge the floor every Sunday.* 2. to soak up or wipe with a sponge (usually followed by "up"). *My dad sponged up the water that had spilled on the floor.* {<u>spuhnj</u>} spongelike, adj.
• **throw in the sponge**

to give up; to admit defeat. *The tennis player threw in the sponge after he lost four games in a row.*

spon·gy *adjective* (spongier, spongiest) like a sponge in being light, full of holes, or able to keep its shape after being pressed or stretched. *We walked over the spongy ground near the swamp.* {<u>spuhn</u> jee}

spon·sor *noun* 1. a person who takes responsibility for someone or something. *The sponsor for the school field trip counted the students on the bus.* 2. a business or a person who pays the cost of a radio or television program in exchange for showing commercials during the program. *Coke and Pepsi are sponsors for many television programs.* 3. a person who presents someone for baptism or confirmation; godparent. *verb* (sponsored, sponsoring, sponsors) to serve as a sponsor for. *The local pizza restaurant sponsored the little league baseball team.* {<u>spŏn</u> sər} sponsorship, n.

spon·ta·ne·ous *adjective* 1. happening in a free way; not forced. *My friend suddenly let out a spontaneous laugh.* 2. happening without outside causes or forces. *There was a spontaneous explosion in the lab.* {spŏn <u>tay</u> nee əs} spontaneously, adv.

spook *noun* (informal) a ghost; phantom. *verb* (spooked, spooking, spooks) (informal) to frighten or cause to be nervous. *A rattlesnake spooked my horse.* {<u>spoohk</u>}

spool *noun* an object shaped like a cylinder with a rim on each end. Thread, tape, wire, and film are wound on spools. {<u>spoohl</u>}

spoon 🔄 *noun* 1. a tool with a small, shallow bowl at the end of a handle, used for eating, stirring, serving, or measuring. 2. the amount that a spoon will hold. *The recipe called for two spoons of sugar.* *verb* (spooned, spooning, spoons) to move by using a spoon; scoop up. *She spooned the medicine into her mouth.* {<u>spoohn</u>}
• **born with a silver spoon in one's mouth** born to rich parents.

spore *noun* a tiny reproductive body made up of one or more cells, produced by certain animals and plants. Ferns and fungi produce spores. {<u>spohr</u>}

sport 🔄🔄 *noun* 1. an athletic event or game played according to rules. Sports often require certain skills and involve two people or teams on opposite sides. *Soccer is my favorite sport.* 2. something done for fun or amusement. *We like to skip stones just for sport.* 3. a person who has a good attitude about difficult situations. *He was a sport about the joke we played on him.* *adjective* 1. of or having to do with sports. *He went out running in his sport shoes.* 2. suited for casual wear. *He went out to dinner in a sport coat.* *verb* (sported, sporting, sports) to amuse oneself through activity; play. *We sported with our friends on the playground.* {<u>spohrt</u>}

sports·man·ship *noun* the qualities and behavior which a person should show when playing a sport or game. *She showed good sportsmanship by shaking hands with the person who won the game.* {<u>spohrts</u> mən shihp}

A
B
C
D
E
F
G
H
I
J
K
L
M
N
O
P
Q
R
S
T
U
V
W
X
Y
Z

 Living World    Physical World   Natural Environment    Economy   Government and Law   691

a
b
c
d
e
f
g
h
i
j
k
l
m
n
o
p
q
r

s

t
u
v
w
x
y
z

spot *noun* 1. a mark, such as a stain, different in color from the area around it. *She has a dark spot on her shirt.* 2. place; position. *His name was written in the first spot on the list.* 3. an uncomfortable position. *If we don't finish on time, we'll be in a spot.* 4. an area or location. *We found a good vacation spot by the lake.* *verb* (spotted, spotting, spots) 1. to cause to be marked with spots. *The street is spotted with oil.* 2. to notice or catch sight of. *He spotted his sister in the crowd.* {spŏt}

• **on the spot**
1. at once; immediately. *The teacher gave us our tests back on the spot.* 2. in a bad or uncomfortable position. *He was on the spot when she finally confronted him.*

spouse *noun* a husband or wife. {spows}

spout *verb* (spouted, spouting, spouts) 1. to force out in a steady stream. *The fountain spouted water.* 2. to flow out in a forced manner. *Hot lava is spouting from the volcano.* *noun* a tube, pipe, or other narrow opening from which a liquid is poured. *The tea poured from the spout on the pot.* {spowt}

sprain ⊕ *verb* (sprained, spraining, sprains) to twist so that ligaments are stretched or torn. *I sprained my left ankle when I tripped on the stairs.* *noun* the twisting of a body joint so that ligaments are stretched or torn. *The sprain in my wrist makes it hard for me to write.* {sprayn}

sprang *verb* a past tense of **spring.** {sprăng}

sprawl *verb* (sprawled, sprawling, sprawls) 1. to lie, sit, or fall with the arms and legs spread out in a loose or relaxed way. *I sprawled on the*

the couch to watch my favorite TV show. 2. to spread in a manner that is not ordered or organized. *The town sprawls from here to the river.* {sprawl}

spray *noun* 1. water or another liquid flying or falling in fine drops; mist. 2. a liquid that is made to be sprayed. *We used bug spray on the plants.* 3. a device used to send out liquid in a mist of tiny drops. *I am using a spray to paint the house.* *verb* (sprayed, spraying, sprays) 1. to send out in a spray. *He sprayed poison on the windows to kill the flies.* 2. to use a spray on or cover with a spray. *She sprayed her throat with medicine. / It's quicker to spray walls with paint than to use a brush.* 3. to come out in a spray. *Water sprayed from a hole in the hose.* {spray} sprayer, n.

spread *verb* (spread, spreading, spreads) 1. to open or stretch out. *He spread the map on the table. / She spread her arms to catch the ball.* 2. to put on in a layer. *She spread some jam on her bread.* 3. to scatter or send forth. *Please spread the news that there will be a meeting tonight.* *noun* 1. the act of spreading. *She stopped the spread of her spilled milk with a paper towel.* 2. a stretch of open space. *They camped on the spread below the mountains.* 3. a cloth covering that is put over furniture such as a bed or table. 4. food that can be spread on crackers, bread, vegetables, or other foods. {sprehd}

spring *verb* (sprang or sprung, sprung, springing, springs) 1. to move upward quickly or suddenly; jump. *The dog sprang to catch the ball.* 2. to change position suddenly. *He*

sprang into action when he went into the game. 3. to close or move quickly. *The trap springs to catch a mouse.* 4. to come into being quickly. *Flowers are springing up in the garden.* 5. to cause to form or develop. *The pipes sprang a leak.* 6. to set free or to give information. *They sprang a bird from the cage. / He sprung the secret that there would be a surprise party.* *noun* 1. an elastic device or object that returns to its original shape after being pressed or stretched out. *The car needs new springs.* 2. a quick and sudden movement; jump. *He made a spring to catch the balloon.* 3. a flow of water from the earth. *We stopped in the woods to drink water from a spring.* 4. a season of the year between winter and summer. *Flowers grow in the spring.* *adjective* 1. having to do with or taking place during the season of spring. *I'm going down south for spring vacation.* 2. used for the season of spring. *She went shopping for spring clothes.* {spring} spring-like, adj.

sprin·kle *verb* (sprinkled, sprinkling, sprinkles) 1. to drop or scatter in small bits. *I always sprinkle nuts on my ice cream.* 2. to drop or scatter small bits upon. *He is sprinkling the lawn. / She sprinkled the salad with cheese.* 3. to rain very lightly (often used with "it"). *It has been sprinkling off and on.* *noun* 1. a slight amount of rain. *The sprinkle only lasted for a few hours before the sun came out.* 2. a small amount or number. *There was a sprinkle of laughter in the classroom.* {spring kəl}

sprint *verb* (sprinted, sprinting, sprints) to run or go at top speed. *He sprinted to the top of*

 Human Body    Human Mind   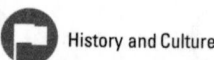 Everyday Life    History and Culture   Communication

the hill to catch the bus. *noun* a short race at top speed. *The coach told us to do several sprints.* {**sprihnt**} sprinter, n.

sprout *verb* (sprouted, sprouting, sprouts) 1. to start to grow. *The buds on the trees sprouted in the spring.* 2. to grow rapidly. *His children sprouted like weeds.* 3. to grow or cause to grow. *Do you expect me to sprout wings and fly? / He sprouted the beans in a large jar.* *noun* a shoot or bud of a plant. {**sprowt**}

spruce[1] ❶ *noun* 1. an ever-green tree with hanging cones and short, thin leaves shaped like needles. 2. the soft wood of this tree. {**sproohs**}

spruce[2] ❓ *verb* (spruced, sprucing, spruces) to make or become neat, or give a new look to (usually followed by "up"). *I spruced up my room with bright wallpaper.* {**sproohs**}

spry *adjective* (spryer or sprier, spryest or spriest) moving in a brisk and lively way; nimble. *The spry young boy moved quickly through the playground.* {**spriy**}

spur *noun* 1. a metal piece with a spike that is attached to the heel of a rider's boot. Spurs are used to make a horse go forward. 2. anything that urges someone or something to action or to greater effort or speed. *My father's praise was a spur to do better in school.* *verb* (spurred, spur-ring, spurs) 1. to poke using spurs. *The rider spurred his horse to jump the fence.* 2. to urge to act (often followed by "on"). *Her support spurred me on.* {**spuhr**}

• **on the spur of the moment** without much thought. *We decided to go camping on the spur of the moment.*

spurt *verb* (spurted, spurting, spurts) 1. to rush or shoot out in a forced or sudden way; spout. *The toothpaste spurted from the tube.* 2. to have a sudden and short burst in speed, amount, or degree. *The runner spurted to the finish line.* 3. to shoot out in a stream or squirt. *The large cut in my finger spurted blood.* *noun* 1. a rush or squirt of liquid or steam; spout; jet. *Give that motor a spurt of oil.* 2. a sudden, short burst of activity, speed, or energy. *My sister had a growth spurt at age thirteen.* {**spuhrt**}

sput·ter *verb* (sputtered, sput-tering, sputters) 1. to spit out saliva or bits of food while speaking in a fast or excited way. *The little boy sputtered and cried about the broken toy.* 2. to make a quick series of popping or spitting noises. *The car engine sputtered and came to a stop.* 3. to say quickly in a confused or angry way. *She sputtered angry words to the policeman.* *noun* the act or sound of sput-tering. *I heard a sputter from the lawn mower.* {**spuh** tər}

spy *noun* (spies) 1. a person who works for a government in secret to watch and get infor-mation about another nation's activities and plans. 2. a person who watches in secret to get information about others. *verb* (spied, spying, spies) 1. to observe in a secret and careful way (usu-ally followed by "on" or "upon"). *I spied on my sister from behind a bush.* 2. to dis-cover or catch sight of. *He

spied a cat under the porch.* {**spiy**}

sq. *abbreviation* an abbreviation for **square**.

sq. ft. *abbreviation* an abbrevia-tion for "square foot" or "square feet."

squad *noun* a small number of persons trained to work together. *The football squad practiced every day. / My brother's army squad is going to Greece.* {**skwahd**}

squall *noun* a sudden, powerful wind that moves in suddenly. Squalls usually bring rain, snow, or sleet. {**skwahl**}

square ❶ *noun* 1. a flat, closed figure with four straight sides of equal length and four angles of equal measure. 2. something that has the form of such a shape. *We drew squares on the sidewalk for a game of hop-scotch.* 3. an out-door space or plaza within a town or city. *We sat by a fountain in the town square.* 4. an instrument with straight edges and a right angle used to draw or test right angles. *He used a square to make his art project.* 5. the result of a number multiplied by itself. *The square of five is twenty-five.* 6. (informal) one who is not aware of fashion or is old-fashioned. *My father is a real square.* *verb* (squared, squaring, squares) 1. to cut or make into a square or similar shape. *The carpenter used a plane to square the boards for our new shelves.* 2. to put straight or even. *He squared the blankets on the bed.* 3. to fit or match with. *Her answer on the test squared with mine.* 4. to multiply by itself. *Ten squared equals one hundred.* 5. to agree (usually followed by

A
B
C
D
E
F
G
H
I
J
K
L
M
N
O
P
Q
R
S
T
U
V
W
X
Y
Z

"with"). *Mike's story does not square with the facts.* *adjective* (squarer, squarest) 1. formed with four equal sides and four right angles. *I looked out through the square window.* 2. having to do with any unit of measure in the form of a square. *Our bedroom has an area of eighty square feet.* 3. having the form of a square. *The neighborhood has five square blocks.* 4. making a right angle. *The room has square corners.* 5. honest; direct. *That store is known for giving a square deal.* 6. having to pay no more money; paid up. *I gave him ten dollars, and now we're square.* 7. (informal) not interested in anything new; old-fashioned. *I have some really square neighbors.* *adverb* (squarer, squarest) 1. at right angles. *We moved the chairs square with the table.* 2. in the shape of a square. *We sat square around the table.* 3. in a direct manner. *The commander spoke square with the soldiers about the dangers of the mission.* {**skwayr**} squareness, n.

square root *noun* a number that, when multiplied by itself, produces another number. *Five is the square root of twenty-five.* {**skwayr rooht**}

squash[1] *verb* (squashed, squashing, squashes) 1. to press, beat, or crush into a flat mass. *I stepped on the ant and squashed it.* 2. to be pressed or crushed into a flat mass. *The flowers were squashed by the dog.* 3. to press or squeeze into a tight space. *Many people were squashed into the subway.* *noun* a racket sport for two or four players. Squash is played in a court with four walls. {**skwŏsh**}

squash[2] *noun* 1. a fruit that grows on a vine and is eaten as a vegetable. Squash grows in many sizes, colors, and shapes. 2. the plant that bears such a fruit. {**skwŏsh**}

> **Word History** *Squash* is a shortened form of the Algonquin word, *askutasquash.*

squat *verb* (squatted, squatting, squats) to sit on one's heels, or to crouch low to the ground with the knees bent. *I squatted to talk to the children.* *adjective* (squatter, squattest) having a low, heavy body or structure. *My mother is squat in her old age.* {**skwŏt**}

squawk *verb* (squawked, squawking, squawks) to give a harsh scream. *My parrot squawks at me when I come home.* *noun* a harsh scream. *The squawk of a bird woke me up this morning.* {**skwawk**}

squeak *noun* a short, high, shrill sound or cry. *I hope that squeak was your shoes and not a mouse.* *verb* (squeaked, squeaking, squeaks) to give off a high, shrill sound. *The child squeaks with delight. / Your bicycle wheels will not squeak if you oil them.* {**skweek**}

• **squeak by [or] through** barely succeed; almost fail. *She did not think she would pass the swimming test, but she squeaked by.*

squeal *noun* a fairly long, loud, shrill sound or cry. *The squeal of tires startled me.* *verb* (squealed, squealing, squeals) 1. to let out a squeal. *The children squealed with delight on the swings.* 2. to say

with a squeal. *My sister squealed the news that she was pregnant.* {**skweel**} squealer, n.

squeeze *verb* (squeezed, squeezing, squeezes) 1. to press firmly together. *He squeezed my hand as he said goodbye.* 2. to put pressure on or crush so as to pull something from. *She squeezed oranges for juice.* 3. to hug. *My mom squeezes me every morning before I leave for school.* 4. to press into a small or crowded space. *He squeezed two more people into the elevator.* 5. to force one's way through a crowd or small space (usually followed by "through" or "in"). *We squeezed through the people to get to the front of the line.* *noun* 1. the act of squeezing. *A squeeze of lemon will add flavor to the food.* 2. a hug. *My teacher gave me a big squeeze when the school year ended.* {**skweez**} squeezable, adj.

squid *noun* (squid or squids) a sea animal with a long, soft body and ten strong tentacles. Squids are carnivores that eat other sea animals. They are mollusks and are closely related to octopuses. Squids range in size from four inches to over sixty feet. {**skwihd**}

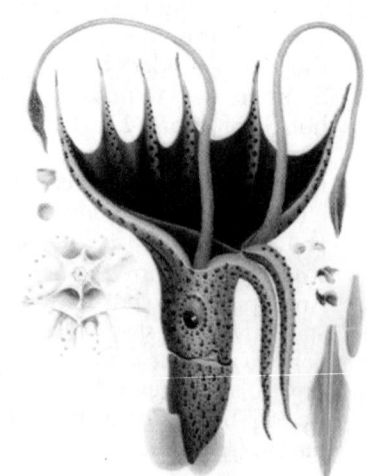

 Human Body   Human Mind   Everyday Life   History and Culture   Communication

squint *verb* (squinted, squinting, squints) to partly close the eyelids. *We squinted in the sun.* *noun* the act or habit of squinting. {skwiht}

squirm *verb* (squirmed, squirming, squirms) 1. to twist the body about; wriggle. *The boy squirmed in his chair because he had to go to the bathroom.* 2. to feel embarrassed or uncomfortable. *Ashton squirmed when the spider moved closer.* *noun* a twisting movement; the act of squirming. *Kenny got out of the tight sweater with a wiggle and a squirm.* {skwuhrm} squirmy, adj.

squir·rel *noun* a small rodent that is active during the day. There are many kinds of squirrels found all around the world. The word "squirrel" is often used to refer to tree squirrels, small rodents with long, bushy tails. Tree squirrels have gray, red, brown, or black fur. {skwuhrl or skwuh rəl}

Word History *Squirrel* comes from two ancient Greek words that mean "shadow" and "tail."

squirt *verb* (squirted, squirting, squirts) 1. to be shot out in a thin jet; spurt. *Water squirts from the fountain.* 2. to shoot out in a thin jet; spurt. *Hoses squirt water.* 3. to wet with liquid shot out in a thin jet or spray. *He squirted me with a* water gun. *noun* 1. the act of squirting. 2. a thin jet or spray of liquid. *I noticed a squirt of oil coming from the bottom of the car.* {skwuhrt}

Sr. *abbreviation* an abbreviation for **Senior**.

St. *abbreviation* 1. an abbreviation for **street**. 2. an abbreviation for **Saint**.

stab *verb* (stabbed, stabbing, stabs) 1. to pierce or wound with or as if with a pointed object. *I stabbed myself with a fork.* 2. to thrust at or into. *The nurse stabbed the needle into my arm.* *noun* 1. the act or an instance of stabbing. 2. a sudden sharp pain or pang. *I felt a stab of pain when the doctor put the needle in my arm.* {stăb} stabber, n.

• **take a stab at**
to try or attempt. *Let's take a stab at climbing to the top of that tree.*

sta·ble[1] *adjective* (stabler, stablest) 1. fixed, firm, or steady in position; not shaky or easily moved. *Please keep the ladder stable.* 2. not easily changed; lasting a long time. *A stable job will help her support her children. / We are lucky to have freedom and a stable form of government.* {stay bəl} stably, adv.

sta·ble[2] *noun* a building where animals such as horses or cows are kept and fed. Stables are often divided into separate stalls. *verb* (stabled, stabling, stables) to put or keep in a stable. *He stabled the bull.* {stay bəl}

stack *noun* 1. a large, neat pile of hay, straw, or grain. 2. a neat pile arranged in layers. *There is a stack of newspapers on the street corner every morning.* 3. a tall chimney; smokestack. *verb* (stacked, stacking, stacks) 1. to put, store, or arrange in a stack or stacks. *She stacked the wood by the stove.* 2. to be put or arranged in a stack. *These chairs will stack easily.* {stăk}

sta·di·um *noun* a place used for sports events and other outdoor activities. Stadiums have rows of seats that rise up around an open field. {stay dee əm}

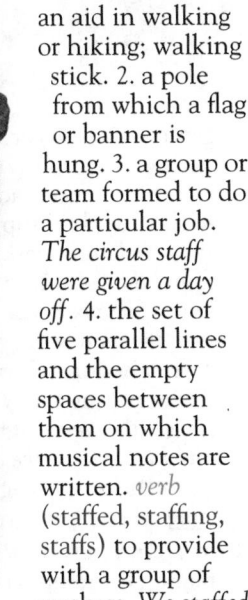

staff *noun* (staffs or staves) 1. a pole or rod often used as an aid in walking or hiking; walking stick. 2. a pole from which a flag or banner is hung. 3. a group or team formed to do a particular job. *The circus staff were given a day off.* 4. the set of five parallel lines and the empty spaces between them on which musical notes are written. *verb* (staffed, staffing, staffs) to provide with a group of workers. *We staffed the event with many young people.* {stăf}

stag *noun* an adult male deer. {stăg}

stage ⬆ 🌐 *noun* 1. a raised platform used for concerts, plays, talks, and other performances. 2. the job of acting in the theater (used with "the"). *He started his career on the stage after finishing school.* 3. a separate period or step in a process of growth or development. *Adolescence is a stage between childhood and adulthood. / The first stage in preparing an oral report is finding a topic.* *verb* (staged, staging, stages) to perform or present on a stage. *The theater club is*

 Living World   Physical World   Natural Environment    Economy    Government and Law

A B C D E F G H I J K L M N O P Q R S T U V W X Y Z

a b c d e f g h i j k l m n o p q r **s** t u v w x y z

going to stage a play by Shakespeare this year. {stayj}

stage·coach *noun* a large coach with four wheels pulled by a team of horses. Stagecoaches were used in the past to carry passengers, mail, and goods. {stayj kohch}

stag·ger *verb* (staggered, staggering, staggers) 1. to walk or stand in an unsteady way or with a need for support. *He staggered in the dark until he found the light.* 2. to shock or stun. *The news that he had won the money staggered him.* 3. to schedule or arrange at different times. *My parents stagger the days that my brother and I have to do the dishes.* *noun* the act of staggering. {stăg ər} staggeringly, adv.

stain *noun* 1. a spot or colored mark. *Dirt stains on the carpet are hard to remove.* 2. a dye used to color something. *We used a dark stain on the floors to make them look nice.* 3. something that causes shame. *The lies he told at school left a stain on his character.* *verb* (stained, staining, stains) 1. to spot or color. *The grass stained my pants.* 2. to cause to take on a new color by putting on a stain. *I stained the old chair in our living room.* 3. to become, or be able to become, stained. *This wood stains nicely.* 4. to mark with shame or dishonor. *Cheating on the exam stained his reputation.* {stayn}

stair *noun* 1. (plural) a set of steps that make up a staircase; flight of steps. 2. one of

the steps that make up such a set. {stayr}

Homophone Note Are you looking for the word *stare* (to look steadily)? *Stair* and *stare* sound alike but have different meanings.

stair·case *noun* a set of steps with a railing that goes from one floor to another in a building. {stayr kays}

stair·way *noun* a staircase, often one walled off from the rest of a building. {stayr way}

stake[1] *noun* a sharpened or pointed post that is driven into the ground. Stakes can be used to mark a place or to support something. *We used stakes to hold our tent in place.* *verb* (staked, staking, stakes) 1. to make a claim to or mark off, using stakes or as if using stakes (often followed by "off" or "out"). *We staked out the area that we would use for our camp.* 2. to tie to or lean against a stake in order to give support. *He staked the bean plant.* 3. to tie or attach to a stake. *We staked the goat in the front yard.* {stayk}

stake[2] *noun* 1. one's share or interest in something. *I have no stake in the family farm since I left home.* 2. (often plural) anything valuable that can be won or lost. *The stakes in this election are very high.* {stayk}

Homophone Note Are you looking for the word *steak*? *Stake* and *steak* sound alike but have different meanings. To learn why you might have trouble with raccoons and bears if you pitch your tent using steaks, look up *steak*.

sta·lac·tite *noun* a rock formation that looks like an icicle and hangs from the roof of a cave. Stalactites are built up

from minerals in dripping water. {stə lăk tiyt *or* stă lək tiyt}

Language Note *Stalactites* and *stalagmites* are two kinds of underground rock formations. Stalactites grow downward from the ceiling of a cave, and stalagmites grow upward from the floor of a cave. Here is a way to help you to remember which is which: stalactite -- ceiling, stalagmite -- ground.

Word History *Stalactite* comes from *stalaktos*, an ancient Greek word that means "dripping" or "trickling."

sta·lag·mite *noun* a rock formation that looks like a cone and is built upward from the floor of a cave. Stalagmites are built up from minerals in dripping water. {stə lăg miyt *or* stă ləg miyt}

Word History *Stalagmite* comes from *stalagma*, an ancient Greek word that means "a drop."

stale *adjective* (staler, stalest) 1. having lost its taste or moisture; not fresh. *We left the bread out while we were away, and now it's stale.* 2. boring because it is no longer new; used too often. *The stories he tells these days are all stale.* {stayl} staleness, n.

stalk[1] *noun* 1. a plant's main stem. 2. any long thin structure that is used to support something. {stŏ k}

stalk[2] *verb* (stalked, stalking, stalks) 1. to walk in a stiff, proud manner. *I stalked in and told her exactly how angry I was.* 2. to track and follow. *A lion will stalk an animal before it makes a kill.* {stŏ k} stalker, n.

 Human Body  Human Mind  Everyday Life  History and Culture  Communication

stall[1] *noun* 1. an area of a barn or stable used for holding a single animal. 2. a booth used by a merchant to show and sell goods. *verb* (stalled, stalling, stalls) to cause to stop running. *He stalled the engine when he pushed the gas pedal.* {**stawl**}

stall[2] *verb* (stalled, stalling, stalls) 1. to delay by certain actions. *Quit stalling and do your homework.* 2. to delay, or cause to go forward only slightly. *He stalled our trip by saying he was very ill.* *noun* something used to avoid or delay. *Her excuse was a stall to keep from going to work.* {**stawl**}

stal·lion *noun* an adult male horse that can produce young. {**stăl** yən}

sta·men *noun* (stamens) the part of a flower that makes and bears the pollen. {**stay** mən}

Stamen
anther
filament

stam·i·na *noun* the strength to handle long effort or disappointment. *He needed stamina to work in the mines for thirty years.* {**stăm** ih nə}

stam·mer *verb* (stammered, stammering, stammers) to speak in an anxious or uncertain way. People who stammer often repeat sounds and stop between words. *He stammered through the poem as he read it to the class.* *noun* a stammering manner of speech. *I speak with a stammer if I'm upset.* {**stăm** ər}

stamp *verb* (stamped, stamping, stamps) 1. to move with force and speed downward upon something. *She stamped her foot on the floor.* 2. to make a stamping motion with the foot. *The child stamped and cried when his mother tried to send him to bed.* 3. to put out, crush, or stop by or as if by moving the foot in such a manner (usually followed by "out"). *She stamped out the fire.* / *He wants to stamp out crime.* 4. to walk in an angry way by stamping the feet. *He stamped out and slammed the door.* 5. to mark with a carved and inked rubber or wooden block that makes a design, letters, or numbers. *My teacher stamped my paper with a star.* 6. to place a postage stamp upon. *I stamped my letter before I put it in the mailbox.* *noun* 1. a small piece of paper printed with a design and attached to mail to show that the fee for mailing has been paid; postage stamp. 2. any similar piece of paper used for decoration or to show that a fee has been paid. *Pam put stamps and stickers on her notebook.* 3. a tool used for stamping or for cutting out uniform shapes. 4. the action or an instance of stamping. *It takes only one stamp of his foot for me to know that my child is angry.* {**stămp**}

stam·pede *noun* 1. the sudden and hurried mass movement of a large group of frightened animals. 2. any similar movement or rush of a crowd. *There was a stampede at the store for goods on sale.* *verb* (stampeded, stampeding, stampedes) 1. to move in or as if in a stampede. *The frightened horses stampeded when the dog ran toward them.* 2. to cause to move in or as if in a stampede. *We stampeded the cows back to the barn before the storm.* 3. to rush on, to, or into. *Spectators stampeded the gates.* {**stăm peed**}

stand ❓ ⭕ *verb* (stood, standing, stands) 1. to get in or be in a position on one's feet (often followed by "up"). *The teacher told the class to stand up.* 2. to cause to be in an upright position. *Stand the ladder by the house.* 3. to remain in effect. *Our offer will stand for another week.* 4. to be located somewhere. *The church stands in the valley.* 5. to hold to an opinion or attitude. *I stand on my record.* 6. to put up with. *He can't stand it when she is late.* 7. to have to go through. *He is standing trial for robbery.* *noun* 1. an ending of activity. *The group came to a stand at the bus stop.* 2. a place where something or someone stands. *The guard took his stand at the gate.* 3. a determined attitude or position. *We must take a stand on this issue.* 4. a raised platform. *A band played on the stand.* 5. a stall, booth, or table on which goods for sale are shown. 6. a witness stand in court. *The witness took the stand and gave her testimony.* 7. a table or rack for holding a certain thing. *He looked over the magazine stand in the waiting room.* / *Her clock is on a night stand by her bed.* 8. (plural) the seats at a playing field or stadium. *We walked through the stands to find our friends.* {**stănd**}

• **stand for**

1. to be a symbol of, or to represent. *The letters stand for numbers in the math problem.* 2. to put up with. *She won't stand for me being late.*

A B C D E F G H I J K L M N O P Q R S T U V W X Y Z

 Living World
 Physical World
 Natural Environment
 Economy
Government and Law

stand·ard *noun* 1. something that is used and accepted as a guide, example, or authority. *This bike helmet meets the government safety standard.* 2. a flag or banner of a nation or ruler. *adjective* 1. serving as a standard or accepted model. *A standard pound is equal to sixteen ounces.* 2. widely accepted as excellent or as an authority. *Many schools have standard science books that teachers must use.* 3. normal; routine; usual. *It is standard for me to go to bed at nine o'clock every night.* {**stăn** dərd}

stan·za *noun* a group of related lines in a poem that make up one section within the poem. Stanzas often have a regular meter and rhyme pattern. {**stăn** zə}

sta·ple¹ *noun* a short, thin piece of stiff wire shaped like a U. Staples are designed to be pushed through several sheets of paper and then bent inward to hold the papers together. *verb* (stapled, stapling, staples) to hold together or attach using a staple or staples; drive a staple or staples into. *We stapled our art work to the classroom wall.* {**stay** pəl}

sta·ple² *noun* 1. a food that is considered very important and used often. *Sugar and flour are two kinds of staples.* 2. one of the most important crops or products of a region. *Rice is a staple in China.* {**stay** pəl}

star 🌟 *noun* 1. any of a vast number of heavenly bodies visible from earth as points of light in the night sky. 2. a design with five or six points that emerge from a center.

The American flag has stars and stripes. 3. a performer or athlete who is considered to be outstanding. *She is a movie star.* 4. one who has a leading role in a play or movie. *My favorite actor was the star of the show.* *verb* (starred, starring, stars) 1. to present in a main role in a film or play. *That TV show stars a new actor.* 2. to perform the lead or be the star in a play or film. *Tonight I will star in the opening of our school play.* 3. to mark with a star or stars. *The teacher starred the correct answers on my test.* {**star**}

star·board *noun* the right side of a ship or aircraft when facing forward from inside. *adjective* of, having to do with, or on the right side of a ship or aircraft. *He fell off the starboard side of the boat.* {**star** bərd}

starch *noun* 1. a white food substance found in many foods. *Potatoes and grains have starch in them.* 2. a substance used to make clothing or other fabric stiff. *verb* (starched, starching, starches) to use starch to make stiff. *I starch my shirts every time I iron them.* {**starch**}

stare *verb* (stared, staring, stares) to look in a steady, fixed way, with the eyes open wide. *Everyone stared at the boy with the ripped shirt.* *noun* a long, hard, steady look. *She gave him a stare.* {**stayr**}
• **stare down**
to try to frighten or make uncomfortable by staring at. *Instead of fighting with her, he tried to stare her down.*
• **stare one in the face**
to be clearly obvious or

impending. *Poverty is staring us in the face.*

Homophone Note Are you looking for the word *stair* (a step or steps)? *Stare* and *stair* sound alike but have different meanings.

star·fish *noun* (starfish or starfishes) a sea animal with a flat body and five or more arms. Starfish live in shallow parts of the ocean. They are carnivores that eat clams and other mollusks. They are also called sea stars. {**star** fihsh}

Stars and Stripes *noun* (used with a singular or plural verb) the national flag of the United States. It has thirteen red and white stripes and a blue field with fifty white stars that stand for the fifty states; Old Glory. {**stars** ənd **striyps**}

start *verb* (started, starting, starts) 1. to begin a movement or activity. *The game will start after school.* 2. to set in motion; cause to begin. *She told me to start the car.* 3. to move suddenly as if by surprise. *The rabbit started at the sound.* 4. to help to begin a project or job. *He started his brother in business.* *noun* 1. the beginning of something. *We can't wait for the start of summer.* 2. a quick or sudden movement. *The siren made him jump with a start.* 3. the place or time something begins. *He knew from the start*

 Human Body   Human Mind 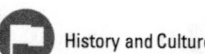 Everyday Life   History and Culture   Communication

that he would win the game. {**start**}

star·tle *verb* (startled, startling, startles) 1. to cause to move suddenly. *The bolt of thunder startled me out of bed.* 2. to alarm suddenly; surprise. *The cat startled me when she jumped up on my lap.* 3. to become surprised or scared. *My mother startles easily if I sneak up on her quietly.* {**star** təl} startlingly, adv.

starve *verb* (starved, starving, starves) 1. to die or suffer from not eating and drinking. *People in Africa are starving.* 2. (informal) to feel a need of food; be hungry. *If you skip breakfast, you'll be starving by lunch time.* 3. to feel a great desire for something one has not had or been given (usually followed by "for"). *I'm starving for your attention.* {**starv**}

state *noun* 1. the condition of a person or thing. *The old house was in a bad state.* 2. the population of an area under a single government. *The president addressed the state by television.* 3. an area of land that with other such areas forms a political unit. *Our nation has fifty states.* *adjective* of or related to the central civil government. *Every year I pay state and federal tax.* *verb* (stated, stating, states) to say or write; express. *He stated his opinion.* {**stayt**}

state·ment *noun* 1. something stated in words. *The company made a statement to everyone about the new work hours.* 2. a report or record of financial matters. *The bank sends my mom a statement every month.* {**stayt** mənt}

states·man *noun* (statesmen) a man who shows skill and wisdom in government. {**stayts** mən}

stat·ic *adjective* 1. without motion; fixed. *The static expression on your face makes me think that you don't care.* 2. without change. *The town center was static for years until new shops and restaurants opened.* 3. of or having to do with electrical charges within an object. *In the winter my hair has static electricity after I dry it.* *noun* 1. the electrical charges within an object; static electricity. 2. noise caused by electricity in the air that interferes with radio or TV reception. {**stăt** ihk}

sta·tion *noun* 1. the place where a person or thing is normally found. *The soldier went to his station.* 2. a place or building used by a business or other organization. *The rescue squad gathered at the fire station.* 3. a regular stopping place on a route or road. *She drove him to the train station.* 4. a radio or television business. *verb* (stationed, stationing, stations) to assign to a particular place. *The soldier was stationed in England.* {**stay** shən}

sta·tion·ar·y *adjective* 1. not moving; still. *The cars on this road have been stationary for over an hour.* 2. not able to be moved; fixed. *I have a stationary bike to use in the winter.* 3. not changing in condition; static. *The price of bananas has been stationary all summer.* {**stay** shə **nayr** ee}

Homophone Note Are you looking for the word *stationery* (writing paper)? *Stationary* and *stationery* sound alike but have different meanings.

sta·tion·er·y *noun* 1. paper used for writing letters. 2. paper, pens, envelopes, and other writing materials. {**stay** shə **nayr** ee}

Homophone Note The words *stationery* and *stationary* (not moving) sound alike but have different meanings.

sta·tis·tics *noun* (used with a plural verb) pieces of data or facts gathered in the form of numbers. *Some statistics show that there are more females in our society than males.* {stə **tih** stihks}

stat·ue 🔊 *noun* a piece of art that is shaped or put together out of stone, metal or other material. Statues are often in the form of a human or animal. {**stă** chooh}

sta·tus *noun* 1. a person's position or rank compared with others. *His status went up when he got the new job.* 2. state of matters; stage of progress. *She is anxious to find out the status of her job application.* {**stă** təs or **stay** təs}

stay[1] *verb* (stayed, staying, stays) 1. to spend time in a place. *She stayed at home for too long.* 2. to continue spending time in a place or with a group. *Stay with us a few more minutes.* 3. to remain for the period of. *She stayed five days at our house.* 4. to live for a short time. *We stayed in town for six months.* 5. to remain in a particular condition or state. *She stayed healthy.* *noun* a visit or short period of living. *Our stay in the city was short.* {**stay**}

stay[2] *noun* an object used to support or steady something; brace. *We used a stay on the ladder.* {**stay**}

A
B
C
D
E
F
G
H
I
J
K
L
M
N
O
P
Q
R
S
T
U
V
W
X
Y
Z

stead·fast *adjective* 1. able to be trusted or relied on; loyal. *I can always count on my steadfast friend.* 2. not likely to change; firmly in place. *He has a steadfast job at the bank.* {<u>stehd</u> făst or <u>stehd</u> fəst}

stead·y *adjective* (steadier, steadiest) 1. firmly fixed in position; stable. *The craftsman built a steady table.* 2. having a regular movement or course of action. *We took a slow but steady pace to get the job done.* 3. not easily upset; calm. *We remained steady when the fire alarm rang.* 4. dependable; one who can be trusted. *He is a steady player on our team.* 5. firm; not shaking. *He has a steady hand with the hammer.* *interjection* "calm yourself"; "control yourself." *Steady! You're getting way too upset over this.* *verb* (steadied, steadying, steadies) 1. to make or keep steady or stable. *We steadied ourselves in the canoe.* 2. to become steady. *The rocking chair steadied when he got up.* *adverb* (steadier, steadiest) in a steady manner. *Hold the board steady while I cut it.* {<u>steh</u> dee} steadily, adv., steadiness, n.

steak *noun* a large, flat cut of meat or fish usually cooked by frying, broiling, or grilling. {<u>stayk</u>}

Homophone Note The words **steak** and **stake** sound alike but have different meanings.

steal  *verb* (stole, stolen, stealing, steals) 1. to take from another without permission or right. *Someone stole my bicycle.* 2. to get in a clever or secret way. *She stole a glance at the comic book.* 3. to move secretly or without being noticed (usually fol-lowed by "in," "from," or "away"). *He stole away from the party and went home.* 4. to run safely to while the pitcher is throwing to the batter. *He was thrown out while trying to steal home.* *noun* 1. (informal) something bought at a very low price; bargain. *At this low price the car is a steal.* 2. an act of stealing a base in baseball. *He had three steals in the game.* {<u>steel</u>} stealer, n.

Homophone Note Are you looking for the word **steel** (a metal)? **Steal** and **steel** sound alike but have different meanings.

steam   *noun* 1. water vapor formed by boiling. *We cooked the vegetables with steam.* 2. the white mist formed in the air when water vapor cools. *The bathroom was full of steam after my hot shower.* 3. (informal) energy; power. *Do you have the steam to climb this hill?* *verb* (steamed, steaming, steams) 1. to give off or produce steam. *The tea kettle is steaming.* 2. to apply steam to in order to cook or clean. *He steamed the fish for five minutes.* 3. to be coated by or covered with mist. *The windows steam up in cold, wet weather.* 4. to be in motion using or as if using steam power. *The train steamed up the mountain.* {<u>steem</u>}

steam·boat *noun* a boat that runs on steam power. {<u>steem</u> boht}

steam engine *noun* an engine which uses steam to supply energy to its mechanical parts. {<u>steem</u> ehn jən} steam-engine, adj.

steam·roll·er *noun* a large truck with a huge roller that is used to smooth and crush the material used in building roads. {<u>steem</u> roh lər} steam-roll, v.

steam·ship *noun* a large ship powered by steam; steamer. {<u>steem</u> shihp}

steed *noun* a lively and sturdy horse used for riding. {<u>steed</u>}

steel *noun* 1. a hard, strong metal made from iron mixed with carbon. Steel is used to make machines, cars, tools, knives, and many other things. 2. something that is as hard or strong as steel. *Superman is called the man of steel.* *adjective* made of or having to do with steel. *verb* (steeled, steeling, steels) to prepare for something difficult; make strong or brave. *She steeled herself for the long hike up the mountain. / Her love steeled him against danger.* {<u>steel</u>}

Homophone Note The words **steel** and **steal** (to take unlawfully) sound alike but have different meanings.

steep[1] *adjective* (steeper, steepest) 1. having a sharp slope or slant. *The goat scampered easily down the steep, rocky slope.* 2. too expensive or high. *Five dollars is steep for an ice-cream cone.* {<u>steep</u>}

steep[2] *verb* (steeped, steeping, steeps) to soak in a liquid. *She steeped the tea in hot water.* {<u>steep</u>}

stee·ple *noun* a tall, narrow tower on top of a building. A steeple often has a pointed spire. {<u>stee</u> pəl}

steer[1] *verb* (steered, steering, steers) 1. to cause to move in a certain direction. *I steered the car toward the exit.* 2. to direct or guide toward a course of action. *He steered*

700

her toward going to college. 3. to be able to be steered. *My car doesn't steer well.* {**steer**}

• **steer clear of**
to keep away from; avoid. *Steer clear of the bumps when you drive on that road.*

steer[2] *noun* a young bull or male ox that is not able to produce young and that is raised for its meat. {**steer**}

stem[1] ❶ *noun* 1. the main part of a plant that grows up from the ground and supports the branches, leaves, flowers, or fruits that may grow from it. 2. a long, thin part. *These wine glasses have delicate stems. verb* (stemmed, stemming, stems) to come from; start from. *His success stems from hard work.* {**stehm**}

sten·cil *noun* 1. a sheet of some material out of which letters or a pattern has been cut. Paint or ink can pass through stencils to form a design on the surface underneath. 2. a design or letter made by using a stencil. *verb* (stenciled, stenciling, stencils) to produce using a stencil. *I stenciled flowers on my living room walls.* {**stayn** səl}

step *noun* 1. the movement made by lifting one foot and putting it down in another place; motion used in walking. *He took a step toward the door.* 2. the distance traveled in one such movement. *My office is three steps down the hall from yours.* 3. a raised surface to place the foot on when going up or down; stair. *He walked up the steps and knocked on the door.* 4. the sound made when walking. *She heard steps on the front porch.* 5. a fixed pace, rhythm, or pattern used in dancing or other types of movement. *We learned a new step in ballet class.* 6. an act or

stage in a series. *Follow the steps carefully in putting together the bicycle. verb* (stepped, stepping, steps) 1. to move by taking one or a few steps. *I stepped to the other side of the room.* 2. to place the foot down. *He stepped on an ant.* {**stehp**}

• **in step**
moving to a rhythm with another person. *They were in step as they crossed the street together.*

step- *prefix* a prefix that means "related because someone married again." *A stepmother is a woman who becomes a mother because she marries the child's father.*

step·fa·ther *noun* the husband of one's mother in a later marriage, not one's natural father. {**stehp** fah thər}

step·moth·er *noun* the wife of one's father in a later marriage, not one's natural mother. {**stehp** muhth ər}

ster·e·o *noun* (stereos) a system of equipment for playing sound that uses separate channels to create a realistic effect. *Our stereo has a CD player and two speakers.* {**stehr** ee oh}

ster·ile *adjective* 1. free of live germs or bacteria. *Dentists use sterile tools.* 2. not able to produce children, plants, or fruit; not fertile. *This soil is sterile from too much use.* {**stehr** əl} sterility, n.

ster·ling *adjective* 1. of or made of the very finest silver, or 92.5% pure. *I have several sterling silver picture frames at home.* 2. excellent or very fine. *He has a sterling record at school. noun* 1. British money. 2. fine silver used in making dishes, silverware, and jewelry. {**stuhr** ling}

stern[1] *adjective* (sterner, sternest) 1. firm and deter-

mined; not flexible. *Our teacher is stern about homework that isn't done.* 2. grim or strict. *My dad had a stern expression on his face when I got home late.* {**stuhrn**} sternly, adj., sternness, n.

stern[2] *noun* the rear or back part of anything. *She sat in the stern of the boat.* {**stuhrn**}

steth·o·scope *noun* an instrument that makes the sounds inside a body louder. Doctors and nurses listen to the heart with a stethoscope. {**stehth** ə skohp}

stew *verb* (stewed, stewing, stews) 1. to cook by boiling slowly in a closed pot. *He stewed the meat until it was tender.* 2. to be worried, or annoyed; fret. *She will stew until the children get home. noun* a dish made of meat or fish with vegetables and boiled slowly. {**stooh**}

stick[1] *noun* 1. a long and thin piece of wood, such as a stem or branch, from a tree or bush. *We used sticks to start the fire.* 2. something shaped like a stick. *The child was given a stick of candy.* {**stihk**}

stick[2] *verb* (stuck, sticking, sticks) 1. to pierce or poke with a pointed object; stab. *She stuck her finger with a piece of glass.* 2. to fix into place by pushing the pointed end of an object into something. *She stuck a tack in the wall.* 3. to be or become attached by having the point enter an object or thing. *The knife stuck in the wall.* 4. to put in a particular place or position. *Stick your coat in the closet.* 5. to remain or become fixed in place. *The tape stuck to the wall.* 6. to remain firmly. *Her words stuck in his mind.* 7. to con-

A B C D E F G H I J K L M N O P Q R S T U V W X Y Z

tinue to hold firmly. *She stuck to her opinion.* 8. to be or become set or caught and unable to move. *Our car got stuck in the mud.* {stihk}

• **stick by**
to remain loyal to. *He sticks by his friends.*

• **stick out**
to stand out; to be easily seen. *That purple suit makes him stick out in a crowd.*

stick·er *noun* a paper label, patch, or sign with sticky material on the back side. {stihk ər}

stick·ler *noun* one who must observe or conform to something (usually followed by "for"). *He's a stickler for details.* {stihk lər}

stick·y *adjective* (stickier, stickiest) 1. tending to stick to or hold on to something when touched. *Glue is sticky.* 2. hot or warm and very humid; muggy. *Let's go swimming on this sticky day.* {stihk ee}

stiff *adjective* (stiffer, stiffest) 1. not easy to bend. *This thick cardboard is really stiff.* 2. not moving or operating easily. *I could hardly open the stiff door. / She complained about her stiff ankles.* 3. not easy in expression or movement; formal. *She gave them a stiff greeting. / I felt uneasy because of her stiff manner.* 4. difficult. *It was a stiff climb up the mountain. / There's some stiff competition for the job.* 5. severe; harsh. *He endured some stiff punishment for stealing.* 6. rather firm or thick. *Beat the egg whites until they are stiff.* 7. very high; above normal. *Stiff prices make it hard for poor families to get by.* *adverb* (stiffer, stiffest) completely; entirely. *I was bored stiff during the meeting. / She was scared stiff by the monster.* {stihf} stiffness, n.

stile *noun* a set or series of steps for climbing over a fence or wall. {stiyl}

Homophone Note The words *stile* and *style* (a way or fashion) sound alike but have different meanings.

still *adjective* (stiller, stillest) 1. not moving. *We were told to be still.* 2. making or having no sound; silent. *The room was still after everyone left.* 3. quiet; calm. *They sat by the still lake and watched the sun set.* *noun* calm; quiet; silence. *In the still of the night, she walked in the moonlight.* *adverb* (stiller, stillest) 1. neither moving nor making sound. *He sat still and waited for her call.* 2. at a particular time; as before; yet. *They still live with their parents.* 3. despite that. *He may be sick, but he still needs to exercise.* 4. to an even greater degree. *Fame is good, but fortune is better still.* *conjunction* and yet. *We were full; still, we wanted dessert.* *verb* (stilled, stilling, stills) 1. to cause to be quiet. *She stilled the class by raising her hand.* 2. to cause to stop moving. *He stilled his bicycle at the corner.* 3. to become still. *The lake stilled after the storm.* {stihl}

stilt *noun* 1. a long, thin pole with a block to rest the foot upon. *With a pair of stilts, a person can walk above the ground.* 2. any of the posts used to support a structure built above the surface of land or water. *The house on that steep hill is built on stilts.* {stihlt} stiltlike, adj.

stim·u·late *verb* (stimulated, stimulating, stimulates) to bring about to activity or action. *That book stimulated his interest in monsters.* {stihm

yə **layt**} stimulatingly, adv., stimulation, n., stimulative, adj., n., stimulator (stimulater), n.

stim·u·lus *noun* (stimuli) 1. something that causes or increases action, feeling, or thought. *Hearing the great pianist perform was a stimulus to practice harder.* 2. something that causes a physical response in a body part. *The electric shock was a stimulus that caused me to jump.* {stihm yə ləs}

sting *verb* (stung, stinging, stings) 1. to pierce, wound, or stick with a stinger. *A bee stung him on the cheek.* 2. to cause to feel a sudden, sharp pain. *Their mean words stung him.* 3. to feel a sudden, sharp pain. *I stung for a long time after the accident.* *noun* 1. the act or an instance of stinging. *The sting of a bee can hurt for a few days.* 2. the smart, pain, or wound caused by or as if by a stinger. *The sting of the rope burn will go away in a couple of minutes.* {sting}

sting·er *noun* 1. one that stings. 2. the sharp, pointed part of certain animals and plants that sometimes carries a poison. The stinger is used to wound. {sting ər}

sting·ray *noun* a broad, flat fish that has a long tail with a poisonous spine on it. Stingrays are a kind of ray. Their tails can cause severe wounds. {sting ray}

stin·gy *adjective* (stingier, stingiest) 1. spending or giving as little as possible. *My stingy boss has not given me a raise in two years.* 2. less than expected or needed; meager. *He gave her a stingy amount of*

Human Body   Human Mind   Everyday Life   History and Culture   Communication

money when she needed help. {**stihn** jee}

stink *verb* (stank or stunk, stunk, stinking, stinks) 1. to give off a strong and bad smell. *The dog stank after he went swimming in the river.* 2. (informal) to be not very good or of very low quality. *His singing stinks.* 3. to cause to have a bad smell (often followed by "up"). *Cigar smoke stank up the room.* *noun* a strong, bad smell. *There was an awful stink in the house after the flood.* {**stingk**}

Word History In Old English, *stink* meant "to give off a smell (of any kind)." By 1200, only a strong and offensive smell was called a "stink."

stir[1] *verb* (stirred, stirring, stirs) 1. to mix or move in a circle with a hand or object. *She stirred her coffee with a spoon.* 2. to put into motion. *The alarm stirred me from my sleep.* 3. to move around with energy; become active; be awakened. *She woke up to find everyone in the house already stirring.* 4. to make excited or full of energy (usually followed by "up"). *Please don't stir up the children right before dinner.* 5. to cause excitement or feelings in. *The music stirred her.* 6. to move slightly. *The wind did not stir.* 7. to move so as to shift position. *She did not stir when I called.* *noun* 1. act of stirring; stirring motion. *He gave the batter a stir.* 2. state of excitement; commotion. *The speech caused a great stir.* {**stuhr**} stirrer, n.

stir·rup *noun* a loop or ring of metal, wood, or leather with a flat bottom that hangs from each side of a saddle. Stirrups are used to support the rider's foot. {**stuh** rəp *or* **steer** əp}

stitch ● *noun* 1. one movement of a needle and thread through cloth or other material when sewing. 2. a single loop of thread or yarn drawn through cloth or other material. 3. a sudden, sharp muscle pain in one's side. 4. the smallest or least little bit. *He didn't have a stitch of clothing on him.* *verb* (stitched, stitching, stitches) to fasten, or join with stitches; sew. *I need to stitch my pants, or the hole will get larger.* {**stihch**}
  • **in stitches**
  (informal) laughing out of control. *I was in stitches after he told us that funny joke.*

stoat *noun* the European name for a weasel, especially for ermines when they have brown fur in summer. {**stoht**}

stock ● ● *noun* 1. a supply ready for use; store. *My parents keep a large stock of food in the house.* 2. the total of goods ready for sale by a merchant or business. *The local store had a large stock of nails.* 3. farm animals; livestock. 4. the shares in the owning of a business or company. *I hold stock in a small local business.* 5. family background of a particular kind. *They come from Polish stock. / She comes from good stock.* 6. a liquid in which meat, fish, or poultry has been cooked. Stock is used as a base for soup or gravy. 7. a base, handle, or frame for certain objects. *You should be careful when holding the stock of a gun.* *adjective* 1. in supply on a regular basis. *The stock newspapers are brought to the local stand every morning.* 2. often used; commonplace. *My friend has a set of stock jokes that he likes to tell.* *verb* (stocked, stocking, stocks) 1. to supply with

goods or livestock. *They stocked the shelves with books.* 2. to keep ready for future use or sale. *We don't stock a large number of shoes.* 3. to keep or collect something for future use (often followed by "up"). *Stock up on cereal while it is still on sale.* {**stŏk**} stocker, n.
  • **in stock**
  present for use or sale. *We have several sizes in stock.*
  • **out of stock**
  not present for use or sale. *The item I was looking for was out of stock.*
  • **take stock in [or] put stock in**
  to consider important. *He took stock of what I said. / She puts stock in what her father says.*

stock·ade *noun* 1. a fence for defense made of upright posts. 2. a military prison. {sto **kăd**}

Stock·holm *noun* the capital city of Sweden. {**stŏk** hohm *or* **stŏk** hohlm}

stock·ing *noun* a knit covering that fits closely on the foot and some part of the leg. {**stŏk** ing} stockinged, adj., stockingless, adj.
  • **in one's stocking feet**
  wearing socks or stockings but no shoes. *We danced around in our stocking feet.*

stock·y *adjective* (stockier, stockiest) thick, sturdy, and often short in build or form; stout. *That football team has many stocky players.* {**stŏk** ee} stockiness, n.

stock·yard *noun* a closed-in lot for keeping livestock before they are slaughtered or shipped. {**stŏk** yard}

stoke *verb* (stoked, stoking, stokes) to add to and stir up the fuel of. *We stoked the fire to warm up the house.* {**stohk**}

stole[1] *verb* past tense of **steal**. {**stohl**}

stole² *noun* a woman's long scarf of fur or cloth. {**stohl**}

stom·ach 🔵 *noun* 1. the organ in the body that receives food that has been swallowed and begins to digest it. 2. the front part of the body below the chest; belly. *verb* (stomached, stomaching, stomachs) to put up with; stand. *I can't stomach your rude behavior.* {**stuh** mihk}

stomp *verb* (stomped, stomping, stomps) 1. to stamp or walk heavily upon so as to smash or otherwise harm. *I stomped the bug until I knew that it was dead.* 2. to walk heavily. *She stomped on my foot by accident.* 3. to stamp heavily. *I will stomp my feet on the floor until someone downstairs hears me.* {**stŏmp**}

stone 🌀 *noun* (stones or stone) 1. hard matter formed from mineral and earth material; rock. 2. a piece of rock shaped naturally or cut for use in building or some other particular use. *We have a sidewalk made of stone.* 3. a small piece of rock; pebble. *She skipped a stone across the water.* 4. a precious mineral; jewel. *Her ring has three emerald stones.* 5. a hard seed or pit. *He ate a peach and threw out the stone. verb* (stoned, stoning, stones) to throw stones at to punish or kill. *The angry crowd stoned the thief.* {**stohn**} stonelike, adj., stoner, n.

• **leave no stone unturned** to use every means possible; consider every choice. *He left no stone unturned when trying to please his parents.*

stone- *prefix* a prefix that means "in a complete way." A *stone-deaf* person is completely deaf.

Stone Age *noun* the stage of human culture when stone tools and weapons were made and used. The Stone Age dates from about two million B.C. to about 3,500 B.C. {**stohn ayj**}

stood *verb* past tense and past participle of **stand**. {**stuud**}

stool 🔵 *noun* 1. a seat without arms or a back. 2. a low piece of furniture for standing on to reach a high place, or for resting the feet on while sitting in a chair. 3. the waste matter that leaves the body during a bowel movement. {**stoohl**}

stoop¹ *verb* (stooped, stooping, stoops) 1. to bend the body forward and downward, as to pick up something. *I stooped to put on my socks.* 2. to stand or walk with shoulders and neck hanging forward. *If you stoop too much, you will hurt your back.* 3. to perform a task or act that lowers oneself or is not honest and upright. *She will never stoop to lying. noun* a way of standing in which the head and shoulders fall forward and downward. *My father walks with a stoop in his old age.* {**stoohp**}

stoop² *noun* a large step or small porch at the entrance to a home, often reached by a short flight of steps. {**stoohp**}

stop *verb* (stopped, stopping, stops) 1. to halt or cause to halt. *The sudden cloudburst stopped our picnic. / My mother stopped the videotape when it was time to eat dinner.* 2. to cease moving, acting, or proceeding. *The car stopped at the red light. / He stopped in the middle of the story.* 3. to do no longer; cease from. *Will you stop yelling?* / 4. to reach an end; cease. *The fun stopped when someone got hurt.* / 5. to close or plug. *He stopped the bottle with a cork.* 6. to block (often followed by "up"). *Grease stopped up the drain.* 7. to prevent from moving or traveling. *The accident stopped traffic.* 8. to pause for a short visit during a course or journey (often followed by "at," "in," or "by"). *We'll stop at your house on our way to Arizona. noun* 1. the act of stopping or state of being stopped. *The car came to a stop in front of our house.* 2. a point where a bus or other public vehicle stops for passengers. *The people waited at the stop for the bus to come.* {**stŏp**}

• **stop over** to make a brief stop before traveling further. *We stopped over and ate dinner.*

stop·per *noun* something that blocks an opening; plug. *Put a stopper in the drain, and the tub will fill up with water.* {**stŏ pər**}

stop·watch *noun* a watch that can be stopped and started instantly. *Stopwatches are used to time runners in a race.* {**stŏp wŏch**}

stor·age *noun* 1. the act of storing or state of being stored. *Will you be responsible for the storage of my furniture?* 2. a place for storing goods. *My things should be safe in storage.* {**stohr ihj**}

store 🔵🌀 *noun* 1. a place where things are sold. *Please pick up some bread at the grocery store.* 2. a supply kept or saved for future use. *The best mothers keep a store of cookies in the cupboard.* 3. a large amount; plenty. *There is a store of talent in this classroom.*

🏃 Human Body ❓ Human Mind 👕 Everyday Life 🚩 History and Culture 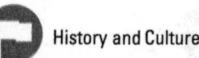  Communication

verb (stored, storing, stores) to gather and keep for future use. *We stored away our winter clothes. / The squirrel forgot where he stored his nuts.* {stohr}

• **in store**
about to happen. *We didn't know what was in store for us at the party.*

sto·rey *noun* a spelling of **story** used in Canada and Britain. See **story.** {stohr ee}

stork *noun* 1. a wading bird with long legs and a long neck and bill. 2. a symbol for the birth of a child. *She wrapped the gift for the new baby in paper covered with pictures of storks.* {stohrk}

storm 🌀 🌍 *noun* 1. a violent disturbance in the atmosphere, that brings rain, snow, wind, thunder, or lightning. 2. an outburst of strong feeling. *On hearing the bad news, the crowd exploded in a storm of anger. verb* (stormed, storming, storms) 1. to blow with heavy rain or snow, and sometimes with thunder and lightening. *It stormed all night.* 2. to move or rush angrily. *We stormed out of the house.* 3. to attack. *The army stormed the enemy position last night.* {stohrm} stormlike, adj.

sto·ry[1] 📖 📚 *noun* (stories) 1. an account of something that happened, either true or made up. *Did I ever tell you the story of when I saw the wolf?* 2. a work of fiction that is shorter than a novel; short story. 3. a lie. *Don't tell stories about where you were.* {stohr ee}

sto·ry[2] 🏢 *noun* (stories) one level of a building; floor. *That building has ten stories.* {stohr ee}

stout *adjective* (stouter, stoutest) 1. having physical strength; sturdy; thick. *Your stout arms are strong enough to carry this heavy load.* 2. firm or full of courage. *With stout hearts, we began our dangerous journey.* 3. having a thick or fat body. *My stout cat eats too much.* {stowt} stoutness, n.

stove 🔥 *noun* a device that uses electricity or burns fuel to provide heat for cooking or warmth. {stohv}

stow *verb* (stowed, stowing, stows) to put away or store in a place or container. *You must stow your bags under the seat on an airplane.* {stoh} stowable, adj.

• **stow away**
a person who hides on a ship, airplane, or train. *The pilot found the stow away who was hiding in the bathroom.*

strag·gle *verb* (straggled, straggling, straggles) to stray from or drop behind a group. *Don't straggle too far, or you will get lost.* {străg əl} straggler, n.

straight *adjective* (straighter, straightest) 1. without a curve or bend. *He drew a straight line.* 2. in the correct order or state. *Our work is now straight.* 3. direct; frank. *I appreciate your straight talk on this sensitive subject.* 4. upright; honest. *The witness gave a straight response to the lawyer's question. adverb* (straighter, straightest) 1. in a straight line or course. *He went straight to the baseball game after dinner.* 2. in an upright position. *The soldier stood straight.* 3. directly. *He came straight to the point.* {strayt} straightness, n.

Homophone Note Are you looking for the word *strait* (a channel of water)? *Straight* and *strait* sound alike but have different meanings.

straight·en *verb* (straightened, straightening, straightens) 1. to make or become straight. *The dentist wants to straighten my teeth.* 2. to put right; repair (often followed by "out"). *Let's straighten the living room before mom comes home.* {stray tən} straightener, n.

strain[1] ⚙️ 🏃 *verb* (strained, straining, strains) 1. to pull or stretch tight. *He strained the rope until it broke.* 2. to pull with energy or force. *The dog strained to break free of the leash.* 3. to stretch to the limit. *Reading in the dark for three hours strained my eyes.* 4. to use the greatest amount of effort; strive. *He strained to reach the finish line first.* 5. to hurt or injure by using too much. *He strained a muscle during practice.* 6. to put one's nerves and muscles under the greatest amount of force or stress. *He strained to lift the heavy box.* 7. to pass through a sieve or filter. *The cook strained the sauce.* 8. to remove by filtering. *I strained the sand from the small pebbles. noun* 1. the act of straining. *It was a strain for her to finish the work today.* 2. the condition of being strained. *The strain of work led to her illness.* 3. a hurt or injury that is the result of putting too much force or stress on some part of the body. *He caused a strain in his*

A
B
C
D
E
F
G
H
I
J
K
L
M
N
O
P
Q
R
S
T
U
V
W
X
Y
Z

 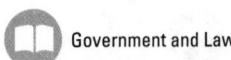

back by lifting the heavy books. 4. a great amount of pressure or force that can cause harm. *The strain of the heavy trucks broke the bridge.* 5. tiring or heavy pressure on the mind. *Her dear friend's sickness is a strain on her.* {**strayn**} strainingly, adv.

strain² ❶ *noun* all the descendants of a common ancestor; race. {**strayn**}

strain·er *noun* a sieve or other device used to strain or filter. {**stray** nər}

strait *noun* 1. a narrow body of water between two larger bodies. 2. (usually plural) a condition or position of trouble or distress. *She lost her job and is in difficult straits.* {**strayt**}

Homophone Note The words *strait* and *straight* (not bending) sound alike but have different meanings.

strand¹ *verb* (stranded, stranding, strands) 1. to beach, or leave behind on the shore. *The bad weather stranded us for several hours.* 2. to place or leave in a helpless or difficult position. *I was stranded in the desert with no water.* {**strănd**}

strand² *noun* 1. a length of fibers, threads, wires, or hairs twisted together to form yarn, rope, or cable. 2. a single fiber from such a length. 3. something that looks like such a length. *You are wearing a very pretty strand of beads.* {**strănd**}

strange *adjective* (stranger, strangest) 1. unusual; odd; peculiar. *He draws strange pictures.* / *The strange behavior of the fox led us to believe that it had rabies.* 2. not known or familiar. *He likes to visit*

strange countries. / *I didn't want to go to a strange new school.* *adverb* (stranger, strangest) in a strange or unusual manner. *He talks strange.* {**straynj**} strangeness, n.

Synonyms
These words share a meaning with *strange*, adjective 1:
unusual, funny, curious, odd, peculiar, queer, weird, eccentric

stran·ger *noun* 1. a person whom one does not know. *He won't talk to strangers.* 2. a person who is new to a region or place. *There are lots of strangers in town during the summer.* {**strayn** jər}

stran·gle *verb* (strangled, strangling, strangles) 1. to kill by stopping the breathing of; choke. 2. to choke or be choked. *The puppy strangled on the leash.* {**străng** gəl} strangler, n.

strap *noun* 1. a thin, flat strip of material used to fasten or hold objects together or in position. Straps often have a buckle at one end. 2. such an object tied in a loop and used to hold, grasp, pull, or lift. *Tighten the shoulder strap on your backpack.* *verb* (strapped, strapping, straps) to fasten together or in place with a strap or straps. *I will strap the bags to the top of the car.* {**străp**}

strat·e·gy *noun* (strategies) 1. a plan, method, or series of actions meant to perform a particular goal or effect. *What is your strategy for winning the game?* 2. the planning and direction of large military movements and actions during war

time. {**stră** tə jee}

strat·o·sphere *noun* a layer of the earth's upper atmosphere from about six miles to about thirty miles above the earth's surface. {**străt** ə sfeer}

straw *noun* 1. the dried stalks of plants such as oats, wheat, or rye that remain after the grain is removed. Straw is used for feeding animals, for weaving hats and baskets, or for packing. 2. a single such stalk of grain. *He likes to chew on straw.* 3. a thin, hollow tube of paper, plastic, or glass used to suck up a drink; drinking straw. {**straw**}

• **draw straws** to choose one person from several by having each choose a partly covered straw, with the shortest straw indicating the chosen person. *We will draw straws to see who gets to go first.*

straw·ber·ry *noun* (strawberries) 1. a red, juicy fruit with seeds on the outside. 2. the stemless plant which grows low to the ground and bears this fruit. {**straw** behr ee}

stray *verb* (strayed, straying, strays) 1. to wander from or go beyond a fixed place, course, or practice, or to wander away from a group. *I strayed from the camp and quickly became lost.* 2. to wander away or drift in thought. *I strayed from what the teacher was saying.* *noun* an animal who has strayed or wandered from its home. *There are many strays in our neighborhood.* *adjective* straying or having strayed; lost or out of place. *My family often feeds stray dogs.* / *There*

 Human Body   Human Mind   Everyday Life   History and Culture    Communication

are stray hairs all over the bathroom floor. {**stray**}

streak *noun* 1. a long, narrow line, mark, smear, or band. *There is a streak of black paint on the wall.* 2. a movement or something that moves very quickly in a long line. *Did you see the streak of lightning across the night sky?* 3. a trace; tendency; strain. *He has a stubborn streak.* 4. a short period or series of events. *We're having a streak of hot weather.* *verb* (streaked, streaking, streaks) 1. to form or make a streak or streaks on or in. *I hope the children won't streak the wet paint.* 2. to form into streaks or form with streaks. *The painter streaked color on the canvas.* 3. to move very quickly or flash by. *The runners streaked down the road.* 4. to be in streaks. *Rain streaked down the window.* {**streek**}

stream  *noun* 1. a small, flowing body of water, such as a brook or creek. *We went fishing in the stream.* 2. a steady flow of a liquid, people, or some other thing. *A stream of lava poured down the volcano. / A stream of fans came up to the stage.* 3. a steady flow of anything. *There was a stream of laughter from the audience.* *verb* (streamed, streaming, streams) 1. to flow, as in a current or stream. *Water streamed off his body when he stepped out of the pool.* 2. to give forth. *His wound was streaming with blood.* 3. to float or wave. *The flag streamed in the wind.* 4. to pour forth beams of light; shine. *Sunshine streamed in through my window.* {**streem**}

street *noun* 1. a public road in a town or city along which vehicles travel. Streets often have sidewalks and buildings along their sides. 2. the people who use, live on, or spend time on a certain street. *Our street had a party last night.* {**street**}

street·wise *adjective* having knowledge about what goes on and the ability to survive in a city. *Homeless people become very streetwise.* {**street wiyz**}

strength *noun* 1. the state, quality, or condition of being strong. *He had no strength after his illness.* 2. the power to hold off wear, damage, or injury. *This rope has enough strength to carry the load.* 3. having a strong effect on the senses. *Her paintings have strength of color.* {**strengkth** *or* **strength** *or* **strehnth**}

strength·en *verb* (strengthened, strengthening, strengthens) to make or grow strong or stronger. *I strengthen my mind by reading lots of books.* {**strengk** thən *or* **streng** thən *or* **strehn** thən}

stress *noun* 1. the importance or special attention given to something; emphasis. *My teacher puts a lot of stress on reading.* 2. the stronger tone placed on a given syllable of a word when it is spoken. *In the word "doctor," the stress is on the first syllable.* 3. physical pressure or force that causes strain on something. *The weight of the books put a lot of stress on the shelf.* 4. a condition of strain or tension. *Lifting heavy boxes put stress on his back.* *verb* (stressed, stressing, stresses) 1. to place importance on or give special attention to; underline. *He stressed the need for more food for people hurt by the war.* 2. to say with a stronger tone. *Stress the first syllable when*

you say the word "favorite." {**strehs**}

stretch *verb* (stretched, stretching, stretches) 1. to spread out or reach out to the full length in order to make loose and flexible. *He always stretches his legs before playing soccer.* 2. to cause to extend or reach from one point to another. *He stretched a wire from the pole to the house.* 3. to reach out or extend. *He stretched his hand out to help me.* 4. to pull or draw tightly. *We stretched the tent over its poles.* 5. to cause to become longer or wider. *He stretched his chewing gum into long strings.* 6. to extend over an area or in a certain direction. *The storm will stretch across the state.* 7. to lie down. *He stretched out on the couch for a nap.* *noun* 1. the act of stretching. *The team sat down for a stretch of the arms and legs.* 2. a continuous area or distance. *We drove over a long stretch of desert land.* 3. the degree to which something can be stretched. *The rope has a short stretch.* 4. a continuous period of time. *He left town for a long stretch.* {**strehch**} stretchability, n., stretchable, adj.

strict *adjective* (stricter, strictest) 1. stern; not yielding; demanding. *Her strict teacher told her to stay after school.* 2. kept or acting within the rules or in an exact way. *Her school has strict rules about what to wear.* 3. perfect or absolute. *There must be strict silence in his classroom.* {**strihkt**} strictly, adv., strictness, n.

stride *verb* (strode, stridden, striding, strides) to walk with long, even steps. *We strode along the river.* *noun* 1. a long walking step, or the manner

of taking long steps in walking. *She has a loose, easy stride.* 2. (often plural) a forward leap; progress. *This class has made great strides this year.* {**striyd**} strider, n.

strike *verb* (struck, struck or stricken, striking, strikes) 1. to hit with the hand or a weapon. *He struck me with the back of his hand.* 2. to smash into. *I struck the telephone pole with my car.* 3. to attack or make an attack upon. *The army struck the enemy lines.* 4. to hurt by biting. *The snake struck his leg.* 5. to have a strong effect on the mind or feelings of; impress. *His plan struck her as a good idea.* 6. to tell by means of sound. *The clock struck one o'clock.* 7. to cause to produce a light or spark by means of rubbing. *Can you please strike the match and then light the fire?* 8. to reach. *Sunlight will strike that hill by six o'clock.* 9. to refuse to continue working. *The union will strike soon.* 10. to come across suddenly. *They finally struck upon oil after searching for months.* *noun* 1. the act or an instance of striking. *The strike of her hand hurt my cheek.* 2. an action taken by a trade union or group of workers to stop work until the things and conditions that they ask for are agreed upon. *The telephone union strike will begin at midnight tomorrow.* 3. an attack. *The strike came as a surprise to the enemy.* 4. a failure to hit a pitched baseball or softball into the fair part of the playing field. 5. the knocking down of all pins with one roll of the ball in bowling. {**striyk**}

• **strike up**
to begin or cause to begin. *I struck up a conversation with my neighbor.*

string ⊙ *noun* 1. a cord or thin rope. *He tied a string to his balloon.* 2. something like a string. *These strings of spaghetti aren't fully cooked.* 3. a necklace made of pearls or beads placed on a cord with a thread. *She wore a string of pearls to the fancy dinner.* 4. a series of things arranged or happening in order. *The string of accidents made me uneasy.* 5. a thin cord or wire on a musical instrument that makes a sound when plucked or played with a bow. *I need to buy a new string for my violin.* 6. (plural) musical instruments that have strings. *The strings are an important part of an orchestra.* *verb* (strung, stringing, strings) 1. to supply with a string or strings. *He strung his guitar.* 2. to thread on a cord or string. *She will string the beads to make a necklace.* 3. to stretch between two points. *We strung the clothesline between two trees.* {**string**}

string bean *noun* a long, green pod that is produced by a bean plant and eaten as a vegetable; snap bean. {**string been**}

stringed *adjective* equipped or furnished with strings. *My cello is a stringed instrument.* {**stringd**}

stringed instrument *noun* any musical instrument that is sounded by bowing, plucking, or strumming the strings. Violins, guitars, and zithers are some stringed instruments. {**stringd ihn** strə mənt}

strip[1] *verb* (stripped, stripping, strips) 1. to take off the outside covering or clothing from. *We stripped the house of paint. / I stripped my clothes to go swimming.* 2. to take away from. *War often strips people*

of all their possessions. 3. to clear out completely. *The thieves stripped the house of its furniture.* {**strihp**}

strip[2] *noun* 1. a long, narrow piece or area of mostly uniform width. *Cut this fabric into strips. / We walked along a strip of beach.* 2. a series of pictures or images joined together in a row that tell a story or show something. *He likes to read that comic strip.* {**strihp**}

stripe *noun* a long, narrow band or strip set apart from the area or surface around it by a different color or material. *Zebras have black and white stripes on their bodies.* *verb* (striped, striping, stripes) to mark with a stripe or stripes. *I striped my car with red and yellow paint.* {**striyp**}

strive *verb* (strove or strived, striven or strived, striving, strives) to try or work hard. *My brother strives to be a better piano player.* {**striyv**}

stroke *noun* 1. an act or instance of striking. *One stroke of the stick knocked the bottle off the table.* 2. an event, idea, or happening that has a sudden, strong effect. *Meeting you on the street was a stroke of good luck.* 3. a single complete movement of part of the body. *I know two kinds of swimming strokes.* 4. a single mark made in writing or painting, or the act of making such a mark. *The artist added a few strokes of yellow to his painting.* 5. a sudden sickness in the brain caused by the breaking or blocking of a blood vessel. A

 Human Body   Human Mind   Everyday Life   History and Culture    Communication

stroke can cause parts of the body to become numb. It can also cause death. *verb* (stroked, stroking, strokes) to touch or brush gently with the hand or a brush. *My mom stroked my face while I lay sick in bed.* {**strohk**}

stroll *verb* (strolled, strolling, strolls) to walk slowly without a clear goal or purpose. *We strolled down the path and enjoyed the flowers.* *noun* a slow and easy walk. *I took a stroll this morning and listened to the birds.* {**strohl**}

strong ✦ ✦ *adjective* (stronger, strongest) 1. having or showing great physical power or strength. *The strong man lifted the heavy log.* 2. having power of mind or character. *He gave a strong objection to the ruling of the court.* / *He has a strong belief that life is sacred.* 3. showing great movement, force, or energy. *A strong wind blew the old barn down.* 4. having a bad or powerful taste or smell. *I hate the strong smell of your feet.* / *Just put a thin slice of cheese on your cracker, because it's very strong.* {**strawng**} strongly, adv., strongness, n.

struck *verb* past tense and past participle of **strike**. {**struhk**}

struc·ture *noun* 1. a thing made up of a number of parts joined together in a certain way. *A human cell is a complicated structure.* 2. the way in which such a thing is joined together. *A carpenter knows about the structure of furniture.* 3. anything that has been built. *They have finished building the new structure for the playground.* {**struhk** chər}

strug·gle *verb* (struggled, struggling, struggles) 1. to resist by waving the arms and legs and wriggling the body. *He struggled to break free of the girls* who were tickling him. 2. to make a strong effort. *He struggled to hold back his tears.* 3. to go forward by using great energy. *They struggled through the deep snow.* *noun* 1. the act or an instance of struggling. *It was a struggle to free myself from my brother's grip.* 2. a fight; combat. *There was a struggle between two boys in the hallway.* {**struhg** əl}

strum *verb* (strummed, strumming, strums) to play by running the fingers in a light way across the strings. *I strum my guitar whenever I feel sad.* *noun* an act, instance, or sound of strumming. *I listened for the strum of the guitar in the next room.* {**struhm**}

strut *verb* (strutted, strutting, struts) to walk in a proud or vain manner. *She strutted down the hallway to show off her new dress.* *noun* a strutting step or manner of walking. {**struht**}

stub *noun* 1. a short part that sticks out; stump. *My dog has a stub of a leg.* 2. a short piece that is left over after the rest has been used. *It is hard to write with the stub of a pencil.* *verb* (stubbed, stubbing, stubs) to strike against something by accident. *I stubbed my toe on the step.* {**stuhb**}

stub·born *adjective* 1. not willing to accept change, help, or control; obstinate. *She is very stubborn and won't do what they tell her.* 2. hard to deal with. *It was hard to remove the stubborn stain from my shirt.* {**stuhb** ərn} stubbornly, adv., stubbornness, n.

stud¹ *noun* 1. a nail with a rounded knob or head that sticks out. Studs were once used as protective devices attached to weapons or armor and are now used to decorate clothing and furni- ture. 2. a small button that is put through a hole to fasten an article of clothing. 3. an upright post in a wall that provides support for paneling, boards, or other kinds of siding. 4. a pin or peg attached to an automobile tire to help it grip a road surface firmly. *verb* (studded, studding, studs) to set with studs or something like studs. *He studded his leather jacket to make it fancier.* / *The sky is studded with stars.* {**stuhd**}

stud² *noun* a male horse or other male animal that is kept for breeding. {**stuhd**}

stu·dent ✦ ✦ ✦ *noun* 1. a person who goes to a school or college. *How many students are in your class?* 2. a person who studies something carefully or in depth. *He is a student of American history.* {**stooh** dənt}

stu·di·o ✦ *noun* (studios) 1. the room or shop where an artist works. 2. a photographer's shop. 3. a special room or building in which films, music, radio, or television shows are produced or broadcast. {**stooh** dee oh}

stud·y ✦ ✦ *noun* (studies) 1. the act of using the mind to learn. *After weeks of study, he passed the test.* 2. a branch of knowledge; subject. *He wants to get into the study of medicine.* 3. (plural) one's own learning. *She does well in her studies.* 4. a close look at something; investigation. *She did a study of insects.* 5. a room set aside for reading and studying. *I have lots of books in my study.* *verb* (studied, studying, studies) 1.

a b c d e f g h i j k l m n o p q r **s** t u v w x y z

to try to gain knowledge or skill. *He studies hard at school.* 2. to try to learn or gain knowledge or skill in. *He is studying art at the university.* 3. to examine in detail. *They will study our report. / He studied his next move in the game.* 4. to commit to memory; learn. *She studied her lines for the next scene.* {**stuh** dee}

stuff *noun* 1. the material or matter from or with which something is made. 2. personal things, or any other type of materials or objects. *Will you keep an eye on my stuff while I'm gone?* 3. (informal) things or ideas of little value. *Don't let that stuff bother you.* *verb* (stuffed, stuffing, stuffs) 1. to pack, or pack into, a container or opening. *Grandmother stuffed cans into the cupboard. / Stuff your laundry down the chute.* 2. to fill with stuffing. *We stuffed the turkey before putting it in the oven. / The pillows were stuffed with cotton.* 3. to put much food into. *We stuffed ourselves at dinner.* {**stuhf**}

stuff·ing *noun* that which is or can be stuffed. *My mom puts stuffing in the turkey for Thanksgiving. / The stuffing is coming out of my pillow.* {**stuhf** ing}

stuff·y *adjective* (stuffier, stuffiest) 1. not having enough fresh air. *When the windows are closed, this room gets stuffy.* 2. having a plugged nose. *It's hard to breathe through my stuffy nose.* 3. dull, boring, or very proper. *The party would be stuffy without music and dancing.* {**stuhf** ee} stuffiness, n.

stum·ble *verb* (stumbled, stumbling, stumbles) 1. to trip or lose one's balance in walking

or running. *He stumbled on a rock and fell down.* 2. to speak or act without grace, or in a clumsy way. *He stumbled over his lines in the play because he was nervous.* 3. to discover, reach, or come across by chance (usually followed by "across," "on," or "upon"). *I stumbled upon a letter from my first boyfriend.* *noun* an act or instance of stumbling. *He took a stumble on the rocks.* {**stuhm** bəl}

stump *noun* 1. a base of a tree that is left standing after the tree has been cut down. 2. a part left over after the rest has been broken, cut off, or eaten; stub. *He came back from the war with a stump of an arm.* *verb* (stumped, stumping, stumps) to puzzle or cause to be at a loss. *The last word on the spelling test stumped him.* {**stuhmp**}

stun *verb* (stunned, stunning, stuns) 1. to cause to be unconscious. *The hard blow to the woman's head stunned her.* 2. to shock or amaze. *The news of my cousin's death stunned me.* {**stuhn**}

stung *verb* past tense and past participle of **sting**. {**stung**}

stunt[1] *verb* (stunted, stunting, stunts) to stop or slow the growth of. *The cold weather stunted the plants.* {**stuhnt**}

stunt[2] *noun* 1. an act of skill, strength, or bravery. *We watched the airplanes perform stunts in the sky.* 2. anything done to attract attention or public notice. *Screaming in the hallway was a stunt to get the teacher out of the room.* {**stuhnt**}

stu·pid *adjective* (stupider, stupidest) 1. dull or slow to learn; not smart. *It was difficult to teach that stupid man anything at all.* 2. having no point or without sense;

foolish. *Selling his car for three dollars was a stupid thing to do.* {**stooh** pihd} stupidly, adv., stupidness, n.

stur·dy *adjective* (sturdier, sturdiest) strong, hardy, or solid. *Your sturdy shelves will hold the weight of these heavy books.* {**stuhr** dee} sturdiness, n.

stut·ter *verb* (stuttered, stuttering, stutters) to repeat sounds when speaking, as if unable to complete or begin certain words. *I stutter when I must speak to a large group of people.* *noun* an act or instance of stuttering. *She has spoken with a stutter since she was a little girl.* {**stuh** tər}

sty[1] *noun* (sties) a pen for pigs; pigpen. {**stiy**}

sty[2] or **stye** *noun* (sties or styes) a small, swollen gland on the edge of the eyelid. {**stiy**}

style *noun* 1. the manner in which something is said or done. *I like the style of her writing.* 2. the special quality or manner in which something is said, done, or made. *I enjoy watching this dancer because he has style.* 3. a state of being in fashion. *Short skirts are back in style.* *verb* (styled, styling, styles) to give a style to; design or fashion in a certain manner. *How would you like me to style your hair?* {**stiyl**} styler, n.

Homophone Note Are you looking for the word *stile* (a series of steps)? *Style* and *stile* sound alike but have different meanings.

sub *noun* 1. (informal) a short form of the word **submarine**. 2. a substitute teacher. *We had a sub in math today.* 3. a sandwich made on a long roll; submarine sandwich. *verb* (subbed, subbing, subs) (informal) to take the place

 Human Body   Human Mind   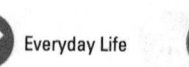 Everyday Life   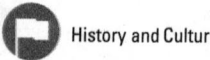 History and Culture    Communication

of another; substitute for another. *Ms. Smith was sick, so Mr. Jones subbed for her.* {**suhb**}

sub- *prefix* 1. a prefix that means "under" or "below." *A subnormal temperature is a temperature that is below normal. / A subway is a way to travel underground.* 2. a prefix that means "secondary" or "lower." *Because a captain is lower in rank than a general, the captain is the general's subordinate.*

sub·di·vide *verb* (subdivided, subdividing, subdivides) 1. to make smaller divisions in something already divided. *We subdivided the pizza slices so that everyone could eat.* 2. to divide into building lots for sale to separate owners. *They subdivided the land around the old farm house into ten parts.* {**suhb** dih **viyd** or **suhb** dih **viyd**} subdivider, n.

sub·ject *noun* 1. the topic of what is said, written, or studied. *The subject of the book was Native Americans.* 2. a person or thing that is looked at in a close and careful way. *We used frogs as subjects for examination in our science class.* 3. a person who is controlled by a leader or by a state. *The queen spoke to her subjects.* 4. an area of study; course. *Her best subject is English.* 5. a noun or noun phrase that is one of the two main parts of a sentence. *A subject usually names the person, place, thing, or condition that the verb explains.* *adjective* 1. under the power of someone or something (often followed by "to"). *We are subject to the teacher's orders.* 2. depending upon (usually followed by "to"). *Our plans are subject to your approval.* 3. likely to have or

to get (usually followed by "to"). *He is subject to sore throats.* *verb* (subjected, subjecting, subjects) 1. to put or bring under power (usually followed by "to"). *The coach subjected us to a long run.* 2. to make open (usually followed by "to"). *He subjected himself to their laughter.* {**suhb** jehkt, n., **suhb** jehkt, adj., səb **jehkt**, v.} subjectable, adj., subjection, n.

sub·ma·rine *noun* a sea vessel that can travel under water. {**suhb** mə **reen** or **suhb** mə **reen**}

sub·merge *verb* (submerged, submerging, submerges) 1. to put underwater or in some other liquid. *The crew submerged the submarine.* 2. to cover completely or cause to overflow with water; flood. *The tide submerged the beach.* 3. to sink or go underwater. *The children submerged in the pool to see who could hold their breath the longest.* {səb **muhrj**}

sub·mit *verb* (submitted, submitting, submits) 1. to give in to the will or power of another. *The boy submitted to his mother's demand that he spit out his gum.* 2. to offer to another to look at. *He submitted the story to the magazine in hope that it would be published.* {səb **miht**} submissible, adj.

sub·or·di·nate *adjective* lower in rank or importance; secondary. *A corporal is subordinate to a colonel.* *noun* one who is lower in rank, or under the control of another. *As a captain, he is the general's subordinate.* *verb* (subordinated, subordinating, subordinates) to put in a position of lesser rank or importance; make less important than (often followed by "to"). *He subordinates his work to his family life.* {sə **bohr** də niht, n.,

sə **bohr** də niht, adj., sə **bohr** də **nayt**, v.} subordinately, adv., subordination, n., subordinative, adj.

sub·scribe *verb* (subscribed, subscribing, subscribes) to agree to pay for a certain number of issues of a publication such as a magazine. *I subscribe to three magazines.* {səb **skriyb**} subscriber, n.

sub·scrip·tion *noun* an agreement to pay for a magazine, newspaper, or tickets to a series of events. *I am buying a subscription to see plays this summer at our town's theater.* {səb **krihp** shən}

sub·set *noun* a mathematical set made up of elements that are in a given set. *Odd numbers are a subset of whole numbers.* {**suhb** seht}

sub·side *verb* (subsided, subsiding, subsides) 1. to become less; decrease. *The baby's tears subsided after his mother picked him up.* 2. to sink to a lower or normal level. *The waves subsided after the storm.* {səb **siyd**}

sub·stance *noun* 1. that of which something is made; matter. *The substance of my shirt is cotton.* 2. a particular kind of matter. *She was covered with a sticky substance.* 3. the important part of something; meaning. *The substance of her phone call was a request for help.* {**suhb** stəns}

sub·sti·tute *noun* a person or thing that takes the place of another. *She was my substitute in the game when I got sick. / Honey is a substitute for sugar.* *verb* (substituted, substituting, substitutes) 1. to put or use in place of another person or thing. *She substituted margarine for butter in the recipe.* 2. to act, serve, or be in the place of another. *He substituted for our usual*

 Living World  Physical World  Natural Environment  Economy   Government and Law

A B C D E F G H I J K L M N O P Q R **S** T U V W X Y Z

teacher. {**suhb** stih **tooht**} sub-stitutable, adj., substitution, n.

sub·tract ❸ *verb* (subtracted, subtracting, subtracts) to take away from a whole or larger amount. *What do you get when you subtract ten from seventeen? / The dentist recommended that I subtract candy from my diet.* {səb **trăkt**} sub-tracter, n.

sub·trac·tion *noun* 1. the taking away of a part of something. *The subtraction of junk food from her diet made her feel healthy and strong.* 2. an oper-ation that finds the differ-ence between two numbers or how many are left when some are taken away. *Joe used subtraction to find out how much weight his puppy gained this month. / The subtraction of five people from the class left only ten.* {səb **trăk** shən}

sub·tra·hend *noun* that number which is taken away from another number in subtrac-tion. *In the equation "13-10=3," "10" is the subtra-hend.* {**suhb** trə **hehnd**}

sub·urb *noun* an area or com-munity located just outside a city or town. *Many people who live in a suburb go to work in the city.* {**suh** bərb}

sub·way *noun* an underground passenger train or rail system in a large city. Subways are powered by electricity. {**suhb** way}

suc·ceed *verb* (succeeded, suc-ceeding, succeeds) 1. to have a good or favorable result; do well. *No one thought his new business would succeed.* 2. to get what is wanted. *He suc-ceeded in getting her to quit smoking.* 3. to follow or come after. *Who will succeed the president if he dies while in office?* {sək **seed**}

suc·cess *noun* 1. a person or thing that does or goes well. *Her book was a huge success, selling millions of copies.* 2. the reaching of something desired or intended. *After years of trying to find a good job, he finally had success.* 3. having become rich or famous. *Her success made her a snob.* {sək **sehs**}

suc·cess·ful *adjective* 1. ending or doing well. *The successful coffee shop was open eighteen hours a day.* 2. having reached a wanted goal. *The firemen were successful in put-ting out the fire.* 3. having gained a lot of money or a high social position. *The suc-cessful doctor drove an expen-sive car.* {sək **sehs** fəl} successfully, adv.

suc·ces·sion *noun* 1. the act or process of following or coming after something or someone else. *The three jets took off in succession.* 2. the persons or things that follow or come after one another. *A succession of birds landed on the roof throughout the day.* {sək **seh** shən}

suc·ces·sive *adjective* following one after another. *He played in eight successive games before he hurt his ankle.* {sək **seh** sihv} successively, adv.

suc·ces·sor *noun* a person or thing that comes after or fol-lows another. *The class presi-dent shook hands with her successor after her good-bye speech.* {sək **seh** sər}

such *adjective* 1. of a certain character or kind. *Such friends as I have are hard to find.* 2. similar to; like. *The factory packs beef, pork, and other such meats.* 3. so much; that much. *We could never wish him such bad luck.* *pro-noun* someone or something of a specific kind. *Such is the nature of man.* {**suhch**}

suck *verb* (sucked, sucking, sucks) 1. to pull into the mouth by using the tongue and lips to make a vacuum. *I sucked the soda through a straw.* 2. to drain the liquid from in this way. *The baby sucked her bottle of juice until it was empty.* 3. to hold in the mouth and squeeze with the tongue. *The baby is sucking her thumb.* 4. to eat by holding in the mouth and licking. *Suck a hard candy if you are hungry.* 5. to take or draw in by suction. *The vacuum cleaner sucked the dirt from the floor.* {**suhk**}

suc·tion *noun* the force that pulls or draws an object or liquid into a vacuum. *The suction of the vacuum cleaner is blocked.* {**suhk** shən}

sud·den *adjective* 1. happening without notice or warning; not expected. *A sudden noise frightened us.* 2. sharp, quick or abrupt. *I made a sudden turn into the traffic. / There was a sudden change in her mood.* {**suhd** ən} suddenly, adv., suddenness, n.

suds *plural noun* water mixed with soap, or the foam that forms on soapy water. {**suhdz**}

sue *verb* (sued, suing, sues) to start a lawsuit against in a court of law; prosecute. *The injured passenger will sue the drunk driver.* {**sooh**}

Homophone Note The words *sue* and *Sioux* (a Native American nation) sound alike but have different meanings.

Suez Canal *noun* a canal in northeastern Egypt. It crosses the Isthmus of Suez and con-nects the Mediterranean Sea with the Red Sea. {**sooh** ehz kə **năl**}

 Human Body

 Human Mind

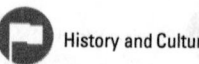 Everyday Life

 History and Culture

Communication

a b c d e f g h i j k l m n o p q r s t u v w x y z

suf·fer *verb* (suffered, suffering, suffers) 1. to feel pain or misfortune. *She suffers from headaches. / He suffered from his mistakes.* 2. to be harmed or hurt in some way. *His grades suffered when he started playing football.* 3. to experience or endure. *She suffered the loss of her job.* {**suhf** ər} sufferable, adj., sufferably, adv., sufferer, n.

suf·fi·cient *adjective* enough; as much as needed. *The amount of food here will be sufficient for the camping trip.* {sə **fih** shənt} sufficiently, adv.

suf·fix *noun* a unit of meaning that is added to the end of a word to make a new word with a slightly different meaning. The "ed" in "wanted" is a suffix. {**suhf** ihks}

suf·fo·cate *verb* (suffocated, suffocating, suffocates) 1. to kill by not allowing to breathe; smother. 2. to die from lack of air. *The animals suffocated in the smoke from the fire.* 3. to be kept from breathing easily or from cool fresh air. *I nearly suffocated on that hot, crowded bus.* {**suhf** ə **kayt**} suffocation, n.

suf·frage *noun* the right to vote or the exercise of this right. {**suhf** rihj}

sug·ar ○ *noun* a sweet substance in a crystal form that comes mainly from sugar cane and sugar beets. Sugar is used to flavor, preserve, and ferment food. {**shuu** gər}

sugar cane *noun* a tall grass of tropical areas that has a thick stalk. Sugar cane is the main source of sugar. {**shuu** gər **kayn**}

sug·gest *verb* (suggested, suggesting, suggests) 1. to put forth for thinking about; propose. *We suggested several ways to raise money.* 2. to bring to mind in a way that is not direct; hint. *The story suggests a deeper meaning.* 3. to call to mind by being similar to. *The rain suggests tears.* {sə **jehst** or səg **jehst**} suggestingly, adv.

sug·ges·tion *noun* 1. the act of suggesting or state of being suggested. *Suggestion does not work on small children; you have to give them commands.* 2. something that is suggested. *The teachers did not like my suggestion that they allow students to chew gum in class.* 3. a small amount; hint; trace. *The delicious soup had a lot of cream with a suggestion of garlic.* {səg **jehs** chən}

su·i·cide *noun* 1. the act of killing oneself on purpose. 2. someone who has committed such an act. {**sooh** ih **siyd**}

suit *noun* 1. a set of clothes with a jacket and trousers or a skirt made of the same material and color. 2. the act or method of bringing an action in a court of law. *He filed suit against the city.* 3. all the playing cards of a single kind in the deck. *The four suits of playing cards are hearts, diamonds, clubs and spades.* *verb* (suited, suiting, suits) 1. to be right for; fit. *The color yellow suits her.* 2. to be acceptable to; satisfy. *The change in plans suits me.* {**sooht**}

suit·a·ble *adjective* right for the situation or purpose; fitting. *I want to buy him a suitable going away gift.* {**sooht** ə bəl}

suitability, n., suitableness, n., suitably, adv.

suit·case *noun* a case in the shape of a rectangle used for carrying clothing and personal items. {**sooht** kays}

suite *noun* 1. several rooms that are connected. *They reserved a hotel suite.* 2. several things that together form a set or series. *They performed a suite of lively dances.* {**sweet**}

Homophone Note The words **suite** and **sweet** (as in taste) sound alike but have different meanings.

sul·fur or **sulphur** *noun* a substance that is one of the chemical elements. It is found in the form of pale yellow crystals or in compounds with other elements. Sulfur is used in making matches, gunpowder, and fertilizer. (symbol: S) {**suhl** fər}

sulk *verb* (sulked, sulking, sulks) to express anger or bad humor by being silent or distant. *He sulked when his mother told him to stop riding his bike.* *noun* (sometimes plural) anger or ill humor shown by sulking. *She's got the sulks this morning.* {**suhlk**}

sul·len *adjective* 1. silently showing anger. *He gave her a sullen look.* 2. dark and filled with gloom. *I awoke under a sullen sky.* {**suh** lən} sullenly, adv., sullenness, n.

sul·phur *noun* another spelling of **sulfur**. {**suhl** fər}

sul·tan *noun* the ruler of an Islamic country. {**suhl** tən}

sum *noun* 1. the number or amount that comes from adding two or more numbers. *The sum of ten and ten is twenty.* 2. an amount of money that is not stated or definite. *He has saved a large*

a
b
c
d
e
f
g
h
i
j
k
l
m
n
o
p
q
r
s
t
u
v
w
x
y
z

sum over the years. {<u>suhm</u>}

• **sum up**
to state or tell again in a short, clear way. *The lawyer summed up his arguments to the jury.*

Homophone Note The words *sum* and *some* (unspecified in number) sound alike but have different meanings.

su·mac *noun* a small tree with pointed leaves and clusters of red or white berries. {<u>sooh</u> măk *or* <u>shooh</u> măk}

sum·mer *noun* the warmest season of the year, falling between spring and autumn. In the northern hemisphere summer continues from late June to September. *verb* (summered, summering, summers) to spend the summer. *They will summer at the beach.* {<u>suhm</u> ər}

sum·mer·y *adjective* like or having to do with summer. *We had summery weather in March.* {<u>suhm</u> ə ree}

sum·mit *noun* the highest part; peak. *We reached the summit of the mountain.* {<u>suhm</u> iht}

sum·mon *verb* (summoned, summoning, summons) 1. to call to appear for a particular purpose. *The principal summoned the students who had been fighting to the office.* 2. to call up; stir up. *She summoned her courage before entering the dark, scary house.* {<u>suhm</u> ən}

sum·mons *noun* (summonses) a notice to appear before a court of law. *The court sent her a summons.* {<u>suhm</u> ənz}

sun 🌐 *noun* 1. the star in the middle of our solar system. The earth and other planets revolve around it and receive heat and light from it. 2. the heat and light energy given off by the sun; sunlight. *Can you feel the sun on your face?* 3. a star. *verb* (sunned, sun-

ning, suns) to expose to the sun's rays. *The lizard sunned itself on the rock.* {<u>suhn</u>} sunlike, adj.

• **under the sun**
in existence; in the world; on earth. *It's the best railway system under the sun.*

Homophone Note Are you looking for the word *son* (a person's male child)? *Sun* and *son* sound alike but have different meanings.

Sun. *abbreviation* an abbreviation for **Sunday.**

sun·bathe *verb* (sunbathed, sunbathing, sunbathes) to bare the body to the sun's rays. *My sister and her friends sunbathe in the back yard in order to get a summer tan.* {<u>suhn</u> bayth} sunbather, n.

sun·burn *noun* a sore redness of the skin caused by staying in the sun too long. *I got a sunburn because I fell asleep on the beach.* *verb* (sunburned or sunburnt, sunburning, sunburns) to cause to get a sunburn. *The sun reflecting off the water sunburned my skin.* {<u>suhn</u> buhrn}

sun·dae *noun* a serving of ice cream topped with syrup, fruit, chopped nuts, and whipped cream. {<u>suhn</u> day *or* <u>suhn</u> dee}

Homophone Note The words *sundae* and *Sunday* (a day of the week) sound alike but have different meanings.

Sun·day *noun* the first day of the week. Sunday comes between Saturday and Monday. {<u>suhn</u> day}

Homophone Note The words *Sunday* and *sundae* (a dessert) sound alike but have different meanings.

Word History *Sunday* comes from an early English word meaning "the day of the sun."

sun·di·al *noun* a device that stands in a garden or on a lawn to show the time of day. A sundial has a flat, round disk with numbers and a pointer that casts a shadow. As the shadow moves across the numbers, the sundial shows what time it is. {<u>suhn</u> diy əl *or* <u>suhn</u> diyl}

sun·flow·er *noun* a tall plant with large, yellow flowers. The seeds in the center of the flower can be eaten. {<u>suhn</u> flow ər}

sun·glass·es *plural noun* a pair of eyeglasses with dark lenses to protect the eyes from bright sunlight. {<u>suhn</u> glăs ihz}

sun·light 🌐 *noun* the light of the sun; sunshine. *The sunlight hurts my eyes.* {<u>suhn</u> liyt}

sun·ny *adjective* (sunnier, sunniest) 1. having much sunlight. *My bedroom is bright and sunny because it has nice, big windows!* 2. cheerful; bright. *He has such a sunny smile.* {<u>suhn</u> ee} sunniness, n.

sun·rise *noun* 1. the moment each day at which the sun first can be seen above the eastern horizon. *I was awake at sunrise today.* 2. the rising of the sun above the eastern horizon and the changes in the colors of the sky and clouds. *What a beautiful sunrise!* {<u>suhn</u> riyz}

sun·screen *noun* an ingredient used in a lotion that is put on the skin to protect against sunburn. {<u>suhn</u> skreen}

sun·set *noun* 1. the moment each day when the sun goes

 Human Body   Human Mind    Everyday Life    History and Culture   Communication

below the western horizon. *The street lamps come on at sunset.* 2. the sun's going below the western horizon and the changes in the colors of the sky and clouds at that time. *There was a beautiful sunset last night.* {**suhn** seht}

sun·shine *noun* the bright light of the sun not hidden by clouds. *We felt the sunshine on our faces all day at the beach.* {**suhn shiyn**} sunshiny, adj.

sun·tan *noun* a dark coloring of the skin as a result of exposure to strong sunlight or a sun lamp. {**suhn** tăn} suntanned, adj.

su·per *adjective* (informal) excellent. *My teacher said I did a super job on my book report.* {**sooh** pər}

su·per- *prefix* 1. a prefix that means "above" or "over." *A supervisor is a person who watches over you.* 2. a prefix that means "beyond" or "greater than." *A nation that is a superpower is one with power beyond its own country. / A supersonic jet is a jet that travels at a speed greater than the speed of sound.*

su·perb *adjective* of the finest kind or quality. *He is a superb musician.* {sə **puhrb** or sooh **puhrb**} superbly, adv., superbness, n.

su·per·in·ten·dent *noun* 1. one who manages or directs something. *She is the superintendent on this job.* 2. one in charge of the care and operation of a building. *The building superintendent will fix the lock.* {sooh pər ihn **tehn** dənt}

su·pe·ri·or *adjective* 1. having a higher position, degree, or rank. *In the navy, an admiral is superior to a captain.* 2. much better than others in quality; excellent. *His work was superior because it was* neat, correct, and complete. 3. showing a sense of being better than others. *She acted superior to her friends because her family was rich.* noun 1. a person who has a higher position or rank than others. *The soldiers received their orders from their superior.* 2. a person who is better than others in skill, talent, or in some other way. *She is his superior in basketball.* {sə **peer** ee ər}

Su·pe·ri·or *noun* Lake Superior, the largest and most western of the Great Lakes. It lies between the U.S. states of Minnesota, Wisconsin, and Michigan and the Canadian province of Ontario. {sə **peer** ee ər}

su·pe·ri·or·i·ty *noun* the quality or state of being better, higher, or greater. *The team showed their superiority by winning the game.* {sə **pee** ree **ohr** ih tee}

su·per·la·tive *adjective* 1. of the finest kind or highest quality. *He is a superlative flute player.* 2. having to do with the form of adjectives and adverbs that indicates the highest or most extreme degree of comparison. *"Newest" and "most readily" are the superlative forms of "new" and "readily."* noun the superlative degree, or a word or form in this degree. *She used the superlative, "best," to describe her opinion of the painting.* {sə **puhr** lə tihv or sooh **puhr** lə tihv, n., sə **puhr** lə tihv or sooh **puhr** lə tihv, adj.}

su·per·mar·ket  *noun* a large store that carries a wide variety of food and household items. {**sooh** pər **mar** kiht}

su·per·nat·u·ral *adjective* having to do with forces separate from or higher than natural laws. *Last night my dreams were full of supernatural creatures such as ghosts and vampires.* {**sooh** pər **nă** chə rəl or **sooh** pər **năch** rəl} supernaturally, adv.

su·per·sti·tion   *noun* a belief that is not based on fact. *It's just a superstition that black cats bring bad luck.* {**sooh** pər **stih** shən}

su·per·vise *verb* (supervised, supervising, supervises) to direct during the carrying out of a task. *She supervises us but doesn't boss us around.* {**sooh** pər **viyz**} supervisor, n.

sup·per *noun* an evening meal. *Please make sure you're home in time to have supper with the family.* {**suhp** ər}

sup·ple *adjective* (suppler, supplest) 1. easily curved or bent; flexible. *We will use these supple branches to make a basket.* 2. able to move with ease; not stiff. *With exercise you will have supple muscles.* {**suhp** əl} suppleness, n.

sup·ply  *verb* (supplied, supplying, supplies) 1. to provide. *The state supplied food to the homeless.* 2. to provide what is wanted or needed (usually followed by "with"). *The teacher supplied the students with pens and paper.* noun (supplies) 1. the act of providing or supplying. *That department is in charge of supply.* 2. an amount of something available for use; stock. *The supply of food was not enough for the whole month.* 3. (plural) materials kept for use as needed. *We packed supplies for our trip.* {sə **pliy**} supplier, n.

sup·port *verb* (supported, supporting, supports) 1. to bear. *I know you're tired, but I can't support your weight, so you will have to walk.* 2. to hold up; brace. *The table is sup-*

ported by four legs. 3. to help during a time of trouble or stress. *She supported me when I was ill.* 4. to provide enough for. *Parents support their families by working.* 5. to provide proof or evidence for. *What other people say supports his story.* noun 1. the act supporting, or the condition of being supported. *Where can he get support?* 2. someone or something that gives support. *He has been such a support to me during this time of trouble.* {sə **pohrt**} supportingly, adv.

sup·pose *verb* (supposed, supposing, supposes) 1. to assume to be true in order to make clear or to explain. *I suppose she loves him, because she married him.* 2. to consider to be possible. *I suppose we might stay until next week. / Suppose your bike was stolen instead of mine.* 3. to believe; think. *I suppose that his plan will work.* {sə **pohz**}

su·preme *adjective* 1. having the highest rank, position, or authority. *The supreme wizard called the other wizards to a meeting.* 2. greatest in character, degree, or importance. *His guitar playing shows supreme skill.* {sə **preem**} supremely, adv.

sure *adjective* (surer, surest) 1. free of doubt as to the truth of something; positive. *I am sure that this water is safe to drink.* 2. certain to be; not possible to avoid. *They are sure winners.* 3. steady and without fail; reliable. *She has a sure hold on his arm. / Is he a sure friend? adverb* (informal) certainly; surely. *It sure is cold today. / Sure, you can use my skate board.* {**shoohr** or **shuhr**}, adj., **shoohr** or **shuhr**, adv.}

sure·ly *adverb* 1. certainly. *That is surely what will happen.* 2. without fail; inevitably. *Slowly but surely they will finish the job.* {**shoohr** lee or **shuhr** lee}

surf *noun* ocean waves that break on the shore or other land barriers. *The surf is calm today.* verb (surfed, surfing, surfs) to ride on the waves of the sea with a surfboard. *They surf on the biggest waves.* {**suhrf**}

Homophone Note Are you looking for the word **serf** (a feudal servant)? **Surf** and **serf** sound alike but have different meanings.

sur·face *noun* 1. the outside of something. *The surface of this ball is smooth.* 2. the outside look of something. *On the surface, his plan looked easy.* verb (surfaced, surfacing, surfaces) 1. to finish by smoothing or leveling. *His dad surfaced the wood for a tree house.* 2. to rise to the top; come up from being submerged below. *The submarine surfaced and the crew came out.* {**suhr** fihs}

surf·board *noun* a long, narrow board on which a person kneels, stands, or lies while riding the waves. {**suhrf** bohrd}

surge *noun* 1. a strong forward motion; rush. *The storm caused a sudden surge of flood water.* 2. a rise, increase, or rush of something. *She felt a surge of anger when she saw the broken window. / There was a surge in the price of gasoline.* verb (surged, surging,

surges) to move or swell in or like a wave; billow. *The king's men surged over the hill.* {**suhrj**}

sur·geon *noun* a medical doctor who does surgery. {**suhr** jən}

sur·ger·y 🌐 *noun* (surgeries) 1. the field of medicine that treats disease and injury by fixing or removing parts of the body. 2. an operation done by a surgeon. *He is going to have surgery for the torn muscle in his leg.* {**suhr** jə ree}

sur·name *noun* the name that tells the particular family that one is a part of; family name; last name. *Smith and Jones are surnames.* {**suhr** naym}

sur·pass *verb* (surpassed, surpassing, surpasses) 1. to be greater or larger than; go beyond. *This year's milk supply surpasses last year's.* 2. to be better than in talent or accomplishment. *She surpassed all others with her excellent teaching skills.* {sər **păs**}

sur·plus *noun* the amount that goes beyond what is needed or required; an extra amount. *There is a surplus of winter wheat this year.* adjective more than what is necessary; extra. *They gave us the surplus apples from their orchard.* {**suhr** pluhs or **suhr** pləs, n., **suhr** pluhs or **suhr** pləs, adj.}

sur·prise *verb* (surprised, surprising, surprises) 1. to catch off guard; come upon or occur to suddenly. *He surprised her with a kiss. / The blizzard surprised the whole town.* 2. to cause a feeling of wonder in; amaze. *Vicky's ability in chess surprised us.* noun 1. the act of surprising. *Tell me what your plan is because I hate surprises.* 2. the state of being sur-

Human Body   Human Mind   Everyday Life   History and Culture   Communication

prised, astonished, or struck with wonder. *He could not hide his surprise at seeing his old enemy after so many years.* 3. that which brings about such a state. *Winning the lottery was a surprise.* {sər **priyz** or sə **priyz**, n., sər **priyz** or sə **priyz**, v.}

Word History When it entered the English language from early French, *surprise* meant "to overtake."

sur·ren·der *verb* (surrendered, surrendering, surrenders) 1. to turn over or yield to the power or control of another. *The general was forced to surrender his troops. / They surrendered their guns.* 2. to give oneself up to someone or something; submit. *The army surrendered at midnight. / We surrendered to the music and danced the night away.* *noun* an act or instance of giving up or surrendering. *He demanded the surrender of their weapons.* {sə **rehn** dər}

sur·round *verb* (surrounded, surrounding, surrounds) 1. to close off all sides of. *The wall surrounds the town.* 2. to form in a circle around; encircle. *Fans surrounded the singer after the concert.* {sə **rownd**}

sur·round·ing *noun* (plural) the environment of anything. *They live in very poor surroundings.* {sə **rown** ding}

sur·vey *verb* (surveyed, surveying, surveys) 1. to have a general look at. *He surveyed the house that is for sale.* 2. to examine carefully or in detail. *She surveyed the report for mistakes before handing it in.* 3. to measure the shape, area, and elevation of with special instruments. *Those men are surveying the land out here because the town wants to build a new road.* *noun* (sur-

veys) 1. the act of finding out the shape, area, and elevation of a piece of land. *They did a survey of the property.* 2. a general look at or review of something. *This class is a survey of American history.* 3. the collecting of information on a particular subject from a small portion of the public. *They did a phone survey of women over forty for their opinions of the new law.* {**suhr** vay or sər **vay**}

sur·viv·al *noun* the act or fact of continuing to be alive or survive. *Our survival depends on taking care of the natural environment.* {sər **viy** vəl}

sur·vive *verb* (survived, surviving, survives) 1. to continue to live following the death of another. *Only three people survived after the terrible crash.* 2. to live or continue beyond or in spite of. *The pioneers survived a terrible winter on the prairie that year.* 3. to continue to exist or be in use. *With enough water, the plants will survive.* {sər **viyv**} survivability, n., survivable, adj.

sus·pect 🌐 💬 *verb* (suspected, suspecting, suspects) 1. to believe to be true. *I suspect that she likes you very much.* 2. to believe the guilt of without enough proof. *They suspect him of stealing just because he's new in town.* *noun* one who is suspected of doing something wrong or of a crime. *She is a suspect in the robbery.* {**suh** spehkt, n., sə **spehkt**, v.}

sus·pend *verb* (suspended, suspending, suspends) 1. to hang from a higher position. *Suspend the lantern from a high branch.* 2. to cause to stop for a period of time. *They suspended the game until the rain stopped.* 3. to exclude as a

punishment. *The principal suspended them from school for fighting.* 4. to cause to hang in a fluid substance such as air or water. *A fly is suspended in the salad oil.* {sə **spehnd**}

sus·pend·ers *plural noun* a pair of straps that hold trousers up. Suspenders are worn over the shoulders and attached to the trousers at the front and back of the waist. {sə **spehn** dərz}

sus·pense *noun* a state of excitement or anxiety that comes from mystery or doubt. *The movie kept us in suspense.* {sə **spehns**} suspenseful, adj.

sus·pi·cion *noun* 1. the act or an instance of not believing or of suspecting. *The clever thief did nothing to cause suspicion while the police searched his house.* 2. the state of being suspected. *Suspicion will follow him wherever he goes.* 3. a belief that something is true. *It's my suspicion that the accident was his fault.* {sə **spih** shən}

sus·pi·cious *adjective* 1. causing questions or doubt. *The police questioned him about his suspicious activities.* 2. without trust. *She is a suspicious person.* {sə **spih** shəs} suspiciously, adv.

SW *abbreviation* an abbreviation for **southwest**.

swal·low[1] 🔊 *verb* (swallowed, swallowing, swallows) 1. to cause food to go from the mouth to the stomach. *The baby swallowed a mouthful of cereal.* 2. to take in and cover completely; make disappear (usually followed by "up").

A B C D E F G H I J K L M N O P Q R S T U V W X Y Z

a
b
c
d
e
f
g
h
i
j
k
l
m
n
o
p
q
r
s
t
u
v
w
x
y
z

Darkness swallowed up the village. 3. (informal) to believe or to accept without questioning. *The principal swallowed Al's story about why he was late.* 4. to hold or keep back. *She swallowed her anger.* *noun* 1. an act or instance of swallowing. *A swallow hurts when your throat is sore.* 2. the amount that is or can be swallowed at one time; gulp. *Take a swallow of water.* {swŏl oh}

swal·low² ⬤ *noun* a small bird with long, pointed wings and often a forked tail. Swallows are known for their graceful flight and move to different areas at certain times of the year. {swŏl oh}

swam *verb* past tense of **swim**. {swăm}

swamp ⬤ ⬤ *noun* a wet, low area of land that is usually covered with water; bog; marsh. *verb* (swamped, swamping, swamps) 1. to weigh down, burden, or overcome; overwhelm. *We were swamped with junk mail.* 2. to cause to sink or fill with water. *The terrible waves swamped our canoe.* 3. to become flooded with water or sink, as a boat. *The ship swamped in the storm.* {swŏmp}

swan *noun* a large water bird, usually white, with a very long neck and webbed feet. {swŏn}

swap or **swop** *verb* (swapped or swopped, swapping or swopping, swaps or swops) to exchange or trade. *The children swapped bicycles. / I will swap my television set for a video camera.* *noun* an exchange or trade. *They made a fair swap.* {swŏp}

swarm *noun* 1. a large number of insects moving together in a group. *I came upon a swarm*

of ants. 2. a colony of bees moving to or settled in a hive. *The swarm built a new hive in the next field.* 3. a group of people, animals, or things in motion; throng. *A swarm of sea gulls landed on the beach.* *verb* (swarmed, swarming, swarms) 1. to come together or move as a large group or mass. *Swallows swarmed in the tree.* 2. to be covered or crowded; teem. *The town swarmed with students.* 3. to crowd or come together over; throng into or over. *The audience swarmed the stage.* {swohrm}

sway *verb* (swayed, swaying, sways) 1. to swing back and forth or from side to side; rock. *She swayed in time to the music.* 2. to cause to swing back and forth or from side to side. *I swayed the cradle until the baby slept.* 3. to change in sympathy or opinion. *He's swaying toward my ideas.* 4. to cause to change a decision or opinion. *Her speech swayed them to change their vote.* *noun* 1. an act or instance of swaying. *We saw how windy it was by the sway of the trees.* 2. control or influence. *The president holds sway over the final decision.* {sway}

swear *verb* (swore, sworn, swearing, swears) 1. to make a serious or solemn promise; vow. *He swore to her that he was telling the truth.* 2. to make a statement under oath (usually followed by "to"). *She has sworn to the truth of what she said.* 3. to use angry or vulgar language. *He swore at the car when it failed to start.* {swayr}

• **swear off**
(informal) to decide or promise to give up. *If he*

would swear off ice cream, he might lose some weight.

sweat ⬤ *verb* (sweated or sweat, sweating, sweats) 1. to give off a salty fluid from the skin pores to cool the body. *I was sweating in the hot lecture hall.* 2. to collect moisture from the surrounding air. *A cold can of soda will sweat in hot weather.* *noun* 1. the liquid given out from sweat glands through the pores of the skin. *After running he was covered with sweat.* 2. the condition of sweating. *She was so nervous, she went into a cold sweat.* 3. drops of moisture that form on a surface. *There was sweat on the pipes in the basement.* {sweht}

sweat·er ⬤ *noun* a knitted shirt, pullover, or jacket. {sweht ər}

sweat·shirt *noun* a knitted pullover shirt with long sleeves. Sweatshirts are often worn during exercise to soak up sweat. {sweht shuhrt}

Swe·den *noun* a country on the Scandinavian Peninsula in northern Europe. Stockholm is the capital of Sweden. {swee dən} Swede, n., Swedish, adj.

sweep *verb* (swept, sweeping, sweeps) 1. to clear of dirt or dust by using a broom or brush. *The maid swept the floor.* 2. to remove by brushing with a broom or brush (usually followed by "away," "up," or "out"). *She swept the dust away.* 3. to move, carry away, or remove with force. *The river swept the child away.* 4. to touch lightly; brush. *Her dress swept the floor. / She swept his face with her hand.* 5. to pass through or over with force or speed. *Fear is sweeping the country.* 6. to pass over by a long, steady motion. *Her eyes swept the room.* 7. to move

 Human Body   ? Human Mind    Everyday Life   History and Culture    Communication

steadily with great force or speed. *The hurricane swept through our village.* noun 1. the act or motion of sweeping. *He cleared the table with one sweep of his hand.* 2. a steady line or motion. *The sweep of the pitcher's leg before he throws is very graceful.* 3. a large, clear area. *The farmer looked out across the sweep of plains.* {sweep}

sweet *adjective* (sweeter, sweetest) 1. having a taste like that of sugar or honey; not bitter, salty, or sour. *I love this sweet chocolate.* 2. not spoiled; fresh. *The milk will stay sweet in the refrigerator.* 3. having no salt. *I prefer sweet butter to salted.* 4. gentle or pleasant. *She is such a sweet girl that she brings her mother flowers every day.* 5. pleasant to the mind or senses. *She told me of her sweet thoughts of me.* / *There are sweet smells in the flower garden.* / *I heard the sweet sound of music.* noun (often plural) food with a sweet taste, such as candy or cookies. *He ate too many sweets.* {sweet} sweetly, adv., sweetness, n.

Homophone Note Are you looking for the word *suite* (connected rooms)? *Sweet* and *suite* sound alike but have different meanings.

sweet·en *verb* (sweetened, sweetening, sweetens) 1. to cause to be sweet or sweeter in taste. *She sweetens her tea with honey.* 2. to become sweet or sweeter. *Apples sweeten as they get ripe.* {swee tən} sweetener, n.

swell *verb* (swelled, swelled or swollen, swelling, swells) 1. to make larger by growth or pressure; expand. *The crowd swelled as the night went on.* / *The balloon swelled.* 2. to

cause to be greater or larger in amount, force, or loudness. *The constant rain swelled the river.* 3. to become greater in amount, force, or loudness. *The sound swelled louder and louder.* 4. to grow within and rise out; spring or well up. *Water swells from a fountain in the park.* / *Feelings of love swelled inside him.* 5. to cause to curve out or bulge. *The bee sting has swelled part of the child's arm.* / *There is no wind to swell the sails.* noun 1. the act of swelling or a swollen state. *The storm caused a swell of water to flood the cellar.* 2. a long wave or series of waves. *The ship was lifted by the swell.* *adjective* fine; excellent; nice. *He is a swell friend.* / *What a swell day!* {swehl}

swell·ing *noun* 1. the act or condition of something that is swelling or swollen. *Ice packs will control the swelling.* 2. a part that is swollen. *She has a large swelling where the bee stung her arm.* {sweh ling}

swept *verb* past tense and past participle of **sweep.** {swehpt}

swerve *verb* (swerved, swerving, swerves) 1. to change direction suddenly; turn quickly; veer. *The car swerved to avoid the child.* 2. to cause to turn or change direction quickly. *She swerved the car off the road.* noun an act of suddenly changing direction; quick turn. *His swerve prevented an accident.* {swuhrv}

swift *adjective* (swifter, swiftest) 1. moving or able to move very rapidly. *She is a swift runner.* 2. happening, coming, or being done quickly. *He made a swift change of plans.* noun a bird with long wings and a short tail that can fly very fast.

There are several kinds of swifts. {swihft} swiftly, adv., swiftness, n.

swim ○ *verb* (swam, swum, swimming, swims) 1. to move through water by moving parts of the body. *My dog swam out into the pond to get a stick.* 2. to glide or flow as though moving through water. *He swam through the sea of people in the crowded streets.* 3. to be in or covered with a liquid. *She gave us peaches swimming in cream.* 4. to feel dizzy or faint. *I think I need to sit down because my head is swimming.* noun the act or a period of swimming. *We decided to go for a swim.* {swihm} swimmer, n.

swim·mer *noun* a person or animal that moves through water using limbs, tail, or fins; one who swims. {swihm ər}

swin·dle *verb* (swindled, swindling, swindles) to cheat out of money or property. *The crook swindled the old man of all his savings.* noun an act of cheating out of money or property. *The victim of his swindle had him arrested.* {swihn dəl} swindler, n.

swine *noun* (swine) pig; hog. {swiyn}

swing *verb* (swung, swinging, swings) 1. to cause to move back and forth around a point or on an axis. *He swung the door open and closed.* / *The old clock swung its pendulum back and forth.* 2. to move back and forth around a point or on an axis, while hanging or suspended. *The tire swing swung from the tree.* 3. to move back and forth while seated on a swing. *My friend and I like to swing on the playground.* 4. to cause to move in a wide motion. *He swung his leg over*

the fence. / He swings his arms as he walks. 5. to cause to move in an arc or circle. *She swung her bag at the robber.* / *The player swung his bat at the pitch.* noun 1. the act of swinging. *We went for a swing on the playground.* 2. a swinging movement. *The batter took a swing at the pitch.* 3. a steady rhythm in music. *This song has a nice swing to it.* 4. a seat hung from ropes or chains on which one sits and moves back and forth for pleasure. *She went to the swings at the playground.* 5. shift; change. *The president experienced a swing in popularity.* {<u>swing</u>}

swirl verb (swirled, swirling, swirls) 1. to move around with a spinning or whirling motion. *The river swirled around the rocks.* 2. to cause to go around and around; cause to whirl. *The washing machine swirls the clothes.* noun 1. a spinning or whirling motion. *The wind raised a swirl of dry leaves.* 2. a curving shape or line. *Her hair hung in swirls.* {<u>swuhrl</u>}

swish verb (swished, swishing, swishes) 1. to move quickly, making a whistling or rustling sound. *Her silk dress swished as she walked.* 2. to cause to move with a rustling sound. *The wind swished a pine branch across the window.* noun a quick motion that makes a whistling or rustling sound; sound of rustling. *I heard the swish of her broom on the sidewalk.* {<u>swihsh</u>}

Swiss adjective of or having to do with Switzerland or its people. *Have you ever tasted Swiss chocolate?* noun (Swiss) a person who was born in or is a citizen of Switzerland. {<u>swihs</u>}

switch noun 1. a thin branch or rod used for whipping. *When my grandfather was a child, he would sometimes get whipped with a switch.* 2. a device that opens and closes an electrical circuit. *Someone turn on the light switch.* 3. a shift; change. *We made a switch in our lives when we moved to the country.* 4. a device for shifting trains from one track to another. *The train went through the switch and changed directions to head south.* verb (switched, switching, switches) 1. to whip with a switch or similar object. 2. to change; shift. *Let's switch the discussion to another topic.* 3. to change or shift course. *The tone of the speech switched from being very cheerful to very sad.* 4. to exchange; trade. *They switched their old car for a new one.* 5. to turn on or off by operating a switch (usually followed by "off" or "on"). *Could you switch the TV off and go to bed, please?* {<u>swihch</u>}

Swit·zer·land noun a country in central Europe. Bern is the capital of Switzerland. {<u>swiht</u> sər lənd}

swiv·el noun a device that allows the object fastened or mounted to it to turn freely or pivot. *His chair is on a swivel.* verb (swiveled, swiveling, swivels) to turn on or as if on a swivel. *The chair in Mom's office swivels.* / *He swiveled in my direction when I called his name.* {<u>swih</u> vəl}

swol·len verb a past participle of **swell**. *The river had swollen to the top of the bank.* adjective made larger by growth, pressure, or inflation; bulging. *He has a swollen finger.* {<u>swoh</u> lən} swollenness, n.

swoop verb (swooped, swooping, swoops) 1. to sweep down suddenly from above, or as if from above in attack (often followed by "down on"). *The bird swooped down to the ground.* / *The army swooped down on the city.* 2. to take, lift up, or remove in a single motion from above; scoop up (often followed by "away," "up," or "off"). *She swooped the papers off the floor with her hand.* noun a fast, sudden motion from above. *The swoop of a bird startled me.* {<u>swoohp</u>}

swop verb or noun another spelling of **swap**. {<u>swŏp</u>}

sword noun a weapon that has a long pointed blade fixed on a handle or hilt. Swords are used to cut or thrust. {<u>sohrd</u>}

sword·fish noun (swordfish or swordfishes) a large fish that has a long, sharp upper jaw that looks like a sword. Swordfish live in warm seas and are used for food or sport. {<u>sohrd</u> fihsh}

Syd·ney noun a city on the southeastern coast of Australia. Sydney is the capital city of a province. {<u>sihd</u> nee}

syl·la·ble noun 1. a unit of speech formed with a single pulse of air pressure. Syllables are made of a single vowel sound with or without surrounding consonants. 2. a written character or group of characters that indicate one syllable. {<u>sihl</u> ə bəl}

sym·bol ❷ noun 1. an object or picture that represents something else. *The rose is a symbol of love.* 2. a sign or figure that represents

Human Body　　Human Mind　　Everyday Life　　History and Culture　　Communication

a particular number, quality, or process. *The plus sign "+" is the symbol for addition.* {**sihm** bəl}

Homophone Note Are you looking for the word **cymbal** (a percussion instrument)? *Symbol* and *cymbal* sound alike but have different meanings.

sym·bol·ic *adjective* 1. of, pertaining to, or represented by a symbol. 2. acting as a symbol (often followed by "of"). *Red is symbolic of anger.* {sihm **bo** lihk} symbolically, adv.

sym·me·try *noun* (symmetries) a state in which both sides of something are balanced in size, form, or arrangement. *Human faces have symmetry.* {**sihm** ə tree}

sym·pa·thet·ic *adjective* 1. feeling or showing understanding. *He is a sympathetic person who listened to me when I was unhappy.* 2. feeling favorable (often followed by "to" or "toward"). *The president is sympathetic to their ideas.* {sihm pə **theh** tihk} sympathetically, adv.

sym·pa·thize *verb* (sympathized, sympathizing, sympathizes) 1. to share in another's emotions (often followed by "with"). *She sympathized with me about the death in our family.* 2. to

feel or express approval of something; be in agreement (often followed by "with"). *We sympathize with the mayor's plans for a new library.* {**sihm** pə **thiyz**} sympathizer, n., sympathizingly, adv.

sym·pa·thy 🔊 *noun* (sympathies) 1. the ability to share another's feelings; compassion. *Her sympathy for others makes her a good listener.* 2. a feeling or expression of approval for something. *I have sympathy for the worker's complaints.* {**sihm** pə thee}

sym·pho·ny 🔊 *noun* (symphonies) 1. a musical piece for an orchestra that has three or four movements. 2. a concert orchestra; symphony orchestra. *We listened to the symphony's new CD.* {**sihm** fə nee}

Word History *Symphony* comes from an ancient Greek word that means "a sounding together."

symphony orchestra *noun* a large group of classical musicians, including string, woodwind, brass, and percussion sections. A symphony orchestra performs symphonies and other orchestral pieces under the direction of a conductor. {**sihm** fə nee **ohr** kə strə}

symp·tom *noun* 1. a sign of something. *Tears can be a symptom of sadness or happiness.* 2. something that happens in the body suggesting that there is a disease or disorder. *Fever is a symptom of the flu.* {**sihmp** təm} symptomless, adj.

syn·a·gogue *noun* a place used by Jews for worship and religious instruction. {**sihn** ə gŏg or **sihn** ə gawg}

syn·drome *noun* a group of signs or symptoms that together indicate a particular disease or condition. {**sihn** drohm}

syn·o·nym *noun* a word having the same or nearly the same meaning as another word of the same language. *"Abundant" and "plentiful" are synonyms.* {**sih** nə nihm}

syn·on·y·mous *adjective* having the same or a similar meaning; expressing the same idea or intent. *The librarian told us that reading a book is synonymous with going on an adventure.* {sih **nŏn** ə məs}

syn·tax 🔊 *noun* 1. the study of the way sentences are formed, and how the words go together. *In English class we are studying syntax.* 2. the word order or pattern of word order in a sentence. *Do you know if the syntax of this sentence is correct?* {**sihn** tăks}

syn·thet·ic *adjective* made with chemicals formed in a laboratory instead of something found in nature; man-made; artificial. *My pants are made of a synthetic material that looks like silk. / Diet soda is made with a synthetic sweetener instead of sugar.* noun a chemical substance made by a laboratory, and not of natural origin. *Plastic and nylon are synthetics.* {sihn **theh** tihk} synthetical, adj., synthetically, adv.

sy·phon *noun* another spelling of *siphon*. {**siy** fən}

syr·up *noun* 1. a solution of sugar in water that contains medicine and flavoring. *She gave him some cherry cough syrup.* 2. a sweet food made by mixing maple sap or sugar and water with other ingredi-

A
B
C
D
E
F
G
H
I
J
K
L
M
N
O
P
Q
R
S
T
U
V
W
X
Y
Z

a
b
c
d
e
f
g
h
i
j
k
l
m
n
o
p
q
r
s
t
u
v
w
x
y
z

ents. The liquid is boiled until it is a very thick syrup. *I put chocolate syrup on my ice cream.* {**seer** əp *or* **suh** rəp}

sys·tem *noun* 1. a group of related things or parts that work together as a whole. *This is a large school system.* 2. a human or animal body as a unit. *The snake bite left poison in his system.* 3. an ordered set of rules, ideas, or principles. *The school has a system for students who cut classes.* 4. a particular way or method of doing something. *We need a better voting system.* / *He's got a system for getting his homework done.* {**sihs** təm} systemless, adj.

 Human Body
 Human Mind
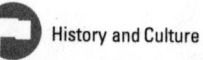 Everyday Life
 History and Culture
Communication

Tt

T is a consonant. When combined with "h," there are two slightly different "th" sounds. The most common "th" sound is the softer "th" found in thanks, then, thing, thousand, thrill or thunder. Some words (such as that, them, this, those, thus) have a harder "th" sound. The word "thyme" has a silent "h."

Tips to help you look up words starting with T: Also look under C for Czechoslovakia and P for pterodactyl.

These words may be hard to look up if you don't already know how to spell them:

technique	thousand
tension	through
thermometer	thumb
thimble	tragedy
thistle	twelfth
thorough	

t or **T** *noun* (t's or T's) the twentieth letter of the English alphabet. {**tee**}

• **to a T**
in a complete or perfect way. *The role of a witch in the play suited her to a T.*

tab *noun* 1. a small loop, strap, or flap, used for pulling, hanging, or opening. *The tab makes it easy to open the can of soda.* 2. (informal) a bill at a bar or restaurant; check. *His generous father paid the tab.* {**tăb**}

• **keep tabs on**
(informal) to keep under close watch; observe carefully. *The police are keeping tabs on the suspect's every move.*

• **pick up the tab**
to pay the bill at a bar or restaurant. *Will you pick up the tab?*

ta·ble 🔄 *noun* 1. a piece of furniture with a flat top, supported by one or more legs. 2. the people seated around a table. *There was laughter coming from the next table.* 3. an organized display of information layed out in rows and columns. *The table in the science book showed the weights of different mammals.* *verb* (tabled, tabling, tables) to put off the discussion of. *City council tabled the new proposal, agreeing to discuss it at a later date.* {**tay** bəl}

• **turn the tables on**
to reverse a situation in order to gain the advantage. *She turned the tables on him when she said she was giving him full responsibility for completing the project.*

ta·ble·cloth *noun* a cloth laid over a dining table to protect its surface during a meal. {**tay** bəl **klaw**th}

ta·ble·spoon *noun* 1. an amount equal to one half of a fluid ounce or three teaspoons. A tablespoon is used in cooking to measure ingredients. (abbreviation: tbs.) *I need three tablespoons of butter in this recipe.* 2. a large spoon used for serving or eating soup or stew. {**tay** bəl **spoohn**}

tab·let *noun* 1. a tiny, flat, hard mass of medicine; pill. 2. a pad made up of sheets of paper bound together at one edge. 3. a flat piece of stone or metal with words or pictures on one surface; plaque. *Each player on the championship team got her name written on a metal tablet that hangs in the gym.* {**tăb** liht}

table tennis *noun* a game like outdoor tennis but played on top of a large table. In table tennis, small, wooden paddles and a small, hollow ball are used. {**tay** bəl **tehn** ihs}

ta·boo ❓🔄 *adjective* forbidden. *Sex was a taboo subject when I was young.* *noun* (taboos) a ban on a subject, action, or behavior. *There is a taboo on certain ways of dressing in some countries.* {tă **booh** *or* tə **booh**, n., tă **booh** *or* tə **booh**, adj.}

tack *noun* 1. a short pin with a flat, wide head. 2. a way of dealing with a problem. *Since your way hasn't worked, let's take a different tack.* *verb* (tacked, tacking, tacks) 1. to fasten or attach with a tack. *She tacked the poster to the bulletin board.* 2. to add as something extra (usually followed by "on"). *He tacked on twenty dollars to my pay.* {**tăk**}

tack·le *noun* 1. equipment or gear used in a sport or hobby such as fishing. 2. a rope and pulley used to lift or move a heavy weight. 3. the act of seizing and throwing a

A
B
C
D
E
F
G
H
I
J
K
L
M
N
O
P
Q
R
S
T
U
V
W
X
Y
Z

a
b
c
d
e
f
g
h
i
j
k
l
m
n
o
p
q
r
s
t
u
v
w
x
y
z

person down. *He made a great tackle to stop the other team's player from scoring a touchdown.* verb (tackled, tackling, tackles) 1. to seize and throw a person to the ground. *He tackled the boy who was stealing his bicycle.* 2. to try to master or solve. *I tackled the arithmetic problem.* {**tăk** əl}

ta·co noun (tacos) a Mexican dish made of a folded tortilla with a filling such as meat or cheese. {**tah** koh}

tact noun the ability to say or do the right thing when dealing with others in a difficult situation. *We need a person with tact to talk to the angry customer.* {**tăkt**}

tac·tics plural noun (used with a plural verb) methods used to bring something about. *His tactics for getting a raise were successful.* {**tăk** tihks}

tad·pole noun a young frog or toad. *A tadpole lives in water and has gills and a tail.* {**tăd** pohl}

Word History *Tadpole* comes from early English words that mean "toad" and "head." A tadpole is a young toad that seems to be all head.

taf·fy noun (taffies) a chewy candy made of molasses or sugar. *Taffy is boiled and then pulled until it holds its shape.* {**tăf** ee}

tag[1] noun a piece of cardboard, thin metal, or plastic, attached to something or someone. *She gave a name tag to each of us. / The price tag shows that this shirt is on sale.* verb (tagged, tagging, tags) 1. to put a tag on. *Tag those books for the yard sale.* 2.

(informal) to follow someone closely (usually followed by "after" or "along"). *My little brother tags along with us when we go to the park.* {**tăg**}

tag[2] noun 1. a children's game in which one player chases the other players until one is touched. The touched player then becomes the pursuer. 2. an act or instance of tagging in the game of baseball. verb (tagged, tagging, tags) 1. to touch in the game of tag, or in a similar game. 2. to touch, in the game of baseball, with the ball or with the hand or glove holding it. *The runner was tagged out before he reached second base.* {**tăg**}

tail ● noun 1. the rear part of an animal's body that sticks out from the backbone. *The dog wags his tail when he is happy.* 2. something that looks like an animal's tail in position or form. *He attached a tail to the kite. / The comet had a long tail.* 3. the rear, bottom, or end part of anything. *You should tuck in the tail of your shirt.* 4. (plural) the reverse side of a coin, opposite the head. *I'll flip a coin, and you call heads or tails.* adjective being in the rear. *We built a porch on the tail end of our house. / I sat in the tail seat on the plane.* verb (tailed, tailing, tails) 1. to follow at the end of. *A large float tailed the parade.* 2. (informal) to follow secretly in order to observe. *The policeman tailed the suspect.* {**tayl**} tailless, adj.

Homophone Note Are you looking for the word *tale* (a story)? *Tail* and *tale* sound alike but have different meanings.

tail·light noun a red warning light at the rear of a vehicle. {**tayl** liyt}

tai·lor noun one who makes, alters, or repairs clothing. *After he had lost some weight, he took his suits to a tailor.* verb (tailored, tailoring, tailors) to make or change for a particular need or purpose. *We tailored the television program for young people.* {**tay** lər}

Tai·pei noun the capital city of Taiwan. {**tiy** pay}

Tai·wan noun an island country in eastern Asia. Taipei is the capital of Taiwan. {**tiy** wahn} Taiwanese, n., adj.

take verb (took, taken, taking, takes) 1. to get through force, skill, or trick; seize; capture. *The army took the city at dawn. / He took first prize at the fair.* 2. to cause to be in one's hands; grasp. *Take the flowers and put them in some water.* 3. to carry away; remove. *Please take some brownies home with you.* 4. to subtract. *If you take five from ten, you get five.* 5. to deal with; do. *He will take his test next week.* 6. to fill. *He took a seat near the window.* 7. to put or bring into one's body. *She took two pills for her headache.* 8. to use for travel. *She takes the bus to school.* 9. to move; to bring. *We will take the lumber by train.* 10. to accept; follow. *Don't take orders from him.* 11. to experience. *I take pleasure in helping you.* 12. to study. *He will take a class in art history.* 13. to put up with. *I can't take the cold weather.* 14. to require. *This job takes a lot of time and effort.* 15. to make or do. *They take pictures when they are on vacation.* 16. to have an effect. *The medicine took, and he is well again.* 17. to become set. *The dye didn't take, so she had to try*

 Human Body   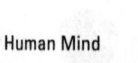 Human Mind    Everyday Life    History and Culture    Communication

again. 18. to gain favor. *The band's new record certainly took, selling over a million copies.* 19. to make worse (usually followed by "from"). *Her poor posture takes from her appearance.* 20. to become. *She took sick and stayed home. noun* 1. the act of taking. *A good friendship is built on give and take.* 2. a thing that is taken. *Their take from the bake sale was ten dollars.* 3. the amount of fish or game taken at a single time. *The hunters came home with a plentiful take.* 4. a scene made without interruption. *The director was pleased to see the actors perform their parts in one take.* 5. a sound recording made in a single attempt. *It took three takes for the band to get the song right.* {tayk}

• **take after**
to look or act like. *She takes after her mother.*

• **take back**
1. to get back something given to another person. *He gave me his bicycle, but then took it back.* 2. to withdraw. *She should take back her comments about our work.*

take·out *adjective* having to do with food that is eaten some place other than where it was made. *We bought a takeout meal. noun* food taken out of a restaurant to be eaten elsewhere. *We ordered takeout for dinner.* {tayk owt}

talc *noun* a soft, mineral material used in making body powder and other products. {tălk}

tale ⊘ ➋ *noun*
1. an account of a real or made-up event; story. *He told a*

funny tale about his trip. 2. a lie; false information. *She tells so many tales that I never believe anything she says.* {tayl}

Homophone Note The words *tale* and *tail* (a part of some animals) sound alike but have different meanings.

tal·ent *noun* 1. a natural skill or ability. *He has a talent for acting, so he will be the star of the play.* 2. a person or group of people who have or show talent. *We've won many trophies because there is a lot of talent on our football team.* {tăl ənt} talented, adj.

talk *verb* (talked, talking, talks) 1. to use spoken words. *Can the baby talk yet?* 2. to discuss. *They talked business at the meeting.* 3. to bring or persuade; convince (usually followed by "into"). *The salesman talked her into buying new shoes, even though she didn't need them. noun* 1. the act of talking; conversation. *They had a long talk about school.* 2. a speech. *The visitor gave a talk on how to stay fit and healthy.* 3. a meeting. *The leaders of the world had a talk in Washington to discuss world trade.* 4. a rumor; gossip. *The talk around town is that he wants to marry her.* {tŏk}

• **talk back**
to answer in a rude manner. *Students must not talk back to the teacher.*

talk show *noun* a radio or television program in which a host talks with famous or interesting people. On a talk show, questions may be taken from people in the listening or viewing audience. {tŏk shoh}

tall *adjective* (taller, tallest) 1. of more than the average height. *She is so tall.* 2. being a certain height. *Mel is four*

feet tall. 3. (informal) hard to believe or made-up. *He told a tall tale.* {tawl}

tal·low *noun* the hard fat from animals such as cattle or sheep. Tallow is used in making soap, candles, lubricating substances, and certain foods. {tăl oh}

tal·ly *noun* (tallies) a total of points scored or debts owed. *Here is the tally of what you owe me. verb* (tallied, tallying, tallies) 1. to find the total of; add up. *At the end of the game we tallied our points.* 2. to enter or record as part of a continuing count. {tăl ee}

Tal·mud *noun* the collection of writings on Jewish civil and religious law {tŏl muud *or* tăl muud} Talmudic, adj.

tal·on *noun* a claw of a bird or animal. {tăl ən}

ta·ma·le
noun a Mexican dish of ground meat wrapped in cornmeal dough. Tamales are cooked in corn husks. {tə **mah** lee}

tam·bou·rine *noun* a small drum that has metal disks attached around the rim. The player shakes the tambourine with one hand and strikes it with other. {tăm bə **reen**}

tame ❶ *adjective* (tamer, tamest) 1. taken from a wild state and made obedient; domesticated. *A tame bear travels with the circus.* 2. still in the wild state but gentle and not afraid of human beings. *Tame deer feed in our yard.* 3. dull or without adventure. *They had a tame vacation. / She grew bored with her tame life. verb* (tamed, taming, tames) to bring under human control;

a
b
c
d
e
f
g
h
i
j
k
l
m
n
o
p
q
r
s
t
u
v
w
x
y
z

domesticate. *He tames lions for the circus.* {**taym**} tamer, *n.*

tam·per *verb* (tampered, tampering, tampers) to meddle in something when one is not asked, and so change or damage it (usually followed by "with"). *Someone tampered with my bicycle and now the brakes don't work.* {**tăm** pər}

tan *verb* (tanned, tanning, tans) 1. to make into leather by soaking in a special solution. *He tans cow skins.* 2. to make brown by exposure to the sun or to a special lamp. *She tans herself under a lamp in the winter months.* 3. to become tanned. *He tans easily.* *noun* 1. a yellowish or light brown color. *The cat is a dark shade of tan.* 2. this color given to skin by exposure to the sun or a special lamp. *Your skin is a lovely tan.* {**tăn**} tannish, *adj.*

   • **tan one's hide**
   (informal) to beat or spank someone very hard. *When my father was a boy, his father tanned his hide for smoking cigarettes.*

tang *noun* a sharp, strong flavor or odor. *There was a tang of lemon in the frosting. / The air near a sea has a salty tang.* {**tăng**}

tan·ge·rine *noun* 1. a citrus that is a type of mandarin orange. A tangerine has loose, reddish orange skin, a slightly flattened shape, and sweet, juicy fruit. 2. the fruit of this tree. {**tăn** jə **reen** *or* **tăn** jə **reen**}

Word History *Tangerines* were called "tangerine oranges" in the 1800s, because they were oranges imported from Tangier, a port city in Morocco.

tan·gle *verb* (tangled, tangling, tangles) 1. to mix or twist into a confused mass. *The cat tangled the yarn.* 2. to be or become mixed up in a confused mass. *My hair tangled in the wind.* 3. to involve in a complicated or confused situation; entangle. *Don't tangle me in your problems.* *noun* 1. a confused, mixed up mass. *Her hair is a tangle of curls.* 2. a complicated or confusing condition or situation. *The boss walked out and left them with a tangle.* {**tăng** gəl}

tank ○ ▣ *noun* 1. a large container used to hold liquid or gas. 2. the amount held by such a container. *Get a full tank of gasoline.* 3. a large vehicle used by the military that has armor and heavy guns. A tank moves on two continuous metal belts instead of wheels. {**tăngk**}

tan·trum *noun* a violent, noisy outburst of angry temper. *The child had a tantrum and threw her food across the table.* {**tăn** trəm}

tap¹ *verb* (tapped, tapping, taps) 1. to strike lightly. *She tapped my head as she walked by.* 2. to strike a surface lightly once or several times. *She tapped on the door before entering.* *noun* 1. one or more light blows or raps. *The bird's taps on the window pane woke me up.* 2. the noise made by such a rap or blow. *I heard a tap on the door.* {**tăp**}

Sometimes a few **taps** on the pipe will fix a clogged water **tap**.

tap² *noun* a device to control the flow of liquid or gas from a pipe; faucet. *verb* (tapped, tapping, taps) 1. to put a hole in, to draw off liquid or gas. *He taps the maple trees in March.* 2. to draw off, or draw off from. *We tapped sap from the tree.* 3. to connect wires to, for the purpose of listening secretly. *The telephone lines were tapped by the police.* {**tăp**}

   • **on tap**
   1. ready to be served from a cask. *The beer is on tap.* 2. on hand; available for use or service. *The store has several new products on tap.*

tap dance *noun* a dance in which the dancer uses the foot, heel, or toe to tap out a rhythm. Tap dancers wear special shoes to sound the taps. {**tăp** dăns}

tape ○ ◑ *noun* 1. a long narrow strip of plastic, cloth, or paper that has glue on one side. Tape is used to stick things together. 2. a long magnetic strip used to record sounds and pictures. *verb* (taped, taping, tapes) 1. to fasten, hold together, or repair with tape. *I'll tape your picture onto the wall.* 2. to record on tape. *They taped her speech.* {**tayp**}

 Human Body   Human Mind   Everyday Life   History and Culture Communication

tape measure *noun* a tool for measuring length made of a long strip of cloth or flexible metal. A tape measure is marked off in inches, centimeters, or other units. {**tayp meh** zhər}

ta·per *verb* (tapered, tapering, tapers) 1. to narrow. *The pants taper at the ankles.* 2. to cause to narrow at one end. *He tapered the stick with his knife.* 3. to slowly come to a complete stop. *The talking tapered into silence.* *noun* a long thin candle. {**tay** pər}

tape recorder *noun* a machine used to record sound onto magnetic tape or to play back the sound recorded. {**tayp** rih **kohr** dər}

tap·es·try *noun* (tapestries) a piece of heavy cloth into which a design or picture has been woven with colored threads. Tapestries are used as wall decorations. {**tăp** ihs tree}

ta·pir *noun* a large mammal that has four short legs with hooves, a round body, and a long flexible snout. Tapirs look like pigs, but they are related to horses and rhinoceroses. They live in the rain forests of southeast Asia and Central and South America. Tapirs eat plants. {**tay** pər}

taps *plural noun* (used with a singular verb) the signal played on a trumpet or drum in the U.S. military forces. Taps are used as a signal for lights to be put out, or at the end of a funeral service. {**tăps**}

tar[1] *noun* a dark, heavy, sticky substance made from wood, coal, or peat. Tar is used to cover roads and protect roofs. {**tar**}

• **beat the tar out of**
1. (informal) to beat or whip severely. *The angry old man beat the tar out of the poor, helpless dog.* 2. to best or outdo by a large amount. *Our players beat the tar out of their team.*

• **tar and feather**
to punish or humiliate by covering with tar and feathers. *A long time ago, people who were caught doing something wrong were sometimes tarred and feathered.*

tar[2] *noun* (informal) a sailor. {**tar**}

ta·ran·tu·la *noun* (tarantulas) a large, hairy spider found in the warmer parts of North, Central, and South America. Some tarantulas have a slightly poisonous bite. {tə **răn** chə lə}

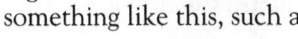

tar·dy *adjective* (tardier, tardiest) late or delayed. *She is never tardy for work, but sometimes leaves early.* {**tar** dee} tardiness, n.

tar·get *noun* 1. an object or mark at which bullets, arrows, or darts are fired or aimed. *With her bow and arrow, she hit the target every time.* 2. a goal; objective. *Her target was to win a raise in pay.* 3. someone or something that is made fun of, criticized or scorned; butt. *They made him a target because he wears clothes that are different from theirs.* {**tar** giht}

Word History *Target* comes from *targe*, a French word for a small round shield, not a large one that covered the whole body.

tar·iff 🌐 *noun* a government tax on goods that come into a country; duty. *They raised the tariff on fuel oil.* {**tar** ihf}

tar·nish *verb* (tarnished, tarnishing, tarnishes) 1. to dull the luster or color of. *Sun and wind tarnished the new car.* 2. to become dull or lose color. *The silverware tarnished.* 3. to spoil or stain. *He told lies that tarnished her character in other people's eyes.* *noun* a dullness or loss of color on a metal surface. {**tar** nihsh}

tart[1] *adjective* (tarter, tartest) sour or acid in taste; sharp; biting. *I like tart fruit.* {**tart**} tartness, n.

tart[2] *noun* a small baked pastry shell with a fruit or other filling. Tarts sometimes do not have a top crust. {**tart**}

tar·tan *noun* woolen cloth woven in a plaid design. Tartans are worn by people of Scottish clans. {**tar** tən}

tar·tar *noun* a hard, yellow substance that forms on the teeth. {**tar** tər}

task *noun* a piece of work to be done; duty. *He gives me a different task to complete every day.* {**tăsk**}

• **take to task**
to reprimand; rebuke; censure. *He took her to task for that cruel remark.*

Tasmanian devil *noun* a mammal with black fur and a tail like a cat's tail. Tasmanian devils live in burrows. They are fierce hunters and will eat almost anything. Tasmanian devils are marsupials that live in Australia. {**tăz may** nih ən **deh** vihl}

tas·sel *noun* 1. an ornament made of a bunch of threads or cords. The threads are tied together at one end and hang free at the other. *Her shawl has tassels along the edge.* 2. something like this, such as

A B C D E F G H I J K L M N O P Q R S **T** U V W X Y Z

the blossom at the top of a corn plant. {tăs əl}

taste 🌐 *verb* (tasted, tasting, tastes) 1. to experience and recognize the flavor of by putting into the mouth. *She tasted the soup to see if it was ready.* 2. to eat a little bit of. *I would like to taste the chocolate cake.* 3. to have a particular flavor. *The sauce tastes bitter.* *noun* 1. the act of tasting food or drink. *I went to a fancy restaurant for a taste of fine food.* 2. the sense by which one can notice flavors. *Taste is dulled when you have a cold.* 3. a small amount tasted. *She had a taste of the soup.* 4. a personal liking. *I have a taste for flying.* 5. the ability to know what is beautiful and good. *She has good taste when it comes to music.* {tayst}

bitter
salt
sour
sweet

taste bud *noun* one of the bumps on the surface of the tongue that form the sense organ of taste. The taste buds sense whether something is sweet, sour, salty, or bitter. {tayst buhd}

taste·less *adjective* 1. having little or no taste or flavor. *She cooks tasteless meals.* 2. marked by poor taste; not appropriate. *His parents thought his behavior was tasteless.* {tayst lihs}

tast·y *adjective* (tastier, tastiest) delicious; having a pleasing flavor. *He makes tasty desserts.* {tay stee} tastiness, n.

tat·ter *noun* 1. a torn and hanging part or piece of cloth; shred. *The dog has a* tatter of the man's pants in his teeth. 2. (plural) ragged, torn clothes. *Many people were dressed in tatters in the poor country we visited.* {tăt ər}

tat·tle *verb* (tattled, tattling, tattles) 1. to tell secrets or give information about another person. *They tattled to the teacher and got the other class in trouble.* 2. to tell or reveal by talking carelessly. *She tattled his secrets to all her friends.* {tăt əl}

• **tattle on**
to betray by telling secrets to another; tell on. *She tattled on me.*

tat·tle·tale *noun* a person who tells the secrets of others. *A tattletale needs someone to listen.* {tăt əl tayl}

tat·too *noun* (tattoos) a picture, pattern, or other marking made on the skin with needles. The needles put colors into the skin. Tattoos are very difficult to remove. *verb* (tattooed, tattooing, tattoos) to make a picture, pattern, or other marking, by pricking with needles that insert colors. *She tattooed a dragon on his shoulder.* {tă tooh}

taught *verb* past tense and past participle of **teach.** {tawt}

Homophone Note Are you looking for the word *taut* (tight)? *Taught* and *taut* sound alike but have different meanings.

taunt *verb* (taunted, taunting, taunts) to make fun of, tease, or challenge in mean language. *They taunted her about* her old, ragged clothing. {tawnt}

taupe *noun* a dark brownish gray color. {tawp *or* tohp}

Tau·rus *noun* 1. a constellation located between Aries and Gemini and near Orion. Taurus is also called the Bull. 2. the second sign of the zodiac, the Bull, which the sun enters about April 21. 3. a person born under this sign, between April 21 and May 20. {taw rəs}

taut *adjective* (tauter, tautest) tightly drawn, pulled, or stretched; not loose. *Pull the rope until it is taut.* {tawt}

Homophone Note The words *taut* and *taught* (past tense of "teach") sound alike but have different meanings.

tav·ern *noun* 1. a place that sells alcohol to drink at a bar. 2. a place that provides rooms for people to sleep for the night; inn. {tăv ərn}

taw·ny *noun* a light brown color having shades of yellow or orange; tan. *adjective* (tawnier, tawniest) having to do with the color tawny. *His skin is tawny.* {taw nee}

tax 🌐 *noun* 1. a sum of money paid to a government and used for its services. *Taxes are charged on what we earn and many things that we buy.* 2. a difficult demand; strain or burden. *The medical bills were a tax on our savings.* *verb* (taxed, taxing, taxes) 1. to place a tax on. *The government taxes gasoline and cigarettes.* 2. to place a difficult demand or burden on. *Working two jobs taxed his strength.* {tăks}

tax·a·tion *noun* the act of taxing. *Money from taxation is used to build roads and schools.* {tăk say shən}

a b c d e f g h i j k l m n o p q r s **t** u v w x y z

 Human Body Human Mind Everyday Life History and Culture Communication

tax·i *noun* (taxis or taxies) a taxicab. *verb* (taxied, taxiing [or] taxying, taxies [or] taxis) to travel slowly on the ground or on the surface of water before taking off or after landing. *The airplane taxied on the runway.* {<u>tăk</u> see}

tax·i·cab *noun* an automobile or other vehicle that carries passengers for a fee that is charged according to the distance traveled. {<u>tăk</u> see kăb}

TBA *abbreviation* an abbreviation for "to be announced."

tbs. *abbreviation* an abbreviation for **tablespoon**, or tablespoons.

T cell *noun* a type of white blood cell that defends the body against certain diseases. {<u>tee</u> sehl}

tea 🌱💧 *noun* 1. an evergreen bush that bears white flowers and that grows mainly in Asia. 2. the dried leaves of this plant. *She poured boiling water over the tea.* 3. a drink that is made by steeping dried tea leaves or herbs in hot water. Tea is served hot or cold. 4. a social gathering at which tea and other food and drink are served. *He invited us to a tea.* {<u>tee</u>}

teach 🏛️ *verb* (taught, teaching, teaches) 1. to show or help to gain knowledge. *He taught his class how to add and subtract.* 2. to offer lessons in. *She teaches Spanish.* 3. to give lessons. *She teaches in a public school.* {<u>teech</u>}

teach·er *noun* one whose job is teaching; instructor. {<u>teech</u> ər}

teal *noun* (teal or teals) 1. a small duck with a short neck that lives in and around fresh water. 2. the color that comes from mixing green, blue, and a small amount of black paint. {<u>teel</u>}

team 🏛️ *noun* 1. a group of people on one of the sides in a sports event or game. 2. a group formed to work together. *A team of scientists worked on the problem.* 3. two or more horses or other animals that are harnessed together to pull a wagon or plow. *verb* (teamed, teaming, teams) to form a team (usually followed by "up"). *Let's team up to play baseball this summer.* {<u>teem</u>}

Homophone Note Are you looking for the word *teem* (to have in abundance)? *Team* and *teem* sound alike but have different meanings.

team·mate *noun* a member of the same team or group. *My teammates agree that we need a new coach.* {<u>teem</u> mayt}

team·work *noun* the working together of a group of people to produce a desired result. *We can get the job done with enough teamwork.* {<u>teem</u> wuhrk}

tea·pot *noun* a covered pot with a spout and handle. A teapot is used to make and serve tea. {<u>tee</u> pŏt}

tear[1] 💧 *noun* 1. a drop of salty liquid that comes from the eye. Tears clean the eye and keep it wet. 2. (plural) the expression of feeling through crying. *I could tell by her tears that she was glad to see me again.* {<u>teer</u>}
• **in tears**
crying. *He was in tears over the death of his pet.*

Homophone Note Are you looking for the word *tier* (a layer)? *Tear* and *tier* sound alike but have different meanings.

tear[2] *verb* (tore, torn, tearing, tears) 1. to pull apart or into pieces. *She tore the old clothes into rags.* 2. to cause or make by ripping. *He tore a hole in the knee of his pants.* 3. to disturb. *His life was torn by bad luck.* 4. to take away with force. *The child tore the toys away from his little sister.* 5. to move rapidly; rush. *He tore around the house looking for his keys.* *noun* the result of tearing; rent. *His shirt has a tear.* {<u>tayr</u>}
• **tear down**
to destroy or demolish. *He tore down the old building.*

tease *verb* (teased, teasing, teases) to make fun of or annoy in a playful way. *He teases his little sister.* *noun* one who teases. *He is such a tease!* {<u>teez</u>}

tea·spoon *noun* 1. an amount equal to one third of a tablespoon. A teaspoon is used in cooking. (abbreviation: tsp.) 2. a small spoon used with tea, coffee, or desserts. {<u>tee</u> spoohn}

tech·ni·cal 🏛️ *adjective* 1. having to do with special skills or techniques. *They hired someone to deal with the technical problems.* 2. mechanical or industrial. *He is going to a technical school to learn how to fix cars.* 3. having terms that have to do with a particular science, art, or profession. *I'm reading a technical book on computer electronics.* {<u>tehk</u> nih kəl} technically, adv.

tech·ni·cian *noun* a person whose work requires special skills. *His father is a medical technician.* {<u>tehk</u> <u>nih</u> shən}

A
B
C
D
E
F
G
H
I
J
K
L
M
N
O
P
Q
R
S
T
U
V
W
X
Y
Z

tech·nique *noun* the particular method or way of doing or performing something. *He learned several techniques for glazing pottery.* {**tehk** **neek**}

tech·nol·o·gy 🔵 *noun* (technologies) 1. a field of knowledge having to do with the use of industry and science for the concerns of everyday life. *Doctors depend on medical technology.* 2. all of the things and ways that can help to solve everyday problems in the material world. *Technology is used to help solve energy problems.* {**tehk** **no** lə jee} technologist, *n.*

teddy bear *noun* a children's toy made to look like a bear. Teddy bears are filled with soft stuffing and covered with furry fabric. {**tehd** ee **bayr**}

teem *verb*
(teemed, teeming, teems) to be full; swarm (usually fol-

lowed by "with"). *The lake teems with fish.* {**teem**}

Homophone Note The words *teem* and *team* (a group working together) sound alike but have different meanings.

teen·ag·er 🔵 *noun* a person of age thirteen through nineteen. {**teen** ay jər}

teens *plural noun* 1. the numbers thirteen through nineteen. *The temperature stayed in the teens for several days.* 2. people of ages thirteen through nineteen; teenagers. *His children are teens.* {**teenz**}

tee·pee *noun* another spelling of tepee. {**tee** pee}

teeth 🔵 *noun* plural of **tooth**. *He has lost all his teeth.* {**teeth**}

teethe *verb* (teethed, teething, teethes) to have teeth growing out through the gums. *The baby can't sleep when she is teething.* {**teeth**}

tel·e·cast *verb* (telecasted, telecasting, telecasts) to broadcast by television. *They will telecast the film this summer.* *noun* a television broadcast. *It was a three-hour telecast.* {**tehl** ə **kǎst**}

tel·e·com·mut·ing *noun* the doing of work at home by using a computer and sending this work back to the office by electronic means. *Much of this dictionary was written by people who are telecommuting.* {**tehl** ə kə **myoo** ting}

tel·e·gram *noun* a message in code sent by electronic means over wires. {**tehl** ə **grǎm**}

tel·e·graph 🔵 *noun* a system by which messages may be sent by electronic means. The telegraph puts messages in code and sends them along wires. *verb* (telegraphed, telegraphing, telegraphs) to send a telegram to. *I telegraphed them about our arrival.* {**tehl** ə **grǎf**}

tel·e·phone 🔵 🔵 *noun* a device used to send sound or some other signal over long distances by wire or radio waves. A telephone has a part for speaking into and a part for listening. *verb* (telephoned, telephoning, telephones) 1. to call on a telephone. *I telephone my mother every week.* 2. to verbally send by using a telephone. *He telephoned the good*

Look at all those teeth! Plant-eaters, like the horse, have teeth for grinding. Meat-eaters, like the lion and the wolf, have teeth for grabbing prey. Rodents, like the beaver, have teeth for gnawing. What kinds of teeth do you have?

 Human Body   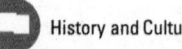 Human Mind   Everyday Life   History and Culture    Communication

news of his baby's birth. {**tehl** ə fohn}

tel·e·scope *noun* an instrument that uses lenses and sometimes mirrors to make distant objects appear larger. {**tehl** ə skohp}

Word History Galileo used the Italian word *telescopio* in 1611 for the instrument that he had built. The word came from an ancient Greek word that means "far-seeing." *Telescope* was first used in English about fifty years later.

tel·e·vise *verb* (televised, televising, televises) to broadcast or receive by television. *They televised the horrible effects of the war.* {**tehl** ə viyz}

tel·e·vi·sion 🌐 ⚙ *noun* 1. the process of sending pictures through the air as electrical waves over distances to be seen on a screen; TV. *Fifty years ago, television was only black and white.* 2. a set with a screen for receiving and viewing such pictures. {**tehl** ə vih zhən}

tell *verb* (told, telling, tells) 1. to express in spoken or written words. *Tell me a story.* 2. to provide with information. *He told me about the accident.* 3. to make known. *He'll never tell the secret.* 4. to command. *Please tell the children to behave.* 5. to recognize; distinguish. *He can't tell the difference between my brother and me.* 6. to give proof of. *Her success tells of her hard work.* 7. to reveal a secret or private matter. *I know the answer, but I won't tell.* {**tehl**}

Synonyms
This word shares a meaning with *tell*, verb 1:
relate

tell·er 〰 *noun* 1. someone or something that tells. *My grandfather was a teller of tales.* 2. an employee in a bank who takes in and pays out money. *The teller opened an account for me.* {**tehl** ər}

tem·per ⚙ *noun* 1. a usual state of mind of manner of feeling. *She has a sunny temper.* 2. a state of mind or emotion at a specific time; mood. *I decided to stay because she was in a good temper for once.* 3. a mood of anger. *His tempers don't last long.* 4. an ability to get irritated or angry. *Be careful how you speak to him, because he has a temper.* 5. sense of calm or patience; control. *She lost her temper with me when I broke her vase.* *verb* (tempered, tempering, tempers) to make softer or less harsh. *The teacher tempered discipline with humor.* {**tehm** pər}

tem·per·ate 🌐 *adjective* having neither extremely hot nor extremely cold temperatures and mild weather. *The United States is in a temperate zone.* {**tehm** pər iht *or* **tehm** priht}

tem·per·a·ture 🌐 ⚙ *noun* 1. the degree of heat or cold of an object or an environment. *The temperature is higher in the afternoon than in the evening.* 2. the measurement of heat or cold as shown in degrees on a thermometer. *Ice melts when the temperature is above zero degrees.* 3. a higher than normal body temperature caused by infection or illness; fever. *John stayed home from school because he had a temperature.* {**tehm** pər ə chər *or* **tehm** prə chər}

tem·pest *noun* a very strong wind along with rain, snow, hail, or sleet. *The barn blew down in last night's tempest.* {**tehm** pihst}

tem·plate *noun* a pattern used as a guide in cutting or shaping pieces of wood or metal. Templates are usually made of thin metal or wood. {**tehm** pliht *or* **tehm** playt}

tem·ple[1] 🔵 🔵 *noun* 1. a building or place where gods and goddesses are worshiped. 2. a Jewish synagogue. {**tehm** pəl}

tem·ple[2] 🌐 *noun* the flat area on either side of the head between the forehead and ear. {**tehm** pəl}

tem·po *noun* (tempos) the speed at which a musical piece is to be played. {**tehm** poh}

tem·po·rar·y *adjective* for a short time; not permanent. *I got a temporary job for the summer.* {**tehm** pə rayr ee} temporarily, adv.

tempt *verb* (tempted, tempting, tempts) 1. to try to get to do something wrong or not wise. *Stop tempting me with that dessert; I'm on a diet.* 2. to be attractive or very appealing to. *The idea of a swim tempts me.* {**tehmpt**}

ten *noun* the number that comes after 9 and before 11 in the sequence of cardinal numbers; 10. *adjective* being ten in number. *I invited ten friends to my birthday party.* {**tehn**}

Ten Commandments *plural noun* the ten laws handed down by God to Moses on Mount Sinai, according to the Old Testament of the Bible. The Ten Commandments are laws of moral conduct in the Jewish and Christian religions. {**tehn** kə **mănd** mənts}

tend[1] *verb* (tended, tending, tends) to be likely; usually do. *He tends to be shy. / The*

A
B
C
D
E
F
G
H
I
J
K
L
M
N
O
P
Q
R
S
T
U
V
W
X
Y
Z

brakes on this car tend to screech. {**tehnd**}

tend² *verb* (tended, tending, tends) 1. to care for or watch over; look after. *I will ask Mrs. Meany to tend the children for a hour or two. / I'll tend the garden while you are gone.* 2. to give one's attention (usually followed by "to"). *Tend to your own work, not the person's next to you.* {**tehnd**}

ten·den·cy *noun* (tendencies) 1. the fact of being likely to move in a certain direction. *The wheel has a tendency to roll to the right.* 2. the fact of being likely to act in some way. *He has a tendency to get angry if he doesn't get his way.* {**tehn** dən see}

ten·der *adjective* (tenderer, tenderest) 1. easily chewed or crushed; not tough; soft. *This is a tender piece of meat.* 2. showing love or kindness in a gentle way. *The father spoke tender words to his crying baby.* 3. easily hurt when touched; sore; sensitive. *The wound is still tender.* 4. not strong; delicate. *Carefully water these tender plants.* {**tehn** dər} tenderly, adv., tenderness, n.

ten·don 🔵 *noun* a cord or band of tough white tissue that connects a muscle with a bone or other body part; sinew. {**tehn** dən}

Ten·nes·see *noun* a state in the southeastern United States. Its capital is Nashville. (abbreviated: TN) {**teh** nə **see**} Tennessean, n., adj.

Word History *Tennessee* is the English spelling of *tanasie*, which means "the meeting place." It was the name of a Cherokee village, but Spanish explorers began calling the whole area *Tenaqui* in the 1500s.

ten·nis *noun* a game that is played on a court by two or four players. In tennis, a small ball is hit back and forth over a low net using rackets. {**tehn** ihs}

ten·or 🔵 *noun* 1. a man's singing voice with the highest natural range, or a singer with such a voice. *Two men in our group sing tenor. / My father is a tenor who sings at weddings.* 2. an instrument, such as a saxophone, with this kind of range. *He plays the tenor in the saxophone quartet.* *adjective* having the range of a tenor voice or part. *You sing the tenor part, and I'll sing bass.* {**tehn** ər}

tense¹ 🔵🔵 *adjective* (tenser, tensest) 1. pulled or stretched tightly. *The strings on a violin must be tense.* 2. unable to relax one's body or emotions. *My father sounds tense when I call him at work.* *verb* (tensed, tensing, tenses) to make or become tense. *He tensed his leg muscles. / The dog tensed at the sound of footsteps outside.* {**tehns**} tensely, adv.

Synonyms
These words share a meaning with *tense*, adjective 1:
tight, stretched, taut

tense² 🔵 *noun* the aspect of verbs that shows when an action takes place. Verbs can be in past, present, or future tense. {**tehns**}

ten·sion *noun* 1. the act of stretching or state of being stretched; strain. *Don't put too much tension on that rope or it will break.* 2. physical, mental, or emotional strain. *I could feel the tension in the exam room. / Massage can help reduce muscle tension.* {**tehn** shən}

tent *noun* 1. a shelter made of canvas, nylon, or plastic. A tent is held up by poles and attached to the ground with stakes. 2. something that is like such a structure in shape or some other way. *He is in an oxygen tent to help him breathe.* {**tehnt**}

ten·ta·cle *noun* a long thin body part on the head or around the mouth of some animals. Tentacles are used for feeling or taking hold of things. *Octopus and squid have tentacles.* {**tehn** tə kəl} tentacled, adj.

tenth *adjective* coming next after the ninth in a series. *I was the tenth runner to finish the marathon.* *noun* 1. one of ten equal parts of a whole; 1/10. *Nine tenths of the students think she is a great teacher.* 2. the number, person, or thing that comes next after the ninth in a series. *Of all the cars we test drove, the tenth was the best.* {**tehnth**}

te·pee or **teepee** or **tipi** *noun* a tent shaped like a cone and made with skins or bark. Tepees were used by some North American Indian peoples who lived on the plains. {**tee** pee}

tep·id *adjective* not quite warm; lukewarm. *Soup is supposed to be hot, not tepid.* {**tehp** ihd}

term *noun* 1. a word or phrase for something that might be known only by people who have a particular job, interest, or hobby. *"Man on" is a term used in soccer to warn that a player is coming to take the ball away from a teammate.* 2. a set period of time during which something

 Human Body    Human Mind   Everyday Life   History and Culture    Communication

happens. *The president's term in office is four years.* 3. a part of the school year; semester. *I received excellent grades during the fall term.* 4. (plural) the parts of an agreement that must be followed if the agreement is to be kept; conditions. *The terms were that if I improved my grades, Mom would buy me a bike.* 5. (plural) relationship. *My sister and I are on good terms with one another.* *verb* (termed, terming, terms) to give a name to; call. *Because the driver was drunk, the crash was termed a crime and not an accident.* {**tuhrm**}

ter·mi·nal *adjective* 1. found at or forming the end of something. *A "terminal leaf" is a leaf that grows at the end of a branch.* 2. ending in death; fatal. *Cancer is not always a terminal illness.* *noun* 1. a device at the end of a wire or cable that allows a connection to be made to an electrical circuit. 2. a station for trains, buses, airplanes, or ships, that is found at one end of an important route. 3. a monitor and keyboard connected to a computer. {**tuhr** mih nəl} terminally, *adv.*

ter·mi·nate *verb* (terminated, terminating, terminates) 1. to bring to an end; put a stop to. *The referee terminated the soccer game after a fight broke out.* 2. to come to an end (often followed by "at," "in," or "with"). *The beach terminates at those cliffs. / The course will terminate in two weeks.* {**tuhr** mih **nayt**}

ter·mite *noun* an insect that eats wood. Termites have pale, soft bodies and look somewhat like ants. They live in large groups in warmer

parts of the world. They can destroy trees, buildings, and other things made out of wood. {**tuhr** miyt}

ter·race *noun* 1. a flat, paved surface outside of a house or other building; patio. *We ate dinner on the terrace on the warm summer evening.* 2. a flat, raised section of ground. *The side of the hill was made into terraces so that the land could be used for farming.* 3. a small balcony with a roof. {**tehr** əs}

ter·rain  *noun* land or ground, or the natural characteristics of its surface. *The mountainous terrain makes this area popular for skiing.* {tə **rayn**}

ter·ra·pin *noun* a turtle that lives in fresh or somewhat salty water. It is found in North America and can be eaten as food. {**tehr** ə pihn}

ter·rar·i·um *noun* (terrariums or terraria) a closed container for growing small plants or keeping small animals. A terrarium is usually made of clear glass or plastic. {tə **rayr** ee əm}

ter·res·tri·al *adjective* 1. of or relating to the planet Earth. *The sun makes terrestrial life possible.* 2. living on or in the ground, rather than in trees, water, or air. *Pigs are terrestrial creatures.* {tə **reh** stree əl}

ter·ri·ble *adjective* 1. causing fear, terror, or horror. *A terrible wave almost swallowed the ship.* 2. very great; extreme. *She has a terrible case of the flu.* 3. very bad; not acceptable. *That's a terrible drawing of a frog.* {**tehr** ə bəl} terribly, *adv.*

ter·ri·er *noun* any of several breeds of dogs. Ter-

riers are small, lively dogs that were originally bred to drive animals from their holes. {**tehr** ee ər}

Word History *Terrier* comes from early French words that together mean "dog of the earth." Terrier dogs were given this name because their prey lives in holes under the ground.

ter·rif·ic *adjective* 1. much greater than the ordinary or usual. *He ran the race at a terrific pace.* 2. very good; fantastic. *A terrific band is playing at the youth center tonight.* 3. causing strong fear or terror. *They hid under the bed after hearing a terrific clap of thunder.* {tə **rih** fihk} terrifically, *adv.*

ter·ri·fy *verb* (terrified, terrifying, terrifies) to fill with great fear or terror; scare. *Big, hairy spiders terrify my dad.* {**teh** rih **fiy**}

ter·ri·to·ry ❶ 🌐 *noun* (territories) 1. an area of land that belongs to and is governed by a country. *The territory of Canada includes the island of Labrador.* 2. an area or region of land. *This is rattlesnake territory, so be careful where you step!* {**tehr** ih tohr ee}

ter·ror ❸ *noun* 1. very great fear. *Big, hairy spiders fill him with terror.* 2. something that causes great fear. *The man-eating tiger was the terror of the village.* {**tehr** ər}

Synonyms
These words share a meaning with
terror, noun 1:
panic, horror, abuse, dread, fright

ter·ror·ism 🌐 *noun* the use of violence or fear by a political

A
B
C
D
E
F
G
H
I
J
K
L
M
N
O
P
Q
R
S
T
U
V
W
X
Y
Z

a
b
c
d
e
f
g
h
i
j
k
l
m
n
o
p
q
r
s
t
u
v
w
x
y
z

group as a way of forcing others to meet its demands. {**tehr** ə rihz əm}

ter·ror·ize *verb* (terrorized, terrorizing, terrorizes) 1. to control by using threats or acts of violence. *An escaped prisoner terrorized a tiny mountain village.* 2. to cause to feel terror. *The little boy was terrorized by the snarling dog.* {**tehr** ə riyz}

test ⊕ ⊙ ⊙ *noun* 1. a trial to find out what something is, what it is made up of, or how good it is. *A blood test is part of a complete physical exam.* / *Tests showed that the water was safe to drink.* 2. a set of questions to find out how much someone knows about something, or their ability to do something. *She gives us a test at the end of every math lesson. verb* (tested, testing, tests) to give a test to or do a test of; examine. *The doctor tested my hearing.* / *The teacher tested us on two chapters of the math book.* {**tehst**}

tes·ta·ment *noun* (capitalized) one of the two main parts of the Bible, the Old Testament or the New Testament. {**tehs** tə mənt}

tes·ti·mo·ny *noun* (testimonies) 1. a statement made under oath before a judge in a court of law. *After listening to the testimony of the witnesses, most of the jury decided that Mr. Goode was not guilty.* 2. any statement or action used to prove something. *This ring is testimony of my love.* {**tehs** tih **moh** nee}

test tube *noun* a thin, hollow, glass tube that is closed at one end. Test tubes are used in scientific experiments. {**tehst** toohb}

tet·a·nus *noun* a disease that affects the muscles of the neck and lower jaw and can cause death. Tetanus is caused by germs that enter the body through a wound. Another name for this disease is lockjaw. *Almost all children in the United States receive a vaccine that protects them from tetanus.* {**teht** ə nəs}

teth·er *noun* a rope, chain, or leash for tying up or holding something that moves. *Our dog is kept on a tether so that she won't escape from the yard. verb* (tethered, tethering, tethers) to tie up or chain with a tether. *He tethered the hawk to his wrist with a cord.* {**tehth** ər}

• **at the end of one's tether** at the limit or end of one's strength or ability.

Tex·as *noun* a state in the southwestern United States. Its capital is Austin. (abbreviated: TX) {**tehk** səs} Texan, n., adj.

Word History *Texas* means "allies" or "friends" in the Hasinai language. The Hasinai were a federation of Caddo tribes living in eastern Texas when Spaniards started exploring the area around 1528.

text *noun* 1. the main part of a printed work, not including such things as the title, headings, and questions. *You can skip the questions at the end of each chapter and read only the text.* 2. the words that appear in anything written or printed. *This dictionary has both text and pictures.* 3. a textbook. *Please remember to bring your text to class every day.* {**tehkst**}

text·book *noun* a book used for teaching a particular subject. *The new history textbook includes a chapter on terrorism.* {**tehkst** buuk}

tex·tile *noun* cloth made by weaving or knitting. *The*

royal robes were made of rich textiles and fur. *adjective* having to do with weaving or making fabric. *My great-grandmother wove silk in a textile mill.* {**tehks** tiyl or **tehk** stəl, n., **tehks** tiyl or **tehk** stəl, adj.}

tex·ture *noun* the feel or look of a surface. *The wood had a rough texture until it was sanded and polished.* {**tehks** chər} textured, adj.

than *conjunction* 1. compared to or with. *Her voice is louder than yours is.* / *It costs more than thirty cents.* 2. except; besides; but. *Who can I tell other than her?* / *There is no warmer coat than this.* {**thăn**}

thank *verb* (thanked, thanking, thanks) 1. to say that one is grateful to. *I'll thank him for all his help.* 2. to give blame or responsibility to. *We have him to thank for this mistake.* {**thăngk**}

thank·ful *adjective* feeling or showing thanks; grateful. *We are thankful for our good health.* {**thăngk** fəl} thankfully, adv., thankfulness, n.

thanks *plural noun* an expression of gratitude. *Please accept our thanks for all you have done. interjection* "thank you." *Thanks. We couldn't have done it without you.* {**thăngks**}

• **no thanks to** without the help of. *We found the house, no thanks to the taxi driver.*

• **thanks to** 1. let thanks be given to. *Thanks to the whole family for their help.* 2. because of; due to. *Thanks to all of you, we finished the job.*

thanks·giv·ing *noun* 1. the act or expression of giving thanks. *Let us offer thanksgiving for the aid our town received after the flood.* 2. (capitalized) a U.S. holiday

 Human Body   Human Mind   Everyday Life    History and Culture   Communication

held on the fourth Thursday in November; Thanksgiving Day. On Thanksgiving, Americans remember the good harvest of the Pilgrims in 1621 and show thanks for what they have now. {**thăngks gihv** ing}

that *pronoun* (those) 1. the person, thing, or matter mentioned or understood. *I said I didn't like her, but that really isn't true.* 2. the one that is less in mind or further away. *This is more interesting that that.* 3. the time or event just mentioned. *Before that, we were happy. / Did you see that?* 4. the one or kind; who; whom; which (used to introduce a clause that describes or narrows down the thing just mentioned). *The friends that I met in first grade are my favorite. adjective* 1. the person, thing, or matter as mentioned or understood. *That woman I was telling you about from the bank is getting married.* 2. the one that is less in mind or further away. *That road is not as direct as this one. / When you said you liked Jim, I didn't know you meant that Jim. adverb* to such a degree or extent. *I can't run that far without losing my breath. conjunction* 1. used to introduce a clause that is the subject or object of the main verb. *We know that she is bored. / His wish is that he will live a long life.* 2. used to introduce a clause showing purpose (often following "so" or "in order"). *We worked so that we could save money.* {**thăt**}

thatch *noun* straw, palm leaves, or other dried plant material used as a roof covering. *The cottage has a roof made of thatch. verb* (thatched, thatching, thatches) to cover with thatch. *Every spring we*

must thatch our cottage again. {**thăch**}

thaw *verb* (thawed, thawing, thaws) 1. to go from being a frozen solid to being a liquid; melt. *The icy river thawed in early April.* 2. to return to a normal temperature after being frozen. *Her fingers soon thawed out over the fire. / The steak is thawing in the refrigerator.* 3. to cause to become unfrozen. *He thawed some chicken so that we could cook it for dinner. noun* a period of weather warm enough to melt ice and snow. *The river flooded during the spring thaw.* {**thaw**}

the[1] *definite article* 1. used before a noun when the noun is something specific or already mentioned. *The scarf I wanted had red tassels.* 2. used before titles. *I read a poem called "The Ancient Mariner."* 3. used before something that is best or in fashion. *Mack's Grill is the restaurant when it comes to family dining.* 4. used before a proper name. *We went swimming in the Mississippi River.* 5. used before a decade. *My parents were born in the sixties.* 6. used to indicate a group. *She's learning all about the Aztecs in her history class.* {**thee**}

Homophone Note The words *the*[1] and *thee* can sound alike, but they have different meanings.

the[2] *adverb* 1. used in comparisons to show that two things happen at the same time. *The older she gets, the better she sings.* 2. used in comparisons to show extent or degree. *He went on a diet and*

looks the better for it. {**thə** or **thee**}

Homophone Note The words *the* and *thee* (you) can sometimes sound alike but have different meanings.

the·a·ter ⭕ ❷ or **theatre** *noun* 1. a building where plays, movies, or concerts are presented. 2. the art or business of writing or performing plays. *Randy wants a career in theatre or ballet.* {**thee** ə tər}

thee *pronoun* you. This word was once in common use, but is now used mostly in literature of the past and religious texts. *How do I love thee?* {**thee**}

Homophone Note The words *thee* and *the* can sometimes sound alike but have different meanings.

theft ⭕ *noun* an act of stealing. *The theft of the golden crown caused great dismay in the kingdom.* {**thehft**}

their *pronoun* done by them, belonging to them, or having to do with them. *We went to their wedding. / Their house is new. / I want to play with their toys.* {**thayr**}

Homophone Note The words *their* and *there*, and the contraction *they're* ("they are"), all sound alike but have different meanings.

theirs *pronoun* the one that belongs to them. *Our car is green, and theirs is red.* {**thayrz**}

Homophone Note The word *theirs* and the contraction *there's* ("there is") sound alike but have different meanings.

them *pronoun* the persons or things already spoken of. *I told them to stay home. / When*

A
B
C
D
E
F
G
H
I
J
K
L
M
N
O
P
Q
R
S
T
U
V
W
X
Y
Z

a b c d e f g h i j k l m n o p q r s **t** u v w x y z

she asked for the books, I gave them to her. {thehm}

theme ⊘ *noun* 1. the main subject or topic. *The theme of his talk was world peace.* 2. a short piece of writing, usually written for a class or in school. *We had to write a theme about what we did on summer vacation.* 3. the main melody in a piece of music. *The theme returns one last time at the end of the piece.* {theem}

them·selves *plural pronoun* 1. used to emphasize the importance of "they." *They built the barn themselves.* 2. their own selves (used to show that an action is done to the same people who are doing the action). *Cats keep themselves clean.* 3. their usual, healthy, or true selves. *After a nice vacation, they are feeling themselves again.* {thehm **sehlvz** or thəm **sehlvz**}

then *adverb* 1. at that past time. *Life was hard then, but we are rich now.* 2. soon after; next. *The game ended, and then we went home.* 3. if that occurs; therefore; as a result. *If she stays, then I will leave.* *noun* that time. *He has not spoken since then.* {thehn}

the·o·ry ⊘ *noun* (theories) 1. a reasonable, widely accepted explanation for why something happens. *After studying plants and animals in South America, Charles Darwin worked out the theory of evolution by natural selection.* 2. the set of rules that forms the basis of an art or science. *This year in math class we will study set theory and number theory.* 3. a view or opinion that has not been proved. *The detective has a theory about what happened to the monkey.* {thee ə ree}

ther·a·py ⊘ *noun* (therapies) treatment meant to cure a disease or heal an injury. *Eric will need months of physical therapy before he can play football again.* {thehr ə pee}

> **Word History** *Therapy* comes from *therapeia*, an ancient Greek word that means "curing or healing."

there *adverb* 1. in, at, or to that place. *Be there by morning, or I'll leave without you.* / *Go there, and you will see for yourself how beautiful it is.* 2. at that point. *There she stopped reading and began to cry.* 3. in that matter. *You are right about some things, but you are wrong there.* *pronoun* used to introduce a sentence or clause in which the verb comes before the subject. *There was once a man named Elmer Brown.* / *There will come a time when you want to leave home.* *noun* that place. *I come from there as well.* *interjection* used when something is finished, or to express a feeling. *There! We're all done.* / *There! I told you this would happen.* {thayr}

> **Homophone Note** The words *there* and *their*, and the contraction *they're* ("they are"), all sound alike but have different meanings.

there·af·ter *adverb* following that; from then on. *I tried spinach for the first time last year and have eaten it every day thereafter.* {thayr **ăf** tər}

there·by *adverb* 1. as a result of that; by that means. *She studied for an hour, thereby making sure she was ready for the test.* 2. connected with

that. *We must try to keep working together because thereby depends our success.* {thayr **biy** or **thayr** biy}

there·fore *adverb* for that reason; as a result. *He went to bed early and was therefore well rested.* {thayr fohr}

there's shortened form of "there is" or "there has." *There's one cookie left.* / *There's been a family gathering every September for years.* {thayrz}

> **Homophone Note** The contraction *there's* and the word *theirs* (the one that belongs to them) sound alike but have different meanings.

ther·mal *adjective* 1. using, resulting from, or producing heat. *Thermal currents in the air lifted the hawk higher and higher.* 2. made to hold in heat. *Skiers wear thermal underwear to stay warm.* {thuhr məl}

ther·mom·e·ter ⊘⊘⊘⊘ *noun* an instrument for measuring temperature. Some thermometers are made of a closed glass tube containing mercury or alcohol that rises or falls as the temperature rises or falls. {thər **mŏm** ət ər}

> **Word History** *Thermometer* comes from two ancient Greek words that mean "heat" and "measure."

Ther·mos *noun* 1. (Trademark) A Thermos is a container that is used to keep food or drink at its original temperature. 2. (lower case) any container used to keep food or drink at its original temperature. {thoohr məs}

ther·mo·stat *noun* a device that controls temperature automatically. Thermostats may be found in houses, cars,

 Human Body   Human Mind   Everyday Life   History and Culture   Communication

ovens, and refrigerators. {**thoohr** mə **stăt**}

the·sau·rus ⦿ *noun* (thesauri or thesauruses) a book that lists words with their synonyms or antonyms. *I looked in a thesaurus for a word that means the same thing as "useful."* {thə **saw** rəs}

Word History *Thesaurus* is a Latin word borrowed from the ancient Greek word *thesauros*, which means "treaure" or "storehouse."

these *pronoun or adjective* plural of **this**. *These aren't my pants. / These are the shoes I want to buy.* {**theez**}

they *pronoun* 1. those people, animals, or things. *They are not as polite as we are.* 2. the people, things, or animals already talked about. *If your parents come, they can stay at our house.* 3. people in general; everyone. *They say it will be a rainy spring.* {**thay**}

they'd shortened form of "they had" or "they would." *They'd promised to be here on time. / They'd have called if there was a problem.* {**thayd**}

they'll shortened form of "they will." *They'll never forget this day.* {**thayl**}

they're shortened form of "they are." *They're good friends of mine.* {**thayr**}

they've shortened form of "they have." *They've been here for years.* {**thayv**}

thick *adjective* (thicker, thickest) 1. large in measurement from one side of a surface to the opposite side; not thin in the smallest dimension of something. *We placed a thick book on the chair so that Sarah could reach her dinner plate.* 2. measured from one side to the other. *The ice is three inches thick.* 3. having parts or particles that are

very close to one other; dense. *I couldn't see through the thick fog. / It was hard to walk through the thick forest.* 4. flowing slowly. *Ketchup is thicker than soy sauce.* *adverb* (thicker, thickest) in a thick way; so as to be thick. *He spread the butter on thick.* *noun* the strongest or most active part. *We were in the thick of an argument when you called.* {**thihk**}

thick·en *verb* (thickened, thickening, thickens) to make or become thick or thicker. *We thickened the soup by adding cream and flour.* {**thihk** ən} thickener, n.

thick·et *noun* a thick patch of shrubs, bushes, or small trees. {**thihk** iht}

thick·ness *noun* 1. the fact or quality of being thick. *The thickness of the soup made it seem very filling.* 2. the measurement of the distance between the two sides of something. *The wall has a thickness of six inches.* 3. a layer. *My new winter jacket is made with two thicknesses of wool.* {**thihk** nihs}

thief *noun* (thieves) someone who steals. *A thief took all our money.* {**theef**}

thigh *noun* the part of the human leg between the hip and the knee. {**thiy**}

thigh·bone *noun* the long bone between the hip and the knee. {**thiy** bohn}

thim·ble *noun* a small cup worn to protect the finger that pushes the needle through cloth when sewing. A thimble is usually made of a hard material such as metal or plastic. {**thihm** bəl}

thin *adjective* (thinner, thinnest) 1. small

in the measure from one side of a surface to the other; not thick. *It's dangerous to walk on thin ice.* 2. having little width; slim. *The young tree has a thin trunk.* 3. having little flesh; lean. *The dog is so thin that its ribs are showing.* 4. not dense; sparse. *The grass is thin under the trees. / The air will be thin on top of the mountain.* 5. liquid; watery. *The cook made a thin sauce out of wine and spices to drizzle over the fish.* 6. without force. *She sang in a thin voice.* 7. not convincing; without substance. *The movie's plot is thin.* *adverb* (thinner, thinnest) in a thin manner. *He sliced the bread thin.* *verb* (thinned, thinning, thins) to make or become thin (often followed by "down" or "out"). *I must thin out the weeds in the garden. / He tried to thin down by going on a diet.* {**thihn**}

Synonyms
These words share a meaning with **thin**, adjective 2:
narrow, slender, slim

thing *noun* 1. that which is spoken of, thought of, or done. *That was a mean thing to say. / The thing that bothers me is that he left without saying goodbye. / Don't do a thing without telling me.* 2. an object that is not a person. *What is that thing in your hand? / These things can be put away.* 3. (plural) personal items; belongings. *She put her things in a trunk.* 4. (plural) matters or affairs. *Things are not very good right now.* 5. an event. *A bad thing happened yesterday.* 6. a creature. *He's a cute little thing.* {**thing**}

think ⦿ *verb* (thought, thinking, thinks) 1. to use the power of the mind. *A philosopher once said, "I think,*

A B C D E F G H I J K L M N O P Q R S T U V W X Y Z

a
b
c
d
e
f
g
h
i
j
k
l
m
n
o
p
q
r
s
t
u
v
w
x
y
z

therefore I am." 2. to judge or reason about a matter. *I thought about the question for a long time.* 3. to recall or remember (usually followed by "of"). *He tried to think of where he'd left his keys.* 4. to remember or have in mind. *She was thinking how happy she had been.* 5. to exercise caution. *Think before you act.* 6. to have an opinion. *I think he is a good man.* 7. to form as an idea; imagine. *He thought he could swim across the river.* {**thingk**}

third *adjective* coming next after the second in a series. *He was the third man to walk on the moon.* *noun* 1. one of three equal parts of a whole; 1/3. *He ate a third of the cake.* 2. the number, person, or thing that comes next after the second in a series. *I was the third of four members that joined the band.* {**thuhrd**}

Third World *noun* countries that are poor and that depend on farming rather than business and industry for income. {**thuhrd wuhrld**}

thirst *noun* 1. a dry feeling in the mouth or throat that is caused by the need or desire to drink. 2. any strong desire. *Mary has a thirst for good books.* *verb* (thirsted, thirsting, thirsts) 1. to feel thirsty. *The farm workers thirsted for a cold drink after being in the sun for hours.* 2. to have a strong desire. *Jane thirsted for peace and quiet in her busy life.* {**thuhrst**} thirstiness, n.

thirst·y *adjective* (thirstier, thirstiest) 1. feeling a need to drink. *Joe was thirsty after his five-mile run.* 2. feeling a strong desire; eager (usually followed by "for"). *Aunt Gertrude was thirsty for adventure when she set out on her trip to*

the rain forest. {**thuhr** stee} thirstily, adv., thirstiness, n.

thir·teen *noun* the number that comes after 12 and before 14 in the sequence of cardinal numbers; 13. *adjective* being thirteen in number. *I have thirteen pencils in my school bag.* {**thuhr teen**}

thir·teenth *adjective* coming next after the twelfth in a series. *The thirteenth time I tried, I finally got the soda machine to accept my dollar.* *noun* 1. one of thirteen equal parts of a whole; 1/13. *She carefully measured out a thirteenth of a cup of oil.* 2. the number, person, or thing that comes next after the twelfth in a series. *Some say the thirteenth is an unlucky day.* {**thuhr teenth**}

thir·ti·eth *adjective* coming next after the twenty-ninth in a series. *The bikers made it to the thirtieth mile.* *noun* 1. one of thirty equal parts of a whole; 1/30. *Her grades were among the top thirtieth of her class.* 2. the number, person, or thing that comes next after the twenty-ninth in a series. *The new moon will come on the thirtieth of this month.* {**thuhrt** ee əth}

thir·ty *noun* (thirties) the number that is equal to three times ten; 30. *adjective* being thirty in number. *My mother is thirty years old.* {**thuhrt** ee}

this *pronoun* (these) 1. the person, thing, or matter that is mentioned, understood, or present. *This is my father.* / *Let's talk about this over a cup of tea.* 2. the person, thing, or matter closer than another in time or space, or the one most in mind. *You take that over there, and I'll take this.* 3. the statement or idea that is about to follow. *Listen to this.* *adjective* 1. used to indicate a

person, thing, or matter that is talked about, understood, or present. *This boat is old; will it carry us?* / *Now, this man had five daughters.* 2. used to show that a person, thing, or matter is closer than another in time or space, or more in mind. *This house and that house are alike.* *adverb* to the degree or extent that is being pointed out. *It is always this cold here.* / *Does it have to take this long?* {**thihs**}

this·tle *noun* a kind of plant with prickly leaves and a head of purple flowers. *The thistle is the national flower of Scotland.* {**thihs** əl}

thong *noun* 1. a narrow strip of leather or similar material that is used to tie or fasten. 2. a sandal held on the foot by a narrow leather, rubber, or plastic strap that passes between the first and second toes. {**thawng** or **thŏng**}

tho·rax *noun* (thoraxes) 1. the part of the body between the neck and the abdomen in humans and in animals with four limbs; chest. It contains the ribs, heart, and lungs. 2. the second or middle part of an insect's body. {**thohr** ăks}

thorn *noun* 1. a short, stiff point on a plant stem or branch. 2. any kind of plant, shrub, or tree that has sharp, stiff points on its stem or branches. {**thohrn**} thorny, adj.

thor·ough *adjective* 1. leaving nothing out; complete. *We found the lost wallet after a thorough search of the class-room.* 2. correct in every detail. *The thorough house-keeper vacuumed under the bed.* {**thuhr** oh} thoroughly, adv., thoroughness, n.

thor·ough·bred *adjective* of a pure breed. *My dog is a thor-*

 Human Body   Human Mind   Everyday Life    History and Culture   Communication

oughbred German shepherd. *noun* 1. an animal of pure breed. 2. (capitalized) one of a breed of horses created by crossing Arabian or Turkish stallions and English mares. {**thuhr** oh brehd}

thor·ough·fare *noun* 1. a street that opens at both ends into other streets. 2. a passage or way through from one place to another. *There is no thoroughfare from the park to our street.* {**thuhr** oh **fayr**}

those *pronoun or adjective* plural of **that**. *Those boxes have to be moved.* {**thohz**}

thou *pronoun* you; the person or god spoken to. This word was once in common use, but is now used mostly in literature of the past and religious texts. {**thow**}

though *conjunction* 1. in spite of the fact that. *Though the sun was shining, it was cold.* 2. even if; but (sometimes used with "even"). *He will continue to climb, though he may never reach the top.* / *I didn't go, even though I wanted to.* *adverb* however. *He likes to read; he's not a good student, though.* {**thoh**}
• **as though** as if. *He looked as though he needed food.*

thought[1] *noun* 1. the act, process, or power of thinking. *He put a lot of thought into choosing a college.* 2. the result of thinking; a single idea. *I just had a thought.* 3. serious or careful attention. *He gave thought to the problem.* {**thawt**}

thought[2] *verb* past tense and past participle of **think**. {**thawt**}

thought·ful *adjective* 1. having or showing careful thought. *I* just read a thoughtful book about the causes of war. 2. giving careful attention to the needs of others; considerate. *How thoughtful of you to bring me a snack!* {**thawt** fəl} thoughtfully, adv., thoughtfulness, n.

thought·less *adjective* 1. not thinking enough; showing little care. *The thoughtless driver sped through the red light.* 2. showing a lack of thought or attention. *There were many thoughtless mistakes on her spelling test.* 3. not giving attention to the needs of others; inconsiderate. *It was thoughtless of you to eat all the sandwiches.* {**thawt** lihs} thoughtlessly, adv., thoughtlessness, n.

thou·sand *noun* (thousands or thousand) 1. the number that is equal to ten times one hundred; 1,000. 2. (plural) the numbers from 1,000 through 999,999. *adjective* being one thousand in number. *This ancient city is a thousand years old.* {**thow** zənd} thousandth, adj., n.

thrash *verb* (thrashed, thrashing, thrashes) 1. to give a beating to; whip. *The mean farmer thrashed the slow old horse.* 2. to move around in a wild, whipping way (often followed by "around"). *The wild pig thrashed around for an hour after it had been caught.* {**thrăsh**}

thread *noun* 1. a fine cord used in sewing, weaving, and the like. Thread is usually made of two or more fibers such as cotton twisted together. 2. something that looks or acts like thread. *There was a fine thread of blood coming from the* cut. / *Are you following the thread of the plot?* 3. the curved ridge on a screw or screwing device. *verb* (threaded, threading, threads) 1. to pass thread through. *He threaded the needle on the sewing machine.* 2. to go along on carefully or with difficulty. *He threaded his way through the forest.* 3. to move in a winding course. *The stream threaded between the mountains.* {**threhd**}

threat *noun* 1. a statement that harm or punishment will follow. *Our neighbor uses threats to frighten us away from his property.* 2. a warning of trouble or harm. *After the emperor was killed, a threat of war hung over the country.* {**threht**}

threat·en *verb* (threatened, threatening, threatens) 1. to say that one will harm or punish; make a threat to. *The judge threatened him with a jail sentence.* 2. to warn or give a sign of. *The cloudy sky threatened snow.* {**threh** tən}

three *noun* the number that comes after 2 and before 4 in the sequence of cardinal numbers; 3. *adjective* being three in number. *I bought three packs of gum.* {**three**}

thresh *verb* (threshed, threshing, threshes) to separate the grain or seeds from. *Farmers used to thresh wheat by hand, but now they use machines.* {**threhsh**}

thresh·old *noun* 1. the piece of wood or stone underneath a door that forms the bottom of the doorway. 2. the point when something starts to happen. *Poor leadership has brought the two countries to the threshold of war.* {**threhsh** hohld or **threhsh** ohld}

A B C D E F G H I J K L M N O P Q R S T U V W X Y Z

 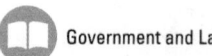

a
b
c
d
e
f
g
h
i
j
k
l
m
n
o
p
q
r
s
t
u
v
w
x
y
z

thrift *noun* wise use and saving of money or other resources. *Because of her thrift and hard work, Mary had enough money to buy a car when she was seventeen.* {**thrihft**} thrifty, adj.

thrill *verb* (thrilled, thrilling, thrills) to cause to feel a sudden, sharp excitement. *It thrills me to ski down a steep mountain at top speed.* noun 1. a sudden, sharp feeling of great excitement. *I felt a thrill as our car raced through the night.* 2. something that gives a feeling of sudden excitement. *It was a thrill to meet the President.* {**thrihl**}

thrive *verb* (thrived or throve, thrived or thriven, thriving, thrives) 1. to do well or be successful. *The business thrived in its new downtown location.* 2. to grow strong and healthy. *This plant thrives in the shade.* {**thriyv**}

throat 🏃 👄 *noun* 1. the narrow passage inside the neck. Food and air pass through the throat to the stomach and lungs. 2. the front part of the neck. *This shirt buttons at the throat.* {**throht**}

throb *verb* (throbbed, throbbing, throbs) to beat or pulse quickly and strongly. *My heart throbbed when I heard the bad news.* / *The runner's legs throbbed with pain.* noun a strong beat or pulse. *George's heart gave a throb when Mary walked into the room.* / *We could hear the throb of the bass guitar.* {**thrŏb**}

throne *noun* 1. the seat used by a ruler or other important person for ceremonies or other special events. 2. the power or rank of a ruler. *The king lost his throne after the civil war.* {**throhn**}

Homophone Note Are you looking for the word **thrown** (past participle of "throw")? **Throne** and **thrown** sound alike but have different meanings.

throng *noun* a large crowd of people. *A throng gathered outside the theater.* *verb* (thronged, thronging, throngs) to gather or move forward as a crowd. *Thousands thronged to the stadium to see the last game of the season.* {**thrŏng** or **thrawng**, n., **thrŏng** or **thrawng**, v.}

through *preposition* 1. in one side or end and out the other. *Water goes through the pipe.* 2. among; between. *The monkey swung through the trees.* 3. by way or means of; because of. *I met them through my father.* / *We learn through experience.* 4. in some parts of; around. *We ran through the woods.* 5. during every part of; for the beginning, middle, and end of. *He slept through the afternoon.* 6. finished; done. *We're through being sad.* 7. up to and including. *My brothers and sisters are ages two through eight.* 8. without stopping for; past. *Don't drive through a red light.* *adverb* 1. in one side or end and out the other. *Water poured through.* 2. from the start to the finish. *She read the book through.* 3. to or at the end. *He had to see the matter through.* *adjective* 1. having no further interest to participate in a particular activity or situation; finished. *He is through with swimming lessons.* 2. passing from one end of a street or area to the other without stopping. *He got on a through train to take him across town.* {**throoh**}

Homophone Note The words **through** and **threw** (past tense of "throw") sound alike but have different meanings.

through·out *preposition* in, to, or during every part of. *The lights were on throughout the town.* / *The party lasted throughout the night.* adverb 1. in, during, or including every part. *The old house is still solid throughout.* 2. from the start to the finish; during the whole time. *They remained friends throughout.* {**throoh owt**}

throw *verb* (threw, thrown, throwing, throws) 1. to send through the air with force by using the arm and wrist; hurl. *He threw the football down the field.* 2. to cause to fall to the floor or ground. *The bucking horse finally threw him.* 3. to put on or take off quickly. *He threw a sweater over his shoulders.* 4. to put suddenly into a given condition. *The drug threw him into a deep sleep.* 5. to cast. *The setting sun threw long shadows on the road.* 6. to lose on purpose, for money or some other reason. *The boxer threw the fight because his family needed the money that he was offered to let the other man win.* noun 1. the act or result of throwing. *He made a strong throw from the outfield.* 2. the distance an object is or can be thrown. *His house was just a stone's throw away.* {**throh**}

thrown *verb* past participle of **throw.** {**throhn**}

thrush *noun* a common songbird that can be found in

🏃 Human Body ❓ Human Mind 🔼 Everyday Life 🏴 History and Culture 📞 Communication

many parts of the world. Many thrushes have a dark upper body and a spotted breast. The robin and bluebird are kinds of thrushes. {**thruhsh**}

thrust *verb* (thrust, thrusting, thrusts) to push or drive with force. *He thrust his fist through the door in anger.* *noun* 1. the act of pushing or driving forward with force. *The knight finished his enemy with one last thrust of his sword.* 2. an attack by the army, navy, or other force. *The officers planned a thrust into enemy lands.* 3. the force that pushes a jet or rocket engine forward as it takes off. *The thrust of my model rocket is tiny compared to the thrust of the rockets that launch the space shuttle.* {**thruhst**} thruster, n.

thru·way *noun* a long highway that crosses one or more states. Cars and trucks can travel quickly on a thruway because there are few entrances and exits. Some states charge drivers for using a thruway. {**throoh** way}

thud *noun* 1. a dull, muffled sound of one thing hitting another. *The backpack landed at the bottom of the stairs with a thud.* 2. a blow, fall, or knock that causes such a sound. *He gave me a thud on the back with his fist.* *verb* (thudded, thudding, thuds) to make the sound of a thud or thuds. *His heart thudded with fear.* {**thuhd**}

thug *noun* a criminal who is rough or uses violence. *We were attacked by thugs who beat us and stole our money.* {**thuhg**}

thumb *noun* 1. the short, thick first finger on humans and other primates. The thumb makes it easy for the hand to pick up things and grasp

them. 2. a cover for this finger, as in a glove. *The thumb on my mitten is torn.* *verb* (thumbed, thumbing, thumbs) to scan by turning pages with the thumb. *I thumbed the book, but I didn't read it.* {**thuhm**}

• **all thumbs**
awkward, especially with the hands; clumsy. *I'm all thumbs with tools.*

• **thumb one's nose**
to treat with contempt or defiance (usually followed by "at"). *He thumbs his nose at danger.*

• **thumbs down**
a sign or gesture of disfavor or disagreement. *Our teacher gave a thumbs down to his idea for the party.*

• **under one's thumb**
under the power of someone; being controlled or very influenced by. *You have to get out from under his thumb if you want to start your own business.*

thumb·tack *noun* a tack with a flat, round head that can be pressed into a wooden or cork board with a thumb. *We used thumbtacks to put up our posters on the bulletin board.* {**thuhm** tăk}

thump *noun* 1. a heavy, dull sound of one thing hitting another. *The heavy backpack made a thump as it landed on the sidewalk.* 2. a blow or knock that makes a heavy, dull sound. *The boxer gave the other fighter a thump with his fist.* *verb* (thumped, thumping, thumps) 1. to beat or strike with a heavy, dull sound. *Their boss thumped the desk with her fist.* 2. to beat, strike, or fall on something with a heavy, dull sound. *The elephant's feet thumped along the forest floor.* 3. to make the sound of a thump. *My heart*

thumped with excitement as the names of the winners were read. {**thuhmp**}

thun·der *noun* 1. the loud cracking noise or low distant rumble that follows a flash of lightning. Thunder is caused by the violent movement of air masses. 2. any sound that is like this noise. *I hear the thunder of the waves.* *verb* (thundered, thundering, thunders) 1. to give forth or produce thunder. *The sky thundered all night.* 2. to make a sound of or like thunder. *The airplane thundered over our heads.* 3. to express oneself loudly and with great force. *The speaker thundered at the audience.* {**thuhn** dər}

• **steal one's thunder**
to get the attention, praise, or applause that someone else expected to receive. *I was supposed to be the star of the play, but he stole my thunder.*

thun·der·cloud *noun* a large, dark storm cloud that makes lightning and thunder. Thunderclouds are charged with electricity. {**thuhn** dər klowd}

thun·der·storm *noun* a storm with thunder, lightning, rain, and wind. *We ran for shelter during the thunderstorm.* {**thuhn** dər stohrm}

Thurs. or **Th.** or **Thu.** *abbreviation* an abbreviation for **Thursday.**

Thurs·day *noun* the fifth day of the week. Thursday comes between Wednesday and Friday. {**thuhrz** day}

Word History *Thursday* comes from an early Scandinavian word that means "Thor's day." *Thor* was the Scandinavian name for the god of thunder.

A
B
C
D
E
F
G
H
I
J
K
L
M
N
O
P
Q
R
S
T
U
V
W
X
Y
Z

a b c d e f g h i j k l m n o p q r s t u v w x y z

thus *adverb* 1. in this way; so. *Turn your head thus.* 2. for this reason; therefore. *We had no heat, and thus we were cold this winter.* 3. to this degree or amount; so. *No one has entered the contest thus far.* {<u>thuhs</u>}

thy *pronoun* your. This word is used mostly in religion and in things written long ago. {<u>thiy</u>}

thyme *noun* 1. a small plant that has fragrant leaves and is related to the mint plant. Thyme is an herb. 2. the leaves of this plant, used to add flavor to food. *The cook added thyme to the soup.* {<u>tiym</u>}

Homophone Note The words *thyme* and *time* sound alike but have different meanings.

Ti symbol of the chemical element titanium.

ti[1] *noun* the syllable that indicates the seventh tone of a musical scale. {<u>tee</u>}

ti[2] *noun* any of several tropical plants resembling a palm, found in Asia and the Pacific, with long, narrow leaves growing in a tuft at the top. {<u>tee</u>}

Ti·bet *noun* a region of southwestern China, north of the Himalayas. Tibet has its own government and has been a center of Buddhism for over 1,500 years. {tih <u>beht</u>}

tick[1] *noun* 1. the quiet, clicking sound of a watch or clock. *The tick of the clock kept me awake all night long.* 2. a small check or other mark made next to an item on a list. *I put a tick next to the words on my spelling list that I need to study. verb* (ticked, ticking, ticks) 1. to make a sound like the tick of a clock. *If you're very quiet, you can hear my watch tick.* 2. to pass, as time.

The minutes ticked away as I waited for the bus. 3. to check or mark (usually followed by "off"). *I ticked off the words on my spelling list when I was sure that I knew them.* {<u>tihk</u>}

• **what makes one tick** what causes one's behavior (often used as a question). *I often wonder what makes my little brother tick.*

tick[2] *noun* a small animal that is related to the spider. Ticks attach themselves to people and other animals and suck their blood.

Ticks are known to spread disease. {<u>tihK</u>}

tick·et 🌎 💬 *noun* 1. a small, narrow slip of paper or thin cardboard that shows that one has paid for something. *You must show your ticket to get into the theater.* 2. a list of candidates supported by one political party in an election. *There are three women on the Republican ticket.* 3. a notice to appear in court or pay a fine. *Joe got a ticket for driving through a red light. verb* (ticketed, ticketing, tickets) to give a ticket to. *The police officer ticketed Joe for driving too fast.* {<u>tihk</u> iht}

tick·le *verb* (tickled, tickling, tickles) 1. to touch or poke so as to cause a tingling feeling or laughter. *My little brother laughed and squirmed when I tickled him.* 2. to fill with pleasure or excitement. *The funny story tickled the children.* 3. to have or cause a feeling of tingling or itching. *My throat tickles. / A feather tickles when brushed across the skin. noun* a feeling of being tickled. *The tickle in my nose*

made me sneeze. {<u>tihk</u> əl}

• **tickled pink** delighted or very pleased.

tick·lish *adjective* 1. sensitive to tickling. *He is a ticklish boy. / The bottoms of his feet are very ticklish.* 2. needing careful, sensitive treatment. *Her parents' divorce was a ticklish subject.* {<u>tihk</u> lihsh} ticklishness, n.

ticktack-toe *noun* a game for two players who take turns marking either an X or an O on a grid of nine squares. The winner is the first player who fills in three squares in a row with the same mark. {<u>tihk</u> tăk toh}

tid·al *adjective* caused by, having, or related to tides. *Many interesting animals live in tidal pools.* {<u>tiyd</u> əl}

tid·dly·winks *plural noun* (used with a singular verb) a table game in which the players press large plastic disks against the edges of small ones in order to make the small ones jump into a cup. {<u>tihd</u> lee wingks *or* <u>tih</u> də lee wingks}

tide 🌎 🌐 *noun* 1. the change in the height of the surface of oceans and other large bodies of water that happens about every twelve hours. Tides are caused by the pull of the moon and sun. 2. the flowing of water away from or back onto the land. *The shells were swept away with the tide.* 3. something like this in its rising and falling current, or drift. *The tide of public opinion turned against the president.* {<u>tiyd</u>}

• **tide over** to support through some temporary difficulty, usually a lack of money. *This money will tide me over until I get a job.*

 Human Body   Human Mind   Everyday Life   History and Culture  Communication

ti·dings *plural noun* (sometimes used with a singular verb) news or information. *Have you heard any tidings of your brother?* {tiyd ings}

ti·dy *adjective* (tidier, tidiest) neat and in order. *It's hard for some people to keep their desk tidy. verb* (tidied, tidying, tidies) to make neat or put in order (usually followed by "up"). *She tidied up her hair. / He tidied up his room before going out.* {tiyd ee} tidiness, n.

tie *verb* (tied, tying, ties) 1. to fasten, secure, or bind with a cord or string. *He tied the boat to the dock.* 2. to fasten by pulling together the sides or parts of and making a knot with a string. *I tied my shoe.* 3. to make by looping together and pulling tight a string or cord. *He tied a knot to hold the flag to the pole.* 4. to make even in a contest. *We tied the score in the second half.* 5. to make or be equal scores in a contest. *The two teams tied in the final minutes of the game. noun* 1. something that brings people or things together. *Our school ties have kept us in contact for years since graduation.* 2. a strip of cloth wrapped around the neck and tied in a knot in front. *He wears a tie to work.* 3. an equal score. *We broke the tie by scoring a goal.* 4. a game in which the final score is the same for each side. *The championship game was close all the way through and finally ended in a tie.* {tiy}

tier *noun* one of several rows or layers placed one above another. *The wedding cake had four tiers. / The stadium had many tiers of seats.* {teer}

Homophone Note. The words *tier*[1] and *tear*[1] (a drop from the eye) sound alike but have different meanings.

ti·ger *noun* a large, very strong mammal with short, yellow-orange fur and black stripes. Tigers are carnivores. They live in several parts of Asia but are endangered in all their habitats. Tigers are the largest of the big cats and are closely related to lions, leopards, and other cats that roar. {tiy gər}

tight *adjective* (tighter, tightest) 1. fastened or shut in a secure way; fixed in place. *I made a tight knot so my shoes would stay tied.* 2. close in fit or timing. *I need new shoes because these old ones are too tight. / I need to rush because I'm on a tight schedule.* 3. closely fitted or made so that nothing can pass through. *This window has a tight seal so that heat cannot escape in the winter.* 4. stretched out; taut. *We used tight ropes to hold down our tent during the storm.* 5. difficult to manage or get out of. *She found herself in a tight position after she lied to her brother.* 6. (informal) not willing to spend or share. *Mr. Scrooge was rich, but he was tight with his money. adverb* (tighter, tightest) in a firm, close, or secure way. *Her eyes were shut tight. / We stretched the rope tight. / She held her baby tight. / The glue held the pieces together tight.* {tiyt} tightly, adv., tightness, n.

• **sit** or **hold tight** to stay and wait for further information or events. *We decided to sit tight until the storm passed before walking home.*

• **sleep tight** to sleep well or soundly. *I slept tight once I was back in my own bed.*

tight·en *verb* (tightened, tightening, tightens) to make or become tight. *She tightened the knot so it would stay tied.* {tiyt ən}

tight·rope *noun* a thick rope or wire that is stretched tight and high above the ground. Acrobats perform on a tightrope at a circus. {tiyt rohp}

• **walk a tightrope** to keep a difficult balance or middle position between opposed people or choices.

tights *plural noun* a piece of clothing made of tight, stretchy material that covers the legs and hips. Tights are worn for exercise, dancing, or as everyday clothing under a skirt. {tiyts}

Ti·gris *noun* a river of southwest Asia. It flows through Turkey and Iraq. It joins the Euphrates River in a valley where some of the most ancient civilizations were located. {tiy grihs}

tile *noun* 1. a flat piece of baked clay or other hard material. Tiles are used to cover floors, walls, or roofs. *The workers tiled our bathroom.* 2. a short pipe of concrete or baked clay used as a drain. *verb* (tiled, tiling, tiles) to cover with tiles.

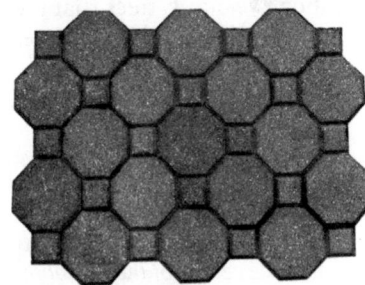

{tiyl}

till[1] *preposition* until. *I'll be gone till Friday. conjunction* 1. up to

Right margin alphabet: A B C D E F G H I J K L M N O P Q R S T U V W X Y Z

the time when; until. *They watched TV till it was time to go to bed.* 2. unless; before (used with a negative sense). *He won't leave till he's eaten.* {<u>tihl</u>}

till² *verb* (tilled, tilling, tills) to prepare for growing crops, especially by plowing. *My great-grandfather used to till the land with a horse-drawn plough.* {<u>tihl</u>}

till·er *noun* a handle that is attached to a rudder and used to steer a boat. {<u>tih</u> lər}

tilt *verb* (tilted, tilting, tilts) 1. to move or place so that one side is higher than the other; tip. *He tilted the chair against the wall. / The dog tilted its head in curiosity.* 2. to lean to one side; slant. *The kitchen floor tilts down here. / The trees tilted in the heavy wind.* *noun* 1. an act or instance of tilting; slope. 2. a leaning or sloping position. {<u>tihlt</u>}

• **at full tilt**
at maximum speed. *He was driving down the highway at full tilt.*

• **tilt at windmills**
to battle against imaginary enemies or offenses.

tim·ber ❶ *noun* 1. trees that are used as wood to build houses and buildings. *They cut the timber into boards.* 2. the wood of such trees. *The timber used to build our garage came from pine trees.* 3. a wooden piece that holds up a roof. *The timbers can be seen near the ceiling of the log cabin.* *interjection* "Look out!" (used by loggers to warn of a falling tree). *When the logger yelled,* "Timber!" *I got out of the way.* {<u>tihm</u> bər}

time ❷ ❶ *noun* 1. the system in which events appear to happen one after the next in a way that can never be turned back; the past, present, and future. 2. the passing of minutes, days, weeks, years, and centuries. 3. the measured period between the beginning and the end of an event. *We waited in line a long time. / How much time until dinner?* 4. (often plural) a period marked by particular events. *Grandfather liked to talk about the old times.* 5. a particular instance or event. *I remember the time you broke your leg. / She called me two times.* 6. the period or instance set aside for a particular activity or event. *It's time for dinner.* 7. a moment or moments as shown on a clock or calendar. *What time does the play start?* 8. the length of the period spent at work in a given day or week. *I work full time.* 9. a speed or type of rhythm or movement. *This song is in waltz time, which means that it has three beats to the measure.* *adjective* 1. of or having to do with time. *I often wonder if time travel is possible.* 2. set to work at a particular time. *The police dog found the time bomb two hours before it was set to explode.* *verb* (timed, timing, times) 1. to record the rate or duration of. *I timed his mile run at 5 minutes 40 seconds.* 2. to set or choose the time for; schedule. *We timed our meeting for after school.* 3. to fix or change the speed or action of. *The bus driver timed*

her arrival perfectly to pick up the passengers from the airport. {<u>tiym</u>}

Homophone Note Are you looking for the word *thyme* (a spice)? *Time* and *thyme* sound alike but have different meanings.

time·ly *adjective* (timelier, timeliest) happening at just the right moment. *The doctor's timely visit saved my life.* {<u>tiym</u> lee} timeliness, n.

tim·er *noun* 1. one who measures or records time. *The timers stood at the finish line with their stopwatches.* 2. a device that measures time. *We used a stopwatch as our timer at the swim meet.* 3. a device that starts or stops a machine or appliance at set times. *The timer turns our lights on and off while we are away from home.* {<u>tiym</u> ər}

time limit *noun* a limit set on the amount or period of time during which some action can or must be taken or completed. {<u>tiym</u> lih miht}

time·ta·ble *noun* a schedule that lists the times at which certain events take place. People read timetables to find out when trains, buses, or airplanes will arrive or leave. {<u>tiym</u> tay bəl}

time zone *noun* a region in which all the clocks are set to the same time. The earth is divided into twenty-four time zones. The time in each zone is one hour earlier than it is in the zone to its east. {<u>tiym</u> zohn}

tim·id *adjective* 1. not bold or confident with other people; shy. *The timid child did not like*

 Human Body    Human Mind    Everyday Life    History and Culture    Communication

A B C D E F G H I J K L M N O P Q R **S** **T** U V W X Y Z

Time

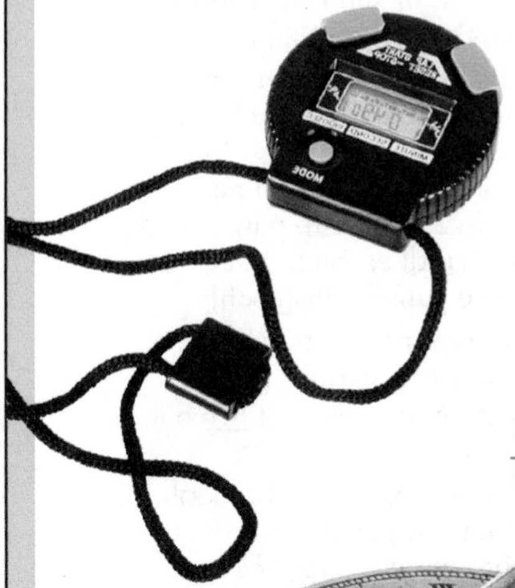

Perhaps there is nothing more mysterious and at once more ordinary than the passage of time. Kindergarten students learn to measure it in minutes, hours, days, weeks, months and years, yet the nature of what exactly it is continues to baffle the greatest minds the world has ever known. Einstein suggested we think of it as a fourth dimension together with the three dimensions of space: length, width, and height. When you ride your bicycle down the street, you are traveling forward in time just as you are traveling forward in distance along the street. Should you decide to go back to the place you started from, you need only turn your bicycle around and go in the opposite direction. Yet, you can never reverse the direction of time. Just as the puddle of wax cannot melt back into a candle, you can never ride your bicycle back to the time you started from.

Time moves relentlessly forward.

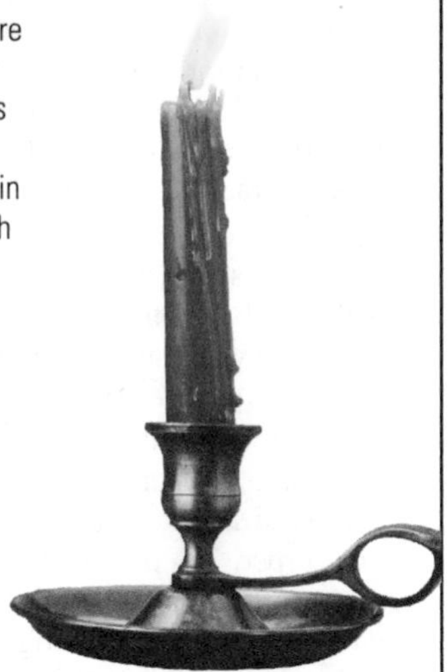

---

to go to parties. 2. not eager or willing to face danger; fearful. *Timid people should not become astronauts.* {**tihm** ihd} timidity, n., timidly, adv., timidness, n.

tin *noun* a soft, light gray metal that is one of the chemical elements. Tin does not rust easily. It can be combined with other metals to form alloys such as bronze or pewter. (symbol: Sn) {**tihn**}

tin·foil *noun* a sheet of tin or aluminum thin enough to be used to wrap things. {**tihn foil**}

tinge *verb* (tinged, tingeing, tinges) 1. to give a slight color to. *The sky was tinged orange by the setting sun.* 2. to leave a trace on; slightly affect. *Sorrow tinged his voice.* *noun* 1. a trace of color; tint. *That cheese is old and has a green tinge.* 2. a slight trace.

We noticed a tinge of mystery in her smile. {**tihnj**}

tin·gle *verb* (tingled, tingling, tingles) 1. to have a light stinging or prickly feeling. *My cheeks tingled when I came inside from the cold.* 2. to cause a light stinging or prickly feeling. *This shampoo tingles.* *noun* a light prickly or stinging feeling. *I felt a tingle when I dove into the freezing water.* {**ting** gəl}

tin·kle *verb* (tinkled, tinkling, tinkles) 1. to make light ringing sounds. *The wind*

chime tinkled in the breeze. 2. to cause to make light ringing sounds. *She tinkled Santa's bells.* *noun* a light ringing sound. *We heard the tinkle of the cat's little bell.* {**ting** kəl}

tin·sel *noun* strips or sheets of foil or other shiny material used as a decoration. *Many people hang tinsel on their Christmas tree.* {**tihn** səl}

tint 🔄 *noun* 1. a shade of a color. *We chose an olive-green tint for our carpet.* 2. a pale or light color, often made by adding white to a paint or using a weak dye. *verb* (tinted, tinting, tints) to give a color or tint to. *We tinted the curtains pink.* {**tihnt**}

ti·ny *adjective* (tinier, tiniest) very small, minute; miniature. *This kitten is tiny. / Her dolls live in a tiny house.* {**tiy** nee}

tip[1] *noun* 1. the end, especially of something pointed, slender, or tapered. *Touch it with the tip of your finger.* 2. the top; peak; summit. *There is snow at the tip of the mountain.* {**tihp**}

tip[2] *verb* (tipped, tipping, tips) 1. to move to a leaning or slanted position; tilt. *She tipped the bowl to get the last drops of soup.* 2. to lean; slant; tilt. *The sailboat tipped in the wind.* 3. to turn over; upset; topple (often followed by "over"). *A dog tipped over my garbage can.* 4. to turn over; topple (usually followed by "over"). *The glass of milk tipped over onto my books.* *noun* the act of tipping. *He greeted her with a tip of the hat.* {**tihp**}

tip[3] *noun* 1. a small gift of money given as a way of thanking someone for a service done. *Let's give the waitress a good tip.* 2. a piece of

secret and useful information. *He gave me a tip on the horse race.* 3. a small, useful idea; hint. *I bought a book full of gardening tips.* *verb* (tipped, tipping, tips) to give a tip to in return for a service. *Tip the waiter, and I'll pay the bill.* {**tihp**}

tip·toe *noun* the end or tip of the toe. *We stood on our tiptoes so we could see over the wall.* *verb* (tiptoed, tiptoeing, tiptoes) to walk quietly or on tiptoes. *We tiptoed out of the sleeping baby's room.* {**tihp** toh}

• **on tiptoe**
1. standing or walking on the toes, especially to proceed quietly or cautiously. 2. filled with eager anticipation; expectant. *The cast was all on tiptoe before the play.*

tire[1] *verb* (tired, tiring, tires) 1. to use up the strength and energy of; make tired. *The long hike tired us.* 2. to cause to lose interest or make bored. *The long speech tired everybody.* 3. to become weak or sleepy. *She tires quickly when we play ball because she never exercises.* 4. to lose interest or become bored (usually followed by "of"). *We tired of her constant complaining.* {**tiyr**}

After the Indianapolis 500 auto race, even the **tires** feel **tired**!

tire[2] *noun* a rubber covering that fits around the rim of a

wheel. Tires are usually filled with air. {**tiyr**}

'tis shortened form of "it is." *My love, 'tis of you I sing.* {**tihz**}

tis·sue 🔄 ⭕ *noun* 1. a group of cells in an animal or plant body that are like each other and do similar things. *Muscle tissue is different from fat tissue.* 2. soft, thin paper used as a handkerchief. 3. see **tissue paper**. {**tihsh** ooh}

tissue paper *noun* very thin, almost transparent paper used for wrapping. {**tihsh** ooh **pay** pər}

ti·tle *noun* 1. a name of a book, film, play, piece of music, or other work of art. *The book has a French title.* 2. a word used with or instead of a name to show a person's position, rank, or occupation. *His title is "Professor," not "Doctor."* 3. a legal right to own something such as property or the document that proves it. *She has the title to this house.* 4. a sports championship. *Our school won the state basketball title.* *verb* (titled, titling, titles) to give a title to. *She titled the story before sending it to press.* {**tiyt** əl}

TN or **Tenn.** *abbreviation* an abbreviation for **Tennessee.**

TNT *noun* a powerful explosive. TNT is an abbreviation for "trinitrotoluene." {**tee ehn tee**}

to *preposition* 1. in the direction of; toward. *We took the road that goes to town. / They're waving to me.* 2. as far as. *We took the elevator to the third level.* 3. with the goal of. *They came to my rescue.* 4. indicating something received or owned. *The towel belongs to her. / The letter is addressed to you.* 5. in connection with. *She is kind to her brother.* 6. used with;

 Human Body  Human Mind  Everyday Life 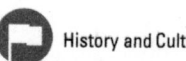 History and Culture  Communication

intended for. *This is the key to the house*. 7. closely on, against, or beside. *Apply a hot pad to the sore spot*. 8. in regard to; concerning. *He is blind to his own mistakes*. 9. resulting in or from. *If he had worked to the best of his ability, he wouldn't have failed. / My heart was torn to pieces when she left*. 10. as compared with. *The score was six to three*. 11. before. *The time is five minutes to eight*. 12. held in; per. *There are sixty marbles to a bag*. 13. used before a verb to show the infinitive, or by itself as an implied verb. *Do you want to sing? Yes, I want to. adverb* 1. into a shut position. *She pulled the door to*. 2. into an awake state. *The wounded man finally came to*. {**tooh**}

Homophone Note The words **to**, **too**, and **two** sound alike but have different meanings.

toad *noun* a small animal that looks like a frog and has dry, rough skin. Toads are amphibians, but live mostly on land rather than in or near water. {**tohd**}

toad·stool *noun* a mushroom shaped like an umbrella. Toadstools are often poisonous. {**tohd stoohl**}

toast[1] *noun* bread that has been sliced and browned in an oven or toaster. *verb* (toasted, toasting, toasts) to make crisp and brown by heating. *We toasted the cheese sandwiches for lunch*. {**tohst**}

toast[2] *noun* a call on other people to drink in honor of someone or something, or

the words of praise before this call. *He made a toast to the graduate. verb* (toasted, toasting, toasts) to drink in honor of, or to the health of. *We toasted the new workers*. {**tohst**}

toast·er *noun* an electric appliance used to heat and brown bread or rolls. {**toh** stər}

to·bac·co *noun* (tobaccos or tobaccoes) 1. a plant with large, sticky leaves that are smoked or chewed. 2. the leaves of this plant, dried and cut for smoking in cigarettes, cigars, or pipes. {tə **băk** oh}

to·bog·gan *noun* a long, narrow, wooden sled that curves up in front. Toboggans have no blades underneath and are difficult to steer. *verb* (tobogganed, tobogganing, toboggans) to ride or coast on a toboggan down a surface covered with snow or ice. *They tobogganed down the icy slope*. {tə **bŏg** ihn}

to·day *noun* 1. the present day. *Today is the first day of school*. 2. the present time in general. *The toys of today are made of plastic. adverb* 1. on or during the present day. *I'm not going to school today*. 2. at or during the present time in general. *Today we no longer live in caves*. {tə **day** or tooh **day**, n., tə **day** or tooh **day**, adv.}

tod·dler *noun* a young child who has just learned to walk. {**tŏd** lər}

toe *noun* 1. one of the parts of the body that extend from the end

of the foot in humans and other animals with backbones. Humans have five toes on each foot. 2. the front part of a shoe, slipper, or sock. *I wore out the toe on my favorite socks*. {**toh**}

• **on one's toes** (informal) alert and ready to act. *Emergency room nurses have to be on their toes*.

• **step on someone's toes** to annoy or anger by trying to take over someone else's job or role. *He was fired because he stepped on the boss's toes*.

Homophone Note The words **toe** and **tow**[1] sound alike but have different meanings. If your car breaks down, asking someone for a "toe" won't get you anywhere.

tof·fee *noun* a hard candy made from butter and brown sugar. {**tawf** ee *or* **tahf** ee}

to·fu *noun* a food made from soybean milk. Tofu looks and feels like soft cheese. {**toh** fooh *or* toh **fooh**}

to·geth·er *adverb* 1. in or into one gathering, group, mass, or place. *She mixed the water and cement together*. 2. in or into agreement or cooperation with one another. *The two sides worked together in order to find a solution*. 3. at the same time. *They arrived together on the train*. {tə **gehth** ər}

toil[1] *noun* long or difficult work. *After a week of toil, the crops were all harvested. verb* (toiled, toiling, toils) 1. to work long and hard. *The farmers toiled in the field from dawn to dusk*. 2. to go or move with great effort. *They toiled through the thick swamp on their way to the mainland*. {**toil**}

A B C D E F G H I J K L M N O P Q R S **T** U V W X Y Z

toil² *noun* (usually plural) something in which one becomes trapped or tangled; snare. *The unlucky sailor was caught in the toils of the octopus. / We were stuck in the toils of government rules and regulations.* {**toil**}

toi·let *noun* 1. a bowl that is filled with water and that has a seat and a drain. A toilet is used for receiving and disposing of human waste. 2. a room that contains this appliance; bathroom. {**toi** liht}

to·ken *noun* 1. a symbol that stands for something larger and greater in value. *The gift was a token of our respect for him.* 2. a piece of metal or plastic shaped like a coin and used in place of money for a specific and limited purpose. *We bought tokens for the bus and subway.* {**toh** kən}
  • **by the same token** for the same reason. *By the same token that you donate money to charity, you should also be kind to beggars.*

To·ky·o *noun* the capital city of Japan. Long ago Tokyo was known as Edo. {**toh** kee oh}

told *verb* past tense and past participle of **tell**. {**tohld**}

tol·er·ance *noun* 1. willingness to accept people whose race, religion, opinions, or habits are different from one's own. 2. the ability to put up with or endure. *He has a great tolerance for the cold.* {**tŏl** ər əns}

tol·er·ant *adjective* willing to accept or respect differences in others, such as their race, opinions, and beliefs. {**tŏl** ər ənt}

tol·er·ate *verb* (tolerated, tolerating, tolerates) 1. to allow or accept; not oppose or attack. *She tolerates her child's messy room, although she does not like it.* 2. not to be bothered by; endure or bear. *He tolerates cold weather well.* {**tŏl** ər ayt}

toll¹ *verb* (tolled, tolling, tolls) 1. to cause to ring with slow, even strokes. *They are tolling the bell for the men lost at sea.* 2. to call or announce by ringing a large bell. *The church bell tolled the hour.* 3. to ring with slow single sounds. *"Ask not for whom the bell tolls…"* *noun* the act of ringing a large bell, or the sound made by ringing a large bell. {**tohl**}

toll² *noun* 1. a charge for using a bridge or a road. 2. a charge for a long-distance telephone call or other service. 3. an amount of damage caused by some action or event. *The flood took a terrible toll in life and property.* {**tohl**}

tom·a·hawk *noun* a light ax with a stone head, once used by some native North American peoples as a weapon or tool. {**tŏm** ə hawk}

to·ma·to *noun* (tomatoes) 1. a red or yellow fruit with a juicy pulp. A tomato is eaten either raw or cooked as a vegetable. 2. the plant that bears this fruit. {tə **mayt** oh *or* tə **maht** oh}

tomb *noun* 1. a hole in which a dead body is buried; grave. 2. a structure built to hold the bodies of one or more dead persons. {**toohm**}

tomb·stone *noun* a piece of stone that marks a grave and may give the dead person's name and dates of birth and death; gravestone. {**toohm stohn**}

to·mor·row *noun* 1. the day after today. *Tomorrow is his birthday.* 2. a future time. *Can you imagine the world of tomorrow? adverb* on the day after today. *I will leave tomorrow.* {tə **mar** oh *or* tə **mohr** oh, n., tə **mar** oh *or* tə **mohr** oh, adv.}

tom-tom *noun* (tom-toms) a small or narrow drum, usually played by beating with the hands. {**tŏm tŏm**}

ton *noun* 1. a unit of weight equal to 2000 pounds or 907.18 kilograms, used in the United States and Canada; short ton. 2. a unit of weight equal to 2,240 pounds or 1,016.06 kilograms, used in Great Britain; long ton. 3. see **metric ton**. {**tuhn**}

tone 🔵 🔵 *noun* 1. a single sound that is thought of as having pitch, strength, or length. *You will hear three high tones in a row when the washing machine is done.* 2. the character of a sound or sounds. *The tone of the old violin is warm and rich.* 3. the sound of words as they show a feeling. *The teacher spoke to the children in a friendly tone.* 4. healthy firmness of the skin, muscle, or organs of the body. *The athlete has excellent muscle tone.* 5. the shade of a color. *The walls were painted in a strange tone of green.* 6. general spirit or mood. *The movie tried to capture the tone of the 1980s.* *verb* (toned, toning, tones) to make firm. *We toned our*

 Human Body  Human Mind  Everyday Life  History and Culture  Communication

muscles by running every day. {tohn}

• **tone down**
to make less harsh, loud, or bright. *We toned down the color of the walls. / Please tone your voices down.*

tongs *plural noun* (usually used with a plural verb) a tool used to grasp small objects. Tongs have two arms that are held together by a hinge and are usually made of metal. {t**ŏ**ngz *or* t**aw**ngz}

tongue ⊕ ⊖ *noun* 1. the movable organ in the bottom of the mouth, used for licking, tasting, swallowing, and human speech. 2. this organ taken from a cow, ox, or other animal and used as food. 3. power or manner of speaking. *She spoke with a sharp tongue.* 4. the language or speech of a particular area. *She spoke in a foreign tongue.* 5. a flap of leather under the laces of a shoe or boot. {tuhng}

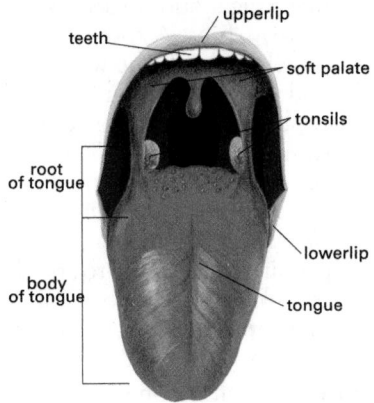

upperlip
teeth
soft palate
tonsils
root of tongue
lowerlip
body of tongue
tongue

ton·ic *noun* 1. something that brings back or refreshes strength or energy. *The warm spring weather was a tonic to us all.* 2. a medicine that brings back or refreshes one's strength or energy. {t**ŏ**n ihk}

to·night *noun* this present or coming night. *Tonight is a good night to see the moon.*

adverb on or during this present or coming night. *She will be here tonight.* {tə **niyt** *or* tooh **niyt**, n., tə **niyt** *or* tooh **niyt**, adv.}

ton·sil *noun* either of two spongy parts which hang in the throat near the back of the tongue. {t**ŏ**n sihl}

ton·sil·li·tis *noun* an illness that causes the tonsils to become red and swollen. {t**ŏ**n sih **liy** tihs}

too *adverb* 1. as well; also; in addition. *He's smart, and she is too.* 2. to a greater degree than is wanted; excessively. *She is too tired to speak.* 3. very; extremely. *I'm not too sure.* 4. indeed (used to oppose a statement seen as a criticism). *I can too read!* {tooh}

Homophone Note The words *too*, *to*, and *two* sound alike but have different meanings.

took *verb* past tense of **take**. {tuuk}

tool *noun* 1. an instrument that is usually held with the hands, such as a hammer or drill. Tools are used for doing work. 2. any instrument, thing, or activity that helps to get something done. *Writing is a good tool for thinking.* *verb* (tooled, tooling, tools) to shape, work, or decorate using a tool. *He tools leather belts.* {toohl}

tool·box *noun* a container for hand tools. A toolbox often has a handle for carrying and several compartments to make it easy to find small tools. {toohl b**ŏ**ks}

toot *verb* (tooted, tooting, toots) 1. to make the quick, short sound of a horn or whistle. *The factory whistle tooted to signal the end of the*

work day. 2. to blow and cause to make a quick, short sound. *Tom tooted his whistle for hours.* *noun* the sound made by a horn or whistle, or the act of making such a sound. *We were awakened by the toot of the horn.* {tooht}

tooth ⊕ *noun* (teeth) 1. one of the hard, white, bony objects that grow in rows in the jaws of people and animals. Teeth are used for biting and chewing. 2. a small, pointed part similar to a human tooth in form or in how it is used. *The teeth of the saw cut into the tree.* 3. a liking or weakness for a particular flavor or type of food. *She has a sweet tooth and eats too much candy.* {tooht**h**} toothless, adj.

tooth·ache *noun* a pain in or close to a tooth. {tooht**h** ayk}

tooth·brush *noun* a brush with a short, narrow head and a long handle used to clean the teeth. {tooht**h** bruhsh}

tooth·paste *noun* a paste used to clean the teeth. {tooht**h** payst}

tooth·pick *noun* a short, thin, pointed piece of wood that is used to remove tiny pieces of food from between the teeth. {tooht**h** pihk}

top[1] *noun* 1. the highest area, point, or surface. *We climbed to the top of the mountain.* 2. a cover, cap, or lid placed over or on something. *Put the top on the jar.* 3. the highest position. *She is at the top of her class.* 4. one who is in or at the highest position. *He is top in his music class.* *adjective* 1. located in the highest place or position. *The bird perched on the top branches of the tree.* 2. first; foremost. *He is the top expert in his field.* *verb* (topped, topping, tops) 1. to provide with or act as a

A B C D E F G H I J K L M N O P Q R S **T** U V W X Y Z

a b c d e f g h i j k l m n o p q r s **t** u v w x y z

top. *Snow topped the trees.* 2. to reach or go over the top of. *They topped the hill after a long climb.* 3. to go beyond. *He topped his brother in the swimming race.* 4. to take away the top of; cut. *He will top all the bushes in the yard.* {tŏp}

• **blow one's top** (informal) to lose control; become angry. *Sam blew his top when his brother broke his radio.*

• **on top of**
1. in total control of. *The doctor was on top of the case of the man with a broken arm.* 2. completely familiar with. *He is on top of the latest advances in computer technology.* 3. in addition to. *We got more homework on top of what we got yesterday.*

top² *noun* a toy shaped like a cone that spins on its point. {tŏp}

to·paz *noun* a clear, crystal stone that is yellow or brown and used in jewelry. {**toh** păz}

top·ic 🌐 *noun* 1. a subject of discussion or conversation. *The teacher assigned each group a topic to discuss.* 2. a subject or theme of an essay, book, or other written work. *The topic of this book is life in the Arctic.* {**tŏp** ihk}

to·pog·ra·phy 🌐 *noun* (topographies) the shape of the earth's surface across an area or region. The topography of an area includes the size and location of hills and dips in the land. *The topography of our region is marked by many lakes and hills.* {tə **pŏg** rə fee} topographic, adj.

top·ple *verb* (toppled, toppling, topples) 1. to sway and fall down; tumble. *The pile of blocks toppled over when it got too tall.* 2. to cause to fall down or fall over. *The child built a tower out of blocks and then toppled it.* {**tŏp** əl}

top·sy-tur·vy *adverb* 1. upside down. *The boat turned topsy-turvy in the waves.* 2. in a state of great confusion. *The police searched the office and left everything topsy-turvy.* *adjective* upside-down. *The furniture seems to be topsy-turvy when I stand on my head.* {**tŏp** see **tuhr** vee}

to·rah *noun* 1. (sometimes capitalized) the whole body of recorded Jewish law and wisdom, in particular the Old Testament and the Talmud. 2. the sacred scrolls that contain the first five books of the Bible. Parts of the Torah are read during religious services. {**tohr** ə or tohr **ŏ**}

torch *noun* 1. a stick or rod with a burning material on one end that is lit and carried for light. 2. a tool that produces a very hot flame for working with glass or metal. *The police used a torch to cut through the metal door.* {**tohrch**}

tore *verb* past tense of **tear²**. {**tohr**}

tor·ment *verb* (tormented, tormenting, torments) 1. to cause to feel great pain or distress. *The cruel guard tormented the prisoners.* 2. to annoy, tease, or cause to feel worry. *The bully tormented the small boy by calling him names.* *noun* a state of great suffering of the body or mind. *I was in torment after falling into a patch of poison ivy.* {**tohr** mehnt, n., **tohr** mehnt, v.}

tor·na·do *noun* (tornadoes or tornados) a storm of very strong winds that form a cloud shaped like a funnel. Although it does not last long, a tornado destroys everything in its path. {**tohr** nay doh}

tor·pe·do *noun* (torpedoes) a long missile that is shaped like a cigar and is used to destroy ships. A torpedo travels through the water under its own power and explodes when it hits something. *In World War Two, torpedoes were launched from both submarines and airplanes.* *verb* (torpedoed, torpedoing, torpedoes) to attack or sink with torpedoes. *The submarine torpedoed the enemy warship.* {**tohr** pee doh}

tor·rent *noun* a heavy flow of water with a strong current, such as a rushing stream, a flood, or a heavy rainfall. {**taw** rənt or **tar** ənt}

tor·so *noun* (torsos) the human body from neck to hips; trunk. {**tohr** soh}

tor·til·la *noun* a Mexican flat bread or thin pancake made of cornmeal. Tortillas are often served hot and filled

 Human Body    Human Mind    Everyday Life    History and Culture   Communication

with beans, meat, or other foods. {tohr **tee** ə}

tor·toise *noun* a turtle that lives on land. {**tohr** təs}

tor·ture *noun* 1. the intentional causing of great physical or emotional pain to a person or animal. *Some governments use torture to find out the secrets of their enemies.* 2. great pain of the emotions or mind; agony. *Speaking in front of a group was torture for him.* *verb* (tortured, torturing, tortures) to cause great physical or emotional pain intentionally. *The cruel soldiers tortured their prisoners until they revealed military secrets.* {**tohr** chər} torturer, n., torturous, adj.

toss *verb* (tossed, tossing, tosses) 1. to throw lightly; fling. *I tossed a few coins into the well for good luck.* 2. to throw back and forth, from one person to another. *Let's go toss the baseball.* 3. to be thrown back and forth. *The ship tossed during the storm.* 4. to throw gently. *Please toss the newspaper over here.* 5. to lift with a sharp motion. *The horse tossed its head.* 6. to mix gently in order to coat with a sauce or dressing. *Please toss the salad.* 7. to move, fling, or throw oneself about. *She tossed in her sleep.* *noun* the act or an instance of tossing; pitch. *A coin toss decides which team gets the ball first.* {**taws** or **tŏs**, n., **taws** or **tŏs**, v.}

tot *noun* a very young child. {**tŏt**}

to·tal *adjective* 1. making up or including the whole; entire; full. *I paid the total amount that I owed.* 2. complete. *He made a total fool of himself by wearing pajamas to work.* *noun* the whole amount; sum. *We spent a total of fifty dollars at the restaurant.* *verb* (totaled, totaling, totals) 1. to add up. *She totaled each team's points.* 2. to amount or add up to. *The day's sales totaled only fifty dollars.* {**toht** əl}

to·tal·ly *adverb* completely; entirely. *The new computer was totally useless after it fell into the bathtub.* {**toht** əl ee}

tote *verb* (toted, toting, totes) to carry on one's back or in one's arms or hands. *We tote our books to school in a backpack.* {**toht**}

to·tem *noun* 1. a living thing, such as an animal or plant, that is taken as the symbol of a family or clan. *The totem of our clan is the bear.* 2. a symbol or image of a totem that is carved or painted. *The masks were decorated with the buffalo totem.* {**toh** təm}

totem pole *noun* a wooden pole that is carved and painted with totem images. Totem poles were raised outside the homes of some native peoples who lived near the Pacific coast in northwestern North America. {**toh** təm **pohl**}

tot·ter *verb* (tottered, tottering, totters) 1. to sway or rock as if about to fall. *Grandpa tottered as he walked down the stairs.* 2. to be shaky or not steady. *The company is tottering on the edge of failure.* {**tŏt** ər}

tou·can *noun* a tropical bird of the Western Hemisphere that is brightly colored and has a very large bill. {**tooh** kăn}

touch *verb* (touched, touching, touches) 1. to put one's hand or fingers on in order to feel. *She touched the cat's soft fur.* 2. to make contact with. *Don't let the paper touch the fire.* 3. to be next to. *Their yard touches ours.* 4. to affect; have an impact on. *This problem touches the lives of many people.* 5. to make changes on; improve (usually followed by "up"). *The artist wants to touch up the painting.* 6. to have an emotional effect on. *The movie on war touched him deeply.* *noun* 1. the act or an instance of touching. *He felt a touch on his arm and turned to find an old friend.* 2. the sense by which a person feels an object or thing. *He used his touch to find his way through the dark tunnel.* 3. contact. *Please keep in touch with the office through the week.* 4. a mild case. *She has a touch of the flu, but she can still work.* 5. a small amount; trace. *This recipe calls for a touch of garlic.* / *He felt a touch of guilt for saying those mean things.* {**tuhch**}

touch·down *noun* 1. the act of scoring six points in football by catching or carrying the ball behind the opponent's goal line. 2. the point or moment at which an aircraft or spacecraft lands. {**tuhch** down}

touch·y *adjective* (touchier, touchiest) easily made angry or upset; sensitive. *Tim is touchy about the size of his ears.* {**tuhch** ee}

tough *adjective* (tougher, toughest) 1. hard to break; strong; lasting a long time. *I have a tough car that's been on the road for over twenty-two*

A
B
C
D
E
F
G
H
I
J
K
L
M
N
O
P
Q
R
S
T
U
V
W
X
Y
Z

a
b
c
d
e
f
g
h
i
j
k
l
m
n
o
p
q
r
s
t
u
v
w
x
y
z

years. 2. difficult to cut up or chew. *He could hardly eat the tough meat.* 3. able to put up with trouble or hardship; strong. *Soldiers are trained to be tough.* 4. hard to control; rough. *Those tough kids down the street are nothing but trouble.* 5. difficult to do or understand. *Road construction is a tough job. / Math is really tough for me.* 6. harsh. *Research in the Arctic makes for tough conditions to work in.* {**tuhf**}

tour *verb* (toured, touring, tours) 1. to journey from place to place. *Her favorite rock band is touring this summer.* 2. to journey through. *We toured the mountains of Spain last summer.* *noun* 1. the act of journeying from place to place. *Seeing the Queen was the high point of our tour of Britain.* 2. a trip that performers take in order to give a series of concerts or shows in different places. *The orchestra's tour included stops in three countries.* 3. a short, guided visit. *We were given a tour of the museum.* {**toohr**}

tour·ist *noun* a person who is travelling for pleasure. *Paris is full of tourists in the summer.* {**toohr** ihst}

tour·na·ment *noun* 1. a contest of skill including a series of games where those who lose one game may no longer take part. *Tammy won the tennis tournament after winning five matches.* 2. a contest in medieval times between knights on horseback carrying lances. Each rider would try to knock the other off his horse as they rode toward each other. {**tuhr** nə mənt *or* **toohr** nə mənt}

tow *verb* (towed, towing, tows) to pull along at the end of a rope or chain; haul. *The truck towed our car to the garage.* *noun* an act or instance of being pulled by a rope or chain. *We needed a tow because our car wouldn't start.* {**toh**}

• **in tow**
as followers or in one's company. *The mother duck had seven ducklings in tow.*

Homophone Note The words ***tow¹*** and ***toe*** (a part of the foot) sound alike but have different meanings.

to·ward *preposition* 1. moving or facing in the direction of. *We walked toward the main street.* 2. just before; close to. *They will leave sometime toward afternoon.* 3. with respect to. *She was friendly toward the new girl in her class.* 4. as partial payment of. *Here is ten dollars toward the amount that I owe you.* 5. leading to having or getting. *The new law is a step toward equal rights for all.* {**tohrd** *or* **twohrd** *or* tə **wohrd**} towards, *prep.*

tow·el *noun* a piece or length of soft cloth or paper used to wipe or dry the face, body, dishes, or other things. *verb* (toweled, toweling, towels) to rub, wipe, or dry with a towel (usually followed by "off"). *I toweled off the dog after his bath.* {**tow** əl}

tow·er *noun* a tall, narrow building or part of a building that rises high above the ground. *We climbed up a lookout tower and saw for miles in every direction.* *verb* (towered, towering, towers) to rise high or far above others; reach a great height. *He towers over his father.* {**tow** ər}

town 🔵 🔵 *noun* 1. an area with streets, houses, and buildings that is larger than a village but smaller than a city. 2. the business or shopping area of a city or town; downtown. *She went to town to get some groceries.* 3. the people who live in a town. *The whole town came to the carnival.* {**town**}

tox·ic *adjective* having to do with or made of a poison; poisonous. *The factory spilled toxic waste into the lake.* {**tŏk** sihk} toxicity, n.

toy 🔵 *noun* any object that can be used in play, especially by children; plaything. *adjective* used as a plaything, especially being a tiny likeness or imitation of a larger object. *He wants a toy truck for his birthday.* *verb* (toyed, toying, toys) to handle or treat something carelessly or idly. *The child toyed with his cereal.* {**toi**}

trace *noun* 1. a mark or sign of a past event or thing. *We saw traces of birds on the sand.* 2. a very small amount of something. *There was a trace of snow, but not enough to play in.* *verb* (traced, tracing, traces) 1. to follow the track or trail of. *We traced our friend to the campsite.* 2. to discover through investigation. *The police were able to trace the location of the missing child.* 3. to follow the history of. *She traced her family tree through three centuries.* 4. to copy by following the lines of as seen through a sheet of paper. *He traced the drawing onto very thin paper.* {**trays**}

tra·che·a *noun* (tracheas) 1. the tube that carries air to the lungs in humans and other

 Human Body   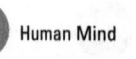 Human Mind    Everyday Life   History and Culture    Communication

animals that breathe air; windpipe. 2. a similar tube in an insect, or a tube that carries water up the stems of some plants. {**tray** kee ə} tracheal, adj.

track noun 1. a mark or series of marks left on the ground by the feet of people or animals, or the wheels of machines; trail. *They saw dog tracks in the mud.* 2. a pair of connected rails on which trains travel. 3. a path or course laid out for running or racing in competitive sports, often in the shape of an oval. *He ran around the track every morning.* verb (tracked, tracking, tracks) 1. to follow the footprints or other traces of. *The wolf tracked the rabbit.* 2. to make a trail with. *The dog tracked mud on the carpet.* {**trăk**} tracker, n.

• **keep track of**
to record the movements or progress of. *The police kept track of where he was at all times.* / *We kept track of our scores on a piece of paper.*

• **off the track**
not related to the point or issue. *Her remarks were off the track.*

track and field noun a set of athletic events that take place on or near a running track. Track and field events include running, jumping, and throwing. {**trăk** ənd **feeld**} track-and-field, adj.

tract noun 1. an area of land or water. *There are large tracts of forest in some parts of our country.* 2. a group of body parts and organs which act together to perform a function. *The lungs and the windpipe are part of the respiratory tract.* {**trăkt**}

trac·tion noun the grip or holding power of a body moving on a surface. *Tires can lose their traction on an icy road.* {**trăk** shən}

trac·tor noun a powerful motor vehicle with large tires used to pull plows and other farm machines. {**trăk** tər}

trade 🌐 noun 1. the act of exchanging or buying and selling goods. *It was a good trade to get a new car for my old one plus a thousand dollars.* 2. a job that involves a particular skill. *He is a mason by trade.* verb (traded, trading, trades) 1. to exchange. *They traded baseball cards.* 2. to buy and sell. *She trades shares in the stock market.* {**trayd**}

trade·mark noun a name, symbol, or other mark used to show who made a product. By law, only the company that makes or sells the product may use its trademark. {**trayd** mark}

trad·er noun a person who buys and sells; dealer; merchant. *My uncle is a trader in Asian cloth.* {**tray** dər}

trading post noun a store in a frontier area or other place far from towns. At a trading post, local products can be traded for goods brought from distant places. *Settlers traded buffalo skins for flour and sugar at the trading post.* {**trayd** ing pohst}

tra·di·tion 🌐 noun 1. the handing down of a culture's beliefs and customs from parents to children over many years. 2. the beliefs and customs thus handed down. *It is a tradition in my family to celebrate the new year with a special meal.* {trə **dih** shən} traditional, adj.

traf·fic 🌐 noun 1. the movement of people or vehicles along a sidewalk, road, or other route of travel. *Traffic on the highway was heavy this morning.* 2. buying and selling; trade. *They work to stop the illegal traffic of stolen jewelry.* verb (trafficked, trafficking, traffics) to buy or sell, especially something that is illegal. *The criminals were caught trafficking in drugs.* {**trăf** ihk} trafficker, n.

Word History *Traffic* comes from an Italian word that means "to carry on trade." By 1825, the word "traffic" was being used for people or vehicles coming and going along a road.

trag·e·dy 🌐🌐 noun (tragedies) 1. a disaster; a very sad event. *It was a tragedy when the ship sank.* 2. a play or story about serious events or ideas that usually ends with the death of the main character or characters. {**trăj** ih dee}

trag·ic adjective 1. having to do with tragedy. *King Lear is a tragic hero.* 2. causing death, destruction, or disaster. *She made a tragic mistake when she rode her bicycle through the red light.* 3. very sad; causing pity. *The film's tragic ending left the audience silent.* {**trăj** ihk} tragically, adv.

trail 🌐 verb (trailed, trailing, trails) 1. to drag along behind on the ground. *The boy trailed his coat as he walked home.* 2. to follow the trace, track, or scent of. *The dogs trailed the fox.* 3. to be behind in a game or event. *Our team trailed by ten points.* 4. to become weaker. *His voice trailed to a low whisper as he fell asleep.* noun 1. a path or course through a forest or other rural place. *He followed the trail to the cabin.* 2. a track or scent left behind by a moving person, animal, or object. *The hounds picked up*

A B C D E F G H I J K L M N O P Q R S **T** U V W X Y Z

the trail of the escaped prisoner. 3. something that trails or hangs. *There was a trail of smoke from the chimney.* {**trayl**}

trail·er *noun* 1. a wagon pulled by a car or truck and used to carry a load. 2. a vehicle that can be pulled and is used as a camper, home, or office. Many trailers have kitchens, bathrooms, bedrooms, furniture, and electricity. {**trayl** ər}

train ❓ 🔄 *noun* 1. a connected series of railroad cars. 2. a long, moving line of persons, animals, or vehicles. *The train of horses climbed the hill.* 3. a series of things or ideas. *He lost his train of thought.* 4. the long part of a gown or robe that trails behind the person wearing it. *The bridesmaids walked behind the bride, carrying the long train from her gown.* *verb* (trained, training, trains) 1. to teach skills or actions. *He trained his dog to heel.* 2. to instruct. *The chess players were trained by a master.* 3. to make fit through a program of exercise and diet. *The coach trained him for the big race.* 4. to prepare oneself to be in an athletic contest. *She trained for the Olympics.* 5. to cause to take a particular shape or form. *I can't seem to train my hair to curl.* {**trayn**}

Word History The word *train* comes from a Latin word that means "to pull or draw."

train·er *noun* a person who trains people or horses so they are strong and ready for competition. *The trainer worked with the athlete for months so she would be ready for the national soccer tournament.* {**trayn** ər}

trait *noun* a characteristic or quality that makes a person or animal different from others. *Kindness is a trait that we look for in our friends.* / *A striped coat is a trait of the tiger.* {**trayt**}

trai·tor *noun* a person who is disloyal to his or her country, his or her friends, or another group. *The traitor gave his country's military secrets to the enemy.* {**tray** tər}

tram *noun* 1. a small railroad or railroad car used for carrying loads in a mine or other small space. 2. a vehicle hung from a cable and used for carrying loads up or down steep hills or across chasms; cable car. {**trăm**}

tramp *verb* (tramped, tramping, tramps) 1. to walk with heavy steps. *We tramped through the mud.* 2. to step on with force (usually followed by "on" or "upon"). *We tramped on the ants.* 3. to walk with steady, even steps; march; hike. *We tramped through the woods and across the fields on our way home.* *noun* 1. a heavy step, or the sound made by a heavy step. *We heard the tramp of the soldiers' boots as they marched down the road.* 2. a long walk at a steady pace; march; hike. *We saw many birds on our tramp through the woods.* 3. a person who travels on foot from town to town and who lives by begging or doing odd jobs. {**trămp**}

tram·ple *verb* (trampled, trampling, tramples) 1. to step on in a heavy or noisy way; to crush with the feet; stamp (usually followed by "on," "upon," or "over"). *The clumsy dancer trampled on her partner's toes.* 2. to step on or with a heavy, noisy, crushing step. *The elephant trampled the undergrowth.* 3. to crush, destroy, or extinguish by or

as if by treading underfoot (usually followed by "out"). *The harsh discipline trampled out all his finer instincts.* *noun* the act or sound of trampling. {**trăm** pəl}

tram·po·line *noun* a sheet of strong canvas attached to a frame by springs. Trampolines are used for jumping and tumbling. {**trăm** pə **leen**}

trance *noun* a condition in which one seems to be asleep and cannot fully control movements or the mind. A trance can be caused by hypnosis or illness. {**trăns**}

tran·quil *adjective* without noise or excitement; calm; steady; peaceful. *We enjoyed a tranquil evening by the lake.* {**trăng** kwəl}

trans- *prefix* 1. a prefix that means "across" or "over." *They took a transcontinental trip, seeing much of Asia.* 2. a prefix that means "through." *Light can appear or go through glass that is transparent.* 3. a prefix that means "change." *To transform a barn into a house is to change the form of the barn to the form of a house.*

trans·ac·tion *noun* 1. the act of doing business. *My transactions at the bank took twenty minutes.* 2. a piece of business, such as a sale or trade. *I earned over a thousand dollars from that transaction.* {**trăn zăk** shən}

trans·at·lan·tic *adjective* 1. going or reaching across the Atlantic Ocean. *We took a transatlantic flight from Boston to Paris.* / *A transatlantic cable allowed people in Europe and North America to telephone each other.* 2. found on the other side of the Atlantic Ocean. *I have to attend a transatlantic business meeting.* {**trănz** ət **lăn** tihk}

trans·con·ti·nen·tal *adjective* going or reaching across a

 Human Body

Human Mind

 Everyday Life

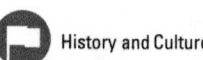 History and Culture

Communication

continent. *The transcontinental railroad joins cities that are thousands of miles apart.* {trănz kŏn tə <u>nehn</u> təl} transcontinentally, adv.

trans·fer *verb* (transferred, transferring, transfers) 1. to move or carry from one person or place to another. *I transferred my books from my locker to my backpack.* 2. to change from one bus or train to another. *In order to get home, I had to transfer at Central Station.* *noun* 1. the act of moving something from one person or place to another. *The transfer of the star player to another team disappointed fans.* 2. a ticket that lets a person change from one bus or train to another free of charge. {<u>trăns</u> fər} transferable (transferrable), adj.

trans·form *verb* (transformed, transforming, transforms) 1. to change the form, look, or shape of. *A fresh coat of paint transformed the old house.*

2. to change the nature, character, use, or condition of. *Months of hard work transformed her into an honor student.* {trăns <u>fohrm</u> or trănz <u>fohrm</u>}

trans·for·ma·tion *noun* a major change in the form, shape, character, or nature of something or someone. *We were surprised by the bird's transformation from ugly duckling to beautiful swan.* {trăns fər <u>may</u> shən or trănz fər <u>may</u> shən}

trans·fu·sion *noun* the transfer of blood from an outside source into the bloodstream of a person or animal. *People who give blood for use in trans-*

fusions are called "blood donors."* {trănz <u>fyoo</u> zhən}

tran·sis·tor 🌐 *noun* a small device used to control the flow of electric current. Transistors use very little energy. They are found in televisions, computers, and other kinds of electronic equipment. {trăn <u>zih</u> stər}

tran·sit *noun* 1. the act of passing over, across, or through; passage. *The train's swift transit across the country made for a pleasant journey.* / *We were very upset that our suitcase was lost in transit.* 2. a system for carrying people or goods by vehicle from one place to another. *Public buses, trains, and subway trains are all forms of transit.* {<u>trăn</u> siht *or* <u>trăn</u> ziht}

tran·si·tive verb *noun* a verb that has a direct object. In the sentence, "My father owns a grocery store," "owns" is a transitive verb and "store" is the direct object. {trăn sə tihv <u>vuhrb</u>}

trans·late 🌐 *verb* (translated, translating, translates) to change into the words of another language. *My mother translated the Korean story into English for me.* {trănz <u>layt</u> or trănz <u>layt</u>} translator (translater), n.

trans·la·tion *noun* 1. the act of changing writing or speech from one language to another. *The company needs people skilled in translation from Japanese to English.* 2. writing or speech that has been changed from one language to another. *After we struggled through the story in Spanish, the teacher handed out an English translation.* {trănz <u>lay</u> shən}

trans·lu·cent *adjective* letting only some light through so that what can be seen on the

other side is not clear. *Our bathroom window is made of translucent glass.* {trănz <u>looh</u> sənt}

trans·mis·sion *noun* 1. the act of transmitting or the fact of being transmitted. *Washing hands slows the transmission of disease.* 2. a system of gears that sends power from the engine to the wheels in an automobile, truck, or other vehicle. 3. the sending of radio waves; broadcast. *Transmission ends at midnight on some channels.* {trănz <u>mih</u> shən}

trans·mit *verb* (transmitted, transmitting, transmits) 1. to send or carry from one person, place, or thing to another. *Please transmit this message to the commander.* 2. to make known or send out; broadcast. *Our local TV station transmits the news every day at six o'clock.* 3. to pass on or spread. *Mosquitos transmit diseases.* {trănz <u>miht</u>} transmittable, adj.

trans·mit·ter *noun* the apparatus that makes and changes radio waves in order to send them out as radio or TV signals. *We could not watch Channel 4 because their transmitter was broken.* {<u>trănz</u> **miht** ər}

tran·som *noun* a small window above a door. A transom is often attached with a hinge so that it can be opened and shut. {<u>trăn</u> səm}

trans·par·ent *adjective* 1. letting light pass through and giving a clear view of objects on the other side. *Most glass used in windows is transparent.* 2. easily seen through; obvious. *His reasons for suddenly being friendly are transparent;*

A B C D E F G H I J K L M N O P Q R S **T** U V W X Y Z

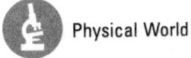 

a
b
c
d
e
f
g
h
i
j
k
l
m
n
o
p
q
r
s
t
u
v
w
x
y
z

he wants an invitation. {**tranz payr** ənt}

tran·spire *verb* (transpired, transpiring, transpires) to give off waste from a surface in the form of vapor. *When green plants transpire, water vapor passes from their leaves into the air.* {**tran spiyr**} transpiration, n.

trans·plant *verb* (transplanted, transplanting, transplants) 1. to pull up and plant again in another place. *We transplanted the rose bushes so they would get more sunlight.* 2. to remove a body organ by surgery and attach it somewhere else on the same body or on another body. *Doctors transplanted skin from the burn patient's leg to her face.* *noun* an act of transplanting. *The doctors did a heart transplant to save the patient's life.* {**tranz plant**}

trans·port *verb* (transported, transporting, transports) to carry from one place to another. *The ferry transports cars across the bay.* *noun* 1. the act of carrying or transporting. *The transport of supplies to the soldiers will require two helicopters.* 2. a means of carrying or transporting. *The subway is this city's public transport.* 3. a ship or plane used to carry soldiers and their supplies. {**trans pohrt**, n., **trans pohrt**, v.} transporter, n.

Word History *Transport* comes from the Latin words *portare*, which means "carry," and *trans*, which means "across."

trans·por·ta·tion ⊙ *noun* 1. the act of carrying or moving something. *Someone must arrange the transportation of our furniture to the new office.* 2. something that carries or transports. *A mule and a*

sports car are both forms of transportation. {**trans** pər **tay** shən or **tranz** pohr **tay** shən}

trap *noun* 1. a device for catching, holding, and often killing wild animals. 2. a trick used to catch or fool someone. *The teacher's question was a trap for those students who hadn't been paying attention.* 3. (plural) the percussion instruments in a band or orchestra; drum set. *I started playing the traps in third grade.* *verb* (trapped, trapping, traps) 1. to catch in a trap. *They trapped a mouse in the attic.* 2. to catch by fooling or tricking. *They trapped her into telling where the gift was hidden.* {**trap**}

trap·door *noun* a door that is fitted into a floor, ceiling, or roof. *Some trapdoors open and close by sliding, and others use a hinge.* {**trap dohr**}

tra·peze *noun* a rope swing with a bar hung high above the ground. *A trapeze is often used by acrobats in a circus.* {**tra peez** or trə **peez**}

trap·e·zoid *noun* a flat, closed figure with four straight sides. Of these sides, only two are parallel. *adjective* shaped like a trapezoid. {**trap** ih **zoid**}

trap·per *noun* a person who traps wild animals and sells their furs. {**trap** ər}

trash ⊙ ⊛ *noun* anything that is thrown away because it is not wanted or considered worthless; garbage; rubbish. *That old furniture is trash. / The garbage truck picked up the trash.* {**trash**}

trau·ma *noun* (traumas) 1. a wound or injury to the body. *The car accident caused serious trauma to my sister's legs.* 2. an emotional shock that has a

deep effect on one's life for a long time. *The terrible tornado caused trauma to everyone who survived it.* {**traw** mə or **trŏ** mə} traumatic, adj.

trav·el *verb* (traveled or travelled, traveling or travelling, travels) 1. to journey from place to place. *My father traveled to many countries.* 2. to journey over. *We traveled twenty miles on yesterday's bicycle trip. / We traveled the country on our vacation.* 3. to move forward in any way. *Cars travel fast on this highway.* *noun* (plural) trips or journeys. *Our travels took us through Europe and the Middle East.* {**trav** əl} traveler, n.

trawl *noun* a large net that is shaped like a cone and is dragged along the bottom of the ocean to catch fish. *verb* (trawled, trawling, trawls) to fish with a trawl net or line. *After trawling for hours, they went home without any fish.* {**trawl**}

tray *noun* 1. a flat, open piece of wood, metal, or plastic used to carry, hold, or display food, drink, or small items. It often has a low rim. 2. such a container and what it holds. *Please pass the tray of cookies.* {**tray**}

treach·er·ous *adjective* 1. betraying or likely to betray trust; false. *The king's treacherous brother betrayed him to his enemy. / Her treacherous friend told her secrets to others.* 2. full of danger or risk; not to be trusted. *They were warned not to ski the treacherous slope.* {**trehch** ər əs}

treach·er·y *noun* (treacheries) a breaking of faith or loyalty; betrayal. *The treachery of his cheating his own brother saddened their family.* {**trehch** ər ee}

 Human Body   Human Mind   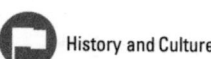 Everyday Life   History and Culture    Communication

tread *verb* (trod or treaded, trodden or trod, treading, treads) 1. to step or walk on, in, or along. *We treaded the leaves as we walked the forest path.* 2. to move on foot; step or walk. *Treading through the puddles, I soaked my shoes.* 3. to crush or press down with, or as if with, the feet. *Don't let the dog tread the flowers in your garden.* *noun* 1. the act, manner, or sound of stepping or walking. *He is a big man who walks with a heavy tread. / I heard his tread in the hall before I saw him.* 2. a surface on which one steps, such as the horizontal surface of a stair. *I fell down the stairs because my foot missed a tread.* 3. that which touches the ground in walking, such as the sole of the foot or shoe, or in rolling, such as the outer surface of a tire or the belt around the wheels of a tank. *The treads of my sneakers are filled with mud. / The tread of the tractor crushed the stones in its path.* 4. the pattern of grooves on a tire, or the depth of the grooves. *There wasn't much tread left on the tire.* {<u>trehd</u>}

• **tread water**
to keep floating in an upright position with just the head above water by moving the legs and feet as though walking. *Since I don't know how to swim, I just tread water.*

tread·mill *noun* a belt or circle of moving steps that, when walked by a person or animal, causes a wheel to turn. Treadmills are used to run machines or to give people exerise. {<u>trehd</u> mihl}

trea·son *noun* the betrayal of one's country by going to war against it or giving information to its enemies. *They*
accused him of treason when he gave the enemy information about the generals' plans. {<u>tree</u> zən}

treas·ure *noun* 1. money or valuable items that have been collected or stored up. *The king has treasures worth millions of dollars.* 2. someone or something that is greatly valued or admired. *My aunt is a treasure to me.* *verb* (treasured, treasuring, treasures) to prize or value greatly; love. *I treasure her friendship.* {<u>trehzh</u> ər}

treas·ur·er *noun* the officer of a club, business, or other organization who is responsible for taking care of the group's money. {<u>trehzh</u> ər ər}

treas·ur·y *noun* (treasuries) 1. the money of a club, business, government, or other group. *We paid for the class trip out of our treasury.* 2. (capitalized) the government department responsible for public money. *The U.S. Treasury is in charge of all the nation's public money.* {<u>trehzh</u> ər ee}

treat *verb* (treated, treating, treats) 1. to behave toward in a particular way. *My mother treats me fairly.* 2. to deal with in a particular way. *He treats the dog badly.* 3. to discuss in speech or writing. *He treated several ideas in his talk.* 4. to attempt to relieve or cure. *She treated her cold with vitamins.* 5. to buy food, drink, or entertainment for at one's own expense. *We treated them to dinner.* 6. to act upon in order to get a particular result. *He treated the wood with polish.* *noun* 1. the act of treating. *He told us that the ice cream was his treat.* 2. anything considered as a source of pleasure. *Chocolate is his favorite treat.* {<u>treet</u>}

treat·ment *noun* 1. the act of behaving in some way toward another. *His treatment of the frightened girl was gentle and caring.* 2. the way in which one behaves toward another. *I hate his mean treatment of his puppy.* 3. giving medicine or using other ways to help cure a disease or heal an injury. *A good treatment for a cold is the old one of chicken soup.* {<u>treet</u> mənt}

treat·y *noun* (treaties) a formal agreement between two or more countries. *The kings signed a treaty that ended the long war.* {<u>treet</u> ee}

tre·ble  *adjective* of, having to do with, or having the highest musical part, voice, range, or instrument. *She sang the treble part in the chorus.* *noun* the treble part or voice, or a treble instrument. *I sing the treble in my quartet.* {<u>treh</u> bəl}

tree  *noun* 1. a woody plant that has a long main trunk and many branches. Trees usually grow quite tall. 2. any object that is like a tree. *You can hang your coat on the clothes tree.* 3. a chart that shows the generations of a family. *Our family tree has five generations.* *verb* (treed, treeing, trees) to force to climb up a tree so as to avoid danger. *A big dog treed our cat.* {<u>tree</u>}

tree ring *noun* the layer of wood made by a tree during a single year; annual ring. It is possible to figure out the age of a tree that has fallen or has been cut down by counting its rings. {<u>tree</u> ring}

trek *verb* (trekked, trekking, treks) to travel or make one's way slowly and with difficulty. *The brave settlers trekked across the western plains.* *noun* a slow or difficult

 Living World   Physical World    Natural Environment    Economy   Government and Law

trip. *Their long trek through the mountains was cold and scary.* {**trehk**} trekker, n.

Word History *Trek* is a word from Afrikaans, the language of the Dutch settlers in South Africa. It meant "to journey or migrate by wagon." This word entered the English language in the mid-1800s. Throughout the 1800s, the British and Dutch struggled for control of South Africa.

trem·ble *verb* (trembled, trembling, trembles) 1. to shake from fear, weakness, or cold. *The little boy trembled when he heard the thunder. / I trembled in the icy wind.* 2. to be shaky. *The trees trembled in the strong wind. / The bride's voice trembled when she said, "I do."* {**trehm** bəl}

tre·men·dous *adjective* 1. very large in degree or size; huge. *A tremendous crowd came to the sale.* 2. excellent; superb. *The young actors did a tremendous job in the play.* {trə **mehn** dəs} tremendously, adv.

Word History *Tremendous* comes from a Latin word that means "to be trembled at."

trem·or ⊕ ⊕ *noun* 1. a shaking or trembling. *I felt tremors of fear when I heard that she was lost.* 2. a shaking caused by an earthquake. *The tremors from the earthquake were felt for miles.* {**trehm** ər}

trench *noun* 1. a deep, narrow ditch. *We dug a trench for a pipe from the gas tank to the house.* 2. a ditch that is packed on one side with the dirt dug from it, used as shelter and a place of protection from enemy fire. *The trench saved the soldiers from the enemy's bullets.* {**trehnch**}

trend *noun* 1. a general course, direction, or tendency. *One*

bad trend is that many young people do not vote. 2. the latest style. *Short skirts are the trend this year.* {**trehnd**}

tres·pass *noun* 1. an act of entering the property of another without permission, which is against the law. *His trespass of the property cost him a fine of one hundred dollars.* 2. a sin. *Stealing is a trespass against the rules of society.* *verb* (trespassed, trespassing, trespasses) to enter upon the property of another without permission. *In our rush to get home, we trespassed into the farmer's field.* {**trehs pǎs** or **trehs** pəs, n., **trehs pǎs** or **trehs** pəs, v.} trespasser, n.

tres·tle *noun* a framework that holds up a bridge or other structure. {**treh** səl}

tri- *prefix* a prefix that means "three." *A triangle has three angles and three sides.*

tri·al ⊕ ⊕ *noun* 1. the act of hearing a case in court to decide whether or not a person has broken a particular law. *She proved at her trial that she had not robbed the bank.* 2. the act or process of testing. *The trial of the new soft drink showed that most people liked it.* 3. suffering, pain, or hardship. *She has had many trials in her life.* *adjective* 1. of or relating to a trial. *The trial records run over one thousand pages.* 2. done by way of a trial or experiment. *The trial run of the new magazine showed that it would be popular.* {**triy** əl}

tri·an·gle *noun* 1. a flat, closed figure that has three straight sides. 2. something that looks like a triangle. One type of triangle is a musical instrument made of a bent metal rod that is struck by another rod

to make a sound like a bell. {**triy** ǎng gəl}

Word History *Triangle* comes from *triangulus*, a Latin word that means "having three angles or corners."

tri·an·gu·lar *adjective* of or shaped like a triangle. *We moved the sofa and chairs into a triangular pattern.* {**triy** ǎng gyə lər}

trib·al *adjective* of or relating to a group of people having the same ancestors, customs, and other characteristics. *The museum had a show of tribal costumes from local Native Americans.* {**triy** bəl}

tribe *noun* a group of people, families, or villages that share the same language, social customs, and ancestors. *She left her tribe to go explore the world.* {**triyb**}

trib·u·tar·y ⊕ *noun* (tributaries) a river or stream that flows into a larger river or stream, or into a lake. {**trihb** yoo **tayr** ee}

trib·ute *noun* something given, done, or said to express respect or thanks. *Her former students held a dinner as a tribute to their favorite teacher.* {**trihb** yoot}

trick *noun* 1. something done to fool or cheat someone. *His lie was a trick to get my money.* 2. a joke or prank. *My brother has played many tricks on me.* 3. an act of skill or magic. *He taught his monkey a new trick. / The gymnast did tricks on the high bar.* *adjective* 1. of or marked by deception or skill. *The football team used a trick play to score the goal.* 2. made for use in tricks. *The magician had a trick deck of cards.* *verb* (tricked, tricking, tricks) to cheat or fool someone. *They tricked me into paying twice what this dress is worth.* {**trihk**}

 Human Body  Human Mind 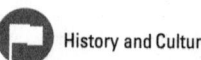 Everyday Life  History and Culture ⊕ Communication

trick or treat *noun* an activity practiced at Halloween when children visit their neighbors and say, "trick or treat!" in order to receive a treat such as candy. {**trihk** ər **treet**}

trick·le *verb* (trickled, trickling, trickles) 1. to fall or flow in drops or in a thin, weak stream. *Juice trickled down the baby's chin.* 2. to go or come slowly, or in small numbers. *Viewers trickled through the museum.* *noun* a thin, weak flow. *Lack of rain reduced the creek to a trickle.* {**trihk** əl}

trick·y *adjective* (trickier, trickiest) 1. using or marked by tricks or lies. *It is hard to trust a tricky person.* 2. needing skill or care; difficult. *We worked hard to solve the tricky problem.* {**trih** kee} trickiness, n.

tri·fle *noun* something that has very little value or importance. *His anger seemed wasted on trifles.* *verb* (trifled, trifling, trifles) to treat something or someone lightly, without proper respect or care (usually followed by "with"). *Don't trifle with a loaded gun.* / *He was angry at her for trifling with his feelings.* {**triy** fəl}

• **a trifle**
a little bit; somewhat; slightly. *He was a trifle jealous.*

trig·ger *noun* a small lever that when pressed or pulled causes a gun to fire. *verb* (triggered, triggering, triggers) to cause, begin, or set off. *The little girl's accident triggered the kindness of strangers.* {**trihg** ər}

trill ❷ *noun* 1. a trembling or quivering sound made by a singing voice or a musical instrument. *The singer's trill was so high that her voice broke a glass.* 2. a trembling or quivering sound made by a bird or insect. *I awoke to the trill of birds.* / *We heard the trill of insects all around the porch.* *verb* (trilled, trilling, trills) to sing, play, or speak with a trembling or quivering sound. *The singer trilled the last note of the song.* {**trihl**}

tril·lion *noun* (trillions [or] trillion) 1. the number that is equal to one thousand times one billion; 1,000,000,000,000. 2. a very large number that is not named exactly. *I have a trillion of these little things to take care of today.* *adjective* 1. being one trillion in number. *It will take over a trillion dollars to pay off our national debt.* 2. being a very large number that is not named exactly. *There must be a trillion grains of sand on this beach.* {**trihl** yən} trillionth, adj., n.

trim *verb* (trimmed, trimming, trims) 1. to make neat or orderly by cutting or clipping away some parts. *I trimmed my bangs, which had been hanging over my eyes.* / *He trimmed the bushes so they were all the same height.* 2. to remove by or as if by cutting. *He trimmed the ripped edges of the wrapping paper.* 3. to decorate. *Our family trimmed the tree on Christmas Eve.* *noun* 1. a fit or ready condition for work or use. *Since he exercises, he is in fine trim.* 2. material added to decorate the edges of clothing, windows and doorways, or automobiles. *I added lace trim to my dress.* / *The red house had white trim around the windows.* 3. an act or instance of trimming hair. *The barber gave him a quick trim.* *adjective* (trimmer, trimmest) 1. having a neat, orderly appearance. *I cleaned my room so that it looks neat and trim.* 2. in good condition; fit. *Her figure is trim thanks to her daily swim.* {**trihm**} trimmer, n.

tri·o ❷ *noun* (trios) 1. a group of three people who sing or play musical instruments together. 2. a piece of music written for either of these groups. 3. a group of three persons or things. *There was a trio of kittens in the basket.* {**tree** oh}

trip *noun* 1. the act of traveling; a journey. *They made a trip to New York.* 2. a short journey from one point to another. *I made two trips to the store today.* *verb* (tripped, tripping, trips) 1. to stumble. *I tripped over a log while I was walking in the forest.* 2. to cause to fall or stumble. *The mean girl tripped her friend by sticking her foot in his path.* 3. to cause to fail (often followed by "up"). *She was doing fine on the math exam until the fractions tripped her up.* {**trihp**}

tri·ple *adjective* 1. three times as much; three times as many. *The price of new cars is triple what it was twenty years ago.* 2. having three parts. *Our bay window has a triple design, with three separate windows.* *noun* 1. an amount or number three times as great as another. *I increased the recipe amounts by triple for my dinner party.* 2. a hit in baseball that allows the batter to advance to third base. *He's hit a triple in each of our last three games.* *verb* (tripled, tripling, triples) 1. to increase to three times the size or amount. *That store has tripled*

A
B
C
D
E
F
G
H
I
J
K
L
M
N
O
P
Q
R
S
T
U
V
W
X
Y
Z

a
b
c
d
e
f
g
h
i
j
k
l
m
n
o
p
q
r
s
t
u
v
w
x
y
z

its sales from five years ago. 2. to become three times as many or as great. *The city's population tripled in less than twenty years.* 3. to hit the ball far enough for the batter to advance to third base in baseball. *She tripled in the ninth inning and drove in two runs.* {trihp əl}

tri·plet *noun* one of three children or animals born at a single birth. *The triplets all grew up to look exactly the same.* {trihp liht}

tri·pod *noun* a stand with three legs used to support a camera or telescope. {triv pŏd}

tri·umph *noun* 1. the winning of a great victory or success. *The nation's final triumph ended the long years of war.* / *Her first novel was a triumph that she'd worked hard for.* 2. the sense of joy that comes from such a victory. *His triumph was heard in the tone of his voice.* *verb* (triumphed, triumphing, triumphs) 1. to win a great victory or success. *She triumphed in her race for mayor.* 2. to win against something or overcome difficulties. *She triumphed over her unhappy childhood.* {triv uhmf}

triv·i·al *adjective* not valuable or important; insignificant. *The clerk was tired of hearing the many trivial complaints.* {trihv ee əl}

troll¹ *verb* (trolled, trolling, trolls) 1. to trail behind a slowly moving boat. *We trolled shiny lures for a long time before we caught a fish big enough to keep.* 2. to try to catch by using a line trailed behind a boat. *The fisherman on television trolled bass all afternoon.* {trohl}

troll² *noun* an ugly dwarf or giant that lives in a cave or under a bridge in Scandinavian folk stories. {trohl}

trol·ley *noun* (trolleys) 1. a street vehicle that uses electricity from a track or overhead wires to move. 2. a pulley wheel held against or traveling on a track or overhead wire. Trolleys conduct electricity from the wire to a vehicle on a track. {trŏl ee}

trom·bone *noun* a brass wind instrument. The trombone is a long tube bent in two loops that ends in a bell shape. It is played with valves or a slide that moves to change tones. {trŏm bohn *or* trŏm bohn}

troop ⊘ ⊙ *noun* 1. a group or gathering of people, animals, or things. *A troop of workers crossed the road.* 2. (plural) soldiers. *We sent thousands of troops to war.* *verb* (trooped, trooping, troops) 1. to join together or assemble in a crowd. *We trooped into groups of five hundred and protested on every street corner.* 2. to travel in a group or throng. *The baboons trooped into the forest and climbed the trees.* {troohp}

troop·er *noun* 1. a soldier who rides a horse. 2. a state police officer. {trooh pər}

tro·phy *noun* (trophies) something given to recognize a win or other accomplishment; award. *The winner of the essay contest took home a gold trophy.* {troh fee}

Word History Why is a *trophy* a sign of victory? The word "trophy" comes from an ancient Greek word, *trope*, which means "to turn." From this word, came another Greek word, *tropaion*, the name for any monument built where an enemy had been turned back in battle.

trop·i·cal *adjective* of, having to do with, characteristic of, or happening near the equator. *The tropical weather made him sweat.* {trŏp ih kəl}

trot *verb* (trotted, trotting, trots) 1. to travel quickly by moving the left front leg at the same time as the right back leg and the right front leg at the same time as the left back leg. *The horse trotted around the pasture.* 2. to go at a pace between a walk and a run; jog. *The toddler trotted in front of his grandfather into the park.* *noun* 1. the gait of an animal with four legs in which the left front leg moves at the same time as the right hind leg, and the right front leg moves at the same time as the left back leg. *The horse's trot was very smooth and efficient.* 2. any gait between a walk and a run; brisk or jogging pace. *That athlete's awkward trot shows that she has a sore ankle.* {trŏt}

trou·ble *verb* (troubled, troubling, troubles) 1. to disturb or worry. *What is troubling you?* 2. to bother. *It troubles me when you don't do your homework.* 3. to cause to do extra work. *May I trouble you to get my coat?* 4. to take great effort or pains. *He troubled over the speech for weeks.* *noun* 1. a state of being disturbed or in need. *The drowning man was in serious trouble.* 2. a source of difficulty or distress. *Her husband has always been trouble.* 3. effort; work. *It is no trouble at all to feed the cat.* {truhb əl}

trou·sers *plural noun* a garment for the lower parts of the body from waist to ankle that covers each leg; pants; slacks. {trow zərz}

⊙ Human Body   ⊙ Human Mind   ⊙ Everyday Life   ⊙ History and Culture   ⊙ Communication

trout *noun* (trout or trouts) a fish that usually lives in fresh water. Some sea trout live in the ocean but lay eggs in fresh water. Trout are related to salmon, have spots on their bodies, and are caught for food or sport. {**trowt**}

trow·el *noun* 1. any hand tool that has a flat blade. Trowels are used to work with plaster and cement. 2. a hand tool with a broad, curved blade used for digging dirt in a garden. {**trow** əl *or* **trowl**}

tru·ant *noun* a person who is absent from school without permission. *adjective* absent from school without permission. *The truant student failed all of her exams.* {**trooh** ənt} truancy, n.

truce ⬤ *noun* a stop or end of war that is agreed upon by all groups that participate; armistice. *The leaders of the world signed a truce to end the war.* {**troohs**}

truck ⬤ *noun* a large motor vehicle used for carrying heavy loads. *verb* (trucked, trucking, trucks) to carry by truck. *He trucks oranges from Florida to New York.* {**truhk**}

trudge *verb* (trudged, trudging, trudges) to walk in a heavy way with much effort or weariness. *The tired mountaineer trudged to the base camp. noun* a long, tiring walk. *It was a long trudge home after losing the game.* {**truhj**}

true *adjective* (truer, truest) 1. in agreement with fact. *The jury had to decide if they believed that the witness had made a true statement.* 2. real or genuine. *I've always wanted to own a true diamond.* 3. faithful; loyal. *You are a true friend because you've always*

been there for me. 4. legitimate or according to law. *I will become the true owner of his estate. adverb* (truer, truest) exactly. *The judge always stayed true to the constitution.* {**trooh**}

trum·pet ⬤ *noun* 1. a brass wind instrument. Trumpets have three valves on a looped tube that ends in a bell shape. Trumpets produce bright, strong, piercing tones. 2. a loud, piercing sound or call, especially that made by an elephant. *verb* (trumpeted, trumpeting, trumpets) to make a trumpetlike sound or call. *The elephant trumpeted at the trespassing baboon.* {**truhm** piht}

trunk ⬤ ⬤ *noun* 1. the main stem of a tree. *There was a sign nailed to the trunk of the tree.* 2. the body of a human or animal, not including the head, neck, arms, and legs. *He waded into the water up to his trunk.* 3. a large, strong container, often with a lock, used to store or transport goods; chest. *She brought her trunk into her new room and unpacked it.* 4. a large compartment in the rear of an automobile used to store items such as packages and tools. *He took the spare tire out of the trunk.* 5. the long snout of an elephant. 6. (plural) a pair of short pants worn in sports such as track, men's swimming, and boxing. *The boxer in the red trunks was winning the fight.* {**trungk**}

trust ⬤ *noun* 1. a belief in the strength or truth of a person or thing. *You have earned my trust because you are always honest.* 2. the charge or care

of a person or thing. *They left the child in the trust of his grandmother.* 3. property managed by one person for the benefit of another. *His parents set up a trust of two thousand dollars that he can have when he turns eighteen. verb* (trusted, trusting, trusts) 1. to rely upon; depend on (usually followed by "in" or "to"). *We trusted in the old bridge to get us safely across the river.* 2. to place confidence in. *I trust your opinion.* 3. to believe. *I trust his word.* 4. to place in the care of. *She trusted her car to her brother while she was away.* 5. to hope. *He trusted that next year would bring better luck.* {**truhst**}

truth *noun* 1. agreement with the facts or what is real. *There is no truth to the claim that the earth is flat.* 2. the state or condition of being true. *The truth of the matter is that he never did the work he was supposed to.* 3. a fact or principle that has been proved. *It is a truth that this world is round and not flat.* 4. what is sincere; honesty. *There was no truth in what he said.* {**troohth**}

truth·ful *adjective* 1. likely to stay with the truth; habitually honest. *A truthful child will not lie even to benefit himself.* 2. keeping to what is real or true. *The reporter gave us a truthful account of the incident.* {**troohth** fəl} truthfully, adv.

try *verb* (tried, trying, tries) 1. to attempt through effort. *She tried fixing the car herself to save money.* 2. to make an effort. *You didn't win, but you tried.* 3. to test the quality or take a taste of. *She tried our apple pie.* 4. to be a hard test for. *The long wait tried his*

A
B
C
D
E
F
G
H
I
J
K
L
M
N
O
P
Q
R
S
T
U
V
W
X
Y
Z

patience. 5. in law, to put on trial. *They tried him for murder.* *noun* (tries) an effort or attempt. *It was a good try, but he did not win the race.* {**triy**}

• **try on**
to put on clothing to see if it pleases or fits. *She tried on four dresses before making a choice.*

• **try out**
1. to compete for a position, as for a job, play, or sport. *She tried out for a part in the play.* 2. to test. *I tried out the bike and bought it.*

tsar *noun* another spelling of **czar.** {**zar** or **tsar**}

T-shirt ⊙ or **tee shirt** *noun* 1. a soft collarless shirt with short sleeves that is often worn under another shirt. 2. a similar outer shirt, often with designs or messages. {**tee shuhrt**}

tsp. *abbreviation* an abbreviation for **teaspoon** or teaspoons.

tub *noun* 1. a large, round container with a flat bottom used for washing, packing, or storing. 2. a bathtub. {**tuhb**}

tu·ba *noun* a large, brass wind instrument with a wide bell that produces deep, full tones. {**tooh** bə}

tube *noun* 1. a long, hollow piece of glass, metal, or rubber used to hold or carry liquids or gases. 2. anything shaped like such a tube. *Long tubes carry heat to all the rooms in the house.* 3. a small, soft container that is sealed at one end and closed with a cap on the other end. The contents of such a tube are removed by squeezing. *This tube of toothpaste is almost empty.* {**toohb**}

tu·ber *noun* an underground stem

that is short, thick, and round. New stems that grow above the ground can grow from buds on tubers. Potatoes are tubers. {**tooh** bər}

tuck *verb* (tucked, tucking, tucks) 1. to gather up and push in or turn under the loose end or edge of so as to secure (often followed by "in" or "up"). *She always tucks in her shirt.* 2. to place in a snug or secure spot. *She tucked the list into her pocket.* 3. to cover with blankets in a snug way. *It's time to tuck the children into bed.* 4. to pull or gather up into or as if into a fold or folds (usually followed by "in" or "up"). *We tucked in the pleats.* *noun* 1. something that has been folded or tucked. *She placed the pillows over the tuck of the sheet.* 2. a flat fold or pleat sewed in place in a garment. *She sewed a tuck into her skirt for a closer fit.* {**tuhk**}

Tues. or **Tu.** or **Tue.** *abbreviation* an abbreviation for **Tuesday.**

Tues·day *noun* the third day of the week. Tuesday comes between Monday and Wednesday. {**toohz** day or **toohz** dee}

Word History *Tuesday* was "Tiw's day" in early English. *Tiw* was an English name for the Roman god of war.

tuft *noun* a group or clump of long strands that are attached at one end and loose at the other. Yarn, hair, and grass are some strands that can form tufts. *The barber started by cutting several large tufts of hair.* {**tuhft**}

tug *verb* (tugged, tugging, tugs) to pull at in a strong way. *The child tugged her mother's skirt to get her attention.* *noun* 1. a strong pull or pulling force.

The tug of the ocean current was too strong to go swimming safely. 2. a tugboat. *A tug came to guide the big ship into port.* {**tuhg**}

tug·boat *noun* a small, powerful boat used to guide, push, or pull larger ships into and out of harbors. {**tuhg** boht}

tu·i·tion *noun* 1. the charge for being taught at a college or private school. *We pay tuition every semester.* 2. instruction or teaching at a college or private school. *I am under tuition at the local community college.* {**tooh** **ih** shən}

tu·lip *noun* 1. a plant that grows from a bulb. Tulips have large leaves shaped like lances and flowers that are shaped like cups. 2. the flower or bulb of this plant. Tulips come in many colors. {**tooh** lihp}

tum·ble *verb* (tumbled, tumbling, tumbles) 1. to roll end over end while falling or while in flight. *The puppies tumbled over each other. / The airplane tumbled out of control.* 2. to perform somersaults, rolls, leaps, and other acrobatic exercises or stunts. *The cheerleader tumbled across the gym.* *noun* 1. an act or instance of falling or tumbling; fall. *He broke his wrist in the tumble.* 2. an acrobatic exercise or stunt. *The next tumble in the routine makes the gymnast look as if she's defying gravity.* 3. a disorderly, confused, or not organized state or collection. *I need to clean up the tumble in this room.* {**tuhm** bəl}

tum·ble·weed *noun* a plant whose rounded, branched tops break off in autumn and are rolled about by the wind. {**tuhm** bəl weed}

 Human Body
 Human Mind
 Everyday Life
 History and Culture
Communication

tu·mor *noun* a mass of extra tissue that grows in or on the body. Some tumors are harmful. {**tooh** mər}

tu·na *noun* (tuna or tunas) 1. a large fish that lives in the ocean. Tuna are used for food. 2. the flesh of this fish, often canned. {**tooh** nə}

tun·dra 🌿 *noun* one of the huge plains in the arctic regions of North America, Europe, and Asia. Trees do not grow on tundras. {**tuhn** drə}

tune 🎵 *noun* 1. a specific series of pleasing musical tones; melody. *He played a tune on the piano.* 2. the correct musical pitch. *She cannot sing in tune.* 3. the state of being made to have the proper musical pitch. *Is the piano in tune?* 4. agreement or harmony. *Her clothes are out of tune with the times.* *verb* (tuned, tuning, tunes) to adjust a musical instrument so that it has proper musical pitch. *He tuned his guitar.* {**toohn**}

• **sing a different tune** to change one's opinion or behavior. *He was singing a different tune about his sister after she helped him pass his exam.*

• **tune in** to adjust to receive TV or radio signals from a certain station, or to select from a number of programs. *He tuned in the baseball game.*

• **tune out** (informal) to break away from or ignore. *He read the newspaper, tuning out the noise from the TV.*

tu·nic *noun* 1. an article of clothing that is loose and hangs to the knees. Tunics sometimes do not have sleeves and are sometimes belted. The ancient Greeks and Romans wore tunics. 2. a short coat with a stiff high collar, worn as part of a uniform by soldiers or the like. {**tooh** nihk}

tuning fork *noun* a small metal device that produces a tone in perfect pitch when it is struck against something. Tuning forks are often used to tune musical instruments or test hearing. {**toohn** ing **fohrk**}

tun·nel *noun* 1. an underground or underwater passage used by cars, trains, or other vehicles. *We get to the city by going through a tunnel under the river.* 2. the hole or den of a burrowing animal. *verb* (tunneled, tunneling, tunnels) 1. to hollow out under or through something. *A mole tunneled a den for her babies to live in.* 2. to construct a tunnel or tunnels. *A rabbit has been tunneling in our garden.* {**tuhn** əl}

tur·ban *noun* a man's head covering worn by Sikhs and Muslims. A turban is a long piece of cloth that is wrapped several times around the head. {**tuhr** bən}

turf *noun* the surface layer of the soil that is held together in a thick mat by grass and other plant roots. {**tuhrf**} turfless, adj., turflike, adj.

tur·key *noun* (turkeys) 1. a large North American bird with brownish feathers and a bare head with fleshy folds of skin hanging under the jaw. Turkeys are now raised in many parts of the world. 2. the flesh of this bird, used as food. *We always have turkey on Thanksgiving.* 3. (slang) a foolish person. *My brother calls me a turkey when I act silly.* {**tuhr** kee}

Tur·key *noun* a country in western Asia and southeastern Europe between the Mediterranean and Black Seas. Ankara is the capital of Turkey. {**tuhr** kee}

Turk·ish *adjective* of or having to do with Turkey, or its people or language. *noun* the language of Turkey. {**tuhrk** ihsh}

tur·moil *noun* a state of great confusion or axiety; commotion. *The assassination of the ruler sent the world into the turmoil of sudden war.* {**tuhr** moil}

turn *verb* (turned, turning, turns) 1. to cause to move around a center point. *Turn the key in the lock to open the door.* 2. to cause to shift from one side to the other by moving in a circle. *She turned the plant toward the sun.* 3. to change the course or direction of. *Turn the car left.* 4. to change the position of by moving in a circle or by moving in reverse. *He turned his desk toward the window.* 5. to change the nature, character, or color of. *The change of season turned the leaves many colors.* 6. to cause to feel sick. *That scary movie turned my stomach.* 7. to direct toward. *After music she turned her attention to art.* 8. to send out, let go, or drive away. *He turned the cat out on the street.* 9. to cause to have a bad feeling about. *He turned the dog against me.* 10. to make into a greater amount. *He turned a penny into a dollar.* 11. to make sour or ferment. *Warm weather turned the milk.* 12. to change one's feelings. *He*

A
B
C
D
E
F
G
H
I
J
K
L
M
N
O
P
Q
R
S
T
U
V
W
X
Y
Z

turned away from his friends. 13. to seek help or support from (followed by "to"). *In times of trouble, he turns to me.* *noun* 1. the act of turning. *He made a left turn at the corner.* 2. a change of direction, position, or condition. *The truck made the turn at a slow speed. / My life has been taking a turn for the better.* 3. a complete revolution of a wheel or other round object. *Tighten the screw by giving it a few clockwise turns.* 4. an angle, bend, or curve. *There are many turns in the path.* 5. a point in time that marks the beginning of a new or different period. *We had a party to celebrate the turn of the century.* 6. an action or service that is given. *She did him a good turn.* 7. a chance for an action to be done in a certain order. *It is your turn to do the dishes.* 8. a short trip or tour. *We took a turn down the street.* {**tuhrn**}

• **out of turn**
not in correct order. *He got into line out of turn.*

• **take turns**
to do one after the other, in order. *We'll take turns on the bicycle.*

Word History *Turn* comes from *tornare*, which means "to turn on a lathe." This Latin word comes from *tornos*, an ancient Greek word that meant "tool for drawing circles."

tur·nip *noun* 1. a plant that is safe to eat and that has a large white root and hairy leaves that are sometimes used as greens. 2. the root of this plant. Turnips are eaten as vegetables. {**tuhr** nihp}

turn·pike *noun* a highway on which drivers are charged a toll. {**tuhrn** piyk}

Word History In the 1400s, a *turnpike* was a spiked barrier built across a road to prevent passage. By the 1700s, "turnpike" meant a road with toll gates.

turn·stile *noun* a device with rotating arms that allows people to pass through one at a time. Turnstiles control movement from one area to another. {**tuhrn** stiyl}

turn·ta·ble *noun* 1. the round plate that holds and rotates the record on a record player. 2. any other rotating plate or platform. *The chef keeps the spices on a turntable so he can reach any of them quickly and easily.* {**tuhrn** tay bəl}

tur·pen·tine *noun* 1. a mixture of oil and resin from certain pines and other related trees. 2. a thin oil made from this mixture and used as a paint thinner or to dissolve other substances. *I used turpentine to get the tar off my skin.* {**tuhr** pihn tiyn}

tur·quoise *noun* 1. a blue or bluish green mineral that is cut and polished for use in jewelry. 2. a bright blue or bluish green color. {**tuhr** koiz *or* **tuhr** kwoiz}

tur·ret *noun* 1. a small tower on a larger building such as a castle. 2. a low, steel structure that carries mounted guns on a tank, plane, or warship. Turrets can be rotated. {**tuhr** iht *or* **toohr** iht}

tur·tle *noun* a reptile with a soft body covered by a hard shell that lives in water or on land. A turtle pulls its head, legs, and tail into its shell for protection. {**tuhr** təl}

tur·tle·neck *noun* 1. a high, snug collar that folds down. Some sweaters have turtlenecks. 2. a sweater or knit shirt with such a collar. {**tuhr** təl nehk}

tusk ❶ *noun* a long, large, pointed tooth that sticks out from the mouth of some animals. Tusks grow in pairs and may be used to find food or fight. Elephants, walruses, and wild boars have tusks. {**tuhsk**} tusked, adj.

tu·tor *noun* a person who gives private instruction to a student. *The tutor comes twice per week to help my son with math.* *verb* (tutored, tutoring, tutors) to teach or instruct individually. *I tutor him in English to make some extra money.* {**tooh** tər}

TV *abbreviation* an abbreviation for **television.**

'twas shortened form of "it was." *'Twas a dark and stormy night.* {**twuhz**}

tweed *noun* a rough, wool cloth woven with at least two colors. Tweed is used to make coats and suits. {**tweed**}

tweez·ers *plural noun* a small metal tool that has two arms, used for picking up or plucking out small objects such as hairs or splinters. {**twee** zərz}

twelfth *adjective* coming next after the eleventh in a series. *The twelfth month of the year is December.* *noun* 1. one of twelve equal parts of a whole; 1/12. *I live only a twelfth of a mile from you!* 2. the number, person, or thing that comes next after the eleventh in a series. My

 Human Body   Human Mind   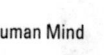 Everyday Life    History and Culture   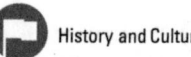 Communication

birthday is on the twelfth of this month. {**twehlfth**}

twelve *noun* the number that comes after eleven and before thirteen in the sequence of cardinal numbers; 12. *adjective* being twelve in number. *There are twelve months in a year.* {**twehlv**}

twen·ti·eth *adjective* coming next after the nineteenth in a series. *The twentieth anniversary of my parents' wedding was a happy event. noun* 1. one of twenty equal parts of a whole; 1/20. *One twentieth of their income goes to charity.* 2. the number, person, or thing that comes next after the nineteenth in a series. *The twentieth was the happiest year of their marriage.* {**twehn** tee ihth}

twen·ty *noun* (twenties) the number that is equal to two times ten; 20. *adjective* being twenty in number. *I gave him twenty dollars for a new pair of jeans.* {**twehn** tee}

twice *adverb* 1. two times; in two instances. *I called her twice.* 2. two times as much. *There are twice the number of people here today.* {**twiys**}

twig *noun* a small branch of a tree or shrub. {**twihg**}

Word History *Twig* comes from an Old English word that means "something divided in two."

twi·light *noun* 1. the faint light in the sky when the sun is below the horizon before sunrise and after sunset. *She could not see who I was in the twilight.* 2. the period of time in which the sky is illuminated in this way. *They planned to set up camp before twilight, but the hike took longer than they expected.* {**twiy** liyt}

twin *noun* 1. either of two children or animals born at the same time to one mother. 2. one of two people or things that are identical or closely resemble each other. *This vase is a twin of the lamp. adjective* 1. being a pair or one of a pair of people or animals born at the same birth. *It was hard to distinguish between the identical twin boys.* 2. being two or one of two persons, animals, or things that are identical or very similar to one another. *I bought a pair of twin lamps for the living room.* {**twihn**}

twine *noun* sturdy string that is made by twisting two or more strands together. *The machine tied hay with twine. verb* (twined, twining, twines) 1. to twist or wind together. *We twined the cords together to keep them from tangling.* 2. to twist, coil, or wrap around. *Ivy was twining the post.* 3. to be or become coiled or twisted (often followed by "around"). *The plant twines around the trunk of a tree as it climbs.* {**twiyn**}

twinge *noun* 1. a sudden, sharp pain that does not last long. *You will feel a twinge when the nurse inserts the needle.* 2. a slight emotional pain; pang. *She felt a twinge of remorse when she thought about her mean comment.* {**twihnj**}

twin·kle *verb* (twinkled, twinkling, twinkles) 1. to shine with a light that flickers or is not steady. *Stars may look like they twinkle, but that is an illusion.* 2. to be bright or shine with enjoyment or amusement. *Her eyes twinkled when she laughed. noun* 1. a short gleam of light; flicker. *I saw the twinkle of the lights from*

the far-off city. 2. a look of amusement or delight in the eyes. *That twinkle in his eye always lets me know when he's joking.* {**twing** kəl}

twirl *verb* (twirled, twirling, twirls) 1. to cause to spin or revolve quickly; rotate. *He twirled the drumstick in the air.* 2. to wrap or wind around something. *The children like to twirl spaghetti around their forks.* 3. to spin or rotate quickly. *The dancers twirled around the floor.* {**twuhrl**} twirler, n.

twist *verb* (twisted, twisting, twists) 1.to combine by winding together in order to make a single thread. *Machines twist wires together to make cable.* 2. to become or be twined together. *The stems twisted until we couldn't tell which plant was which.* 3. to wind, coil, or weave around something else. *I twisted my hair around my finger.* 4. to wind or wrap. *The ivy twisted around the drain pipe.* 5. to make into a coil or spiral. *Flora twisted her hair into a bun.* 6. to operate by turning. *She twisted the door handle and entered the room.* 7. to turn in order to face another direction. *The mountain road twisted and turned. / I twisted to the left and saw you standing there.* 8. to change the shape of; disfigure. *Grief twisted her face.* 9. to change shape or form as the result of having been twisted. *The tree branches twisted into knots.* 10. to change the meaning of. *You twisted my words.* 11. to wrench or sprain. *I twisted my ankle.* 12. to squirm. *His body twisted in pain. noun* 1. some-

 Living World   Physical World    Natural Environment   Economy    Government and Law

A
B
C
D
E
F
G
H
I
J
K
L
M
N
O
P
Q
R
S
T
U
V
W
X
Y
Z

thing twisted, curled, or made into a spiral, such as citrus peel, hair, or yarn. 2. the act or process of twisting. *She gave the lid a twist.* 3. a wrench or sprain of a muscle. *This twist will need some time to heal.* 4. a sudden or not expected change in an otherwise predictable or even pattern. *The movie has a twist at the end.* 5. a negative change of something. *We couldn't believe his twist of events.* {**twihst**}

• **twist someone's arm** to use force or persuasion to cause some action. *I'll go to dinner, but only because you twisted my arm.*

twist·er *noun* (informal) a tornado or cyclone; whirlwind. {**twihst** ər}

twitch *verb* (twitched, twitching, twitches) 1. to move or pull with a quick, sudden motion; jerk. *He was twitching his head from side to side. / Someone twitched the sleeve of my jacket.* 2. to move with a sudden, often repeated jerking motion. *Her left eye twitches when she doesn't get enough sleep. noun* an involuntary, jerky movement of a body part, or a condition marked by such movements. *The twitch in his leg annoyed him.* {**twihch**}

twit·ter *verb* (twittered, twittering, twitters) 1. to make a series of short, light sounds like a small bird; chirp. *The little birds twittered in the trees.* 2. to tremble or quiver from excitement or nervousness. *He twittered around in the kitchen before the important guests arrived. noun* 1. the light chirping of a bird or birds. *We could hear the twitter of finches in the park.* 2. an anxious or agitated state. *The*

pianist was in a twitter before taking the stage. {**twih** tər}

two *noun* the number that comes after one and before three in the sequence of cardinal numbers; 2. *adjective* being two in number. *I'd like two pieces of cake please.* {**tooh**}

Homophone Note The words **two**, **to**, and **too** all sound alike but have different meanings.

TX or **Tex.** *abbreviation* an abbreviation for **Texas.**

ty·coon *noun* a rich, powerful person in business or industry. *The tycoon owns all of the city's television stations.* {**tiy koohn**}

type *noun* 1. a group of things that share certain features or properties that set the group apart from others; kind. *Whole wheat is the only type of bread that she will eat. / That type of dog has pointed ears.* 2. an example of a kind of plant or animal. *That tree was a good type for us to study.* 3. a block with raised letters or figures used in printing. *In the old days, people made and set type by hand to print books. verb* (typed, typing, types) 1. to write using a typewriter or computer. *I typed my report so that it would be neat and easy to read.* 2. to put into a group or class. *He typed the bones according to size.* {**tiyp**}

type·writ·er *noun* a machine that produces type similar to that of print. Keys are pressed with the fingers to activate letters, numbers, or characters. {**tiyp** riyt ər}

ty·phoon *noun* a hurricane that occurs in the western Pacific

area and the China Sea. {**tiy foohn**}

Word History *Typhoon* is the English form of a Chinese word that means "a great wind."

typ·i·cal *adjective* having the distinctive qualities of a particular type of person or thing. *A typical baby walks at about one year old.* {**tihp** ih kəl} typically, adv.

tyr·an·ny ❓ 💬 *noun* (tyrannies) 1. a government in which a single person rules absolutely and in a cruel way. *Tyranny has caused much unhappiness for the people.* 2. the abuse of power, or the government or authority that uses power in this way. *That person thinks she can rule with tyranny in her office.* {**teer** ə nee}

ty·rant *noun* 1. a ruler who governs absolutely with unfairness and cruelty. *The tyrant is responsible for the deaths of millions of his fellow citizens.* 2. a person who exercises authority in a cruel or harsh way. *He's a tyrant with the members of the orchestra that he conducts.* {**tiyr** ənt}

tzar *noun* another spelling of **czar.** {**zar** *or* **tsar**}

 Human Body   Human Mind   Everyday Life   History and Culture   Communication

Uu

U is a vowel that makes several different sounds.

Tips to help you look up words starting with u: Sometimes vowels sound similar to each other. If you can't find the word you're looking for under U, it may start with a, e, or o (especially words with short vowels that sound like "uh," such as alive, earn, or onion).

Some words with a long "u" sound ("yoo") can be found under E (ewe) or Y (you or Yule).

These words may be hard to look up if you don't already know how to spell them:

unanimous
union
usual

u or **U** *noun* (u's or U's) 1. the twenty-first letter of the English alphabet. 2. a grade given for unsatisfactory school work. {<u>yoo</u>}

ud·der ● *noun* a large organ with two or more glands, each with its own nipple. Udders are the organs in mammals such as cows and goats from which the offspring drink milk. {<u>uhd</u> ər}

UFO *abbreviation* an abbreviation for "unidentified flying object."

ug·ly *adjective* (uglier, ugliest) 1. unpleasant to look at; not attractive. *He has an ugly scar on his face. / My aunt buys me ugly dresses.* 2. causing offense; mean in a repulsive way. *That was an ugly thing to say.* 3. likely to cause trouble; very unfriendly. *The mob soon turned ugly.* ugliness, n.

U·kraine *noun* a country in eastern Europe. Kiev is the capital of Ukraine. {yoo <u>krayn</u>} Ukrainian, n., adj.

u·ku·le·le *noun* a musical instrument that looks like a small guitar with four strings. The ukulele was brought from Portugal to Hawaii, where it became very popular. {yoo kə <u>lay</u> lee}

Word History *Ukulele* is a Hawaiian word that means "leaping or jumping flea." The "ukelele" was brought to Hawaii by the Portuguese.

ul·cer *noun* an open sore on the body. Ulcers produce pus and are found on the skin or in the stomach or small intestine. *Many stomach ulcers are caused by bacteria.* {<u>uhl</u> sər}

ul·tra- *prefix* 1. a prefix that means "above" or "beyond." *The word "ultrasonic" refers to sounds beyond those that the average person can hear.* 2. a prefix that means "very" or "extreme." *The word "ultralight" means "very light."* {<u>uhl</u> trə}

umbilical cord ● *noun* a cord that connects an unborn baby to its mother. The umbilical cord supplies nourishment to the fetus and takes away wastes. {uhm <u>bih</u> lih kəl <u>kohrd</u>}

um·brel·la *noun* a screen made of fabric stretched over a folding frame. An umbrella is used to shield against the rain or sun. {uhm <u>breh</u> lə}

Word History *Umbrella* comes from the Italian word *ombrello,* which means "little sunshade."

um·pire *noun* a person who rules on plays in a game; referee. *verb* (umpired, umpiring, umpires) to serve as umpire in. *We still need to find someone who will umpire our game on Saturday.* {uhm <u>pivr</u>}

UN *abbreviation* an abbreviation for **United Nations.**

un- *prefix* 1. a prefix that means "not." *An unhappy person is a person who is not happy. / An unfinished task is a task that is not finished.* 2. a prefix that means "back" or "reverse." *To unload a truck is to remove a load from the truck.*

un·a·ble *adjective* not having the power, skill, or means needed to do something; not able. *She is unable to read. / I am unable to visit you today because I have a doctor's appointment.* {uhn <u>ay</u> bəl}

u·nan·i·mous *adjective* 1. in complete agreement. *The group is unanimous in wanting a new leader.* 2. showing, based on, or characterized by complete agreement. *Hal was elected treasurer by a unani-*

A
B
C
D
E
F
G
H
I
J
K
L
M
N
O
P
Q
R
S
T
U
V
W
X
Y
Z

mous vote. {yoo **nă** nih məs} unanimously, *adv.*

Word History *Unanimous* comes from *unanimus*, a Latin word that means "of one mind."

un·a·ware *adjective* not aware; not realizing. *Until the day we sneaked into his yard, we were unaware that Mr. Griffin had a watchdog.* *adverb* not expected; by surprise; unawares. *The surprise party took me unaware.* {uhn ə **wayr**}

un·a·wares *adverb* by surprise or in a way that was not expected. *We caught the thief unawares.* {uhn ə **wayrz**}

un·be·com·ing *adjective* 1. not attractive or proper on a particular person. *That color is most unbecoming on him.* 2. not proper or correct. *It is unbecoming to brush your hair during dinner. / This is conduct unbecoming of an officer.* {uhn bə **kuh** ming}

un·be·liev·a·ble *adjective* very hard to believe; not at all likely. *Sharon's story about an alligator being in the swimming pool is unbelievable. / The wedding cake was unbelievably high.* {uhn bə **lee** və bəl} unbelievably, *adv.*

un·can·ny *adjective* beyond ordinary human or natural means or ability. *He has an uncanny ability to predict the future.* {uhn **kă** nee}

un·cer·tain *adjective* 1. not known for sure; not definite. *It is uncertain whether eating too much salt causes health problems.* 2. not knowing with certainty; not sure. *Lottie is uncertain what to do next.* 3. likely to change; not predictable. *You shouldn't go sailing in uncertain weather.* {uhn **suhr** tən} uncertainly, *adv.*

un·cle *noun* 1. the brother or brother-in-law of one's father or mother. 2. a familiar form of address to refer to an older man who is not related. {**ung** kəl}

• **say** or **cry uncle** to give up; yield. *He wouldn't stop bothering me until I cried uncle.*

un·clear *adjective* 1. hard to understand; confusing. *His directions to the park were unclear.* 2. dark or cloudy; hard to see; not clear. *I have only an unclear photo of my grandmother.* {uhn **kleer**}

Uncle Sam *noun* 1. a cartoon person that represents the government or people of the United States. Uncle Sam is a tall, thin man with a beard, top hat, and trousers that have red and white stripes. *The Uncle Sam character was based on Sam Wilson, who lived in Troy, New York, in the 1800s.* 2. the U.S. government or people. *Uncle Sam wants people to join the army.* {**ung** kəl **săm**}

un·com·fort·a·ble *adjective* 1. feeling discomfort; not comfortable. *I'm uncomfortable in this tight suit. / Kevin is uncomfortable with people he*

does not know well. 2. causing discomfort. *This cot is very uncomfortable.* {uhn **kuhm** fər tə bəl *or* uhn **kuhmf** tər bəl} uncomfortably, *adv.*

un·com·mon *adjective* unusual or rare. *Aunt Martha found an uncommon beetle in her garden.* {uhn **ko** mən}

un·con·scious *adjective* 1. not conscious or aware. *Unconscious of what lay ahead, they set off on their journey.* 2. having temporary loss of being conscious. *The victim of the car accident was unconscious for a few hours.* 3. done without being aware or in control of what one is doing. *It was an unconscious mistake.* {uhn **kŏn** shəs} unconsciously, *adv.*, unconsciousness, *n.*

un·con·sti·tu·tion·al *adjective* not according to the constitution of a state or country. *In the United States, it is unconstitutional for the government to limit free speech.* {uhn **kŏn** stih **tooh** shə nəl}

un·co·op·er·a·tive *adjective* not willing to work together or cooperate. *When it was time to clean up, some students were uncooperative.* {uhn koh ŏp ər uh tihv}

un·cov·er *verb* (uncovered, uncovering, uncovers) 1. to remove the cover from. *We uncovered the pie before eating it.* 2. to make known; reveal. *The student uncovered a plot to steal the test questions.* {uhn **kuh** vər}

un·de·cid·ed *adjective* 1. not yet decided or settled. *The matter is undecided.* 2. not yet able to reach a decision; uncertain. *He is undecided about whether to go to college.* {uhn dih **siy** dihd}

a b c d e f g h i j k l m n o p q r s t u v w x y z

 Human Body  Human Mind Everyday Life History and Culture Communication

un·der *preposition* 1. below; beneath. *There's a lot of dust under the bed.* 2. beneath the surface of. *We swam around under the ocean to explore a coral reef.* 3. at or in a position farther down or lower than. *The mouth is located under the nose.* 4. smaller or less than. *A pack of gum costs under two dollars.* 5. below in position or importance. *The vice-president is under the president.* 6. subject to the control of. *The country is suffering under its new leader.* 7. subject to the instruction or guidance of. *She studies under famous people.* 8. subject to the conditions or limits of. *He's under oath and must tell the truth.* 9. in the process of. *There's a new plan under discussion.* 10. according to. *Under no circumstances will I go to his house.* *adverb* 1. into or by way of a lower place or position. *Emily lifted up her blankets and climbed under.* 2. below the surface. *The ship hit an iceberg and went under.* / *The farmer plowed his crops under.* 3. fewer or less in number or quantity. *This book is written for children ages eleven and under.* *adjective* 1. located in a lower position; beneath. *The mechanic examined the under parts of the machine.* 2. lower in degree or rank. *He is one of the under officers of the club.* {uhn dər}

un·der- *prefix* 1. a prefix that means "below" or "beneath." *An underground cave is a cave below the ground.* 2. a prefix that means "less" or "not enough." *When people are underpaid, they are not paid enough.*

un·der·dog *noun* a person or team that is expected to lose a contest in sports or politics. *We cheered for the underdogs* because they were from our hometown. {uhn dər dawg}

un·der·go *verb* (underwent, undergone, undergoing, undergoes) to have the experience of; receive; endure. *She'll undergo surgery on her foot next week.* / *Our family underwent major changes last year.* {uhn dər goh}

un·der·ground ❶ *adjective* 1. located, living, or taking place beneath the earth's surface. *The girls found an underground cave.* 2. not in public; hidden. *Many Quaker families worked for the Underground Railroad.* *adverb* beneath the earth's surface. *Moles live underground.* *noun* 1. a place or region beneath the earth's surface. *Many coal miners work in the underground.* 2. a group of people who work in a secret way against a government or enemy. *Many French people worked for the underground after the Nazis invaded their country.* {uhn dər grownd}

un·der·growth *noun* low plant growth beneath and around taller trees. *The dense undergrowth slowed our hike.* {uhn dər grohth}

un·der·hand *adjective* 1. done with the hand below shoulder level. *Softball uses an underhand pitch.* 2. secret and sneaky; in a dishonest way. *I wasn't fooled by the underhand flattery.* *adverb* with the hand held below shoulder level and the palm turned up. *Toss me the ball underhand.* {uhn dər hănd}

un·der·line *verb* (underlined, underlining, underlines) 1. to draw a line under. *The student underlined the spelling words in her workbook.* 2. to emphasize. *The governor underlined the importance of* creating jobs. {uhn dər liyn or uhn dər liyn}

un·der·neath *preposition* 1. below or beneath; under. *She left the doll underneath the table.* 2. hidden by. *The boy is underneath the blanket.* *adverb* under or below. *Beth lifted up the rock and looked underneath.* {uhn dər neeth}

un·der·pants *plural noun* short pants worn under other clothing as underwear. {uhn dər pănts}

un·der·pass *noun* a passage or road that goes beneath another passage or road. *The exit ramp curves around and forms an underpass under the freeway.* {uhn dər păs}

un·der·sea *adjective* having to do with, located, carried on, or used beneath the surface of the sea; underwater. *That camera can take undersea pictures.* / *The undersea drilling will help lower oil prices.* {uhn dər see}

un·der·side *noun* the under or lower side or surface; bottom. *The fish had a white underside and an orange back.* {uhn dər siyd}

un·der·stand ❾ *verb* (understood, understanding, understands) 1. to get the meaning, nature, or importance of. *Do you understand what you're reading?* 2. to know very well the ways and nature of. *She understands computers.* 3. take as settled; assume. *The rules of the game must be understood by all players.* 4. to hear, learn, or

A B C D E F G H I J K L M N O P Q R S T **U** V W X Y Z

be told; gather. *I understand that lunch is free today.* 5. to have sympathy for. *No one understands me.* {**uhn** dər **stănd**}

un·der·stand·ing *noun* 1. the ability to understand; thinking; intelligence. *Her clear understanding makes her a fine leader.* 2. explanation; opinion. *What is your understanding of what happened?* 3. an agreement. *After talking all night, we reached an understanding.* 4. knowledge or skill in a particular area. *She has a good understanding of math.* 5. sympathy or tolerance toward other people. *He was very understanding once I had explained why I was late.* *adjective* feeling or having sympathy. *I'm glad to have such an understanding friend.* {**uhn** dər **stăn** ding}

un·der·stood *verb* past tense and past participle of **understand**. *adjective* on which an understanding has been reached; agreed upon. *The teacher decided to make the understood classroom rules official by writing them on a poster.* {**uhn** dər **stuud**}

un·der·take *verb* (undertook, undertaken, undertaking) 1. to decide or start to do. *She's undertaking a new project.* 2. to promise or obligate oneself to do. *Sure, I'll undertake the job of buying balloons for the party.* {**uhn** dər **tayk**}

un·der·tak·er *noun* a person whose job is to prepare dead bodies for burial and make arrangements for funerals. {**uhn** dər **tay** kər}

un·der·tow *noun* a strong current of ocean water moving in the opposite direction from the waves moving toward shore. *The swimmer was lucky to escape the pull of the undertow.* {**uhn** dər **toh**}

un·der·wa·ter *adjective* located, done, or made for use below the surface of a body of water. *Beavers build underwater houses. / Submarines are built for underwater travel.* *adverb* below the water's surface. *The otter dived underwater.* {**uhn** dər **waw** tər}

un·der·wear ○ *noun* clothing worn next to the skin under other clothing. {**uhn** dər **wayr**}

un·der·weight *adjective* lower in weight than is normal, desired, or necessary. *Brad thinks he is underweight for his age.* {**uhn** dər **wayt**}

un·der·world *noun* 1. the criminal class of society. 2. an imaginary world beneath the earth's surface where dead people and spirits live. {**uhn** dər **wuhrld**}

un·do *verb* (undid, undone, undoing, undoes) 1. to release from or remove wrapping or fastening from. *The captain undid the knot that tied the boat to the dock.* 2. to make useless; reverse. *He undid the good that others had done.* 3. to ruin or destroy. *If the hurricane hits land, it will undo all of the farmers' hard work.* {**uhn** **dooh**}

Homophone Note Are you looking for the word *undue* (too much)? *Undo* and *undue* sound alike but have different meanings.

un·dress *verb* (undressed, undressing, undresses) 1. to remove the clothing or covering from. *The child undressed the doll and put different clothes on it.* 2. to remove one's clothing. *He went into his room, undressed, and went to bed.* {**uhn** **drehs**}

un·due *adjective* too much; more than is right or appropriate. *We protested the undue cruelty shown to prisoners of war.* {**uhn** **dooh**}

Homophone Note The words *undue* and *undo* (to release or reverse) sound alike but have different meanings.

un·earth *verb* (unearthed, unearthing, unearths) 1. to dig up out of the earth. *The archaeologist helped unearth an ancient city.* 2. to find or reveal by searching. *It took hours for my aunt to unearth the recipe we had asked for.* {**uhn** **uhrth**}

un·eas·y *adjective* (uneasier, uneasiest) 1. not comfortable; nervous. *The passengers on the plane were uneasy when the ride got bumpy.* 2. not confident in manner; awkward. *Dale was uneasy at the formal dinner because he didn't know which was the salad fork and which was the dessert fork.* {**uhn** **ee** zee}

Synonyms
These words share a meaning with *uneasy*, adjective 1:
troubled, worried, nervous, anxious

un·em·ployed *adjective* having no job; not employed. *She's unemployed but hopes to find a job soon.* *noun* those people who are out of work or do not have a job (used with "the"). *The president came up*

 Human Body   Human Mind    Everyday Life   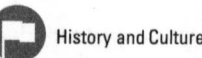 History and Culture    Communication

with a plan to create jobs for the unemployed. {**uhn** ihm **ploid**}

un·e·qual *adjective* 1. not equal, as two or more people, things, or numbers. *The musicians have unequal abilities. / The workers were upset by the unequal treatment they received.* 2. not well balanced or matched. *We watched an unequal fight in the woods between a raccoon and a wolf.* {**uhn ee** kwəl}

un·e·ven *adjective* 1. not smooth, regular, or flat; rough or jagged. *I twisted my ankle while skating on the uneven sidewalk.* 2. not regular or changing in quality; not consistent. *The editor rejected the book because of its uneven writing.* 3. not straight, level, or parallel. *He wasn't paying attention and sewed an uneven hem.* 4. not balanced; unfair; one-sided. *The high school team against the junior high school team was an uneven match.* 5. of a number, odd. *Three is an uneven number.* {**uhn ee** vən} unevenly, adv.

un·fair *adjective* (unfairer, unfairest) 1. against what is just or fair. *Some people think the judge made an unfair decision in that case.* 2. showing bias; not fair. *The principal was unfair to those students.* {**uhn fayr**} unfairly, adv., unfairness, n.

un·fa·mil·iar *adjective* 1. not known or experienced before; unusual; strange. *Unfamiliar faces scare the baby.* 2. not having previous experience or knowledge; not acquainted. *He is unfamiliar with the rules.* {**uhn** fə **mihl** yər}

un·fas·ten *verb* (unfastened, unfastening, unfastens) to release from; undo; separate.

Bonnie unfastened the dog from its leash. {**uhn fa** sən}

un·fold *verb* (unfolded, unfolding, unfolds) 1. to open or spread out from a folded condition. *Please unfold the napkin and put it on your lap.* 2. to become open or spread out. *The paper unfolded in the wind. / This chair unfolds so you can sit on it.* 3. to reveal, develop, or make known or clear by explanation. *We unfolded the mystery of his disappearance.* 4. to be or become revealed or known by explanation. *The plot unfolds slowly at first.* {**uhn fohld**}

un·for·tu·nate *adjective* 1. having bad luck; unlucky. *The unfortunate man lost his glasses again.* 2. causing a difficult or harmful condition. *An unfortunate event led us to believe we'd never reach the summit.* 3. causing regret; sorry. *His unfortunate lack of manners caused him to lose friends.* {**uhn fohr** chə niht} unfortunately, adv.

un·friend·ly *adjective* (unfriendlier, unfriendliest) 1. not friendly; distant, unpleasant, or mean to other people. *The unfriendly dog bit its owner's leg.* 2. leading to a poor or harmful future; not welcoming. *Unfriendly weather caused the polar expedition to turn back.* {**uhn frehnd** lee}

un·hap·py *adjective* (unhappier, unhappiest) 1. not glad or cheerful; sad; full of gloom. *My nephew is unhappy with his new school.* 2. causing results that are not wanted; not fortunate. *He made an unhappy choice of job.* {**uhn hăp** ee} unhappily, adv., unhappiness, n.

un·health·y *adjective* (unhealthier, unhealthiest) 1. in bad health; ill. *The*

unhealthy child missed a lot of school. 2. causing poor health or disease. *Smoking is an unhealthy habit.* {**uhn hehlth** ee}

un·heard-of *adjective* never before known or considered; completely new. *The unheard-of discovery started a revolution in physics.* {**uhn huhrd** əv}

u·ni- *prefix* a prefix that means "one" or "single." *A unicycle is a vehicle with one wheel.*

u·ni·corn *noun* a mythical animal having the body of a horse and a single, long horn extending from its forehead. {**yoo** nih **kohrn**}

Word History *Unicorn* comes from *unicornis*, a Latin word that means "having one horn."

u·ni·form *adjective* 1. always the same; never changing. *She runs at a uniform speed.* 2. very alike; without any difference. *The houses on this block are uniform in their appearance.* *noun* a special suit of clothing worn by all members of a particular group. *All the kids in that school wear a uniform.* {**yoo** nih **fohrm**}

u·ni·fy *verb* (unified, unifying, unifies) to make into a single unit or thing; bring together; unite. *Hard times unified the family.* {**yoo** nih **fiy**}

un·im·por·tant *adjective* 1. not powerful or respected. *He doesn't pay attention to unimportant people.* 2. of no meaning or value; not important. *What she thinks of me is unimportant.* {**uhn** ihm **pohr** tănt}

A
B
C
D
E
F
G
H
I
J
K
L
M
N
O
P
Q
R
S
T
U
V
W
X
Y
Z

un·in·ha·bi·ted *adjective* not lived in or inhabited. *The house on the corner is uninhabited.* {uhn ən **hăb** ih tehd}

un·in·ter·est·ed *adjective* having no interest; indifferent. *The new boy seemed uninterested in making friends.* {uhn ihn tə **reh** stihd *or* uhn **ihn** trə stihd}

un·ion *noun* 1. the act of uniting. *With the union of East and West Germany in 1990, many people were reunited with their friends and family.* 2. the condition of being united. *The union of the two companies was what kept their business successful.* 3. two or more things or people joined together to form something new. *Several English teachers formed a poetry-reading union.* 4. a group of states or countries united under a single government. *The U.S. Civil War began when the northern states refused to allow the southern states to leave the Union.* 5. the act of joining or of being joined in marriage. *Today, we celebrate the union of Toni and Marcus.* 6. an organization of workers; trade union. *The union agreed on a contract that promised fair wages for its members.* {**yoon** yən}

u·nique *adjective* 1. being the only one of its type; sole; single. *The boiling point of water is unique to water.* / *Everyone's fingerprints are unique.* 2. having no equal; different from everything else. *Neil Armstrong was unique in being the first human to walk on the moon.* {yoo **neek**}

u·ni·son *noun* 1. (used with "in") speaking all at the same time, or singing at the same time in the same pitch. *The class chanted "good morning" in unison.* / *The choir sang in unison.* 2. agreement; accord. *The students worked in unison to make their school a hate-free zone.* {yoo nih sən}

u·nit ❶ *noun* 1. a single thing that is one of a group of similar things. *Our apartment building has forty units.* 2. a fixed amount that is used as a standard of measurement. *The foot and the meter are units for measuring distance.* 3. a group of people or things that act together as a whole. *The army unit prepared to go overseas.* 4. the smallest positive whole number; one. *In the number "256," the "6" is in the units place.* {**yoo** niht}

u·nite *verb* (united, uniting, unites) 1. to join together into a whole; combine. *The prime minister united the members of her party.* 2. to be joined together into or act as a whole. *The pack of wolves united against the moose.* 3. to bring together in marriage. *The rabbi united the couple last week.* {yə **niyt**}

United Kingdom *noun* a nation in northwestern Europe on the islands of Great Britain and Ireland and made up of England, Scotland, Wales, and Northern Ireland (usually used with "the"). London is the capital of the United Kingdom. {yoo **niy** tihd **king** dəm}

United Nations *plural noun* (used with a singular or plural verb) an organization of many nations started in 1945 to promote world peace and understanding. {yoo **niy** tihd **nay** shənz}

United States of America *noun* a country in North America (usually used with "the"). Washington, D.C., is the capital of the United States of America. {yoo **niy** tihd **stayts** əv ə **meh** rih kə}

u·ni·ty *noun* (unities) the condition of being united or of acting as one. *The unity of the team is what won the game.* {**yoo** nih tee}

u·ni·ver·sal *adjective* 1. of, having to do with, or characteristic of the whole world or the world's population. *Universal peace seems like an impossible dream.* 2. for or affecting everyone. *The need for food and shelter is universal.* {yoo nih **vuhr** səl}

u·ni·ver·sal re·source lo·cat·or *noun* an address identifying the location of a file on the Internet, commonly called a URL. A URL consists of the the computer on which the file is located, and the file's location on that computer.

 Human Body   Human Mind   Everyday Life    History and Culture   Communication

{yoo nih **vuhr** səl **ree** sohrs **loh** kay tər}

u·ni·verse 🌐 *noun* all matter and energy; all existing things, including the earth and heavens. *Do you think that Earth is the only planet in the universe with intelligent life?* {**yoo** nih vuhrs}

Word History *Universe* comes from a Latin word that means "turned into one."

u·ni·ver·si·ty 🔵 🔴 *noun* (universities) a large school, where people both learn and do research. *A student must finish high school before attending a university. Universities offer several levels of degrees.* {yoo nih **vuhr** sih tee}

un·kind *adjective* (unkinder, unkindest) not kind or sympathetic; harsh. *Her unkind remark about my new haircut hurt my feelings.* {uhn **kiynd**} unkindness, n.

Word History In Old English, the word *unkind* meant "unnatural" or "not what is expected from one's own people or family."

un·law·ful *adjective* not allowed by law; illegal. *It is unlawful to drive through a red light.* {uhn **law** fəl}

un·less *conjunction* except on the condition that. *We won't go unless we're invited.* {uhn **lehs**}

un·like *adjective* not alike or equal; different; unequal. *The country mouse and the town mouse were unlike in many ways.* *preposition* 1. not like; not similar to. *Unlike Mary, I love to swim.* 2. not typical of. *It is unlike you to cry.* {uhn **liyk**}

un·lim·it·ed *adjective* having no limits, bounds, or restrictions. *The climbers had an*

unlimited view from the top of Mount Everest. {uhn **lihm** ə tihd}

un·load *verb* (unloaded, unloading, unloads) 1. to remove the load from. *Unload the truck when it arrives.* 2. to remove. *On the dock, the workers unloaded the cargo from the ship.* 3. to remove the ammunition from. *She unloaded the gun for safety.* {uhn **lohd**}

un·lock *verb* (unlocked, unlocking, unlocks) 1. to open the lock of by turning a key or mechanism. *The janitor unlocks the museum in the morning.* 2. to become unlocked. *The vault unlocks electronically.* 3. to make known; disclose. *They unlocked the mystery at last.* {uhn **lök**}

un·luck·y *adjective* (unluckier, unluckiest) 1. marked by or involving ill fortune or bad luck. *This is the third time that unlucky person has lost his wallet. / It was unlucky when it rained on the day of the class picnic.* 2. likely to bring or indicating ill fortune. *Some say it is unlucky for a black cat to cross your path.* {uhn **luh** kee} unluckily, adv.

un·manned *adjective* not having a human pilot or crew. *NASA sent an unmanned spacecraft to Mars.* {uhn **mänd**}

un·nat·u·ral *adjective* 1. not according to natural laws or processes. *It is unnatural for water to flow uphill.* 2. not honest; pretended or artificial. *Kim has an unnatural smile in her school photograph.* {uhn **näch** rəl}

un·nec·es·sar·y *adjective* not needed or required. *It is*

unnecessary to carry an umbrella on such a fine day. {uhn **neh** sə **sayr** ee} unnecessarily, adv.

un·pack *verb* (unpacked, unpacking, unpacks) 1. to take out of a package, suitcase, or container. *Mr. Wilson unpacked his clothes after he returned from his trip.* 2. to take contents out of. *We spread a blanket on the ground and unpacked the picnic basket.* {uhn **păk**}

un·pleas·ant *adjective* not pleasant or agreeable; distasteful. *The unpleasant odor told us we had forgotten to put the fish in the refrigerator. / What unpleasant manners he has!* {uhn **pleh** zənt} unpleasantly, adv.

un·pop·u·lar *adjective* not liked or approved of by many people. *He makes himself unpopular by saying nasty things about his classmates.* {uhn **pöp** yə lər}

un·rav·el *verb* (unraveled, unraveling, unravels) 1. to undo; reduce from cloth to threads; cause to come apart. *Sylvie unraveled her knitting when she noticed a mistake in it.* 2. to come apart. *I pulled on a thread, and the whole seam unraveled.* 3. to remove tangles or make clear. *I tried to unravel the tangled cords. / The scientist hopes to unravel the mystery of how dinosaurs disappeared.* {uhn **răv** əl}

un·rea·son·a·ble ❓ *adjective* 1. not acting or behaving with good sense; not guided by good judgment or sound thinking. *The unreasonable little boy refused to let go of the cat's tail.* 2. beyond reasonable limits; much more than is fitting. *That's an unreasonable price for a pair of sneakers.* {uhn **ree** zə nə bəl}

A
B
C
D
E
F
G
H
I
J
K
L
M
N
O
P
Q
R
S
T
U
V
W
X
Y
Z

 Living World  Physical World  Natural Environment  Economy Government and Law

un·re·li·a·ble *adjective* not able to be relied on. *Her old car is very unreliable in cold weather. / The worker was fired for being unreliable.* {**uhn** rih **liy** ə bəl}

un·rest *noun* a state of trouble, disturbance, or lack of satisfaction. *The constant unrest in some neighborhoods made it difficult for the mayor to keep order.* {**uhn rehst**}

un·ru·ly *adjective* (unrulier, unruliest) not easy to restrict; difficult or impossible to control; wild. *The baby-sitter tried to calm the unruly child.* {**uhn rooh** lee}

un·sa·tis·fac·to·ry *adjective* not good enough to meet a need or desire; not satisfactory. *The meal we had at that restaurant was unsatisfactory.* {**uhn** să tihs **făk** tohr ee}

un·seen *adjective* not seen, observed, or discovered; invisible; not noticed. *An unseen thief broke into the jewelry store and stole the diamonds.* {**uhn seen**}

un·set·tled *adjective* 1. not fixed, stable, or constant; variable. *The unsettled weather forced us to cancel the picnic.* 2. upset, shaken up, or disturbed. *The unsettled customers demanded their money back.* 3. not decided; not resolved; not determined. *The issue of who gets to use the car tonight is still unsettled.* 4. not paid, adjusted, or closed. *The bill is still unsettled after six months. / The lawsuit is still unsettled, so there will be a trial.* 5. not lived in by many people; not populated. *Most of Antarctica is unsettled.* {**uhn seht** əld}

un·sight·ly *adjective* not pleasant or agreeable to look at; ugly. *The squirrels made an unsightly mess in the shed.* {**uhn siyt** lee}

un·sta·ble *adjective* 1. likely to change suddenly. *Jane is still in the hospital because her condition is unstable.* 2. not steady; not securely fixed. *The unstable chair collapsed when I sat on it.* {**uhn stay** bəl}

un·stead·y *adjective* 1. not stable or secure; not firm. *That old desk is too unsteady to support a computer.* 2. shaky or uneven. *The ballet students looked unsteady when they tried to balance on toe.* {**uhn steh** dee}

un·suit·a·ble *adjective* not proper or appropriate. *The drunk man was thrown out of the restaurant for using unsuitable language.* {**uhn sooh** tə bəl}

un·tan·gle *verb* (untangled, untangling, untangles) 1. to free from a tangled or snarled condition. *Please help me untangle the telephone cord.* 2. to make clear; make order out of; straighten out. *The professor untangled the mystery of the missing monkey.* {**uhn tăng** gəl}

un·tie *verb* (untied, untying, unties) 1. to free from being tied or bound. *The police found the man who had been kidnapped and untied him.* 2. to loosen or undo. *Katya untied the knots in her cat's cradle string.* 3. to come undone. *Jim's shoelace untied and he tripped.* {**uhn tiy**}

un·til *conjunction* 1. up to the time when. *We drove until the sun came up.* 2. before. *She can't watch TV until she does her homework.* 3. to the point that. *Anna danced until her feet hurt.* *preposition* 1. up to the time of. *We worked until evening.* 2. before. *He won't move until summer.* {**uhn tihl**}

un·true *adjective* 1. not correct or accurate; false. *Her stories were all untrue.* 2. without loyalty or devotion; not faithful. *The traitor was untrue to his country.* {**uhn trooh**}

un·u·su·al *adjective* not usual or ordinary; not common; remarkable. *She had never seen such an unusual bird before. / It is unusual for workers in the U.S. to take an afternoon nap.* {**uhn yoo** zhooh əl} unusually, adv.

Synonyms
These words share a meaning with ***unusual***, adjective 1:
strange, remarkable, exceptional, uncommon

un·well *adjective* in poor health; sick; ill. *She stayed home because she was unwell.* {**uhn wehl**}

un·wind *verb* (unwound, unwinding, unwinds) 1. to undo from a wound or twisted state; remove the twists from. *Let's unwind this cord and plug it in.* 2. to become not twisted or coiled. *The thread unwound from the spool.* 3. to free from stress; relax. *A vacation will unwind you.* 4. to free oneself from stress; relax. *She goes running to unwind.* {**uhn wiynd**}

up *adverb* 1. to, toward, at, or in a higher place or position. *The plane flew up among the clouds. / We climbed up to the second floor.* 2. to or in an upright position. *The tent is up.* 3. out of bed; awake. *We got up early.* 4. above the horizon. *The sun came up at six in the morning.* 5. to or at a higher level or amount. *He is moving up at work. / The price of shoes is going up.* 6. entirely; completely. *I filled up my glass. / Button up your coat.* 7. from below a surface. *A few flowers came up.* *preposition* 1. to, at, or toward a

 Human Body  Human Mind  Everyday Life  History and Culture  Communication

higher point on or in. *The train headed up the hill.* 2. at or toward a point further ahead on or in. *She skipped up the path.* 3. toward the source of. *Let's go up the river.* *adjective* 1. going upward. *Take the up staircase to my office.* 2. at a high level. *There's a bird up in the sky.* 3. finished; ended. *He'll pay me when the week is up.* 4. in an upright or vertical position. *The new wallpaper is up.* 5. (informal) taking place; happening. *What's up at the office?* 6. above ground. *The summer crops are up.* 7. in a state of activity, operation, or being ready. *Are you up for dancing?* 8. in the air. *The kite is up.* 9. under consideration; in view. *Is your idea up for discussion?* 10. over; finished. *Your time is up.* *noun* 1. an upward course or movement. *His health is on the up.* / *Life is full of ups and downs.* 2. an upward slope; rise. *verb* (upped, upping, ups) to make better. *What will up our chances of winning?* {**uhp**}

• **up to**
1. busy with; doing. *What are you up to?* 2. the responsibility of. *It's up to us.* 3. as much as; at the most. *A good wrench can cost up to sixty dollars.*

up- *prefix* a prefix that means "up" or "upward." *To go upstairs is to go up the stairs.* / *To uproot a plant is to pull a plant upward by its roots.*

up·bring·ing *noun* the training and rearing of a child or children. *He had a strict upbringing.* {**uhp** bring ing}

up·grade *noun* an upward slope or incline. *The crew used a bulldozer to make the upgrade less steep.* *verb* (upgraded, upgrading, upgrades) to raise to a higher level of quality,

rank, or importance. *She upgraded her computer by adding more memory.* / *The hospital upgraded his condition from fair to good.* {**uhp** grayd or **uhp** grayd, n., **uhp** grayd or **uhp** grayd, v.}

up·heav·al *noun* 1. an act, instance, or condition of being raised or heaved upward. *The upheaval from the earthquake destroyed many buildings.* 2. a sudden, violent change. *The French Revolution caused upheaval in Europe.* {**uhp** heev əl or **uhp** heev əl}

up·hill *adverb* on an upward slope or in an upward direction. *Jack and Jill walked uphill to the well.* *adjective* 1. located on or following along an upward incline. *My car slipped out of gear on the uphill street.* 2. requiring great effort; difficult. *The reporter fought an uphill battle to get information from the president's secretary.* {**uhp** hihl}

up·hold *verb* (upheld, upholding, upholds) 1. to support or decide in favor of, when faced with a challenge. *The court upheld his right to free speech.* 2. to keep from sinking or falling; support. *For years, parts of the old church walls have been upheld by props.* / *His sense of humor upheld him in difficult times.* {**uhp** hohld}

up·hol·ster·y *noun* (upholsteries) 1. materials used to cover furniture. *I like the pattern of the upholstery on that chair.* 2. the work or business of covering furniture. {**uhp** hohl stə ree} upholsterer, n.

up·land *noun* the raised or higher parts of land in a region. *adjective* of, having to

do with, or located in a higher area. *The upland farms did not face the danger of flooding.* {**uhp** lănd}

up·load *verb* (uploaded, uploading, uploads) to send information from one computer to another computer or to a computer network. *I uploaded some photographs to my Web page so that my friends could see them.* *noun* the act or process of sending information from one computer to another computer or to a computer network. *The upload took a long time because of the slow Internet connection.* {**uhp** lohd}

up·on *preposition* 1. on. *She placed her hand upon his shoulder.* 2. up and on, in a high position. *The king sat upon his throne.* 3. at the time or occasion of. *We greeted the guests upon their arrival.* {ə **pŏn**}

up·per *adjective* higher in place, rank, position, or level. *The child climbed to the upper branches of the tree.* / *The upper grades at the high school need more teachers.* *noun* the part of a shoe above the sole. *This boot has a leather upper.* {**uh** pər}

up·per-case *adjective* capital rather than lower-case. *Please write your name in upper-case letters.* {**uh** pər **kays**}

up·per·most *adjective* highest in place, rank, importance, or influence. *Planning winter activities is the committee's uppermost concern.* *adverb* in the highest or most important position or rank. *Repairing the computer is uppermost on the list of jobs for today.* {**uh** pər **mohst**}

up·right *adjective* 1. in a vertical or standing position. *Long ago, these leaning pillars*

 Living World
 Physical World
 Natural Environment
 Economy

Government and Law

775

were upright. 2. having straight posture. *It is easier to breathe when standing in an upright position.* 3. right, honest, and just in actions or morals. *The upright boy refused to cheat on the exam.* *noun* 1. something standing in a vertical position. *The uprights for the building will be in place tomorrow.* 2. a piano with strings vertical to the keyboard. *I practice on an upright.* *adverb* in a vertical or upright position. *Please sit upright in your chair.* {uhp **riyt**}

up·ris·ing *noun* the act or an instance of rebelling or rising up against authority. *About a thousand people were killed by the Chinese government in the Tienanmen Square uprising of 1989.* {uhp **riy** zing}

up·roar *noun* 1. a loud, confused disturbance; commotion. *When stock prices fell, there was an uproar on the floor of the stock exchange.* 2. a very active debate or public disagreement. *The governor's arrest caused an uproar in the press.* {uhp **rohr**}

up·root *verb* (uprooted, uprooting, uproots) 1. to pull up or tear out of the ground by the roots. *The storm uprooted many trees.* 2. to force to leave a home, native land, or natural environment. *War and famine uprooted the people of that region.* {uhp **rooht**}

up·set ❷ ❼ *verb* (upset, upsetting, upsets) 1. to tip or turn over. *He upset the pitcher of water.* 2. to bother or to make uncomfortable. *Their complaints upset her. / Milk upsets his stomach.* 3. to disturb the order of; interfere with. *A loud noise upset the meeting.* 4. to win against when expected to lose to. *The underdog upset the favored team.* *noun* 1. an instance or condition of being upset. *There was great upset in the land after the king died.* 2. the defeat of an opponent considered likely to win. *We celebrated the junior high team's upset of the high school team.* *adjective* 1. tipped or turned over. *After the storm there were many fallen branches and upset mailboxes.* 2. disturbed or bothered. *I have an upset stomach. / Be kind to an upset friend.* 3. not organized; out of order. *Her desk was all upset, with loose papers everywhere.* {uhp **seht**}

Synonyms
These words share a meaning with *upset*, verb 1:

tip over, topple, overturn

upside down *adverb or adjective* with the part that is usually underneath on top; inverted. *My uncle held my brother upside down.* {uhp **siyd down**} upside-down, adj.

up·stairs *adverb* on or toward an upper floor; up the stairs. *She keeps her books upstairs. / He went upstairs.* *adjective* on or having to do with an upper floor of a building. *You can sleep in the upstairs bedroom.* *noun* (usually used with a singular verb) the upper floor or floors of a building. *He showed them the upstairs of the house.* {uhp **stayrz**}

up-to-date *adjective* 1. having the most recent information; current. *We listened to the most up-to-date news report.* 2. following or keeping up with the most current fashions, ideas, or techniques. *Those shoes have an up-to-date look.* {uhp tə **dayt**}

up·ward *adverb* toward or to a higher position or place. *The cat climbed upward in the tree.* *adjective* moving toward a higher position or place. *We watched her upward rise in the company with pride.* {uhp wərd} upwards, adv.

u·ra·ni·um ❶ *noun* a heavy, silver-white radioactive metal that is one of the chemical elements. It is used to produce nuclear energy. (symbol: U) {yə **ray** nee əm}

U·ra·nus *noun* 1. the third largest planet in the solar system and seventh in distance from the sun. 2. the ruler of the heavens in Greek mythology. Uranus was overthrown by his son, who was then overthrown by his own son, Zeus, who became ruler of the Greek gods. {**yoor** ə nəs or yə **rayn** əs}

ur·ban *adjective* of or having to do with a city or town. *This urban area is home to thousands of people and businesses.* {**uhr** bən}

Word History *Urban* comes from *urbs*, a Latin word that means "city."

urge *verb* (urged, urging, urges) 1. to push or drive forward or onward. *We urged the cows back into the barn.* 2. to encourage or try to persuade. *They urged us to stay for dinner.* *noun* a natural desire or impulse to do something. *An urge to eat popcorn came over him after school.* {**uhrj**}

ur·gent *adjective* 1. needing immediate action or attention. *Our need for water*

 Human Body    Human Mind   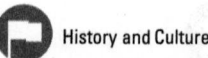 Everyday Life    History and Culture   Communication

became urgent. 2. expressed in a strong way. *The college student sent his parents an urgent request for money.* {**uhr** jənt} urgently, adv.

u·rine *noun* a substance made by the kidneys to carry waste out of the body. Urine comes out as a yellow liquid in mammals and as a partially solid substance in reptiles and birds. {**yuh** rihn}

Word History *Urine* comes from *aurina*, a Latin word that means "color of gold."

URL *abbreviation* the address of documents on the World Wide Web. URL is an abbreviation for **universal resource locator.** *The URL for Wordsmyth is http://www.wordsmyth.net .*

urn *noun* 1. a large vase with a base. *She put the plant in an urn.* 2. a metal container with a spout. Urns are used to make and serve coffee and tea. {**uhrn**}

Homophone Note The words *urn* and *earn* (to receive as pay) sound alike but have different meanings.

Ursa Major *noun* a constellation in the northern sky, also called the Big Dipper. {**uhr** sə **may** jər}

Ursa Minor *noun* a constellation in the northern sky, also called the Little Dipper. {**uhr** sə **miy** nər}

U·ru·guay *noun* a country in southeastern South America. Montevideo is the capital of Uruguay. {**yoor** ə gwiy *or* **yoor** ə gway *or* **ooh** rooh gway}

U.S. *or* **US** *abbreviation* an abbreviation for **United States.**

us *pronoun* 1. a form of "we" used after certain verbs or prepositions; the speaker and another or others. *They took*

us home. / He gave the puppy to us. / She came with us. 2. the person speaking and another or others. *They hired us. / He ate with us.* {**uhs**}

U.S.A. *or* **USA** *abbreviation* an abbreviation for **United States of America.**

us·a·ble *adjective* able or fit for being used. *This printer is old but usable.* {**yoo** zə bəl}

us·age *noun* 1. way or manner of using or treating something. *His little car has had a lot of rough usage.* 2. use. *The government regulates the usage of lead in gasoline.* {**yoo** sihj}

USDA *abbreviation* the government agency responsible for regulations on the safety of food. USDA is an abbreviation for the "United States Department of Agriculture."

use *verb* (used, using, uses) 1. to bring into service. *I used a computer to type my report.* 2. to spend; consume. *He used his last dollar to buy some bread.* 3. used in the past tense with "to," to show a past habit or state. *We used to go shopping every Saturday. / I used to be a baby like you.* *noun* 1. the act or practice of using. *We made use of wood for heating this year.* 2. the fact or condition of being used. *The radio is always in use.* 3. way of using. *I love this writer's use of words.* 4. ability or permission to use. *She lost the use of her thumb. / The neighbors gave us use of their pool while they were on vacation.* 5. benefit; advantage. *There is no use in fighting.* 6. purpose. *This machine has many uses.* {**yoos**, n., **yooz**, v.}

• **make use of**
to use or cause to be used; find a purpose or activity for. *We made use of our free time by calling old friends.*

• **use up**

to use all of; finish. *Someone used up the toothpaste.*

Synonyms
These words share a meaning with *use*, noun 1:
application, employment, usage

used *adjective* 1. having been owned by someone else; not new. *She bought a used car.* 2. familiar with; in the habit of (followed by "to"). *People who live in Louisiana aren't used to shoveling snow. / She got used to her new teacher after only a few days.* {**yoozd**}

use·ful *adjective* able to be used in a helpful, practical, or effective way. *We have a useful book that tells which mushrooms are safe to eat.* {**yoos** fəl}

use·less *adjective* having no good or practical purpose. *It is useless to try to move all this furniture when we're so tired.* {**yoos** lihs}

us·er-·frien·dly *adjective* easy to use or easy to learn how to use. *Most children's software is user-friendly.* {**yooz** ər **frehnd** lee}

ush·er *noun* a person who shows people to their seats in a house of worship, theater, or stadium. *verb* (ushered, ushering, ushers) to lead, escort, or show (usually followed by "into," "in," "out," or "to"). *The servants ushered us into the royal chamber.* {**uhsh** ər}

U.S.S.R. *or* **USSR** *abbreviation* an abbreviation for "Union of Soviet Socialist Republics," the official name of the former **Soviet Union.**

u·su·al *adjective* 1. most common or expected; customary. *My backpack was in its usual place.* 2. ordinary; normal; common. *Hurricanes are usual this time of year.* *noun* that which is usual; something usual. *He comes into this*

A B C D E F G H I J K L M N O P Q R S T **U** V W X Y Z

 Living World  Physical World  Natural Environment  Economy Government and Law

diner every morning and orders the usual. {<u>yoo</u> zhooh əl} usually, adv.

UT *abbreviation* an abbreviation for **Utah**.

U·tah *noun* a state in the western United States. Its capital is Salt Lake City. (abbreviated: UT) {<u>yoo</u> **taw** *or* <u>yoo</u> **tah**}

Word History *Utah* means "hill dwellers." Utah is the English spelling of *yuta*, the Spanish name for the Ute Shoshone people. The Spanish explorers probably learned the name from other Indians who referred to that group of Shoshone as "people of the mountains."

u·ten·sil ⊙ *noun* a device, instrument, or container used in a kitchen. *In our kitchen, the spatula, vegetable peeler, and other utensils are in their own drawer.* {yoo **tehn** sihl}

u·ter·us *noun* (uteri [or] uteruses) the muscular organ of a female mammal in which the fetus develops before birth. {<u>yoot</u> ər əs}

ut·most *adjective* of the highest or greatest degree, amount, or intensity; greatest. *We must make the utmost effort to finish this book before the exam.* *noun* the highest or greatest degree, amount, or effort. *This catalogue advertises the utmost in luxury.* / *He did his utmost to win.* {uht **mohst**}

ut·ter[1] *verb* (uttered, uttering, utters) to give forth with the voice. *He uttered a growl.* / *The baby uttered her first words.* {<u>uht</u> ər}

ut·ter[2] *adjective* complete or total; absolute. *Maia has my utter confidence.* / *He was in utter dismay when his team lost its final game.* {<u>uht</u> ər}

 Human Body  Human Mind   Everyday Life  History and Culture  Communication

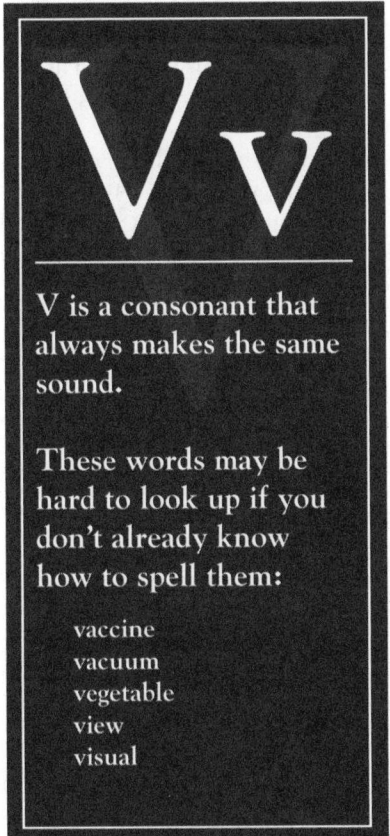

Vv

V is a consonant that always makes the same sound.

These words may be hard to look up if you don't already know how to spell them:

vaccine
vacuum
vegetable
view
visual

v or **V** *noun* (v's or V's) the twenty-second letter of the English alphabet. {vee}

VA *abbreviation* an abbreviation for **Virginia**.

va·cant *adjective* 1. without activity or contents; empty. *The streets were vacant after midnight. / The shelves in the store were vacant after the sale.* 2. not in use; available. *There were no vacant seats on the bus. / The boss interviewed several people for the vacant position in the office.* 3. showing lack of thought or emotion. *When I spoke to Paula in Hungarian, she responded with a vacant stare.* {vay kənt}

va·ca·tion *noun* a period of rest from

school, work, or other activities. *We'll go on vacation as soon as school ends. verb* (vacationed, vacationing, vacations) to take a vacation. *They vacation in Mexico.* {vay kay shən}

Word History *Vacation* comes from a Latin word that means "to be empty, free, or at leisure." See the word history at *school* for an interesting surprise.

vac·ci·nate *verb* (vaccinated, vaccinating, vaccinates) to give a vaccine to, so as to protect from a disease. *The doctor vaccinated the child against measles.* {vak sih nayt} vaccination, n.

vac·cine *noun* germs of a disease that are dead or not active. Vaccines are used to help the immune system protect against the disease. *There is a new vaccine for the flu every year.* {vak seen}

vac·u·um *noun* (vacuums) 1. a space empty of all matter. 2. a space or container from which most of the air has been removed. Outer space and the inside of a light bulb are examples of vacuums. 3. **vacuum cleaner.** *verb* (vacuumed, vacuuming, vacuums) to use, or clean by means of, a vacuum cleaner. *He vacuums twice a week.* {vak yoom}

vacuum cleaner *noun* an electrical appliance that cleans floors, carpets, rugs, and upholstery by means of suction. {vak yoom klee nər}

va·gi·na *noun* (vaginas [or] vaginae) in most female mammals, the passage leading from the uterus to the opening through which a baby is conceived and born; birth canal. {və jiy nə}

vain *adjective* 1. not leading to a desirable or lasting effect.

The climbers made a vain attempt to reach the top of Mount Everest. 2. having too much pride in one's appearance; conceited. *She is very vain about her hair.* {vayn}

Homophone Note The words **vain, vane,** and **vein** sound alike but have different meanings.

val·en·tine *noun* 1. a greeting card or gift sent on Valentine's Day. *I gave my friend a valentine.* 2. a friend or loved one greeted or chosen on Valentine's Day. *Will you be my valentine?* {val ən tiyn}

Valentine's Day or **Valentines Day** *noun* see **Saint Valentine's Day.** {val ən tiynz day}

val·id *adjective* 1. based on truth, fact, or logic. *It's valid to say that cats have whiskers. / His argument is valid.* 2. acceptable by law. *She has a valid license to drive.* {val ihd}

val·ley *noun* (valleys) a long area of low land between mountains or hills. A stream or river often runs through a

valley. {val ee}

val·u·a·ble *adjective* 1. having a great value in money; expensive. *That is a valuable car.* 2. considered to be of great worth; useful; important. *She is a valuable worker. / That is valuable information. noun*

a
b
c
d
e
f
g
h
i
j
k
l
m
n
o
p
q
r
s
t
u
v
w
x
y
z

(usually plural) something worth a lot of money, such as a piece of jewelry. *He keeps his valuables in a safe at the bank.* {**văl** yə bəl}

val·ue 📖 🌐 *noun* 1. the worth, importance, or usefulness of something. *She places great value on education.* 2. the worth of something in money, goods, or services. *What is the value of your car?* 3. (plural) principles considered most important. *Protecting the natural environment is one of his values.* *verb* (valued, valuing, values) 1. to set or guess the worth of. *The book dealer valued the collection of antique books at seven hundred dollars.* 2. to think of as important or valuable. *He valued her help. / I value you as a friend.* {**văl** yoo}

> **Word History** *Value* comes from a Latin word that means both "to be of value" and "to be strong and well." *Valiant* (brave or heroic) and *valor* (heroic courage) come from the same Latin word.

valve *noun* 1. a device that controls the flow of a liquid or gas through a pipe or tube. *The plumber closed the valve before repairing the faucet.* 2. a flap that controls the flow of a liquid in the body. *Heart valves control the flow of blood through the heart.* 3. a device that controls the flow of air in a musical instrument such as the trumpet. A valve

makes the sound of an instrument higher or lower. {**vălv**}

vam·pire *noun* 1. a creature from folk tales that was dead but came back to life. Vampires suck blood from people. 2. a bat native to Central and South America that feeds on the blood of animals. {**văm** piyr}

van *noun* a tall, covered truck or car used to move people or goods. *Workers loaded our furniture into the moving van.* {**văn**}

van·dal *noun* a person who destroys or damages property on purpose. {**văn** dəl}

van·dal·ism *noun* destruction or damage of property that is done on purpose. *Breaking the windows at school was an act of vandalism. / Is grafitti vandalism or art?* {**văn** də lih zəm}

vane *noun* 1. a device set up to turn in the wind. Vanes show the direction of the wind. *Some farmers use vanes to harness the wind's power.* 2. one of the wide flat parts on a machine, such as the windmill or the waterwheel, which catch and direct the energy of wind or water as they turn. {**vayn**}

> **Homophone Note** The words *vane*, *vain*, and *vein* sound alike but have different meanings.

va·nil·la *noun* 1. a tropical orchid that bears a fruit used for flavoring. 2. the fruit of

this plant, used as a flavoring; vanilla bean. 3. the extract of this fruit used as a flavoring or in perfume. {və **nih** lə}

van·ish *verb* (vanished, vanishing, vanishes) 1. to disappear suddenly from sight. *The ghost appeared and then vanished.* 2. to stop existing; to end. *Her smile vanished when she heard the bad news.* {**văn** ihsh}

van·i·ty *noun* (vanities) too much pride in oneself or in how one looks. *He is so filled with vanity that it is hard to talk honestly with him.* {**văn** ih tee}

va·por *noun* 1. tiny particles of a liquid or solid in a gas. *Mist and clouds are made of water vapor.* 2. a liquid or solid that becomes a gas when it is heated or when its pressure drops. {**vay** pər}

var·i·a·ble *adjective* likely to change; not constant. *The weather in the spring is variable.* *noun* something that can change or that has no fixed value. *When deciding which medicine is right, a doctor must look at many variables, such as the age and weight of the patient.* {**vayr** ee ə bəl} variably, *adv.*

va·ri·e·ty *noun* (varieties) 1. change or difference; diversity. *Without variety, the school day would be boring.* 2. a number of different things in a group or class. *There was a large variety of people at the party.* 3. a particular type within a category. *What variety of peppers are these?* {və **riy** ə tee}

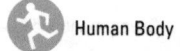 Human Body    Human Mind    Everyday Life   History and Culture    Communication

var·i·ous *adjective* 1. of many different kinds; diverse. *I have various reasons for wanting to quit the team.* 2. several; many. *Various restaurants serve vegetarian dishes.* {<u>vayr</u> ee əs *or* <u>var</u> ee əs}

var·nish *noun* a liquid that is brushed on wood or other surfaces to protect them with a hard, shiny coat. *verb* (varnished, varnishing, varnishes) to cover or coat with varnish. *We varnished the boat before we put it in the water.* {<u>var</u> nihsh}

var·y *verb* (varied, varying, varies) 1. to change; to make different. *She varies the story each time she tells it.* 2. to give variety to. *He varies his daily exercise routine.* 3. to change from time to time or as a result of some other change. *His mood varies depending on the weather.* 4. to be different; contrast. *Opinions varied on whether the mayor had served the city well.* {<u>vayr</u> ee *or* <u>var</u> ee}

Homophone Note Some people say the words **vary** and **very** in exactly the same way, but these two words have different meanings.

vase *noun* an open container of glass or pottery that is taller than it is wide. A vase is used as a decoration or to hold cut flowers. {<u>vayz</u> *or* <u>vays</u> *or* <u>vahz</u>}

vas·sal *noun* a person in the Middle Ages who was given the use of land in return for loyalty and service to a lord. {<u>văs</u> əl}

vast *adjective* (vaster, vastest) 1. very large in size or area. They drove past vast rolling fields. 2. very large in number or amount. *A vast crowd attended the concert.* {<u>văst</u>} vastly, adv.

vat *noun* a very large barrel, tub, or tank, used for holding liq-

uids. *There are several vats of milk at the dairy farm.* {<u>văt</u>}

vault¹ *noun* 1. an arch made of stone, brick, or concrete that forms a roof or ceiling. *The ancient Romans were the first to use vaults in their buildings.* 2. a room, chamber, or passage with a roof or ceiling shaped like an arch. *The underground vault of the old cathedral contains the remains of medieval knights and nobles.* 3. a sturdy room or compartment used to store and protect valuable things. *The bank keeps a lot of money in its vault.* {<u>vawlt</u>}

vault² *verb* (vaulted, vaulting, vaults) to jump, leap, or spring over, using the hands or a pole as a support. *Tom vaulted over the fence.* *noun* a jump, leap, or spring. *His vault carried him across the creek.* {<u>vawlt</u>} vaulter, n.

VCR *abbreviation* an abbreviation for **videocassette recorder**.

veal *noun* the flesh of a calf, used as meat. {<u>veel</u>}

veer *verb* (veered, veering, veers) to change direction; turn quickly. *The car veered to the right to avoid hitting the deer.* {<u>veer</u>}

veg·e·ta·ble 🌳💧 *noun* 1. a plant or part of a plant, such as carrots, beans, or lettuce, that is used for food. 2. any living thing that is a plant. *Some people classify everything in nature as either animal, vegetable, or mineral.* *adjective* 1. coming from or made of vegetables that can be eaten. *The cook made a delicious vegetable stew.* 2. of or having to do with a plant or plants. *There is a lot of vegetable matter at the bottom of the lake.* {<u>vehj</u> tə bəl}

Word History In the 1300s, the word *vegetable* meant "living and growing." The word's modern meaning, "a plant that is cultivated for food," began to be used in the mid-1700s. The origin of the word "vegetable" is the Latin word *vegetabilis*, which means "to give energy to" or "enliven."

veg·e·tar·i·an *noun* a person who eats no meat or fish but only vegetables, fruits, nuts, and grains. *adjective* 1. having to do with vegetarians. *There are a few vegetarian restaurants in town.* 2. made up of vegetables and having no meat. *She made a vegetarian soup for lunch.* {<u>vehj</u> ə <u>tayr</u> ee ən} vegetarianism, n.

veg·e·ta·tion *noun* plants or plant life in a particular place. *We walked through the thick vegetation near the river.* {<u>vehj</u> ə <u>tay</u> shən}

A
B
C
D
E
F
G
H
I
J
K
L
M
N
O
P
Q
R
S
T
U
V
W
X
Y
Z

a b c d e f g h i j k l m n o p q r s t u v w x y z

ve·hi·cle O *noun* 1. something used to carry and move people or things. *Cars, buses, and airplanes are vehicles*. 2. a means of communicating or expressing. *The book served as a vehicle for her ideas about nature.* {**vee** ih kəl}

veil *noun* 1. a thin piece of cloth worn over the head, shoulders, and face. A veil is used as a decoration, or to hide a person's face. 2. something that hides or separates. *The castle stood behind a veil of fog.* *verb* (veiled, veiling, veils) to hide or cover with a veil or something like a veil. *A thick stand of trees near the road veiled the house.* {**vayl**}

vein *noun* 1. a small vessel that carries blood to the heart. 2. one of a series of thin ribs or lines that form the structure of a leaf or insect wing. 3. a body or layer of ore in a mass of rock. *The miners found a vein of silver in the cave wall.* {**vayn**}

Homophone Note The words *vein*, *vain*, and *vane* sound alike but have different meanings.

Vel·cro *noun* a trademark for a device that fastens using strips of nylon tape. One strip is covered with tiny hooks that attach to another strip with tiny loops. Velcro is used on clothing and many other items. {**vehl** kroh}

ve·loc·i·ty *noun* (velocities) 1. speed. *The car is moving with great velocity.* 2. rate of speed or motion. *The velocity of the wind is twenty miles per hour.* {və **lo** sih tee}

vel·vet *noun* a fine cloth made from silk, rayon, or cotton. Velvet has a soft, fuzzy feel on one side. *adjective* 1. made of, covered with, or wearing velvet. *The queen always preferred the velvet crown.* 2. soft or smooth like velvet. *The baby has velvet skin.* {**vehl** viht} velvety, adj.

vend *verb* (vended, vending, vends) to sell or offer for sale in person or through a machine. *He vends produce at the farm market.* / *This machine vends soft drinks.* {**vehnd**} vendor, n.

vending machine *noun* a machine that sells small things such as candy bars or soft drinks. It is operated by putting money into a slot and pressing a button. {**vehn** ding mə **sheen**}

Venetian blind *noun* a window blind made of thin slats connected by a cord. The slats can be tilted to control the amount of air or light let through. A cord is also used to raise and lower the blind. {və **nee** shən **bliynd**}

Ven·e·zue·la *noun* a country in northern South America. Caracas is the capital of Venezuela. {veh nə **zway** lə} Venezuelan, n., adj.

Ven·ice *noun* a city in Italy. Venice is built on many small islands. {**veh** nihs}

ven·om O *noun* the poison that certain snakes, insects, scorpions, and other animals produce. Venom is put into prey by biting or stinging. {**veh** nəm}

vent *noun* an opening through which a gas or vapor can enter, pass through, or exit. *verb* (vented, venting, vents) 1. to let out. *Fireplaces vent smoke through a chimney.* 2. to give expression to suddenly or with force. *Ron vented his anger by shouting and pounding his fist on the table.* {**vehnt**}

ven·ti·la·tion *noun* the circulation of air, or change of air. *Open the window for better ventilation.* {vehn tə **lay** shən}

ven·tri·cle *noun* either of the two lower compartments of the heart. Ventricles receive blood from the upper compartments, called atria, and pump it to the lungs and throughout the body. {**vehn** trih kəl}

ven·tril·o·quism *noun* the skill or act of speaking without moving the lips so that the voice seems to come from a source other than the speaker. {vehn **trih** lə kwih zəm}

ven·ture *noun* an activity or undertaking in which there is risk or the result is not certain. *He entered a business venture with his friend.* *verb* (ventured, venturing, ventures) 1. to go forward in spite of risks; brave the dangers of. *She ventured into the icy water to rescue her friend.* 2. to move, travel, or go in a brave or daring manner. *He ventured out into the world with only a few cents in his pocket.* {**vehn** chər}

Ve·nus *noun* 1. the goddess of love and beauty in Roman

 Human Body   Human Mind   Everyday Life   History and Culture Communication

mythology. In Greek mythology, Venus is called Aphrodite. 2. the sixth largest planet in the solar system and second in distance from the sun. Venus has a dense, cloudy atmosphere. The clouds that cover Venus reflect light and make it the brightest planet. {**vee** nəs}

ve·ran·da or **verandah** *noun* a large, open porch attached to a house. Verandas have roofs and are used for social activities. {və **răn** də}

Word History *Veranda* comes from a word in the Hindi language of India. This word is *varanda*, which means "long balcony." The Hindi word may come from a word in the Portuguese language. The country of Portugal is a long way from India, but the Portuguese, renowned sailors and explorers, had power in India in the 1500s.

verb *noun* a word that expresses a state of being or an action. Verbs usually have different forms to express tense, voice, mood, and number. "Read," "blew," "drives," "seemed," and "skip" are examples of verbs. {**vuhrb**}

ver·bal *adjective* 1. having to do with words. *That poet has wonderful verbal skill.* 2. using the spoken rather than the written word. *The buyer and seller made a verbal agreement before writing up a contract.* {**vuhr** bəl} verbally, *adv.*

ver·dict *noun* 1. the decision of a judge or jury in a law case. *The verdict in Mr. Simpson's trial was "not guilty."* 2. any decision or opinion. *After living with lime-green walls for a week, the verdict in my family was that the color had to go.* {**vuhr** dihkt}

verge *noun* 1. the border or edge of something. *We stopped at the verge of the forest.* 2. the point at which something happens, begins, or comes into effect; brink. *The scientists are on the verge of a major discovery.* *verb* (verged, verging, verges) to come close to or be on the border of (often followed by "on"). *That land verges on the city park. / The child's crying verged on a temper tantrum.* {**vuhrj**}

Synonyms
These words share a meaning with *verge*, noun 1:
edge, bounds, limit, border, margin.

ver·i·fy *verb* (verified, verifying, verifies) to make sure of the truth or correctness of. *We verified his story by talking to his father. / The waiter verified our bill by checking it with a calculator.* {**vehr** ə fiy}

ver·mil·ion *noun* the color that comes from mixing bright red and a small amount of orange paint. {vər **mihl** yən}

ver·min *noun* (vermin) an animal that causes harm or damage or is difficult to control; pest. Rats and cock-roaches are thought of as vermin. *Some people set out poison or traps to kill vermin in their home.* {**vuhr** mihn}

Ver·mont *noun* a state in the northeastern United States. Its capital is Montpelier. (abbreviated: VT) {vər **mŏnt**}

Word History *Vermont* is based on French words that mean "green mountain." In the 1600s, French explorers called the mountains *les verts monts*. Vermont's nickname is "The Green Mountain State."

ver·sa·tile *adjective* 1. able to do many different things well. *Chris is a versatile athlete.* 2. having a number of different uses. *A pocket knife is a versatile tool.* {**vuhr** sə tihl} versatility, n.

verse *noun* 1. poetry or a poem. *He bought a book of verse.* 2. one line or one section of a poem. *We memorized three verses of the poem.* 3. a section of a song. *Most people know only the first verse of "America the Beautiful."* {**vuhrs**}

Word History The word *verse* goes back to the Latin *versus*, which means "a line of writing or poetry." This Latin word came from another Latin word, *vertere*, which means "to turn." What did lines of poetry have to do with turning? Think of the action of a farmer plowing a field, turning around at the end of one plowed row or line to make another line for planting. Note: *Vert-* is an important Latin word-part, or root, in the English language: you can find it in the words *convert* (to turn something into something else), *invert* (to turn something upside-down) and *vertigo*, the word doctors use for "dizziness."

A B C D E F G H I J K L M N O P Q R S T U V W X Y Z

a
b
c
d
e
f
g
h
i
j
k
l
m
n
o
p
q
r
s
t
u
v
w
x
y
z

ver·sion *noun* 1. a description or report in a particular style or from one point of view. *I told the principal my version of the fight.* 2. a particular form of something. *We saw the film version after we read the book.* {**vuhr** zhən}

ver·sus *preposition* 1. against; in opposition to. *It was West High School versus North High School for the city softball championship.* 2. as compared with; in contrast to. *We argued about life in prison versus the death penalty.* {**vuhr** səs}

ver·te·bra *noun* (vertebrae or vertebras) one of the small bones that form the spinal column. {**vuhr** tə brə}

ver·te·brate ❶ *adjective* having a backbone. *A jellyfish is not a vertebrate animal. noun* an animal that has a skeleton with a backbone inside its body. Mammals, birds, amphibians, reptiles, and fish are large groups of vertebrates. {**vuhr** tə **brayt** *or* **vuhr** tə briht, n., **vuhr** tə **brayt** *or* **vuhr** tə briht, adj.}

ver·tex *noun* (vertexes or vertices) 1. the highest point of anything; apex. *After much climbing, we reached the vertex of the mountain.* 2. the point where the sides of an angle or geometric solid come together. *A cube has eight vertices.* {**vuhr** tehks}

ver·ti·cal *adjective* straight up and down; upright. *His shirt has a pattern of vertical stripes.* {**vuhr** tih kəl} vertically, adv.

ver·y *adverb* 1. to a great extent; in a high degree;

extremely. *He is very sad. / It is very cold tonight.* 2. used to make an adjective stronger. *She is the very best student in the class. / He now has his very own car. adjective* (verier, veriest) 1. exact; precise. *Your help was the very thing we needed.* 2. complete; extreme. *He lives at the very end of the street.* 3. same. *This is the very place I saw him yesterday.* 4. by itself; mere. *The very sight of him makes me laugh.* {**vehr** ee}

Homophone Note Are you looking for the word *vary* (to change or be different)? Some people say the words *very* and *vary* in exactly the same way, but these two words have different meanings.

ves·sel *noun* 1. a hollow container for liquids. *This ancient jar is a vessel for olive oil.* 2. a large boat or ship. *We traveled on a sailing vessel.* 3. one of the small tubes that carry blood and other fluids throughout the body. *Veins and arteries are vessels.* {**veh** səl}

vest *noun* a short piece of clothing without sleeves, usually worn over a shirt or blouse and under a jacket. *verb* (vested, vesting, vests) to place in control or possession of someone. *The law vests control of the corporation in a board of directors.* {**vehst**}

vet[1] *noun* (informal) a short form for **veterinarian**. {**veht**}

vet[2] *noun* (informal) a short form for **veteran**. {**veht**}

vet·er·an ❓ 🌐 *noun* 1. a person who has had long experience in a particular activity. *The baseball veteran gave the rookie a few tips.* 2. a person who has served in the armed forces during a war. *His*

grandfather is a veteran of the Korean War. {**veht** ə rən}

Veterans Day *noun* a holiday in the United States that honors veterans of the armed forces. It is held on November 11 and used to be called "Armistice Day." {**veht** ə rənz **day**}

vet·er·i·nar·i·an *noun* a doctor for animals. *We took our dog to the veterinarian to get his rabies shot.* {**veht** ə rih **nayr** ee ən}

ve·to *noun* the power of a government official or group to keep something from taking effect. *The president's veto sent the bill back to Congress. verb* (vetoed, vetoing, vetoes) to prevent from taking effect. *The governor vetoed that law. / My father vetoed my decision to dye my hair green.* {**vee** toh}

Word History *Veto* is a Latin word that means "I forbid." It was used by representatives of the Roman people when they opposed the Roman Senate.

VFW *abbreviation* a national organization made up of Americans who served in the U.S. armed forces during wars fought outside of the United States. VFW is an abbreviation for "Veterans of Foreign Wars."

vi·brate *verb* (vibrated, vibrating, vibrates) 1. to move back and forth very rapidly and steadily. *The floor vibrates when I jump up and down.* 2. to cause to move back and forth very rapidly and steadily. *Sound waves vibrate the diaphragm in a microphone.* {**viv** brayt}

vice *noun* 1. wicked, evil, or criminal behavior. *The police tried to get rid of vice in the neighborhood.* 2. a slight personal fault or weakness. *Her*

 Human Body
 Human Mind
 Everyday Life
 History and Culture
 Communication

vice is eating too much chocolate. {**viys**}

Homophone Note Are you looking for the word *vise* (a gripping tool)? *Vice* and *vise* sound alike but have different meanings.

vice president *noun* 1. an officer who ranks directly below a president. The vice president works as president when the president cannot perform his duties. 2. (capitalized) the title of the elected official of this rank in the U.S. government, who acts as president of the Senate. *Vice President Andrew Johnson became president after Abraham Lincoln was assassinated.* {**viys** **preh** zə dənt} vice presidency, n., vice presidential, adj.

vi·cin·i·ty *noun* (vicinities) an area near or around a place; somewhere nearby. *He lives in the vicinity of the town hall.* {və **sih** nih tee}

vi·cious *adjective* 1. wicked; evil. *They played a vicious trick on me.* 2. likely to be cruel or violent; fierce. *Stay away from the vicious dog.* {**vih** shəs} viciously, adv., viciousness, n.

vic·tim *noun* 1. someone who is hurt, injured, or killed by a person, group, or event. *The murderer stabbed his victim.* / *The orphan was a victim of war.* 2. someone who is tricked or cheated. *He was the victim of a plot to take his land.* {**vihk** tihm}

vic·tor *noun* the winner of a contest, battle, argument, or struggle. *The victors celebrated after the game.* {**vihk** tər}

vic·to·ri·ous *adjective* having won a victory. *The victorious candidate gave a speech after the election.* {vihk **tohr** ee əs}

vic·to·ry *noun* (victories) success in a fight against an enemy, opponent, or something difficult. *The game ended with a victory for the home team.* / *The Russian victory at Stalingrad was a turning point of World War Two.* {**vihk** tə ree}

vid·e·o 🔊 *noun* 1. the picture part of television. *We adjusted the video and the sound before watching the show.* 2. a *videotape*. *adjective* having to do with the picture part of television, or any images shown on a screen. {**vih** dee oh}

vid·e·o·cas·sette *noun* a cassette that holds a videotape. Videocassettes are used to record and play back pictures and sound. {**vih** dee oh kə **seht**}

videocassette recorder *noun* a device that records on and plays videocassettes; VCR. {**vih** dee oh kə **seht** rə kohr dər}

video game *noun* a game played on a television or computer in which players control what happens. {**vih** dee oh gaym}

vid·e·o·tape *noun* 1. a magnetic tape used to record pictures and sound to be played on a television. 2. a recording made on this tape. *verb* (videotaped, videotaping, videotapes) to make a recording of on videotape. *We videotaped our favorite show while we were on vacation.* {**vih** dee oh tayp}

Vi·en·na *noun* the capital city of Austria. {vee **eh** nə}

Vi·et·nam *noun* a country in souteastern Asia. Hanoi is the capital of Vietnam. {**vee** eht **nahm** *or* **vee** eht **năm** *or* vee eht **nahm**}

Vi·et·nam·ese *noun* 1. a person who was born in or is a citizen of Vietnam. 2. the lan-guage of Vietnam. *adjective* of or having to do with Vietnam, or its people or language. {vee **eht** nə **meez**}

VUI MỪNG
KÍNH MỜI

view ❓ *noun* 1. the act of looking at or seeing; examination; survey. *The doctor stepped closer for a better view of her scalp.* 2. one's range of sight. *He walked inside and disappeared from view.* 3. the area that can be seen from a particular point; scene; vista. *There is a beautiful view from the top of Pike's Peak.* 4. (often plural) a way of thinking about something; opinion; perception. *She told us her views on education.* *verb* (viewed, viewing, views) 1. to see; perceive with the eyes. *We viewed the film on the animals of Australia.* 2. to look at with great care; survey. *The police will view the evidence.* 3. to think about or consider. *How do you view the war?* {**vyoo**}

• **in view of**
taking note of; taking into account; considering. *In view of your otherwise good*

A B C D E F G H I J K L M N O P Q R S T U V W X Y Z

 Living World    Physical World    Natural Environment   Economy   Government and Law

behavior, we won't punish you this time.

view·point *noun* an opinion. *This book discusses different viewpoints on the Vietnam War.* {**vyoo** point}

vig·i·lant *adjective* alert and careful about danger. *The duty of a lifeguard is to be vigilant.* {**vihj** j lənt} vigilantly, adv.

Synonyms
These words share a meaning with ***vigilant***, adjective 1:
alert, cautious, attentive, watchful, wary

vig·or *noun* 1. active strength or power. *He spoke with vigor against war.* 2. mental or physical energy or force; enthusiasm. *He is full of vigor, even at eighty years of age.* {**vih** gər}

vi·gour *noun* a spelling of **vigor** used in Canada and Britain. See **vigor**. {**vih** gər}

Vi·king *noun* (sometimes lower case) any of the Scandinavian sea warriors and traders who were active from around A.D. 700 to 1100. The Vikings raided the coasts of Europe and settled parts of Britain, western Europe, Russia, and elsewhere. {**viy** king}

vil·la *noun* a large, luxurious country house or estate. *He lives in the city and has a villa where he spends weekends.* {**vihl** ə}

vil·lage 🟢 🔵 *noun* 1. a small town or community, often in the country. 2. the people who live in a particular village. *The whole village is against the plan for a new highway.* {**vihl** ihj}

vil·lain *noun* 1. an evil person; scoundrel. *The police haven't caught the villain who stole the car.* 2. such a person or creature in a story. Villains cause trouble for the hero or heroine. *The wolf is the villain in the story of Little Red Riding Hood.* {**vihl** ən} villanous, adj.

vine *noun* a plant having a long, thin, woody stem that climbs up a support or creeps along the ground. *Grapes grow on vines.* {**viyn**}

vin·e·gar *noun* a sour liquid formed when wine, cider, or malt ferments. It is used to flavor or preserve food. {**vihn** ə gər}

vine·yard *noun* an area where grapes are farmed. {**vihn** yərd}

vi·nyl *noun* a tough, shiny plastic made from a resin. Phonograph records, floor coverings, and water pipes are some things that are made of vinyl. {**viy** nəl}

vi·o·la *noun* a musical instrument that looks like a violin. It has four strings and is larger than a violin but smaller than a cello. {vee **oh** lə or viy **oh** lə}

vi·o·late *verb* (violated, violating, violates) 1. to break or fail to keep. *She violated the speed limit and got a ticket.* 2. to disturb. *He violated their privacy.* {**viy** ə layt}

vi·o·lence *noun* 1. a strong force that can harm or damage. *The violence of the hurricane lasted a few hours.* 2. an act that causes injury or harm. *The criminal uses violence to* try to get what he wants. {**viy** ə ləns}

vi·o·lent *adjective* 1. acting with great force or ill will. *The violent criminal was sent to prison for twenty-five years.* 2. very strong; harsh. *The violent storm tore off the roof of our house.* 3. having strong emotional force. *He has a violent temper.* {**viy** ə lənt} violently, adv.

vi·o·let *noun* 1. the color of purple violets; the last color in the color spectrum. 2. a small plant that bears purple, white, blue, or yellow flowers. {**viy** ə liht}

vi·o·lin *noun* a musical instrument with four strings and no frets. It is held between the chin and shoulder and is played with a bow. {**viy** ə **lihn**}

vi·per *noun* a poisonous snake with long, hollow fangs. {**viy** pər}

vir·gin *noun* (capitalized) Virgin Mary, the mother of Jesus Christ. *adjective* not touched by humans; natural; not changed. *The virgin forest has many old trees.* {**vuhr** jihn}

Vir·gin·ia *noun* a state in the southern United States on the Atlantic Coast. Its capital is Richmond. (abbreviated: VA) {vər **jihn** yə}

Word History *Virginia* was named for Queen Elizabeth I of England, known as the "Virgin Queen." Parts of the state of Virginia became Kentucky in 1792 and West Virginia in 1863.

Virgin Islands *plural noun* a group of islands in the West Indies in the Caribbean Sea. Part of the Virgin Islands

 Human Body   Human Mind  Everyday Life  History and Culture  Communication

belongs to the United States, and part belongs to the United Kingdom. {**vuhr** jihn **iy** ləndz}

Vir·go *noun* 1. a constellation located between Leo and Libra. Virgo is also called the Virgin. 2. the sixth sign of the zodiac, the Virgin, which the sun enters about August 21. 3. a person born under this sign, between August 21 and September 22. {**vuhr** goh}

vir·tu·al *adjective* not actually being true or real, but seeming to be, or having the same result as if true or real. *By not defending herself in court, the accused woman gave a virtual admission of guilt.* {**vuhr** chooh əl}

vir·tu·al re·al·i·ty *noun* a space created by software such as a computer game that resembles the physical world in sight and sound; cyberspace. *When you enter the virtual reality of some games, you feel like you are in another world.* {**vuhr** chooh ehl ree ăl ih tee}

vir·tue ❷ *noun* 1. right action or thoughts; goodness. *His virtue is shown by the way he treats all people with respect.* 2. a particular type of moral goodness. *Patience is a virtue.* 3. a good quality or characteristic. *She has the virtue of honesty.* {**vuhr** chooh}

vi·rus ❷ ❹ *noun* (viruses) 1. a tiny organism that can reproduce only in living cells. Viruses cause disease in humans, animals, and plants. 2. a disease caused by such an organism. *Measles and the flu are viruses.* 3. see **computer virus.** {**viy** rəs}

vise or **vice** *noun* a tool used to grip objects. Vises have two jaws that are opened and closed by a lever or screw. *The carpenter put the board in the vise before cutting it with a saw.* {**viys**}

Homophone Note The words *vise* and *vice* sound alike but have different meanings. To learn why the carpenter considered it a vice for his children to play with his vise, look up *vice*.

vis·i·ble *adjective* 1. able to be seen. *The skyscraper is visible from across the river.* 2. easily seen; obvious. *There has been no visible change in the patient's condition.* {**vihz** ə bəl} visibly, adv.

vi·sion ❷ *noun* 1. the ability to see; sight. *His vision improved after he started wearing glasses.* 2. the power to see future events or ideas. *His plan for the new playground showed vision.* 3. something present in or felt by the imagination but not actually present or true. *He had visions of lying on a beach in Mexico.* {**vih** zhən}

vis·it *verb* (visited, visiting, visits) 1. to go or come to see. *We visit our cousins every year. / I visited the zoo last week.* 2. to stay with for a short time as a guest. *Our friends visited us in February. noun* 1. an act of calling to see a person or place. *I had a good visit with friends. / Our visit to the city was fun.* 2. the act of staying somewhere as a guest. *I go to my grandparents' house for a visit every year.* {**vihz** iht}

vi·sor *noun* 1. a brim that sticks out from the front of a cap or hat and shades the eyes. 2. a flap above the inside windshield of a vehicle that shields the eyes from glare. 3. the upper front part of a helmet or other item worn on the head. Visors protect the eyes and face. {**viy** zər}

vis·ta *noun* a distant view as seen from a particular point or through an opening such as between buildings or trees. *They enjoyed the vista from*

their cabin on the mountain. {**vihs** tə}

vis·u·al ❷ *adjective* 1. having to do with sight or seeing. *Visual strength is needed to read the small letters on an eye chart.* 2. having to do with or using pictures or video. *The teacher's visual aids made the lesson more interesting.* {**vih** zhooh əl}

vis·u·al·ize *verb* (visualized, visualizing, visualizes) to form a picture of in the mind. *He visualized climbing the mountain.* {**vih** zhooh ə liyz}

vi·tal *adjective* 1. having to do with life. *The nurse checked the patient's heartbeat and other vital signs.* 2. necessary to life. *The heart and lungs are vital organs.* 3. full of life or energy. *The old woman was still vital at ninety years of age.* 4. very important; necessary. *It is vital that you finish high school.* {**viy** təl} vitally, adv.

Synonyms
These words share a meaning with *vital*, adjective 4:
necessary, essential, critical, crucial, indispensable

vi·ta·min *noun* one of a number of natural or human-made substances needed for the health and normal working of the body. Humans get

A B C D E F G H I J K L M N O P Q R S T U V W X Y Z

most of their vitamins from food. {**viy** tə mihn}

viv·id *adjective* 1. bright and strong. *That poster has many vivid colors.* 2.

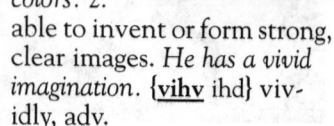

able to invent or form strong, clear images. *He has a vivid imagination.* {**vihv** ihd} viv·idly, *adv.*

vo·cab·u·lar·y 🔊 *noun* (vocabularies) 1. the words of a language. *We study English vocabulary in school.* 2. the words or terms used in a particular field. *He is learning the vocabulary of chemistry.* 3. the words used by or familiar to a particular person or group of people. *She did not understand the vocabulary of skateboarders.* 4. a list of words arranged in alphabetical order with their definitions. *He used a vocabulary to help him understand the science textbook.* {voh **kăb** yə **layr** ee}

vo·cal *adjective* 1. having to do with or produced by the voice. 2. performed by singing. *Franz Schubert is famous for composing vocal music.* 3. given to speaking in an open or strong way. *She is vocal in her support of our school.* {**voh** kəl} vocally, *adv.*

vocal cords *noun* the folds at the top of the windpipe that produce the sounds of the voice. There are two pairs of vocal cords. When air passes over the lower pair, it vibrates and sounds are made. {**voh** kəl **kohrdz**}

vo·ca·tion *noun* a job or career; occupation. *Mel is taking courses for his vocation as an actor.* {voh **kay** shən}

vogue *noun* a popular fashion or style. *The clothing of the 1990s is no longer in vogue.* {**vohg**}

voice 🔊 *noun* 1. the sounds produced through the mouth by a human being. *You have a beautiful voice.* 2. the ability to make such sounds. *He lost his voice from yelling too much at the game.* 3. an expression of desire or interest. *The principal listened to the voice of the students.* 4. the power to express an opinion. *She has a voice in the decision.* *verb* (voiced, voicing, voices) to express with the voice. *He voiced his approval of the plan.* {**vois**}

voice mail *noun* 1. a spoken message that has been recorded electronically and stored on a central computer. The person to whom the message has been sent can listen to it by telephoning the computer. *I can check my voice mail from any telephone.* 2. a telephone system that records spoken messages electronically and stores them on a central computer. A subscriber then listens to the messages by telephoning the main computer. *Our school uses voice mail as a way for teachers and families to stay in touch.* {**vois** mayl}

void *adjective* 1. not containing anything; empty. 2. having no effect; useless. *His work on the project was void.* 3. empty; lacking (usually followed by "of"). *She seems to be void of emotion.* 4. not filled, as an office or position. *His position was left void after he retired.* 5. having no legal power; not valid. *The contract was declared void.* *noun* 1. an empty space or vacuum. *We are still exploring the void of outer space.* 2. a feeling of emptiness or loss. *There was a void in our family when my grandmother died.* *verb* (voided, voiding, voids) to make not valid; cancel. *She voided the check because she had made a mistake.* {**void**}

Synonyms
These words share a meaning with *void*, adjective 1:
empty, bare, vacant

vol·ca·no 🔊 *noun* (volcanoes or volcanos) 1. an opening in the earth's crust through which melted rock, ash, and gases are forced out. 2. a mountain or hill made from melted rock that builds up around such an opening. {vŏl **kay** noh}

Word History In Roman mythology, *Volcanus* was the blacksmith of the Roman gods. He forged thunderbolts from his fire.

vole *noun* a small rodent with gray or brown fur, short legs, and a short tail. Voles are rodents closely related to lemmings and mice. Many kinds of voles are found in Europe, Asia, North America, and northern

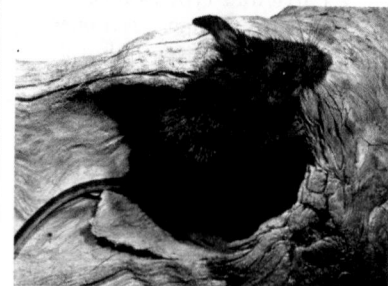

Africa. In North America, voles are sometimes called field mice. {**vohl**}

vol·ley *noun* (volleys) 1. the firing of a number of guns or other weapons at the same time. *The soldiers sent a volley of bullets at the enemy.* 2. a burst of words or acts done together. *The students had a*

 Human Body   Human Mind  Everyday Life  History and Culture  Communication

volley of complaints for their teacher. 3. the act of returning the ball before it touches the ground in sports such as tennis. *He won the point with a good volley.* *verb* (volleyed, volleying, volleys) to return the ball before it touches the ground in sports such as tennis. *She always volleys accurately.* {vŏl ee}

vol·ley·ball *noun* 1. a game in which two teams use their hands to hit a ball back and forth over a high net. Points are scored when the ball hits the ground in the opponent's court. 2. the ball used in this game. {vŏl ee bawl}

volt *noun* a unit of force for measuring electric current. (abbreviated: V) {vohlt}

Word History The Italian physicist Alessandro Volta (1745-1827) invented the first electric battery. It became known as the Voltaic cell. After Volta's death, a unit of measurement was named after him in honor of his contribution to science.

volt·age *noun* the force of an electric current as measured in volts. {vohl tihj}

vol·ume *noun* 1. a collection of pages of writing or print bound together; book. *Our public library has thousands of volumes.* 2. one of the books in a series or set of books. *This encyclopedia has twenty-five volumes.* 3. the size of a three-dimensional space enclosed within or occupied by an object. *The*

volume of the car engine is about two hundred cubic inches. 4. amount; quantity. *Many people in this country waste large volumes of water.* 5. the amount of sound. *Would you please turn up the volume on the CD player?* {vŏl yoom *or* vŏl yəm}

vol·un·tar·y *adjective* 1. acting from or done by choice. *She made a voluntary decision to go back to school.* 2. done or carried out by persons working without pay. *The soup kitchen depends on voluntary help.* {vŏl ən tayr ee} voluntarily, adv.

vol·un·teer *noun* a person who offers to work or help without pay. *adjective* of or having to do with a volunteer or volunteers. *She is a volunteer firefighter.* *verb* (volunteered, volunteering, volunteers) to offer for no pay. *He volunteered an hour a week at the museum.* {vŏl ən teer}

vom·it *verb* (vomited, vomiting, vomits) to throw up food and other contents of the stomach through the mouth. *He vomited all night and didn't go to school the next day.* *noun* matter that is vomited. *He cleaned up the vomit from the floor.* {vŏm iht}

vote ⬭ *noun* 1. a formal expression of a choice in an election or other group decision. *My vote will go to the best candidate.* 2. the way in which such a choice is made known. *She asked for a vote of raised hands from all the children who wanted to go outside.* 3. the right to vote; suffrage. *Women had to fight hard for the vote.* 4. the results of an election. *The vote went against him.* *verb* (voted, voting, votes) 1. to express a choice in an elec-

tion or decision. *Did you vote yesterday?* 2. to decide together. *We voted her our favorite teacher.* {voht}

vouch *verb* (vouched, vouching, vouches) to promise to be true, real, or correct (usually followed by "for"). *He vouched for the results of the scientist's experiment.* {vowch}

vow *noun* a serious promise or pledge. *She made a vow of revenge. / The couple exchanged wedding vows.* *verb* (vowed, vowing, vows) 1. to promise or pledge in a serious way. *The witness vowed to tell the truth in court.* 2. to make a serious promise. *The new mayor vowed to keep the roads in good repair.* {vow}

vow·el ⬭ *noun* 1. in the English alphabet, any of the letters "a," "e," "i," "o," "u," and sometimes "y." 2. any of the speech sounds represented by these letters. These sounds are produced by allowing a free flow of air through the mouth. {vowl *or* vow əl}

voy·age *noun* a long journey by air, land, sea, or outer space. *The voyage to the moon and back took over a week.* *verb* (voyaged, voyaging, voyages) to make or take a long trip or journey; travel. *The scientists voyaged to the South Pole.* {voi ihj} voyager, n.

vs. *abbreviation* an abbreviation for **versus**.

VT *or* **Vt.** *abbreviation* an abbreviation for **Vermont**.

vul·gar *adjective* 1. without good taste or manners. *The vulgar child chewed with her mouth open.* 2. showing bad taste; giving offense; not appropriate. *I don't find that vulgar joke funny. / She turned away from the vulgar*

A B C D E F G H I J K L M N O P Q R S T U V W X Y Z

a
b
c
d
e
f
g
h
i
j
k
l
m
n
o
p
q
r
s
t
u
v
w
x
y
z

painting. {<u>vuhl</u> gər}

vul·ner·a·ble *adjective*
1. able to be hurt or injured. *The plants in the garden are vulnerable to frost.*
2. open to attack or danger. *The towns on the coast are vulnerable to hurricanes.* {<u>vuhl</u> nə rə bəl} vulnerability, n.

vul·ture *noun* a large bird that usually has dark feathers and a bald head and neck. There are many kinds of vulture. These birds are related to hawks and feed on dead animals. {<u>vuhl</u> chər}

Word History *Vulture* comes from a Latin word that means "to tear."

 Human Body
 Human Mind
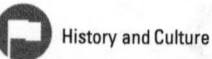 Everyday Life
 History and Culture
Communication

Ww

W is a consonant that always makes the same sound. Words that start with "wr" always have a silent "w" (such as wrap, wreck, wriggle, or wrong). The "w" is silent in some "wh" words (such as who or whole).

Tips to help you look up words starting with w: Also look under O for words like "one" and "once."

These words may be hard to look up if you don't already know how to spell them:

Wednesday	women
weight	won
weird	would
whistle	wrestle
wolf	written
woman	

w or **W** *noun* (w's or W's) the twenty-third letter of the English alphabet. {**duh** bəl **yoo** or **duh** bəl yuu or **duhb** yə}

W or **w** *abbreviation* 1. an abbreviation for **west**. 2. an abbreviation for **watt** or watts.

WA or **Wash.** *abbreviation* an abbreviation for **Washington**.

wad *noun* 1. a small mass or ball. *He chewed a wad of gum.* / *There was a wad of paper on the floor.* 2. (informal) a roll or large amount of paper money. *He walked into the jewelry store with a wad and bought the most expensive necklace there.* *verb* (wadded, wadding, wads) to roll or press into a wad (often followed by "up"). *She wadded up the paper.* {**wahd**}

wad·dle *verb* (waddled, waddling, waddles) to walk using short steps while rocking from side to side. *The penguins waddled into a group.* *noun* a way of walking while rocking from side to side. *He has a waddle we can recognize from far away.* {**wŏd** əl}

wade *verb* (waded, wading, wades) 1. to walk through water or something else that slows a person down. *The soldiers waded slowly through the tall grass.* 2. to move ahead slowly or with difficulty (often followed by "through"). *She waded through the pile of papers, searching for his letter.* {**wayd**}

Homophone Note The words *wade* and *weighed* (past tense of the verb "weigh") sound alike but have different meanings.

waf·fle[1] *noun* a flat cake cooked in a device that leaves a pattern of

squares on the cake. *We had waffles for breakfast.* {**wŏf** əl}

Word History *Wafel*, the German and Dutch word for the *waffle* we eat, may have come from the German word that means "to weave."

waf·fle[2] *verb* (waffled, waffling, waffles) to speak or write in a way that is not clear or direct. *The mayor waffled when asked about the new traffic rules.* {**wŏf** əl}

wag *verb* (wagged, wagging, wags) 1. to cause to move quickly up and down or from side to side. *Our dog wags her tail when we talk to her.* / *My mother wagged her finger at me when I was late coming home from school.* 2. to move quickly up and down or from side to side. *The dog's tail wags.* *noun* the act of wagging. *With a wag of its tail, the dog ran into the house.* {**wăg**}

wage *noun* (often plural) money paid in a regular way to a person for doing work or giving help. *I collect wages every week from my boss.* *verb* (waged, waging, wages) to carry on or take part in. *During World War II, Germany waged war with its neighboring countries.* {**wayj**}

wag·on *noun* 1. a vehicle with four wheels that is used to carry heavy loads. Wagons are usually drawn by horses, tractors, or trucks. 2. a small, open cart with four wheels and a handle, used as a child's toy. {**wăg** ən}

waif *noun* a child without a home or friends. *The waifs hoped to be adopted by a kind family.* {**wayf**}

wail *verb* (wailed, wailing, wails) 1. to make a long, loud cry out of sadness or pain.

A
B
C
D
E
F
G
H
I
J
K
L
M
N
O
P
Q
R
S
T
U
V
W
X
Y
Z

The boy wailed when he fell off his bicycle. 2. to make a sound like such a cry. *The ambulance's siren wailed.* *noun* a long, loud cry of pain or sadness, or a sound like this. *The wail of the wind kept me awake last night.* {**wayl**}

Homophone Note The words *wail* and *whale* (a large marine mammal) sound alike but have different meanings.

waist *noun* 1. the part of the human body between the chest and hips. 2. the part of a piece of clothing that covers this part of the body. *The waist of my pants is loose.* {**wayst**}

Homophone Note Are you looking for the word *waste*? *Waist* and *waste* sound alike but have different meanings.

wait *verb* (waited, waiting, waits) 1. to stay in one place until an expected event happens (often followed by "for" or "until"). *We're waiting for the mail to arrive.* 2. to slow down or stop until another person catches up. *They waited for the little dog who couldn't run very fast.* 3. to remain ready for something. *He waited for a chance to take her out on a date.* 4. to be delayed. *The new house will have to wait until we have more money.* *noun* the act, instance, or period of waiting. *There was a long wait before the movie started.* {**wayt**}

• **lie in wait**
to wait for a chance to make a surprise attack. *She was always afraid that a gang of thieves was lying in wait around the next corner.*

• **wait on [or] wait upon**
1. to attend to the needs of; act as a servant to. *She is tired* from waiting on her family. 2. to meet the wants and needs of in a restaurant. *The waiter has to wait on several tables at once.*

Homophone Note The words *wait* and *weight* (heaviness) sound alike but have different meanings.

wait·er *noun* a man who serves or waits on customers in a bar, restaurant, or cafe. {**wayt ər**}

wait·ress *noun* a woman who serves or waits on customers in a bar, restaurant, or cafe. {**wayt rihs**}

wake[1] *verb* (waked or woke, waked or woken, waking, wakes) 1. to come out of sleep (often followed by "up"). *I usually wake up at eight o'clock.* 2. to cause to stop sleeping (often followed by "up"). *Please wake me up before dinner.* *noun* a watch kept over the body of a dead person before it is buried. *Everyone cried at my grandmother's wake.* {**wayk**}

wake[2] *noun* 1. the track of waves left by something that is moving through water. *It was hard to row the little boat through the wake of the passing ship.* 2. the trail or track left behind by something that has passed. *The big storm left houses destroyed in its wake.* {**wayk**}

• **in the wake of**
following; directly after. *In the wake of the ice storm, all of the lights in our house went off.*

wak·en *verb* (wakened, wakening, wakens) 1. to cause to stop sleeping; awake. *The sun wakened him every morning.* 2. to stop sleeping; become awake; wake up. *He wakened from his nap when the phone rang.* 3. to make more active; stir. *The book wakened his interest in bugs.* {**wayk ən**}

Wales *noun* a country in Europe on the southwestern part of the island of Great Britain. Cardiff is the capital of Wales. {**waylz**}

walk ○ *verb* (walked, walking, walks) 1. to move at a steady pace by steps. *I walked to the bank.* 2. to travel on foot for exercise or fun. *He walks in the park after work.* 3. to move over, through, on, or upon by walking. *She walks the fields.* 4. to cause or help to walk. *He walked the dog.* 5. to lead or go with on foot. *He walked her home after the party.* *noun* 1. an act or instance of walking for exercise or fun; stroll. *Let's take a walk after dinner.* 2. a particular style or rate of walking. *The toddler's wobbly walk made us smile.* 3. distance measured in terms of time needed for walking. *My house is an hour's walk from here.* 4. a path, sidewalk, or other area for walking. *We shoveled the walk leading to the door.* {**wŏk**}

• **walk of life**
job or social position. *He has friends from every walk of life.*

• **walk off with [or] walk away with**
1. to win or get easily. *We were surprised when the youngest contestant walked off with first prize.* 2. to steal. *She walked off with my wallet.*

wall ○ *noun* 1. a structure that forms the side of a building or divides or shuts off a space. *He hung the picture on a wall*

a b c d e f g h i j k l m n o p q r s t u v **w** x y z

 Human Body Human Mind Everyday Life  History and Culture  Communication

in his room. 2. something like a wall that divides, blocks, or shuts in. *Plant cells often have thick walls.* verb (walled, walling, walls) 1. to divide, surround, or separate with or as if with a wall (often followed by "in" or "off"). *I walled in part of the living room to make a closet.* 2. to close with a wall or a structure like a wall. *We walled up the windows so that no one could look inside the old house.* {wŏl}

wal·let noun a pocketbook that is small and flat; billfold. Wallets are used to hold money, cards, or other small personal items. {wŏl iht}

wal·low verb (wallowed, wallowing, wallows) to roll the body in mud, sand, dirt, or water. *Water buffalos and other animals wallow for comfort.* {wŏl oh}

wall·pa·per noun paper printed with colors or colored patterns and pasted onto walls and ceilings. verb (wallpapered, wallpapering, wallpapers) to cover a wall, ceiling, or other surface with wallpaper. *My father wallpapered my bedroom.* {wŏl pay pər}

wal·nut noun 1. a tree that grows nuts and is a source of useful wood. 2. the nut of such a tree, having a hard, brown shell and a seed that can be eaten. 3. the hard, dark

wood of such a tree. Walnut is used to make furniture. 4. the dark, reddish brown color of this wood. {wŏl nuht}

wal·rus noun (walrus or walruses) a large mammal with tusks and thick, brown skin. Walruses are the largest pinnipeds or mammals with four flippers instead of feet. They spend much of their time on beaches or on frozen ocean in Arctic regions. Walruses are closely related to sea lions and seals. {wŏl rəs}

waltz noun 1. a round dance for two people. The waltz is a dance with three beats. 2. a piece of music composed for this dance or in its rhythm. *She played a waltz at the piano recital.* verb (waltzed, waltzing, waltzes) to dance a waltz. *We waltzed across the floor while the orchestra played.* {wŏlts}

wam·pum noun white and dark beads made from polished shells. Some American Indian peoples used wampum as money or decoration. {wŏm pəm}

wan adjective (wanner, wannest) 1. very pale. *His face is wan due to a long illness.* 2. without strength; weak. *He gave a wan smile when I told the bad joke.* {wŏn}

wand noun a thin stick or rod used by people such as magicians. *He waved his wand and pulled a rabbit out of his hat.* {wŏnd}

wan·der verb (wandered, wandering, wanders) 1. to move about with no purpose, aim, or plan; roam. *We wandered through the halls until classes started.* 2. to take a wrong turn or go the wrong way. *Some boys wandered from the group. / My attention wandered during the long movie.* 3. to have trouble thinking

clearly. *His mind is wandering because he is ill.* {wŏn dər} wanderer, n.

wane verb (waned, waning, wanes) 1. to become slowly less in size. *When the moon wanes, it's a better time to look at the stars.* 2. to become less powerful, rich, or strong. *His interest in science is waning.* {wayn}

want verb (wanted, wanting, wants) 1. to desire; wish for. *I want some lunch.* 2. to wish or have a need for (often followed by an infinitive). *I want to go home now.* 3. to have a need or desire. *He worked hard to make sure they never wanted for food, clothing, or a warm house.* 4. to need. *This coat wants mending.* 5. to seek in order to capture. *The police want him for robbery.* noun 1. something that is desired or needed. *He provides for the wants of his children.* 2. lack; not enough. *They starved for want of food.* 3. the state of lacking something; need. *I am in want of a good book.* 4. a lack of the usual necessities of life. *We helped the children in want.* {wŏnt}

Synonyms

These words share a meaning with *want*, noun 2:

need, lack, absence, deficiency

war ◯ noun 1. a state or time of armed fighting between countries, states, or other groups of people. *Many lives were lost in World War II.* 2. a strong effort to achieve something; fight or struggle. *Changes in the laws might help win the war against poverty.* verb (warred, warring, wars) to make or take part in war; fight. *The Soviet Union and Afghanistan warred with one another for many years.* {wohr}

A B C D E F G H I J K L M N O P Q R S T U V W X Y Z

• at war
in a state of active fighting or conflict. *The United States was at war with Germany, Japan, and Italy during World War II.*

• declare war on
to state an intention or plan to make war against. *Our soldiers were sent to fight once we declared war on the enemy.*

Homophone Note The words *war* and *wore* (past tense of "wear") sound alike but have different meanings.

war·bler *noun* a small American songbird that eats insects. There are many kinds of warblers and some are brightly colored. {**wohr** blər}

-ward or **-wards** *suffix* 1. a suffix that means "in the direction of." *If you travel northward, you are going in a northern direction.* 2. a suffix that means "toward." *If you are heading homeward, you are going toward home.*

ward *noun* 1. a large room in a hospital with beds for several patients, or a section for one type of patient. *Patients under the age of sixteen stay in the children's ward.* 2. an area of some cities or towns set apart for the purpose of voting. *Our city is divided into five wards, and each elects its own representative to the city council.* 3. a child or other person who has been placed under control of a person or group other than a parent by a court of law. *A prisoner is a ward of the state. / After her parents died, Anne became a ward of her relatives. verb* (warded, warding, wards) to prevent or turn aside (usually followed by "off"). *He could not ward off the flu. / The*

knight warded off the blow with his shield. {**wohrd**}

war·den *noun* 1. a person who is responsible for or guards someone or something. 2. the person who runs a prison. {**wohr** dən}

ward·robe *noun* 1. a tall closet or cabinet, or a small room where clothes are kept. 2. a collection of clothes or costumes that is the property of one person or of a theater. *He bought some new shirts to expand his wardrobe for summer.* {**wohrd rohb**}

ware *noun* 1. (usually plural) a thing or things offered for sale. *The shop showed some of its wares in the window.* 2. objects of the same kind offered for sale (usually joined with another word to form a longer word). *The shipment of kitchenware arrived at the department store.* {**wayr**}

Homophone Note The words *ware*, *wear*, and *where* all sound alike but have different meanings.

ware·house *noun* a large building or other place where products or private goods are stored. {**wayr** hows}

war·fare *noun* 1. the act of fighting a war. *Many lives were lost in the warfare of the twentieth century.* 2. fighting; conflict. *Refugees fled the country to escape the constant warfare.* {**wohr fayr**}

warm 🔊 *adjective* (warmer, warmest) 1. having or giving off some heat. *Today was a warm day. / He took a warm shower.* 2. serving to hold in body heat. *He wrapped himself in a warm blanket.* 3. having or causing a feeling of very high body temperature. *He was warm from running.* 4. lively; enthusiastic. *The*

musicians received a warm round of applause. 5. full of kindness; friendly. *She took him in a warm embrace. / You have a warm heart to do such kind things.* 6. close to giving the answer or finding something in certain games. *He was getting warmer when he looked under the bed for the ball. verb* (warmed, warming, warms) 1. to make warm or warmer (often followed by "up"). *He warmed up the soup for dinner.* 2. to produce pleasant or kindly feelings in. *Her sympathy warmed me.* {**wohrm**} warmer, n., warmly, adv.

• warm up
to prepare for physical exercise or other activity by practicing. *The band was still warming up when the audience began to arrive.*

warm-blood·ed *adjective* having a body temperature that remains steady and warm, no matter what the outside temperature is. *Many scientists think that dinosaurs were warm-blooded. / Mammals and birds are warm-blooded animals.* {**wohrm bluhd** ihd} warm-bloodedness, n.

warmth *noun* 1. the condition of being warm; heat. *Most plants need warmth to grow.* 2. kindness; friendliness. *People like him for his warmth.* {**wohrmth**}

warn *verb* (warned, warning, warns) 1. to tell of a possible danger; alert. *They warned us about the snowstorm.* 2. to caution about what may happen as a result of a particular action; advise. *He warned the children that they*

 Human Body   Human Mind   Everyday Life   Foreground History and Culture   Communication

would be sorry if they didn't do their homework. {wohrn}

Homophone Note The words **warn** and **worn** sound alike but have different meanings.

warn·ing *noun* 1. the words, sound, or act of a person or thing that warns. *We didn't hear the teacher's warning to be quiet.* 2. a signal or notice of a possibly dangerous situation. *The sign was a warning to keep out of the water.* *adjective* acting as a warning. *We heard a warning siren before the storm hit.* {wohr ning}

warp *verb* (warped, warping, warps) 1. to bend or twist out of shape. *Rain had warped the old, wooden fence.* 2. to distort. *You warped the story of what really happened.* 3. to become bent or twisted out of shape. *The walls warped a little more every time it rained.* *noun* a bend or twist. *We noticed a warp in the floor from the leaky roof.* {wohrp}

war·ri·or *noun* a person who fights or has experience in battle; soldier. {wohr ee ər}

War·saw *noun* the capital city of Poland. {wohr saw}

war·ship *noun* a ship built or equipped for fighting. {wohr shihp}

wart *noun* 1. a small, hard, raised growth on the skin that is caused by a virus. Warts usually grow on hands or feet. 2. a growth like this on the surface of a plant or skin of an animal. {wohrt} warty, adj.

war·y *adjective* (warier, wariest) 1. on guard against threat or danger. *He is wary of dogs because one bit him last year.* 2.

caused by or showing caution. *There was a wary look on his face as he entered the principal's office.* {wayr ee}

was *verb* a past tense of the verb **be** which is used with "I," "he," "she," "it," and with singular nouns. *Can you tell me what time he was here yesterday?* {wuhz}

wash 🌿 ⚙ *verb* (washed, washing, washes) 1. to make clean by using water or soap. *He washed all the cups.* 2. to move by the action of a liquid. *The waves washed shells onto the beach.* 3. to wear away or destroy by the action of moving water. *Rain washed the soil off the field.* 4. to be carried by the action of moving water. *A pail washed up on the beach.* 5. to be removed or worn down by the action of moving water (often followed by "away"). *The paint on the road washed away in the rain.* 6. to clean oneself. *Did you wash before dinner?* 7. to flow over; rush against. *The waves washed over the dock.* *noun* 1. the act or an instance of washing. *He gave the floor a wash.* 2. things washed or to be washed together. *My mother does the wash and hangs the clothes outside to dry.* 3. the movement of waves of water. *The constant wash of waves wore away the rock.* 4. a thin layer spread to cover a surface. *He put a wash of blue paint on the chair.* 5. a liquid used as a medicine. *She prepared a wash to treat the wound.* {wŏsh}

• **come out in the wash** to turn out in a satisfactory way. *Don't worry, these problems will all come out in the wash.*

• **wash down** 1. to clean completely with

water or other liquids. *He washed down the decks.* 2. to drink water or other liquid in order to help to swallow. *He washed down the pill with juice.*

wash·a·ble *adjective* able to be washed without damage. *My new coat is washable.* {wŏsh ə bəl}

wash·er *noun* 1. a person or thing that washes. 2. a machine used for washing clothes. 3. a flat ring of rubber, metal, or other material used with a nut and bolt to make a tight fit. {wo shər}

washing machine *noun* a machine that washes laundry. {wo shing mə sheen}

Wash·ing·ton *noun* 1. a state in the northwestern United States on the Pacific Coast. Its capital is Olympia. (abbreviated: WA) 2. the capital city of the United States. Washington includes all of the District of Columbia. {wo shing tən}

Word History *Washington* was named for George Washington, first president of the United States.

Wash·ing·ton's Birth·day *noun* February 22, the day on which the birthday of George Washington is celebrated. The official U.S. holiday is now called Presidents' Day and occurs on the third Monday in February. {wo shing tənz buhrth day}

wasp *noun* an insect that has four wings and a slender body with a very narrow waist. Some wasps can give a painful sting. {wŏsp}

a
b
c
d
e
f
g
h
i
j
k
l
m
n
o
p
q
r
s
t
u
v
w
x
y
z

waste 🟢 🔵 *verb* (wasted, wasting, wastes) 1. to use or spend in a careless way or for little or no return. *He wasted his money at the carnival.* 2. to fail to use or take full advantage of. *He wasted the chance to go to college.* 3. to cause to become more weak. *The cold weather wasted the old woman.* 4. to become weak or exhausted. *The old man's health was wasting away.* *noun* 1. the act of wasting or state of being wasted. *Going to the sale was a waste of time.* 2. useless matter thrown away during a particular process. *The factory poured its waste into the river.* 3. material given off by the body after food is digested. *There were portable bathrooms at the festival to dispose of human waste.* *adjective* 1. seen as useless or worthless. *We put our waste food in the compost pile.* 2. used for garbage or refuse. *I emptied the waste container.* {**wayst**}

Homophone Note The word *waste* and *waist* (a part of the human body) sound alike but have different meanings.

waste·bas·ket *noun* a small, open container for holding trash. {**wayst** băs kiht}

waste·ful *adjective* using more than is needed. *It is wasteful to take more food than you can eat.* {**wayst** fəl} wastefully, adv., wastefulness, n.

waste·land *noun* land where there are no living things or where nothing will grow. {**wayst** lănd}

watch 🟣 🟢 *verb* (watched, watching, watches) 1. to look closely or carefully. *He watched as the bug crawled across the table.* 2. to look at closely or with continued attention. *I watched the birds build their nest.* 3. to look or wait in anticipation (usually followed by "for"). *Watch for our spring sales.* 4. to be careful. *Watch that you don't cut yourself.* 5. to guard or tend attentively. *Grandmother is watching the children.* *noun* 1. an act or a period of staying awake. *He took the first watch to guard the ship.* 2. the act of guarding or protecting. *She kept a close watch on her brother.* 3. a small device for measuring and showing the time, often worn on the wrist. {**wŏch**}

• **watch it**
to be careful; to have caution. *Watch it when you near the edge of the cliff.*

• **watch out**
to be careful. *Watch out that you don't fall.*

watch·dog *noun* a dog that is trained to guard property. *The watchdog barked loudly at the man who was trying to break into the factory.* {**wŏch** dawg}

watch·ful *adjective* watching closely or carefully; alert. *The cat was watchful as the mouse scampered across the floor.* {**wŏch** fəl} watchfully, adv., watchfulness, n.

watch·man *noun* (watchmen) a person who keeps watch over or guards something. {**wŏch** mən}

wa·ter 🟢 🔵 *noun* 1. a clear liquid that has no taste or odor. Water takes the form of rain, rivers, oceans, and lakes and is a requirement for most forms of life. 2. a body of such liquid such as a lake or sea. 3. a particular kind of water, or a solution that has water. *I drink soda water. / She loves the smell of rose water.* *verb* (watered, watering, waters) 1. to pour or put water on. *He watered the plants.* 2. to provide drinking water for. *She watered the horses.* 3. to produce or give off liquid. *Chopping onions makes my eyes water.* {**waw** tər}

• **by water**
by way of a boat or ship. *They toured the city of Venice by water.*

water buffalo *noun* a large buffalo with dark gray fur that lives in the southern parts of Asia. Water buffalo have curved horns that can be six feet wide. They weigh up to one ton. Water buffalo are very strong, and people often raise them to pull heavy loads. {**wo** tər **buh** fə loh}

wa·ter·col·or *noun* 1. paint made of pigment mixed with water. 2. a painting done with watercolors. *The artist gave us a watercolor of our house.* 3. the art or technique of painting with watercolors. *We learned watercolor in school this year.* {**waw** tər **kuh** lər}

wa·ter·cress *noun* 1. a plant related to mustard that grows in fresh water. 2. the leaves of this plant, which have a sharp taste and are used in salads and other foods. {**wo** tər **krehs**}

wa·ter·fall 🔵 *noun* a stream of water that falls from a higher place; cascade. {**wo** tər **fŏl**}

water lily *noun* 1. a plant that grows in

 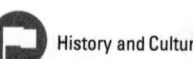

a pond or lake. Water lilies have large, flat, floating leaves and pretty flowers in various colors. 2. the flower of this plant. {**wo** tər **lih** lee}

wa·ter·logged *adjective* 1. flooded so as to be heavy and difficult to manage. *The crew could not move the waterlogged ship.* 2. completely soaked or filled with water. *The land was waterlogged after several days of rain.* {**wo** tər **lawgd** or **wo** tər **lŏgd**}

wa·ter·mel·on *noun* 1. a large, round fruit with a green rind and sweet pulp that is red or pink. Watermelons have many seeds. 2. the plant or vine that bears this fruit. {**wo** tər **meh** lən}

water moccasin *noun* a poisonous snake found in swamps or wet areas of the southern United States. The water moccasin is brown or olive in color and shows the white inside of its mouth when threatened. {**wo** tər **mo** kə sihn}

wa·ter·proof *adjective* not letting water through; not absorbent. *The waterproof jacket kept the rain off her dress.* *verb* (waterproofed, waterproofing, waterproofs) to make waterproof. *I waterproofed my boots with mink oil.* {**wo** tər **proohf**}

wa·ter·shed *noun* 1. the area of land from which water drains into a river, river system, or lake. *Our city is in the Great Lakes watershed.* 2. a ridge of high land that lies between two such drainage areas. {**wo** tər **shehd**}

wa·ter·way  *noun* a long body of water large enough for boats to travel on. *The Erie Canal is a busy waterway.* {**wo** tər **way**}

wa·ter·works *plural noun* (waterworks) (used with a

singular or plural verb) a system that provides water to a city or town. *This waterworks needs to be replaced.* / *These waterworks provide for several towns.* {**wo** tər **wuhrks**}

wa·ter·y *adjective* (waterier, wateriest) 1. having to do with or made of water. *Fish have a watery playground.* 2. having too much water. *He does not like watery oatmeal.* {**wo** tə ree}

watt *noun* a unit for measuring the force of electric power. (abbreviated: w, W) {**wŏt**}

wave  *noun* 1. a moving ridge or swell on the surface of a body of water. *The boat rocked on the ocean waves.* 2. a curve or curves. *Her hair is full of waves.* 3. a motion or signal made by moving the hand up and down or back and forth. *She said goodbye and gave me a wave.* 4. a sudden increase of a feeling, activity, or condition. *She felt a wave of happiness.* / *There was a wave of cold weather.* *verb* (waved, waving, waves) 1. to move up and down or back and forth with ease. *The flag waves at the top of the pole.* 2. to cause to move up and down or back and forth. *I waved my hand.* 3. to make a signal by moving a hand, arm, or object up and down or back and forth. *She waved when she saw us.* 4. to give a sign or direct by moving one's hand up and down or back and forth. *I waved hello.* / *He waved them off the stage.* 5. to be shaped in a series of curves; gently curl. *His hair waves.* 6. to shape into curves. *I waved my hair.* {**wayv**}

wax¹ *noun* 1. a solid yellow substance made by bees for building their honeycombs; beeswax. 2. any substance

like this wax that can be easily shaped when heated. Candles are made from wax. 3. a mixture with wax in it that is used to polish a smooth, hard surface. *verb* (waxed, waxing, waxes) to rub, polish, or coat with wax. *My father waxes his car every Sunday.* {**wăks**}

wax² *verb* (waxed, waxing, waxes) 1. to grow or increase in amount, size or strength. *Her anger waxed as he continued to insult her.* 2. to become brighter. *The moon waxes when the size of its bright areas increases from a crescent to a full moon.* {**wăks**}

way *noun* 1. a road or path leading from one place to another. *Which is the fastest way home?* 2. an opening that is a passage. *The front window is the only way in.* 3. space clear of people or objects. *Make way for the principal.* 4. movement or progress toward a particular end. *I made my way into town.* / *She is on her way to becoming an actress.* 5. a particular direction. *Look that way to see the parade.* 6. distance. *The store is just a short way from here.* 7. manner; way of acting. *He asked in a nice way.* 8. a particular manner of acting or course of action. *We did it his way.* 9. method of thinking or acting; respect. *In some ways, she's right.* *adverb* by or to a large amount or distance; far. *The car costs way too much.* {**way**}

• **give way**
to collapse or fall apart. *The roof gave way after a big snowstorm.*

Homophone Note The words *way*, *weigh*, and *whey* all sound alike but have different meanings.

A
B
C
D
E
F
G
H
I
J
K
L
M
N
O
P
Q
R
S
T
U
V
W
X
Y
Z

 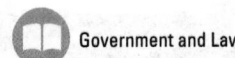

Weapons

Early humans learned to use simple weapons and fire to help them hunt and survive.

Then humans began to use throwing sticks and **bows** and **arrows**. They learned to shape stones to make sharp blades and spear or arrow heads.

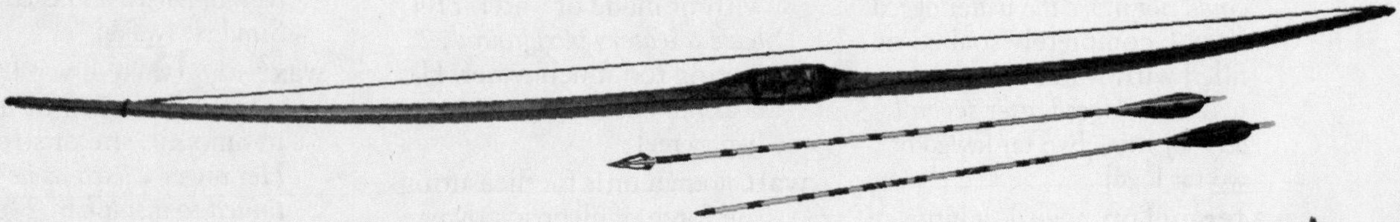

People learned to forge **metal**. They made swords, knives, axes, and arrowheads out of metal. They formed metal into shields and armor to protect themselves.

Gunpowder was invented in China over a thousand years ago. This momentous invention spread throughout the world. This led to the invention of exploding weapons, such as bombs, and guns.

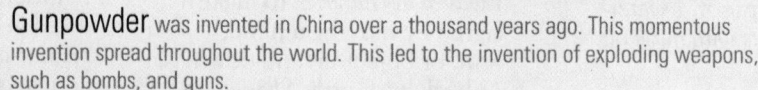

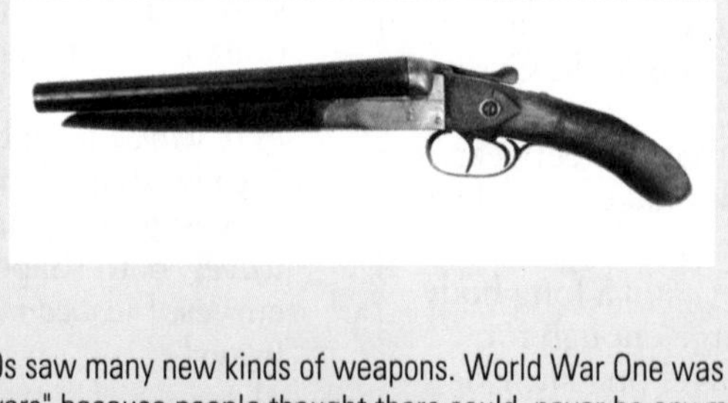

The 1900s saw many new kinds of weapons. World War One was called "the war to end all wars" because people thought there could never be any more powerful weapons. Some of the weapons used in World War One were poison gas, bombs, and machine guns. Blimps, airplanes, battleships, submarines, and tanks provided new mobility to the larger, more powerful weapons. Sadly, this war was not an end. The world moved from gunpowder to nuclear weapons.

Nuclear weapons have the power to destroy all life on Earth.

we *pronoun* the person speaking or writing and one or more others. *We became friends.* {wee}

Homophone Note The words *we* and *wee* (very small or early) sound alike but have different meanings.

weak ◑ *adjective* (weaker, weakest) 1. not having much physical strength or power. *I was too weak to walk after the accident.* 2. likely to break or fail under strain or pressure; not sturdy. *The weak branches on the tree broke off during the storm.* 3. not strong in force; faint. *Her weak voice could not be heard from the back rows.* 4. not having ability or skill in a particular activity. *He is a weak tennis player and prefers to play soccer.* {week}

Homophone Note Are you looking for the word *week* (a unit of time)? *Weak* and *week* sound alike but have different meanings.

weak·en *verb* (weakened, weakening, weakens) to make or become weak or weaker. *He weakened as he climbed the hill.* / *I weakened the juice by adding more water.* {week ən}

weak·ling *noun* a person who is weak in body or character, or an animal that is weak in body. *The poor weakling could not stand up to the bully.* / *The kitten was a weakling and didn't live long.* {week ling}

weak·ness *noun* 1. the quality or condition of being weak. *Weakness kept him from finishing the race.* 2. a personal problem; defect. *Spending too much money was his biggest weakness.* 3. a special liking. *She has a weakness for Italian food.* {week nihs}

wealth ◐ *noun* 1. a large amount of money or property or the state of having such. *As a woman of wealth, she was able to buy a private jet.* 2. a large amount of something; abundance. *He has a wealth of knowledge about science.* {wehlth}

wealth·y *adjective* (wealthier, wealthiest) rich; having wealth. *That wealthy man owns several businesses.* {wehl thee} wealthiness, n.

weap·on ◎ *noun* 1. an object or device used to attack or defend. *Guns, shields, and swords are weapons.* 2. anything used to attack or defend someone or something. *He used cruel words as his weapon.* {weh pən}

wear ◑ *verb* (wore, worn, wearing, wears) 1. to have or carry on one's person. *He wears a suit.* / *She likes to wear jewelry.* 2. to cause to become damaged through long use, friction, or exposure. *Constant kneeling wore the knees of his jeans.* 3. to make by long use, friction, or exposure. *She wore a hole in her sleeve.* 4. to make weak. *This child is wearing my patience.* 5. to pass slowly. *The days wore on as they waited for some good news.* *noun* 1. the act of wearing. *My jacket has many years of wear.* 2. the condition of being worn. *You can tell by the wear on this tire that it wasn't aligned properly.* 3. clothing of a particular kind. *She stocks women's wear at the department store.* 4. damage caused by much use. *The coat showed signs of wear.* {wayr} wearer, n.

• **wear off** to become less or disappear gradually. *The scent wore off after a few days.*

• **wear out** 1. to make useless through much use. *He wore out his sneakers.* 2. to make tired or weary. *The dancing wore us out.*

Homophone Note The words *wear*, *ware*, and *where* sound alike but have different meanings.

wea·ry *adjective* (wearier, weariest) 1. tired in body or mind; fatigued. *He was weary after riding his bicycle all day.* / *Studying for the exam made her weary.* 2. becoming impatient, bored, or unhappy with a particular thing (often followed by "of"). *I am weary of working every day.* *verb* (wearied, wearying, wearies) 1. to make weary; tire. *A long swim wearied the dog.* 2. to become impatient, bored, or unhappy with a particular thing (often followed by "of"). *We soon wearied of his silly stories.* {weer ee} wearily, adv, weariness, n.

wea·sel *noun* (weasels or weasel) a small mammal with brown fur, a long body and neck, and short legs. Various kinds of weasels are found in the northern parts of Europe, Asia, Africa, and North America. Weasels hunt at night for rabbits and rodents. Polecats, ferrets, and mink are closely related to true weasles. Weasels living in very cold regions grow white fur and are called ermine. {wee zəl}

weath·er *noun* the conditions outside at a particular place and time. Sunshine, clouds, temperature, and rain are some of the changing conditions that make up the weather. *What will the weather be like for the picnic?* *verb* (weathered, weathering, weathers) 1. to last through; survive. *Their friendship weathered hard*

 Living World
 Physical World
 Natural Environment
 Economy
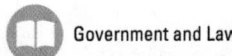 Government and Law

Weather

Weather is caused by the sun's energy acting within the atmosphere. But without the vast amounts of water on planet Earth, our weather would be far different.

When water evaporates into the atmosphere, it causes the air to become less dense. Because that moist air is also usually warmer than the air directly above, it rises rapidly through the atmosphere and begins to cool.

When the moist air cools enough, tiny droplets of water and ice begin to condense. We see this as clouds. Fog is merely a cloud at Earth's surface.

As the air cools more, the tiny droplets combine and begin to fall to the ground as sleet, rain, hail, or snow. As the air grows dryer and cooler, it becomes dense enough to sink back to Earth's surface.

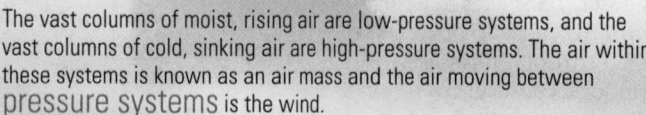

The vast columns of moist, rising air are low-pressure systems, and the vast columns of cold, sinking air are high-pressure systems. The air within these systems is known as an air mass and the air moving between pressure systems is the wind.

The natural electricity we call lightning is very common. Lightning strikes somewhere on Earth more than once every second. Lightning can strike from a cloud to the ground, from one cloud to another cloud, from a cloud to clear air, or within one cloud. The thunder you hear is caused by the rapid expansion of superheated air that lightning has passed through.

Scientists classify lightning by its temperature. Hot lightning strikes for a long time and can easily set trees on fire. It causes long, low rumbles of thunder. Cold lightning strikes for a short time, but with a stronger electrical current than hot lightning. Cold lightning can split tree trunks and melt solid rock. It causes sharp, loud claps of thunder.

Violent weather - the squalls, tornados, thunderstorms, blizzards, typhoons, hurricanes, and monsoons that are capable of turning the human world upside down - are all caused by the action of high-pressure and low-pressure weather systems.

times. 2. to change as a result of being exposed to the weather. *The red wooden deck chairs weathered to a soft pink.* {wehth ər}

• **under the weather** (informal) slightly ill or unhappy. *Take a hot bath if you are feeling under the weather.*

Homophone Note The words **weather** and **whether** (a conjunction) sound alike but have different meanings.

weath·er·man 🔵 🔘 *noun* (weathermen) a person who forecasts weather or reports it on radio or television. {wehth ər măn}

weather vane *noun* a device that swings in the wind to show what direction the wind is blowing. {wehth ər vayn}

weave *verb* (wove or weaved, woven or wove, weaving, weaves) 1. to make by passing threads or strips over and under each other. *She is weaving a beautiful rug.* 2. to create or form something by putting separate parts or ideas together. *He wove a story from from several events in his life.* 3. to put into or include (usually followed by "in" or "into"). *I am weaving a pattern into the cloth. / He wove opinions into his speech.* 4. to spin, like spiders and larvae. *The spider weaves a web to catch insects.* 5. to move from side to side with turns and twists. *She wove her way through the crowd.* *noun* the pattern or construction of a fabric. *That cloth has a rough weave.* {weev}

Homophone Note The word **weave** and the contraction **we've** ("we have") sound alike but have different meanings.

web 🔵 🔵 🔵 *noun* 1. the skin that connects the toes of water birds and water animals. 2. any network that is like woven material. *He has a web of wires behind his computer.* 3. a thin structure spun by spiders and the larvae of certain insects. 4. (sometimes capitalized) see **World Wide Web**. *adjective* (sometimes capitalized) of or pertaining to the World Wide Web. *I installed a new Web browser on my computer.* {wehb}

Word History The word **web** comes from an Old English word that means "woven fabric."

webbed *adjective* 1. having or joined by a web. *Ducks have webbed feet.* 2. made of or formed by a web or webbing. *That chair has a webbed seat.* {wehbd}

web·foot *noun* (webfeet) 1. a foot with the toes connected by skin or a web. *We saw a bird at the beach with a webfoot.* 2. an animal with such feet. *There is a webfoot swimming on the pond.* {wehb fuut} web-footed, adj.

Web page or **web page** *noun* (web pages) a document belonging to a Web site on the World Wide Web. *The band's web page has information on its performance schedule.* {wehb payj}

Web site or **web site** or **website** *noun* a location on the World Wide Web. A Web site contains a home page and other pages that are linked to the home page. {wehb siyt}

we'd shortened form of "we had" or "we would." *We'd eaten all the cake before they got here. / We'd like to go to the park.* {weed}

Homophone Note The contraction **we'd** and the word **weed** sound alike but have different meanings.

wed *verb* (wedded, wed or wedded, wedding, weds) 1. to take as husband or wife in a ceremony; marry. 2. to join in marriage. *The judge wed my parents in their home.* {wehd}

wed·ding *noun* a ceremony of marriage. *My sister's wedding will take place in a church.* {weh ding}

wedge *noun* 1. a piece of wood or metal shaped like a triangle with a thin edge. A wedge is driven or forced between objects to split, lift, or make them stronger. *He split the wood with a wedge. / They leveled out the floor by driving wedges beneath it.* 2. anything in the form of a triangle with two nearly equal sides. *I own a wedge of land in the city. / He ate a wedge of cake.* *verb* (wedged, wedging, wedges) 1. to split or force apart with a wedge (often followed by "open" or "apart"). *She wedged open the window with a hammer. / He wedged apart the two boards.* 2. to fix firmly in place with a wedge. *He wedged the wheels of his truck so that it would not*

A B C D E F G H I J K L M N O P Q R S T U V W X Y Z

a
b
c
d
e
f
g
h
i
j
k
l
m
n
o
p
q
r
s
t
u
v
w
x
y
z

roll. **3.** to force or thrust into a narrow space. *Four people wedged themselves into the phone booth at once.* {<u>wehj</u>}

Wednes·day *noun* the fourth day of the week. Wednesday comes between Tuesday and Thursday. {<u>wehnz</u> day}

Word History *Wednesday* comes from early English words that mean "Woden's day." *Woden* was once the chief god of the peoples of northwestern Europe.

wee *adjective* (weer, weest) **1.** very small or tiny. *The wee boy was hard to find in a crowd.* **2.** very early. *I woke up in the wee hours before dawn.* {<u>wee</u>}

Homophone Note The words *wee* and *we* sound alike but have different meanings.

weed ❶ *noun* any plant that grows wild where it is not wanted, especially in gardens or among farm crops. *We pulled weeds from our lawn.* *verb* (weeded, weeding, weeds) **1.** to clear of weeds. *We weed our vegetable garden every week.* **2.** to remove as not wanted (often followed by "out"). *He weeded out several paragraphs from the story he was writing.* {<u>weed</u>} weeder, n.

Homophone Note The word *weed* and the contraction *we'd* ("we had" or "we would") sound alike but have different meanings.

week *noun* **1.** a unit of time equal to seven days. *On some calendars the first day of the week is Monday, and on others it is Sunday.* **2.** the amount of time spent working during a period of seven days. *A school*

week is usually five days. {<u>week</u>}

Homophone Note Are you looking for the word *weak* (not strong)? *Week* and *weak* sound alike but have different meanings.

week·day *noun* any day of the week except Saturday and Sunday. *We go to school on weekdays.* {<u>week</u> day}

week·end *noun* the part of the week between Friday evening and Sunday evening. {<u>week</u> ehnd}

week·ly *adjective* **1.** done, happening, or printed once a week. *We made our weekly trip to the farmer's market. / Sailing on the lake is a weekly event. / She reads the weekly magazine.* **2.** of or having to do with a week. *He has a weekly schedule for his chores.* *adverb* once a week; each week. *They go out dancing weekly.* *noun* a newspaper or magazine that comes out once a week. *This newspaper is a weekly.* {<u>week</u> lee}

weep ❓ *verb* (wept, weeping, weeps) to show strong feelings by crying. *She wept when she heard that her grandmother had died.* {<u>weep</u>}

weigh *verb* (weighed, weighing, weighs) **1.** to measure the weight of by using a scale. *The grocer weighed the cheese.* **2.** to think about carefully before making a decision. *I'm weighing my choices.* **3.** to have a particular amount of weight. *I weigh a lot more than I did last year.* **4.** to burden the thoughts or feelings of (usually followed by "on" or "upon"). *Feelings of guilt weighed on him.* {<u>way</u>}
• **weigh down**
1. to make heavier. *Her clothes weighed her down as she swam.* **2.** to cause to lower,

bend, or stay down by adding weight. *She weighed down the balloon with a stone.* **3.** to make serious, troubled, or sad. *Her troubles weigh her down.*

Homophone Note The words *weigh*, *way*, and *whey* sound alike but have different meanings.

weight *noun* **1.** the quality of being heavy. *There's a lot of weight to this bowling ball.* **2.** a unit or system of units by which such a quality is measured. *Ounces and pounds are units of weight.* **3.** a particular amount of this quality. *He lifted a weight of five pounds.* **4.** an object used because it is heavy. **5.** importance; influence. *My father's advice had a lot of weight in my decision.* *verb* (weighted, weighting, weights) to make heavier. *He weighted the bag with rocks so that it would sink to the bottom of the lake.* {<u>wayt</u>}
• **carry weight**
to have influence, importance, or authority. *His words carry a lot of weight.*
• **pull one's weight**
to do one's share of work. *He certainly pulls his own weight on the football team.*

Homophone Note The words *weight* and *wait* sound alike but have different meanings.

weight·less *adjective* having, or seeming to have, little or no weight; not controlled by gravity. *He felt weightless as he jumped off the diving board.* {<u>wayt</u> lihs} weightlessly, adv., weightlessness, n.

weird *adjective* **1.** strange or odd; puzzlingly unusual. *His weird behavior has his parents worried.* **2.** mysterious, strange, eerie, or ghostly. *A weird*

 Human Body   Human Mind   Everyday Life   History and Culture   Communication

laugh came from the closet. {**weerd**} weirdly, adv., weirdness, n.

Word History In ancient Norse mythology, a person's destiny was controlled by three sister-goddesses, often called the "weird sisters." In Old English, *weird* (spelled *wyrd*) means "fate" or "destiny." Artists often gave these eerie goddesses a strange, witch-like appearance, which may be why "weird" means what it does today.

wel·come *interjection* used to express warm greetings to someone who has just arrived. *Welcome! We are glad you are here.* *noun* a warm or friendly greeting. *We gave her a warm welcome.* *verb* (welcomed, welcoming, welcomes) 1. to receive with pleasure and friendliness. *We welcomed them into our home.* 2. to be glad to receive or accept. *I would welcome a cold drink right now.* 3. to meet or receive in a particular way. *The farmers welcomed the arrival of warm weather by planting crops.* *adjective* 1. received in a warm or friendly way. *They were welcome guests.* 2. invited; freely allowed. *You are welcome to share this food.* 3. used as a polite answer to an expression of thanks. *You're welcome.* {**wehl** kəm} welcomer, n.

weld *verb* (welded, welding, welds) 1. to join metal or plastic by using heat, followed either by pressure or by adding a melted material. *He welded the broken bicycle back together.* 2. to bring two separate things into complete union. *She welded the two groups into one powerful company.* {**wehld**}

wel·fare *noun* 1. a state of health, happiness, and good fortune. *A good teacher is concerned about the welfare of her students.* 2. public or private aid to people in need. *Welfare helped her family get through a tough time.* / *The business promoted people's welfare by helping them find jobs.* {**wehl** fayr}

Word History The word *welfare* comes from two Old English words that mean "get along" and "well." These same Old English words form the word "farewell."

we'll shortened form of "we will." *We'll never win the talent contest.* {**weel**}

Homophone Note The contraction *we'll* and the word *wheel* (a round frame) sound alike but have different meanings.

well¹ *adverb* (better, best) 1. in a good, proper, or acceptable way. *Her work is going well.* 2. carefully; completely. *He did his job very well.* 3. with skill. *She sings well.* 4. with reason. *You may well ask why I'm taking French lessons.* 5. in a kind way. *They think well of him.* 6. to a great amount or extent. *They live well beyond the border.* 7. in a close or familiar way. *I knew her well.* *adjective* (better, best) 1. healthy; sound. *She is not well today.* 2. right; in a good condition. *All is well with my mother.* 3. fortunate; good. *It is well that you asked before making your decision.* *interjection* 1. used to show surprise, anger or acceptance. *Well! I never expected that he would leave without telling me.* 2. used during a pause in a conversation, or as the start of a sentence. *I feel... well... bad about it to be honest.* / *Well, I*

guess it's time to go. {**wehl**}
• **as well**
besides; also; too. *I ate lots of cake and ice cream as well.*
• **as well as**
and also. *He is honest as well as kind.*

Synonyms
These words share a meaning with *well*, adverb 2:
completely, carefully, thoroughly

well² *noun* 1. a deep hole dug in the ground to get water, oil, gas, or other natural resources. 2. a spring, pool, or other natural source of water. 3. a good source. *She is a well of information.* *verb* (welled, welling, wells) to rise or spring to the surface. *The river welled forth and spilled over its banks.* / *Tears welled up in his eyes.* {**wehl**}

well-bal·anced *adjective* properly controlled. *My mother makes well-balanced meals with plenty of vegetables.* {**wehl băl** ənst}

well-be·haved *adjective* showing good manners. *He was well-behaved at the concert.* {**wehl** bə **hayvd**}

well-known *adjective* known by many; famous; familiar. *He is a well-known actor.* {**wehl nohn**}

well-man·nered *adjective* polite and considerate. *The well-mannered girl waited for her turn to use the computer.* {**wehl măn** ərd}

well-off *adjective* 1. rich; having enough money to be comfortable. *The people who live in that big house are well-off.* 2. in a good position or situation; fortunate. *Our team was well-off when the opponent's star player was kicked out of the game.* {**wehl awf**}

well-read *adjective* having read much in one or a wide range

 Living World   Physical World  Natural Environment ᗯᗯᗯ Economy 📖 Government and Law

of subjects; knowledgeable. *It takes a lot of time and effort to become a well-read person.* {**wehl rehd**}

well-round·ed *adjective* 1. having a proper balance. *It is important to get a well-rounded education.* 2. having an interest or skill in many fields. *She is a well-rounded person who could work at many different jobs.* {**wehl rown** dihd}

Welsh *adjective* of or having to do with Wales, or its people or language. *noun* 1. (used with a plural verb) the people of Wales (usually used with "the"). 2. the language of Wales. {**wehlsh** or **wehlch**}

went *verb* past tense of **go**[1]. {**wehnt**}

wept *verb* past tense and past participle of **weep.** {**wehpt**}

we're shortened form of "we are." *We're the best team in the league.* {**weer**}

were *verb* a past tense of the verb **be** that is used with the pronouns "you," "we," or "they." It is also used with plural nouns. {**wuhr**}

Homophone Note The words *were* and *whir* (to move rapidly) sound alike but have different meanings.

weren't shortened form of "were not." *Weren't you the one that told me not to go there?* {**wuhr** ənt}

west *noun* 1. the direction behind a person facing the rising sun. 2. one of the four major points of direction on the compass. The west is directly opposite the east. 3. (often capital) the western part of a country or area. *He's moving to the west to look for work.* 4. (capital) the western part of the world as distinguished from the East. *This*

cook blends traditions from the East and the West. *adjective* 1. from, of, or in the west. *There's a west wind blowing.* 2. toward or facing the west. *My room is in the west wing of the house. adverb* from, in, or toward the west. *The pioneers traveled west in search of a new home.* {**wehst**}

West Bank *noun* an area in the Middle East between the west bank of the Jordan River and the eastern border of Israel. It was once part of Jordan and was taken over by Israel in 1967. {**wehst băngk**}

west·er·ly *adverb or adjective* 1. of or toward the west. *The river flows westerly. / He headed off in a westerly direction.* 2. blowing from the west. *The sailors hoped the wind would blow westerly. / The captain says we need a strong westerly wind to help us reach our destination. noun* a storm or wind from the west. *A westerly blew us off course.* {**wehst** ər lee}

west·ern *adjective* in, to, from, or having to do with the west. *We watch the sun setting in the western sky. noun* (usually capitalized) a book, film, or play that shows life in the American West and is usually set in the nineteenth century. *We spent Saturday morning watching Westerns.* {**wehs** tərn}

west·ern·er *noun* (often capitalized) a person born in, or living in, the western part of the United States, or in a western area or region. *We could tell that he was a Westerner by the way he talked.* {**wehs** tər nər}

Western Hemisphere *noun* the half of the earth that includes North, Central, and South America. {**wehs** tərn **heh** mih sfeer}

West Germany *noun* a country in central Europe until 1990. West Germany was once known as the Federal Republic of Germany by itself, but is now united with East Germany to form one country, the current Federal Republic of Germany. {**wehst juhr** mə nee} West German, n., adj.

West Indies *noun* a large group of islands in the North Atlantic between North and South America. The West Indies include the Antilles and the Bahamas. {**wehst ihn** deez} West Indian, n., adj.

West Virginia *noun* a state in the eastern United States. Its capital is Charleston. (abbreviated: WV) {**wehst** vər **jihn** yə} West Virginian, n., adj.

Word History *West Virginia* was part of Virginia until 1863. Forty counties formed a new state during the Civil War in order to remain part of the Union (the northern United States). Virginia was named for the "Virgin Queen," Elizabeth I of England.

west·ward *adverb* toward the west. *The house faces westward. / We travelled westward. adjective* in, at, facing, or moving toward the west. *He headed off in a westward direction.* {**wehst** wərd} westwards, adv.

wet *adjective* (wetter, wettest) 1. soaked, made moist, or covered with water or another liquid. *This towel is wet, but there are dry ones in the closet.* 2. not yet dry. *Don't walk on wet cement.* 3. marked by rain, mist, or fog. *We hoped for sun, but it was a wet afternoon. noun* 1. water; moisture. *There was wet all through the rotted wood.* 2. bad weather; rain; snow. *She loves*

 Human Body   Human Mind   Everyday Life   History and Culture    Communication

a b c d e f g h i j k l m n o p q r s t u v **w** x y z

the sun and hates the wet. *verb* (wet or wetted, wetting, wets) to make wet, damp, or moist. *He wet the floor with a mop.* {weht} wetness, n.

• **all wet**
completely wrong. *We told him he was all wet.*

• **wet one's whistle**
to have something to drink. *He wet his whistle at the fountain.*

Synonyms
These words share a meaning with *wet*, noun 1:
moisture, damp, dampness

we've shortened form of "we have." *We've never been to the city.* {weev}

Homophone Note The contraction *we've* and the word *weave* sound alike but have different meanings.

whack *verb* (whacked, whacking, whacks) to hit or smack with a sharp blow. *He whacked the baseball over the fence.* *noun* a blow that makes a sharp sound; smack. *She gave the board a whack with the hammer.* {wăk}

• **out of whack**
(informal) not working properly; out of order. *Would you fix the window that is out of whack?*

whale *noun* a very large mammal that lives in the water. Most kinds of whales live in the ocean. They have a body shaped like a dolphin or porpoise, flippers for front limbs, and a flat, triangular tail. Some kinds of whales have teeth; others feed with baleen. *verb* (whaled, whaling, whales) to hunt whales. {wayl}

Homophone Note The words *whale* and *wail* (a loud cry) sound alike but have different meanings.

whal·ing *noun* the business or work of hunting and killing whales and selling their parts. {wayl ing}

wham *interjection or noun* a word used to imitate the loud noise made by a hard blow, heavy falling object, or explosion. *Wham! His bike crashed into the fence.* {wăm}

wharf *noun* (wharves or wharfs) a structure built along a shore, and often into the water, where boats and ships dock; pier. {wohrf}

what *pronoun* 1. which thing or kind of thing. *What will you wear to the party?* 2. used to ask for information. *What did he say?* 3. that which. *It is important to do what I ask.* 4. anything that. *I'll be there, come what may.* *adjective* 1.

which one or ones. *What brand of cheese shall I buy?* 2. whatever. *Give him what help he needs.* *adverb* how much. *What do you care?* {wuht}

what·ev·er *pronoun* 1. anything or everything that. *Take whatever you like.* 2. no matter what. *Whatever happens, you can count on me.* 3. one or any of several things; anything else. *Please bring forks, cups, plates, or whatever.* *adjective* 1. of any kind or amount. *I will lend you whatever clothes you need.* 2. of any kind. *No animals whatever are allowed in the house.* {wuht ehv ər}

what's shortened form of "what is" or "what has." *What's your name? / What's been happening here?* {wuhts}

wheat *noun* 1. the grain obtained from certain grasses and used in making flour and other foods. 2. the grasses that produce these grains. {weet}

wheel *noun* 1. a round frame that turns on the axle. Wheels are found on cars, trucks, bikes, wagons and other things. 2. any instrument or device that looks or acts like such a frame. *He turned the steering wheel.* 3. (plural) moving forces. *The wheels of industry never stop. / The wheels of justice are slow.* *verb* (wheeled, wheeling, wheels) 1. to cause to turn. *He wheeled his bicycle around the corner.* 2. to move on wheels. *They wheeled the patient into the operating room.* 3. to turn quickly or suddenly so as to face another direction. *The teacher wheeled to*

A B C D E F G H I J K L M N O P Q R S T U V **W** X Y Z

a
b
c
d
e
f
g
h
i
j
k
l
m
n
o
p
q
r
s
t
u
v
w
x
y
z

face the class. {<u>weel</u>}

• **at the wheel**
driving or steering an automobile, ship, or the like. *She was at the wheel when the car crashed.*

Homophone Note The word *wheel* and the contraction *we'll* ("we will") sound alike but have different meanings.

wheel·bar·row *noun* a small cart with one or two wheels in front, two legs at the rear, and handles for pushing. Wheelbarrows are used to carry rocks, soil, leaves, and other materials short distances. {<u>weel</u> **bar** oh}

wheel·chair *noun* a chair on two large wheels that is used by those who cannot walk from place to place. {<u>weel</u> **chayr**}

wheeze *verb* (wheezed, wheezing, wheezes) to breathe with a hoarse or whistling sound. *He was wheezing because he had a bad cold. noun* difficult, whistling breathing or a wheezing sound. *His allergies give him a terrible wheeze.* {<u>weez</u>}

when *adverb* 1. at what time. *When will you come?* 2. at which time. *When is it all right to clap? conjunction* 1. at or during the time that. *He will sleep late when he is on vacation. / It is not wise to travel when you are sick.* 2. every time that; as soon as. *The dog barks when the doorbell rings.* 3. if; considering that. *How can you say I failed, when you know how hard I tried? pronoun* 1. what time. *Since when have you owned this car?* 2. which time. *Until when will you be home?* {<u>wehn</u>}

when·ev·er *conjunction* 1. any time that. *I am ready whenever you are.* 2. at whatever time; when. *Whenever he visited, he brought presents. / Work whenever you can.* {<u>wehn</u> <u>ehv</u> ər}

where *adverb* 1. at or in what location. *Where are you headed?* 2. in what position. *Where does the candidate stand in the race?* 3. toward what end; in what way. *Where does all the money go?* 4. from what source or location. *Where did you get that crazy idea? conjunction* 1. in or at what point or place. *I know where Peter is.* 2. in or at the point or place. *He put a marker where the ball landed.* 3. to whatever place or situation; wherever. *She will follow where he leads.* 4. at which place. *She reached the top of the hill, where she paused to catch her breath. pronoun* what place. *Where does the new student come from?* {<u>wayr</u>}

Homophone Note The words *where*, *ware*, and *wear* sound alike but have different meanings.

where·a·bouts *adverb* in or near what location; about where. *Whereabouts did you park the car? noun* (whereabouts) (used with a singular or plural verb) the place where a person or thing is. *Her whereabouts is a secret.* {<u>wayr</u> ə **bowts**}

where·as *conjunction* 1. while in contrast. *He is kind, whereas she is cruel.* 2. in as much as; because. *Whereas the water was very cold, we decided not to go swimming.* {<u>wayr</u> <u>ăz</u>}

where·upon *conjunction* after which; as a consequence. *I did my homework, whereupon I went outside to play soccer.* {<u>wayr</u> ə <u>pŏn</u>}

wher·ev·er *conjunction* in, at, or toward whatever place or situation. *She leaves a mess wherever she goes. adverb* where. *Wherever did you find such a beautiful hat?* {<u>wayr</u> <u>ehv</u> ər}

wheth·er *conjunction* 1. used to introduce one choice or alternative. *Please find out whether it is snowing.* 2. used to introduce two or more choices or alternatives. *Whether we swim or run, we will get plenty of exercise.* {<u>wehth</u> ər}

Homophone Note The words *whether* and *weather* (conditions outside) sound alike but have different meanings.

whey *noun* the watery part of milk that is left when the curds are separated out in making cheese. {<u>way</u>}

Homophone Note The words *whey*, *way*, and *weigh* sound alike but have different meanings.

which *pronoun* 1. what one or ones. *Which of these coats is yours?* 2. any one or ones; whichever. *She could not decide which she wanted, the blue dress or the red.* 3. used as a relative pronoun to give more information about the person or thing that it refers to. *The back room, which is Laura's office, has a window.* 4. used to represent the thing or things that it refers to. *James wrote five poems, of which the last was the best.* 5. used as a relative pronoun to refer to the word "that." *I gave her that which she asked for. adjective* what particular one or ones of a group of things that have already

 Human Body   Human Mind    Everyday Life   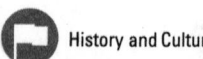 History and Culture    Communication

been talked about. *Which suit do you like?* {**wihch**}

Homophone Note The words *which* and *witch* (a magical woman) sound alike but have different meanings.

which·ev·er *pronoun* whatever or any one that. *Take whichever looks good.* *adjective* no matter which. *I'll go to whichever movie you care to see.* {**wihch** **ehv** ər}

whiff *noun* 1. a faint smell carried on the air. *I got a whiff of roses as I walked past the garden.* 2. a light, short puff of air or smoke. *We needed a whiff of breeze to get the sailboat moving.* {**wihf**}

while *noun* a period of time. *Please stay for a while.* *conjunction* 1. during the time that; as long as. *I will not speak to you while you are angry.* 2. although. *While he can't cook, he cleans very well.* 3. and on the other hand; whereas. *He loves dogs, while she likes cats.* *verb* (whiled, whiling, whiles) to cause to pass in a pleasant, calm and relaxed way (usually followed by "away"). *We whiled away the days of summer.* {**wiyl**}

whim *noun* a sudden desire, thought, or change of mind. *On a whim, she went for a walk at midnight.* {**wihm**}

whim·per *verb* (whimpered, whimpering, whimpers) to cry in weak, broken sounds. *Our dog whimpers whenever we leave the house without her.* *noun* a weak, broken cry. *The baby gave a whimper when I took the bottle away.* {**wihm** pər}

whine *verb* (whined, whining, whines) 1. to make a long, high cry that expresses pain, complaint, or fear. *He whined when his mother told him to*

quit playing and come home for dinner. 2. to complain or protest in a manner that is annoying. *She whined when the coach took her out of the game.* 3. to express or perform with, or as though with, a whine. *The soldier whined his way through basic training.* *noun* the act or sound of whining. *We heard his whine but paid no attention to it.* {**wiyn**} whiner, n.

whin·ny *verb* (whinnied, whinnying, whinnies) to make the sound of a horse; neigh. *noun* the long, high, broken sound made by a horse; neigh. {**wihn** ee}

whip *verb* (whipped, whipping, whips) 1. to strike or beat with quick, repeated strokes with a long, thin strap, or a rod. *You should never whip the dog.* 2. to strike with the motion or force of a whip. *The wind whipped the sheets on the line.* 3. to take off or out with sudden force; pull (usually followed by "off" or "out"). *She whipped out her driver's license.* 4. to beat into a froth. *I whipped the cream for our pies.* 5. (informal) to defeat. *He whipped his opponent in the tennis match.* 6. to move suddenly or quickly; dash. *The dog whipped across the yard.* *noun* a long, thin cord, strap, or rod. *A whip can be used as a weapon, or to prod an animal.* {**wihp**}

whip·poor·will *noun* a bird with gray, black, and white feathers that lives in eastern North America and eats insects. The whippoorwill sings at night, and its call sounds like its name. {**wih** pər **wihl**}

whir *verb* (whirred, whirring, whirs) to move or turn quickly with a humming or buzzing sound. *The blades on*

the mower whirred as I pushed it through the grass. *noun* the act or sound of whirring. *The electric fan makes a whir when it's on.* {**wuhr**}

Homophone Note The words *whir* and *were* sound alike but have different meanings.

whirl *verb* (whirled, whirling, whirls) 1. to turn or spin quickly on a central point. *The bicycle wheel whirled when he lifted it off the ground.* 2. to turn or change direction suddenly; wheel about. *He whirled around to glare at me.* 3. to have a feeling of spinning quickly; reel. *His head whirled from the noise of the city.* 4. to give a quick spinning or turning motion to; cause to revolve. *He whirled his partner on the dance floor.* 5. to drive or carry along very rapidly or in a circular direction. *The wind whirled the newspaper through the park.* *noun* 1. the act or motion of whirling. *He gave the ball a whirl.* 2. a state or feeling of being dizzy or confused. *The roller coaster ride left my head in a whirl.* 3. something that whirls or is whirled. *A giant whirl of wind destroyed the house. / Her ring went down the drain in a whirl.* {**wuhrl**}

whirl·pool *noun* water turning rapidly about a center and pulling downward. *It's dangerous to swim near the whirlpool.* {**wuhrl** poohl}

whirl·wind *noun* 1. a small storm in which a column of air turns rapidly around a central axis as the storm moves forward. Tornadoes are whirlwinds. 2. something that is like such a storm in power or movement. *He is a whirlwind on the soccer field.* *adjective* happening or

A
B
C
D
E
F
G
H
I
J
K
L
M
N
O
P
Q
R
S
T
U
V
W
X
Y
Z

 Living World
 Physical World
 Natural Environment
 Economy
Government and Law

moving with great speed or force. *They went on a whirlwind tour of Europe.* {**wuhrl wihnd**}

whisk *verb* (whisked, whisking, whisks) to brush off or carry off with, or as though with, a quick, light sweep of the hand or a brush. *He whisked the ashes into the rubbish bin. / She whisked the children off to bed.* {**wihsk**}

whisk·er 🌐 *noun* 1. (usually plural) hair growing on the upper lip, cheeks, and chin. 2. one of the long hairs growing near the mouth of a cat, rat, and certain other animals. {**wihs** kər} whiskery, adj.

whis·key *noun* (whiskeys) a liquor made from rye, corn, or other grains. {**wihs** kee}

whis·ky *noun* (whiskies) another spelling of **whiskey**. This spelling is usually used for Scotch or Canadian whiskey. {**wihs** kee}

whis·per *verb* (whispered, whispering, whispers) to speak in a soft, low tone. *Please whisper while the baby is sleeping. noun* 1. a soft, quiet way of speaking. *I heard whispers next to me in the library.* 2. a soft, quiet sound like the whispering of voices; rustle. *Listen to the the whisper of the leaves in the forest.* {**wihs** pər}

whis·tle 🌐 *verb* (whistled, whistling, whistles) 1. to make shrill high sounds by forcing air through a small opening in the lips or a device. *The child learned to whistle yesterday.* 2. to produce by whis-

tling. *She whistled my favorite song.* 3. to make such sounds by forcing steam through a narrow opening. *The tea kettle whistles within five minutes of being heated.* 4. to make such a sound by fast movement through the air. *The baseball whistled past my head.* 5. to signal or give a command by such a sound or sounds. *She whistled for the dog.* 6. to signal, direct, or command by, or as though by, whistling. *The umpire whistled the start of the third quarter. noun* 1. a shrill, high sound produced when air is forced through a narrow opening, such as the lips or a steam vent. *He called the dog with a whistle. / I heard the whistle of the train.* 2. a small instrument or pipe through which air or steam is blown to produce such a sound. *The referee used a whistle to stop the game.* 3. the act or sound of whistling. *The boy called the dog with a whistle. / The whistle of the tea kettle sent her running to the stove.* {**wihs** əl}

white *noun* 1. the color of snow or salt; the lightest color. 2. the white part of something. *The recipe called for six egg whites.* 3. a person who has light skin. *Martin Luther King, Jr. helped bring racial harmony between blacks and whites. adjective* (whiter, whitest) 1. having the color white. *She dreamed of riding a white horse.* 2. nearly the color white; pale. *Her face was white with shock after the accident.* 3. having light or pale skin. *There are not many white families in my*

neighborhood. {**wiyt**} whiteness, n.

white blood cell *noun* a small blood cell with no color that helps protect the body against infections and bacteria. {**wiyt bluhd sehl**}

White House *noun* 1. the official home of the President of the United States in Washington, D.C. (used with "the"). 2. the office of the U.S. president (used with "the"). *The White House gave out copies of the president's schedule.* {**wiyt hows**}

whit·en *verb* (whitened, whitening, whitens) to make or become white. *He whitened his shirt with bleach.* {**wiy** tən} whitener, n.

white-tailed deer *noun* an animal with antlers, long legs, and hooves. White-tailed deer are mammals. They live in woodlands of northern South America, Central America, and the United States, and are very common in the eastern United States. They are closely related to moose and other kinds of deer. {**wiyt tayld deer**}

white·wash *noun* a thin white paint used on walls, fences, or foundations. *verb* (whitewashed, whitewashing, whitewashes) 1. to paint with whitewash. *Tom got his friends to whitewash the fence.* 2. to cover up. *He tried to whitewash his theft so he wouldn't be punished.* {**wiyt wŏsh**}

whit·tle *verb* (whittled, whittling, whittles) 1. to cut small bits or thin layers from, or to trim or shape by so doing. *He whittled a piece of wood into the figure of a cat.* 2. to reduce the size of by, or as if by, cutting (usually followed by "down" or "away"). *We must*

🏃 Human Body   ❓ Human Mind   👕 Everyday Life    History and Culture    Communication

whittle down our spending. / She whittled away inches from her waist by daily exercise. {<u>wiht</u> əl}

whiz *verb* (whizzed, whizzing, whizzes) 1. to make a buzzing or hissing sound by, or as if by, flying swiftly through the air. *The model airplane whizzed above them.* 2. to fly or rush past with such a sound. *He sent the football whizzing through the air.* {<u>wihz</u>}

who *pronoun* 1. what person or persons. *Who are you?* 2. the person or persons that; any person or persons that. *Is it who I think it is?* {<u>hooh</u>}

whoa *interjection* "Stop!" *"Whoa! Don't cross the street until the light turns green."* {<u>woh</u>}

Homophone Note The words *whoa* and *woe* (sadness) sound alike but have different meanings.

who'd shortened form of "who would" or "who had." *Who'd like some watermelon? / I got advice from someone who'd already solved the problem.* {<u>hoohd</u>}

who·ev·er *pronoun* 1. every or any person or persons who; anyone that. *Whoever is the object of your love is very lucky.* 2. no matter who. *Whoever made this mess, we all have to clean it up.* 3. what person. *Whoever would set fire to the school?* {<u>hooh</u> <u>ehv</u> ər}

whole *adjective* 1. having the entire amount or length. *She stayed awake the whole night.* 2. having all the pieces or complete parts. *I put together the whole puzzle.* 3. all in one piece; not divided. *The whole frog was swallowed at once.* *noun* 1. all the pieces or parts of a thing; the entire amount of a thing. *I gave him the whole of my coin collection.* 2.

an entire or complete thing. *He settled for half but would have rather had the whole.* {<u>hohl</u>} wholeness, n.

• **on the whole**
all things considered; in general. *On the whole, I'm very happy.*

Homophone Note The words *whole* and *hole* (an opening) sound alike but have different meanings.

whole number *noun* a counting number or zero. 1, 5, 15, and 258 are examples of whole numbers. {<u>hohl</u> <u>nuhm</u> bər}

whole·some *adjective* good for the health of one's body or mind. *Fruits and vegetables are wholesome foods. / The library has many wholesome books in the children's section.* {<u>hohl</u> səm}

who'll shortened form of "who will." *Who'll come with me to the store?* {<u>hoohl</u>}

wholly *adverb* entirely; completely. *That is not wholly true.* {<u>hohl</u> lee}

Homophone Note The words *wholly* and *holy* (sacred) sound alike but have different meanings.

whom *pronoun* what person or persons (considered as the object of a verb or preposition). *She is the woman with whom I work. / Whom does this concern?* {<u>hoohm</u>}

whom·ev·er *pronoun* whoever; what or which persons (as the object of a verb or preposition). *I will choose whomever I like.* {<u>hoohm</u> <u>eh</u> vər}

whoop *noun* a loud shout or cry. *She gave a whoop of happiness when she hit a home run.* *verb* (whooped, whooping, whoops) to give a loud shout or cry. *She whooped with surprise and joy when she saw her*

new bike. {<u>woohp</u> or <u>wuup</u>, n., <u>woohp</u> or <u>wuup</u>, v.}

Homophone Note The words *whoop* and *hoop* (a large ring) sound alike but have different meanings.

whooping cough *noun* a serious breathing disease in children, marked by heavy coughing and passed easily from one child to another. {<u>hoohp</u> ing **kawf** or <u>huup</u> ing **kawf**}

whooping crane *noun* a large North American bird, now rare, with black and white feathers and a loud, whooping call. {<u>hoohp</u> ing **krayn** or <u>wuup</u> ing **krayn**}

whoosh *noun* a loud rushing or gushing sound, as made by air or water moving rapidly. *I was kept awake by the whoosh of cars on the street in front of my house.* *verb* (whooshed, whooshing, whooshes) to make a rushing or gushing sound, or to move something with such a sound. *Water whooshed down the drain. / She whooshed the pile of papers off the table and onto the floor.* {<u>wuush</u>}

who's shortened form of "who is" or "who has." *Who's that boy in the green sweater? / Who's been here before?* {<u>hoohz</u>}

Homophone Note The contraction *who's* and the word *whose* sound alike but have different meanings.

whose *pronoun* 1. of or belonging to which person or persons. *Whose diamonds are*

A
B
C
D
E
F
G
H
I
J
K
L
M
N
O
P
Q
R
S
T
U
V
W
X
Y
Z

 Living World   Physical World    Natural Environment    Economy   Government and Law

those? 2. of or belonging to which thing, animal, event, or the like. *This has been a vacation whose purpose was to rest.* 3. that which belongs to which person or thing. *Whose horse is winning the race, his or mine?* {**hoohz**}

Homophone Note The word *whose* and the contraction *who's* ("who is") sound alike but have different meanings.

why *adverb* for what reason, purpose, or cause. *Why are you in such a hurry? conjunction* 1. for what reason, purpose, or cause. *I don't know why you didn't call.* 2. because of which; for which. *Tell me the reason why you didn't like the movie. noun* (often plural) the reason or explanation. *Einstein wanted to learn the whys behind the laws of the universe. interjection* used to express surprise or mild annoyance. *Why, I never knew you were once an actor! / Why, Max, you bad dog!* {**wiy** or **hwiy**}

WI or **Wis.** or **Wisc.** *abbreviation* an abbreviation for **Wisconsin.**

wick *noun* a cord in a candle or oil lamp that draws up fuel to be burned at its upper end. {**wihk**}

wick·ed ❓ *adjective* 1. evil in actions or ideas. *Our wicked neighbor enjoyed making others unhappy.* 2. very bad; naughty; mischievous. *The wicked child was sent to bed early.* 3. painful, harmful, or dangerous. *I have a wicked sore throat.* {**wihk** ihd} wickedly, adv., wickedness, n.

Word History *Wicked* comes from an Old English word that means "to give way," "bend easily," or "be weak."

wick·er *noun* 1. a twig or shoot of willow or other long, woody strip that bends easily. 2. a basket or piece of furniture made of such twigs or strips woven together. *The chairs on our porch are wicker. adjective* made of wicker. *The porch is lined with plants in wicker baskets.* {**wihk** ər}

wide *adjective* (wider, widest) 1. reaching across a large area from side to side. *The three of us walked through the wide doorway together. / She likes to wear jeans with wide legs.* 2. having an exact measurement from side to side. *The path is only four feet wide.* 3. having great range or scope. *After years of studying in China, she has a wide understanding of that country. / It seemed that we could see forever across the wide prairie.* 4. completely open. *Surprise showed in her wide eyes.* 5. away or far from a certain point or goal (often followed by "of"). *Robin's arrow landed wide of the target. adverb* 1. over a great distance or area. *He searched far and wide for her.* 2. as fully as possible; completely. *The window was wide open.* {**wiyd**}

-wide *suffix* a suffix that means "all the way through" or "throughout." "Countrywide" means "throughout the country."

wide·ly *adverb* 1. over a wide space or region. *Our products are widely known.* 2. among many people. *His musical gifts are widely recognized.* 3. to a great degree; by a large amount. *Those two have widely different opinions about religion.* {**wiyd** lee}

wid·en *verb* (widened, widening, widens) to make or become wide or wider. *They had to widen the driveway for their second car.* {**wiy** dən}

wide·spread *adjective* 1. happening or scattered over a wide area. *She enjoyed widespread fame after her new film came out.* 2. open or spread out to full width. *The bird's widespread wings cast a large shadow on the water.* {**wiyd sprehd**}

wid·ow *noun* a woman whose husband has died and who has not married again. *verb* (widowed, widowing, widows) to make a widow. *She was widowed by an auto accident.* {**wihd** oh}

wid·ow·er *noun* a man whose wife has died and who has not married again. {**wihd** oh ər}

width *noun* the length of something from one side to the other. *I need a bookshelf with a width of four feet.* {**wihdth** or **wihth**}

wife *noun* (wives) a woman who is married, or the woman to whom a man is married. {**wiyf**}

wig *noun* a head covering made of natural or artificial hair, worn to cover one's own hair. {**wihg**}

wig·gle *verb* (wiggled, wiggling, wiggles) 1. to move with quick, twisting motions from side to side. *The toy snake wiggled across the floor.* 2. to cause to move quickly from side to side. *The child wiggled his loose tooth. noun* a quick movement from side to side or a course of such movements. *We'll move with a wiggle during that part of the dance.* {**wihg** gəl}

 Human Body   Human Mind   Everyday Life   History and Culture   Communication

wig·wam *noun* a Native American shelter, shaped like a dome, made up of poles covered with bark, hides, or mats. {**wihg** wahm}

wild 🌐 🌍 *adjective* (wilder, wildest) 1. living in a natural state; not tamed. *There are wild animals in the jungle.* 2. not cultivated. *I love wild strawberries.* 3. without discipline; unruly. *The teacher could not control the wild students.* 4. crazy; out of control. *He was wild at the awful news.* *adverb* (wilder, wildest) in a wild manner; wildly. *The weeds are growing wild in the field.* *noun* a deserted region; wilderness. *It takes a tough person to live in the wild. / He built a cabin in the wilds of Alaska.* {**wiyld**} wildly, adv., wildness, n.

wild·cat *noun* a bobcat, lynx, ocelot, or other wild cat of medium size. {**wiyld** kăt}

wil·der·ness *noun* a region in its natural state where there are trees and wild animals, but no people living there. {**wihl** dər nihs}

wild·flow·er *noun* a wild, flowering plant that grows in meadows, woods, or other natural areas. {**wiyld** flow ər}

wild·life *noun* wild animals that live free of humans. {**wiyld** liyf}

will¹ *auxiliary verb* 1. used to show the future. *The new pool will open soon.* 2. used to show that something is certain. *It will be finished today.* 3. used to show the intention to. *I will pay you back next Saturday.* 4. used to show purpose or intention. *I will go if you do.* 5. to be able to. *This car will run if you change the oil.* {**wihl**}

will² 🌐 *noun* 1. the power of the mind to choose a course of action or to make a decision. *My father has a strong will.* 2. the act or process of using this power. *A democracy is ruled by the will of the people.* 3. desire; wish. *They took the child against her will.* 4. strength; desire; control. *A good athlete has the will to win.* 5. a legal statement that describes how one wishes to distribute his or her property after death. *When my grandfather died, he left me an accordion in his will.* *verb* (willed, willing, wills) 1. to decide upon. *He can succeed if he wills it.* 2. to give by means of a legal will. *He willed the house to his children.* {**wihl**}

will·ful or **wilful** *adjective* 1. according to one's will; on purpose. *Her staying out all night was a willful act to show her independence.* 2. stubborn; wanting one's own way. *He is a willful child whose favorite word is, "No!"* {**wihl** fəl} willfully, adv., willfulness, n.

wil·ling *adjective* 1. wanting or agreeing to do something; ready. *I am willing to listen.* 2. ready to join in happily or gladly. *Thank you for being such a willing helper.* {**wihl** ing} willingly, adv., willingness, n.

wil·low *noun* a tree or bush that has narrow leaves. The long twigs of willows bend easily and are used in weaving baskets and making furniture. {**wih** loh}

wilt *verb* (wilted, wilting, wilts) to lose freshness and become limp. *The flowers had wilted by the time the party was over. / I am wilting in this heat.* {**wihlt**}

wimp *noun* (informal) a weak person. wimpish, adj., wimpy, adj.

win *verb* (won, winning, wins) 1. to do the best or come first in a contest or game. *Our team won in the state basketball championship.* 2. to get through great effort; finally achieve. *The slaves won their freedom after years of pain and struggle.* 3. to succeed in getting the support or favor of. *His speech won many voters.* *noun* a victory in a race, contest, or other competition. *After losing several games, our team finally had a win.* {**wihn**}

Word History *Win* comes from an Old English word that means "to struggle for or work at."

wince *verb* (winced, wincing, winces) to draw suddenly back or away from something painful or frightening. *I winced when I saw the size of the needle in the doctor's hand.* {**wihns**}

winch *noun* a machine, run by motor or hand, that pulls or lifts objects by a rope or cable that is wound around a drum. {**wihnch**}

wind¹ 🌐 *noun* 1. air as it moves naturally over the surface of the earth. *The wind blew papers across the park.* 2. a stream of air produced by any other means. *The wind from the fan keeps me cool.* 3. breath; breathing. *After running hard he was out of wind.* *verb* (winded, winding, winds) to make short of breath. *The run winded him.* {**wihnd**}
• **get wind of**
to receive hints of or information about. *The police got wind of the crime from talk on the street.*

A
B
C
D
E
F
G
H
I
J
K
L
M
N
O
P
Q
R
S
T
U
V
W
X
Y
Z

 Living World  Physical World   Natural Environment  Economy  Government and Law

a b c d e f g h i j k l m n o p q r s t u v **w** x y z

wind² 🔊 *verb* (wound, winding, winds) 1. to follow or to have a bending or turning course. *The trail wound through the woods.* 2. to turn around a thing. *The snake wound around the tree branch.* 3. to make into a ball or put onto a spool; roll. *She wound the yarn.* 4. to cover with or wrap. *The doctor wound the bandage around his arm.* 5. to turn through a series of motions. *He wound the crank.* 6. to make work by tightening the spring of. *Every night he wound the clock. noun* a single turn or twist. *Give it one more wind.* {wiynd}
• **wind down** 1. to become less strong or intense. *The storm is finally winding down.* 2. (informal) to relax. *They went to the beach to wind down.*
• **wind up** 1. (informal) to bring or come to an end. *Please wind up the party before midnight.* 2. to be in a state of great excitement. *The children were all wound up after the parade.* 3. (informal) to find oneself in a certain place or situation; end up. *He got on the wrong bus and wound up in Pittsburgh. / As usual, I wound up washing the dishes.*

Homophone Note The words **wind²** and **whined** (past tense of "whine") sound alike but have different meanings.

wind·fall *noun* 1. money or another piece of good fortune that is not expected or earned. *He was surprised to inherit a windfall from his grandmother.* 2. a tree or fruit from a tree, blown down by wind. *We had to ride our bikes around the windfall of tree*

branches on the path. {wihnd fŏl}

Word History In the 1400s, the trees on a British nobleman's estate belonged to the king he served. However, trees that had fallen in a storm were free to those who lived on the estate. Such a piece of luck was called a **windfall**.

wind instrument *noun* a musical instrument that is sounded by the force of air blown into it. Flutes, trumpets, and clarinets are some wind instruments. {wihnd ihn strə mənt}

wind·mill *noun* a machine that pumps water by using the energy from a wheel that is placed on top of a tower and turned by the wind. {wihnd mihl}

win·dow 🔊 *noun* 1. an opening in a wall or vehicle that lets in air and light and provides a view out. 2. the glass and frame that fit into such an opening. {wihn doh}

Word History *Window* comes from early Scandinavian words that mean "an eye for the wind."

win·dow-shop *verb* (window-shopped, window-shopping, window-shops) to pass time

by looking at goods in store windows without any intention of buying them. *I like to window-shop at the mall.* {wihn doh **shŏp**} window-shopper, n.

wind·pipe *noun* the tube that carries air between the throat and the lungs in humans and certain animals; trachea. {wihnd piyp}

wind·shield *noun* a curved piece of glass or plastic attached to the front of a car or other vehicle to protect the driver and riders from the wind. {wihnd sheeld}

wind·surf·ing *noun* a sport in which a person stands on a board to which a sail is attached and sails through the water by moving the sail. {wihnd suhr fing}

wind·swept *adjective* exposed to the wind; windy. *The boat landed on a windswept beach.* {wihnd swehpt}

wind·y *adjective* (windier, windiest) having a great amount of wind. *We like to fly kites on windy days.* {wihn dee}

wine *noun* the juice of grapes that has been fermented and contains alcohol. {wiyn}

wing 🔊 🔊 *noun* 1. either of a pair of movable body parts used by birds, bats, or insects to fly. 2. any body part that looks or acts like a wing, but does not enable flight. *Penguins use their wings to swim, but they cannot fly.* 3. something having the shape or use of a wing. *The wing of an*

 Human Body   Human Mind    Everyday Life    History and Culture   Communication

airplane is usually made of metal. 4. a side section of a building. *My class is in the north wing of the school.* 5. (plural) the area on both sides of the stage that is hidden from the view of the audience. *The actors waited in the wings.* *verb* (winged, winging, wings) to move by using or as if by using wings; fly. *The eagle winged over the river.* {wing}

• **under one's wing**
under one's care or protection. *The coach took us under his wing.*

winged *adjective* having wings. *I was bitten by a winged insect.* {wingd or wing ihd}

wing·span *noun* the distance from the tip of one wing of a bird or plane to the tip of the other. *The bird's wingspan measured two feet.* {wing spăn}

wing·spread *noun* the distance from the tip of one wing of a bird or plane to the tip of the other wing when they are spread wide. *The huge bird had a wingspread of four feet.* {wing sprehd}

wink *verb* (winked, winking, winks) 1. to close and open one eye quickly, as a sign of agreement or friendliness. *Uncle Joe always winks at people he likes.* 2. to close and open both eyes quickly; blink. *His part in the play was so small that if you winked you'd miss him!* 3. to express by winking. *He winked his agreement.* *noun* 1. the act or motion of winking or blinking. *I gave my eyes a wink to clear the dust from them.* 2. the short time needed for, or as if for, winking once. *The tired child fell asleep in a wink.* {wingk}

win·ner *noun* one that wins or is likley to win or succeed. *She was the winner of several*

races. / *We picked that puppy because he seems like a winner.* {wihn ər}

win·ning *adjective* 1. being the one that wins; successful or victorious. *They were the winning team this year.* 2. pleasant and attractive. *My husband has a winning smile.* *noun* (usually plural) the money or things won by someone. *She happily counted her winnings.* {wihn ing}

win·ter  *noun* 1. the season of the year between autumn and spring. *It can get very cold in the winter.* 2. cold, often wet or damp, weather. *She wears a heavy coat to withstand the winter.* *verb* (wintered, wintering, winters) 1. to spend the winter. *They would like to winter in a warm climate.* 2. to keep through the winter. *They wintered their cattle in large barns.* {wihn tər}

win·ter·green *noun* 1. a low evergreen found in eastern North America that bears white flowers and red berries. Oil from its leaves is used to make flavoring. 2. the oil of this plant, or a flavoring from or like this oil. {wihn tər green}

win·try *adjective* (wintrier, wintriest) of, or relating to winter. *I could see my breath in the wintry air.* {wihn tree or wihn tə ree}

wipe *verb* (wiped, wiping, wipes) 1. to clean or dry by rubbing lightly with a soft cloth, paper, or one's hand. *I wiped the wet dishes with a towel before putting them away.* 2. to remove by wiping (usually followed by "away," "off," "out," or "up"). *He wiped the crumbs off the table. / She wiped away the tears on her baby's face.* *noun* one light rub or a brief rubbing; act of wiping. *The waitress gave the the table a quick wipe.* {wiyp}

• **wipe out**
1. to destroy. *The flood wiped out the town. / Hungry rabbits wiped out our vegetable garden.* 2. (informal) to kill. *We wiped out the nest of wasps with a can of bug spray.*

wire *noun* 1. a thin rod or thread of metal. *The cows were kept in the pasture by a fence made of wire.* 2. any material made of such rods or threads woven or twisted together. *The wrecking ball swung from a heavy wire on the crane.* 3. the line or cable used in a telephone, telegraph, or electric power system. 4. a telegram; cable. *The president received a wire from the general overseas.* *verb* (wired, wiring, wires) 1. to put an electrical system in. *The electrician wired the house.* 2. to fasten or join with wire. *He wired the muffler up to his car.* 3. to send by telephone or telegraph. *Please wire flowers to your sister.* 4. to send a telegram or cable to. *We can wire him at his office address.* {wiyr}

wire·less *adjective* working or sent without wires. *We use a wireless telephone when we're out of the house.* *noun* a telephone or telegraph set that

works without wires. *You can call her on the wireless.* {**wiyr** lihs}

wir·ing *noun* a system of wires used to carry electricity. *It's a fine old house, but needs new wiring.* {**wiyr** ing}

wir·y *adjective* (wirier, wiriest) 1. like wire in appearance; thin and stiff. *The goat's beard felt rough and wiry.* 2. like wire in being thin and strong. *Her tall, wiry build makes her a natural athlete.* {**wiyr** ee}

Wis·con·sin *noun* a state in the midwestern United States. Its capital is Madison. (abbreviated: WI) {wihs **kŏn** sihn} Wisconsinite, n.

Word History *Wisconsin* comes from *ouisconsink*, an Algonquin name for the Wisconsin River. *Ouisconsink* may mean "grassy place" or "place of the beaver."

wis·dom *noun* 1. the state of being wise. *My grandmother's wisdom comes from years of living and learning.* 2. good judgment and an understanding of that which is true or good. *She had the wisdom to teach her children to respect themselves.* 3. knowledge; learning. *Reading is a good way to gain wisdom.* {**wihz** dəm}

wisdom tooth *noun* the last tooth on each side of both the upper and lower jaws of humans that is the last tooth to appear. A wisdom tooth can cause problems when there is not enough room for it to grow. {**wihz** dəm **toohth**}

-wise *suffix* a suffix that means "in a certain way, direction, or position." *If you turn something clockwise, you turn it the same direction as the hands of a clock.*

wise ⊙ *adjective* (wiser, wisest) 1. having understanding and good judgment about what is true or good. *Years of experience have made her wise.* 2. showing such understanding. *You have made a wise decision.* {**wiyz**} wisely, adv.

wish *verb* (wished, wishing, wishes) 1. to long for; desire; want. *I wish that he would come home soon.* 2. to express wishes to or for. *I wish you good luck.* *noun* 1. a desire or hope for something. *My wish is that you will visit me soon.* 2. a thing wished for or desired. *He got his wish.* {**wihsh**}

wish·bone *noun* a forked bone found in front of the breastbone of most birds. Wishbones from cooked birds are used to make wishes. The two ends of the bone are pulled by two different people until the bone breaks somewhere near the middle. The person with the larger end left from the break is said to have won their wish. {**wihsh** bohn}

wisp *noun* 1. a thin bundle of hay, tuft of hair, or small bit of something else. *The baby has only a wisp of hair on her head.* / *Wisps of smoke rose from the chimney.* 2. a small trace or hint. *I heard a wisp of fear in her voice.* {**wihsp**}

wis·te·ri·a *noun* a woody vine with drooping clusters of purple or white flowers that look like bunches of grapes. {wih **steer** ee ə *or* wih **stayr** ee ə}

wit *noun* 1. (sometimes plural) quick and clever understanding of the world around one, and the ability to use or express this understanding. *The policewoman's sharp wits had gotten her out of many tough spots.* 2. the use of this ability to make other people laugh, or a person who typi-cally does so. *The wit in Shakespeare's plays still makes people laugh.* / *He is the family wit who always has funny things to say.* 3. the ability to understand, think, or know. *By using all their wits, they were the first team to solve the puzzle.* {**wiht**}

witch *noun* a woman who is believed to have magic powers. {**wihch**}

Homophone Note Are you looking for the word *which*? *Witch* and *which* sound alike but have different meanings.

with *preposition* 1. in the company of. *They walked with me.* 2. marked by; having. *Give this to the woman with the straw hat.* 3. by using. *She locks the door with a key.* / *He won her over with his charm.* 4. showing or feeling. *She drove with confidence.* 5. in relation to. *We agreed with the idea that all people should be free.* 6. regarding; toward. *They are happy with him.* 7. in the care or keeping of. *He left his money with us.* 8. in the same group as; among; into. *He mixed sugar with butter for the cake.* 9. in opposition to. *Don't argue with me.* 10. so as to be separated from. *I hate to part with this new book.* 11. of the same opinion as. *I'm with you on this plan.* 12. due to; because of. *He wept with joy.* {**wihth**}

with·draw ⊙ *verb* (withdrew, withdrawn, withdrawing, withdraws) 1. to take out or away; remove. *She withdrew the nail from the board.* / *She withdrew her jewels from the safe.* / *He withdrew $50 from his bank account.* 2. to take back. *He withdrew his support from the project.* 3. to remove oneself from a place or activity. *Two players withdrew*

 Human Body   Human Mind   Everyday Life   History and Culture   Communication

from the game. {wih**th draw**} withdrawable, adj., with-drawer, n.

with·drew *verb* past tense of **withdraw**. {wih**th drooh**}

with·er *verb* (withered, withering, withers) 1. to dry up or wilt. *The flowers in the garden withered from lack of rain.* 2. to cause to dry up or wilt. *The hot sun withered the plant sitting in the window.* 3. to cause to feel embarrassed. *The loud student was withered by the teacher's angry stare.* {wih**th** ər}

Word History *Wither* comes from an early English word that means "to expose to the weather."

with·held *verb* past tense and past participle of **withhold**. {wih**th hehld**}

with·hold *verb* (withheld, withholding, withholds) 1. to hold back; control. *She withheld her anger.* 2. to refuse to give. *They withheld his pay until he returned his uniform.* {wih**th hohld**}

with·in *adverb* into or in the inner part of a room, building, or other space. *The door was closed, but I knew that she sat within.* *preposition* 1. in the inner part of; inside. *The dog stayed within the fence.* 2. not going beyond the limits of. *I will mail the letter to you within the next two weeks.* / *It is within a citizen's rights to organize a protest.* {wih**th ihn**}

with·out *preposition* 1. having none of or no; lacking. *I am without money until Friday.* 2. free of. *She is a person without any worries.* *adverb* with something missing or lacking. *The roses didn't bloom this year, so we'll have to do without.* {wih**th owt**}

with·stand *verb* (withstood, withstanding, withstands) to resist or stand up to; bear. *The boat was sturdy enough to withstand the heavy wind and waves.* / *He withstood the pressure from his friends to drink and smoke.* {wih**th stănd**}

with·stood *verb* past tense and past participle of **withstand**. {wih**th stuud**}

wit·ness ⊕ *verb* (witnessed, witnessing, witnesses) 1. to watch or be present at. *He witnessed the accident.* / *They witnessed their son's college graduation.* 2. to prove that a will or other legal paper was signed properly by signing it oneself. *The old man's two sons witnessed his will.* *noun* 1. a person who sees or hears something that happened. *He was a witness to the fight.* 2. a person who gives evidence in a court of law. *The witness said that the accident was the other driver's fault.* 3. a person who proves a legal paper was signed properly by signing it as well. *They signed as witnesses of their mother's will.* {wiht nihs}

Word History The word *witness* comes from *wit*, which in Old English means "knowledge."

wit·ty *adjective* (wittier, wittiest) showing or characterized by clever humor. *She told witty stories about her travels.* {wiht ee}

wives *noun* plural of **wife**. {wiyvz}

wiz·ard *noun* 1. a person who is believed to have magic powers. 2. (informal) a person who has amazing skill at something. *My brother is a wizard at fixing cars.* {wih zərd}

wk. *abbreviation* an abbreviation for **week**.

wob·ble *verb* (wobbled, wobbling, wobbles) to move or tip from side to side in an unsteady way; be out of balance. *The bike wobbled because its front wheel was bent.* / *Most babies wobble when learning to walk.* {wo bəl}

woe *noun* 1. great suffering or sorrow. *The death of a loved one can cause much woe.* 2. trouble or problem. *His money woes kept him awake at night.* {woh}

Homophone Note The words *woe* and *whoa* (stop!) sound alike but have different meanings.

wok *noun* a large frying pan with a rounded bottom, used for cooking Chinese food. {wŏk}

wok·en *verb* a past participle of **wake**[1]. {woh kən}

wolf *noun* (wolves) a wild mammal that has a pointed nose, pointed ears, and a bushy tail. Wolves are closely related to coyotes, dogs, and foxes. They usually eat birds and other small animals, but they also hunt in packs for larger animals such as deer. Wolves used to be common in Europe, Asia, and North America, but are now extinct or endangered in most areas. *verb* (wolfed, wolfing, wolfs) to eat quickly; to swallow food in large bites. *He wolfed down his breakfast and ran to catch the school bus.* {wuulf}
• **cry wolf**

a
b
c
d
e
f
g
h
i
j
k
l
m
n
o
p
q
r
s
t
u
v
w
x
y
z

to give a false alarm. *If you cry wolf too often, no one will believe you when you are in real danger.*

wol·ver·ine *noun* a mammal with a long, thick body, short legs, and a bushy tail. Wolverines have dark fur with white marks on the face and body. They are the largest kind of weasel, and may grow over three feet long. Wolverines hunt many kinds of animals, including large mammals. They live in the northern parts of North America, Europe, and Asia. {**wuul** və **reen**}

wolves *plural noun* plural of **wolf.** {**wuulvz**}

wom·an *noun* (women) 1. an adult female human. *When a girl becomes a woman, she is expected to decide things for herself.* 2. women in general. {**wuum** ən}

wom·an·hood *noun* the state of being a woman. *At the age of eighteen, she was just reaching womanhood.* {**wuum** ən **huud**}

wom·bat *noun* a mammal with brown fur and short, thick legs. Wombats are Australian marsupials that live in burrows and eat plants. They are closely related to koalas. {**wŏm** băt}

wom·en *noun* plural of **woman.** *There should be ten women at the meeting tonight.* {**wihm** ihn}

won *verb* past tense and past participle of **win.** {**wuhn**}

Homophone Note The words *won* and *one* (the first number) sound alike but have different meanings.

won·der *verb* (wondered, wondering, wonders) 1. to feel admiration, surprise, or amazement (often followed by "at"). *She wondered at his bravery in the war.* 2. to want

to know or be curious about. *I wonder where she is.* *noun* 1. a thing or event that causes admiration, surprise, or amazement. *The mountains in Oregon are natural wonders.* 2. the feeling that is caused by something amazing, impressive, or surprising. *I gazed in wonder at the vast ocean.* {**wuhn** dər}

won·der·ful *adjective* causing feelings of wonder; excellent or amazing. *She has made wonderful progress in school this year.* {**wuhn** dər fəl} wonderfully, adv.

won't shortened form of "will not." *I won't go without you.* {**wohnt**}

wood 🟢 🔵 🌐 *noun* 1. the hard material lying under the bark that makes up the trunk and branches of a tree. 2. such a material cut and dried for use as a building material. 3. such a material burned for fuel; firewood. 4. (usually plural) a collection of trees growing close together in one area; forest. *I took my dog for a walk in the woods yesterday.* {**wuud**}

Homophone Note Are you looking for the word *would* (a helping verb)? *Wood* and *would* sound alike but have different meanings.

wood·chuck *noun* a rodent with a thick body and shaggy brown fur. Woodchucks live in burrows and sleep all winter. They are also called groundhogs. Woodchucks are common in Canada and the northeastern United States {**wuud chuhk**}

wood·ed *adjective* having woods; covered with trees. *They bought some wooded land in the hills.* {**wuud** ihd}

wood·en *adjective* made of wood. *Her wooden hobbyhorse was a favorite toy.* {**wuud** ihn}

wood·land *noun* land covered with woods; forest. {**wuud** lənd}

wood·peck·er *noun* a bird with a hard, pointed bill for making holes in trees to find insects to eat. Their strong claws and stiff tails help them climb trees. Woodpeckers are of many different sizes. {**wuud** pehk ər}

wood·wind *noun* 1. any of a group of musical wind instruments that were originally made of wood. Clarinets, flutes, and oboes are some woodwinds. 2. (plural) the section of an orchestra or band made up of these instruments. {**wuud** wihnd}

wood·work *noun* door and window frames and other wooden parts inside a house, or other objects or parts made of wood. *I love the fine woodwork found in older homes.* {**wuud** wuhrk}

wood·work·ing *noun* the art, act, or process of shaping wood. *He makes wonderful toys with his woodworking.* *adjective* of or used for working in wood. *A saw and a chisel are two kinds of woodworking tools.* {**wuud** wuhr king} woodworker, n.

wood·y *adjective* (woodier, woodiest) 1. filled with trees; wooded. *It is not possible to play ball in our woody backyard.* 2. containing or made of wood. *There are woody plants all over the island.* {**wuud** ee}

wool *noun* 1. the thick, soft, often curly hair of sheep, goats, llamas, and other animals. 2. yarn made from this hair. 3. clothing knitted or made of this yarn. 4. any cov-

 Human Body   Human Mind   Everyday Life   🏴 History and Culture   ☎ Communication

ering or material that looks like sheep hair. *He used steel wool to clean the barbecue grill.* *adjective* made of wool; woolen. *My wool sweater keeps me very warm.* {**wuul**}

• **pull the wool over someone's eyes** (informal) to trick or fool someone. *He was pulling the wool over their eyes when he told them he was a rock star.*

wool·en *adjective* of or made of wool. *We packed woolen jackets and hats for our winter trip.* {**wuul** ihn}

word 🌐 *noun* 1. a sound, group of sounds, or the symbols written for such sounds in writing that have some meaning. Words are a basic unit of language. *We could not understand his words.* 2. a short remark or statement. *I'd like to say a word about that.* 3. a message; news. *We sent word that we had arrived.* 4. a promise. *He gave his word that he would be there for us.* 5. a signal or command. *The chorus walked on stage when she gave the word.* *verb* (worded, wording, words) to choose words to express. *She worded her thoughts carefully.* {**wuhrd**}

• **eat one's words** to admit that something one said was wrong. *She teased her brother when he started taking up the flute, but she ate her words after she heard him play.*

word·ing *noun* the act or manner of putting into words. *The sweet wording of the love letter moved her to tears.* {**wuhr** ding}

word processing *noun* 1. the creation of typed documents with a computer. 2. the skill or act of creating typed documents with a computer. *Many jobs today require word*

processing. {**wuhrd** pro seh sing}

word·y *adjective* (wordier, wordiest) having or using too many words. *Her ideas are good, but her report is too wordy.* {**wuhr** dee} wordiness, n.

wore *verb* past tense of **wear.** {**wohr**}

Homophone Note The words *wore* and *war* (battle) sound alike but have different meanings.

---

work 🌿⚗️🌊 *noun* 1. the use of energy or effort to achieve a result by doing or making something; labor. *It takes a lot of hard work to build a house.* 2. a task or project that uses such effort. *He finished his work at the office.* 3. something made or done as the result of such effort. *His painting was a work of art.* 4. a job. *She enjoys her work with children.* *verb* (worked, working, works) 1. to have a job. *He works at the bank.* 2. to run or act properly. *The car doesn't work.* 3. to use; handle. *I don't know how to work the oven.* 4. to cause to be or happen; bring about. *Her careful teaching worked wonders to improve the student's grades.* 5. to cause to produce, act, or do work. *She works her horses hard.* {**wuhrk**}

work·bench *noun* a sturdy table or bench where a carpenter or other worker works. {**wuhrk** behnch}

work·book *noun* a book for students that has problems or exercises and spaces for written answers or practice. {**wuhrk** buuk}

work·er *noun* 1. someone or something that works. 2. a type of female ant, bee, or termite that cannot lay eggs and does most of the work

for the insect colony it lives in. {**wuhr** kər}

work·man *noun* (workmen) a male worker who works with his hands or with machines. *Many workmen were hired to build the new town hall.* {**wuhrk** mən}

work·man·ship *noun* 1. the art or skill of someone who works with their hands or with machines. *She takes great pride in her workmanship as a carpenter.* 2. the quality of such a person's work. *That potter is widely known for the workmanship of his bowls and cups.* {**wuhrk** mən shihp}

work·out *noun* 1. a period or program of physical exercise. *He does a workout every other day during baseball season.* 2. something difficult to do. *The exam gave the students a real workout.* {**wuhrk** owt}

world *noun* 1. the universe; everything that exists. 2. the earth and all those who live on it. *I would like to travel around the world someday.* 3. a particular area or field of activity, along with all the people and things having to do with it. *The United States is part of the western world.* / *The business world is competitive.* 4. the whole human race; all people. *The world was amazed when men landed on the moon.* 5. a planet or star thought of as being like the earth. *Some people believe in life on other worlds.* 6. a great amount. *It would make a world of difference if you could study harder.* {**wuhrld**}

A
B
C
D
E
F
G
H
I
J
K
L
M
N
O
P
Q
R
S
T
U
V
W
X
Y
Z

 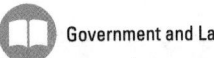

a
b
c
d
e
f
g
h
i
j
k
l
m
n
o
p
q
r
s
t
u
v
w
x
y
z

• out of this world (informal) very good; excellent. *Her chocolate cake is out of this world!*

• think the world of to have a very high opinion of. *She thinks the world of her friend.*

Homophone Note The words *world* and *whirled* (past tense of "whirl") sound alike but have different meanings.

world·ly *adjective* (worldlier, worldliest) 1. of or relating to the material world; not spiritual. *She gave up all her worldly goods when she became a nun.* 2. engaged with and knowing about the people, activities, and ways of the material world; sophisticated. *She seemed far too worldly for a teenager.* {**wuhrld** lee} worldliness, n.

world·wide *adjective* spread or happening all over the world. *There was worldwide interest in who would become the next U.S. president.* {**wuhrld** **wiyd**}

World Wide Web or **web** or **world wide web** *noun* a part of the Internet. The World Wide Web is made of documents called "pages" that are linked to each other. *We searched the World Wide Web for information on pandas.* {**wuhrld** **wiyd** **wehb**}

worm ❶ *noun* 1. an animal with a long, thin, round, or flat body. Worms have no legs and move by creeping or crawling. Worms are invertebrates and have no backbone. 2. (plural; used with a singular verb) a disease caused by worms, or

other animals that look like worms, living as parasites inside other animals. *verb* (wormed, worming, worms) 1. to make one's way slowly or by a winding route. *The puppy wormed through people's legs under the table.* 2. to cause or make by moving in a winding, indirect route. *The motorcycle wormed its way through heavy traffic.* 3. to get by tricky means (usually followed by "out" or "into"). *He tried to worm out of his chores.* 4. to find out by tricky means (usually followed by "out" or "from"). *She couldn't worm the secret plans out of him.* 5. to treat or cure the disease caused by worms. *The veterinarian wormed our cat.* {**wuhrm**}

worn-out *adjective* 1. no longer able to be used because of wear. *I finally put my worn-out shoes in the trash.* 2. very tired. *After a day of shopping, she felt worn-out.*

{**wohrn** **owt**}

wor·ry ❓ *verb* (worried, worrying, worries) 1. to feel anxious, troubled, or uneasy. *Don't worry, I'll take care of the problem.* 2. to cause to feel troubled or anxious. *He worried his mother by staying out so late.* 3. to bite and shake with the teeth. *The dog worried the rat to death.* *noun* 1. the act of worrying. *Worry doesn't*

change anything. 2. the condition of being worried; concern. *I am sad with worry that he won't come home.* 3. a cause of troubled or anxious feelings. *Please try to forget your worries for a while.* {**wuhr** ee} worrier, n.

Word History In Old English, *worry* meant "to strangle." In the English spoken later, in the 1500s, "worry" meant "to treat roughly." The sense of "to annoy or bother" was first used in 1671.

worse *adjective* 1. comparative form of **bad**. 2. more evil or harmful. *He started with shoplifting and went on to worse crimes.* 3. in poorer condition or health. *The patient is worse this week. noun* someone or something that is worse than another. *You may be a bad tennis player, but I've seen worse. adverb* 1. comparative form of **badly**. 2. in a way that is more evil or harmful. *The student behaved worse last year than he did this year.* {**wuhrs**}

wor·ship ❓ *noun* 1. love and devotion shown to a being or an object considered sacred. *Many religions give worship to God on a particular day of the week.* 2. great love or devotion. *His worship of his beautiful wife was known to all. verb* (worshiped, worshiping, worships) 1. to give religious devotion, honor, and love to. *She worshiped God through weekly church services and daily prayers.* 2. to treat with devotion or much love. *The new parents worship their baby.* {**wuhr** shihp} worshiper, n.

worst *adjective* 1. superlative form of **bad**. *It was the worst winter he could remember.* 2. most lacking in good qualities. *He is the worst player on*

 Human Body    Human Mind    Everyday Life   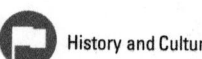 History and Culture    Communication

the team. 3. most likely to result in harm or injury. *That's the worst food to eat when you are sick.* 4. in the most poor condition or health. *That is the worst she has ever felt.* noun someone or something that is worst. *Of all the author's books, that one is the worst.* adverb 1. superlative of **badly** and **ill**. *Of all the patients in the hospital, he felt worst.* 2. in the most evil way; in the worst manner. *He behaved worst out of all the children.* {wuhrst}

• **if worst comes to worst** if the worst happens; if no other way is successful. *If worst comes to worst, we'll stay home from the party.*

worth *preposition* 1. good or important enough for. *It is a film worth seeing.* 2. having a value of. *That jacket is worth fifty dollars, but is on sale for thirty.* 3. having money and property that amounts to. *He is worth at least three million dollars.* noun 1. the value of a thing or person. *His worth to the company cannot be measured.* 2. a number or amount that can be bought with a particular sum. *He bought five dollars' worth of raffle tickets.* 3. value in money or material. *The necklace's worth is about $1,000.* {wuhrth}

worth·less *adjective* without use or value. *The attic was filled with worthless junk.* {wuhrth lihs}

worth·while *adjective* valuable enough to be worth doing. *Many students find it worthwhile to learn how to type.* {wuhrth wiyl}

wor·thy *adjective* (worthier, worthiest) 1. having enough worth or value. *He gives money to children's programs and other worthy causes.* 2. deserving (often followed by

"of"). *He is a kind man worthy of praise for his good works.* {wuhr thee}

would *auxiliary verb* 1. past tense of **will**[1]. *They decided they would go to a movie after dinner. / I said I would help.* 2. used to express some action that depends on something else. *I would fly if I could.* 3. used to form polite questions or requests. *Would you like to sit down? / Would you please stop making that noise?* {wuud}

Homophone Note The words *would* and *wood* (a hard material from trees) sound alike but have different meanings.

would·n't shortened form of "would not." *The horse wouldn't budge. / Wouldn't you like a second raspberry tart?* {wuud ənt}

wound[1] ⊕ *noun* 1. a cut or other injury to a part of the body. 2. an injury to one's feelings. *His anger at her was like a wound to her heart.* verb (wounded, wounding, wounds) to injure or harm by cutting, piercing, or tearing the skin. *He wounded his knee by falling on a rock.* {woohnd}

wound[2] *verb* past tense and past participle of **wind**[2]. {wownd}

wove *verb* past tense and a past participle of **weave**. {wohv}

wo·ven *verb* a past participle of **weave**. {woh vən}

wow *interjection* (informal) a word used to express amazement, pleasure, or enthusiasm. *Wow! Look at the size of that elephant! verb* (wowed, wowing, wows) (informal) to

amaze. *They were wowed by her singing.* {wow}

wran·gle *verb* (wrangled, wrangling, wrangles) 1. to quarrel over. *They wrangled the question back and forth.* 2. to herd or tend. *The cowboys were wrangling the herd of cows.* {răng gəl} wrangler, n.

wrap *verb* (wrapped, wrapping, wraps) 1. to cover by circling or folding something around. *He wrapped his neck with a scarf.* 2. to cover with paper or some other material. *He wrapped the presents in colorful paper.* 3. to hide or cover as if by wrapping. *The house was wrapped in darkness.* 4. to wind, circle, or turn. *The snake wrapped around the branch.* noun 1. that which wraps or is used to wrap. *I chose red and green gift wrap for my Christmas presents.* 2. (plural) clothing, blankets, or some other covering worn outdoors. *The women wore fur wraps against the icy weather.* {răp}

• **keep under wraps** to keep secret or hidden. *They kept the surprise party under wraps.*

A
B
C
D
E
F
G
H
I
J
K
L
M
N
O
P
Q
R
S
T
U
V
W
X
Y
Z

a
b
c
d
e
f
g
h
i
j
k
l
m
n
o
p
q
r
s
t
u
v
w
x
y
z

• **wrap up**
to finish up; complete. *The detective wrapped up the details of the case.*

• **wrapped up in**
completely engaged in; having all of one's attention. *The children were completely wrapped up in the kittens.*

Homophone Note The words *wrap* and *rap* sound alike but have different meanings.

wrap·per *noun* that which is used to cover something. *We were angry to see so many candy wrappers on the beach.* {**răp** ər}

wrap·ping *noun* paper or some other material that is used to cover something. *Such beautiful wrapping promises a wonderful present.* {**răp** ing}

Homophone Note The words *wrapping* and *rapping* (a form of *rap*) sound alike but have different meanings.

wrath ❓ *noun* fierce anger. *He had to face his parents' wrath after crashing the car.* {**răth**}

wreak *verb* (wreaked, wreaking, wreaks) to carry out or cause. *The flood wreaked destruction on the houses by the river.* {**reek**}

Homophone Note The words *wreak* and *reek* (a strong smell) sound alike but have different meanings.

wreath *noun* a band of flowers or leaves woven or twisted together in the shape of a circle and used as a symbol or decoration. *We hung Christmas wreaths on both*

our front and back doors. {**reeth**}

wreck *noun* 1. an action or event that results in great or total destruction. *His careless driving on the icy road caused a car wreck.* 2. what is left of something that has been destroyed or ruined. *The once beautiful ship is now just an old wreck on the bottom of the lake.* *verb* (wrecked, wrecking, wrecks) 1. to ruin or destroy. *The fire wrecked two buildings. / His mean words wrecked their friendship.* 2. to tear down or apart. *The town wrecked two old houses to build a new library.* {**rehk**}

wreck·age *noun* what is left after something has been ruined or destroyed. *Workers cleared the road of wreckage from the accident.* {**reh** kihj}

wren *noun* a small brown songbird with a long bill and an upright tail. {**rehn**}

wrench *verb* (wrenched, wrenching, wrenches) 1. to twist or bend suddenly and with force. *She wrenched the tight ring off her finger.* 2. to damage or hurt by moving in this way. *She wrenched her knee while playing basketball.* *noun* 1. a tool with jaws that is used to

grip and turn a bolt, pipe, or other object. 2. a twisting movement, made suddenly and with force. *The dentist yanked out the rotten tooth with one last wrench.* {**rehnch**}

wrest *verb* (wrested, wresting, wrests) to take away with, or as if with, a twist or pull. *The policeman wrested the gun from the suspect's hand. / The knights wrested power from the king.* {**rehst**}

Homophone Note The words *wrest* and *rest* sound alike but have different meanings.

wres·tle *verb* (wrestled, wrestling, wrestles) 1. to take part in the sport of wrestling, or to struggle to throw and hold another to the ground. *My dad and brother enjoy wrestling together.* 2. to struggle or fight (usually followed by "with"). *He wrestled with the huge Christmas tree. / She is wrestling with a difficult problem.* 3. to force into some position by or as if by wrestling. *He wrestled his brother to the floor. / He wrestled his scattered thoughts into order.* {**rehs** əl} wrestler, n.

wres·tling *noun* an athletic exercise or contest in which two people struggle to throw and hold each other to the ground. {**rehs** ling}

wretch·ed *adjective* 1. unhappy; miserable. *Those wretched people lost everything they owned in the fire. / I feel wretched that I made you so angry.* 2. evil. *That wretched man beats his dog.* {**rehch** ihd}

wrig·gle *verb* (wriggled, wriggling, wriggles) 1. to twist and turn one's body with quick movements from side to side; wiggle. *The excited children wriggled in their seats while waiting for the clowns.*

 Human Body   Human Mind    Everyday Life    History and Culture    Communication

2. to get oneself out of or into by tricky means (usually followed by "into" or "out of"). *She wriggles out of every difficult job.* / *He wriggled into being the teacher's pet by bringing her presents.* 3. to move, or cause to move, with quick, twisting movements. *He wriggled the key into the lock.* {**rihg** gəl} wriggly, adj.

wring *verb* (wrung, wringing, wrings) 1. to twist and squeeze tightly. *Please wring the wet towel over the sink.* 2. to press or force out by or as though by this means. *We wrung the water out of our wet bathing suits.* / *She wrung the truth out of him.* 3. to press and squeeze together because of feeling nervous or troubled. *She wrung her hands as she waited for news of her sick child.* {**ring**}

Homophone Note The words *wring* and *ring* sound alike but have different meanings.

wrin·kle *noun* a fold or ridge on an otherwise flat surface, such as cloth or skin. *You'll need to iron the wrinkles out of your gown.* / *People get wrinkles on their faces as they grow old.* *verb* (wrinkled, wrinkling, wrinkles) to make or cause folds or ridges in. *The baby wrinkled her nose at the smell of the peas.* / *The kitten sat on my lap and wrinkled my skirt.* {**ring** kəl} wrinkly, adj.

wrist *noun* the joint between the arm and hand, or the bones that make up this joint. {**rihst**}

Word History *Wrist* comes from an Old English word that means "to turn."

wrist watch *noun* a watch on a strap or band that is worn around the wrist. {**rihst** wŏch}

write ❷ *verb* (wrote, written, writing, writes) 1. to form on a surface with a pen, pencil, typewriter, or other instrument. *Write your name on the paper.* 2. to express or record by writing. *He wrote his ideas in a notebook.* 3. to be the author or composer of. *She wrote that song.* 4. to produce written material as a job. *She writes for the local newspaper.* 5. to fill in the spaces of or cover with writing. *He wrote six pages.* 6. to send a letter. *Write to me soon.* {**riyt**}

Homophone Note The words *write* and *right* sound alike but have different meanings.

Word History *Write* comes from an Old English word that means "to scratch or carve."

writ·er *noun* 1. one who writes. 2. one whose job is to write books, articles, poems, or other materials; author. {**riy** tər}

writ·ing ❷ *noun* 1. the act, art, or job of one who writes. *Writing is his favorite hobby.* 2. something that is written, such as letters, words, or symbols. *The writing on the old scroll was faded and hard to read.* 3. a written state or form. *Can you put your idea in writing?* 4. a particular literary style. *His writing is very funny.* {**riy** ting}

writ·ten *verb* past participle of **write**. *adjective* done in writing. *The teacher wants a written report, not an oral one.* {**riht** ihn}

wrong *adjective* 1. not true or correct. *Your answer is wrong.* 2. not moral or good; wicked; bad. *Murder is wrong.* 3. acting in a way that is not proper or correct. *She was wrong to tell you that.* 4. not proper or suited. *We added the wrong ingredients.* / *He chose the wrong moment to speak.* 5. not working or operating properly. *There is something wrong with my car.* *adverb* in the wrong way. *I did it wrong again!* *noun* treatment or action that is not fair or just. *They have done him much wrong.* *verb* (wronged, wronging, wrongs) to treat badly. *He was wronged by his friend.* {**rawng**} wrongly, adv.

wrote *verb* past tense of **write**. {**roht**}

wrought iron *noun* a soft iron, used in making garden furniture, candle holders, and other strong objects with fancy shapes and details. {**rawt iy** ərn}

A
B
C
D
E
F
G
H
I
J
K
L
M
N
O
P
Q
R
S
T
U
V
W
X
Y
Z

a
b
c
d
e
f
g
h
i
j
k
l
m
n
o
p
q
r
s
t
u
v
w
x
y
z

wrung *verb* past tense and past participle of **wring**. {rung}

Homophone Note The words ***wrung*** and ***rung*** sound alike but have different meanings.

wt. *abbreviation* an abbreviation for **weight**.

WV or **W. Va.** *abbreviation* an abbreviation for **West Virginia**.

WY or **Wyo.** *abbreviation* an abbreviation for **Wyoming**.

Wy·o·ming *noun* a state in the northwestern United States. Its capital is Cheyenne. (abbreviated: WY) {wiy <u>oh</u> ming} Wyomingite, n.

Word History *Wyoming* is the English version of *macheweaming*, an Algonquin word that means "place of the big flats." When the Territory of Wyoming was created in 1868, it was named after the Wyoming Valley in Pennsylvania.

 Human Body
 Human Mind
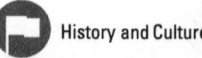 Everyday Life
 History and Culture
Communication

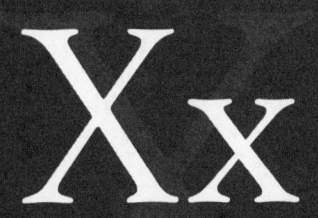

When "x" comes at the beginning of a word, it sounds like "z" (Xerox or xylophone). When the name of the letter X is part of a word, it sounds like "eks" (as in Xmas and X-ray).

Tips to help you look up words starting with X: Look under E for words that start with "eks" sound (such as example, excellent or explain).

x or **X** *noun* (x's or X's) 1. the twenty-fourth letter of the English alphabet. 2. a mark used as a signature by one who cannot write. 3. a mark used to point out a particular place on a map. 4. an unknown number in algebra. {ehks}

xen·o·pho·bi·a *noun* a fear or hatred of foreign people or things. {zeen ə foh bee ə *or* zehn ə foh bee ə} xenophobic, adj.

Xe·rox *noun* 1. (Trademark) Xerox is the name for a process of copying printed material or for the machine used in this process. 2. (lower case) a copy made by a Xerox machine or by a similar machine. *verb* (xeroxed, xeroxing, xeroxes) to copy on a Xerox machine. {zeer ŏks}

Xho·sa *noun* (Xhosa or Xhosas) 1. a member of one of the Bantu peoples living in South Africa. 2. the language of this people. {koh sə *or* koh zə}

Xmas *abbreviation* short for **Christmas**. {krihs məs *or* ehks məs}

x-ray 🌐 *noun* (x-rays) 1. a beam of high-energy radiation that is able to pass through many kinds of solid material. *Scientists have found many uses for x-rays.* 2. a photograph made with such a beam. *The nurse took an x-ray of my leg to see if any bones were broken.* *verb* (x-rayed, x-raying, x-rays) to photograph, treat, or examine using x-rays. *The dentist x-rayed Sam's teeth to check for cavities.* {ehks ray}

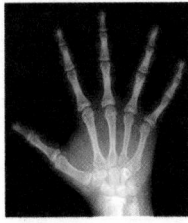

xy·lo·phone *noun* a percussion instrument composed of a series of metal or wooden bars. It is played by hitting the bars with small wooden mallets. {ziy lə fohn}

Word History *Xylophone* is made up of the Greek words *xylon*, which means "wood," and *phone*, which means sound."

a
b
c
d
e
f
g
h
i
j
k
l
m
n
o
p
q
r
s
t
u
v
w
x
y
z

Yy

At the beginning of words, y is almost always a consonant making the "yuh" sound. In the middle or at the end of words, y is often a long vowel making the "ee" sound (as in baby) or the "iy" sound (as in my).

Tips to help you look up words starting with y: Also look for words with a long "u" sound ("yoo") under E (ewe) or U (usual).

These words may be hard to look up if you don't already know how to spell them:

yield

you

young

y or **Y** *noun* (y's or Y's) 1. the twenty-fifth letter of the English alphabet. 2. an unknown number in algebra. {wiy}

-y or **-ey** *suffix* 1. a suffix that means "full of" or "made of."

A *muddy puddle is full of mud.* 2. a suffix that means "like." *A grouchy person is a person who acts like a grouch.* 3. a suffix that means "somewhat." *Coppery hair is hair with a color somewhat like copper.* 4. a suffix that means "likely to." *A sticky substance is something that is likely to stick.*

yacht *noun* a small ship used for private trips or racing. {yaht}

yak *noun* a large, heavy mammal with long hair. Yaks are closely related to cattle. They live in Tibet and Central Asia. People raise yaks to carry loads and for their milk, fur, and leather. Very few yaks are left in the wild. {yăk}

yam *noun* 1. the root of a tropical climbing plant, or the plant itself. The root is eaten as a cooked vegetable. 2. a kind of sweet potato. {yăm}

Word History *Yam* comes from *nyam*, a West African word that means "to eat." Yams are a staple in the diet of many African people, and during difficult times may be the only thing there is to eat.

yank *verb* (yanked, yanking, yanks) (informal) to pull or take out suddenly; jerk. *The dog yanked the hamburger from the little girl's hand.* *noun* (informal) a sudden pull; jerk. *With one yank, he pulled the toy out of the dog's mouth.* {yăngk}

Yan·kee *noun* 1. a person who was born or lives in New England. 2. a Union soldier during the Civil War. 3. a person who was born in or is

a citizen of the United States. {yăng kee}

Word History *Yankee* comes from *Janke*, the Dutch form of "Johnny." The Dutch in colonial New York called the new English settlers "Yankees."

yap *verb* (yapped, yapping, yaps) 1. to bark with sharp, high sounds. *My dog yapped at me until I took her for a walk.* 2. (slang) to talk in a loud and silly way. *My sister yaps on the phone with her friends for hours at a time. noun* a quick, high bark. *He was greeted by the yaps of his two little dogs.* {yăp}

yard[1] *noun* 1. a unit of length equal to three feet or 0.9144 meters. (abbreviated: yd.) 2. a long rod fastened across the mast of a ship to hold a sail. {yard}

yard[2] *noun* 1. an open area next to a house or other building. *We have trees and flowers in our yard. / Students play in the school yard.* 2. an enclosed area used for a particular purpose. *We saw dozens of trains at the railroad yard. / Dad bought building supplies at the lumber yard.* {yard}

yard·stick *noun* 1. a measuring stick three feet long. 2. a rule or standard against which something is compared or judged. *By the yardstick of his family's success in business, he was failing. / Grades are the yardstick of success in school.* {yard stihk}

yarn *noun* 1. a strand of twisted fibers made from silk, cotton, wool, or other materials and used for knitting or weaving. 2. (informal) a long tale that may exaggerate the truth or is hard to believe. *My grandfather likes to tell yarns about his childhood.* {yarn}

 Human Body   ? Human Mind   Everyday Life   History and Culture   Communication

yawn *verb* (yawned, yawning, yawns) 1. to open the mouth while breathing in deeply. People yawn as a sign of feeling tired or bored, or because their brains are not getting enough oxygen. 2. to open wide so as to make a broad or deep space. *The Grand Canyon yawned beneath us.* *noun* the act of opening the mouth wide and breathing in deeply. *The baby's yawns told me it was time for her nap.* {<u>yawn</u>}

yd. *abbreviation* an abbreviation for **yard**, or yards.

ye[1] *pronoun* you. Ye was in common use during the Middle Ages, but today is used mainly in religious and literary writings. *Did ye hear of the attempt on the king's life?* {<u>yee</u>}

ye[2] *definite article* the. Ye is a misreading of an old spelling of "the" in which the letter for the "th" sound looked like a "y." When stores today put "ye" on their signs, they do so in order to look old-fashioned. *The sign on the new store read "Ye Olde Gift Shoppe."* {<u>yee</u>}

year *noun* 1. a unit of time equal to 365 days or, every fourth year, 366 days, from January through December; twelve months. (abbreviated: yr.) 2. the time it takes any planet to go completely around its sun. *A year on Jupiter is much longer than a year on Mercury.* 3. about the length of one year. *We saw each other two years ago.* 4. a part of the year that is set aside for some particular activity. *Our school year begins in early September.* {<u>yeer</u>}

year·ly *adjective* 1. happening once a year or every year. *Our neighborhood party was a*

yearly event. 2. of or relating to a year or each year. *The yearly taxes on this house are very high.* *adverb* once each year. *He cleans his garage yearly.* {<u>yeer</u> lee}

year-round *adjective* throughout the entire year. *The indoor rink offers year-round skating.* {<u>yeer</u> <u>rownd</u>}

yeast ❶ *noun* tiny, single cells of certain fungi that are used to make bread, alcohol, and some medicines. {<u>yeest</u>}

yell ❷ ❸ *verb* (yelled, yelling, yells) to scream out loudly, as in pain, anger, fear, surprise, or excitement. *My mom yelled at me for not cleaning my room.* *noun* a loud cry or shout; scream. *We heard angry yells coming from the barn.* {<u>yehl</u>}

yel·low *noun* the color of an egg yolk or ripe lemon; the color between orange and green on the color spectrum. *adjective* (yellower, yellowest) 1. having the color yellow. *She loved her yellow bird.* 2. cowardly. *When Jim ran away from the bully, his friends said he was yellow.* {<u>yehl</u> oh} yellowish, adj.

yellow jacket *noun* a wasp or hornet that has a black body with bright yellow markings. Yellow jackets live together in large groups in nests close to or under the ground. {<u>yehl</u> oh <u>jăk</u> iht}

yelp *verb* (yelped, yelping, yelps) to cry out or bark

quickly and sharply. *I yelped when I saw I was about to fall. / The puppy yelped when the baby pulled his tail.* *noun* a quick, sharp cry or bark. *I gave a yelp when I stuck myself with the pin. / We heard the yelps of the puppy before we saw him.* {<u>yehlp</u>}

yen[1] *noun* (yen) the main unit of money in Japan. {<u>yehn</u>}

yen[2] *noun* (informal) a yearning or desire. *She has a yen for some spicy food.* {<u>yehn</u>}

yes *adverb* it is as you say or ask (used to express agreement or acceptance). *Would you like some candy? Yes, I would.* *noun* 1. an answer that shows agreement or consent. *Will you say yes if I ask you to dinner?* 2. a vote in favor of something; aye. *Everyone voted yes to having pizza for dinner.* {<u>yehs</u>}

yes·ter·day *adverb* on the day before today. *Did you stop by my house yesterday?* *noun* the day before today. *Yesterday was a busy day for me.* {<u>yeh</u> stər day}

yet *adverb* 1. so far; at this time. *They aren't home yet.* 2. at some time in the future; eventually. *We'll see him yet.* 3. in addition; even. *He had yet another drink.* 4. but; nevertheless. *This morning is sunny, yet cold.* 5. even; still. *The second task was yet more difficult.* *conjunction* in spite of this; even so; nevertheless. *It happened years ago, yet I will never forget it.* {<u>yeht</u>}
• **as yet**
up until now. *They have not as yet learned to read.*

yew *noun* 1. an evergreen tree or shrub that has sharp, flat needles and poisonous red berries. 2. the wood from such a tree or shrub, used in

A
B
C
D
E
F
G
H
I
J
K
L
M
N
O
P
Q
R
S
T
U
V
W
X
Y
Z

a
b
c
d
e
f
g
h
i
j
k
l
m
n
o
p
q
r
s
t
u
v
w
x
y
z

the past to make bows for archery. {yoo}

Homophone Note The words **yew**, **ewe**, and **you** sound alike but have different meanings.

yield *verb* (yielded, yielding, yields) 1. to give forth or produce. *Our garden yielded lots of vegetables this year. / This recipe yields two dozen cookies.* 2. to give up or hand over. *She yielded her wallet to the criminal.* 3. to give way. *The locked door yielded after the policeman gave it a hard kick.* *noun* a thing or amount produced. *Our garden promises an excellent yield of corn and beans.* {yeeld}

YMCA *abbreviation* a national organization that provides sports programs and other recreational activities for young people. YMCA is an abbreviation for "Young Men's Christian Association."

yo·del ➋ *verb* (yodeled, yodeling, yodels) to sing or call out with many quick changes so that the voice moves between the natural chest voice and very high sounds. *noun* a song with many quick changes between the natural voice and a very high voice. Yodeling is popular among the mountain people of the Alps. {yoh dəl} yodeler, n.

yo·ga ➌ *noun* (often capitalized) a Hindu practice made up of a system of physical and mental exercises that free the self from the body and mind to find spiritual peace. {yoh gə}

Word History *Yoga* comes from a Sanskrit word that means "union."

yo·gurt *noun* a soft food that is made from sour milk and often flavored or sweetened with fruit. {yoh gərt}

yoke *noun* 1. a device used to join together a pair of work animals. A yoke is made up of a wooden bar with two U-shaped ends that fit around the animals' heads. 2. a pair of draft animals joined by this device. *The farmer used a yoke of oxen to plow his fields.* *verb* (yoked, yoking, yokes) to attach to a plow, wagon, or some other machine or vehicle. *We yoked the horses to the wagon for a ride through the fields.* {yohk}

Homophone Note Are you looking for the word **yolk** (a part of an egg)? **Yoke** and **yolk** sound alike but have different meanings.

yolk *noun* the yellow part of an egg. The yolk feeds the baby bird until it is hatched. People use egg yolks in many food dishes. *This cake recipe calls for two whole eggs and three yolks.* {yohk}

Homophone Note The words **yolk** and **yoke** (a harnessing device) sound alike but have different meanings.

Yom Kippur *noun* the holiest day in the Jewish religion, observed by praying, not eating, and asking forgiveness for sins. Yom Kippur comes ten days after Rosh Hashanah, the first day of the Jewish year. {yohm kee puhr *or* yŏm kihp ər}

yon·der *adjective* (informal) somewhat distant, but within sight. *Yonder pine is about a quarter mile away.* *adverb*

(informal) in or at a particular place. *He lives yonder.* {yŏn dər}

you *pronoun* 1. the person or persons being spoken or written to. *You will like my friends. / Did I give you the instructions?* 2. a person; people in general; one. *You never know what will happen when those two teams play each other.* {yoo}

Homophone Note The words **you**, **ewe**, and **yew** sound alike but have different meanings.

you'd shortened form of "you would" or "you had." *You'd really enjoy meeting her. / You'd better come in before it starts raining.* {yood}

you'll shortened form of "you will." *You'll really like my mom.* {yool}

Homophone Note Are you looking for the word **yule** (a name for Christmas)? **You'll** and **yule** sound alike but have different meanings.

young ➊ *adjective* (younger, youngest) 1. at an early stage of life or growth. *My sister is still a young child.* 2. in an early stage. *The night is young.* 3. having the qualities of a young person. *My grandfather has a young spirit.* *noun* offspring that have been recently born. *The mother cat is taking care of her young.* {yuhng}

young·ster *noun* a young person; child. *The playground is full of youngsters every Saturday morning.* {yuhng stər}

Word History *Youngster* comes from a German word that means "young sir or lord."

 Human Body
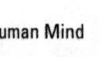 Human Mind
 Everyday Life
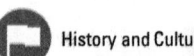 History and Culture
 Communication

you're shortened form of "you are." *You're the best friend I've ever had.* {<u>yoor</u>}

Homophone Note *You're* and *your* sometimes sound alike, but "your" is a possessive form of "you" (is that your coat?).

your·self *pronoun* (yourselves) 1. used to emphasize "you"; your own self. *You yourself must write to them; no one else will do it.* 2. your usual or healthy self. *This medicine will make you feel more like yourself again.* {yohr <u>sehlf</u> *or* yoor <u>sehlf</u>}

yours truly words used to end a letter before it is signed; (informal) I, me, or myself. *As soon as the alarm clock rings, yours truly will be out of bed.* {<u>yohrz</u> <u>trooh</u> lee *or* <u>yoorz</u> <u>trooh</u> lee}

youth *noun* (youths or youth) 1. the quality or state of being young. *The doctor's youth surprised her.* 2. the early stage or period of anything. *Women's professional basketball is still in its youth.* 3. the period between childhood and adulthood. *She was happy in her youth.* 4. young people as a group. *The youth of this country are our future.* 5. any young person. *Some youths from the neighborhood offered to help the old couple.* {<u>yooth</u>}

you've shortened form of "you have." *You've been a very good boy.* {<u>yoov</u>}

yowl *verb* (yowled, yowling, yowls) to make a loud, sad cry. *The cat yowled when his owner left him behind.* *noun* a sad cry or howl. *The baby's yowls told his mother he was tired. / My cat's yowls woke me up.* {<u>yowl</u>}

yo-yo *noun* (yo-yos) a toy made of two thick wooden or plastic disks connected by a peg around which a string is tied. One plays with a yo-yo by holding the end of the string and moving the hand to cause the disk unit to roll up and down the string. {<u>yoh</u> yoh}

yr. *abbreviation* an abbreviation for **year** or years.

Yu·go·sla·vi·a *noun* a country in southeastern Europe. Yugoslavia is also called the Federal Republic of Yugoslavia. Belgrade is the capital of Yugoslavia. {yoo goh <u>slah</u> vee ə} Yugoslavian, n., adj.

Yu·kon *noun* 1. a territory of northwest Canada. It borders Alaska on the west, British Columbia on the south, the Northwest Territories on the east, and the Arctic Ocean on the north. Its capital is Whitehorse. 2. a river of northern North America. It flows from this territory through central Alaska into the Bering Sea. {<u>yoo</u> kŏn}

Word History *Yukon* is the English spelling of the Loucheux Indian word *yu-kun-ah*, which means "greatest river." The territory was named for the Yukon River.

yule *noun* (sometimes capital) Christmas or the Christmas season. {<u>yool</u>}

Homophone Note The word *yule* and the contraction *you'll* ("you will") sound alike but have different meanings.

yule·tide *noun* (sometimes capital) the Christmas holiday season. {<u>yool</u> tiyd}

A
B
C
D
E
F
G
H
I
J
K
L
M
N
O
P
Q
R
S
T
U
V
W
X
Y
Z

 Living World  Physical World Natural Environment Economy Government and Law

Zz

a b c d e f g h i j k l m n o p q r s t u v w x y z

Z is a consonant that makes two sounds. Z usually makes its regular "z" sound, especially at the beginning of words. Z sometimes makes a "zh" sound in the middle of words (such as azure).

Tips to help you look up words starting with z: Also look under X for a few words (such as xylophone) that start with the "z" sound. Also, the word "czar" starts with a silent c.

z or **Z** *noun* (z's or Z's) the twenty-sixth and last letter of the English alphabet. {zee}

Za·ire *noun* 1. See **Congo**. The Democratic Republic of the Congo was formerly called Zaire. 2. a river of central Africa that flows from the southeastern part of the Democratic Republic of the Congo into the Atlantic Ocean; Congo River. {zah **eer**}

Zam·bi·a *noun* a country in south, central Africa. Lusaka is the capital of Zambia. Zambia used to be called Northern Rhodesia. {**zăm** bee ə} Zambian, n., adj.

zap *verb* (zapped, zapping, zaps) 1. (informal) to strike, or kill suddenly. *He zapped the wasp with bug spray.* 2. to strike or hit with laser beams, x-rays, or microwaves. *The heroine zapped the alien with her laser gun. / He zapped the hot dogs in the microwave oven.* {zăp} zapper, n.

zeal *noun* great enthusiasm for a person or cause. *The leader's followers were filled with zeal. / Her zeal for helping the poor was known by everyone in the community.* {**zeel**}

ze·bra *noun* (zebras or zebra) a large mammal with a striped coat, long legs, and hooves. Zebras are closely related to horses but have shorter manes. They live in large herds in Africa. Several kinds of zebras are in danger of becoming extinct. {**zee** brə}

ze·nith *noun* 1. the point in the sky that is directly over the head of the person looking at it. 2. the highest point; peak. *Her fourth book showed her writing skills at their zenith.* {**zee** nihth}

> **Word History** *Zenith* comes from an Arabic word that means "the way over the head."

ze·ro *noun* (zeros or zeroes) 1. the number represented by the Arabic numeral 0. 2. the number that comes before the number one. 3. nothing. *With her family safe and happy, her worries were zero. adjective* being none or nothing in number or quantity. *The store's new owners promised zero change in prices.*

> **Word History** *Zero* comes from an Arabic word that means "empty."

zest *noun* a sense of great pleasure or enjoyment. *The old woman's zest for living made her seem much younger.* {zehst} zestful, adj., zesty, adj.

> **Word History** *Zest* was borrowed into English in the 17th century from the French word *zest* that means "orange or lemon peel." By the end of the18th century, it was being used to mean "keen enjoyment."

Zeus *noun* the ruler of the gods, in Greek mythology. In Roman mythology, Zeus is called Jupiter. {**zoohs**}

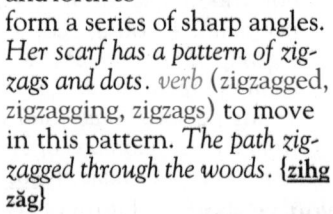

zig·zag *noun* a line or course that moves back and forth to form a series of sharp angles. *Her scarf has a pattern of zigzags and dots. verb* (zigzagged, zigzagging, zigzags) to move in this pattern. *The path zigzagged through the woods.* {**zihg** zăg}

Zim·ba·bwe *noun* a country in south, central Africa. Harare is the capital of Zimbabwe. Zimbabwe used to be called Rhodesia. {zihm **bahb** way} Zimbabwean, n., adj.

zinc ⊕ *noun* a bluish white metal that is one of the chemical elements. Zinc does not rust easily. It can be combined with other metals to form alloys. Zinc is also

 Human Body Human Mind Everyday Life  History and Culture ⊙ Communication

used in making batteries. (symbol: Zn) {**zingk**}

Word History *Zinc* comes from a German word that means "point or spike." When zinc is cooled after heating it looks like spikes.

zin·ni·a *noun* a plant with colorful flowers that is related to the daisy. The zinnia is found in North and South America. {**zihn** ee ə}

zip[1] *noun* 1. a sudden, sharp noise. *The zip of an arrow cut through the silence.* 2. (informal) energy or pep. *At eighty years old, she is still full of zip.* *verb* (zipped, zipping, zips) to move or act quickly and with energy. *He zipped through his chores so he could go out with his friends.* {**zihp**}

Synonyms
These words share a meaning with *zip*, noun 2:
life, energy, vigor, pep

zip[2] *verb* (zipped, zipping, zips) 1. to fasten by closing a zipper. *I zipped my jacket before heading into the cold.* 2. to become fastened by the closing of a zipper. *This purse zips shut easily.* {**zihp**}

Zip Code *noun* (Trademark) Zip Code is a U.S. Postal Service system that uses a code

of five or more numbers to identify every postal delivery area in the United States. Zip stands for "Zone Improvement Plan." {**zihp** kohd}

zip·per ● *noun* a fastener made up of two rows of teeth that lock together and a slide pull that either joins them or pulls them apart. Zippers are used on clothing, handbags, and other articles. {**zihp** ər}

zit *noun* (slang) a **pimple**.

zith·er *noun* a stringed instrument that has a flat sound box and thirty or forty strings. Zithers are played by plucking the strings. {**zih** thər, zih thəm *or* **zih** thər, **zih** thərn}

zo·di·ac ● ● *noun* an imaginary belt in the heavens that includes the paths of the sun, moon, and planets as seen from the earth. The zodiac is divided into twelve equal signs or parts. Each part is named for a constellation that appears within the belt. {**zoh** dee ăk}

zone ● *noun* 1. an area that is divided from other areas because of a particular use or some other special quality. *You'll find a supermarket in the business zone.* / *Houses can be painted only certain colors in the historic zone.* 2. any of the five areas of the earth's surface, marked by latitude lines, and named according to the region's temperature. There are two frigid zones, two temperate zones, and one torrid zone. *verb* (zoned, zoning, zones) to divide or make into particular areas. *The town has zoned this area for houses only.* {**zohn**}

zoo ● *noun* (zoos) a place where living animals, especially wild ones, are kept for people to look at. The word "zoo" is short for "zoological garden." {**zooh**}

zo·o- *prefix* a prefix that means "animal." *Zoology is the study of animals.*

The Signs of the ZODIAC

The word "zodiac" comes from a Greek word meaning "animal signs," although some of the signs of the zodiac are not animals. Each of the twelve signs of the zodiac is named after a constellation, a formation of stars which ancient people associated with an animal, person, or other shape. The sun appears to pass through each constellation at a different time of the year. The constellation that the sun passes through when you are born is your zodiac sign.

Aries the Ram (March 21 - April 19)
Taurus the Bull (April 20 - May 20)
Gemini the Twins (May 21 - June 21)
Cancer the Crab (June 22 - July 22)
Leo the Lion (July 23 - August 22)
Virgo the Virgin (August 23 - Sept. 22)

Libra the Scales (Sept. 23 - Oct. 22)
Scorpio the Scorpion (Oct. 23 - Nov. 21)
Sagittarius the Archer (Nov. 22 - Dec. 21)
Capricorn the Goat (Dec. 22 - Jan. 19)
Aquarius the Water Bearer (Jan. 20 - Feb. 18)
Pisces the Fish (Feb. 19 - March 20)

Some people believe that there are secrets to be learned about a person's personality or future based on his or her zodiac sign and the position of planets in relation to the stars as viewed from Earth. Many ancient cultures combined their myths and religions with this belief, and it can still be found today in daily horoscopes and astrology readings.

A B C D E F G H I J K L M N O P Q R S T U V W X Y Z

 Living World   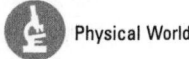 Physical World   Natural Environment    Economy    Government and Law

a
b
c
d
e
f
g
h
i
j
k
l
m
n
o
p
q
r
s
t
u
v
w
x
y
z

zo·ol·o·gy *noun* (zoologies) the science and study of animals. {zooh <u>o</u> lə jee}

> **Word History** The word ***zoology*** is formed from *zoion*, an ancient Greek word that means "animal," and the suffix "-ology," which means "the study of."

zoom *verb* (zoomed, zooming, zooms) 1. to move quickly while making a low humming sound. *The speedboat zoomed over the water.* 2. to climb suddenly and sharply. *The price of beach houses has zoomed over the last few years.* {<u>zoohm</u>}

zuc·chi·ni *noun* (zucchini or zucchinis) a type of summer squash that is shaped like a cucumber and has a smooth, dark green skin. {zooh <u>kee</u> nee}

 Human Body    Human Mind    Everyday Life   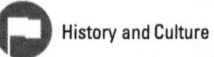 History and Culture    Communication

Introduction to World History Time Line

The time line has two parts. The first part gives an overview of geological, or prehistoric, time from the beginning of the universe to today. The second part shows important eras and events in human history. There are two ways to use this historical time line. First, you can follow developments of a specific world region through time. Each region has its own color, and time progresses from left to right across the pages. Second, you can learn about events by time period. By looking down the page from the time-period heading, you can survey events from every region of the world that happened around the same time. Sidebars on each page give additional information related to the time period featured on that page.

About 15,000,000,000 years ago
The universe may have begun with an explosion known as the "**Big Bang.**"

12,000,000,000 years ago
Our galaxy, the Milky Way, and galaxies throughout the Universe were clouds of gas and dust.

4,500,000,000 years ago
Our moon started orbiting Earth.

3,000,000,000 years ago
Continents began to form.

4,600,000,000 years ago
Our solar system formed.

ARCHEOZOIC ERA:
{ar kee ~ zoh ihk}
4,000,000,000 to
545,000,000 years ago

4,000,000,000 years ago
Life began on Earth.

1,500,000,000 years ago
First life with cells: some kind bacteria evolved in the ocean

Jurassic Period of the Mesozoic Era
from 205,000,000 to
135,000,000 years ago
Reptiles: More kinds developed, including meat-eating ocean reptiles (ichthyosaurs {Ik thi ə sorz}).

250,000,000 years ago
Mass extinction: the greatest catastrophe in the history of life on Earth. Many living things died out. Geologists are not sure why.

MESOZOIC ERA:
250,000,000 to
65,000,000 years ago
New plants and animals appeared. Birds and mammals evolved from reptiles.

200,000,000 years ago
First pterosaurs {ter oh sohrz}: Some evolved into the largest animals that ever grew.

210,000,000 years ago
First mammals: small animals the size of rats.

Triassic Period of the Mesozoic Era.
250,000,000 to
205,000,000 years ago
First dinosaurs.

150,000,000 years ago
Continents shifted: Atlantic Ocean started to form as the continents spread apart.

CENOZOIC ERA
65,000,000 years ago to present
Extinction of dinosaurs. Rise of mammals.

50,000,000 years ago
First primates: earliest ancestors of monkeys, apes, and humans

140,000,000 years ago
First birds

90,000,000 years ago
First sharks

60,000,000 years ago
Australian continent broke off from Antarctica.

18,000 years ago
Peak of most recent Ice Age. Glaciers covered the Northern Hemisphere. Asia and North America became linked by a land bridge.

20,000 years ago
First calendar: People in what is now the Middle East carved notches on bones.

25,000 years ago
Flute: Oldest known musical instrument was carved from a bird bone.

15,000 years ago
People may have begun settling in North America.

Cretaceous Period of the Mesozoic Era
Last dinosaurs, first flowers.
from 135,000,000 to 65,000,000 years ago

10,000 years ago (8000 B.C./B.C.E.)
End of the most recent Ice Age. Gradual melting of the glaciers after the last Ice Age probably caused majo ooding in many parts of the world. Many kinds of reptiles, birds, and mammals became extinct.

12,000 years ago
South America was inhabited. People were now on every continent except Antarctica.

11,000 years ago
Copper: first metal used to make jewelry in Europe and the Middle East

Dates and geologic times are approximate

680,000,000 years ago
First animals: sea worms and jelly fish.

Ordovician Period of the Paleozoic Era. 505,000.000 to 438,000,000 years ago.
First vertebrates

450,000,000 years ago
First simple land plants

Silurian Period of the Paleozoic Era. 438 million to 408 million years ago.

PALEOZOIC ERA: 545,000,000 years ago to 250,000,000 years ago
The development of plants and animals.
Cambrian Period of the Paleozoic Era. 545,000,0000 to 505,000,000 years ago.
Many new kinds of animals developed in the ocean, including corals and sponges.

500,000,000 years ago
First fish

412,000,000 years ago
Ferns: first plants with roots, stems, and leaves

400,000,000 years ago
First insects

330,000,000 years ago
First reptiles

ermian Period of the Paleozoic Era.
86,000,000 to 250,000,000 years ago
More reptiles; first beetles

Carboniferous Period of the Paleozoic Era. 360,000,000 to 286,000,000 years ago
Giant trees; flying insects
First amphibians

Devonian Period of the Paleozoic Era. 408,000,000 to 360,000,000 years ago
Pangea supercontinent began forming when continents collided, then merged.

2,600,000 years ago
First humans: They are called "Homo habilis" (tool-using humans).
Pleistocene Ice Age began: Glaciers advanced and retreated over the northern continents about 50 times.

34,000,000 years ago
Europe and Asia separated from what is now Greenland and North America.

5,000,000 years ago
Australopithecines: Primates that walked on two legs (hominids) developed in Africa.

1,500,000 years ago
Fire: Humans in Africa used it to cook food and keep safe from wild animals.

10,000,000 years ago
Early hominids: Some primates evolved into ancestors of modern humans.

3,200,000 years ago
Australopithecines lived in what is now Ethiopia, Africa.

1,300,000 years ago
Humans settled in Europe and Asia. "Homo erectus" used tools and fire.

30,000 years ago
People started to decorate their bodies with jewelry, beads, shells.

40,000 years ago or earlier
Europe was settled by modern people.

60,000 years ago
Australia began to be settled.

35,000 years ago
Cave art: Earliest known paintings were made in what is now France.

45,000 years ago
Bows and arrows were being used in Africa.

7,000 years ago
5000 B.C./B.C.E.
Travel: Sails were used on boats in the Persian Gulf.

6,000 years ago
4000 B.C./B.C.E.
Medicine: Skull surgery was done in Egypt and other Mediterranean countries and in Peru, South America.

Ancient Peoples and Civilizations

Understanding and Using Systems of Dates

Many of the dates on these two pages and all of the dates on the two pages before these are approximate, because these things happened before people began keeping track of dates. So these dates have been estimated by scientists and historians.

Today all countries use the same dating system for international communication. This system was started by Christians and counts forward from the time Jesus, or Christ, was born just over two thousand years ago. In the Christian calendar system, dates since the birth of Jesus are labeled A.D., for "anno Domini," which means "in the year of our Lord" in Latin. A.D. is written before the numbers (for example, if you were born "in the year of our Lord 1996," it would be written A.D. 1996). Dates before Jesus was born count backward and are labeled "B.C.," for "before Christ," and written with the number first (500 B.C. = "500 years before Christ").

Because most people in the world today are not Christians, some groups have begun using dating labels that don't use Christian terms. In this system the time since Jesus was born is called the Common Era, and dates since then are labeled "C.E." instead of "A.D." Dates before then are labeled "B.C.E.," for "before Common Era." This time line uses both B.C./B.C.E. dates and A.D./C.E. dates.

B4

3500 to 2500 B.C./B.C.E.

Africa

3200 B.C./B.C.E.
Egyptians made writing material from **papyrus**.

3100 B.C./B.C.E.
Menes became the **first Pharaoh** (king) in Egypt, uniting cities along the Nile River.

3000 B.C./B.C.E.
Egyptians first **tamed cats** to catch rats.

3650 B.C./B.C.E.
The **Sphinx**, in Egypt, was the world's largest carved stone head. This was also the beginning of the Age of Pyramids.

Asia

3200 B.C./B.C.E.
The **earliest civilizations in China** formed along the three largest rivers, the Huang He, Chang Jiang, and Xi Jiang.

2700 B.C./B.C.E.
China's first emperor was Huangdi, the Yellow Emperor.

Europe & Western Asia

The Americas

before 3000 B.C./B.C.E.
Pottery was made in Ecuador, Peru, and Colombia.

Oceania

Converting B.C.E./B.C. Dates to "Years Ago"

To figure out approximately how many years ago a B.C./B.C.E. date was, just add 2,000 years. For example, something that happened around 3500 B.C.E. occurred about 5,500 years ago [3,500 + 2,000 = 5,500]. If you know the exact B.C.E. date of an event, calculate "years ago" by adding the current year to that B.C.E. date. So, if you are reading this in the year 2003, something that happened in 46 B.C./B.C.E. occurred 2,049 years ago because 2,003 + 46 = 2,049.

2501 to 1500 B.C./B.C.E.

1500 B.C./B.C.E.
Queen Hatshepsut founded the **Egyptian Empire.**

2000 B.C./B.C.E.
Two huge cities were built by the **Indus River Valley civilization,** in what is now Pakistan. The cities had garbage chutes and sewer system.

1600 to 1500 B.C./B.C.E.
The Chinese people of the **Shang dynasty** developed calligraphy, a writing system using a brush and ink.

1800 B.C./B.C.E.
Abraham founded Judaism in Mesopotamia, what is now Israel and Palestine.

1750 B.C./B.C.E.
King Hammurabi of Babylonia organized the earliest known set of **written laws.**

1500 B.C./B.C.E.
A huge stone circle known as **Stonehenge** was completed in England. It may have been used as a temple and a place to study the stars.

1450 B.C./B.C.E.
The wealthy, highly developed **Minoan culture** on the island of Thera was destroyed by a volcano explosion.

2400 B.C./B.C.E.
The **Chavín people** in what is now Peru were irrigating crops. By 2000 they were building ceremonial centers.

2000 B.C./B.C.E.
The **Lapita** people of New Guinea raised pigs, dogs, and chickens and grew coconuts, yams, and bananas. They made pottery with complicated patterns.

1501 to 500 B.C./B.C.E.

1290 B.C./B.C.E.
Moses led Hebrew slaves in their escape from Egypt.

800 B.C./B.C.E.
The **Nok people** of West Africa farmed, worked metal, and made large clay statues.

600 B.C./B.C.E.
The **Phoenicians sailed around Africa.** They may also have crossed the Atlantic to the Americas.

1250 to 1200 B.C./B.C.E..
According to legend, the Greeks captured the city of Troy, in what is Turkey, by giving the Trojans a **giant wooden horse.** Soldiers hiding in the horse opened the city gates and let the Greek army in.

1900 B.C./B.C.E..
The twelve Hebrew tribes were united under King Saul in what is now Israel and Palestine. **Judaism** was the first religion that worshipped a single god; it later became the basis for Christianity and Islam.

776 B.C./B.C.E..
The **earliest known Olympic Games** were held in Greece.

620 B.C./B.C.E..
The **first known coins** were made from a mixture of gold and silver in Asia Minor (now Turkey).

550 B.C./B.C.E..
Cyrus the Great started the **Persian Empire,** which eventually included what is now the Middle East, Egypt, Afghanistan, and part of India. It lasted more than 200 years.

1200 B.C./B.C.E.
The Olmecas in Central America carved **colossal stone heads,** weighing up to 20 tons.

500 B.C./B.C.E. to A.D./C.E. 200
The **Adena mound builders** built the Great Serpent Mound in the Ohio River Valley of what is today the Midwest United States of America.

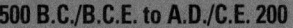

1000 B.C./B.C.E.
Wild dogs called **dingoes** arrived in Australia.

500 B.C./B.C.E. to 500 A.D./C.E.

551 B.C./B.C.E.
Confucius was born in China. His teachings, called **Confucianism,** are based on respect.

528 B.C./B.C.E.
Buddhism was founded in India by Siddharta Gautama, later known as the Buddha.

215 B.C./B.C.E.
The **Great Wall of China** was started by the Ch'in Dynasty to keep out invaders. It was eventually 4,000 miles long.

200 to 100 B.C./B.C.E.
Taoism, a religion based on living in harmony with nature, developed in China.

C.E./A.D.105
The Chinese developed the world's first **paper from woody plants.**

C.E./A.D.105
The Russians invented **chess.**

336 to 323 B.C./B.C.E..
Alexander the Great was only 20 years old when he became king of Greece. He conquered the Persians, and his Greek Empire stretched from Egypt to India.

218 B.C./B.C.E..
A general from Carthage, North Africa, named **Hannibal attacked Rome** by marching soldiers and elephants across Spain and then over the Alps.

6 to 4 B.C./B.C.E.
 Jesus was born in Palestine, probably a few years before the date estimated when the Christian calendar was created. **Christianity** is based on his teachings.

A.D./C.E. 79
Italy's **Mount Vesuvius** erupted, burying the towns of Pompeii and Herculaneum.

A.D./C.E. 476
The **fall of the Roman Empire** came after attacks by nomads from Central Asia.

400 B.C./B.C.E.
The earliest known writing and calendar in the Americas were developed by the Zapotec people in Central America.

A.D./C.E. 300 to 1300
The **Anasazi** lived in what is now the Southwest United States. They built pueblos into the hillsides, some with as many as 800 rooms.

Ancient Times: Some Highlights

About 5000 B.C./B.C.E., the **world's first civilization,** the Sumerians, developed in Mesopotamia, now Iraq. Sumerians lived in the "Fertile Crescent" between the Tigris and Euphrates Rivers, and they traveled the rivers to trade with India and Egypt. Sumerians had legal and medical systems and used carts for transportation. They invented the first known writing, called cuneiform, using picture signs pressed into clay tablets.

Between 2686 and 1550 B.C./B.C.E., approximately, Egyptian pharaohs ("kings") had **pyramids** built as huge tombs for themselves. The pyramids' shape represented the rays of the sun.

The Zhou dynasty (1122 to 221 B.C./ B.C.E.) ruled during **China's "golden age,"** when ironworking was introduced.

The Etruscan civilization (800 to 300 B.C./B.C.E.), in what is today's Italy, was noted for its pottery and sculpture.

The city-states of Hellenic Greece (750 to 338 B.C./B.C.E.) were the **first democracies.** Greek literature, science, philosophy, and art still inspire people.

The **Roman Empire** (27 B.C./B.C.E. to A.D./C.E. 476) controlled most of the lands around the Mediterranean Sea and Europe as far north as Britain. The Romans spoke Latin, which became the basis for many modern European languages. The empire split in two parts in A.D./C.E. 395: the Byzantine and West Roman Empires.

B5

The Middle Ages, or Medieval Times

501 to 750 A.D./C.E

751 to 1000 A.D./C.E

New Cultures, Religions

New civilizations sprang up around the world.

*Many groups in the Americas lived in **tribes**. From 800 until 1500 Mississippian Temple Mound Builders had a class system and made human sacrifices. The Calusa lived in today's Florida from 500 B.C./B.C.E. until they were killed by the Spanish in the 1500s. In what is now the U.S. northwest and British Columbia, Canada, the Makah hunted whales from canoes. The Haudenosaunee nations lived in today's Ontario and New York. Their cooperative ways helped inspire British colonists to form a federation, the United States of America.*

__Feudalism__ was the way of life in Western Europe from around 800 to 1400: there were the highest lords (who usually lived in castles), and under them many nobles. At the bottom were peasants, or serfs, who worked on farms and paid taxes to the lords. In towns, people made crafts or traded goods. Diseases, illiteracy, and dirty conditions were part of life. Priests and monks were the most educated people.

In Europe, the Catholic Church was powerful; Islam spread in Europe, Asia, and Arabia. Other __religions__ grew in Asia, including Buddhism, Shinto, Confucianism, and Hinduism.

B6

Africa

500s
The kingdom of **Aksum** flourished in east Africa near the Red Sea (today's Eritrea and Ethiopia), exporting ivory, crystal, brass, and copper goods.

641
Islamic Arabs took over Egypt, then began taking over much of the rest of North Africa.

750
Northern and western Africans began to use the **camel** to transport goods across the Sahara ("desert" in Arabic).

971
The **world's first university** was founded in Cairo, Egypt, by Arab Muslims.

971
The **kingdom of Ghana** (today's Mali, not today's Ghana) in West Africa took over the Berber city of Awdaghost. Ghana's kings were considered divine, and they inherited rule through their mother's side of the family.

Asia

500
Buddhist monks and merchants brought **Korean and Chinese culture to Japan.** Many Japanese became Buddhists.

800
The **Fujiwara clan** took over the rule of Japan. During their nearly 300-year rule Japan's culture grew on its own, rather than being based on China's or Korea's.

802
The **Khmer Empire** was created by Rajah Jayavarman II in what is now Cambodia. The Khmer built huge temple complexes, and their armies conquered Thailand and what is now southern Vietnam.

868
In China, wooden blocks were used to make the world's **first printed book,** a set of talks by Buddha.

900
A thin pottery, which came to be known as **china** or **porcelain,** was first made in China.

Europe & Western Asia

500
England's **legend of King Arthur** may be based on a Celtic chieftain from this period. Many tales have been told of Arthur and his Knights of the Round Table.

525
The **Christian calendar,** using the birth of Jesus as year one, was proposed by a monk.

570
Muhammad, the prophet who started Islam, was born in Mecca, in what is now Saudi Arabia. He developed a new religion known as Islam; its people were called Muslims. Muhammad and his soldiers spread Islam throughout Arabia.

793
Vikings from Scandinavia began raids on the British Isles. They started colonies in Europe, Iceland, Greenland, and Russia.

800
Charlemagne was crowned Holy Roman Emperor after he conquered Italy, Austria, Hungary, and northern Germany. He was a great lawmaker and encouraged learning and the arts.

The Americas

700s
The first North American towns appeared along the Ohio and Mississippi Rivers.

700s to 900s
By the 700s, in the areas that today are Mexico, Belize, Guatemala, and Honduras, **Mayan culture** had been in existence for more than five hundred years, and the population was at its peak. Mayans were pyramid builders, like early Egyptians. But within the next two hundred years, one Mayan city after another was abandoned, and much of the population disappeared. Nobody knows exactly why.

Oceania

Around A.D./C.E. 900
The ocean-sailing Polynesians settled in Aotearoa (now also called New Zealand) and developed the **Maori culture.**

1001 to 1250 A.D./C.E

1203
The **Soso** people overran Ghana's capital city, Kumbi, bringing that kingdom to an end. The Soso king, Sumaguro Kante, then overcame the Mandingo peoples to the west.

1235
Mandingo leader **Sundiato** killed the Sumaguro Kante and built an empire, called Mali.

1119
The Chinese first understood the use of **magnets,** leading to the invention of the magnetic compass for navigation.

1192
Yoritomo became the first **shogun** ("great general") to rule Japan.

1171
The English took power in **Ireland** for the first time.

1200
The Spanish developed **guitars** from an instrument brought to Spain by the Moors (Arabs from Africa).

1215
King John of England signed the **Magna Carta,** which became the basis for constitutional governments around the world.

1251 to 1500 A.D./C.E

1312
Emperor **Mansa Musa** came to power in Mali. Despite being a Muslim, he was known for his lavish lifestyle.

1347
Bubonic plague (the "Black Death") moved to Europe from Asia, where it had started around 1332. Spread by rats and fleas, this gruesome disease killed up to 75 million people around the world, including one-third of all the people in Europe and one-quarter of all Africans. There were so few people left to do the farming that even more people died of starvation.

1436
The European **"Age of Discovery"** started when the Portuguese began searching for a sea route to India.

1455
In Germany, Johannes **Gutenberg** built a printing press with movable type. Common people could now learn through reading, because it became easier and cheaper to make multiple copies of books.

1492
The Italian explorer **Cristobal Colon** (Christopher Columbus) sailed west from Spain, hoping to find a shortcut route to India. Instead, he arrived in the Caribbean islands.

1325
In what is now Mexico, the **Aztecs** were a warlike people with a strong civilization. They were eventually conquered by the Spanish in 1521.

1438
The **Incas** ruled what is now Peru. They had bridges, tunnels, and paved roads. Their civilization was destroyed by the Spanish in 1532.

1494
Portugal and Spain signed a treaty promising that they would both share the "New World" that Christopher Columbus had "discovered."

1497
While exploring for England, **John Cabot** reached the east coast of what is now Canada.

1499
European map makers started naming the continents of the New World "America" after the Italian **Amerigo Vespucci,** who wrote about his travels there and was the first to let people know that the newly discovered continents were not Asia.

Some Highlights

China was ruled by **dynasties.** The Sui dynasty (581 to 618) was followed by the T'ang (618 to 907). Under the Sung (960 to 1279) the Chinese invented the magnetic compass, gunpowder, and an early movable type. The Sung were defeated by the **Mongols** from north central Asia, who set up the Yuan dynasty (1279 to 1368) and who had the biggest empire of all time. Mongols established the trade route between Europe and Asia called the "Silk Road." The Chinese eventually drove the Mongols out and established the Ming dynasty (1368 to 1644).
In 1096 Christians from western Europe began invading lands of Muslim Turks in a series of wars that lasted almost two hundred years, known as **Crusades,** to take Jerusalem and other historic places they wanted for themselves.

A family of Italian merchants, the Polos, visited China and India starting in 1275. On their return they introduced to Europe some things they had learned about in their travels— including paper money, using coal, and postal services. **Marco Polo** wrote Description of the World, a book that may have inspired Christopher Columbus and other explorers to look for new routes to Asia.

In 1300 Europe was still feudal, and most people lived on land owned by nobles. Slowly kings built up power, and areas similar to modern European countries began to take shape. A time that came to be known as the **European Renaissance** ("rebirth") began in Italy around 1300 and continued until about 1600. During this time Muslim scholars restored ancient texts to Europeans, who had lost or destroyed many of their copies of them. The Europeans, inspired by these works of early Greek, Roman, and Egyptian civilizations, created new and beautiful art, music, and literature. They also built sailing ships and started traveling to other parts of the world.

The Columbian Exchange

For many centuries people had been living in the Americas. But because Europeans learned this only after the 1492 voyage of Christopher Columbus, they called these lands the "New World."

In the years that followed the European discovery of these lands, Europeans took over more and more of the lands of the native peoples of the Americas (although they did not wipe out the people themselves). They found things in the New World that they had never seen before, and they brought things to the New World that the native people had never known, including foods, animals, ideas, and diseases. This came to be called the "Columbian Exchange."

Here are some things that started in the Old World and went to the Americas:

• smallpox • measles • in uenza • typhoid • horses • brown rats • house mice • cattle • goats • apples • wine grapes • wheat • sparrows • bananas • sugar • coffee • rice

Here are some things that were brought from the New World to Europe:

• corn (maize) • potatoes • squash • peanuts • sweet potatoes • chocolate • beans • tomatoes • pineapples • chili peppers • vanilla • tobacco • avocados • sunflowers

B8

The 1500s: the Sixteenth Century

	1501-1525	1526-1550
AFRICA	**1517** Spain began **regular slave trading** (the Portuguese had been doing it since the 1400s).	**1500s** The **Benin Empire** was a military power feared by its neighbors. Its city-states were ruled by obas (kings). It was a major exporter of slaves.
ASIA	**1517** Polish astronomer **Copernicus** said the Earth moves around the Sun, not the other way around. Eventually his idea was accepted.	**1547** **Ivan the Terrible** became the first czar (from the Latin word meaning "king") of all Russia. He was mean and cruel, which is why he got his nickname. He even killed his own son in anger.
EUROPE & WESTERN ASIA	**1517** German priest **Martin Luther** challenged the Roman Catholic Church to reform. It did reform, but Protestant churches also started up. This time became known as the Reformation.	
THE AMERICAS	**1513** **Juan Ponce de Léon** landed in Florida. He was the first Spaniard to explore North America.	**1530** The **Portuguese colonized Brazil**, where they started using African slaves in 1534. **1534** Jacques Cartier tried to start a French colony in **Quebec**, but it didn't work.
OCEANIA		

The 1600s: the Seventeenth Century

	1601-1625	1626-1650
AFRICA		
EUROPE & WESTERN ASIA		**1633** The great Italian scientist **Galileo** was tried by the Inquisition of the Roman Catholic Church for his heretical view that the Earth revolved around the sun. He was sentenced to house arrest for the rest of his life.
ASIA	**1629** The lavish Moghul palace at Agra (in today's India), the **Taj Mahal**, was started. It took 22 years and 20,000 workers to build it; it was a tomb for Shah Jahan's favorite wife, Mumtaz	**1642** The **Irish rebelled against the English** but were brutally crushed by Oliver Cromwell in 1649. **1649** The **English executed their king,** Charles I, after a bloody civil war.
THE AMERICAS	**1604** The first European colonists settled in **Canada.**	**1636** **Harvard College**, the first university in North America, was founded.
OCEANIA	**1620** Protestant English Pilgrims sailed to North America on the **Mayflower** and started the Massachusetts Bay Colony.	

1551–1575

1556
Emperor Akbar succeeded to the throne at age 13. Under him the Moghul Empire stretched from Afghanistan to the east coast of what is India today.

1571
The **Philippine Islands** in the South Pacific became part of the Spanish Empire under King Philip II.

1565
St. Augustine, Florida, was founded by Spanish settlers. Today it is considered the **oldest city in North America.**

1576–1600

1590
A slave named **Amador led a major revolt** against the Portuguese on the island of São Tomé off the west coast of Africa (today part of São Tomé and Príncipe, one of the world's smallest independent countries). Amador was killed, but much of the island was destroyed. The island remained a holding place for slaves bound for the Americas.

1588
Spain sent a fleet of ships, known as the **Spanish Armada,** to invade England, but the English navy beat them back with the help of stormy weather.

1651–1675

1652
Dutch farmers, called **Boers**, settled in southern Africa near the Cape of Good Hope.

1681
The **first time women were allowed to dance in a professional ballet** was in *The Triumph of Love*. Before this, female roles were played by males.

1690
In **the Battle of the Boyne**, in Ireland, supporters of the Protestant King of England, William of Orange, defeated supporters of his Catholic father-in-law; William introduced harsh laws for Catholics.

1676–1700

1689
Peter I, age ten, and his half-brother, Ivan, V, became co-czars of Russia; Peter later seized complete power. He began the work that would later make Russia one of the world's superpowers, and he would become known as **Peter the Great.**

1668 to 1688
Captain Henry Morgan of Wales was a pirate, or buccaneer, who terrorized Spanish ships in the Caribbean. Most of the treasures he stole went to his investors in England. He was later made a knight and then lieutenant governor of Jamaica.

Slavery: The Shameful Sale of Human Beings

West Africa is associated with gold and ivory and with voodoo, the only religion from Africa that is still practiced in the Americas. It is also associated with slavery.

Racial discrimination in the United States can be traced back to the slave trade, which began in the late 1400s and continued for hundreds of years. More than twenty million African men, women, and children were kidnapped and shipped under dreadful conditions across the Atlantic to the Americas, then sold and used as free labor in households and on plantations.

Europeans bene ted from slavery, but so did many African leaders, who became wealthy and powerful as a result of the trade and abuse of their fellow Africans.

The "Age of Reason"

In Europe and the Americas the time of the late 17th century through the 18th century (1600s and 1700s) was known as the "Enlightenment" or the "Age of Reason." Humans were coming out of centuries of ignorance, and they were enlightened by reason, science, and a new respect for the natural rights of people. People also started to believe in humanitarianism, or taking care of and helping people who were less fortunate. This did not, however, apply to slaves or Native Americans.

Important scientific c discoveries of this era included the movement of planets, moons, and stars, and Sir Isaac Newton discovered gravity. During this time people started believing that it was important to achieve happiness and do something worthwhile in life.

The Industrial Revolution

Starting in the middle of the seventeenth century, the Western world was experiencing what came to be known as the "Industrial Revolution," which was not a war but a drastic change in society and the way people lived their lives.

New machines and factories moved people who had once worked on farms into the cities, where they labored mostly in textile production and mining. Workers, including children, often worked twelve to fourteen hours a day, six days a week, in terrible conditions for little money. This is where we get the word "sweatshop."

Machines made more machines, and steam--ships and railroads moved goods quickly and cheaply. Industrial cities grew, and capitalism took hold.

As the Industrial Revolution spread throughout Europe, Asia, and North America, labor movements designed to protect workers grew up gradually. It's hard to imagine now, but in the 1840s New Hampshire became the first state to make the ten-hour day the longest legal workday, and Pennsylvania was among the first to make twelve the minimum age for workers in commercial occupations.

The 1700s: the Eighteenth Century

1701-1725

AFRICA

1701
The **Ashantis** expanded their territory to become one of the largest, wealthiest kingdoms in West Africa—like others, trading in slaves, as well as cola nuts and gold.

Slave auction

1722
A **slaving post** was established by the Dutch at Maputo in the Cape Colony (at what is now Cape Town, South Africa)

ASIA

EUROPE & WESTERN ASIA

1721
German Johannes Sebastian **Bach** composed the Brandenburg Concertos.

THE AMERICAS

OCEANIA

1726-1750

1732
A **mutiny** at the Maputo slave post caused it to be abandoned.

1716
Shogun ruler Yoshimune began to open Japan to outside contacts.

1735
Swedish scientist **Carolus Linnaeus**, the "father of modern botany," developed a way to classify all plants and animals.

The 1800s: the Nineteenth Century

1801-1825

AFRICA

1822
The United States established the **colony of Liberia** in western Africa as a home for freed slaves.

EUROPE & WESTERN ASIA

1825
The **first passenger train service** began in England.

ASIA

THE AMERICAS

1808
Federal law banned bringing new slaves into the United States. Smugglers continued to bring in some slaves until just before the Civil War.

OCEANIA

1826-1850

1835
In South Africa Dutch farmers, known as **Boers**, trekked inland to avoid being ruled by the British.

1845 to 1846
Plant disease caused a devastating **potato famine** in Ireland, where potatoes were the main food for tenant farmers working for rich British and Protestant Irish "gentleman farmers." About a million people died, and another million emigrated to Canada, the United States, Australia, or England.

1848
Under the leadership of **Susan B. Anthony** and **Elizabeth Cady Stanton,** a group of women created and made the Declaration of Women's Rights in Seneca Falls, New York.

1838 to 1839
Thousands of Cherokee Nation people were forced to leave their homes in Georgia and the Carolinas and relocate to Oklahoma. Their trek became known as the **"Trail of Tears"** because not only were they all displaced, but thousands died as well.

1826
Aborigines revolted against English settlers in Tasmania.

1751-1775

1762
Empress **Catherine the Great** started her rule of the Russian Empire. She increased the empire's territory and gave new rights to women.

1769
Scottish inventor **James Watt** patented his improved steam engine.

1752
American inventor and statesman **Benjamin Franklin** used a kite to identify electricity in lightning.

1768
Scientific explorer **Captain James Cook** started his expeditions to learn about the Pacific islands. He later claimed **Australia** and **New Zealand** for England.

1776-1800

1795
The **British took over the Cape Colony**.

1789
In the **French Revolution**, rebels overthrew the monarchy and demanded equal rights.

1797
English doctor Edward Jenner developed a **smallpox vaccination**.

1776
The American **Declaration of Independence** was written by Thomas Jefferson and signed by rebel leaders on July 4.

1788
The United States adopted its **Constitution** and elected **George Washington** its first president; the **Bill of Rights** was added in 1789.

1791
In Haiti, **Toussaint L'Ouverture** led a slave revolt against the French.

1788
England started sending convicts to Botany Bay, the first British colony in **Australia**.

1851-1875

1869
The **Suez Canal** opened in Egypt; it shortened the sea route from Britain to India from three months to three weeks.

1860
The **kingdom of Italy** was united. The next year a national parliament was formed, and all of Italy but Venice and Rome came under one rule.

1860
Florence Nightingale started the world's first nursing school in London.

1851 to 1864
As many as thirty million Chinese were killed in the **Taiping Rebellion**, led by Hong Xiuquan. The rebels wanted to re-create a legendary state in which poor people owned and farmed the land. It took the Chinese army 14 years to defeat them.

1861 to 1865
The **U.S. Civil War** divided people in the North and South. It would take years to heal the wounds.

1865
U.S. president and Civil War leader **Abraham Lincoln** was assassinated by **John Wilkes Booth**.

1876-1900

1899
Boer War started between Dutch and British colonies in South Africa.

1880
Greenwich Mean Time was established at Greenwich Observatory, England.

1884
France presented the **Statue of Liberty** as a gift to the United States.

1889
The **Eiffel Tower** was built in Paris, France.

1875
Alexander Graham Bell invented the **telephone**.

1877
Thomas Alva Edison invented the **phonograph** (first record player); two years later he demonstrated his invention, the **light bulb**.

1886
The **American Federation of Labor** is created to protect American workers. Labor leader Samuel Gompers is named its first president.

1893
Women in New Zealand earned the **right to vote**.

North American Colonists Break Free

The European colonies in North America were controlled from Europe, especially Spain, France, and England—who also fought among themselves and against various Native American tribes. By 1713 the English had taken Acadia (Nova Scotia) from the French and destroyed St. Augustine in Florida, which had been Spanish. In 1759 they won Quebec from the French.

By the late 1700s many colonists were tired of distant rule and "taxation without representation." They got help from the French and some Native American peoples, and in 1775 they started the American Revolution against England. George Washington was commander in chief of the colonial army. To everyone's surprise, the colonists beat the great British Empire, and in 1788 they ratified the Constitution establishing the United States of America.

Setters began to move westward. The new country's prosperity and population grew. The former colonists didn't treat their Native American friends well, forcing many to give up their homelands.

Women's Right to Vote

In the mid-1800s, U.S. women began to protest their lack of suffrage, or the right to vote. Susan B. Anthony and Elizabeth Cady Stanton led a group of women who proposed a general declaration of the rights of women. After the Civil War, one by one, states granted women the right to vote. In 1920 the National Woman's Party had enough voting power to make the U.S. Congress pass the Nineteenth Amendment to the Constitution, granting all American women the right to vote.

In England it was not until after World War I that a group called the Women's Political Union was able to achieve equal voting rights for women—in 1928.

The 1900s: the Twentieth Century

The World at War, Not Once, but Twice

The 1900s brought two devastating wars that affected nearly the entire world. At least ten million people died in World War I, which began in 1914. The "Central Powers"— Germany, Austria-Hungary, and the Ottomans— fought the "Allies," led by England, France, Russia, and the United States. This was the first war with trench fighting, poison gas, and airplanes. In 1918 the Allies won, and the League of Nations was formed in 1920, with hopes of avoiding future wars.

But in 1939 Germany invaded Poland. By 1940 there was war between the Axis powers of Germany, Italy, and Japan and the Allied powers of France, Great Britain, the U.S.S.R., and later the United States. The war ended in 1945, when the United States dropped the world's first two atomic bombs on Hiroshima and Nagasaki in Japan, and the Axis surrendered. The death toll was in the tens of millions, mostly civilians.

Medical Breakthroughs Improve the Quality of Life

The discovery of antibiotics helped doctors around the world fight against diseases like tuberculosis. It also cut the risk of infection from surgery. Vaccines against polio, diphtheria, and other diseases increased childhood life expectancy.

Organ transplant surgery started in the 1950s. Since then lasers, arthroscopy, and other methods have made surgery safer. X-rays, CAT scans, and magnetic resonance imaging (MRI) have made diagnosing illnesses easier. The discovery of DNA in the 1950s led to genetic engineering. By 1974 new techniques allowed medical researchers to change the genetic structure of living things. In 1997 scientists cloned a mammal (the sheep who came to be known as Dolly) for the first time.

1901
The first **Nobel Peace Prize** went to the founder of the International Red Cross, Jean Henri Dunant of Switzerland.

1903
The **Wright Brothers** flew the first powered airplane.

1905
Albert Einstein published his theories of time, space, and motion. His ideas about atoms were the basis for atomic weapons and nuclear power.

1908
Henry Ford started making the inexpensive Model T; soon, driving was very popular.

1912
China became a republic after the overthrow of the last Manchu emperor, a six-year-old boy.

1912
The luxury cruise ship **Titanic** sank on its very first voyage after hitting an iceberg in the North Atlantic; 1513 people drowned.

1916
The **first national child labor law** in the United States protected children from unsafe working conditions.

1917
The **Russian Revolution** ended the Czarist rule in Russia. The new Communist government eventually formed the Soviet Union, or U.S.S.R., which lasted until 1991.

1918 to 1919
A worldwide influenza (flu) epidemic killed 21 million people.

1919
Mohandas Gandhi began "peacefully protesting" British colonial rule in India. Indians would finally gain their independence in 1947. Gandhi's nonviolent methods inspired civil rights movements around the world.

1920
The first **regular radio broadcasts** began in Pittsburgh (KDKA) and Detroit (WWJ).

1927
Charles Lindbergh made the first solo airplane flight across the Atlantic Ocean.

1929
The U.S. stock market "crashed": beginning of the **Great Depression.**

1930
The planet **Pluto** was identified.

1933
Adolf Hitler became dictator of the Nazi German government. He was the most notorious murderer of the twentieth century, responsible for the deaths of millions of Jews and others who did not fit into his philosophy of "Aryan Supremacy."

1936
The British Broadcasting Corporation made the **first television broadcast.**

1937
Pilot **Amelia Earhart** and navigator Fred Noonan disappeared during their attempted flight around the world.

1941
The United States entered **World War II** after the **Japanese bombed Pearl Harbor**, Hawaii.

1942
Thirteen-year-old **Anne Frank** started her diary of life in hiding from the Nazis. She and her family were arrested and sent to a concentration camp two years later. In 1945 she died while a prisoner of the Nazis.

1945
The **United Nations** was formed to promote world peace and cooperation.

1947
Jackie Robinson was the first black person to play major league baseball.

1948
The United Nations helped create **Israel** on traditionally Hebrew land that was part of Palestine.

1949
Communists took control of China (left); **Taiwan** (right) formed a separate republic.

1949
The U.S.S.R. built its first atomic bomb.

1954
The U.S. Supreme Court ruled that separation of people by race or ethnic group, or **segregation, in schools was illegal.**

1957
Sputnik, the first artificial satellite to orbit Earth, was launched by the Soviet Union.

1957
Western European countries formed the **Common Market,** which later became the European Union.

1957
Ghana was the first African country to gain independence from European colonial rule.

1959
Alaska and Hawaii became the 49th and 50th U.S. states.

1959
Communist rebel leader **Fidel Castro** assumed power in Cuba.

1962
Rachel Carson published *The Silent Spring* and brought the environment to people's attention.

1963
The first Catholic U.S. president , **John F. Kennedy,** was assassinated.

1963
Newly independent African countries founded the **Organization of African Unity.**

1964
The U.S. **Civil Rights Act** was passed to lessen legal discrimination against minorities.

1969
Two U.S. astronauts were the first humans to **walk on the moon.**

1970
The first **Earth Day** was organized in Seattle, Washington.

1972
The twin **World Trade Center** towers were built in New York City.

1974
The last European colonies in Africa gained their **independence from Portugal:** Angola, Guinea-Bissau, and Mozambique.

1974
U.S. president **Nixon resigned** after corruption in his 1972 re-election campaign was exposed.

1976
Twenty-six African countries boycotted the Olympics Games in Montreal in protest of **apartheid,** the discriminatory practices against black people in South Africa.

1977
The first **personal computers** were very large and very expensive.

1981
Columbia, **the first space shuttle** to orbit Earth, was jointly launched by NASA and the European Space Agency.

1980
Mount Saint Helens volcano erupted in Washington State.

1984
Geraldine Ferraro was the first female candidate nominated by a major political party for U.S. vice president.

1989
Chinese students led a democracy movement.

1989
East Germany broke its ties with the U.S.S.R. and reunited with West Germany. **The Berlin Wall was torn down**; it had been built in 1961 to keep East Germans in their communist country and others out.

1990
The **Hubble Space Telescope** was launched.

1991
Republics in the Soviet Union (Union of Soviet Socialist Republics) became 15 separate countries again after the Communists lost control of the U.S.S.R.

1991
Apartheid was repealed in South Africa.

1997
An international treaty banned the use of land mines.

1997 to 2000
The **ozone hole** over Antarctica stopped getting bigger. Scientists were optimistic that it might be gone by 2050.

1999
Canada's Inuits were given control over 770,000 square miles reaching from the Northwest Territories into the Arctic Circle.

Age of Communication and Transportation

Radio broadcasting, beginning in 1920, signaled the dawn of telecommunication. Television became widely available in the 1940s Telephone calls, first made using wires, were later carried by fiber optics and satellites. Toward the end of the century, data, sound, and pictures were sent around the globe by the Internet.

The automobile and internal combustion engine dominated land travel, at the same time as diesel and electric engines for trains were developed. Air travel began with the Americans Orville and Wilbur Wright in 1903; commercial air travel began seventeen years later. Jet engines improved air travel after World War II. Space exploration began in earnest in 1957, with both the Soviet Union and the United States trying to be first in doing new things. The Russians put the first person in space, but the Americans were first on the moon. The International Space Station was operational starting in 2000.

The Cold War

What came to be known as the "cold war" began after World War II. The communist Soviet Union and its allies faced off against the capitalist United States and its allies. The two super-powers kept each other on alert by staging an arms race in which each of them built up huge stockpiles of nuclear weapons. Wars broke out between Soviet and U.S. allies around the globe as each side tried to expand its sphere of influence. Long, drawn-out wars were fought in Korea, Vietnam, and Angola.

In the United States families lived in fear of a Communist takeover. Many of them built bomb shelters on their properties in case of an attack. Joseph McCarthy, a senator from Minnesota, led a national witchhunt for suspected communist sympathizers. The Cold War ended in 1989 when the Soviet Union's communist system fell apart.

Symbolic Communication

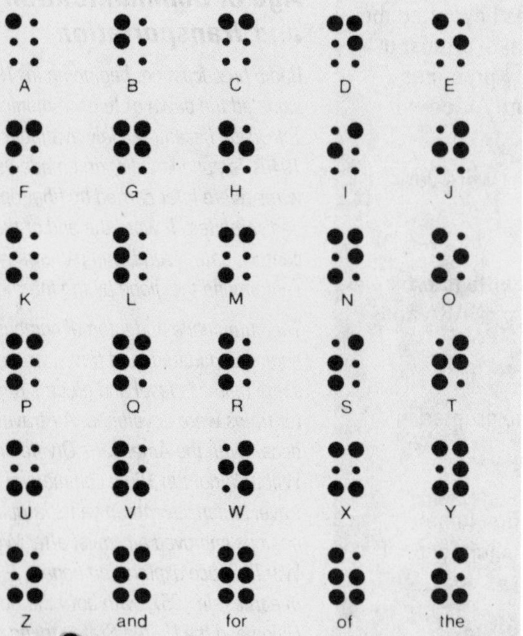

A   B   C   D   E

F   G   H   I   J

K   L   M   N   O

P   Q   R   S   T

U   V   W   X   Y

Z   and   for   of   the

Braille

People who are blind often learn to read Braille, a pattern of raised dots that represent letters and numbers. Braille is read by running one's finger over the raised dots. Braille was invented by Louis Braille (1809-1852).

Zodiac Signs

What's your sign? Some people believe that you can tell a lot about people based on what zodiac sign they were born under. The signs of the zodiac roughly correspond to the months of the year, with a new sign starting around the last week of every month. The symbols represent constellations. People who use the zodiac signs to make predictions are called astrologers.

Body Language

Sometimes you don't have to say a word to let people know how you're feeling—your body language does the talking. The look on your face, the way you move, and whether you stand up straight or slouch can tell people if you are happy or sad, confident or uncertain.

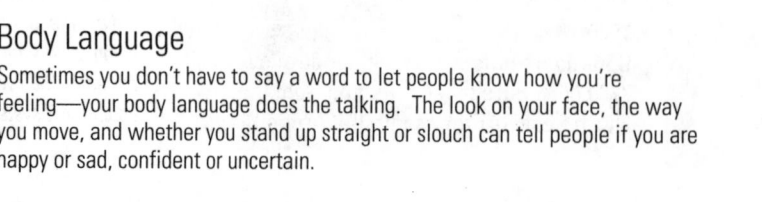

We Can Do It!

Street Signs

Street signs come in many shapes, sizes, and colors, and they have many different functions. Some tell laws for driving, some give information about a place, some are warnings, and some are used just for decoration. Street signs can use pictures, words, numbers, or a combination of all three. Can you guess what these signs mean?

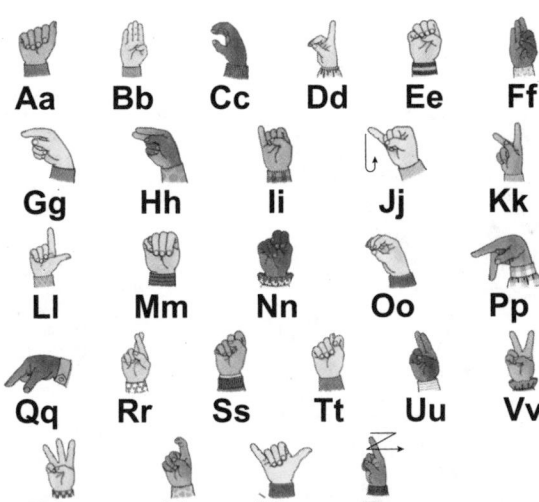

Sign Language

People who can't hear or speak often use sign language to communicate. English words can be spelled out using the American Sign Language alphabet, shown here, but most signs express entire words. Signs usually have three features: the position of the hands, the location of the hands in relation to the body, and the movement of the hands. People in different countries use different sign languages, although many signs are similar in more than one language.

Danger
25000 V.

Democrats

Republicans

World Population Density

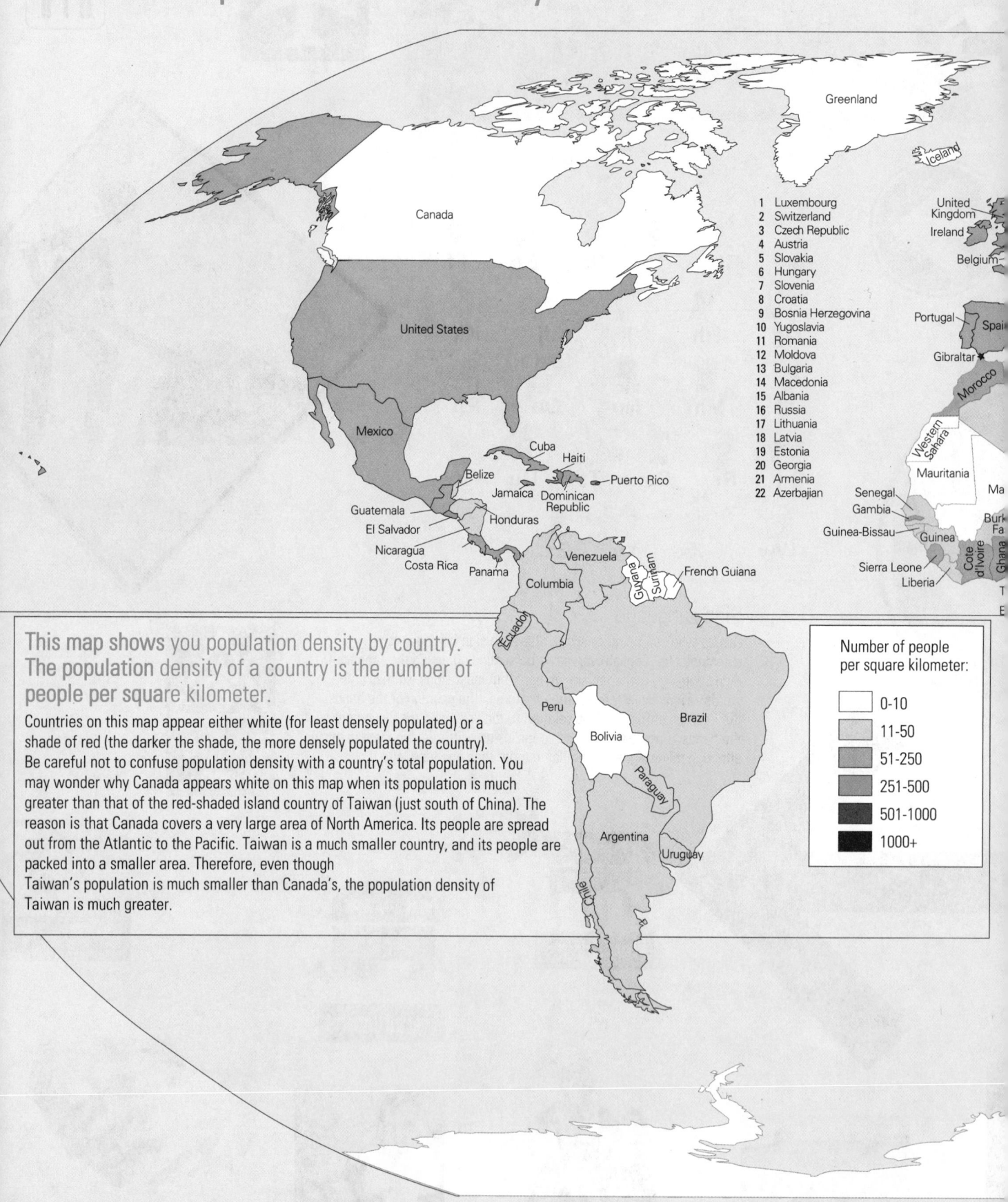

1	Luxembourg
2	Switzerland
3	Czech Republic
4	Austria
5	Slovakia
6	Hungary
7	Slovenia
8	Croatia
9	Bosnia Herzegovina
10	Yugoslavia
11	Romania
12	Moldova
13	Bulgaria
14	Macedonia
15	Albania
16	Russia
17	Lithuania
18	Latvia
19	Estonia
20	Georgia
21	Armenia
22	Azerbajian

This map shows you population density by country. **The population** density of a country is the number of people per square kilometer.

Countries on this map appear either white (for least densely populated) or a shade of red (the darker the shade, the more densely populated the country). Be careful not to confuse population density with a country's total population. You may wonder why Canada appears white on this map when its population is much greater than that of the red-shaded island country of Taiwan (just south of China). The reason is that Canada covers a very large area of North America. Its people are spread out from the Atlantic to the Pacific. Taiwan is a much smaller country, and its people are packed into a smaller area. Therefore, even though
Taiwan's population is much smaller than Canada's, the population density of Taiwan is much greater.

Number of people per square kilometer:

	0-10
	11-50
	51-250
	251-500
	501-1000
	1000+

Russia

Sweden
Finland
19
18
16
17
Poland Belarus
3
5
4
6
11
12
8
9 10 13
15 14
Malta
Greece
Cyprus
Lebanon
Israel
Gaza Strip
Jordan
Libya
Egypt
Turkey
Syria
Iraq
Iran
Kuwait
Bahrain
Qatar
Saudi Arabia
United Arab Emirates
Oman
Yemen
Djibouti

20
21 22
Uzbekistan
Turkmenistan
Kyrgyzstan
Tajikistan
Afghanistan
Kazakhstan
Mongolia
Pakistan
Nepal
Bhutan
India
Bangladesh
Burma
China
North Korea
South Korea
Japan
Taiwan
Hong Kong
Macao
Hainan Dao
Philippines
Laos
Thailand
Vietnam
Cambodia
Sri Lanka

Chad
Sudan
Eritrea
Ethiopia
Somalia
Central Africa Republic
Uganda
Kenya
Congo
Rwanda
Burundi
Democratic Republic of the Congo
Tanzania
Angola
Malawi
Zambia
Mozambique
Madagascar
Namibia
Zimbabwe
Botswana
South Africa
Swaziland
Lesotho

Brunei
Malaysia
Singapore
Indonesia
Indonesia
Papua New Guinea
Australia
New Zealand

It is estimated that the population of our
planet will reach eight billion by the end of the
year 2026. Many are concerned that the world's
natural resources are reaching their limit in supporting so
many people. Almost all of the world's population
growth occurs in poorer and less developed nations,
where unhealthy living conditions cause high death rates
among children. High child death rates make parents want
to have larger families in the hope that some of their
children will survive to carry on the family name. Other
causes of overpopulation in poorer countries include lack
of family-planning education, and political
structures that are oppressive to women. In an effort to
control population growth, some governments have
imposed limits on family size and mandatory sterilizations
(the disabling of reproductive organs). But the more
effective solutions seem to be the more democratic:
education, quality health care, and programs that help
impoverished women to enter social, political, and
business worlds.

Antarctica

North America

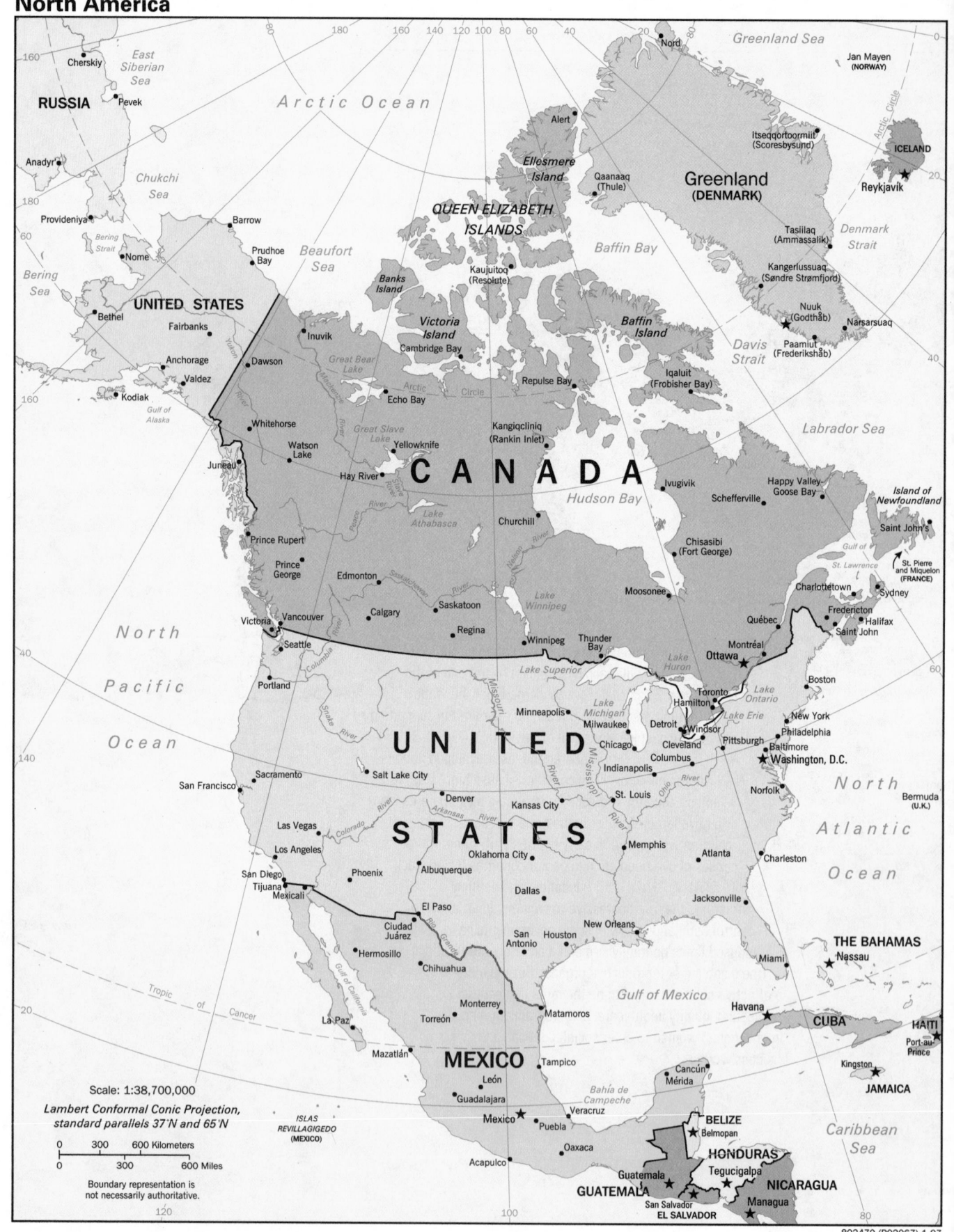

RUSSIA

East Siberian Sea

Arctic Ocean

Greenland Sea

Jan Mayen (NORWAY)

Cherskiy

Pevek

Anadyr'

Chukchi Sea

Providenya

Bering Strait

Barrow

Nome

Bethel

Beaufort Sea

Prudhoe Bay

Fairbanks

UNITED STATES

Anchorage

Valdez

Kodiak

Juneau

Gulf of Alaska

Alert

Ellesmere Island

QUEEN ELIZABETH ISLANDS

Qaanaaq (Thule)

Kaujuitoq (Resolute)

Banks Island

Inuvik

Dawson

Whitehorse

Watson Lake

Great Bear Lake

Mackenzie River

Echo Bay

Cambridge Bay

Victoria Island

Arctic Circle

Repulse Bay

Baffin Island

Iqaluit (Frobisher Bay)

Baffin Bay

Itseqqortoormiit (Scoresbysund)

ICELAND

Reykjavík

Tasiilaq (Ammassalik)

Kangerlussuaq (Søndre Strømfjord)

Nuuk (Godthåb)

Narsarsuaq

Paamiut (Frederikshåb)

Greenland (DENMARK)

Nord

Denmark Strait

Davis Strait

Yellowknife

Great Slave Lake

Hay River

C A N A D A

Kangiqcliniq (Rankin Inlet)

Churchill

Hudson Bay

Ivugivik

Scheffervillle

Happy Valley-Goose Bay

Labrador Sea

Island of Newfoundland

Saint John's

St. Pierre and Miquelon (FRANCE)

Prince Rupert

Prince George

Edmonton

Calgary

Saskatoon

Regina

Lake Athabasca

Nelson River

Lake Winnipeg

Winnipeg

Thunder Bay

Chisasibi (Fort George)

Moosonee

Gulf of St. Lawrence

Charlottetown

Sydney

Fredericton

Halifax

Saint John

Québec

Montréal

Ottawa

Lake Superior

Lake Huron

Toronto

Hamilton

Lake Ontario

Lake Erie

Windsor

Detroit

Cleveland

Pittsburgh

Boston

New York

Philadelphia

Baltimore

Washington, D.C.

Victoria

Vancouver

Seattle

Portland

North Pacific Ocean

Columbia River

Snake River

Minneapolis

Milwaukee

Lake Michigan

Chicago

Columbus

Indianapolis

St. Louis

Norfolk

North Atlantic Ocean

Bermuda (U.K.)

San Francisco

Sacramento

Salt Lake City

Denver

Colorado River

Arkansas River

Kansas City

Missouri River

Mississippi River

Ohio River

U N I T E D

S T A T E S

Las Vegas

Los Angeles

San Diego

Tijuana

Mexicali

Phoenix

Albuquerque

Oklahoma City

Dallas

Memphis

Atlanta

Charleston

Jacksonville

El Paso

Ciudad Juárez

Hermosillo

Chihuahua

San Antonio

Houston

New Orleans

Miami

Rio Grande

Gulf of California

La Paz

Torreón

Monterrey

Matamoros

Gulf of Mexico

Havana

THE BAHAMAS

Nassau

CUBA

HAITI

Port-au-Prince

Kingston

JAMAICA

Mazatlán

León

Guadalajara

MEXICO

Tampico

Veracruz

Cancún

Mérida

Bahía de Campeche

Tropic of Cancer

Mexico

Puebla

Oaxaca

Acapulco

ISLAS REVILLAGIGEDO (MEXICO)

BELIZE

Belmopan

Guatemala

San Salvador

EL SALVADOR

GUATEMALA

Tegucigalpa

HONDURAS

Managua

NICARAGUA

Caribbean Sea

Scale: 1:38,700,000

Lambert Conformal Conic Projection, standard parallels 37°N and 65°N

0   300   600 Kilometers

0   300   600 Miles

Boundary representation is not necessarily authoritative.

802470 (R02067) 1-97

South America

Caribbean Sea

Martinique (FRANCE)
ST. LUCIA
ST. VINCENT AND
THE GRENADINES
BARBADOS
GRENADA

*North
Atlantic
Ocean*

Isla de
San Andrés
(COLOMBIA)

Netherlands
Antilles
(NETH.)

Aruba
(NETH.)

Barranquilla
Cartagena
Maracaibo
Barquisimeto
★ Caracas
Valencia
Port-of-Spain
TRINIDAD AND
TOBAGO

Cúcuta
San Cristóbal
VENEZUELA
Ciudad
Guayana
Georgetown
Paramaribo ★
Cayenne

Medellín
★ Bogotá
GUYANA
SURINAME
French
Guiana
(FRANCE)

Cali
COLOMBIA
Boa Vista
Macapá

*Isla de Malpelo
(COLOMBIA)*

Río Magdalena

Equator
Quito ★
ECUADOR
Guayaquil
Amazon
Río Negro
Manaus
Amazon
Belém
São Luís

Iquitos
Santarém
Fortaleza

Piura
Río Marañón
Teresina
Natal

Trujillo
Huánuco
Río
Branco
Pôrto
Velho
Río Madeira
B R A Z I L
Recife
Maceió

PERU
Río Ucayali
Río Xingu
Río Tocantins

★ Lima
Cusco
Río Beni
Río Mamoré
Trinidad
Río São Francisco

*South
Pacific
Ocean*

Lago
Titicaca
Salvador

Arequipa
★ La Paz
BOLIVIA
Cuiabá
★ Brasília

Arica
Cochabamba
Sucre
Santa Cruz
Goiânia
Río Paraguai

Iquique
Potosí
Campo
Grande
Uberlândia
Belo
Horizonte
Vitória

Antofagasta
PARAGUAY
Río Paraná
Rio de Janeiro

Salta
Asunción ★
São Paulo
Santos

San Miguel
de Tucumán
Curitiba

Resistencia
Florianópolis

*Isla San Félix
(CHILE)*
*Isla San Ambrosio
(CHILE)*
Río Paraná
Pôrto Alegre

CHILE
Córdoba
Santa Fe
Salto

*ARCHIPIÉLAGO
JUAN FERNANDEZ
(CHILE)*
Valparaíso
Mendoza
Rosario
URUGUAY

Santiago ★
Buenos Aires ★
La Plata
Montevideo ★

Concepción
ARGENTINA

*South
Atlantic
Ocean*

Bahía Blanca
Mar del Plata

Puerto Montt
San Carlos de
Bariloche

Comodoro Rivadavia

Scale 1:35,000,000
Azimuthal Equal-Area Projection

Río
Gallegos
*Strait of
Magellan*
★ Stanley
Falkland Islands
(Islas Malvinas)

0   500 Kilometers
0   500 Miles

Punta Arenas
Ushuaia

South Georgia and the
South Sandwich Islands

Boundary representation is
not necessarily authoritative.

B19

Africa

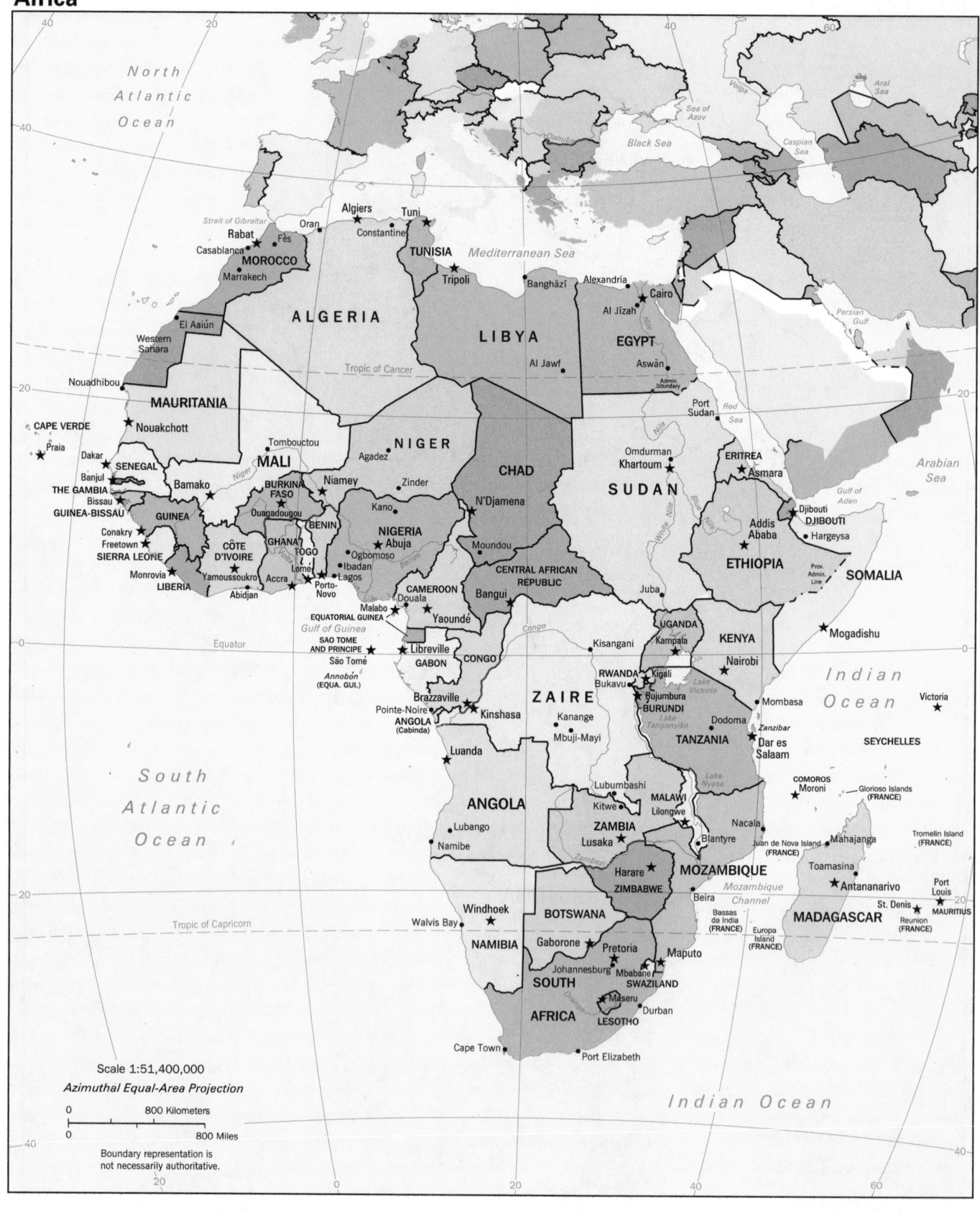

North Atlantic Ocean

Strait of Gibraltar

Algiers Tuni
Oran   Constantine
Rabat   Fès
Casablanca
MOROCCO **TUNISIA**
Marrakech

Mediterranean Sea

Tripoli   Banghāzī   Alexandria
                     Cairo
Al Jīzah
LIBYA **EGYPT**

El Aaiún
Western Sahara
Al Jawf   Aswān

Tropic of Cancer

ALGERIA

Nouadhibou

MAURITANIA

Port Sudan
Red Sea

Persian Gulf

CAPE VERDE
Praia
Nouakchott

Tombouctou
MALI
Agadez
NIGER
Zinder
Omdurman
Khartoum
ERITREA
Asmara

Arabian Sea

Dakar
SENEGAL
Banjul
THE GAMBIA
Bissau
GUINEA-BISSAU
Bamako
BURKINA FASO
Niamey
Ouagadougou
Kano
N'Djamena
CHAD
SUDAN
Moundou
White Nile
Blue Nile
Addis Ababa
Djibouti
DJIBOUTI
Hargeysa
Gulf of Aden

Conakry
Freetown
SIERRA LEONE
Monrovia
LIBERIA
GUINEA
Yamoussoukro
Abidjan
CÔTE D'IVOIRE
GHANA?
TOGO
Accra
Lomé
BENIN
Ibadan
Ogbomoso
Lagos
Porto-Novo
NIGERIA
Abuja
Benue
Bangui
CENTRAL AFRICAN REPUBLIC
Juba
Prov. Admin. Line
ETHIOPIA
SOMALIA

CAMEROON
Douala
Yaoundé
Malabo
EQUATORIAL GUINEA
SAO TOME AND PRINCIPE
São Tomé
Libreville
GABON
Congo
Kisangani
Kampala
UGANDA
KENYA
Nairobi
Mogadishu

Gulf of Guinea
Equator
Annobón (EQUA. GUI.)

Brazzaville
Pointe-Noire
Kinshasa
CONGO
ZAIRE
Kananga
Mbuji-Mayi
Bukavu
RWANDA
Kigali
Bujumbura
BURUNDI
Lake Victoria
Lake Tanganyika
Dodoma
TANZANIA
Zanzibar
Dar es Salaam
Mombasa
SEYCHELLES
Victoria

Indian Ocean

Luanda
Lubango
Namibe
ANGOLA
Lubumbashi
Kitwe
ZAMBIA
Lusaka
Lake Nyasa
MALAWI
Lilongwe
Blantyre
Nacala
COMOROS
Moroni
Glorioso Islands (FRANCE)
Mahajanga
Tromelin Island (FRANCE)
ANGOLA (Cabinda)

South Atlantic Ocean

Zambezi
Harare
ZIMBABWE
Beira
MOZAMBIQUE
Mozambique Channel
Toamasina
Antananarivo
MADAGASCAR
Port Louis
St. Denis
MAURITIUS
Reunion (FRANCE)
Juan de Nova Island (FRANCE)

Tropic of Capricorn

Windhoek
Walvis Bay
BOTSWANA
Gaborone
NAMIBIA
Pretoria
Johannesburg
Maputo
Mbabane
SWAZILAND
Maseru
LESOTHO
Durban
SOUTH AFRICA
Orange
Cape Town
Port Elizabeth
Bassas da India (FRANCE)
Europa Island (FRANCE)

Indian Ocean

Scale 1:51,400,000
Azimuthal Equal-Area Projection

0   800 Kilometers
0   800 Miles

Boundary representation is
not necessarily authoritative.

Asia

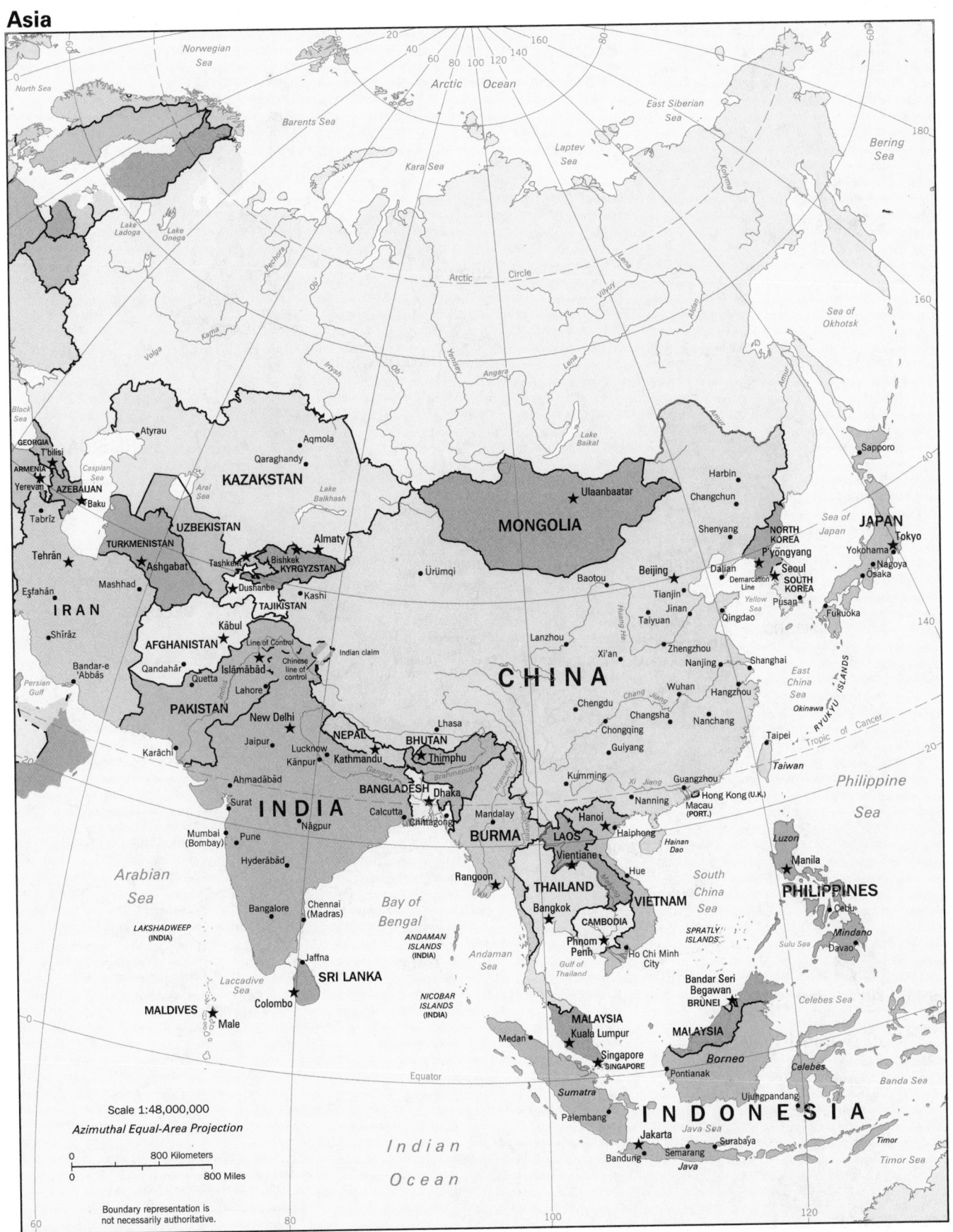

North Sea
Norwegian Sea
Barents Sea
Arctic Ocean
Kara Sea
Laptev Sea
East Siberian Sea
Bering Sea

Lake Ladoga
Lake Onega
Pechora
Ob'
Irtysh
Yenisey
Lena
Vilyuy
Kolyma
Aldan
Amur

GEORGIA
T'bilisi
ARMENIA
Yerevan
AZEBAIJAN
Baku
Tabrîz
Tehrân
Eşfahân
Shîrâz
Bandar-e Abbâs

Black Sea
Caspian Sea
Aral Sea
Persian Gulf

IRAN

Atyrau
Aqmola
Qaraghandy
KAZAKSTAN
Lake Balkhash
UZBEKISTAN
Almaty
Tashkent
Bishkek
KYRGYZSTAN
Ashgabat
TURKMENISTAN
Mashhad
Dushanbe
TAJIKISTAN
Kashi
Ürümqi
AFGHANISTAN
Kâbul
Qandahâr
Quetta
Islâmâbâd
Lahore
PAKISTAN
Karâchi
Ahmadâbâd
Surat
Mumbai (Bombay)
Pune
Hyderâbâd
Bangalore
Chennai (Madras)

Line of Control
Chinese line of control
Indian claim
Lhasa
NEPAL
Kathmandu
Lucknow
Kânpur
New Delhi
Jaipur
BHUTAN
Thimphu
BANGLADESH
Dhaka
Calcutta
Chittagong
Nâgpur

INDIA

Lake Baikal
Ulaanbaatar
MONGOLIA

Harbin
Changchun
Shenyang
NORTH KOREA
P'yongyang
Demarcation Line
SOUTH KOREA
Seoul
Pusan
Dalian
Beijing
Baotou
Tianjin
Jinan
Qingdao
Taiyuan
Zhengzhou
Lanzhou
Xi'an
Nanjing
Shanghai
Chengdu
Wuhan
Hangzhou
Chongqing
Changsha
Nanchang
Guiyang
Kunming
Guangzhou
Nanning
Hong Kong (U.K.)
Macau (PORT.)
Taipei
Taiwan

CHINA

Huang He
Chang Jiang
Xi Jiang

Sea of Japan
JAPAN
Sapporo
Tokyo
Yokohama
Nagoya
Osaka
Fukuoka
Yellow Sea
East China Sea
Okinawa
RYUKYU ISLANDS
Tropic of Cancer

Philippine Sea

Mandalay
Hanoi
Haiphong
Hainan Dao
BURMA
LAOS
Vientiane
Hue
Rangoon
THAILAND
Bangkok
CAMBODIA
Phnom Penh
Ho Chi Minh City
VIETNAM
South China Sea
SPRATLY ISLANDS

Luzon
Manila
PHILIPPINES
Cebu
Mindano
Davao
Sulu Sea

Arabian Sea
LAKSHADWEEP (INDIA)
Laccadive Sea
SRI LANKA
Jaffna
Colombo
MALDIVES
Male

Bay of Bengal
ANDAMAN ISLANDS (INDIA)
Andaman Sea
NICOBAR ISLANDS (INDIA)
Gulf of Thailand

Bandar Seri Begawan
BRUNEI
MALAYSIA
Kuala Lumpur
MALAYSIA
Medan
Singapore
SINGAPORE
Pontianak
Borneo
Celebes Sea
Celebes

Equator

Sumatra
Palembang
Jakarta
Bandung
Semarang
Surabâya
Java
Java Sea
Ujungpandang
INDONESIA
Banda Sea
Timor
Timor Sea

Indian Ocean

Scale 1:48,000,000
Azimuthal Equal-Area Projection

0   800 Kilometers
0   800 Miles

Boundary representation is
not necessarily authoritative.

B21

Europe

Serbia and Montenegro have asserted the formation of a joint independent state, but this entity has not been formally recognized as a state by the United States.

F.Y.R.O.M. - The Former Yugoslav Republic of Macedonia

Greenland (DENMARK)

Jan Mayen (NORWAY)

Greenland Sea

Denmark Strait

Norwegian Sea

Hammerfest

Tromsø

Murmansk

ICELAND

Reykjavík

Arctic Circle

Kiruna

Barents Sea

White Sea

Arkhangel'sk

Severnaya Dvina

NORWAY

Luleå

Oulu

Lake Onega

Lake Ladoga

Tórshavn   Faroe Islands (DENMARK)

Umeå

FINLAND

Tampere

Trondheim

SWEDEN

Gulf of Bothnia

SHETLAND ISLANDS

Bergen

Gävle   Turku   Helsinki   St. Petersburg

Rockall (U.K.)

HEBRIDES   ORKNEY ISLANDS

Oslo   Stockholm   *ALAND ISLANDS*   *Gulf of Finland*   Tallinn

RUSSIA

Volga

North Atlantic Ocean

Stavanger   *Skagerrak*   Göteborg   *Gotland*   ESTONIA   Moscow

Aberdeen   *Kattegat*   *Öland*   *Baltic Sea*   LATVIA   Rīga   Smolensk

Glasgow   Edinburgh   *North Sea*   DENMARK   LITHUANIA   Vitsyebsk   *Dnepr*

Belfast   UNITED   Copenhagen   Malmö   Vilnius   Mahilyow   *Dvina*

Dublin   KINGDOM   *Irish Sea*   Leeds   Manchester   Hamburg   Bremen   Berlin   Kaliningrad   RUSSIA   Minsk   BELARUS   Homyel   Kiev

IRELAND   Isle of Man (U.K.)   Liverpool   Gdańsk   Hrodna   Brest

Cardiff   Birmingham   Amsterdam   NETH.   Poznań   Warsaw

Celtic Sea   London   Rotterdam   Essen   Leipzig   *Oder*   POLAND   Rivne

Guernsey (U.K.)   Brussels   Cologne   Łódź   *Vistula*   L'viv   UKRAINE

Jersey (U.K.)   BEL.   Bonn   GERMANY   Wrocław   Kraków   Chernivtsi   Mykolayiv

English Channel   Lille   Luxembourg   Frankfurt am Main   Prague   CZECH REPUBLIC   Brno   SLOVAKIA   Cluj-Napoca   Chişinău   Odesa

Paris   LUX.   Stuttgart   Munich   Vienna   Bratislava   Budapest   MOLDOVA   Iaşi

Nantes   Strasbourg   LIECH.   AUSTRIA   HUNGARY   ROMANIA

Loire   Zürich   Vaduz   Ljubljana   Zagreb   Bucharest   Constanţa

FRANCE   Bern   SWITZ.   Milan   SLOVENIA   CROATIA   Belgrade   *Danube*   *Black Sea*

Bay of Biscay   Geneva   Lyon   Turin   Venice   *Po*   BOSNIA AND   Serbia   Varna

Bilbao   Bordeaux   Genoa   HERZEGOVINA   BULGARIA

Toulouse   MONACO   SAN MARINO   Sarajevo   Montenegro   Sofia

Porto   Andorra la Vella   Marseille   Florence   Podgorica   Skopje

Zaragoza   ANDORRA   *Ligurian Sea*   ITALY   Tirane   F.Y.R.O.M.   Thessaloníki

PORTUGAL   Madrid   Barcelona   *Corsica (FRANCE)*   Rome   ALB.   *Aegean Sea*

Lisbon   SPAIN   Valencia   VATICAN CITY   Naples

Tagus   *Balearic Sea*   *Sardinia*   *Tyrrhenian Sea*   GREECE   *Rhodes*

Sevilla   *BALEARIC ISLANDS*   Cagliari   Palermo   Athens

Gibraltar (U.K.)   Málaga   *Ionian Sea*   *Crete*

Strait of Gibraltar   *Alborán Sea*   *Mediterranean Sea*   *Sicily*

Scale 1: 19,500,000

Lambert Conformal Conic Projection, standard parallels 40 N and 56 N

MALTA   Valletta

300 Kilometers

300 Miles

Oceania

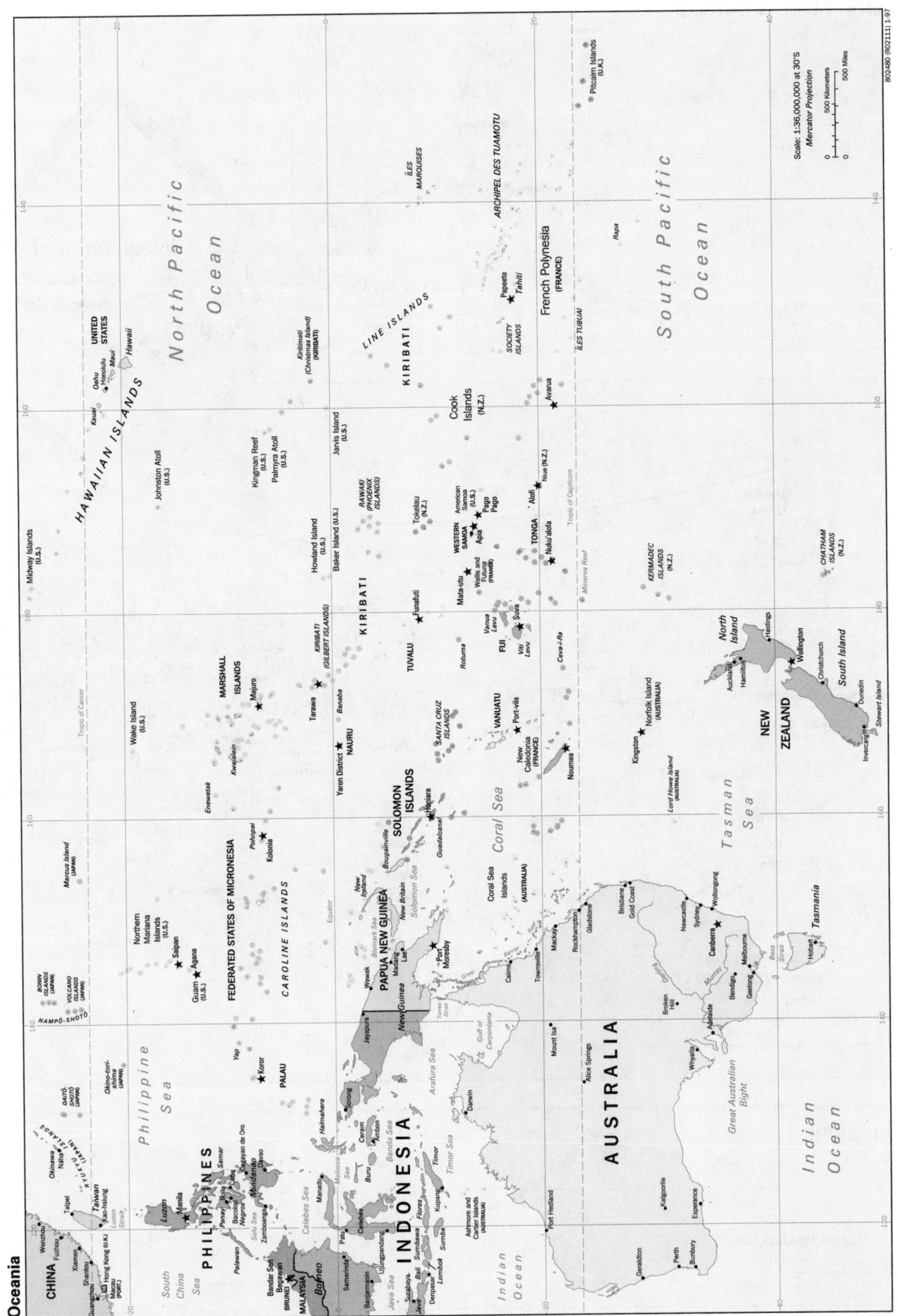

UNITED STATES

Chukchi Sea

Barrow

Prudhoe Bay

70

Arctic Circle

Nome
Bering Strait

Fairbanks

Alaska

60

Bering Sea

Anchorage
Valdez

Bethel

Juneau

Gulf of Alaska

Ketchikan

ALEUTIAN ISLANDS

170

180

170

160

150

140

Scale 1:37,000,000

0   400 Kilometers

0   400 Miles

(R02418)

Scale 1:360,000

0   5 Kilometers

0   5 Miles

White House

Washington, D.C.

The Mall   U.S. Capitol

Virginia

Pentagon

(R02437)

130   120   110   100   90   80

50

Seattle
Olympia
Washington

Salem
Oregon

Montana

North Dakota

Bismarck

Augusta

Maine

Helena

Idaho

Boise

South Dakota
Pierre

Minnesota

St. Paul

Wisconsin

Madison

Michigan

Lansing

Detroit

Toronto

Montpelier
N.H.
Vt.

Concord
Boston

Albany   Mass.
Providence
Hartford   R.I.

New York
Trenton

Conn.

40

Wyoming

Sacramento   Carson City
Nevada

San Francisco

California

Salt Lake City

Cheyenne

Utah

Denver

Colorado

Nebraska

Lincoln

Iowa

Des Moines

Chicago

Illinois   Indiana

Springfield   Indianapolis

Columbus

Ohio

Pennsylvania

Harrisburg

Philadelphia
New Jersey
Dover
Md.   Del.

Washington, D.C.

70

Las Vegas

Santa Fe

Topeka

Kansas

St. Louis
Jefferson City
Missouri

Frankfort

Charleston

West
Virginia

Richmond

Virginia

Raleigh

North Carolina

Los Angeles

Arizona

Phoenix

New Mexico

Oklahoma

Oklahoma City

Arkansas

Little Rock

Memphis

Tennessee

Nashville

Kentucky

Columbia

South
Carolina

North Pacific Ocean

Dallas

Jackson
Mississippi   Alabama

Montgomery

Atlanta

Georgia

North Atlantic Ocean

30

⊙ **State capital**

Scale 1:27,000,000

Albers Equal-Area Projection
standard parallels 28°30'N and 45°30'N

0   500 Kilometers

0   500 Miles

Austin

Texas

Baton Rouge

New Orleans

Louisiana

Tallahassee

Florida

Miami

Houston

Gulf of Mexico

100   90   80

Hawaii

170   180   170   160   150   140

25

Midway Islands (U.S.)

NORTHWESTERN HAWAIIAN ISLANDS

North Pacific Ocean

25

Tropic of Cancer

Scale 1:34,000,000

0   400 Kilometers

0   400 Miles

Kauai
Oahu   Honolulu

Maui

Hawaii

180   170   160   150

20

B24

Canada

ICELAND
Reykjavík
Arctic Circle

Denmark Strait

Greenland (DENMARK)

Nuuk (Godthab)

Davis Strait

Baffin Bay

Baffin Island

Iqaluit (Frobisher Bay)

Labrador Sea

Island of Newfoundland

Saint John's

St. Pierre and Miquelon (FRANCE)

Sydney
Charlottetown
Fredericton
Halifax
Saint John
NOVA SCOTIA

Gulf of St. Lawrence

NEWFOUNDLAND

Happy Valley–Goose Bay

Schefferville

Ivugivik

Chisasibi (Fort George)

QUEBEC

Québec
Montréal
Ottawa
Toronto
Hamilton
Windsor
Lake Ontario
Lake Erie

Washington, D.C.

North Atlantic

Alert

Ellesmere Island

QUEEN ELIZABETH ISLANDS

Kaujjuitoq (Resolute)

Cambridge Bay

Victoria Island

Banks Island

NORTHWEST TERRITORIES

C A N A D A

Kangiqcliniq (Rankin Inlet)

Churchill

Hudson Bay

Moosonee

ONTARIO

Thunder Bay

Lake Superior
Lake Michigan
Lake Huron

Echo Bay

Arctic Circle

Great Bear Lake

Yellowknife

Hay River
Slave River
Great Slave Lake

Mackenzie River

Inuvik

Beaufort Sea

Arctic Ocean

Lake Athabasca

Peace River

SASKATCHEWAN

MANITOBA

Saskatoon
Regina

Winnipeg
Lake Winnipeg
Nelson River

Missouri
Mississippi River
Arkansas River

U N I T E D   S T A T E S

ALBERTA

Edmonton
Calgary

Saskatchewan River

BRITISH COLUMBIA

Prince Rupert
Prince George
Vancouver
Victoria

Whitehorse
Watson Lake
Dawson
Yukon River

UNITED STATES

Gulf of Alaska

Columbia River
Snake River
Colorado River
Ohio River

North Pacific Ocean

RUSSIA

Chukchi Sea

Bering Strait

Bering Sea

Flags of the World

Afghanistan
Capital: Kabul
Currency: afghani
Language: Afghan Persian (or Dari Persian), Pashtu, others
Location: S. Asia

Albania
Capital: Tiranë
Currency: lek
Language: Albanian, Greek
Location: E. Europe

Algeria
Capital: Algiers
Currency: Algerian dinar
Language: Arabic, Berber dialects, French
Location: N. Africa

Andorra
Capital: Andorra la Vella
Currency: euro, French franc, Spanish peseta
Language: Catalan, French, Castilian
Location: W. Europe

Angola
Capital: Luanda
Currency: kwanza
Language: Portuguese, Bantu, other African languages
Location: S. Africa

Antigua & Barbuda
Capital: St. John's
Currency: East Caribbean dollar
Language: English
Location: Caribbean Sea

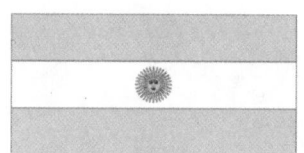

Argentina
Capital: Buenos Aires
Currency: Argentine peso
Language: Spanish, English, Italian, German, French
Location: S. South America

Armenia
Capital: Yerevan
Currency: dram
Language: Armenian
Location: SW. Asia

Australia
Capital: Canberra
Currency: Australian dollar
Language: English, aboriginal languages
Location: Oceania

Austria
Capital: Vienna
Currency: euro, Austrian schilling[1]
Language: German, Slovene, Croatian, Hungarian
Location: C. Europe

Azerbaijan
Capital: Baku
Currency: Azerbaijani manat
Language: Azerbaijani (Azeri), Russian, Armenian
Location: SW. Asia

Bahamas, The
Capital: Nassau
Currency: Bahamian dollar
Language: English, Creole
Location: Caribbean Sea

Bahrain
Capital: Manama
Currency: Bahrain dinar
Language: Arabic, English, Farsi, Urdu
Location: Asia (or Middle East)

Bangladesh
Capital: Dhaka
Currency: taka
Language: Bangla (Bengali), English
Location: S. Asia

Barbados
Capital: Bridgetown
Currency: Barbadian dollar
Language: English
Location: Caribbean Sea

Belarus
Capital: Minsk
Currency: Belarusian rubel
Language: Byelorussian (Belarusian), Russian
Location: E. Europe

Key: 1=former currency, 2=Communauté Financière Africaine (African Financial Community)

Flags of the World

Belgium
Capital: Brussels
Currency: euro, Belgian franc[1]
Language: Dutch, French, German
Location: W. Europe

Belize
Capital: Belmopan
Currency: Belizean dollar
Language: English, Spanish, Mayan, Garifuna (Carib), Creole
Location: Central America

Benin
Capital: Porto-Novo
Currency: CFA franc[2]
Language: French, Fon, Yoruba, other African Languages
Location: W. Africa

Bhutan
Capital: Thimphu
Currency: ngultrum, Indian rupee
Language: Dzongkha, Tibetan and Nepalese dialects
Location: S. Asia

Bolivia
Capital: Sucre and La Paz
Currency: boliviano
Language: Spanish, Quechua, Aymara
Location: C. South America

Bosnia and Herzogovina
Capital: Sarajevo
Currency: marka
Language: Croatian, Serbian, Bosnian
Location: E. Europe

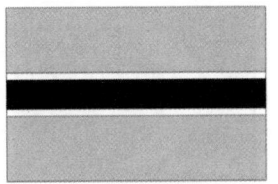

Botswana
Capital: Gaborone
Currency: pula
Language: English, Setswana
Location: S. Africa

Brazil
Capital: Brasilia
Currency: real
Language: Portuguese, Spanish, English, French
Location: E. South America

Brunei
Capital: Bandar Seri Begawan
Currency: Brunei dollar
Language: Malay, English, Chinese
Location: SE. Asia

Bulgaria
Capital: Sofia
Currency: lev
Language: Bulgarian, Turkish
Location: E. Europe

Burkina Faso
Capital: Ouagadougou
Currency: CFA franc[2]
Language: French, Sudanic tribal languages
Location: W. Africa

Burundi
Capital: Bujumbura
Currency: Burundi franc
Language: Kirundi, French, Swahili
Location: C. Africa

Cambodia
Capital: Phnom Penh
Currency: riel
Language: Khmer, French, English
Location: SE. Asia

Cameroon
Capital: Yaounde
Currency: CFA franc[2]
Language: English, French, other African Languages
Location: W. Africa

Canada
Capital: Ottawa
Currency: Canadian dollar
Language: English, French
Location: N. North America

Cape Verde
Capital: Praia
Currency: Cape Verdean escudo
Language: Portuguese, Crioulo
Location: Altantic Ocean off Africa

Flags of the World

Central African Republic
Capital: Bangui
Currency: CFA franc[2]
Language: French, Sangho, Arabic, Hansa, Swahili
Location: C. Africa

Chad
Capital: N'Djamena
Currency: CFA franc[2]
Language: French, Arabic, African languages
Location: C. Africa

Chile
Capital: Santiago
Currency: Chilean peso
Language: Spanish
Location: S. South America

China, People's Republic of
Capital: Beijing
Currency: yuan
Language: Mandarin, Yue, Wu, Minbei, Minnan, Xiang, Gan, Hakka dialects, others
Location: E. Asia

Colombia
Capital: Bogotá
Currency: Colombian peso
Language: Spanish
Location: N. South America

Comoros
Capital: Moroni
Currency: Comoros franc
Language: Arabic, French, Comoran
Location: Indian Ocean off Africa

Congo, Republic of the
Capital: Brazzaville
Currency: CFA franc[2]
Language: French, Lingala, Monokutuba, Kikongo, others
Location: C. Africa

Congo, Dem. Rep. of the
Capital: Kinshasa
Currency: Congolese franc
Language: French, Bantu languages
Location: W. Africa

Costa Rica
Capital: San José
Currency: Costa Rican colón
Language: Spanish
Location: Central America

Côte d'Ivoire (Ivory Coast)
Capital: Yamoussoukro
Currency: CFA franc[2]
Language: French, Dioula, other African languages
Location: W. Africa

Croatia
Capital: Zagreb
Currency: Kuna
Language: Croatian
Location: E. Europe

Cuba
Capital: Havana
Currency: Cuban peso
Language: Spanish
Location: Caribbean Sea

Cyprus
Capital: Nicosia
Currency: Cyprus pound, Turkish lira
Language: Greek, Turkish, English
Location: Mediterranean Sea

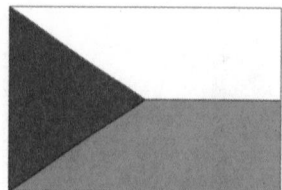

Czech Republic
Capital: Prague
Currency: Czech koruna
Language: Czech
Location: C. Europe

Denmark
Capital: Copenhagen
Currency: Danish krone
Language: Danish, Faroese
Location: N. Europe

Djibouti
Capital: Djibouti
Currency: Djiboutian franc
Language: Arabic, French, Afar, Somali
Location: E. Africa

Key: 1=former currency, 2=Communauté Financière Africaine (African Financial Community)

Flags of the World

Dominica
Capital: Roseau
Currency: East Caribbean dollar
Language: English, French patois
Location: Caribbean Sea

Dominican Republic
Capital: Santo Domingo
Currency: Dominican peso
Language: Spanish, English
Location: Caribbean Sea

Ecuador
Capital: Quito
Currency: U.S. dollar
Language: Spanish, Quéchua
Location: South America

Egypt
Capital: Cairo
Currency: Egyptian pound
Language: Arabic, English, French
Location: Africa

El Salvador
Capital: San Salvador
Currency: Salvadoran colón, U.S. dollar
Language: Spanish, Nahua
Location: Central America

Equatorial Guinea
Capital: Malabo
Currency: CFA franc[2]
Language: Spanish, French, pidgin English, Fang, Bubi, Ibo
Location: W. Africa

Eritrea
Capital: Asmara
Currency: nafka
Language: Tigre, Tigrinya, Afar, Amharic, Arabic, Kunama, others
Location: E. Africa

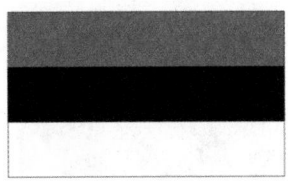

Estonia
Capital: Tallinn
Currency: Estonian kroon
Language: Estonian, Russian, Ukrainian, Finnish, English
Location: E. Europe

Ethiopia
Capital: Addis Ababa
Currency: birr
Language: Amharic, Tigrinya, Oromigna, others
Location: E. Africa

Fiji
Capital: Suva
Currency: Fijian dollar
Language: English, Fijian, Hindustani
Location: Oceania

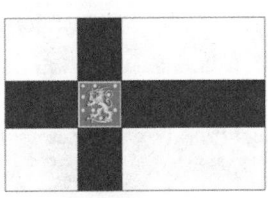

Finland
Capital: Helsinki
Currency: euro, markka
Language: Finnish, Swedish
Location: N. Europe

France
Capital: Paris
Currency: euro, French franc
Language: French
Location: W. Europe

Gabon
Capital: Libreville
Currency: CFA franc
Language: French, Bantu languages
Location: W. Africa

Gambia, The
Capital: Banjul
Currency: dalasi
Language: English, Mandinka, Wolof, Fula
Location: W. Africa

Georgia
Capital: T'bilisi
Currency: lari
Language: Georgian, Russian
Location: S.W. Asia

Germany
Capital: Berlin
Currency: euro, Deutsche mark[1]
Language: German
Location: C. Europe

Flags of the World

Ghana
Capital: Accra
Currency: cedi
Language: English,
  African languages
Location: W. Africa

Greece
Capital: Athens
Currency: euro, drachma[1]
Language: Greek,
  English, French
Location: S. Europe

Grenada
Capital: St. George's
Currency: East Caribbean
  dollar
Language: English,
  French patois
Location: Caribbean Sea

Guatemala
Capital: Guatemala City
Currency: quetzal,
  U.S. dollar, others
Language: Spanish,
  Mayan languages
Location: Central America

Guinea
Capital: Conakry
Currency: Guinean franc
Language: French,
  African languages
Location: W. Africa

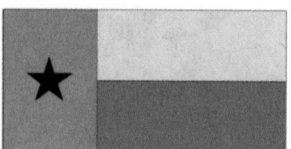

Guinea-Bissau
Capital: Bissau
Currency: CFA franc[2]
Language: Portuguese,
  Crioulo, African languages
Location: W. Africa

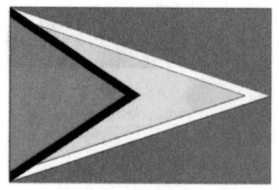

Guyana
Capital: Georgetown
Currency: Guyana dollar
Language: English, Creole,
  Hindi, Urdu, native South
  American languages
Location: N. South America

Haiti
Capital: Port-au-Prince
Currency: gourde
Language: Creole, French
Location: Caribbean Sea

Honduras
Capital: Tegucigalpa
Currency: lempira
Language: Spanish, native
  Central American languages
Location: Central America

Hungary
Capital: Budapest
Currency: forint
Language: Hungarian
Location: C. Europe

Iceland
Capital: Reykjavik
Currency: Icelandic krona
Language: Icelandic
Location: N. Europe

India
Capital: New Delhi
Currency: Indian rupee
Language: Hindi, English,
  many other languages
Location: S. Asia

Indonesia
Capital: Jakarta
Currency: Indonesian rupiah
Language: Bahasa Indone-
  sian, Dutch, English, others
Location: SE Asia

Iran
Capital: Tehran
Currency: Iranian rial
Language: Persian, Turkic,
  Kurdish, others
Location: Middle East (SW.
  Asia)

Iraq
Capital: Baghdad
Currency: Iraqi dinar
Language: Arabic, Kurdish,
  Assyrian, Armenian
Location: Middle East (SW.
  Asia)

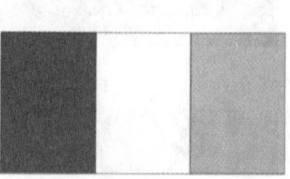

Ireland
Capital: Dublin
Currency: euro, Irish pound[1]
Language: English,
  Irish (Gaelic)
Location: W. Europe

Key: 1=former currency, 2=Communauté Financière Africaine (African Financial Community)

Flags of the World

Israel
Capital: Jerusalem
Currency: new Israeli shekel
Language: Hebrew,
Arabic, English
Location: Middle East (SW.
Asia)

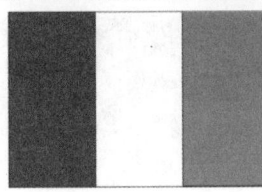

Italy
Capital: Rome
Currency: euro, Italian lira[1]
Language: Italian, others
Location: S. Europe

Jamaica
Capital: Kingston
Currency: Jamaican dollar
Language: English, Creole
Location: Caribbean Sea

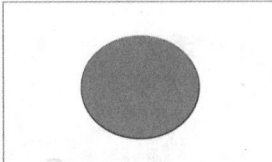

Japan
Capital: Tokyo
Currency: yen
Language: Japanese
Location: E. Asia

Jordan
Capital: Amman
Currency: Jordanian dinar
Language: Arabic, English
Location: Middle East (SW.
Asia)

Kazakhstan
Capital: Astana
Currency: tenge
Language: Russian, Kazakh
(or Qazaq)
Location: C. Asia

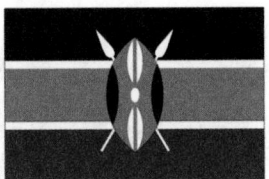

Kenya
Capital: Nairobi
Currency: Kenyan shilling
Language: English,
Kiswahili, others
Location: E. Africa

Kiribati
Capital: Tarawa
Currency: Australian dollar
Language: English, I-Kiribati
Location: Oceania

Korea, North
Capital: P'yongyang
Currency: North Korean won
Language: Korean
Location: E. Asia

Korea, South
Capital: Seoul
Currency: South Korean won
Language: Korean
Location: E. Asia

Kuwait
Capital: Kuwait
Currency: Kuwaiti dinar
Language: Arabic, English
Location: Middle East
(SW. Asia)

Kyrgyzstan
Capital: Bishkek
Currency: Kyrgyzstani som
Language: Kirghiz (or Kyrgyz),
Russian
Location: C. Asia

Latvia
Capital: Riga
Currency: Latvian lat
Language: Latvian (or Lettish),
Lithuanian, Russian
Location: E. Europe

Laos
Capital: Vientiane
Currency: kip
Language: Lao,
French, English
Location: SE. Asia

Lebanon
Capital: Beirut
Currency: Lebanese pound
Language: Arabic, French,
English, Armenian
Location: Middle East
(SW. Asia)

Lesotho
Capital: Maseru
Currency: loti,
South African rand
Language: Sesotho, English,
Zulu, Xhosa
Location: S. Africa

Flags of the World

Libya
Capital: Tripoli
Currency: Libyan dinar
Language: Arabic, Italian, English
Location: N. Africa

Liberia
Capital: Monrovia
Currency: Liberian dollar
Language: English, African languages
Location: W. Africa

Liechtenstein
Capital: Vaduz
Currency: Swiss franc
Language: German, Alemannic dialect
Location: C. Europe

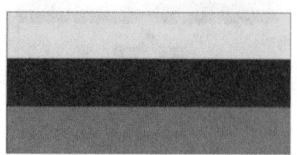

Lithuania
Capital: Vilnius
Currency: litas
Language: Lithuanian, Polish, Russian
Location: E. Europe

Luxembourg
Capital: Luxembourg
Currency: euro, Luxembourg franc[1]
Language: Luxembourgish, French, German
Location: W. Europe

Macedonia
Capital: Skopje
Currency: Macedonian denar
Language: Macedonian, Albanian, others
Location: SE. Europe

Madagascar
Capital: Antananarivo
Currency: Malagasy franc
Language: Malagasy, French
Location: Indian Ocean off Africa

Malawi
Capital: Lilongwe
Currency: Malawian kwacha
Language: English, Chichewa
Location: S. Africa

Malaysia
Capital: Kuala Lumpur
Currency: ringgit
Language: Bahasa Melayu, Chinese, Tamil, English
Location: Asia (South Pacific)

Maldives
Capital: Malé
Currency: rufiyaa
Language: Maldivian Dhivehi
Location: Indian Ocean

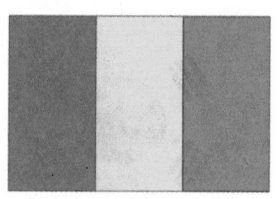

Mali
Capital: Bamako
Currency: CFA franc[2]
Language: French, Bambara, other African languages
Location: W. Africa

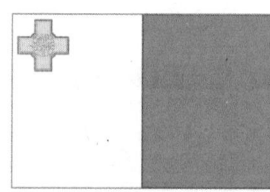

Malta
Capital: Valletta
Currency: Maltese lira
Language: Maltese, English
Location: Mediterranean Sea

Marshall Islands
Capital: Majuro
Currency: U.S. dollar
Language: English, Marshallese dialects, Japanese
Location: Oceania

Mauritania
Capital: Nouakchott
Currency: ouguiya
Language: Arabic, Wolof, French, others
Location: N. Africa

Mauritius
Capital: Port Louis
Currency: Mauritian rupee
Language: English, French, Creole, Hindi, others
Location: Indian Ocean

Mexico
Capital: Mexico City
Currency: Mexican peso
Language: Spanish, native Mexican languages
Location: S. North America

Key: 1=former currency, 2=Communauté Financière Africaine (African Financial Community)

Flags of the World

Micronesia
Capital: Palikir
Currency: U.S. dollar
Language: English, Trukese, Pohnpeian, others
Location: Oceania (South Pacific)

Moldova
Capital: Chisinau
Currency: Moldovan leu
Language: Moldovan (or Rumanian), Russian, Gagauz
Location: E. Europe

Monaco
Capital: Monaco
Currency: euro, French franc[1]
Language: French, English, Monegasque, Italian
Location: W. Europe

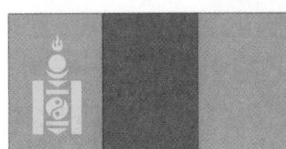

Mongolia
Capital: Ulaanvaator
Currency: togrog or tugrik
Language: Khalka Mongol (or Mongolian), Turkic, Russian
Location: N. Asia

Morocco
Capital: Rabat
Currency: Moroccan dirham
Language: Arabic, Berber dialects, French
Location: N. Africa

Mozambique
Capital: Maputo
Currency: metical
Language: Portuguese, native African languages
Location: Africa

Myanmar
Capital: Rangoon (Yangon)
Currency: kyat
Language: Burmese, Karen, others
Location: SE. Asia

Namibia
Capital: Windhoek
Currency: Namibian dollar, South African rand
Language: Afrikaans, English, German, native African languages
Location: S. Africa

Nauru
Capital: Yaren District
Currency: Australian dollar
Language: Nauruan, English
Location: Oceania (South Pacific)

Nepal
Capital: Kathmandu
Currency: Nepalese rupee
Language: Nepali, others
Location: S. Asia

Netherlands, The
Capital: Amsterdam
Currency: euro, Netherlands guilder[1]
Language: Dutch
Location: W. Europe

New Zealand
Capital: Wellington
Currency: New Zealand dollar
Language: English, Maori
Location: Oceania

Nicaragua
Capital: Managua
Currency: gold cordoba
Language: Spanish
Location: Central America

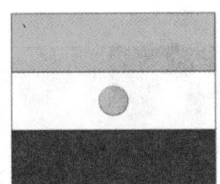

Niger
Capital: Niamey
Currency: CFA franc[2]
Language: French, Hausa, Djerma
Location: W. Africa

Nigeria
Capital: Abuja
Currency: naira
Language: English, Hausa, Yoruba, Igbo (Ibo), Fulani
Location: W. Africa

Norway
Capital: Oslo
Currency: Norwegian krone
Language: Norwegian
Location: N. Europe

Flags of the World

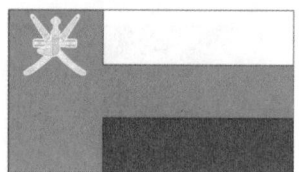

Oman
Capital: Muscat
Currency: Omani rial
Language: Arabic, others
Location: Middle East (SW Asia)

Pakistan
Capital: Islamabad
Currency: Pakistani rupee
Language: Punjabi, Sindhi, Urdu, English, others
Location: Asia

Palau, Republic of
Capital: Koror
Currency: U.S. dollar
Language: Palauan, English, others
Location: Oceania (South Pacific)

Panama
Capital: Panama City
Currency: balboa, U.S. dollar
Language: Spanish, English
Location: Central America

Papua New Guinea
Capital: Port Moresby
Currency: kina
Language: Melanesian and Papuan languages, pidgin English, English
Location: Oceania (South Pacific)

Paraguay
Capital: Asunción
Currency: guarani
Language: Spanish, Guarani
Location: C. South America

Peru
Capital: Lima
Currency: nuevo sol
Language: Spanish, Quechua, Aymara, others
Location: W. South America

Philippines
Capital: Manila
Currency: Philippine peso
Language: Filipino (based on Tagalog), English, regional languages
Location: Asia (South Pacific)

Poland
Capital: Warsaw
Currency: zloty
Language: Polish
Location: C. Europe

Portugal
Capital: Lisbon
Currency: euro, Portuguese escudo[1]
Language: Portuguese
Location: SW. Europe

Qatar
Capital: Doha
Currency: Qatari rial (or riyal)
Language: Arabic, English
Location: SW. Asia (or Middle East)

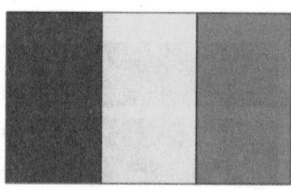

Romania
Capital: Bucharest
Currency: leu
Language: Romanian, Hungarian, German
Location: SE. Europe

Russia
Capital: Moscow
Currency: Russian ruble
Language: Russian, others
Location: N. Asia and E. Europe

Rwanda
Capital: Kigali
Currency: Rwandan franc
Language: Kinyarwanda, French, Swahili, English
Location: C. Africa

Samoa
Capital: Apia
Currency: tala
Language: Samoan (Polynesian), English
Location: South Pacific Ocean

San Marino
Capital: San Marino
Currency: euro, Italian lira[1]
Language: Italian
Location: S. Europe

Key: 1=former currency, 2=Communauté Financière Africaine (African Financial Community)

Flags of the World

Saõ Tomé and Príncipe
Capital: Saõ Tomé
Currency: dobra
Language: Portuguese
Location: Atlantic Ocean off Africa

Saudi Arabia
Capital: Riyadh
Currency: Saudi riyal
Language: Arabic
Location: SW Asia (or Middle East)

Senegal
Capital: Dakar
Currency: CFA franc[2]
Language: French, Wolof, others
Location: W. Africa

Seychelles
Capital: Victoria
Currency: Seychelles rupee
Language: English, French, Creole
Location: Indian Ocean

Sierra Leone
Capital: Freetown
Currency: leone
Language: English, Mende, Temne, Krio
Location: W. Africa

Singapore
Capital: Singapore
Currency: Singapore dollar
Language: Malay, Chinese, Tamil, English
Location: Asia (South Pacific)

Slovakia
Capital: Bratislava
Currency: Slovak koruna
Language: Slovak, Hungarian
Location: C. Europe

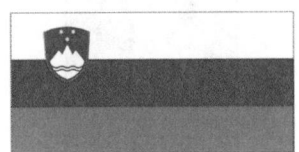

Slovenia
Capital: Ljubljana
Currency: Slovenian tolar
Language: Slovenian, Serbo-Croatian
Location: SE. Europe

Solomon Islands
Capital: Honiara
Currency: Solomon Islands dollar
Language: Melanesian Pidgin, English
Location: Oceania (south Pacific)

Somalia
Capital: Mogadishu
Currency: Somali shilling
Language: Somali, Arabic, English, Italian
Location: E. Africa

South Africa
Capital: Pretoria, Cape Town, Bloemfontein
Currency: rand
Language: Afrikaans, English, Bantu languages
Location: S. Africa

Spain
Capital: Madrid
Currency: euro, Spanish peseta[1]
Language: Castilian Spanish, Catalán, Galician, Basque
Location: SW Europe

Sri Lanka
Capital: Colombo
Currency: Sri Lankan rupee
Language: Sinhala, Tamil, English
Location: Indian Ocean off India

St. Kitts and Nevis
Capital: Basseterre
Currency: East Caribbean dollar
Language: English
Location: Caribbean Sea

St. Lucia
Capital: Castries
Currency: East Caribbean dollar
Language: English, French Patois
Location: Caribbean Sea

St. Vincent and the Grenadines
Capital: Kingstown
Currency: East Caribbean dollar
Language: English, French Patois
Location: Caribbean Sea

Flags of the World

Sudan
Capital: Khartoum
Currency: Sudanese dinar
Language: Arabic, English, African tribal dialects
Location: N. Africa

Suriname
Capital: Paramaribo
Currency: Surinamese guilder
Language: Dutch, English, Sranang Tongo, Hindustani
Location: N. South America

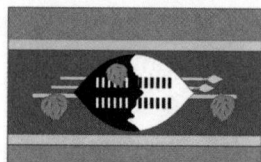

Swaziland
Capital: Mbabane
Currency: lilangeni
Language: Siswati (or siSwati), English
Location: S. Africa

Sweden
Capital: Stockholm
Currency: Swedish krona
Language: Swedish, Finnish, Lappish
Location: N. Europe

Switzerland
Capital: Bern (administrative), Lausanne (judicial)
Currency: Swiss franc
Language: German, French, Italian
Location: C. Europe

Syria
Capital: Damascus
Currency: Syrian pound
Language: Arabic, Kurdish, Armenian, others
Location: SW Asia (or Middle East)

Taiwan
Capital: Taipei
Currency: new Taiwan dollar
Language: Mandarin Chinese, Taiwanese, Hakka dialects
Location: Pacific Ocean off E. Asia

Tajikistan
Capital: Dushanbe
Currency: somoni
Language: Tajik, Russian
Location: C. Asia

Tanzania
Capital: Dar es Salaam
Currency: Tanzanian shilling
Language: Kiswahili or Swahili, English, Arabic, African languages
Location: E. Africa

Thailand
Capital: Bangkok
Currency: baht
Language: Thai, English, others
Location: SE. Asia

Togo
Capital: Lomé
Currency: CFA franc[2]
Language: French, Ewe, Mina, Kabye, Dagomba
Location: W. Africa

Tonga
Capital: Nuku'alofa
Currency: pa'anga
Language: Tongan, English
Location: Oceania (South Pacific)

Trinidad and Tobago
Capital: Port-of-Spain
Currency: Trinidad and Tobago dollar
Language: English, Hindi, others
Location: Caribbean Sea

Tunisia
Capital: Tunis
Currency: Tunisian dinar
Language: Arabic, French
Location: N. Africa

Turkey
Capital: Ankara
Currency: Turkish lira
Language: Turkish, Kurdish, Arabic
Location: SE. Europe and SW. Asia

Turkmenistan
Capital: Ashgabat
Currency: Turkmen manat
Language: Turkmen, Russian, Uzbek
Location: C. Asia

Key: 1=former currency, 2=Communauté Financière Africaine (African Financial Community)

Flags of the World

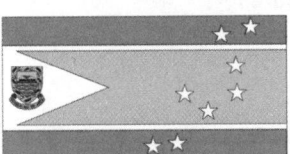

Tuvalu
Capital: Funafuti
Currency: Australian dollar,
Tuvaluan dollar
Language: Tuvaluan, English
Location: Oceania (South
Pacific)

Uganda
Capital: Kampala
Currency: Ugandan shilling
Language: English, Swahili,
Luganda, others
Location: E. Africa

Ukraine
Capital: Kiev
Currency: hryvnia
Language: Ukrainian,
Russian, others
Location: E. Europe

United Arab Emirates
Capital: Abu Dhabi
Currency: Emirati (or U.A.E.)
dirham
Language: Arabic, Persian,
English, Hindi, Urdu
Location: SW. Asia (or Middle
East)

United Kingdom
Capital: London
Currency: British pound (or
pound sterling)
Language: English, Welsh,
Scottish, Gaelic
Location: W. Europe

United States of America
Capital: Washington, D.C.
Currency: U.S. dollar
Language: English, Spanish
Location: North America

Uruguay
Capital: Montevideo
Currency: Uruguayan peso
Language: Spanish,
Portunol, Brazilero
Location: S. South America

Uzbekistan
Capital: Tashkent
Currency: Uzbekistani sum
Language: Uzbek, Russian
Location: C. Asia

Vanuatu
Capital: Port-Vila
Currency: vatu
Language: English, French,
pidgin (Bislama)
Location: Oceania (South
Pacific)

Vatican City
Capital: Vatican City
Currency: euro, Vatican lira
Language: Latin, Italian, others
Location: S. Europe

Venezuela
Capital: Caracas
Currency: bolivar
Language: Spanish, native
South American languages
Location: N. South America

Vietnam
Capital: Hanoi
Currency: dong
Language: Vietnamese, French,
English, Khmer, Chinese
Location: SE. Asia

Yemen
Capital: Sanaá
Currency: Yemeni rial
Language: Arabic
Location: SW. Asia
(or Middle East)

Yugoslavia
Capital: Belgrade
Currency: new Yugoslav dinar
Language: Serbian
Location: SE. Europe

Zambia
Capital: Lusaka
Currency: Zambian kwacha
Language: English,
Bantu languages
Location: S. Africa

Zimbabwe
Capital: Harare
Currency: Zimbabwean dollar
Language: English,
Sindebele, Shona
Location: S. Africa

United States Presidents 1789-2002

1. George Washington

Born: February 22, 1732 in Virginia
In Office: 1789-1797
Party: Federalist
Vice President: John Adams
Married: Martha Dandridge Custis
Died: December 14, 1799
Interesting Facts: only President who didn't live in Washington, D.C. during his presidency, because the capital was located in Philadelphia at the time; only President to be elected unanimously by the electoral college; turned down some of his supporters who wanted to make him King.

2. John Adams

Born: October 30, 1735 in Massachusetts
In Office: 1797-1801
Party: Federalist
Vice President: Thomas Jefferson
Married: Abigail Smith
Died: July 4, 1826
Interesting Facts: first President to live in the White House, although it was not yet called the White House; first Vice President of the United States, under George Washington.

3. Thomas Jefferson

Born: April 13, 1743 in Virginia
In Office: 1801-1809
Party: Democratic-Republican
Vice Presidents: Aaron Burr (1801-1805), George Clinton (1805-1809)
Married: Martha Wayles Skelton
Died: July 4, 1826
Interesting Facts: first President to shake hands with people instead of bowing to them; author of the Declaration of Independence; kept bears on display in cages on the White House lawn.

4. James Madison

Born: March 16, 1751 in Virginia
In Office: 1809-1817
Party: Democratic-Republican
Vice Presidents: George Clinton (1809-1812), Elbridge Gerry (1813-1814)
Married: Dolley Payne Todd
Died: June 28, 1836
Interesting Facts: first President to wear long trousers instead of knee breeches; at 5 feet, 4 inches and about 100 pounds, he was the shortest and lightest President.

5. James Monroe

Born: April 28, 1758 in Virginia
In Office: 1817-1825
Party: Democratic-Republican
Vice President: Daniel D. Tompkins
Married: Elizabeth Kortright
Died: July 4, 1831
Interesting Facts: first President to ride on a steamboat; third of the first five Presidents to die on the 4th of July; first President to have his inauguration outdoors.

6. John Quincy Adams

Born: July 11, 1767 in Massachusetts
In Office: 1825-1829
Party: Democratic-Republican
Vice President: John C. Calhoun
Married: Louisa Catherine Johnson
Died: February 23, 1848
Interesting Facts: first son of a President to become President himself; first President to be photographed.

7. Andrew Jackson

Born: March 15, 1767 in South Carolina
In Office: 1829-1837
Party: Democratic
Vice Presidents: John C. Calhoun (1829-1832), Martin Van Buren (1833-1837)
Married: Rachel Donelson Robards
Died: June 8, 1845
Interesting Facts: first President to be born in a log cabin; first President to ride on a railroad train; only President who served in both the Revolutionary War and the War of 1812; only President to have been a prisoner of war; became a soldier at age 13.

8. Martin Van Buren

Born: December 5, 1782 in New York
In Office: 1837-1841
Party: Democratic
Vice President: Richard M. Johnson
Married: Hannah Hoes
Died: July 24, 1862
Interesting Facts: first President to be born a citizen of the United States; owned two tiger cubs as pets in the White House.

9. William Henry Harrison

Born: February 9, 1773 in Virginia
In Office: 1841
Party: Whig
Vice President: John Tyler
Married: Anna Tuthill Symmes
Died: April 4, 1841
Interesting Facts: served the shortest time in office of any President; first President to die in office. Harrison delivered the longest inaugural address of any President on an extremely cold day and while not wearing a hat. He became ill and died in the White House one month later.

10. John Tyler

Born: March 29, 1790 in Virginia
In Office: 1841-1845
Party: Whig
Vice President: None
Married: Letitia Christian, Julia Gardiner
Died: January 18, 1862
Interesting Facts: had more children than any other President, a total of 15 children; the tradition of playing "Hail to the Chief" whenever a President appears at state functions was started by Tyler's second wife, Julia.

11. James Knox Polk

Born: November 2, 1795 in North Carolina
In Office: 1845-1849
Party: Democratic
Vice President: George M. Dallas
Married: Sarah Childress
Died: June 15, 1849
Interesting Facts: had the first gas lights installed in the White House; survived a gallstone operation at age 17 without anesthesia or antiseptics, as those medical practices were not in use at the time; for the first time, news of the President's nomination was spread using the telegraph.

12. Zachary Taylor

Born: November 24, 1784 in Virginia
In Office: 1849-1850
Party: Whig
Vice President: Millard Fillmore
Married: Margaret Mackall Smith
Died: July 9, 1850
Interesting Facts: never voted until he was 62 years old because he had been a soldier and was always moving from place to place; his was the first presidential election held on the same day in every state.

13. Millard Fillmore

Born: January 7, 1800 in New York
In Office: 1850-1853
Party: Whig
Vice President: None
Married: Abigail Powers, Caroline Carmichael McIntosh
Died: March 8, 1874
Interesting Facts: installed the first permanent library, the first kitchen stove, and the first bathtub in the White House.

14. Franklin Pierce

Born: November 23, 1804 in New Hampshire
In Office: 1853-1857
Party: Democratic
Vice President: William R.D. King
Married: Jane Means Appleton
Died: October 8, 1869
Interesting Facts: installed the first central heating system and the first bathroom with hot and cold water in the White House.

15. James Buchanan

Born: April 23, 1791 in Pennsylvania
In Office: 1857-1861
Party: Democratic
Vice President: John C. Breckinridge
Married: never married
Died: June 1, 1868
Interesting Facts: only President to never be married; first to send a transatlantic telegram.

16. Abraham Lincoln

Born: February 12, 1809 in Kentucky
In Office: 1861-1865
Party: Republican
Vice Presidents: Hannibal Hamlin (1861-1865), Andrew Johnson (1865)
Married: Mary Todd
Died: April 15, 1865
Interesting Facts: writer of the Emancipation Proclamation, which declared slavery unlawful; first President born outside the original 13 Colonies; first President to die by assassination; first president to wear a beard; tallest President.

17. Andrew Johnson

Born: December 29, 1808 in North Carolina
In Office: 1865-1869
Party: Democratic
Vice President: None
Married: Eliza McCardle
Died: July 31, 1875
Interesting Facts: first President to be impeached; first President to be visited by a Queen (Queen Emma of the Sandwich Islands); did not learn to read until he was 17.

18. Ulysses Simpson Grant

Born: April 27, 1822 in Ohio
In Office: 1869-1877
Party: Republican
Vice Presidents: Schuyler Colfax (1869-1873), Henry Wilson (1873-1875)
Married: Julia Boggs Dent
Died: July 23, 1885
Interesting Facts: signed the legislation that created Yellowstone National Park, the country's first national park; first President to have both parents alive when he took office.

19. Rutherford Birchard Hayes

Born: October 4, 1822 in Ohio
In Office: 1877-1881
Party: Republican
Vice President: William A. Wheeler
Married: Lucy Ware Webb
Died: January 17, 1893
Interesting Facts: had the first telephone installed in the White House; first President to graduate from law school; first President whose wife graduated from college.

20. James Abram Garfield

Born: November 19, 1831 in Ohio
In Office: 1881
Party: Republican
Vice President: Chester A. Arthur
Married: Lucretia Rudolph
Died: September 19, 1881
Interesting Facts: last of seven Presidents born in log cabins; first President who could write with either his left hand or his right hand; died of blood poisoning after he was shot and doctors kept trying to remove the bullet with instruments that were not sterile.

21. Chester Alan Arthur

Born: October 5, 1829 in Vermont
In Office: 1881-1885
Party: Republican
Vice President: None
Married: Ellen Lewis Herndon
Died: November 18, 1886
Interesting Facts: destroyed all of his personal papers before he died.

22. Grover Cleveland

Born: March 18, 1837 in New Jersey
In Office: 1885-1889, 1893-1897
Party: Democratic
Vice President: Thomas A. Hendricks (1885), Adlai E. Stevenson (1893-1897)
Married: Frances Folsom
Died: June 24, 1908
Interesting Facts: only President to serve one term, lose an election, and then come back to serve another term; first President to appear in a movie; answered the White House telephone personally.

23. Benjamin Harrison

Born: August 20, 1833 in Ohio
In Office: 1889-1893
Party: Republican
Vice President: Levi P. Morton
Married: Caroline Lavinia Scott, Mary Scott Lord Dimmick
Died: March 13, 1901
Interesting Facts: first President to have electric lights and electricity installed in the White House; grandson of former President William Henry Harrison.

24. Grover Cleveland, second term

25. William McKinley

Born: January 29, 1843 in Ohio
In Office: 1897-1901
Party: Republican
Vice President: Garret A. Hobart (1897-1899), Theodore Roosevelt (1901)
Married: Ida Saxton
Died: September 14, 1901
Interesting Facts: third President to die by assassination; first President to ride in an automobile; first President to use the telephone for campaigning; had a pet parrot in the White House that could whistle "Yankee Doodle."

26. Theodore Roosevelt

Born: October 27, 1858 in New York
In Office: 1901-1909
Party: Republican
Vice President: Charles W. Fairbanks
Married: Alice Hathaway Lee, Edith Kermit Carow
Died: January 16, 1919
Interesting Facts: first President to ride in an airplane, shortly after he left office; youngest person to become President when he took over for McKinley, who had been shot (Kennedy was the youngest person to win a Presidential election); first President and first American to win the Nobel Peace Prize; only President to have a stuffed animal named after him — the teddy bear.

27. William Howard Taft

Born: September 15, 1857 in Ohio
In Office: 1909-1913
Party: Republican
Vice President: James Schoolcraft Sherman
Married: Helen Herron
Died: March 8, 1930
Interesting Facts: first President to own a car; last President to keep a cow for fresh milk on the White House lawn; first to throw out the first baseball of a season; heaviest President at 332 pounds; first President to appoint a woman to a major post in the federal government.

28. Woodrow Wilson

Born: December 28, 1856 in Virginia
In Office: 1913-1921
Party: Democratic
Vice President: Thomas R. Marshall
Married: Ellen Louise Axson, Edith Bolling Galt
Died: February 3, 1924
Interesting Facts: first President to hold a press conference; first President to have earned a Ph.D.; raised a flock of sheep on the White House lawn.

29. Warren Gamaliel Harding

Born: November 2, 1865 in Ohio
In Office: 1921-1923
Party: Republican
Vice President: Calvin Coolidge
Married: Florence Kling De Wolfe
Died: August 2, 1923
Interesting Facts: first President to own a radio and the first to give a speech over the radio airwaves; first President to visit Canada.

30. Calvin Coolidge

Born: July 4, 1872 in Vermont
In Office: 1923-1929
Party: Republican
Vice President: Charles G. Dawes
Married: Grace Anna Goodhue
Died: January 5, 1933
Interesting Facts: was sworn into office by his own father; kept many animals at the White House including numerous dogs and cats, a donkey, a goose, a pet raccoon, a bobcat, lion cubs, a pygmy hippo, a wallaby, and a bear.

31. Herbert Clark Hoover

Born: August 10, 1874 in Iowa
In Office: 1929-1933
Party: Republican
Vice President: Charles Curtis
Married: Lou Henry
Died: October 20, 1964
Interesting Facts: first President born west of the Mississippi River; approved the "Star-Spangled Banner" as the national anthem; first President to donate his salary to charity; had an asteroid named after him.

32. Franklin Delano Roosevelt

Born: January 30, 1882 in New York
In Office: 1933-1945
Party: Democratic
Vice Presidents: John Nance Garner (1933-1941),
Henry A. Wallace (1941-1945),
Harry S. Truman (1945)
Married: Anna Eleanor Roosevelt
Died: April 12, 1945
Interesting Facts: first President to appear on television; was in office longer than any other President.

33. Harry S. Truman

Born: May 8, 1884 in Missouri
In Office: 1945-1953
Party: Democratic
Vice President: Alben W. Barkley
Married: Elizabeth "Bess" Virginia Wallace
Died: December 26, 1972
Interesting Facts: did not have a middle name, only a middle initial; first President to travel underwater in a modern submarine; first President to order the dropping of atomic bombs on another country.

34. Dwight David Eisenhower

Born: October 14, 1890 in Texas
In Office: 1953-1961
Party: Republican
Vice President: Richard M. Nixon
Married: Mary "Mamie" Geneva Doud
Died: March 28, 1969
Interesting Facts: first President to preside over 50 states; first President to appear on color television; first President licensed to pilot a plane; first President to have a helicopter at the White House.

35. John Fitzgerald Kennedy

Born: May 29, 1917 in Massachusetts
In Office: 1961-1963
Party: Democratic
Vice President: Lyndon B. Johnson
Married: Jacqueline Lee Bouvier
Died: November 22, 1963
Interesting Facts: fourth President to die by assassination; the youngest person ever to win an election to become President; first Roman Catholic President; first President to win the Pulitzer Prize; first President who had served in the U.S. Navy; creator of the Peace Corps.

36. Lyndon Baines Johnson

Born: August 27, 1908 in Texas
In Office: 1963-1969
Party: Democratic
Vice President: Hubert H. Humphrey
Married: Claudia "Lady Bird" Alta Taylor
Died: January 22, 1973
Interesting Facts: was sworn in aboard an airplane; first President sworn in by a woman; during his administration first manned spacecraft orbited the moon.

37. Richard Milhous Nixon

Born: January 9, 1913 in California
In Office: 1969-1974
Party: Republican
Vice Presidents: Spiro T. Agnew (1969-1973),
Gerald R. Ford (1973-1974)
Married: Thelma "Pat" Catherine Ryan
Died: April 22, 1994
Interesting Facts: only President to resign to avoid impeachment; first President to visit China.

38. Gerald Rudolph Ford

Born: July 14, 1913 in Nebraska
In Office: 1974-1977
Party: Republican
Vice President: Nelson A. Rockefeller
Married: Elizabeth "Betty" Bloomer Warren
Interesting Facts: first President not elected by the people to become president – he became Vice President when Nixon's elected Vice President, Spiro T. Agnew, resigned, and then became President when Nixon resigned.

39. James Earl Carter, Jr.

Born: October 1, 1924 in Georgia
In Office: 1977-1981
Party: Democratic
Vice President: Walter F. Mondale
Married: Eleanor Rosalynn Smith
Interesting Facts: the first President born in a hospital; first President sworn in using his nickname (Jimmy); first President to send his mother on a diplomatic mission.

40. Ronald Wilson Reagan

Born: February 6, 1911 in Illinois
In Office: 1981-1989
Party: Republican
Vice President: George H.W. Bush
Married: Jane Wyman, 'Nancy Davis
Interesting Facts: the oldest person to ever serve as President and the longest-lived President; the only professional actor to become President; first President to wear contact lenses; survived an attempted assassination.

41. George Herbert Walker Bush

Born: June 12, 1924 in Massachusetts
In Office: 1989-1993
Party: Republican
Vice President: J. Danforth Quayle
Married: Barbara Pierce
Interesting Facts: at one time was the youngest pilot in the Navy; received the Distinguished Flying Cross for heroism; first President to publicly refuse to eat broccoli.

42. William Jefferson Clinton

Born: August 19, 1946 in Arkansas
In Office: 1993-2001
Party: Democratic
Vice President: Albert Gore, Jr
Married: Hillary Rodham
Interesting Facts: the second U.S. President to have been impeached and found not guilty; first President to have been a Rhodes scholar; met President Kennedy as a boy and was inspired to enter a life of public service.

43. George Walker Bush

Born: July 6, 1946 in Connecticut
In Office: 2001-
Party: Republican
Vice President: Richard Cheney
Married: Laura Welch
Interesting Facts: was once a managing general partner of a professional baseball club; second son of a President to become President himself; was a cheerleader in high school.

U. S. State Facts

ALABAMA
Capital: Montgomery
U.S. Postal Abbreviation: AL
Date Admitted: Dec. 14, 1819
Rank: 22nd

Bird: yellowhammer
Tree: southern longleaf pine
Flower: camellia
Nicknames: Yellowhammer State, Heart of Dixie

GEORGIA
Capital: Atlanta
U.S. Postal Abbreviation: GA
Date Admitted: Jan. 2, 1788
Rank: 4th

Bird: brown thrasher
Tree: live oak
Flower: Cherokee rose
Nicknames: Peach State, Empire State of the South

ALASKA
Capital: Juneau
U.S. Postal Abbreviation: AK
Date Admitted: Jan. 3, 1959
Rank: 49th

Bird: willow ptarmigan
Tree: Sitka spruce
Flower: forget-me-not
Nickname: The Last Frontier

HAWAII
Capital: Honolulu
U.S. Postal Abbreviation: HI
Date Admitted: August 21, 1959
Rank: 50th

Bird: nene, or Hawaiian goose
Tree: kukui, or candlenut
Flower: pua aloalo, or hibiscus
Nickname: Aloha State

ARIZONA
Capital: Phoenix
U.S. Postal Abbreviation: AZ
Date Admitted: Feb. 14, 1912
Rank: 48th

Bird: cactus wren
Tree: palo verde
Flower: blossom of the saguaro cactus
Nickname: Grand Canyon State

IDAHO
Capital: Boise
U.S. Postal Abbreviation: ID
Date Admitted: July 3, 1890
Rank: 43rd

Bird: mountain bluebird
Tree: western white pine
Flower: syringa
Nickname: Gem State

ARKANSAS
Capital: Little Rock
U.S. Postal Abbreviation: AR
Date Admitted: June 15, 1836
Rank: 25th

Bird: mockingbird
Tree: loblolly pine
Flower: apple blossom
Nickname: Natural State

ILLINOIS
Capital: Springfield
U.S. Postal Abbreviation: IL
Date Admitted: Dec. 3, 1818
Rank: 21st

Bird: cardinal
Tree: white oak
Flower: violet
Nickname: Prairie State

CALIFORNIA
Capital: Sacramento
U.S. Postal Abbreviation: CA
Date Admitted: Sept. 9, 1850
Rank: 31st

Bird: California, or valley, quail
Tree: California redwood
Flower: California, or golden, poppy
Nickname: Golden State

INDIANA
Capital: Indianapolis
U.S. Postal Abbreviation: IN
Date Admitted: Dec. 11, 1816
Rank: 19th

Bird: cardinal
Tree: tulip tree, or yellow poplar
Flower: peony
Nickname: Hoosier State

COLORADO
Capital: Denver
U.S. Postal Abbreviation: CO
Date Admitted: August 1, 1876
Rank: 38th

Bird: lark bunting
Tree: Colorado blue spruce
Flower: white and lavender columbine
Nickname: Centennial State

IOWA
Capital: Des Moines
U.S. Postal Abbreviation: IA
Date Admitted: Dec. 28, 1846
Rank: 29th

Bird: eastern goldfinch
Tree: oak
Flower: wild rose
Nickname: Hawkeye State

CONNECTICUT
Capital: Hartford
U.S. Postal Abbreviation: CT
Date Admitted: Jan. 9, 1788
Rank: 5th

Bird: American robin
Tree: white oak
Flower: mountain laurel
Nicknames: Constitution State, Nutmeg State

KANSAS
Capital: Topeka
U.S. Postal Abbreviation: KS
Date Admitted: Jan. 29, 1861
Rank: 34th

Bird: western meadowlark
Tree: cottonwood
Flower: sunflower
Nickname: Sunflower State

DELAWARE
Capital: Dover
U.S. Postal Abbreviation: DE
Date Admitted: Dec. 7, 1787
Rank: 1st

Bird: blue hen chicken
Tree: American holly
Flower: peach blossom
Nicknames: First State, Diamond State

KENTUCKY
Capital: Frankfort
U.S. Postal Abbreviation: KY
Date Admitted: June 1, 1792
Rank: 15th

Bird: cardinal
Tree: tulip tree
Flower: goldenrod
Nickname: Bluegrass State

FLORIDA
Capital: Tallahassee
U.S. Postal Abbreviation: FL
Date Admitted: March 3, 1845
Rank: 27th

Bird: mockingbird
Tree: Sabal palmetto
Flower: orange blossom
Nickname: Sunshine State

LOUISIANA
Capital: Baton Rouge
U.S. Postal Abbreviation: LA
Date Admitted: April 30, 1812
Rank: 18th

Bird: eastern brown pelican
Tree: bald cypress
Flower: magnolia
Nickname: Pelican State

U. S. State Facts

MAINE
Capital: Augusta
U.S. Postal Abbreviation: ME
Date Admitted: March 15, 1820
Rank: 23rd
Bird: chickadee
Tree: eastern white pine
Flower: white pine cone and tassel
Nickname: Pine Tree State

NEVADA
Capital: Carson City
U.S. Postal Abbreviation: NV
Date Admitted: Oct. 31, 1864
Rank: 36th
Bird: mountain bluebird
Trees: single-leaf pinon, bristlecone pine
Flower: sagebrush
Nicknames: Sagebrush State, Silver State, Battle Born State

MARYLAND
Capital: Annapolis
U.S. Postal Abbreviation: MD
Date Admitted: April 28, 1788
Rank: 7th
Bird: Baltimore oriole
Tree: white oak
Flower: black-eyed Susan
Nicknames: Old Line State, Free State

NEW HAMPSHIRE
Capital: Concord
U.S. Postal Abbreviation: NH
Date Admitted: June 21, 1788
Rank: 9th
Bird: purple finch
Tree: white birch
Flower: purple lilac
Nickname: Granite State

MASSACHUSETTS
Capital: Boston
U.S. Postal Abbreviation: MA
Date Admitted: Feb. 6, 1788
Rank: 6th
Bird: black-capped chickadee
Tree: American elm
Flower: mayflower
Nicknames: Bay State, Old Bay State

NEW JERSEY
Capital: Trenton
U.S. Postal Abbreviation: NJ
Date Admitted: Dec. 18, 1787
Rank: 3rd
Bird: eastern goldfinch
Tree: red oak
Flower: purple violet
Nickname: Garden State

MICHIGAN
Capital: Lansing
U.S. Postal Abbreviation: MI
Date Admitted: Jan. 26, 1837
Rank: 26th
Bird: American robin
Tree: eastern white pine
Flower: apple blossom
Nickname: Wolverine State

NEW MEXICO
Capital: Santa Fe
U.S. Postal Abbreviation: NM
Date Admitted: Jan. 6, 1912
Rank: 47th
Bird: roadrunner
Tree: pinon
Flower: yucca
Nickname: Land of Enchantment

MINNESOTA
Capital: St. Paul
U.S. Postal Abbreviation: MN
Date Admitted: May 11, 1858
Rank: 32nd
Bird: common loon
Tree: red, or Norway, pine
Flower: pink and white lady's slipper
Nicknames: North Star State, Gopher State

NEW YORK
Capital: Albany
U.S. Postal Abbreviation: NY
Date Admitted: July 26, 1788
Rank: 11th
Bird: bluebird
Tree: sugar maple
Flower: rose
Nickname: Empire State

MISSISSIPPI
Capital: Jackson
U.S. Postal Abbreviation: MS
Date Admitted: Dec. 10, 1817
Rank: 20th
Bird: mockingbird
Tree: magnolia
Flower: magnolia
Nickname: Magnolia State

NORTH CAROLINA
Capital: Raleigh
U.S. Postal Abbreviation: NC
Date Admitted: Nov. 21, 1789
Rank: 12th
Bird: cardinal
Tree: pine
Flower: dogwood
Nickname: Tar Heel State

MISSOURI
Capital: Jefferson City
U.S. Postal Abbreviation: MO
Date Admitted: August 10, 1821
Rank: 24th
Bird: bluebird
Tree: flowering dogwood
Flower: hawthorn
Nickname: Show Me State

NORTH DAKOTA
Capital: Bismarck
U.S. Postal Abbreviation: ND
Date Admitted: Nov. 2, 1889
Rank: 39th
Bird: western meadowlark
Tree: American elm
Flower: wild prairie rose
Nicknames: Peace Garden State, Sioux State, Flickertail State

MONTANA
Capital: Helena
U.S. Postal Abbreviation: MT
Date Admitted: Nov. 8, 1889
Rank: 41st
Bird: western meadowlark
Tree: ponderosa pine
Flower: bitterroot
Nickname: Treasure State

OHIO
Capital: Columbus
U.S. Postal Abbreviation: OH
Date Admitted: March 1, 1803
Rank: 17th
Bird: cardinal
Tree: buckeye
Flower: scarlet carnation
Nickname: Buckeye State

NEBRASKA
Capital: Lincoln
U.S. Postal Abbreviation: NE
Date Admitted: March 1, 1867
Rank: 37th
Bird: western meadowlark
Tree: eastern cottonwood
Flower: goldenrod
Nickname: Cornhusker State

OKLAHOMA
Capital: Oklahoma City
U.S. Postal Abbreviation: OK
Date Admitted: Nov. 16, 1907
Rank: 46th
Bird: scissor-tailed flycatcher
Tree: redbud
Flower: mistletoe

U. S. State Facts

OREGON
Capital: Salem
U.S. Postal Abbreviation: OR
Date Admitted: Feb. 14, 1859
Rank: 33rd

Bird: western meadowlark
Tree: Douglas fir
Flower: Oregon grape
Nickname: Beaver State

UTAH
Capital: Salt Lake City
U.S. Postal Abbreviation: UT
Date Admitted: Jan. 4, 1896
Rank: 45th

Bird: California gull
Tree: blue spruce
Flower: sego lily
Nickname: Beehive State

PENNSYLVANIA
Capital: Harrisburg
U.S. Postal Abbreviation: PA
Date Admitted: Dec. 12, 1787
Rank: 2nd

Bird: ruffed grouse
Tree: eastern hemlock
Flower: mountain laurel
Nickname: Keystone State

VERMONT
Capital: Montpelier
U.S. Postal Abbreviation: VT
Date Admitted: March 4, 1791
Rank: 14th

Bird: hermit thrush
Tree: sugar maple
Flower: red clover
Nickname: Green Mountain State

RHODE ISLAND
Capital: Providence
U.S. Postal Abbreviation: RI
Date Admitted: May 29, 1790
Rank: 13th

Bird: Rhode Island red
Tree: red maple
Flower: violet
Nickname: Ocean State

VIRGINIA
Capital: Richmond
U.S. Postal Abbreviation: VA
Date Admitted: June 25, 1788
Rank: 10th

Bird: cardinal
Tree: American dogwood
Flower: American dogwood
Nickname: Old Dominion State

SOUTH CAROLINA
Capital: Columbia
U.S. Postal Abbreviation: SC
Date Admitted: May 23, 1788
Rank: 8th

Bird: Carolina wren
Tree: palmetto
Flower: Carolina, or yellow, jessamine
Nickname: Palmetto State

WASHINGTON
Capital: Olympia
U.S. Postal Abbreviation: WA
Date Admitted: Nov. 11, 1889
Rank: 42nd

Bird: willow goldfinch
Tree: western hemlock
Flower: coast rhododendron
Nickname: Evergreen State

SOUTH DAKOTA
Capital: Pierre
U.S. Postal Abbreviation: SD
Date Admitted: Nov. 2, 1889
Rank: 40th

Bird: Ring-necked Pheasant
Tree: Black Hills spruce
Flower: pasqueflower
Nicknames: Mount Rushmore

WEST VIRGINIA
Capital: Charleston
U.S. Postal Abbreviation: WV
Date Admitted: June 20, 1863
Rank: 35th

Bird: cardinal
Tree: sugar maple
Flower: rhododendron
Nickname: Mountain State

TENNESSEE
Capital: Nashville
U.S. Postal Abbreviation: TN
Date Admitted: June 1, 1796
Rank: 16th

Bird: mockingbird
Tree: tulip poplar
Flower: iris
Nickname: Volunteer State

WISCONSIN
Capital: Madison
U.S. Postal Abbreviation: WI
Date Admitted: May 29, 1848
Rank: 30th

Bird: American robin
Tree: sugar maple
Flower: wood violet
Nickname: Badger State

TEXAS
Capital: Austin
U.S. Postal Abbreviation: TX
Date Admitted: Dec. 29, 1845
Rank: 28th

Bird: mockingbird
Tree: pecan
Flower: bluebonnet
Nickname: Lone Star State

WYOMING
Capital: Cheyenne
U.S. Postal Abbreviation: WY
Date Admitted: July 10, 1890
Rank: 44th

Bird: western meadowlark
Tree: plains cottonwood
Flower: Indian paintbrush
Nicknames: Equality State, Cowboy State

Sir John Alexander Macdonald

Born: January 11, 1815
In office: 1867-1873, 1878-1891
Party: Liberal Conservative
Died: June 6, 1891

Alexander Mackenzie

Born: January 28, 1822
In office: 1873-1878
Party: Liberal
Died: April 17, 1892

Sir John Joseph Caldwell Abbott

Born: March 12, 1821
In office: 1891-1892
Party: Liberal Conservative
Died: October 30, 1893

Sir John Sparrow David Thompson

Born: November 10, 1845
In office: 1892-1894
Party: Liberal Conservative
Died: December 12, 1894

Sir Mackenzie Bowell

Born: December 17, 1823
In office: 1894-1896
Party: Liberal Conservative
Died: December 10, 1917

Sir Charles Tupper

Born: July 2, 1821
In office: 1896
Party: Conservative
Died: October 30, 1915

Sir Wilfrid Laurier

Born: November 20, 1841
In office: 1896-1911
Party: Liberal
Died: February 17, 1919

Sir Robert Laird Borden

Born: June 26, 1854
In office: 1911-1917, 1917-1920
Party: Conservative
Died: June 10, 1937

Arthur Meighen

Born: June 16, 1874
In office: 1920-1921, 1926
Party: Conservative
Died: August 5, 1960

William Lyon Mackenzie King

Born: December 17, 1874
In office: 1921-1926, 1926-1930, 1935-1947
Party: Liberal
Died: July 22, 1950

Richard Bedford Bennett

Born: July 3, 1870
In office: 1930-1935
Party: Conservative
Died: June 26, 1947

Louis Stephen St-Laurent

Born: February 1, 1882
In office: 1948-1957
Party: Liberal
Died: July 25, 1973

John George Diefenbaker

Born: September 18, 1895
In office: 1957-1963
Party: Progressive Conservative
Died: August 16, 1979

Lester Bowles Pearson

Born: April 23, 1897
In office: 1963-1968
Party: Liberal
Died: December 27, 1972

Pierre Elliott Trudeau

Born: October 18, 1919
In office: 1968 to 1979, 1980 to 1984
Party: Liberal
Died: September 28, 2000

Charles Joseph Clark

Born: June 5, 1939
In office: 1979-1980
Party: Progressive Conservative

John Napier Turner

Born: June 7, 1929
In office: 1984
Party: Liberal

Martin Brian Mulroney

Born: March 20, 1939
In office: 1984-1993
Party: Progressive Conservative

Kim Campbell

Born: March 10, 1947
In office: 1993
Party: Progressive Conservative

Jean Chrétien

Born: January 11, 1934
In office: 1993 to Present
Party: Liberal

Alberta
Capital: Edmonton
Entered Confederation: September 1, 1905

- Home of the annual Calgary stampede.
- Land mass nearly equal to that of Texas.

British Columbia
Capital: Victoria
Entered Confederation: July 20, 1871

- Vancouver cited as the most "livable city in the world" by the United Nations.

Manitoba
Capital: Winnipeg
Entered Confederation: July 15, 1870

- One of the largest Mennonite populations in the world.

New Brunswick
Capital: Fredericton
Entered Confederation: July 1, 1867

- Land is 85% forest.
- Highest percentage of French speakers outside of Quebec.

Newfoundland and Labrador
Capital: St. John's
Entered Confederation: March 31, 1949

- John Cabot claimed "St. John's Isle" in 1497 for Henry VII of England.

Northwest Territories
Capital: Yellowknife
Entered Confederation: July 15, 1870

- Located above the 60th parallel.
- Eight official languages.

Nova Scotia
Capital: Halifax
Entered Confederation: July 1, 1867

- Halifax explosion of 1917 was the deadliest man-made explosion prior to the atomic bomb.

Nunavut
Capital: Iqualit
Entered Confederation: April 1, 1999

- Canada's newest territory, established in 1999.
- Population primarily Inuit.

Ontario
Capital: Toronto
Entered Confederation: July 1, 1867

- First province to enter confederation.
- Most populous province in Canada.

Prince Edward Island
Capital: Charlottetown
Entered Confederation: July 1, 1873

- Smallest province in area.
- Best known for *Anne of Green Gables* by Lucy Maud Montogmery.

Quebec
Capital: Quebec
Entered Confederation: July 1, 1867

- French is the main spoken language.
- Largest province in area.

Saskatchewan
Capital: Regina
Entered Confederation: September 1, 1905

- Elected their first socialist government in North America in 1944.

Yukon Territory
Capital: Whitehorse
Entered Confederation: June 13, 1898

- Experienced Klondike Gold Rush in the late 1800s.

Weights and Measures

The metric system, or international system, is used around the world as the standard system of measurement. The units of this system were decided on by international agreement. These units are known as "SI units," which comes from the French abbreviation for *système international.*

The system of measurement commonly used in the United States is known as the "customary system." You may also hear it called the "British" or "English" system. This system is based on traditional units of measurement that have been handed down over many centuries.

The customary system of measurement has different names for smaller and larger sizes of the basic unit. For example, the foot is the basic unit of length, an inch is one-twelfth of a foot, and a yard is three feet. By contrast, the metric/SI system adds prefixes to the name of the basic unit to show smaller and larger sizes. For example, a meter is the basic unit of length. A centimeter is one-hundredth of a meter, and a kilometer is one thousand meters. The most common prefixes used in the metric/SI system are shown in the table below.

MEASUREMENT

Multiple/fraction		Prefix	Symbol
10^{12}	(x 1,000,000,000,000)	tera–	T
10^9	(x 1,000,000,000)	giga–	G
10^6	(x 1,000,000)	mega–	M
10^3	(x 1,000)	kilo–	k
10^2	(x 100)	hecto–	h
10^1	(x 10)	deka–	da

Example: A kilogram is one thousand grams.

	Prefix	Symbol
1/10	deci–	d
1/100	centi–	c
1/1,000	milli–	m
1/1,000,000	micro–	μ
1/1,000,000,000	nano–	n
1/1/000,000,000,000	pico–	p

Example: A nanosecond is one-billionth of a second.

TIME

Unit	Abbreviation	
second	s	
minute	min.	= 60 s
hour	h	= 60 min = 3,600 s
day	d	= 24 h = 86,400 s

BOILING POINT
K 373
F 212°
C 100°

BODY TEMP.
K 309
F 98.6°
C 36°

FREEZING POINT.
K 273
F 32°
C 0°

TEMPERATURE

There are three systems for measuring temperature. In the United States, we measure temperature in degrees on the Fahrenheit scale. Countries that use the metric system measure temperature in degrees on the Celsius scale. (This used to be called the centigrade scale.) Both systems use a special sign (°) that means degree.

	Fahrenheit	Celsius	Kelvin
steam point (boiling point)	212°F	100°C	373 K
ice point	32°F	0°C	273 K (freezing point)

To change a Fahrenheit temperature to Celsius, start with the number of Fahrenheit degrees, subtract 32, then divide by 1.8.
Example: A cold winter day is 12°F or –11°C
(°F – 32) ÷ 1.8 = °C
(12 – 32) + -20 ÷ 1.8 = –11

To change a Celsius temperature to Fahrenheit, start with the number of Celsius degrees, multiply by 1.8, then add 32.
Example: Normal body temperature is 37°C or 98.6°F
(°C x 1.8) + 32 = °F
(37 x 1.8) = 66.6 + 32 = 98.6

THE KELVIN SCALE
°C + 273 = K

The heaviest insect is the Goliath beetle of the Central and South American rain forests. It weighs 3.5 ounces or 98 grams.

MASS (WEIGHT)

Customary unit	Abbreviation	
ounce (avoirdupois)	oz.	
pound	lb.	= 16 oz.
ton	tn.	= 2,000 lb.

SI unit	Abbreviation	
gram	g	
kilogram	kg	= 1,000 g
ton/tonne	t (Mg)	= 1,000 kg

1 ounce = 28.35 grams	1 gram = 0.0353 ounce
1 pound = 0.45 kg	1 kg = 2.2 lb.

To change ounces to grams, multiply the number of ounces by 28.35.
Example: A loaf of bread weighs 24 ounces or about 680 grams.
$$24 \times 28.35 = 680.4$$

To change pounds to kilograms, multiply the number of pounds by 0.45.
Example: A bag of flour weighs 5 pounds or 2.25 kilograms.
$$5 \times 0.45 = 2.25$$

To change grams to ounces, multiply the number of grams by 0.0353.
Example: A box of pasta weighs 500 grams or 17.65 ounces.
$$500 \times 0.0323 = 17.65$$

To change kilograms to pounds, multiply the number of kilograms by 2.2.
Example: A man weighs 75 kilograms or 165 pounds.

DISTANCE (LENGTH)

Customary unit	Abbreviation	
inch	in.	
foot	ft.	= 12 inches
yard	yd.	= 3 feet = 36 inches
mile	mi.	= 5,280 feet = 1760 yards

SI unit	Abbreviation	
millimeter	mm	= 1/1,000 meter
centimeter	cm	= 1/100 meter = 10 mm
meter	m	= 1,000 mm = 100 cm
kilometer	km	= 1,000 m

1 cm = 0.39 in.	1 in. = 2.54 cm	1 m = 39 in.
1 ft. = 30.48 cm	1 km = 0.62 mi.	1 mi. = 1.6 km

To change inches to centimeters, multiply the number of inches by 2.54.
Example: A sheet of binder paper is 11 inches long or about 28 cm long.
$$11 \times 2.54 = 27.94$$

To change miles to kilometers, multiply the number of miles by 1.61.
Example: The Nile River is 4145 miles or 6673 kilometers long.
$$4145 \times 1.51 = 6673$$

To change centimeters to inches, multiply the number of centimeters by 0.39.
Example: A pencil is 20 centimeters or about 8 inches long.
$$20 \times 0.39 = 7.8$$

To change kilometers to miles, multiply the number of miles by 0.62.
Example: A 5 kilometer race is 3.1 miles.
$$5 \times 0.62 = 3.1$$

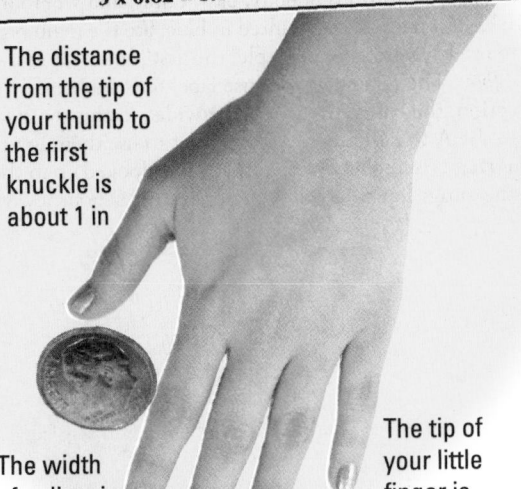

The distance from the tip of your thumb to the first knuckle is about 1 in

The width of a dime is about 1mm

The tip of your little finger is about 1 cm across

The basic unit for measuring capacity or volume in the International System is the cubic centimeter (c3). The liter is a special name for 1,000 cubic centimeters (or one cubic decimeter). The liter is not used for precise scientific measurements. [Use a capital "L" when writing the abbreviation for liter—a lower-case " l" can be confused with the number one (1).]

CAPACITY

Customary unit	abbreviation	
fluid ounce	= oz.	
cup	C	= 8 oz.
pint	pt. / 2 C	= 16 oz.
quart	qt. /2 pt. /4 C	= 32 oz.
gallon	gal. /4 qt.	= 128 oz.

SI unit	abbreviation
milliliter	mL = 1 cubic centimeter (c3)
liter	L = 1000 mL = 1,000 cubic centimeters (c3)

1 oz. = 29.57 mL	1 mL = 0.0338 oz.
1 qt. = 0.946 L	1 L = 1.057 qt.

To change ounces to milliliters, multiply the number of ounces by 29.57.
Example: A container of milk contains 8 oz. or 236.56 mL.
$$8 \times 29.57 = 236.56$$

To change milliliters to ounces, multiply the number of milliliters by 0.0338.
Example: A bottle of shampoo contains 350 milliliters or about 12 ounces.
$$350 \times 0.0338 = 11.83$$

To change quarts to liters, multiply the number of quarts by 0.946.
Example: A jug of cider contains 4 quarts (1 gallon) or 3.784 liters.
$$4 \times 0.946 = 3.784$$

To change liters to quarts, multiply the number of liters by 1.057.
Example: A bottle of soda contains 2 liters or 2.114 quarts.
$$2 \times 1.057 = 2.114$$

Guide to the Wordsmyth Lexipedia Word Explorer

There are two parts to the **Wordsmyth Lexipedia Word Explorer**: the *Index of Topics* and the *Index of Keywords*. Each of them will be explained in this Guide. The **Index of Topics** begins on page B50, and the **Index of Keywords** begins on page B52.

The **Index of Topics** lists groups of words by topic. (It is not a classification of all knowledge, so there are many topics that won't be found in this index.) It is meant to suggest keywords in the same topic area. These keywords can then be looked up in the **Index of Keywords**— or in the A to Z section of the dictionary.

Let's consider the first topic in the Index of Topics, **The Human Body**. Under this topic, we see the subtopics are **Parts of Our Bodies**, **How our Bodies Work**, and **How We Care for Our Bodies**. To the right of these subtopics is a box containing a list of Keywords. You can look these up in the **Index of Keywords** to find related words, pictures, and meanings.

1. **The Human Body**
   - Parts of Our Bodies
   - How Our Bodies Work
   - How We Care for Our Bodies

Keywords

blood, body, cell, digestion, disease, drug, excrete, exercise, face, first aid, foot, hair, head, health, hygiene, injury, muscle, nerve, organ, reproduction, respiration, sense, skeleton, tooth

Once you have scanned the keyword box to get a feel for the range of words that fall under the topic of the human body, you may select one of these words and look it up in the Index of Keywords, beginning on page B52. Let's see what we can learn about the keyword **foot** in this index.

The **Index of Keywords** is arranged in alphabetical order in much the same way as the A to Z section of the dictionary. But instead of finding definitions under the keywords, you will find information on words, pictures, and meanings that relate to the keyword. In our example keyword, **foot**, information is organized in the following way. (Note: the numbers below refer to the numbered information on the diagram.)

1. Keyword: Keywords are in dark maroon type and hang over the edge of the column.

2. Keyword Sense Label: This label appears in parentheses in black type immediately after the Keyword. It tells you which definition of the keyword is being described if you look it up in the A to Z section of the dictionary. We see under the keyword foot that the first noun sense is being described.

3. Icon: Following the Sense Label will be an icon (small picture). Each of the ten icons refers to one of the topics in the Index of Topics. The Icons quickly tell you what topic or topics the keyword falls under if you would like to explore other words under this topic. We see here that **foot** has the **Human Body** icon.

4. Cross References: Sometimes under a keyword the phrase "*see*" or "*see also*" appears: Under foot you will notice the phrase "see also body." These are cross references, telling you which other keywords have information you might be interested in.

5. Picture References: To get to pictures related to a keyword, first find the phrase, "*for pictures see definitions of....*" Look up the words listed there in the A to Z dictionary. Under foot this reference reads, "for pictures see definitions of **body, paw, talon, and webfoot**."

6. Relational Phrases, 7. Related Words, and 8. Related Word Sense Labels: Relational phrases, printed in blue, are the main organizing element of the Index of Key Words. They define the relationship words have to the keyword. For example, the first phrase for foot is "*some kinds of feet,*" under which we find the related words *forefoot, hoof, paw,* and *webfoot*. The related word sense label tells you exactly which sense of that word has a relation to the keyword. If the related word is an inflection, the base entry word is provided in this sense label so that you know which entry word to look up. You should look these words up in the A to Z dictionary if you want to use them in your writing or research. If a related word appears in bold, dark maroon print, this means that it is also a keyword and may be looked up in the Index of Keywords to find other related words. Thus, your exploration of words and meanings can take you on a nearly endless journey of discovery.

2. Keyword Sense Label

3. Icon

1. Keyword

4 . Cross Reference

6. Relational Phrase

5. Picture Reference

Related Words

Sense Label

Base Entry Word

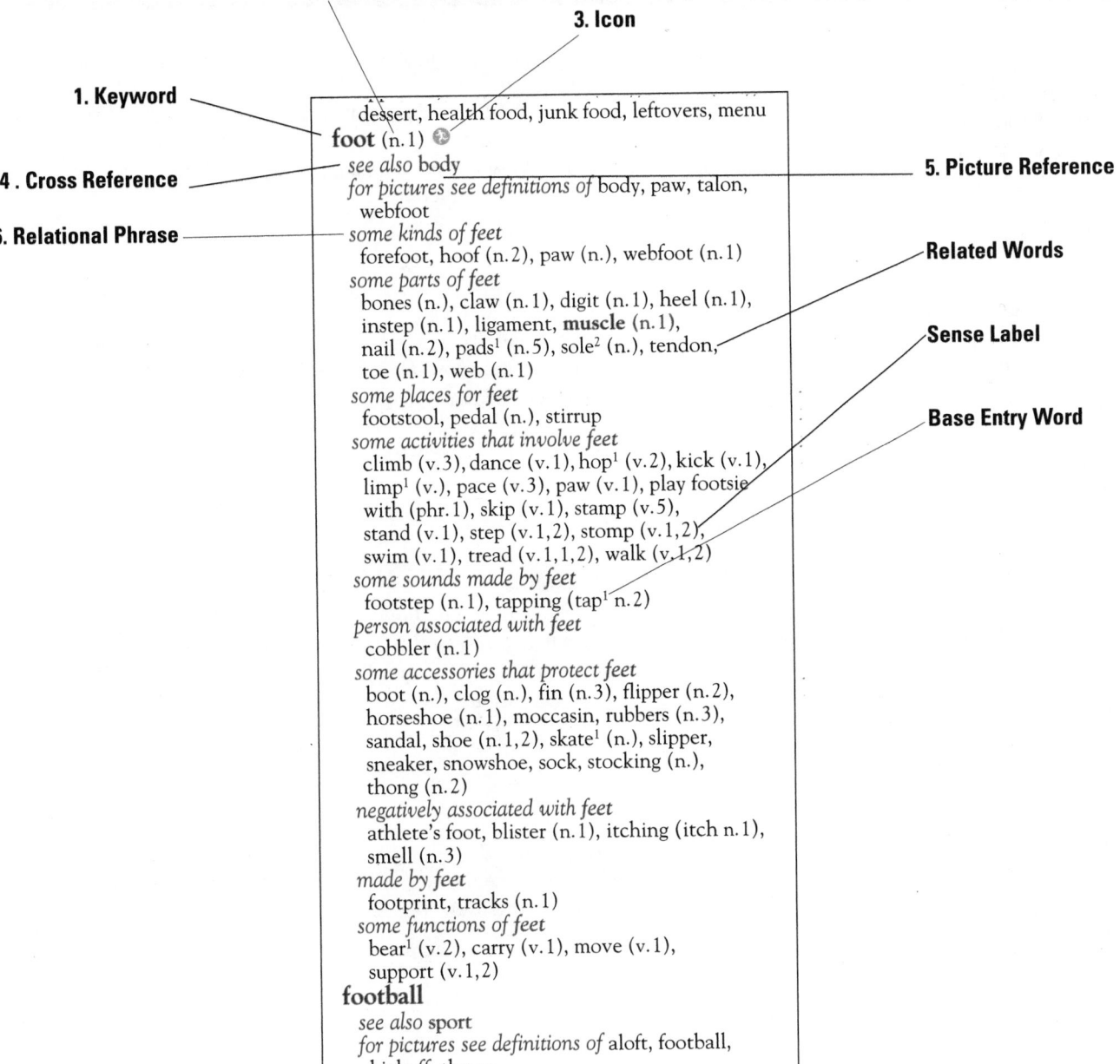

dessert, health food, junk food, leftovers, menu

foot (n.1) ⊕

see also body

for pictures see definitions of body, paw, talon,
   webfoot

some kinds of feet
   forefoot, hoof (n.2), paw (n.), webfoot (n.1)

some parts of feet
   bones (n.), claw (n.1), digit (n.1), heel (n.1),
   instep (n.1), ligament, **muscle** (n.1),
   nail (n.2), pads¹ (n.5), sole² (n.), tendon,
   toe (n.1), web (n.1)

some places for feet
   footstool, pedal (n.), stirrup

some activities that involve feet
   climb (v.3), dance (v.1), hop¹ (v.2), kick (v.1),
   limp¹ (v.), pace (v.3), paw (v.1), play footsie
   with (phr.1), skip (v.1), stamp (v.5),
   stand (v.1), step (v.1,2), stomp (v.1,2),
   swim (v.1), tread (v.1,1,2), walk (v.1,2)

some sounds made by feet
   footstep (n.1), tapping (tap¹ n.2)

person associated with feet
   cobbler (n.1)

some accessories that protect feet
   boot (n.), clog (n.), fin (n.3), flipper (n.2),
   horseshoe (n.1), moccasin, rubbers (n.3),
   sandal, shoe (n.1,2), skate¹ (n.), slipper,
   sneaker, snowshoe, sock, stocking (n.),
   thong (n.2)

negatively associated with feet
   athlete's foot, blister (n.1), itching (itch n.1),
   smell (n.3)

made by feet
   footprint, tracks (n.1)

some functions of feet
   bear¹ (v.2), carry (v.1), move (v.1),
   support (v.1,2)

football

see also sport

for pictures see definitions of aloft, football,
   kickoff, throw

B49

Lexipedia Word Explorer: The Topical Index

1. The Human Body
- Parts of Our Bodies
- How Our Bodies Work
- How We Care for Our Bodies

Keywords

blood, body, cell, digestion, disease, drug, excrete, exercise, face, first aid, foot, hair, head, health, hygiene, injury, muscle, nerve, organ, reproduction, respiration, sense, skeleton, tooth

2. The Human Mind
- How We Feel
- How We Think
- How We Act

Keywords

action, anger, behavior, belief, care, emotion, fear, happiness, hate, knowledge, learn, love, mind, morals, personality, sadness, thought

3. Everyday Life
- Where We Live
- How We Travel
- What We Eat and Wear
- Who We Know
- Having Fun

Keywords

airplane, boat, building, car, city, clothing, community, cooking, drink, family, food, furniture, game, home, jewelry, leisure, relationship, room, school, sport, tool, transportation

4. History and Culture
- What Organizes Society
- What Happened in the Past
- What shapes the future

Keywords

celebration, culture, education, history, myth, religion, science, tradition

5. Communication
- How We Communicate With Language
- How We Communicate Through Art

Keywords

art, book, color, communication, dance, film, grammar, instrument, language, literature, music, photography, theater

6. The Living World
- Kinds of Animals
- Kinds of Plants
- Other Living Things
- The Living World in Action

Keywords
amphibian, animal, arthropod, bacteria, bird, cat, crustacean, diet, dinosaur, dog, endangered species, extinction, fish, flower, fruit, fungus, grain, grass, insect, invertebrate, leaf, life, mammal, milk, mollusk, pet, plant, reptile, rodent, seed, spider, tree, vegetable, virus, worm

7. The Physical World
- How We Study the Physical World
- Some Parts of the Physical World
- What We Create from the Physical World

Keywords
chemistry, computer, electricity, element, energy, geology, Internet, light, mathematics, measurement, number, physics, shape, space, technology

8. Natural Environment
- Some Parts of the Natural Environment
- Structures in the Natural Environment
- What We Do With the Natural Environment
- Processes in the Natural Environment

Keywords
air, conservation, continent, desert, earth, ecosystem, farming, fishing, forest, gardening, geography, hunting, lake, mountain, natural resources, ocean, plain, river, sea, soil, stone, tundra, volcano, water, weather

9. The Economy
- Organization of the Economy
- The Economy in Action

Keywords
advertise, bank, business, economy, industry, money, tax, work

10. Government and Law
- Government Structures
- Structure of the Law

Keywords
country, crime, democracy, government, law, legislature, military, monarchy, politics, power, war, weapon

abacus *for a picture see definition*
abandoned *for a picture see definition*
abdomen
 see also arthropod, body, insect
 for pictures see definitions of body, insect
above *for a picture see definition*
abreast *for a picture see definition*
abuse *see* injury
academy *see* art, school
accelerate *for a picture see definition*
accent *see* language
accessory *for a picture see definition*
accident
 see also car, first aid, injury
 for a picture see the definition of crash
accompaniment *see* music
accountant *see* business, mathematics
accumulate *for a picture see definition*
accusation *see* crime, law
ache *see* disease, injury
acid *see* chemistry, digestion
acoustic
 see also music
 for a picture see the definition of acoustic
acronym *for a picture see definition*
act *see* law, legislature, theater
action (n.2)
 see also behavior
 some kinds of actions
 accidental, careful (adj.1), deft,
 deliberate (adj.1), intentional,
 involuntary (adj.2), steady (adj.2)
 some things that cause action
 command (n.2), direction (n.3), order (n.1),
 pressure (n.2), spur (n.2), stimulus (n.1)
 commitments to action
 agreement (n.2), guarantee (n.2),
 pledge (n.1), promise (n.1)
 postponing actions
 defer¹, delay (n.1), postpone, procrastinate,
 stall² (n.)
 reasons for actions
 policy¹, precedent, principle (n.1),
 purpose (n.1)
 some things that hinder action
 arrest (n.), ban (n.), block (n.7), detention,
 embargo (n.2), taboo (n.)
 some things that regulate action
 law (n.1), rule (n.1)
activity *see* action, energy, exercise
actor *see* theater
actress *see* theater
acupuncture *for a picture see definition*
add *see* mathematics, number
addiction *see* drug, health
adhesive *for a picture see definition*
adjective *see* grammar
admiration *see* behavior, thought
adorn *for a picture see definition*
adult *see* family, life, relationship
advancement *see* technology
adverb *see* grammar
advertisement
 see also business
 similar to advertising
 propaganda, publicity (n.1)
 some kinds of advertisements
 announcement (n.1), circular (n.),
 commercial (n.), display (n.2), flier (n.2),
 handout (n.2), junk mail, leaflet (n.1),
 notice (n.1), poster, Spam (n.2)
 broader category that includes advertising

communication (n.3)
 some parts of advertisements
 caption, cartoon (n.1), graphic (n.),
 jingle (n.2), logo, message (n.1),
 photograph (n.), picture (n.1,3), slogan
 some places for advertising
 billboard, booth (n.2), **Internet**, journal (n.2),
 magazine (n.1), media (n.2), newspaper,
 periodical, publication (n.2), radio (n.2),
 television (n.2), Web site
 some actions associated with advertising
 air (v.2), announce, appear (v.3),
 broadcast (v.1), convince, debut (v.),
 display (v.2), inform (v.1), introduce (v.4),
 market (v.2), notify, persuade (v.2),
 present² (v.2,3), promote (v.3), run (v.15),
 sell (v.2,3), urge (v.2)
 some people associated with advertising
 actor, announcer, candidate, model (n.5)
 some subjects of advertisements
 bargain (n.2), deal (n.2), event (n.1),
 price (n.1), product (n.1), service (n.2)
aerobics
 see also dance, exercise
 for a picture see the definition of aerobics
aeronautics *see* airplane, space, technology
aesthetic *see* art, culture
affection *see* emotion, love
Afghan *for a picture see definition*
afloat *for a picture see definition*
afraid *see* fear
age *see* history, life
agency *see* government
aggression *see* behavior, war
agility *see* action, exercise
agitate *see* behavior, emotion
agony
 see also disease, injury
 for a picture see the definition of agony
agreement *see* belief, thought
agriculture *see* farming, plant
ahead *for a picture see definition*
ail *see* disease, health
air (n.1)
 see also respiration, weather
 broader category including air
 gas (n.1)
 parts of the body associated with air
 lungs, mouth (n.1), nose (n.1), trachea (n.1),
 windpipe
 some components of air
 carbon dioxide, nitrogen, oxygen
 some actions involving air
 blow² (v.3), breathe (v.1), burp (v.1),
 choke (v.3), cough (v.1), exhale, gasp (v.1),
 inhale, puff (v.1), pump (v.1), sneeze (v.),
 sniff (v.1), snort (v.1), whistle (v.3)
 some descriptions of air
 clear (adj.1), damp (n.), foggy (adj.1),
 fresh (adj.6), humid, misty (adj.1),
 steamy (steam v.2), stuffy (adj.1)
 some sounds of air
 swish (n.), whoosh (n.)
 relating to lack of air
 choke (v.1), deflate (v.1), smother (v.5),
 suffocate (v.2,3)
 some instruments that measure air
 barometer, thermometer
 some things that use air
 accordion, air bag, bagpipe, bellows,
 carburetor, duct, fan¹ (n.1), flue, harmonica,
 Jacuzzi, kite (n.1), organ (n.1), pipe (n.3),
 pump (n.), tire², vacuum (n.3), whistle (v.1),
 wind instrument

also associated with air
 air pressure, atmosphere (n.1), breeze (n.1),
 current (n.1), eddy (n.), front (n.4),
 greenhouse effect, hurricane, smog, tornado,
 whirlwind (n.1), wind¹ (n.1)
aircraft *for pictures see definitions of* helicopter,
 jet¹
airplane
 see also technology, vehicle
 for pictures see definitions of jet¹, seaplane
 some examples of airplanes
 airliner, bomber (n.1), jet¹ (n.2), liner¹,
 seaplane, shuttle (n.2), transport (n.3)
 some kinds of airplanes
 commercial (adj.1), private (adj.4)
 broader categories that include airplanes
 aircraft, **transportation** (n.1), **vehicle** (n.1)
 some parts of airplanes
 cabin (n.2), coach (n.3), cockpit (n.1),
 compartment, control (n.1), fin (n.2),
 flap (n.1), fuselage, gear (n.2),
 instrument (n.1), jet engine, nose (n.3),
 porthole, propeller, rudder, tail (n.3), tire²,
 wheel (n.1), wing (n.3)
 some places for airplanes
 airport, hangar, ramp, runway (n.1), sky (n.1),
 terminal (n.2)
 group of airplanes
 fleet¹ (n.2)
 some actions of airplanes
 ascend (v.1), climb (v.1), coast (v.2),
 descend (v.1), fly¹ (v.2), glide (v.), land (v.3),
 pitch¹ (v.5), roll (v.3), thrust (v.), turn (v.3)
 some activities associated with airplanes
 board (v.3), eject (v.2), parachute (v.2), sky
 dive (sky diving), travel (v.1)
 some people associated with airplanes
 aviator, captain (n.2), crew (n.2),
 engineer (n.1), flight attendant, mechanic,
 navigator, pilot (n.1)
 related to airplanes
 glider, helicopter
 some things associated with airplanes
 airline, flight¹ (n.2), propulsion, radar (n.2),
 sonar (n.2), touchdown (n.2), wingspan
 some things typically transported by airplanes
 cargo, freight, luggage, mail¹ (n.2), passenger,
 soldier
airship *for a picture see definition*
alarm *for a picture see the definition of* reluctant
alarm clock *for a picture see the definition of* reluctant
album
 see also book, music
 for a picture see the definition of album
alcohol *see* drink, drug
alfalfa *for a picture see definition*
algae *see* plant
algebra *see* mathematics
alien *see* law, space
allegiance *see* behavior, belief, country
allegory *see* belief, literature, myth
allergy *see* first aid, health
alliance *see* country, war
alligator *for a picture see the definition of* reptile
alloy *see* chemistry, element
almond *for a picture see definition*
aloft *for a picture see definition*
alphabet *see* grammar, language
altitude *see* geography, measurement
alto *see* instrument, music
amazement *for a picture see the definition of* marvel
ambassador *see* government

amber *for a picture see definition*
ambulance *for a picture see definition*
amendment ○ *see* law, legislature
ammunition ○ *see* weapon
amoeba ❶ *see* animal, cell
amount ❸ *see* measurement, number
amphibian (n.1) ❶
see also animal
for pictures see definitions of amphibian, frog,
  newt, salamander, toad
some examples of amphibians
  frog (n.1), newt, salamander, toad
broader categories that include amphibians
  animals (n.1), vertebrates (n.)
some places for amphibians
  aquarium (n.1), bog (n.), land (n.1), mud,
  swamp (n.), water (n.2)
behaviors of some amphibians
  bask, climb (v.1), hop¹ (v.1), sing (v.1),
  swim (v.1)
sounds of some amphibians
  chirp (v.), click (v.1), croak (v.), peep² (v.),
  trill (v.)
young of some amphibians
  tadpole
things that amphibians eat
  insects (n.1), **plants** (n.1), **worms** (n.1)
some characteristics of amphibians
  camouflage (n.), cold-blooded (adj.1), gills,
  metamorphosis (n.1), webfeet (webfoot n.1)
some growth stages of amphibians
  adult (n.2), egg¹ (n.2), larva (n.2)
amphitheater ❷ *see* building, theater
analyze ❸ *see* thought
anarchy ○ *see* government, law
anatomy ❸❶ *see* animal, body, plant
ancient ○ *see* history
anemia ❸ *see* blood, disease
anesthesia ❸ *see* drug, nerve, sense
anger (n.) ❸
see also emotion
broader categories that include anger
  emotion (n.1), feeling (n.3)
some actions involving anger
  argue (v.2), bawl out, bristle (v.2), fly off the
  handle, frown (v.1), glare (v.2), grimace (v.),
  growl (v.1), roar (v.1), scowl (v.),
  scream (v.2), snap (v.5), snarl¹ (v.2),
  sputter (v.3), stamp (v.6), sulk (v.),
  swear (v.3), yell (v.)
some reactions to anger
  cool off, excuse (v.1), forgive (v.1), keep one's
  shirt on, let bygones be bygones, pardon (v.2),
  soothe (v.1)
some actions that cause anger
  annoy, antagonize, bait (v.2), bother (v.1),
  enrage, exasperate, incense² (v.1), incite (v.1),
  infuriate, irritate (v.1), make one's blood boil,
  needle (v.), offend, provoke (v.1), raise the
  hackles of, rub the wrong way, scold (v.), step
  on someone's toes
some people associated with anger
  mob (n.1)
without anger
  friendly, mellow (adj.4), mild (adj.1), tranquil
feeling angry
  bitter (adj.2), black (adj.3), cross (adj.),
  fiery (adj.3), furious (adj.1), hot (adj.4), hot
  under the collar, indignant, irate, livid (adj.2),
  mad (adj.2), on the warpath (phr.2),
  sore (adj.4), sullen (adj.1)
some forms of anger
  bile (n.2), fury (n.1), huff (n.), outrage (n.2),
  rage (n.1), temper (n.3), wrath
some results of anger

contempt (n.2), feud (n.), grudge (n.),
  quarrel (n.), tantrum
animal (n.1) ❸❶❻
see also amphibian, arthropod, bird, crustacean,
  endangered species, fish, insect, invertebrate,
  mammal, mollusk, pet, reptile
for pictures see definitions of armadillo, pair
some examples of animals
  amphibian (n.1), **arthropod**, **bird** (n.),
  crustacean, **fish** (n.1), **insect** (n.1),
  invertebrate (n.), **mammal**, **mollusk**, primate,
  protozoan, **reptile**, vertebrate (n.), **worm** (n.1)
some kinds of animals
  carnivore, herbivore, insectivore (n.1)
some categories of animals
  class (n.7), family (n.4), genus, order (n.6),
  species
parts of some animals
  antler, blubber (n.), bristle (n.1), claw (n.1),
  flipper (n.1), fur (n.1), hoof (n.1), horn (n.1),
  mane, pad¹ (n.5), pouch (n.2), quill (n.3),
  snout (n.), tail (n.1)
study of animals
  zoology
some places for animals
  aquarium (n.1), barn (n.), burrow (n.),
  cage (n.1), cave (n.), circus (n.1), den (n.1),
  desert¹ (n.), farm (n.1), field (n.1), forest (n.),
  hole (n.2), home (n.1), lair (n.1), land (n.1),
  log (n.1), mountain (n.1), nest (n.1),
  pasture (n.1), pen² (n.1), ranch (n.),
  refuge (n.1), sanctuary (n.4), stump (n.1),
  terrarium, underground (n.1), water (n.1),
  wood (n.1), woods (n.4), zoo (n.)
groups of some animals
  band¹ (n.1), brood (n.1), drove² (n.1),
  flock (n.1), herd (n.1), litter (n.2), pack (n.3),
  school², swarm (n.1,2), troop (n.1)
uses of some animals
  carrying (carry v.1), **clothing**, companionship,
  farming (farm v.2), **food** (n.),
  plowing (plow v.2), pulling (pull v.2),
  riding (ride v.1)
behaviors of some animals
  build (v.1), court (v.1), crawl (v.1,2),
  dig (v.1), dive (v.1), feed (v.1), fight (v.1),
  fly¹ (v.1), forage (v.1), gather (v.2), gnaw,
  hibernate, hide¹ (v.1), hop¹ (v.1), hunt (v.1),
  mate (v.), migrate (v.1), nurse (v.2), run (v.2),
  swim (v.1), trot (v.1), tunnel (v.1), walk (v.1)
some people associated with animals
  farmer, fisherman, groom (n.2), jockey,
  naturalist, researcher (research n.), trainer,
  veterinarian
some things animal eat
  animals (n.1), berries (berry n.), **birds** (n.),
  blood (n.1), corn (n.1), eggs¹ (n.2), **fish** (n.1),
  flowers (n.1), **fruit**, game (n.3), grubs (n.),
  honey (n.1), **insects** (n.1), **mammals**,
  plants (n.1), pollen, **rodents**, **worms** (n.1)
animated cartoon *for a picture see definition*
announcer ❷ *see* advertisement, communication
answer ❸❷ *see* language
antelope *for a picture see the definition of* gnu
antenna
see also insect, technology
for a picture see the definition of insect
anthology ❷ *see* book
anthropology ○ *see* culture, science
antibiotic ❸ *see* bacteria, disease, drug
antique
see also furniture, history
for a picture see the definition of antique
antiseptic ❸ *see* disease, drug, first aid

antler
see also mammal
for pictures see definitions of antler, moose
antonym ❷ *see* grammar
anxiety ❸ *see* emotion, fear
aorta *for a picture see the definition of* body
apartment ○ *see* building, home
ape *for pictures see definitions of* chimpanzee,
  frown, gorilla, orangutan
Aphrodite *for a picture see definition*
Apollo *for a picture see definition*
apostrophe ❷ *see* grammar
apparel ○ *see* clothing
appearance ❸ *see* color, hygiene, shape
appendix *for pictures see definitions of* appendix,
  body
apple *for pictures see definitions of* apple, gravity,
  sack¹
appliance ○❸ *see* electricity, technology
apply *for a picture see definition*
apprehend *for a picture see definition*
apprehension ❸ *see* fear
apron *for a picture see definition*
aquarium
see also building, fish, pet
for a picture see the definition of aquarium
Aquarius *for pictures see definitions of* constellation, zodiac
aquatic ❶ *see* fish, lake, mammal, ocean, river
archaeology ○ *see* culture, history, science
architecture ○❸❷ *see* building
arctic ❶❻ *see* tundra, weather
arena ○❷ *see* building, sport
Ares *for a picture see definition*
argue ❸ *see* action, behavior
Aries *for pictures see definitions of* constellation,
  zodiac
arithmetic ❸ *see* mathematics, number
ark *for a picture see the definition of* pair
arm
see also body, muscle, skeleton
for a picture see the definition of body
arm² ○ *see* military, weapon
armadillo *for a picture see definition*
armchair *for a picture see definition*
armor *for a picture see the definition of* medieval
army ○ *see* military, war
arrest
see also crime
for pictures see definitions of apprehend, nab
arrowhead *for a picture see definition*
art (n.2) ○❷
see also color, communication, culture, dance,
  film, literature, music, photography, theater
broader catagory that includes art
  communication (n.1), **culture** (n.1)
some examples of art
  ballet (n.1), bust¹ (n.1), cartoon (n.1), carving,
  collage, drama (n.1), embroidery,
  engraving (n.1), mobile (n.), mosaic, opera,
  picture (n.1,3), piece (n.3), play (n.2),
  portrait (n.1), statue, symphony (n.1)
similar to art
  craft (n.3), graffiti, handicraft (n.2),
  workmanship (n.1)
some kinds of art
  architecture (n.1), **dance** (n.2), drawing (n.1),
  film (n.3), **literature** (n.1), music (n.3),
  painting (n.2), **photography**, poetry (n.2),
  sculpture (n.1), **theater** (n.2),
  woodworking (n.)

some places for art
academy, auditorium, collection (n.2),
exhibition (n.2), gallery (n.2), museum,
stage (n.1), studio, theater (n.1)
some actions of art
act (v.2), carve (v.1), compose (v.2),
dab (v.2), dance (v.1), daub (v.), design (v.1),
doodle (v.), draw (v.1), etch, illustrate (v.2),
mold[1] (v.1), paste (v.1), sculpt, sew (v.),
sing (v.1), sketch (v.2), stitch (v.), stroke (v.),
weave (v.1), weld (v.1), write (v.3)
some descriptions of art
artistic (adj.2), classical (adj.1),
contemporary (adj.2), creative, folk (adj.2),
graphic (adj.1), modern (adj.2), pop[2]
some things used in art
acrylic, brush[1] (n.1), canvas (n.2), chalk (n.2),
charcoal (n.2), clay (n.), color (n.2),
costume (n.2), crayon (n.), easel,
enamel (n.1,2), ink (n.), loom[1] (n.), oil (n.3),
paint (n.2), palette, paper (n.1), pastel (n.2),
pen[1], pencil (n.), pigment (n.2), shape (n.2),
sketch (n.1), sponge (n.2,3), stone (n.2),
style (n.2), texture, thread (n.1),
watercolor (n.1), wood (n.2)
some people associated with art
actor, architect, artisan, artist (n.1), author,
composer, craftsman, critic (n.1), dancer,
dealer (n.1), director (n.2), illustrator,
model (n.4), musician, painter (n.1),
patron (n.2), poet, potter, sculptor,
writer (n.2)
related to art
aesthetic, artifact

artery
see also blood
for a picture see the definition of body
arthropod ◐
see also insect, invertebrate, spider
for pictures see definitions of arthropod,
centipede, crab, millipede
some examples of arthropods
beetle, bug (n.1), centipede, crayfish,
dragonfly, fly[2], gnat, mayfly (n.1), mite[1],
mosquito, moth, shrimp (n.), **spider**, tick[2]
broader categories that include arthropods
animal (n.1), **invertebrate** (n.)
parts of some arthropods
abdomen (n.1), antenna (n.2), claw (n.2),
fang, gill, thorax (n.2), wing (n.1)
some places for arthropods
land (n.1), **water** (n.1)
produced by some arthropods
beeswax, silk (n.1), venom, wax[1] (n.1),
web (n.3)
behaviors of some arthropods
fly[1] (v.1), pollinate, swim (v.1)
growth stages of some arthropods
cocoon, egg[1] (n.2), larva (n.1), nymph (n.2),
pupa
things made from arthropods
dye (n.), **food** (n.), medicine (n.1),
shellac (n.1)
things some arthropods eat
bacteria, insects, leaves, plankton,
plants (n.1), **worms** (n.1)
artichoke *for a picture see definition*
article ◐◑ *see* book, law
artifact ◐ *see* art, history
artisan ◐◑ *see* art
artist ◐◑ *see* art
ascend *for a picture see definition*
ascent *for a picture see definition*
askew *for a picture see definition*
asparagus *for a picture see definition*

assembly ◐ *see* democracy, legislature
asset ◐ *see* business, money
association ◐ *see* business, relationship
assorted *for a picture see definition*
aster *for pictures see definitions of* aster, flower
astrology ◐ *see* belief, space
astronaut
see also space
for a picture see the definition of exploration
astronomer *for a picture see the definition of* exploration
astronomy ◐◑ *see* science, space
Athena *for a picture see definition*
athlete
see also exercise, sport
for pictures see definitions of infield, involve
Atlas *for a picture see definition*
atmosphere ◐ *see* air, earth, weather
atom ◐ *see* element, physics
atrium *for a picture see the definition of* body
attack ◐◑ *see* disease, war
attention ◐◑ *see* care, thought
attentive *for a picture see definition*
attire ◐ *see* clothing
attitude ◐◑ *see* behavior, belief
attorney ◐ *see* crime, law
audience ◐ *see* leisure, theater
auditorium ◐◑ *see* building, theater
auger *for a picture see definition*
auricle *for a picture see the definition of* body
author ◐ *see* literature
authority ◐◑ *see* government, knowledge
automobile ◐◑ *see* car
aviation ◐ *see* airplane, technology
ax *for pictures see definitions of* ax, hatchet, tomahawk
axis *for a picture see the definition of* equator
baby
see also family, life, reproduction
for pictures see definitions of bib, crawl, diaper,
diminutive, infant, mammal
back
see also body
for a picture see the definition of back[1]
backbone ◐◑ *see* personality, skeleton
backgammon *for a picture see definition*
backpack *for a picture see the definition of* knapsack
bacteria ◐◐◑
see also cell, disease, virus
broader categories that include bacteria
germ (n.1), microbe, microorganism, organism
some actions of bacteria
absorb (v.1), multiply (v.3,5), secrete
some descriptions of bacteria
microscopic (adj.1), rodlike (rod n.1),
spiral (adj.)
some products of bacteria
boil[2], enzymes, infection (n.1), medicine (n.1),
pneumonia, soil[1] (n.1), spores, tetanus
some things affected by bacteria
digestion, health (n.1)
conventionally associated with bacteria
culture (n.4), microscope, slide (n.3), test tube
negatively associated with bacteria
plaque (n.2), septic (adj.1)
absence of bacteria
sterile (adj.1)
some effects of bacteria
decay (n.2), **digestion, disease**,
fermentation (n.1)
some things that affect bacteria

antibiotic, antiseptic, disinfectant, heat (n.1),
hygiene, iodine (n.2),
pasteurization (pasteurize), penicillin,
sanitation
badminton *for a picture see definition*
bag *for pictures see definitions of* drawstring, garbage, rubber, sack[1]
bagel *for a picture see definition*
bait ◐ *see* fishing
bake ◐ *see* cooking, food
balance
see also bank, health, mind
for a picture see the definition of balance
bald eagle *for pictures see definitions of* bald eagle,
bird, conservation
ball
see also game, sport
for pictures see definitions of dimple, glove, Ping-
Pong, racket[2], volleyball
ball[2] *see* celebration, dance
ballad ◐ *see* literature, music
ball bearing *for a picture see definition*
ballerina *for a picture see definition*
ballet ◐ *see* dance
balloon *for pictures see definitions of* deflate, inflate
banana *for a picture see definition*
band
see also mammal, music
for a picture see the definition of drum major
band[2] *see* jewelry
bandage
see also first aid, injury
for pictures see definitions of adhesive, bandage
banjo *for pictures see definitions of* banjo, music
bank[1] ◐ *see* river, soil
bank[2] (n.1/v.1) ◐
see also business, money
some kinds of banks
commercial (adj.2), drive-in
broader categories that include banks
economy (n.2), **money**
some parts of banks
ATM, cage (n.2), lobby (n.1), safe (n.),
vault[1] (n.3)
some activities in banking
borrow (v.1), cash (v.), credit (v.2),
deposit (v.2), exchange (v.1), finance (v.),
invest (v.1), lend (v.2), loan (v.2), pay (v.2),
repay (v.2), save[1] (v.2), withdraw (v.2)
some things used in banking
account (n.2), asset (n.2), bill[1] (n.2),
bond (n.3), cash (n.), check (n.2), coin (n.),
credit (n.3,5), credit card, debt (n.1),
funds (n.1,3), **money**, receipt (n.2), slip[2] (n.1),
statement (n.2)
some people associate with banks
cashier (n.2), clerk (n.1), customer,
guard (n.1), manager, teller (n.2)
some actions negatively associated with banking
bankrupt (v.), counterfeit (v.), embezzle,
forge[1] (v.3), rob (v.1), steal (v.1)
bankrupt ◐ *see* business, money
baptism ◐ *see* celebration, religion
barb *for a picture see definition*
barbecue *for a picture see definition*
bar code *for a picture see definition*
bare *for a picture see definition*
bargain ◐ *see* business, money
bark
see also dog
for a picture see the definition of bark
bark
see also plant, tree

for a picture see the definition of bark

barn ○ see building, farming

barrel for a picture see the definition of keg

base[1] ⊙ ○ see chemistry, thought

baseball
  see also leisure, sport
  for pictures see definitions of glove, infield, involve, mound, outfield

BASIC ⊙ ○ see computer, language

basket for pictures see definitions of basket, wicker

basketball ○ see leisure, sport

bass
  see also instrument, music
  for pictures see definitions of bass[1], music

bass drum for a picture see definition

bat for a picture see definition

bat for a picture see definition

bathe ⊙ ○ see hygiene

bathroom ⊙ ○ see home, hygiene

battery
  see also electricity, energy
  for a picture see the definition of battery

battle ○ see military, war

battleship for a picture see definition

bay ⊙ see lake, ocean, sea

beach
  see also lake, ocean, sea
  for pictures see definitions of low tide, shore

beacon for a picture see definition

beagle for a picture see definition

beak for pictures see definitions of beak, bird

beam
  see also happiness, light
  for a picture see the definition of ray[1]

bean ○ see farming, gardening, vegetable

bear
  see also mammal
  for pictures see definitions of bare, endangered species, grizzly bear, growl, polar bear, teddy bear

beard for pictures see definitions of beard, goatee

beat ○ see instrument, music

beauty ⊙ ⊙ see belief, earth, hygiene

beaver for pictures see definitions of beaver, teeth

bed
  see also flower, furniture, gardening
  for pictures see definitions of bed, cradle

bedpan for a picture see definition

bee for pictures see definitions of honeycomb, insect

beef for a picture see definition

beer for a picture see the definition of froth

beetle for pictures see definitions of beetle, ladybug

begonia for a picture see definition

behavior (n.2) ⊙
  see also action, personality
  similar to behavior
    action (n.2), approach (n.3), bearing (n.1), conduct (n.)
  some kinds of behavior
    aggressive (adj.1), apologetic, best (good adj.6), bullying (bully n.), casual (adj.2), childish (adj.1), civil (adj.3), controlling (control n.1), correct (adj.2), courteous, cowardly (adj.2), crazy (adj.2), dangerous, disciplined (discipline n.1), discourteous, disturbing (disturb v.3), eccentric (adj.), formal (adj.1), harsh (adj.3), heroic (adj.2), hysterical (adj.1), improper (adj.2), informal (adj.1), insolent, mischievous (adj.2), natural (adj.3), neurotic, outrageous (adj.2), pious (adj.1), polite, proper (adj.2), strange (adj.1), unruly,

violent (adj.1), wicked (adj.1), wild (adj.3)
  some kinds of repeated behavior
    convention (n.2), custom (n.1), fashion (n.2), habit (n.1), manner (n.2), method (n.2), practice (n.1), procedure, process (n.1), ritual (n.2), routine (n.2)
  study of behavior
    psychology
  some actions in response to behavior
    approve (v.3), change (v.1), deter, forbid, pardon (v.2), permit (v.1), praise (v.1), prohibit (v.2), reward (v.), sanction (v.)
  associated with negative behavior
    act up (phr.1), carry on (phr.2), make a spectacle of oneself, misbehave
  changing one's behavior
    clean up one's act, get one's act together, improve (v.2), reform (v.2), turn over a new leaf
  copying someone's behavior
    imitate (v.1), impersonate, mimic (v.1), parrot (v.)
  some influences on behavior
    attitude (n.1), challenge (n.3), commandment (n.1), conscience, criticism (n.1), dare (n.), discipline (n.1), disposition (n.1), **emotion** (n.1), encouragement (n.1), etiquette, guidance (n.1), manners (n.2), **morals** (n.2), **personality** (n.1), principle (n.1), regulation (n.1), **religion** (n.2), rule (n.1), sportsmanship, taboo (n.), tradition (n.2)
  some ways to influence behavior
    incite (v.2), inspire (v.2), prompt (v.1), provoke (v.1), steer[1] (v.2)

belief (n.1) ⊙ ○
  see also mind, religion, thought
  similar to belief
    bias (n.2), conviction (n.3), delusion (n.2), expectation (n.2), faith (n.2), idea (n.2), opinion (n.1), point of view, prejudice (n.1), trust (n.1), viewpoint
  some kinds of beliefs
    lofty (adj.3), newfangled, obstinate, old-fashioned (adj.2), open (adj.7), orthodox, political, religious (adj.2)
  some actions involving belief
    accept (v.3), assume (v.1), bet your boots, buy (v.2), confirm (v.1), convert (v.3), deny (v.1), dismiss (v.3), disregard (v.), doubt (v.1,2), presume (v.1,3), put stock in, reject
  some actions that cause belief
    assure (v.2), bluff[2] (v.2), convince, deceive, fool (v.1), mislead, persuade (v.2), trick (v.)
  some representations of beliefs
    adage, allegory, creed, doctrine, motto, proverb
  some people associated with belief
    believer (believe v.1), follower
  without belief
    doubtful (adj.1), incredulous, suspicious (adj.2), uncertain (adj.2), up in the air
  some things that influence beliefs
    morals (n.2), **myth** (n.1), philosophy (n.2), **politics** (n.3), **religion** (n.1,3), superstition, tradition (n.2), values (n.3)

bell ○ see instrument, music

bellows for a picture see definition

belly for a picture see definition

belt for a picture see the definition of buckle

bench
  see also furniture
  for pictures see definitions of bench, bleacher

beret for a picture see definition

berry
  see also farming, fruit
  for pictures see definitions of berry, mistletoe, raspberry

beverage
  see also drink
  for a picture see the definition of beverage

bib for a picture see definition

bicycle
  see also exercise, vehicle
  for pictures see definitions of above, bicycle, dazzle, messenger, reflector

bighorn for a picture see definition

bike for pictures see definitions of above, dazzle, messenger, messenger, reflector

bill
  see also business, legislature, money
  for pictures see definitions of bill, Euro, international, money, peso

bill
  see also bird
  for a picture see the definition of bill

bin for a picture see the definition of recycle

binary for a picture see the definition of number

binocular for pictures see definitions of binocular, field glass

biology ⊙ ○ see animal, body, life, plant, science

bird (n.) ○
  see also animal
  for pictures see definitions of bald eagle, beak, bill, bird, blackbird, bluebird, blue jay, buzzard, canary, cardinal, chick, chickadee, chicken, cock[1], cockatoo, conservation, crest, decoy, duck[1], egret, emu, falcon, flutter, fly[1], goose, group, hawk[1], heron, hoot, hover, hummingbird, mallard, mockingbird, owl, parakeet, parrot, partridge, peacock, pheasant, phoenix, quail, rooster, sea gull, soar, sparrow, squawk, toucan, trio, turkey, vulture, waddle, warbler, whooping crane, wren
  some examples of birds
    albatross, auk, blackbird, bluebird, blue jay, bobolink, buzzard, canary (n.1), cardinal (n.2), catbird, chickadee, chicken (n.1), condor, crane (n.1), crow[1] (n.), cuckoo (n.), dodo, duck[1] (n.), eagle, emu, falcon, finch, finch, flamingo, flicker[2], flycatcher, goose (n.1), grackle, grouse, gull, hawk[1] (n.1), heron, hummingbird, jay, kingfisher, kite (n.2), kiwi (n.1), lark[1] (n.), loon, magpie, martin, meadowlark, mockingbird, nightingale, nuthatch, oriole, ostrich, owl, parrot (n.), partridge, peacock (n.1), peafowl, penguin, pheasant, phoenix, pigeon, plover, puffin, quail, quetzal, raven (n.), roadrunner, robin, sparrow, stork (n.1), swallow[2], swan, swift (n.), thrush, toucan, turkey (n.1), vulture, warbler, whippoorwill, whooping crane, woodpecker, wren
  some categories of birds
    fowl, game (n.3), nocturnal (adj.2), songbirds, wading (wade v.1), water (n.2)
  broader categories that include birds
    animal (n.1), vertebrate (n.)
  parts of some birds
    beak, bill[2] (n.), comb (n.3), crest (n.1), crop (n.5), feathers (n.), talon, wings (n.1)
  study of birds
    ornithology
  some places for birds
    cage (n.1), coop (n.), habitat, nest (n.1), refuge (n.1), roost (n.), sanctuary (n.4), **tree** (n.1)
  group of birds

flock (n.1)
produced by birds
eggs[1] (n.2)
used for measuring birds
wingspan, wingspread
some behaviors of birds
breed (v.1,3), court (v.1), feed (v.1,4),
fly[1] (v.1), forage (v.1), mate (v.),
migrate (v.1), mob (v.1), nest (v.), peck[2] (v.1),
perch[1] (v.), sing (v.1)
sounds of some birds
buzz (n.1), caw (v.), chatter (v.2), chirp (v.),
clatter (v.), cry (v.3), gobble[2] (v.), honk (v.1),
hum (v.1), mimic (v.1), peep[2] (v.1), quack[1] (v.),
screech (v.), squawk (v.), squeak (v.),
trill (n.2), twitter (v.1), whistle (v.1)
some male birds
gander, peacock (n.1), rooster
some female birds
goose (n.2), hen
young of some birds
brood (n.1), chick, duckling, gosling
some things that birds eat
fruit, grain (n.1), **insects** (n.1), **seeds** (n.1),
worms (n.1)
characteristics of some birds
feathered (feather n.), warm-blooded, web-
footed (webfoot n.2), **winged** (wing n.1)
some growth processes of birds
hatching (hatch[1] v.3), incubating (incubate)
birth ⊕ ❶ *see* reproduction
birthday ❍ *see* celebration, tradition
biscuit *for a picture see the definition of* cracker
bison *for a picture see definition*
bite ⊕ ❶ *see* first aid, tooth
bitter *for a picture see the definition of* taste
blackbird *for a picture see definition*
blackboard ❍ *see* school
bladder
see also excrete, organ
for a picture see the definition of body
blade *for a picture see definition*
blanket *for pictures see definitions of* Afghan, quilt
blastoff *for a picture see definition*
blaze *for a picture see the definition of* blaze[2]
bleacher *for a picture see definition*
bleed ❍ *see* blood, first aid, injury
blimp *for a picture see the definition of* airship
bliss ⑦ *see* happiness
block
see also sport, thought
for a picture see the definition of ice
blood (n.1) ⊕ ❶
see also body
broader categories that include blood
body (n.1), fluid (n.)
some body parts associated with blood
aorta, artery (n.1), auricle (n.2), blood vessel,
capillary, heart (n.1), kidney (n.1), liver (n.1),
small intestine, spleen, vein (n.1), ventricle,
vessel (n.3)
some parts of blood
corpuscle, plasma, red blood cell, T cell, white
blood cell
some things that compose blood
antibody, hormone, iron (n.1), nutrients,
oxygen, protein, serum (n.1), waste (n.3)
some places for blood
blood bank, **body** (n.1), hospital,
laboratory (n.1)
some actions with blood
donate, draw (v.3), test (v.)
some actions of blood
circulate (v.1), clot (v.), flow (v.1), pulse (v.),

pump (v.1)
some descriptions of blood
red (adj.), sticky (adj.1), warm (adj.1)
some things that eat blood
flea (n.), horsefly, leech, louse, mosquito, tick[2],
vampire
some people associated with blood
doctor (n.1), donor (n.2), nurse (n.1), surgeon
conventionally associated with blood
sweat (n.1), tears[1] (n.1)
some diseases related to blood
anemia, diabetes, leukemia, stroke (n.5)
some terms for loss of blood
bleed (v.1), bloodshed
also associated with blood
bloodstream, Red Cross, transfusion
blossom
see also flower
for a picture see the definition of blossom
bluebird *for a picture see definition*
blue jay *for a picture see definition*
blues ⑦ ❸ *see* music, sadness
boa constrictor *for a picture see definition*
boar *for a picture see the definition of* tusk
board *for a picture see the definition of* palette
boat (n.1) ⊕
see also vehicle, water
for pictures see definitions of battleship, canoe,
capsize, dinghy, freighter, kayak, lifeboat,
propel, rowboat, sailboat, ship, wharf, yacht
some kinds of boats
ark (n.1), barge (n.), canoe (n.), catamaran,
craft (n.4), cruiser (n.1), dinghy, dory[1],
ferry (n.), galley (n.1), gondola (n.1),
houseboat, junk[2], kayak (n.1), launch[2],
lifeboat, motorboat, racer (n.2), raft (n.2),
rowboat, sailboat, sloop, steamboat, tugboat
broader categories that include boats
transportation (n.1), **vehicle** (n.1),
vessel (n.2)
some parts of boats
anchor (n.1), ballast (n.1), boom[2] (n.1),
canvas (n.1), deck (n.1), engine (n.1),
fin (n.2), galley (n.2), hull[2], jib, mast (n.1),
motor (n.), oar, outboard motor, outrigger,
paddle (n.1), prow, rigging (rig n.2), rudder,
sail (n.1), tiller
some places for boats
bay, boathouse, canal (n.1), channel (n.1),
dock (n.1), harbor (n.1), **lake**, levee (n.2),
marina, **ocean** (n.1), pier (n.1), quay,
river (n.1), sea (n.3), waterway, wharf
some actions related to boats
cruise (v.1), launch[1] (v.2), moor[2] (v.2),
paddle (v.1), rock[2] (v.1), roll (v.3), row[2] (v.),
sail (v.1), swamp (v.3), tip[2] (v.3), troll[1] (v.1)
some people associated with boats
admiral, captain (n.2), crew (n.2),
ensign (n.2), pirate (n.1), sailor (n.2)
some terms related to boats
bow[3], port[2], starboard (n.)
also associated with boats
coast guard, **fishing (fish** v.2), navy (n.1),
seasickness (seasick), sonar (n.2)
bob *for a picture see definition*
bob *for a picture see definition*
bobbin *for a picture see definition*
body (n.1) ❍
see also blood, cell, digestion, disease, excrete,
exercise, face, first aid, foot, hair, head, health,
hygiene, injury, life, muscle, nerve, organ,
reproduction, respiration, sense, skeleton,
tooth
for pictures see definitions of appendix, body
some kinds of damage to the body

cripple (n.), frostbite (n.), sore (n.), sprain (n.),
wound[1] (n.1)
some parts of the body
abdomen (n.1), arm[1] (n.1), back[1] (n.1),
bone (n.), brain (n.1), breast (n.1), buttock,
chest (n.1), extremity (n.3), finger (n.1),
foot (n.1), gland, **hair** (n.1), hand (n.1),
head (n.1), hips (n.), joint (n.), lap[1], leg (n.1),
limb (n.2), muscle (n.1), neck (n.1),
nerve (n.1), **organ** (n.2), penis,
shoulder (n.1,2), **skeleton** (n.1), skin (n.1),
thorax (n.1), tissue (n.1), toe (n.1),
trunk (n.2), vagina, waist (n.1)
study of the body
anatomy (n.2)
automatic reactions of the body
allergy, reflex (n.1), shock[1] (n.4)
some activities of the body
digest (v.1), **excrete**, exercise (v.2), perspire,
secrete, sweat (v.1)
some descriptions of the body
burly, muscular (adj.2), short (adj.2),
stout (adj.1,3), strong (adj.1), sturdy,
tall (adj.1), weak (adj.1)
some things that are produced by the body
antitoxin, **cell** (n.1), hormone, insulin (n.1),
lymph, mucus, red blood cell, sound[1] (n.1),
sweat (n.1), waste (n.3), white blood cell
some representations of the body
bust[1], doll, dummy (n.2), statue
some accessories for the body
armor (n.1), **clothing**, cosmetic, **jewelry**, razor
conventionally associated with the body
mind (n.1), soul (n.1)
some conditions of the body
balance (n.3), breakdown (n.2), health (n.2),
hypothermia, illness (n.1), paralysis,
tension (n.1),
unconsciousness (unconscious adj.2)
some movements of the body
bend (v.3), bow[1] (v.1), creep (v.1),
crouch (v.), curtsy (v.), dance (v.1,2),
duck[2] (v.1,3), jump (v.1,3), reach (v.1,2),
shake (v.1,2), somersault (v.), squirm (v.1),
stoop[1] (v.1,2), stroke (v.), twitch (v.1),
wriggle (v.1)
some positions of the body
attention (n.4), attitude (n.2), pose (n.1),
posture
some terms for the shape of the body
build (n.), figure (n.4), form (n.2), frame (n.3)
some things that affect the body
drug (n.1), **exercise** (n.1), **food** (n.),
gravity (n.1), massage (n.), medicine (n.1),
mineral (n.), nutrient, rest[1] (n.2), sleep (n.1),
vitamin, **water** (n.1)
some things that are done to the body
acupuncture, autopsy, burial, checkup,
implant (n.), injection (n.2), spank,
surgery (n.2), transplant (n.)
some things the body is able to do
express (v.1), feel (v.2), gesture (v.),
move (v.1), sense (v.1)
bog ❻ *see* ecosystem, farming, geography
boil
see also anger, cooking
for a picture see the definition of boil[1]
bolt *for a picture see definition*
bomb
see also war, weapon
for a picture see the definition of grenade
bond ❽ ❍ *see* crime, money
bone
see also skeleton
for pictures see definitions of body, skeleton,
skull

bongo *for pictures see definitions of* bongo[2], music
book (n.1) ⚬ ⚬
  see also leisure, literature
  for pictures see definitions of accumulate, album
  some kinds of books
    album (n.1), atlas (n.2), booklet,
    catalogue (n.2), cookbook, diary (n.2),
    dictionary, encyclopedia, handbook,
    journal (n.1), manual (n.), notebook, novel[1],
    pamphlet, paperback, register (n.1),
    scrapbook, textbook, workbook
  broader categories that include books
    art (n.2), **communication** (n.3), **culture** (n.1)
  some categories of books
    biography, fiction (n.1), juvenile (adj.2),
    nonfiction, poetry (n.1), reference (n.2),
    romance (n.2), western (n.)
  some parts of books
    appendix (n.1), caption, chapter (n.1),
    cover (n.1), excerpt (n.), footnote, foreword,
    glossary, illustration (n.1), index (n.),
    introduction (n.2), leaf (n.2), page[1] (n.),
    paper (n.1), photograph (n.), picture (n.1),
    plate (n.3), preface (n.1), quotation (n.2),
    sheet (n.3), spine (n.3), text (n.2)
  some places for books
    bookcase, bookmobile, classroom,
    library (n.1), **school**[1] (n.1)
  some actions associated with books
    autograph (v.), ban (v.), bind (v.1),
    borrow (v.1), browse (v.1), censor (v.), cite,
    critique (v.), leaf (v.2), look up, publish,
    read (v.1), review (v.2), skim (v.3),
    study (v.3), thumb (v.), write (v.1,3)
  some descriptions of books
    classic (adj.1,2), epic (adj.1,2),
    overdue (adj.1), popular (adj.1)
  some people associated with books
    author, bookworm (n.1), critic (n.1),
    editor (n.1), illustrator, librarian, playwright,
    poet, writer (n.2)
boom[1] ⚬ *see* economy
boom[2] *see* boat
boomerang *for a picture see definition*
boot
  see also clothing, computer, foot
  for pictures see definitions of leather, overshoe
bore *for a picture see definition*
bore *for a picture see definition*
bored *for a picture see the definition of* insomnia
boredom ⚬ *see* mind
borrow ⚬ *see* bank, money
botany ⚬ *see* plant, science
bottle *for pictures see definitions of* decanter, flask
bounce *for a picture see the definition of* dribble
bow
  see also action, dance, theater
  for pictures see definitions of bow, curtsy
bow
  see also instrument, weapon
  for pictures see definitions of crossbow, music
bow
  see also boat
  for a picture see the definition of bow
bowel *for a picture see the definition of* immerse
bowl
  see also cooking, food
  for a picture see the definition of bowl
box *for pictures see definitions of* empty, lug, Pandora
box *for a picture see the definition of* jab
boy *for a picture see the definition of* toddler
brain
  see also head, mind, organ, sense, thought

for pictures see definitions of body, brain
brake ⚬ *see* vehicle
branch
  see also plant, tree
  for a picture see the definition of pine
brass
  see also instrument
  for a picture see the definition of music
brave ⚬ *see* action, behavior
bread *for a picture see definition*
break
  see also first aid, injury, skeleton
  for a picture see the definition of shatter
breast
  see also bird, mammal, milk
  for a picture see the definition of body
breathe ⚬ *see* air, exercise, respiration
breed ⚬ *see* animal, plant, reproduction
breeze ⚬ *see* air, respiration, weather
bridge *for pictures see definitions of* bridge, cable
brilliant ⚬ *see* knowledge, thought
broadcast *see* communication
broccoli *for a picture see definition*
broil ⚬ *see* cooking
broke ⚬ *see* money
broken *for a picture see definition*
bronchial tube *for a picture see the definition of* body
brooch *for a picture see definition*
brook ⚬ *see* geography, river
broom *for a picture see the definition of* brush[1]
brush
  see also art, hygiene, tool
  for pictures see definitions of brush[1], hygiene
brush[2] ⚬ *see* plant
Brussels sprouts *for a picture see definition*
buck *for a picture see the definition of* buck[1]
buckle *for a picture see definition*
bud ⚬ *see* flower, plant
buddy *for a picture see definition*
buffalo *for pictures see definitions of* mammal, wallow, water buffalo
buffet *for a picture see definition*
bug
  see also insect
  for pictures see definitions of beetle, housefly, Japanese beetle, ladybug
bugle *for a picture see definition*
build *for pictures see definitions of* inventive, labor
building (n.1) ⚬
  see also community
  for pictures see definitions of cathedral, dilapidated, dome, greenhouse, vault[1]
  some kinds of buildings
    abbey, amphitheater, annex (n.), apartment,
    aquarium (n.2), arena (n.2), auditorium, barn,
    boathouse, capitol (n.1), castle (n.1), chapel,
    church (n.1), coliseum, condominium,
    convent (n.2), courthouse, dormitory,
    embassy (n.2), facility (n.1), factory, firehouse,
    fort, fortress, greenhouse, gymnasium,
    hall (n.2), high-rise, hothouse, house (n.1),
    jail (n.), landmark (n.2), lighthouse, museum,
    observatory, office (n.1), outhouse, penthouse,
    post office, prison, rink (n.3),
    roundhouse, sawmill, **school**[1] (n.1), shack (n.),
    shed[1], silo (n.1), skyscraper, station (n.2),
    temple[1] (n.1), theater (n.1), warehouse
  some parts of buildings
    atrium (n.1), balcony (n.1), belfry,
    buttress (n.), cloister (n.1), court (n.1), dome,

eave, elevator (n.1), escalator, lobby (n.1),
loft (n.1), steeple, terrace (n.1), tower (n.),
turret (n.1), wing (n.4)
some things that compose buildings
  beam (n.1), floor (n.2), girder, wall (n.1)
some places for buildings
  plot[2], site
some people associated with buildings
  architect, custodian (n.2), janitor, mason,
  painter (n.2), plumber
some tools used in making buildings
  backhoe, bulldozer, crane (n.2), scaffold,
  shovel (n.1), steamroller
also associated with buildings
  blueprint (n.1), construction (n.3)
bulb
  see also light, plant
  for pictures see definitions of filament, flower
bulldog ⚬ *see* weapon
bull's-eye *for a picture see definition*
bunch *for a picture see definition*
bunny *for pictures see definitions of* bunny, rabbit
bureau ⚬ ⚬ *see* furniture, government
burn ⚬ ⚬ *see* cooking, first aid, injury
burrow
  see also animal, soil
  for a picture see the definition of den
bus ⚬ *see* vehicle
bush ⚬ *see* leaf, tree
business (n.2) ⚬
  see also industry, money, work
  similar to business
    commerce, company (n.1), enterprise (n.2),
    firm[2]
  some kinds of businesses
    cooperative (n.), corporation, partnership
  broader category that includes business
    economy (n.1)
  some parts of businesses
    accounting (account n.2),
    administration (n.2), distribution (n.2),
    engineering (engineer n.1),
    manufacturing (manufacture n.),
    research (n.), sales (n.1), service (n.4),
    shipping (n.1)
  some places associated with businesses
    bazaar (n.1), **building** (n.1), mall (n.2),
    office (n.1), outlet (n.2), plaza (n.2),
    shop (n.1), shopping center, stall[1] (n.2),
    store (n.1), trading post, warehouse
  some actions of businesses
    advertise (v.1), bargain (v.), bill[1] (v.),
    credit (v.2), employ (v.2), fire (v.4),
    guarantee (v.1), hire (v.1), incorporate (v.2),
    lease (v.1), manage (v.1), manufacture (v.1),
    market (v.2), negotiate, order (v.2),
    patent (v.), pay (v.1), price (v.1,2),
    purchase (v.), stock (v.2)
  some descriptions of businesses
    commercial (adj.1), industrial (adj.1),
    productive (adj.1), professional (adj.1,2),
    profitable (adj.1), retail (adj.)
  some things used in businesses
    computers, desks, files[1] (n.1,2), machines,
    packaging (package n.2), software, **tools** (n.1)
  some people associated with businesses
    accountant, boss (n.), businessman,
    businesswoman, cashier (n.1), clerk (n.1),
    client, consumer, customer, dealer (n.1),
    director (n.1), employee, employer,
    executive (n.1), investor, manager,
    merchant (n.1), salesperson, secretary (n.1),
    staff (n.3), trader, tycoon
  some negative actions of businesses

rip off (phr. 2), swindle (v.)
also associated with businesses
   budgets (n. 1), capital[1] (n. 3, 4), contracts (n. 1),
   cost (n. 2), demand (n. 4), goods (pl. n. 2),
   inventory, merchandise, merger,
   monopoly (n. 1), overhead (n.), payroll (n. 2),
   price (n. 1), profit (n. 1), stock (n. 4),
   supply (n. 2), trademark

bust[1] *see* art, body

butterfly
  see also insect
  for pictures see definitions of butterfly, insect,
   monarch, transform

buttock *for a picture see the definition of* body

button *for a picture see the definition of* insignia

buy *see* business, money

buzzard *for a picture see definition*

cabbage *for a picture see definition*

cabin *see* airplane, building

cabinet *see* furniture, government

cable *for a picture see definition*

caboose *for a picture see definition*

cactus
  see also desert, plant
  for pictures see definitions of cactus, flower

cafeteria *see* food, room, school

cage *see* pet

cake *for pictures see definitions of* cake, layer

calcium *see* element, milk, skeleton, tooth

calculator *see* mathematics, technology, tool

calf
  see also mammal
  for a picture see the definition of calf[1]

calf
  see also muscle
  for a picture see the definition of body

camel *for pictures see definitions of* camel, dromedary, hump

camera
  see also film, photography
  for a picture see the definition of lens

camouflage *for a picture see definition*

campaign *for a picture see the definition of* platform

campfire *for a picture see definition*

canary *for a picture see definition*

cancer *for pictures see definitions of* constellation,
  zodiac

candidate
  see also democracy, politics
  for a picture see the definition of candidate

candle *for a picture see the definition of* wick

candlestick *for a picture see the definition of* menorah

cane *for a picture see the definition of* sugar cane

canine
  see also dog, tooth
  for a picture see the definition of canine

cannon *for a picture see definition*

canoe
  see also boat
  for pictures see definitions of canoe, propel

cantaloupe *for a picture see definition*

canteen *for a picture see definition*

canvas *see* art, boat

canyon *see* geography

cap *for a picture see the definition of* fleece

cape *for a picture see the definition of* cape[1]

capital[1] *see* country, grammar, money

Capricorn *for pictures see definitions of* constellation, zodiac

capsize *for a picture see definition*

car (n. 1)
  see also vehicle
  for pictures see definitions of abandoned,
   accelerate, crash, expensive, racer, tire,
   vehicle, wreck, zoom
  some kinds of cars
   cab (n. 1), compact[1] (n. 2), convertible (n.),
   hatchback, racer (n. 2), sedan, taxicab
  broader categories that include cars
   transportation (n. 1), **vehicle** (n. 1)
  some parts of cars
   air bag, axle, battery (n. 1), brakes (n.),
   bumper (n.), carburetor, chassis, clutch (n. 2),
   dashboard, door (n. 3), engine (n. 1),
   fender (n. 1), gearshift, headlights, hood (n. 3),
   hubcaps, ignition (n. 2), key[1] (n. 1), lock[1] (n. 1),
   piston, radiator (n. 2), radio (n. 1), seat (n. 1),
   seat belt, tires[2], transmission (n. 2), trim (n. 2),
   trunk (n. 4), window (n. 1), windshield
  some places for cars
   garage (n. 1), gas station, highway, lane (n. 2),
   parkway, road (n. 1), service station,
   street (n. 1), thruway
  some actions of cars
   accelerate (v. 2), backfire (v. 1), brake (v.),
   coast (v. 2), cruise (v. 2), drive (v. 4),
   honk (v. 2), idle (v. 2), park (v.), reverse (v. 1),
   ride (v. 1), screech (v.), shift (v. 3), skid (v.),
   speed (v. 2), stop (v. 1)
  some things used in cars
   antifreeze, gasoline, oil (n. 2), **water** (n. 1)
  some people associated with cars
   chauffeur, driver, mechanic, passenger
  some states of cars
   neutral (n.), reverse (n. 3)
  also associated with cars
   accident (n. 1), breakdown (n. 1), carpool,
   exhaust (n. 1), inspection (n. 2), noise (n. 2),
   pollution (n. 2), speeding (speed n. 1),
   ticket (n. 3), traffic (n. 1)

caravan *for a picture see definition*

carbon dioxide *see* air, respiration

card *for pictures see definitions of* concentrate, suit

cardinal *for a picture see definition*

care (n. 1)
  see also behavior, hygiene, thought
  some kinds of care
   custody (n. 1), **hygiene**
  some places associated with care
   asylum (n. 2), clinic, day care, garage,
   home (n. 5), hospital, institution (n. 1), kennel,
   nursery (n. 3), orphanage, stable[2] (n.)
  some actions associated with not caring
   disregard (v.), neglect (v. 2)
  some actions associated with caring
   attend (v. 2), baby (v.), dote, groom (v. 2),
   handle with kid gloves, keep tabs on,
   maintain (v. 2), mind (v. 1), minister (v.),
   mother (v.), nurse (v. 1), pamper, protect,
   support (v. 3, 4), take care of (phr. 1),
   tend[2] (v. 1), keep an eye on, look after,
   trust (v. 4), watch (v. 2, 3)
  some descriptions of one who cares
   alert (adj.), attentive (adj. 1), aware,
   careful (adj. 1), cautious, competent,
   conscientious, exacting (adj. 2), immaculate,
   neat (adj. 2), orderly (adj. 1), precise (adj. 1),
   responsible (adj. 3), scrupulous (adj. 2),
   thorough, vigilant, watchful
  some descriptions of one who does not care
   careless (adj. 2), haphazard, hasty (adj. 2),
   incompetent, indifferent, irresponsible,
   negligent, reckless, slipshod, sloppy (adj. 3),
   thoughtless (adj. 2)
  some people associated with care
   baby-sitter (baby-sit), caretaker,

custodian (n. 1), doctor (n. 1), father (n. 1),
   groom (n. 2), guardian (n. 2), housekeeper,
   janitor, mother (n. 1), nanny, nurse (n. 1),
   parent, pediatrician, shepherd (n. 1),
   superintendent (n. 2), veterinarian
  similiar to care
   attention (n. 2), caution (n. 1), heed (n.),
   pains (n. 3)
  also associated with caring
   ASPCA, Red Cross, SPCA

career *see* work

careful *for a picture see definition*

caress *for a picture see definition*

carnation *for a picture see definition*

carnivore
  see also animal, diet
  for a picture see the definition of carnivore

carob *for a picture see definition*

carriage *for a picture see the definition of* stagecoach

carrot *for a picture see definition*

carry *for pictures see definitions of* lug, resolve

cart *for pictures see definitions of* cart, wheelbarrow

cartoon *see* art, film

cartwheel *for a picture see definition*

carve *for a picture see definition*

cash *see* money

cashew *for a picture see definition*

casket *for pictures see definitions of* casket, coffin

castanet *for a picture see definition*

cast iron *for a picture see definition*

castle *for pictures see definitions of* castle, fortress,
  moat, rook

cat (n. 1, 2)
  see also mammal, pet
  for pictures see definitions of carnivore, cat,
   cheetah, cougar, feline, frolic, glare, jaguar,
   leopard, lick, lion, lioness, lounge, lynx, ocelot,
   peril, scratch, snooze, tiger, unlucky, whisker
  some examples of cats
   bobcat, cheetah, cougar, jaguar, leopard, lion,
   lynx, mountain lion, ocelot, panther, puma,
   tiger
  some kinds of cats
   domestic (adj. 2), purebred (n.), stray (n.),
   wildcat
  broader categories that include cats
   animal (n. 1), carnivore, **mammal**,
   vertebrate (n.)
  some parts of cats
   claws (n. 1), fur (n. 1), mane, pads[1] (n. 5),
   paw (n.), ruff (n. 2), tail (n. 1), whiskers (n. 2)
  some qualities of cats
   agile (adj. 1), independent (adj. 1)
  some behaviors of cats
   breed (v. 3), feed (v. 4), hunt (v. 1), leap (v. 1),
   pounce (v.), stalk[2] (v. 2)
  makes sounds like a cat
   catbird
  some sounds of cats
   growl (v. 1), hiss (v. 2), meow (v.), mew (v.),
   purr (v.)
  female cat
   lioness
  young of cats
   kitten, litter (n. 2)
  conventionally associated with cats
   mouse (n. 1)
  some things cats eat
   birds (n.), **insects** (n. 1), **mammals**,
   snakes (n.)

catch *for a picture see the definition of* Frisbee

caterpillar *for pictures see definitions of* caterpillar,

metamorphosis, silkworm, transform
catfish *for a picture see definition*
cathedral *for a picture see definition*
cattle ❶ *see* farming, mammal
cauliflower *for a picture see definition*
cave ❻ *see* geography, geology
celebration ⊖
  see also leisure, tradition
  similar to celebration
    ceremony (n.1), holiday, memorial,
    ritual (n.1)
  some kinds of celebrations
    ball² (n.1), banquet, barbecue (n.1), clambake,
    dance (n.3), feast (n.), festival (n.1), fiesta,
    function (n.2), gala, honeymoon (n.),
    masquerade (n.1), reception (n.3), social (n.)
  some parts of celebrations
    parade (n.), presentation, procession (n.2),
    speech (n.3), toast² (n.)
  some places for celebrating
    auditorium, church (n.1), hall (n.2),
    home (n.2), monument (n.1), mosque,
    park (n.1), plaza (n.1), temple¹ (n.2),
    yard² (n.1)
  some actions involved in celebrating
    acclaim (v.), anoint, applaud (v.2),
    award (v.1), bestow, bless (v.3), cheer (v.2),
    congratulate, dedicate (v.2), glorify (v.1),
    honor (v.1,2), praise (v.2), rejoice,
    sing (v.1,4), whistle (v.1)
  some things used in celebrating
    balloons (n.3), bonfires, candles (n.),
    champagne, confetti, cornucopias (n.1),
    costumes (n.2), crepe paper,
    decorations (n.2,3), **drink** (n.1,2),
    firecrackers, fireworks, **food** (n.), garlands,
    gifts (n.1), hats, leis, medals, **music** (n.1),
    novelties (novelty n.3), ornaments (n.),
    presents² (n.), tinsel, trophies (trophy)
  some expressions of celebrating
    appreciation (n.1), gratitude, joy (n.1),
    reverence
  some people associated with celebrating
    band¹ (n.2), clown (n.1), marshal (n.2),
    performer, speaker (n.1)
  some occasions for celebration
    anniversary (n.2), baptism, bar mitzvah,
    birth (n.1), birthday, Canada Day,
    Christmas (n.2), confirmation (n.3), Easter,
    Fourth of July, Good Friday, graduation (n.2),
    Memorial Day, New Year's Day, Passover,
    Ramadan (n.1), Rosh Hashanah,
    Thanksgiving (n.2), triumph (n.1), Veterans
    Day, victory, wedding
celery *for a picture see definition*
cell (n.1) ❸❶❹
  see also animal, bacteria, body, plant
  some examples of cells
    corpuscle, egg¹ (n.1), red blood cell, sperm, T
    cell, white blood cell
  some means for categorizing cells
    function (n.1), structure (n.2)
  some parts of cells
    chromosome, cytoplasm, membrane,
    nucleus (n.2), protoplasm
  some things composed of only one cell
    amoeba, **bacteria**, paramecium, protozoan
  some things composed of cells
    blood (n.1), gland, lymph, **organ** (n.2),
    plasma, pus, tissue (n.1)
  includes the study of cells
    biology
  some things that produce cells
    bone marrow (marrow), spleen
  person who studies cells
    scientist

  some tools for studying cells
    microscope, slide (n.3)
  grows in cells
    virus (n.1)
  some things found in cells
    carbohydrate, carbon, DNA, enzyme, fat (n.1),
    gene, hydrogen, nitrogen, oxygen, protein,
    vitamin, **water** (n.1)
cello *for a picture see definition*
census ⊖ *see* government
cent *for a picture see definition*
centaur *for pictures see definitions of* centaur, constellation
centipede *for a picture see definition*
century ❶ *see* history
cereal
  see also food, grain
  for a picture see the definition of granola
ceremony
  see also tradition
  for a picture see the definition of ceremony
cetacean
  see also animal
  for a picture see the definition of cetacean
chain *for pictures see definitions of* chain, link
chair
  see also furniture
  for pictures see definitions of armchair,
  upholstery
chalk ❶❹ *see* art, school
chameleon *for a picture see the definition of* reptile
champion *for a picture see definition*
channel *for a picture see definition*
character ❸❹ *see* art, literature, personality
charge ❶❷⊖ *see* crime, electricity, money
charm *for a picture see definition*
chase *for a picture see the definition of* elude
check
  see also bank, money
  for a picture see the definition of check
checkerboard *for a picture see definition*
checkup ❹ *see* health
cheer ❹ *see* happiness
cheetah *for a picture see definition*
chef
  see also cooking
  for pictures see definitions of apron, present²
chemical ❶ *see* chemistry, element
chemistry ❶ ❹
  see also element, science
  a broader category that includes chemistry
    science
  some places associated with chemistry
    lab, laboratory (n.1)
  some actions associated with chemistry
    analyze, combine (v.), condense (v.3),
    congeal, cool (v.3), dilute, dissolve (v.1),
    experiment (v.), filter (v.2), heat (v.1),
    react (v.3), separate (v.2)
  some things produced using chemistry
    additives, cleaners (n.1), concrete (n.),
    drugs (n.1), fertilizer, gasoline,
    medicine (n.1), paint (n.1), plastic (n.),
    steel (n.1)
  some things used in chemistry
    acid (n.), balance (n.1), base¹ (n.5), beaker,
    Bunsen burner, **computer**, filter (n.1), flask,
    goggles, litmus paper, microscope, reaction,
    test tube
  some people who use chemistry
    baker, chemist, engineer (n.1)
  some aspects of chemistry
    energy (n.1), equilibrium, product (n.2),

    reaction
  some things that are associated with chemistry
    atom (n.1), compound (n.2), **element** (n.4),
    experiment (n.), fluoride, formula (n.4), ion,
    metal, molecule, oxide, salt (n.2)
cherry *for a picture see definition*
chess *for pictures see definitions of* chess, strategy
chest
  see also body, furniture
  for a picture see the definition of body
chew ❹ *see* digestion, tooth
chick *for a picture see definition*
chickadee *for a picture see definition*
chicken
  see also bird, farming
  for pictures see definitions of chick, chicken,
  cock¹, crest, rooster
child
  see also family, life, relationship
  for a picture see the definition of toddler
chili *for a picture see definition*
chilly *for a picture see the definition of* chili
chime *for a picture see definition*
chimpanzee *for pictures see definitions of* chimpanzee, monkey
china *for a picture see definition*
chinchilla *for a picture see definition*
Chinese *for pictures see definitions of* Chinese, language
chipmunk *for a picture see definition*
chisel *for a picture see definition*
chlorophyll ❶ *see* plant
choir *for pictures see definitions of* choir, unison
chopstick *for a picture see definition*
chord *for a picture see the definition of* chord²
chorus
  see also music
  for pictures see definitions of choir, unison
chow *for a picture see the definition of* chow¹
chow *for a picture see the definition of* chow²
Christmas tree *for pictures see definitions of*
  adorn, decorate
chromosome ❸❶ *see* cell, reproduction
chrysanthemum *for a picture see definition*
church
  see also building, religion
  for a picture see the definition of cathedral
cicada *for a picture see definition*
cigarette *for a picture see the definition of* hazardous
cinema ❹ *see* building, film, photography
circuit
  see also electricity
  for a picture see the definition of direct current
circulation *for a picture see the definition of* body
citizen ⊖ *see* country, government
citrus
  see also fruit
  for pictures see definitions of citrus, grapefruit
city (n.1) ❶
  see also community
  similar to city
    town (n.2)
  some kinds of cities
    capital¹ (n.1), metropolis
  broader category that includes cities
    community (n.1)
  some places for cities
    country (n.1), county (n.2), province (n.1),
    state (n.2)
  description of a city
    urban
  some people associated with cities

mayor, police officer, sheriff

some things found in cities
apartment, bus (n.), crowd (n.1), high-rise, museum, office (n.1), park (n.1), pollution (n.1), skyscraper, subway, taxicab, traffic (n.1)

civil ◎ *see* democracy, law

clam *for a picture see definition*

clamp *for a picture see definition*

clarinet *for pictures see definitions of* clarinet, music

clasp *for a picture see definition*

class ❶❷❸ *see* life, money, school

classic ❶❷ *see* art, tradition

claw ❶ *see* animal, foot

clay ❸ *see* soil

clean *for a picture see the definition of* scrub

cleaver *for a picture see definition*

clever ❼ *see* action, thought

cliff
see also geography, geology
for pictures see definitions of cliff, reckless

climate ❻ *see* weather

climb *for a picture see the definition of* ascent

clip *for a picture see definition*

clip *for a picture see definition*

clock *for pictures see definitions of* counterclockwise, pendulum, reluctant

clog *for a picture see definition*

close-up *for a picture see definition*

cloth *for a picture see the definition of* homespun

clothing
for pictures see definitions of overall, overcoat
some examples of clothing
blouse, bonnet, boots (n.), cap¹ (n.1), chaps, coat (n.1), derby (n.2), dress (n.1), dungarees (n.2), garter, gloves (n.1), gown (n.1), hat, jacket (n.1), jersey (n.1), jumper (n.1), jump suit (n.1), leotard, mittens, muffler (n.1), necktie, pajamas, pants (pl.n.), pullover, sari, scarf, shirt (n.), shoes (n.1), shorts (n.3), skirt (n.1), slacks, sneakers, socks, sombrero, stockings (n.), suit (n.1), sweater, sweatshirt, tie (n.2), tights, trousers, trunks (n.6), T-shirt (n.1), turban, turtleneck (n.2), underpants, underwear, uniform (n.), vest (n.)
similar to clothing
apparel, attire (n.), costume (n.1), garment, outfit (n.2)
some parts of clothing
button (n.1), buttonhole (n.), collar (n.1), cuff¹ (n.1), drawstring, fly¹ (n.1), hem (n.), monogram (n.), neck (n.2), pocket (n.1), seam (n.1), seat (n.4), sleeve (n.), waist (n.2), zipper
some places for clothing
cleaners (n.2), closet, dresser, Laundromat, store (n.1), suitcase, wardrobe
some actions associated with clothing
bundle up, change (v.5), clothe, design (v.1), dress up, iron (v.1), launder, mend (v.1), press (v.2), sew (v.), starch (v.), stitch (v.), strip¹ (v.1), try on, undress (v.1), wash (v.1), wear (v.2)
people associated with clothing
model (n.5), tailor (n.)
some accessories for clothing
apron, belt (n.1), bib (n.1), sequin, smock, spangle
without clothing
bare (adj.1), naked (adj.1), nude (adj.1)
negatively associated with clothing
moth (n.2), rip (n.), stain (n.1)

associated with clothing
clothespin, detergent, dryer, fad, fashion (n.1), iron (n.3), line¹ (n.3), sewing machine, style (n.3), vogue, washing machine
some materials for clothing
canvas (n.1), corduroy (n.1), cotton (n.1), denim (n.1), elastic (n.), flannel, fringe (n.1), hemp (n.2), holland, lace (n.1,2), leather (n.), linen (n.1), muslin, rayon (n.2), silk (n.2), Velcro, wool (n.3)

cloud *for a picture see the definition of* ray¹

clover *for pictures see definitions of* charm, clover, shamrock

clown *for pictures see definitions of* clown, juggle

cluster *for a picture see definition*

coach *for a picture see the definition of* stagecoach

coal ❻ *see* energy, natural resources

coast
see also geography, ocean, sea, vehicle
for a picture see the definition of maroon¹

coat *for a picture see the definition of* overcoat

coat of arms *for a picture see definition*

cobra *for a picture see definition*

cock *for pictures see definitions of* cock¹, rooster

cockatoo *for a picture see definition*

cockpit *for a picture see definition*

cockroach *for pictures see definitions of* cockroach, vermin

coconut *for a picture see definition*

cocoon *for pictures see definitions of* metamorphosis, silkworm, transform

code ❶❷❸◎ *see* language, law, tradition

coffee ❶ *see* drink

coffin *for pictures see definitions of* casket, coffin

coil *for a picture see definition*

coin
see also money
for pictures see definitions of coin, international, quarter, shilling

cold-blooded
see also amphibian, fish, reptile
for a picture see the definition of cold-blooded

collapse *for a picture see definition*

collar *for pictures see definitions of* delicate, lace

collie *for a picture see definition*

colon *for a picture see the definition of* body

colonial *see* government, history

colonnade *for a picture see definition*

colony ❶◎ *see* animal, bacteria, government

color (n.1) ❼
see also art, light
some examples of colors
almond (n.3), amber (n.2), aqua, auburn, azure, beige, black (n.1), blue (n.), blush (n.2), bronze (n.2), brown (n.3), buff (n.3), canary (n.2), cherry (n.4), chestnut (n.4), chocolate (n.4), cocoa (n.3), copper (n.2), cream (n.3), crimson, ebony (n.3), ecru, emerald (n.2), gold (n.4), gray (n.), green (n.1), hazel (n.3), indigo (n.3), ivory (n.2), jet² (n.1), khaki (n.1), lavender (n.3), lilac (n.3), magenta, mahogany (n.3), maroon¹, mauve, mulberry (n.3), mustard (n.3), navy (n.3), olive (n.3), orange (n.3), orchid (n.3), peach (n.3), pink (n.1), purple (n.), raspberry (n.3), red (n.), rose¹ (n.3), ruby (n.2), russet (n.1), salmon (n.2), scarlet (n.), silver (n.4), slate (n.3), tan (n.3), tawny (n.1), teal (n.2), turquoise (n.2), violet (n.1), walnut (n.4), white (n.1), yellow (n.)
broader categories that include color
art (n.4), light¹ (n.1)

some actions associated with color
bleach (v.1,2), blend (v.1), clash (v.3), dye (v.), fade (v.1), glow (v.2), mix (v.1), stain (v.1,2), tarnish (v.1,3)
some descriptions of colors
bold (adj.3), bright (adj.2), chromatic (adj.1), creamy (adj.1), dark (adj.2), dingy (adj.2), faint (adj.1), gaudy (adj.2), gay (adj.2), intense (adj.1), light¹ (adj.2), loud (adj.2), neutral (adj.2), pale (adj.1), pastel (adj.1), showy, solid (adj.6), strong (adj.3), visible (adj.1), vivid (adj.1), weak (adj.3)
some people associated with color
artist (n.1), painter
conventionally associated with color
complexion, crayon (n.), dye (n.), ink (n.), light¹ (n.1), makeup (n.1), paint (n.1,2), pigment, prism (n.1), rainbow, spectrum
without color
albino, color-blind (adj.1)
aspects of color
hue, shade (n.4), tinge (n.1), tint (n.1), tone (n.5)

colt *for pictures see definitions of* colt, mammal

columbine *for a picture see definition*

column *for pictures see definitions of* colonnade, upright

comb ❼❶ *see* bird, hair, hygiene

comedy ❼ *see* film, literature, theater

comet *for a picture see definition*

comma ❼ *see* grammar

command ❼ *see* communication, military, monarchy, power

commercial ❼❸ *see* advertisement

commonwealth ◎ *see* country, government

communication (n.1,3) ❼
see also art, grammar, language
some examples of communication
bulletin, call (n.3), conference, conversation, debate (n.), discussion, drawing (n.2), gesture (n.1), graph (n.), leaflet (n.1), letter (n.2), meeting (n.2), message (n.2), note (n.1), notice (n.1), painting (n.1), pamphlet, photograph (n.), play (n.2), speech (n.3), telegraph (n.), transmission (n.3)
some kinds of communication
advertise (v.1,2), advise (v.1), contact (v.), describe, enlighten, express (v.1), inform (v.1), invite (v.2), persuade, promote (v.1,3), reveal, share (v.2,3), speak (v.1), talk (v.1), teach (v.1), tell (v.1,2,3,4,6,7)
some categories of communication
audible, electronic (adj.1), oral (adj.1), silent (adj.1), spoken (adj.), written (adj.)
some descriptions of communication
brief (adj.1,2), clear (adj.3), confidential, difficult (adj.1), direct (adj.1,2), indirect (adj.1,3), interrupted (interrupt v.1), long¹ (adj.2), long distance, mass (n.1), mutual (adj.1), one-sided (adj.1), precise (adj.1), rapid (adj.1), wordy
some things used in communication
art (n.1), code (n.2), language (n.1), mass media, signal (n.1), symbol (n.1), technology (n.2), touch (n.2), voice (n.1)
some people associated with communication
actor, announcer, artist (n.1), audience (n.2), commentator, editor (n.2), journalist, narrator, operator (n.2), playwright, reporter, salesperson, speaker (n.1), teacher, writer (n.2)
some tools of communication
camera, computer, disc (disk n.2,3), fax (n.1),

film (n.3), intercom, interface, loudspeaker, microphone, modem, newspaper, radio (n.2), tape (n.2), telephone (n.), television (n.2), transmitter
some things negatively associated with communication
gossip (n.1), leak (n.2), lie[1] (n.), propaganda
communism ☺ *see* economy, government
community (n.1) ☺
see also government, relationship, city
some examples of communities
borough (n.1), **city**, town (n.1), village (n.1)
some kinds of communities
rural, suburban (suburb), urban
some places for communities
city (n.1), college, **country** (n.1), province (n.1), region (n.1), state (n.2), town (n.1), university, village (n.1)
representation of communities
map (road map)
some people associated with communities
citizens (n.2), council, mayor, officials (n.), police (n.1), representative (n.1)
some things found in communities
block (n.3), **building** (n.1), **business** (n.2), church (n.1), fire department, ghetto (n.2), **home** (n.2), library (n.1), neighborhood (n.1), park (n.1), post office (n.1), precinct, quarter (n.5), restaurant, road (n.1), **school**[1] (n.1), shopping center, store (n.1), street (n.1), waterworks
commute ☺ *see* transportation, vehicle
companionship ☺ *see* family, pet, relationship
compass *for pictures see definitions of* compass, east, exploration
compassion ☺ *see* care
competition ☺ *see* business, game, sport
composer ☺ *see* literature, music
computer ☺☺☺
see also communication, Internet, technology
for pictures see definitions of hardware, laptop computer
some kinds of computers
mainframe, microcomputer, personal computer
broader category that includes computers
technology (n.2)
some parts of computers
CD, disk (n.3), floppy (n.), floppy disk, hard drive, hardware (n.2), joystick (n.), keyboard (n.), memory (n.4), microchip, modem, monitor (n.3), mouse (n.2), printer (n.2), RAM, ROM, software
some actions relating to computers
boot (v.2), compute (v.2), copy (v.1), delete, enter (v.7), file[1] (v.1), input (v.), process (v.), program (v.), save[1] (v.2), scroll (v.), shut down, sort (v.)
some descriptions of computers
desktop (adj.), office (n.1), personal (adj.1), portable
some things computers are used for
artificial intelligence, data processing, desktop publishing, **Internet**, video games, word processing (n.1)
some people associated with computers
hacker, programmer, technician
some things conventionally associated with computers
BASIC, command (n.4), computer virus, cursor, database, interface, loop (n.4), network (n.4), print-out, scan (n.2)
some terms for computer information
data, input (n.1), output (n.2)
some units for measuring computers

bit[3], byte, kilobyte, megabyte
conceive ☺ *see* reproduction, thought
concentrate *for a picture see definition*
concentration ☺ *see* care, thought
concept ☺ *see* belief, thought
concern ☺ *see* care, emotion
concert ☺ *see* dance, leisure, music
conch *for a picture see definition*
condominium ☺ *see* building, home
conduct ☺☺☺ *see* behavior, electricity, music, theater
conductor *for a picture see the definition of* recital
cone *for pictures see definitions of* cone, ice cream
confederate ☺ *see* government, politics
conflict ☺☺ *see* relationship, war
conga *for a picture see definition*
congress ☺ *see* legislature
conifer *for a picture see definition*
conscience ☺ *see* behavior, morals
conservation (n.2) ☺☺
see also endangered species, extinction, natural resources
for a picture see the definition of conservation
similar to conservation
moderate (v.1), preserve (v.1), protect, recycle, save[1] (v.2)
some focuses of conservation
air (n.1), **animals** (n.1), **earth** (n.1,4), **ecosystem**, **energy** (n.1), environment (n.2), **forests**, habitat, minerals (n.), natural gas, **natural resources**, petroleum, **plants** (n.1), **soil**[1] (n.1), **water** (n.1)
some reasons for conservation
endangered species, erosion, **extinction**, pollution, smog, trash, waste (n.2)
consider ☺ *see* thought
console *for a picture see the definition of* console[1]
consonant *for a picture see definition*
constellation
see also space
for a picture see the definition of constellation
constitution ☺ *see* government, law
constrictor *for a picture see definition*
construction *for pictures see definitions of* construction, labor
consumer ☺☺ *see* diet, economy
contemplate ☺ *see* thought
contemporary ☺☺ *see* art, history
contest *for a picture see definition*
continent
see also earth, geography, geology
broader category including continent
earth (n.1), land (n.1)
some parts of continents
continental shelf, divide (n.), mainland
study of continents
geology (n.1), plate tectonics
names of the seven continents
Africa, Antarctica, Asia, Australia (n.1), Europe, North America, South America
contour *for a picture see definition*
control ☺ *see* behavior, power
conversation ☺ *see* language
conviction ☺☺ *see* belief, crime, law
cooking (v.1,2) ☺
see also diet, food
for pictures see definitions of apron, barbecue, boil[1], campfire, cookout, present[2], recipe
broader categories that include cooking
housework, job (n.2)
place for cooking
kitchen

some actions associated with cooking
beat (v.3), chop (v.2), dress (v.4), glaze (v.1), grease (v.2), mash (v.2), mix (v.1), stir[1] (v.1), stuff (v.2)
some things used in cooking
broiler, campfire, casserole (n.1), cookbook, firewood, food processor, gas (n.2), griddle, gridiron (n.1), grill (n.1), microwave, natural gas, oven, pan (n.1), pot (n.1), range (n.6), recipe, saucepan, spatula, stove, tablespoon (n.2), teaspoon (n.2), toaster, wok
some measurements used in cooking
cup (n.3), dash (n.2), ounce (n.2), pinch (n.2), quart, tablespoon (n.1), teaspoon (n.1)
some people associated with cooking
chef, cook (n.)
some ways of cooking
bake (v.1), boil[1] (v.4), broil (v.1), fry (v.), grill (v.1), roast (v.1), scramble (v.4), simmer (v.), smoke (v.3), steam (v.4), stew (v.1)
cookout *for a picture see definition*
coordination ☺ *see* exercise, muscle
copper *for a picture see definition*
coral *for pictures see definitions of* coral, underwater
coral snake *for a picture see definition*
corduroy *for a picture see definition*
core
see also earth, fruit
for a picture see the definition of earth
corkscrew *for a picture see definition*
corn *for pictures see definitions of* ear, Indian corn
corrode *for a picture see definition*
cosmetic
see also color, face, hygiene
for pictures see definitions of cosmetic, made-up, makeup
cosmic ☺ *see* space
cost ☺ *see* business, money
costume *for pictures see definitions of* disguise, imitate, makeup
cottage ☺ *see* building
couch *for a picture see the definition of* plaid
cougar *for a picture see definition*
cough ☺ *see* disease, health, respiration
counterclockwise *for a picture see definition*
country (n.1) ☺
see also culture, government
similar to a country
homeland, kingdom (n.1), nation (n.2), state (n.2), tribe
broader categories that include country
alliance, confederation (n.2), federation, league[1] (n.1), treaty, union (n.4)
some parts of a country
borders (n.2), capital[1] (n.1), **city** (n.1), county (n.1,2), district (n.1), province (n.1), town (n.1), village (n.1)
some actions of a country
administer (v.1), ally (v.), banish (v.1), blockade (v.), defend (v.1), deport, exile (v.), govern (v.1), naturalize, tax (v.1), trade (v.1), war (v.)
some qualities associated with country
domestic (adj.3), federal (adj.2), foreign (adj.1), imperial (adj.2), independent (adj.1), international, national (adj.1), sovereign (adj.2)
some representations of a country
anthem (n.1), customs (n.2), flag (n.), language (n.2)
some people associated with countries

ambassador (n.1), armed forces, citizens (n.1),
countryman (n.1), countrywoman (n.1),
emigrant, exile (n.2), foreigner, immigrant,
king (n.1), minister (n.2,3), patriot,
premier (n.), president (n.2), prime minister,
queen (n.1), rebel (n.2), refugee, traitor
negative action associated with a country
treason
measures a country
census
some feelings for a country
allegiance, patriotism
some foundations of countries
economy (n.2), government (n.3),
history (n.1), laws (n.1), natural resources
couple *for a picture see definition*
courage ⊙ *see* behavior, personality
court ⊙ *see* crime, law
covered wagon *for a picture see definition*
cow
see also farming, mammal, milk
for pictures see definitions of back[1], calf[1], cow,
dewlap, front, inertia, plentiful, warm-blooded
cowboy *for pictures see definitions of* rodeo, wrangle
crab *for pictures see definitions of* crab, crustacean
crack *for pictures see definitions of* crack, yolk
cracker *for a picture see definition*
cradle *for a picture see definition*
craft ⊕ *see* art
crane *for pictures see definitions of* crane, whooping
crane
crash *for a picture see definition*
crater *for a picture see definition*
crawl *for a picture see definition*
crayon ⊙ ⊕ *see* art, color
crazy ⊙ *see* behavior, mind
creative ⊙ ⊕ *see* art, thought
credit ⊗ *see* business, money
creek ⊕ *see* geography, river
creep *for a picture see definition*
crest *for a picture see definition*
cricket *for a picture see the definition of* cricket[1]
crime (n.1) ⊙
see also law
some examples of crime
arson, assault (n.3), manslaughter,
murder (n.), perjury, robbery,
shoplifting (shoplifter), theft, vandalism
some broader categories that include crimes
justice (n.1), law (n.1)
some actions associated with crime
assault (v.), charge (v.2), embezzle, kidnap,
kill (v.1), maim, rob (v.1), steal (v.1)
some reactions to crimes
accuse, arrest (n.), atone, confess (v.3),
convict (v.), fine[2] (v.), incriminate, indict,
interrogate, interview (v.), investigate,
jail (v.), pardon (n.2/v.1), police (v.),
prosecute, punish (v.1)
some people associated with crime
bystander, convict (n.), criminal (n.), gangster,
lawyer, police (n.1), suspect (n.), thug,
victim (n.1), witness (n.2)
some things conventionally associated with crime
alibi (n.1), bail[1] (n.), bond (n.3), case[1] (n.4),
getaway, parole (n.)
some places conventionally associated with crimes
penitentiary, prison, scene (n.1)
critic ⊙ ⊕ *see* art, literature, music, theater
crocodile *for pictures see definitions of* crocodile,
reptile

crop
see also farming, gardening
for a picture see the definition of crop
croquet *for a picture see definition*
crossbow *for a picture see definition*
cross section *for a picture see definition*
crossword puzzle *for pictures see definitions of*
crossword puzzle, puzzle
crown *for pictures see definitions of* crown, velvet
crust *for a picture see the definition of* earth
crustacean ⊙
see also arthropod
for pictures see definitions of crab, crustacean,
lobster
some examples of crustaceans
barnacle, crab, crayfish, lobster (n.1),
shrimp (n.)
broader categories that include crustaceans
animal (n.1), arthropod, invertebrate (n.),
seafood
some parts of crustaceans
antenna (n.2), claw (n.2), shell (n.1)
some places for crustaceans
land (n.1), reef, sand (n.), water (n.1)
affects crustacean
fishing (fish v.2), pollution
behaviors of some crustaceans
claw (v.), crawl (v.1), feed (v.4), hide[1] (v.1),
molt, snap (v.3), swim (v.1), walk (v.1)
person associated with crustaceans
fisherman
some things crustaceans eat
algae, insects (n.1), plankton, plants (n.1)
cry ⊙ ⊕ *see* emotion, injury
crystal *for a picture see definition*
cub *for a picture see the definition of* mammal
cucumber *for a picture see definition*
cultivate ⊕ *see* farming, gardening
culture (n.1) ⊙ ⊕
see also art, celebration, education, history,
language, myth, religion, tradition
some studies of culture
anthropology, archaeology, art (n.4),
history (n.2), humanities (humanity n.3),
literature (n.1)
some actions associated with culture
adapt (v.2), advance (v.5), emerge (v.1),
flourish (v.1), influence (v.), progress (v.2),
thrive (v.1)
some descriptions of cultures
ancient (adj.2), classical (adj.1),
eastern (adj.1), global (adj.1), medieval,
modern (adj.1), political, primitive (adj.2),
tribal, urban, western (adj.)
some people associated with culture
archaeologist (archaeology), artist (n.1),
historian, philosopher
see/see also culture
art (n.2), history (n.2), language (n.1),
tradition (n.1)
some aspects of culture
art (n.1), beliefs (n.3), customs (n.1), dialect,
folklore, history (n.1), ideas (n.1),
language (n.1), legends (n.1), literature (n.1),
music (n.1), myth (n.1), religion (n.1),
rituals (n.1), values (n.3)
cup *for pictures see definitions of* china, goblet, tin
curiosity ⊙ *see* learn
currency
see also money
for pictures see definitions of international, peso
curtsy *for a picture see definition*
custom ⊙ ⊗ *see* tradition
cuticle *for a picture see the definition of* hand

Cyclops *for a picture see definition*
daddy-longlegs *for a picture see definition*
daffodil *for a picture see definition*
dairy ⊙ ⊕ *see* farming, milk
daisy *for pictures see definitions of* daisy, flower
Dalmatian *for a picture see definition*
dance (n.1,2,4) ⊕ ⊕ ⊙ ⊕
see also art
for pictures see definitions of ballerina, Maypole
similar to dancing
march (v.1), prance (v.1), skip (v.1,3)
some kinds of dance
ballet (n.1), conga (n.1), folk dance (n.1),
jig (n.1), polka (n.1), reel[3], tap dance,
waltz (n.1)
broader categories that include dance
art (n.2), culture (n.1)
some parts of dances
movement (n.1), sequence (n.1), step (n.5)
some places for dancing
auditorium, ballroom, concert (n.),
formal (n.1), party (n.1), recital (n.1),
social (n.)
some actions in dancing
bow[1] (v.1), clap (v.3), glide (v.), hop[1] (v.1),
jump (v.1), leap (v.1), prance (v.1),
rock[2] (v.1), skip (v.1,3), stamp (v.5),
sway (v.1), tap[1] (v.2), twirl (v.3), twist (v.10),
whirl (v.1)
some descriptions of dancing
acrobatic (acrobat), classical (adj.2), elegant,
graceful, lively (adj.1), popular (adj.1),
rhythmic
used in dancing
costume (n.1), leotards, tights
some people associated with dancing
ballerina, dancer, partner (n.2), performer
dandelion *for a picture see definition*
dangle *for pictures see definitions of* dangle, upside
down
dart *for a picture see definition*
data processing ⊙ *see* computer, technology
daub *for a picture see definition*
daydream *for a picture see definition*
dazzle *for a picture see definition*
deadly
see also animal, disease, plant, virus
for a picture see the definition of deadly
deal ⊙ *see* business, game
death ⊙ ⊕ *see* life
debate ⊙ ⊕ *see* belief, democracy, thought
debris *for a picture see definition*
debt ⊗ *see* bank, money
debut *for a picture see definition*
decagon *for a picture see definition*
decanter *for a picture see definition*
decibel ⊕ *see* measurement, physics
decide ⊙ *see* action, belief
deciduous
see also leaf, tree
for a picture see the definition of deciduous
decorate *for a picture see definition*
decoration ⊙ *see* jewelry
decoy *for a picture see definition*
decree ⊙ *see* government, power
deed ⊗ *see* bank, home
deep ⊙ ⊕ *see* ocean, sea, thought
deer *for pictures see definitions of* buck[1], deer, doe,
elk, fawn, horn, reindeer, scrawny
defeat ⊙ *see* game, war
defend ⊙ ⊕ ⊙ *see* action, military, sport
deflate *for a picture see definition*

deft *for a picture see definition*
degree ☺ *see* measurement, weather
delegate ☺ *see* democracy, politics, power
deliberate ☺ *see* thought
delicate *for a picture see definition*
delicious *for a picture see definition*
delta *for a picture see definition*
demand ☺ *see* business, power
Demeter *for a picture see definition*
democracy (n.1) ☺
 see also government, politics
 some kinds of democracy
  popular (adj.2), representative (adj.1)
 some broader categories that include democracies
  government (n.3), **politics** (n.2)
 study of democracy
  civics, social studies
 some actions in a democracy
  advise (v.1), consent (v.), debate (v.1),
  elect (v.1), lobby (v.), pass (v.6), poll (v.2),
  ratify, veto (v.), vote (v.1)
 some people associated with democracy
  constituents (n.2), representatives (n.1)
 some things conventionally associated with a
 democracy
  assembly (n.4), congress (n.1), council, House
  of Representatives, majority (n.2),
  opposition (n.3), parliament (n.1),
  poll (n.1,2,3), rights (n.3), senate (n.2),
  vote (n.1,2,3,4)
 some aspects of democracies
  civil rights (pl.n.2), constitution (n.1),
  equality, freedom (n.2,3), justice (n.1),
  law (n.1), liberty (n.3), suffrage,
  tolerance (n.1)
den
 see also room, home
 for a picture see the definition of den
department ☺ ☺ *see* government, school
dependable *for a picture see definition*
deposit ☺ ☺ *see* bank, geology, soil
depression ☺ ☺ *see* economy, emotion, sadness
derrick *for a picture see definition*
descent *for a picture see definition*
desert[1] ☺
 see also ecosystem, geography
 broader category including desert
  ecosystem, land (n.1)
 some parts of deserts
  arroyo, dunes, oasis, sand (n.)
 some descriptioins of deserts
  arid, barren (adj.1), desolate (adj.1),
  dry (adj.1), forsaken (adj.), hot (adj.1)
 plant that lives in deserts
  cactus
 some animals that live in deserts
  camel, lizard, scorpion, snake (n.1)
 also associated with the deserts
  caravan (n.1), mirage, thirst (n.1)
desire ☺ *see* emotion, thought
dessert *for a picture see definition*
develop ☺ ☺ ☺ *see* disease, industry, muscle,
 photography, reproduction
device ☺ *see* technology, tool
devotion ☺ ☺ *see* care, religion
dewlap *for a picture see definition*
diagnosis ☺ *see* disease, thought
dial *for a picture see the definition of* rotary
dialect ☺ *see* language
diameter *for a picture see definition*
diamond
 see also jewelry, stone
 for a picture see the definition of facet

diaper *for a picture see definition*
diaphragm *for a picture see the definition of* body
dice *for a picture see definition*
dictator ☺ *see* government, power
dictionary ☺ *see* book, language
diet (n.1) ☺ ☺ ☺
 see also drink, food, health
 some kinds of diets
  carnivorous, herbivorous, omnivorous,
  vegetarian (adj.2)
 broader categories that include diet
  health (n.1)
 some parts of a diet
  drink (n.1), **food** (n.)
 some activities associated with diet
  digest (v.1), eat (v.1), farm (v.2), forage (v.1),
  harvest (n.), hunt (v.1), slaughter (n.1),
  swallow[1] (v.1)
 diet influences
  body (n.1), development (n.1), **energy** (n.1),
  health (n.2), malnutrition, metabolism,
  nourishment
 also associated with diet
  climate, **ecosystem**, food chain
dig *for a picture see the definition of* excavate
digestion ☺
 see also body, diet, food, organ
 for a picture see the definition of body
 digestion affects
  growth (n.1), **health** (n.1),
  maintenance (n.1), repair (n.1)
 affects digestion
  bacteria, nutrition (n.1)
 used in the process of digestion
  acid (n.), alimentary canal, bile (n.1),
  blood (n.1), bowel, enzyme, esophagus, gland,
  liver (n.1), mouth (n.1), **muscle** (n.1),
  pancreas, saliva, small intestine,
  stomach (n.1), teeth (**tooth** n.1), throat (n.1),
  tongue (n.1), tract (n.2)
 negatively associated with digestion
  indigestion
 some processes in digestion
  absorb (v.1), carry (v.1), chew (v.),
  dissolve (v.4), filter (v.2), flow (v.1),
  form (v.1), mash (v.2), pass (v.4),
  produce (v.2), push (v.1), release (v.2),
  squeeze (v.1), store (v.), swallow[1] (v.1)
 some things obtained from digestion
  energy (n.1), nourishment
 that which is digested
  food (n.)
digital
 see also computer, number
 for a picture see the definition of digital
dilapidated *for a picture see definition*
diminutive *for a picture see definition*
dimple *for a picture see definition*
dinghy *for a picture see definition*
dinner ☺ *see* cooking, food
dinosaur ☺
 see also extinction, reptile
 for pictures see definitions of dinosaur, extinct
 similar to dinosaurs
  alligator, crocodile, lizard
 broader categories that include dinosaurs
  reptile, vertebrate (n.)
 parts of some dinosaurs
  armor (n.3), beak, horn (n.1), scales[1] (n.1),
  tail (n.1), wings (n.1)
 display place for dinosaurs
  museum
 descriptions of some dinosaurs
  enormous, fierce (adj.2)
 some behaviors of dinosaurs

  attack (v.1), defend (v.1), feed (v.4),
  hunt (v.1), mate (v.)
 study of dinosaurs
  paleontology
 conventionally associated with dinosaurs
  evolution (n.2), **extinction**, fossil, prehistoric
 things some dinosaurs ate
  berries (berry n.), **dinosaurs**, eggs[1] (n.2),
  fish (n.1), leaves, **mammals**, **plants** (n.1),
  seeds (n.1)
diplomat ☺ *see* country, government
direct
 see also action, film, music, power, theater
 for pictures see definitions of direct, divert
direct current *for a picture see definition*
director ☺ *see* film, music, theater
dirt ☺ *see* soil
discipline ☺ ☺ *see* behavior, care, education,
 power
disco *for a picture see definition*
discrimination ☺ *see* hate
discussion ☺ *see* communication, language
disease ☺
 see also bacteria, diet, health, hygiene, virus
 some examples of diseases
  AIDS, alcoholism, arthritis, asthma,
  cancer (n.1), chicken pox, croup, diabetes, flu,
  hives, influenza, jaundice, leprosy, leukemia,
  lockjaw, malaria, measles, mumps,
  plague (n.1,2), pneumonia, poliomyelitis,
  rabies, scurvy, tetanus, virus (n.2), whooping
  cough, worms (n.2)
 some kinds of treatment for diseases
  acupuncture, antibiotic, antidote, antiseptic,
  chemotherapy, **drug** (n.1), **first aid**,
  injection (n.1), insulin (n.2), medicine (n.1),
  penicillin, prescription (n.2), remedy (n.1),
  serum (n.2), surgery (n.2), therapy
 some places for treatment of diseases
  clinic, hospital
 some activities associated with diseases
  cure (v.1), heal (v.1), identify (v.1),
  quarantine (v.), treat (v.4)
 some descriptions of diseases
  contagious, deadly (adj.1), fatal (adj.1),
  incurable, infectious (adj.1), mild (adj.2),
  serious (adj.4)
 some things that can cause or spread diseases
  bacteria, chigger, germs (n.1), housefly,
  infection (n.1), louse, mosquito, tick[2],
  virus (n.1), **worm** (n.1)
 some people associated with diseases
  doctor (n.1), intern (n.), medic, nurse (n.1),
  patient (n.), pediatrician, pharmacist,
  physician, resident (n.2), surgeon
 some states of people with diseases
  ailing (ail v.2), ill (adj.1),
  recovering (recover v.3),
  recuperating (recuperate), sick (adj.1,2)
 tools used to study diseases
  stethoscope, test tube
 some means of disease prevention
  booster shot, checkup, **hygiene**, inoculate,
  physical (n.), quarantine (n.), vaccine, vitamin
 some processes involving diseases
  act up (phr.2), plague (n.1), spread (v.3)
 some stages of diseases
  attack (n.2), bout (n.2), epidemic, fit[2] (n.1),
  outbreak (n.2), remission
 some symptoms of diseases
  ache (n.), amnesia, bump (n.2), chill (n.2),
  collapse (n.), coma, convulsion (n.1),
  cough (n.1), fever (n.1), pain (n.1), paralysis,
  rash[2] (n.1), seizure (n.1), shock[1] (n.4),
  sore (n.), sweat (n.2), swell (n.1),

temperature (n.3)

disguise *for a picture see definition*

dish
  see also cooking, food
  for pictures see definitions of china, platter

disheveled *for a picture see definition*

dislocate *for a picture see definition*

disposition ☺ *see* behavior, personality

dissect *for a picture see definition*

distort *for a picture see definition*

distribution ☻☺ *see* business, natural resources

dive *for a picture see the definition of* scuba diving

diver *for a picture see the definition of* underwater

divert *for a picture see definition*

divide ☺ *see* mathematics

DNA ☺ *see* cell, reproduction

Doberman pinscher *for a picture see definition*

doctor ☻☺ *see* body, care, disease, health, injury

doe *for a picture see definition*

dog (n.) ☻
  see also mammal, pet
  for pictures see definitions of animated cartoon, bark, beagle, bulldog, canine, chow², collie, Dalmatian, Doberman pinscher, droop, expectation, Frisbee, Great Dane, greyhound, hairy, heel, hound, husky, loyalty, mammal, pack, pet, pointer, poodle, puppy, retriever, spaniel, terrier, thoroughbred, tilt
  some examples of dogs
    beagle, bloodhound, boxer (n.2), bulldog, chow², cocker spaniel, collie, coyote, dachshund, Dalmatian, dingo, foxhound, German shepherd, Great Dane, greyhound, hound (n.1), husky², Irish setter, mongrel, Pekingese, pointer (n.4), poodle, retriever, spaniel, terrier
  similar to dogs
    fox (n.1), jackal, wolf (n.)
  some kinds of dogs
    domestic (adj.2), purebred (adj.), wild (adj.1)
  broader categories that include dogs
    animal (n.1), carnivore, **mammal**, **pet** (n.1), vertebrate (n.)
  some parts of dogs
    beard (n.2), claw (n.1), dewlap, fur (n.1), muzzle (n.1), pads¹ (n.5), paw (n.), ruff (n.2)
  place for dogs
    kennel
  group of dogs
    pack (n.3)
  uses for some dogs
    hunting (hunt n.1), watchdog
  representation of a dog
    Canis Minor
  behaviors of some dogs
    bury (v.1), circle (v.2), fetch, guard (v.1,2), guide (v.1), herd (v.2), hunt (v.1), hunt (v.2), lick (v.1), pant (v.1), play (v.4), pull (n.1), race¹ (v.1), scratch (v.2), sleep (v.1), sniff (v.2), stalk² (v.2), track (v.1)
  some sounds of dogs
    bark¹ (n.), growl (n.), howl (n.), whimper (n.), whine (n.), yelp (n.)
  young of dogs
    litter (n.2), pup, puppy, runt
  some people associated with dogs
    firefighter, hunter (n.1), owner, police officer, veterinarian
  some accessories for dogs
    bowl¹ (n.1), brush¹ (n.1), collar (n.1), Frisbee, leash (n.), muzzle (n.2), pen² (n.1), run (n.9), tag¹ (n.), toy (n.)
  conventionally associated with dogs
    bone (n.), **cat** (n.1), hydrant, scent (n.2)

some diseases of dogs
    distemper, rabies
some things dogs eat
    animals (n.1), meat (n.1)

doily *for a picture see definition*

doll *for a picture see definition*

dollar
  see also money
  for pictures see definitions of international, money

dolphin *for pictures see definitions of* cetacean, dolphin, mammal

dome *for a picture see definition*

domestic ☻☺ *see* country, pet

domino *for a picture see definition*

donkey *for pictures see definitions of* donkey, overload

door
  see also building, car, room
  for a picture see the definition of entrance¹

dormitory ☺ *see* building, school

dot *for a picture see definition*

dough
  see also cooking, money
  for a picture see the definition of dough

dove *for a picture see the definition of* soar

drab *for a picture see definition*

draft ☻☺ *see* book, military

dragon
  see also myth
  for a picture see the definition of dragon

dragonfly *for a picture see definition*

drama ☺ *see* film, literature, theater

draw ☺ *see* art

drawstring *for a picture see definition*

dread ☺ *see* fear

dreadlocks *for a picture see definition*

dream ☺ *see* mind, thought

drench *for a picture see definition*

dress
  see also clothing
  for a picture see the definition of gown

dribble *for a picture see definition*

driftwood *for a picture see definition*

drill *for a picture see definition*

drink (n.1) ☻
  see also food, milk, water
  for pictures see definitions of beverage, ferment, slurp
  some examples of drinks
    ale, beer (n.1,1,2,2), brandy, buttermilk, cider, cocktail (n.1), cocoa (n.2), coffee (n.2), gin¹, juice (n.), lemonade, liquor, malted milk, **milk** (n.2), orangeade, pop¹ (n.2), punch³, shake (n.2), soda, tea (n.3), **water** (n.1), wine (n.)
  similar to a drink
    beverage, refreshment (n.1)
  broader categories that include drinks
    diet (n.1), **food** (n.)
  some ingredients in drinks
    carbon dioxide, carob (n.2), chocolate (n.2), clove¹, coffee (n.2), flavoring, **fruit**, ginger (n.1), **grain** (n.1), herbs (n.2), hops² (n.2), ice (n.1), leaves (**leaf** n.1), malt, **plants** (n.1), soda water, spice (n.1), sugar
  places to purchase drinks
    bar (n.4), canteen (n.2), restaurant, supermarket, tavern (n.1), vending machine
  some actions with drinks
    bolt (v.2), brew (v.1), chill (v.2), choke (v.3), dilute, down¹ (v.3), drain (v.3), dribble (v.1), drink (v.1,2,3), drip (v.1), dunk (v.1),

flavor (v.), gulp (v.2), gurgle (v.2), heat (v.1), lap³ (v.2), lick (v.2), mix (v.1), pasteurize, serve (v.6), sip (v.), slurp (v.), spill (v.1), steep² (adj.), suck (v.1), swallow¹ (v.1), taste (v.1), toast² (v.), treat (v.5), wash down (phr.2), wet one's whistle
  some descriptions of drinks
    cold (adj.5), fresh (adj.2), hot (adj.1), instant (adj.2), piping hot, sour (adj.1), strong (adj.4), sweet (adj.1), weak (adj.3)
  some people associated with drinks
    waiter, waitress
  some accessories for drinks
    bottle (n.1), can² (n.1), canteen (n.1), cup (n.1), flask, glass (n.2), goblet, kettle, mug (n.1), pitcher¹, straw (n.3), Thermos, tray (n.1)
  without something to drink
    dry (adj.4), parched (parch v.2), thirsty (adj.1)
  associated with drinks
    bubbles (n.1,2), dregs (pl.n.1), froth (n.), sediment (n.1)
  some effects of drinks
    quench (v.1), refresh (v.1)
  units for measuring drinks
    cup (n.3), gallon, glass (n.2), liter, pint, quart, quart

drive ☺ *see* vehicle

dromedary *for a picture see definition*

droop *for a picture see definition*

drowsy *for a picture see definition*

drudgery *for a picture see definition*

drug (n.1) ☺
  see also disease, health
  some examples of drugs
    aspirin (n.1), ether, penicillin
  similar to drugs
    medicine (n.1)
  some kinds of drugs
    anesthetic, antibiotic, antiseptic, herb (n.2), narcotic, preventive (n.), tonic (n.2)
  some places for drugs
    drugstore, pharmacy
  some actions with drugs
    apply (v.2), cure (v.1), dispense (v.1), give (v.1), heal (v.1), inhale, prepare (v.1), prescribe, swallow (v.1), take (v.7)
  some things used to make drugs
    alcohol (n.1), **bacteria**, camphor, cashew (n.1), eucalyptus, peppermint (n.1), resin (n.1), yeast
  people associated with drugs
    doctor (n.1), druggist, pharmacist, physician, psychiatrist
  an amount of drugs
    dose
  some effects of drugs
    anesthesia, grogginess (groggy), healing (heal v.2), numbing (numb adj.1), relaxing (relax v.1), unconsciousness (unconscious adj.2)
  some methods for giving or taking drugs
    capsule (n.1), compress (n.), dressing (n.3), eyedropper, injection (n.1), IV, lozenge, needle (n.3), ointment, pellet (n.2), pill, preparation (n.3), spray (n.2,3), syrup (n.1), tablet (n.1), wash (n.5)

drum *for pictures see definitions of* bass drum, bongo², conga, drum, music, snare drum, tom-tom

drum major *for a picture see definition*

drumstick *for pictures see definitions of* drumstick, music

dryer ☻☺ *see* clothing, hair

duck *for pictures see definitions of* bird, conservation, decoy, duck[1], follow, mallard

dumbbell *for a picture see definition*
dune
see also geography, geology
for a picture see the definition of dune
duty 🔊 🔵 *see* morals, tax
dynamite *for a picture see definition*
eagle *for pictures see definitions of* bird, conservation, fly[1]
ear
see also head, organ, sense
for a picture see the definition of ear
ear
see also plant, seed
for a picture see the definition of ear
earth (n.1) 🔵 🔵
see also ecosystem, geography, geology, natural resources, soil, space, weather, continent, volcano
for pictures see definitions of earth, equator, solar system
similar to earth
globe (n.1)
broader category that includes earth
planet
some parts of the earth
continent, hemisphere (n.1), region (n.2), zone (n.2)
some components of the earth
air (n.1), land (n.1), mineral (n.), **water** (n.1)
study of the earth
geography (n.1), **geology** (n.1), meteorology, plate tectonics
some terms that describe the earth
earthly (adj.1), global (adj.1), terrestrial (adj.1)
some representations of the earth
globe (n.2), map (n.), topography
natural events involving the earth
earthquake, erosion, eruption, landslide (n.1), tremor (n.2)
reference points on the earth
epicenter, equator, latitude, longitude, magnetic pole, meridian (n.1), North Pole, South Pole
some layers of the earth
atmosphere (n.1), bedrock, crust (n.3), magma, mantle (n.2), ozone layer, stratosphere
structures leading into the earth
cave (n.), cavern, chasm, mine[2] (n.1), pocket (n.2)
earthquake
see also earth, geology
for a picture see the definition of earth
earthworm *for a picture see definition*
easel *for a picture see definition*
east *for a picture see definition*
eat
see also diet, digestion, food
for a picture see the definition of reunion
eccentric 🔊 *see* behavior
echo *for a picture see definition*
eclipse
see also light, space
for a picture see the definition of eclipse
ecology 🔵 *see* ecosystem
economy
see also advertisement, bank, business, industry, money, tax, work
some kinds of economies
barter (n.), capitalism, communism, feudalism, socialism
some categories of economies

domestic (adj.3), global (adj.1), local (adj.1), national (adj.2)
some actions associated with economies
consume (v.3), distribute (v.2), export (v.), import (v.), produce (v.2), supply (v.2), trade (v.1)
some descriptions of an economy
sound[2] (adj.3), stable[1] (adj.1), strong (adj.3), unstable (adj.1), weak (adj.2)
some people associated with economics
consumer, producer
some elements of economies
consumption, distribution (n.1), employment (n.2), goods (pl.n.2), production (n.1), services (n.2)
some states of economies
boom[1] (n.2), depression (n.3)
things that influence economies
embargo (n.1), inflation (n.1), shortage (n.1), surplus (n.)
ecosystem 🔵 🔵
see also conservation, life
some examples of ecosystems
cave (n.), **desert**[1], earth (n.3,4), everglade, **forest**, **lake**, marsh, **ocean**, pond, prairie, rain forest, **river** (n.1,2), **sea** (n.1,2), stream (n.1), swamp (n.), **tundra**
some parts of ecosystems
air (n.1,2), **animal**, bacteria (bacterium), microorganism, mineral (n.), nutrient, organism, oxygen, **plant** (n.1), rock[1] (n.1), **soil**[1] (n.1), sun (n.1,2), temperature (n.1), vegetation, **water** (n.1)
the study of ecosystems
ecology
also associated with ecosystems
conservation (n.2), evolution (n.1), food chain, life (n.1), **life cycle**
editor 🔊 *see* book, film
education (n.1) 🔵
see also knowledge, learn, school
similar to education
learning
a broader category that includes education
culture (n.1)
some places associated with education
academy, boarding school, campus, classroom, college, dormitory, elementary school, grammar school, gym (n.1), gymnasium, high school, homeroom, institute (n.1), junior high school, kindergarten, nursery school, primary school, public school, **school**[1] (n.1), schoolhouse, seminary, university
some actions associated with educating
answer (v.4), clarify, enlighten, explain (v.1,3), grade (v.1), illustrate (v.1), instruct (v.1), lecture (v.1), prepare (v.1), question (v.1,2), study (v.1,4), teach
some descriptions of education
academic (adj.1,2), basic (adj.), formal (adj.1), free (adj.6), higher (high adj.3), physical (adj.1), practical (adj.2), well-rounded (adj.1)
some people associated with education
academic (n.), cadet, chancellor (n.2), class (n.4,5), classmate, coach (n.2), faculty (n.3), freshman, graduate (n.), instructor, junior (n.2), mentor, principal (n.1), professor, pupil[1], scholar (n.2), senior (n.3), sophomore, student (n.1), sub (n.2), teacher, tutor (n.)
without an education
ignorant (adj.1), illiterate
egg
see also bird, cooking, reproduction
for pictures see definitions of bird, broken, egg,

metamorphosis, nest, transparent, yolk
egg *for a picture see definition*
eggplant *for a picture see definition*
egret *for a picture see definition*
Egyptian *for a picture see the definition of* language
elbow *for pictures see definitions of* body, body
eldest *for a picture see definition*
election 🔵 *see* democracy, politics
electricity (n.1,2) 🔵
see also energy, light
some broader categories that include electricity
energy (n.1), power (n.5)
some actions related to electricity
amplify (v.1), break (v.4), charge (v.3), conduct (v.3), discharge (v.2), disconnect (v.2), electrocute, ground[1] (v.3), magnetize, plug in, power (v.), shock[1] (v.2), shut off, surge (v.), transform (v.2), wire (v.1)
some things that produce electricity
battery (n.1), cell (n.4), dry cell, dynamo, friction (n.1), generator
some places associated with producing electricity
dam (n.), windmill (n.)
some people associated with electricity
electrician, engineer (n.1), physicist
related to electricity
magnetism (n.1)
some aspects of electricity
charge (n.4), current (n.2), frequency (n.3), resistance (n.2), voltage
some means for transporting electricity
cable (n.2), conductor (n.2), cord (n.2), line[1] (n.6), wire (n.3)
some things associated with electricity
blackout (n.1), circuit (n.4), circuit breaker, direct current, electrode, electromagnet, electron, fuse[2] (n.), insulation (n.2), outlet (n.4), plug (n.2), pole[2] (n.2), short (n.1), signal (n.3), socket (n.1), switch (n.2), terminal (n.1), transistor
some things in nature associated with electricity
aurora australis, aurora borealis, lightning (n.), magnetic pole (n.2), static (n.1,2)
some things that use electricity
amplifiers, appliances, calculators, **computers**, lamps, motors (n.2), radar (n.2), radios (n.2), receivers (n.2), satellites (n.2), telephones (n.), televisions (n.2), toys (n.), transmitters
some units for measuring electricity
kilohertz, kilowatt, volt, watt
electromagnet *for a picture see definition*
electronic 🔊 🔵 *see* electricity, technology
element (n.4)
see also natural resources, stone
some examples of elements
aluminum, arsenic, barium, beryllium, bromine, calcium, carbon, chlorine, cobalt, copper (n.1), fluorine, gold (n.1), helium, hydrogen, iodine (n.1), iron (n.1), krypton, lead[2] (n.1), magnesium, manganese, mercury (n.1), neon (n.), nickel (n.1), nitrogen, oxygen, phosphorus, platinum, plutonium, potassium, radium, radon, silicon, silver (n.1), sodium, sulfur, tin, uranium, zinc
similar to an element
ion
some parts of elements
electron, neutron, proton
some things composed of elements
alloy, compound (n.2), mineral (n.), oxide
some activities associated with elements
analyze, combine (v.), conduct (v.3), oxidize (v.1)
some qualities of elements

dense, gaseous, inert, liquid (adj.),
metallic (adj.2), radioactive, stable[1] (adj.2),
unstable (adj.1)
some representations of elements
formula (n.4), symbol (n.1)
some people who study elements
chemist, physicist
conventionally associated with elements
fission, fusion (n.4)

elementary school ◯ *see* education, school

elephant *for pictures see definitions of* elephant,
hinder, mammal

elk *for a picture see definition*

elude *for a picture see definition*

e-mail ◯ ◯ *see* computer, Internet

embarrassment ◯ *see* behavior, emotion

embassy ◯ *see* building, government

emblem *for a picture see definition*

embroidery *for a picture see definition*

embryo ◯ ◯ *see* life, reproduction

emerald *for a picture see definition*

emergency ◯ ◯ *see* first aid, injury

emotion (n.1) ◯
see also anger, fear, happiness, hate, love,
sadness
some examples of emotions
affection, alarm (n.1), amazement, anguish,
anxiety, awe (n.), compassion, concern (n.2),
contempt (n.1), desperation,
disappointment (n.2), disgust (n.),
doubt (n.1), dread (n.), ecstasy, envy (n.1),
fright (n.1), fury (n.1), grief (n.), guilt (n.2),
hope (n.1), jealousy, joy (n.1), love (n.1),
pity (n.1), pride (n.1), rage (n.1), regret (n.1),
relief[1] (n.1), reverence, satisfaction (n.1),
scorn (n.), shame (n.1), sorrow (n.1),
surprise (n.2), sympathy (n.1),
understanding (n.5), wonder (n.2)
similar to emotion
feeling (n.3)
some kinds of emotions
anger (n.), fear (n.1), **happiness**, hatred,
love (n.1,2), **sadness**
a broader category that includes emotion
mind (n.1)
study of emotion
psychology
some actions associated with emotions
bawl (v.), beam (v.3), blubber (v.), blush (v.),
brood (v.2), cackle (v.), choke up (phr.1),
chuckle (v.), cry (v.2), frown (v.1), giggle (v.),
grin (v.), groan (n.), grumble (v.1), gush (v.2),
howl (v.1), laugh (v.), moan (v.2), mope (v.1),
pout, scowl (v.), scream (v.1), sigh (v.1),
smile (v.), snicker (v.), snort (v.2), sob (v.),
squirm (v.2), sulk (v.), tremble (v.1),
wail (v.1), weep, whimper (v.), whine (v.1)
some qualities of an emotion
deep (adj.3), fiery (adj.3), fleeting, hot (adj.4),
intense (adj.2), keen (adj.3), passionate,
profound (adj.1), shallow (adj.2),
slight (adj.1), violent (adj.3), warm (v.2)
some actions that cause emotions
agitate (v.2), amaze, appall, arouse (v.2),
astonish, astound, bother (v.1,2), bowl over,
cheer (v.2), disturb (v.3), embarrass, excite,
exhilarate (v.2), fluster (v.), horrify, humiliate,
hurt (v.1), inflame (v.1), inspire (v.2), key up,
offend, outrage (v.1), plague (v.1),
provoke (v.1,3), put to shame (phr.1),
rattle (v.4), repel (v.3), revolt (v.2),
rouse (v.2), ruffle (v.2), scare (v.1),
shame (v.1), shock[1] (v.1), stagger (v.2),
stir[1] (v.3), terrorize (v.2), thrill (v.),
torment (v.1), touch (v.4), upset (v.2),

worry (v.2)
without emotions
aloof, cool (adj.4), frigid (adj.2), hard-
boiled (adj.2), hollow (adj.3),
impersonal (adj.2), indifferent, numb (adj.1),
vacant (adj.3)
an element of an emotion
break (n.5), burst (n.2), flicker[1] (n.2),
flutter (n.1), gleam (n.2), glimmer (n.2),
glint (n.2), hint (n.), ray[1] (n.3), spark (n.2,3),
throb (n.), tinge (n.2), trace (n.2),
twinge (n.2)
feeling emotions
afraid (adj.1), aghast, angry (adj.1),
anxious (adj.1), apprehensive, ardent,
breathless (adj.2), content[2] (adj.), cranky,
cross (adj.), depressed (depress), desperate,
envious, expressive, fearful (adj.1),
furious (adj.1), glad (adj.1), gloomy (adj.2),
grateful, guilty (adj.1), happy (adj.1),
hopeful (adj.1), hopeless (adj.2), ill at ease,
indignant, irrational, jealous, joyful,
miserable (adj.1), moody (adj.2),
nervous (adj.2,3), neurotic, on edge, on
tenterhooks, out of sorts (phr.1), pathetic,
proud (adj.1), romantic (adj.2), sad (adj.1),
sensitive (adj.2), sentimental, timid (adj.2),
touchy, upset (adj.2), wretched (adj.1)
some demonstrations of strong emotion
fit[2] (n.2), outburst, scene (n.4), tantrum

employee ◯ *see* business, work

empty *for a picture see definition*

emu *for a picture see definition*

enamel *for a picture see definition*

encyclopedia ◯ *see* book, knowledge

endangered species ◯
see also conservation, extinction
for a picture see the definition of endangered
species
some examples of endangered species
alligator, ass (n.1), bat[2] (n.), bear[2], bison (n.1),
butterfly, cactus, cricket[1], gibbon, gorilla,
leopard, orangutan, orchid (n.1), rhinoceros,
tarantula, tiger, wolf (n.), zebra
someone who studies endangered species
naturalist
some places for endangered species
preserve (n.2), refuge (n.1), reserve (n.3),
shelter (n.1), zoo
some things that affect endangered species
breeding (n.1), conservation (n.1),
destruction (n.1), hunting (hunt n.1),
logging (log v.3), pesticides, pollution,
trapping (trap v.1)

enemy ◯ ◯ *see* hate, war

energy (n.1) ◯ ◯
see also digestion, electricity, light, physics
some kinds of energy
atomic energy (n.1), **electricity** (n.1), nuclear
energy, solar (adj.2)
some sources of energy
carbohydrate, chemical (n.), coal (n.1),
fire (n.1), **food** (n.), fuel, gas (n.2,3), gasoline,
light[1] (n.1), natural gas, oil (n.2), plutonium,
sun (n.2), uranium, **water** (n.1), wind[1] (n.1)
study of energy
physics
some descriptions of energy
atomic (adj.1), chemical (adj.2), electrical,
hydroelectric, mechanical (adj.2),
nuclear (adj.1), solar (adj.1)
some things that produce energy
battery (n.1), engine (n.1), generator,
windmill (n.)
person who studies energy
physicist

conventionally associated with energy
conservation (n.1), effort (n.1),
exhaustion (n.2), force (n.1), health (n.2),
heart (n.5), might[2] (n.), pep (n.), power (n.5),
strength (n.1), vigor, youth (n.1), zip[1] (n.2)
some things that require energy
activity (n.1), concentration (n.2),
electricity (n.1), labor (n.1), life (n.1),
metabolism, play (n.1), work (n.1)
some units for measuring energy
calorie, horsepower, kilowatt, watt

enforce ◯ *see* law, power

engine ◯ ◯ *see* energy, vehicle

engineering ◯ *see* mathematics, science, technology

English
see also language
for a picture see the definition of language

enjoy ◯ *see* happiness

enlighten ◯ *see* knowledge, learn

enrage ◯ *see* anger

entertain ◯ ◯ *see* leisure, thought

entrance *for a picture see the definition of* entrance[1]

envelop *for a picture see definition*

environment ◯ *see* conservation, ecosystem, geography, weather

eon ◯ *see* history

epic ◯ ◯ *see* film, literature

epidemic ◯ *see* disease

epoch ◯ *see* history

equality ◯ ◯ *see* law, measurement, number

equation ◯ *see* mathematics, science

equator *for a picture see definition*

equestrian *for a picture see definition*

era ◯ *see* history

erosion
see also conservation, geology
for a picture see the definition of conservation

erupt *for a picture see the definition of* earth

esophagus *for a picture see the definition of* body

essay ◯ *see* literature

estate *for a picture see the definition of* mansion

etch *for a picture see definition*

etiquette ◯ *see* behavior, tradition

eucalyptus *for a picture see definition*

Euro *for pictures see definitions of* Euro, international

Europe *for a picture see definition*

event ◯ *see* history

everglade ◯ *see* ecosystem

evergreen *for pictures see definitions of* evergreen,
mistletoe

ewe *for a picture see definition*

exaggerate *for a picture see definition*

exam ◯ ◯ *see* health, school

examine ◯ *see* thought

excavate *for a picture see definition*

excel *for a picture see definition*

exchange ◯ *see* business

exclaim *for a picture see definition*

excrete ◯
see also body
some parts of the body involved in excretion
bladder, bowel, colon[2], duct, kidney (n.1),
large intestine, lung, pore[2]
some actions associated with excretion
clean (v.), filter (v.1), perspire, release (v.2),
remove (v.4), secrete, sweat (v.1), transpire
some products of excretion
stool (n.3), sweat (n.1), tears[1] (n.1), urine,
vomit (n.), waste (n.3)

affects excretion
  diet (n.1), **exercise** (n.1)
exercise (n.1) 🔵🔵
  see also health, muscle
  for pictures see definitions of push-up, workout
  some examples of exercise
    bike (v.), dance (v.1), gymnastics (n.1),
    hike (v.), jog (v.3), jump (n.1), push-up,
    run (n.1), sit-up, ski (n.1), swim (n.),
    tumble (v.2), walk (n.1), wrestling, yoga
  some kinds of exercise
    aerobics, **sports** (n.1), workout (n.1)
  some places for exercising
    club (n.3), field (n.3), gym (n.1), trail (n.1)
  some actions associated with exercising
    bend (v.3), breathe (v.1), count¹ (v.5),
    hold¹ (v.9), jump (v.1), kick (v.1), lift (v.1,3),
    lower (v.1), move (v.1,6), raise (v.1),
    run (v.1), straighten (v.1), warm up
  some descriptions of exercise
    aerobic, gentle (adj.2), intense (adj.2),
    moderate (adj.)
  some descriptions of someone exercising
    breathless (adj.1), flushed (flush¹ n.2),
    glowing (glow n.3), hot (adj.1),
    perspiring (perspire), tired (tire¹ v.1)
  some things exercise affects
    cholesterol, circulation (n.2),
    development (n.1), **emotions** (n.1),
    health (n.1), heart (n.1), lungs, metabolism,
    muscles (n.1), weight (n.3)
  some people associated with exercise
    athlete, coach (n.1), dancer, gymnast,
    player (n.1), trainer
  some accessories for exercising
    ball¹ (n.2), bar (n.1), bicycle (n.), jump rope,
    leotard, machine, mat (n.3), racket² (sneakers,
    sweatshirt, tights, trampoline, uniform (n.),
    weights (n.4)
  some effects of exercising
    agility (agile adj.1), coordination (n.2),
    energy (n.3), fitness (fit¹ adj.2),
    flexibility (flexible adj.1), strength (n.1)
exhale 🔵*see* respiration
exhibition *for a picture see definition*
expectation *for a picture see definition*
expense 🔵 *see* business, money
expensive *for a picture see definition*
experiment
  see also science
  for a picture see the definition of experiment
exploration *for a picture see definition*
explosive *for a picture see definition*
export 🔵 *see* business, country
express 🔵🔵🔵 *see* action, behavior, emotion
expression *for a picture see definition*
extinct *for a picture see definition*
extinction 🔵🔵
  see also conservation, endangered species
  some causes of extinction
    destruction (n.1), hunting (**hunt** v.1),
    poison (v.1), pollution (n.1)
  animals that may become extinct
    endangered species
  some animals that are extinct
    dinosaurs, dodo, mammoth (n.), mastodon,
    saber-toothed tiger
  some things that can prevent extinction
    conservation (n.1),
    preservation (preserve v.1), protection (n.1)
eye
  see also face, organ, sense
  for a picture see the definition of eye
fable 🔵🔵 *see* literature, myth

fabric *for a picture see the definition of* homespun
face (n.1) 🔵
  see also body, head
  a broader category that includes face
    body (n.1), **head** (n.1)
  some parts of a face
    brow, cheek (n.1), chin (n.), ear¹ (n.1),
    eye (n.1), eyebrow, eyelash, forehead,
    jaw (n.1), lip (n.1), mouth (n.1), nose (n.1),
    nostril, teeth (**tooth** n.1)
  some actions with faces
    blink (v.1), blush (v.), cry (v.2), express (v.2),
    flush¹ (n.2), frown (v.1), gesture (n.1),
    laugh (v.), smile (v.)
  some descriptions of faces
    beautiful, cute, fair¹ (adj.3), haggard,
    handsome (adj.1), jaundiced, plain (adj.4),
    pleasant (adj.1), pretty (adj.), rugged (adj.1),
    ugly (adj.1), wrinkly (wrinkle n.)
  some accessories for faces
    compact¹ (n.1), cosmetic,
    eyeglasses (eyeglass), eyeliner, goggles,
    handkerchief, lipstick, lotion, makeup (n.1),
    mask (n.1), puff (n.3), rouge, scarf, towel (n.),
    visor (n.2)
  some things found on faces
    acne, beard, dimple (n.1), expression (n.2),
    freckle, moustache (mustache), pimple,
    whiskers (n.1), wrinkle (n.)
  also associated with faces
    complexion, feature (n.1), profile (n.1)
facet *for a picture see definition*
facility 🔵 *see* building
factory 🔵 *see* building, industry
faculty 🔵🔵🔵 *see* education, knowledge, school,
  thought
fad *for a picture see definition*
fair *for a picture see the definition of* exhibition
fairy *for a picture see definition*
faith 🔵🔵 *see* belief
falcon *for pictures see definitions of* conservation,
  falcon
fall *for a picture see the definition of* mishap
family (n.1) 🔵🔵
  see also life, relationship, reproduction
  some descriptions of families
    akin (adj.1), close (adj.2), distant (adj.3),
    domestic (adj.1), maternal (adj.1),
    paternal (adj.1), social (adj.1),
    supportive (support v.3,4)
  some people associated with families
    descendant, relative (n.)
  conventionally associated with family
    coat of arms, heirloom, history (n.4),
    home (n.1), reunion, **tradition** (n.1)
  some members of a family
    aunt (n.1), brother (n.1), brother-in-law,
    child (n.2), cousin, daughter-in-law,
    father (n.1), father-in-law, grandchild,
    grandfather, grandmother, grandparent, great-
    grandchild, great-grandparent, husband,
    mother (n.1), mother-in-law, parent,
    relative (n.), sister (n.1), sister-in-law,
    stepfather, stepmother, uncle (n.1), wife
fan
  see also air
  for a picture see the definition of fan¹
fan
  see also sport
  for a picture see the definition of fan
fanatic *for a picture see definition*
fang
  see also tooth
  for a picture see the definition of fang

fantastic *for a picture see definition*
fantasy *for a picture see definition*
farming 🔵
  see also animal, food, gardening, plant
  similar to farming
    agriculture, aquaculture, culture (n.3),
    gardening (**garden** n.)
  some kinds of farms
    dairy (n.3), hacienda, homestead, orchard,
    plantation, ranch (n.), range (n.4), vineyard
  some parts of farms
    barn, field (n.1), pasture (n.1,2), silo (n.1),
    stockyard
  some places for farming
    bog (n.), grassland, grove
  some activities in farming
    breed (v.1), butcher (v.), cultivate, fertilize,
    fleece (v.), graft (v.), grow (v.5), harvest (v.),
    irrigate, market (v.2), mow, plant (v.1),
    plow (v.1), prune², raise (v.3), reap (v.1),
    shear (v.2), slaughter (v.1,1), sow¹, thresh (v.),
    till², weed (v.1)
  some descriptions of land for farming
    arable, fallow (adj.), fertile (adj.1),
    infertile (adj.1)
  some things used for farming
    airplane, bin, combine (n.), cultivator,
    feed (n.), fertilizer, flail (n.), fodder,
    harrow (n.), harvester (n.2), hitch (n.1),
    hoe (n.), insecticide, manger, mash (n.1),
    pesticide, plow (n.1,1), rake (n.), roost (n.),
    scarecrow, shovel (n.1), spade¹ (n.),
    tractor (n.), trowel (n.2)
  some people associated with farming
    cowboy, cowgirl, farmer, hand (n.2), peasant
  some things that negativly affect farms
    boll weevil, drought, frost (n.2), **fungus**,
    grasshopper, parasite, pest
  gods and goddesses of farming
    Ceres, Demeter, Saturn (n.2)
  some animals that live on farms
    alpaca, cattle, chicken (n.1), cow (n.1),
    donkey, duck¹ (n.1), goat (n.), horse (n.1),
    livestock, llama, ox, pig (n.1), rabbit,
    sheep (n.1), stock (n.3), stud² (n.),
    turkey (n.1)
  some plants grown on farms
    barley (n.1), beans (n.1), buckwheat (n.1),
    coffee (n.1), corn (n.1), cotton (n.1),
    grain (n.1), hay (n.), rice (n.1), rye (n.1),
    soybean, sugar cane, tobacco (n.1),
    vegetables (n.1), wheat (n.1)
fat 🔵🔵 *see* animal, cell, diet, plant
fatigue *for a picture see definition*
faucet *for a picture see the definition of* tap
fawn *for pictures see definitions of* fawn, scrawny
fear (n.2/v.1) 🔵
  see also behavior, emotion
  similar to fear
    anxiety, apprehension (n.1)
  broader categories that include fear
    behavior (n.1), **emotion** (n.1), feeling (n.3)
  some actions related to fear
    faint (v.), flee (v.2), flinch, hide¹ (v.3), make
    one's blood run cold, make one's hair stand on
    end, pale (v.), quake (v.1), quiver¹ (v.),
    run (v.3), scream (v.1), shiver (v.), shriek (v.),
    shrink (v.2), shudder (v.), start (v.2),
    startle (v.2), sweat (v.1), tremble (v.1),
    wail (v.1), whimper (v.), whine (v.1), wince,
    yell (v.)
  some reactions to fear
    convulse, dread (v.1), face (v.2), perspire, stare
    down
  some things that cause fear
    change (n.1), death (n.1), failure (n.1),

loss (n.1,5), pain (n.1,2), separation (n.1), superstition, surprise (n.2)

some people associated with fear
baby (n.3), chicken (n.3), coward, wimp

conventionally associated with fear
banshee, boo (intj.2), ghost (n.1), ghoul, Halloween, monster (n.1), mummy, nightmare (n.1), phantom, scarecrow, spook (n.), vampire (n.1)

without fear
bold (adj.1), brave (v.), calm (adj.2), confident (adj.1), courageous, daring (dare v.1), fearless, secure (adj.1), serene

feeling fear
afraid (adj.1), aghast, anxious (adj.1), apprehensive, breathless (adj.2), frantic, ill at ease, nervous (adj.2,3), shaky (adj.1), timid (adj.2)

some states of fear
alarm (n.1), dread (n.), fright (n.1), horror (n.1), panic (n.), shock[1] (n.1), terror (n.1)

fearless *for a picture see definition*

feat *for a picture see definition*

feather
see also bird
for pictures see definitions of bird, feather

federal ☉ *see* government

feed ☉ ☉ *see* diet, food

feel ☉ ☉ *see* emotion, sense, nerve

feeling ☉ *see* anger, care, emotion, fear, happiness, hate, love, sadness

feet ☉ ☉ *see* foot

feign *for a picture see definition*

feline
see also cat, mammal
for a picture see the definition of feline

fence *for a picture see the definition of* rickety

ferment *for a picture see definition*

fern *for a picture see definition*

Ferris wheel *for a picture see definition*

fertilize ☉ ☉ *see* farming, gardening, reproduction

festival ☉ *see* celebration

festive *for a picture see definition*

feudalism ☉ ☉ *see* economy, government

fiber ☉ ☉ ☉ *see* diet, muscle, plant

fiction ☉ *see* book, literature

fiddle *for a picture see definition*

field
see also farming, geography, sport
for pictures see definitions of crop, lavender, outfield, plentiful, rural, vast, vineyard

field glass *for a picture see definition*

fight *for a picture see the definition of* contest

figure ☉ ☉ *see* body, mathematics, shape

filament *for a picture see definition*

film (n.3) ☉
see also art, photography, theater
for pictures see definitions of negative, reel[1]

similar to film
video (n.2)

some kinds of films
animated cartoon, documentary (n.), feature (n.3), motion picture (n.2)

some categories of film
comedy, drama (n.1), romance (n.2), tragedy (n.2), western (n.)

broader categories that include film
art (n.2), **culture** (n.1)

some places associated with films
cinema (n.2), festival (n.2), marquee,

set (n.2), studio (n.3), theater (n.1)

some actions involved in filming
act (v.2), cast (v.5), direct (v.2), edit, record (v.2), splice (v.1)

some qualities of films
classic (adj.1,2), educational (adj.1), foreign (adj.1), independent (adj.3), silent (adj.1)

some descriptions of films
bomb (n.2), dud, flop (n.2), hit (n.2), sensation (n.4), smash (n.4)

some things used in films
camera, cassette, celluloid, film (n.2), lighting, magnetic tape, microphone, reel[1] (n.1), roll (n.2), screen (n.3), script (n.1), spool

some people associated with films
actor, cast (n.4), crew (n.1), critic (n.1), director (n.2), producer, star (n.4)

some elements of films
background (n.1), close-up, dialogue, foreground, lighting, set (n.2), sound[1] (n.1), stunts[2] (n.1)

also associated with film
matinee, popcorn (n.2)

fin
see also airplane, boat, fish
for a picture see the definition of fin

finale ☉ *see* dance, music, theater

finance ☉ *see* bank, business, money

finch *for pictures see definitions of* bird, trio

finger
see also body
for pictures see definitions of body, finger, hand

fingernail *for a picture see the definition of* hand

fire
see also energy, light
for a picture see the definition of earth

firearm *for a picture see definition*

fire engine *for a picture see definition*

fire escape *for a picture see definition*

firefighter *for pictures see definitions of* fearless, heroic

fireworks *for a picture see definition*

first aid ☉
see also disease, health, injury
for a picture see the definition of first aid

some kinds of first aid
artificial respiration, CPR

some actions in first aid
bandage (v.), breathe (v.1), clean (v.), clear (v.2), cover (v.1), disinfect, dislodge, elevate, loosen (v.2), massage (v.), press (v.1), puff (v.1), push (v.1), support (v.2), wash (v.1), wrap (v.1)

some things used for first aid
antiseptic, aspirin (n.2), bandage (n.), blanket (n.1), compress (n.), dressing (n.3), gauze (n.2), ice (n.1), needle (n.1), patch (n.2), scissors, soap (n.), splint, thermometer, **water** (n.1)

people associated with first aid
doctor (n.1), nurse (n.1), operator (n.2), technician, victim (n.1)

organization associated with first aid
Red Cross

some conditions that require first aid
accident (n.2), allergy, asthma, bite (n.2), bleeding (bleed v.1), blister (n.1), break (n.1), burn (n.), choking (choke v.3), convulsion (n.1), cut (n.1), dehydration (dehydrate v.2), drowning (drown v.1), emergency, fainting (faint n.), fatigue (n.), fire (n.1), fracture (n.), frostbite (n.), hypothermia, inflammation, **injury**, nosebleed, pain (n.1),

poisoning (poison n.1), reaction, scrape (n.2), scratch (n.1), shock[1] (n.3,4), splinter (n.), sprain (n.), sting (n.2), strain[1] (n.3), sunburn (n.), trauma (n.1), unconsciousness (unconscious adj.2), wound[1] (n.1)

some effects of first aid
heal (v.1), help (v.1), save[1] (v.1)

some key things associated with first aid
breathing (breathe v.1), consciousness (n.1), pulse (n.1)

fish (n.1) ☉
see also invertebrate, pet
for pictures see definitions of aquarium, catfish, cold-blooded, flounder, perch, pike, ray[2], salmon, school[2], scuba diving

broader categories that include fish
animal, vertebrate

some examples of fish
anchovy, barracuda, bass, bluefish, catfish, cod, dory, eel, flounder, herring, mackerel, minnow, perch, pickerel, pike, ray, salmon, sardine, sea horse, shark, skate, smelt, sole, stingray, swordfish, trout, tuna, goldfish, guppy

some things that affect fish
fishing (v.2), pollution

group of fish
school[2]

some things fish are used for
bait, food, seafood

some characteristics of fish
aquatic, cold-blooded

some places for fish
aquarium, fishery, hatchery, lake, ocean, pond, preserve, river, sea, water

some growth stages of fish
roe, spawn

some parts of fish
fins, gills, scales[1]

some kinds of fish
bony, flatfish, flying fish, freshwater, game, saltwater

some food that is made using fish
broth, chowder, fillet, soup, steak, stew, stock

some things that fish eat
algae, fish, invertebrates, plants, tadpoles, worms

behaviors of some fish
founder, nibble, swim

representation of a fish
Pisces

fishing (v.2) ☉
some activities in fishing
boating (boat v.), casting (cast v.4), sailing (sail v.4), trawling (trawl v.), trolling (troll[1] v.2)

some things used for fishing
bait (n.1), barb, bob[2] (n.2), fishhook, fishing rod, harpoon (n.), hook (n.2), lure (n.2), net[1] (n.3), pole[1], reel[1] (n.1), rod (n.2), seine, spear[1] (n.), tackle (n.1), trawl (n.)

person associated with fishing
fisherman

also associated with fishing
fishery (n.1), whaling

fission *for a picture see definition*

fit[1] ☉ ☉ ☉ *see* body, exercise, morals

fit[2] ☉ *see* health, mind

flag *for pictures see definitions of* flag, half-mast, Stars and Stripes

flame ☉ *see* energy, light

flare *for a picture see definition*

flask *for a picture see definition*

flax *for a picture see definition*

fleece *for a picture see definition*

flesh ⊕ ◐ *see* fruit, muscle, vegetable

flex *for a picture see definition*

flight[1] ◐ ◐ *see* airplane, bird, insect

flight[2] *see* fear

flipper ◐ *see* fish, mammal

float *for a picture see the definition of* descent

flock ◐ *see* bird, mammal

flood
see also river, weather
for a picture see the definition of earth

flounder *for a picture see definition*

flounder *for a picture see definition*

flour ◐ *see* cooking

flower (n.2) ◐
see also fruit, plant, seed
for pictures see definitions of alfalfa, aster, begonia, blossom, carnation, chrysanthemum, columbine, daffodil, daisy, dandelion, flax, flower, grow, lily, orchid, petal, petunia, pistil, pollinate, profuse, pussy willow, rhododendron, rose[1], stalk[1], stamen, sunflower, tulip, vase
some examples of flowers
alfalfa, anemone, aster, azalea, begonia, buttercup, cacao (n.1), carnation, cattail, chrysanthemum (n.1), clove[1], clover (n.), columbine, crocus, daffodil, daisy (n.), dandelion, dogwood, flax (n.1), forget-me-not, forsythia, gardenia (n.1), geranium, gladiolus, goldenrod, hawthorn, heather, holly (n.1), hollyhock, honeysuckle, hyacinth, indigo (n.2), iris (n.2), jonquil, larkspur, laurel (n.1), lavender (n.1), lilac (n.1), lily (n.1), lily of the valley, locust (n.3), lotus (n.1), magnolia (n.1), marigold, mistletoe (n.1), morning glory, mustard (n.1), myrtle (n.1), narcissus (n.1), nasturtium, orchid (n.1), pansy, peony (n.1), peppermint (n.1), petunia, phlox (n.1), poinsettia, poppy, prickly pear, primrose, pussy willow, rhododendron, rose[1] (n.1), sagebrush, snapdragon, sunflower, thistle, tulip (n.1), violet (n.1), water lily (n.1), wintergreen (n.1), wisteria, zinnia
some kinds of flowers
cross (n.4), herb (n.1), hybrid, native (n.3), wildflower
some categories of flowers
annual (n.), biennial (n.2), perennial (n.)
broader category that includes flowers
plant (n.1)
some parts of flowers
anther, blossom (n.1), bud (n.1), hood (n.2), hull[1] (n.2), ovary (n.2), petal, pistil, pollen, sepal, stamen, stem[1] (n.1)
study of flowers
botany
some places for growing flowers
field (n.1), **garden** (n.)
some activities of flowers
bloom (v.), blossom (v.), flower (v.), grow (v.1), pollinate
qualities of some flowers
beautiful, colorful (adj.1), fragrant, pretty (adj.)
produces flowers
bulb (n.1), **seed** (n.1)
some people associated with flowers
florist, gardener (n.1)
conventionally associated with flowers
bee (n.), gift (n.1), honeybee, romance (n.1)
container for flowers
vase
eats flowers
bird (n.), **insect** (n.1), **mammal**, **reptile**,

rodent
have flowers
plants (n.1), **trees** (n.1), **vegetables** (n.1)
some things made from flowers
bouquet, corsage, garland, honey (n.1), Maypole, medicine (n.1), perfume (n.1), tea (n.3), wreath
things that affect the growth of flowers
bee (n.), insect (n.1), seasons (n.1), sunlight, temperature (n.2), wind[1] (n.1)

fluid ⊕ ◐ *see* blood, drink, water

fluoride ⊕ ◐ *see* element, tooth

flute *for a picture see the definition of* music

flutter *for a picture see definition*

fly
see also airplane, bird, technology
for pictures see definitions of fly[1], soar

fly
see also insect
for pictures see definitions of housefly, insect, mayfly, pester

foal *for a picture see definition*

fog *for a picture see the definition of* mist

foliage
see also leaf, tree
for a picture see the definition of foliage

folk ◐ ◐ *see* art, community, family, music

follow *for pictures see definitions of* follow, heel

food (n.) ◐ ◐
see also cooking, diet, digestion
for pictures see definitions of bread, chow[1]
examples of food
apple (n.1), artichoke, asparagus, bacon, banana, bean (n.1), beef (n.1), beet, bologna, broccoli, burrito, casserole (n.2), cauliflower, chicken (n.2), chili (n.2), chocolate (n.1), citrus (n.), clam (n.), collard (n.1), corn (n.1), crab, cucumber, date[2], drumstick (n.2), egg[1] (n.2), eggplant, flounder[2], grits, ham[1] (n.1), hamburger, hash (n.2), hot dog (n.), jerky[2], lamb, lasagna, legume (n.2), lemon (n.1), lettuce (n.2), lime[2] (n.1), loaf[1] (n.2), lobster (n.2), meatball, mincemeat (n.1), mush (n.1), mushroom (n.), mussel, mutton, nectarine, oatmeal (n.2), olive (n.1), omelet, orange (n.1), parsnip (n.1), pasta, patty (n.1), pea (n.1), peach (n.1), pear (n.1), pepper (n.2), perch[2], pickle (n.), pie, quahog, radish (n.2), raspberry (n.2), ravioli, sardine, scallop (n.1), shrimp (n.), soup, spinach, squash[2] (n.1), stew (n.), strawberry (n.1), tangerine (n.1), tomato (n.1), tuna (n.1), turkey (n.2), turnip (n.2), zucchini
some kinds of foods
bread (n.1), fish (n.2), **fruit**, **grain** (n.1), herb (n.2), meat (n.1), poultry, spice (n.1), staple[2] (n.1), **vegetable** (n.1)
some ingredients in foods
calorie, carbohydrate, fiber (n.2), mineral (n.), nutrient, preservative, protein, starch (n.1), vitamin
some places for buying food
bar (n.4), cafeteria, canteen (n.2), delicatessen, diner (n.2), grocery (n.1), mess (n.3), restaurant, store (n.1), supermarket
some places for storing food
cabinet (n.1), can[2] (n.1), cupboard, freezer, icebox, jar[1] (n.1), kitchen, larder, pantry, refrigerator, sack[1] (n.), shelf (n.1)
some actions associated with food
bite (v.1,1), can[2] (v.), cater (v.1), chew (v.), **cook** (v.2), diet (v.), digest (v.1), dish (v.), fast[2] (v.2), feast (v.), feed (v.4), forage (v.1), freeze (v.1), garnish (v.), gorge (v.),

grind (v.1), harvest (v.), **hunt** (v.1), lap[3] (v.2), nibble (v.1), nourish (v.1), pickle (v.), prepare (v.1), preserve (v.3), refrigerate, salt (v.1), season (v.1), serve (v.6), slurp (v.), snack (v.), spread (v.2), starve (v.1,2), stuff (v.3), swallow[1] (v.1), taste (v.1), treat (v.5), vomit (v.), wolf (v.), wrap (v.2)
descriptions of some foods
cooked (cook v.3), delicious, kosher (adj.1), raw (adj.1), salty, sour (adj.1), sweet (adj.1), tasty, tough (adj.2)
some things that food affects
development (n.1), growth (n.1), **health** (n.1), nutrition (n.1)
some things used for serving food
bowl[1] (n.1), buffet (n.1), cellophane, china (n.2), chopsticks, counter[1] (n.1), dish (n.1), fork (n.1), knife (n.), napkin, pan (n.1), plate (n.1), platter (n.), pot (n.1), saucer, scoop (n.1,2), service (n.8), silverware, spoon (n.1), table (n.1), tablecloth, tray (n.1), utensil
some people associated with food
baker, butcher (n.2), chef, cook (n.), dietician (dietitian), farmer, fisherman, gourmet, grocer, server (n.1), vegetarian (n.), waiter, waitress
accessories that protect from food
apron, bib (n.1)
without food
famine, hunger (n.2), malnutrition
negatively associated with food
mold[2], poison (n.1)
some effects of food
allergy, **energy** (n.1), indigestion (n.1), nourishment
some events associated with food
banquet, barbecue (n.1), breakfast (n.), buffet (n.2), clambake, cookout, dinner, feast (n.), lunch (n.), luncheon, meal[1] (n.1), mess (n.3), picnic (n.1), roast (n.2), snack (n.), supper, tea (n.4)
some means of providing food
farming (farm v.2), fishing (**fish** v.2), gardening (**garden** v.), gathering (gather v.1), hunting (**hunt** v.1), picking (pick[1] v.2), planting (plant v.1)
some terms for portioning food
helping, meal[1] (n.2), provision (n.3), rations (n.2), serving
also associated with food
appetizer, calorie, cocktail (n.2), course (n.6), dessert, health food, junk food, leftovers, menu

foot (n.1) ⊕
see also body
for pictures see definitions of body, paw, talon, webfoot
some kinds of feet
forefoot, hoof (n.2), paw (n.), webfoot (n.1)
some parts of feet
bones (n.), claw (n.1), digit (n.1), heel (n.1), instep (n.1), ligament, **muscle** (n.1), nail (n.2), pads[1] (n.5), sole[2] (n.), tendon, toe (n.1), web (n.1)
some places for feet
footstool, pedal (n.), stirrup
some activities that involve feet
climb (v.3), dance (v.1), hop[1] (v.2), kick (v.1), limp[1] (v.), pace (v.3), paw (v.1), play footsie with (phr.1), skip (v.1), stamp (v.5), stand (v.1), step (v.1,2), stomp (v.1,2), swim (v.1), tread (v.1,1,2), walk (v.1,2)
some sounds made by feet
footstep (n.1), tapping (tap[1] n.2)
person associated with feet
cobbler (n.1)

some accessories that protect feet
boot (n.), clog (n.), fin (n.3), flipper (n.2), horseshoe (n.1), moccasin, rubbers (n.3), sandal, shoe (n.1,2), skate[1] (n.), slipper, sneaker, snowshoe, sock, stocking (n.), thong (n.2)
negatively associated with feet
athlete's foot, blister (n.1), itching (itch n.1), smell (n.3)
made by feet
footprint, tracks (n.1)
some functions of feet
bear[1] (v.2), carry (v.1), move (v.1), support (v.1,2)

football
see also sport
for pictures see definitions of aloft, football, kickoff, throw

force ⏻ *see* energy, physics

forest
see also ecosystem, tree
for a picture see the definition of forest
some kinds of forests
jungle, rain forest, wood (n.4)
some kinds of protected forests
park (n.1), preserve (n.2), reserve (n.3)
broader categories that include forests
ecosystem, environment (n.1), **natural resources**
some activities in forests
camp (v.2), hike (v.), picnic (v.), scout (v.1)
some products of forests
board (n.1), charcoal (n.1), firewood, kindling, log (n.1), lumber[1], paper (n.1), plank, pole[1], timber (n.1,2)
people associated with forests
camper (n.1), guide (n.1), hunter (n.1), lumberjack, ranger (n.1)
some things that live in forests
animals (n.1), **birds** (n.), **fungus**, **insects** (n.1), **plants** (n.1), **trees** (n.1)

fork *for pictures see definitions of* fork, utensil

formula
see also mathematics, science
for a picture see the definition of formula

fortress *for a picture see definition*

fossil
see also geology, history, stone
for pictures see definitions of amber, dinosaur, fossil

foul *for a picture see definition*

fountain *for a picture see definition*

fountain pen *for a picture see definition*

fowl ⏻ *see* bird

fox *for pictures see definitions of* fox, prey

fracture ⏻ *see* first aid, injury, skeleton

franc *for pictures see definitions of* franc, international

fraud ⏻ *see* crime, money

freighter *for a picture see definition*

French *for a picture see definition*

French fries *for pictures see definitions of* French fries, international

French horn *for pictures see definitions of* French horn, music

frequency ⏻ *see* energy, measurement

fret *for a picture see the definition of* chord[2]

friend
see also relationship
for pictures see definitions of buddy, dependable, friend

fright ⏻ *see* fear

frigid ⏻ *see* tundra, weather

Frisbee *for a picture see definition*

frog *for pictures see definitions of* amphibian, dissect, frog, leapfrog

frolic *for a picture see definition*

frond *for a picture see definition*

front *for a picture see definition*

froth *for a picture see definition*

frown
see also anger, sadness
for a picture see the definition of frown

fruit ⏻⏻
see also plant, seed, vegetable
for pictures see definitions of apple, assorted, banana, berry, bunch, cantaloupe, cherry, citrus, cucumber, eggplant, fruit, gourd, grape, grapefruit, gravity, honeydew melon, kiwi, mango, melon, nectarine, orange, papaya, pear, persimmon, pineapple, plantain, plum, pomegranate, produce, pumpkin, radiate, raisin, raspberry, star, tangerine, tomato
some examples of fruits
apple (n.1), apricot (n.1), avocado, banana, blackberry (n.1), blueberry (n.1), cherry (n.1), cone (n.3), crab apple (n.1), cucumber, currant (n.2), date[2], fig, gourd, grape, grapefruit, guava (n.2), huckleberry (n.2), kiwi (n.2), lemon (n.1), lime[2] (n.1), loganberry (n.2), mandarin (n.3), mango, melon, mulberry (n.1), olive (n.1), orange (n.1), papaya, peach (n.1), pear (n.1), pepper (n.2), persimmon, pineapple (n.1), plantain, plum, pomegranate (n.1), prickly pear, pumpkin, raspberry (n.2), squash[2] (n.1), strawberry (n.1), tangerine (n.2), tomato (n.1), vanilla (n.2), watermelon (n.1)
some kinds of fruit
berry (n.), citrus (n.), nut (n.1)
broader categories that include fruit
crop (n.1), **food** (n.), **plant** (n.1), produce (n.)
some parts of fruits
core (n.1), flesh (n.3), hull[1] (n.1), husk (n.), kernel (n.1), meat (n.2), peel (n.), pit[2] (n.), pulp (n.1), rind (n.), **seed** (n.1), skin (n.2)
some places for fruit
bog (n.), farm (n.1), **garden** (n.), grocery (n.1), grove, market (n.1), orchard, store (n.1), supermarket
activities with fruit
cook (v.1), cultivate, eat (v.1), grow (v.1), harvest (v.), hull[1] (v.), peel (v.1), plant (v.1), preserve (v.3), raise (v.3), store (v.)
things that produce fruit
blossom (n.1), flower (n.1), ovary (n.2), **seed** (n.1)
some people associated with fruit
cook (n.), farmer, gardener (n.1), grocer
some things made from fruit
cobbler (n.2), cocktail (n.2), jam[2], jelly, juice (n.), marmalade, pie, preserve (n.1), salad (n.2), sauce (n.2), tart[2], yogurt

fry ⏻ *see* cooking

fuel ⏻⏻ *see* energy, food

full moon *for a picture see definition*

fun ⏻ *see* game, leisure

fungus ⏻
see also disease, plant
for pictures see definitions of fungus, mold[2], mushroom
some kinds of funguses
lichen, mildew, mold[2], mushroom (n.), toadstool, yeast
broader categories that include fungus
organism, **plant** (n.1)
some parts of funguses
cap[1] (n.2), **cell** (n.1), filament (n.1),

---

stem[1] (n.1)
some places for funguses
bog (n.), **forest**, swamp (n.)
some activities of funguses
decay (v.1), decompose, rot (v.1)
some descriptions of funguses
fluffy (adj.1), fuzzy (adj.1), scaly, slimy (adj.1)
produced by funguses
spores
affects the growth of funguses
moisture
things that eat funguses
animal (n.1), human (n.)
process involving funguses
fermentation (n.1)
some diseases involving funguses
athlete's foot, rust (n.2)
some things made with funguses
alcohol (n.1), antibiotic, bread (n.1), medicine (n.1)

fur
see also animal, endangered species, hair, mammal
for a picture see the definition of fur

furniture ⏻
see also room
for pictures see definitions of armchair, bed, bench, plaid, stool, upholstery
some examples of furniture
armchair, bed (n.1), buffet (n.1), cabinet (n.1), chair (n.1), chest (n.2), couch, cradle (n.1), crib (n.1), desk, dresser, footstool, hutch (n.2), rocking chair, sofa, stool (n.1), table (n.1)
parts of some furniture
arm[1] (n.2), back[1] (n.3), cushion (n.1), desktop (n.), headrest, leaf (n.3), leg (n.2), rung[2], seat (n.1)
some places for furniture
house (n.1), museum, office (n.1), **room** (n.2)
descriptions of some furniture
antique (n.), comfortable (adj.2), modern (adj.2)
some materials used in furniture
bamboo (n.2), cherry (n.2), cloth (n.1), cotton (n.1), fiberglass, glue (n.), lumber[1], mahogany (n.2), nails (n.1), paint (n.1), pine (n.2), plastic (n.), plywood, rivets (n.), screws (n.1), shellac (n.1), stain (n.2), stud[1] (n.), stuffing (stuff n.1), upholstery (n.1), walnut (n.3), wicker (n.2), willow, wood (n.2), wrought iron
some people associated with furniture
artisan, carpenter, mover

fury ⏻ *see* anger, emotion

fuzzy *for a picture see definition*

gadget ⏻ *see* technology, tool

gait *for a picture see definition*

galaxy
see also space
for pictures see definitions of galaxy, solar system

game (n.2) ⏻⏻
see also leisure, sport
for pictures see definitions of backgammon, checkerboard, chess, concentrate, croquet, domino, football, Ping-Pong, puzzle, strategy
some examples of games
backgammon (n.2), ball[1] (n.3), billiards, bingo, bowling, cards (n.3), checkers, chess, darts (n.2), dominos (n.2), hide-and-seek, hopscotch, horseshoes (n.2), jacks (n.3), leapfrog, Ping-Pong, poker[2], table tennis, tag[2] (n.1), ticktack-toe, tiddlywinks, video game
similar to games

competition (n.2), event (n.2), match² (n.3), race¹ (n.1), **sport** (n.1,2)
some broader categories including games
entertainment (n.1)
some parts of games
move (n.3), play (n.3), round (n.3), rule (n.1), score (n.4)
some parts of board games
board (n.2), dice (pl.n.), piece (n.2), timer (n.3)
some places for games
arcade (n.2), arena (n.1), court (n.1), field (n.3), park (n.1), playground, stadium
some actions associated with games
beat (v.2), compete (v.2), deal (v.4), defeat (v.1), lose (v.3), play (v.2), tie (v.4,5)
some things used in games
ball¹ (n.2), cards (n.2), checkerboard, **computer**, counter¹ (n.2), dice (pl.n.), equipment (n.1), Frisbee, horseshoe (n.1), joystick, marbles (n.2), playing card, racket²
some people associated with games
athlete, dealer (n.2), player (n.1)
conventionally associated with games
captain (n.5), coach (n.1), league¹ (n.2), referee (n.), team (n.1)
some results of games
defeat (n.1,2), draw (n.), loss (n.5), tie (n.3,4), victory, win (n.)
garage ✪ *see* building, vehicle
garbage
see also conservation
for pictures see definitions of garbage, rubber
gardening ✪ ✪
see also farming
kinds of soil related to gardening
clay (n.), clod (n.1), dirt (n.1), earth (n.3), humus, sand (n.), sod (n.)
some places for gardens
field (n.1), yard² (n.1)
some activities in gardening
cultivate (v.1), dig (v.1), graft (n.1), grub (v.1), harvest (v.), hoe (v.), irrigate, plant (v.1), plow (v.1), prune² (v.1), rake (v.1), reap (v.1), sow¹ (v.1), transplant (v.1), weed (v.1)
some things used in gardening
bulbs (n.1), clipper (n.1), compost, fertilizer, gloves (n.1), hoe (n.), hose (n.1), **plants** (n.1), rake (n.), **seeds** (n.1), shovel (n.1), spade¹ (n.), trowel (n.1), **water** (n.1)
biblical garden
Eden (n.1)
some flowers found in gardens
geranium, hollyhock, marigold, nasturtium, peony (n.1), petunia, snapdragon
gargoyle *for a picture see definition*
garlic *for a picture see definition*
garment ✪ *see* clothing
garnet *for a picture see definition*
gas
see also air, chemistry, energy
for a picture see the definition of **explosive**
gasoline
see also car, energy
for a picture see the definition of **explosive**
gauge *for a picture see definition*
gear *for a picture see definition*
gecko *for a picture see definition*
gem
see also jewelry, stone
for pictures see definitions of gem, ruby
Gemini *for pictures see definitions of* constellation, zodiac
gene ✪ ✪ *see* cell, reproduction

generation ✪ *see* reproduction, tradition
genus ✪ *see* life, relationship
geography (n.1) ✪
see also continent, desert, lake, mountain, ocean, plain, river, sea, volcano
broader category that includes geography
science
some parts of geography
plate tectonics, topography
some topics of study in geography
animals (n.1), **buildings** (n.1), cities (**city** n.1), climate, **culture** (n.1), **deserts**¹, **lakes**, land (n.1), **mountains** (n.1), nations (n.1), **natural resources**, oceans (n.1), **plains** (n.), **plants** (n.1), **rivers** (n.1), **seas** (n.1), terrain, towns (n.1), **transportation** (n.1), waterways
some tools for studying geography
atlas (n.2), globe (n.2), map (n.)
associated with geography
map (v.1), social studies, survey (v.3)
geology ✪ ✪
see also continent, earth, science, stone, volcano
some kinds of geology
marine (adj.1), physical (adj.2), terrestrial (adj.1)
a broader category that includes geology
science
some parts of geology
paleontology, plate tectonics
some processes studied in geology
erosion, eruption
some activities in geology
collect (v.1), measure (v.1)
some tools used in geology
altimeter, binoculars, chisel (n.), compass (n.1), flashlight, hammer (n.1), laser, magnifying glass, map (n.), pick² (n.), radar (n.1), seismograph
some things that affect geology
earthquakes, glaciers, gravity (n.1), precipitation (n.2), time (n.2), **volcanos** (n.1), **water** (n.1), waves (n.1), wind¹ (n.1)
geometry ✪ *see* mathematics, shape
germ ✪ ✪ *see* bacteria, disease, virus
German *for pictures see definitions of* German, language
German shepherd *for a picture see the definition of* thoroughbred
gesture
see also action, communication
for a picture see the definition of interpret
Ghana *for a picture see definition*
gift *for a picture see the definition of* wrapping
Gila monster *for a picture see definition*
gill ✪ *see* fish, respiration
ginger *for a picture see definition*
giraffe *for a picture see definition*
glacier ✪ *see* geology
glad ✪ *see* happiness
gladiator *for a picture see definition*
gland
see also body, organ
for a picture see the definition of body
glare *for a picture see definition*
glass
see also drink
for pictures see definitions of goblet, magnifying glass
glide *for a picture see the definition of* descent
glitter *for a picture see definition*
gloat *for a picture see definition*

global ✪ *see* earth, geography, politics
globe *for pictures see definitions of* equator, inquisitive
glossary ✪ *see* book
glove *for pictures see definitions of* drab, glove
glue ✪ *see* art
gnome *for a picture see definition*
gnu *for a picture see definition*
goalie *for a picture see definition*
goalkeeper *for a picture see the definition of* goalie
goat
see also mammal
for pictures see definitions of goat, kid¹
goatee *for a picture see definition*
goblet *for a picture see definition*
god
see also myth, religion
for pictures see definitions of Apollo, Ares, Hercules, Hermes, Neptune, Zeus
goddess *for pictures see definitions of* Aphrodite, Athena, Demeter
gold ✪ *see* element
golf *for a picture see the definition of* putt
gong *for a picture see the definition of* music
goo *for a picture see definition*
goods ✪ *see* business
goose *for pictures see definitions of* bill, goose
gorilla *for pictures see definitions of* frown, gorilla
gossip ✪ *see* language
gourd
see also fruit, plant
for a picture see the definition of gourd
government (n.1,3) ✪
see also country, democracy, law, legislature, military, monarchy, politics, power, war
some kinds of government
commonwealth (n.1), confederacy (n.1), **democracy** (n.1), empire, federation, **monarchy**, republic (n.1), tyranny (n.1)
some kinds of governmental decisions
decree (n.), judgment (n.), legislation, regulation (n.2), rule (n.3)
some parts of governments
agency (n.3), bureau (n.2), cabinet (n.2), congress (n.1), department, executive (n.2), House of Representatives, judicial (adj.1), **legislature**, military (n.), parliament (n.1), senate (n.2)
some government places
capital¹ (n.1), chambers (n.3), court (n.3), White House (n.1)
representation of the government
constitution (n.1)
some people associated with governments
ambassador (n.1), consul, diplomat (n.1), judge (n.1), justice (n.3), police officer, politician (n.2), representative (n.1), sovereign (n.), vice president (n.2)
some heads of governments
king (n.1), monarch (n.1), president (n.2), prime minister, queen (n.1), sovereign (n.)
also associated with government
justice (n.1), taxation
gown *for a picture see definition*
graceful *for a picture see definition*
graffiti *for a picture see definition*
grain (n.1) ✪
see also grass, plant, seed
for pictures see definitions of grain, granola, Indian corn, rice, straw
some examples of grains
barley (n.2), corn (n.2), Indian corn, oat (n.2), rice (n.2), rye (n.2), wheat (n.1)

broader category that includes *grains*
  plant (n.1)
some activities involving grains
  cultivate (v.2), grind (v.1), harvest (v.),
  plant (v.1), store (v.), thresh (v.)
some things that eat grains
  birds (n.), human (n.), **insects** (n.1), livestock,
  poultry
some people associated with grains
  farmer, miller
tools associated with grains
  combine (n.), grindstone (n.), flail (n.),
  mill (n.2), scoop (n.1), screen (n.1), scythe
some containers for grains
  hopper (n.2), sack[1] (n.), silo (n.1)
some things made from grains
  alcohol (n.1), beer (n.1), broth, cereal (n.2),
  feed (n.), flour (n.), fodder, **food** (n.), gin[1],
  graham, granola, mash (n.1), meal[2],
  oatmeal (n.1), oil (n.1), porridge, soup,
  whiskey
units for measuring grains
  bushel, peck[1] (n.1)
grammar ✪
  see also language
  some places for grammar
    school, essay, speech, writing
  broader categories that include grammar
    communication, language
  some descriptions of grammar
    grammatical, irregular, regular
  some aspects of grammar
    adjective, adverb, antonym, command,
    comparative, complex sentence, compound
    sentence, conjunction, contraction, definite
    article, exclamation, future, homograph,
    homonym, homphone, indefinite article,
    infinitive, interjection, interrogative, linking
    verb, noun, object, past, plural, predicate,
    prefix, preposition, present, pronoun,
    pronunciation, singular, sound, stress, subject,
    suffix, superlative, verb
  some topics of study in grammar
    affix, clause, paragraph, part of speech, phrase,
    sentence, simple sentence, spelling, syllable,
    tense, vocabulary, wording
  study of grammar
    syntax
  some grammatical notation
    apostrophe, bracket, capital, colon, comma,
    dash, exclamation mark, hyphen, letter, lower
    case, mark, parenthesis, period, point, question
    mark, quotation mark, semicolon, slash,
    punctuation
granite *for a picture see definition*
granola *for a picture see definition*
grape *for pictures see definitions of* bunch, grape
grapefruit *for a picture see definition*
graph ✪ ✪ *see* communication, mathematics
graphic ✪ *see* art, photography
grass (n.1) ✪
  see also grain, leaf, plant
  for pictures see definitions of alfalfa, rice, straw
  some examples of grasses
    alfalfa, bamboo (n.1), barley (n.1),
    bluegrass (n.1), reed (n.1), rice (n.1), rush[2],
    rye (n.1), sugar cane, wheat (n.2)
  similar to grass
    sod (n.), tuft
  broader category that includes grasses
    plant (n.1)
  some parts of grasses
    blade (n.3), cane (n.2), joint (n.), **leaf** (n.1),
    root[1] (n.1), shoot (n.2), stem[1] (n.1)
  some places for grasses
    everglade, grassland, lawn, mall (n.1), marsh,

meadow, parkway, pasture (n.1), prairie,
savanna, yard[2] (n.1)
  some descriptions of grasses
    fresh (adj.6), green (adj.1), lush (adj.1),
    short (adj.1), tall (adj.1), thick (adj.3)
  affects the growth of grasses
    fertilizer, **fungus**, lime[1], nitrogen, shade (n.1),
    soil[1] (n.1), sunlight, **water** (n.1), **worm** (n.1)
  some people associated with grasses
    gardener (n.1), mower
  some tools associated with grasses
    lawn mower, mower, rake (n.), scythe,
    shovel (n.1), sickle
  some things done with grasses
    cut (v.3), dry (v.1), edge (v.1), feed (v.2),
    fertilize (v.2), graze[1] (v.1), landscape (v.),
    plant (v.1), rake (v.2), seed (v.1), store (v.),
    water (v.1), weed (v.1)
  some things made from grasses
    basket (n.1), hay (n.), hut, paper (n.1)
grasshopper *for pictures see definitions of* grasshopper, insect
grave *for a picture see the definition of* headstone
gravity
  see also earth, physics, space
  for a picture see the definition of gravity
graze *for a picture see definition*
graze *for a picture see definition*
Great Dane *for a picture see definition*
greenhouse *for a picture see definition*
grenade *for a picture see definition*
greyhound *for a picture see definition*
grief ✪ *see* emotion, sadness
grill
  see also cooking
  for a picture see the definition of cookout
grimace *for a picture see definition*
grin *for a picture see definition*
grizzly bear *for a picture see definition*
grocery ✪ *see* food
ground
  see also soil, thought
  for a picture see the definition of ground
ground *for a picture see definition*
groundhog *for pictures see definitions of* groundhog, woodchuck
group *for pictures see definitions of* group, huddle
grow
  see also farming, gardening, life
  for pictures see definitions of amphibian, grow
growl
  see also animal, behavior
  for a picture see the definition of growl
growth ✪ ✪ *see* life
guitar *for pictures see definitions of* acoustic, guitar,
  music
gull *for a picture see the definition of* sea gull
gun
  see also weapon
  for pictures see definitions of cannon, firearm,
  gun, holster, revolver, rifle
gym ✪ ✪ *see* exercise, school, sport
gymnastics ✪ ✪ *see* exercise, sport
habit ✪ *see* behavior, tradition
habitat ✪ *see* conservation, ecosystem
hacker ✪ *see* computer, Internet
haiku *for a picture see definition*
hail *for a picture see definition*
hail
  see also weather
  for a picture see the definition of hail

hair (n.1) ✪ ✪
  see also body, head
  for pictures see definitions of body, wig
  some kinds of hair
    beard, eyebrow (n.2), eyelash, mane,
    mustache, ruff (n.2), sideburns, whisker
  some parts of hair
    oil (n.1), pigment (n.1), root[1] (n.2),
    shaft (n.3), strand[2] (n.1)
  place for hair care
    salon (n.2)
  some activities that involve hair
    brush[1] (v.1), comb (v.1), cut (v.3), dry (v.1),
    dye (v.), grow (v.5), part (v.2), set (v.1),
    shampoo (v.), shave (v.1), shear (v.2),
    style (v.), trim (v.1)
  some descriptions of hair
    blond (n.), bristle (n.1), brittle (adj.),
    coarse (adj.1), curly, fine[1] (adj.3), fuzz,
    long[1] (adj.2), oily (adj.2), shaggy (adj.1),
    shiny (adj.1), short (adj.1), soft (adj.2),
    straight (adj.1), thick (adj.1,3), thin (adj.1,4),
    unruly
  some things used for hair care
    barrette, brush[1] (n.1), comb (n.1), dryer,
    gel (n.), hairpin (n.), headband, razor,
    ribbon (n.1), roller (n.4), scissors,
    shampoo (n.1), tweezers
  some people associated with hair
    barber, groomer (groom n.2)
  without hair
    bald (adj.1)
  negatively associated with hair
    dandruff
  some arrangements of hair
    clump (n.1), curl (n.1), lock[2] (n.1), part (n.7),
    shock[3], tuft, wisp (n.1)
  some hair colors
    auburn, black (adj.1), blond (adj.2),
    brown (adj.), golden (adj.1), gray (adj.3),
    red (adj.), white (adj.1)
  some functions of hair
    beauty (n.1), protection (n.1), warmth (n.1)
  some hair styles
    bangs, bob[2] (n.1), braid (n.), bun (n.2),
    dreadlocks, permanent (n.), pigtail, ponytail
  some things made from hair
    wig (n.)
  some things that affect hair
    diet (n.1), genes, heredity (n.1), **hygiene**
hairy *for a picture see definition*
half *for a picture see definition*
half-mast *for a picture see definition*
hall ✪ *see* building, room
Halloween
  see also celebration
  for a picture see the definition of Halloween
halve *for a picture see definition*
hamburger *for a picture see the definition of* international
hammer *for a picture see the definition of* tap
hammock *for a picture see definition*
hamster *for a picture see definition*
hand
  see also body
  for pictures see definitions of body, clasp, finger,
  hand, x-ray
hang *for a picture see the definition of* upside down
happiness ✪
  see also emotion
  similar to happiness
    gaiety, glee, joy (n.1), pleasure (n.1)
  broader categories that include happiness
    emotion (n.1), feeling (n.3), mood
  some actions involving happiness

beam (v.3), chuckle (v.), crow² (v.2), frolic, glow (v.3), kick up one's heels, laugh (v.), prance (v.2), purr (v.), radiate (v.4), rejoice, romp (v.), smile (v.), twinkle (v.2)
some reactions to **happiness**
  celebrate (v.1), cheer (v.2), congratulate, delight (v.2), embrace (v.1), praise (v.2)
descriptions of someone who is not **happy**
  blue (adj.2), dejected, dismal, downcast (adj.2), melancholy (adj.1), miserable (adj.1), sad (adj.1), wretched (adj.1)
some descriptions of someone who is **happy**
  aglow (adj.2), bright (adj.4), carefree, cheerful (adj.1), festive (adj.2), gay (adj.1), genial (adj.1), glad (adj.1), good-natured, happy-go-lucky, jaunty, jolly, jovial, joyful, joyous, jubilant, light² (adj.3), lighthearted, merry, overjoyed, playful (adj.1), radiant (adj.2), tickled pink
some causes of **happiness**
  birth (n.1), fortune (n.1,2), graduation (n.1), love (n.1), luck (n.2), marriage (n.2), peace (n.1), retirement (n.1), reunion, success (n.2), triumph (n.1)
some states of **happiness**
  bliss, cheer (n.1), delight (n.1), ecstasy, rapture
also associated with **happiness**
  celebration (n.2), festivity (n.1), holiday, lark² , merrymaking, party (n.1), vacation (n.), wedding
harbor ◐ ◖ *see* boat, thought, water
hardware *for a picture see definition*
hare *for pictures see definitions of* hare, rabbit
harmonica *for a picture see definition*
harmony ◐ ◖ *see* music, relationship
harp *for pictures see definitions of* harp, music
harpsichord *for a picture see definition*
harvest ◐ ◖ *see* farming, gardening
hat
  see also clothing
  for pictures see definitions of askew, beard, beret, corduroy, fleece, fur, hat, made-up
hatchet *for a picture see definition*
hate ◐
  see also emotion
  similar to **hate**
    animosity, contempt (n.1), disgust (n.), hostility (n.1), ill will, malice, scorn (n.)
  some broader categories that include **hate**
    emotion (n.1), feeling (n.3)
  some actions associated with **hate**
    despise, detest, glare (v.2), growl (v.1), loathe, scorn (v.1), scowl (v.), sneer (v.)
  some reactions to **hate**
    anger (n.), contempt (n.1), disgust (n.), dislike (n.), fear (n.1), prejudice (n.2), scorn (n.)
  some descriptions of **hate**
    abominable, blind (adj.2), callous (adj.1), loathsome, malignant (adj.1), nasty (adj.2), vicious
  some people associated with **hate**
    adversary, enemy (n.1), foe, villain (n.1)
  feeling **hatred**
    bitter (adj.2), cold (adj.3), evil (adj.), hateful (adj.2), hostile (adj.1), icy (adj.3), wicked (adj.1)
hawk *for pictures see definitions of* conservation, hawk¹
hawk *for a picture see definition*
hay ◐ *see* farming
hazardous *for a picture see definition*
head (n.1) ◐ ◑
  see also body

for pictures see definitions of body, insect
some parts of human **heads**
  face (n.1), hair (n.2)
some parts of animal **heads**
  antenna (n.2), antler, blowhole (n.1), comb (n.3), crest (n.1), horn (n.1)
some actions of **heads**
  beckon, bow¹ (v.1), butt³ (v.), dive (v.1), nod (v.1), shake (v.1), turn (v.4)
a representation of a **head**
  bust¹
some accessories for **heads**
  bandanna, beret, bridle (n.), cap¹ (n.1), crown (n.1), halo (n.1), halter (n.1), hat, headband, headrest, helmet, hood (n.1), kerchief, muzzle (n.2), pillow, scarf, turban, veil (n.1), visor (n.1,3)
negatively associated with **heads**
  amnesia, concussion (n.2), headache (n.1)
associated with **heads**
  brain (n.1), **mind** (n.1)
headdress *for a picture see definition*
headphone *for a picture see definition*
headstone *for a picture see definition*
heal ◐ *see* disease, health, injury
health (n.1) ◐ ◑
  see also bacteria, body, diet, disease, exercise, hygiene, injury, virus
  similar to **health**
    welfare (n.1)
  some kinds of **health**
    emotional (adj.1), mental (adj.1), physical (adj.1)
  some places associated with **health**
    clinic, gym (n.1), hospital, spa (n.3)
  some activities for checking someone's **health**
    checkup, exam, physical (n.)
  descriptions of somthing that is bad for someone's **health**
    detrimental, harmful, hazardous
  some descriptions of somone in poor **health**
    diseased (**disease**), failing (fail v.2), ill (adj.1), run-down (adj.1), sick (adj.1,4), sickly (adj.1), unhealthy (adj.1), unwell, weak (adj.1)
  some descriptions of somone in good **health**
    energetic, fit¹ (adj.2), flourishing (flourish v.1), hardy (adj.1), healthy (adj.3), hearty (adj.3), lively (adj.1), right (adj.6), robust (adj.1), sane (adj.1), sound² (adj.1), strong (adj.1), thriving (thrive v.2), trim (adj.2), well¹ (adj.1)
  descriptions of something that is good for someone's **health**
    beneficial, healthful, nourishing (nourish), nutritious, wholesome
  some people associated with **health**
    dentist, dietician (dietitian), doctor (n.1), intern (n.), patient (n.), pediatrician, pharmacist, physician, psychiatrist, psychologist, resident (n.2), surgeon, trainer, veterinarian
  things that can negatively affect somone's **health**
    addiction, overeating (overeat), overworking (overwork n.), pollution (n.2), smoking (smoke n.3), stress (n.4), trauma
  some things that affect someone's **health**
    diet (n.1), **disease**, emotion (n.2), environment (n.2), **exercise** (n.1), fitness (fit¹ adj.2), genes, heredity (n.1), **hygiene**, immunization (immunize), nutrition (n.2), oxygen, rest¹ (n.1), sleep (v.1)
  also associated with **health**
    body (n.1), **mind** (n.1), spirit (n.3)
hear ◐ *see* sense
hearing aid *for a picture see definition*
heart

see also blood, muscle, organ
  for pictures see definitions of body, emblem, heart
heartbeat *for a picture see definition*
heat ◐ ◑ ◖ *see* energy, physics, weather
Hebrew *for pictures see definitions of* Hebrew, language
hedgehog *for a picture see definition*
heel *for pictures see definitions of* body, heel
heirloom *for a picture see definition*
helicopter *for pictures see definitions of* helicopter, rotor
helmet *for pictures see definitions of* helmet, reflector
herb ◐ *see* flower, plant
herbivore ◐ *see* diet, plant
Hercules *for a picture see definition*
herd
  see also animal
  for a picture see the definition of herd
Hermes *for a picture see definition*
heroic *for a picture see definition*
heron *for pictures see definitions of* bird, heron
hexagon *for a picture see definition*
hieroglyphic *for a picture see definition*
highway ◐ *see* transportation, vehicle
hike *for pictures see definitions of* forest, top¹
hill *for a picture see the definition of* dune
hinder *for a picture see definition*
Hindi *for pictures see definitions of* Hindi, language
hip *for a picture see the definition of* body
hippopotamus *for a picture see definition*
history (n.1,2) ◐
  includes the study of **history**
    social studies
  some descriptions of periods in **history**
    ancient (adj.2), colonial (adj.2), contemporary (adj.2), modern (adj.1), Paleozoic, prehistoric
  a person associated with **history**
    historian
  conventionally associated with **history**
    book (n.1), past (adj.1), time (n.2)
  some periods in **history**
    ice age, Middle Ages, Renaissance (n.2), Stone Age
  units for measuring **history**
    age (n.4), century (n.1), eon, epoch, era, generation (n.2), millennium, period (n.2)
hockey
  see also sport
  for pictures see definitions of hockey, puck
hold *for pictures see definitions of* caress, lull
holiday ◐ *see* celebration, culture, tradition
holster *for a picture see definition*
holy ◐ ◖ *see* religion
home (n.1,2) ◐
  see also building, community, family
  for a picture see the definition of mansion
  similar to **homes**
    dwelling, residence (n.1)
  some kinds of **homes**
    apartment, bungalow, cabin (n.1), condominium, cottage, house (n.1), hut, igloo, lodge (n.1), loft (n.1), manor, mansion, mobile home, pueblo (n.1), shack (n.), tent (n.1), tepee, trailer (n.2)
  broader category that includes **homes**
    community (n.1)
  some parts of **homes**
    chimney, door (n.1), foundation (n.1), frame (n.1), gutter, roof (n.1), shingles (n.),

injection *for a picture see definition*

injury ☉
   see also **first aid**
   for pictures see definitions of bandage, dislocate
   some examples of injuries
      break (n.1), bruise (n.), burn (n.),
      concussion (n.2), cut (n.1), fracture (n.),
      scrape (n.2), sore (n.), sprain (n.),
      strain[1] (n.3), trauma, wound[1] (n.1,2)
   some kinds of injuries
      emotional (adj.1), fatal (adj.1), minor (adj.1),
      physical (adj.1), serious (adj.4)
   places for treatment of injuries
      clinic, hospital
   some actions related to healing injuries
      bandage (v.), mend (v.3), rally (v.3),
      recover (v.3), recuperate, treat (v.4)
   some reactions to injuries
      clench (v.1), cry (v.1,2), gasp (v.1),
      grimace (v.), gulp (v.1), pout, scream (v.1),
      squirm (v.1), wince
   some descriptions of someone prone to injuries
      delicate (adj.2), fragile, vulnerable (adj.1)
   some descriptions of injuries
      painful (adj.1), sensitive (adj.2), sore (adj.1),
      tender (adj.3)
   some descriptions of someone not prone to injuries
      sturdy, tough (adj.1)
   some causes of injuries
      abuse (n.2), accident (n.2), assault (n.1),
      attack (n.1), blow[1] (n.1,2), fall (n.1),
      shock[1] (n.1,3), strike (n.1), violence
   some people associated with injuries
      doctor (n.1), nurse (n.1), victim (n.1)
   some accessories for healing injuries
      bandage (n.), cast (n.3), crutches (crutch),
      disinfectant, medicine (n.1),
      stitches (stitch n.2)
   conventionally associated with injury
      insult (n.)
   some feelings associated with injuries
      ache (v.1), burn (v.2), hurt (v.4), pain (v.),
      sting (v.3), suffer (v.1)
   some results of injuries
      amnesia, coma, inflammation, paralysis,
      scab (n.1), scar (n.1,2)
   some things for healing injuries
      therapy, treatment (n.3)

inlet
   see also ocean, river
   for a picture see the definition of inlet

inquisitive
   see also knowledge, learn
   for a picture see the definition of inquisitive

insane ☉ *see* mind

insect (n.1) ☉
   see also arthropod, invertebrate, spider, worm
   for pictures see definitions of beetle, butterfly,
      cicada, cockroach, cricket[1], dragonfly,
      grasshopper, housefly, insect, Japanese beetle,
      katydid, ladybug, locust, louse, maggot, mayfly,
      mosquito, moth, praying mantis, termite,
      vermin, wasp
   some examples of insects
      ant, aphid, bee (n.), beetle, bookworm (n.2),
      butterfly, cicada, cockroach, cricket[1],
      dragonfly, firefly, flea (n.), fly[2], glowworm,
      gnat, grasshopper, hornet, housefly, Japanese
      beetle, katydid, ladybug, locust (n.1,2), louse,
      mayfly (n.1), mosquito, moth, praying mantis,
      termite, wasp
   similar to insects
      bug (n.1,2), pest, vermin
   broader categories that include insects
      animal (n.1), **arthropod, invertebrate** (n.)

parts of some insects
   abdomen (n.2), antenna (n.2), feeler,
   stinger (n.2), thorax (vein n.2), wing (n.1)
some places for insects
   hive (n.1), nest (n.2)
some groups of insects
   colony (n.2), swarm (n.1,2)
produced by insects
   beeswax, cocoon, honey (n.1), shellac (n.1),
   silk (n.1), wax[1] (n.1)
used by some insects
   flower (n.1), nectar
behaviors of some insects
   bite (v.2), build (v.1), defend (v.1), feed (v.4),
   fly[1] (v.1), forage (v.), mate (v.), sting (v.1),
   suck (v.1), work (v.5)
some sounds of insects
   buzz (n.1), chirp (n.), hum (n.), trill (n.2)
young of insects
   grub (n.), larva (n.1), nymph (n.2), pupa
some growth stages of insects
   adult (n.2), egg[1] (n.2), larvae (larva n.1)
some things insects eat
   blood (n.1), flowers (n.1), **fruit, insects** (n.1),
   leaves, **plants** (n.1)
some things that affect insects
   insecticide, pesticide
also associated with insects
   plague (n.1)

insectivore ☉ *see* animal, diet, plant

insignia *for a picture see definition*

insomnia *for a picture see definition*

inspiration ☉ *see* mind, thought

install *for a picture see definition*

instinct ☉ *see* behavior

instruct
   see also education, knowledge, learn, school
   for a picture see the definition of instruct

instrument (n.2) ☉ ☉
   see also music
   for pictures see definitions of banjo, bass[1], bass
      drum, bongo[2], bugle, castanet, cello, chime,
      clarinet, conga, fiddle, French horn, guitar,
      harmonica, harp, harpsichord, lute, organ,
      piano, recorder, saxophone, snare drum,
      tense[1], tom-tom, trumpet, viola, violin,
      whistle, xylophone, zither
   some examples of percussion instruments
      bass drum, bell (n.1), bongo[2], castanet,
      chime (n.1), conga (n.2), cymbal, drum (n.1),
      glockenspiel, gong, kettledrum, organ (n.1),
      piano, snare drum, tambourine, tom-tom,
      trap (n.3), triangle (n.2), xylophone
   some examples of brass instruments
      bugle, cornet, French horn, horn (n.2),
      trombone, trumpet (n.1), tuba
   some examples of stringed instruments
      banjo, bass[1] (n.2), cello, guitar, harp, lute, lyre,
      mandolin, ukulele, viola, violin, zither
   some examples of wind instruments
      accordion, bagpipe, harmonica, pipe (n.3),
      whistle (n.2)
   some examples of woodwind instruments
      bassoon, clarinet, English horn, fife, flute,
      oboe, piccolo, recorder (n.3), saxophone
   some kinds of instruments
      brass (n.2), percussion (n.2), string (n.6),
      woodwind (n.1)
   some categories of instruments
      alto (adj.), bass[1] (adj.), soprano (adj.),
      tenor (adj.), treble (adj.)
   some parts of instruments
      bell (n.2), bellows, button (n.3), fret[2],
      joint (n.), key[1] (n.4), keyboard,
      mouthpiece (n.1), neck (n.3), pedal (n.),

peg (n.2), pipe (n.4), reed (n.2), string (n.5),
   valve (n.3)
some actions on instruments
   adjust (adjustment), tune (n.3)
some actions with instruments
   bang (v.1), blow[2] (v.4), bow[2] (v.), pluck (v.3),
   strike (v.1), trill (v.)
some sounds of instruments
   bang (n.1), clang (v.), drone[2] (n.), hum (n.),
   toot (n.), whistle (n.1)
some people associated with instruments
   conductor (n.1), drum major, drum majorette,
   drummer, musician, player (n.2)
some accessories of instruments
   bow[2] (n.2), drumstick (n.1), mallet (n.3),
   mute (n.2), pick[1] (n.4)

intellect ☉ *see* knowledge, mind

interact *for a picture see definition*

interest ☉ ☉ *see* bank, money, thought

international
   see also country, government
   for a picture see the definition of international

Internet ☉ ☉
   see also communication, computer, technology
   some parts of the Internet
      home page, link (n.2), Web page, Web site
   some actions with the Internet
      click (v.3), download (v.), e-mail (n.2/v.1),
      find (v.3), search (v.), spam (v.),
      telecommute (telecommuting), upload (v.)
   some people associated with the Internet
      hacker, programmer
   some accessories for the Internet
      computer, keyboard, modem, monitor (n.3),
      mouse (n.2)
   conventionally associated with the Internet
      electronic mail, network (n.4)

interpret
   see also language, mind
   for a picture see the definition of interpret

interrogate *for a picture see definition*

intersect *for a picture see definition*

intravenous *for a picture see definition*

introduction ☉ *see* book, communication,
   dance

invention ☉ *see* technology

inventive *for a picture see definition*

inventory ☉ *see* business

invertebrate (n.) ☉
   see also animal, arthropod, crustacean, insect,
      mollusk, spider, worm
   for a picture see the definition of invertebrate
   some examples of invertebrates
      abalone, barnacle, beetle, centipede, clam (n.),
      cockle (n.), crab, crayfish, earthworm,
      jellyfish, leech, lobster (n.1), millipede,
      mussel, octopus, oyster, quahog, scallop (n.1),
      scorpion, sea anemone, sea urchin, shrimp (n.),
      slug[1] (n.1), snail (n.1), sponge (n.1), squid,
      starfish, turtle (n.)
   some kinds of invertebrates
      arthropod, insect, mollusk, shellfish, **spider,
      worm** (n.1)
   broader category that includes invertebrates
      animal (n.1)
   lacking in invertebrates
      backbone (n.1)

invest ☉ *see* bank, business, money

investigate ☉ ☉ *see* crime, thought

invisible *for a picture see definition*

involve *for a picture see definition*

iris *for a picture see the definition of* flower

iron ☉ ☉ *see* element

irrational ☉ *see* behavior, thought

irrigate *see* farming, gardening

irrigation *for a picture see definition*

island *for a picture see the definition of* maroon[1]

Italian *for a picture see the definition of* language

IV *for a picture see the definition of* intravenous

ivy *for a picture see definition*

jab *for a picture see definition*

jacket *see* clothing

jack-in-the-box *for a picture see definition*

jackknife *for a picture see definition*

jade *for a picture see definition*

jaguar *for a picture see definition*

jail *see* crime

Japanese *for pictures see definitions of* Japanese, language

Japanese beetle *for a picture see definition*

jar *for a picture see the definition of* jar[1]

jar *for a picture see definition*

jaw
  see also face, head, skeleton, tooth
  for a picture see the definition of fang

jealousy *see* emotion

jeep *for a picture see definition*

jellyfish *for a picture see definition*

jester *for a picture see definition*

jet
  see also airplane, vehicle
  for a picture see the definition of jet[1]

jewel *for pictures see definitions of* gem, jewel

jewelry
  see also clothing, stone
  for pictures see definitions of brooch, garnet, glitter, jewel, necklace, ruby, topaz
  some examples of jewelry
    anklet, band[2] (n.2), bracelet, brooch, chain (n.1), crown (n.1), earrings, necklace, pendant, pin (n.2), ring[1] (n.2), stone (n.4), watch (n.3)
  similar to jewelry
    decoration (n.2), ornament (n.)
  some components of jewelry
    amber (n.1), amethyst, bead (n.1), copper (n.1), diamond (n.1), emerald (n.1), garnet, gems (n.1), glass (n.1), gold (n.1), jade, jewel (n.1), pearl (n.), platinum, ruby (n.1), silver (n.1), sterling (n.2), topaz, turquoise (n.1)
  descriptions of jewelry
    dazzle (v.2), flash (v.3), gleam (v.), glint (v.), glisten, glitter (v.), shine (v.1), sparkle (v.1), twinkle (v.1)
  some people associated with jewelry
    artisan, jeweler
  unit for measuring jewelry
    carat

job *see* work

jockey *for pictures see definitions of* equestrian, jockey

joint
  see also body, skeleton
  for a picture see the definition of body

journal *see* book, communication, literature

joust *for a picture see definition*

jowl *for a picture see definition*

joy *see* emotion, happiness

joystick *for a picture see definition*

judge *see* fruit, thought, vegetable

juggle *for a picture see definition*

jukebox *for a picture see definition*

jump *for a picture see the definition of* equestrian

jump rope *for a picture see definition*

jungle *see* forest

Jupiter *for a picture see the definition of* solar system

jury *see* crime, law

justice *see* government, law

juvenile
  see also family, life
  for a picture see the definition of juvenile

kaleidoscope *for a picture see definition*

kangaroo *for pictures see definitions of* kangaroo, mammal, marsupial

karate *for a picture see definition*

katydid *for a picture see definition*

kayak *for a picture see definition*

keen *see* mind, thought

keg *for a picture see definition*

kettle *for a picture see definition*

key[1] *see* home, instrument, music

key[2] *see* geography, geology

keyboard
  see also computer, instrument
  for pictures see definitions of music

kickoff *for a picture see definition*

kid
  see also animal, family, life
  for a picture see the definition of kid[1]

kid[2] *see* action, mind

kidney
  see also blood, excrete, organ
  for a picture see the definition of body

kill *see* crime, hunting, life

kimono *for a picture see the definition of* obi

king *see* monarchy

kiss *for pictures see definitions of* envelop, passion, smack

kitchen *see* cooking, room

kite *for a picture see definition*

kiwi *for pictures see definitions of* kiwi, radiate

knapsack *for a picture see definition*

knee *for a picture see the definition of* body

kneecap *for a picture see the definition of* body

knife
  see also cooking, tool, weapon
  for pictures see definitions of blade, cleaver, jackknife, knife, pocketknife, utensil

knight *for pictures see definitions of* joust, knight, medieval

knit *for a picture see the definition of* deft

knot *for a picture see definition*

knowledge (n.1,2)
  see also education, learn
  similar to knowledge
    ability (n.2), comprehension, experience (n.3), grasp (n.2), know-how, learning, skill (n.1)
  some kinds of knowledge
    academic (adj.2), common (adj.2), practical (adj.1,2), scientific
  broader category that includes knowledge
    mind (n.1)
  some actions associated with knowledge
    acquire, convey (v.2), convince, declare (v.3), disclose (v.1), enlighten, fathom (v.), gain (v.1), illuminate (v.3), know (v.1,2), learn (v.1,2), possess (v.1), thirst (v.2), transfer (v.1)
  some descriptions of knowledge
    abstract (adj.1,2), basic (adj.), certain (adj.2), current (adj.1), definite (adj.2), essential (adj.), familiar (adj.1), for certain, fundamental (adj.), obscure (adj.2,3), trivial, useful, useless
  some people associated with knowledge

academic (n.), ace (n.2), authority (n.3), doctor (n.2), expert (n.), judge (n.3), master (n.3), philosopher, professional (n.1), sage (n.), scholar (n.1), scientist, specialist, veteran (n.1)
  some things conventionally associated with knowledge
    acquaintance (n.2), basics (n.), discipline (n.3), domain (n.2), education (n.2), field (n.4), given (n.), study (n.2,3), subject (n.4), understanding (n.4), wisdom (n.3)
  absence of knowledge
    ignorant (adj.1), in the dark, unfamiliar (adj.1)
  feeling knowledgeable
    aware, certain (adj.1), current (adj.2), definite (adj.1), familiar (adj.2), learned, literate (adj.2), streetwise, well-read, worldly (adj.2)
  some things that can be known
    deductions (n.2), facts (n.1)

knuckle *for a picture see the definition of* hand

koala *for a picture see definition*

labor *for a picture see definition*

laboratory *see* room, science

lace *for pictures see definitions of* delicate, lace

lacquer *for a picture see definition*

lacrosse *see* sport

ladder *for pictures see definitions of* ladder, rung

laden *for a picture see definition*

ladybug *for a picture see definition*

lagoon *see* lake, ocean, sea

lake
  see also ecosystem, water ocean
  for pictures see definitions of reflection, vacation
  some examples of lakes
    Erie (n.1), Great Lakes, Huron (n.1), Michigan (n.2), Ontario (n.2), Superior
  similar to lake
    lagoon (n.2), pond, sea (n.1)
  some broader categories that include lake
    ecosystem, water (n.1)

lamb *for pictures see definitions of* lamb, mammal

lamp
  see also electricity, light
  for a picture see the definition of lantern

land *see* continent, country, geography, soil

landmark *for a picture see definition*

landscape
  see also art, geography
  for a picture see the definition of scene

lane *see* transportation, vehicle

language (n.1)
  see also communication, grammar
  for pictures see definitions of Chinese, French, German, Ghana, Hebrew, Hindi, interpret, Japanese, language, Russian, Spanish, Vietnamese
  some examples of languages
    American English, Apache, Arabic (n.), BASIC, Cajun (n.2), Chinese (n.2), Danish (n.), Dutch (n.2), English (n.2), Finnish (n.), French (n.2), German (n.2), Greek (n.2), Hebrew (n.2), Irish (n.2), Italian (n.2), Japanese (n.2), Korean (n.), Latin (n.1), Middle English, Mongol (n.2), Norwegian (n.2), Old English, Persian (n.2), Polish (n.), Portuguese (n.2), Russian (n.2), Scottish (n.2), Spanish (n.1), Turkish (n.), Vietnamese (n.2), Welsh (n.2), Xhosa (n.2)
  similar to language
    speech (n.2), tongue (n.4)
  some kinds of written language
    alphabet, code (n.2), hieroglyphic (n.),

shorthand
some broader categories that include **language**
communication (n.1), **culture** (n.1)
some parts of **language**
accent (n.3), consonant (n.2), dialect, figure of speech, gesture (n.1), grammar (n.1), idiom, jargon, pronunciation (n.1), sign (n.2), slang, sound[1] (n.1), vocabulary (n.1), vowel (n.2), word (n.1)
some actions involving **language**
babble (v.1,2), chatter (v.1), communicate (v.3,4), decipher (v.1), decode, gesture (v.), gossip (v.), interpret (v.4), mumble (v.1,2), mutter (v.), program (v.), sign (v.2), speak (v.1,2,4,5), swear (v.3), taunt, translate
some body parts that produce **language**
larynx, lips (n.1), lungs, mouth (n.1), nose (n.1), throat (n.1), tongue (n.1), vocal cords
expressed through **language**
emotion (n.1), feeling (n.3), idea (n.2,3), **knowledge** (n.1), **thought**[1] (n.2)
some people associated with **language**
speaker (n.1), translater (translate)
some forms of **language**
formal (adj.1), informal (adj.2), spoken (adj.), written (adj.)
lantern *for a picture see definition*
laptop computer *for a picture see definition*
larva
see also insect, life, reproduction
for a picture see the definition of **caterpillar**
lathe *for a picture see definition*
laugh ☺ *see* action, happiness
launch *for a picture see the definition of* launch[1]
laundry ○ *see* clothing, room
lavatory ○ *see* hygiene, room
lavender *for a picture see definition*
law (n.1,2) ○
see also crime, government, legislature
similar to **law**
regulation (n.1), rule (n.1)
some kinds of **laws**
civil (adj.1), criminal (adj.1), **military** (adj.2), religious (adj.1)
some broader categories that include **law**
civilization (n.2), **government** (n.3), society (n.2)
some places associated with the **law**
assembly (n.4), bench (n.3), cell (n.2), chamber (n.2,3), court (n.2), courthouse, courtroom, house (n.4), jail (n.), **legislature**, penitentiary, prison
some actions associated with the **law**
acquit, arrest (v.2), authorize (v.2), ban (v.), convict (v.), enforce, execute (v.1,3), forbid, imprison, indict, judge (v.1), license (v.), pardon (v.1), police (v.), prosecute, protect, punish (v.1)
some qualities of the **law**
fair[1] (adj.1), impartial
some people associated with the **law**
advocate (n.), attorney, bar (n.5), counsel (n.2), judge (n.1), jury (n.1), justice (n.3), lawyer, **legislature**, peer[1] (n.1), police (n.1), sheriff, witness (n.2)
conventionally associated with the **law**
case[1] (n.4), lawsuit, sanction (n.3)
state of being without **laws**
anarchy (n.1)
some stages of enforcing the **law**
accusation, appeal (n.3), conviction (n.1), hearing (n.3), pardon (n.2), plea (n.2), probation, sentence (n.2), summons,

testimony (n.1), trial (n.1), verdict (n.1)
some violations of the **law**
crime (n.1), offense (n.1)
lawyer ○ *see* crime, law
layer *for a picture see definition*
lead[1] *see* government, power, theater
lead[2] *see* element
leader
see also government, power, relationship
for a picture see the definition of **leader**
leaf (n.1) ◐
see also flower, plant, tree
for pictures see definitions of **flower, foliage, frond, leaf**
similar to **leaves**
foliage
some kinds of **leaves**
blade (n.3), frond, needle (n.5), tea (n.3), tobacco (n.2)
broader category that includes **leaves**
plant (n.1)
some parts of **leaves**
cells (n.1), chlorophyll, pigment (n.1), pores[2], veins (n.2)
some activities involving **leaves**
burn (v.6), compost, dry (v.1), rake (v.1)
some qualities of **leaves**
color (n.1), form (n.1), **shape** (n.1), texture
produced by **leaves**
oxygen
affects **leaves**
frost (n.1), sunlight, temperature (n.2), **water** (n.1), wind[1] (n.1)
used by **leaves**
carbon dioxide, **energy** (n.1), minerals (n.), **water** (n.1)
some things that eat **leaves**
animals (n.1), **birds** (n.), **insects** (n.1), **reptiles**
processes of **leaves**
photosynthesis, transpiration (transpire)
lean *for a picture see the definition of* lean[1]
leapfrog *for a picture see definition*
learn ⊙
see also education, knowledge, mind, school
similar to **learn**
acquire, discover (v.2), understand (v.1,4)
some broader categories that include **learning**
knowledge (n.3), **mind** (n.1)
some places associated with **learning**
college, laboratory (n.1), library (n.1), **school**[1] (n.1), study (n.5), university
some actions associated with **learning**
ascertain, cram (v.3), determine (v.2), digest (v.2), discover (v.2), examine, experience (v.), experiment (v.), feel (v.1), find out, grasp (v.2), hear (v.2), imitate (v.1), imprint (v.2), inquire, investigate, master (v.1), memorize, observe (v.2), pick up (phr.3), practice (v.2), read (v.1), see (v.1,4), study (v.2,3,4), understand (v.1)
some descriptions of someone **learning**
apt (adj.2), bright (adj.3), curious (adj.1), inquisitive, intelligent, quick (adj.3), slow (adj.3), smart (adj.4), stupid (adj.1)
some actions that cause **learning**
demonstrate (v.1,2,3), discipline (v.1), drill (v.2), educate, inform (v.1), instruct (v.1), lecture (v.1), reinforce, repeat (v.1), teach (v.1,2)
some people associated with **learning**
apprentice (n.), expert (n.), explorer, master (n.3), mentor, novice (n.1), professor, pupil[1], sage (n.), scholar (n.1), student, teacher
conventionally associated with **learning**

aptitude (n.2), association (n.2), awareness (aware), curiosity (n.1), experience (n.2,3), interest (n.1), memory (n.1), observation (n.1), practice (n.1), study (n.1)
without **learning**
automatic (adj.2), inborn, instinctive (adj.1)
some aspects of **learning**
comprehension, memory (n.1), perception (n.1)
some things that are **learned**
fact (n.1), information (n.1), job (n.1), **language** (n.1), lesson, method (n.1), moral (n.1), skill (n.2), subject (n.4), technique, theory (n.1), **tradition** (n.1), trick (n.3)
lease ○ *see* business
leather
see also animal, clothing
for a picture see the definition of **leather**
leek *for a picture see definition*
leg
see also body
for a picture see the definition of **insect**
legislature ○
see also democracy, law
some examples of **legislatures**
assembly (n.4), House of Commons, House of Lords, House of Representatives, senate (n.1)
a broader category including **legislature**
government (n.1)
some actions of **legislature**
convene, debate (v.1), decide (v.1), meet (v.4), vote (v.1)
some products of **legislature**
law (n.1,2), legislation (n.2)
some members of **legislatures**
representative (n.1), senator
legume
see also fruit, plant, seed, vegetable
for a picture see the definition of **legume**
leisure (n.) ○
see also art, game, sport
similar to **leisure**
ease (n.1), rest[1] (n.2)
some places associated with **leisure**
arcade (n.2), arena (n.1), barbecue (n.1), beach (n.), **boat** (n.1,2), carnival, circus (n.1), concert (n.), den (n.2), fair[2] (n.1), field (n.3), hammock, living room, movie (n.2), museum, park (n.1), picnic (n.1), pier (n.1), playground, restaurant, rocking chair, sofa, theater (n.1), yard[2] (n.1)
some activities associated with **leisure**
amble, **fish** (v.2), **garden** (v.), idle (v.1), lounge (v.), muse, picnic (v.), play (v.4), putter[1], read (v.1), relax (v.3), stroll (v.), unwind (v.4)
some ways of describing **leisure**
calm (n.1), lazy (adj.1), peaceful (adj.1), quiet (adj.3), serene
some things conventionally associated with **leisure**
amusement (n.2), entertainment (n.2), recess (n.1), recreation, vacation (n.)
lens *for pictures see definitions of* lens, magnifying glass
leopard *for pictures see definitions of* leopard, lounge
leprechaun *for a picture see definition*
letter
see also communication, grammar, language
for a picture see the definition of mail[1]
lettuce *for a picture see definition*
level *for a picture see definition*

Libra *for pictures see definitions of* **constellation,** zodiac

library ○ ● *see* book, building, community, school

lick *for a picture see definition*

lie[1] ○ *see* behavior, crime, mind

life ●

see also animal, bacteria, fungus, plant, virus
study of **life**
biology, ecology, philosophy (n.1)
some actions associated with **life**
feed (v.4), grow (v.1), move (v.2),
reproduce (v.3)
associated with length of **life**
annual (n.), biennial (n.2), life span,
perennial (n.)
changes in **life**
aging (age n.3), birth (n.1), death (n.1),
growth (n.1), metamorphosis (n.1)
opposite of **life**
death (n.1), **extinction**
some stages of human **life**
adolescent (n.), adult (n.2), baby (n.1),
child (n.1), elder (n.), embryo, infant (n.),
juvenile (n.), newborn (n.), senior citizen,
teen-ager, toddler, tot, youngster, youth (n.5)
some things that affect **life**
food (n.), oxygen, sunlight, temperature (n.1),
water (n.1)
some things that are **alive**
animal (n.1), **bacteria, fungus,** human (n.),
microbe, parasite, **plant** (n.1), protozoan,
virus (n.1)
also associated with **life**
alive (adj.1), lively (adj.1), organic,
vital (adj.1,2,3)

lifeboat *for a picture see definition*

lift *for a picture see the definition of* strain[1]

ligament ○ *see* body, muscle, skeleton

light[1] (n.1) ●

see also energy, physics
for pictures see definitions of filament, lantern
broader categories that include **light**
energy (n.1,2), **physics**
some sources of **light**
bulb (n.3), candle (n.), filament (n.2),
flare (n.1,2), flashlight, floodlight, headlight,
lamp, lantern, light[1] (n.2), lighthouse,
lighting (light[1] n.2), moon (n.1), searchlight,
taillight, torch (n.1)
some actions of creating **light**
burn (v.1), ignite (v.1), illuminate (v.1),
kindle (v.3), light[1] (v.2,4), radiate (v.1), set
fire to
some actions of **light**
dazzle (v.1), fade (v.2), flash (v.1),
flicker[1] (n.1), glare (n.1), gleam (n.1),
glimmer (n.1), glow (n.1), shine (n.2),
sparkle (n.), twinkle (n.1)
some descriptions of **light**
aglow (adj.1), bright (adj.1), dim (adj.1),
fluorescent, incandescent, luminous,
radiant (adj.1), shiny (adj.2), solar (adj.1),
sunny (adj.1)
some things that produce **light**
blaze[1] (n.1), cinder, **electricity** (n.1),
fire (n.1), firefly, fireworks (pl.n.1),
flame (n.1), glowworm, lightning (n.),
lightning bug, northern lights, radiation,
reflection (n.2), spark (n.2), star (n.1),
sun (n.1)
conventionally associated with **light**
dawn (n.1), daybreak, daytime, eclipse (n.),
light-year, luster, sunglasses, sunrise (n.2),
sunscreen, suntan, twilight, window (n.1)

some conditions of being without **light**
blackout (n.1), darkness (n.1), nighttime
negative effect of **light**
sunburn (n.)
some forms of **light**
beam (n.2), daylight, laser, moonbeam,
ray[1] (n.1), sunshine
some things that use or involve **light**
camera, **color** (n.1), dimmer, exposure (n.3),
eye (n.1), mirror (n.), photograph (n.),
prism (n.1), rainbow, shade (n.1),
shadow (n.1), silhouette (n.1,2), spectrum,
sundial, tint (n.1)
some units for measuring **light**
frequency (n.3), volt, watt

lighthouse *for pictures see definitions of* beacon, lighthouse

lightning

see also electricity, weather
for a picture see the definition of lightning

lily *for a picture see definition*

limb ○ ○ *see* body, tree

line *for a picture see the definition of* leader

link *for a picture see definition*

lion *for pictures see definitions of* lion, mammal, teeth

lioness *for a picture see definition*

lip

see also face
for a picture see the definition of tongue

liquid ○ *see* element, water

lira *for pictures see definitions of* international, lira

listen ○ *see* sense

literacy ○ ● *see* book, education, knowledge

literature (n.1) ○ ●

see also art, book
some examples of **literature**
allegory (n.2), autobiography, ballad,
biography, comedy, drama (n.1), epic (n.),
essay, fable (n.2), fantasy (n.2), folk tale,
haiku, limerick, lyric (n.1), narrative, novel[1],
parable, play (n.2), poem, psalm,
romance (n.3), sonnet, story[1] (n.2), tale (n.1),
tragedy (n.2), verse (n.1)
some kinds of **literature**
fiction (n.1), nonfiction, poetry (n.1), prose
broader categories that include **literature**
art (n.2), **communication** (n.1), **culture** (n.1)
some parts of **literature**
character (n.3), climax (n.2), dialogue,
moral (n.1), passage (n.2), plot[1] (n.1),
setting (set n.2), story[1] (n.1), subject (n.1),
theme (n.1), title (n.1), tone (n.6)
some actions associated with **literature**
characterize (v.1), compose (v.2), create (v.1),
critique (v.), depict, describe, entertain (v.1),
examine (v.1), explain (v.1), expose (v.1),
express (v.1), imagine (v.1), influence (v.),
inspire (v.2), portray (v.1), read (v.1),
relate (v.1), rhyme (v.2), tell (v.1), write (v.3)
some descriptions of **literature**
aesthetic, classic (adj.1,2), comic (adj.),
controversial, dramatic (adj.1), heroic (adj.1),
historical (adj.2), humorous, imaginative,
juvenile (adj.2), lyric (adj.),
romantic (adj.1,3), tragic (adj.3)
some things used in **literature**
allegory (n.1), alliteration, conflict (n.1),
description (n.1), humor (n.2), idiom, irony,
metaphor, meter[2] (n.1), rhyme (n.2), simile,
symbol (n.1)
some people associated with **literature**
author, critic (n.1), minstrel, narrator,
playwright, poet, writer (n.2)

litter ● *see* animal, conservation

liver

see also blood, organ
for a picture see the definition of body

livery *for a picture see definition*

living room ○ *see* home, leisure, room

lizard *for pictures see definitions of* gecko, Gila monster, horned lizard, iguana, reptile

llama *for a picture see definition*

loaf *for a picture see definition*

loaf *for a picture see definition*

loan ● *see* bank, business, money

lobby ○ ○ *see* politics, room

lobster *for a picture see definition*

lock[1] ○ *see* building, car, home

lock[2] ○ *see* hair

locomotive *for a picture see definition*

locust *for a picture see definition*

lofty *for a picture see definition*

log *for a picture see the definition of* conservation

logic ○ *see* mind, thought

logo *for a picture see definition*

loin *for a picture see the definition of* body

look ○ *see* sense

loom *for a picture see definition*

loom *for a picture see definition*

lopsided *for a picture see definition*

lounge

see also leisure, room
for a picture see the definition of lounge

louse *for a picture see definition*

love (n.1,2) ○

see also care, emotion
similar to **love**
affection, passion (n.2)
some broader categories that include **love**
emotion (n.1), feeling (n.3)
some actions associated with **love**
adore (v.2), care (v.2), caress (v.), cherish,
court (v.1), cuddle, dote, elope, embrace (v.1),
fancy (v.2), flirt (v.), hug (v.1,3), kiss (v.),
like[2] (v.2), marry (v.1), melt (v.3), pat (v.2),
propose (v.3), treasure (v.), worship (v.1,2)
some descriptions of **love**
ardent, crazy (adj.2), deep (adj.3),
devout (adj.2), everlasting, faithful (adj.1),
intimate (adj.1), lasting, lifelong,
mad (adj.5,6), passing (adj.2), passionate,
pious (adj.1), precious (adj.2),
romantic (adj.2), true (adj.2), warm (adj.5)
some people associated with kinds of **love**
bride, brother, child (n.2), friend (n.1),
grandchild, grandparent, groom (n.1),
idol (n.2), love (n.3), mate (n.1,4), parent,
pet (n.1), relative (n.), sister (n.1), spouse,
valentine (n.2)
some things conventionally associated with **love**
Aphrodite, candy (n.), Cupid, flowers (n.1),
forget-me-not, heart (n.1), jealousy,
narcissus (n.3), ring[1] (n.2), valentine (n.1),
Valentine's Day, Venus (n.1)
feeling **love**
affectionate, close (adj.2), demonstrative,
fond (adj.1), loving (love n.1,2),
tender (adj.2)
some relationships of **love**
attachment (n.2), bond (n.1,2),
brotherhood (n.1), devotion,
engagement (n.3), marriage (n.1),
romance (n.1), sisterhood (n.1)

low tide *for a picture see definition*

loyalty *for a picture see definition*

lug *for a picture see definition*

lull *for a picture see definition*

lumber
  see also building, tree
  for a picture see the definition of lumber
lumber *for a picture see definition*
lunch ○ *see* cooking, food
lung
  see also organ, respiration
  for a picture see the definition of body
lute *for a picture see definition*
lynx *for a picture see definition*
machine ○○ *see* technology
mad ○ *see* anger, mind
made-up *for a picture see definition*
magazine ○ *see* book, literature
maggot *for a picture see definition*
magic *for pictures see definitions of* illusion, magic
magma *for a picture see the definition of* earth
magnesium ○ *see* element
magnet *for a picture see the definition of* electromagnet
magnetize ○ *see* electricity, physics
magnifying glass *for a picture see definition*
mail
  see also communication
  for a picture see the definition of mail[1]
maize *for pictures see definitions of* Indian corn,
  maze
majestic *for a picture see definition*
make-believe *for a picture see definition*
makeup *for pictures see definitions of* apply, cosmetic, makeup
mallard *for a picture see definition*
mammal ○
  see also animal
  for pictures see definitions of armadillo, beaver,
  bighorn, bison, buck[1], bulldog, bunny, camel,
  carnivore, cat, cheetah, chimpanzee,
  chinchilla, chipmunk, collie, colt, cougar, cow,
  Dalmatian, deer, Doberman pinscher, dolphin,
  dromedary, droop, elephant, elk, endangered
  species, ewe, fox, frown, giraffe, gnu, goat,
  gorilla, Great Dane, greyhound, grizzly bear,
  groundhog, growl, hamster, hare, hedgehog,
  hippopotamus, horn, interact, jaguar,
  kangaroo, kid[1], koala, leopard, lion, lioness,
  llama, lounge, lynx, mammal, moose, mouse,
  ocelot, orangutan, otter, pig, pinniped,
  pointer, polar bear, poodle, prairie dog,
  primate, puppy, rabbit, raccoon, ram, rat,
  reindeer, retriever, rhinoceros, scrawny, seal[2],
  sea lion, sheep, sloth, spaniel, squirrel, stripe,
  tiger, tusk, vole, wallow, warm-blooded, water
  buffalo, whale, whisker, wolf, woodchuck,
  zebra
  some examples of mammals
  aardvark, alpaca, anteater, antelope (n.1),
  armadillo, ass (n.1), badger (n.), bat[2] (n.),
  bear[2], bison (n.1), blue whale, boar (n.2),
  bobcat, buffalo, camel, canine (n.1), caribou,
  cat (n.1), cattle, cetacean, chimpanzee,
  chinchilla, cougar, coyote, deer, dingo,
  dog (n.), dolphin, donkey, dormouse,
  elephant, elk (n.1), feline (n.), ferret (n.2),
  fox (n.1), gazelle, gibbon, giraffe, gnu,
  goat (n.), gorilla, guinea pig (n.1), hamster,
  hare, hedgehog (n.1), hippopotamus,
  hog (n.2), horse (n.1), human (n.), hyena,
  impala, jackal, jaguar, kangaroo, koala,
  lemming, leopard, lion, llama, lynx, manatee,
  marsupial, mink (n.1), mole[2] (n.1), mongoose,
  monkey (n.1), moose, mountain lion,
  mouse (n.1), musk ox, nutria, ocelot,
  orangutan, otter, panda (n.1), panther (n.1),

peccary, pig (n.1), pinniped, platypus,
polecat (n.1), porcupine, porpoise (n.1),
primate, puma, rabbit, raccoon, rat (n.1),
reindeer, rhinoceros, rodent, sable (n.1), seal[2],
sea lion, sheep (n.1), shrew, skunk (n.1),
sloth (n.2), sperm whale, tapir, Tasmanian
devil, tiger, walrus, weasel, weasel, whale (n.),
white-tailed deer, wolf (n.), wolverine,
wombat, yak, zebra
  some kinds of mammals
  carnivore, herbivore, insectivore
  broader categories that include mammals
  animal (n.1), vertebrate (n.)
  parts of some mammals
  nipple (n.1), udder
  some groups of mammals
  band[1] (n.1), colony (n.2), drove[2] (n.1),
  flock (n.1), herd (n.1), litter (n.2), pack (n.3),
  troop (n.1)
  produced by mammals
  fur (n.2), meat (n.1), **milk** (n.1)
  some male mammals
  boar (n.1), buck[1], bull (n.), ram (n.1), stag,
  stallion, steer[2], stud[2] (n.)
  some female mammals
  cow (n.1), doe, ewe, lioness, mare, sow[2]
  some young mammals
  bunny, calf[1] (n.1), colt, cub, fawn, filly,
  foal (n.), heifer, kid[1] (n.1), kitten, lamb,
  pup (n.1)
  characteristics of some mammals
  aquatic (adj.2), domestic (adj.2), furry (adj.1),
  hairy (adj.2), nocturnal (adj.2), solitary (adj.1), warm-
  blooded, wild (adj.1)
  some prehistoric mammals
  mammoth (n.), saber-toothed tiger
man *for pictures see definitions of* beard, jowl
manager ○ *see* business, work
mane ○ *see* cat, hair
mango *for a picture see definition*
mansion *for a picture see definition*
mantle
  see also earth, geology
  for a picture see the definition of earth
manual ○ *see* book
manuscript ○ *see* book, literature
map ○ *see* community, earth, geography
maple *for a picture see definition*
marble *for a picture see definition*
march *for a picture see the definition of* drum major
marina ○ *see* boat
market *for a picture see definition*
maroon *for a picture see the definition of* maroon[1]
marriage ○ *see* family, love, relationship
Mars *for a picture see the definition of* solar system
marsupial
  see also mammal
  for pictures see definitions of kangaroo, koala,
  marsupial
marvel *for a picture see definition*
mask *for pictures see definitions of* mask, masquerade
masquerade *for a picture see definition*
massage
  see also body, muscle
  for a picture see the definition of massage
masterpiece ○ *see* art, literature, music
mat ○ *see* exercise
match[1]
  see also energy
  for a picture see the definition of match
match[2]
  see also game, sport

for a picture see the definition of match
mathematics ○
  see also measurement, number, shapes
  some kinds of mathematics
  algebra, geometry (n.1)
  broader category that includes mathematics
  science (n.1)
  some parts of mathematics
  numbers (n.1), operations (n.4)
  some actions in mathematics
  add (v.3), average (v.1), calculate (v.1),
  compute (v.1), count[1] (v.2), deduct,
  divide (v.3), estimate (v.1), factor (v.),
  figure (v.1), graph (v.), multiply (v.4),
  round (v.3), square (v.4), subtract,
  transform (v.1)
  some descriptions of mathematics
  complex (adj.2), linear (adj.1), numerical,
  random
  some terms used in mathematics
  addend, character (n.4), common
  denominator, cube (n.2), decimal point,
  denominator, digit (n.2), dividend (n.1),
  divisor, equation, example (n.4), factor (n.2),
  mean[3] (n.2), median (n.1), minuend,
  minus (n.1), multiple (n.), multiplicand,
  multiplier, **number** (n.2), numerator,
  parenthesis, plus (n.1), power (n.6),
  product (n.3), quotient, ratio, root[1] (n.5),
  set (n.5), slash (n.3), square (n.5), square root,
  subset, subtrahend, sum (n.1), symbol (n.2),
  x (n.4), y (n.2)
  some people who use mathematics
  accountant, astronomer, engineer (n.1),
  mathematician, physicist, scientist
  some things conventionally associated with
  mathematics
  abacus, bar graph, calculator, **computer**,
  graph (n.), problem (n.2), statistics
matter ○○ *see* element, physics, thought
mature ○○ *see* life, thought
mayfly *for a picture see definition*
Maypole *for a picture see definition*
maze *for a picture see definition*
meal
  see also cooking, food
  for a picture see the definition of reunion
meal[2] ○ *see* grain
mean[1] ○ *see* thought
mean[2] ○ *see* behavior, personality
mean[3] ○ *see* mathematics
meander *for a picture see definition*
measure ○○ *see* measurement, music
measurement (n.1) ○
  see also mathematics, number
  for a picture see the definition of measurement
  broader categories that include measurement
  engineering, **mathematics**, science (n.1)
  some actions associated with measuring
  assess (v.3), calculate (v.2), determine (v.2),
  estimate (v.1), figure (v.1), gauge (v.2),
  measure (v.1), pace (v.4), read (v.3),
  reckon (v.1), register (v.3), sound[3] (v.1),
  survey (v.3), weigh (v.1)
  some qualities of measurement
  amount (n.1), degree (n.2), extent (n.1),
  grade (n.1), interval, magnitude (n.1),
  pitch[1] (n.3), quantity (n.1), range (n.1),
  reach (n.2), scope (n.), span (n.1,2)
  some descriptions of measurement
  accurate (adj.2), approximate (adj.),
  astronomical (adj.1), average (adj.1,2),
  comparative (adj.2), cubic (adj.3), digital,
  exact (adj.), linear (adj.2), metric,
  numeric (numerical), precise (adj.2),

scientific, standard (adj.1), thermal (adj.1)
some descriptions of measurements
  big (adj.1), bright (adj.1), close (adj.1), cold (adj.1), deep (adj.1,4), dim (adj.1,2), distant (adj.1), empty (adj.1), enormous, equal (adj.1), equivalent (adj.), fast[1] (adj.1), few (adj.), heavy (adj.1), high (adj.1), hot (adj.1), large, light[2] (adj.1), long[1] (adj.2), loud (adj.1), low (adj.1), many (adj.), massive (adj.1), minute[2] (adj.1), narrow (adj.1), quiet (adj.1), scant (adj.2), shallow (adj.1), short (adj.1,2,3), slender (adj.2,3), slim (adj.2), slow (adj.1), small (adj.1), tall (adj.2), thick (adj.1), thin (adj.1), vast, wide (adj.1,2)
some prefixes used in measurements
  centi- (pfx.1), kilo-, milli-
some people associated with measuring
  architect, astronomer, baker, engineer (n.1), scientist
some tools used in measurement
  altimeter, anemometer, balance (n.1), barometer, clock (n.), Geiger counter, hourglass, level (n.3), plumb (n.), rule (n.4), ruler (n.2), scale[2], seismograph, spoon (n.1), stopwatch, tape measure, thermometer, timer (n.2), yardstick (n.1)
some things conventionally associated with measurements
  charts (n.1,2), diagrams (n.), experiments (n.), gauges (n.2), geography (n.1), geometry (n.1), grades (n.3), logs (n.2), maps (n.), meters[3], metric system, standards (n.1), surveys (n.1), tables (n.3), topography
some things that are measured
  altitude, angle (n.2), breadth, capacity (n.1), circumference (n.2), density, depth (n.2), diameter (n.2,3), distance (n.1), elevation (n.1), energy (n.2), force (n.1), frequency (n.3), girth, height (n.1), latitude, length (n.1), longitude, pace (n.3), power (n.5), pressure (n.1), radioactivity, radius (n.1), size, speed (n.2), temperature (n.1,2), thickness (n.2), time (n.3), velocity (n.2), voltage, volume (n.4), weight (n.2), width (n.)
some units of measurement
  acre, bushel, byte, calorie, carat, centimeter, cord (n.4), cup (n.3), day (n.2), decibel, degree (n.3,3), fathom (n.), foot (n.2), gallon, gram, hectare, horsepower, hour (n.1), inch (n.1), kilohertz, kilometer, knot (n.4), league[2], light-year, liter, measure (n.5), megabyte, meter[1], mile (n.1), minute[1] (n.1), mph, ounce (n.1,2), peck[1] (n.1), pint, pound[2] (n.1), quart, rod (n.3), second[2] (n.1), tablespoon (n.1), teaspoon (n.1), ton (n.1,2), volt, watt, yard[1] (n.1)

meat
  see also cooking, diet, food, hunting
  for a picture see the definition of beef
mechanic *for a picture see the definition of* install
medal *for a picture see the definition of* champion
media ◐ *see* communication
medicine ◔ *see* disease, drug, health
medieval *for a picture see definition*
meditate *for a picture see definition*
megaphone *for a picture see definition*
melancholy ◔ *see* emotion, sadness
melody ◔ *see* music
melon *for a pictures see definitions of* cantaloupe, honeydew melon, melon
membrane ◐◑ *see* body, cell
memorial ◐◔ *see* history, tradition
memory ◔ *see* knowledge, thought

menace *for a picture see definition*
menorah *for a picture see definition*
merchandise ◔ *see* business
mercury *for a picture see the definition of* solar system
mermaid *for a picture see definition*
merry ◔ *see* emotion, happiness
merry-go-round *for a picture see definition*
messenger *for a picture see definition*
metabolism ◔ *see* digestion, energy, food
metal ◔ *see* element
metamorphosis
  see also amphibian, insect, life
  for pictures see definitions of amphibian, metamorphosis, transform
meteor *for a picture see the definition of* flare
meteorology ◔ *see* weather
meter *for a picture see the definition of* meter[3]
metronome *for a picture see definition*
microorganism ◑ *see* bacteria, virus
microscope
  see also science, technology, tool
  for a picture see the definition of microscope
military (adj.2) ◔
  see also country, war, weapon
  kind of military
    militia
  some parts of the military
    battalion, corp (corps n.1), infantry, platoon
  some places associated with the military
    battlefield, battlement, garrison (n.2), headquarters (n.2)
  some activities associated with the military
    attack (n.1), battle (n.1), blockade (n.), bombard (v.1), camouflage (n.), charge (n.5), draft (n.3), enlist (v.1), fight (v.1), furlough, siege, **war** (n.1)
  some things used by the military
    aircraft carrier, armament, armor (n.2), battleship, bomb (n.1), bomber (n.1), destroyer, ship (n.1), submarine, tank (n.3), weapon (n.1)
  some people associated with the military
    admiral, cadet, captain (n.3,4), commander (n.2), ensign (n.2), general (n.), lieutenant, major (n.), major (n.), marine (n.), officer (n.2), sailor (n.1), soldier (n.1), veteran (n.2)
  some divisions of the military
    air force, army (n.1), coast guard, Marine Corps, navy (n.1)
milk (n.1,2) ◑◔
  see also drink, mammal
  broader categories that include milk
    drink (n.1), liquid (n.), nourishment
  some ingredients in milk
    calcium, carbohydrates, cholesterol, fat (n.1), potassium, protein, sodium, sugar, vitamins
  sources of milk
    mammal, nipple (n.1), udder
  some places for milk
    dairy (n.1), grocery (n.1), icebox (n.1), refrigerator, supermarket
  some activities with milk
    beat (v.3), bottle (v.), buy (v.1), churn (v.1), deliver (v.1), drink (v.1), flavor (v.), package (v.), pour (v.1), produce (v.1), refrigerate, sell (v.1), shake (v.1), stir[1] (v.1)
  some animals that produce milk
    cattle, cow (n.1), goat (n.), llama, reindeer, sheep (n.1), yak
  some containers for milk
    bottle (n.1), bucket (n.), carton, cup (n.1), glass (n.2), jug (n.1), mug (n.1), pail (n.1), pitcher[1], Thermos

  some things made from milk
    butterfat, buttermilk, cheese, cottage cheese, cream (n.1), curd, ice cream, whey, yogurt
  some things that affect milk
    bacteria, homogenization (homogenize), pasteurization (pasteurize), sanitation, temperature (n.1,2)
  units for measuring milk
    cup (n.1,3), gallon, liter, ounce (n.2), pint, quart
Milky Way *for a picture see the definition of* constellation
millipede *for a picture see definition*
mind (n.1) ◔
  see also action, anger, behavior, belief, care, character, emotion, fear, happiness, hate, knowledge, learn, love, morals, sadness, thought
  similar to the mind
    brain (n.1)
  study of the mind
    psychology
  some actions of the mind
    associate (v.1), choose (v.2), decide (v.3), desire (v.), direct (v.1), dream (v.1), experience (v.), fancy (v.1), feel (v.2,3,4), imagine (v.1), imprint (v.2), judge (v.3), **learn** (v.3), note (v.3), notice (v.), perceive (v.2), picture (v.1), recall (v.1), regard (v.3), remember (v.2), sense (v.1), think (v.1), understand (v.1), visualize, want (v.1)
  some qualites of the mind
    involuntary (adj.1), voluntary (adj.1)
  some descriptions associated with the mind
    brilliant (adj.2), clear (adj.3), clever (adj.1), insane (adj.1), keen (adj.2), mad (adj.1), rational (adj.2), sane (adj.1), sharp (adj.6), smart (adj.1), sound[2] (adj.1), strong (adj.2)
  some things conventionally associated with the mind
    balance (n.3), consciousness (n.3), discipline (n.1), facility (n.2), humor (n.3), hypnosis, intelligence (n.1), mood, reason (n.2), sanity, self-control, sleep (n.1), trance, will[2] (n.1)
  some aspects of the mind
    capacity (n.2), comprehension, feeling (n.1), imagination, insight (n.1), instinct (n.1), intuition, memory (n.1), perception (n.1), reason (n.2), **thought**[1] (n.1), will[2] (n.1)
mineral
  see also element, geology, natural resources, soil, stone
  for pictures see definitions of mineral, opal, salt, turquoise
miniature *for a picture see definition*
mirror *for a picture see definition*
mischief *for a picture see definition*
miserable ◔ *see* emotion, sadness
mishap *for a picture see definition*
mist *for a picture see definition*
mistletoe *for a picture see definition*
misunderstand *for a picture see definition*
mite *for a picture see the definition of* mite[1]
mitt *for a picture see the definition of* glove
mix-up *for a picture see definition*
moat *for a picture see definition*
moccasin *for a picture see definition*
mockingbird *for a picture see definition*
model
  see also art, clothing, photography
  for a picture see the definition of runway
modem ◔◑ *see* computer, Internet

modern ◗ ◔ *see* art, history, technology
mold
  see also fungus
  for a picture see the definition of mold²
molecule ◔ *see* chemistry, element, physics
mollusk ◔
  see also invertebrate
  for pictures see definitions of clam, mollusk,
    mussel, octopus, oyster, slug¹, snail, squid,
    tentacle
  some examples of mollusks
    abalone, clam (n.), cockle (n.), conch (n.1),
    mussel, octopus, oyster, quahog, scallop (n.1),
    slug¹ (n.1), snail (n.1), squid, starfish
  broader categories that include mollusks
    animal (n.1), **invertebrate** (n.)
  some parts of mollusks
    feeler, gill, membrane, **muscle** (n.1),
    shell (n.1), tentacles, valve (n.2)
  some places for mollusks
    coral (n.1), land (n.1), mud, reef, rocks¹ (n.2),
    roots¹ (n.1), sand (n.), **water** (n.1)
  some descriptions of mollusks
    marine (adj.1), slimy (adj.1), soft (adj.2)
  produced by mollusks
    fossil, mucus, pearl (n.)
  some products made from mollusks
    bait (n.1), beads (n.1), buttons (n.1),
    chalk (n.1), chowder, **food** (n.),
    ornament (n.), shells (n.1)
  some behaviors of mollusks
    bore¹ (v.3), propel, siphon (v.), squirt (v.2),
    sting (v.1), swim (v.1)
  some growth stages of mollusks
    egg¹ (n.2), larvae (larva n.1)
  some things mollusks eat
    crustacean, fish (n.1), sea anemone
monarch *for a picture see definition*
monarchy ◔
  see also government
  similar to a monarchy
    kingdom (n.1)
  a broader category that includes monarchies
    government (n.2,3)
  some places associated with monarchies
    castle (n.1), palace
  some actions associated with monarchies
    abdicate, decree (v.), proclaim, rule (v.1)
  some descriptions of monarchies
    absolute (adj.1,2), imperial (adj.1),
    royal (adj.1), sovereign (adj.1)
  some people associated with monarchies
    count² (n.), countess (n.2), czar, duchess (n.1),
    duke, earl, emperor, empress (n.1), king (n.1),
    lord (n.2), nobility (n.1), prince,
    princess (n.1), queen (n.1), subject (n.3),
    vassal
  some things conventionally associated with
  monarchies
    crown (n.1), robe (n.1), scepter, seal¹ (n.1),
    throne (n.1)
  some aspects of monarchies
    coronation, realm (n.1), reign (n.1),
    succession (n.1)
money ◔
  see also economy
  for pictures see definitions of coin, euro, franc,
    international, lira, money, peso, quarter,
    shilling
  some examples of money
    dime (n.), dollar (n.1), franc, nickel (n.1),
    penny (n.1), pound² (n.2), quarter (n.1),
    shilling (n.2)
  some kinds of money
    bill¹ (n.2), cash (n.), coin (n.), currency (n.1),

dough (n.2), token (n.2), wampum
  some places for money
    bank² (n.1), billfold, mint² (n.1), piggy bank,
    pocketbook, purse (n.1), treasury (n.2), wallet
  some actions with money
    buy (v.1), coin (v.1), donate, pay (v.2), pay off,
    pay the piper (phr.2), pick up the tab,
    purchase (v.), save¹ (v.2), sell (v.1),
    spend (v.1)
  some illegal actions with money
    counterfeit (v.), steal (v.1), swindle (v.)
  some people associated with money
    aristocracy (n.1), breadwinner, cashier, heir,
    heiress, millionaire, miser
  some descriptions of people and their money
    affluent, bankrupt (adj.), broke (adj.),
    frugal (adj.1), greedy (adj.1), middle class,
    pauper, penniless, poor (adj.1), rich (adj.1)
  conventionally associated with money
    class (n.3), interest (n.4), rate (n.3),
    refund (n.), rent (n.), saving (n.2),
    scholarship (n.1), wealth (n.1)
  negatively associated with money
    debt (n.1), fee (n.1), fine² (n.), in
    hock (phr.2), ransom (n.), theft
  associated with family and money
    alimony, allowance (n.), dowry,
    inheritance (n.1)
  some terms associated with business and money
    account (n.2), bond (n.3), capital¹ (n.3,4),
    income, investment (n.3), loan (v.2),
    net² (adj.1/v.1), pension, proceeds,
    profit (n.1), revenue, speculate (v.2),
    stock (n.2,4)
monkey
  see also mammal
  for pictures see definitions of interact, mammal,
    monkey
monopoly ◔ *see* business
mood ◔ *see* behavior, emotion
moon
  see also space
  for pictures see definitions of crater, full moon,
    moon
moose *for a picture see definition*
mope ◔ *see* emotion, sadness
morals (n.2)
  see also belief, culture, religion
  similar to morals
    conscience, principles (n.2), values (n.3)
  broader categories that include morals
    religion (n.1), society (n.1)
  some actions associated with lack of morals
    abuse (v.1), cheat (v.1), lie¹ (v.), sin (v.),
    steal (v.1), tempt (v.1)
  some reactions associated with morals
    atone, bless (v.3), condemn (v.1),
    discipline (v.2), forgive (v.2), guide (v.2),
    impeach, instill, punish (v.1), reform (v.2),
    relapse (v.), remedy (v.2), shape (v.2)
  some people associated with morals
    angel (n.2), cheat (n.), culprit, devil (n.2), liar,
    rogue (n.2), saint (n.2), thief
  some descriptions of people who act morally
    good (adj.2), honest (adj.1), honorable,
    just (adj.1), noble (adj.2), responsible (adj.3),
    scrupulous (adj.1), steadfast (adj.1),
    upright (adj.3)
  some descriptions of people who do not act
  morally
    criminal (adj.1), dishonest, disreputable,
    evil (adj.), immoral (adj.), misguided,
    shady (adj.3), wicked (adj.1), wrong (adj.2)
  some things associated with morals
    adages, allegories (allegory n.2), parables,
    right (adj.1), wrong (adj.2)

mosaic *for a picture see definition*
mosquito *for pictures see definitions of* insect, mosquito
moss ◔ *see* plant
moth *for pictures see definitions of* metamorphosis,
  moth
mother *for a picture see the definition of* mammal
motor ◔ ◔ *see* electricity, technology, vehicle
mound *for pictures see definitions of* dune, mound
mountain (n.1) ◔
  see also geography, geology
  for a picture see the definition of top¹
  some examples of mountains
    Alps, Andes, Himalayas, Olympus, Rocky
    Mountains
  similar to mountains
    hill (n.1), **volcano** (n.2)
  some parts of mountains
    cliff, crest (n.3), foothill, ledge (n.2),
    peak (n.1), ridge (n.3), spine (n.3), summit,
    tip¹ (n.2), top¹ (n.1), zenith (n.2)
  some things mountains are composed of
    earth (n.3), rock¹ (n.1)
  some sciences that study mountains
    geography (n.1), geology (n.1)
  groups of mountains
    mountain range, range (n.5), sierra
  some activities related to mountains
    ascend (v.1), clamber, climb (v.1),
    descend (v.1), hike (v.), scale³ (v.1), ski (v.)
  person associated with mountains
    mountaineer (n.1)
  area between mountains
    valley
  measurements of mountains
    altitude, elevation (n.1)
  natural events involving mountains
    avalanche (n.1), erosion, landslide (n.1)
  some animals that live on mountains
    alpaca, bear² (n.), bighorn, chinchilla, cougar,
    llama, mountain lion, puma
  transportation up mountains
    chairlift
mouse
  see also computer, rodent
  for pictures see definitions of mouse, peril
mouth
  see also face, river
  for pictures see definitions of body, teeth
mouthpiece *for a picture see the definition of* reed
move
  see also body, game, muscle
  for a picture see the definition of direct
movie
  see also film, theater
  for a picture see the definition of negative
mud ◔ *see* soil
muffler *for a picture see definition*
mug ◔ *see* drink
mule *for a picture see the definition of* overload
multiply ◔ ◔ *see* mathematics, reproduction
murder ◔ *see* crime
muscle (n.1) ◔
  see also body, cell, exercise, skeleton
  for a picture see the definition of mussel
  some examples of muscles
    biceps, diaphragm (n.1), heart (n.1)
  broader categories including muscles
    body (n.1), flesh (n.1)
  some parts of muscles
    cell (n.1), fiber (n.1), protein, tissue (n.1)
  some actions with muscles
    bend (v.2), breathe (v.1), contract (v.1),
    cramp¹ (v.), develop (v.2), exercise (v.2),

massage (v.), move (v.1), pull (v.1,5), relax (v.1,3), strain[1] (v.1), support (v.2), tense[1] (v.), tighten, twist (v.7)
some descriptions of someone's **muscles**
frail (adj.2), strong (adj.1), toned (tone n.4), weak (adj.1)
conventionally associated with **muscles**
convulsion (n.1), coordination (n.2), dumbbell, weights (n.4)
some conditions negatively associated with **muscles**
cramp[1] (n.1), influenza, kink (n.2), lockjaw, stitch (n.3), tetanus
some things that affect **muscles**
diet (n.1), **exercise** (n.1)

muse ◔ *see* art, myth, thought
museum ◒◓ *see* art, history
mushroom
see also fungus
for pictures see definitions of fungus, mushroom
music (n.1,2) ◒◔
see also art, dance, instrument, theater
for pictures see definitions of music, score
some examples of **music**
anthem, arrangement (n.4), ballad, carol (n.), chant (n.1), composition (n.3), concerto, folk song, hymn, jingle (n.2), lullaby, medley (n.1), number (n.5), overture (n.2), piece (n.3), psalm, reel[3], song (n.1), symphony (n.1), taps, waltz (n.2), yodel (n.)
some kinds of **music**
bluegrass (n.2), blues (n.2), classical (adj.2), disco (n.2), folk music, jazz (n.), march (n.2), opera, polka (n.2), pop[2], rap[2], waltz (n.2)
broader categories that include **music**
art (n.2), **culture** (n.1)
some categories of ranges in **music**
alto (adj.), bass[1] (adj.), soprano (adj.), tenor (adj.), treble (adj.)
some parts of **music**
act (n.4), chorus (n.3), finale (n.1), lyrics (n.2), movement (n.3), phrase (n.2), refrain[2], scale[3] (n.4), theme (n.3), tune (n.1,2,3), verse (n.3)
some sources of **music**
album (n.2), compact disk, **instrument** (n.2), music box, performance (n.1), phonograph, record (n.2), tape (n.2), voice (n.1)
some groups that perform **music**
band[1] (n.2), chorus (n.1), orchestra (n.1), quartet (n.1), trio (n.1)
some actions of making **music**
beat (v.4), blow[2] (v.4), chant (v.1), drum (v.1), fiddle (v.1), finger (v.), hum (v.1,2), pipe (v.1), play (v.3), pluck (v.3), sing (v.1), strike (v.1), tap[1] (v.1), trill (v.), yodel (v.)
some descriptions of **music**
acoustic (adj.2), melodious, musical (adj.1,3), resonant, shrill
some sounds of **music**
bang (n.2), blare (n.), clang (n.), drone[2] (n.), hum (n.), ring[2] (n.2), tone (n.1), trill (n.1), whistle (n.1)
some people associated with **music**
artist (n.1), composer, conductor (n.1), critic (n.1), disc jockey, drum major, drum majorette, drummer, minstrel, musician, pirate (n.2), player (n.2), rocker (n.3), singer (n.1)
some accessories for **music**
baton (n.1), metronome, stand (n.4), tuning fork
conventionally associated with **music**
accompaniment (n.1), encore (n.2), register (n.4), swing (n.3)

god of **music**
Apollo
illegal use of **music**
piracy (n.2)
some elements of **music**
beat (n.3), harmony (n.3), melody (n.1), rhythm (n.1), tone (n.2)
some notations in **music**
bar (n.6), clef, flat (n.2), half step, key[1] (n.5), measure (n.5), meter[2] (n.2), note (n.3), score (n.2), sharp (n.), staff (n.4)
some performances of **music**
ballet (n.2), concert (n.), opera, recital (n.1), solo (n.1)
some musical scales
chromatic scale, major scale, minor scale
some units for measuring **music**
decibel, meter[2] (n.3), pitch[1] (n.4), tempo, time (n.9), volume (n.5)
mussel *for a picture see definition*
mystery ◒◔ *see* crime, film, literature
myth (n.1) ◒
see also culture, tradition
similar to **myth**
allegory (n.1), ballad, epic (n.), fable (n.1), folk tale, parable, story[1] (n.2), tale (n.1)
some mythological characters
Atlas (n.1), centaur, Cyclops, fairy, giant (n.1), gnome, Hercules, Hermes, hero (n.2), heroine (n.1), Midas, Muse (n.1), nymph (n.1), Orion (n.1)
some gods of Greek **mythology**
Aphrodite, Apollo, Ares, Demeter, Hera, Pan, Pluto (n.1), Poseidon, Uranus (n.2), Zeus
some gods of Roman **mythology**
Ceres, Cupid, Juno, Jupiter (n.1), Mars (n.1), mercury (n.2), Minerva, Neptune (n.1), Saturn (n.2), Venus (n.1)
also associated with **mythology**
cornucopia (n.1), genie, Hades, sphinx (n.1), unicorn
nab *for a picture see definition*
nail ◒◔ *see* body, building, foot
narrate ◒ *see* book
nation ◒ *see* country
natural resources ◔
see also conservation, ecosystem, endangered species, energy, extinction, geology
some examples of **natural resources**
air (n.1), **animals** (n.1), coal (n.1), earth (n.4), **forest**, minerals (n.), oil (n.2), **plants** (n.1), **soil**[1] (n.1), sunshine, **water** (n.1), wood (n.4)
sciences that study **natural resources**
ecology, **geography** (n.1)
some people associated with **natural resources**
naturalist, ranger (n.1)
some things that affect **natural resources**
chemicals (n.), **conservation** (n.2), consumption, disaster (n.1), dump (n.), poison (n.1), pollution (n.2), preservation (preserve v.1), trash, waste (n.2), weather (v.2)
nature
see also ecosystem, geography, geology, life, personality
for a picture see the definition of nature
navel *for a picture see the definition of* body
navy ◒ *see* color, military
neck ◔ *see* body
necklace *for pictures see definitions of* glitter, necklace
nectarine *for a picture see definition*
needle *for pictures see definitions of* acupuncture,

injection, thimble
negative *for a picture see definition*
neon ◔ *see* element
Neptune *for pictures see definitions of* Neptune, solar system
nerve (n.1) ◒◔
see also cell, mind, sense
for a picture see the definition of body
some kinds of **nerves**
auditory, motor (adj.2), optical (adj.1), spinal cord
some body parts associated with **nerves**
brain (n.1), skin (n.1), spinal cord
some parts of **nerves**
cell (n.1), ending (end n.1), fiber (n.1), tissue (n.1)
groups of **nerves**
bundle (n.1), system (n.1)
some actions of **nerves**
feel (v.1), hear (v.1), hurt (v.4), see (v.7), smell (v.1), taste (v.1)
some descriptions of **nerves**
numb (adj.1), sensitive (adj.3)
conventionally associated with **nerves**
impulse (n.2), reflex (n.1), sensor
some conditions related to **nerves**
epilepsy, leprosy, paralysis, poliomyelitis
some things **nerves** *sense*
pain (n.1), pressure (n.1), temperature (n.1)
nest
see also bird, home, insect, rodent
for a picture see the definition of nest
nestle *for a picture see definition*
net[1] *see* clothing, fishing
net[2] ◔ *see* business, money
network ◔ *see* communication, computer
neurotic ◔ *see* fear, mind
newspaper ◔ *see* communication, literature
newt *for a picture see definition*
night *for a picture see the definition of* knight
nipple *for a picture see the definition of* body
nitrogen ◔◕ *see* air, element
nocturnal
see also animal
for a picture see the definition of nocturnal
nomad *for a picture see definition*
nonfiction ◔ *see* literature
noodle *for a picture see definition*
North Star *for a picture see the definition of* constellation
nose ◔ *see* face, organ, sense
note ◔ *see* communication, music
notebook ◒◔ *see* book, school
notice ◔ *see* communication
nourishment ◒◔ *see* digestion, food
novel[1] ◔ *see* book, literature
nuclear ◔ *see* energy, physics
number (n.2,3) ◔
see also mathematics
for a picture see the definition of number
similar to a **number**
numeral, symbol (n.2)
some kinds of **numbers**
Arabic numeral, cardinal number, decimal (n.2), fraction (n.2), improper fraction, integer, mixed number, ordinal number, power (n.6), Roman numeral, root[1] (n.5), whole number
a broader category that includes **numbers**
mathematics
some parts of **numbers**
billions (n.1), billionths (billion n.1), decimal point, digits (n.2), hundreds (n.2),

hundredths (hundred n.2), millions (n.1),
millionths (million n.1), thousands (n.2)
some actions associated with numbers
add (v.3), average (v.1), average out (phr.1),
calculate (v.1), compute (v.1), count¹ (v.2),
divide (v.3), estimate (v.1), figure (v.1),
measure (v.1), multiply (v.4), round (v.3),
square (v.4), subtract
some qualities of numbers
equal (adj.1), infinite, large, maximum (adj.),
minimum (adj.), negative (adj.3),
positive (adj.4), small (adj.1), unequal (adj.1),
zero (adj.)
some people who frequently use numbers
accountant, architect, astronaut, clerk (n.2),
engineer (n.1), mathematician, navigator,
pilot (n.1), scientist
some decriptions of numbers
binary (adj.2), even (adj.6), irrational,
odd (adj.4), prime (adj.3)
some things that contain or use numbers
address (n.2), area code, calendar (n.1),
combination (n.2), coordinate (n.),
countdown, dice (pl.n.), grade (n.3),
index (n.), telephone (n.), Zip Code

nurse
see also care, disease, first aid, health, injury,
milk
for a picture see the definition of mammal
nut
see also fruit, plant, seed
for pictures see definitions of almond, cashew,
peanut, pistachio, source, walnut
nutrient ● ● ● *see* diet, element, food
nutrition ● *see* diet, food, health
oak ● *see* tree
oar *for a picture see the definition of* paddle
oasis
see also desert, water
for a picture see the definition of oasis
oat ● *see* grain, seed
obi *for a picture see definition*
observatory ● *see* building, space
occupation ● *see* work
ocean (n.1) ●
see also ecosystem, geography, sea, water
for pictures see definitions of scuba diving,
underwater
some examples of oceans
Antarctic Ocean, Arctic Ocean, Atlantic,
Indian Ocean, Pacific
broader category including ocean
ecosystem, water (n.1)
some parts of the ocean
bay, deep (n.1), fjord, gulf (n.1), inlet,
lagoon (n.1)
study of the ocean
oceanography
characteristic of the ocean
saltwater
land related to the ocean
beach (n.), coast (n.), continental shelf,
seashore, shoal, shore (n.1)
movements of the ocean
billow (n.), breaker, current (n.1), ebb (n.),
surf (n.), tide (n.1), undertow, wave (n.1)
some means of transportation in the ocean
boat (n.1,2), liner¹, ship (n.1), vessel (n.2)
some natural objects in the ocean
floe, iceberg, reef
some things that live in the ocean
anchovy, barnacle, clam (n.), coral (n.1), crab,
dolphin, fish (n.1), jellyfish, kelp (n.1),
lobster (n.1), microorganisms, oyster,
plankton, porpoise (n.1), quahog,

scallop (n.1), sea horse, seaweed (n.1),
shellfish, snail (n.1), sponge (n.1), turtle (n.),
whale (n.)
ocelot *for a picture see definition*
octopus *for a picture see definition*
offend ● ● *see* anger, crime
office ● ● *see* building, democracy, room, work
offshore *for a picture see definition*
oil ● ● *see* energy, natural resources
oil well *for a picture see definition*
okra *for a picture see definition*
omnivore ● *see* animal, diet
onion *for a picture see definition*
opal *for a picture see definition*
opera ● *see* leisure, music, theater
operation ● *see* disease, health, injury
opinion ● *see* belief, thought
orange *for pictures see definitions of* orange, section
orangutan *for a picture see definition*
orchard ● *see* fruit, tree
orchestra
see also instrument, music, theater
for a picture see the definition of recital
orchid *for a picture see definition*
ordeal ● *see* thought
ore ● *see* element, natural resources, stone
organ (n.2) ● ●
see also body, instrument
for pictures see definitions of music, organ
some examples of organs
bladder, brain (n.1), ear¹ (n.1), esophagus,
eye (n.1), gill, heart (n.1), kidney (n.1), large
intestine, liver (n.1), lung, ovary (n.1),
pancreas, skin (n.1), small intestine, spleen,
stomach (n.1), taste bud, tongue (n.1)
some kinds of organs
gland, **muscle** (n.1), sense organ
broader category that includes organs
body (n.1)
some parts of organs
cell (n.1), membrane, tissue (n.1)
groups of organs
system (n.1,2), tract (n.2)
some descriptions of organs
external, internal (adj.1), vital (adj.2)
some things produced by organs
chemical (n.), egg¹ (n.1), enzyme, hormone
some functions of organs
breathe (v.1), produce (v.2), pump (v.1),
secrete, swallow¹ (v.1), taste (v.1)
also associated with organs
transplant (v.2)
organism ● *see* life
organization ● *see* business, relationship
origami *for a picture see definition*
Orion *for a picture see the definition of* constellation
otter *for a picture see definition*
outbreak ● *see* disease
outburst ● *see* anger, emotion
outfield *for a picture see definition*
outhouse *for a picture see definition*
outlet ● *see* electricity
outline
see also book
for a picture see the definition of invisible
outrage ● *see* anger, emotion
ovary
see also flower, organ, reproduction
for pictures see definitions of body, flower
oven ● *see* cooking
overall *for a picture see definition*

overcoat
see also clothing
for a picture see the definition of overcoat
overhead ● *see* business, money
overload *for a picture see definition*
overshoe *for a picture see definition*
owl *for pictures see definitions of* hoot, nocturnal,
owl
oxen *for a picture see definition*
oxygen ● ● *see* air, element, respiration
oyster *for a picture see definition*
ozone *for a picture see the definition of* earth
ozone layer *for a picture see the definition of* earth
pack *for a picture see definition*
paddle *for a picture see definition*
paddle wheel *for a picture see definition*
pagoda *for a picture see definition*
pain ● ● *see* disease, emotion, first aid, injury,
sense
paint *for pictures see definitions of* daub, expression,
palette
painting ● ● *see* art
pair *for a picture see definition*
palate *for a picture see the definition of* tongue
palette *for a picture see definition*
palm *for a picture see the definition of* hand
pan
see also cooking
for a picture see the definition of skillet
pancreas *for a picture see the definition of* body
panda *for a picture see the definition of* endangered
species
Pandora *for a picture see definition*
panorama *for a picture see definition*
pants
see also clothing
for a picture see the definition of overall
papaya *for a picture see definition*
paper
see also art, book, communication, school
for a picture see the definition of papyrus
papyrus *for a picture see definition*
parade ● *see* celebration, culture
parakeet *for a picture see definition*
parent ● *see* family, relationship
parenthesis ● *see* grammar, mathematics
park
see also game, leisure, sport
for a picture see the definition of meter³
parliament ● *see* legislature
parrot *for pictures see definitions of* cockatoo, parrot, squawk
part of speech ● *see* grammar
partridge *for a picture see definition*
party
see also celebration, politics
for pictures see definitions of refreshment,
reunion
passenger ● *see* airplane, car, vehicle
passion *for a picture see definition*
past ● *see* history
pasta *for a picture see the definition of* noodle
pasture
see also animal, farming
for a picture see the definition of plentiful
patchwork *for a picture see definition*
patent ● *see* business, law
path *for a picture see definition*
patient *for a picture see the definition of* intravenous

patriot ☉ *see* country

pattern *for pictures see definitions of* grain, tile

paw
see also animal, foot
for a picture see the definition of paw

pay ☉ *see* business, money, work

pea *for a picture see the definition of* legume

peace ☉ *see* mind, country

peach *for pictures see definitions of* fuzzy, half

peacock *for pictures see definitions of* peacock, plumage

peanut *for pictures see definitions of* peanut, source

pear *for pictures see definitions of* enamel, pear

pebble ☺ *see* stone

pedestal *for pictures see definitions of* marble, upright

peek *for a picture see definition*

peel ☉ *see* fruit, vegetable

pen
see also art, communication, school
for a picture see the definition of fountain pen

pen² ☉ *see* farming, pet

pencil ☉ ☺ *see* art, communication, school

pendulum *for a picture see definition*

penguin *for pictures see definitions of* conservation, group, waddle

penis *for a picture see the definition of* body

penny *for a picture see the definition of* cent

pension ☺ *see* money, work

pentagon *for a picture see definition*

pepper
see also cooking, fruit, vegetable
for a picture see the definition of variety

perceive ☉ *see* sense, thought

perch *for a picture see definition*

perch *for a picture see definition*

percussion
see also instrument
for a picture see the definition of music

perform ☉ *see* dance, music, theater

peril *for a picture see definition*

period ☉ ☺ *see* grammar, history

perpendicular *for a picture see definition*

persimmon *for a picture see definition*

personality (n.1) ☉
see also behavior
similar to personality
  attitude (n.1), character (n.1),
  disposition (n.1), humor (n.3), nature (n.1),
  temper (n.1)
broader categories that include personality
  behavior, mind (n.1)
some reactions to personalities
  admiration, amusement (n.2),
  annoyance (n.3), attraction (n.1), disgust (n.),
  dislike (n.), enchantment, fancy (n.3),
  friendship (n.2)
some descriptions of personalities
  adventurous (adj.1), affable, aggressive (adj.1),
  agreeable (adj.1), artificial (adj.2),
  belligerent (adj.1), bold (adj.1), charming,
  colorful (adj.2), conservative (adj.2,3),
  dreadful (adj.2), dull (adj.2), enthusiastic,
  fake (adj.), generous (adj.1), genial, good-
  natured, gullible, happy-go-lucky, imaginative,
  impulsive (adj.1), insincere, likable,
  lousy (adj.2), magnetic (adj.2),
  mischievous (adj.2), moody (adj.1),
  nervous (adj.2), nosy, obnoxious,
  plastic (adj.3), playful (adj.1), pleasant (adj.2),
  polite, reckless, reserved (adj.2), rotten (adj.2),
  serious (adj.1), shy (adj.1), silly, sincere,

somber (adj.2), stiff (adj.5), stubborn (adj.1),
  sweet (adj.4), timid (adj.1), unnatural (adj.2),
  unpleasant, warm (adj.5), witty
some people associated with specific personalities
  angel (n.2), brat, bully (n.),
  conservative (n.1), crank (n.3), devil (n.3),
  extrovert, follower, fool (n.1), grouch (n.),
  jerk (n.3), leader, monster (n.3), rascal (n.2),
  rat (n.2), rogue (n.2), snake (n.2), villain (n.1)
some things conventionally associated with
  personality
  breeding (n.2), chip off the old block,
  individuality, take after, tendency (n.2), trait

perspire ☉ *see* excrete

persuade ☉ *see* belief, communication, thought

peso *for pictures see definitions of* international, peso

pest ☉ *see* insect, rodent

pester *for a picture see definition*

pet (n.1) ☉ ☺
see also cat, dog, fish, rodent
for a picture see the definition of pet
some examples of pets
  canary (n.1), **cat** (n.1), chicken (n.1),
  chinchilla, cockatoo, cow (n.1), **dog** (n.),
  duck¹ (n.1), ferret (n.1), frog (n.1), gerbil,
  goose (n.1), guinea pig (n.1), hamster,
  horse (n.1), lizard, mouse (n.1), parakeet,
  parrot (n.), pig (n.1), pigeon, rabbit, rat (n.1),
  snail (n.1), snake (n.1), toad, tortoise,
  turtle (n.)
some ways to categorize pets
  breed (n.), pedigree
broader categories that include pets
  amphibian (n.1), **animals** (n.1), **bird** (n.),
  fish (n.1), **mammal, reptile**
some places for pets
  aquarium (n.1), barn, box¹ (n.1), cage (n.1),
  coop (n.), crate (n.), hutch (n.1), kennel,
  pen² (n.1), run (n.9), terrarium, yard² (n.2)
some descriptions of pets
  affectionate, friendly (adj.1), loving,
  noisy (adj.1), passive (adj.2), playful (adj.1),
  tame (adj.1)
behaviors of some pets
  beg (v.1), fetch, play (v.5), run (v.1)
person associated with pets
  veterinarian
some accessories for pets
  ball¹ (n.2), bell (n.1), biscuit (n.1), bone (n.),
  bowl¹ (n.1), brush¹ (n.1), chain (n.1),
  collar (n.2), harness (n.1), leash (n.),
  muzzle (n.1), perch¹ (n.2), rawhide (n.1),
  saddle (n.1), scoop (n.1), stand (n.4), toy (n.),
  treat (n.2), wheel (n.1)
organization that protects lost pets
  SPCA
some needs of pets
  attention (n.3), companionship,
  exercise (n.1), **food** (n.), kindness (n.2),
  love (n.2), nutrition (n.2), shelter (n.1),
  water (n.1)
sometimes found on pets
  flea (n.), mite¹, parasite, tick²
ways to take care of pets
  bathe (v.1), brush¹ (v.1), clean (v.), clip¹ (v.1),
  feed (v.1), groom (n.1), pet (v.), train (v.1),
  vaccinate, walk (v.1)
also associated with pets
  tricks (n.3)

petal
see also flower
for pictures see definitions of flower, petal

petrify *for a picture see definition*

petunia *for a picture see definition*

pheasant *for a picture see definition*

philosophy ☉ ☺ *see* belief, life, thought

phoenix *for a picture see definition*

phone *for pictures see definitions of* ahead, rotary

phosphorus ☉ *see* element

photography
see also art, film
for a picture see the definition of negative
similar to photographs
  image (n.1), likeness (n.2), picture (n.1),
  print (n.3), slide (n.4), snap (n.5), snapshot
some kinds of photography
  motion picture (n.1), portrait (n.1), x-
  ray (n.2)
broader categories that include photography
  art (n.2,4), **culture** (n.1)
some things that include photographs
  album (n.1), **book** (n.1), booth (n.1),
  catalogue (n.2), gallery (n.2), **Internet**, locket,
  magazine (n.1), newspaper, passport,
  scrapbook, studio (n.2)
some actions associated with photography
  copy (v.1), crop (v.2), develop (v.4),
  distort (v.1), enlarge (v.1), expose (v.3),
  film (v.1), filter (n.1), focus (v.1),
  mount¹ (v.3), pose (v.1), print (v.4),
  project (v.3), sit (v.4)
some descriptions of photographs
  action (n.1), aerial (adj.2), close-up, digital,
  landscape (n.2), panoramic (panorama),
  remote (adj.1,2), satellite (n.2), still (adj.1),
  underwater (adj.)
some people associated with photography
  model (n.4,5), photographer
some elements of photography
  angle (n.4), background (n.1), contrast (n.2),
  focus (n.3), foreground, lighting,
  perspective (n.2), subject (n.2)

photosynthesis ☉ *see* plant

phrase ☉ *see* grammar, music

physical ☉ ☺ *see* body, geography, geology, health

physics ☉
see also electricity, energy, light
some kinds of physics
  advanced (adj.1), atmospheric, basic (adj.),
  fundamental (adj.), nuclear (adj.1),
  optical (adj.1)
broader category that includes physics
  science (n.1)
some actions associated with physics
  accelerate (v.1), analyze, collide (v.1),
  examine, experiment (v.), observe (v.2),
  record (v.2), research (v.), test (v.)
some people associated with physics
  astronomer, engineer (n.1), mathematician,
  meteorologist (meteorology), physicist
some things conventionally associated with
  physics
  electron, neutron, nucleus (n.3), orbit (n.1),
  particle, proton, reactor (n.1)
some aspects of physics
  atoms (n.1), **electricity** (n.1), **energy** (n.1),
  force (n.1,2), friction (n.2), gravity (n.1),
  heat (n.1), inertia (n.1), **light¹** (n.1),
  magnetism (n.1), matter (n.1), motion (n.1),
  nuclear energy, sound¹ (n.1), **space** (n.2),
  time (n.1), work (n.1)
some things that use physics
  computer, electromagnet, generator, laser,
  lever (n.1), microscope, pendulum, pulley,
  pump (n.), radar (n.1), radio (n.1),
  reactor (n.), rocket (n.), telescope, transistor

piano *for pictures see definitions of* music, piano

picture

see also art, film, photography
for a picture see the definition of papyrus
pie *for pictures see definitions of* delicious, dessert
pier *for a picture see the definition of* wharf
pig *for pictures see definitions of* mammal, nestle, pig
pigment ❹ *see* color
pike *for a picture see definition*
pill ❸ *see* drug
pilot
see also airplane, vehicle
for a picture see the definition of cockpit
pin *for pictures see definitions of* brooch, safety pin
pine
see also tree
for a picture see the definition of pine
pineapple *for a picture see definition*
Ping-Pong *for a picture see definition*
pinniped *for pictures see definitions of* pinniped, seal[2], sea lion
pipe ❶❷❸ *see* air, instrument, water
pirate *for a picture see definition*
Pisces *for pictures see definitions of* constellation, zodiac
pistachio *for a picture see definition*
pistil
see also flower, reproduction, seed
for a picture see definitions of flower, pistil
pistol
see also weapon
for a picture see the definition of revolver
pit
see also fruit, seed
for a picture see the definition of pit[2]
pitcher *for a picture see the definition of* mound
pitchfork *for a picture see definition*
plague ❹ *see* disease
plaid *for a picture see definition*
plain (n.) ❻
see also geography, tundra
some kinds of plains
prairie, savanna, **tundra**
some animals that live on plains
antelope (n.1), bear[2], bison (n.1), cheetah, deer, gazelle, giraffe, gnu, horse (n.1), hyena, impala, lion, mustang, prairie dog, zebra
some plants that live on plains
grass (n.1), sagebrush
also associated with plains
arroyo, cowboy, cowgirl, ranch (n.)
plan ❸ *see* thought
planet ❸ *see* space
plankton ❶ *see* animal, ocean, plant
plant (n.1) ❶❻❸
see also flower, fruit, fungus, grain, grass, industry, seed, tree, vegetable
for pictures see definitions of begonia, cactus, fern, grow, houseplant, maple, mistletoe, petunia, poinsettia, seedling
some examples of plants
bramble, bush (n.), cactus, cereal (n.1), conifer, evergreen (n.), fern, **flower** (n.2), **grass** (n.1), herb (n.1), houseplant, insectivore (n.1), ivy (n.2), legume (n.1), lily (n.3), moss, palm[2], seaweed (n.1), shrub, **tree** (n.1), weed (n.)
some kinds of plants
cross (n.4), dwarf (n.2), hybrid, native (n.3)
some categories of plants
annual (adj.1), biennial (adj.1), deciduous, perennial (adj.1)
some parts of plants
blade (n.3), boll, branch (n.1), bulb (n.1),

cell (n.1), chlorophyll, foliage (n.1), **fruit**, **grain** (n.1), **leaf** (n.1), nectar, offshoot (n.1), petal, pore[2], root[1] (n.1), runner (n.4), sap, sepal, sprout (n.), stem[1] (n.1)
study of plants
botany
some places for plants
aquarium (n.1), bed (n.2), border (n.4), crop (n.1), **forest**, **garden** (n.), greenhouse, habitat, heath, hothouse, jungle, moor[1], nursery (n.2), oasis, orchard, terrarium, vase
some activities with plants
browse (v.2), cultivate (v.1), eat (v.1), feed (v.4), **garden** (v.), graze[1] (v.1), hay (v.), implant (v.), landscape (v.), mow (v.2), plant (v.1), root[1] (v.1), sink (v.7), sow[1], transplant (v.1)
some descriptions of plants
fresh (adj.6), green (adj.1), poisonous (adj.1)
produced by plants
bloom (n.1), blossom (n.1), bud (n.1), flower (n.1), **fruit**, **seed** (n.1)
some things plants cause
allergy, hay fever, rash[2] (n.1)
some uses of plants
clothing, **food** (n.), fuel, shelter (n.1)
some behaviors of plants
bloom (v.), creep (v.3), grow (v.1), pollinate, wilt
some people associated with plants
farmer, florist, gardener (n.1)
animals that only eat plants
herbivore, vegetarian (n.)
some growth stages of plants
embryo, seed (n.1)
some things that affect plants
air (n.1), blight (n.1), fertilizer, **insects** (n.1), irrigation, manure, nutrients, pollination (pollinate), **soil**[1] (n.1), sunlight, **water** (n.1), weeds (n.)
plantain *for a picture see definition*
plasma ❸ *see* blood, cell
plate
see also cooking, food
for pictures see definitions of earth, platter
plate tectonics
see also continent, geology
for a picture see the definition of earth
platform *for pictures see definitions of* platform, scaffold
platter *for a picture see definition*
play ❸❹ *see* game, leisure, music, theater
playground ❷ *see* game, leisure
playpen *for a picture see definition*
plea ❸ *see* crime
plentiful ❷ *see* definition
plot[1] ❷ *see* literature
plot[2] ❻ *see* building, farming, gardening
plum *for a picture see definition*
plumage *for a picture see definition*
plumbing ❹ *see* building, water
Pluto *for a picture see the definition of* solar system
plutonium ❹ *see* element
pocketknife *for a picture see definition*
poem *for pictures see definitions of* haiku, sonnet
poetry ❷❹ *see* literature
poinsettia *for a picture see definition*
pointer *for a picture see definition*
point of view ❸ *see* belief, thought
poisonous ❶ *see* animal, first aid, plant
polar bear *for pictures see definitions of* growl, polar bear
Polaris *for a picture see the definition of* constella-

tion
police
see also community, law
for pictures see definitions of apprehend, divert, nab
politics (n.2,3) ❶
see also government
some kinds of politics
international, local (adj.1), national (adj.1)
broader categories that include politics
culture (n.1), history (n.3)
some places associated with politics
capitol, headquarters (n.1), parliament (n.2), White House (n.1)
some groups associated with politics
communist (n.2), conservative (n.2), democrat (n.2), republican(n.2), socialist
some actions associated with politics
advertise (v.1), advocate (v.), campaign (v.), contribute (v.1), debate (v.1), lobby (v.)
some activities associated with politics
block (n.5), boycott (n.1), convention (n.1), demonstration (n.2), election, forum (n.2), hearing (n.3), party (n.3), platform (n.3), primary (n.), protest (v.2), race[1] (n.3), rally (n.), ticket (n.2)
some descriptions of politics
conservative (adj.1), environmental (environment n.2), liberal (adj.3), progressive (adj.3), radical (adj.3), revolutionary (adj.1), social (adj.2)
some people associated with politics
candidate, congressman, congresswoman, delegate (n.), governor, mayor, minister (n.2), nominee, politician (n.1), president (n.2), prime minister, running mate, senator
some activities negatively associated with politics
civil war, rebellion (n.1), revolution (n.1), terrorism, uprising
pollen ❶ *see* flowers, reproduction
pollinate *for a picture see definition*
pollution
see also air, conservation, ecosystem, water
for a picture see the definition of conservation
pomegranate *for a picture see definition*
pond ❻ *see* ecosystem, lake, water
poodle *for a picture see definition*
pool ❶ *see* exercise, leisure, water
pop[1] ❶ *see* drink
pop[2] ❷ *see* art, music
pop[3] ❸ *see* family
population ❶ *see* country
porcupine *for a picture see the definition of* hedgehog
portrait ❹ *see* art, photography
pose ❹ *see* art, photography
poster ❹ *see* advertisement, communication
post office ❶ *see* building, community
posture *for a picture see definition*
pot
see also cooking
for pictures see definitions of boil[1], cast iron, copper, kettle
potassium ❹ *see* element
potato *for pictures see definitions of* potato, tuber
poultry ❹ *see* bird, farming, food
pound *for pictures see definitions of* international, pound
pound *for a picture see definition*
power (n.2) ❶❸
see also energy, government, mathematics, military

convert (v.2), crusade (v.), reform (v.1,2)
some actions associated with religions
 anoint, believe (v.1), bless (v.1),
 celebrate (v.2), fast[2] (v.2), meditate,
 ordain (v.1), practice (v.1), praise (v.2),
 pray (v.2), preach (v.2), profess (v.1),
 worship (v.1)
some ways of describing religions
 divine (adj.1,2), fundamental (adj.),
 holy (adj.1), moral (adj.1), orthodox,
 sacred (adj.1), spiritual (adj.2), supreme (adj.1)
some people associated with religions
 atheist, bishop (n.1), cantor, chaplain, clergy,
 congregation (n.2), heathen, martyr (n.1),
 medicine man, minister (n.1), missionary,
 monk, novice (n.2), nun, pagan, parson,
 pilgrim (n.1), pope, preacher, priest, prophet,
 rabbi
conventionally associated with religions
 Allah, altar (n.), angel (n.1), Bible (n.1),
 candle (n.), ceremony (n.1), Christmas (n.1),
 creator (n.2), crusades (n.1), deity,
 demon (n.1), devil (n.1), Easter, god (n.2),
 gods (n.1), Hades, Hanukkah, hell (n.1),
 idol (n.1), Koran, persecution, pew, pulpit,
 Ramadan (n.1), revival (n.3), ritual (n.1),
 Satan, Scripture (n.3), service (n.7), Talmud,
 torah
feeling religious
 devout (adj.1), heavenly (adj.1), holy (adj.2),
 moral (adj.1), pious (adj.1), solemn (adj.2),
 spiritual (adj.1)
reluctant *for a picture see definition*
remember ⊙ *see* history, knowledge, thought
remote control *for a picture see definition*
representative ⊙ *see* democracy, legislature
reproduction (n.3) ⊙ ⊘
 see also body, life
 for a picture see the definition of body
 some places associated with reproduction
  cocoon, greenhouse, hospital, incubator,
  nest (n.1)
 some activities associated with reproduction
  breed (v.3), conceive (v.3), develop (v.5),
  divide (v.4), fertilize (v.1), hatch[1] (v.1),
  mate (v.), multiply (v.5), pollinate, spawn (v.),
  unite (v.1)
 able to reproduce
  fertile (adj.2)
 associated with reproduction
  brood (n.1), generation (n.1), life (n.1),
  litter (n.2), newborn (n.), offspring, seedling,
  young (n.)
 multiple offspring through reproduction
  quadruplet, quintuplet (n.1), triplet,
  twin (n.1)
 some stages of reproduction
  birth (n.1), conception (n.2), egg[1] (n.1),
  embryo, larva (n.1)
 some things involved with reproduction
  ovary (n.1), penis, pistil, pollen, pouch (n.2),
  seed (n.1), sperm, stamen, umbilical cord,
  uterus, vagina, yolk
 some things passed on through reproduction
  characteristic (n.), chromosome, DNA, gene
 unable to reproduce
  infertile (adj.2), sterile (adj.2)
reptile ❶
 see also animal, dinosaur
 for pictures see definitions of boa constrictor,
  cobra, constrictor, coral snake, crocodile,
  gecko, Gila monster, horned lizard, iguana,
  protrude, rattlesnake, reptile, reptile, snake,
  tortoise, viper
 some examples of reptiles
  adder, alligator, anaconda, boa constrictor,

caiman, chameleon, cobra, constrictor,
  copperhead, coral snake, cottonmouth,
  crocodile, garter snake, gecko, Gila monster,
  horned lizard, horned toad, iguana, lizard,
  monitor (n.4), python, racer (n.3),
  rattlesnake, snake (n.1), terrapin, tortoise,
  turtle (n.), viper, water moccasin
 similar to a reptile
  dragon
 broader categories including reptiles
  animal (n.1), vertebrate (n.)
 parts of some reptiles
  fang, flipper (n.1), hood (n.2), scale[1] (n.1),
  shell (n.1)
 produced by reptiles
  eggs[1] (n.2), venom
 characteristic of reptiles
  cold-blooded (adj.1)
 extinct reptile
  dinosaur
 things some reptiles eat
  fruits, insects (n.1), **plants** (n.1), **rodents,**
  vegetation
republic ⊙ *see* government
research ❶ *see* science
resolve *for a picture see definition*
respect ⊙ *see* behavior, relationship, thought
respiration
 see also body, life
 for a picture see the definition of body
 some activities that stop respiration
  choke (v.1), strangle (v.2), suffocate (v.3)
 some activities that involve respiration
  blow[2] (v.3), breathe (v.1), cough (v.1),
  draw (v.5), exhale, gasp (v.1), gulp (v.1),
  heave (v.3), hiccup (v.1), huff (v.), inhale,
  pant (v.1), puff (v.4), sigh (v.1), sniff (v.1),
  sniffle (v.), snore (v.), snort (v.1), sob (v.),
  suck (v.1), wheeze (v.), yawn (v.1)
 produced by respiration
  carbon dioxide
 some body parts used in respiration
  blowhole (n.1), bronchial tube, gill, lung,
  mouth (n.1), nose (n.1), nostril, throat (n.1),
  trachea (n.1), trunk (n.1), windpipe
 predator that kills by stopping respiration
  anaconda, boa constrictor, constrictor, python
 some tools used for respiration
  Aqua-Lung, snorkel, spacesuit
 involved with respiration
  air (n.1), breath (n.1), oxygen
 some diseases that involve respiration
  asthma, bronchitis, croup, distemper,
  pneumonia, whooping cough
 some things that affect respiration
  aerobics, allergy, anemia, heat (n.1), moisture,
  smoke (n.1), ventilation
 ways to recover someone's respiration
  artificial respiration, CPR
respond ⊙ *see* action, sense, thought
rest[1] ⊙ ⊙ *see* body, leisure, mind
retriever *for a picture see definition*
reunion *for a picture see definition*
revenue ⊘ *see* business, money
reverence *for a picture see definition*
review ⊘ *see* book, theater
revolver *for a picture see definition*
rhinoceros *for pictures see definitions of* mammal,
  rhinoceros
rhododendron *for a picture see definition*
rib *for a picture see the definition of* body
rice
 see also grain
 for a picture see the definition of rice

rich ⊘ *see* money
rickety *for a picture see definition*
ride
 see also transportation, vehicle
 for pictures see definitions of Ferris wheel, rodeo,
  roller coaster
rifle *for a picture see definition*
rigging *for a picture see definition*
ring
 see also jewelry, sport
 for a picture see the definition of emerald
ritual
 see also tradition
 for a picture see the definition of ritual
river (n.1) ❻
 see also boat, ecosystem, geography, water
 for pictures see definitions of inlet, waterfall,
  windmill
 some examples of rivers
  Amazon (n.1), Euphrates, Ganges,
  Jordan (n.2), Mississippi (n.2), Missouri (n.2),
  Mohawk (n.1), Niger (n.2), Nile, Ohio (n.2),
  Potomac, Rhine, Seine, Tigris, Yukon (n.2),
  Zaire (n.2)
 similar to rivers
  brook, creek (n.), inlet, stream (n.1), tributary
 broader categories including rivers
  ecosystem, water (n.1)
 some parts of rivers
  curve (n.2), eddy, estuary, everglade (n.),
  ford (n.2), fork (n.2), headwaters, mouth (n.3),
  pool (n.2), rapid (n.), shoal, waterfall,
  whirlpool
 means of transportation on a river
  barge (n.), canoe (n.), ferry (n.), kayak, paddle
  wheel, raft (n.2), rowboat
 mythical figure associated with rivers
  nymph (n.1)
 some terms for land associated with rivers
  bank[1] (n.2), basin (n.2), divide (n.), sandbar,
  shore (n.1), watershed
 some things that affect the flow of rivers
  dam (n.), embankment, levee (n.1), sandbar
 also associated with rivers
  bridge (n.1), crossing (n.2), dredge (n.),
  flood (n.1)
road ⊙ *see* car, vehicle
robbery ⊙ *see* crime
rock
 see also stone
 for pictures see definitions of crystal, granite,
  mineral, quartz, salt, sandstone, sedimentary
rock[2] ⊘ *see* dance, music
rocket *for pictures see definitions of* launch[1], rocket
rocking horse *for a picture see definition*
rodent ❶
 see also mammal
 for pictures see definitions of chinchilla, hamster,
  hedgehog, mouse, prairie dog, rat, squirrel,
  vole, woodchuck
 some examples of rodents
  beaver, chinchilla, chipmunk, dormouse,
  gerbil, gopher, groundhog, guinea pig (n.1),
  hamster, hedgehog (n.1), lemming,
  mouse (n.1), muskrat, nutria, porcupine,
  prairie dog, rat (n.1), squirrel, vole, woodchuck
 broader categories that include rodent
  animal (n.1), **mammal**, vertebrate (n.)
 some parts of rodents
  bristle (n.1), cheeks (n.1), claws (n.1),
  fur (n.1), tail (n.1), teeth (**tooth** n.1),
  whisker (n.2)
 some places for rodents
  arctic (n.), bog (n.), burrows (n.), cage (n.1),

caves (n.), cliffs, **desert**[1], **forest**, log (n.1),
meadow, mesas, **mountains** (n.1), nest (n.2),
shrubs, swamp (n.), **trees** (n.1), **tundra**,
underground (n.1)
some groups of rodents
colony (n.2), pack (n.3)
descriptions of some rodents
abundant, alert (adj.), nervous (adj.2),
nocturnal (adj.2), quick (adj.2), quiet (adj.1)
produced by some rodents
burrow (n.), dam (n.), mound (n.1),
tunnel (n.2)
uses for some rodents
experiments (n.), research (n.)
some behaviors of rodents
build (v.1), burrow (n.), chew (v.),
collect (v.1), dig (v.1), gnaw, hibernate,
mate (n.3), scamper, scurry, store (v.),
swim (v.1)
some things rodents eat
berries (berry n.), **bird** (n.), bulb (n.1),
cones (n.3), corn (n.1), eggs[1] (n.2), **fruit**,
grains (n.1), **grass** (n.1), **insects** (n.1),
mushroom (n.), nuts (n.1), roots[1] (n.1),
seeds (n.1), **vegetable** (n.1), wood (n.1)
rodeo *for a picture see definition*
roller coaster *for a picture see definition*
rolling pin *for a picture see definition*
romance ⊙ ◑ *see* love, relationship
Roman numeral *for a picture see the definition of*
number
roof *for a picture see the definition of* pagoda
rook *for a picture see definition*
room (n.2) ⊙
see also building, home
some examples of rooms
alcove, ballroom, bathroom, bedroom,
booth (n.1), classroom, closet, courtroom,
den (n.2), dinette, dining room, entry (n.2),
family room, gymnasium, hall (n.3), hallway,
kitchen, laundry (n.2), lavatory (n.1), living
room, lobby (n.1), loft (n.1), lounge (n.1),
nook, nursery (n.1), office (n.1), parlor (n.1),
restroom, salon (n.1), studio (n.1,3),
study (n.5), suite (n.1), vault[1] (n.2),
ward (n.1)
broader category that includes rooms
building (n.1)
some parts of rooms
ceiling (n.1), door (n.2), floor (n.1),
wall (n.1), window (n.2)
some things used in making rooms
brick (n.1), cement (n.1), concrete (n.),
fiberglass, linoleum, lumber[1] (n.),
molding (n.2), nails (n.1), paint (n.1),
pipes (n.1), plumbing (n.1), rivets (n.),
screws (n.1), steel (n.1), tile (n.1), wires (n.3),
wood (n.2)
some things found in rooms
appliance, bathtub, carpet (n.1), fireplace,
furniture, lights[1] (n.2), mirror (n.),
picture (n.1), radiator (n.1), rug, sink (n.),
toilet (n.1)
rooster *for pictures see definitions of* cock[1], crest,
rooster
root
see also plant
for pictures see definitions of carrot, flower,
ginger, radish, root[1]
rope *for pictures see definitions of* knot, rigging,
twist
rose *for a picture see the definition of* rose[1]
rotary *for a picture see definition*
rotor *for a picture see definition*
rowboat *for a picture see definition*

royal ◔ *see* monarchy
rubber *for a picture see definition*
ruby *for a picture see definition*
ruin *for a picture see definition*
rule ⊙ ◑ *see* game, law, mathematics
ruler
see also government, power
for a picture see the definition of measurement
run ⊙ *see* exercise
rung *for a picture see definition*
runway *for a picture see definition*
rural *for a picture see definition*
Russian *for pictures see definitions of* language,
Russian
rye ◑ *see* grain
saber *for a picture see definition*
sack *for pictures see definitions of* drawstring, sack[1]
sacred ◔ *see* religion
saddle *for a picture see definition*
sadness ◔
see also emotion
similar to sadness
anguish, gloom (n.2), grief (n.),
melancholy (n.), misery (n.1), remorse,
sorrow (n.1)
broader categories that include sadness
emotion (n.1), feeling (n.3), mood
some actions related to sadness
bawl (v.), bleed (v.3), blubber (v.),
complain (v.1), cry (v.2), grieve (v.1),
groan (v.), howl (v.1), miss[1] (v.6), mope (v.1),
mourn, pout, sigh (v.1), sniffle (v.), sob (v.),
wail (v.1), weep, whimper (v.), yowl (v.)
some reactions to sadness
cheer (v.1), comfort (v.), console[1] (v.1), ease (v.1),
pity (v.), regret (v.), soothe (v.2),
sympathize (v.1)
some causes of sadness
death (n.1), disappointment (n.2), hurt (n.),
injury, loss (n.3), misfortune (n.1), pain (n.2),
tragedy (n.1)
conventionally associated with sadness
catastrophe, doom (n.), funeral, half-mast,
tragedy (n.1), wake[1] (n.)
feeling sad
black (adj.3), bleak (adj.2), blue (adj.2),
dark (adj.3), dismal, down[1] (adj.1),
downcast (adj.2), dreary, gloomy (adj.2), glum,
heartbroken, heavy (adj.4), lonely (adj.3),
lonesome (adj.1), low (adj.3),
miserable (adj.1), somber (adj.2), sorry (adj.1),
sullen (adj.2), unhappy (adj.1)
some states of sadness
blues (n.1), depression (n.1), mourning (n.1),
woe (n.1)
safety pin *for a picture see definition*
Sagittarius *for pictures see definitions of* constellation, zodiac
sail
see also boat
for pictures see definitions of sailboat,
windsurfing
sailboat *for pictures see definitions of* capsize, sailboat
salamander *for a picture see definition*
salary ◔ *see* money, work
saliva ◔ *see* digestion
salmon *for a picture see definition*
salt
see also chemistry, cooking, natural resources,
ocean
for pictures see definitions of salt, taste
salute *for a picture see definition*

sand ◔ *see* soil
sandstone *for a picture see definition*
sane ◔ ◔ *see* emotion, health, thought
sanity ◔ *see* behavior, emotion, health
satellite
see also space, technology
for pictures see definitions of moon, satellite
Saturn *for a picture see the definition of* solar system
savanna ◔ *see* ecosystem, plain
save[1] ◔ *see* bank, money
saxophone *for pictures see definitions of* music,
saxophone
scaffold *for a picture see definition*
scale
see also fish, reptile
for a picture see the definition of scale
scale
see also measurement
for a picture see the definition of scale
scale[3] ◔ ◔ *see* music
scar ◔ *see* injury
scare ◔ *see* fear
scarecrow *for a picture see definition*
scarf *for a picture see the definition of* muffler
scene
see also film, theater
for a picture see the definition of scene
school[1] (n.1) ◔ ◔
see also building, community, education, learn
some kinds of schools
academy, boarding school, college, elementary
school, grade school, high school,
institute (n.2), institution (n.1), junior high
school, kindergarten, nursery school, primary
school, public school, seminary, university
some parts of schools
auditorium, cafeteria, classroom, department,
dormitory, gym (n.1), homeroom,
laboratory (n.), lavatory (n.1), library (n.1),
lockers, office (n.1), showers (n.4)
some subjects studied in schools
art (n.1), computer science, crafts (n.1),
economics, **geography** (n.1), geometry (n.1),
gym (n.2), **health** (n.1), **history** (n.2),
languages (n.1), **literature** (n.1),
mathematics, **music** (n.2), **religion** (n.1),
sciences (n.1), social studies, **technology** (n.1)
some activities associated with schools
homework, project (n.1), schoolwork
some people associated with schools
aide, child (n.1), class (n.5), classmate,
coach (n.1,2), custodian (n.2), faculty (n.3),
freshman, instructor, janitor, junior (n.2),
librarian, parent, principal (n.1), professor,
pupil[1], secretary (n.1), senior (n.3),
sophomore, staff (n.3), student (n.1),
superintendent (n.1), teacher, tutor (n.)
money that pays for school
scholarship, tuition (n.1)
some things found in schools
blackboard, **book** (n.1), chalk (n.2),
chalkboard, crayons (n.), eraser, glue (n.),
ink (n.), notebook, paper (n.2), paste (n.1),
pen[1], pencil (n.), textbook
some things happening in schools
add (v.3), coach (v.), comprehend,
divide (v.3), drill (v.1,2), examine (v.2),
expel (v.2), fail (v.5,6), flunk out, grade (v.1),
instruct (v.1), learn (v.1), multiply (v.2),
pass (v.2), play (v.2,3,4), practice (v.2),
question (v.1), quiz (n.), read (v.1), rehearse,
school[1] (v.), study (v.1), subtract,
suspend (v.3), teach (v.1,3), test (v.),
tutor (v.), understand (v.1), write (v.1,2)

time periods in schools
  class (n.6), course (n.4), lunch (n.),
  period (n.3), recess (n.1), semester,
  session (n.2), term (n.3)

school
  see also fish
  for a picture see the definition of school²

schooner *for a picture see definition*

science (n.1) 🔵
  see also animal, body, chemistry, geology,
  mathematics, measurement, mind, physics,
  plant, space, technology
  some examples of sciences
    aeronautics, agriculture, anatomy (n.2),
    archaeology, astronomy, aviation, biology,
    botany, **chemistry** (n.1), ecology, economics,
    electronics, genetics, **geology** (n.1), law (n.4),
    medicine (n.2), meteorology, ornithology,
    physics, psychology, zoology
  some places for science
    lab, laboratory (n.1), **school¹** (n.1)
  some activities in science
    examine (v.2), research (v.), study (v.3),
    test (v.)
  college degree in science
    B.S.
  some aspects of science
    argument (n.2), debate (v.1), discussion,
    experiment (n.), hypothesis, law (n.3), logic,
    theory (n.2)
  suffix for science
    -logy

scientist *for a picture see the definition of* technician

score
  see also game, music, sport
  for a picture see the definition of score

Scorpio *for pictures see definitions of* constellation,
zodiac

scorpion *for a picture see the definition of* deadly

scout *for a picture see the definition of* uniform

scrapbook 🔵 *see* book, photography

scratch *for a picture see definition*

scrawny *for a picture see definition*

scream 🔵 *see* anger, fear

scroll *for a picture see definition*

scrub *for a picture see definition*

scuba diving *for a picture see definition*

sculpture
  see also art
  for a picture see the definition of carve

scythe *for a picture see definition*

sea (n.1) 🔵 🔵
  see also geography, ocean, water
  for pictures see definitions of scuba diving,
  underwater
  some examples of seas
    Black Sea, China Sea, Dead Sea,
    Mediterranean Sea, North Sea, Red Sea
  broader categories including sea
    ecosystem, water (n.1)
  some terms for describing the sea
    marine (adj.1), maritime, nautical
  some people associated with the sea
    diver (n.1), mermaid, pirate (n.1), sailor,
    Viking
  gods of the sea
    Neptune (n.1), Poseidon
  measures related to the sea
    knot (n.4), league² , nautical mile
  some terms for location on the sea
    at sea (phr.1), high seas, overseas (adj.2)
  also associated with the sea
    seafaring, sea level

sea gull *for a picture see definition*

seal *for a picture see the definition of* seal²

sea lion *for a picture see definition*

seaplane *for a picture see definition*

search *for a picture see the definition of* unearth

seat
  see also clothing, furniture
  for a picture see the definition of stool

secrete 🔵 *see* digestion, excrete

section *for a picture see definition*

sediment 🔵 *see* geology, soil

sedimentary *for a picture see definition*

see 🔵 *see* light, sense

seed (n.1) 🔵
  see also farming, grain, plant
  for pictures see definitions of almond, coconut,
  seed
  some examples of seeds
    almond (n.2), bean (n.1), buckwheat (n.2),
    cacao (n.2), coconut (n.2), corn (n.2),
    lentil (n.1), lima bean (n.1), nutmeg,
    oat (n.2), pea (n.1), peanut, rice (n.2),
    rye (n.2), soybean (n.2)
  similar to seed
    spore
  some kinds of seeds
    fruit stone (stone n.5), **grain** (n.1),
    kernel (n.2), legume (n.1), nut (n.1), pit² (n.)
  broader category that includes seeds
    plant (n.1)
  some parts of seeds
    bur (n.1), germ (n.2), hull¹ (n.1), husk (n.)
  place for seeds
    furrow (n.1)
  activities involving seeds
    disperse (v.1), fertilize (v.1), hull¹ (v.),
    plant (v.1), thresh (v.)
  produced by seeds
    sapling, seedling
  some behaviors of seeds
    develop (v.2), germinate, grow (v.1),
    sprout (v.1)
  some things that contain seeds
    berry (n.), boll, cone (n.3), ear², **fruit**,
    ovary (n.2), pistil, pod
  some things that affect seeds
    irrigation, moisture, rain (n.1), season (n.1),
    soil¹ (n.1), sunshine, temperature (n.1)
  some things that spread seeds
    airplane, car (n.1), **clothing**, feathers (n.),
    feet **(foot** n.1), fur (n.1), ship (n.1),
    train (n.1), waves (n.1), wind¹ (n.1),
    wings (n.3)
  things that grow from seeds
    blossom (n.1), flower (n.1), **plant** (n.1)

seedling *for a picture see definition*

sell
  see also business, money
  for a picture see the definition of hawk

semicircle *for a picture see definition*

semicolon 🔵 *see* grammar

semitrailer *for a picture see definition*

senate 🔵 *see* legislature

senior 🔵 *see* life, relationship, school

sense (n.1) 🔵
  see also body, life, nerve
  some examples of senses
    hearing (n.1), sight (n.1), smell (n.2),
    taste (n.2), touch (n.2)
  some kinds of senses
    auditory, optical (adj.1), visual (adj.1)
  body parts involved with sensing
    brain (n.1), ears¹ (n.1), eyes (n.1), **nerve** (n.1),
    nervous system, nose (n.1), palate (n.1),

skin (n.1), taste bud, tongue (n.1)
some activities with senses
  experience (v.), feel (v.1), hear (v.1),
  listen (v.1), look (v.1), perceive (v.1),
  see (v.1), smell (v.1), sniff (v.2), taste (v.1),
  touch (v.1), watch (v.1)
some qualities of sensations
  dim (adj.2), dull (adj.4), keen (adj.2),
  sensitive (adj.1), sharp (adj.2), strong (adj.1),
  weak (adj.3)
some descriptions of sensations
  beautiful, bitter (adj.1), bright (adj.1),
  cold (adj.1), creamy (adj.1), delicious,
  dull (adj.4), fishy (adj.1), foul (adj.1), fragrant,
  harsh (adj.1), hot (adj.1), icy (adj.2),
  loud (adj.1), luscious, mild (adj.3), musty,
  plain (adj.3,4), pungent, rank² (adj.1),
  rough (adj.1), salty, sharp (adj.3), shrill,
  smooth (adj.1), sour (adj.1), stale (adj.1),
  sticky (adj.1), strong (adj.4), sweet (adj.1),
  tart¹, tasteless (adj.1), ugly (adj.1),
  warm (adj.1)
some tools for impaired senses
  Braille, contact lens, glasses (glass n.3),
  hearing aid
absence of certain senses
  blind (adj.1), deaf (adj.1), numb (adj.1)
some results of sensing
  awareness (aware), enjoyment, pain (n.1),
  vision (n.1)
some things that affect someone's senses
  anesthesia, blindness (blind adj.1), common
  cold, deafness (deaf adj.1), **diet** (n.1), **disease**,
  health (n.1), illness (n.1), paralysis
some things that are sensed
  aroma, fragrance, matter (n.1), odor,
  pain (n.1), phenomenon (n.1), pressure (n.1),
  scent (n.1), sights (n.3), sound¹ (n.2),
  taste (n.3), temperature (n.1)

sentence 🔵 🔵 *see* crime, grammar

sentiment 🔵 *see* belief, emotion

sequel 🔵 *see* book, film

serious 🔵 *see* behavior, thought

serve *for a picture see definition*

service 🔵 🔵 *see* economy, government, military

sew 🔵 *see* clothing

sewer 🔵 🔵 *see* community, water

shack 🔵 *see* building

shade 🔵 *see* color

shadow *for a picture see definition*

shake *for a picture see the definition of* clasp

shamrock *for a picture see definition*

shape (n.1) 🔵
  see also mathematics
  for pictures see definitions of cone, contour,
  decagon, hexagon, pentagon, semicircle,
  square, trapezoid, triangle
  some examples of shapes
    circles (n.1), cones (n.1), cubes (n.1),
    decagons, diamonds (n.2), hexagons, isosceles
    triangles, octagons, ovals (n.),
    pentagons (n.1), pyramids (n.1),
    quadrilaterals, rectangles,
    rhombuses (rhombus), right triangles, scalene
    triangles, spheres (n.1), squares (n.1),
    trapezoids (n.), triangles (n.1)
  similar to shape
    form (n.1), outline (n.1)
  some kinds of shapes
    ellipses, polygons, solids (n.1)
  some broader categories that include shapes
    art (n.4), geometry (n.1), **mathematics**
  some parts of shapes
    angles (n.1,2), axis (n.1), circumference,
    depth (n.2), diameter (n.1,2),

dimensions (n.1), exterior (n.1), faces (n.5), height (n.1), length (n.1), perimeter, radius (n.1), side (n.1), thickness (n.2), width
some descriptions of **shapes**
circular (adj.1), congruent, cubic (adj.1,2), geometric (adj.2), irregular (adj.1), linear (adj.1), oblong (adj.), oval (adj.), regular (adj.6), square (adj.1,3)
some people associated with **shapes**
architect, engineer (n.1), painter (n.1), sculptor
some things conventionally associated with **shapes**
arcs, lines[1] (n.1), planes[1] (n.3)
some elements of **shapes**
geometry (n.2), size (n.1), symmetry
shatter *for a picture see definition*
shed *for a picture see the definition of* outhouse
sheep *for pictures see definitions of* bighorn, ewe, lamb, mammal, RAM, sheep
shelf ⊙ *see* furniture
shell
see also crustacean, mollusk
for pictures see definitions of conch, mollusk, mussel, shell
shelter ⊙ *see* building
shield *for pictures see definitions of* coat of arms, shield
shilling *for pictures see definitions of* international, shilling
shin *for a picture see the definition of* body
ship
see also boat
for pictures see definitions of battleship, freighter, schooner, ship, wake[2], yacht
shirt ⊙ *see* clothing
shock[1] ⊙⊙⊙ *see* electricity, emotion, first aid, injury
shoe
see also clothing
for pictures see definitions of clog, leather, moccasin, overshoe, worn-out
shore
see also lake, ocean, sea
for pictures see definitions of low tide, shore
shoulder
see also body, skeleton
for a picture see the definition of body
shovel
see also tool
for pictures see definitions of implement, resolve
show ⊙ *see* film, theater
shower ⊙ *see* hygiene
shriek *for a picture see definition*
shrub ⊙ *see* plant, tree
sick ⊙ *see* disease, health
sickle *for a picture see definition*
sieve *for pictures see definitions of* sieve, strainer
sight ⊙ *see* light, sense
sightseeing *for a picture see definition*
sign
see also communication, language, mathematics
for pictures see definitions of intersect, sign, symbol, warning
silhouette *for a picture see definition*
silkworm *for a picture see definition*
silo *for a picture see definition*
silver ⊙⊙ *see* element, jewelry
silverware *for a picture see definition of* utensil
sing
see also music
for pictures see definitions of choir, debut,

impersonate, unison
sink ⊙ *see* water
sister
see also family, relationship
for a picture see the definition of triplet
skate *for a picture see the definition of* graceful
skeleton (n.1)
see also body
for pictures see definitions of body, skeleton
some parts of the human **skeleton**
backbone (n.1), breastbone, brow (n.1), cartilage, collarbone, eyebrow (n.1), hipbone, jawbone, joint (n.), kneecap, rib (n.1), shinbone, shoulder blade, skull, spinal column, teeth (**tooth** n.1), thighbone, vertebra, wrist
some things that compose **skeletons**
bones (n.), cartilage
sciences that involve the study of **skeletons**
anatomy (n.2), paleontology
some places for study of **skeletons**
classroom, museum
some activities with **skeletons**
assemble (v.2), display (v.1), exhibit (v.), find (v.2,3), repair (v.1), research (v.), study (v.3)
some descriptions of **skeletons**
bony (adj.2), brittle (adj.), hard (adj.1), hollow (adj.1), porous, strong (adj.1), white (n.1)
some people associated with **skeletons**
doctor (n.1), intern (n.), medic, paleontologist (paleontology), pediatrician, physician, scientist, surgeon, teacher, veterinarian
tool for viewing **skeletons**
x-ray (n.1)
some tools for repairing **skeletons**
brace (n.2), cast (n.3), splint
conventionally associated with **skeletons**
dinosaur, Halloween
functions of **skeletons**
protection (n.1), support (n.1)
related to **skeletons**
fossil
some things that affect the strength of **skeletons**
calcium, caries, **diet** (n.1), **disease**, nutrition (n.1)
some things that connect **skeletons**
ligament, tendon
ski
see also leisure, sport
for a picture see the definition of balance
skillet *for a picture see definition*
skin ⊙ *see* body, organ, sense
skirt ⊙ *see* clothing
skull
see also skeleton
for pictures see definitions of body, skull
sky ⊙ *see* air
slang ⊙ *see* language
sled *for pictures see definitions of* sled, toboggan
sleep ⊙⊙ *see* body, health, mind
sleepy *for pictures see definitions of* drowsy, insomnia
sleet ⊙ *see* weather
slice *for a picture see the definition of* section
slime *for a picture see definition*
slipper *for a picture see the definition of* moccasin
sloth *for a picture see definition*
slug *for a picture see the definition of* slug[1]
slurp *for a picture see definition*
smack *for a picture see definition*
small intestine ⊙ *see* body, digestion, organ

smell ⊙ *see* sense
smile ⊙ *see* happiness
smoke *for a picture see the definition of* hazardous
snack ⊙ *see* food
snail *for pictures see definitions of* mollusk, snail
snake
see also reptile
for pictures see definitions of boa constrictor, cobra, constrictor, coral snake, exaggerate, rattlesnake, reptile, snake, viper
snare drum *for pictures see definitions of* music, snare drum
snooze *for a picture see definition*
snout ⊙ *see* animal
snow
see also weather
for a picture see the definition of top[1]
snuggle *for a picture see definition*
soak *for a picture see the definition of* drench
soap ⊙ *see* hygiene
soar *for a picture see definition*
soccer *for pictures see definitions of* excel, goalie
social studies ⊙⊙ *see* culture, geography, history
sock *for a picture see the definition of* foul
socket *for a picture see definition*
soda ⊙ *see* drink
sofa ⊙ *see* furniture
softball ⊙ *see* sport
soil[1] (n.1) ⊙
see also conservation, ecosystem, geology, natural resources, stone
some kinds of **soil**
bog (n.), clay (n.), clod (n.1), dirt (n.1), dust (n.1), earth (n.4), grime, humus, mud, sand (n.), silt, sod (n.), turf
some actions involving **soil**
bury (v.1), dig (v.1), grub (v.1), pollute, smudge (v.2), sweep (n.1), wallow, wash (v.1)
some things **soil** *is used for*
anthill, burrow (n.), grave[1], tunnel (n.1)
some **soil** *formations*
clod (n.1), embankment, mound (n.2), trench (n.1)
some natural processes involving **soil**
erosion, landslide (n.1), settlement (n.1), wash (v.5)
solar ⊙ *see* energy, light, space
solar system *for a picture see definition*
soldier ⊙ *see* military
sole *for a picture see definition*
sole *for a picture see definition*
song ⊙ *see* music
sonnet *for a picture see definition*
soprano ⊙ *see* music
sore ⊙ *see* injury, sense
soul ⊙ *see* mind
sound[1] ⊙⊙ *see* language, music, physics
sound[4] ⊙ *see* geography, water
sour *for a picture see the definition of* taste
source *for a picture see definition*
space (n.2) ⊙
see also physics, technology
similar to **space**
cosmos, heavens (n.1), outer space
some broader categories that include **space**
science (n.1), universe
study of **space**
astronomy
some places associated with **space**
observatory, planetarium
some actions associated with things in **space**

burn (v.1), collide (v.1), emit (v.1), erupt,
escape (v.1), expand (v.2), explode (v.1),
flare (v.1,2), jet[1] (v.), orbit (v.), radiate (v.1),
reflect (v.1), revolve (v.1,2), rotate (v.3),
spin (v.1)
some descriptions associated with space
astronomical (adj.1), cold (adj.1), cosmic,
empty (adj.1), expanding (expand v.2),
extraterrestrial, heavenly (adj.1), infinite,
intergalactic, interplanetary, lunar,
nebular (nebula), solar (adj.1), vast (adj.1)
some people associated with space
alien (n.2), astronaut, astronomer, cosmonaut
some things conventionally associated with space
astrology, capsule (n.2), constellation, flying
saucer, light-year, Milky Way, module (n.2),
moon (n.2), NASA, polestar, rocket (n.),
satellite (n.2), shooting star, solar system,
spacecraft, space shuttle, space station,
spacesuit, spacewalk, telescope, vacuum (n.2),
zodiac
some constellations and stars in space
Aquarius (n.1), Aries (n.1), Big Dipper,
cancer (n.2), Canis Major, Canis Minor,
Capricorn (n.1), Dog Star, Gemini (n.1),
Libra (n.1), Little Dipper, North Star,
Orion (n.1), Pisces (n.1), Polaris, ram (n.3),
Sagittarius (n.1), Scorpio (n.1), Sirius,
sun (n.1), Taurus (n.1), Ursa Major, Ursa
Minor, Virgo (n.1), zodiac
some elements of space space
asteroids, black hole, comets, dust (n.),
galaxies (galaxy), gas (n.1), meteors, Milky
Way, moons (n.2), nebulae (nebula), quasars,
satellites (n.1,2), solar system, stars (n.1),
voids (n.1)
some planets in space
earth (n.1), Jupiter (n.2), Mars (n.2),
mercury (n.3), moon (n.1), Neptune (n.2),
Pluto (n.2), Saturn (n.1), Uranus (n.1),
Venus (n.2)
space shuttle *for a picture see the definition of*
blastoff
spaghetti *for a picture see the definition of* noodle
spaniel *for a picture see definition*
Spanish *for pictures see definitions of* language,
Spanish
sparrow *for a picture see definition*
speak ◑ *see* language
species ◐ *see* life
speech
see also language
for a picture see the definition of platform
spice
see also cooking, food
for a picture see the definition of ginger
spider ◐
see also arthropod, crustacean, insect
for pictures see definitions of creep, invertebrate,
spider, tarantula, terrify
some examples of spiders
black widow, tarantula
broader categories that include spiders
arthropod, invertebrate (n.)
some parts of spiders
fangs, legs (n.1)
some places for spiders
burrow (n.), web (n.3)
produced by spiders
cobweb (n.1), cocoon, eggs[1] (n.2), silk (n.1),
venom
some behaviors of spiders
court (v.1), feed (v.4), hunt (v.1), jump (v.1),
mate (v.), nest (v.), prey (v.1), protect,
spin (v.2), trap (v.1), weave (v.4), wrap (v.1)

spiders eat
insects
related to spiders
mite[1], scorpion, tick[2]
spin *for a picture see definition*
spinach *for a picture see definition*
spine ◑ *see* skeleton
spiral *for a picture see definition*
spleen *for a picture see the definition of* body
spoken ◑ *see* language
spool *for a picture see the definition of* reel[1]
spoon
see also food, tool
for pictures see definitions of immerse, utensil
sport (n.1) ◐ ◐
see also exercise, game, leisure
for pictures see definitions of aloft, badminton,
football, hockey, puck, putt
some examples of sports
archery, badminton, baseball (n.1),
basketball (n.1), boxing, cricket[2], croquet,
discus (n.2), diving (dive n.2), fencing,
football (n.1,3), gymnastics (n.2),
handball (n.1), hockey, judo, lacrosse, polo,
racquetball, shot put, sky diving, soccer,
softball (n.1), squash[1] (n.),
swimming (swim v.1), tennis, volleyball (n.1),
windsurfing, wrestling
some kinds of sports
contact (n.1), individual (n.1), team (n.1)
broader category including sports
game (n.2)
some parts of sports
finals (n.1), **game** (n.2), half time, inning,
quarter (n.7), semifinal (n.), set (n.4)
some places related to sports
amphitheater, arena (n.1), coliseum,
course (n.5), dugout (n.2), field (n.3),
grandstand, gym (n.1), gymnasium, park (n.2),
ring[1] (n.4), stadium, track (n.3)
some actions in sports
assist (v.1), bench (v.), block (v.2), bunt (v.),
foul (v.3,4), fumble (v.3), hit (v.1), kick (v.1),
miss[1] (v.1), pass (v.7), score (v.3), serve (v.5),
swing (v.4), tee off (phr.1), trail (v.3), try
out (phr.1), volley (v.)
some people associated with sports
amateur (n.1), athlete, boxer (n.1),
captain (n.5), champion (n.1), designated
hitter, fan[2], finalist, goalie, goalkeeper,
gymnast, player (n.1), professional (n.2),
referee (n.), runner (n.1), runner (n.1),
scout (n.2), umpire (n.), underdog
some accessories for sports
ball[1] (n.2), baseball (n.2), basket (n.3),
basketball (n.2), cup (n.4), discus (n.1),
equipment (n.1), football (n.2), goal (n.2),
handball (n.2), home plate, javelin (n.2),
jersey (n.1), mat (n.3), padding (pad[1] n.1),
puck, sneakers, softball (n.2), spikes (n.3),
uniform (n.), volleyball (n.2)
conventionally associated with sports
draft (n.3), league[1] (n.2), mascot,
sportsmanship
some results of sports
goal (n.3), loss (n.5), penalty (n.2),
point (n.9), run (n.11), touchdown (n.1),
win (n.)
spot *for a picture see the definition of* dot
sprain ◐ *see* first aid, injury
spruce
see also tree
for a picture see the definition of spruce[1]
square
see also mathematics, shape

for a picture see the definition of square
squawk *for a picture see definition*
squid *for pictures see definitions of* squid, tentacle
squirrel *for pictures see definitions of* chipmunk,
squirrel
squirt *for a picture see definition*
stadium *for a picture see the definition of* bleacher
staff *for a picture see definition*
stage ◐ ◑ *see* theater
stagecoach *for a picture see definition*
stair *for a picture see the definition of* path
stalk *for a picture see the definition of* stalk[1]
stamen *for pictures see definitions of* flower, stamen
stand ◐ ◐ *see* belief, furniture, thought
star
see also film, light, space, theater
for pictures see definitions of constellation, star
starfish *for a picture see definition*
Stars and Stripes *for a picture see definition*
statue
see also art
for pictures see definitions of majestic, statue
steal ◑ *see* crime
steam ◐ ◐ *see* anger, cooking, water
steeple *for a picture see definition*
stem
see also plant
for a picture see the definition of stalk[1]
step *for pictures see definitions of* path, rung
stethoscope *for a picture see definition*
stick *for pictures see definitions of* drumstick, staff
sticky *for a picture see the definition of* goo
sting ◑ *see* first aid, injury
stinger ◐ *see* insect
stingray *for a picture see definition*
stitch ◑ *see* art, clothing
stock ◐ ◐ *see* business, cooking, money
stomach
see also body, digestion, organ
for a picture see the definition of body
stone (n.1) ◐
see also element, geology, jewelry, soil
for pictures see definitions of crystal, emerald,
garnet, gem, granite, jade, mineral, petrify,
quartz, ruby, sandstone, sedimentary, topaz,
turquoise
some examples of gem stones
agate (n.1), alabaster (n.), amber (n.1),
amethyst, crystal (n.1), diamond (n.1),
emerald (n.1), garnet, jade, opal, quartz,
ruby (n.1), topaz, turquoise (n.1)
similar to stone
rock[1] (n.1,2)
some kinds of stones
basalt, bedrock, chalk (n.1), gem (n.1),
granite, igneous, limestone, lodestone,
marble (n.1), metamorphic (adj.2),
mineral (n.1,/adj.1), precious (adj.1),
sandstone, sedimentary, shale, slate (n.1)
broader categories that include stones
element (n.4), **natural resources**
sources of stones
lava, magma, sediment (n.2)
study of stones
geology (n.1)
some places stones are found
deposit (n.2), lode, quarry (n.), vein (n.3)
some activities with stones
mining (mine[2] v.1), panning (pan v.2),
prospecting (prospect v.),
unearthing (unearth v.1)
activities with stones as weapons

catapult (v.1), sling (v.1), stone (v.)
some people associated with stones
jeweler, mason, miner, sculptor
some tools used with stones
chisel (n.), pick²
some formations of stone
canyon, cave (n.), cliff, gorge (n.), jetty (n.1), mine² (n.1), **mountain** (n.1), quarry (n.), reef
some forms of stones
boulder, cobblestone, jewel (n.1), meteor, meteorite, ore, pebble, rock¹ (n.1), stalactite, stalagmite
some things that are made of stones
carving, concrete (n.), gravel, grindstone (n.), grit (n.1), headstone, hearth (n.1), **jewelry**, keystone (n.1), masonry, pueblo (n.1), rubble, statue, tablet (n.3), tomahawk, tombstone
unit for measuring stones
carat

stool
see also furniture
for a picture see the definition of stool

store ○ ✿ *see* business

storm ○ ✿ *see* anger, weather

story¹ ○ ✿ *see* literature, myth

story² ○ *see* building

stove ○ *see* cooking

strain
see also emotion, first aid, injury, muscle
for a picture see the definition of strain¹

strainer *for pictures see definitions of* sieve, strainer

strategy *for a picture see definition*

stratosphere *for a picture see the definition of* earth

straw *for a picture see definition*

stream
see also ecosystem, river, water
for a picture see the definition of meander

street ○ *see* community, transportation

stress ○ ○ *see* emotion, health

string *for a picture see the definition of* music

stripe *for pictures see definitions of* stripe, vertical

strong ○ ○ *see* health, muscle, skeleton, thought

student
see also education, learn, school
for a picture see the definition of student

studio ○ *see* art, film, photography

study
see also education, knowledge, learn, school
for a picture see the definition of homework

subtract ○ *see* mathematics

suck *for a picture see the definition of* tick¹

sugar ○ *see* cooking, drink, food

sugar cane *for a picture see definition*

suit *for a picture see definition*

sun
see also light, space
for a picture see the definition of solar system

sundae *for a picture see definition*

sunflower *for a picture see definition*

sunset *for a picture see the definition of* view

supermarket ○ *see* business, food

superstition ○ ○ *see* belief, myth

supply ✿ *see* business

surf *for pictures see definitions of* surf, windsurfing

surfboard *for a picture see definition*

surgery ○ *see* disease, health, injury

suspect ○ ○ *see* belief, crime

suspenders *for a picture see definition*

swallow¹ ○ *see* digestion, food

swallow² ○ *see* bird

swamp ○ ✿ *see* ecosystem, water

sweat ○ *see* excrete

sweater ○ *see* clothing

sweet *for a picture see the definition of* taste

swim ○ *see* exercise, leisure

swing *for a picture see the definition of* dangle

sword *for pictures see definitions of* saber, shield

symbol
see also language, number
for pictures see definitions of emblem, icon, symbol

symmetry *for a picture see definition*

sympathy ○ *see* behavior, emotion

symphony ○ *see* music

syntax ○ *see* grammar

table ○ *see* furniture

table tennis *for a picture see the definition of* Ping-Pong

taboo ○ ○ *see* belief, culture, morals, religion

taco *for a picture see definition*

tadpole *for a picture see the definition of* amphibian

tail ○ *see* animal

tale
see also literature, myth
for a picture see the definition of tale

talon *for pictures see definitions of* bird, talon

tame ○ *see* pet

tangerine *for a picture see definition*

tank
see also home, military, pet, vehicle, weapon
for pictures see definitions of caravan, tank

tap *for a picture see definition*

tap *for a picture see definition*

tape ○ ○ *see* communication, measurement, music

tarantula *for a picture see definition*

tariff ✿ *see* tax

tassel *for a picture see definition*

taste
see also sense
for a picture see the definition of taste

tattoo *for a picture see definition*

Taurus *for pictures see definitions of* constellation, zodiac

tax (n.1) ✿
see also government, money
some examples of taxes
income tax, tariff
similar to a tax
levy (n.1)
some kinds of taxes
custom (n.2), duty (n.3)
broader categories that include taxes
government (n.3), **money**
some actions associated with taxes
assess (v.2), collect (v.3), evade (v.1), impose (v.), levy (v.), pay (v.2), repeal (v.)
some descriptions of taxes
fair¹ (adj.1), federal (adj.1), high (adj.3), local (adj.1), low (adj.2), state (adj.)
some people associated with taxes
accountant, treasurer
conventionally associated with taxes
gross (n.2), net² (adj.1), revenue (n.2)
some things that are taxed
goods (pl.n.2), income, property (n.2), real estate

taxi *for a picture see the definition of* hail

tea ○ ○ *see* drink

teach
see also education, knowledge, learn, school
for a picture see the definition of instruct

team ○ *see* game, sport

teapot *for a picture see the definition of* heirloom

tear¹ ○ *see* emotion, excrete

tease *for a picture see the definition of* gloat

technical ○ *see* technology

technician *for a picture see definition*

technology
see also airplane, car, computer, Internet, science, space
similar to technology
application (n.1), engineering, invention (n.1)
some kinds of technology
agricultural (agriculture), chemical (adj.1), environmental (environment n.1), industrial (adj.1), medical, **military** (adj.1,2), nuclear (adj.1)
some broader categories that include technology
engineering, **science** (n.1)
some places associated with technology
lab, laboratory, launch pad, outer space
some actions relating to technology
apply (v.1), develop (v.1), employ (v.1), improve (v.1), invent (v.1), modify (v.1)
some descriptions of technology
advanced (adj.1), backward (adj.), complicated, convenient, current (adj.1), dangerous, efficient, impractical (adj.1), modern (adj.1), new (adj.1), obsolete, revolutionary (adj.2), up-to-date (adj.1), useful
some products of technology
airplane, artificial intelligence, assembly line, automobile, **computer**, **Internet**, radar (n.2), radio (n.2), satellites (n.2), space station, television (n.2)
some people associated with technology
engineer (n.1), inventor, mechanic, technician
some things conventionally associated with technology
gadget, **industry** (n.1), ingenuity
some industries based on technology
communications (n.3), **energy** (n.1), manufacturing (manufacture n.), **space** (n.2), **transportation** (n.1)

teddy bear *for a picture see definition*

teen-ager ○ *see* life

teeth
see also skeleton
for pictures see definitions of body, teeth, tongue

telegraph ○ *see* communication

telephone
see also communication
for pictures see definitions of ahead, rotary

telescope *for a picture see definition*

television
see also communication
for a picture see the definition of remote control

teller ✿ *see* bank

temper ○ *see* anger, behavior

temperate ○ *see* weather

temperature ○ ○ *see* measurement, weather

template *for a picture see definition*

temple
see also building, religion
for a picture see the definition of pagoda

tendon ○ *see* body, muscle, skeleton

tennis *for pictures see definitions of* racket², serve

tenor ○ *see* instrument, music

tense
see also emotion, muscle
for a picture see the definition of tense¹

tense² ○ *see* grammar

tentacle *for a picture see definition*

termite *for a picture see definition*

terrain ⊕ *see* geography

terrier *for a picture see definition*

terrify *for a picture see definition*

territory ❶ ◌ *see* government

terror ◔ *see* emotion, fear

terrorism ◌ *see* crime

test ⊕ ◌ *see* education, health, school, science

theater (n.2) ⊕ ◔
  see also art, building, culture, dance, film, music
  similar to **theater**
    play (n.2), sketch (n.3), skit (n.1)
  some kinds of **theater**
    comedy, drama (n.1), mystery (n.2),
    tragedy (n.2)
  broader categories that include **theater**
    art (n.2), **culture** (n.1)
  some places associated with **theater**
    amphitheater, auditorium, balcony (n.2),
    hall (n.2), stage (n.1), wings (n.5)
  some actions in **theater**
    act (v.2), bow[1] (v.1), cast (v.5), cue[1] (v.),
    dance (v.1), direct (v.1), enact (v.2),
    enter (v.1), exit (v.), express (v.1),
    improvise (v.1), interpret (v.3), memorize,
    perform (v.2), portray (v.2), produce (v.4),
    prompt (v.2), put on (phr.2), rehearse,
    sing (v.1), stage (v.), star (v.3), take a bow, try
    out (phr.1)
  some actions associated with **theater**
    bomb (v.2), dramatize (v.2), flop (v.2),
    headline (v.), review (v.2)
  some reactions to **theater**
    applaud (v.1), boo (v.), laugh (v.)
  some descriptions of **theater**
    amateur (adj.), classical (adj.1),
    contemporary (adj.2), dramatic (adj.1),
    epic (adj.1), experimental (adj.2),
    modern (adj.2), musical (adj.3), political,
    professional (adj.2)
  some people associated with **theater**
    actor, audience (n.1), cast (n.4), critic (n.1),
    director (n.2), playwright, star (n.4), usher (n.)
  some things conventionally associated with
    theater
    audition (n.), costume (n.2), curtain (n.3),
    debut (n.), dress rehearsal, encore (n.2),
    excerpt (n.2), finale (n.2), hero (n.2),
    heroine (n.2), lead[1] (n.3), marquee, matinee,
    monologue (n.2), opening (n.4),
    pantomime (n.1), part (n.3), preview (n.),
    program (n.3), prop[2], rehearsal, review (n.1),
    revival (n.2), role (n.1), scene (n.3),
    scenery (n.2), script (n.1), set (n.2),
    ticket (n.1), villain (n.2), wardrobe (n.2)
  some elements of **theater**
    character (n.3), dialogue, expression (n.3),
    gesture (n.1), lighting, makeup (n.1),
    plot[1] (n.1), technique

theft ◌ *see* crime

theme ◔ *see* book, literature, music

theory ◔ *see* belief, learn, thought

therapy
  see also disease, injury, mind
  for a picture see the definition of therapy

thermometer
  see also health, measurement, weather
  for a picture see the definition of thermometer

thesaurus ◔ *see* book, language

thief *for a picture see the definition of* menace

thigh *for a picture see the definition of* body

thimble *for a picture see definition*

think ◔ *see* thought

thorax *for a picture see the definition of* insect

---

thoroughbred *for a picture see definition*

thought[1] (n.1,2) ◔
  see also knowledge, mind
  similar to **thought**
    attitude (n.1), **belief** (n.1), concept,
    idea (n.1), impression (n.1), notion (n.1),
    outlook (n.2), perception (n.2), point of view,
    sentiment (n.1), theory (n.3), view (n.4),
    whim
  broader category that includes **thought**
    mind (n.1)
  some actions involving **thinking**
    associate (v.1), assume (v.1), conceive (v.4),
    consider (v.1), contemplate (v.2),
    deliberate (v.), determine (v.2), devise, dream
    up, dwell (v.2), entertain (v.3), evaluate,
    expect (v.2), figure (v.2), guess (v.3), imagine,
    invent (v.2), judge (v.3), meditate, muse,
    picture (v.1), ponder, presume (v.1),
    reason (v.1,2), recall (v.1), reckon (v.2),
    recollect, reflect (v.5), regard (v.1),
    remember (v.1), review (v.3), speculate (v.1),
    suppose (v.3), weigh (v.2)
  some reactions to **thoughts**
    accept (v.3), agree (v.1), approve (v.1),
    concur, hedge (v.2), oppose (v.1), reject, see
    eye to eye, suggest (v.1)
  some descriptions of **thoughts**
    abstract (adj.1,2), clever (adj.2),
    conscious (adj.3), deep (adj.2),
    deliberate (adj.2), eccentric (adj.), illogical,
    incoherent, inconceivable, ingenious,
    logical (adj.2), original (adj.2),
    profound (adj.2), reasonable (adj.3),
    serious (adj.1), sober (adj.2)
  some people associated with **thinking**
    genius (n.2), intellectual (n.), inventor,
    philosopher, psychiatrist, psychologist
  some things conventionally associated with
    thought
    brain (n.1), food for thought,
    humanities (humanity n.3), matter (n.2),
    philosophy (n.1), psychology, sense (n.3,4)
  without **thinking**
    automatic (adj.2), careless (adj.2),
    casual (adj.2), impetuous, impulsive (adj.1),
    offhand, off the cuff, on the spur of the
    moment, regardless (adj.), shallow (adj.2),
    shortsighted (adj.2), thoughtless (adj.1)
  some elements of **thinking**
    concentration (n.2), examination (n.1),
    imagination, **knowledge** (n.1),
    perception (n.2), reflection (n.3)
  some outcomes of **thinking**
    conclusion (n.2), decision,
    determination (n.2), judgment (n.1),
    knowledge (n.1), plan (n.1), proposal (n.1)

thread *for pictures see definitions of* bobbin, reel[1],
  thimble, thread

throat
  see also body, digestion, respiration
  for a picture see the definition of throat

throw *for a picture see definition*

tick *for a picture see the definition of* tick[1]

ticket ◔ ◌ *see* communication, dance, music,
  theater

tide ❶ ⊕ *see* ocean

tiger *for pictures see definitions of* carnivore, tiger

tile *for a picture see definition*

tilt *for a picture see definition*

timber ❶ *see* forest, tree

time
  see also history, measurement
  for a picture see the definition of time

timer *for a picture see definition*

---

tin *for a picture see definition*

tint ◔ *see* color

tire *for a picture see definition*

tire *for a picture see definition*

tissue ⊕ ◌ *see* animal, body, cell, organ, plant

toad *for a picture see definition*

toboggan *for a picture see definition*

toddler *for a picture see definition*

toe
  see also foot
  for a picture see the definition of body

tomahawk *for a picture see definition*

tomato *for pictures see definitions of* close-up, cluster, halve, tomato

tom-tom *for a picture see definition*

tone ⊕ ◌ *see* color, muscle, music

tongue
  see also body, language, organ, sense
  for pictures see definitions of body, tongue,
  tongue

tonsil *for a picture see the definition of* tongue

tool (n.1,2)
  see also art, building, cooking, farming,
    gardening, health, home, science
  for pictures see definitions of auger, ax, bellows,
    chisel, clamp, cleaver, corkscrew, drill,
    hatchet, implement, knife, level, pitchfork,
    rake, rolling pin, scythe, sickle, tomahawk,
    trowel, tweezers, utensil, vise
  similar to **tools**
    device (n.1), gadget, instrument (n.1)
  some parts of **tools**
    blade (n.1), edge (n.3), handle (n.),
    point (n.1), prong (n.1)
  some students' **tools**
    pen[1], pencil (n.), ruler (n.2)
  some places for **tools**
    bench (n.2), shed[1], shop (n.2), toolbox,
    trunk (n.4)
  some actions with **tools**
    chop (v.1), cut (v.1), dig (v.3), file[2] (v.),
    lance (v.), saw[1] (v.), shear
  some carpenters' **tools**
    auger, awl, ax (n.), brace (n.4), chisel (n.),
    clamp (n.), clasp (n.1), clip[2] (n.1), drill (n.1),
    file[2] (n.), hammer (n.1), level (n.3),
    lever (n.1), mallet (n.1,2), plane[2] (n.), pliers,
    punch[2] (n.), saw[1] (n.), screwdriver,
    stamp (n.3), tape measure, vise, wrench (n.1)
  some cooks' **tools**
    cleaver, corkscrew (n.), fork (n.1), knife (n.),
    mixer, scoop (n.1,2), sieve, sieve, spatula,
    spoon (n.1), strainer, tongs
  some gardeners' and farmers' **tools**
    clipper (n.1), harrow (n.), hoe (n.), pick[2],
    pitchfork, rake (n.), shears, shovel (n.1),
    sickle, spade[1] (n.)
  some household **tools**
    broom, comb (n.1,2), funnel (n.1), hanger,
    mop (n.1), nutcracker, opener (n.2), razor,
    scissors, tweezers
  some general purpose **tools**
    brake (n.), bulb (n.3), buzzer, cartridge (n.3),
    clock (n.), crank (n.1), draft (n.5), drain (n.1),
    fan[1] (n.2), fastener, faucet, filter (n.2), heater,
    hinge (n.), hoist (n.), horn (n.3), lamp,
    latch (n.), lock[1] (n.1), mute (n.2),
    needle (n.1), receiver (n.2), recorder (n.2),
    scale[2], shade (n.3), shower (n.4), shutter (n.2),
    signal (n.1), siren, speaker (n.2), spray (n.3),
    spring (n.1), switch (n.2), timer (n.2),
    valve (n.1), watch (n.3), whistle (n.2)
  some painters' **tools**
    brush[1] (n.1), easel

---

some plumbers' tools
blowtorch, gauge (n.2), monkey wrench (n.)

some special purpose tools
abacus, anemometer, balance (n.1), barometer, bellows, camera, cell (n.4), choke (n.), circuit breaker, dimmer, electrode, Geiger counter, guillotine (n.), gyroscope, hearing aid, hourglass, intercom, microscope, periscope, seismograph, square (n.4), stethoscope, telescope

tooth (n.1)
see also body, skeleton
some kinds of teeth
bicuspid, bucktooth, canine (n.2), eyetooth (n.), fang, molar, tusk, wisdom tooth (n.)
broader category that includes tooth
bone (n.)
some parts of teeth
dentine, enamel (n.3), pulp (n.3), root¹ (n.2)
study of teeth
orthodontics
some places for teeth
gum², jaw (n.1), mouth (n.1)
some activities of teeth
bite (v.1), chew (v.), click (v.1), crush (v.1), cut (v.1,4), grind (v.1), rip (v.1), tear² (v.1)
some activities that involve teeth
break (v.1), brush¹ (v.1), chip (v.), clean (v.), fill (v.4), floss (v.1,2), stain (v.1), straighten (v.1), whiten
some descriptions of teeth
hard (adj.1), shiny (adj.1), white (n.1)
some sounds of teeth
chatter (n.2), click (n.1)
some people associated with teeth
dentist, hygienist, orthodontist (orthodontics)
some tools for the care of teeth
braces (n.3), dental floss, drill (n.1), filling (n.1), mouthpiece (n.2), toothbrush, toothpaste, toothpick
some things associated with unhealthy teeth
acids (n.), **bacteria**, caries, cavity, plaque (n.2), sugar, tartar, toothache
some things that affect the strength of teeth
calcium, fluoride, fluorine, **hygiene**

toothache *for a picture see the definition of* lopsided
top *for a picture see the definition of* top¹
top *for a picture see the definition of* spin
topaz *for a picture see definition*
topic *see* book, communication, literature
topography *see* geography
tornado *for a picture see definition*
tortoise *for pictures see definitions of* reptile, reptile, tortoise
totem pole *for a picture see definition*
toucan *for a picture see definition*
touch *see* sense
tournament *for a picture see definition*
tower *for pictures see definitions of* derrick, landmark
town *see* city, community
toy
see also leisure
for pictures see definitions of jack-in-the-box, rocking horse, spin, wooden, yo-yo
trachea *for a picture see the definition of* body
track *for a picture see the definition of* caboose
trade *see* business
tradition (n.1)
see also culture, history
some examples of traditions
ceremony (n.1), costume (n.1), folk dance (n.1), folklore, folk tale, legend (n.1),

myth (n.1)
similar to tradition
convention (n.2), custom (n.1)
some kinds of traditions
ceremonies (ceremony n.1), codes (n.1), institutions (n.2), methods (n.1), practices (n.2), rituals
broader categories that include tradition
culture (n.1), **history** (n.2)
some actions associated with tradition
accept (v.3), adopt (v.2), buck² (v.3), cherish, conform, establish (v.1), follow in the footsteps of, hand down, honor (v.1), ignore, obey (v.1), observe (v.4), rebel (v.1), shun, take root (phr.2), teach (v.1)
some descriptions of traditions
ancient (adj.1), cultural, daily (adj.), ethnic, family (n.2), formal (adj.1), honorable, legal (adj.1), literary (adj.1), modern (adj.1), mythic (mythical adj.1), national (adj.2), oral (adj.1), religious (adj.1), social (adj.2), tribal, written (adj.)
some people associated with traditions
ancestor, community (n.2), family (n.2), forefather, forerunner (n.1), parent
conventionally associated with tradition
costume (n.1), etiquette, folklore, habit (n.1), heirloom, manner (n.1,2), **morals** (n.2), routine (n.1), taboo (n.)
some things that maintain traditions
breeding (n.2), **education** (n.1), example (n.2), inheritance (n.2), prejudice (n.2), upbringing

traffic *see* transportation, vehicle
tragedy *see* emotion, film, literature, sadness, theater
trail *see* sport, transportation
trailer *for a picture see the definition of* semitrailer
train
see also learn, vehicle
for pictures see definitions of caboose, locomotive
transform *for a picture see definition*
transistor *see* technology
translate *see* language
transparent *for a picture see definition*
transportation (n.1)
see also vehicle
for a picture see the definition of locomotive
some places for transportation
air (n.2), highway, **lake**, land (n.1), lane (n.3), **ocean** (n.1), railway (n.2), **river** (n.1), road (n.1), **sea** (n.1), sidewalk, **space** (n.2), trail (n.1), **water** (n.1)
some actions associated with transportation
canter (v.), drive (v.4,5), fly¹ (v.1,2), gallop (v.1,2), motor (v.), ride (v.1,3), run (v.1), sail (v.1,2), steam (v.3), trot (v.1,2), walk (v.1)
some forms of transportation
camel, donkey, elephant, feet (**foot** n.1), horse (n.1), legs (n.1), llama, **vehicle** (n.1)
trapezoid *for a picture see definition*
trash
see also conservation
for a picture see the definition of rubber
treasury *see* business, government, money
treble *see* instrument, music
tree (n.1)
see also forest, plant
for pictures see definitions of bark, conifer, deciduous, evergreen, horizon, lofty, maple, oasis, spruce¹, willow
some examples of trees
alder, almond (n.1), apple (n.2), apricot (n.2),

ash² (n.1), aspen, balsa (n.1), balsam fir, beech, birch, butternut (n.1), cacao (n.1), carob (n.1), cashew (n.1), cedar (n.1), cherry (n.2), chestnut (n.2), coconut (n.1), cork (n.1), crab apple (n.1), cypress, dogwood, ebony (n.2), elm, eucalyptus, fir, guava (n.1), hawthorn, hazel (n.1), hemlock (n.1), hickory (n.1), holly (n.1), juniper, larch (n.1), laurel (n.1), lemon (n.2), lime² (n.2), magnolia (n.1), mahogany (n.1), maple (n.1), mulberry (n.1), oak (n.1), olive (n.2), papaya, peach (n.2), pear (n.2), pecan (n.2), pine (n.1), pistachio (n.2), pomegranate (n.2), poplar (n.1), redwood (n.1), rhododendron, sequoia, spruce¹ (n.1), sumac, walnut (n.1), willow, yew (n.1)
some kinds of trees
citrus (n.), conifer, evergreen (n.), flowering (**flower** n.2), **fruit**, palm²
some categories of trees
deciduous, perennial (adj.1)
broader category that includes trees
plant (n.1)
some parts of trees
bark² (n.), bough, branch (n.1), bud (n.1), crown (n.3), flower (n.1), foliage (n.1), frond, knot (n.2), **leaf** (n.1), needle (n.5), root¹ (n.1), thorn (n.1), trunk (n.1), twig
some places for trees
arbor, brush² (n.1), **forest**, grove, jungle, nursery (n.2), orchard, thicket, wilderness
some activities with trees
blaze² (v.2), cut (v.1), grow (v.1), log (v.1), **plant** (v.1), prune²
some things produced by trees
acorn, camphor, cone (n.3), **fruit**, nut (n.1), resin (n.1)
young trees
sapling, seedling
some people associated with trees
logger, lumberjack
person who studies trees
naturalist
some things built in trees
cocoon, hive (n.1), nest (n.1)
some things trees provide
amber (n.1), beauty (n.1), chocolate (n.1), coffee (n.1), cork (n.2), dyes (n.), ebony (n.1), **food** (n.), fuel, **furniture**, gums¹ (n.2), hardwood (n.2), houses (n.1), log (n.1), lumber¹, maple syrup, medicine (n.1), oils (n.1), oxygen, paper (n.1), plastics (n.), poles¹, resin (n.1), rubber (n.1), shade (n.2), shelter (n.1), spices (n.1), textiles (n.), **tools** (n.1), turpentine (n.1)
also associated with trees
Christmas tree, stump (n.1)

tremor *see* body, earth, emotion
trial *see* crime, law
triangle *for a picture see definition*
tributary *see* river
trick *for a picture see the definition of* dazzle
trill *see* instrument, music
trio
see also music
for pictures see definitions of debut, trio
triplet *for a picture see definition*
troop *see* military
trowel *for a picture see definition*
truce *see* relationship, war
truck
see also vehicle
for pictures see definitions of antique, derrick, fire engine, semitrailer
trumpet

see also instrument
for pictures see definitions of music, trumpet

trunk
  see also body, car
  for a picture see the definition of body
trust ⊙ *see* belief
t-shirt ◐ *see* clothing
tub *for a picture see the definition of* recycle
tuba *for a picture see the definition of* music
tuber *for a picture see definition*
tulip *for pictures see definitions of* flower, tulip
tundra ☺
  see also ecosystem, plain
  broader category including tundra
    plain (n.)
  some descriptions of tundras
    arctic (adj.2), cold (adj.1), frigid (adj.1),
    icy (adj.1,2)
  some things found in tundras
    ice (n.1), lichen, moss, snow (n.1,2),
    wildflower
tune ◐ *see* instrument, music
tuning fork *for a picture see definition*
turkey *for pictures see definitions of* bird, turkey
turnip *for a picture see definition*
turquoise *for a picture see definition*
turtle *for pictures see definitions of* protrude, reptile, reptile
tusk
  see also mammal, tooth
  for a picture see the definition of tusk
TV *for a picture see the definition of* remote control
tweezers *for a picture see definition*
twin *for a picture see the definition of* identical
twist *for a picture see definition*
tyranny ⊙ ▢ *see* government, power
udder ◐ *see* mammal, milk
ulcer *for a picture see definition*
umbilical cord ☺ *see* mammal, reproduction
Uncle Sam *for a picture see definition*
uncooperative *for a picture see definition*
underground ◐ *see* ecosystem, geology, rodent, soil, worm
undersea *for a picture see definition*
understand ⊙ *see* learn, thought
underwater *for a picture see definition*
underwear ◐ *see* clothing
unearth *for a picture see definition*
unhealthy ☺ *see* disease
unicorn ◐ *see* myth
uniform
  see also clothing
  for pictures see definitions of livery, uniform, vertical
unison *for a picture see definition*
unit ◐ *see* measurement, number
universe ☺ *see* earth, space
university ◐ ▢ *see* community, education, school
unlucky *for a picture see definition*
unreasonable ⊙ *see* behavior, thought
upholstery *for a picture see definition*
upright *for a picture see definition*
upset ☺ ⊙ *see* emotion
upside down *for a picture see definition*
uranium ◐ *see* element
Uranus *for a picture see the definition of* solar system
Ursa Major *for a picture see the definition of* constellation

Ursa Minor *for a picture see the definition of* constellation
utensil
  see also food, tool
  for a picture see the definition of utensil
uterus *for a picture see the definition of* body
vacation *for a picture see definition*
vaccine ☺ *see* disease, virus
vacuum ◐ ☺ *see* hygiene, space
vagina *for a picture see the definition of* body
valentine *for a picture see definition*
valley
  see also geography, mountain
  for a picture see the definition of valley
value ⊙ ☺ *see* money, thought
valve *for a picture see definition*
vane *for a picture see definition*
variety *for a picture see definition*
vase *for pictures see definitions of* carnation, vase
vast *for a picture see definition*
vault *for a picture see the definition of* vault[1]
vegetable (n.1) ◐ ◐
  see also cooking, farming, food, fruit, gardening, plant
  for pictures see definitions of artichoke, asparagus, broccoli, Brussels sprouts, cabbage, carrot, cauliflower, celery, eggplant, lettuce, market, okra, potato, produce, radish
  some examples of vegetables
    artichoke, asparagus, bean (n.1), beet, broccoli, cabbage, carrot (n.1), cauliflower, celery, collard (n.1), corn (n.1), cucumber, eggplant, leek, lettuce (n.1), okra (n.1), onion (n.1), parsnip (n.1), pea (n.1), pepper (n.2), potato, radish (n.1), spinach, squash[2] (n.1), string bean, turnip (n.2), watercress (n.2), yam (n.1)
  some kinds of preserved vegetables
    canned (can[2] v.), frozen (adj.1), pickled (pickle v.)
  broader categories that include vegetables
    crop (n.), **food** (n.), **plant** (n.1), produce (n.)
  some parts of vegetables
    flesh (n.3), meat (n.2), peel (n.), **seed** (n.1), skin (n.2), tuber
  some components of vegetables
    calcium, iron (n.1), mineral (n.), nutrition (n.1), starch (n.1), sugar, vitamins
  some places for vegetables
    farm (n.1), field (n.1), **garden** (n.), grocery (n.1), market (n.1), supermarket
  some activities involving vegetables
    cook (v.1), cultivate, eat (v.1), grow (v.1), harvest (v.), hull[1] (v.), peel (v.1), plant (v.1), preserve (v.3), raise (v.3), store (v.)
  some things that produce vegetables
    blossom (n.1), flower (n.1), ovary (n.2), seed (n.1)
  some people associated with vegetables
    cook (n.), farmer, gardener, grocer, vegetarian (n.)
  person who only eats vegetables
    vegetarian (n.)
vehicle (n.1) ◐
  see also airplane, boat, car, transportation
  for pictures see definitions of ambulance, bicycle, caravan, fire engine, jeep, jet[1], locomotive, rotor, rowboat, seaplane, semitrailer, tank, vehicle, zoom
  some examples of vehicles
    airplane, airship, automobile, balloon (n.2), bicycle (n.), blimp, **boat** (n.1), bus (n.), camper (n.2), **car** (n.1), carriage (n.1), cart (n.2), chariot, fire engine, glider, hang

glider, helicopter, jeep (n.2), pickup (n.2), ship (n.1), snowmobile, tank (n.1), tractor, trailer (n.2), train (n.1), tram (n.2), trolley (n.1), truck (n.), van
  broader category that includes vehicles
    transportation (n.1)
  some places for vehicles
    air (n.2), garage (n.1), path (n.3), sidewalk, station (n.3), terminal (n.2), track (n.2), trail (n.1), waterway
  some actions of vehicles
    drive (v.2,4,5), go (v.1), haul (v.2), journey (v.), move (v.2), progress (v.1), tow (v.), transport (v.), travel (v.1)
  some people associated with vehicles
    driver, passenger
  some things typically transported in vehicles
    cargo, freight, person (n.1)
vein
  see also blood
  for a picture see the definition of body
Velcro *for a picture see definition*
velvet *for a picture see definition*
venom ◐ *see* first aid, injury, reptile, spider
ventricle *for a picture see the definition of* body
Venus *for a picture see the definition of* solar system
verb ◐ *see* grammar
verbal *for a picture see definition*
verdict ▢ *see* crime
vermin *for a picture see definition*
verse ◐ *see* literature, music
vertebra *for a picture see the definition of* body
vertebrate ◐ *see* amphibian, animal, bird, dinosaur, mammal, reptile, rodent
vertical *for a picture see definition*
veteran ⊙ ▢ *see* military, war
video ◐ *see* film, game, leisure
Vietnamese *for pictures see definitions of* language, Vietnamese
view
  see also belief, sense
  for pictures see definitions of panorama, view, vista
village ◐ ▢ *see* community
vineyard *for a picture see definition*
viola *for a picture see definition*
violin *for pictures see definitions of* fiddle, music, tense[1], violin
viper *for a picture see definition*
Virgo *for pictures see definitions of* constellation, zodiac
virtue ☺ *see* behavior, personality
virus (n.1) ☺ ◐
  see also bacteria, disease
  broader categories that include viruses
    germ (n.1), microorganism
  some parts of viruses
    gene, protein
  some descriptions of viruses
    deadly (adj.1), infectious (adj.1), microscopic (adj.1)
  some living things that are affected by viruses
    animal (n.1), **bacteria, cell** (n.1), human (n.), **plant** (n.1)
  some things that are affected by viruses
    health (n.1), lungs, nervous system, spinal cord, white blood cell
  results of some viruses
    coma, coughing (cough n.1), death (n.1), epidemic, fever (n.1), indigestion (n.2), rash[2] (n.1), sickness (n.1), sneezing (sneeze n.), suffering (suffer v.1)
  some carriers of viruses

food (n.), germs (n.1), housefly, **insects** (n.1), mosquito, saliva
some conditions resulting from viruses
  AIDS, chicken pox, cold (n.2), **disease**, distemper, infection (n.1), influenza, measles, mumps, pneumonia, poliomyelitis, rabies, wart (n.1)
some processes involving viruses
  develop (v.5), invade (v.1), outbreak (n.2), reproduce (v.2), spread (v.3)
some things that affect viruses
  antibody, booster shot, chemotherapy, **hygiene**, medicine (n.1), sanitation, serum (n.2), shot[1] (n.6), surgery (n.2), vaccine
vise *for a picture see definition*
vision 🌐 *see* light, sense
vista *for a picture see definition*
visual 🌐 *see* art, light, sense
vivid *for a picture see definition*
vocabulary 🌐 *see* language
voice 🌐 *see* communication, language
volcano 🌐
  see also geology
  for a picture see the definition of earth
  similar to volcanoes
    geyser
  some parts of volcanoes
    ash[1], basalt, crater, gas (n.1), granite, igneous, lava (n.1), magma, rock[1] (n.1)
  include the study of volcanoes
    geography (n.1), **geology** (n.1), plate tectonics
  some actions of volcanoes
    erupt, explode (v.1), spew (v.3), spout (v.1,2)
  some descriptions of volcanoes
    active (adj.1), dormant (adj.1), extinct (adj.2)
vole *for a picture see definition*
volleyball *for a picture see definition*
vote 🌐 *see* democracy
vowel 🌐 *see* grammar
vulture *for a picture see definition*
waddle *for a picture see definition*
waffle *for a picture see the definition of* waffle[1]
wage 🌐 *see* money, work
wagon *for pictures see definitions of* cart, covered wagon
wake *for a picture see the definition of* reluctant
wake *for a picture see the definition of* wake[2]
walk 🌐 *see* exercise, foot
wall
  see also building
  for a picture see the definition of wall
wallow *for a picture see definition*
walnut *for a picture see definition*
walrus *for a picture see the definition of* pinniped
war (n.1) 🌐
  see also military, weapon
  similar to war
    conflict (n.2), rebellion (n.1), revolution (n.1)
  some broader categories that include wars
    government (n.2), **history** (n.1), **politics** (n.2)
  some parts of war
    action (n.4), battle (n.1), campaign (n.), invasion (n.1), siege
  some descriptions of war
    bloody (adj.2), civil (adj.1), global (adj.1), tribal
  some people associated with war
    commander (n.2), enemy (n.2), general (n.), POW, soldier, spy (n.1), traitor, veteran (n.2)
  without war
    peace (n.1)
  some acts of war
    assault (v.), attack (v.1), besiege (v.1),

blockade (v.), bomb (v.1), bombard (v.1), defend (v.1), destroy, devastate (v.1), fight (v.1), fire (v.5), retreat (v.1), shell (v.2)
  some mythical figures associated with war
    Ares, Athena
  some things associated with war
    alliance, armistice, bloodshed, casualties (casualty n.1), draft (n.3), loyalty, patriotism, treason, treaty, truce, victory
warbler *for a picture see definition*
warm-blooded *for a picture see definition*
warning *for a picture see definition*
wash 🌐 🌐 *see* clothing, hygiene
wasp *for pictures see definitions of* wasp, yellow jacket
waste 🌐 🌐 *see* conservation, excrete
watch
  see also care, jewelry
  for pictures see definitions of digital, gear, remote control, wrist watch
water (n.1) 🌐 🌐
  see also conservation, drink, geography, natural resources, weather
  some kinds of water
    brine (n.1), broth, freshwater, saltwater
  some actions involving water
    absorb (v.1), bail[2] (v.), bloat, boil[1] (v.1), brew (v.1), dam (v.), dehydrate (v.1), dredge (v.), drown (v.1), float (v.1), flush[1] (v.3), ford (v.), hose (v.), launch[1] (v.2), pour (v.1), scour[1] (v.3), shower (v.1), sink (v.6), slop (v.2), soak (v.1), splash (v.1), sponge (v.1), spray (v.1), squirt (v.3), steep[2], submerge (v.2), swim (v.2), wade (v.1), wallow, wring (v.1)
  some actions of moving water
    deluge (v.1), dribble (v.1), drift (v.1), drip (v.1), drizzle (v.), flush[1] (v.1), gush (v.1), leak (v.2), seethe (v.1), trickle (v.1), wave (n.1)
  some uses for water
    baptize (v.1), bathe (v.1), boat (v.), clean (v.), cook (v.2), drink (v.1), fish (v.2), irrigate, raft (v.), rinse (v.1), sail (v.1), ski (n.2), steep[2], wash (v.1)
  elements in water
    hydrogen, oxygen
  means of transportation on water
    barge (n.), **boat** (n.1), ferry (n.), passage (n.3), ship (n.1), submarine
  some areas of flowing water
    brook, cataract (n.1), channel (n.1), creek (n.), eddy (n.), gully, **river** (n.1), stream (n.1), tributary, waterfall, waterway
  some bodies of water
    bay, inlet, lagoon (n.1), **lake**, moat, **ocean** (n.1), pond, puddle (n.1), **sea** (n.1), swamp (n.)
  some natural processes involving water
    condensation (n.1), erosion, evaporation (evaporate v.1), flooding (v.1), precipitation (n.1), purification (purify), rusting (rust v.), tide (n.1)
  some states of water
    fog (n.1), hail[2] (n.1), ice (n.1), liquid (n.), rain (n.1), sleet (n.), snow (n.1), steam (n.1), vapor (n.1)
  some things that contain water
    basin, bottle (n.1), bowl[1] (n.1), cup (n.1), fountain (n.1), glass (n.1), jug (n.1), kettle (n.1), pail (n.1), pool (n.3), sewer, sink (n.), tub (n.1)
  some things that live in water
    amphibian (n.1), beaver, **crustacean**, **fish** (n.1), lotus (n.1), otter, seal[2], seaweed (n.1), terrapin, turtle (n.), water

lily (n.1)
  things that control the flow of water
    aqueduct (n.1), dam (n.), ditch (n.), embankment, faucet, gutter, levee (n.1), nozzle (n.1), pipe (n.1), siphon (n.), sluice (n.1), valve (n.1)
  units for measuring water
    degree (n.2), fathom (n.), feet (foot n.2), league (n.2), meter[1]
  also associated with water
    undertow, waterlogged (adj.2)
water buffalo *for a picture see definition*
waterfall
  see also geography, river, water
  for a picture see the definition of waterfall
waterway 🌐 *see* transportation, boat
wave 🌐 *see* ocean
weak 🌐 *see* health, mind, muscle
wealth 🌐 *see* money
weapon (n.1) 🌐
  see also hunting, military
  for pictures see definitions of arrowhead, cannon, crossbow, firearm, grenade, gun, holster, jackknife, revolver, rifle, saber, tank, tomahawk, weapon
  some examples of weapons
    arrow (n.1), atomic bomb, ax (n.), bayonet, boomerang, bow[2] (n.1), cannon, catapult (n.1), club (n.1), crossbow, dagger (n.), firearm, flintlock (n.2), grenade, guided missile, gun (n.1), harpoon (n.), hydrogen bomb, javelin, knife (n.), lance (n.1), machine gun, mine[2] (n.1), missile (n.1), missile (n.1), musket, pistol, revolver, rifle, saber, sling (n.2), slingshot, spear[1] (n.), sword (n.), tank (n.3), TNT, tomahawk, torpedo (n.)
  similar to weapons
    arm[2] (n.), armament
  some broader categories that involve weapons
    crime (n.1), hunting (**hunt** v.1), **war** (n.1)
  some parts of weapons
    arrowhead, barrel (n.3), blade (n.1), butt[1] (n.1), chamber (n.5), clip[2] (n.2), cylinder, edge (n.3), fuse[1] (n.1), handle (n.), hilt (n.), magazine (n.2), muzzle (n.3), shaft (n.6), sight (n.6), trigger (n.1)
  some places associated with weapons
    armory, arsenal, blockhouse (n.1), fort, fortress, holster, joust (v.), scabbard, sheath, silo (n.2), stockade (n.1), turret (n.2)
  some actions associated with weapons
    aim (v.1), arm[2] (v.1), bomb (v.1), discharge (v.1), duel (v.), explode (v.3), fell[2] (v.2), fire (v.1), hack (v.1), hit (v.1), hurl, injure, jab (v.2), knife (v.1), load (v.2), puncture (v.), shoot (v.1,5), slash (v.1), stab (v.1), stick[2] (v.1), strike (v.1), thrust (v.)
  some descriptions of weapons
    accurate (adj.2), blunt (adj.1), deadly (adj.1), destructive, explosive (adj.2), **military** (adj.1,2), nuclear (adj.3), powerful, sharp (adj.1)
  some things often used with weapons
    ammunition (n.1), armor (n.1), blank (n.3), bullet (n.), cartridge (n.1), dart (n.1), gunpowder, helmet, mail[2], projectile, ramrod, round (n.5), shell (n.3)
  some people associated with weapons
    archer, criminal (n.), gangster, guard (n.1,2), gunner, hunter (n.1), knight (n.1), minuteman, musketeer, pirate (n.1), policeman, policewoman, ranger (n.1), samurai, sheriff, soldier, trooper, warrior
wear 🌐 *see* clothing

weather (n.)
see also air, geology
for a picture see the definition of weather
some kinds of weather
blizzard, downpour, drizzle (n.), drought, flurry (n.1), hail² (n.1), hurricane, mist (n.), precipitation (n.1), rain (n.1), rainfall (n.1), shower (n.1), sleet (n.), snowstorm
study of weather
meteorology
some descriptions of weather
arctic (adj.2), arid, bleak (adj.1), clear (adj.1), cloudy (adj.1), cold (adj.1), fair¹ (adj.4), foul (adj.3), hot (adj.1), humid, pouring (pour v.2), rainy, sunny (adj.1), temperate, warm (adj.1), windy
some things that protect people from weather
dugout (n.1), house (n.1), igloo, shelter (n.1), sunglasses, sunscreen, windshield
person associated with weather
weatherman
accessories for bad weather
boots (n.), coat (n.1), earmuffs, hat, jacket (n.1), overcoat, overshoe, sweater, umbrella
tools for measuring weather
barometer, thermometer, weather vane
some changes in weather
freeze (n.2), melt (v.1), snap (n.3), spell³ (n.1), thaw (n.)
some ways weather is measured
humidity, temperature (n.2)
also associated with weather
almanac (n.2), autumn, lighthouse, seasons (n.1), spring (n.4), summer (n.), winter (n.1)

weatherman ○ ⑤ *see* weather
web ○ ○ ○ *see* Internet, spider
webfoot *for pictures see definitions of* bird, webfoot
Web page *for a picture see definition*
weed ○ *see* farming, gardening
weep ○ *see* sadness
weight *for a picture see the definition of* dumbbell
well *for a picture see the definition of* oil well
whale *for a picture see definition*
wharf *for a picture see definition*
wheel *for pictures see definitions of* paddle wheel, tire, wheel
wheelbarrow *for pictures see definitions of* laden, wheelbarrow
whisker
see also animal, hair
for a picture see the definition of whisker
whistle
see also communication, instrument
for pictures see definitions of music, whistle
whooping crane *for a picture see definition*
wick *for a picture see definition*
wicked ○ *see* behavior, belief, morals, religion
wicker *for a picture see definition*
wig *for a picture see definition*
wild ○ ⑤ *see* animal, behavior
will² ○ *see* mind
willow *for a picture see definition*
wind¹ ⑤ *see* air, weather
windmill *for pictures see definitions of* conservation, vane, windmill
window ○ *see* car, room
windsurfing *for a picture see definition*
wing
see also airplane, bird, building, insect
for a picture see the definition of insect
winter ⑤ *see* weather

wintry *for a picture see definition*
wise ○ *see* knowledge
withdraw ⑤ *see* bank, money
witness ○ *see* crime
wizard *for a picture see definition*
wolf *for pictures see definitions of* canine, teeth, wolf
wood
see also building, tree
for pictures see definitions of driftwood, petrify
woodchuck *for pictures see definitions of* groundhog, woodchuck
wooden *for a picture see definition*
woodwind *for a picture see the definition of* music
word ○ *see* language
work (n.4) ○ ○ ○
see also business, energy, physics
for pictures see definitions of construction, drudgery, industrial
some examples of people who work
accountant, astronaut, author, barber, bodyguard, cashier, chauffeur, chemist, cowhand, critic (n.1), custodian (n.2), detective, diplomat (n.1), electrician, engineer, flight attendant, janitor, journalist, lawyer, librarian, lumberjack, mail carrier, mathematician, mechanic, miner, musician, optometrist, painter (n.2), pharmacist, photographer, physician, physicist, plumber, programmer, psychologist, ranger (n.1), registered nurse, sailor (n.2), salesperson, scientist, secretary (n.1), singer (n.1), technician
some kinds of work
career, employment (n.3), job (n.2), occupation (n.1), profession (n.1), vocation
some places for work
agency (n.1,2), assembly line, business (n.2), forge¹ (n.1,2), office (n.1), shipyard
some groups associated with work
association (n.1), employees, guild, labor union, personnel, staff (n.3), workers (n.1)
some work activities
administer (v.1), command (v.1), direct (v.2), discipline (v.1), guide (v.2,3), handle (v.1), head (v.1), manage (v.1), operate (v.3), organize (v.2,3), regulate (v.1), run (v.14), supervise, train (v.1,2)
some people associated with work
apprentice (n.), boss (n.), colleague, employee, employer, foreman (n.1), manager
some accessories for working
safety belt (n.2), scaffold, tool (n.1,2), uniform (n.)
conventionally associated with work
carpool, commute (n.), Labor Day, workmanship (n.2)
lack of work
unemployed (adj.)
some forms of payment for work
pay (n.), pension, salary, wage (n.)
also associated with work
slavery (n.1)
workout *for a picture see definition*
worm (n.1) ○
see also invertebrate
for a picture see the definition of earthworm
some examples of worms
earthworm, leech
similar to worms
caterpillar, centipede, inchworm
broader categories that include worms
animal (n.1), **invertebrate** (n.)
some parts of worms
bristle (n.1), fin (n.1), tentacles

some places worms are found
burrow (n.), host¹ (n.2), intestines, mud, **ocean** (n.1), sand (n.), **soil¹** (n.1), **water** (n.1), wood (n.1)
produced by worms
cocoon, eggs¹ (n.1)
some behaviors of worms
burrow (v.1), contract (v.1), crawl (v.2), creep (v.2), dig (v.1), stretch (v.1), suck (v.1), swim (v.1)
some things that worms eat
blood (n.1), **grass** (n.1), **leaf** (n.1), **plants** (n.1), wheat (n.1), wood (n.1)
some things that worms influence
agriculture, compost, **soil¹** (n.1)
worn-out *for a picture see definition*
worry ○ *see* emotion, thought
worship ○ *see* behavior, love, religion
wound¹ ○ *see* first aid, injury
wrangle *for a picture see definition*
wrapping *for a picture see definition*
wrath ○ *see* action, anger
wreath *for a picture see definition*
wreck *for a picture see definition*
wren *for a picture see definition*
wrist watch *for a picture see definition*
write
see also literature
for a picture see the definition of write
x-ray
see also photography, skeleton
for a picture see the definition of x-ray
xylophone *for a picture see definition*
yacht *for a picture see definition*
yam *for a picture see the definition of* tuber
yeast ○ *see* fungus
yell ○ ○ *see* anger, fear
yellow jacket *for a picture see definition*
yodel ○ *see* music
yoga ○ *see* exercise
yolk *for a picture see definition*
young
see also life
for a picture see the definition of mammal
yo-yo *for a picture see definition*
zebra *for pictures see definitions of* mammal, stripe, zebra
zeus *for a picture see definition*
zinc ○ *see* element
zipper ○ *see* clothing
zither *for pictures see definitions of* music, zither
zodiac
see also belief, myth
for a picture see the definition of zodiac
zone ⑥ *see* ecosystem, geography, weather
zoo ○ *see* animal
zoom *for a picture see definition*

Acknowledgments

Wordsmyth would like to acknowledge the photographic work of NASA, NASA and the Hubble Heritage Team (STSCI/AURA), Earth Sciences and Image Analysis Laboratory, NASA Johnson Space Center, ESA and D. Maoz (Tel-Aviv University and Columbia University), Getty Photo Collection, NOAA Photo Library, NOAA Central Library, OAR/ERL/National Severe Storms Laboratory (NSSL), OAR/National Undersea Research Program (NURP), University of North Carolina at Wilmington, U.S. Geological Survey (USGS), U.S. Department of Defense, Hemera Photo Collection, and The McGraw-Hill Companies. Images of the Presidents of the United States are from The Library of Congress, and images of Canadian Prime Ministers are from The National Library of Canada. Additional images are from the ClickArt Collection.